1 MONTH OF
FREE
READING

at
www.ForgottenBooks.com

By purchasing this book you are eligible for one month membership to ForgottenBooks.com, giving you unlimited access to our entire collection of over 700,000 titles via our web site and mobile apps.

To claim your free month visit:
www.forgottenbooks.com/free752210

ISBN 978-0-483-35265-0
PIBN 10752210

THE PACIFIC IRON WORKS
ESTABLISHED IN 1849.

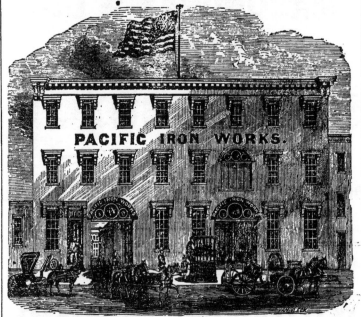

The Proprietors of the above Works invite the attention of all parties interested, to their improved and unequaled facilities for manufacturing

MACHINERY OF EVERY DESCRIPTION.

Our Works are now conceded to be the most extensive and best appointed on this Coast, and the character of our Machinery, we have reason to believe, will bear favorable comparison with that of any similar establishment in the country. Our PATTERN LIST is most complete and extensive, embracing the late improvements in all classes of Machinery adapted to use on this coast.

We would call special attention to the fact that we have secured the exclusive right of manufacture, in this territory, to the Celebrated

GREENE ENGINE,

which is pronounced by Competent Engineers to be the most perfect and the most economical Engine now in use. O.

We are also sole Manufacturers of the Celebrated

BHYAN BATTERY, VARNEY'S AMALGAMATORS AND SEPARATORS,
Austin's Stone Breakers, etc.

All Orders executed with promptness in the most thorough and workmanlike manner.

GODDARD & COMPANY,
125 to 135 First St., and 126 to 144 Fremont St., SAN FRANCISCO.

FEMALE
Collegiate Institute,

SANTA CLARA, CALIFORNIA.

[FEMALE DEPARTMENT UNIVERSITY OF THE PACIFIC.]

Primary, Preparatory and Collegiate Departments under a full corps of efficient instructors.

Music, Painting, Drawing, Wax Work, Embroidery, etc.

References.

REV. J. T. PECK, D.D.,
CAPT. J. B. THOMAS,
HON. J. T. McLEAN,
HON. C. CLAYTON,
HON. ANNIS MERRILL,
                              San Francisco.

REV. M. C. BRIGGS, D.D., Sacramento,
REV. C. V. ANTHONY, Marysville,
HON. H. G. BLASDEL, Governor of Nevada,
HON. J. W. NORTH, Carson City,
REV. T. S. DUNN, Virginia City,
REV. A. N. FISHER, Austin.

UNIVERSITY SCHOOL,

Post Street between Stockton and Powell.

Principal, . . . GEO. BATES, M.A.

(From Magdalen College, Cambridge, England.)

This Institution is designed to give a First class education to a **limited number** of pupils. Constant drilling, and the thorough mastery of the studies undertaken, are considered more important than a superficial and therefore useless acquaintance with a large number of subjects.

The Classical Course comprises all the Greek and Latin languages usually read at Colleges, but it is required that each pupil should become perfectly familiar with the language he is studying.

The Commercial Course embraces the theory and practice of Book-keeping, and all that is necessary for success in business.

Modern Languages.—Pupils are taught both to translate and converse in the French, German and Spanish languages.

Mathematics.—The instruction in this department is most thorough. Great stress is laid on Arithmetic, a complete knowledge of which is essential, both for those who are to be engaged in mercantile pursuits, and for those who wish to pursue higher Mathematical studies. This department is under the sole superintendence of the principal, who gained a high position in the Mathematical lists at Cambridge, and who has had for his pupils some of the most distinguished Mathematicians of that University.

The Premises are very large, and include all that is necessary for a School.

☞ Prospectuses at H. H. Bancroft & Co's, 609 Montgomery Street, or at the School, between the hours of 9 A.M. and 3 P.M.

ST. CATHERINE'S
Academy for Young Ladies,
BENICIA, CAL.

This Institution is conducted by the SISTERS OF ST. DOMINIC, and is situated in the healthy and accessible town of Benicia. The plan of education embraces the various branches of instruction usually taught in the most approved seminaries for young ladies. Pupils of any religious denomination will be received, but for the sake of uniformity, all are required to be present at the regular religious services of the Institution.

The scholastic year, comprising ten months and a half, opens on the twenty-first of August, and ends about the first week of July. No deduction will be made if the pupil is withdrawn during the session, except in case of sickness. Pupils will be received at any time, the fees to commence from date of entrance.

The uniform for Sundays, in Winter, will be black alpaca, white collar, cuffs, black silk apron, white straw bonnet trimmed with white, green vail, and black kid gloves. For the summer uniform inquiry is to be made at the Institution.

Besides the uniform dress, each pupil should be provided with four dresses, six changes of linen, towels, blankets, sheets, pillow-cases, a calico morning gown, parasol, six table napkins, a knife, silver spoon, fork and goblet, a straw bonnet trimmed with green, a white Swiss muslin dress, a dressing and ivory comb, a hair brush, tooth brush, and nail brush. All articles should be marked with the name.

TERMS PER ANNUM—Payable half-yearly in advance.

Board and Tuition	*$225.00*
Entrance	*10.00*
Washing	*45.00*
Pupils remaining at the Academy during vacation, will be charged	*20.00*

DRAWING, PAINTING AND MUSIC FORM EXTRA CHARGES.

There is no extra charge for the French or Spanish Languages, nor for Needle Work.

All correspondence of the young ladies will be subject to the inspection of the Superior.

Letters may be addressed to

Sister LOUISA O'NEILL, O.S.D.,
Prioress.

St. Ignatius' College,

Market Street, between Fourth and Fifth Streets,

SAN FRANCISCO, CAL.

This Institution conducted by the Fathers of the Society of Jesus, was opened for the reception of Students on the 15th of October, 1855. On the 30th of April, 1859, it was incorporated and empowered to confer degrees and academical honors in all the learned professions, and to exercise all the rights and privileges common to any other literary institution in the United States.

THE DESIGN OF THIS INSTITUTION IS TO GIVE A THOROUGH

English, Classical, Mathematical and Philosophical

EDUCATION.

It is intended for day Scholars only.

The Course of Studies embraces the Greek, Latin and English Languages, Poetry, Rhetoric, Elocution, History, Geography, Arithmetic, Book-Keeping, Mathematics, Chemistry, Mental, Moral and Natural Philosophy. The study of Modern Languages is optional.

Besides the CLASSICAL, there is a PREPARATORY DEPARTMENT for the younger students, in which however, none are admitted who have not attained some proficiency in reading, writing and spelling. Its object is to qualify the pupils for the higher studies.

This Institution, provided with a full staff of Professors, presents considerable advantages for the mental and moral training of the students.

A COMPLETE PHILOSOPHICAL APPARATUS

HAS BEEN RECEIVED FROM PARIS.

The Laboratory contains over Two Hundred and Fifty Pure Chemicals, and all that is necessary for the most complicated manipulations and analysis.

THE COLLEGE HAS, MOREOVER, A COMPLETE PHOTOGRAPHIC GALLERY.

A Telegraphic Apparatus has also been provided, which, through the kindness of the California State Telegraph Company, connects St. Ignatius' College with Santa Clara College, Santa Clara County.

TERMS, PER MONTH.

Tuition in the Grammar Department,............$5 00
    do   do   Higher Department,................. 8 00
    do   do   Preparatory Department,........ 3 00

Santa Clara College,

DIRECTED BY, THE FATHERS OF THE SOCIETY OF JESUS.

FOUNDED IN 1851. - - - - - - INCORPORATED IN 1855.

WITH A FULL STAFF,

TWENTY-TWO PROFESSORS AND TUTORS,

AND A

THOROUGH SYSTEM OF INSTRUCTION

IN

Latin,	Mathematics,	History,
Greek,	Natural Sciences,	Geography,
English,	Arithmetic,	Use of the Globes,
Mental Philosophy,	Book-Keeping,	Penmanship.

FRENCH, SPANISH, ITALIAN, GERMAN,

Vocal and Instrumental Music,

AND DRAWING,

DIVIDED INTO TWO REGULAR COURSES:

CLASSICAL AND COMMERCIAL:

BESIDES A

PREPARATORY DEPARTMENT.

TERMS:

Board and Lodging, Tuition in either Classical or Commercial Department, Washing and Mending, Stationery, Medical attendance and Medicines; fuel, baths, per week,...................$8.00

Total per Session, of ten months, $350, payable half yearly in advance.

N. B.—If more than two brothers enter the College, each additional one pays only $200 per Session.

The Fifteenth Annual Session begins August 28th, 1865.

For further information, or for Catalogue of the College, apply to Rev. A. Masnata, President of Santa Clara College, Santa Clara County, or to Rev. A. Maraschi, St. Ignatius' College, Market Street, San Francisco.

B

UNION COLLEGE.

R. TOWNSEND HUDDART, Principal.

JUNCTION OF SECOND AND BRYANT STS.

SAN FRANCISCO.

This Institution has been enlarged during the past year, by the erection of a

SPACIOUS HALL AND RECITATION ROOMS,

Which have been provided with the best kind of PHILOSOPHICAL APPARATUS—with all those modern improvements that tend to facilitate the

PROGRESS OF EDUCATION,

As well as to promote the

HEALTH AND COMFORT OF PUPILS.

THE BUILDINGS ARE COMMODIOUS, THE DORMITORIES LOFTY AND WELL VENTILATED,

And the whole Establishment is provided with every suitable accommodation.

THE GROUNDS FOR EXERCISE AND RECREATION

Occupy a 100-Vara Lot in one of the most desirable parts of the City, near South Park.

DR. HUDDART is assisted by

EFFICIENT INSTRUCTORS

Who co-operate with him in constant supervision over the Education of those intrusted to his care.

THE MODERN LANGUAGES—FRENCH, SPANISH AND GERMAN,

Together with the accomplishments of

MUSIC, PAINTING, DRAWING AND DANCING

Are under the charge of

WELL QUALIFIED TEACHERS.

A Prospectus containing full information can be obtained on application at the College, or at the Bookstores of A. ROMAN & CO. and C. BEACH, Montgomery St.

CALIFORNIA

Insurance Company.

CAPITAL, - - - - - $300,000

Insure against Loss or Damage by Fire, Brick and Frame Buildings, Merchandise, Dwellings, Furniture, and other Insurable property in the State of California, as LOW AS ANY OTHER SOLVENT COMPANY.

ALL LOSSES PAID IN UNITED STATES GOLD COIN.

DIRECTORS:

John Parrott,	J. H. Redington,	R. G. Sneath,	A. H. Titcomb,
Leopold Cahn,	C. J. Deering,	C. F. McDermot,	J. B. Roberts,
E. Baugh,	A. B. McCreery,	J. C. Wilmerding,	F. J. Thibault,
Thomas H. Selby,	C. Duisenberg,	Levi Stevens,	S. Hemenway,
Coghill,	C. J. Janson,	Elias H. Jones,	G. H. Eggers, A. B'I
CK,	Charles Hosmer,	Hall McAllister,	D. Callaghan,
RKER,	J. G. Parker, Jr.,	Albert Miller,	Alex. R. Baldwin.
	H. Heynemann,	B. F. Lowe.	

—224 and 226 California Street.

RKER, Jr., TH BENJ. F. LOWE, agent

Secretary.   President.

PACIFIC
Insurance Company,
436 CALIFORNIA STREET,
SAN FRANCISCO,

Insure against loss or damage by Fire, on Buildings, Merchandise, Wares, and other Personal Property.

CASH CAPITAL, - - - - - - - $750,000.

ASSETS, September 30th, 1865, - - - $1,011,900.65.

ALL LOSSES PAYABLE IN UNITED STATES GOLD COIN.

The Personal Liability of Stockholders, under the law of this State, recognized.

The following List of Directors is a sufficient guarantee of the stability and responsibility of the Company:

Louis McLane,	Wm. Scholle,	Charles Mayne,
W. C. Ralston,	Edward Martin,	Moses Heller,
James Lees,	D. J. Oliver,	G. T. Lawton,
Lloyd Tevis,	Wm. Alvord,	Adam Grant,
Oliver Eldridge,	T. L. Barker,	Morton Cheesman,
Jonathan Hunt,	A. B. Forbes,	G. W. Mowe,
Alpheus Bull,	L. Sachs,	Sacramento:
James DeFremery,	A. G. Stiles,	Edgar Mills,
John Wightman,	Frederick Billings,	Sacramento:
D. O. Mills,	J. G. Kellogg,	C. T. Wheeler,
A. Seligman,	S. J. Hensley,	Sacramento:
A. L. Tubbs,	Geo. H. Howard,	T. R. Anthony,
Charles Meyer,	J. Whitney, Jr.,	Stockton:
Wm. Hooper,	E. L. Goldstein,	J. H. Jewett,
P. L. Weaver,	Moses Ellis,	Marysville:
L. B. Benchley,	Wm. T. Coleman,	D. W. C. Rice,
Wm. Sherman,	John O. Earl,	Marysville:
J. G. Bray,	A. Hayward,	J. C. Ainsworth,
J. B. Newton,	S. M. Wilson,	Portland, O.
S. Steinhart,	H. Hanssmann,	W. S. Ladd,
D. Stern,	G. W. Beaver,	Portland, O.
H. M. Newhall,	Elie Lazard,	William Sharon,
Alfred Borel,	E. W. Leonard,	Virginia, Nevada.

J. HUNT, President.

A. J. RALSTON, Secretary.

NOTE.---This Company added Marine Insurance to its business August 1st, 1865, and now issues Policies on Marine, Inland Navigation and Fire Risks.

The Bank of British Columbia

INCORPORATED BY ROYAL CHARTER.

PAID UP CAPITAL, - - - $1,250,000

In 12,500 Shares, of $100 Each.

WITH POWER TO INCREASE TO $10,000,000.

LONDON OFFICE, 80 LOMBARD STREET.

CHAIRMAN.

T. W. L. MACKEAN, Esq., London, (late of the firm of Turner & Co., China.)

DEPUTY CHAIRMAN.

ROBERT GILLESPIE, Esq., (Messrs. Gillespie, Moffatt & Co., London.)

COURT OF DIRECTORS IN LONDON.

JAS. ANDERSON, Esq., (Messrs. Anderson, Thomson & Co., London.),
JAMES BONAR, Esq., (Messrs. Small & Co., London.)
EDEN COLVILLE, Esq., Fenchurch Buildings, London.
LEWIS FRASER, Esq., (of J. & L. Fraser & Co., London, and of Maclaine,
    Fraser & Co., Singapore.)
DUNCAN JAMES KAY, Esq., (Messrs. Kay, Finlay & Co., London.)
ALEX. MACKENZIE, Esq., (Director of the Oriental Bank, etc., London.)
HENRY McCHLERY, Esq., (Messrs. Cavan, Lubbock & Co., London.)
MARTIN RIDLEY SMITH, Esq., 1 Lombard Street, London, (of Messrs.
    Smith, Payne & Smiths, Bankers.)

BRANCHES:

PORTLAND OREGON, VANCOUVER ISLAND AND BRITISH COLUMBIA.

AGENTS:

New York,.............................AGENCY BANK OF MONTREAL.
Canada and British North American Provinces........BANK OF MONTREAL.
Mexico and South America,..LONDON BANK OF MEXICO & SOUTH AMERICA.
Australia and the East,.....................ORIENTAL BANK CORPORATION.
England,..........................NATIONAL PROVINCIAL BANK OF ENGLAND.
England,.......NORTH AND SOUTH WALES BANK OF LIVERPOOL.
Scotland,.............................BRITISH LINEN COMPANY'S BANK.
Ireland,..UNION BANK OF IRELAND.

This Bank is now open for Business, and is prepared to receive Deposits on Current Account
or on time: to buy and sell Exchange and Bullion: collect Bills: discount Approved Paper:
make advances on good Collateral Securities: grant Credits, and transact a general Banking Business.

SAN FRANCISCO OFFICE, 412 CALIFORNIA ST.

JAMES D. WALKER, Manager.

WM. H. TILLINGHAST, Sub-Manager.

TRAVELERS'
INSURANCE COMPANY

HARTFORD, CONN.

CAPITAL, - - - $500,000.

INSURES AGAINST
ACCIDENTS
OF
EVERY DESCRIPTION.

*The distinctive object and purpose of Accidental Assur-*ance is simply this:—to insure against ALL KINDS OF ACCIDENTS, whether resulting fatally or merely involving disabling personal injury, such as all forms of dislocations, broken bones, ruptured tendons, sprains, concussions, crushings, bruises, cuts, stabs, tears, gunshot wounds, poisoned wounds, burns and scalds, frost bites, bites of mad dogs or serpents, unprovoked assault by burglars, robbers, murderers, etc., the action of lightning or sun-stroke, the effects of explosions, chemicals, floods and earthquakes, suffocation by drowning or choking, *when such accidental injury is the cause of death to the insured, or of disability to follow his usual avocations.*

Agents in all Principal Towns and Cities.

BRANCH OFFICE, SAN FRANCISCO.

Agents appointed, Losses paid, Collections made, Correspondence promptly attended to, and the business of the Pacific States, under the immediate supervision of

R. H. MAGILL, General Agent.

Information furnished applicants, and Policies issued and renewed with promptness and despatch by

L. B. DELL, Resident Agent,

OFFICE—South-west corner of Montgomery and Commercial Streets,
WITH THE "PHŒNIX OF HARTFORD."

c

Savings and Loan Society.

Incorporated, July 23d, 1857.

OFFICE:

No. 619 CLAY STREET,

BETWEEN MONTGOMERY AND KEARNY STREETS.

OFFICERS:

"The only Exclusive House on this Coast!"

J. H. A. FOLKERS,

Sole Agent for GEO. TIEMANN & CO., New York,

Surgical and Dental Instruments,

TRUSSES, ETC.

Direct Importer of

DENTISTS' MATERIALS

Porcelain Teeth, etc., etc.

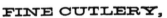

FINE CUTLERY,

London Elastic Stockings, Catheters, Bougies, etc.

218 MONTGOMERY ST.

Opposite the Russ House,   SAN FRANCISCO.

☞ Trusses and Bandages fitted and Warranted. Apparatus for all kinds of deformities made to order.☜

INSTRUMENTS REPAIRED.   GRINDING AND POLISHING DONE.

C. WATERHOUSE, San Francisco. J. W. LESTER, New York.

WATERHOUSE & LESTER,

Importers of

Hard Wood Lumber,

AND ALL KINDS OF

Carriage and Wagon Materials,

Nos. 29 and 31 BATTERY STREET,

SAN FRANCISCO.

17 and 19 Seventh Street, between I and J,

SACRAMENTO.

M. LANZENBERG, Paris. JOHN HAHN, San Francisco.

M. LANZENBERG & CO.

IMPORTERS AND DEALERS IN

French, English and German

BROADCLOTHS, CASSIMERES,

Vestings, Billiard Cloths, Tailors' Trimmings,

French Hats, Plushes, Hat and Cap Trimmings,

No. 628 CLAY STREET, and 633 MERCHANT STREET,

SAN FRANCISCO.

COUNTRY ORDERS PROMPTLY ATTENDED TO.

JOHN C. BELL,

UPHOLSTERY, CARPET

PAPER, OIL CLOTH AND WINDOW SHADE

WAREHOUSE,

American Flags and Regimental Banners constantly on hand and Made to Order.

REMOVED FROM CLAY STREET TO

Cor. Sansom and California Streets, opposite New Bank of California,

SAN FRANCISCO.

NILE & KOLLMYER,

IMPORTERS AND MANUFACTURERS OF

LOOKING GLASS,

PORTRAIT

AND

PICTURE FRAMES

OF EVERY DESCRIPTION,

312 BUSH STREET, RUSS HOUSE BLOCK,

SAN FRANCISCO.

OIL PAINTINGS CLEANED & VARNISHED. OLD FRAMES RE-GILT.

ORDERS PUNCTUALLY ATTENDED TO.

LOCKE & MONTAGUE,

IMPORTERS OF

STOVES, METALS, HOLLOW WARE,

Tinmen's Stock, Tools and Machines,

PLUMBERS' GOODS AND HOUSE-FURNISHING HARDWARE,

ALSO, THE CELEBRATED

DIAMOND ROCK COOKING STOVE,

Now conceded to be the Handsomest, Best Baking, and most Economical Stove ever brought to this market.

Nos. 112 AND 114 BATTERY STREET.

JOHN WINTER,

(ESTABLISHED 1852.)

No. 208 California Street, between Front and Battery,

SAN FRANCISCO, CAL.

MATERIALS FOR BREWERS,

SODA MANUFACTURERS AND TANNERS.

ALSO, CORKS AND CHOICE HOPS, IN BALES AND HALF BALES,

And Agent South Park Malt House.

Orders from any part of the State promptly attended to. Prices given, and samples sent if desired, per return Express Refers to principal Druggists, Brewers, &c., throughout the State.

J. G. KELLOGG.   J. HEWSTON, Jr.   J. H. STEARNS.

KELLOGG, HEWSTON & CO.
ASSAY OFFICE, REFINERY,
AND
CHEMICAL LABORATORY,
416 Montgomery Street, San Francisco.

Deposits for UNREFINED GOLD BARS will be returned in twenty-four hours. The charge will be one-quarter of one per cent. for all amounts over $1,200, and three dollars for any smaller amount. For Silver Bars one per cent. on the value of the Silver, and one-quarter of one per cent. on the value of the Gold contained. No charge being less than three dollars.

Charges of Refining per ounce, gross weight, after melting :

For Bullion under..............300 parts Gold........3 cents.	For Bullion from........501 to 750 parts Gold........7 cents.
For Bullion from........301 to 500 parts Gold.....….5 cents.	For Bullion over....,................parts Gold.......10 cents.

For Bars of our own manufacture, a deduction from the above tariff is allowed, making the Refining charge as follows :

Under 300 fine, 2½ cents per ounce.	Over 750 fine, 8 cents per ounce.
301 to 500 fine, 4 cents per ounce.	No charge for refining less than three dollars.
501 to 750 fine, 5½ cents per ounce.	

Deposits for COINAGE will be refined by us immediately, and deposited in the United States Branch Mint, and returns made to depositors on the same day the returns are made to us. The charge for Coin will be one-half of one per cent., being the same as charged by the United States Branch Mint.

SILVER contained in the deposit will be accounted for to the Depositor, in the manner and at the rate customary at the Mint.

If required, returns will be made in REFINED BARS in four days, at a charge of one-sixteenth of one per cent. on the value of all Gold Bars over $5,000, and one-eighth of one per cent. on all under that amount, and one-half of one per cent. on the value of Silver Bars. No deposit of Gold less than twenty-five ounces, or of Silver less than two hundred ounces, will be returned in Refined Bars.

Analyses of Ores, Minerals, Metals, Soils, Waters, and the Productions of Art,
WILL BE CAREFULLY EXECUTED.
Refer to all the Banks and Gold Dust Dealers in California.

THE BANK OF CALIFORNIA

Incorporated under the Laws of the State.

CAPITAL STOCK, $2,000,000,

(PAID UP IN GOLD COIN)

With the Privilege of increasing to

$5,000,000.

STOCKHOLDERS.

SAN FRANCISCO.

D. O. MILLS,	THOS. BELL,	HERMAN MICHELS,
WM. C. RALSTON,	JNO. O. EARL,	GEORGE H. HOWARD,
R. S. FRETZ,	WM. NORRIS,	H. F. TESCHEMACHER,
J. B. THOMAS,	J. WHITNEY, JR.,	A. HAYWARD,
LOUIS McLANE,	O. F. GIFFIN,	MOSES ELLIS,
ASA T. LAWTON,	A. J. POPE,	H. W. CARPENTIER,
WM. E. BARRON,	JOSEPH BARRON,	WM. ALVORD,
A. B. McCREERY,	A. C. HENRY,	ALPHEUS BULL.
R. M. JESSUP,	J. C. WILMERDING,	P. L. WEAVER.
SAMUEL KNIGHT,		

PORTLAND, OREGON.

JACOB KAMM.

D. O. MILLS, President.   WM. C. RALSTON, Cashier.

Correspondents in New York, LEES & WALLER, No. 33 Pine St.
In London, ORIENTAL BANK CORPORATION.

This institution is prepared to transact a General Banking, Exchange, and Bullion Business in all its branches, and the immediate management of its affairs is committed exclusively to the President and Cashier, to whom, or either of them, the customers of the Bank will apply in all business matters. The regular meeting of the Board of Trustees takes place on the SECOND TUESDAY in each month.

A Branch of this Bank has been established in Virginia City, Nevada, and will take charge of Collections, and attend to any other business in the Banking line.

OFFICE, S. W. CORNER WASHINGTON AND BATTERY STS.

SPRING VALLEY

WATER WORKS

COMPANY.

Incorporated under Act of the Legislature, April 8, 1858.

CAPITAL STOCK, - - - - - - - $6,000,000,

DIVIDED INTO 60,000 SHARES OF $100 EACH.

MAIN RESERVOIR,

LAGUNA HONDA,

Capacity, 16,000,000 Gallons.

Francisco Street Reservoir, Capacity........8,000,000 gallons.
Russian Hill, " " ....*4,000,000* "
Buchanan Street " " ....*1,750,000* "
Brannan Street " " .... *500,000* "

Dam—Pillarcitos Creek, Capacity, - 865,000,000 Gallons.

OFFICERS:

President..W. F. BABCOCK
Vice-President..WM. T. COLEMAN
Superintendent..CALVIN BROWN
Secretary..HENRY WATTSON

TRUSTEES:

LLOYD TEVIS,	W. F. BABCOCK,
CHARLES MAYNE,	N. LUNING,
S. C. BIGELOW,	H. S. DEXTER,

JOHN PARROTT.

OFFICE OF THE COMPANY,

S. E. CORNER OF MONTGOMERY AND JACKSON STS.

JOHN TAYLOR,

IMPORTER AND DEALER IN

DRUGGISTS' AND CHEMISTS' GLASSWARE,

Assayers' Articles, Corks, Twines, Etc.

512 & 514 WASHINGTON ST.,   SAN FRANCISCO.

A FULL ASSORTMENT OF

Crucibles, Furnaces, Muffles, Cupels, Test Tubes; also, Soda Stock, Labels,
PHOTOGRAPHIC MATERIALS, ETC., ETC.

E. T. PEASE.   CHAS. H. GRIMM.

PEASE & GRIMM,

Stock Brokers,

NO. 709 MONTGOMERY STREET,

SAN FRANCISCO.

A. S. LOWNDES,

WINE MERCHANT,

DEALER IN ALL DESCRIPTIONS OF

CALIFORNIA WINES.

AGENT FOR THE

BOSQUEJO VINEYARD, TEHAMA COUNTY, CAL.

311 1-2 BATTERY STREET, CORNER COMMERCIAL
SAN FRANCISCO.

J. & C. SCHREIBER,

DEALERS IN

BEDDING AND FURNITURE,

IMPORTERS OF

PULU, CURLED HAIR, TOW AND MOSS,

BED LACE, SPRINGS, TWINE, ETC.

Sole Manufacturers of FULLER'S PATENT SPRING BED; The
Best in Use; TRY ONE.

406 SANSOM STREET,

SAN FRANCISCO.

UNION IRON WORKS.

HENRY J. BOOTH.   GEO. W. PRESCOTT.   IRVING M. SCOTT.

H. J. BOOTH & CO.,

MANUFACTURERS OF

Locomotives, Marine and Stationary Engines,

FLUE, TUBULAR, CORNISH, AND MARINE BOILERS.

HOISTING MACHINES.

Pumps and Pumping Machinery,

QUARTZ MILLS.

ALL KINDS OF

Stamps and Mortars, Amalgamating Pans and Separators, of the most
Improved Patterns.

ALL KINDS OF SCREENS.

Sole Manufacturers of BLAKE'S QUARTZ CRUSHERS.

Patterns and Pattern Making of all kinds carried on.

OIL MACHINERY OF MOST IMPROVED KINDS.

PLANS and SPECIFICATIONS for Mills and all kinds of Machinery furnished
free of cost.   **H. J. Booth & Co.**

First Street, between Market and Mission, San Francisco.

E

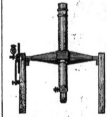

J. C. MERRILL & CO.

COMMISSION MERCHANTS

AND

AUCTIONEERS

AGENTS OF THE

REGULAR DISPATCH LINE OF HONOLULU PACKETS.

PARTICULAR ATTENTION PAID TO

Forwarding and Transhipment of Merchandise, Sale of Whalemen's Bills and other Exchange, Insurance of Merchandise and Specie under Open Policies, Supplying Whale Ships, Chartering Ships, Etc.

Nos. 204 and 206 CALIFORNIA STREET,

SAN FRANCISCO.

Germania Life Insurance Co.

90 BROADWAY, NEW YORK.

ISSUES POLICIES PAYABLE IN U. S. GOLD COIN.

HUGO WESENDONCK, - - - - - - - - President.
FRIEDR. SCHWENDLER, - Vice-President and Act'g Sec'y.

BOARD OF REFERENCE FOR CALIFORNIA.

JOSEPH A. DONOHOE, Esq.
    Of Messrs. Donohoe, Kelly & Co.
C. F. MEBIUS, Esq.
    Consul for Bavaria.
J. W. BRITTAN, Esq.
    Of Messrs. J. W. Brittan & Co.
GUSTAVUS MAHE,
    Director French Savings and Loan Soc'ty.

WM. C. RALSTON, Esq.
    Cashier Bank of California.
ELIE LAZARD, Esq.
    Of Messrs. Lazard Fréres.
EDWARD VISCHER, Esq.
    Consulate of Austria.
HENRY SELIGMAN, Esq.
    Of Messrs. J. Seligman & Co.

General Agent for California and the Pacific Coast,

BERNHARD GATTEL,

No. 510 Montgomery Street,

SAN FRANCISCO.

CITIZENS'
GAS COMPANY

ORGANIZED, 1862.

CAPITAL STOCK, - - $2,000,000

SHARES, - - - - - $100 EACH

This Company has erected extensive works at the junction of Second and Townsend Streets, which are now fully completed. Pipes have been laid through Third, Market and Montgomery Streets, and will be continued through the various streets and thoroughfares contiguous. The operations of this Company will tend to decrease the price of Gas, which, at present rates, is beyond the reach of many.

PRESIDENT,

A. C. WHITCOMB.

SECRETARY,

SAMUEL I. C. SWEZEY.

OFFICE OF THE COMPANY,

No. 702 Washington Street,

CORNER, KEARNY.

UNION

INSURANCE COMPANY

OF SAN FRANCISCO.

Nos. 416 and 418 California Street.

INDIVIDUAL LIABILITY.

CAPITAL STOCK, - - - $750,000.

LOSSES PAID-IN UNITED STATES GOLD COIN.

THIS COMPANY INSURES AGAINST

LOSS OR DAMAGE BY FIRE

*Brick and Frame Buildings, Merchandise, Furniture,
Vessels and their Cargoes while in port, and
other insurable property.*

DIRECTORS:

J. Mora Moss,	C. Christiansen,	J. Underhill,
James Otis,	Joseph Seller,	M. D. Sweeny,
Wm. E. Barron,	L. H Allen,	Moses Ellis,
J. G. Kittle,	Alfred Borel,	James Phelan,
Jos. A. Donohoe,	C. Temple Emmet,	Gustave Touchard,
Jas. C. Conroy,	J. Y. Hallock,	Michael Castle,
P. H. Burnett,	Benjamin Brewster,	Nicholas Larco,
Moses Heller,	Jas. B. Haggin,	N. G. Kittle,
Lafayette Maynard,	Thos. H. Selby,	Wm. C. Talbot,
Chas. L. Low,	Nicholas Luning,	Patrick McAran,
Jacob Scholle,	John Parrott,	Geo. C. Johnson,
	Caleb T. Fay,	
L. Cunningham, } Marysville. William Smith, }		B. F. Hastings, Sacramento.

CHARLES D. HAVEN,
Secretary.

CALEB T. FAY,
President.

F

WM. H. KEITH & CO.

Chemists and Apothecaries,

NO. 521 MONTGOMERY STREET,

Between Clay and Commercial,

Especial attention given to the Compounding of Physicians' Prescriptions, and preparation of Family Medicines. Importers of First Quality of MEDICINES, Chemicals, Surgical and Dental Instruments, Toilet Articles, Perfumery, and Brushes. The Genuine Farina Cologne, Lubin's Extracts, Low's Old Brown Windsor Soap, etc.

☞ Agents for the sale of Mrs. I. J. HOWARD'S Abdominal and Uterine Supporters, which received the FIRST PREMIUM at the LAST MECHANIC'S FAIR.

MANUFACTURERS OF

Wm. H. Keith & Co's Wine of PEPSINE, or Rennet Wine.
A new and efficacious remedy for Dyspepsia, Gastralgia, etc.

Wm. H. Keith & Co's GLUCOLEIN, a new and valuable compound of Cod Liver Oil, put up in glass jars

WM. H. KEITH & CO'S LEMON APERIENT, OR PURGATIVE LEMONADE.
An agreeable, cooling, and active purgative, or mild laxative, as required.

WM. H. KEITH & CO'S SAPONACEOUS TOOTH POWDER.

DEVINE'S PITCH LOZENGES, for the cure of Coughs and Colds.

WM. H. KEITH & CO'S FLORENTINE TOOTH WASH.

Wm. H. Keith & Co's Granular Effervescent Citrate of Magnesia.

WM. H. KEITH & CO'S ROSEMARY AND CASTOR OIL HAIR INVIGORATOR.

Physicians and others, at a distance, ordering goods from us, can depend upon having their orders filled with the same regard to QUALITY and PRICE, as though obtained in person, and we feel confident of giving satisfaction in every case.

SAN FRANCISCO

Stock and Exchange Board.

Rooms N. W. Cor. Montgomery and Washington Streets.

J. B. E. CAVALLIER, President. C. H. GRIMM, Vice President.
FRANKLIN LAWTON, Secretary. HENRY SCHMIEDELL, Treas'r.

MEMBERS.

Adsit, L. B.
Arrington, N. O.
Boilleau, F.
Bradford, C. H.
Brown, L. A.
Bates, Joseph.
Brewster, R. E.
Budd, W. C.
Burling, W.
Child, E. F.
Coursen, G. A.
Critcher, Henry.
Cumming, John.
Cavallier, J. B. E.
Cheeseman, M.
Constantin, J.
Cornwall, P. B.
Darnell, H. Y.
Dewey, E.
Duncan, W. L.
Ehrlich, M.
Elliot, R.
Fitch, J. R.
Freeborn, J.
Felton, C. N.
Gildemeester, A.
Grimm, C. H.
Higgins, Wm. L.
Hill, Thomas.
Hinchman, T. W.
Holt, Z.
Holt, T. H.
Hassey, F. A.
Heath, R. W.
Henriques, David.
Hillyer, M. C.
Hulbert, Thomas F.
Hyman, P. C.
Jenkins, J. S.
Kensey, A. G.
Kunast, A.
Lissak, A. H.
Logan, H. C.
Loveland, L. F.
Lawton, Franklin.
Lent, W. M.
Marina, E. J. de Sta.
Mayer, Simon.
McKenty, J.
Murdock, A. H.
McElwaine, J.
McDonald, M. L.
Mills, S. B.
Pease, E. T.
Peckham, E. P.
Paterson, J.
Page, Robert C.
Rising, D. B.
Roberts, D. S.
Reeve, G. B.
Robbins, J. J.
Schmitt, B. L.
Sparrow, S. J.
Sanborn, T. C.
Schmiedell, Henry.
Shipley, A. J.
Sloss, L.
Smiley, James.
Teackle, E. W.
Tilden, J.
Vinzent, C.
Washburn, E. H.
Whitney, A. W.
Winans, J. C.
Woods, F. H.
Williams, H.

AUTHORIZED SCALE OF COMMISSIONS, ADOPTED JULY 7, 1865.

Miscellaneous.

Legal Tender Notes, on par	¼ per cent.	Steamboat Company Stocks, on par	½ per cent.
Funded Debt, on par	½ per cent.	Telegraph Company Stocks, on par	½ per cent.
Insurance Stock, on par	½ per cent.	Water Company Stocks, on par	½ per cent.
Wharf Stocks, on par	½ per cent.	Bills of Exchange, on net amount	½ per cent.
Gas Stocks, on par	½ per cent.	Mint Certificate, on net amount	½ per cent.
Railroad Stocks, on par	½ per cent.	Specie, on net amount	½ per cent.

Commissions on Mining Shares.

Sale at 1 dollar up to 10 dollars	$ 25 per foot or per share as sold.
Sale at 10 dollars up to 25 dollars	50 per foot or per share as sold.
Sale at 25 dollars up to 50 dollars	1 00 per foot or per share as sold.
Sale at 50 dollars up to 100 dollars	1 50 per foot or per share as sold.
Sale at 100 dollars up to 200 dollars	2 00 per foot or per share as sold.

All over 200 dollars per foot or share, one per cent. on the amount of purchase or sale.

ARTICLE XXXV, OF THE BY-LAWS.

PENALTY FOR DOING BUSINESS FOR LESS THAN REGULAR COMMISSIONS.

Any member doing business for less than the above rates shall, on due conviction, be expelled from the Board.

All Excise Taxes upon the sale of Stocks shall be paid by the Broker.

It is hereby fully and distinctly understood, that the commissions hereafter to be charged shall be upon all purchases and upon all sales, and that the full amount shall be charged and no less sum received, except the principal or customer shall be a Broker belonging to some organized Board of Stock Brokers, with whom a division of commission shall be allowed.

J. B. E. CAVALLIER, President.

FRANKLIN LAWTON, Secretary.

CALIFORNIA LLOYDS.

MARINE INSURANCE.

OFFICE, 418 CALIFORNIA ST.

The Insurers underwriting at the California Lloyds issue

MARINE INSURANCE POLICIES

AGAINST ALL RISKS, ON LIBERAL TERMS.

LOSSES PAYABLE IN UNITED STATES GOLD COIN,

—AND—

PROMPTLY ADJUSTED.

JOHN PARROTT, of Parrott & Co., Bankers.
GEO. C. JOHNSON, of Geo. C. Johnson & Co., Importers.
N. LUNING, of N. Luning & Co., Bankers.
JAMES PHELAN, Capitalist and Importer.
LAFAYETTE MAYNARD, Capitalist.
J. A. DONOHOE, of Donohoe, Kelly & Co., Bankers.
C. L. LOW, Capitalist.
WM. E. BARRON, of Barron & Co., Bankers.
JAMES OTIS, of Macondray & Co., Merchants.
J. MORA MOSS, Capitalist.
J. G. KITTLE, of DeWitt, Kittle & Co., Importers.
THOS. H. SELBY, of Thos. H. Selby & Co., Importers.
J. Y. HALLOCK, of J. Y. Hallock & Co., Importers.

GVE. TOUCHARD,

Secretary.

THE CITY COLLEGE

OF

SAN FRANCISCO.

This Institution is situated at the Corner of

STOCKTON AND GEARY STREETS, OPPOSITE UNION SQUARE,

In the central part of the City. · It furnishes the best facilities for acquiring · · a thorough

ENGLISH, MATHEMATICAL,

COMMERCIAL,

AND

CLASSICAL EDUCATION.

The Course of Studies is the same pursued in the best Colleges.

THE SCIENTIFIC COURSE

Has been adopted with special reference to the wants of California. PROFESSOR PRICE, besides his lectures and instruction in the College, has a Laboratory in the city in which classes are taken through a thorough practical course of.

ASSAYING AND CHEMISTRY,

With special reference to Metallurgy and Mining.- · · · ·

Measures have been taken for the immediate erection of. a Laboratory on the College Premises.

AN ENGLISH EDUCATION

Receives particular and thorough attention. Patient, laborious drilling is the leading feature in the instruction, from the Elementary Classes through all the higher studies.

BOOK-KEEPING is taught with care, and a room is kept for this purpose, fitted up with the fixtures of a complete counting-house.

Nine Instructors are constantly employed, and one hundred and fifty Students are in attendance in the different departments.

On the spacious lot adjoining the College is a fine Gymnasium for the use of the Students.

There is a valuable Philosophical and Chemical Apparatus, in a large hall, kept exclusively for Lectures and Experiments, to which the Students have access. · · · · ·

, For terms and further particulars, address

REV. P. V. VEEDER, -

Principal of the San Francisco City College.

HAYES' PARK,

PAVILION AND GARDEN,

LAGUNA, HAYES, AND GROVE STREETS,

HAYES' VALLEY.

The above Elegant Place of

PUBLIC AMUSEMENT

AND

SUBURBAN RESORT,

Is easily approached by private conveyances, and the cars of the Market Street, and Hayes' Valley Railroad. For those who desire pleasant

Recreation and Healthy Exercise,

The above PAVILION and CONCERT HALL was built, and the spacious

GARDEN

Laid out. All the modern improvements, with apparatus found in a

GYMNASIUM,

Together with a fine

SHOOTING GALLERY,

BILLIARD ROOM, Reception Parlor, Dressing Rooms, etc. Also,

A LARGE AND COMMODIOUS REFRESHMENT SALOON.

One of the features of this Pavilion is a

PROMENADE GALLERY,

Three hundred and twenty feet in length, running round the Concert Hall.

☞ Business communications may be made to

THOMAS HAYES,
PROPRIETOR.

G

SAN FRANCISCO
FIRE

432

MONTGOMERY STREET

S. E. cor. Sacramento.

Donohoe, Kelly

& Co's

Bank Building.

INSURANCE COMPANY

INCORPORATED MARCH, 1861.

OFFICERS:

G. C. BOARDMAN, President.   P. McSHANE, Secretary,

C. D. O. SULLIVAN, Vice President.   E. BIGELOW, Solicitor.

OLDEST LOCAL FIRE INSURANCE COMPANY IN CALIFORNIA.

PERSONAL LIABILITY.

DIRECTORS:

E. W. BURR, (619 Clay Street.)
LUCIUS A. BOOTH, (of Booth & Co., Sacram'to.)
C. D. O. SULLIVAN, (of Sullivan & Cashman.)
HENRY H. HAIGHT, (Attorney at Law.)
WM. BOSWORTH, (Merchant.)
J. DE LA MONTANYA, (Importer Metals & Stoves.)
JOSEPH G. EASTLAND, (Sec. S. F. Gas Co.)
OSCAR L. SHAFTER, (Judge Supreme Court.)
J. ARCHBALD, (Sec. S. F. Savings Union.)
R. B. WOODWARD, (What Cheer House.)
E. F. NORTHAM, (Real Estate, 619 Clay Street.)

GEO. J. BROOKS, (of Geo. J. Brooks & Co.)
JOHN VAN BERGEN, (Merchant, 524 Wash'n St.)
BENJ. D. DEAN, (Physician, cor. Mont'y & Bush.)
GEO. C. BOARDMAN.
CHAS. MAYNE, (with Belloc Freres.)
GILES H. GRAY, (Attorney at Law.)
EDW'D HULL, (of Lindley, Hull & Lohman, Sac.)
E. F. HALL, Jr., (of Chas. W. Brooks & Co.)
J. H. RUTENBERG.
BENJ. BREWSTER, (of Jennings & Brewster.)

BOURS & CO.
BANKERS,
STOCKTON, CAL.

SIGHT DRAFTS on NEW YORK and the PRINCIPAL CITIES in CALIFORNIA.

RECEIVE DEPOSITS, GENERAL AND SPECIAL.

Make Collections throughout California and Nevada Territory,

——AND——

Transact a General Banking Business.

Agency of the Imperial Fire Insurance Company, of London.

REFER TO

Messrs. TALLANT & CO.   Messrs. FALKNER, BELL & CO.

SAN FRANCISCO.

BAEDER & ADAMSON,

Manufacturers of

GLUE, CURLED HAIR,

RAW HIDE WHIPS,

SAND AND EMERY PAPER,

Plasterers' and Saddlers' Hair,

67 BEEKMAN STREET, NEW YORK,

14 S. 4th Street, Philadelphia.

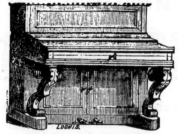

PROGRESS OF THE CITY.

THE *City* of San Francisco was, for the first time, incorporated by the Legislature in May, 1850, the organization of the *County* having been effected in the month previous, by the election of a Sheriff and other officers, thus establishing two distinct systems of government. The Consolidation Act took effect on the first day of July, 1856. Under its stringent provisions our municipal affairs have been administered with energy and fidelity, and a thorough reform has resulted. The enormous outlay consequent on the *dual* system of government has been entirely abolished or seriously reduced, while the checks upon lavish expenditure were so well devised as to defy evasion, and the contraction of debts has been inhibited. The financial history of all this is sufficiently indicated in the subjoined exhibit of the *Aggregate Annual Expenditures* of the City and County of San Francisco, from 1850 to 1865—since the first legislative organization of the government—*exclusive* of the sums paid in liquidation of the principal and interest of the bonded debts:

Assessment and Rates of Taxation from 1850 to 1866.

FISCAL YEARS.	Total Annual Rates.	PARTICULAR CLASS OF ASSESSMENTS.			Total Annual Assessments.
		Real Estate.	Improvements.	Person'l Prop'ty.	
1850–51	$2 00	$16,849,054	In Personal.	$4,772,160	$21,621,214
1851–52	4 10	11,141,463	In Personal.	2,875,440	14,016,903
1852–53	4 41¼	15,676,356	In Personal.	2,805,381	18,481,737
1853–54	3 88½	17,889,850	$6,158,300	4,852,000	28,900,150
1854–55	3 85¼	19,765,285	9,159,935	5,837,607	34,762,827
1855–56	3 85 5-6	18,607,800	8,394,925	5,073,847	32,076,572
1856–57	2 30	17,827,617	8,345,667	4,194,970	30,368,254
1857–58	2 30	15,576,545	7,394,296	12,426,335	35,397,176
1858–59	2 45	13,554,565	5,946,585	11,224,800	30,725,950
1859–60	3 16 9-10	14,172,235	6,523,985	9,323,002	30,019,222
1860–61	2 85	25,283,685	In Real.	10,683,814	35,967,499
1861–62	2 87	31,871,897	In Real.	9,973,222	41,845,119
1862–63	2 74¼	37,016,102	In Real.	29,540,554	66,556,656
1863–64	2 10	43,116,538	In Real.	34,002,027	77,119,165
1864–65	2 98	47,292,903	In Real.	33,443,262	80,736,165
1865–66	3 12	49,137,312	In Real.	39,129,145	88,266,457

The amount absolutely collected on is much less than the aggregate valuations for the last two years. In 1864–5 it was $19,123,450 personal against $35,850,572 assessed, and $43,575,583 real estate against $47,300,718 assessed, in all about $62,700,000 collected on against $83,151,000 assessed. There is about $3,750,000 exempt, $2,380,000 assessed in error, and $14,000,000 delinquent from various causes, among which the most prominent is the resistance to payment of taxes on mortgages.

Annual Municipal Expenditures, 1850 to 1865.

FISCAL YEARS.	CITY.	COUNTY.	TOTAL.
J–51.......................................	$1,694,459	$118,988	$1,813,447
.851–52.....................................	340,628	115,704	456,332
1852–53....................................	716,302	292,727	1,009,029
1853–54....................................	1,440,792	391,033	1,831,825
1854–55....................................	2,167,227	478,993	2,646,190
1855–56....................................	525,633	330,487	856,120
1856–57....................................			353,292
1857–58....................................	The Governments of the City		366,427
1858–59....................................	and County consolidated.		480,895
1859–60....................................	....		706,719
1860–61....................................			512,896
1861–62....................................			475,048
1862–63....................................			700,364
1863–64....................................			785,894
1864–65....................................			813,339
Total for fifteen years...			$13,807,817

Bonded Debt in 1865.

Issued in	By the	Payable in	ANNUAL INTEREST.		Annual Sinking Fund.	Bonds in Circulation.
			Per cent.	Payable in		
1851........	City......................	1871	10	San Francisco...	$50,000	$1,305,500
1854........	School Department......	1865	7	New York......	5,000	32,000
1854........	Fire Department	1866	10	New York......	16,666	174,500
1855........	City......................	1875	6	New York......	21,000	329,000
1858........	City and County	1888	6	San Francisco..	In 1867	1,133,500
1860........	School Department......	1870	10	New York......	5,000	55,500
1861........	School Department......	1870	10	New York......	2,500	18,000
1862–63.....	City and County for San José Railroad..........	1877–8	7	San Francisco...	In 1866	300,000
1863........	City and Co. for City Slip	1883	7	San Francisco...	49,000	968,386
1864........	City and County for San José Railroad..........	1884	7	San Francisco...	2,400	34,008
1864........	Central Pacific R. R. Co.	1894	7	San Francisco...	7,000	400,000
1865........	Western Pacific R. R. Co.	1895	7	San Francisco...	....	250,000
Total Bonds in circulation						$5,000,394

Annual Revenue.

The following is an exhibit of the receipts from State and City and County taxes, licenses, stamps, etc., collected in San Francisco during the fifteen fiscal years ending the thirtieth day of June, 1865:

FISCAL YEARS.	CITY AND COUNTY OF SAN FRANCISCO.				STATE OF CALIFORNIA.
	City Taxes.	County Taxes.	Municipal Licenses.	Total.	
1850–51...................	$163,013	$119,028	$59,591	$341,632	$132,359
1851–52...................	305,661	122,632	276,835	705,128	100,545
1852–53...................	397,033	313,217	328,039	1,038,289	127,682
1853–54...................	592,248	419,378	188,508	1,200,134	204,874
1854–55...................	582,732	389,620	103,784	1,076,136	249,589
1855–56...................	424,766	244,337	33,054	702,157	130,847
1856–57...................	290,846		59,927	350,773	191,311
1857–58...................	510,228	City and Co.	103,048	613,276	257,771
1858–59...................	554,203	governments	25,788	579,991	288,958
1859–60...................	761,711	consolidated.	23,681	785,392	322,935
1860–61...................	737,243	....	23,179	760,422	271,111
1861–62...................	856,087	....	29,167	885,254	303,526
1862–63...................	982,312	....	39,512	1,021,824	520,960
1863–64...................	902,535	....	23,189	925,724	685,712
1864–65...................	1,098,195	....	26,876	1,125,071	952,579

In addition to the above sources of revenue may be enumerated the receipts from fines, rents, harbor dues, and fees collected by the Sheriff, the County Clerk, the County Recorder, Auditor, Tax Collector, Treasurer, etc. The sums received from State and County licenses, and several other sources, are not included.

Population, 1861.*

Believing that the National Census of the City and County of San Francisco, completed during the year 1860, did not truly represent the number of our population, and at the urgent solicitation of numerous patrons of this work, the following exhibit has been carefully prepared from the returns of the different canvassers engaged in collecting information for the present volume. The plan adopted to obtain the necessary data was the same as that so successfully carried into effect in the months of April and May, 1859, the results of which were published in the San Francisco Directory of that year, as follows: "To arrange and classify each sex in three divisions, viz.: MALES: *First Class*—the head of each family, and members thereof over twenty-one years of age; *Second Class*—those between five and twenty-one; *Third Class*—those under five years of age. FEMALES: *First Class*—those over eighteen years of age; *Second Class*—those between five and eighteen; *Third Class*—those under five years of age. Also to collect such other information as would furnish an approximation of the different elements composing our population not included in the foregoing classifications:"

White males over 21 years, names in Register of the present volume (a)	27,100
" " " Residents floating, names not obtained (b)	3,400
" " " Average number boarders, etc., at the hotels, boarding-houses, etc., in addition to the regular boarders (c)	4,100
" " " In the Hospitals	481
" " " U. S. soldiers at the Forts (d)	800
" " " Engaged upon water crafts, ocean, bay, and river, claiming residence in this city (e)	2,500
" " " Foreigners, French, Spanish, etc., names not registered (f)	1,950
" " " Between 5 and 21	5,919
" " " Under 5	6,803
Total white males	53,053
Females over 18	14,783
" Names not registered	500
" Between 5 and 18	4,821
" Under 5	5,136
Total white females	25,240
Chinese males over 21	2,400
" Females over 18	520
" Males under 21 and females under 18	210
Total Chinese	3,130
Colored males over 21	800
" " Under 18	250
" Females over 18	600
" " Under 18	150
Total colored	1,800
Total population of the City and County of San Francisco	83,223

(a) The number of names in the Directory 1861-62 exceeds thirty thousand, of which nearly three thousand are composed of non-resident partners of firms doing business in this city, females, Chinese, and colored.
(b) This is from actual count, and is composed of a class of population who have no permanent place of abode.
(c) This estimate has been arrived at by careful investigation. Number of hotels and lodging-houses in the city, 340.
(d) The number at Fort Point, Alcatraces, and Presidio in June last.
(e) This number is composed of persons sailing from this port who have shipped from this city.
(f) This number has been obtained from actual enumeration.   *From the SAN FRANCISCO DIRECTORY, 1861-62.

National Census, 1860.

From the official returns deposited at the office of the County Clerk. Compiled expressly for the SAN FRANCISCO DIRECTORY, 1861–62.

WHITE MALES.		WHITE FEMALES.		CHINESE.	
Under 1 year	1,730	Under 1 year	1,563	Males of all ages	2,168
" 2 "	777	" 2 "	739	Females of all ages	448
" 3 "	730	" 3 "	677	Total Chinese	2,616
" 4 "	627	" 4 "	600		
" 5 "	645	" 5 "	551	COLORED.	
				Males of all ages	711
Total under 5	4,509	Total under 5	4,130	Females of all ages	435
Between 5 and 10	1,842	Between 5 and 10	1,831	Total colored	1,146
" 10 " 20	2,915	" 10 " 20	3,198		
" 20 " 30	10,184	" 20 " 30	6,226	RECAPITULATION.	
" 30 " 40	9,390	" 30 " 40	3,441	White males, all ages	32,463
" 40 " 50	2,581	" 40 " 50	1,119	White females, all ages	20,610
" 50 " 60	842	" 50 " 60	484		
" 60 " 70	162	" 60 " 70	122	Total whites	53,073
" 70 " 80	36	" 70 " 80	52	Chinese, male and female	2,616
" 80 " 90	2	" 80 " 90	7	Colored, male and female	1,146
Total white males	32,463	Total white females	20,610	Total pop. City and County	56,835

Population, August, 1865.

The following table, compiled from the most reliable data, is presented as an estimate of the population of San Francisco, August 1st, 1865, and in directing attention thereto, it is believed to be as fair an approximation as can be made without an official and accurate canvass:

White males over twenty-one, names in the present volume.......................................40,000
  " Females over eighteen, estimated 25,000
  " Males under twenty-one and females under eighteen, estimated 35,000
  " Males, names refused, and foreigners, estimated 5,000
Chinese, male and female 3,000
Colored, male and female 2,100

.... Total permanent population 110,100

To which should be added a large element of our population known as "floating," which consists of: 1st. Transient boarders, etc., at hotels, boarding-houses, etc. 2d. Soldiers at the fortifications in the harbor. 3d. Persons engaged in navigating the bay, who claim this city as their residence. 4th. A large number of persons in our midst who have no permanent place of abode, together amounting to about 9,000

Total population... 119,100

City Improvements.

During the past year the march of improvement in San Francisco, both within her city limits and its suburbs and adjacent tributary territory, has been onward beyond precedent. A greater number of elegant public and private structures have been erected, new and important manufactures introduced, and improvements of all kinds extended, than during any preceding year. Nothing can repress the energy or discourage the enterprise of our people. It would seem that there is something in the very atmosphere of California that infuses a degree of energy into the most apathetic system, and stimulates into action even the most listless and lethargic institutions. the idle dreamer and speculative theorist, has no business in our active and creative population.

Our capitalists are investing largely in real estate, both within the city limits and the contiguous country. The lands lying along the line of the San José Railroad are becoming a·popular field for investment. Parties who have amassed wealth from the richly-paying gold quartz mines of, California and the unrivaled silver mines of Nevada, regard real estate in San·Francisco as the safest and best paying investment of their surplus means, and steadily remunerating revenue. The prophetic simile of the seer of the Atlantic, uttered more than a century ago—

" Westward the course of empire wends its way "

—holds good in our city's extension, for the march of improvement is rapidly extending in that direction. Places that but a short time ago were regarded as a considerable distance out of town, are now regarded as part and parcel of the city. The conveniencies of travel afforded by the net-work of railroads traversing the city, and leading to every portion of its environs, readily accounts for this. The construction of the bridge, near a mile in length, across Mission Bay, beginning at the foot of Third Street and connecting with the Potrero at Kentucky Street, thus cutting off some miles of travel, has completely revolutionized the face of affairs in those portions of the city heretofore devoted to the active ship and steamboat building.

As before extending improvements in any direction, public thoroughfares must first be projected in a proper manner, we shall commence our sketch of the progress of our city, and the various public and private works that have gone on in all directions, with a review of the street improvements made during the past year. From the full and ample report of Mr. George Cofran, the energetic and eminently practical Superintendent of Public Streets, submitted July 1st, 1865, we learn that from July 1st, 1864, to July 1st, 1865, the following work has been done in his department : grading, 787,593 cubic yards; planking, 1,307,721 square feet; paving 364,502 square feet; macadamizing, 315,739 square feet ; sidewalks, 49,912$\frac{4}{13}$ front feet ; brick sewers, 20,967$\frac{1}{13}$ lineal feet ; redwood sewers, 5,272$\frac{8}{13}$ lineal feet ; crosswalks, 8,161 lineal feet ; curbs, 26,781$\frac{7}{13}$ lineal feet ; piles, 251 lineal feet ; caps, 1,824 lineal feet ; bulkhead, 550 lineal feet. Total length of sewers, 26,239$\frac{9}{13}$ lineal feet. The entire cost of all street work during the year, payable in legal tender notes, amounts to $1,159,257.27.

During the year brick sewers have been laid down in the following streets : Folsom, from First to Fremont ; Stockton, from Sacramento to California ; Stockton, from south half of Sacramento ; Folsom, from Fremont to Beale ; Dupont, from Geary to O'Farrell ; Ellis, from Stockton to Powell ; Dupont, from Post to Geary ; Dupont, from Sacramento to Clay ; Pacific, from Mason to Taylor ; Folsom, from Beale to Main ; Sutter, from Stockton to Powell ; Sansom, Powell, and O'Farrell ; Powell, from Geary to O'Farrell ; Sutter, from Powell to Mason ; Howard, from Fourth to Fifth ; Vallejo, from Dupont to Stockton ; Mason, from Turk to Eddy ; Battery, from Jackson to Pacific ; Mason, from Eddy to Ellis ; Battery, from Pacific to Broadway ; Market, from Seventh to Eighth ; Market, from Mason to Sixth ; Market, opposite Sixth ; Powell, from Post to Geary ; Broadway, from Kearny to Dupont ; Battery, from California to Pine ; Stockton, from Ellis to OFarrell ; Post, from Kearny to Dupont ; Stockton, from Chestnut to Francisco ; Market, from Sixth to Seventh ; Second, from Market to Mission ; Powell, from Bush to Sutter ; Jessie, from Second to Third ; Second, from and to connect with Jessie ; intersection of Market and Seventh ; Howard, from Third to Fourth ; Geary, from Powell to Mason ; Stockton, from Lombard to Chestnut ; Stockton from Post to Geary ; Seventh, from Market to Mission ; Market, opposite Eighth ; Fourth, from Howard to Folsom; Tehama, from Third to Fourth; easterly half of Stockton, opposite Pfeiffer; easterly half of Fourth, opposite Tehama; Bush, from Powell to Mason; Howard, from Second to Third; crossing of Geary and Stockton; Post, from Dupont to Stockton; Filbert, from Dupont to Stockton;—making an aggregate of 20,967½ lineal feet, at a cost of $287,200.29.

We do not deem it necessary to specify the streets and thorougfares graded, paved, and planked, with the accompanying sidewalk improvements, with the details of the work, but will content ourselves with saying that the operations of the departments have been carried on with such vigor that the carriage-ways and sidewalks of our city were never before in so good a condition. That portion of San Francisco fronting on the bay, is daily demanding the more serious attention of the proper authorities from the increasing defects of the planking and the unsafe condition of the streets and wharfs. From the perishable nature of the materials used, it is an impossibility to repair the damages to the planking in the ratio of their occurrence; and the filling in of the city front, and paving the same in a substantial manner, although an expensive remedy, would prove the wisest and most economical policy in the end. The introduction of the Nicolson pavement (of wooden blocks set on asphaltum cement) during the past year, on that portion of Montgomery Street between Sacramento and Commercial, on Bush Street in front of the Cosmopolitan Hotel, has proved a success—standing the test of the wear and tear of vehicles, rendering travel easier, and deadening the sound. The proposed widening of Kearny Street will be an improvement that will add much to the beauty of the city, and the comfort and accommodation of the citizens.

THE LINCOLN SCHOOL BUILDING.—One of the finest architectural ornaments of San Francisco, is the Lincoln School, erected on the spacious lot belonging to the Department on Fifth Street near Market, during the past year. It is a decided improvement on its predecessor, planned by the same architect, the Bush Street School—in itself an elegant and well-arranged building. In fact, it is a matter of doubt whether there is to be found in any city of the United States a more imposing, better built, or more conveniently planned or arranged structure than this model school-building, erected by a community of little more than twelve years' growth. It is a solid brick structure, the exterior and partition walls of which are massive and firm, built upon a solid foundation. All the essentials of safety, health, and comfort of the children, for whose benefit and training it has been called into existence, have been consulted in every detail and its minutest particulars. The building is cruciform in shape, one hundred and forty-one and one-half feet in length, with wings eighteen by thirty-three feet—the whole covering a superficial area of ten thousand one hundred and thirty-seven feet. It comprises two stories with basement and attic, the latter being fitted up as a spacious and well-lighted hall, for the purposes of lectures, school exhibitions, and other literary exercises. The first two stories are elegantly finished in class rooms, fitted up with all the educational appliances of modern times; while the basement, temporarily used for school purposes, in addition to its occupation for the purposes of heating the building, is eventually to be fitted up as a gymnasium, with all the usual appliances for the exercise of the pupils. The means of ventilation is perfect throughout every portion, and such is the admirable arrangment of light that not a dark spot is to be found in any part of the building. Water is also conveyed to every portion, and nothing has been omitted that can in any way conduce to the health, comfort, or convenience of the inmates. The walls of the basement and first story are two feet thick, and, those of the superstructure eighteen inches—and such is the character of the work, that no new building of like extent withstood the shock of the earthquake of the eighth of October, with so little actual damage. The building, which is of the style of architecture known as the Renaissance, which had its origin in the classic age of Louis XIV, is surmounted by a Mansard roof, a style which from its light and airy character being peculiarly adapted to the climate of the coast, is becoming very popular. Above this is a handsome cupola; while an elegant balustrade surrounds the whole. The staircases leading to each story are broad and substantially constructed with frequent landings or resting places—forming altogether four safe and easy avenues of ingress and egress. The building, exclusive of the large hall of the attic, is of sufficient capacity to accommodate with ease nine hundred pupils, based upon the ratio of fifty to each class. The arrangements are such that each class-room forms a school of itself, and can if occasion requires, be entirely isolated from the other portions of the building. A thorough examination of the Lincoln School Building affords the most conclusive proof that a more thorough and complete structure has never been erected here; and the work is alike creditable to Mr. William Craine, the architect who planned and superintended the entire work, and the builders and mechanics engaged in its construction. The building was dedicated to the purposes for which it was designed, on the twenty-ninth of June, 1865, with an address by Edward Tompkins, Esq., and other appropriate exercises.

SYNAGOGUE EMANU EL.—The new church edifice on Sutter Street, between Stockton and Powell, recently erected by this society, is one of the most important additions to the prominent buildings of the city, made during the past season. The lot is one hundred and thirty-seven and a half by one hundred and fifty-seven and a half feet, centrally located, and is most admirably adapted to the purposes to which it is dedicated. The church temple presents an imposing appearance, and when fully completed will be one of the most interesting structures in this city. The auditorium, which will be most beautifully and elegantly finished, is fifty-three feet wide, ninety-seven feet long, and fifty feet high, and is designed to seat twelve hundred persons. The basement is to be devoted to educational purposes and will be arranged to accommodate eight hundred children. The entire cost of the building, ready for use, will be about $150,000.

THE SYNAGOGUE OHAIBA SHALOME.—This handsome edifice, which like the foregoing, gives marked evidence of the prosperity of its founders, and zeal in the faith of their fathers, is located on Mason Street, between Geary and Post. It was consecrated on Friday the fifteenth of September last, with the customary ceremonials of the Jewish Church. It is an elegant, and substantial brick structure erected at a cost of about sixty thousand dollars. The main body of the building is rectangular in form, with a gallery at the two sides, and front end. At the opposite is the altar which is of considerable size, connected with which is the reading desk and preacher's pulpit, the whole surrounded with a carved railing. Above this, high up in the gable end, is a large circular window of stained glass, beneath which, for the whole middle of the end, and about ten feet in depth, is a superb y-carved and polished rosewood frame, heavily gilt in scroll work, the whole forming a border for a slab of white marble, on which are engraved in gold letters the Ten Commandments; beneath this is a very heavy crimson silk Brochas with fringe and tassels, covering the Holy Ark, the whole making a very elegant appearance. All the wood-work of the building, including the pulpits, the benches, the doors, the paneling of the gallery, is in black walnut, beautifully carved and polished. The seats and backs of the pews are uphol-stered in crimson damask, and the floor is covered with Brussels carpet. For the purpose of light, there are beneath the gallery six stained glass windows; on the sides and above them are eight long gothic windows of plain glass, and at the end in a recess is a large circular window with stained glass, whilst from the center of the roof depends a handsome bronze chandelier of sixty lights; a number of other gasoliers surround the walls, while on the altar there are two ornamented bronze stands, eight feet high, surmounted with three lights each. The large hall of the basement below, is fitted up as a school-room, well lighted, ventilated, and conveniently arranged for educational purposes. The entire structure reflects credit upon the Trustees who had the matter in charge, and Mr. Patten, the architect, who designed and superintended its erection.

SAN FRANCISCO SHOT TOWER.—A novel and important feature in San Francisco manufactures has been introduced during the past year, which is no less than the erection by one of our most enterprising citizens, Mr. Thomas H. Selby, of an exten-sive building for the manufacture of bar and sheet-lead, lead-pipe, shot, and bullets, on the corner of Howard and First streets. The main structure which is used for the purposes named, is eighty by seventy feet square, and three stories in hight with a deep basement. The hight of the tower which surmounts this, looming far above the surrounding structures, is two hundred feet from the base. The establishment is fitted up with a first-class engine, machinery, and appliances for the varied operations to be carried on, of the highest order, and in all its arrangements will fully equal any simi-lar enterprise of the Eastern cities—the cost of the whole amounting to not less than seventy-five thousand dollars. This is certainly an important movement toward the further development of the unsurpassed mineral resources of the Pacific coast. Large bodies of galena, yielding a large per centage of the precious metals, abound in the southern portions of our State, where wood, water, and the conveniences of smelting and reduction of ores are within reach. The demand which such a manufactory must create, must eventually result in the profitable working of vast bodies of mineral in the undeveloped lodes of that region. Until this is the case, however, the stock of material for manufacture at the establishment will of necessity be drawn from the Atlantic States and Europe.

ADDITION TO THE OCCIDENTAL HOTEL.—One of the most important as well as spacious and showy private improvements in our city, during the past year, is the extensive addition made to the Montgomery Street front of the Occidental Hotel, by the enterprising owners, J. A. Donohoe and others. This addition comprises a front on Montgomery Street of two hundred and eight feet, is four-stories in hight, and contains one hundred and twenty-five rooms, which with the present capacity of the hotel will afford accommodations for not less than five hundred guests. The main entrance to the hotel, with the ladies' and gentlemen's reception-rooms, will be on Montgomery Street, which portion of the building presents quite an imposing appear-ance. Under the management of the Messrs. Leland, who belong to a race of popular landlords—who are "to the manner born," the Occidental with this important addition will rival in extent and accommodations any similar establishment on either side of the Atlantic. Mr. J. P. Johnson is the architect, who designed and superintended the erection of this extensive structure.

LICK HOUSE ADDITION.—Although the Lick House as originally designed is one of the largest and most commodious hotel buildings of the city, such is the demand for accommodations of this character, that the wealthy owner of this property has erected during the past season an addition to the building but little inferior in size and equal in all its details and arrangements. Its dimensions are one hundred and forty-eight feet on Sutter by the same on Lick Street, and three stories in hight, and contains seventy-five rooms in addition to a large dining hall; the whole to be connected with the main building by bridges running from each floor.

OTHER HOTEL ADDITIONS.—A handsome structure has also been erected by Messrs. Grissim & Henderson on the south side of Bush Street, between Montgomery and Sansom, adjoining the Cosmopolitan Hotel, with a frontage of sixty-eight feet and nine inches, and depth of one hundred and thirty-one feet six inches. The first story of the building, which is fitted up in elegant style, is occupied by the Franco-American Company as a bazaar or sales-room, for the display and disposal of elegant pictures—many of them originals by celebrated masters—statuary, vases, rare mosaics, articles of *vertu*, pianos, and fancy goods of the most elegant description. The second story, which is reached by a spacious stairway from the Bush Street entrance, is occupied for the meetings of the Washoe Club, an association of individuals who have realized largely from the silver drifts of Nevada. The three upper stories of the building, which contain eighty rooms, single and in suits for families, are used by the Reis Brothers, the wealthy proprietors and landlords of the Cosmopolitan Hotel, for the accommodation of their guests—the halls of this portion communicating with those in the hotel building. The basement, which is reached by a broad flight of stone steps at the east side of the front, is fitted up as a first-class bowling saloon. This structure, as well as the large and elegant building of Mr. Cunningham, on the corner of Market and Third streets, was erected under the supervision of Messrs. Kenitzer & Farquharson, architects.

PINE STREET, BETWEEN MONTGOMERY AND SANSOM.—No portion of San Francisco exhibits the rapid march of improvement going on in our midst, more forcibly than that portion of Pine Street situated between Montgomery and Sansom. During the past year a number of spacious and elegant structures have been erected on each side of the thoroughfare within the limits named. During the past year, the proprietor of the Academy of Music has erected an elegant brick on the lot adjoining that handsome structure, formerly occupied by the Engine House of No. 7. Adjoining this, Mr. H. B. Platt has erected a fine brick building; and farther along, near Sansom, Mr. W. S. Clark has built during the past season a spacious brick, five stories in hight—altogether one of the most extensive and best-built structures erected during the year. On the opposite side of the street, a short distance below Montgomery, Messrs. Goetz & Schreiber have erected a handsome brick, which is occupied by themselves as the Eureka Hotel, the upper portion being occupied by the hall of the United Order of Red Men, an association which although of but comparatively recent organization here, is rapidly increasing.

NEW MISSION BRIDGE.—This important enterprise which affords the means of convenient communication with the south-eastern sections of the city, has been fully completed during the past season. Its entire length is nearly one mile and its construction cost nearly $50,000.

CALIFORNIA COTTON MILL.—The articles of incorporation for the erection of the first cotton mill of the Pacific coast, was filed in the San Francisco County Clerk's office, in August, 1865. The association is styled the "Oakland Cotton Manufacturing Company," of which Wm. H. Rector & Sons are the principal stockholders, with a cash capital of $100,000. The work on the first mill, erected by the company, has been completed and fitted up with the requisite machinery for going into successful operaiion. It is eligibly located near the town of Oakland, Alameda County. It is a spacious brick building, ninety by forty feet, and two stories high. The mill contains thirty-two looms, run by a steam engine of forty-horse power, and will give steady employment to about thirty operatives. The company have also erected, contiguous to their factory, three commodious brick buildings for the accommodation of the employés of the establishment, and they have nearly completed a side-wheel steamer of two hundred tons for the transportation of the raw material and manufactured goods to and from the establishment. For the present, it is the intention to manufacture only the heavy articles of goods demanded by the market, such as drillings and sheetings, until the experiments in cotton raising in this State, demonstrate the success of this important branch of agriculture in California, the company will necessarily be obliged to draw their supplies of the raw material from Mexico.

DRIVES IN THE VICINITY OF SAN FRANCISCO.—There are probably few cities that have more grand and beautiful views, fine scenery, and more attractive drives, than are to be found in the immediate vicinity of San Francisco. Take the Point Lobos Road with its sweep around the beach on the north side, passing the hights of Black Point, and taking the Presidio on the way to Fort Point Terminus, and you have a series of the most beautiful landscapes. Take Bush Street and you have a fine road to the cemeteries of the city. Passing these "cities of the dead," a short drive brings you to the Cliff House, where you see the broad Pacific spread before you, in the morning like a vast sheet of silver, and in the evening like one vast mass of molten gold. Sweeping around the curve of the ocean strand, over the new toll road, you reach the Ocean House with the new race track, where those two champions of Kentucky stock, Norfork and Lodi, contested their speed and bottom, and wending your way across the hills, you pass over the new shell road leading to Bay View Park. This popular resort, now under the control of Messrs. Williamson & Hopkins, is one of the most attractive spots in the vicinity of this city. After partaking of the hospitalities of these worthy hosts, you take a beautiful trip overland, Mission-ward, or the graceful bend around Hunters' Point through the Potrero, crossing Mission Bay on its new and substantial bridge, you land at the foot of Third Street, pleased with your entire excursion.

NEW BUILDINGS.—Total number of buildings, August, 1864, 14,443, of which 2,930 are of brick. Number erected from August, 1864 to August, 1865, estimated at 1,075 of which 320 are of brick, making an aggregate in the city and county of 15,518, viz.: wood, 12,268, brick, 3,250.

CHRONOLOGICAL HISTORY OF PRINCIPAL EVENTS,

H

From September 20th, 1864, to November 10th, 1865.

SEPTEMBER 20, 1864. An earthquake occurred at 10:45, A.M., frightening some, but doing no material damage....Michael McDermott, who stabbed and killed Daniel Rolligan two weeks before, was held for trial on a charge of murder.

SEPT. 21. The Mexicans celebrated the victory of their countrymen under Cortinas, over the French, at Matamoras.

SEPT. 22. The new grammar school house, built on the corner of Bush and Taylor streets, was dedicated with appropriate ceremonies....The remains of the late Rev. T. Starr King were removed from the vault at Lone Mountain and entombed in the sarcophagus in front of the Unitarian church.

SEPT. 23. The Pacific Mail Steamer Golden City sailed for Panama with a large number of passengers, among whom were Rev. Dr. Bellows and family, Rt. Rev. Bishop Kip and wife, and other prominent citizens. The treasure shipment amounted to $1,175,208.07.

SEPT. 24. The Spanish-American and Chilean residents celebrated the anniversary of the Independence of Chile.

SEPT. 26. A man named Mordecai Mobley, a native of Springfield, Illinois, aged twenty-nine, and another named N. H. W. Dunn, committed suicide by taking morphine....Salutes fired at 4, P.M., from the U. S. forts and by the volunteer batteries, in honor of Sheridan's victories in the Shenandoah Valley....A whale, about seventy-five feet long, was stranded and came ashore outside the Heads, near the Cliff House.

SEPT. 27. The embargo of the Treasury Department, forbidding the loading of foreign vessels at any portion of Puget Sound, by order of Secretary Fessenden....The Nicaragua steamer Moses Taylor arrived with a large number of passengers.

SEPT. 28. Meeting held at the Mechanics' Pavilion for relieving the distresses of the people of Santa Barbara.

SEPT. 30. The Jewish Holidays, especially the New Year or "Day of Memorial," were celebrated with the accustomed ceremonials, by the large Hebrew population....The fines and penalties collected, during the past month, in the Police Court, amounted to $3,884; number of arrests, seven hundred and nineteen.

OCTOBER 2. Steamship firemen struck for higher wages. An attempt was made to prevent the necessary hands from going on board the steamship Golden Age, which occasioned a riot, rendering necessary the interference of a large body of armed police to restore good order....Board of Military Commission organized for the examination of the defenses in and around San Francisco. The Provost Guard increased to the number of one hundred and sixty men......The thermometer eighty-three degrees in the shade at 2, P.M....The benefit to the Santa Barbara sufferers at the Industrial Fair netted $1,368.30.

OCT. 4. A small frame building on Telegraph Hill was destroyed by fire, about 8 o'clock, A.M.... The great trotting match between Fillmore and Unknown was won by the latter.

OCT. 5. The corner stone of the monument to the late George H. Hossefross was laid at Calvary Cemetery, with appropriate ceremonials......The boiler of Ils' Salt Water Baths, on North Beach, exploded, fatally injuring the engineer.

OCT. 7. A desperado named Roderick, stabbed a woman on Broadway, and attacked a policeman who attempted to arrest him....George Meyers shot a keeper of a saloon on Pacific Street, and afterwards beat her severely on the head with a pistol.

OCT. 9. Eighty-eighth anniversary of the settlement of San Francisco, the Mission of that name being founded October 9th, 1776....Mr. and Mrs. Charles Kean made their first appearance, before a crowded audience, at the Opera House.

OCT. 13. Steamer Brother Jonathan arrived from Victoria and Portland, with a large number of passengers and $369,910 in treasure....Robert Dyson, an old resident of San Francisco, fell in a fit on the street, and died in a short time....The Pacific Mail Steamship Constitution departed for Panama with a large number of passengers, and treasure amounting to $1,204,664.25.

OCT. 15. Patrick Ferris, one of the workmen engaged at the intersection of Greenwich and Leavenworth streets, was killed by the falling of a mass of rock.

OCT. 16. The U. S. gunboat Wateree, Capt. F. H. Murray, Commander, arrived, two hundred and twenty-two days from Hampton Roads.

OCT. 18. The Central American Transit Company's steamer Moses Taylor left for San Juan del Sur with a large number of passengers....The U. S. Courts adjourned out of respect to the memory of Chief Justice Taney.

OCT. 21. A fire occurred on Second Street, near Bryant, doing but little damage.

OCT. 23. The first rain of the season fell to-day ....The opening lecture of the new Medical College, by its founder, Dr. H. H. Toland, was delivered before a large audience....Hypolite Vaduret died suddenly, of disease of the heart.

OCT. 25. The corner stone of the Jewish Synagogue, Emanu El, on Sutter Street, was laid with appropriate ceremonials.

OCT. 26. The British ship Alhambra cleared for Hongkong with treasure shipment amounting to $201,515.94....The C. S. Navigation Co.'s steamer Sophie McLane, running between San Francisco and Suisun, blew up at the latter place about 7 o'clock, A.M., killing and maiming several of the passengers and crew, and making the vessel a total wreck. The following were the parties killed by the explosion, or who subsequently died from its effects: Henry P. Hulburt, Commander; George Folger, Pilot; Charles Yates, Second Engineer; and Wm. Lawlor, deck hand.

OCT. 28. Two more whalers came into port, making twenty-four in number since the thirteenth of the month....The San Francisco Board of Underwriters, in view of the numerous incendiary fires, offer a reward of $1,250 for the apprehension and conviction of parties engaged in house burning.

OCT. 30. First norther of the season, which did considerable damage to the shipping in the harbor ....Wm. H. Keene, a waiter at the New York Restaurant, was drowned while bathing at Point Lobos near the Cliff House.

Oct. 31. A stable on the corner of Stockton and Green streets was set on fire about 10, P.M. and completely destroyed....Fines and penalties of the Police Court for this month, $4,816....John Regan, aged thirty-three years, was found drowned at North Beach.

November 1. A meeting was held at which the certificate of incorporation and constitution of a California Art Union were adopted.

Nov. 5. A fleet of merchantmen and whalers came into port, consisting of eight ships, five barks, five schooners, and three brigs.

Nov. 7. For several days past the city has been visited with severe northers....A bonfire built over a cistern at the intersection of Montgomery and Pacific streets, caused the fire-damp and gases confined in it to explode, throwing the iron cover to a great distance and shattering the walls to pieces.

Nov. 8. The election for President of the United States, members of Congress, and State officers passed off quietly. Nearly all the stores and other places of business were closed during the day.

Nov. 9. The great pacing match between Pacific and Unknown was won by the former.

Nov. 11. Maj. Thomas B. Eastland, a veteran of the Mexican war and an old San Francisco pioneer, died, aged fifty-eight years.

Nov. 12. The steamer Sierra Nevada arrived from the North with a number of passengers, and treasure amounting to $430,073....Dennis Gahagen, a pioneer citizen died, aged fifty-five years. Deceased came to the country as interpreter of the U. S. Boundary Commission under John B. Weller.

Nov. 14. The iron-clad monitor Comanche was successfully launched to-day in presence of thousands of spectators assembled to view the novel and interesting sight. J. P. Buckley, an old and valued citizen, had his ankle caught in a coil of rope during the launch, and so badly crushed as to require amputation.

Nov. 16. A fire broke out at 1, P.M. in a two-story frame building on Market Street near Ellis, destroying it and adjoining buildings, loss $25,000.

Nov. 17. Hon. John P. Buckley died at 5, A.M., of the injuries he received at the launch of the Comanche. Deceased was one of the pioneer business men of San Francisco, having come to this place in 1849. He was foremost in all public enterprises and charities, and his untimely decease was deeply deplored....A fire occurred in a frame building on Pine Street, between Dupont and Stockton, doing slight damage....The P. M. S. Constitution arrived bringing a large number of passengers and six hundred and thirty tons of freight.

Nov. 18. A woman of intemperate habits, known as Mrs. Place, was found burned to death in a basement on the corner of Vallejo and Powell streets.

Nov. 20. A frame shanty in the rear of the Gas Works was burned down, loss trifling.

Nov. 21. A fire broke out at 10, P.M., in the rear of the Antelope Restaurant, 612 Market Street; damage $1,000....The steamer Brother Jonathan arrived from the North with a large number of passengers and treasure amounting to $401,000.

Nov. 22. Over $400,000 in gold dust was deposited in the U. S. Branch Mint, the largest amount deposited in any day since its establishment.

Nov. 23. The P. M. S. Constitution left for Panama with a large number of passengers and treasure amounting to $1,074,203.85.

Nov. 25. Capt. Hiram Fairchild, a pioneer printer, who came to California in 1849 and who had served during the Mexican war died, aged fifty-two years.

Nov. 26. A severe storm occurred in the bay, capsizing and sinking numerous small craft and doing considerable damage to the shipping....At 4

o'clock, P.M., the gauge at the Mint indicated that three inches of rain had fallen up to that time, as much as the entire rain fall of the last season. St. Ann's Valley was completely flooded, and the cellars in the lower part of the city were filled with water.

Nov. 27. Edward E. Powers, a pioneer printer and President of the Eureka Typographical Union, who came to California in 1849, died.

Nov. 28. The rain continues and the weather is exceedingly rough. Considerable damage has been done to the shipping going over the bar outside. Owing to the breaking away of a culvert on the corner of Market and Fremont streets, the extensive basement of Treadwell & Co., filled with hardware, was flooded doing damage estimated at from $30,000 to $40,000.

Nov. 29. An altercation took place on Montgomery Street between Charles F. Curie and Charles Stephens, two mining secretaries, in which the former shot the latter; not, however, dangerously wounding him.

Nov. 30. The fines and penalties of the Police Court for the month amounted to $4,684.75....An Italian fishing boat running in from the Farallones was capsized and lost, the crew being saved by the pilot boat Fanny....The St. Andrew's Society celebrated the anniversary of their patron saint by a dinner at the Cosmopolitan Hotel....The amount of rain which fell during the past week was 6·86 in.

December 2. About 5½, A.M. a fire broke out on Third Street near Stevenson. The fire spread so rapidly that in a short time the whole premises were destroyed. John Hays, a laborer, perished in the flames. The loss of property was only about $3,000.

Dec. 3. The Sacramento sailed for Panama with $765,934.87 in treasure.

Dec. 4. Edward L. Fell, an old citizen of San Francisco, died of typhoid fever. He was one of the most enterprising contractors in the city.

Dec. 6. Frederick D. Kohler, a pioneer citizen of San Francisco, died at the Russ House. Deceased was born in New York in 1810, and filled the offices of First Assistant Engineer of the Fire Department and Alderman of the Sixth Ward of that city. He was elected Chief Engineer of the San Francisco Fire Department at the first election held in 1850, and was subsequently elected County Recorder.

Dec. 9. The second expedition, fitted out under the direction of T. J. L. Smiley, for the recovery of the treasure lost by the burning of the Golden Gate, left for Manzanillo on the steamer Commodore.

Dec. 11. The John L. Stephens arrived from Mexico, with numerous passengers, and $96,359 in specie, and 1,390 bags of silver ore....A fire broke out in an iron building in the rear of Washington and Davis streets, containing about eighty tons of tule hay. The damage was slight....A slight shock of an earthquake was felt about 9, P.M.

Dec. 13. The Golden City left for Panama with a large number of passengers, and treasure amounting to $1,022,188.10.

Dec. 14. The Brother Jonathan arrived from up the Coast with numerous passengers, and $400,200 in treasure.

Dec. 16. The news of the defeat of the rebel commander Hood, by Gen. Thomas, in Tennessee, was celebrated in spirited style.

Dec. 17. A couple of cars ran off the track of the San José Railroad, in the vicinity of School House Station, near the county line. The passengers were but slightly injured, but the Conductor, Mr. E. A. Hudson, aged about thirty years, was crushed to death.

Dec. 20. A fire occurred in a hay warehouse, north-west corner of Clay and Drumm streets. Damage slight.

Dec. 21. A butcher named Henry Schram, a

German, who had a difficulty with his wife, at the Potrero, fired two shots at her, both of which took effect, but not fatally. Supposing that he had killed his wife, Schram shot himself through the head, which killed him instantly.

DEC. 23. The Golden Age left for Panama with $1,053,352.65 in treasure....J. F. Leddy, for several years a clerk in a fashionable dry goods' store, and a pioneer of 1849, committed suicide by swallowing strychnine.

DEC. 24. Some unprincipled parties published a spurious extra, purporting to be issued from the Alta and Bulletin offices, giving an account of the capture of Richmond. Several hundred dollars' worth were sold by the newsboys before the hoax was discovered and the principals arrested.

DEC. 27. The dead body of James Gordon, the mate of a schooner, who had been missing for several days, was found upright in the mud under the wharf on East Street.

DEC. 28. Very dense fogs pervade the city all night, rendering traveling any distance a hazardous operation....James Fitz Maurice, an ex-New York detective, was arrested and held to bail in the sum of $5,000, for an attempt to murder and rob Andrew J. Haight, a gold-pen manufacturer, in his room in broad daylight.

DEC. 30. The U. S. steamer Saginaw, Commander W. E. Hopkins, arrived from Panama, having on board the Salvador pirates, who were immediately transferred to Alcatraz....The San Francisco Fishermen's Association, commonly known as the "Italian Fishermen," inaugurated their new fish market, on the corner of Clay and Leidesdorff streets.

JANUARY 1, 1865. The remains of Capt. S. C. Simmons, a pioneer citizen, who died of hemorrhage resulting from an accident, were followed to the tomb by the Pioneer Association, of which he was a respected member. Deceased was Controller of the Pueblo of San Francisco in 1849-50.

JAN. 2. New Year falling on Sunday, to-day was generally observed with the festivities usual on the occasion. The colored population celebrated the anniversary of the issue of President Lincoln's Emancipation Proclamation.

JAN. 3. A discharged soldier named Michael Callaghan, fell overboard from the steamer Senator, at Broadway Wharf, and was drowned....Joseph Mayer, an old and esteemed merchant of California Street, died suddenly of an attack of asthma.

JAN. 5. A fire occurred in the brick building of James Kelly, 38 California Street. Although promptly extinguished, the damage from fire and water was considerable....The Sacramento arrived with a large number of passengers, among whom was Capt. C. H. Baldwin, U. S. Navy.

JAN. 7. The gold and silver coined at the San Francisco Mint during the year 1864 is reported to be $16,323,186.

JAN. 8. Leon Prudon, ex-Foreman of Lafayette Hook and Ladder Company, and a resident of San Francisco since 1850, died.

JAN. 9. The following officers were chosen for the ensuing year at an election by the Stock Exchange Board: J. B. Cavallier, President; John Perry, Jr., Vice President; Henry Schmeidell, Treasurer; Franklin Lawton, Secretary.

JAN. 10. The America sailed for San Juan del Sur with a large number of passengers.

JAN. 11. The rooms of the California Art Union, No. 312 Montgomery Street, were opened with an elegant collation.

JAN. 12. The trial of Moses Frank for forging an indorsement upon a bill of exchange, drawn by Baum, the Superintendent of the Utah Mining Company, commenced before a jury in the County Court.

JAN. 13. The Sacramento left for Panama with $1,069,465.06 in treasure....Barney Olwell, de-

liberately shot and killed James Irwin. The excuse given was, that the deceased owed his murderer forty-two dollars, which he had the means to pay at the time.

JAN. 14. The Oregon arrived from the North with treasure amounting to $200,000....Steam was for the first time applied to the monitor Comanche, the machinery and turret working admirably.

JAN. 18. The remains of Bernard Hogan, Foreman of Broderick Engine Co. No. 1, were followed to Calvary Cemetery by the members of the Fire Department and numerous citizens, including several carriages filled with the leading Chinese merchants of San Francisco......First Officer Boyd, of the American ship Sir John Franklin, arrived from Pigeon Point, between thirty and forty miles south of the Heads, bringing the news that the vessel had gone ashore at that point, during the fog of the night of the seventeenth. Thirteen of those on board perished, and the vessel and cargo were a total loss.

JAN. 21. The John L. Stephens arrived from Mexican ports with $103,307 in specie, and 1,945 bags of ore....The monitor Comanche, with a number of army and navy officers and invited guests on board, made a successful trial trip to Mare Island.

JAN. 22. The Pacific arrived from the North with treasure amounting to $198,000.

JAN. 23. The Golden City left for Panama with $957,287.58 in treasure.

JAN. 26. A fire occurred about 11 o'clock, P.M., in a frame building occupied by a number of Chinese families, on Sacramento Street, above Kearny. The building was consumed, but the damage was slight. A Chinaman named Tong Yung was suffocated by the smoke.

JAN. 30. The body of James Cunningham, a Norwegian sailor, who had been missing for a month past, was found floating in the Bay.

JAN. 31. M. Schmidt, a native of Germany, aged about thirty years, recently returned from Mexico, in a fit of temporary insanity, shot and dangerously wounded Francis D. Lonneux, in the bar-room of the William Tell House, after which he committed suicide by shooting and stabbing himself. The parties were entire strangers to each other.

FEBRUARY 1. Mr. and Mrs. Charles Kean made their last appearance at the Opera House.

FEB. 2. Frederick Woodworth, an old and highly respected citizen, and the son of Samuel Woodworth, the author of the "Old Oaken Bucket," died to-day.

FEB. 3. The Golden Age left for Panama with treasure amounting to $1,222,311.85.

FEB. 4. The Second and Seventh Regiments of California Volunteers were reviewed by General McDowell, at the Presidio....A young German, name unknown, was drowned off the rocks, near the Cliff House....Lonneux, the man shot by Schmidt, at the William Tell House, Bush Street, died of his wounds.

FEB. 5. The Constitution arrived with a large number of passengers. Preparations had been made to give Gen. Dan. E. Sickles a grand reception, but to the great chagrin of the crowd, he was not on board....A fire occurred, near 12, P.M., in the brick building, 821 Kearny Street, the woodwork and contents of which were entirely destroyed.

FEB. 6. The first pile of the new bridge to connect the Potrero with the city, was driven to-day. ....A fire occurred a little past 1, A.M., in a one-story building, on Third, near Stevenson Street, which was, with its contents, entirely destroyed.... Caroline Lewis, a mulatto woman, who had laid down and gone to sleep, was suffocated by the smoke of the curtains set on fire by the candle.

FEB. 8. Robert Murray, a native of Massachusetts, aged forty-four years, was found dead in his bed.

FEB. 10. Walter S. Denio, Melter and Refiner of

the U. S. Branch Mint, aged thirty-six, died of congestion of the lungs, and operations at the Mint are necessarily suspended until advices are received from Washington.

FEB. 13. The Constitution and Moses Taylor left with a large number of passengers, the former taking $1,325,452.90 in treasure.

FEB. 16. Alexander Barnes, an old citizen of California and one of the original proprietors of the Cosmopolitan Hotel, died of gradual decline.

FEB. 18. The news of the death of Richard M. Jessup, former President of the California Steam Navigation Company, at Panama on the 3d instant, was received to-day.

FEB. 19. Captain Paul and the officers of the ship Great Republic, recently arrived from Boston, were arrested and held to bail for alleged brutal and cruel treatment of the seamen of the vessel....Michael O'Brian, who came to California in 1849, and a well known pioneer butcher of San Francisco, and one of the most warm-hearted and charitable men, died at his residence.

FEB. 21. An old U. S. soldier, named John Jackson, a member of Company B, U. S. Artillery, was drowned between the city and Angel Island.

FEB. 22. The Sacramento left for Panama with treasure amounting to $1,615,156.62....A severe norther in the morning did considerable damage to the shipping in the bay.

FEB. 23. The Oregon arrived from the North with treasure amounting to $145,820....John Herron, a pioneer citizen and for many years the book keeper of the Alta California newspaper, died at his residence in the evening.

FEB. 24. The jury in the case of J. Downes Wilson vs. The San Francisco Bulletin, for alleged slander growing out of remarks in relation to the sale of the Santiago Mine, returned a verdict for plaintiff of $7,500.

FEB. 26. A fire broke out about 6, P.M., in the old Chinese Hospital building, on the corner of Jessie and Ecker streets, destroying the entire establishment.

FEB. 27. The John L. Stephens arrived from the Mexican coast with treasure amounting to $75,581, and a quantity of valuable silver ore.

MARCH 1. March " came in like a lion," bringing snow, hail, and rain within the first twelve hours.

MARCH 2. The Pacific arrived from the Northern Coast with $87,820 in treasure....The cars of the Alameda Railroad made their first through-trip to San Leandro.

MARCH 3. The St. Louis left for Panama with treasure amounting to $1,904,694.75.

MARCH 4. The fall of Savannah, Charleston, and Wilmington, and the second inauguration of Abraham Lincoln were celebrated by military parades and salutes during the day and an illumination and torch-light procession in the evening ....Willard Buzzell, Jack Lott, and William Divers, engaged in whaling at Half Moon Bay, were drowned by the swamping of their boat. The first named was proprietor of the Purissima House, and came to California in 1838.

MARCH 7. The U. S. gunboat Shubrick departed for Sitka, Russian America, with the parties engaged to build the Collins' Russian Overland Telegraph.

MARCH 9. The Golden Age arrived with a large number of passengers, among them Commodore McDougal of the Navy, who is to take command of the Comanche.

MARCH 10. The following rates of fare on the outgoing steamers are lower than have been charged for years. P. M. S. Co. $150, $115, $70, $40; Opposition, $110, $65, $35.

MARCH 12. A fire broke out about 5, A.M., in the grocery of Wm. Wessling on Shipley Street. The building and contents destroyed amounted to $3,000.

MARCH 13. The Golden City and the America left with an unusually large number of passengers, owing to the low rates of fare. The former carried treasure amounting to $1,148,789.78.

MARCH 15. The Sierra Nevada arrived from the North with treasure amounting to $69,200 ....A man named Hill was found buried in the sand at the corner of Scott and Hayes streets, and upon investigation Thomas Byrnes, a butcher, was arrested for his murder.

MARCH 17. The anniversary of the patron saint of Ireland was celebrated by the Irish population of San Francisco with religious, civic, and military exercises.

MARCH 18. The U. S. troops at the Presidio, numbering over three thousand, were reviewed by Gen. McDowell, accompanied by other army and navy officers....The Pacific arrived from the North with treasure amounting to $59,000.

MARCH 21. The ship Derby arrived from Hongkong with two hundred coolies, sixteen of whom were sick with the small pox, and were taken to the pest-house on the Potrero.

MARCH 24. Dr. Oscar L. Cook, Surgeon of the U. S. Army, who came out on the ship Great Republic, fell into the bay from the Alameda Railroad Wharf and was drowned.

MARCH 26. A personal collision took place between Gen. Placedo Vega of Mexico, agent of the Juarez Government, and Señor Francisco Ramirez, editor of El Nueva Mundo, growing out of Mexican affairs.

MARCH 28. Owen Mullin, a private in Company A, Second Regiment of Infantry, C. V., in a fit of intoxication shot and killed his sister in law, Mrs. Jonathan Mullin, at her residence.

MARCH 29. The Oregon arrived from the North with $171,708 in treasure.

APRIL 1. The Brother Jonathan arrived from the North with treasure amounting to $46,000.

APRIL 3. The reception of the news of the surrender of Richmond was hailed with enthusiasm and celebrated in a spirited manner....The Golden Age left for Panama with a large number of passengers and treasure amounting to $654,858.95.

APRIL 6. The John L. Stephens arrived from Mexican ports with $93,440 in specie....A fire occurred at 1, A.M., in the stables of W. H. Richards, west side of Kearny between California and Pine streets; damage trifling.

APRIL 8. The Sierra Nevada arrived from the North with treasure amounting to $109,900.

APRIL 9. Twenty vessels from English, French, South American, British American, Asiatic, Polynesian, and North Atlantic ports came into the harbor to-day.

APRIL 11. General Mason and staff left for Arizona on the steamer Senator.

APRIL 13. The Sacramento and the Moses Taylor sailed with over 1,800 passengers, the former carrying treasure amounting to $1,103,786.68.... The Fire Alarm Telegraph was fully tested and found to work satisfactorily.

APRIL 15. The news of the assassination of President Lincoln clothed the entire city in sadness and gloom. But a short time elapsed before every house was draped with the symbols of mourning. In the afternoon an organized mob proceeded to destroy the type and material of the Democratic Press, Franco Americaine, News Letter, Occidental, and Monitor. After the destruction of the property, military guards were stationed in each of these offices. The utmost excitement prevailed, and but for timely military interference still greater destruction of property might have followed.

APRIL 16. The Pacific arrived from the North, with treasure amounting to $91,000....Impressive services were held in all the churches upon the death of President Lincoln, and a large meeting of citizens was held in Platt's Hall, in the afternoon, at which extensive arrangements were made for celebrating the funeral obsequies in a style worthy the occasion ....Capt. E. C. M. Chadwick, of the California Steam Navigation Co.'s Steamer Chrysopolis, died suddenly about 6 o'clock, P.M....A fire occurred about 9 A.M. in the tannery of William Cole, on Brannan Street, destroying a considerable amount of property.

APRIL 17. A fire occurred about half-past one, A.M., on the south-west corner of Mission and Main streets, destroying four buildings, three of which belonged to Michael Reese.

APRIL 19. The funeral obsequies of President Lincoln, in point of extent and grandeur, surpassed anything ever before seen on the Pacific coast, the procession being some miles in length. The civic and military turn out was immense. An oration, accompanied with appropriate ceremonies, was delivered at the Pavilion....James Lyons, formerly a special policeman, in a fit of intoxication, shot and wounded his wife, and supposing he had killed her, shot himself through the lungs.

APRIL 22. The Golden City sailed for Panama, with treasure amounting to $886,378.84.

APRIL 26. Two shocks of an earthquake occurred near 4 o'clock, P.M.

APRIL 29. The Sierra Nevada arrived from the North with treasure amounting to $113,000.

APRIL 30. Michael Prendergast, a cartman, was instantly killed by the caving in of a high bank on Broadway.

MAY 1. An order was issued from the head-quarters of the Military Department of the Pacific to the occupants of Custom House Block, to vacate the premises by the 9th inst.

MAY 2. A boy named Charles Crane, aged eight years, was drowned in the bay by the upsetting of a boat....Capt. Paul convicted of cruelty to the crew of the Great Republic, was pardoned by the President.

MAY 3. The Constitution left for Panama with treasure amounting to $854,786 21.

MAY 5. The Mexican residents of San Francisco celebrated the anniversary of the victory of Gen. Zaragossa over the French at Puebla.

MAY 8. A fire broke out about half-past three, P.M., in the cooper shop of Joseph Palecki, on Washington near Davis, destroying the entire property and several adjoining buildings. While the fire was progressing, another broke out on the east side of Dupont Street, opposite the Globe Hotel, which destroyed several frame buildings of little value.... The Oregon arrived from the North with treasure amounting to $67,960.

MAY 10. The U. S. war steamer Lancaster, Acting Rear Admiral Pearson, Commander, arrived from Panama, and was saluted by the guns at Alcatraz.

MAY 11. The Del Norte arrived from the North with $3,000 in treasure.

MAY 12. Gen. McDowell and Staff left for San Pedro on the U. S. steamer Saginaw, on a tour of inspection to the military posts in the southern portion of the State.

MAY 14. Up to 3 o'clock, P.M., the thermometer ranged from 75 to 80 degrees in the shade.

MAY 15. A fire at nine o'clock this evening, in a warehouse on Commerce Street, occupied by Bloomingdale & Co. Loss about $50,000.

MAY 16. The municipal election passed off quietly. The entire People's ticket, headed by H. P. Coon, for Mayor, was elected, with the exception of Superintendent of Schools, Harbor Master and Harbor Commissioner, to which offices Messrs. Pelton, Harloe, and Laidley, of the Union Ticket, were chosen. The total vote polled was 14,196.

MAY 18. The Sacramento left for Panama, with treasure amounting to $1,277,447.61....The Orizaba

arrived from the North with treasure amounting to $144,100.

MAY 20. A fire broke out in a frame building on Broadway, between Davis and Front, which was extinguished without material damage.

MAY 23. The long talked of race between Norfolk and Lodi took place at the Ocean House Course, the former winning with ease. Time, 3:43¼; 3:42; 3:5: 3:51; 4:5.

MAY 24. A severe shock of an earthquake, which was also felt some distance down the coast, occurred about 3 o'clock, A.M.

MAY 25. Mr. Thomas H. Jones, Superintendent of Grant's Stone Quarry, on Angel Island, was instantly killed by a piece of rock thrown out by a blast.

MAY 27. The Del Norte arrived from the North with $11,200 treasure.

MAY 31. A. A. C. William, Daniel E. Hungerford, W. W. Bruce, Louis de la Nord, Wm. Berns, Wm. B. Clarke, John Thomas, and Titus Reynolds, were arraigned in the Police Court for an alleged attempt to carry away the Peruvian Dispatch Steamer Colon, and the bail in each case was fixed at $2,500.

JUNE 1. A fire broke out at 1, P.M., on the corner of Jackson and Drumm streets, destroying about thirty frame tenements before the flames were arrested. The entire loss is estimated at not less than $50,000.

JUNE 3. The corner stone of the new Synagogue of the Congregation Ohabai Shalome, on Mason Street, was laid with the usual ceremonials of the Jewish Church....Antonie Mach stabbed and killed Edward Walter at his grocery, 523 Pacific Street, and in the affray wounded the brother-in-law of Walter, named J. Spitz, so severely that his life is despaired of.

JUNE 6. The examination of the parties implicated in the Brontes Colon piracy case concluded before Judge Shepheard to-day. The Court held the parties to bail in the original amount of $2,500 each.

JUNE 7. The Brother Jonathan arrived from the north with treasure amounting to $347,400.

JUNE 8. The Constitution arrived from Panama with a large number of passengers, among whom were ex-Governor Wm. Bigler of Pennsylvania, and Sir James Douglas, ex-Governor of British Columbia....A. C. Campbell, a pioneer lawyer of San Francisco, died of apoplexy, aged forty years.

JUNE 12. The first number of a daily paper, entitled the Examiner, was issued from the office of the Democratic Press.

JUNE 14. There was a slight shock of an earthquake at 12 o'clock, M.

JUNE 16. A German professor of languages, named John Jonkheim, committed suicide.

JUNE 17. The Constitution left for Panama, with treasure amounting to $1,528,836.03.

JUNE 18. The Sierra Nevada arrived from the north with $228,150 treasure.

JUNE 19. A man named Peter McDougall, who came down from Victoria on the Sierra Nevada, committed suicide by cutting his throat with a shoe-knife.

JUNE 20. A fire occurred about 5, P.M., in the new building on Pine Street, owned by H. B. Platt. Loss about five hundred dollars.

JUNE 24. The John L. Stephens arrived from Mexican ports with $148,946 specie.

JUNE 26. The Sacramento arrived from Panama with a large number of passengers. She brought the news of the wreck of the steamer Golden Rule, on Roncador Island, May 30.

JUNE 28. A final decree was entered in the office of the Clerk of the U. S. Circuit Court in favor of the claim of the City of San Francisco to 17,775 acres of pueblo lands, and an order passed for the survey of the same.

JUNE 30. The Brother Jonathan arrived from the north with treasure amounting to $91,685.

JULY 1. Hon. Schuyler Colfax, ex-Speaker U. S. House of Representatives, and party arrived on the Sacramento boat, and were received at the Wharf by the Mayor and a committee of the Board of Supervisors appointed for that purpose....The Pacific Mail Steamship Colorado arrived from New York.

JULY 3. The Sacramento left for Panama, with treasure amounting to $957,571.03.

JULY 4. Rt. Rev. Alonzo Potter, Episcopal Bishop of Pennsylvania, died on board the Pacific Mail Steamship Colorado, of Panama fever, aged sixty-five years.'....The anniversary of the nation's independence was celebrated in a style unsurpassed on any previous occasion—with salutes, a procession in which all the civic and military bodies were largely represented, an oration at the Metropolitan Theater, by John W. Dwinelle, Esq., and an illumination and fireworks in the evening.

JULY 7. Billy Mulligan, while laboring under the effects of delerium tremens, shot Jack McNabb and John Hart, foreman of Eureka Hose Company, at the St. Francis Hotel. After several attempts to capture him alive, he was shot by one of the policemen, and instantly killed.

JULY 9. The funerals of Mulligan's victims, Hart and McNabb, were largely attended.

JULY 10. The Sierra Nevada arrived from the north, with treasure amounting to $274,000.

JULY 12. Salutes were fired from all the U. S. Military and Naval posts in and around San Francisco, in honor of the late Admiral Dupont.

JULY 15. A fire occurred about 12 o'clock, P.M., in a large frame building on Davis Street, occupied as a junk store. Loss about $5,000....The jury in the Broutes Colon piracy case brought in a verdict of acquittal.

JULY 16. A fire occurred about 12 o'clock, P.M., in the Pacific Warehouse, on the corner of Broadway and Battery streets. The building, with the greater portion of its contents, was entirely destroyed. Estimated loss about $100,000.

JULY 18. The Golden City left for Panama, with treasure amounting to $1,474,077.58.

JULY 20. Great excitement was created by the arrival of the whaleship Milo, having on board the crews of the whaleships captured by the pirate Shenandoah in the North Pacific, near two hundred in number....A fire occurred in a furniture establishment, 49 Third Street. Considerable damage was done by fire and water.

JULY 24. A fire broke out about 3 o'clock, A.M., in the Winchester House, 409 Pacific Street. Damage about $5,000, and severely burning a number of the inmates.

JULY 26. The John L. Stephens arrived from the Mexican ports with $99,821.13 in specie.

JULY 27. The Del Norte arrived from the north with treasure amounting to $12,540.

JULY 28. A frame building, corner of Fell and Webster streets, was fired by an incendiary about 9 o'clock, P.M., and burned to the ground.

JULY 29. A grand reception was given to Gen. Rosecrans by the citizens. A procession formed in the evening, marched to the Occidental Hotel where an address of welcome was delivered, and responded to by the distinguished chief.

JULY 31. The Sierra Nevada arrived from the north with a number of passengers, among whom were Hon. Schuyler Colfax and party, considerable freight, and treasure amounting to $282,774.

AUGUST 1. The melancholy news was received by telegraph from Jacksonville, Oregon, that the steamship Brother Jonathan struck on a rock about twenty-five miles north of Crescent City, about 1 o'clock, P.M., July 30, and went down immediately, carrying with her all on board, except fourteen men and one woman. She had on board between two and three hundred passengers, among whom were Brig.-Gen. Wright and family, several Army officers, James Nisbet, Editor of the Bulletin, and a number of other well-known citizens....The barque Gen. Pike arrived in port, having on board the crew of seven more of the whalers captured by the Shenandoah—two hundred and fifty-two in number.

AUG. 4. An immense meeting of citizens opposed to the repeal of the Specific Contract Law, was held at Platt's Hall.

AUG. 6. A fire broke out about 9 o'clock, P.M., in a frame house on Stockton Street, between Union and Filbert. Damage slight.

AUG. 8. The returns of the Census Marshals made to the Board of Education, shows the number of school children of the various districts, to be in the aggregate, 33,354, an increase of 2,475 over the returns of last year.

AUG. 9. The Del Norte arrived from the north with treasure amounting to $5,400.

AUG. 10. The Annual Fair of the Mechanics' Institute opened at the pavilion with an address by the Hon. E. D. Sawyer.

AUG. 17. A grand complimentary dinner to Speaker Colfax and party, was given by the Chinese merchants of San Francisco at the Hang Hung Restaurant 808 Clay Street.... The United States' war steamer Suwanee, ten guns, arrived from Philadelphia, Pa.

AUG. 21. A fire broke out between 4 and 5 o'clock in the old Niantic Hotel, corner of Clay and Sansom, doing considerable damage to that and adjoining buildings. While running to the fire, James H. Washington and Walter J. Bohen, members of the Monumental engine company, were run over by Steam Fire Engine Number 6, and fatally injured.

AUG. 22. The Sierra Nevada arrived from the north with treasure amounting to $779,723.

AUG. 24. The completion of the Alameda Railroad to Hayward's was celebrated in fine style.

AUG. 25. The Golden Age arrived from Panama with a large number of passengers, among whom was Maj. Gen. H. W. Halleck, Commander in Chief of the United States forces of the Division of the Pacific.

AUG. 27. The remains of the late James Nisbet, one of the victims of the wreck of the Brother Jonathan, were followed to their last resting place at Lone Mountain, by a large number of citizens.

AUG. 28. A one-story house on the corner of Townsend and Second streets, took fire about 11, P.M., and burned down. Damage about five hundred dollars.....Mr. Edward Daniels, Impost Clerk in the Custom House, was thrown from a buggy and instantly killed, as he was returning with a friend, from the Ocean House.

AUG. 29. The Orizaba arrived from the north with treasure amounting to $200,555.

AUG. 31. A farewell banquet was given to Hon. Schuyler Colfax at the Occidental Hotel.

SEPTEMBER 1. The funeral of Walter J. Bohen and James H. Washington, who died of injuries received while running to the fire at the Niantic Hotel, was largely attended.

SEPT. 2. The Golden City left for Panama with a large number of passengers, among them, the Colfax party and treasure amounting to $1,759,683.91.

SEPT. 5. Hugh Henderson committed suicide at North Beach.

SEPT. 6. The election for members of the Legislature passed off quietly, a smaller vote than usual being polled.

SEPT. 7. Capt. John Frank Quinley late of the Fifth Infantry C. V., died suddenly of abcess of the brain.

SEPT. 9. The Pioneer Association celebrated the anniversary of the admission of California, into the Union with an oration, poem, and collation....

SEPT. 12. The Sierra Nevada arrived from the north with a number of passengers, among whom was Hon. J. M. Ashley, Member of Congress, a large quantity of Oregon produce, and treasure amounting to $480,759.

SEPT. 13. The Del Norte arrived from the north with $8,000 in treasure.

SEPT. 15. The Mexican residents of San Francisco celebrated the fifty-sixth anniversary of Mexican Independence, in spirited style.

SEPT. 19. The Sonora arrived from Panama with six hundred and twenty-six troops belonging to the Second Artillery, U. S. Army.

SEPT. 21. A fire broke out about one o'clock, A.M., in a saloon on Montgomery Street between Clay and Merchant. Damage slight

SEPT. 22. A fire broke out about seven o'clock, P.M., on the corner of Mason and Chestnut streets. North Beach, occupied as a whisky distillery and petroleum refinery, which was destroyed together with a dwelling-house in the rear. Loss $12,000.

SEPT. 23. The body of a sailor named William Green was found floating in the bay, under one of the city wharfs.

SEPT. 23. A fire broke out about seven o'clock, P.M., in a frame building on Washington Alley, destroying property amounting to about $250.

SEPT. 25. Ground was broken on Sutter Street below Montgomery, for the track of the Front Street, Mission, and Ocean Railroad.

SEPT. 26. The body of a dead soldier named Sullivan was found lying on the road between the city and the Presidio....The first regular rain of the season fell to-day.

SEPT. 27. Cooke performed the promised feat of walking the rope at the Cliff House.

SEPT. 28. The remains of Samuel Woodworth, author of "The Old Oaken Bucket," arrived on the ship Orpheus, for interment with the family dead ....The Sierra Nevada arrived from the North with treasure amounting to $498,772.

SEPT. 29. A fire about 1 o'clock, P.M., at the corner of Howard and Third streets; damage slight.

OCTOBER 1. An affray took place at the Willows, in which Frank Riley, the proprietor of the saloon, was severely wounded by a pistol shot.... Cooke performed his rope-walking feat for the second time, before a large crowd, at the Cliff House.

OCT. 2. The Del Norte arrived with numerous passengers, and the remains of Mrs. Gen. Wright and other victims of the Brother Jonathan disaster.

OCT. 3. The Constitution left for Panama with treasure amounting to $1,141,822.

OCT. 5. The military funeral of Lieut. E. D. Waite, aide-de-camp to Gen. Wright, who perished with the wreck of the Brother Jonathan, took place to-day....A meeting of the Fenians, numbering over five thousand, took place at Union Hall in the evening.

OCT. 6. The Orizaba arrived from the North with treasure amounting to $277,565....The new screw steamer California arrived from New York, through the Straits of Magellan.

OCT. 8. Two severe earthquake shocks occurred at fifteen minutes to 1 o'clock, P.M., throwing down and badly shattering walls of buildings, breaking windows and fragile wares, and doing a large amount of damage. As a large proportion of the people were in attendance at church, no personal injury resulted from this disaster, which extended to a considerable distance in the interior, serious damage having been done to brick buildings in Santa Cruz, San José, and other towns.

OCT. 9. Two distinct earthquake shocks were felt between 9 and 10 o'clock this morning, causing no damage, however.

OCT. 11. A fire occurred at Black Point, between 2 and 3 o'clock, P.M., destroying the stables of Alpheus Bull.

OCT. 12. The Del Norte arrived from the North with numerous passengers and treasure amounting to $9,000. The remains of Gen. Wright and other parties lost on the Brother Jonathan were brought down by the steamer.

OCT. 13. As the steamer Yosemite was leaving the wharf at Rio Vista, on the downward trip, her starboard boiler exploded, blowing off the entire forward portion of the boat, and killing and wounding a large number of passengers. The unfortunate affair cast a universal gloom over the city.

OCT. 15. The Sierra Nevada arrived from the North with treasure amounting to $331,000.

OCT. 16. Gen. Rosecrans returned from his tour among the mines of Nevada, on his way East.

OCT. 17. A difficulty occurred on Kearny Street, between A. G. Hargrove and Peter Campbell, in which the latter shot the former, killing him instantly.

OCT. 18. The Golden City left for Panama with treasure amounting to $1,661,565.29....The Judicial election passed off quietly.

OCT. 20. Mrs. Bridget Baldwin, a respectable widow lady, laboring under depression from unfortunate mining investments, committed suicide.

OCT. 21. The funeral of Gen. Wright and wife took place to-day at Calvary Church. The military escorted the remains to the steamer, by which they were conveyed to their last resting-place, at Sacramento.

OCT. 25. Robert H. Parker, one of the earliest pioneers of California, and well known from his connection with the Parker House in 1849, died at San Diego, on his way from Lower California.

OCT. 26. A fire broke out at 6 o'clock, P.M., on Kearny Street, near California; before the flames were arrested the interior was thoroughly burned out.

OCT. 27. The Orizaba and Del Norte arrived from the North, the former bringing treasure amounting to $232,330.

OCT. 29. The funerals of John S. Benton, one of the officers of the Brother Jonathan, and Charles H. Belden, clerk in the Paymaster's office, victims of the wreck of that steamer, took place to-day.

OCT. 30. The Colorado left for Panama with treasure amounting to $1,141,822.84.

NOVEMBER 1. Amount collected in Police Court for month of October, $2,772.10....The Sierra Nevada arrived from Portland with treasure amounting to $293,000....The Internal Revenue receipts in this city for October were $704,000....A Frenchman named DeKerguidn, committed suicide by taking laudanum, at the California Hotel.

NOV. 4. The California Steam Navigation Co.'s new steamer "Capital" was successfully launched at Hunter's Point....Information received of removal of Collector James, and appointment of J. F. Miller his successor.

NOV. 5. Michael Hynes shot and instantly killed Thomas F. Hayes in Pollard Place....A young man named Slocumb was thrown from a horse and instantly killed, corner Bush Street and Van Ness Avenue....A fire, corner Washington and Davis streets, destroyed property to the value of $8,000.

NOV. 6. Collector Miller filed his official bonds, in the sum of $100,000....The U. S. steamer Suwanee returned from an unsuccessful search after the pirate Shenandoah.

NOV. 8. One of the cars of the Omnibus Railroad was completely demolished at the corner of Montgomery and Bush streets, by a runaway team, injuring several passengers.

NOV. 9. An Italian fishing-boat was run down on the bay, by the Oakland boat, and a man named Tomlinson killed.

NOV. 10. Wm. D. Palmer, a truckman at National Mills, committed suicide with a pistol, at his room, cor Fremont and Folsom streets... Stm Sacramento sailed for Panama, with $1,367,917.48 in treasure.

3

GENERAL REVIEW.

Public Schools.

There is no feature in the history of the advancement of San Francisco to which her citizens can point with a greater degree of pride and pleasure than the ample provision made for the education of her youth. There is no tax which her citizens pay more cheerfully than that which goes into the treasury for the maintenance and support of her Common Schools. During the past year two school edifices have been erected, one of which rivals in extent and appearance many of the first-class colleges of the older States, and various improvements have been made for the increasing number of pupils in this department.

The Public Schools of this city are classified as follows: One State Normal School, for the education and preparation of teachers of the Common Schools: one High School for boys, and one for girls; one Latin School; seven Grammar Schools; nineteen Primary Schools; seven Evening; two Colored; and one Chinese.

The number of Teachers employed in the Department at present is one hundred and forty-four, for the payment of whose salaries there will be required during the present fiscal year the sum of $154,904.85.

With regard to the financial affairs of the schools, the Department was never in a more healthy condition. The total receipts for the year ending June 30th, 1865, amounted to $350,641.78, and the whole amount of disbursements for the same term, for salaries of teachers and employés, buildings, rents, and all incidental expenses of the School Department, is $349,813.26.

Basing the amount of taxes for the benefit of the Public School Fund, upon the assessment roll of $70,000,000, at the School-Tax rate of thirty-five cents on each hundred dollars, the amount raised from this source the present year will be $245,000; apportionment of the State School Fund, $40,000; Poll Taxes, $5,000; rent of School Property, $1,000. Total revenue for the present year, $291,000.

SALARIES OF TEACHERS, 1865-66.

Boys' High School.

One Principal (male)	$2,500
One Teacher of Mathematics (male)	2,100
One Teacher of Belles-Lettres (female)	1,200
One Teacher of Modern Languages (male)	1,200

Girls' High Scool.

One Principal (male)	2,500
One Teacher Mathematics (female)	1,200
One Teacher Belles-Lettres (female)	1,200
One Teacher Modern Languages (female)	1,200

San Francisco Latin School.

One Principal (male)	2,500
One Assistant (male)	1,500

Grammar Schools.

Seven Principals (male) each	2,100
Four Sub-Masters (male) each	1,500
One Special Assistant (male)	960
Five Head Assistants (female) each	1,000
Six Special Assistants (female) each	960
Forty-three Assistants (female) each	810
Two Probationary Teachers (female) each	607

Primary Schools.

Six Principals (female) each	1,200
Five Principals (female) each	1,020
Three Special Assistants (female) each	870
Fifty Assistants (female) each	810
Ten Probationary Teachers (female) each	607
One Principal of Eighth Street School (female)	840
One Principal of Hayes' Valley School (female)	960
One Principal of Pue Street School (female)	840
One Principal of San Bruno School (male)	840
One Principal of Fairmount School (female)	840
One Principal of Six Mile School (female)	840
One Principal of Potrero School (male)	840
One Principal Chinese School (male)	960
One Principal of Broadway Street Colored School (male)	1,050
One Assistant of Broadway Street Colored School (female)	900
One Principal of Fifth Street Colored School (male)	900
One Principal of Evening School (male) $75 per month	
Seven Assistants of Evening School (male) each $62.50 per month	
Two Assistants Evening School (female) each $62.50 per month	
Two Teachers of Music (male) each	1,800
Two Teachers Penmanship and Drawing (male) each	1,800
One Teacher Penmanship (male)	1,200

REPORT OF ATTENDANCE UPON PUBLIC SCHOOLS FOR THE YEAR ENDING JUNE 30TH, 1865.

SCHOOLS.	No. of Boys Enrolled.	No. of Girls Enrolled.	Total No. Enrolled.	Average No. Belonging.	Average Daily Attendance.	Per cent....
Boys' High.......	57·1	....	57·1	54·8	51·7	·943
Girls' High......	....	88·0	88·0	83·8	80·2	·957
GRAMMAR.						
Union	176·6	115·6	292·2	278·8	268·1	·954
Washington......	182·0	200·1	382·1	531·1	338·9	·959
Denman	251·2	314·2	565·4	528·8	496·6	·939
Rincon	230·2	210·6	440·8	416·2	390·2	·937
Mission	49·3	56·6	105·9	98·4	93·1	·946
Spring Valley...	46·0	33·1	79·1	75·5	70·8	·937
Market Street...	24·8	16·8	41·6	38·6	35·8	·927
Greenwich Street	25·0	23·5	48·5	45·7	43·8	·958
PRIMARY.						
Union	282·8	232·2	515·0	476·5	455·2	·955
Denman..........	118·0	43·0	161·0	150·2	136·1	·906
Rincon	45·8	36·6	82·4	76·9	71·6	·931
Mission	122·5	132·0	254·5	232·5	213·6	·918
Spring Valley...	130·5	89·2	219·7	209·5	184·0	·897
Market Street....	259·8	202·8	462·6	433·3	406·3	·937
Fourth Street...	276·5	244·3	520·8	450·3	444·8	·926
Greenwich Street	182·7	147·8	330·5	300·5	279·0	·928
Powell Street...	248·6	245·6	494·2	473·6	440·2	·929
Hyde Street.....	152·5	117·8	270·3	244·9	225·4	·920
Sutter Street....	108·7	134·3	243·0	225·4	208·8	·932
Montgomery St..	143·0	127·6	270·6	250·0	233·4	·933
Second Street...	125·3	131·8	257·1	235·2	222·4	·945
Hayes' Valley...	72·8	54·0	126·8	117·4	109·7	·934
Model	53·0	131·1	184·1	167·9	160·8	·957
Third Street....	144·7	101·3	246·0	224·3	209·8	·935
Eighth Street...	66·2	44·8	111·0	104·9	98·7	·940
Six Mile........	11·7	16·8	22·5	19·0	16·7	·878
Fairmount	23·6	9·6	33·2	28·7	26·8	·923
San Bruno	26·5	25·6	52·1	47·8	43·4	·907
Pacific Street..	59·0	53·3	112·3	99·0	92·9	·938
Tehama Street...	129·8	105·6	235·4	214·4	196·8	·917
Potrero	23·0	21·0	44·0	38·5	25·6	·924
MIXED.						
Evening—Male..	340·5	....	340·6	251·9	197·1	·782
Evening—Female	....	60·6	60·6	49·7	38·3	·770
Colored.........	52·5	41·6	94·1	81·0	70·4	·869
Chinese	40·8	....	40·8	32·4	29·8	·919
Summary of High	57·1	88·0	145·1	138·6	131·9	·951
" Grammar	985·1	970·5	1,955·6	1,835·1	1,735·3	·945
" Primary .	2,807·0	2,442·1	5,249·1	4,850·7	4,516·0	·931
" Mixed...	433·8	102·2	536·0	415·0	335·6	·808
Totals ...	4,283·0	3,602·8	7,885·8	7,239·4	6,718·8	·928

SCHOOLS AND TEACHERS.

BOYS' HIGH SCHOOL.—Theodore Bradley, Thos. C. Leonard, Mrs. C. L. Atwood, and Paul Pioda.

GIRLS' HIGH SCHOOL.—Ellis H. Holmes, Miss Mary L. Bodwell, Miss Minnie F. Austin, and Mme. V. Brisac.

SAN FRANCISCO LATIN SCHOOL. — George W. Bunnell and W. K. Rowell.

STATE NORMAL SCHOOL. — George W. Minns, H. P. Carlton, and Miss Eliza W. Houghton.

LINCOLN SCHOOL.—Ira G. Hoitt, Mrs. Julia B. Hoitt, Andrew E. McGlynn, Philip Prior, Mrs. F. E. Reynolds, Miss L. T. Fowler, Miss Lizzie F. Hitchings, Miss Estelle M. Bullene, Miss Lizzie B. Jewett, Miss L. S. Swain, Miss F. E. Bennett, and Miss Agnes M. Manning.

UNION STREET SCHOOL.—Thomas S. Myrick, T. W. J. Holbrook, Mrs. P. C. Cook, Mrs. C. R. Beals, Miss S. S. Sherman, Miss A. F. Aldrich, Miss E. M. Tibbey, Miss A. L. Eschenburg, Miss C. A. Cummings, Miss Carrie P. Field, Miss Wellie S. Baldwin, Miss Jennie M. Drummond, Mrs. Aurelia Griffith, Miss L. M. Drummond, Miss Annie E. Younger, and Miss Ellen G. Grant.

FRANKLIN DISTRICT SCHOOL (Denman Grammar School).—James Denman, Miss E. M. Baumgardner, Mrs. H. Pearson, Miss H. Augusta Willard, Mrs. L. A. Clapp, Miss C. A. Sherman, Miss C. M. Pattee, Miss May Williams, Miss Margaret Keith, Miss E. A. Shaw, Miss Ada C. Bowen, Miss Lydia A. Clegg, and Miss Laura E. Field.

MONTGOMERY STREET SCHOOL. — Miss A. S. Moses, Miss Lizzie Overend, Miss P. A. Fink, Miss A. M. Hucks, Miss Helen F. Parker, and Miss Helen Satterlee.

WASHINGTON GRAMMAR SCHOOL.—James Stratton, Henry E. McBride, Mrs. H. L. Weaver, Miss D. L. Prescott, Miss H. F. Richardson, Miss S. J. White, Miss Ellen Parker, and Miss M. E. Cheney.

POWELL STREET SCHOOL.—Miss Caroline Price, Miss E. S. Forester, Miss M. A. Casebolt, Miss Maggie Wade, Miss N. M. Chadbourne, Miss S. E. Thurton, Miss C. A. Coffin, and Mrs. M. W. Phelps.

MARKET STREET SCHOOL. — Mrs. C. H. Stout, Miss M. T. Kimball, Miss N. B. Sturtevant, Miss C. J. Neal, Miss L. G. Bunker, Miss Alice Kenny, Miss M. A. Humphreys, and Miss Carry L. Smith.

RINCON SCHOOL.—Ebenezer Knowlton, Joseph D. Littlefield, Miss Helen Thompson, Miss F. Lynch, Miss C. V. Benjamin, Miss M. E. Stowell, Miss S. L. Hobart, Miss M. A. E. Phillips, Miss A. M. Dore, and Miss A. S. Cameron.

STEVENSON STREET SCHOOL.—Mrs. E. C. Burt, Miss Jennie Smith, Miss M. F. Smith, Mrs. L. Deetkin, Mrs. S. N. Joseph, Mrs. J. H. Sumner, Miss Helen Grant, and Miss F. A. E. Nichols.

FOURTH STREET SCHOOL.—Miss L. A. Morgan, Miss E. M. Shaw, Miss M. J. Ritchie, Miss J. C. Haehnlen, Miss E. Cushing, Miss M. J. Bragg, Miss Sarah M. Gunn, Miss A. Louder, Miss S. Davis, and Miss Maggie McKenzie.

MISSION GRAMMAR SCHOOL.—A. Holmes, Miss Jessie Smith, Miss Julia Clayton, Miss Annie Hill, Miss Philena Sawyer, Miss A. A. Rowe, Miss M. O'Connor.

SECOND STREET SCHOOL.—Miss Solome S. Knapp, Miss E. Neville Campbell, Miss E. N. White, and Miss Lydia W. Derby.

SPRING VALLEY GRAMMAR SCHOOL.—B. Marks, Miss M. A. Buffum, Miss H. A. Haneke, Miss J. V. Barkley, Miss M. J. Norton, and Miss D. Hyman.

GREENWICH STREET SCHOOL.—Miss Kate Kennedy, Miss S. M. Scotchler, Miss Fannie M. Cheney, Miss Agnes Chalmers, Miss Lizzie B. Easton, and Miss Fannie Mitchell.

HYDE STREET PRIMARY SCHOOL. — Miss Hannah Cooke, Miss L. A. Humphreys, Miss A. B. Chalmers, and Miss Kate Bonnell.

SUTTER STREET PRIMARY SCHOOL.—Miss Carrie L. Hunt, Miss Jennie M. A. Hurley, Miss Helen S. Arey, and Miss Eve Solomon.

POST STREET PRIMARY SCHOOL. — Miss Kate Sullivan, Miss Mary Goldsmith, Miss Mary A. Salisbury, and Miss Ellen Holmes.

PACIFIC STREET SCHOOL.—Mrs. A. E. Pollock, and Miss H. M. Gates.

EIGHTH STREET SCHOOL. — Miss A. E. Slavan, Miss A. M. Jourdan, and Miss Evlyn Mosse.

TEHAMA STREET SCHOOL.—Miss Bessie Molloy and Miss P. M. Stowell.

HAYES' VALLEY SCHOOL. — Miss L. J. Mastick, Miss Jennie Gunn, and Miss Fannie Stowell.

POTRERO SCHOOL.—T. J. Leonard.

SAN BRUNO SCHOOL.—George S. Pershin.

FAIRMOUNT SCHOOL.—Mrs. H. H. Treat.

SIX MILE SCHOOL.—Mrs. L. Carter.

FIFTH STREET COLORED SCHOOL.—J. B. Sanderson.

COLORED SCHOOL.—S. D. Simonds and Mrs. Georgia Washburn.

CHINESE SCHOOL.—B. Lanctot.

MUSIC.—F. K. Mitchell and Washington Elliott.

WRITING AND DRAWING.—Fulgenzio Seregni, Hubert Burgess, and A. B. Andrews.

PUBLIC SCHOOL CENSUS—TAKEN AUGUST, 1865.

DISTRICTS.	First	Second	Third	Fourth	Fifth	Sixth	Seventh	Eighth	Ninth	Tenth	Eleventh	Twelfth	Totals
Number of Blind Children between four and eighteen years of age													24
Number of Deaf and Dumb Children between four and eighteen years of age													43
Number of Negro Children between four and eighteen years of age													191
Number of Mongolian Children between four and eighteen years of age													279
Number of Indian Children between four and eighteen years of age													69
Number of Children between six and eighteen y'rs of age not attending any School													3,565
Total number of Children reported as attending Private Schools													5,450
Total number of Children reported as attending Public Schools													7,805
Number of Children between four and six years of age attending Private Schools													604
Number of Children between four and six years of age													3,995
Number of White Children under twenty-one born in California													21,123
Number of White Children between eighteen and twenty-one years of age													1,291
Number of White Children under four years of age													11,413
Total number of White Children between four and eighteen years of age													20,661
Number of Girls between four and eighteen years of age													10,577
Number of Boys between four and eighteen years of age													10,004
Application for Public School Accommodations													1,142

Private Educational Institutions.

While the foregoing facts and statistics exhibit abundant and indisputable evidence of the flourishing condition of our Public Schools, there is probably no city of the same number of inhabitants, in the whole American Union—and certainly no community of the same age in the world—that can boast the same number of well conducted Private Educational Institutions. These schools for the proper training of the youth of both sexes, are ample in number, thorough in the course of study pursued, provided with all the apparatus and appliances necessary for pursuing useful scientific investigation, and in every department keeping fully up with the rapid march of improvement characteristic of the age in which we live. While the mental training of pupils is of course the paramount object of these institutions, that physical development so essential to health, happiness, and usefulness in life, is never lost sight of; and, as is the case with the Public Schools, each private institution has its gymnasium, fitted up with all the appliances necessary for healthful exercise, and the highest degree of physical development, with ample room for free and unconstrained movement. Absorbed as the great mass of our citizens are with the cares attendant upon the daily routine of business, and the unceasing rush after "the almighty dollar," too little attention is paid to the examination of and noting the growth and improvement of our educational institutions, public and private. The servants of the people who have the training of the future citizen in the former, as well as the teachers engaged in the latter, are always pleased to receive the intelligent visitor, who can understand and appreciate their efforts, and give countenance and encouragement to the noble work in which they are engaged.

The whole number of private educational institutions in San Francisco is about eighty, with an aggregate attendance of five thousand four hundred and fifty. Of this number twelve are under the control of the Catholic denomination, and the regular aggregate attendance upon the same is thirty-eight hundred.

Being governed in the order of our review by number and attendance, we commence our summary with

CATHOLIC SCHOOLS.

ST. IGNATIUS' COLLEGE.

This well known literary institution, located on Market Street between Fourth and Fifth, which is conducted by the Fathers of the Society of Jesus, was first opened for the reception of students on the fifteenth day of October, 1855, and was incorporated under the law of the State on the thirtieth of April, 1859, and empowered to confer the usual degrees and academical honors. Since its commencement this institution has been attended with the highest degree of prosperity and success. The course of instruction pursued is thorough, and comprises a complete classical, mathematical, and philosophical course of training calculated to prepare the pupil for entering upon the study of any of the professions, or commencing any business vocation. The college is provided with an extensive laboratory, comprising all the necessary appliances for the assaying of metals and making chemical analyses, which is an important feature not generally found in institutions of this character: a spacious building has been erected for a photographic gallery, where all the departments of the Daguerrean art will be practiced and taught. There is a telegraphic room, with an instrument in operation, connecting with a similar station at the Santa Clara College—the use of the California State Line having been granted for this purpose—where the business of operating is taught, forming another novel and important educational feature.

The founders of this institution foreseeing the rapid progress of the Queen City of the Pacific, purchased some years since the property upon which the magnificent college edifice has since been erected. This lot has a frontage of two hundred and seventy-five feet on Market, and the same on Jessie Street, with a depth of three hundred and fifty feet. The college building at present consists of a center and one wing, the former is one hundred and five by fifty-six feet, and the latter, in which is the college Hall—used temporarily as the church, until that building shall be erected in another portion of the grounds—is one hundred and seventy by sixty feet. The present building, the cost of which, independent of the lot, was $120,000, although one of the finest architectural ornaments of the city is only one-third of the extent contemplated. When the extensive additions are made the entire structure will rival anything of the kind to be found in our portion of the country. The present building is admirably adapted to the purposes for which it was designed, being abundantly lighted and well ventilated in every portion; the ceilings are lofty, and spacious halls run through the building. A large play-ground is attached with a commodious shelter from the rain, affording ample means for the physical exercise of the pupils. In fact, nothing has been neglected which is at all conducive to mental and physical training. The number of students in the College at present is four hundred.

ST. MARY'S COLLEGE.

This institution is situated near the county road to San José, at a distance of four miles and a half from this city. The lot on which the building is erected consists of sixty acres; it possesses all the advantages of a salubrious situation, and commands an extensive view of the bay and surrounding scenery. The college building covers a space of two hundred and eighty feet front by a depth of fifty feet, which, in the center, is increased to a depth of seventy feet; one hundred and ten feet of the building will be three stories high, and the remaining portion four stories high. On the northern extremity of the main edifice is situated the refectory, which is forty by eighty feet, and two stories in hight. On the southern extremity is the chapel, forty by one hundred and thirty feet. By this arrangement the greatest advantage is secured for all healthful purposes, as the sun shines during the day on the three principal fronts of the building, and the narrow ends being north and south, during the rainy season the smallest surface is exposed to the inclemency of the weather. Thus the structures form three sides of a quadrangle, and on the eastern front there is a cloister thirteen feet six inches wide, which extends the entire length of the building, so that under any circumstances and at all periods of the year the students can have out-door exercise. The basement will contain the offices of the steward, and all apartments in connection with them; the housekeepers' rooms, servants' rooms, general store rooms, bath rooms, and closets for various purposes.

The chief entrances to the college are in the principal story. These consist of an entrance in the center through a spacious porch, and two side entrances. The center one leads to a hall thirteen feet wide by thirty feet long, on either side of which are the reception rooms. This hall terminates in a corridor which leads to the three chief staircases and the different apartments in this story, namely: Lavatories, Professors' rooms, recreation hall, and library; on the eastern side of this story are the various entrances to the cloister. The second story consists of school rooms, class rooms, music rooms, apartments for natural philosophy and museum. The third story consists of dormitories, bed rooms, bath rooms, and an apartment which will answer as a temporary infirmary. The first story of the refectory building consists of lavatory, refectory, and lunch rooms; the second story is a dormitory. There are three entrances to the chapel—one through the western porch which faces the altar, another through the tower which is situated on the south side, and one on the north side.

The sanctuary is in the east end of the chapel, adjoining to which are sacristies, and organ gallery. The top of the spire is to be one hundred and thirty feet above the surface of the ground, and the south gable of the college building eighty-six feet high. The building will be supplied with gas and water throughout its entire extent. All sewerage and drainage is on the outside. The kitchen, bake-house, and laundry are disconnected with the main buildings; everything has been studied in order to promote the health of the students and give them all accommodation. The portion now in course of erection will accommodate three hundred students. The entire building, when completed, will accommodate seven hundred or eight hundred. The building is designed in the Gothic style of architecture, and in its completeness of outline as well as the faultless elaboration of details, reflects the greatest credit on the professional skill and taste of its architect, Mr. Thomas England. The pension will be exceedingly moderate, not exceeding one hundred and fifty dollars or one hundred and sixty dollars a year for board and tuition, thus placing its advantages within the means of all. Considering the great want of educational facilities in the interior of the State, it must be evident that the Institution will be a great public benefit to the community at large, as children of all denominations will be admitted.

St. Mary's College was opened for the reception of children on the sixth of July, 1863, and has now over two hundred and ten students from all parts of this State and adjoining Territories, under the direction of a large staff of able Professors.

Peter J. Grey, President.

ST. MARY'S SCHOOL.

This school is exclusively for boys, and meets in the basement of St. Mary's Cathedral. It is under the direction of three Brothers of the Third Order of St. Francis and a secular gentleman. The number of children attending this school averages five hundred. The course of studies embraces reading, writing, English grammar, geography, with the use of the globes, arithmetic, algebra, geometry, and the Spanish and Latin languages, if desired. There is a nominal charge of one dollar per month for each pupil able to pay; those not able being educated gratis. As this is a regulation common to all the Catholic parochial schools in the city it will not be necessary to repeat it in referring to the others.

In the class-rooms Sunday school for boys is held from 9 to 11, A.M.

CONVENT OF THE SISTERS OF PRES'

This is one of the largest female city. Located on Powell Street, the Rev. Mother Superior and Presentation. The convent bui' and well adapted to education have cost altogether not less than $70,000, and form a commanding feature of that portion of the city in which they are located. The studies pursued embrace a thorough English course, vocal and instrumental music, French, drawing, embroidery, and other ornamental branches. The number of pupils belonging to this school amounts to nine hundred.

SCHOOL OF ST. FRANCIS.

This is also a male school, conducted in the basement of the Church of St. Francis, on Vallejo Street. The number of pupils is two hundred and sixty, with an average attendance of one hundred and thirty. The course of studies is the same as in St. Mary's School.

SAINT VINCENT'S SCHOOL.

This is a female day school, on Jessie Street between Second and Third, under the direction of Sister Francis McEnnis and ten other Sisters of Charity, who are also in charge of the Roman Catholic Female Orphan Asylum on Market Street. The number of scholars belonging to the school is over five hundred, exclusive of two hundred and fifty orphan children in the asylum. The course of studies is the same as in the school last mentioned, and the noble ladies who conduct it have established a high reputation for ability and devotion to their self-imposed duties. As this school is supported by volunteer contributions, it appeals directly to the liberality of the generous and charitable in our midst. During the past year a commodious frame building has been added, which has been opened as a free school, under the same management.

In addition to the foregoing, the Sisters of Mercy have also a female school under their charge for children thrown upon their care, at which instruction in primary English studies is imparted, and the pupils are taught to be useful in the discharge of household duties.

Other Colleges and Schools.

UNION COLLEGE.

This well-known and highly popular institution, under the charge of Dr. R. T. Huddart, one of the most experienced and successful teachers, under whose tuition some of our most prominent professional and business men were educated on the Atlantic side of the continent, is situated on the corner of Second and Bryant streets. The location is a pleasant one, the buildings commodious, and conveniently arranged, and the grounds ample for exercise and recreation. While a wholesome discipline is practiced in this institution, under the immediate supervision and direction of the Principal, there is an absence of that unnecessary and highly detrimental restraint which tends to dwarf instead of expanding the intellect. The most ample provision being made at this institution for the accommodation of pupils from abroad, a large number of students are in attendance here from the northern States of Mexico and the interior of our own. The average attendance of pupils is over one hundred.

UNIVERSITY SCHOOL.

This institution is under the charge of Mr. George ——, M.A., a graduate of Cambridge University, ——d, where he took a high position as a scholar, ——ially distinguished himself in mathematical ——r. Bates has had large experience in —— in English and American schools, and —— pains nor exertion in the advance- —— . As its name would imply, the —— of the University School is to —— es for those who are preparing ——foreign universities; accord- —— the number of pupils are —— classics. The relative ——is is unusually large—

the terms being fixed rather with a view to educating a limited number thoroughly, than to sending forth a host whose education does not extend below the surface. While this school commends itself to those who are desirous of securing for their sons the watchful care and constant supervision of competent teachers, it avoids the disadvantages attendant upon private tuition.

The University School is located on Post Street between Stockton and Powell. The building is large and commodious, and has an ample play-ground attached. An evening class for adults meets three times a week.

CALIFORNIA COLLEGIATE INSTITUTE.

This popular institution for the education of young ladies is pleasantly located on Silver Street near Third. The building was specially erected for the purpose, is large, commodious, well ventilated, and conveniently arranged, having a large room fitted up as a gymnasium, with all the appliances necessary for healthful as well as graceful exercise for the physical development of the pupils, for here bodily and mental grace are happily combined. Receptions are held on Friday afternoon of each week, which parents, guardians, and visitors desiring to witness the progress of the pupils, and the exercises and course of study of the institute, are cordially invited to attend. While the greater portion of the pupils in attendance are from our own city and State, there are always a number from abroad— the northern States of Mexico, and British America. The institute is under the charge of Miss Lammond, an accomplished lady of great experience in teaching, and formerly the Principal of a popular female institute at Benicia, who gives her personal attention and immediate supervision to every department. She is assisted by the following corps of competent teachers: Madame Villimate, teacher of French; Miss Audubon, Miss Gregory, and Mrs. McGilvray; and Mr. Bentler, teacher of music; Mr. Butman, of oil painting; and Mr. Hartmann.

GRACE FEMALE INSTITUTE.

Occupying the spacious school rooms of Grace Cathedral, was organized by Bishop Kip in March, 1864. The Rev. H. Goodwin was the first Principal. He was succeeded in October, 1864, by the Rev. G. A. Easton. This seminary asks, and thus far has liberally received, the patronage of those parents and guardians who desire especially that the principles of the Gospel be daily and directly taught as the basis of instruction and rule of life. The Principal is assisted by two teachers in the English and two teachers in the French department.

CITY COLLEGE.

This institution, established by Rev. Dr. George W. Burrowes, in the basement of Calvary Church, but at present located on the SE corner of Stockton and Geary Street, is in a flourishing condition, having ten Professors and Teachers constantly employed. The number of pupils receiving instruction at present is one hundred and sixty-five, sixty-three of whom are pursuing the study of the Latin and Greek languages, higher branches of mathematics, mental and moral philosophy, chemistry, etc.

ST. MARK'S GRAMMAR AND ENGLISH DAY SCHOOL.

This school is superintended by a School Board, composed principally of members of the German Lutheran St. Mark's Church. It is situated on Geary Street, between Stockton and Powell, a convenient hall in the basement of St. Mark's Church having been set apart for school purposes. The object of this school is to impart, both in the English and German languages, to children of both sexes, a thorough instruction in all the different branches taught in the public schools of the city, and also to afford to all who desire it, an opportunity for the education of their children in the precepts and doctrines of the Christian religion. Mr. G. H. Labohm, a professionally educated teacher, is Principal. The following gentlemen are the present members of the School Board: J. K. Thomas, I. Everding, P. Mayer, J. Kohlmoos, H. Meese, F. Lauenstein, H. Kohlmoos.

CITY FEMALE SEMINARY.

This institution, which receives the undivided attention of its founder, Rev. Charles Russell Clarke, is located on the corner of Mason and O'Farrell streets, in the immediate vicinity of the routes of the Central and Mission railroads. The Principal is assisted by Mrs. Clarke, who has charge of the general supervision of the Seminary, and by competent and experienced assistants in the different departments. Married and elderly ladies are received temporarily into the institution, which is open at all times to all who desire to select a permanent place for the education of their children, and those interested in the progress of institutions of learning. Number of pupils in attendance, ninety.

SAINT THOMAS' SEMINARY.

This seminary is for the pursuit of clerical studies, and was commenced at its present place (Mission Dolores) in 1854, although prior to that time a few students pursued their ecclesiastical studies at the residence of the Archbishop. The number of students is now fourteen, and seven have been ordained who were educated at the seminary.

SANTA CLARA COLLEGE, SAN JOSE.

This establishment is under the superintendence of the Fathers of the Society of Jesus, and is open to all who choose to avail themselves of its advantages. It is situated in the beautiful valley of Santa Clara, so celebrated for the mildness and salubrity of its climate, and is about three miles distant from San José and quite close to the San José and San Francisco Railroad.

The college was founded in 1851. On the twenty-eighth of April, 1855, it was incorporated, and empowered to confer degrees and academical honors, and to exercise all the rights and privileges common to any other literary institution in the United States. It has a full staff of professors, and presents advantages for the mental, physical and moral training of the students unsurpassed in California. It possesses a complete philosophical apparatus purposely made in Paris for Santa Clara College, and furnished with all necessary instruments for experiments in mechanics, hydraulics, pneumatics, caloric, electricity, magnetism, optics, acoustics, and surveying. New and important additions are being made every year to keep pace with the progress of science.

The chemical laboratory is provided with a full assortment of chemicals, a very good set of furnaces, and all that is necessary for the different kinds of chemical analysis. The museum of natural history comprises a collection of mineralogy of more than one thousand five hundred specimens; also three thousand specimens of shells and other natural curiosities. As an accessory to the scientific department there is a photographic gallery, where the students who wish may learn photography in all its different branches. Practical lessons are given also on the electric telegraph. The college library numbers about ten thousand volumes.

FEMALE COLLEGIATE INSTITUTE, SANTA CLARA.

This institution is known as the Female Department of the University of the Pacific, and is patronized by the California Conference of the Methodist Episcopal Church.

The charter for the university was granted by the legislature in August, 1851. In May, 1852, the Rev. E. Bannister opened a preparatory school for both sexes in the central portion of the Institute edifice. A school, of which this may be considered the outgrowth, was commenced in December, 1850, under the auspices of the Missionary Society of the M. E. Church, by the same Principal.

In December, 1853, the sexes were separated, and for this department, the title "Female Collegiate Institute" adopted. It embraces three departments, primary, preparatory, and collegiate, with a full board of instruction. The collegiate course extends over a period of three years. Ancient and modern languages are thoroughly taught, also all the usual ornamental branches.

The boarding department is limited, there being accommodation for about thirty boarding pupils. Day pupils are also received. The list of graduates is quite extended, though the exact number is not known by the author of this article. It has been successively under the care of Rev. E. Bannister, D.D., Rev. D. A. Dryden, Rev. J. Rogers, Rev. G. S. Phillips, A.M., Rev. E. Bannister, D.D., and Rev. D. Tuthill, A.M. It is at present in successful operation under the last-named principal.

ST. CATHERINE'S ACADEMY, BENICIA.

This institution is conducted by the Sisters of St. Dominic, and is situated in the healthy and accessible town of Benicia. The plan of education embraces the various branches of instruction usually taught in the most approved seminaries for young ladies. Pupils of any religious denomination will be received; but for the sake of uniformity, all are required to be present at the regular religious services of the institution. The scholastic year, comprising ten months and a half, opens on the twenty-first of August, and ends about the first week of July. Pupils will be received at any time, the fees to commence from date of entrance.

Societies—Religious, Benevolent, and Protective.

In another portion of this volume will be found a full list of charitable associations and organizations established for the benefit and improvement of every class of humanity requiring aid and encouragement. It is, however, meet and pleasing to note the continued and regular increase in the number and importance of these indices of modern christian civilization in our midst. There is probably no city in the world of the same population so well supplied with benevolent institutions and elemosynary associations as San Francisco. Every nationality is represented by its charitable association; every want known to humanity is anticipated; every ill that flesh is heir to is ministered to by the kindly hand of benevolence and good fellowship. The vital force and active condition of these praiseworthy associations is the best refutation of the charge sometimes made that our people are absorbed in the worship of mammon. In no community in the world are the calls of distress more fully and liberally responded to. While our numerous benevolent institutions are so liberally sustained by private contribution and individual effort, the State has nobly contributed to the support of a number of this class of our institutions in the following liberal appropriations:

To the Asylum for the Deaf, Dumb, and Blind, $200 per annum for each pupil; Orphan Asylums—Protestant $15,000, and Catholic $10,000; to the Ladies' Protection and Relief Society, $6,000; to the Home of the Inebriate, $2,500, and Magdalen Asylum, $5,000.

SABBATH SCHOOLS.

The Sabbath Schools connected with the different churches continue in a prosperous condition. The report of the average attendance during the past year of the twenty-one schools connected with the Sunday School Union, is as follows:

SUNDAY SCHOOLS.	SUPERINTENDENTS.	Average Attend'e.	Vols. in Library.	Conver- sions.
1st Baptist.........	B. T. Martin	340	1,800	16
2d Baptist.........	Dr. J. C. Spencer..	225	500	
1st Congregational..	L. B. Benchley	350	1,200	3
2d Congregational..	E. D. Sawyer	245	555	10
3d Congregational..	J. W. Cox..........	220	550	
Green St. Cong.	David Cobb, p. tem	201	355	1
Powell Street M. E	E. W. Playter......	206	1,250	34
Mariners'....	H. L. Chamberlain.	75	185	3
Howard St. M. E ...	Charles Goodall....	477	1,500	13
Mission Bethel M.E.	J. B. Firth	97	300	
Folsom St. Ger.M.E.	J. G. Mysell......	131	800	
Broadway Ger. M.E.	M. Kuchenpeisser..	100	855	
First Presbyterian..	S. B. Stoddard....	295	400	3
Hyde and Bush Mis.	John K. Allen....	64	240	
Howard Presbyter'n	W. L. Palmer......	337	1,000	5
St. Paul's Presbyt'n	Warren Holt	75	500	
Industrial School..	George E. Lynde....	135	300	
Larkin St.Presbyt'n	E. R. Waterman ...	120	600	
Potrero Union	Edward Anderson..	25	60	
Central Methodist..	James F. Smith....	200	700	
Montgom'y St. M.E.	M. K. Laudenslager	125	250	
Totals.....		4,043	14,090	89

Protestants not connected with the Union.

Calvary............	J. B. Roberts......	280	1,000	6
Calvary Mission....	H. Bergner........	135	400	
Central Presbyter'n	Stephen Franklin..	40	200	
Grace Cathedral....	F. Smith	200	750	
Trinity...........	B. H. Randolph....	175	1,000	6
Trinity Mission.....	William G. Badger.	300	2,000	
Ch. of the Advent..	E. B. Benjamin....	250	1,500	
St. John's.........	W. O. Andrews	80	750	8
Third Baptist......	William Harris....	25	120	
African Methodist..	J. B. Sanderson....	30	275	
Zion Wesleyan.....	R. T. Houston.....	30	200	
Chinese Mission....	Rev. Mr. Loomis...	25		
German Lutheran..	Rev. Mr. Mooshake	30	200	
St. Mark's Lutheran	Rev. Mr. Buehler..	50	75	
First Ger. Lutheran.	Rev. Mr. Hansen...	25		
First Unitarian....	Samuel L. Cutter..	280	1,100	
Swedenborgian.	James Kellogg....	12	200	
Totals............		1,967	9,770	20

Mission Schools.

Calvary 4th St. Mis.	L. S. Vanwinkle....	60		
Mission St. M. E....	J. H. Lelong.......	88	150	
Howard, Hayes Val.	E. F. Maxfield....	40	150	
Totals		188	300	

Catholic Schools not connected with the Union.

St. Mary's Cathedral	J. McMahan, O.S.F.	400		
St. Francis'.........	Wm. J. Gorman...	120		
St. Patrick's	E. Neale	300		
St. Boniface's.......	Miss Sutkamp.....	60		
St. Ignatius'........	Jesuit Priests ...	330	200	
Mission Dolores.....	Rev. J. Prendergast	130		
St. Joseph's.........	Charles Smith	150	230	
St. Rose's..........	The Sisters........	150	350	
St. Bridget's	Father Aerden.....	150		
Presentation Conv't	Rev. Mother, L. C.	700		
St. Mary's College..	Rev. Father Gray..	100		
Magdalen Asylum...		50		
Catholic Asylum....	Sisters...........	600	450	
Totals....		3,240	1,230	

Israelites.

Cong. Sherith Israel	Dr. Henry.........	80		
Emanu-El	Dr. Cohn..........	300		
Ahabai Shalom.....	E. Blackman	75		
Hebrew School.....	— Stone..........	200		
Total		655		

Average attendance 7,106, which added to the estimated number attending the Catholic 3,240, and the Israelites, 655 make a total of over 11,000 who receive religious instruction on the Sabbath in this city.

YOUNG MEN'S CHRISTIAN ASSOCIATION.

This society was organized in 1853, with a view to the moral, social, and intellectual improvement of young men of all denominations, by means of a reading-room supplied with all the leading religious and secular papers, magazines, and periodicals, domestic and foreign together with a well selected library of over two thousand volumes, embracing nearly every branch of general literature. Of these, about six hundred are religious, two hundred biographical, one hundred poetical, two hundred historical, two hundred travels, and seven hundred miscellaneous, as essays, sermons, classics, fiction, drama, law, philosophy, science, and art, standard works, bound magazines, and periodicals, commentaries, encyclopedias, dictionaries, reference books, public documents, etc. A social prayer meeting is held at the rooms every Saturday evening, from eight to 9 o'clock, and from half-past twelve to 1, P.M. each day is devoted to the same purpose. There is also a literary society conducted under the auspices of the association, which meets at the rooms every Tuesday evening. The association numbers about three hundred and fifty members; of these, five are honorary, seventy-five life, one hundred and thirty-nine active, and one hundred and thirty-one associate. To become a member, the name of the applicant must first be proposed for membership at a regular monthly meeting, by a member of the association, which proposal will be acted upon at the next monthly meeting; *provided*, said applicant has paid the yearly dues, which, for an active member, is five dollars, and for an associate, three. No initiation fee is charged. Members of evangelical churches in good standing, only, may become active members. Life members are constituted by the payment of twenty-five dollars at any one time. Only active and life members are qualified to vote and eligible to office. The rooms of the association are at 526 California Street, nearly opposite the Mechanic's Institute, and are open to the public the year round from 8, A.M. to 10, P.M. The library is open every day (Sundays excepted) from 3 to 10 o'clock, P.M.

LADIES' PROTECTION AND RELIEF SOCIETY.

This institution, organized August 4th, 1863, by the benevolent ladies of San Francisco, and incorporated August 9th the year following, has been productive of a large amount of good in relieving the distress of sick and destitute women and children, and providing employment for females desirous of procuring work. To carry out this praiseworthy object, the society has erected a Home on Franklin Street, between Post and Geary, where protection, aid, and information is cheerfully furnished to all residents and strangers included within the sphere of its benevolent operations. The Legislature of 1863-4, amongst other appropriations for the assistance of the benevolent institutions of the State, allotted this association $6,000, which aided in paying for the Home.

From the organization of the society, till the first of April last, a large part of the work has been caring for families in the city who needed assistance in the way of provisions, fuel, clothing, nurees, medical aid, and medicines, payment of rents, etc. A total of sixty-one families were aided in this manner, during the first seven months of this year, besides the maintenance of the Home. At the time referred to, the San Francisco Benevolent Society commenced its work, and generously assumed the care of the cases then on our hands, and all subsequent out-door work of that kind.

During the p y , one hundred and twenty-two adults and children have been inmates of the Home; of these, eight have been indentured or adopted, leaving the present number seventy-two. The ages of the children range from one to fourteen years.

A school is maintained at the Home, in which all the children old enough are daily taught all the elementary branches. The average number of scholars the past year has been upwards of fifty. Gratifying improvement has been made; but the changes incident to the plan of operations often remove the most promising. Yet this is the only way to secure the highest good of the child, as it has never been any part of the plans of the society to assume the permanent support or education of any.

ORPHAN ASYLUM (PROTESTANT).

This benevolent and praiseworthy institution was organized January 31st, 1851, and incorporated by act of the Legislature on the tenth of the ensuing month. To the almost unaided efforts of a few ladies we are indebted for this noble institution, which now stands as a monument to their charity and goodness of heart. The asylum was first located on the corner of Folsom and Second streets, in a building owned by General H. W. Halleck, from whence it was removed in March, 1854, to the present building, a commodious and elegant stone structure, which was finished at an expense of $30,000. This building occupies the block bounded by Laguna, Octavia, Page, and Webster streets, and is roomy and adequate to the wants of the class for whose benefit it has been founded. Dependent mainly upon private benevolence for support, the institution is one of the proudest monuments of the liberality of the people of San Francisco. In the construction of the building two important matters have been carefully kept in view, which are too often lost sight of in the planning of many public buildings of the present day—ventilation and light. To the abundant supply of fresh air introduced into every portion of the building, combined with the abundant and substantial supply of food furnished the children, and the daily exercise allowed them, may be attributed the unexampled health of the inmates. Every department is thorough and complete, clean, orderly, and well kept; the dormitories are spacious and airy, with everything neat and comfortable; large play-rooms are provided for the exercise of the children, when confined in-doors by the weather; the school room, dining room, kitchen, laundry, wash and bath rooms, are all upon a scale commensurate with the wants of the institution, and everything connected with each is arranged and conducted in the most admirable manner. In the school the children are taught the solid branches, with the addition of drawing and exercises in singing, and in point of aptness and proficiency the pupils will compare favorably with any of the public schools of the city. The elevated location of the asylum commands a view of a great portion of the city and bay, with the opposite shore, and when further improvements are made to the grounds, which are very much needed, a more picturesque and beautiful spot cannot be anywhere found in the vicinity of the city. The Legislature of 1864 appropriated $15,000 for the support of this institution, and for the improvement of the orphan grounds.

The present number of inmates is one hundred and sixty-four, of which seventy-five are girls; and of this number but a very small proportion are from San Francisco. The whole State, and indeed the entire Pacific Coast, claims for its orphans a home and a shelter in the San Francisco Orphan Asylum; and applications constantly being made from even the most remote parts of this and adjoining States and Territories, asking admission sometimes for whole families of orphan children, prove that this institution is being known throughout the land; and through the liberality of its patrons, and the assistance rendered by the State, its managers are enabled to give favorable replies to these numerous calls.

CATHOLIC ORPHAN ASYLUM.

This institution is located on Market Street, near its junction with Kearny, on a lot donated for the purpose by Timothy Murphy of Marin County. The main building, which is a handsome edifice, fronts on Market Street—the school and infirmary buildings being located in the rear. The children, females—the male asylum of the Order being located on the property donated for the purpose by the same testator, at San Rafael, Marin County—number upwards of three hundred. Every attention is paid to the mental and physical training of the children, who are truly healthy and happy. All the solid branches of education are taught in the school, with music and other accomplishments—the asylum being provided with three pianos for the use of the orphans. The rooms are well ventilated, and every attention is paid to the health of the inmates. The play-grounds are ample, and provided with every appliance for healthy exercise. Some of the teachers have been brought up and educated in the institution. Two of the finest globes, terrestrial and celestial, to be found on this coast, belong to this institution. The asylum is supported by the Order under which it was instituted, by donations and private contributions, and by appropriations from the State. The asylum is under the charge of Sister Frances, who is truly a mother to the orphans.

STATE DEAF AND DUMB AND BLIND INSTITUTION.

This admirable institution was organized under the auspices of the State, under an Act of the Legislature of 1860, and under its fostering care is now one of the most flourishing institutions in the land. The buildings were erected upon a large lot at the corner of Mission and Fifteenth streets, and are ample for the accommodation of all the pupils that will be apt to be in attendance for years to come. The Legislature of 1863 passed an Act levying a special tax of one mill on each one hundred dollars, for the support of this institution, and the erection of other buildings. The immediate control of the institution was originally assigned to a board of benevolent ladies; but the last Legislature removed them, and passed a law placing the management under the control of a board of three trustees. At present there are sixty-two pupils, about equally divided. The pupils are under the charge of competent teachers, who instruct them in reading, writing, needle-work, etc.—the blind being also instructed in music. While this is a charitable institution, the benefits of which are denied to none, parents who are able are required to pay a small sum yearly for the care and attention bestowed upon their unfortunate children.

SAN FRANCISCO BENEVOLENT ASSOCIATION.

Of all the benevolent institutions established in our city none have been productive of more real, substantial and lasting good in proportion to the means employed than the San Francisco Benevolent Association. Although less than a year old—filling up, as it has done, a most important hiatus in the benevolent institutions of the day—this association has, in a quiet and unpretentious way, been productive of incalculable good. It was organized at a time when the want of such an institution was most severely felt and its aid most essentially needed. While our City and State were eliciting the admiration of the entire Union for the liberality of their largesses to the various funds for the relief of the sick and wounded soldiers, there was here at home, in our very midst, a large amount of suffering which was unrelieved and unprovided for. This was not so much owing to the apathy or indifference of such of our citizens as were able and willing to relieve the wants of the deserving, as from the fact that such cases were comparatively unknown, or their knowledge in a majority of instances confined to but the few, who were in most cases compelled to seek them out. Hundreds, even in our own active and busy community, able and willing to work—in many cases recently landed upon these shores, penniless, destitute, literally strangers in a strange land—were unable to find employment, and many deserving objects, suffering from destitution and disease, were deterred from seeking aid by that barrier of personal pride and self respect which ever forms a barrier around those who have seen better days. A few public spirited and charitable citizens, fully alive to the work, and seriously desiring to relieve the necessities and procure the means of livelihood for the sensitive and deserving, formed this association and established an agency for carrying out this laudable design, where parties needing assistance and employment might without degradation in their own estimation make such application. The public were requested, through the papers, to send all persons soliciting aid on the street to the agency, and to call the attention of the management to any cases requiring aid or relief, which might come to their knowledge. The benefits of this system were at once made apparent—our citizens were no longer importuned for alms on the public streets, suitable employment was afforded upon application at the office, to all desirous of obtaining work and earning an honest livelihood. No great parade was made, no public appeals for aid, but through assistance quietly rendered the association pursued the even tenor of its way, bestowing its benefits like the dews which fall from heaven, silently and unostentatiously. The only direct appeal made to the public at large for aid was in the placing contribution boxes at the different polling places of the last election, from which source—the voting population having become sensible of the manifold benefits of this organization, and fully assured that their charities would reach the proper objects, which we regret to say is not always the case—quite a handsome sum was realized.

We cannot give a better idea of the practical operations and manifold benefits of this deserving institution than by copying the following statement of its objects and principles, published in the prospectus of the association, for the benefit of members, visitors, and the public at large, who are directly interested:

All who become subscribers are members, and are entitled to the directory and tickets which will enable them to refer applicants to the proper source for relief.

Its arrangements are, first, a division of the city into forty districts, and the appointment of an Advisory Committee; and next, the selection of a general agent to manage the general business of the association, to which all of his time and talents are to be devoted.

The Visitors are distributed so as to cover the entire area of the city. By this minute division of labor and responsibility, the institution is prepared, so far as the means shall be supplied, to meet every proper want of the needy. The laborious and invaluable services of the Visitors, who will be selected with great care, will be entirely gratuitous.

The diversified labors of each district are confided to the prudent supervision and control of a Visitor, whose field of labor is compressed to a limit which admits of his personal attention to all the needy therein.

In whatever part of the city the suffering apply to the members of the association for aid, by means of a directory and printed tickets, they are sent to their appropriate Section and Visitor, whose proximity to the residence of the applicants enables him, by personal visitation and inquiry, to extend, withhold, or modify relief, on clearly defined principles, according to the deserts and necessities of every case.

Assistance is rendered not only with great caution, but with great secrecy and delicacy when necessary. No degradation consequently will follow such relief; nor will it be the means of undermining one right principle, or of enfeebling one well-directed impulse.

As has been already stated, the association is not intended to supersede existing charities, but, so far as is practicable, to make them available to those for whom they are designed.

With this statement of the purposes of the association, the Trustees appeal to the public for aid in this long-needed charity. They especially invite attention to the necessity of avoiding indiscriminate almsgiving, and they request that the bounties of the people be allowed to flow through this or some other regularly authorized channel.

In order that the work of the organization may commence at once, they respectfully invite these who are disposed to contribute to the funds of the association, and thus become members, to present their names, with the amount of their subscriptions, at the office at the earliest possible moment.

The rooms and office of the association are located at No. 410 Pine Street, above Montgomery, where Mr. I. S. Allen, the active agent and manager, can be found to answer the calls made under the foregoing regulations. The following well known citizens comprise the officers of this praiseworthy organization: Robert B. Swain, President; J. W. Stow, Treasurer; Dr. L. C. Gunn, Corresponding Secretary; I. S. Allen, General Agent and Secretary; R. G. Sneath, J. W. Stow, R. B. Swain, and L. Sachs, Advisory Committee; R. B. Swain, R. G. Sneath, Louis Sachs, Capt. Levi Stevens, Moses Ellis, W. C. Ralston, J. W. Stow, Eli Lazard, D. W. C. Rice, M.D., Wm. Norris, and Louis McLane, Trustees.

LADIES' SEAMAN'S FRIEND SOCIETY.

At a time when no one seemed to care for the sailor in this our great commercial city—his wants and necessities, whether in sickness or in health, all uncared for; no home of comfort provided for him, and only the low haunts of vice and dissipation afforded Jack a resting place as he came in from the deep waters—this society was established by a few ladies whose sympathies had been called forth in behalf of this important class of our fellow men. It dates from March 26th, 1856—the object being "to relieve shipwrecked and destitute seamen, to establish a boarding house where they may find a home and protection against the pernicious influences and injustice to which they are subjected in this port; to supply the destitute with clothing, and to place within their reach the means for moral and intellectual improvement." It commends itself as truly philanthropic—its basis, *universal benevolence*, irrespective of sect or country. With unabated zeal and untiring efforts the ladies who are engaged in this meritorious work, notwithstanding the heavy rents to which they are subjected, have sustained a comfortable boarding house, and furnished aid to hundreds of sick and destitute sailors, who otherwise must have suffered, inasmuch as the Revenue Laws of our country precluded their admission (under the circumstances) into the Marine Hospital. Their annual appeal to the Legislature for an appropriation to enable them to purchase a lot and build a Sailors' Home has, as yet, been unheeded.

During the progress of the recent Mechanics'. Institute exhibition, the enterprising managers of the society conducted a New England Kitchen at the Pavilion, the results of which will materially assist them in carrying into effect their very praiseworthy object—to erect a Home in this city that will succor many a weary "Son of the Ocean," and one that will make a worthy addition to the numerous benevolent institutions of this city.

EUREKA BENEVOLENT SOCIETY.

The formation of this society dates back to October, 1850, wh_in, according to the records, to the following gentlemen the credit of establishing this excellent institution is due : J. Jacobs, M. Dittmann, P. Schloss, M. Fishel, A. Helbing, M. Hellman, E. Dittman, S. Lazard, J. Lehman, L. Reinstein, A. Blumenthal, D. Baumfrund, and J. Zeiler.

The management of the affairs of this society is placed in the hands of a Board of Trustees consisting of a President, Vice President, Treasurer, and six Trustees. The Board of Trustees are required to hold regular monthly meetings, and for the purpose of dividing the labors among the several members thereof, the By-Laws provide for the appointment of the following committees : On finance, charity, sick, burial, and real estate. The Secretary, Physician, and Collector are elected by the Board of Trustees, and their compensation is fixed by them.

New members can only be elected at either of the four general meetings held during the months of March, June, September, and December, and it requires a majority consisting of four-fifths of the votes cast to elect, when, after the payment of ten dollars initiation fee and his regular monthly dues of one dollar and twenty-five cents, the applicant is entitled to all the rights and privileges of a member. Life membership can be obtained upon the payment of one hundred and twenty-five dollars, which exempts from payment of dues thereafter. The original object of this society consisted in furnishing assistance to the poor, in attending the sick, and burying the dead ; but in the month of March, 1858, an act was passed at a general meeting establishing a widow and orphan fund, for the benefit of widows and orphans of deceased members. The act provides that one-half of all initiation fees and one-fifth of the monthly dues and one-fourth of all extra ordinary incomes shall be placed to the credit of this fund. The original amount set apart, before any use can be made of its means, was $5,000, which has since been amended, and the By-Laws now require that the fund must reach $20,000 before any part of it can be expended. This fund now amounts to the sum of $15,000, and the general fund possesses about $20,000, making the combined capital of the institution $35,000.

The funds of the society are partly invested in real estate, and in money loaned out on indorsed notes at current rates of interest. The society has now about three hundred and eighty members, and is increasing at the rate of thirty members per year.

Nearly all the society's money for years past has been loaned out upon notes, yet not a dollar has ever been lost, and of the large amount of charity distributed, which will reach a sum perhaps not less than $60,000, not $2,000 has been paid to members, because they have fortunately not required it, and have consequently not asked for it.

Many persons have been relieved with the money of this institution without ever knowing from what source such relief emanated, and hundreds who found themselves here without help and means have been returned to their friends and relatives in the Eastern States or Europe with the assistance of this institution.

The following gentlemen have officiated as presiding officers of this society since its organization : August Helbing for seven years, Dr. I. Reugensberger for one year, H. D. Silverman for one year, L. Tichner for two years, A. Wasserman for two years, B. Schloss for one year, and Henry Regensburger for one year.

In common with the congregation Emanu-El this society is in part owner of the Home of Peace Cemetery, near the Mission Dolores, which is inclosed with a brick wall, and otherwise in a high state of improvement. The books of the institution show an expenditure of upwards of $6,000 towards this very laudable object.

THE INDUSTRIAL SCHOOL.

This reformatory institution is still in successful operation, and is doing a large amount of good in rescuing youth, otherwise uncared for, from evil associations ; breaking up and eradicating bad habits at the outset of life. It has already elicited the gratitude of many a youth of talents and noble impulses, started upon a downward career, but by means of this institution reclaimed, educated, and afforded the means of becoming useful members of society. The whole number of pupils admitted since the first opening of the school, May 3d, 1859, is four hundred and fifty-eight, of whom three hundred and fifty-eight were boys and one hundred girls. The number admitted during the past year was one hundred and twenty-five, of whom eighty-six were boys and thirty-nine girls. Additions have been made to the school building, materially enhancing the comfort and accommodations of the inmates. Among these is a dining room of a capacity sufficient to accommodate over two hundred children. The following are the officers and employés of the institution.

Leonidas B. Benchley, Charles D. Carter, Nathan Porter, Jacob Schreiber, John H. Titcomb, and Gustave Touchard, Managers, 1865-7 ; Charles H. Stanyan, Monroe Ashbury, and James H. Reynolds, appointed from Board of Supervisors, 1865-6 ; John Archbald, Treasurer ; James S. Thomson, Secretary ; George L. Lynde, Superintendent (absent) ; Rufus K. Marriner, Superintendent (temporary) ; Benjamin D. Dean, Physician ; Theodore C. Smith, Nathan J. Stone, and Mrs. Charlotte A. Sawyer, Teachers ; Mrs. Catharine Sheldon, Matron.

PRISONERS' AID SOCIETY.

A new organization has recently been established in this city, having in view the assistance and reformation of men who have been imprisoned for crime, with the following named gentlemen as officers for the ensuing year : Gov. F. F. Low, President ; Dr. J. F. Morse, Vice President ; James Woodworth, Secretary ; M. J. O'Connor, Treasurer.

BRITISH BENEVOLENT ASSOCIATION.

This society was established in July, 1865, with the object of assisting British born subjects in distress or sickness. Meetings are held on the second Tuesday of every month, temporarily at the St. Andrew's Society Rooms, 522 Market Street. Number of members, three hundred and thirty.

Officers—W. Lane Booker, H. B. M. Consul, President ; A. Forbes, First Vice President ; J. B. Wynn, Second Vice President ; John Archbald, Treasurer ; Thomas Hulbert, Secretary ; Edward Briant, Assistant Secretary ; Charles F. H. Gillingham, M.D., Physician ; Jas. Bell, H. A. Fox, Robert Roxby, John Wedderspoon, John Mason, Gomer Evans, John Landale, and Thos. B. Simpson, Board of Trustees ; T. P. Bevans, R. Mayers, C. Ashton, and H. E. Highton, Board of Relief.

GERMAN GENERAL BENEVOLENT SOCIETY.

This association, composed exclusively of Germans, and those who speak the language, was organized January 7th, 1854, for the mutual attendance upon and relief of its members, and especially the protection and aid of newly-arrived German immigrants. The large and commodious Hospital erected by the association on Brannan Street, near Third, where every possible comfort and accommodation adequate to the wants of the sick can be obtained, is an enduring monument of the liberality and philanthropy of this provident class of our citizens.

ST. MARY'S LADIES' SOCIETY.

This society, which was originally founded in 1850 by the Sisters of Mercy for the dissemination of piety among the females of the Catholic Church, and afterwards converted into a mutual benevolent association, holds its meetings in the Hall erected for that purpose adjoining the St. Mary's Hospital, to which its labors are mainly devoted, the officers being selected from the Sisters of Mercy. It is one of the most flourishing of all the benevolent associations, and numbers some six hundred contributing members.

ST. JOSEPH'S BENEVOLENT SOCIETY.

This society is composed of the male members of the Roman Catholic Church, for the aid of those in distress and the consolation and relief of the afflicted. Although mainly devoted to attending to the sick, burying the dead, and relieving the families left in needy circumstances by its own members, its benevolent operations are not exclusively confined to its own limits, but administer to the wants of all such afflicted as come within its notice.

MAGDALEN ASYLUM.

This reformatory institution is located on the San Bruno Road, and is under the charge and direction of the Sisters of Mercy.

During the past year a large and commodious building, three stories in hight, has been erected for the accommodation of the inmates of the asylum. Since the foundation of this institution nearly one hundred females have been received, most of whom have been reformed by the influence and attention of those in charge. At the present time there are sixty penitents, attended by seven Sisters of Mercy.

EUREKA TYPOGRAPHICAL UNION.

This society was organized in 1858, for the purpose of protecting the interests and rendering aid and assistance to distressed members of the " Art Preservative of all Arts. It numbers some three hundred members, and is in a very flourishing condition. An arrangement has been made by this society with the managers of St. Mary's Hospital, by which the sick receive medical attendance and nursing. The society recently purchased a burial lot in Lone Mountain Cemetery, which they design decorating and ornamenting in a becoming manner.

DASHAWAY ASSOCIATION.

This widely-known Temperance organization, originally founded on the twenty-fourth day of May, 1859, by the members of Howard Engine Company, has increased to an astonishing extent, numbering over six thousand members. A large and elegant hall has been erected on Post Street, between Dupont and Kearny, by the Parent association, devoted to the business and social meetings of the members. The affairs of the association are in a most flourishing condition, and the sphere of its usefulness constantly extending. From this parent stock auxiliary societies have sprung up, and are in successful operation all over the State. The name of " Dashaway " has become a household word.

FRENCH BENEVOLENT SOCIETY.

This is a mutual benevolent association, formed in 1851, by a number of French citizens, for the aid and relief of its members, although its action is not confined exclusively to that class. A spacious and commodious hospital, with handsomely laid out grounds, was erected by this association a year since, on Bryant between Fifth and Sixth streets.

LADIES' UNITED HEBREW BENEVOLENT SOCIETY.

This praiseworthy association was established in 1855, by the ladies of the Israelitish faith, for the aid of the distressed among the women of that people, to attend to the sick, bury the dead, aid the poor, and relieve the wants of the distressed. The objects of the association have been carried out with the untiring zeal and philanthropic spirit with which it originated.

ITALIAN BENEVOLENT ASSOCIATION.

This somewhat limited, but industrious, thrifty, and provident portion of our citizens, the Italians, have not been behind other and more numerous classes in their provision for the sick and distressed among their ranks. This society has an arrangement with the managers of St. Mary's Hospital, by which every provision is made for the care of those entitled to its protection and relief.

Hospitals.

There is, perhaps, no city in the world of its age and population better supplied with public and private hospitals than San Francisco. Essentially cosmopolitan in the constituent parts of its population, and embracing as it does representatives from all portions of the globe, each nationality has its benevolent associations, one of the principal objects of which is to make ample provision for the care of its sick. The greater portion of those unfortunates, injured by the casualties constantly occurring in the mines, resort to San Francisco for medical and surgical treatment; hence it is that the public and private hospitals of the city are almost constantly crowded.

The following comprises the leading institutions of this character located here:

THE UNITED STATES MARINE HOSPITAL.

This spacious brick building, two hundred feet long by one hundred feet in width, and four stories high was erected by the U. S. Government on the Government Reserve at Rincon Point, in the year 1853. It is capable of containing several hundred patients, and is devoted exclusively to the use of the sick and disabled belonging to the national and merchant marine service, including landsmen engaged in the inland and coast trade. The number of patients admittted each year is about one thousand, and the number of annual deaths near twenty-two; the average number of patients is about one hundred. The officers in charge of the hospital who are appointed by the Government, are a Surgeon, Apothecary, Steward, and Matron.

THE CITY AND COUNTY HOSPITAL.

This spacious building, which is of brick, and three stories high, located on the corner of Stockton and Francisco streets, was opened for the reception of patients in July, 1857. The lower floor is occupied by the offices of the Resident Physician and attendants, with a surgical ward, and cells for the safe keeping of insane patients. The second floor is occupied by surgical patients, dining hall, apothecary's room, contractor's storeroom, and kitchen. The medical patients are allowed the third floor, a number of small rooms in the rear being set apart for female patients. During the past year important additions have been made, materially enhancing the accommodations. The supplies of the hospital—food, fuel, lights, and washing—are furnished by contract. The officers are one Visiting and one Resident Physician, Apothecary, and Contractor.

The most liberal provisions are allowed by law for the maintenance of this useful institution, viz.: for 1863, contingent expenses, $60,000 per annum; repairs, $6,000; furnishing, $12,000; improvements, $25,000; also, for support of a Small Pox Hospital, $6,000 per annum ; for 1864, to improve and enlarge the present buildings, an addition to the sum now allowed by law of $125,000.

ST. MARY'S HOSPITAL.

This is the most extensive private hospital in the City of San Francisco, and is under the charge of the Sisters of Mercy. The portion completed is one hundred and sixty feet in length by seventy-five in width, built of brick, and four stories high. The ceilings are lofty, the rooms well lighted and ventilated, with warm, cold, and shower baths on each floor, and lighted with gas throughout. In addition to twelve spacious and commodious wards, furnished with all that is to be found in the best regulated sanitary institutions, there are a number of private rooms neatly fitted up and completely arranged for the accommodation of patients. The officers of the hospital are: Sister Mary Russell, Superior; Drs. H. H. Toland, J. P. Whitney, Visiting Physicians; Maximilian Cachot, Resident Physician; Edward O'Doherty, Druggist.

MAISON DE SANTE.

This hospital, founded by the French Mutual Benevolent Society, was opened March 15th, 1858. It is a brick building, situated in the center of a hundred-vara lot, and is surrounded with trees and shrubbery, forming a pleasant promenade and exercising grounds for patients. The building contains two general wards, fitted up with twelve beds each, eight with four beds each, and a large number of private rooms, several of which are appropriated to ladies. The whole is neatly furnished, and heated throughout with hot water—the hospital being also supplied with warm, cold, shower, and steam baths. The officers are two Physicians, a Superintendent, and an Apothecary.

THE GERMAN HOSPITAL.

This is a brick building with a front of one hundred and twelve feet, with a depth of fifty feet, attached to which is a rear wing of one hundred and twenty-two by twenty-three feet, two stories with a basement, with surrounding grounds laid out and arranged, and ornamented with shrubbery and flowers, under careful cultivation, one hundred and thirty-seven by two hundred and eighty-five feet in extent. The two stories are divided into general wards and private rooms for the physicians and attendants in charge. The building is amply supplied with warm, cold, shower, and steam baths, and every appliance for the proper care and treatment of the sick.

Cemeteries.

There is, perhaps, no feature connected with a prominent city that occupies a greater degree of interest in the estimation of strangers and visitors than its cemeteries. One of the most attractive spots to the visitor to the great American metropolis is the "City of the Dead" at Greenwood. The peaceful shades of Mount Auburn have a melancholy charm to those who make a pilgrimage to the great capital of the Bay State, and no one enters the City of Brotherly Love without seeing the classic monuments, tastefully laid out, beautifully adorned, and admirably-kept grounds at Laurel Hill. Other cities of lesser extent and fewer years exhibit equal taste and regard for the depositories of their dead. Spring Grove at Cincinnati, Mount Hope at Rochester, the Albany Cemetery, and numerous

others, are examples of taste in the selection of the location and beauty of adorning and arrangement. In all modern places seelected for the repose of the departed, good taste has retained the primitive forest trees—the monarchs of the grove themselves being fitting monuments "not made with hands." In point of beauty of locality our own Lone Mountain and Calvary cemeteries, situated as they are in full view of that grandest of all monuments, the mighty Ocean, are nowhere surpassed. There is a fitness and sublimity in their contiguity to the waves of the Pacific and the entrance to the Golden Gate, that never fails to impress every beholder. In the way of monuments erected to the memory of the departed by the hand of affection and regard, many may be found in the city cemeteries which are alike models of artistic elegance and pure and refined taste.

MISSION BURIAL GROUND.

The oldest of the city cemeteries is the burial ground of Mission Dolores, which was consecrated by the pious Fathers of the Church as early as the year 1776, the first interment in the consecrated ground being made in September of that year. As the chosen resting place of the early inhabitants of the pueblo, this sacred spot will ever be surrounded with an atmosphere of deep historic interest, reverence, and veneration. The inscriptions to be found on the monuments in this burial place exhibit the varied character and nationalities composing the population of this region, some being composed in the Latin, with which its learned founders were familiar, and others in English, French, Italian, and a still larger number in the Spanish language, the contemplation of which affords the pilgrim to these shores much food for profitable reflection and thought. Several other spots within what have for some years been the city limits, were selected by parties visiting this portion of the Pacific years ago, who little dreaming of the rapid rise and extent of the homes and haunts of the living, selected these grounds for the resting place of their dead. The principal of these grave-yards were located on Russian and Telegraph hills, and a lot on the north-east corner of Powell and Lombard streets. As the march of improvement infringed upon these localities, their occupants were removed to other places of repose where they will not probably again be disturbed until the earth and sea shall give up their dead.

YERBA BUENA CEMETERY.

In order to accommodate the wants of the fast increasing and growing community, so rapidly augmenting at this locality, in February, 1850, the Board other Aldermen of this city set apart the tract bounded by Market, Larkin, and McAllister streets, embracing an area of sixteen acres, as a city burying ground, under the appropriate name of Yerba Buena, the original appellation of the pueblo. The prevalence of the cholera, which swept away such numbers of its victims the season following, rapidly filled the space alotted for interments, and the sudden growth of the city in that direction soon indicated the necessity of more remote and extended grounds for burial purposes. Up to the time of the opening of Lone Mountain Cemetery, seven thousand interments had been made in Yerba Buena. Acting under authority from the Legislature, and in many instances under the direction of the friends of the deceased families, the remains of the dead have been gradually removed, and the grounds will hereafter be dedicated to the uses of a public promenade or park for the use of the living.

LONE MOUNTAIN CEMETERY.

Fully alive to the wants and necessities of the case, a number of public spirited citizens succeeded in securing a tract of one hundred and seventy-four acres in extent—about three miles from the city—which was admirably adapted to the purposes of a rural cemetery. Situated on an elevated plateau at the base of the eminence known as Lone Mountain, from which it derives its name, in full view of the Pacific Ocean, and the opposite Bay, the shores of which their discoverer, Sir Francis Drake, whose name this sheet of water bears—from their fancied resemblance to the white cliffs of Dover, christened New Albion—those solitary centinels of the sea, the Farallones, dimly outlined in the distance, typical of "the Land beyond the river"—the Golden Gate, suggestive of the entrance to the Holy City, with the beautiful Bay of San Francisco, with its cluster of islands—together with an extended view away to the inland, no more beautiful or or appropriate site could have anywhere been found. Since that time the grounds have been laid off into burial lots—with spacious carriage ways winding among its miniature hills and valleys—with walks threading the mazes of the natural shrubbery, which with characteristic taste has been preserved as far as possible—numerous chaste and beautiful monuments, which would do honor to any community, have been erected—every species of ornamental shrubbery and rare flowers planted, and lots inclosed with handsome iron railings—and the evidences of taste and affection of the living is every where apparent in this appropriate resting place of the dead.

Here rest the remains of two illustrious men, whose names and deeds are inseparably interwoven with the history of our State, Senators Broderick and Baker, both of whom fell on the field in the prime of life and the ripeness of manhood. The time will not be long when lofty monuments will be reared to the memory of those illustrious patriots—that of Senator Broderick, which is to be surmounted with a life-size statue in marble, having been commenced some time since. The whole number of interments made in Lone Mountain from its dedication to the present time is about 10,000, daily average five. The management and improvement of these grounds reflect great credit upon the proprietors of the cemetery, Messrs. Nathaniel Gray, J. H. Atkinson, and Charles C. Butler.

CALVARY CEMETERY.

Some four years or more ago, Bishop Alemany purchased an extensive tract of land, comprising eighty acres, adjoining Lone Mountain and possessing like advantages with that cemetery, which was consecrated to the uses of the Catholic Church under the appropriate title of Calvary Cemetery. Since that time numerous improvements have been made in the way of laying out and adorning the grounds, grading avenues for vehicles and walks through the intermediate spaces, under the direction of the Bishop, who has charge of the cemetery. Improvements are constantly in progress, enhancing its beauty and fitness for the sacred sanctuary of the dead. A small but neat chapel has been erected at this cemetery for burial service. Number of burials up to the present time 3,825.

MASONIC CEMETERY.

The "Masonic Cemetery Association of the City and County of San Francisco," was organized on the twenty-sixth of January, 1864, under the Act of the Legislature authorizing the incorporation of rural cemetery associations. The officers are: ———, President; Thomas Anderson, Treasurer; George J. Hobe, Secretary. The association owns sixty-eight acres, thirty of which are already laid out as a Masonic Cemetery. The land lies south of and adjoining Calvary Cemetery. It has a gentle slope towards the east; is sheltered from the prevailing westerly winds by Lone Mountain; is covered in a great measure with shrubbery, and is susceptible of a high state of cultivation. Its situation is equal, if not superior, to the best portion of Lone Mountain Cemetery, and excels it in natural advantages for the improvement and ornamentation of family plots. The association has laid out and macadamized over two miles of road in the cemetery; have spent some $2,000 in excavating for a public vault—said excavation being into solid rock, and so situated that it is entirely sheltered from wind. The grand tour, as well as the avenues running north and south, are all staked, and many of them cut and macadamized. The names of all the avenues are placed on convenient-sized boards, and the individual lots are all staked and numbered. The prices upon the different lots are twenty-five, twenty, and fifteen cents per square foot, according to location, which is about one-half of the prices charged by the Lone Mountain and Calvary cemeteries. The three most eligible plots are Mount Moriah, Fountain Plot, and Forest Hill, and the lots therein contained are the highest priced. The lots facing on what is termed the Grand Tour command the second price, and all other lots the lowest, or fifteen cents. The lots are sold *only* to members of the order of Free and Accepted Masons, or to the blood relations of Masons; and a clause in the deed says: "No conveyance or transfer of a lot shall be made to any but a Free and Accepted Mason, or to the family of one who at the time of his death was a Free and Accepted Mason." But the owner of a lot may permit whomsoever he pleases to be buried upon his ground, provided it is not for a remuneration. A provision has recently been made setting apart a portion of the grounds, which are exempt from this prohibition, and persons of all denominations may now secure lots upon the same terms as members of the order. Number of burials up to the present time, 250. The entrance to the cemetery is from the Point Lobos or Cliff House Road, just beyond the toll gate, over a fine macadamized road recently completed by the association.

HEBREW CEMETERY, GIBBOTH OLOM.

This cemetery, located on Dolores Street, between Nineteenth and Twentieth, was opened and dedicated in 1861. The number buried in the grounds to the present time is two hundred and seventy-four. A considerable portion of these were removed hither from the old Jewish burying ground. The cemetery is surrounded by a high brick wall, has a substantial brick chapel, a portion of which is used for a receiving tomb, and covers an area of five hundred by five hundred and forty feet. The grounds are tastefully laid out with graveled walks and adorned with trees, plants, flowers, and shrubbery. The total cost of the improvements in this cemetery, from the time it was opened, has been from $18,000 to $20,000.

HEBREW CEMETERY—NEVAI SHALOME.

This cemetery is located on Dolores Street, between Eighteenth and Nineteenth, adjoining the Gibboth Olom. The number of interments up to the present time is two hundred and fifty-five, about sixty of which were bodies transferred from the old Jewish Cemetery on the Presidio Road. The grounds, which cover an area of five hundred by five hundred and forty feet, are surrounded by a substantial brick wall, and are laid out in the most artistic style. A stone chapel has been erected at a cost of $6,000.

ODD FELLOWS' CEMETERY.

The Odd Fellows' Cemetery Association have recently purchased twenty-seven acres of land in the immediate vicinity of Lone Mountain Cemetery for cemetery purposes, which was dedicated with appropriate ceremonies on Sunday, Nov. 26th, 1865.

. **Associations—Protective, Literary, Etc.**

For a description of the different associations the reader is referred to the Appendix, page 616, in which will be found the officers and operations of each during the past year. The progress made by many of these associations reflects credit upon the members thereof, and is worthy of the liberality so generously exhibited in their support.

THE MASONIC AND ODD FELLOWS' ORDERS.

Among the most prominent of our public institutions are these benevolent orders. There is, probably, no city in the Union where these associations are in a more flourishing condition than in San Francisco. Each of these orders own a handsome property—fine building with handsome halls for the use of the association. In the elegant building owned by the Masonic Order, built by a joint stock association of the members, there are four large balls for the use of the lodges, and a large banqueting hall, with ante-rooms, committee rooms, and offices. This structure is one of the handsomest public buildings of our city.

The Odd Fellows' Order is also in a most flourishing condition, having recently purchased and fitted up for the use of the order the property on Montgomery Street, between California and Pine, known as Tucker's Hall. The library of this institution is one of the best in the city, abounding in rare works, relating especially to the history of our State.

For list of the different associations, and the officers of each, see Appendix, page 611.

Military.

An unusual degree of activity has been exhibited during the past year in the organization and equipment of our volunteer soldiery. The number of companies now enrolled is fifty, exclusive of the Police organization, with an aggregate effective strength of 3,500 men. Eleven companies have been organized during the past year.

Ample provision has been made by the Legislature of the State to relieve, to some extent, the heavy expense attending these organizations, thereby removing an objection heretofore existing with many to a more general connection with this most important branch of our public service.

Fire Department.

The Department at present consists of eight hundred and twenty-six members, divided into fourteen engine companies, three hook and ladder companies, and three hose companies. For their accommodation there are twenty houses; and for service sixteen fire engines, three hook and ladder trucks, and seventeen hose carriages. Four new and powerful steam fire engines have been recently added to the Department. There are in the city fifty cisterns, capable of holding 1,470,000 gallons of water—many of them substantially built of brick and cement.

We refer our readers to the Appendix, page 587,

for a complete description of the organization of this important branch of the public service, in which will be found a mass of information concerning the different companies, useful to its members and interesting to every citizen.

Railroads.

Extensive improvements have been made in the various railroads laid down in and leading out of San Francisco since the publication of the Directory of last year. In fact, no department of our public improvements more fully indicate the untiring industry and enterprise of our people, or the sagacious employment of capital by those desirous of making profitable and steadily remunerating investments. The benefits to the public by the introduction of street cars, affording a convenient, comfortable, and cheap mode of travel through the various thoroughfares to extreme points of the city, are incalculable. These people's carriages are certainly a great public convenience, and their introduction has doubled and trebled the value of property in the more distant portions, as well as outside of the city. Incredible as it may seem, the carriage distance traveled by some of the street cars, with but three relays of horses, is near a hundred miles a day.

The following is a list of the railroads leading out of and in the vicinity of the city, in operation at present, or in prospective, with a list of the officers, and the action of the same during the past year.

SAN FRANCISCO AND SAN JOSE RAILROAD.

This company was incorporated July 21st, 1860, with a capital stock of $2,000,000. The road was completed in January, 1863, and is pronounced by competent railroad men to be one of the staunchest built roads in the United States. The only funded indebtedness of the company is represented by nine hundred and sixty-eight mortgage bonds of $1,000 each, bearing eight per cent. per annum interest, and issued July 1st, 1864, in p   payment of the contract for constructing the road. These bonds run twenty years, and both principal and interest are payable in United States gold coin. On the seventeenth day of October, 1863, the first train passed over the portion of the road finished from the Mission Dolores to Big Tree Station on the San Francisquito Creek. On the sixteenth day of January, 1864, the road was completed to San José, and trains commenced running to that place; and later, on the fourteenth day of February following, the San Francisco end of the road was extended to the corner of Fourth and Brannan streets, and trains commenced running from that point to San José direct. The company now runs two passenger trains over the road each way daily. One freight train is run each way daily, to which a passenger car is attached. Stages connect at the principal stations and at San José with the morning and evening trains to and from important points. The Board of Directors is composed of the following gentlemen: Henry M. Newhall, Peter Donahue, Chas. B. Polhemus, D. O. Mills, John T. Doyle, S. J. Hensley, and F. D. Atherton. The officers are Henry M. Newhall, President; John T. Doyle, Vice President; D. O. Mills, Treasurer; J. L. Willcutt, Secretary; and C. B. Polhemus, General Superintendent.

THE WESTERN PACIFIC RAILROAD.

This company was incorporated December 11th,

1862, with a capital stock of $5,400,000, for the purpose of constructing a railroad from San José to Sacramento by the way of Stockton. The route is one hundred and twenty miles in length, and connecting with the San Francisco and San José Railroad forms the second link in the great Pacific Railroad chain. Of the capital stock of this road, $400,000 has been subscribed by San Francisco County; $250,000 by San Joaquin, and $150,000 by Santa Clara County. The remainder is furnished by heavy capitalists of San Francisco.

The building of the road is now being pushed forward with commendable energy, and it is confidently expected to be entirely completed to Sacramento by the summer of 1867. The grading of the road from San José to Vallejo Mills, a distance of twenty-three miles, is nearly finished, and cars will be running to that point in May next.

The officers of the company are: Charles N. Fox, President; Erastus S. Holden, Vice President; Charles W. Sanger, Secretary; B. F. Mann, Treasurer; and W. L. Stanroom, Chief Engineer.

SAN FRANCISCO MARKET STREET RAILROAD.

This being the first of the street railroad enterprises, which have inaugurated, and are daily bringing about such important results in our city, is fairly entitled to the honor of being styled the pioneer in this department.

Officers—A. Casselli, President; F. McCoppin, Levi Parsons, R. Bayerque, Henry Pichior, Directors; Henry Pichior, Secretary; J. B. Bayerque, Trustee; F. McCoppin, Superintendent. Secretary's office, south-east corner of Montgomery and Jackson streets; Superintendent's office, west side Valencia near Sixteenth.

OMNIBUS RAILROAD COMPANY.

This is the most extensive in its operations of any of our street railroads. Its capital stock is $1,000,000, divided into 10,000 shares of one hundred dollars each. There are two lines of this road; one running from Powell and Francisco along Powell to Union, Union to Stockton, Stockton to Jackson and Washington, down these streets to Sansom, through these streets to Market, along Market to Second, along Second to Howard, along Howard to Third, and along Third to King Street. The other route is from the intersection of Washington and Montgomery streets, through the latter to Second, through the latter to Howard, Centre, and the Mission Dolores, with a branch from Market through Third to Howard. The cars run northwardly along Montgomery Street to 2½ o'clock, P.M., and southwardly after that time each day. The road is entirely completed, and the rails laid down, if reduced to a single track, would amount to ten miles and one-third. It has twenty-four cars constantly running and eight in reserve for extra service. Ninety men and one hundred and ninety horses are kept constantly employed. The depot on Howard Street, under Union Hall, is one of the largest structures of the city. The extensive stables, built of brick, two stories high, by the company, front on Minna, running back to Clementina Street, one hundred and fifty-seven by one hundred and sixty feet. The officers of this company are: Peter Donahue, President; Eugene Casserly, Vice President; W. H. Lyons, Treasurer; James O'Neil, Secretary; and John Gardner, Superintendent.

FRONT STREET, MISSION, AND OCEAN RAILROAD.

The Legislature of 1862-3 granted to William F. Nelson and others the franchise to lay down a railroad along and upon the following streets: Beginning at or near the intersection of Greenwich with Front Street, and thence along Front Street to Market Street, thence along Market to Sutter Street, thence along Sutter to Larkin Street, thence along Larkin to Pacific Street to the charter limits, with the right of continuation along the said line of Pacific Street to the Ocean Beach, whenever said street is declared open by the proper authorities of the City and County of San Francisco, with an intersecting railroad connecting at the junction of Sutter and Larkin Street, thence running southwardly along Larkin to Market Street, and along and across Market to Johnson Street, thence along Johnson to Mission Street, thence along Mission to Sparks Street, thence along and upon Sparks to Dolores Street, thence along Dolores to Corbet Street, thence along Corbett to Mission Street, thence along Mission to Sparks Street; together with the right to lay and maintain an iron railroad from the intersection of Corbett with Mission Street, along and upon Mission Street to the charter limits of said city and county—making the entire length of the road about one and two-thirds miles.

Under this charter the company having made a contract with H. Casebolt, commenced laying down a double track on the twenty-fifth day of September, 1865, from the corner of Sansom and Sutter streets; and its completion through Sutter, Polk to Broadway is expected by February 1st, 1866. Mr. Casebolt is constructing, under his contract, six first-class twenty-passenger cars. The entire cost of the road, with cars, buildings, and stock will not be less than ninety thousand dollars.

Officers—Henry Haight, President; David Wilder, Secretary; S. S. Tilton, Treasurer.

NORTH BEACH AND MISSION RAILROAD.

This company was organized from a consolidation of two railroad charters granted by the Legislature of California, and approved April 17th, 1861. There are two distinct routes of this company completed and running; one from the corner of Powell and Union through Kearny, etc., to the corner of Fourth and Brannan; another from the corner of California and Montgomery, through Battery, First, and Folsom, to the Willows Race Course, with a branch through Folsom Street to the Willows, making in all five and a half miles of double track, and three-quarters of a mile of single track. The fare on either of these routes is five cents. Twenty-five cars are required to accommodate the regular travel on these routes, and the company have eleven more cars ready for extra occasions, with car-houses, stables, blacksmith shop, work shop, and everything complete for the accommodation of all the rolling stock, horses, etc., required for the prosecution of the business. Their depôt is at the corner of Fourth and Louisa streets. This company was incorporated August 23d, 1862. The capital stock is one million dollars, divided into ten thousand shares of one hundred dollars each. Their annual election for directors takes place on the fourth Monday of August of each year.

The following Board of Directors was chosen at the last election: A. J. Bowie, James T. Boyd, Michael Reese, A. L. Morrison, Henry A. Lyons, Michael Skelly, John S. Hager, and Alpheus Bull, who elected the following officers for the ensuing year: Dr. A. J. Bowie, President; James T. Boyd, Vice President; Michael Reese, Treasurer; Willet Southwick, Secretary; Michael Skelly, Superintendent.

CENTRAL RAILROAD.

The railroad was chartered by Act of the Legislature of 1862. Incorporated in 1862. Capital stock five hundred thousand dollars, in five thousand shares. The route traversed is: from the corner of Davis and Vallejo streets through Davis to Washington, along Washington to Sansom, along Sansom to Bush, and through Bush to Dupont, along Dupont to Post, through Post to Stockton, along Stockton to Geary, through Geary to Taylor, along Taylor

THE

SAN FRANCISCO DIRECTORY

For the Year commencing December, 1865:

EMBRACING A

GENERAL DIRECTORY OF RESIDENTS

AND

BUSINESS DIRECTORY;

ALSO,

A DIRECTORY OF STREETS, PUBLIC OFFICES, ETC.

AND A MAP OF THE CITY:

TOGETHER WITH

The Consolidation Act and its Amendments; the Municipal Government; Societies and Organizations, and a great variety of Useful and Statistical Information,

EXHIBITING AT A GLANCE

The Progress and Present Condition of the City.

EIGHTH YEAR OF PUBLICATION.

COMPILED BY

HENRY G. LANGLEY,

EDITOR OF "STATE REGISTER" AND "STATE ALMANAC."

DEPOTS FOR THE SALE OF THIS WORK:

OFFICE OF THE DIRECTORY, No. 612 Clay Street, up stairs; WM. B. COOKE & Co., 624 Montgomery Street; A. ROMAN & Co., 419 Montgomery Street; GEORGE H. BELL, SW corner Montgomery and Merchant streets; A. GENSOUL, 511 Montgomery Street; C. BEACH, 34 Montgomery Street, and M. FLOOD, 428 Kearny Street.

SAN FRANCISCO:

EXCELSIOR STEAM PRESSES: TOWNE & BACON, BOOK AND JOB PRINTERS,
No. 536 Clay Street, opposite Leidesdorff.

1865.

THE MUTUAL LIFE INSURANCE COMPANY OF — NEW YORK

CASH ASSETS,........$13,500,000.

H. S. HOMANS, General Agent.
609 CLAY STREET.

7347

A FEW COMPLETE SETS
OF THE
San Francisco Directory
FROM 1856 TO 1864,
Eight Volumes Octavo,
The whole forming
A COMPLETE AND RELIABLE HISTORY
OF
THE CITY OF SAN FRANCISCO,
From its first settlement to the present time,
FOR SALE................ Price, $20.00.

Henry G. Langley, Publisher, 612 Clay Street.

PREFACE.

THE present is the eighth volume of the SAN FRANCISCO DIRECTORY, issued by its present compiler, and the fifteenth Directory published in this city.

The first Directory of this city was published in September, 1850, by C. P. Kimball. It was a small pamphlet volume of one hundred and thirty-six pages, containing three thousand, two hundred and eight names, of which fifty-one were Smiths, twelve were Jones, and thirteen were Robinsons. The second was issued in September, 1852, by W. A. Morgan & Co., in an octavo form of one hundred and twenty-five pages, containing about three thousand names, and a classification of trades and professions. In December of the same year, J. A. Parker published the third Directory. It was an octavo volume of one hundred and eighty pages, embracing eight thousand, five hundred names, together with an admirably compiled sketch of the rise and progress of San Francisco, written by Dr. H. Gibbons. The fourth was published by Lecount & Strong, in February, 1854, under the editorial charge of Frank Rivers. It was a volume of three hundred and fifty pages, of octavo size, containing nearly thirteen thousand names, together with extensive references to the municipal government, associations, and other items of valuable information. In December, 1855, Baggett, Joseph & Co. published a Classified Professional and Business Directory, of two hundred and twenty-two pages, octavo, containing the addresses of nearly six thousand business firms. The sixth Directory was issued in October, 1856, under the editorial charge of C. C. Sackett and Samuel Colville. It was a volume of three hundred and fifty pages, in octavo, containing over twelve thousand names, and a large amount of information connected with the rise and progress of the city, and very complete references to the different organizations then in existence. It also embraced a valuable historical sketch of the city, written by Frank Soulé, Esq., and a number of short biographical sketches of the leading firms. In October of the same year, Messrs. Harris, Bogardus & Labatt published a Directory of one hundred and twenty-five pages, octavo, containing about ten thousand names, with a variety of information connected with the city. The eighth, the first of the present series, was issued in January, 1858, by the publisher of the present volume. It was an octavo volume of four hundred and ten pages, containing eighteen thousand, five hundred names. The ninth was published in June, 1859, containing four hundred and ninety pages, and twenty-one thousand, five hundred names. A very valuable historical sketch of the city, written by Clement Ferguson, Esq., accompanied this volume. The tenth was published in July, 1860, containing five hundred and fifty pages, and twenty-six thousand names. The eleventh was published in September, 1861, containing six hundred and twenty-four pages, and twenty-nine thousand names. The twelfth was published in September, 1862, containing six hundred and ninety-four pages, and thirty-four thousand names. The thirteenth was published in October, 1863, containing six hundred and sixty pages, and thirty-eight thousand names. The number of pages of this issue was somewhat reduced from that of the preceding volume, in consequence of the use of a smaller-sized type in the printing of the work. The fourteenth was issued in November, 1864, containing seven hundred and forty pages, and forty-two thousand references.

The foregoing presents an interesting account of the different directories of San Francisco, published since the foundation of the city—exhibiting at a glance the rapid growth of the city, and the progress of an enterprise, which is now regarded as one of the "features" of our metropolis.

The number of references contained in the present volume is nearly forty-five thousand, of which forty thousand are male residents of this city—an increase of eight per cent. over that of last year. In the different departments of the work the same gratifying evidences of the rapid growth of the city will be noticed. The Business Directory contains over thirteen thousand business firms, so arranged as to be of easy reference, to which especial attention is invited. This department has been prepared with unusual care, and it will be found to embrace a mass of information relative to the business of this city, not to be found in any other work.

The present population of San Francisco is estimated at one hundred and nineteen thousand of which thirty-five thousand are whites under the age of twenty-one. The number of females over eighteen, is estimated at twenty-five thousand. These figures are made up from the most reliable data ; and they may be regarded as a fair approximation of the population.

The number of buildings erected during the past year is estimated at one thousand and seventy-five, of which three hundred and twenty are of brick—making an aggregate in the city and county of fifteen thousand five hundred and eighteen.

The thoroughness of the San Francisco Directory may be appreciated to some extent by a comparison with the directories of other cities. The New York Directory gives one name to each seven of the population ; Philadelphia, one to six ; Baltimore, one to five ; Boston (1864), one to four ; and the San Francisco Directory, if the floating population are excluded, one to two and one-half—or nearly three times as many names, in proportion to the population, as are contained in the New York Directory.

Some idea of the cosmopolitan character of the City of San Francisco may be ascertained by comparing the different family names comprised in the present volume with those contained in the New York and Boston directories. The New York Directory, 1864, contains thirty thousand eight hundred and fifty-five family names ; or, estimating the population at one million, one name in thirty-three. Boston, eight thousand eight hundred and twenty-eight ; or, estimating the population at two hundred thousand, one in twenty-two. San Francisco Directory, fourteen thousand four hundred and ninety-four ; estimating the permanent population at one hundred thousand, one in seven. The San Francisco Directory, therefore contains, in proportion to the population of the city, over four times as many different family names as the New York, and three times as many as the Boston Directory.

In the Appendix to the present volume will be found the Consolidation Act with its amendments so arranged that the changes in the law are perceptible at a glance, and a mass of information extremely varied, and much of it very interesting, embracing lists of the Federal, State, and Municipal Officers, notices of Local Societies and Associations, Churches, Military Organizations, etc., etc.

The "Street Directory" has been carefully revised and conforms to the official data of the office of the Assessor of the City and County.

The "General Review" presents a diary of the interesting local events of the year, brief notices of Schools, public and private, Benevolent Associations, Cemeteries, Public Improvements, Railroads, and other subjects worthy of special mention, with historical data of present interest and well calculated to make the book a valuable work of reference to future generations. But the particular features of this department of the Directory are the Tables, presenting a correct census of the city and county for 1861, 1863, and 1865, the compilation of the United States census of the city for 1860, and the statement of the buildings within the city limits.

Prefixed to the Directory is a valuable map of the City of San Francisco carefully revised and corrected to 1865, with the different railroad routes and the new Election Districts.

The compiler would again acknowledge his thanks for the courtesy extended to him during the preparation of the work. The prompt and willing assistance extended by public officers, societies, and others who have been applied to for information, is warmly appreciated. To his numerous advertising patrons, for their substantial evidences of good will, and to Messrs. TOWNE & BACON, to whom the typographical department was intrusted, he would especially offer his thanks.

The SAN FRANCISCO DIRECTORY for 1867 will be issued on the first of January, 1867.

TABLE OF CONTENTS.

NAMES OF ADVERTISERS.

CLASSIFIED LIST OF ADVERTISERS.

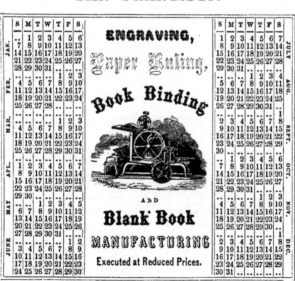

CIRCULAR.

LONDON AND SAN FRANCISCO BANK, LIMITED.

(Incorporated under the Joint Stock Companies' Act of 1862, of Great Britain.)

SAN FRANCISCO OFFICE, 412 Montgomery Street.
LONDON OFFICE, 22 Old Broad Street.   NEW YORK AGENCY, 53 Exchange Place.

CAPITAL, - - $5,000,000,

Of which $500,000 is fully paid up as present Capital, and will be increased as the growth of the business requires.

THE UNDERMENTIONED ARE FOUNDERS AND PROPRIETORS OF THE BANK:

Messrs. BISCHOFFSHEIM, GOLDSCHMIDT & CO.,......................London.
"   FRUHLING & GOSCHEN,..................................."
"   FREDERICK HUTH & CO.,.................................."
"   J. S. MORGAN & CO., (Successors to Messrs. Geo. Peabody & Co.)."
"   STERN BROTHERS,......................................."
INTERNATIONAL FINANCIAL SOCIETY, LIMITED,................"
Mr. FREDERICK RODEWALD,..................................."
THE BANK OF SAXE MEININGEN,...................Saxe Meiningen, Germany.
Mr. JULIUS MAY,..............................Frankfort, on the Main, Germany.
" SIGISMUND SULZBACH,.................................

LONDON BANKERS,...........The London Joint Stock Bank.

SAN FRANCISCO:

Manager, *MILTON S. LATHAM.*   Assistant Manager, *CAMILO MARTIN.*

LOCAL DIRECTORS.

WM. B. JOHNSTON, AGENT LIVERPOOL AND LONDON AND GLOBE INSURANCE COMPANY.
HENRY CARLTON, JR., MERCHANT.
A. EHRHORN, MERCHANT, OF HELLMANN BROS. & CO.

The Bank is prepared to transact ALL KINDS of General Banking and Exchange Business, in London and
an Francisco, and between said cities and all parts of the world.
The San Francisco Office is authorized to draw Bills of Exchange, or issue Letters of Credit, upon either of
he undernamed Founders and Proprietors of the Bank, or, (at the option of the buyer) upon the following
houses, with whom the Bank has established credits, viz:

LONDON,...........................The London Joint Stock Bank, No. 5 Princes Street.
"   ....Messrs. Bischoffsheim, Goldschmidst & Co.
"   ....Messrs. Fruhling & Goschen.
"   ....Messrs. Frederick Huth & Co.
"   ....Messrs. J. S. Morgan & Co. (successors to Messrs. Geo. Pea-
body & Co.)
"   ....Messrs. Stern Brothers.
NEW YORK CITY,..........Messrs. Dabney, Morgan & Co., 53 Exchange Place.
PARIS,.........................Messrs. Bischoffsheim, Goldsdhmidt & Co.
"   ....Messrs. A. J. Stern & Co.
FRANKFORT, on the Main,...Mr. Sigismund Sulzbach.
"   ....Mr. Jacob S. H. Stern.
GERMANY,....................The Bank of Saxe Meiningen.
AMSTERDAM,................Banque de Credit and de Depot des Pays Bas.
ANTWERP,.....................Messrs. Nottebohm Brothers.
"   ....Mr. F. R. Bischoffsheim.
HAMBURG,...................Messrs. John Berenberg, Gossler & Co.
BERLIN,........................Messrs. Moritz Guterbock & Co.
GENOA and NAPLES........The Anglo Italian Bank.
VALPARAISO and LIMA,....Messrs. Fred. Huth, Gruning & Co.
MANILA,.......................Messrs. Russell & Sturgis.
CHINA and JAPAN,..........The Chartered Mercantile Bank of India, London, and China,
and its Branches.
AUSTRALIA, INDIA, and | Asiatic Banking Corporation and its Branches, at
CHINA,...................} Bombay, Calcutta, Colombo, Singapore, Hongkong, Shanghai, Melbourne.
SYDNEY and MELBOURNE,Union Bank of Australia.
IRELAND,.....................Provincial Bank of Ireland, and all its Branches, viz., at

Dublin,	Waterford,	Youghal,	Dungannon,	Kilrush,	Templemore,
Cork,	Galway,	Enniskillen,	Bandon,	Skibbereen,	Carrick-on-Suir,
Limerick,	Armagh,	Monaghan,	Ennis,	Enniscorthy,	Carrick-on-Shan-
Clonmel,	Athlone,	Banbridge,	Ballyshannon,	Fermoy,	non,
Londonderry,	Coleraine,	Ballymena,	Strabane,	Newry,	Clogheen,
Sligo,	Kilkenny,	Parsonstown,	Dungarvan,	Drogheda,	Newcastle, (Co
Wexford,	Ballina,	Cavan,	Mallow,	Nenagh,	Limerick.)
Belfast,	Tralee,	Omagh,	Cootehill,		

SPECIAL attention paid to Selling California Securities in Europe; Collections, Purchases
of Real Estate and Mining Shares, and Investments of all kinds in California.

MILTON S. LATHAM, Manager.

and Sixth to Brannan, and along Brannan to the bridge at Mission Creek. From Taylor Street a branch track runs along Turk to Fillmore, along Fillmore to Post, and along Post to Lone Mountain Cemetery. The entire length of this railroad is five miles of double track, and about one-third of a mile of single track. The car houses and stables of the company are situated at the termini on Brannan Street and at Lone Mountain, and the office is on Taylor Street near Turk. The Central Railroad is completed and has been running for two years, to the great accommodation of the public and the manifest benefit of real estate in the suburbs. ·

The officers of the company are: R. J. VanDe-Water, President; S. C. Bigelow, Vice President; A. J. Gunnison, Treasurer; J. T. Hoyt, Secretary; J. A. McGlynn, Superintendent.

CITY RAILROAD COMPANY.

This company was incorporated by Act of the Legislature, approved April 21st, 1863, and organized May 20th, 1863. The capital stock of one million dollars is divided into ten thousand shares of one hundred dollars each. The first assessment of ten thousand dollars has already been paid in. Dolores to Corbett, and along Corbett to Mission

Portions of this road are under contract, but no work has yet been performed. It is thought, however, that some two miles of road will be built during the coming year. Arrangements have been made with a company of unlimited capital in New York—that has built a number of roads in the Eastern States—to complete this work, which will be commenced early in the sp g.

The officers of the City Railroad are: Isaac Rowell, President; E. W. Casey, Secretary.·

SAN FRANCISCO AND ATLANTIC RAILROAD

The San Francisco and Atlantic Railroad Company was incorporated, under the State law regulating and authorizing incorporations, in July, 1864. Its capital stock is twenty millions, in one hundred-dollar shares. This company proposes to construct a road to run from San Francisco via Stockton, to, or near Folsom, where it will tap the Central Pacific Railroad. Mr. Louis McLane has gone East to negotiate for the required capital to prosecute the work with successful energy.

The officers are: Alpheus Bull, President; Louis McLane, Treasurer; George Wallace, Secretary.

Homestead Associations.

. One of the most important as well as pleasing features in the unexampled progress of our city, is the organization of numerous Homestead Associations, which, by united effort and· consolidated capital, place it within the scope and means of any industrious and prudent individual to secure a tract that he can call his own, and secure to him the proud title of "lord of the soil." In all civilized countries, the moral and healthful effect produced upon communities, and more especially the so-called industrial classes, by the ownership of a fee simple in the soil, has ever been the subject of laudation among the most enlightened statesmen and liberal philanthropists. ·By the organization of Joint Stock Homestead Associations, and the purchase of large and eligibly located tracts of land, every member of the community may become a landholder at a comparatively trifling cost. By the payment of a small sum into the capital stock, and a comparatively trifling amount in stated assessments, every one may, through this medium, which is available to all, in a short time become the possessor of an unincumbered site for a homestead. The healthy and advantageous effect of this system is apparent in the number of elegant and comfortable residences which have sprung up, as if by magic, in the vicinity of the city in all directions within the past year.

For a complete list of the Homestead Associations organized and existing in this city, with the amounts of their capital stock, the dates of their incorporation, names of trustees, with their operations and progress, see Protective Associations, page 616.

Savings Banks.

One of the most healthy and beneficial institutions of a large city is the Savings Banks, which is. emphatically a monetary agent of the people. By receiving on deposit at a remunerative rate of interest, sums, no matter how small, and which would otherwise too often be heedlessly squandered, habits of economy and thrift are inculcated which are productive of the most beneficial results to the entire community. By constant additions, sums insignificant at the outset are gradually swelled to an amount of which the depositors themselves had no definite idea until they gave these institutions a trial, and full and satisfactorily tested the experiment. The loans made by these institutions are generally secured by bond and mortgage, and upon loans mutually advantageous, to all parties. By requiring with the payment of the interest due each month, a sum equivalent to a monthly installment of the original loan, at the time fixed for its maturity, the debt has been entirely extinguished. There are four of these institutions conducted upon the same principle in successful operation in the City of San Francisco, the beneficial effects of which are felt and acknowledged by the community at large. The first of these organized on this coast is the

SAVINGS AND LOAN SOCIETY.

Incorporated July 23d, 1857. Office 619 Clay.· The amount to the credit of the members of the society is $1,333,690.00. A dividend. of one per cent. was declared in July last for the preceding six months, leaving a surplus of $173,834.20 on hand. The management of the Savings and Loan Society reflects high credit upon those who have it in charge, and its advantage to the masses can scarcely be estimated. By its means and under the admirable system devised, depositors are made perfectly secure, thrift is encouraged by accumulations of interest, small capitals are aggregated, and enterprise stimulated by the facilities thus provided. The savings of the laborer thus invested, also aid in producing a general prosperity in which he is himself a sharer, and doubtless it is a conviction of these truths, with confidence in the fidelity of those in charge, which have obtained for this society the unparalleled success of which we have spoken.

HIBERNIA SAVINGS AND LOAN SOCIETY.

Incorporated April 12th, 1859. This association was formed for the mutual benefit of the members, who through it are enabled to find secure and profitable investment for small savings, and on the other hand have an opportunity of obtaining from it at reasonable rates the use of a moderate capital, upon giving good and sufficient security for the same. The affairs of this association have been managed with the utmost prudence and economy, and its business has been gradually increasing. Its success and healthy condition reflects the highest credit upon the management of the concern.

SAN FRANCISCO SAVINGS UNION.

The Legislature having passed an act on the 11th of April, 1862, framed with a special view to the formation of savings societies, a few gentlemen of well-known character and standing in this community took advantage of it to incorporate themselves under the above name. To depositors it offers the security of a guarantee capital of $100,000, to be increased as the business increases by a reserve fund of equal amount, which bears all losses, and neither of which can be withdrawn under any circumstances until every dollar deposited has been repaid to the depositors; in compensation for this guarantee, the stockholders receive a fair share of the net profits, and it is from this share, not from the profits of depositors, that the reserve fund is formed. As, with ordinary prudence, it is all but impossible that the losses should ever amount to $200,000, and as the losses have to be borne by the guarantee capital and reserve fund before they can touch deposits, the latter may be considered as perfectly secure. No dividend is allowed for the first month, as some time is required to find investment for the funds, but after that they are calculated without deduction for broken months, short time, etc., so that their real value is higher than it appears to be. It is a material relief to married women and minors, especially to the former, that when they make deposits in this institution in their own name, they can draw them without the necessity of obtaining the consent of their husbands or guardians. To borrowers it offers the facility of repayment by easy installments, spread over from twelve to forty-eight months, (the law allows six years) according to the circumstances of the case. To men of small means seeking to obtain a homestead, experience has shown this facility to be invaluable. The report of July 3d, 1865, shows the result of the first three years' operations to be—deposits, $380,974.43; guarantee capital paid in, reserve fund, and surplus profits, $; total, $428,696.96. Of this amount there was invested in loans made, $409,016.57; on hand, $18,638.33; balance in stamps on hand and furniture. Profits of the half year (net) $28,065.14.

For list of officers, etc., of the different savings associations, including those not referred to here, see page 616.

Banking Houses.

One of the most notable elements of our prosperity as a City and State, is the consolidating of immense capital under our Banking Law, and the establishment of branch offices in this city of foreign banks and capitalists. Of the former, the Bank of California, corner of Battery and Washington streets, stands first. The capital employed is $2,000,000, with a privilege to increase to $5,000,000. D. O. Mills, President; W. C. Ralston, Cashier....The Pacific Bank, No. 404 Montgomery Street, with a capital of $5,000,000, is another prominent house, embracing in its list of directors some of our wealthiest citizens.

Of the foreign houses we may mention the London and San Francisco Bank, (limited), with a capital of $5,000,000; Milton S. Latham, Manager; office 412 Montgomery Street....The Bank of British Columbia, with a capital of $1,250,000, with power to increase to $10,000,000; James D. Walker, Mana-

ger; office 412 California Street....Bank of British North America, Grain & Sutherland, Agents, office 411 California Street....The Commercial Bank of India, with a subscribed capital of $5,000,000, and $2,500,000 paid-up capital; Richard Newby, Agent, 408 California Street....The British and Californian Banking Company, with head office in London, has established a branch here, with Henry S. Babcock as Manager, and James Ireland, Sub-Manager; office 424 California Street....A number of other institutions founded on a solid basis might be mentioned, did space permit. Suffice it to say, that such large sums of money on deposit here, for commercial and other uses, is a sufficient evidence of our future prospects and stability.

Insurance Companies.

Within the past year several important institutions of this character have gone into successful operation, while those of an older date have largely increased their business. This is an important feature of our domestic policy; and the establishment and successful conduct of home insurance companies exhibits a healthy condition of public contentment, and a feeling of security on the part of our citizens with regard to fire and marine risks. The following is a list of the local institutions of this character in successful operation here, the character of whose officers and managers is a sufficient guaranty of their soundness and reliability in all respects.

HOME MUTUAL INSURANCE COMPANY.

The above company was organized in September, 1864, with a capital of $1,000,000, and is prepared to issue fire, life, and marine policies of insurance upon all insurable property, lives, etc. There are five committees—one on Finance and Loans, one on Insurance, one on Claims and Losses, one Auditing, and one Executive. The Directors are selected from nearly all branches of trade—the industrial classes being particularly well represented. A company of this kind is destined to win its way to public favor and its business soon placed upon an unshaken foundation. The office is at No. 630 Montgomery Street. Geo. S. Mann, President; Wm. H. Stevens, Sec'y.

SAN FRANCISCO INSURANCE COMPANY.

Incorporated March, 1861. Capital and surplus, $240,000.

Officers—George C. Boardman, President; C. D. O. Sullivan, Vice President; P. McShane, Secretary. The capital and surplus of this company are now over $240,000, all paid in gold, and well secured on the best collaterals, and its careful management has made it one of the most reliable offices on the Pacific Coast, bringing with it the reward of a constantly increasing business. Office, No. 432 Montgomery Street, in Donohoe, Kelly & Co.'s Bank Building.

MERCHANTS' MUTUAL MARINE INSURANCE COMPANY.

Organized April 2d, 1863; capital, $500,000. This company, the only California company now exclusively in marine insurance, may be considered in successful and vigorous operation. It offers to the business community a local institution conducted on liberal principles, prompt and energetic in its administration, and offering in its list of stockholders, composed of many of our most reliable merchants, the amplest security to its customers. Its business is conducted entirely on a gold basis, and all losses are paid promptly in United States gold coin.

Officers—James P. Flint, President; J. B. Scotchler, Secretary. Office, south-east corner Front and California.

FIREMAN'S FUND INSURANCE COMPANY.

Organized May 1st, 1863; capital, $500,000, fully paid in gold coin. One-fourth of all the Directors are active or exempt members of the San Francisco Fire Department. One-tenth of its net insurance earnings are divided among the various Fire Departments of the State, to be dedicated to charitable purposes. Having become established on a firm basis the company solicits a share of public patronage, and guarantees that all its losses shall be paid in United States gold coin. Office, No. 238 Montgomery Street.

Officers—S. H. Parker, President; M. Lynch, Vice President; W. H. Patterson, Attorney; C. R. Bond, Secretary.

CALIFORNIA HOME INSURANCE COMPANY.

This company was organized in 1864, under the laws of this State, with a capital of $300,000. It is composed of gentlemen of wealth and standing, and well known to the business community. They insure against loss or damage by fire on all brick and frame buildings, merchandise, dwellings, furniture, etc., and pay all such losses in United States gold coin. From the responsibility of its Directors and the competent business capacity of the officers in charge of its affairs, this company will soon rank second to none of its class on this coast. The office is located at Nos. 224 and 226 California Street.

Officers — B. F. Lowe, President; J. G. Parker, Jr., Secretary.

PACIFIC INSURANCE COMPANY.

This company, which was organized July 14th, 1863, with a capital stock of $750,000, insures against loss or damage by fire. The Board of Directors is composed of the best known and reliable business men and capitalists of the Pacific Coast, and the stockholders represent a larger amount of capital than almost any other company on the continent. The capital is all paid up in gold coin, and recognizing in its fullest extent the law of individual liability, this company offers the best possible guarantee to the insured, and establishes an institution in this important department of which every citizen taking any interest in the welfare and prosperity of Pacific institutions may feel a just pride.

Officers—Jonathan Hunt, President; A. J. Ralston, Secretary. Office 436 California Street.

CALIFORNIA INSURANCE COMPANY.

This company was incorporated February 23d, 1863, with a subscribed capital of $200,000, divided into twenty shares of $10,000 each. It is the pioneer of all the insurance corporations in our city, and the gentlemen owning its stock were the first who had the courage to assume the personal liabilities imposed by our State Constitution on stockholders, in a business supposed to be preëminently hazardous. For the mutual protection of each other and of the insured, with reference to this liability, unusual care was taken to admit only such stockholders as were of undoubted responsibility ; and to prevent sales of stock to irresponsible parties, all the receipts of the company, less taxes, expenses, and losses, are retained on hand, and no dividend can be declared until the entire original capital has been earned from the proceeds of the business. The company has thus far prospered. Its officers are well known and experienced underwriters, and they have won for the office a character for prudence in taking risks and liberality in paying losses. Owing to the substantial character of its stockholders, the peculiarities of our State laws, and of the by-laws of the company, the California Mutual is probably the strongest marine

office in the United States; for not only are its capital and accumulations subject to the claims of creditors and the control of State officers, but after these are exhausted the stockholders remain personally liable for the excess in the same manner as if they had each signed the policy on the plan of the Lloyds of London.

This company divides ten per cent. of its profits on open policies, among the holders of such policies, on the second Monday of January in each year, in lieu of the scrip returns of Eastern marine companies. All its transactions are made only in gold coin. Office 318 California Street. C. T. Hopkins, Secretary.

OCCIDENTAL INSURANCE COMPANY.

Incorporated 1865; capital, $300,000. This company has been but a few months in existence, and it has already accumulated a large amount of business. The directors comprise some of our most active and responsible business men, which cannot fail to secure for its future a reputation for promptness and liberality.

Officers—Henry B. Platt, President; J. Greenebaum, Vice President; R. N. Van Brunt, Secretary. Office south-west corner California and Montgomery streets.

UNION INSURANCE COMPANY.

Incorporated 1865; capital, $750,000. This company, although recently organized, has attained a position equal to any of the home companies. Its affairs are managed with energetic ability, and from the well-known character of its officers, the amplest security is offered to those who desire the protection of the company.

Officers—Caleb T. Fay, President; Charles D. Haven, Secretary. Office 416 California Street.

CALIFORNIA LLOYDS.

This association, organized in 1861, upon the plan of the London Lloyds, includes in its list as underwriters many of our wealthiest citizens. Its risks are exclusively marine; and its losses are promptly paid in gold coin. G. Touchard, Secretary. Office 418 California Street.

Libraries.

It may be set down as a fixed fact that there is no surer indication of the progression and prosperity of a community, than the number and condition of its libraries. In this department San Francisco may safely challenge competition with any city of its age in the range of civilization. The Public Libraries are numerous and respectable, and notwithstanding the activity and energy exhibited by her citizens in every department of life, the statistics of these institutions prove beyond controversy that they are at the same time essentially a reading people. Not physical alone, but mental activity is a prominent characteristic of our population.

In addition to these libraries several of the hotels of the city are provided with large and well selected collections of books for the use of guests. That belonging to the What Cheer House numbers about 5,000 volumes of well selected works, connected with which is an extensive cabinet of specimens in natural history, and a large number of paintings, with a marble bust by Powers, copied by that artist from his statue of California, and a fancy head in marble by Gault, an eminent sculptor, which works of art, selected by the proprietor, Mr. Woodward, during his tour in Europe, reflect credit upon his taste and liberality.

Want of space prevents a reference in detail to the numerous public libraries in this city, prominent among which may be named the Mercantile Library. Association, containing 20,000 volumes; Odd Fellows', 14,000; Mechanics' Institute, 7,500; Young Men's Christian Association, 3,000; California Pioneers, 2,000; San Francisco Verein, 4,000.

The Masonic Fraternity have made arrangements for the foundation of a library in this city. From the well-known character of those who have the enterprise in charge, it must soon take rank with the leading library institutions in the State. For list of officers, etc., of the different literary institutions in the city, see page 619.

Water Companies.

SPRING VALLEY WATER WORKS.

Capital stock $6,000,000, in 60,000 shares of $100 each.

Officers — W. F. Babcock, President; Calvin Brown, Superintendent; Henry Watson, Secretary; Lloyd Tevis, Charles Mayne, S. C. Bigelow, W. F. Babcock, N. Luning, H. S. Dexter, and John Parrott, Trustees.

The present organization is formed by a consolidation of the San Francisco City and Spring Valley Water Works companies, which took place on the first of January, 1865.

The San Francisco Water Works Company filed its certificate of incorporation on the nineteenth day of June, 1857, and on the twenty-seventh day of September of the year following, introduced the water of Lobos Creek into the lower portion of the city, and in January, 1860, the permanent works were completed for the supply of the entire city with water. The Spring Valley Company was incorporated in June, 1858, and in July, 1861, the water from Islais Creek was introduced into the city.

The present works receive their supply from two sources—Lobos and Pillarcitos cieeks. Lobos Creek is a stream of pure fresh water, emptying into the bay near Point Lobos, which supplies two millions of gallons daily. The distance of the stream is three and a half miles in a direct line from the Plaza. The receiving reservoir, with a capacity of 800,000 gallons, is located at Black Point, on the bay, from which the water is elevated by four double-acting pumps, with a capacity of 2,000,000 gallons daily, propelled by two steam engines of two hundred and fifty-horse power each, to the distributing reservoirs on the adjacent hills, the highest being three hundred and fifteen feet above high-water mark, located at the corner of Hyde and Greenwich streets; the second, which is situated immediately below, at the intersection of Hyde and Francisco streets, is one hundred and forty-five feet above high-water mark. The capacity of the first is 5,000,000 gallons, and that of the lower 8,000,000.

Pillarcitos Creek is situated in the coast range of mountains, distant from San Francisco about fifteen miles in a southerly direction. The water is taken at an elevation of seven hundred feet above the level of the sea, through the main coast range by means of a tunnel 1,600 feet in length. A large dam is now being constructed on the Pillarcitos Valley below the tunnel, which dam will be seventy-eight feet in hight and two hundred and twenty-eight feet between the abutments. This will cause the water to cover ninety-two acres of land and make a reservoir that will contain 900,000,000 gallons, which will be filled during the winter season of the year, and

be drawn from as required in the city reservoirs, making this the great retaining reservoir. From the east end of the tunnel the water is conducted around the hills into another large reservoir—Lake Honda, back of the Mission Dolores—by a flume eighteen by thirty inches, with a grade of seven feet to the mile, being thirty-two miles in length. Of this distance six miles are laid of iron pipe, and when the flumes are to be replaced it will probably be done by iron pipe, of which about twelve miles would be required to make the entire route of iron. Lake Honda is a fine natural reservoir, three hundred and seventy feet above the sea, with a capacity of 52,000,000 gallons, from which place the water is brought to another distributing reservoir, corner of Buchanan and Market streets, by means of sixteen and twelve inch cast iron mains. The Market Street Reservoir is constructed on a high bill, two hundred feet above the sea, and is made of brick and cement; capacity 1,750,000 gallons. This is the main distributing reservoir, and supplies four-fifths of the city. The upper part of the city is supplied direct from Lake Honda pressure, which will give a good pressure to almost every section of the city. As to the quality of the water, it is now over two years since it was first introduced, and has been carried to every quarter of the world, and given the greatest satisfaction to all who have used it. The B n Street Reservoir, also used by the company, has a capacity of 500,000 gallons.

The main dam above mentioned, (at this date, first December) is almost completed. The company commenced, in July last, a tunnel under the mountain separating the San Mateo from the San Andreas Valley, which will be 3,350 feet long, and will be completed in April, 1867—it will save nearly eight miles of the present flume—reducing the main line of conduit from thirty-two miles to twenty-four miles in length. This twenty-four miles will eventually be reduced to about eighteen miles—as proved by recent surveys.

The amount of pipe now laid in the city proper, reaches sixty-two miles.

Gas Companies.

CITIZENS' GAS COMPANY.

The Legislature of 1862, on the second of May, granted to Eugene L. Sullivan, Nathaniel Holland, and John Benson, a franchise to lay down pipes through the streets of the City of San Francisco, for the purpose of supplying the citizens with gas; the franchise extending over a period of fifty years. Shortly after the granting of this franchise, the company was organized by the filing of articles of incorporation with the Clerk of this county and the Secretary of State. The articles of incorporation were signed by Eugene L. Sullivan, Nathaniel Holland, John Benson, R. E. Brewster, John Bensley, E. R. Sprague, John A. McGlynn, James Brennan, T. Maguire, Wm. Sherman, A. C. Whitcomb, D. Northrop, W. F. Williamson, and Alfred Barstow, and placed the capital stock at $2,000,000, divided into shares of one hundred dollars each. As soon as the company was completely organized an agent was dispatched east for the purpose of purchasing pipe and material for the erection of the works. An arrangement was soon effected with Mr. Jno. P. Kennedy, a well-known erector of gas works in New York, to furnish the plans and take the superintendence of the erection of their works. The company having purchased between two and three 100-varas of land fronting on the bay at the junction of Townsend and Second streets, work was begun early in the fall of 1863, and has been vigorously pushed to completion. Mr. B. P. Brunner has been elected the permanent superintendent of the works.

It is thought that the company will begin to furnish our citizens with gas about the first of January next. One of the provisions of the company's charter make it imperative upon them to furnish the gas at a cost of not more than six dollars per 1,000 feet. The outcry made against the San Francisco Gas Company in 1862 by San Franciscans was, probably, the origin of the company: but be it what it may, the fact that it will be of vast benefit to the citizens of our city cannot be doubted, for the healthy competition which will result from the struggle of the two companies to furnish us with light, must have the effect to materially reduce the price.

Foundries, Machine Shops, Etc.

There is no department of manufactures and industrial enterprise connected with our city, that has made such rapid progress during the past few years, as that included under this head. The number of establishments engaged in the working of metals is estimated at between three and four hundred, giving steady employment to over two thousand hands.

IRON FOUNDRIES.

The number of Iron Foundries now in operation in this city is fourteen, which give employment to from seven hundred and fifty to one thousand persons.

UNION IRON AND BRASS WORKS.

H. J. Booth & Co., proprietors. This, the pioneer establishment in San Francisco, was founded in 1849, by James and Peter Donahue, brothers, since which time it has steadily increased, ever holding its rank of first in magnitude and importance on the Pacific Coast. The machinery and appliances in these works compare favorably with the best in the world. The superiority of the engines—marine, locomotive, and stationary—built here is admitted, after the severest tests, by the best qualified judges. The first premium for the engine manufactured by H. J. Booth & Co., and exhibited at the Mechanics' Fair, San Francisco, 1865, was awarded to Wm. R. Eckart, the designer. This engine was provided with "Scott & Eckart's Balance-Valve Cut-Off," which for simplicity and effectiveness is unrivaled. The Excelsior Grinder and Amalgamator, patented by Wheeler & Randall, and manufactured here, in its practical workings has fully confirmed the demonstrations of Mr. Randall, as published in the Quartz Operator's Hand Book, that tractory-formed plates possess fully eighty per cent. greater grinding capacity than plane or flat plates. The amount of work done at this establishment can be estimated from the fact that two hundred and seventy-five men are employed.

PACIFIC IRON WORKS.

Goddard & Co., proprietors. Next to the Union, the Pacific is the oldest establishment of the kind in the city, the works having been established on their present site, First Street between Mission and Natoma, in September, 1850, by Messrs. Egery & Hinckley, whose interest was purchased in December, 1853, by the present proprietors, who erected the present spacious buildings and enlarged and increased the works. The daily running expenses of the establishment reach about $1,500; the machinery is driven by an eighty-horse power engine. The melting capacity of the largest cupola is twenty tons; there are two others, the aggregate capacity of which is ten tons, making a total of thirty tons. These works made, during the past year, three steamboat and two propellor engines, two stationary eighty-horse power engines, three sixty-horse power, two forty-five-horse power, thirteen thirty-horse power, six fifteen-horse power, seventeen quartz mills from five to forty stamps each, sixty-four amalgamating pans, thirty-six amalgamating barrels, five thousand six hundred stamp shoes and dies, and seventy steam boilers ranging from twenty to three hundred-horse power each. In addition to the foregoing, a large number of grist, sugar, and saw mills, and castings for agricultural implements were turned out. The average number of hands employed is about one hundred and fifty. About 1,200 tons pig iron consumed per year, with a proportionate amount of wrought iron and boiler plate.

FULTON FOUNDRY.

Hinckley & Co., proprietors, 45, 47, and 49 First Street. Established 1855. Men employed at present fifty-five. The machinery for a large number of steamboats has been manufactured during the past two years. Extensively engaged in the manufacture of saw-mill machinery. Many additions have been made to the stock of tools during the last year, and the facilities at the present time are equal to any shop for manufacture of all kinds of machinery for steamboats, quartz-mills, flouring-mills, etc.

VULCAN IRON WORKS COMPANY.

N. D. Arnot, President; R. Ivers, Treasurer; C. R. Steiger, Secretary; S. Aitken, proprietors. The Vulcan Iron Works, located on First, Natoma, Fremont and Beale, office, First Street, 137-139, were established in August, 1851, by George Gordon & Steen, for the manufacture of steam engines, boilers, and machinery. In January, 1855, they were incorporated as a joint-stock company, and in April, 1857, became the property of the present owners. Steam engines and boilers of every variety are constantly turned out at these works, which have also supplied the machinery for a number of saw, flour, and quartz mills on this coast; all the hydraulic machinery for raising brick buildings in San Francisco was invented and made at these works, and the first locomotive built in the State was built there. The locomotives on the Alameda and San Francisco, Oakland and Napa railroads were built at this establishment. Every class, of mining, pumping, and hoisting machinery can be obtained from this firm, who take especial pride in keeping up with the vast improvements lately made in mining machinery. Hepburn & Peterson's Amalgamating Pan is manufactured here, as also their Separators. This establishment now employs two hundred to two hundred and fifty men, and have during the last year extended their works by the addition of several large shops on the east side of Fremont Street between Mission and Howard, extending to Beale.

MINERS' FOUNDRY.

First Street between Howard and Folsom. This establishment, as its name imports, is engaged principally in manufacturing mining machinery, and during the past year has been largely engaged in supplying the increasing demand caused by the rich development of minerals in Idaho, Reese River, and California. They however are not confined to mining machinery alone, but manufacture all kinds of machinery used on this coast. Quite a notable feature of their business the last year has been the building of sugar machinery for the Sandwich Islands, which has heretofore been manufactured in the Atlantic States and Europe. They employ about one hundred and fifty hands, and melt about two thousand tons of pig iron per annum.

GOLDEN STATE IRON WORKS.

Palmer, Knox & Co., proprietors. This extensive establishment is located on First Street near Market. The operations of this concern have been in the manufacture of steam engines, water wheels, mining pumps, quartz mills, and amalgamators. Among which latter we notice the Knox's Amalgamator, with Palmer's Improved Steam Chest, are being turned out in large numbers. The Golden State gives employment to about fifty men.

CALIFORNIA FOUNDRY.

Brodie, Hubbard & McAdams, proprietors. These works, located at 16 Fremont Street, employ a large number of workmen in the preparation of castings of every description, such as house fronts, leaves, trusses, window caps, sills, quoins, and also light and heavy castings of every descriptions.

PHŒNIX WORKS.

These works, owned by Jonathan Kittredge, are extensively engaged in the manufacture of every description of iron doors, shutters, bank vaults, safes, and every description of blacksmith work. Located 6 and 8 Battery Street.

PIONEER WORKS.

Located corner of Battery and Jackson streets, are manufacturing fire-proof doors, shutters, prison-cells, balconies, etc., and blacksmithing in general. Kittredge & Leavitt, proprietors.

EUREKA WORKS.

William McKibbin, proprietor, 41 and 43 First Street. This establishment manufactures iron stairs, shutters, railings, and house work of every description. The celebrated Eureka Key and Clamp Bridge is also manufactured by Mr. McKibbin.

BOILER WORKS.

The Boiler Works of Messrs. Coffey & Risdon are engaged in an extensive and increasing business, employing a large number of hands, involving a heavy outlay for labor and materials.

PORTLAND BOILER WORKS.

Moynihan & Aitken, proprietors. These works are now established at Nos. 311 and 313 Mission Street. A number of first-class boilers have been built at this establishment during the past year. They employ constantly a large number of hands—consuming a large quantity of material.

There are numerous other establishments engaged in the working of metals, viz.: blacksmith shops, brass foundries, carriage and wagon smiths, coppersmiths, exclusive of those employed in the precious metals.

Metallurgical Establishments.

With the constant discovery of new mines in the Washoe, Humboldt, and Reese River region, and the reclamation of old ones in Mexico, there is of course an increased demand for the best methods and most complete facilities for reducing and extracting the various samples of rock, produced from thousands of sources. In order to avail themselves of every facility and the improvements which are made every day in this department, the owners of many mines ship samples of their ore to this city for reduction and assay. There are several large establishments constantly engaged in reducing ores, the most extensive of which is the San Francisco Gold and Silver Refinery, on Brannan near Seventh. The refinery, a substantial brick structure, is one story in hight, and sixty feet in width, by one hundred and thirty in length. Kellogg, Hewston & Co. proprietors; office 416 Montgomery Street.

Sugar Refineries.

SAN FRANCISCO AND PACIFIC SUGAR REFINERY.

During the year 1862 a new refinery was built, brought into successful operation, and merged into one concern, with the old established "San Francisco Sugar Refining Company." They are incorporated as the "San Francisco and Pacific Sugar Company." Capital, $800,000. George Gordon, Manager; R. Feuerstein, Commercial Agent.

The buildings of the company are located on the corner of Harrison and Eighth streets, and together comprise the largest buildings in the State, with the exception of the U. S. Forts. The buildings consist of a melting house, eighty feet long, forty-five feet wide, and six stories high; a charcoal tank house, eighty-five feet long, twenty-five feet wide, and thirty feet high; a white sugar house, eighty-five feet long, fifty feet wide, and six stories high; a yellow sugar-house, one hundred and twenty-two feet long, seventy-five feet wide, and five stories high; a bone charcoal factory, one hundred feet long, forty feet wide, and thirty feet high; a boiler house, fifty feet square, and twenty-five feet high—with numerous small buildings on the premises for the repair of the machinery, etc.

The company at present are refining 1,000 tons raw sugar monthly; turning out 5,000 barrels white sugar; 2,500 barrels yellow coffee crushed sugar, and 35,000 gallons golden syrup. The works, however, with their present machinery and implements, have sufficient capacity to increase this by one-third, whenever the consumption of refined sugars in the State warrants it. The number of hands employed is about two hundred on the premises, besides giving work to some fifty more outside.

BAY SUGAR REFINERY.

This company have recently erected on the corner of Union and Battery streets extensive works for the refining of sugar. The machinery used is of the most approved description, affording a capacity of about 50,000 pounds per day.

Home Manufactures.

SAN FRANCISCO PIONEER WOOLEN FACTORY.

Incorporated December 2d, 1862. Location, Black Point. Capital $300,000. Heynemann & Co., agents, 315 and 317 California Street. These mills manufacture all kinds of woolen goods, especially blankets, cassimeres, tweeds, and flannels. A great portion of the flannels are worked up into gents' furnishing goods. The number of persons employed are one hundred. Amount of wool used per day is 3,000 pounds, producing from fifteen to two hundred pairs blankets and twenty-five dozen overshirts per day.

MISSION WOOLEN FACTORY.

Located on Folsom between Fifteenth and Sixteenth streets. Lazard & McLennan, proprietors; Lazard Freres, agents. These works were established in 1861. Number of hands employed at the factory are one hundred and forty, and one hundred at other places, in connection with the business. Amount of wool consumed is 800,000 pounds per annum. All qualities and colors of blankets, and all-wool flannels of every description—tweeds, cassimeres, and broadcloths, army and navy cloths manufactured. All these fabrics find a ready market here, and are superior in quality to the same line of imported goods.

These works recently have extended their manufacturing facilities, by the completion of an extensive addition to the main building, thereby affording sufficient room to meet the increasing demand for woolen goods on this coast.

SAN FRANCISCO CORDAGE MANUFACTORY.

This manufactory, which is located at the Potrero, was established in 1856, by Messrs. Flint, Peabody & Co., and Messrs. Tubbs & Co., and has been successfully conducted ever since. The buildings are upon the most extensive scale—that used as the ropewalk being fifteen hundred feet in length, the department devoted to the spinning of the yarn being one hundred feet long by forty feet in width. The material used is Manilla hemp—regular shipments being made for this purpose. This manufactory gives constant employment to fifty hands, who turn out 2,000,000 pounds of cordage during the year—about 6,000 pounds of the raw material being consumed each day in the manufacture. The office is at Messrs. Tubbs & Co.'s, 613 Front Street.

PACIFIC GLASS WORKS.

The Pacific Glass Company was incorporated early in Oct., 1862. Giles H. Gray, Agent, 621 Clay.

This company was incorporated with a capital stock of $50,000, which was afterwards increased to $125,000, and about $10,000 have been levied and paid in on assessments. The factory is situated on a tract of ten acres, purchased by the company, at the Potrero. The first bottle was blown June 16th, 1863.

These works have been ever since in active operation, and is now manufacturing a great variety of green, black, and blue bottles, carboys, fruit jars, etc., of any desired shade of color or shape, and will soon have increased facilities for the manufacture of every description of druggists' ware of a superior quality; also lamp chimneys, retorts, telegraph insulators, and other kinds of blown and pressed glass, at a cost below that of imported ware. Private molds are manufactured and lettered to order. Twenty glass blowers are employed. From forty-five to fifty men and boys receive employment in various capacities at the factory. The increase in the various manufactured articles that require bottles—such as acids, patent medicines, etc., and for putting up pickles, fresh fruits, catsup, mustard, etc., and last, but not least, for the great wine-growing interest in the State—makes this an important branch of manufacture for the Pacific Coast. The new tariff on wines imported here in bottles, will also work very much to the advantage of the company.

DOW'S DISTILLERY.

This establishment is located on Mission Creek, between Brannan and Folsom streets, and is the largest distillery on the Pacific Coast. Barley, wheat, rye, Indian corn, and rice, are used in the manufacture of whisky; the monthly consumption over 1,000,000 pounds of grain, and production of whisky from 60,000 to 75,000 gallons per month; consumption of coal for fuel, about three hundred tons per month. The proprietors have lately altered and refitted the whole establishment and made many improvements, among the principal of which is in the furnaces, whereby they are enabled to use the Mount Diablo California coal exclusively, and with more success and economy than has been heretofore done, thereby enabling them to be independent of foreign coals, and keeping the money that has been heretofore expended for the imported article, at home. They are also rectifiers—the greater portion of their production is made into pure spirits—annually consuming from 6,000 to 7,000 sacks of charcoal in rectifying. They also have the only Column Still on this coast, for the manufacture of high-proof alcohol and spirits—capacity five hundred to six hundred gallons of high-proof alcohol daily. Their barrels are made principally of California or Oregon white oak, and are made for them at the State Prison. In consequence of the partial failure last season of the grain crop in this State, the principal material now used is the Sandwich Island molasses, of which about one hundred barrels per day are consumed.

WIRE ROPE MANUFACTORY.

This enterprise was established by A. S. Hallidie & Co., and has been in successful operation for several years. The consumers of wire rope are princi-

pally the mining and ferry interests of this State and Oregon, it being chiefly used for hoisting, pump, derrick, ferry, and bridge ropes. The longest wire rope made at this manufactory, without splice or joint, was more than one-third of a mile, and three inches in circumference.

These works also manufacture considerable copper and brass wire rope for sash cords, lightning conductors, etc., etc., and iron wire stays for shipping.

The manufactory is located at the foot of Taylor Street, North Beach.

CALIFORNIA WIRE WORKS.

H. T. Graves' Wire Goods Manufactory, 412 Clay Street, was established in 1852, as the Dennis Wire Works, and is one of the oldest manufacturing establishments in San Francisco. It is fully adapted to the manufacture of every article that wire is used for, and in its consumption every style and size of wire is called into use—from the finest wire cloth to the inch-square coal screens made of three-eighth inch wire.

SOAP.

A very superior article of home manufacture, by J. H. C. Portmann, is turned out in large quantities at his works on Mission Creek. Every variety of soap now in use can be had at this manufactory, to meet the demands of a generous public.

The Fluctuations of Trade.

The following table has been prepared for the purpose of showing the changeable character of our business community. Only the leading branches of trade have been included; but these may be regarded as a fair indication of the whole. The yearly changes among the small dealers will not fall short of forty per cent. per annum:

OCCUPATIONS.	No. 1861.	No. 1862.	No. 1863.	No. 1864.	Declined Business.	Remaining in Business.	No. 1865.
Apothecaries........	49	51	58	57	15	42	56
Assayers............	7	6	14	13	3	10	11
Attorneys...........	315	328	343	371	54	317	376
Auctioneers.........	21	18	18	26	4	22	29
Bakeries	67	59	49	60	18	42	68
Bankers	18	18	19	18	...	18	19
Baths	15	15	16	16	3	13	21
Billiard table mak'rs	8	7	6	5	...	5	5
Boarding Houses....	340	444	447	428	193	235	544
Breweries...........	24	23	26	21	4	17	22
Brokers.............	217	216	390	319	82	237	387
Butchers & Markets	230	211	264	245	75	170	332
Cabinet Makers ,...	33	31	28	21	9	12	43
Carpenters..........	109	93	79	91	59	32	84
Cigar Dealers, mk'rs	178	165	158	143	59	84	150
Clothing and Tailors	296	290	304	332	130	202	317
Dress Makers.......	81	93	99	120	80	40	111
Dry Goods	139	120	112	114	26	88	123
Fruits..............	105	122	117	127	66	61	161
Furniture.	53	56	49	65	26	39	63
Groceries.	421	453	460	490	106	384	523
Gunsmiths	15	13	11	11	...	11	15
Hair Dressers.......	102	96	115	72	23	49	107
Hardware...........	34	34	37	40	4	36	44
Hatters.............	21	24	25	27	4	23	29
Liquors, Etc	1,041	1,231	1,315	1,654	552	1,102	1,729
Lumber.............	35	38	32	35	6	29	41
Merchants, Commis'	186	162	149	159	15	144	193
Milliners	74	51	96	86	29	57	85
Painters	84	67	90	89	18	71	92
Physicians	202	209	227	238	53	185	248
Printing Offices. ...;	19	20	19	21	3	18	26
Produce	78	85	84	84	37	47	106
Restaurants	86	89	90	84	24	60	94
Stoves and Tinware.	66	76	60	56	12	44	58
Upholsterers........	27	37	37	36	4	32	37
Watchm'rs & Jew'rs	108	160	161	173	43	130	180
Wood and Coal.	87	88	84	86	30	56	92
Totals.............	4,991	5,300	5,688	6,033	1,869	4,164	6,573

ADDITIONAL NAMES, REMOVALS, CHANGES, ETC.,

RECEIVED TOO LATE FOR REGULAR INSERTION.

ADLER Bar, merchant, dwl 427 Sacramento
Alemania S. M. Co. office 652 Washington
Allardt George F. assistant engineer, Pacific R. R. Co. office 409 California, dwl 421 Powell
Allen A. F. workman, S. F. & P. Sugar Co. dwl 25 Rousch
Altenberg Rosalia Mrs. milliner, 308 Kearny
AMERICAN FLAG, daily and weekly, Daniel O. McCarthy editor and proprietor, office 528 Montgomery, editorial rooms 517 Clay
Ames Henry K. foreman with Bardwell & Co. dwl NW cor Seventh and Jessie
Armstrong Martha Mrs. proprietress Congress House, 314–322 Bush
Anthony John, laborer, dwl 116 Sansom
Aubry Joseph, trunk maker, 713 Clay
Auradou Leon (Spotorno & A.) dwl 507 Merchant
Austin M. E. (Jennings & A.) dwl E s Taylor bet Filbert and Union
Axtell S. B. attorney at law, office 9 Court Block
Ayer Washington, physician, and School Director Third District, office 410 Kearny
Ayres Hiram, news dealer, dwl 121 Bush

BACIGALUPI Theodore, bar keeper, 635 Washington, dwl 623 Broadway
BACON J. S. agent Boston Underwriters (and T. H. & J. S. Bacon) office 216 Front, dwl 1 Vernon Place
BACON T. H. & J. S. shipping and commission merchants and agents Boston Underwriters, office 216 Front, res Boston
Bailey Lewis H. ex-hotel proprietor, dwl 624 Ellis
Baker Henry (Wilson & B.) and cigar inspector U. S. Inter. Rev. dwl 23 Moss
Baker John E. carriages, Russ H, dwl 561 Bryant
BALLARD (Duane) & HALL (Isaac R.) forwarding and commission merchants, 11 Clay
Ballard Joseph H. discharging clerk, dwl 932 Pac
Barker Abner H. (Main St. Wharf Co.) office 708 Montgomery
Barnard Edward, policeman, dwl Summer St. House Summer nr California
Barnard I. D. real estate agent, office 224 Montgomery, dwl Cosmopolitan Hotel
Barnstead Thomas D. policeman, dwl 265 Jessie
Barr Miss, teacher, Fourth St. School, dwl 220 Third
Barrette M. E. (widow) teacher music and languages, dwl 819 Howard
Barron C. J. grainer, dwl 429 Stevenson
Barry (John) & Kennedy (J. F.) house and sign painters, Union Court nr Kearny
Battersby James Mrs. dwl 220 Third
Bechtinger J. physician, office 629 Clay
Beckwith Edward G. Rev. pastor Third Congregational Church, dwl W s Second Av nr Sixteenth
Beers W. J. Plaza Drug Store, 727 Washington, dwl 645 Washington
Behncke Otto, laborer, dwl 308 Beale
Beideman J. C. (estate of) office 240 Montgomery
BELDEN FRANCIS C. wholesale wine, liquors, and teas, 612 Sacramento
Benjamin Charles E. dwl 1 Garden
Bennett Oil Co. (San Mateo County) office 622 Clay room 11

Bent Charles, clerk, 415 Commercial, dwl Benton H
Bernard W. Robert, house and sign painter, 511 Commercial, dwl 1906 Powell
Bernhard Sam. H. (Harris & B.) dwl 317 Dupont
Bert Frederick W. collector, Morning Call, dwl S s Folsom bet Twentieth and Twenty-First
Berthier A. D. physician, office and dwl 814 Wash
Bertram Henry, hairdyeing saloon, Stevenson H
Beseler Charles, mining, dwl 34 Langton
Best & Belcher M. Co. office Pioneer Building
Bettman J. J. (A. Hirschfelder & Co.) dwl 102 Stockton
Bettman Moses, soap dealer, 305 California, dwl 1110 Powell
Bianchi Eugenio, professor music, 714 Vallejo
Bibbins Tracy L. collector and general agent, office 618 Merchant
Bishop (D. M.) & Co. (James B. Faitoute) proprietors The Guide, office 411 Clay
Black George, civil engineer and surveyor, office 528 Clay, dwl N s Eddy bet Devisidero and Broderick
Bloomer Hiram G. painter, 414 Merchant, dwl 1402 Leavenworth
Bloomer Theodore H. book keeper, 321 Front, dwl 1402 Leavenworth
BLOSSOM WILLIAM H. president Sauce M. Co. office with R. N. Van Brunt, Stevenson House, dwl 725 Pine
Blumenthal Guido (Greenhood & B.) dwl NE cor Mission and Ninth
Boland William H. book keeper with James Brokaw, dwl 54 First
Bolke Willhelm (Tiatien & B.) dwl 316 Ritch
Bollo & Brother (Thomas and Vincent) groceries and liquors, SE cor Stockton and Vallejo and NW cor Clay and Stockton
Bollo Vincent (Bollo & Brother) dwl NW cor Clay and Stockton
Bonnaud S. jobber dry goods, 511 Sacramento
Bonney O. sen. collector, dwl 3 Dupont
Borbeck John, liquor saloon, 404 Market
Borella Angiollo, g   and liquors, SE corner Cleaveland and Seventh
Bose John & Co. (Frederick Dahnken) groceries and liquors, NE cor Greenwich and Taylor
Bosler John (Joseph Genth & Co.) dwl 539 Bdwy
BOSTON UNDERWRITERS, T. H. & J. S. Bacon, agents, office 216 Front
BOSWELL (S. B.) & SHATTUCK (D. D.) commission and provision merchants, 317 and 319 Front, dwl 25 Stockton
BOSWORTH (William) & RUSSELL (John B.) stock and exchange brokers, office room 5 Donohoe & Kelly's Building
BOWERS J. T. importer music and musical instruments, 138 Montgomery
Bowman A. S. (Klaus, B. & Co.) dwl 728 Mission
Brackett Cyril H. attorney at law, office 432 Montgomery, dwl Cosmopolitan Hotel
BRAVERMAN (Louis) & LEVY (John) importers and retailers watches, jewelry, diamonds, and silver ware, 621 Wash, dwl 322 Mason
Breslauer B. cigars and tobacco, 302 Sansom, dwl 223 Jessie

Brewer Michael T. *(Laws, B. & Co.)* dwl 22 Langton

Brimblecom Samuel A. poultry, 505 Merchant, dwl 18 South Park

Broderick *(John C.)* & Raphall *(James M.)* attorneys at law, office 614 Merchant

Brooks Robert F. hairdressing saloon, 302 Kearny, dwl NE cor Filbert and Dupont

Brooks Thomas H. *(Newhall & B.)* dwl 310 Jessie

BROWELL JEREMIAH, contractor and builder, 530 Clay, dwl 322 Lombard

Brower A. J. saloon, 543 Jackson, dwl 532 Green

BROWN EDGAR O. real estate agent, office 327 Commercial

BROWN HARVEY S. attorney at law, office 327 Commercial, dwl 1309 Powell

Brown M. J. Mrs. dress maker, 426 Kearny

Brown Sedley. Mrs. actress, Metropolitan Theater, dwl 504 Dupont

Browne J. Ross, office and dwl 85 Mont Block

BRUNS CHRISTIAN, physician, office 434 California, and drugs and medicines, 429 California, dwl cor Taylor and Greenwich

Buckholdt Henry, seaman, dwl 26 Sacramento

Buckingham T. H. boot manufacturer, 416 Battery

Bullock W. H. attorney at law and proctor in admiralty, office 502 Montgomery

BURCKHARDT *(Max)* & HAAS *(Jacob)* importers and dealers in liquors, 130 Third, dwl 1311 Stockton

Burfiend John, bar keeper, Railroad Exchange, dwl SW cor Powell and Francisco

Burke M. & Brother *(William Burke)* produce commission, E s Drumm bet Clay and Sacramento, dwl NW cor Sixth and Brannan

Burks Charles I. carpenter, 108 Leidesdorff, dwl SE cor Second and Market.

Burns John H. *(Maguire & B. Virginia City)* dwl 917 Stockton

Butler Charles, dwl 913 Clay

Butler Matthew *(Dyer, Rokohl & B.)* dwl 867 Folsom

Butler William M. porter with E. G. Mathews & Co. dwl 1015 Mason

CADIZ Joseph G. translator and accountant, 536 Washington, dwl 224 Second

CAHN *(A.)* & CO. *(I. F. Block, Leon Cahn, and H. F. Block)* wholesale groceries and liquors, Portland, Oregon, office 409 California, dwl 547 Folsom

Caldwell E. office 618 Merchant

CALIFORNIA BUILDING AND LOAN SOCIETY, office 405 and 407 California

Callahan John, bar keeper with John Keenan, SW cor First and Stevenson

Calvert William, dentist, office and dwl 19 Post

Campbell A. D. boot maker with Holcombe Bros. & Co. dwl SW cor Dupont and Broadway

CAPITOL FLOURING AND FEED MILLS, Mallory, Leiby & Co. proptrs, 115 Commercial

CAROLIN *(James)* & McARDLE *(Patrick)*. Sun Burst Liquor Saloon, SE cor Market and Second

Carpenter William L. policeman, dwl S s Bernard bet Jones and Leavenworth

Carr M. D. & Co. *(Andrew J. Barkley and A. C. Johnson)* book and job printing, 411 Clay, dwl 1016 Pine

Carrington H. dwl 506 Kearny

Carroll James, clerk, 720 Montgomery, dwl NE cor Montgomery and Pacific

Carson William *(Dolbeer & C.)* res Eureka, Humboldt Co

Casanova Eugene, porter, 419 Jackson, dwl 1115 Montgomery

Cassin Francis, wholesale liquors and manufacturer cordials and bitters, 520 Front, dwl 42 Natoma

Catlin B. T. late adjutant 8th Infantry, C. V. dwl 1 Garden

CAZNEAU THOMAS N. despacheur Underwriters' Rooms, 436 California, dwl E s Thirteenth nr Howard

Central S. M. Co. office Pioneer Building

Cerutti Giovanni B. consul for Italy, office and dwl 907 Jackson

Chabot Remie, sewer pipe manufacturer, office 813 Montgomery, dwl Cosmopolitan Hotel

Chamberlain A. J. book keeper with Charles McCormick, U. S. A. 410 Kearny

Chamberlin Edwin, clerk, dwl 1110 Clay

Chamberlin Joseph P. Congress Hall Exchange Saloon, 318 Bush, dwl 18 Tehama

Chapman Henry *(Hopps & C.)* 628 Commercial

Chappelle Peter, liquor saloon, 611 Jackson

CHARTER OAK INSURANCE CO. Hartford, Henry P. Coon agent, office 2 City Hall

Chase James B. *(DeVries & C.)* dwl E s Mason bet Broadway and Vallejo

CHAUVIN O. agent Union Maritime Society, France, 730 Montgomery, dwl 822 Pacific

Cherry John W. sign painter, 626 Commercial, dwl E s Hyde bet Green and Union

Christie Daniel, furnished rooms, 720 Market

Churchward James, confectionery, 442 Third

Clees P. billiard table manufacturer, 515 Jackson

Coffin Charles G. butcher, dwl NW cor Greenwich and Jackson

Cohen Angelo, mining secretary, 652 Washington, dwl 715 Pine

Cohen *(Isidore)* & Mickales *(Jacob)* pawnbrokers, 650 Market, dwl 226 Fourth

Cohen James, tailor, 1007 Folsom

Cohen J. & Brother *(Jonas Cohen)* clothing, Virginia City, office 307 Battery

Cohn Isaac *(J. & I. Cohn)* dwl 731 Folsom

Cohn J. & I. wholesale clothing and dry goods, 226 Battery, dwl 731 Folsom

Cookesley T. H. *(Green & C.)* dwl Railroad House

Cole Elvin N. *(Tolford & C.)* dwl NE cor Union and Mason

Coleman M. Mrs. dress and cloak maker, 402 Kearny

Coles Thorn, engineer, dwl 416 Stevenson

Collins John W. clerk with Tax Collector, City Hall, dwl 932 Pacific

COMMISSIONERS FOR WIDENING KEARNY STREET, office 410 Kearny

Congress Hall, William Shiel proprietor. 320 Bush

Connell David, commission agent, 647 Sacramento, dwl 4 Drumm

Conner Edward, clerk, dwl N s Bryant nr Grove Av

Cook A. W. *(A. H. Todd & Co.)* dwl 540 Folsom

Coruor C. W. assistant melter, U. S. Branch Mint, and boots and shoes, 26 Fourth, dwl 42 Moss

Coulon A. teacher drawing, 410 Kearny

COWEN *(William J.)* & VANDERBILT *(J. H.)* Temple Saloon, NW cor Montgomery and Post

CRAIG WILLIAM, wholesale and retail wines and liquors, 905 Dupont, dwl 25 John

Crandall Henry R. teacher, Deaf and Dumb Institute, dwl 436 Minna

Crawhall John, clerk, 23 San, dwl 611 Greenwich

Crocker J. H. *(E. L. Smith)* dwl 102 Powell

Crosby Daniel A. assistant librarian Mercantile Library, dwl 1009 Powell

Crosett J. L. & Co. produce commission, 225 Clay

Cullen W. express wagon, dwl S s Sutter nr Larkin

CUNNINGHAM *(J. S.)* & READY *(Thomas G.)* accountants and general agents, 519 Montgomery, dwl 39 Natoma

Cunningham Z. H. blacksmith, 581 Market, dwl 173 Clara

Curran Bernard, merchant tailor, 206 Bush, dwl 201 Powell

Carrier C. H. pump and block maker, 28 Market, dwl 516 Minna

Curtice Samuel *(Haskell & C.)* 420 California

Cutter Thomas A. *(Deming & Co. and Miller & Co.)* dwl W s Hyde bet Pine and California

DAHNKEN Frederick *(Bose & D.)* dwl NE cor Clay and Davis

Dana Martin Van Buren, policeman, dwl NE cor Broadway and Polk

DANERI F. & CO. *(Henry Casanova)* importers and jobbers wines and liquors, 615 and 617 Front, dwl 732 Union

Darrow Henry, carpenter, dwl 626 Kearny

Davis John S. *(Goldsmith & D.)* dwl N s Freelon bet Third and Fourth

DeCASTRO FERDINANDOS, oculist and aurist, office 6 Montgomery

DeHaga John, professor music, 714 Vallejo

DeSequeira A. L. teacher penmanship and book keeping, 204 Montgomery

DEANE CHARLES T. physician, office 314 Bush, dwl 724 Bush

Decker Martin *(Lozier & D.)* 221 Bush

Denman James, principal Denman Grammar School, dwl NW cor Bush and Taylor

Devereux William, bar keeper, 543 Jackson

Dewing Francis & Co. general subscription agents, 509 Sacramento, dwl 1048 Folsom

Diggs Montgomery, farmer, dwl 250 Clara

Dillon James, liquor saloon, 671 Market, dwl 18 Third

DIXON CLEMENT, wines and liquors, S s Summer nr Montgomery

Doane Silas F. printer, dwl 503 Dupont

Doane Wilbur G. salesman with J. W. Davidson & Co. 609 Sacramento

DOLBEER *(John)* & CARSON *(William)* Humboldt lumber dealers, 36 Stewart, dwl Russ H

Donnelly Mary Mrs. fruit, NE cor Silver and Fourth

Dorsey James P. bar keeper with Clement Dixon, dwl SW cor Second and Jessie

Dougherty John, soap stone mills, 311 Market

DOYLE WILLIAM H. ship broker and commission agent, office 423 Wash, dwl 48 Natoma

Drummond W. W. attorney at law, room 22 Exchange Building

Dubourque E. & Co. *(Jules St. Denis and Gustave Soucaze)* house and sign painters, 839 Dupont, dwl W s Pacific Alley, bet Dupont and Stock

Duffield George W. policeman, dwl 333 Vallejo

Duisenberg Charles A. C. Consul for Bremen, office 216 Front

DUISENBERG CHARLES & CO. importers and commission merchants, 216 Front, dwl SE cor Harrison and Sixth

Dundas Thos. Senate Liquor Saloon, 326 Pine, dwl 569 Howard

Dunlap J. D. accountant, dwl 131 Montgomery

DUTTON HENRY & SON *(Henry Dutton Jr.)* hay and grain, Pier 7 Stewart, dwl N s Sutter bet Scott and Devisidero

Dutton Henry jr. *(Henry Dutton & Son)* dwl N s Sutter bet Scott and Devisidero

DYER *(Samuel R.)* ROKOHL *(D.)* & BUTLER *(M.)* auctioneers and commission merchants, NE cor Montgomery and Pine, dwl 625 Post

EARL John O. NE cor Montgomery and Jackson

Eastland A. J. dwl 225 Geary

EATON J. A. & CO. agents North America Life Insurance Co. office 240 Mont dwl 803 Mason

Eel River Oil Co. office 436 Jackson

Ehmann *(Henry)* & Seidenstricker *(Frederick)* beer saloon, SW cor Montgomery and Summer

Eldredge K. C. merchant, office NE cor Front and Pine, dwl 809 Jackson

Elwell Frank, merchant tailor, 316 Bush

EMERY CHARLES G. importer and jobber cigars and leaf tobacco, 518 Battery, dwl 334 Brannan

EMORY F. A. general agent Liverpool, New York, and Philadelphia S. S. Co. office 302 Montgomery, dwl NW cor Dupont and Geary

Estrem Joseph, clothing, 822 Kearny

EVANGEL, Stephen Hilton editor and proprietor, office 528 Clay, dwl 25 Moss

FAIRBANKS & HUTCHINSON *(H. L.)* scales, 334 Montgomery

Faitoute James B. *(Bishop & Co.)* office 411 Clay

Ferris David C. stock broker, 16 Exchange Building, dwl 250 Clementina

Finch W. H. & Co. boots and shoes, 133 Montgomery, dwl Occidental Hotel

Finn Edward, teamster, Stewart St. Wharf, dwl Zoe Place

Fish *(Franklin)* Shehan *(John)* & Co. intelligence office, 522 Montgomery

Fitzgerald Thomas S. dwl with A. T. Ruthrauff, E s Garden nr Bryant

Fleming H. B. Captain, U. S. A., Provost Marshal, office 414 Washington bet Battery and Sansom, dwl Virginia Block cor Pacific and Stockton

FLETCHER ARTEMUS T. agent New York Board Underwriters, office 216 Front, dwl 912 Pine

Fogarty Henry P. policeman, dwl 136 Fourth, rear

Folger Henry, clerk, NE cor Montgomery and Pine

Folks S. *(Wolf & Folks, San Bernardino)* office 207 Battery, dwl 333 Tehama

FONDA ALFRED, auctioneer and commission merchant, 415 Commercial

Forrer Julius, ornamental trees, etc., Gates' Nursery, NW cor Fillmore and Post

Fortune H. W. mining stocks, 605 Montgomery, dwl 1025 Post

Foster Enoch *(J. Foster & Co.)* res Boston

Foster J. & Co. *(Enoch Foster)* importers and manufacturers furniture, etc. 314 Pine, dwl 730 Sutter

Fox John W. physician, office and dwl 12 Mont

Franco-American Commercial Co. J. A. Getze, F. C. Hagedorn, John Bioren, W. H. Clay, and F. A. Gentze, trustees, office 215 Bush

Friedel *(Henry)* & Co. soap manufacturer, Brannan bet Fifth and Sixth

Friend George, porter, dwl S s Tyler nr Buchanan

Frirrchs Henry *(John Stock & Co.)* dwl 627 Pac

GAGER JAMES H. secretary, office 519 Montgomery, dwl Twentieth nr Valencia

Garcelon Harvey, carpenter, Miners' Foundry, dwl S s Tyler bet Buchanan and Fillmore

Gardenier Henry, policeman, dwl Oak bet Mason and Taylor

Gardiner George D. clerk with R. B. Gray & Co. dwl 218 Seventh

Garland W. D. broker, office 618 Merchant

Geinsheimer Gabriel *(S. Goldsmith & Co.)* dwl Lick House

GENTH JOSEPH & CO. *(John Bosler)* wholesale butchers and packers, 539 Broadway, dwl 15 Sutter

Gerhardy Charles *(Dudley & G.)* dwl 2 Milton Pl

Gibb Gaven J. W. & Co. *(G. W. Corbell)* importers and dealers paints, oils, glass, etc. 527 Kearny, and Pacific Color Works foot Taylor, dwl 828 California

Gibbs John, machinist, dwl 47 Natoma

Gihon Thomas, engraver, 613 Sacramento

Gillingham Charles, physician, office 655 Wash

Gird Richard, civil engineer, office 405 Front

GLADWIN BROTHERS *(W. H. and G. S.)* real estate and money brokers, 604 Montgomery, dwl 336 Brannan

Gladwin George S. *(Gladwin Bros.)* dwl N s Howard bet Eighteenth and Nineteenth

GLASER CHARLES & CO. dealers dry goods, hosiery, and Yankee notions, 207 Battery, dwl 568 Mission

Glidden Albert M. ship builder, dwl N s Turk bet Laguna and Buchanan

Godoy José A. consul Republic Mexico, office and dwl 517 Bush

Goffin Adolph, liquor saloon, 12 Fourth

Goldberg Caroline Mme, millinery, 5 Montgomery

Golden William T. groceries and liquors, NW cor Folsom and Eighth

Goldsmith *(Jonathan G.)* & Davis *(John S.)* auctioneers, 6 Fourth, dwl 317 Harrison

Goldsmith S. & Co. *(Gabriel Geinsheimer)* fancy goods, 19 Montgomery, dwl 225 Stevenson

GOMER N. B. druggist and apothecary, SW cor Valencia and Sixteenth

Govovich Pedro, actor, dwl 249 Jessie

Goodsell D. C. M. contractor, dwl 429 First

Graham ———, dwl 225 Clay

Green Thomas, physician, office NE cor Market and Montgomery

GREEN *(C. B.)* & COOKESLEY *(T. H.)* proprietors Railroad House, 318 and 320 Com

Greenhood *(Isaac)* & Blumenthal *(Guido)* Metropolitan Match Factory, NE cor Mission and Ninth, office and depôt NE corner Kearny and Broadway

Gromotka Vincent *(Kuhne & G.)* dwl 717 Clay

Gros Edward, druggist, SE cor Green and Stockton, dwl 839 California

GROVER & BAKER SEWING MACHINE CO. J. W. J. Pierson, agent, 118 Montgomery

GRUBER FERDINAND, naturalist, 626 California, dwl 8 s Hayes bet Gough and Octavia

Grush J. H. & Co. hat and bonnet block makers, 121 Fremont

GUIDE (weekly) Bishop & Co. proprietors, office 411 Clay

GUIDE BOOK of the Pacific, office 405 Front

Guiraud Emily Madame, dress maker, 406 Dupont

Guisti Alphonso, fruits, 823 Dupont

GUNN WILLIAM J. real estate agent and secretary homestead associations, office 502 Washington, dwl 212 Turk

Gurnee C. attorney at law, office 76 Mont Block

HAAS Jacob *(Burckhardt & H.)* dwl 113 Silver

Hagerty James, boot maker, 819 Clay

HAIGHT *(Henry H.)* & PIERSON *(William M)* attorneys at law, office NE cor Montgomery and Pine, rooms 3–6, dwl NE cor Mason and Pac

HALLOCK J. Y. & CO. *(Christian Christiansen)* commission merchants, SW corner Front and Jackson

Hamlin George, salesman, 611 Montgomery, dwl 2 Martha Place

Hammond James, clerk, dwl 1216 Taylor

Hammond William, gents' furnishing goods and tailors' trimmings, 321 Bush

HARDY J. importer and retailer books and stationery, 138 Mont, res Oakland

Harned Alexander, mining stocks, dwl 814 Lombard

Harris *(Eber)* & Bernhard *(Samuel H.)* fruits and vegetables, stall 25 Metropolitan Market, dwl 166 Tehama

HARRIS JAMES, trunk maker, 425 California, factory 639 Market

HARRISON S. L. auctioneer and commission merchant, 23 Sansom, dwl 831 California

Hart Jesse, bricklayer, dwl 116 Sansom

Haskell *(William)* & Curtice *(Samuel)* paper hangers, 420 California

Hayes Jacob F. *(Lipman & H.)* dwl 529 Pine

Hays W. W. physician, office 751 Clay

HEALTH OFFICE, City and County, room 15 second floor City Hall

Heath *(R. W.)* & Langhorne *(M. S.)* Virginia tobacco agency, 609 Front

Heilshorn J. H. office 769 Market

Heury *(C. D.)* & Watson *(S. T.)* painters, 535 Market, bds 4 O'Farrell

Heringhi Bernard, watch maker and jeweler, 826 Kearny, dwl 723 O'Farrell

Hinchman H. E. Miss, millinery, 6 Post

Hinchman T. W. stock and exchange broker, dwl E s Hyde bet Clay and Washington

Hinckley L. M. blacksmith, dwl 116 Sansom

Hoffman Gottlieb, stencil plate cutter, 327 Commercial, dwl 518 Pacific

Hoffman John D. civil engineer and assistant U. S. Engineers, office 728 Mont, res Oakland

Hofman Adolph, mining, dwl 34 Langton

Holbrook C. E. physician, office 320 Kearny

Holdredge S. M. publisher Guide Book of the Pacific, office 405 Front, dwl 639 Market

Holz Louis, stationery, 318 Sansom, dwl St. Nicholas Hotel

HOOPER GEORGE F. shipping and commission merchant and agent Colorado River Line Packets, office 327 Front, dwl 413 Second

Hopps *(Frank W.)* & Chapman *(Henry)* house, sign, and ornamental painters, 628 Commercial

House Jonathan, fruits, 30 Fourth

Hovet Henry R. clerk with J. Van Doren, dwl NE cor Bush and Mason

Howe E. L. with Occidental Insurance Co. Stevenson House

Howard E. T. dwl 913 Clay

Howard I. J. Mrs. manufacturer ladies' supporters, 410 Kearny

Hubbard Charles G. attorney at law, 34 Exchange Building

Hubbard L. physician, office and dwl 324 Kearny

Hubbs Anthony, clerk, San Francisco Directory Office, dwl 908 Broadway

Hurley M. E. Miss, dress maker, 615 Sacramento

Hutchinson H. L. *(Fairbanks & H.)* scales, 334 Montgomery

Hyde James T. physician and druggist, SW cor Folsom and Fremont

IGEL Louis, confectionery, 1319 Stockton

Imbourg Charles, veterinary surgeon, office 403 Kearny

Ingham Richard, policeman, dwl 229 Jessie

IRISH PEOPLE (weekly) office 29 Government H

IRWIN SAMUEL M. & CO. plasterers, office 706 Mission

Isson Sam'l, watch maker and jeweler, 1014 Dupont

JACOBY, *(A.)* COHN *(I. H.)* & SON *(Richard Cohn)* general commission and dealers Eastern produce, 308 Clay

Jacquemot J. carpenter, 814 Sacramento

JENNINGS *(A. A.)* & AUSTIN *(M. E.)* wholesale groceries, 223 Sacramento

Jessup ———, dwl 220 Third

Johnson Asahel C. *(M. D. Carr & Co.)* dwl NW cor Union and Leavenworth

Johnson Elihu, attorney at law, office 618 Merchant

Johnson John, cook, dwl 1305 Powell

Jones W. G. *(Parker & J.)* 532 California

JORDAN ALBERT H. architect, office 410 Kearny, res San Mateo

JORDAN L. J. proprietor Pacific Museum, 320 Montgomery, dwl 211 Geary

KALTSCHMIDT Oscar, artist, studio 410 Kearny

Kaufmann Adam, shoe maker, 216 Pacific

Kavanagh James, policeman, dwl 25 Clementina

Keenan John, liquor saloon, SW cor First and Ste venson

Keil William *(Lehe & K.)* dwl 57 Jessie

Keyes John A. carpenter, dwl 1025 Pacific

Kimball Charles P. real estate agent and house broker, 629 Market opposite Montgomery

King Charles J. clerk with John Sime & Co. dwl 913 Clay

King William F. clerk with John Sime & Co. dwl 913 Clay

Kip W. Ingraham Rt. Rev. D.D. Episcopal Bishop, Rector Grace Cathedral, dwl 338 Second

Kirkpatrick C. A. physician, office 6 Armory Hall, dwl 1 Garden

Klebs Alexander, wholesale wines and liquors, 1023 Dupont, dwl 518 Filbert

KOHLER & FROHLING (*Charles Kohler, Otto Schmitz, and Henry Kohler*) wine growers and dealers native wines, 626 Montgomery, dwl 1313 Stockton

Kohler (*H.*) & Maier (*Charles*) retail boots and shoes, 830 Kearny

Kohler Henry (*Kohler & Frohling*) res Los Angeles

Krause Anna Mrs. millinery, 37 Second

KUHNE ARNOLD, music teacher, office 613 Clay, dwl 1114 Stockton

Kuhne (*William*) & Gromotka (*Vincent*) singing birds, etc. 717 Clay

Kustel Guido, mining, dwl 34 Langton

LADD M. J. Mrs. teacher music, dwl 718 Stockton

Lagatha Domingo, seaman, dwl 26 Sacramento

Lake Henry, New York Oyster and Coffee Saloon, 258 First

Lamping L. G. tinsmith, 4 Sansom cor Market

LANGERMANN WILLIAM, merchant, office 519 Montgomery, dwl 1707 Stockton

Langhorne M. S. (*Heath & L.*) res Lynchburg, Va

Langley Charles, seaman, dwl 26 Sacramento

Larkin Frank R. agent Larkin estate, office 302 Montgomery, dwl 1116 Stockton

Larsen P. C. watch maker, dwl 928 Pine

LASKY (*Levi*) & LAMSON (*George F.*) auctioneers and commission merchants, 524 California, dwl 673 Harrison

LAWS, (*Jeremiah*) BREWER (*Michael T.*) & CO. general agents subscription books, office 409 Jackson and 621 Sansom, dwl E s Gilbert nr Brannan

Lawson William, seaman, dwl 26 Sacramento

Lehe (*E.*) & Keil (*Wm.*) cigars and tobacco, SE cor Second and Market

Leiby G. W. (*Mallory, L. & Co.*) 115 Commercial

Lekens Louis, saloon, 541 Jackson

Leopold Henry, importer and dealer birds and cages, 106 Montgomery

Leopold Henry, waiter, dwl 26 Sacramento

Lester J. W. (*Waterhouse & L.*) res New York

Lester Lisle Miss, dwl 327 Bush

Letcher Giles C. assistant register clerk, Twelfth District Court, dwl 734 Mission

Levy S & Co. produce commission, 225 Washington

LIMBERG GEORGE T. attorney at law, office 302 Montgomery, dwl 369 Jessie

Lindeman F. L. bakery and confectionery, 964 Folsom

LINDLEY CHARLES, attorney at law and solicitor in chancery, office Donohoe, Kelly & Co.'s Building room 1 SE cor Mont and Sac

Lipman Charles F. dwl 872 Mission

Lipman (*Joseph*) & Hayes (*Jacob*) hairdressing saloon, 403 Pine

Lipman Simon W. hairdresser with Lipman & Hayes, dwl 529 Pine

Littler Charles W. auctioneer with J. R. Stewart & Co. dwl NE cor Natoma and Sixth

Loane John M. agent B. D. Wilson & Son's California wines and brandies, SE cor First and Market, dwl NE cor Fifth and Clara

Loehr George W. miner, dwl 26 Sacramento

Loheide Mary M. (widow) dwl 26 Fourth

Lord C. S. (*Nudd, L. & Co.*) dwl Oak Avenue nr Harrison

Lord F. chiropodist, 637 Washington

Low Joseph W. merchant, dwl Cosmopolitan Hotel

LOZIER (*Peter*) & DECKER (*Martin*) bowling saloon, 221 Bush

Lynch Patrick, liquor saloon, 413 Pine

MAAS John G. groceries and liquors, SE cor Fremont and Howard

Mabes August, shoe maker with C. W. Cornor, 26 Fourth

Macdougall W. J. music teacher, dwl 655 Wash

Mace A. A. attorney at law, office 21 Court Block third floor

MAGINNIS E. & CO. produce, 503 Sansom, dwl 112 Austin

Maguire T. G. book keeper, Union Foundry, dwl 22 Tehama

Maier Charles (*Kohler & M.*) dwl 830 Kearny

MALLORY, (*A. P.*) LEIHY (*G. W.*) & CO. proprietors Capitol Flouring and Feed Mills, 115 Commercial, dwl 8 Mary

Mandot J. & Co. stock and money brokers, office 619 Washington

Manna A. dwl 834 Clay

Mansur J. salesman with J. G. Hodge, dwl 1009 Powell

MARSH, (*A. Judson*) PILSBURY (*C. J.*) & CO. hardware, tools, and metals, NE cor Front and Pine, dwl SW cor Stockton and Jackson

MARTENS F. & CO. (*John Quinn*) liquor saloon, 421 Commercial, dwl 712 Washington

Martin Abraham, wholesale groceries, etc. 214 Sacramento, dwl 315 Clementina

MARTIN (*Henry*) & CO. (*J. F. Greenman*) dealers copper and other ores, SW cor Montgomery and California

Martin M. S. stock broker, 16 Exchange Building, dwl 625 Harrison

Martin Susan Miss, dress maker, 45 Stevenson

Mayers Henry, clerk, dwl 1109 Clay

Mayrisch Gustave (*Engelbrecht & Mayrisch Bros.*) dwl 434 Minna

McALLISTER H. & C. attorneys at law, office 540 Clay, dwl 419 First

McCLELLAND J. A. & CO. produce commission, 123 Clay, dwl W s Hyde bet Filbert and Greenwich

McCORMICK CHARLES, surgeon U. S. A. medical director Department California, office 410 Kearny, dwl Cosmopolitan Hotel

McCullough (*Patrick*) & Ferris (*David*) Arcade Saloon, 158 Stewart

McDonald John, employé, Opera House, dwl Bay State House

McGrew William, attorney at law, office Valencia nr Sixteenth, dwl First Avenue bet Fourteenth and Fifteenth

McKENNA J. P. & CO. packers and curers hams, bacon, lard, etc. W s Garden bet Harrison and Bryant and NE cor Harrison and Sixth

McKenty A. Jackson, office 605 Washington

McKeon Patrick, laborer, dwl 8 s Cleaveland nr Seventh

McKinley B. F. laborer, dwl 116 Sansom

McManus Thomas, Broadway Exchange Saloon, 5 Broadway

McNULTY J. M. physician and health officer City and County, office 314 Bush, dwl 222 Post

McQUAID JOHN A. attorney at law, office 649 Clay, dwl 718 Howard

McWilliams William, policeman, dwl 540 Howard

Meacham D. K. keeper Greenwich Dock Warehouse, dwl N s Ellis bet Polk and Van Ness Av

Mead (*William C.*) & Son (*Charles H. Mead jr.*) saddles and harness, 224 Sansom, dwl 436 Minna

MEAGHER, (*Philip*) TAAFFE (*William P.*) & CO. importers and wholesale dry goods, furnishing goods, etc. 107 Battery, and retail 9 Montgomery, dwl Cosmopolitan Hotel

Michaels Benjamin K. book keeper with Ware & Mosher, dwl 127 Fourth

Mickales Jacob (*Cohen & M.*) dwl 650 Market

MILLER J. F. collector port San Francisco, office Custom House third floor, dwl Occidental Hotel

Miller John F. attorney at law, office 204 Mont

Mitchell George H. book keeper with W. M. Hixon & Co. dwl 122 Geary

Moffit A. B. & Co. seeds, 204 Washington

Moneypenny (*Charles*) & Mason (*William*) groceries and liquors, 136 Natoma

Moody S. S. clerk U. S. Bonded Warehouse, dwl 220 Third

Mooney Bedelia Miss, proprietress Niantic Hotel, NW cor Clay and Sansom

Moore B. P. furniture, 314 Pine, dwl W s Hyde bet Eddy and Turk

Moore James, policeman, dwl 222 Fremont

Morehouse George W. clerk with J. VanDoren, dwl 527 Geary

Morse A. C. collector S. F. Benevolent Association, office 410 Pine, dwl 449½ Minna

Morshead Philip, Long Island Livery and Sale Stable, 233 Bush

Mosher Daniel (Ware & M.) dwl 18 Stockton

Müller Jens, Vulcan Saloon, SE cor Fremont and Mission

Murdock A. H. stock broker, 621 Montgomery, dwl 530 Howard

Murdock C. A. clerk, 604 Mont, dwl 530 Howard

Murdock G. H. clerk with Dodge & Phillips, dwl 530 Howard

NATIONAL LIFE AND TRAVELERS' INSURANCE CO. Francis Schultze agent, office NE cor Clay and Battery

Needham John (Needham & Co.) 769 Market

NEEDHAM (W. L.) & CO. (J. Needham) Washoe Stable, 769 Market, dwl 660 Howard

NEW YORK BOARD UNDERWRITERS, office 216 Front, Artemus T. Fletcher agent

NEWHALL (William M.) & BROOKS (Thomas H.) auction and commission merchants, 722 Montgomery

Nicolaus (Julius) & Oester (Charles) blacksmithing, 19 Fremont

Nolan Thomas, policeman, dwl SE cor Pacific and Davis

NUDD, (A. D.) LORD (C. S.) & CO. wholesale liquors, 410 Front, dwl Occidental Hotel

O'BRIEN Thomas, groceries and liquors, 12½ Fourth

O'Donnell Charles, physician, office 537 California

O'Reilly James, fruits and vegetables, dwl N side Jessie bet Seventh and Eighth

Olmsted John C. salesman with A. Roman & Co. 417 Montgomery, dwl 734 Mission

PARDOW George, mining secretary, office 53 Montgomery Block, dwl SW cor Stock and Lombard

Pardow George jr. photographic printer with Addis & Koch, dwl SW cor Stockton and Lombard

PARKER (J. M.) & JONES (W. G.) livery and sale stable, 532 California cor Webb

Paster Samuel E. liquor saloon, 518½ Battery, dwl 536 Howard

PATRICK H. C. publisher and proprietor Record, 538 Market

Patterson James, Placerville Soap Stone Factory, office 420 Market

Peake John, drug clerk, cor First and Howard

Peiser S. clothing, 230 Montgomery

Pennie James C. cooper, dwl 1107 Clay

Perkins Daniel E. seeds, etc. 216 Wash, res Oakland

Pettit ——, dwl 626 California

PIERSON J. W. J. agent Grover & Baker Sewing Machine, dwl 705 Greenwich

Pierson William M. (Haight & P.) attorney at law, office NE cor Mont and Pine, dwl 110 Mason

PIPER EVELINE M as. dress maker and manufacturer gents' shirts and collars, 624 Market

Piper Walter J. H. special policeman, dwl 624 Market

Poole Spencer, policeman, dwl 928 Clay

Pratt Henry, miner, dwl 171 Clara

Price Charles E. conductor, North Beach & M. R. R. Co

PROCUREUR (A. P.) & WENZEL (Edward) watch case and jewelry engravers, 621 Washington, dwl S s Hayes bet Franklin and Gough

Quick John W. San Francisco Screen Works, 137 and 139 First, dwl 673 Mission

Quinlan John. helper, Pacific Foundry, dwl N s Clara bet Fourth and Fifth

Quinn John (F. Martens & Co.) dwl 712 Wash

RAIMER Edward L. nursery, cor Folsom and Twenty-Second

RANDALL A. G. real estate and monetary agent, office 504 Battery

Ranft Henry, book keeper with Jacoby Kohn & Son

RANSOM LEANDER, State land locating agent, office 625 Merchant, dwl 105 Mason

Ransom Samuel (Smith & R.) dwl 748 Harrison

Ready Thomas G. (Cunningham & R.) dwl SW cor Stockton and Washington

RECORD (weekly) H. C. Patrick publisher and proprietor, office 538 Market

Reddington John, laborer, dwl N s Sacramento bet Jones and Leavenworth

Reese's Block, W s Battery bet Pine and Cal

Reinstein S. manufacturer California clothing, SE cor Sansom and Halleck

Richardson S. O. policeman, dwl 559 Market

Riley Hazen K. conductor, Central R. R. Co. dwl E s Fourth bet Mission and Howard

Riley John, butcher, dwl 125 Shipley

ROBBINS JAMES J. agent Nicolson Pavement, office 619 Montgomery, dwl 1008 Bush

Roberts George, bricklayer, dwl 116 Sansom

Robinson E. A. clerk, 318 Bush

Rogers Ford H. book keeper with O. B. Fogle, 617 Montgomery, dwl 115 Dupont

Rokohl D. (Dyer, Rokohl & Butler) dwl Lick H

Roman Richard, ex-State Treasurer, bds NW cor Post and Leavenworth

Robertson J. Donald, photographic gallery, 109 Third

Rostoffzoff Alexander, cigars and tobacco, 1010 Dupont, dwl 821 Filbert

Rudolph William, gunsmith, 216 Pac, dwl 22 Scott

SABBATTON Tyler, superintendent and engineer S. F. Gas Co. dwl Cosmopolitan Hotel

Sackett Frederick A. book keeper with Church & Clark, dwl 1009 Powell

Salomon Otto F. with Hoelscher & Wieland, dwl 217 Howard

Salomons F. P. (Heynemann & Co.) dwl 1125 Powell

Samuels Brothers (David and Julius) dry goods, 630 Market, res New York

Santina Catharine (widow) liquor saloon, 808 Clay

Saulters Simon P. millwright, dwl 116 Sansom

Schallich Lucas, cabinet maker, 8 Fourth

Scharff Henry, groceries and liquors, SE cor Powell and Greenwich

Scheier Gabriel, furniture, 20 Fourth

Schlegel Henry, liquor saloon, 331 Kearny

Schonfeld (Jonas) & Bremer (Herman) manufacturers cigars, 311 Pine, dwl 252 Jessie

SCHULTZE FRANCIS, commission merchant and agent National Life and Travelers' Insurance Co. office NE cor Bat and Clay, dwl 314 Bush

Schumann Herman, cigars and tobacco, SE cor Market and Third

Schwarzbach Bruno, physician, office and dwl 820 Washington

Schweitzer (Bernard) Stiefel (Louis) & Co. importers and jobbers fancy goods, 410 Sacramento, dwl 608 Leavenworth

Searle H. C. attorney at law, 728 Mont room 1, dwl 116 Sansom

Seidenstricker Frederick (Ehmann & S.) dwl 205 Sansom

Sevier (Francis) & Walker (Joseph) liquor saloon, 517 Broadway

Sheffield (Charles P.) & Patterson (James) importers and manufrs saws and files, NE corner Jack and Bat, dwl SW cor Second and Mission

Shehan John *(Fish, S. & Co.)* dwl Russ House
Shepherd Frederick A. miner, dwl 245 Clara
Sheerren Nicholas, bricklayer, dwl S s Cleveland nr Seventh
Sherwood B. F. merchant, office Pioneer Building, bds Lick House
Siebe George *(John Siebe & Brother)* dwl SE cor Powell and Union
Siebe John & Brother *(George Siebe)* proprietors Railroad Exchange Saloon, SW cor Powell and Francisco, dwl SE cor Powell and Union
Sieberst Henry G. clerk with Casserly & Barnes, dwl SW cor Grove and Franklin
Skinner Frank H. clerk, steamer Cornelia, dwl 6 Martha Place
Sloan John W. bricklayer, dwl 231 Stevenson
Smith William J. merchant, dwl 811 Stockton
SMITH *(Alexander)* & RANSOM *(Samuel)* manufacturers doors, sash, and blinds, 22 and 24 California, dwl 623 Howard
Smith Andrew D. clerk Twelfth District Court, dwl N s California bet Leavenworth and Hyde
Smith David, doors, sash, and blinds, NW cor California and Drumm
Snedeker Henry, capitalist, dwl 109 Perry
Soucaze Gustave *(E. Dubourque & Co.)* dwl 424 Powell
Spencer Mary A. boarding, 156 Stewart
Sproul John, policeman, dwl room 11 Summer St. House, Summer nr California
Spruance James *(J. C. Horan & Co.)* dwl 652 Market
Steele Henry, clerk 727 Wash, dwl 11 Brenham Pl
Steinweg Charles, blacksmith and wheelwright, N s Mission nr Beale
Steler P. watch maker and jeweler, 920 Dupont
Stephan John G. butcher, dwl 913 Clay
Stewart Charles, meat market, 1218 Pacific, dwl 1226 Pacific
Stewart Paton jr. fencing academy and teacher art self-defense, 769 Market
Stone Appleton W. policeman, dwl N s California bet Jones and Leavenworth
STONE *(Rockwell)* & HAYDEN *(Peter)* importers and jobbers saddlery, hardware, etc. 418 Battery, dwl 1619 Powell
Stow Henry M. real estate, 325 Montgomery, dwl 816 Mission
STRATMAN JOHN, news agent, periodicals, books, stationery, etc. 506 Wash nr Sansom
Stratton Frank J. book keeper with Russell & Erwin Manufacturing Co. dwl 831 Sutter
Striby Louisa, music teacher, 763 Howard
Striby William, music teacher, 763 Howard
Summerfield S. dry goods, 20 Second, and millinery, 18 Second, dwl 269 Minna
Sutherland James G. wholesale and retail liquors, SW cor Third and Stevenson
Sutliff Henry, salesman, dwl 832 Kearny
Sutliff Thomas, dealer in cigars, tobacco, etc., 832 Kearny
Swasey W. F. dwl NW cor Bush and Mason
SWEENY MYLES D. & CO. *(Upton M. Gordon)* importers wines and liquors, 709 Sansom, dwl 1425 Mason

TAAFFE William P. *(Meagher, T. & Co.)* dwl SW cor Jones and Filbert
Taussig Ludwig, wholesale wines and liquors, 723 Sansom
Tedford Charles J. clerk, dwl 135 Tehama
Terry Caleb C. carpenter, dwl 3 Cleaveland
Thompson H. C. foreman Spirit of the Times, dwl E s Montgomery bet Union and Green
Thompson William T. pilot examiner, dwl N s McLaren Lane bet Mission and Market
Thomson Peter, gents' furnishing goods, 607 Sacramento, dwl 328 Brannan
TOBEY WILLIAM H. petroleum and mining

agent, room 7 Government House 502 Wash, dwl W s Eleventh bet Howard and Folsom
Tolford *(C. Frank)* & Cole *(Elvin N.)* Star Laundry, office 105 Sansom, dwl Stevenson House
TOWNSEND L. R. architect and secretary California Building and Loan Society, office 407 California, dwl 807 Stockton
Treadwell George A. assayer and chemist, 512 Bush
Treadwell John B. clerk, dwl 512 Bush
Treyer Theodore, tailor, 22 Sansom
TRIPP *(Silas G.)* & ROBINSON *(Thomas B.)* pyrotechnists, Howard nr Twenty-Fourth
Tucker Reuben, policeman, dwl 508 Mason

UNDERWOOD .WARREN L. attorney at law, office 302 Montgomery, dwl 320 Bush
UNION MARITIME SOCIETY (France) O. Chauvin agent, office 730 Montgomery

VALENTINE John, produce commission, 3 Merchant, dwl 333 East
Vaillant J. Guibert's Submarine Metallic Varnish, 432 Pacific
VAN BRUNT R. N. agent New York Life Insurance Co. office SW cor Mont and California
VanGulpen Carl, merchant, dwl 1617 Powell
Vanderbilt J. H. *(Cowen & V.)* dwl Shiels' Block
Verdinal D. F. *(J. M. & D. F. V.)* attorney at law, office 636 Clay, dwl 1114 Powell
Voss Carsten, Eagle Coffee Saloon, 637 and 639 Pac

WAINWRIGHT William, oysters and liquors, 219 California, dwl 4 Langton
Walker Joseph *(Sevier & W.)* dwl 517 Broadway
Walton Thomas, annealer, U. S. Branch Mint, dwl 243 Clara
Wanderer Henry, boot maker, 533 Pine
Ward James D. policeman, dwl 196 Clementina
WARD T. M. D. Rev. pastor African M. E. Church, Powell St. dwl 335 Sutter
WARE *(James)* & MOSHER *(Daniel)* manufacturers doors, sash, and blinds, 26 California, dwl 129 Second
WATERHOUSE *(C.)* & LESTER *(J. W.)* importers and dealers carriage and wagon materials, 29 and 31 Battery, dwl cor Howard and Eighteenth
Watmore Edward W. *(James G. Sutherland)* SW cor Third and Stevenson
Warm Swimming Bath Association, NE cor Powell and Filbert
Weigold John, clerk, 106 Montgomery
Weil Henry J. watch maker and jeweler, 1120 Dupont
Wertheimber Philip, merchant, dwl N s Greenwich bet Mason and Taylor
Wetherbee A. K. printer, dwl 116 Sansom
Whipple Willard, street contractor, dwl 1107 Clay
WHITCOMB A. C. attorney at law and president Citizens' Gas Co. office NW cor Wash and Kearny, dwl Armory Hall, fourth floor, room 1
Whitland William, butter, cheese, etc. 45 Wash Mkt
Whitman Henry, North Beach Market, NW cor Greenwich and Janson, dwl NW cor Powell and Union
WHITMORE H. M. real estate, office 618 Merchant
Wiese Peter, upholsterer, 29 Fourth
Wilke *(Louis)* & Lutz *(J. C.)* beer saloon, NE cor Kearny and Bush
WILLIAMS JOHN S. carpenter, dwl 1910 Powell
Willis William, mining secretary, office Pioneer Building
Wood Ann Miss, furnished rooms, 913 Clay
Wood Zephaniah, architect, office 328 Montgomery

YATES M. H. Mrs. boarding, Cunningham's Building, SE cor Market and Third
YOUNG ANDREW, German Coffee Saloon, 614 Montgomery

THE

SAN FRANCISCO DIRECTORY,

For the Year commencing December 1st, 1865.

☞ NOTICE.—*Names too late for regular insertion, removals, changes, etc., which have occurred during the printing of the work, will be found on the pages immediately preceding this.*

For List of Boarding Houses, Hotels, Lodgings, etc., see BUSINESS DIRECTORY, *pp. 488, 505, and 512; for Packets, Sail and Steam, see* p. 518; *for the location of the offices of the different Mining Companies, see* REGISTER OF NAMES.

ABBREVIATIONS.

abv	Above	E	East	off	Office	STREETS.	
acct	Accountant	exch	Exchange	op	Opposite	Bdwy	Broadway
atty	Attorney	F. P	Fort Point	pl	Place	Bat	Battery
av	Avenue	h	House	P. O	Post Office	Cal	California
bdg	Building or Buildings	imp	Importer	Preo	Presidio	Com	Commercial
bds	Boards	lab	Laborer	proptr	Proprietor	Leav	Leavenworth
bet	Between	manuf	Manufacturer	res	Resides or Residence	Leid	Leidesdorff
blk	Block	mec	Mechanic	rms	Rooms	Merch	Merchant
C. H	Custom House	mcht	Merchant	S	South	Mont	Montgomery
clk	Clerk	Mis Dol	Mission Dolores		Side	Pac	Pacific
com	Commission	mkr	Maker	stm	Steamer or Steamship	Sac	Sacramento
cor	Corner	mkt	Market	U.S.B.M	U.S.Br'ch Mint	San	Sansom
dept	Department	N	North	wkm	Workman	Stock	Stockton
dwl	Dwelling	nr	Near	W	West	Wash	Washington

AARON Chalfant, carpenter, dwl with P. L. Murphy, E s Howard bet Fifteenth and Sixteenth

Aaron Joseph, barber, dwl 125 Perry

Aaron S. merchant, dwl 151 Clara

Aaron, see Aron

Abadie François, laborer, dwl S s Polk Alley

Abbecco Mary Mrs. dwl 4 Brown Alley

Abbey Richard, miner, dwl 264½ Folsom

Abbot Charles E. real estate and mining agent, office 302 Montgomery, room 6 third floor, dwl 912 Jackson

Abbot, Downing & Co. manufacturers Concord carriages, Concord, N. H. Hill & Eastman agents, 618 Battery

Abbot Maria C. dwl 25 Rousch

Abbott Andrew J. laborer, dwl S s Eddy nr Van Ness Avenue

Abbott Frank, driver, dwl 823 Greenwich

Abbott Henry B. mariner, dwl SW cor Leavenworth and Filbert

Abbott J. M. mining, dwl 537 Mission

Abbott John, cook, 331 Bush

Abbott Joseph, sash and blind maker with George Robinson & Co. dwl 181 Jessie

Abbott Oscar, commission agent, 723 Montgomery, dwl 858 Mission

Abbott Sophronia E. (widow) dwl 1005 Powell

Abbott William, salesman, 48 Second

Abbott William A. captain, dwl 25 Rousch

Abeel John, farmer Industrial School

Abel Albert, mariner, 32 Stewart

Abel Charles, boatman, dwl 212 Stewart

Abel Conrad, plasterer, dwl N s Bush bet Dupont and Stockton

Abel George, porter with E. G. Mathews & Co. dwl Merchant nr East

Abel H. laborer, dwl 6 Merchant

ABELL ALEXANDER G. grand secretary Grand Lodge F. & A. M. office Masonic Temple, dwl 1027 Washington

Abell Frank, photographic operator with William Shew, dwl 28 Russ

Abell John, farmer, Industrial School, Old Ocean House Road

Abell Martin, ship carpenter, dwl 528 Pacific

Abell Samuel O. Wilson's Circus

Abels S. E. clerk with Joseph Isaac & Co. 513 Sansom

ABEND POST (German daily and weekly) Leo Eloesser & Co. editors and proprietors, office 517 Clay and 514 Commercial

Abendenner A. dwl 266 Minna

Abiel L. C. feeder, dwl with L. B. Hanson

Abraham Gabriel, tailor, 35 Second

Abraham Isaac B. dwl NE cor Geary and Leav

Abraham J. merchant, dwl 626 O'Farrell

Abraham Max, glazier, dwl 50 Jessie

Abrahams David, dwl 154 Minna

Abrahams David, peddler, dwl NE cor Natoma and Jane

Abrahams E. dry goods, 23 Second

Abrahams John, with D. R. Provost & Co. dwl 711 California

Abrahams Louis, clothing, 10 Clay

Abrahamson Peter, stoves and tinware, 439 Bush
Abram Isaac, junk, dwl 270 Stevenson, rear
Abrams *(Jonas)* & Levy *(Bernard)* boots and shoes, 325 East, dwl 120 St. Mark Place
Abrams Marcus, broker, dwl 786 Folsom
Abrams *(Samuel)* & Greenberg *(Henry)* real estate and insurance agents, 321 Montgomery, dwl 307 Clementina
Academic Seminary, Rev. Elkan Cohn, Principal, N s Post bet Dupont and Stockton
ACADEMY OF MUSIC, Thomas Maguire proprietor, N s Pine bet Montgomery and Sansom
ACADEMY OF NATURAL SCIENCES, rooms 622 Clay
ACCIDENTAL INSURANCE CO. New York, Bigelow & Brother, agents, 505 Montgomery
Achiele Louis, compositor, American Flag, dwl 767 Mission
Achille Gregory, laundryman, dwl 604 Broadway
Ackerman August, *(E. F. Strolen & Co.)* dwl 1117 Kearny
Ackerman Brothers *(Samuel S., Hart S., and Hyman S.)* dry goods, 19 Mont, res Germany
Ackerman Charles, carpenter, dwl NW cor McAllister and Buchanan
Ackerman David, butcher with Henry Loeb, dwl SW cor Stockton and Broadway
Ackerman Dora (widow) dwl 747 Howard
Ackerman Hart S. *(Ackerman Brothers)* dwl 746 Mission
Ackerman Henry & Co. *(Joseph Rosenthal)* dry goods, 413 Kearny, dwl 769 Mission
Ackerman Hyman S. *(Ackerman Bros.)* dwl NW Ellis and Powell
Ackerman Hyman S. dry goods, 414 Kearny, dwl W s Mason bet Geary and Post
Ackerman Joseph, *(McElwee & A.)* dwl 416 Post
Ackerman L. S. dwl 722 Green
Ackerson Charles H. carpenter, dwl Harrison bet Fourth and Fifth
Ackerson J. B. laborer, dwl 73 Stevenson
ACKERSON *(John W.)* & RUSS *(J. A.)* lumber, Hathaway's Wharf, res Redwood City
Ackerson Thomas, boatman, Howard Street Wharf, dwl N s Fifteenth near Mission
Ackland *(Edward T.)* & Trickle *(Ezekiel C.)* fish, 19 Occidental Mkt, dwl SW cor Franklin and Fell
Ackley *(George)* & Bergstrom *(John)* parlor, chamber and office furniture, 417 Mission, dwl Second bet Market and Mission
Ackley Henry F. book keeper, dwl SW cor Clay and Jones
Ackley, Lawrence, shoe maker, 114 Kearny, dwl Lincoln Avenue
Adair James, driver, North Beach and South Park R. R. Co. dwl W s Larkin nr Ellis
ADAM THOMAS, liquor saloons, Old Corner, 516 Montgomery, SE cor Com, and Branch Old Corner, junction Market and Mont, dwl 207 Dupont
Adami George, brewer, dwl 637 Broadway
Adami John *(Albrecht & Co.)* dwl 637 Broadway
Adami John, milk depôt, 735 Pacific
Adams A. T. W. printer with Francis, Valentine & Co
Adams Charles, with Reynolds Howell & Ford, dwl Clay nr East
Adams Charles Capt. dwl SE cor Pennsylvania Avenue and Solano
Adams Charles, clerk, NW cor Second and Bryant
Adams Charles S. hide inspector with F. G. Burke, dwl 1529 Dupont
Adams Cyrus, dwl 528 Pine
Adams G. driver, Omnibus R. R. Co
ADAMS *(George G.)* & ROOT *(W. D.)* house brokers and mining secretaries, 410 Montgomery, dwl 136 Shipley
Adams Grove *(Mitchell & A.)* res Virginia City
Adams H. bar keeper, dwl Hall Court
Adams H. Mrs. house keeper Occidental Hotel
Adams H. D. W. machinist, dwl 331 Fourth, rear

Adams H. laborer, Golden Age Flour Mills, 717 Bat
Adams Henry, second lieutenant Comp. C, Cal. Vol Fort Point
Adams Henry Q. searcher records, 420 Montgomery, dwl W s Larkin nr Willow Avenue
Adams Hermann, tailor, dwl N s Jackson bet Montgomery and Sansom
Adams Horace E. waiter, 28 Mont, dwl 636 Com
Adams Howard, carpenter, dwl 333 Fourth
ADAMS HUGH, clerk. 238 Stewart
Adams Isaac, barber, dwl 118 Jackson
Adams James *(Smith & A.)* dwl Augustus nr Green
Adams James, hay dealer, dwl S s Hayes nr Franklin, Hayes Valley
Adams James H. shoe maker, dwl E s Hyde bet Green and Union
Adams John, employé, Cosmopolitan Hotel
Adams John, bill poster with Way & Keyt
Adams John Q. law student with R. H. Waller, dwl E s Hyde bet Union and Green
Adams John W. dwl W s Prospect Avenue nr California Avenue
Adams Joseph, city gauger, office 321 Front, dwl SE cor Front and Oregon
Adams J. S. dwl 559 Market
ADAMS LAWSON S. *(John Arnold & Co. Sacramento)* office 405 Front, dwl 114 Minna
Adams Lizzie E. Miss, principal Protestant Orphan Asylum
Adams Lodice W. (widow) dwl W s Prospect Avenue nr California Avenue
Adams Nelson B. book keeper with B. P. Moore & Co. dwl E s Carlos Place
Adams O. P. surgeon stmr America, dwl 919 Howard
Adams Petroleum Co. (Mount Diablo) office 19 Bat
Adams Q. L. *(Paine & A.)* 522 California, dwl Verona Place
Adams Rhoda. (col'd) dwl 819 Pacific
Adams Richard, butcher, dwl N s Brannan between Eighth and Ninth
Adams *(Robert H.)* & Brother *(Ross M. Adams)* hat and cap manufacturers, 824 Kearny
Adams Ross M. *(Adams & Brother)* 824 Kearny
Adams Roxanna Miss, assistant matron Protestant Orphan Asylum
ADAMS SAMUEL, druggist and apothecary, SE cor Bush and Powell, dwl 814 Bush
ADAMS SAMUEL, wholesale lime, cement, etc. SE cor Market and Main
Adams Warren P. box clerk P. O. dwl 609 Pine
Adams William, stevedore, dwl 331 Green
Adams William H. porter, dwl 15 Harlan Place
Adams William H. clerk, 911 Dupont
ADAMS *(William J.)* BLINN *(Samuel P.)* & CO. lumber and Puget Sound Line Packets, 215 and 217 Stewart, Piers 17 and 18, dwl NW cor Second and Brannan
Adcock William, porter, 212 Cal, dwl Sherwood Pl
Addis Jacob, glassware packer, 303 Third
Addis *(Robert W.)* & Koch *(John)* photographic art gallery, 425 Mont, dwl Cosmopolitan Hotel
Addison *(James H.)* & Macomber *(Horace L.)* painters, cor Bush and Trinity
Addison John E. dwl 49 Belden Block
Addomes Samuel K. clerk with Elam & Howes, dwl 5 Vernon Place
Adelaide Consolidated S. M. Co. office 338 Mont
ADELPHI HOTEL CO. *(Christian, Ferdinand, and Gustavus Reis, and John S. Henning)* proprietors Cosmopolitan Hotel, SW cor Bush and Sansom
ADELSDORFER BROTHERS *(Zachary and Joseph Adelsdorfer)* importers and jobbers fancy goods, cutlery, etc. SE cor Sansom and Sacramento, res Bavaria, Germany
Adelsdorfer Isaac, dwl 270 Jessie
Adelsdorfer Joseph *(Adelsdorfer Bros.)* dwl 1314 Post
Ademar William, with A. Lusk & Co. 524 Clay

Ader Paul, butcher with Eugene Peguillan & Bro. dwl SW cor Utah and Sixteenth
Adkenson L. laundryman Cosmopolitan Hotel
Adler A. bakery, 316 Third
Adler Bennett, tailoring and repairing, dwl 27 Pacific
Adler Charles, book keeper with Reis Brothers, dwl Cosmopolitan Hotel
Adler Charles, salesman, 409 Sac, dwl 534 Tehama
Adler David, meat market, 3 Stock, dwl 237 Minna
Adler Elkan, baker, 316 Third
Adler Henry, merchant, office 207 Battery, dwl 214 Sansom
Adler Jacob (Goldman & A.) dwl 330 Kearny
Adler James, express wagon, cor Market and Second
Adler Jonas (Simon, Dinkelspiel & Co.) dwl 329 O'Farrell
Adler Julius, book keeper with Pollack Bros. dwl 118 Prospect Place
Adler Julius, clerk with M. Heyneman, dwl 526 Ellis
Adler (Leopold) & Stern (Jacob) boots and shoes, 221 Third
Adler Lewis, native wines and liquor saloon, 714 Market
Adler Maurice, Rincon Point Market, 302 Beale
Adler Samuel, miner, dwl 810 Greenwich
Adlington David L. carpenter, dwl 1125 Kearny
Adolph William (col'd) bootblack, 639½ Market, dwl Dupont nr Green
Adolphus Henry, physician and druggist, 511 Jackson, dwl 103 Geary
Adomi Christoph, shoe maker, dwl 532 Broadway
Adowling Edward, hostler with J. G. Scovern
Adrian William, merchant, dwl 629 California
Adriance F. C. & Co. (Henry W. Jones) real estate agents, 537 Washington, dwl 1409 Powell
Adriatic G. & S. M. Co. office 623 Montgomery
Adsit L. B. stock and money broker, office 604 Montgomery, dwl 736 Sutter bet Taylor and Jones
AERDEN JAMES H., O.S.D. Rev. pastor St. Bridget's Church, SW cor Broadway and Van Ness Avenue, dwl 519 Green
ÆTNA INSURANCE CO. Edward H. Parker agent, office 224 California
Afflerbach C. H. Rev. pastor German Methodist Episcopal Church, dwl 728 Broadway
Affron J. W. express wagon, 1775 Mason
Agard George E. book keeper with Flood & Co. dwl 311 Green
AGARD (W. B.) FOULKES (Thomas) & CO. importers and commission merchants, 412 Front, dwl 311 Green
Agatta Peter, workman with P. Somps, Visitacion Valley
Ager James E. clerk with Truman & Co. dwl Fifteenth nr Howard
Ager John E. book keeper, dwl N s Fifteenth bet Howard and Mission
Aggers Henry, mariner, dwl 140 Clara
Agillaro Petrie, dwl 1 Delaware Court
Agnew Gilmore, compositor, Alta California, dwl 917 Market
Agnew Henry, clerk, 26 Kearny
Agnew John, Dashaway Livery and Sale Stables, 26 Kearny
Agnew Luke, receiver Omnibus R. R. Co. dwl 66 Minna
Agnew Thomas, conductor, Omnibus R. R. dwl 549 Mission
Agnew Thomas laborer, Spring Valley W W
AGNEW (Thomas H.) & DEFFEBACH (Thomas B.) book and job printers, SW cor Sansom and Merchant, dwl 209 Ellis
Agrall Ino, assayer, dwl Dresdener House
Aguirra John M. dwl Gardner Alley
Ah Chee (Chinese) washing, 1506 Dupont
Ah Chung (Chinese) washing, S s Brannan nr Seventh

Ah Hing (Chinese) washing and ironing, 762 Clay
Ah Ming (Chinese) garder, NW cor Eighth and Bryant
Ah Sang (Chinese) cigar manufacturer, 712 Dupont
Ah Shin (Chinese) cigar maker, 721 Sacramento
Ah Sing (Chinese) washing, 30 Stewart
Ah Sing (Chinese) washing and ironing, 1020 Bat
Ah Song (Chinese) washing, 504 Pacific
Ah Sun (Chinese) washing, 40 Webb
Ah Yen (Chinese) washing, 214 Bush
Ahern Nellie Miss, domestic with Eliza Faulkner, S s Harrison bet Seventh and Eighth
Ahern Ellen Miss, domestic, 115 Powell
Ahern James, stevedore, dwl cor Mission and Main
Ahern Jeremiah, ship carpenter, 14 Broadway, dwl Serpentine Avenue nr Howard
Ahern John M. teamster, dwl NE cor First and Tehama
Ahern Michael, laborer, Spring Valley Water Works
Ahern Patrick, workman with Wilson & Stevens, dwl N s Brannan bet Sixth and Seventh
Ahern Timothy J. stone cutter, dwl S s Presidio Road nr Scott
Ahlborn William, teamster with J. & C. Schreiber, bds Bootz Hotel
Ahlers Behrend, Bay Sugar Refinery, dwl E s Sansom bet Union and Filbert
Ahlers Edward W. F. salesman, 616 Kearny
Ahlers Joseph H. (F. Wieland & Co.) SW cor Vallejo and Powell
Ahlgreen Charles, baker, New York Bakery
Ahlstrom John, shoe maker, dwl 671 Howard
Ahpel Henry, dwl 1014 Bush
Ahrens Christian, jeweler, 836 Dupont
Ahrens Henry, groceries and liquors, SW cor Post and Kearny
Ahrens John, fruits, SW cor Battery and California, dwl S s California bet Kearny and Dupont
Ahrens John, handcartman, cor Cal and Sansom
Ahrens John H. clerk, NW cor Mission and Fourth
Aibischer Bruno, dwl 1337 Dupont
Aibischer Joseph, dwl 1337 Dupont
Aigeltinger Leopold, furrier, dwl 259 Clara
Aiken John (Beckman A. & Co.) dwl 314 O'Farrell, rear
Aime Guisseppe, fisherman, 33 Italian Fish Market
Aine H. E. carpenter, Eureka Hose Co. 4
Ainsa J. M. warehouse clerk, Naval Office, dwl 405 Lombard
Ainsa Manuel, dwl 405 Lombard
Ainsburry Margaret (widow) dwl 25 Jessie
Ainsworth Lizzie Miss, actress Olympic
Aitken Charles H. (Hall & A.) dwl N s Pacific bet Hyde and Larkin
Aitken James (Moynihan & A.) dwl 308 Second
Aitken Samuel, vice-president Vulcan Iron Works Co. dwl 266 Clementina
Aitken Thomas, stevedore, dwl SW cor Davis and Pacific
Ajaireguy Miguel, carpenter, dwl 1024 Kearny
Ajle Eugene, dwl 208 Third
Alameda August, porter stmr Golden City, dwl 519 Vallejo
Alameda Coal M. Co. office 804 Montgomery
ALBANY BREWERY, Spreckels & Co. proprietors, 71-75 Everett
Albarez J. G. fruits, dwl 1018 Kearny
Albers August, groceries and liquors, 825 Stevenson
Albers (Marcus) & Foege (Frank) groceries and liquors, 641 Pacific
Albert C. Mariner's Saloon, 931 Kearny
Albert John, bar keeper, Continental Hotel
Albert Lewis, teamster, Pier 1 Stewart, dwl 22 Natoma
Albert Louis, musician, dwl SW cor Dupont and Broadway
Albertson Lauritz, seaman, bds 7 Washington
ALBIN LEONCE, book and job printer, 533 Commercial, dwl 904 Powell

Albrecht Andrew, milk ranch, dwl S s Filbert bet Laguna and Octavia
Albrecht C. W. seaman, dwl 20 Commercial
Albrecht George, blacksmith, dwl 627 Broadway
Albrecht John, tailor, 339 Bush
Albrecht Joseph, cook, 218 Bush
ALBRECHT *(Joseph)* & CO. *(John Adami)* Broadway Brewery, 637 Broadway
Albrecht Richard, bakery and confectionery, 1006 Folsom
Alcayaga José, groceries and liquors, NE cor Vallejo and Dupont
Alcock Joshua P. lumber piler, dwl 20 East
Alcovich, dwl 403 California
Alden A. W. Miss, dwl 909 Clay
Alden John, clerk, dwl 202 Second
ALDEN RICHARD C. chief clerk U. S. Com. Dept. office 418 California, dwl 405 Powell
Alden Samuel, drayman, dwl NE cor Sacramento and Jones
Aldred Robert, cokeman, San Francisco Gas Co
Aldrich A. F. Miss, special grammar assistant, Union Grammar School, dwl 101 Prospect Place
Aldrich G. C. upholsterer, 618 Mission, dwl cor Ellis and Stockton
Aldrich Julia A. Miss, teacher, dwl NE cor Freelon and Fourth
Aldrich L. A. Miss, dress maker, dwl 63 Stevenson House
Aldrich Louis, actor, Maguire's Opera House, dwl 913 Montgomery
Aldrich Mary Miss, chambermaid, Russ House
Aldrich William, laborer, dwl 277 Minna
Alemania S. M. Co. office 519 Montgomery
ALEMANY JOSEPH SADOC, O.S.D. Most Rev. Archbishop of San Francisco, dwl 602 Dupont
Alers Augustus, physician, office 521 Pacific
Alexander David G. carpenter, dwl 227 Bush
Alexander Edward, stevedore, dwl 116 Sansom
Alexander Eli, dwl 16 Virginia
Alexander Eli, meat market, 241 Sutter, dwl 22 Stockton Place
Alexander Frederick, painter, dwl Verona Place
Alexander Geo. dwl 435 Brannan
Alexander George, cooper with Handy & Neuman, dwl W s Sansom bet Greenwich and Filbert
Alexander George, treasurer Chelsea Laundry
Alexander Henry P. carpenter, dwl 13 Geary
Alexander Isidor, slipper manufactory, 306 Sansom, dwl 722 Howard
ALEXANDER J. & CO. *(Jacob and Leo Ash)* wholesale clothing, 310 and 312 Sansom, dwl 734 Vallejo
Alexander Jacob, hides, dwl 14 Clay
Alexander Jacob, paper box maker with Levy & Mochet, dwl 8 Polk Lane
Alexander Jacob, saddler, dwl 1231 Dupont
Alexander James, farmer, dwl 733 Folsom
Alexander James B. carpenter, dwl N s California bet Dupont and Stockton
Alexander John, agent, dwl 815 Montgomery
Alexander Joseph D. salesman with George L. Kenny & Co. dwl N s Green bet Jones and Leavenworth
Alexander Julius, dwl W s Folsom bet Twelfth and Thirteenth
Alexander Louis L. superintendent, dwl 818 Post
Alexander Lyman, fancy goods, 16 Second
Alexander Marcus, dwl 161 Perry
Alexander Margaret, domestic, 362 Third
Alexander Mary Miss, domestic, 16 Mason
Alexander Mary (col'd, widow) domestic, 124 Sutter
Alexander Mary Mrs. dwl 733 Folsom
Alexander Mathew, Howard Street House, 504 Howard
Alexander Mendel, shoe maker with Prescott & Israel, dwl 13 Second
Alexander Meyer, French laundry, dwl N s Chestnut bet Stockton and Powell

Alexander Messein, merchant, dwl 811 Harrison
Alexander Robert, ship carpenter, dwl 167 Silver
Alexander Samuel, cap maker, 1110 Dupont
Alexander Samuel, tailor, 144 Stewart
Alexander Samuel O. clothing, SE cor Jackson and Dupont, dwl 115 O'Farrell
Alexander Sarah Miss, domestic, dwl 516 Stockton
Alexander S. H. P. carpenter, dwl 336 Bush
Alexander Simon, dwl 115 O'Farrell
Alexander S. L. cook, Clipper Restaurant, dwl 14 Dupont
Alexander Theodore, auctioneer, 824 Kearny
Alexander Theodore, fancy goods, dwl 1311 Kearny
Alexander Virginia Miss, domestic, dwl 514 Lombard
Alexander William, laborer, dwl 522 Pine
Alferitz Pietro *(Dellapiane & Co.)* dwl SE cor Montgomery and Pacific
Alfter Charles W. clerk with Samuel Adams, dwl 814 Bush
Alger James, salesman with Lawrence & Houseworth, dwl N s Folsom bet Third and Fourth
Alger Thomas H. porter, 422 Battery
Alges James, boot maker, dwl Sherwood Place
Alison Charles, shipwright, dwl NW cor Leavenworth and Union
Alison Charles jr. machinist, dwl NW cor Leavenworth and Union
Aliston David, drayman, dwl 417 Folsom
Alker Thomas, express wagon, Union Place
Allardt George F. assistant engineer, Pacific Railroad Co. office 409 California, dwl 608 Post
Allari Henry, porter, 423 Front, dwl 53 Third
Allari Joseph, dwl 127 Fourth, rear
Allaway John, cooper, S. F. & P. Sugar Co. dwl W s Eighth bet Howard and Folsom
Allen A. C. liquor saloon, 792 Pacific
Allen Addison F. workman, S. F. & P. Sugar Co. dwl 25 Rousch
Allen Albert W. bailiff U. S. Courts, dwl U. S. Court Building.
Allen Alexander, foreman weaving, Mission Woolen Mills, dwl W s Shotwell bet Nineteenth and Twentieth
Allen Alexander, watchman, S. F. P. W. Mills, dwl North Point bet Polk and Van Ness Avenue
Allen Asa, hairdressing saloon, 136 Fourth
Allen Barney, carpenter, dwl 741 Market
Allen Benjamin, salesman with Heuston, Hastings & Co. dwl 207 Tehama
Allen B. K. carpenter, dwl Columbia Hotel
Allen Catharine Mrs. domestic, 314 Post
Allen Charles R. clerk, 21 Battery, dwl 40 Tehama
Allen E. G. wood and coal, 513 Bush, dwl 2 Hardie Place
Allen Ellen (widow) dwl 432 Bush
Allen Ellery, carpenter, dwl 741 Market
Allen Emma (widow) lodgings, 829 Sacramento
Allen Emma E. (widow) dwl 1 Armory Hall
Allen E. W. liquor saloon, 724 Pacific
Allen Frank, lamplighter, San Francisco Gas Co. dwl 15 William
Allen George, carpenter, SW cor Bryant and Ritch
Allen George, clerk, Thomas Roche, dwl New Wisconsin Hotel, 411 Pacific
Allen George, stevedore, dwl 14 Merchant
Allen Henry H. carpenter, S. F. P. W. Mills, dwl North Point bet Polk and Van Ness Avenue
Allen Henry M. merchant, dwl 629 O'Farrell
Allen H. Hastings, millwright, dwl SE cor Jones and Francisco
Allen Isaac P. with Redington & Co. dwl E s Jones bet Pine and California
Allen Isaac S. secretary San Francisco Benevolent Association, 410 Pine, dwl E s Jones bet Pine and California
Allen James, dwl 1009 Kearny
Allen James F. match factory, 201 Beale, dwl Railroad House

Allen James S. deputy constable, Fourth Township, office 230 Bush
Allen J. D. carpenter, 196 Stevenson
Allen J. M. livery and sale stable, 669 Market
Allen John, drayman, cor Vallejo and Front, dwl W s Montgomery cor Moulton Place
Allen John, hardware and boots and shoes, 733 Pac
Allen John, laborer, dwl 180 Jessie
Allen John, molder, Pacific Foundry, dwl 336 Beale
Allen John, professor music, dwl 16 Freelon
Allen John H. (Geo. W. Knight & Co.) dwl W s Gilbert nr Brannan
Allen John K. salesman with A. Roman & Co. dwl 1102 Pine
Allen John R. machinist, Miners' Foundry, dwl Bailey House
ALLEN (Joseph E.) & SPIER (Richard P.) importers and jobbers books and stationery, etc. 542 Clay, resides New York
Allen (L. H.) & Lewis (C. H.) wholesale and commission merchants, Portland Oregon, office NW corner California and Front, dwl 332 Second
Allen L. H. market wagon, 32 Washington Market
Allen Lizzie Miss, dwl 1 Armory Hall
Allen Lorenzo H. oysters and clams, dwl 12 Harlan Place
Allen Lumber S. shipwright, dwl N s Folsom nr Stewart
Allen Nathaniel, seaman, dwl 51 Jessie
Allen Oliver P. general clerk Superintendent U. S. Branch Mint, dwl 630 Sutter
Allen Patrick, laborer, dwl 525 East
Allen Peley, laborer, dwl 840 Market
Allen Peter, cook, 104 Second
Allen Sarah (widow) dwl 26 Stockton
Allen Sheldon (Curtis & A.) res Watsonville
Allen Smith M. drayman, 413 Sac, dwl 28 Third, rear
Allen Theodore H. stevedore, dwl Russ House
Allen W. H. (Fletcher & A.) real estate and attorney at law, office 6 and 7 Armory Hall Building, dwl 2 Garden
Allen William, cook, dwl 1016 Pine
Allen William, molder, Pacific Foundry, dwl 214 Beale
Allen William jr. scroll sawyer, dwl E s Beale nr Folsom
Allen William B. compositor, Evening Bulletin, dwl 812 Stockton
Allen William H. machinist, dwl 569 Mission
Allen William H. A. first mate Brother Jonathan, dwl W s Telegraph Place
Allen William M. clerk with T. Rodgers Johnson, 325 Montgomery, dwl 116 Jackson
Allen William R. slipping agent, 617 Davis, dwl 910 Leavenworth
Allen William S. book binder with Bartling & Kimball, 505 Clay
Allen W. T. laborer, dwl 15 Stewart
Allen W. V. dwl 87 Stevenson House
Allenson Mary (widow) dwl 33 Jackson
Allensworth Thomas, seaman, dwl 11 Pinckney Pl
Allenwyne J. Miss, stevedore, 308 Stockton
Alley William, stevedore, Greenwich bet Montgomery and Sansom
Allias August, butcher with Vincent Lanouche
Allie John, dwl 1611 Powell
Alligess George, deck hand, steamer Julia
Allion Francis & Co. (Andrew Davis) fruits, NE cor Second and Folsom
Allison Frank J. salesman, 621 Washington, dwl Frank's Building W s Plaza
Allison John, carpenter with Geo. Treat, dwl NW cor Twenty-Fourth and San Bruno Road
Allison John P. laborer, dwl Alta nr Sansom
Allison Oscar, dwl 226 Ritch
Allison, see Alison
Allkire Henry J. medical student, dwl 607 Greenwich

Allwell James, street contractor, dwl 76 Natoma
Allwell Susan, dress maker, dwl 72 Natoma
Allyn John, dentist, dwl E s Howard nr Twentieth
Allyn William H. machinist, Union Foundry, dwl 529 Mission
Allyne John W. book keeper with Stanford Bros. dwl 923 Bush
Almaden Quicksilver Mine, S. F. Butterworth agent, office 207 Battery
Almer Robert, laborer, dwl Washoe Place
Almy G. M. produce com, dwl Stevenson House
Almy Moses B. with Dickinson & Gammans, dwl Russ House
Alpen H. captain schooner Alameda, dwl 5 Mission
Alpers Charles, leader Metropolitan Band, dwl 103 Dupont
Alpers John, musician, dwl 9 Stockton Place
Alphonse G. Restaurant du Cariboo, 532 Pacific
Alrutz John, with Loring & Sprague, dwl 608 Bush
Alsenz Jacob, boots and shoes, dwl 914 Washington
Alsgood (Henry) & Miller (W. H.) groceries and liquors, NW cor Jackson and Drumm
Alsina Frederico & Co. fishermen, 29 Italian Fish Market
ALSOP & CO. (Charles B. Polhemus) merchants and agents London and Liverpool Royal Insurance Co. 411 and 413 California. (See Sup. Names)
Alsop John, umbrella maker, 334 Bush
ALSTROM (S.) & JOHNSON (G. S.) proprietors Lick House, W s Mont bet Post and Sutter
Alt Christopher, boot maker, 608 Vallejo
ALTA CALIFORNIA NEWSPAPER (daily, weekly, and steamer) Fred'k MacCrellish & Co. proprietors, office 536 Sacramento
Alta Flour Mills, Stevenson nr First
Altamireno Simona Mrs. dress making, 206 Dupont
Altenberg Ernest, book keeper with A. S. Rosenbaum & Co. dwl 828 Washington
Altenberg Frederick, dwl 415 Bush
Altenberg Rosalia Mrs. millinery, 302 Kearny, dwl 415 Bush
Altenburg Pauline Mrs. French millinery, 828 Wash
Altes George, tailor, dwl 1518 Powell, rear
Althoff Herman, paper ruler with Buswell & Co. dwl 313 Pine
Althoff John, painter with Hopps & Kanary
Altman Frederick, dwl 17 Stockton Place
Altman Isaac, fruit peddler, dwl W s Robbins Place, nr Union
Altmayer Aaron, (Einstein Bros.) dwl 214 San
Altmayer Abraham (Einstein Bros.) dwl 214 San
Alton Jane A. (widow) boarding, 904 Jackson
Altoub Pedro (Louis Peres & Co.) res San José
Altschul Louis, wines and liquors, 723 Sansom
Altshuler H. Mrs. millinery, 234 Kearny and 1105 Dupont
Altshuler Levi, clerk, dwl 234 Kearny
Altvater David, National Mills, dwl cor Pine and Belden
Alvarado J. C. dwl Cosmopolitan Hotel
Alvarez J. M. painter, dwl 634 Pacific
Alves Antonio J. barber, 633 Pacific
Alves Manuel (Jozedeavilar & A.) 114 Jackson
Alvey Charles W. stoves and tinware, 907 Kearny, dwl 1520 Dupont
Alvieo Transportation Co. Bray & Bro. agents, NE cor Clay and Front
ALVORD WILLIAM & CO. (Richard Patrick) importers and jobbers hardware, 122 Battery, dwl 564 Folsom
Amador Consolidated Silver M. Co. office 315 Mont
Amasqui Lorenzo, laborer, dwl N s Dupont Alley
Ambroise Sebastien, Lafayette Market, NE cor Pine and Dupont
Ambrose B. market wagon cor Fifth and Folsom
Ambrose Samuel, dwl 829 Broadway
Amedee Peter, laborer, dwl 409 Post
Amelia M. Co. office 55 Montgomery Block

AMERICAN EXCHANGE HOTEL, John W. Sargent proprietor, 319-325 Sansom
AMERICAN FLAG, daily and weekly, Daniel O. McCarthy editor and proprietor, office 604 Montgomery, editorial rooms 517 Clay
American Home Missionary Society, Rev. James H. Warren agent, office 402 Front
American Pioneer Copper M. Co. (Weaver District Colorado) office 338 Montgomery
American Pioneer G. & S. M. Co. office 338 Mont
AMERICAN RUSSIAN COMMERCIAL ICE CO. office 718 Battery
AMERICAN THEATER, E s Sansom bet California and Sacramento
AMERICAN VINTAGE CO. Milo Hoadley agent, office 617 Montgomery
Amerige George, printer, dwl 100 Stockton corner O'Farrell
Ames Benjamin F. drayman, 410 Front, dwl N s Stevenson bet Sixth and Seventh
Ames Frank M. salesman with Haynes & Lawton, 516 Sansom, dwl 433 Jessie
Ames George H. clerk, 718 Montgomery, dwl 408 Geary
Ames H. stevedore, dwl 111 Minna
Ames Henry K. foreman with Bardwell & Co. dwl NE cor Hyde and O'Farrell
Ames John, fruits, dwl 1438 Pacific
Ames Orpheus N. with Hobbs, Gilmore & Co. dwl with Horace Hawes, cor Folsom and Ninth
AMES ORVILLE T. stock and money broker, 618 Montgomery, dwl 113 Perry
Ames Sophia, stewardess, steamer Senator
Amich Adam, carpenter, dwl Helvetia Hotel
Amis Sophia (col'd) domestic, with Frank M. Pixley
Amme Hermann H. tailor with J. L. Brooks, dwl 510 Front
Ammon Frank, fruit peddler, E s Capp bet Twenty-First and Twenty-Second
Amos Abraham, carpenter, dwl 18 First
AMOS F. R. & CO. dairy and produce commission, NE cor Com and Front, dwl 505 O'Farrell
Amos George W. clerk, Pier 9 Stewart, dwl Folsom bet Beale and Fremont
Amos John, silversmith, 810 Montgomery
Amos John T. millwright, Pier 9 Stewart, dwl SW cor Union and Kearny
AMOS (Zechariah) PHINNEY (Arthur) & CO. (William H. Hooke) lumber, and proprietors Victoria and Puget Sound Packets, 123 Stewart Pier 9, dwl 507 Harrison
Amy Gustave, salesman, 312 Sacramento, dwl 18 Third
Amy Leon (Ekeil & Co.) dwl 619 Kearny
Ancarani Raffaele, with Brignardello, Macchiavello & Co. 706 Sansom
Ancenhofer Louis, farmer, old Ocean House Road, six miles from City Hall
Anderau Joseph, preserved meats, 9 Metropolitan Market, dwl 31 Kearny
Anderfuren John, tailoring, 24 Dupont
Anderson A. seaman, steamer Senator
Anderson Alexander, laborer, dwl W s Jones bet Pacific and Broadway
Anderson Andrew (Rosendahl & A.) dwl 1816 Powell
Anderson Andrew, cook, dwl 228 Commercial
Anderson Andrew, laborer, dwl E s Main bet Market and Mission
Anderson Andrew, laborer, dwl SW cor Louisiana and Sierra
Anderson Andrew, seaman, dwl 44 Sacramento
Anderson Andrew P. laborer, dwl 8 s Bush bet Polk and Van Ness Avenue
Anderson Charles, with Ashton & Gay, dwl 626 Ellis
Anderson Charles, laborer, dwl 56 Stewart
Anderson Charles, pyrotechnist with Tripp & Robinson, dwl Empire Lodgings

Anderson Charles, seaman, dwl 44 Sacramento
Anderson Charles C. porter, S. F. & San José R. R. Co. 302 Mont, dwl E s Sumner nr Howard
Anderson Charles D. with James McDonogh, dwl 121 Jessie
Anderson Daniel, brick maker with William Buckley
Anderson David, watch maker and jeweler, 58 Clay
Anderson David C. actor, Maguire's Opera House, dwl 845 Dupont
Anderson Edward, collector, dwl 1407 Powell
Anderson Edward, watchman, dwl S s Liberty bet Townsend and Brannan
Anderson Edward, wheelwright with Kimball &. Co
Anderson Elias, seaman, dwl 44 Sacramento
Anderson Erick M. tailor, dwl E s Montgomery bet Broadway and Vallejo
Anderson F. B. Cincinnati Brewery, dwl 818 Jack
ANDERSON F. C. & CO. real estate agents, 537 Washington
ANDERSON (George) & HUSHAN (Patrick) Union Restaurant, SE cor Jackson and Drumm
Anderson George, carpenter, dwl N s Vallejo bet Larkin and Polk
Anderson George, seaman, dwl 51 Sacramento
Anderson George, seaman, dwl 228 Commercial
Anderson Gustave, workman, S. F. Cordage Factory, dwl cor Shasta and Michigan
ANDERSON (Henry C.) & ROALFE (William) oysters, 32 Washington Market, dwl E s Vincent nr Union
Anderson Isaac, flour packer, dwl NE corner Bush Sansom
Anderson J. topographical aid, U. S. Coast Survey, office Custom House third floor
ANDERSON JAMES & CO. (Charles Shelton) shippingmasters, Davis cor Pacific, dwl Vernon House
Anderson James, bootblack (colored) dwl 8 Auburn
Anderson James, watch maker with Tucker & Co. dwl 169 Minna
Anderson James H. (colored,) dwl 8 Auburn
Anderson Jane Miss, dwl 220 Tehama
Anderson J. M. dwl Cosmopolitan Hotel
Anderson John, mariner, dwl 223 Ritch
Anderson John, carpenter, dwl 209 Jessie
Anderson John, carpenter, dwl 5 Dixon's Block, Jane
Anderson John, carpenter with Godfrey Hargitt, 17 Geary, dwl 209 Jessie
Anderson John, cook, dwl 20 Commercial
Anderson John, cook with Augustus Lind
Anderson John (col'd) cook, dwl 829 Pacific
Anderson John, laborer, stm Pacific, dwl W s Sansom bet Green and Vallejo
Anderson John, liquors, dwl 8 Jackson
Anderson John, nurse, U. S. Marine Hospital
Anderson John, stock broker, office 622 Clay, dwl E Mariposa nr Carolina
Anderson John, tinsmith with A. Brown, res Oakland
Anderson John, wines and liquors, W s Front bet Vallejo and Broadway, dwl 306 Green
Anderson John F. (colored) upholsterer, dwl 1006 Jackson
Anderson J. P. proptr Ocean House, W s Drumm bet Jackson and Clark
Anderson Lewis, dwl E s Leavenworth bet Pacific and Broadway
Anderson Magnes, waiter, dwl Original House
Anderson Maria (widow) dwl 111 Ellis
Anderson Mary (widow) dwl 37 Jessie
Anderson Mary A. Mrs. dwl S s Liberty bet Townsend and Brannan
Anderson Mathew A. music teacher, dwl 812 Stock
Anderson Matilda Miss, domestic, dwl E s Vincent nr Union
Anderson Neil T. stevedore, dwl W s Sansom bet Green and Union

Anderson Peter (col'd) proprietor and publisher Pacific Appeal and clothes renovator, 541 Merch, dwl E s Sansom bet Green and Union
Anderson Peter W. salesman, 607 Sacramento
Anderson (P. W.) & Pronsergue (A.) importer laces and embroideries, 105 Montgomery
Anderson Rasmus, seaman, dwl 44 Sacramento
Anderson Robert, dwl 1429 Taylor
Anderson Sarah (col'd widow,) dwl 1136 Pacific
Andorson Thomas, Empire Coal Yard, 737 Jackson, dwl 34 Ellis
Anderson Thomas, foreman Lazard Freres' Warehouse, dwl W s Sansom bet Green and Union
Andorson Thomas, laborer with John G. North, dwl SW cor Louisiana and Sierra
Anderson William, contractor, dwl 418 Tehama
Anderson William, engineer, Potrero Rope Walk, dwl cor Humboldt and Kentucky
Anderson William, machinist, dwl Ecker bet Clementina and Folsom
Anderson William, watchman, Market Street R. R. dwl Valencia nr Sixteenth
Anderson William, watchman, U. S. Marine Hospital
Anderson William G. ship carpenter, dwl Illinois nr Lena Place
Anderson William H. dwl 541 Tehama
Anderson William H. calker, dwl 315 Harrison
Anderson William H. contractor, dwl 418 Tehama
Anderson Win. T. dwl 842 Mission
Anderson (Wm. N.) & Kline (Jacob) Fulton Market SE cor Stockton and Washington, dwl 14 John
Andolshek Andrew Rev. assistant pastor, St. Boniface Church, dwl 122 Sutter
Andrade Antonio, dwl 442 Union
Andrade Evaristo, compositor, El Correo de San Francisco, 617 Sansom
Andrade G. mcht, office 403 Jackson, dwl 27 Sixth
Andrade José, dwl W s Margaret Place
Andrade Wm. dwl 27 Sixth
Andre P. pork, etc. 19 Metropolitan Market
Andres Chris. musician, dwl 320 Kearny
Andres Mary (widow) dwl 1314 Powell
Andres Peter, laborer, dwl 315 Bush
Andresen Brothers (Christian and John) carriage making and blacksmithing, 119 Sansom
Andresen John (Andresen Bros.) dwl 119 Sansom
Andrew Guadulupe, machinist, dwl 162 First
Andrews A. B. teacher penmanship Public Schools, dwl 720 Market
Andrews Ann M. (widow) dress making, dwl 1 Howard Court
Andrews Asa (Batchelder & A.) dwl Bryant Pl
Andrews Charles, steward stm Moses Taylor
Andrews Charles N. manuf children's carriages, SE cor Main and Howard, dwl 1025 Pacific
Andrews E. O. Tremont Market, NE cor Fremont and Folsom, dwl 30 Natoma
Andrews Frederick J. workman, Alta Mills, dwl W s Treat Avenue nr Twenty-Second
Andrews George, p i r, dwl 24 Oak
Andrews George B. mixer North Beach & M. R. R. Co. dwl 161 Tehama
Andrews Harry. mail clerk Alta California, dwl Masonic Building
Andrews Henry, dwl NE cor Folsom and Sixth
Andrews H. L. dwl 4 Hardie Place
Andrews H. S. Mrs. electro chemical baths and water cure, 10 Post, Masonic Temple
Andrews J. B. dwl William Tell House
Andrews Jerry, fireman, steamer Chrysopolis
Andrews J. G. machinist, S. F. I. W'ks, dwl 162 First
Andrews John, lodgings, 13½ Second
Andrews John, painter, dwl 229 Sutter
Andrews M. E. Miss, saleswoman, 208 Bush, res Oakland
Andrews Mitchell, seaman, dwl 54 Sacramento
Andrews Nancy H. (widow) dwl 759 Mission
Andrews Oliver, hog butcher, E s Ninth bet Bryant and Brannan

Andrews P. T. dwl 633 Market
Andrews Thomas I. maltster, 432 Brannan, dwl 434 Brannan
ANDREWS W. O. (J. C. Hutchinson & Co.) notary public and commissioner deeds, 626 Montgomery, dwl E s Second Avenue nr Sixteenth
Andrezjowski J. W. Military Headquarters Saloon, NW cor Bush and Montgomery, dwl 702 Bush
Andronetti G. B. dwl 928 Pacific
Angel James R. clerk with John A. Russ, dwl 1117 Montgomery
Angel Oliver, calker, dwl 54 First
Angel Texas, clerk with S. M. & D. S. Wilson, dwl 1117 Montgomery
Angele George, laborer, Pacific Flour Mills
Angeline James, box maker, dwl 537 Howard
Angelis August, tinsmith with M. Prag, dwl 16 San
ANGELIS EDWARD, proprietor German Hall, 16 and 18 Sansom
Angelis Theodore, jeweler with C. Eckart, dwl German Hall
Angelins Richard, workman, Albany Brewery, dwl 129 Fourth
Angell Andrew J. machinist, dwl E s Minna bet Second and Third
Angell H. A. blacksmith, dwl 120 Minna
Angell Horace B. (Howland, A. & King) dwl 11 Clementina
Angell Hyram G. machinist, dwl 47 Clementina
Angell J. W. clerk, Miners' Foundry, dwl 11 Clementina
Angels Charles A. reporter, dwl 155 Third
Anger Louis, instrument maker with Wm. Schmolz, dwl Federal Building
Anger Victor, currier with W. H. Warren, dwl Folsom bet Eighteenth and Nineteenth
Angerer Charles, shoe making, 126 Post
Anges William, wool sorter, S. F. P. W. Mills, dwl cor North Point and Van Ness Avenue
Angh Kee & Co (Chinese) merchants, 738 Sac
Angoustures Antoine, works with Arguelas Bernal
Angoustures François, works with Arguelas Bernal
Anguis C. G. (Catanich & Co.) dwl 525 Davis
Angus John A. superintendent S. F. P. W. Mills, dwl cor North Point and Van Ness Avenue
Annan William, teamster with James McDevitt, dwl W s Sansom bet Broadway and Vallejo
Annie Frederick, varnisher with Goodwin & Co. dwl W s Third bet Jessie and Stevenson
Annis William, boatman, dwl 631 Davis
Anqui Stephen, waiter, Russ House
Ansaldo Frank, drayman, 421 Jackson
Ansbro Thomas, policeman, C. S. N. Co. Broadway Wharf, dwl Zoe Place nr Folsom
Anson Patrick F. painter with James R. Kelly, dwl cor Geary and Larkin
Anson Richard, dwl SW cor Larkin and Geary
Ansorg Charles, dwl 813 Harrison
Ansons Victor, sausage maker, dwl 1418 Stockton
Antelope G. & S. M. Co. office 522 Montgomery
Anthes Anthea (John & A. A.) NW cor Sacramento and Kearny
Anthes Frederick, musician, dwl 27 St. Mark Place
Anthes John & Anthea, liquor saloon, NW cor Sacramento and Kearny
Anthes John (Huber & A.) dwl 805 Bush
Anthes Peter, clerk, 61 Washington Market, dwl E s Mission abv Twelfth
Anthony Edward T. & Co. repackers merchandise, NE cor Sacramento and Battery, dwl N s Oak bet Franklin and Gough
Anthony George W. news dealer, Occidental Hotel
Anthony James M. mariner, dwl N s Minna bet Second and Third
Anthony Julius, waiter, What Cheer House
Anthony M. Mrs. dwl 220 Kearny
Anthony Mary Mrs. nurse, dwl 332 Third
Anthony R. M. book keeper with William Sherman & Co. dwl 729 California

Antoine Lewis (col'd) cook; 630 Commercial
Antonio John, workman with Antonio Flores
Antonio Joseph, liquor saloon, W s Mission bet Twenty-First and Twenty-Second
Antunovich Floro, coffee stand, NW cor Clay and East
Antunovich Nicolas, bar keeper, NW cor Clay and East
Antz Henry, butcher, dwl 37 Third
Anzel Philip, soap manufacturer, dwl SW cor Lombard and Hartman
Apache Chief Mining Co, office 702 Washington
Apel John, architect, dwl 283 Stevenson
APEL'S BUILDING, E s Kearny bet California and Pine
Apeltree John, brewer, dwl 713 Greenwich
Apollo G. & S. M. Co. office 402 Front
Appel Frank, baker, dwl 200 Sutter
Appel John C. cabinet maker, dwl NW cor Vallejo and Polk
Appel Samuel & Co. (B. P. Barnett) manufacturers oil clothing, 322 Commercial, dwl 7 Dupont
Appel Samuel, liquor saloon, SE cor Stockton and O'Farrell, dwl 7 Dupont
Appel Sarah Mrs. millinery, 204 Kearny
Appel Wolf, tailor, dwl 204 Kearny
Appleby Thomas, landscape gardener and nurseryman, cor Valencia and Fourteenth, dwl Cincinnati Brewery, Valencia nr Sixteenth
Appleby William, gardener, Mission, dwl Cincinnati Brewery, Valencia nr Sixteenth
Applegate J. Henry, jr. book keeper with A. Roman & Co. dwl 219 Stevenson
Applegate Josiah H. attorney at law, office 702 Washington, dwl 219 Stevenson
Applegate Uriah, wagon maker, dwl 186 Jessie
APPLETON D. E. & CO. books, stationery, cutlery, etc., 508 Montgomery, and bookstands SE cor Clay and Kearny, NE cor California and Kearny, and NE cor Sacramento and Leidesdorff, dwl 1010 Pine
Appleton Michael, laborer, bds with Joseph Seale, N s Turk nr Fillmore
Appo Junius B. porter stm Pacific, dwl 924 Wash
Apulstil Charles, watch case maker, dwl SW cor Oak and Fillmore
Ar Hing (Chinese) washing, 1213 Dupont
Ar Qnong (Chinese) washing and ironing, dwl E s Sansom bet Broadway and Pacific
Arbitrios Mining Co. office 811 Montgomery, A. Martinon, secretary
Arbogast Frederick, upholsterer with F. G. Edwards
Arcan Charles, apprentice Miner's Foundry, dwl 312 Beale
ARCHBALD JOHN, cashier and secretary San Francisco Savings Union, 529 California, dwl 1312 Powell
Archer Edward (col'd) porter, dwl 927 Broadway
Archer Kate Mrs. actress, Maguire's Opera House
Archer William, machinist, Vulcan Iron Works, dwl 120 Shipley
Archibald James, molder, dwl 129 Jackson
ARCTIC FIRE INSURANCE CO. New York, Bigelow & Brother agents, 505 Montgomery
Arden William, laborer, dwl 3 Lick Alley
Ardito Guiseppe, fisherman, 9 Italian Fish Market
Ardizzi Antonio, cook, 515 Sansom
Arees C. P. Lafayette H. & L. Co. No. 2
Arents Hiram, merchant, dwl 543 Tehama
Areskog Gustave A. tanner, with James Duncan, dwl S s Brannan bet Eighth and Ninth
Arey Charles, captain bark Ocean, office Pier 12 Stewart
Arey Eliza Miss, dwl 41 Everett
Arey Emily F. (widow) matron Deaf, Dumb, and Blind Asylum, SE cor Fifteenth and Mission
Arey Eva Miss, dwl 1024 Stockton
Arey Helen S. Miss, assistant, Sutter Street Primary School, dwl 41 Everett

Arey James A. cigar clerk, International Hotel
Arey Walter W. book keeper with Jacob Underhill & Co. 120 Battery
Arfort John B. blacksmithing, 220 Post, dwl 16 Lewis Place
Argall John, machinist, Vulcan Iron Works, dwl 629 Mission
Argent G. & S. M. Co. office 529 Clay
Argenti Ellen Mrs. toys, 402 Third
Argenti Madaline (widow) dwl 459 Bryant
Argenti Tullio, stencil cutter, dwl 402 Third
Argoz José, adjutant general, Mexican Army, dwl What Cheer House
Argyras Basil, broker, office 423 Front, dwl NE cor Dupont and Chestnut
Arimond Jacob, groceries and liquors, cor Presidio Road and Fillmore
Arimoso Liberal, with Peter Bonzi, 515 Merchant
Arison Henry, carpenter, dwl 828 Union
Arizona Consolidated M. Co. office 611 Clay
Armajin Charles, with Lewis & Neville, 113 Clay, dwl West End Hotel
Armer Robert, laborer, dwl 5 Washoe Place
ARMES (C. W. & G. W.) & DALLAM (Richard B.) manufacturers brooms, 26 and 28 Beale, tub and pail manufactory, 22 and 24 California, and importers wood and willow ware, 215 and 217 Sacramento, dwl 618 Greenwich
Armes George W. (Armes & Dallam) res Oakland
Armes William J. lumber dealer, dwl 540 Second
Armitage John, sail maker, dwl N s McAllister bet Buchanan and Webster
Armond Frank, peddler wagon, cor Market and Third
Armor Joseph G. house and sign painter, 427 California, dwl 7 Prospect Place
ARMORY HALL BUILDING, NE cor Montgomery and Sacramento
Arms Moses C. Waverly Market, NW cor Sacramento and Waverly Place, dwl 627 Union
Arms Richard D. inspector, C. H. dwl SW cor Broadway and Montgomery
Armstrong Catharine (widow) dwl 724 Howard
Armstrong Charles, lab. dwl 27 St. Mark Pl, rear.
Armstrong Charles, steward Vigilant Engine Co. dwl 708 Broadway
Armstrong Charles M. & Co. proptrs Mission Street Brewery, Mission nr Second, dwl 371 Brannan
Armstrong Christopher, sign painter, dwl SW cor Hayes and Octavia
Armstrong Dennis, salesman, 206 Kearny, dwl 7 Morse
Armstrong Elizabeth, domestic, dwl 6 Hodges Place
Armstrong Ellen E. Miss, dwl with Edward G. Beckwith, E s Mission bet Fourteenth and Fifteenth
Armstrong Francis, porter, 120 Bat, dwl 45 Louisa
Armstrong (Henry) & Kelly (William) grainers, 611 Market, dwl 619 Mission
Armstrong J. driver with John Agnew, 26 Kearny
Armstrong James, dwl 735 Market
Armstrong James, bar keeper, Olympic Melodeon, dwl NE cor Clay and Kearny
Armstrong (James) & Bertran (Thomas) tinsmiths Fort Point, dwl 126 St. Mark Place
Armstrong J. I. carpenter, dwl 323 Kearny
Armstrong J. J. contractor, dwl SE cor Mission and First
Armstrong John, clerk, dwl SE cor Taylor and Filbert
Armstrong Kate Miss, domestic, 833 Bush
Armstrong Lewis (Pearson & A.) dwl Russ House
Armstrong Marietta Mrs. boarding, 735 Market
ARMSTRONG (R. B.) SHELDON (John P.) & DAVIS (W. H.) Union Lumber Yard, SE cor California and Davis, dwl S s Wash nr Powell
Armstrong Robert, carpenter, dwl Bay View Park
Armstrong Thomas, hostler, What Cheer Livery Stable, 121 Jackson

Armstrong Trueman B. tinsmith with J. W. Brittan & Co. dwl 616 California

Armstrong W. dwl What Cheer House

Armstrong William, painter, dwl 152 Perry

Arnaud Albert, upholsterer, dwl 205 Sutter

Arnaud Ernest, box maker, dwl 58 Jessie

Arnaud Paul, upholsterer, 205 Sutter

Arndt Gottlieb, boot maker, dwl 631 Broadway

Arnheim Julius, clerk, 332 Mont, dwl 8 Stewart

Arnheim S. clothing, 315 Pacific

Arnheim Samuel S. cigars and tobacco, 332 Montgomery and 8 Stewart

Arnhold Frederick, porter, Bootz Hotel

Arnitz Xavier, Essex Market, SE cor Dupont and Green

Arnold Amelia (widow) liquor saloon, 1211 Dupont

Arnold Ames, teamster with Blyth & Wetherbee

Arnold B. laborer, Bay Sugar Refinery, dwl 220 Pacific

Arnold Benjamin E. wholesale butcher, 536 Kearny, dwl 509 Bryant

Arnold Bernard, laborer, dwl Chicago Hotel, 220 Pacific

Arnold Caspar, hatter, 14 Geary

Arnold *(Cyrus)* & Heywood *(S. J.)* poultry and produce, 11 and 12 Metropolitan Market, dwl 650 Howard

Arnold Edward, barber, dwl Bush nr Lone Mountain

ARNOLD ELBRIDGE F. books, stationery, and periodicals, 538 Market, dwl 51 Natoma

Arnold Emily P. Mrs. dwl 116 Perry

Arnold Ferdinand D. butcher, dwl 737 Howard

Arnold Francis W. cooper, 708 Front, dwl N s Filbert bet Gough and Octavia

Arnold Frank, carpenter, dwl 446 Brannan

Arnold Franklin, watchman Manhattan House, 705 Front

ARNOLD JOHN & CO. *(Lawson S. Adams)* merchants, (Sacramento) office 405 Front

Arnold John, mariner, dwl 737 Howard

Arnold John, tailor, dwl 336 Bush

Arnold John C. butcher with B. E. Arnold, dwl cor Bryant and Tenth

Arnold John F. drayman, 320 Jackson, dwl S s Washington bet Leavenworth and Hyde

Arnold Lewis, grocer, dwl 1318 Jackson

Arnold Mary Ann Miss, domestic, 212 Ellis

ARNOLD N. S. & CO. importers hardware, agricultural implements, washing machines, and clothes wringers, 306 Battery, dwl W s Capp bet Twenty-Third and Twenty-Fourth

Arnold Oscar B. collector, office 626 Clay, dwl SW cor Folsom and First

Arnold Robert (col'd) wood sawyer, dwl N s Green bet Montgomery and Sansom

Arnold Thomas C. porter, 216 Cal, dwl 619 Mission

Arnold Thomas J. *(Cox & A.)* dwl 226 Sixth

Arnold William, varnisher with J. Peirce 415 Cal

Arnot Nathaniel D. president Vulcan Iron Works Co. dwl 947 Howard

Arnstein Eugene, book keeper with Stein, Simon & Co. dwl 1321 Powell

Aron Joseph *(Weil & Co.)* dwl 1018 Bush

Aron Simon, salesman, 226 Front, dwl 1125 Powell

Arons Morris, house and sign painter, 3 Summer, dwl S s Sixteenth bet Valencia and Guerrero

Aronsohn Siegmund, beer bottler, dwl 3 Monroe

Aronson George *(A. P. Craner & Co.)* dwl 110 Kearny

Aronstein Adolf, physician, office and dwl 812 Wash

Arpers John, musician, dwl 911 Greenwich

Arps John, groceries and liquors, NW cor Geary and Hyde

Arrata Pietro, chocolate maker with D. Ghirardelli & Co. 417 Jackson

Arrington A. S. clerk, 626 Mont, dwl 1433 Taylor

ARRINGTON N. O. stock and money broker, 626 Montgomery, dwl 724 Folsom

Arriola Fortunato, artist, studio 338 Montgomery, room 20, dwl 2 Haven Place

Arrivets John, boot maker, 631 Pacific

Arrowsmith D. B. ex-gauger, dwl 834 Clay

Arroyo Seco Copper M. Co. No. 1 (Amador Co.) office 415 Montgomery

Arthur Edwin M. clerk, 512 Cal, dwl 1027 Bush

Arthur George N. with J. D. Arthur & Son, dwl 1027 Bush

Arthur Jacob F. policeman, City Hall, dwl 325 Jessie

ARTHUR J. D. & SON, importers and jobbers agricultural implements, SW cor California and Davis, dwl 1027 Bush

Arthur Thomas, workman with John Henry, dwl Dolores Hall

Arthurs Anna Miss (col'd) domestic, 218 Bush

ARTIGUES LOUIS, butcher, 17 New Market, dwl N s Sixteenth nr Rhode Island

Arzaga Joseph, compositor, American Flag, dwl Gautier's House 516 Pacific

Aschiem William, clerk, dwl 429 Bush

Ash Charles, drayman, SW cor Third and Brannan

Ash David, blacksmith, dwl 917 Jones

Ash Jacob *(J. Alexander & Co.)* dwl 822 Post

Ash James J. with L. Atkinson & Co. dwl 917 Jones

Ash Leo *(J. Alexander & Co.)* dwl 822 Post

Ash Louisa (widow) dwl 49 Jessie

Ash Philip, molder, dwl 421 Natoma

Ash *(William H.)* & Hurley *(Charles)* gents' furnishing goods, 602 Kearny, dwl 917 Jones

Ashburner William, mining engineer, 90 Montgomery Block, dwl Brevoort House

ASHBURY MONROE, real estate and supervisor Fifth District, office and dwl 7 Mercantile Library Building

Ashby Mark T. dwl 516 Greenwich

Ashcom James E. register clerk Fourth District Court, dwl 218 Bush

Ashcroft William, mate stmr Cornelia, dwl 41 Natoma

Ashenheim William, clerk, 25 Metropolitan Market

Asher A. F. clothing, dwl 725 Battery

Asher Edward, waiter, Russ House

Asher Elias, groceries and liquors, NW cor Bush and Battery

Asher S. clothing, dwl 14 Stewart

Ashim Rose Miss, dwl 540 Mission

Ashim Simon, dwl 6 Howard Court

Ashley Augustus F. carpenter, dwl 783 Market

Ashley D. R. attorney at law, dwl 712 Bush

Ashley B. (col'd) waiter stmr Chrysopolis

Ashley S. J. master mason, Engineer's Department, Fort Point

Ashman Richard A. engineer, Miners' Foundry, dwl 336 Ritch

Ashmead G. S. carpenter and builder, 318 Dupont, dwl 320 Dupont

Asholford W. W. dwl What Cheer House

ASHTON CHARLES, agent for physicians, office 415 Pine, dwl N s Ellis bet Hyde and Larkin

Ashton Charles S. clerk with J. J. Robbins, dwl 930 Mission

Ashton George, dwl W s Shotwell nr Fifteenth

Asin William, carpenter, dwl Summer Street House

Askin David, porter with James H. Widber, cor Kearny and Market

Askins Richard, seaman, dwl 132 Folsom

Asmus *(John)* & Folmar *(Philip)* farmers, San Miguel Rancho

Asmus John, porter, Commercial Flour Mill, dwl 415 Powell

Asmussen Peter, drayman, dwl 721 Lombard

Aspen Mary Mrs. dwl 1 Stockton Place

Assembly Hall, NW cor Post and Kearny

ASSESSOR CITY AND COUNTY, office City Hall 22 first floor

ASSESSOR U. S. INTERNAL REVENUE, office NW cor Battery and Commercial

Assion Henry *(Assion & Bro.)* dwl 205 Mont
Assion *(Joseph)* & Brother *(Henry)* merchant tailors, 205 Montgomery, dwl 348 Third
Asamiru Adolph, baker with Engelberg & Wagner
Aston Antonetti (widow) dwl 604 California
Aston Curran, carpenter, dwl 75 Fourth
Aston James, porter, John Sime & Co. dwl S s Jessie bet Fifth and Sixth
Astredo Anthony, bar keeper, Lick House Saloon, dwl 112 Sutter
Astruc Gustave, carpenter, Lafayette H. & L. Co. No. 2
Atattorre Jophilo, laborer, dwl W s Battery bet Vallejo and Green
ATCHINSON B. M. & CO. *(P. A. Rodgers)* butter, cheese, and eggs, 7 Occidental Market, dwl 60 Natoma
Atchison Lewis, with Thomas Varney, 127 First, dwl 728 Folsom
Athearn *(Charles G.)* & Morrison *(Charles W.)* wholesale and retail groceries and provisions, 8 Clay, dwl N s Hayes bet Octavia and Laguna
Athearn Charles M. milk dealer, dwl 147 Tehama
Athearn Joseph H. clerk, 8 Clay, dwl 343 Fremont
Athenæum Building, SE cor Montgomery and Cal
Atherton F. D. office 705 Sansom, res Redwood City
Atherton William F. stoves and tin ware, 15 Second, dwl 16 Sansom
Atherton W. L. medical student, dwl 755 Clay
Atkins Charles, dwl 10 Stevenson House
Atkins Eben, with Dibblee & Hyde, 108 Front, dwl 436 Bush
Atkins Henry B. groceries and liquors, NW cor O'Farrell and Jones
Atkins Robert C. *(Orr & A.)* dwl 607 Pine
Atkinson B. M. dwl 462 Natoma
Atkinson Edward, dyer, S. F. P. Woolen Mills
Atkinson George, wheelwright, S s Vallejo nr Battery, dwl 212 Broadway, rear
Atkinson James, dyer, S. F. P. Woolen Mills
ATKINSON JAMES, Market Exchange Liquor Saloon, 538 Market
Atkinson John P. steward stm Yosemite, dwl 365 Minna
Atkinson Joseph B. *(L. Atkinson & Co.)* res Philadelphia
Atkinson Joseph H. real estate, office 621 Clay, dwl N s Broadway above Taylor
ATKINSON L. & CO. *(Joseph B. Atkinson)* manufacturers and importers shirts, collars, etc. 509 Sacramento
Atkinson Nathan *(S. Hancock & Co.)* office room 2 Mead House
Atkinson Samuel, assistant superintendent S. F. & S. José R. R. dwl S s Sixteenth, second door W of Folsom
Atkinson Thomas, dwl Old San José Road nr Industrial School
Atkinson Thomas F. machinist, Fulton Foundry
Atlantic House, John McManus, proprietor, 210 and 212 Pacific
ATLAS IRON WORKS, Dunn, McHaffie & Co. proprietors, 24 and 26 Fremont
Attridge Edward, porter, 410 Front, dwl N s Filbert bet Jones and Leavenworth
Attridge James, warehouse laborer, dwl SW cor Sansom and Union
Attridge Thomas, porter with Lewis P. Sage, dwl E s Calhoun bet Green and Union
Atwill Albert J. painter, dwl 116 Sansom
Atwood C. L. Mrs. teacher Belles Lettres Boys' High School, dwl 145 Natoma
ATWOOD *(E. A.)* & BODWELL *(H. H.)* windmill manufacturers, 222 Mission, dwl 145 Natoma
Atwood Edward, dwl 9 Dupont
Atwood Edward T. butcher, dwl 5 Martha Place
Atwood Frank H. with Melville Atwood, dwl 722 Bush

Atwood George, mariner, dwl NE cor Broadway and Kearny
Atwood Geo. A. engineer, Golden State Iron Works dwl W s Folsom bet Twenty-First and Twenty-Second
Atwood Lucy S. Mrs. dwl with J. L. Eells, W s Folsom bet Twenty-First and Twenty-Second
Atwood Melville, mining engineer, dwl 722 Bush
Atwood William T. book keeper with Martin & Co. dwl Cosmopolitan Hotel
Au Soos (Chinese) washing and ironing, 841 Dupont
Aub George F. expressman, dwl 323 Pine
Auberlin Augustus, machinist, Fulton Foundry, dwl 10 St. Mark Place
Aubert Albert, butcher with J. Stock, dwl 626 Cal
Aubert Paul, dwl N s O'Farrell bet Laguna and Octavia
Aubinaud Peter, dwl 8 s Polk Alley
Aubrant Constant, blacksmith, dwl N s Pacific bet Dupont and Kearny
Aubrey William H. carpenter, dwl 37 Stevenson
Aubriere Pierre, laundryman, dwl 638 Broadway
Aubry Catherine F. Mrs. books and stationery, 310 Third
Aubry Francis O. cabinet maker, 302 Third, dwl 310 Third
Aubry Joseph, trunk manufacturer, SW cor Stockton and Sacramento
Auction G. & S. M. Co. office 404 Front
Audiffred *(H.)* & Male *(G.)* wood and charcoal, foot Market Street Wharf, dwl S s Bush bet Polk and Van Ness Avenue
AUDITOR CITY AND COUNTY, office 3 City Hall, first floor
Audouin Charles, cook, dwl 821 Kearny
Auer Joseph, tailor, dwl 319 Bush
Auerbach Leopold, shoe maker, NE cor Kearny and Broadway
Auerbach Louis, cigars, What Cheer House, dwl 621 Post
Aufermann August, clerk 219 Montgomery, dwl Lutgen's Hotel
Auger B. Eugene, importer and commission merchant, 704 Sansom, dwl SE cor Gough and Fulton
Auger Mary A. (widow) French laundry, 777 Clay
Augier Caroline Madame, French dress maker, 620 Sacramento
Augusta Louise Miss, waitress, dwl SW cor Dupont and Broadway
Augustine John, vegetable garden, nr Bay View Park
Augustine Morris, book keeper, 316 Sacramento, dwl 1521 Powell
Augustus Joseph, painter, and steward Howard Engine House
Ault Joseph P. freight clerk, dwl 258 Clementina
Aunget Henry, with N. R. Lowell, NW cor Pine and Davis
Auradon *(Jules)* & Bunker *(Robert F.)* curers and dealers in hams, bacon, etc. 507 Merchant, dwl 1310 Pacific
Aureau Frances Miss, French laundry, 26 Post
Aureau L. liquor saloon, SW cor Kearny and Commercial, dwl 25 Post
Auser E. W. clerk, steamer Relief, res Petaluma
Ausserman A. book keeper, dwl Lutgen's Hotel
AUSTIN *(Alexander)* & CO. *(Joseph Austin and Alexander Chisholm)* dry goods, SE cor Montgomery and Sutter
Austin Alvah C. *(Goddard & Co.)* dwl 850 Howard
AUSTIN BENJ. C. importer and jobber stoves, tinware, wire, etc. 324 Clay, dwl 720 Filbert
Austin Augusta (widow) dwl with Gerrard Dehney
Austin Daniel, Wilson's Circus, bds Brooklyn Hotel
Austin Edward, laborer, dwl 35 Sacramento
Austin Edward, oiler, steamer Chrysopolis
Austin Emilins, tinsmith with Osgood & Stetson, dwl Clay nr Stockton

Austin Frank B. office 6 Government House, dwl 1109 Stockton
Austin Henry, carpenter, dwl 327 Dupont
Austin Henry, dentist, 634 Washington, dwl 516 Lombard nr Powell
Austin Henry, drayman, dwl 1513 Larkin
Austin John, second-hand crockery, 212 First
Austin Joseph *(Austin & Co.)* bds Russ House
Austin Joseph, dwl 15 Rousch
Austin Marcus E. with Willard Hodges, 223 Sacramento, dwl E s Taylor bet Filbert and Union
Austin Margaretta (widow) dwl 607 Sutter
Austin Minnie F. Miss, teacher Belles Lettres, Girls' High School, dwl 313 Taylor
Austin Sampson, with R. A. Swain & Co. dwl 826 Broadway
Austin Turner, carpenter, dwl 633 Market
Australian & Melbourne Circular Line of Packets, P. A. Hughes agent, Battery op Custom House
Autagne George, waiter, 647 Commercial, dwl 814 Sacramento
Averell Anson *(Grant, Averell & Co.)* dwl 320 O'Farrell
Averill Chester C. Mexican coast messenger, Wells, Fargo & Co. dwl SE cor Mont and Cal
Averill William, ship carpenter with John G. North, dwl 331 Bryant
Avery Annie L. physician, office and dwl 158 Second cor Howard
Avery Benjamin P. city editor Evening Bulletin, dwl 3 Geary Place
Avery Clark, carpenter, dwl Presidio Road nr Scott
Avery D. R. *(Brown & A.)* dwl 515 Bush
Avery Harris G. tinsmith with Locke & Montague, dwl 436 Fremont
Avery Henry F. helper, Miners' Foundry, dwl 6 Lick Alley
Avery James A. mariner, dwl 309 Bryant
Avery Ophelia (widow) domestic, 621 Bush
Axt Louis, shoe maker, 640 Broadway
Ayala Cipriano, wood dealer, dwl S s Greenwich bet Stockton and Powell
Ayer Henry, clerk, dwl 414 Market
Ayer Joseph G. contractor and builder, dwl W s Folsom bet Twentieth and Twenty-First
Ayer Milo J. carpenter, dwl SE cor O'Farrell and Leavenworth
Ayer Washington, physician and school director, Third District, office and dwl 605 Sacramento
AYERS ELLIS, importer and jobber stoves and tinware, 417 Washington, dwl American Exchange
Ayers Grosvenor P. clerk with Ellis Ayers, 417 Washington, dwl American Exchange
Ayers Henry P. painter, dwl 655 Harrison
Ayers Hiram, carrier, Morning Call
Ayers Ira jr. book keeper with George F. Bragg & Co. dwl 770 Howard
AYERS J. J. & CO. *(Peter B. Forster, Charles F. Jobson and Austin Wiley)* editors and proprietors Daily Morning Call, office 612 Commercial, dwl 25 Turk
Ayers Lionel, works Davis' Laundry, W s Harriet bet Howard and Folsom
Ayhens Leon, butcher, dwl NE cor Pine and Dupont
Ayles Thomas W. driver, North Beach & M. R. R. Co
Ayliffe Sophia (widow) dwl 673½ Mission
Ayres Frank, steward, 111 Washington
Ayres Henry, sash maker with Smith, Ware & Co. dwl 623 Howard
Ayres John C. brass founder, dwl E s Mariposa nr Carolina
Ayres Joseph, carpenter, dwl 636 Commercial
Ayres William, compositor, Daily Examiner, dwl 125 Bush
Ayres W. O. physician, office and dwl 613 Howard

B

Baas Charles, bar keeper, Kihlmeyer's Saloon, dwl 4 Milton Place
Baasar Ferdinand, laborer, dwl 59 Stevenson
Babb Charles, compositor, Evening Bulletin, dwl 34 Second
Babb Thomas, blacksmith with M. P. Holmes, dwl 435 Pine
BABBITT E. B. colonel U. S. A., deputy quartermaster-general and chief Q. M. office 742 Washington, dwl 314 Fremont
Babbitt Hiram, sash and blind maker with George Robinson & Co. dwl 359 Minna
Babcock A. B. Eureka Lodgings, 624 Commercial
Babcock Annie Mrs. furnished rooms, SW cor Wash and Dupont
Babcock Benjamin E. cashier Custom House, office 2d floor, dwl NE cor McAllister and Fillmore
Babcock E. A. engineer, dwl E s Valencia bet Sixteenth and Seventeenth
Babcock George, book keeper, 119 Clay, dwl 548 Mission
Babcock George W. carpenter with John Center, dwl W s Folsom nr Sixteenth
BABCOCK HENRY S. manager British and Californian Banking Co. Limited, office 424 California, dwl 11 Essex
Babcock Jasper, contractor, dwl SE cor Valencia and Sixteenth
Babcock, J. T. machinist, Vulcan Iron Works
BABCOCK WILLIAM F. president Spring Valley W. W. Co. office 414 Montgomery, dwl 11 Essex
Babcox Charles, quartz mill, dwl 225 Second
Baben Patrick, laborer, dwl Russian Hill
Babin Edouard, cook, Telegraph House, W s Battery bet Green and Vallejo
Babson Edward jr. *(C. L. Taylor & Co.)* dwl S s Washington bet Mason and Taylor
Babson William E. purser steamship Moses Taylor, dwl Cosmopolitan Hotel
BABY FRANCIS R. assistant agent Pacific M. S. S. Line, office NW cor Sacramento and Leidesdorff, dwl 524 Pine
BACA *(Pablo)* & CO. *(J. Perea and Paul Dulhorn)* wholesale butchers, Potrero Avenue, office 402 Montgomery, dwl 27 O'Farrell
Baccala Louis, cook, Gamba House
Bacchus Catherine Miss, domestic, 831 Bush
Baccus Charles, salesman, 15 Third, dwl Mason bet California and Sacramento
Baccus John B. physician, dwl NW cor Mason and California
Baccus John B. jr. printer, dwl NW cor Mason and California
Bach Frederick W. clerk with Martin L. Haas, dwl 725 Union
Bach John, gunsmith and sporting materials, 408 Commercial, dwl 116 Virginia
Bach Matilda (widow) dwl 725 Union
Bach R. billiard maker, dwl 323 Pine
Bachelder Henry, porter, dwl 114 Austin
Bachelder Hiram, carrier, Evening Bulletin, dwl 12 Harlan Place
Bachelder John R. carpenter, dwl 511 Jones
Bachelder J. W. *(T. F. & J. W. B.)* attorney at law, office 625 Merchant, dwl 1228 Sacramento bet Taylor and Jones
Bachelder L. L. dwl 1026 Clay
Bachelder *(T. F.)* & *(J. W.)* attorneys at law, office 625 Merchant, dwl 320 Lombard
Bachelder, see Batchelder
Bacher Celestin, piano maker with Jacob Zech, 416 Market
Bacher Edw. driver with Michel & Co. dwl 329 Geary
BACHMAN BROTHERS *(Herman S., Nathan S., and David S.)* importers and jobbers dry goods, 304 and 306 California, res New York

Bachman David S. *(Bachman Bros.)* dwl 327 O'Farrell
Bachman Leopold, clerk, 304 California, dwl 327 O'Farrell
Bachman Nathan S. *(Bachman Bros.)* dwl 327 O'Farrell
Bachmann August, upholsterer with H. Rosenfeld, dwl 604 Dupont
Bacigalupi Louis, gardener, nr Laguna
Bacigalupi Carlo, vegetable garden, nr Bay View Park
Bacigalupi Domingo, fruits and nuts, 910 Dupont
Bacigalupi Joseph, wood carver with J. B. Luchsinger, dwl cor Sacramento and Drumm
Backer John, cabinet maker, dwl 637 Broadway
Backer John R. bar keeper, NW cor Clay and Davis
Backer William, Sandy Hill Bakery, NE cor Clay and Mason
Backhaus Peter, cook, dwl 18 Sansom
Backler Conrad, baker, Clipper Restaurant
Backs Ferdinand, with Henry Frank, 217 Com
Backus Charles E. compositor, dwl NW cor Union and Sansom
Backus Frank, with Martin Kedon, dwl 175 Davis
Backus George, iron finisher, dwl Mason nr cor Cal
Backus Gordon, assistant assessor U. S. Int. Rev. NW cor Battery and Com, dwl W s Larkin bet Pine and California
Backus J. H. steward, dwl 326 Second
Backus Lucy (widow) dwl with James H. Bullard
Backus Oscar J. *(Tay, Brooks & B.)* dwl SE cor Montgomery and Green
Backus Peter, proprietor Mansion House, W s Dolores op Sixteenth, Mission Dolores
Backus Peter F. laborer, What Cheer House Restaurant
Bacon Dean, carpenter, dwl N s Geary nr Leav
Bacon Francis N. machine shop, 113 Pine, dwl First Street House
Bacon Henry, clerk, NE cor Hayes and Octavia
Bacon Horace, bailiff, U. S. Courts, dwl 527 Pine
BACON JACOB *(Towne & B.)* dwl 929 Howard
Bacon James, laborer, Miners' Foundry, dwl 36 Natoma
BACON J. S. agent Boston Underwriters *(and T. H. & J. S. Bacon)* office 308 Front, dwl 1 Vernon Place
Bacon Louis S. sculptor modeler, SW cor Pine and Morse, dwl 5 Quincy Place
Bacon T. F. book keeper with Towne & Bacon, res Oakland
BACON T. H. & J. S. shipping and commission merchants, and agents Boston Underwriters, office 308 Front, res Boston
Bacon William, cook, steamer Amelia
Badarous Camille J. physician and surgeon, office 732 Washington, dwl SW cor Guerrero and Liberty
Badenhop Henry, groceries, W s Mission between Twelfth and Thirteenth
Badger Alexander, warehouse clerk, Quartermaster's Department, dwl 1016 Washington
Badger James, workman, S. F. & P. Sugar Co. dwl 22 Langton
Badger Joseph *(Dyer, B. & Rokohl)* dwl 607 Pine
Badger Oliver B. with Dyer, Badger & Rokohl, dwl 620 Market
BADGER *(William G.)* & LINDENBERGER *(Thomas E.)* importers and jobbers clothing, etc., agents Chickering & Son's piano fortes, 411–415 Battery (and school director Seventh District) dwl 333 Second
Badker Henry, boatman, Pacific Street Wharf, dwl Bone Alley nr Kearny
BADLAM ALEXANDER JR. agent Samuel Brannan, office 420 Mont, third floor, dwl 402 Mont
Badlam Ezra B. money broker, 504 Montgomery, dwl 1317 Powell

Badt Alexander L. book keeper with L. King & Bro. dwl 279 Stevenson
Badt Morris, clothing, 505 and 527 and 529 Commercial, dwl 279 Stevenson
Baebr William *(Pohlmann & Co.)* dwl 242 Clementina
Baettge Charles, drayman, dwl S s Green bet Larkin and Polk
Baettge Peter, workman with J. H. C. Portmann
Baez Carlos, compositor, 622 Clay, dwl NE corner Kearny and Broadway
BAFIEOS JOHN, groceries and liquors, NW cor Union and Dupont
Bagge Charles E. baker, dwl 3 Agnes Lane
Baggs James, laborer, dwl NE cor Mission and Beale
Baggs James E. laborer, dwl Bertha W s Beale
Bagley David T. office 712 Montgomery, dwl 834 Clay
Bagley Hannah Miss, domestic, dwl SE cor Pine and Leavenworth
Bagley J. B. medicated vapor baths, 611 Howard
Bagley Johanna, chambermaid, Lick House
Bagley M. molder, dwl cor Sherman and Corbet
Bagley Townsend, dwl 45 Everett
Bagnall Bridget, liquors, dwl N s Pacific bet Montgomery and Sansom
Bagnell Eliza (widow) dwl 709 Vallejo
Bahlman H. driver, Philadelphia Brewery
Bahls J. F. W. book binder with Buswell & Co. 509 Clay, dwl 407 Pacific
Bahrs Andreas, groceries and liquors, NE cor Jackson and Davis
Bahrs Hermann, driver, Pacific Brewery, 271 Tehama
Bailey Anne (widow) dwl 1423 Kearny
Bailey Catherine Miss, domestic, 508 Sutter
Bailey Charles A. carpenter, dwl 116 Sansom
Bailey Charles P. office 614 Front, dwl 603 Pine
BAILEY *(Charles W.)* & HILLIS *(William H.)* books and stationery, 767 Market
Bailey David, blacksmith with P. Bones, dwl 254 Minna
Bailey *(Edward D.)* & Co. liquor saloon, 320 Montgomery, dwl NE cor Pine and Montgomery
Bailey E. J. engineer steamer Reliance, dwl Ritch nr Brannan
Bailey Frank, liquor saloon, 109 Washington
Bailey George, harness maker with J. M. Hurlbutt & Co. dwl cor Market and Broadway
Bailey Harvey, express wagon, Davis nr Jackson
Bailey Henry, laborer, dwl 776 Harrison
Bailey Henry E. accountant with Edgerly & Wickman, 407 East
Bailey Isaac L. teamster, Genesee Flour Mills, dwl 37 Louisa
Bailey James, gardener, dwl Ecker nr Second
Bailey James D. insurance clerk, dwl 730 Bush
BAILEY JOSEPH H. crockery and glassware, 1513 Stockton, dwl 830 Union
BAILEY LEWIS H. dwl Portsmouth House, cor Clay and Brenham Place
Bailey Lizzie A. music teacher, 613 Clay
Bailey Margaret Miss, tailoress, dwl 44 Jessie
Bailey Martha J. (widow) dwl 1511 Stockton, rear
Bailey Mary J. (widow) dwl 27 Perry
Bailey O. L. *(Emerson & B.)* dwl Original House
Bailey Sally Miss, domestic, dwl 924 Jackson
BAILEY *(Samuel M.)* & HYATT *(John B.)* proprietors Oriental Hotel, SW cor Bat and Bush
Bailey Thomas, foreman Rincon Wool Depôt, dwl 337 Bryant
Bailey Wilber F. photographic artist, dwl W s Jones bet Pacific and Jackson
Bailey William, fireman, dwl Davis Street House
Bailey William I. drayman, dwl 69 Jessie
BAILEY WILLIAM J. proprietor Isthmus House, 54 First
Bailey. See Bayley.

Bailley William (col'd) white washer, dwl cor Jessie and Ann
Baillie Emily P. (widow) dwl 428 Third
Bailly Achille, with François Bailly, 516 Clay, dwl 718 Stockton
Bailly Arthur, clerk, 40 Washington Market, dwl 516 Clay
Bailly François, sausages and pork, 40 Washington Market, dwl 516 Clay
BAILY A. H. proprietor Baily House, 116 and 118 Sansom
Baily David, carpenter, dwl Baily House
BAILY HOUSE, 116 and 118 Sansom
Baily Jacob E. brick layer, dwl Jane nr Mission
Baily William, fruit dealer, 403 Davis, dwl 124 Silver
Baimle Frederic, spinner, Woolen Mill, dwl N s Sixteenth nr Valencia
Bain Frank, tinsmith, dwl Trinity nr Sutter
Bain James, blacksmith, dwl Howard Engine House
Bain John, blacksmith, Vulcan Foundry, dwl 27 Ritch
Balnbridge Arnop, conductor, Central R. R. Co. dwl SE cor Brannan and Seventh
Baine Melinda (widow) dwl 110 Stockton
Baird John H. (Tucker & Co.) dwl Pacific Club
Bairden Eugene, laborer with Wm. J. Kingsley
Baja California S. M. Co. office 611 Clay
Bajo Peter (Alexander Finance & Co.) dwl 837 Dupont
Baker Adolph, book keeper with California Insurance Co. dwl Belden nr Pine
Baker A. J. carrier, Evening Bulletin
Baker Alexander, clerk with G. M. Josselyn, dwl 609 Pine bet Stockton and Powell
Baker Alfred W. stock broker, dwl 1123 Stockton
Baker B. carpenter, Spring Valley Water Works
Baker Catherine F. (widow) boarding, 800 and 802 Howard
BAKER (Charles H.) & RANDAHL (Charles) meat market, SW cor Folsom and Nevada
Baker Charles V. varnisher, dwl 13 Second
Baker Christian, baker with Charles Schroth, 230 Kearny
Baker C. N. machinist, dwl Original House
Baker Colin C. (Stevens, Baker & Co.) office 215 Front
Baker Colin C. jr. dwl 10 Bernard
Baker Conrad, with Kellogg, Hewston & Co. dwl 340 Minna
Baker Copper M. Co. office 611 Clay
Baker David, dwl What Cheer House
Baker E. D. (widow) dwl 1114 Kearny
Baker Edgar G. confectioner, 1126 Dupont
Baker E. G. carrier Alta and Call, dwl W s First Avenue nr Fifteenth
Baker Elizabeth L. (widow) music teacher, 762 Folsom
Baker Ferdinand, shoe dealer, dwl S s Hayes bet Octavia and Laguna
Baker Frank, cabinet maker, dwl 21 Second
Baker Frederick W. cigars and tobacco, dwl 705 Davis
Baker George, laborer, dwl 515 Market
Baker George H. lithographer, office 522 Montgomery, dwl 213 Prospect Place
Baker George J. dwl 132 St. Mark Place
Baker George L. Kellogg, Hewston & Co.'s Refinery, Brannan nr Seventh
Baker G. P. dwl NE cor Market and Montgomery
Baker Henry, laborer, dwl E s Grove Avenue bet Bryant and Harrison
Baker Henry (Wilson & B.) and cigar inspector U. S. Int. Revenue, dwl 316 California
Baker Henry E. auctioneer, 413 Kearny, dwl 607½ Pine
Baker Herman, waiter, Clipper Restaurant
Baker Isaac F. Potrero Daily and City Express, SE cor Montgomery and California, dwl 163 Perry

Baker Isaiah, dwl 312 Green
Baker James G. shipping master, Vallejo bet Front and Davis, dwl SE cor Tehama and Second
Baker Jane B. Miss, with Wheeler & Wilson Sewing Machine Co. 439 Montgomery, dwl 9 Auburn
Baker John, hackman, Russ House, dwl 409 Third
Baker John, hair dresser, dwl 6 Pratt Court nr Cal
Baker John, ranch, Point Lobos, 4½ miles west Plaza
Baker John B. book keeper, dwl 1109 Pine
Baker John H. trunk maker, dwl St. Francis Engine House
Baker John Perry, salesman, 219 Front, dwl Cosmopolitan Hotel
Baker John S. bargeman, C. H. dwl E s Davis nr Vallejo
Baker John S. clerk, San Francisco Directory office, 612 Clay, dwl 131 Montgomery
Baker Joseph, crockery and glass ware, SW cor Dupont and Sutter
Baker Judah jr. (Stevens, Baker & Co.) office 215 Front
Baker L. F. produce and commission, SE cor Washington and Davis, dwl E s Yerba Buena nr Clay
Baker Lizzie Miss, domestic with F. Richling, 930 Folsom
Baker Luther, carpenter, dwl 741 Market
Baker Margaret A. Mrs. dwl 1614 Stockton
Baker Maria, (widow) Golden Gate Ranch, Point Lobos, 4½ miles from Plaza
Baker Mary A. (widow) dwl 764 Howard
Baker M. C. carpenter, dwl 563 Howard
Baker Orrin V. machinist, dwl 11 St. Mark Place
Baker Osborn, bargeman, Custom House, dwl U. S. Barge Office
Baker P. Y. musician, dwl 608 market
Baker Raphael, mcht (Salt Lake) dwl 240 Minna
Baker Richard P. mariner, dwl 303 Davis
Baker Russell, carpenter, dwl 741 Market
Baker Russell, seaman, dwl 10 Stewart
Baker Samuel, delivery clerk, P. O. dwl 609 Pine
Baker S. D. bds 423 Stevenson
Baker Seward W. clerk, What Cheer House
Baker Stephen W. captain of police, City Hall, dwl 108 Silver nr Third
Baker Sylvester C. mariner, dwl 10 Bernard
Bakman John, laborer, dwl 1432 Stockton
Balch Stephen M. (Chamberlin & B.) dwl N s Folsom nr Sixteenth
Balcom William E. carpenter, dwl S s Sixteenth nr Valencia
Baldermann Adolph, cook with Stevens & Oliver, dwl SW cor Pine and Polk
Baldridge M. salesman with William Sherman & Co. 412 Sansom
Baldwin Abel, carrier, American Flag, dwl 327 Bush
BALDWIN ALBERT S. physician and surgeon, office and dwl SE cor Clay and Kearny
BALDWIN (Amos B.) & MOFFAT (Eugene) wholesale butchers, W s Ninth nr Brannan, dwl nr Brannan Street Bridge
BALDWIN A. R. & CO. importers and jobbers wines and liquors, 219 and 221 Front, dwl 923 Jackson
Baldwin Calvin T. solicitor American Flag, dwl S s Perry bet Fourth and Fifth
Baldwin Charles H. (C. Adolphe Low & Co.) U. S. N. res Mare Island
Baldwin Charles M. teamster with Grant, Averell & Co. 44 Sacramento
Baldwin Daniel P. pattern maker, dwl 507 Market
Baldwin Edwin, clerk, dwl 115 Dupont
Baldwin E. J. (widow) dwl 303 Third
Baldwin Elias J. dwl 410 Geary
Baldwin Elihu F. mining, dwl SE cor Fell and Van Ness Avenue
Baldwin Hiram S. physician, office 612 Clay, dwl 609 Sutter

Baldwin James, bar tender with William Worford, dwl 106 Pacific
Baldwin Jeremiah, distiller with J. Dows & Co. dwl E s Florida nr Eighteenth
Baldwin Lloyd, attorney at law, office 10 Montgomery Block, dwl 930 Clay
Baldwin Lucinda N. (widow) dwl 311 Clementina
Baldwin Mary (widow) furnished rooms, 812 Sac
Baldwin M. M. & Co. watch makers and jewelers, 311 Montgomery, dwl 524 O'Farrell
Baldwin Nellie S. Miss, teacher, Union Street Primary School, dwl 403 Union
Baldwin Orville D. confectionery and fruit, 418 Third
Baldwin Otis F. dwl 1335 Pacific
Baldwin S. physician, dwl Oriental Hotel
Baldwin Thomas J. captain schooner Louisa Harker, dwl 356 Third
Baldwin Thomas John, calker, dwl 317 Beale
Baldwin William, ship carpenter, dwl N s Crook bet Townsend and Brannan
Baldwin W. S. Miss, assistant Union Grammar School, dwl 403 Union
Bale James, waiter, U. S. Restaurant
Balfrey Michael, shoe maker with Thomas Healy, dwl 562 Bryant
Balke (William) & Titjen (Henry) groceries and li or , SW cor Ritch and Brannan, dwl 310 Ritch s
Ball Albert, physician, office Government House, cor Washington and Sansom, dwl 717 Clay
Ball Charles, with P. Riley & Co. dwl N s Howard bet First and Second
Ball Charles T. cook, dwl 1016 Montgomery
Ball David H. book binder and paper ruler, 406 Clay, dwl 318 Ritch
Ball Edward, with J. Hirth & Co. dwl 538 Com
Ball Gabriel, milk wagon, San Bruno Road nr Bay View
Ball George A. book keeper with Buswell & Co. dwl 512 Stockton
Ball John, seaman, dwl 12 Commercial
Ball John M. policeman, City Hall, dwl 6 Moss nr Howard
Ball Martha S. Mrs. dress maker, dwl 717 Clay
Ball Randolph D. ship carpenter, dwl 16 Frederick
Ball Richard D. ship carpenter with John G. North Potrero
Ball Thomas, compositor, News Letter, dwl 217 Post
Ballard Charles, Nicaragua Lodgings, SE cor Commercial and Leidesdorff
BALLARD (Duane) & HALL (Isaac R.) forwarding and commission merchants, 224 Clay, dwl 1006 Bush
Ballard George, painter with W. Worthington, dwl 179 Minna
Ballard John, carpenter, dwl Bailey House
Ballard Joseph H. discharging clerk, dwl 715 Bush
Ballaw John, laborer, dwl W s Ohio bet Pacific and Broadway
Ballenberg Nathan, musician, dwl 735 Pine
BALLENTINE JAMES, carpenter and builder, office NE cor Sansom and Halleck, dwl W s Ninth bet Market and Mission
Ballentine John P. brick mason, dwl N s Jessie nr Ninth
Balley E. J. clerk with Forbes Brothers & Co. dwl NE cor South Park and Third
Ballhaus Christian, boot maker, dwl 417 Pacific
Ballhouse Frederick, gardener, dwl W s Leavenworth bet Greenwich and Lombard
Ballinger Andrew, laborer, dwl E s Gilbert bet Bryant and Brannan
Ballinger Patrick (Whelan & B.) dwl E s Gilbert bet Bryant and Brannan
Ballinger Peter, liquor saloon, 545 California
Ballinger William M. printer, dwl S s Francisco bet Kearny and Dupont

Ballou Emerson, cook, Seymour House, 24 Sansom
Ballou S. A. Capt. Commissary Subsistence U. S. A. C. V. office 208 Sansom, dwl 433 Tehama
Balmer Metia (widow) dwl 444 Natoma
Baloun J. L. (Bergholte & B.) dwl 914 Clay
Balowley Guisepe, butcher with Eugene Peguillan & Bro. dwl SW cor Utah and Sixteenth
Baltimore G. & S. M. Co. office 33 Montgomery Block
Baltz Peter (Deuvell & Co.) dwl 627 Broadway
Balzer C. A. (Ziel, Bertheau & Co.) res Hamburg
Balzer C. Henry, clerk with Ziel, Bertheau & Co. dwl 354 Brannan
Bambauer Carrie Miss, domestic, 424 Post
BAMBER JOHN & CO. (C. E. Driscoll and R. L. Taylor) Contra Costa Express, 719 Davis, dwl 928 Montgomery
Bamber Joseph J. with John Bamber & Co. 719 Davis
Bamber W. F. cook, dwl Hall Court
Bamley Fred. spinner, Mission Woolen Mills
Bancroft Albert L. (H. H. Bancroft & Co.) dwl S s Cal bet Franklin and Lafayette Avenue
Bancroft C. A. jr. with H. H. Bancroft & Co. dwl W s Franklin bet Pine and California
Bancroft C. E. dwl W s Franklin bet Cal and Pine
BANCROFT H. H. & CO. (Albert L. Bancroft) importing booksellers and stationers, 609 Montgomery, dwl S s Cal bet Franklin and Lafayette Avenue
Banderen Honore, employé Metropolitan Restaurant, 715 Montgomery
BANDMANN (Julius) NIELSEN (H.) & CO. importers and commission merchants, 210 Front, dwl 514 Lombard
Banfield John F. ship carpenter, dwl 732 Harrison
Bangle Edward, salesman, 509 Sansom, dwl 713 Bush, rear
BANK BRITISH COLUMBIA, James D. Walker, manager, office 412 California
BANK BRITISH NORTH AMERICA, Grain & Sutherland, agents, office 411 and 413 California
BANK CALIFORNIA, SW corner Washington and Battery; after first July, 1866, NW cor California and Sansom
BANK EXCHANGE, George F. Parker proprietor, SE cor Montgomery and Washington
Bank Joseph, billiard maker with M. E. Hughes, dwl 27 St. Mark Place
Banks G. S. & Co. National Livery Stable, 577 Market
Banks James, fireman, stm Washoe, dwl NE cor California and Davis
Banks James, superintendent Lake Honda, Spring Valley W. W. dwl Lake Honda
Banks James, waiter, City Front House, 625 Davis
Banks James, waterman, dwl 13 William
BANKS (Thomas C.) & CO. bankers, 513 Montgomery cor Commercial, dwl 724 California
Banks William, comforter manufacturer, 402 Sacramento, dwl 1001 Mason
Bauman Caroline Miss, domestic, 431 Pine
Bannan John, express wagon, dwl 512 Green
Bannerot Eugene, machinist with L. P. Garem, dwl 234 Jessie
Bannett Harris, boarding, 532 Commercial
Banning John, inspector, Custom House, dwl Oriental Hotel
Bannon Ann Miss, domestic, dwl 1707 Powell
Bannon Catharine Miss, domestic, dwl 1120 Powell
Bannon Edward, drayman with Treadwell & Co. dwl 204 Battery
Bannon Francis, confectioner with Rathbun & Co. 430 Sansom
Bannon P. laborer, Spring Valley Water Works
Bannon Philip, laborer, dwl 308 Minna, rear
Baptiste Jean, vegetable garden, Hunter's Pt. Road
Baptiste Mattoni, laborer with B. Bonnet & Co

Baque P. tailor with Eugene Boucher
Bar David, merchant, dwl 1620 Powell
Bar Jacob, butcher with W. Smith, dwl Potrero Avenue
Baraty François, butcher, 7 Clay Street Market, dwl 237 Stevenson
Barba Joseph, butcher, dwl 1202 Dupont
Barbara Ricardo, hair dressing saloon, 538 Com
Barbat John, physician, dwl 910 Pacific
Barber.Augustine Miss, dwl 431 Sutter
Barber Charles J. (Fisk & B.) dwl NE cor Howard and Fourth
Barber Elizabeth (widow) dwl 109 Montgomery
Barber Enos W. (Lawton & Co.) dwl 741 Market
Barber John A. (colored) plasterer, dwl 1030 Pacific
Barber Mary E. Miss, dwl 122 Geary
Barber Noyes, with Yates & Stevens, dwl Clay-Street House
Barber P. J. builder, dwl 8 s Columbia bet Guerrero and Dolores
Barber Richard (col'd) mining stocks, dwl SW cor Clay and Kearny
Barber Thomas H. boatman, dwl 1222 Pacific
Barber William (Doyle & B.) attorney at law, office 9–11 Wells Bdg 605 Clay, dwl 321 Geary
Barber William, blacksmith, 118 Bush, dwl 5 Calhoun
Barber William, boarding, 215 Broadway
Barber William M. blacksmith, dwl 5 Calhoun
Barbero Angello, laborer, dwl Union Place
Barbetto Frederico, fisherman, 38 Italian Fish Mkt
Barbi Michel, workman with Bergerot & Co. dwl NW cor Sixteenth and Rhode Island
Barbier Andrew, French Laundry, 841 Clay
Barbier Armand, local policeman, dwl 216 Stockton
Barbier Ennis (widow) dress maker, dwl 614 Cal
Barbier Louis, cook, Union Club Rooms
Barbiere Joseph, watchman, steamer Josie, McNear
Barchi C. Rev., S.J. prefect, St. Ignatius' College, S s Market bet Fourth and Fifth
Barciarini Joseph, tinsmith, dwl W s Pacific Alley
BARCKHAUSEN JULIUS, agent German General Benevolent Soc'y, office 625 Merchant, dwl 8 Louisa
Barckley Robert, teamster, dwl 606 Third
Barclay David, laborer, C. H. dwl 836 Union
Barclay J. seaman, steamer Senator
Barclay Robert H. wheelright with Kimball & Co. dwl 902 Market
Barde Constance Mme. millinery, 928 Dupont
BARDE W. L. D. attorney at law, office 604 Merchant, dwl 452 Jessie
Bardeau Paul, tailor, dwl SW cor Dupont and Bdwy
Bardellini Angelo & Co. firshermen, 50 Italian Fish Market, dwl 109 Washington
BARDENHAGEN (Mengels) & CO. (William Schmeelk) groceries and liquors, NE cor Folsom and Sixth
Bardenweiper C. P. drayman, 212 Front, dwl Bitter's Hotel
Bardenweiper D. C. drayman, dwl NW cor Kearny and Jackson
Bardon Briget (widow) dwl 148 Minna
Bardwell (J. L.) & Co. steam bag manufacturer, 105 Clay
Bareis Adolph, butcher, dwl 1202 Dupont
Barer Edward, tailor with Julius Tammeyer, 325 Bush
Baretto Lewis, cook, 20 Sansom
Barfield Martin, miner, dwl 523 Broadway
Bargion M. machinist, dwl Everett bet Third and Fourth
Bargion Peter, machinist and draftsman, San Francisco Iron Works, dwl 108 First
Bargon Martin, tailor, 409 Bush
Bargones Leonardo, drayman with Pascal Dubedat & Co. dwl 8 s Francisco bet Mason and Taylor
Baright George P. carpenter, dwl 120 Natoma
Baright Samuel, carpenter, dwl 120 Natoma

Baringer Peter, carpenter, dwl op King bet Third and Fourth
Bark John, laborer with Louis Ancenbofer
Barkeloo John, real estate, 705 Montgomery, dwl 127 Montgomery
Barker Abel P. policeman, City Hall, and lodgings 39 Second
Barker Abner H. office 708 Montgomery room 3, dwl 14 Kearny
Barker Benjamin F. carpenter, 35 Webb
Barker Ellen M. Miss, assistant, Washington Grammar School, dwl cor Chestnut and Leavenworth
Barker Erastus H. dwl 912½ Sacramento
Barker Frank, carpenter, dwl E s Central Place nr Pine
Barker Frederick, teamster, Pier 3 Stewart, dwl SW cor Oak and Franklin
Barker Grace (widow) dwl SE corner Folsom and Eleventh
Barker Hawley, workman, and dwl San Francisco Cordage Factory
Barker Isaac jr. (Colby & B.) dwl W s Howard bet Eighteenth and Nineteenth
Barker John, dwl Ninth nr Bryant
Barker Joshua, book keeper with J. H. Coghill & Co. dwl 607 Folsom
Barker Stephen, machinist, Vulcan Iron Works, dwl 26 Russ
Barker Thomas, brick layer, dwl 56 Stevenson
Barker T. L. office NW cor Front and Clay, dwl Cosmopolitan Hotel
Barker William, maker, cor Clay and Mason
Barker William F. carpenter, dwl 633 Market
Barker Young W. house and sign painter, 212 Fourth
Barkhans D. (F. W. & D. B.) dwl 10 Turk bet Mason and Taylor
BARKHAUS F. W. & D. German book sellers and importers, 321 Kearny, dwl Ashburton Place
Barkley Andrew J. (M. D. Carr & Co.) dwl 1016 Pine
Barkley James W. printer, dwl 1016 Pine
Barkley Johanna Mrs. domestic, 14 Fifth
Barkley John, apprentice, Pacific Foundry, dwl 349 Minna
Barkley J. V. Miss, assistant, Spring Valley Grammar School, dwl Pacific bet Hyde and Larkin
Barkley William, wood dealer, dwl 1426 Pacific
Barkman Richard H. clerk, dwl cor Mission and Stewart
Barlage Henry, cabinet maker with J. Peirce, dwl 14 Virginia
Barlow Charles, dwl W s First Avenue bet Fifteenth and Sixteenth
Barlow Elisha L. machinist, dwl S s Mission Creek, N Brannan Street Bridge
Barlow Luke B. molder, dwl W s Beale bet Market and Mission
Barlow Samuel, handcartman, cor Jackson and Davis, dwl 214 Commercial
Barlow Susan Miss, domestic with W. O. Andrews, E s Second Av bet Sixteenth and Seventeenth
Barman Charles, tinsmith, dwl 624 Commercial
Barman Jonas, dwl San Bruno Road, 3½ miles from City Hall
Barnan F. express wagon, cor Broadway and Front
Barnard Alfred F. carpenter with Stevens & Rider, dwl 118 O'Farrell
Barnard Chauncey jr. clerk with William T. Coleman & Co. dwl 1014 Stockton
Barnard Edward, ship carpenter, dwl Summer Street House
Barnard Frank, secretary Black Diamond Coal Co. and accountant with B. H. Ramsdell, dwl 23 Hawthorne
Barnard George, drayman with Thomas H. Selby & Co. dwl 114 William
Barnard Isaac D. real estate and intelligence office, 410 Montgomery, dwl Cosmopolitan Hotel
Barnard Mary Mrs. (widow) dwl 149 Shipley

Barnard M. S. stevedore, dwl 145 Silver
Barnard Thomas G. contractor, dwl 23 Hawthorne
Barnat Isaac, express wagon, cor Washington and Sansom
Barnes Alexander, mason, San Francisco Gas Co. dwl Minna Place
Barnes B. tailor, dwl 720 Front
Barnes Charles, tailor with M. Brandhofer, dwl 521 Dupont
Barnes Charles A. plasterer, dwl 415 Stevenson
Barnes, Daniel, carpenter, dwl 5 Hardie Place
Barnes E. D. collector, dwl 532 Commercial
Barnes George Ed. dwl American Exchange Hotel
Barnes George W. carpenter, dwl S s Clay bet Jones and Leavenworth
Barnes Harvey S. farmer, dwl Old San José Road, 6 miles from City Hall
Barnes Monroe, tinsmith with Taylor & Iredale
Barnes William, carpenter, dwl 509 Broadway
Barnes William jr. carpenter, 509 Broadway
Barnes William H. L. *(Casserly & B.)* attorney at law, office 436 California, dwl 30 Laurel Place
Barnett Annie E. Miss, dwl 60 Everett
Barnett B. P. *(Samuel Appel & Co.)*, dwl 322 Com
Barnett Edward, deck hand, steamer Yosemite
Barnett Hannah, domestic, 255 Stevenson
Barnett Isaac *(Goldstone, Barnett & Co.)* dwl 113 Geary
Barnett J. dwl What Cheer House
Barnett J. & Co. *(Joseph Barnett)* clothing, Virginia City, office 314 California, dwl 333 Jessie
Barnett John, baker, SE cor Fourth and Jessie, dwl 264 Stevenson
Barnett Joseph *(J. Barnett & Co.)* res Virginia City
Barnett Joseph, peddler, dwl E s Carlos Place
Barnett Joseph P. oilcloth manuf, dwl 25 Stone
Barnett Julius, clothing, dwl 333 Jessie
Barnett N. W. laborer with Murray & Noble
Barnett Samuel, merchant tailor, dwl 349 Jessie
Barnett Thomas *(Goldstone, Barnett & Co.)* dwl 425 Fourth
Barnett Wolfe, clock maker, dwl W s Gaven nr Filbert
Barney Aurelius, express wagon, 911 Market
Barney David G. porter Howard Warehouse, dwl 1409 Stockton
Barney Getrudes Senora, dwl 17 St. Ann
Barnhisel Epenetus R. newspaper carrier, 609 Market, dwl 415 Pine
Barnister Frederick, dwl 32 Stewart
Barnum William R. clerk with Young & Co. dwl 809 Stockton
Barnstead Thomas S. junk, 113 Com, dwl 26 Jessie
Barnstin G. fruit dealer, 235 Third
Barnum's Restaurant, L. Dingeon proprietor, 621 and 623 Commercial
Baron Victorine Mme. furnished rooms, NE cor Dupont and Jackson
Barquin François, tailor, dwl S s Market bet Sixth and Seventh
Barr Charles, foreman blacksmith, Vulcan Iron Works, dwl SW cor Harrison and Seventh
Barr D. C. seaman, bds 7 Washington
Barr Hannah Miss, domestic, dwl 614 Pine
Barr Jane, domestic with W. L. Underwood, NE cor McAllister and Fillmore
Barr John, mechanic, San Francisco Gas Co
Barr John D. umbrella and parasol manufacturer, 625 Mission
Barr Neil, clk Cal. Steam Nav. Co. dwl 146 Second
Barr Niel, foreman molder Vulcan Iron Works, dwl 125 Fourth
Barr Robert B. asphaltum roofer, dwl 24 Hunt
Barr William, dwl What Cheer House
Barr William H. boatman, Vallejo Wharf, dwl 312 Green
BARRA *(Ezekiel I.)* & GALVIN *(Jeremiah G.)* importers New England rum, 118 First cor Minna, dwl 4 Minna

Barraclough J. & Co. *(George Lauder)* hay, grain, and feed, 39 Clay
Barraco Andrew, express wagon, cor Sansom and Washington
Barraillac Charles, basket maker with Victor Navelet, 221 Leidesdorff
Barrasch Henry, upholsterer, dwl 323 Pine
Barra's Hall, E. I. Barra proprietor, 116 First
Barraud C. L. steward with C. F. Cazotte
Barrel Mary Mrs. dwl 134 Third
Barrell Samuel, with A. H. Lissak jr. dwl E side Stockton nr Pacific
Barrera Antoine, waiter, 546 Clay, dwl Mansion House
BARRETT & SHERWOOD *(Robert Sherwood successor)* importers and dealers watches, diamonds, jewelry, etc. 517 Montgomery
Barrett Abraham, boots and shoes, dwl 528 Pacific
Barrett Alfred, watch maker, 33 Second
Barrett Edward, with Martin Kedon, dwl Manhattan House
Barrett Edward, bar keeper, NW cor Fourth and Folsom
Barrett Edward, boot maker, dwl SW cor Market and Second
Barrett Edward, helper, Union Foundry, dwl 13 Clementina
Barrett Edward, laborer, dwl 22 Clementina
Barrett Edward, laborer, dwl 7 Bay State Row
Barrett Francis, carpenter, dwl Hubbard nr Howard
Barrett George, laborer, dwl 735 Green
Barrett Henry, broker, dwl 639 Market
Barrett Henry, clothing, dwl 528 Pacific
Barrett Henry S. laborer with Stephen S. Tilton
Barrett Horace T. clerk, 309 Clay, dwl 129 Third
Barrett James, dwl N s Seventeenth bet Guerrero and Dolores
Barrett James, apprentice, Pacific Foundry
Barrett James, butcher, dwl NW cor Sixth and Stevenson
Barrett James, clerk, Portland Iron Works, dwl 228 Minna
Barrett James, laborer, dwl 56 Stevenson
Barrett James, painter with John Duff, dwl 2 Rousch
Barrett James, porter, 641 Washington
Barrett James, real estate agent, 420 Montgomery, dwl Seventeenth bet Guerrero and Dolores
Barrett Johanna (widow) dwl W s Mary Lane nr Berry
Barrett John, carrier, Daily Examiner, dwl What Cheer House
Barrett John, conductor, North Beach & M. R. R. Co
Barrett Maggie L. Miss, domestic, dwl 728 Bush
Barrett Margaret Mrs. dwl S s Sacramento bet Davis and Drumm
Barrett Maria Miss, furnished rooms, 1206 Stockton
Barrett Mary (widow) dwl 425 Stevenson
Barrett Michael, boiler maker, Pacific Foundry, dwl 228 Minna
Barrett Michael, ship carpenter, dwl S s Fulton nr Laguna, Hayes Valley
Barrett M. L. book keeper, dwl 54 First
Barrett Patrick, butcher, NE cor Ritch and Harrison
Barrett Patrick, carrier, Evening Bulletin, dwl 166 Minna
Barrett Richard, with Reynolds & Murray, NW cor Clay and Davis
Barrett Richard, pressman with George W. Stevens & Co
Barrett Robert, brick molder, dwl Gilbert bet Bryant and Brannan
Barrett Robert, laborer, dwl E s Gilbert bet Bryant and Brannan
Barrett Simon, tailor with Lesser & Leszynsky, 638 Sacramento
Barrett William, molder, dwl St. Mark Place

Barrett William G. cashier S. F. Gas Co. dwl 607 Howard

Barrett Wm. clerk, NE cor Howard and Third

Barrette Mary E. (widow) teacher music and languages. dwl 12 Stockton

Barretto Pietro, fisherman, 37 Italian Fish Market

Barrigan Philip, with Reynolds, Howell & Ford, dwl Natoma nr Fifth

Barringer F. fireman, stm Petaluma

Barrington William B. store keeper with Dickson, DeWolf & Co. dwl N s Broadway nr Kearny

Barris H. D. Philadelphia Market, 904 Stockton

Barrity Francis, fireman, stm Sacramento

BARROILHET HENRY *(Belloc Freres)* and consul for Peru, office 535 Clay

Barron Cornelius, steward, American Exchange

Barron Cornelius J. painter and grainer, 644 Market

Barron Edward, dwl 829 Mission

Barron Edward, book keeper, dwl NE cor Dupont and Jackson

Barron Henry, express wagon, cor Pine and Montgomery, dwl 319 Bush

Barron James, captain steamer Poco Tiempo, dwl 232 O'Farrell

Barron James C. painter, dwl 79 Everett

Barron John, house painter, dwl SW cor Kearny and Francisco

Barron Joseph,*(Barron & Co.)* dwl 926 Clay

Barron M. with S. S. Culverwell, 29 Fremont

Barron M. D. drayman, Wells, Fargo & Co. dwl 148 Minna

Barron Michael, carpenter, dwl SE cor Bush and Powell

BARRON *(William E.)* & CO. *(Joseph Barron and Thomas Bell)* commission merchants, office NE cor Montgomery and Jackson, dwl 606 Stockton

Barrow Charles W. with W. R. Thomas, 24 Occidental Market, dwl 417 Howard

Barrows William, laborer, with Ackerson & Russ, dwl 40 Natoma

Barrs B. D. express wagon, dwl Clementina bet Second and Third

Barrus Daniel, jeweler with R. B. Gray & Co. dwl 813 Stockton

Barry Bridget, domestic, 256 Fourth

Barry Catherine (widow) dwl 114 William

Barry Charles E. clerk with Richard Tobin, dwl NW cor Taylor and Bernard

Barry David, laborer, dwl 1 Valparaiso

Barry David, laborer, dwl SW cor Mission and Fifth

Barry David, sail maker, dwl SE cor Fifth and Mission

Barry Edward, milk ranch, San Bruno Road 3¼ miles from City Hall

Barry Edward, mining secretary, office 302 Mont

Barry Ellen, domestic, 215 Minna

Barry Ellen Miss, with S. Reinstein, dwl 154 Clara

Barry George, laborer, dwl 59 Everett

Barry H. Mrs. furnished rooms, 200 Stockton

Barry H. J. dwl 200 Stockton

Barry Hannah (widow) dwl 810 Greenwich

Barry J. S.J. St. Ignatius College, S s Market bet Fourth and Fifth

Barry James, wheelwright with Nelson & Doble, dwl 756 Howard

Barry James H. laborer, dwl 22 Rousch

Barry James J. cook, Miners' Restaurant, dwl cor Fifth and Minna

Barry *(John)* & Kennedy *(J. F.)* house and sign painters, 4 Summer

Barry John, dwl S s Stevenson nr Seventh

Barry John, apprentice, Golden State Iron Works, dwl 60 Tehama

Barry John, carpenter, dwl N s Pine bet Leavenworth and Hyde

Barry John, equestrian, Wilson's Circus, dwl Brooklyn Hotel

Barry John, molder, Fulton Foundry, dwl 60 Tehama

Barry John, painter, dwl W s Eighth bet Howard and Clementina

Barry John, laborer, dwl 60 Tehama

Barry John, laborer, dwl 16 Ecker

Barry John, miner, dwl 412 Folsom

Barry John H. delivery clerk, California State Telegraph Co. 507 Montgomery, dwl 752 Howard

Barry John T. foreman Monitor, dwl NE cor Jackson and Montgomery

Barry J. W. machinist, Union Foundry, dwl 12 Perry

Barry Martin, tailor, dwl 227 Post

Barry Mary Miss, domestic, dwl 843 Clay

Barry Mary (widow) dwl 553 Howard

Barry M. C. boot maker, E s Cemetery Avenue bet Sutter and Post

Barry Michael, dwl 35 Valparaiso

Barry Michael, carpenter, dwl 38 Natoma

Barry Michael, miner, bds Franklin Hotel, SE cor Sansom and Pacific

Barry Patrick, laborer, dwl 10 Hunt

Barry P. Oliver, clerk, County Recorder's Office, dwl 923 Pacific

Barry Richard, workman S. F. & Pacific Sugar Co. dwl Harrison nr Eighth

Barry Robt. F. rope maker, dwl N s Bryant bet Sixth and Seventh

Barry Robert M. tailor, Trinity nr Sutter

BARRY *(Theodore A.)* & PATTEN *(Benjamin A.)* wines and liquors, Union Building, 413 Montgomery, dwl 709 Geary

Barry Theresa (widow) music teacher, dwl 28 Ritch

Barry Thomas, butcher with Lux & Miller, dwl cor Ninth and Braunau

Barry Thomas, express wagon, cor Leid and Cal

Barry Thomas, foreman with Edward J. Quirk

Barry Thomas, laborer, dwl Dolores Hall, W s Valencia nr Sixteenth

Barry Thomas, laborer, dwl SW cor Kearny and Bay

Barry Thomas, workman with John Henry, dwl Dolores Hall

Barry William, Eureka Typographical Union, 625 Merchant

Barry William, actor, Maguire's Opera House, dwl 845 Dupont

Barry William, laborer, dwl 458 Natoma

Barry William B. with Philip A. Roach, dwl 200 Stockton

Barry William I. compositor, Alta California, dwl 1515 Leavenworth nr Pacific

Barry Wm. hackman, dwl Jessie bet Third and Fourth

BARSTOW ALFRED *(D. P. & A. Barstow)* attorney at law, notary public, and commissioner of deeds, office 24 Montgomery Block, dwl 81 Montgomery Block

BARSTOW D. P. & A. attorneys at law, office 23 and 24 Montgomery Block, res Oakland

BARSTOW GEORGE, attorney at law, office 8 and 9 Donohoe, Kelly & Co.'s Building, SE cor Mont and Sacramento, dwl Lick House

Barstow Simon F. compositor, Alta California, dwl 510 Taylor

Bartel Henrietta *(Mrs. Synon & Sister)* 318½ Third

Bartell Catharine Miss, domestic, dwl 1607 Powell

Bartelle Mary Miss, domestic, dwl 624 Green

Bartels Conrad, musician, dwl 1518 Powell, rear

Bartels George C. clerk, dwl 61 Second

Barter Augusta B. (widow) dress maker, 715 How

Barters Johanna Miss, domestic, 1109 Pine

Bartet Jean Baptiste Mde. French teacher, dwl 715 Green

Bartet Jean Baptiste, dwl 715 Green

Bartet William, furnished rooms, NW cor Broadway and Kearny

Barthold Eliza (widow) dwl 33 Natoma
Bartholomea John, employer, Bay Sugar Refinery, dwl 813 Battery
Bartholomew Henry G. porter with C. H. Strybing, dwl SW cor Ritch and Bryant
Bartholomew Josephine Mrs. dress maker, dwl 1006 Pacific
Barthrop Edward, canvasser, dwl SW cor Sacramento and Leavenworth
Bartlett B. L. assistant assessor U. S. Int. Rev. NW cor Bat and Com, dwl American Exchange
Bartlett Charles, dwl 736 Market
Bartlett Charles H. dwl 1018 Washington
Bartlett Charles H. paper hanger, dwl 12 Everett
Bartlett Columbus *(W. & C. Bartlett)* attorney at law, office 4 Odd Fellows' Hall, res Oakland
Bartlett Earl, attorney at law, office 34 Montgomery Block, dwl 212 Green
Bartlett Elizabeth (widow) dwl op King bet Third and Fourth
Bartlett Frank A. shipping clerk, dwl cor Natoma and Jane, 1 Dixon's Block
Bartlett George W. laborer, dwl 28 Washington
Bartlett H. A. workman with Casebolt & Co
Bartlett J. C. teamster, dwl 1034 Market
Bartlett J. D. book keeper with J. C. Johnson & Co. dwl 566 Howard
Bartlett Job B. drayman Commercial Mills, dwl 1034 Market
Bartlett John, produce, dwl 200 Stockton
Bartlett Jonathan D. house and sign painter, W s Dolores op Sixteenth, Mission Dolores, dwl NE cor Seventeenth and Church
Bartlett Joseph, drayman, 222 Sutter
Bartlett Pliny *(Bovee, Hallett, B. & Dalton)* 318 Pine, dwl 253 Tehama bet Third and Fourth
Bartlett R. K. ship carpenter, res Oakland
Bartlett Robert, groom, dwl 342 Brannan
Bartlett Robert B. porter with Macondray & Co. 206 Sansom
BARTLETT W. & C. attorneys at law, office 4 Odd Fellows' Hall, 325 Mont, dwl 218 Bush
Bartlett William, hog butcher with Peter Schinkel, dwl cor Tenth and Bryant
Bartlett William C. Rev. editor Pacific, office 536 Clay, res Redwood City
Bartley Kate Miss, domestic, dwl 1021 Washington
Bartling *(William)* & Kimball *(Henry)* book binders, 505 Clay cor Sansom, dwl 10 Clarence Place nr Townsend
Bartman Anthony, carpenter, dwl 506 Union
Bartman Charles, dwl 506 Union
Bartman Ferdinand, carpenter, dwl 522 Filbert, rear
Bartman John C. musician, dwl 506 Union
Barto Cornelius, fruits, 1220 Powell
Barton B. F. & Co. *(Edward Carroll)* proprietors Pioneer Salt Works, depôt 211 and 213 Sacramento, dwl Stevenson House
Barton Charles *(Dexter, Lambert & Co.)* res Boston
Barton E. G. mining, dwl 109 Ellis
Barton J. A. machinist, Vulcan Iron Works,
BARTON *(John)* & BROTHER, proprietors Pacific Salt Works, 218 Sacramento, dwl 15 Laurel Place
Barton Joshua H. with H. W. Bragg & Co. dwl 54 Third
Barton Nancy Mrs. dwl 181 Jessie
Barton P. (widow) silk and woolen dyeing, 33 Kearny
Barton Phineas W. clerk, Pacific Salt Works, dwl 15 Laurel Place
Barton Robert (col'd) whitewasher, dwl 8 Pennsylvania Avenue
Barton Sarah Miss, domestic, 608 Market
Barton William, painter, dwl N s Union bet Hyde and Larkin
Barton William, stevedore, dwl W s Stockton nr Francisco
Bartty John, handcartman, cor Wash and Mont

Baruth Solomon *(Julius Kron & Co.)* dwl 763 Clay
Basan Libordeo, dwl 514 Pacific
Buscombe Annie Miss, dress making, 912 Market
Bascus Joseph, express wagon, cor Broadway and Dupont
Baselina Alexander, nurse, City and County Hospital
BASHAM F. & SON *(Frederick Basham)* modelers and plaster workers, 28 Geary, dwl 936 Folsom
Basham Frederick *(F. Basham & Son)* dwl 936 Folsom
Baskerville R. D. hair dressing saloon, 305 Davis, dwl 342 Fifth
Basler George A. pa e , dwl 274 Tehama
Bass Chester (col'd) shaving saloon, 925 Kearny, dwl W s Virginia nr Pacific
Bass Thomas J. drayman with Cameron, Whittier & Co. dwl 526 O'Farrell
Basse Thomas *(Eggers & Co.)* dwl Sherman nr Folsom
Bassett Alonzo, stone cutter with Charles B. Grant, dwl 415 Vallejo
Bassett Charles F. accountant, 415 Davis, dwl N s Mission nr Twelfth
Bassett John, carpenter, dwl with P. L. Murphy, E s Howard bet Fifteenth and Sixteenth
BASSETT JOSEPH, wholesale flour and grain, 213 Clay, dwl 1108 Bush
Bassett Lewis, seaman, steamer Pacific
Bassett Martin, carpenter, dwl 446 Brannan
Bassett Nathaniel, dwl 420 Stevenson
Bassetti James, waiter, 512 Clay, dwl SE cor Washington and Powell
Basso Andrea, employé Brignardello, Macchiavello & Co. 706 Sansom
Bastable George, dwl 603 Pine
Bastheim Joseph *(Friedlander & B.)* 8 Mont
Bastian Philip, laborer, dwl W s Kearny bet Vallejo and Broadway
Bastiana Zeffero, cook, 515 Merchant
Baston Abner F. teamster with Miller & Hall, dwl 521 Howard
Batchelder C. M. Miss, dwl 638 Howard
Batchelder David F. manager Globe Hotel and local policeman, dwl SE cor Dupont and Pacific
Batchelder *(John R.)* & Andrews *(Asa)* carpenters and builders, Bryant Place
Batchelder Joseph M. shipping merchant, dwl 107 Powell
Batchelder Nathaniel, carpenter, dwl 737 Howard
Batchelder Nathaniel, local policeman, dwl 51 Second
Batchelder William H. porter, 213 Front, dwl Austin nr Polk
Batchelder, see Bachelder
BATCHELOR EDWARD P. attorney at law, office 9 Montgomery Block, dwl 811 Jackson
Bateman David, engineer, Saucileto Water Boat, dwl 329 Val-lejo
Bateman Henry C. book binder and Catholic bookseller, 202 Kearny, dwl 333 Bush
Bateman *(James)* & Phillips *(Edward)* shoe making, 219 Davis
Bateman Maria B. Miss, domestic, dwl 926 Jackson
Bateman M. C. Eagle Bakery, 45 Stevenson
Bateman Michael C. contractor City and County Hospital, dwl 8 s Pacific bet Gough and Octavia
BATEMAN WILLIAM A. milk depôt, 329½ Kearny, dwl 610 Bush
Bates Asher B. attorney at law, office Court Block, 636 Clay, dwl 115 Dupont nr Geary
Bates Catherine (widow) dwl 764 Harrison
Bates E. G. drayman, dwl Sansom nr Bush
BATES GEORGE, principal University School, N s Post bet Stockton and Powell, dwl 413 Brannan
Bates Gustavus E. drayman with David Hays & Co. 224 Sacramento

Bates Henry, miner, dwl 413 Brannan
Bates Henry, molder with Cock & Flynn, dwl Central Hotel
Bates John S. assistant U. S. boarding officer, office E s Davis nr Vallejo, dwl 529 Pine
Bates John W. *(Meeker, James & Co.)* res Marysville
BATES JOSEPH, stock broker, office 524 Montgomery, dwl 413 Brannan
Bates Philip, ship carpenter, dwl cor Mariposa and Indiana
Bates William, porter, dwl 7 Clementina
Bates William H. pattern maker, Union Foundry, dwl SW cor Minna and Jane
Bateson James H. tailor, dwl 7 Clementina
Bath *(Albert L.)* & Morrison *(John B.)* carriage makers, 118 Bush, dwl 29 Third
Bath John, carpenter, dwl 241 Minna
Batopilas Mining Co. office 811 Montgomery, A. Martinon, secretary
Batt Henry, jeweler, dwl 763 Mission
Battams William, salesman 112 Battery, dwl 29 Minna
Battarach André, with John Frarrac, E s Dolores nr Fifteenth
Batteaux Daniel, liquors, SW cor Kearny and St. Mark Place, dwl 114 Fourth
Batten George, steward, dwl St. Lawrence House
Batten Sampson, stone cutter, dwl 216 Ritch
Battermann Christopher C. workman, Pacific Brewery, dwl E s Hyde bet Clay and Washington
Battern William D. box maker with Hobbs, Gilmore & Co. dwl 547 Mission
Batties Sarah, American Laundry, dwl N s Pacific bet Montgomery and Sansom
Battiest José, waiter, dwl Lick House
Battista John, fruits, 235 Jackson
Battles John, waiter steamer Yosemite
Battles Luke, waiter, steamer Yosemite
Battles Winslow *(Bullard & B.)* dwl 731 Harrison
Battles W. Ward, contractor, dwl 652 Market
Batturs Edward T. book keeper with Wightman & Hardie, dwl 728 Howard
Baubeau Mad. (widow) dwl N s Minna nr Eighth
Bauch Peter G. ship and Custom House broker, 508 Battery, dwl 624 Lombard
Bauer August, gardener with Gottleib Fruhling Presidio
Bauer Charles, bar keeper, Harbor View House nr Presidio
Bauer Charles, waiter, dwl 716 Clay
Bauer Charles E. compositor, Morning Call
Bauer Charles H. F. laundryman, dwl 20 Langton
Bauer Edward, porter with Thomas Taylor & Co. dwl 18 Sansom
Bauer Emile *(White & B.)* dwl 824 Vallejo
Bauer G. A. miller, dwl 515 Market
Bauer George, waiter, 506 Montgomery, dwl 106 Montgomery Block
Bauer Henry, upholsterer, dwl 409 Stockton
Bauer Herman, gil , dwl 840 Clay
Bauer John, with dkr B. Thayer, dwl W s Mary Lane nr Berry
Bauer John, cooper, Mason's Brewery, dwl 631 Broadway
Bauer John, lager beer saloon, 47 Third, dwl 243 Minna, rear
BAUER JOHN A. *(F. Vietor)* drugs, medicines, chemicals, etc. 644 Washington
Bauer Mary (widow) dwl E s Dupont bet Francisco and Bay
Baufait Ernest, waiter, 647 Commercial, dwl 626 Cal
BAUGH THEODORE E. proprietor Merchants' Exchange 521 Clay, dwl 25 South Park
Baugh W. Washington, clerk with T. E. Baugh, 521 Clay, dwl 25 South Park
Baulsir Nimrod, block maker with Thomas F. Mitchell, dwl 1332 Washington
BAUM CHARLES, Custom House broker, 510 Battery opposite Custom House, dwl 1705 Powell

Baum George, printer, dwl 20 Mason
Baum Gustave, furniture, 919 Dupont
Baum J. express wagon, cor Battery and Sac
Baum Julius, clothing, 407 and 409 Commercial, and SE cor Com and Leidsdorff, dwl 517 Folsom
Baum Julius & Bro. *(Simon Baum)* clothing, 424 Montgomery, dwl 517 Folsom
Baum Louis, dwl 750 Howard
Baum Simon *(J. Baum & Bro.)* dwl 517 Folsom
Bauman George, tailor with J. R. Mead & Co. dwl Hartman Place
Baumann Mathias, seaman, bds 7 Washington
Baumann Sebastian, milkman, dwl 315 Bush
Baumann Sophie A. Miss, milliner, 40 Fourth
Baumeister Henry, carpenter, dwl 429 Sutter
Baumeister Herman, National Flour Mills, dwl 728 Folsom
BAUMEISTER JOHN & CO. *(George Pfuelb)* proprietors Bootz's Hotel, 435 Pine
Baumgardner E. M. Miss, assistant, Denman Grammar School, dwl 746 Howard
Baumgardner L. I. professor, St. Mary's College
Baumgardner Valentine *(Heerdink & Co.)* dwl 9 Front
Baumman John, musician, dwl 29 St. Mark Place
Baumont Joanna, liquors, 310 Pacific
Bann Mary Miss, assistant cook, Industrial School Old Ocean House Road
Bausch Jacob, boot and shoe maker, dwl SW cor Mason and Jackson
Bausman William, editor, dwl 321 Clementina
Baurhyte Robert H. first engineer steamer Yosemite, dwl 428 O'Farrell
Bauville August, waiter, Union Restaurant, dwl Stewart nr Folsom
Baux F. A. with J. B. Baux, dwl 367 Jessie
Baux Jean B. amalgamator, dwl 367 Jessie
Bavaria Brewery, 622 Vallejo
Bawa Charles, baker, dwl E s Agnes Lane nr Berry
Bawden William G. compositor, Sunday Mercury, dwl E s Dupont bet Post and Sutter
Bawla Louis, waiter, dwl SE corner Vallejo and Kearny
Baxter Annie T. Miss, domestic, dwl 1312 Powell
Baxter Charles E. clerk with Richards & McCracken, dwl 1109 Howard
Baxter Charles M. captain steamer Petaluma, res Petaluma
Baxter Daniel, employé, C. S. Navigation Co. dwl N s Alta bet Montgomery and Sansom
Baxter Edward H. clerk with Crane & Brigham, dwl 1109 Howard
Baxter Ethan A. clerk with Richards & McCracken, dwl 1109 Howard
Baxter Hall W. clerk with Crane & Brigham, dwl 1109 Howard
Baxter John T. carpenter, dwl N s Thirteenth nr Mission
Baxter Joseph G. lamp lighter, San Francisco Gas Co. dwl SW cor Grove and Franklin
Baxter Louisa L. (widow) dwl 1109 Howard
Baxter Mary (widow) dwl SE cor Front and Oregon
Baxter Mary A. Miss, domestic, dwl 818 Howard
Baxter Robert C. shipsmith with W. S. Phelps & Co. dwl Manhattan House
Baxter Samuel, seaman, dwl 132 Folsom
Baxter William H. assistant assessor, U. S. Internal Rev. NW cor Bat and Com. dwl 525 Howard
Baxter William R. waiter, dwl 253 Stewart
Bay City Laundry, 1140 Folsom
Bay of Monterey G. & S. M. Co. office 338 Mont
Bay Shore & Ft. Point Road Co. office 522 Clay
Bay State G. & S. M. Co. office 6 Montgomery Blk
Bay State House, Milo Robinson proprietor, NE cor Front and Sacramento
BAY SUGAR REFINERY, SW cor Battery and Union, office NE cor California and Front
BAY VIEW PARK, Bay View nr San Bruno Road, 5 miles from City Hall

BAY VIEW PARK STOCK ASSOCIATION ROOMS, Harter & Fitch proprietors, 219 Bush
Bay View Turnpike Co. office 528 Clay
Bay Warehouse, James C. King & Co. Sansom nr Lombard
Baye Henry, sailor, dwl 140 Stewart
Bayer Anthony J. baker with Swain & Brown, dwl W s Leroy Place bet Sacramento and Clay
Bayer Julius, express wagon, Dupont Alley nr Broadway
Bayerque Romain, with Pioche & Bayerque, dwl 806 Stockton
Bayhaut Dominique, dwl 1524 Stockton
Bayless Charles, driver, Central R. R. dwl SE cor Brannan and Seventh
Bayless Joseph, architect, 20 Montgomery, dwl Geneva nr Brannan
Bayless Thornton J. book keeper with William Meyer & Co. dwl Stevenson House
Bayless William H. architect, office 20 Montgomery, dwl E s Geneva nr Brannan
Bayley George B. deputy tax collector, City Hall, dwl 30 McAllister
Bayley M. F. photographic gallery, NE cor Kearny and Commercial, dwl 710 Pine
Bayley *(William F.)* & Cramer *(Charles L.)* photographic gallery, 618 Washington, dwl 118 Jones bet Pacific and Jackson
Bayley, see Bailey
Bayliss Thos. F. & Co. *(Joseph S. Cutler and David Sullivan)* proprietors Union Line Packets, office foot Commercial, res Petaluma
Bayly *(Charles A.)* & Tothill *(John)* apothecaries, 512 Kearny
Bayly George, mariner, dwl 32 Stewart
Bayly Mrs. nurse, dwl 163 Tehama
Bayn Christina Miss, domestic, 115 Eddy
Bays Henry, ship carpenter, dwl E s Crook bet Brannan and Townsend
Bayteste S. J. express wagon, Stockton nr Vallejo
Bazille August, butcher, N s Sixteenth nr Rhode Island
Bazille John, wholesale butcher, N s Sixteenth nr Rhode Island, and 29 and 30 Washington Mkt
Bazin Victoire, tailor, 445 Bush
Bazzi Edward, cook, SW cor California and Drumm
Bazzuro Frank, with Ossalino & Co. 524 Market
BEACH CHILION, books and stationery, 34 Montgomery, dwl 908 Broadway
Beach Eliza (widow) dwl 1020 Stockton
Beach George H. clerk with J. W. Brittan & Co. res Oakland
Beach Henry H. book keeper with R. G. Sneath, 408 Front, dwl 27½ Fourth
Beach Henry M. accountant with W. H. Richards & Co. dwl 514 Howard
Beach John C. clerk, Original House
Beach Joseph D. C. drayman with Dickinson & Gammans, dwl 207 Second
Beach Lewis, porter with J. C. Meussdorffer, dwl 3 White Place
BEADLE DONALD *(Bryant & B.)* dwl 515 Bush
Beakey David, tinsmith with J. E. Jorgensen, dwl 624 Commercial
Beakley Absolom, with Adam Cook, 226 Sutter
Beal John, carpenter, dwl Bailey House
Beal Samuel, upholstering, 527 California, dwl SE cor Mason and Eddy
Beals C. R. Mrs. assistant Union Grammar School, dwl 923 Powell
BEALS H. CHANNING, commercial editor Mercantile Gazette, office 536 Clay, dwl 726 Green
Beam Henry, marble cutter, dwl 1607 Leavenworth
Beamish John, shoe maker, dwl 152 First
Bean John, teamster with L. B. Garrison
Bean Moses T. mariner, dwl 519 Greenwich
Bean Redmon, stevedore, dwl 609 Market
Bean William, clerk, dwl 616 Mission

Bean William, machinist, dwl Bailey House
Beanny James, workman with John Henry, dwl Dolores Hall
Beans T. Ellard *(J. R. Whitney & Co.)* bds Lick House
Beanston George, messenger Board Education, 22 City Hall, dwl S s Greenwich nr Dupont
Beanston Peter, blacksmith with Pollard & Carvill, dwl S s Greenwich bet Dupont and Stockton
Beant J. H. express wagon, 751 Mission
Beard Adeline, domestic, dwl N s Greenwich bet Montgomery and Sansom
Beard Charles C. clerk, dwl 800 Howard
Beard George, longshoreman, dwl 1021 Battery
Beard George, Montezuma Saloon, 52 First, dwl 54 First
Beard John, laborer, dwl N s Townsend bet Third and Fourth
Beard Joseph R. broker, office 606 Merchant, dwl 800 Howard
Beard Mathew, helper with David Stoddart, dwl 116 Beale
Beardslee Cyrus W. carpenter, dwl SE cor Leavenworth and Washington
Beardsley *(James S.)* & Wolfe *(James E. jr.)* butter, cheese and eggs, 29 Occidental Market, dwl 633 Market
Beardsley John H. abstract clerk U. S. Branch Mint, dwl 1007 Bush
Bearing Charles, ship carpenter, dwl 439 First
Bearwald Benjamin, tinsmith, dwl 356 Jessie
Bearwald George, job wagon, cor California and Kearny, dwl 257 Minna
Bearwald Gustave, job wagon, 540 California, dwl Jessie nr Third
Bearwald Louis, carpenter, dwl 356 Jessie
Bearwald Tobias, cigars and tobacco, 714 Kearny, dwl 356 Jessie
Beath J. M. premium amalgamators, 311 Market
Beaton William, laborer, dwl cor Fillmore and Pacific
Beattie George, miller Golden Gate Mills, dwl 518 Dupont
Beattie Patrick, with Jos. Peirce, dwl 531 O'Farrell
Beatty James, laborer, dwl W s White Place near Bryant
Beatty John, drayman with Samuel Adams, dwl 509 Mason
Beatty John, waiter, Lick House
Beatty John J. painter, 122 Third
Beatty L. F. actor, Maguire's Opera House
Beatty Robert, White House, W s Mission bet Twenty-Third and Twenty-Fourth
Beatty Samuel G. *(Gunnison & B.)* searcher records, dwl SE cor Mason and Ellis
Beatty Wm. hostler, North Beach & M. R. R. Co
Beauchamp Joseph, furniture and repairing, 215 Second, dwl 155 Third
Beauharnais Sarah A. (widow) NE cor Dupont and Broadway
Beaujardin T. professor music, dwl 731 Broadway
Beaven W. hostler, Omnibus R. R. Co
Beaver George W. *(James Patrick & Co.)* dwl 927 Market
Beaver Samuel C. stamp clerk, office U. S. Internal Revenue, dwl 927 Market
Bec Bartheleny, dwl 1405 Stockton, rear
Bec Pascal, grinder, dwl S s Polk Alley
Becher Henry, cook, dwl 619 Mason
Becherer Charles F. local policeman, dwl NE cor Kearny and Broadway
Becherer Emilia Mrs. proprietress Mountain Lake House, 4 miles W Plaza
Beck A. G. teacher book keeping, office and dwl 116 Stevenson
Beck David L. broker, dwl 18 Stanly Place
Beck E. B. clerk, 205 Front, dwl 18 Stanly Place
Beck F. musician, S. F. Ind. Musical Club

Beck Frank E. S. physician and surgeon, 706 Montgomery, dwl 516 Sutter
Beck George, night clerk, Railroad House
Beck Henry, shoe maker, 320 Dupont
Beck Jacob, bricklayer, dwl 9 Hunt
Beck James G. painter, dwl Trinity nr Sutter
Beck John G. laborer, dwl E s Shotwell bet Nineteenth and Twentieth, rear
Beck Joseph P. broker, dwl 903 Pacific
Beck Nathaniel A. currier, Folsom bet Eighteenth and Nineteenth
Beck Peter, groceries and liquors, NE cor Mission and Beale
Beck Theodore, gas maker, dwl 716 Pacific
Becke Francis, upholsterer with Kennedy & Bell, dwl What Cheer House
BECKER BROTHERS *(B. Adolph and M. Rudolph E.)* cigars and tobacco, NE cor Montgomery and Clay and 714 Washington, dwl 808 California
Becker Caspar, laborer Bay Sugar Refinery, dwl S s Union bet Battery and Sansom
Becker Casper, carriage trimmer with R. S. Eells, dwl 434 Union bet Kearny and Dupont
Becker Christian, baker with Charles Schroth, 230 Kearny.
Becker Martin, clerk, NW cor Brannan and Sixth
Becker Michael, baker, Hamburg Bakery.
Becker M. Rudolph E. *(Becker Bros.)* dwl 808 Cal
Becker Nicholas, porter, 408 Clay, dwl cor Gough and O'Farrell
Becker Peter, baker with William Stohlmann, cor Dupont and St. Mark Place
Becker William, groceries and liquors, NE corner Green and Montgomery
Beckert Ernest, waiter, 424 Sacramento
Beckett Caroline A. Mrs. dwl 227 Pacific
Beckett Joseph, collar maker with Kreitz & Cosbie, dwl 66 First
Beckett Sarah A. Miss, domestic with G. W. Babcock, W s Folsom bet Sixteenth and Seventeenth
Beckford Daniel R. oculist, 731 Clay, dwl 778 Harrison
Beckitt Joseph, harness maker with W. F. Wilmot & Co. 315 Battery
Beckman *(Andrew)*, Aiken *(John)* & Co. *(William J. F. Douglass and John Prior)* sail makers, 516 Davis (up stairs) dwl 1 St. Mary Place
Beckman Charles, with Brennan & Co. dwl 6 Sutter
Beckman Frederick, armorer, 416 Commercial, dwl NW cor Grove and Van Ness Avenue
Beckmann John, clerk, SE cor Sixteenth and Mission
Beckwell E. S. carpenter, dwl 140 Stewart
Beckwell S. L. carpenter, dwl 140 Stewart
Beckwith C. B. dwl What Cheer House
Beckwith Charles, coachman with John P. Manrow
Beckwith Edward G. Rev. pastor Third Congregational Church, dwl E s Mission bet Fourteenth and Fifteenth
Beckwith Elliott S. boat builder with Joseph Gilman, dwl 138 Stewart
Beckwith James R. driver, North Beach & M. R. R. Co
Beckwith Seth L. boat builder with Joseph Gilman, 24 Commercial
Beconarne Frank, vegetable garden, nr Bay View Park
Bedell William, machinist, Vulcan Iron Works, dwl 213 Fremont
BEE HIVE BUILDING, M. Cannavan proprietor, NE cor Washington and Dupont
Bee Silver M. Co. (Reese River) office 404 Mont
Beebe James, musician, Wilson's Circus
Beebe Richard W. wheelwright, dwl NW cor Pine
Beebe William S. cooper, dwl 1125 Kearny and Sansom
Beebee R. F. pattern maker, Vulcan Iron Works, dwl 36 Battery

Beebee Robert M. tinsmith with Osgood & Stetson, dwl 36 Battery
Beec Frederick, shoe maker with George Burkhardt, dwl 4 Milton Place
Beeching M. janitor Washington School
Beeching Robert, blacksmith with J. R. Sims, dwl 1110 Pacific
Beedle Ira, painter, dwl 54 First
Beehan Edward, dwl Shotwell nr Sixteenth
Beekman Charles, porter, 206 Clay
Beer *(Frank)* & Co. *(Benedict Dworzazek)* Chicago Saloon, 547 California, dwl Lewis Place
Beer Gottlieb, book keeper, 226 Front, dwl 430 Greenwich
Beer Julius *(Weil & Co.)* res New York
Beers Barrit *(J. B. Beers & Son)* dwl 813 Bush
Beers Herbert M. shoe manufactory, 313 Pine, dwl 334 Union
BEERS J. B. & SON *(Barrit Beers)* dentists, office 127 Montgomery
Beers W. J. clairvoyant, office 645 Washington
Beettner John, pattern maker, dwl 45 Clementina
Beevan Isaac, job wagon, SW cor Pine and Kearny, dwl 8 s Union bet Polk and Larkin
Begeman *(C. F. Wm.)* & Bonn *(H.)* carriage painters, NE cor Mission and Ninth, dwl NE cor Dupont and Post
Beggs Harry, hook keeper with Webb & Holmies, dwl 59 South Park
Beggs James, assistant superintendent S. F. Gas Co. dwl 59 South Park
Beggs Patrick, baker with James Donnelly, 109 Sansom
Beggs Thomas, laborer, dwl 122 William
Beggs William W. office superintendent S. F. Gas Co. dwl 59 South Park
Begim Joseph B. employé H. Hazeltine & Co. dwl 613 Kearny
Begin Mary, furnished rooms, dwl 613 Kearny
Begley Catharine Miss, domestic, dwl 933 Sacramento
Begley Michael, molder, Miners' Foundry, dwl SW cor Sherman and Seventeenth
Beguhl Adolph, fresco painter, 223 Fourth
Behan Edward, dwl W s Shotwell bet Fifteenth and Sixteenth
Behan James, spinner. S. F. Pioneer W. Mills, dwl North Point bet Polk and Van Ness Avenue
Behen Fenton, dwl S s Mission bet Eighth and Ninth
Behen Henry P. mining engineer, dwl S s Mission bet Eighth and Ninth
Beher Henry, cook, Russ House
Beherns Gottlieb, cabinet maker with Goodwin & Co. dwl SW cor Dupont and Green
Behlow Charles J. *(H. Liebes & Co.)* dwl 325 Pine
Bchuken Martin, express wagon, 1007 Battery
Behr Herman, physician, office 639 Washington, dwl N s Bryant bet Fourth and Fifth
Behr Otto, mate, schooner Amazon, bds 7 Wash
Behre *(Frederick)* & Co. *(Henry Spannhaake)* produce, 515 Merchant, dwl 607 Geary
Behre Henry C. confectionery and coffee saloon, 210 Stockton
Behrens George H. porter with Crane & Brigham, dwl 3 Central Place
Behrens H. C. F. physician, Bee Hive Building, NE cor Washington and Dupont, dwl 10 Sutter
BEHRENS JAMES, agent Cliquot wine, 429 Battery, dwl 1105 Folsom
Behrens Joseph, groceries, wines and liquors, NW cor Brannan and Sixth
Behrman Ernst, carpenter, dwl 115 St. Mark Place
Behrmann Otto H. cooper, Union Brewery
Beideman Jacob C. Estate of, office 315 Mont
Beidenback August, baker, dwl 106 Kearny
Bein J. Frank, tinsmith with D. R. Provost & Co. dwl Trinity nr Sutter
Bein William, machinist, Miners' Foundry, dwl 116 Sansom

Beirbraner Charles, with Erzgraber & Gœtjen, 120 Davis
Beirbraner, John, cabinet maker, dwl 120 Davis
Beirne Patrick *(Cooney & B.)* dwl Ecker bet Market and Stevenson
Beisel Jacob, tanner, Mississippi nr Mariposa
Bela Louis, blacksmith, dwl 16 Lewis Place
Belcher Frederick P. drayman, 318 Battery, dwl S s Union bet Jones and Leavenworth
Belcher James, cabinet maker, dwl 541 Mission
Belcher Robert H. furniture wagon, 433 California, dwl S s Union bet Jones and Leavenworth
Belden Block, SW cor Montgomery and Bush
Belden Charles H. clerk, Paymaster's Department, dwl SE cor Eddy and Mason
BELDEN FRANCIS C. wholesale wines, liquors, and teas, 612 Sacramento, dwl 1018 Stockton
Belden Joseph W. clerk, estate of Jacob C. Beideman, dwl N s Geary bet Polk and Van Ness Av
Belden Josiah, real estate, office, room 10 Mercantile Library Building, res San José
Belden Margaret S. Mrs. dress maker, 32 Second, dwl cor Eddy and Mason
Belding Orrin, assayer, dwl 820 Howard
Belduke *(Joseph)* & Co. *(Rogers Sicott)* Pacific Concord Carriage Manufactory, 820 Folsom, dwl SE cor Sixth and Minna
Belendor Charles, varnisher with J. & J. Easton, dwl 623 Geary
Belfrage John G. seaman, dwl 44 Sacramento
Beliar Clara (widow) dwl 215 Fourth
Beliar Louisa Miss, dwl 215 Fourth
Belinder C. varnisher, 725 Market, dwl 623 Geary
Belknap David P. *(Winans & B.)* attorney at law, off 604 Merch, dwl NW cor Fourth and Mission
Bell Ada, Miss, actress, Olympic, dwl SE cor Bush and Dupont
Bell Agnes Miss, domestic with William H. Brown, N s Fifteenth nr Howard
Bell Amory F. salesman, 606 Clay, dwl 1030 Clay
Bell A. R. plasterer, dwl 227 Sixth
Bell Charles, drayman, W s Front bet Broadway and Vallejo
Bell Charles E. shipwright with J. G. North, dwl 605 Third
Bell Dorcas Miss, dwl W s Folsom bet Eleventh and Twelfth
Bell Ellen (col'd, widow) with James P. Dyer, dwl 1411 Mason
Bell Freeman, plumber, dwl 238 First
Bell George, fruits, 257 Third
Bell George, sailor, dwl 154 First
BELL GEORGE H. bookseller and stationer, 611 Montgomery cor Merchant, dwl 1028 Minna
Bell George W. (col'd) soap maker with James P. Dyer, dwl W s Mason nr Pacific
BELL GERRITT W. assayer, office 512 Cal, and supervisor Eighth District, dwl 1021 Leav
Bell H. plumber, dwl 238 First
Bell Hazellrigge, book keeper, dwl 736 Market
Bell Henry, produce, dwl 121 St. Mark Place
Bell Henry W. book keeper, bank Wells, Fargo & Co. dwl 611 Union
Bell H. H. clerk, dwl SE cor Second and Howard
Bell Jacob, with Edward Palm, SW cor Pine and Montgomery
BELL JAMES *(Falkner; B. & Co.)* dwl N s Folsom bet Eleventh and Twelfth
Bell James (col'd) barber, dwl 1023 Pacific
Bell James H. (col'd) laborer, dwl 1234 Bush
Bell James H. (col'd) whitewasher, 547 Clay
Bell John *(Branson & B.)* dwl N s Clay bet Hyde and Larkin
Bell John *(Kennedy & B.)* dwl SW cor Stockton and Bush
Bell John, carpenter, bds Manhattan House, 705 Front
Bell John, laborer, bds Franklin Hotel, SE cor Sansom and Pacific

Bell John, sail maker, dwl W s Clay bet Hyde and Larkin
BELL JOHN C. carpets, paper hangings, upholstery, etc. SW cor California and Sansom, dwl 504 Greenwich
Bell John C. sr. dwl 504 Greenwich
Bell John P. conveyancer, 23 Exchange Building, dwl W s Mission bet Second and Third
Bell John W. New York Department, Wells, Fargo & Co. dwl 611 Union
Bell Josiah, clerk, Pier 3 Stewart, bds Howard House
Bell Margaret R. (widow) dwl 10 Rousch
Bell Octavius, attorney at law, office with J. P. Hoge, dwl 517 Pine
Bell Philip A. (col'd) editor Elevator, office 9 Phœnix Building, dwl 622 Battery
Bell Richard, bds Franklin House, SW cor Sansom and Broadway
Bell Samuel, dwl 742 Howard
Bell Samuel, ship carpenter, dwl SW cor Lombard and Larkin
Bell Samuel L. carpenter, bds 606 Third
Bell Sarah I. Mrs. boarding, 742 Howard
Bell Thomas *(Barron & Co.)* dwl 606 Stockton
Bell Thomas, gasfitter with McNally & Hawkins, 129 Montgomery
BELL THOMAS, proprietor Bell's Saloon, 218 Clay, dwl 1227 Pacific
Bell William, boiler maker, dwl 146 Stewart
Bell William, brakeman, S. F. & San José R. R., dwl 446 Brannan
Bell William, compositor, Alta California, dwl Filbert bet Hyde and Larkin
Bell William, express wagon, cor Market and Stewart
Bell William, gardener, dwl with N. White, W s Florida nr Twentieth
Bell William, painter, dwl S s Filbert bet Hyde and Larkin
Bell William, porter, 202 Front, dwl 31 Main
Bell William, second mate steamer Golden City, dwl 180 Jessie
Bell William, ship carpenter, dwl SW cor Lombard and Larkin
Bell William, shipwright, dwl SW cor Shasta and Michigan
Bell William H. Col. dwl 306 Seventh
Bell William M. stonecutter, dwl Third bet Townsend and Bryant
Bell Zadoc F. (col'd) clerk, office Elevator, 9 Phœnix Building
Bella Union G. & S. M. Co. office 702 Washington
Bella Union Melodeon, 708 Washington
Bellanger *(Joseph)* & Valory *(Louis)* billiard and liquor saloon, 530 Clay
Bellay Francis, portrait painter, dwl 19 Hinckley
Belle *(E.)* & Coulon *(A.)* professors drawing, 408 Pine
Belle Edward, dentist, office and dwl 408 Pine
Belle Vue House, T. L. Planel proptr, 1018 Stockton
Belleau Ann S. (widow) dwl 820 Bush
Bellemere Augustus *(Pohlmann & Co.)* dwl 613 Kearny
Bellemere Louis, barber, dwl SE cor Eighth and Mission
Bellenger G. Mde. lodgings, 736 Pacific
Bellew John, laborer, dwl 13 Ohio
Bellew John jr. laborer, dwl 13 Ohio
Bellhorn Joseph, carpenter, dwl NW cor Kearny and Jackson
Bellieno Cecil H. book keeper, dwl 736 Market
Belliere Eugene, shaving saloon, 756 Clay
Bellinger Charles, varnisher, dwl 728 Market
Bellisle Francis N. foreman car shop S F. & San José R. R. dwl 261½ Jessie
Bellman Vincent, workman, Potrero Rope Walk, dwl adjoining S. F. Cordage Factory
Bello Vincent, fruits and nuts, 1328 Stockton

Belloc B. *(Belloc Freres)* office 535 Clay
BELLOC FRERES *(I. & B. Belloc)* importers and bankers, 535 Clay, res Paris
Bellocy Alfred, butcher, 1224 Dupont
Bellow Charles, fur maker, dwl 323 Pine
Bellows Henry, clerk with C. A. Low & Co. dwl Brevoort House
Bellstedt John, laborer, Bay Sugar Refinery, dwl 8 s Union bet Battery and Sansom
Belluzzi Pietro, employé, Brignardello, Macchiavello & Co. 706 Sansom
Belou Michael, tailor, dwl 1317 Kearny
Bellville Eli, broom maker, dwl 222 Fremont
Belzar Henry J. upholsterer with J. F. & H H. Schafer, 504 Sansom
Bemak Isaac, cap maker with Wolf Fleisher, dwl 130 Third
Beman Mary E. (widow) clairvoyant physician, dwl N s Washington bet Mason and Taylor
Bemis Charles C. inspector boilers, office third floor Custom House, dwl 417 Bryant
Bemis Stephen A. wood and coal, dwl W s Sixth bet Stevenson and Mission
Benard Alexander, clerk with Auguste Benard, dwl 262 Tehama
Benard Auguste, groceries and liquors, SW corner Fourth and Howard, dwl 262 Tehama
Benas Benjamin, merchant tailor, 13 Kearny
Benchel Gottlieb, tailor, dwl 1705 Mason
BENCHLEY L. B. & Co. *(John Bensley, Francis D. Kellogg, and James McMechan)* importers and jobbers American and foreign hardware, 206 and 208 Battery (after Jan. 1st, 1866 3 Front nr Market) dwl 1019 California nr Taylor
Bendel Herman, salesman with Tillmann & Co. dwl SW cor Washington and Stockton
Bender Charles, importer and dealer leather and shoe findings, 114 Sutter
Bender Franz, boot maker, 29 Ritch
Bender Jacob A. brick layer, dwl SE cor Jones and California
Bender John, piano forte maker with Benjamin Curtaz, 123 Kearny, dwl 266 Stevenson
Bender Josiah P. brick layer, dwl W s Scotland nr Filbert
Bender *(William H.)* & Co. *(Benjamin E. Van Straaten)* meat market, SE cor Hayes and Laguna
Bendit Henry, upholsterer, dwl SW cor Bush and Kearny
Bendit Isaac, peddler, dwl 41 Jessie
Bendit Morris, express wagon, cor California and Montgomery, dwl Bagley Place
Beneaux L. R. prompter, Maguire's Opera House
Benedett Diffarari, gardener, NE cor Laguna and McAllister
Benedict C. S. clerk with Heuston, Hastings & Co. dwl 118 Sansom
Benedict Jacob, Kellogg, Hewston & Co.'s Refinery, dwl 121 Natoma
Benedict John, carpenter, Kellogg, Hewston & Co.'s Refinery, dwl Columbia Hotel 741 Market
Benedict Sophia S. Miss, artist, Shew's Gallery, dwl 212 Powell
Benedict Walker F. dwl with John P. Manrow
Benfield Conrad, seaman, bds 7 Washington
Benheim Sarah (widow) dwl 168 Minna
Benicia Cement Co. office 529 Clay
Bening George F. liquor saloon, SW cor Washington and East, dwl 912 Harrison nr Fifth
Benjamin Charles (color'd) barber, dwl 3 Dupont Place
Benjamin C. V. Miss, special grammar assistant Rincon School, dwl 1109 Stockton
Benjamin Edmund B. *(Cameron, Whittier & Co.)* dwl N s Folsom nr Thirteenth
Benjamin Edward A. clerk, 213 Front, dwl SE cor California and Dupont

Benjamin Frank, clerk, 106 Battery, dwl 1109 Stock
BENJAMIN FREDERICK A. office 605 Montgomery, dwl 1206 Powell
Benjamin Jacob, office 605 Montgomery, dwl 1308 Pine
Benjamin *(Studzinski)* & Brown *(David)* clothing, 305 Kearny
Benjamin William K. treasurer's clerk, Melter and Refiner's Department, U. S. Mint, dwl SW cor Powell and Geary
Benkelmann Adam, Union Restaurant, Brannan Street Bridge
Benker Frederick, groceries and liquors, SW cor Third and Folsom
BENKERT GEORGE F. agent Benkert's Philadelphia boots, and D. R. King & Co.'s ladies' shoes, office 210 Pine, dwl 117 Stockton
Benn Frederick *(William Holtz & Co.)* dwl SW cor Pacific and Montgomery
Benn George, laborer, dwl 1219 Powell
Benn Thomas, hostler, 679 Market, dwl SE cor St. Mary and Pine
Bennan John, beer bottler, dwl 512 Green
Benner Frederick M. Melter and Refiner's Department, U. S. Branch Mint, res Oakland
Bennet Charles A. clerk, 21 Third cor Stevenson
BENNET H. W. drugs and medicines, 21 Third cor Stevenson
Bennett Alvin P. book keeper, dwl 407 Green
Bennett A. T. book keeper with S. B. Whipple
Bennett A. W. dwl What Cheer House
Bennett C. H. molder, Miners' Foundry, dwl United States Hotel
Bennett Charles H. molder, dwl United States Hotel
Bennett Edwin S. book keeper, Fashion Stables, 16 Sutter
Bennett F. E. Miss, assistant, Lincoln School
Bennett Flary, express wagon, dwl N s Union bet Sansom and Battery
Bennett Frederick, laborer, dwl 44 Beale
Bennett George, captain schooner Amazon, bds 7 Washington
Bennett George, dentist, office 653 Clay, dwl International Hotel
Bennett George C. waiter, U. S. Restaurant
Bennett H. C. assistant editor American Flag, 517 Clay, dwl 1131 Clay
Bennett Herbert, with Bowen Brothers, dwl SE cor Sutter and Polk
Bennett James, dwl 812 California
Bennett James, fireman, dwl Davis Street House
Bennett James, laborer, dwl Dolores Hall, W s Valeucia nr Sixteenth
Bennett James, workman with John Henry, dwl Dolores Hall
Bennett James C. carpenter, dwl 108 Sutter
Bennett James C. carpenter and builder, dwl cor Mariposa and Indiana
Bennett John, laborer, dwl Cincinnati Brewery, Valencia nr Sixteenth
Bennett J. P. book keeper with Bulletti & Co. dwl 706 California
Bennett Maria L. dwl with Mrs. M. T. Butler, N s Thirteenth bet Howard and Folsom
Bennett Mary Miss, dwl W s Howard bet Eighteenth and Nineteenth
Bennett Mary Mrs. dwl SE cor Twentieth and Florida
Bennett Morris, laborer, dwl NW cor Bush and Franklin
BENNETT *(Nathaniel)*, C O O K *(Elisha)* & CLARKE *(Daniel)* attorneys at law, office 31–33 Exchange Building, dwl 12 Ellis
Bennett Nicholas, bar keeper, dwl 15 Sutter
Bennett N. P. capt. bark D. C. Murray, off 511 San
Bennett O. D. mechanic with James Brokaw, dwl 10 Anthony
Bennett P. B. fish, 2 Washington Fish Market, dwl 731 Union

BENNETT R. H. produce commission, 3 Clay, dwl Essex Place
Bennett Samuel, furniture, 1019 Dupont
Bennett Stephen, pantryman, Clipper Restaurant, dwl 121 Stevenson
Bennett Thomas, physician. office SE cor Sutter and Montgomery, dwl 716 Pine
Bennett W. dwl What Cheer House
Bennett William, laborer, dwl 308 Fremont
Bennett William F. saddler with Main & Winchester
Bennett William H. Mrs. South Park Laundry, 540 Third
Bennett William J. machinist, Pacific Foundry, dwl 302 Fremont
Bennett W. Leroy, dwl 652 Market
Bennoist E. engineer and chemist, 643 Third
Benns Charles, butcher, dwl S s Twenty-Third nr Mission Road
Benoit A. Mme. lodgings, Wright's Building, NW cor Jackson and Montgomery
Benoit Henry, waiter, German Hospital, Brannan
Benoit Jean M. with Louis Gamba, 518 Sacramento
Benrimo Henry, cigars and tobacco, dwl 416 Bush
Benrimo Joseph, cigars and tobacco, Occidental Hotel
Bensley Daniel, baker, dwl 132 Natoma
Bensley James, plasterer, bds N s Sixteenth bet Guerrero and Dolores
BENSLEY JOHN (*L. B. Benchley & Co.*) dwl 708 Mission
Benson Andrew, longshoreman, dwl W s Sansom bet Greenwich and Filbert
Benson C. A. captain scbr Tolo, Pier 9 Stewart
Benson Henry, clerk, dwl 619 Pine
Benson James, book keeper Fireman's Fund, Ins. Co. dwl W s Sixth bet Brannan and Townsend
Benson Jane, domestic, 913 Folsom
Benson John, trustee, Citizen's Gas Co. dwl 908 Clay
Benson Peter, seaman, dwl 20 Commercial
Benson Richard, proprietor Union City Warehouse and Line Packets, office 64 Clay, res Union City
Benson William, fireman, steamer Orizaba
Benson William, liquors, dwl 815 Montgomery
Benson William, longshoreman, dwl 631 Davis
Bent Edward F. book keeper with Richards & Mc-Cracken, dwl 924 Mission
Bent H. H. with S. S. Culverwell, 29 Fremont
Bente Lewis, driver Winkle's Bakery, dwl cor Battery and Vallejo
Bentley J. H. dwl SW cor Kearny and Pacific
Benton H. A. medical electrician, office and dwl 109 Montgomery
Benton Helen M. (widow) dwl E s Howard bet Twenty-Fifth and Twenty-Sixth
BENTON HOUSE, F. J. Hanlon proprietor, SW cor Mission and First
BENTON JOSEPH A. Rev. pastor Second Congregational Church, Taylor nr Geary, dwl 1032 Pine
Bentz Henry, hair dresser, dwl 18 Harlan Place
Benzen G. A. attorney at law, office 22 Exchange Building
Bepler, Frederick G. coppersmith, 421 Mission
Bepler Justus, distillery, San Miguel Station San José Railroad, 7 miles from City Hall
Beppler John, with Frederick Schwab, 519 Geary
Beque Joseph, collector, Lafayette H. & L. Co. No. 2
Berard Alfred (*Berard Bros.*) dwl 638 Bdwy
Berard Bros. (*Felicien and Alfred*) laundry, 638 Broadway
Berat Edward, with Jules Bouvet
Berbe Louis, groceries and liquors, Potrero Avenue
Berbier François, with François Bailly, 516 Clay
Berdenback August, baker, steamer Orizaba
Berdenger, William, shoe maker, dwl 623 Sutter
Bereaud Brothers (*Lewis and Felix*) bakery, cor Third and Stevenson

Bereaud Felix (*Bereaud Bros.*) dwl cor Third and Stevenson
Berel Jacob, job wagon, dwl 120 Shipley
Beresford John, porter, Cosmopolitan Hotel
Beretta Peter, machinist, Union Foundry, dwl 109 Minna
Berg Carl F. physician and surgeon, office and dwl 904 Kearny
Berg Conrad, laborer, Pacific Flour Mills
Berg Edward, book keeper, dwl 614 California
Berg Edward, waiter, 623 Commercial
Berg John A. tailor, 50 Sacramento
Berg Maurice, gilder with Snow & Co. dwl Harrison opposite Dora
Berg Peter, molder, Jackson Foundry, dwl SW cor Dupont and Broadway
Berge O. Erich, groceries and liquors, S s Green bet Montgomery and Sansom
Bergenheim Alma C. Miss, dwl W s Mission bet Twentieth and Twenty-First
Berger Gabriel, contractor and builder, dwl 212 Post
Berger Julius F. with Edward Cohn, 627 Clay
Bergerot J. A. & Co. (*J. P. Manciet*) produce, 9 and 10 Clay Street Market
Bergerot (*John A.*) & Co. (*C. Etienne*) vegetable gardeners, NW cor Sixteenth and Rhode Island
Berggren August, merchant, office 415 Montgomery, dwl 1109 Stockton
Berggren J. seaman, dwl 44 Sacramento
Berghaeuser John, dwl 1600 Taylor
Berghauser T. O. laborer, dwl NW cor Kearny and Jackson
Berghöfer (*Conrad*) & Dodge (*Daniel*) Crescent Market, 203 Stewart, dwl 542 Folsom
Bergholte (*William*) & Baloun (*J. L.*) tailors and cutters, 819 Clay, dwl 914 Clay
Bergin Daniel (*Olpherts & B.*) dwl NW corner Kearny and Jackson
Bergin Henry, cook, NE cor Clay and Davis
Bergin James J. soap manufacturer, SE cor Green and Powell, dwl 1528 Powell
Bergin John, boiler maker, Pacific Foundry, dwl 36 Natoma
Bergin Margaret Miss, domestic, SW cor Bush and Powell
Bergin Michael, attorney at law, office 40 Exchange Building, dwl 1520 Powell
Bergin Thomas, real estate, dwl 1520 Powell
Bergin T. I. attorney at law, office 23 Exchange Building, dwl SE cor Powell and Green
Bergion Manuel, machinist, Pacific Foundry, dwl 55 Everett
Bergis Pierre (*J. Hirth & Co.*) dwl N s Commercial nr Dupont
Bergland Hans, carpenter, dwl 44 Sacramento
Bergman Anna M. (widow) dwl 746 Market
Bergmann Jacob, book keeper with Adelsdorfer Bros. dwl Steckler's Exchange
Bergner Herman, teacher, City College, dwl 633 O'Farrell
Bergner John, boatman, dwl 212 Stewart
BERGSON OLE, carpenter and builder, 111 Leidesdorff
Berget Louis E. hair dressing saloon, 944 Market, dwl E s Brooks nr Geary
Bergstein Henry, clerk, 311 Battery, dwl 303 Sixth
Bergstein L. dry goods, 303 Sixth, dwl 965 Folsom
Bergstrom John (*Ackley & B.*) dwl E s Mission nr Twenty-Ninth
Berhalt Louis, laborer, dwl 1314 Dupont
Bering John P. foreman with A. S. Hallidie & Co
Berjman Samuel, butcher with L. Miller & Co
Berkowitz Meyer, cloaks, dress trimmings, etc. 626 Sacramento, dwl 262 Minna
Berlemann William, laborer, dwl 20 Clay
Berliner Emil, teacher piano forte, dwl Irving House
Berliner H. A. fancy goods, 414 Sacramento, dwl 836 Market

Berman E. crockery, 127 Third
Bermarento Felicia, handcartman, Drumm nr Wash
Bermingham George C. book keeper, 402 Sansom, dwl 129 Third
Bermingham John, superintendent Oregon and California S. S. Co. office Folsom Street Wharf, dwl 618 Third
Bermingham Thomas, groceries, SE cor Taylor and Turk
Bermingham. See Birmingham
Bermudes Jesus, domestic, dwl 1024 Kearny
Bernal Arguelas, gardener, dwl Old San José Road nr Industrial School
Bernal José Jesus, ranchero, dwl SE cor Seventeenth and Church
Bernard B. furniture, 1120 Stockton
Bernard Barnett, upholsterer with W. G. Weir, dwl 426 Third
Bernard C. A. house and sign painter, 617 Clay, dwl 741 Market
BERNARD CHARLES, manufacturer and dealer Chartres Coffee, 707 Sansom, dwl 217 Stevenson
Bernard Conway, fireman, stm Princess
Bernard Felicien, laundryman, Lafayette H. & L. Co. No. 2
Bernard Isaac, crockery, 426 Third
Bernard John, captain schooner Wm. Frederick, dwl W s Sixth bet Bryant and Brannan
Bernard John, collar maker with Kreitz & Cosbie, 36 Battery
Bernard Joseph, cook, dwl 1303 Dupont
Bernard Lupachet, bar keeper, Bella Union
Bernard Robert, painter with Snow & Co. dwl 1904 Powell
Bernard Ulrick, baker, dwl 26 Second
Bernard Waldamar R. sign painter with J. W. Denny, dwl 1906 Powell
Bernard W. M. workman with Casebolt & Co
Berne Jonathan J. adjuster, Phœnix Insurance Co. office 603 Commercial
Bernede, Jean, butcher, 5 Clay Street Market, dwl Lagoon
Berner, John, watchman, dwl SW cor Louisiana and Sierra
Berney William, saw maker, dwl 17 Minna
BERNHAMMER HENRY, propr City Front House, 625 and 627 Davis
Bernhard Adolph, cap maker with Wolf Fleisher, dwl St. Mark Place nr Kearny
Bernhard Bernhard, hair dresser with Stahle Bros. dwl 9 Tay
Bernhard Bonn, dwl NW cor Fifth and Tehama
Bernhard Minna Mme. dwl 626 California
Bernhard Robert, miner, dwl W s Leavenworth bet Greenwich and Lombard
Bernhard Roth, tailor, 835 Washington
Bernhard Samuel H. (Trickle & B.) dwl 317 Dupont, rear
BERNHEIM MAURICE, wholesale and manufacturing confectioner, 408 Clay
Bernheim Reuben, merchant, office 304 California, dwl 724 Mission
Bernheisel S. Newspaper Carriers' Association
Bernis G. proprietor Bernis Building, 626 California
Bernstein Abraham, fruits, dwl E s Russette Place No. 2
Bernstein Edward, carpenter, dwl 546 Bryant
Bernstein Louis, clerk with Solomon Bernstein
Bernstein M. C. furniture, 841 Pacific
Bernstein Solomon, dress trimmings, 1008 and 1012 Stockton
Beron Fortune, workman at Cole's Laundry, 114 Dora
Berri Emanuel B. (B. Davidson & B.) acting consul for Belgium, office NW cor Montgomery and Commercial, dwl 605 Bush
Berring Hermann, clerk, 504 Montgomery, dwl 719 Broadway
Berring Rudolph, discharging clerk, dwl 118 Freelon

Berroa Andres, cigars and tobacco, 613 Pacific
Berrot B. gardener, French Hospital
Berry Ann Miss, domestic, 1012 Washington
Berry Charles, carpenter, dwl 728 Market
Berry Edward, with O. F. Willey & Co. 316 Cal
Berry Fulton G. groceries and liquors, NW corner Jackson and Stockton, dwl 516 Dupont
Berry George, dwl 36 Valparaiso
Berry Geo. W. drayman, dwl N s Sutter nr Gough
Berry Gideon M. clerk, County Recorder, dwl 116 Stockton
Berry H. H. captain brig Francisco, office Pier 10 Stewart
Berry James, blacksmith with Nelson & Doble, dwl 756 Howard
Berry James, stone cutter, bds Brooklyn House
Berry John, carriage painter with R. S. Eells & Co. dwl S s Welsh nr Fourth
Berry John, seaman, dwl 44 Sacramento
Berry Lewis (colored) white washer, dwl 421 Kearny, rear
Berry Mary Miss, domestic, 18 Mason
Berry S. B. ship joiner, dwl Bitter's Hotel
Berry Thomas, livery stable, 16 Clementina
Berry Victor, seaman, steamer Senator
Berry William, carpenter, Omnibus R. R. Co
Berson A. Mme. French Laundry, 828 Washington
Bert Amelia Miss, milliner, 44 Fourth, dwl 677 Harrison
Bert Augustus, dwl 11 O'Farrell
Bert Bernard (H. Schroder & Co.) res Bordeaux, France
Bert Edward G. theatrical manager, dwl 677 Harrison
Bert Frederick W. dwl with P. B. Forster, W s Shotwell bet Twentieth and Twenty-First
Bertheau Cesar (Ziel, Bertheau & Co.) res Hamburg
Berthelot Charles L. porter with John Flanagan & Co. 421 Front
Berthold Louis (Dinger & B.) dwl 703 Battery
Bertholot A. box maker, dwl Stockton near Sacramento
Berthon Eugene, groceries and liquors, 523 Union
Bertin Louis, laborer, dwl 1712 Mason
Bertody Charles, physician, office and dwl 807 Washington
Bertolio J. M. Rev. S.J. clergyman, St. Ignatius Church, S s Market bet Fourth and Fifth
Berton Francis (Hentsch & B.) dwl 835 Howard
Bertony Angelo, vegetable garden, W s Mission nr Twenty-Sixth
Bertram Theophilus, dwl Bay Shore and Fort Point Road, 3 miles from Plaza
Bertram Thomas, tinsmith with Tay, Brooks & Backus, dwl 459 Clementina
Bertran Thomas (Armstrong & B.) dwl Ft. Point
Bertrand Auguste, workman with Lee & Son, dwl S s Solano nr York
Bertrand Ferdinand, with Goodwin & Co
Bertrand R. (widow) machine sewing, 261 Minna
Bertucci Louis & Co. (Louis Geminiani) Italian Restaurant, 512 Clay
Bertuse L. waiter, dwl Niantic Hotel
Bertz Henry, porter, 226 Front, dwl 21 Scott
Bertz Jacob, clerk, 226 Front, dwl 725 Broadway
Berwick Thomas, sail maker with John S. Blakiston, dwl 1918 Mason
Berwin Aaron (P. Berwin & Bros.) res New York
Berwin Isaac, tailor, 115 Leidesdorff, dwl 211 Clay
Berwin L. D. merchant, dwl 1513 Powell
Berwin Moritz (P. Berwin & Bros.) dwl 828 Post
Berwin P. & Brothers (Aaron and Moritz Berwin) importers and jobbers hats, caps, etc. 319 Sacramento, dwl 828 Post
Besby Henry, bar keeper, 413 Montgomery, dwl 243 Second
Bescheinen William, watch maker with G. C. Shreve & Co. dwl 606 Montgomery

Beschorman Augustus H. furrier, dwl 58 Everett
Beschorman Matilda A. domestic, 220 Seventh
Beslin Daniel, laborer, dwl 40 Clementina
Besou Joseph, gardener, Old San José Road E Industrial School
Besse Joseph O. salesman, 633 Clay, dwl 706 Mason
Bessemer Henry L. manufacturer perfumery, dwl 761½ Mission
Bessett Martin L. carpenter, dwl with P. Murphy, E s Howard bet Fifteenth and Sixteenth
Bessey Albion P. truckman, cor Clay and Sansom, dwl S s Grove bet Franklin and Gough
Bessie J. D. carpenter, dwl 777 Market
Besson Felix & Gustave, coffee saloon, 520 Merchant
Besson Gustave (F. & G. B.) dwl 520 Merchant
Besson (Harriet, widow) & Pons (Charlotte) Mesdames, French corset makers, 629 Sacramento
Best & Belcher M. Co. office 712 Montgomery
Best John, varnisher with John Wigmore, dwl 557 Howard
Best William, painter with Hopps & Kanary
Best William, stair builder with N. P. Langland, dwl 223 First
Best William J. agent Dexter, Lambert & Co. 105 Battery, dwl 1209 Taylor
Beston Elizabeth (widow) furnished rooms, 106½ Clay
Bestor Henry T. draftsman with Patrick Walsh, 104 Sutter
Bestor John, bar keeper, 601 Sacramento, dwl 626 California
Betcold Mathes, maltster with Peter Bush, dwl S s Brannan bet Eighth and Ninth
BETGE ROBERT J. importer and dealer books and stationery, news agent, etc. 217 Montgomery, Russ House, dwl 739 Pine
Betilla R. laborer, dwl 52 Stevenson
Betkowski Peter, job wagon, cor Montgomery and Bush, dwl 23 Silver
Betten Eliza Miss, domestic, 426 Post
Betten Frederica Miss, domestic with Louis Gerstle
Bettman Joseph (Hirschfelder & Co.) dwl Continental Hotel
Bettman Moses, soap dealer, 305 California, dwl 225 Fourth
Bettman Siegmund, merchant, dwl 347 Minna
Betty Joseph, deck hand, steamer Petaluma
Betuel François & Co. (François Veyrat) groceries and liquors, SW cor Pine and Dupont
Betzel Louis, clerk, dwl 114 Stevenson bet Second and Third
Beutler John B. professor music California Institute, dwl 612 Mission
Bevan Benjamin, clerk with William Craig
Bevans Isaac, carpenter, dwl 913 Sacramento
Bevans Thomas P. physician, dwl S s Vallejo bet Hyde and Larkin
Bevans William M. compositor Evening Bulletin, dwl S s Turk bet Jones and Leavenworth
Bevell Richard, dwl E s Park Avenue bet Harrison and Bryant
Beverland William, seaman, dwl 44 Sacramento
Beversen Charles, groceries and liquors, 570 Mission cor Anthony
Bevins William M. printer, dwl 311 Minna
Bevitt John, butcher with Louis Peres & Co. cor Potrero Avenue
Bewley Allen H. salesman with S. W. H. Ward & Son, dwl 1020 Jackson
Beychart George, ship carpenter, dwl 1816 Powell
Beyea J. L. clerk, Pacific Iron Foundry, dwl 823 Montgomery
Beyer Louis, barber, 805 Battery, dwl 625 Vallejo bet Dupont and Stockton
Beyer Michael, job wagon, SW cor Sacramento and Sansom, dwl 621 Pacific
Beziade P. tailor, dwl SW cor Broadway and Dupont

Bianchi Eugeneo, tenor Italian Opera, dwl 804 Montgomery
Bianchini Amedeo, employé, Brignardello, Macchiavello & Co. 706 Sansom
Biarnes Aristide, laundryman with Arsene Lemaitre
Bibb William, carpenter, dwl 532 Commercial
Bibbins (Tracy L.) & Garland (William D.) collectors and general agents, office 540 Clay, dwl 1121 Powell
Bibend Charles, capitalist, 540 Washington, dwl W s Twelfth bet Howard and Folsom
Bibend Ferdinand, machinist, Miners' Foundry, dwl N s Harrison bet Seventh and Eighth
Bibend Frederick, machinist, Miners' Foundry, dwl N s Harrison bet Seventh and Eighth
BICHARD NICHOLAS, importer anchors, chains, etc. 209 Stewart Pier 15, dwl NE cor Harrison and First
Bickel Conrad, dwl NW cor Octavia and Haight
Bickford Anson W. drayman, dwl Eighth bet Howard and Folsom
Bickford L. H. carpenter, bds 411 Pacific
Bicknell James M. steward, dwl SW cor Powell and California
Bidala Nemecia Miss, dwl 1615 Powell
Bidau Peter, real estate, dwl 924 Dupont
Biddell M. Miss, music teacher, dwl 524 Howard
Biddolph James, machinist with Palmer, Knox & Co. dwl 72 Minna
Biden Charles S. editor, dwl N s Jessie bet Fourth and Fifth
Biden Henry M. compositor, Alta California, dwl 619 Market
Bidleman Joseph B. office 605 Montgomery, dwl SW cor Broadway and Dupont
Biebrach Frederick, baker, 819 Sansom, dwl S s Oak nr Buchanan
Biedeman Charles, clerk with H. P. Wakelee, NW cor Howard and Third, dwl 250 Tehama
Biedert Albert, musician, dwl 323 Kearny
Bielawski Casimer, draftsman, office U. S. Surveyor General, dwl 242 Stevenson
Bieler Frank, mining stocks, dwl 315 Bush
Bien Joseph, machinist and locksmith, 322 Commercial, dwl 750 Folsom
Bienenfeld Elias, fancy goods, dwl 1229 Stockton
Biesterfeld Lorenzo, ship carpenter, bds 7 Wash
Biesterfeld Oscar, ironer, New England Laundry, N s Brannan bet Fifth and Sixth
Bigee Terence, laborer, dwl N s O'Farrell between Devisidero and Broderick
Bigelow Elijah, solicitor, S. F. Insurance Co. office 402 Front, res Oakland
BIGELOW GEORGE H. (Bigelow & Brother) dwl 714 Howard
BIGELOW (Henry H.) & BROTHER (George H. Bigelow) fire, life, and marine insurance agents, office Parrott's Building, 505 Montgomery, dwl 1020 Pine
Bigelow J. laborer with E. T. Stein
Bigelow John B. watch maker, 17 Fremont, dwl 18 Eddy
Bigelow Jonathan E. surveyor, Bigelow & Brother, 505 Montgomery, dwl 1020 Pine
Bigelow Oliver E. box maker with Hobbs & Gilmore, dwl 414 Market
BIGELOW (Samuel C.) & BOWMAN (Arthur W.) real estate agents, office room 10 Mercantile Library Building, dwl NW cor Steiner and McAllister
BIGELOW T. B. office SW cor Front and Jackson, res Oakland
Bigger Alexander, pantryman, steamer Orizaba
Bigley Cornelius, groceries, 134 Clay, dwl 323 Kearny
Bigley Daniel, clerk, 134 Clay, dwl 323 Kearny
Bigley George, clerk, 134 Clay, dwl 323 Kearny
Bigley John, repairer Fire Alarm and Police Telegraph, City Hall, dwl W s Larkin nr Ellis

Bigley Margaret Miss, domestic, dwl 527 Green
Bigley Thomas, shipwright and calker, 31 Market, dwl 832 Mission
Biggs A. R. traveling agent, dwl 104 Powell
Biggs Jessie E. house mover, dwl 39 Second
Biggs John E. Flume House, San Bruno Road
Biggs Nancy F. (widow) dwl 120 Silver
Bignami Louis, waiter, dwl 9 Stockton
Bigot Louis, cook, Cosmopolitan Hotel, dwl 10 Sutter
Bigot Esther Mrs. laces and embroideries, 828 Wash
Bigreiss G. Frederick, frame maker with Snow & Co. cor Washington and Sansom
BILAY ANTHONY F. Eureka Bowling Saloon, E s Valencia nr Sixteenth
Biley B. hostler, Omnibus R. R. Co
Bilfinger Mary Mme. dress-maker, dwl 1116 Dup
Bill F. dwl 9½ Montgomery Block
Bill Jacob, brewer, Broadway Brewery
Bill Philip, dwl 338 Third
Billet E. W. (Howe & B.) 423 Washington
Billett Maria (widow) dress making, dwl 419 Stock
Billing Peter, seaman, dwl Western House, Stewart
Billings Edwin P. machinist, Miners' Foundry, dwl 47 Clementina
Billings Frederick, real estate, office 43 Montgomery Block, dwl Occidental Hotel
Billings John F. policeman, City Hall, dwl 626 Vallejo, rear
Billings Peter, seaman, dwl cor Michigan and Napa
Billings P. T. engineer, dwl W s Hartman nr Lombard
Billington C. E. express wagon, cor Third and Howard
Bilsky Morris, clerk with Henry Levy, dwl 523 Pac
Binckley Omer, painter, dwl 315 First
Bine Solomon (Mansbach & B.) dwl 41 Natoma
Bingenheimer Christopher, cooperage, 106 Davis, dwl 654 Mission
Bingham, Albert D. drayman, 225 Clay
Bingham C. Edward, cigars and tobacco, NE cor Sutter and Sansom, dwl 6 Sutter
Bingham C. S. V. seaman, dwl City Front House
BINGHAM JAMES W. clerk Board of Supervisors, office 4 City Hall, second floor, dwl 108 Geary
Bingham John, capt. schooner Glen Ann, dwl 766 Mission
Bingholier John, laborer, dwl 511 Green
Bioren John, Franco-Am. Commercial Co. 215 Bush
Birch Mary J. (widow) dwl 938 Mission
Birch P. machinist, Fulton Foundry
Birch Samuel, laborer, dwl S s Seventeenth bet Church and Dolores
Birch Thomas, plasterer, dwl 310 Tehama
Birch William, machinist, dwl 81 Natoma
Bird Adam, second-hand furniture, 243 Third
Bird Ann S. (widow) dwl 319 Minna
Bird George, carrier, Mazeppa, dwl 12 Commercial
Bird George, propertyman Eureka Theater
Bird George F. dwl 327 Commercial
Bird Herbert, supervisory agent Phœnix Insurance Co. office 603 Commercial, dwl SW cor Commercial and Montgomery
Bird Isabella Mrs. furnished rooms, 820 Wash
Bird John, cook, Empire State Restaurant, dwl NE cor Bush and Sansom
Bird John W. printer, Alta Job Office, dwl 1113 Kearny
Bird Lawrence, brick layer, dwl S s Shipley nr Harrison Avenue
Bird Levi, driver with Edmund H. Knight
Bird Michael, laborer, dwl S s Clementina bet Fifth and Sixth
Bird Robert, jeweler with R. B. Gray & Co. dwl 921 Union
Bird Thomas, dwl W s Battery bet Filbert and Union
Bird Thomas, saloon, 160 First
Bird William, tailor, 126 Bush, dwl 820 Wash

Birdsall George W. local policeman, dwl 223 Ritch nr Brannan
Birdsall Gertrude, dwl E s Davis bet Pacific and Jackson
Birdsall John, dwl S s Shipley nr Harrison Avenue
Birdsall John M. engineer, bds 127 Pacific
Birdsall Z. with Wells, Fargo & Co. dwl NW cor Clay and and Clay Avenue
Birdseye John C. dwl Cosmopolitan Hotel
Birge J. J. dentist, office 1 Mead House, NW cor Montgomery and Pine
Birkmaier George L. salesman, 424 Sansom
Birmaham Bridget Miss, domestic, dwl 930 Clay
Birmingham Edward, engineer, dwl with Charles Clint
Birmingham Patrick, laborer, dwl W s Gilbert bet Bryant and Brannan
Birmingham Peter, student, Mission Dolores Church
Birmingham Thomas, seaman, dwl 54 Sacramento
Birmingham Thomas J. porter, dwl 706 Battery
Birmingham William, bar tender, dwl 21 First
Birmingham W. W. compositor, American Flag, dwl Original House
Birmingham, see Bermingham
Birrell Andrew, dwl 1219 Mason
Birrell Andrew jr. treasurer Metropolitan Theater, dwl 1219 Mason
Birt William, tinsmith with Taylor & Iredale
Birt, see Bert and Burt
Bisagno Bartolomo (Bisagno Bros.) res Chiavori, Italy
Bisagno Brothers (Louis and Bartolomo) importers and jobbers hardware, cutlery, crockery, etc. 420 Battery, dwl 924 Pacific
Bishop B. F. jeweler with J. M. Seamans
Bishop (Duncan M.) & Co. (James B. Faitoute) proprietors The Guide, office 410 Clay
Bishop Gurdon, teamster, dwl W s Florence nr Broadway
Bishop Henry, clerk, NE cor Harrison and Fourth
Bishop Lester, boarding, E s Valencia nr Sixteenth
Bishop Margaret Miss, domestic, dwl 615 Green
Bishop Nimrod, carpenter, dwl 62 Tehama
Bishop Oliver H. butcher with William Buckley, dwl W s Florence nr Broadway
Bishop Ransom B. master mechanic S. F. & San José R. R. dwl SE cor Shotwell and Sixteenth
Bishop Richard, stone cutter with Michael Cronin, dwl 421 Vallejo
Bishop Thomas B. attorney at law, office 620 Washington, room 5, dwl N s Thirteenth nr Mission
Bishop William A. teamster, dwl 89 Everett
Bisilio Joseph, seaman, dwl S s Union bet Sansom and Calhoun, rear
Bissell Edwin C. Rev. pastor Third Cong. Church, dwl NE cor Dupont and Lombard
Biter John, attorney at law, office cor Washington and Brenham Place, bds Bitter's Hotel
BITTER WILLIAM, proprietor Bitter's Hotel, NW cor Kearny and Jackson
Bitzer John, coffee peddler, dwl Gardner Alley near Post
Biven Racy, miner, dwl NW cor Stockton and Pac
Bivens Samuel (col'd) porter, C. H. dwl 16 Scott
Bixby Henry, dwl 284 Minna
Bixby Samuel V. office 410 Montgomery
Bixio Oliver, clerk with Ben Holladay, dwl NE cor Pine and Powell
Bizard Etienne, liquor saloon, 712 Market
Bizard Thomas, dwl 672 Mission
Bjorkman John R. laborer, dwl N s Chestnut bet Stockton and Powell
Black Adam, boot maker, dwl S s Mission bet Eighth and Ninth
Black Amanda F. (widow) furnished rooms, 445 Bush
Black Bess G. & S. M. Co. office 36 Exchange Bdg
Black Charles, blacksmith with Black & Saul, dwl 541 Mission

Black Charles, plumber with J. H. O'Brien & Co. dwl Pacific Engine House
Black Diamond Coal Mine, office 110 Jackson
Black George, surveyor, dwl N s Eddy bet Devisidero and Broderick
Black George C. brick layer, dwl Pacific Engine House, 112 Jackson
Black Hawk M. Co. office 424 Battery
BLACK *(Henry M.)* & SAUL *(Edmond)* carriage manuf, 717 Market, dwl 235 Stevenson
Black Jacob, cook, steamer Orizaba
Black John, boiler maker with Coffey & Risdon
Black John, laborer, dwl NW cor Main and Harrison
Black John, mate, brig Tenor, dwl 238 Stewart
Black John W. book keeper with Thomas H. Selby & Co. dwl 707 Stockton
Black Ledge G. & S. M. Co. office 402 Front
Black Richard, Carpenter, dwl Sixth Street House, NW cor Sixth and Bryant
Black Robert, hostler, Cliff House
Black Rock G. & S. M. Co. office 338 Montgomery
Black Samuel, farmer, dwl 73 Tehama
Black W. K. carpenter, dwl 663 Howard
Black W. W. omnibus, Plaza
Blackum Henry (col'd) seaman, bds 5 Broadway
Blackburn Leslie F. dwl 322 Sutter
Blackman Abraham, dwl 1140 Pacific
Blackman Cassius H. clerk with Fargo & Co. dwl 607 Pine
Blackmore Thomas, boarding, 327 Beale
Blackstone Nathaniel L. dwl E s Lagoon
Blackstone William, seaman, dwl 238 Stewart
Blackwell John, cook, Brooklyn Hotel
Blackwood William, clerk, Quartermaster's Department U. S. A. 742 Washington, dwl cor Grove Avenue and Bryant
Blady Catharine Miss, domestic, dwl 808 Vallejo
Blaikie Andrew, draftsman, Miners' Foundry, dwl 519 Bryant
Blaikie George W. ship joiner, dwl W s Leavenworth bet Washington and Clay
Blaikie James L. Melter and Refiner's Department U. S. Branch Mint, dwl 121 Prospect Place
Blaikie Richard, ship joiner, dwl W s Leavenworth bet Washington and Clay
Blaikie Sarah (widow) dwl W s Leavenworth bet Washington and Clay
Blain George, carpenter, dwl 222 Stevenson
Blain John D. Rev. pastor Central Methodist Episcopal Church, dwl 451 Natoma
Blainey James, bar keeper, SW cor Jackson and Kearny
Blair Chauncy S. pattern maker, Golden State Iron Works, dwl 8 Minna
Blair Jeanette (widow) dwl S s Welch bet Third and Fourth
Blair Joseph F. machinist, Pacific Foundry, dwl 306 Fremont
Blair Laura Mrs. lodgings, 737 Market
Blair *(Mathew)* & Co. hay and grain dealers, 28 Washington, dwl 248 Stevenson
Blair Phineas S. cabinet maker with J. A. Shaber, dwl 633 Market
Blair Samuel, captain bark Rival, office Pier 10, dwl 47 Tehama
Blair Thomas M. special policeman, dwl 108 Post
Blair William, job wagon, dwl S s Welch bet Third and Fourth
Blaisdell E. F. Mrs. fancy and dry goods, 329 Dupont, dwl 1 Harlan Place
Blaisdell Jay P. teamster with John R. Sedgley, dwl SE cor California and Davis
Blaisdell, see Blasdell
Blaise Lapariat, baker, dwl 539 Broadway
Blake B. bar keeper, Eureka Hose Co. No. 4
BLAKE *(Calvin T.)* & CO. *(George W. Blake)* hatters, 524 Montgomery, dwl W s Calhoun bet Green and Union

Blake Charles D. teamster with Reynolds & Co. dwl E s Folsom bet First and Fremont
BLAKE CHARLES E. dentist, SW cor Clay and Kearny, dwl 907 Bush
Blake Charles W. sawyer, dwl cor Pine and Bat
Blake Edward, drayman with Joseph D. C. Beach, 401 Front
Blake Elizabeth (widow) dwl 815 Howard
BLAKE *(Francis)* & MOFFITT *(James)* importers printing papers, inks, etc. 533 Washington, dwl 933 Stockton
Blake George (col'd) cook, 630 Commercial
Blake George H. clerk with J. C. Johnson & Co. dwl 727 Tehama
Blake George M. book keeper, U. S. Sanitary Commission, SE cor Mont and Pine, res Oakland
Blake George O. commission merchant, 609 Front, dwl Cosmopolitan Hotel
Blake George W. *(Blake & Co.)* hatters, dwl 1123 Stockton
Blake Henry C. accountant, office 436 Jackson, dwl 1414 Stockton
Blake Henry R. painter, dwl 709 Greenwich
Blake J. sail maker, dwl 360 Leavenworth
Blake James, laborer, dwl 142 Clara
Blake James, miner, dwl SE cor Sutter and Leav
Blake James, physician, office and dwl 206 Bush
Blake John (col'd) liquor saloon, 734 Pacific
Blake John, tailor with Frank Elwell, 315 Mont
Blake John R. (col'd) calker, dwl 909 Pacific
Blake M. (widow) dwl 121 Shipley
Blake Mary Miss, domestic, NE cor Brannan and Ninth
Blake Mary L. (widow) dwl W s Leroy Place bet Sacramento and Clay
BLAKE MAURICE C. judge Probate Court City and Co. San Francisco, room 18 City Hall second floor, chambers 19 third floor, dwl Russ House
Blake Nicholas laborer, dwl 267 Stevenson
Blake Ozias, ship master bark D. M. Hall, dwl 238 Stewart
Blake Peter, carpenter, Vulcan Foundry, dwl 716 Harrison
Blake Phillip H. toll collector San Francisco & Point Lobos Road nr Cemetery Avenue
Blake *(Sumner C.)* & Myers *(Albert)* books, stationery, etc. 702 Mont, dwl 3 Central Place
Blake T. A. *(Goodyear & B.)* dwl 127 Mont
Blake William G. barber, dwl SE cor Howard and Third
BLAKE *(Wm. H.)* & DENISON *(A. G.)* (col'd) hair dressing saloon, 615 Merchant
Blakely Irvine *(Mosgrove & B.)* dwl 222 Third
Blakely W. H. drayman, cor Battery and Merchant, dwl S s Harrison bet Fifth and Sixth
Blakely William, porter, 211 Bat, dwl 225 Sutter
Blakley William M. laborer, Miners' Foundry
Blakeman A. Noel, clerk, office U. S. Internal Revenue, dwl American Exchange Hotel
Blakeslee Albert, painter, dwl 34 Third
Blakiston John S. sail loft, NW cor Clay and East second floor, dwl 629 Market
Blamine James, drayman, 209 California
Blanc Alexander, dwl NW cor Jackson and Front
Blanc *(Maurice)* & Seran *(Gustave)* liquor saloon, 109 Fourth, dwl 293 Clementina
Blanc Stewart, boot maker, dwl 705 Battery
BLANCH MARIANO editor El Correo de San Francisco, office 617 Sansom
Blanchard A. assistant keeper F. P. Light House
Blanchard A. captain schooner Belle, office 413 East
Blanchard Alexander, mariner, dwl E s Reed nr Washington
Blanchard F. H. messenger, Surveyors' Department Custom House, dwl 405 Post
Blanchard Henry P. merchant, office 214 California, dwl Lick House
BLANCHARD JULES, hardware, etc. 26 Third
Blanchard Lott, keeper Fort Point Light House

Blanchard Louis, wind-mill maker, dwl Lestrade Alley

Blanchard R. S. clerk, dwl 54 First

Blanchard Sarah J. Miss, teacher, private school 528 Bush, dwl 909 Clay

Blanchard Stephen, dwl 54 First

Blanche Augustine Miss, artist, dwl 613 Kearny

Blanche Henry, tailor, dwl 1015 Pacific

Blanchet Henry, tailor, dwl 1337 Dupont, rear

Blanchfield Thomas, carpenter with Steam Paddy Co. dwl N s Oak nr Gough

Blanchon Jean, cartman, dwl 1402 Powell

Blanckardt T. A. clerk, Q. M. Department U. S. A. dwl 3 Brenham Place

BLANCKEART V. J. & CO. (Albert S. Verriez) wines and liquors, 911 Dupont

Blanco Timoteo, boot maker, dwl 47 Jackson

Blanden E. clerk, dwl 81 Natoma

Blanding Edward J. salesman with Bowen Bros. dwl SE cor Second and Natoma

Blanding Lewis, attorney at law, office NE cor Montgomery and California

Blanding Robert H. clerk with Bowen Bros ·

Blanding William, president Ophir Silver Mining Co. office NE cor Mont and Cal, dwl 703 Bush

Blaner Ernest, upholsterer with Goodwin & Co. dwl S s Pine bet Montgomery and Kearny ·

Blaney James A. Pennsylvania Engine Co. No. 12

Blaney John, painter with Hopps & Kanary, dwl 509 Ellis

Blaney John H. mining, dwl 549 Howard

Blankcard Charles, commission merchant, dwl 207 · Minna

Blanken Henry, dwl 6 Mile House, San Bruno Road

Blanken Nicholas, clerk, SW cor Broadway and Kearny

Blao M. waiter, Cosmopolitan Hotel

Blasco Abraham, clerk, dwl 297 Clementina

Blasdell George E. with Lewis & Neville, dwl 307 · Tehama nr Fourth

Blasdell G. W. street contractor, dwl 650 Howard

Blasdell Laurence B. jeweler with Mathewson & Bucklin, dwl 647 Howard

Blasdell, see Blaisdell

Blass Gusson, salesman, 36 Second, dwl 65 Jessie

Blass Meyer, dry goods, 36 Second, dwl 65 Jessie

Blass Morris, clerk, 58 Second, dwl 65 Jessie

Blaszkower Marks, clerk, 303 Kearny

Blatchley Joel S. attorney at law, office 40 Mont·gomery Block, dwl 1008 Taylor

Blattner John J. contractor, dwl 425 Third

Blauer Rudolph, cook, Bootz's Hotel ·

Blauvelt Richard D. jr. clerk, County Recorder's office, dwl 611 Mason nr Ellis

Bleiman Edward, laborer, dwl 2 Vallejo Place

Blenker Jacob, fireman, S. F. Pioneer W. Mills, dwl North Point bet Polk and Van Ness Avenue

Blessman Louis, with Feaster & Co. 213 Pine, dwl 126 Bush

Blethen James H. master stmr Moses Taylor, office NW cor Battery and Pine, dwl 514 Dupont

Blethen James H. jr. mate, steamer Colorado, dwl 514 Dupont

Blettner Nicholas, coachman, Tremont House

Blewitt (Isaac) & Johnson (Edwin H.) gunsmiths, 507 Commercial

Bley H. dwl 214 Sansom

Bleymonn Edward, matress repairer, 521 Market, dwl Vallejo Place

Blick Peter, carpenter, Vulcan Iron Works, dwl 705 Harrison

Bligh Catharine (widow) dwl 528 Union

Blinn Cyrus A. carpenter, dwl 216 Tehama

Blinn Samuel P. (Adams, B. & Co.) dwl 542 Second cor Brannan

Bliss George D. butcher with Johnson & Co. dwl S s Pacific nr Polk

Blitz Bernard S. policeman, City Hall, dwl 1206 Stockton

Bliven James (Fagin, B. & Skelly) NE cor Harrison and Third

Bloch H. F. (A. Cahn & Co.) resides Portland, Oregon

Bloch I. F. (A. Cahn & Co.) dwl 527 Folsom

Bloch John, dry goods, 3 Virginia Block, dwl 708 Vallejo

Bloch William, boots and shoes, 1022 Dupont ·

Blochman Abraham (Uhlfelder & Cahn) dwl 515 Folsom

Block A. B. gents' furnishing goods, 1107 Dupont

Block Abram & Co. (North San Juan) office 300 Battery, dwl 312 Sutter

Block Charles, driver, dwl 190 Stevenson

Block George, laborer, dwl 1013 Pacific

Block James N. book keeper with H. Cohn & Co. dwl 312 Sutter

Block Jane (widow) dwl 2 Dixon's Block, Jane

Block John, gents' furnishing goods, 532 Kearny, dwl cor Geary and Mason

Block William, proprietor Harbor View and Fort Point Omnibus Line, dwl S s Francisco bet Mason and Taylor

Blockmann Emanuel, millinery, 40 Fourth ·

Blodes Theodore, hair dressing saloon, 602 Market, dwl 21 Geary

Blodget Henry, cook, dwl 39 First

Blodgett Edgar C. agent for Wilson & Stevens, dwl W s Potrero Avenue nr Sixteenth

Blohm Peter, groceries and liquors, 42 Webb·

Blom John, ship carpenter, dwl N s Vallejo bet Kearny and Montgomery

Blondell Thomas, job wagon, NE cor Montgomery and Sutter, dwl cor Webster and Fulton

Blondin M. dwl 214 Sansom

Blong Thomas W. butcher, dwl Brannan Street Bridge

Blood James, boatman, dwl NE cor Francisco and Stockton

BLOOD, J. H. attorney at law and commissioner ·. deeds, office 7 Montgomery Block, dwl SE cor Montgomery and California

Blood L. L. commission merchant, 225 Clay, dwl 1104 Powell

Blood Mary Mrs. millinery, 8 Montgomery

Blood Susan E. dwl 265 Minna

Blood William, sail maker, dwl N s Filbert bet Montgomery and Sansom

Bloom Annie Miss, domestic, dwl 732 Vallejo

Bloom Samuel (W. Wolf & Co.) 619 Sacramento

Bloom Samuel, tanner and currier, S s Brannan nr Sixth, dwl Sixth nr Folsom

Bloom William, express wagon, Brannan bet Fifth and Sixth

Bloomer Hiram G. painter, NE cor Jackson and Montgomery, dwl W s Vernon Place nr Jackson

Bloomer (Jacob) & Co. (James Williams) liquor saloon, Oriental Hotel, dwl 3 Tehama

Bloomer Theodore H. book keeper, State Gauger's office, dwl W s Vernon Place nr Jackson

Bloomer William, superintendent Metropolitan Market, dwl 131 Montgomery

Bloomfield Solomon, dwl 518 Filbert

Bloomfield William G. seaman, dwl N s Union bet Battery and Sansom

Bloomingdale E. furniture, dwl 607 Union

Bloomingdale H. salesman with E. Bloomingdale, dwl 607 Union

Bloomingdale Israel, book keeper, 300 Battery, dwl 1022 Stockton

Bloor George W. compositor, Morning Call, dwl N s Jackson bet Leavenworth and Hyde

Blos Joseph, porter with DeWitt, Kittle & Co. dwl 813 Sansom

Blossett Mary Ann Miss, domestic, SW cor Gough and Fulton.

Blote John H. dwl 784 Folsom

Blucher S. C. boot maker, 1504 Stockton
Blue Anchor Boarding House, J. Louis Schroeder proprietor, 7 and 9 Washington
Blue Ledge G. & S. M. Co. office 402 Front
Blue Ledge G. & S. Quartz Co. (El Dorado Cal.) office 7 Government House
Bluemel Leberecht, tailor, dwl 33 St. Mark Place
Blum A. baker, dwl SW cor Fourth and Mission
Blum B. M. glazier, dwl Continental Hotel
Blum Christopher, painter, dwl 235 Sutter
Blum Elias, waiter, dwl 821 Kearny
Blum Ennestine Miss, with Gustave Coblentz
BLUM HERMAN, gents' furnishing goods, 304 Montgomery, dwl Occidental Hotel
Blum Isaac, glazier, dwl 38 Jackson
Blum Isaac, tailoring, 104 Bush
BLUM ISIDOR, clothing and gents' furnish'g goods, 411 Montgomery, dwl 1022 Jackson
Blum Simon, express wagon, SW cor California and Sansom, dwl 315 Fremont
Blum Solomon, book keeper with L. Strassburger, dwl 623 Washington
Blumberg J. F. salt mills, 27 Fremont, dwl E s Howard bet Fifteenth and Sixteenth
Blume Henry, boot maker, dwl 19 St. Mary
Blumenberg J. H. real estate, dwl 315 Pine
Blumenstein Philip, laborer with R. B. Woodward, NW cor Mission and Fourteenth
Blumenthal Abram, clerk with Isaac Harris, dwl Los Angeles
Blumenthal G. paper hanger and decorator, dwl Hall Court
BLUMENTHAL H. M. proprietor Original House Restaurant, dwl 1510 Powell
Blumenthal Martin A. mcht, dwl St. Nicholas Hotel
Blunn Edward, gardener, dwl 46 Silver
Blunt Amelia Mrs. music teacher, dwl NW corner Kearny and Broadway
Blunt John, steward, dwl 630 Green, rear
Blunt John P. salesman with J. R. Hughes, dwl 706 Jones
Blunt Phineas U. dwl 706 Jones
Bluxome Isaac, coal and iron, 206 Front, dwl 656 Folsom
Bly Leander A. carpenter with James Brokaw, dwl 271 Clary
BLYTH (Henry) & WETHERBEE (S. H.) lumber yard, 101 Market, dwl 405 Folsom
Blythe J n, conductor, Central R. R. dwl 427 Sixthoh
Blythe Susan (widow) dwl cor Jones and McAllister
Boag John, workman with E. Morrell, dwl NE cor Twentieth and Florida
BOARD OF CITY ENGINEERS, office 14 City Hall, third floor
BOARD OF COMMISSIONERS WIDENING KEARNY ST. office 410 Kearny
BOARD OF DELEGATES S. F. F. DEPARTMENT, 1 City Hall, third floor
BOARD OF EDUCATION, rooms 22 City Hall, second floor
BOARD OF EQUALIZATION, office 3 City Hall, second floor
BOARD OF FIRE WARDENS S. F. F. DEPARTMENT, 2 City Hall, third floor
BOARD OF PILOT EXAMINERS, office 519 Clay
BOARD OF RELIEF (Masonic) office Masonic Temple
BOARD OF STATE HARBOR COMMISSIONERS, office 302 Montgomery
BOARD OF SUPERVISORS, rooms 2 City Hall, second floor
BOARD OF SUPERVISORS, clerk of, office second floor, City Hall, room 3
BOARDMAN GEORGE C. president San Francisco Fire Insurance Co. office Donohoe, Kelly & Co.'s Building, 432 Montgomery, dwl Cosmopolitan Hotel

Boardman Joseph, architect, dwl NE cor Francisco and Dupont
Boardman Thomas S. jeweler with Geo. C. Shreve & Co. dwl 621 Clay
BOAS Emanuel (Joseph Boas & Co.) res New York
BOAS JOSEPH & CO. (Charles B. Richard and Emanuel Boas) importers and jobbers fancy goods, and agents Hamburg Packet Co. 513 Sacramento, dwl 531 Post
Boas Michael, drayman, 542 Howard
Bobenrieth John, workman Willows Brewery, dwl SW cor Mission and Nineteenth
Bobues John, liquors, dwl Battery bet Filbert and Union
Boccardo Luigi, employé with Brignardello, Macchiavello & Co. 706 Sansom
Boch Rudolph, salesman, 420 Bat, dwl 1217 Powell
Bock Adolph, clerk, dwl SW cor Polk and Hayes
Bock Charles, liquor and billiard saloon, 769 Clay, dwl SE cor Clay and Dupont
Bock Jacob, miner, bds Franklin Hotel, SE cor Sansom and Pacific
Bocke Frank, upholsterer, dwl 132 Sutter
Bockeln Christian, laborer, Bay Sugar Refinery, dwl S s Greenwich bet Jones and Taylor
Bocken Henry, restaurant, 643 Washington, dwl S s Union above Mason
Bockholz Henry, seaman, dwl 44 Sacramento
Bockman Richard H. groceries and liquors, NE cor Folsom and Eighth
Bockmann B. H. clerk, dwl 104 Stewart
Bockmann (Henry) & Mangels (Henry) groceries and liquors, NE cor Freelon and Fourth
Bockmann Henry, drayman, dwl NW cor Kearny and Jackson
Bockrath Henry, produce, dwl 321 Fifth
Bocksch Charles, gardener, N s Presidio Road near Presidio House
Bodden Hugh, stone cutter, dwl 528 Pacific
Bode Frederick, job wagon, corner Sacramento and Montgomery, dwl Powell nr Green
Bode George C. with J. B. Thomas, dwl 826 Mission
Bode Luis, agent Clinton Temperance Hotel, 311 Pacific
Bodecker Bernard, musician, dwl 424 Union
Boden John F. court room clerk, Fourth District Court, dwl 405 Bush
Boden John H. clerk with Henschel & Maurice, dwl 424 Bush
Boden P. (widow) dwl 424 Bush
Bodkin Eliza Miss, dress maker, 246 Sixth
Bodkin Sarah Miss, dress maker, 246 Sixth
Bodkin Thomas, plasterer, dwl 119 Shipley
Bodwell H. H. (Atwood & B.) dwl 237 Minna
Bodwell Mary L. Miss, teacher mathematics, Girls' High School, dwl 17 Tehama
Body William, pantryman, stm Pacific
Boege H. painter, 417 Dupont
Boegler Mary (widow) dwl 737 Broadway
Boehm Andrew, baker, 120 Third
Boehm Daniel (col'd) cook, stm Chrysopolis
Boehm Isaac, clerk, 134 Second
Boehm Philip J. waiter, dwl 35 Jessie
Boehme Frederick, musician, Maguire's Opera H. dwl S s Vallejo bet Montgomery and Kearny
Boehmer Fritz, merchant, dwl 611 Union
Boell Charles L. printer with Calhoun & Son, dwl 817 Vallejo nr Powell, rear
Boenstein Herman, clerk, dwl 61 Stevenson
Boepple Ferdinand, shoe maker with William F. Burke, dwl Meyer's Hotel
Boero Luigi, employé with Brignardello, Macchiavello & Co. 706 Sansom
Boese Julius, clerk, Golden Gate Market, dwl 721 Broadway
BOFER WILLIAM & CO. (August Bultman and Adolph Marquard) importers and retailers hardware, 610 Sacramento

Bofinger Jacob, gold and silver plater, 431 Kearny
Bogan Charles, merchant, dwl S s Union bet Montgomery and Calhoun
Bogardus J. P. *(Californian Publishing Co.)* dwl Delgardo Place
Bogart John M. book keeper, 127 Clay, dwl W s Eleventh bet Market and Mission .
Bogart O. H. book keeper with R. H. McDonald & Co. dwl 1 Milton Place
Bogash Charles, clerk, 634 Commercial, dwl 406 Dupont
Boge Joseph, painter, dwl Lütgen's Hotel
Bogee William, laborer, Lone Mountain Cemetery
Bogel C. H. groceries and liquors, SW cor Waverly Place and Washington
Bogel Theodore *(B. Lefevre & Co.)* dwl 1015 Jackson
Boggs Edwin, dwl 522 Dupont
Boggs P. H. dwl 522 Dupont
Bogle Joseph H. policeman, dwl 9 Front, rear
Bogner Charles, tailor, W s Valencia bet Fifteenth and Sixteenth
Boham Mary Miss, domestic, dwl S s Chestnut bet Stockton and Powell
Bohan Bridget Miss, domestic, dwl 1526 Powell
BOHANAN PATRICK, groceries and liquors, NW cor Natoma and Mary
Bohen Benjamin T. policeman, City Hall, dwl 4 St. Mark Place
Bohen George T. dwl 617 Pine
Bohle Sophia Miss, domestic, 835 Post
BOHLKEN *(John Martin)* & BREMER *(Henry)* groceries and liquors, NW cor Third and Harrison
Bohm S. H. merchant, office 117 Battery, dwl 524 Green
Bohm William, manufacturing jeweler, 614 Merch
Bohme William, conductor, North Beach & M. R. R. Co. dwl 276 Jessie
Bohmer Louis G. Independence H. & L. Co. No. 3
Bohn Adolph, dwl 427 Green
Bohn B. J. seaman, bds 5 Washington
Bohn John, stoves and tin ware, 1218 Dupont, dwl 418 Union
Bohner Charles A. Five Mile House, San Bruno Road
Bohrman H. farmer, dwl 323 Pine
Boice Charles De S. book keeper, American Exchange Hotel
Boie George, packer, Golden Gate Mills, 430 Pine
BOILLEAU FERDINAND, stock broker, office NE cor Montgomery and Jackson, dwl S s Lombard bet Leavenworth and Hyde
Bois John (col'd) cook, bds 5 Broadway
Boise River G. & S. M. Co. office 338 Montgomery
Boisnet Alphonse, cabinet maker, 3 Stockton
Boisnet Prosper, cabinet maker, 3 Stockton
Boisse Eugene, hair dressing saloon, 526 Commercial, dwl 626 Sacramento
Boisse Gaston, Knickerbocker Engine Co. No. 5
Boisse Hermine Madame, dress maker, 625 Sac
Boitano Andrea, boarding, dwl W s Union Place
Boitias Henriette Mrs. dwl 430 Bush
Bokee David McK. cashier Holladay's Steamship Line, SW cor Front and Jackson, dwl 733 Pine
Bolado Joaquin *(Sanjurjo, B. & Pujol)* dwl 526 Sutter
Bolan James, groceries and liquors, 328 Third
Boland James, book keeper, Vulcan Foundry, dwl Hubbard Court
Boland John, butcher, 39 Metropolitan Market, dwl SE cor Taylor and O'Farrell
Boland Nelson, street paver, dwl 116 Jessie
Boland William H. book keeper, dwl 54 First
Bolander Catherine (widow) furnished rooms, 736 Market
Bolander Frederick A. student, dwl 736 Market
Bolander Henry N. professor German Academic Seminary, dwl 60 Second

Bolander Henry N. Mrs. ladies' fancy store, 60 Second
Boldemann Adolph, cook, 28 Montgomery, dwl Pine bet Polk and Van Ness Avenue
Bole James, book keeper with Henry Dreschfeld, dwl 322 Vallejo
Boles John, laborer with C. B. Folsom, dwl S s O'Farrell bet Devisidero and Scott
Bolfrey William, shoe maker, dwl 562 Bryant
Bolger John, boiler maker, Union Foundry, dwl 260 Clementina
Bolger John, plasterer, dwl S s Shipley nr Harrison Avenue
Bolger Miles, liquor saloon, SW cor Davis and Sac
Bolger Thomas, clk, 315 Montgomery, dwl 218 Bush
Bolger, see Bulger
Bolhens William, dwl SW cor Polk and Hayes
Bolian Martin, tailoring, 108 Sansom
Bolinas Petroleum Co. office 611 Clay
Bolinger William A. secretary Crescent Quartz Mill Co. office 311 Clay, dwl 519 Folsom
Bollen George W. machinist, Pacific Foundry, dwl W s Rousch nr Folsom
Bolles Frederick, 1st officer stm Del Norte, dwl NE cor Taylor and Jackson
Bolles, see Bowles
Bollier Paul, tobacconist, dwl 8 Lick Alley
Bolling George K. Mrs. trimmings and fancy goods, 1009 Folsom
Bolling George K. musician, dwl 617 Folsom
Bollinger John C. collector, dwl SW cor Stockton and Greenwich
Bollo Thomas, groceries and liquors, SE cor Stockton and Vallejo
Bolster Thomas, brakeman, Market Street Railroad, dwl junction Hayes Valley and Market
Bolte Henry, Thunderbolt Billiard and Liquor Saloon, 938 Kearny, dwl NE cor Dupont and Broadway
Bolte Wilhelm, clerk, 209 Front
Bolten Jacob, clerk with D. Erichs, dwl SE cor Vallejo and Battery
Bolton Henry, handcartman, corner Drumm and Jackson
BOLTON JAMES R. real estate, office 618 Merchant, dwl NW cor Jones and Greenwich
Bolton John G. butcher, dwl 18 Rousch
Bolton John H. dwl 1104 Taylor
Boltz Albert, steward, dwl E s Sonoma Pl nr Union
Bona Peter, real estate, dwl SW cor Dupont and Broadway
Bonacine Angelo, carver, dwl N s Broadway bet Kearny and Dupont
Bonal John, shoe maker, dwl 740 Vallejo
Bonatti Aquiline, with Henry Ielmini, dwl 445 Bush
Bond Balaam, assistant janitor Masonic Temple
Bond C. waterman, dwl SW cor Dupont and Bdwy
BOND CHARLES R. secretary Fireman's Fund Ins. Co. 238 Montgomery, dwl 819 Wash
Bond George, carpenter, dwl 39 Second
Bond Henry H. apprentice with S. S. Culverwell, res San Antonio
Bond Margaret Mrs. domestic, 121 Sixth
Bond Richard L. carpenter and builder, dwl N s Broadway bet Leavenworth and Hyde
Bond Thomas H. J. real estate agent and collector, dwl N s Broadway bet Leavenworth and Hyde
Bondil P. engineer, French Hospital
Bondon Arthur, clerk; Central American Transit Co. dwl 1018 Stockton
Bonduel Charles, foreman Courier de San Francisco, 617 Sansom, dwl 921 Washington
Bone Yune (Chinese) washing, 162 Minna
Bone Mary (widow) dwl 24 Clara, rear
Boner Margaret Miss, domestic, dwl 1002 Powell
Bones John W. contractor and builder, dwl 40 Minna
Bones Samuel W. dwl 40 Minna
Bonestell J. T. salesman with R. B. Gray & Co. dwl 512 Stockton

Bonestell Louis H. salesman with John G. Hodge & Co. dwl 512 Stockton

Bonetti Giacomo, laborer, dwl S s Polk Alley

Bongert Mitchell, teamster, dwl 639 Broadway

Bonglet Elisa, laundress, dwl S s Hayes bet Octavia and Laguna

Bonher Charles A. ranchero, St. Francis H. & L. Co. No. 1

Bonis Peter, veterinary surgeon, 214 Stevenson

Bonn Henry *(Begeman & B.)* dwl SW cor Tehama and Fifth

Bonnard Charles R. K. printer, Eureka Typographical Rooms, 625 Merchant

Bonnard Francis A. compositor, Morning Call, dwl 1324 Jackson

Bonnard Thomas, dry goods, dwl 425 Fourth

Bonneau Thomas C. hair dressing saloon, Railroad House, dwl SE cor Minna and Sixth

Bonnell A. C. cashier Evening Bulletin, 620 Mont, dwl 711 Bush

Bonnell Edward, clerk, County Recorder's Office, dwl N s Saco bet Hyde and Leavenworth

Bonnell Henry W. clerk with Brooks & Rouleau, dwl 711 Bush

Bonnell Kate Miss, assistant, Hyde Street Primary School, dwl 711 Bush

Bonnell Rufus, clerk with D. J. Oliver, dwl 711 Bush

Bonner Charles, mining engineer, office 804 Mont, room 9, dwl 111 Taylor

Bonner John L. (col'd) porter, 611 Sacramento, dwl 611 Mason

Bonnet *(B.)* & Co. *(John Leotier)* asphaltum workers, SW corner Third and Stevenson, and brick mkrs, W s Larkin bet Bdwy and Vallejo

Bonnet Caroline Mme. dwl 8 Polk Alley

Bonnet Eugene, cook, 526 Clay

Bonnet Isaac, dwl 632 Post

Bonnet Pierre, French Garden, Lobos Creek

Bonney George, broker, SW cor Mont and Clay

Bonney O. mining stocks, dwl 620 Market

Bonney Olpha jr. carpenter, dwl 732 Folsom

Bonney Thomas C. carpenter, dwl 13 Ellis

Bonzi Antoine, with Peter Bonzi, 515 Merchant

Bonzi Peter, Italian Restaurant, 515 Merchant

Boobar E. C. *(Galloway & B.)* dwl 554 Folsom

Boohen Patrick, hostler, 16 Sutter, dwl 814 Mission

Booker H. E. Mrs. *(T. Sullivan & Co.)* dwl 214 Powell

BOOKER W. LANE, H. B. M. consul, office 428 California, dwl Union Club Rooms

Bookmeyer William, seaman, bds 7 Washington

Books Robert F. hair dresser, dwl E s Mason bet Vallejo and Green

Bookstaver *(S. J.)* & Weller *(Peter H.)* butchers, 82 Washington Market, dwl E s Eighth bet Howard and Folsom

Boomsma Albit, clerk, Keystone House, 127 Jackson

Boone William, drayman, cor Cal and Battery, dwl 109 Pine

Boone William H. clerk with Brocas & Perkins, bds International Hotel

Booraem H. Toler, attorney at law, office 519 Mont

Booraem T. L. collector, dwl 116 Perry

Booraem Townsend, teamster, Pacific Glass Works, dwl cor Iowa and Mariposa

Boorman John, milk ranch, dwl N s Broadway bet Franklin and Van Ness Avenue

Boosma Albert, liquor saloon, 923 Kearny

Booth *(Adam)* & Co. produce commission merchants, 36 and 38 Clay, dwl 1713 Mason

Booth Daniel E. clerk, U. S. Land Office, dwl 1711 Dupont

Booth George, works with John Higgins, Lake Merced Ranch

BOOTH H. J. & CO. *(G. W. Prescott and I. M. Scott)* Union Foundry, NE cor First and Mission, dwl SW cor First and Harrison

Booth Hosea, workman with N. Simonds, cor Bay View Park and Hunter's Point Road

Booth Joseph *(William Booth & Co.)* res Newark, N. J

Booth Lucius A. mining, office 402 Front, dwl W s First Avenue nr Fifteenth

Booth N. B. & Co. *(M. Pezold)* manufacturing confectioners, 20 Kearny

BOOTH NEWTON *(Booth & Co. Marysville)* office 405 Front

Booth Samuel, spinner, Mission Woolen Mills, dwl W s Shotwell bet Nineteenth and Twentieth

BOOTH WILLIAM & CO. *(Joseph Booth)* importers and manufacturers hats and caps, 314 Sacramento, dwl 42 Tehama

Booth William, machinist, Union Foundry, dwl NW cor First and Mission

Boothby Ezekiel, workman with Smith & Brown, dwl 6 Columbia nr Sixteenth

Boothby William L. teamster, dwl 308 Folsom

Boothman James, with D. R. Provost & Co. dwl 735 Market

Boothman Jeannette Miss, dwl 735 Market

Boothroyd G. waiter, steamer Senator

Bootz Adam, hotel keeper, dwl N s Page bet Franklin and Gough

BOOTZ'S HOTEL, John Baumeister & Co. proprietors, 435 Pine

Booyer David, dwl Russ House

Böpp Peter, butcher with A. Reiner. dwl Potrero Av

Boquillon A. A. hay and grain, 53 Third

Boradt Henry, butcher with J. Scmadec, NE cor Folsom and Twenty-Second

Borbeck John, liquors, 600 Cal, dwl 514 Geary

Borchard Charles *(Ehrenpfort & Co.)* dwl 24 Stockton

Borchard Louis, clerk, dwl 313 Kearny

Borchelt John, carpenter, dwl W s Larkin bet Green and Union

Borchers Diedrich, dwl 529 Broadway

Borchers Fabian *(Gotze & B.)* dwl N E cor Kearny and California

Borchers *(Henry J.)* & Poska *(Jacob)* foreign and domestic fruits, 423 Davis and 252 Stewart

Borchers J. C. physician, office and dwl 343 Kearny

Borchers Thomas, wool presser with Clark & Perkins, dwl 409 Union

Borchers William, sailor, dwl 20 Frederick

Borde Frederick, express wagon, NW cor Montgomery and Commercial, dwl 1616 Powell

Borde Johanna (widow) dwl 1616 Powell

Bordenave James, bakery, 433 Pacific

BORDEAUX & SAN FRANCISCO MARITIME LINE PACKETS, Alexis DeStoutz agent, 431 Battery

BORDEAUX BOARD OF UNDERWRITERS, Henry Schroder & Co. agents, 811 Montgomery

Border John, laborer, dwl S s Liberty bet Townsend and Brannan

Bordner Jacob, carpenter Russ House

Bordwell George, architect, office 224 Montgomery, dwl 442 Second

BOREL ALFRED, com merchant, NW cor Mont and Jackson, dwl NW cor Cal and Stockton

Borel Antoine, clerk with Alfred Borel, dwl NW cor California and Stockton

Borel Gustave, collector with Z. Hebert, dwl Santa Clara bet Hampshire and Jersey

Borella A. groceries and liquors, NE cor Third and Tehama

Borger Christian, jeweler, dwl 238 Stewart

Borgher Louisa, domestic, dwl 1414 Kearny

Boring Samuel W. cotton raiser, dwl with W. Sublett, San Bruno Road nr Twentieth

BORKER *(Solomon)* & ROSENFELD *(Anthony)* stock and money brokers, office 602 Montgomery, dwl 722 Vallejo

Borkheim Henry, regimental tailor, 236 Sutter

Borle Louis, cook 323 Washington

Born Charles, hair dresser with Henderson & Brown, dwl 417 Post

Born Nicholas, driver with Bernard Raubinger, 130 Geary
Bornemann F. H. assistant book keeper, office U. S. Assistant Treasurer, dwl SW cor Folsom and Thirteenth
Bornemann Francis G. cashier office U. S. Assistant Treasurer, dwl SW cor Folsom and Thirteenth
Bornemann George, laborer with Peter Salmon
Bornheim George, tailoring, 102 Sansom
Bornheimer Francis, fruit, 226 Third
Bornstein Julius, with E. Martin &. Co. dwl NW cor Franklin and Oak
Bornstein Paulina Miss, assistant teacher, Hebrew school, dwl cor Oak and Franklin
Bornstine Henry, retail dry goods, 731 Montgomery
Borren Korm, furniture, 246 Third
Borsch Barbara Miss, domestic with Frederick Beckman, W s Van Ness Avenue nr Grove
Bortfeld E. billard-table maker, dwl Hinckley
Borthwick Robert, porter dwl 229 Bush
BORUCK MARCUS D. *(Chase & B.)* dwl 619 Geary
Bosch Rebecca, domestic, 311 Clementina
Boschen Fabian *(N. Boschen & Co.)* dwl SE cor Minna and Fifth
Boschen Nicholas &. Co. *(Fabian Boschen)* groceries and liquors, SE cor Minna and Fifth
Boschken Jacob *(C. F. Glein & Co.)* dwl 407 Powell
Bose Henry, clerk with C. H. Bogel
BOSE *(John)* & DAHNKEN *(Frederick)* Exchange Liquor Saloon, NE cor Clay and Davis, dwl W s Taylor bet Filbert and Greenwich
Bose John, hog ranch, S s El Dorado nr Nebraska
Bose Richard, house and sign painter, dwl 235 Sutter
Bosquet Andrew, porter, A. P. Hotaling & Co. NE cor Sansom and Jackson
BOSQUI EDWARD & CO. printers, book binders, and blank book manufacturers, 517 Clay and 514 Com, dwl NE cor Greenwich and Dupont
Bosqui Kenneth J. conductor, North Beach & Mission Railroad Co. dwl 334 Seventh
Bosqui William, printer with Edward Bosqui & Co. 517 Clay
Bosselmann H. fireman, steamer Pacific
Boston Copper Mining Co. office 626 Montgomery
BOSTON LINE PACKETS, Glidden & Williams' Line, Meader, Loler & Co. agents, 405 Front
Boston Louis, handcartman, cor Pacific and Davis
Boston Mary W. (widow) dwl 413 Stevenson
BOSTON UNDERWRITERS, T. H. & J. S. Bacon agents, office 308 Front
Bostrom John, shoe making, 305 Davis
Bostwick Henry, real estate, dwl 933 Sacramento
BOSWELL *(S. B.)* & SHATTUCK *(D. D.)* commission and provision dealers, 317 and 319 Front cor Commercial
Boswell William, teamster with F. Glas, 25 Wash
Bosworth Charles W. boot maker, 153 Third, dwl NE cor Harrison and Ritch
Bosworth George F. compositor, American Flag
Bosworth H. M. *(W. B. Frisbee & Co.)* dwl 3 Montgomery
BOSWORTH *(William)* & RUSSELL *(John B.)* stock and exchange brokers, NE cor Montgomery and Merchant, dwl 14 Prospect Place
Botcleven Robert, laborer with Hey & Meyn
Bothe Louis C. dwl SE cor California and Kearny
Bothe Sophie Mrs. midwife, dwl SE cor California and Kearny
Bothmann Frederick, job wagon, cor Second and Market, dwl 9 Clara
Bottcher Richard, liquor saloon, 641 Pacific
Bottnayar, Hebert, vegetable garden nr Bay View Park
Botts C. T. attorney at law, office 19 Montgomery Block, dwl Russ House

Bouchard Hyppolite, crockery and lamps, 1330 Dupont
Boucher Charles, laborer, dwl Bertha W s Beale
BOUCHER EUGENE, merchant tailor, 537 Sacramento, dwl 228 Post bet Dupont and Stockton
Boucher James, porter, 223 California, dwl S s Stevenson bet Sixth and Seventh
Boucher James S. workman with Casebolt & Co. dwl Stevenson bet Sixth and Seventh
Boudan Alcidi, laundry, 2111 Mason
Boudin *(Louis)* & Gleizes *(Benjamin)* French Bakery, 434 Green, rear
Bonette Dominique, dwl 721 Pacific
Bouffé Ernest, waiter, 647 Com, dwl 626 California
Bougart Michael, cartman, 639 Broadway
Bougrand Mme. dwl 1314 Dupont
Boukofsky E. dwl 215 Minna
Bouldoire Mdme. dwl 816 Montgomery
Boulfoir Geodon, employé, Metropolitan Restaurant, 715 Montgomery
Boulin Peter, carpenter, dwl 515 Green
Boulon Etienne, syrup manufacturer, dwl 613 Union
Bouquin Adele Miss, domestic, dwl 709 Commercial
Bourasson Theodore, laundryman with F. P. Coset, Sixth bet Bryant and Brannan
Bourasso T. L. dwl 116 Sansom
Bourdache Jean, dwl 206 Third
Bourdais Miss, dress maker, 15 Second
Bourek W. hostler, Omnibus R. R. Co
Bourgade Cheri, wines and liquors, 247 Third
Bourgeois Alexandre, carriage maker, 630 Broadway
Bourgom Joseph, dwl 8 s Bush bet Buchanan and Webster
Bourn William B. shipping merchant, 222 Sacramento, dwl 537 Third
Bourne Elisha W. book keeper with Macondray & Co. dwl 428 Bryant
BOURNE GEORGE M. water cure physician, 10 Post, Masonic Temple
Bourne John B. book keeper with Jones & Bendixen, dwl W s Jones bet Filbert and Greenwich
BOURQUIN CHARLES, dentist, office 426 Kearny, dwl NW cor Pacific and Dupont
Bourquin Emile, dwl 1507 Dupont
Bourse Geo. R. (colored) steward, dwl 1507 Mason
Boursier Edward, butcher with Hypolite Dereins, 2 Clay Street Market
Bouafield F. H. assayer with Hentsch & Berton, dwl 225 Second
Boushey Stepin, mining, dwl 310 Minna
Bousquet Berrand, baker, 26 Third, dwl 209 Stevenson
Bousquet Mme. dress maker, dwl 1216 Stockton
Boutard Charles, laundry, 178 Jessie
Boutelle C. B. aid, U. S. Coast Survey, office Custom House, third floor
Bouton Francis G. *(Russell & B.)* dwl 307 Sixth
Bouton Wilmot Miss, teacher private school, SE cor Green and Dupont, dwl 718 Green
Bouvel Jules, laundry, N s Bush nr Broderick
Bouwman Bernard, boot and shoe maker, dwl 137 Jessie
Bovee James·S. machinist, dwl E s Taylor bet Filbert and Valparaiso
BOVEE, *(William H.)* HALLETT, *(George H.)* BARTLETT *(Pliny)* & DALTON *(P. E.)* Contra Costa Laundry, office 13 Broadway, res Oakland
Bovee William R. manager U. S. Restaurant, 509 Clay
Boven James, carpenter, dwl N s Broadway bet Leavenworth and Hyde
Bovyer William L. carpenter and builder, 417 Pine, dwl 1014 Pine
Bow Edwin R. W. salesman, 309 Montgomery, dwl 730 Folsom
Bow Frank, brass molder, dwl 33 Baldwin Court
Bow Joseph, broker, dwl 522 Dupont

Bow Kate, domestic, 220 Stevenson
Bow Mary (widow) dwl 730 Folsom
Bovan John, drayman, cor Eighth and Brannan
Bowcher James, cabinet maker with W. G. Weir, dwl 541 Mission
Bowden Charles S. broker, dwl S s Geary bet Dupont and Stockton
Bowden John, second officer steamer Orizaba, office NW cor Battery and Pine
Bowden John, drayman, dwl Folsom bet Fourth and Fifth
Bowden John, laborer, dwl Freelon nr Fourth
Bowden Joseph, house painter, dwl S s Filbert bet Leavenworth and Hyde
Bowden William, house painter, dwl S s Filbert bet Leavenworth and Hyde
Bowen Ada C. Miss, assistant, Denman Grammar School, dwl SW cor Stockton and Jackson
Bowen Archibald J. longshoreman, dwl NE cor Montgomery and Alta
BOWEN BROTHERS (Charles R. and Pardon M.) wholesale groceries and liquors, 425 and 427 Battery, and retail SE cor Montgomery and California, dwl SE cor Sutter and Polk
Bowen (Charles F.) & Hart (Felix L.) books and stationery and circulating library, 620 Market, dwl 608 Market
Bowen Dennis, hostler, 641 Sacramento, dwl 10 St. Mary
Bowen Elizabeth Miss, dwl W s First Avenue nr Sixteenth
Bowen Ezekiel C. Coiner's Department, U. S. Branch Mint, dwl S s Vallejo nr Leavenworth
Bowen George H. driver with Henry H. Edmunds
Bowen Gustave, brass finisher with Morris Greenberg
Bowen Hannah Miss, domestic, dwl 908 Jackson
Bowen James, gardener, dwl E s Park Avenue bet Bryant and Harrison
Bowen James L. house carpenter, dwl 841 Vallejo
Bowen James V. glass stainer, 12 Fourth, dwl 222 Stevenson
Bowen John, gas fitter, dwl 4 Hartman Place
Bowen Kate Miss, cap maker with Kalisher & Diamant, dwl E s Sixth bet Stevenson and Jessie
Bowen Kate Miss, chambermaid, American Exchange
Bowen Maria, chambermaid, American Exchange
Bowen Michael, laborer, dwl W s Mary Lane nr Bush
Bowen Pardon M. (Bowen Bros.) dwl 726 California
Bowen Patrick, hostler, dwl 121 Stevenson
Bowen Reuben W. book binder with Bartling & Kimball, 505 Clay
Bower John, farmer, S s Old Ocean House Road, 6 miles from City Hall
Bower John, porter with H. P. Wakelee, dwl 7 Mary Lane
Bowerman Daniel, sash and blind maker with Geo. Robinson & Co. dwl 13 Perry
Bowers Alexander, dwl 74 Tehama
Bowers Benjamin D. express wagon, cor Bush and Montgomery, dwl Clementina nr Third
Bowers Elisha P. furniture and bedding, 31 Third, dwl 267 Third
Bowers E. P. (E. L. Smith & Co.) dwl 197 Third
Bowers George D. clerk, 131 Montgomery, dwl Clementina nr Third
Bowers Jordan (colored) dwl 333 Sutter
Bowers J. T. importer pianos, harmoniums, melodeons, music, etc. 131 Montgomery, dwl 812 California
Bowers Kate, domestic, dwl N s Bryant bet Second and Stanly Place
Bowers Michael, laborer, dwl 949 Folsom
Bowers P. T. (widow) with Charles S. Eaton
Bowers S. T. dwl 331 Bush

BOWIE AUGUSTUS J. physician and surgeon, office 622 Clay, dwl NW corner Stockton and Sutter
Bowie Henry P. dwl NW cor Stockton and Sutter
Bowker Enoch C. tally clerk, Pier 4 Stewart
Bowlan James, with George Hughes, 501 Sansom
Bowler Mary (widow) dwl 37 Stevenson
Bowles George, carpenter, dwl cor Polk and Bay
Bowles James, clerk, NE cor Leidesdorff and Sacramento, dwl S s Bush bet Kearny and Dupont
Bowles, see Bolles
Bowley S. C. (Holt & B.) dwl 423 Bryant
Bowley Susan (widow) boarding, 54 Third
Bowlin W. F. book keeper, dwl 54 First
Bowman A. clerk, 27 Third, dwl 14 Hunt
Bowman Alex. S. (Klaus & B.) dwl 730 Mission
Bowman Arthur W. (Bigelow & B.) dwl NW cor McAllister and Steiner
Bowman A. S. express wagon, 42 Third
Bowman A. W. broker, dwl Lick House
Bowman Bridget (widow) dwl S s Minna bet Eighth and Ninth
Bowman Caroline (widow) dwl 826 Mission
Bowman C. C. merchant, office and dwl 728 Mont
Bowman Charles, milkman, dwl Buckley Ranch, half mile SW of Lone Mountain Cemetery
Bowman E. B. (col'd) dwl 521 Broadway
Bowman E. P. dwl 8 Vassar Place
Bowman Francis, carpenter, dwl NW cor Broadway and Kearny
Bowman George, gilder, dwl W s Hartman Place nr Lombard
Bowman George F. dwl NW cor Steiner and McAllister
Bowman Gustave, seaman, dwl 20 Commercial
Bowman J. engineer, dwl SW cor Louisiana and Sierra
Bowman James, dwl S s Sacramento bet Powell and Mason
BOWMAN JAMES F. editor Daily Dramatic Chronicle, office 417 Clay, dwl 223 Minna
Bowman James W. engineer, dwl SW cor Montgomery and Jackson
Bowman John, carpenter, Miners' Foundry, boards Revere House
Bowman Peter E. boarding and inspector, C. H. dwl SW cor Broadway and Montgomery
Bowman Thomas, engineer, dwl U. S. Court Building, SW cor Montgomery and Jackson
Bowman William Rev. secretary, St. Mary's Cathedral
Bowman William F. milkman, E s Fourth near Brannan, dwl 446 Brannan
Bowman William O. contractor, dwl NE cor Townsend and Crook
Bowmaster Christian, grocer, dwl 20 Clementina
Bowne William F. shipping merchant, dwl 418 Fremont
Bowos John, blacksmith, dwl W s Salmon between Mason and Taylor
Bowret Jules, laundry, Sixth nr Brannan
Box James, carpenter, dwl E s Hyde bet Tyler and McAllister
Boy George, dwl 14 Lewis Place
Boyce James, dwl 442 Clementina
Boyce John, molder, Union Foundry
Boyce Samuel, with Thomas Boyce, 544 Washington, dwl Benton House
BOYCE THOMAS, advertising and newspaper agency, 544 Washington, dwl 526 Bryant
Boyd (Alexander) & Davis (Jacob Z.) real estate, office 321 Front, dwl 235 Geary
Boyd Anna Miss, furnished rooms, 11 Stockton
Boyd Catharine (widow) lodgings, 325 Dupont
Boyd Colin M. tally clerk, Pier 11 Stewart, dwl 719 Market
Boyd E. T. waiter, Lick House
Boyd George, foreman with William M. White, dwl 32 Ellis

Boyd George W. captain ship Coquimbo, office 8 Stewart Pier 1, dwl S s Columbia bet Dolores and Guerrero

Boyd H. C. engineer, dwl Niantic Hotel

Boyd James, laundry, Capp nr Howard

Boyd James, machinist, Miners' Foundry, dwl 350 Third

BOYD JAMES T. attorney at law, office 8 Wells' Building, 605 Clay, dwl 240 Montgomery

Boyd John, dwl S s Green bet Taylor and Jones

Boyd John, drayman, NW cor Jackson and Sansom, dwl N s Willow Avenue bet Larkin and Polk

BOYD *(John D.)* McAULIFFE *(Florence T.)* & CO. *(Christian Merkle)* varnishers, polishers, and stainers fancy woods, 412 Pine, dwl NE cor Fourth and Mission

Boyd John M. carpenter, dwl 364 Minna

Boyd Joseph, tinsmith, dwl Alta nr Sansom

Boyd Joseph C. clerk, 218 Battery, dwl 142 Clara

Boyd Michael, baker, 1412 Dupont

Boyd Oliver D. proprietor Empire State Restaurant 426 and 428 Sansom, dwl 107 Sansom

Boyd Theodore C. engraver and stationer, 300 Mont, dwl 713 Taylor

Boyd Thomas C. apprentice, Golden State Iron Works, dwl SE cor Geary and Powell

Boyd William, captain bark William H. Gawley, office Pier 1 Stewart

Boyd William A. *(R. S. Cutter & Co.)* dwl 254 Tehama

Boyd W. M. Coiner's Dept. U. S. Branch Mint, dwl 927 Pine

Boye Bernard, laborer, dwl S s Cal bet Polk and Van Ness Avenue

Boye Otto, boarding, 1819 Powell cor Greenwich

Boyer Daniel, handcartman, Clay nr Drumm

Boyer, David, fruits, cor Commercial and East, dwl 35 Sacramento

Boyer Joseph, express wagon, dwl 1008 Dupont

Boyer Michael, cartman, dwl 424 Pacific

Boyer William, shoe maker, dwl 32 Russ, rear

Boyes Charles, merchant tailor, 42 Sutter

Boyban John, carriage trimmer with Pollard & Carvill, dwl 528 Bush

Boylan Bridget Mrs. domestic, dwl 732 Vallejo

Boylan Charles, fruit dealer, Washington Hose Co. No. 1

Boylan James, laborer, dwl N s Fulton nr Octavia

Boylan Michael, gas fitter, San Francisco Gas Co

Boylan Owen, laborer, dwl 140 Stewart

Boylan Patrick, laborer, dwl S s Clementina bet Fifth and Sixth

Boyle Agnes F. Mrs. dwl 124 Jessie

Boyle Arthur, molder, dwl 57 Stevenson

Boyle Bernard, dwl S s Cal bet Van Ness Avenue and Polk

Boyle Bernard, laborer with George D. Nagle

Boyle Bridget Miss, laundry, Lick House

Boyle Edward, furrier with Adolph Muller, dwl 111 Turk, rear

Boyle Edward, porter, 210 Cal, dwl 424 Tehama

Boyle Ellen Miss, domestic, dwl 742 Pine

Boyle Francis R. cigar maker, 705 Davis, dwl 713 Sansom

Boyle George, dwl 212 Harrison

Boyle George S. dentist, office and dwl 625 Clay

Boyle James, hostler, North Beach & M. R. R. Co. dwl S s Perry bet Fourth and Fifth

Boyle James, laborer, dwl 1020 Folsom

Boyle James, laborer, dwl SE corner Brannan and Gilbert

Boyle James, plasterer, dwl Bootz Hotel

Boyle Jane (widow) dwl 219 Minna

Boyle John *(Fraser & Co.)* dwl 404 Geary

Boyle John C. gas fitter with J. H. O'Brien & Co. dwl 4 Hartman Place

Boyle John F. professor, St. Mary's College

Boyle Magloin, restaurant, NW cor Sansom and Merchant

Boyle Mary (widow) dwl with A. Lawson, S s California Avenue nr Folsom

Boyle Mary E. Miss, saleswoman, 16 Second, dwl 124 Jessie

Boyle Michael, miner, bds Marysville Hotel, 414 Pacific

Boyle Patrick, carpenter, dwl S s Vallejo bet Sansom and Montgomery

Boyle Patrick, farmer, dwl 525 Commercial

Boyle Peter, laborer, bds NE cor Sixteenth and Howard

Boyle Robert, musician, dwl 249 Jessie

Boyle Terrence, laborer, dwl 11 Langton

Boyle Thomas, coachman, dwl S s Chestnut bet Stockton and Powell

Boyle Thomas, ship joiner, dwl NE cor Bush and Laguna

Boyle Timothy, laborer, dwl 29 Main

BOYLE W. A. dentist, office and dwl 625 Clay

Boyle William, tailoring, 308 Sansom, dwl S s Filbert bet Mason and Taylor

Boylen Bernard, laborer, Golden Age Flour Mills, 717 Battery, dwl Pacific Temperance House

Boylen Charles, fruits, 1436 Stockton

Boylen Michael, gas fitter, dwl 12 Sutter

Boylen William, tailor, dwl S s Filbert bet Mason and Taylor

Boyling Thomas, mariner, dwl 709 Greenwich

Boyne Joseph, laborer, dwl Codman Place

Boyne Thomas, wines and liquors, dwl 521 East

Boynton Abbott B. coachman with Frank M. Pixley

Boynton Chas. E. *(Gebhard & B.)* dwl 342 Brannan

Boynton C. W. civil engineer, office 240 Mont

Boynton G. F. carpenter, dwl 812 Jackson

Boynton Samuel S. painter, dwl 68 Clementina

Boysen Charles, hatter, 316 Kearny

Boysen Julius, hatter and straw presser, 514 Pine

Boytin T. conductor, Omnibus Railroad

Bozane John, blacksmith, Fort Point

Bozzer Emanuel, wood and coal, dwl 1420 Powell

Bracelyn Bridget, domestic, NW cor Bryant and Grove Avenue

Brack George A. confectionery, 1228 Stockton

Brack Oswald, shoe making, 606 Post

Bracken James, porter, dwl 18 Natoma

Bracken John, nurse, City and County Hospital

Bracken Lawrence, expressman, dwl W s Ritter nr Harrison

Bracken Mary (widow) dwl 820 Jackson

Bracken Peter, cook, dwl 18 Natoma

Brackett Charles A. blacksmith with D. Hewes & Co. dwl S s Harrison bet Seventh and Eighth

Brackett J. George, flour packer, National Mills, dwl O'Farrell nr Jones

Brackett John B. millwright, dwl 83 Everett

Brackett Joseph G. with Nelson Pierce, 321 Front, dwl 508 O'Farrell

Brackett Joseph G. jr. packer, National Flouring Mills, dwl 508 O'Farrell

Brackett William, dwl 115 Dupont

Brackett *(W. L.)* & Keyes *(O. H.)* Stewart Street Market, 50 Stewart, dwl 34 Tehama

Braconnier Louis, clerk, 1117 Dupont

Bradbury George H. captain, Pacific Mail Steam-S. Co. dwl 406 Bryant

Bradbury Thomas, machinist, dwl with A. Guerrera, N s Mission nr Eleventh

Bradbury William B. carpenter, dwl N s Bush bet Polk and Van Ness Avenue

Braddey Mary (widow) dwl 46 Jane

Braddock Ann Mrs. wines and liquors, SE cor Davis and Jackson

Braden Thomas, laborer with Hey & Meyn, dwl Eighteenth nr Florida

Brader Ann (widow) dwl 740 Broadway

Brader Christian, foreman with Henry Brader, 611 Battery, dwl 737 Broadway

Brader Henry, Excelsior Bottling Establishment, 611 Battery, dwl 738 Broadway

Brader Louis, dwl 740 Broadway
Brader Peter, dwl 740 Broadway
Bradford Charles H. stock and exchange broker, 609 Clay, dwl 823 Montgomery
Bradford Edwin J. clerk, dwl S s Tehama nr Fifth
Bradford E. J. bar keeper, 621 Merchant, dwl S s Tehama nr Fifth
Bradford G. waiter, Cosmopolitan Hotel
Bradford George, bill poster, dwl Niantic Hotel
Bradford George B. lumber, dwl 67 Tehama
Bradford John F. seaman, dwl 10 Stewart
Bradford Joseph, salesman with Hawley & Co. dwl 65 Tehama
Bradford Woodbury, printer, dwl Winters Alley bet Union and Green
Bradhower August, laborer, Bay Sugar Refinery, 813 Battery
Bradlee Stephen H. stair builder with B. H. Freeman & .Co. dwl N s Jessie bet Seventh and Eighth
Bradlee Stephen H. jr. with D. R. Provost & Co. dwl N s Jessie bet Seventh and Eighth
Bradley Anna Miss, domestic, 431 Post
Bradley Bernard, laborer, dwl SE cor Ninth and Minna
Bradley Bernard, painter, dwl 65 Natoma
Bradley Charles, retortman, San Francisco Gas Co
Bradley Charles L. clerk with Fulton G. Berry, dwl 808 Jackson, rear
Bradley Dame, news dealer, dwl SW cor .Dupont and Broadway
Bradley David H. salesman, 106 Battery, dwl 652 Market
Bradley Eliza Mrs. furnished rooms. 1014 Stockton
Bradley Ellen Miss, domestic, dwl 837 California
Bradley Ellen Miss, dress maker, dwl SE cor Ninth and Minna
Bradley George, carpenter, dwl 130 Second
Bradley George L. *(C. R. Peters & Co.)* dwl 920 Bush
BRADLEY HENRY W. importer photographic and ambrotype materials, 620 Clay *(and Bradley & Rulofson)* dwl 1112 Bush
BRADLEY *(Henry W.)* & RULOFSON *(William H.)* photographic art gallery, 429 Montgomery cor Sacramento, dwl 1112 Bush
Bradley Hugh, plasterer, dwl 812 Union
Bradley James H. engineer C. S. N. Co. dwl 140 Natoma
Bradley John, painter dwl 13 Second
Bradley John, waiter, dwl 13 Second
Bradley Kate Miss, domestic with Mrs. W. H. Tillinghast, N s Folsom bet Eighth and Ninth
Bradley Margaret, laundry, Lick House
Bradley Michael, gardener, dwl 43 Ecker
Bradley Peter, laborer with John Center, NW cor Sixteenth and Folsom
Bradley Richard (col'd) janitor S. F. Olympic Club Rooms, dwl 1004 Washington
Bradley Robert, plasterer, dwl SE cor Pacific and Polk
Bradley Samuel, pattern maker, Vulcan Iron Works, dwl Quincy Place nr Pine
Bradley Theodore, principal Boys' High School, dwl 1 Bagley Place
Bradley Thomas, bds Brooklyn Hotel
Bradley, Thomas W. *(Savin & B.)* dwl 605 Bdwy
Bradley William, miner, dwl 228 Commercial
Bradley William O. inspector, C. H. dwl 603 Pine
Bradshaw Edward, seaman, dwl 44 Sacramento
Bradshaw George H. clerk, 416 Battery, dwl NE cor Post and Leavenworth
Bradshaw Oliver L. machinist, dwl 619 Market
Bradshaw Richard, blacksmith with M. P. Holmes, dwl 20 Jessie
Bradshaw Samuel C. office 238 Montgomery, dwl NE cor Post and Leavenworth
Bradshaw Samuel C. r. assayer, dwl NE cor Post and Leavenworth

BRADSHAW *(Turell T.)* & CO. *(George F. Bragg)* wholesale and retail grocers, NE cor California and Sansom, dwl 716 Stockton
Bradshaw William R. book keeper with Dewey & Co. dwl 1106 Mason
BRADSTREET J. M. & SON *(Commercial Agency, New York)* W. W. West agent, office SE cor Montgomery and Sacramento
Bradt Gurden G. policeman, City Hall, dwl Miles Place, N s Sacramento below Powell
Bradt Joseph, stock broker, dwl 63 Minna
Bradt S. S. clerk, dwl 1026 Montgomery
Brady Anna Miss, domestic, 227 Geary
Brady, Barney, gardener, dwl 926 Clay
Brady Benjamin, merchant, office 120 California, dwl 628 Vallejo
Brady Bernard *(O'Reilly & B.)* dwl NW cor Mission and Fifth
Brady Catherine, domestic, 754 Mission
Brady Daniel, butcher, SE cor Jessie and Fifth, dwl cor Sixth and Stevenson
Brady Elizabeth, dwl 419 Stockton
Brady Ellen Mrs. domestic, dwl 916 Stockton
Brady Francis R. with Locke & Montague, dwl 405 Kearny
Brady Hannah, domestic, 611 Folsom
Brady Henry J. mining secretary, dwl 612 Pine
Brady James, cook, dwl 538 Market
Brady James, gas fitter, 8. F. Gas Co
Brady James, Market Ex. Restaurant, 625½ Mission
Brady James, metal roofer with John Kehoe, 228 Bush
Brady James, stone cutter, dwl 12 Sutter
Brady James G. printer, dwl 819 Jackson
Brady Jane Miss, domestic, 411 Ellis
Brady Johanna (widow) dwl 7 Brooks
Brady John, boiler maker with Coffey & Risdon, dwl 349 Tehama
Brady John, cooper, S. F. & P. Sugar Co. dwl W s Ninth bet Folsom and Harrison
Brady John, laborer, dwl 308 Pacific
Brady John, laborer, dwl 160 Jessie
Brady John, laborer, dwl SW cor Bush and Stock
Brady John, waiter, Russ House
Brady John B. draftsman, office 423 Washington room 4, dwl 511 Pine
Brady John J. dwl 620 Third
Brady John T. clerk with Langley, Crowell & Co. dwl SE cor Sansom and Washington
Brady Mary Miss, dwl 249 Jessie
Brady Mary Miss, domestic, 912 Washington
Brady Mary Miss, domestic, 932 Bush
Brady Mary O. domestic, 1109 Stockton
Brady Mathew, seaman, dwl S s Grove bet Franklin and Gough
Brady Mathew, steward, dwl 255 Beale
Brady Mathew, stone yard, office and dwl 1812 Powell
Brady Owen, hostler with William Black
Brady Patrick, laborer, dwl W s Dolores bet Twenty-Second and Twenty-Third
Brady Patrick, metal roofer with H. G. & E. S. Fiske, dwl 165 Tehama
Brady Patrick, waiter, Lick House, dwl 631 Post
Brady Patrick F. upholsterer with Goodwin & Co. dwl 625 Bush
Brady Philip, agent Evening Bulletin S. F. & San José R. R. dwl Coso House
Brady Philip, blacksmith, Union Foundry, dwl 349 Tehama
Brady Philip, laborer, dwl E s Gilbert nr Brannan, rear
Brady Philip, with Jones, Wooll & Sutherland, dwl 249 Jessie
Brady Robert, plumber, dwl 127 Fourth, rear
Brady Robert D. workman, Pacific Glass Works, dwl cor Mariposa and Indiana
Brady Rosa C. Miss, with Wheeler & Wilson Sewing Machine Co. 439 Montgomery, dwl 521 Pine

Brady Rosella Miss, dwl 521 Pine
Brady Thomas, dwl SE cor Mission and First
Brady Thomas, brick layer, dwl 113 Tehama
Brady Thomas, clerk with J. D. O'Callahan, dwl E s Jansen bet Greenwich and Lombard
BRADY THOMAS A. editor and proprietor Monitor, office 622 Clay, dwl 619 Pine
Brady William J. boiler maker, Union Foundry, dwl 106 Beale
BRAGG GEORGE F. & CO. commission merchants, 111 California (and Bradshaw & Co.) dwl 822 Washington
BRAGG H. W. & CO. (C. Waterhouse and J. W. Lester) importers and dealers carriage and wagon materials, 29 and 31 Battery, res Sacramento
Bragg M. J. Miss, assistant, Fourth Street School, dwl W s Main bet Harrison and Folsom
Bragg Robert, ship joiner, dwl W s Main bet Folsom and Harrison
Braggadocia G. & S. M. Co. office 6 Mont Block
Braghi Rinaldo, groceries and liquors, NE cor Brannan and Seventh
Brahaney Thomas, waiter, SE cor Mission and First
Brainard Henry C. express wagon, 624 Market, dwl 623 Market
Brainard Richard (Langley, Crowell & Co.) dwl SW cor Second and Minna
Braley George A. fruits, dwl 501 Davis
Bralley Patrick, hair dresser with Thomas C. Bonneau, dwl 7 Rassette Place No. 3
Bralley Patrick, peddler, dwl 221 Beale
BRALY MARCUS A. real estate, office 405 Front, dwl SE cor Geary and Hyde
Brambilla Elvira, artist, Italian Opera, dwl 726 Vallejo
Bramell Aaron, longshoreman, dwl E s Sansom bet Union and Filbert
Bramson Henry A. machinist, Union Foundry, dwl Philadelphia House
Bramstone George, clerk with Cutting & Co
Branch Ellen Mrs. domestic, dwl 775 Market
Branch (William) & Colyer (Washington) Old Georgia Restaurant, 923 Kearny, dwl 1304 Pac
Brand Aristide (Saulnier & Co.) dwl 818 Bdwy
Braud Ernest, cigars and tobacco, Cosmopolitan Hotel
Brand Herman, manufacturer cigars, 408 Clay, dwl 262½ Clementina
Brand H. N. brass finisher, dwl 349 Bush
Brand Isidor, cigar maker with E. Goslinsky, dwl 710 Harrison nr Third
Brand Jonas, jeweler with F. R. Reichel
Brand Lucien, Custom House clerk with Koopmanschap & Co. dwl 818 Broadway
Brand T. O. dwl E s Clinton bet Bryant and Brannan
Brandel George, with Charles Schroth, 230 Kearny, dwl 315 Bush
Brandel Henry, laborer, dwl 315 Pine
Brandenstein Herman, clerk with A. S. Rosenbaum & Co. dwl Mission bet Second and Third
Brandenstein Joseph (A. S. Rosenbaum & Co.) dwl 121 Eddy
Brandenstein Meyer, butcher, dwl 109½ Ellis
Brander Hermann T. clerk, SE cor Mission and Fourth
Brander John S. groceries and liquors, SE cor Mission and Fourth, dwl 107 Fourth
Brander Morris (Johnson & B.) dwl NW cor Jones and Pacific
Brandhofer Michael, merchant tailor, 628 Merchant
Brandon James, bar tender with Jesse Richardson, dwl cor Front and Vallejo
Brandon Joseph R. (Grey & B.) attorney at law, office 522 Montgomery
Brandon William, workman, S. F. & P. Sugar Co. dwl SW cor Dora and Folsom
BRANDRETH WILLIAM F. office with Rubber Clothing Co. 642 Sac, dwl Occidental Hotel

Brands James, foreman molder, Fulton Foundry, dwl Tehama bet Second and Third
Brandt Adolph, clerk, dwl 248 Fremont
Brandt Alonzo B. gold beater, dwl 510 Sacramento
Brandt Bernard L. house and sign painter, 322 Commercial, dwl 622 O'Farrell
Brandt George E. sail maker, dwl 42 Stevenson
Brandt John, cabinet maker with Goodwin & Co. dwl Clinton bet Bryant and Brannan
Brandt Louis (Liebling & B.) dwl Gautier's Home, N s Pacific nr Montgomery
Brandt Louis, shoe maker, dwl 344 Third
Brandt Otto, groceries and liquors, 1040 Market
BRANGER JEAN, Hotel de France, 821 Kearny, dwl 1000 Powell
Brangon Richard M. (Hatch & B.) dwl 1006 Clay
Branlin John H. cook, Empire House, S s Vallejo bet Front and Battery
Brann A. T. driver, dwl 537 Howard
Brann C. H. F. teller with B. Davidson & Berri, dwl 809 Howard
Brann Loring, furniture and job wagon, SW cor Market and Fourth, dwl corner Missouri and Mariposa
Brann Robert C. sail maker with John Harding, dwl 32 Clary
Brannan Bridgett (widow) dwl 916 Montgomery
Brannan Ellen Miss, cook, Protestant O. Asylum
Brannan James, laborer, dwl 46 Louisa
Brannan James, laborer, Spring Valley W. W
Brannan James, upholsterer with Goodwin & Co. dwl 13 Ohio cor Broadway
Brannan J. F. carpenter, dwl St. Lawrence House
Brannan John, boiler maker, dwl National House
Brannan John, laborer, Fort Point
Brannan John, laborer, dwl NW cor Vallejo and White
Brannan John, peddler, dwl 547 Mission
Brannan John, teamster, dwl S s Brannan bet Eighth and Ninth
Brannan Joseph, laborer with Hey & Meyn
Brannan Julia Miss, domestic, Protestant Orphan Asylum
Brannan Martin J. tanner with S. Bloom, dwl 606 Third
Brannan Mary Miss, domestic with D. Stein, S s Fulton nr Gough
Brannan Mary F. (widow) dwl 690 Geary
Brannan Michael, laborer, dwl 30 Fourth
Brannan Patrick, teamster, foot Townsend, dwl 314 Ritch
Brannan Patrick, horse shoeing, cor Spring and Summer, dwl 421 Tehama
Brannan Patrick, salesman, 609 Sacramento, dwl Brooklyn Hotel
Brannan Patrick T. (Newman & B.) dwl Potrero
Brannan Richard, porter with Dell, Cranna & Co. dwl Vernon House
Brannan Richard H. dwl 233 Fourth
Brannan R. W. clerk, dwl cor Jackson and Drumm
BRANNAN SAMUEL, real estate, office 420 Montgomery, third floor, dwl 1319 Powell
Brannan William, laborer with Hey & Meyn
Branschied William (G. Weber & Co.) dwl 820 Pac
BRANSON (Ware) & BELL (John) sail makers S s Broadway bet Battery and Front, dwl 233 Stevenson
Brant George, sail maker, dwl N s Stevenson bet First and Second
Brant John H. drayman, cor Clay and Drumm, dwl 109½ Ellis
Brant William P. policeman, City Hall, dwl E s Jones bet Broadway and Vallejo
Brasche, George H. architect, dwl 129 Jessie
Brascocci Mateo, fisherman, 10 Italian Fish Market
Brash John, printer, dwl 217 Post
Brass John, tinsmith with Tay, Brooks & Backus
Brass J. H. book keeper, National Mills, dwl Oriental Hotel

Brand Etienne, machinist, dwl 441 Bush, rear
Brauer Aloys *(Frederick Hess & Co.)* dwl 1234 Stockton
Brauer Claus W. groceries and liquors, dwl NE cor Sansom and Pacific
Braun Charles, dwl 809 Howard
Braun William, seaman, bds 7 Washington
BRAVERMAN *(Louis)* & LEVY *(John)* importers and retailers watches, jewelry, diamonds, silver ware, 621 Washington
Bray Dennis E. Columbian Engine Co. No. 11
Bray Edward L. broom maker with L. Van Laak, dwl SE cor Mission and First
Bray Henry, with Bray & Brother, dwl 759 Market
Bray Frank, dwl 759 Market
Bray John, book keeper with Bray & Brother, dwl 917 Clay
Bray John A. dry goods, Independence H. & L. Co. No. 3
BRAY *(John G.)* & BROTHER *(W. A. Bray)* commission merchants, and agents Alviso and San José Family Flour Mills, office NE cor Clay and Front, res Santa Clara
Bray Michael, shoe maker, 341 Third
Bray W. A. *(Bray & Brother)* res San Antonio
Brayton Albert P. jr. *(Goddard & Co.)* dwl 434 Second
Brayton C. E. clerk with Brooks & Rouleau, res Oakland
Brazell James, salesman, 106 Sutter, dwl 11 Geary
Brazer John *(Larrabee & B.)* dwl 95 Montgomery Block
Breaden Thomas, laborer with Hey & Meyn
Breadham August, laborer, Bay Sugar Refinery, dwl 813 Battery
Breal Henry, upholsterer, dwl 416 Post
Breant Leon, tailor, dwl 418 Dupont
Brechtel William F. house and sign painter, SW cor Post and Devisidero
Brecken Henry, with Horace Davis & Co. 430 Pine
Brede John, clerk, dwl 423 Washington
Bredenbeck George, farmer, bds 7 Washington
Bredhoff *(Charles)* & Cordes *(John)* liquors, SE cor Pacific and Drumm
Bredhoff Charles *(Martens & B.)* 58 Washington Market
Bredhoff *(Henry)* & Co. *(John Gerves)* billiard and liquor saloon, 423 East, dwl 1506 Powell
Bree Hannah Miss, domestic, dwl 835 Howard
Bree John, brass finisher, dwl 509 Howard
Bree John H. apprentice, dwl 509 Howard
Bree Thomas W. actor, dwl 509 Howard
Breed Daniel C. *(B. & Chase)* dwl 1011 Bush
BREED *(Daniel N. and Daniel C.)* & CHASE *(Andrew J.)* wholesale groceries and provisions, 400 Battery cor Clay, dwl 1213 Powell
Breed Edward A. dwl 1213 Powell
Breed H. L. *(Tilden & B.)* dwl 1003 Stockton
Breed James F. night clerk, Post Office, dwl 652 Howard
Breen John *(T. F. Neagle & Co.)* dwl 682 Post
Breen Michael J. carrier Morning Call, dwl N s Mission bet Twelfth and Thirteenth
Breen Patrick, waiter, Lick House
Breen Thomas, machine and brass foundry, 120 Fremont
Breese Joseph C. with Snow & Co. dwl 226 Stevenson
Breevort House, Mrs. M. H. Yates proprietress, NW cor Mission and Fourth
Breeze Thomas *(Murphy, Grant & Co.)* 401 and 403 Sansom
Breidenstein Emanuel, cook, Golden Gate Hotel
Breidenstein L. manufacturer jewelry boxes, 650 Washington, dwl 1209 Kearny
Breig John, soda maker, dwl 109 Jessie
Breiling Brothers *(Jacob and John)* Franklin Meat Market, 335 Bush
Breiling John *(Breiling Bros.)* dwl 407 Bush

Breithaupht Felix, brewer, Broadway Brewery
Breitwieser Charles W. bar keeper, 218 Clay, dwl 106 First
Bremen Anna Miss, domestic, dwl 1013 Pine
BREMEN BOARD UNDERWRITERS, C. F. Mebius agent, office 223 Sacramento
Bremen Wilhelmina Miss, domestic, dwl 1415 Powell
Bremer Frederick, with Erzgraber & Goetjen, 120 Davis
Bremer Henry *(Bohlken & B.)* dwl NW cor Harrison and Third
Bremer Henry, driver, Brown's Bakery, dwl 1223 Stockton
Bremer Hermann *(Schonfeld & B.)* dwl 529 Pine nr Dupont
Bremer William, teamster with Lyon & Co. dwl 274 Jessie
Bren William, clerk, dwl 10 Kearny
Brendel Christman, agent National Brewery, dwl 421 O'Farrell
BRENHAM C. J. commissioner deeds for all the States and Territories, office 205 Battery, dwl SW cor Howard and Sixteenth
Brennan Annie Mrs. ladies' hair dresser, 705 Howard
Brennan Catharine Miss, domestic, dwl NE cor Dupont and Francisco
Brennan Edward, porter with Taaffe & Co. dwl Santa Clara nr San Bruno Road
Brennan *(James)* & Co. *(John McHugh)* produce commission and agents Santa Cruz steamer Salinas, 206 Clay, res Watsonville
Brennan James *(Brennan & Co.)* 16 Third
Brennan James, dwl 705 Howard
Brennan James E. tailor, 223 Montgomery, dwl 558½ Howard
Brennan James F. bar keeper, 520 California
Brennan John, laborer, dwl 29 Main
Brennan John, salesman with Taaffe & Co. dwl 22 Montgomery
Brennan Martin, porter, 302 California, dwl with G. White W s Montgomery nr Vallejo
Brennan Mary Miss, domestic, 108 Stockton
Brennan Michael T. contractor and builder, dwl 11 Ritch
Brennan *(Patrick)* & Co. *(James Brennan)* dry goods, 16 Third
Brennan Richard, stone mason, dwl SE cor Mission and Lafayette Avenue
Brennan Richard P. Rev. vice president St. Mary's College
Brennan Thomas, carriage maker, dwl 30 Ecker
Brennan Thomas P. *(Newman & B.)* dwl S s Mariposa nr Mississippi
BRENNAN *(Thomas W.)* & RYDER *(George W.)* Old California Exchange Saloon, NE cor Kearny and Clay, dwl 112 Natoma
Brennan William, bar keeper, 206 Leidesdorff
Brenner Anthony *(Brenner Bros.)* dwl 401 Bush
Brenner Brothers *(George and Anthony)* tailors, 401 Bush
Brenner Charles, musician, dwl 443 Bush
Brenner William, dwl E s Brown's Alley
Brenner William H. bar keeper with D. Droger, SE cor Filbert and Battery
Brenning August, with John Howes, dwl 20 Ohio nr Broadway
Brenning John, drayman with Osterhoudt & Harloe, NW cor Washington and Davis
Brereton James, collector, S. F. Gas Co. dwl 640 Second
Breslauer Baruch, cigars and tobacco, 314 Sansom, dwl 224 Jessie
Breslauer Henry & Co. *(Abraham B. Goldstein)* dry goods, 50 Third, dwl 225 Jessie
Breslauer Henry, importer and jobber dry and fancy goods, 310 California, dwl 225 Jessie
Breslauer Nathan, clerk, 310 California, dwl 225 Minna
Breslin Daniel, retortman, S. F. Gas Co

Bresnehan Johanna Miss, domestic, 307 Taylor
Bresnehen Stephen, laborer, dwl 246 Minna
Brearasher *(Solomon)* & Co. *(Frederick Weidemuller)* bakery, 1012 Dupont
Bresse Louis, cook, dwl 20 Minna
Brestat August, cook, dwl 404 Green
Breth Patrick, laborer, bds 127 Pacific
Brett John R. dwl Geary Place
Bretzke Albert, clerk, Adjutant-General's Office, 742 Washington, dwl 323 Dupont
Breuer Charles, bedstead maker, dwl Davis bet Sacramento and Commercial
Brew John, seaman, dwl 44 Sacramento
Brew Nathaniel, ship carpenter, dwl 27 Clara
Brewer Catharine, liquors, SW cor Chambers and Front
Brewer Frederick L. butcher with A. Elias, dwl 538 Market
Brewer Jacob, carpenter, dwl 962 Howard
Brewer Henry W. carpenter, dwl 225 Minna
BREWER JOHN H. attorney at law, office 40 Montgomery Block, res Oakland
BREWER MICHAEL T. subscription books and engravings, 420 Montgomery, dwl 22 Langton
Brewer William, bar keeper, Bella Union, dwl 12 St. Charles
Brewster Benjamin *(Jennings & B.)* dwl 112 Powell
Brewster Edward, ship carpenter, dwl 235 Beale
Brewster J. B. calker, dwl W s Second bet Folsom and Howard
Brewster *(John)* & Son *(John Brewster jr.)* house and sign painters, 237 Bush, and proprietor Summer Street House, Summer nr Montgomery
Brewster John, seaman, dwl 532 Commercial
Brewster John jr. *(Brewster & Son)* dwl Summer nr Montgomery
BREWSTER ROBERT E. treasurer California State Telegraph Co. office 507 Montgomery, dwl 639 Clay
Brewster William C. porter, 419 Clay, dwl What Cheer House
Brewton J. C. lamplighter, dwl 816 Clay
Breyfogle William O. carpenter with W. J. L. Moulton, dwl 8W cor Twenty-Third and Bartlett
Brezzolara George, with Cutting & Co. dwl Filbert nr Dupont
Briant Edward, secretary British Relief Society, dwl 634 Post
Brice Alexander E. purifier, San Francisco Gas Co
Brice James, dwl 315 Montgomery
Brice William, bootcrimper, dwl 24 Dupont
Bricket John B. fruits, 940 Market
Brickle John, real estate, dwl 917 Clay
Brickley James, carpenter, dwl S s Mission nr Center
Brickley Samuel, dwl What Cheer House
Bricknell William, miller, dwl 54 First
Brickwedel Aaron D. groceries and liquors, SW cor First and Market
BRICKWEDEL C. H. & CO. *(F. H. Hegeler)* Steamer Dining Saloon, 253 and 255 Stewart
BRICKWEDEL HENRY & C. *(Otto Kloppenburg)* importers and jobbers wines and liquors, 208 and 210 Front, dwl SE cor Franklin and Fulton
Brickwedel Jacob, groceries and liquors, NE cor Clay and Waverly Place
Brickwedel John, liquor saloon, NE cor Post and Cemetery Avenue
Brideson Catharine, domestic, dwl 1606 Larkin
BRIDGE MATTHEW, mason contractor and builder, office 319 Bush, dwl 683 Harrison
Bridge Samuel J., U. S. appraiser, office C H
Bridge Thomas, costumer, dwl 26 Tehama
BRIDGE WILLIAM E. proprietor Black Hawk Livery and Sale Stable, 317 Pine, dwl 224 Montgomery

Bridgeman John, teamster with Reynolds & Co. dwl 417 Folsom bet First and Fremont
Bridges George R. with S. P. Taylor & Co. dwl Empire Lodgings
Bridges Marshall C. hardware, dwl 826 Jackson
Bridges Thomas L. naturalist, dwl W s Eleventh bet Market and Mission
Bridgewood Samuel, engineer, dwl S s Lombard nr Kearny
Briedling T. P. (widow) dwl 135 Post
Briel August, butcher, dwl E s Ninth bet Bryant and Brannan
Briel Jacob, butcher, dwl E s Ninth bet Bryant and Brannan
Brier Columbus, principal, English Institute, SW cor Geary and Mason, dwl 122 Geary
Brier John W. assistant teacher, English Institute, dwl 122 Geary
Brigaerts Gerard, box maker with J. S. Gibbs, dwl 66 Jessie
Brigandat Nicolas P. bookbinder with H. Payot, 640 Washington
Briggs B. F. *(Hathaway & Co.)* dwl 312 Beale
Briggs Charles F. brick layer, dwl 73 Fourth
Briggs Edgar, salesman, 226 Front, dwl 128 Turk
Briggs George M. milkman, dwl Bailey House
Briggs G. N. pattern maker, Union Foundry
Briggs H. H. carriage maker, dwl 559 Market
Briggs Jesse, contractor, dwl 39 Second
Briggs Joseph W. drayman, 417 Washington, dwl W s Haywood bet Folsom and Louisa
Briggs Oliver F. assistant assessor, U. S. Int. Rev. NW cor Battery and Commercial, dwl 23 Clara
Briggs O. W. Rev. dwl NW cor Mission and Eleventh
Briggs W. H. molder, Vulcan Foundry, dwl 81 Natoma
Briggs William C. engraver with R. B. Gray & Co
Briggs William R. broker, dwl 335 Pine
Brigham C. O. *(Hall & B.)* dwl 844 Mission
Brigham James H. book keeper with Armstrong, Sheldon & Davis, 124 Market
Brigham S. O. importer Paris fashions, 111 Mont, dwl 23 Kearny
Brigham William H. *(Crane & B.)* res New York
Bright John, cartman, dwl 231 Pacific
Bright Robert, dwl 1217 Pacific
Brignardello Gio. Battista, employé, Brignardello, Macchiavello & Co. 706 Sansom
Brignardello Nicola, clerk, 623 Pacific
Brignardello Santiago & Bro. *(Stefano Brignardello)* importers hardware and crockery, 623 Pacific. dwl 703 Stockton
BRIGNARDELLO, *(Stefano)* MACCHIAVELLO *(Giovanni Battista)* & CO. *(N. Larco)* macaroni and vermicelli manufacturers, 706 Sansom *(and S. Brignardello & Bro.)* res Italy
Brika Francoe, workman with L. L. Lanthaieurne, near St. Mary's College
Brill Jacob, wood carver, dwl S s California bet Montgomery and Kearny
Brimblecom Samuel A. poultry dealer, dwl 18 Park Avenue
Brin Victor, porter with Chauche & Martin, 608 Front
Brincatt Salvo, butcher with Wm. Dick & Co. dwl 24 Freelon
Brindle William, stone mason, dwl S s Filbert bet Leavenworth and Hyde
Brines Charles, gardener with J. O'Hara, dwl cor Twentieth and Harrison
Brinkmann Charles, wood carver, dwl NW cor Market and Sansom
Brinkmann John, blacksmith, dwl 631 Broadway
Brinn Rose, domestic, dwl 618 Howard
Brion Nicholas C. employé, Occidental Restaurant, dwl SE cor Broadway and Dupont
Briordy John, groceries and liquors, 60 First cor Lick Alley

Briordy John J. gas fitter with Thomas Ross, dwl N s California bet Stockton and Powell
Briordy Margaret Miss, domestic, 524 Sutter
Briordy Patrick, clerk, 19 Washington Market, dwl 820 California
Brisae Felix, broker, dwl NE cor Pine and Taylor
Brisac V. Mme. teacher modern languages, Girls' High School, dwl NE cor Pine and Taylor
Brisk Julius, clothing, dwl 5 Jackson
Brissacker Solomon *(A. Patek & Co.)* dwl 836 Mission
Brister Andrew, laborer with D. W. Ruggles, 310 Jackson, dwl Mason bet Jackson and Pacific
Bristol Harry, 320 Montgomery
Bristol Harry, cooper with Handy & Neuman, 216 Commercial
Bristol Joseph D. attorney at law, dwl 970 Harrison
BRITISH AND CALIFORNIAN BANKING CO. limited, office 424 California
BRITISH AND FOREIGN MARINE INSURANCE CO. Liverpool, Falkner, Bell & Co. agents, office 430 California
Britt John, house mover, dwl N s Willow Avenue nr Polk
Britt William, seaman, dwl E s Maria nr Market
Brittain William, blacksmith with Black & Saul, dwl 10 Hunt
BRITTAN J. W. & CO. *(A. D. McDonald)* importers and jobbers stoves and metals, 118 and 120 Front, res San Mateo
Brittingham William E. clerk, 12 Second, dwl 540 Mission
Britton George, dwl 819 Montgomery
Britton George W. book keeper with Goodwin & Co. dwl 1313 Taylor
BRITTON *(Joseph)* & CO. *(Henry Steinegger)* lithographers, 533 Commercial, dwl S s Union bet Mason and Taylor
Britton William F. boot black, dwl NW cor Washington and Sansom
Brizolaro Louis, laborer, dwl 425 Filbert
Broad Charles C. butcher, dwl 1222 Bush
Broad James, laborer, dwl E s Taylor, bet Chestnut and Lombard
Broadway Block, Joseph Roster proprietor, NW cor Kearney and Broadway
Broadway Brewery, 637 Broadway
Brocard Eugene, cook, St. Francis Restaurant, dwl 720 Dupont
Brocas *(John W.)* & Perkins *(Chas. C.)* forwarding and commission merchants, 52 Clay and East Street Wharf, dwl International Hotel
Brock Christian C. mariner, dwl 2 Hartman Place
Brock John C. captain bark Mary, 212 Clay
Brockhage Frederick, clerk with C. V. Gillespie
BROCKLEBANK *(Manuel T.)* & CO. real estate agent, office 302 Montgomery, dwl 603 Pine
Brocklebank O. H. dwl 38 Belden block
Brockman Charles, organist, dwl 29 Hunt
Brocq Alfred, nursery, Bay View Park
Brod Emanuel, cook U. S. Marine Hospital
Brodek Bros. *(R. G. & S. B.)* clothing, 339 Kearny
Brodek Gustave *(Brodek Bros.)* dwl 44 Everett
Brodek Samuel *(Brodek Bros.)* dwl 44 Everett
Brodek Samuel *(Saalburg & B.)* dwl S s Stevenson bet Third and Fourth
Broder Gillman, cook, dwl 729 Broadway
Broder Patrick, cook Franklin House, SW cor Broadway and Sansom
Broderick Annie Miss, dwl 283 Stevenson
Broderick Catharine Miss, domestic, dwl 613 Stock
Broderick David, shoe maker, 252 Stewart
Broderick Edward, workman with J. M. Mitchell
Broderick Ellen (widow) dwl 26 Everett
Broderick John, works at S. F. & P. Sugar Co. dwl NW cor Bryant and Park Avenue
Broderick Julia Miss, domestic, 503 Leavenworth
Broderick Lizzie Miss, domestic, White House, San José Road

Broderick Patrick, boiler maker with Coffey & Risdon
Broderick Patrick, hackman, dwl 5 Lafayette Pl
Broderick T. J. boots and shoes, 225 Montgomery, dwl 316 Minna
Broderick Walton, laborer, dwl 414 Market
BRODERICK WILLIAM, agent Singer Manufacturing Co. 139 Montgomery, dwl 22 Perry
Brodersen J. B. mcht, off 611 Clay, dwl 128 Post
Brodie *(James)* & Radcliff *(C. M.)* mechanical draftsman, office 402 Mont. dwl 830½ Harrison
Brodie James, apprentice, Vulcan Iron Works, dwl 830½ Harrison.
Brodie Samuel H. attorney at law, dwl 323 Pine
BRODIE, *(William)* HUBBARD *(Warren)* & McADAMS *(Archy)* proprietors California Foundry, 16 Fremont, dwl 84 Everett
Brodie William jr. engineer, dwl 84 Everett 624 Mission
Brodwolf George, merchant tailor, 319 Bush, dwl 319 Bush
Brodwolf Michael, tailor, dwl 319 Bush
Brody Michael, butcher, dwl Grass Valley House E s Sixth nr Market
Brogan Michael, baker, dwl 313 Fifth
Brokamp Benjamin, upholsterer with J. F. & H. H. Schafer, 504 Sansom
Brokaw Henry V. salesman with James Brokaw, dwl 561 Howard
BROKAW JAMES, sash, door, blind, and molding manufacturer, Mechanics' Mill, SW cor Mission and Fremont, dwl 19 Belden Block
BROKERS' BLOCK (Exchange Building) NW cor Montgomery and Washington
Brokete Hinrich, employé, Bay Sugar Refinery, dwl S s Union bet Battery and Sansom
Brolly D. assistant engineer, P. M. S. S. Co
Brolly John C. waiter, U. S. Restaurant, dwl Niantic Hotel
Bromley Washington L. mining secretary, 436 Jackson, dwl N s Union bet Hyde and Larkin
Bromley William B. dwl 247 Tehama
Bromley William P. pilot, dwl N s Riley nr Taylor
Brommer Claus *(D. Brommer & Bro.)* dwl NE cor Sixth and Bryant
Brommer Diedrich & Brother *(Claus)* groceries and liquors, NE cor Sixth and Bryant and milk ranch, Old San José Road, 5 miles fm City Hall
Brommer Henry, with Croskey & Howard, dwl S s Hayes bet Gough and Octavia
Brommer John, milkman with Brommer & Bro
Bronn Jean F. proprietor Bronn's Hotel, SE cor Stockton and Filbert
Bronn Theodore, assayer, dwl SE cor Stockton and Filbert
Bronsdon Phineas, road master, S. F. & San José R. R. dwl 17 Moss
Bronson J. F. clerk, Lone Mountain Cemetery, dwl 527 Pine
BRONSTRUP WILLIAM, groceries and liquors, SW cor Folsom and Dora
Broock Benjamin, scroll sawyer, Chace's Mills, dwl Beale Street House
Brookbanks M. E. Mrs. milliner, dwl 633 Market
Brooke Thomas, with Cutting & Co
Brookes Samuel M. artist, 611 Clay, dwl W s Old San José Road bet Twenty-Third and Twenty-Fourth
Brooklyn Charles, fireman, dwl Davis Street House
BROOKLYN HOTEL, John Kelly, jr. proprietor, SE cor Pine and Sansom
Brooklyn House, John Gately proprietor, 217 Bdwy
Brooks Aaron, cotton planter, dwl 327 Jessie
Brooks Benj. laborer, Empire Lodgings, 636 Com
BROOKS *(Benjamin S.)* & WHITNEY *(George E.)* attorneys at law, office 10-12 Exchange Buildings, dwl 631 Harrison
Brooks Celia Miss, domestic, 613 Post
Brooks Charles E. box maker with Hobbs, Gilmore & Co. dwl 66 Jessie

BROOKS CHARLES W. & CO. *(W. Frank Ladd and Edward F. Hall jr.)* shipping and commission merchants and agents Hawaiian Packet Line for Honolulu, office 511 Sansom, dwl 1109 Stockton

Brooks David, paper hanger, dwl 50 Stevenson

Brooks Edmund *(Reid & B.)* dwl S s Filbert bet Mason and Taylor

Brooks E. L. B. attorney at law, office 620 Washington room 16, dwl 1020 Montgomery

Brooks Eliphalet C. carriage maker with Pollard & Carvill, dwl 719 Market

Brooks Ezra L. carpenter, 763 Mission, dwl N s Thirteenth bet Mission and Valencia

Brooks Frank, porter, 223 California, dwl 313 Geary, rear

Brooks George, builder, dwl cor Chestnut and Kearny

Brooks H. E. clerk with Bryant & Morrison, dwl 603 Pine

Brooks Henry, printer, dwl 27 Ritch

Brook Henry, workman with W. Hall, Old San José Road nr county line

Brooks Henry B. *(Tay, B. & Backus))* dwl 766 Folsom

Brooks Henry S. agent, dwl 1804 Montgomery

BROOKS *(James)* & LAWRENCE *(Joseph E.)* editors and proprietors Golden Era, office 543 Clay, dwl N s Turk bet Polk and Van Ness Avenue

Brooks James, boot maker, dwl What Cheer House

Brooks James, mate, steamer Amelia

Brooks James H. miller, Golden Gate Mills, dwl Bootz's Hotel

Brooks James M. carpenter, dwl NW cor Chattanoga and Twenty-Third

BROOKS JOHN L. merchant tailor, 710 Montgomery, dwl 212 Post

Brooks Joseph, driver with Cutting & Co. dwl 111 Freelon

Brooks Joseph, salesman, 408 Commercial

Brooks L. B. mining, dwl Tehama House

Brooks L. H. (colored) steward, 630 Commercial, dwl 1208 Powell

Brooks Mary Miss, domestic, 130 Turk

Brooks Mary (widow) dwl 305 O'Farrell

Brooks Nellie Miss, actress, Bella Union

BROOKS NOAH, U. S. Naval Officer, office third floor Custom House, dwl Cosmopolitan Hotel

Brooks Robert C. ship carpenter, dwl 176 Jessie

Brooks Samuel, seaman, dwl 20 Commercial

Brooks *(S. S.)* & Hughes *(David B.)* general contractors, dwl 804 Bush

Brooks T. H. merchant, dwl International Hotel

BROOKS THADDEUS R. civil engineer, office 14 City Hall third floor, dwl 704 Howard nr Third

Brooks Theodore, teamster, dwl 210 Harrison

Brooks Thomas, dwl 111 Freelon

Brooks Thomas H. *(Newhall, B. & Nettleton)* dwl 310 Jessie

Brooks Timothy, seaman, steamer Pacific

BROOKS W. H. stationery, book, and periodical depôt, 51 Third

BROOKS *(W. H. J.)* & ROULEAU *(François A.)* searchers records, office 620 Washington rooms 1 and 2, dwl 729 Harrison

Brooks William P. house carpenter, dwl 1524 Dupont

Brooks William S. steerage steward, steamer Colorado, dwl 208 Third

Brooks W. N. dwl 43 Belden Block

Broom Woolf, wool dealer, dwl 232 Sixth

Broomcraft Salvo, marketman, dwl 824 Harrison

Brophy Michael *(Leonard & B.)* dwl N s Bush bet Van Ness Avenue and Franklin

Broren John, porter, dwl 913 Dupont

Bros George, hair dresser with Henderson & Brown, dwl cor Jane and Mission

Bros Jacob, hair dresser with C. Diehl, dwl 317 Dupont

Brosnan J. D. waiter, Lick House

Brotherson William, mariner, dwl Davis nr Washington

Brotherton Robert, carpenter, dwl S s Broadway bet Polk and Van Ness Avenue

Brotherton Thomas W. Rev. clergyman, St. John's Church, Mission Dolores, dwl W s Eleventh nr Market

Brougham John *(Lebert & B.)* dwl 1902 Dupont

Broughton Nap. L. broker, dwl Russ House

Broust Augustus, laborer, dwl SW cor Dupont and Broadway

Browell Jeremiah, contractor, dwl 322 Lombard

Brower Andrew J. saloon, 532 Green

Brower Celsus, clerk, Commissary Musters' Office, dwl 609½ Howard

Brower Daniel R. bakery, NE cor Vallejo and Stock

Browman Joseph, waiter, Occidental Hotel

Brown A. tinsmith, dwl 672 Harrison

Brown A. B. watchman, Chelsea Laundry

Brown A. C. Broderick Engine Co. No. 1

Brown Adolph, with Horace Porter, dwl Kearny bet Pacific and Broadway

BROWN A. F. fancy goods, 308 Battery, dwl 1107 Folsom

Brown Albert, laborer, 546 Clay

Brown Alexander, engineer, dwl 9 Ritch, rear

BROWN ALEXANDER B. Billiard Hall, 328 Montgomery, dwl 79 Stevenson House

Brown Alexander H. rigger, dwl Mont nr Bay

Brown Andrew, laborer, dwl 140 Stewart

Brown Andrew D. policeman, City Hall, dwl E s Mission bet Twelfth and Thirteenth

Brown Anne Miss, domestic with I. N. Thorne, W s Howard bet Sixteenth and Seventeenth

Brown Ann M. I. Miss, domestic, 1126 Folsom

Brown Anne Mrs. Olympia Saloon, 912 Kearny

Brown Archibald, stoves and tinware, 214 Third

Brown August, seaman, dwl 44 Sacramento

Brown Augustus, machinist with Joseph Brown, dwl 134 Sutter

Brown Benjamin, marker, Davis' Laundry, W s Harriet bet Howard and Folsom

Brown Benjamin B. porter, Vallejo Street Bonded Warehouse, dwl 35 Louisa

Brown Ben W. *(Smith & B.)* dwl E s Columbia nr Sixteenth

Brown Beriah, editor, dwl 655 Washington

Brown Bridget Mrs. fruits, dwl 57 Stevenson

Brown Brown, carpenter, dwl E s Howard bet Fourteenth and Fifteenth

Brown Calvin, chief engineer, Camp Pilarcitos, Spring Valley W. W. Co

Brown Carmine (widow) dwl W s Varennes nr Filbert

Brown C. F. dentist, NE cor Third and Hunt, res Oakland

Brown C. H. upholsterer with Goodwin & Co. dwl E s Larkin bet Union and Filbert

Brown Charles, dwl W s Dolores bet Fifteenth and Sixteenth

Brown Charles, boiler maker, dwl 141 Shipley, rear

Brown Charles, cabinet maker with J. Peirce, bds Oriental House

Brown Charles, carpenter, dwl 1207 Dupont

Brown Charles, carpenter, dwl 134 Minna

Brown Charles, cook, dwl 23 Hinckley

Brown Charles, cook, International Hotel

Brown Charles, express wagon, 34 Kearny

Brown Charles, fruits, 624 Jackson

Brown Charles, handcartman, Market nr Drumm

Brown Charles, laborer, dwl 140 Stewart

Brown Charles, mariner, dwt 32 Stewart

Brown Charles, musician, dwl 545 California

Brown Charles, seaman, steamer Orizaba

Brown Charles, seaman, dwl S s Sacramento bet Davis and Drumm

Brown Charles, seaman, dwl 44 Sacramento
Brown Charles, stoves and tinware, 34 and 36 Kearny, dwl 342 Minna
Brown Charles, waiter, steamer Orizaba
Brown Charles F. (Eureka Soap Co.) office 206 Sacramento, dwl 66 Clementina
Brown Charles F. fruits, 1218 Stockton
Brown Charles H. teamster, dwl E s Larkin bet Union and Filbert
Brown Charles M. boiler maker with Coffey & Risdon
Brown Charles P. coffee stand, 517 East
BROWN (Chester) & WELLS (Asa R.) stair builders, 535 Market, dwl 56 Third
Brown Christian, boatman, dwl 317 Bryant
Brown C. K. (widow) dwl 313 Mason
Brown Daniel T. proprietor Brown's Bakery, 1223 Stockton
Brown Daniel H. wire-rope maker with A. S. Hallidie & Co
Brown David (Benjamin & B.) dwl 305 Kearny
Brown David, teamster with Brocas & Perkins, 52 Clay
Brown David B. policeman, City Hall, dwl 913 Greenwich
Brown David L. pressman with Francis, Valentine & Co. dwl 508 Dupont
Brown Denton D. engineer, dwl 872 Mission
BROWN EDGAR O. real estate agent, office 620 Washington, room 13
Brown Edmund (col'd) barber, dwl 15 Virginia Pl
Brown Edward, dwl N s Folsom nr Sixth
Brown Edward, clerk, NW cor First and Natoma
Brown Edward, clerk, dwl NE cor Sixth and Bryant
Brown Edward, laborer, Fort Point
Brown Edward (col'd) dwl 5 Park Avenue
Brown Eliza Miss, domestic, dwl SE cor Lombard and Jones
Brown E. J. Mrs. dress making, 528 California
Brown Elizabeth, domestic, dwl 318 First
Brown Elizabeth A. (widow) dwl 832 Vallejo, rear
Brown Emanuel, watchman, National Mills, dwl SE cor Market and Sansom
Brown Emma (widow) dwl 10 Stockton Place
Brown Fannie Miss, dwl N s Mission bet Tenth and Eleventh
Brown Fanny Miss, actress, Olympic, dwl American Exchange
Brown Ferdinand, ship carpenter, bds 7 Wash
Brown Frederick, dwl 135 Minna
Brown Frederick, carpenter, dwl 23 Minna
Brown Frederick, musician, dwl 5 Brown Alley
Brown Frederick, seaman, dwl 44 Sacramento
Brown Frederick A. carpenter, dwl 511 Mission
Brown Frederick W. bar tender, dwl 528 Pac, rear
Brown G. A. dwl 627 Commercial
Brown George, dwl What Cheer House
Brown George C. engraver, dwl 532 Commercial
Brown George F. policeman, City Hall, dwl 1332 Pacific
BROWN GEORGE S. superintendent San Francisco Olympic Club Rooms, dwl 603 Taylor
Brown Geo. W. draftsman with S. C. Bugbee & Son
Brown Gideon H. dentist, 137 Third
BROWN GRAFTON T. lithographer, 543 Clay, dwl 727 Clay
Brown Hannah B. (widow) dwl 739 Green
Brown Harry, actor, dwl Oriental Hotel
BROWN HARVEY S. attorney at law and real estate, dwl 1309 Powell
Brown Henry, with Pollard & Carvill, dwl Mission nr Jane
Brown Henry, blacksmith, dwl 136 Fourth
Brown Henry, printer, dwl 8 Jasper Place
BROWN HENRY, proprietor Mariners' Home, 306 Clark
Brown Henry, steward, 424 Sacramento
Brown Henry S. Capt. marine surveyor and pilot examiner, office 504 Battery, dwl 1106 Mont

Brown H. J. express wagon, cor Mont and Merch
Brown (Ireson C.) & Hussey (Albion C.) carpenters, Summer nr Montgomery, dwl W s Guerrero bet Nineteenth and Twentieth
BROWN (Isaac W. W.) & BROWN (John B.) Brown's Market, 406 Folsom, dwl 318 Beale
Brown J. A. clerk, dwl Coso House
Brown J. A. cook with George T. Parker
Brown James, dwl NE cor Mission and Fourth
Brown James, with Jas. Brokaw, dwl 330 Kearny
Brown James, brass molder with Morris Greenberg
Brown James, cartman, cor Union and Battery
Brown James, coal weigher, San Francisco Gas Co
Brown James (col'd) livery stable, dwl 10 Scotland
Brown James, drayman with James McDevitt, dwl NW cor Green and Battery, rear
Brown James, laborer, dwl 83½ Greenwich
Brown James, laborer, San Francisco Gas Co. dwl 210 Minna
Brown James, painter, dwl 305 Montgomery
Brown Ja   , ranchero, bds Cambridge House, 304 Pacifimes
Brown James, waiter, Railroad House
Brown James A. drayman, 313 Front, dwl 9 Riley
Brown James A. C. sergeant U. S. Marines, office and dwl 931 Kearny
Brown James E. (col'd) Custom House Livery Stable, 318 Broadway, dwl 10 Scotland
Brown James F. with Eureka Soap Co. 207 Sac
Brown James F. carpenter, dwl 8 Hardie Place
Brown James H. brass molder, dwl 21 Jessie
Brown James H. (col'd) whitewasher, dwl SW cor Jessie and Annie
Brown James L. book binder with Edward Bosqui & Co. dwl 322 Vallejo
Brown James P. last manufacturer, dwl 114 Geary
Brown James S. dwl N s Folsom nr Sixth
Brown James S. dwl NE cor Sixth and Bryant
Brown James W. (Sherman & B.) dwl NE cor Fourth and Mission
Brown James W. carpenter, dwl 842 Clay
Brown J. Anthony, cook, Bank Exch, dwl 528 Cal
Brown J. D. liquor saloon, 112 First
Brown Jeremiah (col'd) cook, dwl 819 Pacific
Brown Jesse, contractor night work, office 115 Kearny, dwl E s Gardner Alley nr Post
Brown Jesse, fireman, bds 631 Davis
Brown J. Newton, physician and professor Toland Medical College, office and dwl 46 Sutter
Brown Johanna, domestic with C. H. Reynolds, dwl E s Larkin bet Washington and Jackson
Brown John (Warwick & B.) dwl 207 Third
Brown John, baker, dwl 1412 Dupont
Brown John, bar keeper with J. N. Harris, dwl 432 California
Brown John, boatman, dwl 1816 Powell
Brown John, boot maker, dwl 917 Sutter
Brown John, captain schooner W. A. Fisher, Caduc's Line, foot Washington
Brown John, carpenter, 208 Washington, dwl W s Leidesdorff bet California and Sacramento
Brown John, clerk, dwl 131 Tehama
Brown John, cook, NW cor First and Minna
Brown John, laborer, dwl E s Sansom bet Vallejo and Green
Brown John, laborer with John G. North, Potrero
Brown John, longshoreman, dwl N s Oregon near Front
Brown John, milk ranch, nr S. F. Cordage Manuf
Brown John, restaurant, 638 Pacific
Brown John, seaman, dwl 44 Sacramento
Brown John, ship carpenter, dwl 508 Howard
Brown John, shoe maker with James H. Swain & Co. dwl 917 Sutter
Brown John, waiter, What Cheer House Restaurant
Brown John A. distiller with Justus Bepler
Brown John B. (Brown & B.) dwl 318 Beale
Brown John F. compositor with Dewey, Waters & Co. dwl 49 Third

Brown John F. tinsmith with B. C. Austin, dwl NW cor First and Mission

Brown *(John H.)* & Carroll *(Henry)* (col'd) white-washing, 708½ Market, dwl cor Pac and Jones

Brown John K. mate, steamer Josie McNear, res Petaluma

Brown John M. carpenter, dwl 3 Auburn

Brown Joseph A. merchant, dwl 92 Everett

Brown Joseph, dyer, S. F. Pioneer Woolen Mills

Brown Joseph, seaman, dwl 44 Sacramento

Brown Joseph M. carpenter, Jessie bet Fifth and Sixth, dwl 30 Ritch

Brown *(Julius)* & Wagner *(Samuel)* toys and fancy goods, 134 Kearny

Brown Justus, fireman, Sacramento steamer, dwl Crescent Engine Co. No. 10

Brown J. W. captain ship Reviere, office Pier 10 Stewart, dwl 13 Tehama

Brown L. A. stock broker, office 706 Montgomery, dwl N s Clay bet Dupont and Stockton

Brown Lewis M. carpenter, dwl N s Geary bet Leavenworth and Hyde

Brown Louis, Slice Bar Exchange, 204 Stewart

Brown Lucy Mrs. dwl 528 Folsom

Brown Lucy Mrs. nurse, dwl 68 Stevenson House

Brown M. A. Mrs. boarding, 321 Minna

Brown Maggie Miss, domestic, dwl 607 Union

Brown Maggie H. Mrs. laces, 24 Post

Brown Marcus, teamster with James McDevitt, dwl W s Sansom bet Broadway and Vallejo

Brown Margaret (widow) dwl S s Mission bet Twelfth and Thirteenth

Brown Margaret (colored) lodgings, Godchaux's Building, NE cor Mission and Second

Brown Martha A. (col'd, widow) dwl 907 Sac

Brown Mary Miss, domestic, dwl 1215 Clay

Brown Mary Miss, domestic with Jeffery Cullen

Brown Mary (widow) dwl 115 Ellis

Brown Mary R. (widow) dwl 285 Minna

Brown Michael, hay and grain, 204 Washington, dwl NW cor Third and Tehama

Brown Michael, laborer, dwl 138 Silver

Brown Michael, machinist with Singer Manufacturing Co

Brown M. L. (widow) Young Ladies' School, 962 Howard

Brown Morris, merchant, dwl 323 Jessie

Brown Nelson, baker, steamer Pacific

Brown Nelson, carpenter, dwl 116 Sansom

Brown Nicholas, workman, S. F. & P. Sugar Co. dwl 9 Lick Alley

Brown Patrick, laborer, dwl Union Court

Brown Peter, laborer, dwl W s Jansen bet Greenwich and Lombard

Brown Peter N. baker, dwl 1221 Stockton

Brown Philip, boatman, dwl 629 Vallejo

Brown Phillip, hair dresser, Montgomery Baths, dwl Kearny above Union

Brown Richard *(Henderson & B.)* dwl 564 Howard

Brown Richard, laborer, dwl United States Hotel, 706 Battery

Brown Richard, laborer, bds with Joseph Seale, dwl N s Turk nr Fillmore

Brown Robert F. laborer, dwl Market bet Third and Fourth

Brown Robert H. miller, dwl 117 Minna

Brown Samuel, cook, International Hotel, dwl 24 Post

Brown Samuel, washer, Davis Laundry, W s Harriet bet Howard and Folsom

Brown Samuel E. printer, foreman News Letter, dwl 1311 Stockton

Brown Samuel J. cook, International Hotel

Brown Sarah (widow, colored) dwl E s Lagoon

Brown Sedley Mrs. actress, Metropolitan Theatre

Brown Seth, carpenter, dwl SW cor Larkin and Turk

Brown S. L. Miss, dwl S s Columbia bet Guerrero and Dolores

Brown Stephen G. hair dressing saloon, Brooklyn Hotel

Brown Sylvester B. drayman, 313 Front, dwl 9 Riley

Brown Theodore, proprietor Dresdener House, 337 Bush

Brown Thomas, clerk, 21 Washington Market, dwl Bitters' Hotel

Brown Thomas, packer with Wangenheim, Sternheim & Co. dwl 213 Mission

Brown Thomas, salesman with Treadwell & Co. dwl 607 Folsom

Brown Thomas A. iron molder, dwl 63 Clementina

Brown W. deck hand, Cal. S. N. Co

Brown Walter S. dwl E s Dupont nr Francisco

Brown W. B. printer, dwl 625½ Mission

Brown *(W. H.)* & Avery *(D. R.)* fruit and vegetables, 41 and 42 Wash Mkt, dwl 605 Howard

Brown Willard B. compositor, Police Gazette, 424 Battery

Brown William, dwl E s Crook bet Brannan and Townsend

Brown William, blacksmith, dwl U. S. Hotel, 706 Battery

Brown William, boarding, 152 Stewart

Brown William, captain schooner Ann Sophia, dwl W s Main bet Folsom and Harrison

Brown William, clerk, 60 Third

Brown William, crockery and plated ware, 508 Market

Brown William, drayman with A. C. Hichhorn, 325 Front

Brown William, driver, North Beach & M. R. R. Co. dwl 110 Shipley, rear

Brown William, engineer, dwl W s Main bet Folsom and Harrison

Brown William & Co. fancy goods, 106 Third, dwl 243 Second

Brown William, harness maker with Hyde & McClennen, dwl 127 St. Mark Place

Brown William, laborer, Tiger Engine Co. No. 14

Brown William, laborer, dwl SW cor Louisiana and Sierra

Brown William, pail maker, 24 California

Brown William, ship carpenter, dwl E s Beale bet Market and Mission

Brown William, stevedore, dwl NW cor Front and Broadway

Brown William, tinsmith with A. Brown, dwl Mission nr Anna

Brown William, waiter, steamer Pacific

Brown William H. *(Swain & B.)* dwl 5 Kearny

Brown William H. dwl 751 Clay

Brown William H. (colored) boot black, 630 Kearny, dwl E s Dupont bet Filbert and Greenwich

Brown William H. clerk with Treadwell & Co. dwl N s Fifteenth nr Howard

BROWN WILLIAM H. contractor night work, office Rasette Place No. 3 nr Sutter

Brown William H. merchant, dwl 1024 Stockton

Brown William H. whitewasher, dwl SE cor Pacific and Kearny

Brown William P. groceries and liquors, SE cor Clay and Dupont, dwl 1416 Powell

Brown William P. porter, 412 Front, dwl 45 Louisa

Brown William R. carriage builder, W s Grand Avenue nr Mission, dwl N s Mission bet Tenth and Eleventh

Brown W. P. policeman, City Hall, dwl 1416 Pow

Brown W. T. architect, dwl 660 Howard

Browne John M. merchant, dwl 504 Second

Browne Michael, dwl 173 Beale

Browne Theodore, stevedore, Howard Engine Co. No. 3.

Browne Thomas A. molder, dwl 63 Clementina

Browne Thomas J. dwl N s Courtlandt Avenue nr North Avenue

Brownell Hiram, blacksmith, Phœnix Iron Works, dwl 119 Washington

Browning Ann (widow) boarding, 13 Geary
BROWNING *(August)* & McNAMARA *(William)* silver platers, locksmiths, etc. 806 Washington, dwl NE cor Jackson and Leavenworth
Browning Jacob, drayman, cor Pine and Front, dwl 318 Geary
Browning Jeremiah, drayman with Conroy & O'Connor, dwl 318 Geary
Browning *(John)* & Klein *(Richard)* wood, coal, and hay, 620 Broadway
Browning *(William)* & Kohlmoos *(John)* butter, cheese, etc. 505 Washington, dwl 771 Folsom
Brownlee James L. dwl E s First Av nr Fifteenth
Brownlee John, waiter, Empire State Restaurant
Brownstone Isaac, merchant, dwl 513 Leavenworth
Bruce Alexander, metal roofer with H. G. & E. S. Fiske, dwl Folsom nr Main, rear
BRUCE DONALD, book and job printer, 534 Commercial
Bruce Henry, laborer, dwl 170 Minna
Bruce James, lather, dwl 14 Bay State Row
Bruce James H. mariner, dwl 1218 Jackson
Bruce John, calker, dwl 54 First
Bruce Lewis P. painter, dwl 922 Howard
Bruce Mary E. domestic, 752 Folsom
Bruce Richard, painter, dwl 329 Vallejo
Bruce Robert C. book keeper with Agard, Foulkes & Co. dwl 804 Pine
Bruce Thomas, laborer, dwl 56 Stewart
Bruce William, dwl N s Page nr Octavia
Bruder William *(Weinmann & B.)* dwl 612 Pacific
Brueck Herman Rev. pastor German M. E. Church, N s Folsom bet Fourth and Fifth, dwl rear of church
Brueckner William, Reduction Works, 416 Market, dwl NE cor Jackson and Kearny
Bruggemann Adolph, seaman, bds 7 Washington
Bruggemann Henry, cutter with I. Eisenberg, dwl 542 Green
Bruggemann Henry, roofer, dwl W s Folsom Avenue nr Folsom
Bruggy Patrick, laborer, dwl E s Eighth bet Harrison and Folsom
Bruhl Moses, importer diamonds, 623 Washington, dwl Occidental Hotel
Bruhns William, S. F. Dairy & Milk Depôt, 1209 Dupont
Brumagim Jacob, banker, dwl 1315 Mason
BRUMAGIM JOHN W. public administrator and attorney at law, office 36 Montgomery Block, dwl 1019 Jackson
Brumagim Mark, office 36 Montgomery Block, dwl 1019 Jackson
Brumagim Patrick, hostler, Central R. R. Co. dwl W s Gilbert nr Brannan
Brunaido Antonio, peddler, dwl 14 Merchant
Brune Adolph, musician, dwl Harwood Alley
Brune Aug. cigar maker, dwl 619 Pacific
Brunel Gustave, porter, 308 Commercial
Brunell Agathe (widow) dwl Willows Pavilion, NE cor Valencia and Seventeenth
Brunell C. S. (widow) dwl 19 Natoma
Bruner Jacob, salesman, 19 Mont, dwl 428 Folsom
Bruner William H. physician, office NE cor Market and Montgomery, dwl 518 Sutter
Bruning Martin, bar keeper, 324 Montgomery, dwl 707 Mission
Brünings Hermann & Co. *(Claus Mangels)* groceries and liquors, SW cor Third and Mission
Brunjes Diedrich, groceries and liquors, 425 Bush
Brunjes Frederick, porter, 409 Clay, dwl 613 Pow
BRUNJES HENRY, groceries and liquors, NE cor Fourth and Harrison
BRUNK *(Daniel D.)* & ROWLEY *(Charles M.)* attorneys at law, office 7 and 8 Armory Hall third floor, dwl 419 Stockton
Brunn D. (widow) boarding, 1022 Stockton
Brunn T. O. salesman with Andrew Kohler, 424 Sansom

Brunner B. P. superintendent Citizen's Gas Works, dwl Cosmopolitan Hotel
Brunner Leony F. printer, California Demokrat, dwl 1226 Stockton
Brunner Louis, beer saloon, SW cor Montgomery and Summer, dwl SW cor Pacific and Sansom
Brunning William *(Miller & B.)* dwl SW cor Jessie and Annie
Bruns Antoine, with Pacific Distillery Co
BRUNS CHRISTIAN, physician, office 434 California, and drugs and medicines, 429 California, dwl 1217 Mason
Bruns Conrad, laborer, dwl SE cor Sixth and Mission, up stairs
Bruns *(Frederic)* & Bro. *(George Bruns)* groceries and liquors, SW cor Folsom and Spear and SE cor Sixteenth and Mission
Bruns Frederick *(Scanlin & B.)* dwl Mission near Sixteenth
Bruns George *(Bruns & Brother)* dwl SE cor Mission and Fifteenth
Bruns Henry *(Pope & B.)* dwl junction Filbert and Presidio Road
Bruns Henry, groceries, SW cor Old San José Road and Thirtieth
Bruns *(Herman)* & Co. *(George H. Wilson)* groceries and liquors, 201 Commercial
Bruns Hermann C. clerk, dwl W s Sumner near Howard
Bruns Herminia Mrs. dress maker, 713 Folsom
Bruns John D. furniture, dwl 840 Mission
BRUNS NICHOLAS, groceries and liquors, 617 Davis, dwl E s Guerrero bet Sixteenth and Seventeenth
Bruns Peter, capt. schooner Emily Howard, foot Market
Bruns William, carpenter, dwl 713 Folsom
Brunsen Martin, Martin's Exchange Saloon, 612 Montgomery
Brunt William N. butcher, dwl W s Garden bet Harrison and Bryant
Brunton Charles W. printer, dwl 308 Jessie
Brush Albert, blacksmith, dwl 820 Post
Brush Reuben G. book keeper with R. B. Swain & Co. dwl 535 Mission
Brusneshen Margaret Miss, domestic, dwl 411 Dupont
Brusnihan C. driver, Original House
Bryan Bartholomew, works with Cornelius Conahan
Bryan Bonnard, laborer, S. F. & San José R. R. dwl Cook nr cor Townsend and Third
BRYAN BROTHERS *(William and Thomas Bryan)* wines and liquors, 322 and 324 Sansom
Bryan Charles H. with Louis Teese jr. dwl 13 Harlan Place
Bryan D. C. attorney at law, dwl E s Stock nr Clay
Bryan Edwin H. collector, dwl 430 Union
Bryan Frank, clerk, Subsistence Department, Division of the Pacific, office 418 California, dwl 405 Powell
Bryan Frederick F. weighmaster, 313 Davis, dwl 1715 Powell
Bryan Henry, attorney at law, office 611 Clay
Bryan John, watchman, steamer Princess
Bryan John M. liquor saloon, 704 Howard, dwl 216 Minna
Bryan John M. photographic gallery, 611 Clay, dwl SE cor Howard and Third
Bryan Joseph, bar keeper, 230 Commercial
Bryan Thomas *(Bryan Bros.)* dwl 320 Sansom
Bryan William H. surveyor, dwl 509 Bush
BRYAN WILLIAM J. house broker and real estate agent, 420 Montgomery, and drugs and medicines, SW cor Second and Mission, dwl NE cor Howard and Second
Bryans Edward, porter, 106 Battery, dwl 249 Third
Bryant A. H. conveyancer, office 528 Montgomery, dwl 226 Sansom

BRYANT *(A. J.)* & MORRISON *(John C. jr.)* wholesale dealers wines, brandies, porter, etc. 614 Front, dwl 916 Bush

Bryant B. miner, bds Franklin Hotel, SE cor Sansom and Pacific

BRYANT *(D. S.)* & BEADLE *(D.)* produce commission merchants, 316 and 318 Davis, res Oakland

Bryant E. G. physician, office 415 Montgomery

Bryant Frederick, clerk with E. G. Cook & Co. dwl 124 Jessie

Bryant George W. assistant assessor, U. S. Int. Rev. NW cor Battery and Com, dwl 616 Taylor

Bryant James E. clerk with R. A. Swain & Co. dwl 18 Clara

Bryant *(John)* & Co. *(Simon Strahan and Benjamin McCachren)* wood carvers and frame makers, 313 Market, dwl SW cor Eighteenth and Howard

Bryant John, dwl 115 First

Bryant John, compositor, Flag Office, bds New Wisconsin Hotel, 411 Pacific

Bryant Mahala M. Miss, private school, 272 Clementina, dwl 57 Clementina

Bryant Margaret (widow) dwl N s Mission nr Ninth

Bryant M. M. fruit dealer, 203 Third

Bryant Otto, cabinet maker, dwl 178 Stevenson

Bryant Richard, laborer with John Center, NW cor Sixteenth and Folsom

Bryant Robt. W. mining, dwl 425 Third

Bryant Samuel (col'd) carpenter, dwl S s Greenwich bet Larkin and Polk

Bryant Susan J. Mrs. dwl with I. N. Thorne, W s Howard bet Sixteenth and Seventeenth

Bryant Thomas S. painter, dwl 152 Natoma

Bryant W. D. driver, North Beach & M R. R. dwl 133 Shipley

BRYANT WILLIAM F. agent Pacific Mineral Co. office 2 Odd Fellows' Hall, 325 Montgomery, dwl Lick House

Bryant William T. tailor, dwl NW cor Kearny and Broadway

Bryant William W. assistant mailing clerk, Post Office, dwl 616 Taylor

Bryden George, driver, dwl 711 Pacific

Brydges Marshall C. stoves and tinware, 6 Sacramento, dwl Jackson nr Powell

Brynes Charles, stevedore, dwl Vigilant Engine House No. 9

Bryngelson Peter, pile driver, dwl 128 Clay

Buch Jacob S. clerk, dwl SE cor Mont and Cal

BUCHAN *(P. G.)* & WADE *(John)* attorneys at law, office 537 Washington, dwl 947 Mission

Buchanan Catherine (widow) dwl 318 Davis

BUCHANAN HENRY, Third Ward Burton-Ale House, 324 Commercial

Buchanan James, laborer, dwl 412 Post, rear

Buchanan John, carpenter, dwl 729 Union

Buchanan John, grocer, dwl 571 Howard, rear

Buchanan Mary Miss, dress maker, 243 Stevenson

Buchard J. M. Rev. S.J. clergyman, St. Ignatius Church, S s Market bet Fourth and Fifth

Bucher Joseph, painter, dwl NW cor Kearny and Jackson

BUCHHOLTZ *(John)* & KOCK *(Claus)* proprietors New Atlantic Hotel, 619 Pacific

Buchner Christian, lab, bds St. Louis Hotel, 11 Pac

Buck Benjamin (col'd) cook, dwl 11 Scott

Buck George, express wagon, SW cor Montgomery and Clay, dwl 314 Third

Buck John *(Ohland & Co.)* dwl Brannan Street Bridge

Buck John, workman, Albany Brewery

Buck John S. assistant engineer, Pac. Mail S. S. Co

Buck J. W. seaman, dwl 54 Sacramento

Buck Warner, carpenter, dwl 208 O'Farrell

Buck William, ship carpenter, bds Blue Anchor, 7 Washington

Buck ——, salesman with S. W. H. Ward & Son

Buckelew Daniel, boot maker, dwl SW cor Dupont and Broadway

Buckelew Martha (widow) dwl E s Mason nr Green

Buckelew Moses S. book keeper with Rountree & McMullin, dwl 42 Everett

Bucken Lawrence, express wagon, cor Third and Mission

Buckeye G. & S. M. Co. office 436 Jackson

Buckingham Aurelius A. pilot, 805 Front, dwl 717 Bush

Buckingham Charles E. insurance agent, 420 Mont

Buckingham M. dwl What Cheer House

Buckingham Thomas, with John G. Hein, 416 Bat

Buckingham W. H. local policeman, dwl 120 Post

Buckland Sarah, matron Union College

Buckler M. C. (widow) lodgings, 32 Natoma

Buckley Bridget (widow) dwl 3 Hardie Place

Buckley Charles P. watchman, Maguire's Opera House

Buckley Christopher A. bar keeper, 612 Washington, dwl N s Tehama bet Fifth and Sixth

Buckley Daniel J. clerk, 521 Merchant, dwl 72 Tehama

Buckley David, clerk, 318 Clay, dwl 508 Mission

Buckley Edmund, plasterer, dwl N s Bernard bet Taylor and Jones

Buckley Edward, dwl 627 Commercial

Buckley Edward, actor, Bella Union, dwl 9 Bdwy

BUCKLEY EDWARD P. license collector City and County, office 7 City Hall first floor, dwl 2006 Powell

Buckley Francis, builder, W s Fifth bet Howard and Mission, dwl W s Devisidero bet Eddy and Turk

Buckley Francis jr. dwl with F. Buckley, W s Devisidero bet Eddy and Turk

Buckley Hannah, domestic, dwl 10 Silver

Buckley James, brick yard and cabinet maker, N s Vallejo bet Polk and Van Ness Avenue, office 528 Montgomery

Buckley James A. bricklayer, dwl 1221 Pacific

Buckley Jeremiah, milk ranch, N s Cliff House Road, four miles from Plaza

Buckley Jeremiah J. porter, 223 California, dwl 429 Fremont

Buckley John, dwl 530 Tehama

Buckley John, laborer, dwl NW cor Kearny and Broadway

Buckley John P. (widow) dwl SW cor Jackson and Taylor

Buckley Julia Miss, domestic, dwl 1010 Bush

Buckley Michael, clerk, dwl NW cor Folsom and Baldwin Court

Buckley Michael, laborer, dwl 32 Webb

Buckley Michael, machinist helper, Vulcan Iron Works

Buckley Michael, porter with Rockwell, Coye & Co. dwl 38 Natoma

Buckley Patrick, laborer, dwl 925 Broadway

Buckley Patrick, laborer, dwl with Patrick McAntee, N s Mission bet Twelfth and Thirteenth

Buckley Samuel, 115 Dupont, dwl 19 Dupont

Buckley Susan Miss, domestic, SW cor Sixteenth and Clapp

Buckley Thomas, laborer, Spring Valley W. W

Buckley Timothy, proptr Burnet House, 32 Webb

Buckley William, brick yard, dwl NE cor Polk and Green

Bucklin E. P. *(Mathewson & B.)* dwl SW cor Folsom and Fourth

Buckman H. L. office Central American Transit Co. dwl American Exchange

Buekman John, dwl NW cor Folsom and Eighth

Buekman John A. clerk, office Central American Transit Co. NW cor Battery and Pine, dwl Occidental Hotel

Buckmar ary Mrs. dwl SW cor Bdwy and Mont

Buckmast Dorcas, domestic, dwl Mission

Buckmaster John, lather, dwl 12 Sutter
Bucknam Charles, clerk, dwl 522 Pine
Bucknan Ezra T. stoves and tin ware, 20 Stewart, dwl 309 Fremont
Buckner Charles, cabinet maker, dwl 105 Garden bet Sixth and Seventh
Buckner Charles jr. cabinet maker, 719 Mission, dwl 105 Garden bet Sixth and Seventh
Buckner F. A. teacher oil painting, California Collegiate Institute
Buckner Henry, driver, Philadelphia Brewery, dwl 204 Second
Buckner William, cook, Central House, 814 Sansom
Budd Charles P. stock broker, 707 Montgomery, dwl 609½ Howard
Budd James, fireman, steamer Sacramento
Budd J. H. attorney at law, office 625 Merchant, dwl 652 Howard
Budd J. H. Mrs. furnished rooms, 652 Howard
BUDD W. C. & CO. brokers (and member San Francisco Stock and Exchange Board) office 707 Montgomery, dwl Lick House
Budden Hugh, stone cutter, dwl Sierra Nevada Hotel, 528 Pacific
Buddington Walter, pilot steamer Cornelia, dwl Vernon Place bet Mason and Taylor
Buddle William, peddler, dwl cor Beale and Folsom
Budke Hermann, carder, Mission Woolen Mills
Budlong J. B. carpenter, dwl 336 Bush
Buehler Francis, wire worker, dwl 29 O'Farrell
Buehler Jacob M. Rev. pastor German Lutheran Church, dwl 29 O'Farrell
Buel Frederick Rev. depository California Bible Society, 757 Market
Buell R. T. dwl 84 Montgomery Block
Buena Plata Consolidation M. Co. office 6 Montgomery Block
Buena Vista Vinacultural Society, office 604 Clay
Buerfind Hermann, farmer, San Miguel Ranch nr Ocean House Road
Buerkner Charles, clerk with H. Hanssmann, 220 Front
Buerro Girolomo, cook, New World Restaurant, 1013 Dupont
Buetell Augustus, broker, dwl 630 Market
Buetrosvich Filippo, 3 Washington Fish Market
Buettner Hermann, principal private school, 918 Pacific, dwl N s Greenwich bet Dupont and Stock
Buffandeau Emile B. collector, office 528 Clay
BUFFINGTON J. M. secretary mining companies, office 7 and 10 Government House, 502 Washington, dwl 137 Silver
Buffington William, miner, dwl SE cor Sutter and Leavenworth
Bufford Henry, laundryman, dwl E s Mission nr Thirtieth
Bufford James L. painter, 217 Dupont, dwl 505 Sutter
Bufford Samuel F. Bay City Laundry, dwl E s Sixth bet Bryant and Brannan
BUFFUM A. C. physician and surgeon, office 652 Market cor Kearny, bds Russ House
Buffum J. W. collector, dwl 422 Third
Buffum M. A. Miss, assistant, Spring Valley Grammar School, dwl 932 Howard
Buffum R. V. E. Mrs. embroidery goods, 422 Third
Bugbee Charles L. (S. C. Bugbee & Son) dwl 722 Folsom
Bugbee John S. attorney at law, office with Doyle & Barber, 605 Clay, dwl 20 Hawthorne
BUGBEE S. C. & SON (C. L. Bugbee) architects, 74 and 75 Montgomery Block (and school director Tenth District) dwl 20 Hawthorne
Bugbee Sumner W. clerk, 73 Montgomery Block, dwl 20 Hawthorne
Buhl C. C. bds Brooklyn Hotel
Buhler Auguste, clerk with A. Gros, dwl 720 Wash
Buhler John F. boot maker, 529 Jackson
Buhler O. shoe maker, dwl 109 Pine
Buhn Lena Miss, domestic, dwl 614 Jackson

Buhre John H. clerk with Christoph Nobmann
Buhsen Diedrich, groceries and liquors, 727 Davis and NW cor Pac and Davis, res Oakland Point
Buia (Nicholas) & Gliubetich (Michael) restaurant and liquors, 605 Davis
Buislay Adolfo, gymnast, Wilson's Circus, dwl NW cor Turk and Taylor
Buislay Augusto, gymnast, Wilson's Circus
Buislay Esteban, gymnast, Wilson's Circus
Buislay Grenet, gymnast, Wilson's Circus
Buislay Jonquin, gymnast, Wilson's Circus
Buislay Julio, gymnast, Wilson's Circus
BUJAN ANTONIO, toll collector, San Bruno Road, 3 miles from City Hall
Bulger Martin, engineer, dwl 15 Russ
Bulger Raphael R. compositor, Evening Bulletin, dwl 108 St. Mark Place
Bulger Thomas, drayman, U. S. Appraiser's Store
Bulger V. F. printer with Towne & Bacon, dwl 108 St. Mark Place
Bulger, see Bolger
Bulkley Ichabod, clerk with C. A. Hooper & Co. dwl S s Townsend bet Third and Fourth
Bulkley Milton (Sherwood, B. & Co.) dwl SW cor Third and Market
BULL ALPHEUS, president Gould & Curry S. M. Co. office NE cor Montgomery and Jackson, dwl NE cor Leavenworth and Francisco
Bull H. C. major U. S. A. paymaster, office 655 Washington
Bull Thomas, dwl American Exchange
Bullard Deborah (widow) dwl 662 Howard
Bullard Elizabeth A. Miss, domestic, dwl 1219 Clay
Bullard James H. book keeper with O. T. Ames, dwl 518 Powell
Bullard Mary E. Miss, nurse, dwl 1221 Clay
Bullard (Matthew B.) & Battles (Winslow) petroleum cooking stoves, 316 Montgomery, dwl 731 Harrison
Bullen Henry M. ship carpenter, dwl 76 Natoma
Bullen Tupper, millwright, dwl W s Thirteenth nr Valencia
Bullene Estelle M. Miss, assistant, Lincoln School, dwl 1024 Folsom
Bulletti (C.) & Co. (Ubaldo Selna) fruits, Pacific Fruit Market, dwl E s Dupont bet Lombard and Greenwich
Bullian Christian, cook, dwl SE cor Filbert and Dupont
Bullion John, laborer, bds Sacramento Hotel, 407 Pacific
Bullis Edward, with Standard Soap Co. 207 Commercial
Bullivant Herbert E. clerk with R. F. Osborn & Co
Bullock Alice (widow) dwl 105 William
Bullock Frank D. salesman with J. R. Mead & Co. dwl 423 Sutter
Bullock Marion, carpenter, dwl with Nelson Young
Bulmer Frederick, cook, steamer Relief
Bulson John, engineer, Empire Brewery, dwl 232 Stevenson
Bultman August (William Bofer & Co.) dwl 1014 Stockton
Bumm George W. pressman with Edward Bosqui & Co. dwl 20 Mason
Bummer James K. drugs and medicines, NE cor Post and Mason
Bunce William, book keeper with Hobbs, Gilmore & Co. dwl SE cor Sacramento and Leavenworth
Bundy Burrell (colored) porter, dwl 1419 Mason
Bundy Charles S. (colored) hair dresser with Wm. H. Blake, dwl 919 Broadway
Bundy John H. (colored) hog ranch, NE cor Utah and Sixteenth
Bundy Thomas, express wagon, NE cor Clay and Montgomery
Bundy Thomas (colored) hog ranch, NE cor Utah and Sixteenth
Buneman Catherine (widow) dwl 28 Clara

Bunemann Charles, clerk with Schultz & Von Bargen, dwl 905 Larkin

Bunker Albert, butcher, dwl NW cor Bush and Powell

Bunker Frederick R. book keeper with Moore & Co. dwl E s Hyde bet Filbert and Greenwich

Bunker G. F. ship master, dwl S s DeBoom nr Second

BUNKER HENRY S. & CO. Mexican shipping and Custom House Broker, office SE cor Battery and Washington, dwl N s Mission opposite Twelfth

Bunker Paul, foreman Howard Warehouse, dwl 735 Union

Bunker *(R. F.)* & Auradou *(Julius)* pork packers, 9 Clay Street Market, dwl 1505 Leavenworth

Bunker S. G. Miss, special primary assistant, Market Street School, dwl 1305 Stockton

Bunker William, printer with Francis, Valentine & Co. dwl 52 Minna

Bunn Lucy (widow) dwl 618 Lombard

Bunnell A. W. Mrs. adjuster, U. S. Branch Mint, dwl cor Sacramento and Franklin

Bunnell E. F. dentist, office 611 Clay, dwl NW cor Sacramento and Franklin

Bunnell George, dentist, dwl International Hotel

Bunnell George W. principal, S. F. Latin School, dwl NW cor Sacramento and Franklin

Bunnell N. dwl What Cheer House

Bunner Ann (widow) preserved fruits, 727 Mission

Buntielich H. milk wagon, Hayes Valley

Bunting Joseph *(Harvey M. Lockwood & Co.)* dwl 520 Folsom

Buolen John, milkman with Edmund H. Knight

Burbank Caleb, attorney at law, dwl S s Clay be-Leavenworth and Hyde

Burbank David, dentist, office 505 Montgomery, dwl 47 Frederick nr Second

Burbank Eleazer A. upholsterer, 727 and 729 Market, dwl 221 Tehama

Burbank Otto, comedian, Olympic Melodeon, dwl 53 Minna

Burbank Sheldon C. stone cutter, dwl Fort Point

Burbege Lettie, cloak maker, dwl 22 Natoma

Burch H. boatman, dwl cor Battery and Jackson

Burch Frederick R. dwl 731 Clay

Burckes Henry W. carpenter with A. A. Snyder, dwl 606 O'Farrell

Burckes Samuel S. carpenter with A. A. Snyder, dwl 606 O'Farrell

Burckhardt John, peddler, dwl 4 Milton Place

Burckhardt *(Max)* & Klebs *(Alexander)* foreign and domestic wines and liquors, 634 Commercial, dwl 1311 Stockton

Burckhardt, see Burkhardt

Burdeau Antoine, dwl 58 Jessie

BURDELL GALEN, dentist, office and dwl 625 Ciay

Burdell William, machinist, dwl 230 Fremont

Burdet Peter, butcher, dwl N s Minna bet Eighth and Ninth

Burdett William, dwl S s Washington nr Dupont

Burdick Edward F. clerk with H. M. Newhall & Co. dwl 11 Hampton Place

Burdick *(Eugene B.)* & Dooley *(John)* wholesale butchers, Brannan Street Bridge, dwl 418 Tehama

Burdick François, lodgings, 732 Pacific

Burdick J. D. *(Truman & Co.)* res San José

Burditt Henry W. captain, office 511 Sansom

Burditt William W. *(Coleman & B.)* dwl Bee Hive Building

Burdock Henry, pile driver with Galloway & Boobar

Burfiend Chris *(Wagner & B.)* dwl SE cor Corbett and Castro

Burfiend Martin *(Siebe & Co.)* dwl 1812 Mason

Burge Ann (widow) dwl S s Freelon bet Third and Fourth

Burgess Andrew, machinist, Vulcan Iron Works

Burgess Andrew, photographic operator with James Wise, 417 Montgomery

Burgess Charles, photographic copyist, 727 Clay, dwl 1304 Taylor

Burgess C. M. hostler, Cliff House

Burgess George H. artist, studio 423 Montgomery, dwl 1304 Taylor

Burgess Henry, cabinet maker, dwl 759 Folsom

Burgess Hubert, teacher penmanship and drawing Public Schools, dwl 1304 Taylor

Burgess William, cook, City and County Hospital

Burgue George, vegetable garden, nr Bay View Park

Burhans W. D. toll collector Bay Shore and Fort Point Road

Burhans Willett S. pattern maker, Fulton Foundry, dwl 919 Market

Burke Albert, dwl 1016 Stockton

Burke Barbara (widow) dwl NE cor Jones and Filbert

Burke Bridget (widow) dwl 307 Tehama

Burke Catharine (widow) dwl W s Sansom bet Filbert and Greenwich

Burke Charles, boiler maker, dwl 66 Jessie

Burke Daniel, dwl E s Nevada nr Folsom

Burke David, laborer, dwl Union Court

Burke Dennis, soda manufacturer, dwl 27 Valparaiso

Burke Edwin R. mining stock, dwl 320 Minna

Burke Ethelbert, deputy collector Custom House, dwl N s Turk bet Van Ness Av and Franklin

Burke Francis, brass molder with R. F. Rocchiccoli, dwl 65 Natoma

BURKE FRANCIS G. hides, wool, and furs, office 220 Front, res Fruitvale

Burke Gilbert, hostler, 16 Sutter, dwl Davis Street House

Burke Hannah Miss, domestic, dwl 1022 Dupont

Burke Henry, teamster, dwl W s Sansom bet Broadway and Vallejo

Burke Isaac, laborer, dwl S s Eddy bet Jones and Leavenworth

Burke James, farmer, San Miguel Ranch, dwl N s Ocean House Road

Burke James, laborer, dwl Clementina bet Second and Third

Burke James, plasterer, dwl S s Harrison nr Sixth, rear

Burke James, tailor, dwl 22 Lafayette Place

Burke James, workman, Union Foundry, dwl N s Minna nr Eighth

Burke J. C. bar keeper, dwl 33 Second

Burke J. C. engineer S. F. Cotton Mills, dwl 118 Ritch

Burke John, with Reynolds, Howell & Ford, dwl E s Salmon nr Mason

Burke John, foreman What Cheer Livery Stable, 121 Jackson

Burke John, hostler with J. F. Willson, 807 Mont

Burke John, laborer, dwl E s Salmon bet Mason and Taylor

Burke John, shoe maker with I. M. Wentworth & Co. dwl 5 Lick Alley

Burke John, workman, Mt. St. Joseph, San Bruno Road

Burke John J. dwl 32 Jane

Burke Joseph, carpenter, dwl N s Minna bet Seventh and Eighth

Burke Joseph, laborer, dwl S s Seventeenth bet Dolores and Church

Burke J. P. machinist, Miners' Foundry, dwl 571 Howard

Burke Julia Miss, domestic, 524 Sutter

Burke Lewis, molder, Vulcan Iron Works, dwl 418 Green

Burke M. & Brother *(William Burke)* produce commission, 60 Clay, dwl NW cor Sixth and Brannan

Burke Martin, lab with G. H. Peck, dwl 820 San

Burke Martin, laborer, dwl S s Beale bet Market and Mission
BURKE MARTIN J. chief of police City and County S. F. office 11 City Hall first floor, dwl 930 Clay
Burke Mary Miss, domestic with T. N. Cazneau, N s Thirteenth nr Howard
Burke Mary Miss, domestic, dwl 807 Pacific
Burke Mary (widow) dwl N s Olive Avenue nr Van Ness Avenue
Burke Michael, dwl 2 Lafayette Place
Burke Michael, dwl W s Sixth N Brannan
Burke Michael, cigar maker, dwl 150 Clara
Burke Michael, cook, dwl 532 Commercial
Burke Michael, laborer, dwl S s Brannan bet Sixth and Seventh
Burke Michael P. with Stevens & Oliver, dwl 114 Kearny
Burke Nicholas, with Deeth & Starr, dwl cor Dupont and Francisco
Burke Patrick, blacksmith helper, S. F. & San José R. R. Co. dwl cor Twelfth and Folsom
Burke P. J. machinist, dwl 313 Bryant
Burke Richard, machinist, dwl SW cor Dupont and Broadway
Burke Robert, boatman, bds City Front House, 625 Davis
Burke Soren, seaman, dwl 228 Commercial
Burke Thomas, carpenter, dwl 517 Vallejo
Burke Thomas, drayman, dwl First nr Mission
Burke Thomas, finisher, Excelsior Iron Works, dwl 127 Shipley
Burke Thomas, hostler, 257 Clementina
Burke Thomas, machinist, Union Foundry, dwl 64 First
Burke Thomas, painter, dwl E s Park Avenue bet Bryant and Harrison
Burke Thomas L. workman with John Downes Wilson, E s Mission bet Fourteenth and Fifteenth
Burke Vincent, hostler, dwl Davis Street House
Burke Walter, workman, S. F. & Pacific Sugar Co. dwl E s Nevada bet Folsom and Harrison
Burke William, dwl W s Sixth nr Brannan
Burke William (M. Burke & Bro.) dwl NW cor Sixth and Brannan
Burke William, driver, dwl W s Battery bet Vallejo and Green
Burke William, hostler, Omnibus R. R. Co. dwl 124 Shipley, rear
Burke William, laborer, dwl 213 Tehama
Burke William, molder, Vulcan Iron Works, dwl 418 Green
Burke William A pattern maker, dwl S s Clay bet Jones and Leavenworth
BURKE WILLIAM F. importer and retailer boots and shoes, NW cor Montgomery and Pine, dwl 1006 Clay
Burkhardt Adolph, cutler with Michael Price, 110 Montgomery
Burkhardt Alvin, brass finisher, dwl S s Vallejo bet Montgomery and Kearny
Burkhardt Christian, butcher with Wm. K. Dietrich
Burkhardt Christian, Union Bakery, 1516 Stockton
Burkhardt Frederick, carpenter, dwl 209 Pacific
Burkhardt (George) & Faas (William) liquor saloon, 1214 Stockton, dwl 209 Pacific
Burkhardt George, shoe maker, 323 Bush, dwl W s Sixth bet Harrison and Bryant
Burkhardt George, watches and jewelry, 209 Pacific
Burkhardt John G. driver, Union Bakery, dwl 1516 Stockton
Burkhardt R. apprentice, Vulcan Iron Works
Burkhardt, see Burckhardt
Burkhead William N. compositor, Evening Bulletin, dwl 815 Stockton
Burks Charles I. carpenter, dwl 29 Second
Burley John, carpenter, dwl NE cor Pacific and Kearny

BURLING WILLIAM, broker, office NW corner Montgomery and Washington, dwl 318 Jessie
Burlingame Charles S. laborer, dwl Point Lobos Road nr Lone Mountain Cemetery
Burmeister Allerich, groceries and liquors, NW cor California and Leavenworth
Burmeister C. H. groceries and liquors, SW cor Beale and Mission
Burmeister Christian, groceries and liquors, 31 Main, dwl cor Beale and Mission
Burmeister Claus, merchant tailor, 402 Brannan
Burmeister Francis H. carpenter, dwl Cincinnati Brewery, Valencia nr Sixteenth
Burmeister Henry, steward, Zeile's Vapor Baths, 517 Pacific
Burmeister Henry, workman with Adam Wagner
Burmeister, see Buhrmeister
Burnap John, commission merchant and wholesale and retail grocer, 425 Davis, dwl NE cor Larkin and Green
Burnett Frederick A. steward Old Corner, 516 Mont
BURNETT G. G. drugs and medicines, 330 Mont
Burnett George W. butcher, dwl SE cor Polk and Washington
Burnett Henry A. lieut. Second Cav. C. V. office N s Wash bet Bat and Sansom, dwl 5 Fourth
Burnett John M. mining secretary, office 605 Montgomery, dwl 1205 Sacramento
Burnett M. dwl 273 Minna
Burnett M. J. (widow) dwl 410 Bush
Burnett Peter H. president Pacific Bank, office NE cor Montgomery and California, dwl 615 Post
BURNETT W. C. attorney at law, office 21 Court Block 636 Clay, dwl 704 Sutter
Burnett William, supervising inspector steamboats Pacific Coast, office third floor Custom House
Burnham Andrew W. carriage maker, 321 Pine, dwl 539 Market
BURNHAM GILMAN M. merchant, office 509 Clay, dwl 12 Hawthorne
Burnham James W. clerk with McElwee & Ackerman, dwl 526 O'Farrell
Burnham Oscar, engineer, dwl 627 Commercial
Burnham William F. upholsterer with H. J. M. Troutt, dwl cor Steiner and Tyler
Burning Moscow G. & S. M. Co. office 620 Wash
Burningham Margaret Miss, domestic, dwl 1815 Stockton
Burns A. M. captain stm Orizaba, C. S. N. Co. office NE cor Front and Jackson, dwl 915 Powell
Burns Annie, cook, dwl 318 Jessie
Burns Bernard, cartman, cor Geary and Kearny
Burns Bernard, stone cutter, dwl 89 Everett
Burns Bridget Miss, domestic, dwl 512 Stockton
Burns Bryan, laborer, Alcatraces, dwl W s Sansom bet Green and Union
Burns Catherine Miss, dress maker, dwl NE cor Montgomery and Pacific
Burns Christopher, machinist, dwl 277 Minna
Burns Daniel, painter, dwl 12 Sutter
Burns Delia, domestic, dwl 318 Jessie
Burns Edmund, laborer, dwl N s Mission nr Seventh
Burns Edward, express wagon, cor Pacific and Davis, dwl 207 Pacific
Burns Eliza Miss, dress maker, 31 Everett
Burns Ellen, domestic, 234 Sixth
Burns F. J. captain bark Architect, office Pier 10 Stewart
Burns Francis, sailor, dwl Minna Place
Burns Frank, dwl E s Beale bet Mission and Mkt
Burns Hannah Miss, domestic, 730 Bush
Burns H. J. stencil plate cutter, What Cheer House, dwl 9 Dupont
Burns Hugh, dwl SW cor Folsom and Eleventh
Burns Isidor, shipsmith, 33 Market, dwl 921 Bush
Burns James, apprentice with Thomas O'Malley, 646 Market
Burns James, driver with DeVries & Chase, dwl NW cor Calhoun and Union

Burns James, gas fitter, dwl NW cor Jessie and Anna
Burns James, laborer, dwl N s Sixteenth bet Guerrero and Dolores
Burns James, laborer with Hey & Meyn
Burns James, laborer, dwl Sixteenth nr Guerrero
Burns James, stone cutter, dwl 331 Bush
Burns James, washer, Davis' Laundry, W s Harriet bet Howard and Folsom
Burns John, dwl with Michael Burns, Castro nr Thirteenth
Burns John, baker, dwl 9 St. Mary
Burns John, boatman, bds City Front House, 625 Davis
Burns John, fireman, Pacific Glass Works, dwl S s Mariposa nr Mississippi
Burns John, laborer with Edw'd J. Quirk
Burns John, porter, dwl 5 Sonoma Place
Burns John, porter, International Hotel
Burns John Henry, seaman, stm Orizaba
Burns John, steward, Seymour House, 24 Sansom
Burns John, teazer, Pacific Glass Works
Burns John C. carpenter, dwl 108 Sutter
Burns John W. laborer, Golden Age Flour Mills, dwl E s Sansom bet Filbert and Green
Burns John H. saloon keeper, dwl 807 Jackson
Burns Maggie Miss, domestic, 628 Sutter
Burns Margaret, domestic, dwl W s Mont nr Union
Burns Martin, laborer, dwl 110 William, rear
Burns Martin J. carpenter, dwl NE cor Polk and Jackson
Burns Mary Miss, chambermaid, Russ House
Burns Mary Ann Miss, domestic, dwl 820 Pine
Burns Michael, cooper with Lyon & Co. dwl E s Sixth bet Howard and Tehama
Burns Michael, gardener, dwl W s Castro bet Thirteenth and Fourteenth
Burns Michael, laborer, dwl S s Market bet Ninth and Tenth
Burns Michael, porter International Hotel
Burns Patrick, blacksmith with Gallagher & Rodecker, dwl 22 Geary
Burns Patrick, blacksmith, 12 Geary, dwl 675 Mission
Burns Patrick, hostler with P. Benis, dwl 214 Stevenson
Burns Patrick, laborer with Hey & Meyn
Burns Patrick, laborer, dwl 20 Rousch, rear
Burns Patrick, steward, Lick House, dwl 242 Minna, rear
Burns Patrick, steward, steamer Relief
Burns Peter, coachman, Brooklyn Hotel, dwl 126 Bush
Burns Peter, helper, Union Foundry, dwl 243 Tehama
Burns Peter, laborer, dwl 509 Howard
Burns Robert, dwl 517 Pine
Burns Robert, steward, What Cheer House Restaurant, dwl 119 Pine
Burns Sarah A. nurse, dwl 319 Minna
Burns T. laborer, Spring Valley W. W
Burns Thomas, boatman, dwl 617 Davis
Burns Thomas, cartman, dwl 1029 Pacific
Burns Thomas, foundryman, dwl 32 Stewart
Burns Thomas, laborer, dwl 45 Stevenson
Burns Thomas, teamster, dwl U. S. Hotel, 706 Battery
Burns Thomas H. machinist, dwl 240 Sixth
Burns Timothy, waiter, Lick House
Burns William, laborer, Spring Valley W. W
Burns William, laborer, dwl 106½ Clay
Burns William, longshoreman, dwl S s Greenwich bet Montgomery and Sansom
Burns William, teamster with James McDevitt, dwl W s Sansom bet Vallejo and Broadway
Burns, see Byrnes
Burnside S. M. Co. office 436 Jackson
Burnstadt Harris, laborer, dwl SW cor Union and Powell

Burnstine Joseph, furniture, 834 and 838 Market, dwl 37 O'Farrell
Buron Louis, laundryman with Parfait Lemaitre
Burr Amos, brakeman, S. F. & San José R. R. res San José
Burr Clarence C. clerk, dwl with E. Willard Burr
Burr Edmund C. dwl with E. Willard Burr
Burr Ellen Miss, domestic, dwl 1526 Powell
BURR E. WILLARD, president Savings and Loan Society, office 619 Clay, dwl S s Filbert bet Polk and Van Ness Avenue
Burr George W. molder, Fulton Foundry, dwl Polk bet Eddy and Ellis
Burr H. P. captain ship John Jay, dwl 17 Perry
Burr Levi, liquor saloon, Bay bet Kearny and Dupont
Burr M. George, carpenter, dwl 150 Third
Burr William, porter, SE cor Clay and Davis
Burrell John M. (W. F. Wilmot & Co.) 315 Battery
Burrill C., U. S. special examiner drugs, office Custom House, dwl S s Geary above Stockton
Burrill, see Birrell
Burris George R. steward, steamer Sierra Nevada
Burris William (colored) janitor, Fourth Street and Third Street schools, dwl 109 Clara
Burroughs William, with R. A. Swain & Co. dwl 20 Minna
BURROWES GEORGE REV. D.D. president City College, SE cor Stockton and Geary
Burrows Edward M. dwl 223 Minna
Burrows H. W. molder, San Francisco Iron Works, dwl What Cheer House
Burrows John, bar tender, Cordes Exchange, dwl 135 Stewart
Burrows Jonathan, carpenter, 763 Mission, dwl 759 Mission
Burscough Henry, laundry, 505 Third
Burson James N. deputy superintendent streets, dwl N s Berry nr Dupont
Burt Ann E. Mrs. house keeper with W. H. Scoville, W s Shotwell bet Twenty-First and Twenty-Second
Burt Charles, boiler maker with Coffey &.Risdon, dwl 54 First
Burt E. C. Mrs. principal Stevenson Street School, dwl 830 Pacific
Burt Hiram, cooper, S. F. &' P. Sugar Co. dwl E s Rousch nr Folsom
Burt Howard, salesman with Snow & Co. dwl 511 Vallejo
Burt Silas S. fireman, U. S. B. M. dwl 830 Pacific
Burt William J. laborer, dwl S s Twentieth nr San Bruno Road
BURTON CHALES H. merchant, office 405 Front, dwl 1018 Washington
Burton Elizabeth Mrs. (colored) dwl 1614 Powell
Burton James A. machinist, dwl 41 Natoma
Burton John, hat and bonnet bleacher and dresser, 1317 Stockton
Burton John, pattern maker, Miners' Foundry, dwl SW cor Minna and Fourth
Burton L. A. (widow) dwl 612 California
Burton Matilda (col'd, widow) dwl 12 Virginia Pl
Burton R. J. clerk, dwl 133 Tehama
Burton Theodore L. (McNeil & B.) dwl E s Taylor bet Filbert and Union
Burtsell John M. book keeper with Murphy, Grant & Co. dwl W s Shotwell bet Fifteenth and Sixteenth
Buscelle James, bag maker, dwl 535 California
Busch Henry, clerk, dwl 408 Folsom
Bush Alonzo, driver with Wells, Fargo & Co. dwl NW cor Montgomery and California
Bush Charles, hair dresser with Ciprico & Cook, Cosmopolitan Hotel, dwl NE cor Taylor and Geary
Bush Emma Miss, governess, dwl 839 Mission
Bush Ephraim, pattern maker, Vulcan Iron Works, dwl 24 Minna

Bush Frederick, clerk, NE cor Ellis and Powell
Bush Henry, photographic gallery, Shiels' Block, 5 Post
Bush John, boiler maker, Pacific Foundry, dwl 324 Green
Bush John, coachman with R. J. Van Dewater
Bush Jonathan P. physician, office and dwl 605 Sac
Bush (*Louis*) & McAllister (*William B.*) dentists, office 606 Kearny, dwl 45 Clementina
Bush Nathan, furniture, 708 Pacific, and groceries and liquors, NW cor Pacific and Kearny, dwl 708 Pacific
Bush Norton, book keeper, San Francisco Gas Co. dwl 149 Tehama, E Third
Bush Peter, Union Malt House, S s Brannan bet Eighth and Nineth
BUSH STREET HOUSE, James McNamara proprietor, 331 and 333 Bush
Bush Thomas H. book binder with Buswell & Co. dwl 62¼ Yerba Buena
Bush William, driver with Dames & Lohse, bds New England House
Bush, see Busch
Bushman John, bar tender, dwl 44 Stewart
Bushman W. (*Grush & Co.*) dwl 250 Jessie
Bushman William (*Sanders & B.*) dwl 250 Jessie
Bushman William, peddler, dwl Pacific W Taylor
Bushnell Horace (*Jack & B.*) dwl 8 Hardie Place
Bushnell J. H. painter, dwl Summer Street House
Bushnell William E. master steamer Oakland, res Brooklyn
Bushway John, coppersmith, dwl 1 Agnes Lane
Businger Ferdinand, engineer, dwl 20 Minna
Buss J. musician, dwl E s August Alley nr Union
Busse Albert (*E. G. Cook & Co.*) dwl 124 Jessie
Busse August, shoe maker with John Schade, 16 Sansom
Bussett H. N. ship carpenter, dwl 555 Mission
Busson James P. clerk. dwl 234 Stevenson
Buster Hiram C. blacksmith, dwl 131 Montgomery
Buster Mary Mrs. furnished rooms, 131 Mont
BUSWELL (*Alexander*) & CO. book binders, paper rulers, etc. 509 Clay and 508 Commercial, dwl SW cor Union and Jones
Buswell Francis, dwl 40 Silver
Buswell William T. pattern mkr, Fulton Foundry
Butcher George H. imp and manuf hardware, office 421 Battery, dwl Cosmopolitan Hotel
Butenop Alexander, clerk, 625 Pacific
Butenop Henry, groceries and liquors, 625 Pacific
Butenop Peter, with Marden & Folger, dwl 625 Pac
Buthe Christian L. clerk, SE cor Pine and Battery
Buthe Henry, butcher with Wilson & Stevens, dwl N s Brannan bet Eighth and Ninth
Butler Alfred, dwl 149 Perry
Butler Ann Mrs. domestic, 615 Post
Butler Annie Miss, domestic, 615 Harrison
Butler B. F. (widow) dwl SW cor Cal and Mason
Butler Charles, carpenter, dwl 28 Sansom
Butler Charles, waiter, steamer Senator
Butler Charles C. dwl NE cor Sutter and Steiner
Butler Daniel, with Cal. Steam N. Co. Bdwy Wharf
Butler Edward, blacksmith helper, Vulcan Iron Works, dwl Volunteer Engine House
Butler Frederick S. with M. F. Butler, dwl N s Thirteenth bet Howard and Folsom
Butler George, bar keeper, 112 Leidesdorff
Butler George, laborer, dwl SW cor Turk and Fillmore
Butler Henry, captain schooner Enterprise, office Pier 11
Butler Henry W. newspaper clerk, Post Office, dwl 1009 Powell
Butler James, hostler, SW cor Howard and Fourteenth
Butler James, soda bottler, dwl 190 Stevenson
Butler James, waiter, 35 Natoma
Butler J. D. janitor Market St. and Stevenson St. schools

Butler J. H. carpenter, dwl W s Kearny bet Pacific and Jackson
Butler John, with J. Hirth & Co. 539 Com
Butler Joseph, cook, steamer Yosemite
Butler Joseph B. book keeper, dwl 1417 Powell
Butler Joseph D. dwl 503 Sutter
Butler M. Miss, principal S. F. Female Seminary, NE cor Mason and Jackson
Butler M. A. Mrs. millinery, 136 Montgomery, dwl W s Sixth bet Folsom and Howard
Butler Mary Mrs. dress making, 503 Sutter
Butler Mary A. (widow) dwl 809 Jackson
Butler Matthew, book keeper with Dyer, Badger & Rokohl, dwl 867 Folsom
Butler M. F. architect, 73 Montgomery Block, dwl N s Thirteenth bet Howard and Folsom
Butler Michael, laborer, dwl Filbert nr Mont
Butler Patrick, laborer, dwl Dolores Hall, N s Valeucia nr Sixteenth
Butler Patrick, nail maker with Nelson & Doble, dwl 503 O'Farrell
Butler Patrick, workman with John Henry, dwl Dolores Hall
Butler Patrick F. dwl W s Sixth bet Folsom and Howard
Butler Richard, workman, S. F. & P. Sugar Co. dwl 14 Russ
Butler Robert, groceries and liquors, NE cor Harrison and Eighth
Butler Robert, laborer, dwl 12 St. Charles
Butler Robert B. proprietor Union House, 511 and 513 Mission
Butler Rudolph J. accountant British and Californian Banking Co. 424 California, res Oakland
Butler Samuel S. lodgings, 525 and 528 Commercial, and 511 Washington, dwl SE cor Leavenworth and Lincoln
Butler T. J. carpenter, dwl 120 Natoma
Butler T. R. assistant assayer U. S. Branch Mint, dwl Russ House
Butler Walter A. teamster with John R. Sedgeley, dwl with John R. Sedgeley, S s Twelfth bet Howard and Folsom
Butler Warren C. Coiners' Department U. S. Branch Mint, dwl 1417 Powell
Butler William, laborer, 31 Metropolitan Market, dwl 636 Commercial
Butler William, steward, dwl Manhattan Engine House
Butler William M. porter with E. G. Mathews & Co. dwl 209 Clara
BUTMAN FREDERICK A. landscape painter, studio 240 Montgomery, dwl 806 Howard
Butt Christopher C. (*Frederick W. Lange & Co.*) dwl SW cor Stockton and Bush
Butt (*Peter N.*) & Kuchmeister (*Henry W.*) groceries and liquors, SE cor Pacific and Kearny, dwl SE cor Powell and Pacific
Butte G. & S. Mining Co. office 623 Montgomery
Butter Charles, engineer with C. S. Navigation Co
Butter M. laborer, Spring Valley W. W
Butterfield O. stock broker, bds Meyer's Hotel, 814 Montgomery
Butterfield Charles B. (*Butterfield & Bro.*) dwl 408 Pine
Butterfield Rodney, shoe maker, dwl 737 Pacific
BUTTERFIELD WILLIAM & BROTHER (*C. B. Butterfield*) auctioneers and commission merchants, 408 Pine
Butters James A. with J. W. Brittan & Co. 120 Front
Butters John S. captain steamer Pacific, dwl S s Sacramento bet Leavenworth and Jones
Butterworth James, tinner, dwl S s Folsom bet Beale and Main
BUTTERWORTH SAMUEL F. agent Quicksilver Mining Company, office 205 Battery, res New Almaden
Buttmann John, tinsmith, dwl 323 Pine

Buttner Charles, works S. F. Chemical Works, NW cor Valencia and Fifteenth
Buttner Henry, drayman, NE cor California and Front, dwl N s Brannan bet Fifth and Sixth
Büttner Henry, driver, Philadelphia Brewery, dwl 232 Second
Büttner John, pattern maker, Miners' Foundry, dwl 46 Clementina
Button Sophia B. Miss, clairvoyant and physician, office and dwl 3 St. Mark Place
Butts Benjamin F. milkman, dwl 14 Stockton Place
Butts Harvey D. dwl cor Mission and Stewart
Butts R. W. drayman with C. H. Harrison, 517 Front, dwl 635 Broadway
Buxton George, engineer, dwl 608 Post
Buyer (C.) & Reich (Leopold) fancy goods, SW cor Stockton and Jackson
Buzzolini D. commission merchant, office 417 Jackson, dwl 301 Clementina
By Sing Hing (Chinese) washing, 429 Third
Byas William (col'd) porter, 406 Pine, dwl 1212 Sacramento
Byatt William, gardener, SE corner Chestnut and Jones
Bycroft Thomas B. blacksmith with H. Steele, dwl cor Ritch and Clara
Byers J. M. (J. McDonough Foard & Co.) dwl 10 Ellis
Byers John P. stevedore, dwl N s Union bet Battery and Sansom
Byfield Augustus N. consul for Portugal, dwl 607 Dupont
Byington H. W. (May & B.) dwl 826 Sutter
Byles George, dwl 160 Perry
Byring O. H. repacker case goods, dwl 6 Merch
BYRNE & CASTREE (David B.) groceries and liquors, SW cor Howard and Twelfth
Byrne Bernard, clerk with Croskey & Howard, dwl E s Grove nr Van Ness Avenue, Hayes' Valley
Byrne Bridget, domestic, dwl 148 Minna
Byrne Charles & Co. sail makers, 7 Clay, dwl [E s Harriet nr Folsom
Byrne Charles J. seaman, Vigilant Engine Co. No 9
Byrne Dennis, waiter, 605 Commercial, dwl 1118 Kearny
Byrne Ellen Miss, domestic, 405 Powell
Byrne Felix, carpenter, dwl 7 Park Avenue
Byrne Francis, cooper with Handy & Neuman, dwl 510 Sacramento
Byrne Francis E. painter, dwl 510 Sacramento
Byrne Garrett J. (Kerby, Byrne & Co.) dwl 12 O'Farrell
BYRNE (Henry H.) & FREELON (Thomas W.) attorneys at law, office 27-30 Court Block 636 Clay
Byrne James, dwl 148 Minna
Byrne James, drayman with Locke & Montague, dwl 3 Berry
Byrne James, harness maker, dwl 79 Stevenson
Byrne J. O. dwl 440 Clementina
Byrne John M. importer, 426 Jackson, dwl 533 Sutter
Byrne Julia, domestic, dwl 139 Townsend
Byrne Maggie Miss, saleswoman, 518 Kearny, dwl 127 Second
Byrne Mary Miss, domestic, 621 Leavenworth
Byrne Mary J. (widow) saloon S s Sacramento bet Davis and Drumm
Byrne Michael, laborer, Union Foundry, dwl 34 First
Byrne Michael, salesman with Kerby, Byrne & Co. dwl 108 Minna
Byrne Patrick, with Crane & Brigham, dwl 148 Minna
Byrne Patrick, laborer, dwl with Nicholas McDonald
Byrne Rosalie (widow) dwl 120 Perry
Byrne Thomas, dwl 47 Minna
Byrne Thomas, contracter, dwl 511 Mission
Byrne Thomas, laborer, dwl 1025 Pacific

Byrne Thomas, merchandise broker, office 308 Front, dwl 658 Folsom
Byrne Thomas K. merchant (Oregon) dwl 257 Stevenson
Byrnes Barney, teamster, dwl 26 Hunt
Byrnes Edward, expressman, dwl 207 Pacific
Byrnes Edward P. laborer, dwl 158 Perry
Byrnes Ellen, dwl NW cor O'Farrell and Devisidero
Byrnes John, fireman, steamer Cornelia, dwl 1226 Kearny
Byrnes Kate Miss, domestic, 14 Stockton
Byrnes Kate Mrs. dwl 247 Stevenson
Byrnes Patrick, hotel keeper, dwl NW cor O'Farrell and Devisidero
Byrnes Patrick, poultry dealer, dwl 18 Ecker
Byrnes Peter, blacksmith, California Engine Co. No. 4
Byrnes Thomas, porter with McAran & Kelly, dwl N s Broadway bet Montgomery and Sansom
Byrnes Thomas E. (Feehan, B. & Co.) dwl 304 Jessie
Byrnes William, stevedore, dwl 549 Howard
Byron John, bricklayer, dwl 249 Minna
Byron Michael, bricklayer, dwl 338 Minna
Byron Peter, hostler, Omnibus R. R. Co
Byron Thomas, carpenter, dwl 728 Market
Byrum Ann (widow) dwl S s Brannan bet Seventh and Eighth
Byxbee John F. book keeper with H. B. Tichenor & Co. dwl 210 O'Farrell nr Powell
Byxbee Robert G. (H. B. Tichenor & Co.) dwl 26 Essex

C

Cabana Theopolis, boot maker, dwl 1213 Dupont
Cabannes Eugene, restaurant, NW cor Sansom and Merchant
Cabannes Joseph, wholesale butcher, Potrero Av
Cabery Cormack, carpenter, dwl NW cor Jessie and Anna
Cabery Patrick, carpenter, dwl NW cor Jessie and Anna
Cables Lewis H. with George Hughes, dwl 325 Sixth
Cachot M. physician, St. Mary's Hospital
Cachrovestini Angelo, deck hand, stm Sacramento
Cadel James, machinist, Miners' Foundry
Cadel Peter, real estate, dwl 508 Union
Cadenice Maurice, vegetable garden, Hunter's Point Road
Cadenice Nicolas, vegetable garden, Hunter's Point Road
Cadesi John, fruit dealer, 204 Second
Cadieu Andrew M. with Heuston, Hastings & Co. dwl Lick House
Cadin Fannie, domestic, 542 Bryant
Cadiz Eugenia (widow) dwl 909 Jackson
Cadogan James J. book keeper with M. O'Connor, res Oakland
Cadogan Patrick, workman S. F. & P. Sugar Co. dwl Eighth nr Howard
Cadogan Timothy, helper S. F. Sugar Refinery, dwl W s Ritter nr Harrison
CADUC PHILIP, proprietor Caduc's Packet Line and American Cobble Stone Depôt (agent Am. Russ. Com. Co. and Napa Soda, Sacramento City) office North Point Dock, dwl 722 Sutter
CADUC'S SAN FRANCISCO, FREEPORT AND SACRAMENTO LINE PACKETS, office foot Washington
Cady John, boiler maker, Union Foundry, dwl 36 Moss
Cady John, hostler, 115 Kearny
Cady John J. job wagon, NW cor Bush and Mont, dwl Mission bet Eighth and Ninth
Cady Lorenzo, contractor, dwl N s Folsom between Eighth and Ninth

Caeder A. mate stm Clinton, foot Vallejo
Caffall George, longshoreman, dwl W s Vincent nr Union
Cafferato *(Antonio)* & Larebarde *(John Baptiste)* wood and coal, 1823 Powell
Caffery Mary Miss, milliner, dwl 54 Third
Catfiero Frank, mariner, dwl 109 Washington
Caffrey Dennis, Tower Saloon, 210 First
Caffrey James, picture frame maker, dwl 331 Bush
Caffrey Michael, porter, dwl 128 First
Caffrey Patrick, laborer with Edw'd J. Quirk
Cafrey Timothy, laborer, Omnibus R. R. Co
Cagliere George, clerk, dwl 611 Dupont
Cagney John, drayman, dwl Howard nr Fourth
Cagney Martin, teamster, dwl 213 O'Farrell
Cagney Timothy, waiter, dwl 116 Stevenson
Cahalan John, shoe maker, 831 Washington
Cahalan John L. carpenter, dwl 728 Market
Cahalen John, porter, 211 Bat, dwl 271 Stevenson
Cuhen Edmond, clerk, 226 Front, dwl cor Stockton and Broadway
Cahill Anna Miss, domestic with Frank M. Pixley
Cahill Anthony, drayman, cor California and Davis
Cahill Edward, waiter, dwl W s Stanford corner Townsend
Cahill Ellen, domestic, dwl 1312 Pine
Cahill Ellen (widow) dwl 30 Jessie
Cahill James, laborer, dwl S s Folsom bet Van Ness Avenue and Franklin
CAHILL *(James F.)* & McELROY *(James)* liquor saloon, SE cor.Bush and Kearny, dwl NW cor Seventh and Howard
Cahill J. C. liquor saloon, NW cor Dupont and St. Mark Place
CAHILL JOHN, liquor saloon, NE cor Brannan and Fourth
Cahill John, painter, dwl W s Hyde bet Union and Filbert
Cahill Mary Miss, domestic with J. Conway, W s Alemeda nr El Dorado
Cahill Mary (widow) dwl 311 O'Farrell
Cahill Michael, wood and coal, Waverly Place, dwl 131 St. Mark Place
Cahill Patrick, drayman with Dickson, De Wolf & Co. dwl S s Cal bet Leavenworth and Hyde
Cahill Patrick, laborer, dwl 505 Howard
Cahill Patrick, molder, Union Foundry
Cahill Patrick, waiter, Russ House
Cahill Patrick, workman, S. F. & P. Sugar Co. dwl W s Chesley nr Harrison
Cahill William, porter, 212 Battery, dwl 78 Natoma
CAHN *(A.)* & CO. *(I. F. Bloch, Leon Cahn, and H. F. Bloch)* wholesale groceries and liquors, Portland, Oregon, off 205 Cal, dwl 547 Folsom
Cahn David, with Lazard Freres, dwl 115 Battery
Cahn Israel *(Uhlfelder & Cahn)* dwl 513 Folsom
Cahn Jerome, dry goods, 226 Third
Cahn Leon *(Cahn & Co.)* dwl 547 Folsom
Cahn Leopold *(Uhlfelder & C.)* dwl 515 Folsom
Cahn M. dwl 214 Sansom
Cahn Sylvain *(Lazard Freres)* dwl 1018 Bush
Cahrey William W. peddler, dwl NE cor Howard and Seventh
Cain Ann Miss, at Cole's Laundry, 114 Dora
Cain Edward, pressman with Agnew & Deffebach, dwl Howard Engine House
Cain James, molder, Union Foundry, dwl 427 Union
Cain John, mariner, dwl 17 Fourth
Cain John, shipsmith with W. S. Phelps & Co. dwl Oriental Hotel
Cain Michael, laborer, dwl cor Greenwich and Powell
Cain Rufus K. brick layer, dwl 411 Dupont
Caire Adrien *(Caire Bros.)* res Paris, France
Caire Brothers *(Justinien and Adrien)* importers and jobbers hard ware, 530 Washington and 1028 Dupont, dwl 313 Green
Cairns Daniel, machinist, Union Foundry, dwl 32 Everett

CAIRNS JOHN, dwl 111 Perry
Cairns Matthew, laborer, dwl Union Court
Cairns Robert, salesman with Joseph Peirce, dwl N s Guy Place
Calaly Michael, laborer, dwl 218 Dupont
Caldwell Andrew, porter, 401 Battery, dwl 12 Oak
Caldwell Charles, molder, Golden State Iron Works, dwl Jane
Caldwell Charles M. carpenter, 607 Market, dwl St. Lawrence House
Caldwell David, dwl Farmers' Exchange, Old San José Road op St. Mary's College
Caldwell Edwin, office 540 Clay, dwl 437 Minna
Caldwell Eugene J. Rev. assistant pastor St. Bridget's Church, SW cor Bdwy and Van Ness Av
Caldwell G. & S. M. Co. *(Cove District, Tulare Co.)* office 7 Stevenson House
Caldwell Isaac (col'd) cook, dwl 16 Hawthorne
Caldwell James, plasterer, dwl 11 William, rear
Caldwell Joseph, blacksmith with N. W. Spaulding, dwl Second Av bet Sixteenth and Seventeenth
Caldwell William, machinist, Fulton Foundry, dwl Bernal Heights
Caledonia Series G. & S. M. Co. office 338 Mont
Caledonia Tunnel & M. Co. *(Gold Hill)* office 7 Government House, 502 Washington
CALEF JONATHAN S. physician, office 726 Washington, dwl 312 Post
Calender John T. (col'd) boarding, 907 Pacific
Caler Isabella (widow) dwl 27 Freelon
Calgin John, dwl 109 First
CALHOUN C. A. & SON. *(William A.)* book and job printers, 320 Clay, dwl 215 Mason bet Ellis and O'Farrell
Calhoun Sarah Miss, domestic with John Satterlee, W s Folsom bet Eleventh and Twelfth
Calhoun William, laborer, S. F. & San José R. R
Calhoun William, seaman, ship Constitution, dwl S s Pinkham Place nr Eighth
Calhoun William A. *(Calhoun & Son)* dwl 1117 Folsom
CALIFORNIA ART UNION, rooms 312 Montgomery
California Bible Society, office 757 Market
California Borax Co. office 205 Battery
California Brewery, A. Schuppert proprietor, NE cor Stockton and Jackson
CALIFORNIA BUILDING, LOAN, AND SAVINGS SOCIETY, office 406 Montgomery
CALIFORNIA CHRISTIAN ADVOCATE (weekly) office 711 Mission
CALIFORNIA CHRONIK (weekly) Charles Ruehl publisher, NW cor Kearny and Sac
California City Letter Express Co. office 316 Mont
California Coal M. Co. office SE cor Montgomery and Jackson
California Collegiate Institute, Miss Margaret L. Lammond principal, 64 Silver
California Copper Smelting Works, Antioch Contra Costa Co. office 602 Front
CALIFORNIA DEMOKRAT (daily, German) Frederick Hess & Co. proprietors, NW cor Kearny and Sacramento
CALIFORNIA FARMER (weekly, agricultural) Warren & Co. editors and proprietors, office 320 Clay
CALIFORNIA FOUNDRY, William Brodie & Co. proprietors, 16 Fremont
CALIFORNIA HOME INSURANCE CO. B. F. Low president, office 224 and 226 California
California Homestead Association, office 305 Montgomery room 6
CALIFORNIA HOTEL, Gailhard Bros. proprietors, SE cor Commercial and Dupont
CALIFORNIA INSURANCE CO. Albert Miller president, C. T. Hopkins secretary, office 318 California
CALIFORNIA LEADER, Theobalds & Co. proprietors, office 625 Merchant

CALIFORNIA LLOYD'S MARINE INSURANCE CO. G. Touchard secretary, office 418 California

CALIFORNIA, OREGON, AND MEXICAN STEAM SHIP LINE, office SW cor Front and Jackson

California Petroleum Co. office 620 Washington

California Petroleum Rectifying Co. office 1 Government House

CALIFORNIA PIONEERS, rooms 808 Montgomery bet Jackson and Pacific

CALIFORNIA POLICE GAZETTE, F. S. Harlow & Bro. publishers and proprietors, office 424 Battery

CALIFORNIA POWDER WORKS, Santa Cruz, John F. Lohse agent, office 318 California

CALIFORNIA RURAL HOME JOURNAL, T. Hart Hyatt & Co. publishers and proprietors, office 306 Sansom

California Sheep Raisers' & Wool Growers' Association, office NE cor Front and Clay

CALIFORNIA STATE TELEGRAPH CO. H. W. Carpentier president, George S. Ladd superintendent and secretary, office 507 Montgomery

CALIFORNIA STEAM NAVIGATION CO. office NE cor Front and Jackson

California Straw Works *(J. D. Kersey and Miss M. J. Little)* office 45 Third

CALIFORNIA TEACHER (monthly) office 536 Clay

CALIFORNIA WINE COOPERAGE CO. depôt SW cor Drumm and Commercial

CALIFORNIA YOUTHS' COMPANION, Smith & Co. publishers and proptrs, office 505 Clay

CALIFORNIAN PUBLISHING CO. *(A. A. Stickney, John Collner, and J. P. Bogardus)* publishers Californian, office 532 Merchant

CALIFORNIAN (weekly) office 532 Merchant

Calish Raphael S. express wagon, cor Dupont and Broadway

Calkin Milo, clerk, office U. S. Internal Revenue, dwl 814 Bush

Call Jonas, dwl Oriental Hotel

Callabotta Sylvester, coffee saloon, 47 Jackson

CALLAGHAN D. manufacturer Donnolly & Co.'s Yeast Powders, 121 Front, dwl NW cor Howard and Fourteenth

Callaghan Ellen Miss, domestic, dwl 1028 Pine

Callaghan Eugene, dwl 331 Bush

Callaghan George W. longshoreman, dwl 116 Jackson

Callaghan James, laborer, dwl N s Filbert bet Montgomery and Sansom

Callaghan James, steward, 532 Commercial

Callaghan Jeremiah, merchant, office 421 Front, dwl SE cor Mission and Fourteenth

Callaghan John, groceries, etc. 121 Front, dwl NE cor Pacific and Laguna

Callaghan John, liquors, dwl 130 Pacific

Callaghan M. captain brig George Emery, office Pier 10 Stewart

Callaghan Philip, molder, bds 127 Pacific

Callaghan Thomas, laborer, Custom House, dwl Filbert bet Larkin and Polk

Callaghan's Building, N s Dupont bet Clay and Washington

Callagher Alice Miss, domestic, dwl 905 Pacific

Callahan Bernard, chief engineer S. F. & P. Sugar Co. dwl 16 Russ

Callahan Bridget Miss, domestic, dwl 1020 Pine

Callahan Cornelius, laborer, dwl E s White nr Vallejo

Callahan Daniel, laborer, dwl with John J. Wiseman, W s Twelfth bet Folsom and Harrison

Callahan David, laborer, dwl 170 Minna

Callahan Delia Miss, domestic, dwl 1815 Stockton

Callahan Dennis, carpenter, dwl 12 Sutter

Callahan D. O. collector, Daily Examiner, dwl SW cor Stockton and Pacific

Callahan Ellen Miss, domestic, 117 Taylor

Callahan Ellen Miss, domestic, 600 Sutter

Callahan James, dwl 331 Bush

Callahan James, hostler, 655 Sacramento, dwl Kearny nr California

Callahan James, porter, Occidental Hotel

Callahan James K. blacksmith with Samuel F. Ross, bds Columbia Hotel

Callahan J. J. clerk with J. R. Stewart & Co. dwl 235 Stevenson

Callahan Joanna Miss, domestic, dwl 1309 Mason

Callahan John, grocer, dwl NE cor Chestnut and Hyde

Callahan John, laborer, S. F. & San José R. R

Callahan John, liquor saloon, cor Jones and Francisco

Callahan Julia Miss, domestic, dwl 516 Green

Callahan M. driver, Omnibus R. R. Co

Callahan Mary Miss, domestic, St. Mary's Cathedral

CALLAHAN *(M. B.)* & SANDERSON *(Samuel A.)* importers and jobbers crockery and glass ware, 310 and 312 Battery, dwl 431 Sixth

Callahan Michael, workman, S. F. & P. Sugar Co. dwl E s Harrison Avenue nr Folsom

Callahan Patrick, laborer, Spring Valley W. W

Callahan Timothy, boiler maker, dwl 511 Mission

Callahan Timothy, laborer, dwl N s Allen nr Hyde

Callahan William, steamboatman, dwl SE cor Fifth and Shipley

Callan Kate Miss, domestic, 222 Post

Callan Thomas, laborer, dwl 230 Sutter

Callan Thomas, wood and coal, W s Fifth nr Howard, dwl 315 Minna

Callau W. A. carpenter, dwl 2 Sherwood Place

Callard F. D. dwl 115 Dupont

Callehe Daniel, laborer with Hey & Meyn

Callender H. A. jeweler with R. B. Gray & Co

Callender John *(Simons & C.)* S s Clark bet Front and Davis

Callihan Daniel, mangler, Chelsea Laundry

Callinan Hannah Miss, domestic, dwl 1425 Stockton

Callinan John, hair dresser with R. D. Baskerville, dwl First Street House

Callott Oliver S. pilot (opposition) office W s Front bet Vallejo and Broadway, dwl 606 Mont

Callsen Anna Miss, seamstress, dwl S s Pacific bet Larkin and Hyde

Callsen Peter, carpenter, dwl Pacific nr Larkin

Callundan Christian F. local policeman, dwl SW cor Battery and Vallejo

Calnan Julia Miss, domestic, 463 Clementina

Calnan Patrick, handcartman, cor Mission and Beale

Calnen Daniel, cartman, 751 Mission

Calnon Johanna Miss, cloak maker, dwl 12 Sutter

CALNON PATRICK, The Old Stand Saloon, SW cor First and Mission, dwl 143 Natoma

Calsby James, employé with Hill & Eastman, dwl NE cor Dupont and Sutter

Calsing Martin, machinist, Miners' Foundry, dwl 520 Merchant

Calvert John, bricklayer, dwl 423 Post

Calvert William, dentist, office 109 Montgomery, dwl 564 Howard

Camaiano Andrea, fisherman, 15 Italian Fish Market

Camaiano Benedetto, fisherman, 20 Italian Fish Mkt

Camaiano Giacomo, fisherman, 1 Italian Fish Market

Caman A. physician, office and dwl, 106 Fourth

Camargo G. & S. M. Co. office 402 Front

Cambournac John, tailor, Lafayette H. & L. Co. No. 2

Cambridge House, Laurence McKeone proprietor, 304 Pacific

Cambridge Silas, teamster with Reynolds & Co. dwl 417 Folsom

Camerden Michael, pork and sausages, 36 Occidental Market, dwl SW cor Fillmore and Pacific

Cameron *(Angus)* & Kuenzi *(John R.)* wood turners and scroll sawyers, 309 Market, dwl 264 Minna

Cameron A. S. Miss, assistant, Rincon School, dwl 435 Tehama
Cameron Daniel, ship carpenter, dwl 264 First
Cameron (Duncan) & Worth (W. E.) Neptune Iron Works, 46 Fremont, dwl Hampton Court bet Second and Third
Cameron Elizabeth Mrs. boarding, 312 Beale
Cameron Hannah H. (widow) dwl 672 Harrison
Cameron James, U. S. Bakery, 509 Third
Cameron John, driver, Omnibus R. R. Co
Cameron John B. pattern maker, dwl 302 O'Farrell
Cameron Robert, clerk, dwl 312 Beale
CAMERON, WHITTIER (W. Frank) & CO. (Edmund B. Benjamin and Silas W. Johnson) importers and jobbers paints, oils, window glass, etc. 425 and 427 Front
Cameron William, bar keeper with James M. Houck, dwl 312 Beale
Cameron William, carpenter, dwl Sierra Nevada Hotel, 528 Pacific
Cameron William, fruit dealer, dwl 119 Natoma
Cameron William, weigher, Washington Street Wharf, dwl Beale nr Mission
Cameron William G. teamster with J. W. Gale & Co. 409 Davis
Camfield Richard, laborer with Hey & Meyn
Camman Augustus capt. Pier 11 Stewart, dwl 261 Clary
Camman Augustus W. dwl 236 Minna
Cammet John, dwl cor Howard and Thirteenth
Camner John, butcher with C. Schmitt, dwl Potrero Avenue
Camp Sarah (widow) dwl 811 Vallejo
CAMPBELL, (Alexander) FOX (Charles N.) & CAMPBELL (Henry C.) attorneys at law, office 710 Montgomery, dwl 26 Turk
Campbell Alexander, attorney at law, office 540 Clay, dwl Tehama House
Campbell Alexander, porter with A. Roman, dwl 423 Post, rear
Campbell Alice J. Miss, dwl 616 Sacramento
Campbell Allen D. boots and shoes, 519 Kearny, dwl 128 Third
Campbell B. H. Coiner's Department, U. S. B. M
Campbell Charles, wire worker with H. T. Graves, 412 Clay
Campbell Colin, clerk with Campbell, Fox & Campbell, dwl 26 Turk
Campbell C. Stuart (Dunn & C.) 538 Market, opposite Second
Campbell Delia (widow) domestic, NW cor Mission and Seventeenth
Campbell Donald, dwl Flume House, San Bruno Road
Campbell Duncan, rigger, dwl 1306 Montgomery
Campbell Edward, laborer, dwl 26 Natoma
Campbell Edwin R. attorney at law, dwl NW cor Stockton and Pacific
Campbell Elbridge G. molder, Miners' Foundry, dwl 511 Mission
Campbell Eliza T. Mrs. millinery, 128 Third
Campbell E. Neville Miss, assistant Second Street School, dwl 145 Natoma
Campbell Francis, dwl SE cor Dolores and Twentieth
Campbell G. & S. M. Co. (Boise Co. Idaho) office 7 Government House
Campbell George (Dickson, DeWolf & Co.) resides London
Campbell Henry C. (Campbell, Fox & C.) attorney at law, office 710 Mont, dwl 26 Turk
Campbell Isaac, baker, dwl 627 Third
Campbell J. A. with Nathaniel Gray, dwl 641 Sac
Campbell James, dwl 113 Ellis
Campbell James A. receiver North Beach and Mission R. R. Co
Campbell James O. dwl NE cor Eddy and Larkin
Campbell John, book keeper, Pier 12 Stewart, dwl 314 Brannan

Campbell John, jeweler, 335 Kearny, dwl 516 Bush
Campbell John, porter, Brooklyn Hotel
Campbell John, ranchman, Lake Merced
Campbell John A. carpenter, dwl SW cor Valencia and Columbia
Campbell John W. (colored) laborer, dwl N s Green bet Mason and Taylor
Campbell (Joseph) & Fairbanks (H. T.) commission produce, SE cor Front and Washington, dwl 4 St. Mary
Campbell Joseph, hair dresser, 426 Folsom
Campbell J. T. book keeper, 669 Market
CAMPBELL J. W. H. grain and produce storage, Cunningham's Warehouse, dwl NE cor Green and Montgomery
Campbell Mary Miss, domestic, 1112 Bush
Campbell Mary Miss, domestic, 726 Green
Campbell Murdock, calker, dwl 504 Howard
Campbell Nicholas, carpenter, dwl 1 Bagley Place
Campbell Patrick, contractor, dwl 325 Fourth
Campbell Patrick, engineer, dwl with J. McGill, S s Market bet First and Second
Campbell Patrick, laborer, dwl SW cor Seventeenth and Dolores, rear
Campbell Patrick, laborer, dwl Mission nr Twenty-First
Campbell Patrick, laborer with Hey & Meyn
Campbell Peter, laborer, dwl W s Second bet Brannan and Townsend
Campbell Peter H. dwl 1502 Leavenworth
Campbell Philip, purifier, San Francisco Gas Co. dwl 513 Minna, rear
Campbell Sarah Miss, dwl 710 Washington
Campbell Sarah T. Mrs. furnished rooms, 642 Sac
Campbell Thomas, blacksmith, NW cor Bush and Market, dwl N s Brannan bet First and Second
Campbell Thompson, attorney at law, office 35 Montgomery Block, dwl 1519 Mason
Campbell Thompson jr. commissary musters U. S. A. dwl 1519 Mason
Campbell T. R. architect and civil engineer, dwl 323 Minna
Campbell W. C. pattern maker, Vulcan Iron Works, dwl 361 Minna
Campbell William, architect and civil engineer, dwl 323 Minna
Campbell William, blacksmith, dwl 27 Ritch
Campbell William H. carpenter, dwl 829 Greenwich
Campbell William H. conductor, Central R. R. Co
Campbell William H. porter, 412 Clay, dwl SE cor Greenwich and Taylor
Campbell W. J. with Geo. F. Bragg & Co. 111 California, dwl 759 Market
Campe Henry, clerk with Geo. F. Huneman, dwl SE cor Second and Brannan
Campe Henry, groceries and liquors, NW cor Tehama and Second
Campe John & Magnus, groceries and liquors, NE cor First and Folsom
Campe Magnus (John & Magnus C.) NE cor First and Folsom
Campion Thomas, drayman with Wm. Horr, dwl 123 Turk
Campioni Emile, costumer, 712 Washington
Campioni Samuel, pressman with Francis, Valentine & Co. dwl 710 Washington
Campodonico John, drayman, Washington Hose Co. No. 1
Camps Joaquin, drayman, dwl 26 Lewis Place
Campton George (Wm. Dick & Co.) dwl American Exchange Hotel
Cañas Manuel, porter with Webb & Holmes, dwl Union bet Montgomery and Sansom
Canavan Bartley, cabinet maker with J. Strahle, dwl 521 Howard
Canavan Patrick, driver, dwl 315 First
Canavan P. H. (T. Leroy) dwl 921 Stockton
Canavan, see Cannavan
Canbaur Elizabeth W. dwl N s Cal nr Franklin

Candi Louis, vegetable garden, Hunter's Point
Candy Wm. machinist, dwl 408 Market
Cane Michael, express wagon, cor San and Bush
Cane Patrick, carpenter, dwl 67 Stevenson
Cane, see Cain and Kane
Cañedo Eugenio, cook, dwl 10 Stewart
Canfield Patrick, boiler maker, Vulcan Iron Works, dwl 23 Natoma
Canfield Patrick, laborer, bds 127 Pacific
Canfield Patrick, waterman, dwl 140 Minna
Canfield Rufus J. Collection Department Wells, Fargo & Co. dwl 1608 Mason
Canham Charles, cook, dwl SW cor Dupont and Broadway
Canham William F. painter and paper hanger, dwl N s Cal bet Van Ness Avenue and Franklin
Canham William J. with Stevens & Oliver, 28 Montgomery
Cann Thomas, carpenter, dwl 128 St. Mark Place
Canna Robert, clerk, dwl 1050 Mission
Cannavan James, milk wagon. dwl 418 Jessie
Cannavan John, laborer, dwl W s Vincent nr Union
Cannavan Margaret, machine sewer, 262 Minna
CANNAVAN MICHAEL, importer dry goods, Bee Hive Building, NE cor Washington and Dupont, branch 803 and 805 Kearny nr Washington, dwl NE cor Kearny and Lombard
Cannavan, see Canavan
Canner John, butcher with Smith & Co. dwl S s El Dorado nr Potrero Avenue
Canney Christopher C. shoe dresser with I. M. Wentworth & Co. 210 Pine
Canngina Augnst, baker, dwl cor Dupont and Stockton Place
Canning William, stevedore, dwl NW cor Front and Broadway
Cannon Frank, molder, Union Foundry, dwl 557 Mission
Cannon James, with Charles Harley & Co. dwl foot Stockton
Cannon J. H. dwl International Hotel
Cannon John, express wagon, dwl 18 Natoma
Cannon John, wheelwright with Kimball & Co. dwl 308 Jessie
Cannon Oliver F. teamster, NW cor Front and Pine, dwl NE cor Folsom and Shotwell
Cannon Patrick, laborer, dwl 138 Stevenson
Cannon Patrick, porter with J. Peirce, 417 Cal
Cannon Thomas, bar keeper, dwl 64 Natoma
Cannon William, butcher with Mrs. M. O'Brian
Canny Thomas, teamster with James McDevitt, dwl W s Sansom bet Broadway and Vallejo
Canoi Guiseppe, Vegetable Garden nr Bay View Park
Canon Catharine Mrs. dwl 34 Hinckley
Cantes George, bar keeper, dwl NW cor Kearny and Jackson
Cantfield Richard, laborer, dwl S s Twelfth nr Folsom
CANTIN (J. P.) & EVERETT (A. F.) stock and exchange brokers, 614 Mont, dwl 6 Garden
Cantrell George, machinist, Fulton Foundry, dwl 260 Tehama
Cantrell Joseph B. tinsmith with Locke & Montague, dwl 260 Tehama
Cantrell Thomas G. machinist with Devoe, Dinsmore & Co. dwl E s Larkin bet Bush and Pine
Cantrell Wm. B. sash maker with Jas. Brokaw, dwl 220 Tehama
Cantrowith Joseph, porter with H. Cohn & Co. dwl 3 William
Cantus George, bar keeper, dwl Vigilant Engine House
Cantwell Kate Miss, domestic, dwl 1413 Powell
CANTY (Daniel) & WAGNER (William) manufacturing and retail confectioners, 113 Montgomery, dwl 3 Mason
Canty John, cook, dwl 212 Third
Canty Michael, laborer, dwl 28 Louisa

Canty Thomas, laborer, dwl 328 Third, rear
Canty Timothy, tailor. 548 Wash, dwl 536 Wash
Canty William W. boiler maker with Coffey & Risdon, dwl 408 Market
Cany Edward. dwl 552 Mission
Capatorno G. fish, 2 Washington Fish Market
Caplice John, laborer, dwl 217 Jessie
Capp Charles S. attorney at law, office 543 Clay, dwl SE cor Monroe Avenue and McAllister
Cappell J. R. conductor, Omnibus Railroad Co
Capprice Joseph (Gould & C.) dwl 17 Bernard bet Taylor and Jones
Caprera Charles, porter, 204 Battery
Captoe William, blacksmith, dwl 323 Pine
Capurro Giuseppe, engineer with D. Ghirardelli & Co. 417 Jackson
Caradine Sarah Mrs. dwl 34 Folsom
Caraffa Dominico & Co. (Raggio Girolamo) Genoa Bakery, 1309 Dupont
Caraso Charles, gardener nr Bay View Park
Carazo Luis, clerk with Hellmann Brothers & Co. dwl 18 Ellis
Carberry John, tailor with Archibald McArthur, dwl 290 Jessie
Carbine Patrick shoe maker, dwl W s Kearny bet Sutter and Bush
Carbray John, dwl 560 Howard
Card George, driver, dwl SE cor Harrison and Main
CARD R. & CO. poultry and game, 62 and 63 Washington Market, dwl 321 Sutter
Card Stephen, president Saucelito Water and Steam Tug Co. office 326 Clay
Cardenasso Joseph (Maulette & C.) dwl SE cor Merchant and Sansom
Cardiff Miles, boots and shoes, 513 Bryant
Cardiff Richard J. (Kerrigan & C.) dwl NW cor Minna and Jane
Cardillo Guiseppe, 7 Washington Fish Market
Cardinell John A. deputy constable Sixth Township, Mission Dolores, office and dwl W s Valencia nr Sixteenth
Carduell W. Henry, calker, dwl 30 Frederick
Cardinet Emile H. fish, 25–28 Washington Market, dwl NE cor Taylor and Lombard
Carera Francolini, dwl 1114 Stockton
Carete Jean Baptiste, laundryman with Parfait Lemaitre
Carew Thomas, drayman, 300 Battery, dwl NE cor Fell and Octavia
Carey Ann Miss, domestic with William P. Taaffe
Carey Annie Miss, domestic, dwl 704 Powell
Carey Cornelius, drayman, U. S. Appraiser's Store, dwl E s Taylor bet Post and Geary
Carey Eliza Miss, domestic, 923 Howard
Carey Ellen Miss, domestic with Selden S. Wright
Carey Henry M. wagon maker with Casebolt & Co. dwl W s Dora nr Harrison
Carey John, laborer, Spring Valley W. W. Co
Carey Joseph W. boatman, dwl 429 Union
Carey Kate Miss, domestic, SE cor Ellis and Mason
Carey M. A. Miss, dress maker, 127 Montgomery
Carey Margaret Miss, dress maker, dwl 8 Everett
Carey Michael, laborer, Fort Point
Carey Michael, teamster with M. P. Sessions, dwl 12 Clarence Place
Carey Michael, waterman, dwl 8 Everett
Carey Peter, bricklayer, dwl 48 Clementina
Carey Sarah Miss, domestic with Selden S. Wright
Carey Thomas, bricklayer, dwl cor Lombard and Franklin
Carey, see Cary
Carick Richard, fireman, dwl 1150 Folsom
Carignan Adolph, dwl NW cor Jane and Minna
Carity Madelaine Mrs. dress maker, 212 Third
Carl Kate Miss, domestic, dwl 1100 Pine
CARLE (A. J.) & GORLEY (H. A.) auction and commission merchants, 724 and 726 Montgomery, dwl W s Montgomery between Pacific and Broadway

Carle Edward, porter with Scholle & Brothers, 409 Sacramento, dwl 615 Market
Carlin Daniel, porter with Dickinson & Gammans
Carlin Hugh P. machinist, San Francisco Iron Works, dwl 50 Natoma
Carlin Margaret Miss, domestic, 728 Sutter
Carlin William, blacksmith, 704 Broadway, dwl 440 Union
Carlin William, porter with Dickinson & Gammans, dwl N s Turk nr Polk
Carlisle George, bar keeper, dwl S s Bernard bet Taylor and Jones
Carlisle M. W. waiter, steamer Pacific
Carlisle S. real estate, dwl 5 Dixon's Block
Carlisle W. E. steward, steamer Pacific
Carlo William, gymnast, Wilson's Circus, dwl American Exchange
Carlos Tiburcio, saddlery, 525 Pacific
Carlson Gustav A. boot maker, dwl 638 Pacific
Carlson Hans H. T. seaman, bds 7 Washington
Carlson John, seaman, dwl 20 Commercial
Carlton C. A. machinist, dwl 318 Davis
Carlton Charles, laborer, dwl 318 Davis
CARLTON *(Charles C.)* & HARRIS *(Edwin)* Carlton's Warehouse, 16–22 Beale, dwl 820 Howard
Carlton Cook, dwl St. Lawrence House
Carlton E. B. (widow) dress and cloak maker, dwl 129 Second
Carlton F. D. capitalist, office 39 Montgomery Block, dwl Lick House
Carlton George W. clerk, Carlton's Warehouse, dwl 64 Tehama
Carlton Harriet C. (widow) furnished rooms, 327 and 329 Bush
CARLTON HENRY jr. agent Bay Sugar Refinery, office NE cor California and Front, dwl 570 Harrison
Carlton H. P. assistant State Normal School, dwl 428 Natoma
Carlton *(Oliver B.)* & Co. *(George W. Kimball)* fish, 34 Metropolitan Market, dwl 321 Ritch
Carlton Silas M. *(Healy, Carlton & Co.)* 429 Pine
Carlton William B. clerk with L. B. Benchley & Co. dwl 329 Bush
Carlton, see Carleton
Carlyle John, dwl 331 Bush
Carmach Bernard, peddler, dwl 132 Sutter, rear
Carmach Herman, dwl 132 Sutter, rear
Carmach Lotta (widow) dwl 132 Sutter, rear
Carmach Louis, tailor, dwl 132 Sutter, rear
Carman B. book keeper, office and dwl 719 Clay
Carman Mary, dwl SW cor Pacific and Front
Carman Walter, propertyman, Wilson's Circus
Carman William, physician, office and dwl 616 Howard
Carmany Cyrus W. secretary Savings and Loan Society, dwl 621 Clay
Carmany John H. printer with Towne & Bacon, dwl 621 Clay
Carmatz Adolph, watchmaker, 707 Clay, dwl 627 Green
Carmelich Frank, cook, dwl 515 Sacramento
Carmelich George, saddler and harness maker, 230 Sansom, dwl 513 Pine
Carmichael John, contractor, dwl 131 Stevenson
Carmichael William, blacksmith, dwl E s Brooks nr Geary
Carmichael William, drayman, Battery nr Green
Carn Daniel, dwl 407 Tehama
Carnap Robert F. book keeper, dwl W s Garden bet Harrison and Bryant
Carnaud Julius, teacher music, dwl 1013 Stockton
Carnaud S. musician, dwl 1013 Stockton
Carnduff Samuel, laborer, dwl S s Clary nr Fifth
Carnell Richard, fruits, 129 Kearny, dwl 321 Pine
Carnepa Augustus, with Vincent Squarza, 120 Leid
Carnes George A. City Letter Express, office SE cor Sansom and Wash, dwl 528 Bush, rear

Carnes Thomas, roofer, dwl Manhattan Engine House
Carney Isabella Miss, domestic, dwl 1502 Taylor
Carnody Joseph, laborer, bds Franklin House, SW cor Sansom and Broadway
Caro Heyman, dwl 54 Third
Caro Louis *(Nichols & Co.)* dwl 642 Mission
Caro Samuel, clothing, 54 Third, dwl 708 Howard
Caro Wolf, dwl 263 Stevenson
CAROLIN *(James)* & McARDLE *(Patrick)* Sun Burst Liquor Saloon, dwl 215 Tehama
Carothy J. B. cook, Cosmopolitan Hotel
Carothy Joseph, butcher, Cosmopolitan Hotel
Carpenter A. D. master steamer Princess, dwl 1020 Jackson
Carpenter Charles, driver, North Beach & M. R. R
Carpenter Daniel, painter, dwl 327 Dupont
Carpenter Dyer A. clerk with Samuel I. C. Swezey, dwl 1020 Jackson
Carpenter Edmund P. jeweler with R. B. Gray & Co. dwl 32 John
Carpenter Geo. W. brass finisher, dwl 1109 Kearny
Carpenter G. W. book keeper, Pier 4 Stewart, dwl 331 Second
Carpenter Isaac W. compositor, Hebrew, dwl Morse nr Bush
Carpenter James M. machinist, Pacific Foundry, dwl 118 Natoma
Carpenter Kate, domestic, 757 Howard
Carpenter Noah, dwl 1107 Kearny
Carpenter P. printer, dwl 4 Brown Alley
Carpenter Sarah F. dwl 1112 Leavenworth
Carpenter William L. compositor, Evening Bulletin, dwl S s Bernard nr Leavenworth
Carpenter William H. saloon keeper, dwl 402 Stock
Carpenter William L. *(T. C. Hanson & Co.)* dwl 832 Market
Carpenter W. T. machinist, dwl 109 Minna
Carpentier Edward R. *(Clarke & C.)* attorney at law, office 606 Washington, dwl NE cor Montgomery and Market
CARPENTIER H. W. president California State Telegraph Co. office 507 Montgomery, res Oakland
Carpin J. drayman, 623 Sansom
Carpine Patrick, dwl 219 Kearny
Carr Ann Miss, domestic, dwl 1019 Washington
Carr Annie Miss, with John Searls, dwl S s Union bet Hyde and Larkin
Carr Charles, butcher with W. D. Litchfield, dwl cor Folsom and First
Carr C. L. dwl International Hotel
Carr Henry, porter, 219 Front, dwl 1407 Powell
Carr J. I. carpenter, dwl 116 Sansom
Carr John, hostler, dwl 1432 Stockton
Carr John F. book keeper with G. B. & I. H. Knowles, dwl 315 Geary
Carr Joseph, machinist, Vulcan Iron Works
Carr J. Thurston, salesman with Stone & Hayden, dwl 224 Minna
Carr J. Tyler *(Littlefield, Webb & Co.)* dwl 509 Bush bet Dupont and Stockton
Carr Mary Miss, domestic, dwl 810 Vallejo
Carr M. D. & Co. *(Andrew J Barkley)* book and job printing, 410 Clay, dwl 1016 Pine
Carr Michael, deckhand, stm Cornelia
Carr Michael, fireman, stm Cornelia
Carr Osmar, cook, stm Golden City, dwl 234 Minna
Carr Patrick, soap maker, dwl 22 Valparaiso
Carr Samuel, with Wm. J. Cowen, 500 Battery
Carr Sarah Miss, domestic, 206 Eddy
Carr Thomas, longshoreman, dwl SW cor Kearny and Bay
Carr William, gardener, dwl 818 Folsom, rear
Carr William, waiter, Occidental Hotel, dwl 2 Clemcutina
Carr William B. contractor, dwl 542 Bryant
Carrabene John, plasterer, dwl N s Brannan near Sixth

Carran *(Joseph)* & Rosa *(Adolph)* butchers, 8 New Market, dwl 1229 Mission
Carrens Thomas, seaman, stm Senator
Carrere Adolphus, clerk with H. Schroder & Co. dwl N s Vallejo bet Dupont and Stockton
Carrick Daniel, sailor, dwl 134 Stevenson
Carrick James R. lather, dwl 312 Clementina
Carrick John, lather, dwl 312 Clementina
CARRIE JOSEPH A. & CO. books, blank books, stationery, etc. 402 and 404 Battery, dwl 803 Folsom
CARRIERS' UNION ASSOCIATION, rooms 528 Clay
Carrigan Adolphe, clerk with M. Keller, dwl 130 Minna
Carrigan Andrew jr. salesman with Conroy & O'Connor, dwl 608 Geary
Carrigan Daniel, workman, S. F. & P. Sugar Co. dwl E s Kate nr Bryant
Carrigan Edward, cooper, dwl W s Chesley nr Harrison
Carrigan Ellen, domestic, dwl 840 Mission
Carrigan John, laborer, dwl S s Stevenson bet Sixth and Seventh
Carrigan Patrick, laborer, dwl 8 Lick Alley
Carrigan Peter, boiler maker, Vulcan Iron Works, dwl 24 Perry
Carrigan Simon, carpenter, dwl NE cor Hyde and Union
Carrigan Susan A. Miss, milliner with Mrs. M. A. Butler, dwl W s Chelsey nr Harrison
Carrigan, see Corrigan and Kerrigan
Carrillo R. P. molder, Vulcan Iron Works, dwl 38 Tehama
Carrington William, real estate, dwl W s Oneida Place
Carrion Rosallio, waiter, dwl N s Vallejo bet Kearny and Montgomery
Carrique Edward, messenger, Phœnix Insurance Co. 605 Commercial, dwl 168 Silver
Carristy Rena, liquor saloon, S s Sixteenth between Guerrero and Dolores
Carrol James, workman with W. Hall, Old San José Road, county line
Carrol Patrick *(Winkleman & C.)* dwl Beale bet Bryant and Harrison
Carrol Patrick, laborer, dwl NE corner Pacific and Front
Carroll A. G. Miss, millinery, 24 Kearny
Carroll Andrew, fireman, Moses Taylor, dwl Central House, 814 Sansom
Carroll Ann Miss, domestic, dwl 933 Sacramento
Carroll Ann (widow) dwl 24 Kearny
Carroll Anna Miss, domestic, dwl 1419 Taylor
Carroll Bridget, domestic, 403 Folsom
Carroll Dennis, Pacific Engine Co. No. 8
Carroll David, laborer, dwl N s Pine nr Kearny
Carroll Dennis, laborer, dwl E s Cemetery Avenue bet Sutter and Post
Carroll Edward *(B. F. Barton & Co.)* dwl 331 Folsom
Carroll Eliza Miss, domestic, 106 O'Farrell
Carroll Eliza Miss, domestic, dwl 522 Third
Carroll Ellen Miss, domestic, 869 Mission
Carroll Frank, waiter, Clipper Restaurant, dwl 214 Green
Carroll Henry (col'd) *(Brown & C.)* dwl NE cor Third and Stevenson
Carroll James, clerk, bds Tremont House
Carroll James, laborer with Hey & Meyn
Carroll James, liquor saloon, dwl 215 Tehama
Carroll James, salesman with W. W. Traylor, dwı 539 California
Carroll J. B. boiler maker, Vulcan Iron Works, dwl 3 Berry
Carroll Jeremiah, boiler maker with Coffey & Risdon, dwl N s Fulton nr Jefferson Avenue
Carroll John, dwl 331 Fremont
Carroll John, Tiger Engine Co. No. 14

Carroll John, with J. W. Brittan & Co. dwl Union Place
Carroll John, with Thomas Connolly, dwl 920 Howard
Carroll John, blacksmith, dwl Washington Hose Co. No. 1
Carroll John, blacksmith, N. B. & Mission R. R. Co
CARROLL JOHN, importer and jobber wines and liquors, 305 and 307 Front, dwl 12 Clementina
Carroll John, laborer, dwl 331 Bush
Carroll John, laborer, dwl SW cor Madison Avenue and Hayes
Carroll John, laborer, dwl E s Jasper Place
Carroll John, lamp lighter, San Francisco Gas Co. dwl 509 Howard
Carroll John, peddler fruit and vegetables, dwl N s Vale bet Guerrero and Dolores
Carroll John A. dwl 731 Clay
Carroll John C. Eureka Bakery, 5 Jessie
Carroll John F. with R. A. Swain & Co. dwl Tiger Engine House
Carroll Joseph, book keeper, dwl cor Clay and Brenham Place
Carroll Katie Miss, dwl 272 Minna
Carroll Luke W. marble cutter, 67 Fourth, dwl 324 Vallejo bet Sansom and Montgomery
Carroll Margaret Miss, domestic, NW cor Stockton and Sutter
Carroll Margaret (widow, col'd) dwl 7 Brooklyn Place
Carroll Martin, drayman with J. W. Brittan & Co. dwl 1521 Dupont
Carroll Martin, laborer with Conroy & Tobin
Carroll Mary Mrs. domestic, NW cor Grove and Polk
Carroll Mary Mrs. domestic, dwl 252 Fourth
Carroll Mary E. Mrs. assistant matron, Protestant Orphan Asylum
Carroll Michael, boatman, Fort Point
Carroll Michael, boot mkr, 646 Com, dwl 2 Varenne
Carroll Michael T. stone cutter, dwl 324 Vallejo bet Montgomery and Sansom
Carroll Owen, machinist, Pacific Foundry, dwelling Hubbard bet First and Second
Carroll *(Pctrick)* & Brother *(Thomas Carroll)* groceries and liquors, NE cor Third and Minna, dwl 119 Third
Carroll Patrick, book keeper with Daniel Jordan, dwl 132 Fourth
Carroll Patrick, hostler with F. Collier, dwl 550 Geary
Carroll Patrick, laborer, dwl W s Second nr Market
Carroll Patrick, laborer, dwl cor Greenwich and Montgomery
Carroll Patrick, stone cutter, dwl 324 Vallejo, rear
Carroll Patrick, track repairer, San Francisco & San José R. R. Co
Carroll Patrick, watchman, 655 Sacramento, dwl 695 Geary
Carroll P. N. laborer, S. F. & San José R. R. Co
Carroll Richard, groceries and liquors, SW cor Harrison and Garden
Carroll Richard T. salesman with John Carroll, dwl 12 Clementina
Carroll Thomas *(Carroll & Bro.)* dwl 119 Third
Carroll Thomas, laborer with Conroy & Tobin
Carroll Thomas Mrs. with Dr. Henry Austin
Carroll William, book keeper with John Carroll, dwl 12 Clementina
Carroll William, driver with William P. Henderson, 1 Metropolitan Market
Carroll William, laborer, dwl 335 Broadway
Carroll William, livery stable, dwl 815 Broadway
Carruth Frank, photographer with Bradley & Rulofson, 429 Montgomery
Carruthers George *(Eckert & C.)* dwl E s Yerba Buena nr Clay
Carruthers John, with John S. Manson, dwl Yerba Buena nr Clay

Carruthers Matthew, produce, 203 Washington, dwl 115 Kearny
Carson Bernard, card engraver, 539 Sacramento, dwl 115 Post
Carson Frederick, cook, dwl 923 Kearny
Carson James G. clerk with E. J. Pringle, dwl 115 Post
Carson John, dwl 19 Natoma
Carson John, boarding, 10 and 12 Anthony
Carson John, groceries and liquors, op Pre'o House
Carson John, propertyman, Wilson's Circus
Carson John G. blacksmith, Pennsylvania Engine Co. No. 12
Carson Matthew N. carpenter, dwl 22 Ritch
Carson M. T. Mrs. dwl 110 Taylor
Carson Ruth A. (widow) dwl 5 Fourth
Carson William *(Dolbeer & Co.)* dwl Eureka Hotel
Carson William, plumber, dwl 225 Minna
Carson W. S. Eureka Restaurant, 116 Jackson
Carss Robert, dwl 49 Louisa
Carsten Frederick, employé, Bay Sugar Refinery, dwl S s Union bet Battery and Sansom
Carsten Frederick, groceries and liquors, NW cor Bush and Dupont
Carsten Peter, laborer, Bay Sugar Refinery, dwl 19 Hinckley
Carswell David, painter, dwl 103 Dupont
Carswell George W. salesman with Tubbs & Co. dwl 7 Ritch
Carswell John D. printer with Frank Eastman, dwl 117 Second
Cartage Edward, laborer, dwl 26 Stewart
Carter Abraham, clerk, S. F. Gas Works, dwl 7 Ritch
Carter Brainard, baker, dwl 18 Natoma
Carter C. C. dwl 820 Howard
Carter Charles, plasterer, N s Olive Avenue nr Van Ness Avenue
CARTER CHARLES D. real estate agent, office 610 Merchant, dwl 1307 Taylor
Carter Charles W. seaman, dwl 238 Stewart
Carter Chester, dwl 1705 Dupont
Carter Edward, laborer with Edward J. Quirk
Carter Frederick S. mining secretary, office 315 Montgomery, dwl 610 Mason
Carter George (col'd) dwl 1512 Mason
Carter George (col'd) waiter, N s Dupont Alley
Carter George B. (col'd) waiter, stm Chrysopolis
Carter George R. *(Treadwell & Co.)* res Oakland
Carter George W. carpenter, dwl N s Green bet Mason and Taylor
Carter H. employé, Occidental Hotel
Carter Henry, salt packer, dwl 115 First
Carter Hyland K. dwl 777 Market
Carter James, millwright, dwl 1514 Dupont
Carter James E. produce, bds Tremont House
Carter James M. carpenter, dwl NE cor Lombard and Jones
Carter James W. (col'd) messenger, U. S. Clothing Depôt, 34 California
Carter John, dwl 210 Harrison
Carter John, dwl 1415 Dupont
Carter John, bar tender, cor O'Farrell and Dupont
Carter John, calker, dwl 605 Third
Carter John, groceries and liquors, NW cor Dupont and O'Farrell
Carter John, hostler, dwl 1332 Stockton
Carter John T. book keeper, 310 Battery, dwl 610 Mason
Carter John Warren, book keeper with R. & J. Morton, dwl 610 Mason
Carter L. Mrs. principal Six Mile School, Old San José Road
Carter Louis, real estate, dwl 405 Hyde
Carter M. H. drayman with Armes & Dallam, 217 Sacramento, dwl 663 Mission
Carter Peter, book keeper, Spring Valley W. W. Co. dwl 1213 Kearny
Carter Richard, tailor with Frank Elwell, dwl 567 Mission

Carter Robert W. house broker and real estate agent, 713 Montgomery, dwl NW cor Jones and Pine
Carter Simon, laborer, dwl 141 Shipley, rear
Carter William H. drayman, 217 Sansom
Carteron Constance, liquors, 605 Sansom
Cartheut James L. *(Handy & C.)* dwl 27 Stone
Cartier *(Victor)* & Co. *(E. Laerampe)* lapidaries, 532 Broadway, rear
Cartmell James, with B. Morris & Co. dwelling 16 Ecker
Cartmell Margaret (widow) dwl 16 Ecker
Carto Benjamin, carpenter, dwl N s Hayes nr Octavia
Carton James, clerk, 1 Washington Market, dwl Brooklyn Hotel
Cartwright Thomes, driver with Bradshaw & Co. dwl 633 Market
Carty Anthony, dwl 216 Washington
Carty Paul, local policeman, dwl cor Montgomery and Chestnut
Carubino *(P.)* & Louis *(Frank)* coffee saloon, 939 Kearny
Carvalho Charles T. Chinese interpreter, dwl 1120 Howard
Carver John, clerk, NW cor Dupont and O'Farrell
Carvill Orrin S. *(Pollard & C.)* 37 and 39 Webb
Cary Bridget Miss, dwl N s Harrison nr Sixth
Cary E. W. dwl 260 Clary
Cary Isaac G. (col'd) barber, 640 Clay
CARY JAMES C. attorney at law, office NW cor Montgomery and Merchant, dwl 20 Tehama
Cary John, porter, 215 Front, dwl 617 Geary
Cary J. W. teacher assaying, dwl 77 Fourth
Cary M. Miss, seamstress, dwl 662 Howard
Cary Mary (widow) dwl 151 Natoma
Cary Mary (widow) dwl 108 Pacific
Cary S. D. solicitor, Union Insurance Co. 416 California, dwl Vallejo nr Taylor
Cary William, groom with G. S. Banks & Co. dwl St. Charles Hotel
Cary, see Carey
Casa Martin, dwl nr Bay View Park
Casanova Eugene, porter with F. Daneri & Co. 419 Jackson, dwl 502 Vallejo
Casanova Henry *(F. Daneri & Co.)* dwl S s Union bet Jones and Leavenworth
Casares Peter, blacksmith with Mangeot & Richard, dwl E s Stockton bet Jackson and Pacific
Casares Thomas, blacksmith with Mangeot & Richard, dwl E s Stockton bet Jackson and Pacific
Casassa Andrea, bar keeper, 120 Leidesdorff, dwl Garibaldi House
Case Charles A. coal oil, dwl 728 Market
Case Elijah, merchant, dwl 502 Sutter
Case George A. book keeper with Stephen Smith, dwl 502 Sutter
Case George A. job wagon, SW cor Washington and Montgomery, dwl 1606 Larkin
Case George F. clerk, 42 Clay, dwl 1606 Larkin
Case Oscar L. painter, dwl 223 Sacramento
Case Russell, clerk with Hooker & Co. 117 California, dwl 114 Geary
CASEBOLT GEORGE T. & CO. importers and jobbers carriage materials, coach trimmings, and hardware, 212 and 214 Pine, dwl NW cor Fifth and Stevenson
Casebolt H. & Co. car builders and manufacturers and importers carriages, SW cor Market and Fifth
Casebolt Ira J. blacksmith with H. Casebolt & Co. dwl 145 Fourth
Casebolt J. D. salesman, 214 Pine, dwl 3 Howard Court
Casebolt M. A. Miss, assistant, Powell Street School, dwl NW cor Fifth and Stevenson
Casedebeck Joseph, workman with P. Somp, Visitacion Valley
Caseli Alexander, office Pioche & Bayerque, dwl 403 California

Casen Isaac, laborer, dwl W s Washington Avenue nr Precita Avenue
Caser William, dwl 447 Natoma
Casey Bridget (widow) dwl 209 Tehama
Casey Daniel, with H. Casebolt & Co. dwl 267 Clara
Casey Daniel, laborer, dwl N s Broadway bet Montgomery and Kearny
Casey Daniel J. blacksmith with Black & Miller, dwl W s Washington Avenue bet Mission and Howard
Casey Daniel H. hatter with W. F. Coupland, dwl NW cor Ellis and Leavenworth
Casey Edward W. secretary City Railroad Co. office 326 Clay, dwl 325 Fifth
Casey Ellen Miss, domestic, dwl 315 Clementina
Casey Eugene M. plumber, dwl 12 Everett
Casey Frank, laborer, dwl N s Liberty nr Guerrero
Casey Henry, clerk, County Recorder, dwl 435 Eddy
Casey James, job wagon, NW cor Mission and Third, dwl 129 Stevenson
Casey James, laborer, dwl 52 Everett
Casey James, watchman, steamer Orizaba
Casey Jennie Miss, domestic, dwl W s Crook bet Brannan and Townsend
Casey Johanna (widow) dwl 49 Everett
Casey John, laborer with George Hotte
Casey John, milker with Murray & Noble
Casey John, painter with J. Donovan, 312 Davis
Casey John, stevedore, dwl 511 Mission
Casey John, teamster with Heman W. Massey, 32 Market
Casey Joseph, tailor, dwl NW cor Ellis and Leavenworth
Casey Margaret Miss, domestic, Franklin House, SW cor Sansom and Broadway
Casey Margaret (widow) dwl W s Salmon bet Mason and Taylor
Casey Mary Miss, domestic, 22 Hawthorne
Casey Mary Miss, domestic, 33 Natoma
Casey Mary Miss, dress maker with Madame Augier, dwl 38 Natoma
Casey Michael, carpenter, dwl 610 Leavenworth
Casey Michael, porter, St. Mary's College
Casey Owen, carpenter, S. F. & P. Sugar Co. dwl S s Harrison nr Eighth
Casey Owen, groom, dwl 62 Minna
Casey Patrick, workman, S. F. & P. Sugar Co. dwl E s Nevada nr Eleventh
Casey Patrick J. painter with James R. Kelly, dwl 38 Natoma
Casey P. C. liquor saloon, 930 Market
Casey Richard, carpenter, dwl 38 Natoma
Casey Robert, waterman, 609 Market
Casey Sarah Miss, domestic, dwl 716 Pine
Casey Thomas, carpenter with S. S. Culverwell, dwl 267 Third
Casey Thomas, brick contractor, dwl 139 Shipley
Casey Thomas, cooper, S. F. & P. Sugar Co. dwl Harrison nr Eighth
Casey Thomas, laborer, S. F. & San José R. R. Co
Casey Thomas, tinsmith, dwl 736 Market
Casey William, helper with David Stoddart, dwl cor Second and Minna
Cash George, with E. White & Co. 114 Dupont
Cash Samuel, bolt cutter, Miners' Foundry, dwl S s Howard bet First and Second
Casha Kate, chambermaid, American Exchange
Casham Benjamin, laborer with W. H. Kentzel, dwl S s Vallejo bet Montgomery and Kearny
Cashell Frank, laborer, Mission Street Wharf, dwl S s Vallejo bet Kearny and Montgomery
Cashman D. conductor, Omnibus R. R. Co
Cashman Dennis, laborer, dwl 8 Silver
Cashman John, dwl 905 Howard
Cashman John sr. dwl 905 Howard
Cashman Theodore, machinist apprentice, Vulcan Iron Works, dwl 905 Howard

Cashman William, metal roofer with John Kehoe, 228 Bush
Cashman William F. (Sullivan & C.) dwl 626 California
Casinolo Antonio, laborer, dwl Garibaldi House, NE cor Broadway and Sansom
Caskey John, ship carpenter, dwl 630 Second
Casner Jonas (L. Gensler & Co.) dwl 221 Minna
Cason Joseph (colored) hair dresser with Robert C. Franklin, dwl 308 Third
Caspar Israel & Co. (Julius Lippmann) cigar manufacturers, 526 Merchant
Casper John C. painter, dwl 28 Sansom
Casperson Martin, upholsterer, dwl 626 California
Cass Margaret Miss, domestic, 200 Ellis
Cassaccia Henry, laborer, dwl Union bet Green and Vallejo
Cassans Henry, job wagon, cor Market and Geary, dwl 607 Greenwich
Cassns F. B. delivery clerk P. O. dwl 1009 Powell
Cassassa Charles, dwl 515 Union
Cassassa Rolando, drayman, dwl E s Union Place
Cassebeer Herman, cashier Pacific Museum, dwl 607 Pine
Cassebohm William, accountant with Morris Speyer, dwl 139 Silver
Cassell Joseph, bricklayer, dwl 49 Clementina
Cassen Henry, furniture wagon, dwl 607 Greenwich, rear
Cassen Isaac, laborer, dwl Presidio Valley
CASSERLY (Eugene) & BARNES (William H. L.) attorneys at law, office 436 California, dwl 410 Harrison
Casserly Patrick, contractor, dwl SW cor Fulton and Laguna
Casserly Patrick, hackman, Plaza
Casserly Patrick, liquor saloon, dwl SW cor Clinton Avenue and Fulton
Cassey James, express wagon, cor Mission and Third
Cashnel Maximilian, physician, St. Mary's Hospital
Cassiara Dominick, porter, 623 Commercial
Cassidy B. stone cutter, Eureka Hose Co. No. 4
Cassidy Catherine (widow) furnished rooms, 110 Kearny
Cassidy Edward, butcher with W. D. Litchfield, dwl 116 St. Mark Place
Cassidy Ellen (widow) dwl E s Vincent nr Union
Cassidy Frank, miner, dwl 213 Tehama
Cassidy Hugh, carpenter, dwl N s Presidio Road nr Fillmore
Cassidy Hugh, fireman, Mission Woolen Mills
Cassidy Hugh, laborer, dwl W s Ritter nr Harrison
Cassidy James, metal roofer with John Kehoe, 228 Bush
Cassidy John, hostler, 328 Bush
Cassidy John, laborer, dwl 25 Everett
Cassidy John, waiter, dwl 3 Hunt
Cassidy John C. dwl 634 Sacramento
Cassidy John J. waiter, Empire State Restaurant, dwl 126 Bush
Cassidy Margaret Miss, domestic, E s Montgomery bet Green and Union
Cassidy Mary Miss, domestic, 704 Howard
Cassidy Mary Miss, domestic, dwl 531 Union
Cassidy Philip, job wagon, cor Mission and Stewart, dwl E s Gilbert nr Brannan, rear
Cassidy Richard, fireman, Crescent Engine Co. No. 10
Cassidy Sarah, employé, Occidental Hotel
Cassie William, waterman, dwl 69 Stevenson
Cassimer Jean, dwl 102 St. Mark Place
Cassin Ann Miss, domestic, SE cor Jones and Sutter
Cassin Francis, wholesale wines and liquors and manufacturer syrups and cordials, 620 Front, dwl 42 Natoma
Cassin Mary Miss, music teacher, dwl 42 Natoma
Cassin Martin, sexton St. Bridget's Church, SW cor Broadway and Van Ness Avenue
Cassln Martin, shoe maker, 910 Market

Cassin Mary Ann Miss, domestic, 721 Geary
Cassin Michael, spinner, Woolen Mills, dwl with P. L. Murphy, E s Howard bet Fifteenth and Sixteenth
Cason John P. workman with Levi Bros. Bay View
Cusson Peter & Co. *(Vincent Pefaur)* milk ranch, nr Bay View Park
Casson Pierre, workman with Levi Bros. Bay View
Cassou P. importer cigars, 711 San, dwl 536 Wash
Cassuben Ernest, with Louis Frincke, 423 Bush
Cassule Jean, gardener, N s Tyler nr Webster
Castagnet Dominique, groceries and liquors, 709 Broadway
Castagnetto Pietro, liquor saloon, 609 Pacific
Castagnino Emanuel, carpenter, dwl 8 Harwood Alley
Castagnino Lazzaro, carpenter, dwl 8 Harwood Al
Castañeda Jesus, dwl 1125 Powell
Castany Antonio, saddles and harness, 583 Market
Castegnetto Peter, drayman, dwl 506 Green
Castel F. C. furniture, 811 Clay
Castello W. mason, Spring Valley Water Works
Castelo Cipriana C. dwl 826 Vallejo
Castelow William, confectioner with C. H. Mercer, 518 Kearny, dwl 126 Minna
Castera Charles, hair dressing saloon, 1026 Dupont
Casterlo Bridget, domestic, dwl 264½ Stevenson
Castillo T. dwl 8 O'Farrell
CASTLE BROTHERS *(Frederick L. and Michael Castle)* wholesale grocers, 213 and 215 Front, dwl 1115 Stockton
Castle Charles, engineer Vulcan Iron Works, dwl W s Second nr Brannan
Castle Dwight H. stencil cutter, 260 First
Castle Michael *(Castle Bros.)* dwl S s Lombard bet Stockton and Powell
Castle Nicholas, carrier, Alta California, dwl E s Capp bet Nineteenth and Twentieth
Castle Stephen W. dry goods, 819 Montgomery
Castleas John, teamster, Mission Express, bds with James Dorland
Castner Frederic S. laborer, dwl W s Tennessee nr Solano
Castner William H. ship carpenter with John G. North, dwl W s Tennessee nr Solano
Casto J. E. cooper, dwl 32 Rousch
Castorene Pasquale, bar keeper, Lafayette Hook and Ladder Co. No. 2
Castree David B. *(Byrne & C.)* dwl SW cor Howard and Twelfth
Castro Grabel, dwl SW cor Guerrero and Sixteenth
Castro Luis, surveyor, dwl 469 Jessie
Castro Manuel, dwl cor Clay and Brenham Place
Castro Timothy, cooper, S. F. & P. Sugar Co. dwl Rousch nr Folsom
Caswell Alfred M. fruits, 267 Third
Caswell George E. salesman, 308 Battery, dwl 42 Everett
Caswell Samuel P. merchant, dwl 632 Market
Caswell William, laborer, dwl N s Bryant bet First and Fremont
Catalina Consolidated G. & S. M. Co. office 53 Montgomery Block
Catania Joseph, seaman, dwl 109 Washington
Catanich Peter & Co. *(C. G. Anguis)* fruits, 525 Davis
Catarina Hernandez, dwl 1303 Dupont
Cate Charles, bricklayer, dwl SW cor Mary and Minna
Cathcart Henry, dwl 18 Dupont
Cathcart James, cooper, S. F. & P. Sugar Co. dwl E s Chesley nr Harrison
Cathcart Thomas, house and sign painter, 670 Howard
CATHCART *(William)* & COFFIN *(J. W.)* ship chandlers and captain bark W. B. Scranton, 415 East, dwl 552 Folsom
Cathcart William S. mariner, dwl 1104 Pacific
Cathroy William, machinist, Union Foundry

Catlin B. T. adjutant Eighth Infantry C. V. Fort Point
Catlin J. H. express wagon, 39 Third
Catlin Preston H. fruits, 13 Fourth, dwl SE cor Bush and Dupont
Caton Emanuel, cook, dwl 115 First
Caton Thomas, boot mkr, N s Sixteenth nr Valencia
Catton John C. broker, dwl 403 Green
Catton William, clerk with Dickson, DeWolf & Co. dwl 403 Green
Caubrey Kate Miss, domestic, 124 Geary
Caughell Peter, captain schooner J. R. Whiting, dwl NE cor Filbert and Polk
Caugtlin John, printer, dwl SE cor Mission and First
Caulfield James, hostler, dwl 712 Broadway
Caulfield John, shoemaker, dwl 120 Sutter, rear
Caulfield Patrick, laborer, dwl W s Mission nr Thirteenth
Cauru Etienne *(Bergerot & Co.)* dwl NE cor Sixteenth and Rhode Island
Cavalletti Charles, liquor saloon, 537 Broadway
Cavalli Paul, blacksmith, Phœnix Iron Works, dwl Sutter above Montgomery
CAVALLIER J. B. E. real estate and stock broker and president S. F. Stock and Exchange Board, office 619 Washington, dwl 521 Post
Cavallier Jules P. clerk, 619 Wash, dwl 521 Post
Cavalry Ann (widow) dwl NW cor Vallejo and Montgomery
Cavan George, ship joiner, dwl 822 Union
Cavan Patrick, drayman, cor Pacific and Drumm
Cavanagh Dora (widow) dwl E s Ninth bet Mission and Minna
Cavanagh Ellen Miss, domestic, dwl 510 Stockton
Cavanagh J. carpenter, dwl 331 Bush
Cavanagh J. D. dwl 331 Bush
Cavanagh John, cutter with I. Joseph & Co
Cavanagh John, laborer, dwl 12 Commercial
Cavanagh Mary Miss, domestic, dwl 932 Bush
Cavanagh Patrick, laborer, dwl 1511 Larkin
Cavanagh Patrick, painter, dwl 721 Market
Cavanagh Richard, laborer North Beach & M. R. R. Co
Cavanagh Sarah Mrs. dwl 937 Folsom
Cavanagh Thomas, cooper, dwl 19 Harlan Place
Cavanagh, see Kavanagh
Cave Alfred, drayman, 614 Front
Caverley Ann (widow) dwl 20 Jessie
Caverly J. M. first officer Pacific Mail steamer Colorado
Caverly Richard, boiler maker Union Foundry, dwl 20 Jessie
Cavinyar Joseph, gardener, SE cor Guerrero and Fifteenth
Cawley Edward H. porter, 62 Clay, dwl 42 Clara near Folsom
Cayton Eliza Miss, domestic, dwl 1001 Powell
Cayton Ellen Miss, domestic, dwl 615 Pine
Cayton William W. clerk, Quartermaster's Dept. U. S. A. dwl 403 Folsom
Cazalis Eugene, commission merchant, 308 Commercial, dwl W s Gough bet Hayes and Grove
Cazaux B. French boot maker, 710 Pacific
Cazeau Dominique *(J. Hirth & Co.)* dwl 533 Com
Cazegrand Bartoley, vegetable garden, SW cor Twentieth and Florida
Cazneau Augusta Mrs. dwl 1709 Dupont
CAZNEAU THOMAS N. despacheur, Underwriters' Rooms, 504 Battery, dwl E s Thirteenth nr Howard
Cazneau William, shipmaster, dwl with T. N. Cazneau, E s Thirteenth nr Howard
Cazneau William L. clerk County Recorder's Office, dwl 1709 Dupont
Caznoll Estelle, lodgings, 303 Sutter
Ceaser John, boot fitter, dwl 311 Bush
Cecil John, book keeper Sailors' Home, SW cor Battery and Vallejo

Cedar M. Miss, dress maker, dwl 777 Market
Cederblom John, boiler maker, Vulcan Iron Works, dwl 429 Clementina
Ceillesen Heindrich, workman with Frank Rodgers
Celepo Powley, house and sign painter, dwl 12 Stockton Place
Cella Alexander, bar keeper with Ricci & Co. dwl Coso House
Cella Luca, liquor saloon, NW cor Dupont and Vallejo, dwl 713 Filbert, rear
CELLE EUGENE, physician, office and dwl 829 Washington
Celle John B. paper box maker with Henry Manneck, dwl Margaret Place
Celler Michael, driver with Bloomingdale & Co. dwl 766 Howard
Center David, carpenter and builder, dwl W s Folsom bet Twentieth and Twenty-First
Center James, dwl W s Howard nr Fifteenth
CENTER JOHN, real estate, office 535 Clay, dwl NW cor Sixteenth and Folsom
Center John jr. salesman with R. A. Swain & Co. dwl 8 O'Farrell
Center, see Senter
Centlivre Charles, painter, dwl SE cor Union and Kearny
Centlivre Eliza (widow) dwl E s Sansom bet Vallejo and Green
Centlivre Mary J. domestic, dwl E s Sansom bet Vallejo and Green
CENTRAL AMERICAN TRANSIT CO. I. W. Raymond agent, office NW cor Battery and Pine
Central Flour Mills, office 117 Clay
Central House, James Cornynn, proprietor, 814 San
Central Park Homestead Associat'n, office 302 Mont
CENTRAL RAILROAD CO. John A. McGlynn, superintendent, office 116 Taylor bet Turk and Eddy
Central S. M. Co. office 712 Montgomery
Central (No. 2) G. & S. M. Co. office 712 Mont
Central Wharf Co. foot Commercial, office 523 Montgomery
Cepf Henry, hose maker, dwl Eighteenth nr York
Cephas Joseph (col'd) waiter, dwl 823 Sacramento
Ceran John, laborer, Union Foundry, dwl Shipley nr Sixth
Cerelli Sebastian, with Mauletti & Cardenasso, cor Merchant and Sansom
Cereni Frank, bottle dealer, 207 Davis, dwl 541 Tehama
Cerf Julius, agent A. Dennery & Bro. Sacramento, office 517 Sacramento, dwl 407 Taylor
Cerruti Giovanni Batista, dwl 907 Jackson
Cervante Germain, gardener, Old San José Road nr Industrial School
Chabot Anthony, office 728 Montgomery, bds Occidental Hotel
Chabot Justin, carpenter, dwl 106 Kearny
Chabot Remie, sewer pipe manufacturer, SW cor Francisco and Mason, office 118 Montgomery, dwl Cosmopolitan Hotel
Chace Fidelia Miss, dwl 733 Folsom
CHACE'S MILLS, Macdonald Bros. proprietors, SW cor Market and Beale
Chadbourne Charles F. drayman, 216 California, dwl NE cor Washington and Dupont
CHADBOURNE JABEZ, attorney at law, office 4 and 5 Armory Hall, dwl 723 Sutter
Chadbourne Joseph, steam cracker bakery, 433 Jackson, dwl W s Folsom bet Eleventh and Twelfth
Chadbourne Joshua (Rider, Somers & Co.) dwl Treat Avenue bet Twenty-First and Twenty-Second
Chadbourne Levi, clerk with John Burnap, dwl NE cor Larkin and Green
Chadbourne N. M. Miss, assistant Powell St. School, dwl NE cor Green and Larkin

Chadbourne (Thomas J.) & Co. (C. H. Murch) Eclipse Bakery, 1412–1418 Dupont
Chadd R. Varick, compositor, American Flag, dwl Gautier House
Chadwick John L. clerk with George F. Hooper, dwl 204 Montgomery
Chadwick Korah, machinist, Pacific Foundry, dwl NE cor Second and Natoma
Chadwick Nathaniel G. carpenter, dwl W s Buchanan bet Greenwich and Lombard
Chaffee Charles, dwl rear City Hall
Chaffey George W. dwl What Cheer House
Chaignaud Frank, tailor with Wm. Germann, dwl SW cor Clay and Dupont
Chaigneau Alfred, compositor, 533 Commercial, dwl 621 Pacific
Chaiver John, express wagon, cor Dupont and Pac
Chalmers A. B. Miss, assistant Hyde St. Primary School, dwl 805 Hyde
Chalmers Agnes Miss, assistant Greenwich Street School, dwl 805 Hyde
Chalmers James B. contractor, dwl 805 Hyde
Chalmers James C. photographer with J. M. Bryan, dwl NW cor Sutter and Hyde
Chalmers William, drayman, 319 Washington, dwl 240 Clara
Chaloner John, gardener, dwl E s Second between Brannan and Townsend
Chambariere Isadore, merchant, 426 Jackson, dwl 626 California
Chamber John, mariner, dwl 224 Ritch
CHAMBER OF COMMERCE, rooms 521 Clay, William R. Wadsworth secretary, office 402 Front
Chamberlain Albert, carpenter, Union Foundry, dwl SW cor Market and Third
Chamberlain Henry L. foreman with Locke & Montague, dwl 1106 Taylor
Chamberlain Joseph C. barber with G. Sichel, dwl 274 Minna
Chamberlain Louisa (widow) private boarding, 115 Dupont
Chamberlin A. L. (George L. Kenny & Co.) res New York
Chamberlin Andrew J. book keeper with Charles McCormick, 408 Market
Chamberlin C. C. (widow) authoress, dwl 166 Tehama
Chamberlin Edwin, clerk, dwl 405 Post
Chamberlin James, waterman, dwl 8 s Liberty bet Brannan and Townsend
Chamberlin Joseph P. saloon, 113 Second, dwl 18 Tehama
Chamberlin P. F. clerk with Littlefield, Webb & Co. bds What Cheer House
Chamberlin (Romeo M.) & Balch (Stephen M.) produce commission merchants, 210 Clay, dwl 850 Mission
Chamberlin William, salesman, 417 Montgomery, dwl 405 Post
Chambers Charles, baker, dwl NW cor Filbert and Taylor
Chambers Charles H. butcher with A. J. Shrader, dwl cor Ninth and Brannan
Chambers Frank W. pattern maker, Union Foundry, dwl 158 Tehama
Chambers George, messenger U. S. Surveyor General, dwl 409 Washington
Chambers M. C. laborer, dwl 505 Howard
Chambers T. J. A. mining stocks, office 411 Mont, dwl N s Greenwich bet Powell and Mason
Chamblin John, dwl 566 Howard
Chamon Eugene (Neuval & C.) dwl 842 Wash
Champion A. D. A. professor St. Mary's College
Champlin J. A. lodgings, dwl 524 Howard
Champlin J. A. (widow) dwl 21 Stockton Place
Champlin John L. clerk, What Cheer House
Champney Harriet (widow) dwl 137 Clara
Chandler A. S. bar tender, steamer Sacramento.

Chandler C. (widow) music teacher, dwl 638 How
Chandler Charles, dwl 77 Clementina
Chandler George C. painter with James R. Kelly, dwl 629 Vallejo
Chandler John, dwl 77 Clementina
Chandler Richard D. clerk, C. S. Navigation Co. cor Front and Broadway, dwl 408 Eddy
Chandler Robert H. pilot steamer Cornelia, dwl NE cor Dupont and Lombard
Chandler William S. dwl W s Eleventh bet Harrison and Bryant
Chanel Jaque, blacksmith, dwl 630 Broadway
Chaney Orlando, laborer with Wm. J. Kingsley
Chang Doy Hang (Chinese) washing, 618 Jackson
Chang Ning Tuck Kee (Chinese) mcht, 704 Dupont
Changero Nicholas, musician, dwl 1328 Stockton
Chantry David, hostler, dwl 16 Sutter
Chapel Roderick, broker, dwl 5 Calhoun
CHAPELLE A. MARIUS, real estate agent, office 619 Merchant, dwl 1018 Stockton
CHAPIN GEORGE W. real estate agent, office 338 Montgomery rooms 12 and 13, dwl 1022 Pine
Chapin Samuel F. physician, office 338 Montgomery rooms 12 and 13, dwl 1022 Pine
Chaplin Hiram, boot maker, 1150 Folsom
Chaplin James, clerk with C. V. Gillespie, dwl 268 Clementina
Chapman Charles C. real estate, dwl 509 Stockton
Chapman Charles D. dwl 509 Stockton
Chapman C. M. Mrs. millinery and dress making, 218 Third, dwl NW cor Third and Tehama
Chapman Cyrus C. salesman with J. C. Horan & Co. dwl 217 Sixth
Chapman Frederick, clerk, Pacific Glass Works, dwl Potrero
Chapman George W. furnished rooms, NW cor Third and Tehama
Chapman G. W. furnished rooms, NW cor Third and Tehama
Chapman Henry, house and sign painting, 114 Sansom
Chapman Henry, proprietor Frank's Building, Brenham Place, W s Plaza
Chapman Howard (George Robinson & Co.) dwl 32 California
Chapman Ira H. engineer, dwl N s St. Charles nr Kearny
Chapman Jacob W. hay merchant, dwl NE corner Broadway and Kearny
Chapman John B. paper hanger, dwl S s Berry nr Mary Lane
Chapman J. Warren, clerk, 512 Montgomery, dwl Central Place
Chapman R. J. express wagon, cor Market and Montgomery, dwl 3 Martha Place
Chapman Robert, fruits, 147 Second, dwl 574 Mission
Chapman Samuel, boarding, Bay bet Kearny and Dupont
Chapman Sarah Mrs. music teacher, dwl 574 Mission
Chapman S. C. carpenter, dwl 1624 Stockton
Chapman William, clerk with J. Goodwin, dwl W s Tennessee nr Solano
Chapman William S. dealer scrip, 76 Montgomery Block, dwl 530 Harrison
Chappell Jacob G. policeman, City Hall
Chappell James A. carpenter, dwl 9 Vassar Place
Chappelle Peter, liquors, 936 Kearny
Chappelle, see Chapelle
Chapple Thomas, jeweler, dwl N s San José Railroad nr Guerrero
Chappler William, harness maker with Main & Winchester, dwl 3 Central Place
Chard Ann (widow) dwl 1617 Dupont
Chard Joseph W. dwl 9 Pollard Place
Chardine Armand, proprietor St. Francis Restaurant, SW cor Dupont and Clay
Charie Alfred, pantryman, Miners' Restaurant, dwl 149 Kearny

Charie Francis, pantryman, Miners' Restaurant, dwl 149 Kearny
Charkkert Charles, with Erzgraber & Goetjen, 120 Davis
Charlemagne College, Anatole Hamel director, 628 Broadway
Charles Cany Mining Co. office 338 Montgomery
Charles François, employé, Metropolitan Restaurant, dwl 730 Vallejo
Charles Henry, boatman, dwl 711 Lombard
Charles Hermann (Isidor & H. C.) dwl 153 Fourth
Charles Isidor & Hermann, dry goods, 153 Fourth
Charles James M. carpenter, dwl S s Shipley nr Harrison Avenue
Charles M. baker, New York Bakery, dwl Original House
Charles Marshall, dwl 4 Virginia Place
Charles Thomas C. broker, dwl NE cor Greenwich and Dupont
Charles William, laborer, NE corner Valencia and Seventeenth
Charlier Emile, cook, 647 Com, dwl 814 Sacramento
Charlton Frank (colored) bootblack with Aaron Creamer, dwl Mason nr Jackson
Charlton Joseph, cabinet maker with John Wigmore, dwl Whitehall Exchange
Charpentier Adolphe, cigars and tobacco, 710 Market
Charpiot Madaline Mrs. furnished rooms, 938 Dupont
Charruau Meline (widow) sausages, preserved meats, etc. 6 New Market, dwl 1207 Powell
Chart Obed, gardener, S s Presidio Road, opposite Presidio House
Chart Sophie Miss, domestic, 222 Stockton
Charter James U. H. dwl 361½ Minna
Chartier Auguste, dwl 721 Pacific
Chartrey Ralph, machinist, Golden State Iron Works, dwl 224 Stevenson
Chary Hannah Miss, domestic with J. W. Towne, N s Thirteenth nr Howard
Chase Alexander, topographical aid U. S. Coast Survey, office Custom House, third floor
Chase Andrew J. (Breed & C.) dwl S s California bet Larkin and Polk
Chase Andrew M. with Heuston, Hastings & Co. dwl Lick House
Chase Charles, laborer, dwl E s Selina Place
Chase Charles F. laborer, Golden Age Flour Mills, 717 Bat, dwl W s Bat bet Bdwy and Vallejo
CHASE (Charles M.) & BORUCK (Marcus D.) editors and proprietors Spirit of the Times and Fireman's Journal, office SW cor Sansom and Jackson, dwl 1007 Washington
CHASE E. JACOB, superintendent Washington Market, office 532 Clay, dwl NE cor Montgomery and Broadway
Chase Elbridge G. printer with Frank Eastman, dwl 33 Turk
Chase Ellen (widow) dress maker, 127 Fourth
Chase George L. dwl 313 Fremont
Chase George W. Mrs. (widow) dwl 525 Howard
Chase G. W. mining stocks, dwl 503 Dupont
Chase Henry A. printer with George W. Stevens & Co. dwl 4 Monroe
Chase James A. dwl 1707 Mason
Chase James B. (De Vries & C.) office W s Battery nr Broadway, dwl 275 Clary
Chase Jennie M. (widow) dwl 510 Pine
Chase John, milkman with Eben Johnson
Chase John A. oil bleacher, bds Chicago Hotel, 220 Pacific
Chase John E. porter, 117 California, dwl 222 Fremont
Chase Quincy A. salesman, 424 Sansom, dwl N s DeBoom nr Second
Chase R. P. physician, office 436 Bush, dwl 110 Powell
Chase Russell, engineer, San Francisco & San José R. R. dwl W s Folsom bet Sixteenth and Seventeenth

Chase Thomas F. coal oil dealer, dwl 728 Market
Chase William A. janitor Second Street and Tehama Street schools, dwl 34 Second
Chase William T. carpenter, dwl 33 Tehama
Chase William W. clerk with George Morrow, dwl 222 Fremont
Chateau Christian, painter, dwl 26 Geary
Chateau Maria Madam, midwife, dwl 26 Geary
Chatham Roland, miller, Pioneer Mills, dwl 8 s Mariposa nr Carolina
Chatterton James, apprentice with John S. Blaikiston, bds Pacific Temperance House
Chatterton John, dwl 408 Dupont
CHAUCHE (Adrien George) & MARTIN (Louis Grellett) French importers wines, brandies, liquors, etc. 608 Front, dwl 1022 Dupont
CHAUVIN O. agent Union Maritime Society France, office 421 Jackson, dwl 822 Pacific
Chauvon Eulie Mrs. furnished rooms, 403 Cal
Chanvou Jules, mariner, dwl 403 California
Chaves Juan, cigar maker with Herman Brand, 230 Commercial, dwl Pinckney Place
Cheany C. driver, Omnibus R. R. Co
Cheeney Aaron, carpenter, dwl 5 Trinity
CHEESMAN DAVID W. treasurer U. S. Branch Mint and assistant treasurer U. S. office 608 Commercial, dwl 100 O'Farrell
CHEESMAN MORTON (Woods & C.) dwl 17 Stanly Place
Cheesman R. B. pile driver with Galloway & Boobar, dwl 240 Fremont
Cheever Henry A. mariner, dwl 26 Essex
Chell John W. cook, dwl 35 Webb
Chelon Michel, butcher with Joseph Cabannes, dwl Potrero Avenue
Chelsea Laundry, James Laidley proprietor, 542 Brannan
Chely Louis, machinist, dwl 815 Battery
Cheminant Alex. S. clerk with Koopmanschap & Co. dwl 25 Ellis
Chemingham Jane (col'd, widow) dwl W s Jones bet Ellis and O'Farrell
CHENERY RICHARD, dwl Lick House
Cheney D. B. Rev. D.D. pastor First Baptist Church, dwl 1417 Taylor
Cheney Fannie M. Miss, assistant Greenwich Street School, dwl 1417 Taylor
Cheney George A. clerk with C. J. Hawley & Co. dwl 219 Mason
Cheney M. E. Miss, assistant Washington Grammar School, dwl 1417 Taylor
Chenot Adele Miss, domestic, dwl 826 Union
CHENOT EUGENE, cigars and liquors, NW cor Fourth and Folsom
Cherekeno Angelo, workman, Vegetable Garden, W s Mission nr Twenty-Sixth
Cherokee G. & S. M. Co. office 804 Montgomery
Cherry Eliza J. Miss, domestic, dwl 817 Mason
Cherry John M. painter, dwl 718 Broadway
Cherry John W. sign painter, 500 Battery, dwl E s Hyde bet Green and Union
Cherry Susan Miss, dress maker, dwl 8 s Mission bet Eighth and Ninth
Chesi Pietro, fish, 5 Washington Fish Market
Chesley Charles P. dentist, office 12 Montgomery, dwl 238 Minna
Chesley William, with George S. Haskell & Co. 514 Market
Chesnut Kate, domestic, Franklin Hotel, cor Sansom and Pacific
Chester Frederick, salesman with Kerby, Byrne & Co. dwl 739 Howard
Chester Henry (Hyde & C.) dwl 619 Mission
Chester James, mariner, dwl 32 Stewart
Chester John, hostler, 26 Kearny
Chettonari A. laborer, dwl E s Margaret Place
Chevalier J. B. professor French, Union College
Chevalier John M. seaman, Lafayette H. and L. Co. No. 2

Chevalier Madame, French dress making, 213 Dupont
Chevalier Nneval, laundryman, dwl 213 Dupont
Chevallier Reuben, washer, Chelsea Laundry
CHEVALLIER VICTOR, druggist, Pharmacie Francaise, 739 Clay
Chevance Julius, cook, Russ House
Chevassus Edward, accountant with J. E. René, 716 Montgomery
Chevelier Louise (widow) dwl 828 Washington
Chevers William H. dwl 620 Greenwich
Chevesich Henry, accountant with D. Ghirardelli & Co. 417 Jackson
Chewning Emma Mrs. millinery, 44 Fourth
Chewning Montgomery, butcher, dwl 44 Fourth
Cheyne Robert, fruits, 140 First, dwl SE cor Mission and First
Chiapparo Salvador, seaman, dwl 109 Washington
Chicago G. & S. M. Co. office 402 Front
CHICAGO HOTEL, E. W. Heimburg & Co. proprietors, 220 Pacific
Chichester James, varnisher, dwl 307 O'Farrell
Chick Elwell, carpenter, dwl 1610 Larkin
Chick Harrison, book keeper with Wm. Horr, dwl 1612 Larkin
Chick Henry, carpenter, dwl Lutgen's Hotel
Chicop William, vegetable gardener, nr Bay View Park
Chiebaut Charles, gardener, Lafayette H. & L. Co. No. 2
CHIEF ENGINEER S. F. FIRE DEPARTMENT, office 6 third floor City Hall
CHIEF OF POLICE City and County, office 10 first floor City Hall
CHIELOVICH ANDREW, Bocatyr Restaurant and Liquor Saloon, SW corner California and Drumm
Child Anna Miss, teacher, dwl E s Stanford bet Townsend and Brannan
CHILD E. F. stock broker and member S. F. Stock & Exchange Board, office 602 Washington cor Montgomery, dwl 930 Mission
Child Thomas T. book keeper, 538 Washington, dwl SW cor Dupont and Bay
Childress Henry J. miner, dwl 334 Seventh
Childress S. S. P. Sacramento messenger with Wells, Fargo & Co. dwl 354 Seventh nr Folsom
Childs Charles W. collector, 526 Montgomery, dwl 522 Dupont
Childs George, deputy sheriff, City Hall, dwl 718 O'Farrell bet Hyde and Larkin
Childs George E. book keeper, Occidental Hotel
Childs James (Menzies Loury & Co.) dwl SW cor Fulton and Devisidero
Chilesian Louis, gardener with Henry H. Byrne, dwl W s Thirteenth nr Howard
Chinese See Yup Asylum, 512 Pine
Chinese Theater, NW cor Dupont and Jackson
Chinn J. W. (A. J. Shipley & Co.) dwl 740 Folsom
CHIOUSSE (Joseph) & SALMON (Peter) florists, 716 Washington
Chipchase John, pattern maker, Miners' Foundry, dwl 320 Folsom
Chipchase John M. with Buswell & Co. dwl 320 Folsom
Chipchase William, pattern maker, Pacific Foundry, dwl 320 Folsom
Chipioneña Mining Co. office 318 California
Chipman Edward S. attorney at law, office 17 Exchange Buildings, dwl 527 Greenwich
Chipman John S. atty at law, dwl 527 Greenwich
CHIPMAN WILLIAM W. attorney at law, office 17 Exchange Buildings, dwl 527 Greenwich
Chipman W. T. dwl 323 Sutter
Chiquel John, gardener, Old San José Road E Industrial School
Chisholm Alexander (Austin & Co.) dwl 118 Post
Chisholm Duncan, tailoring, 414 Pine, dwl 8 Central Place

Chisholm G. D. carpenter, dwl 416 Bush
Chisholm Stephen, blacksmith with George W. Knight & Co. Potrero Avenue
Chisholm William, pressman, Alta California, dwl 19 Filbert
Chismell Daniel, laborer, dwl 541 Mission
Chittenden Arthur, portrait painter and teacher painting, Union College, dwl 10 Sutter
Chittenden Charles R. sash and blind maker with S. S. Culverwell, dwl 408 Market
Chittenden H. W. Mrs. furnished rooms, 408 Market
Chittenden Joseph G. with Hobbs & Gilmore, dwl 45 Minna
CHITTENDEN N. W. attorney at law, office 804 Montgomery, dwl 921 Stockton
Chitsick Johnson, laborer, dwl W s Russ bet Folsom and Howard
Chincovich P. wines and liquors, SW cor Drumm and Pacific
Chlemens Henry, longshoreman, dwl N s Polk Alley
Chloride Ledge G. & S. M. Co. office 606 Mont
Cbolet Joseph, pork, sausages, etc. 75½ Washington Market, dwl SW cor Dupont and Broadway
CHOLLAR POTOSI MINING CO. office 706 Montgomery
Chong Long & Co. (Chinese) washing, 233 Jackson
Chong Loong (Chinese) washing, 313 Bush
Chopart Joseph, liquor saloon, 4 Market
Choppat Louis, compositor, Courier de San Francisco, 607 Sansom
Choy Yik (Chinese) cigar manufacturer, 711 Dupont
Choynski I. N. antiquarian books, SW cor Market and Second, dwl 540 Mission
Chreghino Antone, wood and coal, dwl Crescent Engine House
Christen John, laborer, dwl cor Douglas Place and Seventeenth
Christensen F. Henry, carpenter, S. F. & San José R. R. dwl W s Folsom bet Sixteenth and Seventeenth
Christenson Jurgen, foreman with Charles Bernard, dwl S s Union bet Montgomery and Calhoun
Christian E. J. hotel keeper, dwl 108 Sutter
Christian Louis, liquor saloon, 1420 Stockton
Christian Richard R. dyeing and scouring, 808 Market, dwl NW cor Grove and Fulton
Christiansen Christian *(J. Y. Hallock & Co.)* and acting consul for Sweden and Norway, office 615 and 617 Front, dwl cor First Avenue and Fifteenth
Christiansen Christian, mariner, dwl 5 Mission
Christiansen Hans B. cook, Continental Hotel
Christiansen Max, seaman, dwl 44 Sacramento
Christianson John, mariner, dwl 32 Stewart
Christie Charles, compositor, California Farmer
Christie Daniel, dwl 535 California
Christie Henry, with William A. Hughes, 515 Clay, dwl 714 California
Christie Mary Miss, domestic, dwl 1809 Stockton
Christie Robert, carpenter, dwl 116 Sansom
Christie Robert F. blacksmith, dwl Knickerbocker Engine Co. No. 5
Christin Charles, melter with Hentsch & Berton, dwl S s Hayes bet Franklin and Gough
CHRISTIN *(Louis)* & PONS *(Theoffried)* managers Union Club Rooms, NW cor Montgomery and California
Christmas Frank, milker with S. C. & L. H. Talcott
Christmas L. milkman with S. C. & L. H. Talcott
Christmas William, cook, U. S. Marine Hospital, dwl 302 Fremont
Christofferson Peter, capt. schooner Frances Ellerhorst, dwl 26 Stewart
Christy George, painter with John Duff
Christy James, shipsmith with Coleman & Gardiner, dwl W s Mississippi nr Mariposa
CHRISTY *(S. P.)* & WISE *(J. H.)* wool commission merchants, office 610 Front, dwl 820 Washington

Chroniger Susan Miss, dress maker, dwl 161 Second
Chrysopolis G. & S. M. Co. office 607 Washington
Chu Lung (Chinese) washing, 326 Commercial
Chue Antoine, cook, 721 Pacific
Chung Hing (Chinese) washing, 615 Pacific
Chung Shun & Co. (Chinese) merchants, 806 Sac
Chung Sung (Chinese) washing, NE cor Montgomery and Washington
Chung Wo Tong (Chinese) drugs, 931 Dupont
Chung Yek (Chinese) washing, 615 Jackson
Church Albert R. book keeper with McNear & Bro. dwl cor Sherman and Howard
CHURCH *(Andrew S.)* & CLARK *(Seymour B.)* importers and jobbers fruits, nuts, etc. 407 Front and manufacturers fireworks S s Market nr Seventh, dwl 107 Sansom
Church Charles C. clerk with Griffith & Ellis, dwl N s Union nr Montgomery
Church E. W. (widow) dwl 339 Second
Church Isaac S. impost book keeper, Custom House, dwl 10 Ellis
Church Luther, driver with Stillman Hendricks
Church Robert, clerk with Eisen Bros. dwl 720 Market
Church Samuel R. teamster with E. Judson, dwl W s First Avenue nr Fifteenth
Church Thomas R. salesman, 223 Montgomery, dwl 1104 Powell
Church W. A. proptr Empire Lodgings, 636–640 Com
CHURCH WILLIAM S. sign painter, 823 Montgomery, dwl 816 Montgomery
Churchill Joseph, cooper, dwl N s Oregon between Front and Davis
Chute R. clerk with Samuel C. Harding, dwl 723 Vallejo
Chy Lung & Co. (Chinese) toys and fancy goods, 640 Sacramento
Cichi A. Rev. S.J. professor Natural Philosophy St. Ignatius College, S s Market bet Fourth and Fifth
Cieffo Marian, fish, 12 Washington Fish Market
Cienega Masedonio, tailor, dwl 927 Pacific
Cignione Pasquale, fisherman, 17 Italian Fish Mkt
Cills James H. computation clerk, U. S. Branch Mint, dwl 415 Filbert
Cimmino D. accountant with Pascal, Dubedat & Co. 426 Jackson
Cincinnati Brewery, Adam Meyer proprietor, E s Valencia bet Sixteenth and Seventeenth
Cipriano Raffo, musician, dwl 619 Broadway
CIPRICO *(George)* & COOK *(John)* hair dressing saloon Cosmopolitan Hotel, dwl SE corner Valencia and Seventeenth
Ciprico George M. assistant book keeper, 106 Battery, dwl SE cor Valencia and Seventeenth
CIRCUIT COURT U. S. rooms SW corner Montgomery and Jackson
Citizen George H. carpenter, dwl 263 Clementina
CITIZENS' GAS CO. works King nr Third, office 702 Washington
Citizens' Homestead and Road Association, office 606 Montgomery
Citron M. L. clothing, 131 Pacific, dwl 30 John
CITY AND COUNTY ASSESSOR, office 13 City Hall first floor
CITY AND COUNTY ATTORNEY, office 13 City Hall third floor
CITY AND COUNTY AUDITOR, office 3 City Hall first floor
CITY AND COUNTY HOSPITAL, SW cor Francisco and Stockton
CITY AND COUNTY JAIL, N s Broadway bet Dupont and Stockton
CITY AND COUNTY PHYSICIAN, office County Hospital
City Assembly Rooms, 727 Market
CITY COLLEGE, Rev. George Burrowes president, Rev. P. V. Veeder principal, SE cor Stockton and Geary

CITY FEMALE SEMINARY, Rev. Charles R. Clarke principal, SE cor Mason and O'Farrell
CITY HALL BUILDING, for City and County offices, Kearny op Plaza
City Homestead Association, office 5 Government House, 502 Washington
CITY LETTER AND PACKAGE EXPRESS, office SE cor Washington and Sansom
CITY POUND, NE cor Union and Van Ness Avenue
CITY RAILROAD CO. office 326 Clay
Civrat Edona, dwl 721 Pacific
Clabrough John P. gunsmith with Liddle & Co. dwl N s Vallejo bet Montgomery and Sansom
Claffee Thomas, carpenter, dwl 749 Market
Claffey James, porter with Conroy & O'Connor, dwl 505 Third
Claffey John, fruits, SW cor Fourth and Tehama
Claffy Hubert D. carpenter, dwl Market nr Fourth
CLAFLIN AARON & CO. importers and jobbers boots and shoes, 406 Front
Clahan Mary (widow) lodgings, dwl 24 Minna
Clain William, seaman, dwl 20 Commercial
Clancey John, dwl What Cheer House
Clancey John, teamster, dwl S s Brannan nr Sixth
Clancey Michael, boatman, dwl S s Union bet Calhoun and Sansom
Clancey Patrick, cooper with Timothy Lynch, 219 Washington, dwl SW cor Sansom and Bdwy
Clancey Thomas B. drayman with L. B. Benchley & Co. dwl Vernon House
Clancy Michael, fireman, steamer Yosemite
Clancy Patrick, coachman with William P. Taaffe
Clancy Patrick, laborer, dwl N s Lynch bet Leavenworth and Hyde
Clancy Thomas, blacksmith with Casebolt & Co
Clancy Thomas, fireman, steamer Pacific
Clancy Thomas C. express wagon, NW cor Sansom and Merchant, dwl 9 Perry
Clannan Annie T. (widow) dwl 309 Clementina
Clapp Francis W. wagon maker, dwl Tiger Engine Co. No. 14
CLAPP GEORGE H. physician and druggist, SE cor Howard and Sixth
Clapp George W. dwl cor Clay and Brenham Place
Clapp Jason (*Winall & C.)* dwl 532 Howard
Clapp John C. assistant mailing clerk, Post Office, dwl 520 Stockton
Clapp L. A. Mrs. assistant, Denman Grammar School, dwl 814 Bush
Clapp Michael, carpenter, Leidesdorff nr California, dwl NW cor Third and Stevenson
Clar John, clerk, office U. S. Surveyor General, dwl 503 Dupont
Clara G. & S. M. Co. office 338 Montgomery
Clara Thomas, waiter, dwl 28 Ecker
Clare Charles, blacksmith, Golden State Iron Works, dwl 215 Stevenson
Clare John, tailor, dwl 115 Pacific
Clare Mary Miss, domestic, dwl 1806 Stockton
Claresy Victoria Mme. liquor saloon, 607 Jackson
Clark Alfred, cook, dwl 636 Commercial
Clark Alonzo D. waiter, What Cheer House
Clark Anna Miss, domestic, 628 Sutter
Clark Benjamin, dwl St. Lawrence House
Clark Bernard, carpenter with John N. Clark, dwl S s Shotwell bet Twenty-First and Twenty-Second
Clark Bridget E. Miss, domestic with John D. Wilson, E s Mission bet Fourteenth and Fifteenth
Clark Burnett, carpenter, dwl 319 Stockton
Clark C. watchman, Omnibus R. R. Co
Clark Carrie F. (widow) dwl 136 Sutter
Clark Catherine Miss, seamstress, Morse bet Pine and Bush
Clark Charles, books and stationery, 149 Fourth, dwl 331 Tehama
Clark Charles H. jr. clerk, dwl SW cor Clay and Taylor

Clark Charles K. book keeper, 205 Front, dwl 728 Howard
Clark Charles P. dwl 255½ Clementina
Clark Charles W. dwl 7 Harrison Avenue
Clark Charles W. toll collector, Jackson Street Wharf, dwl W s Polk bet Sac and Clay
Clark Daniel J. laborer, dwl SE cor Fell and Webster
Clark David S. accountant, 613 Montgomery, dwl 512 Bush
Clark Edward, carpenter, dwl E s Hyde bet Ellis and O'Farrell
Clark Edward, carriage painter, dwl SE cor Jessie and Fifth
Clark Edward, painter, dwl Tehama bet Fir stand Second
Clark Edward B. broker, dwl 39 Second
Clark Edward J. captain schooner Sarah Ann, dwl 26 Stewart
Clark Edwin P. carpenter, dwl SW cor Sacramento and Prospect Place
Clark E. F. clerk, 417 Battery
Clark Elizabeth (widow) dwl 223 Minna
Clark Elizabeth (widow) with John D. Feldbush
Clark Elizabeth (widow) dwl 1918 Mason
Clark Ellen (widow) lodgings, 815 Dupont
Clark Ellen (widow) lodgings, dwl 67 Clementina
Clark Emma Miss, dwl with John A. Snook, N s Thirteenth nr Mission
Clark Frank, coffee saloon, dwl 12 Stewart
Clark George, boiler maker, Union Foundry, dwl 7 Baldwin Court
Clark George, laborer, dwl cor Bdwy and Sansom
Clark George, ship carpenter, dwl 64 Tehama
Clark George, shipping clerk with J. G. Baker, dwl 118 Geary
Clark George, watchman, dwl 106½ Clay
Clark George D. potter with V. Wackenreuder, San Bruno Road
Clark George W. carpenter, S. F. Cotton Mills, dwl SW cor Market and First
Clark George W. importer and jobber paper hangings, 500 Sansom, dwl 720 Union
Clark George W. jr. S. F. Cotton Mills, dwl 136 Sutter
Clark G. G. Sacramento messenger, Wells, Fargo & Co
Clark H. furniture and bedding, 625 Market, dwl 26 Montgomery
Clark Henry, apprentice, Pacific Foundry
Clark Hugh, plasterer, dwl E s Gilbert bet Bryant and Brannan
Clark Hugh R. plasterer with Samuel Kellett, dwl S s Natoma bet Fifth and Sixth
Clark Hugh W. carpenter, dwl 625 Sutter
Clark Jackson, milkman with Henry H. Edmunds
Clark James, dwl Stevenson 134 nr Second
Clark James, with Donald Bruce, dwl 815 Dupont
Clark James, boatman, dwl 514 Mission
Clark James, butcher, dwl NE cor Stock and Wash
Clark James, laborer, dwl 160 First
Clark James, teamster with Reynolds & Co. dwl E s Folsom bet First and Fremont
Clark James A. milkman with Henry H. Edmunds
Clark James E. tinner, dwl 12 Everett
Clark James H. clerk, dwl 27 Hinckley
Clark James R. clerk with H. S. Love, dwl 44 Second
Clark Jesse, with Lyon & Co. 159 Jessie, dwl 541 Mission
Clark John, dwl 1107 Kearny
Clark John, cabinet maker with Goodwin & Co. dwl 775 Clary
Clark John, carpenter, SE cor Third and Harrison
Clark John, cook, steamer Orizaba
Clark John (col'd) laborer, dwl 418 Dupont
Clark John, seaman, dwl W s Sansom bet Filbert and Greenwich
Clark John, wood turner, dwl 765 Mission

Clark John, wood turner, dwl SE cor Hyde and Leavenworth
Clark John G. teller, Bank California, dwl NE cor Jones and Washington
Clark John H. importer and dealer saddlery and harness, 107 Sansom
Clark John L. upholsterer with C. M. Plum, dwl 608 Market
Clark John N. carpenter, E s Harrison nr Third, dwl 14 Hawthorne
Clark Joseph, calker, dwl SW cor Louisiana and Sierra
Clark Joseph, pile driver, dwl SE cor Pine and Bat
Clark Joseph E. stocks, office 46 Exchange Building, dwl Lick House
Clark J. P. stocks, office 46 Exchange Building, dwl 1107 Kearny
Clark Judson, baker, New York Bakery, dwl 7 Scott
CLARK (J. W.) & PERKINS (J. E.) wool commission merchants, office NE cor Front and Clay, warehouse N s Commerce nr Battery, dwl 615 Harrison
Clark Kate, domestic, dwl 653 Howard
CLARK L. S. attorney at law, office 14 and 15 Court Block 636 Clay, dwl W s Nevada near Folsom
Clark Maria (widow) dwl 242 Stevenson
Clark Margaret Miss, domestic, 1029 Bush
Clark Margaret Miss, domestic, 110 Hyde
CLARK MARTIN (Martin & Horton) dwl 922 Vallejo
Clark Mary E. Miss, teacher of English, City College, dwl 607 Sutter
Clark M. E. carpenter with F. N. Giles, 435 Jackson
Clark Michael E. bricklayer, dwl W s Fillmore bet Fell and Hayes
Clark Nathan, hairdresser, 624 Wash, dwl 1106 Pac
Clark Olive J. Miss, dwl Lick House
Clark Orange Rev. D.D. dwl NE cor Washington and Jones
Clark Patrick, workman, S. F. & P. Sugar Co. dwl 33 Rousch
Clark Patrick F. shoe maker, 110 Sutter, rear, dwl 141 Shipley
Clark Patrick J. porter with D. N. & E. Walter, 305 California
Clark P. B. commission merchant, office 520 Montgomery, dwl Lick House
Clark Peter F. dwl 202 Montgomery
Clark P. G. clerk, Naval Office Custom House, dwl 627 California
Clark Rachel, Rebecca, and Sarah, Misses, dress makers, 962 Howard
Clark R. Frank, warehouse book keeper, Custom House, dwl 223 Minna
CLARK RICHARD S. dwl 903 Sacramento
Clark Robert, newspaper carrier, dwl E s Mission nr Thirty-First
Clark Robert, ship carpenter, dwl 72 Tehama
Clark Rodney, millwright, Fulton Foundry
Clark Rodney, real estate agent, SE cor California and Montgomery, dwl 535 California
Clark Sallie Miss, actress, Maguire's Opera House
Clark Sarah (widow) dwl with William H. Brown, N s Fifteenth nr Howard
Clark Sarah E. (widow) dress maker, 715 Howard
Clark Seymour B. (Church & C.) res New York
Clark Simon P. (colored) hair dresser, 159 Second
Clark Terrence, laborer, dwl 113 St. Mark Place
Clark Thomas, cabinet maker, dwl 138 Minna
Clark Thomas, laborer, dwl SW cor Polk and Eddy
Clark Thomas, plumber, 641 Market, dwl SE cor Fifth and Minna
Clark Treat P. with Locke & Montague, dwl 429 Greenwich
Clark William, bar tender with M. O'Brien, dwl SW cor Vallejo and Davis

Clark William, boarding, 71 Tehama
Clark William, nurse, City and County Hospital
Clark William, workman, S. F. & P. Sugar Co. dwl Downey nr Bryant
Clark William E. conductor, Omnibus R. R. Co
Clark William H. T. watch maker, gilder, and silver plater, 228 Kearny
Clark William S. proprietor Clark's Point Warehouse, cor Broadway and Battery, dwl 316 Pine
Clarke Alfred, policeman, City Hall, dwl 1213 Clay
Clarke Alonzo N. (Knowles & C.) dwl 920 Stock
Clarke Benjamin, laborer, dwl 65 Stevenson
Clarke Charles Russell Rev. principal City Female Seminary, dwl SE cor Mason and O'Farrell
Clarke Daniel (Bennett, Cook & C.) attorney at law, dwl 323 First
Clarke Francis, job printer, 520 Merchant, res Santa Clara
Clarke Francis M. stevedore, dwl Meek Place
CLARKE (H. K. W.) & CARPENTIER (Edward R.) attorneys at law, office 606 Washington, dwl 913 Bush
Clarke Howland, carpenter, dwl 54 First
Clarke James, laborer, dwl W s Sansom nr Filbert
Clarke Jeremiah, attorney at law, office 11 Court Block 636 Clay, dwl 1517 Mason
Clarke John, laborer, Greenwich Warehouse, dwl W s Sansom nr Filbert
Clarke John, wood turner, dwl S s Pacific bet Leavenworth and Hyde
Clarke John E. dwl W s Seventh nr Folsom
Clarke Samuel J. jr. attorney at law, office 604 Merchant
Clarke Thomas, blacksmith, Union Foundry, dwl S s Howard nr Fremont
Clarke Thomas, plumber, 641 Market
Clarke W. carpenter, dwl 331 Bush
Clarke William, workman, S. F. & P. Sugar Co dwl W s Seventh nr Brannan
Clarke William H. attorney at law, dwl 834 Clay
Clarkson Henry C. mining stocks, dwl 131 Second
Clarkson Louisa Miss, actress, Eureka Theater, dwl 131 Second
Clarsey Ellen Miss, washwoman, Mt. St. Joseph nr San Bruno Road
Clary Mary Miss, domestic with Mrs. W. H. Tillinghast, N s Folsom bet Eighth and Ninth
Clary Peter, laborer, dwl 59 Minna
Clary T. waiter, Cosmopolitan Hotel
Clary Thomas, dwl N s Fulton nr Octavia
Clary William H. mining, office 605 Montgomery, dwl American Exchange
Clasby James, dwl 238 Sutter
Clasby John, laborer, dwl N s Filbert bet Jones and Leavenworth
Classen Benjamin, laborer, Griffing's Warehouse, dwl cor Geary and Taylor
Classen Henry, bar keeper, dwl 107 Ellis
CLASSEN (J. Milton) & CO. (John F. Rohe) proprietors Pacific Soda Works and importers soda stock, 115 Jessie, dwl Lick House
Classen John C. carpenter and builder, dwl E s Jones bet Greenwich and Filbert
Clatworthy Frank, agent with John H. Scott, cutlery, 29 and 31 Battery, dwl Brevoort House
Claude Frank, coppersmith, dwl 1 St. Mary
Claughlin Rufus, with Jas. H. Hoadley, SW cor Bush and Lyons nr Lone Mountain Cemetery
Clausen Charles, boatman, dwl 18 Frederick
Clausen Francis (Peterson & Co.) dwl 656 Mission
Clauss Morris R. molder, dwl 809 Washington
Clausse Jacob, dwl 119 St. Mark Place
Claussen Henry (Mangels & C.) dwl S s Geary bet Kearny and Dupont
Claussen H. H. veterinary surgeon, 211 Pine, dwl 137 Sansom
Claussen John, cigars and tobacco, 121 Kearny
Claveau Anthony, scenic artist, dwl 1508 Mason, rear

Clay Albert H. clerk, 401 Battery, dwl 608 Sutter
Clay Jabez P. brick maker, dwl E s Dolores near Sixteenth
CLAY STREET MARKET, 524 Clay
Clay Street Wharf Co. office 526 Merchant
Clay W. H. trustee Franco Am. Com. Co. 215 Bush
Clay William, laborer, dwl NE cor Pac and Front
Clayburgh Albert & Co. (M. Clayburgh) clothing, 418 Montgomery and 523 Sac, dwl 202 Ellis
Clayburgh Morris (A. Clayburgh & Co.) dwl NE cor Sacramento and Sansom
Clayes Joseph R. groceries, 913 Washington
Claypoole William, painter, SE cor Commercial and Davis
Clayson C. captain schooner William, office 413 East
CLAYTON CHARLES & CO. produce commission, agents Santa Clara Flour Mills, 223 Clay, (and Supervisor Tenth District) dwl 558 Folsom
Clayton C. T. carpenter, Pacific Glass Works, dwl Potrero
Clayton Francis, clerk, dwl 1206 Stockton
Clayton Frank, dwl SW cor Taylor and Clay
Clayton Furman, engineer steamer Amelia, dwl 1223 Mason
Clayton Gilbert, gas fitter with Thomas Day, 732 Montgomery, dwl 1023 Mason
Clayton H. A. employé, Cosmopolitan Hotel, dwl 109 Sansom
Clayton Henry, civil engineer, office 543 Clay
Clayton Joshua C. mining engineer, dwl 474 Jessie
Clayton Julia Miss, assistant, Mission Grammar School, dwl 1223 Mason
Clayton William, dwl NE cor Folsom and Fourth
Clayton William, fruits, etc. NE cor San and Bush
Cleary Edward, molder, Union Foundry, dwl 32 Tehama
Cleary Francis D. book keeper with Taaffe & Co. dwl 1306 Pine
Cleary Mary Miss, domestic, 1419 Taylor
Cleary Patrick, merchant, dwl 1306 Pine
Cleary Patrick, shoe maker with Charles L. Rowe, dwl 21 Stevenson
Cleary Peter, express wagon, Mission nr Third
Cleary Thomas, engineer, dwl 1015 Pacific
Cleary Thomas, mechanic, San Francisco Gas Co
Cleary Thomas J. waterman, 609 Market
Cleary Thomas P. plasterer, dwl junction Market and Turk
Cleaveland Edwin, broker, dwl SE cor Jessie and Fourth
Cleaveland Henry W. architect, office 505 Montgomery, dwl Occidental Hotel
Cleburne Joseph, physician, office and dwelling 1234 Stockton
Clees, Peter, billiard table manuf, 510 Jackson
Clegg Lydia A. Miss, assistant, Denman Grammar School, dwl 425 Bryant
Clemens Charles S. laborer, dwl N s Bryant bet First and Fremont
Clemens John, pressman with Dewey, Waters & Co. 505 Clay, dwl Chambers nr Front
Clemens Samuel S. reporter, dwl 44 Minna
Clement Caroline Mrs. dress making, 415 Powell
Clement Charles, dwl 415 Powell
Clement Daniel, carpenter, dwl Trinity nr Bush
CLEMENT EPHRAIM B. searcher of records, office 710 Washington, dwl 526 Green
Clement Jabish (Collins & C.) attorney at law, dwl SW cor Montgomery and Broadway
Clement John, dwl What Cheer House
CLEMENT JOSEPH, searcher of records, 710 Washington, dwl 526 Green
Clement Lucius G. tally clerk, Pier 10 Stewart, dwl 807 Union
CLEMENT R. P. (Collins & C.) attorney at law and supervisor Second District, office 58 Exchange Building, dwl 807 Union
Clement Rufus H. salesman with H. W. Bragg & Co. 31 Battery

Clement William L. M. carpenter, dwl N s Bush bet Sansom and Battery
Clements Daniel, carpenter, Columbian Engine Co. No. 11
Clements George sen. seaman, dwl 20 Commercial
Clements John, dwl What Cheer House
Clements John, captain schooner Mighell, Caduc's Line, foot Washington
Clements John, printer, Liberty Hose Co. No. 2
Clements Matilda Miss, dry goods, 152 Third
Clements William, seaman, dwl 20 Commercial
Clendennen Alexander G. dwl with F. Gracier, W s California Avenue nr Isabella
Clendennen James B. book keeper with John Kentfield, Pier 10 Stewart, dwl 209 Second
Cleopatra Co. (fishermen) 30 Italian Fish Market
Clerc Pierre (Kleinclaus & C.) dwl 634 Vallejo
CLERK BOARD OF SUPERVISORS, office 3 second floor City Hall
Clerks' Relief Society, rooms SE cor Sansom and California
Cleveland Elizabeth A. Miss, private school, W s First Avenue nr Sixteenth, dwl 22 First Avenue
CLIFF HOUSE, Junius G. Foster proprietor, terminus S. F. & Point Lobos Road, 6 miles from City Hall
Clifford Bridget Miss, domestic, dwl 819 Vallejo
Clifford Daniel, laborer, dwl 19 Langton
Clifford Ella F. nurse, dwl 329 Jessie
Clifford George, commission merchant, office 200 Front, dwl Union Club Rooms
Clifford Patrick, laborer, S. F. & San José R. R
Clifford Thomas C. (Davis & C.) dwl 712 O'Farrell
Clifford Z. hostler with Isaac Stone
Cliffron Bridget Miss, domestic, 427 Sacramento
Clinch Thomas, drayman, SE cor Clay and Davis, dwl Continental Hotel
Cline H. groceries and liquors, 5 Mission
Cline Henry, brick maker with E. Morrell, dwl 253 Jessie
Cline Henry, clerk, Mission Street Wharf
CLINE HENRY, liquors, Mission Street Wharf
Cline John F. porter, Bank Exchange, dwl N s Washington nr Leavenworth
Cline Martin, brick maker with E. Morrell, dwl 253 Jessie
Cline Peter, laborer, dwl E s Hyde bet Jackson and Pacific
Cline Simon, clothing, 409 East
Cline, see Kline, Kliene, and Kleine
Clinkinbeard N. Medora Miss, dwl with Mrs. N. W. Spaulding, W s First Avenue bet Fifteenth and Sixteenth
Clint Charles, longshoreman, dwl W s Sansom bet Greenwich and Filbert
Clinton Arthur, carpenter, dwl 67 Minna
Clinton C. R. Ethiopian minstrel, Academy Music
Clinton James, coal passer, steamer Orizaba
Clinton James, laborer, dwl 411 Natoma
Clinton James J. bag maker with C. Meyer & Co. dwl cor Union and Van Ness Avenue
Clinton John, seaman, dwl E s Sullivan nr Courtlandt Avenue
Clinton Mary Mrs. dress maker, 15 Ritch
Clinton Temperance House, 311 and 313 Pacific
Clodi Louis, printer, California Demokrat, dwl 1 St. Mary bet California and Pine
Cloffey James, laborer, 505 Third
Cloherty Anna, domestic, 754 Folsom
Clom Sen (Chinese) cigar manuf, dwl 535 Pacific
Clooney Dennis, blacksmith, dwl 510 Minna
Clooney John P. pressman, dwl 58 Stevenson
Close Harriet A. (widow) dress making, 828 Market
Close Lewis A. apprentice with Isaac H. Small, dwl 828 Market
Close William, local policeman. dwl 828 Market
Cloud Mary E. (widow) dwl 131 Second
Cloud William, waiter, dwl 47 Jessie
Clough Amos, seaman, dwl 21 Langton

Clough E. E. dwl What Cheer House
Clough Elijah, printer with Towne & Bacon, dwl 245 Minna
Clough Frances Miss, dress maker, dwl 21 Langton
Clough John F. laborer, dwl 21 Langton
Clough *(Richard W.)* & Ellis *(John)* painters, 85 Everett, rear
Clough Sidney A. driver with A. S. Hallidie & Co. 412 Clay
Clough *(William W.)* & Somers *(Austin P.)* market, SE cor Ritch and Bryant, dwl 422 Third
Clue John P. baker, Eclipse Bakery, 1412 Dupont
Clune Thomas, merchant, dwl N s Grove bet Laguna and Octavia
Clynes Margaret, ironer, Chelsea Laundry
Coabortita (Sinaloa) G. & S. M. Co. office 505 Mont
Coacibicci Antonio, fisherman, 3 Italian Fish Market
Coad Alfred, machinist, dwl 12 Sixth
Coad Harry, comedian, Bella Union, dwl N s Geary bet Leavenworth and Hyde
Coad Samuel, teacher music, dwl 561 Mission
Coady James K. trunk maker, dwl 282 Stevenson
Coakely Kate Mrs. with Kennedy & Bell, dwl 307 First
Coal Creek Coal M. Co. (Sonoma Co.) office 28 Government House
Coaly Timothy, laborer, dwl 30 First
Coates Caleb *(Hay & C.)* dwl 204 Montgomery
Coates Joseph, butcher, dwl N s Mission bet Beale and Main
Coates Moses H. builder, dwl 610 Third
Coates Theodore H. clerk with R. J. Tiffany, dwl 610 Third
Cobb Charles, jeweler with R. B. Gray
Cobb David, photographic operator with William Shew, 423 Montgomery
Cobb Henrietta Miss, dwl with Thomas A. Hughes
COBB *(Henry A.)* & SINTON *(Richard H.)* real estate auctioneers, 406 Mont, dwl 1413 Powell
Cobb Henry A. jr, with Cobb & Sinton, 404 Montgomery, dwl 1413 Powell
Cobb John P. workman with N. Simonds, cor Bay View Park and Hunter's Point roads
Cobb Lym , steward, steamer Josie McNear
Cobb Moses G. *(Tyler & C.)* attorney at law, office 31 Court Block 636 Clay, res Stockton
Cobbledick James *(Meekery James & Co.)* res San Antonio
Cobleigh *(Charles E.)* & Spencer *(William V.)* milk ranch, N s Clay bet Polk and Van Ness Av
Cobleigh John L. milk ranch and drayman, N s Clay bet Larkin and Polk
Coblentz D. *(Coblentz & Bro.)* 1023 Dupont
Coblentz *(G.)* & Brother *(D. Coblentz)* dry goods, 1023 Dupont, dwl 1105 Mason
Coblentz Joseph, salesman, 618 Kearny, dwl Mason nr Washington
Cobliner Aaron, jobbing merchant, 422 California
Coburn Francis H. carpenter, E s Leroy Place
Coburn Loring, livery stable, 1016 Stockton
Coburn Parker, carpenter, dwl Washington Hose Co
Cocamunga M. Co. office 1 Government House, 502 Washington
Cochran Alexander (col'd) messenger, office Navy Agent, dwl 1404 Leavenworth
Cochran John, dwl N s Grove bet Laguna and Octavia
Cochran John, dwl SW cor Treat Avenue and Twentieth
Cochran John, porter with William P. Harrison, dwl S s Vallejo bet Montgomery and Kearny
Cochran Joseph P. weigh clerk U. S. Branch Mint
Cochran Maggie Miss, dwl 74 Natoma
Cochran William, teamster, cor Mission and Stewart, dwl 914 Sacramento
Cochrane George, waterman, 609 Market, dwl 646 Mission
Cochrane John, contractor, 223 Fourth
Cochrane John, hostler, dwl 628 Pacific

Cochrane John, lab, dwl cor Lombard and Fillmore
Cochrane Kate, domestic, 735 Harrison
Cochrane Mary Ann Miss, domestic, 210 Powell
Cochrane Mary (widow) dwl 161 Silver
Cochrane Robert, carpenter, dwl 1309 Kearny
Cochrane Robert N. butcher with David Adler, 3 Stockton
Cochrane Thomas, porter, 211 Bat, dwl 673 Mission
Cock *(William)* & Flynn *(James F.)* Empire Iron Works, 221 Mission, dwl 606 Howard
Cockrill Theodore G. salesman with Bryant & Morrison, dwl 30 Natoma
Cocks Barzilla, ship carpenter, dwl 46 Tehama
Cocks Oliver C. pressman with Thompson & Co. dwl 104 Fourth
Cocks William H. butter, cheese, etc. 104 Mission, dwl 104 Fourth
Cocoran Timothy, laborer, dwl 256 Third
Coddington George, deck hand, steamer Yosemite
Code John, carriage stables, 818 Mission, dwl 285 Minna
Code Philip D. with D. R. Provost & Co. dwl 10 Bernard
Cody Wm. with Pollard & Carvill, dwl 186 Jessie
Codington William H. book keeper with Miller & Lux, dwl 509 Taylor
Cody Allen J. carpenter, bds Baily House
Cody John, tanner, dwl W s Clinton nr Brannan
Cody Mathew, laborer, dwl 49 Jessie
Cody Michael, dwl NE cor Chestnut and Hyde
CODY PATRICK J. Morning Light House, SW cor Mission and Twenty-Ninth
Cody Thomas, local policeman, dwl 428 Green
Coe Edward H. inspector, Custom House, dwl W s Calhoun bet Union and Green
Coe Lawrence W. president Imperial G. M. Co. dwl 34 Essex
Coes George H. musician, dwl 813 Stockton
Coey David N. box maker, dwl 66 Jessie
Cofer Elliot M. book keeper, dwl 30 Natoma
Coffay Daniel, laborer, S. F. & San José R. R
Coffee B. house mover, dwl 59 Stevenson
Coffee Hannah (widow) dwl 4 Jessie
Coffee John, carriage maker, dwl NW cor Jessie and Anna
Coffee Joseph, laborer, dwl 11 Sherwood Place
Coffee William H. clerk, dwl 1 Bagley Place
Coffey Daniel, cooper, S. F. & P. Sugar Co. dwl 31 Moss
Coffey Esther (widow) dwl 1604 Stockton
Coffey James, employé, Cosmopolitan Hotel
Coffey Jeremiah, brass finisher, dwl N s Bush bet Sansom and Battery
Coffey John, policeman, City Hall, dwl 57 Everett
Coffey John, stevedore, dwl W s Dupont nr Francisco
COFFEY *(Lewis)* & RISDON *(John N.)* boiler makers, NW cor Market and Bush, and Main Street Wharf Co. dwl 516 Stockton
Coffey Mary (widow) dwl S s Stevenson bet Sixth and Seventh
Coffey Patrick, boiler maker, Union Foundry, dwl 6 Jessie bet First and Ecker
Coffey P. J. carriage painter with Kimball & Co
Coffin A. G. *(Redington & Co.)* res New York
Coffin Albert, cooper with Alexander Coffin, dwl 43 Everett
Coffin Alexander, State inspector provisions, junction Pine and Market, dwl 217 Minna
Coffin Benjamin, cooper with Alexander Coffin
Coffin Benjamin, porter, Howard Warehouse, W. s Dupont bet Pacific and Broadway
Coffin C. A. Miss, assistant, Powell Street School, dwl 530 Folsom
Coffin Catherine Mrs. dwl 132 First
Coffin C. C. drayman with Edward H. Parker, dwl Howard bet Eleventh and Twelfth
Coffin Charles, laborer, dwl SW cor Dupont and Broadway

Coffin Charles G. butcher, dwl 822 Broadway
Coffin E. laundryman, Cosmopolitan Hotel
Coffin Edward A. stevedore, dwl 20 Clara
Coffin Frank, watchman, dwl 143 Natoma
Coffin Frederick S. carpenter, dwl 218 Stockton
Coffin George, stevedore, dwl 530 Folsom
Coffin George F. cashier with J. C. Merrill & Co. dwl 530 Folsom
Coffin Miss Hannah, domestic, 111 O'Farrell
Coltin Henry, cooper with Alexander Coffin, dwl 518 O'Farrell
Coffin H. printer, dwl 231 Stevenson
Coffin James H. compositor with Agnew & Deffebach, dwl 735 Union
COFFIN *(Jarvis B.)* & RUDMAN *(John)* lumber dealers, Pier 14 Stewart, dwl 609 Harrison
Coffin J. L. clerk with Wheeler Martin, bds Isthmus House
Coffin John F. mineral water works, dwl 143 Natoma
Coffin J. W. *(Cathcart & C.)* dwl 822 Broadway
Coffin Peter F. porter, 408 Front, dwl N s Bernard nr Jones
Coffin Robert G. cooper, dwl 143 Natoma
Coffin Rodolphus W. druggist with W. E. Mayhew, SW cor Valencia and Sixteenth
Coffin Zenas, assistant weigher and measurer, office Custom House dwl S s Francisco bet Leavenworth and Hyde
Coffy Mary Miss, domestic with Francis T. Eisen, NW cor Guerrero and Seventeenth
COFRAN GEORGE, superintendent streets and highways, office 12 City Hall, first floor, dwl 14 Quincy
Cog Fy (Chinese) physician, 639 Jackson
Cogan James, broker, dwl 405 Post
Cogan John, mariner, dwl 809 Mason
Cogan John R. laborer, dwl E s Sansom bet Green and Union
Cogan Morris, carpenter, dwl SW cor Ritch and Folsom
Cogan Thomas, stone mason, dwl 12 Sutter
Coggeshall J. H. druggist, dwl 1518 Mason
Coggeshall Sarah Miss, housekeeper with N. Simon, cor Bay View Park and Hunter's Point roads
Coggshall W. A. book keeper, dwl Cosmopolitan Hotel
Coggshall William A. lumber surveyor, dwl Bailey House
Coghill Andrew J. & Co. *(Owens, Moore & C. Stockton)* office 313 Front, dwl 1215 Clay
COGHILL, J. H. & CO. *(Wm. N. Coghill)* importers and jobbers groceries and provisions, SW cor Front and Commercial, res New York
Coghill Thomas B. salesman with J. H. Coghill & Co. dwl 1231 Washington
Coghill William N. *(J. H. Coghill & Co.)* dwl 1231 Washington
Coghlin Daniel C. shipwright, dwl 236 Fremont
Cogill John, teacher dancing, dwl 1410 Powell
Cogle M. L. machinist, dwl 546 Mission
Cogswell Henry D. real estate, office and dwl 610 Front
Cogswell James L. dentist, office and dwl 117 Second
Cogswell James P. *(Standard Soap Co.)* dwl 247 Second
Cogswell's Building, 610 Front
Cohalau Daniel, livery stable, dwl 16 Virginia
Cohane Lawrence, carpenter, 687 Market, dwl 12 Everett
Cohea Edward U. conductor Market Street R. R. dwl W s Valencia bet Sixteenth and Seventeeth
Cohen Abraham, laborer, dwl 626 Kearny
Cohen Abraham, tailor, dwl 123 Jackson
COHEN ALFRED A. attorney at law, office SW cor Sansom and Jackson
Cohen Angelo, clerk with B. Gattel, 519 Montgomery, dwl NE cor Stockton and Greenwich

Cohen Benjamin L. salesman, dwl 138 Silver
Cohen Bernard *(Morris & C.)* dwl 552 Tehama
Cohen David, peddler, dwl 41 Jessie
Cohen Frederick, dwl SW cor First and Stevenson
Cohen Frederick, drayman, 215 Battery, dwl cor Second and Mission
Cohen Harris, dwl 134 Sutter
Cohen Harris, job wagon, dwl 137 Third
Cohen Henry, clothing, dwl 812 Kearny
Cohen Henry, book keeper with A. A. Cohen, dwl 730 Howard
Cohen Henry, truckman, cor California and Sansom, dwl Howard bet Fifth and Sixth
Cohen Henry L. book keeper, 313 Sacramento, dwl cor Dupont and Francisco
Cohen Henry M. dwl 557 Mission
Cohen Isadore, dwl 38 First
Cohen Jacob, clerk, dwl 253 Minna
Cohen James, brick maker, dwl W s Dolores bet Fifteenth and Sixteenth
Cohen King, cigar manufacturer, dwl 942 Kearny
Cohen L. M. merchant, dwl 1513 Stockton
Cohen Louis, salesman, 4 Montgomery, dwl N s Jessie bet First and Second
Cohen Louis, tailor, 70 First, dwl 229 Sixth
Cohen Louis, variety store, 743 Pacific
Cohen Louis M. salesman, 530 Kearny, dwl 805 Bush
Cohen Martin, book keeper with Heynemann & Co. dwl 1120 Stockton
Cohen Meyer, clothing, 516 Com, dwl 35 Everett
Coben N. cabinet maker, W s Clara nr Bush
Cohen Samuel, clerk, 427 Montgomery, dwl 1117 Kearny
Cohen Samuel H. collector, dwl 1505 Stockton
Cohen Selig A. market wagon, dwl 508 Post
Cohen Simon, salesman, 320 Kearny
Cohen Simon, tailor, 110 Leidesdorff
Cohen Solomon, glazier, dwl E s Rassette Place No 2
Cohen Thomas *(S. Snapper & Co.)* dwl SE cor Stockton and Sacramento
Cohen Thomas, clerk, dwl 718 Stockton
Cohen Waldow Madame, pianoforte teacher, dwl 1505 Stockton
Cohen William, clothing, dwl 912 Kearny
Cohen William, laborer with Hey & Meyn
Cohen William, waiter, dwl 323 Pine
Cohn Abraham, glazier, dwl 23 Jessie
Cohn Abram, brewer, dwl 1049 Howard
Cohn Alexander, salesman, 509 Commercial
Cohn D. physician, office 642 Washington
Cohn Edward, cigars and tobacco, 627 Clay
Cohn Edward, cigars and tobacco, dwl 515 Pine
COHN`ELKAN Rev. pastor congregation Emanu El and principal Academic Seminary 235 Post, dwl 117 Taylor
Cohn H. drayman, 308 California
COHN H. & CO. *(Jacob and Herman Greenebaum and Henry Woodleaf)* importers and jobbers clothing, 413 and 415 Sacramento, res New York
Cohn Harris, job wagon, dwl 137 Third
Cohn Henry, book keeper with I. H. Cohn & Son, dwl W s Sansom bet Bush and Pine
Cohn Hermann, dwl 227 Stevenson
Cohn I. H. & Son *(Richard Cohn)* wholesale butter, eggs, and cheese, 607 Sansom, res Petaluma
Cohn I. N. bakery, 27 Dupont
Cohn Isaac *(J. & I. Cohn)* office 220 California, dwl 731 Folsom
Cohn Isaac, cigars and tobacco, 622 Kearny, dwl 615 Commercial
Cohn Isadore, dwl 226 Fourth
Cohn J. & I. merchants, office 220 California, dwl 731 Folsom
Cohn Jacob, boots and shoes, 37 Pacific, dwl SE cor Broadway and Front
Cohn Jacob, merchant, dwl 331 Fourth
Cohn Jacob D. salesman, 431 Mont, dwl 253 Minna

Cohn James, tailor, dwl 16 Lafayette Place
Cohn Julius, cigars and tobacco, 228 Battery, dwl 525 Pine
Cohn Louis, dwl 206 Eddy
Cohn Louis, clothing, 417 Commercial
COHN LOUIS, merchant, office 207 Battery, dwl 1201 Sacramento
Cohn Louis, tailor, 312 Pacific, dwl 207 Pacific
Cohn Louis B. clothing, 921 Kearny
Cohn M. A. shells and fancy goods, 822 Market
Cohn Manuel, clothing, 413 Commercial
Cohn M. B. clothing, dwl 131 Jackson
Cohn M. D. salesman, 651 Wash, dwl 253 Minna
Cohn Morris (Levy & C.) dwl 45 Second
Cohn Morris, broker, office 218 Battery, dwl Continental Hotel
Cohn Nathan, tailor, 672 Mission
Cohn Richard (I. H. Cohn & Son) dwl 109 Sansom
Cohn Salmun, tailor, 312 Pacific, dwl E s Battery bet Pine and Bush
Cohn Samuel, clerk with Chas. Sutro, St. Francis H. & L. Co. No. 1
Cohn Samuel A. vegetables and fruit, dwl 508 Post
Cohn Simon (Basch, Cohn & Co.) dwl 628 O'Farrell
Cohn Simou, cap maker with Wolf Fleisher, dwl 202 Second
Cohn Simon, clothing, 509 and 525 Commercial, dwl New York Hotel
Cohn S. S. clerk with M. L. Citron, dwl 131 Pacific
Cohn William, compositor, Abend Post, dwl 533 Mission
Cohn W. M. clothing, dwl 666 Mission
Cohn ——, upholsterer, dwl 1 St. Mary Place
Cohrn Edward, cigars and tobacco, dwl 913 Stockton
Coit Benjamin B. physician, office NE cor Market and Montgomery
Cokely Ellen, domestic, dwl 267 Stevenson
Cokely Ellen Miss, domestic, NW cor Franklin and Post
Cokely Ellen Miss, domestic, 314 Stockton
Cokely James, laborer, bds Phœnix House, 721 San
Cokley Julia, domestic, 1069 Howard
Colbert Daniel, laborer, S. F. & San José R. R
Colbert John, dwl Broderick Engine House
Colborn A. D. (widow) dwl 604 Pine
Colburn Alfred, clerk, 62 Washington Market, dwl with Capt. Rollins
Colburn Charles H. driver, Wells, Fargo & Co. dwl 536 Pine
Colburn George L. superintendent Home of the Inebriate
Colburn George W. painter, dwl Sumner St. House
Colburn Reuben B. conductor, Central R. R. Co. dwl NW cor Sixth and Brannan
Colburn Richard, clerk, dwl SW cor Union and Calhoun
Colburn Thomas, night watchman, Lick House
COLBURN THOMAS W. secretary mining companies, office 505 Mont, dwl 1825 Stockton
Colby (Benjamin F.) & Barker (Isaac jr.) brick manufacturers, office Third Street Wharf, dwl W s Howard bet Eighteenth and Nineteenth
Colby Charles A. compositor, Our Mazeppa, dwl 1102 Pacific
Colby Hiram H. waterman, 609 Market
Colby James, ship calker, dwl W s Thirteenth nr Market
Colby J. P. drayman with Bryant & Beadle, dwl Sailors' Home, Davis
Colby Jonathan, drayman, dwl 318 Davis
Colby Z. F. fruits, Meiggs' Wharf, dwl NE cor Francisco and Mason
Colcord M. J. (widow) dwl 663 Mission
Coldwell Charles, carpenter, dwl 258 Minna
Coldwell Charles, molder, dwl 48 Jane
Coldwell Edward L. with N. Davidson, Glen Ranch, Potrero Nuevo
Cole C. with Eisen Bros. dwl 515 Market
Cole C. H. second steward, Lick House

Cole Cornelius, attorney at law, dwl 1030 Bush
Cole Edmund C. house painter, dwl S s Filbert bet Leavenworth and Hyde
Cole Edward, boot maker, dwl 1240 Dupont
Cole Edward, porter with Agard, Foulkes & Co. 412 Front
Cole Elvin N. clerk, What Cheer Laundry
Cole G. carpenter, dwl 559 Market
Cole H. drayman, dwl 163 Minna
Cole Henry W. millwright, dwl NW cor California and Larkin
Cole James (col'd) waiter, stm Chrysopolis
Cole J. L. carpenter, Maguire's Opera House
Cole John, boiler maker, Union Foundry, dwl 12 Moss
Cole John, harness maker with J. C. Johnson & Co. dwl 632 Second
Cole John, laborer, dwl 934 Kearny
Cole John, stone cutter, dwl 24 Sansom
Cole John H. helper, Columbian Engine Co. No. 11
Cole Josiah L. dwl 1020 Jackson
Cole Levi F. boiler maker, Union Foundry, dwl E s Geneva bet Sixth and Seventh
Cole Lyman, painter, dwl 815 Montgomery
Cole Martin, expressman, bds Telegraph House
Cole Mary (widow) dwl W side Grove bet Laguna and Octavia
COLE N. P. & CO. (O. W. Merriam) importers and wholesale dealers furniture, mahogany, etc. 518 Front, dwl 730 Sutter
Cole N. W. carpenter with S. S. Culverwell, 29 Fremont, dwl 903 Sacramento
COLE R. BEVERLY, physician, office 1234 Stockton, dwl 649 Howard
COLE R. E. surgeon dentist, 715 Clay, res Oakland
Cole Silver M. Co. office 123 California
Cole Thomas, stone cutter, dwl 24 Sansom
Cole Thomas jr. traveling agent, Wells, Fargo & Co. dwl Brevoort House
Cole William, dwl 6 Montgomery
Cole William, engineer, dwl 181 Jessie
Cole William, laundry, office 108 Dupont, dwl 114 Dora
Cole William, stone cutter, dwl 24 Sansom
Coleman Agusta Miss, 156 Third
Coleman A. J. bar keeper, Hygeian Bowling Saloon, Francisco bet Powell and Mason
Coleman A. N. (Hayward & C.) dwl Occidental Hotel
Coleman Andrew, receiver, Central R. R. Co. dwl 116 Taylor
Coleman B. shoe maker, dwl 216 Second
Coleman C. S. surgeon, stm Moses Taylor, res San Leandro
Coleman David M. book binder with Edward Bosqui & Co. dwl S s Montgomery Court near Broadway
Coleman David R. ship smith, 706 Front, dwl 609 Powell
Coleman E. envelope manufacturer, 775 Market, dwl 777 Market
Coleman Eliza, domestic, dwl 322 Fremont
Coleman James N. cooper, dwl 13 Auburn
Coleman James S. employé, Pacific Mail S. S. Co. dwl 114 Freelon
Coleman Jane (widow) produce, dwl W s Battery bet Filbert and Union
Coleman J. E. W. house and sign painter, dwl 412 Tehama
Coleman John, shoe maker, 1020 Market, dwl Hayes Valley
Coleman John H. collector, Alta California, dwl St. Charles, bet Broadway and Pacific
Coleman John P. lager beer saloon, 1005 Kearny
Coleman Joseph, laborer, dwl W s Chesley nr Harrison
Coleman Joseph W. dwl 446 Third
Coleman Josias M. clerk with Armes & Dallam, 217 Sacramento

Coleman M. Mrs. cloak and dress maker, 659 Clay, dwl 120 Ellis
Coleman Maggie Miss, domestic, dwl 1221 Clay
Coleman Margaret Miss, domestic, 742 Howard
Coleman Michael, laborer, dwl E s Diamond near Seventeenth
Coleman Milton, carpenter, dwl SW cor Sixteenth and Capp
Coleman Morris, clothing, 110 Third, dwl 156 Third
Coleman P. hostler, Omnibus R. R. Co
Coleman Patrick, laborer, dwl 9 Clara
Coleman Patrick, helper, Union Foundry, dwl 135 Clara
Coleman Robert, asphaltum roofer, dwl 145 Post
Coleman Susan, domestic with John M. Bogart, W s Eleventh nr Market
Coleman Thomas, boot fitter, dwl 710 Bush
Coleman Thomas, salesman, 510 Market, bds Fisher House
Coleman Thomas, saloon, dwl 1308 Kearny
Coleman Thomas, workman, S. F. & P. Sugar Co. dwl Ritter nr Seventh
Coleman Thomas jr. clerk, dwl 777 Market
Coleman (Thomas S.) & Burditt (W. W.) Idaho Liquor Saloon, 650 Sac, dwl 1308 Kearny
Coleman William, seaman, dwl 109 Jackson
COLEMAN WILLIAM T. & CO. (George Platt) importing, shipping, and commission merchants, office 417 Battery cor Merchant, dwl Union Club Rooms
Coleman, see Colman
COLEMAN'S CALIFORNIA LINE CLIPPER SHIPS, office 417 Battery cor Merchant
Coles Albert, lather, dwl 803 Howard
Coles Edward, waiter, 28 Montgomery
Coles Robert J. driver, Omnibus R. R. Co. dwl 803 Howard
Coleson A. A. clerk, dwl E s Kearny bet Greenwich and Lombard
COLEY (H. C.) & DEARBORN (J. P.) fruit, confectionery, etc. 121 Fourth
Coley Hiram M. porter with R. Hall & Co. dwl 23 Clara
Colfer Patrick, hostler, 317 Pine, dwl Main near Market
Colgan Michael, saddle and harness, dwl 822 Vallejo
Colgrove George L. teamster with R. T. Reynolds & Co. dwl 417 Folsom bet First and Fremont
Colier Charles E. bar keeper, 530 Clay
Collen James, workman, woolen factory, dwl E s Mission nr Fifteenth
Colleran Mary Miss, domestic, dwl 627 Union
Collerty Margt. Miss, domestic, dwl 115 Prospect Pl
Collett C. baker, Russ House
Collett John, baker, Brown's Bakery, dwl 1223 Stockton
Collibeaux Pauline Madame, French Laundry, 335 Bush
Collie Thompson, captain schooner Fairfield, office 7 Stewart
COLLIE (William M.) & STEWART (Henry) nursery and florists, 27 Geary
Collier August, jeweler with F. R. Reichel
Collier Charles W. Old Georgia Restaurant, 923 Kearny, dwl 518 Pacific
Collier Dell Miss, milliner with Mrs. E. McCrum, 604 Kearny
COLLIER FREDERICK, livery and sale stable, 655 Sacramento, dwl 642 Sacramento
Collier J. M. carpenter with S. S. Culverwell, 29 Fremont, dwl 404 Bush
Collier W. J. compositor, American Flag, bds New Wisconsin Hotel, 411 Pacific
Colligan Torrence, laborer, dwl Vallejo nr Larkin
Colligin John, laborer with William Buckley
Collin Charles, machinist, Pacific Foundry, dwl Tehama nr First
Collin Henry, salesman with William Sherman & Co. dwl 1307 Pacific

Collin Sarah L. Mrs. midwife, dwl 1307 Pacific
Collin William, clerk, dwl 58 Shipley
COLLINS (A. L.) & CLEMENT (R. P. and Jabish) attorneys at law, office 58 Exchange Building, dwl 618 Green
Collins Alvina Miss, domestic with James R. Bolton
Collins Andrew, miner, dwl 253 Clementina
Collins Bartholomew, tailor, 416 Folsom
Collins Benjamin, carpenter, 627 California, dwl 248 Jessie
Collins Benjamin, waiter, dwl 106½ Clay
Collins Bernard, seaman, bds Blue Wing, Front nr Vallejo
Collins B. R. teamster, Pier 9 Stewart, dwl 206 Fifth
Collins Catharine Miss, domestic, 962 Mission
COLLINS C. E. watch maker and jeweler, 602 Montgomery, dwl 755 Clay
Collins Charles (colored) waiter, stmr Chrysopolis
Collins Charles E. clerk, 413 Montgomery, dwl Brooklyn Hotel
Collins Charles E. minstrel, Academy Music
Collins Cornelius, bricklayer, dwl 151 Natoma
Collins Cornelius, builder, W s Fifth nr Minna, dwl 1211 Bush
Collins Daniel, deck hand, steamer Princess
Collins David, dwl 206 Fifth
Collins David, laborer, dwl 1332 Washington
Collins Dennis, butcher, dwl W s Gilbert bet Bryant and Brannan
Collins D. J. furniture repairer, 613 Mission
Collins D. R. molder, Miners' Foundry, dwl 53 Natoma
Collins Edward, clerk, Assistant Weigher, Custom House, dwl 407 Hyde
Collins Edward, boiler maker helper, Vulcan Iron Works
Collins Edward, seaman, dwl S s Greenwich bet Montgomery and Sansom
Collins Elizabeth (widow) dwl 6 Lick Alley
Collins Ellen M. Miss, laundress, Protestant Orphan Asylum
Collins E. S. plumber and gas fitter, 825 Montgomery, dwl 202 Green
Collins George, attorney at law, dwl 268 Tehama
Collins George H. salesman with Newhall, Brooks & Nettleton, dwl 22 Minna
Collins J. Capt. dwl 140 Stewart
Collins James, boiler maker, Pacific Foundry, dwl 15 Ecker
Collins James, deck hand, steamer Chrysopolis
Collins James, laborer, dwl with Patrick McAntee, N s Mission bet Twelfth and Thirteenth
Collins James, painter, dwl 7 Trinity
Collins James C. hatter, dwl 114 Prospect Place
Collins Jane Miss, domestic, 934 Howard
Collins John, bar keeper, 614 Montgomery
Collins John, boot black with C. Diehl, 533 Sac
Collins John, brass finisher, dwl 93 Jessie
Collins John, cutler with Michael Price, dwl 18 Marsh
Collins John, express wagon, cor Clay and Davis, dwl 66 Stevenson
Collins John, tailor, dwl 63 Stevenson
Collins John, watchman, Golden State Iron Works, dwl Beale nr Market
Collins John Mrs. dwl 1224 Jackson
Collins John C. hair dresser with Steffen & Bro. dwl 173 Minna
Collins John W. clerk with Tax Collector, City Hall, dwl 715 Bush
Collins Joseph C. proprietor Government House, 502 Washington, office 5, dwl room 31
Collins M. laborer, dwl 316 Fourth
Collins Maggie Miss, domestic with William H. Hyde, E s Mission bet Fourteenth and Fifteenth
Collins Margaret, domestic with William Kerr, dwl 903 Battery
Collins Margaret Miss, domestic, dwl 1304 Pine

Collins Matthew, second officer steamer Pacific
Collins Michael, driver, California Powder Works, dwl S s Boyd nr Eighth
Collins Michael, laborer, dwl N s Washington bet Larkin and Polk
Collins Michael, laborer. S. F. & San José R. R
Collins Michael, plasterer, dwl W s Russ bet Folsom and Howard
Collins Patrick, dwl 428 Clementina
Collins Patrick, dwl 145 Natoma
Collins Patrick, deck hand, steamer Julia
Collins Patrick, laborer, dwl S s Folsom bet Beale and Main
Collins Patrick, laborer, dwl 419 Stevenson
Collins Patrick, laborer, dwl 949 Folsom
Collins Pauline (widow) dress maker, 627 Sac
Collins Peter, clerk with Robert Page, dwl 20 Dupont
Collins Richard, carpenter, 627 Cal, dwl 248 Jessie
Collins Richard, fireman, Mission Woolen Mills
Collins Richard, laborer, dwl E s First Avenue bet Fourteenth and Fifteenth
Collins Richard W. wharfinger, Broadway Wharf, dwl 122 Geary
Collins Silas H. teamster, Pier 9 Stewart, dwl 206 Fifth
Collins Solomon J. mariner, dwl 1906 Mason
Collins Salvin P. dwl 815 Mission
Collins Timothy, builder, dwl 548 Tehama
Collins Timothy, laborer, dwl 331 Bush
Collins Timothy, messenger, 37 Montgomery Block, dwl 41 South Park
Collins William, deck hand, steamer Chrysopolis
Collins William, night watchman, S. F. & San José R. R. dwl Florida nr Twentieth
Collischonn Charles, clerk with Abel Guy, dwl 110 Eddy
Collison James, boiler maker, Vulcan Iron Works, dwl 10 Jessie
Collinson John A. chief adjuster Coiner's Department, U. S. Branch Mint, dwl 1 Harlan Place
Collner John (California Publishing Co.) dwl 12 Natoma
Collombe G. & S. M. Co. office 607 Washington
Collopy Michael, with Stillman Hendricks, N W cor Larkin and Pine
Collopy Timothy, miner, dwl N s Minna nr Seventh
Colman Abraham (Colman Bros.) dwl 427 Sac
Colman A. F. druggist with James H. Widber, cor Kearny and Market
Colman Brothers (Solomon, Morris, Abraham, and Charles) wholesale and retail clothing, SW cor Montgomery and Wash, res New York
Colman Charles (Colman Bros.) dwl 427 Sac
Colman James M. (Glidden C. & Co.) Pier 22 Stewart
Colman Morris (Colman Bros.) dwl 427 Sac
Colman Michael, peddler, dwl Hinckley
Culopal S. M. Co. office 305 Montgomery room 6
Colorado River Line Packets, George F. Hooper agent, office 308 Front
Colson Alexander, tinware, 930 Dupont, dwl E s Jasper Place
Colson Andrew, seaman, dwl 44 Sacramento
Colson Edward A. messenger, Custom House, dwl NE cor Kearny and Greenwich
Colson John, seaman, dwl 44 Sacramento
Colston G. I. lather, dwl 28 Sansom
Colter D. laborer, Spring Valley W. W
Colter John, policeman, City Hall, dwl S s Pfeiffer nr Stockton
Colting E. P. mariner, dwl N s Chestnut bet Dupont and Stockton
COLTON (David D.) & HARRISON (Ralph C.) attorneys at law, office 402 Montgomery rooms 11-13 third floor, dwl 220 Third
Colton William, laborer with Hey & Meyn
Colton William, teamster, cor Stewart and Mission, dwl W s Hawes nr Folsom

Colton's Building, NW cor Third and Tehama
Colt J. C. dwl Niantic Hotel
COLUMBIA FIRE INSURANCE CO. New York, R. B. Swain & Co. agents, 206 Front
Columbus Amiel, cook, City Front House, 625 Davis
Columpio G. & S. M. Co. office 606 Montgomery
Colvan Kate Miss, domestic with Sam'l L. Theller
Colvin James A. gas fitter with Thomas Day, 732 Montgomery, dwl S s Greenwich bet Leavenworth and Jones
Colvin Lydia Mrs. dress maker, 644 Mission
Collwell William, machinist, Vulcan Foundry, dwl E s Folsom nr Precita Avenue
Colyer Washington (Branch & C.) dwl 923 Kearny
COMBES J. C. Blue Wing, 526 Montgomery, dwl 1027 Dupont
Comeiford Mary Theresa Miss, superioress Presentation Convent, cor Stockton and Lombard
Comer Bartley, sawyer, dwl 118 Minna
Comerford Edward, seaman, dwl 44 Sacramento
Comerford Patrick, express wagon, Meiggs' Wharf
Comerford Patrick, liquor saloon, dwl 719 Francisco
Comeron James, bakery, 509 Third
Comet Petroleum Co. office 36 Exchange Building
Comford John, laborer with John Center, N W cor Sixteenth and Folsom
Comings John H. clerk, Piers 17-18 Stewart, dwl 23 Minna
Comins Paschal B. mechanic, 1067 Broadway dwl 68 Bernard
Comiskey Patrick, groom, dwl 62 Minna
Commatti Dominic, clerk, 21 Washington Market, dwl E s Dupont bet Greenwich and Lombard
Commerce S. M. Co. office 529 Clay
COMMERCIAL BANK CORPORATION OF INDIA AND THE EAST, Richard Newby agent, office 408 California
Commercial Building, cor Pine and Battery
COMMERCIAL FLOUR MILL, Grosh & Rutherford proprietors, 143 and 145 First
Commercial Hotel, W. H. Norton proprietor, 123 and 125 Pacific
Commercial Printing Office, Francis, Valentine & Co. proprietors, 517 Clay
Commeseel Herman L. importer and commission merchant, 307 California, dwl 823 Sutter
Commins Edward (P. Riley & Co.) dwl NW cor Mission and Eleventh
Commissioners (Board of) Funded Debt, office Parrott's Building
Compes H. cabinet maker, dwl 316 Jackson
Compostino Frederick, laborer, dwl 1214 Kearny
Compton H. N. wheelwright with J. C. H. Matthai, 607 Battery
Compton Kenneth, cigar maker, dwl 30 Third
Compton L. F. miller, Golden Age Flour Mills, dwl NE cor Bush and Sansom
Comstock Arnold M. broker, dwl 810 Vallejo
Comstock Mary (widow) adjuster, U. S. Branch Mint, dwl N s Pine bet Powell and Stockton
Comyns John, calker, dwl 3 Liberty
Couahan Cornelius, milk ranch, Lake Merced
Conahan John, works with Cornelius Conahan
Conaff Kate Miss, domestic, dwl 1707 Stockton
Conant B. H. molder, Vulcan Iron Works, dwl 212 Second
Conant Hartwell, molder, dwl 81 Natoma
Concannon Lawrence, core maker, Golden State Iron Works, dwl 43 Clementina
Conch Alfred A. Bay City Laundry, 1140 and 1142 Folsom
Concordia Club Room, NE cor Bush and Kearny
Condel Joseph D. book keeper with Samuel Kellett, dwl 316 Fourth
Couden E. W. teamster with Reynolds & Co. dwl E s Folsom bet First and Fremont
Conden James, machinist, Vulcan Iron Works
Condett Edward, cook, dwl S s Dupont Alley

Condon Kate Miss, domestic with Robert J. Polk
Condon Margaret Miss, domestic, Summer Street House
Condon Mary (widow) dwl 1710 Mason, rear
Condon Morris, porter, 404 Front, dwl 510 Front
Condon Patrick, shoe maker with Dennis A. Healey, dwl 12 O'Farrell
Condray Otis, stevedore, dwl 308 Folsom
Condrick John, longshoreman, dwl Filbert nr Mont
Coudrin James, machinist, Union Foundry, dwl 355 Minna
Cone Jessie B. clerk with S. P. Whitman, 313 Mont
Cone Scott, dwl 845 Dupont
Cone William H. salesman, 34 Montgomery, dwl 8 Virginia Place
Coneo *(John)* Pizello *(Frank)* liquor saloon, 1313 Dupont
Conery John, laborer, dwl 8 Pollard Place
Coney Alexander, pawnbroker, 813 Dupont
Coney Ellen Miss, domestic with D. Stern, S s Fulton nr Gough
Confert Zundell, waiter, 506 Montgomery dwl 812 Green
Confidence Silver M. Co. (Gold Hill) office 415 Mont
Cong Wa (Chinese) washing, S s Sixteenth bet Valencia and Mission
Congdon Charles, seaman, dwl 54 Sacramento
CONGDON GEORGE, mining secretary, office 606 Montgomery, bds Occidental Hotel
Congdon Henry B. mining secretary and commissioner deeds for Nevada, office 620 Washington, dwl N s Thirteenth nr Mission
Conge C. French Hospital, Bryant nr Sixth
Conger *(Benjamin T.)* & Gray *(William O.)* produce commission, 212 Wash, dwl 212 Minna
Conger Charles C. first lieutenant Co. K California Volunteers, Fort Point
Congiato N. Very Rev.; S.J. clergyman, St. Ignatius' Church, S s Market bet Fourth and Fifth
Congrahs Pehr, tailor, dwl 631 Broadway
Conkelman Benjamin, traveling agent, Wheeler & Wilson's Sewing Machine Co. dwl 920 Stockton
Conklin Enoch, captain steamer Julia, C. S. Navigation Co. office NE cor Front and Jackson
Conklin Henry B. waiter, Lick House
Conklin Nathaniel G. machinist, dwl 1111 Dupont
Conkling David, book keeper with B. C. Horn & Co. dwl 555 Harrison
CONKLING G. W. auction salesroom, 714 Montgomery, dwl 962 Mission
Conlan John, laborer, dwl 307 First
Conlan John, waiter, dwl 759 Market
Couland Bernard, waiter, dwl 18 Sherwood Place
Conland Francis, laborer, dwl 18 Sherwood Place
Conley Arthur, laborer with Wm. Kerr, dwl 903 Bat
Conley Daniel, laborer, dwl E s Main bet Harrison and Bryant
Conley Elizabeth (widow) dwl 1025 Washington
Conley Frank, bar tender, 339 Third cor Verona
Conley James, groom, dwl 449 Jessie bet Fifth and Sixth
Conley James, packer, dwl 17 Main
Conley John, cartman, dwl 137 Minna
Conley John, laborer, dwl S s Brannan bet Sixth and Seventh
Conley Lawrence, liquors, SE cor Geneva and Brannan
Conley Michael, laborer, dwl 37 Baldwin Court
Conley Patrick, waiter, Magnolia Restaurant, dwl 8 s Tehama nr Fifth
Conlin Catherine Miss, domestic, 22 Montgomery
Conlin Elizabeth Miss, domestic, dwl 835 Howard
Conlin James, laborer, S. F. & San José R. R. dwl
Conlin Jas. metal roofer with H. G. & E. S. Fiske, dwl 407 Tehama
Conlin John, contractor, dwl 129 Clara, rear
Conlin John, retortman, S. F. Gas Co
Conlin John C. carpenter, dwl W s Seventh nr Harrison

Conlin John F. street contractor, dwl 113 O'Farrell
Conlin John J. carpenter, dwl Clara bet Fourth and Fifth
Conlin Mary Miss, domestic, 610 Ellis
Conlin Michael, laborer, S. F. & P. Sugar Co. dwl W s Gilbert bet Brannan and Townsend
Conlin Patrick, with J. Hirth & Co. dwl 517 Vallejo
Conlin Terrence, laborer, dwl 17 Sherwood Place
Conlin Winnie Miss, domestic, 631 Sutter
Conlon Bernard, waiter, Miners' Restaurant, dwl 159 Minna
Conlon Martin, cartman, dwl Brannan bet Fifth and Sixth
Conlon Mathew, laborer with William Kerr, dwl 903 Battery
Conlon Thomas, laborer with William Buckley
Conly Sarah Miss, domestic, 925 Howard
CONNECTICUT MUTUAL LIFE INSURANCE CO. Hartford, Bigelow & Brother agents, 505 Montgomery
Conneff James, laborer, dwl W s Sansom bet Greenwich and Filbert
Connegan Maria, domestic, dwl 320 Jessie
Connell Charles, waiter, Russ House
Connell Charles, plasterer, dwl 204 Montgomery
Connell Charles D. first assistant engineer S. F. Fire Department, and inspector, Custom House, dwl Vigilant Engine House
Connell David, commission agent, 4 Drumm (
Connell Ellen, domestic, dwl 416 Second
Connell Hannah Miss, nurse, dwl NW cor Stockton and Pacific
Connell James, steward, Willows, SW cor Mission and Eighteenth
Connell James D. carpenter and builder, office and dwl 1026 Pacific
Connell John, cartman, dwl Ellis nr Van Ness Av
Connell John, porter, 223 Front, dwl 28 Clementina
Connell Julia (widow) dwl 17 Hunt
Connell M. A. laborer, Custom House.
Connell Margaret Miss, domestic 317 Powell
Connell Mary Miss, domestic, dwl 618 Third
Connell Mary Ann Miss, domestic, dwl with Edward LeBreton
Connell Michael, groceries and liquors, NW cor Moss and Folsom
Connell Michael, laborer, S. F. & San José R. R
Connell Michael, laborer, dwl W s Geneva bet Bryant and Brannan
Connell Michael, lab, dwl E s Rassette Place No. 2
Connell Philip, stone mason, dwl 119 Stevenson
Connell Richard, carrier, Bulletin and Call, dwl E s Russ nr Folsom
Connell Richard, hackman, dwl 12 Clara
Connell Thomas, boiler maker, dwl N s Frederick
Connell Thomas, cartman, 69 Jessie
Connell Thomas, laborer, dwl 50 Beale
Connell Thomas, laborer, Golden State Iron Works
Connell Thomas L. laborer, dwl 551 Market
Connell Timothy, boiler maker with Coffey & Risdon
Connell Timothy, waiter, Russ House
Connell W. C. G. conductor, North Beach & M. R. R. Co
Connell William, workman with Casebolt & Co
Connell William, workman with A. Tait, Old San José Road nr St. Mary's College
Connell William F. plasterer, dwl 633 Market
Connell see Cornell
Connelly Ann Miss, with Lesser Leszynsky, dwl 5 O'Farrell
Connelly Bridget (widow) dwl 127 Perry
Connelly Catharine (widow) dwl NE cor Taylor and Union
Connelly D. W. real estate, dwl 634 Sacramento
Connelly Ellen Miss, domestic, 627 Sutter
Connelly James E. dwl Clementina bet First and Second
Connelly James J. molder, Union Foundry, dwl 1 Boston Place nr First

Connelly Jane Miss, cloak maker with L. Leszynsky, dwl 5 O'Farrell
Connelly John, Manhattan Engine Co. No. 2
Connelly John, laborer, dwl Devisidero bet Tyler and McAllister
Connelly John, laborer, dwl 266 Jessie
Connelly Kate Miss, domestic, 211 Powell
Connelly Lawrence, liquors, dwl Harrison nr Sixth
Connelly Margaret Miss, domestic, dwl 1119 Pine
Connelly Martin, dwl N s Brannan bet Fifth and Sixth
Connelly Martin, boiler maker, Union Foundry, dwl 648 Mission
Connelly Martin, ship carpenter with John G. North, Potrero
Connelly Mary Miss, domestic, dwl 1004 Bush
Connelly Mary Miss, domestic, dwl 843 Clay
Connelly Mary Miss, domestic, dwl 920 Bush
Connelly Michael, laborer, dwl 29 Ritch
Connelly Patrick, cartman, dwl 137 Minna
Connelly Patrick, driver, North Beach & M. R. R. Co
Connelly Patrick, laborer, dwl 29 Ritch
Connelly Patrick, laborer, U. S. Appraiser's Store
Connelly Patrick, laborer, dwl 3 Sherwood Place
Connelly Peter, driver, dwl SE cor Fourth and Jessie
Connelly William, driver, North Beach & M. R.R. Co
Connelly William, laborer, dwl S s Filbert bet Leavenworth and Hyde
Conner Edward, clerk with J. J. Robbins
Conner Francis, capt. stm Sierra Nevada, office SW cor Front and Jackson, dwl 560 Folsom
Conner J. dwl 219 Mason
Conner John, collector, dwl 110 Perry
Conner John, seaman, dwl 44 Sacramento
Conner M. workman with Casebolt & Co
Conner Patrick, works with Herman Buerfind
Conner Patrick, laborer, dwl 71 Jessie
Conner S. L. W. carpenter, dwl SW cor Minna and Mary
Conner W. George, butcher, dwl 410 Folsom
Conners Dennis, porter, 400 Battery
Conners James, soda bottler, dwl Manhattan Engine House
Conners James, teamster, dwl 368 Brannan
Conners Kate Miss, dress maker, dwl 16 Natoma
Conners Margaret (widow) dwl 3 Sherwood Place
Conners Patrick, laborer with Hey & Meyn
Conners Patrick, retortman, San Francisco Gas Co
Conners Robert T. carpenter with Hobbs, Gilmore & Co. dwl 1 Haywood
Connerton Martin, porter, 423 Front, dwl 5 Washoe Place
Connerty Catharine Miss, domestic, dwl 1213 Clay
Connerty Frank, night nurse, St. Mary's Hospital
Connery Patrick, driver with John Agnew, 26 Kearny
Conness Margaret Miss, domestic, dwl 831 Jackson
Conniff Michael, carpenter, dwl 422 Third
Conniff Nicholas, carpenter and contractor, dwl S s Bryant bet Fifth and Sixth
Conniff William, butcher, SW cor Howard and Sumner
Conniff William, clerk, 329 Bush
Connolly Bridget Miss, domestic, 1050 Union
Connolly Bridget Miss, domestic, 926 Jackson
Connolly Edward A. bricklayer, dwl SE cor Ellis and Larkin
Connolly James, dwl 12 Sutter
Connolly James, dwl NE cor El Dorado and Nebraska
Connolly James, mining, dwl 5 O'Farrell
Connolly James, upholsterer with J. F. & H. H. Schafer, dwl 828 Broadway
Connolly James E. calker, dwl Crescent Engine House
Connolly John, bar keeper, Occidental Hotel
CONNOLLY JOHN, Rotunda Liquor Saloon, junction Market, O'Farrell, and Dupont, dwl 5 O'Farrell

Connolly Kate Miss, dress maker, dwl 812 Mont
Connolly Mary (widow) dwl with Mrs. Kate Hobe W s Mission bet Twenty-First and Twenty-Second
Connolly Mary, chambermaid, Lick House
Connolly Mary A. Miss, cloak maker, dwl 12 Sutter
Connolly Michael, helper, Union Foundry, dwl 37 Baldwin Court
Connolly Michael, laborer, dwl 441 Bush, rear
Connolly Michael, hog ranch, near Toll Gate San Bruno Road
Connolly Michael L. hog ranch, York nr Solano
Connolly Nicholas, wholesale butcher, Potrero Avenue, dwl S s Bryant bet Seventh and Eighth
Connolly Nicholas, works with O. F. Swett
Connolly Owen, butcher, SE cor Laguna and Waller
Connolly Patrick, laborer, dwl cor Berry and Mary Lane
Connolly Patrick, porter, 7 Montgomery, dwl Annie nr Eddy
Connolly Peter, contractor, dwl NE cor Howard and Sumner
Connolly Thomas, carpenter, dwl N s Broadway bet Montgomery and Kearny
Connolly Thomas, laborer, dwl W s Fillmore opposite Kate
Connolly Thomas, poultry, butter, eg, etc. 4 and 5 New Market, dwl 920 Howard
Connolly Timothy, lieutenant, U. S. A. dwl 351 Minna
Connolly William, waiter, Occidental Hotel
Connolly, see Conolly
Connor Anna S. Mrs. domestic with Frederick Belcher
Connor Bridget Miss, domestic, dwl 1217 Wash
Connor Hannah Miss, domestic, dwl 835 California
Connor Hester (widow) fancy goods, SW cor Harrison and Chesley
Connor James, laborer, dwl 28 Dupont
Connor John, dwl 213 Stevenson
Connor John, boiler maker with Coffey & Risdon
Connor John, mariner, dwl 138 Fourth
Connor John, steamboatman, dwl W s Mowry Al
Connor John O. workman, dwl with John M. Mitchell
Connor Kate, servant, dwl 1306 Kearny
Connor Maria (widow) dwl N s Seventeenth bet Guerrero and Dolores
Connor Mary Miss, domestic, dwl 1030 Jackson
Connor Patrick, broker, dwl 407 Dupont
Connor Rosa Miss, domestic, 536 Ellis
Connor Thomas, plasterer, bds Manhattan House
Connor William, molder, Golden State Iron Works, dwl 48 Louisa
Connor William B. jeweler with Lemme Bros. dwl 22 Sansom
Connors David, job wagon, dwl 264 Clementina, rear
Connors David, marble worker with John Daniel, 421 Pine, dwl 319 Bush
Connors Edward, purifier, San Francisco Gas Co
Conners Jeremiah, stone cutter, Fort Point
Connors John, peddler, dwl Sixth nr Brannan
Connors John, stevedore, dwl NW cor Front and Broadway
Connors Lawrence, bricklayer, dwl 848 Folsom, rear
Connors Michael, laborer, dwl 266 Jessie
Connors Thomas, laborer, dwl with C. Peterson, N s Courtlandt Avenue, nr North Avenue
Connors William, molder, Golden State Iron Works, dwl 48 Louisa
Conofry Ann Miss, domestic, 917 Howard
Conolly William J. assistant book keeper, Hibernia Savings and Loan Society, dwl 431 Bryant
Conover Edgar, painter, dwl S s Brannan bet Clinton and Geneva
Conrad Andrew, carpenter and cabinet maker, 414 Pine, dwl Chatham Place

Conrad Christian Mrs. (widow) dwl 641 Mission
Conrad Christian, clerk, 535 Commercial, dwl 641 Mission
Conrad David (J. & D. Conrad) dwl 14 Tehama
Conrad Henry, metal roofer with H. G. & E. S. Fiske, dwl 641 Mission
Conrad J. & D. wholesale fruits, 419 Washington, res Philadelphia
Conrad William A. cabinet maker with N. P. Langland, dwl W s Larkin bet Turk and Tyler
Conrades (Ferdinand) & Co. (Charles Haake) Antelope Oyster Saloon, 612 Market, dwl 129 Jessie
Conradi William, musician, dwl 1513 Stockton, rear
CONRO F. D. & CO. proprietors Golden Age Flour Mills, 717 Battery, office 127 Clay, dwl 751 Howard
Conro George A. clerk, 127 Clay, dwl 751 Howard
Conroy B. physician, office and dwl 503 Pacific
Conroy Francis, laborer, dwl cor Presidio Road and Van Ness Avenue
Conroy James, stone cutter, dwl nr Mountain Lake House, Point Lobos
CONROY (James C.) & O'CONNOR (John F. Michael J. and Thomas H. O'Connor) importers and jobbers metals and. hardware, 107–113 Front and 204–214 Pine, res New York
Conroy (John) & Tobin (Richard) farmers, Ocean House Valley
Conroy John, glass maker, 26 Stevenson
Conroy John, janitor Lincoln School
Conroy John, laborer, dwl Bartol bet Broadway and Vallejo
Conroy John C. job wagon, SE cor Market and Fourth, dwl 18 Louisa
Conroy Julia Miss, domestic, dwl 820 Filbert
Conroy Martin, teamster with J. Barraclough & Co. dwl cor Drumm and Sacramento
Conroy Martin, workman, S. F. & P. Sugar Co. dwl cor Ninth and Mission
Conroy M. C. night clerk, P. O. dwl 1912 Mason
Conroy Michael, laborer, dwl 210 Ritch
Conroy Thomas, machinist, Union Foundry, dwl 243 Tehama
Conry Mathew, workman, S. F. & P. Sugar Co. dwl SE cor Ninth and Mission
Conry Patrick, laborer with Conroy & Tobin
Considine Ann Miss, domestic, 1213 Taylor
Considine Edward, butcher, dwl 37 Third
Consolacion Silver M. Co. office 220 Montgomery
Consolez D. carpenter and builder, 949 Howard
Consolidated Silver Hill M. Co. office 522 Mont
Constant Madame, French millinery, 634 Vallejo, dwl 634 Vallejo
Constantin John, broker, dwl 819 Montgomery
Constin Margaret Miss, dwl 618 Third
Conte Vicenzo, fisherman, 11 Italian Fish Marke
Contet (Alexander) & Plege (Louis) hatters, 721 Clay
Conti Charles, finisher with R. F. Rocchiccoli, 523 California
Conti G. (G. Lucchesi & Co.) dwl E s Dupont bet Broadway and Pacific
Contic M. A. bottle depôt, dwl W s Jasper Place nr Filbert
Continental Hotel, Tandler & Lang proprietors, SE cor Sansom and Commercial
CONTINENTAL INSURANCE CO. New York, C. A. Low & Co. agents, office 426 California
CONTRA COSTA EXPRESS, Bamber & Co. proprietors, 739 Davis
CONTRA COSTA FERRY, foot of Broadway
CONTRA COSTA LAUNDRY, office 13 Broadway, branches 624 Commercial, 318 Pine and 677 Market
Converse Dennison, paper dealer, SW cor Sansom and Merchant, dwl 820 Washington
Couvrey Patrick, laborer, bds Washington House
Couvry John, coachman, 25 Stockton

Conway Cornelius, laborer, dwl Lincoln Avenue bet Sutter and Post
Conway D. J. gardener with George Hotte
Conway Edward, chief clerk office U. S. Surveyor General, dwl 618 Third
Conway Elias N. mining stocks, dwl 404 Eddy
Conway Ellen Miss, domestic, dwl 807 Pacific
Conway James, bar keeper, SW cor Jackson and Kearny
Conway James, laborer, Miners' Foundry
Conway James, laborer, dwl 49 Stevenson
Conway James, tailor, dwl 116 Stevenson
Conway James H. policeman, City Hall, dwl N s Filbert bet Kearny and Dupont
Conway James N. engineer with Hobbs, Gilmore & Co. dwl 42 First
Conway John (Thomas & C.) dwl 226 Jessie
Conway John, dwl S s Stevenson bet Sixth and Seventh
Conway John, carpenter, dwl 728 Market
Conway John, laborer, dwl E s Vincent nr Green
Conway John, painter, dwl Brannan bet Sixth and Seventh
Conway John, wholesale butcher, Brannan Street Bridge, dwl W s Alameda nr El Dorado
Conway John H. with Hoogs & Madison, 316 Montgomery, dwl 106 Ellis
Conway John R. physician, dwl 404 Eddy
Conway John R. policeman, City Hall, dwl 272 Minna
Conway Mary Miss, domestic, dwl 807 Stockton
Conway Michael, helper, dwl N s Mission bet First and Second
Conway Michael, laborer, bds Sacramento Hotel, 407 Pacific
Conway Michael, laborer, dwl E s Geneva bet Bryant and Brannan
Conway Michael G. saddler, 721 Market, dwl W s Jones bet Sacramento and California
Conway Morris, laborer, dwl N s Austin bet Gough and Octavia
Conway Patrick, laborer with George D. Nagle
Conway Phillip, plasterer, dwl W s Clinton bet Brannan and Bryant
Conway Richard, Surveyor General's office, dwl 618 Third
Conway Thomas, cabman, dwl S s Jackson bet Leavenworth and Hyde
Conway Thomas, harness maker with Main & Winchester, dwl 35 Louisa
Cony Daniel, weigher and measurer, office Custom House, dwl S s Filbert bet Hyde and Larkin
Coogan William H. sutler's clerk, Presidio
Coogen Richard, boarding, dwl 541 Mission
Cook A. express wagon, cor Stockton and Vallejo
Cook Aaron, merchant, dwl 715 Post
Cook Adam, furniture, 226 Sutter
Cook Algeron M. teamster with Wetherbee & Cook, dwl NW cor Fulton and Laguna
Cook Anna Miss, domestic, SW cor Sutter and Hyde
Cook A. W. (A. H. Todd & Co.) dwl 630 Howard bet Second and Third
Cook Camille (widow) dwl 120 Perry
Cook Caroline Mrs. dwl 431 Pine
Cook Charles, policeman, City Hall, dwl 1116 Taylor nr Clay
Cook Charles E. coachman, dwl 807 Greenwich
Cook Charles F. dwl 809 Union
Cook Charles G. painter, dwl 410 Bush
COOK (Charles W.) & PECKHAM (E. P.) notaries public, conveyancers and stock brokers, office 607 Clay, dwl SW cor Lombard and Taylor
Cook Clarissa Mrs. manuf hair jewelry, 645 Clay
Cook David S. secretary San Bruno Turnpike Co. office 409 California, res San Mateo
Cook D. D. dwl International Hotel
COOK E. G. & CO. (Albert Busse) groceries and liquors, SE cor Second and Minna, dwl NE cor Seventh and Bryant

Cook Elisha *(Bennett, C. & Clarke)* attorney at law, dwl 323 First
Cook E. N. broker, dwl International Hotel
Cook Frederick, blacksmith with Larkins & Co. dwl 443 Bush
Cook Frederick, cabinet maker with J. J. Easton, dwl 725 Market
Cook George, with Herman Brand, dwl S s Green bet Kearny and Dupont
Cook George, workman with W. Hall, Old San José Road nr county line
Cook Gilman G. fireman, bds City Front House, 625 Davis
Cook Horatio N. *(Cook & Son)* dwl 1517 Taylor
Cook Ira, laborer, U. S. Sub. Dept. 208 Sansom, dwl 119 Natoma
Cook Isaac *(Wetherbee & C.)* dwl NW cor Fulton and Laguna
Cook Jacob, canvasman, Wilson's Circus
Cook James, engineer Commercial Flour Mills, dwl 305 Bryant
Cook James, waiter, 12 Sutter
Cook John *(Ciprico & C.)* dwl NE cor Geary and Taylor
Cook John, dwl 608 Market
Cook John, drayman, cor Front and Sacramento, dwl S s Jackson bet Leavenworth and Hyde
Cook John, molder, bds Sacramento Hotel, 407 Pac
Cook John, seaman, dwl Shiels' Block
Cook John, steward, dwl Crescent Engine House
Cook John, waiter, dwl 515 Merchant
COOK JOHN H. game, 48 and 49 Washington Market, dwl 733 Union
Cook Julia (widow) furnished rooms, 6 Sansom
Cook Louis, merchant, dwl 718 Vallejo
Cook Marcus M. milk ranch, SW cor Pierce and Bush
Cook *(Mathew M.)* & Son *(Horatio N. Cook)* hose and collar manufacturers, NW cor Broadway and Battery, dwl 1517 Taylor
Cook Michael, dwl 431 Pine
Cook Michael, laborer, bds 606 Third
Cook Michael, laborer, dwl N s Point Lobos Road, 3 miles from Plaza
Cook M. S. laborer, Lone Mountain Cemetery
Cook N. B. sash, blind, and door maker with J. McGill & Co. dwl E s Howard nr Sixteenth
Cook Nelson (col'd) porter with Sather & Co. dwl 1526 Dupont
Cook Pardon A. milk ranch, dwl SW cor Pierce and Bush
Cook P. C. Mrs. head assistant, Union Grammar School, dwl 762 Mission
Cook Peter, compositor, Evening Bulletin, dwl 1319 Kearny
Cook Philip, compositor, American Flag, dwl SW cor Stockton and O'Farrell
Cook Samuel M. tin plate worker with Cutting & Co. dwl E s Larkin bet Green and Union
Cook S. B. molder, Jackson Foundry, dwl Sacramento Hotel
Cook Thomas, dwl 443 Bush
Cook Thomas, coal passer, stm Chrysopolis
Cook Thomas, job wagon, cor Sacramento and Montgomery, dwl cor Leidesdorff and Halleck
Cook Thompson, dwl 319 Bush
Cook William, carpenter, dwl NE cor Stockton and O'Farrell
Cook William A. special policeman, dwl W s Carlos Place
Cook William P. broker, dwl 202 Second
Cook William S. dwl 529 Green
Cooke Geo. B. stevedore, dwl 953 Folsom
Cooke Hannah Miss, principal Hyde St. Primary School, dwl 313 Taylor
Cooke James, equestrian and jester, Wilson's Circus, dwl 524 Howard
Cooke Mary M. (widow) lodgings, 32 Second
Cooke Peter *(Wm. B. Cooke & Co.)* res New York

Cooke Robert C. First California Guard, N s Pine nr Sansom
COOKE WILLIAM B. & CO. *(Peter Cooke)* importing stationers and law blank publishers, 622 and 624 Montgomery, Montgomery Block, dwl 1116 Powell
Cookingham Amanda Miss, dwl 1218 Jackson
Cooley John, laborer, dwl 15 Hunt
Cooley L. P. milk ranch, dwl NW cor Valencia and Twenty-Third
Cooley Michael, mariner, dwl 1 Park Avenue
Coolidge Charles C. dwl 319 Geary
Coolidge Joseph A. justice of the peace, fifth township, office 613 Market, dwl 420 Second
Coombs Edward, clerk, 645 Washington
Coombs Joseph, attorney at law, dwl NE cor Montgomery and Pacific
Coombs William jr. real estate agent, office 626 Clay
Coombs, see Combs
Coon Charles D. book keeper with Thomas Hill, dwl 1010 Bush
Coon Eliza Miss, domestic, 306 Stockton
Coon George W. blacksmith with Larkin & Co. dwl Whitehall Exchange
COON HENRY P. mayor, City and Co. and ex officio president Board of Supervisors, office 2 City Hall first floor, dwl N s Geary near Larkin
Coon Jacob *(Grant & C.)* dwl NW cor Mission and First
Coon Sing (Chinese) washing, 4 Front
Coonen Michael, stevedore, dwl 58 Stewart
Cooney *(John)* & Beirne *(Patrick)* retail wines and liquors, 417 Powell
Cooney John jr. house and sign painting, 830 Market, cor Union and Montgomery
Cooney John sen. groceries, S s Union bet Montgomery and Calhoun
Cooney Margaret Miss, domestic, dwl 618 Pine
Cooney Michael, cooper, S. F. & P. Sugar Co. dwl 15 Rousch nr Howard
Cooney Thomas, laborer, dwl 183 Jessie
Coons Alonzo, carpenter, Vulcan Iron Works, dwl Bailey House
Coons Charles A. bricklayer with George D. Nagle, dwl 7 Kearny
Coons John H. ship carpenter, dwl 113 Natoma
Coony John, butcher with Henry O. Hill, dwl 1113 Clay
Coop J. G. tinman, dwl 116 Sansom
Cooper A. F. *(Misgill & C.)* dwl 245 Second
Cooper Ann E. (col'd, widow) dwl 1433 Dupont
Cooper Archibald, foreman Melter and Refiner's Department U. S. Branch Mint, dwl NE cor Washington and Dupont
Cooper Colden, Forwarding Department, Wells, Fargo & Co. dwl Brevoort House
Cooper Cyrus (col'd) waiter, stm Chrysopolis, dwl W s Mowry Alley
Cooper David L. clerk, Main Street Wharf, dwl SW cor Howard and First
Cooper Eugene T. book keeper with E. J. Crane, dwl 137 Silver
Cooper Ezekiel, laborer, dwl NE cor Sacramento and Leavenworth
Cooper F. *(Strobel, Fleig & Co.)* dwl 1129 Folsom
Cooper Frances J. (col'd, widow) dwl 909 Pacific
Cooper Grace S. (widow) dwl 515 Pine
Cooper Henry, bricklayer, dwl 14 Harlan Place
Cooper James, with Warren Haley, Oriental Hotel Restaurant
Cooper J. B. R. office 523 Montgomery, dwl 821 Bush
Cooper James K. express wagon, 68 Natoma
Cooper John A. driver, Omnibus R. R. Co. dwl 215 Tehama
Cooper Joseph, sailing master, dwl 347 First
Cooper Oliver *(Griffin & C.)* dwl Quincy nr Cal
Cooper Randolph *(Derry & C.)* (col'd) dwl 1403 Mason

Cooper Theodore, cook, stm Princess
Cooper Thomas (col'd) laborer, dwl 907 Sac
Cooper William, bar tender, stm Relief
Cooper William, boot fitter, dwl 253 Clementina
Cooper William, seaman, dwl 32 Stewart
Coose Bay Coal Co. office 606 Montgomery
Cooty P. H. Eureka Hose Co. No. 4
COPE *(W. W.)* DAINGERFIELD *(William P.)* & HAMBLETON *(J. Douglas)* attorneys at law, office 5-7 U. S. Court Buildings, dwl 115 Dupont
Copeland Thomas, painter with Swett & Gadsby, dwl 110 William, rear
Copeland William, seaman, dwl 20 Commercial
Copeland William M. Capt. dwl 329 Beale
Copeman Margaret, domestic, 760 Mission
Copiapo S. M. Co. office 605 Clay
Copithorne Jane (widow) dwl 10 Rousch
Copithorne Richard, with Locke & Montague, dwl 10 Rousch
Coplan Willis, compositor, Dramatic Chronicle, dwl Irving House
Copp D. H. ship joiner, dwl 21 Belden Block
Copp John G. tinsmith with Tay, Brooks & Buckus, bds Bailey House
Copp N. P. *(Vandervoort & Co.)* dwl 30 Third
Coppage John, cooper, S. F. & P. Sugar Co. dwl 32 Rousch
Coppi Giacomo *(Pezzoni & C.)* dwl W s Taylor bet Lombard and Chestnut
Coppi Victor, ivory and wood turner, 309 Pine, dwl 613 Kearny
Coptch, Charlotte E. dwl with Thomas L. Bridges, W s Eleventh bet Market and Mission
Coquens Kate Miss, chambermaid, Russ House
Cora, J. H. salesman, dwl 532 Pine
Corbell George W. *(Gavin W. Gibb & Co.)* dwl 8 Virginia
Corbett Alexander C. plasterer, dwl 710½ Taylor
Corbett D. E. groceries and liquors, SW cor Mason and O'Farrell
Corbett Edward W. dwl W s Fifth bet Howard and Folsom
Corbett Ellen, domestic with J. Roome Lewis
Corbett *(E. W.)* & Rounds *(Samuel A.)* wood and coal, 735 Brannan, dwl 195 Prospect Place
Corbett James, engineer, dwl 1425 Mason
CORBETT JAMES, liquor saloon, 10 Sutter, dwl 34 Clary
Corbett John, salesman with Agard, Foulkes & Co. dwl SW cor First and Folsom
Corbett John, Head Quarters Saloon, 565 Market, dwl 739 Howard bet Fourth and Fifth
Corbett John C. dwl N s Sixteenth nr Guerrero
Corbett Lawrence, dwl N s Hayes nr Larkin
Corbett Malachi, laborer, dwl N s Salmon bet Mission and Taylor
Corbett Patrick, laborer, dwl 1721 Leavenworth
Corbett Patrick J. hackman, Plaza, dwl 24 Perry
Corbett Richard, dwl What Cheer House
Corbett Thomas, clerk with Hooker & Co. dwl 816 Bush
Corbitt William, dwl 81 Clementina
Corby Joseph, groceries and liquors, SW cor Stevenson and Sixth
Corbyn Harry, laborer, Volunteer Engine Co. No. 7
Corbyn Sheridan, theatrical manager, dwl 213 Ritch
Coreetia François, dwl 721 Pacific
Corcoran Daniel, laborer, dwl 266 Jessie
Corcoran Daniel P. tailoring, 4 California
Corcoran David, porter, 309 Sacramento, dwl 361 Minna
Corcoran Dennis, mariner, dwl Beale Place
Corcoran Frank E. stocks and money, office 605 Montgomery, dwl 1801 Stockton
Corcoran John, laborer, dwl 529 Mission
Corcoran John, laborer, dwl 5 Lafayette Place
Corcoran Mary Miss, domestic, 810 Folsom

Corcoran Michael, express wagon cor California and Montgomery
Corcoran Patrick, laborer with Thomas Corey, dwl 12 Broadway
Corcoran William, contractor and builder, dwl 323 Pine
Corcoran William, porter, 116 Cal, dwl 1334 Pacific
Corcory William, laborer, dwl 1120 Kearny, rear
Cord George W. furniture, dwl 92 Everett
Cordan Anton C. hair dresser, 129 Third, dwl E s Montgomery bet Broadway and Vallejo
Cordes Allrich J. F. groceries and liquors, NE cor Pacific and Powell, dwl SW cor Broadway and Octavia
Cordes C. H. Union Saloon, 17 Fremont, dwl 20 Natoma
Cordes Claus H. Blue House Exchange, 1007 Bat
Cordes Hermann *(L. Feldmann & Co.)* 211 California, dwl E s Calhoun bet Green and Union
Cordes John *(Bredhoff & C.)* SE cor Pacific and Drumm
Cordes John, groceries, cor Powell and Pacific, dwl cor Broadway and Octavia
Cordes *(William)* & Vinken *(Frederick)* groceries and liquors and restaurant, cor King and Third, dwl cor Bush and Pierce
CORDES WILLIAM, liquor saloons, 145 Stewart SE cor King and Third and W s Main nr Harrison, and groceries and liquors NW cor Bush and Pierce
Cordillera G. & S. M. Co. office 321 Washington
Cordiner C. L. merchant tailor, 208 Montgomery
Cordiviola Stefano, tailor, 1106 Dupont
Cordona Antonio, vegetable garden, Visitacion Valley
Cordouan Felix, wines and liquors, 643 Broadway
Cords Henry, laundryman, dwl E s Jansen bet Lombard and Greenwich
Cordy Mathew, laborer, dwl 29 Jessie
Core Thomas, liquor saloon S s Folsom bet Beale and Main
Coret F. P. laundryman, E s Sixth bet Brannan and Bryant
Coret Mme. dwl 1314 Dupont
Corey Oliver, seaman, steamer Pacific
Corey Thomas, stoves and tinware 204 Pacific, dwl 813 Harrison
Corey William, coachman, dwl W s Wetmore Place
Corfield Thomas, laborer with William Buckley
Corgill G. dwl Original House
Corkey Elizabeth Miss, domestic, dwl 620 Green
Corkey Hannah Miss, domestic, dwl 620 Green
Corkey Mary Miss, domestic 719 Post
Corkry William, stone mason, dwl SE cor Vallejo and Kearny
Corlett William, pilot steamer Chrysopolis, dwl 221 Green
Corley Lewis, laborer, boards with Joseph Seale, N s Turk nr Fillmore
Corley William *(Stewart & C.)* dwl S s Geary bet Kearny and Dupont
Corliss A. carpenter with James Brokaw, dwl 566 Mission
Corliss Ellen A. (widow) dwl 408 Folsom
Corliss William B. house painter, 156 Perry
Corli Jerry, laborer, boards with Joseph Seale, N s Turk nr Fillmore
Corlut Frank, cook, 104 Second
Cornahrens Herman, groceries and liquors, NE cor Howard and Sixth
Corneen Richard, driver with John Agnew, 26 Kearny
Cornelissen Edward *(John Offerman & Co.)* dwl NE cor Dupont and Pacific
Cornelius Gustav, clerk, 520 Broadway
Cornelius John F. dwl 424 Fremont
Cornelius Louis, waiter, 407 Cal, dwl 20 Everett
Cornell Charles M. carpenter, NW cor Second and Tehama

CORNELL CHAUNCEY, justice of the peace third township, office 526 Montgomery, dwl 1226 Sacramento

Cornell George, painter, dwl 1 Noble Place

Cornell Herbert S. salesman, 411 Montgomery, dwl 47 Belden Block

Cornell Jacob H. master steamer Sacramento, res Alameda

Cornell Meriba Miss, matron Deaf, Dumb, and Blind Institution, SE cor Fifteenth and Mission

Cornell Patrick, deck hand, steamer Yosemite

Cornell Richard, carrier, Alta California

Cornell William C. clerk with G. H. Grey, 621 Clay, dwl 1226 Sacramento

Cornell, see Connell

Corneps Hermann, packer, Golden Gate Mills, 430 Pine, dwl 629 Green

Corner J. H. laborer, Bay Sugar Refinery, dwl SW cor Battery and Green

Cornfoot David, molder, apprentice, Vulcan Iron Works, dwl N s Mission nr Third

Cornfoot Henry, mariner, dwl S s Shipley nr Fifth

Corning Burr W. tinsmith with J. W. Brittan & Co. dwl 126 St. Mark Place

Corning James, canvasman, Wilson's Circus

Cornish Henry C. (col'd) second hand furniture, 622 Battery

Cornish S. C. commercial reporter Evening Bulletin, dwl American Exchange

Corno Paul, captain steam tug Rabboni, dwl 406 Eddy

Cornor C. W. Melter and Refiner's Department U. S. Branch Mint, dwl 1048 Folsom

Cornor Charles W. shoe maker, 304 Pine, dwl NW cor Seventh and Folsom

Cornwall George, fireman, S. F. & San José R. R. dwl 456 Jessie

CORNWALL PIERRE B. stock broker, office 608 Merchant, dwl 1121 Stockton

Cornwall W. A. attorney at law, room 48 Exchange Building, dwl 1423 Kearny

Cornwell Morris A. deputy gauger, dwl 17 Dupont

CORNYNN JAMES, proprietor Central House, 814 and 816 Sansom

Cornynn Mortimer, Central House, 113 and 115 First

Cornyns Laurence, calker, dwl W s Gilbert bet Brannan and Townsend

CORONER CITY AND COUNTY SAN FRANCISCO, Stephen R. Harris, office 7 Court Block 636 Clay

CORPORATION YARD, Fire Department, City and County San Francisco, Wm. Free superintendent, 15 and 17 First

Corr David, with Painter & Co. dwl 2 Clementina

Corr William, gardener, dwl 818 Folsom

Corrard Eugene, New York Baths, 738 Pacific

Correll John J. carpenter, dwl 2 Winter Place

Corrigan Andrew, laborer, dwl W s White Place nr Bryant

Corrigan Ann Miss, domestic, dwl 918 Stockton

Corrigan Eliza (widow) dwl E s Bower Place

Corrigan John, works with James Glasgow

Corrigan Mary (widow) dwl 238 Jessie

Corrigan William, dwl 720 Market

Corsen Charles, laborer, dwl W s August Alley nr Green

Corson H. dwl What Cheer House

Cortaye Edward, stevedore, dwl 26 Stewart

Cortes Benjamin V. assistant receiver, Spring Valley W. W. Co. dwl 2 Chatham Place

Cortez American Silver M. Co. office 8 Stevenson House

Cortez Charles, drayman, dwl 13 Hinckley

Cortez G. & S. M. Co. office 36 Exchange Building

Corthay Louis C. (Deloche & C.) dwl Market bet Sixth and Seventh

Corthey C. J. calker, dwl 54 First

Cortis A. J. book binder, 522 Montgomery, dwl 1819 Stockton

Corwin James, plasterer, dwl 331 Bush

Corwin Joseph R. clerk with James McCabe, 625 Merchant, dwl 420 Dupont

Cory Isaac H. salesman with Hooker & Co. 117 Cal

Cosala Charles, dwl nr Bay View Park

Coshie H. S. C. collar maker with Kreitz & Cosbie, dwl 36 Battery

Cosbie William (Kreitz & C.) dwl 36 Battery

Cosette S. & C. M. Co. office 804 Montgomery

Cosgriff Charles, blacksmith with W. Shear, dwl SW cor Mission and Sixteenth

Cosgriff Charles P. blacksmith, dwl 24 Kearny

Cosgriff Henry, hostler with Dr. H. S. Gates, dwl S s Sutter bet Devisidero and Broderick

Cosgrove Bernard J. blacksmith, dwl Vigilant Engine House

Cosgrove Bridget Miss, domestic, 809 Stockton

Cosgrove Daniel, driver, Central R. R. Co. dwl S s Brannan bet Sixth and Seventh

Cosgrove Edward, clerk, International Hotel

Cosgrove Edward, laborer, dwl 511 Mission

Cosgrove Edward, warehouseman, New Orleans Warehouse, dwl Union House

Cosgrove Elizabeth Miss, domestic, dwl 847 Howard

Cosgrove Eveline (widow) dwl NE cor Union and Kearny

Cosgrove F. conductor, Omnibus R. R. Co

Cosgrove Felix, butcher, dwl SW cor Bryant and White Place

Cosgrove Hugh, plasterer, dwl W s Jansen bet Greenwich and Lombard

Cosgrove Jacob, fireman, steamer Julia, dwl 617 Davis

Cosgrove James, furniture wagon, cor Montgomery and California, dwl United States Hotel

Cosgrove James, speculator, dwl 558 Howard

Cosgrove James B. painter, dwl NE cor Union and Kearny

Cosgrove John, apprentice, 620 Merchant, dwl NE cor Union and Kearny

Cosgrove John, assistant engineer, P. M. S. S. Co

Cosgrove John, fireman, steamer Julia

Cosgrove John, longshoreman, bds 123 Jackson

Cosgrove John, painter, dwl 112 Jackson

Cosgrove Joseph, painter with B. L. Brandt, 322 Commercial

Cosgrove Kate Miss, domestic, 528 Ellis

Cosgrove Maria Miss, domestic, 1231 Stockton

Cosgrove Martin, driver, dwl 310 Folsom

Cosgrove Mary Miss, dwl 50 Silver

Cosgrove Mary Miss, domestic, 113 Stockton

Cosgrove Patrick, express wagon, cor Bush and Sansom

Cosgrove Patrick, fruits, 356 Third

Cosgrove Patrick, milk ranch, E s Folsom nr Precita Avenue

Cosgrove Patrick, packer with Haynes & Lawton, dwl 118 Ellis

Cosgrove Patrick, teamster with Stanyan & Co. dwl NE cor Polk and Austin

Cosgrove Philip, contractor, dwl 50 Silver

Cosgrove Thomas, laborer, Fort Point

Cosgrove William J. stone mason, dwl 9 Berry, rear

Coskery William, painter, dwl 624 Commercial

Cozla James, dwl 532 Bryant

COSMOPOLITAN HOTEL, Adelphi Hotel Co. proprietors, SW cor Bush and Sansom

Coso House, L. J. Ewell proprietor, 627 and 629 Commercial

Cossasa Andrea, bar keeper, dwl NE cor Broadway and Sansom

Coseboon Enoch T. driver Central R. R. dwl SE cor Sixth and Folsom

Costa Antoine, with J. Hirth & Co. 533 Com

Costa Frank, barber, 703 Front, dwl N s Vallejo bet Montgomery and Sansom

Costa G. liquors, 314 Pacific

Costa John, express wagon, dwl Union nr Powell

Costa John, fireman, dwl 29 Commercial

Coste L. dwl 631 Broadway
Costello Edward, lather, dwl 12 Sutter
Costello Samuel, proprietor Half Way House, Ocean House Road
Costello Thomas, repairer umbrellas, 118 Minna
Costello William H. confectioner, Eureka Hose Co. No. 4
Coster Thomas, coachman with James Bell, W s Folsom bet Eleventh and Twelfth
Costigan John, messenger, Cigar Inspector U. S. Int. Rev. Dept. dwl 319 Battery
Costigan Thomas, blacksmith, dwl 78 Natoma
Costlo Johanna (widow) dwl 303 Folsom
Coston John, miner, dwl 814 Sansom
Costudia Gabriel, coffee stand, NE cor Commercial and Leidesdorff
Cota John, with H. Casebolt & Co. dwl John near Pacific
Cotanato Peter, laborer, dwl W s Bower Place
Cotta Manuel, waiter, stmr Yosemite
Cotter Benjamin (col'd) whitewasher, dwl cor Jessie and Annie
Cotter Cornelius, cartman, dwl S s Eddy bet Polk and Larkin
Cotter Edward B. dwl 745 Clay
Cotter Frank, painter, dwl W s Leroy Place
Cotter Hannah (widow) dwl 429 Sutter
Cotter Jeremiah, laborer, dwl Union Court
Cotter John, laborer, dwl W s Larkin bet McAllister and Tyler
Cotter John C. merchant, dwl 518 Powell
Cotter William, laborer, dwl 1504 Mason
Cottle Franklin D. carpenter and builder, 42 Fremont, dwl 932 Howard
Cottle John, plasterer, dwl N s Pine bet Leavenworth and Hyde
Cotton Thomas J. clerk stmr Julia
Cotton Westerly, seaman, dwl 111 Washington
Cottrell Edward M. salesman with Wm. Meyer & Co. 636 Clay, dwl 734 Green
Cottrell Henry, cook, Sailors' Home, SW cor Battery and Vallejo
Coty John, carpenter, dwl 8 Bay State Row
Couch John, Mission Express, office 716 Kearny, dwl W s Guerrero bet Sixteenth and Seventeenth
Couch Thomas, machinist, Vulcan Iron Works, dwl 541 Mission
Coughlan Catharine Mrs. dwl 1118 Kearny, rear
Coughlan Patrick, laborer, dwl 13 Ohio
Coughlan Thomas, laborer, dwl 212 Fremont
Coughlen Ellen (widow) dwl nr S. F. Cordage Factory, Potrero
Coughlen Michael, laborer with Hey & Meyn
Coughlin Anna Miss, domestic, 112½ Pine
Coughlin Jeremiah, express wagon, dwl S s Brannan nr Sixth
Coughlin John, boiler maker, Union Foundry, dwl Empire House
Coughlin John, boot maker, dwl N s Sutter bet Montgomery and Kearny
Coughlin John, butcher with James Hurley, dwl 12 Sutter
Coughlin John, express wagon, SW cor Folsom and Eighth
Coughlin John I. cartman, 813 Sansom
Coughlin Michael, retortman, S. F. Gas Co
Coughlin Thomas, laborer, S. F. Gas Co
Coughlin William, laborer, dwl NW cor Vallejo and Sansom
Coughlin William B. laborer, dwl 1224 Jackson
Coughran Ann Miss, domestic, 626 Sutter
Cougot Charles, waiter, dwl 821 Kearny
Coulon Alphonse (Belle & C.) 408 Pine
Coulon Edmond, tailor, 1213 Dupont
Coulson Robert, paper hanger with Frank G. Edwards, dwl 717 Folsom
Coulter David, laborer, dwl E s Hyde bet Lombard and Greenwich

Coulter J. D. cabinet maker, dwl 647 Howard
Coulter Joseph, store keeper, International Hotel
Coulter M. Mrs. dwl SE cor Sixth and Clary
COUNTY ASSESSOR, office 22 first floor City Hall
COUNTY AUDITOR, office first floor City Hall
COUNTY CLERK, office 18 first floor City Hall
COUNTY CORONER, office 7 Court Block, 636 Clay
COUNTY JAIL, N s Broadway bet Kearny and Dupont
COUNTY JUDGE, office second floor City Hall
COUNTY RECORDER, office SE cor Kearny and Washington
COUNTY SURVEYOR, office third floor City Hall
COUNTY TREASURER, off first floor City Hall
County William, laborer, dwl 27 Stevenson
Coupland William F. hatter, 540 California
Courcelle Achille, wholesale and retail furniture, 820 Washington
Courier Joseph, boot maker, dwl 414 Market
Courley Ann Miss, domestic with John Wigmore
Cournel Louis, dwl 721 Pacific
Courneen Dennis, spinner Mission Woolen Mills, dwl with P. L. Murphy, E s Howard bet Fifteenth and Sixteenth
Courheen James, wool washer Mission Woolen Mills, dwl with P. L. Murphy, E s Howard bet Fifteenth and Sixteenth
COURRIER DE SAN FRANCISCO (Daily, Weekly, and Steamer) off 617 and 619 Sansom
Coursen Charles, laborer, dwl 1515 Dupont
Coursen G. A. salesman, dwl W s Leavenworth bet Sacramento and California
Courson Alfred, boatman, foot Market
COURT BLOCK, 636 Clay and 641 Merchant
COURT CIRCUIT U. S. rooms SW cor Montgomery and Jackson
COURT COMMISSIONER Fourth Judicial District, James M. Taylor, office 636 Clay
COURT COMMISSIONER Twelfth Judicial District, Robert C. Rogers, office 604 Merchant
COURT COMMISSIONER Fifteenth Judicial District, Harlow S. Love, office 540 Clay
COURT COUNTY, room 8 second floor City Hall
COURT DISTRICT FOURTH, room 8 second floor City Hall
COURT DISTRICT TWELFTH, room 2 second floor City Hall
COURT DISTRICT FIFTEENTH, room 16 second floor City Hall
COURT DISTRICT U. S. rooms SW cor Montgomery and Jackson
Court Job, compositor, Alta California
COURT JUSTICE'S First District, rooms 536 Pac
COURT JUSTICE'S Second District, rooms 623 Merchant
COURT JUSTICE'S Third District, rooms 528 Montgomery
COURT JUSTICE'S Fourth District, rooms 230 Bush
COURT JUSTICE'S Fifth District, rooms 613 Market
COURT JUSTICE'S Sixth District, rooms Valencia nr Sixteenth
COURT POLICE JUDGE'S, room 13 first floor City Hall
COURT PROBATE, room 18 second floor City Hall
COURT SESSIONS, room 8 second floor City Hall
Courtade Joseph, butcher, dwl 1402 Stockton
Courtaine Henry, actor, dwl 783 Market
Courtal Dominique, carpenter, dwl cor Pacific and Kearny
Courtenay Charles, house, sign, and ornamental painter, 10 Sutter, dwl 806 Union
Courtenay John E. sail maker with James A. Wright, 211 Sacramento, dwl 305 Montgomery
Courtis Thomas, real estate, dwl 515 Bush
Courtney John, stone cutter, dwl Minna bet Third and Fourth

Courtney Martin, tailor with Archibald McArthur, dwl 15 Everett
Courts John W. salesman, 651 Clay, dwl 3 Dupont
Consens Caleb N. sexton First Unitarian Church, dwl Julia Court
Consens George W. fruits, 817 Clay
Cousin Nicholas, dwl 1823 Stockton
Cousins C. laborer, dwl Original House
Cousins Charles S. assistant melter and refiner, U. S. Branch Mint, dwl 811 Stockton
Cousins James, ship carpenter, dwl S s Francisco bet Dupont and Stockton
Cousins William, brick mason, dwl S s Broadway bet Taylor and Jones
Couttolenc J. A. contractor and builder, dwl 9 Pinckney Place
Couture Joseph, porter with W. H. Keith & Co. dwl 528 Vallejo
Cove Robert, porter with Edward H. Parker, dwl ·W s Lafayette Avenue nr Howard
Covert Abraham M. dwl E s Valencia nr Thirteenth
Covert Stephen H. painter, dwl 556 Bryant
Covet F. P. laundry, Sixth bet Bryant and Brannan
Covey Harris R. (Porter & C.) dwl Russ House
Covington Elam, office 604 Merchant third floor
Cowan Bennett, clothing, dwl 13 Natoma
Cowan Charles, peddler, dwl 943 Kearny
Cowan H. A. dwl 12 Sutter
Cowan Hugh, restaurant, dwl 8 Broadway
Coward H. G. dwl Russ House
Cowell Ellen Miss, domestic, 113 O'Farrell
Cowell Henry (Davis & C.) office 11 Phœnix Building SW cor Sansom and Jackson
Cowell J. G. accountant with Davis & Cowell, dwl SE cor Montgomery and Vallejo ·
Cowen Annie (widow) dwl 662 Howard
Cowen B. (H. & B. Cowen) dwl 13 Natoma
Cowen H. & B. clothing, 327 East
Cowen Marks. tailor, dwl 408 Pacific
COWEN WILLIAM J. Custom House Exchange, 500 Battery cor Washington
Cowes J. C. (col'd) steward, dwl 355 First
Cowes Robert N. (col'd) dwl 355 First
Cowie James S. cook, Davis Laundry, W s Harriet bet Howard and Folsom
Cowing Turner, dwl 323 First
Cowles Charles P. clerk, dwl 311 Brannan
Cowles Juan, vegetable gardener, W s Mission nr Twenty-Sixth
COWLES SAMUEL, judge County Court, room 8 City Hall second floor, chambers 18 third floor, dwl S s Erie bet Howard and Mission
Cowley Edward J. jr. clerk with George H. Butcher, dwl 439 Minna
Cowper William H. clerk with J. W. Sullivan
Cox & Rose G. & S. M. Co. office 302 Montgomery
Cox Abraham (col'd) (Peck & C.) dwl 5 Bdwy
Cox Anna M. Mrs. boarding, 138 Fourth
Cox Benjamin, with Treadwell & Co. 204 Battery
Cox Catharine Miss, domestic, 904 Jackson
Cox Cecilia Madame (col'd) hair dresser, 441 Bush
Cox Daniel, dwl 202 Davis
Cox Edward D. paper carrier, dwl NW cor Dupont and St. Mark Place
Cox Edwin, engineer steamer Sacramento
Cox Emma Mrs. dwl 757 Mission
Cox George, clerk, Pier 19 Stewart, dwl 31 Everett
Cox H. J. dwl 115 First ·
Cox James F. mariner, dwl 138 Fourth
COX (James W.) & NICHOLS (A. C.) commission hides, leather, oils, and tallow, 422 Battery, dwl N s Thirteenth nr Howard ·
COX (Jerome B.) & ARNOLD (Thomas J.) contractors Western Pacific Railroad, office 240 Montgomery, dwl 1109 Folsom
Cox John, bricklayer, dwl 13 Front
Cox John, laborer, dwl 10 Jessie
Cox John, laborer, San Francisco Gas Co

Cox Joseph, cigars and tobacco, 210 Montgomery, dwl 211 Bush
Cox Leander, assistant engineer steamer Pacific, dwl 938 Dupont
Cox Maria, chambermaid, Railroad House
Cox Mathew B. superintendent Pacific Mail Steam Ship Co. Folsom St. Wharf, dwl 566 Howard
Cox Palmer, artist, dwl 40 Tehama
Cox Patrick, paver, North Beach & M. R. R
Cox William B. groceries and liquors, SE cor Third and Bryant
Cox William J. dwl 318 Davis ·
Coye Hiram L. (Rockwell, C. & Co.) dwl 807 Greenwich
Coye Lewis, miner, dwl 532 Commercial
Coyle Henry, boot maker, 356½ Third
Coyle Hugh, lab, dwl N s Thirteenth nr Valencia ·
Coyle James, drayman, Pier 5 Stewart, dwl 629 Post
Coyle James W. with H. Casebolt & Co. dwl cor Clay and Larkin
Coyle John, laborer, dwl 779 Folsom
Coyle Mary, domestic, dwl 430 Bryant
Coyle Mathew, box maker, dwl 9 Natoma
Coyle Peter, morocco leather dresser with J. J. Grady, dwl cor Folsom and Eighteenth
Coyle Michael, machinist, Pacific Foundry, dwl 24 Natoma
Coyne John, tinsmith with M. Prag, dwl 109 Minna
Crabb Alexander, compositor, Evening Bulletin, dwl 122 Silver
Crabb Pierre, laborer, dwl S s Liberty bet Townsend and Brannan
Crach P. capt. schooner Artful Dodger, off 413 East
Craddock Charles F. clerk with Judge H. J. Wells, dwl 623 Merchant
Craff Henry, miner, dwl 219 California
Craffrey Edward, waiter, dwl 21 Stevenson
Craft John, dwl SW cor Kearny and Pacific
Crafts Ellen B. assistant teacher, Grace Institute, dwl 1020 Stockton
Crafts Henry, dwl W s Howard nr Thirteenth
Cragin Martin, laborer, dwl 129 Pacific
Craig Alexander, driver with Craig, Golden & Yung, dwl 108 Powell
Craig Benjamin F. carpenter, dwl 574 Folsom
Craig Bridget, domestic, 731 Folsom
Craig H. dwl What Cheer House
Craig James, carpenter, dwl 19 Silver
Craig John, carriage maker, dwl Bryant Place
Craig John, salesman, dwl N s Townsend bet Second and Third
Craig John, ship joiner, dwl 150 Silver
Craig Julia Miss (col'd) domestic, 235 Geary
Craig J. W. (P. C. Craig & Co.) dwl 305 Third
Craig Louisa Miss, domestic, 712 Pine
Craig Michael, lather, dwl 351 Tehama
Craig P. C. & Co. (J. W. Craig) New England Sewing Machines, 305 Third
Craig Robert, laborer, dwl 141 Shipley
Craig (Peter) Golden (Thomas) & Yung (Nicholas) undertakers, 705 Market, dwl 108 Powell
CRAIG WILLIAM, wholesale and retail wines and liquors, 305 Dupont, dwl 25 John ·
Craig William H. carpenter, bds 423 Stevenson
Craik John, clerk with Dickson, De Wolf & Co. 412 Battery
CRAINE WILLIAM, architect, office 634 Washington ·
Craiten Peter, laborer, dwl 27 Battery
Cram Elizabeth (widow) dwl 815 Bush
Cram Mary A. Mrs. seamstress, dwl NE cor Fifth and Clara
Cram William R. harness maker, 557 Market, dwl 60 Jessie
Cramer Charles L. (Bayley & C.) dwl 239 Jessie
Cramer John, butcher, dwl 32 Everett, rear
Cramer V. & Co. merchants, 310 Sacramento,· dwl 1231 Stockton

Cramers Olivia Miss, domestic, dwl 852 Mission
Cramp Martha S. (widow) dwl 331 Beale
Crandall Henry B. teacher Deaf, Dumb, and Blind Institute, SE cor Fifteenth and Mission
Crandall Charles, dwl 608 Third
Crane Albert E. merchant and stock broker, dwl 1314 Washington
Crane A. M. *(Tompkins & C.)* attorney at law, office 620 Merchant, res Alameda
Crane Catherine Miss, domestic, 28 Rincon Place
Crane Erwin J. commission merchant, office 321 Front, bds 532 Pine
Crane George, dwl 5 Hardie Place
CRANE *(Henry A.)* & BRIGHAM *(William H.) (James Riddel and George W. Fisher)* importers and wholesale druggists, SE corner Front and Clay, dwl 719 Sutter
Crane Israel, commission merchant, 308 Commercial, bds Lick House
Crane James C. clerk, dwl 534 Kearny
Crane James H. silver plater, dwl S s Pacific bet Powell and Mason
Crane Jeremiah, shoe maker, dwl E s Main bet Folsom and Harrison
Crane John, compositor, California Farmer, dwl 23 Main
Crane S. E. broker, dwl 834 Clay
Crane Thomas, merchant, dwl Cosmopolitan Hotel
Crane William, book keeper, dwl 561 Howard
Crane William, laborer, dwl 48 Louisa
Crane William T. laborer with William J. Kingsley
Crane W. W. jr. attorney at law, office 6 Wells' Building, 605 Clay, res Oakland
Crane, see Craine
Craner A. P. & Co. *(George Aronson)* pawnbrokers, 110 Kearny, dwl 339 Tehama
Cranert Frederick, hatter, 510 Bush
Cranford George, dwl with Jason Wight
Crangle William C. boatman, foot Market
Cranna William R. *(Dell, C. & Co.)* dwl 33 Park Avenue
Crannell Nicholas, tinsmith, W s Valencia bet Sixteenth and Seventeenth
Cranston A. B. office 622 Montgomery, dwl What Cheer House
Cranz Theodore D. cabinet maker with Goodwin & Co. dwl 505 Green
Crary J. O. B. merchant, dwl 1016 Stockton
Craven Anna Miss, domestic, 334 Beale
Craven Peter, boiler maker with Coffey & Risdon, dwl 117 Pine
Craver Jeremiah, carpenter, dwl S s Sixteenth bet Mission and Valencia
CRAWFORD A. & CO. ship chandlers and sail makers, 27 Market, dwl 508 Greenwich
Crawford Alice Mrs. lodgings, SW cor Stevenson and Second
Crawford Charles, driver, Omnibus R. R. Co. dwl 119 Jessie
Crawford George, laborer, Spring Valley W. W
Crawford *(James S.)* & Dutch *(William)* dentists, office 415 Montgomery
Crawl William, clerk, dwl 31 Main
CRAWLEY GEORGE W. Pacific R. R. House, 446 Brannan
Cray Patrick, laborer, dwl 116 Stevenson
Creagh Michael, boot maker, dwl NE cor Dupont and Francisco
Creamer Aaron, hair dressing saloon, American Exchange, dwl SE cor Sutter and Taylor
Creamer C. merchant, dwl 1231 Stockton
Creamer James, drayman with E. Martin & Co. dwl NW cor Washington and Hyde
Creamer Thomas, U. S. Revenue Cutter Wm. L. Marcy, dwl SE cor Fourth and Brannan
Creber Walter, brewer, Cincinnati Brewery
Creegan James, dwl 23 St. Ann
Creegan Peter, laborer, dwl 23 St. Ann
Creery J. J. collector, dwl 108 Virginia

Creigh J. D. attorney at law, office 604 Merchant, dwl 629 Sutter
Creigh S. W. clerk, steamer Yosemite, dwl S s Bush bet Mason and Taylor
Creighton Bridget (widow) domestic with Charles Welsh
Creighton Derby, mate, steamer Yosemite
Creighton James, deck hand, steamer Yosemite
Creighton Patrick, butcher, 240 Fourth, dwl 315 Tehama
Creighton Patrick, laborer, Ft. Alcatraz, dwl 1413 Kearny
Creighton Robert, real estate, dwl E s Hyde bet Clay and Washington
Creighton Terrence, seaman, dwl 24 Stevenson
Creighton William, bag maker, dwl 225 Minna
Crellim John *(Morgan & Co.)* res Oysterville, W. T
Crellin Thomas *(Morgan & Co.)* res Oysterville, W. T
Cremar John P. H. cooper, dwl N s Post bet Laguna and Buchanan
Cremer John, laborer, dwl S s Sixteenth bet Valencia and Mission
Crenan Michael, coach driver, International Hotel, dwl 8 Milton Place
Creon Amandos, book keeper, dwl 23 Dupont, rear
CRESCENT CITY LINE STEAMERS, California Steam Navigation Co. office NE cor Front and Jackson, and Ben Holladay, SW cor Front and Jackson
Crescent Quartz Mill Co. (Plumas Co.) office 311 Clay
Cressy Theodore S. clerk, 319 Washington, dwl 242 Clara
Crest Maghars, seaman, steamer Del Norte
Cretzer G. W. Monumental Engine Co. No. 6
Creuziger Hugo, upholsterer, dwl 317 Ritch
Crevling George W. cooper with Handy & Neuman, dwl Bay State House
Cribbin Patrick, hostler, 328 Bush
Crichton William, with Lewis & Neville, 113 Clay
Criggins Thomas, fruits, 125 Third cor Minna
Crim George L. dwl W s Howard bet Nineteenth and Twentieth
CRIM SAMUEL, live stock dealer, cor Washoe and Twenty-Second, dwl W s Howard bet Nineteenth and Twentieth
Crimmens William, blacksmith with Albert Folsom, dwl 23 Everett
Crinns William H. jr. salesman with Newhall, Brooks & Nettleton, dwl 22 Minna
Crippel John, stevedore, dwl 36 Stewart
Crippen Frederick I. clerk with J. H. Tobin, dwl 623 Howard
Crispin Thomas, helper, Pacific Foundry, dwl 224 Second
Critcher Henry, broker, office 606 Merchant, res Oakland
Crittenden Charles S. livery stable, 814 Mission
Crittenden Jane M. (widow) dwl 115 Perry
Croak Mary Miss, nurse, dwl 816 Filbert
Croce *(Peter E.)* & Giamboni *(Natale)* fruits and confectionery, SE cor Stockton and Clay
Crockard Hugh, shipsmith, dwl 910 Harrison
Crocker Charles W. reporter, dwl 1308 Powell
Crocker J. cabinet maker with J. Peirce, 417 California, dwl 744 Howard
Crocker John A. ship carpenter, dwl 327 Beale
Crocker Winslow, dwl 214 Powell
Crockett Consolidated G. & S. M. Co. office 728 Montgomery
CROCKETT, *(J. B.)* WHITING *(W. P. C.)* & WIGGINS *(W. W.)* attorneys at law, office 3-5 Exchange Building, res Alameda Co
Crockett John, clerk with Crockett, Whiting & Wiggins, res Alameda Co
Crofoot David O. photographic printer, Selleck's Gallery, 415 Montgomery, dwl 409 Green
Croftin Samuel, third pilot steamer Yosemite

Crofton James, deck hand, steamer Cornelia
Crofton John, blacksmith, bds Franklin Hotel, SE cor Sansom and Pacific
Crogan Ellen Miss, domestic, 121 Eddy
Crogan James, painter with Hopps & Kanary, dwl 331 Bush
Croke James Very Rev. rector St. Mary's Cathedral, cor Cal and Dupont, dwl 602 Dupont
Croly Jeremiah, laborer, dwl N s Seventeenth bet Dolores and Church
Croman Robert, works with Hermann Buerfind
Cromar James, dwl 331 Bush
Crombie John H. tinsmith with J. W. Brittan & Co. dwl 233 First
Cromer Henry, Melter and Refiner's Department, U. S. Branch Mint, dwl 769 Folsom
Cromer Jacob, carpenter, dwl NW cor Third and Stevenson
Cromer Nathaniel, butcher, dwl Potrero nr Brannan Street Bridge
Cromode Edward, carpenter, dwl 545 Mission
Crompton John, fireman, steamer Cornelia, dwl 15 Everett
Cromwell Charles P. dwl 320 Lombard
Cromwell R. G. (col'd) hairdresser, dwl 524 Folsom
Cron (Adalbert) & Co. fruits, 18 Occidental Market, dwl 673 Mission
Cronan Cornelius, shoe maker with Thomas Dolliver, dwl 84 Stevenson
Cronan Daniel, laborer, dwl 14 Jessie
Cronan David, laborer, bds Franklin House
Cronan Edward, miner, dwl SE cor Union and Calhoun
Cronan John, helper, Pacific Foundry, dwl 541 Mission
Cronan John, miner, bds Franklin House, SW cor Sansom and Broadway
Cronan John, wines and liquors, 710 Battery, dwl 207 Pacific
Cronan Michael, butcher, Folsom Street Market, SW cor Folsom and Folsom Avenue
Cronan Michael, laborer, dwl 131 Shipley
Cronan Peter, carriage painter with Stein, Link & Scherb, dwl SE side Dale bet McAllister and Tyler
Cronan Thomas, liquor saloon, 119 Kearny
Cronan William, metal roofer with John Kehoe, 228 Bush
Croner Hannah Miss, domestic with Thos. Stealey
Cronin Cornelius, molder, Pacific Foundry, dwl E s First bet Howard and Mission
Cronin Dennis, hostler, 960 Howard
Cronin Ellen Miss, domestic, 926 Jackson
Cronin Hannah Miss, domestic, 1002 Pine
Cronin James, baker, Love's Bakery, dwl 76 Jessie
Cronin John, dwl W s Capp bet Eighteenth and Nineteenth
Cronin John, laborer, dwl Filbert nr Montgomery
Cronin John, lab, dwl SW cor Capp and Nineteenth
Cronin Josephine Miss, liquor saloon, 249 Third
Cronin Martin, machinist, Union Foundry, dwl 18 Baldwin Court
Cronin Michael, clerk, American Bakery, dwl 1027 Dupont
Cronin P. J. harness maker, 219 Davis, dwl Franklin House
Croning Margaret, domestic, dwl 637 Folsom
CRONISE TITUS F. editorial department Mercantile Gazette and proprietor Stock Circular, office 536 Clay, dwl 103 Powell
Cronise W. H. V. office 536 Clay, dwl 526 Green
Crook Mary Miss, domestic, 456 Natoma
Crook Richard, drayman, dwl N s Sutter bet Larkin and Polk
Crooker William, professor music, dwl Lutgen's Hotel
Crooker W. L. dwl 226 Sutter
Crooks (D. W.) & Magilton (Thomas) lumber, SW cor Folsom and Main, dwl 311 Beale

Crooks James, dwl NE cor Post and Octavia
Crooks John, clerk, 8 Occidental Market, dwl NE cor Post and Octavia
Crooks Mathew, real estate, dwl W s Crook bet Brannan and Townsend
Crooks Richard, drayman with Samuel Adams, dwl Sutter nr Polk
Crooks Robert, drayman, 11 Clay, dwl N s Stevenson nr Third
Crooks Samuel, dwl Bush Street House
Crooks Samuel M. hackman, dwl 627 Commercial
Crooks Sarah Miss, dwl 13 Ellis
Crooks William, dwl 512 Hyde
Croon Francis, store keeper with Koopmanschap & Co. dwl S s Vallejo bet Mont and Sansom
Cropper T. B. teamster with Justus Bepler
Crosbey George, dwl What Cheer House
Crosby Daniel A. attorney at law, dwl 619 Bush
Crosby F. W. & Co. impts and jobbers watches, diamonds, jewelry, etc. 638 Clay, dwl 519 Folsom
Crosby George, clerk with Humphrey & Co. 104 Clay, dwl 727 O'Farrell
Crosby George O. produce, 104 Clay, dwl 727 O'Farrell
Crosby Henry R. clerk Twelfth L. H. District, C. H. dwl Brooklyn Hotel
Crosby James, cook, dwl 215 Broadway
Crosby John, tailoring, 610 Montgomery
CROSBY L. stock broker, office 36 Exchange Building, dwl with Wm. W. Knight
Crosby Peter, express wagon, corner Kearny and Market
Crosby William, farmer, dwl corner Valencia and Eighteenth
Crosett James F. compositor with Dewey & Co
Crosett James L. (H. T. Felton & Co.) dwl E s Second bet DeBoom and Bryant
Croshe Pierre, proprietor garden, Old San José Road E Industrial School
CROSKEY (Robert) & HOWARD (Irwin) groceries and liquors, SE cor Franklin and Hayes, Hayes' Valley
Crosley John W. salesman with Treadwell & Co. dwl 509 Bush
Croslow James, laborer, dwl 16 Taylor, rear
CROSS (Alexander) & CO. (John Wedderspoon) commission merchants, 625 Sansom, warehouse 611-615 Battery, res Valparaiso, S. A
Cross Donald, machinist, dwl 54 First
Cross Frederick L. salesman 217 Montgomery, dwl 550 Mission
Cross Frank, laborer, dwl 114 Jackson
Cross Horatio, miner, dwl 704 Folsom
Cross Richard, teamster with Dickson, DeWolf & Co. dwl 327 Broadway
Cross Thomas, lithographic printer, dwl 327 Bdwy
Cross William, clerk, dwl Central House, 814 San
Cross William, driver Central R. R. Co. dwl NW cor Brannan and Sixth
Crossin John, butcher with B. E. Arnold, dwl cor Tenth and Bryant
Crothers James, miner, dwl 931 Kearny
Croty Annie Miss, domestic, 532 Pine
Crouch Daniel L. foreman molder San Francisco Iron Works, dwl 54 First
Crouch James, cigar maker, dwl W s Jasper Place nr Filbert
Croué A. superintendent French Hospital
Croughwell Eugene, harness maker with C. H. Mead, dwl 115 Washington
Crouse John R. importer and dealer groceries, SE cor Sansom and Clay, dwl 246 Fourth
Croutzeille Adolph, butcher, dwl N s Minna bet Eighth and Ninth
Crouz (Charles) & Littlebridge, wood and coal yard, dwl 737 Green
Crovat Maria (widow) dwl 314 Minna
Crow Allen D. with Cameron, Whittier & Co. dwl Columbia Hotel

Crow Hubert F. clerk with Castle Bros. dwl 316 Fourth

Crow James, plasterer, dwl 313 Geary, rear

Crow Johanna, housekeeper with John McNamara, E s Valencia nr Thirteenth

Crowe D. H. book keeper, Pacheco Warehouse Co. 402 Front, dwl SW cor Stockton and Ellis

CROWE (John) & FARRELL (Michael) undertakers, 709 Market

Crowe Margaret (widow) dwl 6 Brown Alley

Crowe Timothy, locksmith and bell hanger, 659 Mission

Crowell Charles I. book keeper with Hosmer, Goewey & Co. dwl 724 Howard

Crowell Eugene (Langley, C. & Co.) resides New York

Crowell George E. machinist, dwl 419 Fremont

Crowell Harris, cigars, dwl 314 Sixth

Crowell Henry, with Feaster & Co. dwl 126 Bush

Crowell Hiram, carpenter, dwl W s Leavenworth bet Sacramento and California

Crowell Horatio, seaman, dwl 10 Stewart

Crowell James P. dentist, dwl 139 Fourth

Crowell Mary A. Mrs. dwl 19 Natoma

Crowell Prentiss Capt. wharfinger Rincon Point Dock, dwl SW cor Third and Market

Crowell William L. salesman with A. Roman & Co. dwl 930 Clay

Crowell Zenas, book keeper California Insurance Co. 318 California, dwl 530 Pine

Crowl James, plumber with Thomas Day, 732 Montgomery, dwl cor Lombard and Stockton

Crowlan Michael, stone cutter, dwl 176 Minna

Crowlen James, laborer, dwl 541 Mission

Crowley Ann (widow) dwl 334 Third

Crowley Bridget Miss, domestic, dwl 10 John

Crowley Bridget M. Miss, domestic, dwl 828 Pacific

Crowley Catharine Miss, domestic, 634 Broadway

Crowley Catherine, domestic, 762 Howard

Crowley Charles, laborer, American Exchange

Crowley C. J. machinist, dwl 426 Folsom

Crowley Cornelius, fruits, SW cor Clay and Battery, dwl 334 Third

Crowley Daniel, blacksmith Omnibus R. R. Co. dwl W s Leroy Place bet Sacramento and Clay

Crowley Daniel, laborer, dwl NE cor Washington and Leavenworth

Crowley Daniel, laborer Market St. R. R. dwl N s Seventeenth bet Mission and Howard

Crowley Daniel A. teacher, dwl 213 Beale

Crowley David, teamster with James McDevitt, dwl W s Sansom bet Broadway and Vallejo

Crowley Ellen Miss, domestic, 114 Mason

Crowley Ellen T. (widow) dwl 21 Clementina

Crowley Florence, carpenter, dwl 670 Harrison

Crowley James, lab, North Beach & M. R. R. Co

Crowley James F. prompter Italian Opera, Academy Music

Crowley James F. carpenter, dwl 331 Bush

Crowley Joanna, domestic with P. E. Bowman, dwl SW cor Broadway and Montgomery

Crowley Johanna Miss, domestic with A. Dott, N s Oak bet Franklin and Gough

Crowley Johannah Miss, domestic, 1208 Sac

Crowley John, boiler helper, Pacific Foundry, dwl 75 Natoma

Crowley John, calker, dwl Manhattan Engine H

Crowley John, cartman, dwl Natoma nr Fifth

Crowley John, cartman, dwl 443 Minna

Crowley John, deck hand, steamer Yosemite, dwl 20 Rousch, rear

Crowley John, groom, dwl 23 Jessie

Crowley John, laborer, dwl 115 First

Crowley John, laborer, dwl 239 Minna, rear

Crowley John, laborer, dwl 269 Stevenson

Crowley John, letter carrier, Post Office, dwl 55 Clementina

Crowley John, waiter, Occidental Hotel

Crowley John, watch maker, 422 Folsom

Crowley John C. miner, dwl W s Laskie bet Eighth and Ninth

Crowley John D. carpenter, dwl 157 Shipley

Crowley John D. pantryman steamer Julia

Crowley John J. meat market, N s Sixteenth nr Valencia, dwl S s Sixteenth nr Valencia

Crowley Julia Miss, domestic, 617 Bush

Crowley Julia Miss, domestic, 209 Jones

Crowley Margaret Miss, domestic with P. Johnson, Serpentine Avenue nr San Bruno Road

Crowley Margaret Miss, domestic with Mrs. Michael Graney, S s Brannan bet Seventh and Eighth

Crowley Mary, domestic, 732 Howard

Crowley Mary Miss, domestic, 311 Stockton

Crowley Michael, laborer, dwl N s Bernard bet Jones and Leavenworth

Crowley Michael, seaman, dwl 405 Green

Crowley M. J. pantryman steamer Yosemite

Crowley Patrick, constable First Township, office 536 Pacific, dwl 314 Green

Crowley Richard, with C. S. Nav. Co. Broadway Wharf

Crowley Richard, blacksmith, dwl E s Sansom bet Broadway and Pacific

Crowley Richard, stevedore, dwl 516 Mission

Crowley Timothy, cartman, dwl 25 Rincon Place

Crowley Timothy, drayman, dwl W s Rassette Place No. 1

Crowley Timothy, laborer, dwl 126 Pacific

Crown Charles, mariner, dwl 32 Stewart

Crown Harris, cigars, 414 Sac, dwl 314 Sixth

Crown Lead G. M. Co. office 406 Montgomery

CROWN POINT G. & S. M. CO. office 708 Montgomery

Crown Point Ravine G. & S. M. Co. (Gold Hill) office 7 Government House

Crownan Cornelius, laborer, dwl 156 First

Crowne E. clerk with Livingston & Hickey, dwl 178 Minna

Crowninshield Jacob, with Louis R. Lull, dwl 927 Washington

Crowninshield William B. express wagon, cor Clay and Sansom

Crowt John, harness maker with J. M. Hurlbutt & Co. 407 Battery

Crowther George T. dwl 22 Clara

Croz Peul, butcher with Z. Hebert, dwl Hampshire nr Santa Clara

Crozade Alphonse, billiard saloon, 713 Pacific, dwl 1027 Dupont

Crozat P. jobber cigars and tobacco, 613 Sansom, dwl W s Dupont bet Jackson and Wash

Croze Auguste, laundry, 231 Ritch

Crudden William, butcher with Crummie & O'Neill, dwl NW cor Jackson and Larkin

Cruise John, clerk with Stephen S. Smith, dwl E s First nr Bryant

Crummer H. B. clerk, 300 Montgomery, bds Brooklyn Hotel

Crummie James, butcher, dwl S s Folsom bet Ninth and Tenth

CRUMMIE (John) & O'NEILL (Hugh) wholesale butchers, Brannan Street Bridge, dwl S s Folsom nr Ninth

Crump William, cellarman with B. D. Wilson & Son

Cruse William, laborer, dwl 30 Jane

Crussell Frank, locksmith, Summer St. House

Crutchley Mary E. (widow) dwl 1027 Minna

Cruver Henry, drayman, dwl cor Leavenworth and Jackson

Cruz Henry, groceries, 56 Clay, dwl SE cor Turk and Larkin

Cruz Pedro, with Cutting & Co. dwl 402 Green

Cruze (Charles) & Co. (Sheffield Lillibridge) wood and coal, 531 Pine, dwl 737 Green

Cryer Charles, engineer, dwl 231 Minna

Cryer Clara Miss, cloak maker with L. Leszynsky, dwl 231 Minna

Cuba G. & S. M. Co. office 606 Montgomery

Cubbins Thomas, mason, dwl cor Virginia Avenue and Lundy Lane
Cuddy Francis, boiler maker, dwl 61 Natoma
Cuddy James, driver with Guttridge & Curtin, dwl NE cor Sixth and Jessie
Cuddy Patrick J. laborer with P. Taggert, dwl W s Florida nr Solano
Cuddy William, sail maker with James A. Wright, 211 Sacramento
Cudworth Abel W. dwl 1109 Kearny
Cudworth J. W. milk ranch, S s Presidio Road nr Laguna
Cue Mary, domestic, dwl 1312 Pine
Cue William, with Tay, Brooks & Backus, dwl 23 Stevenson, rear
Cuff Dennis, boot maker, N s Brannan bet Sixth and Seventh
Cuff Hannah Miss, domestic, 823 Post
Cuff Thomas, workman with I. Peirson, N s Sixteenth nr Nebraska
Culbert Alexander, mariner, dwl 32 Stewart
Culbert James, cook, Original House Restaurant
Culfer Patrick, groom, dwl E s Main nr Market
Cullen Charles, conductor, North Beach & M.R.R. Co. dwl 207 Fourth
Cullen J. laborer, Spring Valley W. W
Cullen James, dyer, Mission Woolen Mills
Cullen Jeffery, with B. Davidson & Berri, dwl N s Lombard bet Leavenworth and Jones
Cullen Lizzie Miss, domestic with A. Hollub, SW cor Laguna and Tyler
Cullen Lizzy Mrs. with Samuel Hill, 111 Montgomery, dwl 526 Pine
Cullen Margaret Miss, domestic with A. Hollub, SW cor Laguna and Tyler
Cullen Michael, laborer, dwl S s Fourteenth nr Folsom
Cullen Patrick, helper, Union Foundry, dwl E s Gilbert bet Sixth and Seventh
Cullen Philip, laborer, dwl 22 Jessie
Cullen Philip, retortman, S. F. Gas Co
Cullen Thomas, gunsmith with N. Curry & Bro. dwl 319 Bush
Cullen Thomas, liquor saloon and ball court, 543 Market
Cullen Thomas, machinist, Union Foundry, dwl National House
Cullens J. W. second hand furniture, 30 First
Culligan J. O. express wagon, dwl cor Third and Folsom
Culligan John, gardener, dwl 422 Brannan
Culligan T. laborer, Spring Valley W. W
Cullimore John, workman with John B. Wooster, SW cor Mission and Lafayette Avenue
Cullinan D. dwl 331 Bush
Cullinan John, O.S.F. teacher, St. Mary's Cathedral
Cullinane James, carpenter, dwl Meek Place
Cullum Frank, laborer, dwl 304 Jessie
Culon John L. carpenter, dwl 759 Mission
Culshaw William, cooper, dwl 52 Sacramento
Culver C. B. dwl 428 Bush
Culver Charles F. carpenter, dwl 636 Commercial
Culver James H. pattern maker, Pacific Foundry, dwl 4 Gustavus
Culver Willet, ornamental shrubbery, San Souci Valley, 3 miles W City Hall
Culver William H. attorney at law, dwl 722 Wash
Culver William H. sen. dwl W s Sixth bet Stevenson and Jessie
Culverwell Joseph E. teamster, 29 Fremont, dwl 227 Sixth
CULVERWELL STEPHEN S. manufacturer doors, sash, blinds, moldings, etc., 20, 29 and 31 Fremont, dwl 234 Sixth
Culverwell William, agent and accountant, 619 Merchant, dwl with W. M. Higgins
Cum Chong (Chinese) washing, 8 Stevenson
Cum Kee (Chinese) washing, 922 Kearny
Cum Sin (Chinese) washing, 327 Pine

Cumsky Alice (widow) dwl 810 Howard
Cumisky Henry, baker, dwl 1715 Leavenworth
Cummer George, seaman, dwl 52 Clay
Cumming George, machinist, Vulcan Iron Works, dwl 362 Third
Cumming James M. with P. F. Loughran & Co. dwl 506 Howard
Cumming John, lumber dealer, dwl 23 Minna
Cumming John, stock broker, 622 Montgomery, res Twelve Mile House
Cumming William H. deputy gauger, Custom House, dwl NE cor Natoma and Second
Cummings Alfred H. real estate, dwl 146 Silver
Cummings A. M. (widow) lodgings, 17. Third
Cummings C. A. Miss, assistant, Union Grammar School, dwl NE cor Stevenson and Third
Cummings C. F. clerk with Way & Keyt, 525 Merch
Cummings Daniel B. express wagon, cor Montgomery and Clay
Cummings Daniel F. carpenter, dwl Mariposa nr Carolina
Cummings Edward (Riley & Co.) dwl W s Eleventh bet Market and Mission
Cummings Edwin J. clerk with James McDonough, dwl 616 California
Cummings F. G. (W. B. Cummings & Co.) dwl 719 California
Cummings George F. dwl 414 Market
Cummings George S. book binder with Bartling & Kimball, dwl N s Folsom nr Fourth
Cummings G. Parker, architect, office 131 Mont
Cummings Harrison R. (Field & C.) dwl 10 Bagley Place
Cummings Henry K. commission fruit dealer, 415 and 417 Davis, dwl 517 Post
Cummings James, dwl What Cheer House
Cummings James, spinner, S. F. P. Woolen Mills, dwl Bay bet Larkin and Polk
Cummings James M. carpenter, dwl S s Union bet Taylor and Jones
Cummings Jane (widow) dwl N s Harrison bet Seventh and Eighth
Cummings John, coachman with W. Blackwell, NW cor Bryant and Grove Avenue
Cummings Joseph (col'd) laborer, dwl W s August Alley bet Green and Union
Cummings Loren, teamster, dwl N s Sixteenth nr Dolores
Cummings Mathew, laborer, dwl 12 Sutter
Cummings Patrick, clerk, NE cor Fifth and Clara
Cummings Patrick, foreman laborers, Donohue's Foundry, dwl 14 Mason
Cummings Patrick, horse shoer with Thomas Donlan, dwl 2 Berry
Cummings Patrick, laborer, dwl 12 Sherwood Place
Cummings Plympton, carpenter, dwl 1011 Mason
Cummings Richard, salesman, 6 Clay, dwl 8 Clay
Cummings Rose Ann, domestic, 510 Howard
Cummings Timothy, driver, Omnibus R. R. Co
Cummings Timothy, porter with Conroy & O'Connor, dwl 12 Sutter
CUMMINGS W. B. & CO. (F. G. Cummings) importers and commission merchants, 124 California, dwl 719 California
Cummings William, dwl 82 Natoma
Cummings William, deck hand, stm Chrysopolis
Cummings William C. stevedore, dwl 322 Green
Cummings William F. dwl 202 Second
Cummins James, spinner, Pioneer Woolen Mills, NW cor Beach and Larkin
Cummins Theresa (col'd) stewardess, dwl 1408 Mason
Cummisky Patrick, engineer, dwl 118 Minna
Cundliff James, porter, 538 Merchant
Cunihan Patrick, teamster, dwl 266 Stevenson
Cunio John, gardener, NE cor Laguna and McAllister
Cunito Charles, cook, dwl 939 Kearny
Cunliffe James, glass blower, Pacific Glass Works, dwl Potrero

Cunniff John, with Reynolds, Howell & Ford, dwl 1304 Powell
Cunniff Patrick, dwl Hubbard nr Howard
Cunningham A. H. (widow) dwl 456 Natoma
Cunningham Andrew, Banks O'Clyde Liquor Saloon, NE cor Sutter and Sansom
Cunningham Barbara Mrs. Oregon House, 238 Stewart
Cunningham Catharine Miss, domestic 959 Folsom
Cunningham Charles, laborer, dwl 330 Bush
Cunningham Charles C. steward Occidental Hotel
Cunningham D. hostler, Omnibus R. R. Co
Cunningham David, finisher, Excelsior Iron Works, dwl S s Third bet Howard and Folsom
Cunningham Francis, real estate, office 675 Market, dwl 623 Commercial
Cunningham James, boatman, dwl E s Main bet Folsom and Harrison
Cunningham James, engineer steamer Julia, dwl SW cor Louisiana and Sierra
Cunningham James, clerk, Daily Examiner, dwl 246 Tehama
Cunningham James, laborer, C. H. dwl 55 Jessie
Cunningham James, laborer, dwl 39 Clay
Cunningham James, miller, City Flour Mills, dwl 15 Ecker
Cunningham James, poultry and game, 14 Metropolitan Market, dwl 946 Mission
Cunningham James, real estate, dwl 652 Market
Cunningham John, with Levi Shilling
Cunningham John, bricklayer, dwl 30 Hunt
Cunningham John, carpenter, dwl S s Market bet Sixth and Seventh
Cunningham John, engineer, dwl with Frank Houston, E s Calhoun nr Green
Cunningham John, fruits, dwl 944 Kearny
Cunningham John, groom, dwl 12 Jessie
Cuaningham John, hide inspector, dwl NW cor Clay and Drumm
Cunningham John, horse shoer with S. B. Stickle
Cunningham John, laborer, dwl 32 Clementina
Cunningham John, mason, S. F. Gas Co
Cunningham John J. book keeper, 11 Montgomery, dwl 318 Minna
Cunningham Kate Miss, domestic, 1028 Bush
Cunningham Lindsey, collector with John G. Hodge & Co. dwl 456 Natoma
Cunningham Mary Miss, domestic, 407 O'Farrell
Cunningham Michael, ironer, Chelsea Laundry
Cunningham Michael, laborer, dwl NE cor Pacific and Kearny
Cunningham P. book keeper with M. Nolan, dwl 58 Minna
Cunningham Palmer, with James Brokaw, dwl Natoma bet First and Second
Cunningham Parlan R. carpenter, dwl 29 Minna
Cunningham Patrick, laborer, dwl 152 Shipley
Cunningham Patrick, silversmith, bds Franklin Hotel, SE cor Sansom and Pacific
Cunningham Peter, printer with Painter & Co. dwl 38 First
Cunningham Peter, waiter, St. Nicholas Hotel
Cunningham Robert, calker, dwl S s Sutter bet Dupont and Kearny
Cunningham Robert, clerk, Falkner, Bell & Co. dwl 456 Natoma
Cunningham Rose, dress maker, dwl 707 Mission
Cunningham Rose Miss, domestic, dwl 1820 Powell
Cunningham Samuel, engineer, dwl 15 Howard Court
Cunningham Simon D. watchman, U. S. Branch Mint, dwl W s Priest bet Clay and Washington
Cunningham Theodore B. real estate, office 55 Montgomery Block
Cunningham Thomas (Virginia City) dwl 318 Minna
Cunningham Thomas, clerk, dwl E s Havens Place
Cunningham Thomas, waiter, 626 Kearny, dwl 405 Dupont

Cunningham Thomas L. clerk, dwl 102 St. Mark Pl
Cunningham T. J. express wagon, cor Washington and Sansom
Cunningham William, New York Department Wells, Fargo & Co. dwl 456 Natoma
Cunningham William C. harness maker with Main & Winchester, dwl E s Capp bet Eighteenth and Nineteenth
Cunningham William W. dwl 1226 Bush
Cunningham William W. agent Daily and Weekly Examiner, dwl 246 Tehama
CUNNINGHAM Z. H. & CO. blacksmiths, 581 Market, dwl 137 Shipley
Cunningham ——, cabinet maker, dwl 29 Minna
Cunnington Margaret (widow) dwl 11 Pinckney Pl
Cunningworth John B. druggist and apothecary, 228 Pacific
Cnnnio Stephen, laborer, dwl W s Gaven nr Filbert
Cuong Chun (Chinese) washing, 816 Mission
Curley Bridget Miss, cook, 516 Sutter
Curley Bridget D. Miss, domestic, 868 Mission
Curley Cornelius, carpenter, dwl 657 Mission
Curley Cornelius, job wagon, cor Post and Montgomery, dwl N s Harrison bet Fifth and Sixth
Curley James, dwl N s Minna bet Fifth and Sixth
Curley James, deck hand, steamer Chrysopolis
Curley James, job wagon, cor Sansom and California, dwl N s Minna bet Fifth and Sixth
CURLEY JAMES, proprietor Roxbury House, 318 Pacific
Curley John, boiler maker, dwl 15 Natoma
Curley John, butcher, dwl Crowley House, Brannan
Curley John, laborer, dwl N s Linden nr Laguna
Curley John M. teamster, dwl NW cor Union and Eliza
Curley Margaret Miss, dwl 9 Lick Alley
Curley Mary Miss, dwl 6 Lick Alley
Curley Mary Miss, domestic, 1050 Mission
Curley Michael, lather, dwl 11 Sherwood Place
Curley Patrick, drayman, cor Mission and Sixteenth
Curley Patrick, laborer, dwl 213 Tehama
Curley Patrick, laborer, dwl 10 Lewis Place
Curley Patrick C. proprietor United States Hotel, 706 Battery
Curley Thomas, laborer, dwl 31 Louisa
Curley Thomas, pantryman, Brooklyn Hotel
Curley Thomas, waiter, What Cheer House Restaurant
Curley William, laborer with John Center, dwl E s Shotwell bet Nineteenth and Twentieth
Curley William, laborer, Fort Point
Curley William, laborer, dwl 31 Louisa
Curran Bernard, tailor, dwl 201 Powell
Curran Bridget Miss, domestic, 1019 Bush
CURRAN HUGH, proprietor Franklin Hotel, SE cor Sansom and Pacific
Curran Joseph, cooper, S. F. & P. Sugar Co. dwl 32 Rousch
Curran Mary (widow) dwl 52 Shipley
Curran Michael, baker, dwl cor Brannan and Gilbert
Curran Patrick, workman, S. F. & P. Sugar Co. dwl Hinckley nr Broadway
Curran Patrick H. lab, dwl N s Grove nr Gough
Curran Thomas, Eureka Employment Office, 138 Sutter
Curran William, laborer, dwl 180 Jessie
Currey John, judge, Supreme Court, chambers 535 Clay, dwl 47 South Park
Currey, see Kurre
Currie James, gas fitter, dwl 319 Bush
Currie Robert K. machinist, Vulcan Iron Works, dwl E s Main bet Folsom and Harrison
Currier A. laborer, Spring Valley W. W
Currier (Amos) & Winter (Daniel) sign painters and picture frame makers, 620 Market, dwl 708 Larkin
Currier Benjamin, carpenter, dwl 561 Bryant, rear
Currier C. H. pump and block maker, 29 Market, dwl 516 Minna

Currier Joseph, boot maker, dwl Sutter bet Montgomery and Sansom
Currier Nathaniel, dwl 9 Moss
Currigan Susan Mrs. dwl W s Gilbert bet Bryant and Brannan
Curry Celia (widow) dwl SW cor Kearny and Bay
Curry Charles A. bar keeper with Brennan & Ryder, dwl N s Jackson above Stockton
Curry Elias L. carpenter, office and dwl 808 Jackson, rear
Curry Francis J. boiler maker, Pacific Foundry, dwl 61 Natoma
Curry James, plasterer, dwl 204 Montgomery
Curry John (N. Curry & Brother) res Monroe Co. Ohio
Curry John, dwl 609 Battery
Curry John (col'd) with Henry C. Cornish, 622 Bat
Curry Luke, groceries and liquors, 734 Market, dwl Serpentine Avenue bet Folsom and Howard
Curry N. & Brother (John Curry) guns, pistols, and sporting materials, 317 Battery
Curry Patrick, dwl 278 Minna
Curry Patrick, laborer, dwl W s Powell nr Sac
Curry Samuel T. carpenter, dwl 633 Market
Curry William, dwl 18 First
Curry William, stevedore, dwl 38 Jessie
Curtain James, guardsman, San Quentin, dwl 1336 Pacific
Curtain Thomas, painter with Sweett & Gadsby
Curtas Peter, bar keeper, SE cor Pine and Kearny, dwl Belden nr Pine
Curtaz Benjamin, manufacturer piano fortes, 123 Kearny, dwl SE cor Sutter and Leavenworth
CURTIN CALLAHAN, importer and dealer dry goods, 48 Second, dwl 241 Jessie
Curtin Cornelius (Guttridge & C.) dwl W s Eighth bet Folsom and Howard
Curtin David, salesman, 36 and 38 Third, dwl 760 California
Curtin Mary Miss, domestic, 829 Howard
Curtis Bartholomew, drayman, dwl 13 Louisa
Curtis Catherine, domestic, 305 Fremont
Curtis Catherine (widow) furnished rooms, 118 Post
Curtis Charles, cartman, dwl 10 Hinckley
Curtis Charles, laborer, dwl 133 Folsom
Curtis Charles H. sash and blind maker with Geo. Robinson & Co. dwl 14 Natoma
Curtis Charles W. dwl SW cor Post and Kearny
Curtis E. S. shipmaster, W s Front bet Broadway and Vallejo, dwl 17 Third
Curtis George, Melter and Refiner's Department, U. S. Branch Mint, dwl Russ House
Curtis James M. laborer, dwl 17 Fourth
Curtis Jarvis B. stock broker, dwl 10 Sutter
CURTIS (J. M.) & ALLEN (Sheldon) commission merchants, 313 Davis, dwl S s Chestnut bet Jones and Leavenworth
Curtis John P. carpenter and builder, 320 Jackson, dwl 133 Stevenson
Curtis Joseph, boot maker, 264 Third
Curtis Lewis W. painter, dwl 256 Tehama
Curtis Lucien, dwl 1223 Washington
Curtis Margaret Mrs. teacher dress cutting, 27 Stock
Curtis Margaret (widow) dwl W s Battery bet Vallejo and Green
Curtis Michael, blacksmith, dwl 447 Clementina, rear
Curtis Murray, law student with Tompkins & Crane, res Oakland
Curtis Richard, currier with W. H. Warren, dwl 525 Mission
Curtis Richard, laborer with Hey & Meyn
Curtis Richard, laborer, dwl 525 Mission
Curtis Thomas, laborer with Hey & Meyn
Curtis Thomas, laborer, dwl W s Hawes nr Folsom
Curtis Thomas, porter, 217 Front, dwl 333 Bush
Curtis William, seaman, dwl 238 Stewart
Curtis William F. carpenter, dwl 915 Jones
Curtiss Samuel, paper hanger with G. W. Clark, dwl W s Mary nr Mission

Curtoys William J. laborer, dwl S s Sacramento bet Drumm and Stewart
Curty J. attendant, French Hospital
Cusack Thomas, calker, dwl Prospect Place
Cushing Benjamin F. shipwright with Joseph Ringot, dwl 126 Beale
Cushing Charles A. book keeper, Novelty Iron Works, dwl 516 Seventh
Cushing Charles B. collector, Spring Valley W. W. dwl SW cor Montgomery and Broadway
Cushing Charles D. collector with Main & Winchester, dwl 18 Stanly Place
Cushing Charles H. clerk with E. T. Steen, dwl 516 Seventh
Cushing E. Miss, assistant, Fourth St. School, dwl 106 Stockton
CUSHING G. H. state gauger, office 321 Front, dwl 652 Howard
Cushing John, cartman, dwl 416 Post
Cushing John D. (Mangels & Co.) SE cor Howard and Fourth
Cushing Robert, contractor, dwl 106 Stockton
Cushing T. H. Columbia Engine Co. No. 11
Cushing Thomas Rev. assistant pastor Mission Dolores Church
Cushing Volney, captain steamer Cornelia, office NE cor Front and Jackson
Cushman Charles D. corresponding clerk with C. W. Brooks & Co. dwl NW cor Steiner and Fulton
Cushman Zacheus, inspector, Custom House; dwl NW cor Steiner and Fulton
Cusick James, groom, dwl 413 Market
Cnaick William, laborer, dwl 410 Folsom
Cusolle John, dwl N s Minna nr Seventh
CUSTOM HOUSE BLOCK, SE cor Sacramento and Sansom
Cutler Acors S. machinist, Miners' Foundry, dwl 429 Clementina
Cutler L. S. clerk, 632 Washington, dwl SW cor Market and Third
Cutrell William E. (Mangels & C.) dwl NE cor Fourth and Silver
Cutter Albert J. carpenter and builder, 806 Clay
Cutter David S. (William H. Tobey & Co.) dwl 115 Perry
Cutter Ephraim P. agent, office 30 Exchange Buildings, dwl 510 Dupont
Cutter Henry M. salesman with William T. Cutter, 111 California, dwl 809 Stockton
Cutter Horace F. office 523 Montgomery, dwl 1309 Mason
CUTTER JAMES H. wholesale grocer and Treasurer S. F. Fire Department Charitable Fund, 511 Front, dwl SW cor Hyde and Sutter
Cutter Joseph S. (T. F. Bayliss & Co.) resides Petaluma
Cutter R. S. & Co. (William A. Boyd) Howard Market, NE cor Second and Howard
CUTTER SAMUEL L. jr. attorney at law, office 30 Exchange Building, dwl 510 Dupont
Cutter Thomas A. (Deming & Co. and Miller & Co.) dwl 114 Geary
Cutter William T. agent Cutter's Whisky, 111 California, dwl 652 Market
Cutter William W. sr. dwl 652 Market
Cutting Calvin, brakeman, S. F. & San José R. R
Cutting Edwin, painter, 759½ Mission
Cutting Eugene O. plasterer with Samuel Kellett, dwl 759 Mission
CUTTING (Francis) & CO. manufacturers pickles, preserves, etc. 21 and 31 Main, office and salesroom 202 Front, dwl 330 Bryant
Cutting Lewis, with Cutting & Co. dwl 334 Bryant
Cutts James M. hatter with K. Meussdorffer, dwl Quincy Place
Cuvelier Alexander, dwl nr San Bruno Road 3½ miles from City Hall
Cypiot Ferdinand, merchant, dwl 632 Market
CZAPKAY'S BUILDING, 651–657 Washington

D

D'ANGELO Anthony, hair dresser with J. Lipman, dwl Washington nr East

D'Arcy Anne, domestic, 733 Harrison

D'Arcy John, bakery, SW cor Perry and Third

D'ASSONVILLE V. physician, office and dwl 1030 Dupont

D'Este J. pantryman Clipper Restaurant

D'Haro Alonzo, dwl N s Seventeenth bet Guerrero and Dolores

D'Lucca Francisco, fisherman, 48 Italian Fish Market

D'Oliveira Emanuel, physician, office and dwl 812 Washington

Dabovich Elia, fruits, 1122 Stockton

Dabovich N. foreign and domestic fruits, 420 Davis, dwl 1108 Taylor

Dace Joseph, molder, Pacific Foundry, dwl N s Broadway nr Kearny

Dacey C. laborer, Spring Valley W. W

Dacey James, dwl N s Bryant bet Fifth and Sixth, rear

Dacey John, groceries and provisions, 1426 Stock

Dacey Kate Miss, domestic, 1010 Powell

Dacker Charles, mariner, dwl 32 Stewart

Dacota S. M. Co. office 24 Government House

Dady Edward, gardener, dwl SE cor Stevenson and Ecker

Dafarel Benedict, gardener, NE cor Laguna and McAllister

Daffis Maximin, shoe maker with James H. Swain & Co. 204 Bush

Dager Joseph W. dwl E s Jones bet Jackson and Pacific

Daggan Charles, plasterer, dwl SW cor Dupont and Broadway

Dagger Charles, hair rope maker, 521 Market, dwl Vallejo Place

DAHLEN FRANCIS, groceries and liquors, NW cor Dupont and Sutter and NW cor Ritch and Clara, dwl 28 Ritch

Dahlmann Charles & Co. (Adolph Roos) clothing, 520 Sacramento, dwl 324 Geary

Dahncke Frederick, groceries and liquors, SW cor Washington and Drumm

Dahnken Frederick (Bose & D.) dwl NE cor Taylor and Valparaiso

Dailey B. hostler, Omnibus R. R. Co.

Dailey H. carpenter, dwl Cincinnati Brewery, Valencia

Dailey James, laborer with Hey & Meyn

Dailey John, tailor, dwl 212 Harrison

Dailey Thomas, tailor, dwl SE cor Harrison and Main

Daily Aeneas, fruits, 546 Mission

Daily Daniel, spinner, S. F. P. Woolen Mills, dwl North Point bet Polk and Van Ness Avenue

Daily John, tin and sheet iron worker, dwl SE cor Powell and Pacific

Daily Lawrence H. messenger, Custom House, dwl 112 Vallejo

Daily William, bar keeper, dwl W s White Place nr Bryant

Daingerfield Charles H. S. (col'd) porter, dwl Bernard nr Jones

Daingerfield William P. (Cope, D. & Hambleton) attorney at law, office 6 U. S. Court Block, dwl 915 Sutter

Daise John, laborer, dwl E s August Alley nr Union

Dake Edmund C. clothing, 541 and 543 Washington, dwl 634 Mission

Dakin Edward, bag factory, 33 Clay, dwl 129 Third

Dakin James, laborer, S. F. & P. Sugar Co. dwl W s Eighth bet Howard and Clementina

Dakin William, plasterer, bds 411 Pacific

Dalamore John, hostler, dwl Central House, 814 Sansom

Dalchy Peter, blacksmith, Miners' Foundry

Daleth Nicholas (Conrad Wieland & Co.) dwl 172 Jessie

Daley Agnes Miss, domestic, 622 Greenwich

Daley Barkley, laborer, dwl 25 Stevenson

Daley Cornelius, laborer, dwl 84 Stevenson

Daley Daniel, laborer, dwl Spear nr Harrison

Daley David, blacksmith, dwl 254 Minna

Daley Dennis A. laborer, Market St. R. R. dwl NE cor Market and Stockton

Daley Edward, peddler, cor Sixteenth and Mission

Daley Elizabeth Miss, domestic, 31 Minna

Daley Francis, vegetable peddler, dwl W s White Place nr Bryant

Daley Frank, blacksmith helper, Vulcan Iron Works

Daley James, laborer, dwl 327 Vallejo, rear

Daley James, laborer, dwl 1107 Pine

Daley J. H. proprietor West End Hotel, Brenham Place W s Plaza

Daley J. L. laborer, Pacific Engine Co. No. 8

Daley John, laborer with Wm. J. Kingsley

Daley John H. (Stewart & D.) dwl West End Hotel

Daley Julia E. Miss, domestic with Edmund Benjamin, W s Folsom bet Twelfth and Thirteenth

Daley Margaret, dwl 545 Folsom

Daley Mary, domestic, 421 Harrison

Daley Mary Miss, domestic, 711 Leavenworth

Daley Michael, groceries and liquors, SW cor Greenwich and Sansom

Daley Michael, apprentice, dwl 148 Mission

Daley Michael A. coal passer, dwl 269 Stevenson

Daley Patrick, drayman, S s Broadway nr Leavenworth

Daley Patrick, fruit peddler, dwl 133 Stevenson

Daley Peter, laborer, dwl 15 Ohio

Daley Thomas, cigars, dwl 321 Pacific

Daley, see Dailey and Daly

Dall Christopher C. (Hunter, Parker, Crowell & Co.) dwl 733 Broadway

Dull Cornelius, carpenter, dwl 140 Clara

Dall Edward R. sutler's clerk, Presidio

Dall John H. Capt. superintendent S. F. & Oakland R. R. Co. office 535 Clay, dwl 417 Mont

Dall ——, carpenter, dwl 31 Second

Dallam Richard B. (Armes & D.) dwl 616 Greenwich

Dalley W. J. dwl SW cor Kearny and Pacific

Dalliba Henry S. book keeper Daily Examiner, dwl 218 Minna

Dallmand Albert, salesman with Rosenbaum & Friedmann, 316 Sacramento

Dalrymple (Geo. L.) & Irvin (James) Neptune Exchange, 32 Stewart

Dalton Daniel, laborer, dwl S s Turk nr Fillmore

Dalton Eugene, stone cutter, Lone Mountain Cemetery

Dalton John, laborer, dwl W s Main bet Harrison and Bryant

Dalton John P. gardener, NW corner Folsom and Sixteenth

Dalton Michael, painter, dwl NE cor Fulton and Pierce

Dalton P. Edward (Bovee, Hallett, Bartlett & D.) Contra Costa Laundry, dwl NE cor Stevenson and Third

Daly Annie Miss, dress maker, 422 Third

Daly Catharine Miss, domestic with George J. Griffing

Daly Catharine (widow) dwl 518 Dupont

Daly Charles, salesman with Hawley & Co. dwl 716 Howard

Daly Daniel J. stoves and tinware, 814 Market

Daly Dennis, laborer, dwl 4 O'Farrell Alley

Daly Dennis, laborer, dwl 331 Fourth, rear

Daly Edward, Ned's Market, N s Sixteenth bet Valencia and Guerrero

Daly Felix, stoves and tinware, 36 Sutter, dwl 30 Montgomery

Daly Frank, blacksmith, bds St. Louis Hotel
Daly George, compositor, 417 Clay, bds Russ House
DALY *(James)* & HAWKINS *(Michael)* real estate agents, office 220 Montgomery, dwl 30 Montgomery
Daly James, with Edward Dakin, 33 Clay, dwl Pine nr Jones
Daly James, laborer, dwl Higgins Place
Daly James, laborer, dwl S s Serpentine Avenue nr Folsom
Daly James, teamster with James McDevitt, dwl Ohio nr Pacific
Daly Jeremiah, laborer, Central R. R. Stables, dwl E s Garden bet Harrison and Bryant
Daly John *(Richardson & D.)* dwl SW cor Oak and Franklin
Daly John, cartman, dwl E s St. Ann nr Ellis
Daly John, cartman, cor Bdwy and Leavenworth
Daly John, hostler, 16 Sutter, dwl Bootz's Hotel
Daly John, plasterer, dwl 13 Ellis
Daly John, teamster, dwl NE cor Franklin and Oak
Daly Mary Miss, domestic, 407 Taylor
Daly Mary A. Miss, domestic, 24 Rousch
Daly Michael, blacksmith with Patrick McGivern, 148 Minna
Daly Michael, laborer, dwl 178 Stevenson
Daly P. H. dwl 209 Clay
Daly Rosa (widow) dwl 10 Harlan Place
Daly Sarah Mrs. dwl 148 Fourth
Daly Simon, laborer, dwl 178 Stevenson
Daly Thomas, laborer, dwl 321 Stockton
Daly Thomas, laborer, dwl NE cor Harrison and Main
Daly William, laborer, dwl 19 St. Mark Place
Daly William, laborer, dwl 840 Market
Daly William D. dwl 148 Fourth
Daly, see Dailey, Daley, and Dayley
DAM GEORGE W. real estate agent, 422 Montgomery, dwl 1419 Taylor
Dame Milton S. clerk Western Pacific Railroad Co. office 409 California, dwl 47 South Park
DAME TIMOTHY, Western Pacific Railroad Co. office 409 California, dwl 47 South Park
Dameron James P. attorney at law, office 35 Exchange Building, dwl 11 Minna
Dames *(Wm.)* & Lohse *(Theodore F.)* importers and jobbers wines and liquors, 609 Sansom, dwl 419 Bryant bet Second and Third
Damkroeger Gottlieb, carpenter, dwl 1111 Pacific
Damkelly Joseph, spinner, S. F. P. Woolen Mills, dwl Bay bet Larkin and Polk
Damm Kosmos, upholsterer, dwl 401 Bush
Dammann Andrew, seaman, dwl 620 Lombard, rear
Damon Dexter, with James E. Damon, dwl 928 Folsom
Damon Fannie Miss, music teacher, 928 Folsom
Damon James E. & Co. wholesale stationers, 421 and 423 Sansom, dwl 928 Folsom
Damon Newton Mrs. operator with Samuel Hill, dwl W s Downey nr Bryant
Damon Newton F. *(Perry & D.)* dwl W s Downey nr Bryant
Damon Seth T. workman with Samuel Hill, dwl W s Downey nr Bryant
Damonte Lorenzo, salesman, 531 Washington, dwl 534 Filbert
Damour Ferdinand, physician, office and dwl 402 Kearny cor Pine
Damrell Daniel, assistant foreman Alta California, dwl 419 Tehama
DANA BROTHERS *(William A. and Henry F. Dana)* & CO. real estate, office 326 Clay cor Battery, dwl 33 South Park
Dana *(George)* & Dick *(Stephen W.)* proprietors Central Warehouse, 210 Sacramento, dwl NE cor Clay and Battery
DANA GEORGE S. proprietor Pacific Glue Manufactory, E s Lagoon, dwl cor Gough and Lombard

Dana Henry F. *(Dana Bros. & Co.)* res Boston
Dana Martin V. B. with George S. Dana, dwl SE cor Union and Van Ness Avenue
Danaher P. H. salesman, 300 Montgomery, dwl 507 Bryant
Danahey Timothy, laborer, dwl 264½ Stevenson
Danary John, vegetable wagon, dwl 1506 Stockton
Daneal Francis, mason, dwl NW cor Guerrero and Sixteenth
Daneri Bartolomeo, Garibaldi House, NE cor Broadway and Sansom
DANERI F. & CO. *(Henry Casanova)* importers and jobbers wines and liquors, 419 and 421 Jackson, dwl 732 Union
Daneri Lorenzo, with D. R. Provost & Co. dwl cor Sansom and Pacific
Daney G. & S. M. Co. office 607 Washington
Daney Michael, liquor saloon, 616 Broadway
Daney Richard, gilder, dwl 13 Second
Danforth George S. carpenter, dwl 68 Tehama
Danforth Solomon, dwl 759 Howard
Danforth William, carpenter, Chelsea Laundry
Danforth William, with Goodwin & Co. dwl 432 Bush
Danglada Antoine, hatter, 641 Commercial, dwl N s Fifteenth bet Guerrero and Dolores
Danglada Domingo, dwl N s Fifteenth bet Guerrero and Dolores
Danglada Eugenio, dwl N s Fifteenth bet Guerrero and Dolores
Danglada Ignacio, clerk, 324 Washington, dwl N s Fifteenth bet Guerrero and Dolores
Danglada Manuel, dwl N s Fifteenth bet Guerrero and Dolores
Danglada Manuela Miss, dwl N s Fifteenth bet Guerrero and Dolores
Dangler Jennetta (widow) furnished rooms, 413 Kearny
Danhauzer M. tailor, dwl W s Bower Place
Daniel John, marble works, 421 Pine, dwl SW cor Pine and Stockton
Daniel Joseph, dwl 632 Market
Daniel R. P. carpenter, dwl 64 Tehama
Daniell Thomas, ship and house joiner, dwl 826 Filbert
Daniell William H. book keeper, dwl 610 Mason
Daniels Benjamin, gardener, dwl S side Hayes bet Gough and Octavia
Daniels Charles, engineer, dwl King bet Third and Fourth
Daniels Charles D. butcher, SW corner Bryant and Rincon Place
Daniels J. M. superintendent Ocean Race Course
Daniels John H. M. picture frame maker with D. Hausmann & Co. dwl 1222 Kearny
Daniels Laura Miss, teacher, dwl St. Lawrence H
Daniels Patrick, expressman, W s Thirteenth near Harrison
Danielson Daniel, machinist with Palmer, Knox & Co. dwl 22 Dupont
Danielwitz Isidor, student with Yale & McConnell, dwl 732 Vallejo
Dankemeier Henry, with Thurnauer & Zinn, dwl W s Harriet nr Folsom
Dann *(Frederick P.)* & Landesman *(John)* attorneys at law, office 604 Merchant, residence San Leandro
Dannenbaum Moses *(Dannenbaum, Katzenstein & Co.)* res New York
DANNENBAUM *(Salomon)* KATZENSTEIN *(Isaac)* & CO. *(Moses Dannenbaum)* fancy goods, 20 Montgomery, dwl 22 Montgomery
Dannenberg Amelia Mrs. infants' clothing, embroideries, etc. 618 Sacramento
Dannenberg Joseph, merchant, dwl 618 Sacramento
Danner Frederick A. carpenter, 757 Mission, dwl S s Brannan bet Fifth and Sixth
Dannheimer Louis, merchant tailor, 310 Mont
Danos J. B. butcher, NE cor Laguna and Waller

Danove Dominco, drayman, 430 Jackson, dwl N s Green bet Dupont and Stockton

Danzel Gustavus, clerk with R. Feuerstein & Co. 212 Front

Danziger Henry *(S. Jaffe & Co.)* dwl 640 Mission

Danzin Charles, carrier, Le National, dwl 1 Adona Place

Daoty Kate Miss, domestic, 35 Essex

Darby Thomas, clerk with C. J. Brenham, 205 Battery, dwl 224 Second

Darcey Cornelius, laborer with Hey & Meyn

Darcy James, plasterer, dwl 250 Tehama, rear

Darcy Patrick, tanner, dwl 132 Townsend

Dardanne Charles, butcher, dwl 942 Pacific

Dargan William, laborer, Custom House, dwl 50 Natoma

Dargie John, porter, 205 Front, dwl W s Scotland nr Greenwich

Darien Catherine Miss, domestic, 514 Sutter

Darile Edouard, dwl 625 Clay

Dark Albert T. pork packer, dwl 54 Beale

Darling Abram F. mining, dwl 720 Market

Darling George, workman with G. Treat, S s Twenty-Fourth bet Folsom and Howard

Darling John, carpenter, dwl 59 Minna

Darling Richard, painter, dwl 308 Minna

Darling W. H. bond clerk, Custom House, dwl 2 Vernon Place

Darnanvilly Joseph, waiter, St. Francis Restaurant

Darnell Henry Y. stock broker, dwl N s Nineteenth bet Guerrero and Dolores

Darrell E. F. carpenter, dwl 315 Montgomery

Darrimon Leone, laundry, N s Fern Avenue bet Polk and Van Ness Avenue

Darrow William, janitor Denman Grammar School, dwl cor Jones and Geary

Darry Frank, laborer, dwl S s Hayes bet Franklin and Gough

Dart J. laborer, dwl Original House

DART PUTNAM C. merchant, office 419 Front, dwl 570 Harrison

Dartois W. G. porter, dwl 616 Post

DARYES RICHARD, saloon, 21 First, dwl 518 Stockton

Dase John, porter, London & S. F. Bank, dwl Union Alley nr Powell

DASHAWAY HALL, S s Post bet Kearny and Dupont

Dashea Louis, vaquero with David Mahoney, dwl SE cor Pacific and Polk

Dastugue Gabriel, butcher, 4 New Market, dwl cor Polk and Bush

Daufield Abraham, porter, dwl 323 Pine

Daum George, supt Nevai Shalome (Jewish) Cemetery, dwl S s Day bet Guerrero and Dolores

Dauphin Joseph, dwl 613 Mission

Davega *(Benj. F.)*, Joseph *(Jacob J.)* & Labatt *(J. J.)* auctioneers and commission merchants, 318 Pine, dwl 1521 Stockton

Davenport Andrew J. painter, dwl 402 Geary

Davenport John, laborer, dwl 150 Natoma

Davenport Thomas, book keeper, Bank California, res Encinal, Alameda Co

Davenport Thomas, laborer, dwl E s Lagoon

Davenport William, dwl 629 Clay

Davenport Wm. H. merchant, dwl 719 California

Daver Alexander, harness maker with Main & Winchester, dwl 417 Stockton

Davey John, laborer, dwl N s Market nr Third

David August, stoves and tinware, 1204 Stockton

DAVIDSON & CO. commission merchants, 338 Montgomery, room 5

Davidson Alexander, cooper, dwl 305 First

Davidson Alonzo, milkman, dwl 419 Natoma

DAVIDSON B. & BERRI *(Emanuel)* bankers, NW cor Montgomery and Commercial, resides London

Davidson David, carpenter, dwl N s Twentieth bet Guerrero and Dolores

DAVIDSON DONALD & CO. mining stocks and shippers ores, 338 Montgomery room 5, dwl Union Club Rooms

Davidson Douglas N. (col'd) barber, 640 Clay, dwl 612 Powell

Davidson Esther (widow) dwl 264 Jessie

Davidson George, book keeper with James Patrick & Co. dwl SW cor Broadway and Montgomery

Davidson Hugh, salesman, 609 Sacramento

Davidson *(Jacob)* & Poppe *(Charles)* cigars and tobacco, NE cor Com and Bat, dwl 37 Minna

Davidson John, gardener, SW cor Sixteenth and Howard

DAVIDSON J. W. & CO. *(Raphael Weill and George H. Huntsman)* importers and retail goods, 609 Sacramento, res Paris

Davidson Lewis, dwl 407 Third

Davidson M. merchant (Mokelumne Hill) office 314 California

Davidson Nathan, milkman, Glen Ranch, nr S. F. Cordage Factory

Davidson S. N. jeweler with Lemme Bros. dwl 134 Sutter

Davidson Thomas, porter, Express Bdg, dwl E s Fifteenth bet Howard and Mission

Davidson Walter P. porter, Bank California, dwl N s Jessie bet Fifth and Sixth

Davidson William, book keeper, 609 Sacramento

Davidson William, broker, dwl 627 Commercial

Davidson W. P. clerk, dwl 450 Jessie

Davies John R. job wagon, cor Pine and Montgomery, dwl N s Cal bet Hyde and Leavenworth

Davies John S. broker, office 723 Montgomery, dwl NW cor Stockton and Pacific

Davies Shadrach, cabinet maker, 904 Clay, dwl N s Washington nr Leavenworth

Davis Abraham, glazier, dwl W s First nr Natoma

Davis Alex. musician, dwl 215 Stevenson

Davis Alfred, tanner and currier with Jones & Co. dwl What Cheer House

Davis Alfred E. mining, dwl 331 Minna

Davis Alvin H. dwl 711 California

Davis Andrew *(Allion, Francis & Co.)* dwl NE cor Second and Folsom

Davis Andrew, laborer. Golden Age Flour Mills, 717 Battery, dwl 7 Clay

Davis Anna P. boarding, 746 Howard

Davis Benjamin, paper carrier, dwl 111 Ellis

Davis Bernard, glazier with James Brokaw, dwl 59 Stevenson

Davis Calvin W. millwright with James Brokaw, dwl E s Capp bet Eighteenth and Nineteenth

Davis Catharine A. Davis Laundry, W s Harriet bet Howard and Folsom

Davis C. E. dentist, Dolan's Building, NE cor Hunt and Third

Davis Charles (col'd) boot black, dwl SW cor Green and Dupont

Davis Charles F. tinner, dwl 319 Bush

Davis Charles W. contractor and builder, dwl SW cor Howard and Eighteenth

Davis Daniel, cigars, 612 Wash, dwl 1022 Stockton

Davis Daniel L. (col'd) drayman, 400 Battery, dwl cor Clay and Hyde

Davis David, second officer stmr America

Davis David H. molder, Fulton Foundry, dwl 431 Tehama

Davis Dominick, coffee stand, dwl 107 Pacific

Davis D. S. brick molder, dwl St. Lawrence House

Davis D. W. coiner's dep't U. S. Branch Mint, dwl 1211 Pacific

Davis Edward, seaman, dwl NW cor Green and Bat

Davis Edward, workman, S. F. Cordage Factory, dwl nr S. F. Cordage Factory

Davis Emma M. (widow) dwl SW cor Folsom and Twentieth

Davis E. N. dwl What Cheer House

DAVIS ERWIN, capitalist, office 44 Montgomery Block, dwl SW cor Powell and California

Davis (E. W.) & Clifford (Thomas C.) teamsters, Golden Gate Mills, dwl 712 O'Farrell
Davis Franklin A. (Sedgley & D.) dwl Mission Creek nr Mariposa
Davis Gabriel, dwl 623 Post
Davis G. C. dyer, S. F. P. Woolen Mills
Davis George, carpenter, dwl 629 Third
Davis George, laborer with David B. Hughes, dwl S s Lombard bet Taylor and Jones
Davis (Geo. B.) & Schafer (H. H.) Quincy Hall Clothing, 545-549 Washington, dwl 1118 Sac
Davis George E. Rev. dwl S s Geary nr Octavia
Davis George H. (Horace Davis & Co.) dwl 27 South Park
Davis G. F. clerk with C. J. Hawley & Co. dwl 906½ Howard
Davis Griffith, bricklayer, dwl E s First Avenue nr Fifteenth
Davis H. clerk with S. Froomberg, dwl 214 Clara
Davis Henry, dwl 3 Garden
Davis Henry F. Miners' Foundry
DAVIS HENRY L. sheriff City and County San Francisco, office 8 City Hall second floor, dwl 1028 Clay
Davis Henry P. job wagon, NE cor Bush and Sansom, dwl NE cor William and Geary
Davis Herbert J. salesman with Wightman & Hardie, dwl Lick House
DAVIS HORACE & CO. (George H. Davis) proprietors Golden Gate Flour Mills, 430 Pine, dwl 27 South Park
Davis Isaac. with. Theodore Van Tassell, dwl 3 Garden
Davis Isaac, tailor, 722 Dupont
DAVIS (Isaac E.) & COWELL (Henry) lime, cement, and plaster, NE cor Front and Washington, dwl 28 South Park
Davis Isidore, merchant tailor, 635 Market
Davis J. A. dwl 151 Tehama
Davis (Jacob) & Koffel (Solomon) hair dressing saloon, 44 Sutter, dwl 6 Hardie Place
Davis Jacob Z. (Boyd & D.) res Sacramento City
Davis James, machinist, San Francisco Iron Works, dwl 16 Ecker
Davis James, plasterer, office 338 Montgomery
Davis Jefferson (col'd) plasterer, dwl 1337. Dupont, rear
Davis Job C. dwl W s Harriet bet Folsom and Howard
Davis John, broker, dwl NW cor Stockton and Pac
Davis John, carpenter, dwl W s Mariposa nr Carolina
Davis John, hackman, Plaza
Davis John, merchant, dwl 632 Market
Davis John, paper hanger, dwl 318 Davis
Davis John, ship carpenter, dwl N s Broadway bet Van Ness Avenue and Franklin
Davis John B. F. assistant assessor, U. S. Internal Rev. NW cor Bat and Com, dwl 282 Stevenson
Davis John H. butcher with William J. Tighe, NW cor O'Farrell and Mason
Davis John S. fruits, E s Sixth nr Tehama
Davis Joseph, salesman, 431 Mont, dwl 14 Freelon
DAVIS JOSHUA P. mining secretary, office 103 California, dwl 331 Fremont
Davis Lazarus, peddler, dwl 7 Hinckley
Davis Lemuel B. with Clark & Perkins, 402 Front, dwl 609½ Howard
David Louis, dwl 14 Freelon
Davis Louis, merchant, dwl 227 Post
Davis M. (widow) dwl 315 Taylor
Davis Marks, furniture, 1316 Dupont
Davis Marks, seaman, steamer Orizaba
Davis Mary (widow) dwl E s Seventh bet Brannan and Townsend
Davis Max. with Manheim, Schonwasser & Co. dwl 411 O'Farrell
Davis Max, clothing, 607 Pacific. dwl 1023 Kearny
Davis Max, waiter, dwl Irving House
Davis Morris, job wagon, dwl 506 Post

Davis Moses, butcher, dwl W s Carlos Place
Davis Moses C. engineer, San Francisco Gas Co. dwl SE cor First and Natoma
Davis Mrs. (widow) dwl 746 Howard
Davis N. P. Mrs. lodgings, proptr St. John's House, 629 Clay
Davis N. R. physician, office 131 Montgomery, dwl 933 Sacramento
Davis Patrick, fruit peddler, dwl cor Mission and Beale
Davis Peter P. milkman, Battery near Broadway
Davis Rebecca Mrs. (widow) dwl 222 Ritch
Davis Richard, butcher, NW cor Ellis and Scott, dwl N s Eddy bet Scott and Devisidero
Davis Richard, carpenter, dwl 728 Market
Davis Richard E. painter and paper hanger, 731 Mission
Davis Robert, laborer, bds 412 Vallejo, rear
Davis Robert, lumber stevedore, dwl 642 Howard
Davis Rosalia Miss, dwl 811 Harrison
Davis R. P. rigger, dwl 343 Harrison
Davis Russell (col'd) drayman, 400 Battery, dwl N W cor Clay and Hyde
Davis S. Miss, assistant Fourth Street School, dwl 166 Tehama
Davis S. A. book keeper, dwl Oriental Hotel
Davis Samuel, dwl 1016 Washington
Davis Samuel, deck hand, steamer Oakland, res Brooklyn, Alameda Co
Davis Samuel, ship carpenter, dwl 308 Beale
Davis Samuel S. (col'd) porter, dwl 1804 Mason
Davis Samuel T. compositor, Golden Era, dwl 327 Broadway
Davis Sarah A. (widow) dwl 9 Belden
Davis S. D. carpenter, dwl 414 Market
Davis S. G. box maker with Hobbs, Gilmore & Co. dwl National House
Davis Shubael, cooper, dwl 218 Mission
Davis (Solon H.) & Witham (William L.) produce and flour, SW cor Clay and Davis, dwl E s Leavenworth nr Green
Davis Sturges, foreman with R. B. Gray & Co. dwl 813 Stockton
Davis Thomas, butcher with O. H. Willoughby, dwl N s Sixteenth nr Nebraska
Davis Vernon, machinist, Union Foundry, dwl 63 Natoma
Davis Virgil, machinist, Pacific Foundry
Davis W. E. boatman, dwl Jackson bet Davis and Drumm
Davis. W. H. (Armstrong, Sheldon & D.) dwl 8 Hubbard
Davis William, calker, dwl 217 Beale
Davis William, carpenter, dwl 545 Mission
Davis William, gas fitter with Thomas Day, 732 Montgomery, dwl 1024 Montgomery
Davis William, nurse, U. S. Marine Hospital
Davis William, turner, dwl S s Oak bet Franklin and Gough
Davis William, wines and liquors, 717 Davis
Davis William P. book keeper with Stevens, Baker & Co. dwl 1410 Leavenworth
Davis William W. stone cutter with Phil. Caduc, bds Franklin Hotel cor Pacific and Sansom
Davis W. R. clerk, International Hotel
Davis W. W. wool sorter, S. F. P. Woolen Mills, dwl North Point between Polk and Van Ness Avenue
Davison Elizabeth (widow) dress maker, dwl 751 Mission
Davison Margaret Miss, dwl NE cor Folsom and Tenth
Davisson M. P. cook, Sailor's Home, SW cor Battery and Vallejo
Davisson Robert G. (Tobin Bros. & D.) dwl E s Dupont, bet Chestnut and Lombard
Davock Michael E. salesman with Simon, Dinkelspiel & Co. dwl 921 Pacific
Davoto Francisco, fruits, dwl 533 Pacific

Davou Henry F. bargeman, Custom House, dwl 216 Prospect Place
Davoue William O. Letter Department Wells, Fargo & Co. dwl 522 California
Dawes Elizabeth Miss, dwl 316 Fourth
Dawes James, butcher, dwl SE cor Pac and Larkin
Dawes John G. book keeper with Roberts, Morrison & Co. dwl NE cor Second and Minna
Dawsey John, dwl 57 Minna
Dawson Charles S. clerk with H. P. Wakelee
Dawson Charlotte (widow) dwl 636 Howard
Dawson George W. cattle dealer, dwl 542 Mission
Dawson Henry, dwl 22 Kearny
Dawson James, carpenter, dwl 504 Howard
Dawson Thomas, blacksmith, bds 127 Pacific
Dawson William, miner, dwl SW cor Union and Sansom
Day Daniel, stone cutter, dwl 323 Dupont
Day D. W. dwl What Cheer House
Day Franklin H. with Kellogg, Hewston & Co. dwl NE cor Washington and Dupont
Day George A. pattern maker, Fulton Foundry, dwl Noble Place nr Third
Day James (col'd) steward, dwl 1606 Powell
Day John, with Owen Keating
Day John, confectioner with Salomon & Co. 211 Sutter
Day John, deck hand, steamer Oakland, res Brooklyn, Alameda Co
Day John, superintendent Masonic Cemetery
DAY JOHN S. & CO. *(Lovell White)* wholesale groceries, provisions, etc. 306 and 308 Clay, dwl S s Sixteenth bet Howard and Folsom
Day Kate Miss, actress, Bella Union
Day Margaret Miss, domestic, 509 Bush
Day Maria L. Miss, domestic, 609 Bush
Day Michael, drayman, dwl 228 Clay
Day Patrick, washing, N s Lombard bet Montgomery and Kearny
Day Robert & Co. paper hangings, 823 Montgomery, dwl 18 Ecker
Day Sarah M. (widow) dwl with J. S. , S s Sixteenth bet Folsom and Howard Day
Day Sherman, mining engineer, office 57 Montgomery Block, res Oakland
DAY THOMAS, importer and jobber gas fixtures, gas pipes, etc., 732 Mont, dwl 630 Harrison
Day Thomas O. drayman, 616 Front, dwl W s Folsom Avenue bet Folsom and Harrison
Day Thomas S. with Thomas Day, 732 Montgomery, dwl 630 Harrison
Day Wellington F. calker, dwl 44 Stewart
Dayball Martin, laborer, dwl 16 Rousch
Dayley James, laborer, dwl 44 Stevenson
DAYLEY JAMES C. mining secretary, office 338 Montgomery, res Oakland
Daysman Dennis, teamster, dwl N s Market bet Oak and Page
Dayton Edward, dwl 129 Third
Dayton John B. book binder with Edward Bosqui & Co. dwl International Hotel
Dazet John, butcher, with John Bazille, dwl N s Sixteenth nr Nebraska
Dazet Joseph, butcher, dwl N s Chestnut bet Dupont and Stockton
DeAguylar Francisco T. handcartman, NW corner Front and Sacramento, dwl 21 Ohio
DeAngelis John, comedian, dwl 527 Green
DéArce L. Pontin, book keeper with M. Lanzenberg & Co. dwl 323 Geary
DéArcy William F. ship carpenter, dwl 351 First
DeBack Josias, teamster, 402 Sansom, dwl 830 Harrison
DeBerrio William, astrologer, 816 Stockton
DeBlois *(George L.)* & Co. *(Thomas Whaley)* produce and commission merchants, 421 Davis, dwl W s Stockton bet Washington and Clay
DeBray William, molder, dwl 335 Second
DeBuck Louis, express wagon, cor Wash and Kearny

DeCamp J. K. drayman, cor Market and Sac
DeCASTRO FERDINANDOS, oculist and aurist, office 620 Market
DeCAZOTTE CHARLES F. consul of France, office 434 Jackson, dwl 19 South Park
DeClairmont R. teacher languages, dwl 1518 Stock
DeCosta Jacob N. groceries, dwl S s Green bet Larkin and Polk
DéFiennes Henry A. pressman, Alta California, dwl 1528 Stockton
DeFOREST J. commission merchant and produce dealer, 221 Clay, dwl SW cor Jackson and Powell
DeFREMERY H. S. ship and Custom House broker, 413 Washington, dwl 1007 Washington
DeFREMERY JAMES, commission merchant and consul for Mecklenburg-Schwerin, and the Netherlands, office 407 Merchant, res Oakland
DeFremery William C. B. with James DeFremery, 407 Merchant, res Oakland
DeFrevelle Eugene, fish dealer, dwl 18 Rousch
DeGarcelon Joseph, clerk, dwl 16 Drumm
DeGiougeou Louise Mme, dwl 907 Clay
DeGroote D. A. watchman, dwl St. Francis Engine House
DeGroote Leon, dwl N s Merchant nr Kearny
DeHaga John, professor music, dwl 224 Sansom
DeHann William M. dwl S s Clementina nr Eighth
DeKirwary William, mining stocks, dwl 1024 Stock
DeLafontaine Joseph, cooper with Handy & Neuman, dwl 19 Harlan Place
DeLaguna A. DeLeo, professor modern languages City College, dwl 633 O'Farrell
DeLaMONTAGNIE J. E. secretary Lumber Dealers' Association, Pier 3 Stewart, dwl 719 Clay
DeLaMontanya George, tinsmith, 216 and 218 Jackson, dwl E s Taylor bet Pacific and Broadway
DeLaMontanya Hudson, dwl 1107 Kearny
DeLaMONTANYA JAMES, importer stoves and metals, 216 and 218 Jackson, dwl E s Taylor bet Pacific and Broadway
DeLaMontanya Mathew, dwl 1107 Kearny
DeLand Alfred, merchant, dwl 864 Mission
DeLange Conrades, laborer, dwl W s Shotwell bet Twenty-First and Twenty-Second
De Lanty William, laborer, dwl 21 Minna
DeLarrie Manuel S. compositor, Nuevo Mundo, dwl Rock Building, NE cor Broadway and Kearny
DeLaverre Emanuel T. local policeman, Vallejo Wharf, dwl Moulton Place nr Montgomery
DeLeon Edward P. student at law with Alfred Rix and clerk 226 Montgomery
DeLong Frank C. salesman with Rockwell, Coye & Co. dwl 807 Greenwich
DeLuce George, musician, Metropolitan Theater, dwl 920 Stockton
DeMontpreville Cyrille, lithographer, Wright's Bdg, room 7, NW cor Jackson and Montgomery
DePass Charles B. book keeper with John J. Marks & Co. dwl 540 Washington
DePass J. M. real estate and money broker, office 55 Exchange Building, dwl 203 Dupont
DePee Thomas (col'd) laborer, dwl 907 Pacific
DePrefontaine J. J. R. editorial department Alta California, office 423 Wash, dwl 123 Jessie
DePrefontaine Mary L. (widow) dwl 546 Howard
DePuche Julia (col'd, widow) dwl 720 Broadway
DePuis Paul, jewelry box maker, 650 Washington
DeRamirez Concepcion F. Mrs. dwl 1153 Mission
DeRo Charles, office 428 Cal, dwl 23 South Park
DeRoos Frances Mrs. ladies' nurse, dwl 309 Dupont
DeRoos Jacob, merchant, dwl 309 Dupont
DeRussy René E. col U. S. Engineers, fortifications Fort Point, Angel Island, etc. office 37 Montgomery Block, dwl 41 South Park
DeRutte Edward (estate of) importer wines and liquors, 431 Battery
DeSequeira Anthony, book keeper, Phœnix Insurance Co. 605 Commercial, dwl 413 Tehama

DeSequeira Antonio Lorenzo, physician, dwl 413 Tehama
DeSilva J. H. core maker, San Francisco Iron Works, dwl Harrison bet Main and Stewart
DeSoto G. & S. M. Co. office 605 Montgomery
DeSt. Dennis M. dwl 626 California
DeSTOUTZ ALEXIS, salesman and vice consul for Switzerland, office 431 Battery
DeSucca B. dwl 622 Pacific
DeSucca James, molder, 541 Mission
DeTavel A. veterinary surgeon, office 427 Pine
DeValk Henry, with Edward McDevitt, 216 Davis
DeVaul John, butcher with Mrs. M. O'Brian, dwl Government House
DeVecque Joseph, laborer, dwl 1717 Powell
DeVries *(Thomas)* & Chase *(James B.)* stevedores and ballasters, office W s Battery bet Broadway and Vallejo, dwl 1514 Mason
DeWard M. (widow) laundress, dwl 118 Minna
DeWITT *(Alfred)* KITTLE *(Nicholas G.)* & CO. *(Jonathan G. Kittle)* shipping and commission merchants, NW cor California and Front, res New York
DeWitt Andrew, carpenter, dwl N s Welch bet Third and Fourth
DeWitt William, bar keeper, Sanders' Hotel, 44 Sacramento
DeWitte John J. interpreter, dwl 625 Merchant
DeWolf Samuel J. Mrs. dwl 423 Harrison
DeYoung Amelia (widow) dwl 422 Bush
DeYoung Charles *(G. & C. DeYoung)* dwl 422 Bush
DeYOUNG G. & C. proprietors Daily Dramatic Chronicle, office 417 Clay, dwl 422 Bush
DeYoung John, captain sloop W. R. Allen, dwl 26 Stewart
DeYoung Michel, carrier, Daily Dramatic Chronicle, dwl 422 Bush
DeYoung Morris, broker, dwl 949 Mission
Deacon James, workman, S. F. & P. Sugar Co. dwl Brannan nr Potrero
Dead Whale Asphaltum Co. office 404 Montgomery
DEAF, DUMB, AND BLIND ASYLUM, SE cor Fifteenth and Mission
Deagan Patrick, stone cutter, bds 541 Mission
Deaks John, carpenter, dwl 17 Frederick
Dean Benjamin *(Hostetter, Smith & D.)* dwl 608 Sutter
Dean Benjamin D. physician, office room 10 Belden's Block, SW cor Bush and Montgomery, dwl 104 Stockton
Dean Eunice (widow) dwl 6 Langton
Dean F. W. stevedore, dwl NW cor First and Folsom
Dean George A. straw hat presser, dwl 538 Mission
DEAN H. C. butcher, 1 Occidental Market, dwl Russ House
Dean James O. auditor Savings and Loan Society, 619 Clay, dwl 104 Stockton
Dean J. B. molder, Pacific Foundry, dwl 538 Mission
Dean John, job wagon, cor Sansom and Clay, dwl N s Clay bet Hyde and Larkin
Dean Joseph (col'd) barber, dwl 923 Broadway
Dean J. T. merchant, office 314 Washington, dwl 516 Folsom
Dean Oliver, clerk with Aaron Claflin & Co. 406 Front, dwl 1106 Powell
Dean Preston, miner, dwl 6 Langton
DEAN W. E. secretary, Chollar-Potosi M. Co. 706 Montgomery, dwl 103 Powell
DEANE CHARLES T. physician, office 26 Montgomery, dwl 724 Bush
Deane George A. molder, dwl 537 Mission
DEANE JAMES R. importer and jobber paints, oils, window glass, etc. 318 Clay, dwl Serpentine Avenue, nr San Bruno Road
Deane John *(Murphy, Grant & Co.)* dwl Occidental Hotel

Deane William, carpenter, dwl 219 Kearny
Deane, see Deen
Dearborn J. P. *(Coley & D.)* dwl 121 Fourth
Dearien William H. carpenter, dwl W s Langton nr Folsom
Dearinger Jerry, plasterer, dwl 113 William
Dearlove George, house agent, dwl 6 Pollard Place
Deas Zephaniah, produce, dwl Verona nr Third
Deaven Ann (widow) dwl W s Bernal nr Precita Avenue
Deaves Edwin, artist and engraver, 224 Fourth
Deb\'{a}ck Josiah, express wagon, dwl 830 Harrison
Debernardi Louis, cook, 512 Clay
Debernardi Natale, cook, 512 Clay
Debije John, ranch, W Jewish Cemetery, Mission Dolores
Dehney Gerrard, mariner, dwl E s Hyde bet Washington and Clay
Debus Matilda Mrs. dwl SW cor Seventeenth and Dolores, rear
Decalso Luca, drayman, cor Davis and Washington
Deck Frederick, oysterman, 605 Commercial
Decker Barbara (widow) dwl 268 Jessie
Decker Christian, dwl 3 Harrison Avenue
Decker Christian J. upholsterer, dwl Morse nr Bush
Decker Frederick A. with Martin Hashagan, dwl 102 Sacramento
Decker Henry & Co. *(J. H. Tum Suden)* Cosmopolitan Exchange Liquor Saloon, NW cor Bush and Sansom, dwl 273 First
Decker Henry, apprentice with Thomas O'Malley, 646 Market
Decker Henry M. clerk, NW cor Folsom and Twelfth
Decker Jacob, liquor saloon, SE cor Bush and Cemetery Avenue
Decker Martin *(Toby & D.)* dwl SW cor King and Third
Decker Peter Mrs. dwl Brevoort House
Decker Peter, seaman, dwl 238 Stewart
Decker Robert, clerk with Allerich Burmeister
Decker Susan (widow) dwl 531 Union
Deckert Constance, cook, dwl 716 Pacific
Deckodan Raymond, fruits, dwl 916 Montgomery
Dee Hannah Miss, domestic, 911 Jackson
Dee Mary M. Miss, domestic, 803 Mason
Deede Alexander, handcartman, cor Stockton and Pacific, dwl SE cor Broadway and Powell
Deeds George, dwl W s Mason bet Valparaiso and Greenwich
Deegan Patrick, stone cutter, Fort Point
Deely Dennis, warehouseman, U. S. Clothing Depôt, dwl 331 Fourth nr Folsom
Deen H. F. dwl St. Francis Engine House
Deen James E. steward St. Francis H. & L. Co. dwl St. Francis Engine House
Deering Charles J. merchant, office 419 Clay, dwl 819 California
Deering James H. *(Deering Bros. Tuolumne Co.)* wholesale boots and shoes, 419 Clay, dwl 819 California
Deering Mathew, milk ranch, dwl junction Old San José Road and San José Railroad
Deeth Dexter, book keeper with Russell & Erwin Manufacturing Co. dwl 418 Geary
Deeth *(Jacob)* & Starr *(Thomas N.)* ship bread and cracker bakery, 203 and 205 Sacramento, and State Stamp Inspector, office 424 Battery, dwl 562 Howard
Deetkin E. Mrs. assistant, Stevenson St. School, dwl 60 Natoma
Deffebach Thomas B. *(Agnew & D.)* dwl 827 Wash
Deffeny Mary Miss, domestic, 1022 Jackson
Defraw Madame, dress maker, dwl 1314 Dupont
Degear George W. carpenter, 104 Beale
DEGEN PHILIP, tanner, Old San José Road nr Industrial School
Deidrickson Christopher, rigger, bds 606 Third
Deihl Conrad, beer saloon, dwl 532 Broadway

Deininger Christian F. Rev. Merriman's Hall, 635 Mission, dwl 251½ Clementina
Deirs John, laborer, dwl 617 Davis
Deiterle J. (widow) dwl 215 Kearny, rear
Deitz Adam, hair dresser, 416 Folsom
Deitz Andreas, dwl 123 Tehama
Deitz Charles, bar keeper, W s Main bet Harrison and Bryant
Deitz George, book keeper with Wheelan & Co. dwl 15 Tehama
Deitz Henry, cartman, dwl Rousch nr Folsom
Deitz Jacob, barber, dwl SE cor First and Jessie
Deitz Louisa (widow) dwl 560 Howard
Dejean Louis, fruits, 430 Kearny
Dejonghe Peter, tailoring, 104 Sutter
Dejort Albert, fruits, 1620 Stockton
Dejout Marie Miss, domestic, 708 Howard
Delabigne J. B. produce commission and leather and flour depôt, 323 Clay, dwl 642 Sacramento
Delafont Leopold, bar and billiard saloon, SW cor Pine and Kearny
Delahanty Bridget Miss, domestic, 214 Ellis
Delahanty Michael, private boarding, 127 St. Mark Place
Delaney Anne Miss, domestic with Mrs. W. L. Perkins, E s Eleventh bet Market and Mission
Delaney Bridget Miss, dwl W s August Alley near Union
Delaney Daniel, musician, Maguire's Opera House, dwl W s Mary Lane nr Sutter
Delaney Isabella (widow) dwl 510 Folsom
Delaney James, laborer, dwl 817 Vallejo, rear
Delaney Michael, veterinary surgeon, 733 Market, dwl N s Washington bet Gough and Octavia
Delaney Patrick, laborer, dwl 764 Howard
Delaney Wm. D. ship carpenter, dwl 816 Folsom, rear
Delano Charles M. book keeper with Sullivan & Cashman, dwl SE cor Eddy and Mason
Delano Robert T. calker, dwl 221 Harrison
Delano Silas L. wheelwright, 713 Mission, dwl SW cor Folsom and Folsom Avenue
Delano Thomas S. wood and coal, 233 Fourth
Delano Walter H. wood and coal, 326 Geary, dwl 783 Market
Delano Warren, hay merchant, dwl NE cor Broadway and Kearny
Delanty William, laborer, dwl 511 Mission
Delanty William, warehouseman, New Orleans Warehouse, dwl 21 Minna
Delany A. L. butcher, W s Sixth bet Harrison and Bryant
Delany Charles, porter with Abel Guy, dwl 411 Washington
DELANY CHARLES McC. attorney at law, office 519 Montgomery, dwl 324 Sutter
Delany Edward, cooper, dwl cor Sutter and Mary Lane
Delany Edward, stevedore, dwl 50 Natoma
Delany Ephraim (col'd) porter, dwl with James Sampson
Delany James, laborer, dwl 214 Commercial
Delany John, cabinet maker, dwl 15 Geary
Delany Margaret Miss, cook, Mt. St. Joseph
Delany Mary Miss, domestic, 748½ Market
Delapierre F. fireman, Cosmopolitan Hotel
Delarnevelle Gustave, bar tender, dwl 18 St. Charles nr Kearny
Delatour Alexander, book keeper, dwl E s Jansen bet Lombard and Greenwich
Delaunay H. painter, 632 Pacific, rear
Delavan John, pilot, 5 Vallejo, dwl 826 Union
Delay Julia, domestic, 345 Fourth
Delbanco Fanny Madame, midwife, dwl 232 Kearny
Delbanco N. clerk with S. Herrmann & Co. dwl S s California bet Dupont and Kearny
Deletti Vicente, fisherman, 3 Italian Fish Market
Delex Eleanor, dwl W s Valencia bet Seventeenth and Eighteenth

Delf Marcus, seaman, dwl 705 Battery
Delfert Johan, hairdresser, 9 Jackson
Delic Juan, vegetable garden, nr Hunter's Point
Dell John E. carpenter with James Brokaw, dwl 31 Second
DELL (L. B.), CRANNA (William R.) & CO. importers lamps, kerosene, alcohols, and oils, 511½ and 513 Front
DELL LEWIS B. resident agent Phœnix Insurance Co. Hartford, and Traveller's Insurance Co. Hartford, office 605 Commercial cor Montgomery, dwl 358 Brannan
Dellahan John, soda wagon driver, dwl NE cor Harrison and Third
Dellahan Michael, laborer, 30 Jessie
Dellahanty Cornelius, with H. Casebolt & Co. dwl 30 Jessie
Dellahanty Richard, laborer, dwl Beale Place
Dellahanty William, laborer, dwl 28 Natoma Place
Dellapaine (Joseph) & Co. (Pietro Alferitz) wholesale and retail grocers, 426 Battery cor Washington, dwl SE cor Montgomery and Pacific
Dellwig Theodore (Dellwig & Bro.) dwl SW cor Mission and Fourth
Dellwig (Louis A.) & Bro. (Theodore Dellwig) fancy bakery, SW cor Mission and Fourth
Delmaestro Gulielmo, dwl 431 Pine
Delmore Ann Miss, domestic, dwl 1018 Clay
Deloche (Jean B.) & Corthay (Louis) poultry, butter, cheese, and eggs, 9 New Market, dwl 712 Harrison bet Ritch and Third
Delpodiot Jean, tailor, dwl 528 Vallejo
Delsol August, waterman, 609 Market, dwl N s Vallejo bet Dupont and Stockton
Delventhal Jos. musician, SW cor Jack and Davis
Delventhal William, groceries, SW cor Jackson and Davis
Demangeon Auguste, with Cameron, Whittier & Co. dwl 1622 Stockton
Demarest Jacob D. physician, office NE cor Jackson and Kearny, dwl W s Shotwell bet Twentieth and Twenty-First
Demartinni Joseph, laborer, dwl W s Union Place
Demas John, dwl 317 Jessie
Demay Andrew, coal passer, stm Yosemite
Deme Augustus, carriage painter with Black & Saul, dwl 330 Kearny
Demerest James H. jail keeper, County Jail, dwl N s Broadway nr Jones
Démeritt Eldridge J. teamster with Peter Sesser, dwl NW cor Minna and Sixth
DEMING (H. A.) & CO. (Thomas A. Cutter) agents Howe's Sew'g Machines, 3 Montgomery, Masonic Temple, dwl 122 Geary
Deming John T. dwl 532 Commercial
Demmick Henry, foreman molder Union Foundry, dwl 66 Natoma
Demming Charles, conductor, Omnibus R. R. Co
Demming J. conductor, Omnibus R. R. Co
Demming John, steward, Pacific Mail S. S. Co
Demont Lorenzo, clerk, dwl 427 Filbert
Demousset M. (Paulin Huant & Co.) dwl 735 Green
Dempsey Ellen Miss, domestic, 121 Eddy
Dempsey James, laborer, dwl 119 Commercial
Dempsey Jeremiah, marble worker, dwl 10 Sutter
Dempsey John, shoe maker, N s Brannan nr Sixth, dwl Sixth nr Brannan
Dempsey Patrick, bakery, 127 Fourth
Dempsey Patrick, waiter, What Cheer House Restaurant
Dempsey Peter, attorney at law, office 604 Merch
Dempsey William, bar keeper, Willows, SW cor Mission and Eighteenth
Dempster C. J. (Ross, D. & Co.) dwl S s Twelfth bet Mission and Howard
Denca Stephen, porter, dwl 1018 Stockton
Deney A. & Co. importers wines and liquors, 623 Sansom, dwl NW cor Sansom and Jackson

Deney Ernest M. porter with A. Deney & Co. dwl 623 Sansom
Denegri Andrea, fruits, 329 Kearny
Denegri Joseph, fruits, dwl 1508 Dupont
Denehy Patrick, proprietor Winthrop House, 524 Mission
Denett Joseph, lather, dwl 23 Natoma
Denham William, Mechanics' Saloon, SW corner Kearny and Pacific, dwl 934 Kearny
Denier Jean, housesmith, dwl S s Pine bet Dupont and Kearny
Denigan Thomas C. book keeper with Christy & Wise, dwl American Exchange
Denike Wm. J. house painter, 805 Washington, dwl cor Leavenworth and Vallejo
Denis Modiste, first cook Miners' Restaurant, dwl California Hotel
Denis Zocchi, fruits, 1307 Dupont
Denison A. G. *(Blake & D.)* (col'd) dwl 615 Merch
Denmark *(Jacob H.)* & Horning *(Diedrick J.)* groceries and liquors, NW cor Taylor and Pacific
Denman James, principal Denman Grammar School, dwl Lick House
Denn John, dwl 13 Moss
Denn Thomas, waiter, Russ House
Dennahay Daniel, laborer, dwl 306 Minna
Dennan Patrick, laborer, dwl W s Church nr Seventeenth
Dennehy D. shoe making, 7 Sansom
Denner Peter, cook, dwl N s Heron nr Eighth
Denney Alexander, bar keeper, 616 Montgomery, dwl Powell nr Broadway
Denney Ellen Miss, dwl 26 Louisa
Denney John, seaman, dwl 26 Louisa
Denney John, ship carpenter, dwl 116 Sansom
Denney J. P. calker, dwl 116 Sansom
Denney Samuel D. ornithologist, dwl N s Union bet Hyde and Larkin
Denning Hannah (widow) fancy goods and fruits, 938 Market
Dennis George H. property man, Olympic Melodeon, dwl SW cor Dupont and Filbert
Dennis George W. express wagon, Montgomery nr Washington, dwl 919 Post
Dennis Jacob, liquor saloon, 616 Pacific
Dennis James S. bar keeper, 616 Montgomery, dwl 21 Ritch
Dennis Jean B. butcher, dwl 645 Pacific
Dennis John R. stone cutter with Francis Williams, dwl SE cor Pine and Battery
Dennis Joseph, deck hand, stm Relief
Dennis Mary Miss, domestic, 1007 Washington
Dennis Mary A. Miss, domestic, 27 Post
Dennis Michael, laborer, stm Orizaba
Dennis Nelson, carpenter, S. F. & San José R. R. dwl cor Brannan and Ninth
Dennis Ozies, carpenter, dwl 605 Third
Dennis Peter, lumber piler with Hobbs, Gilmore & Co. dwl 629 Vallejo
DENNIS S. W. dentist, office 652 Market corner Kearny, bds Russ House
Dennis Thomas W. molder, dwl 274 Jessie
Dennis William E. jr. dwl with M. S. Gill, SE cor Hayes and Pierce
Dennison Benjamin T. bar keeper, dwl 145 Fourth
Dennison B. Frank, dwl 1409 Kearny
Dennison Ezra F. ranchero, dwl N s Sixteenth bet Valencia and Guerrero
Dennison James R. clerk with Wm. Lindsey, 536 Washington, dwl W s Sansom bet Greenwich and Filbert
Dennison James W. dwl W s Main nr Folsom
Dennison Maria J. (widow) boarding, 704 Howard
Dennison Richard, tinsmith, dwl E s Kearny bet Union and Filbert
Denniston Isaac V. farmer, dwl N s Seventeenth bet Guerrero and Dolores
Denniston James G. dwl W s Dolores bet Fifteenth and Sixteenth

Denniston Richard, coppersmith with G. & W. Snook, dwl 1408 Kearny
Dennoe Alfred, book keeper, dwl 139 Jessie
Dennoe Elizabeth (widow) dwl 139 Jessie
Denny Bridget (widow) dwl S s Pinkham Place nr Eighth
Denny Charles W. local policeman, dwl 5 Harrison Avenue
Denny Daniel, laborer, dwl 282 Stevenson
Denny Edward, clerk, 413 Sansom, dwl S s Sixteenth bet Folsom and Shotwell
Denny J. Gideon, broker, dwl 423 Harrison
DENNY G. J. marine and landscape painter, studio 238 Montgomery, dwl 423 Harrison
Denny John W. house and sign painter, 617 Montgomery, dwl 276 Minna
Denny Margaret (widow) dwl 737 Broadway
Denny Mary Miss, domestic, 722 Folsom
Denny Mary A. Miss, domestic with Charles L. Bugbee
Denny Timothy, carpenter, dwl 465 Minna
Denny W. (widow) Potomac House, S s Folsom bet Main and Spear
Denny W. J. brass molder, dwl 140 Natoma
Dense Julia A. (widow) dress maker, 619 Mission
Denslow Mellville, printer with Towne & Bacon, 536 Clay
Densmore G. B. Golden Era office 543 Clay, dwl 663 Howard
Dent George W. dwl E s Howard bet Fifteenth and Sixteenth
Dent Henry S. dwl E s Howard bet Fifteenth and Sixteenth
Dent Patrick, cooper, S. F. & P. Sugar Co. dwl S s Heron nr Eighth
Dentler Alice (widow) nurse, dwl 1308 Kearny
Deoatht Henry, laborer, dwl cor Douglass and Corbett
Depken G. clerk with Charles Baum, dwl 321 Dupont
Deppermann Gustave, clerk, 111 Clay, dwl 526 Post
Deprette August, workman with C. Deprette, Hunter's Point Road nr St. Mary's College
Deprette Charles, vegetable garden, Hunter's Point Road nr St. Mary's College
Dupue P. H. express wagon, dwl 1305 Broadway
DERBEC ETIENNE, editor Courier de San Francisco, office 617 Sansom, dwl 907 Clay
Derby Charles W. teamster with S. J. Hopkins, dwl 253 Stevenson
Derby E. M. commission merchant, office 402 Front, res Brooklyn, Alameda Co
Derby George B. drayman, 730 Sacramento, dwl 608 Bush
Derby John L. school furniture, N s Mission bet Second and Third, dwl 247 Second
Derby L. N. dwl 145 Natoma
Derby Lydia W. Miss, assistant, Second St. School, dwl 145 Natoma
Derby William, drayman, dwl 608 Bush
Dereins Hypolite, butcher, 2 Clay St. Market
Derham Edward, butcher with Deeth & Starr, dwl cor Second and Brannan
Derham Hyacinthus Rev. O.S.D. assistant pastor St. Francis Church, N s Vallejo bet Dupont and Stockton
Derham James, porter with D. J. Oliver, dw 417 Tehama
Derham William, blacksmith, dwl 777 Folsom
Derham William, porter with D. J. Oliver, dwl 417 Tehama
Deri Lorenzo, laborer with Hentsch & Berton
Dermody James W. sawyer with Hobbs, Gilmore & Co. dwl 113 Jones
Dermody Michael, laborer, dwl NW cor Tyler and Franklin
Dermot John, carpenter, dwl 765 Howard
Dern Christina Mrs. dwl 1016 Stockton

Derognat Louis, laborer, Lafayette Brewery, Lafayette H. & L. Co. No. 2

Derondel Pierre, dwl 721 Pacific

Deroni Peter, pantryman Clipper Restaurant

Derrick Michael L. compositor, Alta California, dwl 1215 Pacific

Derrickson William, dwl 734 Mission

Derringer Jeremiah, plasterer, dwl 113 William

Derry August, clerk, dwl 1207 Dupont

Derry Patrick, laborer, dwl N s Oak nr Taylor

Derry *(W. R.)* & Cooper *(Randolph)* (colored) bootblacking, 225 Kearny

Derx Jacob, boot fitter, 319 Bush

Descaleo Luca, drayman, 324 Davis, dwl NW cor Turk and Polk

Descalzo Antonio *(Pietro, Sinne & Co.)* dwl 1013 Dupont

Desch Charles, physician, office and dwl 814 Washington

Deschaseaux Francis, restaurant, 507 Washington, dwl S s Washington nr Dupont

Descy Cornelius, fireman, City Water Works

Desebrock Frederick *(Dow & D.)* dwl SE cor Fourth and Brannan

Desera M. with François Bailly, 516 Clay

Desert Mining Co. office 529 Clay

Desman James, porter, dwl 116 Sansom

Desmeu Henry with Horace Porter, dwl Hayes' Park Pavilion

Desmond Cornelius, hatter, SW cor Bush and Sansom

Desmond Cornelius P. porter, American Exchange

Desmond Daniel, laborer, San Francisco Gas Co. dwl Meek Place

Desmond Daniel, wheelwright, dwl 212 Ritch

Desmond Edward, stevedore, dwl W s Main bet Folsom and Harrison

Desmond Felix, carpenter, dwl 1521 Mason

Desmond James, workman with C. V. Stuart, dwl N s Seventeenth bet Howard and Capp

Desmond Joanna Miss, milliner, 157 Third

Desmond Joseph D. painter, dwl 34 Second

Desmond Julia Miss, domestic, SW cor Howard and Fifteenth

Desmond Margaret Miss, milliner, 157 Third

Desmond Patrick, hostler with J. G. Scovern, dwl 120 William

Desmond Patrick, porter with Geo. C. Johnson & Co. dwl Bailey House

Desmond William, cabinet maker with W. G. Weir, dwl Gorden nr Harrison

Desmu Joseph, Prospect Market, 1202 Dupont, dwl 1207 Dupont

Desneufbour Leopold, dwl 843 Clay

Desnoufbour Mme, French dress maker, 843 Clay

Desprez Constant, billiard and liquor saloon, 520 Clay

Desprez Philip, workman with A. Brocq, Bay View

Dessaa John, agent and collector, office 617 Clay

Dessol August, cartman, dwl 1402 Powell

Destago Peter, sailor, dwl 816 Clay

Desty Robert, dwl 231 First

Desucca James, molder, Pacific Foundry, dwl Empire House

Desurlle Guiseppo, peddler, Bannam Place nr Green

Detels Henry *(Hagermann & D.)* dwl 521 Bryant

DETELS MARTEN, groceries and liquors, SE cor Harrison and Main

Detjens Henry, Eagle Saloon, 919 Kearny

Detjens William, bar keeper, 919 Kearny, dwl 619 Pacific

Detrick Henry, express wagon, cor Bush and Kearny

Detrick Jacob S. foreman machine shop Union Foundry, dwl 566 Howard

Detruit Charles, hair dresser, 509 Kearny

Dettelbach S. M. with Lazard Freres, dwl SE cor Stockton and Jackson

Dettelbrach Morris, junk dealer, 417 Brannan

Dettmar Henry, machinist, dwl 227 Kearny

Dettmer Anna Miss, domestic, 113 Taylor

Dettmer Henry, tailoring, 104 Sutter

Dettmer *(John)* & Luhrsen *(Frederick)* groceries and liquors, SE cor Montgomery and Filbert

Dettner George, cook, 706 Market, dwl 19 St. Mark Place

Deucher August, shoe maker, 704 Pacific

Deuber Alphouse, liquor saloon, 819 Kearny

Deussing Titus, salesman, 623 Clay, dwl 10 Virginia

Dentcher Michael, waiter, 614 Clay

Deutsch Jacob, boots and shoes, 1325 Stockton

Deuwel *(Joseph)* & Co. *(Peter Baltz)* New Orleans Bakery, 627 Broadway, dwl 634 Pacific

Devaurs François, laborer with B. Bonnet & Co

Develin Edward, laborer, dwl Battery near Vallejo

Devey Patrick, fruit dealer, dwl Bertha W s Beale

Deviercy Eugene *(Frontier & D. and Otto Wiedero & Co.)* dwl 740 Commercial

Devine Ann (widow) dwl W s Battery bet Vallejo and Broadway

Devine Benj. polisher, Chelsea Laundry

Devine Henry, job wagon, dwl 275 Minna

Devine John, box maker, dwl Western Hotel

Devine John, tailor, cor Spring and Summer

Devine Kate (widow) private school, 938 Market

Devine Margaret Miss, domestic, 119 Powell

Devine Mary Miss, dwl with William McCrossen, S s Stevenson bet Seventh and Eighth

Devine Owen, baker, dwl 108 First

Devine Patrick, blacksmith helper, dwl 1116 Howard

Devine P. J. marble cutter, dwl 28 Stanford bet Townsend and Brannan

Devine Thomas, janitor Spring Valley School

Devine Thomas, laborer, dwl 617 Geary

Devine Thomas, laborer, dwl SE cor Filbert and Van Ness Avenue

Devine Thomas, miner, dwl 533 Post

Devine William, local policeman, dwl Jansen nr Greenwich

Devinne Margaret Miss, dwl with Mrs. Nicholas Connolly, S s Bryant bet Seventh and Eighth

Devinney Joseph, stevedore, dwl 1528 Stockton

Devire Jeremiah, laborer, dwl 129 Pacific

Devis Ellen Mrs. (widow) dwl NW cor Townsend and Third

Devitt Edward, porter City Hall, dwl 510 Sac

Devitt Felix, cooper with T. Landy, dwl N s Tyler bet Hyde and Larkin

Devitt Frank, boatman, dwl N s Union bet Montgomery and Calhoun

Devlin Edward, laborer, dwl W s Battery bet Vallejo and Green

Devlin Mark, gardener, SE cor Union and Franklin

Devlin Mary Miss, dwl 223 Stevenson

Devlin Mathew, butcher, dwl SE cor Sixth and Clara

Devlin Sarah (widow) dwl 17 Hunt

Devlin Thomas, dwl 223 Stevenson

Devlin Thomas, laborer, dwl 206 Harrison

Devney Margaret, domestic with Isaac Cook, NW cor Fulton and Laguna

Devoe B. O. real estate, dwl 917 Clay

Devoe *(James)* Dinsmore *(Samuel)* & Co. *(James Devoe jr.)* San Francisco Machine and Iron Works, NE cor Mission and Fremont, dwl 874 Mission

Devoe James jr. *(Devoe, Dinsmore & Co.)* dwl 652 Market

Devoe Thomas H. clerk, dwl 627 Commercial

Devoto Antonio, fruits, 802 Kearny, dwl W s Kearny bet Washington and Jackson

Devries Thomas, stevedore, dwl 1514 Mason

DEWAR JOHN, commission merchant and agent Pioneer Line Victoria Packets, office 311 East, dwl 112 Natoma

Deweese William H. dwl 607 Greenwich

DEWEY *(A. T.)* & CO. *(Warren B. Ewer and C. W. M. Smith)* proprietors and publishers Mining and Scientific Press and patent agents, 505 Clay, dwl cor Mission and Thirteenth

Dewey *(A. T.)* Waters *(E. D. jr.)* & Co. *(W. B. Ewer and C. W. M. Smith)* book and job printing, 505 Clay

Dewey Eugene E. *(S. P. Dewey & Sons)* dwl Occidental Hotel

Dewey James, boatman, dwl NW cor Clay and Davis

Dewey John H. horse trainer, dwl 97 Stevenson

DEWEY S. P. & SONS *(William P. and Eugene E.)* real estate and stocks, office 410 Montgomery, dwl Occidental Hotel

Dewey William P. *(S. P. Dewey & Sons)* dwl 522 California

Dewing *(Francis)* & Laws *(Jeremiah)* importers subscription books, off 511 Sac, dwl 1048 Folsom

Dexter Albert G. locksmith, 108 Kearny

Dexter Charles, apprentice, 614 Market

DEXTER CHARLES H. saloon, 320 Montgomery, dwl 22 Montgomery

Dexter Charles H. jr. with McNally & Hawkins, dwl 22 Montgomery

Dexter Franklin, salesman with Locke & Montague, dwl 904 Jackson

DEXTER *(George R.)* LAMBERT *(C.)* & CO. *(Charles Barton)* manufacturers and dealers ribbons and trimmings, 105 Battery, resides Boston

Dexter Granville M. porter with Voizin, Ris & Co. dwl N s Riley nr Taylor

Dexter Henry S. dwl 557 Harrison

Dexter Peter B. recording secretary and librarian Mechanics' Institute, 529 California, dwl Sophie Terrace

Dexter R. master J. B. Lawrence, dwl 238 Stewart

Deyheigen Louis, waiter, dwl 150 Stewart

Dezou Paul; dwl 626 California

Dhaoo Mary Miss, domestic, 510 Third

Dhaw Mary, domestic, dwl NE cor Green and Union

Dhue John, stone cutter, Fort Point, dwl NE corner Green and Hyde

Diamant Bernard *(Kalisher & D.)* dwl 256 Jessie

Diamant Leopold, book keeper with W. & I. Steinhart, 321 Sacramento, dwl 129 Stevenson

Diamond Carrie Miss *(Mrs. and Miss D.)* dwl 404 Kearny

Diamond Dominic, plaster, dwl NE cor Third and Mission

Diamond John, drayman, dwl 10 Ritch

Diamond Joseph P. laborer, Union Foundry, dwl 10 Ritch

Diamond Mrs. & Miss *(Martha and Carrie)* millinery, 404 Kearny

Diana G. & S. M. Co. office 402 Front

Dias A. H. L. dwl 270 Tehama

Dias Amelia Miss, dwl NE cor Guerrero and Eighteenth

Dias Cebera Miss, dwl NE cor Guerrero and Eighteenth

Dias Florinda Miss, dwl NE cor Guerrero and Eighteenth

Dias Juana (widow) dwl N s Sixteenth bet Guerrero and Dolores

Dias Thomas, dwl NE cor Guerrero and Eighteenth

Dias Thomas, laborer, dwl W s Sonoma Place nr Green

Diaz Antonio C. clerk La Voz de Mejico, dwl 1821 Stockton

Diaz Tiburcia (widow) dwl 1606 Mason

Dibbern Henry, porter with Thomas Taylor & Co. 413 Clay, dwl SW cor Dupont and Greenwich

Dibbern J. drayman, dwl 1615 Dupont, rear

Dibble William S. book keeper with J. W. Brittan & Co. dwl 126 Perry

DIBBLEE *(Albert)* & HYDE *(William C.)* shipping and commission merchants, 108 Front, dwl Lick House

DICAUD JOSEPH H. groceries and liquors, SW cor Dupont and Vallejo

Dick David *(J. Vantine & Co.)* dwl NE cor Dupont and Washington

Dick Johnston Petroleum Co. (Humboldt) office 526 Washington

Dick Robert D. machinist, Vulcan Foundry, dwl 8 Brooks

Dick Stephen W. *(Dana & D.)* dwl SE cor Ellis and Franklin

Dick Theodore, baker, Lick House

Dick William & Co. *(George Campton)* pork packers, 65 Washington Market, dwl E s Second Avenue bet Sixteenth and Seventeenth

Dick William, laborer, dwl S s Commercial bet Drumm and East

Dickens Sarah M. Miss, photographic card mounter with Jacob Shew, dwl SE cor Second and Natoma

Dickenson Stanhope, dwl 607 Howard

Dickenson Francis R. (col'd) mariner, dwl 1804 Mason

Dickerman Lyman, boots and shoes, dwl 811 Jackson

Dickerson David E. carpenter, dwl NW cor Hayes and Webster

Dickey Eugene G. bar keeper, Ocean House

DICKEY GEORGE S. druggist, NW cor Third and Folsom, dwl 128 Fifth

DICKEY JAMES R. proprietor Ocean House, 6$\frac{1}{2}$ miles SW City Hall

Dickins Thomas W. dwl 7 Vassar Place

Dickinson Charles, with Wilson & Baker, 550 Clay

Dickinson Harvey, dwl NW cor Taylor and Green

Dickinson James G. clerk, 61 Washington Market, dwl 313 Kearny

DICKINSON *(O. jr.)* & GAMMANS *(George B.)* wholesale groceries and provisions, etc. 401 and 403 Front cor Clay, dwl 1020 Stockton

Dickinson S. mining secretary, office 423 Wash

Dickinson Seth J. first lieut. Co. I, C.V. Fort Point

Dickison C. C. lumberman, bds Franklin Hotel, SE cor Sansom and Pacific

Dickman Peter, laborer, Bay Sugar Refinery, dwl S s Union bet Battery and Sansom

Dickman William, photographic gallery, 121 Mont

DICKSON, DeWOLF & CO. *(George Campbell)* importing, shipping, and commission merchants, office 410–414 Battery

Dickson George R. agent William Shiels, dwl 319 Bush

Dickson James C. waterman, 609 Market

Dickson John T. cabinet maker with Crowe & Farrell, dwl 207 Third

Didas William, barber, dwl 243 Stevenson

Dieber Alfred V. sail maker, dwl 266 Minna

Diedech Jean, mixer, Pacific Glass Works, dwl Potrero Nuevo

Diedrich Conrad, baker, dwl 226 Pacific

Diederichsen Charles, Coloseum Saloon, 540 Jackson, dwl 826 Broadway

Diederickson William, tug boat Columbia, dwl 734 Mission

Diefenbacher Jacob, wig maker with C. Hubert, dwl 603 Montgomery

DIEHL CHRISTOPHER, baths and hair dressing saloon, 533 Sacramento, dwl 6 Pratt Court

Diehl *(Conrad)* & Hauser *(Bernard)* beer saloon, 1126 Dupont, dwl 532 Broadway

Diel Valentine, dwl 936 Mission

Diercks Elizabeth, domestic, 568 Bryant

Dierking Charles Rev. pastor German Meth. E. Church, 858 Folsom

Dierks John, seaman, bds 7 Washington

Dietch Leah Mrs. fancy dry goods, 312 Third

Dietch Samuel, tailor, 312 Third

Dietrich H. B. physician, office S s Bush above Kearny, dwl 511 Pine

Dietrich Henry, job wagon, NE cor Bush and Kearny, dwl Webb nr Sacramento

Dietrich Hugo B. hair dresser with Chretien Pfister, dwl 511 Pine

Dietrich John, groceries and liquors, SE cor Vallejo and Mason

Dietrich Richard, dwl N s Sutter bet Polk and Van Ness Avenue

DIETRICH WILLIAM K. curer and packer provisions, 54 and 55·Washington Market, dwl N W cor Union and Larkin

Dietterle Christopher, wagon maker, dwl E s Capp bet Twenty-Third and Twenty-Fourth

Dietterle Helena Mrs. clairvoyant, dwl E s Capp bet Twenty-Third and Twenty-Fourth

Dietz A. C. & Co. oil and camphene, office 519 and 521 Front, branch SW cor Clay and Kearny, resides Oakland

Diez Cayetano, cigar maker with E. Goslinsky, dwl 515 Filbert

Diggins Augustus, dwl N s Sutter bet Devisidero and Broderick

Diggins Byron, dwl N s Sutter bet Devisidero and Broderick

Diggins J. C. sawyer with James Brokaw, dwl 623 Howard

Diggins Wesley, mining stocks, dwl N s Sutter bet Devisidero and Broderick

Diggs William H. Capt. mariner, dwl S s Seventeenth bet Guerrero and Dolores

Dikeman Daniel S. deputy superintendent streets, City Hall, dwl 2 Clarence Place

Diller George W. cigars and tobacco, 621 Montgomery, dwl cor First and Folsom

Dillmann George F. Monitor Saloon, 825 Kearny, dwl 1009 Kearny

Dillmann Mathias, bar keeper, 825 Kearny, dwl 1009 Kearny

Dillon Ann Miss, dwl 72 Natoma

Dillon Catharine (widow) dwl 366 Minna

Dillon James (Ryan & D.) dwl 28 Third

Dillon James, coachman, dwl E s Laguna nr Hayes

Dillon James H. boot maker, dwl N s Vallejo bet Montgomery and Sansom, rear

Dillon John P. salesman, SE cor Post and Kearny

Dillon Joseph, steward, 331 Bush

Dillon Luke, job wagon, 315 Battery, dwl 406 Third

Dillon M. & Co. liquor saloon, 212 Bush

Dillon Margaret Miss, domestic with J. R. Deane, Serpentine Avenue nr San Bruno Road

Dillon Mary A. Miss, domestic, Deaf, Dumb, and Blind Asylum, SE cor Fifteenth and Mission

Dillon Mary Ann Mrs. dress maker, 406 Third

Dillon Mary E. Mrs. dress maker, dwl 265½ Tehama

Dillon (Michael) & Chandler (Charles) liquor saloon, 212 Bush

Dillon Michael, fruit peddler, NW cor Montgomery and Vallejo

Dillon Michael, laborer, dwl 4 Hunt

Dillon Michael J. wagon maker with Gallagher & Rodecker, dwl 227 Sansom

Dillon Nicholas, dwl 9 Baldwin Court

Dillon P. (Bacca & Co.) dwl Potrero Avenue

Dillon Patrick, molder, Union Foundry, dwl Folsom nr First

Dillon Robert, butcher, S s Harrison bet Seventh and Eighth

Dillon Robert, salesman, SE cor Post and Kearny

Dillon Sarah Miss, domestic with Adolph Pavillier, E s First Avenue nr Fifteenth

Dillon (Thomas) & Hanlon (John) stair builders, 406 Natoma, dwl 404 Natoma

Dillon Thomas, hardware, SE cor Post and Kearny

Dillon William, with Dyer, Badger & Rokohl, 300 Montgomery

Diltz Austin M. laborer, Lone Mountain Cemetery

Dilyes Conrad, waiter, dwl 633 Broadway

Dimler Charles, sail maker with John Harding, 215 Front, dwl 266 Minna

Dimmer Nicholas, groceries and liquors, dwl 815 Pac

Dimmick Henry, molder, dwl 47 Natoma

Dimon Jacob S. merchant, dwl 566 Bryant

Dimon John, workman with Bergerot & Co. dwl NW cor Sixteenth and Rhode Island

Dimond Hugh (Sullivan & Cashman) dwl 604 , Sutter

Dimond James, dwl 44 Ritch

Dimond John, dwl 123 Shipley

Dimpfel Josephine Miss, music teacher, dwl 1221 Clay

Dinan Jeremiah B. with Fred Collier, dwl NW cor Pine and Mason

Dinan Timothy, laborer, dwl 13 St. Mary

Dineen Jerry, hostler, North Beach & M. R. R. Co

Dinegan Margaret Mrs. dwl Hinckley Alley nr Vallejo

DINGEON LEON, proprietor Barnum Restaurant, 621 and 623 Commercial

Dinger (Philip) & Berthold (Louis) Fell's Point Market, 703 Battery

Dingle George (col'd) with Lee & Williams, dwl Merchant nr Montgomery

Dingle George R. D. engineer, dwl 227 Green

Dingle Nelson H. driver, Central R. R. Co. dwl NW cor Brannan and Sixth

Dingley Charles L. captain bark Adelaide Cooper, office Pier 9 Stewart, dwl 343 Fremont

Dingley William H. dwl 466 Jessie

Dinkelspiel Lazarus (Simon, D. & Co.) dwl 730 Post

Dinkelspiel Samuel B. importer watches, jewelry, etc. 607 Washington, dwl 233 Sixth

Dinklage Joquina (widow) dwl 1418 Powell

Dinneen Catherine (widow) dwl E s Dora nr Harrison

Dinneen Margaret Miss, hairdresser, dwl E s Dora nr Harrison

Dinniene J. H. glass cutter, dwl SW cor Beale and Mission

Dinsmore Samuel (Devoe, D. & Co.) dwl 37 Fifth

Dios Padre G. & S. M. Co. (Sonora, Mexico) office 1 Government House

DIRECTORY CITY AND COUNTY SAN FRANCISCO, office 612 Clay, Henry G. Langley proprietor

DIRECTORY OF THE PACIFIC STATES, office 612 Clay, Henry G. Langley proprietor

Dirking August, importer watches and materials, 621 Washington

Disaway Cornelius D. bds with Simeon F. Smith, N s Fourteenth nr Guerrero

Dischenger William, butcher, dwl 617 Jackson

Discorni Louis, gardener, SE cor Guerrero and Fifteenth

Disney Mordecai, dwl 204 Stockton

Diss F. A. J. merchant, dwl 122 Natoma

Dissat Antoine, hairdresser with C. Hubert

Dissosway H. P. (Winant & Co.) dwl 35 Clara

DISTRICT ATTORNEY City and County San Francisco, office 20 second floor City Hall

DISTRICT ATTORNEY U. S. office 3 U. S. Court Building, SW cor Montgomery and Jackson

DISTRICT COURT California, Fourth District, room 14 second floor City Hall

DISTRICT COURT California, Twelfth District, room 1 second floor City Hall

DISTRICT COURT California, Fifteenth District, room 16 second floor City Hall

DISTRICT COURT U. S. rooms SW cor Montgomery and Jackson

Disturnell N. F. clerk, Merchants' Mutual Marine Insurance Co. dwl 465 Clementina

Disturnell Richard O. conductor, Central R. R. Co. dwl 465 Clementina

Dithmar Augustus C. machinist, Miners' Foundry, dwl 331 Fourth, rear

Dithmar H. F. machinist, Miners' Foundry
Dittes Michael, barber, dwl 243 Stevenson
Dittmer Charles, proprietor Golden Eagle Hotel, 219 Kearny
Dittmer, Frederick, tailor, dwl N s Vallejo bet Stockton and Powell
Ditty Frances (widow) dwl 1036 Folsom, rear
Diver John, baker, dwl 108 First
Diverdy John, cook, American Bakery, dwl 1027 Dupont
Dividend G. & S. M. Co. office 338 Montgomery
Divine Belle Miss, actress, Metropolitan Theater
Divine Lawrence, waiter, steamer Yosemite
Divine William, special policeman, dwl W s Jansen bet Greenwich and Lombard
Divisich Stephen, steward, dwl 711 Pacific
Dix Casper, clerk, cor Presidio Road and Fillmore
Dix George, dwl 10 Scott
Dixey Francis, merchant tailor, 625 Washington, dwl N s Sutter bet Polk and Van Ness Avenue
Dixon Block, SW cor Natoma and Jane
Dixon Clement, ship carpenter, dwl 313 Fifth
Dixon *(Elizabeth Miss)* & Putnam *(Elizabeth Mrs.)* milliners and millinery goods, 615 Clay
Dixon *(James E.)* & Vagts *(George)* lamps, oils, crockery, and glassware, 144 Fourth and drayman with Stanford Brothers, dwl 616 Lombard
Dixon John *(Jones, Dixon & Co.)* res New York
Dixon John, carpenter, dwl 828 Union
Dixon John, tinsmith with M. Prag, 125 Clay
Dixon John G. laundryman, Davis' Laundry, W s Harriet bet Howard and Folsom
Dixon John J. plumber with Thomas Day, 732 Montgomery, dwl 46 Clary
Dixon Richard, laborer, San Francisco Baths, 636 Washington, dwl 1223 Pacific
Dixon Robert, salesman, 411 Sacramento, dwl American Exchange
Dixon Samuel *(Peter Thomson & Co.)* dwl 605 Sac
Dixon Thomas J. clerk with J. H. O'Brien & Co. 706 Montgomery, dwl 46 Clary
Doane Jefferson, blacksmith, Fulton Foundry, dwl SW cor First and Stevenson
Doane J. G. teamster, 50 Stewart, dwl Turk nr Laguna
Doane John O. book keeper with Kerby, Byrne & Co. dwl S s Stevenson bet Sixth and Seventh
Doane Joshua G. teamster, Pier 4 Stewart, dwl S s Turk bet Laguna and Buchanan
Doane Lucy J. (widow) dwl 42 Hawthorne
Doane Marshall, hay press manufacturer, W s Shotwell bet Twenty-First and Twenty-Second
Doane Micah, drayman with Chas. F. Chadbourne, dwl 1420 Dupont
Doane Soloman, dwl SW cor Gough and Geary
Doane Wilber G. salesman, 119 Montgomery, dwl SW cor Market and Third
Dobbie James B. tinsmith with D. S. Weaver, dwl 115 Dupont
Dobelmana *(Philip)* & Einsfield *(Peter)* hairdressers, 9 Second, dwl 26 Jessie
Dober Joseph W. B. carpenter, dwl 536 Tehama
Doberer Henry W. photographic printer, dwl 526 Merchant
Doble Abner *(Nelson & D.)* dwl cor Pierce and Greenwich
Doble John, book keeper, 321 Pine
Dobnsbeck Sarah A. (widow) lodgings, 13 Third
Dobrzensky Julius, gas meter maker, dwl 429 Stevenson
Dobrzensky Julius, peddler, dwl 162 Minna
Dobrzensky Morris, gas meter maker and brass finisher, 417 Mission, dwl 347 Jessie
Dobrzensky Phœbe Miss, domestic, 162 Minna
Dobson George, seaman, dwl 333 East
Dockendorff Amiel, with Henry Kohn, cor Turk and Leavenworth
Dockendorff George C. employé, S. F. Chemical Works, NW cor Valencia and Fifteenth

Dockery Jennie L. Miss, domestic, dwl 1415 Powell
Dockham Daniel S. hog ranch, dwl 106 Dora
Dodd Benjamin, longshoreman, bds 133 Folsom
Dodd James H. driver, Presidio Omnibus, dwl 16 Turk
Dodd R. C. Pacific Engine Co. No. 8
Dodeene James, workman with L. L. Lefebore, dwl W s Florida nr Twentieth
Dodge Ansel H. carpent, dwl Stevenson House
DODGE BROTHERS *(J. C. and H. L.)* & CO. *(John Sroufe)* California and Eastern wholesale dealers provisions, 406 Front, dwl 821 California
Dodge Charles F. office with H. S. Bunker, 24 Bat
Dodge Robert K. dwl 107 Leidesdorff
Dodge Daniel *(Berghofer & D.)* dwl 611 Howard
Dodge David, carpenter, dwl 64 Tehama
Dodge David F. *(S. D. Wilson & Co.)* dwl 619 Pine
Dodge E. J. with Blair & Co. 28 Washington, dwl 21 Minna
Dodge Eleazer E. Excelsior Market, SE corner Sixteenth and Mission
Dodge *(Francis)* & Ziegler *(J. Louis)* house movers, 669 Mission
Dodge H. L. *(Dodge Bros. & Co.)* dwl 821 Cal
Dodge Josiah W. purser steamer America, dwl W s Second Avenue bet Camp and Seventeenth
Dodge Martha Mrs. lodgings, dwl 243 Second
Dodge Nathan, clerk with J. E. Wolfe, dwl 525 Geary
Dodge Thomas H. carpenter, dwl 30 Battery
Dodge William H. dwl 325 Folsom
DODGE *(W. W.)* & PHILLIPS *(D. L.)* wholesale groceries and provisions, 325 Front, dwl 15 Rincon Place
Dodson Griffin (col'd) porter, dwl 908 Pacific, rear
DOE B. & J. S. importers and jobbers doors, windows, and blinds, junction Market and California, res Boston
Doe Charles, with B. & J. S. Doe, dwl 13 Anthony
Doe John, hostler, dwl 712 Broadway
Doe J. S. *(B. & J. S. Doe)* dwl 521 Pine
Doe Mark H. pattern maker, Miners' Foundry, bds 770 Howard
Doerfler Joseph, boot maker, NW cor Howard and Eighth
DOERGER CHARLES & CO. *(Charles Kurre)* ivory turners, 539 Sacramento, dwl 1027 Pacific
Dogan Lary, mechanic, dwl 200 Front
Dogget Richard, laborer, dwl 105 William
Dohaney James, carpenter, dwl W s Sumner bet Howard and Folsom
Doheny Michael, laborer, dwl 117 Shipley
Doherty A. & H. bag dealers, 215 Davis, dwl cor Turk and Taylor
Doherty Alexander, laborer, dwl 110 Freelon, rear
Doherty Barnaby B. contractor, dwl 1 Sherwood Pl
Doherty Barney, farmer, Laguna de Puerca, near Ocean House
Doherty Edward, laborer, dwl N s Union bet Hyde and Larkin
Doherty Ellen Miss, domestic, 126 Turk
Doherty Francis, laborer, dwl E s Larkin between Broadway and Vallejo
Doherty George, contractor, dwl 416 Lombard
Doherty H. *(A. & H. Doherty)* dwl cor Turk and Taylor
Doherty James, hack driver, dwl 1008 Pacific
Doherty James, hostler, dwl 706 Commercial
Doherty Jane Miss, domestic, Jackson bet Larkin and Hyde
Doherty John, hack driver, dwl 820 Dupont
Doherty John, retortman, San Francisco Gas Co
Doherty John, workman, S. F. & P. Sugar Co. dwl N s Bryant nr Eighth
Doherty John C. furniture, dwl 762 Howard
Doherty Josephine Miss, domestic, Brevoort House
Doherty Kate Miss, domestic with John W. Harker

Doherty Margaret Miss, domestic, 113 Prospect Pl
Doherty Maria, domestic, 750 Howard
Doherty Mary, domestic, 566 Bryant
Doherty Michael, mechanic, San Francisco Gas Co
Doherty Patrick, retortman, San Francisco Gas Co
Doherty Rosa Miss, domestic, NW cor Twenty-Fourth and Mission
Doherty Timothy, workman, S. F. & P. Sugar Co., dwl 16 Rousch
Doherty William K. physician and surgeon, SE cor Sacramento and Leidesdorff, dwl 109 Sansom
Doherty, see Dougherty, O'Doherty, and O'Dougherty
Dohoney John, drayman, cor Stewart and Mission, dwl 117 Shipley
Doboty Matthew, frame maker, dwl 17 Fourth
Dohrmann J. H. professor piano, dwl 706 Bush
Doig George F. machinist, Grover & Baker Sewing Machine Co. dwl SE cor Second and Natoma
Dolan Annie (widow) seamstress, dwl 933 Sac
Dolan Ellen Miss, domestic, 421 Stockton
Dolan James, bricklayer, dwl 331 Bush
Dolan James, laborer, dwl 35 Sacramento
Dolan John, furrier with A. Muller, dwl Manhattan Engine House
Dolan John, laborer with Malachi Norton
Dolan John, laborer, Union Foundry, dwl 258 Clementina
Dolan John, tinsmith with Osgood & Stetson, dwl 810 Sansom
Dolan Katy Miss, domestic, 1412 Mason
Dolan M. & Co. (Otto Kaeding) dealers and jobbers foreign and domestic fruits, 538 Wash
Dolan Mary Miss, domestic, 1109 Folsom
Dolan Mary Miss, domestic, 516 Stockton
Dolan Mary Ann Miss, domestic, 121 Stockton
Dolan Michael, fruits, dwl 7 Scotland
Dolan Michael, job wagon, 300 California, dwl 107 Perry
Dolan Michael, laborer, dwl cor Kearny and Francisco
Dolan Michael, ship carpenter, 14 Broadway, dwl W s Seventh bet Folsom and Harrison
Dolan M. J. wheelwright, Eureka Hose Co. No. 4
Dolan Patrick, dwl 211 Pine
Dolan Patrick, laborer with Sedgley & Davis, dwl Mission Creek nr Mariposa
Dolan Patrick, painter, dwl 21 Lafayette Place
Dolan Patrick, tanner with Davis & Sedgley, dwl Mission Creek nr Mariposa
Dolan Rosanna Miss, domestic with Michael Cannavan
Dolan Thomas, fruits, NE cor Davis and Pacific, dwl N s Oregon bet Davis and Front
Dolan Thomas, helper, Pacific Foundry, dwl 28 Battery
Dolan Thomas, laborer, dwl 310 Ritch
Dolan Thomas, laborer, dwl N s McAllister bet Leavenworth and Hyde
Dolan Thomas J. carpenter, dwl NE cor Clay and Mason
Dolan Timothy, carpenter, bds Franklin Hotel, SE cor Sansom and Pacific
Dolan William, hackman, Plaza, dwl 1614 Stockton
DOLAN WILLIAM B. dwl NE cor Third and Hunt
Doland Patrick, house painter with J. W. Denny
Doland Thomas, laborer, Union Soap Factory, S s Braunan bet Fifth and Sixth, dwl Brannan bet Sixth and Seventh
DOLBEER (John) & CARSON (William) Humboldt lumber dealers, 36 Stewart, dwl American Exchange
Dolben David, milkman, dwl 14 Stockton Place
Dolchy John H. blacksmith, dwl 254 First
Dole Daniel N. porter, 206 California, dwl 505 O'Farrell
Dole Frank B. clerk, dwl 449 Minna
Dole John S. merchant, dwl 115 Prospect Place

Dolet August, butcher, 18 New Market, dwl S s Francisco bet Dupont and Stockton
Dolet Jean Baptiste, housesmith, dwl 713 Dupont
Dolbeguy B. importer liquors and provisions, 507 and 509 Front, dwl 421 Sutter
Dollah Frederick, watch maker, dwl 200 Sutter
Dollabanty Ann Mrs. domestic with John Armitage
Dollard John, drayman, 121 Front
Dolling Henry, laborer, dwl S s Filbert bet Leavenworth and Hyde
Dolliver Thomas, ladies' shoe manufacturer, 106 Sutter
Dolores Hall, W s Valencia bet Fifteenth and Sixteenth
Dolson Adelia E. Miss, music teacher, dwl E s Laskie bet Eighth and Ninth
Dolson Dewitt C. messenger, Custom House, dwl E s Laskie bet Eighth and Ninth
Dolson Theophilus, works with Michael Kenny
Domarus Otto, porter, 411 Sansom, dwl 30 Eddy
Dombrell James H. job wagon, dwl S s King bet Third and Fourth
Domett Charles H. proprietor Union Livery Stables, 13 and 15 Stevenson, dwl Domett Alley nr Bush
Domett J. W. saddle and harness, 20 First, dwl 523 Bush
Domett William E. pilot, 805 Front
Dominata Rocco, laborer, dwl N s Broadway bet Montgomery and Sansom
Domingo José, barber, 506 Mission
Domingus Antoine, waiter, Clipper Restaurant
Dominique (John) & Gonella (Zaverio) fruits and nuts, 1112 Dupont
Dominique Marseille, workman with Levi Bros. Bay View
Donahue Catharine Miss, domestic, dwl 618 Cal
Donahue Daniel, compositor, Monitor, dwl 624 Commercial
Donahue Dennis, drayman, cor First and Howard
Donahue Dennis, laborer, dwl 42 Natoma
Donahue Edward, laborer, dwl Rassette Place No. 3
Donahue James, cartman, cor Fourth and Brannan
Donahue James, fireman, steamer Julia, dwl 509 Mission
Donahue James, retortman, San Francisco Gas Co
Donahue Jeffrey, laborer, dwl Union Court
Donahue Jeremiah, laborer, dwl Rassette Place No. 3
Donahue Jeremiah, steward, dwl Zoe Place
Donahue John, laborer, Volunteer Engine Co. No. 7
Donahue John, laborer, San Francisco Gas Co
Donahue John C. laborer, dwl S s Broadway nr Leavenworth
Donahue Joseph, laborer, dwl N s Tehama nr Sixth
Donahue M. C. book keeper, dwl Oriental Hotel
Donahue Michael, hostler, dwl Bay View
Donahue Patrick, dwl S s Harrison nr Sixth
Donahue Patrick, hostler, 818 Mission
DONAHUE PETER, president Omnibus R. R. Co. dwl NE cor Second and Bryant
Donahue Peter, painter with John Duff
Donahue Philip, fireman, Pacific Distillery
DONAHUE PHILIP, proprietor Phil's Exchange and Restaurant, 417 Front, rooms 122 Montgomery Block
Donahue Thomas, scroll sawyer with James Brokaw, dwl 210 Pacific, Pacific Temperance House
Donahue Timothy, laborer, dwl N s Ellis bet Van Ness Avenue and Franklin
Donahue William, blacksmith, dwl 8 Pratt Court
Donahue William, miner, dwl S s Mariposa near Mississippi
Donahue, see Donohoe, Donohue, O'Donohoe, and O'Donohue
Donalan Michael, waiter, Occidental Hotel
Donalds Daniel, bar keeper, SW cor Market and Ecken
Donaldson E. J. Mrs. seamstress, dwl 3 St. Charles

Donaldson James, clerk with Cross & Co. 625 Sansom
Donaldson John, saloon, SW cor Market and Ecker
Donaldson William G. carpenter, dwl 504 Howard
Donaldson W. James, clerk, dwl 916 Stockton
Donalty Augustus P. bricklayer, dwl 28 Sansom
Donart Pierre, butcher with John Bazille, dwl N s Sixteenth nr Nebraska
Doncaster, Henry, clerk with C. V. Gillespie
Dondero Charles, printer, dwl 534 Green
Donegan Mary Miss, domestic, dwl S s Chestnut bet Stockton and Powell
Donegan Michael, laborer, dwl 514 Front
Donegan Patrick, painter, Volunteer Engine Co. No. 7
Doner Peter, laborer, Union Soap Factory, S side Brannan bet Fifth and Sixth
Doney Laurence, machinist, Vulcan Iron Works
Donlan Anna Miss, domestic, SW corner Green and Leavenworth
Doulan Bridget Miss, domestic, 515 Geary
Donlan Catherine Miss, domestic, 312 Ellis
Donlan Esther Mrs. dwl 1903 Dupont
Donlan James, stone cutter, dwl 27 Geary
Donlan Thomas, horseshoer, 3 Powell, dwl N s Haight nr Buchanan
Donlan Thomas, hostler, dwl 183 Jessie
Donlan William, boiler maker, dwl NW cor Jessie and Annie
Donley James, lather, dwl Gardner Alley nr Post
Donley John, laborer, dwl 126 Bush
Donlin Thomas, teazer, Glass Works, dwl 322 Ritch
Donnecliff T. teamster, dwl West End Hotel
Donnegan Michael, teamster, dwl U. S. Hotel 706 Battery
Donnell Oliver, handcartman, cor Broadway and Davis
Donnellan B. C. carpenter, dwl 14 Harlan Place
Donnelly Andrew, workman, S. F. & P. Sugar Co. dwl N s Harrison nr Eighth
Donnelly Anne Miss, dwl SW corner Eighth and Minna
Donnelly Bernard, workman, S. F. & P. Sugar Co. dwl Harrison nr Eighth
Donnelly Daniel, Washington House, 412 and 414 Davis
Donnelly Edward, street contractor, dwl N side Filbert bet Jones and Leavenworth
Donnelly Hannah Miss, domestic, 929 Howard
Donnelly James, carpenter, dwl W s Sumner near Howard
Donnelly James, proprietor Donnelly's Bakery, 109 Sansom
Donnelly James, stone cutter, dwl 29 Geary
Donnelly James H. workman, S. F. & P. Sugar Co. dwl E s Sumner nr Howard
Donnelly Jane Miss, domestic, 530 Ellis
Donnelly John (P. Donnelly & Bro.) dwl 60 Tehama
Donnelly John, book keeper with John Flanagan & Co. dwl S s Bryant bet Third and Fourth
Donnelly John, butter, cheese, and eggs, 119 Occidental Market, dwl N s Clementina bet Fourth and Fifth
Donnelly John, driver, North Beach & M. R. R. Co. dwl 277 Minna
Donnelly John, gardener with Michael Burnes
Donnelly John, laborer, dwl S s Brannan bet Sixth and Seventh
Donnelly John, pressman, dwl E s Montgomery bet Green and Union
Donnelly John, tinsmith with Tay, Brooks & Backus, dwl E s Montgomery bet Green and Union
Donnelly John, Washington House, 412 and 414 Davis
Donnelly John F. baker with James Donnelly, 109 Sansom
Donnelly Luke, cooper with John R. Regan, dwl S s Lewis Place nr Taylor

Donnelly Luke E. salesman, 306 California, dwl Howard Court
Donnelly Michael, laborer with William Kerr, dwl 903 Battery
Donnelly Michael, workman, S. F. & P. Sugar Co. dwl NE cor Fourth and Silver
Donnelly P. & Bro. (John Donnelly) butter, cheese, bacon, etc. 20 Occidental Market, dwl 60 Tehama
Donnelly Patrick, baker, St. Mary's Hospital
Donnelly Patrick, laborer, bds Western Hotel
Donnelly Patrick, laborer with Wm. J. Kingsley
Donnelly Patrick, laborer, dwl S s Hayes nr Laguna
Donnelly Robert, laborer, dwl 11 Baldwin Court
Donnelly Sarah (widow) dwl W s Harrison Place nr Harrison
Donnelly Thomas, miner, dwl Central House, 814 Sansom
Donnelly Thomas F. miner, dwl S side Mary near Chelsea Place
Donnigan Annie Miss, ironer, Chelsea Laundry
Donnigan Lizzie Miss, ironer, Chelsea Laundry
Donnigan P. laborer, North Beach & M. R. R. Co
Donnigan Eliza Miss, domestic, 317 Mason
Donnolly Thomas, with Daniel Callaghan, 121 Front, dwl 1611 Mason
Donnolly Thomas C. dwl 1611 Mason
Donnot Peter, vegetables, 1306 Dupont
Donovan Ann Miss, domestic, 1206 Mason
Donovan Ann (widow) dwl 6 Turk
Donovan Ann (widow) dwl S s Stevenson near Seventh
Donovan Daniel, laborer, Fort Point, dwl S s Vallejo bet Hyde and Larkin
Donovan David, laborer, 546 Clay, dwl 544 Clay
Donovan Dennis, gardener, dwl S s Pine between Leavenworth and Hyde
Donovan Dennis, laborer, dwl 29 Geary
Donovan Elizabeth Miss, domestic, 116 Eddy
Donovan Ellen Miss, domestic, 113 Eddy
Donovan Eugene, dwl NW cor Bryant and Park Av
Donovan Honoria (widow) dwl 258 Tehama
Donovan James, laborer with George D. Nagle
Donovan Jeremiah, laborer, dwl N s Fulton bet Gough and Octavia
Donovan Johanna Miss, seamstress with J. C. Horan
Donovan John, blacksmith, Union Foundry, dwl 84 Jessie
Donovan John, coach painter with A. Folsom, dwl 20 Howard Court
Donovan John, laborer, dwl 319 Tehama
Donovan John, painter, dwl 208 Fourth
Donovan John, ship carpenter, dwl N s Crook bet Townsend and Brannan
Donovan Joseph, laborer, dwl Rassette Place No. 3
Donovan Maggie Miss, chambermaid, Continental Hotel
Donovan Mary Miss, chambermaid, Continental Hotel
Donovan Mary Miss, domestic, 1417 Taylor
Donovan Michael, carriage painter with Albert Folsom, dwl 20 Howard Court
Donovan Michael, laborer, dwl 350 Jessie
Donovan Michael, laundryman City and County Hospital
Donovan Nancy (widow) dwl 210 Minna
Donovan Richard, laborer, dwl SW cor Page and Steiner
Donovan Thomas, laborer, dw 164 Minna
Donovan Timothy, laborer, dwl S s Clay bet Polk and Van Ness Avenue
Donovan Winifred A (widow) dwl E s Mary Lane nr Sutter
Donoghue Jeremiah P. laborer, dwl 3 Rassette Alley nr Sutter
Donoghue Margaret, domestic, dwl 311 Union
Donoghue Michael, conductor, North Beach & M. R. R. Co.

Donoghue Patrick J. agent, dwl 1112 Kearny
Donohoe James, liquor saloon, dwl 88 Stevenson
Donohoe Jane Miss, chambermaid, Russ House
Donohoe Jane Miss, domestic, 1001 Washington
Donohoe John, carman, dwl 8 s Freelon bet Fourth and Fifth
DONOHOE, *(Joseph A.)* KELLY *(Eugene)* & CO. bankers, SE cor Montgomery and Sacramento, dwl 526 Harrison
DONOHOE, KELLY & CO.'S BUILDING, SE cor Montgomery and Sacramento
Donohoe Mary Miss, domestic, 106 Turk
Donohoe Owen, shoe maker, 629 Merchant
Donohoe Thomas, blacksmith, dwl 1718 Stockton
Donohoe William, blacksmith with James' Glenden, dwl Pratt Court
Donohue Francis, salesman with Taaffe & Co. dwl cor Sixth and Folsom
Donohue Frank, dwl 'W s Guerrero, bet Figg and Duncan
Donohue Hugh, painter, dwl 125 Shipley, rear
Douohne Hugh, plasterer, NW cor Sixth and Bryant
Donohue James, baker, Ellis' Bakery, dwl 6 Noble Place
Donohue James, blacksmith, S. F. Gas Co, dwl 147 Natoma
Donohue James, laborer, S. F. Gas Co. dwl 541 Mission
Donohue John, plasterer, dwl Sixth St. House, NW cor Sixth and Bryant
Donohue John, ship carpenter, dwl 24 Minna
Donohue M. folder, Chelsea Laundry
Donohue Michael, conductor, North Beach & M. R. R. Co. dwl 774 Folsom
Donohue Patrick, contractor, dwl 905 Folsom
Donohue Patrick, wagon dealer, dwl 304 Vallejo
Donohue *(Thomas)* & Phelan *(Patrick)* liquor saloon, 31 Second
Donohue Thomas, carpenter, dwl Moulton Place nr Montgomery
Donovan Annie Miss, domestic, 806 Bush
Donovan Cornelius, steward, American Exchange
Donovan Daniel, laborer with Hey & Meyn
Donovan Daniel, laborer with John Center, dwl W s Florida nr Twentieth
Donovan Daniel, laborer, dwl 352 Jessie .
Donovan Dennis S. gardener, dwl N s Pine nr Leavenworth
Donovan Eugene, laborer, dwl N s Bryant nr Sixth
Donovan James, house, ship, sign, and ornamental painter, 312 Davis, dwl 14 Turk
Donovan Jeremiah, laborer, dwl Hinckley Place nr Vallejo bet Montgomery and Kearny
Donovan John, laborer with Hey & Meyn
Donovan John, laborer, dwl E s Eighth bet Bryant and Brannan
Donovan John jr. plasterer, dwl E s Eighth bet Bryant and Brannan
Donovan Kate Miss, domestic with C. J. Janson, W s Mission bet Twentieth and Twenty First
Donovan Maria (widow) dwl E s Jasper Place
Donovan' Michael, laborer, dwl 350 Jessie, rear
Donovan Patrick, hostler, dwl Mission bet First and Second
Donovan Thomas, laborer, dwl 636 Commercial
Donovan Timothy, porter with J. Peirce, dwl 210 Minna
Donovan, see Donnovan and Dunnovan
Douzat Pierre, dwl 721 Pacific
Douzel Aime J. clerk, steamer Amelia, dwl 913 Jackson
Donzelmann J. H. driver with Kobler & Frohling, dwl E s First nr Brannan
Donzelmahn John F. groceries and liquors, 409 Pine, dwl 415 Pine
Doody Sarah Miss, domestic, 310 Stockton
Doolan Thomas, bricklayer, dwl 176 Minna
Doolan William, clerk with Haggin & Tevis, dwl 917 Clay

Dooley Andrew, gardener with R. B. Woodward, dwl N s Mission bet Twelfth and Thirteenth
Dooley Catharine (widow) dwl W s Gaven nr Filbert
Dooley John *(Burdick & D.)* dwl Brannan St. Bridge
Dooley John, bar keeper, dwl W s Buchanan bet Bush and Sutter
Doolittle A. J. map agent, dwl 638 Howard
Doolittle F. fruits, 668 Howard
Doolittle W. G. accountant and teacher penmanship, 328 Montgomery
Doonin Jennie Miss, domestic with J. Chadbourne, W s Folsom bet Eleventh and Twelfth
Dopmann Ann, seamstress, dwl 864 Mission
Doran A. F. farmer, bds Franklin Hotel, SE cor Sansom and Pacific
DORAN E. C. paymaster and acting navy agent, office 434 California, res Mare Island
Doran Hugh J. conductor, Central R. R. Co. dwl 242 Sixth
Doran *(James)* & Ford *(Thomas)* horseshoeing, 121 Bush, dwl 112 Freelon
Doran John, milk ranch, cor Folsom and Kosciusko
Doran Julia Mrs. dress maker, 242 Sixth
Doran Michael, laborer, dwl Union Court
Doran Richard E. molder, Fulton Foundry, dwl 255 Third
Doran Timothy, bar keeper with Stewart & Daley, dwl West End Hotel
Doran William, conductor, Omnibus R. R. Co. dwl 1009 Pacific
Dorcey John, wagon maker with Mangeot & Richard, dwl SE cor Howard and Ninth
Dore A. M. Miss, assistant, Rincon School, dwl 19 Tehama
Dore Benjamin, contractor, office 728 Montgomery, dwl 19 Tehama
Dore Edward W. drayman with Jennings & Brewster, dwl 773 Folsom
DORE MAURICE & CO. *(William A. Quarles and Augustus P. Flint)* real estate, stock, and general auctioneers, 327 Montgomery, dwl SW cor Washington and Taylor
Doren David, ship carpenter, dwl W s Clay Avenue
Doren James, drayman, dwl 6 Scott
Doreton Augusta (widow) dwl 320 Beale
Dorety B. R. laborer with Justus Bepler
Dorgan Timothy, laborer, S. F. & P. Woolen Mills, dwl North Point bet Polk and Van Ness Avenue
Dorgan William, porter, dwl 50 Natoma
DORGELOH *(Louis)* & MEYER *(Anton)* Harmonie Hall, 775 Clay
Doriot Louis, cook, Phil's Exchange, 417 Front
Doris Cornelius, dwl 518 Market
Dorland Henry S. *(J. F. & H. S. D.)* dwl N s Sixteenth nr Guerrero
Dorland James F. & Henry S. Mission Express, office 716 Kearny, dwl N s Sixteenth nr Guerrero
Dorland Nathan, driver, 207 Sansom
Dorland Thomas *(H. Hazeltine & Co.)* dwl W s Dolores bet Seventeenth and Eighteenth
Dorland Thomas A. C. assistant book keeper with H. H. Bancroft & Co. dwl SW cor Dolores and Dorland
Dorland Thomas G. salesman with William Shew, dwl 32 Russ nr Folsom
Dorman Charles, carpenter with James Brokaw, dwl 31 Second
Dorman *(W. F.)* & Wolf *(J. W.)* produce commission, 101 Clay, dwl NE cor Howard and Fifteenth
Dormer Charles, cook, 323 Washington
Dormer Julia (widow) dwl 572 Folsom
Dormitzer Ludwig P. salesman with Adelsdorfer Bros. SE cor Sansom and Sacramento

Dorn John, cartman, 6 Scott
Dorn Marks, salesman, 308 Sac, dwl 223 Jessie
Dorn Michael, drayman, dwl 1420 Dupont
Dorn Peter, shoe maker, 34 Genry
Dorn Richard & Co. commission merchants, NW cor Pine and Battery, dwl 444 Jessie
Dornau George, with D. Buhsen & Co. dwl NW cor Pacific and Davis
Dornay Patrick, bar keeper, 3¼ Mile House, San Bruno Road
Dornay Patrick, fruits, SE cor Bush and Kearny
Dorr Cæsar, butcher, Lick House, dwl 252 Tehama
Dorr Henrietta Miss, cloak maker, dwl 709 Greenwich
Dorr Herbert C. author, dwl 760 Clay
DORR J. B. & CO. (C. E. Hazeltine) livery and sale stable, 408 and 410 Bush, dwl Cosmopolitan Hotel
Dorr Joseph A. bds Brooklyn Hotel
DORR RALPH S. legal tender broker, 605 Montgomery, dwl NE cor Mission and Second
Dorr Ralph S. jr. dwl SW cor First and Folsom
Dorrow H. dwl 315 Montgomery
Dorser Jacob, laborer, dwl 728 Market
Dorsett Edward, porter steamer Chrysopolis
Dorsey Amelia Miss, domestic, dwl Mechanics' Hotel
Dorsey B. Johnson, purser, Pacific Mail S. S. Co. dwl 20 Perry
Dorsey Edward Mrs. liquor saloon, 133 Folsom
Dorsey George, liquors and billiards, 7 Broadway
Dorsey George, laborer, dwl 56 Stevenson
Dorsey John, waiter, 523 Clay, dwl Niantic Hotel
Dorsey Sarah Miss, chambermaid, Russ House
Doscher Albert, handcartman, cor Clay and Battery, dwl Bartol nr Vallejo
Doscher Frederick, bar keeper, NE cor California and Davis
Doscher George H. miner, dwl 338 Third
Doscher Henry (Scanlin & D.) NW cor Bush and Jones
Doscher Henry, driver, Albany Brewery, dwl Jessie bet Fifth and Sixth
Doscher Henry F. liquor saloon, SE cor Brannan and Ninth
Doscher (Herman) & Co. (Nicholas Wiebalk) groceries and liquors, 138 Second
Doscher H. Henry, groceries and liquors, SE cor Brannan and Seventh
DOSCHER JOHN D. groceries and liquors, SE cor Bush and Sansom
Doscher Nina Miss, domestic, 832 Mission
Doston Edmund (col'd) hair dresser, dwl 110 Sutter
Dott Andrew, ship chandler, dwl N s Oak bet Franklin and Gough
Dotter William C. lamplighter, S. F. Gas Co. dwl N s Hayes nr Van Ness Avenue
Doty John, house painter with J. W. Denny, dwl 415 Pine
Doty John L. carpenter with Edwin O. Hunt, dwl W s Sansom bet Pine and Bush
DOTY W. R. & CO. (Decatur Marden) agents eastern manufacturers hardware, etc. 113 Pine, res Sonoma
Doublet Francis, gardener with W. J. Shaw, Thirteenth E Folsom
Douboison Louis, laborer, Russ House
Doud Aaron, furniture and bedding, 113 Sansom, dwl S s Seventeenth nr Dolores
Doud Bernard, workman, S. F. & P. Sugar Co. dwl Gilbert
Doud Francis, dwl 325 First
Doud Hugh, hackman, Russ House
Doud James, cooper, dwl NE cor Pac and Franklin
Doud Philo, Franklin bakery, 256 First
Douddal Julia, domestic, dwl 220 Fremont
Dougall William, tinsmith with Locke & Montague, dwl Original House
Dougart John I. butcher, Golden Gate Market, dwl N s Bush bet Pierce and Scott

Dougherty Bridget, domestic, 785 Folsom
Dougherty Brien, helper, Union Foundry, dwl 34 First
Dougherty Catharine, laundry, Lick House
Dougherty Cornelius, boiler maker with Coffey & Risdon
Dougherty Daniel, dwl 153 Minna
Dougherty Edward, boiler maker apprentice, Vulcan Iron Works, dwl 41 Berry
Dougherty Edward, carpenter with McGinn & Finnegan, dwl N s Tehama bet Third and Fourth
Dougherty Ellen Miss, domestic, 30 Geary
Dougherty George, engineer, Montgomery Bath House, dwl 36 Battery
Dougherty George, rigger, dwl 265 Clary
Dougherty Hannah Miss, domestic with O. P. Fitzgerald
Dougherty Henry, laborer, dwl 59 Shipley
Dougherty James, boiler maker with Coffey & Risdon
Dougherty James, laborer, dwl Ecker bet First and Second
Dougherty James, retortman, S. F. Gas Co
Dougherty John, blacksmith with Nelson & Doble, 321 Pine
Dougherty John, blacksmith with Nutting & Upstone, dwl Central House
Dougherty John, gas fitter with Thomas Ross, 319 Bush, dwl 217 Post
Dougherty John, hackman, dwl 820 Dupont
Dougherty John, laborer, Vulcan Iron Works, dwl 413 Filbert
Dougherty John, ship carpenter, dwl 1 Sherwood Place
Dougherty John, soap stone mills, 521 Market, dwl Broadway nr Battery
Dougherty John H. saloon, dwl 57 Minna
Dougherty Joseph, painter, dwl 153 Minna
Dougherty Kate Miss, dwl 110 William
Dougherty Kate Miss, domestic, 110 Stevenson
Dougherty Mary Miss, domestic, 522 Stockton
Dougherty Matthew, frame maker with Nile & Kollmyer, bds 333 Bush
Dougherty Michael, miner, dwl 53 Natoma
Dougherty Morris, tailor, dwl 17 Sherwood Place
Dougherty Patrick, dwl W s California Avenue nr Winslow
Dougherty Patrick, laborer, dwl Bertha W s Beale
Dougherty Patrick, bag maker, dwl 153 Minna
Dougherty Rebecca (widow) dwl S s Market bet Sixth and Seventh, rear
Dougherty Roger, laborer, dwl 36 Eddy
Dougherty Thomas, with Reynolds & Murray, dw Ohio nr Broadway
Dougherty W. C. secretary P. O. dwl Geary Place above Taylor
Dougherty William, carpenter, dwl 39 First
Dougherty William, laborer, dwl 16 Taylor, rear
Dougherty William, laborer, S. F. Gas Co
Dougherty William H. master brig Gen. Jessup, dwl 238 Stewart
Dougherty, see Doherty, O'Doherty, and O'Dougherty
Doughney William, dwl cor Jessie and First
Douglass Agnes (widow) dwl 121 Shipley
Douglass Edward, compositor, dwl 111 Ellis
Douglass Edward, pressman with Agnew & Deffebach, dwl 232 Third
Douglass Frederick, with McGarvey & Co. res Oakland
Douglass George W. carpenter, Omnibus R. R. Co. dwl 161 Tehama
Douglass Jacob, clerk with Douglass, Wise & Co. dwl 220 Stevenson
Douglass James, lumber surveyor, dwl 35 Tehama
Douglass James H. laborer with J. Center, NW cor Folsom and Sixteenth
Douglass John, fireman, dwl E s Tyson Place near Washington

Douglass Joseph, boot maker, 429 Kearny
Douglass Peter (col'd) dwl N s Dupont Alley
Douglass Robert, second officer stm Sierra Nevada, office SW cor Front and Jackson
Douglass Thomas H. superintendent I. Friedlander's Warehouse, Rincon Point, dwl 507 Powell
Douglass William A. physician, office 804 Mission, dwl 813 Mission
Douglass William F. (Beckman, Aiken & Co.) dwl W s Harriet bet Fifteenth and Sixteenth
Douglass William Y. captain of police, City Hall, dwl 20 Geary
Douillard Frank, Orient Market, 1224 Dupont
Dove Alexander (col'd) steward, dwl NW cor Sacramento and Tay
Dove William H. carriage painter with M. P. Holmes, dwl 320 Third
Dow Francis A. dwl 46 Second
Dow George, laborer, dwl 671 Mission
Dow George G. cabinet maker with John Wigmore, 423 California
Dow George W. book keeper, dwl 281 Stevenson
Dow James G. broker, dwl 337 Jessie
Dow (J. Blake) & Desebrock (Frederick) liquors and billiards, SE cor Fourth and Brannan, dwl 603 Pine
Dow Martin & Co. lamps and oils, etc. 62 Second, dwl 46½ Second
Dowd Bernhard, dwl SW cor Brannan and Gilbert
Dowd John, cooper, dwl NE cor Pac and Franklin
Dowd Mary Miss, domestic, 1415 Taylor
Dowdell Grace (widow) dwl 11 William
Dowdell Robert, pressman with Francis, Valentine & Co. dwl Original House
Dowley Michael, carpenter, dwl 310 Seventh
Dowling Bridget (widow) dwl W s Salmon bet Mason and Taylor
Dowling Daniel, workman, S. F. & P. Sugar Co. dwl Langton nr Folsom
Dowling James, laborer, dwl 909 Folsom
Dowling James, spinner, S. F. P. Woolen Mills, dwl cor Francisco and Van Ness Avenue
Dowling James, stage manager Metropolitan Theater, dwl 1120 Kearny
Dowling James, waterman, 609 Market, dwl 625 Geary
Dowling John H. brass finisher and locksmith, dwl 113 Post
Dowling Kate Miss, domestic with James Bell, W s Folsom bet Eleventh and Twelfth
Dowling L. Jenny Miss, domestic with James Bell, W s Folsom bet Eleventh and Twelfth
Dowling Mary Miss, domestic with John R. Robinson, 924 Mission
Dowling Mary Miss, domestic, 19 Prospect Place
Dowling Michael, coachman, dwl 835 Clay, rear
Dowling Patrick, stone cutter, dwl N s Green bet Leavenworth and Hyde
Dowling Richard, foreman with Main & Winchester, dwl 322 Beale
Dowling Richard, hackman, Plaza
Dowling William M. bricklayer, dwl S s McAllister bet Devisidero and Broderick
Down John, bricklayer, dwl 528 Pacific
Downer Abner J. mining agent, office 7 Government House, 502 Washington, dwl 825 Bdwy
Downer Thomas P. deputy wharfinger Pacific Wharf, dwl NE cor Pacific and Davis
Downes Charles, apprentice, dwl 66 Minna
Downes Edward, retortman, S. F. Gas Co. dwl 66 Minna
Downes George W. clerk, dwl 33 Everett
Downes G. W. drayman, cor Hunt and Third
Downes John, ship carpenter, dwl 312 Beale
Downes Margaret Miss, domestic, 35 O'Farrell
Downes William, workman S. F. & P. Sugar Co. dwl Nevada nr Eleventh
Downey Hannah Miss, domestic with F. G. Bornemann, S s Thirteenth nr Folsom

Downey James H. carpenter, SE cor Harrison and Third, dwl E s Ritter bet Bryant and Harrison
Downey John (Sweeney & D.) dwl Stevenson nr Third
Downey John, blacksmith helper, San Francisco Iron Works, dwl 25 Stevenson
Downey John, laborer, Lone Mountain Cemetery
Downey John, laborer, dwl N s Twentieth bet Valencia and Guerrero
Downey John H. machinist, dwl 4 Quincy Place
Downey Kate Miss, domestic, 963 Folsom
Downey Margaret Miss, domestic with George J. Griffing
Downey Patrick, carpenter, dwl 921 Sutter
Downey Patrick B. plasterer, dwl 270 Minna
Downey Thomas, blacksmith, dwl 625½ Mission
Downey Timothy, bar keeper, Occidental Hotel
Downey William C. compositor, American Flag, dwl 73 Natoma
Downing Edward, with Lewis & Neville, dwl West End Hotel
Downing Henry C. (Jones & Bendixen) dwl NE cor Fillmore and Grove
Downing Margaret, ironer, Chelsea Laundry
Downing Matthew, plasterer, dwl 23 Louisa
Downing Richard, plasterer, dwl N s Ash nr Larkin
Downing Theodore H. carpenter, dwl S s Day nr Guerrero
Downing Thomas (Hopps & D.) dwl 110 Sutter
Downing Timothy, bar keeper, Occidental Hotel
Downs Alva, laborer, dwl 115 William
Downs Charles, gas fitter with McNally & Hawkins, dwl 51 Minna
Downs George W. clerk, dwl 210 Fourth
Downs Helen M. (widow) dwl 624 Bush
Downs Joshua, groceries and liquors, SE cor Fourth and Stevenson
Downs Mary, domestic with Albert S. Evans
Downs Thomas D. dwl N s Brannan bet Sixth and Seventh
DOWS J. & CO. (James Mairs) proprietors Dows' Distillery, Mission Creek, office 208 Sacramento, dwl 36 South Park
Dowsett George, stevedore, 315 Beale
Dox Peter, bar keeper, 320 Montgomery
Doyle Andy, butcher with Johnson & Co. dwl cor Brannan and Ninth
Doyle Dennis B. carpenter, dwl N s Hayes bet Gough and Octavia
Doyle Dennis E. silver plater, dwl cor Folsom and Nineteenth
Doyle Edward, ship carpenter, dwl S s Twentieth bet Guerrero and Dolores
Doyle Edward H. night watch, dwl 709 Stockton, rear
Doyle Ellen (widow) dwl 36 Clementina
Doyle Eugene G. boarding, 308 Beale
Doyle Fanny, chambermaid, Lick House
Doyle James, driver, North Beach & M. R. R. Co. dwl SE cor Folsom and Fourth
Doyle James, helper, Union Foundry, dwl 24 Stevenson
Doyle James, laborer, dwl W s Buchanan bet Haight and Kate
Doyle James, porter with J. D. Farwell & Co. dwl 415 Pine
Doyle James, silversmith, 810 Montgomery, dwl Mission Dolores
Doyle James F. seaman, dwl 20 Commercial
Doyle James J. contractor and builder, 812 Pacific, dwl 1902 Powell
Doyle James P. plumber and gas fitter with J. K. Prior, dwl W s Shotwell bet Fifteenth and Sixteenth
Doyle James R. proprietor Pacific Coal Yard, 413 and 415 Pacific, dwl N s O'Farrell bet Hyde and Leavenworth
Doyle John, blacksmith, bds Marysville Hotel 414 Pacific

Doyle John, carriage painter, 507 Broadway, dwl 430 Clementina
Doyle John, clerk, dwl 737 Market
Doyle John, laborer, dwl E s Larkin bet Union and Filbert
Doyle John, porter, dwl 50 Natoma
Doyle John, proprietor Seymour House, 24 Sansom
Doyle John Mrs. (widow) dwl 432 Bryant
DOYLE *(John T.)* & BARBER *(William)* attorneys at law, office 9–11 Wells' Building 605 Clay, dwl 430 Bryant
Doyle Joseph, dwl E s Clinton nr Brannan
Doyle Kate Miss, domestic, 508 Mason
Doyle Margaret Miss, domestic, 729 Harrison
Doyle Martin C. laborer, dwl 113 Shipley, rear
Doyle Mary Miss, domestic, 768 Harrison
Doyle Mary A. (wi   ) dwl 458 Natoma, rear
Doyle Michael, dwl Leidesdorff and Commercial
Doyle Michael, groceries and liquors, NE cor Hayes and Van Ness Avenue
Doyle Michael, laborer, dwl 50 Natoma
Doyle Morris, blacksmith, dwl SE cor Geary and William
Doyle Patrick, express wagon, 153 Minna
Doyle Patrick, harness maker, dwl 136 Natoma
Doyle Patrick, laborer, Spring Valley W. W
Doyle Peter, liquor saloon, dwl Crescent Engine House
Doyle Peter, bar keeper, 533 Kearny
Doyle Richard, carpenter, dwl Ws Mary nr Minna
Doyle Richard, steamboatman, dwl 639 Washington
Doyle Robert E. office 112 California, dwl Occidental Hotel
Doyle Rody, blacksmith, 320 Third, dwl E s Mission bet Eighteenth and Nineteenth
Doyle Thomas, dwl S s Cemetery Alley bet Dolores and Church
DOYLE THOMAS, liquors and passengers' stores, 535 Sacramento, dwl 244 Stevenson
Doyle William, laborer with John Center, NW cor Sixteenth and Folsom
Doyle William, trunk maker with E. Galpen & Co. dwl N s Perry bet Fourth and Fifth
Doyle William, workman with John Henry, dwl N s Vallejo bet Montgomery and Sansom
Doyle William H. ship broker and commission agent, office SE cor Washington and Sansom
Doyle William R. mining superintendent, dwl 50 Natoma
Draddy Ellen Miss, saleswoman, 609 Sacramento
Dragri Joseph, seaman, dwl 44 Sacramento
Draheim Minna Miss, dress maker, 8 Clara
Drain Daniel, ship carpenter, dwl 308 Beale
Drain James, ship carpenter, dwl 54 First
Drake Alexander, laborer with Conroy & Tobin
DRAKE EUGENE B. attorney at law, office 420 Montgomery third floor, dwl 325 Dupont
Drake George W. driver, Easton's Laundry W s Lagoon
Drake Hattie A. Mrs. dwl 502 Washington
Drake H. B. glass blower, Pacific Glass Works, dwl W s Tennessee nr Mariposa
Drake John, carpenter, dwl 26 Geary
Drake *(Samuel)* & Emerson *(J. A.)* commission fruits, 312 Washington, dwl 363 First
Drake Stephen, carpenter, dwl 741 Market
DRAMATIC CHRONICLE (Daily) G. & C. De-Young, proprietors, office 417 Clay
Drapnick Ferdinand, watch maker, 622 Clay, dwl 262 Jessie, rear
Drathmann William F. book keeper with Tillman & Co. dwl NW cor Dupont and Pine
Drayeur August, clerk, Miners' Restaurant, dwl 825 Jackson
Dreane John, bricklayer, Manhattan Engine Co. No. 2
Dreg John, boots and shoes, 1126 Dupont
Drell Frederica (widow) dwl 409 Stockton

Drennan James, engineer, steamer Oakland, res Brooklyn Alameda Co.
Drennan John, carpenter, dwl cor Hawthorne and Folsom
Drentwehl Henry, clerk, dwl 520 Vallejo
DRESCHFELD HENRY, money and real estate agent and notary p   i ; general agent London and Lancashire Fire Insurance Co. office 623 Montgomery, dwl 606 Pine
Dresdener House, Theodore Brown proptr, 337 Bush
Dresher Valentine, compositor, Monitor, dwl 10 Bush
Dresser T. E. teacher music, dwl 507 Bush
Dreux Edward, cook, Lafayette H. & L. Co. No. 2
Drew Edward F. laborer, dwl 721 Market
Drew Henry P. collector, office 604 Merchant, dwl 74 Clementina
Drew Hiram M. *(W. H. Smith & Co.)* dwl N s Fell nr Franklin
Drew Horace, dwl 70 Clementina
Drew John, bar keeper, Bay View Park
Drew J. R. stair builder, dwl 229 Clary
Drew Thomas, bar keeper, Bay View Park
Dreyer *(Diedrick)* & Ebbighausen *(Frank)* groceries and liquors, cor Gilmore and Kentucky
Dreyer John, liquor saloon, SW cor Clay and East
Dryfoos Adolfo, teacher penmanship, dwl 240 Minna
Dryfous Jules, dry goods, dwl 1313 Kearny
DREYFUS BENJAMIN, agent United Anaheim Wine Growers' Association and Landing Co. office 321 Montgomery
Dreyfus Bernhard, clerk with D. Hausmann & Co. 537 Clay, dwl 255 Third
Dreypoelcher Frederick, billiard maker with M. E. Hughes, dwl 512 Leavenworth
Drinan James, laborer, dwl N s Mission bet Main and Beale
Drindheimer Matilda Mrs. dwl 527 Filbert
Drinkhouse Edward J. accountant, 228 Front, dwl 221 Ritch
DRINKHOUSE J. A. wholesale cigars and tobacco, 228 Front, dwl 42 South Park
Drinkwater Thomas, furniture, 437 Bush
Drinkworth John, seaman, dwl 513 Broadway
Drinnin John, carpenter, dwl 170 Minna
Driscoll Catherine Miss, domestic, 208 Stockton
Driscoll Catherine (widow) dwl 23 Geary
Driscoll C. E. *(John Bamber & Co.)* 719 Davis
Driscoll Charles, boatman, Vallejo Wharf, dwl 404 Vallejo
Driscoll Cornelius, with Charles Harley & Co. dwl Francisco nr Dupont
Driscoll Cornelius, laborer, dwl 512 Mason
DRISCOLL *(Dan.)* & JELLINGS *(Edward)* proprietors Brokers' Exchange Saloon, 426 Montgomery, dwl 22 Stockton
Driscoll Dennis, deck hand, steamer Yosemite
Driscoll Dennis, laborer, Greenwich Warehouse, dwl 804 Geary
Driscoll Dennis, stone mason, dwl E s Mary Lane nr Sutter
Driscoll Dennis O. *(Kennedy & D.)* 108 Third
Driscoll Frank, porter, dwl cor Filbert and Mont
Driscoll Giles, laborer, dwl E s Treat Avenue nr Twenty-First
Driscoll James, waiter, Russ House
Driscoll James N. glass cutter, dwl 252 Stevenson
Driscoll Jeremiah, gardener, dwl 48 Jessie
Driscoll Jeremiah, ship carpenter, dwl Washington Hose Co. No. 1
Driscoll Johanna (widow) dwl 809 Mason
Driscoll Johanna (widow) liquors, 512 Mission
Driscoll John, blacksmith, dwl NE cor California and Prospect Place
Driscoll John, deck hand, steamer Chrysopolis
Driscoll John, express wagon, cor Eighth and Folsom
Driscoll John, laborer, bds Golden Age Hotel
Driscoll Kate, domestic with P. E. Bowman, dwl SW cor Broadway and Montgomery

Driscoll Michael, laborer, dwl 333 Bush
Driscoll Timothy, core maker, Vulcan Iron Works, dwl NE cor California and Prospect Place
Driscoll Timothy, feed, wood, and coal, NW cor Mission and Sixteenth
Driscoll William H. porter with B. C. Horn & Co. dwl 238 Sutter
Drish John M. salesman with Henston, Hastings & Co. dwl 407 Sutter
Drobaz Mateo *(Luzich & D.)* dwl 503 East
Droege Peter, carpenter. dwl 26 St. Mark Place
Droge *(August)* & Vessing *(Henry F.)* groceries and liquors, NE cor Natoma and Jane
Droge Gustavus F. C. groceries and liquors, cor Natoma and Jane
Droge Henry, groceries and liquors, cor Pacific and Front
Droge J. C. pile driver, dwl 160 Stewart
Droger D. North Point Saloon, dwl SE cor Battery and Filbert
DROGER H. & CO. *(Henry Wuhrmann)* groceries and liquors, SE cor Pine and Battery
Drohen John, laborer, bds 606 Third
Drollet John A. groceries and liquors, 1336 Dupont
Drossell Joseph H. clerk, 429 California, dwl 434 Cal
Droste Barnard, dwl NW cor Jackson and Drumm
Droste Henry, clerk, Chicago Hotel
Droste Herman *(E. W. Heimburg & Co.)* dwl Chicago Hotel
Drouet Joseph, canned fruits, dwl 1622 Stockton
Drouet Victor, canned fruits, 1622 Stockton, rear
Drought Robert, tailor, 304 Pine
Drown A. N. law student, office Sharp & Lloyd, dwl S s Filbert bet Polk and Van Ness Avenue
Drucker Albert, groceries and liquors, 624 Mission
Drucker August, proprietor Eureka Baths, 328 Pacific, dwl 919 Montgomery
Drucker Eilert, groceries and liquors, NE cor Clay and Stockton
Drucker, John, clerk with Albert Hosing, dwl NE cor Fifth and Mission
Druffel Francis H. Empire Bakery, SW cor Bush and Mason
Drugon Samuel, plasterer, dwl 37 Moss
DRUHE JOHN G. saloon, NE cor Eighteenth and Mission
Druhe John H. groceries and liquors, SW cor Market and Stewart, dwl NW cor Eighth and Folsom
Drum F. J. dwl What Cheer House
Drum Maggie Miss, teacher private school, Prospect Place, dwl 22 John
DRUM RICHARD C. colonel U. S. A. assistant adjutant general and chief of staff, office 742 Washington, dwl Occidental Hotel
Drum Thomas J. attorney at law, office 606 Washington, dwl 10 Ellis
Drummond Jeannie M. Miss, assistant, Union Grammar School, dwl 704 Howard
Drummond Joseph, boiler maker, dwl 309½ Clementina
Drummond Joseph H. boiler maker with Coffey & Risdon, dwl 309½ Clementina
Drummond L. M. Miss, assistant, Union Street Primary School, dwl 704 Howard
Drummond W. W. attorney at law, office 620 Washington room 16
Drury James, joiner, dwl 215 Ritch
Drury Jane Miss, domestic, dwl 921 Jackson
Drury John, tobacconist, dwl NW cor Mission and Jane
Drury Peter, laborer, dwl W s Mont nr Filbert
Drury Samuel, dwl 315 Sutter
Drury William, tailor with Davis & Schafer, dwl E s Valencia nr Willows
Druyea E. dwl What Cheer House
Dryer Annie Miss, domestic, 738 Green
Dryer Charles, proprietor Fashion Restaurant, 820 Clay, dwl 112 St. Mark Place

Dryer Charles J. clerk, 228 Front
Dryer Henry, seaman, dwl 44 Sacramento
Dryer John, with Stevens & Oliver, dwl 1019 Kearny
Dryer W. T. bar keeper, Shakspeare Saloon, NW cor Montgomery and Washington
Drynen John, mining stocks, dwl 716 California
DuBois James L. clerk with Charles W. Brooks & Co. dwl SE cor Mission and Second
DuCruet M. laundryman, dwl 341 Third
DuPRAT JOSEPH J. commercial reporter Alta California, office 423 Washington, dwl 304 Mason
DuRose Francis F. wool carder, dwl 812 Union
Duane Charles P. dwl 284 Minna
Duane John, bricklayer, dwl 113 St. Mark Place
Duane William R. compositor, Alta, California, dwl Sansom nr Pine
Dubbs Anna J. (widow) boarding, SW cor Stockton and Jackson
Dubedat Eugene *(Pascal, D. & Co.)* dwl 1209 Powell
Dubois August P. book keeper, Cal. State Tel. Co. 507 Mont, dwl S s Folsom nr Precita Avenue
Dubois Julia A. (widow) lodgings, Wright's Building, NW cor Jackson and Montgomery
Dubois Julia P. (widow) dwl E s Folsom nr Precita Avenue
Dubois Edmund, with J. Hirsch & Co. dwl 329 Kearny
Dubosq Pierre, dwl 721 Pacific
Dubourque E. & Co. *(Jules St. Dennis)* house and sign painters, 703 Sacramento, dwl W s Pacific Alley bet Dupont and Stockton
Dubuque G. & S. M. Co. office 611 Clay
Ducatel A. Mrs. fruits and vegetables, 10 Washington Market, dwl W s Kearny bet Washington and Jackson
Duchanger H. express wagon, cor Broadway and Dupont
Duchatel Francis, porter, 321 Montgomery, dwl S s Post bet Kearny and Dupont
Duchemin Jane A. M. dwl Greenwich bet Montgomery and Sansom
Duck J. A. compositor, American Flag, dwl 814 Pac
Duck William B. & Co. *(T. W. Manchester)* Tehama Market, NE cor Second and Tehama
Ducker William, boatman, dwl SW cor Washington and East
Duckett Edward, waiter, What Cheer House
Ducoing Eugene, laborer with J. B. Neulens, dwl S s Filbert bet Taylor and John
Ducoing John, lab. dwl SE cor Jones and Filbert
Ducommun *(S. W.)* & Lowney *(Timothy)* carriage mkrs, 535 and 537 Market, dwl 792 Folsom
Ducsoquet Ernest, Bay City Laundry
Ducy Edmund, gardener, Hayes' Park, Hayes' Valley
Duden Fréres & Co. (manufacturers laces and white goods, Brussels, Bel.) Alfred Esch agent, office 629 Clay
Dudett John (col'd) whitewashing, 771 Howard
Dudgeon Eneas, portable hydraulic press maker, NW cor Eighth and Minna
DUDLEY *(E. T.)* & GERHARDY *(Charles)* importers and dealers leather and shoe findings, 422 Battery, dwl 506 Market
Dudley George, mechanic with Nutting & Upstone, dwl S s Everett nr Howard
Dudley Thomas, clerk, 13 Stewart, dwl Leidesdorff bet Sacramento and California
Duerden James B. boat builder, dwl 567 Bryant, rear
Dueuwald Charles F. *(I. Raphael & Co.)* dwl Trinity nr Bush
Duewold Frank, cigar maker, dwl W s Varennes nr Filbert
Dufau John T. dwl 524 Merchant
Duff Andrew, bar keeper, Sazurac Exchange, dwl 413 Green

Duff Andrew, ship carpenter, dwl W s Gilbert bet Brannan and Townsend
Duff James R. mining, dwl S s DeBoom nr Second
Duff J. M. stock broker, dwl NE cor Dupont and Jackson
Duff John, paper hangings and painter, 642 Clay, dwl 5 DeBoom
Duff John J. clerk, 642 Clay, dwl 5 DeBoom
Duff Robert, dwl 433 Stevenson
Duff Sarah E. teacher private school, dwl 413 Green
Duff Thomas, French Laundry, 705 Commercial
Dufficy Peter, plumber, dwl 2 Margaret Place
Duffie Henry, waiter, Russ House
Duffield George W. boatman, dwl 333 Vallejo
Duffy Ann Miss, dwl S s Stevenson bet Sixth and Seventh
Duffy Bernard, porter with Myles D. Sweeny, dwl 905 Broadway
Duffy Bridget, laundress, Lick House
Duffy Catherine, dwl 178 Minna
Duffy Delia Miss, domestic, 759 Market
Duffy Edward, carpenter with S. S. Culverwell, 29 Fremont, dwl E s Dupont bet Lombard and Chestnut
Duffy Edward, handcartman, dwl S s Chambers bet Battery and Front
Duffy Edward, plumber with McNally & Hawkins, d 1 16 Sutter
Duffy Henry, express wagon, 706 Broadway
Duffy Henry steward, dwl S s Stevenson bet Sixth Seventh
Duffy Hugh, upholsterer, dwl 706 Broadway
Duffy Hyacinth, with Cutting & Co. dwl 741 Vallejo
Duffy James (Goodwin & D.) dwl 657 Washington
Duffy James, book keeper with Cameron, Whittier & Co. dwl 9 Tehama
Duffy James, compositor, Evening Bulletin, dwl 741 Vallejo
Duffy James, janitor public school cor Jackson and Virginia, dwl 912 Powell
Duffy James, painter, dwl 111 Geary
Duffy Joanna M. domestic with G. H. Tay, W s Calhoun
Duffy John, baker, dwl 32 Rousch
Duffy John, furnished rooms, 10 Sutter
Duffy John, laborer, dwl 14 Jessie
Duffy John, workman, S. F. & P. Sugar Co. dwl Rousch nr Folsom
Duffy Lizzie Miss, domestic, 1027 Bush
Duffy Mary Miss, domestic with Mrs. S. A Sanderson, E s Howard bet Fifteenth and Sixteenth
Duffy Mary A. Miss, domestic, 1513 Stockton
Duffy Patrick, ballaster, dwl 110 Freelon, rear
Duffy Patrick, waiter, Cosmopolitan Hotel
Duffy Peter, butcher with Metzger & Co. dwl cor Brannan and Ninth
Duffy Peter, laborer, dwl 180 Jessie
Duffy Philip, laborer, dwl S s California bet Mason and Taylor
Duffy Philip, watchman, steamer Yosemite
Duffy Rose Miss, domestic with William N. Meeks
Duffy Thomas, carpenter, dwl N s Filbert bet Larkin and Polk
Duffy William, laborer, bds 761 Mission
Duffy William, butcher, W s Ninth bet Bryant and Brannan
Duffy William, helper, Union Foundry, dwl 3 Minna
Duffy William, teamster, dwl 229 Minna
Duffy William, wagon maker with Belduke & Co
Duffy William E. painter, Columbian Engine Co. No. 11
Duffy Winefred Miss, domestic, dwl 412 Post
Dugal Samuel, carpenter, 633 Market
Dugan Charles, seaman, dwl 44 Sacramento
Dugan Charlotte L. Miss, milliner, dwl 1 Martha Place
Dugan Elizabeth Miss, dwl 520 Geary
Dugan Ellen Miss, domestic, 803 Union

Dugan Hannah Miss, domestic, 816 Sutter
Dugan Hugh, molder, Union Foundry, dwl S s Market bet Fifth and Sixth
Dugan Jeremiah, Columbian Engine Co. No. 11
Dugan, Jeremiah, teamster with Moses Marsh, SW cor Folsom and Eleventh
Dugan John H. painter with Hopps & Kanary, dwl S s Folsom bet Main and Spear
Dugan Julia, domestic, 1300 Pine
Dugan Margaret (widow) dwl 903 Folsom
Dugan Mark M. boot maker, 102 Second, dwl 754 Howard
Dugan Patrick, laborer, dwl 312 Fifth, rear
Dugan Patrick S. shoe maker, 110 Leidesdorff, dwl SW cor California and Mason
Dugan William, express wagon, dwl 212 Tehama
Dugan William, laborer, dwl 171 Jessie
Dugan William, marble polisher, dwl 175 Jessie
Dugan William, waiter, Occidental Hotel
Duggan Mannes Rev., O.S.D. assistant pastor St. Bridget's Church, cor Van Ness Av and Bdwy
Duggan Patrick, carpenter, dwl 505 Howard
Duggan Robert, laborer, dwl cor Gough and Pacific
Duggan Thomas J. tanner with Davis & Sedgley, dwl Mission Creek nr Sixteenth
Duggan William C. ironer, Chelsea Laundry
Duhem August, florist, dwl 716 Washington
Duhue Catherine Miss, domestic, 424 Post
DUISENBERG CHARLES & CO. importers and commission merchants, office 205 California, dwl SE cor Harrison and Seventh
Duisenberg Charles A. C. consul for Bremen, office 205 Cal, dwl SE cor Harrison and Seventh
Duisenberg Jacob, merchant, dwl New York Hotel
Duke George, blacksmith with Flintoff & O'Neill, dwl 124 Natoma
Duke John, carpenter with A. A. Snyder, dwl 133 Tehama
Duker James M. bar keeper, 429 Montgomery
Dulea Charles, lab. dwl S s McAllister, nr Franklin
Dulbom (Pablo) & Barker (Pablo) butchers, dwl 1510 Dupont
Dulhom Paul (Baca & Co.) dwl Potrero Avenue
Dulion G. P. butcher, dwl W s Washoe Place
Dulion Leon (P. & L. Dulion) dwl 636 Pacific
Dulion Mary L. Miss, domestic, 521 Post
Dulion Paul & Leon, New Orleans Market, 705 Pacific, dwl W s Washoe Place
Dulip (J. P.) & Waddington (F.) groceries and liquors, SW cor Dupont and Broadway, and feed, 534 Bdwy, dwl NE cor Dupont and Bdwy
Dulking Frederick, works with Liepsic & Loudon
Dullan M. Mrs. nurse, dwl 739 Market
Dumartheray Francis, real estate, 34 Montgomery Block, dwl 88 Montgomery Block
Dumas Lucian, French Laundry, 416 Dupont
Dumbrell James H. job wagon, SE cor Clay and Montgomery, dwl King nr Ritch
Dumeste Alexander, butcher with J. B. Danos, NE cor Laguna and Waller
Dumfries Patrick, teamster, bds N s Geary nr Leav
Dumont Adolph, domestic with C. Duval, N s Seventeenth bet Guerrero and Dolores
Dumont Pierre, lithographer with Britton & Co. dwl 9 Harlan Place
Dumont Victor, dwl 619 Vallejo
Dumphy Edward, bricklayer, dwl 434 Stevenson
Dunan Daniel, laborer, Golden Age Flour Mills, dwl W s Havens Place
Dunand A. French Laundry, SW cor Stockton and Jackson
Dunare Francis, laborer, dwl E s Sansom bet Broadway and Pacific
Dunbar J. Wesley, sawyer with Hobbs, Gilmore & Co
Dunbar Samuel, draftsman, Fulton Foundry, dwl Oriental Hotel
Dunbar William A. teamster, dwl N s Post nr Larkin

Dunbar William F. *(Giles & D.)* dwl 221 Dupont
Dunbar William H. *(Hobart, D. & Co.)* res Boston
Duncan A. J. deck hand, steamer Chrysopolis
Duncan George *(Skinner & D.)* dwl S s Sixteenth nr Guerrero
Duncan George E. (col'd) hairdresser with N. A. Godfrey, dwl 924 Washington
Duncan Henry, dwl 49 Frederick
Duncan Isabella, domestic, 704 Howard
Duncan Isabella (widow) dwl W s Duncan Court
Duncan James, carpenter, dwl E s Anthony nr Mission
Duncan James, ship joiner W s Drumm nr Jackson, dwl 518 Bryant
Duncan James, tanner and currier, S s Brannan bet Eighth and Ninth
Duncan James E. carpenter, dwl 716 Larkin
Duncan James W. carpenter and builder, 1216 Taylor, dwl N s Vallejo bet Leavenworth and Hyde
Duncan John, engineer, dwl 761 Folsom
Duncan John, ship joiner with James Duncan, dwl South Park
DUNCAN JOSEPH C. manager Franco-American Commercial Co. office 215 Bush
Duncan Joseph Wylie, office 329 Sansom, dwl 772 Mission
Duncan Peter, salesman, 224 Battery, dwl Howard Court
Duncan Robert, with I. S. Van Winkle & Co. dwl Frederick nr Bryant
Duncan Robert, carpenter, dwl S s California bet Leavenworth and Hyde
Duncan Robert T. laborer, S. F. & San José R. R. dwl 446 Brannan
DUNCAN WILLIAM L. stock and real estate broker, and member San Francisco Stock and Exchange Board, office 605 Montgomery, dwl 810 Montgomery
Duncliff Thomas, teamster, dwl 414 Tehama
Duncum Henry, saw maker and locksmith, 114 Dupont
Dundas Lizzie Miss, milliner, 40 Fourth, dwl 569 Howard
Dundas Thomas R. dwl 569 Howard
Dundas William, dwl 569 Howard
Dundon John, laborer, dwl 15 Hunt
Dundon Patrick F. boiler maker, dwl 30 Clementina
Dungan Anna (widow) trimmings, dwl 623 Howard
Dunham A. M. photographic printer with William Shew, dwl 216 Stevenson
Dunham Benjamin F. salesman with Conroy & O'Connor, dwl 530 Pine
Dunham Clara (widow) dwl 216 Stevenson
Dunham Ephraim G. with William Shew, dwl 216 Stevenson
Dunham George A. local policeman, dwl SE cor Main and Harrison
Dunham W. H. dwl 21 Stockton Place
Dunham William, beer saloon, Mechanics' Hotel, dwl 934 Kearny
Dunham Woodruff, wood dealer, dwl 123 Clementina
Dunbard A. A. carrier, Morning Call
Dunkelly Edward, spinner, Pioneer Woolen Mills, dwl NW cor Beach and Larkin
Dunker Chris. *(Henry Kohn & Co.)* dwl 408 Folsom
Dunker Ernest, dwl NE cor Stockton and Sutter
Dunkin Louis, clerk with William Frederick, dwl SW cor Battery and Broadway
Dunlap David, cigars and tobacco, dwl 1014 Clay
Dunlap D. L. dwl International Hotel
Dunlap Maria Mrs. dress maker, dwl SW cor Dupont and Broadway
Dunlap Perley, hackman, Lick House, dwl S s O'Farrell bet Stockton and Powell
Dunlap William, employé with Lyon & Co. dwl 510 Jackson
Dunlay John, porter with Molloy & O'Connor, dwl Bay State Row

Dunleevy Jeremiah, harness maker with John O'Brien, dwl cor Mason and Market
Dunleevy Mary Ann Miss, domestic, 833 Bush
Dunlevy Andrew J. ship carpenter, dwl 933 Folsom
Dunlevy James, physician, SW cor Kearny and Dupont
Dunmire S. S. carriage maker, dwl 625 Third
Dunn Ann Miss, domestic, 1415 Taylor
Dunn Barney, hostler, dwl 706 Commercial
Dunn Barney, private watchman, dwl W s Vincent nr Green
Dunn Benjamin H. upholsterer, dwl 311 Bush
Dunn C. C. carpenter, dwl 331 Fremont
DUNN *(Charles D.)* & CAMPBELL *(C. Stuart)* book and job printing, 538 Market op Second, dwl 574 Mission nr Second
Dunn Daniel, fruit dealer, 414 Folsom
Dunn Daniel P. drayman, 323 Front
Dunn Dennis, blacksmith helper, Vulcan Iron Works, dwl 34 Frederick
Dunn Dennis, boiler maker with Coffey & Risdon
Dunn Edward, drayman, 706 Battery
Dunn Edward, laborer, dwl cor Folsom and Twelfth
Dunn Edward, wood and coal, 502½ Third
Dunn Elizabeth (widow) lodgings, dwl 421 Dupont
Dunn Ellen Miss, domestic, 302 Stockton
Dunn Frank, laborer, dwl 8 Lafayette Place
Dunn Horace D. clerk (Sacramento) dwl 52 Silver
Dunn James *(Henry & D.)* dwl W s Powell near Filbert
Dunn James, blacksmith, dwl 308 Jessie
Dunn James, express wagon, cor Cal and Mont
Dunn James, teamster, 17 California, dwl W s Eighth bet Howard and Clementina
Dunn *(John)* & McDonald *(David)* blacksmiths and boiler makers, S s Oregon bet Davis and Front, dwl 124 Jessie
DUNN, *(John)* McHAFFIE *(John)* & CO. *(Rees Llewellyn)* Atlas Iron Works, 24 and 26 Fremont, dwl 29 Jane
Dunn John, with William Hoffman & Co. 427 Sacramento, dwl S s Riley nr Jones
Dunn John, blacksmith, dwl 36 Frederick
Dunn John, book keeper, S. F. & P. Sugar Co. 310 Commercial
Dunn John, helper Fulton Foundry, dwl 14 Jessie
Dunn John J. pattern maker, Union Foundry, dwl 29 Jane
Dunn Joseph, cartman, dwl S s Bernard bet Taylor and Jones
Dunn Lawrence, machinist, Pacific Foundry, dwl 29 Jane
Dunn Margaret (widow) domestic with Mrs. J. Stanton, W s Mission nr Fifteenth
Dunn Martin, stone mason, dwl 314 O'Farrell, rear
Dunn Mary Miss, domestic with Theodore A. Barry
Dunn Mary Mrs. dwl 113 Tehama
Dunn Mary (widow) dwl W s Guerrero bet Thirteenth and Fourteenth
Dunn Mary (widow) dwl with Edward Long, W s Second Avenue bet Sixteenth and Seventeenth
Dunn Mary (widow) dwl 1 Graham Place
Dunn Michael, letter clerk with John Bamber & Co. dwl S s Vallejo bet Montgomery and Kearny
Dunn Patrick, drayman, dwl N s Turk bet Van Ness Avenue and Franklin
Dunn Patrick, U. S. A. dwl 178 Stevenson
Dunn Thomas M. engineer with Jones, Wooll & Sutherland, dwl 514 O'Farrell
Dunn Timothy, laborer, dwl Rassette Place No. 3
Dunn Willet *(Schlam & W.)* dwl 818 Montgomery
Dunn William, dwl E s Zoe bet Bryant and Brannan
Dunn William, blacksmith apprentice, Vulcan Iron Works, dwl 29 Jane
Dunn William, contractor, dwl nr Bay View Park Road first toll gate
Dunn William, groceries and liquors, SW cor Pacific and Leavenworth
Dunn William C. cartman, dwl 24 Ritch

Dunn William W. machinist, dwl 1013 Sacramento
Dunnaham Joseph, dwl 118 Harrison
Dunnavent Alex C. dwl 136 Minna
Dunne Edward, laborer with Hey & Meyn
Dunne John, boot maker, dwl SW cor Mission and Thirteenth
Dunne Mathew, laborer, dwl S s Natoma nr Seventh
DUNNE P. F. boot and shoe manufacturer, 316 Battery, dwl S s Chestnut bet Stockton and Powell
Dunnicliff Thomas, drayman with D. J. Oliver, dwl S s Tehama bet Fifth and Sixth
Dunnie James, laborer, dwl SW cor Jessie and Annie
Dunnigan David, laborer, dwl S s Folsom bet Beale and Main
Dunnigan Frank, laborer, dwl 55 Shipley, rear
Dunnigan Mary Mrs. domestic, 942 Mission
Dunnigan Michael, marble polisher, dwl N s Harrison nr Sixth
Dunnigan (Patrick) & Flynn (Thomas) blacksmiths, 573 and 575 Market, dwl cor Sacramento and Jones
Dunnigan Rose Miss, domestic, 426 Post
Dunning J. W. painter, dwl Oriental Hotel
DUNNING ORSON, physician and oculist, office and dwl 515 Sacramento
Dunning Ralph, clerk, U. S. Engineers, 37 Montgomery Block, dwl 86 Montgomery Block
Dunning Thomas, laborer, dwl S s Perry bet Fourth and Fifth
Dunning Thomas, groceries and liquors, 253 Clara
Dunning Wilfred, painter, dwl Original House
Dunning Zophar (Hubert & D.) dwl 44 Market
Dunnivan James, laborer, dwl 519 Mission
Dunnivan James, laborer, dwl 459 Jessie
Dunnivan James, express wagon, cor Folsom and Stewart
Dunnivan Jeremiah, laborer, dwl S s Folsom bet Beale and Main
Dunnivan John, blacksmith, dwl 76 Jessie
Dunnivan John, grainer, dwl 155 Third
Dunnivan Patrick (Brennan & D.) dwl S s Sacramento bet Jones and Leavenworth
Dunphy Catharine Miss, dwl 2 Trinity
Dunphy Mary C. Miss, chambermaid with Isaac Stone
Dunphy T. James, painter with Hopps & Kanary, dwl 407 Hyde nr Ellis
Dunphy William, dwl 111 Mason
Dunshee Cornelius E. carpenter, dwl S s Pine bet Van Ness Avenue and Franklin
Dnuton E. boot maker, dwl 218 First
Duparque Emille, hairdresser with C. Hubert
Duparque Louis, tailor, E s Powell bet Chestnut and Francisco
Duperu Numa, clerk, Pier 22 Stewart, dwl 28 Rincon Place
Dupont J. H. boots and shoes, 822 Washington
Dupouey Henri, professor French, Grace Institute, dwl 719 California
DUPRE EUGENE, French notary and mining president, office 606 Merchant, dwl Midway nr Francisco
Duprey Joseph, dwl 522 Dupont
Dapuy (John) & Co. (Martin Kametto) blacksmiths and wheelwrights, 528 Broadway
Dupuy Pedro, butcher with Louis Peres, dwl Potrero Avenue
Dupuytron Jacob, laborer, dwl N s Chestnut bet Kearny and Dupont
Dupy Victor, laborer, dwl E s Leroy Place bet Sacramento and Clay
Duquemy Augustine Miss, milliner, dwl 260 Minna
Duquemy J. B. carver, 260 Minna
Duran Edward, clerk, dwl 822 Pacific
Duran John, butcher, 14 New Market, dwl 515 Merchant
Durand A. clerk with O. Chauvin, dwl 822 Pacific

Durand Adrien, clerk French Benevolent Society, 649 Sacramento, dwl 639 Broadway
Durand Anson P. gymnast, dwl 77 Fourth
Durand Frederick, cook, dwl SW cor Dupont and Broadway
Durand Joseph, fireman, steamer Clinton
Durand Nicholas, cook, 718 Market, dwl cor Bush and Broadway
Durant F. dwl What Cheer House
Durant G. & S. M. Co. office 620 Washington
Durant John, cabinet maker with Goodwin & Co. dwl 10 Lafayette Place
Durbrow Alfred K. Gibb & Vallejo St. Bonded Warehouses, cor Front and Vallejo, dwl SW cor Market and Third
Durbrow Joseph jr. with Parrott & Co. NW cor Montgomery and Sacramento, dwl 320 Mason
Duren George G. carriage maker, dwl E s Quincy nr Pine
Durgin E. G. carpenter, dwl 112 Stewart
Durgin John, cook, Willows, SW cor Mission and Eighteenth
Durham Frank, laborer, dwelling N s Union near Kearny
Durham Hyacinth Rev. assistant pastor St. Francis Church, dwl 519 Green
Durham James, laborer, dwl Union Court
Durham William (colored) seaman, dwl 11 Pinckney Place
Durian Victor, employé Government House Restaurant, 504 Washington
Durie Pauline (widow) dwl 25 Turk, rear
DURKEE JOHN L. fire marshal, office and dwl 7 City Hall third floor
Durken Anthony, laborer, San Francisco Gas Co. dwl 64 Natoma
Durkin A. & Co. proprietors Mission St. Brewery, 608 and 610 Mission, dwl E s Guerrero near Eighteenth
Durkin Bridget Miss, domestic with James Center, W s Howard nr Fifteenth
Durkin Edward (Tully & D.) dwl 526 Tehama
Durkin James, hostler, Central R. R. Co. dwl 109 Dora
Durnen James, carpenter, dwl 777 Market
Durney Alfred F. dwl 603 Geary
Durning Thomas, children's and fancy goods, 10 Second
Durose John, machinist, Union Foundry
Duross W. machinist, Vulcan Iron Works
Durphy James, carpenter, dwl 39 First
Durr John, salesman with Taaffe & Co
Durr Joseph, clerk, dwl 21 Jessie
Duschee Henry, driver, dwl 477 Jessie
Dussol Gustave, attorney in fact Abel Guy, dwl 611 Bush
Dussol Madeline (widow) dwl 9 Hardie Place
Dustin Thomas (col'd) dwl 241 Minna
Dustin Thomas J. (col'd) steward, dwl 1134 Pacific
Dustow Mary J. Miss, nurse, City and County Hospital
Dutard Bernard, produce commission, 217 Clay, dwl 15 Valparaiso nr Mason
Dutard Eugene, with B. Dutard, 217 Clay, dwl 15 Valparaiso nr Mason
Dutard Hypolite, with B. Dutard, dwl 15 Valparaiso nr Mason
Dutch William (Crawford & D.) dwl American Exchange
Dutcher John M. sawyer with Macdonald Bros. dwl 67 Clementina
Dutcher Sarah Mrs. (widow) dwl 110 Freelon
Dutertre Baptiste, meat market, 2 O'Farrell
Dutertre Louis, lodgings, NE corner Dupont and Broadway
Dutton Cyrus H. (col'd) hair dresser with N. A. Godfrey, dwl Bee Hive Building
DUTTON HENRY & SON (Henry Dutton, jr.) hay and grain, Pier 7 Stewart, dwl 801 Union

Dutton Henry jr. *(Henry Dutton & Son)* dwl Sutter bet Scott and Devisidero

Dutton Jane Miss, proprietress Clay St. House, 62 Clay

Dutton Joseph, carpenter, dwl W s Fillmore opposite Kate

Dutton Samuel E. book keeper, Pier 7 Stewart, dwl Sutter bet Scott and Devisidero

Duval Caroline Mrs. dwl N s Seventeenth bet Guerrero and Dolores

Duval James, clerk with Reynolds, Howell & Ford, dwl 615 Pine

DUVENECK CHARLES & CO. *(Richard Strothoff)* Shakspeare Liquor Saloon, Exchange Building, dwl Mission bet Seventeenth and Dolores

Duvivier Eugene, employé, Metropolitan Restaurant, 715 Montgomery

Duyne Ann (widow) notions, 14½ Fourth

Dwann James, miller, bds Sacramento Hotel, 407 Pacific

DWINELLE JOHN W. *(Shafter, Goold & D.)* attorney at law, office 11 Montgomery Block, res NW cor Clay and Fifth, Oakland

DWINELLE SAMUEL H. Judge Fifteenth District Court, room 17 City Hall second floor, chambers 17 third floor, dwl SW cor Leavenworth and Ellis

Dworzazek. Benedict *(Beer & Co.)* dwl S s Pine bet Leavenworth and Hyde

Dwyer Alice (widow) domestic, dwl 1116 Stockton

Dwyer Anna (widow) dwl 1420 Powell

Dwyer Anthony, carpenter, dwl E s Valencia bet Twelfth and Thirteenth

DWYER *(David)* & CO. *(Bartholomew Haley)* coal, 539 California, dwl 114 Ellis

Dwyer Edward *(Philip J. & E. D.)* dwl 552 Mission

Dwyer Jeremiah, dry goods, 104 Third, dwl 39 Everett

Dwyer John, machinist, dwl 54 First

Dwyer John, shoe maker with John Johnson, dwl cor Market and Ecker

Dwyer John E. machinist, Vulcan Iron Works, dwl 216 Minna

Dwyer Joseph, drugs and medicines, 2 Sacramento

Dwyer Kate Miss, dwl 18 Jessie

Dwyer Kate Miss, domestic, 652 Market

Dwyer Kate (widow) dwl 74 Natoma

Dwyer Lawrence, painter, dwl E s Clinton S Brannan

Dwyer Margaret Miss, domestic, 329 O'Farrell

Dwyer Michael, laborer, dwl 11 St. Mary

Dwyer Michael, stove mounter, 112 Battery, res Oakland

Dwyer Philip J. & E. Faneuil Hall Market, 56 First, dwl Central House

Dwyer Robert, stableman, dwl 712 Broadway

Dwyer Thomas, apprentice, Golden State Iron Works, dwl Isthmus House

Dwyer Thomas, finisher, S. F. P. Woolen Mills, dwl North Point bet Polk and Van Ness Av

Dwyer Thomas, waiter, Russ House, dwl 52 Everett

Dwyer Timothy *(Enright & D.)* dwl 183 Jessie

Dwyer William, merchant, dwl 115 First

Dyas John, oiler, steamer Orizaba

Dyberg Alfred V. sail maker with John Harding, dwl 266 Minna

Dyckman John, wood dealer, dwl 726 O'Farrell

Dye William M. book keeper with Koopmanschap & Co. dwl 804 Pine

Dyer Ann (widow) dwl NE cor Haight and Laguna

Dyer Columbus, ship carpenter with John G. North, dwl SW cor Louisiana and Sierra

Dyer Frank E. overland mailing clerk, Post Office, dwl 22 Kearny

Dyer George F. book keeper with H. M. Newhall & Co

Dyer Henry, clerk, 546 Clay, dwl 928 Clay

Dyer James, laborer, dwl 440 Clementina

Dyer James, silversmith, dwl 6 Brenham Place

Dyer James A. carpenter, dwl W s Eighth bet Mission and Howard

Dyer James B. laborer, dwl W s Sansom bet Green and Vallejo

Dyer James J. *(Whitcombe & D.)* dwl 205 Third

Dyer John B. apprentice with S. S. Culverwell, dwl Broadway nr Montgomery

Dyer Joseph, dwl 1330 Dupont

Dyer J. P. *(Hardenberg & D.)* office 25 Belden Block, dwl 621 Bush

DYER JAMES P. (colored) proprietor New England Soap and Tallow Works, NW cor Nebraska and Sixteenth, dwl 1413 Mason

Dyer J. S. gardener, S s Presidio Road nr Spring Valley School

Dyer Michael, boot fitter, dwl 1119 Sacramento

Dyer M. P. box maker, dwl S s Sacramento bet Mason and Taylor

Dyer Richard, teamster, 315 Davis, dwl S s Bush nr Polk

Dyer Rodolphus C. dwl 121 Fourth

DYER, *(Samuel R.)* BADGER *(Joseph B.)* & ROKOHL *(D.)* auctioneers and commission merchants, NE cor Montgomery and Pine, dwl 625 Post

Dyer Spencer S. engineer, dwl W s First Avenue nr Fifteenth

Dyer William C. cooper, 1019 Battery, rear, dwl E s Bartol nr Broadway

DYER *(Wm. D.)* & LUDERS *(Edward T.)* proprietors Dyer's Photographic Gallery, 612 Clay, dwl 40 Minna

Dykeman Paul, boatman, dwl 79 Jessie

Dynan Timothy, with Porter & Covey, dwl St. Mary

Dyson Mary Mrs. dress making, 112 Dupont

Dyson Thomas, paper hanger, dwl 112 Dupont

E

EADE William, laborer, Golden Age Flour Mills, dwl 320 Vallejo

Eades William, Our Bakery, 1434 Stockton

Eadon William H. with Crane & Brigham, dwl SW cor Eddy and Jones

Eagan Ann (widow) dwl 3 Minna

Eagan Charles H. painter, dwl 415 Pine

Eagan Edward, blacksmith, C. S. Nav. Co

Eagan Eliza Miss, domestic, 1519 Taylor

Eagan George L. clerk, 415 Pine

Eagan Michael, carpenter with Francis Buckley

Eagan Patrick, carpenter, dwl NE cor Pacific and Front

Eagan Timothy, laborer, dwl U. S. Hotel, 706 Bat

Eagan William, bar keeper, SW cor Howard and Third, dwl 13 Ritch, rear

Eagan William E. carpenter, dwl 633 Market

Eager John, porter, dwl 64 Natoma

Eager W. T. pressman with John A. T. Overend, dwl Original House

Eagle G. & S. M. Co. office 15 Montgomery Block

Eagle Warehouse, N. R. Lowell, proprietor, NW cor Davis and Pine

Eagle William C. car builder, S. F. & San José R. R. dwl 10 O'Farrell

Eagler Frederick, handcartman, cor Pac and Dupont

Eagles M. P. Mrs. cloak and dress maker, 10 O'Farrell

Eagles William C. car builder, dwl 10 O'Farrell

Eago Frederick, pistol gallery, dwl 162 Tehama

Eakins Isaiah, messenger, C. H. dwl 115 Geary

Ealy Nicholas, water tender, steamer Sierra Nevada, dwl 547 Mission

Eamech Charles M. tinsmith with Edward Hagthrop, dwl S s Sutter bet Taylor and Jones

Eangonner Auguste, baker with Peter Job, dwl Dupont bet Pine and Bush

Eardman John, tinsmith, dwl 816 Filbert
Earl A. C. clerk, Tremont House, 418 Jackson
Earl Enoch, cooper with Henry Shuman, dwl 802 Stockton
Earl Henry, porter, 312 Bush, dwl 551 Folsom
Earl Thomas J. barber, dwl 608 Stockton
Earle George, lumber surveyor, Pier 11 Stewart, dwl 59 Clementina
Earle George F. clerk with Redington & Co. dwl 815 Hyde
Earle George Frederick, salesman, 616 Kearny, dwl 59 Clementina
Earle Halford, clerk with Sinclair & Moody, dwl 815 Hyde nr Bush
Earle Henry, butcher, W s Sixth bet Harrison and Bryant
Earle Henry G. clerk, 113 Davis, dwl Howard Engine House
Earle Henry H. clerk with Redington & Co. dwl 815 Hyde
Earle James H. local policeman, dwl SW cor Dupont and Pacific
EARLE JOHN H. liquors, NE cor Clay and Drumm, dwl 1317 Mason
Earley James, laborer, dwl 7 Eddy
Earley James, machinist, Union Foundry, dwl 54 First
Early, John, hackman, Manhattan Engine Co. No. 1
Early S. G. delivery clerk, California State Telegraph Co. dwl 110 Silver
Easly Benjamin, dwl 8 s Jessie bet First and Second
East Range G. & S. M. Co. office 712 Montgomery
Easter John, express wagon, Clay nr Davis
Eastham Henry F. mariner, dwl 109 Perry
EASTLAND JOSEPH G. secretary S. F. Gas Co. office SE corner First and Natoma, dwl 225 Geary
Eastman Augustine, dwl 50 Tehama
Eastman Charles F. paymaster's clerk, dwl 18 First
Eastman Cyrus A. miner, dwl 2 Melvina Place
EASTMAN CYRUS A. mining secretary, 728 Montgomery, dwl 28 Hawthorne
Eastman Cyrus Alvah, dwl 11 Ewer Place
Eastman Edward H. porter with William P. Harrison, dwl 528 Pine
EASTMAN FRANK, Franklin Book and Job Printing Office, 415 Wash, dwl 1117 Taylor
Eastman Harrison, artist and wood engraver, 338 Montgomery rooms 21 and 22, dwl 1133 Clay
Eastman Thomas S. (Hill & E.) dwl 1010 Taylor
Eastman Webster, carpenter, dwl 633 Market
Eastman William H. carpenter and builder, 637 California, dwl 528 Pine
Easton George R. stevedore, dwl 302 Vallejo
Easton James (Easton & Bro.) cabinet makers, 725 Market, dwl N s Minna bet Eighth and Ninth
Easton Giles A. Rev. assistant pastor, Grace Cathedral, and principal Grace Female Institute, dwl 1006 Pine
Easton (John) & Brother (James Easton) cabinet makers 725 Market, dwl 522 O'Farrell, rear
Easton John, cabinet maker with Easton & Brother, dwl 522 O'Farrell
Easton Lizzie B. Miss, assistant, Greenwich Street School, dwl 803 Union
Easton O. W. asphaltum roofer and patent weather strip, office 316 Montgomery, dwl 803 Union
Easton Richard, carpenter, dwl 522 Broadway
Eaton Alexander, blacksmith with Gallagher & Farren, dwl W s Mission Avenue bet Sixteenth and Seventeenth
Eaton Benjamin B. carpenter, dwl S s Shipley nr Harrison Avenue
EATON CHARLES S. employment and real estate agent, office 708 Kearny, dwl 1206 Mason
Eaton Cornelius J. mining secretary, office 523 Montgomery, dwl 330 Fremont
Eaton E. B. physician and druggist, SE cor Folsom and Caroline

Eaton Henry, general freight agent, S. F. & San José R. R. dwl 28 Stanly Place
EATON I. WARD (J. L. Riddle & Co.) dwl NE cor Essex and Laurel Place
EATON J. A. & CO. general agents North America Life Insurance Co. office 240 Montgomery, dwl 929 Howard
Eaton Lemuel P. mining, dwl SW cor Post and Taylor
Eaton Noble H. clerk, 19 Sansom, dwl cor Essex and Laurel Place
Eaton S. T. Miss, private school, N s Folsom near Sixth, dwl 770 Howard
Eaton William L. Melter and Refiner's Dept U. S. Branch Mint, dwl 1219 Pacific
Eaves Patrick, fireman, dwl Davis St. House
Eayrs Henry P. clerk, 538 Market, dwl 655 Harrison
Ebbesen Herman, cook, 126 California
Ebbets Arthur M. coal depôt, 115 Sacramento bet Davis and Drumm, dwl 1405 Jones
Ebbinghausen Frank (Dreyer & E.) dwl cor Gilmore and Kentucky
Ebbinghausen George, clerk with H. Koster, dwl SE cor Third and Howard
EBBINGHAUSEN HENRY, groceries and liquors, SW cor Folsom and Fourth
Ebeling Philip, jeweler with Lawrence Brothers, dwl 520 Green
Eberhart Adolphe, wines and liquors, dwl 2 Telegraph Place
Eberline Margaret (widow) with Isaac D. Holt, W s Folsom bet Sixteenth and Seventeenth
Ebert Ernest, boot maker, 648 Washington
Ebrell William (col'd) seaman, dwl 7 Broadway
Ebright H. carpenter, Spring Valley W. W
Ebson Edward, laborer, Bay Sugar Refinery, dwl 1021 Battery
Ecclas John, plumber and gas fitter, 667 Mission
Eccles Christopher, blacksmith, dwl E s Mission bet First and Second
Eccles William, tinsmith, dwl 1526 Stockton
Echart Henry, manuf billiard tables, 821 Mont
Echter F. crimper, 533 Broadway
Eck Florent, cooperage, 1235 Stockton
Eckart Christian, jeweler, 620 Merchant
Eckart William R. draftsman, Union Foundry, dwl 608 Post
Eckel Frederick, salesmen, 411 Sansom, dwl 162 Tehama
Eckel J. N. homeopathic physician, office and dwl 226 Post
Eckenroth Joseph, wagon maker with Charles Steinweg, dwl Washington Avenue
Ecker George O. (Tucker & Co.) dwl 505 Montgomery
Eckert (Frederick M.) & Carruthers (George) carpenters and builders, N s Summer nr Mont
ECKFELDT JOHN M. melter and refiner U. S. Branch Mint, office 608 Commercial, dwl 404 Eddy
Eckhard William, laborer, dwl 327 Vallejo, rear
Eckhardt Henry, Leavenworth Market, NE cor Jackson and Leavenworth
Eckhardt Henry, piano maker with Jacob Zech, dwl 522 Filbert
Eckhoff Herman, clerk with H. Doscher, SE cor Seventh and Brannan
Eckley George R. teller with Sather & Co. dwl 826 Folsom
ECKMANN JULIUS R. Rev. editor and proprietor Hebrew Observer, office 511 Sacramento, dwl 725 California
Eckstein Alfred, cigars and tobacco, 15 Montgomery, Lick House
Eckstram Charles A. musician, dwl 1113 Dupont
Eclipse Tunnel Co. office 420 Montgomery
Edams George F. machinist, Fulton Foundry, dwl 641 Mission
Eddick Peter, blacksmith, dwl 416 Folsom

Eddy *(James)* & Williams *(William)* liquors, SE cor Pacific and Montgomery, dwl 906 Vallejo

Eddy J. Frank, bds American Exchange

Edelkamp Bernard, wood yard, SW cor Stewart and Folsom, dwl 424 Third

Edelkamp Bernard Mrs. fancy dry goods, 424 Third

Eden John *(Heins & E.)* dwl S s Winters Alley nr Mason

Eden Line Packets, Clay St. Wharf

Eden Samuel, importer, dwl 117 Stockton

Edgar Catherine (widow) dwl N s Grove nr Van Ness Avenue, Hayes' Valley

Edgar John, boot maker, dwl 705 Battery

Edgar Michael J. compositor, Sunday Mercury, dwl E s Dupont bet Post and Sutter

Edger Catherine (widow) dwl 14 Natoma

Edgerly C. L. carpenter, 319 Bush, bds What Cheer House

Edgerly Harry, Harry's Saloon, 6 Merchant, dwl 920 Sutter

EDGERLY *(N. Bona)* & WICKMAN *(William)* ship chandlers, 407 East, dwl 920 Sutter

Edgerton George H. carpenter, dwl W s Capp bet Twenty-First and Twenty-Second .

Edmand R. A. butcher with Owen Connolly, SE cor Laguna and Waller

Edmands L. R. P. clerk with Moore & Co. dwl 711 California

Edmonds Charles, musician, dwl Stockton bet Green and Union

Edmonds George H. musician, Olympic Melodeon

Edmonds Henry, teamster, Pier 2 Stewart, dwl 120 William

Edmonds Marcus A. attorney at law, dwl 310 Jessie

Edmonds William (colored) steward, steamer Amelia

Edmonds William, Melter and Refiner's Department U. S. Branch Mint, dwl 522 Howard

Edmondson John (colored) dwl N s Bernard nr Leavenworth

Edmondson T. J. storage, office 705 Sansom, res Haywood's, Alameda County

Edmondston B. B. carpenter, dwl 721 Sutter

Edmunds Henry H. milk ranch, W s Presidio Road nr Presidio House

Edmunds Sophia (widow) dwl 1412 Dupont

Edole William, miner, dwl 323 Pine

Edouart Alexander, artist and photographic gallery, 634 Washington, dwl N s Chestnut bet Leavenworth and Hyde

Edson C. A. store keeper with Cross & Co. 613 Battery, dwl 20 Sixth

Edstrom Anna Mrs. dress making, 113 Dupont

Edstrom Thomas, trunk maker with E. Galpin & Co. dwl 113 Dupont

Edwards Allen, seaman, dwl S s Union, rear, bet Sansom and Calhoun

Edwards, *(A. S.)* Olney *(James N.)* & Co. auction and commission, 626 Montgomery, dwl 128 Silver .

Edwards Edward, liquors, dwl N s Twelfth bet Howard and Folsom

Edwards Eliza Miss, dwl with John Satterlee, W s Folsom bet Eleventh and Twelfth

Edwards Eliza Mrs. ladies' and children's furnishing goods, 557½ Mission

EDWARDS FRANK G. importer and dealer in carpets, paper hangings, window shades, etc. 646 Clay, dwl 12 John .

Edwards Frederick *(Mallett & E.)* dwl 803 Stock

Edwards George W. salesman with George B. Hitchcock & Co. dwl 560 Bryant

Edwards Harry B. waiter, 28 Montgomery

Edwards Henry, salesman with Roberts, Morrison & Co. dwl 618 Market

Edwards Henry F. *(Koopmanschap & Co.)* dwl Union Club Rooms

Edwards James, laborer with John G. North, Potrero Nuevo

Edwards James, laborer, dwl 1819 Powell

Edwards John, carpenter, dwl N s Boyd nr Chesley

Edwards Joseph C. clerk, County Recorder's Office, dwl 748 Howard

Edwards Justin, ship joiner, dwl 319 Beale

Edwards L. B. wharfinger Cowell's Wharf, dwl 619 Bush

Edwards Louis, expressman, dwl 930 Montgomery

Edwards Lowell, cooper with T. F. Neagle, 221 Washington

Edwards Mathias, fisherman, 4 Italian Fish Market

Edwards Sarah (widow) dwl 139½ Fourth

Edwards Thomas M. clerk with William C. Miller, dwl International Hotel

Edwards William P. copyist, dwl NE cor Kearny and Broadway

Edwards William P. salesman with John G. Hodge & Co. dwl 557 Mission

Edwards W. S. assistant, U. S. Coast Survey, office Custom House third floor

Eells Allen M. dwl 519 Folsom

Eells John S. *(R. S. Eells & Co.)* dwl N s Folsom bet Twenty-First and Twenty-Second

EELLS R. S. & CO. *(John S. and Thomas S. Eells)* importers, jobbers, and manufacturers carriages and carriage materials, NW cor Pine and Front, dwl 519 Folsom .

Eells Thomas S. *(R. S. Eells & Co.)* dwl 519 Folsom

Eells William, dwl 316 Fourth

Effinger George, carpenter, dwl 121 Prospect Place

Efford N. C. groceries and liquors, 309 East, dwl E s Dupont bet Lombard and Chestnut

Efner George W. carriage painter with C. D. Henry & Co. dwl 210 Broadway

Efner William G. painter, dwl Wright's Hotel, 210 Broadway

Egan Bridget Mrs. domestic with Jas. Brooks, N s Turk bet Polk and Van Ness Avenue

Egan Edward, blacksmith, dwl N s Green bet Montgomery and Kearny

Egan Edward, helper, Union Foundry, dwl 164 Jessie

Egan Edward, plasterer, dwl nr cor Union and Hyde

Egan Henry, plasterer, dwl N s Bernard bet Jones and Leavenworth

Egan Isaac, dwl 115 Geary

Egan James, dwl 124 Shipley, rear

Egan John *(Kelly & E.)* dwl 228 Jessie

Egan John, teacher, dwl 32 Third

Egan John Mrs. millinery, 32 Third

Egan John W. clerk, 411 Sacramento, dwl 625½ Mission bet First and Second

Egan Michael, laborer, dwl S s Turk nr Polk

Egan Patrick, bricklayer, dwl S s Natoma bet Fifth and Sixth

Egan Patrick, laborer, dwl 436 Jessie

Egan Richard, clerk, dwl 7 O'Farrell

Egan Richard, clerk, 4 Third, dwl SE cor Hyde and Geary

Egan Thomas H. dwl 910 Market

Egan Timothy, laborer, Union Foundry, dwl U. S. Hotel

Egan William, laborer with James Brokaw, dwl 13 Dupont

Egan William, oyster stand, SW cor Third and Howard, dwl 15 Ritch

Egar William, pressman, 511½ Clay, dwl Original House

Egery Artemus J. physician, dwl 627 Commercial

Egery B. D. clerk with L. J. Ewell, dwl 514 Filbert

Eggers Caroline L. Miss, dwl SW cor Twelfth and Folsom

Eggers Ferdinand, grocer, SE cor Dupont and Vallejo, dwl 1424 Dupont

EGGERS FREDERICK, groceries and liquors, SE cor Vallejo and Dupont

Eggers George, varnisher with Goodwin & Co. dwl N s Jackson bet Stockton and Powell

EGGERS *(George H.)* & CO. *(Christian H. Voigt and Thomas Basse)* wholesale groceries, provisions, etc. 210 California, dwl SW cor Folsom and Twelfth
Eggers John C. *(Precht & E.)* dwl 123 Dora
Eggers Hinrich, employé, Bay Sugar Refinery, dwl Pacific bet Davis and Drumm
Eggert William W. deck hand, steamer Julia
Eggleton George, proprietor What Cheer Livery Stable, 121 Jackson, dwl Black Point
Eh Chung & Co. (Chinese) washing, N s Sixteenth bet Guerrero and Dolores
Eh Chung (Chinese) washing, S s Clark nr Davis
Ehlers Brune, dwl 1423 Mason
Ehlers C. F. book keeper with A. Fenkhausen, dwl Lutgen's Hotel
Ehlers Winchen, groceries and liquors, 19 Hinckley
Ehlert Barbara (widow) dwl 1009 Kearny
Ehlin E. *(A. Waldstein & Co.)* dwl 407 Mission
Ehmann George E. baker, Hamburg Bakery, SE cor Mission and Fourth
Ehmann Henry, liquor-saloon, 525 Kearny
Ehrchs Frederick *(Wm. Meyerholz & Co.)* dwl 702 Bush
Ehrenberg Armin, book keeper with Otto Wiedero & Co. dwl S s Geary bet Dupont and Stockton
Ehrenberg Herman, mining stocks, dwl 1024 Stock
Ehrenpfort Andreas, dwl 77 Everett
Ehrenpfort Edward, upholsterer with Goodwin & Co. dwl ·77 Everett
Ehrenpfort *(Frederick)* & Co. *(Charles Borchard)* confectioners, 22 and 24 Stockton and 435 Kearny, dwl 14 Third
Ehrenpfort Minna Miss, domestic, dwl 812 Howard
Ehrenpfort William, dwl 14 Third
Ehrenwerth Morris, clerk, 638 Sac, dwl 12 Second
Ehret John M. shoe maker, 230 Sutter
Ehrhard Adam, cloak and mantilla maker, 645 Sacramento, dwl 519 Kearny
Ehrhardt Christian, shoe maker, 1332 Dupont
Ehrhart *(David)* & Hemmer *(Henry)* boots and shoes, 542 California ·
Ehrhorn Adolphus *(Hellmann Brothers & Co.)* dwl 28 Ellis
Ehrich Caleb, soap manufacturer, dwl 25 Stone
Ehrich Ernest, musician, Academy Music
Ehrichs D. wines and liquors, dwl SE cor Battery and Vallejo
Ehrlich Louis, auctioneer, 130 Third, dwl 13 Everett
EHRLICH MEYER, stock broker, office 20 Montgomery Block, dwl 1607 Powell
Ehrlich Theodore, carrier, Abend Post, dwl NW cor Dupont and St. Mark Place
Ehrman George, upholsterer with Charles M. Plum, dwl 154 Natoma. nr Second
Ehrman L. *(Ehrman & Bachman)* office 309 Sac
Ehrmann Valentine, carpenter, 229 Sutter
Eichel Christian, furniture and upholstery, 108 Fourth, dwl 56 Everett
Eichenkotter Edward, waiter, dwl 719 California
Eichers John, express wagon, NW cor Stockton and Pacific, dwl 1117 Sacramento
Eickoff J. Henry, clerk, S. F. & P. Sugar Co. dwl Dora nr Folsom
EIDENMULLER GEORGE, physician, office cor Washington and Brenham Place, dwl 1712 Union
Einsfield Peter *(Dobelmann & E.)* dwl 89 Stevenson
Einstein Abraham *(Einstein Bros.)* res Boston
EINSTEIN. BROTHERS *(Zadock and Abraham Einstein, and Aaron and Abraham Altmayer)* importers and jobbers boots and shoes, 207–211 Battery, dwl 7 Mason
Eipper Thomas, barber, 328 Pacific, dwl Charles nr Pacific
Eiseman A. fancy goods, 648 Market, dwl 610 Post
Eiseman Jacob, auctioneer, dwl 610 Post
Eisen Aug. F. architect, office 338 Montgomery room 17, dwl NW cor Grove and Franklin

EISEN BROTHERS *(Francis T. and George)* proprietors Pioneer Flour Mill, 515 Market, dwl W s Guerrero bet Sixteenth and Seventeenth
Eisen Frederick, cigar maker, dwl 619 Pacific
Eisen George *(Eisen Bros.)* dwl 515 Market
Eisen *(Nathan)* & Co. *(Julius Levine)* cloaks, 104 Montgomery
Eisenberg E. manufacturer cigars, 723 Sansom, dwl SE cor Washington and Sansom
Eisenberg Isaac, merchant tailor, 617 Washington
Eisenberg Morris, dwl 642 Sacramento
Eisenhamer Adam, express wagon, 416 Battery
Eisenworth (widow) nurse, dwl 5 Dixon Blk, Jane
Eisle Charles A. butcher, dwl 736 Market
Eisler Martin, watchman, dwl 515 Market
Eitel Henry, clerk, 111 Second
Eitel John M. clerk, 5 Stewart
Ekelman John, barber, dwl 207 Post
Ekelund E. electro gilder and silver plater, 733 · Washington, dwl 147 Jessie
Ekenberg H. F. laborer, dwl 436 Fremont
Eklof S. Louis, book keeper, 623 Clay, dwl 649 Clay
Ekstrom Augusta Mrs. millinery, 1118 Dupont
Ekstrom Charles, musician, dwl 1118 Dupont
EL CORREO DE SAN FRANCISCO (French daily and steamer) office 617 and 619 Sansom
El Dorado G. & S. M. Co. office 529 Clay
EL NUEVO MUNDO (Spanish tri-weekly) F. P. Ramires & Co. proprietors, office 609 Front
El Taste S. M. Co. office 1 Government House
ELAM *(Robert H.)* & HOWES *(Edward K.)* importers, jobbers, and manufacturers brooms, wood, and willow ware, etc. 310 and 312 Clay, dwl 621 Leavenworth cor Post
Elan James, driver, dwl 3 Hampton Place
Elbrecht S. S. shipmaster, dwl 238 Stewart
Elder John, baker with Philip Thorn, 22 Dupont
Elder William, merchant, dwl 38 First
Eldredge Albert S. dwl 809 Jackson
Eldredge Kimball C. dwl 809 Jackson
Eldridge Charles H. clerk with J. C. Johnson & Co. dwl 820 Howard
Eldridge *(George C.)* & Morshead *(Philip)* proprietors Long Island Livery and Sale Stable, 233 Bush, dwl 216 Stockton
Eldridge Horace P. clerk, 210 Clay
Eldridge Jacob, barber, dwl 507 Dupont
Eldridge J. Oscar *(H. M. Newhall & Co.)* dwl 336 Second
Eldridge Kate Mrs. dwl 421 Dupont
Eldridge L. A. carpenter, dwl Original House
ELDRIDGE OLIVER, agent Pacific Mail Steamship Line, office NW cor Sacramento and Leidesdorff, dwl 609 Sutter
Eldridge Sylvester A. commercial reporter Alta California, office 423 Washington, dwl W s Guerrero bet Sixteenth and Seventeenth
Eldridge Warren H. Collection Department Wells, Fargo & Co. dwl 904 Jackson
Eldridge William, boiler maker with Coffey & Risdon ·
Elevator (weekly, col'd) office SW cor Sansom and Jackson
Elfelt, *(A. B.)* Weil *(David)* & Co. *(S. Goldsmith)* merchants (Portland, Oregon) office 308 Front, res Portland
Elfenlexin Henry, merchant tailor, dwl 323 Pine
Elfers A. D. *(Michaelsen & E.)* dwl SW cor Jackson and Davis
Elgutter Morris, laces, 18 Second, dwl 224 Jessie
Elgutter Solomon, salesman, 18 Second, dwl 224 Jessie
Elias A. butcher, 100 Occidental Mkt, dwl 215 Post
Elias Jacob, merchant, dwl 903 Hyde
Elias Manus, book keeper with Wormser Brothers, dwl 515 Pine
Elias Raphael, bag factory, 116 Clay, dwl 945 Howard

Elias *(Simon)* & Kutner *(Adolph)* dry goods, 136 Kearny, dwl 68 Everett
Eliaser Abraham, cigars and tobacco, 929 Kearny
Elitch John, dwl 116 Jessie
Eliza Minna Miss, dwl 1157 Mission
Elk Horn Petroleum Co. office 606 Merchant
Elkington James, machinist, Pacific Foundry, dwl 8 Brook
Ellacott John, seaman, dwl 26 Stewart
ELLERHORST H. D. & CO. *(A. C. Teitman)* produce commission and agents R. Benson's Union City Boats, 64 Clay, res Eden, Alameda County
Ellery Epes, mining, office 338 Montgomery room 11, dwl 736 Folsom
Elles Michael, laborer with Hey & Meyn
Ellich John, coffee stand, SW cor Com and East
Ellingham John, blacksmith, bds 761 Mission
Elliot Charles, city superintendent Spring Valley W. W. Co. dwl 258 Cleary
Elliot Edward S. civil engineer, dwl 14 Quincy
Elliot Gardner, carpenter, dwl 14 Quincy
Elliot George H. Capt. U. S. Engineers, fortifications Alcatraz, office 37 Montgomery Block, dwl 18 South Park
Elliot John, miner, dwl 431 Pine
Elliot John N. job wagon, NE cor California and Drumm, dwl 43 Stewart
Elliot S. F. physician, office 7 Court Block
Elliot William, carpenter, Olympic Melodeon, dwl NE cor Clay and Kearny
Elliott Charles W. clerk, 17 California, dwl S s Ellis bet Larkin and Polk
Elliott Edward E. Melter and Refiner's Department U. S. Branch Mint, dwl 942 Mission
Elliott Everett W. trunk maker with E. Galpen & Co. dwl 12 Stanford
Elliott Frederick A. real estate, office 522 Clay, dwl N s Sixteenth nr Valencia
Elliott H. C. teamster, Pier 14 Stewart, dwl S s Ellis bet Larkin and Polk
Elliott Joseph, hostler, Wells, Fargo & Co. dwl 7 Milton Place
Elliott Orson H. bookseller, dwl W s Leavenworth bet Washington and Jackson
Elliott R. broker, dwl 505 Montgomery
Elliott Sarah (widow) dwl 565 Mission
Elliott Thomas, laborer, dwl S s Austin bet Franklin and Gough
Elliott Thomas L. teamster, 17 California, dwl S s Ellis bet Larkin and Polk
Elliott Thomas W. physician, office and dwl 574 Mission
Elliott Washington, teacher music, Public Schools, dwl NW cor Howard and Second
Ellis Abraham, peddler, Davis nr Clark
Ellis Alexander, dwl 644 Sacramento
Ellis Alfred J. merchant, dwl 737 Green
Ellis Ardin, laborer, dwl NW cor Lombard and Leavenworth
Ellis Bernard, dwl 561 Tehama
Ellis Charles, weigher with Hathaway & Co. dwl 39 Clay
Ellis Clement B. surveyor and draftsman, 49 Montgomery Block, dwl 213 California
Ellis Daniel J. teamster with Stanyan & Co. 17 Cal
Ellis Edward, carpenter, dwl nr cor Sierra and Tennessee
Ellis George, bakery, 26 Second
Ellis Henry H. policeman, City Hall, dwl 404 Lombard nr Dupont
Ellis H. W. porter, Original House
Ellis James *(Griffith & E.)* dwl 25 Fifth
Ellis John *(Clough & E.)* dwl 85 Everett, rear
Ellis John, waiter, steamer Orizaba
Ellis John F. salesman with Taaffe & Co. dwl 739 Howard
Ellis John H. cook, with W. J. Shaw, Thirteenth E Folsom

Ellis Joseph V. with Treadwell & Co. dwl cor Indiana and Sierra
Ellis Mary Mrs. dwl 737 Green
Ellis Michael, laborer, dwl 2 Pollard Place
ELLIS MOSES, merchant, office 218 Front, dwl Lick House
Ellis Samuel C. deputy sheriff, City Hall, dwl City Hall
Ellis Thomas D. mariner, dwl 32 Stewart
Ellis Valentine, dwl Mariposa nr Carolina
Ellis William, dwl 423 Harrison
Ellis William, teamster, dwl Dolores Hall, W s Valencia nr Sixteenth
Ellison Thomas, laborer, dwl W s Third nr Brannan
Ellison William, boatman, dwl N s Francisco nr Stockton
Ellmaker Frederick S. dwl E s Guerrero bet Eighteenth and Nineteenth
Ellsworth A. M. *(Whitney & Co.)* office 405 Front, dwl 894 Sutter
Ellsworth Michael, machinist, Miners' Foundry, dwl 519 Mission
Ellsworth Stephen R. dwl 810 Folsom
ELLSWORTH TIMOTHY, redwood and Puget Sound lumber, office SE cor Market and East, dwl 39 South Park
Ellwanger John D. electric machinist with Raneri F. Rocchiccoli, dwl S s Bush bet Dupont and Stockton
Elmore Abbie C. (widow) dwl 1013 Washington
ELMORE M. GAGE, mining secretary, office room 7 Stevenson House, dwl W s Sixteenth bet Folsom and Howard
Elmquist John, machinist, Union Foundry, dwl 243 Tehama
Eloesser Arthur, clerk with Heynemann & Co. dwl 817 Vallejo
Eloesser Hugo, salesman, 111 Battery, dwl 817 Vallejo
ELOESSER LEO & CO. *(Ernest Lomler)* editors and Proprietors Abend Post and job printing, office 517 Clay and 514 Com, dwl 817 Vallejo
Elonjimi Isaac, seaman, dwl 20 Commercial
Elsasser Jonas, clerk, 207 Sansom
Elston Samuel, Bryant St. Market, SW cor Bryant and Rincon Place
Elton J. E. marketman, bds Tremont House
ELVEENA CHARLES, contractor and real estate agent, 610 Clay
Elvey Charles, tinsmith, dwl 1520 Dupont
Elwell Charles, hairdressing saloon, 530 California, dwl 531 California
Elwell D. A. & Co. merchants (Marysville) office 405 Front, bds Cosmopolitan Hotel
Elwell Frank, merchant tailor, 315 Montgomery, dwl 125 Tehama
Elwell Lot, tin roofer, dwl 22 Clara
Elwell William, dwl Mercantile Library Building
Elwert Andrew, cooper, dwl 622 Vallejo
Elwood Frederick H. fruits, 262 Third
Elworth William, engineer, dwl 606 California
ELY ALEXANDER, attorney at law, office 15 and 16 Wells' Building, dwl Occidental Hotel
Ely Benjamin, bar keeper, steamer Senator
Ely Hubbard C. M. book keeper, dwl 916 Stockton
Ely Margaret Miss, domestic, 271 Minna
Ely William, dwl 633 Market
Elze Charles, musician, dwl 315 Bush
Emanuel E. salesman with W. J. Stringer, dwl 48 South Park
Emanuel Francis, deck hand, steamer Petaluma
Emanuel Isaac, speculator, dwl 463 Bryant
Emanuel Lewis, bedstead factory, Beale bet Market and Mission, dwl 48 South Park
Emanuel Louis, dwl 214 Sansom
Emeric Joseph, real estate, dwl 209 Post
Emerson Charles F. carpenter, dwl 100 Stockton
Emerson D. E. traveling agent, Bigelow & Brother, 505 Montgomery, res Oakland

Emerson J. A. *(Drake & E.)* dwl 929 Washington
Emerson James, stone cutter, Fort Point
Emerson Joshua, carriage painter with Walter Welsh, dwl 106 Natoma
Emerson Ralph, mining secretary and professor languages, office 540 Clay, dwl 618 California
Emerson *(William L.)* & Bailey *(O. S.)* Original, wines and liquors, 531 Sacramento, dwl SE cor Hampshire and El Dorado
Emerton John W. milkman, E s Fourth nr Brannan, dwl 446 Brannan
EMERY CHARLES G. importer and jobber cigars and leaf tobacco, 518 Battery, dwl 417 Post
Emery John G. conductor, Central R. R. Co. dwl NW cor Sixth and Bryant
Emery Joseph S. deputy constable, dwl N s Bay bet Leavenworth and Hyde
Emery J. S. mining secretary, office 424 Battery
Emery Robert, apothecary and druggist, 760 Clay
Emery S. S. cigars and tobacco, 614 Montgomery
Emery Thatcher, teamster with William Palmer, dwl 3 Front
Emery Thomas, calker, dwl 1 Central Place
Emery William, drayman, 103 California, dwl Jessie bet First and Second
Emich Charles N. tinsmith, dwl 721 Sutter
Emick Adam, carpenter, dwl 431 Pine
Emmerick Frederick, cigar maker, dwl 1422 Pacific
EMMET C. TEMPLE, attorney at law, office NW cor Montgomery and Commercial, dwl NW cor California and Powell
Emmons Gilbert W. carpenter with E. Galpen & Co. dwl St. Francis Hook & Ladder Co.
Emmons Lewis, carpenter, dwl 636 Commercial
Emmundson Auguste, upholsterer with Kennedy & Bell, dwl SW cor Pine and Kearny
Empire Block, S s California bet Sansom and Bat
EMPIRE BREWERY, Lyon & Co. proprietors, 159 Jessie
Empire G. & S. M. Co. (San Bernardino) off 611 Clay
Empire House, Turner & Lewis proprietors, S s Vallejo bet Front and Battery
Empire Iron Works, Cock & Flynn proprietors, 221 Mission
Empire Lodgings, W. A. Church proptr, 636 Com
Empire Mill & M. Co. (Gold Hill, Nevada) office 240 Montgomery
Empire Petroleum Co. (Colusa) office 605 Mont
Empire State Copper M. Co. office 620 Washington
Emslie Charles, machinist, California Foundry, dwl W s Dale nr Tyler
Enas J. D. carrier, Evening Bulletin, dwl 816 Mont
Enberg Julius, dwl 323 Clementina
Engel Henry G. boatman, dwl S s Union bet Leavenworth and Hyde
Engel Philip, shoe maker, dwl Bootz's Hotel
Engel W. waiter, 156 Second
ENGELBERG *(Emile A.)* & WAGNER, *(Frederick)* German bakery and coffee saloon, 416 Kearny
ENGELBRECHT *(Herman)* & MAYRISCH BROTHERS *(Adolph and Gustave)* importers and jobbers cigars and tobacco, 312 and 314 Front cor Commercial, dwl N s Greenwich bet Mason and Taylor
Engelhardt Frederick, compositor, Hebrew Observer, dwl 336 Bush
Engelhardt George, cooper, Mason's Brewery, dwl N s Green nr Powell
Engelke Lewis A. assayer, dwl W s Jansen bet Greenwich and Lombard
Engelken Frank, mariner, dwl 621 California
Engell B. tailor, dwl SW cor Kearny and Pacific
Engelman E. R. *(Wilber & E.)* 535 and 537 Market
Engels Charles H. tinsmith, 602 Mission
Engels Henry A. tin ware, 602 Mission
Engerham William, dwl 121 Natoma
Engert Alexander F. C. salesman, 205 Front, dwl 1111 Stockton

England *(Thomas)* & Turnbull *(Thomas)* architects, office 528 Clay, dwl SE cor Hyde and Chestnut
Englander Emil, musician, dwl 776 Folsom
Englander Frank, musician, dwl 6 O'Farrell Alley
Englander H. (widow) dress maker, dwl 35 Natoma
Englander Leopold, policeman, City Hall, dwl 34 Turk cor Taylor
Englander Max, drayman, 100 Battery, dwl 36 Turk
Englander W. fruits, 105 Fourth
Englander William, auctioneer, dwl 368 Jessie
Engle Jacob P. millwright, dwl cor Francisco and Fillmore
Engle Henry, barber, dwl 807 Mission
Englehardt Frederick B. mariner, dwl 212 Stewart
Engler Frank, waiter, stmr Senator
Engleskind Louis, butcher, NW cor Beale and Mission, dwl 222 Mission
English Ann Miss, domestic, 763 Mission
English Ann (widow) domestic, 808 Bush
English Edward, bricklayer, dwl 29 Minna
English George A. painter, dwl 559 Market
English James, carpenter, dwl SW cor Sutter and Kearny
English James W. wines and liquors, dwl 614 Howard
English *(Jerome A.)* & Lothrop *(John J.)* blacksmiths, 203 San, dwl SE cor Franklin and Fell
English John, butcher, Liberty Hose Co. No. 2
English John F. peddler, 203 Sansom
English Matthew, harness maker with R. W. Rowland, 105 Sansom
English Michael, house painter, dwl 44 Stevenson House
Engstrom James, dwl 23 Geary
Ennis John, carpenter, dwl 447 Clementina
Ennis William J. conductor North Beach & M. R. R. Co. dwl Vigilant Engine House
Enos A. T. brick mason, dwl Oriental Hotel
Enquer William, baker with Engelberg & Wagner, dwl 827 Vallejo
Enqvist Alfred A. wines and liquors, NW cor Davis and Clark, dwl 505 Sutter
Enright Bridget Miss, domestic, N s California bet Larkin and Hyde
Enright Daniel, laborer with R. A. Thompson, dwl E s Sonoma Place nr Vallejo
Enright John, calker, dwl W s Second bet Howard and Folsom
Enright John, laborer, dwl 233 Minna
Enright *(Patrick)* & Dwyer *(Timothy)* Golden City Restaurant, 706 Market, dwl 11 Everett
Enright William, engineer, St. Mary's Hospital
Enright William, plumber, Spring Valley W. W. Co. dwl S s Ellis bet Larkin and Polk
Ensbury William, with Thomas Adam, cor Montgomery and Market
Ensign George H. real estate, dwl NE cor Montgomery and Market
Enterprise G. & S. M. Co. office 338 Montgomery
Entoine Eugene, paper box maker, SE cor Kearny and California
Enyoung Charles, machinist, Market St. R. R. Co. dwl Valencia bet Fifteenth and Sixteenth
Ephraim Alexander B. merchant, dwl 360 Minna
Epley John W. dwl 413 Stevenson
Epley Minerva Mrs. dwl 774 Mission
Eppes George, plumber with Locke & Montague, 112 Battery
Eppler John, cook, bds Meyer's Hotel, 814 Mont
Eps Charles (col'd) porter, dwl 914 Sacramento
Epstein Simon, dwl 321 Taylor
Epting Frederick, paper hanger, dwl 343 Kearny
EQUITABLE LIFE INSURANCE CO. New York, Bigelow & Brother, agents, 505 Mont
Erb Manuel, tailor, 1416 Stockton
Erbe Adam, varnisher with E. Bloomingdale & Co. dwl SW cor Pine and Kearny
Erbe Catharine Miss, domestic, 616 California

Erenberg Louis, tailoring, 202 Bush
Ericson Casimir, rope maker, S. F. Cordage Factory
Ericson Olof, stair builder with B. H. Freeman & Co. dwl 619 Mission
Ericson Steven O. liquors, dwl 10 Jackson
Erkins William, cabinet maker, 611 Jackson, dwl 10 Natoma
Erkson Alexander C. dwl NW cor Post and Devisidero
Erland N. captain schr Abe Lincoln, office 413 East
Erle Frederick, machinist, Miners' Foundry, dwl 551 Folsom
Ernandes Philip, porter, dwl 1231 Dupont
Ernst Ekert, baker, dwl NW cor Hartman Place and Greenwich
Ernst Harry, laborer, bds with Joseph Seale, N s Turk nr Fillmore
ERNST HERMAN, dealer hides and wool, etc. and tallow factory, Potrero, office 15 Davis, dwl 362 Brannan
Ernst Jacob, bar keeper, 230 Commercial
Ernst L. H. dwl 510 Pine
Ernst Oswald H. Lieut. U. S. Engineers, office 37 Montgomery Block
Ernst Peter, shoe maker, dwl E s Mission nr Precita Avenue
Ernst Victorine Mrs., Cariboo Saloon, E s Mission nr Precita Avenue
Erskine John, laundryman, 305 Davis
Erskine M. C. mate, stmr Pacific, dwl 551 Howard
Ervin Henry J. ship carpenter, dwl N s Frederick
Erwin C. G. carpenter, dwl N s Harrison bet Fifth and Sixth
Erzgraber Robert, with Erzgraber & Goetjen, 120 Davis
ERZGRABER (William) & GOETJEN (Nicholas) manufacturers cider, vinegar, pickles, etc. 120 and 122 Davis, dwl NW cor Webster and McAllister
ESBERG M. & CO. manufacturers and dealers cigars, SE cor Sac and Front, dwl 13 Stockton
Escaig Jean, with Jean Ortet, 223 Leidesdorff
Escalle Josephine Miss, domestic, 324 Geary
Esch Alfred, agent Duden Fréres (Brussels, Bel.) office 629 Clay
Eschen James, seaman, bds 7 Washington
Eschenburg A. L. Miss, assistant, Union Grammar School, dwl 314 Sutter
Eschenburg John, book keeper, dwl 314 Sutter
Eschenburg M. M. adjuster, U. S. Branch Mint, dwl 314 Sutter
Esmeralda Silver M. Co. office 522 Montgomery
Esnault Augustus (Alexander Finance & Co.) dwl 825 Dupont
Esselbsam Abraham, carpenter, dwl W s Washington Avenue nr Precita Avenue
Essman Ernst, salesman, 720 Montgomery, dwl 612 Stockton
Estabrook Charles D. clerk with Harvey & Co. dwl 234 Third
Estabrook John, pork packer, 145 Second, dwl 95 Second
Estall James, tinner, dwl 71 Tehama
Este A. S. laborer, Miners' Foundry
Ester Orrin, laborer, dwl 66 Jessie
Esterbrook James A. clerk with Samuel Platt, dwl 628 Merchant
Esterle B. M. mechanical and surgical dentist, office Belden Block room 13, SW cor Mont and Bush
Esterling John, musician, dwl 522 Filbert, rear
Estes Eben, drayman with Frederick P. Belcher
Estrem Joseph, clothing, 506 Washington
Esty Aaron S. helper, dwl 66 Jessie
Etienne Brunet, bar keeper, SE cor Kearny and Clay
Etienne, (T.) & Co. (Edward Rovere) restaurant, 825 and 827 Dupont
Etienne T. Metropolitan Restaurant, Metropolitan Block, 715 Montgomery

Etique John P. blacksmith, Phœnix Iron Works, dwl 416 Folsom
Ettell John, machinist, dwl N s Perry bet Fourth and Fifth
Etting William A. clerk, 111 Third
Ettinger Morris, fringe maker with Daniel Norcross, dwl W s Seventh nr Brannan
Ettlin Leonhardt, wagon maker with Gallagher & Rodecker, dwl Helvetia Hotel
Ettling Harry, clerk, 126 Third, dwl 6 Prospect Pl
Ettling Marcus, cigars and tobacco, dwl 6 Prospect Place
Ettlinger Max, clerk, dwl Ellis bet Leav and Hyde
Eude Marie Mme. French Laundry, 1320 Stockton
Eudinur Martin, carpenter, dwl 114 William
Eugster John F. (Schmierer & Co.) dwl 427 Kearny
Euler Frederich (Kruse & E.) dwl 129 Third
Euler Henry, carpenter, dwl SE cor Ellis and Leav
EUREKA BENEVOLENT SOCIETY, M. Mayblum treasurer, office SE cor Front and Sac
Eureka Camphene and Oil Works
Eulers Henry, clerk, dwl Lutgen's Hotel
Eureka Hotel, Jacob Levy proprietor, 20 Sansom
EUREKA IRON WORKS, William McKibbin proprietor, 41 and 43 First
EUREKA MATCH FACTORY, W. H. Jessup & Co. proprietors, SW cor Market and Fifth
Eureka Patent Blasting Powder Co. Charles A. James agent, office 327 Commercial
Eureka Petroleum Coal Oil Works, office 511 Front
Eureka Soap Co. (Charles F. Brown) office 207 Sac
EUREKA THEATER, Charles Wheatleigh proprietor, 320 Montgomery
Eureka Turn Verein, Felix Marcuse president, rooms 541 Bdwy between Dupont and Kearny
EUREKA TYPOGRAPHICAL ROOMS, 625 Merchant
Eustace I. second officer steamer Senator
Eustice Joseph, carpenter, dwl 545 Mission
Eustis Helen (widow) nurse, dwl 228 Minna
Evan Louis, seaman, dwl 44 Sacramento
Evangel (semi-monthly) Stephen Hilton editor, office 29 Turk
Evannonch A. handcartman, cor Broadway and Davis
EVANS ALBERT S. editorial department Alta California, dwl S s Green bet Leav and Hyde
Evans C. H. draftsman, Vulcan Foundry, dwl 52 Minna
Evans Charlotte Miss, ironer, Chelsea Laundry
Evans C. L. machinist, Miners' Foundry, dwl 40 Natoma
Evans Francis, blacksmith, Crescent Engine Co. No. 10
Evans George, horse trainer, Bay View Park
Evans George, laborer, dwl Original House
Evans George A. blacksmith, dwl 327 Ritch
Evans George T. professor music, dwl NW cor Mason and O'Farrell
Evans Georgie Miss, ironer, Chelsea Laundry
Evans Gomer, adjuster averages and accountant, 406 California, dwl 1913 Stockton
Evans J. steward, steamer Clinton
Evans James, machinist, dwl 40 Natoma
Evans John, laborer, dwl 414 Market
Evans John, machinist, Vulcan Iron Works, dwl 41 Minna
Evans John, proprietor Spring Valley House, Presidio Road nr Union
Evans John, sampler, U. S. Branch Mint, res Clinton
Evans John jr. carpenter, dwl SW cor Kearny and Pacific
Evans John R. (Wilson & E.) 513 Clay
Evans John R. liquor saloon, 621 Pacific
Evans Joseph, foreman California Leader, dwl NE cor Montgomery and Pacific
Evans Otholo, folder, Chelsea Laundry
Evans Peter J. fruits, 513 Broadway, dwl N s Green bet Kearny and Dupont

Evans Thomas, book keeper, Railroad Iron Works
Evans Westley, contractor, office 306 Clay, dwl 13 Clementina
Evans William (Mills & E.) dwl 6 Jane
Evans William H. blacksmith, Miners' Foundry, dwl 9 Vassar Place
Evatt John M. policeman, City Hall, dwl 152 Silver nr Fourth
Evatt William J. special officer Gilbert's Olympic, dwl 152 Silver
Eveleth Dwight, porter with Fargo & Co. dwl NW cor Pacific and Hyde
Evely James, cartman, dwl Perry bet Third and Fourth
EVENING BULLETIN (daily, weekly, and steamer) San Francisco Bulletin Co. publishers and proprietors, office 620 Montgomery, editorial rooms 517 Clay
Evens John, laborer, dwl S s Market bet Second and Third
Evensen John N. with J. D. Arthur & Son, 101 Cal
Everard William, Steamship Exchange, 214 Stewart
Everding Charles, drayman, 56 Clay, dwl SW cor Scott and Tyler
EVERDING J. & CO. starch manufacturers and produce commission, 56 Clay
Everett A. F. (Cantin & E.) dwl SE cor Montgomery and Vallejo
Everett A. P. auctioneer, dwl 22 Stanly Place
Everett Lewis, watchman, bds 127 Pacific
Everett M. V. B. stock dealer, dwl N s Sacramento bet Van Ness Avenue and Franklin
Everett Rufus H. agent B. D. Wilson, dwl 536 Howard
Everhardt Adolph (B. D. Wilson & Son) dwl 2 Telegraph Place
Everhardt Ernst, clerk, NE cor O'Farrell and Hyde
Evers Babette (widow) dwl 78 Clementina
Evers Charles D. drayman, SW cor Sacramento and Front, dwl 18 Lewis Place
Evers Herman C. groceries and liquors, SE cor Vallejo and Montgomery
Evers James, boot maker, dwl 721 Sansom
Evers Joseph, workman with Harrington Bros. dwl Brannan St. Bridge
Everson William H. (col'd) barber, dwl 612 Powell
Evoca Consolidated Copper M. Co. office 302 Mont
Evrard James, policeman, City Hall, dwl 735 Broadway nr Powell
Ewald Charles S. dwl W s Howard bet Thirteenth and Erie
EWALD EDWARD, Montgomery Baths and Hair Dressing Saloon, 621 Montgomery, dwl W side Howard nr Thirteenth
Ewald Frederick, musician, St. Francis H. & L. Co. No. 1
Ewald Jacob, dwl Belden nr Pine
Ewald John, hair dresser with Ciprico & Cook, Cosmopolitan Hotel
EWELL L. J. produce and fruit, SW cor Washington and Sansom and proprietor Coso House, 629 Commercial, dwl 514 Filbert
Ewer Warren B. (Dewey & Co. and Dewey, Waters & Co.) dwl 8 Clarence Place nr Townsend
Ewes John, molder, dwl E s Tyson Place
Ewing Andrew, clerk, dwl NW cor Kearny and Francisco
Ewing Calvin, leather collar maker, 324 Davis
Ewing Charles G. salesman with Levison Brothers, dwl 455 Bryant
Ewing Frank (col'd) pantryman, stm Chrysopolis, dwl 13 Scott
Ewing M. (widow) dwl 352 Third
EXAMINER (daily and weekly) William S. Moss, publisher and proprietor, office 535 Washington
EXCELSIOR MATCH FACTORY, N s Minna bet Fifth and Sixth
EXCELSIOR PRINTING OFFICE, Towne & Bacon proprietors, 536 Clay, opp Leidesdorff

EXCHANGE BUILDING, NW cor Montgomery and Washington
Exchequer M. Co. office 712 Montgomery
Expert Armand, groceries and liquors, NW cor Leavenworth and Pacific
Express M. Co. office 529 Clay
EXPRESS BUILDING, NE cor Montgomery and California, Samuel Brannan proprietor

F

FAAS William (Burkhardt & F.) dwl 1214 Stock
FABENS F. A. attorney at law, office 47 Montgomery Block, dwl 8 Essex
Fabens George C. clerk with Philip Caduc, dwl 8 Essex
Faber F. A. conductor, Omnibus R. R. Co
Faber Joseph, baker, dwl 140 Second
Fabre M. E. (widow) dwl N s Nineteenth between Guerrero and Dolores
Fabre James, clerk, dwl NE cor Dupont and Jack
Fabriani Guiseppe, fish, 15 Washington Fish Market
Fabry Leopold, market, NE cor Mission and Annie
Faccio Joseph, watch maker with William H. T. Clark, dwl S s Polk Alley nr Stockton
Face, Edward, drayman, dwl Post nr Mason
Fackler John G. Rev. pastor, Central Presbyterian Church, Mission nr Fifth, dwl 37 Fifth
Fadden Mary Miss, domestic, 529 Green
Fader Isadore, tailor, dwl S s Dupont Alley
Fagan Catharine Miss, domestic, 829 Washington
Fagan Catharine (widow) dwl 1309 Powell
Fagan Charles, baker, What Cheer H. Restaurant
Fagan James, drayman, dwl 143 Perry
Fagan James, laborer, dwl 13 St. Mary
Fagan John, laborer, dwl 112 Jones
Fagan Mary (widow) liquor saloon, 585 Market
Fagan Mary (widow) dwl 729 Folsom
Fagan Mary Ann Mrs. dwl 207 Pacific
Fagan, (Michael) Bliven (James I.) & Skelly (Michael) Empire Soda Works, NE cor Harrison and Third
Fagan Michael, clerk, dwl 414 Market
Fagan Michael, clerk with R. Lewellyn, dwl 1008 Pacific
Fagan Peter, butcher, dwl 538 Howard
Fagan Terrence, stone cutter, dwl 119 Minna
Fagan Thomas, workman, Pacific Glass Works, dwl cor Mariposa and Indiana
Fagan William, molder, Union Foundry, dwl 309 Dupont
Fagerholm Ferdinand, seaman, dwl 20 Commercial
Fahan Catharine Miss, domestic, 30 John
Fahay Bridget, domestic, Occidental Hotel
FAHLSTEN C. J. E. & CO. importers wines, liquors, and cigars, 434 Jackson, dwl NE corner Powell and Clay
Fahrbach Emma (widow) dwl 905 Jackson
Fahrback George, musician, dwl 1703 Dupont
Fahrenkrug Frederick C. painter, dwl 704 Sac
Fahrenkrug John, cigar maker with Inslee & Joseph, dwl 704 Dupont
Fahrenkrug William, groceries and liquors, SW cor Tehama and Third
Fair Samuel, dwl 103 Dupont
Fairbanks Hiram T. (Dodge Bros. & Co.) dwl 611 Mason, rear
Fairbanks H. T. (Campbell & F.) res Petaluma
Fairchild Geo. W. sawyer with Hobbs, Gilmore & Co. dwl Hubbard bet Howard and Tehama
Fairfield Chauncey P. Capt. Co. B Second Infantry, C. V. Presidio
Fairfield Josiah, seaman, dwl NE cor Washington and Hyde
Fairfield Marshall, laborer, Pacific Glass Works, dwl NW cor Townsend and Third
Fairfowl James G. stevedore, dwl SW cor Thirteenth and Folsom

Fairman Edward, civil engineer, dwl 733 Wash
FAIRMAN WILLIAM B. *(McKenzie & F.)* dwl 641 Washington
Fairmount Homestead Association, office 302 Mont
Fairweather Alfred J. salesman, 4 Third, dwl N s Stevenson bet Sixth and Seventh
Fairweather Julian, carpenter with James Brokaw, dwl N s Stevenson bet Sixth and Seventh
Fairy Catherine, domestic, 263 Stevenson
Faisandieu Emile, collector, dwl NW cor Kearny and Broadway
Faitoute James B. *(Bishop & Co.)* office 410 Clay
Fake George S. miner, dwl N s Union bet Jones and Leavenworth
Fake John S. assistant city and county surveyor, City Hall, dwl 754 Folsom
Falco Alexander, watch case maker with P. A. Giannini, dwl 728 Washington
Falconbridge Thomas, laborer, Golden Age Flour Mills, 717 Battery
Falconer Henry, cigars, SW cor Market and Third, dwl SW cor Mason and O'Farrell
Falconer Robert S. book keeper with Haynes & Lawton, 516 Sansom
Falcy James, wagon maker, 220 Post
Fales Edward, wood and coal, 419 Post, dwl 731 California
Fales Johanna Miss, domestic, 1707 Stockton
Fales William, seaman, dwl 44 Sacramento
Faline Albert, apprentice, Miners' Foundry, dwl New Branch Hotel
Falk Adolph *(Freund & Co.)* dwl 333 Geary
Falk K. laborer, dwl 108 Dupont
Falk N. H. *(Glidden, Colman & Co.)* Pier 22 Stewart
Falk Samuel, peddler, dwl 112 St. Mark Place
FALKENAU BROTHERS *(Ignace and Frederick)* importers watches, jewelry, silver ware, and fancy goods, 629 Washington, dwl SW cor Taylor and O'Farrell
Falkenau Frederick *(Falkenau Brothers)* dwl SW cor Taylor and O'Farrell
Falkenberg Henry, boarding, NW cor Jessie and Anna
Falkenberg Robert, machinist, Union Foundry, dwl 337 Bush
Falkenberg William, dwl 619 Bush
Falkenburgh A. B. clerk, U. S. Branch Mint, dwl 742 Howard
Falkenstein Gustavus, proprietor San Francisco Cotton Mill, N s King bet Third and Fourth, dwl 360 Brannan
FALKENSTEIN *(Henry)* & CO. *(Moses Meyerfeld and Charles L. Heller)* importers and jobbers cigars and tobacco, 315 and 317 Clay, res New York
Falkman P. T. miner, dwl cor Bush and Baker
FALKNER, BELL *(James)* & CO. *(Henry D. Harrison)* commission merchants, insurance agents, and agents Lloyds, office 430 California
Falkner M. Mrs. house keeper, American Exchange
Falkstrom John, mariner, dwl 32 Stewart
Fall George, book keeper, dwl 439 Union
Fall John C. merchant, dwl 26 O'Farrell
Fall W. H. H. dwl 1421 Stockton
Fallen Catherine Miss, domestic, 865 Mission
Fallen Edward, laborer, dwl SE cor Brannan and Stanford
Fallen Michael, boatman, dwl 1407 Powell
Fallen Michael C. workman, Vulcan Foundry, dwl S s Stevenson bet Seventh and Eighth
Fallon Christopher, dwl 18 Moss
Fallon Daniel G. Center Market, NE cor O'Farrell and Jones, dwl SW cor O'Farrell and Larkin
Fallon Hannah Miss, domestic, 803 Bush
Fallon James, boots and shoes, dwl 50 Tehama
Fallon Thomas G. butcher, dwl SW cor O'Farrell and Larkin
Fallon John, clerk, 208 Bush, dwl 816 Bush

Fallon John, laborer, S. F. & San José R. R
Fallon Kate Miss, domestic with Mrs. Edward G. Beckwith, E s Mission bet Fourteenth and Fifteenth
Fallon Martin C. laborer, bds with Theodore Schulte, W s Valencia bet Fifteenth and Sixteenth
Fallon Michael, dwl 439 Jessie
Fallon Michael, workman, S. F. Glass Works, dwl S s Mariposa nr Mississippi
Fallon Sarah Miss, domestic, 814 Powell
Fallon Thomas, clerk with Brooks & Rouleau, dwl 414 Market
Fallon Thomas, laborer, dwl 24 Sansom
FALLS OF CLYDE CONSOLIDATION G. & S. M. Co. office 605 Montgomery
Falls Thomas J. chief engineer steamer America
Falsting Frederick, seaman, bds 7 Washington
Falter Clements, cook, German Hospital, Brannan
Fancher Charles, butcher, dwl 30 Natoma
Fanen James, teamster with James McDevitt, dwl Vallejo bet Montgomery and Sansom
Fannagan Andrew, express wagon, cor Battery and Pine
Fannell John, workman, S. F. & San José R. R
Fannie Rayne G. & S. M. Co. office room 1 Government House, 502 Washington
Fanning Bridget Miss, domestic, 1715 Mason
Fanning Edward, street contractor, dwl N s Chestnut bet Stockton and Powell
Fanning John, dwl NW cor Mason and Green
Fanning John jr. drayman, dwl NW cor Mason and Green
Fanning Patrick, laborer, dwl NW cor Mason and Green
Fanno Henry, steward Eureka Hotel, dwl E s Vincent nr Green
Fannon Thomas, laborer, dwl W s Van Ness Avenue nr Post
Fantini J. physician, office 1020 Dupont
Fapid Pilar, laborer, dwl N s Oregon nr Front
Faruher John, laborer, dwl N s Stevenson bet Sixth and Seventh
Farara Dominick, laborer, dwl 308 Pacific
Farelly John A. assistant book keeper Hibernia Savings and Loan Society, 506 Jackson
FARGO *(C. F.)* & CO: *(J. C. Wilmerding and C. W. Kellogg)* wholesale liquors, 214 and 216 Front, dwl 16 Belden Block
Fargo J. C. *(Field & Co.)* dwl 1111 Folsom
Fargo Jerome B. dwl 1111 Folsom
Fargo John, assistant engineer steamer Chrysopolis, dwl 723 Vallejo
FARISH A. T. & CO. wool and hide brokers, 221 Davis, dwl NW cor California and Larkin
Farish James R. with A. T. Farish & Co. dwl 749 Market
Farish Thomas E. clerk, 221 Davis, dwl W s Taylor bet Filbert and Greenwich
Farland Henry L. machinist, Vulcan Iron Works, dwl S s Broadway bet Jones and Leavenworth
Farland William, with E. Ayers, dwl Niantic Hotel
Farley Bernard, proprietor Old Home Saloon, E s Sixth nr Brannan
Farley Edward, miner, dwl S s Mission Creek nr Brannan St. Bridge
Farley Edward, workman with Smith & Brown, dwl New Potrero
Farley F. H. watchman, steamer Relief
Farley Henry, porter, SE cor California and San
Farley Hugh, dwl with John Crummie, E s Folsom bet Ninth and Tenth
Farley James, butcher, dwl 24 Minna
Farley James, laborer, S. F. & San José R. R. Co
Farley James, laborer, dwl 27 Freelon
Farley James, laborer, dwl 19 St. Mark Place
Farley James, laborer, dwl N s Filbert bet Sansom and Montgomery
Farley Joseph F. printer, 742 Washington, dwl Bailey House

Farley Martin B. machinist, Pacific Foundry, dwl 29 Second
Farley Mary (widow) liquor saloon, dwl 193 Beale
Farley Mathew, machinist, Pacific Foundry
Farley Michael, machinist, Vulcan Foundry
Farley Owen, laborer, dwl 541 Mission
Farley Patrick, bricklayer, dwl 119 Minna
Farley Patrick, laborer, dwl S s Filbert bet Montgomery and Simsom
Farley P. H. hackman, Plaza, dwl 228 Ritch
Farley Thomas, express wagon, dwl NW cor Front and Broadway
Farley Thomas, hog ranch, N s Chestnut bet Polk and Van Ness Avenue
Farlin J. driver, Omnibus R. R. Co
Farmar Richard B. clerk with J. Bamber & Co. dwl 1713 Stockton
Farmer John, laborer, A. R. C. Ice Co. dwl S s California bet Hyde and Larkin
Farmer Thomas, silversmith, dwl Mission bet Dolores and Valencia
Farn John, laborer with William Kerr, dwl 903 Battery
Farnam Edward, with Woods & Cheesman, dwl 233 Seventh
Farnam O. J. clerk, 414 Washington, dwl SW cor Geary and Powell
Farnen Sarah Miss, dwl NE cor Sixth and Folsom
Farnham John N. shipwright, Mission nr Stewart, dwl 340 Fremont
Farnham J. W. captain bark Gold Hunter, office Pier 1 Stewart, dwl S s Columbia bet Guerrero and Dolores
Farnholts John, deck hand, steamer Amelia
Farnsworth (David L.) & Glynn (Emerson) draymen, 210 California, dwl 29 Turk
Farnsworth E. S. captain P. M. S. S. Sacramento, dwl 20 Laurel Place
Farnsworth Isaac L. carpenter with J. S. Gibbs, dwl 609 Pine
Farnsworth John D. clerk, 39 Market, dwl 805 Geary
Farnsworth William O. book keeper with J. K. Prior, dwl 650 Howard
Farnum W. H. (Stephen Otis & Co.) res Oakland
Farquhar G. draftsman, U. S. Coast Survey, office Custom House third floor
Farquharson David (Kenilzer & F.) dwl 200 Ellis
Farquharson James, clerk, office 50 Exchange Building, dwl 129 Montgomery
Farr Alonzo, liquors, N s King bet Third and Fourth
Farrac John, gardener, dwl E s Dolores nr Fifteenth
Farrai Domino, laborer with William Buckley
Farral Michael, laborer, dwl 331 Tehama
Farrall Simon, laborer, dwl 119 Stevenson
Farran Charles J. clerk with E. H. Parker, dwl SW cor Jessie and Second
Farran James, teamster with William Kerr, dwl 320 Vallejo
Farran John, clerk with A. Crawford & Co. dwl 259 Clara
Farran Samuel M. assistant City and County Surveyor, City Hall
Farran, see Farren
Farrar Albert, sawyer with Hobbs, Gilmore & Co. dwl 633 Market
Farrar Edward, physician, office and dwl 4 Brenham Place
Farrar Owen, brakeman, S. F. & San José R. R. res San José
Farrell Ann Miss, domestic with W. F. Herrick, S s Erie nr Howard
Farrell Ann (widow) dwl Washoe Place
Farrell Anna Miss, domestic, 317 Geary
Farrell Catharine Miss, domestic with A. C. McKean, S s Geary nr Gough

Farrell David, steward, dwl 522 Union
Farrell Edward, carpenter, dwl 828 Union
Farrell Edward, laborer, dwl 10 Front
Farrell Edward G. bag maker with C. Meyer & Co. dwl 318 Davis
Farrell Hannah (widow) dwl 208 Post
Farrell James, with Lyon & Co. dwl 274 Jessie
Farrell John M. cork cutter, dwl 606 Powell
Farrell James, laborer, dwl 1624 Stockton, rear
Farrell James W. drayman with Geo. C. Johnson & Co. dwl E s Caroline nr Sixth
Farrell John, painter, dwl 114 William
Farrell John, seaman, dwl E s Main bet Harrison and Bryant
Farrell John, stone cutter, dwl 115 Geary, rear
Farrell John, workman, S. F. & P. Sugar Co. dwl 37 Everett
Farrell John D. drayman, 223 Front, dwl S s Minna bet Eighth and Ninth
Farrell John J. carver, dwl 1120 Sacramento
Farrell John M. cork cutter, dwl 606 Powell
Farrell John W. wheelwright, dwl 316 First
Farrell Joseph, foreman with D. R. Provost & Co. dwl NW cor Gaven and Filbert
Farrell Maggie C. Miss, dress maker with Pauline Collins, dwl 115 Geary
Farrell Margaret Miss, domestic, 304 Stockton
Farrell Mark, laborer, dwl 156 First
Farrell Mary Miss, domestic, 304 Stockton
Farrell Mary J. (widow) dwl N s Alta nr Sansom
Farrell Michael (Crowe & F.) dwl 255 Jessie
Farrell Michael, butcher, dwl E s Ninth bet Bryant and Brannan
Farrell Michael, laborer, dwl 331 Tehama
Farrell Michael, painter, Columbian Engine Co. No. 11
Farrell Michael, tobacconist, dwl E s Howard bet Eighteenth and Nineteenth
Farrell Morris, drayman, Drumm bet Pacific and Jackson
Farrell Patrick, bricklayer, dwl W s Scotland nr Greenwich
Farrell Patrick, horse trainer, Ocean Race Course
Farrell Patrick, second hand clothing, 322 Pacific
Farrell Peter E. Farrell's Exchange, NW cor Valencia and Sixteenth
Farrell P. J. clerk, 409 Battery, dwl 1920 Mason
Farrell Sylvester, driver with McMillan & Kester, dwl 714 Front
Farrell Thomas, foreman with L. R. Myers & Co. dwl 650 Mission
Farrell Timothy A. teamster, Pier 5 Stewart, dwl N s McAllister bet Leavenworth and Hyde
Farrell Walter, compositor, dwl 28 Sansom
Farrell William, blacksmith, North Beach & M. R. R
Farrell William, gas fitter, dwl S s First bet Harrison and Bryant
Farrell William, laborer, dwl W s Fifth Avenue bet Bryant and Harrison
Farren Anna Miss, domestic, 535 Howard
Farren Catharine Miss, domestic, 716 Stockton
Farren John (Gallagher & F.) dwl 316 First
Farren John, laborer with James McDevitt, dwl Battery bet Broadway and Vallejo
Farren John, watchman, Kellogg, Hewston & Co.'s Refinery, dwl E s Seventh nr Brannan
Farren John W. watchman, dwl 70 Clementina
Farren M. laborer, Vulcan Iron Works
Farren Mary Miss, domestic, 535 Howard
Farren Mary Mrs. domestic, NW cor Bryant and Grove Avenue
Farren Mary (widow) dwl 535 Howard
Farren Michael, express wagon, corner Front and Green
Farren, see Farran
Farrere Manuel, with Joseph Silva
Farrier Hiram L. with W. Wolf & Co. 115 Cal
Farrington Bernard, porter with H. M. Newhall, dwl E s Zoe Place

Farrington Charles L. assistant assessor U. S. Internal Revenue, NW cor Battery and Commercial, dwl 14 Dickson Block, Jane

Farrington E. D. assayer with A. J. Haight, res Oakland

Farrington H. L. machinist, Union Foundry, dwl 357 Bush

Farrington Lola (widow) dwl NW cor Dupont and Filbert

Farron Fannie, domestic, 86 Everett

Farry Thomas, molder, Monumental Engine Co. No. 6

Farwell George, job wagon, 419 Washington, dwl SW cor McAllister and Larkin

FARWELL J. D. & CO. (William H. Farwell) ship chandlers, 307 Clay, res Alameda

Farwell Joseph A. book keeper, 307 Clay, dwl 532 Geary

Farwell Willard B. (late U. S. Naval Officer) office 26 Exchange Building, dwl 213 Geary

Farwell William H. (J. D. Farwell & Co.) dwl 532 Geary

Farwell William, painter, dwl 551 Market

Fary Thomas, molder, Union Foundry, dwl 263 Tehama

Fass Henry, chicken ranch, San Bruno Road nr Santa Clara

FASSETT N. C. (Pacheco Warehouse Co.) office 402 Front, dwl 754 Folsom

Fastert T. dwl Lutgen's Hotel

Fatz Jacob, waiter, Golden City Restaurant, dwl 66 First

Faubel Philip, butcher, 307 Sixth

Faujoy William H. painter, dwl 4 Winters Place

Faulhaber Francis, merchant, dwl 417 Post

Faulkner Andrew, laborer, bds Golden Age Hotel, 127 Pacific

Faulkner Eliza (widow) dwl S s Harrison bet Seventh and Eighth

Faulkner George Mrs. dwl Brevoort House

Faulkner George H. clerk with Charles W. Brooks & Co

Faulkner George L. (William Faulkner & Son) res Oakland

Faulkner James, carder, S. F. Cotton Mill, dwl N s King bet Third and Fourth

Faulkner James, pilot, stm Julia, dwl 332 Green

Faulkner James, teamster with Haste & Kirk, 515 California

Faulkner John, seaman, dwl cor Drumm and Jack

Faulkner Samuel T. dwl 5 Stockton

Faulkner Thomas, porter, 116 California, dwl N s Townsend bet Second and Third

FAULKNER WILLIAM & SON (George L. Faulkner) importers cards, printing materials, etc. 411 Clay, res Clinton, Alameda

Faulner Adam, barber with Charles Frank

Faulstich Thaddeus, clerk, dwl 220 First

Fauss O. (C. Kleinclaus & F.) dwl SW cor Mission and Nineteenth

Fautsch Francis, landscape painter, dwl 630 Ellis

Faver Enocence, produce peddler, dwl 1004 Pacific

FAVOR KIMBAL, physician, surgeon, and accoucheur, office and dwl 131 Third

Favre (A. R.) & Mendessolle (B.) importers and wholesale dealers wines and liquors, 605 Front, dwl NE cor Kearny and Jackson

Favre Cesarine Miss, dress maker, 435 Bush

Favre Julius, cook, 507 Washington

Favre Louis, laborer with Bergerot & Co. Potrero

Favre Marie Madame, dwl 435 Bush

FAY CALEB T. president Union Insurance Co. office 416 California, dwl 730 Post

Fay Catherine, domestic, dwl 39 Fifth

Fay Edward, engineer, steamer Petaluma

Fay Elizabeth Miss, domestic, 928 Bush

Fay Ellen Miss, domestic, 615 Stockton

Fay Frederick, cook, Brooklyn Hotel

Fay Henry, cook, 619 Market

Fay James G., S. F. Cordage Factory, dwl SW cor Shasta and Michigan

Fay John, engineer, dwl 577 Howard

Fay John, steam soap manufactory, N s Chestnut bet Mason and Taylor, dwl 201½ Powell

Fay John, with D. Brommer & Bro

Fay John F. chief engineer steamship Sierra Nevada, office SW cor Front and Jackson

Fay M. H. steward U. S. Restaurant, 507 Clay, dwl 26 Louisa

Fay Michael, whip maker with Main & Winchester, dwl 19 Clara, rear

Fay Newton, folder, Chelsea Laundry

Fay Patrick, laborer, dwl W s Vallejo Place

Fay Philip S. clerk, 616 Front, dwl 13 O'Farrell

Fay Stephen, contractor, dwl 1705 Dupont

Fay Thomas, dyer, Mission Woolen Mills, dwl Mission Creek nr Sixteenth

Fay Thomas, laborer, Pacific Foundry, dwl 512 Mission

Fay Thomas P. laborer, dwl 5 Hayward

Fayard Jean B. perfumery, 711 Clay, dwl 605 Sac

Fazackerley Joseph, porter with E. Bloomingdale & Co

Feaster (John J.) & Co. (John P. Hawkins) contractors night work, 213 Pine

Featherby J. H. clerk, 2 Washington Market

Featherly Sarah (widow) dwl 1011 Pacific

Featherstone Daniel, works with Jacob A. Maison

FECHHEIMER, (Marten S.) GOODKIND, (Henry) & CO. (Henry Kronthal) importers and jobbers clothing, 521 Sacramento, res New York

Feder Louis, merchant, dwl 31 Turk

Feder Reuben, clothing, 254 Stewart

Federal Building, Battery opposite Post Office

Fee William, waiter, dwl 26 Stewart

Feehan (John) Byrnes (Thomas E.) & Co. groceries and liquors, NW cor Fourth and Jessie, dwl cor First and Natoma

Feehan John, groceries and liquors, NW cor First and Natoma

Feehan William, packer with Wangenheim, Sternheim & Co. dwl NW cor First and Natoma

Feely James, cook, 104 Second

Feely John, painter, dwl N s Liberty nr Dolores

Feely Michael, dwl 12 Sutter

Feely Thomas, coachman, dwl 1808 Powell

Feeney Ellen Miss, domestic, 963 Howard

Feeney Ellen M. Miss, with Max Waizmann, dwl 315 Montgomery

Feeney James, laborer, Custom House, dwl 46 Natoma

Feeney James, maltster with Thomas Lee, dwl Volunteer Engine House

Feeney James, metal roofer with John Kehoe, 228 Bush, dwl 624 Commercial

Feeney John, hackman, Plaza, dwl 8 Brooks, rear

Feeney John, laborer, W s Leavenworth bet Washington and Jackson

Feeney John, seaman, dwl 20 Commercial

Feeney Joseph, boat maker, 948 Howard

Feeney Margaret Miss, domestic, cor White Place and Jones

Feeney Mary Mrs. domestic, dwl 724 California

Feeny James, bricklayer, dwl Hinckley Place nr Vallejo bet Montgomery and Kearny

Feeny John, cartman, cor Hyde and Pacific

Feeny Patrick, laborer, dwl 130 Stevenson

Feeny William, dwl 938 Mission

Fehlmann Edward, clerk with H. Schroder & Co. dwl NE cor Washington and Dupont

Fehnemann Bernard, groceries and liquors, NW cor Larkin and Green

Feider Rachel (widow) dwl 264 Jessie

Feig Alexander, furniture, 49 Third

Feig Benjamin, salesman, 417 Commercial

Feig Louis, merchant tailor, 10 Sansom

Feige Albert, driver, New York Brewery

Feige Henry, carpenter, dwl 315 Bush
Feige John, carpenter, dwl 409 Bush
Feisel F. T. *(McLaughlin & F.)* 121 Bush, dwl cor Pine and Sansom
Feiter F. machinist, Vulcan Iron Works, dwl E s Natoma nr First
Feix John, melter, U. S. Branch Mint, dwl 825 Greenwich
Felberg Chester, carpenter, Lick House
Felco John, wheelwright, dwl N s Washington bet Kearny and Dupont
Feldbush John D. Railroad bakeries, SE cor Dupont and Berry and S s Pacific bet Hyde and Leavenworth
Feldbush John H. groceries and liquors, 108 Sutter
Feldbush *(J. H. D.)* & Co. *(F. M. L. Peters)* wholesale toys and fancy goods, 307 California and retail 207 Montgomery, dwl 322 O'Farrell
Feldine Louis, engineer Pacific Distillery
FELDMAN L. & CO. *(Hermann Cordes)* importers and jobbers wood and willow ware, 211 and 213 California, res New York
Feldtman Peter N. clerk, 642 Jackson
Feley John, hostler, dwl 408 Bush
Felix Daniel, carpenter, dwl E s Sixth nr Market
Felix David, porter with Ross, Dempster & Co. dwl 210 Broadway
Felix Frederic, butcher, W s Ninth nr Brannan
Felix Gustave A. bar keeper, 322 Montgomery, dwl 610 Washington
Felker L. M. mariner, dwl 1924 Mason
Fell C. (widow) costumer, 710 Washington, dwl 1107 Mason
Fella Charles, printer with Charles F. Robbins, 416 Battery
Fella Placidus, books and stationery, 224 Kearny, dwl 115 Geary, rear
Felleot Frank, laborer, dwl 811 Pacific
Feller Michael, laborer, dwl 907 Jones
Fellbeimer Bernhard, boot maker, 215 Fourth
Fellows David, dwl S s Presidio Road, opposite Presidio House
Fellows Everett, porter, 11 Montgomery, dwl Minna nr Second
Fellows George W. milkman, E s Fourth S Brannan, dwl 961 Folsom
Fellows James, carpenter, bds Franklin Hotel, SE cor Sansom and Pacific
Fellows Quartz M. Co. office 804 Montgomery
Felon Adela Miss, dwl SW cor Guerrero and Sixteenth
Felon Ann Miss, domestic, 1502 Taylor
Felsenthal Philip, merchant, dwl 6 Oak
Felske Godfrey, rope maker. dwl N s Bryant bet Sixth and Seventh
Felt I. W. salesman with Helbing, Greenebaum & Co. dwl 5 Stockton nr Ellis
Felt J. J. real estate, dwl 17 Rincon Place
Felt Orson, drover, dwl Mariposa nr Carolina
Felton Charles N. office 505 Montgomery, dwl Cosmopolitan Hotel
Felton H. F. & Co. *(James L. Crosett)* commission merchants, 225 Clay
FELTON JOHN B. attorney at law, office 4-6 Court Block 336 Clay, dwl 123 Stockton cor Geary
Felvey L. cooper, S. F. & P. Sugar Co
Fenderich Charles, portrait painter, dwl 445 Bush
Fenelon Ann Miss, domestic, 913 Bush
Fengeler Henry, boot maker, 527 East, dwl NE cor Front and Oregon
FENKHAUSEN A. importer and dealer wines and liquors, 809 Montgomery, dwl 773 Mission
Fenn F. C. M. engraver and silver plater, 637 Howard
Fenn Lyman, carpenter, dwl E s Shotwell bet Twenty-First and Twenty-Second
Fenn William, assistant, Dr. H. H. Toland, dwl SW cor Montgomery and Merchant

Fenn William jr. clerk, dwl 760 Harrison
Fennell Denis, harness maker and military equipments, 520 Battery, dwl 18 Harlan Place
Fennell Henry, shoe maker, 511 Mason
Fennell Katy Miss, domestic, 1515 Powell
Fennell Martin, constable Sixth Township, and conductor, Market St. R. R. dwl W s Valencia bet Fifteenth and Sixteenth
Fennell Michael, mason, dwl W s First Avenue nr Sixteenth
Fennally Richard, butcher, dwl Brannan St. Bridge
Fenner Byron, clerk, SW cor Mission and Second, dwl 358 Jessie
Fenning Anton, miner, dwl 431 Pine
Fenning Ellen, domestic, dwl 324 Fremont
Fenno Henry, waiter, 20 Sansom
FENSTERMACHER MARTIN, proprietor William Tell House, 315 and 317 Bush
Fenton Edward, machinist, dwl 527 Mission
Fenton James, tinsmith with Caleb M. Sickler
Fenton Johanna (widow) dwl W s Eleventh nr Harrison
Fenton John J. drayman, dwl 415 Pine
Fenton Martin, brakeman S. F. & San José R. R. dwl 633 Market
Fenton Samuel, foreman California Foundry, dwl 527 Mission
Fenton William, compositor, Evening Bulletin, dwl 1621 Powell
Ferber A. J. upholsterer, dwl What Cheer House
Fere Juan, dwl Hunter's Point
Ferguson George, carpenter, dwl SE cor Union and Mason
Ferguson Henry, plasterer, dwl S s Market bet Sixth and Seventh
Ferguson James, dwl 131 Montgomery
Ferguson James P. shipwright, dwl 638 Second
Ferguson John, pantryman, stmr Cornelia
Ferguson John P. claim agent, dwl 327 Bush
Ferguson John W. laborer, dwl Whitehall Exchange
Ferguson L. carpenter, dwl 323 Pine
Ferguson Mary H. teacher, dwl 1018 Kearny
Ferguson W. H. (col'd) dwl N s Dupont Alley
Ferguson William, tanner, dwl S s Brannan near Sixth
Fern John, laborer with James McDevitt, dwl 212 Broadway, rear
Fernald E. Maria Miss, adjuster, U. S. Branch Mint, dwl 27 Silver
Fernández B. Señora, private boarding, 7 O'Farrell
Fernandez Ramondo, dwl 65 Minna
Fernbach Joseph, shoe maker, 420 Market
Fernier Mary (widow) Olive Branch Saloon, E s Powell bet Chestnut and Francisco
Ferr Charles, laborer, dwl N s Broadway bet Jones and Leavenworth
Ferrall Kate Mrs. dwl 353 Jessie
Ferrand Charles, clerk, W s Kearny bet Bush and Sutter
Ferrar Louis, vegetable garden, SW cor Twentieth and Florida
Ferrari Angelo, hat maker with McGann & Co. 654 Washington
Ferrari George, clerk with Scalmanini & Frapolli
Ferraro Angelo, vegetable garden, cor Twenty-Second and Florida
Ferraro John, second steward stmr Yosemite
Ferreira Antonio, dwl 528 Bush, rear
Ferrell Thomas, supt Rincon Warehouse, dwl 260 First
Ferrenbach L. H. Mrs. millinery, 804 Washington
Ferrenbach Otto H. reporter, dwl 804 Washington
Ferrer M. Y. professor guitar and singing, dwl 1710 Mason
Ferrie John, clerk with H. C. Logan, 706 Montgomery, dwl 1013 Washington
Ferriere Ann Madame, liquor saloon, 620 Jackson
Ferris Daniel, laborer, Spring Valley W. W

Ferris David, boots and shoes, dwl 336 Union
Ferris David C. broker, room 6 Maguire's Building, dwl 250 Clementina
Ferris John, clerk, 23 Washington Market, dwl Coso House
Ferris John A. dwl 243 Second
Ferris M. waiter, U. S. Restaurant, dwl 30 Jessie
Ferris Michael, phonographic reporter, dwl 11 Geary
Ferris Richard, clerk with D. E. Appleton, dwl 1010 Pine
Ferron Augustus, accountant, dwl 336 Bush
Ferry Eunice, nurse, dwl 318 Jessie
Ferry John, deck hand, stmr Josie McNear
Ferry Mary Miss, domestic, St. Mary's Hospital
Ferry M. B. surveyor Firemen's Fund Ins. Co. dwl 711 California
Fertig George, gardener, German Hospital, Brannan
Fessenden Mary C. Miss, secretary Ladies' Protection and Relief Society, dwl 615 Harrison
Fety Claude B. engraver with F. R. Reichel, dwl S s Green bet Montgomery and Kearny
FEUERSTEIN R. & CO. *(Fred. Roeding)* importers and dealers hides and wool, and agents San Francisco & P. Sugar Co. 212 Front, dwl S s Harrison bet Sixth and Seventh
Feusier E. D. *(Feusier & Son)* dwl 625 Green
Feusier *(Henry)* & Son *(E. D. Feusier)* commission merchants, 221 Clay, dwl 625 Green
Feusier Louis, clerk, Overland Telegraph Office, dwl 625 Green
Fey Henry, shoe maker, dwl 12 Hinckley
Ffripp William R. clerk, dwl 5 Stockton
Fichen John, groceries and liquors, NW cor Dupont and Pacific
Fichner August, sausage maker, dwl N s Fell near Laguna
Fichtner Charles, sausage maker, dwl N s Fell near Laguna
Fichtner Gustavus, paper ruler with Edward Bosqui & Co. dwl N s Fell nr Laguna
Fick John F. porter, 417 Battery, dwl 37 Geary
Ficke Frederick, with Stevens & Oliver, 28 Mont
Fickett C. R. carpenter, dwl 559 Market
Fiedler Ferdinand, assayer, dwl 225 Stevenson
Field Albert E. clerk, Pacific Mail S. S. Co. dwl 332 Vallejo
Field Carrie P. Miss, assistant, Union Grammar School, dwl 323 Taylor
Field *(Charles)* & Shaber *(John A. and William R.)* bedstead manufactory, 407 Mission, dwl 112 Sutter
Field E. X. office 526 Montgomery
Field Fannie Miss, dwl 270 Jessie
Field H. E. Market St. Restaurant, 619 and 621 Market
Field Laura E. Miss, head assistant Denman Grammar School, dwl 305 Taylor
Field Richard, waiter with Lloyd Tevis, dwl 1316 Taylor
FIELD *(Samuel S.)* & CO. *(J. C. Fargo)* importers and wholesale wines and liquors, 422 California cor Leidesdorff, dwl Sophie Terrace
Field S. J. operator, Fire Alarm Telegraph, City Hall
FIELD STEPHEN J. Associate Justice United States Supreme Court, and ex officio United States Circuit Judge Tenth Circuit, office and chambers 1 and 2 U. S. Court Building, dwl 20 Ellis nr Powell
Field Thomas, third officer stmr Pacific
Field *(William)* & Cummings *(Harrison R.)* produce, 16 Occidental Market, dwl 122 Geary
Field William, captain schr Falmouth, office Pier 4 Stewart
Fielden Fielden, cabinet maker, dwl NE cor Brannan and Gilbert
FIELDING *(Samuel M.)* & OSGOOD *(H. P.)* commission merchants and agents Star Soap and Candle Works, 221 Sacramento, dwl 529 Green

Fielding Thomas, assistant engineer Pacific Mail S. S. Co
Fields Alfred, clerk, Crescent Engine Co
Fields Arthur, clerk, dwl E s Florida nr Solano
Fields Charles, peddler, dwl 119 Stevenson
Fields H. (col'd) whitewashing, dwl 319 Bush
Fields Ira (col'd) domestic, 1022 Stockton
Fields Thomas, Emmet Market, SE cor Stockton and Greenwich, dwl 538 Howard
Fields Thomas, express wagon, cor Sansom and Broadway
Fields William H. molder, dwl S s Minna bet Eighth and Ninth
Fielitz William, groceries and liquors, NE cor Fourth and Folsom
Fieney Thomas, deck hand, steamer Yosemite
Fierro Felipe *(F. P. Ramirez & Co.)* dwl Green bet Dupont and Kearny
Fife Ellen Miss, domestic, 1030 Bush
Fife John, laborer, dwl cor Lombard and Fillmore
Fifield Samuel, with John Howes, 502 Sansom, dwl Ohio nr Broadway
Figari L. baker, Russ House
Figaro Louis, dwl W s Geneva bet Bryant and Brannan
Figel Joseph, salesman, with I. Joseph & Co. dwl 14 Stockton
Figel Samuel, with C. A. Fletcher, 1 Montgomery, dwl 122 Ellis
Figure Lewis, dwl W s Larkin nr O'Farrell
Filbert Peter, tinsmith, dwl 515 Sacramento
Filburn Thomas, laborer, dwl SW cor Mission and Beale
File John, cooper, dwl N s Broadway bet Dupont and Stockton
Fillebrown James, carpenter, dwl 429 Tehama
Fillmore George H. assistant assayer, U. S. Branch Mint, dwl 814 Powell
Filz William, laborer, dwl S s Greenwich bet Montgomery and Sansom
Finan Bartholomew, boot maker, 777 Folsom
FINANCE ALEXANDER & CO. *(Augustus Esnault and Peter Bojo)* French rotisserie, 825 Dupont, dwl 636 Pacific
Finberg Abraham, watch maker and jeweler, 911 Kearny
Finberg Louis, jeweler with B. Morris, dwl 913 Kearny
Finch Bridget Miss, domestic, NE cor Folsom and Tenth
Finch Duncan B. Capt. dwl 917 Howard
Finch Frances Mrs. seamstress, dwl 130 Second
Finch William G. real estate, dwl 311 Stockton
Finck Charles, laborer with H. Finck, 117 Jackson
Finck Henry, driver with James Donnelly, 109 Sansom
Finck Henry, meat market, 117 Jackson
Finck Henry, porter, 217 Front, dwl Bitter's Hotel
Finck John, butcher with Louis Rosenberg, SW cor Post and Taylor
Finck Julius *(Will & F.)* dwl 504 Vallejo
Finck Teresa (widow) dwl N s Berry nr Mary Lane
Findlay Robert, stationer, Custom House Place, dwl Wetmore Place
Fine John, carrier, Abend Post, dwl Trinity bet Sutter and Bush
Finegan Ann Miss, nurse, dwl 540 Third
Finegan Bridget, domestic with W. L. Underwood, NE cor McAllister and Fillmore
Finegan Catherine Miss, cook, South Park Laundry, 540 Third
Finegan James C. tinsmith with J. W. Brittan & Co. dwl 6 Minna
Fingeler Henry, shoe maker, dwl 514 Front
Fingland Robert, blacksmith with Gallagher & Farren, 112 Bush
Finigan Holmes, physician, office and dwl 608 Jackson
Finigan James, hackman, Plaza

Finigan Margaret Miss, domestic with T. N. Cazneau N s Thirteenth nr Howard
Finigan Peter, undertaker, dwl 254½ Minna
Finigan Peter, handcartman, dwl Scott nr Pacific
Finigan Thomas, laborer, dwl Chambers bet Front and Battery
Finirk John B. vegetable garden, Bay View
Fink Charles, laborer, dwl 442 Union
Fink Frederick, clerk with Leonhart Iffert, SE cor Dolores and Sixteenth
FINK HENRY & CO. *(John Plath)* groceries and liquors, SW cor Powell and Union
Fink James L. salesman with Henston, Hastings & Co. dwl 407 Sutter
Fink John F. porter, dwl 37 Geary
Fink P. A. Miss, assistant, Montgomery St. School, dwl Stockton bet Lombard and Greenwich
Finke August, maltster, Mission St. Brewery, dwl 365 Brannan
Finke William, maltster, Union Brewery
FINKLER CARL C. attorney at law and consul for Nassau, 637 Washington, dwl W s Jones bet Filbert and Greenwich
Finlayson Alexander, salesman, 11 Montgomery, dwl 29 Second
Finley David, pile driver, dwl 30 Natoma
Finley Hamilton, plasterer, dwl S s Valparaiso nr Jones
Finley John, hostler, 532 California, dwl 16 Sutter
Finley John, laborer, dwl E s Main bet Market and Mission
Finley John, porter, 22 Battery
Finley John, waterman, 609 Market, dwl 106 Mason
Finley Margaretta Miss, dwl 505 Howard
Finley Richard, butcher, dwl 204 Fifth
FINLEY THOMAS E. wines and liquors, 113 Leidesdorff, dwl 911 Larkin bet Geary and Post
Finley William, laborer, S. F. P. Woolen Mills, dwl North Point bet Polk and Van Ness Avenue
Finley William F. gas fitter with McNally & Hawkins, dwl 6 Eddy
Finley William P. dwl St. Lawrence House
Finn Alonzo, dwl 506 Market
Finn Augustus, printer, dwl Washington Hose Co
Finn David A. pressman, dwl 322 Vallejo
Finn Edmund, helper, Union Foundry, dwl N s Berry bet Bush and Sutter
Finn Ellen Miss, domestic with Mrs. Wheeler Martin, S s Thirteenth nr Howard
Finn James, laborer, dwl 262 Jessie
Finn James, teamster, 12 Stewart, dwl 417 Natoma
Finn Jeremiah, drayman, dwl NE cor Chesley and Boyd
Finn John T. attorney at law, office 36 Montgomery Block, dwl 917 Clay
Finn Margaret Miss, domestic, 614 Pine
Finn Mary Miss, domestic, 933 Bush
Finn Patrick, laborer, S. F. Gas Co
Finn Thomas, book keeper, 48 Clay, dwl 322 Vallejo
Finn Timothy W. meat curer with Wilson & Stevens, dwl E s Gilbert nr Brannan
Finnercy John, steward, Russ House
Finnerty Ann Miss, nurse with Samuel L. Theller
Finnerty Patrick, laborer with B. Bonnet & Co
Finnerty Peter, bricklayer, dwl 423 Natoma
Finnerty Peter, express wagon, dwl cor McAllister and Broderick
Finnerty Thomas, third assistant engineer S. F. Fire Department and inspector, Custom House, dwl 737 Union
Finnerty William, bricklayer, dwl 423 Natoma
Finnesee James, tailor, dwl 9 Natoma
Finnigan Catherine Miss, domestic, 210 Powell
Finuigan Edward, plasterer, dwl 11 Sherwood Pl
Finnigan Eliza Mrs. dwl SE cor Pine and Jones
Finnigan James, hack driver, 737 Market
Finnigan James C. tinsmith, dwl 6 Minna
Finnigan Julia, domestic, dwl 320 Jessie
Finnigan Mary Miss, ironer, Chelsea Laundry

Finnigan Peter, barber, dwl 549 Howard
Finnigan Peter A. omnibus, What Cheer House, dwl 10 Prospect Place
Finnigan Rosa Miss, domestic, dwl 209 Powell
Finnigan Theodore, with Standard Soap Co. 207 Commercial, dwl 247 Stevenson
Finnigan Thomas, laborer, dwl S s Chambers bet Battery and Front
Finnin Patrick, fireman, dwl 40 Clementina
Finton Joseph, laborer, S. F. & San José R. R. Co
FIRE ALARM AND POLICE TELEGRAPH, office 11 City Hall 2d floor
FIRE BOARD UNDERWRITERS, office 412 California, W. H. Tillingbast secretary
FIRE DEPARTMENT BOARD CHARITABLE FUND, James H. Cutter treasurer, office 511 Front
FIRE DEPARTMENT BOARD DELEGATES, office 3d floor City Hall
FIRE DEPARTMENT BOARD FIRE WARDENS, office 3d floor City Hall
FIRE DEPARTMENT BOARD FOREMEN, office 3d floor City Hall
FIRE DEPARTMENT CHIEF ENGINEER, office room six 3d floor City Hall
FIRE DEPARTMENT CORPORATION YARD, 17 First
FIRE DEPARTMENT SECRETARY BOARD DELEGATES, office room two 3d floor City Hall
FIRE MARSHAL, office room seven 3d floor City Hall
FIREMAN'S FUND INSURANCE CO. San Francisco, office 238 Montgomery, S. H. Parker president, Charles R. Bond secretary
FIREMAN'S JOURNAL (weekly) Chase & Boruck proprietors, office SW corner Sansom and Jackson
Firmin F. A. dwl 6 Prospect Place
Firnkast John, furniture varnisher, 314 Jackson
First National Petroleum Co. (Visalia) office 617 Montgomery
Firth Joseph B. machinist, Pacific Foundry, dwl Union Court
Fischback Henry, clerk, SE cor Sixth and Natoma
Fischback Hermann *(Fischback & Brother)* dwl 1017 Pacific
Fischback *(John R.)* & Brother *(Hermann)* groceries and liquors, NW corner Pacific and Mason, dwl 1019 Pacific
Fischel Benjamin, porter, 316 Sacramento, dwl 127 Montgomery
Fischer Henry, salesman, 634 Clay
Fischer Martin, sail maker, bds 7 Washington
Fischer Max, wagon maker with Charles Steinweg, dwl 634 Clay
Fischer *(Nicholas)* & Koch *(Martin)* hair dressing saloon, 408 Kearny, dwl 417 Kearny
Fish Charles, shoe maker, 555 Market, dwl 559 Market
Fish Edward P. printer with Francis, Valentine & Co. dwl 51 Government House
Fish Franklin & Co. employment office, 537 Sacramento, dwl N s Carlos Place nr O'Farrell
Fish H. B. cook, dwl Niantic Hotel
Fish James H. real estate, office 606 Montgomery
Fish Nathaniel, dwl Central House 814 Sansom
Fish William H. compositor with Agnew & Deffebach, 511 Sansom
Fishbourne Eliza (widow) dwl N s Tyler bet Leavenworth and Hyde
Fishel William *(M. Kohn & Co.)* dwl 19 Hawthorne
Fisher A. musician, Metropolitan Theater, dwl Dupont bet Sacramento and Commercial
Fisher Amelia (widow) furnished rooms, 812 Clay
Fisher Benard, teacher, dwl 114 St. Mark Place
Fisher Benjamin A. blacksmithing and wagon making, 115 Bush

Fisher Beriah P. carpenter, dwl 7 William
Fisher B. H. carman, 618 Battery
Fisher B. P. janitor Boys' High, Post Street, and Chinese Schools
Fisher B. V. Q. teacher German and English school, 135 Post
Fisher Charles, musician, dwl SW cor Dupont and Bay
Fisher Charles (col'd) steward, dwl 16 Scott
Fisher D. clerk with Henry E. Lea
Fisher Emeline Mrs. (col'd) domestic, 927 Bush
Fisher Emil A. silversmith with F. R. Reichel, dwl 280 Minna
Fisher Frederick, laborer, Bay Sugar Refinery, dwl 10 Hinckley
Fisher George, carpenter, dwl 323 Pine
Fisher George, hair dresser, 102 Pacific, dwl 622 Battery
Fisher George N. barber, 136 Fourth, dwl What Cheer House
Fisher George W. (Crane & Brigham) dwl 714 Filbert
Fisher Godfrey, clerk, 413 Sacramento, dwl 20 San
Fisher Henry B. cook, dwl Niantic Hotel
Fisher Henry E. plasterer, office 338 Montgomery, dwl Presidio Road op Half Way House
Fisher Henry J. melter with G. W. Bell, dwl SW cor Clay and Franklin
Fisher Henry P. general agent, dwl 715 Vallejo
Fisher James L. seaman, dwl 38 Jackson
Fisher John, paints, etc. Brannan between First and Second
Fisher John, tailor with Simon Gray, 112 Kearny
Fisher John M. melter with G. W. Bell, 512 Cal
FISHER LUTHER P. newspaper and advertising agency, office 629 Washington, res Oakland
Fisher Martin, sail maker, East bet Washington and Jackson, dwl 9 Washington
Fisher Mendall, carpenter, dwl 607 Sutter
Fisher Michael, boot maker, 802 Dupont, dwl S s Pacific bet Dupont and Kearny
Fisher Milton, dwl 561 Mission
Fisher Morris, job wagon, cor Jackson and East, dwl 707 Jones, rear
Fisher Peter, lumber piler with Hobbs & Gilmore
Fisher Philander, boarding, 777 Market
Fisher Philip I. book keeper, 317 Sacramento, dwl 20 Sansom
Fisher Robert A. machinist, Union Foundry, dwl SE cor Second and Natoma
Fisher Robert S. bar keeper, Phil's Exchange, dwl cor Sansom and Market
Fisher Samuel, clothing, 527 Jackson
Fisher Sidney A. Forwarding Department Wells, Fargo & Co. dwl 614 California
Fisher William W. teamster with R. G. Sneath & Co. dwl 777 Market
Fisher W. T. dwl 127 Montgomery
Fisher, see Fischer
FISK (Josiah M.) & BARBER (Charles J.) groceries, NE cor Howard and Howard Court, dwl 3 Howard Court
Fisk Royal, commission merchant, office 402 Front, dwl 1221 Washington
Fiske A. dwl Original House
Fiske Charles H. cartman with William Buckley
Fiske Edward S. (H. G. & E. S. F.) dwl 807 Market
Fiske Henry G. & Edward S. metal roofers, 807 Market, dwl 817 Mason
Fiske William H. carpenter, dwl 549 Howard
Fistar Charles, express wagon, cor Kearny and Pac
Fitch Frederick G. Mexican Loan Office, 420 Montgomery, dwl 109 Sansom
Fitch George, job wagon, NW cor Pine and Sansom, dwl O'Farrell nr Taylor
Fitch George jr. driver with J. Henry Wood, dwl 813 Stockton
FITCH GEORGE K. (S. F. Bulletin Co.) dwl 317 Sutter

Fitch George W. merchant, dwl N s California bet Powell and Mason
Fitch Henry S. miner, 619 Merchant
FITCH (J. Benjamin) & MERRITT (Stephen F.) Eureka Billiard Saloon, 314 Montgomery (and Harter & F.) dwl 910 Washington
Fitch J. Ives, dwl 5 Hardie Place
Fitch James R. dwl 636 Sutter
Fitch Mary H. (widow) dwl 241 Minna
Fitch William S. attorney at law, dwl Ocean House
Fite John, carpenter, dwl SE cor Mission and First
Fitschen George, bar keeper, Castle Saloon cor venson and Market
Fitschen Henry (Grosbauer & F.) SW cor Folsom and Haywood
Fitschen John H. groceries and liquors, NE cor Stevenson and Fourth
FITTER EIBE H. California Star Saloon, SW cor Clay and Davis
Fitter Henry, clerk with Ritchard Teitgen, dwl NE cor Pacific and Broadway
Fitz Ann M. (widow) dwl 1111 Kearny
Fitzgerald Austin, tailor, 619 Sacramento, dwl E s Robbins Place nr Union
Fitzgerald Catharine E. Miss, dwl cor Chestnut and Montgomery
Fitzgerald Charles, laborer, Union Foundry, dwl 200 First
Fitzgerald Christopher, bricklayer, dwl 421 Natoma
Fitzgerald Eleanor A. Miss, dwl cor Chestnut and Montgomery
Fitzgerald Eliza Miss, dress maker, dwl NE cor Montgomery and Pacific
Fitzgerald Eliza (widow) dwl cor Montgomery and Chestnut
Fitzgerald Ellen Miss, domestic, 329 O'Farrell
Fitzgerald Francis, laborer, dwl Seventh bet Harrison and Fourth
Fitzgerald Garrett, blacksmith with Nelson & Doble, dwl 135 Natoma
Fitzgerald George, lodgings, 815 Kearny
Fitzgerald George R. rigger, dwl 44 Louisa
Fitzgerald Hannah Miss, domestic, 333 Sixth
Fitzgerald Henry, keeper, County Jail, dwl 1305 Stockton
Fitzgerald James, cartman, dwl 111 William
Fitzgerald James, laborer, dwl W s Battery bet Union and Filbert
Fitzgerald James, seaman, steamer Orizaba
Fitzgerald John, laborer, Lone Mountain Cemetery, dwl cor Fillmore and Jackson
Fitzgerald John, laundryman, dwl 914 Broadway
Fitzgerald John, seaman, dwl 54 Sacramento
Fitzgerald Michael, laborer, dwl E s Salmon bet Mason and Taylor
Fitzgerald Michael, laborer, dwl 156 First
Fitzgerald Michael, machinist, Fulton Foundry, dwl 4 Pennsylvania Avenue
Fitzgerald M. J. ship carpenter with John G. North, Potrero
Fitzgerald Morris, laborer, dwl 237 Sutter
Fitzgerald Morris, laborer, dwl cor Tyler and Leav
Fitzgerald Morris, tinsmith with G. & W. Snook, dwl 622 Battery
Fitzgerald Nicholas, laborer, dwl N s Linden nr Laguna
Fitzgerald O. P. Rev. pastor Minna St. Methodist Church, dwl S s Francisco bet Dupont and Stockton
Fitzgerald Patrick, dwl 4 Pennsylvania Avenue
Fitzgerald Patrick, blacksmith, dwl 137 Pacific
Fitzgerald Patrick, laborer, dwl 146 Clara
Fitzgerald Patrick, laborer, dwl Minna Place
Fitzgerald Patrick, molder, Jackson Foundry, dwl Sacramento Hotel
Fitzgerald Stephen, laborer with B. H. Ramsdell, dwl 136 Silver
Fitzgerald Thomas, blacksmith, North Beach & M. R. R. Co. dwl Minna Place

Fitzgerald Thomas, deck hand stm Cornelia, dwl S s Chambers bet Battery and Front
Fitzgerald Thomas W. porter, dwl W s August Alley nr Union
Fitzgerald Timothy, shoe maker with I. M. Wentworth & Co. dwl 15 Ecker nr Stevenson
Fitzgerald William, waiter, dwl 405 Dupont
Fitzgerrald William, waiter, dwl NW cor Second and Stevenson
Fitz Gibbon David, teacher dancing, Assembly Hall cor Post and Kearny, dwl SW cor Third and Mission
Fitzgibbon John M. ship carpenter, dwl 545 Howard
FITZ-GIBBON M. E. manufacturer asphaltum sidewalks and roofs, office 204 Bush, dwl 107 Minna
Fitzgibbons David, porter with J. H. Coghill & Co. dwl Revere House
Fitzgibbons M. lamplighter, S. F. Gas Co
Fitz Henry, Michael, goldsmith, dwl S s Grove bet Laguna and Octavia
Fitzhugh P. secretary S. F. & Oakland R. R. Co. office 535 Clay, dwl 510 Stockton
Fitzkerl Patrick, molder, bds Sacramento Hotel
Fitzler Joseph, laborer, dwl E s Eighth mr Mission
Fitzmorris George, teamster, 406 California, dwl cor Jackson and Devisidero
Fitzpatrick Arthur G. carpenter and builder, dwl E s Bartlett bet Twenty-Third and Twenty-Fourth
Fitzpatrick Elizabeth Miss, domestic, 116 Shipley
Fitzpatrick James R. W. collector, S. F. Gas Co. dwl 66 Minna
Fitzpatrick Jeremiah, oysters, Occidental Hotel, dwl 4 Brown Alley
Fitzpatrick John, contractor, dwl junction Market and Valencia
Fitzpatrick John, stone cutter, Fort Point, dwl E s Hyde bet Filbert and Greenwich
Fitzpatrick John, trunk maker with Galpen & Co. dwl 106 Sixth
Fitzpatrick John Mrs. fruits, 106 Sixth
Fitzpatrick John E. (Turner & Co.) dwl 529 Union
Fitzpatrick Michael, engineer, Golden Age Flour Mills, dwl 335 Broadway
Fitzpatrick Michael, tanner with Davis & Sedgley, dwl Mission Creek nr Sixteenth
Fitzpatrick Patrick, dwl 189 Beale
Fitzpatrick Patrick, conductor, North Beach & M. R. R. Co. bds Franklin House, SW cor Sansom and Broadway
Fitzpatrick Patrick D. tinsmith with Johnston & Reay, 319 California
Fitzpatrick Simon, laborer, dwl S s Cemetery Alley bet Dolores and Church
Fitzpatrick Thomas, cartman, dwl 106 Beale
Fitzpatrick Thomas, laborer, S. F. Gas Co
Fitzpatrick Thomas, stevedore, dwl 12 Scott
Fitzpatrick Timothy, foundryman, dwl 511 Minna
Fitzpatrick W. carpenter, dwl 177 Minna
Fitzpatrick William, contractor, dwl W s Valencia junction Market
Fitzsimmons Ellen Miss, dwl W s Sansom bet Greenwich and Filbert
Fitzsimmons James, laborer, Union Foundry
Fitzsimmons John, bar tender, dwl 115 First
Fitzsimmons Margaret (widow) dwl W s Sansom nr Filbert
Fitzsimmons Patrick, stone mason, dwl E s Harriet bet Fifteenth and Sixteenth
Fitzwilliam Daniel, bar keeper, NW cor Dupont and Washington
Flach Joseph, dwl 73 Tehama
Flack Joseph, Greenwich Market, 721 Greenwich
Flager John, lodgings, 551 Market
Flagg Henry, wood turner, 307 Market, dwl 15 Belden
Flagg Lucius, broker, dwl 919 Clay
Flagg Thomas, dwl 608 Market
Flaglor Amasa P. clerk with William Shew, dwl E s Larkin bet Green and Union

Flaglor Gilbert, dwl 23 Natoma
Flaglor Permilla (widow) dwl 254 Clementina
Flaglor William G. grainer, dwl 254 Clementina
Flahaut James, laundry, dwl 522 Pacific
Flahaven Michael, tinsmith with Tay, Brooks & Backus, bds 12 Sutter
Flaherty Anna Miss, domestic with Louis Sloss
Flaherty Catharine Miss, domestic, 1308 Pine
Flaherty Dennis, hackman, Plaza, dwl NW cor Gough and Grove
Flaherty Edward, local policeman, dwl NE cor California and Leidesdorff
Flaherty John, laborer, Spring Valley W. W
Flaherty John, laborer, dwl 109 William
Flaherty Kate, domestic with James M. Curtis
Flaherty Margaret Miss, domestic with Louis Sloss
Flaherty Michael, soap maker with John Fay, dwl 1922 Mason
Flaherty Patrick, carpenter with S. S. Culverwell, 29 Fremont
Flaherty Thomas, cartman, dwl Geneva nr Brannan
Flaherty Thomas, laborer, dwl 618 Post
Flanagan Daniel, hostler with Central R. R. Co. dwl E s Eighth bet Bryant and Brannan
Flanagan Edward, stock broker, dwl 1708 Dupont
FLANAGAN EDWARD, real estate agent, secretary Citizens' Homestead and Road Association and agent Coose Bay Coal Mines, office 606 Montgomery, dwl 1708 Dupont
Flanagan J. B. laborer, Spring Valley W. W
FLANAGAN JOHN & CO. importers and jobbers wines and liquors, 421 Front, dwl 223 Green
Flanagan John, bds Phoenix House, 721 Sansom
Flanagan John, salesman with Armes & Dallam, dwl 29 Third
Flanagan Lawrence, apprentice, Pacific Foundry, dwl 66 Jessie
Flanagan Michael, oysterman, Phil's Exchange, dwl 436 Jessie
Flanagan Michael, steward, Central House, 814 San
Flanders Ephraim, calker, dwl SW cor Louisiana and Sierra
Flanders Isabel (widow) dwl 212 Minna
Flanders Nathan, engineer, dwl 1225 Pacific
Flauedy P. Joseph, dwl 1142 Folsom
Flanelly Patrick M. driver, dwl 439 Jessie
Flangan Terrence, laborer, dwl Dolores Hall W s Valencia nr Sixteenth
Flanigan P. blacksmith, dwl 331 Bush
Flanigan Patrick, boot maker, dwl SW cor Dupont and Broadway
Flanigan Thomas, drayman with Sullivan & Cashman, dwl E s Kearny nr California
Flannagan Andrew J. express wagon, cor Pine and Bat, dwl S s Austin bet Polk and Van Ness Av
Flannagan Anne Miss, domestic, 711 Bush
Flannagan Bridget, domestic, 1109 Stockton
Flannagan Edward, cook, Magnolia Restaurant
Flannagan Eugene, porter, Academy Music, dwl 206 Kearny
Flannagan John, waiter, 626 Kearny
Flannagan Mary Miss, domestic with George R. Turner
Flannagan Michael, horseshoer with John Hart, dwl 333 Bush
Flannagan Thomas, drayman with Sullivan & Cashman
Flannelly P. F. peddler, dwl 439 Jessie
Flannelly William, laborer, dwl Union Court
Flannery Patrick, driver with John McDevitt, dwl N s Broadway bet Stockton and Powell
Flannery Roger, with Reynolds, Howell & Ford, dwl N s Filbert bet Stockton and Powell
Flannigan James, laborer, dwl 231 Sutter
Flannigan James, laborer, dwl 11 Bay State Row
Flannigan James, laborer, Courtlandt Avenue nr North Avenue
Flannigan James D. coupé, Plaza, dwl E s Dupont nr Sutter

Flannigan Lawrence, boiler maker, dwl 66 Jessie
Flannigan Mary Miss, domestic, 1001 Powell
Flannigan M. Mrs. dwl E s Reed nr Clay
Flannigan Michael, clerk with Thomas Dunning, 253 Clara
Flannigan William, cartman, cor Bdwy and Battery
Flannigan William, laborer, dwl 210 Pacific
Flannigan Winifred, domestic, dwl 427 Third
Flannigan, see Flanagan
Flary J. deck hand, steamer Petaluma
Flathman Claus, clerk, N W cor Howard and Fifteenth, dwl SE cor Folsom and Main
Flattly John, cartman, dwl 253 Clementina
Fleetfoot Thomas, clerk, dwl SW cor Kearny and Pacific
Fleetwood Thomas A. book keeper, 316 California, dwl 537 California
Fleig Casimer *(Shobel F. & Co.)* dwl 1129 Folsom
Fleischman Charles, drayman, Davis bet Pacific and Broadway
Fleischman David, salesman, 304 California, dwl St. Nicholas Hotel
Fleischmann Rachel Miss, domestic, dwl 900 Vallejo
Fleishel Charles *(Markt & F.)* dwl cor Dupont and Berry
Fleisher Wolf, cap manufacturer, 405 California
Fleishhacker Aaron *(Fleishhacker & Meyer, Carson City, Nev.)* office SE cor Montgomery and Sacramento room 3, dwl 119 Powell
Fleishman Benjamin, merchant, dwl 318 Sutter
Fleishman Charles, dwl E s Larkin bet Jackson and Pacific
Eleishman John, furnished rooms, Shiels' Block
Fleishmann Leopold, butcher, 48 Metropolitan Market, dwl Continental Hotel
Fleming Bartholemew, book keeper with E. V. Joice, dwl 239 Minna
Fleming Charles, gardener with John Rosenfeld
Fleming Charles, upholsterer with Wightman & Hardie
Fleming David, apprentice, Fulton Foundry, dwl 51 Clementina
Fleming David J. ship carpenter, dwl E s Rousch nr Howard
Fleming Edward, miner, dwl 308 Beale
Fleming H. B. Capt. U. S. A. acting ass't provost marshal, office 414 Washington, dwl N W cor Stockton and Pacific
Fleming James, driver, Pioneer Soda Works, dwl E s Stockton bet Broadway and Pacific
Fleming James H. driver, dwl cor Clay and Stock
Fleming John, teamster, dwl cor Buchanan and Greenwich
Fleming Josephine (widow) dwl W s Sonoma Place nr Green
Fleming Mary Miss, domestic, 712 Union
Fleming Patrick, bricklayer, dwl 12 Sutter
Fleming Patrick, laborer, dwl 9 Front, rear
Fleming P. H. steward California Engine No. 4, dwl 412 Market
Fleming Robert, laborer, Spring Valley W. W. dwl E s Hyde bet Union and Filbert
Fleming S. C. local policeman, dwl 8 s Clay nr Davis
Fleming William, driver with Fortman & Co. dwl Front nr Market
Fleming William, ship carpenter, dwl 51 Clementina
Fleming William S. machinist, dwl S W cor Folsom and Fremont
Flemming Albert C. clerk, dwl 114 Broadway
Flemming F. B. carpenter, dwl 616 California
Flemming James, hostler, 679 Market, dwl 12 Dupont
Flemming Samuel, clerk with DeWitt, Kittle & Co. cor California and Front
Flemming Sarah (widow) dwl with W. G. Bloomfield, N s Union bet Battery and Sansom
Flemming William, machinist, Miners' Foundry
Flemming William, teamster with James McDevitt, dwl W s Sansom bet Broadway and Vallejo

Flenniken Robert, salesman with Newhall, Brooks & Nettleton, dwl 1306 Montgomery
Fleres Antonio, hairdresser, 624 Washington, dwl 1121 Powell
Fletcher A. P. carrier, Alta California, dwl 2104 Mason
FLETCHER ARTEMUS T. agent New York Board Underwriters, office 308 Front, dwl cor Tenth and Folsom
Fletcher Barney (col'd) janitor Exchange Buildings room 13, dwl 908 Pacific, rear
Fletcher C. A. clothing, 1 Mont, Masonic Temple
Fletcher Edward, lithographer, 308 Front, dwl W s Leroy Place
Fletcher F. A. dwl What Cheer House
FLETCHER *(J. A.)* & ALLEN *(W. H.)* attorneys at law, office 6 and 7 Armory Hall Building
Fletcher John H. painter with Sweet & Gadsby, dwl 308 Mason
Fletcher L. carpenter, bds Franklin Hotel, SE cor Sansom and Pacific
Fletcher Lemuel, molder, Miners' Foundry, dwl Benton House
Fletcher Livinia (colored, widow) dwl 1604 Mason
Fletcher Robert, pantryman, steamer Amelia
Fletcher Samuel J. upholsterer with Wightman & Hardie, dwl 512 Jones
Fletcher Thomas H. painter, dwl NE cor McAllister and Leavenworth
Fletcher William, carrier, Alta California and Evening Bulletin, dwl 2104 Mason
Fleury Adolph, laborer with McMillan & Kester, dw N s Sacramento bet Dupont and Stockton
Fleury Alexander, French Laundry, dwl 916 Powell
Fleury Desire Mme. furnished rooms, 921 Stockton
Fleury John, dwl 921 Stockton
Fleury Julien, music teacher, dwl 607 Dupont
Fleury Paul, housesmith, 713 Dupont, dwl N W cor O'Farrell and Octavia
Flewres Antonio, dwl N W cor Main and Harrison
Flicca Nancy (widow) dwl with Antonio Flores
Flick William, driver with Deeth & Starr, 205 Sacramento, dwl 331 Jessie
Flinn Mary, cook, dwl 232 Stevenson
Flinn Patrick T. groceries and liquors and hay and grain, SW cor Howard and Eighth
Flinn Randall P. physician and druggist, 5 Stewart
Flinn, see Flynn
Flint Alexander B. carpenter, dwl SE cor Fourth and Louisa
Flint Augustus P. *(Maurice Dore & Co.)* dwl SE cor Pine and Leavenworth
Flint Charles, clerk with Eisen Bros. dwl 515 Market
Flint Edward P. *(Flint, Peabody & Co.)* res Oakland
Flint George C. book keeper with J. Peirce, dwl N s Townsend bet Second and Third
Flint Harlan P. waterman, 609 Market, dwl 106 Mason
FLINT, *(James P. and Edward P.)* PEABODY *(Alfred)* & CO. *(George H. Kellogg)* shipping and commission merchants and agents Glidden & Williams' California Packet Line, office 716 Front, res Oakland
Flint Jane H (widow) treasurer Ladies' Protection and Relief Society, dwl 1312 Powell
Flint John P. waterman, 609 Market, dwl 106 Mason
Flint Milford M. carpenter, dwl SE cor Louisa and Fourth
Flint Thomas, steward, dwl 1003 Stockton
Flint Thomas, book keeper, Pioneer Mills, dwl 632 Market
Flint Thomas P. painter with Hopps & Kanary, dwl 26 Post
Flint William C. dwl N s Market bet Laguna and Buchanan
Flint William K. acct with Flint, Peabody & Co
Flintje George F. with Wormser Bros. dwl N W cor Union and Kearny

Flintoff *(Joseph)* & O'Neill *(Francis)* blacksmiths, cor Halleck and Leidesdorff, dwl 646 Howard
Flint's Warehouse, cor Battery and Greenwich, Thomas B. Ludlum proprietor
Flood Christopher, stevedore, dwl 56 Jessie
Flood Daniel, cook, Franklin House, dwl 212 Broadway, rear
Flood Edward, plasterer, dwl 53 Tehama
Flood H. S. & Co. importers and jobbers staple and fancy dry goods, 306 Cal, dwl Lick House
Flood Hugh, dwl 170 Minna
Flood Isaac (col'd) steward, steamer Sacramento
Flood James, hatter with Charles Nickerson, dwl E s Powell bet Pacific and Broadway
Flood James, plasterer, dwl 53 Tehama
FLOOD *(James C.)* & O'BRIEN *(William S.)* auction lunch, 509 Washington, dwl 15 John
Flood James, retortman, S. F. Gas Co
Flood Jeremiah, pattern maker, Jackson Foundry, dwl N s Austin bet Franklin and Van Ness Avenue
Flood John, plasterer, dwl 521 Geary, rear
Flood John, purifier, S. F. Gas Co. dwl 56 Jessie
Flood John jr. retortman, S. F. Gas Co. dwl 56 Jessie
FLOOD M. importer Catholic books and stationery, 428 Kearny, dwl 17 Harlan Place
Flood Noah, student, dwl 362 Jessie
Flood William A. stone cutter, dwl 28 Clara
Florence Ada (widow) dwl NE cor Dupont and Jackson
Florence Edwin, shoe maker with Thomas Dolliver, 110 Sutter, rear
Florence G. & S. M. Co. office 1 Government House
FLORENCE SEWING MACHINES, Samuel Hill agent, 111 Montgomery
Flores Antonio, farmer, Old Ocean House Road, 6 miles from City Hall
Flores Frank, tinsmith with M. Prag, dwl 816 Filbert
Flores Manuel, with Charles Storm, dwl Union bet Kearny and Dupont
Flores Mary A. (widow) dwl 1419 Stockton
Florida G. & S. M. Co. (Reese River) office 619 Merchant
Florine O. N. bricklayer, dwl 10 Oak
Flote George, seaman, dwl 44 Sacramento
Floto John H. physician, office and dwl 400 Kearny cor Pine
Flower Charles H. laborer, dwl 46 Beale
Flowers Edward, dwl 727 Union
Flowers J. M. (col'd) whitewasher, 761 Clay
Floyd A. B. Mrs. dress making, 302 Dupont
Floyd Alexander, cooper, S. F. & P. Sugar Co. dwl Rousch nr Folsom
Floyd R. D. dwl Gautier's House, 516 Pacific
Floyd William, liquors and billiards, 511 Pacific, dwl Gautier's House 516 Pacific
Floyd Zaccheus, gas fitter, S. F. Gas Co. dwl 29 Everett
Flubacker Emile, shoe maker, dwl 714 Broadway
Fluffum Martin, lumber piler, dwl 40 Stewart
Fluhr Charles, hairdresser with Stahle Bros. dwl 9 Tay
Flynn Andrew, with I. D. Thompson, 321 Mont
Flynn Ann (widow) domestic, NE cor Twentieth and Florida
Flynn Annie Miss, domestic, 514 Dupont
Flynn Anthony, carpenter, dwl N s Clay bet Leavenworth and Hyde
Flynn Bridget Miss, domestic, 1518 Mason
Flynn Delia T. (widow) nurse, dwl 15 Monroe
FLYNN EDMOND, groceries and liquors, NE cor Bryant and Fourth
Flynn Edward, boatman, Pacific St. Wharf
Flynn Ellen (widow) dwl N s Bryant bet Fifth and Sixth, rear
Flynn Ellen (widow) dwl 1220 Powell, rear
Flynn Hannah Miss, dwl SE cor Fourth and Jessie

Flynn Henry, captain Company A, Second Infantry, Cal. Vol. Presidio
Flynn Hugh *(O'Grady & F.)* dwl 803 Howard
Flynn Hugh, steward, dwl 711 Pine
Flynn James, boot maker, 47 Second, dwl 65 Everett
Flynn James, gardener, dwl 517 Dupont
Flynn James, seaman, dwl 44 Sacramento
Flynn James, with Goodwin & Co. dwl 1219 Kearny
Flynn James F. *(Cook & F.)* dwl 4 Beale Court
Flynn John, baker, dwl 12 Sutter
Flynn John, carpenter, dwl 249 Clary
Flynn John, furner, dwl Solano nr York
Flynn John, groceries, NW cor Hyde and Ellis
Flynn John, laborer, dwl 110 Tehama
Flynn Julia (widow) dwl 45 Everett
Flynn Margaret Miss, domestic, 349 Fremont
Flynn Martin, storekeeper, Union Warehouse, dwl 833 Howard
Flynn Maurice, laborer, dwl 245 Jessie
Flynn Maurice W. butcher, SW cor Brannan and Sixth
Flynn Mary Miss, chambermaid, Russ House
Flynn Mary Miss, domestic, NW cor Post and Leavenworth
Flynn Mary Miss, domestic, dwl 858 Mission
Flynn Mary Miss, domestic, 1016 Bush
Flynn Mary Miss, domestic, 1116 Stockton
Flynn Mary Miss, millinery, 940 Dupont
Flynn Mary F. Miss, dwl 28 Rousch
Flynn Michael, carpenter, dwl N s Oak bet Franklin and Gough
Flynn Michael, carpenter, dwl N s Green bet Leavenworth and Hyde
Flynn Michael, melter, Union Foundry, dwl N s Mission bet First and Ecker
Flynn Michael M. tinsmith, dwl 11 Geary
Flynn Morris, laborer, Miners' Foundry
Flynn Patrick *(Dunnigan & F.)* dwl 589 Stevenson
Flynn Patrick, blacksmith, Omnibus R. R. Co. dwl 255 Clementina
Flynn Patrick, butcher, SW cor Brannan and Sixth
Flynn Patrick, cook, dwl 184 Stevenson
Flynn Patrick, cook, Richard's Restaurant, dwl 11 Bay State Row
Flynn Patrick, laborer with Owen Keating
Flynn Patrick T. groceries and liquors, SW cor Howard and Eighth
Flynn Peter, beamster, foot Townsend, dwl E s Gilbert bet Sixth and Seventh
Flynn Thomas, blacksmith, dwl 83 Stevenson
Flynn Thomas, job wagon, SW cor Market and Third, dwl 41 Ritch
Flynn Thomas, laborer, dwl E s Florida nr Eighteenth
Flynn Thomas, stone cutter, Fort Point
Flynn Timothy, dwl 531 Union
Flynn Timothy, plasterer, dwl 252 Minna
Flynn Timothy, workman with E. Morrell, dwl NE cor Twentieth and Florida
Flynn William *(Morse & Co.)* dwl 22 Kearny
Flynn, see Flinn
Foa Julius, real estate, dwl SW cor Broadway and Dupont
Foard Jeremiah W. entry clerk, Custom House, dwl 759 Market
FOARD J. MACDONOUGH & CO. *(J. W. Shaeffer and J. M. Byers)* publishers and proprietors Sunday Mercury, office and editorial rooms 420 Mont up stairs, dwl 4 Hardie Place
Foard T. J. compositor, Sunday Mercury, dwl 10 Ellis
Foard William W. carpenter, dwl S s Green bet Larkin and Polk
Foege Frank *(Albers & F.)* dwl 641 Pacific
Foerster Eliza (widow) dress making, 124 Post
Fog Ludwig, dwl 109 Pine

Fogarty Ann (widow) dwl 476 Jessie
Fogarty David, blacksmith, 671 Mission, dwl 476 Jessie
Fogarty Eliza Miss, domestic, 323 Geary
Fogarty James, butcher, 55 Metropolitan Market, dwl 79 Clementina, rear
Fogarty James, coachman, dwl 1122 Pine
Fogarty Martin, laborer, dwl 314 Vallejo
Fogarty *(Michael)* & O'Ronrke *(John)* restaurant, 204 Fourth, dwl cor Jessie and Sixth
Fogarty Michael. laborer with Hey & Meyn
Fogarty Michael, laborer, dwl Union bet Powell and Mason
Fogarty Michael, laborer, dwl N s Erie nr Mission
Fogarty Patrick, conductor, Omnibus R. R. Co. dwl 136 Fourth
Fogarty Patrick C. carpenter, dwl NW cor Haight and Fillmore
Fogarty Philip, porter with George Morrow, dwl E s Montgomery bet Pacific and Broadway
Fogarty William, laborer, dwl 4 Stockton Place
Fogel Benjamin, tailor, dwl 14 Scott
Fogg George W. foreman machine shop Pacific Foundry, dwl 118 Natoma
Fogg James S. carpenter, Pacific Foundry
Fogle George, tailor, dwl 506 Davis
Fogle O. B. agent soldiers' claims, 617 Montgomery, dwl 714 Mission
Fogler George P. shoe maker, 4 Sutter, bds 414 Market
Fogler Joseph, mechanic with James Brokaw, dwl 15 Tehama
Fogler Philip, shoe maker, 4 Sutter
Fojada D. drayman, dwl S s Bush bet Polk and Van Ness Avenue
Fokin Hi (Chinese) washing, 424 Dupont
Foley Ann, ironer, Chelsea Laundry
Foley Anna Miss, domestic, 538 Howard
Foley Annie Miss, domestic with C. N. Freeman, E s Howard bet Twenty-First and Twenty-Second
Foley Charles, clerk, dwl 214 First
Foley Christopher, engineer steamer Washoe, dwl Moulton Place
Foley Cornelius, milkman, dwl S s Greenwich bet Jones and Leavenworth
Foley Daniel B. compositor, dwl 515 Taylor
Foley David, Camanche Liquor Saloon, Presidio Road cor Octavia
Foley Edward, dwl 106 William
Foley Edward, laborer, steamer Yosemite, dwl E s Montgomery bet Filbert and Greenwich
Foley Ella Miss, dwl 36 Natoma
Foley Ellen (widow) dwl 119 Stevenson
Foley Francis, with R. Feuerstein & Co. dwl 336 Seventh
Foley Francis, laborer, dwl 21 Moss
Foley James, clerk, dwl 519 Bush
Foley James, workman, S. F. Cordage Factory, dwl Michigan nr Sierra
Foley Jeremiah, glass blower, Pacific Glass Works, dwl cor Mariposa and Indiana
Foley Jeremiah, salesman with Kerby, Byrne & Co. dwl 519 Bush
Foley Johanna Miss, domestic, SW cor Twelfth and Mission
Foley John, bar keeper, dwl 214 First
Foley John, blacksmith helper, Vulcan Iron Works
Foley John, deck hand, steamer Clinton
Foley John, drayman, dwl 321 Brannan
Foley John, machinist, dwl 538 Howard
Foley John, nurse, City and County Hospital
Foley Maggie Miss, dwl 36 Natoma
Foley Margaret (widow) dwl 140 Minna
Foley Margaret, domestic, 782 Harrison
Foley Maria Miss, lodgings, 36 Natoma
Foley Mary Miss, domestic, 123 Stockton
Foley Mathew, laborer, dwl 308 Dupont, rear
Foley Michael, baker, dwl 140 Second

Foley Michael, groceries and liquors, SE cor Stevenson and Ecker
Foley Michael, laborer, Fulton Foundry
Foley Michael, laborer, dwl 214 First
Foley Michael, machinist, dwl 129 Pacific
Foley Patrick, drayman, cor Washington and Sansom, dwl 22 Geary
Foley Patrick, laborer, cor Jones and Francisco
Foley Patrick, laborer, dwl 508 Mission
Foley Terrence, apprentice, Pacific Foundry
Foley Thomas, with Louis Jafee, dwl 133 Sutter
Foley Thomas, laborer, Spring Valley W. W
Foley Timothy, boot and shoe maker, dwl S s Sixteenth bet Valencia and Second Avenue
Foley Timothy, carman, dwl 17 Hunt
Foley T. J. dwl Niantic Hotel
Folger Alanson, stair builder with William H. Smith, dwl S s Bryant bet Seventh and Eighth
Folger Daniel W. with C. S. Eaton, 708 Kearny, dwl 1215 Mason
Folger Frederic W. teamster, Spring Valley W. W. dwl S s Bryant bet Seventh and Eighth
Folger James A. *(Marden & F.)* dwl 722 Filbert
Folger James S. druggist with R. H. McDonald & Co
Folger Seth, weigher, dwl 1030 Market
Folger Shubael M. assistant storekeeper, Bonded Store Custom House, dwl S s Post bet Taylor and Mason
Folger Susan (widow) dwl S s Bryant bet Seventh and Eighth
Folbarbor Antonio, laborer with B. Bonnet & Co
Folk S. dwl 529 Howard
FOLKERS J. H. A. agent Tiemann & Co. surgical and dental instruments and trusses, 218 Montgomery, dwl 232 Sutter
Folkert Adolph, workman, Willows Brewery, dwl SW cor Mission and Nineteenth
Folkman Charles M. laborer, dwl 1414 Kearny
Folks William, merchant, dwl 1010 Market
Follacio Louis, cabinet maker with John Wigmore, 423 California
Follan John, laborer, dwl W s Salmon bet Mason and Taylor
Follansbee Joshua, contractor, dwl St. Lawrence House
Follansbee T. H. painter, dwl 115 First
Folleau A. anatomical machinist, office and dwl 624 Washington
Folley Calixte, artist, dwl 626 California
FOLLMER R. A. & CO. *(G. F. G. Wuth and Niels G. Johnson)* proprietors Point San Quentin House, SW cor Louisiana and Sierra, Potrero Nuevo
Folmar Philip *(Asmus & F.)* farmer, San Miguel Rancho
FOLSOM ALBERT, carriage manufactory, 531 California, dwl 418 Post
Folsom Charles, job wagon, 648 Market, dwl S s California bet Larkin and Polk
Folsom Franklin T. blacksmith with Albert Folsom, dwl 418 Post
Folsom George F. carpenter, dwl 4 Pollard Place
Folsom George T. solicitor, Pacific Insurance Co. 436 California, dwl 121 O'Farrell
Folsom W. F. dwl 612 Post
Foncke Frederick, tanner, dwl Chicago Hotel, 220 Pacific
Fonda Alfred, groceries and liquors, NE cor Howard and Third, dwl 631 Folsom
Fonda John, dwl 22 Montgomery
Fonemann William *(Haussler & F.)* 231 Jackson
Fook On (Chinese) merchant, 731 Commercial
Fook Wah (Chinese) employment office, 738 Com
Foorman Saul, butcher with Leopold Fleishman, dwl 20 Sansom
Foot Mathew M. carpenter, dwl N s Fifteenth near Valencia
Foote Elizabeth Mrs. domestic, 607 Sutter

Foote George, engineer, dwl Oriental Hotel
Footman John, waiter, Occidental Hotel
FORBES ANDREW B. with Wells, Fargo & Co. office NW cor Montgomery and California, dwl NW cor Montgomery and Sacramento
FORBES BROTHERS *(Alexander and Charles)* & CO. importers and commission merchants, W s Front nr Vallejo, dwl NE cor South Park and Third
Forbes Charles *(Forbes Brothers & Co.)* dwl NE cor South Park and Third
Forbes David, ship joiner with John G. North, dwl W s Iowa nr Solano
Forbes George W. carpenter, dwl W s Iowa near Solano
Forbes Hugh W. salesman, 327 Sansom, dwl 461 Minna
Forbes J. A. Mrs. millinery, 410 Third
Forbes James, boiler maker with Moynihan & Aitken, dwl 4 Haywood
Forbes James H. dwl W s Iowa nr Solano
Forbes James W. clerk with H. P. Wakelee, NW cor Howard and Third
Forbes Jane (widow) dwl 914 Pacific
Forbes Jennie, furnished rooms, 614 Mission
Forbes Jennie A. Miss, dwl with Robert J. Polk
Forbes John, stevedore, dwl NW cor Front and Broadway
Forbes Pliny, watchman, Occidental Hotel
Forbes Thomas, painter, dwl 318 Davis
Forbes William H. mining treasurer, office room 20 Stevenson House, dwl Lick House
Forcade Jacob, stock broker, dwl SE cor Third and Hunt
Ford Allen, clerk with William Sherman & Co. dwl 528 O'Farrell
Ford Charles, drayman with Charles F. Chadbourne, dwl 1420 Dupont
Ford Daniel, hostler, Omnibus R. R. Co. dwl 255 Clementina
Ford Dennis, marble polisher, 618 Market, dwl 254 Jessie
Ford Elisha, carpenter and proprietor Old Seal Rock House, 6 miles from City Hall
Ford Ellen (widow) dwl 239 Bush
Ford Frank W. deck hand, stmr Cornelia
Ford Henry, stevedore, dwl E s Vincent nr Union
Ford J. dwl What Cheer House
Ford Jane (widow) dwl 349 Fourth
Ford John, boot maker, dwl 12 Jackson
Ford Joseph C. assistant secretary Stock and Exchange Board and mining secretary, office 21 Exchange Building, dwl 309 Clementina
Ford Kate Miss, dwl 130 Dora
Ford Martin, laborer, dwl W s Battery bet Green and Vallejo
Ford Mary M. dwl SE cor Minna and Second
Ford Michael, blacksmith with James Glinden, dwl 336 Bush
Ford Michael, boot maker, dwl 12 Jackson
Ford Michael, laborer, dwl Clementina bet Second and Third
Ford Nathan V. driver, Central R. R. Co. dwl cor Brannan and Eighth
Ford Phineas, dwl Oriental Hotel
Ford Thomas *(Doran & F.)* dwl Sansom nr Green
Ford Thomas, blacksmith, dwl 729 Ellis
Ford Thomas, horseshoer with Patrick Brannan, dwl cor Union and Sansom
Ford Timothy, laborer, dwl 13 Berry, rear
Ford William *(Reynolds, Howell & F.)* dwl 615 Pine
Ford William, plumber, dwl 71 Natoma
Ford William H. mining secretary, office 605 Montgomery, dwl 920 Stockton
Fordahl James, collector, dwl E s Stockton bet Vallejo and Green
Forde Timothy, butcher, E s Ninth bet Bryant and Brannan, dwl 126 Dora

FORDHAM *(R. B.)* & JENNINGS *(C. B.)* jobbing and retail grocers, NE cor Front and Jackson, dwl 1210 Mason
Fore Eliza E. (widow) lodgings, 73 Natoma
Forest Antoine, chancellor French consulate, dwl Union Club Rooms
Forest, see Forrest
Forester E. S. Mrs. special primary assistant Powell Street School, dwl 830 Pacific
Forester Henry B. book keeper with Edmund Marks & Co. dwl 614 Powell
Forks of Matole Oil Company (Humboldt) office 519 Montgomery
Formant Francis, tailor with I. Eisenberg, dwl S s Pacific bet Kearny and Dupont
Formhals Ferdinand, tinsmith with Ellis Ayers, dwl Bitter's Hotel
Forner Jacob B. policeman, City Hall, dwl 420 Green
Fornos John, laborer, dwl NW cor Davis and Chambers
Forrest C. T. *(Russell & Co.)* office 509 Clay
Forrest James M. *(Pacific Straw Works Co.)* dwl 150 Perry
Forrest William D. salesman, 607 Sac, dwl 605 Sac
Forrest W. L. clerk, dwl 873 Mission
Forrester Annie Miss, seamstress, dwl 749 Market
Forrester James, gas fitter with McNally & Hawkins, dwl 5 Stanford
Forrester John F. conductor, Omnibus R. R. Co
Forrester Peter, dwl Stanford bet Townsend and Brannan
Forret *(Jacob)* & Mortier *(Edward)* restaurant, 620 Pacific
Forsaith *(Edward W.)* & Tyler *(George W.)* produce commission, 309 Com, dwl 639 Market
Forsbery William, blacksmith, dwl 334 Third, rear
Forster Frederick, dwl Original House
Forster M. F. dwl Original House
Forster Peter B. *(J. J. Ayers & Co.)* dwl W s Shotwell bet Twentieth and Twenty-First
Forster William, driver, A. R. C. Ice Co. dwl S s Broadway bet Front and Davis
Forsyth *(Alexander)* Morrison *(A.)* & Co. *(John Thompson)* wood and coal, Howard St. Wharf, dwl 47 Tehama
Forsyth George C. *(Forsyth & Son)* dwl N s Jessie between Seventh and Eighth
Forsyth George W. with S. F. Cotton Factory, dwl SE cor Third and King
Forsyth William A. C. tinsmith with W. W. Walmsley, dwl N s Jessie bet Seventh and Eighth
Forsyth *(William K.)* & Son *(George C. Forsyth)* boots and shoes, 803 Market, dwl N s Jessie bet Seventh and Eighth
Fortayon Peter, workman with P. Somps, Visitacion Valley
FORTHMAN JOHN A. liquor saloon, 160 Stewart
Fortmann Frederick, hatter, dwl 323 Pine
FORTMANN FREDERICK, proprietor Pacific Brewery, 271 Tehama
Fortmann Henry, Western House, 138 and 140 Stewart
Fortuna G. & S. M. Co. office 611 Clay
Fortune H. W. mining stocks, office 605 Montgomery, dwl 31 Perry
Fortune James A. salesman, 223 Cal, dwl 1023 Post
Fortune Lewis (col'd) waiter, steamer Chrysopolis
Fortune Silver M. Co. office 8 Stevenson House
Fortune, No. 2, Silver M. Co. office 8 Stevenson House
Fosbery William, blacksmith, S. F. & San José R. R. Co. dwl W s Third bet Harrison and Folsom
Foss Christian W. carpenter, dwl 272 Clementina, rear
Foss Henry, drayman, cor Sacramento and Davis, dwl cor Second and Brannan
Foss Hiram C. carpenter, dwl 605 Sacramento
Foss Levi, assessor Virginia City, dwl 214 Powell

Foss Oscar *(Perkins & F.)* dwl 606 Kearny
Fossard Maria Miss, dwl 6 Valparaiso
Fossas Pedro, compositor, Courrier de San Francisco, dwl 704 Dupont
Fossat Charles, garden, Presidio Road S s Lagoon
Foster Albert, captain steamer Chrysopolis, office NE cor Front and Jackson, dwl 408 Lombard
Foster Alden B. clerk, Pier 2 Stewart, dwl W s Howard bet Twelfth and Thirteenth
Foster Charles C. mining, dwl Railroad House
Foster C. H. ship carpenter, dwl 66 First
Foster Daniel, shipwright, 164 Stewart, dwl Beale Place
Foster Edward, engineer and machinist, dwl 240 Green
Foster Edward M, cook, Union Restaurant, Brannan St. Bridge
Foster Edwin J. dwl Cliff House, 6 miles from City Hall
Foster Elisha F. clerk with Wilson & Bro. dwl 522 California
Foster George J. printer, dwl S s Tyler nr Polk
Foster Henry A. ship carpenter, dwl 33 Tehama
Foster Herman, carpenter, dwl 36 Rousch
Foster J. clerk, dwl 522 Dupont
Foster James, salesman with William F. Burke, 301 Montgomery, dwl 522 Dupont
Foster John R. with John A. Shaber, 622 Market
Foster J. S. dwl What Cheer House
FOSTER JUNIUS G. proprietor Cliff House, terminus S. F. & Point Lobos Road, 6 miles from City Hall
Foster M. Miss, private school, 124 Perry
Foster Nellie Miss, with Julius Merzbach, 412 Kearny, dwl 1017 Powell
Foster Robert, boiler maker, Vulcan Iron Works, dwl Clementina nr Fourth
Foster Samuel, book keeper with F. R. Amos & Co. dwl 505 O'Farrell
Foster Samuel F. dwl 633 Market
Foster Thomas (col'd) waiter, steamer Chrysopolis, dwl 5 Broadway
Foster Whitney, printer, dwl 809 Mission
Foster William, workman, S. F. & P. Sugar Co. dwl Gordon bet Folsom and Harrison
Foster William M. dwl 522 California
Foster William W. clerk, U. S. Clothing Depôt, 34 California, dwl 754 Folsom
Foster Winthrop F. carpenter, dwl W s Fillmore bet McAllister and Tyler
Foster W. W. clerk, dwl 129 Third
Fosum Levert, carpenter, dwl Potrero Nuevo
Fotheringham John, pattern maker, Vulcan Iron Works, dwl 650 Mission
Foubert Eugene, jeweler with E. Perrochon, dwl 343 Tehama
Fouchery Benoit, engineer, dwl 128 St. Mark Place
Fougerou Nicholas *(Patrick Kearns & Co.)* dwl 36 Fourth
Foujere G. Charles, engineer, Market St. R. R. Co. dwl E s Valencia between Fifteenth and Sixteenth
Foulds Andrew, seaman, dwl 132 Folsom
Fouler J. S. builder, dwl 652 Market
Foulk Levi, clothing, 261 Third
Foulkes Thomas *(Agard, F. & Co.)* res London
Foulon Louis, jeweler, dwl E s Larkin bet Broadway and Vallejo
Fountain John, janitor Industrial School, Old Ocean House Road
Fountain John Mrs. matron Industrial School, Old Ocean House Road
Fountain Washington A. tobacconist, dwl Point Lobos
Fouque Jules, carpenter, dwl 532 Broadway
Fouratt Enos, pilot, stm Yosemite, dwl 1706 Mason
Fouratt John R. pilot, stm Julia, dwl 1706 Mason
FOURGEAUD V. J. physician, office 325 Bush, dwl 514 Sutter

Fourness Dyson, machinist with E. F. Steen, dwl 159 Tehama
Fousbee Thomas, painter, dwl 17 Third
Fouts Daniel L. dwl 1023 Powell
FOUTS MARIA Mrs. millinery, 1018 Stockton, dwl 1023 Powell
Foutz Elizabeth Miss, domestic, 607 Sutter
Fouz William *(Mangels & Co.)* dwl 721 Lombard
Fowkes Richard, porter, Cunningham's Warehouse, dwl 318 Taylor
Fowler Albert G. contractor, office 413 Sansom, dwl 718 Union
Fowler Fred R. with Church & Clark, dwl N s Stevenson bet Seventh and Eighth
Fowler George, seaman, dwl 54 Sacramento
Fowler George H. foreman with Church & Clark, dwl N s Stevenson bet Seventh and Eighth
Fowler James (col'd) seaman, dwl W s Bower Place
Fowler John, office NE cor Clay and Front, resides Oakland
Fowler John B. with Addison Martin & Co. dwl 718 Union
Fowler L. T. Miss, assistant, Lincoln School, dwl 915 Market
Fowler Monmouth H. druggist with R. H. McDonald & Co. dwl Third nr Bryant
Fowler Thomas S. chop house, SE cor Third and King
Fowler William C. bar keeper, Hayes Park
Fox Charles, bar keeper, 314 Montgomery
Fox Charles J. *(Tay, Brooks & Backus)* res New York
Fox Charles N. president Western Pacific R. R. Co. office 409 California *(and Campbell, Fox & Campbell)* res Redwood City
Fox Eliza T. (widow) dwl 226 Ritch
Fox Emma Mrs. dwl 10 O'Farrell
Fox Hannah Miss, domestic, 723 O'Farrell
Fox H. B. surgical and mechanical dentist, 515 East
FOX *(Henry A.)* & PORTER *(David)* wholesale and retail wines and liquors, 531 and 533 Clay, dwl 520 Third
Fox Henry L. book keeper with Rockwell, Coye & Co. dwl 1109 Howard
Fox Horatio N. carpenter, dwl 419 Harrison
Fox Johanna Miss, domestic, 933 Bush
Fox John, hostler, 431 California, bds 14 Sutter
Fox John, laborer, dwl 35 Sacramento
Fox John, varnisher with Boyd, McAuliffe & Co. 412 Pine
Fox John J. gas fitter, dwl 144 Natoma
Fox John W. physician, office and dwl 643 Com
Fox Leroy, clerk, dwl 10 O'Farrell
Fox Louis, waiter, SE cor California and Sansom
Fox Michael, miner, dwl 309 Minna
Fox Morris, fruits, S s Union bet Stock and Powell
Fox Peter F. engineer, dwl N s Bernard bet Taylor and Jones
Fox Philip, porter with Redington & Co. dwl 113 Shipley
Fox Richard, janitor Odd Fellows Hall, 325 Mont
Fox Thomas, coppersmith with William Neil, dwl 4 Priest
Fox Thomas H. night inspector, C. H. dwl 145 Fourth
Fox W. actor, Maguire's Opera House
Fox William C. hide curer, dwl 256 Tehama, rear
Foy John J. drayman, dwl 417 Folsom
Foy William, laborer, dwl NW cor Sac and Drumm
Foye Charles E. captain schooner Brilliant, office Pier 11 Stewart, dwl 16 Ellis
Foye Frank, wines and liquors, W side Battery bet Green and Union
Foye George W. captain schooner Mendocino, office Pier 11
Foye Jane R. dwl with A. Holmes, W s First Avenue bet Fifteenth and Sixteenth
Foye Warren, seaman, dwl 238 Stewart
Foye William, house carpenter, dwl W s Sansom bet Filbert and Greenwich

Frae John, laborer, dwl cor Douglass and Seventeenth
Frael Eunice Miss, domestic, 127 Ellis
Frael Maurice, boiler maker, dwl 46 Clementina
Fraher Philip, laborer, dwl 40 Clara, rear
Franc Alexander, liquor saloon, 1021 Dupont
France Henry, iron molder, dwl 242 Fremont
Francesca Fortunato, fisherman, 16 Italian Fish Market
Francioni Marco, engineer, 706 Sansom
Francis, (D. B.) Valentine (S. D.) & Co. book and job printing, 517 Clay, dwl 102 St. Mark Place
Francis George, deck hand, stm Cornelia
Francis George G. clerk with Rockwell, Coye & Co. dwl 507 Powell
Francis Henry dwl E s Mason nr Green
Francis Henry, foreman Excelsior Restaurant, dwl 668 Mission
Francis H. L. employé I. H. Cohn & Son, 607 Sansom, dwl N W cor Ellis and Stockton
Francis James C. (col'd) bootblack with Henderson & Brown, dwl Auburn
Francis John (col'd) cook, stm Chrysopolis, dwl 200 Front
Francis John, marble mason, dwl 25 Fifth
Francis John H. workman, S. F. & P. Sugar Co. dwl N s Boyd nr Chesley
Francis John M. principal Deaf, Dumb, and Blind Asylum, SE cor Fifteenth and Mission
Francis Joseph, bakery, 1412 Dupont
Francis Joseph, shoe maker, N s Market nr East, dwl NW cor Montgomery and Vallejo
Francis J. W. book keeper, dwl 102 St. Mark Place
Francis Robert C. (col'd) hairdressing saloon, 234 Bush, dwl 555 Howard
Francis Samuel, upholsterer, dwl 272 Clementina
Francis William, bar keeper, 14 Clay
Francis William, laborer, dwl Spear nr Harrison
Francisco Matthew & Co. (Joseph Vrangnizan) liquors and coffee, SE cor Pacific and Davis
FRANCO AMERICAN COMMERCIAL CO. office and salesroom 215 Bush
Franco Americana S. M. Co. office 652 Washington
Franco Charles, express wagon, 626 Market
Francoeur Germain, compositor, Alta California, dwl Jackson bet Hyde and Larkin
François Adele Mme. dress maker, dwl 516 Market
François Charles, seeds, 605 San, dwl 516 Market
FRANCONI LOUIS, mining secretary, office 804 Montgomery room 16, dwl 718 Filbert
Frank Abraham, drayman, dwl 420 Post
Frank Abraham L. book keeper with Scholle & Bros. dwl 640 Folsom
Frank August, butcher, dwl 1007 Folsom bet Sixth and Seventh
Frank August Wm. sign painter, 507 Kearny, dwl 511 Dupont
Frank Charles, German Bakery, Belden nr Pine, dwl 326 Kearny
Frank Ephraim, clothing, 213 Pacific, dwl 207 Pac
Frank Francis, milk ranch, dwl 1012 Kearny
Frank Frederick, dwl What Cheer House
Frank Henry, furniture and bedding, 217 Com
Frank Henry L. clerk with Michael Reese, dwl 717 Stockton
Frank Isaac, stock dealer, dwl 764 Folsom
Frank Isaac Capt. solicitor Phœnix Insurance Co. 605 Commercial, dwl 748 Folsom
Frank Jacob, baker with William Stohlman
Frank Jacob J. salesman, 406 Sacramento, dwl E s Second nr Market
Frank James, waterman, 609 Market
Frank John, clerk, 50 and 51 Washington Market, dwl 707 Mission nr Third
Frank John, flour packer, dwl S s Howard bet First and Fremont
Frank John, seaman, dwl 54 Sacramento
Frank Joseph, merchant, office Falkenstein & Co. 315 Clay, dwl 615 Taylor

Frank (Joseph H.) & Co. importers and jobbers stationery, 406 Sacramento, dwl 1713 Stockton
Frank Morris, salesman, 316 Sacramento, dwl 407 O'Farrell bet Taylor and Jones
Frank Moses J. clerk, 413 Sacramento
Frank Reinhard, milk ranch, nr Bay View Park
Frank Wm. oysters, dwl NW cor Kearny and Broadway
Frankel Solomon, drayman, cor Jackson and Front, dwl Clementina bet Second and Third
Frankenau S. A. (Seller, Frankenau & Co. Portland, Oregon) off 217 Front, dwl 329 O'Farrell
Frankenberg Joseph, saddles and harness, 1108 Dupont
Frankenburg Julius, shoe making, 20 Post
Frankenheimer Joseph (Menges & F.) dwl 30 Ellis
Frankenthal Max, salesman with Adelsdorfer Bros. dwl 314 Post
Frankl L. merchant, office 321 Washington
Franklin Abram, pawnbroker, 809 Kearny
Franklin Adolph, proprietor Government House Restaurant, 514 Washington, dwl 430 Union
Franklin Albert, porter, steamer Orizaba
FRANKLIN BOOK AND JOB PRINTING OFFICE, Frank Eastman proprietor, 415 Wash
Franklin Charles, laborer, Bay Sugar Refinery, dwl W s Calhoun bet Union and Green
Franklin Edward. real estate, office 7 Montgomery Block, dwl 626 California
Franklin G. clothing, 511 Davis
Franklin Hotel, Hugh Curran proprietor, SE cor Sansom and Pacific
Franklin House, Cornelius Maloney proprietor, SW cor Sansom and Broadway
Franklin James, clerk, dwl 631 Mission
Franklin John, clerk, dwl 809 Kearny
Franklin Louis M. book keeper, dwl 20 Sansom
Franklin M. J. (Klaus, Bowman & Co.) dwl 728 Mission
Franklin Roderick P. Melter and Refiner's Department U. S. Branch Mint, dwl 522 Howard
Franklin Stephen, corresponding clerk, Bank California, dwl 115 Stockton
Frank's Building, Brenham Place, W s Plaza
Franks Frederick, actor Maguire's Opera House
Franks George, seaman, dwl 54 Sacramento
Fransen John, ship carpenter, dwl S s Francisco bet Taylor and Jones
Fransky George, dwl 77 Stevenson House
Frantz Henry, book keeper, dwl SW cor Dupont and Bay
Franz Charles C. carpenter, Independence H. & L. Co. No. 3
Frapolli Batista (Scalmanini & F.) dwl S s Filbert bet Taylor and Jones
FRASER (A. Edward) & CO. (John Boyle and Charles A. Sankey) mercantile agency and collecting office, 326 Clay cor Battery, dwl 857 Folsom
Fraser Clinton W. salesman with I. C. Mayer & Son, 129 Montgomery
Fraser Donald, dwl Union Club Rooms
Fraser Henry, seaman, dwl 60 Clay
Fraser Henry A. carriage maker with Albert Folsom, dwl Rincon Hill
FRASER JOSEPH, agent Rubber Clothing Co. 118 Montgomery
Fraser Josephine Mrs. dwl 102 Dupont
Fraser Thomas, porter, 106 Battery, dwl 211 Ritch
Frater Joseph D. deck hand, steamer Julia
Fratinger A. M. salesman, 626 Sacramento
Fratres Manuel, deck hand steamer Sacramento
Frau Tomaso, fish, 11 Washington Fish Market
Frauenholz Philip, brewer, dwl 624 Vallejo
Frauley John, laborer, dwl 1413 Kearny
Frawley Frederick, laborer, dwl Franklin House, SW cor Sansom and Broadway
Frawley Patrick, laborer with Nichols & Co. bds Franklin House

Frawley Richard, driver, North Beach, & M. R.;R. Co.
Frawley William, dwl NE cor Geary and Leav
Frazackerley Joseph, laborer, dwl 135 Minna
Frazee Charles D. clerk with Geo. S. Dickey, NW cor Third and Folsom
Frazer James S. molder, dwl NE cor Bryant and First
Frazer Joseph, dwl 407 Stevenson
Frazer Joseph J. contractor, dwl 740 Mission
Frazer Robert S. workman with Stratton Bros. dwl 28 Ritch
Frazer William A. salesman with Carle & Gorley, dwl 326 Clay
Frazier S. dwl SW cor Kearny and Pacific
Frazier Thomas, truckman with I. H. Cohn & Son, dwl NW cor Montgomery and Sutter
Frechette John, meat market, 735 Pacific
Frechette Joseph, carpenter, bds 737 Pacific
Frechette Louis, carpenter with Pratt & Jacobs, 118 Washington
Frederic Louisa Mme. music teacher, 712 Wash.
Frederick Charles A. gilder, dwl 422 Filbert
Frederick (*Valentine*) & Lorber (*John*) Central Beer Saloon, NE cor Pine and Kearny, dwl 1 St. Mary
Frederick William, groceries and liquors, dwl SW cor Battery and Broadway
Fredericks John, tailor, dwl 625 Pacific, rear
Fredericks William, local policeman, dwl 217 Third
Fredoya H. painter, 571 Mission
Frederickson Anthony H. cook Empire State Restaurant, dwl 916 Montgomery
Free Benjamin, apprentice with Morris Greenberg
FREE WILLIAM H. machinist, hose maker, and superintendent corporation yard S. F. Fire Department, 15 and 17 First, dwl NE cor Lombard and Jones
Freeborn I. S. mining, dwl Tahama House
Freeborn James, merchant, dwl Lick House
Freeborn William, butcher, NW cor Jessie and Ecker
Freeborn Wm. H. Star Market, NW cor Kearny and Union
Freelon Thomas G. (*Byrne & F.*) attorney at law, office 28 Court Block, dwl N s Greenwich nr Stockton
Freem J. A. produce, 2 Occidental Market, dwl 72 Natoma
Freeman Benjamin H. surveyor, Union Insurance Co. office 416 California, dwl NW cor Dupont and California
FREEMAN B. H. & CO. (*Geo. W. B. McDonald*) stair builders, scroll sawyers, and wood turners, Chace's Mill, SW cor Market and Beale, dwl 603 Dupont
Freeman Calvin N. mariner, dwl E s Howard bet Twenty-First and Twenty-Second
Freeman Charles, bar keeper, 18 Clay
Freeman Charles, confectioner, dwl 601 Stockton
Freeman Charles N. captain, dwl 516 Folsom
Freeman Charles W. printer with Charles F. Robbins, dwl E s Polk bet Bush and Pine
Freeman Edward, shoe maker, 646 Commercial
Freeman Elisha, captain bark Helen W. Almy, office 405 Front, dwl 516 Folsom
Freeman Emanuel S. salesman with M. Heller & Bros. dwl 812 Howard
Freeman George, porter with Wormser Bros. dwl SE cor Kearny and Union
Freeman Henry, painter, dwl 371 Jessie
Freeman Isadora (*Miss Hubbard and Miss Freeman*) dwl 23½ Second
Freeman (*J. A.*) & Co. (*William F. Wells*) fruits, etc, 2 Occidental Market, dwl 212 Second
Freeman (*Jacob*) & Wrin (*Michael J.*) stoves, 342 Third, dwl S s Hayes bet Laguna and Octavia
Freeman James, cook steamer Senator
Freeman J. E. civil engineer, dwl 327 Bush

Freeman John, laborer, dwl 60 Stewart
Freeman John, seaman, dwl 44 Sacramento
Freeman Josiah, dwl 72 Natoma
Freeman Louis, tailor, 34 Sutter
Freeman Peter, hairdresser, dwl 236 Stewart
Freeman Thomas, laborer, Bay Sugar Refinery, dwl 30 Fremont
Freeman Thomas, stevedore, dwl 23 Baldwin Court
Freeman William (col'd) cook, steamer John L. Stephens, dwl 3 Dupont Place
Freeman William, job cart, 507 Washington, dwl 631 Broadway
Freeman William L. compositor, Alta California
Frees Daniel, machinist, Pacific Foundry, dwl Isthmus House
Freese Christian A. stevedore, dwl W s Main bet Folsom and Harrison
Freeser Christoph, boatman, dwl 1816 Powell
Freeston William, tinsmith, dwl 126 St. Mark Place
Frei Andrew (*Seaborn & F.*) dwl 409 Mission
Freidel Frederick, shoe maker, 104 Stewart
Freidle Rudolph, peddler, dwl 516 Pacific
Freie Frey, cutler with Will & Fink, dwl 205 San
Freie Henry, groceries and liquors, SE cor Sacramento and Dupont
Freiermuth George A. carrier, Morning Call, dwl E s Carlos Place
Freiney J. P. laborer, Vulcan Iron Works
Freiter Peter (col'd) cook, steamer Chrysopolis
Freley Eilert, cook, dwl 26 Stewart
Fremory Michel, porter, dwl 520 O'Farrell
French A. with F. Smith & Co. 210 Sacramento, res Oakland
FRENCH BOARD UNDERWRITERS, J. E. René agent, office 716 Montgomery
French Charles H. book keeper with Morse & Co. dwl 22 Kearny
French Enoch, fruits, SW cor Fifth and Stevenson
French George, lab, What Cheer House Restaurant
French George W. carpenter, dwl W s Leavenworth, bet Vallejo and Broadway
FRENCH HOSPITAL, S s Bryant bet Fifth and Sixth
French Jane Mrs. dwl 411 Green
French John B. teamster, Pier 7 Stewart
FRENCH JOSEPH M. (*French & Gilman, Dalles, Oregon*) office 419 Front, dwl 25 Hawthorne
French Louis, engineer, dwl 820 Dupont
French (*Moses B.*) & Hall (*R. H.*) butter, cheese, and eggs, 7 and 8 Washington Market, dwl 812 California
FRENCH MUTUAL BENEVOLENT SOCIETY (Société Francaise de Bienfaisance Mutuelle) office 649 Sacramento
French Norman G. mining secretary, dwl Tehama House
FRENCH SAVINGS AND LOAN SOCIETY, office 533 Commercial
French Stephen, carpenter, dwl 516 Greenwich
French Wheeler N. drayman, 200 Front, dwl 30 Perry
French William, cartman, dwl 117 Folsom, rear
Frenchman D. with S. S. Culverwell, 29 Fremont
Frere James, vegetable garden, W s Mission nr Twenty-Sixth
Frere Julius, gardener, dwl W s Fillmore nr Geary
Frese Christian, baker, dwl 325 Pine
Frese Emil, clerk with Redington & Co. dwl 318 Clementina
Frese John, clerk with Christoph Nobmann
Freshmood Charles, baker, American Bakery, dwl 1027 Dupont
Fretillaire Louis, carpenter, dwl Meek Place
Fretz F. H. (*Schmidt & F.*) dwl 644 Clay
Fretz R. S. dwl 1 Harlan Place
Freud Morris, fruits, 124 Second
Freudenberg Mathias, with Schultz & Von Bargen, dwl 905 Larkin

Freund Frank M. barber, 430 Third, dwl 144 Silver
FREUND (Philip) & CO. (Adolph Falk) blank books and stationery, 511 Clay, dwl 333 Geary
Frey Andreas, wood carver, dwl 315 Montgomery
Frey Catherine Miss, domestic, 710 Folsom
Frey Charles, cutler, dwl 205 Sansom
Frey Henry J. portrait painter, 649 Clay
Frey Jacob, hairdresser, dwl W s Clara nr Bush
Frey Samuel, cigars and tobacco, 46 Fourth, dwl 46 Jessie
Frey Simon, cigars, 46 Fourth, dwl 260 Jessie
FREY WILLIAM A. musical instruments, fancy goods, etc. 404 Kearny
Friand Jennie Miss, laundry, 807 Howard
Frick Alfred, dwl E s Second Avenue bet Sixteenth and Seventeenth
Frick Augustus, stair builder, Delgardo Place, dwl NE cor Hyde and Green
Frick D. chemist, dwl W s Valencia bet Sixteenth and Seventeenth
Fricken Charles, laborer, Bay Sugar Refinery, dwl 11 Pacific
Frickens Henry, shooting gallery, North Beach, dwl Hall Court
Fricker John H. dwl 1017 Kearny
Fricker Louis, fringe maker with Daniel Norcross, dwl 114 Fourth
Frickner Charles, sausage maker, dwl SW cor Dupont and Broadway
Frid John, dwl 1822 Stockton
Fridach P. fruits, dwl 619 Davis
Fried David, hairdresser with Charles Storm, dwl 247 Stevenson
Fried Jacob, merchant, dwl SE cor Stockton and Lombard
Friedberg (Abraham) & Rosenshine (Matthias) cigar manufacturers, 214 Pacific
Friedberg Charles, book keeper, dwl 735 Pine
Friedberg M. carpenter, dwl 1514 Dupont
Friedberg Morris, cigars, 56 Third
Friedricks Ferdinand, salesman, 14 Third, dwl 228 Sutter
Friedhofer Aug. cooper, Philadelphia Brewery
Friedlander Adolph (Friedlander Bros.) dwl 424 Sacramento
Friedlander Brothers (Meyer and Adolph) dry goods, 628 Sacramento, dwl 20 Sansom
Friedlander Herman (Triest & F.) res New York
Friedlander (Herman) & Bastheim (Joseph) fancy goods, 8 Montgomery, dwl 748 Folsom
FRIEDLANDER I. commission merchant, 112 and 114 California, dwl 30 South Park
Friedlander Julius, salesman, 414 Commercial
Friedlander M. dry goods, 2 Mont, dwl 20 San
Friedlander Philip, cigars and tobacco, SW cor Market and Fourth, dwl 822 Mission
Friedlander Samuel, clerk, 2 Montgomery, dwl 424 Sacramento
Friedlander Samuel J. salesman, 218 Battery, dwl 20 Sansom
Friedlander William, jeweler, 41 Third, dwl 619 Mission
Friedle Rodolph, clerk, SE cor Montgomery and California, dwl 516 Pacific
Friedman George, butcher, NE cor Union and Mason
Friedman Henry, book keeper with H. Levi & Co. dwl 1206 Stockton
Friedman Isaac, fruit and vegetable peddler, dwl Larkin bet Pacific and Broadway
Friedman Jacob, drayman, 505 Clay, dwl W s Leavenworth bet Sacramento and California
Friedman Joseph S. dwl W s Downey nr Bryant
Friedman Nathan, dwl St. Nicholas Hotel
Friedman Simon, with Augustus Strasser, dwl 526 Vallejo
Friedman Solomon, stationery, 1108 Stockton
Friedmann Edward (Rosenbaum & F.) dwl 711 Leavenworth

Friedrich John G. groceries and liquors, SE cor Sixteenth and Second Avenue
Friel Abraham, printer, Alta job office, dwl 113 Kearny
Friel Anna Mrs. dwl 1113 Kearny
Friel (William) & Mann (Jacob) stoves and tinware, 69 Fourth
Friel William H. cooper with Lyon & Co. dwl 1113 Kearny
Friend Charlotte Mrs. dwl 415 Powell, rear
Friend Frank, miner, dwl 315 Pine
Friend John I. captain ship Caroline Reed, 212 Clay
Friend William H. accountant with Armes & Dallam, dwl 82 Everett
Fries Ellen, domestic, dwl 14 Essex
Fries Otto, brewer, Philadelphia Brewery
Friesenhausen John, groceries and liquors, 220 Sutter
Frieser John B. carpenter, dwl 57 Sacramento
Frincke Louis, paper hangings, 423 Bush
FRINK GEORGE W. proprietor Tehama House, 410 California, dwl 118 Perry
Frink Henry, workman with H. Schwerin, Visitacion Valley
Frink W. R. manuf chemicals, dwl 32 Silver
Frisbee Filbert (col'd) dwl Hinckley Place
Frisbee John, express wagon, cor Washington and Montgomery
Frisbee W. B. & Co. (H. M. Bosworth) music and musical instruments, 3 Montgomery Masonic Temple, dwl 10 O'Farrell Alley
Frisch Henry (David Levitzky & Co.) dwl 35 Natoma
Frisch John G. merchant, dwl W s Taylor bet Union and Filbert
Frisch John W. groceries and liquors, SE cor Fifth and Mission
Frischmuth Carl, baker, dwl 717 Pacific
Frisher John, dwl What Cheer House
Frishholz M. boots and shoes, 546 Washington
Frisius Antonio, dwl 166 Silver
Frisius Frederick A. importer and commission merchant (successor to M. Frisius & Co.) office 524 Washington, dwl 784 Folsom
Frisk P. Gustave, machinist, Union Foundry, dwl 44 Sacramento
Frit Igenloub, workman, St. Mary's College
Fritas Peter, workman with Joseph Silva
Fritch George, clerk with James R. Doyle, dwl 6 Martha Place
Fritsch George, cooper, S. F. & P. Sugar Co. dwl N s Harrison nr Eighth
Fritsch J. Eureka Hose Co. No. 4
Fritz H. W. clerk with Charles McCormick, 408 Market, dwl Original House
Fritz Casper, laborer, dwl 24 Howard Court
Fritz D. H. blacksmith with Charles Steinweg, dwl 313 Geary
Fritz John, miner, dwl E s Rassette Place No. 2
Fritz Samuel, dwl 5 Hardie Place
Frixen August, boot maker, 426 Dupont
Frodsham Edward, flour packer, dwl NE cor Dupont and Francisco
Frodsham John, watch maker, dwl 531 Greenwich
Froell Conrad, shaving saloon, NW cor Dupont and Clay
Frohling Amelia (widow) dwl 464 Clementina
Frohmann Susmann, boots and shoes, 156 Third
Fromheim William, groceries and liquors, NW cor Townsend and Third
Fromm William, merchant, dwl 623 Dupont
FRONT STREET MISSION & OCEAN R. R. CO. office 529 Clay
FRONTIER (Pierre) & DEVIERCY (Engene) (and Otto Wiedero & Co.) manufacturing jewelers, 740 Commercial, dwl W s Valencia bet Sixteenth and Seventeenth
Frontman Emile, cook, Occidental Hotel
Froomberg Abram (Froomberg Bros.) dwl 312½ Minna

Froomberg Bros. *(Isaac and Abram)* auctioneers, 813 Kearny and clothing 419 Commercial, dwl 312½ Minna
Frost Charles, bar keeper, dwl 1027 Dupont
Frost Christian, laborer, dwl 511 Green
Frost C. L. Miss, adjuster, U. S. Branch Mint, dwl 113 Ellen
Frost Frank F. book keeper, 532 California, dwl 116 Sansom
Frost Henry, seaman, bds 7 Washington
Frost *(Horatio)* & Richards *(Calvin)* house and sign painters, 13 Post, dwl 635 Sutter
Fruchey J. C. clerk, 624 Commercial, dwl Coso House
Fruchtnicht John, Eureka Saloon, 200 Stewart, dwl 51 Fifth
Fruhling Gottleib, garden, S s Presidio Road nr Scott
Fruhling William, garden, S s Presidio Road nr Steiner
Frumbeler Louis, coppersmith with Locke & Montague, 112 Battery
Fraud F. M. hairdresser, dwl 352 Third
Fry Cary H. Maj. paymaster U. S. A. 724 Washington, dwl Occidental Hotel
Fry Louis, baker, dwl 836 Mission
Fry William, butcher, dwl 63 Minna
Fryer William, drayman, 310 Front
Fuche Louis, tinsmith, dwl 6 Virginia Place
Fuchs Susan Miss, domestic with Louis Gerstle
Fudge Henry, carpenter, dwl 116 Sansom •
Fuegelesberger Andrew, wood and coal, SE cor Broadway and Kearny, dwl W s Kearny bet Broadway and Pacific
Fuentes Charles, carriage painter with R. S. Eells & Co. dwl 508 Broadway
Fugaze John F. barber, 509 Kearny, dwl 329 Bdwy
Fuhr Charles A. furniture, bedding, and upholstery, 626 Market
Fuhrman Adolph, wire worker with H. T. Graves, dwl 26 Dupont
Fuhrman Henry, tailor, 26 Dupont
Fuld Fannie, domestic, dwl 40 Fourth
Fulda Henry C. apprentice, Golden State Iron Works, dwl 80 Everett
Fulda Lamartine, cooper, California Wine Cooperage Co. dwl 80 Everett
FULDA MARTIN, cooper, California Wine Cooperage Co. SW cor Commercial and Drumm, dwl 80 Everett
Fulford Robert, compositor, Varieties, dwl 726 Bdwy
Fullam Edward, molder, Vulcan Iron Works, dwl 3 Tehama
Fullam Thomas, workman, S. F. & P. Sugar Co. dwl 146 Clara
Fullard William, shipmaster, SW cor Market and Stewart, dwl 55 Mission
Fuller Albert P. *(Geo. W. Menomy & Co.)* dwl N s Bush bet Dupont and Kearny
Fuller Alexander (col'dl porter, dwl N s Dupont Alley
Fuller Charles H. express wagon, cor Broadway and Davis, dwl N s Francisco bet Stockton and Powell
Fuller David, carpenter, dwl 615 Mission
Fuller E. J. meat market, NE cor Geary and Taylor, dwl SW cor Taylor and Post
Fuller Francis, agent Napa Soda, dwl 777 Market
Fuller Frederick O. policeman, City Hall, dwl NW cor O'Farrell and Leavenworth
Fuller George W. dwl 44 Belden Block
Fuller Jennie (widow) dwl 630 Mission
Fuller John (col'd) waiter, steamer Chrysopolis
Fuller Joseph G. dwl 1153 Mission
Fuller Josiah, mining Secretary, office 326 Clay, dwl 719 California
Fuller J. P. carpenter and builder, dwl 411 Tehama
Fuller *(J. W.)* & McCarty *(Dennis)* dancing academy, 727 Market, dwl 124 St. Mark Place
Fuller Mary Mrs. dress maker, 615 Mission

Fuller Orlando, furniture, dwl E s Stanford bet Townsend and Brannan
Fuller Rosalie (widow) dwl 1153 Mission
Fuller Thomas, harness maker with J. M. Hurlbutt & Co. dwl Central Place
FULLER *(William P.)* & HEATHER *(Seaton)* importers and jobbers paints, oils, glass, etc. 223 Front, dwl 335 Beale
Fullerton John, laborer, dwl 206 Harrison
Fulmer James G. wire worker with H. P. Graves, dwl 114 Kearny
Fulton Adonica, with Rodmond Gibbons & Co. dwl NW cor Shasta and Illinois
Fulton Alonzo, cook, 546 Clay, dwl 7 Central Place
Fulton David, machinist, Pacific Foundry, dwl 665 Mission
FULTON FOUNDRY, Hinckley & Co. proprietors, 45–49 First
Fulton James M. Oriental Meat Market, 451 East, dwl Pacific nr Larkin
Fulton J. J. hose and belt manuf, dwl 132 Townsend
Fulton John B. foreman spinning room S. F. Cordage Factory, dwl cor Iowa and Humboldt
Fulton John J. foreman Sixth St. Tannery, dwl 132 Townsend
Fulton Robert C. waiter, steamer Orizaba, dwl 3 Brown Alley
Fulton William, butcher, 80 Washington Market, dwl 106 O'Farrell
Fulton William G. grainer, 13 Post, dwl E s Park Avenue bet Bryant and Harrison
Fultz Augustus, stevedore, dwl Howard Engine House
Funded Debt Commissions, 1851, office NW cor Montgomery and Sacramento
Fung Sheuk (Chinese) physician, 744½ Washington
Funk C. C. sail maker, East bet Washington and Jackson, dwl 9 Washington
Funk J. B. dwl Original House
Funk *(Nicholas)* & Smith *(Henry C.)* fruits, 104 Pacific
Funkenstein J. importer and jobber dry goods, 308 California, dwl 35 O'Farrell
FUNKENSTEIN J. & CO. *(Fitel Phillips)* importers and jobbers wines and liquors, 323 California, dwl 35 O'Farrell
Funkenstein Julius, pawnbroker, 843 Dupont, dwl N s O'Farrell bet Stockton and Dupont
Funkenstein Peter, clerk, dwl 843 Dupont
Fuquay *(Franklin F.)* & Richardson *(S. S.)* house and sign painters, 19 Geary, dwl N s California Avenue nr Isabella
Furbush Ellis M. salesman, 542 Clay, dwl E s Taylor bet Filbert and Greenwich
Furbush Moses, dwl E s Taylor bet Filbert and Valparaiso
Furger Mary A. (widow) dwl 615 Mission
Furley John F. gold beater, 641 Commercial, dwl 8 Varenne
Furlong Andrew, Albion House 206 Stewart
Furlong George, rigger and stevedore, dwl S s Union bet Battery and Sansom
Furlong George I. carpenter, dwl 519 Mission
Furlong James, dwl 118 Shipley
Furlong James, mariner, dwl 206 Stewart
Furlong Joseph, butcher with R. O'Neill
Furlong Kate Miss, domestic, 11 O'Farrell
Furman M. H. Mrs. dwl 709 Stockton, rear
Furst Martin I. merchant, dwl 708 Post
Furstenthal Goodman R. traveling agent with I. S. Josephi & Co. dwl 15 Stockton
Furter Samuel with F. Tillman, dwl NE cor Pine and Montgomery
Fury Michael, cook, Lick House
Fusari *(Jacob)* & Gregovich *(Samuel)* fruits, NW cor California and Kearny
Fusilier Antoine, cook, 427 Sacramento
Fusilier John, groceries and liquors, SW cor Geary and Jones

Fuss Louis, waiter, dwl SW cor Dupont and Bdwy
Futter Jacob, tailor, 1210 Stockton
Fyfe Alexander, seaman, dwl 54 Sacramento

G

GABB William M. geologist, 90 Montgomery Block, res Oakland
Gabbs Priscilla Miss, music teacher, 209 Fourth
Gabbs William H. sawfiler, 116 Kearny bet Sutter and Post, dwl 209 Fourth
Gabel J. Jacob, laborer with John J. Hucks, dwl 911 Greenwich
Gabeldu (Samuel) & Meyer (Mathias) Glasgow Iron Co. 25 and 27 Fremont, dwl cor Larkin and Bush
Gabriel Delilah Miss, dwl W s Sixth nr Brannan
Gabriel Lagrave, workman with Bergerot & Co. dwl NW cor Sixteenth and Rhode Island
Cabriel William, plasterer, dwl 509 Dupont
Gadel F. Ephraim, dwl 32 Rousch
Gadhart Margaret, nurse, St. Mary's Hospital
Gadlin A. deck hand, steamer Clinton
Gadsby Elijah H. (Sweett & G.) dwl 25 Fifth
Gaeney Ellen Mrs. dwl W s Mary Lane nr Bush
Gaetz Daniel, shoe maker, 103 Stewart, dwl SE cor Dupont and Greenwich
Gaffney James, gas fitter, S. F. Gas Co. dwl 38 Jessie
Gaffney James, laborer, dwl 109 Clara
Gaffney Mathew, porter, 215 Clay
Gafke Heinrich, employé, Bay Sugar Refinery, dwl S s Allen bet Harrison and Folsom
Gage G. W. mariner, dwl 81 Natoma
Gage Helen E. Miss, branch Madame Demorest's, dress making and patterns, 12 Montgomery
Gage M. D. Mrs. dress making, 12 Montgomery
Gagen Philip, lab, dwl cor Mont and Greenwich
Gager James H. secretary, office Sacramento Valley R. R. Co. SE cor Montgomery and Jackson, dwl 8 Powell
Gagin Philip, laborer, dwl NE cor Montgomery and Greenwich
Gahagan Michael, coachman, dwl 1315 Mason
Gable Anton, bar keeper, 331 Kearny
Gaidon Mark, hatter, 239 Sutter
Gailey Calvin, office 24 Government House, res Alameda
GAILHARD BROTHERS (Charles and Gabriel) proprietors California Hotel, SE cor Commercial and Dupont
Gailhard Gabriel (Gailhard Brothers) dwl California Hotel
Gain Hugh, workman with John Henry
Gaines Charles, waiter, steamer Pacific, dwl 665 Mission
Gairdner Thomas, book keeper, 404 Battery, dwl 808 Folsom
Gaitely Delia Miss, domestic with John Clarke, W s Seventh nr Folsom
Galan Charles F. attorney at law, 9 Mont Block
Galavotti Elise, milliner, 725 Market
Galavotti Silvio, employé with G. Venard, 625 Front, dwl 725 Market
Galavotti Theodore, teacher dancing, 725 Market
Gale A. B. office 402 Front
Gale Albert, boiler maker with Coffey & Risdon
Gale Horatio, engineer, Market St. R. R. Co. bds with Theodore Schulte, W s Valencia bet Fifteenth and Sixteenth
GALE JEREMIAH W. & CO. (Robert Howe) commission fruit dealers, 409 and 411 Davis, dwl 1069 Howard
Gale John, carpenter, 17 Fourth
Gale Thomas M. dwl 210 O'Farrell
Gale, see Gayle
Galeano Antonio, cigar maker, dwl 711 Union, rear
Galigari Peter, gardener, nr Bay View Park

Gulinger Joseph (Kohlman & G.) dwl 637 Market
Galinger Meyer, salesman, 637 Market
Gallagher Andrew, wood sawyer, dwl 716 Folsom
Gallagher Ann (widow) dwl S s Sixteenth bet Valencia and Mission
Gallagher Anne, laundress, Cole's Laundry, 114 Dora
Gallagher Barney, boiler maker with Coffey & Risdon
Gallagher (Bernard) & Farren (John W.) wagon makers, 112 Bush, dwl SE cor Perry and Third
Gallagher Bridget (widow) dwl 415 Powell
Gallagher Bridget C. (widow) boarding, N s Fifteenth nr Howard
Gallagher Charles, carpenter, dwl 29 Louisa
Gallagher Charles, lab, dwl E s Chesley nr Harrison
Gallagher Charles, plumber, Kellogg, Hewston & Co.'s Refinery, dwl 1038 Folsom
Gallagher Charles, workman, S.F. & P. Sugar Co
Gallagher Charles F. blacksmith with Pollard & Carvill, dwl 333 Bush
Gallagher D. watchman, Custom House
Gallagher Daniel, deck hand, steamer Chrysopolis
Gallagher Daniel, lab, dwl N s Minna nr Seventh
Gallagher Edward, dwl 106 Tehama
Gallagher Edward A. T. repacker provisions, etc. 17 Beale, dwl 307 Bryant
Gallagher Edward M. (Noble & G.) dwl Reed Pl
Gallagher Ellen Miss, dress maker, 753 Mission, dwl Mission nr Sixth
Gallagher F. D. clerk, bds Pacific Temperance House
Gallagher Frank, hostler, 317 Pine
Gallagher Henry, carpenter, dwl SW cor Hyde and Filbert
Gallagher Hugh, produce, dwl NE cor California and Mason
GALLAGHER HUGH P. Rev. pastor St. Joseph's Church, W s Tenth bet Howard and Folsom
Gallagher (James) & Rodecker (Elias) blacksmiths and wheelwrights, 115 Pine, dwl 826 Harrison bet Fourth and Fifth
Gallagher James, laborer, dwl 29 Hunt
Gallagher James H. carriage painter with Gebhard & Boynton, dwl Leroy nr Sacramento
Gallagher (James J.) & Kenney (Peter) Excelsior Iron Works, 712 Sansom, dwl 721 Union
Gallagher J. B. collector S. F. Gas Co. dwl SE cor First and Natoma
Gallagher John, cooper with E. A. T. Gallagher, dwl W s Main bet Harrison and Folsom
Gallagher John, employé, Cosmopolitan Hotel
Gallagher John, laborer, dwl Beale Place
Gallagher John, laborer, dwl 24 Jessie
Gallagher John, plumber with McNally & Hawkins, dwl 420 Dupont
Gallagher John A. groceries and liquors, SE cor Shipley and Sixth
GALLAGHER, (John P.) WEED (Joseph H.) & WHITE (Samuel) California Brass Foundry, 125 First, dwl SW cor Hyde and Filbert
Gallagher Joseph A. Rev. pastor St. Joseph's Church, cor Tenth and Howard, dwl W s Tenth bet Howard and Folsom
Gallagher Margaret Miss, domestic, 703 Stockton
Gallagher Margaret Miss, domestic, W s Tenth bet Folsom and Howard
Gallagher Mary Miss, dwl with Rev. H. P. Gallagher, W s Tenth bet Howard and Folsom
Gallagher Mary Miss, domestic, 1910 Mason
Gallagher Mary Miss, domestic, 618 California
Gallagher Mary Miss, domestic, 1019 Folsom
Gallagher Michael, baker, dwl 717 Pacific
Gallagher Michael, warehouseman, U. S. Branch Mint
Gallagher Michael J. artist, dwl NW cor Dupont and Sutter
Gallagher (P.) & Gaven (P. T.) produce, 25 and 26 Occidental Market

Gallagher Patrick, driver, Central R. R. Co. dwl 19 Natoma

Gallagher Patrick, laborer. dwl 27 Commercial

Gallagher Patrick, paper hanger with George W. Clark, 500 Sansom

Gallagher Patrick, tailor, 229 Bush

Gallagher Peter, blacksmith, dwl N s Grove bet Franklin and Gough

Gallagher Robert, coppersmith with William Neil, dwl N s Sac bet Jones and Leavenworth

Gallagher S. C. *(Wheeler & G.)* 302 Montgomery

Gallagher Thomas, blacksmith helper with G. W. Knight & Co. dwl Brannan nr Ninth

Gallagher Thomas J. clerk with C. Temple Emmett, dwl 915 Jones

Gallagher William, marble cutter with L. R. Myers & Co. dwl cor Market and Mason

Gallagher William R. stock broker, office 728 Montgomery, dwl 200 Stockton

Gallagher Winifred Miss, dwl 302 Sutter

Gallagher Winifred (widow) dwl W s Leroy Place bet Sacramento and Clay

Gallahan Patrick, laborer, dwl SW cor Jessie and Annie

Galland Abraham, stock broker, office 411 Montgomery, dwl 522 California

Galland Benno, dry goods, 60 Third

Galland Francisca Mrs. dwl 253 Minna

Gallat Louis, carpenter, dwl 716 Pacific

Gallatin R. (widow) dwl 162 Jessie

Gallego R. C. bag maker, dwl 216 Commercial

Gallene John, carpenter, dwl S s Market bet Sixth and Seventh

Galleppi Felix, laborer with Pietro Juri, dwl W s Scott nr Turk

Gallick William, miner, dwl 261 Clary

Galligan Margaret Miss, dwl 736 Howard

Galligan Patrick, laborer, dwl NW cor Leroy Place and Sacramento

Gallovan Bridget Mrs. domestic, 420 Post

Galloway Edmund, broker, dwl 639 Market

Galloway Isabel (widow) dwl 308 Vallejo

Galloway James, fireman, stmr Princess

Galloway James D. ship joiner, 10 Broadway, dwl S s Broadway nr Taylor

GALLOWAY *(Joseph)* & BOOBAR *(E. C.)* pile drivers and dock builders, SW cor Stewart and Howard, dwl SW cor Powell and Vallejo

Galloway Nicholas, ship calker, dwl 34 Folsom

Galloway Robert M. book keeper, Pier 14 Stewart

Galloway William, captain stmr Amelia, dwl 211 Stevenson

Galloway William P. clerk with J. P. Lecount & Co. dwl 211 Stevenson

Galotti Carlo, liquor saloon, dwl 718 Stockton

Galpen Edward & Co. *(William A. Steele)* trunk manufacturers, 222 Sansom, dwl 741 Folsom bet Third and Fourth

Galtier Louis, with Vincenot & Gautier, 523 Mcht

Galvert James, laborer, dwl 49 Stevenson

Galvin Garet, tailor with C. A. Fletcher, dwl 9 Milton Place

Galvin James, laborer, Market St. R. R. Co. dwl S s Stevenson bet First and Second

Galvin Jeremiah, driver, dwl N s Hayes nr Polk

Galvin Jeremiah G. *(Barra & G.)* dwl 16 Natoma

Galvin Morris, engineer, dwl Original House

Galvin William, hostler with J. F. Willson, 807 Montgomery

Galway James, second lieut. Co. E Second Infantry C. V. Presidio

Gamage Armstrong, superintendent Salt Works, dwl Verona Place

Gamba Frances Mrs. proprietress Gamba House, 518 Sacramento

Gamba Louis, supt Gamba House, 518 Sacramento

Gambert Felix *(Lemoine, Gambert & Co.)* res San José

Gambill A. Jackson, mining stocks, dwl 615 Com

Gamble Alexander, mining, office 522 Montgomery, dwl 607 Harrison

GAMBLE JAMES, general superintendent United States and Pacific Telegraph Co. office 2 Armory Hall, dwl 1000 Pine cor Taylor

Gamble William H. receiving clerk, State Telegraph Co. dwl 740 Howard

Gamboa de Ackley Ignacia (widow) dwl 902 Jackson

Game Matthew F. mining secretary, dwl Brevoort House

Gammans George B. *(Dickinson & G.)* dwl 708 Stockton

Gammans Martin B. ship joiner, 14 Broadway, dwl SE cor Pacific and Stockton

Gammel Christian, wheelwright with Kimball & Co. dwl 219 Kearny

Gampper John, butcher, dwl 617 Jackson

Gancovich George, liquors, dwl 523 Davis

Ganegan William E. foreman Examiner, dwl 218 Minna

Gang David, carpenter, dwl N s Green bet Stockton and Powell

Gang Herman, carpenter, 636 Broadway

Ganion Eugene, cook, Russ House

Gannel James, laborer, bds N s Jessie bet Third and Fourth

Gannon Ann (widow) dwl 520 Stockton

Gannon Ann (widow) dwl 2 Stockton Place

Gannon Edward, laborer, dwl N s Minna bet Fifth and Sixth

Gannon James, dwl N s Union bet Hyde and Larkin

Gannon John, fireman, dwl 133 Folsom

Gannon Michael, laborer with Daniel McGlynn, dwl 30 Ritch, rear

Gannon Peter, waiter, Russ House, dwl E s Harrison Avenue nr Folsom

Gannon Peter T. clerk with E. W. Moss, dwl 319 Kearny

Gannon Thomas, bar keeper with Wm. Hodgkins, dwl 49 Everett

Gans Isidor, butcher with Daniel Harris, dwl 271 Minna

Gans Samuel, butcher with Daniel Harris, dwl 271 Minna

Gansberg George, dwl 838 Vallejo, rear

Gansener Florence, miner, dwl 16 Langton

Gantner Richard, wheelwright, dwl N s St. Charles bet Montgomery and Kearny

Gap Philip, laborer, dwl S s Spring Valley Road 3 miles from City Hall

Garabine Bartiano, peddler, dwl Union bet Stockton and Dupont

Garbade Charles, dwl 722 Pacific

Garbarino Antonio, laborer, dwl W s Union Place

Garcelon Harris, ship carpenter, dwl S s Twentieth bet Guerrero and Dolores

Garcelon Harvey, carpenter, Miners' Foundry, dwl E s Tyler bet Laguna and Buchanan

GARCIA FRANCISCO, proprietor Frank's Saloon, 718 Montgomery, dwl 120 Prospect Place

Garcia Incarnation, printer, dwl 1430 Stock, rear

Garcia José, porter with Cross & Co. dwl Pinckney Place

Garcia Joseph S. captain schooner Lewis Perry, office 321 Front

Garcia Petroleum Co. (Mendocino County) office 28 Government House

Garcier Emanuel, porter, 16 Clay

Garcin L. P. Vulcan Forges, 34 Sutter

Gardiner B. F. clerk, 633 Market

Gardiner George D. clerk with R. B. Gray & Co. dwl 441 Minna

Gardiner Henry, collector, Market St. Wharf, dwl 14 Oak nr Mason

Gardiner James J. deputy city and county surveyor, dwl 710 Washington

Gardiner John H. salesman with William Alvord & Co. dwl 46 Sutter

Gardiner John H. N. dwl 441 Minna

Gardiner Thomas, with Thomas Doyle, 535 Sacramento, dwl 244 Stevenson
GARDNER CHARLES, attorney at law, office 604 Merchant, dwl N s Union bet Hyde and Larkin
Gardner Charles A. collector, 604 Merchant, dwl N s Union bet Hyde and Larkin
Gardner Francis, hostler, dwl 617 Mission
Gardner George, clerk, steamship John L. Stephens, dwl 3 Martha Place
GARDNER *(George M.)* & CO. *(W. R. Hartshorne)* wines and liquors, 707 Davis, dwl 926 Montgomery
Gardner Henry, coppersmith, bds United States Hotel
Gardner Henry H. minstrel, Eureka Hose Co. No. 4
Gardner J. sprinkler, Spring Valley W. W
Gardner James H. Custom House broker, C. H
Gardner J. M. melter, U. S. Branch Mint, dwl 1305 Stockton
GARDNER JOHN, superintendent Omnibus R. R. Co. office Union Hall Howard nr Third, dwl 721 Howard
Gardner Joseph, ship joiner, dwl 33 Tehama
Gardner Joseph W. with Lyon & Co. 159 Jessie, dwl SE cor Mission and First
Gardner Rowland B. clerk, 327 Montgomery, dwl with William C. Mead
Gardner Samuel, Sazarac Exchange Liquor Saloon, 765 Clay
Gardner Sandford T. stock broker, dwl 627 Bush
Gardner S. W. dwl 718½ Union
Gardner William N. G, driver, Central R. R. Co. dwl NW cor Brannan and Sixth
Garecht Daniel, baker, dwl 31 Kearny
Garfield John Q. pail turner with Armes & Dallam
Garfield M. J. carpenter, dwl W s Howard nr Erie
Gargan Patrick, stove mounter with Locke & Montague, dwl cor Ecker and Lick
Garbaga Kate, chambermaid, American Exchange
Garibaldi Bartolomeo, employé with Brignardello, Macchiavello & Co. 706 Sansom
Garibaldi Francisco, saloon, dwl W s Bower Place
Garibaldi Gita, vegetable garden, Visitacion Valley
Garibaldi Guiseppe, drayman, 420 Battery, dwl Card Alley
Garibaldi John, wood and coal, 8 Pollard Place
Garibaldi Joseph, cook, dwl 822 Pacific
Garibaldi Munwella, vegetable garden, Visitacion Valley
Garissere Francis, hairdresser, 532 Jackson, dwl 508 Broadway
Garity James, workman with Casebolt & Co
Garity John, lodgings, dwl 629 Davis
Garity Peter, hackman, Russ House
Garity William, laborer, dwl S s Market bet Sixth and Seventh
Garland Annie Miss, seamstress, dwl 749 Market
Garland H. P. dwl What Cheer House
Garland John, dwl 765 Market
Garland Milton H. confectioner, 765 Market
Garland William D. *(Bibbins & G.)* dwl 449 Minna
Garling Henry *(Hotop, G. & Co.)* 116 Jackson
Garlisch Frederick, waiter, New England House
Garneau Gaspard, dwl S s Cliff House Road, 4 miles from Plaza
Garner Francis B. hostler, 117 O'Farrell, dwl Mission nr First
Garner John, farm hand with Jason Wight
Garner Margaret (widow) dwl 255 Third
Garner William, waiter, steamer Orizaba
Garnery John, dwl 610 Lombard
Garness Mary A. (widow) dwl 15 Battery
GARNESS WILLIAM H. clerk with Dr. E. Trenkle, dwl 611 Washington
Garnett Louis A. stock broker, dwl 35 Essex
Garnisch William, carriage maker, dwl 323 Pine
GARNISS JAMES R. commissioner deeds and agent Guardian Life Insurance Co. office 526 Washington, dwl 1423 Stockton

Garra José, porter with Cross & Co. 613 Battery
Garratt Joseph, foreman with W. T. Garratt, dwl N s Fifteenth nr Howard
Garratt Rebecca (widow) dwl 1112 Leavenworth
GARRATT WILLIAM T. brass and bell founder, 507 and 509 Market, dwl E s Sixth nr Harrison
Garraty Bridget Mrs. laundress, dwl 134 Stevenson
Garraud John, dwl 719 Clay
Garren Louis, cap maker with Wolf Fleisher, dwl N s Ellis bet Polk and Van Ness Avenue
Garrett Berry, laborer, dwl NW cor Shipley and Fifth
Garrett Christine, with William Barnes, dwl S s Ewer Place
Garrett Francis, boot maker, dwl 312 Pacific
Garrett James D. lab, dwl NE cor San and Vallejo
Garrett James H. commission, dwl 546 Tehama
Garrety John, stone cutter, Fort Point
Garrety Philip, dwl N s Day bet Guerrero and Dolores
Garric Osmin, dwl 718 Stockton
Garrigan Laughlin, ballastman, dwl S s Filbert bet Montgomery and Sansom
Garrigan Patrick, cartman, cor Broadway and Bat
Garrioch Alexander, merchant, dwl 325 Geary
Garrison Benjamin, ship carpenter, dwl 41 Clementina
Garrison Lewis B. teamster, office 215 Front, dwl 403 Third
Garrissere Frank, barber, dwl 508 Broadway
Garrity John, laborer, dwl E s Salmon bet Mason and Taylor
Garronne *(Felix)* & Hutaf *(Henry)* groceries and liquors, SE cor Dupont and Cal, dwl 722 Cal
Gars Mary (widow) dwl 19 Virginia
Gartenburg Adolph, peddler, dwl W s Jones bet Ellis and O'Farrell
Garthorne Charles, book keeper, 223 California, dwl N s Eddy bet Hyde and Larkin
Garthorne Charles A. printer with T. J. Higgins, dwl N s Eddy bet Hyde and Larkin
Garthwaite Harry, accountant, dwl NW cor Sacramento and Leavenworth
Gartland Mary Miss, dwl 73 Tehama
Gartland Philip, bricklayer, dwl 73 Tehama
GARTNER NICHOLAS, proprietor Meyers' Hotel, 814 Montgomery
Garvey Annie S. dress maker with Madame Augier, dwl cor Howard and Eighth
Garvey Catherine (widow) dwl 14 Silver
Garvey Christopher, clerk with J. P. Garvey, dwl 14 Silver
Garvey James, bell hanger with Marwedel & Otto, dwl 67 Minna
Garvey James, porter, dwl 39 Jane
Garvey Joanna Miss, domestic, 33 O'Farrell
GARVEY J. P. searcher records, office 618 Merchant, dwl 14 Silver
Garvey Patrick, boiler maker, Union Foundry, dwl Gilbert nr Brannan
Garvey Peter, fireman, steamer Orizaba, dwl 417 Greenwich
Garvey William, clerk, dwl 14 Silver
Garvey William, hostler, dwl 7 Trinity
GARVEY WILLIAM V. insurance broker, 519 Montgomery room 4, res Oakland
Garvin James, porter with Parrott & Co. dwl 29 Jane
Garvin John, saloon keeper, dwl 29 Freelon
Garvin Thomas, laborer with David B. Hughes, dwl S s Lombard bet Taylor and Jones
Garvis John, saloon, dwl W s Hyde bet Geary and O'Farrell
Garwood Daniel S. office 84 Washington Market
GARWOOD GEORGE M. & CO. butchers, 84 Washington Market, dwl 228 Green
Garwood J. H. clerk, 687 Market
Garwood Wm. T. resident physician City and County Hospital

GAS COMPANY CITIZENS', office NW cor Washington and Kearny
GAS COMPANY S. F. office and works NE cor Howard and First
GAS METER INSPECTOR STATE, office 612 Commercial
Gascker Methias, laborer, South Park Malt House, bet Fifth and Sixth
Gaskell R. C. United States mail agent, office Post Office, basement
Gaskin Charles M. local policeman, dwl 424 Bat
Gasley Melanie (widow) liquor saloon, 418 Brannan
Gaspar August, shoe maker, dwl 375 Jessie
Gaspar Conrad, gardener, nr Mountain Lake House
Gasper John, butcher, dwl 627 Vallejo
Gass Frances R. Miss, actress, Maguire's Opera House
Gass George V. dwl N s Pinkham Place nr Eighth
Gass William C. machinist, Union Foundry, dwl 211 Minna
Gassert William, groceries, NW cor Mission and Ninth
Gassmann John B. laundry, 406 Union
Gately B. Miss, dwl 322 Geary
Gately John, groceries and liquors, SW cor Mason and Geary
Gately John, proprietor Brooklyn House, 217 Bdwy
Gately Mary Miss, domestic, 15 Ecker
Gately Mary E. Miss, domestic, 215 Jones
Gately Michael, real estate agent, office 19 Geary, dwl W s Gough bet Grove and Fulton
Gately Patrick, with A. Lusk & Co. dwl Davis nr Chambers
Gately Patrick, laborer, dwl S s Broadway bet Polk and Van Ness Avenue
Gately Thomas J. merchant, dwl 618 O'Farrell
Gately William, real estate, dwl 618 O'Farrell
Gately William jr. carpenter, dwl 618 O'Farrell
Gates Daniel, shoe maker, dwl 1615 Dupont, rear
Gates H. M. Miss, assistant, Pacific St. School, dwl 223 Seventh
Gates Horace, Eagle Coffee and Spice Mills, 110 Fremont, dwl 223 Seventh
Gates Horace D. salt packer, dwl 223 Seventh
GATES HORATIO S. physician and real estate, office 526 Merchant, dwl NE cor Sutter and Steiner
Gates James R. (R. Hall & Co.) dwl 115 Dupont
Gates Louis, carriage trimmer with Casebolt & Co. dwl cor Market and Brooks
Gatier Celeste (widow) dwl Folsom nr Kosciusko
Gatin John, laborer, dwl W s Beale bet Howard and Folsom
Gatinelle Louis, restaurant, 1222 Stockton
Gatt (Antonio) & Gionazzo (Angelo) wood and coal, 510 Green
GATTEL BERNHARD, general agent Germania Life Insurance Company and commissioner deeds for New Jersey, office 519 Montgomery, dwl 113 Taylor
Gatz Emil, baker with Nolton & Spreen, 640 Mkt
Gatzert John, dwl 631 Broadway
Gaubert Joseph, fancy goods and toys, 1312 Stock
Gauchet Alphonse, salesman, Alta Mills, dwl 414 Natoma
Gauchet Henry, dwl 414 Natoma.
GAUGER OF LIQUORS, office 405 Front
Gaughagan Thomas, baker, U. S. Bakery, dwl 1152 Folsom
Gaughran James, stevedore, dwl E s Gilbert bet Bryant and Brannan
GAUGHRAN PETER, butter, eggs, etc. 44 Washington Market, dwl 1006 Clay
Gaul John, laborer, Miners' Foundry, dwl E s First bet Harrison and Bryant
Gauley James A. real estate agent, office 625 Merchant, dwl 611 Stockton
Gaussail Bernard, liquor saloon, 630 Pacific
Gautier Anatole (Vincenot & G.) dwl SW cor Sansom and Pacific

Gautier François, garden, Presidio Road S s Lagoon
Gautier L. M. wines and liquors and furnished rooms, 516 Pacific
Gautier L. P. physician, office 402 Montgomery, dwl SW cor Dupont and Post
Gautier Rose Miss, domestic, 512 Union
Gautner Richard, drayman, Mission St. Wharf
Gauvreau B. Oliver, dwl Mariposa nr Kentucky
Gauvreau Oliver, dwl Mariposa nr Kentucky
Gavard Peter, real estate, dwl 1213 Sacramento
Gaven Dominick, real estate, office 520 Mont
Gaven James, varnisher with J. Peirce, dwl 61 Jessie
Gaven Patrick, laborer, dwl 1305 Jackson
Gaven P. T. (Gallagher & G.) 25 Occidental Mkt
Gaven Samuel, laborer, dwl cor Lombard and Fillmore
Gavidy Joseph, produce, dwl 1027 Dupont
Gavie Ellen Miss, domestic, 1019 Folsom
Gavigan Martin, laborer, Pacific Foundry, dwl 437 First bet Harrison and Bryant
Gavigan Thomas, laborer, dwl 112 Bush
Gavigan William, wood dealer, Commercial Wharf, dwl N s Turk bet Jones and Leavenworth
Gavin Annie Mrs. domestic, 1209 Powell
Gavin John, laborer, Fort Alcatraz, dwl W s Leavenworth bet Sacramento and California
Gavin John, laborer, bds Commercial Hotel
Gavin Keran D. book keeper, Commercial Hotel
Gavin Margaret Miss, domestic, 1309 Taylor
Gawley William H. (Meigs & G.) dwl 417 Harrison
Gay Albert C. carpenter, dwl S s Minna bet Eighth and Ninth
Gay Charles, general agent, office 415 Pine, dwl 608 Ellis
Gay Daniel C. second pilot stmr Yosemite
Gay John, clerk, dwl 105 Second
Gay John, miner, dwl S s Oregon nr Davis
Gayetty E. P. janitor San Bruno and Potrero schools
Gayetty P. C. mining broker, dwl cor Shasta and Wisconsin
Gaylord William H. with N. P. Hopkins, dwl S s Minna nr Eighth
Gayner Thomas, dwl 636 Commercial
Gayner William, retortman, S. F. Gas Co. dwl 21 Natoma
GAYNOR J. P. architect, office 402 Montgomery, dwl W s Sixth Avenue bet Bryant and Harrison
Gaynor Matthew, laborer with B. H. Ramsdell, dwl E s Robbins Place nr Union
Ge Loy (Chinese) washing, 905 Howard
Geantit Alphonse, Lyon Market, 621 Pacific
Geary Annie Miss, domestic, 819 Howard
Geary Annie Miss, domestic, 307 Clementina
Geary Daniel, longshoreman, dwl N s Union bet Montgomery and Calhoun
Geary Edward B. grainer, 10 Sutter, dwl 36 Everett bet Third and Fourth
Geary Henry H. laborer, dwl 112 William
Geary Jeremiah, currier with S. Bloom, dwl NE cor Fourth and Bryant
GEARY J. F. physician and surgeon, office and dwl 632 Howard
Geary John, book binder with Bartling & Kimball, dwl NE cor Fourth and Bryant
Geary John, laborer, dwl 6 Jessie
Geary John W. trunk maker with E. Galpen & Co. dwl N s Perry bet Fourth and Fifth
Geary Mary Miss, domestic, 915 Market
Geary Mary Miss, dwl 229 Bush
Geary Michael, drayman, 217 Davis
Geary Patrick, with Hugh McGrea
Geary Patrick, laborer, dwl 605 Third
Geary William, salesman with Hostetter, Smith & Dean, dwl 921 Powell
Geaune Marie (widow) dwl NW cor Sixteenth and Rhode Island

Gaurado Bernard, apprentice, dwl 115 First
GEBHARD *(Frederick)* & BOYNTON *(Charles E.)* carriage makers, 113 Bush
Gebhardt Wendell, upholsterer, dwl 838 Clay
Gebler Theodore, tin and hardware, 825 Clay
GEDDES CHARLES, architect, office 315 Montgomery room 14, dwl 1024 Minna
Gedge Frank J. salesman, 11 Montgomery, dwl NW cor California and Mason
Gedge George, mining superintendent, dwl NW cor Mason and California
Gedge George F. clerk, dwl NW cor California and Mason
Gee Ashon (Chinese) washing, dwl W s Front bet Broadway and Pacific
Gee John, seaman, bds with T. Langford, Front nr Vallejo
Gee Lee (Chinese) washing, 107 First
Gee Sing (Chinese) washing, 106 Bush
Geffke Henry, laborer, Bay Sugar Refinery dwl W s Mariposa nr Harrison
Gegax Samuel, bag maker, dwl 303 Mission
Geggus Charles, butcher, SW cor Third and Everett, dwl 5 Everett
Geggus Louis, butcher, dwl 5 Everett
Gehrels W. A. groceries and liquors, NE cor Mission and Sixth
Gehret Christian, porter, dwl W s Mason bet Sacramento and Clay
Gehricke Otto, clerk, dwl 143 Perry
Gehrig Ferdinand, brewer, New York Brewery
Gehrman William, sash maker with Smith, Ware & Co. dwl Chicago Hotel
GEIB *(Jesse)* & LUDORFF *(August)* auction and commission, 15 Third
Geiger Adam C. laborer with John Smith
Geiger J. George, bar keeper with Brennan & Ryder, dwl 5 Milton Place
Geigerman Solomon, clerk, 428 Montgomery, dwl 760 Mission
Geils H. H. groceries and liquors, SW cor Sutter and Kearny
Geimann William, fashionable and military tailor, 633 Washington, dwl 835 Pacific
Geirrine Charles, clerk, 738 Market
Geishaker Andrew, sawyer, 307 Mkt, dwl 7 Belden
Geisman Charles, carpenter with J Luger, 205 Com
Geissendorfer Frederick, clerk with Weil & Levi, 401 Battery
Geist William, watch maker and jeweler, 205 Montgomery, dwl 250 Minna
Gelbels Bertha (widow) dwl 710 Washington
Geldfelder Owen, upholsterer with Goodwin & Co. dwl 613 Union
GELIEN RUDOLPH G. manufacturer and dealer tobacco, SE cor California and Front, dwl 623 California
Gellanders Robert, porter, 419 Washington, dwl Market bet Dupont and Kearny
Gem of Sierra S. M. Co. office 40 Montgomery Block
Gemianini Louis *(Louis Bertucci & Co.)* dwl 512 Clay
Genard Ida Mrs. dwl 431 Pine
Gendar Ann Maria Mrs. dress making and patterns, 810 Market
Gendar Edward F. salesman with Church & Clark, dwl 810 Market
Gendar John, with N. B. Booth & Co. 20 Kearny
Generlich Julius, tailor, 409 Bush
Genessee Flour Mills, Gold nr Sansom
Genessy Alexander, broker, dwl 1337 Dupont, rear
Geneva G. & S. M. Co. office 338 Montgomery
Genie John, barber, dwl 182 Stevenson
Genot Fannie Mme. milliner, dwl 638 Vallejo
Genot Sebastian, seal engraver, 622 Clay
Geusberger Max, salesman, 420 Sacramento, dwl 610 Green
Gensler Herman, clerk, 505 Commercial, dwl 230 Minna

Gensler L. & Co. *(Jonas Casner)* cigar manufacturers, 309 East, dwl 230 Minna
Gensler Michael, salesman, 537 Commercial, dwl 221 Minna
GENSOUL ADRIEN, importer and retailer foreign and American books, stationery, fancy goods, etc. 511 Montgomery, dwl 423 Post
Genth Joseph *(C. Smith & Co.)* dwl 539 Bdwy
Gentze F. A. trustee, Franco Am. Com. Co. 215 Bush
Gentzen Peter, baker with Henry Bocken, dwl 628 Merchant
Genung Amanda M. (widow) dwl 239 Jessie
Genung A. W. deputy surveyor, office second floor Custom House, dwl 417 O'Farrell
Geofin Joseph, bootblack, 609 Commercial
Geofin Joseph jr. with Joseph Geofin, 609 Com
Geohagan Bartho, drayman, 300 Battery, dwl S s Folsom bet Fifth and Sixth
Geohagan Margaret (widow) dwl S s Folsom, rear, bet Fifth and Sixth
George Benoit *(Rice & G.)* dwl 225 Pacific
GEORGE *(David)* & SMITH *(John)* wood and coal, 430 Pine, dwl 270 Clementina
George David, carpenter, dwl 248 Jessie
George Henry, painter, dwl 313 Sixth cor Shipley
George Henry A. foreman Fashion Stables, dwl 24 Bush
George John J. carpenter with James Brokaw, dwl W s Eighth bet Howard and Folsom
GEORGE *(Julius)* & LOUGHBOROUGH *(Alexander H.)* attorneys at law, office 505 Montgomery, dwl 717 Sutter
George Levi F. carpenter, 905 Stockton, dwl 842 Clay
George Nelson, carpenter, dwl 629 California
George Peter, liquor saloon, Old San José Road, opposite St. Mary's College
George Washington G. & S. M. Co. (Silver Mountain, Cal.) office 410 Montgomery
Geper John, miner, dwl S s Sixteenth nr Valencia
Geraghty Bernard, groceries and liquors, NW cor Mason and Turk
Gerard Victor, agent Saltzman, Jacot & Co. New York, office 629 Clay
Gerb C. cook, dwl SW cor Kearny and Pacific
Gerber Agathe Mrs. domestic, 622 Vallejo
Gerber J. B. French boot maker, 507 Jackson, dwl 651 Washington
Gerberding C. O. (widow) dwl 1218 Clay
Gerberding Frederick, clerk with Falkner, Bell & Co. dwl 1218 Clay
Gerdes Alexander, groceries and liquors, NW cor Third and Stevenson
Gerdes Carson, express wagon cor Kearny and Post, dwl W s August Alley nr Union
Gereau George, clerk, dwl S s California bet Larkin and Polk
Gereau William B. ship carver, W s Drumm bet Pacific and Jackson, dwl 1505 California
Gerema Charles, cook, 623 Com, dwl 621 Pine
Gehard Berthold, confectionery, 12 Dupont
Gerhardy Charles *(Dudley & G.)* dwl 249 Minna
Gerbardy Philip, San Francisco Market, 323 Kearny
GERHOW FREDERICK, groceries and liquors, cor Mission and East, dwl 1 Lincoln Place
Gerke Henry, farmer, dwl 107 Mason
Gerken Charles, clerk, SW cor First and Bryant
Gerken Claus *(Schroder & G.)* SW cor Fifth and Stevenson
Gerken George, dwl NW cor Mission and Main
Gerken Peter, groceries and liquors, NW cor Mission and Main
Gerlach Conrad, boot maker, 335½ Kearny, dwl 107 O'Farrell
Gerlach John, carpenter, dwl 431 Pine
Gerlich John H. clerk, NW cor Folsom and Sixth
German John, machinist, Union Foundry
German Club, rooms NW cor Kearny and Sac

GERMAN GENERAL BENEVOLENT SOCIE-TY, office 625 Merchant
German Hall, Edward Angeles proprietor, 16 and 18 Sansom
GERMAN HOSPITAL, 427 Brannan nr Third
German Mutual Fire Insurance Co. office 58 Montgomery Block
German Society Natural Sciences, 517 Clay
Germane Henry, laborer, dwl 410 O'Farrell
GERMANIA LIFE INSURANCE CO. B. Gattel agent, office 519 Montgomery
Gernaud Andre, boots and shoes, 1310 Dupont
Gerner Charles, cook, 308 Montgomery
Gernich Augustus, carriage maker with Gebhard & Boynton, 113 Bush
Gernsheimer G. (S. Goldsmith & Co.) dwl cor Market and Geary
Gerran John, clerk with I. N. Choynski, SW cor Market and Second, dwl 641 Commercial
Gerrard Hugh, boatman, bds City Front House, 625 Davis
Gerrau John, porter, 643 Commercial
Gerrity Ellen Mrs. nurse, dwl 1513 Stockton
Gerry F. F. (Robert Pennell & Co.) dwl 737 Howard
GERRY S. RUSSELL, physician and surgeon, office and dwl 819 Washington
Gerson Edward, waiter, dwl 323 Pine
Gerstenbach Henry, porter with Crane & Brigham, dwl 313 Pine
Gerstle Lewis (Louis Sloss & Co.) dwl 98 O'Farrell
Gerstner Antoine, butcher, dwl 45 Clara
Gerstner Emma Miss, dress maker, dwl 45 Clara
Gertzen Otto H. carpenter, dwl 323 Pine
Gerves John (Bredhoff & Co.) 423 East
Geacher Gustav, clerk, office Mustering Department U. S. A. dwl 619 Pacific
Geslin Prosper, waiter, California Hotel
Getchel Louis, book keeper, dwl 223 First
Getchell John C. tinsmith with M. Prag, dwl SW cor First and Stevenson
Getchell Wales L. clerk with Palmer, Knox & Co. dwl 27 Minna
Getchell Washington, carpenter, Golden State Iron Works, dwl Pier 4 Stewart
Getchell, see Gitchell
Getello Dominick, peddler, dwl cor Montgomery and Vallejo
Gethings James A. laborer, Volunteer Engine Co. No. 7
Getleson Bernard (L. E. Weck & Co.) 415 Clay
Getliffe C. J. book keeper with B. Davidson & Berri, dwl 603 Pine
Getz Nicholas, seaman, bds 7 Washington
Geurin Nicolas, cook, Clipper Restaurant
Geyer Johanna C. (widow) dwl 614 Ellis
Ghee Hap (Chinese) washing, 603 Sutter
Gheen Wesley T. cooper with Handy & Neuman, dwl 327 Bush
Ghilardi Louis & Co. (D. Mancarini) manufacturers punches and liquor saloon, 534 Commercial, dwl Dupont Alley nr Dupont
Ghio August & Co. (Fortunato Razzato) wines, liquors, and punches, 527 Washington, dwl cor Broadway and Ohio
Ghio John, cigar maker with E. Goslinski, dwl 535 Filbert
GHIRARDELLI D. & CO. (Angelo Mangini) importers, jobbers, and manufacturers chocolate and coffee, 415 and 417 Jackson, res Oakland
Ghogerty Ellen Miss, domestic, Brevoort House
Giacomazzi Guiseppe, clerk, 445 Bush, dwl 431 Pine
Giacomonazzi Antonio, porter with A. E. Sabatie & Co. 617 Sansom
Giamboni Natale (Croce & G.) SE cor Stockton and Clay
Giambony Frederick, waiter, 512 Clay
Giandoni John, liquor saloon, 1402 Dupont

Giannini Joshua, dwl 572 Folsom
Giannini Peter A. watch case manufacturer, 622 Clay, dwl 19 Lafayette Place
Giavonini & Brother (Daniel and Joseph) wood and coal, 816 Pacific
Givonini Joseph (Giavonini & Bro.) dwl 816 Pacific
Gibb Gaven J. W. & Co. (G. W. Corbell) importers and dealers paints, oils, glass, etc. 527 Kearny and Pacific Color Works, 206 Commercial, dwl 828 California
GIBB JAMES, proprietor Cosmopolitan Saloon, 617 Merchant, dwl 19 John nr Powell
GIBBON J. F. physician and dispensary 617 Kearny, bds American Exchange
Gibbon Patrick, laborer, dwl 213 Tehama
Gibbons Alfred, book keeper, 413 Front, dwl 733 Pine
Gibbons Charles P. jeweler, dwl W s Leavenworth bet Washington and Jackson
Gibbons Francis W. policeman, City Hall, dwl 373 Jessie
GIBBONS HENRY, physician and professor of materia medica, Medical Department University Pacific, office 6 Montgomery, dwl 730 Howard
Gibbons Henry jr. physician, office 6 Montgomery, dwl 730 Howard
Gibbons John, meat market, SW cor Taylor and Greenwich
Gibbons John J. canvasser, dwl W s Leavenworth between Washington and Jackson
Gibbons Patrick, baker, What Cheer House Restaurant
Gibbons Robinson, draftsman, office U. S. Surveyor General, dwl 240 Jessie
GIBBONS RODMOND & CO (Sampson Tams) agents Dupont Powder Co. office 214 California, res Oakland
Gibbons Sarah Miss, domestic, 1211 Taylor
GIBBONS THOMAS, proprietor Golden Age Hotel, 127 Pacific
Gibbons William, molder, dwl 511 Mission
Gibbs Amos, bricklayer with George D. Naglee, dwl 808 Clay
Gibbs Charles, Melter and Refiner's Department U. S. Branch Mint, dwl 55 Second
Gibbs Charles E. forwarding and commission, (agent W. L. Perkins, Sacramento City) office 404 Front, dwl 122 Eddy
Gibbs C. V. S. secretary New York Board Underwriters, office 308 Front, dwl 122 Eddy
Gibbs Eugene R. captain Company E Second Infantry Cal. Vol. Presidio
Gibbs George W. (Geo. C. Johnson & Co.) dwl 400 Harrison cor Second
Gibbs John S. box factory, Chace's Mill, 307 Market, dwl cor Beale and Harrison
Gibbs P. Henry, machinist, Vulcan Foundry, dwl 368 Jessie
Gibbs Reuben F. sawsmith with N. W. Spaulding, 113 Pine
Giblen Timothy, liquor saloon, SE cor Folsom and Beale
Giblin Michael, bricklayer, dwl 1021 Pacific
Giblin Thomas, plasterer, dwl 823 Broadway
Giblon Patrick, waiter, Russ House
Gibney James S. hackman, Tremont House
Gibney John, laborer, dwl W s Sansom bet Greenwich and Filbert
Gibney Margaret (widow) dwl 239 Sutter
Gibney Patrick, deck hand, steamer Yosemite
Gibney Peter J. metal roofer with John Kehoe, dwl 23 Hunt
Gibney Thomas Rev. assistant pastor St. Patrick's Church
Gibson Adolph B. compositor, dwl 433 Pine
Gibson Alexander, porter with Fargo & Co. dwl 459 Jessie

Gibson C. J. Miss, private school, N s Howard bet Twelfth and Thirteenth, dwl S s Sixteenth bet Valencia and Mission
Gibson Charles, junk, dwl E s Scotland nr Filbert
Gibson H. baker, Occidental Hotel
Gibson James, saddler with W. J. Tillmann, dwl 759 Mission
Gibson James A. drayman, 430 California, dwl NW cor Pine and Polk
Gibson John, carpenter, dwl 30 Ritch
Gibson Joseph, cook, United States Hotel
Gibson Peter, cook, NW cor Merchant and East
Gibson P. J. carpenter, dwl with E. O. West, S s Sixteenth bet Valencia and Mission
Gibson William H. (col'd) hairdresser with N. A. Godfrey, dwl 49 Clara
Giddings James, clerk, dwl 670 Mission
Giddons John, laborer, dwl 154 Clara
Gielow John, captain schooner San Joaquin, dwl 319 Jessie
Gienjras Joseph, blacksmith, dwl 417 Market
Giermann C. dwl W s August Alley nr Union
Gierrine Mary (widow) dwl 130 Stevenson
Gies Adam, hairdressing saloon, 315 Kearny
Gies Kilian, hairdresser, 822 Montgomery, dwl W s Montgomery bet Pacific and Broadway
Gieseman Henry, tailor, 204 Dupont
Giffin Coleman J. tinsmith, dwl 1415 Stockton
Giffin H. E. *(O. F. Giffin & Bro.)* res New York
Giffin John, tinsmith, NW cor Stock and Card Pl
Giffin Lizzie Miss, private school, N s Linden bet Octavia and Laguna
GIFFIN O. F. & BROTHER *(H. E. Giffin)* President Empire Mill and Mining Co. office 240 Montgomery, dwl 605 Harrison
Giffing Isaac M. plasterer, dwl 321 Bush
Gifford C. B. artist, 103 California
Gifford Paul J. miner, dwl 109 Perry
Gignoux Cesar, broker, dwl 626 California
Gibon Thomas, engraver, office 522 Montgomery, dwl 420 Bryant
Gilbert Christopher J. boiler maker with Coffey & Risdon, dwl SW cor Sierra and Louisiana
Gilbert C. L. sawyer with Hobbs, Gilmore & Co. dwl NW cor Sacramento and Stockton
Gilbert D. M. ship joiner, dwl 116 Sansom
Gilbert Edward, stone cutter, dwl 408 Dupont
Gilbert Edward Y. compositor, Alta California
Gilbert Elizabeth, dwl N s Twelfth bet Folsom and Howard
Gilbert Ferdinand, proprietor Gilbert's Museum, N s Market bet Montgomery and Sansom and Willows cor Mission and Eighteenth
Gilbert G. I. W. compositor, Evening Bulletin, dwl 23 Minna
Gilbert Isaac, clerk, 22 Third, dwl 87 Everett
Gilbert James, physician, dwl 503 Davis
Gilbert John W. baker, dwl 1138 Folsom
Gilbert M. & Co. clothing, 58 Third
Gilbert M. shipjoiner with John G. North, Potrero
Gilbert Michael, clothing, 22 Third, dwl 87 Everett
Gilbert Samuel W. liquors, dwl SE cor Vallejo and Montgomery
Gilbert Stephen, cook, dwl Benton House, SE cor Mission and First
Gilbert Victor, barber, dwl Vigilant Engine House No. 9
GILBERT'S OLYMPIC, Kearny op Plaza
Gilbertson Emma Miss, seamstress, dwl 533 Mission
Gilchrist Ira, carpenter, dwl W s Shotwell nr Fifteenth
Gilchrist James, carpenter, dwl Original House
Gilcrest Frank M. clerk with Bradshaw & Co. res Oakland
GILDEMEESTER ADRIAN H. stock and exchange broker, office 605 Washington, dwl 411 Lombard
Gildemeester J. P. H. office NW cor Montgomery and Jackson, dwl NE cor Wash and Dupont

Gildemeister Henry A. book keeper with Hellmann, Brothers & Co. dwl 117 Stockton
Gildemeister William, commission merchant, 540 Washington, dwl SW corner California and Front
Gildersleeve *(George W.)* & Co. *(A. Walker)* Occidental Wood and Coal Yard, 607 Market, dwl Guerrero nr Twenty-Fifth
Giles A. J. seaman, dwl 228 Commercial
Giles A. M. razor strop dealer, bds City Front House, 625 Davis
Giles Edward, stone cutter, dwl Zoe Place
Giles F. N. carpenter and builder, 435 Jackson
Giles James, handcartman, Pacific between Davis and Drumm
Giles Newell J. carpenter, 435 Jackson
Giles Robert, stone cutter, dwl Zoe Place
Giles *(William M.)* & Dunbar *(William F.)* house, sign, and ornamental painters, 403 Bush, dwl 221 Dupont
Gilfeather Francis T. blacksmith, S. F. & San José R. R. Co. dwl 707 Mission
Gilfeather James, laborer, dwl 1108 Pacific, rear
Gilfeather Owen, upholsterer, dwl 613 Union
Gilferry James, laborer, S. F. Gas Co
Gilfillan John, machinist, Union Foundry, dwl 32 Everett
Gilfillan John, workman with N. H. Roy & Bro. San Bruno Road
Gilfillan Jonas C. *(Z. W. Moore & Co.)* dwl 537 California
Gilgen James, express wagon, dwl E s Hyde nr Geary
Gilkerson James, laborer, dwl NW cor Jessie and Annie
Gill Celia Miss, domestic, 801 Union
Gill Fred W. book keeper with L. B. Benchley & Co. dwl 823 California
Gill H. B. clerk with R. D. Chandler, dwl 633 California
Gill James, retortman, San Francisco Gas Co
Gill Margaret Miss, domestic, 959 Howard
Gill Margaret (widow) dwl 121 Minna
Gill Mary Miss, dwl 11 Sansom
Gill Mary Miss, domestic, 864 Mission
Gill Martin, California Straw Works, dwl 121 Minna
Gill M. S. clerk with Rodgers, Meyer & Co. dwl SE cor Hayes and Pierce
Gill Owen, Phœnix Saloon, SW cor Folsom and Stewart, dwl 64 Natoma
Gill Robert, fruit stand, 326 Sansom, dwl 11 Bay State Row
Gill Terence, seaman, dwl 44 Sacramento
Gill Thomas, laborer, dwl 7 Bay State Row
Gill Thomas E. & Co. *(J. T. Kersey and Miss M. J. Little)* California Straw Works, 45 Third, dwl 121 Minnie
Gill W. B. carpenter, dwl NW cor Vallejo and Stockton
Gillaspia Horace N. drayman, 216 Battery
Gillan Annie, domestic, Brevoort House
Gillan Francis, hackman, Plaza
Gillan John, dwl What Cheer House
Gillan John, laborer, Spring Valley W. W. dwl Lake Honda
Gillan Margaret Miss, domestic, 25 Stockton
Gillan Michael, longshoreman, dwl SW cor Green and Sansom
Gillan Patrick, bricklayer, dwl N s Washington bet Larkin and Polk
Gillan Patrick, waiter, Russ House
Gillan Roger, waiter, What Cheer House
Gillen Bernard, with Henry Bocken, dwl S s Broadway bet Stockton and Powell
Gillespie Agnes Miss, domestic, 894 Sutter
Gillespie Barbara (widow) dwl E s Jane Place
Gillespie Charles, painter, dwl SE cor Clay and Dupont

GILLESPIE C. V. attorney at law and searcher records, 655 Washington, dwl NW cor Kearny and Chestnut
Gillespie James *(Palmer, G. & Co.)* dwl 229 Minna
Gillespie James, laborer, dwl 29 Hinckley
Gillespie Jane (widow) dwl 912 Dupont
Gillespie Lawrence, carpenter, Union Foundry, dwl N s Minna bet Seventh and Eighth
Gillespie Mary (widow) fruits, 241 Sutter
Gillespie Patrick, laborer, dwl E s Varenne nr Union
Gillespie Robert H. broom maker, dwl 518 Green
Gillespie William, longshoreman, dwl 618 Lombard, rear
Gillet Aristede, laundryman with Parfait Lemaitre
Gillett Frederick, maltster, 159 Jessie, dwl 541 Mission
Gillett George, broker, dwl 1123 Stockton
Gillett Isaac C. with H. Casebolt & Co. dwl 551 Market
Gillett Jaques, basket maker, dwl 1428 Stockton, rear
Gillette Francis lather and plasterer, E s Willow bet Folsom and Shipley
Gillette John, plasterer, dwl E s Willow bet Folsom and Shipley
Gillette Mathew M. cooper with A. Murdock, Oregon nr Davis
Gillette Michael, wagon maker, dwl 551 Market
Gillfeather Ellen Miss, domestic, 707 Mission
Gillfeather Frank, blacksmith, S. F. & San José R. R. Co. dwl 707 Mission
Gillfeather Margaret Miss, seamstress, dwl 707 Mission
Gillfoile Cornelius, bricklayer, dwl 458 Natoma
Gilliard Charlotte A. stewardess steamer Cornelia
Gilliard James (colored) barber, dwl 1407 Mason
Gilligan Christy, dairy, Visitacion Valley
Gilligan James, laborer, dwl SE cor Austin and Van Ness Avenue
Gilliland William, tailor with Wm. Meyer & Co. dwl 64 Stevenson
Gillingham Charles, physician, dwl 29 Second
Gillis Angus, furnished rooms, 44 Minna
Gillis Stephen E. printer, dwl 44 Minna
Gilliway Bridget (widow) dwl W s Sumner nr Howard
Gilliway John G. lather, dwl W s Sumner nr Howard
Gillmire Joseph, miner, dwl S s Dupont Alley
Gillon Patrick, hostler with Daniel McGlynn, dwl 213 Tehama
Gillott Louis, laborer with B. Bonnet & Co
Gillony Delia A. (widow) furnished rooms, dwl 803 Howard
Gillony John, painter, Omnibus R. R. Co
Gillooley Hugh, porter with Conroy & O'Connor, dwl 257 Clary
Gillson Susan Miss, domestic, 804 Bush
Gilman Alden C. mining, dwl 6 Jane
Gilman A. M. merchant, office 409 Front, dwl Cosmopolitan Hotel
Gilman Benjamin F. mechanic with J. S. Gibbs, dwl 11 Front
Gilman Charles, pressman with Francis, Valentine & Co. dwl cor Montgomery and Vallejo
Gilman Charles H. carpenter, dwl 22 Clarence Pl
Gilman Henry, clerk, steamer Yosemite
Gilman Joseph, boat builder, 20 Commercial, dwl 65 Natoma
Gilman J. S. seaman, dwl 10 Tehama Place
Gilman M. Capt. dwl 14 Kearny
Gilman Owen, fireman, steamer Oakland, res Brooklyn
Gilman Tristram C. carpenter, dwl SW cor Montgomery and Vallejo
Gilmartine Bezy, domestic with P. E. Bowman, dwl SW cor Broadway and Montgomery

Gilmor J. W. A. merchandise broker, office NW cor California and Front, dwl N s Mission between Twelfth and Thirteenth
Gilmore Anna Miss, domestic, 1212 Clay
Gilmore Annie Mrs. nurse, Protestant Orphan Asylum
Gilmore Charles H. *(Parkel &. G.)* NW cor Clay and Sansom
Gilmore Elijah S. sawyer with Hobbs, Gilmore & Co. dwl E s Clementina nr Sixth
Gilmore Francis (col'd) seaman, dwl SW cor Kearny and Pacific
Gilmore G. D. carpenter with James Brokaw, dwl 52 Minna
Gilmore George W. *(Hobbs, G. & Co.)* dwl 547 Howard
Gilmore James, job wagon, cor Fremont and Folsom, dwl 234 Fremont
Gilmore J. B. Mrs. private school, 336 Fifth
Gilmore J. H. *(Stilwell & Co.)* dwl 215 Second
Gilmore John, engineer, dwl 229 Minna
Gilmore John, seaman, dwl NW cor Green and Battery
Gilmore John B. dwl 336 Fifth
Gilmore John J. engineer, dwl 282 Minna
Gilmore Mary Miss, milliner, dwl SW cor Dupont and Broadway
Gilmore Robert, engineer, Vulcan Foundry, dwl 715 Howard
Gilmore Robert G. cooper, dwl 145 Fourth
Gilmore Samuel, carpenter, dwl 1811 Mason
Gilmore Stephen D. *(Hobbs, G. & Co.)* dwl 518 Folsom
Gilmore Thomas, miner, dwl 464 Jessie
Gilmore W. D. carpenter, dwl 633 Market
Gilmour Thomas, liquors, dwl NE cor Grove and Laguna
Gilot Louis, brick maker, dwl NW cor Larkin and Broadway
Gilpatrick Joseph G. clerk, Pier 13 Stewart, dwl 223 First
Gilroy Mary Miss, domestic, 431 Minna
Gilson James, express wagon, SE cor Montgomery and Sacramento, dwl 21 Bush
Gim Lee (Chinese) washing, 1009 Pacific
Gimmerans Vasco, speculator, dwl Lick House
Ginardini Paul, waiter, 407 California
Ginardini Peter, waiter, dwl W s Pacific Alley
Gincosta Antonio, dwl 27 Commercial
Gindred Patrick, molder, Vulcan Iron Works
Ginger Charles, brewer, dwl 622 Vallejo
Gingg John, bar keeper, William Tell House
Gingras Mary (widow) lodgings, 7 Stevenson
Ginkel Richard, steward, dwl 323 Pine
Ginley J. M. conductor, Omnibus R. R. Co
Gingsbury Osher, glazier, dwl W s Main bet Folsom and Harrison
Ginty Ann Miss, domestic, 19 Minna
Gionazzo Angelo *(Gatt & G.)* dwl 510 Green
GIORGIANI A. wholesale fruits and commission, 421 Washington, dwl 627 O'Farrell
Giovanari Giacomo, employé with Brignardello, Macchiavello & Co. 706 Sansom
Giovanni Mariana, porter, 623 Commercial
Girard Edward, waiter, dwl 1314 Dupont
Girard L. dwl Union Club Rooms
Girard Thomas, butcher with C. Kerr, dwl N s Brannan bet Eighth and Ninth
Giraud Eugene, clerk with Caire Brothers, dwl 313 Green
Giraux Adelaide Mme. (widow) physician, dwl 732 Vallejo
Gird Richard, civil engineer, office 302 Montgomery, dwl 744 Howard
Girod Jacque, furnished rooms, 809 Clay
Girolamo Raggio *(Dominico Caraffa & Co.)* dwl 1309 Dupont
Girot F. *(Paulin Huant & Co.)* dwl 735 Green
Girot Stephen, carman, dwl 533 Broadway

Girvin *(Alexander)* & Morter *(William)* black-smiths, 322 Third, dwl 21 Clara
Girzikowsky *(William)* & Zeh *(John)* groceries and liquors, 20 Hinckley
Gisi C. barber, dwl 919 Montgomery
Gitchell J. M. special agent U. S. Treasury Department, office third floor Custom House, dwl Russ House
Gittlings James, laundryman, Occidental Hotel
Guisti Joseph, oysters, 26 Metropolitan Market, dwl 12 Harlan Place
Givans William, molder, Miners' Foundry, dwl Union House
Given C. N. (widow) dwl 509 Bush
Gives John, stevedore, dwl 322 Green
Gladden John J. shoe maker, 18 Stewart
Gladwin George S. money broker, office 604 Montgomery, dwl N s Howard bet Eighteenth and Nineteenth
Gladwin W. H. broker, office 604 Montgomery, res Alameda
Glancey William, bricklayer, dwl 19 Harlan Place
Glancy Cecilia Miss, dwl 123 Perry
Glands Catherine, ironer, Chelsea Laundry
Glary Hannah (col'd, widow) dwl N s Card Place
Glas Frank, coal yard, 25 and 27 Washington
Glasby Jessie K. millwright and carpenter, Union Foundry, dwl 34 Ritch
Glaser Andrew, butcher, 244 Third
Glasford P. S. salesman with Ackerman Bros. dwl NE cor Eddy and Mason
GLASGOW IRON AND METAL COMPANY, 25 and 27 Fremont, Gabeldu & Meyer agents
Glasgow James, farmer, Ocean House Road, 1 mile from Ocean House
Glasgow Thomas William, carpenter, dwl E s Sixth nr Market
Glasham W. coal passer, steamer Senator
Glaskin William, dwl 416 Second
Glass *(Charles)* & Levy *(Morris)* importers and jobbers fancy and dry goods, 305 Battery, dwl 347 Minna
Glass James, ship joiner, dwl SW cor Louisiana and Sierra
Glass Joseph, hats, caps, etc. 1016 Dupont
Glass Marks, tailor with L. Goodman, dwl 922 Kearny
Glass Thomas, carpenter, dwl NW cor Kearny and Jackson
Glasson Benjamin, dwl 506 Geary
Glasson M. A. Mrs. dwl 415 Bryant
Glave *(Dora)* Miss & Co. *(Lucy Glave)* worsted and fancy goods, 11 Second
Glave Lucy *(Miss D. Glave & Co.)* dwl 11 Second
Glavigni Luca, fisherman, 41 Italian Fish Market
Glaze A. C. Mrs. dress making, 116 Dupont
Glaze Leroy N. compositor, American Flag, dwl 116 Dupont
Glazebrook John, express wagon, 424 California, dwl N s Clementina bet First and Second
Glazier Isaac & Bro. *(S. W. Glazier)* merchants, office 311 Clay, dwl Cosmopolitan Hotel
Glazier S. W. *(Isaac Glazier & Bro.)* dwl Lick House
Glazier W. W. sawyer with J. McGill & Co. dwl 28 Sansom
Gleason Ellen (widow) dwl 334 Kearny
Gleason George, dwl E s Hyde bet California and Pine
Gleason Horace, waiter, Bailey House
Gleason James D. molder, San Francisco Iron Works, dwl 60 First
Gleason Joanna Miss, domestic, 321 Geary
Gleason John, laborer, dwl 153 Shipley
Gleason John, waiter, Cliff House
Gleason Katy Miss, domestic, 829 Broadway
Gleason M. miner, dwl 559 Market
Gleason *(Patrick)* & Hurley *(Charles)* groceries and liquors, NE cor O'Farrell and Dupont

Gleason Patrick, laborer, dwl S s Sutter bet Laguna and Buchanan
Gleason P. H. proprietor Fort Point Saloon, Francisco bet Powell and Mason
Gleason Thomas, carpenter, dwl 916 Montgomery
Gleason Thomas, laborer, bds 336 Bush
Gleason Timothy M. miner, dwl 345 Fourth
Gleason William, dwl 916 Montgomery
Gleason William, broiler, Russ House
Gleason William H. clerk, dwl 219 Tehama
Gleeson M. E. (widow) furnished rooms, 22 Mont
Gleeson William, carpenter, dwl N s Mission bet First and Second
Gleeson William H. jeweler with Lemme Bros. dwl Brooklyn Hotel
Glein C. F. & Co. *(J. Boschken)* hardware, 317 Kearny, dwl 6 Mason
Gleizes Benjamin *(Boudin & G.)* dwl 434 Green, rear
Glemm Martin, butcher, dwl NE cor Broadway and Kearny
Glenn James, dwl SW cor Kearny and Francisco
Glenn Thomas, waiter, Lick House
Glennan John W. harness maker with J. M. Hurlbutt & Co. dwl 59 Jessie
Glennan Kate Miss, domestic, NW cor Thirteenth and Howard
Glennan Martin, butcher with Jacob Wray
Glenning Bridget Miss, laundress, Lick House
Glennon Rose Miss, domestic, 518 Bush
Glespy John, carman, Filbert nr Jones
Glick K. cigars and tobacco, 254 Third
GLIDDEN, *(A. K. P.)* COLMAN *(James M.)* & CO. *(N. H. Falk)* lumber, spars, and piles, Pier 22 Stewart, dwl 742 Folsom
Glidden Albert M. ship carpenter, dwl 222 Jessie
Glidden George W. lab, dwl cor Church and Ridley
Gliddon Charles E. principal clerk records U. S Surveyor General's office, dwl 160 Silver
Glinden James, blacksmith, 38 Webb, dwl 716 Harrison
Glinn Catherine Miss, domestic, 361 Jessie
Glinn Patrick, laborer, Mission Woolen Mills, dwl N s Fifteenth bet Howard and Folsom
Glinn Timothy, laborer, dwl 26 Ritch, rear
Gliubetich Michael *(Buia & G.)* dwl 605 Davis
Glover Andrew, policeman, City Hall, dwl 204 Green
Glover Charles (col'd) bootblack, SE cor Second and Market, dwl 15 Pacific
Glover George F. M. *(Scott & G.)* dwl 683 Harrison
Glover John, dwl 618 Market
Glover Martin C. refiner, Kellogg, Hewston & Co.'s Refinery
Glück *(John F.)* & Hansen *(Charles E.)* National Brewery, NW cor O'Farrell and William
Gluesing Peter, machinist, Vulcan Iron Works, dwl SE cor Sixth and Minna
Gluyas George E. C. attorney at law, office 625 Merchant, dwl 813 Howard
Gluyas George K. with C. S. Navigation Co. NE cor Front and Jackson, dwl 813 Howard
Gluyas Reese W. clerk, dwl 813 Howard
Glynn Catharine Miss, domestic, 517 Dupont
Glynn Daniel, carman, dwl Shipley bet Fifth and Sixth
Glynn Emerson *(Farnsworth & G.)* dwl 29 Turk
Glynn James, bricklayer, dwl 324 Tehama
Glynn John, laborer, dwl SW cor Leavenworth and Vallejo
Glynn John, wool worker, Broadway Wool Depôt, dwl cor Vallejo and Leavenworth
Glynn Kate Miss, domestic, 926 Pacific
Glynn Mary (widow) dwl 115 Shipley
Glynn Mary (widow) boarding, 79 Jessie
Glynn Michael, laborer, dwl 108 Mason
Glynn Patrick, driver with Haste & Kirk, dwl N s Stevenson bet Seventh and Eighth

Glynn Patrick, laborer, Mission Woolen Mills, dwl with Bridget Gallagher, N s Fifteenth nr Howard

Glynn Thomas, marble worker with John Daniel, dwl 417 Powell

Glynn, see McGlynn

Gnialo Martin L. liquors, 3 Broadway

Goan P. carpenter with S. S. Culverwell, 29 Fremont, res Oakland

Gobbee Joseph, pattern maker, Miners' Foundry, dwl 535 Folsom

GOBENER G. H. groceries and liquors, SW cor Brannan and Third

Gobernadora S. M. Co. office 6 Montgomery Block

Gobert E. D. (Koster & Co.) dwl SW cor Jones and O'Farrell

Gobertz Adam, dwl W s Dolores bet Twenty-First and Twenty-Second

Gochey Thomas A. carpenter, dwl 126 Perry

Godart Albert, laundry, 1015 Sutter and SE cor Hyde and Pacific

Godchalx Charles, stone cutter, dwl 53 Clementina

GODCHAUX BROTHERS (Adolph and Joseph) & CO. (Henry and Charles Schmitt) importers and jobbers fancy dry goods, 109 Battery, res 10 Rue des Petites Ecuries, Paris

Godchaux Buildings, NE cor Second and Mission

Godchaux Joseph (Godchaux Bros. & Co.) dwl 331 O'Farrell

Godchaux Joseph (Godchaux, Weil & Co.) dwl 61 Second

GODCHAUX, (Lazard) WEIL (Abraham) & CO. (Joseph Godchaux) importers and retailers dry goods, 61 Second cor Mission, dwl 325 Minna

Godeau Alex. groceries, 1220 Dupont

GODDARD & CO. (Ira P. Rankin, Albert P. Brayton jr. and A. C. Austin) proprietors Pacific Iron Works, 127–133 First

Goddard Henry K. clerk, dwl 9 Minna

Goddard Louis, laundry, 807 Howard

Goddard Riley M. dwl 316 Jessie

Goddard Squire B. salesman with Cutting & Co. dwl NW cor Bryant and Rincon Place

Godding (Warren) & Koons (Ephraim) tub and pail makers for Armes & Dallum, 22 and 24 Cal

GODEFFROY (Alfred) & SILLEM (William) agents Mendocino Saw Mills, office 535 Clay, dwl 1411 Powell

Godfred Raisch, stone cutter, dwl W s Eighth bet Natoma and Howard

Godfrey Charles, garden, N s Presidio Road nr Halfway House

Godfrey Dennis, deck hand, steamer Chrysopolis, dwl 180 Jessie

Godfrey Dennis, laborer, dwl 14 St. Mark Place

Godfrey Edward A. book keeper with Crane & Brigham, dwl 1114 Clay

Godfrey George, real estate, dwl 821 Howard

Godfrey James T. dwl 315 Geary

Godfrey Julia Mrs. groceries, 614 Broadway

Godfrey N. A. (col'd) hairdressing saloon, Occidental Hotel, dwl 1016 Pacific

Godfrey Samuel (col'd) bootblack with N. A. Godfrey

Godfrey Willard, dwl 28 Sansom

Godfrey William A. H. shirts, etc. 105 Second

Godfrey William H. dwl 1114 Clay

Godfrey William H. 712 Montgomery, res Alameda

Godfroy Joseph, clerk, 207 Kearny

Godicke Charles, butcher with C. Kerr, dwl Brannan St. Bridge

Godkin Thomas, blacksmith, 715 Folsom, dwl 629 Vallejo

Godley Mary Miss, dwl 508 Brannan

Godley Montgomery, with Parrott & Co. dwl 767 Mission

GODOY JOSE A. consul Republic of Mexico, 525 Front, bds Lick House

Godsell Julia Miss, dwl with Mrs. Robert O. Oakley S s Mission bet Eighth and Ninth

Goebel F. W. porter with Heynemann & Co. 313 California

Goerres William, express wagon, Cal nr Kearny

Goetjen Nicholas (Erzgraber & G.) dwl N s McAllister bet Webster and Buchanan

Goetsihe John, fruits, NE cor Davis and Pacific, dwl cor Clark and Davis

Goetter Charles, carpenter, S. F. & San José R. R. Co. dwl W s Folsom bet Sixteenth and Seventeenth

Goetz Joseph, restaurant, 631 Davis

GOETZ (Leopold) & SCHREIBER (John) Eureka Bowling Saloon, 335 Pine, dwl W s Sonoma Place nr Green

Goewey James M. (Hosmer, G. & Co.) dwl 508 Folsom

Goff Dwight, captain ship Dublin, dwl 327 Union

Goffe Theodore A. engineer, S. F. & San José R. R. Co. dwl Sixteenth nr Valencia

Goffin Adolph, steward, SW cor Cal and Drumm

Gogarty Owen, carpenter, dwl 231 Jessie

Goger Charles, tinsmith with Joseph Bien, dwl 13 St. Mark Place

Goggin Catharine Miss, with R. J. Tiffany, dwl 813 Greenwich

Going Elizabeth Mrs. domestic, 1020 Jackson

Goings Mary (widow, col'd) dwl E s Havens Place

Gold August, with Stevens & Oliver, dwl cor Green and Stockton

Gold Cañon Consolidated M. Co. office 702 Wash

Gold Hill G. & S. M. Co. office 338 Montgomery

Gold Hill Tunneling G. & S. M. Co. office 415 Mont

Gold Mark, clerk, dwl Howard Engine House

Goldarcena Raymond, machinist, Vulcan Iron Works, dwl Minna bet Second and Third

Goldbaum Lewis, cigar manufacturer, dwl Hampton Court bet Second and Third

Goldberg Caroline Mme. millinery, 124 Kearny

Goldberg David, tailor, dwl 917 Dupont

Goldberg Israel, salesman, 124 Kearny, dwl 340 Kearny

Goldberg Philip, clothing, 421 East

Goldberg Solomon, dwl N s Pac bet Larkin and Polk

Goldberg Solomon, trader, dwl 521 Geary

Golden Age and Empire G. & S. M. Co. office 522 Montgomery

Golden Age Brewery, S s Union bet Broadway and Stockton

Golden Age Flour Mills, F. D. Conro & Co. proprietors, 717 Battery, office 127 Clay

Golden Age Hotel, Thomas Gibbons proprietor, 127 Pacific

Golden Charles, seaman, stmr Orizaba

Golden City Homestead Association, office 734 Mont

Golden Daniel, porter, dwl 201 Sacramento

Golden Eagle Hotel, Charles Dittmer proprietor, 219 Kearny

GOLDEN ERA (weekly) Brooks & Lawrence proprietors, office 543 Clay

Golden Gate Brewery, S s Greenwich bet Powell and Mason

GOLDEN GATE FLOUR MILLS, Horace Davis & Co. proprietors, 430 Pine

Golden Gate Hotel, Henry H. Meyer proprietor, 728 Market

Golden Jane Miss, seamstress, dwl 59 Minna

Golden John W. clerk with Craig, Golden & Yung, dwl 20 Turk

Golden Rule G. & S. M. Co. office 622 Montgomery

Golden State House, J. W. McCormick proprietor, 135 Jackson

GOLDEN STATE IRON WORKS, Palmer, Knox & Co. 19–25 First

Golden Thomas (Craig, G. & Yung) dwl 20 Turk

Golden Thomas H. painter with W. Worthington, dwl 20 Turk

Golden William T. Mrs. dwl 129 Second

Golding J. barber, dwl Niantic Hotel

Golding James, broker, dwl 845 Dupont

Goldman I. A. dry goods, 634 Mkt, dwl 631 Sutter
Goldman Jacob, Stockton St. Market, 1202 Stockton, dwl 426 Kearny bet Pine and California
Goldman Joseph *(Stetson & Co.)* dwl 4 Eddy Place
Goldman Max, clerk with L. Strauss, dwl 714 Vallejo
Goldman Solomon, boots and shoes, 72 First
Goldmann *(I. W.)* & Adler *(Jacob)* boots and shoes, 330 Kearny, dwl 426 Kearny
Goldschmidt Abraham, peddler, dwl 323 Pine
Goldschmidt Israel, boot maker, 807 Clay
Goldschmidt Julius, commission merchant, 313 Sacramento, dwl NE cor Sacramento and Sansom
Goldschmidt Moses, peddler, dwl 323 Pine
Goldschmidt Rosa Miss, domestic, 1105 Mason
Goldmidt Nathan, dry goods, 651 Clay, dwl 518 Sacramento
Goldsmith Aaron, merchant, dwl 115 Eddy
Goldsmith Anna (widow) dwl NE cor Union and Hyde
Goldsmith Anson, broker, Monumental Engine Co. No. 6
Goldsmith Bernard *(Goldsmith Bros.)* res Portland, Oregon
GOLDSMITH BROTHERS *(Amson, Bernard, and Isaac)* assayers and importers assayers' materials, 422 Montgomery, dwl 113 Mason
Goldsmith E. clerk, 316 Sac, dwl Continental Hotel
Goldsmith Edward, fancy goods, 318 Kearny, dwl 359 Jessie
Goldsmith Gustav, fancy goods, 318 Kearny, dwl 352 Jessie
Goldsmith Henry, cloaks and mantillas, 625 Sac
Goldsmith Isaac *(Goldsmith Bros.)* dwl 113 Mason
Goldsmith Isaac, merchant, dwl W s Jones bet Ellis and O'Farrell
Goldsmith Isaac, salesman, 628 Market
Goldsmith James, janitor Montgomery St. School
Goldsmith Joseph, mariner, dwl 721 O'Farrell
Goldsmith Julius, clothing, dwl Continental Hotel
Goldsmith Leon, dwl 315 O'Farrell
Goldsmith Louis, dry goods, 612 Sacramento, dwl 341 Minna
Goldsmith Mary Miss, assistant, Post St. Primary School, dwl W s Jones bet O'Farrell and Ellis
Goldsmith Meyer, fruits, 826 Market
Goldsmith Meyer, job wagon, cor Bush and Kearny, dwl 14 Louisa
Goldsmith Philip, assayer with Goldsmith Bros. dwl 113 Mason
Goldsmith Rosa (widow) dwl 352 Jessie
Goldsmith S. *(Elfelt, Weil & Co.)* res Portland, Oregon
Goldsmith S. & Co. *(G. Gernsheimer)* ladies' fancy goods, 630 Sacramento and 19 Montgomery, dwl 746 Mission
Goldsmith William E. card and seal engraver, 505 Mont, dwl W s Seventh bet Brannan and Bryant
Goldsmith William H. miner, dwl N s Pacific bet s Polk and Van Ness Avenue
Goldstein Abraham B. *(H. Breslauer & Co.)* dwl 14 O'Farrell
Goldstein Abram S. stoves and tin ware, 213 Fourth
Goldstein Anna Miss, assistant teacher, Hebrew School, dwl 213 Fourth
Goldstein Charles, dry goods, dwl 121 Perry
Goldstein E. L. *(Taaffe & Co.)* dwl W s Powell nr Market
Goldstein Eli, clerk, dwl 1015 Kearny
GOLDSTEIN *(Emanuel L.)* & SELLER *(Joseph)* importers and wholesale grocers, 217 Front, dwl 115 Powell
Goldstein Moses, tailor, 625 Com, dwl 270 Jessie
Goldstein Seelig, cigars and tobacco, 302 Sansom, dwl Continental Hotel
Goldstein William, dwl 631 O'Farrell
Goldstone Charles *(Myers, G. & Co.)* dwl 121 Perry
Goldstone John B. teamster with Blyth & Wetherbee, dwl Howard nr Seventh

Goldstone, *(Michel)* Barnett *(Isaac)* & Co. *(Thomas Barnett)* importers and jobbers gents' furnishing goods, 314 California, res New York
Goldwater Joseph, dwl 227 Jessie
Goller John C. cabinet maker with E. Bloomingdale & Co. dwl 1509 Leavenworth
Golly Alfonzo, peddler, dwl 1004 Pacific
Golly Ambroise, watch maker, 717 Clay, dwl 520 Filbert
Golly John, hairdresser, dwl 520 Filbert
Golly John B. clerk, 631 Clay, dwl 520 Filbert
Goma Raphael, fireman, dwl 33 Commercial
Gomear Julius, ranchman, dwl 3 Pollard Place
Gomez J. seaman, stmr Senator
Gomez Vincent, dwl cor Clay and Brenham Place
Gompertz Charles F. teacher languages, Union College, dwl 148 Silver
Gondalo John, laborer with William Buckley
Gonella Zaverio *(Dominique & G.)* dwl 1112 Dupont
Gones David, dwl 18 First
Gong Long (Chinese) washing, 432 Green
Gonley James, butcher, dwl Continental Hotel
Gonley Margaret Miss, domestic, 1413 Larkin
Gonzales John, saddler with Tiburcio Carlos, dwl 1119 Kearny
Gonzales Josepha Miss, lodgings, 1211 Powell
Gonzales Manuel, shoe maker with Joseph Francis, dwl East bet Washington and Clay
GOOD CHRISTIAN & CO. *(Jacob A. Meuli)* Swiss Confectionery and Ice Cream Saloon, 738 Washington
Good John, carpenter, dwl 633 Market
Good John M. bond clerk, Custom House, dwl 1414 Taylor
Good L. C. clerk with Redington & Co. dwl 827 Bush
Good M. Mrs. dwl 11 Minna
GOODALL CHARLES, agent Saucelito Water Co. office SW cor Merchant and East, dwl W s Sixth bet Brannan and Bryant
Goodall Edwin, book keeper, Saucelito Water Co. dwl 37 Natoma
Goodchild Edward, dwl 1705 Stockton
Goodhue John, watch maker, dwl Hall Court
Goodhue Oliver P. *(C. W. Weston & Co.)* dwl 1922 Taylor
Goodkind Henry *(Fechheimer, G. & Co.)* dwl SE cor Taylor and Ellis
Goodman Charles, furrier with Adolph Muller
Goodman David *(Hart & G.)* dwl N s O'Farrell nr Taylor
Goodman *(Frederick)* & Lindner *(Marx)* clothing, 235 Kearny, dwl 412 Post
Goodman George (col'd) porter, dwl Miles Court nr Sacramento
Goodman G. S. book keeper, 317 Sacramento, dwl 20 Sansom
Goodman Isaac, express wagon, corner Washington and Kearny, dwl S s Turk bet Webster and Buchanan
GOODMAN *(James P.)* & DUFFY *(James)* El Dorado Saloon, 657 Washington, dwl S s Page bet Laguna and Buchanan
Goodman J. H. & Co. bankers (Napa) office 33 Montgomery Block
Goodman Lewis, clerk with Oppenheimer & Bro. dwl 536 Ellis
Goodmann Louis, with Ziegenhirt Bros. dwl Bootz's Hote
Goodman Louis, tailoring, 922 Kearny
Goodman Max *(J. & M. Goodman)* dwl 407 O'Farrell
Goodman Simon, wholesale dry goods, 517 Sacramento, dwl 722 Post
Goodmansen Nelson, laborer with William Buckley
Goodrich Charles F. mining stocks, dwl 963 Folsom
Goodrich Jesse B. professor music, dwl 1024 Stock
Goodrich John A. professor music, dwl 1024 Stock

Goodrich John H. with H. Casebolt & Co. dwl 3 Howard Court

Goodrich L. office Mercantile Library Bdg room 18

Goodrich Richard, laborer, dwl Minna Place

Goodrum George, shipping merchant, office 424 Battery, dwl E s Twelfth nr Mission

Goodue Alex. upholsterer with Goodwin & Co. dwl E s Dupont bet Broadway and Green

Goodwin Alonzo A. furniture wagon, 729 Market, dwl 417 Post

Goodwin Charles, butcher, 6 Occidental Market, dwl Minna nr Second

Goodwin George, seaman, dwl 54 Sacramento

Goodwin H. Rev. pastor Grace Cathedral, dwl 710 Taylor

GOODWIN *(James P.)* & CO. *(Philip B. Holmes)* importers and manufacturers furniture, bedding, etc. 510 and 528 Washington and 636 Market, dwl 1313 Taylor

Goodwin James P. jr. salesman with Goodwin & Co. dwl 1313 Taylor

Goodwin Lewis, saddler with J. C. Johnson & Co. dwl 113 Dupont

Goodwin Patrick, blacksmith with Gallagher & Farren, 112 Bush

Goodwin Robert, salesman with Goodwin & Co. dwl 536 Washington

Goodwin S. B. (widow) dwl 409 Green

Goodwin Susan Miss, domestic, NE cor Turk and Franklin

Goodyear *(W. A.)* & Blake *(T. A.)* civil and mining engineers, office and dwl 127 Montgomery

Goold Edmond L. *(Shafter, G. & Dwinelle)* attorney at law, office 11 Montgomery Block, dwl Brevoort House

Gooley Ellen (widow) dwl 1326 Pacific

Goolnick M. handcartman, 307 Dupont

Goran William, laborer with Isaac Stone

Goraud Benjamin, laborer with B. Bonnet & Co.

Gordon A. C. *(Whitney & Co.)* res Sacramento

Gordon Albert, cooper, dwl 6 Sansom

Gordon E. E. Miss. domestic, 305 Union

GORDON GEORGE, manager S. F. & P. Sugar Co. office cor Eighth and Harrison, res Mayfield, Santa Clara Co

Gordon George, bootblacking, 520 Market, dwl cor Stockton and Pacific

Gordon George, cook, dwl SE cor Sacramento and Drumm

Gordon Isabella Mrs. (col'd) lodgings, NE cor Second and Mission

Gordon James E. clerk with L. B. Benchley & Co. dwl 708 Mission

Gordon John, stair builder, dwl 12 Quincy

Gordon John H. *(Lane & G.)* dwl S s Bush bet Buchanan and Webster

Gordon John H. groceries, 243 Minna, dwl 259 Minna

Gordon Joseph, dwl 7 Howard Court

Gordon Joseph, clerk, London & San Francisco Bank, 412 Montgomery, dwl 638 Folsom

Gordon Joseph S. G. milkman, dwl 147 Tehama

Gordon Louisa Mrs. dwl 38 Stevenson House

Gordon Mary Miss, domestic with L. M. Kellogg, E s Montgomery bet Green and Union

Gordon Michael, hostler, 328 Bush

Gordon Noah M. engineer, Genesee Flour Mills, dwl 305 Union

Gordon Samuel, cokeman, S. F. Gas Co. dwl 544 Folsom

Gordon Sheldon S. policeman, City Hall, dwl 730 Green

Gordon Thomas Mrs. dwl 428 Bush

Gordon Upton M. *(M. D. Sweeny & Co.)* 709 Sansom, dwl E s Fillmore bet Hayes and Fell

Gordon William (col'd) bootblack with Peter Anderson, 541 Merchant

Gore Benjamin B. book keeper with Ross, Dempster & Co. dwl 739 Howard

Gore Charles, beer saloon, 129 Third

Gorfinkel Aaron, merchant, dwl 1136 Dupont

Gorfinkel Sarah Mrs. dry goods, 1136 Dupont

Gorfinkel William, hairdresser, 105 Jackson, dwl 1136 Dupont

Gorham C. E. commission buyer, dwl 1810 Mason

Gorham Daniel, clerk with John Stratman & Co. dwl 528 Green

Gorham Dennis, machinist, dwl 414 Market

GORHAM GEORGE C. clerk U. S. Circuit Court and ex officio clerk U. S District Court, office 15–17 U. S. Court Building, dwl 429 Bryant

Gorham John E. delivery clerk, Post Office, dwl 528 Green

Gorham Thomas, clerk with John Stratman, dwl Government House

Gorhey Michael, porter with Joseph Peirce, dwl Stevenson bet First and Second

Gori Nicholas, fisherman, dwl Merchant bet Drumm and East

Gori Ottaviano, artist and sculptor, dwl 363 Jessie

Gorley H. A. *(Carle & G.)* dwl SW cor Montgomery and Broadway

Gorman Catharine (widow) dwl 820 Vallejo

Gorman David *(George W. Stevens & Co.)* dwl 435 Jessie bet Fifth and Sixth

Gorman Edward, salesman, 411 Montgomery, dwl 820 Vallejo

Gorman Ellen Miss, domestic with Mrs. J. R. Stewart, W s Shotwell bet Fifteenth and Sixteenth

Gorman G. B. first officer steamer Senator

Gorman James, fireman, steamer Golden City, dwl 21 Langton

Gorman Johannah Miss, domestic, 1027 Washington

GORMAN JOHN *(Huefner & G.)* notary public, 619 Merchant, dwl NW cor Howard and Second

Gorman John, drayman with Oakley & Jackson, dwl Union Place

Gorman John, laborer, dwl W s Bower Place

Gorman John, laborer, dwl S s Filbert bet Mason and Taylor

Gorman John, stevedore, dwl E s Sansom bet Green and Vallejo

Gorman Kate Miss *(Misses M. F. & Kate Gorman)* dwl 1221 Stockton

Gorman Lawrence, hostler, 126 Fourth, dwl 61 Everett

Gorman Lawrence, tinsmith, dwl E s Sansom bet Green and Vallejo

Gorman Mary Miss, domestic, 809 Jackson

Gorman Mary F. & Kate Misses, millinery, 1221 Stockton

Gorman Patrick, job wagon, SE cor Montgomery and Pine, dwl S s Turk nr Larkin

Gorman Patrick, lab, dwl N s Filbert nr Sansom

Gorman Patrick, porter, dwl 811 Union

Gorman Simon, laborer, Golden State Iron Works, dwl 4 California

Gorman Susan Miss, milliner, dwl 820 Vallejo

Gorman Timothy, laborer, bds Western Hotel

Gorman William, seaman, dwl 47 Jackson

Gorman William J. principal St. Francis School, NE cor Montgomery and Broadway

Gormfly J. F. plasterer, dwl E s Taylor bet Filbert and Valparaiso

Gormley Isabella Miss, domestic, 122 Sutter

Gormly Patrick, book keeper, 38 Clay, dwl 811 Union

Gorrsin Christian, laborer, dwl NE cor Lombard and Taylor

Gosliner Simon, tailor, dwl 607 Davis

Gosling James, carpenter, dwl 58 Third

Gosling Joseph, architect, Mercantile Library Building, room 17

Goslinsky Elias, manufacturer cigars and dealer leaf tobacco, 316 Front

Goslyn Thomas, laborer with Edward J. Quirk

Goss Peter, bricklayer, dwl 616 California

Goss Samuel, bricklayer, dwl 3 Hardie Place

Gossel Eliza Miss, domestic, 716 Union

Gosson Annie Miss, dwl with J. C. Horan, W s Fillmore bet Fulton and McAllister

Gostorfa Leopold B. book keeper, Bank California, dwl 627 California

Gotiness Joseph, vegetable gardener, Bay View Park

Gotiness Nicola, vegetable gardener, Bay View Park

Gotte Henry, clerk with A. S. Rosenbaum & Co. dwl 332 Kearny

Gottgetreu Henry, meat market, NE cor Hyde and Union

Gottig (Lawrence) & Schoemann (Otto) merchants, (La Paz, L. C.) office 220 Front, dwl 1112 Stockton

Gottlieb Louis, shoe maker with Hinders & Kast, dwl 4 Milton Place

Gottschalk Charles, stone cutter, dwl 53 Clementina

Gottschalk Charles, watch maker with C. E. Collins, dwl Gough bet Grove and Franklin

Gottschalk Jacob, dwl 32 Hinckley

Gottschalk John F. A. boatman, dwl Greenwich bet Sansom and Montgomery

Gotze (Henry) & Borchers (Fabian) groceries and liquors, NE cor Kearny and California

Gouch George, hair dresser with Theodore Blodes, dwl S s Francisco bet Mason and Taylor

Gougerty Jennie, saleswoman, 16 Second, dwl 530 Bush

Gough Arthur, blacksmith, Union Foundry, dwl 28 Battery

Gough Charles H. contractor, dwl 1226 Stockton

Gough E. F. (widow) dwl 1010 Stockton

Gough Henry O. contractor, dwl 1226 Stockton

Gough J. T. butter, eggs, etc. 20 Washington Market, dwl N s California bet Mason and Jones

Gough Mary Miss, domestic, 632 Market

Gough Mary (widow) dwl 1153 Mission

Gough William, gas fitter, 641 Market, dwl 468 Jessie, rear

GOULD & CURRY S. M. CO. office NE cor Montgomery and Jackson

Gould Alexander, rigger, dwl 1306 Montgomery

Gould Alfred B. carpenter with E. Galpen & Co. dwl St. Francis H. & L. Co

GOULD ALFRED S. notary public and commissioner deeds, office 528 Clay, dwl 619 Mission

Gould Charles B. conductor, S. F. & San José R. R. Co. res San José

Gould (E.) & Co. (S. M. Keeler) groceries and liquors, NW cor Third and Silver, dwl 427 Third

Gould (Frank) & Capprise (Joseph) billiard and liquor saloon, 18 Clay, dwl 30 Silver

Gould George O. laborer, S. F. & San José R. R. Co. dwl 117 Dora

Gould James G. broker, office 526 Montgomery, dwl Coso House

Gould Joseph, carpenter, dwl 108 Beale

Gould Lewis, dwl St. Lawrence House

Gould Orville, San José R. R. Depôt, dwl 117 Dora

Gould Peter, cook, steamer Julia

Gould Peter F. laborer, dwl 212 Stewart

Gould Petroleum Co. office 528 Clay

Gould W. B. (Truman & Co.) dwl NW cor Polk and Broadway

Goulet Isidore, merchant tailor, 415 Montgomery, dwl 1103 Montgomery

Goux John B. dyeing and scouring, 212 Third and 1132 Dupont, office 735 Clay

Gove A. B. Capt. office Pier 3 Stewart

Gove Andrew J. harbor commissioner, dwl 1014 Montgomery

Gove West, master bark Nahumkeag, dwl 238 Stewart

Gove W. H. salesman with Rockwell, Coye & Co. dwl 24 Geary

GOVERNMENT HOUSE, 502 Washington cor Sansom

Governor Downey G. & S. M. Co. office 404 Front

Governor Seymour G. & S. M. Co. office 228 Front

Govet Robert (col'd) bootblack, 653 Merchant, dwl W s Broadway bet Kearny and Dupont

Gowan Edward (Malcom & G.) dwl 529 Pine

Gowdy William, carpenter, dwl 109 Third

Gowdy William, carpenter, dwl 276 Tehama

Gowenlock Robert, dwl 803 Greenwich

Graff Samuel & Co. (Frederick Licker) cigars and tobacco, 539 Clay and 1102 Dupont, dwl 14 Scott

Grab Conrad, cabinet maker, dwl W s Garden bet Harrison and Bryant

Grace Female Institute, Rev. H. Goodwin principal, SE cor Stockton and California

Grace William, driver, North Beach & M. R. R. Co. dwl 13 St. Mary

Gracier Francis J. bung maker, 31 Fremont, dwl W s California Avenue nr Isabella

Grader Francis, upholsterer, dwl S s Fulton bet Polk and Larkin

Gradona Giovanni, vegetables, dwl NE cor Clay and Drumm

Grady Augustus, salesman with H. M. Lockwood & Co. dwl 624 Clay

Grady Dennis, stone mason, dwl W s Gilbert bet Brannan and Townsend

Grady Henry, stevedore, Crescent Engine Co. No. 10

Grady James, clerk with Colman Bros. dwl 626 Clay

Grady James, miner, dwl W s White Place nr Bryant

Grady James, waiter, Clipper Restaurant

Grady James J. morocco leather manufacturer, cor Eighteenth and Folsom, dwl 18 Jessie, rear

Grady Jno. waiter, Russ House

Grady John, laborer, dwl 12 O'Farrell Alley

Grady John, workman, Mission Woolen Mills, dwl N s Fifteenth nr Howard

Grady Michael, clerk with H. Earle, W s Sixth bet Harrison and Bryant

Grady Michael, shoe maker, 204 Davis

Grady William, dwl 7 Lick Alley

Graefner Mark, Monitor Saloon, S s King bet Third and Fourth

Graf A. paper hanger, dwl 502 Kearny

Graf Herman, bar keeper, SW cor Kearny and Pac

Graf W. Emil L. superintendent German Hospital, 427 Brannan

Graff E. D. accountant, 625 Front, dwl Frank's Building

Graff Joseph, hostler, 26 Kearny

Graff William, express wagon, 747 Mission

Graffaw Benjamin C. glass blower, Pacific Glass Works, dwl W s Tennessee nr Mariposa

Graft Lewis, laborer, dwl 9 St. Charles

Gragg Frank E. dwl Broderick Engine House

Graham Alexander, painter, dwl 752 Harrison

Graham Ann Miss, domestic, 831 California

Graham Daniel, ship calker, dwl E s Sansom bet Green and Union

Graham Edward, upholsterer, 806 Market

Graham Eliza (widow) dwl 1122 Sacramento

Graham Elizabeth Miss, dwl 311 Stockton

Graham Elizabeth Mrs. proprietress Golden Gate House, 510 Davis

Graham Ellen (widow) dwl 233 Kearny

Graham George, carpenter, dwl NW cor Kearny and Jackson

Graham George, workman with John Henry, dwl Dolores Hall

Graham James, drayman, 211 Battery, dwl 515 Bush

Graham James (McDermott, G. & McCarty) dwl Benton House

Graham John, chief engineer Pacific Mail S. S. Co

Graham John, laborer, S. F. & San José R. R. Co.

Graham John S. dwl San Bruno Road, 3 miles from City Hall

Graham J. R. drayman, Custom House

Graham J. W. carpenter, bds New Wisconsin Hotel, 411 Pacific

Graham M. (Schuyler, Hartley, G. & Co.) resides New York

Graham Margaret Mrs. domestic, 1405 Jones
Graham Nelson, carpenter, dwl 27 Clara
Graham R. elder, Dashaway Hall, Post nr Dupont]
Graham R. J., U. S. Drayman, office Appraiser's Store, dwl 417 Stevenson
Graham Robert, clerk, dwl SW cor Broadway and Montgomery
Graham Roderick, 225 Clay
Graham Thomas, carpenter with S. S. Culverwell, 29 Fremont, dwl 59 Second
Graham Thomas, clerk with N. Curry & Bro. 317 Battery
Graham Thomas, laborer, dwl cor Jones and Market
Graham William M. clerk with C. H. Bradford
Graham S. T. dwl 540 Clay
GRAIN (Francis H.) & SUTHERLAND (Wm. S.) agents Bank British North America, office 411 and 413 California, dwl 1009 Powell
Graler Louis, brewer, Pacific Brewery, 271 Tehama
Grauly Delia Miss, domestic with Mrs. John Searle, E s Eighth bet Howard and Folsom
Grancourt J. B. porter, 422 Cal, dwl 1006 Pacific
GRAND JURY ROOMS, 21 third floor City Hall
Grandant August, lab, dwl W s Gaven nr Greenwich
Grandi George, hairdressing saloon, 508 Clay, dwl Washington opposite Plaza
Grandi Joseph, hairdresser with Pierre Puyoon, dwl cor Pine and Kearny
Grandona August, porter, 413 Front, dwl Greenwich bet Powell and Mason
Grandona Giacomo, chocolate maker with G. Ghirardelli & Co. 417 Jackson
Graney George P. blacksmith, dwl SE cor Fifth and Shipley
Granger Arthur, clerk, dwl 737 Jackson
Grannen John, bar keeper, SW cor Fourth and Market, dwl 110 Natoma
Granniss George W. with Halleck, Peachy & Billings, 43 Montgomery Block, dwl 229½ Minna
Graut Adam (Murphy, Grant & Co.) 401 and 403 Sansom
GRANT (Alfred N.), AVERELL (Anson) & CO. (Andrew Sproul) hay and grain, 41 Sacramento, dwl W s Shotwell bet Twenty-First and Twenty-Second
Grant Barbara Miss, dwl 19 Lafayette Place
Grant Charles B. stone yard, N s King bet Third and Fourth, dwl 322 Fremont
Grant Charles W. book keeper, Pacific Insurance Co. dwl Occidental Hotel
Grant Curtis, milker with Isaac Stone, NW corner Geary and Cemetery Avenue
Grant D. W. (Knapp & G.) dwl 327 Bush
Grant Ellen, chambermaid, Lick House
Grant Ellen Miss, domestic, 845 Dupont
Grant Ellen Mrs. domestic, 734 Green
Grant Ellen G. Miss, assistant, Union St. Primary School, dwl 533 Green
Grant Ennis Miss, domestic, 510 Dupont
Grant George, carpenter, dwl 206 Stewart
Grant (George W.) & Coon (Jacob) shipsmiths, 136 Stewart, dwl 117 Bryant
Grant Helen A. Miss, assistant, Stevenson Street School, dwl 655 Howard
Grant Horace A. seaman, dwl 238 Stewart
Grant James, dwl 426 Bush
Grant James, carpenter, dwl 13 Geary
Grant John, carpenter, 623 Dupont, dwl 223 Stevenson
Grant John, Columbia Marble Yard, E s Cemetery Av bet Post and Sutter, dwl 141 Townsend
Grant Joseph, dwl 605 Geary
Grant Robert, porter with W. J. Stringer, 520 Wash
Grant Robert P. mechanic, dwl E s Capp bet Eighteenth and Nineteenth
Grant Samuel T. tailor, dwl 226 Sutter
Grant Sylvester, carpenter, dwl 223 Stevenson
Grant Thomas C. surveyor Pacific Ins. Co. 436 Cal, dwl Guerrero bet Nineteenth and Twentieth

Grant William B. bargeman, Custom House, dwl U. S. Barge Office
Grant William M. clerk with Samuel A. Wood, dwl 202 Second
Grapil John, laborer, dwl 34 Stewart
Grapp George, harness maker, dwl 429 Pacific
Grard Edward, porter, 518 Sacramento
Graser Philip H. clerk, 230 Kearny, dwl 512 Bush
Grasse Frederick, seaman, dwl 20 Commercial
Grasshoff F. carpenter, dwl 1510 Powell
Grasso Constantino, blacksmith, dwl 615 Sansom
Grattan Margaret (widow) lodgings, 18 Minna
Grattan William, butcher, 203 Stewart
Graubs Henry, carpenter, bds 814 Montgomery
Graue Peter, dwl 621 California
Gravel Felix E. carriage maker with William R. Brown, dwl W s Rousch nr Folsom
Graves Augustus B. salesman with Hiram T. Graves, dwl 1603 Mason
Graves Converse L. stage manager Maguire's Opera House, dwl W s Wetmore Place
Graves (Edmund S.) & Smith (C. W.) coppersmiths and plumbers, 520 Davis, dwl 1221 Clay
Graves George, dwl 34 Essex
Graves George W. clerk with R. Hall & Co. dwl W s Wetmore Place
GRAVES HIRAM T. importer, jobber, and manufacturer wire goods, 412 Clay, (and A. S. Hallidie & Co.) and school director Second District, dwl 1605 Mason
Graves Lucius S. book keeper with Hiram T. Graves, dwl 1605 Mason
Graves Margaret A. (widow) boarding, N s Brannan bet Eighth and Ninth
Graves Samuel, office 412 Clay, dwl 1605 Mason
Gravy John, express wagon, SW cor Dupont and Pacific, dwl N s Kent nr Mason
Gray A. M. contractor and builder, dwl 18 First
Gray Arthur, dwl E s Wallace Place nr California
Gray Asaph, mining stocks, office 402 Front, dwl 740 Pine
Gray C. furniture wagon, 623 Montgomery
Gray (Cyril V.) & Brandon (Joseph R.) attorneys at law, office 522 Montgomery, dwl SE cor Taylor and Eddy
Gray Edward C. Contra Costa Laundry, office 624 Commercial, res Oakland
Gray Edwin George, clerk, 511 Montgomery
Gray George O. job wagon, dwl 936 Market
GRAY GILES H. attorney at law, office 621 Clay, dwl 831 California
Gray Henry A. books and stationery, junction Market and O'Farrell
Gray Henry H. pattern maker, Pacific Foundry, dwl S s California nr Dupont
Gray Henry M. with Nathaniel Gray, 641 Sacramento, dwl 939 Sacramento
Gray James, spinner, Mission Woolen Mills
Gray James, teamster with John Center, NW cor Sixteenth and Folsom
Gray James N. machinist, Union Foundry
Gray Joel, carpenter and builder, dwl 616 Powell
Gray John, dwl 1219 Kearny
Gray John, grocer, dwl 653 Folsom
Gray John I. with J. P. Pennell, Pier 11 Stewart, dwl 520 Minna
Gray John T. plumber with J. H. O'Brien & Co. dwl S s Pacific bet Front and Davis
Gray Joshua, with A. S. Hallidie & Co. dwl 1008 Jackson
Gray M. Mrs. dwl 610 Filbert
GRAY MATHIAS, importer and retailer music, musical instruments, etc. 613 Clay, dwl 1032 Clay
Gray Michael, foreman fulling Mission Woolen Mills, dwl Mission Creek nr Sixteenth
GRAY NATHANIEL, undertaker, importer, and manufactu'r coffins, warerooms 641 Sacramento, dwl 939 Sacramento

GRAY R. B. & CO. importers, jobbers, and manufacturers watches, jewelry, etc. 616 Merchant, dwl 720 Bush
Gray Rush M. clerk with Byrne & Castree, dwl W s Folsom bet Sixteenth and Seventeenth
Gray Samuel, dwl What Cheer House
Gray Simon, tailoring, 112 Kearny
Gray Thomas Mrs. dwl N s Filbert nr Jones
Gray William, butcher, 29 Metropolitan Market, dwl cor Fulton and Franklin
Gray William, laborer, S. F. & P. Sugar Refinery, dwl S s Harrison bet Seventh and Eighth
Gray William, steward, stm Oakland, res Brooklyn
Gray William F. printer, dwl E s Wallace Place nr California
Gray William J. *(L. Miller & Co.)* dwl 826 Jack
Gray William O. *(Conger & G.)* dwl 419 Stevenson
Gray William T. carpenter with John Center, dwl W s Folsom nr Sixteenth
Gray Willis, laborer, dwl 205 Market
Gray W. Vallance, artist with Britton & Co. dwl 921 Union bet Taylor and Jones
Gray, see Grey
Grayles Thomas, laborer, dwl 414 Market
Grayliss John, waiter, Lick House
Grayson A. H. dwl N s Presidio Road nr Octavia
Graze T. J. carriage maker, 539 Market, dwl First bet Market and Mission
Gready Frank, blacksmith with Black & Saul, dwl 129 St. Mark Place
Gready John, fuller, Mission Woolen Mills
Greany Michael, contractor, dwl S s Brannan bet Seventh and Eighth
Great Basin M. Co. office 622 Montgomery
Great Boise Consolidated G. & S. M. Co. office 338 Montgomery
Great Republic G., S. & C. M. Co. office 702 Wash
Greaves Benjamin H. Mexican, shipping office 424 Battery, dwl 121 Virginia
Greaves B. Hudson, commission merchant, dwl 111 Virginia
Greb Conrad, cabinet maker with W. G. Weir, dwl Garden nr Harrison
Greed John, laborer with Reynolds, Howell & Ford, dwl W s Salmon bet Mason and Taylor
Greed Mary Miss, domestic, W s Salmon bet Mason and Taylor
Greed Patrick, laborer with Reynolds, Howell & Ford, dwl W s Salmon bet Mason and Taylor
Greeley A. D. attorney at law, office SE cor Montgomery and Sacramento
Greeley C. C. carpenter, dwl 10 Sutter
Greeley Robert F. associate editor Sunday Mercury, office 420 Montgomery, dwl 248 Third
Green Adam T. salesman with Taaffe & Co. 107 Battery, dwl 516 O'Farrell
Green A. F. & Brother *(J. C. G.)* milkmen, 110 Fourth
Green Alfred A. mining, dwl 310 Clementina
GREEN ALONZO, produce commission, 107 Clay, dwl 413 First
Green Benjamin S. carpenter, dwl N s Nineteenth bet Valencia and Guerrero
Green Charles, cook, City and County Hospital
GREEN CHARLES B. proprietor Railroad House, 319 and 321 Clay and 318 and 320 Commercial
Green Charles G. workman with H. Owens, dwl Shasta nr Michigan
Green Daniel, dwl 230 Fourth
Green Daniel, laborer, dwl E s Gilbert bet Bryant and Brannan
Green Edward, laborer, dwl N s Welch bet Third and Fourth
Green Ellen Miss, dress maker, 6 Turk
Green Frederick *(Samuel Price & Co.)* dwl SW cor Stockton and Washington,
Green Frederick P. agent Sacramento Line Packets, office NE cor Sacramento and Front, dwl 516 Howard

Green G. & S. M. Co. office 606 Montgomery
Green Gardner, shoe maker, dwl 205 Sansom
Green George deck hand, steamer Josie McNear
Green George, driver, Central R. R. Co
Green George M. dwl 310 Clementina
GREEN GEORGE W. Green's Exchange Saloon, 616 Montgomery, dwl 867 Mission
Green Harris, clothing, 105 Pacific
Green Harris V. merchant, dwl 705 Vallejo
Green Harry, boatman, dwl 1027 Dupont
Green Henry, stone cutter, dwl 27 Geary
Green Hetty C. (widow) dwl cor Vallejo and Laguna
Green Isaac N. broker, dwl 326 Mason
Green James, cook, 32 Stewart
Green James (col'd) steward Knickerbocker Engine Co. No. 5
Green James, workman with H. Lein, dwl cor Folsom and Eighteenth
Green Jesus, plasterer with Samuel Kellett, dwl 22 Kearny
Green John, carriage painter with Kimball & Co
Green John, dyer, Mission Woolen Mills, dwl NE cor Howard and Sixteenth
Green John, laborer, dwl W s Montgomery bet Greenwich and Filbert
Green John, laborer, steamer Oregon, dwl 28 Moss
Green John, longshoreman, dwl S s Vallejo bet Montgomery and Sansom
Green John, porter, Howard Warehouse, dwl E s Montgomery bet Filbert and Greenwich
Green John, workman, S. F. Cordage Factory, dwl SW cor Shasta and Michigan
Green John L. agent, office 10–13 Exchange Building, dwl Third bet Howard and Folsom
Green Joseph, clerk with L. F. Baker, dwl E s Yerba Buena nr Clay
Green Julius C. *(A. F. & J. C. G.)* dwl 110 Fourth
Green Lawrence, butcher with R. O'Neill, dwl 11 Russ
Green Lawrence, packer with E. T. Anthony & Co. dwl NE cor Sacramento and Battery
Green Leander D. clerk with R. A. Swain & Co. dwl 308 Jessie
Green Louis, with J. & C. Schreiber, dwl N s Stevenson bet Sixth and Seventh
Green M. A. (widow) dwl 132 Geary
Green Maria (colored, widow) dwl E s Haven Pl
Green Marks, clerk, 213 Battery, dwl 1027 Dupont
Green Mary Miss, domestic with H. S. Gates, NE cor Sutter and Steiner
Green Nancy (widow) dwl 762 Folsom
Green Oliver (col'd) cook, dwl 1503 Powell
Green Rebecca Miss, dwl 15 William
Green Robert, carpenter, dwl 120 Natoma
Green Sarah Miss, domestic, dwl 824 Mission
Green S. F. dwl 921 Stockton
Green Thomas, physician, office and dwl 738 Mission
Green William, blacksmith, dwl What Cheer House
Green William, clerk, 538 Kearny, dwl SW cor Dupont and Pacific
Green William, drayman, cor Mission and Stewart
Green William, laborer, dwl 24 Jessie
Green William, proptr Green's House, 1027 Dupont
Green William, rigger, dwl 58 Stewart, rear
Green William, watch maker, 538 Kearny, dwl 1027 Dupont
GREEN WILLIAM A. proptr Greenwich Dock Warehouse, foot Greenwich, dwl 918 Market
Green William H. farmer, Ocean House Flat near Ocean House
Green, see Greene
Greenberg Charles, groceries, 12½ Fourth
Greenberg Henry *(Abrams & G.)* dwl 828 Pacific
Greenberg Leon, book keeper with Morris Greenberg, dwl 661 Harrison
Greenberg *(Leopold)* & Mandel *(Manuel)* importers and retail crockery and glassware, 524 Sacramento, dwl 1517 Stockton

Greenberg M. & Co. proprietors Pacific Cotton Mill, 120 Bush
Greenberg Morris, Eagle Brass Foundry, 120 Bush, dwl 661 Harrison
Greene Abbie L. Miss, teacher, dwl NE cor Freelon and Fourth
Greene A. P. broker, office 605 Montgomery
Greene David, boarding, dwl 308 Jessie
Greene S. H. merchant, dwl Cosmopolitan Hotel
Greene Thomas, Jackson Brewery, 223 First, dwl 26 Natoma
Greene William, real estate, dwl Ashland Place S s Mission bet Eleventh and Twelfth
Greene, see Green
Greenebaum A. cigars, dwl 423 O'Farrell
Greenebaum Alfred, clerk with M. Esberg & Co. dwl 424 Sacramento
Greenebaum Herman (H. Cohen & Co.) res New York
Greenebaum Jacob (H. Cohen & Co.) dwl 426 Post
Greenebaum Jacob, book keeper, 113 Battery, dwl SW cor Pacific and Stockton
Greenebaum Morris, clerk, dwl 819 Montgomery
Greenebaum Moses (Helbing, G. & Co.) dwl 426 Post
Greenebaum S. dwl 214 Sansom
Greenebaum Sigmund, book keeper with Steinhart Bros. 302 California
Greenenger Jacob, blacksmith with August Pretzel, 416 Market
Greenewald George, boatman, dwl SW cor Washington and East
Greenewald Julius, dwl 1519 Stockton
Greenewald Simon (Louis Sloss & Co.) SE cor Montgomery and Sacramento
Greenhalgh R. P. machinist, dwl 843 Clay
Greenhan Frederick, wharfinger, dwl 916 Harrison
Greenhood George, capt. schooner Coquette, Caduc's Line foot Washington
Greenhood Henry, captain schooner M. Robinson, Caduc's Line foot Washington
Greenhood Herman (Weaverville) office 207 Sansom, dwl 453 Bryant
Greenhood Isaac, waiter, What Cheer House Restaurant
Greenhood Otto, book keeper, 521 Sacramento, dwl Rassette House
GREENHOOD, (William W.) NEWBAUER (Joseph) & KLEIN (Susman) coal dealers, depôt S s Market bet Spear and Main, office 207 and 209 Sansom, dwl 113 Eddy above Mason
Greenleaf Charles, dwl St. Lawrence House
Greenleaf William, express wagon, cor Folsom and Stewart, dwl 309 Folsom
Greenleaf William C. captain barque Oak Hill, dwl 168 Perry
Greenlow John W. night inspector Custom House, dwl SE cor Hunt and Third
Greenman J. F. (Martin & Co.) dwl 940 Mission
Greenman Nelson, driver, Chelsea Laundry
Greenough John R. produce dealer, dwl 15 Monroe
Greentree John D. civil engineer and millwright, dwl 2 Adona Place
Greenwell W. E. triangulation assistant U. S. Coast Survey, office Custom House third floor, dwl 926 Mission
GREENWICH DOCK WAREHOUSE, cor Battery and Greenwich, William A. Green proprietor
Greenwood Elizabeth (widow) dwl 1411 Stockton
Greenwood Frank, deck hand steamer Amelia
Greenwood Henry, butcher, dwl W s Sonora Place, nr Union
Greenwood James, agent Williams & Orvis' Sewing Machines, NE cor Battery and Jackson, dwl 313 Union
Greenwood John, carpenter dwl 210 Ellis
Greenwood Joseph W. boot maker, dwl S s Sixteenth bet Valencia and Mission

Greenwood Monroe, operator Fire Alarm and Police Telegraph, City Hall, dwl 213 Prospect Place
GREENWOOD WILLIAM M. with Dickson De Wolf & Co. 412 Battery, and proprietor India Rice Mills, 39 and 41 Beale, dwl Union Club Rooms
Greer James, plasterer, dwl 422 Powell
Greer John, policeman, City Hall, dwl 4 St. Mark Place
Greer Robert, carpenter, dwl Sacramento bet Larkin and Hyde
Greffoz Julian, watch maker with Robert Sherwood, dwl 514 Bush
Greffoz Louisa Miss, domestic, 825 Post
Gregg Isaac N. coppersmith, dwl 9 Louisa
Gregg John, vocalist, dwl N s Green bet Dupont and Stockton
Gregg Joseph W. carpenter, dwl E s Polk bet Broadway and Vallejo
Gregg Michael, proprietor United States Hotel, 306 Beale
Greggins Thomas, peddler, cor Powell and Bdwy
Grego George, with George Hughes, dwl Niantic Hotel
Gregoire Bastain, cook, Occidental Hotel
Gregoire Louis, salesman with H. Payot, 640 Washington
Gregory Elizabeth Mrs. dress maker, 211 Tehama
Gregory Henry, merchant, dwl Tehama House
Gregory Henry R. book keeper with Palmer, Knox & Co. dwl Isthmus House
Gregory L. A. Mrs. assistant teacher California Collegiate Institute, dwl 64 Silver
Gregory M. Capt. dwl 652 Market
Gregory Paul, machinist, Vulcan Iron Works, dwl 1025 Minna
Gregory Richard, dwl 211 Tehama
Gregory William F. pattern maker, Pacific Foundry, dwl 52 Tehama
Gregovich Samuel (Fusari & G.) dwl NW cor California and Kearny
Greif John, proprietor San Francisco Baths and Hair Dressing Saloon, 636 Washington, dwl 405 Union
Greiner Frederick (Merz & G.) dwl SE cor Sutter and Powell
Greirless Thomas, laborer, dwl 414 Market
Gremke Henry, groceries and liquors, SW cor Clark and Davis
Grenarde Eucher, drayman, cor Clay and Liedesdorff
Greninger Daniel, stoves and tin ware, 116 Third
Grenouilleau Peter, baker, dwl 9 Pinckney Place
Grenzback Esther Mrs. dwl 300 Fourth
Gress L. blacksmith, dwl 1123 Dupont
Gressler Charles A. hairdressing saloon, 307 Pine
Grete C. upholsterer with McElwee & Ackerman, dwl Mission Dolores
Grethen John, dwl 409 Bush
Grethen Placide Mme. French laundry, 409 Bush
Grey Alexander M. painter, dwl 1031 Kearny
GREY (Cyril V.) & BRANDON (Joseph R.) attorneys at law, office 522 Montgomery, dwl SE cor Taylor and Eddy
Grey Giles H. attorney at law, office 621 Clay, dwl 831 California
Grey James, spinner woolen mills, dwl with Ph. Murphy E s Howard bet Fifteenth and Sixteenth
Grey John, dwl West End Hotel
Grey Joseph H. seaman, dwl 238 Stewart
Grey Julia Miss, dwl 127 Perry
Grey Margaret (widow) dwl 162 Minna
Grey Patrick, fuller, S. F. P. Woolen Mills, dwl North Point bet Polk and Van Ness Avenues
Grey Peter J. Rev. pastor Market St. Church, S s Market bet Second and Third
Grey see Gray

Gribben William, boatman, dwl 328 Vallejo
Gridley Joseph C. dwl SE cor Union and Van Ness Avenue
Griebel A. J. butcher with R. J. Stringer, dwl cor John and Dolores
Griére Pierre C. with Tallant & Co. 321 Battery
Griff Josephine (widow) laundry, 293 Clementina
Griffen John, merchant, dwl NW cor Turk and Larkin
Griffin Edward S. sexton Lone Mountain Cemetery, dwl E s Devisidero bet Sutter and Post
Griffin Ellen (widow) dwl E s Hyde bet Vallejo and Green
Griffin Elmina Mrs. dress maker, dwl 1112 Pacific
Griffin Hannah Miss, dwl with John Todd, N s Brannan bet Eighth and Ninth
Griffin James, laborer, dwl Washoe Place
Griffin Jeremiah, machinist, Union Foundry, dwl Continental Hotel
Griffin Jeremiah, seaman, steamer Pacific
Griffin (John) & Cooper (Oliver) boat builders, Clark bet Davis and Drumm, dwl 316 Vallejo
Griffin John, carpenter, dwl 24 Sansom
Griffin John, dwl NW cor Dupont and O'Farrell
Griffin John, salesman with Tobin Brothers & Davison
Griffin John W. (A. P. Hotaling & Co.) dwl 843 Howard
Griffin Mary (widow) dwl 56 Minna
Griffin Lynch, Salt Fish Depôt, 321 Davis, dwl SW cor Filbert and Verona Place
Griffin Margaret Miss, boarding, Virginia. Block, NW cor Stockton and Pacific
Griffin Mary Miss, domestic, 1010 Pine
Griffin Mary Miss, domestic, 837 California
Griffin Mary Miss, domestic, 613 Pine
Griffin Mary (widow) dwl NW cor Green and Calhoun
Griffin Mary (widow) dwl E s Hyde bet Turk and McAllister
Griffin Mathew, laborer with Hey & Meyn
Griffin Michael, waiter, Lick House
Griffin Michael B. salesman with Stein, Simon & Co. dwl 319 Sixth
Griffin Patrick, dwl N s Grove nr Gough
Griffin Patrick, handcartman, dwl Jansen nr Greenwich
Griffin Patrick, machinist, Union Foundry, dwl S s Mission bet First and Second
Griffin Patrick, tailor, dwl 619 Sacramento
Griffin Peter, dwl 206 Fourth
Griffin William W. watchman, S. F. & San José R. R. Co. dwl E s Valencia bet Sixteenth and Seventeenth
Griffin W. T. merchant, cor O'Farrell and Market, dwl 187 Jessie
GRIFFING GEORGE J. office Griffing's Bonded Warehouse NW cor Battery and Filbert, dwl SW cor Chestnut and Kearny
Griffith Alexander, painter, dwl N s Willow Avenue bet Van Ness Adrien and Franklin
Griffith Aurelia Mrs. principal Union St. Primary School, dwl N s Union nr Montgomery
Griffith Fanny (widow) nurse with James Bell, W s Folsom bet Eleventh and Twelfth
Griffith J. B. painter, dwl 120 Natoma
Griffith John, cook, dwl 11 St. Mary
Griffith John W. gilder with Jones, Wooll & Sutherland, dwl 914 Sutter
Griffith Mary Ann Miss, dwl 422 Greenwich
Griffith Millen, mariner, dwl 569 Harrison
Griffith (Milton) & Ellis (James) produce commission, 225 Washington, dwl N s Union nr Mont
Griffith Thomas F. spinner, dwl S s Washington bet Stockton and Powell
Griffiths Charles, farmer, dwl 314 Fifth
Griffiths David T. clerk, Wright's Hotel, 210 Bdwy
Griffiths James, propertyman, Maguire's Opera House

Griffiths Thomas H. captain schooner C. T. Wilson, Caduc's Line foot Washington
Griggens Philip, stevedore, dwl 657 Mission
Griggins Thomas, dwl E s Clinton bet Bryant and Brannan
Grilliet Edmond, collector French Benevolent Society, 649 Sacramento, dwl E s Taylor nr Bdwy
Grimbel Eide Miss, domestic, Butchers' Home, Potrero Avenue
Grimes George T. commission merchant, office 708 Montgomery room 4, dwl 18 John
Grimes James (Hayes & G.) dwl 85 Stevenson
Grimes James, blacksmith, dwl 9 Stevenson
Grimes Mary H. (widow) with George T. Grimes
Grimes, Michael, laborer with B. H. Ramsdell, dwl 438 Union
Grimes Nathan E. stock broker, office 7 Government House, 502 Washington, dwl 137 Silver
Grimes Patrick, horseshoer with George Knight, dwl 445 Natoma
Grimes William, engineer, dwl 304 Fremont
Grimler Mary Mrs. liquor saloon, 331 Kearny
Grimm Adam hairdressing saloon, 17 Montgomery Lick Block, dwl 34 Third
Grimm C. H. (Pease & G.) office 709 Montgomery, dwl 833 Bush cor Taylor
Grimm Charles, beer and billiard saloon, 1421 Pacific
Grimm Emile, baker, American Exchange, dwl NE cor Pacific and Kearny
Grimm Frederick W. groceries and liquors, NW cor Fourth and Clementina
Grimm Henry, clerk, dwl 823 Vallejo
Grimme William H. jeweler with K. B. Gray & Co
Grimsted John, seaman, steamer Orizaba
Grimwood Adolphus D. attorney at law, office 16 City Hall, dwl 1018 Jackson
Grinbaum Morris S. book keeper with Rosenstock & Price, dwl 815 Montgomery
Grinnell Henry B. clerk with Bigelow & Brother, 505 Montgomery, dwl 1020 Pine
Grinnell Henry P. jail keeper, Broadway, dwl 560 Bryant bet Third and Fourth
Grinnin John, California Soda Works, dwl 115 First
Gripp Gottlieb, laborer, dwl with Louis Ancenbofer
Grisar Emil. (McLennan, Whelan & G.) dwl 11 Harlan Place
Grisel Cecile (widow) dwl 124 Geary
Grissim & Walker, petroleum company, office 607 Clay
Grissim Wilson T, real estate, dwl NE cor Market and Montgomery
Griswold George, drugs and medicines, etc. 106 First
Griswold James A. music teacher, dwl 1129 Folsom
Griswold John C. assayer, dwl 622 Clay
Griswold Josiah, carriage painter with R. S. Eells & Co. dwl 106 First
Griswold Julia Miss, dwl 306 Mason
Griswold Maria (widow) dwl 306 Mason
Griswold Mary Miss, dwl 306 Mason
Grixon Thomas, cook with W. Thompson, 112 Pac
Grizar Adrien X. waiter, Union Club Rooms
Grob Herman G. professor music, dwl 106 Geary
Grob Trautman, architect, office SW cor Dupont and Harlan Place
Grobbin Samuel, machinist, Union Foundry
Groesbeck John, constable Fifth Township, office 613 Market, dwl 743 Mission
Groezinger Charles, with G. Groezinger, NW cor Pine and Battery, dwl 219 Kearny
GROEZINGER G. wholesale native wines and liquors, NW cor Pine and Battery, dwl 230 Stevenson
Groffman C. P. stoves and tin ware, 48 Jackson bet Davis and Drumm
GROGAN ALEXANDER B. real estate, office NW cor Sansom and Jackson
Grole John, baker, dwl 319 Bush, rear
Grollman Julius, job wagon, cor Cal and Kearny
Gronadel Bertrand, dwl 721 Pacific

Groom Henry, with Wilson & Evans, 513 Clay, dwl 835 Clay
Groom Lydia Mrs. dress maker, dwl 835 Clay
Groom William, laborer, dwl Old San José Road nr Industrial School
Groosz George, beer saloon, 538 Broadway, dwl 628 Green
Groper Charles, mariner, dwl 1205 Dupont
GROS ALFRED, apothecary and chemist, 720 Washington
Gros Edward, druggist, dwl 839 California
Grosbauer *(John)* & Fitschen *(Henry)* groceries and liquors, NW cor Folsom and Haywood
GROSH *(Samuel)* & RUTHERFORD *(Thomas L.)* Commercial Flour Mill, 143 and 145 First, dwl 220 Seventh nr Folsom
Grosber A. laborer, S. F. P. Woolen Mills
Grosleicht Charles, job wagon, cor Sansom and Sacramento, dwl 413 Natoma
Gross Catherine Miss, dwl N s Grove nr Van Ness Avenue
Gross Elisha S. mining stocks, dwl NW cor Washington and Taylor
Gross Frank W. local editor Evening Bulletin, dwl 731 Harrison
Gross James, laborer, dwl 140 Stewart
Gross John, dwl S s Willow Avenue nr Polk
Gross John F. painter and grainer, dwl W s Eighth bet Howard and Clementina
Gross John F. wines and liquors, dwl SE cor Front and Broadway
Gross Joseph, cigar maker, dwl 605 Kearny
Gross L. boot maker, dwl 533 Pacific
Gross Rachael (widow) dwl 257 Minna
Grossi E. stage manager Academy Music
Grossman George, dwl 21 Louisa
Grossman John, bar keeper, Pony Saloon, dwl 423 East
Grote Frederick, barber, 906 Kearny, dwl 908 Kearny
Grote Frederick, groceries and liquors, NE cor Geary and Broderick
Grote G. Mrs. dry goods and trimmings, dwl 908 Kearny
Grotheer Henry, grocery and liquors, NW cor Brannan and Fourth
Grothy Fred. drayman, dwl E s Bower Place
Grotjan George W. with Kellogg, Hewston & Co. dwl 311 Stockton
Gronard Isabella Miss, milliner, dwl 406 Kearny
Grougery Margaret, domestic, dwl 3 Natoma
Grove Charles, dwl 570 Howard
Grove Timothy, dwl 286 Stevenson
GROVER AND BAKER SEWING MACHINE COMPANY, J. W. J. Pierson agent, 329 Montgomery
Grover Eliphet *(J. B. Wright & Co.)* dwl 418 Filbert
Grover M. S. capt. Company D, Eighth Infantry, C. V. Fort Point
Grover Samuel, laborer, Lone Mountain Cemetery, dwl SW cor Pacific and Fillmore
Grover William A. physician and school director Fifth District, office and dwl 27 Post
Groves Charles, farmer, dwl 54 Sacramento
Groves Edward, brass finisher with M. Greenberg, dwl 125 Shipley
Gruaz Marc, cigars and tobacco, 1438 Stockton
Gruba John H. gardener, dwl 150 Tehama
Grubb John, locksmith, dwl 2 Agnes Lane
Grubb Samuel N. gas fitter with James K. Prior, dwl 5 Hartman Place
Grubb William, machinist, Union Foundry
Grube William, clerk, German General Benevolent Society, dwl 620 Vallejo
Gruber Ferdinand, naturalist, office 223 Sacramento, dwl S s Hayes bet Gough and Octavia
Gruber Jacob C. F. job wagon, cor Davis and Oregon

Gruber Lawrence, laborer, Mason's Bewery
Gruenewald George, miner, dwl 411 Post
Gruenhagen Caroline (widow) dwl 1619 Dupont
Gruenhagen Charles, wireworker with H. T. Graves, 412 Clay, dwl 1619 Dupont
Gruenhagen Martin, accountant, dwl 1619 Dupont
Grugen Annie Miss, dwl 142 Clara
Grumaldi Charles, laborer, Clipper Restaurant
Gruner Ferdinand, engraver, dwl 513 Vallejo
Gruner Francis, jeweler, dwl 515 Vallejo
Grunenwald Anton, tailor, 654 Pacific
Grush *(J. H.)* & Co. J. A. Peer *(and W. Bushman)* hat and bonnet block makers, 29 Fremont, dwl S s Austin bet Polk and Van Ness Avenue
Grush William, dwl Bootz's Hotel
Grussel F. locksmith, dwl Summer St. House
Gschwind Remi, Swiss Pavilion, E s Valencia bet Sixteenth and Seventeenth
Gsell John, cook with Alexander Lemore
Gsbarau David, carpenter, Vulcan Iron Works
Guaile P. plasterer, dwl 331 Bush
Guasaparis Mining Co. office 40 Montgomery Block
GUAYMAS LINE PACKETS, Rodgers, Meyer & Co. agents, 314 Washington
GUAYMAS LINE STEAMERS, Ben Holladay proprietor, office SW cor Front and Jackson
Gude William, cabinet maker, dwl Bootz's Hotel
Gudehaus F. & Co. *(Richard Hottendorf)* groceries and liquors, cor Clara and Berry
Gudehus Christian, clerk, NW cor Bush and Bat
Gudopp Ringolf, laborer, dwl NW cor Hyde and Allen
Guehrin Louis, machinist, dwl N s Ellis nr Van Ness Avenue
Guelfo Bartolomeo, employé with Brignardello, Macchiavello & Co. 706 Sansom
Guenand Cornelius, bar keeper, dwl Manhattan Engine House
Guerim Felix, bakery, 1510 Dupont
Guerin Dennis, cutler with Michael Price
Guerin John, clerk, NE cor Harrison and Dora
GUERIN MICHAEL, boots and shoes, NW cor Commercial and Battery, dwl 461 Bryant
Guerin Patrick, laborer, 414 Brannan, dwl 601 Third
Guerin William, plasterer, dwl 270 Minna
Guerra E. handcartman, cor Jackson and Dupont
Guerrera Augustine, dwl N s Mission nr Eleventh
Guerrier M. H. professor, St. Mary's College
Guertin Alfred, laborer with William Buckley
Guess Henry W. (col'd) porter, dwl 23 Virginia
Guest William, janitor Toland's Medical College
Guhn Marx H. laborer, dwl S s Union bet Calhoun and Sansom
Guibert Placide, hairdresser with Chretien Pfister
GUIDE (weekly) James B. Faitoute proprietor, office 410 Clay
Guider Annie Miss, chambermaid, Russ House
Guidi Joseph A. with Bulletti & Co. dwl NE cor Pacific and Dupont
Guido Santos, second steward stmr Julia
Guignard John, book keeper with August Dirking, dwl 709 Stockton
Guikenheimer Marx, butcher, 4 Clay St. Market, dwl 427 Sacramento
Guilbert Catharine J. (widow) dwl 818 Green
Guilford John, sail maker, 36 Stewart
Guilfoyle John J. harness maker with Main & Winchester, dwl 525 Mission
Guillee Alexander, carpenter, dwl 1213 Dupont
Guillemin Jacques N. wines and liquors, 207 Kearny
Guillemin Paul E. liquors, Lafayette H. & L. Co. No. 2
Guillen Manuel, Mexican consul, rooms 2 and 3 Government House 502 Washington, dwl 110 Stockton
Guillot Jaques, tailor, 606 Vallejo
Guinde Stephen, painter, dwl 707 Vallejo

Guinee Cornelius, morocco dresser with J. J. Grady, dwl cor Folsom and Eighteenth
Guion George W. hardware, 9 Post and 606 Market, dwl 610 Market
Gnion Henry, ship joiner, dwl Oriental Hotel
GUIRADO R. C. drugs and medicines, 210 Bush
Guiraud Joseph, porter with Pascal, Dubedat & Co. dwl 626 California
Guiraud Madame, dress maker, 626 California
Guisti Joseph, oysters, 26 Metropolitan Market, dwl 12 Harlan Place
Gulielmi Alessandro, with V. Squarza, 120 Leid
Gulley Margaret (widow) dwl 127 Townsend
Gulliver Elizabeth (widow) house keeper, dwl W s Folsom Avenue nr Folsom
Gulliver Hannah (widow) dwl W s Valencia bet Fifteenth and Sixteenth
Gulliver Stephen, carpenter with A. A. Snyder, dwl 24 Stone
GULLIXSON (Henry A.) & NELSON (John G.) carpets, upholsterers, and paper hangers, 336 Kearny, dwl 147 Jessie
Gullman Charles, jeweler with Lemme Bros. dwl S s Bryant nr Eighth
Gum Lung (Chinese) washing, 514 Mission
Gum Lung (Chinese) washing, S s Sixteenth bet Guerrero and Dolores
Gumbinner S. (E. White & Co.) dwl 114 Dupont
Gummer Frederick C. salesman with Wm. B. Cooke & Co. dwl 1109 Stockton
Gummer Sarah (widow) dwl 1109 Stockton
Gump Gustave, salesman with H. Cohn & Co. dwl 313 Geary
Gump Solomon (D. Hausmann & Co.) dwl 313 Geary
Gumpertz Gustave, cigars and tobacco, 650 Sacramento, dwl 424 Sacramento
Gun Wao (Chinese) washing, 423 Bush
GUNDLACH JACOB, Bavaria Brewery, 620 and 622 Vallejo
Gundlach Max, merchant, dwl 944 Mission
Gunn Chester, machinist, Pacific Foundry
Gunn Dennis, molder, Miners' Foundry, dwl 28 Minna
Gunn Douglas, inspector, Custom House, dwl N s Geary above Hyde
Gunn Felix, engineer, dwl 28 Minna
Gunn Frank, salesman with Carle & Gorley, dwl S s Clementina bet Third and Fourth
Gunn Jennie Miss, assistant, Hayes Valley School, dwl Union bet Kearny and Montgomery
Gunn John, cooper, 608 Battery, res Alameda
Gunn John, dentist, office and dwl room 1 Armory Hall Building
Gunn John M. longshoreman, dwl 118 Freelon
GUNN LEWIS C. assessor United States Internal Revenue, office NW cor Battery and Commercial, dwl N s Geary above Hyde
Gunn Martin R. blacksmith, Miners' Foundry, dwl 47 Clementina
Gunn Patrick, hostler, 532 Cal, dwl 915 Mont
Gunn Robert D. machinist, Miners' Foundry
Gunn Sarah M. Miss, assistant, Fourth St. School, dwl cor Hyde and Geary
Gunn William, cap maker, dwl 48 Jessie
Gunn William, cooperage, 608 Bat, dwl 321 Union
GUNN WILLIAM J. real estate agent and secretary San Francisco, City, San Miguel, and Mutual Homestead associations, office 5 Government House, dwl 215 Turk
Gunnaud Cornelius, J. bar tender, dwl Manhattan Engine House
Gunner Char es, carpenter, 421 Sansom. dwl Ada Court nr O'Farrell
Gunning Alfred H. draftsman, dwl 60 Tehama
Gunnion Patrick, laborer, dwl 25 Hinckley
GUNNISON (Andrew J.) & BEATTY (Samuel G.) attorneys at law, office 604 Merchant, dwl 421 Harrison

Gunnison A. R. solicitor Home Mutual Ins. Co. 630 Montgomery, dwl 1615 Dupont
Gunther August, workman, S. F. & P. Sugar Co. dwl 33 Rousch
Gunther Ernst, baker, 506 Montgomery, dwl Montgomery Block
Gunther Joseph, groceries and liquors, 1421 Dupont
Gunthorpe Henry A. book keeper Bank of British Columbia, res Oakland
Guntrum Cornelius, butcher, dwl 1819 Powell
Guntz Jeanette (widow) dwl with Peter Shinkel, W s Eleventh nr Harrison
Guntz Leon, upholsterer, 740 Washington, dwl S s St. Charles
Gurmendez D. Mrs. dress maker, dwl 810 Stockton
Gurmendez Eloy, waiter, dwl 810 Stockton
Gus John, upholsterer, dwl 228 Sutter, rear
Gushee F. A. collector, office 526 Montgomery ... ,
Gussman T. with Saulmann & Lauenstein
Gussmann Joseph, laundryman, dwl W s Sonoma Place nr Union
Gust Frank, job wagon, cor California and Montgomery, dwl 511 Mason, rear
Gustafson Charles, seaman, dwl 44 Sacramento
Gustafson Nelson, carriage painter with Larkins & Co. dwl cor Davis and Sacramento
Gutberlet Joseph, boot maker, 648 Washington
Gutereax Philip, boiler maker, Union Foundry
Guth Francis, pattern maker, Pacific Foundry
Guthrie A. with Lewis & Neville, 113 Clay
Guthrie Claude, with Atkins Massey, dwl 6 Brooklyn Place
Guthrie Jonathan (Williams & G.) dwl 6 Brooklyn Place
Guthrie Samuel, machinist, dwl 603 Post
Gutierrez Frank N. night clerk, Post Office, dwl 214 Sansom
Gutowsky Louis, watch maker with Otto Wiedero & Co. dwl Belden nr Pine
Gutte Isidor, book keeper with S. Herrmann & Co. dwl N s Perry bet Fourth and Fifth
Guttel Adolph, waiter, dwl 633 Broadway
Guttman Samuel, second hand clothing, 522 Pacific
Guttridge (William) & Curtin (Cornelius) produce commission, 128 Clay, dwl 12 Bagley Place
Gutzeit Henry, shaving saloon, 631 Kearny
Gutzkow Frederick, superintendent Kellogg, Hewston & Co.'s Gold and Silver Refinery, NW cor Brannan and Seventh, dwl 48 Belden Block
GUY ABEL, banker and commission merchant, 411 Washington
Guyamard G. L. dealer sacks, 112 Sacramento
Guyod Victor, shaving saloon, 712 Pacific
Guyon Henry, ship joiner, dwl 446 Brannan
Guyote G. miner, dwl 314 Pacific
Gwin Alexander, packer, Golden Gate Mills, bds Whitehall Exchange
Gwin F. P. dwl W s Fifth nr Folsom
Gwin William, watchman, dwl 77 Natoma
Gwinn John R. broker, Pacific Board Brokers
Gwong Mow (Chinese) garden, N s Brannan bet Eighth and Ninth
Gwynneth J. M. W. clerk with George D. Nagle, 302 Mont, dwl SE cor Harrison and Park Av

H

HAAENSON Stilan, laborer, dwl 357 First
Haafe Jacob, contractor, dwl S s Willow Av nr Polk
Haake Charles, (Conrades & Co.) dwl 129 Jessie
HAAKE JOHN C. groceries and liquors, 100 Stewart, dwl 104 Stewart
Haar Henry, clerk, NW cor Kearny and Green
Haas Abraham (Samuel Haas & Co.) res Nevada, California
Haas David (Samuel Haas & Co.) res Virginia, Nev
Haas George, baker with John D. Feldbush, dwl 336 Bush

Haas Henry, porter with Redington & Co. dwl 433 Bryant
Haas Jacob, dwl 433 Bryant
Haas Kalman *(Haas Bros.)* dwl 652 Market
HAAS MARTIN L. & CO. *(Leopold Rosenbaum)* importers and jobbers foreign and domestic stationery, blank books, etc. SW cor Front and Sacramento, res New York
HAAS SAMUEL & CO. *(Henry M. Levy, David Haas, and Abraham Haas)* clothing, 428 Montgomery, dwl 760 Mission
Haas Salomon, merchant, office 322 Commercial, dwl 317 Geary
HAASE FREDERICK, groceries and liquors, NE cor Folsom and Beale
Habenich Louisa Miss, domestic, 724 Post
Habenicht Fritz, with Rodgers, Meyers & Co. dwl N s Bryant bet Sixth and Seventh
Haberlin James, spinner, Pioneer Woolen Mills, dwl S s Francisco bet Taylor and Jones
Haberlin John, shipsmith with W. S. Phelps & Co. dwl 86 Stevenson
Habert Hypollite *(Lansezeur & H.)* dwl 10 Eddy nr NW cor Market and Powell
Habien G. glazier, dwl 112 Stewart
Habisch William, assayer, dwl 205 Sansom
Huck J. F. laborer, C. H. bds Western Hotel Bdwy
Hacke C. W. groceries and liquors, NE cor Sac and Waverly Place, dwl NE cor Larkin and Eddy
Hacke Mary Miss, domestic, 1018 Stockton
Hackett Cornelius, porter, dwl NW cor Kearny and Jackson
Hackett Edward, master stm Washoe, res Oakland
Hackett Luke, laborer, dwl 174 Stevenson
Hackett Mary Ann Miss, domestic with George Hudson, N s Sixteenth nr Valencia
Hackett Patrick, laborer, dwl S s Vallejo bet Sansom and Montgomery
Hackett Thomas W. book keeper with Restcome Perry, 103 California
Hackett William, cigars, dwl 34 St. Mark Place
Hackmer George, carman, dwl St. Charles near Kearny
Hadeler John, clerk, NW cor Clay and Mason
Hadler Claus, groceries and liquors, NW cor Clay and Mason
Hadler Hermann, dwl 1715 Stockton
Hadley Dyckman L. dwl 778 Harrison
Hadley M. F. butter, cheese, etc. 64 Washington Market, dwl 627 Mason
Hadlock William, waterman, 609 Market
Haedrich Herman, waiter, dwl 523 Bush, rear
Haehnlen Jacob, dwl 231 Sutter
Haehnlen J. C. Miss, assistant, Fourth St. School, dwl 231 Sutter
Haehnlen Louis, carver, dwl 507 Vallejo
Haffert Thomas, carpenter, dwl N s Liberty nr Dolores
Hufflitt Benjamin, laborer, 626 Kearny
Hutley Margaret A. (widow) dwl 755 Howard
Hafner Charles *(Wunnenberg & Co.)* dwl SE cor Powell and Francisco
Hagan Anna B. (widow) dwl 713 Stockton
Hagan Benjamin, salesman with Steinhart Bros. dwl 724 Post
Hagan Bernard, dwl S s Precita Avenue nr San Bruno Road
Hagan George, seaman, dwl 54 Sacramento
Hagan James Mrs. (widow) dwl 34 Minna
Hagan John, lamplighter, S. F. Gas Co
Hagan John, marble worker, dwl 36 Minna
Hagan M. E. (widow) private boarding, 1009 Powell
Hagan Michael, painter with Hopps & Kanary
Hagan Patrick, miner, dwl 120 Sutter, rear
Hagan, see Hagen and Hagin
Hagedorn F. C. trustee, Franco Am. Com. Co. 215 Bush
Hagelstein Anthony, optician with John C. Sack, dwl 5 Central Place

Hagely Michael, brewer, New York Brewery
Hageman Peter, dwl 6 Sansom
Hagemann Frederick, office 707 Mont, dwl 119 Silver
Hagemann George, with Goetz & Schreiber, 335 Pine, dwl 8 Hardie Place
Hagemann William, off Cogswell's Bdg, 610 Front
Hagen Casper, workman with J. H. C. Portmann
Hagen Henry, clerk with Kohler & Frohling, dwl 1313 Stockton
Hagen Peter, clerk with Kohler & Frohling, dwl 1313 Stockton
Hagenkamp Adolph, dwl 218 Clary
Hager George D. lodgings, 559 Market
Hager Jacob, tailor, 318 Third
Hager John S. attorney at law, dwl Union Club Rooms
Hagermann *(Henry W.)* & Detels *(Henry)* liquor saloon Niantic Hotel, dwl 9 Washington
Hagerty James, boot maker, 515 Kearny
Hagerty John, laborer, bds Phœnix House
Hagerty John F. express wagon, cor Folsom and Third, dwl N s Seventeenth bet Valencia and Guerrero
Hagerty Michael, handcartman, cor Oregon and Davis
Hagerty Peter, calker, dwl 948 Howard
Haggerty Hannah Miss, cloak maker with L. Leszynsky, dwl 38 Tehama
Haggerty John, hostler with Leonard & Brophy, 527 Pacific
Haggerty J. W. with Samuel Hill, 111 Mont
Haggerty Michael, laborer, dwl N s Oregon bet Front and Davis
Haggett Thomas, mariner, dwl 14 Ohio
HAGGIN *(James B.)* & TEVIS *(Lloyd)* attorneys at law and real estate, office 1 and 2 Court Block 636 Clay, dwl 1019 Jackson
Hagstrom Charles M. carriage trimmer with O. F. Willey & Co. 316 California
Hagthrop Edward, stoves and tin ware, 510 Sansom, dwl 626 Sutter
Hahn Alfred, music teacher, dwl 153 Third
Hahn *(August)* & Vizina *(C.)* blacksmiths and wheelwrights, 516 Front, dwl S s Bush bet Buchanan and Webster
Hahn Carsten C. clerk, 138 Second
Hahn Charles, musician, dwl 155 Third
Hahn Ferdinand, physician, office and dwl 122 Post
Hahn Henry, butcher, dwl E s Wetmore Place
Hahn Henry, musician, dwl 524 Vallejo
Hahn Jacob, real estate, dwl 636 Mission
Hahn John *(M. Lanzenberg & Co.)* dwl 323 Geary
Hahn John, driver with Herman Rossbach, 40 Occidental Market
Hahn Seligman *(Hahn, Block & Co.)* office 302 California, dwl 102 Stockton
Hahn William, Harbor View Market, 1000 Pacific, dwl Lombard nr Lagoon
Hahn William B. groceries and liquors, dwl 1016 Clay
Hahne Augustus, with A. J. Plate, 411 Sansom, dwl 110 Sutter
Haight Andrew J. gold pen manufacturer, 434 California, dwl 1916 Taylor
Haight A. V. compositor, dwl 815 Montgomery
Haight Harrison, carpenter, 14 Broadway, dwl 503 Leavenworth
HAIGHT HENRY, notary public, office 607 Clay, dwl 824 Mission
HAIGHT *(Henry H.)* & PIERSON *(William M.)* attorneys at law, office 622 Clay, dwl NE cor Mason and Pacific
Haight Marshall, carpenter, dwl 503 Leavenworth
Hain Carl H. & Co. *(Charles Hine)* watch makers and jewelers, 321 Montgomery, res Geneva, Switzerland
Haine Arthur, lieutenant, C. V. dwl 132 Geary
Haine Joseph, physician, office and dwl 132 Geary bet Dupont and Stockton

Haines George, laborer with Jason Wight
Haines Jacob, porter with William Bailey, dwl 403 Davis
Haines James (col'd) waiter, stm Chrysopolis
Haines M. A. (widow) dwl 831 Clay
Haines Margaret (widow) dwl SE cor Pine and Leavenworth
Hainque Martial, machinist, Vulcan Iron Works, dwl 67 Clementina
Hald Ernest, barber, dwl 153 Tehama
Hale & Norcross S. M. Co. office 60 Exchange Bdg
Hale Henry, mining secretary, dwl 1004 Leav
HALE HENRY M. auditor city and county S. F. office 3 City Hall first floor, dwl 41 Tehama
Hale Hubbard A. tinsmith with Tay, Brooks & Backus, dwl 5 Stevenson
Hale James A. bricklayer, bds Bailey House
Hale Mary Miss, domestic with J. Paul, W s San Bruno Road nr Five Mile House
Hale Thomas T. dwl with Joseph Wood
Hale William, dwl S s Cliff House Road 3 miles W from Plaza
HALE WILLIAM, atttorney at law, office 1 and 2 Exchange Building, dwl 1106 Clay
Hale William jr. student with William Hale, dwl 1106 Clay
Hale William F. laborer, Miners' Foundry
HALE WILLIAM F. physician, office and dwl 520 Kearny
Haley Ann (widow) dwl 112 Dora
Haley Antoine, waterman, dwl 18 Everett
Haley Bartholomew (Dwyer & Co.) dwl Bernal cor Serpentine Avenue
Haley Charles M. & Co. money and exchange brokers, office 604 Montgomery, dwl 813 Broadway
Haley D. paver, Omnibus R. R. Co
Haley Dennis, laborer, dwl 1723 Leavenworth
Haley Dennis J. with T. McCarthy, 612 Washington, dwl S s Minna bet Fourth and Fifth
Haley Eliza Miss, domestic, 714 O'Farrell
Haley F. dwl Coso House
Haley Honora (widow) dwl E s Mary Lane near Sutter
Haley Hugh, porter, 112 Battery, dwl 83 Stevenson
Haley James, carriage maker with H. Casebolt & Co. dwl 1723 Leavenworth
Haley James, laborer, Miners' Foundry
Haley James, laborer, Spring Valley W. W. dwl 1032 Folsom
Haley J. D. express wagon, cor Mont and Cal
Haley Jeremiah, bootblacking, 228 Mont, dwl N s Grove bet Van Ness Avenue and Franklin
Haley Jeremiah, porter, 927 Bush
Haley John, dwl SE cor Ellis and Fillmore
Haley John, calker, dwl 255 Beale
Haley John, hackman, dwl 631 Broadway
Haley John, hackman, dwl 1226 Stockton
Haley John, hackman, Plaza, dwl Rassette Pl No. 3
Haley John, laborer, dwl E s Mary Lane nr Sutter
Haley John, shoe maker, dwl 15 Ecker
Haley (John J.) & Moss (S.) petroleum agency, 604 Montgomery
Haley John J. stock and exchange broker, office 604 Montgomery, dwl 813 Broadway
Haley Margaret (widow) dwl 412 Folsom
Haley Mary A. Miss, saleswoman, 10 Montgomery, dwl 321 Minna
Haley Michael, waiter, Russ House
Haley Morgan, longshoreman, dwl W s Dupont nr Francisco
Haley Patrick, boat builder, dwl NE cor Francisco and Montgomery
Haley Patrick, miner, dwl 411 Post
Haley Patrick, stone cutter, Fort Point, dwl Presidio Road nr Devisidero
Haley Peter, porter, 112 Battery, dwl Burnell nr Serpentine Avenue
Haley P. W. stone cutter, dwl N s Presidio Road nr Scott

Haley Robert, Capt. dwl N s Eddy bet Jones and Leavenworth
Haley Robert, employé, Kellogg, Hewston & Co.'s Refinery, dwl W s Downey nr Bryant
Haley Timothy, laborer, dwl 414 Market
Haley Timothy, laborer, dwl 24 Sansom
Haley Warren, steward, Oriental Hotel Restaurant
Haley William, laborer, Omnibus R. R. Co
Haley William, laborer, dwl S s Broadway nr Leav
Hsley William, shoe maker, dwl 15 Ecker
Haley William, shoe maker with I. M. Wentworth & Co. dwl 4 Lick Alley
Haley, see Healey
Half Moon Bay and Pescadero Express, M. G. Kennedy proprietor, 679 Market
Hall Abraham (Miller & H.) dwl 115 Silver
Hall Alonzo, shipsmith, dwl 235 Beale
Hall Benjamin, dwl 428 Brannan
Hall Benjamin, mining secretary, dwl 603 Pine
Hall Charles A. wood sawyer, dwl W s Robbins Place
Hall Charles E. clerk, 73 Washington Market, dwl 409 Ellis
Hall Charles H. blacksmith, dwl SE cor Montgomery and Jackson Place
Hall Charles R. (Walter S. Pierce & Co.) dwl 26 Montgomery
Hall C. M. inspector, Custom House, dwl 529 Pine
Hall Daniel C. machinist, dwl N s Fourteenth near Guerrero
Hall David C. laborer, dwl Ocean House
Hall David W. painter, dwl 12 Lewis Place
Hall D. C. proprietor Idaho Iron Works, 9 First
HALL EDWARD & CO. importers and jobbers drugs, chemicals, etc. 309 and 311 Front, dwl 315 Second
Hall Edward (colored) dwl 8 Auburn
Hall Edward, file cutter, dwl 419 Fremont
Hall Edward, machinist, S. F. Iron Works, dwl NW cor Davis and Jackson
Hall Edward, second hand furniture, 106 Jackson
Hall Edward B. upholsterer with McElwee & Ackerman, dwl 129 Second
Hall Edward F. jr. (Charles W. Brooks & Co.) dwl 12 Essex
Hall Edward K. compositor, American Flag, dwl Market opposite Montgomery
Hall Edward L. clerk with tax collector, City Hall, dwl SE cor Sacramento and Taylor
Hall E. J. Mrs. physician, dwl 633 Third
Hall Elbridge G. W. with Charles Wilson, 15 Montgomery, dwl 5 Central Place
Hall Eldridge, book keeper with Edouard H. Hirtel, dwl 1014 Stockton
Hall E. M. waterman, dwl 646 Mission
Hall Emma Miss, domestic, 346 Beale
Hall Francis, miner, bds What Cheer House
Hall Francis L. machinist, dwl Tiger Engine House
Hall Frederick W. blacksmith with David Stoddart, dwl 235 Beale
HALL, (Gardner S.) HUNT (John A.) & MALONE (John) proprietors New York Bakery and Restaurant, 626 and 628 Kearny, dwl Old San José Road bet Twenty-Third and Twenty-Fourth
Hall George, brakesman, S. F. & San José R. R. Co. res San José
Hall George, machinist, Pacific Foundry, dwl 129 Second
Hall George, teamster, Pier 1 Stewart, dwl 20 Ritch
Hall George D. dwl 4 Liberty
Hall Hannah (col'd, widow) dwl 27 John
Hall (Harvey) & Aitken (Charles H.) meat market, 6 Washington, dwl Second nr Brannan
Hall H. D. bedstead maker, dwl 223 Bea e
Hall Henry, engineer, dwl 132 Natoma
Hall Henry, painter, dwl 719 Market
Hall Hugh F. shoe maker with William R. McElroy, 339 Bush

HALL *(Isaac M.)* & BRIGHAM *(C. O.)* fruits and vegetables, 73 and 74 Washington Market, dwl 409 Ellis
Hall Isaac R. *(Ballard & H.)* res Petaluma
Hall James (col'd) dwl 1118 Taylor
Hall James, milk dealer, dwl 313 Third
Hall James, saw filer, Baldwin Court, dwl SE cor O'Farrell and Leavenworth,
Hall James M. carpenter, dwl 511 Mission
Hall J. Lyman *(John Hall & Son)* 11 and 13 Cal.
Hall J. M. dwl What Cheer House
HALL JOHN & SON *(J. Lyman Hall)* doors, windows, and blinds, 11 and 13 Cal, res Boston
Hall John, clerk with D. J. Oliver, dwl 518 Mission
Hall John, cooper with Handy & Neuman, dwl 11 Front
Hall John, helper, Pacific Foundry, dwl Mission St. House
Hall John, porter, Occidental Hotel
Hall John, surveyor, dwl Hall Court
Hall John, waiter, 546 Clay
Hall John C. sexton First Baptist Church, N s Washington nr Stockton
HALL JOHN F. stencil cutter and engraver, office 308 Front, dwl 1505 Taylor
Hall John J. broker, dwl 106 O'Farrell
Hall John P. laborer, dwl 514 Mission
Hall Joseph F. dwl 4 Liberty
Hall Josiah S. clerk, SE cor Third and Bryant
Hall J. S. Mrs. school teacher, dwl 111 Virginia
Hall Julia Mrs. dwl 275 Jessie
Hall Lawrence, captain bark Ella Francis, dwl 238 Stewart
Hall Lemuel, ship carpenter, dwl 235 Beale
Hall L. P. seaman, dwl Oregon House
Hall Mary Miss, domestic, 251 Stevenson
Hall Mary Miss, domestic, dwl 822 Mission
Hall Milton jr. watchman, Custom House, dwl 129 Second
Hall M. W. job wagon, SE cor Clay and Montgomery, dwl NW cor Kearny and Broadway
Hall N. H. clerk with David Henriques, 612 Merch
HALL OF RECORDS, SE cor Kearny and Washington
Hall Peter, dwl 515 Taylor
HALL R. & CO. *(James R. Gates)* importers and jobbers drugs, medicines, and fishing tackle, NW cor Sansom and Commercial, dwl W s Taylor bet Greenwich and Lombard
Hall Richard A. (col'd) with Henry H. Wells
Hall Richard H. *(French & H.)* dwl 767 Howard
Hall Robert, book keeper with Gale & Co. dwl SE cor Montgomery and Jackson Place
Hall S. A. carpenter, dwl 546 Mission
Hall Samuel *(Scott & H.)* dwl 114 Perry
Hall Samuel Hastings, physician, office and dwl 402 Montgomery
Hall Samuel M. Club Rooms 534 Kearny, dwl 1229 Pacific
Hall Sarah B. teacher private school Mariners' Church, dwl with Rev. J. Rowell
Hall Sydney, tinsmith with A. Brown, dwl 114 Perry
Hall Thomas, butcher, dwl 114 Perry
Hall T. L. grocer, dwl 56 First
Hall William, farmer, old San José Road, nr county line
Hall William, handcartman, cor Clay and Mont
Hall William D. L. clerk with J. DeForest, dwl 820 Dupont
Hall William H. (col'd) store keeper, stmr John L. Stephens, dwl 1227 Clay
Hall Wm. J. with H. Casebolt & Co. 111 Virginia
Hall Winslow, contractor, dwl 1402 Leavenworth
Hall W. J. carriage maker with H. Casebolt & Co. dwl 111 Virginia
Hall W. K. dwl 720 Market
Hallagher John, seaman, dwl NW cor Green and Battery
Hallahan Eugene, blacksmith, dwl 21 Sherwood Pl

Hallahan Patrick, painter, dwl 46 Tehama
Hallahan Thomas, blacksmith, Pacific Foundry, dwl E s Fremont nr Mission
Hallam James, butcher with J. B. Danos, NE cor Laguna and Waller
Hallam John, stevedore, dwl NW cor Front and Broadway
Hallanan Patrick, laborer, dwl 252 Third, rear
Hallaran Bessie Miss, domestic, 1313 Taylor
HALLECK HENRY W. major general U. S. A. commanding Military Division of the Pacific, headquarters 418 California, dwl 326 Second
HALLECK, PEACHY & BILLINGS, real estate, office 43 Montgomery Block
Halleck Robert, butcher with Harrington Brothers, N s Brannan bet Seventh and Eighth
Halleck Thomas, boiler maker, dwl 50 Natoma
Hallegan Catherine Miss, domestic, 847 Howard
Hallel C. junk, 111 Washington, dwl 1108 Clay
Haller H. G. attorney at law, dwl Lutgen's Hotel
Haller John, blacksmith, dwl 1606 Stockton
HALLER *(Lucas)* & SWARBRICK *(Robert)* wood turning and scroll sawing, 31 Fremont, dwl E s Taylor bet Eddy and Ellis
Haller Peter, blacksmith, NE cor Stockton and Union, dwl 1606 Stockton
Hallett George H. *(Bovee, H., Bartlett & Dalton)* dwl 613 Mission
Hallett Oliver G. agent Contra Costa Laundry, dwl 613 Mission
Hallett Walter, with Blyth & Weatherbee, dwl 405 Folsom
Hallett Winslow L. with Contra Costa Laundry, dwl 613 Mission
HALLIDIE A. S. & CO. *(Hiram T. Graves)* patent wire-rope manufacturers and suspension bridge builders, factory foot Taylor, office 412 Clay, dwl 707 Greenwich
Hallinen Nathaniel, blacksmith, dwl 4 St. Mary
Hallisy Ann Mrs. dwl 214 First
HALLOCK J. Y. & CO. *(Christian Christiansen)* importers window glass, soap, starch, etc. 615 and 617 Front
Halloran Owen, blacksmith, Fulton Foundry, dwl 21 Sherwood
Halloran Thomas, blacksmith, dwl Minna Place
Halloway S. C. carpenter, dwl 741 Market
Halphau Alexander, dwl 13 Minna
Halpin John J. with Treadwell & Co. 204 Battery, dwl 6 Sutter
HALSEY CHARLES, attorney at law, office 42 Exchange Building, dwl SW corner Hyde and Greenwich
Halsey Edward, clerk with Henry Carlton jr. dwl SW cor Hyde and Greenwich
Halsey William F. book keeper with Meiggs & Gawley, dwl 307 Fourth
Halsey William M. collector, dwl 508 Broadway
Halsey William R. builder, dwl Fern Av nr Polk
Halstead John, clerk with Conroy & O'Connor, bds Brooklyn Hotel
Halsted Henry C. chief sutler's clerk, Presidio
Halsted *(Joel)* & Pray *(I. C.)* lumber, 26 Market, dwl 608 Bush
Haltirn T. *(H. Siegfried & Co.)* Odeum Garden and Hall, Mission Dolores
Halton John, stock broker, bds Brooklyn Hotel
Halvorson Ingea Miss, domestic, 713 Greenwich
Halwert George, baker, Oriental Hotel Restaurant
Ham Abigail K. (widow) dwl with William H. Hyde, E s Mission bet Fourteenth and Fifteenth
Ham C. W & Co. *(C. E. Webber)* produce and fruit, 1 Washington Market, dwl 44 Tehama
Ham Frederick, lather, dwl 414 Market
Ham I. H. wholesale flour, 211 Clay, dwl W s Howard nr Twenty-First
Ham James H. salesman with George W. Clark, dwl 215 Prospect Place
Ham Joseph T. dwl W s Clay Avenue

Ham P. B. workman with H. Casebolt & Co
Ham R. K. *(Renton Smith & Co.)* res Santa Clara
Haman John, shipsmith with W. S. Phelps & Co.
dwl 447 Jessie
Hambleton J. Douglas *(Cope, Daingerfield & H.)*
attorney at law, office 6 U. S. Court Block, bds
Occidental Hotel
Hamblin Charles C. spar maker, dwl nr cor Shasta
and Illinois
Hambly S. T. druggist, Tiger Engine Co. No. 14
Hambly Thomas C. attorney at law, office 402 Mont
Hambly William G. printer, dwl N s Mission near
Second
HAMBURG AND BREMEN FIRE INSUR-
ANCE CO., M. Speyer agent, 526 Washington
Hamburg Charles, carpenter, dwl Grove Avenue
bet Harrison and Bryant
Hamburg Gustave, tailor, dwl 44 Clementina
HAMBURG PACKET CO. Joseph Boas & Co.
agents, office 513 Sacramento
Hamburger A. *(B. Hamburger & Brother)* resides
New York
Hamburger B. & Brother *(A. Hamburger)* import-
ers and jobbers millinery and fancy dry goods,
306 and 308 Sacramento, dwl 720 Mission
Hamburger Charles, carpenter, dwl 52 Beale
Hamburger Charles, express wagon, Beale nr Mis-
sion
Hamburger Morris, tailor, dwl 261 Clara
Hameister Charles, ship carpenter, bds 7 Wash
Hamel Anatole, director, Charlemagne College, 628
Broadway
Hamelin Louis, physician, office and dwl 224 Ste-
venson
Hamill James, laborer, dwl N s Clay bet Van Ness
Avenue and Franklin
Hamill John, laborer, dwl N s Clay bet Van Ness
Avenue and Franklin
Hamill William, book keeper, Hibernia Savings and
Loan Society, dwl S s Pacific nr Van Ness Av
Hamilton Alfred (col'd) steward, steamer Washoe
Hamilton Caroline Mrs. dwl 531 Howard
Hamilton Caroline E. (col'd) lodgings, 6 John
Hamilton Charles, coachman, Russ House
Hamilton Charles, miner, dwl with William Mar-
tin, N s Stevenson bet Seventh and Eighth
HAMILTON *(Charles F.)* & KELLOGG *(An-
drew J.)* photographers, 513 Montgomery, dwl
S s Folsom bet Tenth and Eleventh
Hamilton Edward G. clerk, dwl 403 Lombard
Hamilton George, gas fitter, Wilson's Circus
Hamilton Henry, carpenter, dwl 336 Bush
Hamilton James, express wagon, cor Washington
and Montgomery, dwl 9 Harrison Avenue
Hamilton James, miner, dwl 1302 Powell
Hamilton James, sash and blind maker with George
Robinson & Co. dwl Bailey House
Hamilton James H. teacher, Union College, dwl 270
Clementina
Hamilton John, baker, What Cheer House Restau-
rant
Hamilton John, seaman, dwl SW cor Davis and Pac
Hamilton John, workman, S. F. & P. Sugar Co.
dwl 16 Rousch
Hamilton Joseph, saddle and harness maker, 245
Third, dwl 732 Folsom
Hamilton Mary Miss, dwl 9 Harrison Avenue
Hamilton Matilda E. Miss, domestic, 327 Bush
Hamilton R. clerk, dwl 403 Lombard
Hamilton Rob. A. lather, dwl 445 Minna
Hamilton Samuel, San José Wood Yard, 414 Bran-
nan
Hamilton Sarah Miss (col'd) domestic, 940 Mission
Hamilton Southgate, clerk, 214 Cal, res Oakland
Hamilton Thomas, painter, dwl W s Stockton nr
Washington
Hamilton W. B. actor, dwl 403 Lombard
Hamilton W. H. actor, Eureka Theater, dwl 403
Lombard

Hamilton W. H. (widow) dwl 636 Howard
Hamilton William, boatman, dwl 6 Hodges Place
Hamilton William, hackman, dwl 522 Dupont
Hamilton William D. farmer, dwl 103 Dupont
Hamlin A. blacksmith with E. T. Steen
Hamlin Charles C. ship carpenter with John G.
North, Potrero
Hamlin Edward, contractor · and builder, dwl 207
Powell
Hamlin George, engineer, Easton's Laundry, W s
Lagoon
Hamlin George, salesman, 611 Montgomery, dwl
710 Washington
Hamlin J. conductor, Omnibus R. R. Co
Hamlin Philo, miller, dwl 448 Brannan
Hamlin Sumner H. engineer, S. F. & San José R. R.
Machine Shop, dwl Mission Hotel cor Mission
and Sixteenth
Hamlin William B. engineer, Chelsea Laundry
Hamm Louis, clerk with William H. Tillinghast,
dwl Clay Avenue nr Clay
Hamma John B. snuff manufacturer, 604 Battery
Hamma T. B. musician, dwl 604 Battery
Hamman John H. groceries and liquors, 828 Clay
(and Heinsohn & Co)
Hammer Christian, cook, Sacramento Hotel, 407
Pacific
Hammer Edward H. salesman with Thomas H. Sel-
by & Co. dwl 44 Silver
Hammer L. F. baker with Stevens & Oliver, dwl
114 Kearny
Hammers Albert, harness maker with Geo. Carme-
lich, 230 Sansom
Hammers Diedrich, blacksmith with Charles Stein-
weg, 109 Pine
Hammerschmidt A. J. musician, dwl 626 California
Hammerschmidt H. A. glass painting, 230 Sutter
Hammerschmidt *(John)* & Huck *(Valentine)* hair-
dressing saloon, 129 Third, dwl S s Oak bet
Franklin and Gough
Hammersly Alfred, with Henry Buchanan, 324 Com
Hammersmith Jeannette Mrs. furnished rooms, Bel-
den Block and Stevenson House
Hammersmith John E. salesman, 207 Montgomery,
dwl Belden Block
Hammersmith Simon, furnished rooms, Belden Block
and Stevenson House
Hammill John, carman, Bush nr Polk
Hammell John, carpenter, dwl 5 Market
Hammond A. C. Mrs. dwl 208 Jones
Hammond Andrew E. carpenter, dwl S s Alta bet
Montgomery and Sansom
Hammond Bartlett, clerk, dwl 87 Stevenson
Hammond Charles, miner, dwl 619 California
Hammond Harry, seaman, dwl 54 Sacramento
Hammond Jennie, dwl 240 Jessie
Hammond John, laborer, dwl 412 Natoma
Hammond John, mariner, dwl 22 Drumm
Hammond Joseph H. tailor, 24 California, dwl 250
Stevenson
Hammond Richard P. petroleum, office 517 Jackson,
dwl 11 Laurel Place
Hammond T. laborer, Spring Valley W. W
Hammond Thomas, dwl W s Van Ness Av nr Turk
Hammond Thomas, laborer, dwl 252 Third, rear
Hammond William, drayman, dwl 421 Folsom
Hammond William, physician, office 202 Bush, dwl
859 Mission
Hammond William A. watches and jewelry, 57 Sec-
ond, dwl 533 Mission
Hammond William B. N. porter with J. W. Gale &
Co. 409 Davis
Hammond William T. machinist, Fulton Foundry,
dwl 250 Stevenson
Hammuck Ada Mrs. dwl 633 Market
Hampe Frederick, waiter, Clipper Restaurant
Hampshaw William H. liquor saloon, 220 Wash
Hampshire William, rigger, dwl 40 First
Hampton Edward, waiter, steamer Cornelia

Hampton Robert, grocer, dwl 306 O'Farrell
Hams Albert. seaman, bds 7 Washington
Hanaberry Michael C. cartman, dwl Ellis bet Hyde and Larkin
Hanafin Louis, varnisher with Goodwin & Co. dwl Everett bet Fourth and Fifth
Hanagan Patrick, deck hand, steamer Cornelia
Hanmer Moses, merchant, dwl 264½ Minna
Hanavan Alice Miss, dress maker, dwl 312 Tehama
Hanavan Bridget Miss, dress maker, dwl 312 Tehama
Hanavan Catherine (widow) dwl 323 Clementina, rear
Hanavan John, butcher, NW cor Tehama and Sixth
Hanavun Patrick, groceries and liquors, NW cor Tehama and Sixth, dwl N s Tehama nr Sixth
Hancke Wollers, clerk, NW cor Kearny and Sutter
Hancks John, lock maker, dwl St. Louis House
Hancock John, foreman Evening Bulletin, dwl SW cor Hyde and Vallejo
HANCOCK S. & CO. (Nathan Atkinson) real estate agents, Mead House room 2, dwl 763 Mission
Hancock Sarah A. (colored, widow) furnished rooms 102 Dupont
Hand John, waiter, Occidental Hotel
Hand Josiah, clerk Griffing's Warehouse, dwl N s Pine bet Kearny and Dupont
Hand William M. salesman with Bowen Bros. dwl International Hotel
Handerkin William, Stewart St. House, 146 Stewart
Handley John, carpenter, dwl 553 Mission
Handlin James S. Melter and Refiner's Department U. S. Branch Mint, dwl 507 Dupont
Hands Joseph, painter, dwl 741 Market
Handy Douglass, dwl SE cor Howard and Third
Handy J. machinist, dwl 43 Jane
Handy Joseph K. teller Hibernia Savings and Loan Society, dwl 822 Bush
Handy (Lucian N.) and Carthout (James L.) cooperage, 41 Commercial, dwl 27 Stone
Handy Thomas, steward, Brooklyn Hotel
Handy (William L.) & Neuman (James B.) cooperage, 216 Commercial and NE cor Battery and Commerce, dwl 122 Turk
Hanecke Auguste, cook, 336 Bush
Haneke H. A. Miss, special grammar assistant Spring Valley Grammar School, dwl Pacific bet Hyde and Larkin
Haney Edward, laborer, dwl 528 Folsom
Haney James, farmer, San Miguel Rancho, N s Ocean House Road
Haney John, boot maker, Jackson nr Sansom, dwl 1302 Kearny
Haney John, oysters, Snug Saloon, 612 Wash
Haney Joseph, assayer, dwl 337 Bush
Haney Mary Miss, domestic with Henry Schmiedell, N s Bryant bet Sixth and Seventh
Haney Richard, matrees maker, dwl 270 Stevenson
Haney William, drayman, Market nr East, dwl S s Chestnut bet Kearny and Montgomery
Haney William, tinsmith, 208 Commercial
HANEY WILLIAM W. Gem Saloon, NE cor Sacramento and Front, dwl 19 Minna
Hanford Edward, contractor, dwl W s Florence nr Broadway
Hanford J. H. waterman, 609 Market
Hanford Thaddeus, student, dwl Florence nr Bdwy
Hang Frederick, cheese maker, dwl NW cor Kearny and Jackson
Hanifin James. printer with Towne & Bacon
Hanifin Jeremiah J. (Scott & Co.) dwl S s Vallejo nr Front
Haning John, painter with A. & T. Torning, 528 California
Haning William J. painter, dwl 112 Dupont
Haniver William, clerk, dwl 1230 Sacramento
Hanks Fanny Miss, actress, Gilbert's Melodeon, dwl 116 Natoma

HANKS HENRY G. assayer and chemist, 622 Clay
Hanlay Daniel M. blacksmith with Kimball & Co. dwl 68 Stevenson
Hanley Catharine Miss, domestic, 821 Greenwich
Hanley Charles R. dwl SW cor Market and Third
Hanley George W. stevedore with Capt. Batchelder, dwl E s Folsom nr Precita Avenue
Hanley John, laborer, dwl 213 Tehama
Hanley Martin, waiter, Occidental Hotel
Hanley Mary (widow) dwl 16 Merchant
Hanley Mary (widow) dwl 42 Ecker
Hanley Michael, lather, dwl 14 Sansom
Hanley Patrick, dwl SW cor First and Bryant
Hanley Patrick, laborer, dwl N s Green bet Mason and Taylor
Hanley Patrick, laborer, dwl cor Montgomery and Filbert
Hanley William, lather, dwl 14 Sansom
Hanlon Daniel, shipwright, dwl S s Serpentine Avenue bet Mission and Howard
HANLON F. J. proprietor Benton House, SE cor Mission and First
Hanlon Hall, trader, dwl NW cor Taylor and Vallejo
Hanlon John (Dillon & H.) dwl 122 Fifth
Hanlon Margaret Miss, domestic, NW cor Fifth and Tehama
Hanlon Michael, lather, dwl 229 Minna
Hanlon Stephen (Kelly & H.) dwl 903 Howard
Hanlon T. waiter, Cosmopolitan Hotel
Hanlon Timothy, laborer, dwl E s Polk bet Turk and Tyler
Hanlon Valentine, drayman, cor Davis and Pac
Hanly Thomas J. mail clerk Morning Call, dwl 42 Ecker
Hanmar Margaret Miss, domestic, 511 Lombard
Hanna Aquila W. law student, dwl 221 Seventh
Hanna John, cement and plaster, dwl 716 Green
Hanna John, deputy tax collector, City Hall, dwl 20 Mason
Hanna John jr. merchant, 215 Clay, dwl 716 Green
Hanna Patrick R. ship carpenter, dwl 543 Howard
Hanna William, driver, Oriental Hotel, Cresent Engine Co. No. 10
Hanna William, tailor, dwl 329 Kearny
Hannaford John H. waterman, dwl 238 Clary
Hannagan Patrick, laborer, dwl NW cor Davis and Chambers
Hannagan William, lab, dwl SW cor Green and San
Hannah Fanny Miss, domestic, 123 Stockton
Hannah Harriet, boarding. 734 Mission
Hannah Robert, dwl 231 Sutter
Hannah Thomas, gas fitter, dwl 627 Commercial
Hannahan Edward, workman, S. F. & P. Sugar Co. dwl 262 Clara
Hannan Bartlett, porter with Michael Nolan, dwl S s Stevenson bet First and Second
Hannan Bridget Miss, domestic, 1421 Stockton
Hannan Daniel, liqnors, dwl S s Broadway bet Montgomery and Sansom
Hannan Daniel, plumber with J. K. Prior, dwl Franklin House
Hannan James, boiler maker, Pacific Foundry, dwl 228 First
Hannan John, farmer, N s Cliff House Road, 4 miles from Plaza
Hannan Mary (widow) dwl S s Stevenson bet Seventh and Eighth
Hannan Winefried Miss, domestic, 618 Greenwich
Hannath Charles J. laborer, Mason's Brewery
Hannegan Patrick, carpenter, dwl 54 Jessie
Hannena Luckel, cook, 546 Clay, dwl 544 Clay
Hannes William W. carpenter, dwl W s Laskie bet Eighth and Ninth
Hanniver John, hostler, North Beach & M. R. R. Co
Hannon Mary Miss, domestic, 633 O'Farrell
Hannon Mary (widow) dwl 18 Freelon
Hannon William, drayman, dwl S s Stevenson bet Seventh and Eighth

Hanrahan Edmund, workman, S. F. Sugar Refinery, dwl 262 Clara
Hans Jacob, groceries and liquors, SW cor Stockton and Greenwich
Hans Joseph, book keeper, dwl 532 Pine
Hans William, clerk with Jacob Hans
Hansbury Peter, laborer, dwl 9 Clara
Hansbury Thomas, laborer, dwl 328 Third, rear
Hansch Gottlieb, dress maker, 733 Clay, dwl 411 O'Farrell
Hansch Henry, clerk with A. H. Heidhoff
Hanscom John O. dwl 116 Ellis
Hanscom William W. mechanical engineer with Palmer, Knox & Co. dwl 612 O'Farrell
Hansell William E. carpenter, dwl 710 Larkin
Hansen Albert, cabinet maker, dwl SW cor Sacramento and Davis
Hansen August, cabinet maker with Goodwin & Co. dwl 919 Washington
Hansen Casper, laborer, dwl Rincon Point
Hansen Charles, boarding officer, Custom House, dwl SW cor Vallejo and Davis
Hansen Charles E. (Gluck & H.) dwl 416 O'Farrell
Hansen F. Rev. pastor First German Evangelical Lutheran Church, S s Greenwich nr Stockton
Hansen Frederick, cigars and tobacco, 525 East
Hansen Hansen, cook, Blue Anchor, 7 Washington
Hansen James, workman with J. H. C. Fortmann
Hansen Louis, harness maker, 201 Sansom
Hansen Peter, boatman, dwl 1526 Stockton
Hansen Peter, mariner, dwl 340 Ritch
Hansen Peter, seaman, bds 7 Washington
Hansen Peter, stevedore, dwl 26 Stewart
Hansen Theodore, carpenter, Pacific Distillery
Hansen Thomas, laborer, dwl Pier 15 Stewart
Hansen William, mariner, dwl 32 Stewart
Hansom John, carpenter, dwl 308 Minna, rear
Hanson A. G. confectioner, 826 Washington
Hanson Asmus, workman, Kellogg, Hewston & Co.'s Gold and Silver Refinery, dwl W s Dora near Harrison
Hanson Charles, lumber, 54 Stewart, dwl 409 First
Hanson Charles, ship carpenter, bds Sacramento Hotel, 407 Pacific
Hanson Charles, ship carpenter, dwl cor Shasta and Michigan
Hanson Christian, seaman, dwl 44 Sacramento
Hanson Frank, carpenter, dwl 308 Minna, rear
Hanson G. W. attorney at law, dwl SE cor Stockton and Jackson
Hanson Fannie A. (widow) dwl 315 Sutter
Hanson Hans, bar keeper, dwl 320 Green
Hanson H. P. ship carpenter, dwl 3 Hartman Place
Hanson James, captain schr Mongee, dwl N s Union bet Sansom and Battery
Hanson John, laborer, dwl Meek Place
Hanson John C. pump and block maker, 6 California, dwl 765 Mission
Hanson John O. seaman, bds 7 Washington
Hanson John P. cabinet maker, 1502 Stockton
Hanson Martin, boatman, foot Market
Hanson Peter, drayman, cor Mission and Stewart, dwl N s Filbert bet Taylor and Jones
Hanson Richard, pump and block maker with John C. Hanson, dwl 765 Mission
Hanson Stephen B. drayman with William Alvord & Co. 122 Battery, dwl W s Juniper nr Folsom
Hanson T. C. & Co. (Wm. L. Carpenter) butter, cheese, and eggs, 832 Market
Hanson William, teller Bank British North America, 413 California
Hanson William H. driver, Central R. R. Co. dwl Cemetery Avenue
HANSSMANN H. commission merchant and consul Prussia and Oldenburg, office 220 Front, dwl 1118 Powell
Hanzo August, cook, Occidental Hotel, dwl 325 Tehama
Haplinger John (Chas' Stulz & Co.) dwl 627 Green

Happel Frederick, house mover, dwl S s Howard below Fremont
Happers Frank, porter, 408 Battery, dwl 20 O'Farrell
Happsburg Frank, clerk, dwl 20 O'Farrell
Hara J. O. steward stmr Petaluma
Harant Edouard (Huerne & Co.) dwl 262 Clementina
Harant Peter, architect, dwl 1516 Dupont
Haraszthy Charles, dwl 128 Silver
Harbach Daniel L. teamster with Wetherbee & Cook, dwl 16 Clara
Harbidge William, workman, S. F. Cordage Factory, dwl cor Shasta and Michigan
Harbison Samuel, carpenter, dwl Original House
Harbor Police, Office SW cor Jackson and East
HARBOR VIEW HOUSE, Frederick Hermann proprietor, Bay Shore and Fort Point Road 2½ miles from Plaza
Harbourne Henry, shoe maker with John G. Hein, dwl 112 Tehama
Harby Horace, book keeper, dwl 912 Pacific
Harby Julien, collector, dwl 737 Broadway
Hardekopf Adolph B. bar keeper, Potrero Hotel, cor Louisiana and Sierra
Hardenberg (James R.) & Dyer (J. P.) office room 25 Belden Block, dwl Cosmopolitan Hotel
Hardenberg S. B. clerk, Occidental Hotel
Hardenbergh C. L. dwl Russ House
Hardenburg William, wood turner, dwl Frank's Building, Brenham Place
Harder Teis, seaman, bds 7 Washington
Harders Timothy F. drayman, dwl 36 Clara
Hardestey Anderson, liquor saloon, 4 Sansom
Hardie Claus, laborer, dwl Chicago Hotel, 220 Pac
Hardie Dietrich (Wightman & H.) res New York
Hardigan Patrick, groceries and liquors, 162 First
Hardiman Ann (widow) dwl E s Grove Avenue bet Bryant and Harrison
Hardiman George, carrier, Call and Bulletin, dwl S s California Avenue nr Folsom
Hardin George, seaman, dwl 44 Sacramento
Harding Alfred, carpenter, dwl NW cor Annie and Jessie
Harding Benjamin, drayman, dwl 807 Hyde
Harding Daniel C. machinist, bds Roxbury House, 318 Pacific
Harding Edward B. painter, dwl N s Sacramento bet Powell and Mason
Harding George (Voss & H.) dwl 637 Pacific
Harding George, laborer with William Kerr, dwl 903 Battery
Harding George S. custom house broker, dwl 845 Dupont
Harding Isaac, miner, dwl 463 Minna
Harding James, carpenter, dwl Golden Gate House 510 Davis
Harding John, sail loft, 215 Front, dwl 603 Dupont
Harding James W. teacher English, City College and law student with W. C. Burnett, dwl 930 Clay
Harding Lucien, laborer, bds Roxbury House 318 Pacific
HARDING SAMUEL C. constable Second Township, office 623 Merchant, dwl 1415 Taylor
Hardis Timothy F. drayman, dwl 36 Clara
Hardman James H. gold smelter with Kellogg, Hewston & Co
Hardwick E. B. mariner, dwl 319 Seventh
Hardwick Edward, captain sch. Josephine Wilcott, Main St. Wharf
HARDY BENJAMIN F. physician, office and dwl 762 Mission
Hardy Claus, laborer, Bay Sugar Refinery, dwl 220 Pacific
Hardy D. & G. W. storage and commission merchants, Rincon Warehouse, dwl 43 Frederick
Hardy G. W. (D. & G. W. Hardy) dwl 43 Frederick

HARDY J. books and stationery, 208· Bush, res Oakland
Hardy John A. boatman, Pacific Engine Co. No. 8
Hardy Samuel, dwl 608 Market
Hare Alexander, plasterer, dwl 811 Hyde
Hare Andrew, cook, 626 Kearny
HARE CHARLES, anchors, chains, ship stores, etc. 34 and 36 Stewart, dwl 431 Harrison
Hare Elijah (col'd) porter, dwl W s Varenne nr Filbert
Hare Frank C. plasterer, dwl Larkin bet Pacific and Broadway
Hare Richard, laborer, dwl 107 Dora
Hare Thomas, pattern maker, Union Foundry, dwl w s Stockton nr Francisco
Harford C. M. Mrs. dwl 109 Montgomery
Harford Edmund C. jr. calker, dwl Western House
Harford Hiram, calker, dwl Clementina nr Second
Hargan Catharine (widow) dwl N s Stevenson bet Sixth and Seventh
Hargan Daniel D. laborer, bds N s Stevenson bet Sixth and Seventh
Hargan John, laborer, bds N s Stevenson bet Sixth and Seventh
Hargitt Godfrey, carpenter and builder, 17 Geary, dwl 23 Geary
Hargrave Anthony, laborer, dwl Union Court
Hargrave Edward J. car builder, S. F. & San José R. R. Co. dwl E s Alabama bet Fifteenth and Sixteenth
Hargrave Elizabeth A. Mrs. dress making, Union Court
Hargrave Henry, machinist, Pacific Foundry, dwl 15 Tehama Place
Hargrave Mary E. Miss, dwl E s Alabama bet Fifteenth and Sixteenth
Hargrove Joel, merchant, dwl with John Anderson E s Mariposa nr Carolina
Harjes Frederick, groceries and liquors, SE cor Greenwich and Jones
Harkens Bernard, laborer, dwl 110 Tehama
Harkens Patrick, laborer, dwl 31 Ecker
Harker Asa, merchant, dwl 692 Geary.
Harker G. & S. M. Co. office 402 Front
Harker George M. pastor Wesleyan Church E s Lundy Lane nr Virginia, dwl nr cor Hickory and North Avenue
Harker John W. commission merchant, office 402 Front, dwl NE cor Jones and Green
Harkins Bernard, purifier, S. F. Gas Co. dwl 70 Clementina
Harkins Michael, boots and shoes, 151 Fourth
Harkins Robert, brass finisher with Gallagher & Weed, dwl Santa Clara, Potrero
Harkness C. laborer, Vulcan Iron Works
HARKNESS JOHN J. Cropper's Oyster and Terrapin Saloon, SW cor Second and Tehama, dwl 66 Tehama
Harlan Mary (widow) domestic with Mrs. Oliver Taylor W s Seventh nr Howard
Harlan Samuel, night clerk, Original House
Harlbent G. D. laundryman, Cosmopolitan Hotel
HARLEY CHARLES & CO. (George Harley) junk dealers, 116 and 118 Davis, dwl cor Langton and Howard
Harley David, clerk with Francis G. Burke, dwl 7 Langton nr Howard
Harley Edmund J. book keeper with Henry B. Williams, dwl 614 Mission
Harley Frank J. porter, dwl 31 Hinckley
Harley George (Charles Harley & Co.) res New York
Harley James, clerk with Charles Harley, dwl 12 Langton
Harley Janet (widow) dwl 7 Langton
Harlick Absalom, workman with G. Treat S s Twenty-Fourth bet Folsom and Howard
Harlock E. boiler maker with Coffey & Risdon
Harlock Henry, boiler maker with Coffey & Risdon

Harlock Margaret (widow) nurse, 29 Hunt
Harlock Robert, butcher with Harrington Bros. dwl cor Brannan and Ninth
Harlock Thomas, boiler mkr with Coffey & Risdon
Harloe Archibald, captain schooner Pride of the West, dwl 530 Bryant
Harloe John, mariner, dwl 530 Bryant
HARLOE MARCUS, harbor master, office SW cor Merchant and East, dwl 530 Bryant
Harloe William, captain schooner Wm. Ireland, dwl 530 Bryant
Harlow Delia, cook, Western Hotel, 306 Broadway
HARLOW F. S. & BROTHER (Josiah C. Harlow) publishers and proprietors California Police Gazette, office SW cor Front and Jackson, dwl 256 Jessie
Harlow James, contractor and builder, 109 O'Farrell
Harlow James W. laborer, Clipper Restaurant
Harlow (J. O.) & Parker (A. P.) produce commission, NW cor Wash and Davis, dwl 608 Market
Harlow Josiah C. (F. S. Harlow & Bro.) res Virginia City
Harlow William S. editor Police Gazette, office 424 Battery, dwl 211 Tehama
Harman C. Mrs. matron Ladies' P. & Relief Society, E s Franklin bet Post and Geary
Harman Morris, miner, dwl 502 Dupont
Harmon A. K. P. president Chollar-Potosi M. Co. office 706 Montgomery, bds Occidental Hotel
Harmon Ellis, carpenter, dwl S s King bet Third and Fourth
Harmon G. & S. M. Co. office 728 Montgomery
Harmon George, local policeman, dwl 25 Stone
Harmon Henry, with E. C. Dake, dwl 711 Howard
Harmon James A. (Sanborn & H.) dwl 22 Minna
HARMON J. B. attorney at law, office 1 Donohoe, Kelly & Co.'s Building, SE cor Montgomery and Sacramento, dwl Sophie Terrace
Harmon S. dwl 22 Stockton Place
Harmon Samuel H. (Heywood & H.) dwl 331 Second
Harms (Charles) & Joost (Hermann) butter, cheese, eggs, etc. 410 Clay
HARMS HENRY, groceries and liquors, NW cor Folsom and Twenty-Second
HARMS HERMAN, liquor saloon, 2 California
Harms John (Schultze & H.) dwl SE cor Kearny and Union
Harms John, cook, 219 California, dwl 1019 Kearny
Harmstead Joseph B. machinist, U. S. Branch Mint, dwl E s Howard bet Eighteenth and Nineteenth
Harnan Michael, with A. A. Louderback, dwl N s Green bet Mason and Taylor
Harnden Frederick A. bar and coinage clerk Wells, Fargo & Co. dwl SW cor Guerrero and Twenty-First
Harnden William H. with Sather & Co. res Alameda
Harneaur Paul, matrass maker, Lafayette H. & L. Co. No. 2
Harned Alex. mining, dwl 549 Tehama
Harnet Michael, wood yard, 30 Fourth, dwl 32 Fourth
Harnett Daniel, laborer, dwl cor Broadway and Montgomery
Harnett Edward, lithographer, 543 Clay
Harney Daniel, laborer, dwl N s Lynch bet Leavworth and Hyde
Harney James, fruit, dwl SW cor Guerrero and Twentieth
Harney John, blacksmith, dwl 12 Sutter
Harney Patrick, salesman, 211 Montgomery
Harney W. E. waterman, N s Broadway bet Dupont and Stockton
Harney William, court room clerk, County Court, dwl 210 Bush
Harnick Henry, dwl N s Pinkham Place nr Eighth
Harnkin S. H. (Jensen & H.) dwl NW cor Francisco and Midway
Harold William, teamster, Pier 3 Stewart, dwl SW cor Oak and Franklin

Harpending A. dwl Cosmopolitan Hotel
Harper Edward, stone mason, dwl S s Alta between Montgomery and Sansom
Harper James, second engineer stm Julia
Harper John, drayman, corner Battery and Vallejo, dwl S s Moulton Place nr Montgomery
Harper Thomas J. night watchman, Oregon S. S. Co. dwl 525 Mission
Harper William, compositor, Morning Call, dwl SW cor Sacramento and Leavenworth
Harper William (col'd) hairdresser, 916 Kearny, dwl 19 Scott
Harper William, watchman, Bert's New Idea
Harra Theodore, dwl 613 Union
Harragan John, laborer, dwl 6 Sonoma Place
Harren Kate (widow) domestic, dwl 1812 Stockton
Hurri John, cook, 218 Clay
Harrigan Andrew, dwl 1507 Powell
Harrigan Daniel, laborer, dwl S s Post bet Polk and Van Ness Avenue
Harrigan Dennis, hostler, dwl 8 Prospect Place
Harrigan John, hostler, dwl 266 Jessie
Harrigan Kate, chambermaid, American Exchange
Harrigan Michael, laborer, bds with Joseph Seale N s Turk nr Fillmore
Harring James, blacksmith, dwl 741 Market
Harrington Alice Miss, proprietress Mission House, 520 Mission
Harrington Almeda S. with George T. Grimes
Harrington Benjamin G. musician, dwl 28 Green
Harrington Benjamin W. stone mason, dwl S side Ewer Place
Harrington Brothers (Timothy and Daniel) wholesale butchers, Potrero Avenue
Harrington Cornelius, rigger and stevedore, dwl S s Union bet Battery and Sansom
Harrington Cornelius, workman, S. F. Sugar Refinery, dwl E s Eighth bet Bryant and Brannan
Harrington Daniel (Harrington Brothers) dwl SE cor Brannan and Seventh
Harrington Daniel, deck hand stm Yosemite
Harrington Daniel, laborer, North Beach & M. R. R. Co. dwl N s Seventeenth bet Valencia and Guerrero
Harrington Daniel, longshoreman, dwl W s Sansom bet Filbert and Greenwich
Harrington Ellen Miss, domestic, 607 Bush
Harrington Frank B. jeweler with Pohlmann & Co. dwl Ewer Place nr Mason
Harrington Isaac, teamster, dwl 11 Moss
Harrington J. A. with J. W. Brittan & Co. dwl Union Place
Harrington James, hackman, dwl 1016 Stockton
Harrington Jeremiah, stone cutter, dwl S s Tyler bet Jones and Leavenworth
Harrington J. J. assistant collector Morning Call, dwl 726 Broadway
Harrington John, blacksmith with Pollard & Carvill, dwl 333 Bush
Harrington John, laborer, dwl E s Jasper Place
Harrington John, laborer, dwl NE corner Ellis and Laguna
Harrington John C. machinist, Pacific Foundry, dwl 617 Market
Harrington John F. Rev. assistant pastor St. Mary's Cathedral
Harrington John W. captain bark Calotta, dwl 548 Mission
Harrington Margaret C. lodgings, dwl 29 Second
Harrington Marlyn B. (widow) dwl 45 Everett
Harrington Owen, workman, S. F. & P. Sugar Co. dwl Eighth nr Brannan
Harrington Patrick, laborer, dwl Gardner Alley
Harrington Timothy, butcher, dwl W s Gilbert bet Brannan and Townsend
Harrington Timothy, proprietor Phœnix House, 721 Sansom
Harris A. tailor, 504 Mission
Harris Abram (col'd) laborer, dwl 14 Auburn

Harris Albert H. (Morison, Harris & Co.) dwl Occidental Hotel
Harris Avery T. deputy City and County Treasurer, City Hall, dwl 14 Stanly Place
Harris Ben E. foreman stables North Beach & M. R. R. Co. dwl 314 Jessie
Harris Bernard, second hand furniture, 253 Third
Harris Cecilia (widow) dwl 6 Hardie Place
Harris Charles, dwl cor Post and Leavenworth
Harris Charles, cigar maker, dwl 182 Jessie
Harris Charles W. secretary Newport Land Co. office 338 Montgomery
Harris Daniel, butcher, 1 and 3 Clay St. Market, dwl 712 Green
Harris David, foreman with Richard Merriman, dwl 2 Oak
Harris D. C. mason, dwl Original House
Harris Edward, clerk, dwl 6 Prospect Place
Harris Edwin (Carlton & H.) Carlton's Warehouse, dwl 1309 Taylor
Harris Edwin R. dwl 329 Pine
Harris Enon, propertyman, dwl NW cor Third and King
Harris George, dwl SW cor Franklin and Austin
Harris George A. accountant, A. R. C. Ice Co. 718 Battery
Harris George W. carman, 708 Sansom, dwl 1503 Larkin nr Sacramento
Harris Henrietta (widow) dwl 132 Sutter, rear
Harris Henry, merchant (Virginia City) dwl 226 Minna
Harris Herman, cigar maker, dwl 182 Jessie
Harris Hermann, seaman, dwl N s Washington bet Leavenworth and Hyde
Harris Isaac (col'd) porter, 630 Commercial
Harris Isaac, clothing, 613 Davis
Harris Isaac, manufacturer hats and caps, 716 Mkt
Harris Jacob, clerk with William Meyer, dwl 1227 Stockton
Harris Jacob, tailor, dwl 241 Minna
Harris James, bricklayer, dwl 509 Dupont
HARRIS JAMES, trunk manufactory, 513 Kearny
Harris J. F. clerk with Wheeler Martin, dwl 265 Third
Harris J. Freeman, toys and fancy goods, 265 Third
Harris J. L. dwl 22 Montgomery
Harris John (col'd) dwl 837 Broadway
Harris John, cigar maker, 419 Brannan, dwl 184 Jessie
Harris John, laborer, dwl E s Main nr Market
Harris John, peddler, dwl 12 St Mary
Harris John, steward steamer Senator
Harris John F. porter with A. C. Peachy, dwl 726 Harrison
HARRIS JOHN N. wines and liquors, Sample Rooms 432 California
Harris Joseph, dwl 113 Fifth
Harris Joseph, dwl 51 Jessie
Harris Lewis, waiter, Richards' Restaurant, dwl 37 Jessie
Harris Mark, gentlemen's furnishing goods, 802 Kearny, dwl 6 Prospect Place
Harris Marks, tailor, dwl 326 Pacific
Harris Marks, tailor, dwl 1414 Powell
Harris Mary (widow) dwl 17 Third
Harris Mary R. Miss, private school, 410 Stockton
Harris Michael, tailor, 646½ Pacific
Harris Mitchell, tailor, dwl 845 Clay
Harris Mitchell, tailor, dwl 8 Prospect Place
Harris Morris, fancy goods, 153 Second
Harris Moses, glazier, dwl 37 Jessie
Harris P. clerk, dwl S s Sacramento bet Leavenworth and Hyde
Harris Pincus, porter, SE cor Sansom and Sac
Harris Rebecca (widow) domestic, dwl 618 Cal
Harris Robert L. civil engineer, office 72 Montgomery Block, dwl NE cor Brannan and Second
Harris Samuel, clothing, 212 Stewart
Harris Simon, cartman, dwl 50 Clementina

Harris Simon, salesman with Stein, Simon & Co. 632 Sacramento
Harris Stephen M. restaurant, 30 Clay, dwl N s Howard bet.Second and Third
HARRIS STEPHEN R. physician and county corone, office and dwl room 12 Court Block, 636 Clay
Harris Thomas, boot maker, dwl 726 Harrison
Harris Thomas R. with Lewis & Neville, 113 Clay
Harris Timothy, coppersmith, dwl Vigilant Engine House, No. 9
Harris William & Co. gun and locksmith, 208 Leidesdorff, dwl W s Jones bet Sac and Cal
Harris William, tailor with W. Harris, dwl 17 Pac
Harris William, waiter, Original House Restaurant
Harris William J. dwl E s Sansom bet Broadway and Pacific
Harris Yetta (widow) 182 Jessie
Harrison Anthony, ship carpenter, dwl 135 Townsend
Harrison Benjamin, teamster, Monumental Engine Co. No. 6
Harrison Benjamin F. porter, 425 Battery
Harrison Charles A. laborer, dwl 33 John
HARRISON CHARLES H. Phœnix Oil Works, Benicia and Mare Island pilot and Harrison's Steam Pumps, office 517 Front, dwl S s Francisco bet Dupont and Kearny
Harrison David, waiter, Empire 'State Restaurant, dwl cor Bush and Sansom
Harrison Eugene, porter, dwl SW cor Dupont and Broadway
Harrison Frank, laborer, dwl 206 Ritch
Harrison H. E. lodgings, NE cor Broadway and Kearny
Harrison Henry D. (Falkner, Bell & Co.) res London
Harrison James S. merchant, dwl N s Sutter bet Stockton and Powell
Harrison James V. book keeper with Tucker & Co. dwl 1623 Mission
HARRISON JOHN, Boomerang Saloon, NW cor Washington and Dupont, dwl W s Telegraph Place nr Greenwich
Harrison John M. clerk, 406 Front, dwl 921 Stockton
Harrison John T. hairdresser, dwl N s Grove nr Laguna
Harrison Ralph C. (Colton & H.) attorney at law, office 402 Montgomery, dwl 115 Dupont
Harrison Randolph, clerk U. S. Engineers, 37 Montgomery Block, dwl 509 Powell
Harrison Robert, cashier with Forbes Brothers & Co. dwl N s Sutter bet Stockton and Powell
Harrison Samuel S. auctioneer with Voizin, Ris & Webster, dwl 831 California
Harrison Thomas (col'd) dwl 709 Stockton, rear
Harrison Thomas, oiler, steamer Pacific
Harrison William B. tailor with A. McArthur, dwl 306 Dupont
HARRISON WILLIAM P. paper warehouse and printing materials and agent San Lorenzo Paper Mills, 421 Clay, res Oakland
Harrison William S. decorator with Jones, Wooll & Sutherland, dwl E s Prospect Avenue nr Precita Avenue
Harrod W. J. with S. S. Culverwell, 24 Fremont
Harrold James, commission merchant, 619 Front, dwl N s Chestnut bet Dupont and Stockton
Harrold John (Lyon & Co.) dwl 145 Jessie
Harrold Richard, brewer, Empire Brewery, dwl 149 Jessie
Harrold, see Harold
Harron James, painter, dwl S s Cliff House Road nr Lone Mountain Cemetery
Harrop John, laundryman, dwl 19 Clara
Harry Baltimore & Co. fish, 23 and 24 Washington Market, dwl W s Drumm bet Wash and Clay
Harry George, tailor with George L. Reynolds, dwl Chili Hall

Harshall Gerson, tailor, 219 Third
Harshall Gustof, tailor, 144 Third
Hart Angie (widow) dwl 337 Jessie
Hart Bernard, tailor, dwl Adelaide Place nr Taylor
Hart Bridget, cook, Roxbury House
Hart Charles B. searcher records, office 21 Exchange Bdg, dwl S s Clementina bet Fourth and Fifth
Hart David, cartman, cor Mission and Third
Hart Daniel, job wagon, cor Clay and Davis, dwl cor Lombard and Fillmore
Hart Dominick, cartman, cor Sutter and Dupont
Hart Felix L. (Bowen & H.) dwl 620 Market
Hart Francis, plasterer, dwl 40 Natoma
Hart Frederick J. clerk, 300 Montgomery
Hart F. V. clerk, 619 Market
Hart Hugh, cartman, dwl O'Farrell bet Taylor and Jones
Hart J. B. attorney at law, office 20 Exchange Building, dwl N s Minna bet First and Second
Hart John, cartman, dwl 53 Third
Hart John, Eureka Shades Liquor Saloon, SW cor Post and Powell
Hart John, horseshoeing, 419 Pine, dwl 155 Tehama
Hart John, workman, S. F. & P. Sugar Co. dwl S s White Place nr Bryant
Hart John L. porter, Russ House, dwl 235 Jessie
Hart Lewis, dwl 4 Dupont Place
Hart Maria Miss, domestic, 35 Essex
Hart Melvina Miss (col'd) domestic, 404 Eddy
Hart Michael, bricklayer, S. F. Gas Co. dwl 40 Natoma
Hart Michael, workman, S. F. & P. Sugar Co. dwl N s Minna bet Fifth and Sixth
Hart Nancy F. Miss, dress maker, 34 Third
Hart (Simon) & Goodman (David) game, 66 Washington Market, dwl Continental Hotel
Hart Thomas, boiler maker with Coffey & Risdon
Hart Thomas, laborer, dwl 44 Natoma
Hart Thomas, manager Pacific Lodgings, 525 Com
Hart William, laborer, dwl Wetmore Place N s Clay bet Powell and Mason
Hart William, second officer John L. Stephens, dwl 551 Folsom
Hart Wolf, peddler, dwl Kearny nr Pacific
Harte Frank Bret, secretary Superintendent U. S. Branch Mint, office 610 Com, dwl 609 Folsom
Hartee Bridget Miss, domestic, 505 Sutter, rear
Harter Henry, blacksmith with Kimball & Co. dwl 256 Clara
HARTER (I. M.) & FITCH (J. Benjamin) proprietors Bay View Park Stock Association, rooms 219 Bush
HARTFORD FIRE INSURANCE CO. Hartford, Bigelow & Brother agents, 505 Montgomery
Hartford John, laborer, dwl N s Union bet Calhoun and Sansom
Hartford John W. carpenter, dwl 5 Oak
Harting Henry, bar keeper, 540 Jackson, dwl 637 Pacific
Harting Jacob, cartman, dwl 634 Pacific
Hartley John, carpenter, dwl 156 Natoma
Hartley M. (Schuyler, Hartley, Graham & Co.) res New York
Hartley William, preserved meats, 2 Merchant
Hartley William S. B. dwl 418 Greenwich
Hartman Charles, groceries and liquors, SW cor Dupont and St. Mark Place
Hartman Christian, carpenter, dwl 1211 Clay
Hartman Christian, porter, William Tell House
Hartman George, laborer, Pacific Glass Works, dwl Potrero
Hartman Henry, tinsmith, dwl 2021 Mason
Hartman Isaac, attorney at law, dwl 735 Howard
Hartman Jacob, machinist, Miners' Foundry, dwl 202 Dupont, rear
Hartman James, melter, Kellogg, Hewston & Co.'s G. & S. Refinery, dwl S s Hardie Place nr Kearny
Hartman John W. carpenter, dwl 145 Post

Hartman Nicholas, blind maker with S. S. Culverwell, 29 Fremont, dwl 61 Stevenson
Hartman R. J. dress maker, dwl 256 Clary
Hartmann Adolph, book keeper with Andrew Kohler, dwl 735 Pine
Hartmann Adolph, cook, Blue Anchor, 7 Wash
Hartmann Adolph E. jeweler with Lemme Bros. dwl 22 Belden
HARTMANN (*Christian*) & HILLEBRANDT (*Fabian*) groceries and liquors, NW cor Brannan and Third
Hartmann Edward, painter, dwl 719 Greenwich
Hartmann Ernest, teacher instrumental music, California Collegiate Institute, dwl 522 Dupont
Hartmann Frederick, book keeper with Godchaux Bros. & Co. dwl 326 O'Farrell
Hartmann Frederick G. harness maker with Henry Weaver, dwl 326 O'Farrell
Hartmann William, blacksmith with Jonathan Kittredge, dwl N s Folsom bet Main and Spear
Hartmeyer Louis, Monroe Meat Market, NE cor Post and Dupont
Hartnagle Hermann J. (*Morgan & Co.*) dwl SW cor Bryant and Third
Hartnell John, laborer, dwl 318 Broadway, rear
Hartnett Edmund, hostler, 655 Sacramento, dwl Kearny nr California
Hartnett John, hostler, 655 Sacramento, dwl Kearny nr California
Hartnett Michael, foreman S. F. Gas Co
Hartnett Michael, wood and coal, 30 Fourth
Hartney Stephen, club room and dwl 534 Kearny
HARTOG EDWARD, agent and interpreter, office with W. M. Zabriskie, rear City Hall, dwl 522 California
Harton Robert L. brass founder, dwl E s Carolina nr Mariposa
Hartsburg William, blacksmith, Fulton Foundry, dwl 115 First
Hartsel Mina, proprietor Clinton Temperance Hotel, 311 Pacific
Hartshorne Benj. M. vice president C. S. Navigation Co. office NE cor Front and Jackson, dwl 14 Essex
Hartshorne Eldridge, bar keeper with Thomas Adam, cor Mont and Market, dwl 311 Third
Hartshorne Robert, dwl Russ House
Hartshorne William R. (*Gardner & Co.*) dwl U. S. Court Building SW cor Mont and Jackson
Hartson Samuel, with George F. Parker, dwl 115 Montgomery Block
Harttlet Lawrence, butcher with W. Oswald, dwl N s Broadway bet Mason and Taylor
Hartung Charles F. driver with Bowen Bros. dwl 402 Post
Hartung Emily Miss, domestic, 24 O'Farrell
Hartung Fritz, NW cor Fourth and Clementina
Hartung Gustave, porter, NW cor Front and Sac
Hartung Theodore, watch maker and jeweler, 216 Kearny, dwl 272 Jessie
Hartung Wilhelmina (widow) midwife, dwl 207 Dupont
Hartvig William, compositor, American Flag, dwl E s Taylor bet Eddy and Ellis
Hartwell Frank, machinist, dwl 1107 Kearny
Hartwell M. dwl SE cor Mission and First
Hartwell Thomas J. (col'd) dwl N s Sutter bet Larkin and Polk
Hartwig Fritz, driver, Philadelphia Brewery
Hartwig Theodore, marble carver with M. Heverin, dwl N s Hayes nr Polk
Hartz J. butcher, 146 Second
Hartzel C. A. with Snow & Co. SE cor Washington and Sansom
HARVEY ALFRED A. (*Turner & H.*) dwl 722 Washington
Harvey Charles C. (*North British and Mercantile Insurance Co.*) office 414 California, dwl N s Howard bet Sixth and Seventh

Harvey Charles L. carpenter, 114 Dupont, dwl 755 Howard
Harvey David B. dwl 732 Mission
Harvey Edward, laborer, dwl 16 Merchant
Harvey Edward C. sail maker with John Harding, dwl 215 Sansom
Harvey (*Edward E.*) & Co. pork packers, 234 and 236 Third
Harvey Eliza (widow) dwl 417 Greenwich
Harvey Elizabeth (widow) dwl E s First Avenue nr Fifteenth
Harvey Francis P. engineer, Galloway & Boobar, dwl 51 Natoma
Harvey James C. Coiner's Department U. S. Branch Mint, dwl 1005 Clay
Harvey John R. laborer, dwl 547 Mission
Harvey Jonah, brick setter with William Buckley, dwl 810 Stockton
Harvey Joseph, fish, 19 Occidental Market, dwl 20 Geary
Harvey Louise, private school, E s First Avenue nr Fifteenth
Harvey Miles M. with Tay, Brooks & Backus, cor Washington and Front
Harvey Patrick, boot maker, dwl W s Sansom bet Union and Filbert
Harvey William C. plasterer, California Engine Co. No. 4
Harvey William H. compositor, Evening Bulletin, dwl 813 Stockton
Harvey, see Hervey
Harville John W. physician, office and dwl S s Sixteenth bet Valencia and Guerrero
Harwood Eliza Miss, teacher Deaf, Dumb and Blind Institution, SE cor Fifteenth and Mission
Harwood Rufus, ship carpenter with John G. North, Potrero, dwl 13 Front
Harwood Thomas, carpenter, dwl N s Greenwich bet Kearny and Dupont
Hary Ellen Mrs. dwl N s Bryant bet Second and Stanly Place
Hasbach Frederick, teacher modern languages, dwl 719 Vallejo
Hasbach Henry, with Otto Hasbach, dwl 308 Sixth
Hasbach Henry, waiter, dwl 323 Pine
Hasbach Otto, Custom House broker, office 502 Battery, dwl 1014 Stockton
Haseler David, express wagon, dwl SW cor Franklin and Fulton
Haseltine Charles E. & Co. (*Jason B. Dorr*) stevedores, 36 Stewart, dwl 9 Front, rear
Haseltine, Hazen & Co. (*Thomas Dorland*) ship stores. 710 Front, dwl 613 Dupont
Haseltine Hazen jr. clerk, Howard Engine Co. No. 3
Haseltine William, merchant, office and dwl 524 California
Hasen William, conductor, North Beach & M. R. R. Co. dwl 21 Louisa
Hash Samuel, drayman with Thomas F. Northey, 120 California
Hasbagen John, groceries and liquors, NW cor Broadway and Stockton
Hasbagen John H. (*Schroder & H.*) NW cor Stockton and Vallejo
HASHAGEN MARTIN, junk, 102 Sacramento cor Drumm
Hashagen, see Hasshagen
Haskell Andrew, carpenter, dwl 331 Jessie
Haskell A. W. secretary Napoleon Copper M. Co. office 19 Stevenson House
Haskill Charles L. saddler, dwl 77 Stevenson
Haskell D. H. dwl 945 Mission
Haskell George A. blind maker, dwl First St. House
HASKELL GEORGE S. & CO. groceries, 514 Market and 15 Sutter, dwl 545 Folsom
Haskell George S. book keeper with J. & D. Conrad, dwl 320 O'Farrell
Haskell Gilbert W. carpenter, dwl SW cor Guerrero and Columbia

Haskell James H. painter, dwl 356 Third
Haskell J. E. salesman, 819 Montgomery, dwl DeBoom nr Second
Haskell John L. dwl 1231 Stockton
Haskell N. watchman, U. S. Branch Mint, dwl Federal Building
Haskell Phinens, sash and blind maker, dwl N s Fell bet Octavia and Laguna
Haskell Sarah L. (widow) dress maker, 356 Third
Haskell William, with Edward Dakin, 33 Clay, dwl S s Minna bet First and Second
Haskell William, paper hanger with George W. Clark, dwl 331 Jessie
Haskell William F. engineer, dwl SE cor Broadway and Montgomery
Haskell William H. salesman, Carle & Gorley, dwl DeBoom nr Second
Haskin Charles A. Paymaster's Department U. S. A. dwl 345 Fremont
Haskin Henry R. compositor, Evening Bulletin, dwl cor Polk and Tyler
Haskins H. driver, Omnibus R. R. Co
Haskins James, dwl NE cor Greenwich and Leav
Haskins John, farmer, Ocean House Flat nr Ocean House
Haslam James, with D. Seagleken
Haslan Henry A. stove mounter with James DeLa Montanya, dwl 1222 Jackson
Hassam Henry, cabinet maker with R. R. Lloyd, dwl Summer St. House
Hassard Richard, foreman Spring Valley W. W. Co. dwl NE cor Minna and Second
Hassebach George *(John C. Moritz & Co.)* dwl NW cor Powell and Filbert
Hassel *(Henry)* & Huber *(Caspar)* fruit and vegetables, 47 Washington Market, dwl S s Montgomery Court nr Montgomery
Hassen William, conductor, North Beach & M. R. R. Co
Hassett Andrew, fireman, dwl 146 Stewart
Hassett Dennis, miner, bds Franklin Hotel, SE cor Sansom and Pacific
Hassett Julia Miss, domestic, 317 Lombard
Hassett Patrick, peddler, dwl 455 Clementina
HASSEY F. A. stock and real estate broker and notary public, office 524 Mont, dwl Lick House
Hasshagen J. & Co. *(William Helmke)* groceries and liquors, 322 Jackson
Hassitt James, miner, dwl 8 Bay State Row
Hasslinger John, barber, dwl 627 Green
Hasson H. dwl 633 California
Hasson James C. clerk, C. S. Navigation Co. Broadway Wharf, dwl 633 California
Hasson William, blacksmith, Golden State Iron Works, dwl Hubbard nr Howard
HASTE *(John H.)* & KIRK *(Christian)* coal and iron, 515 California, storage 25 and 31 Beale, dwl 734 Post
Haster William, cook, 506 Montgomery
Hasting Joseph, contractor, E s Webb bet California and Sacramento
Hastings B. F. *(John Sime & Co.)* res Sacramento
Hastings C. C. *(Heuston, H. & Co.)* res 265 Broadway New York
Hastings Edward S. ornamental japanning, 203 Commercial, dwl 1 Bagley Place
Hastings E. L. salesman with McAran & Kelly, bds SE cor Market and Third
Hastings E. O. F. dwl 963 Howard
Hastings Frances M. Miss, dwl 311 Clementina
Hastings Francis, dwl 3 Hardie Place
Hastings Francis S. salesman with Heuston, Hastings & Co. dwl 212 Powell
Hastings Frank, artist, dwl with H. B. Congdon, N s Thirteenth nr Mission
Hastings George A. carpenter, dwl 264½ Clementina
Hastings Horace M. *(Taylor & H.)* attorney at law, office 621 Clay

Hastings John, resident physician and superintendent U. S. Marine Hospital, office 420 Montgomery, dwl Rincon Point bet Main and Spear
Hastings Mary P. assistant principal Grace Female Institute, dwl SW cor Stockton and Jackson
Hastings Nathaniel, carpenter and builder, dwl 1011 Bush
Hastings N. P. Miss, teacher, Grace Female Institute, dwl 909 Clay
Hastings R. S. attorney at law, dwl 607 Folsom
HASTINGS S. CLINTON, real estate, office 6 Court Block 636 Clay
HASTINGS WILLIAM, attorney at law and proctor in admiralty, office 436 Jackson, dwl 1226 Sacramento
Hasty Alonzo P. salesman with H. W. Bragg & Co. 31 Battery
Haswell J. C. compositor, Evening Bulletin, dwl 526 Greenwich
Hatch A. D. dwl 1014 Sutter
Hatch B. dwl What Cheer House
Hatch Charles E. clerk with Shafter, Goold & Dwinelle, dwl 1014 Sutter
Hatch Frederick, clerk with S. M. & D. S. Wilson, dwl 1014 Sutter
Hatch James, sawyer with S. S. Culverwell, 29 Fremont, dwl 15 Tehama
HATCH T. H. & CO. *(Richard M. Brangon)* wholesale commission produce, 319 Washington, dwl 811 Hyde nr Bush
Hatch Thomas, cabinet maker, dwl 15 Tehama
Hatch William P. silver plater with W. H. T. Clark, dwl 255 Third
Hathaway & Co. *(B. F. Briggs and E. G. Lamb)* produce commission, 7 Clay
Hathaway A. M. *(Rutherford & H.)* dwl S s Twentieth bet Guerrero and Dolores
Hathaway B. W. physician, dwl 82 Mont Block
Hathaway Charles B. drayman, Drumm nr Pacific, dwl 1332 Pacific
Hathaway E. V. Rincon Point Warehouse foot Main, dwl 38 South Park
Hathaway Job, drayman with Stephen B. Hanson
Hathaway Nathan, carpenter, dwl E s Capp bet Eighteenth and Nineteenth
Hathorne Henry W. clerk C. S. Navigation Co. Broadway Wharf, dwl 70 Minna
Hatman George W. milk ranch, S s Lagoon Presidio Road
Hatt Joseph, gold beater, dwl 601 Sutter
Huttich Joseph, boot maker, dwl 817 Pacific, rear
Haub John, broom maker with L. Van Laack, dwl 26 Stewart
Haubrich William, steward, Barnum Restaurant, 623 Commercial
HAUCK *(Louis)* & MARQUARD *(Frederick)* liquor saloon, 541 Clay, dwl 1306 Powell
Haug Christ, bar keeper Mazurka Hall, dwl 621 Cal
Haugh John A. janitor Mercantile Library Association, dwl 202 Montgomery
Hanghy Francis, employé with J. M. Johnson, dwl 6 Minna
Hauk Christian, cook, 336 Bush
Haun John, cooper with Henry Shuman, 120 Sac
Haun William, merchant, dwl 13 Second
Haupp George, laborer, dwl 7 Virginia Place
Haupt Mathias, stair builder with B. H. Freeman & Co. dwl 11 Belden
Haurcade John, laundry, S s Bush bet Polk and Van Ness Avenue
Hauschild Francis E. carver, dwl 114 Silver
Hause John, waiter, Occidental Hotel
Hauser Bernard *(Diehl & H.)* dwl 522 Vallejo
Hauser David, boots and shoes, SW cor Kearny and Bush and 504 and 506 Com, dwl 769 Mission
Hauser Frederick, watch maker and jeweler, 504 Market
Hauser Henry, professor music, dwl S s Union bet Hyde and Larkin

Hauser Jacob, porter, 324 Sansom
Hauser John C. dwl 637 Broadway
Hauser Joseph L. carpenter, dwl 1100 Stockton
Hauser Victor, jeweler with Lemme Bros. dwl 78 Everett
Hausmann D. & Co. (Solomon Gump) importers and manufacturers moldings, mirrors, etc. 535 and 537 Clay, res New York
Hausmann Frederick, cigar maker, dwl N s Green bet Montgomery and Kearny
Haussey H. E. dwl 331 Bush
Haussler (Leonard) & Fonemann (William) cabinet makers, 231 Jackson
Haussmann Adolph, merchant, dwl 1403 Kearny
Haussmann Isaure Miss, dress maker with Mme. Angier, dwl cor Union and Kearny
Haust Henry, porter with Rogers, Meyer & Co. dwl 1220 Kearny
HAVEN CHARLES D. secretary Union Insurance Co. office 416 California, res Oakland
Haven Jamas M. real estate with George, W. Chapin, 338 Montgomery
Haven Jeremiah, laborer, dwl 721 Market
Haven William S. book keeper, Pacific Mail S. S. Co. res Oakland
Havener E. C. ship carpenter, dwl 58 Stewart
Haveumeyer Frederick, baker, Philadelphia Bakery, dwl 528 Pacific, rear
Havens Francis D. laborer, dwl W s Hyde bet Turk and Eddy
Havens Henry T. deputy assessor City and County, dwl 17 Tehama
Havens Howard, book keeper Donohoe, Kelly & Co. dwl 610 Ellis
Havens Wickbam S. jr. book keeper, Savings and Loan Society, dwl Frank's Building Brenham Place
Havey Michael, laborer with Cornelius Conahan
Haviland John, seamen, dwl 60 Clay
Haviland John T. (Haynes & Lawton) NE cor Sansom and Merchant, dwl 625 Clay
Haviland Walter, book keeper with Dodge & Phillips, dwl Powell nr Clay
HAWAIIAN PACKET LINE to Honululu, Charles W. Brooks & Co. agents, office 511 Sansom
Hawes Charles M. carpenter, dwl NE cor Napa and Shasta
HAWES HORACE, attorney at law, office and dwl cor Folsom and Ninth
Hawes Miner, drayman, dwl 417 Folsom
Hawes Oliver, cupeller, Assayer's Department U. S. Branch Mint, dwl 770 Howard
Hawkins A. K. book keeper, S. F. Gas Co. dwl 931 Howard
Hawkins George W. hatter with LeGay & Co. dwl 28 Sansom
Hawkins James, machinist, dwl 931 Howard
Hawkins James jr. (McNally & H.) dwl 931 Howard
Hawkins John, laborer, dwl 38 St. Mark Place
Hawkins John P. (Feaster & Co.) dwl E s Mission bet Twenty-Fifth and Twenty-Sixth
Hawkins Joseph, mariner, dwl E s Main bet Howard and Folsom
Hawkins Michael (Daly & H.) dwl 931 Howard
Hawkins Michael, dwl 234 Stevenson
Hawkins William, baker, Brooklyn Hotel
Hawkins William, mining, dwl 931 Howard
Hawks Jabez D. salesman with Castle Bros. dwl 750 Mission
Hawks Joseph, laborer, dwl N s Fulton nr Webster
Hawks Ynes, machinist, Union Foundry, dwl NW cor Mission and First
Hawley Applebee, express wagon, Pier 1 Stewart
Hawley Charles A. salesman with H. Avery & Co. dwl 313 Second
HAWLEY C. J. & CO. (Jacob C. Hawley and Ossian C. Mitchell) family groceries, etc. 42 Second cor Jessie, dwl 219 Mason

HAWLEY (David N.) & CO. (Walter N. Hawley) importers and jobbers hardware, SE cor Cal and Battery, res Oakland
Hawley Ebenezer R. (Pacific Straw Works) dwl 324 Ritch
Hawley Edward A. book keeper, Mission St. Brewery, dwl 608 Mission
Hawley Edward A. salesman with Hawley & Co. dwl 32 South Park
Hawley Farm Oil Co. office 519 Montgomery
Hawley Florence, laborer, Fulton Foundry, dwl 4 Jessie
Hawley Francis L. brass finisher, dwl Tiger Engine House
Hawley George T. with Hawley & Co. dwl 32 South Park
Hawley Jacob C. (C. J. Hawley & Co.) dwl SW cor Turk and Laguna
Hawley Michael, molder, Fulton Foundry, dwl 4 Jessie
Hawley Nathan E. carpenter, dwl 311 Bush
Hawley Walter N. (Hawley & Co.) dwl 960 Howard
Hawley Wilson, ship carpenter, dwl 308 Beale
Hawthorn Edward, milkman, dwl 638 Mission
Hawthorn William H. dwl 920 Stockton
Hawthorne Henry J. stone cutter, dwl N s Bush bet Scott and Pierce
Hawver William, foreman molding shop, Pacific Foundry, dwl 24 Stevenson
Haxe George J. butcher, 4 Metropolitan Market, dwl 27 Belden Block
Haxter A. S. Montgomery Block, dwl 536 Wash
HAY (Alexander) & COATES (Caleb) family liquor store, 37 Sutter, dwl NW cor Geary and Dupont
Hay Alexander, boiler maker apprentice, Vulcan Iron Works, dwl 543 Mission
Hay August, French laundry, 1419 Dupont
Hay Henry, compositor, dwl Bay View Park
Hay J. McHardy, clerk with C. W. Weston & Co. dwl Eighth bet Folsom and Howard
Hay John, molder, Fulton Foundry, dwl 511 Mission
Hayburn James C. groceries and liquors, SE cor Fifth and Shipley
HAYCOCK (Judson) & MILLER (Carleton W.) attorneys at law, office 622 Clay
Hayden Daniel, book keeper, Franklin Hotel, SE cor Sansom and Pacific
Hayden Edwin (Kennedy & H.) dwl 146 Fourth
Hayden Edwin, bar keeper, dwl 177 Minna
HAYDEN GRENVILLE G. dentist, office 727 Clay, dwl 126 St. Mark Place
Hayden James, capitalist, dwl 829 Howard
HAYDEN JAMES G. Fashion Saloon, 552 Washington cor Montgomery
Hayden John, steward, dwl 146 Stewart
Hayden (John J.) & Zander (Jacob) hairdressing saloon, 550 Washington, dwl 544 Washington
Hayden John J. butcher, dwl 456 Mission
Hayden Lawrence, bar keeper, 538 Market, dwl 161 Silver
Hayden L. M. (widow) female physician, dwl 67 Jessie
Hayden Nathan, with Adam Smith, 536 Market
Hayden Peter (Stone & H.) res New York
Hayden Peter, laborer, Market St. R. R. Co. bds N s Sixteenth bet Guerrero and Dolores
Hayden Washington, with J. W. Brittan & Co. dwl 616 California
Hayden William, blacksmith helper, Vulcan Iron Works, dwl 134 Stevenson
Hayden William, clerk with J. G. Hayden, dwl 552 Washington
Hayes Alexander, dwl 103 Dupont
Hayes Anna Miss, domestic, 817 Bush
Hayes Bartholemew D. groceries and liquors, SW cor Clementina and Eighth

Hayes Benjamin W. clerk, 638 Clay, dwl 211 Seventh
Hayes Bridget (widow) 268 Minna
Hayes Charles D. book keeper with F. W. Crosby & Co. dwl 1805 Powell
Hayes Curley, laborer, dwl W s Clara nr Sutter
Hayes Daniel, laborer, dwl 695 Geary, rear
Hayes Dennis, carpenter, dwl 114 Hyde
Hayes Dennis, coachman, dwl 1212 Clay
Hayes Dennis, laborer, dwl S s Fulton nr Laguna, Hayes' Valley
Hayes Dennis, laborer, dwl 268 Minna
Hayes Eliza (widow) ladies' nurse, dwl 210 Third
Hayes Ellen Miss, domestic, 706 California
Hayes Ellen C. Mrs. private boarding, 14 Sansom
Hayes E. Rock, jeweler with R. B. Gray & Co. dwl Portsmouth House
Hayes George, law student with Wm. Hayes, 604 Clay, dwl 504 Dupont
Hayes H. S. pantryman, Richards' Restaurant, dwl 637 Kearny
Hayes Jacob F. hairdresser with Lipman & Korn, 406 Pine, dwl 529 Pine
HAYES (James) & PRITCHARD (James A.) marble warehouse, 536 and 538 California, dwl 961 Folsom
Hayes James, dwl 527 Mission
Hayes James, hostler, Central R. R. Co. dwl W s Downey nr Bryant
Hayes James, molder, Union Foundry, dwl 9 Natoma
Hayes Johanna (widow) dwl 109 William
Hayes John, dwl N s Hayes bet Van Ness Avenue and Polk
Hayes John, dwl 527 Mission
Hayes John, blacksmith, dwl 697 Geary, rear
Hayes John, laborer, Fort Point
Hayes John, laborer, dwl 268 Minna
Hayes John, laborer, dwl Union Court
Hayes John, molder, dwl 511 Mission
Hayes John, seaman, dwl 72 Jessie
Hayes Mary (widow) dress making, 433 Bush
Hayes Mary (widow) dwl SW cor Post and Kearny
HAYES MICHAEL, real estate, dwl W s Van Ness Avenue bet Hayes and Grove
Hayes Michael, spinner, Mission Woolen Mills, dwl with P. L. Murphy, E s Howard bet Fifteenth and Sixteenth
Hayes Owen, laborer, dwl N s Fulton bet Gough and Octavia
HAYES' PARK PAVILION AND CONCERT HALL, Hayes, Laguna, Grove, and Buchanan, Thomas Hayes proprietor
Hayes Patrick, salesman with Kerby, Byrne & Co. dwl 108 Minna
Hayes Philip, grocer, dwl NE cor Union and Larkin
Hayes Richard, carpenter, dwl 728 Market
Hayes Robert, dwl 116 Post
Hayes Robert, clerk, SW cor Jones and O'Farrell
Hayes Robert, marble worker with Hayes & Pritchard, dwl 413 Union
Hayes Thomas, carriage trimmer, dwl 14 Sansom
Hayes Thomas, gardener with Samuel C. Bigelow, dwl NE cor McAllister and Steiner
HAYES THOMAS, real estate, dwl W s Van Ness Avenue bet Hayes and Grove, Hayes' Valley
Hayes Thomas F. with Hunter & Myers, dwl 522 Vallejo
Hayes Thomas R. (Main & Winchester) dwl 716 Filbert
Hayes Timothy, laborer, dwl 268 Minna
Hayes William, dwl 414 Market
HAYES WILLIAM, attorney at law, office 604 Clay cor Montgomery
Hayes William, carpenter, dwl Dresdener House
Hayes William, seaman, dwl SE cor Lombard and Montgomery
Hayes (William C.) & Grimes (James) blacksmithing, 17 Battery, dwl Bryant Place

Hayes William J. salesman with Conroy & O'Connor, dwl 646 Mission
Hayes W. S. dwl What Cheer House
Hayes, see Hays
Hayne A. P. physician, office 748 Washington, dwl 1018 Stockton
Hayne, see Haine
Haynes A. S. merchant, dwl 314 Fifth
HAYNES (Benjamin) & LAWTON (Orlando) (and John F. Haviland) importers and jobbers crockery and glass ware, NE cor Sansom and Merchant, dwl 127 Montgomery
Haynes John E. seaman, dwl 44 Sacramento
Haynes John W. jobber teas and mining secretary, office 404 Front, dwl SW cor Twelfth and Mission
Haynes N. mariner, dwl SE cor Taylor and Sac
Haynes Patrick, job wagon, 409 California, dwl 35 Louisa, rear
HAYNES THOMAS J. merchant, office 404 Front, res Oakland
HAYS DAVID & CO. (Bishop Sheldon) draymen, office NE cor Sacramento and Front, dwl 516 Howard
Hays Edward F. carpenter, dwl 602 Powell
Hays James H. straw hat finisher, dwl 527 Mission
Hays Michael, deck hand, stmr Yosemite
Hays Robert, stone cutter, dwl 413 Union
Haysen William, porter, 835 Post
HAYWARD (A.) & COLEMAN (A. N.) importers oils and lamps, etc. 414 Front, res San Mateo
Hayward Charles F. salesman, 216 Battery, dwl Russ House
Hayward George, teller with Sather & Co. dwl 1011 Bush
Hayward L. dwl NW cor Bush and Market
Hayward S. O. (John F. Pynch & Co.) dwl 113 Ellis
Haywood Louisa Mrs. (col'd) dwl W s Tyson Place
Haywood Louisa A. (widow) dwl 114 Dupont
Haywood William (col'd) handcartman, NE cor Sansom and Merchant, dwl 1410 Mason, rear
Haywood, see Heywood
Hazard John, carpenter, dwl 111 Geary
HAZARD POWDER CO. Edward H. Parker agent, office 224 and 226 California
Hazazer Moses, porter, 439 Mont, dwl 28 Sansom
Hazel Stewart, farmer, dwl 20 Louisa
Hazel William, groom, Ocean Race Course
Hazilquist Louis, lodgings, 812 Jackson
Hazleton William, dwl 433 Green
Hazen George, dwl N s Stevenson bet Sixth and Seventh, rear
Hazzard Edward, laborer, dwl 50 Silver
Head A. E. real estate, office 32 Montgomery Block, dwl Lick House
Head E. F. attorney at law, office 46 Mont Block
Head Samuel, engineer and machinist, dwl 312 Shipley
Headspeth John, laborer, dwl 13 Stockton Place
Heald Edward P. associate principal Pacific Business College, 747 Market
Heald George, carpenter with J. Brokaw, dwl Benton House
HEALD JOHN, dentist, office and dwl Stevenson House, room 12
Healey Allen, dwl NW cor Sixteenth and Whitney
Healey Charles S. northern coast messenger, Wells, Fargo & Co. dwl 612 Greenwich nr Stockton
Healey Christopher W. painter, dwl S s Liberty bet Townsend and Brannan
Healey David, molder, Volunteer Engine Co. No. 7
Healey Dennis A. shoe maker, 818 Market
Healey George, miner, dwl N s Austin bet Polk and Van Ness Avenue
Healey Mary Miss, domestic, 613½ Stockton
Healey Michael, expressman, dwl 113 Jessie
Healey Peter, workman with Locke & Montague, dwl W s Bernal nr Precita Avenue

Healy Anna Miss, domestic, 317 Sutter
Healy Bartlett, workman, Dwyer's Coal Yard, dwl W s Bernal nr Precita Avenue
Healy Charles, civil engineer, dwl Oriental Hotel
Healy James W. janitor Mason and Powell Street schools, dwl 715 Hyde
Healy John, baker with Deeth & Starr, dwl 818 Market
Healy John, driver, North Beach & M. R. R. Co
Healy, (Joseph) Carleton (Silas M.) & Co. (George W. Pierce) wood and coal, 429 Pine, dwl 58 Lorquin's Building
Healy Lucian B. civil engineer, dwl NW cor Sixteenth and Whitney
Healy Mark, groceries and liquors, SW cor Leavenworth and Jackson
Healy Thomas, shoe maker, 105 Kearny
Healy, see Haley, Heley, and Hely
Heaney Ann (widow) dwl 514 Minna
Heaney Edward, retortman, S. F. Gas Co
Heaney John, oysterman, 612 Wash, dwl 24 Stone
Heaney Patrick, metal roofer, 825 Montgomery, dwl S s Jessie bet Fourth and Fifth
Heaney Thomas H. contractor, dwl NE cor Polk and Hayes
Heany John, boot maker, dwl 1302 Kearny
Hearn Mary A. (widow) dwl 574 Mission
Hearst George, real estate, office 712 Montgomery, dwl SW cor Leavenworth and Chestnut
Heart Morris, laborer, Golden State Iron Works, dwl 228 Folsom
Hearwig James, blacksmith with Kimball & Co. dwl 741 Market
Heath Elander, machinist with Hobbs, Gilmore & Co. dwl NW cor Polk and Fell
Heath Henry C. with Kellogg, Hewston & Co. dwl 527 Pine
Heath James, collector, dwl 253 Stevenson
Heath Jemimah (widow) dwl 1617 Dupont
Heath J. L. Mrs. dwl 1 Chatham Place
Heath Patrick, milk ranch, nr cor Courtlandt and North avenues
Heath Richard W. commission merchant and dealer tobacco and consul for San Salvador, office 609 Front, res Oakland
Heather Seaton (Fuller & H.) res New York
Heathfield Edwin, salesman with Redington & Co. dwl 827 Bush
Heatley Edward D. with Dickson, DeWolf & Co. 412 Battery
Heaton Samuel C. with J. D. Arthur & Son, dwl Empire Lodgings
Hebbord Charles, machinist helper, Vulcan Iron Works
Hebding Francis E. shoe maker with Philip Schwerdt, 708 Market
Heberling J. C. varnisher with Goodwin & Co. dwl N s Mission bet Third and Fourth
Hebert A. waiter, dwl Lafayette H. & L. Co. No. 2
HEBERT ZEPHIRIN, wholesale butcher, Santa Clara bet Hampshire and Jersey
Hebrard Theodore, florist, dwl N s Hayes nr Octavia
HEBREW (weekly) Philo Jacoby publisher and proprietor, office 509 Clay
HEBREW OBSERVER, Rev. Julius Eckmann publisher and proprietor, office 511 Sacramento
HEBREW YOUNG MEN'S LITERARY ASSOCIATION, rooms N s Pacific nr Stockton
Hecht A. E. book keeper with Hecht Bros. dwl 114 Mason
HECHT BROTHERS (Jacob H. and Isaac Hecht) & CO. (Louis Hecht) importers and jobbers boots and shoes, 417 and 419 Sacramento, dwl 114 Mason
Hecht Isaac (Hecht Brothers & Co.) dwl 114 Mason
Hecht Joseph, clerk with Steinhart Bros. dwl 118 Prospect Place
Hecht Louis (Hecht Bros. & Co.) dwl 114 Mason

Heck Jacob, liquor saloon, 619 Jackson
Heck Joseph, carpenter, dwl 336 Bush
Hecker Adolph, machinist, Miners' Foundry, dwl 152 Clara
Hecker Henry, boots and shoes, 328 Commercial, dwl NE cor California and Kearny
Hecker Lizzie Miss, domestic, 746 Mission
Hecker Mary Miss, domestic, 714 Vallejo
Hecker Peter, box maker, dwl 4 Virginia
Heder John, bar keeper, dwl 18 Sansom
Hedge William, machinist, Miners' Foundry, dwl 540 Howard
Hedge Patrick, laborer, dwl 551 Market
Hedges George W. machinist, Vulcan Iron Works, dwl 135 Beale
Hedrich Hermann, waiter, 626 Kearny
Hee Wah (Chinese) butcher, 735 Sacramento
Heenan Dennis, laborer, dwl 1618 Dupont, rear
Heenan John C. cooper, S. F. & P. Sugar Co. dwl Rousch
Heeny Ann (widow) dwl 514 Minna
Heerdink (John) & Co. (Valentine Baumgardner) manufacturers tobacco, 31 Fremont, dwl 3 Harrison Avenue
Heesch John, seaman, bds 7 Washington
Heeseman George F. groceries and liquors, SW cor Brannan and Second
Hefer Samuel, bar keeper, dwl SW cor Dupont and Broadway
Heffernan Annie Miss, with Henry Lund
Heffernan Arthur, with A. F. Sawyer, dwl Jansen nr Greenwich
Heffernan Elizabeth (widow) dwl W s Jansen bet Greenwich and Lombard
Heffernan Ellen Miss, domestic, 1605 Mason
Heffernan Michael, tailor, cor Spring and Summer, dwl Reese Place
Heffernon Johanna Miss, domestic, 820 Union
Heffernon Patrick, laborer, dwl SW cor Filbert and Montgomery
Heffron Michael, bar keeper, 37 Sutter
Heffron Michael, merchant, dwl 904 Jackson
Heffron Michael, tailor, dwl 12 Hinckley
Hefley William, dwl 204 Stockton
Hefter Charles B. bakery, 776 Folsom
Hegarty Daniel, carpenter, dwl E s Folsom Avenue nr Folsom
Hegarty Joanna Miss, domestic, 1810 Stockton
Hegarty P. L. conductor, North Beach & M. R. R. Co
Hegarty Timothy, carpenter, dwl 10 Broadway
Hegeler F. H. (C. H. Brickwedel & Co.) dwl 253 Stewart
Hegeman Samuel J. clerk, dwl 214 Powell
Hegen Patrick, lab, dwl NE corner Pac and Front
Heideman Adolph, merchant, dwl 431 Pine
Heider Christopher, hairdresser, International Hotel, dwl S s California bet Montgomery and Kearny
Heidhoff A. H. groceries and liquors, SW cor Stockton and Sacramento
Heigel Nicholas, molder, dwl 433 First
Heil Constantine, baker with Charles Schroth, 230 Kearny
Heilborn Bros. (Morris and Julius) basket manuf, 27 Third, dwl Mission bet Third and Fourth
Heilborn Julius (Heilborn Bros.) dwl Mission bet Third and Fourth
Heilman N. drayman, 526 Washington
Heilmann Henry, Union Soap Manufactory, S side Brannan bet Fifth and Sixth, dwl N s Brannan bet Sixth and Seventh
Heim Adam, with Thurnauer & Zinn, dwl 633 Mission
Heim Charles, cook, What Cheer House Restaurant
Heim John G. baker, dwl 910 Kearny
Heiman Leopold, cigars and tobacco, American Exchange
Heimburg Emil, waiter, St. Louis Hotel, 11 and 13 Pacific

HEIMBURG E. W. & CO. *(Herman Droste)* Chicago Hotel, 220 Pacific and saloon N s Grove bet Octavia and Laguna

Heimburg *(Henry)* & Schroeder *(Louis)* proprietors St. Louis Hotel, 11 and 13 Pacific

Heimerle Frederick, shoe maker, dwl 24 Jane

Hein George, salesman with John G. Hein, dwl S s Mission nr Eighth

HEIN JOHN G. importer and jobber leather and shoe findings, etc. 416 Battery, dwl S s Mission nr Eighth

Heinau Michael, hairdresser with Joseph Lipman, dwl SW cor Bush and Monroe

Heineberg Abram, merchant, dwl 343 Minna

HEINIMAN MICHAEL, physician, office 804 Montgomery rooms 7 and 8, dwl S s McLaren Lane nr Folsom

Heinle Henry, cook, NW cor Kearny and Jackson

Heinrich J. J. clerk with H. S. DeFremery, 413 Washington

Heinrich Louis, cutler, dwl 1518 Stockton

Heinrisch Henry, cigars and tobacco, dwl 621 Union

Heins *(Harmon)* & Eden *(John)* groceries and liquors, NW cor Battery and Broadway, dwl S s Winter Alley nr Mason

Heinsohn *(Jacob)* & Hammann *(John H.)* wines and liquors, NE cor Washington and Davis and 828 Clay

Heintz August, shooting gallery, Willows, dwl W s Valencia bet Sixteenth and Seventeenth

Heinz Jacob, liquor saloon, 636 Pacific

Heinze Fred, watchmaker and jeweler, 848 Wash

Heinzenberger Henry, blacksmith, bds Telegraph Hotel 407 Pacific

Heinzenberger Julius A. cabinet maker, SE corner Union and August Alley

Heise Edward, acct with Charles Baum, dwl 28 Ellis

Heise Mary (widow) ladies' nurse, dwl 319 Bush

Heiser Philip, laborer, dwl 532 Broadway

Heissenbüttel Heinrich, clerk, corner Shasta and Michigan

Heisener Frank, carpenter, dwl 258 Tehama

Heister Amos, dwl 724 Howard

Heister William, Keller's Meat Market, 513 Pacific

Heiter Christopher, hairdresser, dwl 545 California

Heitkamp Conrad, laborer, Bay Sugar Refinery, dwl 19 Hinckley

Heitmann Charles, waiter, Oriental Hotel Restaurant, dwl 420 Bush

Heitmann Hinrich, laborer, Bay Sugar Refinery, dwl 813 Battery

Heitmann Nicholas, drayman, dwl 26 St. Mark Pl

Heitmeiller F. blacksmith, Spring Valley W. W

Heitshu Samuel, book keeper with Hostetter, Smith & Dean, dwl 621 Clay

Heizman John, watch maker and jeweler, 408 Commercial, dwl 125 Post

Heizman Lorenz, watch maker, 521 Kearny

Hekman Ludwick, teacher music, dwl 1624 Dupont

Helb George, porter with Boswell & Shattuck, dwl Bay State House

Helb Jacob, cigar maker with Elias Goslinsky, dwl Bay State House

HELBING, *(August)* GREENEBAUM *(M.)* & CO. *(E. Straus)* importers and jobbers crockery, glassware, etc. NE cor Pine and Battery, dwl 1409 Powell

Held Brothers *(B., Simon J. and David)* importers and jobbers millinery goods, 416 Sacramento, res New York

Held David *(Held Brothers)* dwl 1022 Stockton

Held Ernest *(George Held & Bro.)* dwl 163 Tehama bet Second and Third

Held George & Brother *(Ernest Held)* hairdressing saloon, 331 Pine, dwl 163 Tehama bet Second and Third

Held Simon J. *(Held Brothers)* dwl 1022 Stockton

Hele N. L. lithographic printer with Britton & Co. 533 Commercial

Heley Christopher W. painter, dwl 5 Crook

Heley John, tailor, dwl SW cor Cal and Larkin

Helford William, blacksmith, dwl Central House, 814 Sansom

Helgoth Henry, plasterer, dwl 353 Minna

Helke Charles, harness and saddle maker, 139 Third

Hellenschmidt Frederic, butcher, dwl E s Hampshire nr Sixteenth

Heller Charles L. *(Falkenstein & Co.)* dwl 1628 Stockton

Heller Frank, driver, Mason's Brewery, dwl 815 Greenwich

Heller Jonas *(M. Heller & Bros.)* res New York

Heller Karl, dwl 1021 Kearny

HELLER M. & BROTHERS *(Martin and Jonas Heller)* importers and jobbers fancy and staple dry goods, 425 Sacramento, dwl 524 Ellis

Heller Martin *(M. Heller & Bros.)* dwl 9 Mason

Heller Mary Miss, domestic, 1515 Stockton

Heller William *(L. & M. Sachs & Co.)* res New York

Helley Lawrence, laborer, dwl E s Leroy Place bet Sacramento and Clay

Helling Frederick, drayman, 3 Clay, dwl 1717 Leavenworth

Helling Henry, tanner, dwl 464 Clementina

Hellman Jacob, salesman with Taaffe & Co

HELLMANN BROTHERS *(Richard, Edward, and George Hellmann)* & CO. *(Adolphus Ehrhorn)* importing and commission merchants, SW cor Front and Jackson

Hellmann Edward *(Hellmann Brothers & Co.)* res London

Hellmann George *(Hellmann Brothers & Co.)* res Tacna, Peru

HELLMANN HENRI J. agent French Relief and Benevolent Society and secretary Odd Fellows' Savings & Homestead Association, office and dwl 252 Jessie

Hellrich Paul, cabinet maker with W. G. Weir, dwl 119 Prospect Place

Hellweg Henry, tanner with John King, dwl cor Santa Clara and Connecticut

Helmar John J. G. cabinet maker with J. & J. Easton, dwl 502 Dupont

Helmers N. S. teacher piano forte, dwl 704 Folsom

Helmke Henry, clerk with J. N. Harris, dwl 445 Bush

Helmke William *(J. Hasshagen & Co.)* dwl 322 Jackson

Helmken Frederick, clerk, dwl 521 Green

HELMKEN J. THEODORE, importer and retailer hardware, 516 Kearny, dwl 1223 Clay

Helms Anne Miss, domestic, SE cor Sixteenth and Howard

Helms Chris. groceries and liquors, SW cor Folsom and Sixteenth

Helms E. A. groceries and liquors, NE cor O'Farrell and Hyde

Helmson Edward, dwl 810 Jackson

Helnke Frederick, workman, Albany Brewery

Helstrom Charles, seaman, dwl 44 Sacramento

Helstrom John, seaman, dwl 44 Sacramento

Helstrup Edward, seaman, pilot boat Fannie

HELVETIA HOTEL, Jacob Schmid proprietor, 431 and 433 Pine

Helwig August, musician, dwl 417 Sutter

Helwig Eliza Miss, domestic, 411 Sixth

Helwig Heury, bar keeper, dwl 323 Pine

Hely John K. book keeper with George Hughes, dwl 778 Harrison

Hemaby John P. plasterer, dwl 441 Clementina

Hemenway Henry C. book keeper, 215 Sacramento, dwl N s Lombard bet Jones and Leavenworth

Hemenway Oliver, with Hemenway & Merrill, dwl Lombard bet Jones and Leavenworth

Hemenway *(Sylvester)* & Merrill *(A. D.)* wholesale coal oil, groceries, etc. 215 Sacramento, dwl N s Lombard bet Jones and Leavenworth

Hemenway William P. carpenter, dwl S s Bush nr Franklin
Hemme August *(Riehn, H. & Co.)* dwl 839 Mission
Hemmer Henry *(Ehrhart & H.)* dwl 4 Milton Place
Hemmer Louis, waiter, 416 Kearny
Hempel F. shoe maker, 409 Bush
Hemphill Thomas S. clerk with Voizin, Ris & Co. dwl SE cor Montgomery and Green
Hemprich Louis, hairdressing saloon, 18 Kearny, dwl 107 Post
Hempsted Dennison, captain bark Onward, office 511 Sansom
Henabry Michael, cartman, dwl 630 Ellis
Henan John B. waiter, dwl 269 Stevenson
Henarie D. V. B. *(E. Martin & Co.)* dwl 429 Tehama
Hencke *(William)* & Co. *(August Pistolesi)* groceries and liquors, SW cor Washington and Dupont
Hencken *(Carson)* & Spellmeyer *(Charles)* groceries and liquors, 719 Pacific
Hencken Claus *(Rosenberg & H.)* dwl 743 Vallejo
Hencken *(John)* & Muller *(William)* groceries and liquors SE cor Vallejo and Powell
Hencken Martin, porter, 208 Front, dwl 633 Minna
Hencken William H. groceries and liquors, 417 Third cor Perry
Hendemeyer George, butcher, Washington Market, dwl Oriental Hotel
Henderer Benjamin, steamboat fireman, Crescent Engine Co. No. 10
HENDERSON & BROWN *(Richard)* proprietors Cochituate Baths and Hairdressing Saloon, 215 Sansom
Henderson A. cook, Clipper Restaurant
Henderson A. H. porter, City Hall, dwl City Hall third floor
Henderson A. W. brick work, plastering, etc. 561 Mission
Henderson Charles, laborer, dwl 244 Kearny
Henderson David, dwl St. Lawrence House
Henderson David, carpenter, dwl 89 Everett
Henderson Edwin R. baggage master San José R. R. Station, dwl 20 Montgomery
Henderson Frank, manager with James Milburn & Co. 313 Sacramento, dwl 1028 Pine
Henderson Heuston, laborer, dwl N s Chestnut bet Stockton and Powell
Henderson Isabella Mrs. (widow) dwl 325 Ritch
Henderson John, operator Cal. State Telegraph Co. dwl 519 Bush bet Stockton and Dupont
Henderson John, wood and coal, 836 Washington, dwl E s Twelfth bet Howard and Mission
Henderson John jr. dwl E s Twelfth bet Mission and Howard
Henderson Justus *(Marion & H.)* dwl 321 East
Henderson Margaret Mrs. dress making, 430 Geary
Henderson Samuel, dry goods, 105 Fourth
Henderson Thomas, proprietor Palace Saloon, 2206 Powell, dwl 525 Greenwich
Henderson Thomas H. clerk, County Recorder's Office, res Oakland
Henderson W. H. dwl Cosmopolitan Hotel
Henderson William, hairdressing saloon, International Hotel, dwl NE cor Broadway and Mont
Henderson William P. butcher, 1 Metropolitan Market, dwl 867 Mission
HENDLEY A. C. & CO. wholesale provisions, 204 Front, dwl 19 Prospect Place
Hendley George W. clerk with Dibblee & Hyde, dwl 19 Prospect Place
Hendren James R. clerk S. F. & P. Sugar Co. dwl 5 Tay
Hendrick Charles S. contractor, Chestnut nr Kearny
Hendricks Elizabeth C. (widow) stamping, embroidery, etc. 629 Mission
Hendricks Joseph (col'd) dwl 17 Lafayette Place
Hendricks Stillman, milk ranch, N W cor Larkin and Pine

Hendrickson Charles, book keeper News Letter Office, dwl 436 Bush
Hendrickson Henry W. local policeman, dwl 125 Jessie
Hendrickson William, real estate, dwl 331 Minna
Hendrie J. W. office 624 Clay, dwl 1005 Powell
Hendry Charles J. porter with G. M. Josselyn, 34 Market
Hendry George W. porter with G. M. Josselyn, 34 Market
Hendry James, fireman, steamer Relief
Hendry Samuel, house carpenter, dwl 938 Dupont
Hendry William M. shipsmith, foot Second, dwl E s Second bet Brannan and Townsend
Hendy James, drayman, 421 Clay
Hendy John A. *(Storck & H.)* dwl 202 Fourth
Hendy Joshua, agent Hendy's Circular Saws, office 402 Mont, dwl N s Jane bet Natoma and Minna
Heney Jane A. Miss, seamstress, dwl 1300 Kearny
Heney Richard, with J. & C. Schreiber, dwl 270 Stevenson
Heney Richard jr. waiter, 28 Montgomery, dwl 270 Stevenson
Heney William, clerk, 406 San, dwl 270 Stevenson
Henig John, silversmith, dwl 623 Clay
Henings Martin A. Russian Hill Market, NE cor Mason and Broadway
Henke Herman, foreman with Henry Hoesch, 614 Clay
Henkel Edward, tailor, dwl 315 Pine
Henken Henry, clerk with John D. Doscher, SE cor Bush and Sansom
Henken Hinrich, laborer, Bay Sugar Refinery, dwl 150 Second
Henken John, dwl 911 Greenwich
Henkenius Herman, physician and surgeon, office 639 Washington, dwl 306 Sixth
Henkry Henry, dwl 845 Dupont
Henley Patrick, laborer, dwl S s Filbert bet Mason and Taylor
Henley Thomas J. farmer (Mendocino Co.) dwl SW cor Washington and Powell
Henn John Mrs. teacher music, dwl 423 Stevenson
Henna William, with Erzgraber & Goetjen, 120 Davis
Henneberg Mary Mrs. domestic with Robert J. Polk
Henneberg M. C. laborer, dwl Ellis nr Larkin
Hennecart Jean, chorus singer, Academy Music
Hennecken Nicholas, porter with Thomas Taylor, dwl 1114 Stockton
Hennell Abbie (widow) dwl 74 Clementina
Hennessy Andrew, marble works, 507 O'Farrell
Hennessy Bridget M. (widow) dwl 25 Hinckley
Hennessy David, workman, S. F. & P. Sugar Co. dwl W s Ritter nr Harrison
HENNESSY JAMES, clerk, 653 Sacramento, dwl 445 Bush
Hennessy John, marble polisher, dwl S s Harrison bet Seventh and Eighth
Hennessy Lawrence, workman, S. F. & P. Sugar Co. dwl N s Twelfth nr Folsom
Hennessy Mary Miss, domestic, 508 Sutter
Hennessy Mathew, laborer, bds Phœnix House, 721 Sansom
Hennessy Morris, currier, Sixth St. Tannery, dwl 132 Townsend
Hennessy Patrick, laborer, dwl 277 Minna
Hennessy Peter, carpenter, dwl 510 Front
Hennessy Thomas, laborer with Edward J. Quirk
Hennessy William, laborer, dwl Union Court
Hennessy William H. first officer stmr Pacific, dwl 317 Broadway
Hennig William, machinist, dwl 417 Sutter
Henning John S. *(Adelphi Hotel Co.)* dwl Cosmopolitan Hotel
Henning Joseph, dwl What Cheer House
Henning Otto, foreman Pacific Oil and Camphene Works, dwl S s Chestnut bet Mason and Taylor

Henning W. machinist, Union Foundry
Henning T. F. clerk with D. Bubsen, dwl 727 Davis
Hennons Henry, dwl Niantic Hotel
Henrici Ernest, jeweler with Pohlmann & Co. dwl 807 Bush
Henrihan Mary Miss, domestic, 619 Leavenworth
Henriksen Benjamin A. chimney tops, 28 Third, dwl 328 Kearny
HENRIQUES DAVID, real estate, stock, and money broker, office 612 Merchant, dwl 1206 Stockton
Henry & Bernard Con. G.,' S. & C. M. Co.; R. Merriman secretary, office 639 Mission
Henry Alexander (Ralph Moss & Co.) res New York
Henry Alexander, carpenter, dwl 23 Ritch
Henry Augustus K. printer with Francis, Valentine & Co. dwl 518 California
Henry Benjamin, fireman, steamer Yosemite
Henry C. D. & Co. (J. D. Lawlor) carriage painting, 932 Market, dwl 257 Stevenson
Henry Charles, cartman, cor Kearny and Bush
Henry Ellen, dwl 843 Clay
Henry George B. distillery, 42 Commercial, dwl Codman Place
Henry H. A. Rev. pastor Congregation Sherith Israel, dwl 736 Green
Henry Henry, boot maker, E s Mission bet Twenty-Eighth and Twenty-Ninth
Henry Henry, tailor, cor Spring and Summer, dwl S s Shipley bet Fourth and Fifth
Heufy Isaac, laborer, dwl 227 Post
Henry James, ship carpenter with John G. North, Potrero, dwl 814 Montgomery
Henry (John) & Dunn (James) wood and coal, 1626 Powell
Henry John, dwl 8 s Turk bet Webster and Buchanan
Henry John, contractor, dwl Dolores Hall, W s Valencia bet Fifteenth and Sixteenth
Henry John B. distiller, dwl Codman Place
Henry (Joseph) & Kaskell (B. J.) fruits, 614 Washington, dwl 8 s Post bet Dupont and Stock
Henry L. J. physician and surgeon, office 745 Clay, dwl Occidental Hotel
Henry Lucinda (widow) dwl 518 Callifornia
Henry M. J. Miss, dwl 518 California
Henry R. ship joiner, 23 Ritch, rear
Henry Samuel, furniture, 707 Pacific, dwl 1027 Dupont
Henry Samuel H. attorney at law, office 606 Montgomery, dwl 736 Green
Henry Sarah E. Mrs. actress, rooms 20 and 21 Government House, 502 Washington
Henry Simon, carpenter and builder, dwl SE cor Dupont and Jackson
Henry Sylvanus H. book keeper with Oakley & Jackson, dwl 549 Folsom
Henry Thomas, dwl 327 Bush
Henry Thomas, billiard keeper with Pearson & Armstrong, Russ House
Henry Thomas, milkman, 313 Ritch, dwl W s White nr Vallejo
HENRY W. A. dwl 11 Minna
Henry William, clerk, dwl 315 Beale
Henry William, discharging clerk, dwl SW cor Dupont and Broadway
Henry William, hostler, 414 Kearny, dwl 405 Kearny
Henry William W. (Palmer, Gillespie & Co.) dwl 229 Minna
Hensberry Thomas, with James Brokaw, dwl 328 Third
HENSCHEL (H. L.) & MAURICE, ship and custom house brokers, 508 Battery, dwl 317 First
Henschen John, clerk, NW cor Third and Stevenson
Hensey Cristopher, musician, Wilson's Circus
Hensh Charles, varnisher, dwl NW cor Kearny and Jackson

Henshaw J. S. accountant with Fargo & Co. 214 Front, dwl 1011 Stockton
Henshilwood Thomas R. salesman with Kerby, Byrne & Co, dwl 471 Jessie
Hensing Otto, merchant, dwl 273 Stevenson
Hensley Isaac L. driver, dwl 7½ Milton Place
HENSLEY SAMUEL J. merchant, office 205 Battery, res San José
Hensley William, bar keeper steamer Pacific
Hent Reuben W. attorney at law, office 22 Exchange Building, dwl 1013 Washington
Hentrich Lewis, clerk, 54 Washington Market, dwl 914 Post
HENTSCH (Henry) & BERTON (Francis) bankers and assayers and consul for Switzerland, office SW cor Clay and Leidesdorff, dwl 607 Pine
Hentz Carl, blacksmith with James Brokaw, dwl 555 Mission
Hentz Henry, laborer, dwl 204 Stewart
Hentze Caroline, cook, dwl 26 Stewart
Hepburn J. dwl Union Club Rooms
Hepp Valentine, carpenter, dwl 52 Minna
Heppern Annie (widow) cloak maker, dwl 120 Natoma
Heppert Henry, steward Golden Gate Hotel
Hepworth John M. dwl 9 Auburn
Herald John, plasterer, dwl 707 Mission
Herant Edward P. architect, dwl 262 Clementina
Herardo David, porter, dwl 319 Dupont
Herbe Eugene, dwl 222 Stevenson
Herberger Charles, upholsterer, dwl 307 Dupont
Herbert (Allen) & Dunning (Zophar) proprietors National House, 414 Market
Herbert Harriet (widow) dwl 613 Pine
Herbert Henry V. clerk with Cobb & Sinton, dwl N s Folsom bet Eighth and Ninth
Herbert James, clerk, Young America Engine Co
Herbert L. contractor, dwl E s Wallace Place near California
Herbert Peter, lab. with William Kerr, dwl 903 Bat
Herden Jerry, drayman, dwl 127 Market
Herdges William, farmer, dwl 323 Pine
Herding Conrad, tailor, dwl 920 Montgomery
Herdrick Charles W. with Conrades & Co. dwl N s Folsom bet Fremont and First
Herdt Christian, hairdresser with Adam Grimm, dwl 337 Bush
Heren Jane (widow) lodgings, 154 First
Hereringer John C. jeweler, dwl N s Geary bet Laguna and Buchanan
Herget John, lock and gunsmith, 114 Pacific, dwl 18 Ohio
Herigozen Michél, butcher with John Bazille, dwl N s Sixteenth nr Nebraska
Heringhi Bernard, jeweler, 635 Kearny, dwl S s O'Farrell bet Hyde and Larkin
Heritage John, laborer, Lone Mountain Cemetery
Herker Galiel, laborer, Bay Sugar Refinery, dwl 813 Battery
Herlehy Maurice, cooper, S. F. & P. Sugar Co. dwl Rousch
Herliby John, laborer, dwl N s Filbert bet Larkin and Polk
Herlin John, carpenter, dwl SW cor Kearny and Pacific
Herman Catherine (widow) dwl 642 Mission
Herman John, seaman, dwl 532 Commercial
Herman Peter, seaman, dwl 44 Sacramento
Hermand Adolphe, laundryman, dwl 711 Vallejo
Hermann Alexander, musician, dwl 18 Sansom
Hermann Charles, tailor, dwl 76 Jessie
Hermann Christian, confectioner, bds Meyer's Hotel 814 Montgomery
Hermann Frederick, waiter, Bootz's Hotel
Hermann Isaac, groceries and liquors, 619 Post
Hermann James W. cook, S. F. & San José R. R. Co
Hermann John, dwl 447 Jessie
Hermann John, baker, dwl W s San Bruno Road nr California Avenue

Hermann John, cook, Booth's Hotel
Hermann John W. engraver with Lemme Bros. dwl 1412 Stockton
Hermann Kate Miss, domestic with Mrs. Wallets, Fourth nr Market
Hermann Otto W. ship joiner, dwl nr cor Michigan and Napa
HERMANN RUDOLPH, proprietor Harbor View House, Bay Shore and Fort Point Road near Presidio
Hermann S. importer, dwl 312 Stockton
Hermann Samuel, dwl E s Taylor bet Ellis and Eddy
Hermann, see Herrmann
Hern Patrick, with Wilson & Stevens, dwl E s Gilbert bet Bryant and Brannan
Hernas Edward, cook, 530 Merchant, dwl Pacific
Herndeen Edward P. Capt. dwl 238 Stewart
Herney John, blacksmith with Lawton & Co. dwl 12 Sutter
Hernster George, tailor, dwl 506 Kearny
Herold Philip H. blacksmith, 907 Folsom, dwl San Bruno Road 4¼ miles from City Hall
Herold Rudolph, professor music, dwl 211 Post
Heron James, Forwarding Department Wells, Fargo & Co. dwl W s Folsom bet Twenty-Second and Twenty-Third
Heron John M. drayman, dwl 6 Tehama
Heron William (col'd) whitewasher, dwl W s Salmon bet Mason and Taylor
Heron, see Herron
Herr Edward, coachman, American Exchange
Herr John J. book keeper, C. S. Nav. Co. NE cor Front and Jackson
HERRERA FRANCISCO, books and stationery and consul U. S. Colombia, 126 Second, dwl 438 Second
Herrera M r Mrs. Young Ladies' Seminary, 438 Seconda y
Herrguth A. butcher, dwl 208 Jessie
Herrguth Samuel F. cabinet maker, dwl 607 Dupont
Herrick Alfred H. with Langley, Crowell & Co. dwl 306 Mason
Herrick E. I. Mrs. millinery, 106 Kearny
Herrick Hazard P. wharfinger Clay St. Wharf, dwl SW cor Washington and Larkin
Herrick James R. civil engineer, dwl with Nelson R. Herrick
Herrick Lansan D. tinsmith, dwl 106 Kearny
Herrick Nelson R. proprietor Gold Hill Foundry, (Gold Hill, Nevada) dwl Presidio Road opposite Half Way House
Herrick William, laborer, dwl 140 Stewart
Herrick William F. accountant with Dibblee & Hyde, dwl cor Howard and Erie
Herrin John, carrier, Morning Call, dwl cor Valencia and Temple
Herring John, waiter, dwl 323 Pine
Herritage John, laborer, dwl E s Van Ness Avenue nr Hayes
Herrmann H. fancy goods, 205 Battery, dwl 427 Sacramento
Herrmann John, farmer, dwl NW cor Noe and Seventeenth
Herrmann O. W. ship joiner, dwl Illinois, Potrero
Herrmann Peter A. carpenter, dwl 8 Margaret Place
Herrmann S. & Co. importers and jobbers dry goods and groceries, 310 Sacramento, dwl 312 Stock
Herrold Bridget Miss, dwl DeBoom nr Second
Herron David, clerk with William Nicol, dwl 221 Sacramento
Herron James, painter, dwl nr Point Lobos 2 miles from Plaza
Herron Jerry, laborer, dwl NW cor Jessie and Anna
Herron Lizzie Miss, domestic, 828 Post
Herron Susan A. (widow) dwl 49 Clementina
Herron Thomas, dwl 614 Mason
Herron Thomas W. steward, steamer Del Norte
Herron, see Heron
Herschron Charles, bar keeper, St. Nicholas Hotel

Hersee George, dwl Flume House, San Bruno Road
Hersey Edgar, blacksmith, Pacific Foundry, dwl 564 Mission
Hersey Joseph, tinsmith, dwl E s Davis bet Washington and Clay
Hert Frederick, miner, dwl E s Montgomery bet Vallejo and Green
Hertel Edward, painter, dwl 303 Davis
Hertel George, hairdressing saloon, 20 Clay
Herteman Eugene, liquor saloon, 622 Pacific
Herting Eliza Miss, dress maker, 416 Stevenson
Herting Frederick, butcher with Louis Hartmeyer, cor Post and Dupont
Hertwig L. teacher, dwl 515 Pine
Hertz Adolph, wood turner, dwl 118 Prospect Pl
Hertz Alexander, with Peter Lozier, dwl 410 Market
Hertz Hermann, meat market, NE cor Stevenson and Ecker
Hertz Louis, butcher with M. Rosenberg & Co. 3 Occidental Market
Hertz Moses, dwl NE cor Stevenson and Ecker
Hertzfelder Herman, express wagon, dwl 456 Jessie
Hervagault Albert, salesman, dwl 423 Post
Hervagault Mary (widow) dwl 423 Post
Hervey C. B. Mrs. dress making, 10 Stockton
Hervey Eugene, harness maker, dwl 222 Stevenson
Hervey Samuel, boot fitting, NE cor Post and Dupont, dwl 10 Stockton
Herzag Christian, blacksmith, dwl 705 Broadway
Herzberg Julius, accountant, 815 and 817 Sansom, dwl 821 Greenwich
Herzberg Martin, fancy goods, 414 Sacramento, dwl 3 Eddy Place
Herzberg William (Michael Schenk & Co.) dwl 1610 Stockton
Herzer Hermann, dwl 3 St. Mark Place
Herzer Hugo, compositor, Abend Post, dwl 3 St. Mark Place
Herzfelder Herman, express wagon. cor California and Sansom
Herzog (Joseph) & Cahn (Morris) cigars and tobacco, 304 Battery, res Oakland
Herzog Herman, dwl 1022 Stockton
Herzog Michaelis, clerk with I. & J. Cohn, dwl 731 Folsom
Hesh Joseph, shoe maker, dwl 637 Mission
Heshell N. watchman, U. S. Branch Mint
Hesketh George, rope maker, S. F. Cordage Factory, dwl Indiana nr Potrero Rope Walk
Hesketh W. H. laborer, dwl 63 Minna
HESLEP AUGUSTUS M. attorney at law, office 3 and 4 Armory Hall third floor, dwl 239 Seventh
Hess Andrew J. carpenter, dwl SE cor Clay and Dupont
Hess August, laborer, dwl 624 Market
Hess Charles, merchant, dwl St. Nicholas Hotel
Hess Charles, optician, 425 Kearny
Hess Conrad, laborer, dwl 5 Virginia Place
HESS FREDERICK & CO. (Th. G. Koehler and Aloys Brauer) proprietors and publishers German Demokrat, NW cor Sacramento and Kearny, dwl SW cor Dupont and Green
Hess Frederick, bar keeper, NW cor Kearny and Jackson
Hess George B. Portsmouth House Saloon, NW cor Clay and Brenham Place
Hess Henry, clerk, 2 Montgomery, dwl St. Nicholas Hotel
Hess Henry U. salesman, 628 Sacramento, dwl St. Nicholas Hotel
Hess Jacob, boots and shoes, 746 Market
Hess Joseph, book keeper with L. & E. Wertheimer, dwl St. Nicholas Hotel
Hess Joseph S. drayman, Pacific Mail S. S. Co. cor Sacramento and Leidesdorff, dwl cor Washington and Larkin
HESS LEVI, proprietor St. Nicholas Hotel, SW cor Sansom and Commercial

Hesse Christian, works Union Brewery, Clementina nr Fourth
Hesse James H. policeman, City Hall, dwl room 5 third floor, City Hall
Hesse William (Pacific Distillery Co.) dwl 1810 Stockton
Hseser D. L. dwl Original House
Hesselgreen N. mariner, dwl SE cor Sac and Drumm
Hessions Michael, dwl NE cor Bdwy and Larkin
Hessler Charles, salesman with Sbarboro & Bro·dwl 8 Louisa
HESSLER WILLIAM, proprietor American Bakery, 715 Pacific
Hester Martin, steward, What Cheer House Restaurant, dwl Milton Place
Hestler Davis, express wagon, corner Second and Market, dwl SE cor Franklin and Fulton
Hetherington Henry, assistant engineer, stm Oregon, dwl 26 Moss
Hetkes John, last manufacturer, NW cor Broadway and Dupont
Hettinger N. waiter, Cosmopolitan Hotel
Hetzett Charles, machinist, dwl 54 First
HEUCK HERMAN H. cigars, tobacco, and snuff, 233 Kearny
HEUER (George) & KOOP (William) Young America Saloon, NE cor Stewart and Howard
Heuer Philip, groceries and liquors, SE cor Jansen and Lombard·
Heumann Alexander, musician. dwl 18 Sansom
Heurlin O. W. book keeper with Dickson, DeWolf & Co. 412 Battery
Heustis W. F. deputy clerk U. S. Circuit Court and U. S. commissioner, office 15 U. S. Court Block, dwl 915 Market
Heuston Adolph, porter, 311 Com, dwl 321 Front
Heuston Ellen Mrs. dwl Government House room 44
HEUSTON, (H. M.) HASTINGS (C. C.) & CO. clothing, SW cor Montgomery and Sutter, dwl 912 Bush
HEVERIN MICHAEL, marble yard, 783 Market, dwl 13 Fourth
Hevios James, seaman, steamer Senator
Hewer C. physician, dwl SW cor Dupont and Bwdy
Hewes Daniel, mechanic with David Hewes
HEWES DAVID, steam paddy and railroad contractor, office and dwl SW cor Market and Third
Hewes Jesse (col'd) whitewasher, dwl 1403 Mason
Hewes Samuel, clerk with James H. Cutter, 511 Front, dwl with Benj. Shellard E s Montgomery bet Green and Union
Hewes, see Hughes
Hewett Henry, clerk with Falkner, Bell & Co. dwl cor Folsom and Seventh
Hewett Joseph G. hack driver, Howard Engine Co. No. 3
Hewitt Agnes (widow) dwl 947 Howard
Hewitt Amos L. captain sloop P. M. Randall, dwl 20 Everett
Hewitt Charles, captain schr Sarah, dwl 524 Bryant
Hewitt Joshua, porter, American Exchange
Hewitt Mary C. Mrs. seamstress with Galpen & Co. 54 Third
Hewson Robert, carpenter, dwl W s Third bet Folsom and Harrison
Hewston George, physician, office and dwl 652 Folsom
Hewston John jr. (Kellogg, H. & Co.) chemists, dwl 416 Montgomery
HEY (John) & MEYN (Peter) groceries and liquors and contractors, NW cor Folsom and Twelfth, dwl N s Folsom bet Seventh and Eighth
Hey William, clerk, SW cor Folsom and Nevada
Heyberger Carl, upholsterer with Goodwin & Co. dwl 307 Dupont
Heydenfeldt Anna Mrs. adjuster, Coiner's Department U. S. Branch Mint, dwl 1114 Powell

Heydenfeldt Solomon, president Exchequer M. Co. 712 Montgomery
Heydenfeldt Solomon jr. with Edward Bosqui & Co. dwl 613 Stockton
Heye Emile, clerk, 825 Kearny
HEYE (Henry) & LUTTIG (Frank) groceries and liquors, NE cor Lombard and Mason
Heyer Albert, groceries and liquors, NW cor Third and Bryant, dwl 70 Silver
Heyfron Matthew, wood and coal, 716 Folsom
Heyfron Patrick, wood sawyer, dwl 716 Folsom
Heyfron Peter, wood sawyer, dwl 716 Folsom
Heyl George, pork packer, 129 Fourth
Heyn Ernest, agent H. M. Lockwood & Co. 624 Clay, dwl S s Clay nr Leavenworth
Heynemann H. (Heynemann & Co.) dwl 807 Pac
HEYNEMANN (Leonard D.) & CO. (H. Heynemann and F. P. Salomons) importers and jobbers dry goods and agents S. F. & P. Woolen Factory, office 311 and 313 California, res Manchester, England
HEYNEMANN MARTIN D. importer and jobber crockery and glass ware, 409 California, dwl 807 Pacific
Heywood Calvin, office Chace's Mill, 311 Market, dwl Fifth bet Harrison and Folsom
Heywood Frank (Heywood & Harmon) dwl 1121 Kearny
Heywood George, teller with Sather & Co. dwl 906 Leavenworth
Heywood Silas (Arnold & H.) dwl E s Hyde bet Washington and Clay
Heywood William B. (Heywood & Harmon) dwl W s Mary nr Minna
HEYWOOD (Zimri B.) & HARMON (Samuel H. and Frank and William B. Heywood) wholesale and retail lumber, Pier 4 Stewart, dwl 1121 Kearny
Hezlep James, carrier, American Flag, dwl 410 Third
Hezlep Melvina A. Mrs. dress maker, 410 Third
Hibberd H. I. stair builder with B. H. Freeman & Co. dwl 613 Pine
Hibberd Phineas S. carpenter, dwl 613 Pine
HIBERNIA SAVINGS AND LOAN SOCIETY, office 506 Jackson
Hibrard Charles, fireman, dwl Hayes' Valley
Hichhorn A. C. drayman, 325 Front, dwl SW cor Third and Folsom
Hichhorn John E. (E. W. Linsley & Co.) dwl 63 Natoma
Hick Joseph, carpenter, dwl Philadelphia House, 336 Bush
Hickey Catherine Miss, domestic, NE cor Post and Leavenworth
Hickey Cornelius, carpenter, dwl S s Shipley near Harrison Avenue
Hickey Ellen Miss, domestic, dwl 520 Third
Hickey James, laborer, dwl W s Battery bet Broadway and Pacific
Hickey James, packer, Glass Works, dwl S s Precita Avenue nr California Avenue
Hickey John, fruits, 805 Market
Hickey Julia Miss, domestic with Alexander Buswell
Hickey Margaret Miss, domestic, 746 Howard
Hickey P. J. (Livingston & H.) dwl 632 Market
Hickey Thomas, laborer, dwl United States Hotel, 706 Battery
Hickey Thomas, laborer, dwl 227 Sutter
Hickey William, carpenter, dwl 73 Stevenson
Hickie E. T. waiter, Niantic Hotel
Hickie Henry, poll tax collector, City Hall, dwl 654 Minna
Hickman Edward, barber, 154 Perry
Hickman Thomas, butcher, dwl 327 Fourth
Hickox A. D. Wesley, clerk with Bowen Bros. dwl with J. B. Harmstead E s Howard bet Eighteenth and Nineteenth

Hickox Albert A. clerk with William Shew, dwl E s Howard bet Eighteenth and Nineteenth
HICKOX *(George C.)* & SPEAR *(John I. jr.)* bullion and money brokers, NE cor Montgomery and Sacramento, dwl NW cor Mason and Sutter
Hickox Seth, book keeper, dwl 20 Tehama
Hicks *(Daniel)* & Co. *(John R. Wesby and Edward Westall)* book binders, 543 Clay, dwl 1417 Kearny
Hicks J. L. machinist and sewing machines, 47 Second, dwl 165 Minna
Hicks Mary (widow) dwl 28 Annie
Hicks Peter, conductor, Omnibus R. R. Co
Hicks R. M. dry goods, 110 Second
Hicks William B. blacksmith, 118 Bush, dwl Minna nr Third
Hickson Henry, First St. Market, 104 First, dwl 509 Mission
Hickson, see Hixon
Hidalgo Manuel, porter, Gibb's Bonded Warehouse, dwl SE cor Montgomery and Union
Hiekrich Charles, express wagon, cor Oregon and Davis
Hiestand John C. carpenter and builder, dwl SW cor Louisiana and Sierra
Hiester Amos C. compositor, Evening Bulletin, dwl 724 Howard
Hieth Albert, tailor with M. Brandhofer, dwl N s Broadway nr Powell
Hifti Regala Mrs. dress making and embroidery, 717 Clay
Higal Nicholas, molder, Vulcan Iron Works, dwl 433 First
Higarty Cornelius, laborer, dwl Spear nr Harrison
Higbee Rufus B. clerk with Favre & Mendessolle, 605 Front
Higbie George, laborer, dwl Bailey House
Higel Alois, molder, Union Foundry, dwl 520 Mission
Higginbottom James, porter, 22 Battery
Higgins Bennett, dwl 708 Taylor
Higgins Bernard, tinsmith with Locke & Montague, dwl Yerba Buena nr Sacramento
Higgins Bridget Mrs. domestic, 237 Seventh
Higgins Charles S. City Flour Mills, 845 Harrison, dwl 422 Fremont
Higgins Daniel, carpenter, dwl S s Nineteenth bet Capp and Howard
Higgins Daniel, coal oil miner, dwl 215 O'Farrell
Higgins E. J. (widow) furnished rooms, 506 Mkt
Higgins Elisha, wood dealer, dwl 510 Greenwich
Higgins Ellen (widow) dwl 1315 Powell
Higgins E. R. pattern maker, dwl 509 Market
Higgins H. D. Mrs. private school, 1051 Howard
Higgins Honora (widow) dwl 8 Anthony
Higgins James, laborer, dwl 1220 Powell, rear
Higgins James, teacher, dwl 520 Geary, rear
Higgins James S. mariner, dwl 51 Greenwich
Higgins J. B. real estate agency, office 624 Merchant, dwl SE cor Market and Fourth
Higgins Johanna, domestic, 255 Minna
Higgins Johanna (widow) ladies' nurse, dwl Lincoln Avenue
Higgins John, cooper, S. F. & P. Sugar Co. dwl cor Folsom and Eighth
Higgins John, dairyman, Lake Merced Ranch nr Ocean House
Higgins John, laborer, Spring Valley W. W
HIGGINS JOHN, proprietor Western Hotel, 306 Broadway
Higgins John, well borer, dwl 205 Sansom
Higgins John, workman with S. Crim, dwl W s Honora bet Nineteenth and Twentieth
Higgins Mark W. *(Moore & H.)* dwl Minnie nr Sixth
Higgins Michael, hackman, dwl SW cor Jackson and Leavenworth
Higgins Michael, laborer, dwl Chestnut nr Laguna
Higgins Monica Miss, private school, 8 Anthony

HIGGINS *(Patrick)* & SIPPLES *(Richard)* proprietors Shakspeare Hotel, 219 Pacific
Higgins Patrick, cooper, S. F. & P. Sugar Co. dwl NE cor Folsom and Eighth
Higgins Rosa Miss, domestic, 1010 Bush
Higgins Solomon, teamster, 17 California, dwl 1051 Howard nr Sixth
Higgins Thomas, annealer, U. S. Branch Mint, dwl 7 Tay
Higgins Thomas J. photographic gallery, 659 Clay, dwl 708 Taylor bet Bush and Sutter
Higgins Walter B. machinist, Wheeler & Wilson Sewing Machine Co. dwl 242 Third
Higgins William, laborer, dwl W s Salmon bet Mason and Taylor
Higgins William, laborer, S. F. Gas Co
Higgins William, reporter, Police Gazette, dwl 11 Geary
Higgins William L. stock and exchange broker, 723 Montgomery, res Oakland
Higgins William M. druggist and apothecary, 534 Sacramento, dwl Jackson Place
Higgins *(William T.)* & Ladd *(William W.)* wines and liquors, 711 Montgomery, dwl 131 Montgomery
Higgins Wilson, mariner, dwl 13 Howard Court
Higgs Henry W. dwl 119 Dupont
Highton Edward, cashier with Pease & Grimm, 709 Montgomery, dwl 370 Brannan
Highton Edward R. real estate, office 540 Clay room 6, dwl 422 Greenwich
HIGHTON HENRY E. attorney at law, office 540 Clay room 6, dwl 422 Greenwich
Hiher Frank, finisher, Jackson Foundry, dwl 14 Dupont
Hiland Patrick, dwl Franklin House SW cor Sansom and Broadway
Hildburghauser Louis, book keeper with D. N. & E. Walter, dwl St. Nicholas Hotel
Hildebrand Alexander, musician, dwl 507 Bush
Hildebrand Charles H. workman with P. Johnson, Serpentine Avenue nr San Bruno Road
Hildebrand Conrad, trunk maker, N s Thirteenth bet Mission and Howard
Hildebrand Edward H. tailor, dwl 324 Dupont
Hildebrand George, private German school, 753 Mission
Hildebrand J. H. beer saloon, 505 Pacific
Hildebrand Martin, miller, dwl 315 Bush
Hildebrand Michael, baker, What Cheer House Restaurant, dwl N s Thirteenth bet Mission and Howard
Hildebrandt August, brass finisher, dwl Oriental Hotel
Hildebrandt *(Carstin)* & Knop *(Elfert)* groceries and liquors, dwl SE cor Broadway and Mont
Hildebrandt Conrad, baker, dwl 637 Broadway
Hildebrandt Fabian, pile driver, office 2 California, dwl S s Grove bet Laguna and Octavia
Hildebrandt George, varnisher with Goodwin & Co. dwl N s Jackson bet Stockton and Powell
Hildebrandt George, miner, dwl 9 Virginia Place
Hildebrandt Henry, groceries and liquors, NW cor Kearny and Sutter
Hildebrandt Marie Miss, dwl 303 Clementina
Hildebrandt Martin, clerk with Frederick Schroder, SE cor Sacramento and Drumm
Hildebrandt Mary Miss, governess, dwl 307 Clementina
Hildebrandt P. musician, dwl 631 Broadway
Hildebrandt William C. clerk, SW cor Clementina and Fourth
Hildreth James, laborer, dwl 26 Stewart
Hildreth Richard, bar keeper with Martin & Horton, 545 Clay, dwl 9 Park Avenue
Hildreth W. H. teacher, Independence H. & L. Co. No. 3
Hilken John, dwl 1518 Powell
Hill A. B. clerk, steamer Sacramento

Hill Andrew E. clerk, Bank California, dwl 28 O'Farrell
Hill Annie A. Miss, assistant, Mission Grammar School, dwl Fillmore bet Hayes and Fell
Hill Anthony D. carpenter, dwl E s Fillmore bet Fell and Hayes
Hill Benjamin, ship carpenter, dwl 28 O'Farrell
Hill Charles E. drayman, 120 California, dwl Fifth Avenue
Hill Edward, artist, dwl 406 Geary
Hill Elizabeth Miss, domestic, NE cor Folsom and Fourth
Hill Ephraim P. printer, dwl N s Ellis nr Larkin
Hill George A. real estate agent, 622 Montgomery, dwl 518 Seventh bet Brannan and Bryant
Hill Henry O. proprietor Alta Market, 1113 Clay
Hill Horace L. with William Burling, NW cor Montgomery and Washington
Hill James, laborer, dwl S s Perry bet Fourth and Fifth, rear
Hill James K. accountant, dwl N s McAllister bet Laguna and Buchanan
Hill James S. watchman, dwl Perry bet Fourth and Fifth
Hill James W. ship joiner, dwl 1211 Clay
Hill J. Bryant, broker, dwl 616 O'Farrell
HILL (J. C. A.) & EASTMAN (T. S.) agents Abbott, Downing & Co.'s Carriages, 618 Battery, dwl 510 Dupont
Hill J. F. watchman, Miners' Foundry
Hill John, ex-deputy sheriff, City Hall, dwl S s Card Place
Hill John, laborer, S. F. P. Woolen Mills, dwl North Point bet Polk and Van Ness Avenue
Hill John, stock broker, dwl 613 Jones
Hill John, waiter, steamer Pacific
Hill John B. Rev. pastor Central M. E. Church, cor Sixth and Minna, dwl 524 Tehama
Hill John J. clerk, dwl 1121 Sacramento
Hill Joseph J. painter, dwl 512 Bryant
Hill Kate Miss, private school, dwl E s Fillmore bet Fell and Hayes
Hill Margaret (widow) dwl NE cor Folsom and Fourth
Hill Mary Miss, domestic, NE corner Folsom and Fourth
Hill Matilda (widow) dwl 713 Broadway
Hill O. W. Mrs. dress maker, 79 Clara
Hill Richmond, porter with Tucker & Co. dwl 79 Clara
Hill Robert, bakery, 1320 Dupont
HILL SAMUEL, agent Florence Sewing Machines, 111 Montgomery, dwl NE corner Mason and O'Farrell
Hill Samuel, compositor, American Flag, dwl 224 Stockton
Hill Samuel, with George F. Parker, dwll 119 Sacramento
Hill S. W. ship joiner with John G. North, Potrero
Hill Thomas, artist, room 16 Mercantile Library Building, dwl 1123 Folsom
Hill Thomas, stock broker, 622 Montgomery, dwl 435 Natoma
Hill Thomas F. clerk, dwl 321 Minna
Hill William, dwl 1 Martha Place
Hill William, clerk with Nicholas Bruns, dwl 617 Davis
Hill William B. carpenter, 217 Dupont
Hill William H. gilder with Jones, Wooll & Sutherland, dwl S s Geary bet Jones and Leavenworth
Hillard Benjamin, dwl NW cor Green and Taylor
Hillard Frederick, contractor, dwl 114 Silver
Hillard Mary Mrs. domestic with Adam T. Farish
Hillard Richard, captain schooner Lear, dwl W s First nr Bryant
Hillebrandt Carston, groceries and liquors, SW cor Brannan and Gilbert
Hillebrandt Fabian (Hartmann & H.) dwl NW cor Brannan and Third

Hillebrandt John, clerk, SW cor Folsom and Sixteenth
Hiller Edward C. amalgamator, bds American Exchange
Hiller John R. dwl N s Fell nr Franklin
Hiller Mary Miss, domestic, 1005 Stockton
Hiller Richard M. blacksmith with Albert Folsom, dwl Brooklyn Hotel
Hiller Rosina (widow) dwl 15 Stockton
Hiller Rudolph, printer, California Democrat, dwl 1 St. Mary nr California
Hillis William H. (Bailey & H.) 767 Market
Hillman Albert F. blacksmith with Gallager & Rodecker, dwl Albion House
Hillman Edward, stevedore, dwl Greenwich bet Montgomery and Sansom
Hillman F. blacksmith, dwl 559 Market
Hillman Henry, drayman, NE cor California and Davis, dwl cor Front and Market
Hillman (Isaac) & Severence (Jasper) Fountain of Health, 151 Shipley
Hillman John, fireman, steamer Pacific
Hillmann John, miller, Alta Mills, dwl 722 Harrison
Hills Austin, ship carpenter with J. G. North, dwl SW cor Louisiana and Sierra
Hills Henry & Co. employment office, 5 Second
Hills Henry, cook, Hayes' Park Pavilion
Hills Robert D. dwl 735 Market
Hills Sanford M. carpenter, dwl 842 Clay
Hillstrom Matthew, seaman, dwl 20 Commercial
Hillyer E. W. lieut. col., U. S. A. judge advocate, office 742 Washington, dwl 53 Belden Block
Hillyer M. C. & Co. stock brokers, office 706 Montgomery, dwl SW cor Gough and Sutter
Hilman Henry, laborer, dwl 33 Geary
Hilton Charles, dwl 813 Stockton
Hilton Charles W. stock broker, dwl 626 Clay
Hilton C. W. teamster, dwl 116 Sansom
Hilton George K. printer, dwl 625 Bush
Hilton John Wesley, clerk, 13 Fourth, dwl 275 Stevenson
Hilton Joshua, constable Fourth Township, office 230 Bush, dwl 625 Bush
Hilton Prince E. with N. R. Lowell, NW cor Pine and Davis
Hilton Samuel, dwl 34 Silver
Hilton Stephen, carpenter, dwl 741 Market
Hilton Stephen, editor Evangel, office 29 Turk, dwl 25 Moss
Hilton William H. secretary Pioneer Land & Loan Association, office 626 Clay, dwl 17 Third
Hilton, see Hylton
HIMMELMAN ANDREW, real estate and money broker, office 637 Wash, dwl 308 O'Farrell
Himmelman John, cook, 718 Market, dwl cor Hinckley and Pinckney
Himrod Frank D. foreman track repairer, S. F. & San José R. R. Co
Hinchey Lawrence, carpenter, dwl U. S. Hotel, 706 Battery
HINCHMAN A. F. attorney at law, office 19 Exchange Building, dwl 617 Bush
Hinchman C. H. (Hinchman & Co.) dwl NW cor Leavenworth and Sacramento
Hinchman H. E. Miss, milliner, 637 Sacramento, dwl 564 Howard
Hinchman (T. W.) & C (C. H. Hinchman). stock and exchange brokers, 723 Montgomery, dwl 1118 Bush
Hinck John H. bar tender, Thunderbolt Saloon, 938 Kearny
Hincken Sophia (widow) dwl 28 Russ
Hinckley Barney, real estate, office 205 Battery, res Oakland
Hinckley Charles, painter, dwl 545 Mission
HINCKLEY CHARLES E. & CO. chemists and apothecaries, SE corner Clay and Kearny, dwl 1013 Clay

HINCKLEY *(Daniel B.)* & CO. proprietors Fulton Foundry and Machine Works, 45–49 First, dwl 528 Howard
Hinckley Frank, assistant engineer, Western Pacific R. R. office 409 California
Hinckley George, actor, dwl 604 Mission
HINCKLEY GEORGE E. physician, office and dwl NW cor Second and Stevenson
Hinckley Maria P. (widow) dwl 906 Stockton
Hinckley Sarah Miss, actress, Maguire's Opera House, dwl 921 Sacramento
Hinckley William H. furniture and bedding, 823 Clay
HINDERS *(Henry)* & KAST *(L. S.)* boots and shoes, 332 Kearny
Hindman E. dwl International Hotel
Hinds Ambrose, shipping clerk, dwl 1216 Jackson
Hinds Patrick, laborer, dwl 551 Howard
Hine Charles *(Carl H. Hain & Co.)* 321 Montgomery, dwl SE cor Taylor and Sutter
Hine Henry, teamster, Ocean House Race Course, dwl 636 Commercial
Hine Nelson M. bar keeper with Luther R. Mills, dwl 323 Tehama
Hines James, dwl 227 Bush
Hines Michael, fireman, steamer Senator
Hines Patrick, laborer with James McDevitt, dwl W s Montgomery bet Broadway and Pacific
Hing Chong (Chinese) washing, 730 Pacific
Hing Yet (Chinese) washing, 303 Third
Hink Gustavus, clerk, NW cor Brannan and Fourth, dwl NE cor Mission and Eleventh
Hinkel Charles, carpenter, dwl 208 Minna
Hinkle Morris, express wagon, cor Broadway and Dupont, dwl N s Jackson bet Mont and San
Hinkle Philip, centrifugal amalgamators and separators, 29 and 41 Fremont, dwl 1809 Stockton
Hinkley Edward N. book keeper with Wilson & Stevens, 506 Market
Hinman Louis A. broker, dwl NW cor Mission and Laskie
Hinton W. M. *(Thompson & Co.)* dwl 1425 Pacific
Hintz Augustus H. shooting gallery Willows, dwl W s Valencia bet Sixteenth and Seventeenth
Hintze Isaac, clothing and gents' furnishing goods, 20 Sutter
Hinz Adolph, salesman, 633 Clay, dwl 228 Sutter
Hinz Charles E. blacksmith, dwl 555 Mission
Hinz John, broom maker with L. Van Laak, dwl 14 Drumm
Hip Hing & Co. (Chinese) merchants, 711 Sac
Hip Wo (Chinese) washing, 111 Leidesdorff
Hip Wo & Co. (Chinese) merchants, 739 Sacramento
Hirleman George, butcher, dwl 238 Fremont
Hirleman Philip, New York Market, SE cor Mission and Stewart, dwl 238 Fremont
Hirsch *(Joseph)* & Marks *(Jacob C.)* boots and shoes, 50 Second, dwl 637 Mission
Hirsch Leopold, dry goods, 1122 and 1124 Dupont
Hirsch Marks, waiter, Continental Hotel, dwl 246 Stevenson
Hirschfeld Benjamin, fruit peddler, dwl 235 Minna
Hirschfeld *(Julius)* & Maleton *(Henry)* hairdressing saloon, 15 Mead House, dwl 613 Bush
Hirschfeld Philip, salesman with Martin L. Haas & Co. dwl 744 Folsom
Hirschfelder A. & Co. *(J. J. Bettman)* importers and manufacturers mirrors, frames, etc. 427 Montgomery, dwl 325 Sutter
Hirshfeld Benjamin, peddler, dwl 256 Minna
Hirshfeld *(Peter)* & Moritz *(Michael)* ladies' hairdressers 32 Montgomery, dwl 613 Bush
Hirshfield Dora Miss, dwl with Moses B. Lichtenstein
HIRSTEL EDOUARD H. wholesale and retail cigars and tobacco, SE cor Montgomery and Clay, dwl 615 Green bet Stockton and Powell
Hirstel N. A. cigars and tobacco, 213 Montgomery Russ House, dwl 615 Green

Hirth J. & Co. *(Pierre, Bergis, and Dominique Cazeau)* proprietors Miners' Restaurant, 531 and 533 Commercial, dwl 539 Vallejo
Hirtzel Minna, Mrs. with Adolph Müller, 107 Montgomery, dwl 323 Pine
Hishon Mary, domestic, dwl 9 Howard Court
Hislop Robert, upholsterer with John C. Bell, dwl NW cor Howard and First
Hitch Samuel P. coffee grinder with Marden & Folger, dwl NW cor Second and Tehama
Hitchcock Charles, salesman with Roberts, Morrison & Co. dwl 1005 Clay
Hitchcock Charles E. *(Lord & Co.)* consul Hawaiian Islands, office 405 Battery, dwl 9 Laurel Pl
Hitchcock Charles M. physician, office 214 Bush, bds Cosmopolitan Hotel
HITCHCOCK GEORGE B. & CO. counting house stationers, 413 and 415 Sansom cor Commmercial, dwl 1010 Powell
Hitchcock Irving W. clerk, Marysville Hotel, 414 Pacific
Hitchcock W. F. book keeper, 425 Battery, res Oakland
Hitchens James, broker, dwl 809 Harrison
Hitchens Thomas H. driver, Central R. R. Co. dwl SE cor Seventh and Brannan
Hitchings Edward W. salesman with Kennedy & Bell, dwl 921 Stockton
Hitchings Lizzie F. assistant, Lincoln School, dwl 921 Stockton
Hitchins Thomas, broker, dwl 299 Clementina
Hite Ormsby jr. clerk, C. S. Navigation Co. Broadway Wharf, dwl 628 Harrison
Hittell John S. editorial department Alta California, dwl 629 Mission
Hittell Theodore H. attorney at law, office 11 Court Block 636 Clay, dwl 726 Folsom
Hixon Omri, dwl 11 William
HIXON WILLIAM M. importer and jobber carpets, oil cloth, paper hangings, etc. 606 and 608 Clay, dwl 710 Vallejo
Hoadley James H. dwl SW cor Bush and Lyon nr Lone Mountain Cemetery
HOADLEY *(Milo)* & CO. *(Silas Hoadley)* sample rooms and native wines, 617 Montgomery, dwl NE cor Bush and Cemetery Avenue
Hoadley Silas *(Hoadley & Co.)* res New York
Hoag Albert B. clerk, 404 Battery, dwl 808 Folsom
Hoag Caroline Miss, domestic, 711 Leavenworth
Hoag George, porter, 110 Ellis
Hoag Horace, house and sign painter, dwl W s Garden bet Harrison and Bryant
Hoagland Alexander G. salesman, 514 Market, dwl 234 Stevenson
Hoagland Jane (widow) dwl SW cor Twenty-Fourth and Bartlett
HOAGLAND *(William C.)* & NEWSOM *(John J.)* architects, office 328 Mont, dwl 313 Taylor
Hoaninghus A. Julius, carpenter, dwl 52 Beale
Hoare Michael H. blacksmith, Brannan St. Bridge, dwl W s Gilbert nr Brannan
Hobart Allen P. dwl 250 Clementina
HOBART *(Benjamin)* DUNBAR *(William H.)* & CO. importers and jobbers boots and shoes, 223 California, dwl Cosmopolitan Hotel
Hobart John A. office SW cor Davis and Oregon, res Oakland
Hobart John H. drayman, 225 Clay, dwl 16 Stanford
Hobart John R. tally clerk, Pier 19 Stewart, dwl 808 Howard
Hobart S. L. Miss, assistant, Rincon School, dwl 156 Perry
Hobbat Henry, newsdealer, 247 Third
HOBBS, *(Caleb S.)* GILMORE *(George W.)* & CO. *(Stephen D. Gilmore and David Pomeroy)* planing mill and box factory, 217 Market, dwl 51 Second
Hobbs J. K. C. box maker, dwl 51 Second

Hobbs William, waiter, steamer Orizaba
Hobe Adolphus A. groceries and liquors, NE cor Eighth and Minna
HOBE *(George J.)* & WEIHE *(August)* cigars and tobacco, NE cor Washington and Dupont, dwl 910 Vallejo
Hobern Emile, broker, dwl 8 Telegraph Place
Hobi Kate (widow) liquor saloon, W s Mission bet Twenty-First and Twenty-Second
Hobkark Peter, carpenter, bds Cambridge House 304 Pacific
Hobler Francis, attorney at law, dwl 523 Bush, rear
Hobron William, mariner, dwl 1 Perry
Hobson Abraham, boot maker, 543 Kearny, dwl 7 Prospect Place
Hobson Thomas, porter with Thomas Day, 732 Montgomery, dwl NE cor Leav and Pacific
Hoburg Joseph, laborer with Hobbs, Gilmore & Co. dwl Bootz's Hotel
Hoburg William H. dwl 448 Natoma
Hochgurtel Nicholas, saloon, dwl 1624 Powell
Hochheimer Amiel, salesman, 100 Kearny, dwl 26 Howard Court
Hochholzer Hugo, civil engineer, dwl 1015 Powell
HOCHKOFLER RUDOLPH, merchandise broker and consul for Austria, office 203 Front cor California, dwl 30 Hawthorne
Hochstadter E. *(Hochstadter & Bro. Marysville)* office 418 Sacramento, dwl 1021 Powell
Hock Henry, proprietor Mission Railroad Brewery, E s Valencia bet Fifteenth and Sixteenth
Hock John, liquor saloon, dwl NE cor Washington and Dupont
Hock Tobias, hairdressing saloon, 532 Jackson, dwl 6 Milton Place
Hockins Charles, laborer, dwl 1336 Dupont
Hodapp Theodore, porter with L. E. Ritter & Co. dwl 417 Dupont
Hoddif August, broom maker, dwl 228 Mission
Hodes August, cutlery and fancy goods, 321 East
Hodgden Joseph B. local policeman, dwl 277 Stevenson
Hodgdon Alexander, brakeman, S. F. & San José R. R. Co. res San José
Hodgdon Ambrose P. carpenter, dwl N s Sixteenth bet Valencia and Mission
Hodgdon Charles, pattern maker, Miners' Foundry, dwl 7 Harrison Avenue
Hodgdon Charles H. teamster with J. B. Holmes & Co. 108 Market
Hodge Alexander, fruits, 304 Third
Hodge Benjamin O. sheriff's keeper, dwl NW cor Second and Minna
Hodge Charles, paper hanger, NW cor Second and Minna
Hodge John, bar keeper, 52 Third, dwl Jessie bet Fourth and Fifth
HODGE JOHN G. & CO. importers and jobbers books, stationery, etc. 418 and 420 Clay, res New York
Hodge Joseph, hostler, 16 Sutter
Hodge Michael, drayman, 223 Clay, dwl 338 Union
Hodge William, gilder with Snow & Co
Hodges Albert, machinist, Pacific Foundry, dwl E s Selina Place nr California
Hodges James, peddler, dwl 7 Trinity
Hodges John, carpenter, dwl Hodges Place
Hodges Mary E. P. (widow) teacher, dwl NE cor Montgomery and Pacific
Hodges Sylvester, carpenter, dwl E s Selina Place
Hodges Willard, wholesale grocer, 223 Sacramento
Hodges William, carpenter, dwl 446 Brannan
Hodgkin J. E. carpenter with S. S. Culverwell, 29 Fremont, dwl 509 Dupont
HODGKINS WILLIAM, liquor saloon, SW cor Third and Howard
Hodis Augustus, hairdresser with Louis Hemprich, 18 Kearny
Hodkins J. H. dwl 331 Bush

Hodnett J. W. express wagon, cor Sansom and Pine
Hodnett Mary Miss, dress maker, 15 Ritch
Hodnett William, warehouseman, U. S. Clothing Depôt, dwl 1205 Bush
Hoeber Henry, temporary inspector, Custom House, dwl 143 Perry
Hoeckele Louis, clerk, SW cor Folsom and Dora
Hoefer Henry G. gilder, dwl 840 Clay
Hoefler Joseph, lithograph printer with George H. Baker, dwl 746 Market
Hoeg George C. captain bark Mary, 212 Clay, dwl 42 Everett
Hoehler Nicolaus, bowling saloon, 627 Pacific, dwl cor Sansom and Commercial
Hoekenboner Peter, boiler maker helper, Vulcan Iron Works
Hoelscher Anton, brewer, Philadelphia Brewery
HOELSCHER *(August)* & WIELAND *(John)* proprietors Philadelphia Brewery, 232 Second, dwl 236 Second
Hoelscher *(Ernest)* & Rau *(John)* groceries and liquors, SE cor Eddy and Mason, dwl 11 Mason
Hoelscher Werner, clerk with Hoelscher & Rau, SW cor Eddy and Mason
Hoelscher William, with Hoelscher & Wieland, dwl 236 Second
HOESCH HENRY, proprietor Hoesch's Coffee and Dining Saloon, 614 Clay, dwl 1214 Clay
Hoey Patrick, cartman, dwl Perry bet Third and Fourth
Hoey Robert, oiler, steamer Yosemite
Hoey Thomas, laborer, dwl E s Clinton bet Brannan and Townsend
Hoey William, painter, dwl 3 Sherwood Place
Hoff John W. dwl S s Willow Avenue nr Polk
Hoff William C. real estate, dwl 323 First
Hoff, see Hough and Huff
Hoffelman T. H. carrier, Evening Bulletin
Hofferkamp Herman, laborer, Bay Sugar Refinery, dwl W s Jones bet Greenwich and Filbert
Hofferminer W. painter, dwl 31 St. Mark Place
Hoffman Abraham, salesman, 626 Sacramento, dwl 1526 Powell
Hoffman Charles, cabinet maker with J. & J. Easton
Hoffman Charles, porter, 421 Sacramento
Hoffman Charles F. topographer, office 90 Montgomery Block, res Oakland
Hoffman Charles W. beer saloon, 525 Pacific
Hoffman Frank, boot maker, 737 Mission
Hoffman Frank, brewer with Mangels & Co
Hoffman Gottlieb, machinist with Theodore Kallenberg, dwl 518 Pacific
Hoffman Henry, clerk, dwelling 48 Government House
Hoffman H. F. W. clerk Supt. Indian Affairs, dwl 27 Silver
Hoffman H. William *(Plege & H.)* dwl NW corner Post and Taylor
Hoffman J. D. civil engineer, office 728 Montgomery
Hoffman John A. & Co. collectors and gen'l agents, 604 Merchant room 3, dwl W s Florence near Broadway
Hoffman John D. with Jones, Wooll & Sutherland, dwl 58 Minna
Hoffman Joseph, salesman with Hoffman & Co. 312 Sacramento
Hoffman Joseph, workman, S. F. & P. Sugar Co. dwl cor Folsom and Eighth
Hoffman L. A. compositor, American Flag, dwl Original House
Hoffman Lazarus *(Hoffman & Co.)* dwl 528 Ellis
Hoffman Mathias, proprietor Sacramento Hotel, 407 Pacific
Hoffman Mina Mrs. children's clothing and ladies' furnishing goods, 22½ Montgomery
HOFFMAN OGDEN, district judge U. S. Northern District California, office, chambers, and dwl rooms 12 and 13 U. S. Court Building
Hoffman R. C. Mrs. dwl 910 Market

Hoffman *(S.)* & Co. *(L. Hoffman)* importers and jobbers staple and fancy dry goods, 312 Sacramento, dwl 532 Ellis
Hoffman William & Co. importers and jobbers straw and millinery goods, 427 Sac, res New York
Hoffman William *(Teubner & H.)* dwl 7 St. Mary
Hoffman William, cabinet maker with J. & J. Easton, dwl SE cor Page and Octavia
Hoffman William T. clerk with DeWitt, Kittle & Co. dwl 1308 Pacific
Hoffmann Charles H. job gardener, dwl W s Mission bet Twelfth and Thirteenth
Hoffmann Christian, carpenter, dwl 275 Stevenson
Hoffmann Conrad, blacksmith, dwl 639 Bdwy, rear
Hoffmann George, merchant, dwl 1425 Kearny
Hoffmann Henry, cellarman, Mason's Brewery
Hoffmann Henry, salesman, 623 Clay, dwl 2004 Powell
Hoffmann Rudolph, brewer, dwl 809 Clay
Hoffmann Simon, cigars, 338 Third
HOFFMANN *(Victor)* & SCHMIDT *(P. R.)* architects, office 240 Montgomery room 6, dwl N s Oak nr Laguna
Hoffschneider William, type founder, dwl 230 Sutter
Hoffsommer William H. A. painter, dwl 31 St. Mark Place
Hoffstardt ——, teacher piano forte, dwl 1005 Powell
Hofman Joseph A. salesman with A. Roman & Co. dwl 657 Howard
Hogan Alan Miss, domestic, 525 Green
Hogan Annie Miss, domestic, 841 Mission
Hogan Bridget Miss, domestic with John M. Burtsell, W s Shotwell bet Fifteenth and Sixteenth
Hogan Bridget Miss, domestic, NW corner Stockton and Sutter
Hogan Catharine Miss, domestic, 1011 Pine
Hogan Daniel, handcartman, dwl Ritter nr Seventh
Hogan Dennis E. stone cutter, dwl 25 Everett
Hogan Dennis J. laborer, Custom House, dwl 433 Tehama
gan Edward, painter with Hopps & Kanary, dwl Ho 10 Moss
Hogan Ellen A. (widow) private school, dwl 219 Sixth
Hogan Eugene, laborer, dwl 154 Clara
Hogan Frank, laborer, dwl W s Shipley bet Fifth and Sixth
Hogan Frank; gas fitter, dwl NW corner Jessie and Anna
Hogan Foster, teamster with John R. Sedgeley, S s Twelfth bet Howard and Folsom
Hogan Frederick, bar tender, NW cor Folsom and Beale
Hogan George, dwl 521 Mason
Hogan James, shoe maker with H. M. Beers, dwl Franklin Hotel
Hogan John, with Charles Harley & Co. dwl cor Leidesdorff and Commercial
Hogan John, fireman, S. F. & San José R. R. Co. res San José
Hogan John, laborer, dwl W side Mission near Thirteenth
Hagan John, laborer, dwl 146 Minna
Hogan John, laborer, dwl N s McAllister bet Leavenworth and Hyde
Hogan John, laborer, dwl 1312 Kearny
Hogan John, liquor dealer, dwl E s Howard bet Fourteenth and Fifteenth
Hogan John, machinist, Pacific Foundry, dwl 18 Anthony
Hogan John, pressman with Francis, Valentine & Co. dwl cor Montgomery and Broadway
Hogan John, seaman, dwl 132 Folsom
Hogan Margaret Miss, domestic, 125 Silver
Hogan Mary Miss, domestic with Alexander Edouart
Hogan Mary Miss, domestic, 327 O'Farrell
Hogan Matthew, laborer, dwl S s Bernard bet Taylor and Jones
Hogan M. C. seaman, dwl 54 Sacramento

Hogan Michael, carpenter, dwl S s Second bet Brannan and Townsend.
Hogan Michael, fish, 45 Metropolitan Market, dwl 1312 Kearny
Hogan, Michael, laborer, S. F. & San José R. R. Co
Hogan Michael, laborer, dwl 312 Fifth, rear
Hogan Michael, laborer, dwl E s Stanford between Townsend and Brannan
Hogan Michael, laborer with William Kerr, dwl 903 Battery
Hogan Michael P. helper, dwl 36 Natoma
Hogan Patrick, deck hand, stm Chrysopolis
Hogan Patrick, deck hand, stm Yosemite
Hogan Patrick, laborer, dwl Atlantic House 210 Pacific
Hogan Patrick, porter, 112 Bat, dwl 86 Stevenson
Hogan Patrick, waiter, dwl Manhattan House
Hogan Patrick S. laborer, dwl Ocean Flat
Hogan Robert, express wagon, cor Davis and Com
Hogan Robert, laborer, Miners' Foundry
Hogan William, laborer, dwl Original House
Hogan William, laborer, dwl N s Sacramento bet Jones and Leavenworth
Hogan William, miner, dwl 431 Pine
Hogan William H. carpenter, dwl 10 Tehama
Hogan William J. dwl 14 Harlan Place
Hoge George G. W. attorney at law, office 625 Merchant, dwl 30 John
HOGE JOSEPH P. attorney at law, office 4 and 5 Montgomery Block, dwl 26 Ellis
Hogeboom Lawrence V. engineer, stm Pacific, dwl 342 Tehama
Hogelsdorff, Jacob, cigars and tobacco, dwl 28 Tehama
HOGER ERNEST, groceries, 525 Washington
Hogg Augustus, milkman, dwl NW cor Valencia and Nineteenth
Hogle George, carpenter, dwl 123 Tehama
Hogquist Charles, tanner with James Duncan, dwl S s Brannan bet Eighth and Ninth
Hohenschild George, fruits and vegetables, 21 and 22 Washington Market, dwl 23 Valparaiso
Hohenschild Henry, waiter, 718 Market, dwl 720 Market
HOHENSCHILD *(Louis)* & MELSTEDT *(August)* proprietors Taylor's Restaurant, 718 and 720 Market
Hohendorff Henry, Mazurka Hall Beer Saloon, NE cor Pine and Montgomery
Hoin Felix J. *(Hoin & Bro.)* dwl 914 Jackson
Hoin Isador N. clerk, International Saloon, 530 Jackson, dwl 914 Jackson
Hoin *(Peter P.)* & Brother *(Felix N.)* books and stationery, NW cor Jackson and Montgomery, dwl 914 Jackson
Hoin Peter P. sen. Tremont Saloon, 418 Jackson, dwl 914 Jackson
Hoin Theodore E. salesman with W. B. Frisbee & Co. dwl 914 Jackson
Hoire James, laundryman, Chelsea Laundry, dwl Third nr Folsom
Hoit Christian, hairdresser, dwl Dresdener House
Hoit Ezra D. dwl E s Columbia nr Sixteenth
Hoitt Ira G. principal Lincoln School, dwl 804 Bush
Hoitt James, baker with J. Chadbourne, dwl 804 Bush bet Stockton and Powell
Hoitt Julia B. Mrs. head assistant Lincoln School, dwl 804 Bush
Holahan Misses E. & M. millinery, 424 Kearny
Holahan M. Miss *(Misses E. & M. Holahan)* dwl 424 Kearny
Holbrook Benjamin F. salesman, 633 Clay, dwl 115 Sixth
Holbrook E. watchman, Custom House
Holbrook L. E. (widow) boarding, 1123 Stockton
Holbrook Robert, seaman, dwl 54 Sacramento
Holbrook T. W. J. submaster, Union Grammar School, dwl 41 Everett
Holbrook William H. horsetrainer, dwl 533 Jackson

Holchier I. C. liquor saloon, 142 Stewart
Holcomb Franklin, real estate, dwl 324 Vallejo
Holcomb Wesley B. book keeper, Pier 11 Stewart, dwl 118 Perry
Holcombe Atkinson H. *(Holcombe Bros.)* dwl NW cor Washington and Kearny
HOLCOMBE BROTHERS *(Samuel E. and Atkinson Holcombe)* & CO. *(F. X. Kast)* importers and dealers boots and shoes, NW cor Washington and Kearny, dw 1610 Mason
Holcombe Charles, musician, Wilson's Circus
Holden Edward, painter with James Donovan, dwl cor Broadway and Battery
Holden Hannah (widow) dwl Meecham Pl nr Post
Holden James, dwl NW cor Nineteenth and Howard
Holden James, drayman, dwl 818 Folsom, rear
Holden James, laborer with Hey & Meyn .... ,
Holden John A. dwl 749 Market
Holden Martin, boot maker, dwl 824 Green
Holden Theresa Mrs. boarding, 749 Market
Holden Thomas, shipsmith, dwl Broadway bet Montgomery and Kearny
Holden William, laborer, dwl Mission Bay Bridge
Holderegger William, carpenter, dwl 431 Pine
Holderness S. M. commission merchant, office 402 Front, dwl 927 Washington
Holdredge Henry A. porter with Treadwell & Co. dwl 639 Market
Holdredge Ransom G, draftsman, dwl 639 Market
Holdredge Stirling M. publisher Guide Book, Pacific, office 302 Montgomery, dwl 639 Market
Holdredge William, president Home Insurance Co. office 630 Montgomery, dwl 639 Market
Holes John, shoe maker, 915 Pacific
Holing William, clerk, dwl 318 Clementina
Holje Henry & Co. *(P. Johnson and J. B. Holje)* Steamboat Exchange, SW cor Jackson and East, dwl SW cor Sutter and Devisidero
Holje John B. *(H. Holje & Co.)* dwl 28 Clay
HOLLADAY BEN, proprietor California, Oregon, and Mexican Steamship Line, office SW cor Front and Jackson, res New York
HOLLADAY JESSE, agent California, Oregon, and Mexican Steamship Line, office SW cor Front and Jackson, bds Occidental Hotel
Holladay John, fruit dealer, dwl 135 Third
Holladay Joseph, office SW cor Front and Jackson, dwl Cosmopolitan Hotel
Holladay Samuel W. *(Porter & H.)* attorney at law, office and dwl 614 Pine
Hollahan John, hostler, North Beach & M. R. R. Co
Hollahen Eliza Mrs. boarding, 18 Third
Hollahen John, dwl 18 Third
Holland Andrew, laborer, S. F. P. Woolen Mills, dwl North Point bet Polk and Van Ness Av
Holland Andrew, teamster with H. J. Booth & Co. dwl 12 Sutter
Holland Bridget Mrs. domestic, 104 Stockton
Holland Cornelius F. boatman, U. S. Boarding Office, Custom House, dwl Union Place
Holland Henry, liquor saloon, 541 Broadway
Holland Honora Mrs. domestic with S. H. Dwinelle
Holland Honoron, domestic, dwl 451 Bryant
Holland James, express wagon, dwl 209 Beale
Holland James, laborer, dwl cor Jane and Mission
Holland James, musician, dwl 702 Pacific
Holland James, pressman, Alta California, dwl cor Montgomery and Broadway
Holland James, steward, dwl 416 Stevenson
Hollands James E. Columbian Engine No. 11
Holland John, cartman with B. Bonnet & Co
Holland John, fruits, SE cor Montgomery and Jackson, dwl Elizabeth nr Harrison
Holland James, molder, dwl 111 Geary
HOLLAND JOSEPH G. proprietor Holland's Saloon, 621 Merchant, dwl 625 Merchant
Holland Miss Mary, domestic, 1021 Leavenworth
Holland Mary Miss, dress maker, dwl N s Bernard bet Taylor and Jones

Holland Michael, laborer, S. F. P. Woolen Mills, dwl cor Lombard and Franklin
Holland Michael H. bricklayer, dwl 427 Greenwich
HOLLAND NATHANIEL, attorney at law, office 12 Well's Building 605 Clay, dwl 1414 Taylor
Holland Nicholas, wagon maker, dwl 44 Louisa
Holland Patrick, handcartman, cor Montgomery and Post, dwl N s Oregon nr Front
Holland Rose, ironer, Chelsea Laundry
Holland S. M. engineer Golden Gate Mills, dwl Bootz's Hotel
Hollaran Bridget Miss, dwl 12 Howard Court, rear
Hollenbeck James C. merchant, office 523 Front, dwl SE cor Chestnut and Taylor
Holling Charles H. clerk, 6 Stewart, dwl 2 Beale Place
Holling William, clerk with Bradshaw & Co. dwl 318 Clementina
Hollings Henry *(Kruger & H.)* dwl NW cor Mason and Geary
Hollins James E. molder, Jackson Foundry, dwl 111 Geary
Hollinshead Jeremiah V. miner, dwl W s Howard nr Thirteenth
Hollinshead Joseph B. carpenter, dwl W s Howard nr Thirteenth
Hollinshead Margaret (widow) dwl W s Howard nr Thirteenth
Hollis Joseph, drayman with J. Chadbourne, dwl 433 Jackson
Hollis William, grand scribe Sons of Temperance and mining secretary, office 302 Montgomery, dwl 20 Taylor
Hollmann Claus, bar keeper, Precito Valley House
HOLLUB A. & CO. *(S. Seelig)* importers oils, lamps, etc. 501 and 503 Front, dwl SW cor Laguna and Tyler
Holly Kate Miss, domestic, 224 Jessie
Hollywood Ann Miss, domestic, 320 Sansom
Hollywood Catherine Miss, domestic, 402 Eddy
Holm H. house and sign painter, 305 Pine
Holm Thomas, groceries and liquors, SE cor Sutter and Stockton, dwl 908 Pine
Holman Edward, longshoreman, dwl 327 Vallejo, rear
HOLMAN F. A. physician and visiting surgeon City and County Hospital, office SE cor Sutter and Montgomery, dwl 313 Sutter
Holman Fred S. clerk with Gardner & Co. res Oakland
Holman John, hostler, dwl 323 Pine
Holman R. L. clerk, dwl 840 Mission
Holman Thomas W. foreman with N. B. Jacobs & Co. dwl 900 Clay
Holmberg George, wood dealer, dwl W s Montgomery bet Green and Union
HOLMES AARON, real estate agent, office 304 Montgomery, dwl 510 Hyde
Holmes Ahira, principal Mission Grammar School, dwl First Avenue bet Fifteenth and Sixteenth
Holmes Charles S. book keeper, Pier 3 Stewart, dwl 217 Third
Holmes Cornelius, mason, office 523 Montgomery, dwl 913 Union
Holmes Daniel W. clerk with Feaster & Co. 213 Pine
Holmes E. A. clerk, pier 3 Stewart, dwl 217 Third
Holmes E. B. secretary Savage Mining Co. 712 Montgomery, dwl 1120 Powell
Holmes Edward, molder, Vulcan Iron Works, dwl 3 Tehama
Holmes Edward, salesman, 521 Sacramento, dwl 712 Howard
Holmes Ellen Miss, assistant, Post St. Primary School, dwl 510 Hyde
Holmes Ellis H. principal Girl's High School, dwl 16 Prospect Place
Holmes George A. dwl SW cor California and Leavenworth

Holmes Henry, harness maker with Main & Winchester

Holmes Henry J. book keeper, dwl W s Howard bet Nineteenth and Twentieth

Holmes Henry T. *(Webb & H.)* dwl 759 Market

Holmes Jacob, wagon maker with Gallagher & Farren, dwl 112 Bush

Holmes James, dwl 223 Montgomery

HOLMES J. B. & CO. *(John A. Moore)* hay and grain, 5 and 7 California, and 108 and 110 Market, dwl 35 Clementina

Holmes J. J. dwl Occidental Hotel

Holmes John, steward, dwl 933 Sacramento

Holmes John A. carpenter, Pacific Foundry, dwl 119 Natoma

Holmes John E. pattern maker, dwl 119 Natoma

Holmes John W. salesman, 609 Sacramento, dwl 207 Minna

Holmes Milo P. blacksmithing and carriage making, 417 Pine, dwl 219 Tehama

Holmes Philip B. *(Goodwin & Co.)* res New York

Holmes Richard T. salesman with R. S. Eells & Co. cor Pine and Front

Holmes S. physician, office 646 Washington

Holmes Sarah D. Miss, furnished rooms, 522 Cal

Holmes Thomas, clerk, dwl 614 California

Holmes Thomas, Ivy Green Saloon, E s Cemetery Avenue bet Sutter and Post

Holmes William, dwl 712 Howard

Holmes William, cook, dwl 803 Stockton

Holst Christian *(George Grierson & Co.)* dwl 321 Montgomery

HOLST J. C. cigars and tobacco, 321 Montgomery, dwl Summer St. House

Holst John H. butcher, 45 Jackson, dwl Monumental Engine House

Holstrom J. E. seamen, dwl 44 Sacramento

Holstrom John, seaman, dwl 44 Sacramento

Holt Charles, carpenter, dwl with R. N. Holt, W s Mission bet Fifteenth and Sixteenth

Holt Charles E. deputy surveyor Custom House, dwl 214 Sansom

Holt H. painter, dwl 670 Mission

Holt Isaac D. carpenter, S. F. & San José R. R. Co. dwl W s Folsom bet Sixteenth and Seventeenth

Holt James, laborer, dwl 24 Howard Court

Holt Mary J. Mrs. dwl Brevoort House

Holt Robert N. contractor, dwl W s Mission bet Fifteenth and Sixteenth

Holt Sylvanus W. carpenter, dwl 277 Stevenson

Holt Thomas, carman, dwl 649 Mission

Holt Thomas G. express wagon, cor California and Montgomery

Holt *(Thomas H.)* & Bowley *(S. C.)* brokers, 605 Montgomery, dwl 1803 Stockton

HOLT WARREN, maps, atlases, school apparatus, and furniture, 2 Mead House

HOLT Z. broker, office 618 Merchant, dwl 626 California

Holten Lewis, bar tender, NW cor Folsom and Stewart

Holterman Ernst H. book keeper with John G. North, dwl Point San Quentin, Potrero

Holtmier Henry, groceries and liquors, NE cor Filbert and Taylor

Holton Alva C. salesman, 624 Market, dwl 16 Geary

Holton Henry, mate, steamer Petaluma

Holton Lewis, dwl N s Tehama bet Eighth and Ninth

Holton Margaret Miss, dress maker, dwl 742 Vallejo

Holts John, seaman, dwl 44 Sacramento

Holtz Louis F. clerk with C. V. Gillespie, dwl 520 O'Farrell

Holtz William & Co. *(Frederick Benn)* groceries and liquors, dwl SW cor Pacific and Mont

Hold Louis, stationery, 311 Battery, dwl St. Nicholas Hotel

Holzer Martin, clerk with William Spreen, NE cor Brannan and Ninth

Holzhauer Hermann, music teacher, dwl 69 Everett

Holzscheiter Paul, sutler's clerk, Fort Point

HOMANS HARRY S. general agent Mutual Life, Universal Life, and Widows and Orphans Benefit Life Insurance Co.'s and notary public, office 607 Clay, dwl 1419 Taylor

Homana John N. clerk with Harry S. Homans, dwl 1419 Taylor

Homberger M. & Co. *(Gustave Koenigsberger)* ladies' dress trimmings, NE cor Kearny and Bush res New York

Homberger M. & Co. *(Max Straus)* fancy dry goods, 30 Second

HOME INSURANCE CO. New York, Bigelow & Brothers agents, 505 Montgomery

HOME MUTUAL INSURANCE CO. office 630 Montgomery, W. Holdredge president, W. H. Stevens secretary

HOME OF THE INEBRIATE, NW cor Stockton and Chestnut

Homeier Max, musician, dwl 521 Greenwich

Homer Charles Mrs. NW cor Taylor and Broadway

Homer John W. with William Newell, dwl 530 Merchant

Hometz John, cabinet maker, 757 Mission

Hommaich Christian, tailor, dwl 1319 Kearny

Hon Mon (Chinese) carver and painter, NE cor Sacramento and Dupont

Honest Miner G. & S. M. Co. office 402 Front

Honeywell John, carpenter, dwl 308 Beale

Hong Chun (Chinese) washing, NW cor Clay and Mason

Hong Chung (Chinese) washing, 35 Third

Hong Hing (Chinese) washing, 603 Broadway

Hong Lee (Chinese) washing, 113 Jackson

Hong Lee (Chinese) washing, 730 Market

Hong Sang (Chinese) washing, 917 Washington

Hong Sang (Chinese) washing, 108 Dupont

Hong Sing (Chinese) washing, 619 Market

Hong Sun (Chinese) washing, 731 Market

Hong Sung (Chinese) washing, 33 Kearny

Hong Wha (Chinese) washing, 106 Jessie

Hong Wha (Chinese) washing, 625 Mission

Hong Yune Chueng Hee (Chinese) mchts, 708 Sac

HONGKONG LINE PACKETS, via Honolulu, Koopmanschap & Co. agents, office cor Battery and Union

Honisch Gottlieb, dress maker, dwl 411 O'Farrell

HONOLULU HAWAIIAN PACKET LINE, Charles W. Brooks & Co. agents, office 511 Sansom cor Merchant

HONOLULU "REGULAR DISPATCH" LINE PACKETS, J. C. Merrill & Co. agents, office 204 California

Honorado Guevara, dwl 1314 Dupont

HONS FREDERICK, Eureka Saloon, 200 Stewart

HOOGS *(Octavian)* & MADISON *(John H.)* house brokers and real estate agents, 316 Montgomery, dwl 106 Ellis

Hoogs William H. hackman, dwl 34 Louisa

Hoogstädt Abraham, boatman, dwl 53 Sacramento

Hook Ann (widow) dwl 8E cor Midway and Bay

Hook Charles, proprietor Gen. Taylor Market, NE cor Union and Mason

Hook Henry, gas fitter, dwl Bay bet Stockton and Dupont

Hook Valentine. barber, dwl 853 Folsom

Hooke William H. *(Amos Phinney & Co.)* dwl 318 First

HOOKER *(Charles G.)* & CO. importers and jobbers hardware, 117 and 119 California, dwl 523 Folsom

Hooker Fred, fireman, dwl 20 Commercial

Hooker George, waiter with Stevens & Oliver, dwl 311 Bush

Hooker John D. clerk with Hooker & Co. dwl 742 Howard

Hooker William D. machinist, Union Foundry, dwl 250 Stevenson

Hoong Ga (Chinese) washing, 537 Sacramento
Hooper A. J. meat market, SW cor Twenty-Fourth and Mission
Hooper Ambrose J. select school, 5 Monroe
HOOPER CHARLES A. & CO. *(William H. Hooper)* lumber, doors, blinds, and sash, S s Townsend bet Third and Fourth, dwl 512 Folsom
Hooper Edward N. clerk with Cross & Co. 625 Sansom. dwl 1312 Taylor
HOOPER F. P. & J. A. lumber dealers, 49 Market, dwl 512 Folsom
HOOPER GEORGE F. commission and shipping merchant and agent Colorado River Line Packets, office 308 Front, dwl 413 Second
Hooper George W. clerk, 49 Market, dwl 512 Folsom
Hooper John, miner, dwl 512 Folsom
Hooper John, tailor with M. Brandhofer, dwl 337 Bush
Hooper John A. *(F. P. & J. A. Hooper)* dwl 512 Folsom
Hooper John M. bag maker with Lewis & Neville, dwl 111 Virginia
Hooper Louisa M. Mrs. music teacher, dwl 5 Monroe
Hooper W. B. captain U. S. A. dwl 345 Fremont
Hooper William, commissioner Funded Debt 1851 and secretary, office NW cor Montgomery and Sacramento, dwl 1312 Taylor
Hooper William H. *(C. A. Hooper & Co.)* dwl 30 Rincon Place
Hoops John F. liquors, 2 Jackson
Hoover Jackson, bricklayer, dwl 6 Sansom
Hop Gun (Chinese) washing, 13 Jessie
Hop Kee & Co. (Chinese) merchants, 705 Dupont
Hop Lee (Chinese) merchant, 715 Sacramento
Hop Lee (Chinese) washing, 236 Fourth
Hop Lee (Chinese) washing, S s Sacramento bet Davis and Drumm
Hop Long (Chinese) washing, 527 Broadway
Hop Sing (Chinese) physician, 616 Jackson
Hop Sing (Chinese) washing, 553 Market
Hop Wo Co. (Chinese) merchants, 738 Commercial
Hop Wo & Co. (Chinese) merchants, 744 Sac
Hop Yuen (Chinese) merchant, 734 Sacramento
Hope G. & S. M. Co. office 804 Montgomery
Hopkins Alexander, laborer, Pier 7 Stewart
Hopkins A. S. dwl What Cheer House
HOPKINS CASPAR T. secretary California Insurance Co. office 318 California, res Alameda
Hopkins Charles H. dwl 729 California
Hopkins D. Mrs. wines and liquors, 35 Jackson
Hopkins Delia Miss, domestic, 116 Ellis
Hopkins Edward, laborer, dwl W s Gilbert bet Bryant and Brannan, rear
Hopkins George W. painter with John Duff, dwl 3 Auburn
Hopkins Isaac H. cooper, S. F. & P. Sugar Co. dwl 131 Fourth
Hopkins James, laborer, dwl 266 Jessie
Hopkins Jessie P. dwl 610 Powell
Hopkins John L. editor and proprietor World's Crisis, office NE cor Clay and Montgomery, dwl 1613 Powell
Hopkins Lemuel B. mining superintendent, dwl 607½ Pine
Hopkins Marcius, carpenter, dwl Oriental Hotel
Hopkins Mary (widow) dwl 13 Pinckney Place
Hopkins Mary Ann (widow) dwl 131 Fourth
Hopkins Michael, with Haste & Kirk, 515 Cal
Hopkins Mortimer, policeman, City Hall, dwl W s Valencia bet Sixteenth and Seventeenth
Hopkins Nathan P. livery and sale stable, 679 and 681 Market
Hopkins Peter, dwl 1123 Powell
Hopkins Peter, stone cutter, dwl 12 Sutter
Hopkins Rufus C. keeper archives U. S. Surveyor General's Office, dwl N s Mission bet Twelfth Thirteenth
Hopkins Samuel, butcher, dwl 4 Oak

Hopkins Samuel J. lumber, doors, and sash, 112 Washington, dwl S s Sacramento bet Franklin and Van Ness Avenue
Hopkins Samuel J. jr. teamster with Stanyan & Co. dwl S s Sac bet Van Ness Avenue and Franklin
Hopkins Thomas with Reynolds, Howell & Ford, dwl NW cor Filbert and Powell
Hopkins Timothy, apprentice, Pacific Foundry, dwl S s Bryant bet Sixth and Seventh
Hopkins T. R. *(Kennedy & H.)* dwl SW cor Broadway and Montgomery
Hopkins Wirt, assistant assayer U. S. Branch Mint, dwl S s Sac bet Van Ness Avenue and Franklin
Hopkinson Charles L. clerk, 504 Sansom, dwl 127 Montgomery
Hopkinson George, waiter, Clipper Restaurant
Hopkinson Martha (widow) boarding, dwl 29 Minna
Hoppe Charles, clerk, 814 Jackson
Hoppe Lucy (widow) dwl 338 Ritch
Hoppe William, groceries and liquors, 814 Jackson, dwl S s Washington nr Powell
Hoppee Edwin, glass blower, Pacific Glass Works, dwl Potrero
HOPPER GARRITT H. wines and liquors, SE cor Davis and Pacific
Hopper John E. workman, S. F. Cordage Factory, dwl SW cor Michigan and Napa
Hoppinworth Louis, tanner with S. Bloom, S s Brannan E Sixth
HOPPS *(Charles)* & KANARY *(David)* house, sign, and ornamental painters, 216 Sansom, dwl 406 Geary
Hopps *(Charles E.)* & Downing *(Thomas)* house, sign, and ornamental painters, 110 Sutter, dwl 911 Post
Hopps Frank W. painter, dwl 406 Geary
Hopps George W. painter, dwl 406 Geary
Hopwood Sophia (widow) dwl 182 Stevenson
Horabin Thomas, wood and coal, S s Washington nr Stockton
Horan Bridget Miss, domestic, 302 Stockton
HORAN J. C. & CO. *(James Spruance)* importers and jobbers wines and liquors, 415 Front, dwl SW cor McAllister and Fillmore
Horan Julia Miss, domestic, 438 Clementina
Horan Mary Miss, domestic, W s Duncan Court
Horan P. T. boiler maker, Union Foundry, dwl 549 Mission
Horan Thomas, blacksmith with Kimball & Co. dwl 32 Everett, rear
Horber John, real estate and proprietor Horber's Building, 315 Montgomery
Hord George L. clerk, 106 First, dwl Seventh nr Folsom
Hord John R. photographic gallery, 143 Fourth, dwl E s Seventh bet Folsom and Howard
Horeis Meta Miss, domestic, 1205 Pacific
Horgan Frank, plumber with Thomas O'Malley, 646 Market
Horgan *(John)* & Kenny *(John)* blacksmiths, 665 Howard, dwl Folsom nr Seventh
Horgan John, laborer, dwl N s Stevenson bet Sixth and Seventh
Horgan John J. laborer, dwl 36 St. Mark Place
Horgan Julia Miss, domestic, 719 Sutter
Horgan Timothy, stone cutter, dwl E s Cemetery Avenue bet Sutter and Post
Horigau Cornelius, laborer, dwl N s Bernard nr Leavenworth
Horley P. G. tinsmith, dwl St. Lawrence House
Horn Adelbert, watch maker with John Uszynski, 406 Kearny
HORN BARNEY, wholesale butcher, Potrero Avenue, dwl SW cor Mariposa and Florida
HORN B. C. & CO. importers and jobbers cigars and tobacco, SW cor Front and Clay, dwl 555 Harrison
Horn Edward, milkman, dwl 54 First
Horn Elida A. Miss with James DeLaMontanya

Horn George H. clerk, 218 Jackson, dwl E s Taylor bet Pacific and Broadway
Horn Henry F. carpenter. dwl 111 Sixth
Horn John, driver with Nathaniel Gray, 641 Sac
Horn Mary A. (widow) dwl with James DeLa Montana
Horn Philip, stevedore, dwl 40 Tehama
Horn Thomas L. with L. & E. Wertheimer, dwl Cosmopolitan Hotel
Horn W. J. carpenter, dwl 559 Market
Horne Thomas, groom with G. S. Banks & Co
Horner Horatio G. Paymaster's Department U. S. A. dwl Lick House
Horner John C. physician, office and dwl 644 Pacific
Horner Robert H. captain Pacific Mail S. S. Co. office NW cor Sacramento and Leidesdorff
Horner William dwl SE cor Howard and Erie
Horner William E. V. professor Latin and Greek City College, dwl Lick House
Hornet G. & S. M. Co. office 402 Front
Horning Diedrick J. *(Denmark & H.)* dwl NW cor Taylor and Pacific
Hornsman Andrew, cotton factor, dwl 727 Davis
Horr William, ship bread and cracker baker, 719 and 721 Battery, dwl 123 Turk
Horrax Catharine (widow) dwl 438 Union, rear
Horriege' Charles, painter, bds Sacramento Hotel 407 Pacific
Horrigan James, express wagon, dwl W s Ninth nr Mission
Horrigan John, blacksmith, dwl 1050 Folsom
Horrigan John, employé, Franklin House, SW cor Sansom and Broadway
Horrop Samuel, boiler maker with Coffey & Risdon
Horsch John, job wagon, cor Pine and Montgomery, dwl N s Brannan bet Fifth and Sixth
Horst Henry, porter, 314 Washington
Horstmann Christian, job wagon, SE cor Montgomery and Pine, dwl NW cor Bush and Powell
HORSTMANN H. & CO. *(F. Hufschmidt)* importers and dealers furniture and upholstery goods, 740 Washington, dwl 118 Virginia
Horstmann Henry, *(Sneider & H.)* dwl 731 Vallejo
HORSTMANN JOHN, groceries and liquors, NW cor Bush and Powell, dwl 613 Powell
Hort Samuel *(C. Adolphe Low & Co.)* dwl 729 Sutter
Hortkorn Charles, boots and shoes, 528 Kearny, dwl 628 Merchant
Hortnett Morris, dwl 63 Jessie
Horton Alexander, book keeper, Bank of California, dwl 641 Folsom
Horton Charles W. dwl S s Pinkham Pl nr Eighth
Horton Daniel B. carpenter, dwl 31 Kearny
Horton G. & S. M. Co. office 302 Montgomery
Horton George, carpenter with John N. Clark, dwl 210 Green
Horton H. L. gardener, dwl 54 First
Horton Homer, contractor, dwl S s Brannan nr Seventh
Horton Richard, real estate broker, dwl 102 Jessie
Horton Richard, jr. paper hanger, NW cor Jessie and Second
Horton Robert L. *(Nichols & H.)* dwl 467 Tehama
Horton Thomas R. *(Martin & H.)* dwl 711 Cal
Horton William, U. S. inspector, Custom House
Hosey Lawrence, retortman, S. F. Gas Co
Hosford William, bricklayer, dwl SW cor Hayes and Webster
Hosing Albert, groceries and liquors, NE cor Fifth and Mission
Hoskin George, dwl 320 O'Farrell
Hoskins Edwin, carpenter, dwl 509 Dupont
HOSMER *(Charles)* GOEWEY *(James M.)* & CO. *(John H. Hough)* importers and jobbers wines and liquors, 409 and 411 Front, dwl 718 California
Hosmer Christian, express wagon, cor Pine and Montgomery

Hosmer Granville, assistant adjuster, Coiner's Department U. S. Branch Mint, dwl 830 Pacific
Hosmer Horace B. conductor, North Beach & M. R. R. Co. dwl 164 Perry
Hosmer Thomas, machinist, Pacific Foundry, dwl 64 Tehama
HOSPITAL CITY AND COUNTY S. F. SW cor Stockton and Francisco
HOSPITAL FRENCH, Brannan bet Fifth and Sixth
HOSPITAL GERMAN, Brannan nr Third
HOSPITAL SISTERS OF MERCY, cor Bryant and First
HOSPITAL U. S. MARINE, Rincon Point nr cor Main and Spear
Hoss John, cabinet maker with Goodwin & Co
Hossefross George H. Mrs. (widow) dwl 550 Vallejo
Hossett John, wheelwright with Kimball & Co
Hossban Louis, handcartman, corner Jackson and Drumm
Hosslin Thomas, book binder, dwl 245 Stevenson
HOSSTETTER, *(David)* SMITH *(George W.)* & DEAN *(Benjamin)* importers proprietary medicines, druggists' sundries, etc. 401-405 Battery cor Clay, res Pittsburg, Pa
Hostkamper E. proprietor Keystone House, 127 and 129 Jackson
HOTALING A. P. & CO. *(John W. Griffin)* jobbers wines and liquors, NE cor Sansom and Jackson, dwl N s Howard nr Twelfth
Hotchkiss Alexander, brakeman, S. F. & San José R. R. Co. res San José
Hotchkiss T. B. watchman, S. F. & San José R. R. Co. dwl Depôt, Brannan nr First
Hotop *(A.)* Garling *(H.)* & Co. *(H. A. Roesler)* manufacturers and dealers brooms, brushes, etc. 116 Jackson, dwl 226 Mission
Hotte George, farmer, dwl Old San José Road 7 miles from City Hall
Hotte William, porter, 321 Montgomery, dwl Belden nr Bush
Hottendorf Peter *(Melbourn & Co.)* dwl 1421 Mason
Hottendorf Richard *(F. Gudehaus & Co.)* dwl cor Clara and Berry
Hotzel Charles, blacksmith, Vulcan Iron Works, dwl Isthmus House
HOUCK JAMES M. Exchange Saloon, 126 California and South Beach Bathing House, S s King bet Third and Fourth, dwl 2 Hardie Place
Houck William, jeweler, dwl SW cor Broadway and Montgomery
Hough Frank W. clerk, dwl 720 Bush
Hough James F. book keeper with Edward H. Parker, dwl 623 O'Farrell
Hough John H. *(Hosmer, Goewey & Co.)* dwl 720 Bush
Hough Myron B. W. law clerk with Winans & Belknap, dwl 314 Sutter
Houghtaling Abraham I. with William Shew, 421 Montgomery, dwl 505 Bryant nr Third
Houghton Charles L. carpenter, dwl W s Second Avenue bet Seventeenth and Camp
Houghton Eliza W. Miss, assistant, State Normal School, dwl 1018 Clay
Houghton Joseph B. *(Norman & Co.)* dwl W s Second Avenue bet Sixteenth and Seventeenth
Houghton Samuel, silversmith, dwl SE cor Mission and First
Hougse Louis, carpenter, dwl Sierra Nevada Hotel, 528 Pacific
Houkit E. hostler, Omnibus R. R. Co
Houkit J. hostler, Omnibus R. R. Co
Houlton S. W. waterman, dwl W s Second Avenue nr Seventeenth
Hourcade Adolphe, florist, dwl 1333 Dupont
Hourlihan James, laborer, dwl N s Broadway bet Van Ness Avenue and Franklin
Hourihan Jeremiah, hostler, Fort Point

House Isaiah (col'd) waiter, dwl 6 John
Housechild Louisa, domestic, 323 Jessie
Houseman James S. ship carpenter, dwl 41 Clementina
Housewell William, carpenter, bds 761 Mission
HOUSEWORTH THOMAS *(Lawrence & H.)* dwl 402 Eddy
Housken George, captain schooner Reliance, office 413 East
Housley Edward, laborer, dwl Beale Pl nr Main
Housting William, clerk, dwl 6 Brown Alley
Houston A. H. contractor, office 302 Montgomery, dwl 20 Rincon Place
Houston Frank, first assistant engineer steamer Orizaba, dwl E s Calhoun nr Green
Houston George, clerk, dwl 4 Central Place
Houston Joseph, farmer, Ocean House Flat nr Ocean House
Houston Richard T. tailor and clothes' renovator, 645 Merchant
Houston Robert, chief engineer steamer John L. Stephens, office SW cor Front and Jackson
Houston Thomas R. sail maker with John Harding, dwl 28 Sansom
Houston William, clerk, 638 Market
Howard & Martin Petroleum Co. office 620 Wash
Howard Annie, seamstress, Occidental Hotel
HOWARD *(Benjamin C.)* & POOL *(I. Lawrence)* Bonded City Warehouse cor Lombard and Battery and Howard's Bonded Warehouse cor Front and Broadway, dwl 30 Laurel Place
Howard C. Greenwich, attorney at law, dwl 305 Montgomery
Howard Charles A. dwl 1520 Stockton
Howard David, dwl 845 Dupont
Howard Edward T. clerk, Howard's U. S. Bonded Warehouse SW cor Broadway and Front, dwl Russ House
Howard E. H. book keeper with John B. Newton & Co. dwl 204 Montgomery
Howard Fannie Miss, domestic, 734 Folsom
Howard Frederick, freight clerk, Pacific Mail S. S. Co. dwl 413 Dupont
Howard Garrett, liquors, S s Broadway bet Montgomery and Sansom
Howard George *(H. McFarlane & Co.)* dwl 407 Dupont
Howard George *(Tolles & H.)* dwl 724 Market
Howard George A. painter, dwl 704 Dupont
HOWARD GEORGE H. real estate, office 523 Montgomery, res San Mateo
Howard Hattie Miss, domestic, 928 Bush
Howard Henry C. broker, dwl Lick House
Howard Henry O. office and dwl 523 Montgomery
Howard I. J. Mrs. ladies' supporters, 305 Montgomery room 7
Howard Irwin *(Croskey & H.)* dwl SE cor Franklin and Hayes
Howard James, folder, Chelsea Laundry
Howard James, upholsterer, dwl NW cor Pine and Sansom
Howard James G. *(Wade & H.)* attorney at law, office 606 Montgomery
Howard James H. tinsmith, dwl 515 Sacramento
Howard J. L. dwl 822 Folsom
Howard John, boiler maker with Coffey & Risdon
Howard John, driver, Omnibus R. R. Co. dwl 136 Fourth, rear
Howard John, hairdresser, 37 Jackson
Howard John, machinist, dwl 510 Sacramento
Howard John F. carpenter, dwl NE cor Bush and Sansom
Howard Matthew, carpenter, dwl 728 Market
Howard Michael (col'd) proprietor Howard's Hair Restorative, 315 Mont, dwl 1410 Mason
Howard Michael E. dwl E s Reed nr Washington
HOWARD P. physician and surgeon, office 648 Washington
Howard Patrick, seaman, dwl 132 Folsom

Howard R. cigars and tobacco, dwl SW cor Dupont and Broadway
Howard Rebecca A. (widow) physician, office and dwl 220 Stockton
Howard Richard, with Deeth & Starr, 205 Sac
Howard Robert, corporation yard keeper, dwl Broderick Engine House
Howard Rose Miss, domestic with C. S. Lord, Grove Avenue nr Bryant
Howard S. (col'd) hydraulic hose maker, 326 Davis
Howard S. W. carpenter, dwl 28 Sansom
Howard W. D. M. estate of, office 523 Montgomery
Howard William, gas fitter with J. K. Prior, 730 Montgomery, dwl NE cor Mission and Beale
Howard William G. baker, 719 Battery
Howard William J. baker, dwl 17½ Dupont, rear
Howard William P. mariner, dwl 16 Ohio
Howard W. L. dwl 31 Belden Block
HOWARD'S BONDED WAREHOUSE, SW cor Broadway and Front
Howden James, chemist with Charles McCormick, dwl 408 Market
Howds Catherine Miss, domestic, 227 Geary
Howe Albert M. book keeper with C. J. Hawley & Co. dwl 1207 Clay
Howe Arabella (widow) dwl 228 Post
Howe A. W. cartman, dwl Main nr Market
Howe *(C. E. B.)* & Billet *(E. W.)* passenger agents, office 423 Washington
Howe Charles W. clerk, dwl 730 Bush
Howe D. J. reporter, American Flag, dwl 166 Tehama
Howe George L. salesman with Badger & Lindenberger, dwl 730 Bush
Howe G. W. compositor, Morning Call, dwl E s Polk bet Clay and Washington
Howe Harriet A. (col'd, widow) dwl 1009 Wash
Howe Henry P. collector with Wightman & Hardie, dwl 730 Bush
Howe Martha Miss, dwl 1106 Pine
Howe Montgomery, miner, dwl 1106 Pine
Howe M. P. mariner, dwl 152 Minna
Howe Robert *(J. W. Gale & Co.)* dwl E s Howard bet Twentieth and Twenty-First
Howe Susan Mrs. dwl 30 Lewis Place
Howe William, contractor, dwl 730 Bush
Howe William S. seaman, Pennsylvania Engine Co. No. 12
Howe, see Howes
Howell Joseph L. salesman with Wm. B. Cooke & Co. dwl 1018 Powell
Howell L. V. H. *(Reynolds, H. & Ford)* dwl E s Eleventh nr Market
Howell M. C. cigars and tobacco, 616 Montgomery, dwl 1018 Powell
Howell M. D. broker, dwl 892 Sutter
Howell Thomas Rev. pastor Third Baptist Church
Howell Thomas, stoves, 260 Third, dwl 1 Oak near Taylor
Howenstein W. M. dentist, NE cor Hunt and Third
Hower Joel, carpenter, dwl 677 Mission
Howes Edward K. *(Elam & H.)* dwl 619 Leav
Howes Egbert, mariner, dwl W s Devisidero bet Post and Sutter
Howes Enoch, laborer, dwl W s Leavenworth bet Sacramento and California
HOWES GEORGE & CO. *(Jabez Howes)* shipping and commission merchants, 309 Clay, res New York
Howes Harriet (widow) dwl 309 Stockton
Howes Jabez *(George Howes & Co.)* dwl 619 Leavenworth
Howes John, wholesale produce, 502 Sansom and 23 Washington, dwl 1014 Taylor
Howes Joseph, dwl 319 Bush
HOWES SAMUEL P. secretary Refugio Mining Co. office 3 Odd Fellows' Hall, dwl 634 Post
HOWES' SEWING MACHINES, Deming & Co. agents, 3 Montgomery

Howgate George, laborer, dwl W s Main bet Folsom and Harrison
Howitt H. T. dwl What Cheer House
Howland Capt. dwl 537 Sacramento
Howland *(B. F.)* & Vasconcellos *(J. J.)* photographic gallery, 25 and 27 Third, dwl 716 Stock
Howland Darius, mariner, dwl 777 Market
Howland E. B. machinist, dwl 532 Commercial
Howland Edward D. shipwright, dwl 318 Beale
Howland Frederick P. marine railway, foot Second
Howland Henry A. pattern maker, Miners' Foundry, dwl N s Howard bet Third and Fourth
Howland L. L. dwl 5 Stockton
Howland Robert, miner, dwl 54 First
Howland Rufus, pattern maker, Miners' Foundry, dwl 545 Howard
Howland Stephen W. copper crushing and sampling, 22 and 24 California, dwl E side Howard bet Eleventh and Twelfth
Howland W. Fred. P. Billiard Hall, 328 Montgomery, dwl 731 Clay
HOWLAND, *(William H.)* ANGELL *(Horace B.)* & KING *(Ervin T.) (and Cyrus Palmer)* proprietors Miners' Foundry and Machine Shop, 247-257 First, dwl 319 First
Howschild ——, paper box maker, dwl 114 Silver
Howser George, waiter, What Cheer House
Hoy Alexander, stoves and tin ware, 730 Jackson, dwl 1114 Leavenworth
Hoyd Susan E. (widow) lodgings, 202 Second
Hoydt Olmsby jr. dwl 628 Harrison
Hoye Isaac (col'd) baker, 719 Battery, dwl Scott bet Pacific and Broadway
Hoye Thomas, boiler maker, Union Foundry, dwl Brannan nr Sixth
Hoyer Cornelius, deputy license collector, dwl 1608 Larkin
Hoyt Andrew J. policeman, City Hall, dwl 26 Tehama
Hoyt Calvin S. stevedore, dwl Rincon Point
Hoyt C. D. hostler, Omnibus R. R. Co
Hoyt Emily Miss, domestic, 867 Mission
Hoyt H. C. boatman, cor Vallejo and Front, dwl cor Stockton and Bay
Hoyt Henry I. *(Morison, Harris & Co.)* res Norwalk, Conn
Hoyt Hoffman, boatman, cor Vallejo and Front, dwl Stockton and Bay
HOYT JAMES T. Capt. U. S. A. Assistant Q. M. office 34 California, and secretary Central R. R. Co. dwl 1024 Folsom
Hoyt John, insurance broker, dwl 610 Mason
Hoyt John M. storekeeper U. S. Clothing Depôt, 34 California, dwl E s Russ bet Howard and Folsom
Hoyt L. D. tinsmith with W. W. Walmsley, dwl 761 Mission
Hoyt Marcus F. clerk with Locke & Montague, 112 Battery
Hoyt Nathan B. laborer, Custom House, res Oakland
Hoyt Samuel, merchant, dwl 309 Stockton
Hoyt Stanley W. assistant book keeper. Union Foundry
Huant Paulin & Co. *(M. Demousset and F. Girot)* proprietors Lafayette Brewery, 735 Green
Huard Alexander N. visiting physician, French Hospital, dwl 830 Jackson
Hub Peter, waterman, 609 Market
Hubash Joseph, manufacturing jeweler, 409 Sansom, dwl 7 Berry
Hubbard *(Aroline F. Miss)* & Freeman *(Isadora Miss)* milliners, 23½ Second
Hubbard D. H, waiter, dwl 12 Stewart
Hubbard George, waiter, 626 Kearny
Hubbard Hannah (widow) dwl 224 Second
Hubbard Henry W. tailor, 333 East
Hubbard J. F. attorney at law, dwl 7 Hampton Place

Hubbard John, teamster, dwl W s Mission bet Twenty-Fourth and Twenty-Fifth
Hubbard John C. painter, dwl 9 Tehama Place
Hubbard Lydia A. (widow) dwl 70 Minna
Hubbard Marshall, clerk, office Navy Agent, 434 California, dwl NE cor Pacific and Mont
Hubbard Samuel, clerk, Pacific Mail S. S. Co. dwl 25 Laurel Place
Hubbard Thomas, cabinet maker, dwl 51 Shipley
Hubbard Warrin *(Brodie, H. & McAdams)* dwl 1412 Larkin
Hubbell DeWitt, reporter, Police Gazette, 424 Battery
Hubbs Anthony, book keeper, dwl 250 Clara
Hubbs George F. dwl 554 Folsom
Huber Caspar *(Hassel & H.)* dwl S s Montgomery Court nr Montgomery
Huber Edward A. harness maker with C. H. Mead, dwl 352 First
Huber Frederick, cook, William Tell House
HUBER *(F. X.)* & ANTHES *(John)* Philadelphia Saloon, 603 Kearny, dwl 609 Pine
Huber John, tailor, dwl Dresdener House
Huber Joseph, molder, Jackson Foundry, bds Sacramento Hotel
Huber Nicholas, porter, dwl 219 California
HUBERT CHARLES & CO. ship chandlers, 517 Davis, dwl 721 Broadway
Hubert Constant, hairdresser and wig manufacturer, 603 Montgomery
Hubert Jean, tailor, 1220 Stockton
HUBERT NUMA, attorney at law, office 51 Montgomery Block
Hublon John F. E. longshoreman, dwl Alta nr Sansom
Huby Elie J. miner, dwl SE cor Stock and Vallejo
Huchthansen Johanna Miss, domestic, dwl 1218 Clay
Huck D. captain schr Clara L. West, office 413 East
Huck John, mariner, dwl 25 Dupont
Huck Volentine *(Hammerschmidt & H.)* dwl Folsom bet Third and Fourth
Hucks A. M. Miss, assistant, Montgomery St. School, dwl Minna bet Third and Jane
Hucks James, foreman with John J. Hucks, dwl 145 Minna
HUCKS *(John J.)* & LAMBERT *(William)* manufacturers patent axle grease, 146 and 148 Natoma and 145 Minna, depôt 320 Jackson, dwl 145 Minna
HUCKS JOHN J. manufacturing chemist, S s Francisco bet Mason and Taylor
HUDDART R. TOWNSEND Dr. principal Union College, 501 Second cor Bryant
Huddy William, musician, dwl 8 St. Mark Place
Hudson Catherine S. (widow) boarding, dwl 234 Stevenson
Hudson David, farmer, Bay View nr San Bruno Road
Hudson G. B. carpenter, dwl 413 Pine
HUDSON GEORGE, secretary Bay Shore and Fort Point Road Co. office 522 Clay, dwl N s Sixteenth nr Valencia
Hudson Grace Miss, domestic, 312 Stockton
Hudson George B. & Co. American Clothing Store, 327 Sansom, dwl 461 Minna
Hudson Harry, bar tender, dwl Oriental Hotel
Hudson H. C. & Co. *(Charles H. Williams)* spice and mustard manufactory, SE cor Pine and Front, dwl 22 Minna
Hudson Henry, laborer with David B. Hughes, dwl S s Lombard bet Taylor and Jones
Hudson Henry D. calker, dwl S s Jessie bet Fourth and Fifth
Hudson Henry S. with Dickson, DeWolf & Co. res Oakland
Hudson I. N. *(A. N. Rood & Co.)* dwl 200 Stock
Hudson James, watch maker, 15 Fourth

Hudson John, waiter, Empire State Restaurant, dwl Vallejo nr Stockton

Hudson John M. with H. C. Hudson & Co. dwl 22 Minna

Hudson Nelson, importer boots and shoes, dwl 1206 Mason

Hudson P. jr. salesman, 325 Sansom, dwl 339 Jessie

Hudson Phineas, ship carpenter with John G. North, dwl 339 Jessie

Hudson Pliny E. salesman with Wilson & Stevens, dwl 506 Market

Hudson Samuel, usher, Wilson's Circus, dwl Bay View Park

Hudson Thomas, ship carpenter, dwl 54 First

Hudson William, Captain, dwl 520 Harrison

Huefner Otto, clerk, dwl NW cor Folsom and Fifth

HUEFNER *(William)* & GORMAN *(John)* notaries public, 619 Merchant, dwl. cor Folsom and Fifth

Huellmandel Barnett, tailor, dwl 319 Bush

Huen William F. C. Four Mile House, W s Mission nr Thirty-First

Huenert F. Aug, salesman, dwl 914 Dupont

HUERNE *(Prosper)* & HARANT *(Edouard)* architects, office SE cor Montgomery and Sacramento, dwl NW cor Eighteenth and Sanchez

Huesmann Louis, clerk with Tillmann & Co. dwl 913 Sacramento

Huestis Wilbur F. clerk, dwl 915 Market

Huet Engene *(Charles Tence & Co.)* res Paris

Huff Oliver B. *(Stevens & O.)* dwl 615 Mason

Huff William B. clerk, 28 Montgomery, dwl 615 Mason

Huffaker J. student, bds Marysville Hotel, 414 Pacific

Huffschneider William, electrotyper with Wm. P. Harrison, dwl 230 Sutter

Hufschmidt Frederick *(Horstmann & Co.)* dwl 116 Virginia

Hug Joseph, real estate, dwl 710 Howard

Hugg Henry, broker, office 108 Cal, dwl 513 Post

Hugh Augustus, trunk maker, dwl 718 Stockton

Hughes Abraham, longshoreman, dwl 11 Lafayette Place

Hughes Andrew, carpenter, bds Manhattan House, 705 Front

Hughes Catherine Miss, domestic, 517 Sutter

Hughes Charles J. pressman, Alta California, dwl 610 Geary

HUGHES DAVID, steam paddy and railroad contractor, office and dwl SW cor Market and Third

Hughes David B. *(Brooks & H.)* dwl W s Jones bet Lombard and Chestnut

Hughes David T. assayer with Thomas Price, dwl 47 Clementina

Hughes E. dwl What Cheer House

Hughes Edward, driver, North Beach & M. R. R. Co

Hughes Ellen, domestic, 767 Mission

Hughes Ellis, drayman, dwl S s Brannan bet Eighth and Ninth

Hughes F. J. broker, dwl 321 Sixth

HUGHES GEORGE, importing and commission fruit dealer, NW cor Sansom and Clay, dwl 325 Sixth

Hughes Harvey, house mover, dwl 615 Mission

HUGHES HENRY, importer English, French, and German dry goods and gents' furnishing goods, 220 Battery, dwl S s DeBoom nr Second

Hughes Henry, laborer, Fort Point

Hughes J. Miss, boarding, 15 Ecker

Hughes James, boots and shoes, 47 Second, dwl 677 Mission

Hughes James, clerk, dwl 126 St. Mark Place

Hughes James, laborer, S. F. Gas Co

Hughes James, laborer, dwl 254 Jessie

Hughes James, waiter, Cosmopolitan Hotel, dwl 801 Geary

HUGHES JAMES, wines and liquors, 14 Clay

Hughes Jesse (col'd) bootblack, 639¼ Market, dwl cor Mason and Pacific

Hughes John, blacksmith, dwl 130 Second

Hughes John, deck hand, steamer Cornelia

Hughes John, laborer, bds NE cor Sixteenth and Howard

Hughes John, laborer, S. F. & P. Sugar Co. dwl E s Nevada nr Folsom

Hughes John, molder, dwl Tyson Place bet Stockton and Powell

Hughes John, molder, Pacific Foundry, dwl SE cor Tehama and Hubbard

Hughes John, seaman, dwl 1520 Dupont

Hughes Joseph, with J. Hirth & Co. dwl Empire Lodgings

Hughes J. R. boots and shoes, NE cor Montgomery and Sutter, dwl 612 Pine

Hughes Margaret Miss, domestic, 15 Taylor

Hughes Mary Miss, domestic, 712 Folsom

Hughes Matthew, blacksmith with M. P. Holmes, dwl 648 Mission

HUGHES MATTHEW E. importer and manufacturer Phelan's Billiard Tables, 730 Montgomery, dwl SE cor Hayes and Gough

Hughes Michael, watchman California Foundry, dwl N s Market bet Front and Davis

Hughes Owen, machinist, dwl 114 Tehama

Hughes Owen E. porter 642 Sacramento, dwl 31 Rousch nr Folsom

Hughes P. express wagon, 215 Third

Hughes Patrick, driver, dwl Mission St. Brewery

Hughes Patrick, laborer, dwl 20 Hunt

Hughes Patrick, laborer, dwl N s Stevenson bet Sixth and Seventh

Hughes Patrick, machinist, Miners' Foundry

Hughes Philip, teamster, dwl Dolores Hall W s Valencia nr Sixteenth

Hughes Rienzi, stoves and tin ware, 213 Third, dwl 217 Tehama

Hughes Thomas, with Peter Job, dwl 519 Bush

Hughes Thomas, silversmith, dwl 741 Market

HUGHES *(Thomas A.)* & HUNTER, ship brokers and general agents, office 504 Battery, dwl 806 Bush

Hughes Thomas T. book keeper, dwl SW cor Kearny and Pacific

Hughes William, blacksmith, Miners' Foundry

Hughes William, boot fitter, dwl 311 Bush

Hughes William, boot maker, dwl 729 Clay

Hughes William, captain sloop Caroline, office 410 East, dwl 157 Perry

Hughes William, mariner, dwl N s Eleventh near Mission

Hughes William, painter, dwl 57 Jessie

HUGHES WILLIAM A. wines and liquors, 515 Clay

Hughes William G. contractor, dwl W s Jones bet Lombard and Chestnut

Hughes William R. accountant with William Kerr, dwl NW cor Vallejo and Battery

Hughes, see Hewes

Hughson William S. assistant assessor, U. S. Internal Rev. NW cor Battery and Commercial, dwl N s Union bet Hyde and Larkin

Hughston George J. with Chamberlin & Balch, 210 Clay, dwl Central Place

Huguenin Vuillemin J. importer watches, 619 Mont

Huie Hattie M. Miss, domestic, 636 Sutter

Hulbert Henry P. (widow) dwl 172 Clara

Hulbert Thomas F. clerk with F. Boilleau and secretary British Benevolent Society, NW cor Mont and Jackson, dwl SE cor Union and Stock

Hull Asa, book keeper with Samuel Adams, dwl 243 Second

Hull Benjamin F. driver with Wells, Fargo & Co. dwl 711 California

HULL EDWARD *(Lindley, Hull & Lohman, Sacramento)* office 405 Front, dwl Essex Place

Hull George S. book keeper with Thomas H. Selby & Co. dwl 15 Powell

Hull Isaac D. ship joiner, dwl 73 Tehama

Hull Michael J. machinist with Trendwell & Co. dwl 526 Pine

Hull Richard, dwl 632 Market

Hull V. F. job wagon, Davis bet Wash and Clay

Hull William, steward, dwl N s McAllister bet Hyde and Larkin

Hull William, waiter, Lick House

Hull W. M. carpenter, dwl 73 Tehama

Hulme James P. clerk, 117 Clay, dwl 812 Cal

Hulsey Joseph, bricklayer, dwl 306 Dupont

Humbert J. E. S. pressman with John A. T. Overend, dwl Original House

Humbert John J. printer, California Demokrat, dwl 1 St. Mary bet California and Pine

Humboldt Canal Co. office 716 Montgomery

Humboldt Oil Co. office 28 Government House 502 Washington

Humboldt Petroleum Co. (Humboldt) office 206 Jackson

Humboldt and Puget Sound Line Packets, S. L. Mastick & Co. agents, Pier 10 Stewart

Humboldt Stephen, laborer, dwl 140 Stewart

Humburg August, upholsterer with Charles A. Fuhr, dwl 407 Bush

Hume James N. clerk with tax collector, City Hall, dwl NW cor Mission and Fourth

HUME J. N. physician and apothecary, NW cor Mission and Fourth, dwl 802 Mission

Humenick Francis, cook, 308 Montgomery

Hummeltenberg Monroe, machinist, Miners' Foundry, res Oakland

Hummitzsch William, carpenter, dwl W s Larkin nr Ellis

Humphrey Ervin, carrier, Alta California and Call, dwl 206 Fourth

Humphrey (George) & Co. (William B. Swain) produce commission, 104 Clay, dwl Pine bet Kearny and Dupont

Humphrey James, groceries and liquors, NE cor Geary and William

Humphrey John, laborer, bds Meyer's Hotel, 814 Montgomery

Humphreys A. N. porter with J. H. Coghill & Co. dwl 537 California

Humphreys James, machinist, dwl 115 First

Humphreys Julius, dwl 803 Leavenworth

Humphreys Laura A. Miss, assistant, Hyde St. Primary School, dwl 803 Leavenworth

Humphreys Mary A. Miss, assistant, Market St. School, dwl 803 Leavenworth

HUMPHREYS WILLIAM P. surveyor, 49 and 50 Montgomery Block

Hund Catherine (widow) midwife, dwl 337 Fourth

Hund Frederick, barber, SE cor First and Jessie, dwl 243 Stevenson

Hund Fritz, laborer, dwl 323 Pine

Hung Gee (Chinese) washing, 537 Sacramento

Hung Kee (Chinese) washing, 133 Second

Hung Lee (Chinese) cigar manufacturer, Washington Alley

Hung Son (Chinese) butcher, 731 Sacramento

Hung Wo Tong (Chinese) druggist, 641 Jackson

Hung Woa (Chinese) merchant, 734 Commercial

Hung Yun (Chinese) washing, 217 Second

Hungerford Daniel E. Col. dwl 626 California

Hungerford Eveline Mrs. teacher French and Spanish, dwl 626 California

Hunsacker James, assayer, dwl 839 Mission

Hussenbaum Michael, ship carpenter, dwl with John G. North

Hunt C. A. & Co. produce commission, 222 Clay, dwl 823 Post

Hunt Carrie L. Miss, principal Sutter St. Primary School, dwl 1004 Powell

Hunt Charles, calker, dwl 238 Stewart

Hunt Charles E. photographer, dwl 606 Kearny

Hunt David W. machinist and engineer, dwl 28 Second

Hunt D. D. clerk with W. E. Mayhew, dwl 1 Clarence Place

Hunt Dennis, drug clerk, NW cor Mission and Fourth, dwl 760 Folsom

Hunt Edward, entry clerk, Naval Office Custom House, res Oakland

HUNT EDWIN O. patent wind mill, horse power, and pump manufacturer, 28 Second and 110 Jessie, dwl 129 Tehama

HUNT HARVEY, physician and surgeon, office and dwl 12 Montgomery

Hunt James, deputy state gauger, 321 Front, dwl 1808 Mason

Hunt James S. ship calker, dwl W s Fifth Avenue bet Bryant and Harrison

Hunt John, hatter, dwl S s Broadway bet Taylor and Jones

Hunt John, ship carpenter, dwl Wright's Hotel 210 Broadway

Hunt John jr. clerk with George F. and William H. Sharp, dwl S s Broadway nr Jones

Hunt John A. (Hall, H. & Malone) dwl N s Vallejo bet Stockton and Dupont

Hunt John D. merchant, dwl 1004 Powell

HUNT JONATHAN, president Pacific Insurance Co. office 436 California, dwl SE cor Pine and Leavenworth

Hunt Mary Ann (widow) dwl E s Carlos Place

Hunt Mary J. (widow) furnished rooms, 522 Dupont

Hunt Michael, laborer, dwl 51 Stevenson

Hunt Patrick, dwl 509 Pine

Hunt Samuel O. paying teller Pacific Bank, 400 Montgomery, dwl SE cor Pine and Leavenworth

Hunt William, with Conroy & O'Connor, dwl 165 Silver

Hunt William, laborer, dwl 29 Ecker

Hunt William, machinist with David Stoddart, dwl 64 Stevenson

Huntemann Christopher A. bar keeper, NW cor Washington and Kearny, dwl 8 Scotland

Huntemann Richard, plasterer, dwl 1819 Powell

Huntenberg August, clerk with Henning Menke, dwl NE cor Battery and Commercial

Hunter (Alexander) & Myers (Samuel) liquor saloon, 332 Montgomery, dwl 439 Green

Hunter Andrew, proptr Hunter's Grain Separator and Concentrator, off SE cor Clay and Drumm

Hunter Charles C. flour commission merchant, dwl Gautier's House 516 Pacific

Hunter David, dwl NW cor Ellis and Van Ness Av

Hunter David, plasterer, dwl W s Carlos Place nr O'Farrell

Hunter David H. compositor, Alta California, dwl 511 Howard

Hunter Edward, dwl 577 Howard

Hunter George, laborer, dwl 315 Union, rear

Hunter George, tailor, 619 Sacramento

HUNTER, (James) WAND (Thomas N.) & CO. (Michael Kane) wholesale liquors, 612 Front, dwl 531 Bryant

Hunter John, manager sail loft, 211 Sacramento, dwl 17 Clementina

Hunter John, milkman, Hunter's Point

Hunter Louis C. (Scott & Co.) dwl 8 Powell

Hunter P. Schuyler, farmer, Hunter's Point

Hunter Robert A. plasterer, dwl W s Carlos Place nr O'Farrell

HUNTER ROBERT E. farmer, Hunter's Point

Hunter William, dwl St. Lawrence House

Hunter William, waiter, What Cheer House Restaurant

Huntington Charles, dwl 29 Third

Huntington George G. engineer, India Rice Mills, dwl SE cor First and Broadway

Huntington H. A. lieut. U. S. A., A. D. C. Division of the Pacific, office 418 California, dwl Occidental Hotel

Huntington J. S. blacksmith, dwl What Cheer H

Hunton Lewis F. steward, Richard's Dining Saloon, dwl N s California bet Mason and Taylor

Hautsman George H. *(J. W. Davidson & Co.)* dwl 609 Sacramento

Hunzelmann William, tailor, 409 Bush

Hunzen William G. clerk with C. W. Hacke

Huon Charles, gasman Maguire's Opera House

Hup Lee (Chinese) washing, 661 Mission

Huppert Thomas, cabinet maker with E. Bloomingdale & Co. dwl 51 Shipley

Hurd Horatio, book keeper with Ballard & Hall, 224 Clay

Hurd J. M. pressman with Thompson & Co. dwl Dolores bet Sixteenth and Seventeenth

Hurdis Samuel, painter, dwl Hall Court

Hurl James, longshoreman, dwl NW cor Union and Sansom

Hurlbert Henry M. tinsmith with Locke & Montague, dwl 116 Silver

Hurlburt Isaiah jr. real estate agent, 420 Montgomery, dwl 11 Minna

Hurlbutt J. M. & Co. *(Theodore A. Kelsey)* saddlery and harness makers, 407 Battery, dwl cor Turk and Larkin

Hurle John H. cook, 28 Montgomery, dwl New Atlantic Hotel

Hurley Annie Miss, chambermaid, Russ House

Hurley Charles *(Ash & H.)* dwl 603 Pine

Hurley Charles *(Gleason & H.)* dwl NE cor O'Farrell and Dupont

Hurley Charles T. clerk with L. J. Ewell, dwl 514 Filbert

Hurley Daniel, laborer, S. F. & San José R. R. Co.

Hurley Daniel, teamster, dwl W s Sansom bet Broadway and Vallejo

Hurley Daniel J. boarding, 704 Front

Hurley D. D. wood and produce, SW cor Mission and Seventeenth

Hurley Ellen (widow) dwl 23 Natoma

Hurley James, butcher, 4 Occidental Market, dwl 27 Third

Hurley James, laborer, dwl 126 Beale

Hurley Jeremiah, laborer, dwl 158 Jessie

Hurley J. M. A. Miss, assistant teacher, Sutter St. Primary School, dwl NW corner Gough and Pacific

Hurley John, boatman, Fort Point

Hurley John, cartman, dwl Bryant bet Third and Fourth

Hurley John, helper, Union Foundry

Hurley John, laborer, dwl W s McCormack nr Pac

Hurley Michael, laborer, dwl 7 Trinity

Hurley Michael, laborer, dwl 77 Stevenson

Hurley Michael, laborer, dwl 7 Bush

Hurley Michael, workman, dwl SW cor Mission and Seventeenth

Hurley Michael, workman, S. F. & P. Sugar Co. dwl 208 Fourth

Hurley Patrick, carpenter, dwl E s Gough bet Pacific and Broadway

Hurley Patrick, laborer, dwl 267 Stevenson

Hurley Patrick, laborer, dwl 446 Natoma

Hurley Patrick, laborer, dwl W s Summer nr Howard

Hurley Thomas, laborer, dwl cor Mariposa and Minnesota

Hurley William, pressman with Francis, Valentine & Co. dwl 266 Jessie

Hurlls A. R. Miss, dress maker, dwl 209 Second

Hurst F. laborer, dwl Pacific Exchange

Hurtado Joseph, express wagon, cor Clay and Dupont

Hurtado Nicolas, saddler, dwl 522 Battery

Hushan Patrick *(Anderson & H.)* dwl SE cor Sansom and Broadway

Husing John, clerk with Frederick Carsten

Husing Rathye, clerk, Young America Engine Co. No. 13

Husing Rogers *(Schwartz & H.)* dwl SE cor Mission and Eighteenth

Hussey Albion *(Brown & H.)* dwl 32 Clara

Hussey Francis F. teamster, S. F. & P. Sugar Co. dwl 777 Market

Hussey Frank, Ethiopean Comedian, dwl Brooklyn Hotel

Hussey H. E. wood turner, dwl 238 Sutter

Hussey Henry J. sawyer, Chace's Mill, dwl 331 Bush

Hussey Joseph, tailor, cor Spring and Summer

Hussey Lawrence, laborer, dwl N s Perry bet Fourth and Fifth

Hussey Patrick, merchant, dwl 415 Sixth

Hussey Simon, laborer, dwl 326 Green

Husson Matilda Mrs. dwl 36 Government House

Huset John, employé, Metropolitan Restaurant, 715 Montgomery

Hutaf Henry *(Garonne & H.)* dwl 643 California

Hutaf Henry, liquors, 230 Com, dwl 114 Eddy

Hutchings Thomas, groom, Wilson's Circus

Hutchings U. P. office 712 Mont, dwl 639 Clay

Hutchins George H. clerk, Pacific Insurance Co. 436 California, dwl Occidental Hotel

Hutchins John, broker, office 320 Montgomery

Hutchins Lemuel W. butcher, dwl 256 Clementina

Hutchins Thomas, waiter, steamer Orizaba

Hutchinson Brothers *(Daniel & James)* milkmen, E s Fourth nr Brannan

Hutchinson C. & W. carpenters and builders, 304 Pine, dwl 16 Ritch

Hutchinson Charles H. dwl 805 Bush

HUTCHINSON C. I. office 608 Montgomery, dwl 725 California

Hutchinson D. S. dentist, office and dwl 107 Natoma

Hutchinson Ezra I. books and stationery, NW cor Kearny and Geary, dwl 270 Clementina

Hutchinson James *(Hutchinson Bros.)* E s Fourth nr Brannan

Hutchinson James, blacksmith with H. Casebolt & Co. dwl Fourth St. House

Hutchinson James S. cashier with Sather & Co. dwl SW cor Howard and Fifteenth

Hutchinson Jane P. Miss, domestic with Rev. Joseph Rowell

HUTCHINSON J. C. & CO. *(W. O. Andrews)* real estate agents, 626 Montgomery, dwl Second Avenue nr Sixteenth

Hutchinson John, broker, dwl W s Battery bet Vallejo and Green

Hutchinson John F. druggist with W. K. Doherty, dwl 12 Tehama

Hutchinson John J. clerk, Golden Era office, dwl S s Sacramento bet Leavenworth and Jones

Hutchinson Joseph, dwl SW cor Howard and Fifteenth

Hutchinson Richard, with Yates & Stevens, dwl Montgomery nr Broadway

Hutchinson Thomas, laborer with John G. North, Potrero

Hutchinson William *(C. & W. Hutchinson)* dwl 752 Howard

Hutchinson William L. teamster, dwl 710 Sutter

Hutchinson William T. hay and grain, dwl 930 Montgomery

Hutchson Daniel, laborer, What Cheer House Restaurant

Hutchson C. farmer, bds Franklin Hotel

Hutchson William, boarding, 110 Prospect Place

Huter Gustave, porter with L. & E. Wertheimer, dwl 1811 Stockton

Huth Charles, shoe maker, 504 Green

Hutter Gustave, clerk, dwl 1811 Stockton

Hüttner H. J. draftsman, Vulcan Foundry, dwl 555 Mission

Hutton Catherine (widow) dwl 345½ Third

Hutton Henry, butcher, dwl 1817 Mason

Hutton Hugh S. reporter, Evening Bulletin, dwl N s Green nr Leavenworth

---

Hutton James H. miner, dwl W s Leavenworth bet Vallejo and Broadway
Hutton John, drayman with E. G. Mathews & Co. dwl SW cor Larkin and Union
Hutton John T. waiter, dwl 107 Beale
Hutton Patrick, laborer, bds Londonderry House, 12 Broadway
Huxley Thomas, seaman, dwl 54 Sacramento
Huyck John A. fireman, steamer Yosemite
Hyams George J. S. clothing, 431 Mont, dwl 316 First
Hyams Leopold, physician, office and dwl 659 Clay
Hyamson Morris, stationer, dwl Bailey House
Hyans Henry, express wagon, cor Dupont and Wash
Hyans John, lab, with William Kerr, dwl 903 Bat
Hyatt Caleb, architect, office and dwl Shiels' Block, 5 Post
Hyatt Elisha, express wagon, SW cor Market and Fourth, dwl s Austin bet Franklin and Van Ness Avenue
Hyatt J. B. (Bailey & H.) dwl Oriental Hotel
HYATT T. HART & CO. publishers and proprietors California Rural Home Journal, office 306 Sansom
Hyatt T. Hart jr. office Mercantile Gazette, 536 Clay, dwl 55 Second cor Mission
Hyatt William, dwl 820 Dupont
Hyde George, attorney at law, dwl 721 Geary
Hyde Henry, clerk, City and County Attorney, 13 City Hall third floor, dwl Brevoort House
Hyde Isaac, manager What Cheer House
Hyde James T. physician, office and dwl 6 Phœnix Building SW cor Sansom and Jackson
Hyde Jennie (widow) dwl 231 Post
Hyde John, cook, American Exchange
Hyde John B. painter, dwl 145 Fourth
Hyde Michael, dwl N s Thirteenth nr Mission
HYDE (R. E.) & McCLENNEN (Edward D.) saddlery and harness, 227 Mont, dwl 112 Mason
Hyde William, reporter, dwl 636 Commercial
Hyde William C. (Dibblee & H.) dwl 121 O'Farrell
Hyde William C. Capt. mariner, dwl 1618 Powell
HYDE (William H.) & CHESTER (Henry) contractors, 619 Mission, dwl E s Mission bet Fourteenth and Fifteenth
Hydeliff M. J. merchant, dwl 22 Mary
Hyer Albert, grocer, dwl 70 Silver
Hyer Peter, machinist, Union Foundry, dwl 159 Shipley
Hyland Ann (widow) dwl 669 Harrison
Hyland Bernard, coachman with Mrs. J. P. Buckley
Hyland Henry J. (O. F. Von Rhein & Co.) dwl NW cor Mission and Ninth
Hyland Michael, laborer, dwl 158 Minna
Hyland William J. clerk with Spencer & Jarboe, dwl 764 Howard
Hylphers William, mariner, dwl 32 Stewart
Hylton T. de M. physician and editor and proprietor Our Mazeppa, office 423 Wash, dwl 1807 Powell
Hyman Abraham, glazier, 644 Mission
Hyman D. Miss. assistant, Spring Valley Grammar School, dwl 333 Jessie
Hyman Henry, pawnbroker, 741 Washington
Hyman Morris, furniture, 606 Broadway
Hyman Moses, book keeper with M. Heller & Bros. dwl 812 Howard
Hyman P. C. stock broker, office 712 Montgomery, dwl 30 Hawthorne
Hyman Rachel S. Miss, assistant teacher, Academic Seminary, dwl 333 Jessie
Hyman Wolf, pawnbroker, 25 Kearny
Hymes Charles (Lucy & H.) dwl 609 Howard
Hynaud Jacob, laborer, dwl 311 O'Farrell
Hynes John, laborer, Omnibus R. R. Co. dwl W s Guerrero bet Market and Ridley
Hynes John, store keeper Lick House, dwl 409 Post
Hynes Patrick, laborer, dwl 14 Sherwood Place
Hynes Michael P. baker, dwl 3 Pollard Place
Hynes William H. carpenter, 77 Fourth
Hyslop William, teamster, Mission Woolen Mills

I

I X L G. & S. M. Co. office 338 Montgomery
Iaeck Adam, butcher, dwl S s Vallejo bet Montgomery and Sansom
Iagels C. H. clerk, SW cor Howard and Second
Ibbach Adolph, book keeper, 637 Clay, dwl 3 White Place
Iher Thomas, barber, dwl 528 Pacific, rear
Ibstrom L. J. dwl What Cheer House
Iburg William, groceries and liquors, NW cor Pine and Kearny
Icher Francis, blacksmith, dwl 14 Dupont
Iches Robert jr. sawyer with J. S. Gibbs, dwl 10 Jane
Ichon Edward F. clothing, 325 San, dwl 608 Sac
Icke Jacob, upholsterer, dwl 829 Pacific
Ickelheimer Herman, house and sign painter, 15 Dupont
Ide Charles A. metallurgist with Kimball & Murphy, dwl 73 Fourth
Ide James A. merchant, room 96 Stevenson House
Ide John, blacksmith, dwl 812 Sansom
Ide Paulinus, mason, dwl 317 Minna
Ielmini Henry, fruits and confectionery, 445 Bush
Iffert Leonhard, butcher, SE cor Dolores and Sixteenth
Igoa Ellen Miss, domestic with I. F. Blumberg, E s Howard bet Fifteenth and Sixteenth
IKEN FREDERICK, commission merchant, office 525 Front, dwl 117 Stockton
Ikmann William, butcher with Albert Meyer, 55 Sac
Ilgan Margaret Mrs. dwl Hubbard bet Howard and Folsom
Illig William, confectioner, 833 Washington, dwl 140 Second
Ils John G. importer and manufacturer stoves and tin ware, 628 Washington
Ilse William A. with Kellogg, Hewston & Co. res Oakland
Imbler Benjamin, clerk with J. B. Cunningworth, dwl 632 Mission
Imbrie Augustus C. tailor, 215 California, dwl Manhattan Engine House
Imhaus Louis, cigars and tobacco, NE cor Commercial and San, dwl SW cor Mason and Chestnut
Imbaus Louis A. clerk, 106 Battery, dwl SW cor Mason and Chestnut
IMPERIAL FIRE AND LIFE INSURANCE CO. London, Falkner, Bell & Co. agents, office 430 California
Imperial G. & S. M. Co. (Moss Ledge) office 338 Montgomery
Imperial S. M. Co. office 708 Montgomery
Independent G. & S. M. Co. office 402 Front
INDEPENDENT ORDER OF ODD FELLOWS HALL, 325 Montgomery nr California
INDEPENDENT ORDER RED MEN, rooms 333 Pine
Inderstroth Julius, groceries and liquors, SE corner Bryant and Rincon Place
INDIAN AFFAIRS SUPERINTENDENT FOR CALIFORNIA, office 423 Washington
INDUSTRIAL SCHOOL, Old Ocean House Road 5 miles from City Hall, office secretary rooms nine and ten 3d floor City Hall
Ines Manuel, laborer with N. C. Walton, dwl 114 Jackson
ING ANDREW D. leather and depôt Santa Cruz Tannery, 312 and 314 Com, dwl 639 Mission
Ingals George P. carpenter, dwl 218 Stockton
Ingargiloa Lawrence, dwl 1611 Powell
Inge S. W. attorney at law, dwl 408 Stockton
Ingersoll William B. photographer, dwl NW corner Shipley and Fifth, up stairs
Inglis Alexander, waiter, Oriental Hotel Restaurant, dwl 114 Bush

Inglis Francis P. steward Crescent Engine Co. No. 10
Inglis Nelson, captain schooner Roscoe, dwl 148 Silver
Ingoldsby L. D. mining secretary, office 2 and 3 Armory Hall Building
Ingols George, bar keeper, stm Helen Hensley
Ingols James E. with Kellogg, Hewston & Co. dwl 311 Brannan bet Second and Third
Ingols N. Lombard, accountant, 32 Montgomery Block, dwl 311 Brannan
Ingraham Almira Mrs. dwl NW corner Green and Calhoun
Ingraham Frederick, handcartman, dwl 22 Stewart
Ingraham John, driver, North Beach & M. R. R. Co
Ingraham John S. sawsmith with N. W. Spaulding, 113 Pine, dwl 121 Natoma
Ingraham Joseph, cooper, dwl 207 Clara
Ingraham Ossian, driver with D. S. Weaver, 507 San
Ingram Christopher, farmer, Old San José Road 6 miles from City Hall
Ingram Joseph, cooper with Erzgraber & Gœtjen, 120 Davis
Ingram William, weigher, dwl 1218 Kearny
Innd Thomas, carpenter, dwl 523 Mission
Innes J. C. lieut. C. V. assistant commissary musters, 420 Washington, dwl 509 Bush
Inslee (George W.) & Joseph (Michael J.) importers and dealers cigars and tobacco, 326 Montgomery, dwl 302 Mason
INSPECTOR BOILERS (U. S.) office Custom House 3d floor
INSPECTOR COAL, office Cowell's Wharf
INSPECTOR GAS METERS, office 612 Commercial
INSPECTOR HULLS (U. S.) office Custom House 3d floor
INSPECTOR (STATE) STAMPS, office 424 Battery
INSPECTOR STEAMBOATS (U. S.) office Custom House 3d floor
INTERNAL REVENUE, office NW cor Commercial and Battery
INTERNATIONAL HOTEL, F. E. Weygant proprietor, 530–534 Jackson
Inwood George, real estate, dwl 1621 Powell
Iowa Mining Co. office 8 Stevenson House
Iredale Alfred S. (Taylor & I.) dwl 957 Mission
Iredell Joseph B. carpenter, dwl N s Francisco bet Powell and Mason
Irelan William, shipwright, 164 Stewart, dwl 534 Folsom
Irelan William jr. clerk, dwl 534 Folsom
IRELAND JAMES, sub-manager British and Californian Banking Co. Limited, office 424 California, dwl 18 Hawthorne
Ireland Louis F. clerk with Charles W. Brooks & Co. dwl cor Montgomery and Washington
Irish Charles B. dwl 44 Jane
IRISH NEWS (weekly) Jeffrey Nunan editor and proprietor, office 510 Clay
Irons Amos A. teamster, Pier 15 Stewart, dwl 534 Pacific
Irons William, engineer, dwl 17 Powell
Irvin Brown, ex-steamboat captain, 220 Vallejo bet Sansom and Battery
Irvin James (Dalrymple & I.) 32 Stewart
Irvin Robert, laborer, dwl W s Eighth bet Howard and Tehama
Irvine A. W. jeweler with R. B. Gray & Co
Irvine George, cigars and tobacco, 704 Market, dwl 721 Market
Irvine George, salesman with L. J. Ewell, dwl N s Stevenson bet Sixth and Seventh
IRVINE (James) & CO. (John Lyons) wholesale grocers, 224 Front
Irvine Walter (W. Irvine & Co.) 34 Second
Irvine W. & Co. (Walter Irvine) dry goods, 34 Second

Irving Andrew W. jeweler, dwl 32 John
Irving Christopher, baker, Commercial Hotel 123 Pacific
Irving David, tailor, dwl 347 Tehama
Irving H. A. carpenter, Eureka Hose Co. No. 4
Irving Henry P. attorney at law, office 604 Merchant
Irving House, 568 Mission
Irving James, bar. keeper, 534 California, dwl NE cor Grove and Laguna
Irving James D. clerk, Pier 2½ Stewart, dwl S side Hayes bet Gough and Octavia
Irving Lizzie Miss, private school, NE cor Grove and Laguna
Irving Robert (Smith & I.) dwl cor Santa Clara and Carolina
Irving Samuel, salesman with Murphy, Grant & Co. dwl 1 Chelsea Place
Irving W. K. porter with H. H. Bancroft & Co. res Oakland
Irwin Ellen Mrs. dwl 19 Dupont
Irwin Francis, seaman, dwl SW corner Sansom and Greenwich
Irwin George W. waiter with James B. Haggin, dwl 1019 Jackson
Irwin Henry F. warehouseman, dwl 216 Clara
Irwin James, laborer, dwl 35 Sacramento
Irwin James, wholesale and retail wines and liquors, 30 Montgomery, dwl 28 Geary
Irwin John, shoe maker, 12 Clay, dwl SW corner Third and Mission
Irwin Mary Miss, furnished rooms, 173 Minna
Irwin Robert, salesman, 411 Sacramento, dwl 1503 Leavenworth
Irwin Samuel M. & Co. (W. McKinney and George A. Morgan) p   rs, office 702 Market
Isaac Aaron, peddler, dwl 125 Perry
Isaac Christian, furniture, dwl 56 Everett
Isaac Harris, shoe maker with Rudolph Meiners, dwl 41 Jessie
ISAAC JOSEPH & CO. (Oscar Schlesinger) importers and jobbers paper and stationery, 513 Sansom cor Merchant, dwl 1307 Stockton
Isaac Marcus, express wagon, dwl W s Gaven near Filbert
Isaac Michael, tailor, 233 Third
Isaac Morris, tailoring, 7 Summer
Isaackson Wolfe, job wagon, 424 Sansom, dwl 458 Minna
Isaacs Albert, clothing, 903 Kearny
Isaacs Anna Mrs. dwl W s Leavenworth bet Sacramento and California
Isaacs Benjamin, book keeper, 222 Sansom, dwl 366 Jessie
Isaacs Jacob, glazier, dwl 25 Jessie
Isaacs Kate S. (widow) proprietress Identical Saloon SE cor Sacramento and Battery
Isaacs Manuel, with Martin Kedon, 319 Davis
Isaacs Morris, clothing, 1032 Dupont
Isaacs R. & Brother (Ezra Isaacs) dwl 728 Union
Isaacs Samuel, dwl 202 Dupont, rear
Isaacs Simon, tailor, 16 First
Isaacs Solomon, butcher with Wm. Fulton
Isaacs William B. salesman, 106 Battery, dwl 528 Harrison
Isaacson B. clerk with Henry Cohen, 812 Kearny, dwl 714 Green
Isadore Isaac, furniture, 740 Pacific
Isart H. F. musician, dwl W s Margaret Place
Isenhauer Adam, express wagon, dwl 915 Broadway
Isham J. B. G. Capt. dwl 1024 Stockton
Islieber Fred. driver, Bay City Laundry, 1142 Folsom
Isola Jovanni, laborer, dwl 517 Union
Israel Harris H. tailor, dwl 128 Pacific
Israel Isaac G. dwl 841 Mission
Israel Isaac G. jr, saloon, Cosmopolitan Hotel, dwl 841 Mission
Israel Joseph, cooper, S. F. & P. Sugar Co. dwl Rousch

Israel Julius *(Prescott & I.)* dwl 114 Stevenson
Israel Meyer, clerk, 1125 Stockton, dwl 815 Mont
Israeli HarryC. purser, Pacific Mail S. S. Co. office NW cor Sacramento and Leidesdorff
Isson Samuel, watchmaker and jeweler, 639 Pacific
Isthmus House, W. J. Baily proprietor, 54 First
Italia Josie, vegetable garden, nr Bay View Park
ITALIAN BENEVOLENT SOCIETY, office NW cor Montgomery and Jackson
ITALIAN FISH MARKET, SE cor Clay and Leidesdorff
Itasca Silver Mining Co. office 24 Government House
Itchings Thomas, driver, Central R. R. Co. dwl SE cor Brannan and Seventh
Ivancovich John & Co. *(M. Vulicerich)* foreign and domestic fruit, 405 and 407 Davis, dwl E s Dupont bet Washington and Jackson
Ivers Richard, treasurer Vulcan Iron Works Co. dwl 251 Stevenson
Iverson Jurgen, seaman, bds 7 Washington
Iverson L. boatman, dwl 23 Frederick
Ives Charles S. clerk with Joseph M. Johnson, dwl 1410 Leavenworth
Ives George I. book keeper with Peters & Co. North Point Warehouse, dwl 535 Green
Ives James, clerk, dwl 18 Sansom
Ivory Joseph T. carpenter, dwl 26 Stockton
Ivory Joseph T. carpenter, 571 Mission

J

Jack Alexander, U. S. Restaurant, dwl Niantic Hotel
Jack R. Edgar, book keeper with Frank Eastman, dwl 9 Minna
Jack *(William)* & Bushnell *(Horace)* liquor saloon, 300 Dupont
Jacking Daniel W. engineer, S. F. & San José R. R. Co. dwl E s Columbia nr Sixteenth
Jackman Jehiel B. teamster with Wm. K. Dietrich, dwl E s Larkin between Green and Union
Jackman O. M. carpenter, dwl 67 Minna
Jacks Charles C. clerk, U. S. Quartermaster's Department, dwl 603 Pine
Jacks George, waiter, Willows, SW cor Mission and Eighteenth
Jacks John, express wagon, dwl Cresent Engine House
Jackson Alexander, proprietor Mount Hood House, 54 Sacramento
Jackson Andrew, deck hand, steamer Julia
Jackson Andrew, hatter with Calvin Blake, dwl Jackson Place
Jackson Andrew M. liquor saloon, 214 Commercial
Jackson Anna (colored) domestic, 26 Ellis
Jackson Archibald (colored) laborer, dwl NW cor Filbert and Taylor
Jackson A. W. salesman, Pier 12 Stewart, dwl 29 Minna
Jackson Benjamin S. express wagon, NW cor Mont and Com. dwl NE cor Green and Stockton
Jackson Charles *(Oakley & J.)* dwl 1006 Pine
Jackson Charles, bar keeper, dwl 230 Jessie
Jackson Charles, salesman with H. Bornstine, 731 Montgomery
Jackson Charles, seaman, dwl 44 Sacramento
Jackson David B. clerk, Central American Transit Co. NW cor Battery and Pine
Jackson Foundry, 628 Wash, John G. Ils proprietor
Jackson Francis R. with Pollard & Carvill, dwl 304 Sutter
Jackson George, cigar maker, 419 Brannan, dwl 870 Mission
Jackson George, clerk, dwl 23 Geary
Jackson George W. (colored) cook, dwl 1410 Dupont
Jackson George Z. clerk, 129 Kearny, dwl 25 Geary
Jackson Harriet (col'd) stewardess, steamer Amelia

Jackson Henry, coal passer, steamer Orizaba
Jackson Henry, hairdressing saloon, 22 Sansom
Jackson James, assistant, Home of the Inebriate
Jackson James, carpenter, dwl 28 Sansom
Jackson James, physician, dwl 622 Battery
Jackson James, seaman, dwl 44 Sacramento
Jackson June Miss. laundress, Bay City Laundry, 1140 and 1142 Folsom
Jackson Jane Mrs. (colored) dwl 913 Pacific
Jackson Jane Mrs. (colored) dwl 911 Sacramento
JACKSON J. G. & CO. *(William E. Wood)* wholesale and retail lumber, 25 Stewart Pier 2, dwl 911 Sutter
Jackson J. H. cook, steamer Senator
Jackson John, bricklayer, dwl Manhattan House, 705 Front
Jackson John, carpenter, dwl Sailor's Home, SW cor Battery and Vallejo
Jackson John, deck hand, steamer Princess
Jackson John, milk ranch, N s Lombard nr Fillmore
Jackson John H. (col'd, cook) dwl 1503 Powell
Jackson John S. engineer, dwl 3 Telegraph Place
Jackson Joseph, book keeper, dwl 54 Sacramento
Jackson Lucy Miss (colored) domestic, 412 Dupont
Jackson Lydia (widow) dwl W s Beule bet Howard and Folsom
Jackson Mary Miss, domestic, 411 Sixth
Jackson Moses A. (colored) fruits and boot blacking, junction Market and Geary, dwl 12 Geary
Jackson Richard (col'd) waiter, steamer Chrysopolis
Jackson St. Wharf, foot Jackson
Jackson W. driver, Omnibus R. R. Co
Jackson Wesley, druggist, dwl 1303 Mason
Jackson William, porter, steamer Amelia
JACKSON WILLIAM, proprietor Pacific Temperance House, 109–113 Pacific
Jackson William, waiter, steamer Pacific
Jackson William C. conductor, dwl SW cor Stevenson and Second
Jackson William H. clerk, 647 Clay
Jackson William H: dish washer, Willows, SW cor Eighteenth and Mission
Jackson William N. dwl 707 Howard
Jackson William T. cartman, cor Clay and Sansom
Jacob Aaron, tailor, 504 Pine
Jacob Ephraim, dwl 15 Everett
Jacob Jacob, dwl 110 Sutter
Jacob Morris, second hand clothing, 531 Pacific
Jacobi Leopold *(Waller & J.)* dwl 306 Kearny
Jacobi Michael, with J. Seligman & Co. 111 Battery, dwl 1710 Stockton
Jacobs A. & Co. importers and jobbers hats and caps, 325 Sacramento, dwl 329 Jessie
Jacobs A. clothing, 227 Pacific
Jacobs Abraham, express wagon, cor Dupont and Broadway
Jacobs Albert, fruits and produce, 217 Washington *(and Pratt & J.)*
Jacobs Benjamin F. photographic printer with Wm. Shew, dwl 924 Mission
Jacobs Charles, groceries and liquors, SE cor Stockton and Green
Jacobs Charles, pawnbroker, 708 Dupont
Jacobs Davis, tailoring, 315 East, dwl SW cor Commercial and East
Jacobs E. groceries, NW cor Dupont and Harlan Place
Jacobs Elias, merchant, dwl 14 O'Farrell
Jacobs *(Gabriel)* & Rosenfield *(Solomon)* hoop manufactory, 24 Second, dwl Irving House
Jacobs Henry, clerk with I. & A. Froomberg, 428 Commercial
Jacobs I. express wagon, dwl E s August Alley nr Union
Jacobs Joseph, tailor, dwl 1327 Dupont
Jacobs Julius, commission merchant, office NW cor Front and Washington, dwl 204 Ellis
Jacobs Lewis N. telegraphic operator, dwl 14 O'Farrell

Jacobs Max, crockery and glass ware, 208 First
Jacobs Morris, merchant, dwl 230 O'Farrell
Jacobs Morris E. clerk, dwl 14 O'Farrell
Jacobs Nathan, clerk, dwl 54 Third
JACOBS N. B. & CO. *(William T. Reynolds)* importers and jobbers liquors and native wines, 423 Front
Jacobs Nellie Miss, dwl 22 John
Jacobs P. dwl 151 Minna
Jacobs P. Mrs. dry goods, 203 Kearny
Jacobs Rachael (widow) dwl 511 Filbert
Jacobs Samuel B. dwl 427 Greenwich
Jacobs Solomon, drayman, 304 Battery, dwl 624 O'Farrell
Jacobs Solomon, dry goods, 203 Kearny
Jacobs Wolf *(A. Lusk & Co.)* dwl 429 Green
Jacobsen Peter, groceries and liquors, 2019 Mason
Jacobsohn Raphael, laborer, dwl 225 Post
Jacobson A. peddler, dwl 323 Pine
Jacobson Christian, mariner, dwl E s Zoe bet Bryant and Brannan
Jacobson Ferdinand, cigar maker, dwl N s Brannan bet Second and Third
Jacobson George, laborer, dwl 44 Stockton
Jacobson Lauretz, iron filer, Jackson Foundry
Jacoby Augustus *(A. Fridenberg & Co. Virginia)* office 219 Front, dwl 1431 Taylor
Jacoby George, cigars and tobacco, NE cor Front and Sacramento, dwl 1431 Taylor
Jacoby Jacob, pawnbroker, 615 Kearny
Jacoby Jacob, tailor, 714 Commercial
Jacoby J. H. clerk, 213 Mont, dwl 1108 Stockton
Jacoby Louis, with Morris Speyer, 526 Washington, dwl 833 Post
Jacoby Philo, publisher and proprietor Hebrew and job printer, office 509 Clay
Jacoby Samuel, variety store, 1108 Stockton
Jacquenot V. (widow) furnished rooms, 745 Clay
Jacques Joseph J. (col'd) bootblack, 649 Merchant
Jacquot August, varnisher with Boyd, McAuliffe & Co. dwl 7 Dupont
Jacquot Constant, waiter, dwl 1323 Stockton
Jaffe Louis, agent Mount Diablo Coal Mining Co. and wood and coal, 133 Sutter, dwl 527 Post
Jaffe Patrick, laborer, Vulcan Iron Works, dwl 11 Baldwin Court
Jaffe Solomon & Co. *(H. Danziger)* pawnbroker, 341 Kearny, dwl Fourth bet Harrison and Bryant
Jageling Henry, porter with Crane & Brigham, dwl Central Place
Jagmette Siro, dwl 641 Pacific
Jagoe Mary Miss, domestic, 1405 Jones
Jahns Carl, contractor, dwl 21 Everett
Jahraus Jacob, cook, City and County Hospital
Jakman B. deck hand, stmr Julia
Jakowski Morris, tailor, dwl 112 St. Mark Place
Jakubowski Ignatz, salesman, 538 Clay
Jakubowski *(Louis)* & Warszaur *(Herman)* clothing, 342 Kearny and 538 Clay
Jallu François, bakery, 613 California
James J. dwl 153 Clara
JAMES CHARLES, collector and disbursing agent United States port San Francisco, office third floor Custom House, dwl Cosmopolitan Hotel
James Charles A. agent Eureka Patent Blasting Powder Co. office 327 Commercial
James David, blacksmith, dwl SW cor Kearny and Pacific
James E. wagon maker, 415 Third
James Ellen (widow) nurse, dwl 8 Central Place
JAMES GEORGE F. attorney at law, office 624 Merchant, dwl 511 Howard
James George H. C. bar tender, Olympia Saloon, bds Coso House
James J. dwl 153 Clara
James James, dwl U. S. Court Building, SW cor Montgomery and Jackson

James John, stair builder, dwl 763 Mission
James Joseph L. broker, dwl 557 Mission
James Samuel, lodgings, 538 Commercial
James Wallace T. butcher, 317 Fifth, dwl 319 Fifth
James Thomas, carpenter, dwl 15 Geary
James William *(Meeker, James. & Co.)* resides Newark, N. J
James William S. cook, dwl 711 Lombard
Jameson Charles, pyrotechnist, dwl 145 Fourth
Jameson Henry A. blacksmith with Benjamin A. Fisher, 115 Bush
Jameson Horace D. harness maker, S s Brannan bet Seventh and Eighth
Jameson John, waiter, dwl 558 Howard
Jameson Mary (widow) domestic, 1817 Stockton
Jamieson James R. clerk with Riley & Vest, dwl 558 Howard
Jamison John, job wagon, NW cor Pine and Montgomery, dwl W s Carlo nr Powell
Jamison John, lamplighter, S. F. Gas Co. dwl 60 Clay
Jamison Percival, tinsmith, dwl 1114 Leavenworth
Janes Eunice L. (widow) dwl 513 Minna
Janes Henry B. attorney at law, office 622 Clay, dwl 511 Minna
Janes J. C. driver, Omnibus R. R. Co. dwl 513 Minna
Janes Joseph L. broker, dwl 513 Minna
Janes, see Jaynes
Janin Albert C. student with S. L. Johnson, dwl 824 Washington
JANIN HENRY, mining engineer, office NE cor Montgomery and Jackson, dwl Occidental Hotel
Janin Louis B. jr. mineralogist. dwl 85 Mont Block
Janke Charles A. proprietor Turn Verein Hall, N s Bush bet Stockton and Powell
Janney Theodore, shoe maker with J. R. Hughes, dwl 414 Market
Jansen Auguste W. silversmith, 810 Montgomery
Jansen Christian, barber, dwl 619 Pacific
Jansen Henry, boatman, dwl 1816 Powell
Jansen Herman, cook, 416 Kearny
Jansen H. P. miner, dwl 1819 Powell
Jansen Romberg, silver plater, dwl 4 St. Mark Place
Janson Charles J. merchant, office 210 Pine, dwl cor Valencia and Twentieth
Janson Mary Mrs. millinery, 240 Third
Janson William, dwl 240 Third
Jantzen Eliza (widow) laundry, 615 California
Janus William, liquor saloon, S s Sixteenth near Dolores
Jauvin George M. with James Brokaw, dwl First St. House
Jaquelin Emil H. clerk, dwl 745 Clay
Jaques Campin, with Arguelas Bernal
Jaques S. P. bathman, Original House
Jaquillard Theobald, machinist with Kittredge &. Leavitt, dwl S s Stevenson bet Seventh and Eighth
Jaquith William K. stevedore, dwl S s Greenwich bet Montgomery and Sansom
Jaquot Augustus, varnisher, dwl 7 Dupont
Jarboe John R. *(Spencer & J.)* attorney at law, office 24 Court Block 636 Clay, dwl 706 Taylor
Jardon Mary (widow) laundry, dwl 922 Stockton
Jarpa Michael, fruits, NE cor Vallejo and Powell
Jarrett Thomas, shoe maker, dwl N s Oregon near Front
Jarvis Charles, expressman, dwl 414 Market
Jarvis Charles H. bailiff U. S. Courts, dwl U. S. Court Building
Jasephi R. watch maker with M. M. Baldwin & Co. 311 Montgomery
Jasper Gustave B. shoe maker with Francis Worth, dwl SE cor Fifth and Jessie
Jaszynsky Louis, broker, 612 Merchant, dwl NW cor Stockton and Pacific
Jaudin E. & Co. *(G. Kennedy)* dealers California wines and liquors, 523 Front, dwl 1130 Pine

Jandin Ulysse, clerk, French Savings and Loan So-
ciety, 533 Commercial, dwl 1130 Pine
Jaurez Maria I. Miss, dwl W s Duncan Court
Jay David, blacksmith with H. Casebolt & Co. res
San Antonio
Jaynes George, carman, dwl 24 Hunt
Jaynes W. carpenter, dwl 638 Howard
Jean Furcat, butcher with Bacca & Co. dwl Potre-
ro Avenue
Jeandre François, tailor, dwl 528 Vallejo
Jeanean Pierre, butcher Miners' Restauran
Jeannin August, shoe maker, 229 Bush
Jeantrout Pierre, dwl 257 Jessie
Jee Arthur W. commission mcht, office 523 Front
Jeffers Adam W. carpenter, dwl 17 Fourth
Jeffers John, drayman with David Hays & Co. 224
Sacramento
Jeffers M. S. salesman, 135 Montgomery, dwl NE
cor Jones and Turk
Jeffers Robert, laborer, dwl E s Main nr Market
Jefferson G. & S. M. Co. office 402 Front
Jefferson James, laborer with William Kerr, dwl
903 Battery
Jefferson Park Homestead Association, office 302
Montgomery
Jefferson Thomas, compositor, Golden Era, dwl
1013 Pacific
Jeffress John T. workman, S. F. & P. Sugar Co.
dwl E s Howard bet Eighteenth and Nineteenth
Jeffress Thomas W. salesman, dwl W s Howard bet
Eighteenth and Nineteenth
Jeffrey Oil Mining Co. office 528 Clay
Jefts James M. dealer limes, office 419 Washington,
dwl 761 Howard
Jefts Susan (widow) dwl SE cor Greenwich and
Leavenworth
Jeghers A. J. court room clerk Probate Court, dwl
NE cor Powell and Ellis
Jebu Nathaniel L. policeman, City Hall, dwl 275
Jessie
JELLINEK ALBERT, wood and ivory turner, 14
California, bds Ennen House
Jellings Edward (Driscoll & J.) dwl 63 Tehama
Jellings William, with Driscoll & Jellings, dwl 63
Tehama
Jelmini Horace, piano maker with Woodworth &
Schell, dwl Clay Avenue
Jenet Andres, tailor, dwl 636 Pacific
Jenkins A. Mme. millinery, 1130 Dupont
Jenkins Benjamin P. milk ranch, N s Presidio Road
nr Scott
Jenkins Charles, first assistant engineer stm Sierra
Nevada, office SW cor Front and Jackson
Jenkins E. W. Central American Transit Office, dwl
Occidental Hotel
Jenkins Ignatius S. broker, 723 Montgomery, dwl
724 Green
Jenkins John C. second lieut. Co. G, Second Infan-
try C. V. Presidio
Jenkins Mary (widow) dwl 31 Perry
Jenkins Nelson, machinist, Union Foundry
Jenkins Rees, tinsmith, dwl 268 Jessie
Jenkins Reuben F. wood dealer, dwl 30 Moss
Jenkins Samuel J. laborer, dwl NE cor Sacramento
and Drumm
Jenkins Thomas, marble cutter with Hayes &
Pritchard, dwl 8 Virginia
Jenkins William, waiter, dwl 129 St. Mark Place
Jenkins William J. machinist, Union Foundry, dwl
1307 Taylor
Jenkins William L. Vigilant Engine Co
Jenner W. A. dwl 45 Jane
Jenney Enoch S. painter, dwl Bailey House
Jennings Augustus A. produce, dwl 235 Stevenson
Jennings Charles B. (Fordham & J.) dwl 1210
Mason
Jennings David A. secretary Imperial S. M. Co.
office 708 Montgomery, dwl 1210 Mason
Jennings Elisha E. tailor, dwl 535 Green

Jennings Frederick A. painter, dwl 3 Martha Pl
Jennings Isaac, groceries, NW corner Polk and
Austin
Jennings James H. salesman, 402 Sansom, dwl 425
O'Farrell
Jennings John, book keeper, Cunningham's Ware-
house, dwl NE cor Chestnut and Dupont
Jennings John T. dwl 549 Bryant
JENNINGS (Oliver B.) & BREWSTER (Benja-
min) importers and wholesale clothing, 222 and
224 Battery, res New York
Jennings Patrick, waiter, steamer Yosemite
Jennings Peter, farmer, nr Laguna Honda
Jennings T. H. plasterer, dwl 633 Market
Jennings Thomas, plasterer, dwl 336 Bush
JENNINGS THOMAS, wholesale grocer, 402 San-
som, dwl 225 O'Farrell
Jennings W. A. book keeper with R. B. Fordham,
dwl 1210 Mason
Jennings William, tailor, 404 Folsom
Jennings William M. stair builder with N. P. Lang-
land, dwl Tehama bet Fifth and Sixth
Jennison George, cabinet maker with Ackley &
Bergstrom, dwl 116 Sansom
Jenny Maria (widow) dwl 17 Stockton Place
Jensen Asmus, gardener, dwl S s Day bet Guerrero
and Dolores
Jensen Charles, seaman, bds 7 Washington
Jensen Charles H. boarding, 32 Rousch
Jensen (Fritz) & Harnkin (S. H.) groceries and
liquors, NW cor Francisco and Midway, dwl
S s Francisco bet Dupont and Stockton
Jensen P. clerk, SE cor Bryant and Rincon Place
Jensen T. C. cooperage, 154 Second, dwl 150 Second
Jenzen Christ, hairdressing saloon, 633 Pacific
Jeremias G. & Co. (James Joseph) fancy goods,
207 Battery, dwl 257 Mission
Jerkowski Samuel, clerk, 220 California
Jernegan William L. foreman Daily Examiner, dwl
218 Minna
Jerome Edward B. delivery clerk, Post Office, dwl
1114 Kearny
Jerome Frederick, mariner, dwl 1600 Mason
Jerome Theodore, hostler, A. R. C. Ice Co. dwl W s
Battery nr Vallejo
Jerome Theodore F. accountant, dwl 1114 Kearny
Jerome W. S. job wagon, 37 Commercial
Jess Wm. F. millwright, dwl 181 Jessie
Jesse George R. stair builder with N. P. Langland,
dwl 411 Dupont
Jessen Paul, porter, 409 Clay, dwl Lutgen's Hotel
Jessett Sarah (widow) boarding, 286 Stevenson
Jessop John, carpenter, dwl E s Nevada nr Folsom
Jessop John W. dwl 744 Howard
Jessup Andrew J. foreman with Marden & Folger,
dwl 1510 Leavenworth
Jessup Austin, hides and wool, dwl 740 Folsom
JESSUP WM. H. & CO. Eureka Match Factory,
NW cor Harrison and Nevada, dwl SE cor
Folsom and Twelfth
Jester William D. laborer, dwl Beale Place
Jesto Francis, hostler with J. G. Scovern, dwl W s
Taylor bet Post and Sutter
Jesus Louis, brick molder with B. Bonnet & Co
Jete Joseph, laborer with B. Bonnet & Co
Jewell George H. engineer, dwl 202 Second
Jewell Stephen P. oil refiner, dwl 506 Brannan
Jewett G. & S. M. Co. (Gold Hill) office 509 Clay
Jewett James C. driver, North Beach & M. R. R.
Co. dwl 532 Commercial
Jewett Jarvis, agent Palmer's Artificial Leg, 629
Washington, dwl 522 Pine
Jewett Lizzie B. Miss, assistant, Lincoln School,
dwl 20 Stanford
Jewett Miles, with F. Smith & Co. 210 Sacramento
dwl 117 Mason
Jewett Stephen, carpenter, dwl 20 Stanford
Jewett Thomas M. clerk with Lake & Morrison,
dwl 1315 Kearny

Jewett William S. portrait painter, 612 Clay, dwl 507 Stockton
Jillard Marcella (widow) boarding and lodging, 111 Washington
Jillson D. C. carpenter with James Brokaw, dwl 684 Market
Jinati Albert, with R. F. Rocchicoli, 523 California
Joachim Torres, painter, dwl Gautier House 516 Pac
Joaquin Manuel, farmer, Old Ocean House Road, 6 miles from City Hall
Job Frederick, miner, dwl 323 Pine
Job Peter, restaurant and ice cream saloon, SW cor Bush and Montgomery, dwl 518 Bush
Jobson Charles F. *(J. J. Ayers & Co.)* dwl 726 Broadway
Jobson David, real estate, dwl 1010 Montgomery
Joe Lane G. & S. M. Co. office 402 Front
Joel Albert M. book keeper, 218 Battery, dwl 1618 Powell
Jolli William, laborer dwl SE cor Laguna and McAllister
Johanie M. handcartman, Market nr Sansom
Johannson Martin, carpenter, dwl 619 Pacific
John Som Chung (Chinese) washing, 535 Pacific
Johns Edward, refiner, Kellogg, Hewston & Co.'s Refinery, dwl 7 Bagley Place
Johns Owen, seaman, steamer Orizaba
Johns T. Lanyon, editor Puck, office 617 Clay, dwl 180 Minna
Johnson Aaron, mining secretary, off and dwl 625 Clay
Johnson Abraham, proprietor Coasters' House, 117 Sacramento
Johnson Adam, deck hand, steamer Clinton
Johnson Adam, stevedore, dwl 10 Stewart
Johnson Albert, miner, dwl 558 Bryant
Johnson Alfred, jeweler with Lemme Bros. dwl 39 Second
Johnson Andrew, drayman with David McKay, dwl 1012 Leavenworth
Johnson Andrew, porter, NW cor Merch and East
Johnson A. P. photographic gallery, 649 Clay
Johnson Asahel C. dwl 172 Silver
Johnson Augustus, cook, 619 Market
Johnson Brock, clerk, dwl 152 Minna
Johnson C. A. attorney at law, office SE cor Montgomery and Sacramento, dwl 461 Clementina
Johnson Catharine Mrs. (col'd) stewardess, dwl 911 Sacramento
Johnson Charles, captain Brig Hidalgo, office Pier 10 Stewart, dwl 238 Stewart
Johnson Charles, carpenter, dwl 411 Post
Johnson Charles, laborer, Bay View
Johnson Charles, laborer, dwl 140 Stewart
Johnson Charles, laborer, dwl E s Leavenworth bet Broadway and Vallejo
Johnson Charles, seaman, dwl 44 Sacramento
Johnson Charles, seaman, bds 7 Washington
Johnson Charles, stevedore, dwl W s Buchanan bet O'Farrell and Geary
JOHNSON CHARLES E. boarding, SW cor Third and Market
Johnson Charles E. book keeper with Rockwell, Coye & Co. dwl 204 Montgomery
Johnson Charles G. jr. printer with Calhoun & Son, dwl 36 Louisa
Johnson Charles S. student at law with S. L. Johnson, dwl 932 Clay
Johnson Christian, cabinet making, 213 Kearny
Johnson Daniel, molder, Pacific Foundry, dwl 1127 Kearny
Johnson *(E. A.)* & Peterson *(Ludwig)* liquors and coffee, 531 East
Johnson Eben, milk ranch, S s Presidio Road nr Devisidero
Johnson Edgar C. clerk, dwl 522 Dupont
Johnson Edward, carpenter, dwl 541 Mission
Johnson Edward, employé, dwl 122 Commercial
Johnson Edward, express wagon, dwl cor Scott and Filbert

Johnson Edward C. bag maker, NE cor Jackson and Battery
Johnson Edwin H. *(Blewitt & J.)* dwl 348 Third
Johnson Eli, cooper, S. F. & P. Sugar Co. dwl 31 Moss
Johnson Elihu, attorney at law, dwl 204 Stockton
Johnson Elizabeth (widow) dwl W s Scotland nr Filbert
Johnson Evan, shoe making, 50 Sacramento
Johnson Frank, merchant dwl 868 Mission
Johnson Frederick, dwl 403 California
Johnson Frederick, crockery and glass ware, 231 Kearny and 109 Second, dwl N s O'Farrell bet Dupont and Stockton
Johnson Frederick, laborer, dwl NE cor Pacific and Front
JOHNSON GEORGE C. & CO. *(G. W. Gibbs and Robert C. Johnson)* importers iron and steel and consul for Sweden and Norway, 33 Battery
Johnson George (col'd) porter, dwl 605 Clay
Johnson George, rigger, dwl 258 Folsom
Johnson George, sailor, dwl 551 Folsom
Johnson George H. photographer, dwl 645 Clay
Johnson G. O. oyster stand Terminus Saloon, NW cor Powell and Francisco
Johnson G. S. *(Alstrom & J.)* dwl Lick House
Johnson Gustave, seaman, dwl 44 Sacramento
Johnson G. W. dwl 317 Fifth
Johnson Hans J. sail maker, W s Drumm nr Wash
JOHNSON *(Henry)* & BRANDON *(Morris)* groceries and liquors, NW cor Jones and Pacific
Johnson *(Henry)* & McCann *(Peter)* wholesale butchers and drovers, NW cor Brannan and Ninth
Johnson Henry, teacher dancing, dwl 407 Dupont
Johnson Henry, seaman, dwl 44 Sacramento
Johnson Henry, seaman, dwl 117 Sacramento
Johnson Henry, special detective, dwl 1809 Dupont
Johnson Henry B. salesman with Rowland, Walker & Co. dwl 1414 Stockton
Johnson Henry F. watch maker, dwl 39 Second
Johnson Henry W. cook, 30 Clay
Johnson Charles E. dwl SW cor Market and Third
Johnson Mary (widow) domestic, NW cor Stockton
Johnson Niels G. *(Fallmer & Co.)* SW cor Louisiana and Sierra, Potrero Nuevo
Johnson Thomas, club rooms, dwl 616 Sacramento
Johnson Isabella Miss, domestic, 11 O'Farrell
Johnson Jacob, laundryman, Bay City Laundry, 1140 and 1142 Folsom
Johnson James, boot maker, 23 Fourth, dwelling 2 O'Farrell
Johnson James, express wagon, cor Wash and Bat
Johnson James, fruit, W s Fifth nr Folsom
Johnson James, molder, Pacific Foundry, dwl SW cor Kearny and Vallejo
Johnson James (col'd) porter, 712 Montgomery, dwl 918 Washington
Johnson James, shoe maker, dwl 4 Dupont
Johnson James W. dwl 625 Clay
Johnson Jane Miss (col'd) dwl 516 Pine
Johnson Jane Miss, domestic, 1803 Stockton
Johnson Jane Miss, domestic with Samuel Cowles, 8 s Erie nr Mission
JOHNSON J. B. hat and bonnet block, wind mills, manufacturer, etc. NE cor Fremont and Mission, dwl 24 Rousch
JOHNSON J. C. & CO. *(John M. Johnson)* importers and manufacturers saddles and harness, 520 and 522 Sansom
Johnson J. E. express wagon, Folsom nr Willows' Park
Johnson J. E. Neptune Baths and Boarding House, NW cor Larkin and Beach
Johnson J. E. Mrs. boarding, SW cor Market and Third
Johnson Jeremiah, fruits, NW cor Washington and Battery, dwl cor Franklin and McAllister

Johnson Jeremiah, porter with Meeker, James & Co. 14 Pine

Johnson J. H. manufacturer ale and porter, dwl 1610 Stockton

Johnson John, broker, office 436 Jackson, res Oakland

Johnson John Capt. room 41 Government House

Johnson John, boarding, cor Sierra and Georgia

Johnson John, compositor, Golden Era, dwelling 17 Fourth

Johnson John, cook, dwl 105 Washington

Johnson John, cook, 30 Clay

Johnson John, cook, steamer Pacific

Johnson John, handcartman, cor Davis and Wash

Johnson John, laborer, dwl 60 Stewart   •

Johnson John, longshoreman, dwl 636 Commercial

Johnson John, painter with Hopps & Kanary

Johnson John, proprietor Scandinavian House, 39 and 41 Jackson

Johnson John, real estate, office 625 Clay

Johnson John, shoe maker, 40 Sutter

Johnson John F. proprietor Brunswick House, 759 and 761 Mission

Johnson John H. carpenter, dwl W s Hyde bet Union and Filbert

Johnson John M. (J. C. Johnson & Co.) dwl 1214 Sansom

Johnson John P. steward, dwl 404 Union

Johnson John R. blacksmith with Kimball & Co. dwl 522 Dupont

Johnson John S. (col'd) whitewashing, 778 Mission

Johnson John W. cabinet maker, dwl Bailey House

Johnson John Z. ship joiner, dwl 640 Second

Johnson Joseph F. carpenter, dwl W s Valencia bet Temple and Navy

JOHNSON JOSEPH M. coal dealer and agent Pittsburg Coal Mining Co. 215 and 217 Jackson and Oregon opposite C. H. dwl 19 Rousch

Johnson Joshua E. contractor and builder, dwl E s Folsom bet Twenty-First and Twenty-Second

Johnson Josiah G. butcher, NW cor Brannan and Ninth, dwl E s Ninth bet Bryant and Brannan

Johnson J. Sproat, dwl American Exchange

Johnson Leander B. paper hanger with C. W. Clark, dwl 21 Stevenson

Johnson Louis, seaman, bds 7 Washington

Johnson Margaret (widow) dwl 417 Filbert

Johnson Mary Mrs. dwl 4 Hardie Place

Johnson Michael, laborer, dwl W s Battery bet Vallejo and Green

Johnson Miles, cabinet maker, dwl NE cor Filbert and Polk

Johnson Nelson G. (Follmer & Co.) dwl cor Louisiana and Sierra

Johnson Nicolay T. artist, 429 Montgomery, dwl Cosmopolitan Hotel ●

Johnson N. P. tailor, dwl S s Jackson nr East

Johnson Olivia B. (widow) boarding, NW cor Tenth and Bryant

Johnson Olof, mariner, dwl Stewart nr Folsom

Johnson Oscar E. book keeper with Stone & Hayden, dwl 719 California •

Johnson Perry C. mariner, dwl W s Seventh bet Folsom and Harrison

Johnson (Peter) & Holje (John B.) billiard and liquor saloon, 28 Clay

Johnson Peter, dwl N s Filbert bet Leavenworth and Hyde

Johnson Peter, dwl Serpentine Avenue nr San Bruno Road

Johnson Peter, cooper with Cutting & Co. dwl N s Bryant bet Fifth and Sixth

Johnson Peter, gardener with L. R. Mills, junction Old San José Road and San José Railroad

Johnson Peter, nurse, U. S. Marine Hospital

Johnson Peter, seaman, dwl 44 Sacramento ∶

Johnson P. R. painter, dwl 124 Dora

Johnson R. C. bar keeper, dwl 532 Commercial

Johnson Richard, baker, dwl Roxbury House 318 Pacific

Johnson Richard, waiter, 626 Kearny

Johnson Richard E. cooper, S. F. & P. Sugar Co. dwl 31 Moss

Johnson Richard M. liquor saloon, 614 Montgomery, dwl Railroad House

Johnson Richard T. engineer, 719 Battery

Johnson R. M. (Marshall & J.) dwl E s Montgomery bet Broadway and Pacific

Johnson Robert, glass engraver, dwl W s Buchanan bet Eddy and Ellis

Johnson Robert C. (Geo. C. Johnson & Co.) dwl cor Folsom and Essex

Johnson Robert F. painter, dwl 12 St. Mary   •

Johnson R. P. dwl Brenham Place W s Plaza

Johnson S. captain schr Sine Johnson, office 413 East, dwl 133 Frederick

Johnson Samuel, contractor night work, 33 Geary

Johnson Samuel, second cook steamer Pacific

Johnson Samuel L. mason, dwl 28 Sansom

JOHNSON SIDNEY L. attorney at law, office 523 Montgomery, dwl 932 Clay

Johnson Silas W. (Cameron, Whittier, & Co.) bds 117 Second

Johnson Sophia (widow) dwl with Josiah G. Johnson E s Ninth bet Bryant and Brannan

Johnson Theophilus, carpenter, dwl S s Austin bet Polk and Van Ness Avenue   •

Johnson Thomas, carpenter, dwl N s Jackson bet Larkin and Polk

Johnson Thomas C. butcher, dwl 4 Dupont

Johnson Thomas J. club room and dwl 534 Kearny

Johnson Thomas J. P. printer with Charles F. Robbins, dwl 417 Filbert

JOHNSON T. RODGERS, manufacturer regalia and military goods, 325 Montgomery and grand secretary Grand Lodge I. O. O. F. office room 1 Odd Fellows' Hall, dwl NW cor Polk and Grove

Johnson Walter J. carrier, Bulletin and Call, dwl S s Filbert bet Leavenworth and Hyde

Johnson William, with Samuel Johnson, 33 Geary

Johnson William, hostler, Willows, SW cor Mission and Eighteenth

Johnson William, laborer, Atlas Foundry, dwl 24 Natoma Place

Johnson William, laborer, dwl W s Guerrero bet Fifteenth and Sixteenth

Johnson William, seaman, dwl 44 Sacramento

JOHNSON WILLIAM C. assistant assessor, U. S. Internal Revenue, NW cor Battery and Commercial, dwl 3 Central Place

Johnson William H. carpenter, dwl NW cor Folsom and Twenty-Second

Johnson William H. carrier, Alta and Call, dwl N s Filbert bet Leavenworth and Hyde

Johnson William M. carpenter, dwl SW cor Franklin and Hayes, Hayes' Valley

Johnson W. S. salesman with Edward Hall & Co. dwl 506 Dupont

Johnson W. T. miner, dwl 10 Stockton Place   '

Johnston Ann Mrs. ladies' nurse, dwl S s Natoma nr Seventh

Johnston Charles G. boot and shoe maker, dwl 36 Louisa

Johnston E. G. (widow) dwl 24 Mary

Johnston George Pen attorney at law, dwl U. S. Court Building, SW cor Mont and Jackson

Johnston Henry J. sup't Oregon and Crescent City S. S. Line, office SW cor Front and Jackson, dwl 332 Brannan

Johnston (James) & Reay (Alfred W.) stoves and tinware, 319 California, dwl 251 Jessie

Johnston James, waiter, dwl 64 Natoma

Johnston James S. capitalist, office 712 Montgomery, res Oakland

Johnston James W. photographer, dwl S s Natoma nr Seventh

Johnston Jeremiah, express wagon, dwl NW cor McAlister and Franklin
Johnston *(John)* & Co. lumber dealers, 39 Market, dwl 932 Bush
Johnston John, clerk, dwl What Cheer House
Johnston Joseph F. carpenter, dwl W s Valencia bet Twenty-Fifth and Twenty-Sixth
Johnston S. M. clerk, Metropolitan Theater, dwl West End Hotel
Johnston Thomas, carpenter, dwl Morse nr Pine
Johnston Thomas J. architect, Shiels' Block room 2
Johnston William, stone cutter, dwl Summer St. H
JOHNSTON WILLIAM B. agent Liverpool, London & Globe Insurance Co. office 414 Montgomery, up stairs, dwl 338 Second
Johnstow William H. boot maker, 306 Third
JOICE E. V. notary public, office NE cor Battery and Washington, dwl 807 Stockton
Joice Frank, with Samuel Johnson, 33 Geary
Joice John, deck hand, steamer Yosemite
Joice, see Joyce
Joinct Victor, machine shop, 520 Clay, dwl 520 Merchant
Joiner John J. engraver, 648 Sacramento, dwl N s Seventeenth nr Dolores
Jokel Conrad, cabinet maker with W. G. Weir, dwl 336 Bush
Jolliet August, waiter, Union Club Rooms
Jolliffe William H. pilot, 805 Front, dwl 311 Union
Jolly Kate Miss, domestic, 517 Post
Jolly Mary, domestic, 716 Mission
Jonas Alfred, waiter, Magnolia Restaurant, 149 Third
Jonas Bernard, tailor, 337 Kearny
Jonas Emanuel, butcher with L. Miller & Co. dwl 119 Pacific
Jonas Isaac A. watch maker, dwl 119 Pacific
Jonas Nathan, waiter, steamer Yosemite
Jonassen Meyer *(Meyer & J.)* dwl 3 Eddy Place
JONES & BENDIXEN *(Thomas J. Poulterer, Wm. M. Rundell, and Henry C. Downing)* auctioneers and commission merchants, 207 and 209 California
Jones Ann, Miss, domestic, 508 Taylor
Jones Catherine (widow) dwl SW cor Folsom and Spear
Jones C. F. box maker with J. S. Gibbs, dwl 116 Stewart
Jones Charles, saddlery, 741 Folsom, dwl N s Clementina bet Fifth and Sixth
Jones Charles C. merchandise broker, office 323 Front, dwl 330 Stockton
Jones Charles F. Capt. dwl 14 Quincy
Jones Charles J. trimmer with E. Galpen & Co. dwl 38 Clementina
Jones Claude, dwl 1314 Dupont
Jones C. W. *(Pease & Grimm)* office 709 Mont
Jones *(Cyrus G.)* & Starr *(E. S)* mil coalers, 429 Third, dwl 217 Third
Jones Daniel, dwl 319 Ritch
Jones Daniel, carpenter, 208 Wash, dwl 31 Clara
JONES, *(David)* WOOLL *(John)* & SUTHERLAND *(Edwin)* gilders, picture frame makers, and artists' materials, 312 Montgomery
Jones David, real estate, dwl 18 First
Jones David, seaman, dwl 54 Sacramento
Jones E. A. (col'd) porter, 314 Montgomery
Jones Edward, attorney at law, dwl 827 Howard
Jones Edward, seaman, dwl 423 East
Jones E. E. clerk with Moses Ellis & Co. dwl 1310 Kearny
JONES *(Elias H.)* DIXON *(John)* & CO. *(Jas. Pullman and Chas. Newton)* importers and jobbers millinery and fancy goods, NE cor Sacramento and Sansom, res Oakland
Jones Emma Mrs. housekeeper with Sam'l Bigelow, NW cor Steiner and McAllister
Jones Evan E. clerk with Weaver, Wooster & Co. dwl 1310 Kearny

Jones Frank (cook) Mission Dolores Church
Jones Franklin L. painter and paper hanger and president S. F. Fire Department, 604 Jackson
Jones Frederick, watchman, Mission Woolen Mills
Jones Frederick Eugene, with George B. Hitchcock & Co. dwl American Exchange
Jones Frederick W. machinist, Miners' Foundry, dwl 128 Fourth
Jones George, machinist, Vulcan Iron Works, dwl 1317 Stockton
Jones George M. express wagon, 31 Clara
Jones George P. tinsmith with J. G. Ils
Jones George W. wheelwright; dwl S s Lombard bet Taylor and Jones
Jones Georgiana, stewardess, steamer Pacific
Jones Hannah, cook, Wright's Hotel
Jones Harrison, saddle and harness maker, 437 Kearny, dwl N s Austin bet Polk and Van Ness Avenue
Jones Henry, dwl 504 Howard
Jones Henry, seaman, dwl 118 Harrison
Jones Henry B. teacher University School, dwl SE cor Stockton and Filbert
Jones Henry W. *(F. C. Adriance & Co.)* dwl NW cor Powell and Union
Jones Henry W. book keeper with E. Bosqui, dwl 1715 Leavenworth
Jones Hezekiah, dwl 34 Everett
Jones Hugh, longshoreman, dwl Wright's Hotel, 210 Broadway
Jones Isaac, dwl SE cor Mission and First
Jones Isaac Watt, fruit, 205 Fourth
Jones James, laborer, dwl S s Riley nr Taylor
Jones James, porter with Cobb & Sinton, 406 Mont
Jones James Jay, carpenter and builder, dwl 1116 Kearny
Jones James S. engineer, dwl Front nr Pine
Jones Jane Miss, teacher, dwl 664 Howard
Jones J. H. mining secretary, dwl Occidental Hotel
Jones J. L. dwl International Hotel
Jones J. L. with J. R. Mead & Co. dwl 29 Frank's Building
Jones John, dwl 319 Minna
Jones John, laborer, What Cheer House Restaurant
Jones John, laborer, S. F. & San José R. R. Co. dwl NW cor Townsend and Third
Jones John, real estate agent, dwl 245 Stevenson
Jones John, shoe maker, dwl 414 Stevenson
Jones John, waiter, steamer Cornelia
Jones John C. carriagesmith, dwl NE cor Fifth and Stevenson
Jones John D. laborer, dwl 26 Stewart
Jones John J. boot maker, NW cor Pacific and Sansom, dwl N s Stevenson bet Fifth and Sixth
Jones John P. delivery clerk, S. F. & San José R. R. Co. dwl 35 Freelon
Jones John S. laborer, dwl Minna Place
Jones John T. broom maker, dwl What Cheer House
Jones John T. stevedore, dwl 116 Jackson
Jones John W. machinist, Miners' Foundry
Jones John W. salesman with Ackerman Bros. dwl 1209 Taylor
Jones Joseph, bricklayer, dwl 129 Perry
Jones Joseph D. mason, dwl 260 Clementina
Jones Joseph H. commission merchant, office 708 Montgomery, dwl 834 Clay
JONES J. T. & CO. *(Charles J. Willey)* Jones' Sample Rooms, SE cor Montgomery and California
Jones J. W. jeweler with J. M. Seamans
Jones Kate A. (widow) lodgings, dwl 53 Clementina
Jones Mary (widow) boarding, 120 Fourth
Jones M. C. metal roofer with H. G. & E. S. Fiske, dwl Wisconsin House
JONES *(M. P.)* & CO. wholesale groceries and provisions, 205 and 207 Front, dwl 626 Harrison
Jones Nathan, cooper with Handy & Newman, dwl N s Clay bet Davis and Drumm

Jones N. B. bar keeper, NW cor Sac and East
Jones Orrin, dwl 20 Minna
Jones Owen, mariner, dwl 32 Stewart
Jones Patrick, calker, dwl 313 Eddy
Jones Patrick H. calker, dwl Turk nr Taylor
Jones Paul, helper, dwl N s Natoma nr Second
Jones Rebecca Mrs. (col'd) dwl 1409 Mason
Jones Robert, seaman, dwl 44 Sacramento
Jones Robert H. carpenter, dwl 241 Minna
Jones Samuel, express wagon, 815 Battery
Jones Samuel, mariner, dwl 32 Stewart
Jones Samuel D. ex-deputy naval officer, office 26
  Exchange Building, dwl 213 Geary
Jones Samuel Duffield, book keeper, 408 Battery,
  dwl 1314 Washington
Jones Samuel H. dwl 213 Geary
Jones Samuel H. delivery clerk, P.O. dwl 614 Mission
Jones Seneca, pattern maker, Miners' Foundry, dwl
  8 Garden
Jones Simon, tanner and currier, S s Precita Avenue
  nr Bernal
Jones Simon, driver with George Hughes, dwl 325
  Sixth
Jones Thomas, carpenter, dwl 110 Shipley
Jones Thomas, carpenter, dwl 76 Natoma
Jones Thomas, carpenter, N s California nr Mason
Jones Thomas, hostler, Ocean House
Jones Thomas, laborer, dwl 152 Stewart
Jones Thomas A. painter, dwl Scotland nr Taylor
Jones Thomas E. clerk, What Cheer House Restaurant
Jones Thomas J. broker, 728 Montgomery, dwl 421
  Stevenson
Jones Thomas J. clerk, dwl 626 Commerial
Jones Thomas W. carpenter, dwl NW cor Nineteenth and Howard
Jones Warren, clerk, dwl 12 Third
Jones Warren, confectioner, 77 Fourth
Jones W. H. oysterman, dwl Hayes' Valley
Jones William, with Horace Porter, dwl cor Scott
  and Tyler
Jones William, engineer, dwl cor Clay and Brenham Place
Jones William, groceries and liquors, NE cor Fourth
  and Silver
Jones William, laborer, dwl W s Sansom bet Green
  and Vallejo
Jones William, sail maker, dwl 116 Jackson
JONES WILLIAM CAREY, attorney at law, office 20 Exchange Building, dwl SW cor Geary
  and Broderick
Jones William G. manufacturer resin and turpentine, depôt 221 Sacramento, dwl 550 Mission
Jones William H. broker, dwl 627 Commercial
Jones William L. miner, dwl 245 Stevenson
Jones Winfield S. clerk, Fund Commissioners, 505
  Montgomery, dwl 824 Washington
Jones W. Jones, bds 1209 Taylor
Jones W. S. engineer, dwl Portsmouth House
Joost Behrend (Joost Brothers) dwl NE cor Mission and Eleventh
JOOST BROTHERS (Tonjes, Fabian and Behrend) groceries and liquors, NE cor Eleventh
  and Mission
Joost Constant, clerk with Plege & Hoffman, cor
  Post and Taylor
Joost Fabain (Joost Brothers) dwl NE cor Mission
  and Eleventh
Joost Hermann (Harms & J.) dwl 410 Clay
Joost John, clerk, SW cor Dupont and Union
Joost Marten, clerk, NE cor Eleventh and Mission
JORDAN ALBERT H. architect, office 402 Kearny cor Pine, res San Mateo
Jordan August, millinery, 1016 Stockton
Jordan Charles G. cooper, S. F. & P. Sugar Co.
  dwl E s Eighth nr Folsom
Jordan Daniel, contractor and builder, office NW
  cor Kearny and Geary
Jordan Dennis E. builder and mason, dwl 618 Ellis

Jordan Eben, mate steamer Sacramento
Jordan James, gardener with James Otis
Jordan John, cooper, S. F. &. P. Sugar Co. dwl cor
  Fourth and Harrison
Jordan John, express wagon, cor Mont and Filbert
Jordan John, jeweler, dwl Brenham Pl W s Plaza
Jordan John, upholsterer, NE cor Filbert and Mont
Jordan John F. teacher, St. Francis School, dwl 96
  Davis
Jordan Judith (widow) dwl 1809 Stockton
Jordan J. W. book keeper with C. Clayton & Co.
  dwl 322 Fifth
Jordan Leslie A. printer with J. F. Pynch & Co.
  dwl 10 Anthony
JORDAN L. J. physician and proprietor Pacific
  Museum, S s Pine bet Sansom and Montgomery,
  office and dwl 211 Geary
Jordan Michael, laborer, dwl S s Oregon bet Front
  and Davis
JORDAN MORRIS, watches, jewelry, etc. 625
  Montgomery, dwl 619 Montgomery
Jordan Nelson, wharfinger, S. F. & Oakland R. R.
  Wharf, dwl 26 Government House
Jordan Otto, clerk with Fred Iker, dwl 784 Folsom
Jordan William, dwl 63 Clementina
Jorgensen J. Edward, plumber, 28 Third, dwl 522
  Bryant
Jorres George, carpenter with William Jorres, dwl
  SW cor Dolores and Dorland
Jorres William, carpenter and builder, 525 Cal, dwl
  E s Thirteenth bet Howard and Mission
Jose Nathan T. stevedore, dwl 336 Main
Joseph Antonio, deck hand, steamer Cornelia
JOSEPH BROTHERS (Lionel B. and Josephus B.
  J.) importers and manufacturers watches, diamonds, silver ware, jewelry, etc. 607 Montgomery, dwl 4 Brenham Place
Joseph Charles, boots and shoes, 804 Kearny
Joseph Elizabeth Miss, domestic, 336 Fifth
Joseph Frank, deck hand, steamer Sacramento
Joseph H. dwl 634 Howard
Joseph Harry, laborer, dwl 313 Tehama
Joseph I. & Co. clothing, SW cor Montgomery and
  Pine, dwl 821 Post
Joseph (Isaac) & Co. (Lewis Joseph) dry goods,
  643 Clay, dwl 817 Post
Joseph Isaac, tailor, dwl NE cor Pacific and Front
Joseph James, (G. Jeremias & Co.) dwl 257 Mission
Joseph J. J. (Davega, Joseph & Labatt) 318 Pine
Joseph John, miner, Lafayette H. & L. Co. No. 2
Joseph John, waiter, dwl 526 Merchant
Joseph Josephus B. (Joseph Bros.) 607 Montgomery
Joseph Lewis (Joseph & Co.) dwl 337 Tehama
Joseph Lizar, stock and exchange broker, dwl 1521
  Stockton
Joseph Michael J. (Inslee & J.) dwl 302 Mason
Joseph Peter, second steward steamer Cornelia
Joseph Peter H. (col'd) steward, steamer Cornelia
  dwl E s Jansen nr Lombard
Joseph S. N. Mrs. assistant, Stevenson St. School,
  dwl 545 Mission
Josephi David E. (Isaac S. Josephi & Co.) dwl
  1114 Stockton nr Jackson
Josephi Isaac S. & Co. (David E. Josephi) importers
  and jobbers watches, diamonds, etc. 641 Washington, dwl SE cor Mont and Sac room 7
Josephine M. Co. (Coso) office 404 Montgomery
Josephine Copper M. Co. office 1 Government House
  502 Washington
Josephs Mary (widow) dwl 16 Rassette Place No. 2
Joslin F. M. dwl What Cheer House
Jossand Benjamin, employé with Lyon & Co. dwl
  510 Jackson
Josse Eugene, meat market, 1318 Stockton
Josselyn Albert S. captain schooner Fairway, dwl
  1023 Washington
JOSSELYN BENJAMIN F. physician, (Dr. J. C.
  Young's Institute) 540 Washington, dwl 513
  Geary

JOSSELYN G. M. ship chandlery and stores, 34 and 36 Market, bds Russ House
Josselyn Henry, laborer, dwl 148 Silver, rear
Josselyn Henry C. carpenter, dwl Summer St. H
Josselyn J. B. carpenter, 152 Tehama, dwl 651 Howard
Josselyn Joel S. dwl 513 Geary
JOSSELYN JOSEPH H. Electropathic Institute and physician, office and dwl 645 Washington
Josselyn Lucy N. (widow) dwl 1314 Dupont
Josset J. French teacher, dwl 634 Vallejo
Jost Charles, merchant. dwl 807 Mission
Jost Edward, waiter, dwl 18 Sansom
Jourdan A. M. Miss, assistant, Eighth St. School, dwl N s Shipley nr Fifth
Jourdan John P. clerk with A. H. Titcomb, dwl N s Shipley nr Fifth
Jourdan William B. dwl N s Shipley bet Fifth and Sixth
Jourden Joseph T. driver, Central R. R. Co. dwl 63 Clementina
Journe John M. physician, dwl NW cor Sixth and Stevenson
Journet Adelaide Mme. furnished rooms, 120 Post
Joy Edwin F. clerk with Locke & Montague, dwl Codman Place nr Washington
Joy Hartford, keeper Alcatraz Light House
Joy Margaret Miss, domestic with H. L. Bunker, N s Mission nr Twelfth
Joy Reuben M. dwl 1030 Market
Joy Robert B. with Cyrus Arnold, 12 Metropolitan Market, dwl 1030 Market
Joyce John, cartman, Oregon bet Front and Davis
Joyce John, rigger and stevedore, dwl NW cor Green and Battery
Joyce John, waiter, steamer Senator
Joyce Mary Miss, domestic, 1111 Stockton
Joyce Mary Miss, domestic with T. N. Starr, S s Sixteenth bet Folsom and Howard
Joyce Mary Mrs. liquor saloon, S s Folsom bet Spear and Main
Joyce Mary (widow) dwl N s Oregon nr Front
Joyce Mathew, seaman, dwl S s Folsom bet Spear and Main
Joyce Michael, laborer, dwl W s Hyde, bet O'Farrell and Ellis
Joyce M. M. acting treasurer Academy of Music, dwl 765 Mission
Joyce Sarah (widow) dwl E s Nevada nr Folsom
Joyce Thomas, laborer, dwl N s Linden bet Gough and Octavia
Joyner William, dwl N s Ellis between Larkin and Post
Joyner William F. painter, dwl N s Ellis bet Larkin and Polk
Jozedeavilar *(Manuel)* & Alves *(Manuel)* boarding, 114 Jackson
Juan Seth, dwl 845 Dupont
Judah Charles D. attorney at law, dwl 657 Howard
Judah Edward D. driver, A. R. C. Ice Co. dwl Niantic Hotel
Judah Henry R. clerk with A. Roman & Co. dwl 657 Howard
Judd William B. ship carpenter with J. G. North, Potrero Nuevo
JUDGE COUNTY COURT, chambers 18 third floor City Hall
JUDGE DISTRICT (FOURTH) COURT, chambers third floor City Hall
JUDGE DISTRICT (TWELFTH) COURT, chambers third floor City Hall
JUDGE DISTRICT (FIFTEENTH) COURT, chambers 17 third floor City Hall
Judge Henry, harness maker with Main & Winchester, dwl 8 John
Judge Hillyer, dwl 26 O'Farrell
Judge Maria Miss, domestic, 919 Market
JUDGE POLICE COURT, rooms first floor City Hall

JUDGE PROBATE COURT, chambers 19 third floor City Hall
JUDGE UNITED STATES DISTRICT COURT, room 12 U. S. Court Building
JUDGE UNITED STATES (TENTH) CIRCUIT, chambers 1 and 2 U. S. Court Building
Judson Charles C. dwl W s Valencia bet Fourteenth and Fifteenth
JUDSON EGBERT, *(San Francisco Chemical Works Co.)* office 327 Commercial, dwl W s Valencia bet Fourteenth and Fifteenth
Judson Henry C. with S. F. Chemical Works, dwl W s Valencia bet Fourteenth and Fifteenth
Judson James, dwl W s Valencia bet Fourteenth and Fifteenth
Juglis John B. seaman. dwl 327 Bryant
Juguet *(Antoine)* & Perrin *(Pierre)* harness makers, 208 Kearny
Julian Philipe, compositor, 533 Commercial, dwl 22 Brooklyn Place
Julitz Herman, Berlin White Beer Brewery, 511 Green
Jullion John B. blacksmith, 421 Kearny, rear, dwl 105 St. Mark Place
Jump E. artist, 116 Montgomery Block, dwl 1425 Dupont
Jung J. W. clerk with Ziel, Bertheau & Co. dwl 1908 Powell
Jung William, hair dresser, 43 Second, dwl 25 Anthony
Jungcurt Theodore, apothecary, 1317 Dupont
Jungle Julius, waiter, 506 Montgomery
Jungman George, waiter, 417 Front
Junker August R. musician, dwl 1511½ Mason
Juntell August, seaman, dwl 20 Commercial
Jurgens Antonio, tobacco and cigars, 10 First
Jurgens Henry *(Urband & Co.)* dwl NW cor Howard and Fifteenth
Jurgensen Jurgen, seaman, bds 7 Washington
Jurga Peter, bar tender, 16 Stewart
Juri Pietro, milkman, dwl W s Scott nr Turk
Jursch Otto, cabinet maker with A. Conrad, dwl 525 Pine
Jury Jeremiah, with John Jury and Bro. dwl 524 Merchant
Jury John & Brother *(Louis Jury)* Helvetia Coffee Saloon, 524 Merchant
Jury Louis *(John Jury & Brother)* dwl 524 Merch
Jury Louis & Co. *(Antonio Moni)* dairymen, dwl N s Page ¼ mile W Protestant Orphan Asylum
Jusset Charles, laundry, 11 Virginia
Just Francis, job wagon, SE cor Montgomery and California, dwl Mason nr Sutter
Just Herman, bar keeper, dwl 200 Sutter
Juste Anthony, jeweler with John Uszynski, 406 Kearny
Justice Patterson C. drayman with N. P. Perrine, dwl SE cor Harrison and Fifth Avenue

K

KABBE August, driver, 115 Jessie
Kabler Mary (widow) dwl 1 Bagley Place
Kadien Patrick, plasterer, dwl 3 Margaret Place
Kaeb J. A. meat market, NW cor Union and Montgomery dwl 8 Virginia
Kaeding Charles *(R. Liddel & Co.)* 538 Wash
Kaeding Otto *(M. Dolan & Co.)* res Mazatlan, Mexico
Kaeler Frederic, foreman North Beach & M. R. R. Co. dwl S s Fifteenth nr Howard
Kaen John F. machinist, dwl 313 Bryant
Kaen Peter, machinist, dwl 175 Beale
Kaen Thomas L. machinist, Union Foundry, dwl 173 Beale
Kearnay William, marble polisher, dwl W s Fifth Avenue bet Bryant and Harrison
Kafer John, hairdresser, dwl Dresdener House

Kafka John M.D., physician, office and dwl 343 Kearny
Kafka Joseph, collector, Ladies' Hebrew Society, dwl 221 Sutter
Kafka L. T. salesman, 107 Mont dwl 324 Jessie
KAHMAN J. G. groceries and liquors, NW cor Post and Kearny, dwl 404 Bush
Kahn Gabriel, drayman, cor Front and California, dwl 513 Union
Kahn Hyman, porter with Godchaux & Bro. dwl 627 Post
Kahn John, upholsterer, dwl 1 St. Mary
Kahn Leopold, dwl 951 Mission
Kahn *(Louis)* & Strauss *(Jacob)* importers watches, jewelry, etc. 619 Washington
Kahn Solomon, dwl 433 Union
Kahn Teresa (widow) dwl 613 Bush
Kahrs Charles, clerk with Hermann Schroder, dwl 330 Vallejo
Kahrs John, clerk, SW cor Market and First
Kain James, laborer, dwl 6 Brown's Alley
Kain Peter M. machinist, Union Foundry, dwl 163 Beale
Kaindler Gustave *(Verdier, K., Scellier & Co.)* res Paris
Kairns Maggie Miss, domestic, 104 O'Farrell
Kaiser Alexander, clerk, 643 Clay, dwl 337 Tehama
Kaiser Joseph, tailor with M. Brandhofer, dwl Bootz's Hotel
Kaiser Louis, butcher with M. Selig & Co. dwl E s Hampshire nr El Dorado
Kaiser M. collector, office 604 Merchant, dwl 1510 Dupont
Kaiser William, clerk, 630 Sacramento
Kaissen John, longshoreman, dwl 106½ Clay
Kalaher Ann Miss, domestic, 961 Folsom
Kalaher Catherine Miss, domestic, 517 Sutter
Kalaher Michael, laborer, dwl 316 Beale
Kalas Louis, joiner, dwl 716 Pacific
Kalbin Charles, saloon, 200 Sutter
Kalhar John, laborer, dwl 16 Freelon
Kalish Arnold *(Bley & Co.)* dwl 16 Eddy
Kalish R. Samuel, express wagon, dwl S s Sacramento bet Leavenworth and Hyde
Kalisher M. laborer, dwl E s Mission bet Twenty-Eighth and Twenty-Ninth
Kalisher *(Simon)* & Diamant *(Bernard)* cap manufacturers, 414 Sacramento, dwl 55 Shipley
Kalisky Louis, fruits, dwl E s Rassette Place No. 2
Kalisky Samuel, tailor, 333 Kearny
Kallenberg Theodore, model maker, 416 Market, dwl 217 Dupont
Kallner Samuel, tailor, 403 Pine dwl 204 Kearny
Kalmbach Augustus, musician, dwl 1505 Dupont
Kalmuk M. manufacturer cigars, 414 Sacramento, dwl 261 Tehama
Kalstrom Herman, boatman, dwl N s St. Charles nr Kearny
Kalthoff August, crockery, 352 Third and porter with Hayward & Coleman, dwl 354 Third
Kaltschmidt Oscar, artist, studio 606 Market
Kamahsi J. employé, Washington Baths, dwl SE cor Dupont and Jackson
Kamana Herman, clerk, dwl 514 Filbert
Kametto Martin *(J. Dupuy & Co.)* dwl 528 Bdwy
Kaminski Simon, drayman, 323 California, dwl 114 Jones
Kamlade Charles, clerk, NE cor Howard and Sixth
Kamps William, California Saloon, NE cor California and Davis
Kameler Jacob, pawnbroker, 729 Washington, dwl 404 Stockton
Kan W. H. carpenter, dwl 741 Market
Kanaka G. & S. M. Co. office 611 Clay
Kanalay John, laborer, dwl 112 Dora
Kanalay Mary (widow) dwl W s Mission bet Twenty-First and Twenty-Second
Kanary Anna Miss, domestic, 608 Market
Kanary David *(Hopps & K.)* dwl 148 Second

Kanny Owen, cabinet maker with Hobbs, Gilmore & Co. dwl 414 Market
Kane Charles H. butter, cheese, and eggs, 8 Occidental Market, dwl 514 Minna
Kane Daniel, waiter, dwl 405 Third
Kane David, butcher, dwl 641 Vallejo
Kane David, waiter, Empire State Restaurant
Kane Elizabeth (widow) private boarding, 530 Bush
Kane Ellen Mrs. domestic, 1707 Stockton
Kane Frank, apprentice with John Grant, Columbia Marble Works
Kane Frank E. accountant with Hunter, Wand & Co. dwl St. Charles Place nr Kearny
Kane Hugh, longshoreman, bds Golden Age Hotel 127 Pacific
Kane James, bottles and sacks, S s Commercial bet Drumm and East
Kane James, gas fitter, 641 Market, dwl Fourth bet Minna and Howard
Kane James, hackman, Plaza, dwl Mecham Place nr Post
Kane James, painter, dwl 12 Sutter
Kane James J. tanner, dwl 132 Townsend
Kane John, express wagon, dwl 217 Commercial
Kane John, laborer, S. F. Gas Co
Kane John, laborer, dwl 318 Tehama
Kane John, laborer, dwl 323 Clementina, rear
Kane John, porter, Pacific Mail S. S. Co. dwl NW cor Sacramento and Leidesdorff
Kane John F. machinist, Union Foundry, dwl 313 Bryant
Kane John F. pressman with Towne & Bacon, dwl 304 Sansom
Kane Lawrence, waiter, dwl 619 Market
Kane Margaret Miss, domestic, 909 Union
Kane Mary Miss, domestic, 1030 Bush
Kane Mary Miss, domestic, 821 Post
Kane Matthew, packer with Haynes & Lawton, 516 Sansom
Kane Michael *(Hunter, Wand & Co.)* dwl St. Charles Place
Kane Michael, carpenter, dwl Chestnut bet Dupont and Stockton
Kane Michael, express wagon, dwl N s Harrison nr Sixth
Kane Michael, lab, dwl W s Gaven nr Greenwich
Kane Michael, laborer with James McDevitt, dwl E s Sansom bet Broadway and Pacific
Kane Michael, saloon, 125 Fremont
Kane Patrick, laborer, dwl 525 East
Kane Patrick, laborer, dwl 1 Hartman Place
Kane Roger, retortman, San Francisco Gas Co
Kane Thomas, hackman, Plaza, dwl Mecham Place nr Post
Kane Thomas, laborer with David B. Hughes, dwl S s Lombard bet Taylor and Jones
Kane William, retortman, San Francisco Gas Co
Kane W. P. cabinet maker with Goodwin & Co
Kane, see Cane, Caine, Kean, and O'Kane
Kanitz Moritz, dwl SW cor Taylor and O'Farrell
Kannavan James, laborer, dwl 346 Ritch
Kannavan John, laborer, dwl 48 Beale
Kannaven James, painter, dwl N s Lombard bet Montgomery and Kearny
Kanneuly Patrick, laborer, dwl W s Larkin near Post, rear
Kanzee Robert *(Plagemann, K. & Co.)* res New York
Kaplan Louis, merchant, dwl 238 Stevenson
Kapler Adam, carpenter, dwl 728 Market
Kappke H. F. groceries and liquors, SE cor Union and Mason
Karbel Anthony, machinist, dwl 559 Howard
Kardel Theodore, cook, bds 7 Washington
Karn Frederika Mrs. clothing, NW cor Pacific and Montgomery
Karnes Jasper, drayman with Yates & Stevens, 208 Clay
Karnes Patrick, boiler maker, dwl 511 Mission

Karo Samuel, fruits, dwl E s Rassette Place No. 2
Karr Charles, dwl W s Eighth bet Howard and Te-
hama
Karr William, clerk with August Frank, dwl cor
Sixth and Bryant
Karstens Heury *(Whitland & K.)* dwl SW cor
Sansom and Pacific
Kasel William, cooper, dwl 47 Davis
Kaselean John, carpenter, dwl 803 Mission
Kashell B. I. express wagon, corner Dupont and
Broadway
Kaskal Adolph, hatter with Moritz Kaskal, dwl
1120 Leavenworth
Kaskal Moritz, hats and caps, 617 Commercial, dwl
1120 Leavenworth
Kaskell Benjamin, fruits, dwl Manhattan Engine
House
Kaskell B. J. *(Henry & K.)* dwl S s Harrison bet
Second and Third
Kassen Chester S. clerk, dwl 1014 Stockton
Kasson Joe, fisherman, 43 Italian Fish Market
Kast Francis X. *(Holcombe Bros.)* dwl 944 Mission
Kast L. S. *(Hinders & K.)* dwl 261 Stevenson
Kate G. & S. M. Co. office 804 Montgomery
Kathe John B. carpenter with Goodwin & Co. dwl
407 Pacific
Kather William, clerk with Becker Bros. dwl NW
cor Jackson and Kearny
Katz Abraham, shoe maker, 100 Dupont
Katz Alexander, miller, dwl 411 Sutter
Katz Benjamin, clerk, dwl 31 St. Mark Place
Katz Frederick, Jackson Market, 617 Jackson, dwl
N s Union bet Jackson and Leavenworth
Katz Israel, tailor with Lohmann & Moesta, dwl
102 Dupont
Katzenstein Isaac *(Dannenbaum, Katzenstein &
Co.)* res New York
Kauce Francis, dwl 1008 Clay
Kaufman Charles, carpenter, NE cor Stockton and
and Bush, dwl 623 Geary
Kaufman Constant, carpenter, dwl 623 Geary
Kaufmann August, musician, dwl 1509 Powell
Kaufmann Frederick, musician, dwl 5 Tay
Kaufmann Henry, musician, dwl 1009 Mason
Kaufmann Sebastian, cook, 308 Montgomery
Kaul Samuel, tailor, 324 Commercial, dwl 40 First
Kavanagh Catherine Miss, domestic, 6 Montgomery
Kavanagh Edward, with William Lundberg, dwl
937 Folsom
Kavanagh George, baker, dwl 105 Geary
Kavanagh John. tailor, dwl 15 Battery
Kavanagh Michael, with R. Card & Co. dwl cor
Market and Jones
Kavanagh, see Cavanagh
Kavanaugh Charles *(Delany & K.)* dwl 30 Langton
Kavanaugh James, dwl 25 Clementina
Kavanaugh John, bricklayer, 226 Stevenson
Kavanaugh Mary Miss, domestic, 807 Greenwich
Kavenaugh Daniel, boiler maker, dwl 414 Market
Kawton Michael, blacksmith, Market St. R. R. Co.
dwl Fulton, Hayes' Valley
Keady John J. expressman, dwl S s Mission' bet
Eighth and Ninth
Keagel Frank, tailor, 136 First
Keale Simon, waiter, dwl 323 Pine
Kean John, cooper, S. F. & P. Sugar Co. dwl 522
Geary
Keane Daniel, waiter, Lick House
Keane George, dwl 619 Green
Keane J. tinsmith, dwl 625½ Mission
Keane James, book keeper with Fred. Marriott, dwl
510 Mason
Keane John, conductor, North Beach & M. R. R.
Co. dwl 145 Fourth
Keane Malachi, harness maker with Main & Win-
chester, dwl 333 Bush
Keane Thomas, salesman, 138 Mont, dwl 633 Cal
Kearee Patrick, laborer, dwl Lincoln Avenue
Kearn Ann Miss, domestic, 25 Stevenson

Kearn Bernard, laborer, dwl N s Mission bet Sec-
ond and Third
Kearn Patrick, teamster, dwl Jessie bet Third and
Fourth
Kearn Samuel, laborer, dwl SW cor Jessie and
Annie
Kearnan James, porter, St. Mary's Hospital
Keurnan Patrick, laborer, dwl 671 Mission
Kearney Anna Miss, domestic, 703 Stockton
Kearney Arthur, carpenter, dwl W s Hyde bet
Union and Filbert
Kearney Daniel, drayman, dwl 138 Shipley
Kearney James, tailor, dwl N s Harrison bet Sev-
enth and Eighth
Kearney John, cartman, dwl 176 Jessie
Kearney Mary Miss, domestic, 1213 Sacramento
Kearney Mary Miss, dress maker, dwl 208 Fourth
Kearney Michael, laborer, dwl cor Francisco and
Jones
Kearney Richard M. clerk, 104 Third, dwl 39
Everett
Kearney Samuel, hostler, dwl 14 Sutter
Kearney Walter, laborer, bds Western Hotel
Kearney William, laborer, dwl 225 Sutter
Kearney William, shoe maker with Dennis A. Healy,
818 Market
Kearns Alice Miss, domestic, 716 Green'
Kearns Bernard H. sail maker with James A. Wright,
dwl 16 Anthony
Kearns Ellen Miss, domestic, 692 Geary
Kearns James, baker with Swain & Brown, 5
Kearny
Kearns James, cook, Empire State Restaurant, dwl
What Cheer House
Kearns Michael, laborer, dwl W s Varenne near
Union
Kearns Patrick & Co. *(Nicholas Fougeron)* New
York Market, 36 Fourth, dwl 255 Jessie
Kearns Thomas, seaman, dwl Manhattan Engine
House
Kearns, see Kerns
Kearny Celia, domestic, 903 Hyde
Kearny Daniel, drayman, 6 Clay, dwl 138 Shipley
Kearny James, dwl 153½ Second
Kearny James M. plasterer, dwl 166 Minna
Kearny Julia Mrs. dwl 8 Jessie
Kearny M. labror, Spring Valley W. W
Kearny Thomas, laborer, dwl 19 Stevenson
Keates George, butcher, 811 Fifth
Keating E. laborer, Spring Valley W. W
Keating Edward, laborer, dwl 34 June
Keating George, Market St. W. W. 609 Market, res
Watsonville
Keating James, core maker, Miners' Foundry, dwl
523 Howard
Keating John, dwl 18 Taylor
Keating John M. teamster with Peter Sesser, dwl
Sixth nr Market
Keating Michael, laborer, dwl 412 Post, rear
KEATING M. JAMES, proprietor Ivy Green Sa-
loon, 624 Merchant, dwl 211 Pine
Keating Owen, farmer, San Miguel Ranch, S s
Ocean House Road
Keating Patrick, laborer, Golden State Iron Works,
dwl 61 Everett
Keating Patrick, liquors, 71 Stevenson
Keating Robert H. *(Lee & K.)* (col'd) dwl Union nr
Kearny
Keating William, with Joseph M. Parker, 532 Cal
Keating William, musician, dwl 215 Stevenson
Keatley Thomas, carpenter, dwl NE cor Folsom
and Sixth
Keay Carrie Miss, dwl 117 Dora
Keckmann Hermann, clerk, NE cor Broadway and
Stockton
Kedon Martin, merchandise, 319 Davis, dwl 240
Ritch
Kee John, (Chinese) cigar manufactory, 639 Jackson
Kee Song Tong (Chinese) teas, 742 Sacramento

Keech Arnold P. driver with C. B. Folsom, bds Columbia House
Keedy John D. agent Pacific Barrel Factory and with J. Dows & Co. dwl 21 Rousch
Keefe Cornelius. drayman, 218 Front, dwl S s Stevenson bet Sixth and Seventh
Keefe David, laborer, dwl 45 Jessie
Keefe Edward, clerk, dwl 87 Stevenson
Keefe Jane Miss, domestic, 23 Hunt
Keefe Jeremiah, local policeman, dwl E s Park Av bet Harrison and Bryant
Keefe John, driver, Mason's Brewery, dwl 609 Union
Keefe Michael, dwl 12 Natoma
Keefe Patrick, milker with S. C. & L. H. Talcot
Keefe Patrick, miner, dwl N s Folsom nr Sixth
Keefe Timothy, laborer, Fort Point, dwl E s Hyde nr Filbert
Keefe, see Keeffe and O'Keefe
Keefer John, hairdresser with Stable Bros. dwl 337 Bush
Keefer Ralph, teacher, dwl 124 Silver
Keefer Sarah Mrs. dwl 1016 Stockton
Keeffe Daniel, policeman, City Hall, dwl 519 Filbert
Keegan Anna Miss, domestic, 828 Post
Keegan James, gas fitter with J. H. O'Brien & Co. dwl NW cor Mission and Second
Keegan John, with Porter & Covey, dwl 12 Sutter
Keegan John W. painter, dwl 266 Jessie
Keegan Michael, laborer, dwl 57 Everett, rear
Keegan Peter, laborer with Hey & Meyn
Keegan Rosa Miss, domestic, 2 Graham Place
Keeler John, cook, dwl N s Van Ness Av nr Turk
Keeler John, nurse, City and County Hospital
Keeler Ralph, teacher French and German, dwl 124 Silva
Keeler Sol. M. (*E. Gould & Co.*) and purser Pacific Mail S. S. Co
Keeley John, brick mason, dwl SE cor Mission and First
KEELY JOHN, groceries and liquors, SE corner Leavenworth and Pacific
Keely Margaret (widow) dwl 29 Natoma
Keely Rose Miss, domestic, 14 Hawthorne
Keena Edward, engineer with R. B. Gray & Co
Keenan Bernard R. boiler maker, Pacific Foundry, dwl S s Broadway bet Leavenworth and Jones
Keenan Bernard T. gas fitter, dwl Minna bet Second and Third
Keenan Delia Miss, domestic, 1023 Post
Keenan Ellen Miss, domestic with A. M. Hathaway
Keenan John, restaurant, Oriental Hotel
Keenan Julia Miss, domestic, NW cor Grove and Van Ness Avenue
Keenan Patrick, laborer, dwl E s Beale bet Market and Mission
Keenan Patrick, shoe maker, 105 First, dwl 225 Mission, rear
Keenan Sarah Miss, domestic with T. N. Wand, E s Sixth nr Brannan
Keene C. C. musical instrument maker, 103 Montgomery, dwl 819 Howard
Keene J. dwl 842 Clay
Keene James R. clerk with Cope, Daingerfield & Hambleton, 5-7 U. S. Court Block
Keeney Charles C. surgeon, U. S. A. dwl 562 Folsom
Keeney Charles W. with J. M. Bradstreet & Son, dwl Russ House
Keep George, marble cutter with L. R. Myers & Co. dwl NE cor Fourth and Mission
Keep George M. clerk with Pliny Bartlett, dwl NE cor Fourth and Mission
Keepler Charles, laborer, dwl 208 Fifth
Keer Henry, box maker, dwl 4 Virginia
Keese D. waiter, Cosmopolitan Hotel
Keese John, carpenter, dwl 749 Market
Keesing Barnett, real estate, dwl 1012 Bush
Keever John, brewer, Jackson Brewery, dwl 9 Baldwin Court

Kegg F. hostler, Spring Valley W. W
Kehoe Bridget Miss, domestic, SE cor Pine and Leavenworth
Kehoe John, metal roofer tin and sheet iron worker, 228 Bush, dwl 625 Union
Kehoe Patrick, dwl S s O'Farrell nr Gough
Kehoe Peter, boots and shoes, 238 Third
Kehoe Thomas, express wagon, cor Davis and Jackson
Kehoe Thomas, proprietor New England Laundry, N s Brannan bet Fifth and Sixth
Kehrlein Valentine, painter, dwl 232 Green
Keifer Carrie Miss, domestic, 1605 Powell
Keiffer Sarah (widow) furnished rooms, 607 Jackson
Keigan John, laborer with Hey & Meyn
Keightley Mary (widow) dress maker, dwl 608 Green
Keil David, dwl 34 Third
Keil Edward & Co. (*Leon Amy*) East India Tea Co. 631 Washington
Keil Minna Mrs. midwife, 34 Third
Keile Kate Miss, domestic, 934 Kearny
Keiler John, porter, SW cor Battery and Vallejo
Keily Mary Ann Miss, domestic with William B. Heywood, W s Mary nr Minna
Keintz Peter, hairdresser, 50 Fourth, dwl 272 Jessie
Keirnan James, laborer, dwl 117 Shipley
Keirnan Michael, machinist, Singer Manufacturing Co. dwl 43 Ritch
Keiser Joseph, tailor, dwl Bootz's Hotel
Keith Ann (widow) dwl 40 First
Keith E. G. carpenter, dwl 351 First
Keith John, laborer, dwl 266 Jessie
Keith John W. carpenter, 730 Harrison
Keith Margaret Mrs. special grammar assistant Denman Grammar School, dwl 804 Bush
Keith Mathew, laborer, dwl 115 First
Keith Samuel D. engineer, S. F. & San José R. R. Co. dwl W s Folsom bet Sixteenth and Seventeenth
Keith William (*Van Vleck & K.*) dwl 20 Clarence Place nr Townsend
KEITH WILLIAM H. & CO. chemists and apothecaries, 521 Montgomery, dwl 1421 Powell
Kelaber Daniel, laborer, Spring Valley W. W. dwl 1230 Bush
Kelaher James, carriage maker, with M. P. Holmes, dwl 435 Pine
Kelbing Charles, beer saloon, NW cor Sutter and Kearny
Keleher Cornelius, cook, dwl E s Montgomery bet Filbert and Greenwich
Keleher John, laborer, dwl S s Chambers, bet Battery and Front
Keleher Michael J. dwl 29 Moss
Keleher Timothy, laborer, dwl 12 Sutter
Kellaher Cornelius, cook, 28 Montgomery
Kellcost Mary, domestic, 349 Jessie
Kelleher Annie Mrs. dwl NE cor Sixth and Folsom
Kelleher Daniel, blacksmith, Excelsior Iron Works, bds Central House
Kelleher John, workman, S. F. & P. Sugar Co
Kelleher Michael, workman, S. F. & P. Sugar Co. dwl Mission bet Eighth and Ninth
Kellem Daniel, laborer, dwl 753 Mission, rear
Kellen T. workman with Casebolt & Co
Keller Andrew, shipmaster, dwl 238 Stewart
Keller Conly, cook, dwl 200 Sutter
Keller Eliza (widow) dwl 1314 Dupont
Keller Ellen Miss, domestic, 1008 Bush
Keller Frank, driver, Mason's Brewery, dwl Greenwich, bet Mason and Powell
Keller Fred, meat market, 513 Pacific
Keller Henry, paper hanger, dwl 1417 Kearny
Keller Henry, porter, dwl Bootz's Hotel
Keller Jacob, blacksmith, 210 Sutter
Keller James, wagon maker, dwl Bootz's Hotel
Keller James W. laborer, 307 Market, dwl 43 Jessie
Keller Leonard, repairer furniture, 305 Pine

KELLER LEVI, auctioneer and commission merchant, 535 California and 124 Third, dwl 231 First

KELLER M. native wines, brandies, bitters, etc. 609 Front, res Los Angeles

Keller Mary F. (widow) dwl SW cor Post and Kearny

Keller Michael, machinist, Vulcan Iron Works, dwl 1314 Dupont

Keller Thomas, drayman, dwl 155 Leavenworth

Keller Timothy, waiter, 42 Market

Keller William, driver with Stephen C. Story, Occidental market

Kellett Bridget Miss, domestic, 1028 Pine

Kellett Charles, molder, dwl E s Bartlett between Twenty-Second and Twenty-Third

Kellett Robert J. with Cameron, Whittier & Co. dwl 357 Minna

KELLETT SAMUEL, manufacturer plaster decorations, 761 and 763 Market

Kellett William F. plaster worker and decorator, 627½ Market, dwl 633 Market

Kelley Elizabeth Miss, domestic, 926 Jackson

Kelley Hannah Miss, domestic, 506 Third

Kelley Margaret Miss, domestic, NE cor Washington and Jones

Kelley Michael, blacksmith with McGlauflin & Moholy, dwl S s Natoma bet Second and Third

Kelley Michael, coupé, Plaza

Kelley N. P. teamster, dwl W s Valencia nr Sixteenth, Dolores Hall

Kelley Owen, hackman, Plaza, dwl 550 Tehama

Kelley Patrick, milkman, Hunter's Point

Kelley Perry, butcher, Metropolitan Market, dwl cor Montgomery and Market

Kelligan Patrick, seaman, dwl W s Main bet Folsom and Harrison

Kellog Creek Petroleum & M. Co. (Contra Costa Co.) office 7 and 10 Government House 502 Washington

Kellogg Albert, electrotyper, cor Montgomery and Jackson, dwl 523 Bush, rear

Kellogg Andrew J. (Hamilton & K.) dwl 416 Mont

Kellogg Charles D. clerk, dwl 531 Tehama bet Fifth and Sixth

KELLOGG CHARLES L. seeds and agricultural tools, 427 Sansom, dwl 507 Stockton

Kellogg Charles W. acct with Tubbs & Co.and secretary Board Pilot Commissioners, res Oakland

Kellogg C. W. (Fargo & Co.) dwl 414 Bush

Kellogg E. A. book keeper Pacific Insurance Co. 436 California, dwl 652 Howard

Kellogg Francis D. (L. B. Benchley & Co.) res Oakland

Kellogg George H. (Flint, Peabody & Co.) res San Mateo County

Kellogg James, with Kellogg, Hewston & Co. dwl 212 Powell

Kellogg James, cashier London and San Francisco Bank, 412 Montgomery, dwl 416 Tehama

KELLOGG, (John G.) HEWSTON (John jr.) & CO. (J. H. Stearns) assayers, 416 Montgomery, and gold and silver refinery, cor Brannan and Seventh, dwl 416 Montgomery

Kellogg Levi M. deputy collector Custom House, dwl Clarence Place nr Townsend

Kellogg Lorenzo, machinist, Union Foundry, dwl 200 Stockton

Kells W. F. carpenter and builder, 408 Jackson, dwl Clark Alley bet Pacific and Broadway

Kellum Charles D. carpenter, dwl 836 Market

Kellum Edward M. carpenter, dwl N s Harrison nr Sixth

Kellum Harvey T. molder, Miners' Foundry, dwl 320 Beale

Kellum W. C. dentist, office 649 Clay

Kelly Alice Miss, domestic, 20 Ellis

Kelly Alice Miss, domestic with O. J. Preston, S s Mission nr Eleventh

Kelly Ambrose, miner, dwl 419 Pine

Kelly Ann Miss, domestic, dwl 215 Green

Kelly Ann Miss, domestic, SW cor Pine and Mason

Kelly Ann (widow) dwl 45 Sacramento

Kelly Ann (widow) dwl 325 First

Kelly Anna Miss, domestic, 1012 Bush

Kelly Anne (widow) dwl NE cor El Dorado and Nebraska

Kelly Archibald, dwl 78 Natoma

Kelly Barney, carriage maker, dwl 523 Mission

Kelly Bernard, express wagon, NW cor Washington and Sansom, dwl 817 Greenwich

Kelly Bernard J. tinsmith with E. Ayers, dwl S s Bush nr Battery

Kelly Bernard K. blacksmith with Kimball & Co. dwl 523 Mission

Kelly Bridget Miss, cook Mt. Hood House, 54 Sac

Kelly Catharine Miss, domestic, 610 Green

Kelly Catherine, dwl SE cor Corbett and Castro

Kelly Charles, carpenter, dwl N s McAllister bet Leavenworth and Hyde

Kelly Charles, deck hand, steamer Cornelia

Kelly Charles E. (Lane & K.) dwl W s Guerrero nr Sixteenth

Kelly Charles E. hackman, dwl 419 Pine

Kelly Daniel, coachman with Edmund B. Benjamin, W s Folsom bet Twelfth and Thirteenth

Kelly Edward, barber, dwl 426 Folsom

Kelly Edward, clerk, dwl Portsmouth House

Kelly Edward, express wagon, dwl Brannan near Ninth

Kelly Edward, laborer, dwl NW cor Davis and Chambers

Kelly Edward, laborer, dwl cor Greenwich and Webster

Kelly Edward, waiter, steamer Yosemite

Kelly Edward, wines and liquors, 533 Kearny, dwl 420 Bush

Kelly Edward B. stevedore with Moore & Folger, dwl 145 Silver

Kelly Ellen (widow) dwl 1 Thompson Avenue

Kelly Eugene (Donohoe, Kelly & Co.) res New York

Kelly Francis, stone cutter, dwl 60 First

Kelly Frank, Willows, SW cor Mission and Eighteenth, dwl 538 Market

Kelly George, foreman S. F. Gas Co

Kelly George, peddler, dwl W s Bower Place

Kelly George W. miner, dwl 419 Pine

Kelly H. A. compositor, Alta California

Kelly Henry, boatman, schooner Sarah Pratt

Kelly Henry, hostler, dwl 1407 Dupont

Kelly Henry S. laundryman, dwl 22 Oak

Kelly H. P. shoe maker, 112 San, dwl 38 Stevenson

Kelly Hugh, laborer, dwl 53 Stevenson

Kelly Hugh, laborer, dwl W s Second bet Brannan and Townsend

Kelly James, dwl 226 Dupont

Kelly James, carpenter, dwl N s Green bet Mason and Taylor

Kelly James, cooper with Handy & Neuman, res Oakland

Kelly James, deck hand, steamer Chrysopolis

Kelly James, hostler, North Beach & M. R. R. Co. dwl 254 Clara

Kelly James, laborer, Market St. R. R. Co. dwl New York House, 840 Market

Kelly James, laborer, dwl 56 Stevenson

Kelly James, laborer, dwl 14 Bay State Row

Kelly James, laborer, dwl NW cor Sixteenth and Nebraska

Kelly James, laborer, dwl W s Salmon bet Mason and Taylor

Kelly James, longshoreman, dwl cor Alta and San

Kelly James, porter, American Exchange

Kelly James, ship carpenter, dwl Niantic Hotel

Kelly James, superintendent St. Mary's Hospital, dwl W s First bet Harrison and Bryant

Kelly James, waiter, Original House Restaurant

Kelly James D. book keeper with J. C. Horan & Co. dwl Brooklyn Hotel
Kelly James F. porter with N. R. Lowell, dwl 67 Everett
Kelly James L. glass blower, Pacific Glass Works, dwl nr cor Iowa and Mariposa
KELLY JAMES R. importer and dealer paints, oils, varnishes, etc. 38 California, dwl 442 Jessie
Kelly Jeremiah, butcher with Z. Hebert, dwl Hampshire, nr Santa Clara
Kelly Jeremiah J. marble cutter, Columbian Engine Co. No. 11
Kelly John, dwl 232 Clara
Kelly John, dwl SW cor Third and Brannan
Kelly John, beamster, foot Townsend, dwl 314 Ritch
Kelly John, blacksmith with A. Folsom, dwl 415 Pine
Kelly John, blacksmith, dwl 13 Second
Kelly John, boot maker with W. K. Forsyth & Son, dwl Central House
Kelly John, boot maker, 23 Fourth
Kelly John, carpenter, dwl 326 Geary, rear
Kelly John, currier, dwl 314 Ritch
Kelly John, engineer, dwl 13 Second
Kelly John, hog ranch, S s El Dorado nr Utah
Kelly John, horse trainer, Bay View Park
Kelly John, hostler, 679 Market, dwl NW corner Kearny and Sutter
Kelly John, lab, with P. Kelly, University Mound
Kelly John, laborer, Fort Point, dwl S s Union bet Hyde and Larkin
Kelly John, laborer with Hey & Meyn
Kelly John, laborer, dwl 19 Hunt
Kelly John, laborer, dwl 29 Main
Kelly John, laborer, dwl 14 Brooks, rear
Kelly John, laborer, dwl 207 Pacific
Kelly John, laborer, dwl 19 Sherwood Place
Kelly John, laborer, dwl bet Lake Honda and Central Gravel Road
Kelly John, laborer, dwl Bartol Place
Kelly John, laborer, dwl W s Eleventh nr Harrison
Kelly John, laborer, dwl S s Bush bet Laguna and Buchanan
Kelly John, mason, Fort Point
Kelly John, mining stocks, dwl 900 Powell
Kelly John, molder, Union Foundry, res Oakland
Kelly John, porter with McNear & Bro. 39 Clay
Kelly John, tailor with Henry Gieseman, dwl SE cor Vallejo and Dupont
KELLY JOHN jr. proprietor Brooklyn Hotel, SE cor Pine and Sansom
Kelly John H. carpenter, dwl 818 Folsom
Kelly John H. porter with Kelly & Egan, dwl 1333 Pacific
Kelly John J. machinist with David Stoddart, dwl 43 Ritch
Kelly John J. printer with Towne & Bacon, dwl 1120 Sacramento
Kelly John M. butcher with Charles Goodwin, dwl 721 Market
Kelly John P. (McAran & K.) dwl 13 O'Farrell bet Dupont and Stockton
Kelly John R. blacksmith with Albert Folsom, dwl 415 Pine
Kelly Jonathan, laborer, dwl 50 Sacramento
Kelly (Joseph) & Hanlon (Stephen) butchers, Libe y Market 903 Howard
Kelly Joseph P. drayman with R. A. Swain & Co. dwl Seventh nr Harrison
Kelly Julia Miss, domestic, 945 Howard
Kelly Julia Miss, domestic, SE cor Jones and Sutter
Kelly Julia Miss, domestic with Theodore A. Barry
Kelly Kate Miss, domestic, SE corner Sixteenth and Capp
Kelly Kieran, laborer, Point Lobos Road Co
Kelly Lawrence, laborer with Macdonald Brothers, dwl 147 Natoma
Kelly L. C. book keeper with Sather & Co. dwl 42 Hawthorne

Kelly Lewis, molder, Golden State Iron Works, dwl 66 Natoma
Kelly Luke, butcher with Burdick & Dooley, dwl Brannan St. Bridge
Kelly Luke, machinist, Union Foundry, dwl 51 Stevenson
Kelly Martin, conductor, Omnibus R. R. Co. dwl 319 Tehama
Kelly Maggie Miss, chambermaid, Brooklyn Hotel
Kelly Malech, laborer, dwl Bartol bet Broadway and Vallejo
Kelly Margaret (widow) dwl W s Varenne nr Union
Kelly Margaret (widow) dwl 419 Pine
Kelly Marks, plasterer, dwl 529 Pine
Kelly Martin, boarding, 112 Jessie
Kelly Martin, painter, dwl NW cor Jessie and Anna
Kelly Mary Miss, domestic with G. W. McNear, S s Folsom bet Sixth and Seventh
Kelly Mary Miss, domestic with Theodore A. Barry
Kelly Mary Miss, domestic with William Kerr, dwl 903 Buttery
Kelly Mary Miss, domestic, 313 Green
Kelly Mary Miss, domestic, 606 Filbert
Kelly Mary Miss, domestic, 120 Prospect Place
Kelly Mary Miss, dwl SE cor Corbett and Castro
Kelly Mary (widow) 402 Third
Kelly Mary (widow) dwl 4 Sherwood Place
Kelly Mary (widow) dwl 316 Beale
Kelly Mary (widow) domestic, 623 Powell
Kelly Mathew, bricklayer, dwl 25 Stockton Place
Kelly M. B. mason, Eureka Hose Co. No. 4
KELLY (M. H.) & EGAN (John) wholesale wines and liquors, 604 Battery, dwl S side Hayes bet Franklin and Gough
Kelly Michael (John Wagner & Co.) dwl 131 St. Mark Place
Kelly Michael, dwl 18 Oak
Kelly Michael, carriage painter, dwl N s Hickory bet Franklin and Gough
Kelly Michael, express wagon, 116 Minna
Kelly Michael, hackman, Plaza, dwl NW cor Washington and Mason
Kelly Michael, hackman, dwl E s Sixth nr Jessie
Kelly Michael, machinist, Union Foundry, dwl Oak bet Mason and Taylor
Kelly Michael, mastic roofer, dwl 830 Market
Kelly Michael, workman with Casebolt & Co
Kelly Murty, hackman, Plaza
Kelly Patrick, with Helbing, Greenebaum & Co. dwl Hayes' Valley
Kelly Patrick, blacksmith, Vulcan Foundry, dwl 13½ Stevenson
Kelly Patrick, boot and shoe manuf, 729 Clay
Kelly Patrick, cartman, cor Battery and Union
Kelly Patrick, coupé, Plaza
Kelly Patrick, hackman, dwl Manhattan Engine House
Kelly Patrick, helper, dwl 516 Mission
Kelly Patrick, hog butcher, SE cor Alameda and Nebraska
Kelly Patrick, laborer, Fort Point, dwl Green nr Larkin
Kelly Patrick, laborer, dwl 306 Vallejo
Kelly Patrick, laborer, dwl 69 Stevenson
Kelly Patrick, laborer, dwl E s Sansom bet Union and Filbert
Kelly Patrick, laborer, dwl 39 First
Kelly Patrick, laborer, Miners' Foundry
Kelly Patrick, laborer, dwl S s Hickory bet Franklin aud Gough
Kelly Patrick, marble yard, 67 Fourth, dwl 1245 Sacramento
Kelly Patrick, milk ranch, University Mound
Kelly Patrick, store keeper, Russ House
Kelly Penny, dwl 538 Market
Kelly Peter, with Helbing, Greenebaum & Co. dwl S s Fell nr Octavia
Kelly Peter, hog butcher, E s Alameda bet Nebraska and El Dorado

Kelly Peter, hostler, 532 California
Kelly Peter, waiter, 626 Kearny
Kelly Peter R. porter, 219 Bush
Kelly Peter R. porter, NW cor Stockton and Sutter
Kelly Philip, boiler maker, Union Foundry, dwl 138 Natoma
KELLY R. G. butter, cheese, and eggs, 24 Occidental Market, dwl 26 Stockton •
Kelly Rhody, marble worker with Patrick Kelly
Kelly Richard, tailoring, 549 Merchant, dwl SW cor Green and Sansom
Kelly Robert D. dwl 26 Stockton
Kelly Simon, miner, dwl 419 Pine
Kelly Stephen, laborer, dwl 116 Stevenson
Kelly Thomas, dwl E s Alameda bet Nebraska and El Dorado
Kelly Thomas, drayman, Davis nr Washington, dwl 555 Leavenworth
Kelly Thomas, job wagon, Davis nr Washington, dwl N s Austin bet Franklin and Van Ness Avenue
Kelly Thomas, S. F. Gas Co. dwl 549 Mission
Kelly Thomas, miner, dwl 419 Pine
Kelly Thomas, painter with J. W. Denny, dwl N s Brannan bet Third and Fourth
Kelly Thomas, liquor saloon, cor Fourth and Market, dwl 48 Clara
Kelly Thomas, seaman, steamer Pacific
Kelly Thomas, seaman, steamer Senator
Kelly Timothy, fireman, Crescent Engine Co. No. 10
Kelly Timothy, gardener with T. N. Cazneau, dwl NW cor Fulton and Octavia
Kelly Timothy, laborer with Alexander Lemore
Kelly W. H. employé with J. R. Sims, dwl S s Mission bet Eighth and Ninth
Kelly William (Armstrong & K.) dwl 611 Market
Kelly William, engraver, dwl 65 Natoma
Kelly William, harness maker, dwl Lincoln Avenue
Kelly William, laborer, dwl N s Tyler nr Broderick
Kelly William, tailor, St. Mary's College
Kelly William H. teamster, dwl 513 Hyde, rear
Kelly William J. harness maker with W. F. Wilmot & Co. dwl 1 Lincoln Avenue
Kelly, see Kelley
Kelsey Bryant, salesman, 106 Battery, dwl 18 Silver
Kelsey Melville, miner, dwl 18 Silver
Kelsey Theodore A. (J. M. Hurbutt & Co.) dwl 59 Jessie •
Kelso John, street sprinkler, 609 Market
Kelt John M. workman, S. F. & P. Sugar Co. dwl Harrison nr Eighth
Kelton Jacob, seaman, dwl 44 Sacramento
Kelton Samuel B. plasterer, dwl 633 Market
Kem Elizabeth Mrs. music teacher, dwl 155 Third
Kem Wa (Chinese) washing, E s Sonoma Place
Kemble E. C. Maj. paymaster, U. S. A. office 742 Washington
Kemena Hermann, truckman with L. J. Ewell, dwl 514 Filbert
Kemme George, waiter, German Hospital, Brannan
Kemmet Frederick, employé with J. Chadbourne, dwl cor Sacramento and Waverly Place
KEMP (Charles L.) & OWEN (James H.) livery and sales stable, 126 Fourth, dwl 126 Fourth
Kemp Christopher M. (col'd) shipsmith with W. S. Phelps, dwl 1433 Dupont
Kemp Henry N. D. jr. clerk, dwl SW cor Folsom and Spear
Kemp I. W. laborer, dwl Bay State House
Kemp James C. 29 Third
Kemp Johanna Miss, domestic, 518 Howard
Kemp John H. with B. L. Solomon & Sons, dwl 432 Natoma
Kemp J. W. laborer, Bay Sugar Refinery, dwl N s Union bet Battery and Sansom
Kemp William J. stevedore, dwl Union nr Battery
Kemper Peter, cook, dwl 26 Stewart
Kempf George W. (Williams & K.) dwl 244 Clementina

Kempney Philip, furniture, 1311 Dupont
Kenaday Alexander M. printer, dwl 412 Green
Kench Edward W. cook, dwl 1016 Leavenworth
Kendall James K. musician, dwl W s Fifth nr Tehama
Kendall Jerome, carpenter with S. S. Culverwell, 29 Fremont, dwl S s Valparaiso nr Jones
Kendall John, liquors, dwl 10 Broadway
Kendall Thomas, soda peddler, dwl 334 Vallejo
Kendall W. A. reporter, Morning Call, dwl 609 Davis
Kendall William, carpenter, dwl 315 Sutter
Kendig Daniel Rev. chaplain Second Infantry, C. V. Presidio
Kendrick Thomas, stone cutter with C. B. Grant, dwl 775 Market
Kene (Daniel) & Ryan (Dennis) New York Laundry, 123 Silver
Kenefick Bart, deck hand, steamer Chrysopolis
Kenefick Patrick, deck hand, steamer Chrysopolis
Kenerson William, engineer, steamer Relief, dwl cor Francisco and Sansom
Kenfeg William, laborer, dwl 200 Sutter
Kenfield Addie S. dwl 15 Langton
KENITZER (Henry) & FARQUHARSON (David) architects, office 428 California, dwl 436 Greenwich
Kenkel Charles A. gardener, dwl E s Guerrero bet Fifteenth and Sixteenth
Kenmore John, laborer, Lone Mountain Cemetery
Kenna John J. laborer, Bay City Laundry, dwl E s Sixth bet Bryant and Brannan
Kenna Margaret (widow) fancy goods, S s Brannan nr Seventh
Kennard George W. drayman, 218 Front, dwl 513 Hyde
Kennay William B. dwl N s Folsom bet Fifth and Sixth
Kenneally Edward, laborer, dwl 919 Greenwich
Kennedy Albert, grainer, dwl W s Buenaventura nr California
Kennedy B. (widow) dwl 519 Bush
Kennedy Barnard, carpenter, dwl 911 Larkin
Kennedy Bartholemew, blacksmith, dwl 351 Jessie
Kennedy Bernard, carpenter, dwl Bailey House
Kennedy Bridget Miss, domestic, 3 Natoma
Kennedy Bryan, groceries and liquors, SW cor Ellis and Larkin
Kennedy Byron C. physician, off and dwl 12 Mont
Kennedy (Catherine) & Cunning (Lizzie) millinery and fancy goods, 62 Third
Kennedy Catherine (widow) dwl SW cor Folsom and Spear
Kennedy Charles, laborer, dwl 29 Main
Kennedy Charles, machinist, Pacific Foundry, dwl 911 Larkin
Kennedy Daniel, hostler, dwl Bay View
Kennedy Dennis, fireman, dwl SW cor Folsom and Beale
Kennedy Dennis, laborer, dwl 111 William
KENNEDY (Edward) & HOPKINS (T. R.) proprietors Genessee Flour Mills, Gold bet Montgomery and Sansom, dwl SW cor Green and Montgomery
Kennedy Edward, clerk, 535 Clay, dwl 911 Larkin
Kennedy Edward, cutter with G. F. Walter & Co. dwl 7 Prospect Place
KENNEDY (Edward C.) & BELL (John) carpet warehouse, SW cor Montgomery and California, res New York
Kennedy Eliza (widow) furnished rooms, dwl 1006 Clay
Kennedy Francis, laborer, dwl 26 Jessie
Kennedy Frank B. boiler, Assayer's Department U. S. Branch Mint, dwl NW cor Wash and Priest
Kennedy George (E. Jaudin & Co.) dwl 517 Bryant
Kennedy Henry, deck hand, steamer Cornelia
Kennedy Hugh, blacksmith with English & Lothrop, dwl 319 Clementina

Kennedy Hugh, boatman, dwl N s Jackson bet Davis and Drumm
Kennedy Hugh, machinist, Miners' Foundry, dwl SE cor Natoma and June
Kennedy Humphrey, fireman, S. F. & P. Sugar Co. dwl W s Eighth nr Howard
Kennedy James, cartman, dwl W s Clinton bet Brannan and Bryant
Kennedy James, dwl W s Ninth nr Folsom
Kennedy James, blacksmith with P. Bonis, dwl N s Seventeenth bet Guerrero and Dolores
Kennedy James, carpenter, dwl 251 Tehama
Kennedy James, cartman, 526 Broadway
Kennedy James, confectioner with M. Bernheim, 408 Clay
Kennedy James, helper, Vulcan Foundry, dwl Central House
Kennedy James, hostler, Omnibus R. R. Co. dwl 20 Moss
Kennedy James, laborer, dwl 24 Sansom
Kennedy James, molder, Pacific Foundry, dwl 911 Larkin
Kennedy James S. inspector, office U. S. Internal Revenue, dwl 340 Seventh
Kennedy Jane Miss, dwl NW cor Stock and Sutter
Kennedy Jane Miss, domestic, SE cor Polk and Sutter
Kennedy J. F. *(Barry & K.)* 4 Summer
Kennedy *(J. O. B.)* & Bro. *(P. B. Kennedy)* groceries, SW cor Taylor and O'Farrell and SW cor Larkin and Ellis
Kennedy John, dwl SE cor Geneva and Brannan
Kennedy John, bricklayer, dwl 119 Minna
Kennedy John, laborer, S. F. & San José R. R. Co
Kennedy John, laborer, dwl 115 First
Kennedy John, laborer, dwl 554 Tehama
Kennedy John, waiter, Brooklyn Hotel
Kennedy John, workman, S. F. & P. Sugar Co. dwl Natoma nr Eighth
Kennedy John, workman, S. F. & P. Sugar Co. dwl W s Ninth nr Folsom
Kennedy John F. painter, S. F. & P. Sugar Co. dwl N s Drury Lane nr Seventh
Kennedy John W. machinist, Union Foundry
Kennedy Julia Miss, private school, 563 Bryant
Kennedy Kate Miss, principal Greenwich Street School, dwl 1006 Clay
Kennedy Kate Miss, domestic, SE cor Cal and San
Kennedy Kate Miss, domestic, dwl 54 Sacramento
Kennedy Kate A. seamstress, dwl 816 Filbert
Kennedy Lawrence, laborer, dwl N s Main nr Folsom
Kennedy Lizzie Miss, dwl 1006 Clay
KENNEDY L. W. Pacific Hardware agency, 210 Bush, dwl 816 Bush
Kennedy Martin, stone mason, dwl 109 Post
Kennedy Mary Miss, dwl with T. J. Broderick
Kennedy Mary Miss, domestic, 808 Taylor
Kennedy Mary Miss, domestic, 614 Third
Kennedy Mary (widow) dwl 237 Minna, rear
Kennedy Mary J. Miss, domestic, SE cor Filbert and Mason
Kennedy Mary J. Miss, teacher, dwl 563 Bryant
Kennedy Matthew, cooper with J. Polecki, dwl SE cor Sacramento and Davis
Kennedy M. G. San Francisco & San José Baggage Express, 679 Market, dwl 308 Jessie
Kennedy Michael, machinist, Tiger Engine Co. No. 14
Kennedy Michael, workman, S. F. & P. Sugar Co
Kennedy M. J. waiter, International Hotel
Kennedy Patrick, laborer, dwl 1121 Folsom
Kennedy Patrick, laborer with R. B. Woodward, dwl S s Thirteenth nr Mission
Kennedy Patrick, marble cutter with M. Heverin, dwl 336 Minna
Kennedy Patrick, plasterer, dwl 1048 Folsom
Kennedy Patrick, shoe maker with T. J. Broderick, 225 Montgomery

Kennedy P. B. *(Kennedy & Bro.)* dwl SW cor Taylor and O'Farrell
Kennedy *(Philip)* & Driscoll *(Dennis O.)* dry goods, 108 Third
Kennedy Richard, tailor with A. Kramer
Kennedy Sarah Miss, domestic, 831 Bush
Kennedy Sarah Miss, dress maker, NE cor Mission and Fifth, dwl 237 Minna, rear
Kennedy Thomas, dwl W s Ninth nr Folsom
Kennedy Thomas, clerk, dwl E s Garden bet Harrison and Bryant
Kennedy Thomas, fireman, steamer Julia, dwl 508 Kearny
Kennedy Thomas, shoe maker, 204 Second
Kennedy Thomas H. salesman with Taaffe & Co
Kennedy *(Thomas J.)* & Hayden *(Edwin)* fruits, 146 Fourth
Kennedy Thomas J. clerk with P. & T. Moran, dwl 146 Fourth
Kennedy Timothy, cook, 626 Kearny
Kennedy Timothy, works with Thomas Leonard
Kennedy V. B. dwl 331 Bush
Kennedy William, dwl 13 Oak
Kennedy William, groom, dwl E s Second bet Brannan and Townsend
Kennedy William, shoe maker with M. Guerin, 315 Battery
Kennedy William, tinsmith with Osgood & Stetson, 219 Commercial
Kennell Margaret Miss, domestic, 1815 Stockton
Kennell Philip, carpenter, dwl 24 Clementina
Kennelly David, marble cutter with L. R. Myers & Co. dwl 23 Jane
Kennelly Patrick, blacksmith, dwl NW cor Post and Jones
Kenness John, stone mason, dwl W s Sansom nr Green bet Green and Vallejo
Kenney Ann (widow) lodgings, 526 Pine
Kenney Edward, carpenter, dwl 509 Hyde
Kenney Edward, laborer with Smith & Williams
Kenney James, with Kellogg, Hewston & Co. dwl Minna nr Eighth
Kenney James, gas fitter with Thomas Day, dwl 526 Pine
Kenney James, laborer, dwl S s Minna nr Eighth
Kenney James, pressman, Alta California, dwl 921 Kearny
Kenney John, gold pen maker with W. B. J. Kenney, 2 Armory Hall
Kenney John, machinist, Union Foundry, dwl 18 Minna
Kenney John, proprietor Union Livery Stable, 724 Union
Kenney John E. compositor with Towne & Bacon, dwl First nr Minna
Kenney Joseph W. contractor and builder, dwl NE cor Post and Dupont
Kenney Julia Miss, domestic, SE cor Filbert and Mason
Kenney Lydia (widow) dwl 1067 Broadway
Kenney Margaret Miss, domestic, 813 Jackson
Kenney Mary Miss, domestic, 34 Langton
KENNEY MICHAEL, proprietor Court Exchange, rear City Hall, and state inspector gas meters, 612 Commercial
Kenney Michael, laborer, dwl 423 Fremont
KENNEY PATRICK, Knickerbocker Liquor Saloon, 112 Leidesdorff cor Halleck
Kenney Patrick, laborer, dwl 150 Shipley
Kenney Patrick, shoe maker, dwl with A. D. Campbell
Kenney Samuel, tailor, dwl 503 Sutter
Kenney Thomas *(Ward & K.)* 522 Market
KENNEY W. B. J. manufacturer gold pens, 1 and 2 Armory Hall Building
Kenney William, apprentice, dwl Dunbar Alley
Kenney William Dalton, dwl 437 Clementina
Kenney William J. carpenter, dwl 509 Hyde
Kenney, see Kenny

Kennison William, engineer, steamer Relief, dwl cor Chestnut and Montgomery
Kenniston Charles H. ship carpenter with John G. North, Potrero
Kenny Alice Miss, assistant, Market St. School, dwl 526 Pine
Kenny, (F. G.) Maroney (John) & Co. wholesale liquors, 623 Front, dwl 111 O'Farrell
KENNY GEORGE L. & CO. (R. T. Van Norden and A. L. Chamberlin) importers and jobbers books and stationery, 608 Montgomery, dwl SE cor Green and Leavenworth
Kenny James, driver, North Beach & M. R. R. Co. dwl 851 Folsom
Kenny James, liquor saloon, 925 Kearny
Kenny James, stevedore, dwl NW cor Front and Broadway
Kenny John (Horgan & K.) dwl cor Filbert and Sansom
Kenny John, blacksmith, cor Third and Howard, dwl S s Filbert between Montgomery and Sansom
Kenny John, carpenter, dwl 909 Folsom
Kenny John, groceries and liquors, SE cor Sixth and Minna
Kenny John, laborer, dwl 147 Natoma
Kenny John (col'd) porter, dwl 6 John
Kenny Katie Miss, domestic, 507 Greenwich
Kenny Mary Miss, domestic, SW cor Howard and Fourteenth
Kenny Mary A. Miss, domestic, 720 Filbert
Kenny Michael, dairyman, dwl S s Cliff House Road nr Lone Mountain Cemetery
Kenny Michael, retortman, S. F. Gas Co
Kenny Michael, shoe maker, 110 Leidesdorff
Kenny Owen, cabinet maker, dwl National House
Kenny Patrick, with C. O'Donnell, S s Brannan bet Fifth and Sixth
Kenny Peter (Gallagher & K.) dwl 509 Pine
Kenny Thomas, painter, dwl SW cor Kearny and Pacific
Kenny, see Kenney
Kensman Louis B. dwl 46 Ritch
Kent Alice Miss, domestic, 206 Stockton
Kent Edwin, steward, dwl 305 O'Farrell
Kent Joshua, clerk with H. P. Wakelee, dwl 303 O'Farrell
Kent Mary (widow) dwl 14 Natoma
Kent Mary (widow) dwl N s Grove nr Van Ness Avenue, Hayes' Valley
Kent O. F. dwl What Cheer House
Kent Richard, painter, dwl NE cor McAllister and Leavenworth
Kent Samuel H. ship joiner, dwl 120 Silver
Kent Sydney, baker with J. Chadbourne, 433 Jackson
Kent Thaddeus B. porter, 329 Mont, dwl 326 Mason
Kentfield George, captain schooner Ocean Spray, office Pier 10 Stewart
Kentfield John, lumber dealer, office Pier 10 Stewart, dwl 333 Fremont
Kentucky Copper M. Co. office 644 Washington
Kentzel James W. gas fitter with Thomas Day, dwl SW cor Broadway and Hyde
KENTZEL WILLIAM H. wood and coal, N s Broadway bet Montgomery and Sansom, dwl SW cor Hyde and Broadway
Kenyon M. dwl What Cheer House
Kenyon W. P. (hardware, Petaluma) office 14 First
Keo Thomas, expressman, dwl 516 Davis
Keogh Henry, shearer, S. F. P. Woolen Mills, dwl North Point bet Polk and Van Ness Avenue
Keogh James R. steward, St. Mary's College
Keogh Timothy, steward, Bailey House
Kerby E. Mrs. ladies' nurse, dwl 32 Geary
Kerby Ellen (widow) dwl W s Mary Lane nr Sutter
Kerby John, porter, dwl 108 Minna
Kerby Joseph W. with George F. Parker, dwl 12 Central Place

KERBY, (Patrick) BYRNE (Garrett J.) & CO. importers and retail dry goods, 7 Montgomery, res New York
Kerby Washington L. clerk, dwl 9 Belden
Kerby, see Kirby
Kercheval G. H. with William M. White, 431 Cal
Kerchhoff Lawrence, ship carpenter, dwl 1816 Powell
Kerguidu Henri, waiter, 526 Clay, dwl California Hotel
Kerlin George B. clerk, C. S. Nav. Co. Broadway Wharf, dwl 114 Second
Kerlin P. driver, Omnibus R. R. Co
Kerlin Rebecca Mrs. fancy trimmings, 114 Second
Kermode Edward, carpenter, dwl 566 Mission
Kern Benjamin F. printer, dwl 606 Third
Kern John, dwl 231 Pacific
Kern Morris, clerk, What Cheer House, dwl 351 Tehama
Kern River G. & S. M. Co. (Cove District, Tulare Co.) office 7 Stevenson House
Kern Samuel F. boiler maker, Pacific Foundry, dwl 416 Green
Kern William M. works with L. P. Cooley, Old San José Road nr junction San José R. R
Kernahan William, clerk, Asst. A. General's office, dwl Fort Point
Kernan Eliza, domestic, 770 Howard
Kernan James, dwl 331 Bush
Kernan John C. compositor, Daily Examiner, dwl 111 O'Farrell
Kerner Mary Miss, domestic, 127 Eddy
Kerner Peter, cabinet maker, 132 Sutter
Kerns James, cook, Crescent Engine Co. No. 10
Kerns Patrick, butcher, dwl 255 Jessie
Kerr Alexander, dwl What Cheer House
Kerr Andrew, overseer with William Kerr, dwl S s Lombard bet Kearny and Montgomery
Kerr Andrew, porter with Conroy & O'Connor, dwl W s Vincent nr Green
KERR CHARLES, wholesale butcher, Brannan St. Bridge, dwl Mission Creek nr Brannan Street Bridge
Kerr Charles, workman, S. F. & P. Sugar Co. dwl W s Eighth nr Howard
Kerr David, blacksmith with H. Casebolt & Co. dwl 10 Fifth
Kerr David, topographical with U. S. Coast Survey, office Custom House third floor
Kerr Edward, blacksmith with W. S. Phelps & Co. dwl nr cor Tehama and Prospect Place
Kerr Frederick, drayman, dwl 417 Folsom
Kerr John, workman, S. F. & P. Sugar Co. dwl E s Eighth bet Mission and Minna
KERR JOSEPH W. liquor saloon, SW cor Jackson and Kearny
Kerr Martin, watchman, What Cheer House
Kerr Thomas, clerk with Alsop & Co. dwl 344 Jessie
Kerr Thomas, porter, What Cheer House
Kerr William, carpenter, dwl 1014 Pacific
Kerr William, wheelwright and blacksmith, dwl NW cor Vallejo and Battery
Kerr William, workman, S. F. & P. Sugar Co. dwl W s Eighth nr Howard
Kerrigan Ann Miss, domestic, 21 Post
Kerrigan Charles, butcher, dwl with John Kerrigan
Kerrigan. (Edward) & Cardiff (Richard J.) butchers, NW cor Minna and Jane
Kerrigan John, express wagon, cor Market and East, dwl S s Clara bet Fifth and Sixth
Kerrigan John, St. Ann's Meat Market, 1038 Market, dwl SE cor Sixth and Market
Kerrigan Kate Miss, domestic, Brevoort House
Kerrigan Mary Miss, domestic, 115 Stockton
Kerrigan Patrick, laborer, dwl N s Harrison bet Seventh and Eighth
Kerrigan, see Carrigan
Kerrin Kate A. Miss, dwl 415 Fremont
Kerrison George G. dwl 721 Green

Kerrison Robert E, plumber with Thomas Day, 732 Mont, dwl E s Howard near Twenty-Seventh
Kerrison William H. apprentice with T. Day, dwl E s Howard bet Twenty-Second and Twenty-Third
Kerruish Edward, ship carpenter, dwl 24 Clementina
Kersey John D. *(California Straw Works)* dwl 74 Minna
Kershaw Henry J. gardener, dwl SE cor Jones and Vallejo
Kershaw Marsden, wood and coal yard, E s Valencia near Sixteenth, dwl SW cor Fifteenth and Mission
Kerst F. waiter, Cosmopolitan Hotel
Kervan Thomas L. house carpenter, dwl 611 Powell
Kerwan E. clerk, Cosmopolitan Hotel
Kerwin Annie Miss, domestic, 448 Natoma
Kerwin John, handcartman, cor Mont and Market
Kerwin John, laborer, Central R. R. Co. dwl E s Devisidero bet Post and Sutter
Kerwin Richard, painter, dwl 412 Tehama
Kerwin Thomas, express wagon, dwl Jansen near Lombard
Keseberg Louis, distiller, dwl 713 Union
Kesel William, cooper with B. H. Kramer, dwl Ecker nr Market
Kesler D. dwl What Cheer House
Kesmodel Frederick, cutler and surgical instrument maker, 817 Kearny, dwl 533 Mission
Kesper Michael, tailor, 611 Mission
Kesseler Francis, marble cutter, dwl 436 Jessie
Kesseler Joseph, marble cutter, dwl 436 Jessie
Kessing J. H. fish, 7 Clay Market, dwl 1312 Kearny
Kessing John B. with J. H. Kessing, dwl 8 Bay State Row
Kessing John F. produce commission, 56 Clay, dwl SE cor Howard and Twenty First
Kessler F. pastry cook, Cosmopolitan Hotel
Kester Levi B. *(McMillan & K.)* dwl 435 Second
Kestler E. A. merchant, dwl 665 Mission
Ketchum Frank, whitewasher, 627½ Market, dwl 633 Market
Ketchum William, carpenter, dwl 213 Minna
Ketelsen Augustus, seaman, bds 7 Washington
Keton Robert H. *(Lee & K.)* (colored) dwl 339 Union
KETTELL THOMAS P. financial editor Alta California, office 423 Washington, dwl 522. Pine cor St. Mary
Kettleman J. R. blacksmith, dwl 37 Clementina
Kettler Louis H. baker, Sandy Hill Bakery, dwl NE cor Clay and Mason
Keulen Hendrik V. groceries and liquors, NW cor Union and Mason
Keuscher Frederick, Bensley Water Co. dwl W s Fifth, nr Howard
Keville James, cook, dwl 107 Leidesdorff
Kewin William, foreman pattern maker Union Foundry, dwl 17 First Avenue bet Fifteenth and Sixteenth
Keyes Arthur, butcher with Bracket & Keyes, dwl 60 Stewart
Keyes E. D. Gen. dwl 1010 Stockton
Keyes John A. carpenter, SW cor Mason and Jackson
Keyes Joseph W. brick mason, dwl N s Shipley nr Harrison Avenue
Keyes O. H. *(Brackett & K.)* dwl 126 Turk
Keyes Rosanna Mrs. liquors, 930 Kearny
Keys George, commission merchant, 110 Clay, dwl 820 Dupont
Keys Mary Miss, domestic, 216 Clara
Keyser Ezra F. architect, dwl N s Union bet Hyde and Larkin
Keyser George, butcher with G. M. Garwood & Co
Keyser Morris, tailor, 231 Bush
Keyser, see Keiser
Keystone Copper M. Co. (Calaveras Co.) off 326 Clay

Keystone House, E. Hostkamper proprietor, 127 and 129 Jackson
Keyt Abner C. *(Way & K.)* dwl 527 O'Farrell
Khoe Martin, boarding, 41 Minna
Kiarnin Thomas, dwl with P. Johnson, Serpentine Avenue nr San Bruno Road
KIBBE MILLARD, liquor saloons, Old Corner 516 Montgomery SE cor Commercial and Branch, Old Corner junction Market and Montgomery, dwl 1112 Powell
Kichler Christian, silversmith with F. R. Reichel
Kidd Alexander, musician, dwl 511 Mason, rear
Kidd John, wool grader, Broadway Wool Depôt, dwl 212 Pacific
Kidder Mary T. Miss, seamstress, Protestant Orphan Asylum
Kidder Susan (widow) dwl W s First Avenue bet Fifteenth and Sixteenth
Kie Wo (Chinese) employment office, 714 Com
Kieber Joseph, tailor with M. Brandhofer, dwl 628 Merchant
Kiefendorf John W. miller, bds Sacramento Hotel, 407 Pacific
Kiefer Barbara (widow) dwl 61 Shipley
Kieffer Sarah (widow) dwl 421 Dupont
Kiernan Catharine (widow) dwl N s Fell bet Gough and Octavia
Kiernan Francis, salesman, 654 Market
Kiernan Mary Miss, domestic, S s Union bet Mason and Taylor
Kiernan Michael, machinist, Singer Manufacturing Co. dwl 43 Ritch
Kiernan Patrick, dwl S s Ash nr Polk
Kiernan Peter, dwl 24 Howard Court
Kiernan Peter, 329 Sansom, dwl 333 Bush
Kiernan Peter, blacksmith with McLaughlin & Feasel, 121 Bush
Kiernan Philip, carpenter, dwl 409 Third
Kierski Adolph, salesman with Julius Merzbach, dwl 638 Sacramento
Kiersted Edward L. book keeper American Flag, 604 Mont, dwl S s Perry bet Fourth and Fifth
Kiblmeyer Jacob, maltster, Philadelphia Brewery
KIHLMEYER LOUIS, billiard and liquor saloon, NW cor Jackson and Kearny, dwl 606 Jackson
Kilburn Carroll, clerk with John Hall & Son, dwl 325 Third
Kilcline Michael, laborer, dwl 112 William
Kilday Honora (widow) dwl 81 Stevenson
Kilday James, waiter, dwl 4 Sonoma Place
Kilday Michael, box maker, dwl 23 Hunt
Kilday William, boarding, 23 Hunt
Kildey Edward, laborer, dwl SE cor Gustavus and Sacramento
Kildorf Charles, laborer, dwl 140 Stewart
Kilduff William M. chief engineer, Pacific Mail S. S. Co
Kildey James, waiter, International Hotel
Kilgariff John, apprentice, Pacific Foundry, dwl 108 Freelon
Kilgour James Y. gas fitter with Thos. Day, 732 Montgomery, dwl N s Broadway bet Mason and Taylor
Kilham Horace, dwl 1065 Howard
Killaan Martin, harness maker with M. G. Conway, dwl W s Jones bet Sacramento and California
Killeon Ann Miss, domestic, 26 O'Farrell
Killey Charles H. milk ranch, S s Presidio Road nr Webster
Killian Frederick, porter, City Hall, dwl W s Clinton nr Brannan
Killian George, blacksmith with Nelson & Doble, dwl Dupont bet Pine and Bush
Killien Dennis, waiter, 523 Clay, dwl 126 Natoma
Killigan James, laborer, Custom House, dwl N s Filbert bet Larkin and Polk
Killilea Bryan, dwl 4 Delaware Court
Killilea Patrick, laborer, dwl N s Minna bet Fifth and Sixth

Killion Frank, painter, dwl 19 St. Mark Place
Killion Luke, waiter, What Cheer House Restaurant
Killip, *(Jasper N.)* & O'Connor *(Hugh)* livery stable, 704–708 Commercial, dwl 125 St. Mark Place
Killpack Jonathan, teamster, Mission St. Wharf, dwl N s Heron nr Eighth
Killpatrick Francis, merchant tailor, 25 Sansom
Killpatrick George, tailor with Charles O'Neil, 210 Leidesdorff
Kiloh John, book keeper with George L. Kenny & Co. 608 Montgomery, dwl 921 Union
Kilpatrick Hugh, laborer with S. Bloom, S s Brannan nr Sixth
Kilroy Mary Miss, domestic, dwl 1018 Washington
Kiltev Patrick, laborer, dwl N s Thirteenth nr Mission
Kim Woh (Chinese) washing, N s Market opposite Stewart
Kimb William H. painter, dwl Oriental Hotel
Kimball Ariadne L. assistant teacher, Protestant Orphan Asylum
Kimball Brothers *(L. W., W. C. & F. A. K.)* contractors and builders, 122 Natoma
Kimball Charles, drayman, cor Clay and Davis, dwl 11 Mason
Kimball Charles H. *(Ripley & K.)* dwl 114 Geary
Kimball Charles P. real estate agent, 620 Market, dwl S s Hayes bet Octavia and Laguna
Kimball F. A. *(Kimball Bros.)* dwl 122 Natoma
Kimball Fidelia (widow) dwl 321 Ritch
Kimball Frank, machinist, dwl 40 Natoma
Kimball George H. brick mason, dwl 1301 Mason
Kimball George P. & Co. *(William H. Knight)* importers and manufacturers carriages, 769 Market, dwl 64 Mission cor Third
Kimball George W. *(Carlton & Co.)* dwl 321 Ritch
Kimball George W. dwl NE cor Folsom and Main
Kimball Harvey, machinist, dwl 40 Natoma
Kimball Hazen, carrier, Morning Call, dwl 1301 Mason
Kimball Henry *(Bartling & K.)* dwl 11 O'Farrell
Kimball Mathew H. machinist, Pacific Foundry, dwl 40 Natoma
Kimball Moses C. deputy wharfinger Pacific Wharf, dwl NW cor Pacific and Jones
Kimball M. T. Miss, assistant, Market St. School, dwl 527 Howard
Kimball *(Solomon P.)* & Co. Metallurgical Works, 539 and 541 Bryant, dwl 329 Fremont
Kimball Theodore, carriage painter with Pollard & Carvill, dwl 1112 Clay
Kimball Thomas D. calker, dwl 415 Harrison
Kimball Thomas L. clerk with S. M. & D. S. Wilson
Kimball W. C. *(Kimball Bros.)* dwl 122 Natoma
Kincaid Charles A. dwl Occidental Hotel
Kincaid Hartley D. pile driver, dwl 308 Beale
Kincaid William, boiler, dwl N W cor Mission and First
Kinchela James, furnished rooms, dwl SW cor Mission and Second
Kincheloe Julius, sub-assistant, U. S. Coast Survey, office Custom House third floor
Kinchler Patrick, with Coffey & Risdon, dwl 517 Taylor
Kind M. butcher, 35 Natoma
Kind Richard C. T. cabinet maker, 612 Battery, dwl cor Hinckley and Pinckney
Kind Richard W. paper hanger, dwl 213 Post
King Anthony *(L. King & Co.)* res New York
King August, dwl SW cor Filbert and Powell
King Augustus, clerk, SW cor Twenty-Fourth and Mission
King B. hairdresser, 235 Pacific, dwl NE cor Jackson and Buttery
King Benjamin, Crescent Engine Co. No. 10
King Bridget Miss, domestic, 716 Pine
King C. parasol maker, dwl 816 Clay
King Catherine Miss, domestic, 33 Geary

King Charles, helper, Union Foundry, dwl 761 Clay
King Charles J. clerk with Ross, Dempster & Co. dwl 704 Powell
King David, pile driver, bds U. S. Hotel
King Edward H. molder, Miners' Foundry, dwl W s Seventh bet Harrison and Bryant
King Elizabeth Mrs. dwl with Michael King W s Seventh nr Harrison
King Ervin T. *(Howland, Angell & K.)* dwl N s McAllister bet Webster and Fillmore
King Ezra, carpenter, dwl 10 Quincy
King Frances, helper, dwl cor Seventh and Bryant
King Francis, hotel runner, dwl W s Battery bet Vallejo and Green
King Francis, laborer, Miners' Foundry
King Frank, cook, Shakspeare Hotel, 219 Pacific
King Frederick W. tailor, dwl 130 Geary
King George, (col'd) barber, 925 Kearny
King G. C. miner, office 611 Clay, dwl 1118 Leav
King George, tailor with Francis Dixey, dwl 1307 Pacific
King George T. tailor, dwl 1112 Pacific
King Henry, blacksmith, dwl 423 Natoma
King Henry, hairdresser, 3 Stewart
King Henry, laborer, dwl E s Chesley nr Harrison
King Henry, workman, S. F. & P. Sugar Co. dwl Silver nr Second
King Henry L. carpenter, dwl 1002 Powell
King Henry L. jr. deputy superintendent streets, dwl 1002 Powell
KING JAMES C. & CO. shipping and commission, SW cor Battery and Filbert, dwl 40 South Park
King John, assistant propertyman, Maguire's Opera House
King John, boiler maker, dwl 115 First
King John, fireman, Russ House
King John, laborer, dwl E s Gilbert nr Brannan
King John F. tannery and dwl cor Santa Clara and Connecticut
King John H. seaman, dwl 44 Sacramento
King John L. clerk, Evening Bulletin 620 Montgomery, dwl 523 Ellis
King John M. blacksmith and wheelwright, W s Mission nr Sixteenth, dwl cor Fifteenth and First Avenue
KING L. & BROTHER *(Anthony King)* importers and jobbers clothing, 213 and 215 Battery, dwl 30 Geary
King Lewis C. clerk with J. W. Sullivan, dwl 523 Ellis
King Malcom G. draftsman, City and County Surveyor
King Marcus, carpenter, dwl 4 Oak
King Mathew, stone mason, dwl 12 Sutter
King Michael, laborer, dwl S s Tyler bet Hyde and Larkin
King Michael, molder, California Foundry, dwl W s Seventh nr Harrison
King Michael L. molder, dwl 43 Clementina
King Minor, dwl N s McAllister bet Webster and Fillmore
King Patrick, laborer, dwl 30 Sacramento
King Patrick, painter, dwl N s Fulton nr Franklin
King Richard, carpenter, dwl 523 Ellis
King R. J. (widow) Sulphur Vapor Baths, 174 Minna
King Robert W. laborer, dwl 504 Howard
King Samuel, mariner, dwl 228 Commercial
King Samuel B. clerk with C. E. Abbot, dwl 908 Broadway
King Stephen T. life insurance agent, 712 Montgomery, dwl N s Hayes bet Franklin and Gough
King Thomas, policeman, City Hall, dwl 1407 Kearny
King Thomas B. cooper, California Wine Cooperage Co. 101 Davis, dwl W s Selina Place
King Thomas J. carpenter, dwl 523 Ellis
King Thomas Starr Mrs. (widow) dwl 831 Bush
King T. L. cabinet maker, dwl 728 Market
King Wallace, dwl 726 Mission

King William, laborer with Hey & Meyn
King William, laborer, Bay Sugar Refinery, dwl 504 Howard
King William, seaman, dwl S s Welch bet Third and Fourth
King William, teamster, bds 761 Mission
King William B. carriage maker with Lawton & Co. dwl Columbia Hotel
King William F. clerk with John Sime & Co. dwl NW cor Powell and Pine
King W. S. cooper, dwl 215 Sansom
Kingau Eliza Miss, domestic, SW cor Bush and Powell
Kingdutra J. stevedore, dwl Greenwich bet Montgomery and Sansom
Kingman Charles F. hostler. dwl 1808 Powell
Kingon Arthur, clerk, 123 Occidental Market, dwl 148 Silver
Kingon Robert, butter, cheese, and eggs, 123 Occidental Market, dwl 148 Silver
Kingsbury Albert, carpenter with Henry L. King, dwl N s Jessie nr Ninth
Kingsbury Elisha, dwl 722 Washington
Kingsbury George W. drayman, 415 Front, dwl 916 Howard
Kingsbury Thomas, conductor, Omnibus R. R. Co. dwl 230 Third
Kingsley Everett B. drayman, 14 Pine, dwl W s Capp bet Twenty-Second and Twenty-Third
Kingsley John L. photographic operator with Wm. Shew, dwl 26 Frank's Building
Kingsley Omar, equestrian, Wilson's Circus
Kingsley S. O. Wilson's Circus, bds Brooklyn Hotel
Kingsley William J. contractors' foreman, bds Oriental Hotel
Kingsly Delia Mrs. dwl 430 Green
Kingston Henry, mariner, dwl S s Columbia bet Guerrero and Dolores
Kingston John, steward Benton House, dwl SE cor Mission and First
Kingston Mary Miss, domestic, 1016 Stockton
Kingston William, collector, dwl 41 Minna
Kingwell James, porter 212 Battery, dwl W s Sixth bet Howard and Folsom
Kingwell Joseph F. carriage painter with Thomas Stackpole, dwl Sixth nr Folsom
Kingwell Thomas V. brass finisher, dwl 238 Sixth
Kinkel Philip, cooper, dwl 631 Broadway
Kinne Henry, teamster with Reynolds & Co. dwl E s Folsom bet First and Fremont
Kinne William H. teamster, dwl 306 Fremont
Kinnear John, laborer, Custom House
Kinneston C. H. ship carpenter, dwl SW cor Louisiana and Sierra
Kinney Ann Miss, domestic, 554 Folsom
Kinney Christina, domestic, dwl 1109 Stockton
Kinney John, machinist, dwl 41 Minna
Kinney Michael, laborer, dwl 1029 Pacific
Kinney Owen, carpenter, dwl 414 Market
Kinney Patrick, cartman, Lincoln Place
Kinney William, workman with W. Hall, Old San José Road county line
Kinsey Esther (widow) John, dwl 631 Third
Kinsey Kerst, miner, dwl NE cor Stock and Wash
Kinsey ——, dwl 315 Montgomery
Kinsle Michael J. saloon, SW cor First and Tehama
Kinsman Charles, builder, dwl 315 Fifth
Kinsman Franklin, carpenter, dwl 72 Tehama
Kinsman James, carpenter, dwl 81 Natoma
Kinsman John H. assistant surgeon U. S. A. office 408 Market, dwl 1108 Powell
Kinsman J. W. carpenter, dwl SE cor Natoma and Second
Kinsman Lewis B. porter Central Warehouse, dwl Ritch nr Folsom
Kinsman Nicholas W. watchman, Dow's Distillery, dwl NW cor Tenth and Bryant
Kinson George G. cook, 640 Market
Kinzer George W. stock broker, dwl 12 Essex

Kipp Henry, with Lyon & Co. dwl 162 Jessie
Kipp Joseph, 8E cor Front and Pacific
Kipps Alfred K. portrait painter with Bayley & Connor, dwl 737 Pine
Kirby Edward C. messenger Bank British North America, dwl N s Fifteenth bet Howard and Mission
Kirby James, boiler maker, dwl Manhattan Engine House
Kirby John, tailor, 190 Jessie
Kirby Joseph, book keeper, dwl 12 Central Place
Kirby Thomas, boatman, bds City Front House 625 Davis
Kirby William H. janitor P. O. dwl 833 Greenwich
Kirby W. L. secretary, office 611 Clay, dwl 317 Taylor
Kirby, see Kerby
Kirchhoff Bernhard, book keeper, 209 Front
Kirk Christian (*Haste & K.*) dwl 1017 Bush
Kirk Edward, tinner with Locke & Montague, dwl 509 Howard
Kirk Francis, oil well borer, 611 Clay, dwl 37 Geary
Kirk Hiram, molder, Union Foundry, dwl 24 Natoma
Kirk John, fireman, S. F. & P. Sugar Co. dwl Dora nr Folsom
Kirk John, laborer, dwl 11 Langton
Kirk Robert, stock broker, dwl 744 Howard
Kirk Samuel B. packer, Pacific Glass Works, dwl W s Tennessee nr Mariposa
Kirk William, carpenter, dwl 19 Langton
Kirk William H. produce commission, 46 Clay, dwl 86 Natoma
Kirkauldie William, laborer, dwl E s Gilbert near Brannan
Kirke Margaret Miss, domestic with James McM. Shafter
Kirkham R. W. major U. S. A., quartermaster and chief commissary subsistence, office 742 Washington, res Oakland
Kirkland W. P. janitor National Democratic Association Reading Room, dwl 14 Stewart
Kirkpatrick Andrew, calker, dwl Zoe Place
Kirkpatrick Charles A. surgeon Eighth Infantry C. V. Fort Point
Kirkpatrick James, clerk with Charles L. Kellogg, dwl 1316 Powell
Kirkwood Nicholas, assistant engineer, steamer Del Norte
Kirnan Frank, porter with W. B. Johnston, dwl S s Jessie bet Second and Third
Kirnan Sarah F. Miss, dress maker, dwl 513 Pine
Kirrene Mary Miss, domestic, 1210 Mason
Kirsch Joseph, hairdresser, 636 Washington, dwl 405 Union
Kirsch Michael, blacksmith, bds Sacramento Hotel
Kirsky (*Isador*) & Brother (*Moritz Kirsky*) clothing, 617 Pacific
Kirsky Moritz (*Kirsky & Bro.*) res Weaverville
Kirvey Grace Miss, domestic, NW cor Chestnut and Dupont
Kirvig Mary, domestic, dwl 6 Hodge Place
Kirwan John, carpenter, dwl Golden Gate Hotel
Kirwell James, laborer, dwl N s Presidio Road nr Fillmore
Kiser Daniel, physician, dwl 1714 Dupont
Kisfy Z. S. physician, office and dwl 809 Kearny
Kispert Christoph, cartman, dwl 27 Hinckley
Kissam J. J. A. clerk with C. D. Carter
Kissane Henry, teamster, Pier 11 Stewart, dwl 1008 Folsom
Kissling Adolph (*W. Von Ronn & Co.*) dwl 905 Kearny
Kiszler Henry, groceries and liquors, 619 Bdwy
Kittelberger Charles, bar keeper with V. Squarza, dwl SW cor Bush and Taylor
Kitterman James, cook, dwl 11 Baldwin Court
Kittle Henry M. clerk with DeWitt, Kittle & Co. dwl 332 Second

Kittle Jonathan G. *(DeWitt, Kittle & Co.)* dwl 505 Montgomery

Kittle Nicholas G. *(DeWitt, Kittle & Co.)* dwl 332 Second

Kittlewell J. R. blacksmith, 269 First, dwl 37 Clementina

Kittredge C. W. annealer, U. S. Branch Mint, dwl Stockton nr Pine

Kittredge Edward H. accountant with Robert Pennell & Co. dwl 935 Howard

Kittredge George, dwl What Cheer House

Kittredge George S. dwl 935 Howard

KITTREDGE *(J. G.)* & LEAVITT *(Charles H.)* Pioneer Iron Works, 308 Jackson and 603 Battery, dwl 935 Howard

Kittredge John R. *(Smith & K.)* dwl 935 Howard

KITTREDGE JONATHAN, proprietor Phœnix Iron Works 6 and 8 Battery, dwl 110 Ellis

Kittredge Joseph, dwl 28 Sansom

Kittredge Joseph G. jr. blacksmith, Phœnix Iron Works, 8 Battery

Kittridge George, dwl 1027 Dupont

Klaber George, wood and coal, 566 Howard, dwl 61 Tehama

Klaber Michael, workman, S. F. & P. Sugar Co. dwl S s Mission bet Eighth and Ninth

Klain N. M. photographer, dwl 430 Green

Klammer Hermann, laborer, dwl 619 Pacific

KLAPPERICH JOHN S. blacksmith, W s Washington Avenue bet Howard and Mission

Klare Radolph, shoe maker with H. Kobler, dwl 110 Sutter

Klatt Fred, dwl SW cor Mary and Minna

Klatzel Joseph, steward, Gem Saloon, dwl 805 Bush

Klaus, *(John)* Bowman *(A. S.)* & Co. *(M. J. Franklin)* junk, 728 Mission

Klebs Alexander *(Burckhardt & K.)* dwl 518 Filbert

Kleber Ellen Miss, domestic, 843 Clay

Klein Brothers *(Moses and Henry)* groceries and liquors, NE cor Broadway and Kearny

Klein Ernst *(Henry A. Thomford & K.)* NW cor Powell and Filbert

Klein Gabriel, dwl 504 Taylor

Klein Henry *(Klein Brothers)* dwl NE cor Broadway and Kearny

Klein Henry, blacksmith, dwl 233 Sutter

Klein John, laborer, dwl 620 Broadway

Klein John, liquor saloon 634 Pacific

Klein Louisa Miss, domestic with William Hale, dwl 1106 Clay

Klein Moses, Pennsylvania Engine Co. No. 12

Klein Richard *(Browning & K.)* dwl 620 Bdwy

KLEIN S. proprietor Washington Salt Mills 29 Fremont, office 225 Clay, dwl 2012 Powell

Klein Susman *(Greenhood, Newbauer & K.)* dwl 504 Taylor

Klein William, brewer, dwl 637 Broadway

Klein William, driver, Omnibus R. R. Co. dwl 3 Brooks

Kleinclaus *(Balthazar)* & Clerc *(Pierre)* machinists, Agnes Lane, dwl 634 Vallejo

Kleinclaus *(C.)* & Fauss *(O.)* Willows' Brewery, SW cor Mission and Nineteenth

Kleinclaus Gustave, machinist, dwl 634 Vallejo

Kleine Henry, carpenter with S. S. Culverwell, 29 Fremont, dwl Clara nr Sixth

Kleine Henry, groceries and liquors, 5 Mission

Kleinhaus John *(A. Lusk & Co.)* dwl 109 Mont

Kleinschroth *(John)* & Mohr *(Charles)* wines and liquors, 650 Com and SW cor Kearny and Bush

Klemeier *(Hermann)* & Stamer *(Julius)* groceries and liquors, NW cor Jackson and Battery

Klenzer Herman, steward, dwl 238 Stewart

KLEPZIG I. C. E. manufacturer and dealer guns and sporting material, 733 Washington

Klevesane Ernst, milkman, dwl NW cor Guerrero and Duncan

Klevesane John, with Ernst Klevesane

Kline August *(Kline & Co.)* dwl 322 Geary

Kline Benjamin, boot maker, 812 Montgomery, dwl S s Jackson bet Battery and Front

Kline Benjamin, plasterer, dwl 331 Vallejo

Kline Carl F. hardware, dwl 6 Mason

Kline Daniel W. machinist, Union Foundry, dwl Ridley bet Valencia and Mission

Kline Ferdinand, cigar maker with I. K. White, 221 Sacramento

Kline George N. receiving teller with John Sime & Co. dwl NE cor Montgomery and Kearny

Kline George W. clerk with H. M. Newhall & Co. dwl W s Thirteenth nr Mission

Kline Isaac, cigar maker with Inslee & Joseph, dwl E s Dupont bet Sacramento and Commercial

Kline Jacob S. *(Anderson & K.)* dwl SW cor Stockton and Washington

Kline *(Louis)* & Co. *(August Kline)* importers and jobbers hats and caps, 420 Sac, dwl 610 Green

Kline Louis, dry goods 1004 Stockton, dwl 1123 Stockton

Kline Matthew M. express wagon, dwl Bryant bet Seventh and Eighth

Kline Philip, butcher with J. Cabannes, dwl W s Potrero Avenue nr Sixteenth

Kline Philip, waiter, 20 Sansom

Kline Robert, plasterer, dwl N s Bush bet Dupont and Stockton

Kline, see Cline and Klien

Klinefelter George W. dwl 863 Folsom

Kling Frank, fruits, steamer Washoe, dwl cor Davis and Vallejo

Kling O. W. watch maker, 227 Jackson, dwl 112 Virginia

Klingeman C. music teacher, dwl 1007 Powell

Klinkofstrom Martin *(Rowland, Walker & Co.)* vice consul for Russia, office 505 Front, dwl 29 South Park

Klinsmith William, captain sloop Whipple, dwl 203 Stewart

Klint Henry, boatman, bds Sacramento Hotel, 407 Pacific

Klippel Valentine, boot fitter, 134 Sutter

Klokow Luco, fruits, dwl 107 Leidesdorff

Kloos John, laborer, Bay Sugar Refinery, dwl 42 Julia

KLOPENSTINE ANDREW J. *(Klopenstine & Co. Sacramento)* office 405 Front, dwl Russ House

Kloppenberg J. F. lab, Custom House, dwl 226 Pac

Kloppenberg Otto *(Henry Brickwedel & Co.)* dwl E s Franklin bet Fulton and Grove

Kloppenburg Charles, clerk with Edward Vischer, dwl 226 Pacific

Klos Philip H. contractor, dwl N s Turk nr Fillmore

Klose Adolph, book keeper, dwl 1 St. Mary

Klose Christian A. book keeper, dwl 119 Dora

Klostermann Frederick, salesman, 210 California

Klotz Frederick, maltster, Pacific Brewery, 271 Tehama

Kloz John, miner, dwl 323 Pine

KLUMPKE JOHN G. real estate, office 522 Clay, dwl 1205 Sacramento

KLUMPP WILLIAM, engraver, 637 Washington, dwl 248 Clementina

Knack George F. captain schooner Minie G. Atkins, dwl 101 Prospect Place

KNACK JOHN, proprietor Philadelphia House, 336 Bush

Knackstedt Henry, clerk with Bernard Woolfe, dwl 1626 Stockton

Knaga Samuel, with S. Crim W s Howard bet Nineteenth and Twentieth

Knapp A. *(M. McNamee & Co.)* dwl 762 Howard

Knapp James G. insurance broker with H. S. Homans, dwl 212 Powell

KNAPP *(J. B.)* & GRANT *(D. W.)* commission merchants, 310 Washington, dwl S s Bryant bet Downie and Seventh

Knapp J. K. marble works, dwl 212 Powell
Knapp Joel B. book keeper with C. R. Peters & Co. 22 Battery, dwl Oriental Hotel
Knapp Sarah A. (widow) dwl 927 Greenwich
Knapp Solome S. Miss, principal Second St. School, dwl 932 Pacific
Knapp William H. salesman with M. Lanzenberg & Co. dwl 521 Pine
Kuechler Martin, cabinet maker with Craig, Golden & Yung, dwl N s Minna bet Eighth and Ninth
Kneedler George W. brick mason, dwl S s Sacramento bet Jones and Leavenworth
Kneidler John, brick mason, dwl 1318 Jackson
Knell Jacob, bar and billiard saloon, SW cor California and Kearny
Knell John D. musician, dwl 917 Sacramento
Kneller William M. salesman, 113 Battery, dwl 1419 Pacific
Knese William, bds Blue Anchor, 7 Washington
Knibbe H. W. dry goods, 206 Kearny, dwl 214 Second
Knight Daniel, clerk, P. M. S. S. Co. dwl 104 O'Farrell
Knight David, machinist, dwl Oriental Hotel
Knight Edmund H. milk ranch, SE cor Filbert and Fillmore
KNIGHT GEORGE W. & CO. (John H. Allen) blacksmiths and wagon makers, Potrero Avenue, dwl Butchers' Home, Potrero Avenue
Knight John, dwl 104 O'Farrell
Knight Louis F. upholsterer with Frank G. Edwards, dwl E s Garden bet Harrison and Bryant
Knight Luther, drayman, 110 California
Knight Robert, merchant, dwl Russ House
KNIGHT SAMUEL, superintendent Wells, Fargo & Co.'s Express and Bank, office NW cor Montgomery and California, dwl 32 Minna
Knight Stephen, book keeper, dwl 32 Minna
Knight William, book keeper, dwl N s Chestnut bet Dupont and Stockton
Knight William H. (Geo. P. Kimball & Co.) dwl 39 Fifth
KNIGHT WILLIAM W. mining secretary, office 36 Exchange Building and book keeper with Nudd, Low & Co., dwl W s Chestnut between Dupont and Stockton
Knight Wm. H. clerk with H. H. Bancroft & Co. dwl 1015 Clay
Knights L. teamster, dwl 13 Anthony
Knipe Thomas Capt. mariner, dwl 819 Greenwich
Knippenberg E. R. (Meier & K.) dwl SW cor Stevenson and Ecker
Knobloch Jacob, job wagon, SW cor Third and Howard, dwl N s Missouri bet Mariposa and Santa Clara
Knoche Henry (Schuldt & K.) dwl 120 Second
Knoll Charles F. tailoring, 420 Market
Knoll John, with Zwick & Loeven, 725 Vallejo
Knoll Theodore, musician, dwl 727 Broadway
Knop C. F. Shakespeare Saloon, NW cor Montgomery and Washington
Knop Elfert (Hildebrandt & K.) dwl SE corner Broadway and Montgomery
Knop Ferdinand, oysterman, dwl 18 Sansom
Knop (Henry) & Co. (Henry Wuhrman) liquor saloon, SE cor Market and Beale
Knopf Michael, baker, dwl W s Guerrero nr Sixteenth
Knoploch Charles, hairdresser with Aaron Creamer, dwl Bootz's Hotel
Knorp Charles, clerk with Morgan & Co. dwl German Hall
Knorp Frank, matress maker, Easton's Laundry
Knott John M. freight conductor, S. F. & San José R. R. Co. res San José
Knower John, policeman, City Hall, dwl 417 Folsom
Knowland Joseph, clerk with Blyth & Wetherbee, dwl 308 Fremont
Knowles A. E. book keeper, Pier 15 Stewart

KNOWLES (C. C.) & CLARKE (Alonzo N.) surgeon dentists, 121 Montgomery, dwl 25 Silver
Knowles Charles E. clerk with G. B. & I. H. Knowles, dwl 226 Sansom
KNOWLES G. B. & I. H. lumber, 17 California and Piers 13 and 19 Stewart, dwl 909 Taylor
Knowles George, insurance solicitor, dwl 813 Vallejo
Knowles George H. book keeper with W. H. Stowell, dwl 813 Vallejo
Knowles I. H. (G. B & I. H. Knowles) dwl American Exchange
Knowles James, San José Market, 154 First
Knowles Joseph E. salesman, 508 Montgomery
Knowles S. H. dwl 113 Minna
Knowlton Ebenezer, principal Rincon School, dwl Mercantile Library Building room 31
Knowlton George W. soda water manufacturer, dwl S s Townsend bet Third and Fourth
KNOWLTON JAMES J. & CO. advertising agents, 402 Montgomery, res Oakland
Knowlton W. H. watch maker, 648 Sacramento, dwl N s Thirteenth bet Howard and Mission
Knowlton William, dwl N s Thirteenth bet Mission and Howard
Knowmburg John, wheelwright with Kimball & Co. dwl 418 Stevenson
Knox Amariah L. conductor, North Beach & M. R. R. Co
Knox Edward, workman, Casebolt & Co. dwl 361 Minna
Knox Elias, gardener with H. Schmiedell, N s Bryant bet Sixth and Seventh
Knox G. & S. M. Co. (Silver Mountain) office 3 Odd Fellows' Hall
KNOX GEORGE T. notary public and commissioner of deeds, 613 Montgomery, dwl 824 Clay
Knox H. E. surgeon dentist, 715 Clay, res Oakland
Knox Israel W. (Palmer, K. & Co.) res Oakland
Knox John, clerk, dwl 112 Sutter
Knox Oscar, salesman with Tubbs & Co. dwl 117 Second
Knox Samuel, miner, dwl 631 Vallejo
Knudson Louis, lumber piler with Hobbs, Gilmore & Co. dwl 612 California
Koalcer Anthony, barber, dwl 9 Howard Court
Koaster Henry, laborer, bds N s Sixteenth bet Guerrero and Dolores
Kobicke Christian (Mysell & K.) dwl N s Sixteenth bet Guerrero and Dolores
Koch Anna Miss, cook, 835 Post
Koch Edmund L. modeler with John Paterson, dwl 443 Bush
Koch Edward, coppersmith with Graves & Smith, dwl 443 Bush
Koch John (Addis & K.) dwl Cosmopolitan Hotel
Koch John, tailor, dwl 113 Dora
Koch John, waiter, St. Mary's College
Koch John C. upholsterer, dwl 719 Union
Koch Margaretti (widow) dwl 443 Bush
Koch Martin (Fischer & K.) dwl 408 Kearny
Koch William, clerk with F. Scherr, 511 Sacramento, dwl 521 Bryant
Koch William, upholsterer with E. Bloomingdale & Co. dwl S s Pine bet Montgomery and Sansom
Koch William G. sign painter with Frederick Nutz, dwl 719 Union
Kochenrath Albert, with William Meyer & Co. dwl Tyson Place
Kochenrath Charles, photographer with Joseph T. Silva, dwl S s Wash bet Stockton and Powell
Kock Claus (Buchholtz & K.) dwl 619 Pacific
Kock Martin, shaving saloon, 417 Kearny
KOEHLER AUGUST, truss manufacturer, 718 Washington, dwl 523 Green
Koehler Brothers (Frederick and John) cigars and tobacco, 804 Market
Koehler Frederick, car builder, North Beach & M. R. R. Co

Koehler John *(Koehler Brothers)* dwl 804 Market
Koehler T. G. *(F. Hess & Co.)* dwl W s Mason bet Lombard and Greenwich
Koellner A. F. phrenologist, dwl 621 California
Koelzer Anthony, hairdresser, 136 Fourth, dwl 17 Everett
Koen Charles, groceries and liquors, 926 Folsom
Koenig A. Mrs. laces, 817 Washington
Koenig Arnold, stock broker, office NE cor Montgomery and Jackson, dwl S s Lombard bet Leavenworth and Hyde
Koenig Brothers *(A. and F.)* boots and shoes, 817 Washington
Koenig F. *(Koenig Brothers)* dwl 506 Filbert
Koenig Jacob, shoe maker with Conrad Staib, dwl 113 Geary
Koenig William, clerk, 417 Third cor Perry
Koenige August, driver with Aaron Messinger, dwl 685 Geary
Koenigsberger F. book keeper with M. Mayblum, dwl 435 Green
Koenigsberger Gustave *(M. Homberger)* & Co. dwl 333 Minna
Koenigsberger Z. A. cashier with Ackerman Bros. dwl 333 Minna
Koeppel William, saloon and boarding, S s Sixteenth bet Guerrero and Dolores
Koffel Solomon *(Davis & K.)* dwl 224 Jessie
Kofman Edward, tinsmith, dwl W s Bower Place
Kofoed Paul, stevedore, dwl 230 Fremont
Kohl Frederick, clerk, bds Sacramento Hotel, 407 Pacific
KOHLER ANDREW, importer music, musical instruments, fancy goods, and toys, 424 Sansom and 622 Washington, dwl 20 Ritch
Kohler Brothers S. M. Co. (Lower California) office 415 Montgomery
KOHLER *(Charles)* & FROHLING, AND OTTO SCHMITZ, wine growers and dealers native wines, 626 Montgomery, dwl 1313 Stockton
Kobler Dominick, cabinet maker with J. Strahle, dwl 422 Green
KOHLER GEORGE F. Blue Wing Saloon, 526 Montgomery
Kobler Gottheid, foreman with F. R. Reichel, dwl 27 Stone
Kohler H. boots and shoes, 514 Commercial, dwl Bootz's Hotel
Kobler Henry, clerk, dwl 511 Mason
Kobler Jacob, importers and jobbers stoves, ranges, tin plate, etc. Lazard's Building foot Battery, dwl 1604 Clay nr Clay
Kohler Jacob, musician, dwl Larkin nr Clay
Kobler John J. mariner, dwl 526 Montgomery
Kohler Louis G. printer, dwl 1226 Stockton
Kohler Ranemons, mining, dwl 914 Post
Kohler Sophie Miss, milliner, dwl 224 Green
Kohler Theodore G. *(Frederick Hess & Co.)* W s Mason bet Lombard and Greenwich
Kohlman Carl, dry goods, 915 Dupont
Kohlman *(Solomon)* & Galinger *(Joseph)* clothing and dry goods, 637 and 639 Market, dwl 220 Stevenson
Kohlman, see Coleman
Kohlmoos Christian, groceries and liquors, NW cor Mission and First
Kohlmoos Henry, grocery, NW cor Fourth and Tehama
Kohlmoos Herman, musician, dwl 903 Larkin
Kohlmoos John *(Browning & K.)* dwl 903 Larkin
Kohlwin Bernhardt, Railroad Saloon, 440 Bush
Kohn Charles, salesman with M. Kohn & Co. dwl 19 Hawthorne
Kohn David *(M. Kohn & Co.)* dwl 19 Hawthorne
Kohn Emile S. clothing, 651 Washington, dwl 821 Vallejo
Kohn Gabriel, drayman, SW cor Cal and Front
Kohn Henry & Co. *(Chris. Dunker)* groceries and liquors, 408 Folsom

KOHN *(Henry)* & CO. *(Charles Metzger)* dry goods, 8 Fourth, dwl corner Turk and Leavenworth
Kohn Henry L. (No. 2) dry goods, 628 Market, dwl NW cor Turk and Leavenworth
Kohn Isaac, merchant, office 308 Front, dwl 616 Folsom
Kobn John, trimmer with Kimball & Co. dwl 1 St. Mary
KOHN M. & CO. *(William Fishel and David Kohn)* importers and jobbers clothing, blankets, etc. SW cor Sacramento and Battery, res Europe
Kohn, see Cohen and Cohn
Kohncke Adelaide (widow) dwl SW cor Chestnut and Mason
Kohrn William M. laborer, dwl S s Oak nr Gough
Kohstamm Emil, book keeper with Helbing Greenebaum, dwl 1409 Powell
Kolk Joseph, carpenter, dwl 132 Sutter
Kolbe William A. baker, 230 Kearny, dwl 927 Folsom
Kolkmann Hermann, clerk, NW cor San and Sutter
Koller John H. groceries and liquors, 916 Wash
Kollmyer W. A. *(Nile & K.)* dwl 612 Bush
Komer Emanuel, shoe maker, 611 Mission
Kominsky Simon, drayman, dwl 114 Jones
Kone DeWitt C. metal roofer and jobbing, 126 Sutter
Kong Chun (Chinese) washing, 513 East
Kong Chung (Chinese) washing, 821 Kearny
Kong Hang (Chinese) washing, NW corner Vallejo and Mason
Kong Wau (Chinese) washing, 224 Sutter
Kong Yuen & Co. (Chinese) merchants, 728 Com
Konig Frederick, clerk with Henry Umbsen
Konig Gasper, domestic, 1411 Powell
Koning Max, dwl 507 Filbert
Koons Ephraim *(Godding & K.)* dwl 24 California
Koop Adam, butcher with William Van Housen, dwl 124 Ellis
Koop William, *(Heuer & K.)* dwl NE cor Stewart and Howard
Koopman H. captain schooner Hattie Porter, office 413 East
Koopman Henry, groceries and liquors, SW cor Franklin and Austin
KOOPMANSCHAP *(Cornelius)* & CO. *(Henry F. Edwards)* commission merchants and proprietors Union Warehouse, NW cor Battery and Union, dwl 25 Ellis
Kopman John, seaman, dwl E s Main bet Folsom and Harrison
Kopp Francis, clothing, 723 Clay, dwl 819 Clay
Kopp George J. baker, dwl 1314 Dupont
Kopp Jacob, baker, 1314 Dupont
Koppitz George, professor music, dwl 32 Everett
Kopsch A. J. dwl 111 Leidesdorff
Korb John C. boatman, dwl 28 Natoma
Korb Louis F. drayman, dwl 28 Natoma
Korb Louisa Mrs. midwife, dwl 23 Natoma
Korbel Anthony, machinist, dwl 559 Howard
Korbel Francis, cigar box manufacturer, 29 Fremont, dwl 559 Howard
Korbel Joseph, machinist, Miners' Foundry, dwl 559 Howard
Korber August, clerk, 722 Pacific
Korber Henry, liquor saloon, 722 Pacific
Korff Mary (widow) groceries and liquors, NE cor Mission and Thirteenth
Korgan Frederick, clerk, 409 Pine
Korn A. I. *(Lipman & K.)* dwl 68 Everett
Korn Louis, butcher, dwl 532 Ellis
Kornabrens Henry, clerk with Hildebrandt & Knop, dwl SE cor Broadway and Montgomery
Kornell John, laborer, dwl Lutgen's Hotel
Kornfeld Charles, dress making, 733 Clay
Korser Louis, waiter, Telegraph House SW cor Battery and Green
Korten Behrend, groceries and liquors, SW corner Greenwich and Mason

Korts Henry, clerk with H. Koster, dwl SE cor Third and Howard

Koshland Simon, merchant, dwl 530 Ellis

Kosminski H. dwl 214 Sansom

Kostello Kate Miss, domestic, 517 Pine

Koster Albert & Bro. *(Ludwig Koster)* proprietors Union Brewery, Clementina bet Fourth and Fifth

Koster *(Albert)* & Co. *(E. D. Gobert)* groceries and liquors, SW cor Jones and O'Farrell

KOSTER H. groceries and liquors, SE cor Third and Howard

Koster Henry. clerk, NW cor Bryant and Third

Koster Henry W. L. trimmer with Kimball & Co. dwl W s Harriet bet Folsom and Howard

Koster Hermann, groceries and liquors, NE cor Townsend and Crook

Koster John L. *(Plagemann, Kanzee & Co.)* res Austin, Reese River

Koster Joseph, lodgings, NW cor Kearny and Bdwy

Koster Lena Miss, domestic, dwl W s Crook bet Braunan and Townsend

Koster Ludwig *(Albert Koster & Bro.)* Union Brewery, Clementina nr Fourth

Koster Peter, milkman, San Bruno Road near Twenty-Third

Kostneyer Valentine, salesman with Hobe & Weihe, dwl 756 Washington

Kote William, druggist, SW cor Montgomery and Merchant, up stairs

Kotzbuch August, architect, dwl 308 Minna

Kough Bridget (widow) domestic, dwl 1713 Powell

Kower Emile, real estate broker, 605 Montgomery

Kowng On (Chinese) washing, 716 Dupont

Kozminsky Brothers *(H. and C.)* cigars and tobacco, 322 Sansom

Kozmiusky C. *(Kozminsky Bros.)* 322 Sansom

Kraft Francis J. soap maker, Star Soap Works, N s Austin bet Larkin and Polk

Kraft Louis, cartman, Charles bet Dupont and Bdwy

Kraft *(Philip)* & Rosenstein *(Henry)* Montgomery Beer Saloon, NE cor Montgomery and Sacramento, dwl 4 Broadway Block

Kragen Samuel, wood turner, 307 Market, dwl 43 Jessie

Krager Charles, with Kobert Kingou, 123 Occidental Market

Krager Ferdinand, carpenter, dwl nr Flume House, San Bruno Road

Krakauer Morris, tailor with Aaron Wolf

Krakauer Nathan, clerk with Glass & Levy, 305 Battery

Kraker Michael, book keeper with Falkenstein & Co. 315 Clay, dwl 632 Market

Kramar Frederick, shoe maker, 157 Second

Kramer August, tailor, 526 Merchant

Kramer B. H. cooperage, 206 Davis

Kramer Casper, carpenter, dwl 431 Clementina

Kramer Frederick, shoe maker, 217 Davis, dwl SW cor Pine and Sansom

Kramer Frederick, shoe maker with F. Ohm, dwl 3 Chatham Place

Kramer Henry, shoe making, 232 Commercial

Kramer Jacob, groceries and liquors, SW cor Greenwich and Dupont

Kramer John P. laborer, dwl 619 Pacific

Kramer John W. gardener, dwl W s Shotwell bet Twenty-Fifth and Twenty-Sixth

Kramer Philip, clerk, 540 Commercial, dwl SE cor Dupont and Greenwich

Kramer William, gas fitter, dwl SW cor Greenwich and Dupont

Kraner Philip H. merchant, office with Dickinson & Gammans, dwl 20 Belden Block

Kraner Theodore, watch maker, dwl SE cor Hyde and Lombard

Kraner William, book keeper, dwl SE cor Hyde and Lombard

Kratz Henry, tailor, 409 Bush

Kratz John, porter, 226 Montgomery

Kratzenstein Charles E. clerk, 525 Washington, dwl 7 Auburn

Kraus Daniel. hairdresser with George Held & Bro. dwl 337 Bush

Kraus Frank, porter with H. P. Wakelee, dwl 1008 Clay

Kraus Frederick, Castle Billiard and Liquor Saloon, NE cor Montgomery and Market, dwl NE cor St. Ann and Eddy

Kraus Frederick, cigar maker, dwl 120 Dupont

Kraus Jacob, barber, 14 Jackson, dwl 318 Davis

Krause Carl, North Star Restaurant, 535 Merchant

Krause Charles, fruits and vegetables, dwl 242 Clara

Krause John, blacksmith, dwl 507 Pacific

Krause Joseph, dwl 34 Turk

Krause William E. F. agent A. Rowland & Sons London, toilet articles, SW cor Front and Jackson, dwl 124 Silver

Krauser Charles, blacksmith, dwl 626 Green

Krauth Fred. K. printer with Charles F. Robbins, 416 Battery, dwl 8 Virginia Place

Krauth Frederick jr. compositor with B. F. Sterett, 553 Clay

Krauth T. K. dwl 331 Bush

Krebs C. F. E. job wagon, 701 Sacramento, dwl Liberty nr Townsend

Kreger William, carpenter, dwl 312 Folsom

Kreitz *(John B.)* & Cosbie *(William)* leather collar manufactory, 36 Battery

Kreinan Thomas, laborer, Vulcan Iron Works, dwl S s Stevenson nr First

Krenz Oswald, tanner with Henry Von Seggen

Kress John, blacksmith, dwl 323 Pine

Kress Julius, locksmith with Marwedel & Otto, dwl 903 Bush

Kretschmer Herman. hairdresser with Chretien Pfister, dwl 904 Clay

Kreuser Mme. embroiderer, 730 Washington

Kreiger Samuel, clerk, Contra Costa Laundry, 677 Market

Kriens James, laborer, Saucelito Water Works, dwl Washington nr East

Kriete Henry, groceries and liquors, NW cor Pine and Larkin

Krite George, laborer, Bay Sugar Refinery, dwl 26 Stewart

Kroag Frederick, cabinet maker with J. & J. Easton

Kroder Frederick, laborer, dwl S s Bush bet Polk and Van Ness Avenue

Kroger *(Christian)* & Muioch *(Ernst)* proprietors Palms House, 633 Broadway

Krohn Frederick, cigars and tobacco, 317 Pacific

Krohn John, clerk, NE cor Grove and Gough

Krohna Charles, seaman, bds 7 Washington

Kromer William, book keeper with L. Feldmann & Co. dwl SE cor Hyde and Lombard

Kron *(Julius)* & Co. *(Solomon Baruth)* tailors, 763 Clay

Krone Henry, locksmith, dwl 17 Fremont

Krone Louis, trimmings, 1018 Stockton

Kronig Raphael, laborer with William Buckley

KRONING WILLIAM, groceries, NW cor Sacramento and Kearny, dwl S s Sacramento bet Powell and Mason

Kronthal Henry *(Fechheimer, Goodkind & Co.)* dwl SE cor Taylor and Ellis

Krook Peter O. porter, 400 Front, dwl 7 Stevenson

Kropp Henry, clerk, NW cor Everett and Third

Krous Philip, dwl 522 Filbert, rear

Krouse Charles, express wagon, dwl 507 Pacific

Krueckmann Fred. A. physician, dwl 633 Bdwy

Krug August, German apothecary, 1125 Dupont, dwl SW cor Powell and Filbert

Krug William with L. Feldmann & Co. dwl 234 Jessie

Kruger August, flour packer, dwl NW cor First and Natoma

Kruger Carl, dyer, S. F. P. Woolen Mills
Kruger Charles, boot maker, dwl 607 Battery
Kruger Charles, liquor saloon, 648 Pacific
Kruger Charles, tailor, 704 Pacific
Kruger *(Louis)* & Hollings *(Henry)* groceries and liquors, NW cor Mason and Geary
Kruger William, seaman, dwl 54 Sacramento
Krumbec John C. clerk with Henry Bradenhop, N s Mission bet Twelfth and Thirteenth
Krus J. hairdresser, dwl 316 Davis
KRUSE *(Edward)* & EULER *(Emil Rohte and Friedrich Euler)* wholesale grocers, 209 and 211 Front
Kruse Frank *(Dreyer & K.)* dwl 619 Vallejo
Kruse Frank, Globe Livery Stable, 628 Pacific
Kruse Frederic I. tanner with John King, dwl cor Santa Clara and Connecticut
Kruse Henry, dwl 111 Ellis
Kruse Lewis, driver, A. R. C. Ice Co. dwl S s Broadway bet Front and Davis
Kruse Louis, photographer, dwl 1921 Mason
Kruse Peter, stone cutter, dwl 323 Pine
Kruser Constance, embroidering, 732 Washington
Krutcher Elias, carpenter, dwl N s Folsom bet Fifth and Sixth
Kubly F. H. dwl 7 Telegraph Place
Kuch Arnold P. drayman, dwl 741 Market
Kuch Mary Miss, domestic, 30 Eddy
Kuchel Louisa (widow) dwl 127 Silver
Kuchhoff George, tanner with S. Bloom, S s Brannan nr Sixth
Kuchmeister Henry W. *(Butt & K.)* dwl 528 Pac
Kuchenpeiser Frederick, iron door and shutter maker with John R. Sims, dwl 1109 Pacific
Kuechler August, groceries and liquors, NW cor Jessie and Annie
Kuechler Charles, draftsman, dwl 117 Second
Knehn Albin, jewelry engraver with B. Morris & Co. dwl SW cor Kearny and Pine
Knenzi John R. *(Cameron & K.)* dwl 315 Mont
Kuetner Leopold, cigars, corner Jackson and Kearny, dwl 137 Natoma
Kuffer Bernard, driver, Golden Gate Brewery, dwl 713 Greenwich
Kuffer Frederick, waiter, Union Club Rooms
Kuhirt Herman, wood turner, dwl SW corner Pine and Sansom
Kuhirt Pauline Miss, dwl SW cor Oak and Franklin
Kuhl Frederick G. bar keeper, dwl 221 Sacramento
Kuhlmann Hermann, clothing, dwl 217 Pacific
Kuhlmeyer Henry, cigar manufacturer, 229 Third
Kuhn Babet Miss, domestic, 414 Dupont
Kuhn L. melter with Goldsmith Bros. dwl 113 Mason
Kuhn Samuel, gents' furnishing goods, 200 Kearny
KUHNE ARNOLD, music teacher, office with M. Gray 613 Clay, dwl 1010 Stockton
Kull Dorathea (widow) dwl 616 Ellis
Kull John, baker, dwl N s Berry nr Mary Lane
Kunast August, stock broker, 540 Washington, dwl 1415 Powell
Knne Catharine (widow) domestic, 144 Shipley
KUNER ALBERT, seal engraver, office 621 Washington, dwl 246 Clementina
Kuney Dominique (widow) dwl W s Union Place
Kunhardt Fabian, compositor, Nuevo Mundo, dwl 1511 Powell
Kuniu Dora Miss, domestic, 10 St. Mark Place
Kunkall Jonathan, laborer, Golden State Iron Works, dwl Union House, Mission
Knnreuther Adelaide (widow) dwl 40 Fourth
Kunz Andrew, cooper, dwl 716 Pacific
Kunz Catharine (widow) dwl 352 Third
Kunz Christian, baker, Sandy Hill Bakery, dwl NE cor Clay and Mason
Kunz Henry, carriage painter with Andresen Bros. dwl cor Second and Stevenson
Kunze John, tailor, dwl 628 Green
Kurlander Hannah (widow) dwl 12 Hunt
Kurlbaum H. W. captain schooner, dwl 124 Beale

Kurre Charles *(C. Doerger & Co.)* dwl 1027 Pac
Kurre, see Currey and Kurrie
Knrth William, baker, dwl 219 Kearny
Kurtz Andrew, door keeper, U. S. Branch Mint, dwl 624 Commercial
Kushar F. laborer, Spring Valley W. W
Kusher Fred, ship carpenter, dwl N side Pinkham Place nr Eighth
Kusick Patrick, carpenter, dwl 39 First
Kuster Louis, upholsterer with H. Rosenfeld, dwl 20 Russ
Kutner Adolph *(Elias & K.)* dwl 68 Everett
Kutner Louis, cigars and tobacco, NW cor Kearny and Jackson
Kutter Henry, oysters, S s Bush bet Montgomery and Sansom, dwl Kearny nr Pine
Kuttner Charles, deck hand, stm Amelia
Kuttner Naphtaly, fancy dry goods, 350 Third
Kutzbock A. architect, office room 30 Mercantile Library Building
Kwang Chang (Chinese) washing, 1148 Folsom
Kwong Hop & Co. (Chinese) pork butchers, 633 Jackson
Kwong Yee & Co. (Chinese) merchants, 734 Sac
Kyar Christian, seaman, dwl 44 Sacramento
Kyle George, clerk with C. V. Gillespie
Kyle Robert, carpenter, dwl W side Sumner near Howard
Kyle Robert, laborer with William Kerr, dwl 903 Battery
Kyle Thomas, cartman, dwl Jones nr Geary
Kyle Thomas, stone cutter, dwl Brannan nr Second
Kyle William, clerk, dwl 509 Bush
Kysor E. F. builder, 604 merchant

L

L'ECUYER Maurice, liquor saloon, 752 Market
L'Hote Eugene, boots and shoes, 902 Dupont, dwl 1305 Mason
L'Hote René, dwl NE cor Dolores and Twentieth
L'INDEPENDANT (French weekly) Neuval & Chamon editors and proprietors, office 617 Commercial
LaAmistad Silver M. Co. office 804 Montgomery
LaEsperanza Mining Co. office 728 Montgomery
LaFavorita Mining Co. office 429 Sacramento
LaLibertad S. M. Co. office 36 Exchange Building
LaPlace Julien, waiter, City and County Hospital
LaPreux Charles, dwl 1020 Stockton
LaProvidencia S. M. Co. office 613 Montgomery
LaRue James B. dwl 114 Geary
LaRue Lucas B. superintendent San Antonio Ferry, dwl 209 Second
LaSever Salvo, fruits, 720 Dupont
LaSolidad of St. Dimas, office 519 Montgomery
LaTournelle Thomas, farmer, junction San Miguel and Ocean House Road
LaVictoire Copper M. Co. office 29 Exchange Bdg
LaVielle Daniel, bag maker, dwl S s California bet Leavenworth and Hyde
LA VOZ DE MEJICO (tri-weekly, Mexican Liberal) Antonio Mancillas editor and proprietor, office NW cor Montgomery and Jackson
Labateu Varnis, dwl 636 Pacific
Labatt J. J. *(Davega, Joseph & L.)* dwl 5 Fourth
Labatt John, porter, St. Francis Hotel, SW cor Dupont and Clay
Labbe Louis, dwl S s Lombard between Mason and Powell
Labbe Peter, drayman with Chauche & Martin, dwl SW cor Octavia and O'Farrell
Label Henry, fruits, NE cor Dupont and Bush
Label Jacob, job wagon, cor California and Sansom, dwl 20 Lewis Place
Labenthal Hannah Miss, with Mark Livingston
Labinski William, Flag Saloon 322 Montgomery, dwl 621 California

Labohm Henry G. teacher, St. Marcus' School, S s Geary bet Stock and Powell, dwl 217 Dupont
Labouchere Peter, works for Argnelus Bernal
Lacarce Julius C. book keeper with A. Giorgiani, 421 Washington, dwl NE cor Wash and Stock
Lacey Charles, carpenter and builder, 714 Sansom
Lacey H. clerk, dwl 210 Jackson
Lacey, see Lacy
Lachelle John B. workman, Pioneer Woolen Factory, dwl 1011 Kearny
Lachman Louis, tailor, 610 Mont, dwl 128 Jessie
Lachman Samuel, dwl 717 Post
Lackey Margaret Mrs. 196 Stevenson
Lackman George, waiter, Lick House
Laclaverie Paul, book keeper with John Saulnier & Co. 719 Sansom, dwl 1018 Stockton
Lacombe Eulalie (widow) dwl 228 Ritch
Locombe Louis, cook, Miners' Restaurant, dwl W s Clara nr Bush
Lacoste François, waiter, Union Club Rooms
Lacoste Honore, bar keeper, SW corner Pine and Kearny
Lacoste John, butcher, dwl N s Chestnut bet Dupont and Stockton
Lacoste Thomas, gardener, NW cor Sixteenth and R'ode Island
LACOUR LOUIS & CO. importers and wholesale dealers brandies, champagnes, and wines, 206 and 208 Jackson, dwl 431 Post
Lacrampe Ernest, Lafayette H. & L. Co. No. 2
Lacrosse John, surveyor, dwl NE cor Washington and
Lacua François, barber, dwl 1026 Dupont
Lacy John G. tinsmith with J. W. Brittan & Co. dwl 34 Louisa
Lacy Nicholas, laborer, dwl W s Salmon bet Mason and Taylor
Lacy Robert J. carpenter, dwl 511 Vallejo
Lacy Robert P. dwl S s Twentieth bet Guerrero and Dolores
Lacy T. J. P. deputy city and county surveyor, dwl 1009 Jackson
LADD & WEBSTER'S SEWING MACHINES, J. L. Willcutt agent, 32 Montgomery
Ladd Charles J. cabinet maker with J. B. Luchsinger, dwl 719 California
Ladd Clarissa (widow) nurse, dwl 516 Bush
Ladd David W. jeweler, dwl 1011 Mason
LADD GEORGE S. superintendent and secretary California State Telegraph Co. office and dwl 507 Montgomery
Ladd H. J. assistant book keeper California State Telegraph Co. dwl 507 Montgomery
Ladd J. E. clerk, Bigelow & Brother, 505 Montgomery, dwl 22 South Park
Ladd J. W. (Ladd, Reed & Co. Portland, Oregon) office 419 Front
Ladd W. Frank (Charles W. Brooks & Co.) dwl 22 South Park
Ladd Wilbur J. (Slosson & L.) SW cor First and Folsom
Ladd Wililam H. real estate, dwl SW cor First and Folsom
Ladd William W. (Higgins & L.) dwl St. Francis Hotel
Laddy James, waiter, Willows, SW cor Mission and Eighteenth
Laderer S. W. clerk, dwl 553 Mission
LADIES' PROTECTION AND RELIEF SOCIETY, building E s Franklin bet Post and Geary
LADIES' SEAMEN'S FRIEND SOCIETY, office W s Front bet Pacific and Broadway
LADIES' UNITED HEBREW SOCIETY, Mme. Waldow Cohen secretay, 1505 Stockton
Ladourade Leon, cook, 407 California
Lady Bryan G. & S. M. Co., H. O. Howard secretary, office 523 Montgomery
Lady Elizabeth G. & S. M. Co. office 604 Merchant room 3

Lady Franklin G. & S. M. Co. office 305 Montgomery room 6
Lady of the Lake G. & S. M. Co. office 420 Cal
Laemlein Edward, manufacturer Gregory's Bitters, dwl 1816 Mason
Laerampe Ernest (Cartier & Co.) dwl 532 Broadway, rear
Lafargue J. B. ship and produce broker, 306 Davis
Lafayette Brewery, 735 Green
Lafee Jacob, job wagon, cor Pine and Montgomery, dwl 454 Minna
Lafferty Bernard, bar keeper, junction Market and Geary
Lafferty Charles, laborer, dwl 365 Brannan
Lafferty Madalaine Miss, dress mkr, dwl 165 Silver
Lafferty Mary Miss, dress maker, dwl 165 Silver
Lafferty Owen, market, 546 Third, dwl 606 Third
Lafferty Patrick, teamster, dwl United States Hotel, 706 Battery
Lafitte Charles B. secretary, office 424 Battery, dwl SW cor Dupont and Broadway
Laflin James (Pinner & L.) dwl N s Francisco nr Stockton
Laflin John. laborer, dwl 32 Webb
Lafontaine Anton J. book and job printer, office 627 Merchant, dwl 625 Merchant
Laforcade Alexander, butcher with A. Reiner, dwl Potrero Avenue
Lagarde August (Lemoine, Gambert & Co.) res San José
Lage Henry, porter, 616 Kearny, dwl 704 Dupont
Lagoarde Bernard, gun maker, 730 Washington
Lagomarsino Gio. Batta, vegetable garden, SW cor Twentieth and Florida
Lagomarsino Giovanni, vegetable garden, cor Twenty-Second and Florida
Lagomarsino Jean B. with Peter Bonzi, 515 Merch
Lagomarsino L. laborer, dwl 331 Union, rear
Lagomarsino Luigi, vegetable garden, SW cor Twentieth and Florida
Lagomarsino Thomas, vegetable garden, S s Serpentine Avenue nr Folsom
Lagore Joseph (col'd) bootblack, Washington near Montgomery, dwl E s Scott bet Pacific and Broadway
Lagrare Bernare, butcher with Vincent Larrouche
Lague Abraham, blacksmith, dwl 851 Folsom
Lahaney Patrick W. collar maker with Cook & Son, dwl 361 Broadway, rear
Lahey John B. cook, 12 Sutter, dwl 814 Sansom
Lahey Mary, domestic, 236 Jessie
Lahey Thomas, dwl 220 Sutter
Lahn Louis, tanner, E s Folsom bet Fourteenth and Fifteenth
Lahner Anthony, dwl 3 Brooks, rear
Lahommedieu Adolphus, cabinet maker, dwl 15 Tehama
LAHUSEN HENRY, oyster saloon, 324 Montgomery, dwl 128 Geary
Laib Anton, boot and shoe maker, dwl 906 Pacific
Laib Joseph, boot and shoe maker, SW cor Jackson and Stockton
Laibe William, mechanic, dwl 315 Bush
Laidlaw Walter, swimming school, Meiggs' Wharf, North Beach, and salesman, 417 Montgomery, dwl 817 Mason
Laidlaw Walter jr. clerk, 417 Mont, dwl 817 Mason
Laidley Henry, clerk with Henry Cruz, 56 Clay
LAIDLEY JAMES, proprietor Easton's Laundry, N s Presidio Road nr Octavia, and Chelsea Laundry, Brannan nr Third, and State Harbor Commissioner, office 321 Sansom
Laigh Patrick, laborer, Fort Point
Laime Louis, waiter, dwl 737 Vallejo
Laine R. W. Mrs. dwl 515 Pine
Laird D. W. jeweler, 620 Merchant, dwl 1011 Mason
Laird James D. ship clerk, dwl 702 Vallejo
Laird Thomas, gas fitter, dwl Manhattan House, 705 Front

LAKE *(Delos)* & MORRISON *(Robert F.)* attorneys at law and District Attorney United States, office rooms 3 and 4 Court Building, dwl 829 Broadway

Lake Fannie Miss, dress maker, 732 Folsom

Lake George, pressman with Agnew & Deffebach, dwl 826 Broadway

Lake Henry, boot maker and restaurant, dwl 813 Montgomery

Lake Harvey, dwl 524 Howard

Lake J. S. (widow) dwl Rock House, NE corner Kearny and Broadway

Lake Rachael (widow) 732 Folsom

Lake William B. newspaper advertising agency, Government House, room 28, 502 Washington, dwl 535 Tehama

Lakeman Charles, job wagon, SW cor Sansom and Pine, dwl W s Shotwell nr Sixteenth

Lakemann Charles, clerk, 516 Kearny

Lakens Peter, carpenter, dwl 611 Jackson

Lakin Thomas, deck hand, steamer Princess

Lakmann Herman A. dwl 811 Union

Laland John, bottle washer with Kohler & Co. dwl 641 Pacific

Lalande Arsene, jeweler with Pohlmann & Co. dwl cor Clay and Yerba Buena

Lalanne Etienne, hairdresser with Chretien Pfister

Lallemand Henry, liquor saloon, 1017 Dupont

Lallemont Charles, wheelwright, dwl E s Stockton bet Pacific and Broadway

Lally Edward, laborer, dwl 8 St. Mary

Lally John, cartman, 14 St. Mark Place

Lalmant Charles, carriage maker, dwl 8 Polk Alley

Lamaison Martin, meat market, 523 Pine, dwl 433 Bush

Lamar R. C. carrier, Daily Examiner, dwl Welch bet Bryant and Brannan

Lamarche Aline, Madame, dress making, 113 Post

Lamarche E. Madame (widow) French dress maker, 22 Montgomery

Lamanre Theodore, watch maker, 526 Commercial

Lamb Amasa, carpenter, dwl 116 Jessie

Lamb A. S. carpenter, dwl 542 Mission

Lamb Edward, hostler, Easton's Laundry

Lamb E. G. *(Hathaway & Co.)* dwl 690 Geary

Lamb F. B. agent Edson's Washing Machine, dwl 116 Jessie

Lamb George, butcher, dwl 905 Sacramento

Lamb H. broker, Pacific Board Brokers

Lamb Irwin S. poll tax collector, City Hall, dwl W s Second Avenue nr Sixteenth

Lamb James, dwl What Cheer House

LAMB MARTIN W. justice peace Sixth Township, office W s Valencia nr Sixteenth, dwl W s Second Avenue bet Sixteenth and Seventeenth

Lamb Philip, machinist, dwl 830 Market

Lamb Richard, carpenter, dwl W s Dupont bet Washington and Jackson

Lamb Sarah (widow) dwl 13 Bay State Row

Lamb Thomas J. secretary Ophir Silver Mining Co. office NE cor Montomery and Cal, dwl 612 Cal

Lamb W. H. watch maker, dwl NE cor Montgomery and Pacific

Lamb William P. assayer, dwl 905 Sacramento

Lamb Z. E. sawyer with Hobbs, Gilmore & Co. dwl 43 Ecker

Lamback Christian, job wagon, dwl W s Clinton nr Brannan

Lambert C. *(Dexter, L. & Co.)* res New Jersey

Lambert Edward, dwl N s DeBoom nr Second

Lambert Edward A. machinist with Cock & Flynn, dwl 518 Sacramento

Lambert Edward E. dwl 518 Sacramento

Lambert Edward H. clerk, dwl 1302 Taylor

Lambert J. dwl Cosmopolitan Hotel

Lambert John S. merchant, dwl N s DeBoom nr Second

Lambert Major, clerk, 319 Commercial

Lambert P. engineer, Cosmopolitan Hotel

Lambert Rebecca H. dwl 29 Rousch

Lambert V. B. cooper with Handy & Neuman, dwl 824 Filbert

Lambert William *(Hucks & L.)* dwl 146 Natoma

Lambert William, butcher, dwl 631 Vallejo

Lambert William, hackman, dwl 285 Minna

Lambert W. T. dwl W s Margaret Place

Lambeth A. miner, dwl 414 Market

Lambie John, nurse, City and County Hospital

Lamborn Stephen M. carpenter, dwl E s First Avenue bet Fourteenth and Fifteenth

Lamburth A. express wagon, cor Market and Fourth, dwl cor Mariposa and Minnesota

Lameroux Daniel, driver with Nathaniel Gray, 641 Sacramento

Lameroux Samuel D. painter, dwl W s McCormack nr Pacific

LAMMERS *(Deidrick)* & LILIENTHAL *(Henry)* grocers, SE cor Hyde and Filbert

Lammers Henry, drayman, SE cor Sansom and Clay, dwl E s Leavenworth bet Geary and O'Farrell

Lammers Neil, miner, dwl SE cor Hyde and Filbert

Lammers Theodore H. A. porter with Ben Holladay, dwl 1114 Kearny

Lammier Louis, clerk, dwl 1418 Stockton

LAMMOND M. Miss, principal California Collegiate Institute, 64 Silver

Lammot Alfred V. deputy sheriff City Hall, dwl N s Haight bet Fillmore and Steiner

Lammot Henry D. deputy sheriff, City Hall, dwl N s Haight bet Fillmore and Steiner

Lamont Charles L. cook, dwl 935 Kearny

Lamont Jennie Miss, actress, Olympic, dwl 535 Mission

Lamorque Jermain, milkman with Jacob A. Maison

Lamp Peter, seaman, dwl 617 Davis

Lamping L. G. bds Franklin Hotel, SE cor Sansom and Pacific

Lampkins Sampson, foreman, Bay View Park

Lampman Henry, chief engineer steamer Del Norte, office SW cor Front and Jackson

Lampman Robert, compositor with Agnew & Deffebach, 511 Sansom

Lampman Sarah Mrs. dwl with Jas. M. Cummings

Lampson Joseph, mariner, dwl 522 Union

Lamson ——, broker, dwl 632 Market

Lamson George F. *(Lasky & L.)* dwl 618 Cal

Lancaster Canal Mill & M. Co. (Humboldt) office 420 Montgomery

Lancaster Charles E. dentist, office and dwl 912 Dupont

Lancaster Jesse, drayman, dwl 417 Folsom

Lancaster Joseph, tailor with Francis Dixey, dwl S s California bet Kearny and Dupont

Lancaster Margaret M. (widow) dwl 36 St. Mark Pl

Lancaster William, clerk with George H. Parker, 303 Montgomery, dwl 333 O'Farrell

Lanctot B. principal Chinese School, dwl NE cor Montgomery and Broadway

Lancy Thomas C. house and sign painter, 822 Montgomery, dwl 1814 Taylor

Land Chauncey B. (quartz mill, Gold Hill) dwl 1117 Pine

Land Isabel Miss, actress, dwl 25 Prospect Place

Land Philip, machinist, Vulcan Iron Works

Landaeta George, porter Empire State Restaurant

Landale John, mining engineer, dwl 29 Second

Lande Martin J. clerk, 322 Sansom, dwl 88 Everett

Lande Raphael M. merchant, dwl 88 Everett

Landenberger Adam C. *(Walther & Co.)* dwl E s Harrison Avenue nr Folsom

Landenberger C. A. printer, 621 Sansom, dwl E s Harrison Avenue nr Folsom

Lander Edward, book keeper, dwl 331 Jessie

Lander G. & S. M. Co. office 36 Exchange Building

Lander J. laborer, Spring Valley W. W

Lander P. C. real estate, office 17 Exchange Building, dwl 1123 Stockton
Landergin Patrick, gardener, Willows, SW cor Mission and Eighteenth
LANDERS DAVID, dry goods, 4 Third, dwl SE cor Hyde and Geary
Landers Edward, assistant book keeper with Goodwin & Co. dwl 331 Jessie
Landers George, express wagon, cor Davis and Washington
Landers James, dwl Sixteenth nr Guerrero
LANDERS JOHN, agent Manhattan Life and Niagara Fire Insurance companies, office SW cor Montgomery and Clay, dwl 331 Jessie
Landers John, butcher with Richard Davis, NW cor Ellis and Scott
Landers Michael, apprentice with Blake & Co. 524 Montgomery
Landers Patrick, merchant, dwl 619 Geary, rear
Landers Thomas, seaman, dwl 131 Folsom
Landesman John (Dann & L.) attorney at law, office 604 Merchant, dwl 327 Geary
Landesman Mary Mrs. millinery and millinery goods, 141 Montgomery, dwl 327 Geary
Landesman Oscar, millinery goods, 141 Montgomery, dwl 327 Geary
Landis G. C. clerk with Morris Speyer, 526 Washington, dwl 51 Minna
Landkraft August, porter St. Nicholas Hotel
Lando Harris, salesman, 509 Commercial, dwl 115 St. Mark Place
Lando (Joseph) & Marks (S.) slipper manufacturers, 327 Sac, dwl E s Hyde bet Cal and Pine
Landon W. E. Mrs. dwl 783 Market
Landrau Raoul, gardener, dwl Farmers' Exchange, Old San José Road
Landry Ann Mrs. dwl 105 Washington
Landry Norbert, collector with Abel Guy, dwl 423 Washington
Landry Terence, cooperage, 110 Davis, dwl N s Tyler bet Hyde and Larkin
Landsberger Adolph, clerk, 112 Third, dwl 734 Folsom
Landsberger Isidore, office 519 Montgomery, dwl 1415 Powell
Landsberger Joseph, variety store, 606 Mission
Landschneider Henry, miller, dwl 515 Market
Landy John, printer with Towne & Bacon
Lane Andrew, engineer, dwl S s Chestnut bet Montgomery and Kearny
Lane Bridget E. Miss, domestic, 916 Bush
Lane Catherine (widow) dwl Hinckley Place near Vallejo bet Montgomery and Kearny
Lane Charles, barber, dwl 730 Union
Lane Charles, flour packer, National Mills
Lane Charles H. ironer, Davis Laundry W s Harriet bet Howard and Folsom
Lane Charles W. oysterman, Blue Wing, dwl 730 Union
Lane Cornelius, porter, 411 Front
Lane (Edmund) & Gordon (John H.) plumbers and gas fitters, 11 Post
Lane Elizabeth (widow) millinery, 749 Clay
Lane Francis, hostler, Omnibus R. R. Co
Lane Frederick, laborer, dwl 511 Mission
Lane Henry C. bar keeper, dwl 41 Belden Block
Lane James, teamster, Pier 12 Stewart, dwl Hampton Place
Lane Jeannette Miss, dwl 736 Market
Lane Johannah Miss, domestic, 440 Battery
Lane John, cook, steamer Yosemite
Lane John, keeper museum, Willows, SW cor Mission and Eighteenth
Lane John C. blacksmith, dwl S s Perry bet Fourth and Fifth
Lane Kate Miss, domestic, 1313 Stockton
LANE LEVI C. professor anatomy and physiology, Toland Medical College, and physician and surgeon, office and dwl 664 Mission

Lane Mary M. domestic, dwl N s Pacific bet Montgomery and Sansom
LANE (N. B.) & KELLY (C. E.) produce commission, 124 Clay, dwl 17 Powell
Lane O. L. attorney at law, office 4 and 6 Armory Hall, dwl 109 Montgomery Block
Lane P. A. James, dwl N s Vallejo bet Dupont and Stockton
Lane Patrick, laborer, dwl 12 Sutter
Lane Philip P. hairdresser with George Held & Bro. dwl 56 Tehama
Lane Richard (Quinton & L.) 217 Fourth
Lane Robert, carpenter, dwl S s Harrison bet Main and Spear
Lane S. F. painter, dwl Bootz's Hotel
Lane S. J. (widow) dwl 17 Powell
Lane Thomas A. superintendent with Daniel C. McGlynn, dwl S s Stevenson bet Seventh and Eighth
Lane Thomas P. porter 313 Sacramento, dwl 409 Natoma
Lane Timothy, laborer, dwl 282 Stevenson
Laney Michael, laborer, dwl 11 Langton
Lang Alexander, furniture, dwl W s Leavenworth bet Geary and O'Farrell
Lang Augusta Miss, dwl 270 Jessie
Lang Catharine Mrs. hats and caps, 728 Wash
Lang Charles E. sign painter, 216 Washington, dwl 1714 Mason
Lang Ernest, watch maker, 102 Pac, dwl 728 Wash
Lang Ferdinand, cigar maker, dwl 318 Davis
Lang George, wood carver with J. B. Luchsinger, 116 Bush
Lang Harris, salesman, 22 Second, dwl SW cor Stevenson and Second
Lang Henry, butcher, Lick House
Lang Jacob L. (Tandler & L.) dwl Continental Hotel
Lang James, conductor, North Beach & M. R. R. Co. dwl 148 Minna
Lang John F. repairer musical instruments, 1306 Stockton, dwl 1513 Stockton
Lang Margaret Miss, domestic. 1014 Bush
Lang Victor, dwl 728 Washington
Langan Thomas, soda maker, dwl 510 Sacramento
Langdon Richard, tailor and repairer, 651 Merchant
Lange Adolph, laborer, dwl 16 Everett
Lange Frederick, upholsterer with Goodwin & Co. dwl 1520 Dupont
LANGE FREDERICK W. & CO. (Christopher C. Butt) groceries and liquors, SW cor Stockton and Bush
Lange Herman, carriage maker with Andresen Brothers, 119 Sansom
Lange Peter N. dwl SW cor Kearny and Pacific
Lange William, clerk, NW cor Powell and Post
Langensee Philip, wood carver with J. B Luchsinger, dwl 411 Sutter
Langermann August, blacksmith with Casebolt & Co. dwl 375 Jessie
LANGERMANN WILLIAM, merchant, office 510 Montgomery, dwl 1707 Stockton
Langevin C. waiter, Original House Restaurant
Langfeld August, salesman with S. Herrmann & Co. dwl 905 Larkin
Langford Thomas, boarding, Front nr Vallejo
Langhorn Consolidation G. & S. M. Co. office 1 Government House, 502 Washington
LANGLAND NELSON P. stair builder, 49 Beale, dwl 1215 Mission
Langlers Thomas, waiter, Occidental Hotel
LANGLEY, (Charles) CROWELL (Eugene) & CO. (Richard Brainard) importers and jobbers drugs, chemicals, and druggists' glass ware, etc. SW corner Clay and Battery, dwl 662 Harrison
Langley Charles, laborer, dwl 138 Stewart
Langley David, tradesman, dwl 11 Louisa
Langley G. A. (widow) dwl 908 Clay

LANGLEY HENRY G. publisher and proprietor San Francisco City Directory, Pacific Coast Business Directory, State Register, State Almanac, etc. office and dwl 612 Clay bet Montgomery and Kearny
Langstadter Seligman, dry goods, 211 Fourth
Langston Jesse, teamster, dwl E s Folsom bet First and Fremont
Langstriff Richard, gardener with Joseph M. Wood
Lanius Philip, hostler, 669 Market
Lankenau Frederick, groceries and liquors, NE cor Ellis and Powell
Lankershim Isaac, merchant, office 409 Sacramento, dwl SE cor Polk and California
Lanahan Patrick, teamster with James McDevitt, dwl W s Sansom bet Broadway and Vallejo
Lannay Peter, machinist, dwl 444 Third
Lannay Victoire E. (widow) teacher French, 444 Third
Lannergan Lawrence, miner, dwl 209 Broadway
Lannergan William, carpenter, dwl 207 Broadway
Lannes Sullivan, butcher, dwl 433 Bush
Lannigan Mary (widow) dwl 757 Folsom
Lannigan Patrick, liquor saloon, S s Folsom bet Beale and Main
Lannon Bernard, laborer, dwl 119 Fourth
Lannon Mary Miss, domestic, 1716 Mason
LANPHER CHARLES A. dwl NE cor Brannan and Ninth
Lanpher Walter A. butcher with Wilson & Stevens, dwl Brannan St. Bridge
LANSEZEUR (Felix) & HABERT (Hypolite) florists and gardeners, St. Ann's Garden, 10 Eddy nr NW cor Market and Powell
Lansing Henry J. with Kellogg, Hewston & Co. dwl Ellis junction Stockton and Market
Lanszweert Louis, analytical chemist, dwl 32 Silver
Lantheaume Ferdinand, with L. L. Lantheaume nr St. Mary's College
Lantheaume Louis L. vegetable garden nr St. Mary's College
LANZENBERG M. & Co. (John Hahn) importers and dealers French and English cloths, cassimeres, etc. 628 and 630 Clay and 631 Merchant, res Paris
Lapfgeer August W. music teacher, dwl 659 Howard
Lapham Charles H. dwl cor Union and Webster
Lapham William, laborer, bds Atlantic House 210 Pacific
Lapidge W. F. captain Pacific Mail S. S. Golden City, dwl 639 Clay
Lapidge William F. Mrs. proprietress St. John's House, 639 Clay
Lapier Charles, dwl 109 Pine
Laplace Fernand, butcher, dwl 415 Powell
Laplaine Frank, vegetable garden nr Bay View Park
Laporte John B. cigars and tobacco and fruits, 706 Market
Lapouble Frank, liquor saloon, 1304 Dupont
Larbig Nicholas, pilot, steamer Chrysopolis
Larbig Theodore, collector with Samuel Brannan, dwl 420 Montgomery
Larco Andrea, fisherman, 44 Italian Fish Market,
LARCO NICHOLAS, importer provisions, coffee, etc. 430 Jackson (up stairs) (and Brignardello, Macchiavello & Co.) dwl 317 Green
Larcombe Joseph B. clerk with T. E. Finley, dwl cor Stockton and Ellis
Lardner William, boots and shoes, 211 Pacific
Larebarde John Baptiste (Cafferato & L.) N s Vallejo bet Dupont and Kearny
Largary Louis, vegetable garden nr Bay View Park
Large Henry, porter with Redington & Co. dwl 15 Geary
Large William, gilder with Snow & Co. dwl 15 Geary
Larimer Asenith (widow) branch Swain's Bakery, 913 Stockton

Lark Cyrus, plasterer, dwl NW cor Bryant and Third
Lark Cyrus A. clerk with T. E. Bangh, 521 Clay
Larkey James, laborer, dwl N s Presidio Road nr Fillmore
Larkin Dennis, laborer, dwl N s Broadway bet Montgomery and Kearny
Larkin Frank R. agent Larkin Estate, dwl 1116 Stockton
Larkin George B. drayman, cor Battery and Pine, dwl 417 Folsom
Larkin George K. dwl 423 Sixth
Larkin Henry, carpenter with S. S. Culverwell, 29 Fremont
Larkin James, carpenter, dwl 8 Bay State Row
Larkin James, laborer with Hey & Meyn, dwl E s Twelfth nr Folsom
Larkin Mary Miss, domestic, 812 Bush
Larkin Mathew, cartman, cor Battery and Bdwy
Larkin Michael, express wagon, cor Washington and Davis
Larkin Rachel M. (widow) dwl 1116 Stockton
Larkin Stephen, cook, dwl 64 Natoma
Larkin Thomas, drayman, dwl 32 Ritch
Larkin Thomas, roofer, dwl 336 Bush
Larkin Thomas O. dwl 345½ Third
Larkin William, money broker, dwl W s Leavenworth bet Washington and Clay
Larkin William H. printer, dwl 741 Howard
LARKINS (William) & CO. (George McLeod) carriage makers, cor Spring and Summer, dwl S s Dorland bet Dolores and Guerrero
Larmit Julius, porter, dwl 738 Pacific
Larmon James, laborer, S. F. & San José R. R. Co
Larnen Patrick, bricklayer, dwl 108 Shipley
Laroche Abel, dwl 835 Howard
Laroche Alfred, clerk with Hentsch & Berton, dwl 529 Clay
Laroche François, Quincy Market, 1524 Stockton, dwl 1512 Stockton
Laroche William M. real estate, dwl NW cor Hyde and Filbert
Larrabee (John F.) & Brazer (John) book stand, 514 Montgomery
Larrabee Rhoda V. Mrs. dwl 404 Bush
Larrimore Richard, carpenter and builder, dwl 617 Union
Larroche Vincent, wholesale butcher, Potrero Av
Larrondo Faustina, dwl 628 Vallejo
Larsen Mads, carpenter with O. Bergsen, dwl W s Mason bet Lombard and Greenwich
Larsen P. C. watch maker, dwl 636 Pacific
Larsen Peter C. watch maker, dwl 642 Howard
Larseneur Louis, stone cutter with C. B. Grant, dwl 53 Clementina
Larseneur Peter (Paltenghi & L.) dwl 318 Bdwy
Larson Hans, shoe maker, W s Belden, dwl E s Downey nr Bryant
Larson Paul, wagon maker, bds Pacific Temperance House 109 Pacific
Lartigan Jerome, with Lemoine, Gambert & Co. dwl 433 Pacific
Larue Alfred, French laundry, Quincy Place bet Kearny and Dupont
Las Chureas S. M. Co. office 519 Montgomery
LASAR E. & L. proprietors Original House, 531 and 533 Sacramento, dwl 808 Vallejo
Lasar Leopold (E. & L. Lasar) dwl 1522 Powell
Lascouts Henry, wig maker, dwl W s Haven Pl
Lascouts Honoré, hairdresser with Pierre Puyoou, dwl 13 Virginia
Lasher Valentine, shoe maker with Charles Hottkorn, dwl 628 Merchant
Lasbier Francis H. dwl Columbia Hotel
Lask Lewis, merchant, dwl 918 Stockton
LASKY (Levi) & LAMSOM (George F.) auctioneers and commission merchants, 524 California, dwl 673 Harrison
Lassalle Jean, dwl 721 Pacific

Lassana Nicholas, butcher with O. H. Willoughby, dwl N s Sixteenth nr Nebraska
Lassell Louis, book keeper, dwl 655 Howard
Lassen Frederick, dwl 18 Dupont
Lassen James, captain brig Crimea, office Pier 9 Stewart
Lasswell Montreville D. plumber, 725 Mission
Lastreto Louis, cashier with N. Larco, 430 and 432 Jackson, dwl 311 Green
LASTRETO LUCA, coffee saloon and chop house, 513 Commercial, dwl 317 Broadway
Lataille Alfred, waiter, 721 Pacific
Latham James K. S. general book keeper, Wells, Fargo & Co. dwl 1002 Powell
LATHAM MILTON S. manager London and San Francisco Bank, Limited, office 412 Montgomery, dwl 636 Folsom
Lathan John H. C. machinist, dwl Mission near Second
LATHROP (A. B.) & WHIPPLE (Willard) contractors, office 402 Montgomery
Lathrop Elisha H. carriage trimmer with A. Folsom, dwl 719 Market
Lathrop Lydia A. boarding, 719 Market
Lathrop Martin, clerk, dwl 1 Bagley Place
Laton Charles A. book keeper, Pacific Insurance Co. 436 California, dwl 212 Ellis
Latotlu Luca, vegetable garden, nr Bay View Park
Latson Abram C. contractor, dwl 477 Jessie
Lattimore Robert, correspondent Mining and Scientific Press, office 505 Clay
Lattimore William, weigher's clerk, Custom House, dwl 105 Prospect Place
Latz Jacob, cigars and tobacco, 413 Montgomery, dwl 116 Post
Latz Simon, clothing, dwl 319 Pacific
Lau Henning, clerk, 637 Market, dwl 24 Louisa
Lauda John B. apprentice with Alfred J. Smith, dwl 20 Russ nr Howard
Laudenslager Conrad, carpenter, dwl E s Octavia bet Fell and Hayes
LAUDENSLAGER M. K. president Pacific Business College, dwl 747 Market
Lauder George (Barraclough & Co.) dwl 706 Jones
Lauder Silas, driver with Addison Martin & Co
Lauenstein Frederick L. (Saulmann & L.) dwl 835 Post
Lauenstein W. O. cashier with William T. Coleman & Co. dwl 241 Fremont
Laufer Erhart, baker, dwl 1516 Stockton
Langel Andrew, bar keeper, 1232 Dupont
Laugberty David, blacksmith with David Stoddard, dwl 50 Beale
Laughlin Bernard, laborer, dwl S s Brannan bet Fifth and Sixth
Laughlin Bridget, laundress, U. S. Marine Hospital
Laughlin Hannah Miss, domestic, 1615 Dupont
Laughlin Hugh, carpenter, dwl SE cor Hyde and Lombard
Laughlin John, laborer, dwl 266 Jessie, rear
Laughlin John, teamster with John Fay, dwl S s Greenwich bet Mason and Taylor
Laughlin John, waiter, Clipper Restaurant
Laughlin Mary Miss, domestic, 35 Essex
Laughlin Orrin, wagon maker, dwl N s Bryant bet First and Fremont
Laughlin S. O. machinist helper, Vulcan Iron Works
Laughran Mary A (widow) dwl 654 Filbert
Laughton James, carpenter, dwl 632 Green
Launinger John B. waterman, dwl 9 St. Charles
Launinger Mary A. Miss, seamstress, dwl 9 St. Charles
Laura Johnson C. M. Co. (Los Angeles Co.) office 302 Montgomery
Lauerberg Lauritz (Niggle & L.) dwl Sierra Nevada Hotel 528 and 530 Pacific
Laurens M. waiter, dwl 539 Vallejo
Laurent Andre, hatter, 1222 Stockton
Laurent Ange, book bindery, 522 Clay

Laurent Celestine Madame, milliner, 407 Bush
Laurent M. (Marchund & L.) dwl 607 Kearny
Lauricella Joseph, Fisherman's Retreat, 16 Wash
Lauricella R. Fisherman's Retreat, 16 Washington
Laurie Blair, conveyancer and U. S. Commissioner, office 55 Exchange Building, dwl 1018 Stockton
Laurie John, clerk with Daly & Hawkins, dwl 238 Jessie
Lauterwasser (Christian) & Peters (Joseph C.) wood and coal, E s Sixth bet Clementina and Tehama
LAUTERWASSER FREDERICK P. proprietor Golden Gate Market, SE cor Clark and Davis
Lauze Stephen clerk, dwl 6 Virginia Place
Lavagge John, gardener, SW cor Gough and Fell
Lavagge Michael, gardener, SW cor Gough and Fell
Lavarello G. dwl N s Vallejo bet Mont and Kearny
Lavaren James, laborer, dwl 637 Mission
Lavelle John, shoe maker with Mathew White, dwl 227 Minna
Lavelle Michael, boot maker, dwl 763 Howard
Lavcuhurg Samuel, fruit, 134 Third
Lavender Thomas, clerk, India Rice Mills, dwl 411 Filbert
Lavergne Anthony, boot manufacturer, SW cor Sacramento and Kearny
Lavery Margaret (widow) dwl 709 Howard
Lavielle Daniel, bag factory, 318 Davis, dwl California nr Hyde
Lavielle Edward, with Daniel Lavielle, dwl California nr Hyde
Lavielle Samuel jr. with Daniel Lavielle, dwl California nr Hyde
Laville R. hairdressing saloon, 13 Washington
Lavin John P. liquors, dwl 811 Battery
Laviosa Joseph (Pascal, Dubedat & Co.) dwl NW cor Montgomery and Jackson
Lavorini Charley, vegetable garden, nr Hunter's Point
Lavrock George, carriage trimmer with N. P. Holmes, dwl SE cor Mason and Eddy
Lavrock George Mrs. dress maker, 106 Third, dwl SE cor Mason and Eddy
Law Henry, plumber, dwl 514 Bryant
Law William (Williams & L.) NW cor Front and Broadway
Lawhead John B. brick maker, office Third Street Wharf
Lawl William, gold pen maker with W. B. J. Kenny, 2 Armory Hall
Lawler Annette P. (widow) dwl SW cor Green and Leavenworth
Lawler Charles, clerk, dwl 238 First
Lawler Dennis, local policeman, dwl 19 Harlan Place
Lawler James, pertyman Maguire's Academy Music, dwl 816 Montgomery
Lawler James B. confectioner with Ehrenpfort & Co. dwl Summer nr Montgomery
Lawler John, passenger agent, dwl 337 Tehama
Lawler John, workman, Mount St. Joseph
LAWLER JOSEPH, wholesale butcher, Potrero Av, dwl SE cor Santa Clara and Hampshire
Lawler Maria Miss, domestic, 1316 Taylor
Lawler Peter H. armorer, 577 Mkt, dwl 54 Louisa
Lawless James, harness maker, dwl S s California bet Mason and Taylor
Lawless John, carpenter, Occidental Hotel, dwl 506 Kearny
Lawless John, laborer, dwl 1005 Pacific
Lawless Joseph, harness maker with M. Lawless, 508 Sansom
Lawless Lawrence, laborer, dwl 754 Howard
Lawless M. saddle and harness maker, 508 Sansom, dwl S s California bet Mason and Taylor
Lawless Richard, harness maker with M. Lawless, 508 Sansom
Lawless Thomas, stone cutter, dwl E s Sixth nr Harrison

Lawlor David, trunk maker with James Longshore, 208 Bush
Lawlor George, clerk, Lick House
Lawlor George W. butcher, 432 Third, dwl 708 Harrison
Lawlor Patrick, with Greenhood & Newbauer, dwl 4 Trinity
Lawlor Peter, laborer, dwl 51 Louisa
Lawrence Albert, with M. M. Cook, SW cor Pierce and Bush
Lawrence Benjamin B. laborer, Golden Age Flour Mills, 717 Battery
Lawrence Charles, teamster, dwl 645 Mission
LAWRENCE CHARLES B. commission merchant, office 304 Montgomery, dwl Presidio
Lawrence E. A. attorney at law, office 620 Washington room 3, dwl Cosmopolitan Hotel
Lawrence Edward, harness maker, dwl 2 Stockton Place
Lawrence Elizabeth Mrs. dress maker, dwl 1024 Kearny
Lawrence Francis, carpenter, dwl 1024 Kearny
Lawrence Francis, drayman, 11 Washington, dwl Verona nr Third
Lawrence Frank S. Letter Department Wells, Fargo & Co. dwl 9 Verona Place
Lawrence Frederick W. dwl 5 Garden
LAWRENCE (George S.) & HOUSEWORTH (Thomas) opticians, stereoscopic goods, cutlery, etc. 317 and 319 Montgomery, res New York
Lawrence Henry H. assistant assayer U. S. Branch Mint, dwl 909 Union
Lawrence H. S. mariner, dwl W s Beale nr Folsom
Lawrence John, tinsmith, dwl 615 Union
Lawrence John S. carrier, American Flag, dwl Coso House
LAWRENCE JOSEPH E. (Brooks & L.) dwl Occidental Hotel
Lawrence Manuel, steamboat hand, dwl W s Sansom bet Green and Vallejo
Lawrence Mary Miss, domestic, 342 Seventh
Lawrence Paul, engineer with C. S. Nav. Co
Lawrence Rollins, salesman, dwl 536 Washington
Lawrence Samuel, stone cutter with Phil Caduc, dwl 1021 Battery
Lawrence Susan (widow) dwl 133½ Shipley
Lawrence T. W. inspector, C. H. dwl 5 Garden
Lawrence, W. H. cook, steamer Cornelia
Lawrence W. H. foreman, Spring Valley W. W. Co. Camp Pilarcitos
Lawrence William (col'd) cook, Bailey House
Lawrence William, mason, dwl 419 Tehama
Lawrence William B. salesman with Bray & Bro. dwl 608 Market
Lawrence William H. foreman City Warehouse, dwl Selina Place
Lawrenson Edward, harness maker with John O'Kane, dwl 520 Stockton
Lawrenson Thomas, with D. R. Provost & Co. dwl 520 Stockton
Laws Ann (col'd, widow) 1425 Dupont
Laws George, inspector, Custom House, dwl 105 Prospect Place
Laws James, waiter, steamer Pacific
Laws Jeremiah, subscription agent, dwl E s Gilbert nr Brannan
Laws (John) & Co. (George Stone) produce, 8 Metropolitan Market, dwl 25 Fifth
Lawson Albert, plasterer, dwl N s California Avenue nr Mission
Lawson Andrew, deck hand, steamer Princess
Lawson George Dudley, agent Puck, 617 Clay, dwl 286 Stevenson
Lawson Henry, watch maker, dwl 642 Howard
Lawson James D. book keeper, dwl 929 Greenwich
Lawson James L. sub-assistant U. S. Coast Survey, office Custom House third floor
Lawson John C. (Little & L.) dwl S s California bet Montgomery and Kearny

Lawson Larse, with S. S. Culverwell, 29 Fremont
Lawton Abial S. C. with S. B. Hanson, W s Hawes nr Folsom
Lawton Asa T. office NE cor Mont and Jackson
Lawton Elburton, carriage maker with Lawton & Co. 932 Market
LAWTON FRANKLIN, secretary S. F. Stock and Exchange Board, dwl 428 Post
Lawton Gardner T. broker, dwl Lick House
Lawton George W. clerk, 516 Kearny, dwl 1 Eddy Place
Lawton G. H. machinist, Miners' Foundry, dwl 154 Minna
Lawton Irving, dwl 329 Pine
Lawton J. D. (C. D. Henry & Co.) dwl 1 Eddy Pl
Lawton John, laborer, dwl W s Bower Place
Lawton John, waiter, International Hotel
Lawton (John H.) & Co. (Enos W. Barber) carriage and wagon makers, 932 Market
Lawton Michael, blacksmith, dwl N s Fulton nr Gough
Lawton Orlando (Haynes & L.) NE cor Sansom and Merchant
Lawton Selina W. Miss, ladies' hairdressing, 319 Powell
Lawton Theodore, clerk, dwl 643 Folsom
Lawton William, notary public and mining secretary, office 404 Montgomery, dwl 935 Sacramento
Lay James, dwl What Cheer House
Layden Michael, spinner, Woolen Mills, dwl NE cor Sixteenth and Howard
Layton Francis, porter with John G. Hodge & Co. dwl E s Jansen bet Greenwich and Lombard
Layton J. C. engineer, dwl 33 Second
Layton John, tinsmith, dwl 414 Market
Layton, see Leighton
Lazalier William B. drayman, office 401 Front, dwl 425 Bryant
Lazard A. dwl 626 California
Lazard Elie (Lazard Freres) dwl 1018 Bush
LAZARD FRERES (Alexander, Simon, and Elie Lazard, Alexander Weil, and Sylvain Cahn) importers and jobbers staple and fancy dry goods and agents Mission Woolen Mills, 115 Battery, res Paris
Lazard Simon (Lazard Freres) res Paris
Lazard's (formerly Griffing's) Warehouse, cor Battery and Filbert
Lazarque Francisco, wines and liquors, dwl NW cor Pacific and Montgomery
Lazarus Abraham, fruit peddler, dwl 40 First
Lazarus Hermann (S. & H. Lazarus) NW cor Third and Minna
Lazarus Samuel & Hermann, dry goods, NW cor Third and Minna
LeBiel Louis, hunter, dwl S s Cliff House Road, 3 miles from City Hall
LeBlanc John B. boot maker, dwl 1215 Dupont
LeBreton Edward, book keeper with Hentsch & Berton, dwl NE cor Hyde and Chestnut
LeClerc Nicolaus, cook, dwl 827 Dupont
LeCount Arthur, laundryman, dwl 331 Ritch
LeCount, see Lecount
LeCroq Oscar, express wagon, Brannan bet Second and Third
LeGay Charles (LeGay & Co.) dwl 614 Commercial
LeGAY (John B.) & CO. (Charles LeGay) importers, retailers, and manufacturers hats and caps, 614 and 616 Commercial
LeMare James J. collector, office 626 Clay, dwl 1108 Sacramento
LeNational (Republican French Weekly) Theodore Thiele & Co. editors and proprietors, office 533 Commercial
LePesque Anna (widow) dwl 42 Hawthorne
LeRay Joseph, liquor saloon, 11 Sutter
LeRoy James, equestrian, Wilson's Circus
LeROY T. wholesale wines and liquors, 540 Washington

LeROY THEODORE, real estate and first vice president Société Francaise de Secours, office 716 Montgomery
LeRoy William, clerk, 712 Mont, dwl 535 Folsom
LeRoy see Leroy
LeTroduce Henry, employé, Metropolitan Restaurant, 715 Montgomery
Lea Henry E. tinsmith, dwl N s Jackson bet Leavenworth and Hyde
Lea S. Harry, machinist, Golden State Iron Works, dwl 312 Montgomery
Lea Thomas, feed mills and maltster, 430 Pine, rear, dwl NE cor Buchanan and Webster
Lea William, molder, Union Foundry, dwl 25 Natoma
Lea, see Lee
Leach Harry, Letter Department Wells Fargo & Co. dwl 720 Market
Leach James, steamship Sacramento, dwl 112 Shipley, rear
Leach Mary Mrs. saleswoman, 139 Montgomery, dwl S s Railroad Avenue
Leach Robert, florist, dwl S s Railroad Avenue bet Guerrero and Dolores
Leach Stephen W. professor music, dwl 607 Folsom
Leadbeater Edward H. with Taaffe & Co. 9 Montgomery, res New York
Leahy Daniel, butter, cheese, and eggs, 17 Metropolitan Mkt, dwl NE cor Harrison and Seventh
Leahy Daniel F. operator, California State Telegraph Co. 507 Montgomery, dwl 716 Howard
Leahy David, clerk, 17 Metropolitan Market, dwl 840 Market
Leahy Jeremiah, laborer, dwl SW cor Harrison and Garden
Leahy Mary (widow) dwl W s Jane Place
Leahy Mary (widow) dwl 29 Ecker
Leahy Mary Miss, dwl 716 Howard
Leahy Mary Mrs. dry goods, 154 Third, dwl 716 Howard
Leahy T. T. laborer, dwl 13 Stewart
Leahy William, agent Irish News, office 510 Clay
Leamey John, laborer, dwl 102 Dora
Leamey John W. with Reynolds, Howell & Ford, dwl cor Filbert and Union Place
Lean Cornelius, laborer, dwl E s White nr Green
Lear Thomas, glass blower, dwl N s Townsend bet Third and Fourth
Learned Kate E. (widow) dwl 47 Clementina
Learned Wm. H. H. drayman, dwl 456 Jessie
Leary Bernard, shoe maker, dwl 60 Beale
Leary Daniel, cabinet maker with Goodwin & Co. dwl NW cor Gough and Pine
Leary Daniel, laborer, dwl cor Mary Lane and Berry
Leary Dennis, painter with Hopps & Kanary, dwl 567 Mission
Leary James, groom, dwl Halleck Alley
Leary Johanna Miss, domestic, 263 Stevenson
Leary John, dwl W s Polk bet Clay and Sac
Leary John, laborer, dwl 67 Stevenson
Leary John, porter with Goodwin & Co. dwl Bitter's Hotel
Leary Julia (widow) dwl 457 Jessie
Leary M. A. baker with Chas. Schroth, 230 Kearny
Leary Margaret Miss, domestic, dwl 145 Post
Leary Mary Miss, domestic with J. O. Taplin, San Bruno Road
Leary Mary Miss, domestic, 957 Howard
Leary Patrick, laborer, dwl 145 Post
Leatch John, operator, California State Telegraph Co. 507 Montgomery
Leautier Jean, brick maker, dwl NE cor Vallejo and Polk
Leavenworth John, photographer, dwl 633 Market
Leavitt Charles H. (Kittredge & L.) dwl 118 Geary
Leavitt Harriet N. (widow) dress maker, 43 Second
Leavitt John, carpenter, dwl Bootz's Hotel
Leavitt Joseph W. engineer, dwl 248 Jessie
Leavitt Samuel, deck hand, stmr Amelia

Leavy (Charles M.) & Brother (L. A. Leavy) cigars and tobacco, 526 Mont, dwl 536 Wash
Leavy L. A. (Leavy & Brother) dwl 536 Wash
Lebars J. Madame, dress making, 8 Sansom
Lebatard Alphonse (Lebatard & Brother) dwl 513 Washington
LEBATARD (Michel) & BROTHER (Alphonse) groceries, 513 Washington
Lebbe Piere, drayman, dwl SW cor Octavia and O'Farrell
Leber Edward, wheelwright with Kimball & Co. dwl New England House
Leberski Anton, shoemaker, 425 California, dwl Ennen House
Lebert (Christian) & Brougham (John) shaving saloon, 918 Dupont
Leboue Felix, paper hangings and paints, 1131 Dupont
Lebourg August, cook, dwl 8 Polk Alley
Lec Emile (Lec & Son) dwl S s Solano nr York
Lec (John) & Son (Emile) vegetable garden, Solano nr York
Lechard Louisa (widow) furnished rooms, 8 and 14 Kearny
Lechaud Jacques, steward, 605 Bush
Lecher Frank, oysterman, Blue Wing, 526 Mont
Lecholl John, laborer, dwl 1011 Kearny
Leckmann Henriqna Miss, domestic, 518 Third
Leclere Alphonse, butcher, dwl 621 Pacific
Leclere John, merchant, dwl 421 Lombard
Lecomte E. draftsman with Huerne & Harant
LECOUNT J. P. & CO. importers and retailers stationery, SE cor Montgomery and Sacramento, dwl 616 Powell
Lecount, see LeCount
Lecroque Gustave, dwl N s Chestnut bet Stockton and Powell
Ledden James, laborer, dwl 46 Natoma
Ledden John A. clerk, 335 Jessie
Leddy John, boots and shoes, 119 Fourth
Leddy John, saloon, foot Powell, dwl 815 Mont
Leddy Owen, bricklayer, dwl 72 Jessie
Ledeite Madeleine, with Peter Job, dwl Perry near First
Lederer D. L. (Taussig & L.) 723 Sansom
Lederer Simon W. clerk with M. Homberger & Co. dwl 553 Mission
Ledger Anthony H. cook, dwl SE cor Mission and First
Ledlie William, copyist County Clerk's Office, dwl 2002 Powell
Ledwith Anna F. (widow) midwife, dwl 504 Bush
Lee Abram (col'd) laborer, dwl 8 Auburn
Lee Alfred W. tinsmith with Osgood & Stetson, dwl Montgomery House
Lee Amanda Miss, actress. Olympic, dwl 815 Mont
Lee Andrew, express wagon, dwl 3 Douglass Court
Lee Anna (widow) dwl W s Jones bet Sutter and Post
Lee Anthony (col'd) laborer, dwl 907 Sacramento
Lee Benj. F. sash maker with S. S. Culverwell, dwl SW cor Washington and Taylor
Lee Charles, mariner, dwl 326 Vallejo
Lee Charles H. equestrian, dwl N s Sixteenth near Howard
Lee Daniel, employé with Wilson & Moulton, dwl SE cor Pacific and Davis
Lee (David C.) & Keating (Robert H.) (col'd) boot blacking, 547 Clay, dwl 6 John
Lee Dennis, boiler maker, Union Foundry, dwl Sumner bet Seventh and Eighth
Lee Edward, carpenter, dwl N s Harrison bet Seventh and Eighth
Lee Ellen Miss, dress maker, 713 Folsom
Lee Francis, with R. & J. Morton, cor Taylor and Ellis
Lee Francis, farmer, dwl 1715 Stockton
Lee Franklin V. brick mason, dwl S s Washington bet Taylor and Jones

Lee George H. driver, Central R. R. Co. dwl SE cor Sixth and Brannan
Lee Harry, dwl 204 Montgomery
Lee Harry, workman with Turner & Rundle, dwl Pacific House Stewart nr Market
Lee Henry, upholsterer with J. F. & H. H. Schafer, dwl Bootz's Hotel
Lee Henry C. book keeper with Sather & Co. dwl 422 Second
Lee Herman H. (col'd) steward, dwl E s Adelle Al
Lee James, carpenter, dwl W s Polk bet Hayes and Fell
Lee James, cooper, S. F. P. Sugar Co. dwl NE cor Clara and Fifth
Lee James, laborer, dwl S s Thirteenth bet Valencia and Guerrero
Lee John, with George & Smith, dwl Bootz's Hotel
Lee John, cook, 143 Montgomery, dwl 208 Third
Lee John, sash and blind maker with George Robinson & Co. dwl Harrison bet Seventh and Eighth
Lee John S. express wagon, dwl Beale Place nr Fremont
Lee Josephine Miss, dwl 26 Rousch
Lee Llewellyn J. assistant register clerk Fourth District Court, dwl 212 Bush
Lee M. A. Mrs. furnished rooms, 823 Montgomery
Lee Mary Miss, domestic, 317 Mason
Lee Michael, spinner, S. F. P. Woolen Mills, dwl North Point
Lee N. A. liquor saloon, SE cor Clay and Waverly Place
Lee R. H. waiter, Cosmopolitan Hotel
Lee Robert, porter, 619 Front, dwl N s Riley bet Taylor and Jones
Lee Robert P. accountant, Navy Agent's Office, 434 California, dwl Cosmopolitan Hotel
Lee Thomas, laborer, Spring Valley W. W.
Lee Thomas, traveling agent, dwl 918 Vallejo
Lee Thomas F. apprentice with M. O'Brien, dwl N s Fifteenth nr Howard
Lee Tsze Quan (Chinese) physician, 732 Sacramento
Lee Virginia Miss, domestic with Mrs. Samuel Williams
Lee William, hostler, Four Mile House, San Bruno Road
Lee William, job wagon, 413 Sansom, dwl 263 Tehama
Lee William, molder, dwl 48 Jane
Lee William, painter, dwl SE cor Turk and Polk
Lee, see Lea
Leedes (John) & Rolen (Henry) Columbia House, 46 Stewart, dwl 147 Minna
Leedham L. dwl 1016 Stockton
Leeds Josiah B. captain schooner Wm. F. Bowne, office 54 Stewart, dwl 552 Folsom
Leege Ferdinand, clerk, NW cor Sac and Kearny
Leege William (Schlueter & L.) SE cor Third and Hunt
Leek Mary Mrs. furnished rooms, SE cor Sacramento and Davis
Leeks Martin, engineer, S. F. Cordage Factory
Leely John, porter, dwl Hall Court
Leeman Christopher, carpenter, dwl N s Geary nr Larkin
Leening J. N. machinist, Vulcan Iron Works
Leeper Andrew, laborer, dwl NW cor Townsend and Second
Lees Isaiah W. captain police, City Hall, dwl Clay Avenue nr Clay
Lefebvre Antoine, baker, dwl 613 California
Lefebvre Louis L. vegetable garden, W s Florida nr Twentieth
Lefevre Alexander, mechanic, dwl NE cor Taylor and Lombard
Lefevre B. & Co. (Theodore Bogel) druggists and apothecaries, SE cor Washington and Dupont
Lefevre Mary D. (widow) dwl 51 Natoma
LEFFINGWELL HENRY, real estate agent, 25 Montgomery Block, res Oakland

LEFFINGWELL WILLIAM, real estate agent, 619 Montgomery, dwl Occidental Hotel
Lefsky Frederick, washing, dwl N s Washington bet Mason and Taylor
Legall Louis, calker, dwl 54 First
Legardo Romulus, bag maker, dwl 308 Jessie
Legeay Peter, washing, 338 Union, rear
Legge James E. foreman with Dewey & Co. dwl 121 Prospect Place
Leggett Mary (widow) dress maker, 31 Everett
Leggett Matthew H. with Bayley & Cramer, 618 and 620 Washington
Leguer T. boot crimper, Lafayette H. & L. Co. No. 2
Legoff Pierre, dwl 721 Pacific
Legue Peter, laborer, Miners' Foundry
Lehan Mary Miss, domestic, 509 Lombard
Lehane John, laundryman, dwl cor Third and Stevenson
Lehany Patrick, laborer, dwl 113 Shipley, rear
Leheny Michael lab. North Beach & M. R. R. Co
Leheuzey Emanuel, cook, dwl 821 Kearny
Lehey Julia Miss, dwl 155 Clara
Lehman Albert, boot maker, 1111 Dupont
Lehman Rica Miss, domestic with William Erzgraber, N s McAllister bet Webster and Fillmore
Lehman William, shoe maker, dwl 219 Dupont, rear
LEHMANN GEORGE, watch maker and jeweler, What Cheer House 525 Sacramento, dwl 25 Minna
Lehmann Joseph, laborer, Miners' Foundry, dwl 25 Clementina
Lehmann Lipman (Weidenrich, L. & Co.) dwl NE cor Taylor and Tyler
Lehmkuhl Ernest, clerk with D. Buhsen, dwl 727 Davis
Lehmkuhl Herman, groceries and liquors, NE cor Fourth and Minna, dwl 254 Minna
Lehnhardt Henry, machinist, Fulton Foundry, dwl 546 Mission
LEHRKE HENRY, boarding, groceries, and liquors, cor Mariposa and Indiana
Leby Thomas, foreman spinning room S. F. P. Woolen Mills, dwl North Point bet Polk and Van Ness Avenue
Leibe William, brass finisher, 4 St. Mark Place
Leibert B. dwl N s Oak nr Laguna
Leichter Charles, book keeper, dwl 622 Vallejo
Leidstrum Charles, book keeper, Mason's Brewery
Leighton A. V. carpenter, dwl 411 Tehama
Leighton C. A. book keeper, dwl 212 Second
Leighton Charles Francis, plasterer, dwl 40 Moss
Leighton John A. engineer, dwl W s Polk bet Hayes and Fell
Leijus August, upholsterer, dwl 218 Tehama
Leimert Louis, confectioner, 142 Third
Lein Christian, tanner, dwl cor Folsom and Eighteenth
Lein Henry, tannery, cor Folsom and Eighteenth
LEIPNITZ GUSTAVE, druggist and apothecary, 312 Kearny
Leipzig Isaac, job wagon, dwl cor Pine and Van Ness Avenue
Leisen Frank, sash and blind maker with J. McGill & Co. dwl 919 Sacramento
Leisen Garry, clerk, SW cor Howard and Twelfth
Leisen Meus, dwl NW cor Thirteenth and Howard
Leiser John A. boot maker, dwl 1422 Dupont
Leishman James, molder, Vulcan Iron Works, dwl 43 Jessie
Leisner Christopher, Pacific Distillery Co
Leisner Nicholas, cigar maker, dwl S s Hayes bet Laguna and Buchanan
Leith Louisa (widow) dwl 112 Taylor
Leland Ellen Mrs. dwl N s Kent nr Mason
Leland G. & S. M. Co. office 302 Montgomery
LELAND LEWIS & CO. proprietors Occidental Hotel, SE cor Montgomery and Bush
Leland Sarah A. (widow) private boarding, 618 California

Leland W. J. caterer, Occidental Hotel
Lelevier Toussaint, boarding, 725 Pacific
Leliévre Adolphe E. *(Verdier, Kaindler, Scellier & Co.)* dwl 717 Vallejo
Lelong Joseph, confectioner, 413 Davis, dwl SW cor Howard and Twenty-Third
Lelong Joseph H. express wagon, dwl SW cor Howard and Twenty-Third
Lelouedec Rene, tailor, dwl 507 Green
Lem John H. painter with Hopps & Kanary, dwl 417 Sutter
Lemaitre Arsene, French laundry, E s Lagoon
Lemaitre Fleurisse, butcher, 1402 Stockton, dwl 711 Vallejo
Lemaitre Parfait, French laundry, E s Lagoon
Leman Benjamin, dwl 1515 Stockton
Leman Jacob, laborer, Pacific Distillery
Leman Walter M. actor, Maguire's Opera House, dwl SE cor Powell and John
Lembecke Charles, night clerk, Post Office, dwl NW cor Fourth and Tehama
Lembecke Christian, cartman, cor East and Wash
Lembeye Nicolas, workman with Bergerot & Co. dwl NW cor Sixteenth and Rhode Island
Lemeteyer Hippolyte, tinsmith with Tay, Brooks & Backus, dwl 631 Broadway
Lemire Julius, trunk maker, dwl 718 Stockton
Lemkau A. Henry, groceries and liquors, SW cor First and Minna
Lemke Charles H. hair dressing saloon, 1430 Stock
Lemman Thomas, captain schr Wild Pidgeon, dwl E s Mission nr Erie
Lemman William, dwl E s Mission nr Erie
Lemme Brothers *(Charles and Ferdinand)* manufacturing jewelers, 534 Commercial, dwl Hubbard nr Howard
Lemme Ferdinand *(Lemme Bros.)* dwl N s Geary bet Hyde and Leavenworth
Lemmen George, mariner, dwl 368 Minna
Lemmerman Herman, laborer, Bay Sugar Refinery, dwl 8 s Union bet Battery and Sansom
Lemmon William, miner, dwl 126 St. Mark Place
Lemoine, *(Jean B.)* Gambert *(Felix)* & Co. *(August Lagarde)* butter, cheese, eggs, poultry, etc. 1 and 2 New Market, dwl 433 Pacific
Lemon Charles, salesman with Murphy, Grant & Co. dwl American Exchange
Lemon F. H. & Co. livery and sale stable, 115 Kearny
Lemon James, grainer, dwl 81 Natoma
Lemon Samuel (col'd) clerk with Peck & Cox, dwl 5 Broadway
Lemon Sarah Miss, domestic, 111 Mason
Lemon William H. grainer, 110 Sutter
Lemore Alexander, brick yard, cor Polk and Union
Lempp Paul, machinist, Miners' Foundry, dwl 48 Ritch
Lenahan Patrick, with Goodwin & Co
Lenay Henry, baker, dwl S s Brannan bet Fifth and Sixth
Lendrum George, book keeper with Galloway & Boobar, dwl 444 Clementina
Lendy Mary Miss, seamstress, dwl NE cor Townsend and Crook
Lener Joseph, with Saulmann & Lauenstein
Lenfest Elizabeth Mrs. dress maker, 52 Tehama
Lengenfelzer Joseph, boot maker, 418 Bryant
Lengfeld Louis, merchant, office 302 California, dwl 732 Mission
Lenhardt Adam, carpets, 1232 Stockton
Lenhardt Charles, job wagon, SW cor Pine and Sansom, dwl 546 Mission, rear
Lenhart James M. foreman Fashion Stables, 16 Sutter, dwl 4 Howard Court.
Lenighan J. laborer, Spring Valley W. W
Lenling Charles, laborer, dwl 140 Stewart
Lennan Henry, carder, S. F. P. Woolen Mills, dwl North Point bet Polk and Van Ness Avenue
Lennon Bridget Miss, domestic, 15 Powell

Lennon Bridget (widow) dwl 1232 Pacific
Lennon Joanna (widow) dwl 8 s Oak nr Taylor
Lennon John A. clerk with Bernard Geraghty, NW cor Mason and Turk
Lennon Margaret Miss, domestic with L. B. Benchley
Lennon Maria G. (widow) dwl 33 Rousch
Lennon Sabina Miss, domestic, 20 Laurel Place
Lennox Jarvis B. driver with John McKew, dwl NW cor Calhoun and Union
Leno Rosa (col'd) domestic, dwl 826 Mission
Lenormund Emil, dwl Adelaide Place
Lenouvel Jules, laborer, dwl 1307 Kearny
Lent Dittilef N. ship carpenter, dwl 2109 Mason
Lent Silas, engineer, dwl 2105 Mason
LENT WILLIAM M. president Savage M. Co. office 712 Montgomery, dwl 810 Washington
Lentz Daniel, seaman, bds 7 Washington
Lentz William, usher, Maguire's Opera House
Lentz William H. photographer with C. E. Watkins, dwl 509 Dopont
Lenz William, tailor with I. Eisenberg, dwl 409 Bush
Lenzen J. J. shoe maker, 200 Sutter
Leob Henry, butcher, cor Stockton and Broadway, dwl 21 Scott
Leon Caroline Mrs. fancy goods, 568 Howard
Leon Daniel, gymnast, Wilson's Circus
Leon Fidele, waiter, Union Club Rooms
Leon John T. dwl 43 Second
Leon Mary (widow) dwl with J. F. Penny, cor Solano and Kentucky
Leon Patrick, carpenter, dwl E s Seventh bet Bryant and Brannan
Leon Rafela (widow) dwl 1309 Stockton
Leon Sarah Mrs. fancy goods, 214 Second
Leon Ynes Mrs. dwl 1019 Powell
Leonard Anna Miss, saleswoman, 140 Second
Leonard Annette Miss, dwl 26 Belden Block
Leonard Cornelius, pattern maker, Union Foundry, dwl 115 Perry
Leonard Daniel, laborer, dwl 219 Dupont, rear
Leonard Edward, laborer, dwl N s Townsend bet Third and Fourth
Leonard Ellen Miss, domestic, 404 Eddy
LEONARD EPHRAIM W. office 19 Parrott's Building, 505 Montgomery, dwl Lick House
Leonard F. J. principal Potrero School, dwl 347 Fourth
Leonard *(George)* & Brophy *(Michael)* livery stable, 527 Pacific, bds New Atlantic Hotel
Leonard Hiram, lieut. col. U. S. A. and deputy paymaster general, office 742 Wash, dwl 1817 Stock
Leonard James, gardener, dwl 66 Shipley
Leonard James, laborer, dwl W s Sansom bet Broadway and Vallejo
Leonard J. B. produce commission, 5 Washington
Leonard Jeremiah, laundryman with John Erskine, 305 Davis
Leonard John, fireman, dwl 64 Natoma
Leonard John, house painter, dwl E s Yerba Buena nr Clay
Leonard M. A. molder, Vulcan Iron Works, dwl NW cor Second and Tehama
Leonard Mark, carriage maker, dwl N s Market bet Gough and Franklin
Leonard Mary Miss, domestic, 738 Mission
Leonard Mathew, molder, NW cor Second and Tehama
Leonard P. J. waiter, SE cor Mission and First
Leonard Robert, laborer, dwl 343 Harrison
Leonard Thomas, milk ranch, W s Old San José Road opposite St. Mary's College
Leonard Thomas C. teacher mathematics, Boy's High School, dwl 347 Fourth
Leonard Willard, real estate, office 402 Front, res Oakland
Leonhardt Charles, shoe maker, 125 Bush, dwl Bryant Place

Leopold Charles, dwl 202 Dupont
Leopold Henry, waiter, 44 Sacramento
Leutier John *(B. Bonnet & Co.)* dwl W s Larkin bet Broadway and Vallejo
Lepe Pomposo, compositor, American Flag, dwl Gautier House
Lepercq Henry, hay and grain, N s Pacific bet Taylor and Jones
Lepier Stephen, drayman, Liberty Hose Co. No. 2
Lepper Augustus, clerk with Jacob Brickwedel
Leppien Frederick, salesman with Wightman & Hardie, dwl N s Green nr Larkin
Lepreux Charles, office with P. Maury, jr. dwl 1020 Stockton
Leritter John *(Charles Stulz & Co.)* dwl 202 Dupont
Lermitte François, coffee saloon, 526 Clay
Lermond A. J. ship carpenter, bds United States Hotel 304 Beale
Lermond G. W. laborer, bds United States Hotel 304 Beale
Lerond Annise Mme. lace mending, 22 Post
Leroux Alfred, express wagon, dwl 506 Filbert
Leroux Amadee, soda manufactory, 311 Dupont
Leroux Charlemagne, wines and liquors, 1008 Dupont
Leroux Octave, workman, Five Mile House, San Bruno Road
Leroux Theophil, laborer, dwl Pacific St. Marlo Restaurant
Leroy James, dwl 815 Montgomery
Leroy Philip, dwl 530 Tehama
Leroy, see Le Roy
Lesarte Mme. dress maker, dwl 1518 Stockton
Leschell John, picker, Mission Woolen Mills
Leslie Angus, seaman, dwl 20 Sherwood Place
Leslie Alice A. Miss, domestic, Brevoort House
Leslie Robert, steward, dwl 408 Dupont
Lesney Richard, bar tender, Pacific Engine Co. No. 8
Lessen William, dwl 327 Bush
Lessmann Frank, shoe maker, bds Meyer's Hotel, 814 Montgomery
Lester Charles, shoe maker, 18 Stewart
Lester J. W. *(H. W. Bragg & Co.)* res New York
Lestrange Margaret Miss, domestic, 603 Taylor
Lestrange Thomas, fireman, steamer Orizaba
Leszinsky Alexander, dry goods, 21 Kearny
Leszinsky Henry *(Wood & L.)* dwl cor Fillmore and Presidio Road
Leszinsky Isaac H. brick maker, dwl 171 Minna
Leszinsky Samuel, clerk, 540 Kearny, dwl 12 Second
Leszynsky Abraham, clerk, 130 Third
Leszynsky Charles, clerk with Stolz Bros. dwl 145 Natoma
Leszynsky Lesser, cloaks, shawls, and furs, etc. 638 Sacramento
Leszynsky Morris S. carman, dwl 145 Natoma
Letcher Giles C. assistant register clerk, Twelfth District Court, dwl 321 Sixth
Letellier Alexander, jeweler, 620 Merchant
Letker Adam, carriage maker, dwl 22 Langton
Letrosne Felix, shoe maker, dwl 718 Stockton
Letson Thomas, carpenter, dwl 18 Turk
Lette Genaro, hairdresser, 161 Second
Lette George, book keeper, London and San Francisco Bank, 412 Montgomery, dwl 124 Fourth
Letterer Christopher, box maker with Hobbs, Gilmore & Co. dwl Keystone House
Letters Christopher, with Hart & Goodman
Letunell Mary Mrs. laundress, Industrial School, Old Ocean House Road
Leu Valerian, finisher, Jackson Foundry, dwl 513 Filbert
Leuze John, beer saloon, dwl Belden nr Pine
Level Leon, merchant, office 109 Battery, dwl Russ House
Level Nathan, merchant, dwl Bee Hive Building
Levell John, boots and shoes, dwl 763 Howard

Leventritt Marion, salesman, 212 Battery, dwl S s Post bet Jones and Leavenworth
Leverone Francisco, bar keeper, 513 Commercial
Leverone Phillip, cartman, 50 Broadway
Levet John B. D. carpenter, dwl 409 Dupont
Levi A. merchant tailor, dwl 507 Davis
Levi Abraham, clothing, 403 Com, dwl 215 Sixth
Levi Albert A. salesman, 111 Battery, dwl 624 Green
Levi Cecelia Miss, waitress, NW cor Kearny and Broadway
Levi Charles, laborer, dwl 7 Hunt
Levi David, laborer, 641 Market
Levi Eliza Miss, dwl 716 Dupont
LEVI H. & CO. *(Leopold Loupe)* wholesale groceries, provisions, etc. 222 California, dwl 20 Sansom
Levi Jacob, tailor, dwl 37 Hinckley
Levi Morris, laborer, dwl 5 Hunt
Levi Nathan G. clerk, dwl 244 Mina
Levi S. dwl 72 Jessie
Levi Seligman, groceries and liquors, 220 First, dwl 83 Clementina
Levi W. express wagon, cor Post and Dupont
Levin Jacob, book keeper, 310 California, dwl 320 Minna
Levin Louis, saloon, 29 Fourth
Levin Louis tailor, 733 Mission
Levine Julius *(Eisen & Co.)* dwl 104 Montgomery
Levingson Joseph, merchant, dwl 1524 Powell
Levingston John, captain schooner Franklin Adams, dwl 1323 Stockton
Levingston L. J. groceries and liquors, SW cor Dupont and Geary
Levington William, law student with R. R. Provines, dwl 765 Mission
Levinson Henry, merchant, dwl 115 Mason
Levinson M. (widow) dwl E s Salmon bet Mason and Taylor
Levique John, gardener, dwl Farmer's Exchange, Old San José Road.
Levis Ellen Miss, domestic, 1008 Clay
LEVISON BROTHERS *(Lewis and Hermann)* importers watches, jewelry, diamonds, silver ware, watch materials, etc. 629 Washington, res New York
Levison Hermann *(Levison Bros.)* dwl 629 Wash
Levison J. clerk with Levison Bros. dwl 116 Shipley
Levison Joseph A. salesman, 638 Sacramento, dwl 309 Stockton
Levison Lewis, physician, dwl 608 Greenwich
Leviston William, clerk with Sloan & Provines, 38 and 39 Exchange Building
Levitzky, David & Co. *(Henry Frisch)* crockery and glass ware, 54 Second and 614 Market, dwl 35 Minna
Levy Abert, clerk with J. Seligman & Co. dwl 624 Green
Levy Abraham, glazier, dwl 256 Jessie
Levy Adolph, boots and shoes, 19 Second, dwl 47 Stevenson
Levy Alexander, dwl 324 Clementina
Levy A. N. furniture, 33 Market, dwl 113 O'Farrell
Levy Ascher N. fancy goods, 26 Fourth
Levy B. dwl 255 Jessie
Levy Barnard, clerk with Adams & Bro. dwl S s Jackson nr Battery
Levy Benjamin, salesman, 307 Bat, dwl 165 Minna
Levy Benjamin, tailor, 613 Pacific
Levy Bernard *(Abrams & L.)* dwl 120 St. Mark Pl
Levy Bernard, job wagon, cor Clay and Dupont, dwl 145 Post
Levy Bernard, salesman with Godchaux Bros. & Co. 109 Battery
Levy B. L. merchant, dwl 316 O'Farrell
Levy B. W. tailor, dwl 619 Pacific
Levy David, furniture, 607 Mission
Levy David P. bar keeper, Identical Saloon, SE cor Sacramento and Battery

Levy Emanuel, book keeper, 309 Sacramento, dwl 1022 Stockton
Levy Edward, policeman, City Hall, dwl S s Post nr Dupont
Levy Elias, salesman, 112 Third, dwl 521 Howard
Levy F. Mrs. proprietress Eureka Lodging House, 335 Pine
Levy Ferdinand, clerk, 535 California, dwl 7 Hunt
Levy Gustave, fancy and dry goods, 307 Battery, dwl 165 Minna
Levy H. dwl 171 Minna
Levy H. clerk with Harris Myers, dwl 1819 Stock
Levy Henry, dwl 617 Green
Levy Henry, clothing, 110 Third
Levy Henry, groceries and liquors, 523 Pacific
Levy Henry M. (Sam. Haas & Co.) dwl 760 Mission
Levy H. L. (M. B. Levy & Bro.) dwl 333 East
Levy I. S. clerk, dwl 113 O'Farrell
Levy Isaac (J. Levy & Bro.) dwl 1106 Stockton
LEVY ISAAC & CO. (Michael. Levy) dry goods, 618 Kearny, dwl 617 Green
Levy Isaac, dwl 214 Sansom
Levy Isaac, tailor, dwl E s Battery bet Broadway and Pacific
Levy Jacob (M. Levy & Bro.) dwl 119 Perry near Harrison
Levy Jacob, clerk, SE cor Jackson and Dupont ·
Levy Jacob, proprietor Eureka Hotel, 20 Sansom
Levy James, cartman, dwl St. Mary nr California
Levy John (Braverman & L.) dwl 654 Folsom
Levy John, peddler, dwl 844 Folsom
Levy Julius & Bro. (Isaac Levy) dry goods, 1106 Stockton
Levy Julius, broker, dwl 1513 Powell
Levy Julius, cigars, 262 Jessie
Levy Lazard, dwl 313 Clementina
Levy Leon, clerk, dwl 833 Vallejo
Levy (Louis) & Mochet (François) paper box manufacturers, 408 Sac, dwl 2 William
Levy Louis, butcher, dwl 214 Sansom
Levy Louis, dry goods, 12 Second
Levy Louis, dry goods, dwl S s Bryant bet Seventh and Eighth
Levy Louis, tailor, dwl 208 Pacific
Levy M. tailor, 91 Stevenson
Levy M. & Brother (Jacob Levy) dry goods, 4 Montgomery
Levy M. B. & Brother (H. L. Levy) clothing, 333 East, dwl 1157 Mission nr Eighth
Levy Marcus, clothing, 11 Jackson
Levy Mark, clothes cleaner, dwl 12 Pacific
Levy Marquis, commission merchant, 414 Sacramento room 1, dwl 1111 Leavenworth
Levy Mary Miss, dwl SE cor Sac and Battery
Levy Michael (Isaac Levy & Co.) dwl 617 Green
Levy Michael, clerk with A. Jacobs, dwl 227 Pac
Levy Michael, express wagon, dwl Brannan bet Fifth and Sixth
Levy Michel, cloths and cassimeres, 608 Sacramento, dwl 829 Vallejo
Levy Morris (Glass & Levy) res New York
Levy Morris, express wogon, cor Clay and Kearny, dwl 1013 Kearny
Levy Morris, merchant (Folsom) dwl 18 Mason
Levy Nathan, auctioneer, 823 Kearny
Levy Nathan, butcher with Joseph Cabannes, dwl Potrero Avenue
Levy Nathan, Eureka Saloon, NE cor Montgomery and California, dwl 264 Stevenson
Levy Nathan, merchant, dwl 961 Howard
Levy Philip, salesman, 403 Com, dwl 244 Jessie
Levy R. junk, dwl 134 Natoma
Levy Rosa Mrs. furnished rooms, 214 Sansom
Levy Rudolph, milkman with A. W. Owen
Levy Samuel, furniture, 26 Geary
Levy Samuel, merchant, dwl 404 Stockton
Levy Simon, furniture, 37 Second, dwl 114 Jessie
Levy Simon W. dwl 22 Fifth

Levy Solomon, tailor, 235 Jackson
Levy Solomon, express wagon, dwl 318 Davis
Levy Solomon, salesman, 628 Market, dwl 20 San· nr Dupont
Levy Solomon A. (Weil & L.) dwl St. Nicholas Hotel
Levy S. T. dwl 815 Montgomery ·
Levy S. W. (Levy & Fechheimer, Portland, O.) office 302 California, dwl 22 Fifth
Levy Sylvain, salesman, 633 Clay, dwl 833 Vallejo
Levy (T.) & Cohn (M.) dry goods, 45 Second
Levy Thomas S. architect, office room 2 Odd Fellows' Hall, dwl 22 Stanford
Levy U. boots and shoes, 414 Commercial
Levy Wolff, tailor, dwl 46 Jessie
Levy, see Levi
Lew Peter, peddler, dwl 24 Louisa
Lewald George, book keeper, 217 Front, dwl 20 San
Lewald Louis, express wagon, cor California and Battery, dwl 137 Natoma
Lewellyn Robert, groceries and liquors, 1008 Pacific
Lewin Jonas, dwl 255 Stevenson
Lewinsohn Simon, book keeper, 319 Sacramento, dwl 214 Sansom
Lewis A. B. wines and liquors, dwl 32 Geary
Lewis A. J. market, 240 Sixth, dwl 469 Tehama
Lewis Arnold, fireman, stm Amelia
Lewis Augustus Capt. dwl 909 Bush
Lewis Brothers (Joseph and Samuel) manufacturers cigars and importers tobacco, 421 Clay
Lewis Caribien, express wagon, N s Kent nr Mason
Lewis C. H. (Allen & L.) res Portland, Oregon
Lewis Charles, engineer, dwl 505 Bryant
Lewis Charles, laborer with Edward J. Quirk
Lewis Charles F. miner, dwl 151 Tehama
Lewis Cloelia (widow) dwl 865 Mission
Lewis Daniel C. pattern maker. dwl 164 Tehama
Lewis David M. dwl NE cor Broadway and Scott
Lewis D. G. printer with Towne & Bacon, dwl 29 Minna
Lewis Edwin (Turner & L.) dwl S s Vallejo bet Front and Battery
Lewis Edwin, commission merchant and flour and grain, 124 Clay, dwl 913 Jones
Lewis E. Warren, carpenter, dwl S s Green bet Larkin and Polk
Lewis Frederick Clinton jr. clerk with Cross & Co. 625 Sansom.
Lewis Frederick R. clerk with H. M. Newhall & Co. dwl 662 Harrison
Lewis Freeman H. mariner, dwl 151 Tehama
Lewis George, machinist, Vulcan Iron Works, dwl 162 First
Lewis George, mariner, dwl 20 Commercial
Lewis Henry (col'd) dwl 21 Dupont, rear
Lewis Henry, chief engineer U. S. Branch Mint, dwl 829 Washington
Lewis Henry (col'd) porter with Pioche & Bayerque, dwl 927 Greenwich
Lewis Henry E. local policeman, dwl 111 Turk
Lewis Henry L. commission merchant and jobber groceries and provisions, 209 Sacramento, dwl 770 Harrison
LEWIS HENRY M. & MITCHELL M. watch makers and jewelers, 655 Clay
Lewis Henry R. tinsmith, dwl 49 Ritch
Lewis H. J. local policeman, dwl S s Broadway bet Powell and Mason
Lewis Isaac, clerk with L. Auerbach, dwl E s Montgomery bet Vallejo and Green
Lewis James E. mate, Monumental Engine Co. No. 6
Lewis John, cigar maker with I. K. White, 221 Sac
Lewis John, tailor, dwl 10 Brooks
Lewis John (col'd) whitewasher, dwl E s Dupont nr Market
Lewis John, with D. R. Provost & Co. dwl 27 Jessie
Lewis John B. clerk with J. W. Sullivan ·
Lewis John B. real estate, dwl 559 Bryant

LEWIS *(J. Roome)* & NEVILLE *(J. M.)* Clay St. Bag Factory, 113 Clay, dwl NW cor Pine and Leavenworth
Lewis Josiah, carriage painter, dwl 309 O'Farrell
Lewis L. driver, Franklin House, SW cor Broadway and Sansom
Lewis Libby (widow) dwl E s Montgomery bet Vallejo and Green
Lewis Louis, liquor saloon, 29 Fourth, dwl 293 Clementina
Lewis Louis, merchant, dwl 21 Geary
Lewis Lyon, teacher Hebrew, dwl E s Montgomery bet Vallejo and Green
Lewis M. A. butter and eggs, 30 Occidental Market, dwl 144 Valencia
Lewis Mary C. (widow) dwl 56 Stevenson
Lewis *(Milton A.)* & Kearns *(Patrick)* butchers, 36 Fourth
Lewis Mitchell M. *(H. M. & M. M. L.)* dwl 416 Bush
Lewis Morris, furniture, 1302 Dupont
Lewis Nicholas, porter, dwl E s Leavenworth bet California and Pine
Lewis Oscar, pattern and model maker, 509 Market, dwl 164 Tehama
Lewis Oscar, saloon, Cosmopolitan Hotel, dwl NE cor Eddy and Larkin
Lewis Philip, hairdresser with Andrew C. Simpson, 520 Market
Lewis Philip, merchant, office 207 Battery, dwl 1029 Bush
Lewis Prince D. dwl 164 Tehama
Lewis Robert G. dwl 31 O'Farrell
Lewis R. P. secretary Board Kearny Street Com. office 410 Kearny, dwl 17 Langton
Lewis Sabin F. dwl 1131 Folsom
Lewis Samuel *(Lewis Bros.)* res Nevada City
Lewis Solomon, bar keeper, 29 Fourth, dwl 811 Harrison
Lewis Solomon, pawnbroker, 15 Kearny
Lewis Thomas, laborer, dwl E s Beale bet Market and Mission
Lewis Thomas, melter with Riehn, Hemme & Co
Lewis Thomas O. clerk, office Custom House, dwl 1217 Sutter
Lewis W. H. clerk, 706 Kearny
Lewis William, clerk, 602 Montgomery
Lewis William, propertyman, dwl, Manhattan Engine House
Lewis William J. chief engineer Western Pacific Railroad, dwl 461 Natoma
Lewis, see Louis
Lewthwaite Alexander, clerk with S. P. Taylor & Co. 322 Clay
Lewy Raffi, sack dealer, dwl 463 Jessie
Lewzer John, bar keeper, NE cor California and Kearny, dwl Belden nr Pine
Leyba P. miner, dwl NE cor Prospect Place and Sac
Leyden Michael, spinner, Mission Woolen Mills
Lhuomme Louis, cook, dwl 8 Polk Alley
Li Po Tai (Chinese) physician, 744 Washington
Libbey Josiah, carpenter, dwl S s Union bet Hyde and Larkin
LIBBEY M. L. dentist, office and dwl 109 Mont
Libby Augusta Miss, dwl 23 Ritch
Libby E. G. weigher with I. Friedlander, dwl SE cor Geary and Larkin
Libby Eliam, driver, Omnibus R. R. Co. dwl 23 Ritch
Libby Joel, calker, dwl 10 Tehama Place
Libby Joseph, calker, dwl 10 Tehama Place
Libby William H. teamster with Stanyan & Co. 17 California
LICENSE COLLECTOR, City and County, office 7 City Hall first floor
Licht Louis, handcartman, SE cor Sansom and Sacramento, dwl 3 Minna
Lichtenberg Charles B. watch maker, dwl 519 Davis
Lichtenfels Gottlieb, waiter, 712 Kearny

Lichtenstein M. cigar manufacturer, 19 Pacific
Lichtenstein Moses B. pawnbroker, 629½ Commercial, dwl 1224 Hyde
Lichtenstein Moses H. clerk, 629½ Commercial, dwl 1224 Hyde
Lichtenthaler Catharine Miss, domestic, 624 Green
Lichthardt George, clerk with John Dietrich
LICK HOUSE, Alstrom & Johnson proprietors, W s Montgomery bet Sutter and Post
LICK JAMES, proprietor Lick's Flour Mills and Lick House, office 422 Clay, res Santa Clara
Licker Frederick *(Samuel Graaff & Co.)* dwl 1604 Jones bet Pacific and Bernard
Liddle Clara Miss, dwl 256 Stevenson
Liddle Joseph, office 612 Clay
Liddle R. & Co. *(Charles Kaeding)* guns, sporting material, etc. 538 Wash, dwl 256 Stevenson
Liddy James, waiter, 143 Montgomery
Liddy Mary Miss, dwl 208 Third
Lieb Charles F. tailor, dwl E s Mississippi nr Mariposa
Lieb Charles W. printer, dwl E s Mississippi nr Mariposa
Lieb William F. printer, dwl E s Mississippi nr Mariposa
Liebenberg Auguste, clerk with Charles Liebenberg, SE cor Pacific and Battery
Liebenberg Charles, groceries and liquors, SE cor Pacific and Battery
Lieber William, cook, dwl W s Mowry Alley
Lieberman Theodore, book keeper with S. A. Peyser & Co. dwl 822 Mission
Liebert Bruno, music teacher, dwl 265 Minna
LIEBES H. & CO. *(Charles J. Behlow)* manufacturers furs and skin dressers, 105 and 413 Montgomery, dwl 325 Pine
Liebieg F. capt. schooner Anna Beck, office 413 East
Liebling *(Frank)* & Braudt *(Louis)* liquors and billiards, NE cor Pac and Kearny, dwl 409 Post
Liekefeld August, Washoe Saloon, 404 Montgomery
Lieker Frederick, cigar manuf, dwl 909 Vallejo
Liephart Francis, Challenge Soap Factory, W s Ritch nr Third, dwl 115 Perry
Liepsic *(Lyon)* & Loudon *(Meyer)* milk ranch, San Miguel Ranch
Liés Eugene, attorney at law, office 18 Exchange Bdg, dwl N s Hayes bet Gough and Octavia
LIESENFELD PHILIP, billiard table manufacturer, 612 Battery, dwl NE cor Stock and Bush
Light House Department Pacific Coast, office Custom House third floor
Light J. Wolf, job cart, NW cor Commercial and Battery, dwl 707 Jones
Light Louis, handcartman, dwl 3 Minna
Light Samuel, teamster, 307 Battery, dwl 707 Jones
Lighthall Joseph, carpenter, dwl 741 Mission
Lightner C. A. superintendent Ophir M. Co. dwl 632 Market
Lightner Joel F. secretary Potosi and Hale & Norcross S. M. companies, office 60 Exchange Building, dwl N s Filbert bet Jones and Taylor
Lilan Joseph, drayman, dwl W s Capp bet Eighteenth and Nineteenth
Liljequist Andres, seaman, dwl 50 Commercial
Lille Philippi, blacksmith, dwl 630 Broadway
Lillibridge Sheffield *(Charles Cruze & Co.)* dwl 2 Quincy Place
Lilly James S. carriagesmith, dwl New England House
Lilly T. dwl 24 Sansom
Limbacher Peter, barber, dwl 9 Second
Limpert Michael, machinist, dwl 205 Sansom
Lin War (Chinese) washing, 1431 Dupont
Linahan Kate Miss, domestic, 1 Auburn
Linahen Patrick, laborer, dwl 50 Louisa
Linari John, laborer, dwl 1015 Washington
Lincoln B. B. fruits, 712 Washington
Lincoln George W. foreman Griffing's Bonded Warehouse, dwl S s Clay bet Larkin and Polk

Lincoln Henry, engineer with Justus Hepler
Lincoln Jerome, with British & Californian Banking Co. office 424 California, dwl 13 Laurel Pl
Lincoln Jonas, salesman, 424 Mont, dwl 417 Green
Lincoln L. H. propertyman, Maguire's Opera House
Lincoln Rufus W. conductor, dwl 172 Minna
Lincoln Vita, laundry, Spring Valley House, rear
Lincoln Warren, conductor, North Beach & M. R. R. Co
Lincoln William, dwl W s Jones bet Filbert and Greenwich
Lind Augustus, farmer, Old Ocean House Road 1 mile from Ocean House
Lind Frank G. seaman, dwl 32 Stewart
Lind John, contractor, dwl 29 Hunt
Lind John, watchman, stm Amelia, dwl E s Vincent nr Union
Lind John O. contractor, cor Mason and Geary, dwl 211 Tehama
Lind J. Y. physician, office and dwl 759 Market
Lindauer A. office SE cor Montgomery and Sacramento room 3, dwl 521 Green
Linde C. F. paper hanger, dwl Hall Court
Lindell Martin, captain schooner Helen, Caduc's Line, foot Washington
Lindeman Charles, steward, Stevenson House
Lindeman T. baker, International Hotel
Lindemann Diedrich, with D. Brommer & Bro
Lindemann John, clerk, NE cor Green and Stock
Linden John. seaman, dwl 111 Washington
Lindenberg Isaac, clothing, 52 Stewart
Lindenberger Thomas E. (Badger & L.) dwl 345 Beale cor Harrison
Linderman Louisa Miss, domestic with Edwin F. Bunnell
Lindheimer Mier, policeman, City Hall, dwl 1022 Washington
Lindley David S. ship joiner, dwl 284 Minna
LINDLEY, HULL & LOHMAN, merchants (Sacramento) office 405 Front
Lindley Reuben, waiter, Russ House
Lindley William, laborer, dwl S s Filbert bet Montgomery and Sansom
Lindner Conrad (Pless & L.) dwl 708 Union
Lindner Marx (Goodman & L.) dwl 319 O'Farrell
Lindop William, physician, office NW corner Front and Jackson, dwl E side Main bet Folsom and Harrison
Lindow John, tailor, dwl 919 Pacific
Lindsay John M. wood carver with J. B. Luchsinger, 116 Bush
Lindsay Phebe (col'd, widow) dwl 908 Clay
Lindsay Thomas, fruits, SW cor Sansom and Merchant, dwl 248 Minna
Lindsey Dougal, dyer, Mission Woolen Mills
Lindsey James W. molder, Miners' Foundry, dwl 152 Natoma
Lindsey Joseph H. groceries and liguors, dwl W s Sansom bet Greenwich and Filbert
Lindsey William, real estate agent, 536 Washington, dwl W s Sansom bet Greenwich and Filbert
Lineger Charles, laborer, dwl E s Laskie bet Eighth and Ninth
Linehan Br   Mrs. chambermaid, Continental Hotel idget
Linehan C. boots and shoes, 27 Ecker
Linehan Daniel, milkman with David Ring
Linehan Edward, laborer, dwl 10 Jessie
Linehan Frank, milkman with David Ring
Linehan John, laborer, dwl Minna Place
Linehan Mary Miss, domestic, 909 Jackson
Linehan Patrick, stevedore, dwl 518 Mission
Linehan Patrick, teamster with Wolf Brothers, dwl 8 s Louisa nr Ritch
Linehan Timothy, laborer, dwl 10 Jessie
Linekin N. M. (widow) dwl 207 Powell
Linen James, dwl N s Fulton bet Octavia and Laguna
Linen James, author, dwl 225 Geary

Linen Rosa Miss, domestic, 722 Filbert
Linforth Alfred, saw maker 318 Jackson
LINFORTH JAMES. commission merchant, office 208 Battery, dwl NE cor Page and Laguna
Ling Sing (Chinese) washing, 652 Pacific
Lingard Samuel, workman S. F. & P. Sugar Co. dwl W s Harrison Place nr Harrison
Lingren Charles G. seaman, dwl 20 Commercial
Link Ferdinand, dwl 567 Bryant, rear
Link Jacob, merchant, dwl 56 Clay
Link Mary Miss, domestic, 824 Folsom
Link Valentine (Stein, L. & Scherb) dwl 315 Bush
Linman Daniel, seaman, dwl 20 Commercial
Linn Henry, seaman, dwl S s Sacramento bet Davis and Drumm
Linn H. T. F. collector, office 35 Exchange Building, dwl 765 Mission
Linn Jacob (Robinett & L.) dwl 520 Vallejo
Linne Henry, locksmith, dwl 604 Pacific
Linne Stephen, drayman, with Giuseppe Giovanini
Linnett Christopher, carpenter, dwl 741 Market
Lino Domingo, tailor, dwl SW cor Dupont and Broadway
Linon Sarah, domestic with Luis Castro, 469 Jessie
Linscott Russell S. porter with Murphy, Grant & Co. 401 Sansom
Linsey Caroline Mrs. dwl SW corner Dupont and Broadway
Linsley E. W. & Co. (John H. Hichborn) commission produce, 225 Clay, dwl NE cor Montgomery and Pacific
Linthal Henry, porter with Jones, Dixon & Co. dwl 18 Turk
Linton John, dwl 633 Market
Lintrup Charles, stevedore, dwl NE cor Calhoun and Union
Lion Henry, laborer, Custom House
Lion Julia Miss, infants' clothing, 657 Clay, dwl 727 Vallejo
Lion Kate (widow) dwl SW cor Gough and Fulton
Lion Leopold, clerk, 657 Clay, dwl 17 Dupont
Lion Samson, melter, U. S. Branch Mint, dwl 17 Dupont
Lion, see Lyon
Lions Cæsar, porter, 403 California
Lipe Eli, teamster with McKenna Brother & Co. dwl 66 Drumm
Lipman Charles F. dwl 933 Sacramento
Lipman Henry, peddler, dwl Belden nr Pine
Lipman Isaac, cigars and tobacco, NE cor Clay and Kearny
Lipman Joseph, hairdressing saloon, What Cheer House, dwl 110 Hyde bet Eddy and Turk
Lipman Morris, peddler, dwl Belden nr Pine
Lipman Simon, hairdresser, dwl N s Sacramento E Kearny
Lipman Solomon, dry goods (Sacramento City) dwl 113 O'Farrell
Lipman (S. W.) & Korn (A. I.) bath house and hairdressing saloon, 406 Pine, dwl 78 Everett
Lipman Y. brewer, dwl 14 Clara
Lipp William, miner, dwl 45 Jessie
Lippincott A. carpenter with S. S. Culverwell, dwl 807 Geary nr Hyde
Lippincott W. P. engineer, Alta Mills
Lippman Israel (Israel Caspar & Co.) dwl 526 Merchant
Lippman Joseph, importer and retail watches, diamonds, jewelry, etc. 203 Mont dwl 694 Geary
Lippold Bernerd, tanner, dwl SE cor Mariposa and Mississippi
Lipsett Thomas, laborer with W. Horr, dwl NW cor Mason and Sixth
Lipsitch John, express wagon, dwl cor Pine and Van Ness Avenue
Lipson Jacob, cap maker, 619 Sacramento
Lishman John, molder, dwl 43 Jessie
Lisk Henry, laborer, dwl 39 First

Lisman J. boots and shoes, 102 Second
Lisner Jacob W. bar keeper, NW cor Bush and Montgomery
Lissak A. H. jr. stock and money broker, 613 Montgomery, dwl 320 Jessie
Lissner Louis, clerk, 15 Kearny
Litchfield August, dwl 518 Stockton
Litchfield Charles A. bricklayer, dwl 919 Union
Litchfield Hartwell, produce and fruits, S s Harrison, bet Fifth and Sixth
Litchfield W. D. butcher, 53 Washington Market, dwl 347 Fremont
Litner Samuel, bricklayer, dwl W s Buenaventura nr California
Little C. C. N. harness maker with J. C. Johnson & Co. 520 Sansom
Little D. (widow) dwl 1511 Stockton
Little (E. J.) & Lawson (John C.) stoves and tin ware, 214 Jackson, dwl 719 Lombard
Little Ellen E. Miss, dwl with.W. T. Little, N s Fifteenth nr Howard
Little Francis, laborer, dwl 937 Mission
Little Henry S. blacksmith, Pacific Foundry, dwl SW cor Mission and Main
Little John, cook, 339 Third cor Verona
Little John, fruit dealer, dwl SW cor Dupont and Broadway
Little John D. drayman, dwl First nr Mission
Little John G. ship carpenter with John G. North, dwl 320 Ritch
Little Joseph W. mining stocks, dwl 527 Green
Little Martha (widow) dwl 312 Beale
Little Mary (widow) dwl N s Seventeenth bet Guerrero and Dolores
Little M. J. Miss (T. Gill & Co.) dwl 320 Ritch
Little Richard, butcher, dwl 749 Market
Little Robert, baker with W. Horr, dwl 320 Vallejo
Little Samuel, petroleum miner, dwl 358 Jessie
Little Samuel, wood turner, N s California nr Davis, dwl 15 Langton
Little Thomas, apprentice, dwl Washington bet Stockton and Powell
Little William, local policeman, Pacific Mail S. S. Co. dwl 253 Stewart
Little William C. book keeper with Parrott & Co. res Oakland
Little William D. ship carpenter with John G. North, dwl 5 Liberty
Little William T. brass molder with W. T. Garratt, dwl N s Fifteenth nr Howard
Little W. S. sawyer with J. McGill & Co. dwl 609 Market
Littlefield D. C. superintendent Occidental Market, dwl 418 Geary
Littlefield John W. shipwright and calker, 4 Merchant, dwl 19 Perry
Littlefield Joseph D. sub-master Rincon School, dwl 41 Everett
LITTLEFIELD, (Sheldon) WEBB (Peter L.) & CO. (J. Tyler Carr) commission merchants, fruits, and produce, 202 Washington
Littleford John T. (B. Morris & Co.) dwl 114 Shipley
Littler Charles W. auctioneer with J. R. Stewart & Co. dwl 328 O'Farrell
Littleton Amelia (widow) dwl Brevoort House
Litton Thomas, clerk with S. C. Harding, dwl 911 Jackson
Litton William H. stevedore, dwl 920 Stockton
Litzius August, upholsterer with Goodwin & Co. dwl 218 Tehama
Livermore H. P. (Redington & Co.) dwl Cosmopolitan Hotel
Livermore Obadiah, with Pioche & Bayerque, dwl SW cor Kearny and Lombard
Livermore W. G. dwl Russ House
LIVERPOOL AND LONDON & GLOBE INSURANCE CO. Liverpool, W. B. Johnston agent, 414 Montgomery, up stairs

LIVERPOOL, NEW YORK AND PHILADELPHIA S. S. CO. F. A. Emory agent, office 302 Montgomery rooms 1 and 2
Liverpool Petroleum Co. office 28 Government H
Livesey Thomas, with N. W. Spaulding, dwl 8 Oak
Livingston Abraham, crockery and glass ware, 8 and 10 Kearny
Livingston Chauncey (colored) assistant steward, steamer Yosemite, dwl 3 Dupont Place
Livingston Francis, driver, Central R. R. Co. dwl 10 Gilbert
LIVINGSTON FRANK, mining stocks, office 32 Montgomery Block, dwl 1713 Powell
Livingston George H. clerk with J. P. Treadwell, 528 Clay
LIVINGSTON HENRY B. Editorial Department, Alta Californian, dwl Occidental Hotel
Livingston Isaac, dwl 783 Folsom
Livingston (L.) & Hickey (P. J.) importers and jobbers wines and liquors, 221 California, dwl 1715 Powell
LIVINGSTON MARK, mining stocks, office 32 Montgomery Block, dwl 1715 Powell
Livingston Robert, plasterer, dwl Brannan Street Bridge
Livingston Violet Miss, domestic 408 Stockton
Livingston William, cabinet maker, dwl 29 Minna
Lizzie G. & S. M. Co. (Reese River) office 6 Armory Hall
Llewellyn Rees (Dunn, McHaffie & Co.) dwl Beale bet Howard and Mission
Lloyd Hannah (widow) dwl SE cor Stockton and Jackson
Lloyd John, cook, dwl 26 Stewart
Lloyd Peter, blacksmith, Union Foundry, dwl Jackson
Lloyd R. H. (Sharp & L.) attorney at law, office 17-19 Court Block, dwl 1008 Folsom
Lloyd Robert, Pacific Engine Co. No. 8
Lloyd Robert R. & Co. furniture and bedding, 727 and 729 Market, dwl 815 Mission
Lloyd William O. cabinet maker with R. R. Lloyd & Co. dwl 89 Everett
Loane Frank M. bricklayer, dwl N s Minna bet Eighth and Ninth
Loane Henry, ship carpenter, dwl 29 Clara
Loane Henry S. ship joiner with J. G. North, dwl N s Minna bet Eighth and Ninth
Loane John M. driver, dwl NE cor Fifth and Clara
Lob Alexander, butcher, dwl 619 Pacific
Lob Simon, dwl 323 Taylor
Lobner Morris, salesman, 628 Market, dwl cor Market and Stewart
Lobree Elias, tailoring, 530 Commercial, dwl 127 Kearny
Lobree Isaac, dwl 515 Minna
Lods Charles L. foreman carpenters, Spring Valley W. W. dwl Fort Point
LOCAN (Frank) & CO. (Herman Siering) importers and retailers fancy and zephyr worsted goods, 623 Clay, dwl NE corner Francisco and Midway
Lochbann Mathias, baker, dwl E s Larkin bet Green and Union
Locher Sophia, Miss, dwl 330 Stevenson
LOCHHEAD JOHN, machine and steam engine works, 111 Beale, dwl 2 Priest nr Clay
Lochry Edward, with H. Casebolt & Co. dwl cor Post and William
Locke Elisha, with Henderson & Brown, 215 Sansom
Locke Josiah H. miller, Golden Gate Mills, dwl 58 Clementina
Locke Royal P. compositor, dwl 317 Sixth
Locke Silas M. real estate, dwl 1034 Market
LOCKE (S. Morris) & MONTAGUE (W. W.) importers and jobbers stoves, ranges, metals, tinners' stock, etc. 112 and 114 Battery, res New York

Locker John, laborer, dwl 7 Lick's Alley
Lockhart Albert, E. with Atkins Massey, dwl 436 Bush
Lockhart George A. with Atkins Massey, 651 Sacramento, dwl 436 Bush
Lockhart Thomas, carpenter, dwl 54 First
Lockman John M. mariner, dwl W s San José R. R. near Thirtieth
Lockman Louis, clerk, 325 Sansom, dwl 128 Jessie
Lockrow Charles, bricklayer, Columbian Engine Co. No. 11
Lockwood Christine (widow) lodging house, 284 Minna
LOCKWOOD HARVEY M. & CO. *(Joseph Bunting)* gents' and boys' clothing, 624 Clay, res New York
Lockwood T. Warren, printer, dwl E s Union Place nr Union
Loeb Gabriel, clerk, 113 Battery, dwl SE cor Broadway and Stockton
Loeb Henry, Jefferson Market, SW cor Stockton and Broadway, dwl 21 Scott
Loebenstein Jacob, clothing, 220 Kearny
Loeher Jacob, painter, dwl 431 Pine
LOEHR FERDINAND, physician and editor California Demokrat, dwl NW cor California and Dupont
Loessel Theodore, book keeper, San Francisco Savings Union, dwl 555 Howard
Loeven Emil *(Zwick & L.)* dwl 725 Vallejo
LOEWE BROTHERS *(M. H. & L. H.)* importers and jobbers wines and liquors, 309 California, dwl 806 Green
Loewe L. H. *(Loewe Bros.)* dwl 345 Jessie
Loewenstein Jacob H. proprietor. Metropolitan Laundry, 906 Powell
Loewy Herman *(J. Lowenhelm & Co.)* dwl 1125 Powell
LOEWY WILLIAM, county clerk, office 18 City Hall, first floor, dwl 26 Rincon Place
Loftus Ann (widow) domestic, 910 Pacific
Loftus Bridget Miss, domestic, 36 Clay
Loftus James, laborer, Vulcan Iron Works, dwl N s Jessie bet Sixth and Seventh
Loftus James, teamster with James McDevitt, dwl W s Sansom bet Broadway and Vallejo
Loftus John, boot maker, dwl 225 Pacific
Loftus Julia, chambermaid, Occidental Hotel
Loftus Louisa Miss, domestic, 36 Clay
Loftus Michael A. clerk, SW cor Bryant and Ritch
Log Gee (Chinese) washing, NE cor Fourth and Clara
Logan Alexander, collar maker with William Trumbull, dwl 1304 Kearny
Logan Andrew J. watch maker with C. E. Collins, dwl 222 Stockton
Logan B. J. laborer, dwl 118 Minna
Logan H. C. stock broker, 706 Montgomery, dwl 14 Kearny
Logan John, cartman, dwl Sutter nr Kearny
Logan Joseph, baker, dwl 412 Folsom
Loge Charles, tailor, dwl 612 Battery
Logue James, express wagon, cor Bush and Sansom
LOHAUS *(Frederick)* & WICKAN *(Carsten)* groceries and liquors, 42 Stewart
Lohaus William, bar keeper, SW cor Washington and East
Lohe Emma Miss, domestic, 607 Howard
Loheide Mary M. (widow) dwl NE cor Freelon and Fourth
Lohman John, with Raneri F. Rocchiccoli, 523 Cal
Lohmann *(Henry)* & Moesta *(John P.)* clothing and furnishing goods, 644 Clay, dwl 346 Third
Lohmann Henry, cook, Blue Anchor, 7 Washington
Lohr Charles C. carrier, Abend Post, dwl 439 Union
Lohry John H. apprentice, dwl NW cor Mission and First
LOHSE JOHN F. agent California Powder Works, office 318 California, dwl 125 Silver

Lohse Nicholas, carrier, Daily Examiner, dwl SW cor Buchanan and McAllister
Lohse Theodore F. *(Dames & L.)* dwl 537 Bdwy
Loisean Adolph, compositor, Courrier de San Francisco, 617 Sansom
Loker John, watchman, stmr Chrysopolis
Lolor Charles P. *(Meader, L. & Co.)* dwl 852 Mission
Lombard Charles C. clerk, Golden Gate Flour Mills, dwl Bootz's Hotel
Lombard Dock, continuation Lombard St. bet Sansom and Battery
Lombard Jerome, mariner, dwl 24 Sansom
Lombard Joseph, farmer, Old San José Road, nr St. Mary's College
Lometti Charles, machinist with Victor Joinet, 520 Clay
Lometti Joseph, salesman, 531 Washington, dwl 821 Vallejo, rear
Lomler Charles W. collector Abend Post, dwl 562 Mission
Lomler Ernest *(Leo Eloesser & Co.)* dwl 1302 Taylor
LONDON AND LANCASHIRE FIRE ASSOCIATION, office 623 Montgomery.
LONDON AND SAN FRANCISCO BANK, LIMITED, M. S. Latham manager, office 412 Montgomery
London L. A. painter, dwl 551 Tehama
Lone Barney, laborer with William Kerr, dwl 903 Battery
Lone Mountain Cemetery Co. office 6 Government House, 502 Washington
Lonergan George M. salesman, 119 Montgomery, dwl 757 Folsom
Lonergan Henry, blacksmith, Union Foundry, dwl 757 Folsom
Lonergan James, porter, 7 Mont, dwl 757 Folsom
Lonergan John, molder, Pacific Foundry, dwl 757 Folsom
Lonergan William, butcher with John Borland, dwl 757 Folsom
Long Claude, importer and dealer hardware, 604 Washington, dwl 30 Stone
Long Claude jr. clerk, 604 Wash, dwl 30 Stone
Long David, driver, A. R. C. Ice Co. dwl U. S. Court Building SW cor Montgomery and Jackson
Long Edward, sail rigger, dwl 523 Howard
Long Edward, saloon, dwl W s Second Avenue bet Sixteenth and Seventeenth
Long Frederick, upholsterer, dwl 1520 Dupont
Long Frederick A. cane worker, dwl 1703 Dupont
Long Hannah Miss, domestic, 1130 Pine
Long James S. ranchero with W. S. Johnson, Half Moon Bay, dwl E s First Avenue, nr Fifteenth
Long John, laborer, dwl 112 Stewart
Long John (col'd) porter, dwl 914 Sacramento
Long Lydia (widow) dwl E s First Avenue nr Fifteenth
Long Mary, domestic with Patrick H. Tiernan
Long Mary Miss, domestic, 894 Sutter
Long Mathew, engineer, stmr Julia
Long M. H. shipwright, dwl SW cor Shasta and Michigan
Long Michael, foreman with E. Galpen & Co. dwl 12 Stanton
Long Peter, gardener, dwl S s Mary nr Chesley
Long Suwarrow (col'd) handcartman, cor Front and Clay
Long William, with N. R. Lowell, dwl 14 William
Long William, laborer, dwl 425 Fremont
Long Won (Chinese) washing, 947 Folsom
Longewa John, painter, dwl Franklin Hotel cor Sansom and Pacific
Longfellow Alvin J. carpenter, dwl 117 Mason
Longfield August, dry goods, dwl 905 Larkin
Longley A. C. & Son *(Otis A.)* house and sign painters, 922 Howard
Longley Otis A. *(L. & Son)* dwl 922 Howard

Longlitz John, groceries, fruits, and liquors, 906 Pac
Longshore James, trunk manufacturer, 208 Bush, salesroom 304 Sansom, dwl 258 Minna
Loodn Vong, washing, dwl 835 Broadway
Looke Mary (widow) dwl 134 Sutter
Loomis Amanda Miss, music teacher, 317 Minna
Loomis A. W. Rev. Chinese Missionary, dwl NE cor Sacramento and Stockton
LOOMIS (Pascal) & SWIFT (James F.) proprietors and publishers Puck, and wood engravers, office 617 Clay
Loomis Roland, teamster with T. Ellsworth, dwl 368 Brannan
Loomis William, plasterer, dwl Oriental Hotel
LOOMIS WILLIAM E., news agent and stationer, SE cor Washington and Sansom, dwl 622 Greenwich
Looney William, S. F. Cordage Factory, dwl SW cor Shasta and Michigan
Loop (S. J.) & Somers (D. C.) groceries and provisions, NW cor Second and Bryant, dwl N s DeBoom nr Second
Lopez Angel, cigar maker with Plagemann, Kauzee & Co. dwl E s Mont bet Union and Filbert
Lopez Carlos, dwl W s Margaret Place
Lopez Jesus, clerk, 4 Kearny, dwl E s Montgomery bet Union and Filbert
Lopez Manuel, deck hand, steamer Yosemite
Loppin Anna C. Miss, domestic, 107 Powell
Loppin Maggie E. Miss, domestic, 510 Hyde
Lorber John (Frederick & L.) dwl cor Leavenworth and Pine
Lord Andrew J. painter, Summer nr Montgomery, dwl 33 Geary
Lord Charles S. (Nudd, Low & Co.) dwl W s Oak Grove Avenue nr Bryant
Lord (Daniel S.) & Co. (Charles E. Hitchcock and Granville A. Mendon) merchants, office 405 Battery, dwl NE cor Bush and Hyde
Lord Elijah, ship carpenter, dwl 559 Market
Lord Francis, hairdresser, 636 Washington, dwl 706 Bush
Lord Joseph, dwl SE cor Second and Brannan
Lord Joseph D. merchant, dwl 1213 Powell
Lord Philip, rigger, dwl SW cor Clay and Davis
Lord Robert F. waiter, Lick House
Lord T. H. carpenter, dwl 559 Market
Lord William C. machinist, Golden State Iron Works, dwl 308 Fremont
Lore Louis, tailor, dwl SW cor Dupont and Bdwy
Lorenson F. August, salesman, 623 Clay, dwl 1001 Stevenson
Lorenzen Daniel, waiter, German Hospital, Brannan nr First
Lorenzen Lorenz, carpenter, dwl S s Francisco bet Mason and Taylor
Lorenzen Peter, seaman, bds 7 Washington
Lorenzi Pierre, vegetable garden, nr Bay View Park
Lorenzo Fernando, painter, dwl W s August Alley nr Green
Lorentzen Hans, local policeman, dwl 13 Stewart
Lorentzen Harrold, cabinet maker, dwl 206 Kearny
Lorigan Bartholomew, carpenter, dwl Meeks Place
Loring George Y. grocer, dwl 603 Pine
Loring Simeon D. dwl 2 Hardie Place
Loring William H. clerk, 216 Battery, dwl 532 Howard
LORING (William P.) & SPRAGUE (Adna) wines and liquors, 534 Merchant, dwl S Quincy
Lorings G. V. carpenter, dwl 606 Powell
Lorquin E. F. taxidermist, 522 Pine
Los Angeles & Mohican M. Co. office 702 Washington
Losano Alphonso, cigar maker with I. Raphael & Co. 430 Kearny
Losse Louis, miner, dwl 219 Kearny
Losse Philip H. tailor with C. Stahlmann, dwl 219 Kearny
Lothrop Horatio J. hatter with Theodore Van Tassell, dwl 200 Stockton

Lothrop John J, (English & L.) dwl 1006 Leav
Lothrop W. R. carrier, Daily Examiner, dwl Valparaiso bet Filbert and Greenwich
Lott Enoch, ship joiner, dwl E s Hubbard between Second and Third
Lott Jessie (widow) dwl 506 Greenwich
Lotto August, express wagon, cor Mont and Jackson
Lotto Charles, express wagon, dwl E s Varenne nr Filbert
Lottritz John, beer saloon, S s Sixteenth bet Valencia and Mission
Lotus Copper M. Co. office 338 Montgomery
Lotwhommer Charles, organ builder with J. Mayer, dwl S s Oak nr Laguna
Loucitat (Chinese) physician, 626 Jackson
Loucks Adam, hostler, 211 Pine
Loucks Charles J. R. waiter, dwl 116 Post
Loucks Orlando & Co. produce commission, 108 Clay, dwl N s Filbert bet Hyde and Leav
Loucks Peter G. clerk, 108 Clay, dwl N s Filbert bet Hyde and Leavenworth
LOUD ALFRED C. with Aaron Holmes, 304 Montgomery, dwl 620 Market
Loud John, cook, St. Mary's College
Loud John, machinist, dwl 316 Fourth
Loud Warren, merchant, dwl 321 Sutter
Loudeman William, express wagon, 5 Market
Loudenslager Thomas J. dwl 527 Green
LOUDERBACK ANDREW A. game, 5 and 6 Washington Market, dwl NE cor Eddy and Leavenworth
Louderback Charles, dwl 511 Mason
Louderback Davis, with A. A. Louderback, dwl 14 Virginia
Louderback Davis jr. prosecuting attorney Police Court, office 17 City Hall first floor, dwl 14 Virginia
Louderback Sophia M. (widow) dwl E s Hyde bet Clay and Washington
Loudon Alexander, painter, dwl 38 Clara
Loudon Meyer (Liepsic & L.) San Miguel Ranch
Lougee Charles, carpenter, dwl 24 Geary
Lougee James W. sign painter, 516 Davis, dwl 901 Stockton
Longee John, pattern maker, Golden State Iron Works, dwl 24 Geary
Lougee Jonathan P. molder, Pacific Foundry, dwl 24 Geary
Lough James, clerk, 405 Commercial
Loughborough Alex. H. (George & L.) attorney at law, office 505 Mont, dwl 717 Sutter
Loughery Hugh, teamster, foot of Townsend, dwl 135 Stevenson
Loughlin John, laborer, dwl 147 Minna
Loughlin John, soap maker, dwl 823 Greenwich
Loughlin John, waiter, dwl 147 Minna
Loughlin John, laborer with Malachi Norton
Loughlin Stephen O. foundryman, dwl 911 Battery
Loughran Edward, hostler, dwl 724 Union
LOUGHRAN P. F. & CO. (Murphy, Grant & Co.) importers and jobbers carpets, oil cloths, etc. 405 and 407 Sansom, dwl 1109 Stockton
Loughran Thomas, laborer, dwl 24 Sansom
Loughran Thomas, workman, S. F. & P. Sugar Co. dwl Harrison nr Eighth
Loughrey Edward, dwl 106 William
Louis Clementina, laundress, dwl 168 Tehama
Louis Frank (Carnbino & L.) dwl 939 Kearny
Louis Henry, cabinet maker, dwl 23 Brooklyn Pl
Louis Jean B. L. lapidary, dwl Clay Avenue bet Stockton and Powell
Louis John, cook, dwl 27 Jessie
Louis Joseph C. baker, Hamburg Bakery, dwl 413 Powell
LOUIS M. boot and shoe maker, 536 Commercial
Louis, see Lewis
Louison Louis, laborer, dwl cor Filbert and Mont
Louisson Moritz, salesman with Julius Baum, dwl 25 Minna

Louisson Morris, salesman with Neustadter Bros. dwl 822 Post
Loukinin, John, seaman, dwl 20 Commercial
Loumes Joseph, butcher, dwl N s Sixteenth nr Nebraska
Loundes Francis, street contractor, dwl 1407 Stockton, rear
Loundgrist S. captain schooner Star of the Union, office 413 East
Lounsberry J. R. jeweler with R. B. Gray & Co
Lount Daniel S. miner, dwl 811 Stockton
Loupe Leopold *(H. Levi & Co.)* dwl 608 Market
Loux Catharine Miss, domestic, 1600 Taylor
Loux Evans M. seaman, steamer Orizaba
LOVE HARLOW S. attorney at law and court commissioner Fifteenth Judicial District, office 540 Clay, dwl 16 Tehama
Love James, apprentice, Pacific Foundry, dwl 115 Washington
Love James H. ship carpenter with John G. North, dwl 224 Ritch
Love John C. teller, Bank California, dwl 613½ Stockton
Love John Lord, attorney at law, office 540 Clay, dwl 16 Tehama
Love William, bakery, 120 Third
Lovegrove George H. collector S. F. Gas Co. dwl 629 Sutter
Lovejoy Alphonso J. with Truman & Co. dwl NW cor Union and Larkin
Lovejoy William E. artist, Edouart's Gallery, 634 Washington, dwl N s Bush bet Montgomery and Sansom
Lovekin H. S. Miss, adjuster, U. S. Branch Mint, dwl cor Leavenworth and Francisco
Loveland Harvey S. clerk with M. Prag, 125 Clay, dwl 1063 Clay
LOVELAND I. & CO. clothing and gents' furnishing goods, 211 Montgomery, dwl 812 Howard
Loveland Lafayette F. stock and exchange broker, 707 Mont, dwl SW cor Greenwich and Larkin
Lovell Ardine (widow) dwl 8 O'Farrell
LOVELL EDWARD C. mining secretary, office 436 Jackson, dwl SW cor Hyde and Greenwich
Lovell Henry, brick maker, dwl 116 Sansom
Lovell James, dwl 1010 Powell
Lovell William, omnibus, Original House
Lovell William, stock broker, dwl 33 Second
Lovely George S. boarding, 607 Pine
Lovely Horace, dwl 506 Dupont
Lovely M. H. pressman, with Francis, Valentine & Co. dwl 506 Dupont
Lovely Noble, pressman with Francis, Valentine & Co. dwl 506 Dupont
Lovett Charles J. captain bark Smyrniote, office 511 Sansom
Lovett Hannah (col'd, widow) dwl 9 Scott
Lovich Charles, clothing, 40 First
LOW C. ADOLPHE & CO. *(Charles H. Baldwin, Samuel Hort, and George A. Low)* commission merchants and insurance agents, office 426 California
LOW CHARLES L. office 803 Montgomery room 3, dwl 553 Harrison
Low Conrad, laborer, dwl 639 Broadway, rear
Low George A. *(C. Adolphe, Low & Co.)* 426 California, dwl 1010 Stockton
Low James C. inspector, Custom House, dwl International Hotel
Low John, mariner, dwl 16 Ohio
Low Joseph W. *(Nudd, Low & Co.)* dwl Cosmopolitan Hotel
Low L. ± analytical physician, dwl 528 Folsom
Low William R. machinist, dwl N s Townsend bet Second and Third
Lowback William, shoe maker, 6 First
Lowberg N. salesman, dwl 53 Second
Lowder A. Miss, special primary assistant Fourth St. School, dwl 818 Powell

LOWE BENJAMIN F. president California Home Insurance Co. office 224 and 226 California, dwl 609 Bush
Lowe Erestein Miss, domestic, 850 Howard
Lowe Gerald A. clerk with B. F. Low, 226 California, dwl 609 Bush
Lowe *(Seligman)* & Mansbach *(Emanuel)* fancy goods, 116 Second
Lowe William E. clerk with B. F. Lowe, 226 California, dwl 609 Bush
Lowell Arthur D. with N. R. Lowell, NW cor Pine and Davis
LOWELL N. R. Eagle Warehouse, NW cor Pine and Davis, dwl 523 Howard
Lowen John, fisherman, dwl SW cor Washington and Drumm
Lowenberg Isador *(Meyerstein & L.)* dwl 456 Clementina
Lowenberg Sampson, dwl 437 Green
LOWENHELM J. & CO. *(Herman Loewy)* importers and commission merchants, 220 Front, res Europe
Lowenstein Isaac, boots and shoes, 1208 Stockton
Lowering William H. salesman, dwl 532 Howard
Lowery Joseph, bar keeper, dwl 1322 Kearny
Lowery William, fireman, dwl S s Folsom bet Spear and Main
LOWNDES ALFRED S. wine merchant and agent Gerke Wine, 311½ Battery, dwl NE cor Mission and Seventeenth
Lowney John, blacksmith with Albert Folsom, dwl 22 Sansom
Lowney Timothy *(Ducommon & L.)* dwl N s Clementina bet Eighth and Ninth
Lowrey Peter, carpenter, dwl 7 William
Lowry Elizabeth Mrs. dwl S s Francisco bet Taylor and Jones
Lowry George M. clerk with W. J. Lowry, dwl 86 Everett
Lowry John, blacksmith with Albert Folsom, dwl W s Dupont bet California and Pine
Lowry Joseph, hostler, 739 Folsom
Lowry Margaret Miss, 226 Minna
Lowry Margaret Miss, domestic, 118 Perry
Lowry Richard, stevedore, dwl W s Telegraph Pl
Lowry *(William)* & McLagan *(John)* carpenters, 129 Second, dwl 47 Second
Lowry William, fireman, steamer Senator
Lowry W. J. commission produce, SW cor Washington and Davis, dwl 86 Everett
Lowth John, machinist, Vulcan Iron Works, dwl NW cor Fourth and Louisa
Loy Kee (Chinese) cigar manufacturer, 615 Jackson
Loyer George, hairdresser with J. Lipman, dwl N s Berry nr Bush
Lozano T. T. barber with G. Sichel, dwl 620 Green
LOZIER PETER, bowling saloon, 221 Bush bet Mont and San, dwl NE cor Market and Mont
Lübben Elizabeth Miss, domestic, dwl 1213 Mason
Lubbert Henry, seaman, dwl 57 Sacramento
Lubeck C. W. dwl 783 Market
Lubeck John, dwl 319 Bush
Lubeck S. stock broker, office 529 Clay
Luboah John B. workman with E. Morrell dwl NE cor Twentieth and Florida
Lubosh Louis, junk, dwl 241 Minna, rear
Luby William, upholsterer, dwl 12 Sutter
Lucas B. F. dwl 11 Bay State Row
Lucas Jacob, helper, dwl 424 Fremont, rear
Lucas John, carpenter, dwl W s Montgomery nr Vallejo
Lucas John, laborer, Miners' Foundry
Lucas John (col'd) shipsmith with W. S. Phelps & Co. 24 Drumm
Lucas Samuel L. salesman with Stone & Hayden, dwl International Hotel
Lucchesi G. & Co. *(G. Conti)* modelers and plaster workers, N s Summer nr Montgomery
Luce Maggie (widow) dwl 45 Jessie

Lucetti Hannah Miss, domestic, 914 Stockton
Luchsinger Henry, cabinet maker with Goodwin & Co. dwl 345 inna
Luchsinger John M B. furniture manufactory, 116 Bush, dwl 749 Mission
Lucian Simon, cook, 407 California
Lucke Henry, importer and maker French boots and shoes, 648 Washington
Lucy Dennis J. express wagon, cor Fourth and Mission, dwl E s Clinton bet Bryant and Brannan
Lucy (George R.) & Hymes (Charles) soap makers, 181 Beale, dwl Beale St. House
Lucy Margaret Miss, domestic, 28 Tehama
Lucy Samuel C. soap maker, dwl 181 Beale
Luddy William, laborer, bds U. S. Hotel, 706 Bat
Ludeman Adolph, clerk, 587 Market, dwl Post bet Laguna and Buchanan
Ludeman Mary (widow) dwl S s Post bet Laguna and Buchanan
Ludeman O. sash and blind maker, dwl 220 Pacific
Ludeman Otto, painter, dwl 226 Pacific
Ludeman William, junk, 587 Market, dwl Post bet Laguna and Buchanan
Ludemann Henry, boot maker, dwl 309 Pacific
Luders Edward T. (Dyer & L.) dwl 618 California
Ludlam Anthony, oyster dealer, dwl 624 Howard
Ludlam Cornelius, assistant wharfinger, Broadway Wharf, dwl N s Jessie E Second
Ludlam James C. oyster dealer, dwl 624 Howard
Ludlow Charles H. clerk with Blyth & Wetherbee, dwl Pacific Exchange
Ludlow James, dwl 545 Mission
Ludlow James P. Rev. pastor Post St. Baptist Mission Church, dwl W s Hyde bet Bush and Sutter
Ludlow Thomas B. Knickerbocker Engine Co. No. 5
Ludlow William, laborer, dwl E s Harrison bet Main and Beale
Ludlow William B. conductor, Central R. R. Co. dwl 427 Sixth
Ludlum C. toll collector, C. S. Navigation Co. Broadway Wharf
LUDLUM THOMAS B.. proprietor Flint's Warehouse, cor Battery and Greenwich and New Orleans Warkhouse, cor Davis and California, dwl 92 Stevenson
Ludlum Edward, clerk, New Orleans Warehouse, dwl 92 Stevenson
Ludorff August (Geib & L.) 15 Third
Ludorff Julius & Co. (Bernhard Mersing) groceries and liquors, SW cor Montgomery and Jackson
Ludwick Charles, carpenter, dwl 505 Minna
Ludwig John A. cabinet maker, 757 Mission
Ludwigbeck John, waterman, dwl 609 Market
Ludwigeen Frederick C. porter with Morris Speyer, dwl 710 Green
Ludwigsen Minna Miss, milliner, dwl 826 Union
Luedke Rudolph, watch maker, dwl 529 Tehama
Luesmann E. beer saloon, 326 Dupont
Lufkin Joseph, contractor, S s Merchant bet Drumm and East, dwl W s Taylor bet Sac and Cal
Lufkin Thomas, carpenter, dwl 10 O'Farrell
Lugarte Maricio, cooper, dwl NE cor Greenwich and Jones
Luger J. carpenter, 205 Commercial
Luhmensen Henry, with Henry Frank, 217 Com
Luhmensen John, clerk, NE cor Harrison and Sixth
Luhmensen William, groceries and liquors, NE cor Harrison and Sixth
Luhr Conrad, dwl 639 Broadway, rear
Luhr Ernst, painter and glazier, 238 Ritch
Luhrs Albert (McCormick & L.) dwl W s First bet Stevenson and Mission
Luhrs Christopher F. ranchman, dwl NW cor Powell and Filbert
Luhrs Edward F. clerk, NW cor Larkin and Pine
Luhrs John, clerk, NW cor Broadway and Dupont
Luhrs John C. clerk with John Hashagen

Luhrs Louis, laborer, Bay Sugar Refinery, dwl E s Montgomery bet Union and Filbert
Luhrs Nicholas, porter, 406 Front, dwl 1008 Leav
Luhrsen Frederick (Dettmer & L.) dwl SE cor Montgomery and Filbert
Luhrsen Henry, clerk, SE cor Vallejo and Dupont
Luigetto Joe Rogers, fisherman, 7 Italian Fish Mkt
Luke Richard, driver with McMillan & Kester, dwl 53 Mission
Lukin Adolph, dwl 20 Rousch
LULL LOUIS R. inspector state stamps, office SE cor Battery and Washington and secretary California Pioneers, dwl 1009 Powell
Lulofs B. merchant, dwl 620 Market
Lum C. H. sexton Calvary Church, dwl 212 Second
Lum Harry, fireman, steamer Petaluma
Lumbard Charles, broker, dwl 417 O'Farrell
LUMBER DEALERS' ASSOCIATION, J. E. de la Montagnie secretary, office Pier 3 Stewart
Lumbert Francis, printer with F. Clarke, dwl 824 Filbert
Lumes Xavier, wholesale butcher, N s Sixteenth nr Rhode Island
Lumetti Charles, blacksmith, dwl 819 Vallejo, rear
Lumley George, ales, wines, and liquors, 1024 Battery
Lumsden Alexander, dwl 516 Taylor
Lumsden John E. salesman, 643 Merchant, dwl 516 Taylor
Lumsden William, importer and jobber leather and shoe findings, 643 Merchant, dwl 516 Taylor
Lun Sing & Co. (Chinese) merchants, 706 Sac
Lun Wo & Co. (Chinese) merchants, 716 Sac
Luna Francisco, helper with Bacca & Co. dwl Potrero Avenue
Lund Charles, bar keeper, 638 Pacific
Lund Charles, workman, S. F. Cordage Factory, dwl nr cor Humbolt and Kentucky
Lund Henry, mariner, dwl 32 Stewart
Lund Henry, with Cross & Co. dwl N s Chestnut bet Dupont and Stockton
LUND HUGH N. Fair Exchange Liquor Saloon, NE cor Stockton and Geary
Lund Peter, seaman, bds 7 Washington
Lundberg Peter T. carrier, Evening Bulletin and Call, dwl N s Broadway nr Jones
Lundberg William, manufacturing electrician, 810 Mont, dwl W s Mont bet Union and Filbert
Lundblad Frederick, with Thomas B. Ludlum, dwl Union House
Lundborg J. A. W. dentist, office 131 Montgomery
Lundquist John H. carver with Jones, Wooll & Sutherland, dwl 619 Mason
Lundy William, mariner, dwl 36 Battery
Lung Ty & Co. (Chinese) tailors, 716 Dupont
Lunhaust Lewis, baker, Occidental Hotel
Luniewski C. L. inspector, Custom House, dwl SW cor California and Drumm
LUNING NICHOLAS & CO. bankers, 428 California, dwl 623 Powell
Lunis José, waiter, steamer Chrysopolis
Lunnay James, laborer, dwl 1023 Clay
Lunney William, workman, Potrero Ropewalk, dwl cor Shasta and Michigan
Lunny James W. painter, dwl 16 Oak
LUNT DANIEL, secretary Board Education, 22 City Hall, dwl SE cor California and Franklin
Lunt D. S. (Ring & L.) dwl 14 Quincy
Lunt George K. plasterer, dwl SW cor Clay and Davis
Lunt Linda T. (widow) dwl S s Riley nr Taylor
Lunt O. A. teacher dancing, Union Hall, dwl 255 Tehama
Lupton Charles, cook, Manhattan House, 705 Front, dwl SW cor Dupont and Broadway
Lupton Samuel L. attorney at law, office 604 Clay, dwl N s John nr Mason
Luquin Jacinta Mrs. dwl 518 Pacific
Lusen Alfred, dwl 20 Sherwood Place

LUSK A. & CO. *(Wolf Jacobs and John Klein-hans)* wholesale commission fruits, Pacific Fruit Market, dwl 563 Tehama
Lusk C. D. International Livery Stable, 533 Jackson, dwl 1025 Kearny
Lusk George, coachman, dwl 1117 Stockton
Lüsmann H. dwl Lutgen's Hotel
Lussey John, interpreter French, Police Court, dwl 604 Dupont
Lust Simon, cap manufacturer, 408 Sacramento, dwl 250 Minna
Lustenberger Hubert, milk ranch, nr Mission Church
Lustig Isaac, merchant, dwl 462 Natoma
Lutgen's Hotel, H. A. Siegfried proptr, 228 Mont
Luther George E. clerk, Pier 9 Stewart
Luther H. W. jeweler with R. B. Gray & Co. dwl 1108 Powell
Luther John B. auctioneer with Voizin, Ris & Co. dwl 822 Clay
Lutolf Joseph, helper, dwl 507 Market
Luttge C. A. waiter, 506 Mont, dwl 127 Mont
Luttig Frank *(Heye & L.)* dwl NE cor Lombard and Mason
Luttig Lisette Miss, domestic, 1119 Stockton
Luttringer Antone, blacksmith, dwl 1606 Stockton
Luttringer Joseph, liquor saloon, 810 Clay
Luty John S. professor book keeping, 305 Montgomery room 6, dwl 7 O'Farrell
Lutz G. C. butcher, dwl 273 Stevenson
Lutz Jacob, baker, dwl 140 Second
Lutz Jacob, clothes marker, Custom House Place, dwl 106½ Clay
Lutzen Peter H. tanner, dwl 626 Vallejo, rear
Luvisi Cherubino, express wagon, SW cor Market and Fourth, dwl NW cor Mason and Union
Lux Charles *(Miller & L.)* dwl 45 South Park
Lux Fred, assistant assessor, U. S. Internal Revenue, NW cor Battery and Commercial, dwl N s Jackson bet Leavenworth and Hyde
Luxich *(Andrew)* & Drobaz *(Matteo)* coffee stand, 503 East
Luyster T. G. W. steward, U. S. Marine Hospital
Lybby E. H. carpenter, dwl 741 Market
LYCEUM BUILDING (now Exchange Building) NW cor Montgomery and Washington
Lycke Hermann, mariner, dwl 32 Stewart
Lydon John H. watchman, North Beach & M. R. R. Co
Lydon M. Mrs. dwl SW cor Natoma and Fifth
Lyford John S. mason, dwl 1119 Clay
Lykins Jane E. (widow) furnished rooms, 109 Mont
Lyle Albert F. dwl NW cor Howard and Washington Avenue
Lyle Elizabeth A. C. music teacher, dwl NW cor Howard and Washington Avenue
Lyle Freeman B. salesman with Badger & Lindenberger, dwl 632 Market
Lyle George F. clerk with J. B. Thomas, dwl NW cor Howard and Washington Avenue
Lyle Joshua B. dwl NW cor Howard and Washington Avenue
Lyle William S. salesman with Jennings & Brewster, dwl NW cor Howard and Washington Av
Lyman Charles, book keeper with Wetherbee & Cook, dwl S s McAllister bet Laguna and Buchanan
Lyman Charles, laborer with Wm. J. Kingsley
Lyman Charles D. clerk, dwl Tremont House
Lyman Joseph, book keeper with Wetherbee & Cook, dwl S s McAllister bet Laguna and Buchanan
Lymprich John, student, Mission Dolores Church
Lynard Martin, laborer, dwl E s Octavia bet Post and Sutter
Lynch Andrew, cook, dwl SE cor Sac and Davis
Lynch Andrew E. teamster, dwl Sixteenth nr Potrero
Lynch Catharine, domestic, dwl 228 Green
Lynch Celia Miss, domestic, 615 Mason

Lynch Daniel, laborer, Fort Point, dwl NE cor Larkin and Salmon Place
Lynch Dennis J. laborer with W. H. Warren, dwl Folsom bet Eighteenth and Nineteenth
Lynch Dominick Mrs. dwl 228 Ritch
Lynch Edward, laborer, dwl 146 Stewart
Lynch Ellen Miss, cloak maker, dwl 18 Minna
Lynch Ellen Miss, domestic with Mrs. N. W. Spaulding, W s First Avenue bet Fifteenth and Sixteenth
Lynch Ellen (widow) dwl 25 Stockton Place
Lynch Ellen (widow) furnished rooms, Mercantile Library Building
Lynch F. Miss, assistant, Rincon School, dwl 735 Market
Lynch Francis, furniture, 522 Broadway
Lynch Francis E. merchant, office 430 Jackson, res Oakland
Lynch George A. teamster with L. B. Hanson, dwl E s Eleventh bet Folsom and Howard
Lynch George F. box maker with Hobbs, Gilmore & Co. dwl 66 Jessie
Lynch Hannah (widow) dwl 775 Market
Lynch Henry, tinsmith with Taylor & Iredale, dwl 8 s Stevenson bet Fourth and Fifth
Lynch Henry, waiter, 619 Market
Lynch Herbert T. sash maker with Smith, Ware & Co. dwl 528 Bush
Lynch James, apprentice with John Hart, dwl 155 Tehama
Lynch James, butcher with Lux & Miller, dwl cor Ninth and Brannan
Lynch James, mariner, dwl 463 Natoma
Lynch Jeremiah, dwl SW cor Howard and Fourteenth
Lynch J. N. straw worker, dwl Pine bet Kearny and Montgomery
Lynch John, bar keeper, dwl Allen W s Hyde bet Union and Filbert
Lynch John, boiler maker with Coffey & Risdon
Lynch John, cook, dwl 610 Montgomery
Lynch John, cook, dwl 18 Taylor
Lynch John, laborer, dwl 775 Market
Lynch John, laborer, dwl 282 Minna
Lynch John, laborer, dwl 13 Jessie
Lynch John, laborer, Miners' Foundry
Lynch John, painter, dwl Manhattan Engine H
Lynch John, ship carpenter, dwl cor Sansom and Greenwich
Lynch John, steward, International Hotel, dwl 7 Sonoma Place
Lynch John, wool puller, dwl SW cor Fifteenth and Valencia
Lynch John C. carpenter, dwl E s Hyde bet Broadway and Pacific
Lynch John E. laborer, dwl 4 Lick Alley
Lynch John F. musician, dwl St. Francis H. & L. Co. No. 1
Lynch John T. furniture, 814 Pacific
Lynch John W. painter, dwl Manhattan Engine H
Lynch Joseph, harness maker with W. F. Wilmot & Co. 315 Battery
Lynch Joseph, laborer, dwl W s Gilbert bet Bryant and Brannan
Lynch Kate Miss, teacher music, dwl SW cor Broadway and Montgomery
Lynch Margaret Miss, domestic, 128 Turk
Lynch Margaret Miss, domestic, 900 Powell
Lynch Mary Miss, domestic, 266 Folsom
Lynch Mary Miss, domestic, 766 Folsom
Lynch Mary Mrs. dwl W s Margaret Place
Lynch Michael, printer with Francis, Valentine & Co
Lynch Michael, saloon, SW cor Broadway and Davis, dwl W s Mary Lane nr Sutter
LYNCH MICHAEL, secretary S. F. Fire Department and school director Eleventh District, office 2 City Hall third floor, dwl Dolores nr Sixteenth

Lynch Michael, wool puller, dwl nr mouth Mission Creek
Lynch Morris, laborer with Conroy & Tobin
Lynch Patrick, laborer, dwl S s Stevenson bet Sixth and Seventh
Lynch Patrick, laborer, dwl 8 Anthony
Lynch Patrick, laborer, dwl E s Salmon bet Mason and Taylor
Lynch Patrick, laborer, Spring Valley W. W
Lynch Patrick, laborer, Spring Valley W. W
Lynch Patrick, packer with Martin D. Heynemann, dwl SE cor Battery and Pacific
Lynch Patrick, teamster with Herman W. Massey, dwl Stevenson nr Sixth
Lynch Patrick, waiter, International Hotel
Lynch Patrick B. dwl 112 Minna
Lynch Peter, waterman, dwl 53 Clara
Lynch Thomas, bar keeper, NE cor Sutter and San
Lynch Thomas, drayman, dwl 519 Mission
Lynch Thomas, laborer with William Kerr, dwl 903 Battery
Lynch Thomas, plasterer, dwl W s Sixth bet Stevenson and Mission, rear
Lynch Thomas F. hostler, St. Mary's College
Lynch Timothy, cooperage, 219 Washington, dwl 140 Minna
Lynch Timothy, laborer, dwl 6 Haywood
Lynch Timothy, laborer, dwl 268 Jessie
Lynch Timothy, tinsmith, dwl 630 Green, rear
Lynch T. J. plasterer, dwl 529 Pine
Lynch William, deck hand, steamer Chrysopolis
Lynde George L. superintendent Industrial School, Old Ocean House Road 5 miles from City Hall
Lynde John E. with John Howes, 502 Sansom, dwl 5 Fourth
Lynde Joseph B. salesman with Taaffe & Co. 107 Battery, dwl 25 Howard Court
Lynde Lawrence, with Taudler & Lang, Continental Hotel
Lynde William C. clerk, 502 Sansom, dwl 5 Fourth
Lynde ——, dwl 765 Mission
Lynden Isabella Miss, domestic, 510 Stockton
Lyne William, agent Hall's Separator, 424 Davis, dwl 904 Broadway
Lynes Benjamin S. house raiser, dwl 29 Rousch
Lyng James, boot maker, 238 Third
Lynn DeWitt, miller, dwl 559 Market
Lynn George, engineer, dwl N s Vallejo bet Montgomery and Sansom
Lynn Harry, seaman, dwl 117 Sacramento
Lynn Jacob, inspector, Custom House, dwl 419 Powell
Lynn John, deck hand, stm Relief
Lynn Patrick, seaman, dwl 117 Pacific
Lynn Patrick, workmen with Casebolt & Co
Lynne William, tailor with S. Reinstein, 21 Sansom
Lynngreen J. W. cook, dwl NW corner Pine and Kearny
Lynsky Ellen (widow) dwl 208 Third
Lynsky Maria, domestic with Mrs. James L. Kennedy, 340 Seventh
Lyon B. E, express wagon, cor Jessie and Jane
Lyon Charles H. folder, Easton's Laundry, W side Lagoon
Lyon George, stone cutter, dwl W side Sansom bet Greenwich and Filbert
Lyon Henry, dwl 17 Dupont
Lyon I. W. dentist, office and dwl 663 Howard
Lyon James, clerk, Gilbert's Museum, dwl 120 Fifth
Lyon John, bricklayer, dwl Hinckley Place S side Vallejo bet Montgomery and Kearny
Lyon John, laborer, dwl Spring Valley House, rear
Lyon Michael E. shutter maker with J. R. Sims, dwl SW cor Battery and Jackson
Lyon M. L. *(M. & A. L. Mayers & Co.)* dwl Union bet Dupont and Kearny
Lyon Patrick A. blacksmith with Kimball & Co. dwl 741 Market
Lyon Petroleum Co. office 620 Washington

Lyon Samuel, dwl 17 Dupont
Lyon S. B. mechanic with James Brokaw, dwl 500 Mission
Lyon Walter W. dwl 761 Mission
Lyon William, dwl Original House
LYON *(William H.)* & CO. *(John Harrold)* proprietors Empire Brewery, 159 Jessie, dwl Russ House
Lyon Worthington S. with Kellogg, Hewston & Co. dwl 212 Powell
Lyon, see Lion
Lyons Adele (widow) dwl 315 O'Farrell
Lyons Alexander, printer with Towne & Bacon, dwl N s Leavenworth bet Bdwy and Vallejo
Lyons Annie (widow) dwl 83 Clementina
Lyons B. saddle and harness maker, dwl 724 Union
Lyons Bryan, miner, dwl N s Hayes nr Market
Lyons Charles, deck hand, stm Cornelia
Lyons Charles, omnibus driver, boards with Thomas Holmes
Lyons Cornelius. bootblacking, 327 Sansom, dwl N s Mission bet Second and Third
Lyons Cornelius, laborer, dwl NW cor Stevenson and Ecker
Lyons Dennis, dwl 1900 Powell
Lyons Dennis, laborer, dwl 26 Freelon
LYONS E. G. & CO. *(Jules Mayer)* wines and liquors, and manufacturers syrups and cordials, 510 Jackson, dwl SE cor Chestnut and Powell
Lyons Elizabeth Miss, domestic, 73 Clementina
Lyons Elizabeth Miss, domestic, 322 Mason
Lyons Ellen Miss, domestic, 20 Mason
Lyons H. A. dwl Occidental Hotel
Lyons Harriet Mrs. dwl 514 Front
Lyons James, dwl W s Fifth nr Natoma
Lyons James, carder. Woolen Mills, dwl with P. L. Murphy E side Howard bet Fifteenth and Sixteenth
Lyons James, hostler, 126 Fourth, dwl S s Minna bet Third and Fourth
Lyons James, laborer, S. F. & San José R. R. Co
Lyons James D. marble cutter with M. Heverin, dwl 286 Stevenson
Lyons John *(Irvine & Co.)* dwl 1019 Bush
Lyons John, laborer, dwl 520 Geary, rear
Lyons John, lamplighter, dwl 33 Louisa
Lyons John, teamster with Ackerson & Russ, dwl N s Natoma bet Eighth and Ninth
Lyons John, workman, S. F. & P. Sugar Co. dwl 109 Dupont nr Seventh
Lyons John F. printer, Washington Hose Co. No. 1
Lyons Joshua, dwl 1006 Powell
Lyons Julia (widow) boarding, 17 Fourth
Lyons Kate Miss, domestic with Robert J. Tiffany
Lyons Lazarus, salesman, 312 Sacramento, dwl 315 O'Farrell
Lyons Lewis, lamplighter, S. F. Gas Co
Lyons Louis, compositor with T. G. Spear, dwl Leavenworth bet Broadway and Vallejo
Lyons M. Mrs. boarding, dwl 17 Fourth
Lyons Martin, laborer, S. F. & San José R. R. Co
Lyons Martin, shoe maker with H. M. Beers, 313 Pine
Lyons Mary, domestic, dwl 1112 Kearny, rear
Lyons Michael, laborer, dwl NE cor Laguna and Ash, Hayes' Valley
Lyons P. waiter, Cosmopolitan Hotel
Lyons Patrick, dwl NE cor Van Ness Avenue and Fern Avenue
Lyons Patrick, blacksmith, dwl 741 Market
Lyons Patrick, hostler, 431 California, dwl 60 Stevenson
Lyons Thomas, workman with I. O. Taplin, San Bruno Road
Lyons William, express wagon, cor Broadway and Davis, dwl S s Folsom bet Beale and Main
Lyons William, law student with Shafter, Goold & Dwinelle, dwl E s Powell nr Filbert
Lyser Julius, dwl 67 Everett

Lysett James *(Lysett & Co.)* dwl 12 Harlan Place
Lysett *(John P.)* & Co. *(James Lysett)* produce, 27 Metropolitan Market, dwl 12 Harlan Place
Lysnar John R. deutist, 634 Washington, dwl 1913 Stockton
Lytle Stanley A. compositor, Monitor, dwl Coso House

M

MAAHEN Charles, plumber, dwl 1324 Kearny
Maas George, helper, dwl Morey Alley nr Bdwy
Maass Henry F. boot and shoe store, dwl 1817 Powell
Maass Hinrich, laborer, Bay Sugar Refinery, dwl SE cor Howard and Fremont
Mabatt Charles, cook, dwl 64 Natoma
Mac Albert, student, dwl 27 Minna
MacCann Edward *(William MacCann & Co.)* dwl 419 Green
MacCann Robert, clerk with William MacCann & Co. dwl 419 Green
MacCann Telford *(William MacCann & Co.)* dwl 419 Green
MacCANN WILLIAM & CO. *(Edward and Telford MacCann)* ship and commission merchants, office 402 Front, dwl 419 Green
MacCann William, book keeper with Lazard Freres, dwl 419 Green
MacCRELLISH FRED'K & CO. *(William A. Woodward)* publishers and proprietors daily, weekly, and steamer Alta California, office 536 Sacramento, dwl SW cor Pine and Mason
MacDonald John, hostler, Willows, SW cor Mission and Eighteenth
MacDonough N. B. cook, Original House Restaurant
MacDougall W. J. professor music, dwl NE cor Montgomery and Pacific
MacKay Angus A. laborer with Cutting & Co
MacKay Jessie Miss, domestic, 1104 Taylor
MacKeon Bernard, clerk with Donohoe, Kelly & Co. dwl 309 Kearny
MacKINLEY EDWARD, attorney at law, office 4 and 5 Armory Hall, dwl 415 Bryant
MacNee Mary (widow) dwl 36 Ritch
MacPhun William, shipwright, 40 Clay, dwl 63 Shipley
Macabee Alexander, carpenter, dwl 406 Geary
Macartney Amos, commission merchant, dwl 110 Tehama
Macatee Alexina M. Mrs. books and stationery, 352 Third
Macatee John F. teacher, dwl 352 Third
Macauley John, retortman, S. F. Gas Co
Macbeth Alex. stone cutter, dwl Central House, 814 Sansom
Macchiavello Antonio, fisherman, 14 Italian Fish Market
Macchiavello Giovanni B. *(Brignardello, M.& Co.)* res Italy
MACDONALD BROTHERS *(Donald A. and John H. Macdonald)* proprietors Chace's Saw and Planing Mill, 311 Market, dwl 218 Prospect Place
Macdonald Colin, clerk with Alsop & Co. 411 Cal
Macdonald John, workman, S. F. & P. Sugar Co. dwl Seventh bet Brannan and Townsend
Macdonald John A. clerk with Langley, Crowell & Co
Macdonald John A. C. salesman, 607 Sacramento, dwl 605 Sacramento
Macdonald John H. *(Macdonald Brothers)* dwl 209 Seventh
Macdonald Timothy, laborer with C. O'Donnell
Mace Herbert E. collector, dwl 820 Washington
Mace B. F. watchman, Mission Woolen Mills
Macfarlan Franklin J. salesman, 727 and 729 Market, dwl 12 Hubbard
Macgovren James, lamp maker, 108 Leidesdorff
Machado Beatrice (widow) dwl 1106 Powell

Machado Rudolph, clerk, dwl 1106 Powell
Machin Francis, salesman, dwl 202 Second
Macboltt Henry, cabinet maker, dwl NE cor Lombard and Mason
Maciel Joseph, groceries and liquors, dwl 200 Front
Macigalupo Charles, vegetable garden nr Bay View Park
Mack Dennis, teamster, dwl 3 Boston Place
Mack George, fireman, dwl 146 Stewart
Mack Hannah Miss, domestic, 1153 Mission
Mack John, laborer with Andrew Fuegelesberger, dwl 12 Hinckley Place
Mack Joseph H. dwl W s Thirteenth nr Valencia
Mack Margaret, domestic, dwl 749 Market
Mack Patrick, farmer, Ocean House Flat nr Ocean House
Mack William J. *(R. A. Swain & Co.)* dwl 1028 Bush
Mack William, book keeper, dwl 27 Minna
Macken Francis, salesman, 111 Battery
Macken James, coppersmith, 226 Fremont, dwl 224 Fremont
Macken John M. coppersmith, dwl 224 Fremont
MACKENZIE JOHN S. mining secretary, office 522 Montgomery, dwl 1715 Mason
Maker Richard D. driver, Central R. R. Co. dwl SE cor Seventh and Brannan
Mackey Philip, clerk, bds Brooklyn Hotel
Mackie A. G. dwl 532 Commercial
Mackie Clara (widow) furnished rooms, 177 Minna
Mackie David J. liquor saloon, 400 Third
Mackie James W. clerk with D. E. Appleton & Co. dwl 502 Montgomery
Mackie Kate Miss, domestic, 409 Ellis
Mackie Peter, first officer stmr Orizaba, dwl Shotwell nr Sixteenth
Mackie Richard, driver, Central R. R. Co. dwl SE cor Brannan and Seventh
Mackin James, laborer, dwl SW cor Hyde and O'Farrell
Mackin Mary Miss, domestic, 461 Minna
Mackintosh Robert, physician, office and dwl 128 Second
Macklin James F. with J. R. Mead & Co. dwl 709 Howard
Macklyn H. actor, Maguire's Opera House
Macomber Horace L. *(Addison & M.)* dwl SW cor Bush and Trinity
Macomber Joseph jr. with Eureka Soap Co. dwl 60 Clementina
MACONDRAY & CO. *(James Otis, W. A. and Frederick W. Macondroy)* importing, shipping and commission merchants, 204 and 206 Sansom
Macondray Frederick W. *(Macondray & Co.)* dwl 605 Harrison
Macondray Lavina S. (widow) dwl 1003 Stockton
Macondray W. A. *(Macondray & Co.)* dwl 614 Folsom
MACPHERSON *(A. W.)* & WETHERBEE *(Henry)* lumber, and proprietors Albion and Noyo Mills, office 229 Stewart Pier 20, dwl 420 Beale
MACY ALBERT, wharfinger, Third St. Wharf, dwl S s DeBoom nr Second
Macy Daniel F. drayman, dwl 111 Silver
Macy Henry C. architect, office 315 Montgomery, dwl 1215 Mason
Macy Lucy (widow) dwl 514 Howard
Macy Lydia F. (widow) dwl 542 Bryant
Macy O. messenger, U. S. Assistant Treasurer
Macy Robert B. dwl 619 Bush
Macy Thomas, dwl 17 Third
Macy W. H. with Francis, Valentine & Co
Macy William, cashier U. S. Assistant Treasurer, dwl 17 Third
Macy Wm. W. drayman, dwl 111 Silver
Madden David, laborer, dwl 27 Stevenson
Madden Delia Miss, domestic, 829 Mission
Madden Dennis, helper, dwl 27 Stevenson

Madden Frank, marble cutter with M. Heverin, dwl 251 Clementina
Madden James, workman with James Stanton, dwl E s Harriet bet Fifteenth and Sixteenth
Madden James F. night clerk P. O. dwl 265 Tehama
Madden John, laborer, dwl SE cor Sixteenth and Mission
Madden John, junk, NE cor Mission and Annie
Madden John, laborer, dwl SE cor Fulton and Webster
Madden John, laborer, S. F. P. Woolen Mills, dwl North Point bet Polk and Van Ness Avenue
Madden John, plasterer, dwl W s Jane Place
Madden Kate Miss, dress maker, 27 Stevenson
Madden Margaret (widow) saloon, 30 Sacramento
Madden Mary Miss, domestic, SW cor Gough and Sutter
Madden Peter, carpenter, dwl 61 Stevenson
Madden Thomas, farmer, dwl 446 Jessie
Madden Thomas, Grass Valley House, E s Sixth nr Market
Madden Thomas, miner, dwl Allen W s Hyde bet Union and Filbert
Madden Thomas, wheelwright with Stein, Link & Scherb, bds Philadelphia House
Madden Thomas P. office 7 Court Block, dwl Occidental Hotel
Maddern Henry, plumber, dwl 5 Noble Place
Madel Peter & Co. *(Henry T. Tietjen)* groceries and liquors, NE cor Mission and Stewart, dwl 23 Everett
Madero Clodomiro *(F. P. Ramirez & Co.)* dwl S s Geary bet Kearny and Dupont
Madero Jesus, compositor, Nnevo Mundo, dwl Prospect Place
Madge Frederick, assistant secretary Central R. R. Co. office 116 Taylor, dwl 1210 Folsom
Madigan Garrett, stone cutter, dwl 446 Brannan
Madigan John, stone cutter, dwl 446 Brannan
Madigan Margaret Miss, domestic, 30 McAllister
Madigan Thomas, stone cutter, dwl 446 Brannan
Madigan William, stone cutter, dwl 446 Brannan
Madison Benjamin, boatman, dwl 23 Frederick
Madison Benjamin, captain schr Clara, foot Merch
Madison G. & S. M. Co. office 402 Front
Madison James, boiler maker, Pacific Foundry, dwl 15 St. Mark Place
Madison John, carrier, Sacramento Union, dwl 206 Stockton
Madison John H. *(Hoogs & M.)* dwl 206 Stockton
Madison Joseph *(C. Jacobson & Co.)* dwl S s Brannan bet Sixth and Seventh
Madison Merritt, laborer, dwl 230 First
Madley William, carpenter, dwl 209 Jessie
Madrigal Pascual, carpenter, dwl 21 Valparaiso
Madtfeldt William, express wagon, cor Washington and Davis
Maesquere Alexander, saddler, 613 Sansom, dwl SW cor Dupont and Vallejo
Maessen W. with Saulmann & Lauenstein, dwl 631 Broadway
Magagnos J. A. collector, Evening Bulletin, 620 Montgomery, dwl 120 Perry
Maguber Dennis, laborer, dwl SE cor Seventeenth and Dolores
Magaby James, carpenter, dwl 446 Brannan
Magall Charles, driver, dwl 657 Mission
Magary John E. local policeman, dwl Ocean House
Magauran Patrick H. stationery and cigars, 252 Fourth
Magee Adam *(Theobalds & Co.)* dwl N s Francisco nr Dupont
Magee John, blacksmith with Black & Saul, dwl W s Priest bet Clay and Washington
Magee Thomas, printer, dwl 17 Fourth
Magee Wiliam H. compositor, dwl E s Wallace Place nr California
Maggie G. & S. M. Co. office 712 Montgomery
Magocio Paoli, fisherman, 12 Italian Fish Market

Maghar Peter, laborer, dwl 208 Stevenson
MAGILL ROBERT H. general agent Phœnix Insurance Co. Hartford and Travelers' Insurance Co. Hartford, office 603 Commercial cor Montgomery, dwl 19 Stanly Place
Magilton Thomas *(Wesson & M.)* dwl W s Main bet Folsom and Harrison
Maginnis Christopher, pattern maker, Union Foundry, dwl 32 Louisa
Maginnis Eliphas *(Mortimer & M.)* dwl 112 Austin
Maginnis James A. job wagon, NE cor Howard and Fourth, dwl 32 Louisa
Maginnis James R. dwl 209 Ellis
Maginnis John, pattern maker, Union Foundry, dwl 32 Louisa
Maglone Catherine Miss, domestic, 115 Perry
Magne F. express wagon, dwl Bush nr Powell
Magner Anna Miss, dress maker, 246 Minna
Magner Dennis, porter with George C. Johnson & Co. dwl N s Valparaiso nr Jones
Magner John, laborer, dwl 137 Jessie
Magner M. I. clerk, dwl 179 Jessie
Magner Michael, waiter, 619 Market
Magner Thomas, groceries and liquors, NE cor Broadway and Scott
Magnes Abraham, boots and shoes, 6 and 115 Second, dwl 58 Minna
Magnes David, clerk, dwl 58 Minna
Magnus Peter A. watch maker and jeweler, SE cor Davis and Sacramento
Mago Peter, employé, Occidental Restaurant, 536 Washington
Magoreny James, molder, Pacific Foundry, dwl 24 Stevenson
Magorty William, job wagon, 350 California, dwl Shipley bet Seventh and Eighth
Magrane Kate, actress, dwl room 19 Government House, 502 Washington
Magrane Mathew, laborer, dwl S s Filbert bet Mason and Taylor
Magrath James Joseph, dwl 921 Folsom
Magrath Margaret Miss, domestic, 1322 Stockton
Magrath Martin, cooper, S. F. & P. Sugar Co. dwl Shotwell nr Twenty-First
Magrath Michael, carpenter, dwl SE cor Fulton and Steiner
Magrath Peter, mason, dwl N s Haight bet Buchanan and Webster
Magruder Daniel, blacksmith, dwl 716 Sansom
Maguire Bridget, domestic, 528 Bryant
Maguire Catharine (widow) boarding 613 Pine
Maguire Dennis F. cooper. dwl E s Ritter nr Harrison
Maguire Edward, dwl 230 Jessie, rear
Maguire Edward, dwl 156 Second
Maguire Edward, shoe maker, cor Main and Mission
Maguire F. F. clerk, Pacific Temperance House, 109–113 Pacific
Maguire Frank, tinsmith with Marshall C. Brydges, dwl Dolores nr Sixteenth
Maguire James, laborer, bds Western Hotel
Maguire James, machinist, Union Foundry
Maguire James, metal roofer, dwl 1040 Market
Maguire James, stone cutter with Phil Caduc, bds Franklin Hotel
Maguire John, Club Rooms, 510 Kearny
Maguire John P. cartman, dwl S s Grove nr Franklin
Maguire Margaret Miss, domestic, 945 Howard
Maguire Margaret (widow) dwl 133 Minna
Maguire *(Michael)* & Co. *(Owen Maguire)* wood, coal, hay, grain, and feed, SE cor Hayes and Van Ness Avenue
Maguire Michael, laborer, dwl 260 Minna
Maguire Owen *(Maguire & Co.)* SE cor Hayes and Van Ness Avenue
Maguire Patrick, laborer, dwl E s Montgomery bet Chestnut and Lombard
Maguire Roger, hostler, 431 California, dwl 35 Webb
Maguire Thomas, driver, dwl 230 Jessie, rear

Maguire Thomas, laborer with Hey & Meyn
Maguire Thomas, proprietor Maguire's Opera House
   and Academy Music, dwl 616 Washington
Maguire Thomas G. book keeper, Union Foundry,
   dwl 568 Bryant
MAGUIRE'S ACADEMY OF MUSIC, N s Pine
   bet Sansom and Montgomery
MAGUIRE'S OPERA HOUSE, N s Washington
   bet Montgomery and Kearny
Mahagan Jeremiah, laborer, dwl 695 Geary, rear
Mahan Henry & Co. (John W. Nye) produce com-
   mission merchants, 219 Wash, dwl 68 Natoma
Mahnu Henry W. jeweler with R. B. Gray & Co
Mahan Hugh, with Henry Mahan & Co. dwl 68
   Natoma
Mahan John, laborer, dwl 422 Brannan
Mahan John, pilot 5 Vallejo, dwl W s Dupont nr
   Francisco
Mahan Margaret Miss, domestic, 1022 Jackson
Mahan William, bathman, Railroad House, dwl
   Minna nr Second
Mahaney Thomas, laborer, dwl S s Fell nr Laguna
Mabanny John A. printer with Francis, Valentine
   & Co. dwl 906 Stockton
Mahany Dennis, tailor, dwl 672 Mission
Mahany John, laborer, dwl 49 Stevenson
MAHE GUSTAVE, director, French Savings and
   Loan Society, office 533 Commercial, res San
   Mateo
Maher Ann Mrs. dwl S s Vallejo bet Montgomery
   and Kearny
Maher Edward, marine telegraph operator, Point
   Lobos
Maher James, bar keeper, dwl 112 Sutter
Maher James, drayman, 101 Battery, dwl S s Har-
   rison nr Third
Maher James, laborer, Mission Woolen Mills cor
   Fifteenth and Shotwell
Maher James, teamster, dwl W s Shotwell nr Fif-
   teenth
Maher John T. student with James Mee, dwl 222
   Clara
Maher Margaret Miss, domestic, 821 Bush
Maher Mary Miss, domestic, 821 Bush
Maher Mary (widow) furnished rooms, 3 Hardie Pl
Maher M. H. bar keeper, Fashion Saloon, 16 Sutter
Maher Michael, hostler with C. J. Janson, W s Mis-
   sion bet Twentieth and Twenty-First
Maher Michael J. trunk maker with E. Galpen &
   Co. dwl S s Folsom bet Fourth and Fifth
Maher Patrick H. student, Mission Dolores Church
Maher Walter, dwl 3 Hardie Place
Maher William, cook, 414 Market
Maher William, shoe maker, dwl 12 Sutter
Maherm Thomas, florist, bds Brooklyn Hotel
Mahl Christian, book keeper with E. Boucher
Mahler, Henry, clerk, SW cor Brannan and Third
Mahlstedt John, contractor, dwl NW cor Kearny
   and Greenwich
Mahlstedt Richard, dwl 18 Sansom
Mahnke Otto, waiter, 605 Commercial
Mahon Bernard, cartman, dwl St. Mark Place near
   Kearny
Mahon Bridget Miss, laundress, Bay City Laundry
   1142 Folsom
Mahon Frank (Thompson & Co.) 505 Clay
Mahon Henry, express wagon, 201 Washington,
   dwl 68 Natoma
Mahon Patrick, laborer, dwl N s Pine bet Larkin
   and Polk
Mahon William, laborer, dwl 120 Minna
Mahoney Anna Miss, domestic, 826 Sutter
Mahoney Cornelius, laborer with Hey & Meyn
Mahoney Daniel, laborer, Rich's Warehouse Bat-
   tery, bds Telegraph House
Mahoney Daniel, proprietor Sixth St. House, NW
   cor Sixth and Bryant
MAHONEY DAVID, real estate, dwl SW cor
   Pacific and Larkin

Mahoney Dennis, butcher, dwl S s Pacific bet Polk
   and Larkin
Mahoney Dennis, lab, dwl W s Mary Lane nr Bush
Mahoney Dennis, tailor, dwl 419 Sutter
Mahoney Eliza Miss, domestic, 532 Ellis
Mahoney Elizabeth (widow) dwl 425 Stevenson
Mahoney Ellen Miss, dwl 319 Tehama
Mahoney J. S.J. St. Ignatius College S s Market
   bet Fourth and Fifth
Mahoney James, laborer, Spring Valley W. W.
Mahoney Jeremiah, carpenter, dwl 425 Stevenson
Mahoney Jeremiah, laborer, dwl 631 Vallejo
Mahoney Jeremiah, laborer, dwl S s Post bet Polk
   and Van Ness Avenue
Mahoney Jeremiah A. carriage painter with Samuel
   F. Ross, dwl SE cor Gough and Hickory
Mahoney Jeremiah D. laborer, dwl 266 Stevenson
Mahoney John, gardener, dwl 1102 Washington
Mahoney Kate Miss, domestic, 1009 Powell
Mahoney Margaret Miss, domestic, 204 Fifth
Mahoney Margaret (widow) dwl N s Filbert bet
   Stockton and Powell
Mahoney Mary Miss, domestic, 123 Turk
Mahoney Michael, laborer, dwl United States Hotel
   706 Battery
Mahoney Nellie Miss, domestic, 732 Post
Mahoney Stephen, gardener with William Greene,
   S s Mission bet Eleventh and Twelfth
Mahoney Timothy, boarding, Union Court
Mahoney Timothy, laborer, Market St. R. R. Co. dwl
   N s Hayes nr Polk
Mahoney William, laborer, dwl Gardner Alley
Mahoney William, with Henry Bocken, dwl 710
   Union
Mahony Bartholomew, carpenter, dwl 459 Clemen-
   tina
Mahony Daniel, currier, dwl Zoe bet Bryant and
   Brannan
Mahony Daniel, waterman, dwl 16 Moss
Mahony Daniel J. teamster with Ackerson & Russ,
   dwl N s Minna bet Seventh and Eighth
Mahony Henry, porter with Knapp & Grant, dwl
   13 Second
Mahony John, dwl 212 Stewart
Mahony John, teamster, dwl N s Minna nr Eighth
Mahony John J. (Parkinson & M.) dwl 425 Ste-
   venson
Mahony John J. laborer, Spring Valley W. W. dwl
   S s Vallejo nr Kearny
Mahony Stephen, gardener, dwl N s Hayes bet
   Polk and Van Ness Avenue
Mahony Thomas, agent M. Keller, 609 Front, dwl
   716 Howard
Mahony Thomas, laborer, dwl 267 Stevenson
Mahony Thomas, tailor, dwl 14 Sherwood Place
Mahony T. A. job wagon, Pier 5 Stewart
Mahony William, gardener, dwl E s Filbert near
   Brannan
Maier Charles, shoe maker with J. G. Werlin, dwl
   6 St. Mary
Maige F. N. decorative plasterer, dwl 8 O'Farrell
   Alley
Mailer John, engineer, dwl 515 Market
Maillia William, laborer, dwl N s Geary W Larkin
Mails Isaac, dwl 9 Monroe
Main Benjamin, laundryman, Davis' Laundry, dwl
   255 Third
MAIN (Charles) & WINCHESTER (Ezra H.)
   (and Thomas R. Hayes) importers and manu-
   facturers saddles, harness, whips, etc. 214 and
   216 Battery
MAIN STREET WHARF CO. (J. N. Risdon,
   Lewis Coffey, William Ware, Abner H. Barker,
   and Geo. H. Prescott) office cor Main and Bryant
Maine Henry, laborer, dwl E s Lagoon
Mains Benjamin, shoe maker with H. M. Beers, 313
   Pine
Mains J. Riley, photographer with Jacob Shew, dwl
   709 Greenwich

Mairs James *(J. Dows & Co.)* dwl NW cor Tenth and Bryant

Maisch John, wood and coal yard, 36 and 38 Geary, dwl 34 Geary

Maison George, dwl E s Grove Avenue nr Bryant

Maison Jacob A. dairyman, San Miguel Ranch near Ocean House Road

Maitre Balthazar, dwl 626 California

Maitre Therese Mrs. furnished rooms, 626 California

Major John, lithographer, dwl Sixteenth bet Howard and Folsom

Makin Catherine (widow) dwl N s Mission nr Ninth

Makin Cornelius, pressman with B. F. Sterett, dwl N s Mission bet Ninth and Tenth

Makin Joseph, coachman, bds 336 Bush

MAKIN JAMES N. *(Powers & Co.)* dwl 525 Pine

Malagamba Camillo, dwl Dupont bet Pacific and Broadway

Malany James, upholsterer with Goodwin & Co. dwl 322 Vallejo

Malatesta Joseph, coffee caloon, 1015 Dupont

Malatesta Louis, Italian bakery, 427 Pacific

Malay Mary E. Miss, dress maker, dwl N s Market bet Kearny and Dupont

Malbo François, laborer, dwl W s Dupont bet Jackson and Pacific

Malcesar Philip, engineer, dwl SW cor Dupont and Broadway

Malcom Robert, store keeper with Forbes Brother & Co. dwl 1216 Kearny

Male James *(Andeffred & M.)* dwl S s Bush bet Polk and Van Ness Avenue

Malech Gustave, physician, office and dwl 105 Post

Malet Henry, cartman, dwl N s Pacific bet Taylor and Jones

Maleton Henry *(Hirschfeld & M.)* dwl 213 Dupont

Maley John, seaman, dwl Hinckley Place nr Vallejo bet Kearny and Montgomery

Maley Margaret (widow) dwl W s San nr Filbert

Mall Adam *(Scholl & M.)* and boarding, 13 Geary nr Kearny

Mallen Patrick, brick maker, dwl 26 Rincon Place

Mallett *(Joshua J.)* & Edwards *(Frederick)* wood and coal, 803 Stockton

Mallie William, dwl N s Geary nr Van Ness Av

Mallon Henry, carpenter, dwl 14 Sansom

Mallon John & Co. *(Thomas O'Neil)* glass cutters, 14 Beale, dwl 459 Tehama

Mallon John, groceries and liquors, NE cor Pacific and Scott, dwl 1417 Mason

Mallon Patrick, brick dealer, Third St. Wharf

Mullon Patrick, stone cutter, bds Western Hotel

Mallory Dennis, laborer, dwl 314 Clementina

Mallory Egbert M. dwl 603 Post

Mallory George, carpenter, dwl 1010 Stockton

Mallory Henry C. chief clerk, U. S. Internal Revenue, office NW cor Battery and Commercial, dwl 341 Bryant

Mallot Michael, junk, dwl N s Vallejo bet Leavenworth and Hyde

Malloy James, laborer, dwl Central House, First

Malmgren *(Niles M.)* & Nordgren *(E. Henry)* diamond setters, 608 Sac, dwl 1114 Taylor

Malmgren Niles P. salesman, 610 Sacramento, dwl 1114 Taylor

Malone Elizabeth Miss, domestic, 756 Folsom

Malone James, molder, Union Foundry, dwl 53 Natoma

Malone John *(Hall, Hunt & M.)* dwl 4 Milton Pl

Malone John, molder, Union Foundry, dwl 53 Natoma

Malone Michael, laborer, dwl 27 Louisa

Malone Patrick, wood sawyer, dwl Louisa nr Fourth

MALONEY CORNELIUS, proprietor Franklin House, SW cor Sansom and Broadway

Maloney Daniel, salesman with William F. Burke, dwl 74 Natoma

Maloney David, painter with Hopps & Kanary

Maloney Edward, laborer, dwl 5 Central Place

Maloney Ellen Miss, dwl N s Grove nr Van Ness Avenue Hayes' Valley

Maloney Jeremiah, workman, S. F. & P. Sugar Co. dwl 122 Shipley

Maloney John, blacksmith, dwl St. Charles Hotel

Maloney John, dwl Franklin House, SW cor Sansom and Broadway

Maloney John, clerk, Franklin House, SW cor Broadway and Sansom

Maloney John J. stone mason, dwl NW cor Kearny and Jackson

Maloney Lawrence, waiter, steamer Senator

Maloney Mary Miss, dress maker, dwl 161 Second

Maloney Michael, laborer, dwl N s Salmon Place E Larkin

Maloney Michael, stone cutter, dwl SW cor Laguna and Page

Maloney Patrick, carpenter, dwl cor York and Solano

Maloney Patrick, clerk Pier 10 Stewart, dwl cor York and Solano

Maloney Patrick, steward Franklin House, SW cor Broadway and Sansom

Maloney Peter, machinist, dwl St. Charles Hotel

Maloney Richard, coachman, dwl NE cor Pacific and Mason

Maloney Thomas, blacksmith, dwl 26 Ritch

Maloney Thomas, laborer, Fort Point, dwl N s Presedio road nr Fillmore

Maloney Thomas, saloon, 309 Third

Maloy Daniel, waiter, Lick House

Maloy James, sail maker, dwl 333 Bush

Maloy Maggie L. dwl with Edward Ewald W s Howard bet Thirteenth and Erie

Maloy Maria Miss, domestic, 215 Jones

Maloy Patrick, fireman, dwl 26 Ecker

Maloy Thomas, mason, Eureka Hose Co. No. 4

Malta Antonio, fisherman, 36 Italian Fish Market

MALTBY CHARLES, superintendent Indian Affairs, office 423 Washington, dwl International Hotel

Maltby C. C. carpenter, dwl Original House

Mamlock W. upholsterer, 416 Third

Mammoth G. & S. M. Co. office 410 Montgomery

Mammoth G. & S. M. Co. (San Bernardino) office 611 Clay

Man Lee & Ting Kee (Chinese) 731 Commercial

Manaco Antonio, driver with Bulletti & Co. Pacific Fruit Market

Manahan Edward, drayman, dwl N s Turk near Larkin

Manahan Frank P. with Bryan Brothers, 324 San

Manahan Henry, book keeper, dwl 160 First

Manahan John, dwl 512 Mission

Mancarini D. & Co. *(Steffano Pierucini)* modelers and plaster workers, 421 Pine, dwl Franklin Place nr Stockton

Mancarini D. *(L. Ghilardi & Co.)* 534 Commercial

Mancarini Domiano, modeler and plaster worker, 743 Clay

Manchester Benjamin S. calker, dwl cor Virginia Avenue and Buena Vista

Manchester Frederick A. workman with D. R. Provost, dwl cor Virginia Av and Buena Vista

Manchester G. W. dwl 1710 Stockton

Manchester *(Isaac)* & O'Neil *(John)* liquor saloon, 627 Pacific

Manchester Isaac, laborer, Golden State Iron Works, dwl 226 Mission

MANCHESTER J. B. attorney at law, office NE cor Mont and Jackson room 11, dwl NW cor Stockton and Pacific

Manchester J. F. junk, dwl NW cor Main and Harrison

Manchester John B. lather, dwl 25 Louisa

Manchester Lyman H. clerk, 408 Front, dwl 463 Minna

Manchester T. W. *(William B. Duck & Co.)* dwl NE cor Second and Tehama

Manciet J. P. *(J. A. Bergerot & Co.)* 10 Clay St. Market

Manciet J. P. liquor saloon, 448 Brannan

MANCILLAS ANTONIO, publisher and proprietor La Voz de Mejico, office NW cor Montgomery and Jackson, dwl 629 Clay

Mandege Peter, chop house, NW cor Stewart and Mission

Mandel Emanuel *(Greenberg & M.)* dwl 529 Post

Mandevas Charles, dwl 113 Commercial

Mandeville Edward, manufacturer blacksmiths' bellows, 218 Mission,dwl E s Folsom bet Twenty-First and Twenty-Second

Mandeville Margaret (widow) dwl 413 Dupont

Mandeville Samuel, machinist, Union Foundry, dwl Original House

Mandeville Simon V. sash maker with Smith, Ware & Co. dwl E s Folsom bet Twenty-First and Twenty-Second

Mandigo Stephen, with Charles Harley & Co. dwl Pacific Temperance House

Mandlebaum Frank, dwl 1016 Bush

Mandot Copper M. Co. office 508 Battery

Mandron Jaques, boot maker, 729 Pacific

Manes Mary Miss, domestic, 719 Sutter

Mangan Patrick, ship carpenter, dwl W s Gilbert bet Brannan and Townsend

Mangel Philip, upholsterer, dwl 1503 California

Mangela Christopher, porter with John Van Bergen & Co. dwl SW cor Mission and Third

Mangels Claus *(Spreckels & Co. and H. Brunings & Co.)* dwl 70 Everett

Mangels George D. clerk, NE cor Townsend and Crook

Mangels *(Henry)* & Claussen *(Henry)* groceries and liquors, 313 Dupont

Mangels Henry *(Bockman & M.)* dwl NE cor Freelon and Fourth

Mangels *(Herman)* & Cutrell *(William)* Sebastopol Liquor Saloon, NW cor Clay and Davis

Mangels *(John)* & Co. *(John D. Cushing)* groceries and liquors, SE cor Howard .and Fourth, dwl NE cor Tehama and Fourth

MANGELS *(Martin)* & CO. *(W. Fouz)* proprietors Washington Brewery, SE cor Lombard and Taylor, dwl 721 Lombard

Mangels *(Martin)* & Steffens *(Dedrich)* groceries and liquors, SE cor Folsom and Main

Mangels Peter, clerk, NW cor Mont and Sutter

Mangeot Charles, blacksmith and wagon maker, SE cor Howard and Ninth, dwl W s Washington Avenue nr Mission

Mangeot George, hats and caps, 423 Kearny

Mangin Daniel, laborer, dwl 277 Minna

Mangini Angelo *(D. Ghirardelli & Co.)* dwl 841 Howard

Mangolette John, workman with L. Somps, Visitacion Valley

MANHATTAN COAL CO. Mount Diablo, Wolf Bros. agents, office 212 Battery

MANHATTAN FIRE ISURANCE CO. New York, R. B. Swain & Co. agents, 206 Front

Manhattan House, Daniel McCarthy proprietor, 705 Front

MANHATTAN LIFE INSURANCE CO. New York, John Lander agent, SW cor Montgomery and Clay

Manheim Edward *(Manheim, Schonwasser & Co.)* res New York

MANHEIM *(Isaac)* SCHONWASSER *(Samuel)* & CO. *(Edward Manheim)* importers and jobbers millinery and fancy goods, 113 Battery, dwl 825 Post

Manifold S. D. employé, International Hotel

Manion James, butcher, dwl E s Larkin bet Bush and Pine

Manion Michael, laborer, dwl 188 Stevenson

Manion Patrick, laborer, dwl N s Bryant bet Eighth and Ninth

Manion Patrick, laborer, 1514 Stockton

Manke August, with Jacob J. Smith, dwl Louisa bet Third and Fourth

Manley B. straw-hat presser, dwl 732 Folsom

Manley George, workman, Pacific Glass Works, dwl cor Mariposa and Indiana

Manley Solomon, dwl 724 Pacific

Mann Alexander, cigars and tobacco, 232 Mont

Mann Bartlett, retortman, San Francisco Gas Co

Mann Charles H. book keeper, with Henston, Hastings & Co. dwl 272 Stevenson

Mann C. N. Mrs. boarding, dwl 218 Bush

Mann David, tailor, 108 Stewart

MANN GEORGE S. hard wood lumber, 205 Market, dwl 31 South Park

Mann Jacob *(Friel & M.)* 69 Fourth

Mann Joel F. laborer, dwl 528 Folsom

Mann John, dwl N s Tehama nr Sixth

Mann Levi, merchant, dwl 272 Stevenson

Mann Peter, with Justus Bepler nr San Miguel Station

Mann Robert T. porter, dwl 1819 Powell

MANNECK HENRY, paper box manufacturer and importer and dealer colored paper and star board, 210 Pine, dwl 782 Harrison

Mannen Eliza Miss, domestic, 431 Post

Mannie Marcelle, engineer, steamer Clinton

Manning Agnes M. Miss, special grammar assistant Lincoln School, dwl 739 Howard

Manning Alfred W. with Martin & Horton, dwl 10 O'Farrell

Manning Daniel, carpenter, dwl NW cor Jessie and Anna

Manning Dennis R. molder, Vulcan Iron Works, dwl 910 Brannan

Manning Francis, carpenter, dwl 550 Tehama

Manning James, dwl SE cor Clementina and Sixth

Manning James F. waiter, Lick House

MANNING JAMES M. Eighth Ward Exchange, NE cor Market and Powell, dwl SE cor Sixth and Clementina

Manning James W. rope maker, S. F. Cordage Factory, dwl nr cor Humboldt and Kentucky

Manning John, porter, Lick House, dwl E s Mary nr Natoma

Manning John, produce, dwl 70 Jessie

Manning Joseph G. printer, dwl 912 Market

Manning Kate Miss, domestic with E. Burke, N s Turk nr Franklin

Manning Maggie Miss, domestic, 113 Mason

Manning Mary A. Miss domestic, 330 Bryant

Manning Michael, hackman, Plaza

Manning Michael, molder, Jackson Foundry, dwl 706 Battery

Manning Patrick, workman, S. F. & P. Sugar Co

Manning T. G. bricklayer, dwl W s Main nr Folsom

Manning Thomas, porter, Wells, Fargo & Co. dwl N s Broadway bet Montgomery and Kearny

Manning Walter, workman and dwl S. F. Cordage Factory

Mannon Patrick, laborer, dwl 213 Tehama

Manow Hester D. dwl SW cor Fifteenth and Mission

Manrow J. P. real estate agent, office 606 Merchant, dwl NE cor Larkin and Chestnut

Mansbach *(Emanuel)* & Bine *(Solomon)* fancy goods, 56 Second *(and Lowe & B.)*

Mansel Michael, laborer, S. F. & San José R. R. Co

MANSELL FREDERICK, sign and ornamental painter, 420 California

Mansfield Joseph, waiter, Empire State Restaurant

Mansfield J. P. express wagon, dwl cor Turk and Van Ness Avenue

Mansfield Myer, book keeper, 423 Battery, dwl 1304 Pine

Manslet Jean, carpenter, NW cor Pine and Quincy

Manson ——, carpenter, dwl 73 Natoma

Manson John S. real estate, office 206 Front, dwl 713 Broadway

Mansur Joseph, salesman with John G. Hodge & Co. dwl 619 Bush

Manthey Gus A. with Edward Bosqui & Co. dwl 110 Montgomery Block

Manton John, teamster, dwl 32 Rousch

Mantz J. tinner, dwl 215 Third

Manwaring Henry, clerk, 38 California, dwl SW cor First and Stevenson

Manx Patrick, mason, dwl 414 Market

Manzanilla Mining Co. office 1 Government House, 502 Washington

Manzer L. M. delivery clerk, U. S. Appraiser's Store, dwl SW cor Devisidero and Sutter

Manzilla José, with W. Wolf & Co. dwl Pacific bet Dupont and Stockton

Maradina Regina (widow) meat market, 645 Pacific

Marais Clarisse, cabinet maker, dwl St. Charles Hotel

Maran Frank, dwl 24 Sansom

MARASCHI A. Rev., S.J. treasurer St. Ignatius' College, S s Market bet Fourth and Fifth

Marat M. W. hatter, dwl 15 Harlan Place

Marathon G. & S. M. Co. office 1 Government House, 502 Washington

Marazzi Eugene, clerk with E. Mestre

Marble Abbey L. Mrs. adjuster, U. S. Branch Mint, dwl 26 Essex

Marble Frederick, with Francis G. Burke, dwl cor Beale and Mission

Marble Nelson, carpenter, dwl N s Sacramento bet Polk and Larkin

Marcasea Domingo, baker, 509 Third

Marcel Auguste, liquor saloon, 132 Fourth

Marcelin Aurignac, porter, 323 Geary

March Adam, cabinet maker, dwl 606 California

March Charles E. carpenter, W s Clara nr Bush, dwl 314 Sutter

March Launidas, works with Argulas Bernal

March William F. carpenter, dwl 119 Natoma

Marchand Anicet, laborer, dwl 735 Green

Marchand Constant, butcher, dwl 825 Jackson

Marchand (E.) & Laurent (M.) restaurant, 607 Kearny

Marchand Joseph E. accountant with Charles H. Harrison, dwl S s Chestnut bet Dupont and Kearny

Marchant Christopher, butcher, dwl 177 Minna

Marchant (George H.) & Smith (E. L.) matrass makers, 104 Dupont, dwl 177 Minna

Marchebout C. Mme. furniture, 1115 and 1117 Dupont

Marchebout Auguste jr. clerk, 1115 Dupont

Marchoud John, ship carpenter, dwl 825 Jackson

Marcial Augustus, cook, Cliff House

Marcloot Edward, machinist, dwl 54 First

Marco Eugene, carpenter, dwl 17 Hunt

Marcott Edward, machinist with Palmer, Knox & Co. dwl 637 Mission

Marcuet Edward (Tchants, Tenthorey & Co.) dwl 558 Mission

Marcuse Felix, salesman, 618 Sacramento, dwl 824 Folsom

Marcuse Heiman L. tailor, 1314 Stockton

Marden Calvin, clerk, dwl E s Jones bet Greenwich and Filbert

Marden Decatur (W. R. Doty & Co.) resides New York

MARDEN (Ira) & FOLGER (James A.) manufacturers coffee and spices, 220 Front, dwl NW cor Filbert and Jones

Marden Robert A. machinist, Vulcan Iron Works, dwl S s Minna bet Third and Fourth

Maret Eugene, cook, dwl 1013 Sutter

Margarita S. & C. M. Co. office 804 Montgomery

Marggraf Joseph, cabinet maker with J. Peirce, dwl 679 Mission

Marggraff Ernst, waiter, dwl 628 Merchant

Marggraff Leopold, laborer, dwl W s Devisidero bet Post and Geary

Marggraff Nicholas, painter, dwl 315 Montgomery

Margot Henry D. porter with Lazard Freres, dwl 236 First

Maria S. M. Co. office 540 Washington

MARIANI (G. D.) & STEFFANI (C.) wholesale and retail dealers hardware, crockery. etc. 1006 Dupont

Marianni Joseph, painter. W s Gaven nr Greenwich

Marietich Andrea, cook, dwl 105 Washington

Marina E. J. DeSta, broker, office 607 Clay

Marina Joseph G. DeSta, stock broker, office 607 Clay, dwl 555 Tehama

MARINE BOARD UNDERWRITERS OF SAN FRANCISCO, James P. Flint president and C. T. Hopkins secretary, office 318 California

MARINE HOSPITAL U. S. NW cor Harrison and Spear

Mariner Rufus K. dwl 731 Harrison

Marion Auguste, liquors, 107 Jackson

Marion Marten, purifier, S. F. Gas Co

MARION (Samuel) & HENDERSON (Justus) Whitehall Liquor Saloon, 321 East

Marion Samuel, restaurant, 335 East

Marion William L. blacksmith, dwl S s Harrison bet Seventh and Eighth

Maritiese Francisco, vegetable garden nr Bay View Park

Markley George W. carpenter with N. P. Langland

Markes Joseph, laborer, dwl 40 Stewart

MARKET AND MISSION R. R. CO. office SE cor Montgomery and Jackson

Market Frank, vegetable peddler, dwl 1004 Pacific

Market Street. Wharf Co. office foot Market

Markewitz Jacob, tinsmith with Charles Brown, dwl 749 Market

Markey Andrew, laborer, Pacific Foundry, dwl 527 Mission

Markey Bridget Miss, domestic, 1023 Bush

Markey John, teamster, dwl 523 Mission

Markey Philip, salesman, 119 Montgomery, dwl 548 Mission

Markey Richard, baker, Original House Restaurant, dwl 308 Broadway, rear

Markham Henry, butcher with W. D. Litchfield, dwl 116 St. Mark Place

Markham John, driver with L. Racouillat, dwl S s Mission bet First and Second

Markham Olivia, domestic, 724 Mission

Markham Willard, gate keeper, Bay Shore and Fort Point Road, foot Fillmore

Markley Levi, produce commission, 107 Clay, dwl 808 Bush

Markley Washington, dwl 200 Stockton

Marks Aaron, book keeper, 515 California, dwl 515 Howard

Marks Adolph, fancy goods, 1018 Dupont

Marks August, carrier, Abend Post, dwl SW cor Green and Vallejo

Marks Augusta (widow) dwl 647 Commercial

Marks Augustus, grinding and polishing, 416 Market, dwl SE cor Jones and Greenwich

Marks Benas, dwl 1519 Powell

Marks Bernhard, principal Spring Valley Grammar School, dwl S s Sac bet Larkin and Polk

Marks Cornelia Mrs. assistant teacher, Academic Seminary, dwl S s Sac bet Larkin and Polk

Marks David, salesman with Stein, Simon & Co. 632 Sacramento

Marks David, salesman, 317 Sacramento

MARKS EDMUND & CO. wholesale grocers, 311 Commercial, dwl 618 O'Farrell

Marks Emil, cap maker with Simon Lust, dwl 46 Fourth

Marks Frederick, watch maker and jeweler, 1024 Dupont

Marks Harris, glazier, dwl 14 Hinckley

Marks Harris, junk, dwl 253 Jessie

Marks Harris, tailor, 604 Market

Marks Henry, clothing, 24 Stewart
Marks Isaac, salesman, 516 Commercial
Marks J. butcher, dwl 205 Sansom
Marks J. tailor, dwl 231 Pacific
Marks J. A. dwl 515 Howard
Marks Jacob, clerk, dwl 323 Kearny
Marks Jacob, salesman, 317 Sacramento
Marks Jacob C. (Hirsch & M.) dwl 561 Mission
Marks James, dwl 331 Bush
Marks James, with John J. Marks & Co. 6 Clay, dwl 865 Mission
Marks James, painter with Hopps & Kanary
Marks John, tailor, 809 Wash, dwl 1016 Kearny
Marks John H. butcher with Crummie & O'Neill, dwl nr Brannan St. Bridge
MARKS JOHN J. & CO. ship chandlers, 4 and 6 Clay, dwl 510 Third
Marks (Joseph) & Brother (Robert Marks) auctioneers and commission merchants, 521 California, dwl 515 Howard
Marks Joseph, clerk, 617 Sacramento
Marks Louis. with R. Elias, 116 Clay, dwl Eddy nr Jones
Marks Louis, tinner with Charles Brown, dwl 266 Jessie, rear
Marks M. Mrs. dwl NW cor Kearny and Bdwy
Marks Moses, with Marks & Bro. dwl 515 Howard
Marks Morris, peddler, dwl 72 Jessie
Marks Robert (Marks & Bro.) dwl 515 Howard
Marks S. (Lando & M.) 327 Sacramento
Marks S. Mrs. milliner and millinery goods, 617 Sacramento and 414 Kearny
Marks Samuel, tailor, 809 Washington
Marks Saul, merchant, dwl 613 Post
Marks Simon, bleacher and presser, 617 Sacramento
Marks Simon, groceries and liquors, 658 Mission
Marks Simon, job wagon, cor California and Kearny, dwl 15 Rassette Place No. 2
Marks Thomas, with John Marks, dwl 510 Third
Marks William, clerk, bds Sacramento Hotel 407 Pacific
Markt (Frederick) & Fleishel (Charles) locksmiths and bell hangers, 18 Post, dwl W s Capp bet Twenty-First and Twenty-Second
Markus Louis, clerk with E. Frank, dwl 214 Pac
Markwood Wilson, carpenter, bds 761 Mission
Marlen John, with John Higgins, Lake Merced Ranch
Marlett C. W. dwl What Cheer House
Marlin Daniel, assistant engineer, Pacific Mail S. S. Co
MARLOW OWEN, groceries and liquors, NE cor Mission and Third
Marois Charles, brick maker, dwl NE cor Pacific and Larkin
Maroney J. waiter, 626 Kearny
Maroney John, laborer, dwl 18 Freelon
Maroney Thomas, laborer, dwl 52 Louisa
Marony John, liquor saloon, S s Brannan bet Sixth and Seventh
Marot Julius, hatter with K. Meussdorffer, dwl 15 Harlan Place
Marquard Adolph (William Bofer & Co.) dwl 608 Sacramento
Marquard Frederick (Hauck & M.) dwl 910 Washington
Marquard Frederick, express wagon, cor California and Kearny
Marquardt Adolphus F. clerk, 15 Metropolitan Market, dwl 18 Sansom
Marque Emile, compositor, Courrier de San Francisco, 607 Sansom
Marquet Frank, job wagon, N s Pacific bet Stockton and Powell
Marquis John (McDougall & M.) dwl 1117 Folsom
Marran Margaret Miss, domestic with Jas. Adams, S s Hayes nr Franklin
Marren Mary Miss, domestic, 39 Natoma

MARRIOTT FREDERICK, editor and proprietor San Francisco News Letter and California Advertiser, office 528 Clay, dwl N s Filbert bet Jones and Leavenworth
Marron Ann (widow) dwl E s Mason bet Vallejo and Green
Marron John, butcher, SE cor Second and Tehama
Marron M. C. blacksmith, dwl 414 Market
Marron Patrick, mason, dwl 414 Market
Marsack Charles, carpenter, dwl NW cor Third and Stevenson
Marschell Joseph, milk wagon, 230 Broadway
Marsden George, tutor with John Searles, E s Eighth bet Howard and Folsom
Marsen Elk, express wagon, dwl Bush nr Larkin
MARSH, (A. Judson) PILSBURY (C. J.) & CO. hardware, tools, and metals, SE cor Market and First, dwl 716 Stockton
Marsh Albert, policeman, City Hall, dwl 531 Vallejo
Marsh Andrew Jackson, photographic reporter Fourth and Twelfth District Courts, office 607 Washington, dwl 741 Howard
Marsh Creek Petroleum Co. office 617 Montgomery
Marsh E. B. (Turner & M.) dwl 1011 Pine
Marsh John, wood and coal, 38 Geary, dwl 34 Geary
Marsh Moses, chicken ranch, SW cor Folsom and Eleventh
Marsh Nathaniel F. drayman, 117 California, dwl 313 Beale
Marsh Robert, book keeper, dwl 333 Bryant
Marshall Alexander, boot maker, 218 First, dwl 248 Clara
Marshall Caroline (widow) dwl 909 Bush
Marshall David P. lamplighter, S. F. Gas Co. dwl SE cor Howard and Fifth
Marshall Frederick, dwl What Cheer House
Marshall George W. (col'd) porter, dwl 1507 Mason
Marshall Henry, assistant appraiser, U. S. office Custom House, dwl 657 Howard
Marshall Henry H. bar keeper, 615 Washington
Marshall Horatio S. gasman Academy Music, dwl 26 Tehama
Marshall James D. shoe maker with John Irwin, 12 Clay, dwl 449 Jessie
Marshall James G. miner, dwl 611 Greenwich
Marshall James N. weigher, S. F. & P. Sugar Co. dwl 12 Langton
Marshall J. B. treasurer Academy Music
Marshall John, laborer, dwl Spear nr Harrison
Marshall Joseph, restaurant, 304 Front
Marshall Joseph W. drayman, SE cor Washington and Battery, dwl 518 O'Farrell
Marshall L. lamplighter, S. F. Gas Co
Marshall Lavene, laborer, dwl 22 Jessie
Marshall Levine, cap maker, 414 Sacramento, dwl 266 Jessie
Marshall Martin, drayman with L. B. Garrison, dwl 403 Third
Marshall Nicholas, clerk with E. H. Cardinet, dwl NE cor Taylor and Lombard
Marshall Robert, liquor saloon, 733 Howard
Marshall Thomas, machinist, Pacific Foundry, dwl 150 Third
Marshall Thomas, spinner, Mission Woolen Mills, dwl E s Columbia nr Sixteenth
Marshall W. H. (col'd) porter, dwl 23 Virginia
Marshall William, dwl What Cheer House
Marshall William, clerk, Railroad House
MARSHALL (William B.) & JOHNSON (R. M.) Chrystal Palace Saloon, 614 Montgomery, dwl 626 Market
Marsland Edward D. chief engineer, Pacific Mail S. S. Co
Marston C. A. (Jacob Shew) dwl 315 Montgomery
Marston Frank, dwl 233 First
Marston Levi H. carpenter, dwl 275 Jessie
Marston P. F. carpenter, dwl 233 First

Martein John E. seaman, dwl 1022 Mont, rear
Martel J. L. real estate broker, 636 Clay, dwl 446 Natoma
Martell Adam, bar keeper, dwl NW cor Kearny - and Broadway
Martell Ellie Miss, actress, Bella Union
Martell John, butcher, 53 Everett, dwl 50 Everett
MARTELL JOHN, silver plater, 619 Kearny, dwl 50 Everett
Martell Louis, blacksmith with Belduke & Co. dwl Mission nr Fourth
Martencourt L. *(Castorine, Pascal & Co.)* dwl 1127 Dupont
Martenet *(Jefferson)* & Schley *(Daniel)* booksellers and stationers, 633 Market, dwl N s Mission nr Ninth
Martens Christian *(D. Martens & Brother)* NW cor Stockton and Sacramento
Martens D. & Brother *(Christian Martens)* groceries and liquors, NW cor Stockton and Sac
Martens *(Frederick)* & Bredhoff *(Chas.)* butter, cheese, etc. 57 and 58 Washington Market, dwl 822 Union
Martens Martin, Alhambra Liquor Saloon, 18 Sutter, dwl 15 Sutter
Martenstein Daniel, apprentice, dwl 117 Minna
Martenstein Daniel, miller, dwl 559 Market
MARTENSTEIN JACOB & CO. *(Austin Walrath)* proprietors National Flour Mills, 561 and 563 Market, dwl 115 Minna
Martenstein John, miller, National Mills, dwl 106 Minna
Martin Abraham, merchant, dwl 315 Clementina
MARTIN ADDISON & CO. *(Thomas D. Pearson)* fruits, Pacific Fruit Market, dwl 324 O'Farrell
Martin Albert, paying teller with Tallant & Co. dwl 505 Powell
Martin Alexander, book keeper with Donald Davidson & Co. 338 Montgomery
Martin Alexander H. assistant assayer, U. S. Branch Mint, dwl 733 Broadway
Martin Ann (widow) nurse with Mrs. W. L. Perkins, E s Eleventh bet Mission and Market
MARTIN BENJAMIN T. assayer, U. S. Branch Mint, office 608 Commercial, res Oakland
Martin Bridget Miss, domestic, 219 First
Martin Bridget (widow) dwl 946 Mission
MARTIN CAMILLO, assistant manager London & San Francisco Bank and consul for Spain, office 412 Montgomery, dwl 343 Jessie
Martin C. H. dwl Original House
Martin Charles, deck hand, stm Julia
MARTIN *(Clark)* & HORTON *(Thomas R.)* wines and liquors, 545 Clay and 534 Montgomery, dwl Lick House
Martin Cornelius, policeman, City Hall, dwl 1115 Folsom
Martin Daniel, cartman, Harrison bet Fifth and Sixth
Martin Daniel, engineer, stm Sacramento, dwl N s Perry bet Fourth and Fifth
Martin Daniel E. superintendent A. R. C. Ice Co. office 718 Battery, dwl 717 Green
MARTIN EDWARD & CO. *(D. V. B. Henarie)* importers and jobbers wines and liquors, 604 and 606 Front, dwl 863 Mission
Martin Edward, deck hand, stm Chrysopolis.
Martin Edward, handcartman, dwl 214 Commercial
MARTIN EDWARD, treasurer Hibernia Savings and Loan Society, office 506 Jackson
Martin Ellen Miss, domestic with Dan'l Welsh, N s Turk bet Fillmore and Steiner
Martin Ellen T. Miss, dwl with John Martin, S side Folsom nr Eighth
Martin F. F. tinsmith with Locke & Montague, dwl Original House
Martin Frederick, modeler with Samuel Kellett
Martin George, job wagon, cor Market and Geary

Martin George, watchman, S. F. Cordage Factory, dwl nr S. F. Cordage Factory
Martin George W. rigger, dwl Beale Place
MARTIN *(Henry)* & CO. *(J. F. Greenman)* dealers copper and other ores, office SW cor Montgomery and Commerial room 20, res New York
Martin Henry, porter, dwl 500 Vallejo
Martin Jacob, with C. Meyer & Co. dwl 510 Post
Martin James, dwl 330 Sutter
Martin James, laborer, Spring Valley W. W. dwl Laguna Honda
Martin James P. book keeper, Bank California, bds 728 Howard
Martin Jennie (widow) dwl 330 Sutter
Martin John, dwl with William Martin, N s Stevenson bet Seventh and Eighth
Martin John, dwl E s Fifth Avenue bet Bryant and Harrison
Martin John, bar keeper, NW cor Washington and Kearny.
Martin John, boots and shoes, 419 East, dwl S side Harrison bet Fifth and Sixth
Martin John, carpenter, dwl 207 Post
Martin John, cook, 647 Com, dwl 640 Vallejo
Martin John, deputy state ganger, 321 Front, dwl SE cor Folsom and Eighth
Martin John, drayman, 413 Front
Martin John, laborer with Hey & Meyn
Martin John, laborer, bds 318 Pacific
Martin John, produce, dwl Stevenson bet First and Second
Martin John J. assistant auditor, Custom House
Martin John M. clothing, 528, Sac, dwl 809 Bush
Martin John W. bds 728 Howard
Martin Joseph, tailor, dwl 1030 Dupont
Martin Lewis, boatman, dwl Filbert, Telegraph Hill
Martin Lewis, laborer, dwl Bay State House
MARTIN LEWIS, Pacific Billiard Saloon, SE cor Stockton and Jackson
Martin Lloyd, miner, dwl SW cor Post and Kearny
Martin Louis Grellet *(Chauce & M.)* dwl 609 Greenwich bet Stockton and Powell
Martin M. dwl 12 Sutter
Martin Maggie Miss, domestic, 113 Mason
Martin Maria J. dwl 1312 Powell
Martin Mary Miss, domestic; 649 Broadway
Martin Mary Miss, domestic, 687 Market
Martin Mary (widow) nurse with J. C. Horan
Martin Michael, bar keeper, 565 Market
Martin Michael, book keeper, dwl 15 Geary
Martin Michael, groceries, NE cor Hyde and Pac
Martin M. S. stock broker, dwl 625 Harrison
Martin Nicholas, carpenter, dwl 15 Virginia
Martin Patrick, dwl S side Union bet Stockton and Powell
Martin Patrick, teamster, dwl 308 Mason
MARTIN PHILIP, Pony Liquor Saloon, 510 Kearny, dwl 517 Bush
Martin Rebecca (widow) dwl 510 Post
Martin Robert S. conductor, Omnibus R. R. Co. dwl N s Francisco bet Kearny and Dupont
Martin Simon, dwl 315 Clementina
Martin Susan Miss, seamstress, dwl E s Larkin bet Pacific and Broadway
Martin Theodorin B. gardener with W. J. Shaw, dwl 1327 Dupont
Martin Thomas, with Stevens & Oliver, 28 Mont
Martin Thomas, laborer, dwl 835 Clay, rear
Martin Thomas, painter, bds Brooklyn Hotel
Martin Thomas, workman, S. F. & P. Sugar Co. dwl S s Clementina nr Eighth
Martin W. H. registrar U. S. Branch Mint, res Oakland
MARTIN WHEELER, groceries and liquors, SE cor Howard and Second, dwl S s Thirteenth bet Howard and Folsom
Martin William, dwl S s Minna nr Seventh
Martin William, carpenter, dwl N s Stevenson bet Seventh and Eighth

Martin William, machinist, Union Foundry
Martin William, policeman, City Hall, dwl N s Pacific above Taylor
Martin William, workman with I. O. Taplin, San Bruno Road
Martin William A. cooper, dwl 304 Sansom
Martin William H. dwl N s Tehama bet Eighth and Ninth
MARTIN WILLIAM H. secretary mining companies, office 732 Washington, dwl 914 Jackson
Martin William K. dwl 214 Sansom
Martin William L. mariner, 32 Stewart
Martin W. L. bridge builder, dwl 327 Bush
Martincout E. D. molder, Miners' Foundry, dwl 915 Stockton
Martineau J. (widow) dwl 915 Stockton
Martinez Antonio, cigar maker with Herman Brand, dwl 522 Filbert
Martinez Joseph, laborer, dwl 425 Filbert
Martinez Joseph M. cigar maker, 705 Davis, dwl 522 Filbert
Martini B. barber, dwl 756 Clay
Martini Iami, vegetable garden, Bay View
Martini L. A. musician, dwl 917 Sacramento
Martini Rudolph, fruits. 104 Stewart, dwl 636 Pac
Martinon August, commission merchant and mining secretary, office 811 Montgomery, dwl 245 Jessie
Martins Joseph, seaman, dwl 18 Geary
Martins R. (widow) dwl 18 Geary
Martins William, seaman, dwl 617 Davis
Marvin John H. dwl NW cor Third and Tehama
Marwedel *(Charles F.)* & Otto *(Charles)* hardware, locksmiths, and bell hangers, 329 Bush, dwl 6 Vassar Place
Marwin George. mariner, dwl 313 Bryant
MARX ADOLPH, groceries and liquors, NE cor Green and Stockton
Marx David, dwl 316 Third
Marx Flora (widow) dwl 227 Geary
Marx Isaac, news dealer, SW cor Kearny and Pine
Marx Jacob, bottle dealer, dwl 946 Howard
Mary Stewart G. & S. M. Co. office 404 Front
Marysville Hotel, Edward McNabb proprietor, 414 Pacific
MARYSVILLE LINE STEAMERS, California Steam Navigation Co. foot Broadway, office NE cor Front and Jackson
Marzicano Nerino, real estate, dwl SW cor Dupont and Broadway
Marzicano Patrick, real estate, dwl SW cor Dupont and Broadway
Masden George, drayman, dwl 113 Stevenson
Maskell John, clerk with John Rosenfeld, dwl 131 Clara
Maskell Michael, marble cutter with L. R. Myers & Co. dwl 7 Sherwood Place
Mason Casper H. dwl 310 Sixth
Mason Charles, carpenter, dwl 37 Fifth
Mason Charles, secretary H. B. M. Consul, office 428 California
Mason David B. painter, 613 Sansom, dwl What Cheer House
Mason Edmond Y. *(McCoy & M.)* dwl 4 William
Mason Elizabeth Miss, seamstress, dwl W s Morey Alley bet Stockton and Powell
Mason Frances (widow) dwl 641 Broadway
Mason Frederick, real estate agent, 34 Montgomery Block, dwl Lick House
Mason George, farmer, dwl Oriental Hotel
Mason J. Howel, clk, NE cor Jackson and Kearny
Mason John, carpenter, dwl 73 Minna
Mason John, cook, dwl 631 Broadway
Mason John, laborer, dwl 504 Market
Mason John, laborer, dwl 162 Minna
MASON JOHN, proprietor Mason's Brewery, brewery N s Chestnut bet Powell and Mason
Mason John, shoe maker, 7 Second, dwl 629 Mission
Mason John L. engineer, dwl S s Sixteenth bet Valencia and Guerrero

Mason John R. salesman with Jones, Dixon & Co. dwl 557 Leavenworth
Mason Joseph, book keeper, 232 Bush, dwl SE cor Second and Natoma
Mason J. Warren, U. S. storekeeper, Howard's Bonded Warehouse, SW corner Broadway and Front, dwl 512 Bush
Mason Nathaniel, master schooner Hannah Louise, dwl 238 Stewart
Mason Robert T. (col'd) porter, 413 Montgomery, dwl cor Jessie and Ecker
Mason William, carpenter, dwl S s Sixteenth nr Dolores
Mason William C. clerk with C. J. Hawley & Co. dwl 532 Howard
Mason William H. carpenter, dwl S s Sixteenth nr Dolores
MASONIC HALL BUILDING, 418–422 Montgomery, Samuel Brannan proprietor
MASONIC TEMPLE, junction Montgomery, Market, and Post
Mass Peter, butcher, dwl 323 Kearny
Massard Jules, real estate, dwl SW cor Dupont and Clay
Masse Martin *(Millsner & Co.)* dwl 907 Dupont
Massen Christian, laborer, dwl cor California Avenue and San Bruno Road
MASSEY ATKINS, coffin warehouse and undertaker, 651 Sacramento, dwl 606 Sutter
Massey Charles P. jr. book keeper with McElwee & Ackerman, dwl 33 O'Farrell
Massey Herman W. stabling and wood and coal, 1014 Market and teamster, Pier 13 Stewart, dwl 337 Jessie
Massey Joseph, laborer with Peter Salmon
Massey Richard L. painter, Volunteer Engine Co. No. 7
Masson Francis P. *(Salomon & Co.)* dwl 7 Harlan Place
Masson George, carpenter, dwl 31 Kearny
Masson L. D. attorney at law, dwl SE cor Third and Hunt
Masson Madame, teacher French, dwl SW corner Broadway and Montgomery
Masson Marius V. tinsmith with Tay, Brooks & Backus, dwl Clay Avenue
Masson Victor B. salesman, 506 Washington, dwl 635 Washington
Massone Pietro, employé with Brignardello, Macchiavello & Co. 706 Sansom
Massoni Henry F. cook, dwl 259 Minna
Mast Hermann, Butchers' Home, Potrero Avenue
Masten N. K. real estate agent, 619 Montgomery, dwl 21 South Park
Master C. bar keeper, dwl 636 Pacific
Masterson Anna Miss, domestic, 405 Taylor
Masterson Bridget Miss, domestic, 713 Post
Masterson Elizabeth A. (widow) dwl NW cor Townsend and Third
Masterson George, driver, North Beach & Mission R. R. Co
Masterson Hugh, driver with Daniel McGlynn, dwl 112 Jessie
Masterson John, hackman, Plaza, dwl N s Stevenson bet Sixth and Seventh
Masterson Patrick, silversmith with Vanderslice & Co. 810 Montgomery
MASTICK E. B. attorney at law, office 520 Montgomery, res Alemeda
Mastick Levi B. *(S. L. Mastick & Co.)* and school director First District, dwl W s Montgomery bet Vallejo and Green
Mastick L. J. Miss, principal Hayes Valley School, dwl W s Montgomery nr Green
MASTICK S. L. & CO. *(Levi B. Mastick)* lumber and proprietors Humboldt & Puget Sound Packets, 129 Stewart Pier 10, dwl 343 Beale
Mastie James, miner, dwl 522 Pine
Maston Maggie (widow) dwl 633 California.

Mata Claude, workman with L. L. Lantbeaume nr St. Mary's College
Matasci Severino, fruit peddler, dwl W s Pacific Al
Matayron Julius C. tailor, 614 Sacramento
Math John, butcher with Louis Peres & Co. dwl Potrero Avenue
Mather John, dwl 113 Minna
Mather J. W. secretary Quicksilver M. Co. office 205 Battery, dwl 25 Laurel Place
MATHER *(Robert)* & SINCLAIR *(Archy)* hooks and stationery, Metropolitan Market and junction Market and Geary, dwl 248 Jessie
Matheson John, plasterer, dwl Bailey House
Matheson Mark J. steward, stmr Constitution, dwl E s Mission nr Twelfth
Mathet Anna Miss, with Grover & Baker Sewing Machine Co. dwl N s Merchant bet Montgomery and Sansom
Mathews Ann (widow) dwl 459 Bryant
Mathews Barney, hostler, dwl Bay View
Mathews Bernard O.S.F. teacher, St. Mary's School, St. Mary's Cathedral
Mathews Charles, painter, dwl 56 Tehama
Mathews Edward, laborer with C. L. Place & Co. dwl S s Jackson bet Hyde and Larkin
Mathews E. G. & Co. *(H. Allen Mayhew)* produce commission, NW cor Clay and Drumm, res Clinton, Alameda Co
Mathews *(E. J.)* & Fall *(W. H. H.)* stock brokers, office 723 Montgomery
Mathews Henry E. acct, 112 Cal, dwl 1207 Taylor
Mathews James, butcher, dwl 408 Natoma
Mathews James, purifier, S. F. Gas Co. dwl 36 Natoma
Mathews L. C. Mrs. dwl 27 Clementina
Mathews Mary Mrs. dress making and pattern depôt, 25 Geary, dwl 729 Bush
Mathews Patrick, dwl 540 Howard
Mathews Ralph, clerk, dwl 130 Second
Mathews Samuel A. book keeper, dwl NE cor Bernard and Jones
Mathews Thomas, boot maker, dwl 817 Battery
Mathews Thomas, mariner, dwl 214 Stewart
Mathews Thomas, waiter, stmr Orizaba
Mathews William, stone cutter, dwl 29 Natoma
MATHEWSON *(James)* & BUCKLIN *(E. P.)* importers and manufacturers jewelry, 519 Montgomery, dwl 647 Howard
Mathewson John, plasterer, dwl 22 Sansom
Mathewson M. J. (col'd) steward, Pacific Mail S. S. Co
Mathewson Nelson, machinist, Fulton Foundry, dwl 55 Beale
MATHEWSON THOMAS D. real estate agent and broker, office 606 Montgomery, dwl 865 Mission
Mathina Charles, wood and coal, 114 Washington, dwl 705 Vallejo
Mathieson John, boatman, dwl Hodges Place, N s Vallejo bet Montgomery and Sansom
Mathieu Alphonse, proprietor St. Francis Hotel, SW cor Dupont and Clay
Mathieu Gaston, jeweler, 724 Washington
Mathiot Antoine, boots and shoes, 1120 Dupont
Mathis J. V. P. assistant liquidating clerk, Custom House, dwl Russ House
Mathison Andrew C. hay, feed, etc. SE cor Leavenworth and Broadway, dwl 1715 Leavenworth
Mathison Pauline Madame, proprietress Mansion House, 615 Dupont
Matich M. liquors, Jackson St. Wharf
Matich Nicholas, coffee stand, cor Market and East, dwl 211 Clay
Matlack Levi B. book keeper with N. S. Arnold & Co. 306 Battery
Matlar Frank, waiter, dwl 107 Pacific
Matone Patrick, handcartman, Davis nr Wash
Matron Joseph, butcher, 1622 Stockton
Matson George, porter with C. Hubert & Co. dwl NE cor Green and Stockton

Mattas Philip, laborer with Louis Ancenhofer
Mattat George, clerk, 916 Dupont
Mattat Mathieu, cigars and tobacco, 916 Dupont
Matte Henry, shoe maker, dwl 1426 Dupont
Matté Madame, nurse, French Hospital
Mattern Hermann, boot maker, dwl S s Pacific bet Taylor and Jones
Matterson John, plasterer, dwl 22 Sansom
Matteson Charles E. blacksmith with Gallagher & Farren, 112 Bush, dwl 333 Fourth
Mattfeld William, express wagon, cor Davis and Jackson
Matthai John C. H. carriage and wagon maker, 607 Battery
Matthews Henry, real estate office, 338 Montgomery, dwl 317 Mason
Matthews John, longshoreman, dwl W s Sansom bet Greenwich and Filbert
Matthews Lizzie Miss, domestic, SE cor California and Sansom
Matthews Mary Miss, domestic, 403 Green
Matthews Peter, gardener, dwl Presidio Road near Scott
Matthias Isidor, book keeper, 428 Montgomery, dwl 417 Montgomery
Matthias Louis, groceries and liquors, SE cor Dupont and Union, dwl 420 Union
Matthieu C. A. book keeper with Koopmanschap & Co
Mattiesen Otto, seaman, bds 7 Washington
Matting Edward, stone cutter, bds Manhattan House
Mattingly Philip, miner, dwl 335 Jessie
Mattison Betsey (widow) dwl E s Salmon bet Mason and Taylor
Mattole Petroleum Company, office 620 Washington
Mattovich Marco, fruits, 746 Washington
Mattovich Simeon, fruits, 624 Kearny
Mattson Olof, proprietor Scandinavian House, 39 and 41 Jackson
Matzen Henry, boatman, Fort Point
Matzen James, clerk, 44 Washington Market, dwl 18 Sansom
Matzenbach Wm. B. Enterprise House, 18 First
Mau A. merchant, dwl 608 Market
Maubec Charles, book keeper with A. E. Sabatie & Co. 617 and 619 Sansom
Maubec Henry *(A. E. Sabatie & Co.)* res Paris, France
Mauber H. driver, Omnibus R. R. Co
Maubert Joseph, works S. F. Chemical Works Co. NW cor Valencia and Fifteenth
Mangé A. Madame, furnished rooms, NE cor Kearny and Jackson
Mangé Alexander, dwl NE cor Kearny and Jackson
Maule Anton, laborer with V. Wackenreuder, San Bruno Road
Mauletti *(Anthony)* & Cardenasso *(Joseph)* coffee stand, SE cor Merchant and Sansom
Maume Joanna (widow) groceries and liquors, 150 First
Maurer John, brewer, Mason's Brewery, N s Chestnut bet Powell and Mason
MAURER LEO, proprietor Whitehall Exchange, NW cor Spring and Summer
Maurice Frank, cook, 520 Merchant
Maurin John, musician, dwl 636 Pacific
MAURY P. jr. importer French brandies and commission merchant, 710 Sansom, dwl Union Club Rooms
Mavagliano Luigi, fisherman, 6 Italian Fish Market
Maw Thomas M. drayman cor Clay and Front
Mawrey W. A. molder, Miners' Foundry, dwl 61 Tehama
Mawson Edwin R. ship joiner, dwl nr cor Shasta and Illinois
Maxey James R. miner, bds Franklin Hotel SE cor Sansom and Pacific
Maxfield E. F. pattern maker with James Brokaw, dwl 87 Natoma

Maxfield O. Lawrence, engineer, S. F. & San José
R. R. Co. dwl SE cor Valencia and Sixteenth
Maximilian Perpoli, dyer, dwl 1132 Dupont
Maxson W. B. attorney at law, office 604 Merchant
Maxwell Albert, carpenter, dwl SE cor Howard
and Sixteenth
Maxwell Creek G. M. Co. office SE cor Montgom-
ery and Jackson
Maxwell George, laundryman, City and County
Hospital
Maxwell John J. hostler, 739 Folsom
Maxwell John S. dwl E s Fillmore bet Fell and Hayes
Maxwell Patrick, blacksmith with Flintoff &
O'Neill, dwl 113 Geary
MAXWELL RICHARD T. physician and surgeon,
office 124 Sutter, dwl 21 Post
Maxwell Susan M. (widow) dwl 41 South Park
Maxwell Walter, carpenter, dwl 153 Silver
MAY (A. W.) & BYINGTON (H. W.) livery and
sale stable, 328 Bush
May George B. salesman with Goodwin & Co. dwl
1313 Taylor
May Harry W. clerk, Old Corner, 516 Mont
May Ida Miss, actress, Bella Union
May Jacob J. dwl 1521 Powell
May John, blacksmith with Albert Folsom, dwl
Webb nr California
May John, boot maker, 507 Jackson
May John, laborer, dwl N s Eddy bet Franklin and
Van Ness Avenue
May John A. pilot dwl 915 Union
May John H. Our Opera Saloon, 615 Washington,
dwl 112 Sutter
May Maria Mrs. nurse, dwl SW cor Dupont and
Broadway
May Noel, blacksmith apprentice, Vulcan Iron W
May Peter, fish dealer, 23 Italian Fish Market
May Peter, job wagon, cor Drumm and Merchant
MAY PROSPER, wholesale and retail liquors, 725
Clay and 712 Commercial
May Solomon, proprietor Bay City Laundry, 1140
and 1142 Folsom
May William B. physician, dwl 1114 Clay
Maybal Hans, captain schooner Stina Nicolaison,
Caduc's Line foot Wash, dwl 1816 Powell
Maybell John, real estate, dwl 18 Turk, rear
Mayberry E. L. carpenter, dwl 120 Natoma
Mayberry J. W. carpenter, dwl 118 Natoma
MAYBLUM MORRIS, importer and jobber cigars
and tobacco, 230 Front, dwl 1515 Powell
Maybury S. carpenter, dwl What Cheer House
Mayer Charles H. dwl 1813 Stockton
Mayer Frederick K. foreman Spring Valley W. W.
dwl cor Market and Buchanan
MAYER I. C. & SONS (S. D. & James C.) la-
dies' furs, carriage robes, etc. 129 Montgomery,
dwl Brevoort House
Mayer Jacob, tailor, 226 First
Mayer James C. (I. C. Mayer & Sons) dwl Bre-
voort House
Mayer John L. blacksmith, 4033 Mission
Mayer Joseph (S. Mayer & Bros.) res Oakland
MAYER JOSEPH, organ builder, S s Page near
Octavia
Mayer Joseph, stoves and tin ware, 155 Second
Mayer Joseph, tailor, 613 California
Mayer Jules (Lyons & Co.) 510 Jackson, dwl SE
cor Chestnut and Powell
Mayer Leon, watch maker, 1020 Dupont
Mayer Louis, steward, dwl NW cor Kearny and
Jackson
Mayer Philip, carpenter, dwl 226 First
Mayer Richard, hay and grain, 120 Fourth
Mayer S. & Brothers (Joseph and Samuel) import-
ers and jobbers clothing, 307 Cal, res New York
Mayer Samuel (S. Mayer & Bros.) res Philadelphia
Mayer S. D. (I. C. Mayer & Sons) res New York
Mayer Simon, stock broker, 623 Montgomery, dwl
SW cor Dupont and Harlan Place

MAYERHOFER FRANCIS V. physician, office
and dwl NW cor Stevenson and Third
Mayerhofer John C. compositor, Spirit of the Times,
dwl NW cor Stevenson and Third
Mayerhoff Peter, machinist, dwl S s Olive Avenue
bet Polk and Van Ness Avenue
Mayers A. L. (M. & A. L. Mayers & Co.) dwl
828 Vallejo
Mayers Alfred, salesman, 242 Montgomery, dwl S s
Lombard bet Stockton and Powell
Mayers Brooks, carpenter, San Francisco Cordage
Factory
Mayers Emile, steward, dwl E side Varenne near
Union
Mayers Frederick A. dwl 823 Howard
Mayers Henry, clerk, dwl 736 Harrison
Mayers Henry, carrier, Evening Bulletin
Mayers M. and A. L. & Co. (M. L. Lyon) glaziers,
828 Vallejo
Mayers Phillip, contractor, dwl 823 Howard
MAYERS ROBERT, Mayers' Bazaar, 242 Mont-
gomery, dwl S s Lombard between Stockton and
Powell
Mayers, see Meyers and Myers
Mayes George (Spence, Tesmore & Co.) dwl 11
Bagley Place
Mayher Thomas C. machinist, dwl 24 Sansom
Mayhew H. Allen (E. G. Mathews & Co.) dwl
1207 Taylor
Mayhew Henry H. clerk, SW cor Valencia and
Sixteenth
Mayhew John H. captain ship Saracene, office Pier
9 Stewart
Mayhew Seth, bricklayer, dwl 49 Clementina
Mayhew William B. upholsterer with John A. Sha-
ber, dwl 14 Perry
Mayhew William B. cabinet maker, dwl 633 Market
MAYHEW WILLIAM E. druggist and apothe-
cary, NW cor Howard and Fourth
Maynard D. D. solicitor Fireman's Fund Insurance
Co. 238 Montgomery
Maynard Ernest, shoe maker, 18 Stewart
Maynard George H. clerk, 213 Clay, dwl NW cor
Montgomery and Pine
Maynard H. G. (Gold Hill) dwl Lick House
Maynard J. C. dwl Occidental Hotel
MAYNARD LAFAYETTE, real estate, office 205
Battery, dwl 326 Second
Maynard Laura Miss, actress, Bella Union
Mayne Charles, office with Belloc Freres, 535 Clay
Mayne Fanny (widow) dwl 15 St. Mary
Maynes Francis. porter, 405 Sansom, dwl SW cor
Clara and Ritch
Maynes Patrick, gas fitter, S. F. Gas Co
Mayo Charles, pilot (old line) 5 Vallejo, dwl 408
Vallejo
Mayo William, carrier, Alta, dwl 415 Pine
MAYOR CITY AND COUNTY, office 2 first floor
City Hall
Mayre George T. real estate, dwl Occidental Hotel
Mayrisch Adolph (Engelbrecht & Mayrisch Bros.)
dwl 738 Howard
MAYRISCH ERNST, Kunstler Hall Beer Saloon,
619 Kearny, dwl 821 Broadway
Mayrisch Gustave (Engelbrecht & Mayrisch Bros.)
dwl 925 Howard
Mayrisch Rudolph, dwl 738 Howard
MAZATLAN LINE PACKETS, N. Larco agent,
432 Jackson
MAZATLAN LINE STEAMERS, Ben Holladay
proprietor, office SW cor Front and Jackson
Maze Montgomery, second lieut. Co. A Second In-
fantry C. V. Presidio
Mazzini Lewis, (Samengo & M.) dwl E s Drumm
bet Clay and Washington
McAdams Archibald (Brodie, Hubbard & McA.)
dwl 511 Hyde
McAdams Edward, copper plate printer, dwl 2
Haywood

McAdams Patrick, bricklayer, dwl E s Clinton 8 Brannan

McAfee William foreman with Coffey & Risdon, dwl 144 Sixth

McAleavey Mary Miss, domestic, 915 Clay

McAleer Andrew, assistant storekeeper, U. S. Subsistence Department, 208 Sansom

McAleer Catherine Miss, domestic, NE cor Folsom and Eleventh

McAlester, William F. dwl 614 Third

McAllany Ellen Miss, domestic, 759 Market

McAllister Amelia Miss, domestic, 423 Second

McAllister Benjamin B. machinist, Union Foundry, dwl N s McAllister bet Buchanan and Webster

McAllister Cutler *(H. & C. McAllister)* attorney at law, office 540 Clay, dwl 421 First

McAllister Elizabeth, domestic, dwl 423 Second

McAllister F. Marion, rector Church of the Advent S s Howard bet Second and Third, dwl 421 First

McAllister George, machinist, Pacific Foundry, dwl 362 Jessie

McALLISTER H. & C. attorneys at law, office 540 Clay, dwl 926 Jackson

McAllister H. H. collector, 613 Market

McAllister John H. clerk with Ross, Dempster & Co. dwl 58 Natoma

McAllister M. Hall, ex-judge U. S. Circuit Court, dwl 423 First

McAllister Richard, dwl 511 Mission

McAllister Samuel, hatter with LeGay & Co. dwl 305 Montgomery

McAllister Thomas, furniture, dwl 768 Mission

McAllister William B. *(Bush & McA.)* dwl 606 Kearny

McAlpin Thomas, house and sign painter, 3 Broadway, dwl NW cor Jones and Lombard

McAlpine M. B. (widow) seminary, 108 Powell

McAnally John, laborer, dwl 48 Everett

McAnany John, laborer, dwl 57 Stevenson

McAndrew Thomas, molder, S. F. Iron Works, dwl 27 Ritch

McAndrews John, drayman, Broadway Wharf, dwl NW cor Green and Montgomery

McAneny George B. office 712 Mont, dwl 810 Wash

McAnhill John, hostler, 814 Mission, dwl Brannan bet Third and Fourth

McAntee Owen, blacksmith, 322 Third, dwl 855 Folsom

McAntee Owen, boot maker, 683 Market

McAntee Patrick, contractor, dwl W s Mission nr Thirteenth

McARAN *(Patrick)* & KELLY *(John P.)* importers and jobbers wines and liquors, 616 and 618 Front, dwl 13 O'Farrell bet Dupont and Stockton

McArdle Bernard, workman, Union Foundry, dwl N s Minna nr Eighth

McArdle James, laborer, dwl N s Pacific bet Front and Davis

McArdle Michael, boarding, 57 Stevenson

McArdle Patrick *(Carolin & McA.)* dwl 160 Minna

McArdle Thomas, longshoreman, dwl NW cor Sansom and Vallejo

McArron Charles *(Sprung & McA.)* dwl Valencia Mission Dolores

McArthur Archibald, merchant tailor, 431 Bush

McArthur J. dwl What Cheer House

McArthur Thomas, boot maker, 510 Jackson, dwl 24 Dupont

McArthur William E. assistant entry clerk, Naval office C. H. dwl Russ House

McArver Murdie, laborer, Mission Woolen Mills

McAtee Patrick, contractor, dwl Mission nr Ridley

McAteer George, clerk, Cunningham's Warehouse, dwl 58 Clementina

McAuley John, laborer, dwl S s Stevenson bet First and Second

McAuley Mary (widow) dwl 34 Langton

McAuley Timothy, carpenter, dwl 30 Louisa

McAuliffe Anne Mrs. domestic with A. Bujan, San Bruno Road nr first toll gate

McAuliffe Florence T. *(Boyd, McA. & Co.)* dwl 1061 Howard

McAuliffe Jeremiah, paper hanger with George W. Clark, dwl 21 Stanford

McAuliffe Owen, drayman with Molloy & O'Connor, 64 Clay

McAvary Bernard, boot maker, Washington Hose Co. No. 1

McAvoy Cornelius, lather, dwl 315 Bryant

McAvoy Daniel, lather, dwl 315 Bryant

McAvoy Dennis, plasterer, dwl 315 Bryant

McAvoy James, cartman, dwl Stevenson bet Sixth and Seventh

McAvoy James, lather, dwl 315 Bryant

McAvoy James, longshoreman, dwl NW cor Green and Battery

McAvoy John, dwl 315 Bryant

McAvoy John, pile driver, dwl N s Harrison bet Seventh and Eighth

McAvoy Joseph, laborer, dwl 1020 Folsom

McAvoy Joseph, plasterer, dwl Meeks Place

McAvoy Margaret (widow) dwl 315 Bryant

McAvoy Mary Miss, domestic, 9 Mason

McAvoy Peter, seaman, dwl 9 Everett

McAvoy Thomas, laborer, dwl 46 Stevenson

McAvoy William, carpenter, dwl 1315 Stockton

McBean John, clerk, dwl 10 Noble Place

McBoden Allen, advertising agent, dwl 315 Mont

McBowen Samuel, miner, dwl 1818 Stockton

McBoy Ellen Miss, domestic, 153½ Second

McBoyle Alexander, drug clerk, cor Clay and Sansom, dwl 111 Ellis

McBoyle M. C. clerk with Richards & Whitfield, dwl 101 O'Farrell

McBrearty James, carriage maker, dwl Albion House

McBreirty Patrick, tanner with C. O'Donnell, dwl 316 Ritch

McBride Anne Miss, domestic, 332 Seventh

McBride Dennis, dwl W s Fifth Avenue bet Bryant and Harrison

McBride Edward, waterman, 609 Market

McBride Eliza, domestic, 275 Clara

McBride Henry E. submaster Washington Grammar School, dwl 1110 Mason

McBride Jane Miss, domestic, E s Mason bet Vallejo and Green

McBride John, engineer, Pacific Foundry

McBride Patrick, waterman, 609 Market, dwl 315 Montgomery

McBride Willim, dwl 434 Bush

McBurnie Willim, dwl NE cor Mission and Ecker

McCaaver John, laborer, dwl W s Folsom bet Fourteenth and Fifteenth

McCabe Andrew J. broker, dwl 121 Montgomery

McCabe Bernard, laborer, dwl 331 Bush

McCabe Bernard, groceries and liquors, SE cor Jessie and Anthony

McCabe Charles, clerk, 34 Fourth, dwl Jessie bet First and Second

McCabe Delia (widow) dwl 1011 Pine

McCabe Hugh, dwl Liberty Hose House

McCabe James, attorney at law, office 625 Merch

McCabe James, saloon, steamer Chrysopolis

McCabe James, laborer, dwl 311 Sutter

McCabe James F. boiler maker, Union Foundry, dwl SE cor Market and Sixth

McCabe John, laborer, dwl W s Clara nr Sutter

McCabe John, molder, Union Foundry, dwl 38 Everett

McCabe John H. stage manager Bella Union Melodeon and theatrical agent, office 620 Wash

McCabe Jonas, porter, 510 Kearny

McCabe J. T. clerk with I. N. Choynski, dwl S s Harrison bet Seventh and Eighth

McCabe Margaret, domestic, dwl 34 Essex

McCabe Mary Mrs. dress maker, dwl 522 Pine

McCabe Mary (widow) dwl S s Harrison bet Seventh and Eighth
McCabe Mary Catharine Mrs.'dress maker, dwl S s Market bet Sixth and Seventh
McCabe Patrick, fruits, 34 Fourth, dwl S s Market bet Sixth and Seventh
McCabe Patrick, porter, 306 Cal, dwl 333 Bush
McCabe Richard, lithographer with Britton & Co. 533 Commercial
McCachren Benjamin *(Bryant & Co.)* dwl NE cor Sixth and Mission
McCafferty Daniel, bar keeper, SW cor Fourth and Minna
McCafferty Frank, steward, American Exchange
McCaffrey Dennis, engineer, dwl 210 First
McCaffrey Ellen Miss, domestic, 1519 Mason
McCaffrey Frank, foreman S. F. P. Woolen Mills, dwl N s Bay bet Leavenworth and Hyde
McCaffrey Hugh, blacksmith, dwl W s Varenne nr Union
McCaffrey James, dwl 331 Bush
McCaffrey John, laborer, dwl 30 Natoma Place
McCaffrey Margaret (widow) private boarding, 14 Sutter
McCaffrey Thomas, laborer, dwl 7 Noble Place
McCaffrey T. M. conductor, dwl NW cor Jessie and Anna
McCain J. S. merchant, dwl Lick House
McCall Mary (widow) dwl W s Morey Alley
McCall William, bricklayer, dwl 432 Greenwich
McCallum Hugh, carpenter, dwl S. F. Cordage Factory
McCallum William, harness maker with John S. Wilson, 310 Davis, dwl Pacific Temperance House
McCann Andrew, cooper, S. F. & P. Sugar Co. dwl S s Harrison nr Eighth
McCann Bernard, laborer with N. Davidson, Glen Ranch nr S. F. Cordage Factory
McCann Charles, bar keeper, dwl Crescent Engine House
McCann Frederick, fireman, dwl SW cor Third and Mission
McCann Frederick, machinist, dwl W s Mary Lane nr Bush
McCann Garrett, laborer, dwl 237 Sutter
McCann James, boarding, N s Washington bet Davis and Drumm
McCann John, with D. R. Provost & Co. dwl SE cor Pine and Dupont
McCann John, laborer, dwl SE cor Brannan and Third
McCann Joseph, marble polisher, dwl 909 Folsom
McCann Margaret, domestic, 526 Bryant
McCann Mary Miss, domestic, 510 Pine
McCann Michael, wool sorter, dwl W s Treat Avenue nr Twenty-Second
McCann Nicholas, plumber, dwl 35 Webb
McCann Owen, stevedore, dwl S s Filbert nr Sansom
McCann Patrick, engineer, dwl SW cor Third and Mission
McCann Peter *(Johnson & McC.)* dwl S s Brannan bet Sixth and Seventh
McCann Robert, mason, dwl 618 Ellis
McCann Thomas, plumber, dwl 641 Market
McCann William, gas works, dwl 541 Mission
McCann, see MacCann
McCanna Alié Miss, dwl with Bernard McDonald, S s Minna nr Eighth
McCanna Bridget Miss, dwl with Bernard McDonald, S s Minna nr Eighth
McCanna Catherine (widow) dwl 28 Tehama
McCanney Francis, bar keeper, 1522 Stockton, dwl E s Sonoma Place nr Green
McCardle Patrick, boot maker, 618 Pacific
McCardle William J. contractor, dwl S s Ewer Pl nr Mason
McCardy James, laborer, S. F. & San José R. R. Co
McCardy John, laborer, S. F. & San José R. R. Co

McCarfrey Timothy, mechanic, bds Atlantic House 210 Pacific
McCargle Thomas, stevedore, dwl E s Sansom bet Green and Vallejo
McCurran James, laborer, dwl 110 Freelon, rear
McCarrick Isma Miss, with S. Rosenblatt, dwl 615 Bush
McCarrick John, laborer, Lone Mountain Cemetery, dwl E s Devisidero bet Sutter and Post
McCarrick Kate Miss, dwl 615 Bush
McCarrom William, laborer, S. F. Gas Co
McCarthy Arthur, tailor, dwl 15 Berry
McCarthy B. conductor, Omnibus R. R. Co
McCarthy Bartholomew, laborer, dwl W s Mary Lane nr Bush
McCarthy Bridget Miss, domestic, 1801 Stockton
McCarthy Charles, ironer, Davis Laundry, W s Harriet bet Howard and Folsom
McCarthy Charles, waiter, U. S. Restaurant, dwl Niantic Hotel
McCarthy Cornelius, job wagon, cor Geary and Market, dwl Rousch nr Folsom
McCarthy Cornelius, tinsmith, with Taylor & Iredale
McCarthy Daniel, carder, Mission Woolen Mills, dwl with P. L. Murphy, E s Howard bet Fifteenth and Sixteenth
McCarthy Daniel, express wagon, 705 Front
McCarthy Daniel, fruits, dwl E s O'Farrell Alley nr O'Farrell
McCarthy Daniel, groom, dwl 267 Stevenson
McCarthy Daniel, laborer, dwl 206 Sutter
McCARTHY DANIEL, proptr Manhattan House, 705 and 707 Front
McCarthy Daniel, watchman, S. F. P. Woolen Mills, dwl North Point bet Polk and Van Ness Avenue
McCARTHY DANIEL O. editor and proprietor American Flag, office 528 Mont, dwl 1429 Taylor
McCarthy David C. real estate, office 610 Merchant, dwl 426 Bush
McCarthy E. carpenter and builder, dwl 733 Vallejo
McCarthy Ellen (widow) dwl 441 Bush, rear
McCarthy Eugene, broker, dwl 20 Post
McCarthy Eugene, drayman, 204 Battery
McCarthy Florence, clerk, dwl NW cor Sixteenth and First Avenue
McCarthy Florence, entrance and clearance clerk, Custom House, dwl 905 Pacific
McCarthy Florence, laborer, dwl Dolores Hall W s Valencia nr Sixteenth
McCarthy J. grainer, 205 Kearny
McCarthy James, blacksmith, 815 Market, dwl Sansom House
McCarthy James, laborer, North Beach & M. R. R. Co
McCarthy Jeremiah, laborer, dwl 417 Sutter
McCarthy Jeremiah, laborer, dwl 227 Post
McCarthy Johanna Miss, domestic, 933 Sacramento
McCarthy John, fruit stand, 539 Sacramento, dwl 228 O'Farrell
McCarthy John, laborer, North Beach & M. R. R. Co
McCarthy John, laborer, dwl 223 Sutter
McCarthy John, laborer, dwl 23 Geary
McCarthy John, laborer, dwl 428 Geary
McCarthy John D. liquor saloon, 1009 Dupont
McCarthy Joseph, porter, dwl Bay State House
McCarthy Kate Miss, domestic with Peter Anthes, E s Mission nr Twelfth
McCarthy Kate Miss, domestic, 820 Pine
McCarthy Kate Miss, domestic, 321 Taylor
McCarthy Kate Miss, domestic, NW cor Stockton and Pacific
McCarthy Kate Miss, domestic, 892 Sutter
McCarthy Margaret Miss, domestic, 327 Geary
McCarthy Mary Miss, domestic, 835 Mission
McCarthy Mary Miss, domestic, 337 Jessie
McCarthy Mary Miss, domestic, 506 Greenwich
McCarthy Mary Miss, domestic, 619 Leavenworth

McCarthy Mary (widow) dwl 414 Tehama
McCarthy Michael, plasterer, dwl W s Hyde bet Union and Filbert
McCarthy Michael, trackman, Market St. R. R. Co
McCarthy Miles, boot maker, dwl 6 Brown Alley
McCarthy Mortimer, shoe maker, with David Hauser, dwl 1219 Sacramento
McCarthy Owen, boarding, Union Court nr Kearny
McCarthy Patrick, boot maker, 227 Jackson
McCarthy Patrick, job wagon, SW cor Market and Third
McCarthy Patrick, laborer, dwl N s Tyler bet Taylor and Jones
McCarthy Patrick, laborer, dwl 206 Sutter
McCarthy Patrick, workman, S. F. & P. Sugar Co. dwl S s Harrison bet Eighth and Ninth
McCarthy Patrick H. butcher with Joseph Lawler, dwl Potrero Avenue
McCarthy Redmond, laborer, dwl 343 Jessie
McCarthy Silas, laborer, dwl 11 Bay State Row
McCarthy Thomas, apprentice with Morris Greenberg
McCarthy Thomas, workman with John M. Mitchell
McCarthy Timothy, dwl 223 Sutter
McCarthy Timothy, job wagon, 503 Clay, dwl cor Folsom and Rousch
McCarthy Timothy, laborer, North Beach & M. R. R. Co
McCarthy Timothy, wines and liquors, 612 Washington, dwl 905 Pacific nr Powell
McCartney James, clerk, 616 Sacramento
McCartney M. broker, dwl Occidental Hotel
McCartney Samuel, laborer, Masonic Cemetery
McCary Andrew J. lamps and coal oil, 850 Washington, dwl 1024 Stockton
McCary B. conductor, Omnibus R. R. Co. dwl 721 Howard
McCarty Bartholomew, laborer, dwl W s Buchanan bet O'Farrell and Geary
McCarty Bartholomew, laborer, dwl E s Main bet Folsom and Harrison
McCarty Bridget (widow) dwl S s Filbert bet Mason and Taylor
McCarty C. laborer, Spring Valley W. W
McCarty Catherine Mrs. dwl 16 Natoma
McCarty Charles, laborer, dw 27 Baldwin Court
McCarty Charles, laborer, dwl Filbert nr Mont
McCarty Charles, waiter, Magnolia Restaurant
McCarty Cornelius, expressman, dwl W s Rousch nr Folsom
McCarty Cornelius, laborer, dwl W s Garden bet Harrison and Bryant
McCarty Daniel, furniture, 223 Sutter, dwl 225 Sutter
McCarty Daniel, laborer, dwl 267 Stevenson
McCarty Daniel, laborer, dwl 210 Harrison
McCarty Daniel, teacher dancing, dwl 52 Clementina
McCarty Daniel J. baker, dwl 238 Jessie
McCarty Dennis (*Fuller & McC.*) dwl Tehama bet First and Second
McCarty Dennis, bell hanger, dwl cor Minna and Third
McCarty Dennis, tailor with J. R. Mead & Co. dwl 319 Vallejo
McCarty Edmund D. liquor saloon, 608 Howard, dwl 40 Natoma
McCarty Edward, seaman, dwl 18 Baldwin Court
McCarty Ellen (widow) dwl 52 Clementina
McCarty James (*McDermott, Graham & McC.*) dwl Benton House
McCarty James, laborer, dwl 20 Jessie
McCarty James, teamster, dwl 52 Clementina
McCarty Jeremiah, laborer, dwl 227 Post
McCarty Jeremiah, painter, dwl 75 Jessie
McCarty Jeremiah, porter, dwl N s Folsom bet Gough and Octavia
McCarty Jeremiah P. milkman, cor Santa Clara and Connecticut
McCarty Jerrard, teamster with James McDevitt, dwl W s Sansom bet Broadway and Vallejo

McCarty Johanna (widow) milkman, nr cor Napa and Shasta
McCarty John, baker with R. R. Swain, dwl 8 Haywood
McCarty John, bricklayer, dwl 414 Market
McCarty John, cook, Ocean House
McCarty John, lab, dwl SW cor Beale and Folsom
McCarty John, laborer, Fort Point
McCarty John, laborer, Spring Valley W. W
McCarty John, laborer, dwl 6 Hunt
McCarty John, laborer, 255 Beale
McCarty John, laborer, dwl 28 Ritch, rear
McCarty John, laborer, dwl Higgins Place
McCarty John, laborer, dwl SW cor Folsom and Beale
McCarty John, laborer, dwl NW cor Folsom and Twelfth
McCarty John, laborer, dwl N s Stevenson bet Sixth and Seventh
McCarty John, mason, dwl 414 Market
McCarty John, porter, St. Nicholas Hotel
McCarty John, wheelwright, dwl 113 Minna
McCarty John D. saloon, dwl St. Francis H. & L. Co. No. 1
McCarty Kate Miss, domestic, 563 Tehama
McCarty Kate Miss, laundress, dwl 133 Stevenson
McCarty L. P. commission merchant and business manager American Flag, office 604 Montgomery, dwl 40 Minna
McCarty Martin, blacksmith with Kimball & Co. dwl 21 Sherwood Place
McCarty Mary Miss, domestic with Dennis J. O'Callaghan
McCarty Mary Miss, domestic, 1902 Powell
McCarty Michael, butcher, dwl W s Van Ness Avenue bet Broadway and Vallejo
McCarty Michael, lab, dwl cor Vallejo and Kearny
McCarty Michael, laborer, Fort Point
McCarty Michael, tailor, 713 Folsom
McCarty Michael jr. butcher, dwl with Michael McCarty sen
McCarty Neil, hostler, Custom House Livery Stable, 318 Broadway
McCarty Patrick, laborer, Spring Valley W. W
McCarty Patrick, laborer, dwl 141 Jessie
McCarty Peter, laborer, dwl W s Bryant Avenue nr Eighth
McCarty Richard, seaman, dwl 47 Jackson
McCarty Timothy, book keeper, 641 Market, dwl Frank's Building
McCarty Timothy, laborer, dwl 44 Ecker
McCarty William, lab, dwl E s Folsom Av nr Folsom
McCarty William, mason, Spring Valley W. W. Camp Pilarcitas
McCarvell Patrick, laborer, dwl 31 Frederick
McCary Susan Miss, nurse, 869 Mission
McCaughey Kate Miss, domestic, 807 Stockton
McCauley Charles, wines and liquors, 425 Pacific
McCauley John, apprentice with John H. O'Brien & Co. dwl 7 Harlan Place
McCauley John F. fireman, dwl 166 Minna
McCauley Thomas, laborer, dwl 266 Jessie
McCauley Thomas, porter, Wells, Fargo & Co. dwl 510 Sacramento
McCaull Michael, wood and coal, 631 Green, rear
McCausland J. S. dwl Original House
McCauslin William (*Metzger & Co.*) dwl Ninth nr Brannan
McCeney J. attorney at law, dwl Tehama House
McClaffrey Bridget (widow) dwl 77 Jessie
McClaggin James, carpenter, dwl 315 Sutter
McClaggin John, carpenter, dwl 315 Sutter
McClary James, carpenter, dwl S s Bryant bet Seventh and Eighth
McClary John, hostler, dwl 12 Sutter
McCleaman Ann, ironer, Cole's Laundry, 114 Dora
McCleary Daniel (col'd) bootblack, 636 Washington
McCleary Robert, stevedore, dwl S s Folsom bet Beale and Main

McCleary W. W. dwl SE cor Sixth and Clara
McClellan C. B. artist, studio 240 Montgomery
McClellan D. D. broker, dwl 108 Virginia
McClellan Flora Miss, dwl 916 Harrison
McClellan Richard, mining stocks, dwl 1024 Stock
McCLELLAND J. A..& Co. (J. W. Thurman) produce commission, 11 Clay, dwl W s Hyde bet Filbert and Greenwich
McClellen Robert, carpenter, bds Enterprise House
McClennen Edward D. (Hyde & McC.) dwl 112 Mason
McClinton Michael, laborer, dwl with F. Gracier W s California Avenue nr Isabella
McClinton Samuel, laborer, Pier 7 Stewart
McClister Alexander, groom, dwl 29 Jessie
McCloskey James (J. P. Sweeney & Co.) dwl 127 Ellis
McCloskey Mathew, carpenter, dwl 644 Howard
McCloskey Michael, blacksmith, dwl 26 Ritch
McCloskey Owen, blacksmith, dwl 10 Jessie
McCloskey Patrick, water sprinkler, dwl cor Kearny and Green
McClosky William J. drayman, 408 Front, dwl 330 Tehama
McCloud Alexander, boiler helper, Pacific Foundry
McCloud Joseph, drayman, dwl 34 Vulparaiso
McCloud Joshua H. job wagon, 539 Clay, dwl W s Jones bet Jackson and Pacific
McClure Gaylord, clerk, dwl Original House
McClure James W. saddler with George Carmelick, 230 Sansom
McClure P. L. waterman, 609 Market
McCluskey Dennis, plasterer, dwl 336 Bush
McCluskey Henry, engineer stm Oakland, resides Brooklyn
McCluskey Owen, helper, Miners' Foundry
McCluskey Patrick, blacksmith, dwl 705 Front
McCoffey Edward, waiter, Occidental Hotel
McColgan Daniel, laborer, S. F. Gas Co
McColgan Edward, laborer with James McDevitt, dwl W s Sansom bet Broadway and Vallejo
McColgan Michael, saddlery and harness maker, 223 Washington, dwl 822 Vallejo
McColgan Susan Miss, domestic, 240 Jessie
McCOLL WILLIAM, produce commission, 62 Clay, dwl NW cor Minna and Sixth
McColla Catharine (widow) domestic, dwl 1107 Kearny
McColliam Thomas W. sail maker, dwl 220 Eddy
McColligan Daniel, laborer, dwl 132 First
McCollnell Ellen Miss, dress maker, dwl 18 Third
McCOMB EPHRAIM C. mining secretary, office 1 Government House NW corner Sansom and Washington, res Oakland
McComb James, clerk, 121 Front, dwl SW corner Howard and Fourteenth
McComb James, laborer, dwl NW cor Beach and Larkin
McComb John, assistant wharfinger Market Street Wharf, dwl 808 Greenwich
McComb John, foreman compositors Alta California, dwl 1423 Leavenworth
McComb John groceries and liquors, NE cor Sixth and Jessie
McCombs John, dwl SW cor Mission and Stewart
McConahey James, bricklayer, dwl 50 Louisa
McConaby Theodore, porter, 109 Montgomery
McConathy John, distiller, dwl NW cor Tenth and Bryant
McCondrin Patrick, fireman, stm Golden City, dwl W s Sansom bet Green and Vallejo
McConliffe Eugene, drayman, cor Clay and Drumm
McCoulock Edward, laborer, dwl S side Vallejo bet Montgomery and Sansom
McConlogue Charles, laborer, dwl S s McAllister bet Steiner and Pierce
McConnell Eliza Mrs. furnished rooms, 820 Dupont
McConnell James H. cutler, 613 Jackson, dwl 248 Minna

McConnell J. R. (Yale & McC.) attorney at law, office 520 Montgomery, dwl 728 Bush
McConnell John, flour packer, dwl 19 Sherwood Place
McConnell John, hostler, 13 Broadway, dwl 820 Dupont, rear
McConnell Margaret (widow) groceries and liquors, 81 Stevenson
McConnell William (Quinn & McC.) dwl SE cor Mission and Eleventh
McConnell William J. pattern maker, Pacific Foundry, dwl 72 Tehama
McConville James W. bar keeper, 716 Kearny, dwl 510 Sacramento
McConville Nathaniel, cokeman, S. F. Gas Co
McCoort Ellen Miss, domestic, 1116 Stockton
McCOPPIN FRANK, superintendent Market St. R. R. and supervisor Eleventh District, office Valencia nr Sixteenth, dwl SW corner Valencia and Seventeenth
McCord Edward S. with C. S. Navigation Co
McCord James, driver, North Beach & M. R. R. Co. dwl 333 Fourth
McCord Selby, ship carpenter, dwl 236 Ritch
McCord Thomas, carpenter, dwl 314 Third, rear
McCorkell Alexander, painter, 317 Third
McCormack Alexander, cooper with Handy & Neuman, dwl S s Frederick bet First and Second
McCormack Bridget Miss, domestic, 803 Leav
McCormack C. cartman, dwl Zoe bet Bryant and Brannan
McCormack Catherine Miss, cloak maker, 113 Silver
McCormack John, steamboatman, dwl N s Vallejo bet Montgomery and Sansom
McCormack John, oysters, NE cor Mont and Wash, dwl W s Fillmore bet Greenwich and Lombard
McCormack Mary (widow) dwl W s Mary Lane nr Berry
McCormack Mary E. (widow) 113 Silver
McCormack Neil, dwl 249 Clary
McCormack William, dwl 312 Sutter
McCormick Alice Miss, domestic, SE cor Stockton and Jackson
McCORMICK CHARLES, surgeon, U. S. A. medical director Department Pacific, office 408 Market, dwl Occidental Hotel
McCormick Felix, laborer, dwl SE cor Ninth and Minna
McCormick Francis, dwl S s Fell bet Octavia and Franklin
McCormick Francis, blacksmith with M. P. Holmes, dwl 537 Kearny
McCormick Francis, coachman with Wm. Brooks, dwl N s Bryant bet Seventh and Eighth
McCormick Francis, laborer, E s Fell bet Gough and Franklin
McCormick Hugh, amalgamator, dwl 441 Jessie
McCormick Hugh, laborer, S. F. P. Woolen Mills, dwl North Point bet Polk and Van Ness Av
McCormick James, clerk 335 East
McCormick James, laborer with William Kerr, dwl 903 Battery
McCormick James, machinist, Union Foundry, dwl S s Perry bet Fourth and Fifth
McCormick John, dwl Perry bet Fourth and Fifth
McCormick, John, machinist, Pacific Foundry, dwl National House
McCormick John, workman, S. F. & P. Sugar Co. dwl Sumner
McCormick John W. proprietor Golden State House, 135 Jackson
McCormick Mary Miss, domestic, SE cor Stockton and Jackson
McCormick Mary Miss, domestic, 20 Post
McCormick Michael, carpenter, bds 336 Bush
McCormick Patrick, laborer, dwl W s Laskie bet Eighth and Ninth
McCormick Patrick, policeman, City Hall, dwl 623 Union

McCormick *(Peter)* & Luhrs *(Albert)* Stag Saloon, 521 Merchant and teamsters, dwl 64 First
McCormick Robert, stone cutter, dwl Bush Street House, 333 Bush
McCormick William, stoves and tinware, 820 Market
McCormick William L salesman with Conroy & O'Connor, dwl 530 Pine
McCorray Barney, helper, Vulcan Iron Works, dwl Jessie nr First
McCorrister Hugh, blacksmith with Nutting & Upstone, dwl 120 Jessie
McCottrey Robert, engineer, stm Sacramento, dwl W s Montgomery bet Vallejo and Green
McConghtry Henry H. book keeper with Wm. B. Cooke & Co. dwl 716 Stockton
McCouliffe Eugene, drayman, Clay St. Wharf, dwl W s Sherwood bet Folsom and Harrison
McCourt James, tailor, dwl 502 Third
McCourt Patrick, laborer, dwl SE cor Leavenworth and Pacific
McCourtney E. J. calker, dwl 4 Lafayette Place
McCourtney J. F. artist with M. F. Bayley, resides Oakland
McCourtney John, sail maker, dwl 11 Minna
McCovey Margaret Miss, domestic with R. Feuerstein, S s Harrison bet Sixth and Seventh
McCowan Bridget (widow) dwl 319 Kearny
McCowen E. shoe maker, dwl 229 Pacific
McCoy Ann Miss, domestic, 30 McAllister
McCoy Ann Miss, domestic, 1423 Stockton
McCoy Daniel, teamster, Golden State Iron Works, dwl 16 Stanford
McCoy James, longshoreman, dwl NW cor Union and Sansom
McCoy Mary, chambermaid, St. Nicholas Hotel
McCoy Owen, laborer, dwl 745 Mission
McCoy *(William)* & Mason *(Edmund Y.)* house and sign painters, 611 Market, dwl 305 Pine
McCracken Arthur, stevedore, dwl 412 Vallejo
McCracken Henry, laborer, dwl W s Sansom near Filbert
McCracken Hugh, ship carpenter with John G. North, Potrero
McCracken Orrin C. street contractor, dwl 310 Jessie
McCracken William, laborer, dwl S s Vallejo bet Montgomery and Sansom
McCraith Dennis, groceries and liquors, NE cor Pacific and Front
McCraith John, policeman, City Hall, dwl NE cor Hyde and Broadway
McCraken John *(Richards & McC.)* res Portland, Oregon
McCready Mrs. seamstress, dwl 323 Pine
McCready Richard, boiler maker, dwl 274 Jessie
McCready Samuel, baker with Deeth & Starr, dwl 114 Bush
McCreary John M. foreman with Calhoun & Son, dwl Washington nr Stockton
McCreary W. H. driver, A. R. C. Ice Co. dwl S s Broadway bet Front and Davis
McCreery A. B. real estate, Edmund Scott agent, office 602 Commercial
McCrink Peter, blacksmith, Vulcan Iron Works, dwl 60 Tehama
McCrossen Bridget Miss, domestic, 740 Harrison
McCrossen William, waiter, dwl S s Stevenson bet Seventh and Eighth
McCrum Emily Mrs. millinery, 604 Kearny
McCrum Hugh, saloon keeper, 611 Kearny, dwl 604 Kearny
McCue James, steward, American Exchange
McCue Mary Miss, domestic, 728 Vallejo
McCue Patrick, blacksmith, S. F. & San José R. R. Co. dwl with P. L. Murphy E s Howard bet Fifteenth and Sixteenth
McCue, see McHugh
McCulley John, laborer, dwl 67 Stevenson
McCulley John L. laborer, dwl 309 Folsom
McCulloch John, analytical chemist, dwl 713 Filbert

McCulloch John, cooper with Lyon & Co. dwl 32½ Clara
McCullogh & Preston Petroleum Co. office NE cor Clay and Battery
McCullough Mary Miss, domestic, 25 Minna
McCullough Owen, teamster, dwl W s Battery bet Vallejo and Broadway, rear
McCullough Patrick, bar keeper, junction Market and O'Farrell
McCullough Rose Burns (widow) dwl S s Minna bet Eighth and Ninth
McCullough Samuel, contractor, dwl SE cor Garden and Harrison
McCullough Thomas, laborer, dwl 23 Geary
McCullough Thomas, liquor dealer, dwl 210 Fourth
McCullough William, seaman, stm Pacific
McCully John, saloon, SW cor Second and Minna, dwl 105 Minna
McCully William, harness maker, bds Pacific Temperance House 109 Pacific
McCulo Charles, miner, dwl S s Bernard bet Jones and Leavenworth
McCulpha Patrick, driver with G. H. Peck, dwl 820 Sansom
McCumber Joseph, pile driver with Galloway & Boobar
McCummus A. V. Mrs. dwl 537 Howard
McCUNE JAMES N. produce commission merchant, agent Star Line Packets, 117 Clay, dwl 1123 Stockton
McCune John B. *(Sahnke & McC.)* dwl SW cor Howard and Sumner
McCurdy James, foreman with John Henry, dwl E s Valencia bet Fifteenth and Sixteenth
McCurdy James, laborer, S. F. & San José R. R. Co
McCurrie Charles, clerk with M. Gray, 613 Clay, dwl 260 Stevenson
McCusker Catharine Miss, domestic, 1517 Mason
McCusker C. E. clerk with C. J. Hawley & Co. dwl 78 Natoma
McCusker Mary, domestic with Alpheus Bull
McCutten Daniel, laborer with William Kerr, dwl 903 Battery
McDade Edward, workman, S. F. & P. Sugar Co. dwl 1152 Folsom
McDade George, fruits, 335 Fourth
McDade James, workman, S. F. & P. Sugar Co. dwl 109 Dora, rear
McDade Julia Miss, domestic, 506 Greenwich
McDaniel James, clerk with Hughes & Hunter, dwl SE cor California and Dupont
McDaniel James, workman, Miners' Foundry, dwl 249 Clementina
McDermott A. capitalist, bds Brooklyn Hotel
McDermott A. express wagon, cor Stock and Pac
McDermott Alice (widow) dwl W s Thirteenth nr Mission
McDermott Barney, machinist, Pacific Foundry, dwl 78 Fifth
McDermott Bernard, express wagon, Davis Street Ferry
McDermott Bridget Miss, domestic, 692 Geary
McDermott Bridget Miss, domestic, 411 Ellis
McDermott Charles, dwl 1820 Stockton
McDermott Ellen Miss, domestic, 3 Natoma
McDermott Frank, printer with Frank Eastman, dwl S s California bet Mason and Taylor
McDermott Hugh, painter with Hopps & Kanary
McDermott J. bricklayer, dwl 220 Minna
McDermott, *(James)* Graham *(James)* & McCarty *(James)* glass cutters, 120 Fremont, dwl Benton House
McDermott James T. gilder with Jones, Wooll & Sutherland, dwl 12 O'Farrell Court
McDermott John, bricklayer, dwl 220 Minna
McDermott John, driver, North Beach & M. R. R. Co. dwl NE cor Folsom and Fourth
McDermott John, driver Omnibus R. R. Co. dwl 504 O'Farrell

McDermott John, hostler, dwl 444 Clementina
McDermott John, hostler, 16 Sutter, dwl 41 Clementina
McDermott John, ship carpenter, dwl 24 Minna
McDermott Martin, finisher, S. F. P. Woolen Mills, dwl North Point bet Polk and Van Ness Ave
McDermott Mary Miss, domestic, 829 Broadway
McDermott Mary Miss, domestic, 1212 Mason
McDermott Michael, steward, dwl 1117 Stockton
McDermott Michael, tailor, 73 Stevenson
McDermott Patrick, cartman, dwl N s Filbert near Sansom
McDermott Patrick, laborer, dwl 525 Mission
McDermott Patrick, laborer, dwl SW cor Battery and Green
McDermott Patrick, laborer, bds Western Hotel
McDermott Patrick, spinner, Mission Woolen Mills, dwl S s Fourteenth nr Folsom
DeDermott Robert, laborer, dwl 57 Stevenson
McDermott Thomas, dwl SW cor Harrison and Ritter
McDermott Thomas, laborer, Spring Valley W. W
McDermott Thomas, laborer, dwl 19 Everett
McDermott Thomas, pipe fitter S. F. & P. Sugar Co. dwl 1038 Folsom
McDermott Thomas, spinner, S. F. P. Woolen Mills, dwl North Point bet Polk and Van Ness Av
McDermott William, boatman, Folsom St. Wharf, dwl Spear nr Folsom
McDermott William, steward, dwl 149 Second
McDermott Winifred Miss, domestic, 617 Green
McDevitt Ann Miss, laundress, St. Mary's College
McDevitt Anthony, fireman, dwl cor Vallejo and Sansom
McDevitt Edward, dealer sacks, 216 Davis, dwl 153 Minna
McDevitt Eliza Miss, domestic, 626 Ellis
McDevitt Harry, clerk, dwl W s Battery nr Green
McDevitt James, bakery, 108 First
McDevitt James, contractor, dwl W s Sansom bet Broadway and Vallejo
McDevitt Jane Miss, domestic, 469 Minna
McDevitt John, hackman, dwl 1208 Broadway
McDevitt John, proprietor Washington Livery and Sale Stable, 712 Broadway
McDevitt Michael, teamster with James McDevitt, dwl 105 Freelon
McDevitt Patrick, laborer, dwl SW cor Battery and Green
McDevitt Peter, hostler with Porter & Covey
McDevitt Susan Miss, laundress, St. Mary's College
McDevitt William, with Atkins Massey, 651 Sac
McDonald A. D. (J. W. Brittan & Co.) dwl 750 Howard
McDonald A. G. laborer, dwl NW cor Union and Montgomery
McDonald Albert R. stair builder, dwl 1714 Mason
McDonald Alexander, boiler maker with Coffey & Risdon, dwl 258 Clementina, rear
McDonald Archibald, carpenter, dwl 553 Mission
McDonald Archibald, foreman carding room Pioneer Woolen Mills, dwl 1920 Taylor
McDonald Archibald R. physician, dwl 518 Green
McDonald Bernard, boiler maker with Coffey & Risdon, dwl S s Minna nr Eighth
McDonald Bridget, cook, U. S. Hotel, 706 Battery
McDonald Bridget Miss, domestic, 1114 Clay
McDonald Catherine (widow) dwl 118 Geary
McDonald Catherine M. Miss, dwl SW cor Sixteenth and Howard
McDonald C. B. editor American Flag, 517 Clay, dwl Railroad House
McDonald Charles, waiter, What Cheer House
McDonald (Charles C.) & Co. (George P. Rowane) oyster saloon, SE cor Clay and Leidesdorff, dwl N s Vallejo bet Hyde and Leavenworth
McDonald Charles E. S. dwl 928 Folsom
McDonald David (Dunn & McD.) dwl 124 Jessie

McDonald David, book keeper, dwl 518 Folsom
McDonald Donald, carpenter, dwl S s Austin bet Van Ness Avenue and Franklin
McDonald Duncan F. dwl 113 Leidesdorff
McDonald Edward, bottle dealer, dwl E s Jansen bet Greenwich and Lombard
McDonald Edward, clerk, dwl 749 Market
McDonald Edward, poultryman, dwl 13 Berry
McDonald Edward, workman with R. Card, dwl Milton Place
McDONALD EVA A. Mrs. proprietress Union Block, 652 Market cor Kearny
McDonald George, assistant warehouse entry liquidating clerk, Custom House, dwl 4 Garden
McDonald George, clerk, Pier 5 Stewart, dwl Minna nr Third
McDonald George W. foreman with Thomas Day, 732 Montgomery, dwl 1026 Montgomery
McDonald G. W. B. (B. H. Freeman & Co.) dwl 907 Vallejo
McDonald Hannah M. Miss, domestic, SW cor Sixteenth and Howard
McDonald Hugh, horse shoer with Levi Wells, 19 Sutter, dwl Portsmouth House
McDonald J. A. clerk, dwl 148 Minna
McDonald James, handcartman, cor Sac and Drumm
McDonald James, hostler, 431 California, dwl 145 Shipley
McDonald James, laborer with Edward J. Quirk
McDonald James, laborer, Miners' Foundry, dwl 249 Clementina
McDonald James, laborer, dwl 3 Brooks
McDonald James, painter, dwl 57 Jessie
McDonald James, ship carpenter with John G. North, dwl cor Sierra and Michigan
McDonald James, waiter, dwl 523 Bush
McDonald James, workman with R. Card, dwl Milton Place
McDonald John, with Brown & Avery, dwl 515 Bush
McDonald John, blacksmith, dwl cor Clay and Brenham Place
McDonald John, carpenter, dwl 319 Bush
McDonald John, cook, What Cheer House Restaurant
McDonald John, foreman with Wm. Horr, dwl N s Mission bet Tenth and Eleventh
McDonald John, laborer, Spring Valley W. W
McDonald John, laborer, dwl 20 Howard Court
McDonald John, laborer, dwl 529 Mission
McDonald John, painter, dwl 1213 Bush
McDonald John, seaman, steamer Pacific
McDonald John, seaman, steamer Senator
McDonald John, ship carpenter with John G. North, dwl nr cor Michigan and Napa
McDonald John, shoe maker, dwl N s Bernard bet Jones and Leavenworth
McDonald John C. laborer, dwl E s Seventh bet Brannan and Townsend
McDonald John D. shoe maker, dwl NE cor California and Sansom
McDonald John F. clerk, 41 Washington Market, dwl SE cor Bush and Dupont
McDonald John J. foreman, Jackson Foundry
McDonald Joseph, laborer, dwl 308 Folsom
McDonald Margaret Miss, ironer, Chelsea Laundry
McDONALD MARK L. stock and money broker, 621 Montgomery, dwl Cosmopolitan Hotel
McDonald Martin, butcher, Russ House
McDonald Mary Miss, domestic, 112 Perry
McDonald Mary (widow) dwl cor Pacific and Buchanan
McDonald Michael, carpenter, dwl 38 St. Mark Pl
McDonald Michael, clerk, Manhattan House, 705 Front
McDonald Michael, gardener with Michael Cannavan
McDonald Michael, laborer, dwl S s Serpentine Avenue nr Old San José Road

McDonald N. cartman, dwl 120 Post
McDonald Nicholas, contractor, dwl s Clay bet Larkin and Polk
McDonald Patrick, clerk, U. S. Engineers, 37 Montgomery Block, dwl Fort Point
McDonald Patrick, hostler, dwl 15 Stevenson
McDonald Patrick, tinsmith, dwl 65 Stevenson
McDONALD R. H. & CO. *(J. C. Spencer)* importers and jobbers drugs, chemicals, and dental goods. SE cor Pine and Sansom, res Sacramento City
McDonald Richard, dwl 18 Hunt
McDonald Robert, porter with B. Dolbeguy, dwl 425 Powell
McDonald Ronald, miller, National Flour Mills, dwl 6 Margaret Place
McDonald T. G. book keeper with Drake & Emerson, dwl S s Clementina bet Fourth and Fifth
McDonald Thomas, driver with John Agnew, 26 Kearny
McDonald Thomas, seaman, dwl 54 Sacramento
McDonald Thomas A. clerk, 19 Third, dwl 13 Berry
McDonald Timothy, laborer, dwl E s McCormick nr Pacific
McDonald William, driver, North Beach & M. R. R. Co
McDonald William, laborer, dwl 314 Beale
McDonald William, laborer, dwl Lincoln Avenue
McDonald William, porter, dwl W s Jansen bet Lombard and Greenwich
McDonald Winnifred J. Miss, laundress, Bay City Laundry, 1142 Folsom
McDonald, see MacDonald
McDonnald Bessie Miss, domestic, 1020 Wash
McDonnald Patrick, clerk with Edmund Scott, dwl NE cor Montgomery and Jackson
McDonnell Annie Miss, finisher with Addis & Koch, dwl 333 Bush
McDonnell James, handcartman, NE corner Sac and Sansom, dwl E s Jones bet Turk and Eddy
McDonnell James jr. with Jones, Dixon & Co. dwl 210 Jones
McDonnell John, dwl 210 Jones
McDonnell John C. merchant, dwl 260 Stevenson
McDonnell Maria Miss, domestic, 621 Bush
McDonnell Mary Mrs. domestic, 617 Mason
McDonnell William, boatman, dwl 12 Clay
McDonnell William, laborer, dwl 1220 Pacific
McDonnell William, porter with William H. Richards & Co. dwl W s Janseu nr Lombard
McDonogh James, fruits, Pacific Fruit Market, dwl 335 O'Farrell
McDonogh John, laborer, dwl W s Jansen bet Greenwich and Lombard
McDonough James, waiter, dwl 519 Bush
McDonough Julia Miss, domestic, 113 Powell
McDonough Patrick, laborer, dwl N s Presidio Road nr Fillmore
McDonough Patrick, workman, S. F. & P. Sugar Co. dwl 132 Dora
McDonough Richard, laborer, dwl 161 Silver
McDonough Robert G. B. porter, 216 California, dwl 3 Central Place
McDougall Annie M. Miss, dwl 272 Minna
McDougall *(Barnett)* & Marquis *(John)* architects, office 328 Montgomery, dwl 320 Ellis
McDougall Daniel, blacksmith with Henry Steele, dwl North Point
McDougall Duncan, carpenter, dwl SE cor Folsom and Beale
McDougall James, real estate agent, office 604 Merch
McDougall James A., U. S. senator, office with Sharp & Lloyd, Court Block 636 Clay
McDougall John, house painter, dwl S s Stevenson bet Sixth and Seventh
McDougall John, carpenter, dwl 553 Mission
McDougall Mathew, laborer, California Foundry
McDougall William C. miner, dwl King bet Third and Fourth

McDougall, see MacDougall
McDowell Anna Miss, domestic, W s Hyde bet Bush and Sutter
McDowell George (col'd) bootblacking, 327 Sansom, dwl E s Stockton bet Vallejo and Green
McDowell Henry, gas fitter, 641 Market, dwl Minna bet Second and Third
McDOWELL IRVIN, maj. gen. U. S. A. commanding Department California, office and headquarters 742 Washington, res Oakland
McDowell Lilian A. Miss, domestic with Rev. Jas. P. Ludlow
McDowell Samuel, upholsterer, dwl 5 Dixon's Blk, Jane nr Natoma
McDowell William, painter with John Cooney, dwl 410 Pacific
McEachran Benj. F. picture frame maker, dwl NE cor Sixth and Mission
McEleny Ann Miss, boarding, 277 Minna
McEleny Mary Miss, dwl 277 Minna
McElbany Mary Miss, domestic with R. Feuerstein, S s Harrison bet Sixth and Seventh
McElheran W. C. blacksmith, dwl 671 Mission
McElheran W. D. machinist, dwl 671 Mission
McElbinney John, gardener, dwl NW cor Vallejo and Larkin
McElhinney John J. clerk with H. & C. McAllister, dwl NW cor Larkin and Vallejo
McElhinney Michael A. clerk with T. Rodgers Johnson, dwl NW cor Larkin and Vallejo
McElhinney Patrick H. clerk with Kashland Bros. dwl NW cor Larkin and Vallejo
McElrath John, drayman, 305 Front, dwl 1328 Jackson
McElroy James *(Cahill & McE.)* dwl S s Mission nr Eleventh
McElroy James, street sprinkler, cor Green and Kearny
McElroy John, cartman, 3 Perry
McElroy John, laborer, dwl 11 Natoma
McElroy John, printer, dwl cor Clay and Brenham Place
McElroy John, waiter, U. S. Restaurant, dwl cor McAllister and Larkin
McElroy Oscar, dwl 39 Second
McElroy Robert, agent Christian Advocate, 711 Mission, dwl 917 Howard
McElroy William C. miller, dwl cor Gough and Presidio Road
McElroy William R. shoe maker, dwl 339 Bush
McElvanna Patrick, engineer, dwl N s Mission bet Beale and Main
McElwain James, broker, 626 Mont, dwl 834 Clay
McELWEE *(John V.)* & ACKERMAN *(Joseph)* carpets and upholstery, etc. 236 Montgomery, dwl 33 O'Farrell
McElwin Agnes (widow) dwl 546 Folsom
McEntee Ann Miss, domestic with L. B. Benchley
McEntee John F. machinist, Vulcan Iron Works, dwl 855 Folsom
McEntee Joseph A. bar keeper, 225 Kearny, dwl SW cor Prospect Place and Sacramento
McEntire Margaret, domestic, dwl 520 Harrison
McEntire Patrick, assistant weigher and measurer, office Custom House
McEntyre John, miner, dwl 173 Jessie
McErdle O. waiter, Cosmopolitan Hotel
McErlain Patrick, wood and coal, 159 Shipley
McEvoy James, longshoreman, dwl N s Union bet Montgomery and Calhoun
McEvoy Joseph, laborer with Wilson & Stevens, dwl N s Folsom bet Sixth and Seventh
McEvoy Michael, express wagon, cor Dupont and Jackson
McEwen Benjamin *(C. L. Place & Co.)* dwl 414 Beale
McEwen J. A. (widow) dwl 729 Broadway
McEwen James, California Soda Works, 194 Stevenson, dwl 190 Stevenson

McFadden B. C. laborer, dwl SW cor Eddy and Polk
McFadden Benjamin, dwl 19 Natoma
McFadden Edward, laborer, dwl 20 William
McFadden Fannie (widow) dwl 16 Sherwood Place
McFadden Grace, domestic, 611 Folsom
McFadden John, contractor, dwl 28 Everett
McFadden John, laborer, 207 Sansom
McFadden M. (widow) W s Gaven nr Greenwich
McFadden Mary (widow) dwl NW cor Guerrero and Eighteenth
McFadden Patrick, laborer, dwl 1819 Powell
McFadden Patrick C. lumberman, dwl S s Eddy nr Polk
McFadden Peter, with C. S. Nav. Co. Broadway Wharf
McFadden Peter, watchman, dwl 18 Third
McFadden Sophie Miss, domestic, 1115 Stockton
McFadden Thomas, teamster, 58 Stewart, dwl 761 Mission
McFall John, laborer, dwl 915 Pacific
McFallen Michael, blacksmith helper, Vulcan Iron Works, dwl Stevenson bet Seventh and Eighth
McFannin James, deck hand, steamer Chrysopolis
McFarland Andrew, cigars and tobacco, 635 Pac
McFarland Benjamin, cartman, dwl Dup nr Filbert
McFarland Bernard L. painter, 624 Front, dwl W s Dupont bet Union and Filbert
McFarland Charles B. clerk, 606 Clay, dwl 1519 Dupont
McFarland D. C. dwl What Cheer House
McFarland Fanny (widow) dwl S s Ewer Place
McFarland F. J. furniture dealer, dwl 12 Hubbard Court
McFarland Francis, helper, Union Foundry, dwl 525 Mission
McFarland George K. carpenter, dwl 4 St. Mary
McFarland Gilbert, merchant, dwl 817 Mission
McFarland John, laborer, dwl 525 Mission
McFarland Kate S. Mrs. finisher with Wm. Shew, dwl 627 Union
McFarland Owen, hackman, Plaza, dwl 1119 Folsom
McFarland Owen Mrs. dress and cloak maker, 1119 Folsom
McFarland Thomas, boiler maker, dwl 541 Mission
McFarland Thomas, laborer, dwl 706 California
McFarland Thomas H. engineer, Market St. R. R. Co. bds with Theodore Schulte W s Valencia bet Fifteenth and Sixteenth
McFarland William, lamplighter, S. F. Gas Co
McFarlane John (Howard, McF. & Co.) dwl N s Green bet Dupont and Stockton
McFarlin James (McKenna Bro. & Co.) dwl Railroad House
McFaul John, laborer, dwl W s John nr Powell
McFee Benjamin (colored) Union Restaurant, 742 Pacific
McFee John, carpenter, dwl 154 First
McFehish John, compositor, Daily Examiner, dwl 729 Bush
McFetridge John, steward, American Exchange
McFoley Mary Miss, domestic, 839 Mission
McGahan John, laborer, dwl 13 Ohio
McGall Thomas, dealer, dwl 657 Mission
McGann Henry, machinist, Union Foundry, dwl N s Stevenson nr Ecker
McGann Maggie Miss, dwl 10 O'Farrell
McGann Malachi, clerk, dwl 807 Jackson
McGann Patrick & Co. hat and cap manufacturers, 654 Washington, dwl 127 Tehama
McGann Thomas, confectioner, 442 Brannan
McGarr Patrick, drayman, cor Clay and Battery
McGarry M. Miss, dress maker, dwl 568 Howard
McGarry Robert, stevedore, dwl W s Sansom bet Green and Union
McGarry William, express wagon, dwl 433 Stevenson
McGarrity Bridget Miss, laundress, dwl 834 Vallejo

McGarvey Margaret, domestic, 746 Mission
McGarvey Mary Miss, domestic, 717 Post
McGARVEY WILLIAM & CO. bacon, hams, and lard, cor Third and Minna and 433 Stevenson
McGarvin Jane (widow) dwl 32 Tehama
McGarvin Mary Miss, domestic, 527 Folsom
McGattigan Edward, express wagon, Battery near California
McGavin Michael, longshoreman, dwl NW cor Davis and Broadway
McGeary Henry, tailor, 126 Bush
McGeary John, carpenter, dwl S s Mission near Seventh
McGeary John, teamster, Pier 5 Stewart, dwl Geary bet Hyde and Larkin
McGeary Margaret Miss, domestic, 1409 Powell
McGeary Michael, drayman, dwl S s Mission near Seventh
McGee Bridget Mrs. domestic, dwl 5 Auburn
McGee Charles, first engineer steamer Senator
McGee Eliza (widow) dwl W s Priest bet Clay and Washington
McGee James, machinist, dwl 156 Tehama
McGee James J. blacksmith with Casebolt & Co. dwl W s Priest bet Clay and Washington
McGee John, blacksmith, dwl W s Priest bet Clay and Washington
McGee Mary Miss, compositor, Christian Advocate, dwl 211 Minna
McGEE PATRICK, groceries and liquors, 1014 Jackson
McGee Peter, workman with P. Heath nr corner Courtlandt and North avenues
McGee Thomas, painter, dwl 320 Dupont
McGee, see Magee
McGeeny Thomas, teamster, dwl S s Jackson bet Hyde and Larkin
McGennis James, employé with J. R. Sims, dwl 414 Market
McGeoghegan John T. receiving teller with Donohoe, Kelly & Co. dwl N s Seventeenth bet Guerrero and Dolores
McGeoghegan Thomas, dwl N s Seventeenth bet Guerrero and Dolores
McGibbon Archibald, drayman, 401 Front, dwl 116 Tehama
McGiffin James, cabinet maker with J. Peirce, 417 California
McGiffin James, laborer, dwl 451 Jessie
McGiffin Joseph, solicitor, What Cheer House
McGILL JOSEPH & CO. (Samuel Williams) doors, sash, and blind manufacturers, SW cor Market and Beale, dwl 526 Eighth
McGill John, plasterer, dwl S s Market bet First and Second
McGill William H. molder with J. McGill & Co. dwl W s Nevada nr Folsom
McGilley Patrick, dwl S s Sutter bet Jones and Leavenworth
McGillicoddy Jeremiah, laborer, dwl 267 Stevenson
McGillicoddy Owen, express wagon, Second nr Market, dwl 818 Folsom
McGillin Francis, hackman, Plaza, dwl 24 Moss
McGillivray Duncan, clerk with Murphy, Grant & Co. 401 Sansom
McGinley Mary M. Miss, domestic, 59 Tehama
McGinley Timothy, laborer, dwl W s Battery bet Vallejo and Green
McGinn Anna Miss, photographic gallery, 2 O'Farrell cor Market
McGinn Ellen Miss, domestic, 1013 Clay
McGinn Henry, St. Ignatius College, dwl 126 Dora
McGinn (James B.) & Mullins (Jeremiah H.) undertakers, 733 Mkt, dwl NE cor Pac and Hyde
McGinn P. hostler, North Beach & M. R. R. Co
McGinn Patrick J. carpenter, dwl 781 Folsom
McGinnerty John, brass finisher with Raneri F. Rocchiccoli, dwl 131 Shipley
McGinness Patrick, express wagon, 19 Virginia

McGinnis Christopher, pattern maker, Donohoe's Foundry, dwl 32 Louisa
McGinnis Edward, molder, Union Foundry,
McGinnis James, cabinet maker, dwl 414 Market
McGinnis J. M. express wagon, cor Fourth and Howard
McGinnis John, boiler maker with Coffey & Risdon
McGinnis John F. gilder, dwl 619 Geary, rear
McGinnis Mary Mrs. dwl 54 First
McGinnis Patrick, dwl 32 Louisa
McGinnis Patrick, boot maker, 723 Mission
McGinnis Patrick, waterman, dwl SW cor Fifteenth and First Avenue
McGinnis Robert, liquor saloon, SW cor Beale and Howard
McGinnis T. F. hostler, bds 336 Bush
McGirr Bernard, bar keeper, Half-way House Ocean House Road
McGittigan Edward, carman, dwl 116 Beale
McGiveney Edward, laborer, dwl 249 Tehama
McGivern Patrick, carriage maker, 29 and 31 Webb, dwl E s Dolores bet Sixteenth and Seventeenth
McGivner Mary Miss, domestic, 35 Essex
McGladen Mary Miss, assistant matron, S. F. Ladies' Protection and Relief Society
McGlanchy Bridget Miss, domestic, 126 Silver
McGlansey Francis, clerk, dwl 319 Kearny
McGlanflin *(Lewis)* & Moholy *(Jeremiah)* blacksmiths and wheelwrights, S s Brannan nr Seventh, dwl S s Brannan nr Seventh
McGlaudin L. W. clerk with C. V. Gillespie, dwl S s Brannan nr Seventh
McGlaughlin Michael, hackman, Plaza
McGlaughlin P. laundryman, Cosmopolitan Hotel
McGlaughlin Peter, laborer, dwl S s Vallejo bet Montgomery and Sansom
McGlauthlen A. M. (widow) inspectress, Custom House, dwl 112 Taylor
McGlew Thomas, machinist, dwl 143 Silver
McGlinchy Anthony, laborer with William Kerr, dwl 903 Battery
McGlinchy Frank, dwl 319 Kearny
McGlinchy John, teamster with John Center, NW cor Sixteenth and Folsom
McGlinchy Patrick, storekeeper, dwl 313 Davis
McGlinchy William, express wagon, dwl E s Mission bet Eighteenth and Nineteenth
McGloin James, butcher with R. O'Neill
McGlone Anna Mrs. domestic, 224 Stockton
McGlone James, laborer, dwl W s Scott bet Oak and Page
McGlone Margaret Miss, domestic, 1312 Taylor
McGloughlin Henry, hackman, Plaza
McGlynn Andrew E. submaster Lincoln School, dwl Jessie nr Fourth
McGlynn Daniel C. contractor, office and stables 246 Third, dwl 615 Stockton
McGlynn Edward, butcher, S E cor Harrison and Fifth Avenue, dwl 24 Jane
McGlynn Frank, merchant, dwl NW cor Ellis and Octavia
McGlynn Hugh, hostler, 414 Kearny
McGLYNN JOHN A. superintendent Central R. R. Co. office 116 Taylor, and proprietor Presidio, Seal Rock, and Lone Mountain Omnibuses, dwl 869 Mission
McGlynn Patrick, peddler, 609 Mission
McGlynn Patrick, teamster, dwl Dolores Hall W s Valencia nr Sixteenth
McGonagle Michael, laborer, dwl Continental House
McGonigal Isabella Miss, domestic, 213 Powell
McGonigal John, driver, 207 Sansom
McGonigal Michael, laborer, 207 Sansom
McGonigal Neal, driver, 207 Sansom, dwl cor Jessie and Ecker
McGonigal Rosa Miss, domestic, 703 Taylor
McGonigal Sarah Miss, domestic, 28 Ellis
McGonigle John, boatman, dwl 238 Stewart
McGonigle John, laborer, dwl cor Ecker and Jessie

McGonigle Patrick, laborer, dwl Pine above Sansom
McGoolin James, laborer, bds with Joseph Seale N s Turk nr Fillmore
McGorty William, expressman, dwl S s Shipley nr Harrison Avenue
McGory John, laborer, dwl N s Clay bet Van Ness Avenue and Franklin
McGory Michael, hostler, 126 Fourth, dwl First Avenue Mission Dolores
McGory Thomas, laborer, dwl 312 Vallejo
McGory Thomas, teamster with Smith & Adams, dwl 322 Vallejo
McGory Thomas A. with Martin Kedon, dwl 322 Vallejo
McGough James, stone cutter, dwl N s Broadway bet Sansom and Battery
McGough Susan Miss, domestic, 8 Powell
McGovern Bridget Miss, dwl 209 Tehama
McGovern Catherine, domestic with John Downes Wilson, E s cor Mission bet Fourteenth and Fifteenth
McGovern Ellen (widow) dwl S s El Dorado nr Potrero Avenue
McGovern Frank, miner, dwl 333 Bush
McGovern John, dwl 319 Bush
McGovern John, coachman, Oriental Hotel
McGovern John, garden, NW cor Lombard and Polk
McGovern Letitia Miss, domestic, 230 Green
McGovern Mary (widow) domestic, 527 Pine
McGovern Mathew, lather, dwl NW cor Jessie and Anna
McGovern Philip, hostler, dwl 706 Commercial
McGOVERN PHILIP liquor saloon, junction Market and Geary, dwl 317 O'Farrell
McGovern Philip, night watchman, S. F. & San José R. R. Co
McGovern Thomas, miner, dwl E s Church nr Cemetery Alley
McGowan Andrew, shoe maker with Charles Hortkorn, dwl 106 Kearny
McGowan Augustus, porter, Vallejo St. Bonded Warehouse, dwl 46 Clara
McGowan Bartley, drayman, Market St. Wharf, dwl N s Post bet Laguna and Buchanan
McGowan James, tinsmith with G. Moenning, dwl Tehama bet Fifth and Sixth
McGowan John, laborer, dwl 520 Geary
McGowan John S. workman, S. F. & P. Sugar Co. dwl 16 Rousch
McGowan Julia Miss, domestic, SE cor Fifth and Harrison
McGowan Lee, dwl 231 Stevenson
McGowan Lydia Miss, milliner, dwl 16 Rousch
McGowan Matilda Miss, cloak maker, dwl 913 Greenwich
McGowan Matthew, laborer, dwl 11 Bay State Row
McGowan Michael, bathman, Montgomery Baths, dwl 16 Sherwood Place
McGowan Michael, laborer, dwl S s Ewer Place
McGowan Michael, marble worker, 673 Market, dwl 319 Bush, rear
McGowan Patrick, vegetable peddler, dwl 320 Tehama
McGowan Peter, express wagon, cor Broadway and Davis, dwl SW cor Dupont and Bay
McGowan William, confectioner with Canty & Wagner
McGowan William, stone cutter, dwl 227 Stevenson
McGrade Thomas, merchant (Austin, Nevada) dwl N s Fifteenth nr Mission
McGran William, seaman, steamer Pacific
McGrath Ann Miss, domestic, 921 Jackson
McGrath Catharine (widow) dwl S s Oregon nr Davis
McGrath Daniel, laborer, dwl W s Crook bet Brannan and Townsend
McGrath Daniel, waiter, dwl 18 Natoma
McGrath George, stevedore, dwl NW cor Front and Broadway

McGrath Hannah Miss, domestic, 816 Filbert
McGrath James, cooper, S. F. & P. Sugar Co. dwl 32 Rousch
McGrath J. B. stock dealer, bds Brooklyn Hotel
McGrath John, boatman, dwl Commercial between Drumm and East
McGrath John, carpenter, dwl 54 Sacramento
McGrath John, driver, Omnibus R. R. Co. dwl 252 Clara
McGrath John, hostler, North Beach & M. R. R. Co
McGrath John, spinner, Mission Woolen Mills, dwl E s Howard bet Fourteenth and Fifteenth
McGrath John, vegetable peddler, dwl N s Lombard bet Montgomery and Kearny
McGrath Joseph E. carriage painter with Kimball & Co. dwl cor Franklin and Hayes
McGrath Martin, cooper, S. F. & P. Sugar Co. dwl W s Shotwell bet Twentieth and Twenty-First
McGrath Michael, laborer, bds Western Hotel
McGrath Patrick, laborer, dwl S s Stevenson bet Sixth and Seventh
McGrath Patrick, molder, dwl 38 Tehama
McGrath Peter, butcher with Z. Hebert, dwl Franklin Plaza
McGrath Thomas, hostler, Custom House Livery Stable, bds Franklin House
McGrath Thomas, porter with Goodwin & Co. dwl 23 Natoma
McGravy Bernard, shoe maker, dwl Washington Hose Co
McGravy John, boot maker, 217 Battery
McGraw Ann (widow) dwl Bertha W s Beale
McGraw Bernard, dwl 204 Montgomery
McGraw Patrick, dwl S s Stevenson nr Sixth
McGraw Roderick, carpenter with S. S. Culverwell, dwl N s Geary bet Devisidero and Broderick
McGraw William, baker, dwl 140 Second
McGrea H. milkman, dwl SW cor Guerrero and Figg
McGrea Sarah Miss, domestic with Richard O'Neill
McGreeney Thomas, job wagon, Pier 5 Stewart
McGreevy John, boiler maker with Coffey & Risdon, dwl 141 Shipley
McGreevy Richard, boiler maker, Volunteer Engine Co. No. 7
McGregor James, engineer, S. F. & P. Sugar Co. dwl 15 Rousch
McGregor James, painter, dwl S s Washington bet Stockton and Powell
McGREGOR JOSEPH, proprietor San Francisco Observatory and watch maker, 409 Sansom, dwl 215 Green
McGregor Mrs. (widow) dwl 12 Sherwood Place
McGregor Richard, dwl 527 California
McGregor William, laborer, dwl 35 Sacramento
McGreth Catherine M. T. (widow) dwl 29 Everett
McGrew William H. attorney at law, office W s Valencia nr Sixteenth, dwl NW cor Guerrero and Tracy
McGrew W. K. attorney at law and city editor Morning Call
McGrewrey John, waiter, dwl 47 Natoma
McGrury Sarah Miss, domestic, 78 Everett
McGuckin Sarah Miss, domestic, 319 First
McGugin P. C. salesman with Cornelius Desmond
McGuinnis Annie Miss, chambermaid, Russ House
McGuire Andrew, bds Franklin Hotel, SE cor Sansom and Pacific
McGuire Arthur, stair builder, dwl 16 Eddy
McGuire Arthur J. dwl E s Dolores bet Sixteenth and Seventeenth
McGuire Bridget Miss, domestic, 694 Geary
McGuire C. bellman, Occidental Hotel
McGuire Edward, shoe maker, dwl E s Beale bet Market and Mission
McGuire Eliza Mrs. fruits, 812 Market
McGuire Ellen, domestic, 708 Mission
McGuire Frank, apprentice with M. C. Brydges, tinsmith, dwl E s Dolores bet Sixteenth and Seventeenth

McGuire Honora Miss, domestic, 717 Bush
McGuire Hugh, laborer, dwl S s McAllister nr Franklin
McGuire James, driver Lick House Coach, dwl 117 O'Farrell
McGuire James, metal roofer with John Kehoe, dwl 2 Mason
McGuire James, seaman, dwl 238 Stewart
McGuire James, stone cutter, bds Franklin Hotel SE cor Sansom and Pacific
McGuire James J. apprentice, Union Foundry, dwl E s Dolores bet Sixteenth and Seventeenth
McGuire John, laborer, dwl 25 Dupont
McGuire John, laborer, dwl W s Clinton bet Brannan and Bryant
McGuire John, laborer, dwl 553 Mission
McGuire John P. drayman, cor Clay and Battery
McGuire Margaret Miss, domestic, 702 Lombard
McGuire Mary Mrs. furnished rooms, 522 Union
McGuire Patrick, laborer, dwl 212 Clara
McGuire Peter, fireman, stm Chrysopolis, dwl N s Howard bet Eighth and Ninth
McGuire Philip, laborer, dwl 41 Jane
McGuire Philip, steward, dwl 926 Clay
McGuire Roger, hostler with W. M. White, dwl 32 Webb
McGuire Thomas, plasterer with D. Mulrein, dwl 28 Battery
McGuire William, cartman, dwl Louisa nr Fourth
McGuire William (col'd) barber, dwl Broadway bet Dupont and Kearny
McGuire, see Maguire
McGuirk Hugh, carpenter, dwl 50 Natoma
McGUIRK (James) & PARRY (George) Market St. Sample Rooms, 518 Market, dwl 110 Natoma
McGuirk Lawrence, bar keeper, 313 Montgomery, dwl 62 Everett
McGuirk Michael, plasterer, dwl 728 Market
McGukian Francis, laborer with William Kerr, dwl 903 Battery
McGunnigle Dennis, teamster, dwl SE cor Jessie and Ecker
McGunnigle Hugh, laborer, San Francisco Gas Co. dwl 23 Anthony
McGunnigle John, hostler, North Beach & M. R. R. Co
McGunnigle Maggie Miss, laundress, Bay City Laundry, 1140 and 1142 Folsom
McGunnigle Michael, dwl 519 Mission
McGunny Thomas, vegetable peddler, dwl 817 Pac
McGurder Lawrence, waiter, steamer Yosemite
McGurren Arthur, bar keeper, 30 Montgomery, dwl 409 Post
McHaffie John (Dunn, McH. & Co.) dwl 940 Folsom
McHale Anthony, laborer, dwl 160 Shipley
McHale Peter, painter, dwl 73 Jessie
McHall Anna Miss, domestic, 127 Eddy
McHattan Franklin, painter with Patrick J. O'Brien, dwl King bet Third and Fourth
McHenry Adeline (widow) dwl 1711 Mason
McHenry Daniel, marble cutter, Volunteer Engine Co. No. 7
McHenry Edward G. watchman, U. S. Clothing Depôt, dwl 17 Fourth
McHenry John, attorney at law, dwl 212 Broadway
McHenry John, coachman with J. C. Horan
McHenry Mary (widow) dwl SE cor Taylor nad Valparaiso
McHenry Nathan, driver, Central R. R. Co. dwl SE cor Seventh and Brannan
McHenry R. M. reporter, Daily Examiner, dwl 218 Minna
McHenry (Samuel) & Smith (O.B.) produce commission, 11 Washington
McHugh Hugh V. teamster, dwl 820 Dupont
McHugh John (Brennan & Co.) dwl 817 Bush
McHugh John, shoe maker, dwl 7 Margaret Place
McHugh John, tailor, dwl 323 Clementina

McHugh John, teamster, dwl 60 Jessie
McHugh Patrick, conductor, North Beach & M. R. R. Co
McHugh Philip, polisher with Goodwin & Co. 510 Washington
McHugh Thomas, fireman, S. F. & San José R. R. Co. res San José
McHugh William, workman with Casebolt & Co
McHugh, see McCue
McIlwain J. & Co. (Alexander McIlwain) butter cheese, and eggs, 21 Metropolitan Market, dw 548 Folsom
McIlwain William, watch maker, dwl 524 Battery
McInerney Thomas, San Rafael Market, 311 Bdwy
McInrow Michael, laborer, dwl S s Pacific nr Davis
McIntee Owen, dwl 414 Market
McIntire Edward, laborer, dwl cor Larkin an Francisco
McIntire Patrick, laborer, dwl cor Larkin and Francisco
McIntosh Daniel, laborer, Custom House, dwl 529 Greenwich
McIntosh Daniel, seaman, dwl 26 Sacramento
McIntosh Donald, seaman, dwl 238 Stewart
McIntosh R. pattern maker apprentice, Vulcan Iron Works, dwl 128 Second
McIntosh Wells B. boiler maker, Vulcan Iron Works, dwl 510 Sacramento
McIntyre Bridget (widow) domestic, 1115 Stockton
McIntyre James, captain bark Massachusetts, office Pier 10 Stewart
McIntyre James, plasterer, dwl NE cor Howard and Twenty First
McIntyre John, carpenter, dwl E s Zoe bet Bryant and Brannan
McIntyre John, wagon maker, dwl S s Winter Alley nr Mason
McIntyre John B. conductor, Omnibus R. R. Co. dwl 721 Howard
McIntyre Mathew, cooper, 508 Front, dwl 1114 Pac
McIntyre Patrick, laborer, dwl S s Fella Place
McIntyre Robert, machinist, Pacific Foundry
McIntyre Robert, porter, Wells, Fargo & Co. dwl 233 Minna
McIntyre Rose Miss, domestic, 1520 Mason
McIntyre Sarah Miss, domestic, 927 Market
McIver John, helper, dwl 45 Ecker
McIver M. laborer, dwl 134 Natoma
McKalan J. C. tinsmith, dwl S s Pine bet Dupont and Kearny
McKann Bridget Miss, domestic, 631 Harrison
McKaon William, with Thomas Leonard
McKay Aleck, laborer, dwl 233 Stevenson
McKay Alexander, carpenter, bds 336 Bush
McKay Angus A. with Cutting & Co. dwl Benton House
McKay Charles M. clerk with Addison Martin & Co. dwl 1012 Montgomery
McKay David, wholesale grocer, 427 Davis, dwl 618 Howard
McKay Edward, boot maker with John Leddy, dwl 135 Natoma
McKay Elizabeth (widow) dwl NW cor Fifth and Mission
McKay Henry, calker, dwl 116 Perry
McKay James, carpenter with Stevens & Rider, dwl 268 Stevenson
McKay John, with Sinclair & Moody, 212 Clay
McKay Robert, bricklayer, dwl junction Market and Turk
McKay, see MacKay
McKean Alexander C. book keeper, Bank California, dwl S s Geary nr Gough
McKean Robert, bricklayer, dwl 15 Tehama Place
McKean, see McKeon and McKune
McKearnan James, wood sawyer, dwl 171 Jessie
McKearns Owen, workman, Pacific Glass Works, dwl S s Mariposa nr Mississippi
McKearny Ellen Miss, domestic, 227 Jessie

McKee Annie Miss, dress maker, dwl 1 Howard Court
McKee Charles, engineer, stm Contra Costa
McKee David R. clerk with Tallant & Co. 321 Bat
McKee James, express wagon, Clay nr Drumm
McKee James, laborer, dwl E s Seventh bet Brannan and Townsend
McKee John (Tallant & Co.) 321 Battery, dwl 5 Howard Court
McKee John, laborer with Cutting & Co. dwl 50 Beale
McKee John, produce commission, 48 Clay, dwl W s Polk bet Hayes and Grove
McKee Redick, mining, dwl 29 Tehama
McKee William R. real estate, office SW cor Mont and Clay, dwl cor Twenty-Second and Shotwell
McKeever John, pattern maker, bds St. Charles Hotel
McKenley Grace, dwl 172 Minna
McKenley Rose (widow) midwife, dwl 172 Minna
McKenna Alice Miss, domestic, 527 Post
McKenna Catherine Miss, domestic, 105 Mason
McKenna Felix, hackman, Plaza, dwl E s Jones bet Post and Geary
McKenna Francis, hairdresser, dwl 24 Post
McKenna Francis, nursery, N s Precita Avenue nr San Bruno Road
McKenna Henry, mate, stm John L. Stephens, dwl 312 Union
McKenna Hugh, boiler maker, Union Foundry, dwl 81 Jessie bet First and Second
McKenna James, hackman, Plaza, dwl E s Jones bet Post and Geary
McKenna James, tailor, cor Spring and Summer, dwl 23 Hunt
McKenna (John) & Tunsted (Thomas) tannery, W s Lagoon
McKenna John, porter, 422 Battery
McKENNA J. P. & CO. packers and curers hams, bacon, lard, etc. W s Garden bet Harrison and Bryant
McKenna Mary Miss, domestic with John McDonald, nr cor Michigan and Napa
McKENNA (M. F.) BROTHER (T. D. McKenna) & CO. (James McFarlin) hay and grain, NW cor Clay and Drumm, dwl NW cor First and Mission
McKenna Patrick, groom, dwl 415 Market
McKenna Philip, hackman, Plaza
McKenna Susan Miss, domestic, 14 O'Farrell
McKenna T. D. (McKenna Bro. & Co.) dwl Railroad House
McKenna Thomas, deck hand, stm Yosemite
McKenna Thomas F. sash maker with Smith, Ware & Co. dwl Stevenson bet First and Second
McKennan Hugh, dwl SW cor Jones and Jackson
McKennelly Bridget Miss, dwl 38 Everett
McKenney J. laborer, Vulcan Iron Works
McKenney Patrick, night watchman with L. Coburn, 1016 Stockton
McKenny William, plasterer, dwl W s Nevada nr Folsom
McKenty A. Jackson, broker, 605 Washington, dw NE cor Second and Mission
McKenzie Albert, dwl SE cor Clementina and Sixth
McKENZIE (Alexander) & FAIRMAN (Wm. B.) Plaza Exchange Saloon, 716 Kearny cor Merchant, dwl 1009 Washington
McKenzie Andrew, laborer, dwl 1717 Stockton
McKenzie David, laborer, dwl NE cor Folsom and Fremont
McKenzie David, molder, dwl 63 Clementina
McKenzie George R. book keeper with Tobin Bros. & Davisson, dwl 28 O'Farrell
McKenzie John, dwl Mariposa nr Kentucky
McKenzie John, clerk, cor Geary and William
McKenzie John, mariner, dwl 32 Stewart
McKenzie John, tailor with Frank Elwell, dwl 15 Clara

McKenzie John A. boiler maker, dwl 319 Minna
McKenzie John W. notary public, office 406 Montgomery, dwl 606 Filbert
McKenzie J. T. captain stm Clinton
McKenzie Maggie Miss, assistant, Fourth St. School, dwl 15 Clara
McKenzie W. D. dwl 731 Clay
McKenzie William, dwl 9 Howard Court
McKenzie William, laborer with Edward J. Quirk
McKenzie William, seaman, dwl 26 Sacramento
McKenzie William, shipwright, dwl 1021 Battery
McKeon Thomas, miner, bds Franklin Hotel, SE cor Sansom and Pacific
McKEONE LAWRENCE, proprietor Cambridge House, 304 Pacific
McKerren Catharine (widow) dwl W s Fifth near Howard
McKew James, waiter, American Exchange, dwl 35 Webb
McKew John, wood and coal, 431 Union, dwl 1316 Kearny
McKewen Ann (widow) dwl N s Bryant bet Fifth and Sixth
McKewen John, foreman Spring Valley W. W. dwl SE cor Montgomery and Green
McKewen Jonathan C. (Anderson & Co.) 209 Jackson
McKewen Peter & Son (Peter McKewen jr.) plumbing and gas fitting, 618 Clay, dwl SE cor Montgomery and Green
McKewen Peter jr. (McKewen & Son) dwl SE cor Montgomery and Green
McKewn Robert, gas fitter with P. McKewen & Son, dwl SE cor Montgomery and Green
McKewn Thomas, gas fitter with Peter McKewen & Son, dwl SE cor Montgomery and Green
McKibbe William, boiler maker, dwl 669 Harrison
McKibbin Thomas, housesmith, dwl S s Natoma nr First
McKIBBIN WILLIAM, Eureka Iron Railing Works, 41 and 43 First, dwl 1711 Mason
McKiernan John, butcher with William Gray, dwl 15 Sutter
McKinley David A. with Walter H. Delano, 326 Geary, dwl 554 Tehama
McKinley F. fireman, stm Clinton
McKinley Finley, cutler, dwl 522 Market
McKinley Henry, 3½ Mile House, San Bruno Road
McKinley James, dwl 521 Market
McKinley John, street sprinkler, dwl 54 First
McKinley John S. laborer, dwl 107 Leidesdorff
McKinney Daniel, salesman with John Taylor & Co. dwl 12 Ellis
McKinney George, shoe maker with George Spanagle, dwl 119 Fourth
McKinney Peter B. express wagon, cor Jones and O'Farrell
McKinney T. F. cabinet maker, dwl 414 Market
McKinney W. (Irwin & Co.) dwl W s Nevada bet Folsom and Harrison
McKinney William R. boiler maker, Eureka Hose Co. No. 4
McKinnon Daniel A. teamster, Pier 5 Stewart, dwl 803 Geary
McKinnon James J. clerk, Pier 5 Stewart, dwl 711 Hyde
McKinnon John, general agent, Bay View Park
McKinnon John J. (Preston & McK.) dwl S s Geary bet Hyde and Leavenworth
McKinstry (E. W.) & Van Voorhees (William) attorneys at law, office 434 Jackson, dwl 44 South Park
McKnapp Thomas, dwl 716 Dupont
McKnight Ellen (widow) dress making, dwl 1405 Stockton
McKnight Frederick, teller with B. Davidson & Berri, NW cor Montgomery and Commercial
McKoon Adelia (widow) dwl with William L. Perkins, E s Eleventh bet Market and Mission

McKown Joseph O. salesman, 211 Montgomery, dwl 436 Bush
McKune Bernard, book keeper with Donohoe, Kelly & Co. dwl 319 Kearny
McLagan John (Lowry & McL.) dwl 213 Minna
McLaine J. dwl 6 Harriet
McLane Andrew, Beach House, foot Fillmore
McLane Andrew N. builder, dwl SW cor Guerrero and Horner
McLane Catherine Mrs. Half-Way House, Presidio Road
McLane Christina, domestic, dwl 49 Minna
McLane Edward, merchant, dwl 8 Howard Court
McLane John, boiler maker, dwl 8 Natoma
McLane John, foreman Molder Department, Miners' Foundry
McLane John, laborer, dwl W s Stanford bet Townsend and Brannan
McLane Jos. waiter, steamer Yosemite
McLANE LOUIS, general agent Wells, Fargo & Co.'s Express and Banking House, office NW cor Montgomery and California, dwl 438 Bryant
McLane Patrick B. carpenter, dwl 8 Natoma
McLane Peter, housesmith, dwl 1217 Sacramento
McLane Robert, dwl 435 Bryant
McLane William, carpenter, dwl 636 Commercial
McLane, see McLean
McLaren Daniel, deputy superintendent streets, dwl 1310 California
McLaren Deborah A. (widow) dwl 462 Jessie
McLaren P. carriage maker, dwl Howard Engine House
McLarry John, contractor's foreman, dwl Dolores Hall W s Valencia nr Sixteenth
McLary Robert (col'd) barber. dwl 1118 Taylor
McLatchie Margaret, nurse, dwl 752 Harrison
McLaughlin Ann Miss, domestic, 715 Bush
McLaughlin Ann Miss, domestic, S s Lombard bet Stockton and Powell
McLaughlin Barney, laborer, dwl 258 Clementina
McLaughlin Bridget Miss, domestic, 777 Market
McLaughlin Catharine Miss, domestic, N s Lombard bet Taylor and Jones
McLaughlin Charles, dwl Lick House
McLaughlin Charles, boot fitter, dwl 510 Mission
McLaughlin Charles, contractor Western Pacific Railroad Co. office 409 Cal, bds Lick House
McLaughlin Daniel, laborer, dwl 132 Stevenson
McLaughlin Dennis, dwl 1600 Mason
McLaughlin David, baggage master, S. F. & San José R. R. Co. dwl 103 Freelon
McLaughlin Duncan, molder, dwl Mission St. House
McLaughlin Edward, workman with W. Hull, Old San José Road nr county line
McLaughlin Ellen Miss, domestic with John Downes Wilson, E s Mission bet Fourteenth and Fifteenth
McLaughlin Frank, laborer, dwl 234 Fourth
McLaughlin George, baker, dwl What Cheer House
McLaughlin George, Londonderry House, 12 Bdwy
McLaughlin Harry, hostler, dwl 814 Sansom
McLaughlin Henry, hack driver, dwl 838 Vallejo, rear
McLaughlin (Hiram) & Feisel (F. T.) blacksmiths and wagon makers, 121 Bush, dwl S s Bush bet Devisidero and Broderick
McLaughlin Hugh, laborer with John Henry, dwl N s Valencia bet Fifteenth and Sixteenth
McLaughlin Hugh, laborer, dwl 141 Shipley
McLaughlin Hugh, retortman, S. F. Gas Co
McLaughlin James, dwl N s Boyd nr Chesley
McLaughlin James, drayman, dwl E s Carlos Place
McLaughlin James, machinist, dwl 54 First
McLaughlin John, blacksmith, dwl E s Mary Lane nr Sutter
McLaughlin John, boiler maker with Coffey & Risdon
McLaughlin John, laborer, dwl 115 First
McLaughlin John, laborer, dwl Union Court
McLaughlin John, porter, dwl 423 Vallejo

McLaughlin John A. conductor, North Beach & M. R. R. Co. dwl N s Boyd nr Chesley
McLaughlin Lizzie Miss, ironer, Davis Laundry, W s Harriet bet Howard and Folsom
McLaughlin M. waiter, Russ House
McLaughlin Margaret Miss, domestic, 777 Market
McLaughlin Margaret Miss, domestic, 720 Bush
McLaughlin Margaret Miss, domestic, SW cor Gough and Sutter
McLaughlin Margaret (widow) dwl S s Alta bet Montgomery and Sansom
McLaughlin Mary Miss, domestic, 602 Sutter
McLaughlin Mary (widow) dwl 21 Frederick
McLaughlin Michael, dwl S s O'Farrell bet Larkin and Polk
McLaughlin Michael, hostler, 317 Pine, dwl S s Mission nr Second
McLaughlin Michael, hostler, dwl 732 Folsom
McLaughlin Michael, laborer, dwl SW cor Howard and Sumner
McLaughlin Michael, laborer, dwl W s Sansom bet Broadway and Vallejo
McLaughlin Michael, laborer with James McDevitt, dwl W s Battery bet Vallejo and Green
McLaughlin Michael, laborer, Vulcan Iron Works, dwl First bet Stevenson and Jessie
McLaughlin Michael, local policeman, dwl 613 Kearny
McLaughlin Michael, saloon, N s Presidio Road nr Fillmore
McLaughlin Michael, workman, S. F. & P. Sugar Co. dwl Sumner cor Howard
McLaughlin M. P. collector, 604 Merchant, dwl 707 Mission
McLaughlin Neill, laborer, dwl 437 Jessie
McLaughlin Patrick, boot maker, dwl 519 Mission
McLaughlin Patrick, cokeman, S. F. Gas Co
McLaughlin Patrick, job wagon, NW cor California and Sansom, dwl NE cor Harrison and Ritch
McLaughlin Patrick, laborer, dwl 10 Hunt
McLaughlin Patrick, laborer, dwl 231 Beale
McLaughlin Patrick, workman, S. F. & P. Sugar Co. dwl W s Downey between Bryant and Brannan
McLaughlin Patrick, workman, S. F. & P. Sugar Co. dwl Dora nr Harrison
McLaughlin Peter M. broker, dwl 701 Mission
McLaughlin Rosa Mrs. domestic, 1112 Bush
McLaughlin Sarah Miss, dwl 431 Clementina
McLaughlin Thomas, hostler, 431 California, dwl 9 St. Mary
McLaughlin Thomas, painter with Wilson & Moulton, dwl NW cor Calhoun and Union
McLaughlin William, laborer, S. F. Gas Co. dwl 26 Ritch, rear
McLaughlin William, melter, Vulcan Iron Works, dwl 23 Jessie
McLaughlin, see Laughlin
McLEA DONALD, wines and liquors, 534 California cor Webb, dwl 742 Mission
McLean Alexander, tailor with Duncan Chisholm, 414 Pine, dwl 119 Pine
McLean Anthony, tailor, dwl 308 Broadway
McLean Charles, waiter, Russ House
McLean Duncan, with H. Casebolt & Co. dwl 263 Clara
McLean Edward, surveyor, Fireman's Fund Insurance Co. res Oakland
McLean Edward R. apprentice with Dewey & Co. dwl 8 Howard Court
McLean J. A. Miss, adjuster, U. S. Branch Mint, dwl 8 Howard Court
McLean John, conductor, Central R. R. Co. dwl 260 Clary
McLean John, express wagon, 233 Fourth
McLean John T. office NW cor Montgomery and Washington room 26, dwl 1228 Washington
McLean William, blacksmith, Miners' Foundry, dwl 7 Howard Court

McLeary Daniel C. (col'd) bootblack with George Held & Bro. dwl N s Pac bet Mason and Taylor
McLellan R. Guy, attorney at law, office 305 Montgomery room 9
McLennan, (Donald) M. Whelan (John R.) & Grisar (Emil) Broadway Wool Depôt, NW corner Sansom and Broadway, dwl N s Folsom bet Eleventh and Twelfth
McLennan John, clerk, Chelsea Laundry, dwl Crook bet Third and Fourth
McLeod Andrew, boiler maker, Pacific Foundry
McLeod Daniel, book keeper with Jones, Dixon & Co. dwl NE cor Montgomery and Pacific
McLeod George (Larkins & Co.) dwl cor Spring and California
McLeod Hugh S. printer with Charles F. Robbins, dwl Western Hotel
McLeod James, drayman, cor Front and Clay
McLeod James, plasterer, dwl 17 Fourth
McLeod Robert, engineer, dwl 8 Bay State Row
McLeod Thomas M. porter, 521 Clay, dwl 1112 Kearny, rear
McLeod Walter, chip carpenter, dwl 446 Brannan
McLerie Henry J. carpenter, dwl 178 Stevenson
McLester Alexander, hostler, dwl S s Jessie bet First and Second
McLaughlan Timothy, pastry cook, SE cor Mission and First
McLure Andrew, pattern maker, California Foundry, dwl 36 Ritch
McLure John, foreman molder Miners' Foundry, dwl 363 First
McMahan Catherine T. domestic, dwl 426 Second
McMahan John, laborer, dwl SW cor Larkin and Geary
McMahan Margaret Miss, domestic with J. Poorman, S s Geary nr Van Ness Avenue
McMahon Ann Miss, domestic, 1117 Stockton
McMahon Ann widow) dwl 5 Bernard
McMahon Ann (widow) nurse, dwl with M. Murphy, W s Bartlett bet Twenty-Second and Twenty-Third
McMahon Archibald W. butcher with Wm. Wood
McMahon Bernard, butcher with Crummie & O'Neil, dwl NE cor Sixteenth and Humpshire
McMahon Bridget Miss, domestic, 610 Mason
McMahon Charles, blacksmith, dwl 510 Sacramento
McMahon David, machinist, Union Foundry
McMahon Felix, laborer with Macdonald Bros. dwl Stevenson nr Ecker
McMahon F. P. & Co. importers and jobbers oils, 404 Front, dwl SE cor Tehama and First
McMahon James, furniture wagon, cor Montgomery and California, dwl 733 Howard, rear
McMahon James, laborer, dwl 923 Broadway
McMahon James, laborer, dwl 811 Greenwich
McMahon John, with Agnew & Defiebach, dwl 811 Greenwich
McMahon John, with May & Byington, bds Philadelphia Hotel
McMahon John, clerk, 104 Third, dwl 39 Everett
McMahon John, harness maker with C. H. Mead, dwl SE cor Bush and Stockton
McMahon John O.S.F. principal St. Mary's School, St. Mary's Cathedral
McMahon Joseph T. porter, 205 Front, dwl Market nr Sixth
McMahon Kate Miss, dwl 53 Jessie
McMahon Mathew, laborer, dwl E s Sumner nr Howard
McMahon Michael, with D. R. Provost & Co. dwl NE cor Fifth and Minna
McMahon Michael, cartman, dwl Bernard above Taylor
McMahon Patrick, laborer, dwl E s Clinton nr Brannan
McMahon P. J. liquor saloon, Russ House
McMahon Richard F. upholsterer with Gullixon & Nelson, dwl 28 Ritch

McMahon Thomas, butcher with Joseph Lawler, dwl Potrero Avenue
McMahon Thomas, carpenter, dwl 143 Shipley
McMamara Hannah, domestic, 1224 Hyde
McManomy Catherine Mrs. domestic, Protestant Orphan Asylum
McMann Bernard, teamster, dwl 233 Beale
McMann Edward, cartman, Beale nr Folsom
McMann Felix, sawyer, dwl 26 Stevenson
McMann Hugh, cartman, dwl cor Beale and Folsom
McMann John, paper hanger with Frank G. Edwards, dwl 422 O'Farrell
McMann Margaret Mrs. dwl E s Scotland nr Filbert
McMann Mary (widow) 234 Fourth
McMann Michael, dwl 374 Minna
McMann William, drayman with Tay, Brooks & Backus, dwl 37 Ritch
McManma Thomas, saloon, NW cor Stevenson and Ecker
McManus Alice Miss, domestic, 721 Broadway
McManus Alice Miss, domestic, 911 Union
McManus Bernard, with Porter & Covey, dwl 8 s Natoma bet Eighth and Ninth
McManus C. laborer, S. F. Gas Co
McManus Frank, sawyer, dwl 911 Market
McManus James, plumber, 641 Market, dwl Natoma bet Second and Jane
McManus James, waiter, What Cheer House Restaurant
McMANUS JOHN, proprietor Atlantic House, 210 and 212 Pacific
McManus Kate Miss, dress maker, dwl 10 Wright's Building
McManus Mary Miss, domestic, 1018 Powell
McManus M. J. accountant with Louis Lacour, dwl 911 Market
McManus Patrick, builder, dwl 911 Market
McManus Patrick, clerk, NW cor Moss and Folsom
McManus Patrick, steward, Wright's Hotel, 210 Broadway
McManus Patrick, tinsmith with M. Prag, dwl Jessie bet Fifth and Sixth
McManus Patrick, waiter, Miners' Restaurant, dwl 16 Harlan Place
McManus T. D. gas fitter, dwl 148 Minna
McManus William, bar keeper, NW corner Kearny and Commercial, dwl 22 O'Farrell
McMeachan James (L. B. Benchley & Co.) dwl Russ House
McMennamy James, with Atkins Massey, dwl Webb nr Sacramento
McMenomy Daniel, laborer, dwl N s Grove bet Van Ness Avenue and Franklin
McMenomy James W. butcher, 343 Fourth, dwl 145 Fourth
McMenomy John H. butcher with Stephen C. Story, Occidental Market
McMenomy Michael, coachman, 962 Mission
McMenomy William, cartman, dwl N s Stevenson bet Sixth and Seventh
McMichael Theodore, stevedore, dwl 32 Market
McMichaels Charles, laborer, dwl 352 Brannan
McMillan Angus, boiler maker with Coffey & Risdon, dwl 751 Folsom
McMillan Angus, carpenter, dwl 711 Hyde
McMillan Angus, laborer, dwl 76 Jessie
McMillan Charles, dwl 269 Stevenson
McMillan Charles E. policeman, City Hall, dwl 1107 Kearny
McMillan Daniel (Williamson & McM.) dwl N s Townsend bet Third and Fourth
McMillan Daniel, contractor and builder, dwl E s Howard bet Fourteenth and Fifteenth
McMILLAN (Donald) & KESTER (Levi B.) manufacturers syrups and cordials, 714 Front, dwl 636 Second
McMillan Gustavus A. waterman, 609 Market, dwl 56 Shipley
McMillan Robert, physician, off and dwl 722 Wash

McMillan William, carpenter, dwl 13 Ritch
McMonagle John H. Rev. hospital chaplain Presidio, dwl 109 Powell
McMonigle Ann Miss, domestic, 516 Sutter
McMuhon James, dwl Russ House
McMullen Daniel, wood and coal, NE cor Silver and Third, dwl 143 Silver
McMullen Hugh, book keeper, Enterprise Soda Works, dwl 61 Stevenson
McMullen John, teamster with Wolf Bros. dwl 17 Stevenson
McMullen Susan Mrs. domestic with S. T. King, N s Hayes bet Franklin and Gough
McMullin Ernest C. metal roofer with John Kehoe, 228 Bush
McMullin George O. (Rountree & McM.) dwl 923 Sacramento
McMullin Jared C. printer, dwl 117 Second
McMullin John, laborer, dwl N s Camp bet Second Avenue and Guerrero
McMurchy Donald, miner, dwl 50 Natoma
McMurray Hugh J. with P. Riley & Co. dwl 4 Telegraph Place
McMurray John P. plasterer with Samuel Kellett, dwl cor Howard and First
McMurtry Ellen (widow) lodgings, 609½ Howard
McMurtry George, book keeper with Francis G. Burke, dwl 926 Clay
McNabb Bridget (widow) dwl 1364 Kearny
McNabb Edward, proptr Marysville Hotel, 414 Pac
McNaughton William, shoe maker with J. G. Hein, dwl 11 Geary
McNair James, receiving clerk, Bonded Warehouse North Point Dock, dwl 23 Stockton Place
McNair Michael, dwl What Cheer House
McNally Anna Miss, domestic, 123 Powell
McNally Anne (widow) washing, dwl W s White Place nr Bryant
McNally Francis, laborer, dwl E s Main bet Harrison and Bryant
McNally James, dwl 230 Clara
McNally John, boot maker, dwl 8 Ecker
McNally John, laborer, dwl 48 Everett
McNALLY (Lawrence) & HAWKINS (James) plumbers and gas fitters, 104 Montgomery and 28 Sutter, dwl 112 Sixth
McNally Richard, fireman, dwl 39 Clementina
McNally Thomas Y. book keeper with Kennedy & Bell
McNamara Julia Miss, domestic, 1029 Bush
McNamara Andrew, boot maker, dwl 12 Sutter
McNamara Daniel, machinist, Union Foundry, dwl 182 Stevenson
McNamara Dennis, dwl 331 Bush
McNamara Hugh, workman, S. F. Cordage Factory, dwl NW cor Sierra and Indiana
McNAMARA JAMES, proprietor Bush St. House, 331 and 333 Bush
McNamara James, laborer, dwl 158 Shipley
McNamara James, sealer weights and measures, office 321 Front, dwl 61 Minna
McNamara John, carpenter, dwl E s Valencia near Thirteenth
McNamara John, clerk, 535 Commercial, dwl 1022 Montgomery
McNamara John, cook, Pacific House, 35 Pacific
McNamara John, laborer, dwl S s Sixteenth near Valencia
McNamara Kate, domestic, dwl 749 Howard
McNamara Martin, laborer, U. S. Appraiser's Department, Custom House
McNamara Mary Miss, domestic, dwl 1213 Powell
McNamara Michael, laborer, dwl E s Garden bet Harrison and Bryant
McNamara Patrick, laborer, Market St. R. R. Co. dwl cor Valencia and Sixteenth
McNamara Patrick, laborer, dwl 182 Stevenson
McNamara Patrick, laborer, dwl 550 Tehama
McNamara Robert, dwl 1022 Montgomery

McNamara Walter, butcher with Philip Seibel, 35 Geary, dwl 761 Mission
McNamara William *(Browning & McN.)* dwl 1204 Powell
McNamara William, marble cutter with L. R. Myers & Co. dwl 816 Sacramento
McNamee Morris & Co. *(A. Knapp)* bottlers ale and cider, 129 Pacific, dwl SE cor Tyler and Buchanan
McNamee Michael, blacksmith with Henry Steele, dwl 17 Fourth
McNamee Patrick, laborer, dwl cor Third and Minna
McNanney Michael, blacksmith with Charles Steinweg, dwl 318 Pacific
McNaughten John, laborer with David B. Hughes, dwl S s Lombard bet Taylor and Jones
McNaughton Thomas, carpenter, dwl Howard Engine House
McNay William, waiter, Lick House
McNeil Augustus (colored) hairdresser, N s Folsom nr Sixth
McNEAR *(G. W.)* & BROTHER *(John A. McNear)* produce commission, 37 Clay, dwl cor Sherman and Folsom
McNear John A. *(McNear & Bro.)* res Petaluma
McNearny John, calker, dwl 255 Beale
McNeely Hugh, boatman, dwl 1613 Dupont, rear
McNeeve Anna Miss, domestic, 620 Sutter
McNeil Thomas, blacksmith, Manhattan Engine H
McNeil Catherine Miss, domestic, 663 Mission
McNeil Charles, deck hand, steamer Cornelia
McNeil Daniel, dwl NW cor Leavenworth and Bay
McNeil *(James)* & Burton *(Theodore)* gas fitters and plumbers, 817 Kearny, dwl 1626 Dupont
McNeil James, inspector, Custom House, dwl 628 Howard
McNeil John, molder, Union Foundry, dwl N s Mission bet First and Second
McNeil Laughlin, longshoreman, dwl NE corner Leavenworth and Francisco
McNeil Marian Mrs. dwl 513 Broadway
McNeil Thomas, stone cutter, dwl W s Sansom bet Filbert and Greenwich
McNeily P. dwl Russ House
McNelley John M. cook steamer Del Norte, dwl 6 Harrison Avenue
McNerny John, molder, dwl 8 Sherwood Place
McNerny Martin, with R. K. Rogers, milk ranch W Mission Dolores
McNevin Patrick W. tailor, dwl 3 Quincy Place
McNichol Elizabeth, domestic with Charles Bogan, 8 s Union bet Montgomery and Calhoun
McNichol Patrick, waiter, Russ House
McNickess Ann Miss, dwl 20 Langton
McNiel John, shoe maker with I. M. Wentworth & Co. dwl 64 Stevenson
McNiff Thomas, blacksmith with McGlauflin & Moholy, dwl 268 Stevenson
McNish Wickham C. *(Roberts, Morrison & Co.)* res Boston
McNulty Bertrand, copyist, County Clerk's Office, dwl 119 Mason
McNulty Bridget Miss, domestic, 822 Folsom
McNulty Charles A., U. S. Examiner, office Custom House, dwl 119 Mason
McNulty Ellen (widow) domestic, 724 California
McNulty Hugh, hostler, 16 Sutter, dwl 32 Webb
McNulty James, porter, Russ House
McNULTY J. M. physician, office 121 Montgomery, dwl 222 Post
McNulty John, stone cutter, dwl 24 Howard Court
McNulty Michael, calker, dwl 312 Beale
McNulty Thomas, laborer, S. F. Gas Co
McNulty Thomas, laborer with Edward J. Quirk
McNutt Jacob M. carpenter, dwl 123 Dora
McParland Michael, liquor saloon, 225 Kearny, dwl S s Greenwich nr Jones
McPeake James, farmer, Spring Valley W. W
McPeake Robert, butcher, dwl Union House

McPhee William, boiler maker, dwl 441 Sixth
McPherson Angus, civil engineer, dwl SE cor Vallejo and Taylor
McPherson David L. salesman with Wilson & Stevens, dwl 506 Market
McPherson Elizabeth (widow) dwl E s Sansom bet Vallejo and Green
McPherson Horatio, book keeper, bank Wells, Fargo & Co. dwl 510 Stockton
McPherson John, mate, dwl 13 Natoma
McPherson Robert, rigger, dwl 302 Union
McPherson Samuel G. *(Sellers & McP.)* dwl SW cor Union and Taylor
McPherson William, fruits, E s Davis bet Broadway and Pacific, dwl 1314 Powell
McPhillamy Charles, laborer, dwl 111 First
McPYKE HENRY W. proprietor Tontine Saloon, 631 Merchant
McQuade Catherine Miss, dwl 150 Minna
McQuade Catherine L. Miss, dress maker, dwl 816 Mission
McQuade Ellen Miss, domestic, 825 Washington
McQuade Francis N. laborer, dwl 1047 Howard bet Sixth and Seventh
McQuade Hannah, ironer, Chelsea Laundry
McQuade James, laborer with Edward J. Quirk
McQuade John, clerk, County Recorder, dwl NE cor Third and Stevenson
McQuade Margaret Miss, chambermaid, Tehama H
McQuade Michael M. liquor saloon, SW cor Fourth and Minna
McQuade Patrick, laborer, dwl 541 Mission
McQuade Peter, clerk with David McKay, 427 Davis
McQuade Peter, carder, Mission Woolen Mills, dwl SW cor Folsom and Fourteenth
McQueen Jane (widow) dwl 82 Everett
McQueen Robert, carpenter, 14 Broadway, dwl 434 Jessie
McQueeny James, marble worker with Hayes & Pritchard, dwl 147 Shipley
McQuillan Arthur, cook, dwl 34 St. Mark Place
McQUILLAN BERNARD, importer pictures and frames, 209 and 211 Leidesdorff manufactory 508 Commercial, dwl 214 Minna
McQuillan Edward, picture frame maker with B. McQuillan, dwl 214 Minna
McQuillan James, boiler maker, Pacific Foundry, dwl 35 Main
McQuillan Joseph, cartman, 313 Market
McQuillan Joseph, laborer, dwl S s Vallejo bet Montgomery and Sansom
McQuillan Margaret, dwl 214 Minna
McQuillan Peter, boiler maker, Pacific Foundry, dwl 363 Jessie
McQuillan Robert, ship joiner with John G. North, Potrero
McQuilty Andrew, carpenter, dwl 17 Fourth
McQuinn Mathew, liquor saloon, 234 First
McQuinn Patrick, laborer, Union Foundry, 64 First
McQuinn Robert, glazier, dwl S s Mary nr Chesley
McQuinnan William, dwl 319 Bush
McQuithy Andrew, cabinet maker with W. G. Weir, dwl 17 Fourth
McQuoid Joseph, mason, dwl NW cor Columbia and Valencia
McRae F. runner, Original House
McRae J. dwl What Cheer House
McRae John, stevedore, dwl 238 First
McRavey John, shoe maker, N s Union bet Calhoun and Sansom
McRuer Donald C. merchant, office 204 California, dwl 18 Laurel Place
McShaffer Rose Miss, ironer, New England Laundry, Brannan nr Fifth
McShane Christopher, boiler helper, Pacific Foundry, dwl 832 Vallejo
McShane Phillip, secretary S. F. Insurance Co. office 432 Montgomery, dwl 626 California

McShea William, laborer, dwl 312 Beale
McSherry Hugh, teamster, dwl Presidio Road nr Fillmore
McSorley Isabella Miss, domestic, 1715 Powell
McSorley John F. cooper, S. F. & P. Sugar Co. dwl N s Folsom bet Seventh and Eighth
McSorley Peter, dwl E s Jones, bet Sac and Clay
McSweeney Dennis, shoe maker with Rudolph Meiners, dwl 831 Washington
McSweeney Mary (widow) dwl E s Eighth nr Howard
McSweeney Susan Miss, domestic, 1013 Pine
McSwegan James, blacksmith, Union Foundry, dwl 539 Howard
McSwegan Thomas, plasterer, Liberty Hose Co. No. 2
McTag Mary Miss, domestic, 872 Mission
McTanney John, cooper with Handy & Neuman, dwl 515 Kearny
McTavish Elizabeth, dwl 713 Howard
McTernan H. (T. & H. McTernan) NE cor Drumm and Commercial
McTernan T. & H. blacksmithing, NE cor Drumm and Commercial
McTiernan Edward, wool puller, dwl Brannan bet Third and Fourth
McTigue Michael, harness maker with J. C. Johnson & Co. dwl 104 Kearny
McTurner Hugh, blacksmith, dwl 116 Jackson
McUsin Mary Miss, domestic, 349 Fremont
McVay Patrick, deck hand, steamer Washoe
McVea James, cabinet maker, dwl 909 Stockton
McVerry Thomas, dwl NE cor Hyde and Greenwich
McVicar Ann (widow) dwl 1211 Pacific
McVincey Patrick, marble polisher, 635 Market, dwl Battery House, Battery nr Clay
McWain Michael, laborer, dwl United States Hotel, 706 Battery
McWilliams Francis, express agent, dwl 29 Perry
McWilliams James, express agent, dwl 29 Perry
McWilliams John, express agent, 29 Perry
McWilliams William, blacksmith with John G. North, Potrero
Meacham A. D. accountant with Wellman, Peck & Co. dwl 319 Taylor
Mead Allen, workman with S. C. & L. H. Talcott
Mead B. F. & Co. hatters, 309 Montgomery, dwl 54 Minna
Mead Charles H. saddle and harness maker, SE cor Front and Jackson, dwl 350 First
Mead Charles H. jr. (Mead & Son) dwl 1002 Market
Mead Hamilton, driver with R. B. Fordham, 600 Front
Mead H. C. with J. R. Mead & Co. NW cor Washington and Sansom, dwl Lick House
Mead House, NW cor Montgomery and Pine
Mead James, paper hanger, dwl 104 Sutter
MEAD J. R. & CO. importers and jobbers and retail clothiers, NE cor Montgomery and Bush and NW cor Washington and Sansom, bds Occidental Hotel
Mead Lewis, book keeper with Coffey & Risdon, dwl 1 Bush
Mead L. G. book keeper with L. J. Ewell, dwl 514 Filbert
Mead Michael, blacksmith with Larkins & Co. dwl 46 Bush
Mead William, waiter, What Cheer House
Mead (William C.) & Son (Charles H. Mead, jr.) saddle and harness makers, 224 Sansom, dwl 1002 Market
Mead William H. salesman with Blake & Co. dwl 924 Pine
Meadau George, clerk, SW cor Stock and O'Farrell
Meade Catharine Mrs. dwl NW cor Kearny and Broadway
Meade Charles F. dwl 631 Vallejo

Meade Frederick, drayman, dwl 522 Union
Meade Mary A. Miss, domestic, 1315 Mission
Meader Alexander J. stevedore, dwl 8 s Vallejo bet Montgomery and Kearny
MEADER (Charles T.) LOLOR (Charles P.) & CO. importing, shipping and commission merchants, office 405 Front, res Stockton
Meaeu James H. ship carpenter with John G. North, Potrero
Meagher Bridget Miss, domestic, N s Chestnut bet Dupont and Stockton
Meagher Dennis, dwl NE cor Seventeenth and Dolores
Meagher Ellen, domestic, 531 Mission
Meagher Henry, teamster, dwl S s Chambers bet Battery and Front
Meagher James, carpenter, dwl W s Shotwell nr cor Twentieth
Meagher James, drayman, dwl 671 Harrison
Meagher James, laborer, Mission Woolen Mills
Meagher John, policeman, City Hall, dwl 67 Clementina
Meagher John F. professor, St. Mary's College
Meagher Martin, laborer, dwl 35 Valparaiso
Meagher Mary Miss, domestic, 531 Mission
Meagher Michael, laborer, dwl 115 Sixth
Meagher Michael, laborer, dwl 9 Natoma
Meagher Michael, plasterer, dwl Dupont bet Washington and Clay
Meagher Patrick, laborer, dwl 85 Broadway
Meagher William, teamster with J. Peirce, 417 Cal
Meagher William F. shoe maker, 313 Pine, dwl 12 Sutter
Mean John, tinsmith, dwl 323 Pine
Meany Patrick, tailor, dwl 1407 Powell
Mearns George, clerk with C. V. Gillespie, dwl 369 Jessie
Mears James, ale and porter bottler, 717 Francisco
Mebanca A. dwl SE cor Mission and First
MEBIUS C. F. importer and commission merchant, consul for Bavaria, Lubeck and Hesse Cassel, acting consul for Hanover and agent Bremen Board Underwriters, office 223 Sacramento, dwl 1019 Folsom
MECARTNEY AMOS, commission merchant, 220 Davis, dwl 108 Tehama bet Second and Third
Mechanics' Hotel, Richard Williams proprietor, SW cor Kearny and Pacific
MECHANICS' INSTITUTE PAVILION, W s Stockton bet Post and Geary
MECHANICS' INSTITUTE ROOMS, 529 Cal
Mechler John J. hair dresser, dwl 512 Vallejo
MEDAU JOHN & PETER, cigars and tobacco, SE cor Dupont and Pacific
Medau Joseph J. cigars and tobacco, SW cor Davis and Broadway, dwl Bartol nr Vallejo
Medan Peter (John & P. M.) SE cor Dupont and Pacific
Medbery Edwin R. dwl 527 Pine
Medel Peter, groceries and liquors, cor Mission and Stewart, dwl 23 Everett
Medina Frank, musician, dwl 953 Howard
Medina William, machinist with Small & Redmond, dwl Mission Dolores
Medley Fanny Miss, domestic, 331 Beale
Medowcroft James, porter, dwl 621 Mission
MEE JAMES, attorney at law, office 625 Merchant, dwl 222 Clara
Mee John, laborer, dwl W s Willow Avenue bet Van Ness Avenue and Franklin
Meegan Ann (widow) furnished rooms, 417 Stockton
Meegan John, hostler with John Agnew, 26 Kearny
Meehan Charles, tinsmith with G. & W. Snook, dwl E s Kearny bet Green and Union
Meehan Edward, with Robinett & Linn, dwl 8 Valparaiso bet Mason and Taylor
Meehan Francis, varnisher with J. Peirce, 417 Cal
Meehan John, workman, S. F. & P. Sugar Co. dwl Downey

Meehan Lizzie Miss, domestic, 26 Turk
Meehan Michael, with George & Smith, dwl Helvetia Hotel
Meehan Patrick, gardener, NW cor Stockton and Sutter
Meehan Peter, laborer, dwl 10 Sherwood Place
Meehan Peter, waiter, steamer Yosemite
Meehan William, Shades Liquor Saloon, NE cor Kearny and Commercial
Meehlig William, varnisher with E. Bloomingdale & Co. dwl 132 St. Mark Place
Meek William, dwl 707 Mission
MEEKER, (David) JAMES (William) & CO. (James Cobbledick and John W. Bates) importers and jobbers carriage and wagon materials, 12 and 14 Pine, dwl NE cor Sacramento and Hyde
Meeker William A, builder, dwl 19 Silver
Meeks Washington, attorney at law, office 523 Montgomery, dwl 947 Mission
Meeks William N. real estate, office 804 Montgomery, dwl 947 Mission
Meese Herman, president Bay Sugar Refinery, dwl 269 Jessie
Meeteer M. L. carpenter, dwl SE cor Seventeenth and Castro
Meetz (Theodore) & Co. (Benjamin Simon) groceries and liquors, SE cor Post and Dupont
Megannon James, merchant, dwl 652 Market
Megerle Henry C. salesman with Edward Hall & Co. dwl 586 Dupont
Meginly Joseph, conductor, Omnibus R. R. Co. dwl 25 Turk
Meglone E. W. clerk, dwl 164 First
Mehan Edward, Crescent Engine Co. No. 10
Mehan Johanna Miss, domestic, 1019 Jackson
Mehan John, laborer, dwl W s Downey nr Bryant
Meherin Thomas, nursery agent, NE cor Battery and Oregon, dwl 32 Clementina
Mehevy Michael, laborer, bds 336 Bush
Mehrtens August, groceries and liquors, NE cor Filbert and Mason
Mehrtens Henry, groceries and liquors, NE corner Front and Oregon
Mehrtens Martin, tobacconist, dwl 9 Hartman Alley
Meier George, carpenter and builder, dwl 905 Jackson
Meier Henry, groceries and liquors, NW cor Francisco and Stockton
Meier John H. bar tender, dwl 1607 Battery
Meier (L. H.) & Knippenberg (E. R.) groceries and liquors, SW cor Stevenson and Ecker
Meierdierks (Christian) & Co. (Henry Vorrath) groceries and liquors, NW cor Post and Powell
Meighan Patrick, engineer, St. Mary's College, Bernal Heights
Meighan Rebecca A. (widow) bakery, 148 Fourth
MEIGS (George A.) & GAWLEY (William H.) lumber and Puget Sound Packets, Pier 19 Stewart, res Port Madison, W. T
Meiklehaugh Daniel, porter, dwl 1423 Pacific
Meiklem James, laborer with David B. Hughes, dwl 8 s Lombard bet Taylor and Jones
Mein Jacob, laborer, Bay Sugar Refinery, dwl 206 Green
Meincer Lewis, dwl N s Shipley nr Harrison Av
MEINECKE CHARLES, commission merchant and importer foreign wines and brandies, office 215 Front, dwl 1213 Mason
Meinecke George, cook, dwl 18 Sansom
Meinecke Johanna Miss, domestic, 29 O'Farrell
Meiners Rudolph, shoe making, 406 Market
Meininger Louis (N. D. Popert & Co. Marysville) office 426 Sacramento, dwl 147 Turk
Meinke John F. book keeper with Falkenau Bros
Meiraldi Luigi, employé with Brignardello, Macchiavello & Co. 706 Sansom
Meiran Dennis, laborer, dwl 140 Stewart
Meirton John, dwl 9 Hartman Place

Meisnel Louis, with Stevens & Oliver, dwl 1019 Kearny
Meister Christian (Miller & M.) dwl 329 Bryant
Meister Gustave, tailor, dwl 329 Bryant
Mejasson Leon, attorney in fact of Abel Guy, dwl 15 Taylor
Mel George, clerk with W. B. Johnston, dwl 307 Taylor
Mel Henry, clerk with Charles Baum, dwl 307 Taylor
Mel John, importer, SW cor Front and Jackson, dwl 307 Taylor
Mel Louis, clerk with Dickson, DeWolfe & Co. dwl 307 Taylor
Mela Guiseppe, 8 Washington Fish Market
Melander Gustave, seaman, dwl 20 Commercial
Melarky William, laborer, dwl N s Jessie bet Second and Jane
MELBOURN J. & CO. (P. Hottendorf) dealers wood, coal, and feed, dwl 1219 Powell
Melbourne Jacob, dwl 806 Vallejo
Melcher Henry, fireman, dwl St. Louis Hotel, 11 Pac
Melchert A. F. W. shoe making, 429 Bush
Melehan Patrick, Dublin House, 228 First
Melendy H. B. house and sign painter, 341 Bush
Meley Jane (widow) dwl 619 Union
Melick Chichester, furnished rooms, 300 and 302 Fourth
Melin Charles, dwl E s Valencia bet Twentieth and Twenty-First
Melle Jacob, wood turner, bds What Cheer House
Mellen John, laborer, dwl Main nr Folsom
Mellen John, express wagon, cor Clay and East
Mellen W. P. clerk, Folsom St. Wharf, dwl 335 Jessie
Melletz Geo. D. dwl SW cor Brannan and Ritch
Mellis Charles, laundry, dwl 622 Lombard, rear
Mellish William A. seaman, dwl 32 Stewart
Mellon John, vegetables, dwl 23 Clara
Mellon John S. painter, dwl 419 Bush
Mellot Michael, laborer, dwl cor Vallejo and Hyde
Melboy Francis, cooper, dwl Natoma bet Second and Third
Melloy James, workman, S. F. & P. Sugar Co. dwl Natoma
Mellus Gustavus B. clerk, dwl NE cor Freelon and Fourth
Mellus Henry J. local policeman, dwl 1303 Stockton
Melone Drury, office 698 Montgomery, dwl 725 Cal
Melones & Stanislaus G. & S. M. Co. office 606 Montgomery
Meloney Edmund B. workman with J. Pierson, N s Sixteenth nr Nebraska
Meloney M. mason, Spring Valley W. W
Meloney Michael, waiter, Russ House
MELONEY WILLIAM B. jr. saloon keeper, NE cor Brannan and Sixth
Meloy Margaret Miss, domestic, 703 Lombard
Melse Edward G. conductor, Omnibus R. R. Co. dwl 221 Tehama
Melstedt August (and Hohenschild & M.) dwl Metropolitan Hotel
Melters R. S. deck hand, C. S. Navigation Co
Melvets Henry, seaman, dwl S s Main bet Harrison and Bryant
Melville Charles, marble worker, 673 Market
Melville John, drayman, dwl 8 s Francisco bet Taylor and Jones
MELVILLE JOHN, importer wines and liquors, 613 Commercial, dwl 324 Sutter
Melville Michael, cartman, dwl S side, Chestnut bet Mason and Taylor
Melville William, laborer with David B. Hughes, dwl 8 s Lombard bet Taylor and Jones
Melvin John, dwl S s Mary nr Chesley
Menant Lombard, wines and liquors, SE cor Kearny and Clay (and Pacific Asphaltum Co.)
Menckhoff Gustave (Tiedemann & M.) dwl Lombard nr Sansom

Mendazon Marcus, musician, dwl SW cor Dupont and Broadway
Mendel David, dwl 931 Kearny
Mendel Morris, job cart, cor Sacramento and Montgomery, dwl 204 Second
Mendell William H. clerk, 211 Clay, dwl 916 Stock
Mendelson E. clothing, 233 Pacific
Mendelson Goodman, tailor with Isaac Hintze, dwl New Atlantic Hotel
Mendelson Louis, salesman, 138 Montgomery
Mendelson Morris, tailor, 6 Sutter, dwl 132 Sutter
Mendelson Peter, tailor, dwl 132 Sutter
Menderson William & Co. importers and jobbers shirts and collars, 304 Battery, dwl 20 Mont
Mendes Charles, hairdresser with Stable Bros. dwl NE cor Montgomery and Broadway
MENDES DAVID, Red Lion Liquor Saloon, 319 Commercial
Mendessolle Benjamin *(Favre & M.)* dwl 933 Howard
Mendez Teodoro, cigar maker with E. Goslinsky, dwl 535 Vallejo
MENDHEIM H. & CO. importers and retailers German and foreign books, gilt moldings, etc. 631 Clay, dwl 540 Stockton
Mendheim Moritz, importer and commission merchant, office 631 Clay, dwl 540 Stockton
Mendiondon Peter, vegetable gardener, nr Bay View Park
MENDOCINO PACKETS, Pier 11 Stewart, John T. Pennell agent
Mendon Granville A. *(Lord & Co.)* res New York
Mendoza A. jeweler, 622 Clay
Mendoza John, workman with Antonio Flores
Menegey Charles, printer, dwl 518 Union
Menesses Jesus J. clerk, dwl 630 Vallejo
Menews Charles, bar keeper, dwl 1027 Dupont
Mengel John, St. Louis Meat Market, NE cor Sutter and Stockton
Mengel Philip, upholsterer with E. Bloomingdale & Co. dwl 766 Howard
Mengelkamp Bernard, tailor, SE cor Pine and Bat
Menges *(Adam)* & Frankenheimer *(Joseph)* butchers, 30 Metropolitan Market, dwl 502 Market
Menges Frank, butcher with L. Miller & Co. dwl 106 Geary
Menges Louisa Miss, domestic, SW cor Twelfth and Folsom
Menke Henning, groceries and liquors, NE cor Battery and Commerce
Menken J. E. seaman, dwl 54 Sacramento
Mennan Patrick, dwl 177 Beale
Menne Clement, tailor, 533 Jackson
Menomy Edward F. mason, dwl 1709 Stockton
Menomy George W. & Co. *(Albert P. Fuller)* butter, cheese, etc. 3 Wash Market, dwl 813 Montgomery
Menomy Harry C. butcher with Veasey & Robinson, dwl 1123 Taylor
Mensing Henning E. clerk with Louis Berbe, Potrero Avenue
Mentel Gottfried, drayman, 115 Battery, dwl S s Union bet Powell and Mason
Mentel Gustave, truckman, 115 Battery, dwl Union Alley
Mentel William, groceries and liquors, NE cor Broadway and Stockton
Mentz Carl, seaman, bds 7 Washington
Mentz John, dwl What Cheer House
Menu Armand, clerk with Pascal, Dubetat & Co. dwl 330 Sutter
Menu Jacques H. importer wines, office 728 Mont
Menwyer Isidore, butcher with Louis Peres & Co. dwl Potrero Avenue
Meny Toussaint, hay and grain, S s Brannan bet Eighth and Ninth
Menzemer Stephen A. foreman with Cook & Son, dwl E s Sansom bet Broadway and Vallejo
Menzer F. carpenter, Cosmopolitan Hotel

Menzies Stewart, stevedore, dwl S s Francisco bet Kearny and Dupont
MERCADO *(Felix)* & SEULLY *(Firmin)* Sansevain's Wines and Bitters, 506 and 508 Jackson, dwl 728 Bush nr Mason
MERCANTILE GAZETTE AND SHIPPING REGISTER (tri-monthly) E. D. Waters proprietor, office 536 Clay
MERCANTILE LIBRARY ASSOCIATION, rooms NE cor Montgomery and Bush
MERCER CHARLES H. manufacturing confectioner, 127 Second and 518 Kearny, dwl 127 Second
Mercer Frank T. stevedore, dwl 419 Fremont
Mercer Virginia Miss, dwl N s Market bet Oak and Page
Merchant Christopher, butcher, dwl 14 Everett
Merchant Joseph, carpet cleaner, dwl S s Clay bet Polk and Van Ness Avenue
Merchant Thomas S. Virginia Market, 822 Jackson
MERCHANTS' ASSOCIATION, office 623 Montgomery
MERCHANTS' EXCHANGE ROOMS, 521 Clay bet Montgomery and Sansom
MERCHANTS' EXPRESS LINE, New York, DeWitt, Kittle & Co. agents, office NW cor California and Front
Merchants' Line Packets for Victoria and Portland, R. F. Pickett agent, 214 Sacramento
MERCHANTS' MUTUAL MARINE INSURANCE COMPANY, San Francisco, office 206 Front cor California, J. B. Scochler secretary
Merchants' Transportation Co. office 326 Clay
Mercier François *(Roberts & Co.)* 249 Fourth
Mercier Pierre, waiter, Miners' Restaurant, dwl cor Fifth and Minna
Merini Nicol, vegetable garden nr Bay View Park
Meriol Joseph, dwl 1230 Dupont
Meritbew Joseph C. dwl 1910 Mason
Merithew R. S. ship carpenter, dwl 825 Jackson
Merkelbach William, butcher, 51 Everett, dwl SE cor Stewart and Mission
Merker John, dwl 239 Stevenson
Merker Margaret Miss, 607 Jackson
Merker Otto, hairdresser with Henderson & Brown, dwl Pratt Court
Merkle Charles A. employé with Charles Bernard, dwl W s Sansom bet Green and Union
Merkle Christian *(Boyd, McAuliffe & Co.)* dwl 20 Langton
Merle Adrien, clerk with Caire Brothers, dwl 313 Green
Merle Peter, dwl 834 Broadway
Mermond Francis, porter with Stein, Simon & Co. *(and T'schants, Tenthorey & Co.)* dwl 560 Mission
Mermoud Louis, dwl 558 Mission
Mero Alexander, saddler, dwl 3 Howard Court
Mero James, blacksmith with Casebolt & Co. dwl 3 Howard Court
Mero John, blacksmith with Casebolt & Co. dwl 3 Howard Court
Merriam Andrew J. carrier, Evening Bulletin, dwl E s Tay nr Sacramento
Merriam B. driver, dwl 633 Market
Merriam Dana R. melter, Kellogg, Hewston & Co.'s Refinery, dwl S s Stevenson nr Third
Merriam George, bar keeper with Martin & Horton, 545 Clay
Merriam George B. blacksmith, Pacific Foundry
Merriam G. H. tinsmith, dwl S s Commercial bet Montgomery and Kearny
Merriam O. W. *(N. P. Cole & Co.)* res Boston
Merriam William P. clerk, County Recorder's Office, dwl Tay nr California
Merrida Ephraim (col'd) dwl N s Point Lobos Road 2 miles from Plaza
Merrifield A D. insurance agent, 626 Montgomery, dwl 737 Green

Merrifield Charles, milkman with Mills & Evans, dwl 6 June
Merrifield Henry P. compositor, Evening Bulletin, dwl 8 s Green bet Mason and Powell
Merrill A. D. *(Hemenway & M.)* dwl 5 Vassar Pl
Merrill Albion P. real estate, dwl N s Point Lobos Road 2 miles from Plaza
Merrill Annis, attorney at law, office 58 Exchange Building, dwl 932 Pacific
Merrill Arthur, seaman, dwl 26 Sacramento
Merrill Charles A. real estate, dwl N s Point Lobos Road 2 miles from Plaza
Merrill Charles R. clerk with J. C. Merrill & Co. dwl 628 Howard
Merrill Frank, Frank's Exchange, NE cor Pacific and Stockton
Merrill George, clerk with H. K. Cummings, dwl 8 O'Farrell Alley
MERRILL GEORGE B. attorney at law, office 520 Montgomery, dwl 748 Howard
Merrill Jane (widow) dwl 113 Minna
MERRILL J. C. & CO. auction, shipping, and commission merchants, and agents Honolulu Regular Dispatch Line Packets, 204 and 206 California, dwl 14 Stanly Place
Merrill John, drayman, NE cor California and Drumm, dwl 117 Dora
Merrill John R. supt Steam Paddy Company, dwl 808 Howard
Merrill Joseph W. clerk with R. A. Merrill, 14 First
Merrill Maria (widow) dwl 542 Green
Merrill Parker, lodgings, 27 Minna
Merrill R. A. hardware, 14 First, dwl 914 Clay
Merrill Robert, merchant, dwl 240 Stevenson
Merrill Sylvester, book keeper, 518 Front, dwl 730 Sutter
Merriman Meyer, laborer, dwl 5 Pollard Place
Merriman Richard, house mover, 639 Mission, dwl 639 Mission
Merrion G. B. blacksmith, dwl 663 Mission
Merritt Ambrose, with Nathaniel Gray, dwl 718½ Union
Merritt Benjamin C. laborer, Flint's Warehouse, dwl Sierra Nevada Hotel, 528 Pacific
Merritt Enos W. lumberman, dwl W s Florence nr Broadway
Merritt Frederick A. clerk with Samuel Merritt, 240 Montgomery, res Oakland
Merritt Henry, cabinet maker, dwl S s Jessie bet Fifth and Sixth
Merritt Jarvis (col'd) laborer, bds 5 Broadway
Merritt Martin, carpenter, dwl SE cor Pine and Bat
Merritt Phineas G. real estate agent, dwl 1918 Taylor
MERRITT SAMUEL M. D. merchant, office 240 Montgomery, res Oakland
Merritt Stephen F. *(Fitch & M.)* 314 Montgomery
Merritt William H. teamster with Riley & Vest
Merritt Z. T. printer with Dewey, Waters & Co. dwl E s Taylor bet Union and Filbert
Merron John, meat market, SE cor Second and Tehama
Merry Thomas, drayman, dwl Brannan nr Ninth
Merry William Laurence, master stm America, office NW cor Battery and Pine, dwl cor Post and Mason
Mersing Bernhard *(Ludorff & Co.)* SW cor Montgomery and Jackson
Mertage John, seaman, dwl 238 Stewart
Mertle Charles A. laborer, dwl W s Sansom bet Green and Union
Merton John A. porter with Goodwin & Co. dwl E s Montgomery bet Broadway and Vallejo
Mervey John, wood and coal, 1417 Stockton, dwl W s Sonoma Place nr Green
Mervy J. A. drug clerk, dwl 4 Brenham Place
Merz Emil, drayman, 220 Davis, dwl Welch near Fourth
MERZ *(William)* & GREINER *(Frederick)* groceries and liquors, SE cor Sutter and Powell

MERZBACH JULIUS, importer and dealer laces, embroideries, fancy goods, etc. 412 Kearny
Méschévsky Robert, with F. & G. Besson, dwl Revere House
Mesenburg Henry, clerk, NE cor Jessie and Ecker
Meserve James L. cabinet maker with Goodwin & Co. dwl W s Mary bet Mission and Minna
Meserve John S. engineer, 215 Sansom, dwl W s Mary nr Mission
Meserve Theodore, compositor, Alta California, dwl Dupont nr Chestnut
Meseth C. jeweler with R. B. Gray & Co
Meshaw John P. (col'd) boot maker, 539 California, dwl 1234 Bush
Mesick John, book keeper, 220 Battery
Meskal Thomas, workman with Smith & Brown, dwl New Potrero
Mess Henry, butcher, dwl West End Hotel
Messer James, waiter, Lick House
Messer William D. commission merchant, office 206 Front, dwl 408 Market
Messerle Charles, hairdressing saloon. 1212 Stockton
Messersmith A. baker, Occidental Hotel
Messersmith George, National Restaurant, 826 Market, dwl 723 Mission
Messerve E. Mrs. furnished rooms, 612 California
Messeth Charles, jeweler, dwl 827 Vallejo, rear
Messick John, with Hughes & Hunter, dwl 652 Mkt
Messinger Aaron, clerk, 33 Metropolitan Market, dwl 685 Geary
Messinger Simon, produce, 33 and 34 Metropolitan Market, dwl 685 Geary
Mestayer Augustus, with S. P. Collins, dwl Russ H
Mestre E. upholsterer, SW cor Stockton and Jackson
Metastazio Alexander, cook, 614 Clay
Metcalf A. B. Mrs. dwl 212 Broadway
Metcalf Alfred, mate, stm Salinas, dwl 114 Silver
Metcalf Emma Miss, dwl 212 Broadway nr Sansom
Metcalf George, express wagon, 414 Geary
Metcalf Peter, confectioner, 414 Geary
Metcalf Samuel A. sawing and planing mill, SW cor Mission and Fremont, dwl N s Howard nr Sixteenth
Metemore Margaret, domestic, 756 Harrison
Methvern D. C. dwl Original House
Metlen Joseph C. porter, 306 Clay
METROPOLITAN BLOCK (now Exchange Building) NW cor Montgomery and Washington
Metropolitan Coffee and Spice Mill, 25 Second
METROPOLITAN MARKET, N s Market bet Montgomery and Sansom
METROPOLITAN THEATER, William H. Lyon proprietor, 719 and 721 Montgomery
Metson Annie Miss, dwl W s Gavin nr Filbert
Mette Felix J. dwl 1807 Stockton
Metz August, carpenter, dwl 2 Trinity
Metz Frederick, steward, Bootz's Hotel
Metzenrood Jacob, driver with John Maisch, 38 Geary
Metzer Peter, captain bark Perkins, dwl 238 Stewart
Metzger Adolph, bar keeper, 619 Kearny, dwl 616 California
Metzger Charles *(Kohn & Co.)* dwl 8 Fourth
Metzger Charles, dry goods, 134 Second
Metzger Charles L. straw worker, dwl 121 Minna
Metzger *(George)* & Co. *(Patrick Quinn and William McCauslin)* wholesale butchers, Ninth nr Brannan
Metzger George, boot maker, 39 Jackson
Metzger Jacob, butcher with Barney Horn, dwl Potrero Avenue
Metzger Joseph, piano maker with Jacob Zech, dwl 627 Green
Metzger L. F. carpenter, dwl 21 Hunt
Metzger Mary Miss, domestic, 333 Minna
Metzger Valentine G. butcher, dwl E s Ninth bet Bryant and Brannan
Metzger William, molder, Pacific Foundry, dwl 162 First

Metzler Charles, proprietor Golden Gate Brewery, 713 Greenwich

Metzner Catherine (widow) dwl W s Rassette Place No. 1

Meuli Anton, miner, dwl 431 Pine

Meuli Jacob A. *(Christian Good & Co.)* dwl 738 Washington

Meuser Frederick, clerk, 16 Stewart

Meussdorffer C. H. with J. C. Meussdorffer, dwl 3 White Place

MEUSSDORFFER JOHN C. importer and jobber hats, caps, and hatters' materials, 637 Clay and 628 Commercial, dwl 752 Folsom

MEUSSDORFFER KONRAD, hat and cap manufacturer, 635 and 637 Commercial

Mewer Amos, tinsmith, dwl W s Jones bet Filbert and Greenwich

Mewes Charles, lager beer saloon, 611 Pacific

Mexican Emigration Co. office 430 Montgomery

Mexican Loan Office, 420 Montgomery

Mexican Sea Island Cotton Co. office 410 Sansom

Meyer Aaron, cigars and tobacco, 629 Kearny, dwl 31 Stone

MEYER ADAM, Cincinnati Brewery, E s Valencia bet Sixteenth and Seventeeth

Meyer Albert, Golden City Meat Market, 55 Sac

Meyer Ale ander, book keeper with H. Horstman & Co x

Meyer Andrew, teamster with Lux & Miller, dwl W s Ninth nr Brannan

Meyer Anton *(Dorgeloh & M.)* 616 California

Meyer August, musician, dwl NW cor Kearny and Broadway

Meyer August F. *(Meyer & Bro.)* dwl 515 Sac

Meyer August F. clerk with H. F. Kappke, SE cor Union and Mason

Meyer Augustus, musician, dwl 414 Union

MEYER BROTHERS *(Peter, Louis, and Henry J. Meyer)* groceries and liquors, NW cor Folsom and Fremont

Meyer B. W. captain schooner Sky Lark, office 413 East, dwl 24 Stewart

Meyer C. & Co. bag factory, 314 Davis, dwl 531 Mission

Meyer Carl, waiter, 324 Montgomery, dwl N s Post bet Kearny and Dupont

Meyer *(Charles)* & Jonasson *(Meyer)* cloak and mantle manufacturers, 10 Montgomery, dwl 118 St. Mark Place

MEYER *(Charles)* & MOLK *(Henry)* groceries and liquors, NW cor Dupont and Green

Meyer Charles, with J. N. Stand, 211 Dupont

Meyer Charles, boot maker, 1111 Dupont

Meyer Charles, cook, dwl 431 Pine

Meyer Charles, tobacconist, dwl 531 Mission

Meyer Charles C. H. clerk with John G. Ils, dwl 241 Stevenson

Meyer Charles H. J. gunsmith, 604 Pacific

Meyer Claus R. clerk with F. Bruns & Bro. dwl cor Battery and Green

Meyer Conrad, job wagon, 206 Davis

Meyer Conrad, laborer, Bay Sugar Refinery, dwl 11 Pacific

Meyer Constant, clerk with Cobentz & Bro

MEYER DANIEL *(Jonas & Moritz Meyer)* merchants, office 207 Battery, dwl 906 Broadway

Meyer Eleanora Miss, domestic, 832 Folsom

Meyer Ernst, dwl E s Eighth nr Mission

Meyer Franz, clerk, SW cor Mission and Third

Meyer Frederick, teamster with Ross, Dempster & Co. dwl 8 s Twelfth bet Mission and Howard

Meyer G. model instrument maker, 531 Market, dwl 546 Mission

Meyer George, clerk, SE cor Minna and Fifth

Meyer George, clerk with John Horstman, dwl 700 Bush

Meyer George, cook, dwl 54 First

Meyer George F. H. jeweler with Lemme Bros. dwl N s Mary nr Chesley

Meyer George G. cook, Butchers' Home, Potrero Av

Meyer Gustave, butcher with Felix Uri, 16 New Market

Meyer H. furrier, dwl 323 Pine

Meyer Henry, carrier, Evening Bulletin, dwl W s Vincent nr Union

Meyer Henry. cigar maker with E. Goslinsky, dwl Rassette Place No. 2

Meyer Henry, express wagon, 58 Everett

Meyer Henry, groceries and liquors, SW cor Filbert and Dupont

Meyer Henry H. proprietor Golden Gate Hotel, 728 Market

Meyer Henry J. *(Meyer Bros.)* dwl 248 Fremont

MEYER H. W. groceries and liquors, 210 Stewart

Meyer Isaac, salesman with Prosper May, dwl 821 Vallejo

Meyer J. dry goods, dwl 162 Perry

Meyer James S. physician and mining secretary, office 311 Pine, dwl 77 Clementina

Meyer J. G. H. manufacturer billiard balls, 228 Montgomery, dwl 241 Stevenson

Meyer Johanna E. (widow) dwl S s Hayes nr Octavia

Meyer John, lab, Bay Sugar Refinery, dwl 1021 Bat

Meyer John C. butcher, E s Gilbert bet Bryant and Brannan

Meyer John C. clothing, 915 Kearny

Meyer John H. groceries and liquors, NW cor Powell and Washington

Meyer John P. cooperage, NW cor Broadway and Battery, dwl N s Green bet Powell and Mason

Meyer Jonas *(Daniel Meyer)* dwl 810 Vallejo

Meyer Joseph, boot maker, dwl 936 Kearny

Meyer Joseph, clerk, 328 Kearny

Meyer Joseph, tailor, 311 Davis

Meyer J. W. clerk, dwl 619 Pacific

Meyer L. bookseller, dwl 17 Third

Meyer Lena Miss, domestic, 1808 Stockton

Meyer Louis, butcher, W s Larkin bet Pine and California, dwl E s Larkin bet Pine and California

Meyer Louis, express wagon, cor Washington and Kearny, dwl N s California bet Leavenworth and Hyde

Meyer Louis, fruit and vegetables, 61 Washington Market, dwl 313 Kearny

Meyer Louis, tailor, 347 Third

Meyer Mathias *(Gabeldn & M.)* dwl 24 Tehama

Meyer Moritz *(Daniel Meyer)* dwl 526 Ellis

Meyer Moses, dwl 522 Minna

Meyer Moses jr. dwl SW cor Sixth and Mission

Meyer Peter, express wagon, cor Second and Market

Meyer Peter, secretary Bay Sugar Refinery *(and Meyer Bros.)* office cor Battery and Union, dwl 24 Silver

Meyer Pinkus, glazier, dwt 235 Jessie

Meyer Robert, waiter, dwl 323 Pine

Meyer Samuel, boots and shoes. 926 Dupont

Meyer Simon, merchant, dwl 1 Harlan Place

Meyer Solomon, butcher with Eli Alexander, dwl 22 Stockton Place

Meyer Thomas, butcher, dwl 323 Kearny

MEYER T. LEMMEN, importing and commission, 815 and 817 Sansom, res Menlo Park

Meyer Wentley, bar keeper, NW cor Washington and Kearny

Meyer W. F. groceries and liquors, NW cor Mission and Mary

MEYER WILLIAM & CO. *(Simon, Isidor, and Louis Wormser)* manufacturers, importers, and jobbers clothing, SW cor Sacramento and Sansom and 616 Clay, res New York

Meyer William *(Rodgers, M. & Co.)* dwl 1007 Mason

Meyer William, butcher, 258 Third

Meyer William, dry goods, dwl 1227 Stockton

MEYER WILLIAM, gardener and nursery, Post nr Lone Mountain Avenue

Meyer William, waiter, German Hospital, Brannan nr First

Meyer *(William W.)* & Brother *(August F. Meyer)* cigars and tobacco, 335 Pine, dwl 515 Sac
Meyer, see Mayer, Mayers. Myer, and Myers
MEYERBACK SOLOMON, clerk, dwl SE corner Green and Mason
Meyerfeld Moses *(Falkenstein & Co.)* dwl 688 Geary
Meyerhoff Robert, iron door and shutter maker with J.'R. Sims, dwl Ellis bet Polk and Van Ness Av
Meyerholz William & Co. *(Frederick Ehrchs)* King Philip Market, 702 Bush, dwl 704 Bush
Meyerpeter A. H. employment agent, dwl 11 Minna
Meyers Anthony, carpenter, shop and dwl 729 Pac
Meyers Charles, tailor, 602 Broadway, dwl 612 Broadway
Meyers Charles A. laborer, dwl 115 William
Meyers Christian W. ship carpenter, dwl 514 Bryant
Meyers Ephraim, machinist with Hawley & Co. dwl cor Second and Howard
Meyers Henry, steward Eureka Hose Co. No. 4
Meyers Henry, upholsterer with Kennedy & Bell, dwl 108 Austin bet Polk and Van Ness Avenue
Meyers Henry B. carrier, Evening Bulletin, dwl 8 s Filbert bet Hyde and Leavenworth
Meyers' Hotel, N. Gartner proprietor, 814 Mont
Meyers Israel, shirts, 36 and 38 Third, dwl 771 Mission
Meyers *(John)* & Strebost *(William)* boots and shoes, 13 Third
Meyers John, hatter, dwl 749 Market
Meyers Joseph, dwl N s Bryant bet Second and Stanly Place
Meyers L. dwl 430 Post
Meyers Leonard, musician, dwl 427 Greenwich
Meyers M. & A. L. & Co. *(M. L. Lyon)* glaziers, 716 Washington, dwl 828 Vallejo
Meyers Mitchell J. tailor, 805 Clay, dwl N s Ellis bet Polk and Van Ness Avenue
Meyers Oscar, merchant, dwl 356 Minna
Meyers Patrick, upholsterer with Kennedy & Bell, dwl N s Austin bet Polk and Van Ness Avenue
Meyers William, seaman, dwl 26 Sacramento
Meyers William H. dwl 55 Natoma
Meyerstein Henry, clothing, 313 Kearny, dwl 364 Minna
Meyerstein Joseph, junk, dwl 113 Freelon
Meyerstein *(Louis)* & Lowenberg *(Isador)* clothing, 301 Kearny, dwl 456 Clementina
Meyn Hermann, carpenter, dwl NW cor Kearny and Jackson
Meyn John, clerk, NW cor Everett and Third
Meyn Peter *(Hey & M.)* dwl NW cor Folsom and Twelfth
Mezzara P. cameo cutter and sculptor, studio 436 Jackson
Mezzari John, laborer, 546 Clay
Mibelli Luigi, fisherman, 46 Italian Fish Market
Michael Aaron, pawnbroker, 835 Dupont, dwl 51 Clara
Michael Augusta R. (widow) dwl 20 South Park
Michael Herman, tailor, 739 Pacific
Michael Isaac, fancy goods, 200 Fourth
Michael James Mrs. (widow) dwl 20 South Park
Michael Joseph, cigars and tobacco, dwl 515 Kearny
Michael Lewis, clothing, 129 Pacific
Michael Louis, tailor, 607 Davis
Michael Morris, express wagon, corner Market and Second
Michaelis Borchert, tailor, 1432 Stockton
Michaelis Frederick, groceries, 238 Kearny
Michaels Benjamin, sash and blind maker with Smith, Ware & Co. dwl 127 Fourth
Michaels Charles, saddler, dwl 612 Pacific
Michaels Henry, book keeper with Langley, Crowell & Co. dwl 27 Silver
Michaelsen *(A.)* & Elfers *(A. D.)* cigar and tobacco manufacturers, 300 Jackson
Michaelsen Christian, clerk with Charles A. C. Duisenberg, dwl SE cor Harrison and Seventh

Michalofsky Lewis, fruits, N s Folsom nr Sixth
Michel Abram, tailor, 221 Pacific
Michel *(Charles)* & Co. *(John Wuthrich)* Eighth Ward Market, 329 Geary
Michel Heiman, tailor, dwl Davis bet Washington and Clay
Michel Joseph H. *(Myers, Goldstone & Co.)* 36 and 38 Third
Michel M. tailor, dwl 418 Davis
Michel Morris, tailor, dwl 122 Minna
Michelais Bertha (widow) millinery, 46 Second
Michell Daniel, dwl 567 Mission
Michells Michael, butcher, Third nr Brannan
Michels A. W. & Brother *(Louis M. Michels)* importers and jobbers fancy goods, 304 Battery, dwl 427 Sacramento
MICHELS' BUILDING, NE cor Montgomery and Market
Michels Herman, real estate and consul for Saxony, office and dwl NE cor Market and Mont
Michels Isaac, salesman, 304 Battery, dwl 427 Sac
Michels Louis M. *(A. W. Michels & Bro.)* resides New York
Michels Michael, truckman, cor California and Front
Michelsen Frederick, groceries and liquors, SW cor Davis and Jackson
Michelsen Henry, porter, 209 Front
Michelsen Peter, captain sloop Amanda, Pier 15 Stewart
Michelson Christopher, clerk with Hermann Cordes, NE cor Green and Calhoun
Michelson Michael, laundry wagon, dwl 358 Minna
Michelson Peter, cook, dwl 33 Jackson
Michelssen Edwin, merchant, office 327 Front, dwl 425 Sixth
Michkus Jacob, laborer, dwl 553 Bryant
Mickle Edward, secretary Spring Valley W. W. Co. office SE cor Mont and Jackson, dwl 1008 Bush
Mickle Etting, cashier with Barron & Co. dwl 1008 Bush
Micklehaugh Daniel, porter, 221 California, dwl 1423 Pacific
Mickolsen Jacob, captain schooner A. R. Forbes, Caduc's Line foot Washington
Middlehoff Gerret, liquor saloon, NW cor Grove and Laguna, Hayes' Valley
Middlemis George, carpenter, dwl What Cheer H
Middleton Ernst, clerk, Pacific Mail S. S. Co. dwl 112 Mason
Middleton Francis, stevedore, C. A. Transit Co. dwl 315 Union
MIDDLETON JOHN & SON *(Samuel P. Middleton)* real estate auctioneers, 404 Montgomery, dwl 443 Bryant
Middleton John jr. with Newhall & Co. dwl 443 Bryant
Middleton Joseph H. carpenter, dwl N s Tehama nr Sixth
Middleton S. P. *(John Middleton & Son)* dwl 443 Bryant
Middleton William H. carpenter and builder, dwl 466 Clementina
Middlewood George, carpenter with Godfrey Hargitt, 17 Geary
Miel Charles, French and English Female Institute, 54 and 55 South Park
Miesegaes Henry H. clerk Golden Gate Mills, dwl 54 Third
Migbell William, capt. bark Glimpse, dwl 724 Bush
Mikkelson Rasmus, refiner, Kellogg, Hewston & Co.'s Refinery, dwl E s Russ bet Howard and Folsom
Milan John, porter Montgomery Block, dwl 110 Montgomery Block
Milatovich Antonio, dwl 8 s Alta bet Montgomery and Sansom
Milatz Henry, clerk, dwl Potrero Avenue
Milbourne Richard, bootblack, dwl 8 s Bernard bet Jones and Leavenworth

MILBURN JAMES & CO. importers and jobbers dry goods, 313 Sacramento, dwl SW cor Francisco and Dupont
Milburn James (col'd) porter, 231 Post
Milbury Samuel, ranchman, dwl 815 Union
Miles Bernard, with Marden & Folger, dwl W s Thirteenth bet Harrison and Folsom
Miles Charles, groom, Wilson's Circus
Miles Charles E. wharfinger, Dewey's Wharf foot Third, dwl 253 Stevenson
Miles Cornelius, student, dwl 767 Clay
Miles Edward, employé, Keystone House
Miles Edward M. clerk, Spring Valley W. W. Co. dwl 144 Silver
Miles Francis, blacksmith, dwl E s Kate nr Bryant
Miles Harriet (widow, col'd) dwl W s Gilbert bet Brannan and Townsend
Miles J. L. (widow) dwl 14 St. Mary
Miles Mary (widow) dwl 4 O'Farrell
Miles Michael, contractor, dwl 106 Stockton
Miles William F. policeman, City Hall, dwl 110 Kearny
Miley Andrew, cartman, dwl S s Natoma nr Seventh
Milholm M. L. carpenter, dwl 741 Mission
Milks Ezra, ship carpenter with John G. North, dwl nr cor Sierra and Michigan
Mill William, hostler with John Satterlee, W s Folsom bet Eleventh and Twelfth
Millan Edward, cook, dwl 10 Anthony
Millan William, painter with James R. Kelly, dwl Bernal Heights
Millar John, saddler with Hyde & McClennen, dwl 655 Washington
Millar Margaret (widow) dwl with Philip Rodgers, E s Market bet Twelfth and Thirteenth
Millard L. B. dwl What Cheer House
Millen John S. machinist, dwl N s Hayes near Franklin
Millen William J. painter, dwl 721 Mission
Millener John D. melter. S. F. Iron Works
Millener M. molder, dwl 559 Market
Miller Abraham D. teamster with George Morrow, dwl Fella Place nr Powell
Miller Adam, carpenter, N s Leavenworth bet California and Sacramento
Miller Adam jr. carpenter, W s Leavenworth bet California and Sacramento
Miller Adolph, tailor, 200 Sutter, dwl 204 Sutter
Miller Agnes Mrs. liquor saloon, 603 Kearny
MILLER ALBERT, president California Insurance Co. office 318 California, dwl 1208 Sacramento
Miller Alexander, upholsterer with E. Bloomingdale & Co. dwl 21 Second
Miller Anthony, cook, 626 Kearny
Miller Arno T. painter, dwl W s Kearny bet Broadway and Pacific
Miller Augustus C. clerk, 231 Kearny
Miller Bartwell, shoe maker, dwl E s Jasper Place
Miller Bernard, poultry, 6 Metropolitan Market, dwl 27 Hunt
Miller B. H. merchant, dwl 438 Jessie
Miller Caspar, gardener, N s Mission bet Eighth and Ninth, dwl W s Laskie bet Eighth and Ninth
Miller Catharine Mrs. nurse, 816 Filbert
Miller C. B. florist and aquarian, dwl SE cor Fillmore and Grove
Miller C. G. laborer, dwl SW cor Folsom and Spear
Miller (Charles) & Meister (Christian) merchant tailors, 426 Third
Miller (Charles) & Rose (Charles) Last Chance Saloon, 106 Stewart
Miller Charles, butcher, What Cheer House Restaurant
Miller Charles, clerk, 542 Kearny, dwl 626 Cal
Miller Charles, upholsterer, dwl 215 Kearny, rear
Miller Charles A. coppersmith, dwl 110 Silver
Miller Charles E. carpenter, dwl 51 Clara
Miller Charles F. gardener with Alphens Bull
Miller Charles G. lab, dwl SW cor Folsom and Spear

Miller Charles J. compositor, dwl What Cheer H
Miller Charles L. steward with Driscoll & Jellings, dwl 16 Harlan Place
Miller Christopher, clk, SW cor Sutter and Kearny
Miller Cornelius B. plants and flowers, 206 Bush, dwl SE cor Bush and Steiner
Miller C. W. attorney at law, office 622 Clay, dwl 139 Minna
Miller David, dwl What Cheer House
Miller David, with Arthur M. Ebbets, dwl 125 Fourth
Miller Edward, engineer, dwl Dresdener House
Miller Edward J. painter, dwl W s Seventh near Howard, rear
Miller E. J. painter, dwl 459 Minna
Miller E. L. teacher music, dwl 708 Sutter
Miller Eliza (widow) dwl 520 Bryant
Miller Elizabeth Miss (col'd) domestic, 912 Bush
Miller Elizabeth H. Miss, teacher Primary Department, City Female Seminary, dwl with Edward Hagthrop
Miller Ernest, jeweler, dwl N s Lombard bet Mason and Taylor
Miller Francis A. bricklayer, dwl 409 Bush
Miller Frederick, cartman, dwl 17 Scott Place
Miller Frederick, coppersmith, dwl 110 Silver
Miller Frederick, laborer, dwl 1024 Pacific
Miller Frederick W. with Gluck & Hansen, dwl cor O'Farrell and William
Miller Frederick W. blacksmith with Gebhard & Boynton, dwl 108 Bush
Miller F. W. dwl What Cheer House
Miller G. Vulcan Saloon, SE cor Mission and Fremont
MILLER (George) & BROTHER (Thomas) sacks and bottles, 655 Mission
Miller George, with Charles Schroth, 230 Kearny, dwl 219 Kearny
Miller George, carrier, Evening Bulletin
Miller George, driver, dwl 45 Stevenson
Miller George, hatter, dwl 327 Dupont
Miller George, miller, dwl 515 Market
Miller George, molder, dwl Mechanics' Hotel
Miller George W. carpenter with S. S. Culverwell, 29 Fremont, dwl 363 First
Miller George W. hatter with R. J. Tiffany, dwl SW cor Bush and Dupont
Miller George W. poll tax collector, City Hall, dwl 332 Brannan
Miller Gideon L. steward, steamer Julia
Miller Hans, seaman, dwl 113 Commercial
MILLER (Henry) & LUX (Charles) cattle dealers and wholesale butchers, office 536 Kearny, res Gilroy, Santa Clara Co
Miller Henry, baker, New York Bakery
Miller H. M. appraiser, U. S. office Custom House, dwl 13 Hampton Place
Miller Isaac, melter, Fulton Foundry, dwl 24 Clementina
Miller Isaac, pattern maker, Union Foundry, dwl 731 Washington
Miller Jacob, expressman, cor Wash and Kearny
Miller Jacob F. amalgamator, dwl 832 Harrison
Miller James, cabinet maker with J. Peirce, bds 333 Bush
Miller James, conductor, North Beach & M. R. R. Co
Miller James, hatter with K. Meussdorffer, dwl 248 Tehama
Miller James, teamster with Wm. H. Green
Miller James M. carpenter, dwl N s Fell nr Laguna
Miller J. E. clerk with C. V. Gillespie, dwl 655 Clay
Miller Jeremiah, mining superintendent, dwl 232 Sixth
MILLER J. FRANK, deputy collector and auditor, Custom House, res Oakland
MILLER J. H. collector, office 404 Montgomery, dwl 574 Mission
Miller J. H. engineer with S.S. Culverwell, 29 Fremont, dwl 777 Market

Miller *(J. L.)* & Washburn *(J. M.)* groceries and liquors, 131 Third, dwl 617 Mason
Miller J. L. purser steamer Senator, dwl 928 Clay
Miller John, dwl Bryant nr Third
Miller John, baker, Sandy Hill Bakery, dwl NE cor Clay and Mason
Miller John, bedstead factory, 307 Market, dwl 17 Belden
Miller John, butcher with Abram Newman, dwl 553 Mission
Miller John, clerk, dwl 520 Bryant
Miller John, deck hand, steamer Chrysopolis
Miller John, foreman, dwl 9 Vassar Place
Miller John, jeweler with R. B. Gray & Co. dwl SE cor Dupont and Filbert
Miller John, matress maker with Goodwin & Co. dwl E s Franklin bet Bush and Austin
Miller John, model maker, dwl SE cor Austin and Franklin
Miller John, saddler, dwl 655 Washington
Miller John, stevedore, dwl 308 Folsom
Miller John, steward, Ocean House
Miller John F. (col'd) porter, dwl 821 Vallejo
Miller John H. (col'd) porter, dwl W s Selina Place
Miller John J. armorer, dwl SW cor First and Mkt
Miller John J. groceries and liquors, SE cor Sutter and Leavenworth
Miller John J. laborer, dwl Original House
Miller John L. engineer, Chace's Mill, dwl 777 Mkt
Miller John M. cabinet maker, 329½ Kearny, dwl Hayes' Valley
Miller Joseph H. carpenter, dwl 39 Second
Miller *(J. W.)* & Hall *(Abraham)* hay and grain, 418 Market, dwl 553 Leavenworth
Miller *(Louis)* & Brunning *(William)* groceries and liquors, SW cor Jessie and Annie
MILLER L. & CO. *(William J. Gray)* butchers, stalls 12, 59, and 60 Wash Mkt, dwl 732 Vallejo
Miller L. physician, dwl St. Lawrence House
Miller L. dwl 4 St. Mark Place
Miller L. H. jeweler, 210 Clay, dwl St. Lawrence House
Miller Louis & Co. *(Benjamin Tienken)* groceries and liquors, 725 Jackson, dwl NW cor Jessie and Annie
Miller Louis, cook, What Cheer House Restaurant
Miller Louis, jeweler, 614 Sac, dwl 26 Geary
Miller Louis, laborer, dwl S s Bernard bet Taylor and Jones
Miller Margaret (widow) domestic, 616 Sacramento
Miller Mary Mrs. dwl 29 Commercial
Miller Mary E. Miss, with Grover & Baker Sewing Machine Co. dwl Natoma bet Second and Third
Miller Mary J. (widow, col'd) dwl W s August Alley bet Green and Union
Miller M. J. clerk, dwl NE cor Clementina and Third
Miller Nancy M. (widow) dwl N s Camp bet Second Avenue and Guerrero
Miller Nicolaus, cabinet maker, dwl 1510 Powell
Miller Peter, book keeper with Donohoe, Kelly & Co. dwl Geary bet Gough and Octavia
Miller Peter, cook, 619 Market
Miller Peter, tailor, dwl 728 Market
Miller Peter C. stevedore, dwl 411 Folsom
MILLER *(Peter P.)* & CUTTER *(Thomas A.)* What Cheer Laundry, What Cheer House, 125 Leidesdorff, dwl 17 Langton
Miller R. J. carpenter, dwl First St. House
Miller Robert B. compositor, Morning Call, dwl SW cor Sacramento and Leavenworth
Miller Rose Miss, dress maker, dwl St. Lawrence H
Miller R. S. recording clerk, Custom House, dwl 13 Hampton Place
Miller Salvador F. clerk with Haight & Pierson, dwl 1006 Clay
Miller Samuel, dwl What Cheer House
Miller Samuel, with B. Miller, 6 Metropolitan Market, dwl 215 Fourth

Miller Samuel, seaman, dwl 238 Stewart
Miller Samuel, teacher writing, dwl 67 Minna
Miller Sophus, seaman, dwl 44 Sacramento
Miller Stephen, baker, SE cor Mission and Fourth
Miller Stephen, baker, dwl 13 Pinckney Place
Miller Stephen G. accountant with Edward Hall & Co. dwl 126 Silver
Miller S. W. Miller's Bakery, NE cor Clementina and Third
Miller Thomas *(Miller & Bro.)* dwl 655 Mission
Miller Thomas, captain sloop Thomas Brown, office Pier 7 Stewart
Miller Thomas S. broker, dwl 823 Bush
Miller Thomas S. hardware, 729 Davis, dwl 823 Bush
Miller W. cooper, dwl Fulton bet Twenty-Second and Twenty-Third
Miller Washington (col'd) coachman with James B. Haggin, 1019 Jackson
Miller W. G. wood turner, dwl 233 Sutter
Miller W. H. *(Alsgood & M.)* dwl NW cor Jackson and Drumm
Miller William, dwl 317 Clementina
Miller William, dwl 766 Mission
Miller William, barber, dwl 701 Davis
Miller William, coal, dwl 5 Calhoun
Miller William, drayman, 430 California
Miller William, fur maker, dwl 323 Pine
Miller William, hackman, Plaza, dwl W s White nr Green
Miller William, porter, 408 California, dwl S s Sutter bet Laguna and Buchanan
Miller William, wig maker, dwl N s Pine bet Leavenworth and Hyde
Miller William B. shoe making, 413 East, dwl Hinckley nr Kearny
MILLER WILLIAM C. druggist and apothecary, SE cor Pacific and Stockton, dwl SW cor Taylor and Broadway
MILLER WILLIAM H. collector, office Pacific Fruit Market, dwl NE cor Union and Mason
Miller William X. butcher, NE cor Mason and Broadway
Miller *(W. J.)* & Co. commission merchants, 123 Clay
Miller W. N. carpenter, dwl 361 Minna
Miller W. P. architect, office room 27 Mercantile Library Building, dwl 4 Geary Place
Millerton and Owens River Valley Transportation and Road Co. office 1 Government House
Millertz Charles, with Henry Bocken, dwl New Atlantic Hotel
Millet M. (widow) dress maker, dwl 115 Third
Millett M. T. (widow) dwl 318 Sutter
Millett Olive (widow) dwl 57 Natoma
Milligan Ellen Miss, saleswoman, 20 Montgomery, dwl 616 Mission
Milligan Mary Ann Miss, domestic, 312 Stockton
Milliken Frank C. teamster with Robert Pennell & Co. dwl 140 Silver
Milliken George E. carpenter, dwl 121 Natoma
Milliken Henry, dwl 218 Stockton
Milliken Isaac T. notary public and mining secretary, office 608 Merchant, dwl 327 Bush
Milliken John M. office 405 Front room 4, dwl 538 Second
Milliken Seth *(R. Stewart & Co.)* dwl 218 Stock
Milliken William H. machinist, Vulcan Foundry, dwl 218 Stockton
Milliken John *(Millikin Brothers, Sacramento)* office 405 Front, dwl 538 Second
Milliman Delos P. bakery and groceries, SW cor Broadway and Scott
Mills Alfred, mate, steamer Reliance
Mills *(David J.)* & Evans *(William)* milk dealers agents Green Brothers, 6 June, dwl 638 Mission
MILLS D. O. president Bank California, office SW cor Washington and Battery, dwl 1117 Stockton
Mills Gilbert E. blacksmith, dwl Golden Gate Hotel

Mills Henry, blacksmith, Phœnix Iron Wolks, dwl 45 Third
Mills John, night clerk, Russ House
Mills John C. driver with Henry H. Edmunds
Mills John J. attorney at law, dwl 509 Bush
Mills Joseph, dwl 438 Natoma
Mills Louise E. (widow) dwl 75 Natoma
Mills Luther R. liquor saloon, 16 Sutter, dwl Roadside cor Valencia and Twenty-First
Mills Martha Mrs. dress maker, dwl 130 Second
Mills Philo, with L. B. Benchley & Co. dwl 613 Pine
Mills Robert, glass stainer, 12 Fourth, res San Mateo
Mills Robert, laborer, dwl 629 California
Mills Robert, plumber, dwl Mills Place nr Dupont
Mills Thomas, tinsmith, dwl N s Filbert bet Sansom and Montgomery
Mills Thomas G. manufacturer stereoscopes, dwl N s Mission bet Fifth and Sixth
Mills W. conductor, Omnibus R. R. Co
Mills William, blacksmith, dwl 728 Market
Millsner L. & Co. (M. Masse) pawnbrokers, 752 Washington, dwl 629 Sutter
Millsner Leopold, watch maker, 707 Clay, dwl 627 Sutter
Millspaugh George, laborer, 414 Brannan, dwl 220 Ritch
Milmo Anne, domestic with William R. Brown, N s Mission bet Tenth and Eleventh
Milne David, sail maker, dwl S s Perry bet Fourth and Fifth
Milne George, plumber with J. K. Prior, 730 Montgomery, dwl 1026 Montgomery
Milne John A. clerk, 228 Bush, dwl 216 Minna
Milnes William, conductor, dwl 59 Tehama
Milnor George, painter, dwl 636 Commercial
Milwain Alexander, carpenter, dwl E s Howard bet Twenty-First and Twenty-Second
Milzner M. boots and shoes, 322 Kearny, dwl 114 Stevenson
Mina Rica D'Los Flores G. & S. M. Co. office 423 Washington
Mindermann Henry, groceries and liquors, 520 Broadway
Mineban T. dwl 414 Market
Miner Butler B. law student with Williams & Thornton, dwl 18 First
Miner Ellen Miss, 735 Harrison
Miner George W. painter, dwl SE cor Linden and Franklin Hayes' Valley
Miner James, bricklayer, dwl 125 Shipley, rear
Miner John, carpenter, dwl 8 Bay State Row
Miner John B. carpenter, dwl NE cor Tehama and Fourth
Miner Loran, S. F. Laundry, 1130 Folsom, dwl 227 Sixth
Miner Terrence, waiter U. S. Restaurant, dwl cor California and Drumm
Miner Thomas E. hay dealer, cor Commercial and East, dwl 735 Harrison
Miner William H. compositor, Alta California, dwl 511 Howard
MINERS' FOUNDRY AND MACHINE WORKS, 247-251 First, Howland, Angell & King proprietors
Minerva House, F. W. Paupitz proprtr, 123 Jackson
Mingute William, ship carpenter, dwl 308 Beale
Mini Wakan S. M. Co. office 24 Government House, 502 Washington
MINING AND SCIENTIFIC PRESS (weekly) Dewey & Co. proprietors and publishers, office 505 Clay
Minney Frank, fireman, S. F. & San José R.R. Co. dwl SE cor Valencia and Sixteenth
Minney William, fireman, S. F. & San José R. R. Co. dwl SE cor Valencia and Sixteenth
Minnie Lottie Petroleum Co. (Los Angeles) office 613 Merchant
Minnigan James, news collector with T. E. Baugh, NW cor Francis and Lombard

Minns George W. principal State Normal School, dwl 709 Taylor
Minor John, spinner, S. F. P. Woolen Mills, dwl North Point bet Polk and Van Ness Avenue
Minor Richard (col'd) miner, dwl 1214 Pacific
Minot Joseph, professor music, dwl S s Polk Alley
Minseng Nicholas, maltster, Albany Brewery
Minson Charles, policeman, City Hall, dwl 1016 Stockton
Minturn Charles, president Contra Costa Steam Navigation Co. office Vallejo nr Davis, dwl 913 Battery
Minturn John, stock broker, office 528 Montgomery
Minturn Mathew A. glass blower, Pacific Glass Works. dwl nr cor Gilmore and Kentucky
Minturn William B. purser steamer Pacific
Miranda Manuel, harness maker with Hyde & McClennen, dwl 19 Stone
Mirandette Pierre, workman with L. Artigues, dwl NW cor Sixteenth and Rhode Island
Mirando Antonio, vegetable garden, Visitacion Valley
Mirando Mikelo, vegetable garden, Visitacion Valley
Mires John C. (Perkins & M.) dwl Francisco bet Powell and Mason
Mirth George, blacksmith, dwl W s Morey Alley
Misgill (Timothy F.) & Cooper (A. F.) veterinary surgeons and blacksmiths, 815 Market, dwl 414 Post, rear
Mish Barrow, student, dwl 208 Eddy
Mish Meyer, bar keeper, 420 Commercial
Mish Phineas, dwl 6 Kearny
Mish Sarah Mrs. millinery, 6 Kearny
MISH WOLFF, liquor saloon, 420 Commercial
Miskel Michael, laborer, dwl 7 Sherwood
Mission Street Brewery, Durkin & Co. proprietors, 608 Mission
MISSION WOOLEN MILLS, Donald McLennan and Simon Lazard proprietors, office 115 Battery
Mistre Simon, coppersmith, 417 Kearny, dwl 716 Washington
Mitchell A. F. jeweler, bds American Exchange
Mitchell Alexander, waiter, 25 Third
Mitchell B. F. dwl 557 Mission
Mitchell B. J. stationery, 414 Sacramento
Mitchell Catharine Mrs. dwl cor Greenwich and San
Mitchell Charles, clerk, dwl 1009 Mason
Mitchell Charles, pickle manufactory, 114 Sacramento, dwl SE cor Stockton and Filbert
Mitchell Charles, shipping merchant, dwl 1024 Bat
Mitchell Charles F. porter, 404 Front
Mitchell Charles H. with George L. Murdock, 24 Battery
Mitchell Daniel H. stock broker, dwl International Hotel
Mitchell David, teller Bank California, bds 246 Jessie
MITCHELL DAVID C. & CO. ship chandlers, S s Broadway bet Battery and Front, dwl N s Vallejo nr Mason
Mitchell D. H. dwl International Hotel
Mitchell E. J. (widow) dwl 5 Martha Place
Mitchell E. J. (widow) dwl 9 Dupont
Mitchell Elizabeth Mrs. (col'd) dwl 1214 Pacific
Mitchell Erastus, vegetables, 1409 Dupont
Mitchell Fannie Miss, assistant, Greenwich Street School, dwl 739 Pine
Mitchell F. K. teacher music, Public Schools, dwl 131 Montgomery
Mitchell Fred. seaman stm Orizaba
Mitchell George, actor, Maguire's Opera House
Mitchell George H. book keeper, 606 Clay, dwl 1111 Montgomery
Mitchell George W. seaman, dwl 54 Sacramento
Mitchell Henry M. boiler maker, Union Foundry, dwl N s Mission bet First and Ecker
Mitchell James, clerk, stm Oakland, res Brooklyn
Mitchell James, pressman, Alta California, dwl 1805½ Stockton

Mitchell James, wines and liquors, 609 Battery

Mitchell James H. porter, dwl W s Howard bet Eighteenth and Nineteenth

Mitchell Jaques, carpenter, dwl 315 Bush

Mitchell J. E. tobacco and cigars, 4 Second, dwl 633 Market

Mitchell Jennie Miss, domestic, 618 California

Mitchell John, express wagon, dwl Seventh nr Harrison

Mitchell John, groceries and liquors, 174 Stevenson, dwl 25 Everett

Mitchell John, hostler, dwl Bay View

Mitchell John, laborer, dwl 25 Everett

MITCHELL *(John C.)* & PLEGE *(Henry)* butter, cheese, etc. 50 and 51 Washington Market, dwl 1717 Mason

Mitchell John F. groceries and liquors, NW cor Post and Hyde

Mitchell John H. book binder with Edward Bosqui & Co. dwl 1805½ Stockton

Mitchell John H. workman with Turner & Rundle, dwl Solano nr Potrero Avenue

Mitchell John M. farmer, Ocean House Road 3 miles from Mission Dolores

Mitchell Joseph, dwl 35 Sacramento

Mitchell Joseph, porter, dwl 36 Miles Court

Mitchell Joseph, porter with Hoadley & Co

Mitchell Lawrence, hostler, 211 Pine

Mitchell Louis, boot maker, dwl 402 Bush

Mitchell Lydia G. (widow) dwl with Wm. H. Mead

Mitchell Lydia W. Mrs. dwl 329 Minna

Mitchell Maria Miss, domestic, 513 Minna

Mitchell Mrs. & Mrs. Graham Paris Millinery, dwl 59 Second

Mitchell Murray, blacksmith, 350 Ritch

Mitchell Ossian C. *(C. J. Hawley & Co.)* dwl W s Eleventh bet Market and Mission

Mitchell Patrick, drayman, bds 761 Mission

Mitchell Patrick, hostler, 532 California, dwl E s Clara nr Bush

Mitchell Peter, asphaltum worker, office SW cor Post and Kearny, dwl 541 Mission

Mitchell Peter, seaman, dwl E s Main nr Market

Mitchell Richard W. night watchman, Pacific Mail S. S. Co.'s Wharf, dwl 31 Rousch

MITCHELL *(Robert)* & ADAMS *(Grove)* wholesale wines and liquors (Virginia City) office 405 Front, dwl Cosmopolitan Hotel

Mitchell Robert, dwl N s Willow Avenue bet Van Ness Avenue and Franklin

Mitchell Robert, laborer, dwl 35 Sacramento

Mitchell T. dry goods, dwl 21½ Hunt

Mitchell Thomas, carpenter, dwl Broderick Engine House

Mitchell Thomas, workman with John M. Mitchell

Mitchell Thomas F. pump and block maker, 22 Drumm, dwl 739 Green

Mitchell Thomas S. dwl 614 Taylor

Mitchell William, contractor night work, dwl 140 Sutter

Mitchell William, farmer, dwl bet Ocean House Road and Lake Honda

Mitchell William, mail clerk, Evening Bulletin, 620 Montgomery, dwl 1807 Stockton

Mitchell William, spice manufacturer, Howard Engine Co. No. 3

Mitchell William H. wholesale and retail wines and liquors, 12 Oregon, dwl NW cor Bush and San

Mitcheson Charles (col'd) dwl 1328 Pacific

Mitchler Gottlieb, dwl S s Riley W s Taylor

Mitrovich Peter & Co. proprietors Ferry House, 715 Davis

Mittlen James, laborer, dwl 140 Stewart

Mix Warren, tin roofer, dwl What Cheer House

Mizker Philip, cook, dwl SW cor Dupont and Bdwy

Mobery Peter, laborer, NE cor Filbert and Leav

Mochet François *(Levy & M.)* dwl 8 Polk Lane

Mocker Rudolph, tinsmith, dwl 4 St. Mark Place

Mocker William sen. dwl 4 St. Mark Place

Mocker William, meat market, NW cor O'Farrell and Mason, and furnished rooms, NW cor Kearny and St. Mark Place, dwl 10 St. Mark Place, rear

Modry Marcus, cigar maker, cor Bush and Devisidero

Moebus Frederick, shoe maker, dwl 6 Broadway

Moeller George, hatter, dwl 708 Pine

Moeller Jacob, waiter, 308 Montgomery

Moenning Gunther, stoves and tinware, 140 Fourth

Moesta John P. *(Lohmann & M.)* dwl 644 Clay

MOFFAT EUGENE *(Baldwin & M.)* dwl W s Ninth nr Brannan

Moffat Henry, butcher with A. J. Shrader, dwl N s Brannan bet Eighth and Ninth

MOFFAT W. P. attorney at law, Dunbar Alley nr Merchant, dwl 1124 Sacramento

Moffatt George, salesman, 229 Mont, dwl 548 Mission

Moffatt John, gas fitter, dwl NW cor Jessie and Anna

Moffett Albert B. carpenter, nr cor Hickory and North avenues

Moffett George M. carpenter, dwl nr cor Hickory and North avenues

Moffett Orson, livery stable, 325 Mission

Moffitt George, clerk, SW cor Montgomery and Pine, bds Brooklyn Hotel

Moffitt James *(Blake & M.)* dwl 1010 Clay

Moffitt John W. clerk with W. H. Keith & Co. dwl NE cor Montgomery and Broadway

Moffitt Margaret (widow) dwl NE cor Montgomery and Broadway

Moffitt Thomas S. with Redington & Co. dwl 54 Third

Mogan *(Antonio)* & Co. *(Joseph R. Mogan)* furniture and bedding, 900 Market, bds 124 Natoma

Mogan John, butcher, 47 Metropolitan Market, dwl S s O'Farrell bet Polk and Van Ness Avenue

Mogan John P. calker, dwl 41 Louisa

Mogan Joseph R. *(Mogan & Co.)* dwl 124 Natoma

Mogan Patrick, clerk, 47 Metropolitan Market, dwl S s O'Farrell bet Polk and Van Ness Avenue

Moger Abraham, book keeper with G. M. Garwood & Co. dwl 235 Seventh bet Howard and Folsom

Moholy Jeremiah *(McGlauflin & M.)* dwl S s Harrison bet Seventh and Eighth

Mohr Charles *(Kleinschroth & M.)* dwl SW corner Kearny and Bush

Mohrhardt P. F. manufacturer hair jewelry 251 Third and cutter with Davis & Schafer

Mohrig C. F. watches and jewelry, 613 Washington

Mohrmann Frederick, groceries and liquors, SW cor Broadway and Kearny

Moigneu L. J. F. *(Salomon & Co.)* dwl 211 Sutter

Moise Henry, gilder and carver and restorer old paintings, 181 Jessie, dwl 7 Mary

Mojica D. guitar and violin maker, 1026 Kearny

Moldrup A. drayman, Jackson St. Wharf

MOLINIER JOHN Rev. pastor Notre Dame des Victoires, N s Bush nr Stockton

MOLITOR AUGUST P. assayer, office 611 Commercial, dwl 804 Stockton

Molitor Julius, assayer with A. P. Molitor, dwl 804 Stockton

Molitor Titus, assayer with A. P. Molitor, dwl 804 Stockton

Molk Henry *(Meyer & M.)* dwl NW cor Dupont and Green

Molk Henry, drayman, Pacific Flour Mills

Moller J. L. C. bar keeper, 228 Montgomery

Molloy Bessie Miss, assistant, Tehama St. School, dwl 314 Sutter

Molloy Hugh, maltster with Durkin & Co. dwl 248 Minna

Molloy Hugh Mrs. milliner and dress maker, 248 Minna

Molloy James, laborer, dwl 1107 Pacific

Molloy *(John)* & O'Connor *(John)* produce commission, 64 Clay

Molloy Patrick, cooper, dwl 218 Washington
Molloy Paul, dwl W s Howard nr Thirteenth
Moloch Charles, baker, dwl 202 Dupont
Moloch Frederick, produce, dwl 834 Harrison
Moloney Thomas, blacksmith, dwl 26 Ritch
Molony David, painter with Hopps & Kanary, dwl NE cor Van Ness Avenue and Pacific
Molony Patrick, tailor, dwl 319 Bush
Moloy Ann Miss, domestic, SW cor Jackson and Larkin
Moloy Mary Miss, domestic, 620 Sacramento
Molt John P. South Park Market, 432 Third, dwl 428 Third
Monaghan Bernard, apprentice, Pacific Foundry
Monahan Anna Miss, domestic, 1000 Pine
Monahan Bridget Miss, domestic, S s Sixteenth bet Folsom and Howard
Monahan Bridget Miss, domestic, 1121 Stockton
Monahan Daniel, carpenter, City Water Works, dwl Fort Point
Monahan Elizabeth Miss, domestic, 320 Mason
Monahan Francis, carpenter, dwl W s Russ bet Folsom and Howard
Monahan Henry, book keeper, 620 Clay
Monahan Hugh, helper, Union Foundry, dwl 320 Tehama
Monahan James, laborer, dwl 31 St. Mark Place
Monahan John, dwl 430 Bush
Monahan John, box maker, dwl 23 Hunt
Monahan Joseph, lab, dwl E s Mary Lane nr Sutter
Monahan Mary Miss, dwl NW cor Sixth and Minna
Monahan Michael, laborer, dwl 726 O'Farrell, rear
Monahan Michael, laborer, dwl 213 Tehama
Monahan Patrick, boot maker, 620 Mission
Monahan Patrick L. workman with Horace Hawes
Monahan Thomas, laborer, dwl 426 Clementina
Monahan Thomas, plumber with John Kehoe, dwl 149 Minna
Monahan William, salesman, 34 Second, dwl 5 Jane
Monan Stephen, waiter, steamer Orizaba
Moubrone Baptiste, butcher, 310 Fifth
Moncharmont Prosper, compositor, Courrier de San Francisco, dwl 628 Mission
Monchaut Cyprian, job wagon, dwl 519 Geary
Mondelet *(François)* & Etienne *(T.)* restaurant, 837 Dupont, dwl 1018 Stockton
Moneigh Francis, cook, 524 Merchant
Monell George I. N. book keeper with I. S. Van Winkle, NE cor Battery and Bush
Monell Walter J. tailor with G. F. Walter & Co. dwl 931 Market
Moneypenny Charles, boarding, 136 and 138 Natoma bet Third and Fourth
Mong Kee (Chinese) washing, 605 Sansom
Monge François, butcher with Baptiste Monbrone, 308 Fifth
Moni Antonio *(Luis Jury & Co.)* dwl N s Page W Protestant Orphan Asylum
Monie Giraud, hairdresser and wig maker, 307 Montgomery, dwl 613½ Stockton
Monier Peter, champagne inspector, dwl 271 Stevenson
Monitor G. & S. M. Co. office 402 Front
MONITOR (weekly, Catholic) Thomas A. Brady editor and proprietor, 622 Clay
Monje A. G. groceries and liquors, 13 Stewart Pier 1
Monkcon Charles, ship carpenter, dwl 38 Frederick
Monks Richard B. policeman, City Hall, dwl 117 Perry
Monks Samuel, hairdresser, 816 Washington, dwl S s Broadway nr Hyde
Monks Sarah (widow) dwl S s Broadway bet Hyde and Larkin
Monmonier William B. merchant, dwl 937 Howard
Monnier George, porter, 431 Battery
Monnier Peter, porter, 423 Bat, dwl 271 Stevenson
Monnin George, shoe maker, dwl 3 Quincy
Monotti Vincent, soda maker, dwl NE cor Green and Dupont

Monotti Frederick, soda maker, dwl 115 First
Monroe Annie (widow) dwl 518 Pine
Monroe Charles F. engineer, dwl 777 Market
Monroe George, longshoreman, dwl W s Sansom bet Green and Union
Monroe Henry R. cook 612 Market, dwl 31 Geary
Monroe James, miller, dwl 608 Market
Monroe June (widow) dwl 308 Folsom
Monroe John, helper, dwl 225 Minna
Monroe M. dwl 559 Market
Monroe Petroleum Co. office 611 Clay
Monroe William R. book keeper, Cal. State Telegraph Co. dwl E s Larkin bet Green and Union
Monroe W. S. painter, dwl 228 Stevenson
Monsess Carsten, drayman, 517 Sacramento, dwl 247 Clara
Monster Hill G. & S. M. Co. office 1 Government House 502 Washington
MONSTERY THOMAS H. fencing and sparring academy, 534 Kearny cor Sacramento
Montag Peter, butcher, dwl Brannan St. Bridge
Montague Ann Mrs. dwl 60 First
Montague James, machinist with David Stoddart, dwl NW cor Mission and Third
Montague Michael, plasterer, dwl 127 Tehama
Montague W. W. *(Locke & M.)* dwl Lick House
Montano Francisco, compositor, dwl S s Vallejo bet Dupont and Kearny
Monte Cristo G. & S. M. Co. office 338 Mont
Montebelda John, dwl 518 Pacific
Monteiro Antonio P. book keeper with John Middleton & Son, dwl 323 Sutter
Montell Andres, seaman, dwl 20 Commercial
Montell Edgar, mariner, dwl with Nathan Rogers
Montgomery A. assistant engineer, Spring Valley W. W. Co. dwl cor Polk and Beach
MONTGOMERY BLOCK, E s Montgomery bet Clay and Washington
Montgomery Edward, seaman, dwl N s Broadway bet Polk and Van Ness Avenue
Montgomery Frank, molder, Jackson Foundry, dwl 2 California
Montgomery Henry, dwl N s Eddy bet Polk and Larkin
Montgomery Isabella Miss, hoop maker, 24 Second, dwl 326 Beale
Montgomery James, porter, Donohoe, Kelly & Co
Montgomery John (col'd) dwl 805 Stockton
Montgomery Lewis H. molder, S. F. Iron Works, dwl Clara bet Sutter and Bush
Montgomery Margaret Miss, domestic with O. H. Willoughby, N s Sixteenth nr Hampshire
Montgomery Petroleum Co. office 302 Montgomery
Montgomery William, molder, Union Foundry, dwl 464 Jessie
Montlezun Alexander, cook, Clipper Restaurant
Monton T. engineer, dwl 34 Third
Montpellier Albert L. professor French, Union College, dwl 912 Clay
Montpellier M. L. Madame, teacher French, City Female Seminary, dwl 912 Clay
Montrose John B. real estate, dwl 1011 Taylor
Montweller Henry, potter, dwl SW cor Dupont and Broadway
Monumental Petroleum Co. (Colusa) office 611 Clay
Monz Susan, domestic, 720 Mission
Monznla Domini, stone cutter, dwl N s Riley nr Taylor
Mooar George Rev. editor Pacific, office 536 Clay
Moody Charles, with Starr & Riddle, 16 Drumm
Moody Charles, laborer, dwl 26 Sacramento
Moody Charles, pile driver, dwl 504 Howard
Moody Edwin, artist and engraver, dwl King bet Third and Fourth
Moody Francis, dwl 1420 Powell
Moody George P. dwl S s Market bet Seventh and Eighth
Moody H. K. carpenter, dwl 223 Beale
Moody J. A. carpenter and builder, dwl 915 Jackson

Moody James, sail maker, dwl 62 Clay
Moody John C. clerk with C. E. Hinckley & Co. dwl 310 Sutter
Moody Joseph L. *(Sinclair & M.)* dwl SE cor Lombard aud Jones
Moody S. S. laborer, North Point Warehouse, dwl 687 Market
Moody Thomas G. dwl 687 Market
Moody William E. book keeper with Uhrig & Co. dwl 8W cor Montgomery and Green
Moody William G. printer with Towne & Bacon, dwl 645 Third
Moon Adam B. carpenter, dwl 329 Pine
Moon Andrew J. dwl 3 Park Avenue
Moon Andrew J. book keeper with Coffey & Risdon, dwl W s Brannan bet Fifth and Sixth
Moon Benjamin F. dwl 535 Merchant
MOON GEORGE C. real estate agent, office 625 Merchant, dwl 102 Montgomery Block
Moon John, carpenter, dwl 329 Pine
Moon J. W. attorney at law, dwl 668 Harrison
Mooney Arthur, walter, dwl cor Stock and O'Farrell
Mooney B. D. Miss, house keeper, Niantic Hotel.
Mooney Catherine (widow) dwl NE cor Clay and Drumm
Mooney C. H. machinist, dwl 39 First
Mooney Charles, laborer, dwl 411 Pacific
Mooney Cornelius, Pony Express Saloon, NW cor Kearny and Commercial and second assistant Engineer S. F. Fire Department
Mooney Henry, laborer, Vulcan Iron Works
Mooney Hugh, seaman, dwl 25 Clementina
Mooney J. machinist, dwl 39 First
Mooney James, keeper with S. C. Harding
Mooney June Miss, domestic, dwl 260 Clementina
Mooney John H. repairing sewing machines, 111 Montgomery
Mooney Mary Miss, domestic, 1325 Powell
Mooney Michael, seaman, dwl 30 Sacramento
Mooney Patrick, laborer, dwl W s Taylor bet Filbert and Greenwich
Mooney Rose, stewardess steamer Yosemite
MOONEY THOMAS, president California Building Loan and Savings Society, office 404 Montgomery, dwl S s Fulton nr Larkin
Moor James, dwl 630 Commercial
Moor William H. with C. S. Navigation Co. NE cor Front and Jackson
Moorcroft Thomas C. drayman, 116 California
Moore Albert, dwl International Hotel
Moore Alfred *(Moore & Co.)* dwl Cosmopolitan Hotel
Moore Amanda E. dwl 1102 Pacific
Moore Andrew, wood and coal yard, 1210 Powell
Moore Ann Mrs. express wagon, Oak Mrs.
Moore Bartholomew, laborer, Market St. R. R. Co. dwl N s Grove bet Gough and Octavia
Moore B. C. ship clerk, dwl 18 Clarence Place
Moore Benjamin, sash and blind maker with J. McGill & Co. dwl 612 Pine
Moore B. F. attorney at law, office 522 Montgomery, dwl 439 Sixth
Moore Carrie Miss, dwl 204 Seventh
Moore Catharine Miss, domestic, S s Pine bet Mason and Taylor
Moore Catharine (widow) dwl E s Salmon bet Mason and Taylor
Moore Charles, dwl 22 Park Avenue
Moore Charles, seaman, steamer Senator
Moore Charles H. with B. & J. S. Doe, dwl 13 Anthony
Moore Charles W. physician, office and dwl 643 Com
Moore David, drayman with Hawley & Co. dwl N s Folsom bet Tenth and Eleventh
Moore Delaney C. with N. Davidson, Glen Ranch nr S. F. Cordage Factory
Moore Edmund, carpenter, dwl 777 Market
Moore Edward E. seed store, 425 Washington, dwl 8W cor Florida and Twenty-First

Moore Edward F. carriage trimmer, 111 Bush, dwl 118 Ellis
Moore E. L. engineer, Spring Valley W. W
Moore Elliott J. attorney at law, office 77 Montgomery Block, dwl 908 Clay
Moore Ezekiel J. average adjuster, 425 Washington, dwl SW cor Florida and Twenty-First
Moore Francis, laborer, Lone Mountain Cemetery
Moore George, liquor saloon, junction Sacramento and Market
Moore George, plasterer, dwl W s Gilbert bet Bryant and Brannan
Moore George A. drayman, 310 Commercial, dwl 505 O'Farrell
Moore George C. dwl 102 Montgomery Block
MOORE *(George H.)* & CO. *(Alfred Moore)* shipping and commission merchants, 17 Davis and Rincon Dock, dwl 1117 Pine
Moore George W. tinsmith with Osgood & Stetson, 219 Commercial
Moore Henry, dwl 657 Howard
Moore Henry J. plumber, 406 Mont, dwl 48 Minna
MOORE HENRY K. attorney at law, office with Sidney V. Smith, dwl 657 Howard
MOORE HORACE H. librarian, Mercantile Library Association, dwl 822 Bush
Moore Isaac, carpenter with S. S. Culverwell, dwl 270 Clementina
Moore Isabella Miss, dress maker, dwl NE corner Fourth and Bryant
Moore James, dwl 938 Mission
Moore James, broker, dwl 624 Sacramento
Moore James, carder, Mission Woolen Mills, dwl W s Treat Avenue nr Twenty-Second
Moore James, coppersmith, dwl 222 Fremont
Moore James, engineer, dwl 63 Minna
Moore James B. book keeper with Dodge Bros. & Co. dwl 821 California
Moore *(James H.)* & Higgins *(Mark W.)* 671 Howard, dwl 8W cor Sixth and Stevenson
Moore James S. drayman, 103 California, dwl N s Ellis nr Van Ness Avenue
Moore J. H. clerk with Moore & Co. dwl 119 Natoma
Moore John, dwl 668 Harrison
Moore John, driver with John T. Newman, dwl W s Ritter nr Harrison
Moore John, gas fitter, S. F. Gas Co
Moore John, groom, dwl 342 Brannan
Moore John, laborer, dwl 1020 Pacific
Moore John, laborer, bds 606 Third
Moore John, laborer, S. F. Gas Co. dwl E s Zoe bet Bryant and Brannan
Moore John, wood and coal, 662 Mission, dwl 1020 Pacific
Moore John A. *(J. B. Holmes & Co.)* dwl 804 Howard
Moore John A. policeman, City Hall, dwl 473 Jessie
Moore John C. salesman with N. B. Jacobs & Co. 423 Front, dwl 634 Mission
Moore John F. drayman with David B. Sherman, dwl 237 Beale
Moore John J. Rev. (col'd) pastor Zion Church, dwl 331 Union
Moore John J. well borer, dwl SE cor Folsom and Twenty-Second
Moore John M. broker, office 77 Montgomery Blk, dwl 630 Market
Moore John W. private watchman, dwl 719 Davis
Moore Joseph *(Vulcan Iron Works Co.)* superintendent, dwl 642 Second
MOORE JOSEPH H. attorney at law, office 77 and 78 Montgomery Block, dwl 668 Harrison
Moore Joseph John, carpenter, dwl S s Fulton nr Van Ness Avenue
Moore J. Preston, broker, dwl 33 Hawthorne
Moore Justin, lumber dealer, dwl 714 Howard
Moore Kate (widow) dwl 9 Stockton Place
Moore Lilly Miss, actress, Olympic, dwl 116 Natoma

Moore Margaret (widow) dwl 204 Seventh
Moore Martha Miss, dwl 204 Seventh
Moore Mary (widow) dwl 10 Stockton Place
Moore Mary A. Miss, domestic, 1209 Kearny
Moore Mary J. (widow) dwl NW cor Powell and Lombard
Moore Nathan W. private school, 725 Bush
Moore Nathaniel, salesman with Taaffe & Co. 107 Battery, dwl 736 Folsom
Moore Nathaniel, ship carpenter, dwl W s Jane Pl
Moore Patrick, laborer, dwl 1410 Taylor
Moore Philip C. sawyer, Chace's Mills, dwl 28 San
Moore Phillip P. carpenter, dwl SE cor Sansom and Bush
MOORE R. C. superintendent Alta Job Printing Office, 538 Sacramento, dwl 635 Second
Moore Richard, marble cutter, 67 Fourth, dwl Winthrop House
Moore Robert, baker, 719 Battery, dwl E s Rousch nr Howard
Moore Robert S. phonographic reporter, 425 Washington, dwl SW cor Twenty-First and Florida
MOORE SAMUEL W. seed warehouse, 414 California, dwl 812 Powell
Moore Stewart, cooper, S. F. & P. Sugar Co. dwl 155 Shipley
Moore Thomas *(Zeglio & M.)* dwl SW cor Fifth and Stevenson
Moore Thomas, wool grader with Clark & Perkins, N s Commerce nr Battery, dwl 308 Jessie
Moore Thomas, wood and coal, 662 Mission
Moore Thomas L. merchant, dwl 204 Seventh
Moore William, laborer, Bay Sugar Refinery, dwl S s Union bet Battery and Sansom
Moore William, mariner, dwl King bet Third and Fourth
Moore William, Miners' Exchange Saloon, 40 Jackson
Moore William, plasterer, Volunteer Engine Co. No. 7
Moore William, plumber with Taylor & Iredale
Moore William, seaman, dwl 54 Sacramento
Moore William, teamster with C. L. Place & Co
Moore William H. dwl N s Union bet San and Bat
Moore William H. dwl Occidental Hotel
Moore William H. tinsmith with Felix Daly, dwl 12 Sutter
Moore William T. gents' furnishing goods, 250 Third
Moore Z. W. & Co. *(Jonas C. Gilfillan)* fruit and vegetables, 9 Washington Market, dwl NE cor Montgomery and Pacific
Moore, see More
Moorman John, seaman, dwl 20 Commercial
Moors H. C. & Co. *(John D. Swett)* street contractors, office 423 Washington room 1, dwl S s Jessie bet Third and Fourth
Moose John, handcartman, Pacific St. Wharf
Mooser William, architect, office 28 Exchange Building, dwl NW cor Folsom and Thirteenth
Mooshake Frederick Rev. pastor First German Evangelical Lutheran Church, dwl 245 Stevenson
Morairty Eliza Miss, domestic with Jeffery Cullen
Moralas E. Mrs. liquor saloon, 728 Pacific
Morales Juan, compositor, dwl S s Broadway bet Dupont and Stockton
Moran Annie Miss, domestic, 804 Stockton
Moran Annie Miss, milliner, 764 Howard
Moran Barney, painter with Sweett & Gadsby, dwl 110 William
Moran Benjamin, dwl 10 Stewart
Moran Edward, dwl W s Jones bet Filbert and Greenwich
Moran Edward, hostler, 532 California, dwl Clara nr Bush
Moran Edward, painter, dwl SW cor Franklin and Austin
Moran Esther Miss, domestic, 435 Natoma
Moran Felix, laborer, dwl 409 Sutter, rear

Moran Frank, dwl 24 Sansom
Moran Hannah, laundress, Lick House
Moran Harrison, with O. F. Swett, milk ranch, Old San José Road 3 miles from City Hall
Moran *(John)* & Co. produce commission, 114 Clay, dwl 335 Tehama
Moran John, dwl E s Nevada nr Folsom
Moran John, laborer with Hey & Meyn
Moran John, laborer, dwl 528 Union, rear
Moran John, porter, dwl NE cor Pine and Gough
Moran John, stone cutter, bds E s Cemetery Avenue bet Sutter and Post
Moran Maria Miss, domestic, NW cor Chestnut and Dupont
Moran Michael, laborer, dwl 154 Shipley
Moran Nellie, laundress, 114 Dora
Moran Patrick, workman, S. F. & P. Sugar Co. dwl S s Mary nr Chesley
Moran Peter & Thomas, tobacconists, 708 and 710 Battery
Moran Thomas *(P. & T. Moran)* 710 Battery
Moran Thomas, boot maker, dwl 402 Bush
Moran Thomas, carpenter, dwl 304 Pine
Moran Thomas, groom, dwl NE cor Mission and Jane
Moran William, laborer with Edward J. Quirk
Moran William, waiter, Occidental Hotel, dwl 62 Stevenson
Morante Joseph, store keeper, Miners' Restaurant
Morarty Dennis, laborer, dwl 16 Ecker
Morasky C. laundryman, dwl 20 Langton
Moraty John, laborer, dwl 24 Howard Court
Morchio Giacomo, with Lemoine, Gambert & Co. dwl Sansom bet Pacific and Broadway
Mordaunt H. waiter, Cosmopolitan Hotel
Mordecai Isaac T. carrier, Evening Bulletin and Call, dwl E s Mississippi nr Mariposa
More Samuel, salesman with Nudd, Low & Co. 410 Front, bds Russ House
Moreal DeBrevans Adolph, dwl 759 Mission
Moreau Eugene, machinist, Union Foundry, dwl Mason bet Bush and Pine
Moreau George, salesman, 633 Clay, dwl 635 Clay
Moreeno Francisco, fisherman, 5 Italian Fish Mkt
Moreeno José M. physician, office and dwl Mead House room 4
Morehead James, with S. Rosenblatt, 125 Montgomery, dwl Perry
Morehouse Annie (widow) dwl 361½ Minna
Morehouse George W. clerk with J. VanDoren, dwl E s Taylor bet Ellis and Eddy
Morehouse William P. assistant secretary S. F. Benevolent Association, dwl E s Taylor bet Ellis and Eddy
Morel Charles, vocalist, Maguire's Academy Music, dwl 1009 Powell
Morell A. J. agent estate J. S. Garwood, dwl 206 Ellis
Morell George, cook, Franklin Hotel, SE cor Sansom and Pacific
Morelli Jayicinth, fruit peddler, dwl N s Dupont Alley
Morelli Santi, vegetable garden, nr Bay View Park
Morelos Antonio, cigars and tobacco, 646 Pacific
Morenek John, handcartman, cor Vallejo and Dupont
Moreno Philip, laundryman, dwl SW cor Dupont and Broadway
Morey Henry S. machinist, dwl S s Sacramento bet Leavenworth and Hyde
Morey Henry S. machinist, Union Foundry, dwl 1117 Bush
Morey Simon B. dwl 1101 Clay
Morgan Addison, carpenter with A. A. Snyder, dwl 225 Minna
Morgan *(Amasa)* & Co. *(Herman J. Hartnagle)* fruits, SW cor Bryant and Third
Morgan Amasa, fruits and confectionery, 512 Montgomery, dwl 228 Stevenson
Morgan Benjamin, restaurant, SE cor Fourth and Clementina

Morgan Charles B. clerk with. Henry B. Williams, dwl Cosmopolitan Hotel
Morgan Charles B. driver with Wells, Fargo & Co. dwl 1018 Stockton
Morgan C. M. (widow) dwl 809 Pacific
Morgan Cynthia H. (widow) dwl 7 Hartman near Greenwich
Morgan David jr. salesman, Pier 10 Stewart, dwl 8 Scott
Morgan Edward, gardener, dwl 414 Market
Morgan Edward H. salesman with Badger & Lindenberger, dwl 1715 Dupont
Morgan E. M. first clerk, steamer Pacific
Morgan George, clerk with C. V. Gillespie
Morgan George A. (Irwin & Co.) dwl W s Stanford nr Brannan
Morgan George E. cashier, bank Wells, Fargo & Co. dwl 121 O'Farrell
Morgan George N. plasterer, dwl W s Stanford bet Townsend and Brannan
Morgan Henry H. book keeper with C. Clayton & Co. dwl 558 Folsom
Morgan James, dwl Lick House
Morgan James, watchman, S. F. & P. Sugar Co. dwl N s Grove bet Van Ness Av and Franklin
Morgan John, baker, dwl 140 Second
Morgan John, longshoreman, bds Telegraph House
Morgan John A. dwl 1811 Powell
Morgan John C. local policeman, City Hall, dwl Howard bet Twenty-First and Twenty-Second
Morgan (John S.) & Co. (John and Thomas Crellin) oysters, 31 Washington Market, dwl cor Mission and Temple
Morgan Joseph, handcartman, cor Kearny and California
Morgan Joseph A. sail loft, 221 Davis, dwl 32 Minna
Morgan L. A. Mrs. principal Fourth St. School, dwl 609 Folsom
Morgan Levi, brick maker, dwl E s Dolores nr Sixteenth
Morgan Lewis E. assistant assessor, U. S. Int. Rev. NW cor Battery and Commercial, dwl 1011 Bush
Morgan M. J. store keeper, U. S. Subsistence Department 208 Sansom, dwl 433 Tehama
Morgan Patrick, painter, dwl S s Tyler bet Hyde and Larkin
Morgan Peter, porter, dwl 129 St. Mark Place
Morgan Philip, grainer, dwl 625½ Mission
Morgan Richard, dwl 124 Natoma
MORGAN, (S. G.) STONE (Edward F.) & CO. commission merchants, 108 Front, res New Bedford, Mass
Morgan William, carpets, 1224 Stockton
Morgan William W. mail clerk, Alta California, dwl 808 Taylor nr Bush
Morganthau Max, importer and jobber gents' furnishing goods, cigars, etc. 418 Sacramento, dwl 1119 Stockton
Morgenstern A. accountant with S. Morgenstern, dwl SE cor Front and Broadway
Morgenstern Meyer, cloaks and mantillas, 410 Kearny
Morgenstern Robert, book keeper, Bank California, dwl 511 Lombard
Morgenstern Samuel, clothing, SW cor Pacific and Front, dwl SE cor Broadway and Front
Moriarti John, laborer, dwl 24 Howard Court
Moriarty Con, waiter, Occidental Hotel
Moriarty Jeremiah, job wagon, 423, Washington, dwl cor Ecker and Market
Moriarty Johanna Miss, domestic, 21 Ellis
Moriarty John, dwl 835 Broadway
Moriarty John, workman with W. Hall, Old San José Road
Moriarty Morris, laborer, S. F. & San José R. R. Co
Morice Margaret Miss, dwl S s Vallejo bet Hyde and Larkin
MORISON JAMES, physician, office and dwl 219 First

MORISON SAMUEL A. real estate, office NE cor Montgomery and Pine room 6 third floor, dwl 607 Sutter
MORISON, (Thomas A.) HARRIS (Albert H.) & CO. (Henry I. Hoyt and Thomas H. Morison) importers and manufacturers Star Brand shirts, collars, drawers, etc. 329 Sansom cor Sacramento, res New York
Morison Thomas H. (Morison, Harris & Co.) res New York
Morison, see Morrison
Moritz John C. & Co. (George Hassebach) Camanche Market, NW cor Powell and Filbert
Moritz Mark, commission merchant, office and dwl 209 Sansom
Moritz Michael (Hirshfeld & M.) dwl 902 Clay
Morken Herman F. Frank's Saloon, 316 Pine, dwl 630 O'Farrell
Morlock Frederick, butter, cheese, and eggs, 23 Metropolitan Market, dwl 89 Harrison
Morley Carmini, tenor, Italian Opera, dwl SW cor Washington and Breuham Place
MORNING CALL (daily) J. J. Ayers & Co. proprietors and publishers, office 612 Commercial
MORON (Benjamin) & RATTO (Charles) Golden City Coffee Saloon, 10 Stewart
Moroni Emilio, tailor, 1231 Dupont
Morony John, clerk, 423 Front, dwl 315 Minna
Morr Bertha (widow) dwl 921 Washington
Morrell Alexander, propertyman, Wilson's Circus
Morrell Charles, dwl 1009 Powell
Morrell Charles, musical instrument maker, dwl 321 Stockton
Morrell Charles, peddler, Dupont Alley nr Dupont
Morrell Ebenezer, brick maker, NE cor Twentieth and Florida
Morrell Frank D. carpenter, dwl 710 Pine
Morres (S.) & Cohen (Bernard) Excelsior Matches, N s Minna nr Fifth
Morrice William R. clerk, dwl Wright's Hotel, 210 Broadway
Morrill Joseph, coachman, Russ House, dwl 561 Bryant
Morrill O. C. buyer, American Exchange, dwl 634 Sutter
Morrill Warren P. printer with Towne & Bacon, dwl 602 Sutter
Morrill W. H. D. dwl Russ House
Morris A. dwl 632 Market
Morris Abraham, merchant, office 310 California, dwl 102 O'Farrell
Morris Anna Mrs. seamstress, dwl 509 Howard
MORRIS B. & CO. (John T. Littleford) manufacturing jewelers, 643 Sacramento, dwl 1010 Sutter
Morris Charles, book keeper with L. P. Fisher, dwl 811 Jackson
Morris Charles S. dwl 725 Broadway
Morris D. (Strelitz & Co.) dwl 25 Second
Morris Ellen (widow) produce, 10 Metropolitan Market, dwl SE cor Green and Sansom
Morris Frank, dwl 1114 Powell
Morris George H. salesman, Pier 12 Stewart, dwl NE cor Second and Brannan
Morris Henry, laborer, dwl NW cor Front and Pac
Morris Henry, machinist, dwl Manhattan House 705 Front
Morris Henry S. (col'd) pantryman steamer Chrysopolis, dwl 1110 Pacific
Morris Hermann, tailor, 125 Fourth
Morris Hertz, furniture wagon, cor Washington and Montgomery, dwl 118 Jessie
Morris J. (col'd) steward, dwl 355 First
Morris James, paver, dwl N s Geary bet Taylor and William
Morris James R. printer, Morning Call, dwl 906 Stockton
Morris John, tanner with Davis & Sedgley, dwl S. F. & San José R. R. nr Mariposa

Morris John W. ship joiner, dwl SW cor Pine and Kearny

Morris Joseph, dwl Original House

Morris Julius, cigar manufacturer, 744 Commercial, dwl 106 Natoma

Morris L. A. dress maker, 1110 Pacific

Morris Lawrence, handcartman, SW cor Market and Stewart

Morris Lewis, boot maker, dwl SW cor Dupont and Broadway

Morris M. P. variety stall, 9 and 10 Occidental Market, dwl 569 Mission

Morris Patrick J. grainer, 38 California, dwl 23 Howard Court

Morris Peter, express wagon, dwl 134 Natoma

Morris Peter, workman, S. F. & P. Sugar Co. dwl W s Nevada bet Folsom and Harrison

Morris Preston, mining secretary, office 526 Montgomery, dwl NW cor Fillmore and Hayes

Morris Reuben E. laborer, dwl W s Sansom bet Greenwich and Filbert

Morris Robert D. carpenter, dwl N s Sixteenth nr Rhode Island

Morris Robinson (col'd) cook, Bailey House

Morris R. S. (widow) furnished rooms, 720 Market

Morris R. W. auctioneer, dwl SW cor Kearny and Pacific

Morris S. clerk with E. Abrahams, dwl 23 Second

Morris Siegmund, match manufacturer, dwl 552 Tehama

Morris Theodore, machinist apprentice, Vulcan Iron Works

Morris Thomas, carpenter, S. F. & San José R. R. Co. dwl cor Sixteenth and Folsom

Morris William, dwl 225 Minna

Morris William, dwl 308 Beale

Morris William, cartman, dwl Fifth bet Folsom and Shipley

Morris William, engineer with C. W. Thomas, bds Bailey House

Morris William, machinist, dwl 509 Howard

Morris William, ship joiner, dwl 446 Brannan

Morrisey Margaret Miss, domestic, 220 Seventh

Morrisey P. H. groceries and liquors, NW cor Fifth and Tehama

Morrison A. (Forsyth, M. & Co.) dwl 168 Perry

Morrison Andrew J. assistant assessor U. S. Internal Revenue, NW cor Bat and Com, dwl Guy Place

Morrison Andrew L. dwl 508 Second

Morrison Archibald, boot maker, NE cor Brannan and Ninth

Morrison Augustus C. wood and coal, Howard St. Wharf, dwl 168 Perry

Morrison Benjamin, workman, S. F. & P. Sugar Co. dwl W s Eighth nr Howard

Morrison Carlton J. with Halsted & Pray, dwl 16 Turk

Morrison Charles W. (Athearn & M.) dwl SE cor Larkin and Washington

Morrison Daniel, mariner, dwl 117 Mason

Morrison David, cartman, dwl 26 Hunt

Morrison Edward, boiler maker, dwl 513 Mission

Morrison Eliza Miss, domestic, 610 Walter

Morrison Frank, core maker, dwl 511 Mission

Morrison George, ship carpenter, dwl 308 Beale

Morrison G. H. salesman, dwl 312 Brannan

Morrison Hector, carpenter, dwl 1811 Dupont

MORRISON HORACE, with California Steam Navigation Company, NE cor Front and Jackson, dwl NW cor Powell and Jackson

Morrison Hugh, boatman, dwl 913 Market

Morrison Jacob A. bar tender, Manhattan Engine Co. No. 1

Morrison James, boatman, dwl 913 Market

Morrison James, weaver, Mission Woolen Mills, dwl E s Harriet bet Fifteenth and Sixteenth, rear

Morrison James B. dwl 815 Montgomery

Morrison James W. (Roberts, Morrison & Co.) res Boston

Morrison John, express wagon, cor Market and Mont

Morrison John B. (Bath & M.) dwl 12 Russ

Morrison John C. jr. (Bryant & M.) dwl 817 Howard

Morrison John M. drayman, 404 Front, dwl 679 Harrison

Morrison (John W.) & White (Michael P.) draymen, 217 Market, dwl 805 Geary

Morrison Joseph H. drayman, 219 Front, dwl SE cor Jackson and Larkin

Morrison J. Z. coal oil and lamps, dwl S s Bryant nr Sixth

Morrison Margaret, dress maker, 687 Market

Morrison N. G. porter, 408 Front, dwl 19 Ritch

Morrison Patrick, hostler, 16 Sutter

Morrison Patrick, laborer, dwl 2 Sacramento

Morrison R. dwl What Cheer House

Morrison Robert F. (Lake & M.) attorney at law, 3 and 44 Court Building, dwl Russ House

Morrison Samuel, dwl 760 Folsom

Morrison Thomas H. teller, Bank California, dwl 14 Guy Place nr First

Morrison ———, printer, dwl 906 Stockton

Morrison, see Morison

Morrisey Anna Miss, cloak maker with L. Leszynsky, dwl 157 Tehama

Morrisey Jeremiah, porter with Badger & Lindenberger, dwl 38 Clementina

Morrisey John, bricklayer, dwl 57 Jessie

Morrisey Mary (widow) dwl 159 Tehama

Morrisey Michael, coachman, dwl 345 Beale

Morrisey Thomas, laborer, dwl 49 Stevenson

Morrisey William, boot maker, dwl 236 Jackson

MORROW GEORGE, hay and grain, 21 Clay and 28 Commercial, dwl 814 Filbert

Morrow James C. tailor with Heuston, Hastings & Co. dwl 12 Third

MORROW R. F. real estate, office 32 Montgomery Block, dwl Occidental Hotel

Morrow Thomas H. salesman with Hayward & Coleman, dwl 115 Fifth

Morrow William, dwl 50 Natoma

Morrow William W. debenture clerk, Auditor's Office, Custom House, dwl 815 Mission

Morsch Frederick, sign and ornamental painter, 527 Kearny, dwl 130 St. Mark Place

Morse A. C. collector, San Francisco Benevolent Association, office 410 Pine, dwl 107 Hyde

Morse Catherine Miss, domestic, 121 Stockton

Morse Eben E. drayman, 111 Battery, dwl 652 Mission

Morse Edward A. accountant with A. Hollub & Co. NW cor Front and Washington

Morse Elijah, carpenter, dwl 361½ Minna

Morse Ezra, shipping clerk, dwl E s Jones bet Jackson and Pacific

Morse George, artist, 648 Howard

Morse George, seaman, dwl 238 Stewart

Morse George A. seaman, dwl 32 Stewart

Morse George D. photographic operator with William Shew, 423 Montgomery

Morse George W. laborer, dwl 143 Silver

Morse Henry J. express wagon, cor Market and Beale, dwl 71 Tehama

Morse James, clerk with Thomas Day, 732 Montgomery, dwl 361 Minna

MORSE JOHN F. physician, office and dwl 10 Brenham Place

Morse Joseph, butcher, What Cheer H Restaurant

Morse Leonard, watchman, Custom House, dwl Crescent Engine House

Morse M. G. confectioner, dwl 119 Third

Morse Patrick, waiter, Russ House

Morse Peter, watchman, dwl 26 Freelon

Morse P. S. waterman, 609 Market

Morse Sarah Miss, domestic, dwl 856 Mission

Morse Theodore, mining stocks, dwl 1024 Stockton

Morse Thomas, dwl W s Sansom bet Greenwich and Filbert

Morse Thomas H. watchman with Chace & Mc-
  Donald, dwl 11 Mason
Morse Thomas J. & Co. *(William Flynn)* Lick
  House Coaches, dwl and stable 17 O'Farrell bet
  Stockton and Powell
Morshead Philip *(Eldridge & M.)* dwl 233 Bush
Mortensen Eliza Mrs. teacher embroidery, 212
  Fourth
Mortensen William, gardener, dwl 739 Mission
Morter William *(Girvin & M.)* dwl 21 Clara
Mortier Edward *(Forret & M.)* dwl 620 Pacific
Mortimer John, seaman, dwl 26 Sacramento
Mortimer *(Lewis)* & Maginnis *(E.)* produce, 503
  Sansom, dwl Verona nr Third
Morton A. G. salesman with J. Peirce, dwl 57 Clem-
  entina
Morton Alfred maj. U. S. A. provost marshal De-
  partment California, office 416 Washington, dwl
  522 California
Morton Barnard, brick molder with William Buckley
Morton Daniel, teamster with R. & J. Morton, dwl
  318 Ellis
Morton Charles C. wharfinger, India Dock, dwl
  1621 Leavenworth
Morton Edward C. Delivery Department Wells,
  Fargo & Co. dwl 522 California
Morton Edward H. stevedore, office 621 Front and
  watchman, U. S. Branch Mint, dwl 1138 Pacific
Morton Henry, barber, dwl 320 Vallejo
Morton Henry J. dwl cor Mission and Twenty-Fifth
Morton Henry R. hairdresser, 109 Pacific, dwl 410
  Vallejo
Morton J. B. carpenter, 404 Pine, dwl NW cor Cal-
  ifornia and Van Ness Avenue
Morton John *(R. & J. Morton)* dwl 305 Taylor
Morton Kate, seamstress, dwl 815 Montgomery
Morton Nathaniel S. conductor, Central R. R. Co.
  dwl 427 Sixth
Morton Patrick. cartman, dwl cor Larkin and Bdwy
MORTON R. & J. teamsters, office 205 Battery
  cor California, dwl 318 Ellis
Morton Samuel P. cigars and tobacco, 226 Montgom-
  ery, dwl NE cor Ninth and Mission
Morton Sargent, foreman with R. & J. Morton, 205
  Battery, dwl 312 Ellis
Morton Thomas, molder, Union Foundry, dwl 214
  Kearny
Morton William, carpenter, dwl 258 Jessie
Morton William H. captain brig Curlew, office 321
  Front. dwl 632 Sutter
Mosbacher Gerson, shoe maker with Adolph Levy,
  dwl 47 Stevenson
Moser *(Frederick)* & Smith *(Joseph)* liquor saloon,
  W s Valencia bet Fifteenth and Sixteenth
Moser G. E. clerk with C. V. Gillespie, dwl 1510
  Dupont
Moser George, clerk with A. Popp, dwl 1703 Stock
Moses Abram, vender, dwl 1318 Kearny
Moses A. S. Miss, principal Montgomery St. School,
  dwl 60 Natoma
Moses Charles, peddler, dwl 631 Broadway
Moses L. second hand clothing, dwl 824 Montgomery
Moses Lewis (col'd) barber, dwl 117 Virginia
Moses Noah, compositor with Towne & Bacon, dwl
  558 Bryant
MOSGROVE *(Samuel)* & BLAKELY *(Irvine)*
  dry goods, 222 Third, dwl 243 Second
MOSHEIMER JOSEPH, proprietor Pacific Metal-
  lurgical Works, cor Francisco and Mason, of-
  fice 238 Montgomery, dwl 1910 Powell
Mosher Daniel, carpenter, dwl 22 Stockton
Mosher John, seaman, dwl 26 Sacramento
Mosher William H. with S P. Whitman, dwl 28 Eddy
Mosier John, seaman, dwl 44 Sacramento
Moskiman Robert H. compositor, Evening Bulletin,
  dwl Pfeiffer Place
Mosquito G. & S. M. Co. office 15 Montgomery Blk
Moss Alice Ann Miss, domestic, NW cor Post and
  Leavenworth

Moss Elizabeth Miss, dwl 312 Minna
Moss Ellis W. cigars and tobacco, Bank Exchange,
  SE cor Mont and Washington, dwl 320 Fremont
Moss G. & S. M. Co. office 45 Exchange Building
MOSS J. MORA, president American Russian Com-
  mercial Co. office 418 California, res Oakland
Moss John, miner, room 56 Government House, 502
  Washington
Moss John, mining, office 712 Montgomery, dwl Oc-
  cidental Hotel
Moss Kate Miss, domestic, 742 Folsom
Moss Peter, dwl S s Clary nr Fifth
Moss Ralph & Co. *(Alexander Henry)* importers
  and jobbers millinery, fancy, and dry goods, 207
  Battery, dwl 520 Howard
Moss S. *(Haley & M.)* 604 Montgomery
Moss William S. publisher and proprietor Examiner,
  office 535 Washington, res Stockton, Cal
Moss W. T. dwl 28 Annie
Mossa Charles, bootblack, dwl W s Pacific Alley
Mosse D'Alva *(Mosse & Son)* dwl 639 Kearny
MOSSE *(D. H. T.)* & SON *(D'Alva Mosse)*
  books, stationery, and newspapers, 639 Kearny
  and 618 Washington, dwl 1151 Mission
Mosse Evlyn Miss, assistant Eighth St. School
Mosseman Samuel, with Kellogg, Hewston & Co.
  dwl S s Ellis nr Powell
Mott Gordon N. attorney at law, dwl 911 Jackson
Mott Mary J. (widow) dwl NW cor Gough and Hayes
Mott Mary J. (widow) dwl S s Riley nr Taylor
Mott Mary J. (widow) dwl 21 Perry
Mott Peter, assistant engineer U. S. Branch Mint,
  dwl 829 Washington
Mott Thomas R. dwl 911 Jackson
Mott William, laborer, Spring Valley W. W
Motta Charles, boot and shoe maker, 815 Wash
Motzenbecker Paul, tailor, 22 Sansom
Mou Heng (Chinese) washing, 239 Third
Mouchet Josephine Mme. dress maker, dwl 634
  Vallejo
Moulin Alfred, bds California Hotel
Moulthrop Charles, miner, dwl 721 Greenwich
Moulthrop Charles W. pattern maker, Miners'
  Foundry, dwl 512 Howard
Moulthrop John L. book keeper, Miners' Foundry,
  dwl 512 Howard
MOULTON *(Benjamin F.)* & STEWART *(John
  W.)* real estate agents, office 522 Clay, dwl SW
  cor Valencia and Twenty-First
Moulton Brothers *(E. S. and G. H.)* commission
  merchants, 5 Washington, dwl 1509 Leav
Moulton Charles S. drayman with Baldwin & Co.
  dwl NE cor Broadway and Polk
Moulton C. Smith, drayman, 219 Front, dwl SE cor
  Jackson and Larkin
Moulton Garry H. *(Moulton Bros.)* dwl 1509 Leav
Moulton Henry, seaman, dwl 44 Sacramento
Moulton James, special policeman, dwl SW cor
  Dupont and Broadway
Moulton Joseph, ship joiner with John G. North,
  dwl SW cor Louisiana and Sierra
Moulton Josiah *(Wilson & M.)* dwl 607 Harrison
Moulton William J. L. civil engineer and agent
  steam dredger, dwl 323 Seventh
Mounake Charles, with Henry Bocken, 1013 Kearny
Mount Davidson G. & S. M. Co. office 15 Mont Blk
Mount Diablo Freestone Quarrying Co. office 338
  Montgomery
Mount Hood House, Alexander Jackson proprietor,
  54 Sacramento
Mount J. Harvey, salesman, 514 Market, dwl 314
  Sutter
Mount St. Helena Quicksilver M. Co. (Lake Co.
  Cal.) office 7 Government House
Mount Sylvester T. carpenter, dwl N s Austin bet
  Van Ness Avenue and Franklin
Mount Zion G. S. & C. M. Co. office 338 Mont
Mountain John J. upholsterer with H. J. M. Troutt,
  dwl cor Steiner and Tyler

Mountain Top G. & S. M. Co. office room 1 Government House, 502 Washington
Mourney Lawrence, seaman, dwl 132 Folsom
Mouser C. drayman, 517 Sacramento
MOUSER S. M. physician and surgeon, office 324 Bush, dwl 719 Bush
Moutardier Antoine, dwl 1114 Stockton
Mouton August, pantryman, stm Princess
Mouton Jules, machinist, Vulcan Foundry, dwl 34 Third
Moutry James. liquor saloon, 313 East
Mow Frederick, superintendent Lone Mountain Cemetery, dwl SE cor Bush and Cemetery Av
Mowatt Commodore, butcher, dwl 43 Natoma
Mower Amos H. tinsmith with D. S. Weaver, dwl W s Jones bet Filbert and Greenwich
Mower George W. harness maker with C. H. Mead, dwl 116 Sansom
Mower P. W. Mrs. dwl 49 Natoma
Mowry Barton, real estate, dwl 1418 Powell
Mowry Charles E. shipmaster, office 728 Montgomery, bds Cosmopolitan Hotel
Mowry George B. butcher, dwl Hayes' Park Pavilion
Mowry Laura A. Mrs. dwl 1412 Powell
Mowry Lyman, student, dwl 329 Pine
Mowry Mary A. (widow) dwl 329 Pine
Mowry Nathan B. miner, dwl 28 Sansom
Mowry N. B. Mrs. furnished rooms. 28 Sansom
Mowry R. E. dwl Cosmopolitan Hotel
Mowry S. B. Coiner's Department U.S. Branch Mint, dwl cor Clay and Mason
Mowsam E. R. ship joiner with John G. North, Potrero
Moxley C. G. *(C. H. Reynolds & Co.)* dwl 721 Sutter
Moy Eugene, tailoring, 116½ Dupont
Moyle James W. dwl NE cor Market and Laguna
Moynahan Cornelius, workman, S. F. & P. Sugar Co. dwl Harrison nr Ninth
Moynihan Kate Miss, dwl 30 Clementina
Moynihan Mary (widow) dwl 127 Perry
Moynihan Michael, laborer, dwl N s Stevenson, bet Third and Fourth
MOYNIHAN *(T. J.)* & AITKEN *(James)* Portland Boiler Works, 311 and 313 Mission, dwl S s Clementina bet First and Second
Mucaby Elizabeth Miss, dwl 351 Tehama
Muche William, miller, NE cor Fremont and Folsom
Mudge Benjamin W. mining agent, office 528 Clay, dwl 909 Jackson
Mudge Theodore A. deputy license collector, City Hall, and mining secretary, office 528 Clay, dwl 404 Bush
Mudoon Peter, express wagon, Davis Street Ferry
Mudrogna Antonio, fruits, 28½ First
Muecke G. importer and commission merchant, office SW cor Front and Jackson, dwl 117 Stockton
Mueckenhoff Alois, liquor saloon, 516 Pacific
Mueller Albert, musician, dwl 323 Pine
Mueller C. teacher music, dwl 828 Vallejo
Mueller Ernest, jeweler with Fred. Heinze
Mueller George, cabinet maker, dwl 315 Bush
Mugan Catherine Miss, domestic, Willows, SW cor Mission and Eighteenth
Mugan Dennis, drayman, 211 Clay, dwl N s Turk nr Larkin
Mugan John, porter, Pacific Bank, dwl 321 Dupont
Mugan Mary Miss, domestic, 822 Filbert
Muh Nicolaus, proprietor Muh's Hotel, 716 Pacific
Muhl Andres, carpenter, dwl 1518 Powell, rear
Muhlenbrink *(William)* & Rohde *(H. B.)* groceries and liquors, SE cor Sutter and Taylor and SE cor Post and Taylor
Muhlendorfer A. millinery, dwl 214 Sansom
Muhlendorfer Robert, merchant, dwl 305 Mont
Mühlig William, cook, Columbian Engine Co. No. 11
Muhr Adam, dwl 107 Leidesdorff
Muhs David, carpenter, 501 Bdwy, dwl 716 Union

Mnioch Ernst *(Kröger & M.)* dwl 633 Broadway
Muir Adam, shipsmith, 1015 Battery, dwl W s Leidesdorff bet California and Sacramento
Muir Alexander C. carpenter, dwl 807 Filbert
Muir David, tanner, E s Ninth bet Bryant and Brannan
Muir W. M. calker, dwl S s Harrison bet Main and Spear
Mulaney Michael, laborer, dwl Union House
Mulcahy Bridget Miss, domestic, 764 Folsom
Mulcahy Catharine Miss, domestic, 233 Sixth
Mulcahy Cornelius, miner, dwl Franklin Hotel cor Sansom and Pacific
Mulcahy Edward, carpenter, dwl 551 Market
Mulcahy Hannah Miss, domestic, 712 Howard
Mulcahy James, bricklayer, S. F. & P. Sugar Co. dwl 331 Bush
Mulcahy James, workman with Kimball & Co
Mulcahy Lott, cokeman, S. F. Gas Co. dwl 507 Minna
Mulcahy Mathew, cartman, dwl E s Zoe bet Bryant and Brannan
Mulcahy Mathew, steward Liberty Hose Co. dwl 145 Fourth
Mulcahy Patrick, with Standard Soap Co. 207 Com
Mulcahy Thomas, saloon keeper, dwl 239 Bush
Muldonney James, fireman, steamer Amelia
Muldoon Dominick, laborer, bds Commercial Hotel, 123 Pacific
Muldoon Ellen (widow) dwl 23 Ritch, rear
Muldoon James, hostler, 655 Sacramento, dwl Kearny nr California
Muldoon Mary Miss, domestic, 751 Howard
Muldoon Thomas J. brass finisher, dwl 507 and 509 Market
Muldowney James, engineer, dwl SE cor Vallejo and Powell
Mulheron Patrick, dwl 8 Hunt
MULHOLLAND J. & CO. hides and wool, 11 Davis, dwl S s Filbert bet Hyde and Larkin
Mulholland James, workman, S. F. & P. Sugar Refinery, dwl S s Harrison bet Seventh and Eighth
Mulin Bridget Miss, domestic with Charles D. Cushman, NW cor Fulton and Steiner
Mulkean Margaret Miss, domestic, SW cor Sixteenth and Howard
Mull William, clerk with Brooks and Rouleau, dwl 729 Harrison
Mullally John, pork packer with Auradou & Co. dwl 1310 Pacific
Mullally Mary Miss, domestic, 527 Greenwich
Mullally Thomas, seaman, dwl Pacific Exchange
Mullaly Elizabeth Miss. domestic, 709 Taylor
Mullan James, blacksmith, Miners' Foundry
Mullan Patrick, trackman, Market St. R. R. Co
Mullana Michael, tailor, dwl Dupont bet Broadway and Vallejo
Mullane Timothy J. steward, dwl 1013 Pine
Mullaney Michael, laborer, dwl 511 Mission
Mullarkey Susan Miss, domestic, 116 Eddy
Mulleeny Susan Miss, domestic, 911 Bush
Mullen Alice (widow) domestic, SW cor Mission and Lafayette Avenue
Mullen Andrew, cartman, cor Battery and Vallejo
Mullen Andrew, lab. dwl E s Geneva nr Brannan
Mullen Andrew, nurse, U. S. Marine Hospital
Mullen Bridget Miss, furnished rooms, dwl 633 Cal
Mullen Harriet (col'd, widow) dwl 1006 Jackson
Mullen Henry, butcher with Edward Daly, dwl S s Brannan nr Seventh
Mullen Hugh, conpé, Plaza, dwl S s Jackson bet Leavenworth and Hyde
Mullen James, laborer, Golden State Iron Works, dwl cor Market and Ecker
Mullen John, laborer, Miners' Foundry
Mullen Kate (widow) dwl 1708 Dupont
Mullen Mary Miss, domestic, 873 Mission
Mullen Mary E. Miss, domestic with James R. Bolton
Mullen Michael, fireman, dwl Davis St. House

Mullen Michael, stone cutter, dwl 216 Ritch
Mullen Patrick, blacksmith, dwl 541 Mission
Mullen Peter, clerk with Singer Manufacturing Co. 139 Montgomery, dwl 18 First
Mullen Thomas, laborer, dwl 23 Jessie
Mullen William E. book keeper with Meader, Lolor & Co. 405 Front, dwl Brooklyn Hotel
Mullen William G. book keeper, dwl 234 Stevenson
Mullen, see Mullin and McMullen
Mullens Patrick, laborer, Market St. R. R. Co. dwl N s Hayes nr Franklin
Müller A. A. musician, dwl 325 Pine
MULLER ADOLPH, importer and manufacturer furs, 107 Montgomery, dwl and factory NE cor Hyde and Clay
Muller August, baker, Lombard bet Mason and Taylor
MULLER C. optician, 3 Montgomery Masonic Temple, dwl 252 Clementina
Muller Charles, baker with Charles Frank
Muller Charles, druggist, dwl 522 Pine
Muller Charles, upholsterer with Goodwin & Co. dwl 219 Kearny
Muller Charles, waiter, 623 Commercial
Muller Edward, teamster, dwl S s Montgomery Court nr Montgomery
Muller Ferdinand, blacksmithing, 212 Sutter
Muller Frank, butcher with Menges & Frankenheimer, dwl 18 Sansom
Muller Frederick, furrier with I. C. Mayer & Sons, dwl 277 Stevenson
Müller George, bar keeper, dwl 431 Pine
Muller George, driver, Eagle Bakery, dwl 247 Clementina, rear
Maller Gottlieb, cheese maker, dwl 431 Pine
Muller Gustavus, teacher German private school, dwl 1514 Powell
Müller Henry, brick molder with Alexander Lemore
Muller Henry, hairdresser with Chretien Pfister, dwl 132 Sutter
Muller Herman, liquor saloon, 917 Kearny
Muller Hermann G. attorney at law and local editor California Demokrat, dwl 228 Montgomery
Maller James, laborer, dwl 14 Ecker
Müller John, musician, dwl 610 Bush
Müller Joseph W. wood turner with A. Jellinek, dwl 233 Sutter
Müller Louisa Mrs. dwl rooms 54 and 55 Government House, 502 Washington
Müller Michael, laborer, dwl 323 Pine
Muller Peter, jeweler, dwl 610 Bush
Muller Philip, brewer, dwl 716 Pacific
Muller Rudolph, steward, dwl 606 Stockton
Muller William (Hencken & M.) dwl NE cor Vallejo and Powell
Muller William, cooper with C. T. Jensen, dwl W s Folsom nr Twenty-Third
Muller William, laborer, Bay Sugar Refinery, dwl SE cor Hinckley and Pinckney
Mullerick Ellen Miss, domestic, 364 Minna
Mullie Annie Miss, domestic, 118 Perry
Mulligan Francis, molder, Fulton Foundry, dwl Hubbard bet Second and Third
Mulligan Frank, blacksmith, dwl 130 Second
Mulligan James, bar keeper, SW cor Tehama and Second, dwl 44 Ecker
Mulligan John, steerage steward stm Orizaba
Mulligan John H. hatter, dwl Bertha W s Beale
Mulligan Kate Miss, domestic with Charles Halsey
Mulligan Kate Miss, laundress, Cole's Laundry, 114 Dora
Mulligan Owen, workman, S. F. & P. Sugar Co. dwl 246 Tehama
Mulligan Patrick, molder, Fulton Foundry, dwl 120 Minna
Mulligan Thomas, farmer, dwl S s Fifteenth near Valencia
Mulligan Thomas, quarryman, dwl Central House 814 Sansom

Mulligan Thomas, laborer with Owen Keating
Mulligan William, artist, dwl 625½ Mission
Mullikin Joseph D. dwl N s Broadway bet Franklin and Gough
Mullin Bernard, laborer, Golden Gate Market, cor Clark and Davis
MULLIN DANIEL, clerk, 634 Sacramento, dwl 424 Stevenson
Mullin Eugene, jeweler with Pohlmann & Co. dwl 44 Morse
Mullin Michael, express wagon, dwl N s Liberty bet Guerrero and Dolores
Mullin Patrick, milker with Murray & Noble, dwl NW cor Thirtieth and Old San José Road
Mullin William J. dwl 44 Moss
Mullins Dennis, hackman, dwl SW cor Jackson and Leavenworth
Mullins James, fruits, dwl 1304 Powell
Mullins Jeremiah H. (McGinn & M.) dwl SW cor Jackson and Leavenworth
Mullins Joseph, coupé, Plaza, dwl S s Jackson bet Leavenworth and Hyde
Mullins Michael, drayman, dwl 1616 Powell
Mullner Charles, musician, dwl 323 Kearny
Mullot Aine, carpenter, dwl Lestrade Place
Mulloy Charles, carpenter, dwl S s Welch bet Third and Fourth
Mulloy Hugh, cartman, 244 Mission
Mulloy James, dwl 331 Bush
Mulloy James, soda maker, dwl 115 First
Mulloy James, wines and liquors, NW cor Broadway and Davis
Mulloy James jr. bar keeper, NW cor Broadway and Davis
Mulloy John, baker stm Sacramento, dwl 213 Stevenson
Mulraney Bridget Miss, domestic, 137 Silver
Mulrein David, plasterer, 406 Montgomery, dwl 704 Larkin
Mulrenen Patrick, furnaceman, Jackson Foundry
Mulroy Michael, laborer, Lone Mountain Cemetery
Mulvaney John, bricklayer, dwl 186 Stevenson
Mulvey Mary Miss, domestic, 728 Bush
MULVILLE N. B. attorney at law, office 604 Merchant, dwl 910 Taylor
Mulvy Thomas, with Edward McDevitt, dwl 45 Powell
Mumfrey Edward, pressman with Francis, Valentine & Co. dwl 609 Pine
Mun Woa (Chinese) washing, rear City Hall
Munay Philip, pantryman, steamer Orizaba
Mund Christian F. carpenter, dwl 846 Folsom, rear
Mund Henry, jeweler with R. B. Gray & Co
Mund William, watch maker and jeweler, 750 Market
Mundegle Mary Miss, domestic, Cincinnati Brewery, Valencia
Mundwyler Balthazar, musician, dwl 708 Bush
Mundwyler Frederick, musician, dwl 708 Bush
Mundwyler J. Louis, dwl 708 Bush
Mundwyler John jr. musician, dwl 708 Bush
Mundwyler John J. musician, dwl 708 Bush
Mung Sing (Chinese) washing, 22 Clay
Munich Amelia, domestic with E. T. King, N s McAllister bet Webster and Fillmore
Munies Placida Senora, dwelling Gardner Alley nr Post
Munk Richard, compositor, Abend Post, dwl Steckler's Exchange
Munk William R. waiter, dwl 323 Pine
Munnin Brothers (John B. George and Frank Munnin) manufacturers and retailers boots and shoes, 820 Kearny
Munnin Frank (Munnin Bros.) 820 Kearny
Munnin George (Munnin Bros.) 820 Kearny
Munns William, carpenter with J. McGill & Co. dwl S s Columbia bet Guerrero and Dolores
Munro John, ship carpenter, dwl 37 Commercial
Munroe Andrew, tinner, dwl 558½ Howard

Munroe George R. wood and coal, 16 Stockton
Munroe James jr. porter, Montgomery Block, dwl 307 O'Farrell
Munroe William, waiter, steamer Pacific
Munson B. H. printer with Francis, Valentine & Co. dwl 809 Mission
Munson Eliza, dwl W s Eleventh nr Market
Munson *(James)* & Wheelock *(Jay)* saw filing, 28 Kearny
Munson John, carriage maker with H. Casebolt & Co. dwl 317 Jessie
Munson Samuel, bricklayer, dwl 315 Sutter
Muntag Peter, butcher with Crummie & O'Neill, dwl S s Mission Creek nr Brannan St. Bridge
Montanaro Giacomo, clerk, dwl 910 Dupont
Muntel Joseph, blacksmith with Gebhard & Boynton, 115 Bush
Munter Jacob, tailor, 214 First
Murasky August, porter with B. Eugene Auger, dwl N s Ellis bet Van Ness Avenue and Franklin
Murasky Bernhard, polisher, Davis' Laundry, dwl E s Washington Avenue nr Precita Avenue
Murasky Gay, chicken ranch, N s Precita Avenue nr Mission
Murasky William, laundryman, dwl 355 Minna
Murburry Robert, baker, bds 127 Pacific
March Albert F. driver, Eclipse Bakery, 1412 Dupont
March Caleb H. *(Thomas J. Chadbourne & Co.)* dwl 1412 Dupont
Murchison James, night watchman, dwl Oriental Hotel
Murcio John, laborer, dwl N s St. Charles near Kearny
Murdil John, carpenter, bds Cambridge House, 304 Pacific
Murdoch Henry H. clerk, 73 Washington Market, dwl 410 Stockton
Murdoch Hugh M. carpenter and builder, dwl 415 Pine
Murdoch Robert *(P. Smith)* dwl 647 Sacramento
Murdoch William, carpenter, dwl 133 Townsend
Murdoch William, manager with Lafayette Maynard, 205 Battery
Murdock A. H. stock broker, 621 Montgomery, dwl 522½ Howard
Murdock Alexander, cooperage, Oregon below Davis, dwl S s Filbert bet Dupont and Stockton
Murdock Charles A. clerk, dwl 522½ Howard
Murdock George H. clerk with Dodge & Phillips, dwl 522 Howard
MURDOCK GEORGE L. boarding and lodging, 24 Battery
Murdock George L. purser, stm Sierra Nevada, dwl Occidental Hotel
Murdock Hervey H. with Hall & Brigham, dwl 619 Bush
Murdock John, carpenter, dwl 74 Natoma
Murdock William J. porter with Irvine & Co. dwl 411 Bryant
Murfey S. S. notary public, office 520 Montgomery, dwl W s Montgomery bet Vallejo and Green
Murken Martin, groceries and liquors, SE cor Clementina and Ecker
Murphy Andrew, liquor saloon, 36 First
Murphy Ann Miss, domestic, 252 Jessie
Murphy Ann (widow) dwl W s Ritter nr Harrison
Murphy Anna Miss, domestic, 8 O'Farrell
Murphy Annie Miss, domestic, 704 Howard
Murphy Annie Miss, dress maker, dwl 532 Folsom
Murphy Arthur, dwl 6 Thomson Avenue
Murphy Arthur, calker, dwl 342 Ritch
Murphy Barney, confectioner, dwl 127 Second
Murphy Barney, laborer, City Bonded Warehouse, dwl S s Union bet Montgomery and Sansom
Murphy Bartholomew, employé, Cosmopolitan Hotel
Murphy Bartholomew, laborer, dwl 234 Clara
Murphy Bernard D. attorney at law, office 18 Court Block, dwl 219 Minna

Murphy Bridget Miss, domestic, 802 Howard
Murphy Bridget Miss, domestic, 1050 Mission
Murphy Bridget (widow) dwl 157 Tehama
Murphy Catherine Miss, dwl SW cor Mariposa and Florida
Murphy Catherine Miss, domestic. 611 Pine
Murphy C. E. cabinet maker, dwl 15 Tehama
Murphy Charles, laborer, dwl 129 Pacific
Murphy Charles J. hairdressing saloon, 214 Fourth, dwl 247 Clementina
Murphy Cornelius, carpenter, dwl E s Larkin bet Union and Filbert
Murphy Cornelius, teamster with Peter Schinkel, dwl cor Tenth and Bryant
Murphy Cornelius J. with Taaffe & Co. 9 Mont
Murphy Daniel, painter, dwl 440 Jessie
Murphy Daniel, real estate, office 338 Montgomery, dwl 460 Clementina
Murphy Daniel J. with Taaffe & Co. dwl S s Folsom bet Fifth and Sixth
Murphy Daniel J. attorney at law, dwl West End Hotel
Murphy Daniel J. furniture, 732 Market, dwl 11 Geary
MURPHY, *(Daniel T.)* GRANT *(Adam)* & CO. *(Thomas Breeze and John Deane)* importers and jobbers foreign and domestic dry goods, 401 and 403 Sansom cor Sacramento *(and P. F. Loughran & Co.)* res New York
Murphy David, clerk with P. H. Morrissey, NW cor Fifth and Tehama
Murphy D. B. *(Nichols & Co.)* dwl 819 Sansom
Murphy Dennis, hostler, dwl 1016 Stockton
Murphy Dennis, plumber, dwl 140 Stevenson
Murphy Dennis, shoe maker, 158 First
Murphy Dennis H. hairdresser, dwl 261 Clementina
Murphy Dennis W. whip maker with Main & Winchester, dwl 12 First
Murphy D. J. variety store, 646 Mission
Murphy Edward, dwl 1428 Stockton, rear
Murphy Edward, laborer, dwl 29 Jessie
Murphy Edward, molder, Jackson Foundry, dwl 32 Tehama
Murphy Edward, painter, dwl 215 Sansom
Murphy E. F. foreman Western Pacific Railroad, office 409 California
Murphy Eliza Miss, domestic with A. Thompson, Sixth bet Harrison and Bryant
Murphy Eliza Miss, domestic, 442 Second
Murphy Elizabeth Miss, nurse with J. C. Horan
Murphy Ellen (widow) dwl 512 Minna
Murphy Fanny Mrs. cook Bay City Laundry, 1140 and 1142 Folsom
MURPHY FRANCIS L. stove molder, dwl NW cor Sixteenth and First Avenue
Murphy Frank, fruit dealer, dwl S s Turk bet Jones and Leavenworth
Murphy Frank, laborer, dwl 116 Stevenson
Murphy Frank, pilot, dwl S s Pfeiffer nr Stockton
Murphy Frank, waiter, Occidental Hotel
Murphy Frank S. bar keeper, NW cor Pacific and Kearny
Murphy Garrett, dwl E s Howard bet Twelfth and Thirteenth
Murphy George, boatman, dwl 212 Harrison
Murphy George, waiter, steamer Orizaba
Murphy G. J. drayman, Tiger Engine Co. No. 14
Murphy Hannah Miss, domestic, 929 Sacramento
Murphy Henry, waiter, 626 Kearny
Murphy Henry M. salesman with Murphy, Grant & Co. dwl 865 Mission
Murphy Hugh, laborer, dwl N s Greenwich bet Larkin and Hyde
Murphy Hugh, workman with A. Tait, Old San José Road nr St. Mary's College
Murphy Hugh H. laborer, dwl 16 Ecker
Murphy James, bar keeper, 30 Mont, dwl 76 Minna
Murphy James, hairdresser with Ciprico & Cook, dwl Fourth nr Market

Murphy James, hostler, 427 Pine
Murphy James, machinist, Miners' Foundry, dwl 532 Folsom
Murphy James, packer with Callahan & Sanderson, dwl E s Bartol nr Broadway
MURPHY JAMES, physician and surgeon, office and dwl SE cor Clay and Kearny
Murphy James, stamp clerk Post Office, dwl 37 Tehama
Murphy James, steward, Pacific Temperance House, 109 Pacific
Murphy James, stone mason, dwl 507 O'Farrell, rear
Murphy James, whip maker, 12 First
Murphy Jeremiah, hostler, Tremont Livery Stable, dwl 1035 Kearny
Murphy Jeremiah, peddler, dwl Clementina bet Third and Fourth
Murphy John, dwl N s Fulton nr Laguna
Murphy John, dwl 440 Jessie, rear
Murphy John, dwl 909 Folsom .
Murphy John, assistant engineer Pacific Mail S. S. Co
Murphy John, baker, St. Mary's College
Murphy John, brick maker with William Buckley
Murphy John, coal passer, steamer Pacific
Murphy John, engineer, dwl 7 Natoma
Murphy John, groceries and liquors, NW cor Folsom and Baldwin Court
Murphy John, hostler, dwl 915 Sacramento, rear
Murphy John, laborer, dwl 19 Stevenson
Murphy John, laborer, dwl 133 Minna
Murphy John, laborer, dwl N s Bernard bet Jones and Leavenworth
Murphy John, office 402 Montgomery, room 3, dwl N s Fulton nr Laguna
Murphy John, painter, bds Winchester House
Murphy John, saddler, dwl 510 Mission
Murphy John, salesman, 214 Montgomery
Murphy John, watchman, Omnibus R. R. Co
Murphy John B. hostler, 117 O'Farrell
Murphy John D. carpenter, dwl 4 Brown Alley
Murphy John F. painter, dwl 440 Jessie
Murphy John H. porter, Rockwell, Coy & Co. dwl E s Capp bet Nineteenth and Twentieth
Murphy John L. stock broker, dwl 805 Mason
Murphy John M. machinist, dwl 132 Stevenson
Murphy John R. dwl SE cor Harrison and Fourth
Murphy Julia Mrs. sewing, 263 Tehama
Murphy Julia (widow) dwl 14 Anthony
Murphy Kate Miss, domestic, 512 Dupont
Murphy Lizzie, chambermaid, Lick House
Murphy M. (widow) dwl 136 Minna
Murphy Margaret Miss, domestic, 219 Minna
Murphy Margaret Miss, domestic, 915 Sutter
Murphy Margaret Miss, domestic, 557 Leavenworth
Murphy Margaret Miss, domestic, 513 Leavenworth
Murphy Margaret Miss, domestic, 1065 Howard
Murphy Margaret Mrs. dwl 120 Fourth
Murphy Margaret (widow) dwl W s Ohio bet Broadway and Vallejo
Murphy Margaret (widow) dwl 254 Clara
Murphy Mary Miss, dwl NE cor El Dorado and Nebraska
Murphy Mary Miss, domestic, 859 Mission
Murphy Mary Miss, domestic, 321 Geary
Murphy Mary Miss, domestic, 770 Howard .
Murphy Mary. (widow) dwl 1202 Powell
Murphy Mary (widow) dwl 813 Washington
Murphy Mary (widow) dwl 909 Folsom
Murphy Mary A. Miss, domestic, 1115 Stockton
Murphy Mathew, farmer, dwl SW cor Fourth and Mission
Murphy Mathew, house mover, dwl E s Sixth bet Howard and Mission
Murphy Matthew, laborer, dwl 227 Fourth
Murphy Michael, bricklayer, dwl W s Bartlett bet Twenty-Second and Twenty-Third
Murphy Michael, coachman with John W. A Gilmor, N s Mission bet Twelfth and Thirteenth

Murphy Michael, hostler, 655 Sac, dwl 59 Stevenson
Murphy Michael, laborer, dwl 154 Clara
Murphy Michael, laborer, dwl 115 First
Murphy Michael, laborer, dwl 316 O'Farrell, rear
Murphy Michael, laborer, dwl NE cor Pac and Front
MURPHY MICHAEL C. groceries and liquors, NW cor First Avenue and Sixteenth
Murphy Michael D. laborer, dwl N s Geary nr Cemetery Avenue
Murphy Michael J. seaman, dwl Ocean House
Murphy Morris, wheelwright with Kimball & Co. dwl 234 Stevenson
Murphy O. L. boarding, E s Howard bet Fifteenth and Sixteenth
Murphy Owen, dwl N s Stevenson bet Sixth and Seventh
Murphy Patrick, brick maker with C. Bonnet & Co
Murphy Patrick, clerk, dwl SE cor Jessie and Anthony
Murphy Patrick, deck hand, steamer Chrysopolis
Murphy Patrick, express wagon, cor Bush and Franklin
Murphy Patrick, lab with Lyon & Co. 159 Jessie
Murphy Patrick, laborer, Miners' Foundry
Murphy Patrick, laborer, dwl 444 Natoma
Murphy Patrick, laborer, dwl SW cor Jessie and Annie
Murphy Patrick, laborer, dwl N s Bush bet Franklin and Gough
Murphy Patrick, laborer, dwl with P. Slaven, E s Mission bet Seventeenth and Eighteenth
Murphy Patrick, laborer, dwl Dolores Hall, W s Valencia nr Sixteenth
Murphy Patrick, porter, Occidental Hotel
Murphy Patrick, porter, Central House, 814 Sansom
Murphy Patrick, shoe maker with David Hauser, dwl 417 Sutter
Murphy Partick, stone cutter, dwl 310 Fremont
Murphy Patrick, workman with John Henry, dwl Dolores Hall
Murphy Patrick L. carder, Woolen Factory and boarding, dwl E s Howard bet Fifteenth and Sixteenth
Murphy Peter, cartman, dwl E s Sansom bet Vallejo and Green
Murphy Peter, express wagon, cor Bdwy and Davis
Murphy Peter, longshoreman, bds Telegraph House
Murphy Peter, workman with N. H. Roy & Bro. San Bruno Road 3 miles from City Hall
Murphy P. H. clerk, dwl cor Jessie and Anthony
Murphy Philip, vegetable wagon, dwl SE cor Alameda and Nebraska
Murphy P. J. book keeper, Savings and Loan Society, bds Brooklyn Hotel
Murphy P. L. dwl Young America Engine Co
Murphy Richard, butcher with Daniel G. Fullon
Murphy Richard, marble worker, 673 Market, dwl Golden Gate Hotel
Murphy Rosa Miss, chambermaid, NW cor Kearny and Jackson
Murphy Sarah Miss, domestic, 249 Jessie
Murphy Thomas, with N. Dabovich, 420 Davis
Murphy Thomas, bricklayer, Volunteer Engine Co. No. 7
Murphy Thomas, carpenter, dwl 319 Bush
Murphy Thomas, gardener, dwl 720 Bush
Murphy Thomas, gas fitter with Thomas Day, 732 Montgomery
Murphy Thomas, groom, dwl 8 Anthony .
Murphy Thomas, laborer with John Warburton
Murphy Thomas, laborer, dwl W s Seventh nr Howard, rear
Murphy Thomas, laborer, dwl 35 Frederick
Murphy Thomas, marble worker with Hayes & Pritchard, dwl 415 Powell
Murphy Thomas F. waiter, Cosmopolitan Hotel, dwl 258 Clementina
Murphy Thomas P. laborer, dwl S s Perry between Fourth and Fifth

Murphy Timothy, laborer, S. F. Gas Co
Murphy Timothy, laborer, W s Gaven nr Greenwich
Murphy Timothy, laborer, dwl 558½ Howard
Murphy Timothy, laborer, dwl N s Austin between Gough and Octavia
Murphy William, laborer, Omnibus R. R. Co. dwl 9 Langton, rear
Murr Charles H. Sand Hill Meat Market, 215 Kearny, dwl 64 Everett
Murr Christopher, dwl 339 Kearny
Murray Ann (widow) dwl 4 Stockton Place
Murray Bridget (widow) dwl S s Brannan E Seventh
Murray Catherine Miss, domestic, 841 Howard
Murray Catherine Miss, domestic, 24 Ellis
Murray Catherine (widow) dwl 10 Oak, rear
Murray Charles, cook, dwl 8 Hardie Place
Murray Charles, entry clerk with Conroy & O'Connor, dwl NW cor Scott and Bush
Murray Charles, ship carpenter with John G. North, Potrero
Murray E. dwl St. Lawrence House
Murray Edward A. bar keeper with J. T. Jones & Co. dwl Russ nr Howard
Murray Eugene, carpenter, dwl S s Moore Place nr Union
Murray Fanny (widow) furnished rooms, 116 Post
Murray Francis H. carpenter, dwl 208 O'Farrell
Murray Francis J. miner, dwl W s Folsom Avenue nr Folsom
Murray Frank, miner, dwl N s Allen nr Hyde
Murray George m with Barton & Bro. dwl Market bet First and Second
Murray (George N.) & Noble (Alonzo T.) milk ranch, dwl Old San José Road NW cor Thirteenth
Murray George W. baker, dwl 11 Noble Place
Murray Henry, seaman, dwl 111 Washington
Murray Hugh (Reynolds & M.) NW cor Clay and Davis, dwl 319 Kearny
Murray James, hackman, dwl 48 Sacramento
Murray James, laborer, dwl 28 Dupont
Murray Johanna (widow) dwl 813 Greenwich
Murray John, dwl 415 Fremont
Murray John, boiler maker, Vulcan Foundry, dwl 27 Ritch, rear
Murray John, boiler maker, Pacific Foundry, dwl S s California bet Hyde and Leavenworth
Murray John, carpenter, dwl E s Kearny bet Sutter and Post
Murray John, laborer, dwl 541 Mission
Murray John, laborer, dwl N s Hayes bet Polk and Van Ness Avenue
Murray John, plasterer, dwl 504 Howard
Murray John, stevedore, dwl W s Montgomery bet Greenwich and Filbert
Murray John, tailor, dwl N s Grove nr Gough
Murray John B. clerk, dwl NE corner Dupont and Broadway
Murray John J. dwl Oriental Hotel
Murray John K. stone cutter, dwl N s Allen near Hyde
Murray Lawrence, laborer, dwl Manhattan Engine House
Murray Margaret Miss, domestic, 927 Market
Murray Margaret Miss, domestic, 1753 Powell
Murray Margaret Miss, domestic, 1206 Mason
Murray Martin, liquors, 216 Washington, dwl Stevenson bet First and Second
Murray Mary Miss, domestic, 322 Geary
Murray Mary Miss, domestic, dwl 215 Green
Murray Mary (widow) dwl 45 Ecker
Murray Mary (widow) dwl 28 Clementina
Murray Mary (widow) dress maker, dwl 1608 Powell
Murray Mary A. (widow) dwl with James Murray, S s Minna nr Eighth
Murray Matthew, laborer, dwl 721 Market
Murray Matthew, watchman, Brooklyn Hotel
Murray Michael, coppersmith, dwl 308 Beale
Murray Michael, laborer, dwl 28 Louisa

Murray Michael, laborer, dwl 438 Jessie
Murray Michael, stone cutter, dwl 326 Beale
Murray Michael. wood sawyer, dwl 171 Jessie
Murray Morris, laborer, dwl 409 Sutter, rear
Murray Owen, janitor Greenwich St. School, dwl N s Allen nr Hyde
Murray Owen, miner, dwl N s California bet Powell and Mason
Murray Patrick, boatman, dwl 206 Harrison
Murray Patrick G. boiler maker, Union Foundry, dwl 517 Mission
Murray Richard, dwl 225 Third
Murray Richard, laborer, dwl Russette Place No. 3
Murray Richard. porter, 213 Geary
Murray R. J. carpenter, 670 Mission, dwl S s Howard bet First and Second
Murray Robert, dwl St. Lawrence House
Murray Robert, laborer, dwl 102 Sacramento
MURRAY ROBERT, surgeon U. S. A. and medical purveyor, office 805 Sansom, dwl 504 Third
Murray Sarah (widow) dwl W s Wetmore Place
Murray Thomas, brakeman, Market St. R. R. Co. dwl Hayes nr Market
Murray Thomas, butcher, dwl 307 Beale
Murray Thomas, horse shoer, dwl Halleck bet California and Sacramento
Murray Thomas, laborer, dwl N s Hayes bet Polk and Van Ness Avenue
Murray Thomas, laborer, dwl 29 Ecker
Murray Thomas A. drayman with W. B. Lazelier, 401 Front
Murray Thomas F. dwl Bryant bet Main and Beale
Murray Timothy, laborer with Hey & Meyn, dwl W s Sumner nr Howard
Murray William, with A. J. Sweetser, dwl National H
Murray William, carpenter, dwl N W cor Front and Broadway
Murray William, compositor, Alta California, dwl 1232 Bush
Murray William, fishmonger, dwl 414 Market
Murray William, gardener, S W cor Gough and Fulton
Murray William, laborer with Hey & Meyn
Murray William, laborer, dwl 4 Auburn
Murray William, laborer, dwl N s Fulton bet Octavia and Laguna
Murray William M. dwl 255 Third
Murry Andrew J. dwl S s Ellis bet Webster and Fillmore
Murry Barney, watchman, Willows SW cor Mission and Eighteenth
Murry Elizabeth J. (widow) dwl N s Folsom bet Tenth and Eleventh
Murtha Bernard, confectioner with Charles H. Mercer, dwl Broderick Engine House
Murtha Ellen Miss, domestic, 318 Beale
Murtha John, porter with Edward Hall & Co. dwl 719 Howard
Murtha Kate Miss, with William Banks, 402 Sacramento, dwl 815 Montgomery
Murtha Patrick, workman, Donohue's Foundry, dwl 277 Minna
Murtha William O. stoves and tinware, NE cor Market and Powell, dwl N s Pine bet Franklin and Gough
Murto Dennis, hostler, 317 Pine
Mury Louisa (widow) dwl 215 Dupont
Musgrave Simpson, painter, dwl 633 Market
Musgrave William, carpenter with S. S. Culverwell 29 Fremont, dwl 136 Natoma
Mushe William, miller, dwl NE cor Folsom and Fremont
MUSIC HALL, Henry B. Platt proprietor, E s Montgomery bet Pine and Bush
Musie Sophia Miss, dwl E s Shotwell bet Nineteenth and Twentieth
Mussche Charles, with Bollette & Co. Pac Fruit Mkt
Mussot Louisa Mrs. clerk, dwl SW cor Dupont and Broadway

Mustard David, carpenter, dwl 443 Minna
Mustein Henry, clothing, dwl 364 Minna
Mutual Homestead Association, office 5 Government House 502 Washington
MUTUAL LIFE INSURANCE CO. H. S. Homans agent, 607 Clay
Muyano José, bandcartman, dwl 1231 Dupont
Myer Bernard, salesman, 646 Sac, dwl 1821 Powell
Myer Frederick, liquors, 611 Jackson, dwl 528 Pacific, rear
Myer Nathan, dry goods, 646 Sac, dwl 1821 Powell
Myers Albert (Blake & M.) dwl N s Post bet Powell and Mason
Myers Augusta (widow) dwl 117 Dupont
Myers Benjamin (Toothaker & M.) dwl N s Pacific bet Leavenworth and Hyde
Myers Benjamin K. bottler beer and cider, cor Santa Clara and Connecticut
Myers Charles, waiter, Occidental Hotel
Myers Eastburn N. contractor, dwl W s Howard bet Twelfth and Thirteenth
Myers Edward, baker, dwl 636 Commercial
Myers Frank, boot maker with James Noble, dwl SE cor Market and Ecker
Myers Harris, pawnbroker, 632 Com, dwl 255 Minna
Myers Harris, pawnbroker, 818 Kearny
Myers Henry, clerk, 632 Com, dwl 255 Minna
Myers Henry, conductor, North Beach & M. R. R. Co
Myers Henry B. carrier, Evening Bulletin and Call, dwl S s Filbert bet Leavenworth and Hyde
Myers Henry E. contractor, dwl N s Fifteenth bet Howard and Mission
Myers, (Israel) Goldstone (Charles) & Co. (Joseph H. Michel) shirts, 36 and 38 Third, dwl 771 Mission
Myers Jacob, pawnbroker, 827 Dupont, dwl 414 Post
MYERS JOHN, Capitol, 226 Montgomery, dwl 657 Folsom
Myers John, carpenter, dwl Sixth St. House, NW cor Sixth and Bryant
Myers John C. laborer with Wilson & Stevens, dwl E s Gilbert bet Bryant and Brannan
Myers Katie Miss, domestic, 620 Pine
Myers Leon R. & Co. (James N. Block) marble yard, 747 Market, dwl 748½ Market
Myers Mitchell G. tailor, dwl N s Ellis nr Van Ness Avenue
Myers Philip H. blacksmith, dwl 226 Ritch
Myers Samuel (Hunter & M.) dwl 569 Howard
Myers William, seaman, dwl 44 Sacramento
Myers William, ship carpenter, dwl 446 Brannan
Myers, see Mayer, Mayers, Meyer, and Meyers
Mylas Francis, horse shoer with George Knight, dwl W s Kate nr Bryant
Myle James, carpenter, dwl Sierra Nevada Hotel 528 Pacific
Mylott Andrew E. clerk with Conroy & O'Connor, dwl SE cor Pine and Scott
Myrick Frederick W. book keeper with Marden & Folger, 220 Front, dwl NW cor Filbert and Jones
Myrick Ira L. stock drover, dwl Russ House
Myrick Thomas S. principal Union Grammar School, dwl 652 Market
Myrisch Gustave, dwl 925 Howard
Myron Daniel, laborer, dwl Western House, Stewart
Myrtetus Christopher, ship joiner, Folsom St. Wharf, dwl 253 Stewart
Mysell (Joseph G.) & Kobicke (Christian) Mission Dolores Bakery, N s Sixteenth bet Guerrero and Dolores

N

NAAL Seraphin, cook, 530 Merchant, dwl 1013 Pac
Nachtigall Frederick, carpenter, Post near Lone Mountain Avenue
Nachtigall Henry L. real estate, dwl 920 Pacific

Nachtrieb Henry, watchman, Miners' Foundry, dwl 232 Jessie
Nackey John R. dwl 56 Everett
Nacoeari G., S. & Copper Co. office SW cor Front and Jackson
Nagan Mary Miss, domestic, N s Pacific bet Montgomery and Sansom
Nagel Jacob, boots and shoes, 222 Kearny, dwl SW cor O'Farrell and Stockton
Nagel Jacob, porter, dwl 1024 Stockton
Nagel John, painter, dwl S s Ewer Place
Nagel Louis, lithographer, dwl King bet Third and Fourth
Nagel Mortimer, clerk, Contra Costa Laundry, dwl S s King bet Third and Fourth
Nagel (William) & Rothermel (Philip) El Dorado Meat Market, NE cor Dupont and Green
Nagle Edward, soap maker with Henry Heilmann, dwl 441 Jessie
Nagle Ellen Miss, domestic with F. McCoppin, SW cor Valencia and Seventeenth
NAGLE GEORGE D. contractor and brickmaker, office 302 Mont room 5, dwl 16 Rincon Place
Nagle Jacob (Simon & N.) dwl 631 Pacific
Nagle James, lather, dwl 23 Natoma
Nagle James, retortman, S. F. Gas Co
Nagle John, plasterer, dwl NW cor Laguna and Fell
Nagle John, porter, 222 California, dwl SW cor Sutter and Laguna
Nagle Mary, dress maker, 713 Howard
Nagle Mary (widow) dwl S s Oregon bet Front and Davis
Nagle Richard, baker, dwl NE cor Clementina and Third
Nagle Richard, laborer, dwl S s Brannan bet Seventh and Eighth
Nagle Thomas S. plasterer, dwl N s Stevenson bet Sixth and Seventh
NAGLEE'S BUILDING, SW cor Montgomery and California
Nahl Brothers (H. W. Arthur and Charles) artists and lithographers, 121 Mont, dwl 824 Bush
Nahl Charles (Nahl Bros.) dwl 818 Bush
Nahmens B. Jurgen, seaman, bds 7 Washington
Nahten S. express wagon, dwl 338 Vallejo
Nally Eliza T. millinery goods, 1221 Stockton
Nalond John H. house mover, dwl 621 Mission
Namur Pius, restaurant, California Hotel
Napa City Flouring Mills, J. P. Raymond & Co. agents, office 119 Clay
Napa City Packet Line, office foot Commercial
NAPA CITY STEAMER, foot Broadway
NAPA RAILROAD, office 420 Montgomery
Naphtaly Joseph, office clerk, County Court, dwl 228 Sixth
Napidge Frank, dwl NE cor Clay and Dupont
Napier Frances (widow) dwl 722 Pine
Napier Stephen, teamster, dwl Folsom bet Fifth and Sixth
Napoleon Copper M. Co. office 19 Stevenson House
Napoleon Louis (col'd) dwl Ocean Race Course
Napolitano Guiseppe A. fish, 14 Washington Fish Market
Narey James, laborer, dwl 319 Vallejo
Narisemene A. laborer, dwl E s Margaret Place
Narizano Charles, book keeper, 420 Battery, dwl Powell bet Pacific and Broadway
Narkey Adolphus, clerk with Hansohn & Hammann, dwl 828 Clay
Nary Nicholas, shoe maker, dwl 16 Stockton Place
Nary Patrick, laborer, dwl 77 Stevenson
Nash Anastasia Miss, dwl Central House, 814 San
Nash Hannah Miss, domestic, 305 Taylor
Nash James N. baker, dwl S s Welch bet Third and Fourth
Nash J. M. superintendent Swimming Bath Association, NE cor Powell and Filbert
Nash Peter E. carpenter, dwl NE cor Howard and Sixteenth

Nash Thomas W. carpenter, dwl 196 Stevenson
Nash William, Letter Department Wells, Fargo & Co. dwl SE cor Third and Stevenson
Natane Brunette Miss, domestic, 1018 Bush
Naten Louis, machinist, dwl 319 Jessie
NATHAN BERNHARD, importer and retail China ware, crockery, glass ware, cutlery, etc. 616 Kearny, dwl 617 Kearny
Nathan Edmund, salesman, 513 Sac, dwl Russ H
Nathan Samuel C. pilot, office cor Vallejo and Davis, dwl 327 Union
Nathan Samuel J. clerk, 124 and 126 Third
Nathan Solomon, clothing, 112 Stewart
National Brewery, Gluck & Hansen proprietors, NW cor O'Farrell and William
NATIONAL FLOUR MILLS, J. Martenstein & Co. proprietors, 561 and 563 Market
National House, Dunning & Herbert proprietors, 414 Market
Nauland (Frederick) & Whitman (Henry) Buffalo Market, NW cor Union and Powell
Naulty James, plasterer, dwl Lincoln Avenue
Naulty Nicholas, molder, Pacific Foundry, dwl 45 Stevenson
Nauman Amelia Mrs. butter, cheese, eggs, produce, etc. 507 Sansom, dwl SE corner Folsom and Twenty-First
Nauman Charles, clerk with Mrs. Amelia Nauman, 507 San, dwl SE cor Folsom and Twenty-First
Nanman Edward, locksmith, 218 Commercial, dwl Dupont bet Vallejo and Green
Nava John, cook, dwl 1435 Taylor
Navarre Alfred, clerk with D. Ghirardelli & Co. 417 Jackson
Navarro Henrique, saddle maker, dwl N s Filbert bet Stockton and Powell
Nave Mary (widow) dwl 1012 Kearny
Navel Bridget Mrs. laundress, City Laundry, 1140 and 1142 Folsom
Navel Thomas, laborer, dwl W s Mission nr Thirteenth
Navelet Victor, willow basket maker, 521 Kearny and 221 Leidesdorff
Naverrete Mary (widow) dwl 828 Broadway
NAVY AGENT'S OFFICE, E. C. Doran acting navy agent and paymaster United States Navy, office 432 California
Naylor   eter (Thomas H. Selby & Co.) res New York
Ne Plus Ultra G. & S. M. Co. office 338 Montgomery
Neaf Maria Mrs. domestic, 1000 Market
Neagle T. F. & Co. (John Breen) cooperage, 221 Washington, dwl 1306 Pacific
Neal C. J. Miss, assistant, Market St. School, dwl 8 Minna
Neal Daniel, cabinet maker, dwl 562 Bryant
Neal Daniel. carpenter, Russ House
Neal Daniel F. pattern maker, Golden State Iron Works, dwl 8 Minna
Neal Fannie Miss, dwl 562 Bryant
Neal Henry R. shipping clerk, dwl E s Montgomery bet Chestnut and Lombard
Neal Michael, driver with John Agnew, 26 Kearny
Neal William W. captain tug boat Merrimac, office 407 East, dwl 711 Taylor
Neal, see Neil and Neill
Nealan Patrick, painter, dwl W s Jones bet Union and Filbert
Nealand John, house mover, dwl 617 Mission
Neale George W. clerk, dwl 528 Pacific, rear
Neall Samuel, clerk with Judge Field, dwl SW cor California and Leavenworth
Nealy J. R. carpenter, dwl 515 Kearny
Nealy William, dwl E s Lagoon
Neary James, laborer, Omnibus R. R. Co
Neary John, blacksmith with Patrick Burns, dwl Golden Gate Hotel
Neary Nicholas, shoe making, 7 Sutter, dwl W s Stockton bet Union and Filbert

Neary Thomas, foreman, Market St. R. R. Co. dwl Guerrero bet Nineteenth and Twentieth
Neath William, salesman, Occidental Market, dwl 259 Jessie
Neau Henry, washing, 11 John
Neeb Henry, tailor, 629 Merchant
Needham Festus, laborer, dwl S s Vallejo bet Sansom and Montgomery
Needham William L. furniture, dwl 9 Dupont
Neelan John, laborer, bds 127 Pacific
Neelan William, painter with Hopps & Kanary
Neely Robert, carpenter, dwl 515 Pine
Neely Robert J. drayman, 533 Clay, dwl 713 Howard
Neff Charles, notice server with City and County Treasurer
Neff Ella (widow) dwl 216 Post
Nehrlich Frederick, cooper, dwl E s Beale bet Market and Mission
Neibir Auguste Mrs. dwl 137 Clara
Neidinger W. A. music teacher, dwl 617 Union
Neil Catherine Miss, domestic, 323 Taylor
Neil Daniel F. pattern maker, dwl 8 Minna
Neil David, foreman Golden Gate Nursery, dwl 825 Folsom
Neil James, express wagon, cor Market and Second, dwl 10 Lick Alley
Neil Washington, captain stmr Josie McNear, res Petaluma
Neil William, coppersmith and plumber, 35 Sacramento, dwl 16 Silver
Neilan Bridget Miss, domestic, 405 Powell
Neill James, dwl SE cor Bush and Powell
Neill P. agent marble works, 635 Market, dwl Brooklyn Hotel
Neill Patrick, marble cutter, dwl 26 Mary
Neimeyer Gottlieb, tailor with Wm. Geimann, dwl 1314 Dupont
Neiner Aaron, clothing, dwl 236 Minna
Nelle George, clerk, 423 Battery, dwl 42 South Park
Nelligan William H. boot maker, dwl 705 Battery
Nellis William M. machinist, S, F. Iron Works, dwl 206 Fourth
Nelon Timothy, laborer, dwl 926 Pine
Nelson A. N. & Co. (Charles Peterson) Union Restaurant 1025 Dupont, dwl 1027 Dupont
Nelson Andrew, captain schr Emma Adelia, dwl 12 Ritch
Nelson Andrew, carpenter, dwl 32 Stewart
Nelson Andrew, matress maker, bds 336 Bush
Nelson C. Frank, painter with James Donovan
Nelson Charles, blacksmith, Phœnix Iron Works, dwl 511 Mission
Nelson Charles, captain bark Monitor. office Pier 10, dwl 142 Silver
Nelson Charles, seaman, dwl 26 Sacramento
Nelson Christian, captain Water Boat, office SW cor Merchant and East, dwl 939 Mission
Nelson Consolidated G. & S. M. Co. office 210 Pine
Nelson Daniel, seaman, dwl 44 Sacramento
Nelson Edward, dwl Beale Place
Nelson Elias, seaman, dwl 26 Sacramento
Nelson Elizabeth (widow) dwl 517 Bush
Nelson Frank, house painter with J. W. Denny, dwl SE cor Jones and Post
Nelson Fred, seaman, dwl 26 Sacramento
Nelson George, captain schr I. P. Harms, Caduc's Line foot Washington
Nelson George, printer with A. J. Lafontaine, dwl Pacific Temperance House
Nelson George H. book keeper with John Sime & Co. dwl S s Folsom bet Fifth and Sixth
Nelson George, tinsmith, dwl 210 Dupont
Nelson Hans, longshoreman, dwl Alta nr Sansom
Nelson Henry, pilot, steamer Petaluma
Nelson Henry, ship carpenter, dwl 20 Frederick
Nelson Henry, truckman, cor Clay and Davis, dwl 4 Drumm

Nelson Isaac M. groceries, N s Twentieth bet Guerrero and Dolores
Nelson Jacob, calker, dwl 34 Frederick
Nelson James, carpenter, dwl 15 Geary
Nelson James, carpenter, dwl 207 Clara
Nelson James, cashier with Charles Minturn, dwl 830 Washington
Nelson James, cook, dwl 923 Kearny
Nelson John, dwl 410 Bush
Nelson John, carpenter, dwl 207 Minna
Nelson John, deck hand, steamer Julia
Nelson John, seaman, dwl 26 Sacramento
Nelson John G. (Gullixson & N.) dwl 149 Jessie
Nelson John P. porter, 417 Battery, dwl 418 Bryant
Nelson Josiah, miner, dwl 15 Noble Place
Nelson L. M. Miss, dwl 1028 Clay
Nelson M. captain schr Don Leandro, office Pier 4 Stewart
Nelson Nicholas, seaman, dwl 26 Sacramento
Nelson N. P. boot maker, 640 Pacific
Nelson Ole, carpenter, dwl 336 Bush
Nelson Ole, cartman, cor Powell and Greenwich
Nelson Peter, captain, dwl 26 Stewart
Nelson Peter, seaman, dwl 26 Sacramento
Nelson Robert, boatman, dwl 140 Stewart
NELSON (Thomas) & DOBLE (Abner) blacksmiths, 321 Pine, dwl 22 Oak nr Mason
Nelson Thomas, mariner, dwl 209 Clay
Nelson William, dwl 208 Harrison
Nelson William, laborer, dwl 226 Mission
Nelson William L. clerk, dwl 1108 Powell
Nelstein Bertha (widow) dwl 234 Commercial
Nemire Amiel, inspector. Custom House, dwl E s Calhoun bet Green and Union
Nepier Stephen H. teamster with Benjamin Collins, dwl N s Folsom bet Fifth and Sixth
Neppe Jacob, drayman, dwl NE cor Pine and Polk
Neppert John D. merchant, dwl SW cor Howard and Langton
Neppert Philip, upholsterer with Wightman & Hardie, dwl S s Dupont Alley
Neppit John D. carpets, E s Stockton bet Pacific and Broadway
NEPTUNE IRON WORKS, Cameron & Worth proprietors, 46 Fremont
Neri J. Rev. S.J. clergyman, St. Ignatius Church, S s Market bet Fourth and Fifth
Nesbit Benjamin R. dwl What Cheer House
Nesbitt Anna J. (widow) dwl 46 Sutter
Nesbitt Robert, molder, Union Foundry, dwl 414 Market
Nesbitt Samuel, baker with Picket & Co. dwl 1016 Montgomery
Nesmith William, waiter, Richards' Restaurant, dwl 27 Anthony
Nessian William, molder, Vulcan Iron Works, dwl 154 First
Nestel August, hairdresser with Adam Grimm, dwl 133 Kearny
Netter Augustus, drayman, Sacramento nr Front, dwl 707 Post
Netterville William, molder, dwl 44 Stevenson
Nettle William, packer, 819 Sansom, res San José
Nettleton H. S. (Newhall, Brooks & N.) dwl 22 Minna
Nenget Michael, painter, dwl 1027 Dupont
Neuhaus Charles (Tillmann & Co.) dwl 411 Sixth
Neuhoff John F. with Lyon & Co. dwl 124 Natoma
Neuland Edward, marker, Chelsea Laundry
Neulens Buessard, wholesale and retail liquors, 811 Dupont, dwl 517 Green
Neulens J. Beussard, coal dealer, E s Sansom bet Pacific and Broadway
Neuman James B. (Handy & N.) dwl American Exchange
Neuman Marie, French milliner and millinery, 612 Kearny
Neumann F. cabinet maker, bds New England H
Neumann Isidor, merchant, dwl 469 Clementina

Neumann Joseph, dwl 469 Clementina
Neumann Louis, groceries and liquors, SW cor Stockton and O'Farrell
Neumann Paul, attorney at law, 803 Montgomery room 4, dwl SW cor Dupont and Bay
Neumann Solomon, dwl NW cor Sixth and Clementina
Neumuller Jacob, blacksmith with Gebhard & Boynton, dwl 336 Bush
Neunaber (Henry) & Co. (D. Puckhaber) groceries and liquors, SW cor Folsom and Beale
Neustadt Adolph, reporter, dwl 212 Minna
Neustadt Louis, Telegraph Meat Market, 505 Bdwy
Neustadter Bernard, cigars and tobacco, 113 Pacific
NEUSTADTER BROTHERS (Louis W. and Henry) importers and jobbers gents' furnishing goods, 300 Battery cor Sac, res New York
Neustadter Henry (Neustadter Bros.) dwl Steckler's Exchange
Neustadter Jacob H. book keeper with Neustadter Bros. dwl 621 California
NEUVAL (August) & CHAMON (Eugene) editors and proprietors L'Independant, office 617 Commercial, dwl 518 Union
Neuval Frank, groceries and liquors, 518 Union
Nevada G. & S. M. Co. office 402 Front
Nevada Gold Quartz M. Co. office 712 Montgomery
Nevel Michael, fireman stm Pacific, dwl 522 Union
Neveu Alfred, French laundry, dwl 835 Broadway
Neville Charles, laborer, dwl 429 Pacific
Neville James T. bar keeper, dwl Manhattan Engine House
Neville J. M. (Lewis & N.) dwl 1004 Bush
Neville Michael, mariner, dwl W s Jasper Place nr Union
Nevin Charles W. compositor, Daily Examiner, dwl 218 Minna
Nevin James, ship carpenter, dwl 327 Bryant
Nevins Jemima H. (widow) dwl with Wm. Bunce
Nevins Moris, hostler, dwl 826 Green
NEW AGE (weekly) John F. Pynch & Co. proprietors, office 532 Merchant
New Almaden Quicksilver M. Co. (now Quicksilver M. Co.) office NW cor Battery and California
New Atlantic Hotel, 619 Pacific, Buchholts & Kock proprietors
NEW BRANCH HOTEL, Michael O'Neil proprietor, 12 Sutter
NEW ENGLAND HOUSE, Jacob Schleicher proprietor, 205 Sansom
New Henry J. waiter, 25 Third, dwl 538 Com
NEW IDEA THEATER, Michael Reese proprietor, S s Commercial bet Kearny and Dupont
New Joseph, boot maker, dwl SW cor Dupont and Broadway
NEW MARKET, 518 Clay nr Sansom
NEW ORLEANS WAREHOUSE, T. B. Ludlum proprietor, NW cor California and Davis
New Wisconsin Hotel, Sincock & Trembath proprietors, 411 Pacific
New York & Grass Valley G. M. Co. office 20 Stevenson House
New York and Marsh Landing Line Packets, Mission St. Wharf
New York & Nevada S. M. Co. office 20 Stevenson House
New York & Reese River S. M. Co. office 20 Stevenson House
NEW YORK AND SAN FRANCISCO STEAMSHIP LINE (Pacific Mail Steamship Co.) office NW cor Sacramento and Leidesdorff
NEW YORK AND SAN FRANCISCO STEAMSHIP LINE (Central American Transit Co.) office NW cor Pine and Battery
New York & Santa Fe S. M. Co. office 20 Stevenson House
New York & Washoe S. M. Co. office 20 Stevenson House

NEW YORK BAKERY, Hall, Hunt & Malone proprietors, 626 and 628 Kearny
NEW YORK BOARD UNDERWRITERS, office 308 Front, A. T. Fletcher agent
NEW YORK BREWERY, Wunnenberg & Co. proprietors, SE cor Powell and Francisco
New York Hotel, SW cor Battery and Commercial
New York House, John Tucker proptr, 840 Market
NEW YORK LIFE INSURANCE CO. J. B. Scotchler agent, office 206 Front
NEW YORK LINE PACKETS, William T. Coleman & Co. office NW cor Battery and Merchant, Ross, Dempster & Co. SW cor Battery and Pacific, DeWitt, Kittle & Co. NW corner California and Front, George Howes & Co. 309 Clay, and Henry B. Williams 305 Front, agents
Newbauer Joseph (Greenhood, N. & Klein) dwl 115 Taylor bet Eddy and Turk
Newberger Bernard, shoe maker, dwl 221 Third
Newburger Elias, real estate, dwl 68 Minna
Newburgh Oscar, news dealer, SW cor Market and Second, dwl 68 Jessie
Newby David, blacksmith, dwl 115 First
Newby Misses (J. H. & S. H.) millinery, 1006 Stockton
NEWBY RICHARD, agent Commercial Bank Corporation of India and the East, office 408 California, dwl Cosmopolitan Hotel
Newby S. H. Miss (J. H. & S. H. N.) dwl 1006 Stockton
Newcomb C. Lemuel, with C. W. Weston & Co. dwl Tremont House
Newcomb George W. porter, 119 Clay
Newcomb James P. foreman American Flag, dwl 151 Tehama nr Third
Newcomb Margaret (widow) dwl W s Jansen bet Greenwich and Lombard
Newcomb Thomas, mining secretary, 617 Mont
Newcomb William, varnisher, dwl 409 Mission
Newdorfer Henry, boots and shoes, 524 Commercial, dwl 1 Hardie Place
Newell Charles J. baker with James Donnelly, 109 Sansom
Newell Edward E. dentist with H. J. Paine, dwl 506 Dupont
Newell Edwin, mariner, dwl 32 Stewart
Newell Horace, salesman with Oakley & Jackson, dwl 1803 Mason
Newell J. A. mariner, dwl 1024 Bush
Newell L. W. stock broker, office 626 Montgomery
Newell Margaret (widow) dwl 615 Geary
Newell Mary (widow) dwl 2 Dixon Block, Jane
Newell Mary L. (widow) dwl 18 Eddy
Newell William, printing roller manufacturer, 530 Merchant
NEWELL WILLIAM A. physician, office and dwl 632 Mission
Newfelder Mrs. dwl 210 Bush
Newfield Aaron, dwl 272 Tehama
Newfield Joseph, peddler, dwl 272 Tehama
Newfield Louis, dwl 736 Vallejo
Newfield Marcus, clerk, 636 Clay, dwl 272 Tehama
Newhall H. C. attorney at law with J. B. Felton, office 4 Court Block, dwl 10 Ellis
NEWHALL H. M. & CO. (J. Oscar Eldridge and Gilbert Palache) auction and commission merchants, SW cor Sansom and Halleck (and president S. F. & San José R. R. Co.) dwl 334 Beale
Newhall John F. maltster, dwl 124 Natoma
Newhall S. W. surveyor, dwl 217 Third
NEWHALL (Wm. M.) BROOKS (Thos H.) & NETTLETON (H. S.) auction and commission merchants, 722 Montgomery, dwl 323 Fremont
Newhoff Edward C. printer with Edward Bosqui & Co. 517 Clay
Newhoff Ellen (widow) dwl 119 Third
Newhoff Francis, gunsmith, 208 Leidesdorff, dwl NE cor Third and Minna

Newhouse Charles, drayman, 516 Sacramento, dwl 914 Stockton
Newhouse (M.) & Schuline (N.) merchants, Idaho City, dwl 411 Hyde
Newkirk Isaac J. furniture, dwl 1207 Bush
Newkom Solomon, boots and shoes, 42 Fourth
Newland John, laborer, dwl cor Mission and Jane
NEWMAN ABRAHAM, butcher, 2 and 3 Metropolitan Market, dwl 553 Mission
Newman Adolph, dwl S s Card Place
Newman Arthur, seaman, dwl 255 Beale
NEWMAN B. B. (Van Arman & N.) attorney at law, office cor Washington and Brenham Place, dwl nr Lone Mountain
NEWMAN BROTHERS (Thomas and Edward) manufacturers brushes and importers and jobbers wood and willow ware, etc. 406 and 408 Battery, res New York
Newman (Carleton) & Brannan (Patrick T.) S. F. Flint Glass Works, SW cor Ritch and Townsend, dwl E s Crook between Townsend and Brannan
Newman Charles, drayman with A. C. Deitz & Co. 519 Front, dwl 228 Post
Newman Charles W. miner, dwl 621 Bush
Newman C. L. hardware, 111 Third, dwl 252 Fourth
Newman Dorice Miss, domestic, 325 Sutter
Newman Edward (Newman Bros.) dwl 117 O'Farrell
Newman George, workman with G. Treat, S side Twenty-Fourth bet Folsom and Howard
Newman Henry, watches and jewelry, 13 Second
Newman Isaac, upholsterer, dwl 1136 Folsom
Newman Jacob, cabinet maker with W. G. Weir, dwl W s Allen nr Hyde
Newman James, cooper, dwl 327 Dupont
Newman John T. teamster, 511 Market, dwl W s Ritter nr Harrison
Newman John W. clerk with Cameron, Whittier & Co. 425 Front
Newman Julius, merchant (Grass Valley) office 308 California, dwl 213 Minna
Newman Margaret Miss, dwl 21 Langton
Newman Margaret Miss, domestic with John Satterlee, W s Folsom bet Eleventh and Twelfth
Newman Matilda (widow) dwl 325 Sutter
Newman Michael, butcher with Abram Newman, dwl 553 Mission
Newman Michael, laborer, dwl 14 Sansom
Newman Otto, miner, dwl SW cor Kearny and Pac
Newman Philip, butcher with A. Dolet, dwl S side Francisco bet Dupont and Stockton
Newman Philip, butcher with Abram Newman, dwl 553 Mission
Newman Samuel, deputy constable, dwl Crescent Engine House
Newman T. printer, Eureka Typographical Union, 625 Merchant
Newmah Thomas, dwl 117 O'Farrell
Newman Thomas, helper, Pacific Foundry, dwl Battery St. House
Newman William, butcher, dwl SW corner Dupont and Broadway
Newman William, seaman, dwl 26 Sacramento
Newmark Joseph P. commission merchant, office 401 Sacramento, dwl 830 Post
Newmark M. J. attorney at law, office 529 Clay
Newmark Simon, cigars and tobacco, dwl 205 Pac
Newmeyer William, garden, Presidio House, rear
Newport Land Co. office 402 Montgomery
Newsbaum Joseph, workman with I. Paul, San Bruno Road nr Five Mile House
Newsham John, foreman blacksmith Union Foundry, dwl 25 Clara
Newsom John J. (Hoagland & N.) res Clinton, Alameda Co
Newsom William, cook, dwl 423 East
Newton Benjamin (John B. Newton & Co.) res New York

Newton Charles *(Jones, Dixon & Co.)* res Brooklyn, Alameda County
Newton Isaac jr. book keeper with Meader, Lolor & Co. bds International Hotel
Newton John, dwl 25 Stockton Place
NEWTON JOHN B. & CO. *(Benjamin and L. H. Newton)* commission merchants, 108 and 110 California, dwl 909 Clay
Newton L. H. *(John B. Newton & Co.)* 110 Cal
Newton Thomas, millwright, dwl 54 First
Newton William, brick layer, dwl 25 Stockton Pl
Newton William, laborer, bds Roxbury House 318 Pacific
Newton William J. confectioner with Rathbun & Co. 430 Sansom
Ney J. L. cloaks and mantillas, 14 Montgomery
NIAGARA FIRE INSURANCE COMPANY, New York, John Lander agent, SW cor Montgomery and Clay
Niagara S. M. Co. office 529 Clay
Niantic Hotel, Miss B. Mooney proprietress, NW cor Sansom and Clay
Nibbe *(Jacob)* & Gibson *(Charles)* drayman, cor Front and California, dwl cor Pine and Polk
Nichol A. E. Mrs. matron, City and County Hospital
Nicholas Joseph D. fruits, 26 Sansom
Nicholas Julius & Co. *(Charles Oester)* blacksmiths, 19 Fremont, dwl 563 Beale
Nicholas Kate Miss, domestic, 713 Post
Nicholas N. G. fruits, SW cor Battery and Jackson, dwl 306 Jackson
Nicholas Philip, handcartman, cor Mont and Sac
Nicholls George, assistant machinist, Maguire's Opera House
Nichols Amos R. agent Dr. Tisdale's Vegetable Syrup, 225 Clay, and carpenter, 210 Washington, dwl 225 Clay
Nichols Andrew W. book keeper, bank Wells, Fargo & Co. dwl 924 Jackson
Nichols Asa C. *(Cox & N.)* school director, Sixth District, dwl 835 California
Nichols B. C. Miss, teacher private school, SE cor Powell and Washington, dwl 1006 Powell
Nichols Charles, mastic roofer, dwl Fifth Avenue bet Harrison and Bryant
Nichols Charles M. clerk, 142 Fourth, dwl 154 Silver
Nichols Edwin B. painter, dwl 636 Commercial
Nichols *(Elam)* & Horton *(Robert L.)* butter and cheese dealers, 142 Fourth, dwl 154 Silver
Nichols Elijah, clerk with Byrne & Freelon
Nichols F. A. E. Miss, assistant, Stevenson St. School, dwl 432 Filbert
Nichols Frederick C. porter with J. R. Stewart & Co. dwl 668 Mission
Nichols G. M. Mrs. milliner and millinery goods, 661 Clay
Nichols *(H. C.)* & Co. *(D. B. Murphy)* ship bread bakers, 819 Sansom, dwl SE cor Fourth and Stevenson
Nichols J. laborer, dwl N s Washington bet Drumm and East
Nichols Jacob, sash and blind maker with J. McGill & Co. dwl 13 Kearny
NICHOLS JAMES, attorney at law, office 614 Merchant, dwl 429 Filbert
Nichols Jirah S. ship carpenter, dwl S s Shipley bet Fifth and Sixth
Nichols John, fruits, 1438 Pacific
Nichols Margaret (widow) furnished rooms, 29 Post
Nichols Mary, domestic, 257 Tehama
Nichols Moses, captain schr Caroline Mills, dwl 219 Main
Nichols *(Richard)* & Co. *(Louis. Caro)* produce, 31 Metropolitan Market, dwl Montgomery House
Nichols Richard J. wharfinger, Vallejo St. Wharf, dwl 1006 Powell
Nichols Watson, keeper with S. C. Harding, dwl 154 Silver

Nichols William, book seller, dwl 110 Tehama
NICHOLS WILLIAM M. North Beach Terminus Saloon, NW cor Powell and Francisco
Nicholson Jacob, captain schr Annie Forbes, dwl 548 Bryant
Nicholson J. H. teller, Bank California, dwl 338 Brannan
Nicholson John, dry goods, dwl NW cor Stockton and Green
Nicholson John, painter, dwl E s Harriet bet Fifteenth and Sixteenth
Nicholson John J. book keeper with P. J. White & Co. dwl 765 Mission
Nicholson John Y. Custom House broker, office Davis bet Pacific and Clark, dwl 814 Lombard
Nicholson Joseph A. carrier, Bulletin and Alta, dwl SW cor Pine and Kearny
Nicholson Michael, plasterer, dwl 18 Clara
Nicholson N. seaman, dwl 140 Stewart
Nicholson William H. plasterer, dwl E s Harriet bet Fifteenth and Sixteenth
Nickelofsky L. lamplighter, S. F. Gas Co
Nickelsburg S. H. salesman with M. Heller & Bros. dwl 524 Ellis
NICKERSON CHARLES, City Hat Store, 209 Montgomery, dwl 463 Clementina
Nickerson L. H. salesman, 209 Montgomery, dwl 463 Clementina
Nickerson Mulford, dwl Russ House
Nickerson Stafford S. carpenter, dwl 706 Larkin
Nickerson Zenas P. carpenter, dwl W s Nevada bet Harrison and Folsom
Nickleson John, waiter, Cosmopolitan Hotel
Nickols Sheldon K. clerk warehouse, Quartermaster's Department, dwl 1016 Washington
Nicol William, cigars and tobacco, 532 Sacramento, and book stands NE cor Clay and Mont and NW cor Clay and East, dwl 108 Tehama
Nicol William, laborer, dwl W s Bat nr Vallejo, rear
Nicolaus Julius, blacksmith, dwl 48 Beale
Nicolay Louis, shoe maker, 112 Dupont
Nicoli Henrietta Mrs. dwl 529 Jackson
NICOLSON PAVEMENT, J. J. Robbins agent, office 619 Montgomery
Nieblas Felix, job cart, SW cor Montgomery and Sacramento, dwl 1220 Dupont
Niebour Theodore, teamster with J. Peirce, dwl 606 Montgomery
Niedt Edward, soap maker with Henry Hillman, Brannan nr Sixth
Niefert Frank, machinist with S. S. Culverwell, 29 Fremont, dwl New England House
Nielsen H. *(Bandmann, N. & Co.)* dwl 514 Lombard
Nielsen L. N. laborer, dwl Gautier's House 516 Pac
Nier Henry, oysterman, dwl 18 Sansom
Niff Samuel, carpenter, dwl Western Hotel
Niggle *(George)* & Laurberg *(Lauritz)* proprietors Sierra Nevada Hotel, 528 and 530 Pacific
Nightingale George, seaman, dwl S s Union bet Sansom and Calhoun, rear
NIGHTINGALE JOHN, agent and wharfinger, Market Street Wharf, office foot Market, dwl 113 Stockton
Nightingale William J. engineer, steamer Cornelia
Nihan James, laborer, dwl with John Brady W s Ninth nr Folsom
NILE *(M. D.)* & KOLLMYER *(W. A.)* gilders and picture framers, 312 Bush, dwl 633 Market
Nilege George, cook, dwl Mission nr cor Stewart
Niles James M. mariner, dwl NW cor Clay and East
Nimo James, cook, New York Bakery
Ninas John, works with Joseph Silva, Ocean H Flat
Nisbet James, estate of *(S. F. Bulletin Co.)* 620 Montgomery
Nissen William, molder, dwl 154 First
Nissler Henry, cook, 706 Market, dwl Summer nr Montgomery
Nixon A. H. sail maker, dwl W s Beale nr Mission

Nixon James, fireman, steamer Chrysopolis, dwl E s Sonoma Place nr Green
Nixon John L. carpenter, dwl E s, Howard bet Fourteenth and Fifteenth
Nixon Mary (widow) nurse, dwl 228 Minna
Noah Joel, tyler Masonic Lodges, dwl 118 Geary
Noah John, dwl 417 Folsom
NOAH M. M. Editorial Department Alta California, dwl 812 Stockton
Noble Alonzo T. (Murray & N.) dwl Old San José Road NW cor Thirtieth
Noble A. P. machinist, Miners' Foundry, dwl 63 Clementina
Noble Ellen Miss, chambermaid, Russ House
Noble Hamden H. clerk with G. W. Clark, 500 San
Noble James, boot maker, City Hall, rear, dwl Jessie nr Fourth
Noble John, dwl 1508 Dupont, rear
Noble John, tailor, dwl 60 Miles Court·
Noble (Thomas) & Gallagher (Edward M.) sign painters, 437 Jackson, dwl Reed Place
Noble Warham M. clerk, S W cor Howard and Twelfth
Noblet B. dwl What Cheer House
Noblet Jules, driver, laundry, 293 Clementina
Noblett John, billiardman, Lick House
NOBMANN CHRISTOPH, groceries and liquors, NE cor Bush and Mason and SE cor Leavenworth and Sacramento
Nobmann Frederick & Co. (E. E. Seibeik) meat market, NE cor Sacramento and Leavenworth
Nobmann Henry, carrier, Abend Post, dwl 319 Bush
Nobmann John, groceries, Francisco nr Powell
Nocey J. boatman, dwl 1314 Dupont
Nocken Alexander, dwl 417 Sutter
Nodop Claus, brewer, New York Brewery ·
Noe Jesus, farmer, Old San José Road 3 miles from City Hall
Noe Miguel, stock dealer, Old San José Road 3 miles from City Hall
Noe Vincent, farmer, Old San José Road 3 miles from City Hall
NOEL A. mining secretary, office and dwl 607 Wash
Noel Louis, bricklayer, dwl Elizabeth nr Louisa
Nogues Bernard, laborer with J. S. Gibbs, dwl Dupont bet Vallejo and Broadway
Nohl Ad. book keeper with Spencer & Jarboe, dwl 812 Jackson
Noiset Alphonse, editor L'Independent, dwl 622 Pac
Nolan Bridget Miss, domestic, 59 Minna
Nolan Bridget Miss, domestic with John T. Newman, W s Ritter nr Harrison
Nolan David A. waiter, dwl 349 Fourth
Nolan Edward, miner, bds Franklin Hotel, cor Sansom and Pacific
Nolan George, molder, dwl with John Donelly, E s Montgomery between Green and Union
Nolan James, furrier, dwl Manhattan Engine House
Nolan James, painter with Hopps & Kanary, dwl S s California bet Leavenworth and Hyde
Nolan James, tanner with W. H. Warren, dwl Folsom bet Eighteenth and Nineteenth
Nolan James H. laundryman, Chelsea Laundry, dwl 9 Noble Place
Nolan Jane Miss, domestic, 736 Folsom
Nolan John, baker, dwl 636 Commercial
Nolan John, laborer, bds with Joseph Seale N s Turk nr Fillmore
Nolan Joseph, boot maker, dwl S s Francisco bet Kearny and Dupont
Nolan Joseph, porter, Hibernia Savings and Loan Society, dwl S s Francisco bet Dupont and Kearny
Nolan Julia Miss, domestic, 1306 Pine
Nolan Margaret Miss, domestic, 1203 Pacific
Nolan Maria Miss, domestic, 221 Seventh
Nolan Mary Miss, domestic, 312 Post
Nolan Mary (widow) dwl E s Beale bet Market and Mission

Nolan Michael, groceries and liquors, 87 Stevenson, dwl 507 Minna
Nolan Michael, laborer, dwl 248 Tehama, rear
Nolan Michael N. conductor, dwl 112 Sutter
Nolan M. M. conductor, S. F. & San José R. R. Co. dwl 112 Sutter
Nolan M. P. first officer stm Golden City, dwl 637 Folsom
Nolan Ona, laborer, dwl U. S. Hotel, 706 Battery
Nolan Patrick, boot maker, 205 Stevenson
Nolan Patrick, teamster, 58 Stewart. dwl 1424 Pac
Nolan Patrick F. boot maker, dwl 519 Kearny
Nolan Peter, teamster with Davis and Sedgley, dwl Mission Creek nr Sixteenth
Nolan Peter, teamster, dwl S s Camp nr Second Av
Nolan Thomas, boatman, bds City Front House, 625 Davis ·
Nolan Thomas, boiler maker, Union Foundry, dwl N s Mission bet Fremont and Main
Nolan Thomas, hostler, North Beach & M. R. R. Co
Nolan Thomas, laborer, dwl 6 Shipley, rear
Nolan Thomas, night inspector Custom House, dwl Crescent Engine House
Nolan Thomas, plasterer, dwl E s Folsom Avenue nr Folsom
Nolan Thomas, produce, SE cor Anna and Ellis
Noland David, waiter, 626 Kearny
Noll George, tailor with Eugene Boucher, dwl 25 Anthony
Nollner Bernard, tobacconist, dwl Summer St. H
Nolstein Edward, dwl 214 Sansom
Nolte Charles R. groceries and liquors, NW cor Mission and Twenty-Fourth
Nolte William, watch maker and jeweler, 103½ Mont, dwl S s Minna bet Seventh and Eighth
Noltemeyer Frederic, groceries and liquors, SE cor Harrison and Chesley
NOLTING J. C. A. bar and billiard saloon, NW cor Washington and Kearny, dwl 420 Kearny
Nolting (William H.) & Spreen (William) oyster saloon and chop house, 640 Market, dwl 238 Sutter
Nolting (William H.) & Wilke (Louis) beer saloon, NE cor Bush and Kearny, dwl 238 Sutter
Noly Victor, stock agent, LeNational, office 533 Commercial, dwl SW cor Pine and Kearny ·
Nonan John, drayman, 739 Sacramento
Nonan Michael, laborer, dwl Morey Alley nr Powell
Nonnenmann Charles, butcher with Selig & Co. dwl nr Brannan St. Bridge
Noon Mark, shoe maker, dwl 15 Geary
Noon Martin, carriage maker with Stein, Link & Scherb, dwl 64 First
Noon Mary (widow) dwl 508 Mission
Noon Patrick, laborer, dwl N s Valencia nr Market
Noonan Ann Mrs. dwl E s Eighth nr Howard
Noonan Dennis B. laborer, S. F. Gas Co. dwl 44 Baldwin Court
Noonan James, dwl E s Eighth nr Howard
Noonan James, boiler maker, Union Foundry, dwl Empire House
Noonan Jeremiah, harness mkr with John O'Kane, 14 Sutter
Noonan John, laborer, dwl 38 Everett
Noonan John, laborer, dwl W s Salmon bet Mason and Taylor
Noonan Margaret Miss, domestic, 1015 Powell
Noonan Matilda Mrs. domestic, 920 Sutter
Noonan Michael, with Starr & Riddle, 16 Drumm, dwl 26 Sacramento
Noonan Patrick, box maker with Hobbs, Gilmore & Co. dwl 907 Folsom
Noonan Patrick, laborer, dwl 60 Stevenson
Noonan Patrick, laborer, dwl W s Valencia near Market
Noonan Patrick, sawyer with. Hobbs, Gilmore & Co. dwl 20 Hunt
Noonan Thomas, dwl E s Eighth nr Howard
Noonan Timothy, carpenter, dwl 914 Powell ·

Noonan William, lodgings, 114 Bush
Noonan William, marble worker, 10 Sutter, dwl 920 Sutter
Noonan, see Nunan
Nooney James, mining, dwl 327 Bush
Norak Caroline Miss, laundry, 904 Clay
Noran Alfred, porter, dwl 111 St. Mark Place
NORCROSS DANIEL, military goods and regalia, 5 Masonic Temple Mont, dwl 415 O'Farrell
Norcross Frank, painter, dwl 569 Mission
NORCROSS HARRIET N. Mrs. ladies dress trimmings, 5 Masonic Temple Montgomery, dwl 415 O'Farrell
Norcross Wesley F. dwl 11 Ellis
Norcross W. F. Mrs. teacher music, 11 Ellis
Nordblom Henry, actor, dwl 525 Greenwich
Norden Henry, laborer, Bay Sugar Refinery, dwl Sansom bet Union and Filbert
Norden N. G. stair builder, dwl NE cor Stockton and Market
Nordgren E. Henry (Malmgren & N.) res Saratoga, Santa Clara County
Nordon C. (Frederick H. Rosenbaum & Co.) res Germany
Noriega Pedro, hatter with Cornelius Desmond, dwl 23 Stevenson
Norlund Peter, liquor saloon, 32 Sacramento
Norman (Frank G.) & Co. (Joseph B. Houghton) groceries and liquors, SE cor Valencia and Sixteenth
Norman George, painter with John G. North, dwl 14½ Fourth
Norman M. (widow) fruits, N s Sixteenth bet Valencia and Mission
Normand E. V. wool packer, dwl 134 Minna
Norrey Anna Miss, domestic with Henry L. Kohn (No. 2)
Norring Albert F. porter, County Recorder's Office
Norris Charles, engineer, steamer John L. Stephens, dwl 214 Stewart
Norris Charles, workman with A. Fulton, cor Shasta and Illinois
Norris David, assistant foreman Evening Bulletin, dwl Harlan Place
Norris Edward, painter with A. & T. Torning, dwl 510 Sacramento
Norris George, well sinker, dwl 37 Commercial
Norris George N. apprentice, dwl 115 First
Norris James C. clerk, Bank California, dwl 939 Howard
Norris Michael, stone cutter, dwl 270 Clementina
Norris William, cooper with Henry Shuman, 120 Sacramento
NORRIS WILLIAM, office California Steam Navigation Co. SE cor Front and Jackson, dwl NW cor Stockton and Jackson
NORTH AMERICAN FIRE INSURANCE CO. New York, C. Adolphe Low & Co. agents, office 426 California
NORTH AMERICAN LIFE INSURANCE CO. J. A. Eaton & Co. general agents, office 240 Montgomery
NORTH BEACH & MISSION RAILROAD, office and depôt SW cor Fourth and Louisa
NORTH BRITISH AND MERCANTILE INSURANCE CO. W. H. Tillinghast agent, office 414 California
NORTH CHINA MARINE INSURANCE COMPANY, Koopmanschap & Co. agents, office NW cor Union and Battery
North Eclipse M. Co. office room 1 Government House 502 Washington
North John Mrs. dwl Oriental Hotel
NORTH JOHN G. proprietor North's Ship Yard, Point San Quentin, Potrero
North Point Dock, continuation Sansom bet Lombard and Chestnut
NORTH POINT WAREHOUSE, C. R. Peters & Co. proprietors, North Point Dock

North Potosi G. & S. M. Co. office 712 Montgomery
North San Francisco Railroad and Homestead Association, office 24 Montgomery Block
North Star G. & S. M. Co. office 228 Front
North Superior Copper M. Co. office 338 Mont
NORTHERN ASSURANCE FIRE AND LIFE INSURANCE CO. London, W. L. Booker agent, office 428 California
Northey Thomas F. (Souther & N.) dwl 714 O'Farrell
NORTHROP D. B. attorney at law, office 42 Montgomery Block
Northrop John, molder, dwl 520 Mission
NORTHUP (C. B.) & SHAW (E. B.) butter, cheese, etc. 76 Washington Market, dwl 200 Stockton
Norton A. dwl What Cheer House
Norton B. R. book keeper and salesman with R. B. Gray & Co. dwl 11 O'Farrell
Norton Catharine (widow) dwl 1304 Pine
Norton D. N. dwl Oriental Hotel
NORTON EDWARD, ex-judge Supreme Court, office NE cor Montgomery and Pine
Norton Ellen Miss, domestic, 408 Eddy
Norton Frank, with D. R. Provost & Co. dwl 735 Market
Norton G. & S. M. Co. office 8 Stevenson House
Norton George, with Lewis & Neville, dwl Tremont House
Norton George F. (Smith & N.) (col'd) dwl Lombard nr Franklin
Norton George M. mining, dwl 348 Fremont
Norton Henry, Forwarding Department Wells, Fargo & Co. dwl N s Sacramento bet Montgomery and Kearny
Norton Henry, miner, dwl S s Alta bet Montgomery and Sansom
Norton J. laborer, dwl SE cor Eighth and Mission
Norton James, carpenter, bds Commercial Hotel, 123 Pacific
Notton J. H. machinist apprentice, Vulcan Iron Works, dwl 348 Fremont
Norton John, porter with L. B. Benchley & Co
Norton John W. jr. teamster, Pier 1 Stewart, dwl 9 Hampton Place
Norton Joseph, dwl SW cor Polk and Pacific
Norton Joshua (Emperor) dwl 624 Commercial
Norton Julia (widow) dress making, dwl 208 Fourth
Norton Kate, domestic, 276 Mission
Norton Kearney, hostler, 115 Kearny, dwl 606 Post
Norton Malachi, farmer, Ocean House Flat
Norton Margaret Miss, domestic with Charles H. Stanyan
Norton Michael, driver, dwl 87 Stevenson
Norton M. J. Miss, assistant, Spring Valley Grammar School, dwl cor Pacific and Polk
Norton Patrick, hostler, dwl 706 Commercial
Norton Peter, cooper with Henry Shuman, 120 Sac
Norton R. C. with O. F. Willey & Co. 316 Cal
Norton Robert, cook, Franklin Hotel, SE cor Sansom and Pacific
Norton Rose Miss, domestic, 730 Filbert
Norton Samuel, dwl What Cheer House
Norton William H. proprietor Commercial Hotel, 123 and 125 Pacific
Norvall Edward, butcher, dwl S s Cemetery Alley bet Dolores and Church
Norwald P. Miss, dress making, 13 St. Mark Place
Norwood William E. book keeper, Russ House
Noslay F. R. seaman, dwl 26 Sacramento
Nothig William, driver, Philadelphia Brewery
Nouberger Salomo, physician, dwl NW cor Kearny and Jackson
Nougues Joseph, contractor and builder, dwl 318 Green
NOURSE JOSEPH P. mining secretary, office 620 Washington room 8, dwl 621 Harrison
NOVELTY IRON WORKS, E. T. Steen proprietor, 39 and 41 Fremont

Noyes Amos, marine surveyor, office NE cor Washington and Battery, dwl S s Guy Place
NOYES *(C. G.)* & WHITNEY *(A. W.)* stock and money brokers, office 608 Montgomery, bds Cosmopolitan Hotel
Noyes George H. drayman with Irvine & Co. dwl 10 Howard Court
Noyes James M. drayman with Redington & Co. dwl 10 Howard Court
Noyes J. D. pilot steamer Princess
Noyes John, brass molder, dwl 125 First
Noyes Leonard W. dwl 319 Kearny
Noyes Moody, laborer, dwl 937 Mission
Noyes Richard B. insurance broker, dwl S s Guy Pl
Noyes William F. dwl 10 Sutter
Noyes William N. dwl S s Guy Place
Noyo and Albion River Packets, A. W. Macpherson agent, Pier 20 Stewart
NUDD, *(A. D.)* LOW *(Joseph W.)* & CO. *(Charles S. Lord)* importers and wholesale dealers wines and liquors, 410 Front, dwl Occidental Hotel
Nuestra Señora de Guadalupe S. M. Co. office 620 Washington
NUEVO MUNDO (Spanish, tri-weekly) F. P. Ramirez & Co. proprietors, office SW cor Sansom and Jackson
Nugent Abigail (col'd, widow) dwl W s Varenne nr Union
Nugent Ellen (widow) dwl Clementina bet Second and Third
Nugent Mary, dwl 210 Jackson
Nugent Owen, laborer, dwl United States Hotel, 706 Battery
Nugent Peter, cook, dwl NW cor Jessie and Anna
Nugent Susan Miss, domestic, 720 Howard
Nugent Thomas, millwright, dwl 83 Everett
Nugent W. laborer, Spring Valley W. W
Nugent William H. calker, dwl Pacific Exchange
Nunan Bridget (widow) dwl E s Vallejo Place
Nunan Edward, carpenter and builder, 321 Pine, dwl 426 Geary
Nunan Edward, laborer, dwl 411 Post
Nunan Henry, carpenter and builder, dwl 426 Geary
Nunan James, laborer, bds with Joseph Seale, N s Turk nr Fillmore
NUNAN JEFFREY, editor and proprietor Irish News, office 510 Clay, dwl What Cheer House
NUNAN MATHEW, groceries and liquors, SW cor Bryant and Ritch ▪
Nunan Thomas, carriage trimmer with Larkins & Co. dwl First nr Stevenson
Nunan Thomas W. wheelwright with Casebolt & Co. dwl 914 Powell
Nunan Timothy, carpenter, dwl 914 Powell
Nunes Antonio, cook, dwl 725 California
Nungassar Saloma (widow) dwl with P. Muntag, S s Mission Creek nr Brannan St. Bridge
Nunn Joanna Mrs. dwl N s Folsom bet Fifth and Sixth
Nutson Charles, engineer, steamer Belle
Nutt John C. teamster with J. McGill & Co. dwl E s Eighth nr Minna
Nuttall John, engineer, Steam Paddy Co. dwl S s Harrison bet Seventh and Eighth
Nutting A. B. machinist, Vulcan Iron Works, dwl 31 Natoma
Nutting *(Calvin)* & Upstone *(John)* Pioneer Iron Works, 123 Bush, dwl NE cor Greenwich and Randall Place
Nutting Joseph E. contractor and builder, 714 Sansom, dwl SW cor Clay and Powell
Nuttman James E. carpenter, dwl Russ House
Nutz Frederick, sign and ornamental painter, 525 California, dwl 111 Dora nr Folsom
Nutzhorn Henry, laborer, dwl 26 Stewart
Nye A. R. clerk with Geo. W. Chapin
Nye John W. *(Henry Mahan & Co.)* dwl 68 Natoma

Nye Thomas, dwl 217 Third
Nyhan Thomas, driver, Omnibus R. R. Co. dwl W s Eleventh nr Folsom
Nyholm E. G. miner, dwl 20 Commercial
Nyland C. J. dwl What Cheer House
Nyland Mary Miss, with Kennedy & Bell, dwl E s Louisa bet Third and Fourth

O

O'BAVIN John, drayman, bds Clinton Temperance Hotel, 311 Pacific
O'Brian George, seaman, steamer Pacific
O'Brian James, drayman, dwl 822 Howard, rear
O'Brian Jeremiah, carpenter, dwl 321 Clementina
O'Brian John, butcher with Mrs. M. O'Brian, dwl 1217 Washington
O'Brian Michael Mrs. butcher, 13 and 14 Washington Market, dwl 1217 Washington
O'Brian P. carpenter, dwl 331 Bush
O'Brian Peter, deck hand, steamer Chrysopolis
O'Brian Peter, waiter, What Cheer House Restaurant
O'Brien Abbie Miss, domestic, 317 Powell
O'Brien Ann Miss, domestic, 632 Market
O'Brien Ann (widow) dwl 333 O'Farrell
O'Brien Aunie Miss, dress maker, dwl Spear bet Market and Mission
O'BRIEN BROS. *(Daniel and Michael)* groceries and liquors, SW cor Stockton and Vallejo
O'Brien Catharine (widow) dwl W s Leroy Place
O'Brien Catherine, boarding, 64 and 66 First
O'Brien Catherine L. Miss, dress making, 112 Post
O'Brien Charles, shoe maker, dwl 9 Berry, rear
O'Brien Cornelius, laborer, dwl United States Hotel, 706 Battery
O'Brien Cornelius, laborer, dwl E s Gough bet Bush and Pine
O'Brien Cornelius, porter, Howard Warehouse, dwl E s Battery bet Pacific and Broadway
O'Brien D. waiter, Cosmopolitan Hotel
O'Brien Daniel, dwl 1616 Dupont
O'Brien Daniel, dwl 107 Tehama
O'Brien Daniel, baker with Deeth & Starr, dwl 21 Clementina
O'Brien Daniel, drayman, cor Front and Jackson
O'Brien Daniel, laborer with John Center, dwl W s Florida nr Twentieth
O'Brien Daniel, rope maker, dwl W s Bryant bet Sixth and Seventh
O'Brien Daniel, scroll sawyer, dwl 74 Tehama
O'Brien Daniel, waiter, Russ House, dwl S s Turk bet Polk and Van Ness Avenue
O'Brien David, laborer, dwl 213 Tehama
O'Brien Dennis, confectioner, dwl 127 Second
O'Brien Dennis, laborer, dwl 411 Stevenson, rear
O'Brien Dennis, painter with Hopps & Kanary, dwl 333 Bush
O'Brien Edward, dwl 3 Central Place
O'Brien Edward, stone cutter, dwl 32 Webb
O'Brien Edward N. tailor, dwl 524 Battery
O'Brien Ellen (widow) dwl 550 Tehama
O'Brien E. M. (widow) female employment, office 110 Montgomery
O'Brien Felix, carpenter, dwl N s Geary nr Van Ness Avenue
O'Brien Felix, laborer, dwl E s Main nr Market
O'Brien Francis, hostler, dwl 814 Mission
O'Brien George, deck hand, steamer Pacific, dwl S s Vallejo bet Front and Davis
O'Brien James, boot maker, dwl 108 Pacific
O'Brien James, express wagon, corner Howard and Third
O'Brien James, clerk, U. S. Clothing Depôt, 34 Cal
O'Brien James, Enterprise Saloon, NW cor First and Stevenson, dwl 32 Tehama
O'Brien James, fruits, NE cor Pacific and Larkin
O'Brien James, laborer with George D. Nagle

O'Brien James, laborer, Fulton Foundry, dwl 547 Mission
O'Brien James, laborer, S. F. Gas Co. dwl 6 Turk
O'Brien James, laborer, S. F. Gas Co. dwl 128 First
O'Brien James, laborer, dwl 122 Shipley
O'Brien James, laborer, dwl 182 Stevenson
O'Brien James, laborer, dwl E s Crook bet Brannan and Townsend
O'Brien James, oysterman, 324 Sansom, dwl SW cor Washington and Sansom
O'Brien James K. teamster, Sutler's Store, Presidio
O'Brien Jeremiah, laborer, Union Court
O'Brien J. J. carpenter, Manhattan H. 705 Front
O'Brien Joanna Miss, domestic, 607 Bush
O'Brien (John) & Rice (John) furniture and bedding, 107 Second, dwl 314 Beale
O'BRIEN (John) & WARD (James) employment office, NE cor Montgomery and Clay, dwl N s Chestnut bet Powell and Stockton
O'Brien Kate Miss, domestic, 320 O'Farrell
O'Brien Kate, domestic, 451 Bryant
O'Brien John, laborer, dwl 314 O'Farrell, rear
O'Brien John, dwl 314 Beale
O'Brien John, baker with Deeth & Starr, dwl NE cor Pacific and Kearny
O'Brien John, blacksmith, S. F. Gas Co
O'Brien John, boot maker, 817 Battery, dwl 75 Fourth
O'Brien John, carpenter, dwl 728 Market
O'Brien John, cartman, cor Jones and Taylor
O'Brien John, cartman, dwl 614 Post
O'Brien John, calker, dwl 251 Tehama
O'Brien John, express wagon, corner Second and Mission
O'Brien John, express wagon, corner Third and Folsom
O'Brien John, laborer, S. F. Gas Co
O'Brien John, laborer, dwl 313 Sixth
O'Brien John, laborer, dwl nr cor Prentice and Courtlandt Avenue
O'Brien John, laborer, stm Cornelia, dwl W s Sansom bet Green and Union
O'Brien John, laborer, dwl S s Brannan bet Seventh and Eighth
O'Brien John, liquor saloon, Brannan St. Bridge, dwl N s Bryant bet Seventh and Eighth
O'Brien John, molder Union Foundry, dwl 52 Shipley
O'Brien John, molder, Fulton Foundry, dwl 547 Mission
O'Brien John, porter, 222 Cal, dwl 268 Clara
O'Brien John, saddler and harness maker, 240 Kearny, dwl SE cor Bush and Kearny
O'Brien John shoe maker, dwl 404 Green
O'Brien John D. brick mason, dwl 52 Louisa
O'Brien John D. contractor, dwl Manhattan Engine Co. No. 2
O'Brien John E. liquor saloon, Brannan St. Bridge, dwl W s Kate nr Bryant
O'Brien John H. & Co. gas fitters and plumbers, 706 Montgomery, dwl 209 Jones
O'Brien Joseph, dwl 2 Noble Place
O Brien Joseph, laborer, dwl 273 First
O Brien Joseph, porter with Blake & Moffitt, dwl 230 Jessie
O'Brien Lydia Miss, bds Franklin Hotel, SE cor Sansom and Pacific
O'Brien Margaret Miss, domestic, 843 Mission
O'Brien Margaret Miss, domestic, 960 Howard
O'Brien Margaret Miss, domestic, 811 Bush
O'Brien Margaret Miss, domestic, 323 Geary
O'Brien Margaret Miss, dress maker, dwl 245 Tehama
O'Brien Martin, butcher, SE cor Mission and Ninth
O'Brien Mary Miss, domestic, 420 Bryant
O'Brien Mary Miss, domestic, 1117 Pine
O'Brien Mary Miss, domestic, 526 Sutter
O'Brien Mary Miss, domestic, 606 Third
O'Brien Mary (widow) dwl 104 Minna

O'Brien Mary (widow) nurse with Mrs. John W. A. Gilmor, N s Mission bet Twelfth and Thirteenth
O'Brien M. bellman, Occidental Hotel
O'Brien Mathew, lodgings, 47 Jackson
O'Brien Mathew J. clerk with Martin O'Brien, dwl NW cor Laguna and Fell
O'Brien Mathias, gas fitter, 641 Market, dwl 265 Stevenson
O'Brien Michael, hostler, North Beach & M. R. R. Co. dwl cor Hayward and Louisa
O'Brien Michael, hostler with Louis McLane
O'Brien Michael (O'Brien Bros.) dwl SW corner Stockton and Vallejo
O'Brien Michael, laborer, dwl 128 First
O'Brien Michael, laborer with Edward J. Quirk
O'Brien Michael, laborer, dwl N s Allen nr Hyde
O'Brien Michael, laborer, dwl E s Salmon bet Mason and Taylor
O'Brien Michael, laborer, dwl E s Seventh bet Brannan and Townsend
O'Brien Michael, laborer, dwl United States Hotel 706 Battery
O'Brien Michael, porter with Fargo & Co. dwl 33 Valparaiso nr Taylor
O'Brien Michael, waiter, Market St. Restaurant, dwl 253 Jessie
O'BRIEN MICHAEL, wines and liquors, SW cor Vallejo and Davis, dwl 847 Howard
O'Brien Michael, waiter, 706 Market, dwl N s Jessie bet Third and Fourth
O'Brien Morris, confectioner with Charles H. Mercer, 518 Kearny, dwl 126 Minna
O'Brien Mortimer, laborer, dwl E s Guerrero bet Thirteenth and Fourteenth
O'Brien Patrick, carpenter, dwl SE cor Polk and Geary
O'Brien Patrick, gas fitter, dwl 265 Stevenson
O'Brien Patrick, handcartman, cor Folsom and Third
O'Brien Patrick, helper, Pacific Foundry, dwl Schaffer Place
O'Brien Patrick, laborer, dwl Higgins Place
O'Brien Patrick, liquor saloon, NW cor Folsom and Stewart
O'Brien Patrick, porter, 506 Market
O'Brien Patrick A. gas fitter with J. H. O'Brien & Co. 706 Montgomery, dwl 619 Geary
O'Brien Patrick J. carriage painter, SW cor Morse and Pine, dwl N s Bryant bet Seventh and Eighth
O'Brien Peter, laborer, dwl 207 Pacific
O'Brien P. J. janitor Eighth St. School
O'Brien P. R. plumber and gas fitter, 641 Market, dwl 265 Stevenson
O'Brien Rosanna Miss, domestic, St. Mary's Cathedral
O'Brien Rose Miss, domestic, 16 Prospect Place
O'Brien Thomas, dwl 5 Lick Alley
O'Brien Thomas, dwl E s Beale bet Market and Mission
O'Brien Thomas, blacksmith, dwl E s Varenne nr Union
O'Brien Thomas, collector, S. F. Gas Co. dwl 335 Tehama
O'Brien Thomas, gas fitter with P. R. O'Brien, dwl 13 Second
O'Brien Thomas, laborer, dwl Zoe Place
O'Brien Thomas, laborer, dwl 11 Hunt
O'Brien Thomas, local policeman, City Hall
O'Brien Thomas, miner, dwl N s Perry bet Fourth and Fifth
O'Brien Thomas, porter, Carlton's Warehouse
O'Brien Timothy, drayman, dwl SW cor Kearny and Pacific
O'Brien Timothy, gardener, dwl 54 Shipley
O'Brien Timothy, laborer, dwl SW cor Fifth and Stevenson
O'Brien Timothy, miner, dwl SW cor Folsom and Dora

O'Brien William, bar keeper, dwl 32 Tehama
O'Brien William, drayman, 36 Clay, dwl N s Sutter nr Franklin
O'Brien William, hostler, North Beach & M. R. R. Co
O'Brien William, laborer, dwl 6 Haywood
O'Brien William, mining, dwl 323 Stockton, rear
O'Brien William, wholesale butcher, Ninth near Brannan, dwl W s Ninth nr Folsom
O'Brien Willliam James, drayman with H. Casebolt & Co
O'Brien William S. (Flood & O'B.) dwl Washington opp Stone
O'Brien, see Brien, Bryan, and O'Brian
O'Bryan M. dwl What Cheer House
O'Byrne Felix, editor, dwl 622 Green
O'Callaghan Daniel, collector Daily Examiner, dwl Brooklyn Hotel
O'Callaghan D. J. commission merchant, 106 Clay, dwl S s Chestnut bet Dupont and Kearny
O'Carroll Kate Miss, chambermaid, Occidental Hotel
O'Connell Anthony F. drayman, dwl 1610 Mason
O'Connell Charles, deck hand, steamer Julia
O'Connell Christopher, laborer, dwl 330 Green, rear
O'Connell Cornelius, laborer, dwl 208 Harrison
O'Connell Daniel, carpenter, dwl N s Fell nr Octavia
O'Connell Dauiel, machinist, dwl 65 Stevenson
O'Connell Daniel A. waiter, dwl 181 Jessie
O'CONNELL DANIEL A. watch maker, 155 Third
O'Connell James, packer, dwl W s Main bet Market and Mission
O'Connell James, porter, 612 Sacramento, dwl S s Clementina bet Third and Fourth
O'Connell James, wood yard, Mission St. Wharf, dwl NW cor Tehama and Fifth
O'Connell Jane Miss, domestic, SE cor Shotwell aud Sixteenth
O'Connell John, express wagon, cor Montgomery and Sutter, dwl N s Mission nr Sixth
O'Connell John, laborer, dwl 32 Langton
O'Connell John, porter, 612 Sacramento, dwl S s Clementina bet Third and Fourth
O'Connell Julia (widow) dwl W s Tyson Place
O'Connell Laurence, laborer, dwl 263 Clementina
O'Connell Maggie Miss, domestic, 1118 Bush
O'Connell Margaret, Tri Mountain House, 545–549 Market
O'Connell Martin, gas fitter, dwl 63 Stevenson
O'Connell Mathew, express wagon, cor Bat and Sac
O'Connell Michael, laborer, dwl 43 Baldwin Court
O'Connell Michael, laborer, dwl 230 Minna
O'Connell Patrick, laborer with Augustus Lind
O'Connell Thomas, laborer, dwl 156 Natoma
O'Connell Thomas, soap maker, dwl Beale St. House
O'Connell William, boot maker, dwl 152 First
O'Conner B. clerk, dwl 103 Second
O'Conner Bridget, chambermaid, Occidental Hotel
O'Conner Hugh, porter, 214 California
O'Conner James, soda bottler, Empire Soda Works, dwl NE cor Harrison and Third
O'Conner Jeremiah, stone cutter, bds Market bet Third and Fourth
O'Conner Margaret Mrs. saloon, 156 Third
O'Conner Michael, foreman with R. Feuerstein & Co. dwl Oak Park nr Bryant
O'Conner Michael, machinist, Union Foundry, dwl 26 Anthony
O'Conner Patrick, butcher, Liberty Hose Co. No. 2
O'Conner Patrick, laborer, dwl SE cor Stevenson and Ecker
O'Conner Patrick, molder, Union Foundry, dwl Geary nr Market
O'Conner Patrick, teamster, dwl N s Brannan bet Seventh and Eighth
O'Conner Timothy, hostler, Central R. R. Co. dwl W s Gilbert bet Bryant and Brannan
O'Conner Timothy, laborer, dwl 20 Jessie
O'Conner William, shoe maker, 152 First, dwl 156 First

O'Conners Dennis, driver, dwl 45 Stevenson
O'Conners Dennis jr. baker, dwl 45 Stevenson
O'Conners John, boiler maker, dwl 518 Mission
O'Connor Bridget Miss, domestic, 827 Bush
O'Connor Catherine, domestic, 250 Fourth
O'Connor Cornelius, contractor and builder, dwl 34 Natoma
O'Connor Daniel, boarding, 26 Fourth
O'Connor Daniel, laborer, dwl 40 Louisa
O'Connor Daniel, transcript clerk, P. O. dwl Russ House
O'Connor Dennis, laborer, dwl SE cor Drumm and Commercial
O'Connor Dennis, porter, Pacific Engine Co. No. 8
O'Connor Edward, S.J., St. Ignatius College, S s Market bet Fourth and Fifth
O'Connor Francis, drayman, cor Mission and Stewart
O'Connor Frank, dwl N s Brannan nr Sixth
O'Connor Frank, coupé, South Park Livery Stable
O'Connor Frank, waiter, steamer Yosemite
O'Connor Hannah (widow) dwl 775 Market
O'Connor H. T. attorney at law, office 45 Montgomery Block, dwl 331 Bush
O'Connor Hugh (Killip & O'C.) dwl 515 Post
O'Connor James & Bro. (John O'Connor) jobbers and wholesale dealers wines and liquors, 512 Battery, dwl 517 Mason
O'Connor James, dwl 1016 Stockton
O'Connor James, express wagon, cor Third and Stevenson
O'Connor Jane, chambermaid, Occidental Hotel
O'Connor Jeremiah, dwl N s Harrison, rear, bet Seventh and Eighth
O'Connor Jeremiah, printer with Towne & Bacon, dwl 547 Market
O'Connor Johanna Miss, domestic, 939 Sacramento
O'Connor John (James O'Connor & Bro.) 512 Bat
O'Connor John (Molloy & O'C.) dwl SE cor Gough and Pacific
O'Connor John, carpenter, dwl 111 Fourth
O'Connor John, gardener with J. C. Horan
O'Connor John, laborer, dwl 11 Langton
O'Connor John, laborer, dwl SE cor Pac and Gough
O'Connor John, laborer, dwl S s Greenwich nr Stockton
O'Connor John, steward, Pacific Mail S. S. Co
O'Connor John F. (Conroy & O'C.) res New York
O'Connor Kate Miss, domestic, 517 Dupont
O'Connor M. Miss, assistant, Mission Grammar School, Seventeenth nr Dolores
O'Connor Margaret Miss, domestic, 833 Post
O'Connor Margaret Miss, domestic, 820 Mission
O'Connor Margaret Miss, domestic, 616 O'Farrell
O'Connor Mary, ironer, Chelsea Laundry
O'Connor Mary Miss, dwl N s Union bet Sansom and Calhoun
O'Connor Mary Miss, dwl 209 Ellis
O'Connor Mary Miss, domestic, 315 Fifth
O'Connor Mary Miss, domestic, 517 Dupont
O'Connor Mary Mrs. lodgings, 188 Stevenson
O'Connor Michael, bricklayer, bds Franklin House SW cor Sansom and Broadway
O'Connor Michael, butcher with J. Conway, dwl W s Alameda nr El Dorado
O'Connor Michael, express wagon, cor Front and Jackson
O'Connor Michael, laborer, dwl 7 Ecker
O'Connor Michael J. (Conroy & O'C.) dwl 845 Mission
O'Connor Moses, importer and jobber wines and liquors, NW cor Front and Jackson, res San Lorenzo, Alameda Co
O'Connor Patrick, handcartman, dwl W s Gilbert bet Brannan and Townsend
O'Connor Patrick, laborer, S. F. & San José R. R. Co
O'Connor Patrick, laborer, dwl 840 Market
O'Connor Patrick, sash and blind maker with Geo. Robinson & Co. dwl S s Stevenson bet First and Second

O'Connor Patrick M. cartman, dwl Gilbert near Brannan
O'Connor P. J. architect, dwl 571 Howard
O'Connor Simon, waiter, steamer Yosemite
O'Connor Terence, real estate, dwl 316 Fourth
O'Connor, Thomas, bar keeper, Russ House, dwl N s Minna bet Third and Fourth
O'Connor Thomas, clerk with A. Giorgiani, dwl SW cor Hyde and O'Farrell
O'Connor Thomas H. (Conroy & O'C.) res New York
O'Connor Thomas J. clerk with Conroy & O'Connor, dwl 731 California
O'Connor Timothy, brass finisher with M. Greenberg
O'Connor Timothy, carpenter, dwl N s Welch bet Third and Fourth
O'Connor Timothy, drayman, dwl 7 Jane
O'Connor Timothy, hackman, dwl 413 Bryant
O'Connor Timothy, miller, 110 Fremont, dwl 21 Beale
O'Connor William, cartman, cor Mont and Sansom
O'Connor William, laborer, dwl N s Union bet Calhoun and Sansom
O'Daniel Bryan, laborer, dwl E s Salmon bet Mason and Taylor
O'Day Dennis J. teamster with Sinclair & Moody, dwl 208 Ritch
O'Day Michael, drayman, cor Front and Jackson
O'Day Thomas, drayman with McAran & Kelly, dwl Folsom Avenue
O'Day Thomas, laborer, dwl Church bet Green and Lombard
O'Day William, varnisher, dwl 114 Bush
O'Dea Bridget Miss, cook, 522 Sutter
O'Dea Martin, horse shoer with Patrick Brannan, dwl 174 Stevenson
O'Dea Michael, laborer, dwl 308 Vallejo
O'Dea Thomas, teamster, dwl N s Church Place
O'Dell Alonzo, blacksmith, bds 840 Market
O'DOHERTY GEORGE, official reporter, Fourth and Twelfth District courts, office City Hall room 15 second floor, dwl Occidental Hotel
O'Doherty William, drayman, 401 Sansom, dwl cor Mission and Fifth
O'Donahue Patrick, miner, dwl 2 Trinity
O'Donahue Thomas, shutter maker with J. R. Sims, dwl E s Stock bet Filbert and Greenwich
O'Donald James, United States Nursery, NE cor Fifth and Folsom
O'Donald John, printer, dwl 179 Minna
O'Donnell Bernard, proprietor North Beach Livery Stable, 1808 Powell
O'Donnell Charles, hostler, 807 Montgomery
O'Donnell Charles, physician, office 32 Kearny, dwl 544 Third
O'Donnell Cornelius, tanner, S s Brannan bet Fifth and Sixth
O'Donnell Cornelius, trunk maker with E. Galpen & Co. dwl S s Harrison bet Fourth and Fifth
O'Donnell Dennis, job wagon, corner Howard and Fourth, dwl 256 Clementina
O'DONNELL HUGH, real estate, dwl NE corner Dupont and Vallejo
O'Donnell James, tailor, dwl 112 First
O'DONNELL JAMES, wines and liquors, 6 Drumm, dwl SE cor Front and Oregon
O'Donnell John, machinist, bds 606 Third
O'Donnell John, tailor with S. Hass & Co. dwl 112 First
O'Donnell Julia Mrs. dwl cor Bdwy and Gough
O'Donnell Margaret (widow) dwl NE cor Union and Mason
O'Donnell Margaret (widow) dwl 12 O'Farrell Alley
O'Donnell Martin, butcher, dwl 10 Central Place
O'Donnell Michael, laborer, dwl 28 Silver
O'Donnell P. waiter, Cosmopolitan Hotel
O'Donnell Patrick, miner, dwl N s Hayes nr Market
O'Donnell Thomas, handcartman, cor Davis and Broadway

O'Donnell Timothy, tanner, dwl Western Hotel
O'Donoghue Jeremiah J. teacher, dwl 75 Fourth
O'Donoghue J. H. L. clerk, dwl 16 Sansom
O'Dougherty Andrew B. professor classics and belles lettres, Union College
O'Dougherty Edward, student, St. Mary's Hospital
O'Dougherty William, drayman, cor San and Sue
O'Douf Eleanor (widow) dwl SW cor Utah and Sixteenth
O'Dowd John, porter with DeWitt, Kittle & Co. dwl cor Pacific and Franklin
O'Dowd Michael, fruits, 924 Market
O'Dwyer James, salesman, 48 Second, dwl 137 Tehama
O'Farrell Andrew, dwl with Michael O'Farrell, 607 Geary, rear
O'Farrell Catherine (widow) dwl 12 Natoma
O'Farrell Michael, dwl 607 Geary, rear
O'Farrell T. laborer, dwl S s Harrison bet Main and Spear
O'Ferrall Francis, book keeper with Brennan & Co. dwl 613 Mason
O'Ferrall M. Rev. S.J. professor rhetoric St. Ignatius' College, S s Market bet Fourth and Fifth
O'Ferrall M. J. clerk, NW cor Second and Howard
O'Flaherty Dennis, hackman, Plaza
O'Flaherty Richard, asphaltum worker, dwl 5 Mason
O'Flaherty Thomas, dwl E s Geneva nr Brannan
O'Garra Ann Mrs. domestic with E. Corbett, W s Fifth bet Howard and Folsom
O'Gorman Thomas, porter, dwl 27 Jane
O'Grady Anne Miss, dwl S s Mission bet Second and Third
O'Grady Coleman, stone mason, dwl S s Vallejo bet Taylor and Jones
O'Grady (James) & Flynn (Hugh) wood and coal, 831 Howard, dwl 362 Clementina bet Third and Fourth
O'Grady James, waiter, dwl 10 Jessie
O'Grady Patrick, butcher, dwl 1005 Pacific
O'Grady Thomas, tailor, dwl 504 Minna
O'Gray George, express wagon, 625 Montgomery
O'Halloran Florence, molder, Union Foundry, dwl 326 Tehama
O'Halloran Timothy, laborer, dwl 1013 Mason
O'Hanlon Felix, drayman, cor Market and Stewart, dwl 17 Hunt
O'Hanlon James, marble worker, dwl 202 Dupont, rear
O'Hara Bridget (widow) 764 Harrison
O'Hara (Charles) & Co. (P. Henry Rice) wood and coal, 133 Post, dwl 110 Kearny
O'Hara Edward, machinist, Union Foundry, dwl 248 Tehama
O'Hara James, laborer, dwl 9 Clara
O'Hara John, waiter, Russ House
O'Hara Thomas, tinsmith, dwl N s Lynch bet Leavenworth and Hyde
O'Hara William G. newspaper carrier, dwl 145 Fourth
O'Hare Edward, molder, dwl 75 Jessie
O'Hare James, watchman with Dinsmore & Co. dwl W s Gilbert bet Bryant and Brannan
O'Hare John, California Nursery, cor Twentieth and Harrison
O'Hare Kate Miss, domestic, 515 Ellis
O'Hea Richard, mariner, dwl 522 Filbert
O'Heron John, laborer, dwl 459 Jessie
O'Herran Daniel, laborer, Spring Valley W. W
O'Herron Thomas, laborer, dwl NW cor Stevenson and Ecker
O'Kane John, express wagon, 217 Commercial
O'KANE JOHN, harness, saddles, etc. 526 Kearny and 14 Sutter, dwl 508 Brannan
O'Kane Margaret Miss, domestic with Edward Kirby, N s Fifteenth bet Howard and Mission
O'Keefe Abbey Miss, domestic, 831 Jackson
O'Keefe Cornelius, drayman, dwl N s Stevenson bet Sixth and Seventh

O'Keefe Daniel, clerk with H. P. Wakelee, dwl cor Folsom and Sixth
O'Keefe Daniel, policeman, City Hall, dwl 519 Filbert
O'Keefe David, handcartman, cor Broadway and Battery
O'Keefe Dennis, laborer, steamer Pacific
O'Keefe Dennis, laborer, dwl W s Battery bet Filbert and Union
O'Keefe John, driver, Mason's Brewery
O'Keefe John, seaman, dwl 132 Folsom
O'Keefe Joseph, cabinet maker with W. G. Weir, dwl 15 Natoma
O'Keefe Michael, waiter, Cosmopolitan Hotel, dwl 801 Geary
O'Keefe William, clerk with H. P. Wakelee, dwl 515 Taylor
O'Keeffe Daniel, groceries and liquors, NE cor Harrison and Dora
O'Keeffe Thomas F. dwl 311 Stockton
O'Keeffe Thomas J. dwl 311 Stockton
O'Kerr Matt. waiter, Cosmopolitan Hotel
O'Kune J. W. collector, S. F. Gas Co. dwl SE cor First and Natoma
O'Laughlin Stephen, laborer, dwl W s Battery bet Vallejo and Green
O'Leary Daniel, painter with James R. Kelly, dwl SE cor Jessie and Anthony
O'Leary Dennis, drayman with A. E. Sabatie & Co. dwl W s Jones bet Post and Sutter
O'Leary Johanna Miss, domestic, 935 Sacramento
O'Leary Patrick, marble polisher, dwl United States Hotel 706 Battery
O'Loan John, driver, Central R. R. Co. dwl SE cor Sixth and Shipley
O'Lordan Daniel, hostler, Central R. R. Co. dwl S s Mary nr Chesley
O'Loughlen Edmund, watchman with P. Tiernan, dwl cor Mariposa and Minnesota
O'Malley James, plumber with Thomas O'Malley, 646 Market
O'Malley James J. machinist, Union Foundry, dwl E s Jones nr Geary
O'Malley John, watchman, Metropolitan Theater, dwl 917 Jackson
O'Malley Michael, molder, Union Foundry, dwl 518 Jones
O'Malley Patrick, upholsterer with Goodwin & Co, dwl 23 Natoma
O'Malley Thomas, plumber and gas fitter, 646 Market, dwl 727 Ellis
O'Marley James, plumber, dwl 36 Natoma
O'Meara Bridget (widow) dwl 1110 Pine
O'Meara Margaret Miss, cloak maker with L. Leszynsky, dwl W s Buenaventura nr Cal
O'Meara Mary (widow) dwl 518 Bryant
O'Meara Mary (widow) dwl N s Lynch bet Leavenworth and Hyde
O'Meara Mary Ann Miss, domestic, 7 Mason
O'Meara Michael, drayman, cor Mission and Stewart, dwl 16 Hunt
O'Neal James B. machinist, Pacific Foundry, dwl 549 Mission
O'Neal Smith, chimney sweep, 339 Bush
O'Neil Anne Miss, chambermaid, St. Nicholas Hotel
O'Neil Arthur, express wagon, NE cor Clay and Kearny, dwl SW cor Jessie and Third
O'Neil Catharine Miss, domestic, 331 Fourth
O'Neil Charles, dwl 23 Fremont
O'Neil Charles, molder, dwl Washington Hose H
O'Neil Charles, tailor, 210 Leidesdorff, dwl Bartol Place nr Vallejo
O'Neil Daniel, laborer, dwl 1020 Folsom
O'Neil David, locksmith, dwl 420 Dupont
O'Neil Dennis, helper, Vulcan Foundry, dwl Brown Alley nr Dupont
O'Neil Dennis, laborer, dwl 135 Sutter
O'Neil E. Miss, milliner, dwl 130 Second
O'Neil Edward, clerk, steamer Chrysopolis

O'Neil Edward, with Cutting & Co. dwl Sutter bet Kearny and Dupont
O'Neil Edward, laborer, Vulcan Iron Works
O'Neil Edward, machinist, Union Foundry, dwl 78 Natoma
O'Neil Eugene, draftsman, dwl N s Bryant bet First and Fremont
O'Neil Felix, foreman with M. E. Hughes, 730 Montgomery, dwl 30 Moss
O'Neil James, bookbinder with Buswell & Co. dwl 121 St. Mark Place
O'Neil James, fireman, dwl 8 Natoma
O'Neil James, job wagon, SW cor Market and Third, dwl SE cor Chesley and Mary
O'Neil James, laborer, dwl W s Main, bet Market and Mission
O'Neil James, laborer, dwl W s Clara nr Sutter
O'Neil James, laborer, dwl E s Chesley nr Harrison
O'Neil James, retortman, S. F. Gas Co
O'Neil James, seaman, steamer Senator
O'Neil James F. saloon keeper, dwl NE cor Stockton and Geary
O'Neil Jeremiah T. house, sign, and ornamental painter, 10 Sutter, dwl New Branch Hotel
O'Neil John (Manchester & O'N.) dwl 627 Pacific
O'Neil John, assistant propertyman, Maguire's Opera House
O'Neil John, blacksmith, dwl Empire House
O'Neil John, fireman, S s Folsom bet Spear and Main
O'Neil John, house painter, dwl SW cor Kearny and Francisco
O'Neil John, laborer, dwl 46 Beale
O'Neil John, liquor saloon, SW cor Kearny and Pac
O'Neil John, longshoreman, bds Golden Age Hotel 127 Pacific
O'Neil John, machinist, dwl 29 Hinckley
O'Neil Julia (widow) dwl S s Fella Place
O'Neil Lawrence, laborer, dwl 541 Mission
O'Neil Margaret (widow) dwl 16 Anthony
O'Neil Mary Miss, dress maker, 46 Beale
O'NEIL MICHAEL, proprietor New Branch Hotel, 12 Sutter, and livery and sale stable, 17 Sutter
O'Neil Michael S. clerk, dwl 12 Sutter
O'Neil M. J. wholesale liquors, 312 Jackson, dwl 403 Lombard
O'Neil Morris, pantryman, steamer Yosemite
O'Neil O. H. professor mathematics, Union College
O'Neil Patrick, laborer, dwl W s Mary Lane nr Bush
O'Neil Patrick, laborer, Market St. R. R. Co. dwl W s Dolores nr Seventeenth
O'Neil Peter (D. Sullivan & Co.) dwl NE cor Fifth and Clara
O'Neil Solomon, laborer, dwl SW cor Pacific and Fillmore
O'Neil Thomas (John Mallon & Co.) dwl S s Mary bet Seventh and Eighth
O'Neil Thomas, drayman, Wash Hose Co. No. 1
O'Neil Thomas, drayman, 311 Com, dwl 535 Howard
O'Neil Thomas, driver, North Beach & M. R. R. Co
O'Neil Timothy, laborer, dwl 12 First
O'Neil William, laborer, S. F. Gas Co
O'Neil William, laborer, dwl N s Clay bet Van Ness Avenue and Franklin
O'Neil William, seaman, dwl SE cor Alta and Calhoun
O'Neill Anne Miss, domestic with John Anderson, E s Mariposa nr Carolina
O'Neill Bernard, boiler maker with Coffey & Risdon, dwl 159 Silver
O'Neill Charles, carpenter, dwl W s Eliza bet Taylor and Jones
O'Neill Charles, laborer, dwl S s Grove nr Larkin
O'Neill Cornelius, varnisher with Goodwin & Co. dwl N s Market bet Third and Fourth
O'Neill Edward W. clerk, C. S. Navigation Co. dwl 753 Howard
O'Neill Francis (Flintoff & O'N.) dwl 13 Ann

O'Neill Hugh *(Crummie & O'N.)* dwl NE cor Sixteenth and Hampshire
O'Neill James, butcher with R. O'Neill, dwl 11 Russ
O'Neill James, job wagon, cor Montgomery and Sacramento, dwl 220 Dupont
O'Neill James, secretary Omnibus R. R. Co. office S s Howard bet Third and Fourth, dwl 351 Minna
O'Neill James, workman with John Sheridan, dwl Serpentine Avenue nr San Bruno Road
O'Neill James jr. teamster, dwl 220 Dupont
O'Neill John, butcher with W. Smith, dwl Potrero Avenue
O'Neill Patrick, express wagon, cor Clay and Kearny
O'Neill Patrick, milkman, dwl N s Alta bet Montgomery and Sansom
O'Neill P. F. blacksmith, dwl 28 Second
O'Neill Richard, butcher, 15 and 16 Washington Market, dwl 11 Russ
O'Neill Sarah Miss, domestic, 226 Sixth
O'Neill Thomas Rev. O.S.D. pastor St. Bridget's Church, cor Van Ness and Broadway
O'Neill Thomas, salesman with Taaffe & Co
O'Niel Annie (widow) dwl SW cor Sixth and Mkt
O'Niel Mary Miss, domestic, 1015 Jackson
O'Niel Michael, proprietor New Branch Hotel, 12 Sutter
O'Niel Michael, trunk maker with E. Galpen & Co. dwl 46 Beale
O'Niel Sarah Miss, domestic, 227 Fourth
O'Niel William, laborer, dwl 528 Union, rear
O'Pitz Frederick, blacksmith, dwl 741 Market
O'Regan Patrick, hog butcher, dwl W s Eleventh bet Folsom and Harrison
O'Regan Patrick, ship carpenter, dwl 60 Beale
O'Regan P. D. bakery, SE cor Fourth and Jessie
O'Reilly F. J. bar keeper, 509 Washington, dwl 713 Howard
O'Reilly *(James)* & Brady *(Bernard)* groceries and liquors, NW cor Mission and Sixth
O'Reilly John, painter, dwl NE cor Kearny and Filbert
O'Reilly John, laborer, dwl 504 Vallejo
O'Reilly Joseph, boiler maker, dwl SW cor Louisiana and Sierra
O'Reilly Michael, painter, dwl NE cor Kearny and Filbert
O'Reilly Michael, porter, bds Franklin Hotel, SE cor Sansom and Pacific
O'Reilly Michael, stone cutter, dwl 29 Geary
O'Reilly Michael R. assistant, St. Mary's Cathedral
O'Reilly Peter, machinist, Pacific Foundry, dwl Larkin nr Turk
O'Reilly Peter, brick layer, dwl 111 Geary
O'Reilly Philip, waiter, Lick House
O'Riley Jeremiah, laborer, S. F. & San José R. R. Co
O'Riley Patrick, hostler with Central R. R. Co. dwl SE cor Clinton and Brannan
O'Rourke Bernard, dwl S s Pine bet Pierce and Scott
O'Rourke Hugh, clerk with Feehan, Byrnes & Co. dwl SE cor Jessie and Fourth
O'Rourke James, boiler maker, dwl 200 Bush
O'Rourke John *(Fogarty & O'R.)* dwl 10 Sherwood Place
O'Rourke John, well borer, dwl S s Fourteenth nr Folsom
O'Rourke John, wood turner with A. Jellinek, dwl Jessie nr Third
O'Rourke Lawrence, conductor, Omnibus R. R. Co. dwl 307 Minna
O'Rourke Michael, carpenter, dwl 26 Ritch
O'Rourke Patrick, butcher, SW cor Minna and Jane, dwl 112 Jessie
O'Rourke Patrick, laborer, dwl 120 Austin
O'Rourke Peter, hackman, Lick House, dwl S s O'Farrell bet Stockton and Powell

O'Rourke T. porter, Cosmopolitan Hotel
O'Shaughnessy William J. butcher, dwl NW cor Grove and Octavia
O'Shea Daniel, bricklayer, dwl 15 Tehama Place
O'Shea James J. stoves and tin ware, 1324 Stockton, dwl 1526 Stockton
O'Shea Kate (widow) dwl 11 Hunt
O'Shea Patrick, laborer, dwl 121 Commercial
O'Shea Thomas, carpenter, dwl 12 Sutter
O'Shea Thomas, contractor, dwl cor Ellis and Hyde
O'Shea William, contractor, dwl S s Ellis bet Jones and Leavenworth
O'Sullivan Abbey, domestic, 965 Howard
O'Sullivan Catharine Miss, dwl 106½ Clay
O'Sullivan Timothy, workman, S. F. & P. Sugar Co. dwl W s Dora nr Harrison
O'Sullivan William, with Reynolds, Howell & Ford, dwl 24 Sansom
O'Toole James, boot maker, W s Davis nr Broadway, dwl SE cor Dupont and Francisco
O'Toole John, shoe maker with T. J. Broderick, dwl SE cor Jones and Sacramento
Oaks James, carpenter, dwl 728 Market
Oakes John engineer, bds Franklin Hotel, SE cor Sansom and Pacific
OAKLAND AND SAN ANTONIO STEAM NAVIGATION CO. foot Pacific
Oakland Homestead Association, office 305 Montgomery room 6
Oakley Oliver B. silver plater, 108 Leidesdorff, dwl E s Market bet Twelfth and Thirteenth
Oakley Robert O. book keeper, 219 Sansom, dwl S s Mission bet Eighth and Ninth
OAKLEY *(Samuel E.)* & JACKSON *(Charles)* salt, cider, vinegar, etc. 320 Front, dwl 706 Folsom
Oaktree James, dwl 320 Fifth
Oatley George W. carpenter, dwl with P. L. Murphy, E s Howard bet Fifteenth and Sixteenth
Oatley Joseph, seaman, dwl 113 Commercial
Obenauer Geo. hairdresser, 43 Second, dwl 80 Jessie
Obernauer John, dwl 524 Vallejo
Obenduer George, tailor, dwl 1624 Dupont
OBER BENJAMIN, homeopathic physician, office and dwl 109 St. Mark Place
Oberg Charles M. laborer with Moore & Co. dwl E s Clinton nr Brannan
Obergh John A. stationer, 158 Third
Oberhoff Henry, seaman, bds 7 Washington
Obermeier Francis, shoe fitter, 10 Dupont
Ocaranza Jesus, compositor, La Voz De Mejico, dwl Vallejo bet Powell and Stockton
Occidental Copper M. Co. office 302 Montgomery
OCCIDENTAL HOTEL, Lewis Leland & Co. proprietors, SE cor Montgomery and Bush
OCCIDENTAL INSURANCE CO. San Francisco, office SW cor Montgomery and California
OCCIDENTAL MARKET, Market to Sutter bet Sansom and Montgomery
Ocean Beach M. T. Road Co. office 605 Montgomery
OCEAN HOUSE. James R. Dickey proprietor, 6½ miles SW City Hall
OCEAN RACE COURSE, J. M. Daniels proprietor, 6½ miles SW City Hall
Oche Battes, workman with E. Morrell, dwl NE cor Twentieth and Florida
Ochne F. upholsterer, dwl 29 Third
Ochs Solomon, meat market, 10 Dupont, dwl 9 Dupont, rear
Ochs Sophie (widow) boarding, 427 Sacramento
ODD FELLOWS' CEMETERY ASSOCIATION, office 325 Montgomery
ODD FELLOWS' HALL, 323–327 Montgomery
ODD FELLOWS' SAVINGS AND HOMESTEAD ASSOCIATION, office 325 Mont
Odell Jacob, insurance broker, office 206 Front, dwl SE cor Fifth and Mission
Odell Jacob, watchman, U. S. Branch Mint, dwl 873 Mission

Odenheimer William, boot maker with Henry Rose, dwl 54 First

Odermatt Franz, machinist, Pacific Foundry, dwl E s Second nr Tehama

Odero Maria (widow) dwl W s Galatin bet Fifteenth and Sixteenth

ODEUM GARDEN AND CONCERT HALL, NW cor Dolores and Fifteenth Mission Dolores, H. A. Siegfried & Co. proprietors

Odgman Henry, tinner, dwl 120 Natoma

Odlund Erick, seaman, dwl 26 Sacramento

Oeding John, cigar maker, dwl 1 Montgomery Pl

Oeffinger Chr. cooper, Philadelphia Brewery

Oehlert Henry, cigars, tobacco, and fruit, 7 Stewart

Oehm Englebard, carpenter with S. S. Culverwell, dwl N s Geary nr Larkin

Oester Charles (Julius Nicholas & Co.) dwl 513 Davis

Oestermann Louis, clerk, 435 Kearny

Oesting Paul, garden, S s Presidio Road nr Steiner

Offenbehr Elizabeth Mrs. dwl 639 Bdwy, rear

Offenberg John L. pastry cook Russ House, dwl N s Tyler bet Hyde and Larkin

Offerman Henry C. clerk, SW cor Third and Tehama

Offerman (John) & Co. (Edward Cornelissen) groceries and liquors, NE cor Dupont and Pacific, dwl 1111 Dupont

Offerman John H. groceries and liquors, NE cor Fourth and Mission

Offo (Chinese) physician, 639 Jackson

Offt George, seaman, bds 7 Washington

Ogburn Henry U. tinsmith with B. C. Austin, dwl 764 Howard

OGDEN FREDERICK, mining, office 338 Montgomery room 7, dwl 427 Second

Ogden George S. with C. Meyer & Co. 314 Davis

Ogden H. W. dwl What Cheer House

Ogden Margaret, stewardess steamer Julia

Ogden Richard L. office SE cor Montgomery and California room 7

Ogilvie John, job wagon, cor Montgomery and Sacramento, dwl 1013 Bush

Ogilvie M. (widow) dwl 22 Silver

Ogle (James) & Schriefer (Diedrick H.) groceries and liquors, 155 Natoma

Oglesby James, boiler, Assayer's Department U. S. Branch Mint, dwl 1018 Pine

Oblandt Henry & Nicholas, groceries and liquors, NW cor Pacific and Powell

Ohlandt (Nicholas) & Co. (John Buck) proprietors bone factory, New Potrero (and H. & N. Ohlandt) dwl nr Brannan St. Bridge

Ohlandt Richard, clerk with H. & N. Ohlandt

Ohlendorff Louis J. H. clerk with Becker Bros. 600 Montgomery

Ohlsol P. H. sailor, dwl 27 Frederick

Ohlson Marcus, carpenter, dwl S s Nevada bet Eleventh and Twelfth

Ohm Charles, laborer, S. F. & San José R. R. Co. dwl 46 Silver

Ohm Edward F. watches and jeweler, 615 Montgomery, dwl 211 Geary, rear

Ohm Frederick, shoe maker, 103 Sansom

Ohm Louis, porter steamer Sierra Nevada, dwl 262 Jessie

Ohman John, boatman, dwl Third St. Wharf

Ohmans William, upholsterer with Wightman & Hardie, 416 Clay, dwl 514 Pine

Ohmeis George E. wood turner with Cameron & Kuenzi, dwl 325 Pine

Ohn Gee (Chinese) employment office, 630 Jackson

Ohnstein Oscar, waiter, 416 Kearny

Ohrt Christian, cigars and tobacco, 521 Clay, dwl 28 O'Farrell

Oipel Jules, cabinet maker with J. Peirce, dwl 724 Harrison

Olbrecht Augustus, real estate, office 338 Montgomery, dwl 1212 Kearny

Olcovich Bros. (Joseph, Bernhard, and Heyman) commission merchants, office 403 California

Olcovich Bernhard (Olcovich Bros.) dwl 403 Cal

Olcovich Heyman (Olcovich Bros.) dwl 403 Cal

Oldham Caleb (col'd) laborer, dwl 821 Pacific

Oldham Charles W. whitewasher, NW cor Pine and Sansom

Oldman Henry, tailor, dwl 27 Jessie

Olds Julia R. (widow) dwl 533 Union

Oliff M. laundryman with John Erskine, 305 Davis

Oliva Juan B. vegetable garden, nr Hunter's Point

Oliver Anthony, distiller, dwl E s First Avenue nr Fifteenth

Oliver Christian, mariner, dwl 32 Stewart

OLIVER D. J. importer and wholesale dealer paints, oils, glass, varnishes, etc. 318 Wash

Oliver Elizabeth P. (widow) 308 Third

Oliver James, custodian California Art Union, 312 Montgomery, dwl 308 Third

Oliver James L. musician, 613 Clay

Oliver J. C. barber, dwl 741 Market

Oliver (John) & Warfield (John) (col'd) bootblacking, etc. 508 Kearny

Oliver John B. with D. J. Oliver, 318 Washington, dwl 243 Jessie

Oliver John C. hairdresser, dwl 138 Fourth bet Minna and Howard

Oliver Robert, engineer, dwl NW cor Broadway and Davis

Olivia Antoine, gardener with Milo Hoadley

Olligan William H. laborer, Golden State Iron Works, dwl 4 Quincy

Olmstead Fred L. dwl Brevoort House

Olmstead James M. lumber surveyor, dwl 639 Mission

Olmstead Louis, furnished rooms, SE cor Third and Hunt

Olmstead Sarah (widow) boarding, 759 Market

Olmsted John C. clerk, Cosmopolitan Hotel, dwl 803 Bush

Olmsted John C. salesman, 34 Mont, dwl 734 Mission

Olmsted Rowland, dwl 327 Bush

Olney Charles C. book keeper with Wm. K. Dietrich, dwl 17 Hampton Place

Olney James N. (Edwards, O. & Co.) dwl 17 Hampton Place

Olney James N. jr. architect, office 630 Sacramento, dwl 17 Hampton Place

Oloan John, driver, Central R. R. Co. dwl 315 Sixth

Olof John H. seaman, bds 7 Washington

Olonier Xavier, bell founder, dwl 22 St. Charles nr Kearny

OLPHERTS (Robert) & BERGIN (Daniel) Bob's Saloon, NW cor Kearny and Jackson, dwl 512 Broadway

Olsen Andrew, seaman, dwl 26 Sacramento

Olsen Bartlett C. seaman, dwl 26 Sacramento

Olsen H. photographic gallery, 650 and 652 Washington, dwl 617 Kearny

Olsen H. C. (D. Sweeney & Co.) dwl NE cor Fell and Webster

Olsen John, cooper with Henry Shuman, 120 Sac

Olsen John E. liquor saloon, 107 Washington

Olsen L. W. cooper with Cutting & Co. dwl Second bet Howard and Mission

Olsen Martin, laborer, dwl Golden Eagle Hotel

Olsen Mary Miss, domestic, 438 Natoma

Olsen Nicholas, seaman, dwl 26 Sacramento

Olsen Peter, oiler, steamer Orizaba

Olsen Peter, seaman, dwl 26 Sacramento

Olsten John, cook with David B. Hughes, dwl S s Lombard bet Taylor and Jones

Olston Christopher, pile driver with Galloway & Boobar

Oltmanns Conrad, porter, dwl 54 Stewart

Olufs Henry, bar keeper, 9 Washington

Olwell James, contractor, dwl 76 Natoma

Olwell William G. book keeper with Frank G. Edwards, dwl 1612 Stockton

OLYMPIC CLUB ROOMS, 8 s Sutter nr Mont
Omburg Joseph, hairdresser with Aaron Creamer, American Exchange
OMNIBUS RAILROAD CO. office Union Hall, 721-731 Howard bet Third and Fourth
On Lung (Chinese) washing, dwl 1407 Pacific
On Wo (Chinese) washing, 646 Market
Oneota S. M. Co. office 24 Government House
Oneste Joseph, peddler, dwl 1002 Powell
Onfray Mme. groceries, 1204 Dupont
Ontario G. & S. M. Co. office 405 Front
Openheimer William, shoe maker, 647 Merchant
Openshaw Joseph, dwl 105 Freelon
Ophir of the Colorado No. 1 G. & S. M. Co. office 338 Montgomery
OPHIR SILVER MINING CO. office NE corner Montgomery and California
Opitz Frederick, blacksmith with Kimball & Co. dwl 290 Dupont
Oppenheim Benjamin, crockery, 1111 Dupont
Oppenheim Michael, perfumery manufacturer, 412 Union
Oppenheimer Emanuel, shaving saloon, NW corner Union and Powell, dwl 436 Union
OPPENHEIMER *(Henry)* & BROTHER *(Max Oppenheimer)* importers and jobbers cigars and tobacco, 311 Clay, dwl 536 Ellis
Oppenheimer Joseph, clerk, SW corner Bush and Kearny
Oppenheimer Louis, clerk with Oppenheimer & Bro. dwl 536 Ellis
Oppenheimer Max *(Oppenheimer & Bro.)* dwl 536 Ellis
Oppenheimer Max, clerk, 413 Mont, dwl 531 Cal
Oppermann Christian, musician, dwl 1505 Powell
Oram John, laborer, dwl 113 William
Oramas Theodore, clerk, 103 Montgomery, dwl 927 Washington
Orange Flouring Mills, J. P. Raymond & Co. agents, office 119 Clay
Ordenstein Bernard, salesman with Unger & Bro, dwl 4 Custom House Block
Ordenholt Frederick, porter, 205 Sansom
Ordner Louis, bar keeper, SW cor Kearny and Pac
Ordway J. clerk with Ackerson & Russ, dwl 308 Beale
Ordway Robert J. upholsterer, dwl N s Vallejo bet Larkin and Polk
OREGON AND CALIFORNIA LINE PACK- ETS, Richards & McCraken agents, office 405 Front
Oregon and Mexican Lines Steamers, Ben. Holla- day proprietor, office SW cor Front and Jackson
Oregon G. & S. M. Co. office 402 Front
OREGON, VICTORIA AND SAN DIEGO STEAMSHIP LINE, California Steam Nav. Co. proprietor, office NE cor Front and Jackson
Orem John, messenger Twelfth L. H. District, dwl 113 William
Orford Robert, stone cutter, dwl 6 Central Place
ORIENTAL HOTEL, SW cor Bush and Battery
Original Buckeye M. Co. office 702 Washington
ORIGINAL HOUSE, 531 and 533 Sacramento, E. & L. Lasar proprietors
Orion G. & S. M. Co. office 338 Montgomery
Orleans G. & S. M. Co. office 622 Clay
Orley John, gardener, Tyler nr Webster
Orlich John, seaman, dwl 26 Sacramento
Ormsby Charles W. carpenter, dwl NE cor Bush and Sansom
Orney A. F. machinist, 120 Fremont, dwl Bush bet Sansom and Battery
ORPHAN ASYLUM (Protestant) Laguna, Bu- chanan, Haight, and Kate, 2 miles SW Plaza
ORPHAN ASYLUM (Roman Catholic) 8 s Market bet Second and Third
Orphant Robert, blacksmith, Vulcan Iron Works, dwl 42 Jessie
Orr James, stevedore, dwl 329 Green

ORR *(John K.)* & ATKINS *(Robert C.)* gents' furnishing goods, 417 Mont, dwl 745 Clay
Orr Joseph N. baggage master, S. F. & San José R. R. Co. res San José
Orr William H. groceries and liquors, SW cor Har- rison and Fifth Avenue
Orresto G. express wagon, dwl Clementina near Fourth
Orrick Mary (widow) dwl 22 Clementina
Orris John, laborer, dwl 55 Stevenson
Orteig Joseph, stone mason, dwl N s Pacific bet Du- pont and Kearny
Ortelli Joseph, drayman, 538 Washington, dwl N s Filbert bet Taylor and Jones
Ortet Jean, cutlery, 223 Leidesdorff
Orth August, cook, Occidental Restaurant 536 Wash
Orth George, clerk with J. F. Blumberg, dwl 18 First
Ortiz Manuel, waiter, steamer Yosemite
Ortiz Vicente, clerk, dwl 25 Sixth
ORTMANN JOHN F. groceries and liquors, 815 Jackson, dwl 1202 Mason
Osberg Charles E. jeweler with W. Bohm, dwl N s Bush bet Kearny and Dupont
Osborn Anthony (col'd) dwl 19 Stone
Osborn C. Mahlon, with Lewis & Neville, dwl 1004 Bush
Osborn Frank H. clerk, 8 Clay
Osborn *(G. W.)* & Seasions *(E. C.)* real estate agents, 619 Merchant, dwl Erie nr Howard
Osborn H. E. clerk with Crane & Brigham, dwl 1517 Dupont
Osborn Henry, water tender, stm John L. Stephens, dwl NW cor First and Frederick
Osborn Henry A. pile driver, 554 Folsom
Osborn Homer B. carrier, Golden Era, dwl 1715 Dupont
Osborn Jasper B. merchant, dwl 620 Pine
Osborn John, clerk, Pier 3 Stewart, dwl Mission Dolores
Osborn John, laborer, dwl SE cor Pac and Kearny
Osborn John, laborer, dwl E s Shotwell bet Twenty- First and Twenty-Second
Osborn Joseph, mining, dwl 412 Geary
Osborn Maria Mrs. ranch, W s Old San José Road nr St. Mary's College
Osborn R. F. & Co. *(W. G. Osborn)* importers and dealers hardware, 751 Market
Osborn William B. cook, dwl 532 Commercial
Osborn William G. *(R. F. Osborn & Co.)* dwl 115 Ellis
Osborne Catharine (col'd) dwl 2 Brooklyn Place
Osgood Ambrose, ship calker, SW cor Powell and Greenwich
Osgood Archer, carriage painter with G. P. Kim- ball, dwl 64 Third
OSGOOD *(George)* & STETSON *(James B.)* tin can and box manufactory, 219 Commercial, dwl 1045 Howard
Osgood Henry, stevedore, dwl 26 Stewart
Osgood H. P. *(Fielding & O.)* dwl 1021 Wash
Osgood Jane Miss, dwl with J. W. Towne, N s Thirteenth nr Howard
Osgood J. K. (widow) dwl 208 Jones
Osgood John F. *(Osgood & Co.)* res Roxbury, Mass
Osgood Porter, flour packer, National Mills, dwl 242 Minna
Osgood *(William H.)* & Co. *(John F. Osgood)* commission merchants, office 214 California
Osmer Charles *(George Osmer & Co.)* dwl 318 Folsom
Osmer, George & Co. *(John G. W. Schulte and Charles Osmer)* Ensign Liquor Saloon, 1 Mar- ket and NE cor Folsom and Stewart, dwl 218 Folsom
Osorio Francisco, compositor, Flag, dwl Gautier House 516 Pacific
Ossalino *(Salvatore)* & Co. *(G. Tavalaro)* Omni- bus Restaurant, Metropolitan Market

Ossiander Julius, with Thurnauer & Zinn, dwl 805 Bush
Osterhaus Joseph A. cigar maker, dwl 310 Ritch
Osterholt Mary Miss, domestic with Frederick Katz
Osterhoudt Madison S. clerk with A. Lusk & Co. dwl SE cor Folsom and Beale
Ostermann Louis, confectioner with Ehrenpfort & Co. dwl 13 Noble Place
Ostheimer John, laborer, dwl 637 Broadway
Ostrander Catherine (widow) dwl with A. Robinson San Bruno Road nr Santa Clara
Ostrander Peter, express wagon, dwl N s Geary bet Devisidero and Broderick
Ostrander Stephen. salesman with Davis & Schafer, dwl 309 Harrison
Oswald James, laborer, dwl Point Lobos Road nr Lone Mountain Cemetery
Oswald William, proprietor Harbor View Market, 1005 Pacific, dwl 908 Broadway
Otis Charles, builder, dwl 225 Second
Otis James *(Macondray & Co.)* dwl 1105 Taylor
Otis Stephen & Co. *(W. H. Farnum)* real estate and stocks, 509 Clay, dwl SW cor Larkin and Green
Ott August, cook, dwl 1707 Dupont
Ott George W. .shoe maker with Francis Worth, dwl 1204 Powell
Ott John & Co. *(Joseph Ott)* Pacific Bakery, 1017 Pacific
Ott Joseph *(John Ott & Co.)* dwl 1017 Pacific
Ott Josephine Miss, domestic, 1100 Stockton
Ott Mary Miss, domestic, 323 Pine
Otten Victor, dwl 434 Union
Ottenheimer William, merchandise broker, 322 Commercial, dwl 229 Fourth
Ottignon J. L. Melter and Refiner's Department U. S. Branch Mint, dwl 2 Quincy
Otto Charles *(Marwedel & O.)* dwl 713 Sutter
Otto Frederick, molder with S. S. Culverwell, 29 Fremont, dwl 55 Fifth
Otto Gustavus, physician, office SW cor Pine and Belden, dwl 3 St. Mark Place
Otto John, dwl 639 Clay
Otto John, tailor, dwl 818 Pacific
Otto Philomena Mrs. ladies' nurse, dwl 55 Fifth
Otto William, cartman, dwl Clark nr Bush
Ottoway Thomas, laborer, dwl 3 Lick Alley
Ottway Thomas, engineer, dwl 3 Natoma
Otzberger Martin, painter, dwl N s Bush bet Franklin and Gough
Ould — & Co. groceries, NE cor Third and Silver
Oulif Alexis, salesman, 514 Sac, dwl 611 Sac
OUR MAZEPPA, T. de M. Hylton editor and proprietor, office SE corner Washington and Sansom
Ontman Tobias, tailor, 731 Pacific
Overend Alfred, pressman, 511¼ Clay, dwl E s Calhoun bet Green and Union
Overend John A. T. steam power presses, 511¼ Clay, dwl E s Calhoun bet Green and Union
Overend Lizzie Miss, assistant, Montgomery Street School, dwl E s Calhoun bet Green and Union
OVERLAND MAIL COMPANY, office Wells, Fargo & Co. NW cor Montgomery and Cal
OVERLAND TELEGRAPH CO. office 507 Mont
Overman S. M. Co. office 619 Montgomery
Overton Elias P. carpenter, dwl Tyson Place
Overton J. P. dwl cor Filbert and Van Ness Av
Oviedo Visente, dwl 1521 Dupont
Owen A. W. milk ranch, S s Presidio Road opposite Presidio House
Owen Charles, book keeper with Morgan, Stone & Co. dwl 733 Harrison
Owen Charles L. laborer, dwl 46 Silver
Owen E. D. machine hand with S. S Culverwell, 29 Fremont, dwl 623 Howard
OWEN JAMES H. *(Kemp & O.)* dwl 733 Harrison
Owen James H. mining superintendent, dwl 810 Howard

OWEN LAWRENCE C. grand secretary Grand Chapter R. A. M. office Masonic Temple, dwl 696 Geary
Owen Mary Miss, dress maker, dwl 353 Jessie
Owen Michael, blacksmith, dwl 1217 Kearny, rear
Owen P. H. office 610 Merchant
Owen R. B. clerk with Rienzi Hughes, dwl 118 Third
Owens Anna Mrs. dwl 513 Howard
Owens Daniel, painter with Noble & Gallagher, 437 Jackson
Owens David, with Thomas Lea, 430 Pine
Owens Hannah Miss, domestic, 710 Vallejo
OWENS HENRY, ship builder, cor Michigan and Shasta
Owens James, laborer, dwl Greenwich bet Sansom and Montgomery
Owens John, dwl 734 Howard
Owens John A. miller, National Flour Mills, dwl Oriental Hotel
OWENS JOHN B. coal oil and lamps, 10 Third
Owens John M. orderly with Col. Scott, dwl Pres'o
Owens Martin, workman with A. Tait, dwl San José Road nr St. Mary's College
Owens Mary Miss, domestic, 417 O'Farrell
Owens Mary Mrs. domestic, 14 Sutter
Owens M. C. painter, dwl NW cor Sac and Stock
Owens Nancy Miss, domestic, 608 Sutter
Owens O. R. porter, 223 Clay, dwl 237 Bush
Owens Owen W. ship carpenter, dwl cor Shasta and Michigan
Owens P. A. freight clerk, S. F. & San José R. R. Co. dwl 919 Folsom
Owens Patrick, boot maker, dwl 33 Jackson
Owens Patrick, clerk, dwl 845 Dupont
Owens Patrick, laborer, dwl 207 Pacific
Owens Peter, laborer, dwl E s William nr Geary
Owens Philip, boot maker, dwl SE cor Front and Oregon
Owen's River G. & S. M. Co. office 1 Government House, 502 Washington
Owens Robert, porter, dwl 229 Bush
Owens Samuel, with Lewis & Neville, dwl 515 Sac
Owens Thomas (col'd) porter, dwl Hall Court
Owens Thomas J. clerk, 10 Third, dwl 12 Third
Owens William, carpenter with Isaac D. Holt, W s Folsom bet Sixteenth and Seventeenth
Owens William P. dwl 54 First
Oxenham A. H. importer and jobber guns, pistols, and notions, 19 Sansom
Oxer John, carrier, Bulletin, dwl W. s Leavenworth bet Vallejo and Broadway
Oxland Robert, F.C.S. and professor chemistry Toland Medical College, dwl 1014 Stockton
Ozanne Marceline (widow) dress maker, 713 Dupont

P

Pacaud Mary, French laundry, 178 Jessie
Pace Charles, chronometer and watch maker, 613 Battery, dwl 1018 Jackson
Pacheco Jesus M. clerk, NE cor Vallejo and Dupont
Pacheco Line Packets, J. A. McClelland & Co. agents, office 11 Clay
PACIFIC (weekly) Revs. J. A. Benton, George Mooar, W. C. Bartlett, and E. C. Bissell editors, office room 1 NE cor Clay and Front
PACIFIC AND ATLANTIC TELEGRAPH CO. office 507 Montgomery
PACIFIC BANK, P. H. Burnett president, Edward W. Smith cashier, 400 Montgomery cor California
Pacific Barrel Factory, John D. Keedy agent, 313 and 315 Davis
PACIFIC BOARD BROKERS, 606 Washington
PACIFIC BREWERY, Frederick Fortmann proprietor, 271 and 273 Tehama
PACIFIC BUSINESS COLLEGE, 747 Market, M. K. Laudenslager president

PACIFIC CLUB ROOMS, 633 Commercial and 634 Sacramento
PACIFIC COAST BUSINESS DIRECTORY, Henry G. Langley proprietor, office 612 Clay
Pacific Distillery Co. (William Hesse, Henry Voorman, Frederick Putzmann, George Schultz, and Henry Von Bargen) Bay Shore and Fort Point Road, 2¼ miles from Plaza
Pacific Flour Mills, 508 Pacific
PACIFIC FRUIT MARKET, Graves & Williams proprietors, 532 and 534 Clay
Pacific G. & S. M. Co (Esmeralda) office 321 Wash
Pacific G. & S. M. Co. (Santa Cruz Co.) office 338 Montgomery
PACIFIC GLASS WORKS, Mariposa nr Mississippi, Potrero, office 621 Clay
PACIFIC GLUE FACTORY, George S. Dana proprietor, cor Gough and Lombard
Pacific Guano Co. office 509 Clay
PACIFIC HARDWARE AGENCY, L. W. Kennedy agent, office 409 California
Pacific House, Pinner & Laflin proprietors, 35 Pac
PACIFIC INSURANCE CO. office 436 Cal, Jonathan Hunt president, A. J. Ralston secretary
PACIFIC IRON WORKS, Goddard & Co. proprietors, 127-133 First
PACIFIC MAIL STEAMSHIP CO. Oliver Eldridge agent, office NW cor Sacramento and Leidesdorff
PACIFIC MEDICAL AND SURGICAL JOURNAL AND PRESS (bi-monthly) Thompson & Co. publishers, 505 Clay
PACIFIC METALLURGICAL WORKS, North Beach, office SE cor Montgomery and California
Pacific Mineral Co. off Odd Fellows' Hall, 325 Mont
PACIFIC MUSEUM OF ANATOMY, L. J. Jordan proprietor, Eureka Theater, 318 Mont
Pacific Ore Co. office 240 Montgomery
Pacific Petroleum Refining Co. cor Chestnut and Taylor, Stanford Bros. proprietors, 121 Cal
PACIFIC SALT WORKS, Barton & Brother proprietors, 218 Sacramento
Pacific Straw Works (Ebenezer R. Hawley, James M. Forest, Henry W. Thompson, and Edward Ralston) office 603 Market
Pacific Temperance House, William Jackson proprietor, 109-113 Pacific
Pack J. engineer with G. Venard, dwl NW cor Sansom and Merchant
Packard Alonzo O. machinist, Pacific Foundry, dwl 54 First
Packard Cyrus, carpenter, 320 Jackson, dwl corner Coso Avenue and Cherubusco
Packard Edward H. sash and blind maker with Geo. Robinson & Co. dwl 27 Minna
Packard Oscar L. machinist, Pacific Foundry, dwl 54 First
Packard William, dwl 531 Tehama
Packer Elizabeth (widow) dwl S s Francisco bet Kearny and Dupont
Packer James, clerk, dwl S s Francisco bet Kearny and Dupont
Packer John, gardener, dwl cor Wash and Octavia
Packer John, laborer, Fort Point
Packer William H. clerk with John C. Bell, dwl S s Francisco bet Dupont and Kearny
Padderatz, Henry, waiter, 612 Clay, dwl 41 Baldwin Court
Paddock George, painter, dwl 166 Tehama
Paddock N. C. office 606 Front, dwl 915 Clay
Padilla Theodore, miller, dwl 52 Stevenson
Padre George, varnisher with Goodwin & Co. dwl 821¼ Vallejo
Padua Nicola, vegetable garden, S s Serpentine Avenue nr Folsom
Pagannini (Antonio) & Valente (Louis) liquors, NE cor Mont and Pac, dwl 523 Broadway
Paganini Pietro, musician, Gilbert's Museum, dwl 309 Broadway

Page Benjamin F. book keeper with S. L. Mastick & Co. dwl 804 Howard
Page Charles S. carpenter, dwl 319 Geary
Page E. M. mason, Spring Valley W. W
Page Francis H. fruits, 605 Market, dwl 329 Pine
Page Francis S. book keeper, 36 Stewart, dwl 919 Clay
Page Frank, clerk, dwl 17 Third
Page George, longshoreman, dwl 1021 Battery
Page Henry C. teamster, dwl 329 Pine
Page J. H. (John Taylor & Co.) dwl 1015 Clay
PAGE JOSEPH M. crockery, glass, and hardware, 42 Clay, dwl 820 Filbert
Page Maxy B. street sprinkler, 679 Market
Page Nathaniel, real estate, office 206 Front
Page Peter, ship carpenter, dwl 14 Louisa
Page R. B. dwl 113 Dupont
Page Robert C. (Price & P.) stock broker, 626 Clay, dwl 515 Ellis
Pages Jules F. jewelry engraver, 622 Clay, dwl 732 Washington
Pages R. machinist, dwl SW cor Dupont and Bdwy
Paget George W. real estate, dwl 608 Third
Pahl Richard, boot maker, 77 Fourth
Paige Calvin, real estate, office 205 Battery
Pailloz Charlotte Madame, lace mender, 110½ Sutter
Paine E. P. clerk, 9 Washington Market, dwl cor Second and Jessie
Paine F. A. driver, Chelsea Laundry
Paine George C. carpenter, dwl 18 Third
PAINE (Horace J.) & ADAMS (Quincy L.) dentists, office 522 California
Paine John, carpenter, Sumner bet Howard and Mission
Paine L. B. clerk, steamer Josie McNear
Paine William, waiter, International Hotel
Paine, see Payne
PAINTER (Jerome B.) & CO. (John M. and Theodore P. Painter) printers and printers' furnishing goods, 510 Clay, dwl SE cor Powell and Jackson
Painter John M. (Painter & Co.) dwl SE cor Powell and Jackson
Painter Theodore P. (Painter & Co.) dwl SE cor Powell and Jackson
Painter Thomas Ross, dwl S s Clementina nr Sixth
Pajeken Edward, clerk, 217 Front, dwl 7 Prospect Pl
Palache Gilbert (H. M. Newhall & Co.) dwl 321 Fremont
Palache James, book keeper with DeWitt, Kittle & Co. dwl S s Thirteenth bet Valencia and Mission
Palacio Ellen L. Miss, dwl 1511 Powell
Palecki Joseph, cooperage, N s Washington bet Front and Davis, dwl 11 Lafayette Place
Pall Cornelius, seaman, steamer Orizaba
Pallier John G. (col'd) cook, 219 Bush, dwl 21 Lewis Place
Pallies Alexander, porter, 323 Clay, dwl E s Powell bet Chestnut and Francisco
Palm Edward, bowling saloon, 403 Pine Russ Block, dwl N s California bet Kearny and Dupont
Palmer Charles C. Vigilant Engine Co. No. 9
PALMER CYRUS (Howland, Angell & King) dwl 315 Second
Palmer Ed. C. mailing clerk, S. F. Post Office, dwl 509 Powell
Palmer Elisha P. dwl 228 Stevenson
Palmer George B. carpenter, dwl 615 Market
Palmer James, lumberman, dwl 150 Clara
Palmer Jane B. (widow) dwl N s Riley nr Taylor
Palmer John, boatman, dwl 38 Jackson
Palmer John C. with William Shew, 421 Mont
Palmer John L. dwl 211 Minna
Palmer John L. carpenter, dwl 49 Third
Palmer Laura Mrs. dwl W s Sonoma Pl nr Union
Palmer, (L. W.) Gillespie (James) & Co. (William W. Henry) broom manufactory, 205 Davis, dwl Tyler nr Buchanan

Palmer Mary (widow) dwl E s Main bet Folsom and Harrison
Palmer Richard, carpenter, dwl N s Bernard bet Jones and Leavenworth
Palmer Samuel L. salesman with Treadwell & Co. dwl 3 Front
Palmer Sophia T. Miss, dwl 329 Second
Palmer Thomas, boatman, dwl E s Davis bet Pacific and Jackson
PALMER, (Wales L.) KNOX (Israel W.) & CO. (William A. Palmer) proprietors Golden State Iron Works, 19–25 First, dwl 327 Second
Palmer Walter W. mining, dwl 520 Sutter
Palmer William, carpenter, Board Education, dwl 422 Stevenson
Palmer William A. (Palmer, Knox & Co.) dwl 329 Second
Palmer William D. teamster, 563 Market, dwl 7 Front
Palmer W. J. T. carpenter, dwl 422 Stevenson
Palmerston Adelbert R. R. porter, 30 Clay
Palmi Nicoli, laborer with B. Bonnet & Co
Palmieri Agostin, fisherman, 2 Italian Fish Market
Palmtag Andrew, shoe maker, 18 Stewart
PALTENGHI (Andrea) & LARSENEUR (Peter) marble yard, 422 Jackson, dwl 416 Union
Panario Frank, porter with Goodwin & Co. dwl Washington Hose House
Pancho O. fish, 13 Washington Fish Market
Pander Ezekiel, tinsmith with Charles Brown, dwl 32 Geary
Pandora G. & S. M. Co. office 6 Montgomery Block
Panelli Peter, porter, 420 Battery, dwl S s Union bet Powell and Mason
Panitz Frederick, laborer, Bay Sugar Refinery, dwl 813 Battery
Paoletti Guiseppe, fisherman, 45 Italian Fish Market
Paolnelli G. A. peddler, dwl 1112 Dupont
Pape Augustus, stoves and tin ware, 1328 Dupont
Pappe Lizzie Miss, domestic, 117 Taylor
Papy J. J. attorney at law, office 604 Merchant
Paquette A. F. porter with Hunter, Wand & Co. dwl 240 Green
Paradise J. George, porter, 116 California, dwl W s Leavenworth bet Pine and California
Paragon Petroleum Co. office 206 Jackson
Parburt George R. attorney at law, office 41 Exchange Building, dwl 808 Green
Parcells John J. dock and wharf builder, dwl 18 Tehama
Parcells William H. carpenter, Tiger Engine Co
Pardee Eli H. physician, office 767 Clay, dwl 56 Fourth
Pardee Enoch H. oculist, office 767 Clay, dwl 256 Fourth
Pardee George, draftsman, Pacific Foundry, dwl 117 Natoma
Pardessus Rena M. dwl S s Twenty-Third bet Valencia and Bartlett
Pardies Jean, workman with L. Artigues, dwl NW cor Sixteenth and Rhode Island
Pardini Narciso, fish dealer, 32 Italian Fish Market
Pardow George, mining secretary, office 15 Montgomery Block, dwl 1310 Powell
Pardow George jr. photographic printer with Addis & Koch, dwl 1310 Powell
Parent C. L. ship joiner, dwl 232 Fremont
Paret Cornelius W. L. paper hanger, dwl E s Tyson Place nr Washington
Pargo Anthony, cigars, 717 Montgomery, dwl S s Mission bet First and Second
Parice Richard A. (col'd) cook, Bailey House
Paris Frank, handcartman, cor Pacific and Dupont
Paris James, handcartman, dwl Trinity nr Bush
Parie José, brick maker with William Buckley
Parish D. C. box maker with J. S. Gibbs, 307 Mkt
Parish L. W. foreman, Spring Valley W. W
Parish Norman, machinist with S. S. Culverwell, 29 Fremont, dwl 623 Howard

Park Alvah W. stone cutter, dwl 12 St. Mark Place
Park Edmund M. sash maker with Smith, Ware & Co. dwl 221 Second
Park E. W. carrier, Alta California, dwl NW cor Twenty-Fourth and Mission
Park G. & S. M. Co. office 6 Montgomery Block
Park J. dwl Bay State House
Park John C. policeman, dwl 107 Pacific
Park Susan (widow) seamstress, dwl 17 Third
Park Thomas C. seaman, dwl 423 East
Parkell Henry H. dwl 318 Pine
Parkell H. H. Mrs. furnished rooms, 318 Pine bet Montgomery and Sansom
Parker Abraham H. dwl SE cor Sixth and Clara
Parker A. C. (widow) dwl 839 California
Parker A. H. dentist, office and dwl 3 Brenham Pl
Parker Alonzo F. clerk, dwl SE cor Third and Hunt
Parker A. P. (Harlow & P.) dwl 256 Stevenson
Parker Benjamin, trunk maker with E. Galpen & Co. dwl E s Mission bet Twenty-First and Twenty-Second
Parker Charles, seaman, dwl 26 Sacramento
Parker Charles C. P. clerk with R. C. Rogers, 614 Merchant
Parker Charles F. builder, dwl NW cor Leavenworth and Green
PARKER CHARLES H. attorney at law, office 8 and 9 Montgomery Block, dwl NW cor Broadway and Taylor
Parker E. stone cutter, dwl 18 First
PARKER EDWARD H. importer and agent Hazard Powder Co. and Ætna Insurance Co. office 226 California, dwl 1118 Howard
Parker Edward W. (col'd) boot maker, 414 Third, dwl 786 Harrison
Parker Elmira (widow) dwl 757 Mission, rear
Parker Emeline E. (widow) private school, S side Twentieth nr Dolores
Parker Francis L. dwl 514 Minna
Parker Frederick, porter with Boswell & Shattuck, dwl 323 Sutter
Parker F. Warren, shoe cutter with H. M. Beers, dwl 7 O'Farrell
Parker G. plasterer, dwl 315 Bush
Parker George, carpenter, dwl 206 Stewart
Parker George A. with B. C. Horn & Co. dwl 834 Clay
PARKER GEORGE F. proptr Bank Exchange, SE cor Mont and Wash and wholesale wines and liquors, 632 Montgomery, dwl 1212 Powell
Parker George H. American Clock Store, 303 Montgomery, dwl 323 Jessie
Parker Hale P. book keeper, Bank Exchange, dwl 407 Post
Parker Harvey D. with George F. Parker, dwl 1716 Mason
Parker H. C. merchant, dwl Lick House
Parker Helen F. Miss, assistant, Montgomery Street School, dwl 43 Clara
Parker James, clerk with Thomas Magnes, NE cor Broadway and Scott
Parker James, steward, dwl 624 Commercial
Parker James W. clerk, dwl NW cor Minna and Fourth
Parker Johanna (widow) dwl 62 Stevenson
Parker John, compositor, Hebrew, dwl 250 Beale
Parker John, hackman, American Exchange
Parker John C. Fair Wind Liquor Saloon, NW cor Sacramento and East
Parker John E. dwl 201 Powell
PARKER JOHN G. jr. secretary California Home Insurance Co. office 224 and 226 California, dwl NE cor Turk and Franklin
Parker John H. baker with Swain & Brown, 5 Kearny
Parker John W. dwl 407 Post
Parker Joseph M. with Geo. F. Parker, dwl 407 Post
PARKER JOSEPH M. livery and sale stable, 532 California cor Webb, dwl Russ House

Parker J. W. machinist apprentice, Vulcan Iron Works, dwl 407 Post
Parker Louis, wheelwright with Kimball & Co. dwl 446 Clementina
Parker Melvina H. dwl 1520 Stockton
Parker Milan, with Stephen W. Howland, dwl SW cor Stevenson and First
Parker Ralzemond, apothecary, 164 First, dwl 54 Tehama
Parker R. J. (widow) furnished rooms, 216 Stockton
Parker Robert, porter with R. H. McDonald & Co. SE cor Pine and Sansom
Parker Robert A. dwl 43 Clara
PARKER SAMUEL H. president Fireman's Fund Insurance Co. 238 Montgomery, dwl Lick House
Parker Susan Mrs. (widow) dwl 338 Minna
PARKER T. H. surgeon dentist, office 3 Brenham Place on Plaza
Parker William, dwl 608 Greenwich
Parker William, engineer, dwl 633 Market
Parker William, physician, dwl 548 Folsom
Parker William, seaman, dwl 206 Stewart
PARKER WILLIAM C. notary public, office 517 Jackson, dwl 121 Silver
Parker William E. engineer, 609 Market, dwl 630 Howard
Parker W. T. plasterer, dwl 728 Market
Parkhurst Elbridge, express wagon, 633 Market
Parkin Thomas, carpenter, dwl 313 Taylor
Parkins Ann M. (widow) dwl 39 Louisa
Parkinson *(James C.)* & Mahony *(John J.)* gilders, 415 Kearny, dwl Jessie bet Third and Fourth
Parkinson Thomas D. civil engineer, office 14 City Hall third floor, dwl 14 Quincy
Parkqner F. F. seaman, dwl 12 Perry
Parks E. W. carrier, Alta California
Parks Rebecca (widow) dwl 820 Washington
Parks William, weaver, Mission Woolen Mills, dwl N s Treat Avenue nr Twenty-Second
Parma Bartolo, vegetable garden, nr Bay View Park
Parmasano Luigi, fisherman, 8 Italian Fish Market
Parpe Richard, gardener with Dr. C. J. Badarous, SW cor Guerrero and Liberty
Parra Antoine, laborer, dwl Vallejo bet Montgomery and Kearny
Parris S. cigar maker, dwl 323 Pine
Parrish Daniel Mrs. (widow) dwl 251 Clara
Parrish Nathan, planer with James Brokaw, dwl 133 Tehama
Parrish Ransom, fruit dealer, dwl 623 Howard
Parrish William H. sash maker with Smith, Ware & Co. dwl 623 Howard
Parrot *(Frederick)* & Pechin *(Charles)* sparkling lemonade makers, 713 Green
Parrott Charles, dwl cor Octavia and Greenwich
PARROTT *(John)* & CO. bankers, NW cor Montgomery and Sacramento, dwl 620 Folsom
Parrott M. Co. office 6 Montgomery Block
Parrott Tiburcio, with Parrott & Co. dwl 620 Folsom
PARROTT'S BUILDING, NW cor Mont and Sac
Parry George, *(McGuirk & P.)* dwl 504 Market
Parry George, clerk, Treasurer's Department U. S. Branch Mint, res Clinton
Pars John (col'd) sailor, dwl 27 John
Parson A. B. box maker, dwl S s Stevenson bet Seventh and Eighth
Parsons Adonijah, boat builder with Thomas Vice, dwl 226 Third
Parsons Asa E. porter, 111 California
Parsons E. B. dwl What Cheer House
Parsons James B. with Bradshaw & Co. dwl 761 Mission
Parsons Jemima (widow) dwl NW cor Howard and Nineteenth
PARSONS LEVI, attorney at law, office 702 Washington, dwl 807 Stockton
Parsons Wick D. foreman Hebrew Observer, dwl cor Sixteenth and Folsom
Partington John J. dwl SE cor Ritch and Bryant

Partridge Mathew, sailor, dwl 803 Stockton
Partridge Peter G. real estate, office with A. Borel NW cor Mont and Jackson, dwl Frank's Bdg
Partz A. F. W. mining engineer, dwl 607 Pine
Pascal *(Castorine)* & Co. *(L. Martencourt)* liquor saloon, 1127 Dupont
PASCAL *(Emile)* DUBEDAT *(Eugene)* & CO. *(Joseph Laviosa)* importers French Brandies and wines, 426 and 428 Jackson, dwl 826 Union
Pascalaqua Benedetto, fisherman, 13 Italian Fish Market
Pascoe John, miner, dwl 152 Natoma
Pasley Mathew, harness maker with Main & Winchester, dwl 186 Stevenson
Pasmore E. J. professor piano forte, Union College, dwl 39 Natoma
Pasquale Benoit, toys, perfumery, etc. 650 Wash
Passolt Louis, porter, 625 Market
Pastah Antonio, peddler, dwl Powell nr Post
Patata Co. fishermen, 22 Italian Fish Market
Pastene Antonio, groceries, 20 Lewis Place
Patch George, clerk, dwl 920 Stockton
Patch Mary Miss, dwl 345 Fremont
Pate Ellen, lodgings, 670 Mission
Patek Samuel J. porter, dwl 535 Post
Patek *(Abraham)* & Co. *(Solomon Brissacker)* milk bread bakery, 836 and 838 Mission
Paten George, machinist, dwl 53 Natoma
Paterson George, carpenter, S. F. & P. Sugar Co. dwl Ninth nr Folsom
Paterson James, stock and money broker, office 602 Montgomery, dwl 300 Stockton
Paterson John, modeler, sculptor, and ornamental plaster worker, 316 Dupont
Paton George, molder, dwl 53 Natoma
Paton Robert, stone cutter, dwl 24 Folsom
Paton Theophilus, molder, California Foundry, dwl 259 Clementina
Patraarche Francis, mining secretary, dwl 152 Clara
Patre George, varnisher, dwl 819 Vallejo, rear
Patrick George (col'd) hairdressing saloon, N s Folsom nr Sixth
Patrick Holmes C. *(Rice & Co.)* dwl 107 Natoma
Patrick James & Co. *(George W. Beaver)* importers and commission merchants, 617 and 619 Battery, res London
Patrick James C. hardware, 122 Battery, dwl 629 Folsom
Patrick James D. professor music, dwl 326 Mason
Patrick Richard *(William Alvord & Co.)* resides New York
Patrick W. C. hairdressing saloon, 1503 Stockton
Patrick William H. (col'd) waiter, steamer Chrysopolis
Patridge Hiram C. contractor, office 604 Merchant, dwl W s Fifth nr Harrison
Patridge Warren, livery stable, dwl SE cor Mission and First
Patsch August, baker with Engelberg & Wagner
Pattee C. M. Miss, assistant, Denman Grammar School, dwl 1020 Stockton
Pattee Solon, dwl 7 Belden Block
Patten Amelia (widow) boarding, 174 Jessie
Patten Benjamin A. *(Barry & P.)* dwl 709 Geary
Patten David R. book keeper, Pacific Bank, 400 Montgomery, dwl 1030 Pine
Patten E. A. book keeper with G. W. Conkling, 714 Montgomery, dwl E s Dupont bet Cal and Pine
Patten John, laborer, dwl N s Minna nr Eighth
Patten Philip H. store keeper, 22 Battery
Patten William P. waiter, Railroad House
Patten, see Patton
Patterson Charles, sash and blind maker with J. McGill & Co. dwl S s Jessie between First and Second
Patterson Charles, saw and file manufacturer, dwl 729 Broadway
Patterson Crosby, carpenter, dwl 59 Jessie
Patterson D. W. attorney at law, dwl 665 Mission

Patterson George, proprietor The Cottage, 2195 Powell
Patterson George, workman, S. F. & P. Sugar Co. dwl W s Ninth nr Folsom
Patterson James (Sheffield & P.) NE cor Jackson and Battery
Patterson James, third officer, C. S. Navigation Co. office NE cor Front and Jackson
Patterson James, waiter, Russ H, dwl 657 Mission
Patterson John W. first officer steamship Moses Taylor, dwl cor Thirteenth and Valencia
Patterson Margaret, domestic, 750 Mission
Patterson Nancy (col'd) laundress, dwl 665 Mission
Patterson William, driver with Louis Jaffe, 133 Sutter
Patterson William, Golden Acre Nursery, San Bruno Road 3 miles from City Hall
PATTERSON, (William H.) WALLACE (William T.) & STOW (William W.) attorneys at law, 513 Jackson, dwl 605 Merchant
Patton Albert F. clerk, NW cor Clay and East
Patton Charles, farmer, dwl nr St. Mary's College
Patton George, molder, Miners' Foundry
Patton John, helper, Vulcan Iron Works, dwl Minna bet Seventh and Eighth
PATTON JOHN H. bricklayer and jobber, dwl NW cor Folsom and Sixteenth
Patton P. H. assistant store keeper, Battery St. Bonded Warehouse, 22 Battery
Patton Theodore, molder, Vulcan Iron Works
Patton William, architect, office 620 Washington rooms 14 and 15, dwl 415 Pine
Pattridge R. K. wharfinger and lumber dealer, Meigg's Wharf, dwl 34 John
Pauba Adelbert, tailor, 409 Bush
Paul Caspar, laborer, dwl E s Rassette Place No. 1
Paul George R. dwl E s Dupont nr Francisco
Paul James, mining, dwl W s San Bruno Road nr Five-Mile House
Paul James I. carriage maker with P. McGivern, dwl 21 Minna
Paul John C. laborer, Omnibus R. R. Co. dwl 335 Green
Paul John H. blacksmith, dwl 26 Sansom
Paul Joseph, express wagon, cor Bdwy and Davis
Paul Joseph, harness maker with Louis Hansen, 201 Sansom
Paul Richard, boot maker, 77 Fourth
Paul Rosa Miss, dwl 122 Fourth
Paul William, carpenter, dwl N s Head nr Octavia
Paul William P. drayman, dwl 24 Ritch
Pauline Raphael, cook, New World Restaurant, dwl 1013 Dupont
Paulissen H. fresco painter, dwl N s Chestnut bet Dupont and Stockton
Pauls Christian, butcher, dwl 205 Sansom
Paulsen Henry, ship carpenter, bds 7 Washington
Paulsen Hermann, clerk, NE cor Fourth and Everett
Paulus Louis, butcher, Brannan St. Bridge
Pauncefort George, actor, Metropolitan Theater, dwl 820 Washington
Paupitz F. W. Minerva House, 123 Jackson
Pausch George, cook, 605 Commercial, dwl Dupont bet Bush and Sutter
PAVILION, HAYES' PARK, cor Hayes and Laguna
PAVILLIER ADOLPH, merchandise broker, 610 Front, dwl E s First Avenue nr Fifteenth
Pawlicki L. physician, office 617 Commercial, dwl Brooklyn Hotel
Paxson Charles H. deputy city and county treasurer, City Hall, dwl SE cor Howard and Second
PAXSON JOSEPH S. treasurer city and county, office 3 City Hall first floor, dwl 20 Stanly Pl
Payne Robert T. attorney at law, office 522 Montgomery, dwl 110 Stockton
Payne Samuel T. plasterer, dwl 280 Minna
Payne Theodore F. clerk with William Burling, NW cor Montgomery and Wash, dwl Lick H

Payne Theodore Mrs. dwl Lick House
Payne Warren R. real estate, office 618 Merchant, dwl Lick House
Payne, see Paine
PAYOT HENRY, publisher and dealer foreign books and stationery, 640 Wash, dwl 509 Lombard
Payson C. N. stair builder, 1216 Taylor, dwl 741 Market
Paz Costodio, porter, dwl 343 Jessie
Peabody Alfred (Flint, P. & Co.) res Boston
Peabody James C. sash and blind maker with J. McGill & Co. dwl 28 Sansom
Peabody Sarah C. (widow) 295 Clementina
Peabody Thomas J. teamster with R. & J. Morton
Peabody William G. poll tax collector, City Hall, dwl W s Galinto bet Fifteenth and Sixteenth
Peach Augustus L. rope maker, S. F. Cordage Factory
Peach James, bootblack, 318 Sansom, dwl N side Fell bet Gough and Octavia
Peachy A. C. real estate, office 43 Montgomery Blk, dwl 118 Montgomery Block
Peacock John H. clerk, 306 Kearny, dwl 306 Third
Peake Albert A. carrier, Call and Bulletin, dwl 815 Post
Pearce Charles, commission merchant, dwl 74 Clementina
Pearce Charles G. ivory turner and cane maker, 837 Washington
Pearce George T. ship joiner, dwl 316 Taylor
Pearce Henry, machinist, Vulcan Iron Works, dwl N s Jessie bet Seventh and Eighth
Pearce Henry D. gold pen manufacturer, 606 Mont, dwl E side Dupont bet Lombard and Chestnut
Pearce James, book keeper, dwl 308 Beale
Pearce James, bricklayer, dwl 61 Tehama
Pearce John, laborer, dwl 45 Stevenson
Pearce Patrick, laborer, dwl NW cor Florida and Twentieth
Pearce Thomas, shoe maker with M. Guerin, dwl 120 Dora
Pearce William, hostler. dwl cor Jane and Mission
Pearce, see Peirce and Pierce
Peare Daniel, cook, Lick House, dwl 153 Perry
Pearkes George, attorney at law, dwl E s Selina Place
Pearl Francis, waiter, U. S. Restaurant, dwl S side Linen bet Laguna and Buchanan
Pearse Charles H. (Schetter & P.) dwl 74 Clementina
Pearson Benjamin, miner, dwl 26 Sacramento
Pearson B. W. seaman, SW cor Market and Stewart, dwl Sebastopol Hotel
Pearson Charles T. office 423 Wash, warehouse 523 Fourth, dwl E side Stock bet Post and Geary
Pearson George, longshoreman, bds 129 Folsom
PEARSON H. H. & CO. proprietors Russ House, W s Montgomery bet Pine and Bush
PEARSON (H. H.) & ARMSTRONG (Lewis) billiard saloon, Russ House
Pearson H. Mrs. assistant, Denman Grammar School, dwl 404 Geary
Pearson Isaac, express wagon, cor Clay and Mont
Pearson John, hog ranch, dwl Sixteenth E Brannan
Pearson John H. clerk, Adjt General's Office, dwl cor Larkin and Vallejo
Pearson J. W. broker, dwl junction San José R. R. and Old San José Road
Pearson Robert H. mariner, office 606 Merchant
Pearson Samuel A. carpenter with R. B. Woodward, NW cor Mission and Fourteenth
Pearson Thomas D. (Addison Martin & Co.) dwl 603 Stockton
Pearson William, register clerk, C. H. res Oakland
Pearson William H. master schooner Isabella, dwl 238 Stewert
Pearson William S. with Pearson & Armstrong, Russ House
Pearson, see Pierson

Pearsons Hiram, real estate, office 22 Montgomery Block, dwl Russ House
Pease Cornelius B. carpenter, dwl 988 Howard
Pease Daniel, cook, Lick House, dwl 222 Ritch
Pease Elijah, laborer, dwl 1011 Mason
PEASE *(E. T.)* & GRIMM *(C. H.)* and C. W. JONES, stock brokers, 709 Montgomery, dwl 37 South Park
Pease John H. carpenter, dwl 29 Valparaiso
Pease L. S. book keeper with Parrott & Co. dwl Brevoort House
Pease Nelson L. dwl 512 O'Farrell
Pease William C. builder, dwl S s Lombard nr Taylor
Peasley Charles C. with Stephen W. Howland, dwl cor Stevenson and First
Peasley John, fireman, S. F. & P. Sugar Co. dwl E s Sumner nr Howard
Peasley Matthew, saddler, 186 Stevenson
Peat John F. merchandise broker, office 327 Commercial, dwl 121 Ellis
Peat William H. clerk, SE cor Montgomery and Bush, dwl 777 Market
Pebele Cecilia (widow) dwl 602 Filbert
Pechin Charles *(Parrot & P.)* dwl 713 Green
Pechin David, dwl 713 Green
Peck Charles E. carriage maker with Albert Folsom, dwl 533 California
Peck Charles S. drayman, 723 Sacramento, dwl 568 Howard
Peck C. M. book keeper, office and dwl 338 Mont
Peck David, salesman, 404 Front, dwl cor Twenty-Fourth and Bartlett
Peck Elisha T. *(J. R. Stewart & Co.)* dwl 116 Eddy
PECK GEORGE H. wood and coal dealer, SE cor Broadway and Sansom, dwl 924 Sacramento
Peck George W. H. painter, dwl 623 Howard
Peck James B. *(Ramsdell & P.)* dwl 451 Natoma
Peck Jesse T. Rev. pastor Howard St. M. E. Church, dwl Hubbard nr Howard
Peck John M. *(Wellman, P. & Co.)* dwl 750 Howard
Peck Jonas L. blacksmith with Geo. P. Kimball & Co. dwl 409 Powell
Peck Levi P. clerk, office Probate Court, dwl 713 Bush nr Mason
Peck Lewis, dwl 509 Bush
Peck Martin, dwl W s Folsom Avenue nr Folsom
Peck *(William)* (col'd) & Cox *(Abraham)* (col'd) boarding, 5 Broadway
Peckford J. watch maker, 309 Sixth
Peckham B. F. measurer lumber, dwl 116 Sansom
Peckham E. L. petroleum secretary, office 607 Clay, dwl 924 Lombard
PECKHAM E. P. *(Cook & P.)* notary public and stock broker, 607 Clay, dwl 924 Lombard bet Hyde and Leavenworth
Peckins Samuel, watchman with Hobbs, Gilmore & Co
Pecqueux *(Adonis)* & Watterlot *(Louis)* importers and manufacturers feathers and millinery goods, 511 Sacramento, dwl 1111 Kearny
Pedichio Domenico, wines and liquors, S s Vallejo lejo bet Davis and Front
Pedler Thomas C. clerk, Main St. Wharf Co. dwl 71 Natoma
Pedroncini Basilio, dwl W s Pacific Alley
Pedrick William, machinist, dwl S. F. Cordage Factory
Peebles Jane Miss, dwl 1138 Folsom
Peebles John, clerk with Wm. M. Hixon, dwl 1030 Clay
Peebles William, with Cross & Co. 625 Sansom, dwl 607 Washington
Peel Jonathan, real estate, dwl 546 Folsom
Peel Jonathan jr. collector, dwl 546 Folsom
Peel Thomas, dwl 286 Stevenson
Peer John A. *(Grush & Co.)* dwl 209 Minna
Peers Joseph, employé, International Hotel

Peers Richard, employé, International Hotel
Peet *(Francis)* & Son *(Francis Peet jr.)* importers and manufacturers saddlery and harness, 508 Battery, res New York
Peet Francis jr. *(Peet & Son)* res Brooklyn, Alameda Co
Pefanr Vincent *(Peter Casson & Co.)* dwl near Bay View Park
Peguillan Emile *(Eugene Peguillan & Bro.)* dwl SW cor Utah and Sixteenth
PEGUILLAN EUGENE & BRO. *(Emile Peguillan)* wholesale butchers, SW cor Utah and Sixteenth, dwl S s Santa Clara nr Hampshire
Peguillan François, cook, dwl SW cor Stockton and Sacramento
Peigne Hypolyte, brick maker with B. Bonnet & Co
PEIRCE JOSEPH, importer, jobber, and manufacturer furniture, 415–419 California, dwl 21 Prospect Place
Peirce Otis S. furniture, (Victoria, V. I.) office 415 California, dwl 109 Montgomery
Peiser Henry, drayman, cor Sacramento and Sansom, dwl 130 Jessie
Peiser I. & N. clothing, 201 Mont, dwl 108 Post
Peiser Jacob, tailor, 241 Third
Peiser Joseph, express wagon, cor Washington and Dupont
Peiser Louis, salesman, 201 Mont, dwl 9 Harlan Pl
Peiser Michael, tailor, dwl 1318 Jackson
Peiser N. *(I. & N. Peiser)* dwl 108 Post
Pell Charles, agent, dwl 815 Montgomery
Pell Elijah W. dwl with Antonio Oliver, E s First Avenue nr Fifteenth
Pell Philip, farmer, dwl cor Green and Laguna
Pell Seba (widow) dwl cor Green and Laguna
Pell Thomas T. book keeper, Chelsea Laundry
Pelletier Alex. workman with A. Brocq, Bay View
Pelletier Henry, dwl S s Cliff House Road 4 miles from Plaza
Pellett Lucius, boot fitter, dwl N s St. Charles near Kearny
Pellmer Frederick, hostler, dwl 939 Folsom
Pelouze William S. merchant, dwl 313 Minna
Pelt Everett, student, Toland College, dwl 1809 Stockton
PELTON JOHN C. superintendent public schools, office 23 City Hall second floor, dwl 26 Silver
Peltret Peter G. clerk, Internal Revenue and Proprietary Stamps, 315 Battery, dwl W s Sixth nr Harrison
Peltz Henry, laborer, dwl 140 Stewart
Pemble Henry, book keeper with Bowen Bros. bds American Exchange
Pemental Joseph, barber, dwl 406 Vallejo
Pementell M. with Bradley & Rulofson, dwl 6 Vallejo
Pena Antonio D. with William Meyer & Co. dwl 13 Clara
Penario Frank, drayman, Washington Hose Co. No. 1
Pencho Jeana Miss, domestic, 1231 Dupont
Pendel August, vegetable garden, San Bruno Road nr Twenty-Fourth
Pendel Moses, workman with A. Pendel, San Bruno Road nr Twenty-Fourth
Pendergast Frank, cook, 204 Fourth, dwl 206 Fourth
Pendergast James, molder, Golden State Iron Works, dwl 42 Louisa
Pendergast Joseph H. molder, Golden State Iron Works, dwl Union House
Pendergast Jane (widow) dwl N s Filbert nr Mont
Pendergast Mary Miss, domestic with J. R. Sedgeley, S s Twelfth bet Howard and Folsom
Pendergast Michael, dwl Commercial Hotel 125 Pac
Pendergast Michael, tinsmith, dwl N s Austin near Van Ness Avenue
Pendergast Thomas, foreman Golden State Iron Works, dwl cor Twenty-Second and Washoe
Pendergast William, stevedore, dwl 14 Sutter
Pendergast, see Prendergast

Pendergrast George, wood worker, dwl W s Hinckley Place
Pendleton Edwin S. carpenter, dwl 130 Minna
Pendleton Frederick H. sawyer with Hobbs, Gilmore & Co. dwl 116 Kearny
Pendleton George, machinist, dwl 513 Howard
Peneton Solomon (col'd) porter, dwl 3 Dupont Pl
Penlington George, molder, Fulton Foundry
Penlington Thomas, molder, Miners' Foundry, dwl 513 Howard
Penne David H. clerk with Woodworth, Schell & Co. dwl 524 Minna
PENNELL JOHN T. wholesale and retail lumber dealer, Pier 11 Stewart, dwl 43 Tehama
PENNELL ROBERT & CO. (F. F. Gerry) lumber, 30 and 32 Market, dwl 121 Natoma
Penner John, teacher, dwl 5 Dixon's Block, Jane
Penney George, coalman, Pacific Glass Works, dwl Potrero
Penny George, laborer, dwl E s Main bet Harrison and Bryant
Penny John F. ship builder, dwl cor Solano and Kentucky
Penny N. S. mariner, dwl 319 Beale
Penny S. C. driver with Isaac Stone
Penny Wm. carpenter, bds Bitters' Hotel cor Kearny and Jackson
Penniman John, wood and coal, 645 and 647 Mission, dwl 417 Post
Penniman Thomas, dwl Oriental Hotel
Penniman Thomas jr. clerk, County Recorder's Office, dwl SW cor Stockton and Pacific
Pennington Enols H. (col'd) dwl 434 Green
Pennycook John, baker, dwl 652 Second
Pennypacker Joseph J. printer, dwl Clara nr Bush
Pennypacker William, printer, dwl 323 Pine
Penrose C. James, straw hat and bonnet presser, Pacific Straw Works
Penrose William, dealer ores, office 238 Montgomery, dwl 1018 Stockton
Pensam John J. butcher, W s Eighth bet Howard and Tehama
Peoples George, equestrian, dwl St. Lawrence House
Pepper Augustus, sawyer with Hobbs, Gilmore & Co. dwl W s Guerrero nr Twenty-Second
Pepper Edwin S. carpenter, dwl E s Polk bet Clay and Washington
Peppin James, blacksmith with Sprung & McAran, dwl NE cor Folsom and Fourth
Peralta Antonio, cook, 617 Bush
Perata B. Tremont Livery Stable, dwl E s Calhoun bet Green and Union
Perault Joseph, clerk, 311 Davis
Perch Charles, painter, dwl 25 Turk
Percival R. dwl What Cheer House
Percy Frederick, actor, Metropolitan Theater
Perea J. (P. Baca & Co.) 402 Montgomery
Pereau Joseph H. miner, dwl 309 Fourth
Pereau S. E. (widow) dwl 734 Harrison
Peres Antonio, vegetable garden, S s Serpentine Avenue nr Folsom
PERES LOUIS & CO. (Pedro Altoube) wholesale butchers, Potrero Avenue, dwl 114 Post
Perey (Peter) & Stepf (Michael) coppersmiths, 114 Bush, dwl 636 Pacific
Perez Nator, dwl 1118 Kearny, rear
Perez Pedro, carpenter, dwl E s Margaret Place
Perez Ramon, with Barry & Patten, dwl 270 Jessie
Perich John, fruits, NE cor Clay and Dupont
Perine N. P. & Co. (James I. Walker) Boston Mastic Roofing, manufactory 821 Harrison, office 135 Montgomery, dwl S s Guy Place
Perinne Munwell, vegetable garden, nr Bay View Park
Perkins A. C. clerk, Pier 17 and 18 Stewart, dwl 85 Everett
Perkins (A. J.) & Foss (Oscar) photographic gallery, 606 Kearny, dwl 108 Powell

Perkins A. J. ship carpenter, dwl 312 Beale
Perkins Albert, hostler, 317 Pine
Perkins Ann Miss, domestic, 319 Sixth
Perkins Charles, dwl 23 Dupont, rear
Perkins Charles, drayman, U. S. Appraiser's Store, dwl E s Taylor bet Post and Geary
Perkins Charles C. (Brocas & P.) dwl N s DeBoom nr Second
Perkins Dearborn, contractor, dwl cor Montgomery and Broadway
Perkins Edward W. salesman with Kerby, Byrne & Co. 7 Montgomery, dwl 613 Mission
Perkins Edwin S. assistant assessor U. S. Int. Rev. NW cor Battery and Commercial, dwl N s Bush bet Polk and Van Ness Avenue
Perkins Frank, amalgamator, office 127 First
Perkins G. & S. M. Co. office 404 Front
Perkins (George F.) & Mires (John C.) Hygeian Bowling Saloon, dwl Francisco bet Powell and Mason
Perkins George M. conductor, Central R. R. Co. dwl cor Downey and Bryant
Perkins Hiram F. planer with J. S. Gibbs, dwl 613 Mission
Perkins James E. (Clark & P.) dwl 623 Harrison
Perkins James H. carpenter, bds 761 Mission
Perkins John, clerk, dwl 670 Mission
Perkins John B. clerk with Brocas & Perkins, dwl N s DeBoom nr Second
Perkins Joseph A. statistical clerk, Custom House, dwl 748 Howard
Perkins Joseph G. foreman pattern maker, Pacific Foundry, dwl 117 Natoma
Perkins Luke H. wharfinger, Washington St. Wharf, dwl 430 Minna
Perkins O. M. (O. F. Gerrish & Co. Port Townsend, W. T.) office 308 Battery, dwl N s Chestnut nr Hyde
Perkins P. H. mining engineer, dwl W s Priest bet Clay and Washington
Perkins Richard, seaman, dwl 33 Commercial
PERKINS RICHARD F. postmaster San Francisco, office NW cor Battery and Washington, dwl 1009 Powell
Perkins Samuel, lumber dealer, Pier 11 Stewart, dwl 22 Hawthorne
Perkins William, carpenter, dwl E s Capp between Eighteenth and Nineteenth
Perkins William, proptr Montgomery House, 623 Market
Perkins William S. dwl 131 Montgomery
Perkins W. L. forwarding merchant, office 404 Front, dwl E s Eleventh bet Mkt and Mission
Perl John, steward New York Hotel
Perlenbach David, carpenter, dwl 323 Pine
Perley A. S. with Armstrong, Sheldon & Davis, 124 Market
Perman James, carpenter, dwl 207 Post
Perosso Giuseppe, waiter, dwl 1013 Dupont
Perozz John, gardener, NE cor Laguna and McAllister
Peroxide G. & S. M. Co. office 508 Battery
Perrault J. physician, office 9-11 Armory Hall, dwl 113 Prospect Place
Perri Leon, porter with Fox & Porter, 533 Clay
Perrier Hippolyte, liquor saloon, 206 Third
Perrin François, dwl 926 Pacific
Perrin Pierre (Jugnet & P.) dwl 208 Kearny
Perrin R. physician, office and dwl 109 Montgomery
Perrine William Capt. dwl 323 Pine
Perrochon Edward, jeweler, 622 Clay
Perrott James, dwl N s Minna nr Seventh
Perry Alphonso B. clerk, 204 Washington, dwl 615 Market
Perry Benjamin F. plasterer and whitener, 13 Post
Perry Catherine Miss, dwl with W. Collins, E side Florida nr Twentieth
Perry Charles, policeman, City Hall, dwl 731 O'Farrell

Perry David, laborer, dwl S s Broadway nr Leav
Perry E. W. jr. artist, Mercantile Library Building room 15, bds 218 Bush
Perry George, dwl 506 Market
PERRY H. E. contractor, office 619 Market
Perry *(Horace)* & Dumon *(Newton F.)* boot and shoe makers, 604 Mission
Perry James, ship carpenter, dwl 314 Ritch
Perry James, seaman, dwl 26 Sacramento
Perry J. B. blacksmith, dwl 270 Jessie
Perry J. Frank, messenger, Custom House, dwl 463 Natoma
Perry John, cook, steamer Julia
Perry John, cook, American Exchange
Perry John, laborer, dwl 266 Jessie
Perry John, salesman with John C. Bell, dwl S s Chestnut bet Larkin and Polk
Perry John F. assistant assessor, U. S. Int. Rev. NW cor Battery and Commercial, dwl 463 Natoma
Perry John R. carpenter, dwl NE cor Howard and Sixteenth
Perry L. H. butcher, dwl 32 Clara
Perry M. B. machinist, San José Machine Shop, bds with Theodore Schulte, W s Valencia bet Fifteenth and Sixteenth
Perry Restcome, merchant, office 103 California, dwl 425 Sutter
Perry Richard, truckman, 117 Clay, dwl 11 Harrison Avenue
Perry Sarah S. (widow) dwl 253 Stevenson
Perry Thomas, laborer, S. F. & San José R. R. Co
Perry Thomas, mariner, dwl 32 Stewart
Perry W. waiter, dwl SE cor Mission and First
Perry Willard B. machinist, S. F. & San José R. R. Co. dwl W s Valencia bet Fifteenth and Sixteenth
Perryman E. G. Rev. teacher languages Cal. Collegiate Institute, dwl 510 Stockton
Pershin George S. principal San Bruno School, dwl 327 Minna
Pesinger John H. book keeper Contra Costa Laundry, dwl NE cor Stevenson and Third
Persinger Theodore, baker. dwl 18 Sansom
Person Michael, lab, dwl E s Gaven nr Greenwich
Persons Walter (col'd) plasterer, dwl 1328 Pacific
Pestner Ernst, groceries and liquors, SW cor Clementina and Fourth
PETALUMA LINE STEAMERS, foot Vallejo
Petaluma Mill & M. Co. office 620 Washington
Petaluma steam packet Josie McNear, office 3 Clay
Petarchi G. Francis, mining secretary, office 29 Exchange Building, dwl 152 Clara
Petch Richard H. driver, A. R. Com. Co. dwl W s Selina Place
Peter Augustine, vegetable garden, near Bay View Park
Peter Domingo, vegetable garden, near Bay View Park
Peter Samuel, bar tender, 717 Mont, dwl 810 Mont
Peter Sereryer, vegetable garden, near Bay View Park
Peteri John, shoe maker, 8 Summer
Peters Adolphus, machinist, Union Foundry, dwl 944 Mission
Peters Albert, musician, dwl 323 Kearny
Peters Arthur S. clerk with Conroy & O'Connor, res Oakland
Peters Charles, driver, Washington Brewery, dwl SW cor Broadway and Kearny
PETERS CHARLES R. & CO. *(George L. Bradley)* bonded warehouses, 16–22 Battery and North Point Dock, dwl 736 Mission
Peters F. M. L. *(Feldbush & Co.)* dwl 1916 Mason
Peters George, cook, dwl 619 Market
Peters Jane (widow) dwl 660 Howard
Peters John, machinist with J. R. Sims, dwl N s Broadway bet Stockton and Powell
Peters John, waiter, Occidental Hotel
Peters John M. dwl 217 Post

Peters Joseph C. *(Lauterwasser & P.)* dwl E side Sixth bet Clementina and Tehama
Peters W. cook Telegraph House, SW cor Battery and Green
Peters William B. *(Lord & P. Oakland, Oregon)* office 308 Battery, res Oakland
Peters Wyman, dwl E s Sixth nr Market
Petersen Charles, machinist, Pacific Foundry
Petersen Charles A. groceries and liquors, SW cor Montgomery and Union
Petersen Charles J. book keeper with Kohler & Frohling, dwl E s Calhoun bet Union and Green
Petersen George C. agent James Lick, office 422 Clay, dwl Lick House
Petersen Henry, boatman, Pier 15 Stewart
Peterson Albert, seaman, dwl 26 Sacramento
Peterson Andrew, cook, 26 Sacramento
Peterson Andrew, seaman, dwl 26 Sacramento
Peterson Andrew G. liquors, 504 Davis
Peterson Charles *(Nelson & Co.)* dwl 1027 Dupont
Peterson Charles, billiards and liquors, 10 Sac
Peterson Charles, cook, 640 Market
Peterson Charles, cook, dwl 238 Stewart
Peterson Charles, deck hand, steamer Relief
Peterson Charles, express wagon, cor Bdwy and Vallejo, dwl N s Courtlandt Av nr North Av
Peterson Charles, express wagon, cor Market and Sacramento, dwl Main nr Folsom
Peterson Charles, laborer with John G. North, Potrero
Peterson Charles, machinist, Pacific Foundry, dwl 64 Natoma
Peterson Charles, seaman, dwl 26 Sacramento
PETERSON *(Charles J.)* & TIETJEN *(Henry)* grocers, SW cor Leavenworth and Broadway, dwl S s Vallejo bet Hyde and Larkin
Peterson Francis, laborer, dwl 10 St. Mark Pl, rear
Peterson F. W. dwl 13 Tehama
Peterson George K. *(Hepburn & P.)* dwl W s Eleventh nr Market
Peterson George K. mining, dwl 33 Clementina
Peterson Hans, boatman, dwl 6 Hartman Place
Peterson Henry, butcher, dwl 1440 Stockton
Peterson Henry, laborer with William Buckley
Peterson Henry, laborer, dwl E s Lagoon
Peterson Henry, photographer, 25 Third, dwl 210 Stewart
Peterson Jacob, boatman, dwl 1816 Powell
Peterson Jacob, carpenter, dwl Serpentine Avenue nr San Bruno Road
Peterson James, house mover, dwl E s Willow bet Folsom and Shipley
Peterson James, laborer, Bay Sugar Refinery, dwl 56 Minna
Peterson John, clerk, NE cor Folsom and Beale
Peterson John N. drayman, cor Market and First, dwl 410 Tehama
Peterson Lewis, tinsmith with Tay, Brooks & Backus, dwl S s Sac bet Jones and Leav
Peterson Louis, coffee stand, 528 Broadway
Peterson Ludwig *(Johnson & P.)* dwl 531 East
Peterson Maria Miss, domestic, 730 Sutter
Peterson Nicolaus, laborer, Mason's Brewery
Peterson Olof, seaman, dwl 107 Washington
Peterson Oscar, waiter, Lick House
Peterson Paul, laborer, dwl 320 Dupont
Peterson Peter, groceries and liquors, NW cor East and Washington, dwl 615 Mission
Peterson Peter, machinist, dwl 147 Jessie
Peterson Robert L. clerk, 415 East, dwl 27 Minna
Peterson Samuel O. carpenter, dwl E s Valencia bet Sixteenth and Seventeenth
Peterson S. B. & Co. *(Francis Clousen)* Golden State Market, SW cor Market and Stewart, dwl Rincon Place
Peterson S. B. clerk, Williams' Line Packets, dwl 21 Rincon Place
Petit Alexander P. carpenter, dwl cor Hayes and Franklin

Petit Charles, laundry, cor Bush and Broderick
Petitjean J. B. C. shoe maker with Charles Motta
Petre Charles, carpenter, dwl S s Merchant, bet Drumm and East
Petrie W. R. machinist, dwl 11 Front
Petrissent Louis, workman with L. Artigues, dwl NW cor Sixteenth and Rhode Island
Pettee John, clerk, City and County Auditor, City Hall, dwl W s Folsom bet Thirteenth and Fourteenth
Pettengill John A. dentist, dwl 1104 Pine
Petterman Henry, groceries and liquors, 533 California, dwl 5 Spring
Petterson Clous, bar keeper, NW cor Second and Townsend
Petterson Peter, blacksmith, Phœnix Iron Works, dwl 228 St. Mark Place
Petterson P. M. tinsmith with Caleb M. Sickler, dwl SE cor Jones and Bernard
Pettijohn Charles, machinist, Pacific Foundry, dwl 227 Stevenson
Pettinos Charles, student, 803 Montgomery room 2, dwl S s Howard bet Third and Fourth
Pettinos George F. music teacher, dwl 426 Second
Pettinos Peter, dwl 426 Second
Pettinos William T. clerk with Langley, Crowell & Co. dwl 323 Dupont
Pettis John E. salesman with G. W. Conkling, 714 Montgomery, dwl SW cor Bdwy and Mont
Pettis Valentine, shoe maker with Thomas Dolliver, dwl 12 Sutter
Pettit A. book keeper, dwl 522 Union
Pettit A. M. A. (widow) dwl 32 Natoma
Pettit Edwin, cabinet maker, dwl 514 Bush
Pettit Horatio N. dwl 615 Larkin bet Eddy and Ellis
Pettit N. S. assistant store keeper, Appraiser's Store, Custom House, dwl 522 Union
Pettit O. B. agent, office 420 Montgomery
Pettit William H. book keeper, Sutler's Store, Presidio, dwl 519 Bush
Pettit ——, dwl 626 California
Petty David, mustard maker with H. C. Hudson & Co. dwl 18 Stanford
Petty John S. sail maker, dwl W s Gilbert bet Bryant and Brannan
Petty William H. sail maker, dwl S s Hayes nr Laguna
Peyrau Dominique, butcher with Bacca & Co. dwl Potrero Avenue
Peyraud P. physician, office 904 Kearny
Peyser Alexander, clerk, 643 Clay, dwl 337 Tehama
Peyser Henry, drayman, corn Sansom and Merch
Peyser Hermann, clothing, 405 Pacific
Peyser Louis, tailor, dwl 514 Mission
Peyser Michael, tailor, SE cor Pine and Dupont
Peyser Morris A. (S. A. Peyser & Co.) res New York
Peyser S. A. & Co. (Morris A. Peyser) importers and jobbers straw millinery and fancy goods, 424 Sacramento, dwl 822 Mission
Peyser, see Peiser
Peyton Bernard (R. A. Thompson & Co.) dwl 618 Sutter
Peyton Bernard jr. dwl 618 Sutter
Pezold M. (N. B. Booth & Co.) dwl 20 Kearny
Pezzoni (Giuliano) & Coppi (Giacomo) wood and coal, W s Taylor bet Lombard and Chestnut
Pfaff George, flute maker, 614 Sacramento
Pfaff Henry, cabinet maker, dwl SE cor Jackson and Stockton
Pfaff Henry, porter with Thomas Taylor & Co. dwl 18 Sansom
Pfaff William, express wagon, cor Sutter and Mont, dwl S s Sutter bet Polk and Van Ness Avenue
Pfeiffenberger Vincent, waiter, dwl 323 Pine
Pfeiffer Albert, seaman, dwl 140 Stewart
Pfeiffer Caspar, porter with John Taylor & Co. 514 Washington
Pfeiffer E. J. German druggist, 210 Post

Pfeiffer Frederick, shoe maker, dwl E s Rassette Place No. 1
Pfeiffer John, dwl 119 St. Mark Place
Pfeiffer John, butcher with Charles Murr, 215 Kearny
Pfeiffer John W. locksmith, 759 Clay
Pfeiffer Louis, shoe maker, dwl 6 Gardner Alley
Pfeiffer William A. merchant, dwl NW cor Dupont and Francisco
Pfersdorff H. dwl 1205 Dupont
Pfirter D. clerk, 520 Montgomery, dwl 950 Howard
Pfirter J. J. dwl 950 Howard
Pfister Chretien, hairdressing saloon, 221 Mont
Pfister Conrad, dwl 619 Pacific
Pfohl Peter, hostler, Philadelphia Brewery
Pforr Henry, dwl 270 Jessie
PFORR JOHN, real estate agent and broker, office 328 Montgomery, dwl 270 Jessie
Pfuelb George (John Baumeister & Co.) dwl Bootz's Hotel
Phaff January, carpenter, dwl 61 Clementina
Phair Eliza Mrs. liquor saloon, Bay Shore Road 2½ miles from Plaza
Phair Thomas, accountant, dwl Bay Shore and Fort Point Road 2½ miles from Plaza
Phair Thomas, gardener, dwl 268 Tehama
Phalan James E. porter, 406 Front
Phalon Daniel G. salesman with Charles G. Emery, 518 Battery, dwl 535 Howard
Phalon Louis, hairdresser with Stable Bros. dwl 1103 Stockton
Phayer Robert, plasterer, dwl 208 Third
Phelan Anne Miss, domestic, Deaf, Dumb, and Blind Asylum, SE cor Fifteenth and Howard
Phelan Bridget Miss, domestic, dwl 1201 Sac
Phelan Edward, waiter, dwl 47 Jane
Phelan Edward, workman, S. F. & P. Sugar Co
Phelan James, real estate, office 616 Front, dwl 13 O'Farrell
Phelan James, toll collector, Point Lobos Road cor Bush and Broderick
Phelan John, laborer with Arthur M. Ebbets, dwl 1226 Clay
Phelan John J. laborer, dwl 1226 Clay
Phelan Joseph, clerk with C. McC. Delany, dwl cor Bush and Broderick
Phelan Mary J. Miss, domestic, SW cor Mission and Lafayette Avenue
Phelan Michael, carpenter, dwl 13 Ritch, rear
Phelan Patrick (Donohue & P.) dwl 31 Second
Phelan Patrick, printer, dwl 20 Clara
Phelan Peter, boiler maker, dwl 136 First
Phelan Richard H. clerk, dwl American Theater
Phelan Thomas, dwl 905 Folsom
Phelan William, night watchman, International H
Phelps Abner, attorney at law, dwl ½ mile W Protestant Orphan Asylum
Phelps A. E. (W. S. Phelps & Co.) dwl 1203 Pacific
Phelps Alanson H. salesman with Thomas H. Selby & Co. dwl 1105 Pacific
Phelps A. R. actor, dwl 125 Tehama
Phelps C. F. machinist, Vulcan Iron Works
Phelps C. W. inspector, C. H. dwl 830 Pacific
Phelps Daniel T. shipsmith with W. S. Phelps, dwl W s Jones nr Pacific
Phelps Edwin, dwl with Abner Phelps, Page nr Devisidero
Phelps Fanny Morgan Mrs. comedienne, dwl Stevenson House
Phelps John D. teamster with Stanyan & Co. 17 Cal
Phelps M. W. Mrs. assistant, Powell St. School, dwl 830 Pacific
Phelps N. D. Washington Hose Co. No. 1
Phelps Ralph, theatrical agent, dwl Stevenson House
Phelps Samuel E. agent, dwl 28 Sansom
Phelps Tracy, dwl 5 Graham Place
Phelps William, cartman with William Buckley
Phelps William H. hostler, dwl Bay View

Phelps William S. & Co. *(A. E. Phelps)* ship-smiths, 24 Drum, and supervisor Fourth District, dwl 1203 Pacific
PHENIX FIRE INSURANCE COMPANY, New York, Bigelow & Brother agents, 505 Montgomery
PHILADELPHIA BREWERY, 228–238 Second, Hoelscher & Wieland proprietors
Philadelphia House, John Knack proprietor, 336 Bush
Philbrick William H. tinsmith with J. W. Brittan & Co. dwl 515 Sacramento
Philbrook A. K. dwl SE cor Sansom and Pacific
Philbrook Elizabeth (widow) dwl 1112 Kearny
Phillippi Abraham, carpenter, Miners' Foundry, dwl 116 Sansom
Phillippi Anthony, locksmith, dwl E s Grove Avenue nr Bryant
Phillippi John, dwl 658 Folsom
Phillips Aaron F. (col'd) bootblacking, 308 Sansom, dwl 763 Harrison
Phillips Abraham, painter, 208 First
Phillips Allen S. milker with Murray & Noble
Phillips Benjamin, mariner, dwl 34 Second
Phillips Charles, drayman, dwl SW cor Hayes and Franklin
Phillips Charles J. drayman, cor Market and East
Phillips D. L. *(Dodge & P.)* dwl 1025 Washington
Phillips Edward *(Bateman & P.)* dwl 219 Davis
Phillips Eliza (widow) dwl 319 Seventh
Phillips Elizabeth (widow) dwl 708 Sutter
Phillips Fitel *(J. Funkenstein & Co.)* dwl 506 Bush
Phillips G. W. waterman, 609 Market
Phillips Henry S. dwl W s Second Avenue bet Camp and Seventeenth
Phillips James S. mining stocks, dwl 704 Market
Phillips Jane (widow) dwl 1709 Mason
Phillips Jane V. (widow) Mission Exchange, N s Nineteenth bet Guerrero and Dolores
Phillips J. Burke. deputy surveyor port San Francisco, office Custom House second floor, dwl 532 Tehama
Phillips John, coachman with John E. Weeks
Phillips John, hostler, dwl 333 Bush
Phillips John, librarian, Odd Fellows' Hall, 325 Montgomery, dwl NE cor Pine and Kearny
Phillips John, rigger and stevedore, dwl 340 Union
Phillips John, sail maker, dwl 116 Jackson
Phillips J. M. dwl 18 First
Phillips John C. painter, dwl 4 Noble Place
Phillips John D. mariner, dwl SW cor Folsom and Twentieth
Phillips John L. clerk, dwl SW corner Folsom and Twentieth
Phillips Joseph, dwl nr cor Texas and Napa
Phillips Joseph, boiler maker with Coffey & Risdon
Phillips Joseph, bricklayer, dwl 306 Dupont
Phillips Joseph, drayman, 407 East, dwl 29 Lewis Place
Phillips J. S. dwl 12 Sutter
Phillips Julia Miss, seamstress, dwl 29 Minna
Phillips Julius, tailor, 305 Pine
Phillips Lawrence, commission merchants, dwl 728 Harrison
Phillips M. waterman, dwl 559 Market
Phillips M. A. E. Miss, assistant, Rincon School, dwl 607 Folsom
Phillips Margaret (widow) dwl S side Mission bet Eighth and Ninth
Phillips Margaret Ann (widow) dwl 111 St. Mark Pl
Phillips Murray, painter with Hopps & Kanary
Phillips Peyton T. (col'd) laborer, dwl 1230 Pacific
Phillips Philip, carrier, Weekly Record, dwl 728 Harrison
Phillips R. B. (col'd) hairdresser with N. A. Godfrey, dwl 49 Clara
Phillips S. boots and shoes, 15 Pacific
Phillips Samuel, with Field & Co. 422 California

Phillips Samuel G. dwl 113 St. Mark Place
Phillips Sophia M. Mrs. dwl SW cor Folsom and Twentieth
Phillips Thomas, seaman, dwl 35 Pacific
Phillips Thomas G. blacksmith, dwl 633 Market
Phillips William G. machinist, Miners' Foundry, dwl 242 Minna
Phillips William O. engineer, dwl 504 Bush
Phinney Arthur *(Amos P. & Co.)* res Port Ludlow, W. T
Phinney Joseph M. stair builder, dwl 152 Natoma
Phinnūps Edward, painter, dwl 650 Second
Phipps A. B. salesman with Newball, Brooks & Nettleton, dwl 22 Minna
Phipps William H. laborer, dwl 126 Beale
Phister Andrew, bar keeper with Vincent Squarza, dwl 323 Kearny
PHŒNIX BUILDING, SW cor San and Jackson
PHŒNIX INSURANCE CO. (Hartford) R. H. Magill general agent, L. B. Dell local agent, office 603 Commercial cor Montgomery
PHŒNIX IRON WORKS, Jonathan Kittredge proprietor, 6 and 8 Battery
PHŒNIX OIL WORKS, Charles H. Harrison proprietor, office 517 Front
Phol Oliver, machinist, Vulcan Foundry, dwl 228 Fourth
Picarde B. Rev. S.J. professor ancient and modern languages St. Ignatius' College, S s Market bet Fourth and Fifth
Pichoir Henry, cashier with Pioche & Bayerque, dwl NE cor Montgomery and Pacific
Pickens John A. printer, dwl Beale bet Harrison and Brannan
Pickering James F. carpenter, dwl 809 Harrison
Pickering Loring, dwl Lick House
PICKERING WILLIAM, apothecary, SE corner Broadway and Stockton, dwl 1312 Powell
Pickett Charles E. office with Thornton & Williams
Pickett Don C. clerk with Mercado & Seully, dwl N s Taylor bet Washington and Jackson
Pickett Elhanan W. proprietor Market St. Restaurant, 619 Market
Pickett R. F. forwarding merchant, office 214 Sac, dwl E s Capp bet Sixteenth and Seventeenth
Pickett Thomas, laborer, dwl 519 Mission
Pickett William, compositor, American Flag, dwl 1108 Pacific
Pickwick Hall, William Berney proprietor, 31–37 Fourth
Picot J. H. Mme. millinery, 22 Montgomery
Pidwell Cyril T. salesman with Wightman & Hardie, dwl SE cor Mason and Ellis
Pieber Catharine (widow) dwl NW cor Franklin and Fulton
Pieper Henry C. express wagon, NW cor Sansom and Merchant, dwl cor Franklin and Fulton
Pieper Wilhelmenia (widow) dwl 1615 Powell
Pierce Ann Miss, domestic, NE corner Pacific and Mason
Pierce Bridget Miss, domestic, 412 Second
Pierce Charles, bricklayer, dwl 9 Harlan Place
Pierce Charles, carrier, Our Mazeppa
Pierce Charles, laborer, dwl 120 Sutter, rear
Pierce Ellery G. drayman with Knapp & Grant, dwl Jane bet Mission and Jessie
Pierce F. C. salesman with Joseph Peirce, dwl 724 Pine
Pierce George M. tinsmith, Eureka Match Factory, dwl NW cor Pine and Kearny
Pierce George W. *(Healy, Carleton & Co.)* 429 Pine
Pierce George W. L. dwl 113 Natoma
Pierce H. clerk, dwl 559 Market
Pierce Harry, drayman, dwl 569 Mission
PIERCE HENRY & WILLIAM, loan and commission, office 728 Montgomery, dwl 712 Pine
Pierce Ignatius, captain brig J. B. Ford, office 321 Front, dwl 711 Greenwich

Pierce James M. supt Rincon Point Warehouse, dwl 308 Beale
Pierce James P. miner, dwl SW cor Sixteenth and Capp
Pierce Jason B. collector, Mechanics' Institute, dwl 606 Montgomery
Pierce Lewis, carpenter, dwl 229 Jackson
Pierce Mary, domestic, 770 Harrison
PIERCE NELSON, shipping and commission merchant, proprietor Southern Dispatch Line Packets and state pilot examiner, office 321 Front, dwl 711 Greenwich
Pierce Patrick, marble worker with John Daniel, 421 Pine
Pierce Peter, baker with J. Chadbourne, dwl corner Washington and Powell
Pierce Samuel, teamster with Sedgley & Davis, dwl W s Shotwell bet Fifteenth and Sixteenth
Pierce S. J. bricklayer, dwl 564 Mission
Pierce Walter S. & Co. (Charles R. Hall) piano fortes, 26 Montgomery
Pierce William (Henry & William P.) dwl 712 Pine
Pierfort Henry, barber, 712 Pacific
Pieritz Gustave, ship carpenter, bds 7 Washington
Pierman Tobias, laborer, Lone Mountain Cemetery
Pieroni Lorenzi, vegetable garden, nr Bay View Park
Pierre Henry, cook, 526 Clay
Pierre John, laborer, What Cheer House Restaurant
Pierron Pierre, mason, dwl N s Sixteenth bet Guerrero and Dolores
Pierson C. Mrs. flag maker, dwl 110 Mason
Pierson Edward, engineer, dwl N s Bernard bet Taylor and Jones
Pierson Frederick, boiler maker with Coffey & Risdon
Pierson Isaac (col'd) express wagon, NW cor Mont and Clay, dwl SE cor Jackson and Larkin
Pierson J. D. Rev. pastor Friends of Progress, NE cor Fourth and Jessie
Pierson John, hog ranch, N s Sixteenth nr Nebraska
Pierson John, laborer, dwl SE corner Vallejo and Larkin
Pierson Jos. B. laborer, S. F. & San José R. R. Co
Pierson Joseph D. cabinet maker, SW cor Pacific and Taylor, dwl 110 Mason
Pierson Joseph T printer with Agnew & Deffebach, dwl 1334 Washington
PIERSON J. W. J. agent Grover & Baker's Sewing Machine Co. 329 Montgomery, dwl 705 Greenwich
Pierson Lawrence, artesian well borer, dwl 336 Bush
Pierson Mary (widow) dwl 1116 Powell
Pierson Samuel, carpenter, boards with Theodore Schulte W s Valencia bet Fifteenth and Sixteenth
Pierson William E. mariner, dwl 303 Davis
Pierson William M. (Haight & P.) dwl 110 Mason
Pierson, see Pearson
Pierucini Steffano (D. Mancarini & Co.) dwl 912 Sacramento
Piesser Joseph, express wagon, dwl 1406 Dupont
Pigne Dupuytren J. B. physician, office and dwl 1007 Stockton
Pigott James, real estate agent, 619 Merchant, dwl 727 Folsom
Pike Albion A. ship joiner with John G. North, dwl 114 Silver
Pike Charles, workman with Edward Barry, San Bruno Road 3¼ miles from City Hall
Pike Charles R. ship carpenter, dwl 313 Taylor
Pike Elias W. harbor policeman, dwl City Hall third floor
Pike James F. captain bark Delaware, 512 Bush
Pike James N. clerk with Flint, Peabody & Co. dwl 512 Bush
Pike Thomas, books and stationery, SE cor Leidesdorff and Commercial, dwl 518 Green

Pilitzer Isaac, cigars, 209 Fourth
Pilitzer Marcus, cigars, 209 Fourth
Pilkington Charlotte Miss, adjuster, U. S. Branch Mint, dwl 129 Silver
Pilkington James, dwl 129 Silver
Pilliner W. H. photographic gallery, 14 Second
Pilling John, hairdresser, 105 Jackson, dwl SE cor Pacific and Cemetery Avenue
Pillsbury Samuel, local agent, North America Life Insurance Co. 240 Montgomery, dwl 803 Mason
PILOT EXAMINERS, BOARD OF, office 521 Clay
Pilots (Old Line) office 5 Vallejo
Pilots (Opposition) office W s Front bet Broadway and Vallejo
Pilsbury C. J. (Marsh, Pilsbury & Co.) dwl 117 Second
Pimentel Francis, barber, 218 Pac, dwl 314 Vallejo
Pimentel Joseph, barber, 218 Pac, dwl 314 Vallejo
Pimentel Juana (widow) dwl 6 Pollard Place
Pinaglia Lorenzo, coffee grinder with D. Ghirardelli & Co. 417 Jackson
Pinckney David, clerk, U. S. Paymaster's Department, bds 8 W cor Broadway and Montgomery
Pinckney Joseph, teamster, dwl NE cor Polk and Jackson
Pinckney Micojah, clerk, 204 Battery
Pinckney Richard, carpenter, dwl 90 Stevenson
Pinckney William J. laundry, 36 Clay
Pincoll Samuel, collector with J. Peirce
Pincus Morris, tailor, 302 Pacific
Pindell Annie Miss, music teacher, dwl NW corner Kearny and Broadway
Pinderkess Kate Miss, domestic with Joseph Lando
Pinget John, laborer, Bay Sugar Refinery, dwl 813 Battery
Pink John C. broker, dwl 20 Sansom
Pink Margaret (widow) dwl 1519 Dupont
Pinkerton Charles W. dwl 103 Dupont
Pinkham Benjamin F. printer, dwl 1303 Stockton
Pinkham Byron C. carpenter, dwl 23 Kearny
Pinkham C. L. B. furnished rooms, 23 Kearny
Pinkham Frederick W. carpenter, 818 Clay, dwl 823 Clay
Pinkham George, carpenter, dwl 151 Tehama
Pinkham George A. paper carrier, dwl Mississippi nr Mariposa
Pinkham Jonathan C. tanner, dwl Mississippi near Mariposa
Pinkham Seth, accountant with William B. Bourn, res Clinton
Pinkles M. tailor, 204 Second
Pinner J. C. teacher, 8 Anthony
Pinner (Robert) & Laflin (James) proprietors Pacific House, 35 Pacific
Pinnick Harry, butcher with Crummie & O'Neill, dwl cor Folsom and Ninth
Pinnix Edward H. dwl Union Club Rooms
Pinto J. musician, dwl 211 Post
Pinto Jacob, mail clerk, American Flag, dwl 329 Bush
PIOCHE (F. L. A.) & BAYERQUE (J. B.) importers, Mont cor Jackson, dwl 806 Stockton
Pioda Charles, clerk, dwl 512 Union
Pioda Charles, office with G. Venard, 625 Front, dwl 512 Union
Pioda Paul, teacher modern languages Boys' High School, dwl 112 Perry
Pioneer Hotel, SW cor Louisiana and Sierra
Pioneer Land and Loan Association, office 626 Clay
PIONEER PAPER MILLS, S. P. Taylor proprietor, office 322 Clay
Pioneer Salt Works, B. F. Barton & Co. proprietors, office 213 Sacramento
PIONEER WOOLEN FACTORY, Black Point, Heynemann & Co. agents, 311 and 313 California
Piotrowski R. Korwin, assistant store keeper, Bonded Warehouse, dwl 920 Market
Piper Andrew W. confectioner, dwl 19 Clara

Piper Asahel D. real estate agent, dwl 52 First
PIPER EVELINE Mrs. manufacturer gents' premium shirts and collars, 126 Kearny
Piper Henry C. express wagon, cor Merch and San
Piper *(J. B.)* & Rice *(Joseph B.)* brick makers, office Rincon Dock, dwl 52 First
Piper John O. real estate, office 606 Montgomery, dwl 82 Natoma
Piper Joseph, groceries and liquors, SW cor Second and Howard
Piper Stephen L. carpenter and builder, dwl 1022 Pine
Piper Walter J. H. local policeman, dwl 126 Kearny
Piper William A. real estate, office 606 Montgomery
Pipes James G. restaurant, 603 Market, dwl 138 Stevenson
Pippey Henry J. mariner, dwl N s Townsend bet Third and Fourth
Pippey John, dwl N s Townsend bet Third and Fourth
Pippey Robert N. mariner, dwl 333 Ritch nr Townsend
Pique Edward, professor music, dwl 748½ Market
Piratsky George, laborer, dwl S s Oak bet Gough and Franklin
Pirre Pirre, coppersmith, dwl 636 Pacific
Pisani Camilo, fisherman, dwl Merchant bet Drumm and East
Pisani D. *(L. Ghilardi & Co.)* 534 Commercial
Pisani Rafaele, fruits, 230 Montgomery
Pisodo Manuel, cook, dwl 514 Pacific
Pissis Joseph E. physician, dwl 316 Sutter
Pistolesi August *(Wm. Hencke & Co.)* SW cor Washington and Dupont
Pistolesi Guiseppe, porter with Hentsch & Berton, dwl 1214 Kearny
Pitman A. B. porter with A. H. Todd & Co. 45 Clay
Pitmar G. T. snake tamer, dwl 140 Stewart
Pitt Annie A. (widow) dwl NW cor Clay and Clay Avenue
Pitt John, ship carpenter, dwl 308 Beale
Pitt William, with Daniel Norcross, dwl 415 O'Farrell
Pittner Andrew, dwl 5 St. Mary
Pitts Henry A. books and stationery, 408 Third
Pitts W. R. engineer, steamer Paul Pry, dwl Jackson Place
Pittsburg G. & S. M. Co. office 338 Montgomery
Pittsinger Eliza A. Miss, poetess, dwl NW cor Green and Calhoun
PIXLEY *(Frank M.)* & SMITH, *(G. Frank)* attorneys at law, office 52 Exchange Building, dwl S s Presidio Road nr Steiner
Pixley Isaac, dwl S s Presidio Road, nr Steiner
Pixley W. B. clerk with C. C. Riley, NW cor Howard and Second
PIXLEY WILLIAM, wood and coal, 216 Sutter, dwl cor Presidio Road and Fillmore
Pixley W. J. assistant entry clerk, Custom House
Pizello Frank *(Coneo & P.)* dwl 1313 Dupont
PLACE CORNELIUS L. & CO. *(Albert W. Scott and Benjamin McEwen)* hay and grain, SW cor Stewart and Folsom, dwl 322 Folsom
Place Gilbert J. dwl NE cor Dolores and Fifteenth
Place Jonah W. car builder, S. F. & San José R. R. Co. dwl SW cor Stevenson and Sixth
Plagemann *(Henry)* Kanzee *(Robert)* & Co. *(John L. Koster)* cigars and tobacco, 4 Kearny, dwl 30 Everett
Planchar Lavary, washing, dwl 535 Pacific
Planchard Andre, hairdresser with Chretien Pfister, 221 Montgomery, dwl 25 Second
Planel Theophile L. proprietor Belle Vue House, 1018 Stockton
Planet Copper M. Co. office 626 Montgomery
Plank Philip, machinist, dwl 1813 Mason
Planz Henry, tailoring, 319 Commercial, dwl cor Pacific and Auburn
Plass Philip, clerk with George Stewart

Plastrik Charles *(Plastrik & Bro.)* 248 Third
Plastrik *(Simon)* & Bro. *(Charles)* variety store, 248 Third
PLATE A. J. importer and dealer guns, pistols, trimmings, and sporting materials, 411 Sansom, dwl 30 Eddy
Plate Charles, sawyer with Hobbs, Gilmore & Co. dwl 306 Minna
Plate Richard W. painter, bds 761 Mission
Plath Hermann, groceries and liquors, 421 Union
Plath John *(Henry Fink & Co.)* dwl SW cor Powell and Union
Plato David, clothing, 307 East, dwl 572 Bryant
Plato Gabriel D. salesman, 307 East
Plato Samuel, cap maker with Wolf Fleisher, dwl NW cor Broadway and Kearny
Platshek *(Julius)* & Co. *(Samuel Platshek)* clothing, 537 Commercial, bds Continental Hotel
Platshek Samuel *(Platshek & Co.)* bds Continental Hotel
Platt Abraham, clerk, 405 California, dwl 910 Leav
Platt Charles H. first lieut., U. S. A. dwl 320 Pine
Platt Eliza R. (widow) boarding, 248 Fourth
Platt G. sausage maker, 1231 Dupont
Platt George *(William T. Coleman & Co.)* dwl 525 Folsom
PLATT HENRY B. proprietor New Music Hall and Eureka Theater and president Occidental Insurance Co. office 9 Mercantile Library Building, dwl 320 Pine
Platt J. Madison, secretary Dashaway Association
Platt John C. clerk Occidental Ins. Co. dwl 320 Pine
Platt Philip S. watchman Eureka Theater
Platt R. W. laborer, S. F. Gas Co
Platt Samuel, attorney at law, office 628 Merchant, dwl E s Mission bet Twelfth and Thirteenth
PLATT'S MUSIC HALL, E s Montgomery bet Pine and Bush
Plaw Joseph, clerk with Macondray & Co. 206 San
Playter E. W. with Conroy & O'Connor, dwl Occidental Hotel
Ple Edward, cook, Union Restaurant, dwl Polk Al
Pleacher William, second cook Golden Eagle Hotel
Pleasant Henry, laborer, dwl NW cor Folsom and Tenth
Pleasant John, cook, steamer Orizaba
Pleasant View Homestead Association, office 619 Merchant
Plege *(Henry)* & Hoffman *(H. William)* groceries and liquors, NW cor Post and Taylor
Plege Henry *(Mitchell & P.)* dwl NW cor Post and Taylor
Plege Louis *(Contet & P.)* dwl 721 Clay
PLESS *(Henry)* & LINDNER *(Conrad)* liquor saloon, 425 Sansom, dwl 260 Jessie
Plette Henry, seaman, dwl S s Brannan foot Eighth
Pliley E. R. physician, dwl 107 Leidesdorff
Plimpton D. C. proprietor St. Charles Hotel, 39 First
Plotchett L. fruit peddler, dwl W s Salmon bet Mason and Taylor
Plouf Felix, boot and shoe maker, 1205 Dupont
Plover Patrick, carpenter, dwl S s Market, W Sixth
Plum Charles M. importer and jobber carpets and upholstery, 22 Montgomery, and school director Twelfth District, dwl NW cor Post and Franklin
Plum James, sailor, dwl Bay State House
Plum M. Mrs. midwife, dwl 635 Howard
Plume Kate C. (widow) dwl 526 Green
Plumer E. J. (widow) dwl 608 California
Plumer William P. stair builder, dwl 309 Stockton
Plummer Alden, ship carpenter, dwl 223 Beale
Plummer Anthony, dwl N s Clementina nr Eighth
Plummer George, dwl 62 Tehama
Plummer P. mason, Spring Valley W. W
Plummer Richard H. student medicine, dwl 11 Minna
Plummer Sewell, ship carpenter, dwl 223 Beale
Plunkett Delia Miss, dwl 335 Union
Plunkett James, plasterer, dwl W s Telegraph Pl

Plunkett Jane (widow) dwl 335 Union
Plunkett Joseph, boiler maker, Union Foundry, dwl 122 Third
Plunkett Lucia Mrs. millinery, 122 Third
Plunkett M. employé, Cosmopolitan Hotel
Plunkett William A. attorney at law, office 22 Court Block 636 Clay, dwl 335 Union
Plunty Mary Ann Miss, domestic, 762 Mission
Plympton G. P. carpenter, dwl 320 Kearny
Poalk James L. bulletin board reporter, office 516 Montgomery
Pockwitz Louis, clerk, dwl 1513 Stockton, rear
Podd Jessie, fruits and vegetables, 601 Post and 739 Broadway
Podesta Angelo, employé with Brignardello, Macchiavello & Co. 706 Sansom
Poe Alonzo M. topographical engineer, dwl 1511 Stockton, rear
Poehlman William, baker and confectioner, 104 Second
POETT ALFRED, civil engineer, office and dwl 728 Montgomery
POETZ JOHN C. California Restaurant, 405 and 407 California, dwl 32 Rousch nr Folsom
Pogi John, miner, dwl 14 Ohio
Pogue Robert A. carpenter, dwl W s Hyde bet Broadway and Vallejo
Pohl Henry, cooper, S. F. & P. Sugar Co. dwl 8 Langton nr Howard
Pohl Oliver, machinist, Vulcan Foundry, dwl 275 Stevenson
Pobley Joseph, vinegar manufacturer, S s Brannan bet Seventh and Eighth
Pobley William, with Joseph Pobley, dwl S s Brannan bet Seventh and Eighth
Pohlmann Augustus, jeweler with Pohlmann & Co. dwl 807 Bush
POHLMANN (Henry) & CO. (Augustus Bellemere and William Baehr) manufacturing jewelers, 516 Clay, dwl 807 Bush
Poindexter C. W. student, dwl 409 Mason
Point Arena Petroleum Oil and Coal Co. office 12 Phœnix Building
POINT LOBOS AND SEAL ROCK OMNIBUSES, John A. McGlynn proprietor, office nr Lone Mountain Cemetery
POINT SAN QUENTIN HOUSE, R. A. Follmer & Co. proprietors, SW cor Louisiana and Sierra, Potrero Nuevo
Poiro Louis, salesman, 618 Kearny, dwl Powell bet Vallejo and Broadway
Polack Abraham, salesman, 525 Commercial
Polack J. S. real estate agent, office 420 Montgomery up stairs, dwl 115 Dupont
Palack Samuel, clerk, 1012 Stockton, dwl 812 Stock
Poland Frank S. painter, dwl W s Ninth bet Howard and Mission
Poland Nabum, painter, dwl W s Ninth bet Howard and Mission
Polacci Petro, gardener, W s Fillmore nr Market
Polasky Louis, merchant, dwl 55 Bryant
POLASTRI VINCENT, physician and druggist, office and dwl 619 Vallejo
Polatsek Adolphus, salesman, 614 Market, dwl 149 Clara
Polatsek Ephraim, merchant, dwl 149 Clara
POLHEMUS CHARLES B. superintendent San Francisco & San José Railroad, office SE cor Sansom and Halleck
Polhemus Henry D. ticket clerk, S. F. & San José R. R. Co. dwl 704 Howard
Poli Peter, produce peddler, dwl 1004 Pacific
Poli S. bottle and sack dealer, E s Pacific Alley
POLICE ARMORY, room 2 basement City Hall cor Dunbar Alley
POLICE ATTORNEY, office 17 second floor City Hall
POLICE CAPTAIN, room 1 basement City Hall
POLICE CHIEF OF, office 11 first floor City Hall

POLICE COMMISSIONERS, office first floor City Hall
POLICE GAZETTE, (weekly) F. S. Harlow & Brother publishers and proprietors, office SW cor Front and Jackson
POLICE HARBOR, office cor Pacific and Davis
POLICE JUDGE, office 13 second floor City Hall
POLICE JUDGE'S CLERK, office 17 first floor City Hall
POLICE JUDGE'S COURT, office 13 first floor City Hall
Polison Henry, painter, Russ House
Polk Robert T. computation clerk, U. S. Branch Mint, dwl W s Hyde bet Filbert and Greenwich
Polker John H. produce, dwl W s Howard bet Twenty-First and Twenty-Second
POLLACK BROTHERS (Leopold and Joseph Pollock) importers and jobbers fancy goods, 421 Sacramento, dwl Steckler's Exchange
Pollack Joseph (Pollack Brothers) res New York
Pollak John, book keeper with Treadwell & Co. dwl Stockton nr Union
Pollard Aaron, dwl 514 Lombard
POLLARD (Isaac) & CARVILL (Orrin S.) carriage makers, 37 and 39 Webb, dwl 704 Sutter
Pollard John C. machinist, dwl 515 Pine
Pollard John M. bricklayer, dwl 26 Eddy
Pollard Thomas, book keeper with Macpherson & Wetherbee, dwl 639 Mission
Pollock Adolph, express wagon, cor Sac and Bat
Pollock David, boots and shoes, dwl 139 Minna
Pollock David H. salesman, 417 Sacramento, dwl 658 Folsom
Pollock George W. merchant, dwl 1133 Clay
Pollock G. W. Mrs. principal Pacific St. School, dwl 1133 Clay
Pollock James, dwl 337 Jessie
Pollock James, tailor with C. L. Cordiner, dwl 921 Union
Polwarth John A. carpenter, dwl 6 Freelon
Poly Solomon, boarding, 424 Sacramento
Pomelin August, seaman, dwl 20 Commercial
Pomeroy David (Hobbs, Gilmore & Co.) dwl N s Oak bet Van Ness Avenue and Franklin
Pomeroy G. W. dwl 427 Third
Pomeroy J. T. with E. Gould & Co. dwl 427 Third
Pomeroy Sheldon, bar keeper steamer Julia
Pomier Alphonse, mining and civil engineer, dwl 1213 Sacramento
Pomroy Samuel S. salesman with Tobin Brothers & Davisson, dwl 227 Geary
Pond Milo B. physician and apothecary City and County Hospital
Ponjol Charlotte (widow) dwl 30 Everett
Pons Charlotte Madame (Besson & P.) dwl 625 Merchant
Pons Theoffried (L. Christin & P.) Union Club Rooms
Ponti Anton, musician, dwl S s Dupont Alley
Pool Charles W. broker, 605 Sacramento
Pool I. Lawrence (Howard & P.) dwl Brevoort H
Poola John, seaman, dwl 54 Sacramento
Poole Edward A. captain steamer Yosemite, C. S. Navigation Co. office NE cor Front and Jackson
Poole J. F. dwl St. Lawrence House
Poole John H. clerk C. S. Navigation Co. dwl 915 Powell
Poole Marcus M. salesman with Kennedy & Bell, dwl 528 Pine
Poole Nathan A. express wagon, cor Clay and Davis, dwl NE cor Hayes and Octavia
Poole Paterson, bar keeper steamer Yosemite
Poole Spencer, clerk, 546 Clay, dwl 928 Clay
Poole William, dwl 226 Sutter
Pooler Henry, laborer, Fort Point, dwl NE corner Jones and Filbert
Pooley Edward, dwl 34 Russ
Poore Walter S. salesman with Dickinson & Gammans, dwl 726 Washington

POPE *(Andrew J.)* & TALBOT *(William C.)* lumber and proprietors Victoria & Puget Sound Packets, 149 Stewart Pier 12, dwl 614 Folsom
Pope August, cook, dwl 253 Stewart
Pope *(Charles)* & Bruns *(Henry)* groceries and liquors, junction Filbert and Presidio Road
Pope Charles, laborer, dwl 227 Sutter
Pope Ebenezer R. with Alonzo Green, 107 Clay, dwl 413 First
Pope E. M. (widow) dwl 819 Mission
Pope Fowler W. engineer, S. F. & San José R. R. Co. res San José
Pope Francis, clerk with James K. Bummer, dwl SE cor Broadway and Stockton
Pope Hiram, with William E. Bridge, 317 Pine
Pope Jacob, butcher, with Stevens & Oliver, dwl 543 Bush
Pope John F. mining secretary, office 103 California, dwl 1412 Mason
Pope Mary (widow) dwl 252 Stevenson
Pope Overton C. assayer with Thomas Price, dwl 1412 Mason
Popp August, proprietor Alcatraz Market, 1703 Stock
Poppe Charles *(Davidson & P.)* dwl 20 Stock Pl
Popper Charles, commission mcht, dwl 427 Bryant
Popper L. dwl 427 Bryant
Popper Lotti Mrs. dry goods, 101 Third, dwl 427 Bryant
Porcher Peter, tailor, dwl 223 Seventh, rear
Porcheron E. D. wagon maker, NE cor Union and Stockton
Porep Louis, watch maker with G. Lehmann, dwl NE cor Folsom and Fourth
PORT ORFORD LINE STEAMERS, Ben Holliday proptr, office SW cor Front and Jackson
Port Orford, Navarro, and Russian River Packets, H. B. Tichenor & Co. agents, Pier 21 Stewart
PORT WARDEN'S OFFICE, 716 Front
Portal A. cook, Cosmopolitan Hotel
Portal Julius J. B. Folsom Laundry, office SE cor Cal and Kearny, dwl E s Folsom Av nr Folsom
PORTER ASA A. wines and liquors, 520 California, dwl 618 California
Porter Charles Epps (col'd) porter, California State Telegraph Co. dwl N s Sacramento abv Stockton
Porter David *(Fox & P.)* dwl Union Club Rooms
Porter G. & S. M. Co. office 622 Clay
Porter George S. port warden, office 716 Front, dwl 1506 Leavenworth
Porter Henry, waterman, 609 Market, dwl 106 Mason
PORTER HORACE, proprietor Clayton House and wines and liquors, 605 Commercial, dwl N s Mission bet Tenth and Eleventh
Porter J. A. machinist with David Stoddart, dwl Beale St. House
Porter James, broker, dwl W s Mason bet Vallejo and Green
Porter James K. compositor, Daily Examiner, dwl 1619 Mason
Porter John, hostler, dwl 3 Brown Alley
Porter John G. wool sorter, S. F. P. Woolen Mills, dwl North Point bet Polk and Van Ness Av
Porter John W. box maker, dwl 436 Bush
PORTER *(Nathan)* & HOLLADAY *(Samuel W.)* attorneys at law, office 620 Washington, rooms 4-6
PORTER NATHAN, district attorney city and county, office 20 second floor City Hall *(and Porter & Holladay)* dwl 437 Natoma
Porter Nathaniel D. cigars and tobacco, dwl 1815 Powell
Porter T. H. peddler, 114 Clay
PORTER *(Wadsworth)* & COVEY *(Harris R.)* Fashion Livery and Sale Stable, 16 Sutter
Porter W. H. carpenter, dwl SE corner Mission and First
Porter William, blacksmith, dwl E s Zoe bet Bryant and Brannan
Porter William, carpenter, dwl NW cor Filbert and Taylor

Porter W. S. dwl What Cheer House
Portis William, blacksmith, Miners' Foundry, dwl Zoe nr Bryant
PORTLAND BOILER WORKS, Moynihan & Aitken, 311 and 313 Mission
Portland Line Packets, Richards & McCraken agents, 405 Front
PORTLAND LINE STEAMERS, Ben Holladay SW cor Front and Jackson, and C. S. Navigation Co. NE cor Front and Jackson agents
Portley James, laborer, dwl N s Market nr Gough
PORTMANN J. H. C. soap manufacturer, E s Mission Creek bet Sixteenth and Brannan St. Bridge
Portois Peter, architect, 620 Merchant
Portram Ferdinand, cabinet maker, dwl 1326 Dupont
PORTSMOUTH HOUSE, cor Clay and Brenham Place
Poska Jacob *(Borchers & P.)* 423 Davis
Post Benjamin, boot maker, dwl SW cor Dupont and Broadway
Post Edward, laborer, California Engine Co. No. 4
Post Frederick L. property clerk, Police Office City Hall, dwl 1112 Taylor
Post George W. L. butcher with Crummie & O'Neill, dwl N s Brannan bet Seventh and Eighth
Post Hannah (widow) dwl 274 Jessie
Post Nicholas, boot maker with J. H. Swain, dwl SW cor Dupont and Broadway
POST OFFICE U. S. NW cor Battery and Wash
Post St. House, John Schumacher proprietor, 207 Post
Post Victor B. salesman with James Irvine & Co. dwl 1425 Taylor
Post Victor C. machinist, Miners' Foundry, dwl 1421 Taylor
Post William, dwl S side Chestnut bet Powell and Stock
Postel Isaac, cabinet maker with John Wigmore, dwl 223 Kearny
Postel Mary Miss, domestic, 122 Natoma
Postel Peter J. groceries and liquors, NE cor Fourth and Everett
Postel William, job wagon, 520 Sansom, dwl 47 Second
Potesta John, employé with Little & Lawson, dwl 235 Jackson
Potett H. gardener, NW cor Hayes and Van Ness Avenue
Potier E. S. upholsterer, dwl 8 Polk Alley
Potier M. O. Madame, dwl 527 California
Potier Numa, clerk, 714 Montgomery, dwl 527 Cal
Potosi G. & S. M. Co. office 60 Exchange Building
Petter E. A. (widow) lodgings, 225 Second
Potter Ellen F. (widow) furnished rooms, 6 Sutter
Potter F. T. *(A. G. Randall & Co.)* dwl 697 Geary
POTTER GEORGE C. surveyor city and county, office 11 third floor City Hall, dwl 119 Stockton
Potter Henry B. miner, dwl 27 Perry
Potter Jane (widow) furnished rooms, 22 Kearny
Potter John, clerk, 116 Davis, dwl SE cor Sacramento and Davis
Potter J. R. mariner, dwl 117 Sixth
Potter Lyman G. carpenter, dwl 13 Perry
Potter William, liquors, dwl 124 Fourth
Potthoff Augustus, seaman, bds 7 Washington
Potts Izatus, clerk with H. M. Newhall & Co. dwl 845 Dupont
Potts Thomas, laborer, dwl S s Stevenson bet Sixth and Seventh
Poudon Narsic, laborer, dwl S s Grove bet Laguna and Octavia
Pougel Celestin, boot fitter, dwl 18 St. Mary
Pougel Lucien, boot fitter, dwl 18 St. Mary
Pougel Jennie (widow) French laundry, 604 Bdwy
Pougol Louis, laborer, dwl 517 Union
Poulet Paul, furnished rooms, 540 Washington
Poulin Emile, dwl 634 Pacific
Poulsen John, stevedore, dwl 26 Stewart

Poulterer Thomas J. *(Jones & Bendixen)* dwl 1502 Taylor
Poulterer Thomas R. clerk with Jones & Bendixen, dwl 820 Washington
Poultney *(George)* & Smith *(Joseph)* South Park Livery Stable, 342 Brannan
Pound Keeper, office cor Union and Van Ness Av
Pourchasen Edward D. blacksmith, dwl Franklin Hotel cor Sansom and Pacific
Pourcho Frederick, with Jacob Stoerk, dwl Mansion House
Poursillié Adrien, importer brandies, office NW cor Sansom and Jackson, dwl 130 Sutter
Pout Frederick, attorney at law, 21 Montgomery Blk
Pouzadoux Louis *(John Stock & Co.)* dwl 17 Government House
Powell Catherine (widow) dwl SE cor Folsom and Twenty-Second
Powell C. F. Mrs. lodgings, 819 Montgomery
POWELL CHARLES F. Esmeralda Saloon, 610 Clay, dwl 819 Montgomery
Powell Fannie Miss, domestic, 874 Mission
Powell Ferree, brickmason, dwl E s Florida near Twentieth
Powell John, molder, Miners' Foundry, dwl Natoma Place bet Beale and Fremont
Powell Joseph, cook, Phil's Exchange, dwl Broadway Block
POWELL *(L. F.)* & TRIPP *(P. F.)* Magnolia Restaurant, 143 Third, dwl NE cor Third and Hunt
Powell M. dwl International Hotel
Powell R. carpenter, dwl Original House
Powell Richard C. drayman, 417 Battery, dwl 51 Clara
Powelson Peter, express wagon, cor Montgomery and Merchant, dwl SE cor Clay and Leav
Powelson W. L. engineer, Occidental Hotel
Power *(Edward)* & Warren *(James L.)* wood carvers, 27 Fremont, dwl 104 Natoma
Power Ellen Miss, laundress, Bay City Laundry, 1140 and 1142 Folsom
Power James, calker, dwl Albion House Stewart
Power James, tinsmith with Osgood & Stetson, dwl 23 Jane
Power Johanna, domestic with S. Crim, W s Howard bet Nineteenth and Twentieth
Power Lawrence, machinist, Pacific Foundry, dwl 19 Dupont
Power William, carpenter, res Clinton Alameda Co
Powers Charles, sail maker, dwl 158 Silver
Powers Charles, seaman, steamer Orizaba
Powers Charles A. machinist, dwl 609 Folsom
POWERS *(Charles E.)* & CO. *(James N. Makins)* Fremont Market NE cor Folsom and Fremont, dwl 525 Pine
Powers Charles H. painter, dwl S s Ewer Place
Powers Daniel, machinist with S. A. Metcalf, dwl 13 Clara, rear
Powers Elias, ship carpenter, dwl 243 Fremont
Powers Frederick H. salesman, 125 Montgomery, dwl 609 Folsom
Powers G. H. house mover, dwl 613 Mission
Powers James, with Taaffe & Co. 9 Montgomery
Powers James W. carpenter, dwl 28 Rousch
Powers Johanna Miss, domestic with S. Crim, dwl W s Howard bet Nineteenth and Twentieth
Powers John, dwl S s Folsom bet Beale and Main
Powers John, attaché, Maguire's Opera House, dwl 1608 Stockton
Powers John, carpenter, dwl 323 Minna
Powers John, cooperage, 117 Pine, dwl 921 Jones
Powers John, groceries and liquors, NW cor Union and Hyde
Powers John, laborer, Spring Valley W. W
Powers John, laborer, dwl S s Vallejo nr Mont
Powers John, porter, 319 Front, dwl 46 Clementina
Powers John, varnisher, dwl Ecker bet First and Second nr Folsom

Powers John D. weigher, 64 Clay, dwl 56 Tehama
Powers John L. varnisher with Goodwin & Co. dwl SW cor Folsom and Ecker
Powers Maggie Miss, domestic, 534 Ellis
Powers Mary Miss, domestic with W. M. Higgins, Jackson Place
Powers Mary C. Miss, dwl with Thomas H. Powers S s Fourteenth nr Folsom
Powers Michael, laborer, dwl W s Gaven nr Filbert
Powers Michael, wkm with S. C. & L. H. Talcott
Powers Nicholas, baker with Nichols & Co. 819 Sansom
Powers Patrick, laborer, dwl Laguna nr Bush
Powers Robert, laborer, Union Foundry, dwl Mission St. House
Powers Thomas, seaman, dwl 131 Folsom
Powers Thomas H. miner, dwl S s Fourteenth nr Folsom
Powers W. laborer, Spring Valley W. W
Pozzi Pasquale, laborer with Pietro Juri, W s Scott nr Turk
PRACY GEORGE T. machinist and blacksmith, 109 and 111 Fremont, dwl 216 Harrison
Prag Martin, stoves and tinware, 125 Clay, dwl 816 Filbert
Prager Abraham J. merchant, dwl 25 Hunt
Prager Lewis, clerk, dwl 25 Hunt
Prahl Emil, clerk with Falkner, Bell & Co. dwl 6 Quincy
Prairo John M. blacksmith, Pacific Foundry, dwl 23 Sherwood Place
Pram Henry, musician, Wilson's Circus
Pratt Adelia (widow) dwl Verona Place
Pratt Benjamin, policeman, City Hall, dwl 229 Kearny
Pratt Daniel W. carriage painter, S s Market nr First, dwl 1123 Howard
Pratt Frederick H. *(Simpson & P.)* dwl 1042 Folsom
Pratt George H. deputy pound keeper, dwl 760 Harrison
Pratt George H. jr. dwl 760 Harrison
Pratt Henry, mining, dwl 124 Turk
Pratt Henry E. wood turner, dwl Second nr Mission
Pratt *(Henry G.)* & Jacobs *(Albert)* carpenters and builders, 118 Washington, dwl 6 Front
Pratt James, attorney at law, office 41 Exchange Building
Pratt James, clerk, dwl 106 Natoma
Pratt James, printer, dwl N s Stevenson bet Sixth and Seventh
Pratt James N. druggist with W. H. Keith, dwl 14 Natoma
Pratt Nathan, cigars and tobacco, 112 Sansom, bds Bailey House
Pratt Orville C. judge Twelfth District Court, room 1 City Hall second floor, chambers 15 third floor, dwl 213 First
Pratt S. K. express wagon, cor Sansom and Wash
Pratt Tasker S. assistant store keeper Bonded Warehouse, dwl NE cor Montgomery and Pacific
Pratt William H. carpenter with Pratt & Jacobs, bds 6 Front
Pratt William P. *(H. A. Nash & Co. Stockton)* office 216 and 218 Cal, dwl Occidental Hotel
Pray Benjamin C. machinist, dwl 12 Sutter
Pray I. C. *(Halsted & Pray)* dwl 608 Bush
Pray Joseph C. machinist with Small & Redmond
Preble Augustus, dwl cor Pacific and Davis
PRECHT CARL, physician, office and dwl 913 Dupont
Precht Edward, merchant, dwl 913 Dupont
Precht *(Frederick)* & Eggers *(John C.)* fruits, Pacific Fruit Market, dwl 123 Dora
Preda G. billiard and liquor saloon, 727 Mont
Prediger John G. bar keeper, SW cor Pine and Montgomery, dwl Belden nr Bush
Pregel August, metal spinner, 620 Merchant, dwl W s Taylor bet Green and Union

Prendergast James F. blacksmith, dwl 541 Mission
Prendergast John, plumber, dwl E s Harriet bet Howard and Folsom
PRENDERGAST JOHN J. Rev. pastor St. Francis Church, and rector St. Thomas' Seminary, Mission Dolores
Prendergast William, Howard Engine Co. No. 3
Presbury William W. receiving clerk, California State Telegraph Co. 507 Mont, dwl 904 Leav
Presby Elijah, carpenter, Vulcan Iron Works, dwl S s Austin bet Polk and Van Ness Avenue
Presch George, clerk with J. Vokitch, dwl 715 Davis
Prescott D. S. Miss, special grammar assistant, Washington Grammar School, dwl 618 Cal
Prescott Frank, actor, Maguire's Opera House
Prescott Frank, driver with A. W. Owen
Prescott Frederick A. road master, S. F. & San José R. R. Co. dwl E s Capp bet Twenty-First and Twenty-Second
PRESCOTT GEORGE W. superintendent Main St. Wharf, dwl 1024 Bush
Prescott George W. dwl 36 Valparaiso
Prescott G. W. (H. J. Booth & Co.) res Marysville
Prescott (Jacob) & Israel (Julius) boots and shoes, 400 Kearny cor Pine, dwl 279 Stevenson
Prescott John C. mate Revere, dwl 238 Stewart
Prescott Joseph D. driver with I. G. Knowles, dwl 14 Stockton Place
Prescott Minnie Mrs. actress, Maguire's Opera H
Prescott W. P. foreman laboratory U. S. Branch Mint, dwl 313 Pine
Presho Solomon A. clerk, 10 Occidental Market, dwl 569 Mission
PRESIDIO AND FORT POINT OMNIBUSES, John A. McGlynn proprietor, office 714 Kearny
Pressey Benjamin F. carpenter, dwl opposite King bet Third and Fourth
Preston Denzil, book keeper, Pier 5 Stewart, dwl S s Mission nr Eleventh
Preston Edgar F. straw hat presser, dwl 32 Second
Preston J. H. dwl E s Carlos Place
Preston John, machinist with Palmer, Knox & Co. dwl 637 Mission
Preston Margaret, domestic, 14 Stanly Place
PRESTON (Otis J.) & McKINNON (John J.) lumber, 53 Stewart Pier 5, dwl S s Mission nr Eleventh
Preston Robert J. copyist, dwl NE cor Kearny and Broadway
Preston William, carpenter, dwl 567 Mission
Preston William H. janitor Dashaway Hall, dwl 36 St. Mark Place, rear
Pretorius Frederick, boiler maker, Vulcan Iron Works
Pretorius Godfred, carpenter, dwl 565 Bryant
Price Benjamin (Rosenstock & P.) dwl 719 Post
Price Benjamin, barber, dwl 1503 Stockton
Price Caroline Miss, principal Powell St. School, dwl 1112 Clay
Price Charles, seaman, dwl 26 Sacramento
Price David, carpenter, dwl Oriental Hotel
Price David jr. carpenter, dwl NW cor Post and Hyde
Price Edward M. dwl W s Prospect Avenue nr Virginia Avenue
Price Ellen (widow) dress maker, dwl 757 Mission, rear
Price Henry, painter, dwl 12 Sutter
Price Henry F. conductor, North Beach & M. R. R. Co
Price Hugh, express wagon, cor Sutter and Sansom
Price James, seaman, dwl 26 Sacramento
Price J. C. boarding, W s Battery nr Vallejo
Price John M. clerk with L. H. Woolley, dwl 1101 Clay
Price John R. proptr Rincon House, NW cor First and Folsom
Price (Johnson) & Page (Robert C.) stock brokers, 626 Clay, res Oakland

Price Lawrence, deck hand, steamer Chrysopolis
Price Michael, manufacturer cutlery, 110 Montgomery, dwl SE cor Hayes and Octavia
Price Michael sen. with Michael Price, 110 Montgomery, dwl SE cor Hayes and Octavia
Price Michael E. gas fitter, Pennsylvania Engine Co. No. 12
Price Peter, second officer steamer Del Norte, office SW cor Front and Jackson
Price Richard, miner, dwl SW cor Kearny and Pac
Price Robert, laborer, dwl N s Lombard bet Larkin and Polk
Price Samuel & Co. (Frederick Green) commission merchants, office 436 Jackson, dwl S s Pine bet Stockton and Powell
Price Sarah Miss, dwl with Martha N. Thurston nr SE cor Folsom and Twenty-Second
PRICE THOMAS, assayer with Kellogg, Hewston & Co. commission merchant and Professor City College, office 406 Cal, dwl 508 Taylor
Price William, drayman, dwl Pacific Engine House, 112 Jackson
Price William, laborer, dwl E s Folsom nr Precita Avenue
Price William B. (col'd) waiter, steamer Chrysopolis
Prichard Frank H. clerk, dwl 1028 Minna
Prichard John, carrier, Alta California, dwl 604 Merchant
Prichard L. A. Miss, assistant, Hyde St. School, dwl Minna bet Seventh and Eighth
Prichard Robert, dwl 606 Montgomery
Prichard Timothy, carrier, Bulletin, dwl 604 Merch
Priebatch Amelia Miss, dress maker, 46 Everett
Priebatch Julius, tailor, NE cor Bush and Stockton, dwl 46 Everett
Pries R. F. bookseller, 750 Washington, dwl SE cor Sacramento and Prospect Place
Priet Pierre, waiter, dwl 821 Kearny
Prieto Frank, with Peter Bonzi, 515 Merchant
Pril August, butcher with Lux & Miller, dwl cor Ninth and Brannan
Prince A. E. drayman, 211 Clay, dwl 337 Bryant
Prince Allan G. carpenter, dwl 107 Montgomery Blk
Prince Carmen (widow) dwl 708 Pine
Prince Charles H. hostler with John Clarke, W s Seventh nr Folsom
Prince George, driver, Omnibus R. R. Co
Prince George S. dwl 128 St. Mark Place
Prince Imperial G. & S. M. Co. office 804 Mont
Prince Jacob, slipper manufactory, 224 Sansom, dwl 12 Sansom
Prince John, carpenter, dwl 40 Natoma
Prince Levi M. house carpenter, dwl S s Union bet Hyde and Larkin
Prince Mary Miss, domestic, 317 Powell
Prince Robert, molder, Vulcan Iron Works, dwl 708 Pine
Prince Stephen, hostler, dwl Bay View Park
Prince T. shoe maker, dwl Federal Building
Prince T. P. machinist, Fulton Foundry, dwl Oriental Hotel
Princely William, carpenter, dwl 116 Dupont
Princivalle Giacoma, groceries, N s Sixteenth near Dolores
Prindle Ben. A. photographic printer with James Wise, dwl 106 Silver
Prindle Charles W. clerk, 300 Montgomery, dwl 862 Mission
Prindle D. S. contractor raising and moving buildings, 109 Kearny, dwl 862 Mission
Prindle Jane (widow) dwl 106 Silver
Prine Moses S. boatman, dwl SW cor Market and East
PRINGLE EDWARD J. attorney at law, office 8 Court Block 636 Clay, dwl 1018 Stockton
Pringle Miles, carpenter with S. S. Culverwell, 29 Fremont
Pringle S. W. box maker, dwl 812 Sacramento
Priniville Maurice, stone cutter, dwl 270 Clementina

PRINZ JOHN, wines, cigars, and tobacco, 49 Second, dwl 7 Anthony
Prior Charles, wood and coal, 911 Folsom
Prior Edward, butcher with John Conway, dwl E s Ninth nr Folsom
Prior Elizabeth Miss, dwl with Henry Pinnick, W s Ninth nr Folsom
Prior James, porter, Lick House
PRIOR JAMES K. importer gas fixtures and plumbing material, 730 Montgomery, dwl 13 Mason bet Eddy and Turk
Prior James W. job wagon, SW cor Washington and Battery, dwl Natoma bet Sixth and Seventh
Prior John *(Beckman, Aiken & Co.)* dwl N s California bet Dupont and Kearny
Prior Philip, male assistant, Lincoln School, dwl 616 California
Prior William, washer, Chelsea Laundry
Pritchard James A. *(Hayes & P.)* dwl 311 Fourth
Pritchard John H. messenger Savings and Loan Society, 619 Clay, dwl 520 Bryant
Pritchard M. George, interpreter, dwl 902 Jackson
Pritchard Thomas, workman, Spring Valley W. W. Co. dwl NW cor Harrison and Seventh
Pritchard, see Prichard
Pritzel August, machinist, 416 Market
Probasco John W. gauger, Custom House, dwl 307 Third
PROBATE COURT, room 18 City Hall second floor
Probst Louis, cook, Cliff House
Proctor John, carpenter, dwl N s Geary nr Leavenworth
Proctor Joseph, joiner, dwl 413 Folsom
PROCUREUR *(A. Peter)* & WENZEL *(Edward)* watch case and jewelry engravers, 622 Clay, dwl S s Hayes bet Franklin and Gough
Prodger Charles M. assistant newspaper clerk, Post Office, dwl 152 First
Prodo Henry, seaman, dwl 20 Clay
Proetel Aaron, hairdresser, 50 Fourth, dwl 777 Market
Profom Joseph, vegetable garden, Bay View
Prohl Frederick, tailor, dwl 401 Bush
Prohl Louis, carpenter, dwl W s Webster bet McAllister and Tyler
Proll Henry, real estate, dwl 424 Kearny
Proll John, carpenter, Hardie Place, dwl 106 Geary
Prosper Max, porter, dwl 1509 Stockton
Proschold *(Charles)* & Rauch *(Jacob)* hairdressing saloon, 310 Bush, dwl 106 Sixth
Prosso Gregorio, gardener, NE cor Laguna and McAllister
Prost Philemon, brick molder with B. Bonnet & Co
Protois Fanny Mme. dress maker, 749 Clay
Protolongo William, dwl 626 California
Protsch John, waiter, What Cheer H Restaurant
Prow Delaphine (widow) dwl 602 Filbert
Proudfoot George, clerk, 745 Clay
Prouse James E. compositor, Sunday Mercury, dwl 34 Everett
Prousergue Antoine *(Anderson & P.)* dwl 456 Jessie
Providence G. & S. M. Co. (Nevada, Cal.) office 7 Government House
Providencia M. Co. (Reese River) office 6 Montgomery Block
Provines Alexander B. book keeper with E. Stevens & Co. dwl 270 First
Provines R. R. *(Sloan & P.)* attorney at law, office Exchange Building, dwl S s Washington bet Taylor and Jones
Provinze William, cabinet maker, 303 Third
Provoncher Emanuel, carpenter, S. F. Gas Co. dwl 5 Baldwin Court
PROVOST D. R. & CO. importers and manufacturers concentrated vinegar, pickles, preserves, 413 Front, res Oakland
PROVOST MARSHAL U. S. A. Southern District California, office 416 Washington

Provost N. dwl What Cheer House
Prucitano Luigi, fisherman, 39 Italian Fish Market
Prudepe Jean, bootblacking, 748 Washington
Pruett Louisa Mrs. dwl 746 Market
Prunty Francis, barber, dwl N s Broadway nr Sansom
Prunty John, drayman, 102 Clay, dwl N s Tyler bet Polk and Van Ness Avenue
Pruvost E. druggist, French Hospital
Prydz William I. N. butcher with Zimmerman & Co. dwl Brannan St. Bridge
PUBLIC ADMINISTRATOR, J. W. Brumagim, office 36 Montgomery Block
Public Pound, John Short jr. keeper, SE cor Union and Van Ness Avenue
PUCK (monthly) Loomis & Swift proprietors, office 617 Clay
Puckhaber D. *(Neunaber & Co.)* res Boise River
Puckhaber John, groceries and liquors, NW cor Mason and Post, dwl 519 Mason
Pudd Jesse, fruits, 739 Broadway
Puffer William W. drayman, dwl 231 Pacific
PUGET SOUND LINE PACKETS, Adams, Blinn & Co. Pier 17 Stewart, and W. H. Gawley, Pier 1 Stewart, agents
PUGH EDMUND, commission merchant and dealer drugs, chemicals, etc. office 210 Bush, dwl 462 Natoma
Pugh Frederick, clerk with R. Hall & Co. dwl 314 Broadway
Pugh Henry, musician, dwl 314 Broadway
Pugh Henry, painter, dwl 314 Broadway
Pugh Mary Miss, domestic, 1214 Mason
Pugh Thomas E. clerk, 536 Market, dwl 1413 Pac
Puis Lawrence, cooper, dwl 331 Bush
Pujol Domingo *(Sanjurjo, Bolado & P.)* res San Luis Obispo
Pullen Augustus, engineer, Fulton Foundry, dwl 421 Folsom
Pallen F. A. engineer, Spring Valley W. W. dwl 421 Folsom
Pullin Christian, cook, 530 Merchant, dwl cor Dupont and Filbert
Pullman James *(Jones, Dixon & Co.)* dwl S side Geary bet Polk and Van Ness Avenue
Pulsifer Frederick, pile driver, bds United States Hotel
Pulsipher Orrin, carpenter, dwl 265 Tehama
Pult John G. sash maker, dwl 120 Sutter, rear
Pulvermacher Francis, merchant, dwl 1816 Mason
PULVERMAN BENNET, collector, office 526 Montgomery, dwl 635 Market
Punch Simon, hostler, dwl 1016 Stockton
Purcell Charles, blacksmith with Kimball & Co
Purcell Charles, gas fitter with Thomas O. Malley, 646 Market, dwl 1102 Washington
Purcell David, laborer, dwl S s Folsom bet Beale and Main
Purcell George, dwl 527 Mission
Purcell James, laborer, dwl S s Stevenson bet Seventh and Eighth
Purcell John, plasterer, dwl W s Folsom Avenue nr Folsom
Purcell Julia A. Miss, teacher, dwl 77 Minna
Purcell Michael *(Ryan & P.)* and street contractor, dwl 21 Ann
Purcell Michael, wool worker, Broadway Wool Depôt, dwl Powell bet Filbert and Greenwich
Purcell Thomas, with Taaffe & Co. 9 Montgomery, dwl Anna nr Eddy
Purcell Thomas, liquor saloon, 210 Commercial
Purcell Z. B. truckman, Oakland Ferry
Purdon Thomas J. jeweler with Lemme Bros. dwl SW cor Stockton and Vallejo
Purdon William H. musician, dwl Trinity bet Bush and Sutter
Purdy C. T. with J. R. Mead & Co. dwl 5 Milton Place
Purdy Daniel, carpenter, dwl 161 Tehama

Purdy Emeline V. (widow) dwl 530 Bush
Purdy J. Elbridge, book keeper with Hooker & Co. 117 California, dwl 629 O'Farrell
Purdy J. H. inspector, Custom House, dwl 105 Prospect Place
Purdy Joseph W. H. conductor, Central R. R. Co. dwl SE cor Brannan and Seventh
Purdy Wilson, mason, dwl NW cor Sacramento and Waverly Place
Purinton Byron, machinist, Market St. R. R. Co. dwl NE cor Guerrero and Twentieth
Purkitt John H. mining secretary, dwl 1014 Stock
Putman Charles B. salesman with Murphy, Grant & Co. dwl DeBoom nr Second
Putman Jacob, seaman, dwl 26 Sacramento
Putnam Elizabeth Mrs. *(Dixon & P.)* dwl 615 Clay
PUTNAM SAMUEL OSGOOD, secretary C. S. Nav. Co. office NE cor Front and Jackson, dwl 1012 Washington
PUTZMANN FREDERICK, importer and jobber wines and liquors, 213 Jackson *(and Pacific Distillery Co.)* dwl 1808 Stockton
Putzmann Fritz, salesman, dwl NW cor Kearny and Jackson
Puvogel John, groceries and liquors, SW cor Mason and Filbert
Puyoou Bernard, hairdresser with Pierre Puyoou, dwl 610 Kearny
Puyoou Pierre, hairdressing saloon, 610 Kearny, dwl 49 Minna
PYNCH JOHN F. & CO. *(S. O. Hayward)* proprietors New Age, office 532 Merchant, dwl 52 Second
Pyne Robert, painter, dwl 212 Ritch
Pyser Michael, tailor, SE cor Pine and Dupont

Q

QUACKENBUSH Edward, mining secretary, office room 24 Government House 502 Washington
Quackenbush John, dwl 1026 Montgomery
Quackenbush Thomas M. carpenter and builder, 534 Jackson, bds International Hotel
Quade Patrick S. bar keeper, SE cor Market and Fourth
Quaid David, with John Higgins, Lake Merced Rancho
Quaid Kate Miss, domestic, 321 Sixth
Quaid Timothy, workman with P. Kelly, University Mound
Quaid William, stone cutter, Fort Point
Quail Catherine Miss, domestic, SW cor Sutter and Hyde
Quailey John F. oil stocks, dwl 314 Kearny
Quale Francis, laborer, dwl cor McAllister and Van Ness Avenue
Quarles William A. *(Maurice Dore & Co.)* office 327 Montgomery
Quast John, cook Blue Anchor, 7 Washington
Quast Charles, superintendent What Cheer House Restaurant, dwl What Cheer House
Queen Charles (col'd) barber, dwl 1516 Powell
Querillacq John, book keeper with Lyons & Co. dwl 510 Jackson
Quesada Ramon, dwl W s Jones bet Ellis and O'Farrell
Quevedo Vicente, teacher music, dwl 519 Vallejo
Quick J. W. manuf quartz screens, dwl 673 Mission
Quick Robert P. shutter maker with J. R. Sims, dwl 673 Mission
QUICKSILVER MINING CO. Samuel F. Butterworth agent, office 205 Battery
Quigley Daniel, foreman S. F. Gas Co. dwl SE cor Fifth and Minna
Quigley Dennis, laborer with William Kerr, dwl 903 Battery
Quigley Ellen Miss, ironer, South Park Laundry, 540 Third

Quigley James, laborer, bds Boston House, Minna nr Fourth
Quigley James, tailor, dwl 70 First
Quigley John, laborer, dwl NE cor Bryant and Fourth
Quigley John, laundryman, dwl 540 Third
Quigley Margaret A. Mrs. dress maker, dwl SW cor Stevenson and Sixth
Quigley Michael, plasterer, dwl SE cor Union and Larkin
Quigley P. stock dealer, bds Brooklyn Hotel
Quigley Philip, carpenter, dwl SE cor Jessie and Fifth
Quigley Thomas, boiler maker with Coffey & Risdon, dwl 15 Ecker
Quill Michael, laborer, dwl 266 Jessie
Quill Peter, clerk, NW cor Mission and Twenty-Fourth
Quillen Miles, baker, dwl E s Vincent nr Green
Quilligan Michael, cokeman, S. F. Gas Co. dwl S s Brannan bet Fourth and Fifth
Quimby Jason, carpenter, dwl Adelaide Place near Taylor
Quimby M. Miss, dress maker, 608 Market
Quinan James A. clerk, 423 Front
Quince Charles C. painter and paper hanger, dwl 1321 Stockton
Quince Sarah Mrs. dress maker, dwl 811 Union
Quinchard Julius, book keeper with B. Dolheguy, dwl 252 Clara
Quinlan Daniel, driver, Omnibus R. R. Co
Quinlan James, laborer, dwl 28 Ritch
Quinlan John, helper, Pacific Foundry, dwl E side Fillmore nr Turk
Quinlan John, laborer with John G. North, dwl 26 Annie
Quinlan P. B. registrar, Spring Valley W. W. Co. dwl 613 Lombard
Quinley Joseph M. mining, dwl 605 Howard
QUINLIN ALBERT G. physician and surgeon, office and dwl 610 Front
Quinliving Elizabeth Miss, domestic, 1517 Mason
Quinn Ann (widow) dress maker, 20 Montgomery
Quinn Anna Miss, domestic, 109 Ellis
Quinn Arthur, proprietor National Hall and Restaurant, W s Dolores bet Sixteenth and Seventeenth
Quinn Bridget Miss, domestic, SW cor Treat Avenue and Twentieth
Quinn Bridget Miss, domestic, 505 O'Farrell
Quinn *(Charles)* & McConnell *(William)* carpenters and builders, 450 Natoma
Quinn Edward, dwl SW cor Leavenworth and Vallejo
Quinn Edward, wharfinger, Commercial St. Wharf, dwl E s Vincent nr Union
Quinn Hugh, drayman with James H. Cutter, dwl 629 California
Quinn James, dwl 829 Sacramento
Quinn James, bricklayer, dwl 12 Sutter
Quinn James, druggist, dwl 32 Rousch
Quinn James, laborer, dwl 235 Jessie
Quinn James, laborer, dwl 37 Frederick
Quinn James, sash and blind maker with George Robinson & Co. 32 California
Quinn James, workman, S. F. & P. Sugar Co. dwl 32 Rousch
Quinn James C. wood and coal, 325 O'Farrell
Quinn James H. boarding, 206 Pacific
Quinn John, boiler maker with Coffey & Risdon, dwl 97 Stevenson
Quinn John, Bull's Head Liquor Saloon, junction Sutter and Market, dwl 18 Minna
Quinn John, laborer, bds Washington House
Quinn John, laborer, dwl 154 Tehama
Quinn John, laborer, dwl 46 Stevenson
Quinn John C. dwl 325 O'Farrell
Quinn John J. carpenter, dwl Cincinnati Brewery, Valencia nr Sixteenth

Quinn Kate Mrs. fruits, 14 Dupont
Quinn Mary Miss, domestic, 913 Jackson
Quinn Mary Miss, domestic, 764 Harrison
Quinn Mary Miss, domestic with Henry P. Coon
Quinn Mathew, boiler maker, dwl 8W cor Louisiana and Sierra
Quinn Michael, apprentice boiler maker, dwl W s Main bet Harrison and Spear
Quinn Michael E. driver with Dwyer & Co. dwl 83 Stevenson
Quinn Nancy (widow) dwl E s Main bet Harrison and Bryant
Quinn Nicholas, express wagon, 216 Sansom, dwl 222 Tehama
Quinn Patrick, baggage master steamer Yosemite, dwl 410 Vallejo
Quinn Patrick (Metzger & Co.) dwl N s Brannan bet Eighth and Ninth
Quinn Patrick, porter, stmr Yosemite, dwl SW cor Mason and Pacific
Quinn Patrick, workman, S. F. & P. Sugar Co. dwl W s Seventh nr Harrison
Quinn Peter, laborer, dwl 212 First
Quinn Peter, workman, S. F. & P. Sugar Co. dwl W s Seventh nr Harrison
Quinn Q. drayman with P. Riley & Co. dwl SE cor Mason and Post
Quinn Richard, boot and shoe maker, 244 Sixth
Quinn Rose Miss, domestic, 1316 Taylor
Quinn Stephen, engineer, 819 Sansom
Quinn Thomas, groom, dwl 342 Brannan
Quinn Thomas, marble polisher with Zeglio & Moore, dwl 23 Jane
Quinn Thomas L. hackman, dwl 1226 Stockton
Quinn William H. salesman, 106 Bat, dwl 532 Pine
Quinsigamond M. Co. office 6 Montgomery Block
Quint George, brick maker, dwl E s Dolores bet Fifteenth and Sixteenth
Quintanne Miguel, dwl 310 Clementina
Quintel Peter, painter, dwl 507 Broadway
Quinto José M. waiter, steamer Julia
Quinton (Henry) & Lane (Richard) dry goods, 217 Fourth
Quinton John B. builder, dwl 1021 Powell
Quinton William H. clerk, dwl SE cor Harrison and Main
Quirk Edward J. contractor, dwl 8 s Eighteenth nr Diamond
Quirk Michael, laborer, dwl N s Natoma nr Seventh
Quirk Patrick, laborer, 668 Howard
Quitty Andrew, carpenter, dwl 17 Fourth
Qun Fod (Chinese) washing, NW cor Jackson and Virginia
Quong E. Long (Chinese) washing, S s Sixteenth nr Guerrero
Quong Shay Lung & Co. (Chinese) merchants, 812 Dupont
Quong Sow Thong & Co. (Chinese) Li-Po-Tai's drug store, 707 Jackson
Quong Sung (Chinese) merchants, 711 Commercial
Quong Tong Yon (Chinese) merchant, 703 Dupont
Quong Ying Kee & Co. (Chinese) merchants, 718 Commercial
Quong Yuen (Chinese) washing, 28 Stockton
Quonn Mark (col'd) bootblack, 12 First

R

Raabe George A. butcher, SW cor Ritch and Folsom
Raabe John H. clerk, Chicago Hotel, 220 Pacific
Raabe Otto, bar keeper, Jones' Sample Rooms, dwl 103 Prospect Place
Rabbit M. M. dwl Federal Building
Rabel Louis, driver with Chas. Schroth, 230 Kearny
Rabeux Louis, plasterer, dwl 723 Broadway
Rabeux Louise Mrs. corset and dress maker, 723 Broadway

Rabjohn Edwin, car builder, S. F. & San José R. R. Co. dwl 124 Dora
Racine Josephine Mrs. with Mrs. A. Ducatel, dwl 723 Sansom
Raclet William, merchant tailor, 1206 Dupont
Racord Edward, ship joiner, dwl SW cor Louisiana and Sierra
Racouillat August, foreman with L. Racouillat, SW cor Market and Beale
Racouillat L. (Louis Soussingeas & Co.) SW cor Market and Beale
Racouillat Ludovic, box factory, SW cor Market and Beale, dwl 4 Perry
Radcliffe C. M. (Brodie & R.) dwl 402 Mont
Raddeman John, driver, dwl SE cor Third and Howard
Raddington John, laborer, dwl N s Sacramento bet Jones and Leavenworth
Raddy Isma Miss, dwl 520 Stockton
Rading Frederick, bedding, 735 Washington
Radovich Antoine, restaurant, Mission cor Stewart
Radston Jacob, gas fitter, S. F. Gas Co
Rae Charles, cook, dwl 133 Kearny
Raenert Elizabeth (widow) dwl 510 Kearny
Raffen John, molder, Pacific Foundry
Rafferty John, clerk, Vulcan Foundry, dwl 72 Tehama
Rafferty John P. currier with Main & Winchester, dwl 405 Stevenson
Rafferty Peter, pattern maker, Union Iron Works, dwl 159 Shipley
Rafferty Thomas, U. S. A. dwl 1421 Mason
Rafferty William, carpenter, dwl 517 Jones
Raffetto Luiggi, groceries, 623 Broadway
Raffo Francisco, wood dealer, dwl 165 Beale
Raffour L. (Ricaud & R.) dwl Bryant Place
Ragan Anne Miss, domestic with Mark J. Matheson, E s Mission nr Twelfth
Ragan James, clerk, dwl S s Ellis bet Devisidero and Broderick
Ragan William, laborer. dwl 136 First
Raggett Michael, molder, Union Foundry, dwl Welsh bet Third and Fourth
Ragner Adam, hairdresser, dwl Dresdener House
Rahders Henry, porter with Simon, Dinkelspiel & Co. dwl 200 Pine
Rahilt Mary C. (widow) dwl 226 O'Farrell
Rahn Hermann, seaman, bds 7 Washington
Rahwyler Abraham, watch maker and jeweler, 927 Kearny
Raidy John, laborer, dwl N s Filbert bet Larkin and Polk
Railroad Homestead Association, office 543 Clay
RAILROAD HOUSE, Charles B. Green proprietor, 319 Clay and 320 Commercial
RAILROAD IRON WORKS, N. Yung proprietor, 28 Fremont
Raily Owen, laborer, Golden State Iron Works, dwl St. Charles Hotel
RAIMOND R. E. shipping and commission merchant, 515 Front, dwl 924 Stockton
Rain Michael, brass cleaner, dwl 507 Market
Rain William, ranchero, nr S. F. Cordage Factory
Rainey Bridget (widow) furnished rooms, 303 Davis
Rainey John, bar keeper, dwl 6 Sutter
Rainey Samuel, bar keeper, dwl 524 Bryant
Rainey William, salesman with Taaffe & Co. dwl 417 Bryant
Rainford Thomas, seaman, dwl 26 Sacramento
Rainow Lyman, laundryman, dwl 836 Market
Rakow Francis, reporter, California Demokrat, dwl 4 St. Mark Place
Rale Thomas, laborer, dwl 414 Market
Ralle Mathew, fruit dealer, N s Folsom nr Stewart, dwl S s Folsom nr Main
Rally Michael, waiter, Miners' Restaurant, 531 Commercial
Ralph G. H. sawyer with Macdonald Brothers, dwl 541 Jessie

Ralph William, cooper with John R. Regan, dwl N s Washington bet Mason and Taylor

RALSTON ANDREW J. secretary Pacific Insurance Co. office 436 California, dwl 324 Fremont

Ralston Edward, Pacific Straw Works, 603 Market

Ralston Gavin, pattern maker, San Francisco Iron Works, dwl Tyson Place

Ralston (H. A.) & Co. (John Simond) produce commission, 507 Sansom, dwl cor Wash and San

RALSTON W. C. cashier, Bank California, office SW cor Washington and Bat, dwl 324 Fremont

Ram Frederick, carpenter, dwl 3 Sonoma Place

Ramage George W. with Schafer & Brother, 509 Sacramento, dwl 115 Dupont

Ramband Ferdinand, laborer with B. Bonnet & Co

RAMIREZ FRANCISCO P. & CO. (Filipe Fierro and Clodomiro Madero) proprietors Nuevo Mundo, office 603 Front, dwl Geary bet Kearny and Dupont

Ramm John, seaman, bds 7 Washington

Ramon Anton, with Johanna McCarty, dwl corner Napa and Shasta

Ramon Frank, with Johanna McCarty, dwl corner Napa and Shasta

Ramos M. watchman, nr Franconia House, San Bruno Road

Ramsay George, laborer, Russ House

RAMSDELL (B. H.) & PECK (James B.) shipping merchants, office 110 Jackson, res Alameda

RAMSDELL B. H. coal dealer and agent Black Diamond Coal Mine, office 110 Jackson

Ramsey Alexander A. scroll sawyer, dwl 7 Central Place

Ramsey James D. plasterer, dwl N s California bet Leavenworth and Hyde

Ramsfeld John, cabinet maker with J. Peirce, dwl 840 Pacific

RAND CHARLES W., U. S. Marshal Northern District California, office 13 and 14 U. S. Court Building, dwl 324 Jessie

Rand David H. policeman, dwl 8 Central Place

Rand Oliver H. contractor and builder, dwl 808 Taylor

Rand William B. clerk with Haste & Kirk, 25 Beale, dwl 749 Market

Randal Charles (Baker & R.) dwl SW cor Nevada and Folsom

RANDALL A. G. real estate and monetary agent, office 536 Washington, dwl S side Mission bet Twelfth and Thirteenth

Randall Charles F. joiner, dwl 311 Bush

Randall Charles W. clerk with H. P. Wakelee, dwl 311 Harrison

Randall Ephraim (col'd) porter, Wells, Fargo & Co. dwl 8 Brooklyn Place

Randall F. H. (widow) dwl 442 Greenwich

Randall Frank G. student at law with J. P. Hoge, dwl 52 Second

Randall George, dwl 721 Davis

Randall George, clerk with H. P. Wakelee, dwl 311 Harrison

Randall H. B. molder, Miners' Foundry, dwl 61 Tehama

Randall Mary (widow) fruits, dwl 254 Stewart

Randall Nathaniel, wood turner with B. H. Freeman & Co. dwl 21 Perry

Randall P. M. amalgamator, dwl 221 First

Randall Samuel F. clerk, dwl 27 Minna

Randall Sylvanus, dwl 174 Jessie

Randall Sylvester, cook, Pacific Temperance House, 109 Pacific

Randall Thomas, carpenter, dwl 200 Stockton

Randall William F. carpenter, bds Meyer's Hotel, 814 Montgomery

Randell Alfred (col'd) whitewasher, dwl 406 Dupont

Randle P. W. physician and inspector Internal Revenue, dwl 737 Harrison

Randolph B. H. real estate, office 315 Montgomery, dwl 727 Bush

Randolph John H. dwl 815 Montgomery

Randolph Martha Mrs. (col'd) cook, dwl 742 Pacific

Randolph Richard F. ship joiner with John G. North, dwl W s Tennessee nr Solano

Randolph William, laborer, dwl 156 Shipley

Ranft Henry, book keeper with James Behrens, dwl 610 Greenwich

Ranger Alfred N. porter with M. Keller, dwl 130 Minna

Rank C. P. & Co. (I. N. Sloanaker) importers and jobbers fancy and dry goods, 314 Sacramento, dwl 18 First

RANKEN (Herman) & RYAN (W. P.) groceries and liquors, SE cor Tehama and Sixth

Rankin Charles, clerk, SE cor Tehama and Sixth

Rankin David, porter, 424 Sacramento

Rankin E. B. Mrs. adjuster, U. S. Branch Mint and boarding, 728 Howard

Rankin Ira P. (Goddard & Co.) office 127 First, dwl 416 Harrison

Rankin William, cooper, dwl 723 Union

Rannahau Edmund, laborer, dwl 357 First

Rannie William M. miller, dwl W s Eleventh near Bryant

Ransom Elizabeth (widow) dwl N s California bet Leavenworth and Hyde

Ransom François, florist, dwl 7 Jasper Place

Ransom John, laborer, dwl Central House, 814 San

RANSOM LEANDER, state land locating agent, office 302 Montgomery, dwl 105 Mason

Ransom Lee J. with Leander Ransom, 302 Montgomery, dwl 105 Mason

Ransom Samuel (Smith, Ware & Co.) dwl 748 Harrison

Ransom W. A. attorney at law with Casserly & Barnes, dwl 225 Second

Rantz Anna Miss, domestic, 1122 Pine

Raphael Aaron, fruit peddler, dwl 605 Greenwich

Raphael Abram, tailor, 129 Fourth

Raphael I. & Co. (Charles F. Duenwald) cigars and tobacco, 430 Kearny, dwl Trinity nr Bush

Raphael Isaac, clothing, dwl 505 Davis

Raphall James M. (Broderick & R.) attorney at law, office 614 Merchant, dwl 735 Howard

Rapheld Levy, clerk with E. Mendelson, bds Chicago Hotel

Rapp Jacob, baker, dwl 711 Pacific

Rapp Julius, foreman Montgomery Baths, dwl 514 Green nr Stockton

Rappez Maurice, waiter, Gamba House

Rappold John, boot maker, dwl 3 Haywood

Rasche Charlotte (widow) dwl 709 Mission

Rasche Henry, piano tuner with J. T. Bowers, dwl 709 Mission

Rasmussen James, seaman, dwl 113 Commercial

Raspinges Eugene, cook, dwl 709 Stockton

Rassette E. (widow) boarding, 630 Market

Rasso Charles, fisherman, bds 16 Washington

Rat John, laborer, dwl 613 Pacific

Rathbun (H. B.) & Co. wholesale confectioners, 430 Sansom, dwl 626 California

Rathjen Hermann H. clerk, NE corner Mission and Sixth

Rathman Edward, carpenter, dwl 31 St. Mark Pl

Ratigan James, workman, S. F. & P. Sugar Co. dwl SW cor Howard and Sumner

Ratigan John, painter, dwl 1522 Dupont

Ratliff Henry, Rip Van Winkle Saloon, SW cor Davis and Pacific

Rattie Giovanni, vegetables, SE cor Sansom and Merchant

Rattiman Charles, cigar maker, dwl E s Valencia bet Fifteenth and Sixteenth

Rattler Lewis, comedian, dwl 467 Jessie

Ratto Charles F. Golden City Coffee Saloon, 10 Stewart, dwl E s Sumner nr Howard

Rau John (Hoelscher & R.) dwl SW cor Jones and Eddy

Raubinger Bernard, wood and coal, 130 Geary

Raubinger William, with Bernard Raubinger, 130 Geary
Rauch Jacob *(Proschold & R.)* dwl SE cor Sacramento and Leavenworth
Rauck Frederick W. dyer and scourer, 148 Third
Rauerts Henry, porter with H. P. Wakelee
Raughen Henry, tailor, dwl NW cor Kearny and Broadway
Rausche Conrad, laborer, Market St. R. R. Co. dwl Mission Railroad Brewery
Rauscher Martin, hairdresser, 624 Washington
Ravekes David, salesman, 223 Front, dwl E s Harriet nr Sixteenth
Ravenna Michele, employé with Brignardello, Macchiavello & Co. 706 Sansom
Ravenna Vincenzo, employé with Brignardello, Macchiavello & Co. 706 Sansom
Ravest Louis, butcher, dwl 1303½ Dupont
Ravey Hugh, baker, dwl W s Stanford bet Townsend and Brannan
Raw Frederick, shoe maker, 17¼ Dupont
Rawitte John, carpenter, dwl N s Seventeenth bet Valencia and Second Avenue
Rawle Mathew, express wagon, dwl NE cor Folsom and Stewart
Rawson George B. teamster, 39 Clay, dwl N s Clay bet Davis and Drumm
RAWSON JULIUS A. real estate agent, office 338 Montgomery room 11, dwl 24 Silver
Rawson N. dwl 121 Montgomery Block
Ray Alexander, longshoreman, dwl SE cor Sacramento and Davis
Ray Barzillai, carpenter, dwl 1030 Market
Ray F. J. mariner, dwl 121 Natoma
Ray James H. real estate, office 15 Mont Block
Ray Margaret (widow) dwl 508 Bush
Ray Robert, porter with Luning & Co. dwl E s Union Place nr Union
Ray William A. mariner, dwl 140 Silver
Raye Albert P. upholsterer with Charles M. Plum, dwl 228 Post
Raye Bayard V. R. printer with Edward Bosqui & Co. dwl 228 Post
Raye Rosa (widow) dwl 228 Post
Raye William H. sign painter, dwl 512 Post
Raye, see Reay
Rayer Charles E. laundryman, dwl 3 Pollard Place
Raymond C. B. superintendent United Reese River M. Co. office 402 Front, dwl Cosmopolitan Hotel
Raymond Charles, liquor saloon, 51 Sacramento
Raymond David, laborer, dwl W s Main bet Folsom and Harrison
Raymond D. T. secretary Contra Costa S. Navigation Co. office Vallejo nr Davis, dwl S s Union bet Calhoun and Sansom
RAYMOND I. W. agent Central American Transit Co. office NW cor Battery and Pine, dwl Occidental Hotel
RAYMOND J. P. & CO. *(William P. Raymond)* produce commission merchants, 119 Clay, res Oakland
Raymond Richard, handcartman, corner Clay and Drumm
Raymond William P. *(J. P. Raymond & Co.)* dwl 810 Bush
Raynaud Felix, silver plater, 131 Kearny
Raynes John Capt. stevedore, dwl 1012 Montgomery
Raynor Joel, engineer, dwl 639 Mission
Raynor William S. salesman, 204 Bat, dwl 1006 Clay
Razzatto Fortunato *(A. Ghio & Co.)* 527 Wash
Read Charles, folder, Chelsea Laundry
Read Edward B. salesman with William Alvord & Co. 122 Battery
Read James G. book keeper, 151 Third
Read Mary S. (widow) manufacturer skirt supporters, 109 Montgomery
Read Samuel *(H. Rosekrans & Co.)* dwl 908 Leav
Read Samuel, weigher, Washington St. Wharf, dwl Bay State Row

Read W. D. with Bradshaw & Co. res Oakland
Read W. H. dwl 655 Washington
Read, see Reed and Reid
Readen Henry, brewer with Mangels & Co
Reading Fielding (col'd) porter with Kellogg, Hewston & Co
Reading George, express wagon, Mission Creek nr Sixteenth
Reading James, express wagon, 920 Dupont
READING ROOM OF THE NATIONAL DEMOCRATIC ASSOCIATION, 622 Clay, W. D. Sawyer president, Frank V. Scudder secretary
Ready Francis, porter, Medical Purveyor's Office, 805 Sansom, dwl 3 William
Ready Kate Miss, domestic, 915 Stockton
Ready Thomas, Pioneer Soda Works, dwl E s Union Place
Ready Thomas G. accountant, dwl 749 Market
Ready W. W. book keeper with William T. Coleman & Co. dwl 749 Market
Reagan John, with Henry Bocken, dwl 1103 Clay
Reagan Julius R. workman with Turner & Rundle, dwl Solano nr Potrero Avenue
Reagan William, teamster, dwl S s Chambers bet Battery and Front
Real Del Monte Consolidated G. & S. M. Co. office 522 Montgomery
Real Patrick, steward, dwl 12 Sutter
Real Philip, wool worker, Broadway Wool Depôt, dwl 520 Mission
Reanard L. E. Mrs. assistant teacher, California Collegiate Institute, dwl 64 Silver
Reanhare Charles, oysters and clams, dwl S s Chambers bet Front and Davis
Reardon Dennis, groceries and liquors, NE cor Washington and Leavenworth
Reardon James, cook with Hoadley & Co. dwl 617 Montgomery
Reardon James, salesman, dwl 1009 Powell
Reardon Johanna Miss, domestic with M. Castle
Reardon John, deck hand, steamer Yosemite
Reardon John, laborer with Cornelius Conahan
Reardon John J. porter, 213 Front, dwl 333 Bush
Reardon John M. dealer bottles, 2008 Powell
Reardon Julia Mrs. domestic, 1119 Pine
Reardon Margaret Mrs. boarding, 97 Stevenson
Reardon Patrick, dwl 336 Bush
Reardon Peter, deck hand, steamer Washoe
Reardon Samuel, salesman, dwl 1009 Powell
Reardon Timothy, laborer with Lyon & Co. dwl 73 Tehama
Reardon Timothy H. clerk, Melter and Refiner's Department U. S. Branch Mint, dwl 1009 Powell
Reasler Henry, laborer, dwl N s St. Charles nr Kearny
Reasoner Antoine, cabinet maker with Goodwin & Co. dwl 1207 Dupont
Reavey Peter, blacksmith, Vulcan Iron Works, dwl 224 Mission
Reavis W. H. H. confectioner with Rathbun & Co. 430 Sansom
Reay Alfred W. *(Johnston & R.)* dwl 658 Mission
REBARD BROTHERS *(Claude)* hat and cap manufacturers, 630 Washington
Rebhan Andrew, barber, dwl 320 Pacific
Rebinaeick George, dwl 39 Moss
Rebmann Josephine (widow) dwl 15 Stockton Place
Rebmenn August, butcher with C. Kerr, dwl SE cor Brannan and Gilbert
Rebstock John, tailor, dwl 449 Bush
Rebstock Josephine Mrs. millinery, SE cor Bush and Dupont
Reck Henry, dwl 269 Clara
Reckman John, porter, 425 Sac, dwl Post St. House
Reckmann Amandus, grocer, Pacific Engine Co. No.8
RECORD (weekly) RICE & CO. publishers and proprietors, office 538 Market
Record James E. ship joiner with John G. North, Potrero

RECORDER CITY AND COUNTY, office SE cor Kearny and Washington
Rectowald Jacob, laborer, dwl E s Webster bet Fulton and McAllister
Recum C. H. boot maker, dwl 309 Sixth
Reddick James, porter, 618 Kearny, dwl Reese's Building
Reddin Andrew, laborer, dwl 65 Clementina
Redding Elizabeth Miss, domestic, 730 Post
Redding Fielding (col'd) porter, dwl 3 Dupont Place
Redding F. W. invoice clerk, Custom House
Redding George, alcohol dealer, Mariposa nr Mission Creek
Redding George C. teamster, U. S. Appraiser's Store, dwl N s Oak nr Taylor
Redding Patrick, hostler, 427 Pine
Redding Philip, laborer with Haynes & Lawton, 516 Sansom
Redding William (col'd) porter, 406 Pine
Reddish Thomas J. pilot, Old Line 5 Vallejo, dwl International Hotel
Reddy John, laborer, dwl 16 Hinckley
Redfield F. S. captain brig Manuella, office 54 Stewart
Redgrave Charles, machinist, Vulcan Iron Works, dwl Chicago House
Redican Bernard, plasterer, dwl 1618 Dupont, rear
Redington Charles C. receiving clerk, Appraiser's Store, Custom House, dwl 226 Sansom
REDINGTON (John H.) & CO. (H. P. Livermore, D. W. C. Rice, and A. G. Coffin,) importers and jobbers drugs, medicines, oils, etc. 416 and 418 Front
Redington William, drayman, dwl E s Mason nr Green
Redington William P. clerk with Redington & Co. dwl 915 Market
Redington ——, dwl N s Sacramento bet Jones and Leavenworth
Redman Elizabeth M. (widow) dwl W s Franklin nr Grove
Redman Lee, clerk, 706 Kearny, dwl 655 Wash
REDMAN R. A. attorney at law, office 402 Montgomery, dwl 11 Minna
Redman Sarah E. (widow) dwl 19 Perry
Redmond Anna Miss, domestic, 536 Ellis
Redmond John, carpenter, dwl 121 Stevenson
Redmond John B. (McWilliams & Co. Sac. City) dwl 1023 Clay
Redmond John J. salesman with Taaffe & Co
Redmond Joseph H. (Small & R.) dwl 424 Fremont
Redon Claus, dwl N s Geary, rear bet Devisidero and Broderick
Redstone Jacob, employé, S. F. Gas Co. dwl 232 Sixth
Reed Alexander, night watchman, dwl 333 Ritch
Reed Annie Miss (Misses M. & A. Reed) 231 Third
Reed C. H. captain brig Deacon, dwl 548 Howard
Reed Charles, mariner, dwl St. Francis Engine H
Reed Charles, waterman, dwl 9 William
Reed Charles G. clerk, 224 Battery, res Oakland
Reed Charles W. captain Night Inspectors, Custom House, dwl 326 Green
Reed Diana (widow) domestic, 113 Ellis
Reed Edward, ship carpenter with J. G. North, dwl SW cor Louisiana and Sierra
Reed Edward B. clerk, dwl 325 Dupont
Reed Francis, clerk, dwl NW cor Clay and Davis
Reed George, salesman with Macondray & Co. dwl 25 Stockton
Reed George H. (col'd) steward, steamer John L. Stephens, dwl 429 Union
Reed George K. machinist, dwl 515 Pine
Reed George M. carriage maker with Larkins & Co. dwl cor Spring and Summer
Reed Hans, ship joiner with J. G. North, dwl SW cor Louisiana and Sierra
REED HENRY R. forwarding and commission merchant, office 321 Washington
Reed Hilaria S. (widow) dwl 827 Washington

Reed James, carpenter, dwl 4 Natoma
Reed James, coal passer, steamer Pacific
Reed James, laborer, Market St. R. R. Co. dwl N s Post bet Dupont and Stockton
Reed James, steward, American Exchange
Reed James G. book keeper, dwl 211 Minna
Reed John, boat builder, dwl cor Howard and Main
Reed John, carpenter, dwl Summer St. House
Reed John, runner Sailors' Home, SW cor Battery and Vallejo, dwl SW cor Kearny and Bay
Reed John jr. boat builder, dwl cor Howard and Main
Reed John W. carpenter, dwl 925 Broadway
Reed John W. fruits, dwl 140 Shipley
Reed Joseph, tinsmith with Thomas Howell, dwl 1 Oak
Reed Joseph B. driver with J. S. Day & Co. dwl SW cor Hawthorne and Harrison
Reed Joseph L. real estate agent, 526 Montgomery, dwl 110 Tehama
Reed M. & A. Misses, milliners and dress makers, 231 Third
Reed Michael, teamster with M. P. Sessions, dwl 12 Clarence Place
Reed Olof, ship carpenter with J. G. North, dwl W s Kentucky nr Mariposa
Reed Paul, tailor, dwl 1419 Kearny
Reed Richard, groceries, dwl 455 Jessie
Reed Robert, broker, dwl 1018 Powell
Reed Samuel B. inspector, Custom House, dwl SW cor Leavenworth and Filbert
Reed Thomas, contractor, dwl Solano nr York
Reed Thomas, teamster, dwl Bernard nr Taylor
Reed Thomas J. foreman Morning Call, dwl 419 Vallejo
Reed William, carpenter with McMillan & Kester, dwl 651 Mission
Reed William, paper hanger, 509 San, dwl 414 Post
Reed William Capt. toll collector Mission Bay Bridge
Reed William C. miner, dwl 706 Powell
Reed William M. with Cameron, Whittier & Co. dwl 706 Powell
Reed, see Read and Reid
Reeder James H. (col'd) laborer, dwl 8 Auburn
Reemer William T. calker, dwl 54 First
Rees Catharine, theatrical costumer, dwl N side St. Charles nr Kearny
Rees Charles, seaman, dwl 26 Sacramento
Rees John E. laborer, dwl Beale Place
Rees Rowland, miner, dwl 115 Virginia
Reese Antonio, cigars and tobacco, dwl 1016 Stock
Reese Charles, seaman, dwl 44 Sacramento
Reese Evan A. carpenter and builder, 19½ Geary, dwl E s Capp bet Twenty-Third and Twenty-Fourth
Reese George, dwl 765 Clay
Reese Henry, groceries and liquors, SW cor Powell and Greenwich
Reese Henry, salesman with Heynemann & Co. dwl 241 Fremont
Reese James E. painter, dwl 153 Shipley
Reese Maria (widow) dwl with John Satterlee, W s Folsom bet Eleventh and Twelfth
REESE MICHAEL, real estate, office 410 Montgomery up stairs, dwl 717 Stockton
Reese River M. Co. office 3 Odd Fellows' Hall
Reese's Building, 720 Washington bet Kearny and Dupont
Reesenberg Fred, laborer, bds St. Louis Hotel 11 Pacific
Reeve Allan (G. B. Reeve & Co.) res Sacramento
REEVE G. B. & CO. (Allan Reeve) brokers, office 33 Montgomery Block, dwl 420 Second
Reeve William, clerk with Holcombe Bros. dwl 408 Dupont
Reever Frank, laborer with Edward J. Quirk
Reeves Charles, laborer, dwl 140 Stewart
Reeves E. actor, Metropolitan Theater, dwl 113 St. Mark Place

Reevey Hugh, foreman with Deeth & Starr, 205 Sacramento
REFUGIO MINING CO. (Chihuahua, Mex.) office 3 Odd Fellows' Hall
Regan Abram, fancy and dry goods, 52 Fourth
Regan Brothers (Patrick and Timothy) wholesale butchers, cor Tenth and Bryant, dwl W s Eleventh nr Folsom
Regan Cornelius, laborer, dwl Dolores Hall W side Valencia nr Sixteenth
Regan Ellen Mrs. millinery, 129 Second
Regan Hannah Miss, domestic, 606 Sutter
Regan Helena (widow) with M. Welton W s Larkin nr Post
Regan James, clerk with Richard Tobin, 2 Federal Building
Regan Jeremiah, butcher with Regan Brothers, dwl W s Eleventh nr Folsom
Regan Joanna Miss, domestic with Adolph Muller
REGAN JOHN, furniture, 29 Second, dwl 129 Second
Regan John, vegetable dealer, dwl 706 Jones
Regan John, with George & Smith, dwl Whitehall Exchange
Regan John R. cooperage, 215 Washington, dwl 102 St. Mark Place
Regan Patrick, teamster, dwl 110 Chamber
Regan Thomas, laborer, Spring Valley W. W
Regan Thomas, porter, dwl 140 Stevenson
Regan Thomas J. machinist, dwl 12 Sutter
Regan Timothy (Regan Bros.) dwl Eleventh near Harrison
Regan William, confectioner with Canty & Wagner
Regan William, laborer, Vulcan Foundry
Regelbaupt Philip, tailor, 504 Market
Regensberger Simon, book keeper, Anaheim Wine Growers' Association, 321 Montgomery
Regensburger Henry Mrs. (widow) dwl 522 Stock
Regensburger Jacob, physician, office 652 Washington, dwl 914 Stockton
Regensburger Sigmund, salesman, 401 Commercial, dwl 906 Powell
REGISTER U. S. LAND OFFICE, John F. Swift, office 625 Merchant
Regle John, baker, dwl 220 Shipley
Regli Carl F. workman with H. Schwerin, Visitacion Valley
Regna Michael, laborer, dwl E s Kearny bet Pacific and Broadway
Regner Frank A. hairdresser with Aaron Creamer, dwl 337 Bush
Reh Frederick A. paper hanger, 24 Third
Rehen M. dwl SE cor Mission and First
Rehm Peter N. fruits, 27 Fourth
Reibig John, cook, steamer Chrysopolis
Reich Henry, laborer with James Brokaw, dwl Bootz's Hotel
Reich Leopold (Bryer & R.) SW cor Stockton and Jackson
Reichart Jacob, laborer with Alexander Lemore
Reichart Robert, dwl NE cor Kearny and Pine
REICHEL FREDERICK R. manufacturer jewelry and silverware, 620 Merchant, dwl 914 Dupont
Reichel William, dwl SE cor Tehama and Sixth
Reichenbach J. J. porter with Alsop & Co. dwl SE cor Filbert and Larkin
Reichert Adelbert, cook, 706 Market, dwl Pacific, bet Kearny and Dupont
Reichert John A. office 24 Court Block 636 Clay, res Alameda, Alameda Co
Reichert Theodore, salesman, dwl N s Brannan bet Ritch and Fourth
Reichert William, brewer, Philadelphia Brewery
Reichling Francis, dwl 930 Folsom
Reichwagen William, hatter with W. F. Coupland, dwl 205 Sansom
Reid Caroline Miss, milliner, dwl 764 Howard
Reid Charlotte Miss, 764 Howard

Reid G. waiter, steamer Senator
Reid George, butcher, bds Meyer's Hotel 814 Mont
Reid George E. plumber with J. H. O'Brien & Co. 706 Montgomery, dwl 73 Minna
Reid John W. conductor, North Beach & M. R. R. Co. dwl 316 Fourth
Reid (William) & Brooks (Edmund) importers and jobbers crockery and glassware, 524 Sansom, dwl 805 Filbert
Reid, see Read and Reed
Reider Charles, compositor, Abend Post, dwl SW cor Dupont and Broadway
Reider Philip, baker, dwl 12 Hinckley
Reidout Cyrus, calker. dwl 238 Stewart
Reidy Daniel, shoe maker, dwl S s Folsom nr Beale
Reiff Anthony jr. conductor orchestra, Maguire's Opera House, dwl 612 Mason
Reigaud Francis, cooper with Timothy Lynch
Reihm Mathias, machinist, Miners' Foundry
Reiley Michael, porter with D. J. Oliver, dwl E s Montgomery bet Jackson and Pacific
Reiley Patrick, waiter, dwl 64 Natoma
Reillay Patrick, vegetables, 775 Folsom
Reilley Charles J. gas fitter, dwl 4 Graham Place
Reilley James. engineer, dwl 57 Minna
Reilley Mary Miss, domestic, 336 Bush
Reilley Susan (widow) dwl 1108 Powell
Reilly Bernard, groceries and liquors, SE cor Sixth and Clara
Reilly Catharine Miss, domestic, S s Chestnut bet Stockton and Powell
Reilly Edward, saloon, NW cor Fourth and Freelon
Reilly Hannah Miss, domestic, 743 Howard
Reilly Hugh (Rooney & R.) dwl S s Sixteenth nr Rhode Island
Reilly James, dwl 1 Margaret Place
Reilly James, cook, Chelsea Laundry
Reilly James, teamster, Omnibus R. R. Co.
Reilly James S. wood and coal, 751 Mission, dwl NW cor Bryant and Fourth
Reilly John, carpenter, dwl 757 Mission, rear
Reilly John, groom, dwl 186 Stevenson
Reilly John, helper, Fulton Foundry, dwl Central H
Reilly John H. clerk with Edwin Lewis, dwl 1004 Pine
REILLY JOHN L. liquor saloon, SE cor Market and Fourth
Reilly Lawrence, express wagon, cor Wash and Battery, dwl 31 Federal Building
Reilly Maggie Miss, domestic, 8 Essex
Reilly Margaret Miss, domestic, 416 Post
Reilly Margaret Mrs. dress maker, NE cor Fourth and Bryant
Reilly Margaret (widow) dwl 425 Powell
Reilly Mary Mrs. domestic, 914 Stockton
Reilly Michael, laborer, dwl 3 Lick Alley
Reilly Michael, laborer, dwl N s Washington, bet Leavenworth and Hyde
Reilly Michael, stone cutter, dwl 29 Geary
Reilly Philip, cook, dwl 48 Stevenson
REILLY P. J. M.D. importer and jobber drugs and medicines, 535 Commercial, dwl 236 Jessie
Reilly Rose, cook, Chelsea Laundry
Reilly Thomas, gold beater, 641 California, dwl NE cor Battery and Washington
Reilly Thomas, hostler, dwl 710 Broadway
Reilly Thomas, laborer, dwl 230 Jessie
Reilly Thomas, plasterer, dwl 313 Geary, rear
Reilly Thomas N. driver, Davis Laundry, dwl E s Sixth bet Clementina and Folsom
Reilly William T. assistant assayer, U. S. Branch Mint, dwl W s Larkin bet Pine and California
Reilly see Riley
Reimann Henry A. cabinet maker, dwl N s California bet Mason and Taylor
Reimer Edward, laborer, dwl 204 Stewart
REIMER EDWARD L. San Francisco Nursery, cor Folsom and Nineteenth
Reimers Adolph, clerk, NE cor Mason and O'Farrell

Reimers Claus, groceries and liquors, NE cor Mason and O'Farrell

Reimers Henry, hostler, Six Mile H, San Bruno Road

Reineck Philip, carpenter, dwl 532 Broadway

Reineke John, porter, dwl 619 Pacific

Reiner Anton, wholesale butcher, Potrero Avenue, dwl Potrero Avenue

Reiners Charles *(Tuhte & R.)* 26 Stewart

Reiners John, with Erzgraber & Goetjen, 120 Davis

Reiners John H. *(Schwarze & Co.)* dwl NW cor Kearny and Geary

Reinfeld Charles, paper hanger, dwl 516 Vallejo

Reinhardt Charles, mining stocks, dwl N s Stevenson bet Third and Fourth

Reinhardt J. laborer, Spring Valley W. W

Reinhardt John, scroll sawyer with B. H. Freeman & Co. SW cor Market and Beale

Reinhardt John B. dwl 90 Everett

Reinhardt Joseph, plumber, dwl 8 s Thirteenth nr Guerrero

Reinhardt William, porter with P. F. Loughran & Co. 405 Sansom, dwl 1513 Mason

Reinhart B. merchant, office 218 Battery, dwl 710 Folsom

Reinhart Eli, dwl 736 Market

Reinhart John, workman with H. Schwerin, Visitacion Valley

Reinherst J. dwl What Cheer House

Reinkelleurs Henry, tinsmith, dwl 49 Ritch

Reinken Frederick, seaman, bds 7 Washington

Reinle Frederick, pork, etc. 32 Metropolitan Market, dwl 172 Jessie

Reinstedter Godless, butcher with Lux & Miller, dwl cor Ninth and Brannan

Reinstein Louis, tailor with S. Reinstein, dwl 14 Sutter

Reinstein Oscar, with S. Reinstein, 21 Sansom, dwl 449½ Minna

Reinstein S. manufacturer home made clothing, 21 Sansom, dwl 7 Stockton

Reinstein Samuel, conductor, North Beach & M. R. R. Co

Reis Bernard, porter, 633 Clay

Reis Christian *(Adelphi Hotel Co.)* res Sonoma, Sonoma County

Reis Ferdinand *(Adelphi Hotel Co.)* res Sierra Co

Reis Gustavus, dwl 21 Ellis

Reis Julius C. real estate, dwl with Geo. W. Dent E s Howard bet Fifteenth and Sixteenth

Reis Thomas L. dwl 103 Powell

Reiser Mark, dwl 1108 Clay

Reist Frederick, baker, 623 Commercial

Reith Paul, tailor with J. H. Tobin, dwl 1419 Kearny

Remar Isaac, calker, dwl SW corner Louisiana and Sierra

Remington John C. driver, Alta Flour Mills, dwl 5 Dixon Block

Remmers Hermann, clerk with Andreas Babrs, dwl NE cor Davis and Jackson

Rémond Auguste, assistant, 90 Montgomery Block

Remson Rolland, carpenter, dwl E s Selina Place

Renaldo Hermann O. clerk, dwl N s Ash nr Polk

Renard Henry, clerk, dwl 147 Second

Renault Charles, real estate, dwl S s Dupont Alley

Renault Jean, laundryman, Bay City Laundry, 1142 Folsom

Renault John, wood and coal, 712 Pacific, dwl 632 Broadway

Rendlesban Charles, machinist, Vulcan Iron Works, dwl 42 Folsom

Rendsburg John, peddler, dwl 535 Bryant

René J. Ernest, importer and agent French Board Underwriters, office 716 Montgomery

Renee Alexander, employé, Metropolitan Restaurant, 715 Montgomery, dwl St. Charles Place

Renfrew Bourber H. with James Brokaw, dwl 561 Howard

Renfrew Robert, machinist, dwl 561 Howard

Rennehan E. lamplighter, S. F. Gas Co

Rennell Charles, steward, Young America Engine Co. No. 13

Renner Simon, butcher, dwl 282 Minna

Renney William, dwl 1604 Mason

Rennie George, book keeper, 22 Montgomery, dwl cor Sutter and Polk

Rennie Gilbert, with Charles Plum, dwl N s Sutter nr Polk

Rennilson James, spinner, Mission Woolen Mills

Renoult John P. cabinet maker, 610 Vallejo

Rensellaer James, waiter, Occidental Hotel

RENTON *(William)* SMITH *(S. E.)* & CO. *(R. K. Ham)* wholesale and retail lumber, 39 Stewart Pier 3, res Port Blakely, W. T

Repenn Frederick, boots and shoes, 639 Commercial

Repensky Philip, tailor, 909 Kearny

Repiton R. A. J. physician, dwl 816 Montgomery

Rerden Dennis, groceries, NE cor Wash and Leav

Reservoir G. & S. M. Co. (Boise County) office 7 Government House

Resing John, proprietor Farmers' Exchange, W s Old San José Road opposite St. Mary's College

Ressegieu Anna (widow) dwl W s Wetmore Place

Reth Richard, seaman, dwl 20 Commercial

Rethers Charles, tailor with I. Eisenberg, dwl cor Washington and Spofford

Reticker Jacob A. dwl W s White Place nr Bryant

Rety F. Louisiana Rotisserie, 907 Dupont

Reuben George, fancy goods, 17 Dupont

Reubold Michael, shoe maker, 135 Kearny

Reumann Ide, handcartman, SE cor Clay and Battery, dwl SE cor Pine and Battery

Reurboff Herman, stair builder with N. P. Langland, dwl SW cor First and Stevenson

Reurick Azariah, carpenter, dwl 20 Commercial

Reusche August, waiter, 506 Mont, dwl 106 Mont Blk

Reussner Albert, jeweler with Lemme Bros. 534 Commercial

Reuter Gustave S. boots and shoes, 215 Second

Reuter Jacob, dwl 532 Broadway

Reuter William, baker with Engelberg & Wagner

Revalk John, watchmaker and jeweler, 510 Montgomery, dwl 715 Filbert

Revard L. A. waiter, 619 Market

Revello Joseph, cartman, 50 Broadway

Revenue G. & S. M. Co. office 420 California

REVERE HOUSE, John Steinmann proprietor, 323 and 325 Pine

Rex Augusta (widow) dwl 1 St. Mary

Rey Jaques J. office with Britton & Co. dwl S s Union bet Mason and Taylor

Reyerne Eugene, miller, dwl 315 Bush

Reynier Jean, laborer with B. Bonnet & Co

Reynolds Albert R. compositor, Golden Era, dwl 312 Howard

Reynolds Annie Miss, nurse, dwl E s Taylor bet Pacific and Broadway

Reynolds Carmi, pail maker with Godding & Koons, dwl cor Fourth and Howard

Reynolds C. H. & Co. *(C. H. Moxley)* real estate agents, 344 Montgomery, dwl E s Larkin bet Washington and Jackson

Reynolds Charles (col'd) whitewasher, dwl 1604 Mason

Reynolds Cornelius, gardener with James Riley

Reynolds Edward A. book keeper, dwl 126 St. Mark Place

Reynolds Edward B. captain bark Charles Devens, dwl 513 Jones

Reynolds Edward W. S. clerk, dwl 1309 Mason

Reynolds Ellen Miss, domestic with J. S. Day, S s Sixteenth bet Folsom and Howard

Reynolds F. E. Mrs. assistant, Lincoln School, dwl Fifteenth bet Howard and Mission

Reynolds Frank B. with Hosmer, Goewey & Co. dwl 918 Bush

Reynolds Frederick Mrs. (widow) dwl 305 Fremont

Reynolds George, carpenter, dwl N s McAllister bet Polk and Larkin

Reynolds George, laborer, dwl 233 Fourth
REYNOLDS *(George A.)* & MURRAY *(Hugh)* produce commission, NW cor Clay and Davis, bds 1016 Stockton
Reynolds George A. mining superintendent, dwl 822 Filbert
Reynolds George L. merchant tailor, 518 California, dwl S s Washington bet Leavenworth and Hyde
Reynolds Henry D. dwl 959 Howard
Reynolds James H. liquor saloon, SE cor Third and Jessie, and supervisor Tenth District, dwl 147 Jessie
Reynolds James M. laundry, E s Jones bet Pacific and Broadway
Reynolds Jane Mrs. dress maker and milliner, 141 Third
Reynolds Jennie (widow) dwl 431 Minna
Reynolds John *(S. F. & J. Reynolds)* attorney at law, dwl 816 Powell
Reynolds John, miner, dwl 32 Webb
Reynolds John P., Kellogg, Hewston & Co.'s Refinery, dwl W s Seventh nr Brannan
Reynolds Leonard, clerk with S. F. & J. Reynolds, dwl 1100 Pine
Reynolds Louis E. architect, office 328 Montgomery, dwl 1425 Pacific
Reynolds Mack, dwl 333 Sutter
Reynolds Madame, fortune teller, 335 Dupont
Reynolds Mary, domestic, dwl 115 First
Reynolds Michael, coppersmith, dwl 1523 Mason
Reynolds Michael, engineer, dwl 718 O'Farrell
Reynolds Michael, helper, Vulcan Iron Works, dwl 76 Jessie
REYNOLDS, *(Nicholas)* HOWELL *(L. V. H.)* & FORD *(William)* commission merchants, 313 and 315 Davis, dwl 1753 Powell
Reynolds Orson A. dwl 1226 Clay
Reynolds Patrick, laborer with Edward J. Quirk
Reynolds Peter T. waiter, dwl 43 Ritch
Reynolds *(Robert T.)* & Co. *(Leonard Washburne)* teamsters, office NW cor Battery and Bdwy, dwl 407 Folsom bet Fremont and First
Reynolds Samuel S. mason, dwl N s O'Farrell bet Stockton and Powell
REYNOLDS S. F. & J. attorneys at law, office 6 and 7 Exchange Building, dwl 1100 Pine cor Jones
Reynolds Thomas, boiler maker with Coffey & Risdon
Reynolds Thomas, coppersmith and plumber, 506 Front, dwl 1523 Mason
Reynolds Thomas, harness maker with J. C. Johnson & Co. dwl 224 Montgomery
Reynolds Thomas, helper with E. T. Steen, dwl N s Stevenson bet Third and Fourth
Reynolds Thomas, laborer, dwl 130 Stevenson
Reynolds Thomas R. bond clerk Naval Office Custom House, dwl N s Fifteenth nr Mission
Reynolds Thomas V. sail maker with A. Crawford & Co. dwl 65 Clementina
Reynolds William, carpenter, dwl 2 Pollard Place
Reynolds William, mining, office with T. F. & J. W. Bachelder, 625 Merchant
Reynolds William, physician, office and dwl SE cor Kearny and Sutter
Reynolds William O. drayman, dwl E s Larkin bet Union and Filbert
Reynolds William T. *(N. B. Jacobs & Co.)* dwl 1309 Mason
Reynoldson John, workman, Mission Woolen Mills, dwl with A. Allen W s Shotwell bet Nineteenth and Twentieth
Rhawl John, gas fitter with Thomas Day, 732 Montgomery, dwl Dupont nr Green
Rhawl Michael, plumber with Thomas Day, 732 Montgomery, dwl SE cor Bush and Sansom
Rheem Elizabeth (widow) dwl 47 Louisa
Rheen Charles F. dwl 4 Martha Place
Rheide Antony, carpenter, dwl 266 Jessie

Rheinlander Frederic, foreman with J. H. C. Portmann
Rhine Christian, importer and jobber leaf tobacco, 407 Merchant
Rhine Patrick, laborer, bds with Joseph Seale, N s Turk nr Fillmore
Rhoades Charles B. musician, Olympic Melodeon
Rhoades Frank, machinist, dwl 29 Minna
Rhoades Thomas, carpenter, dwl N s Folsom bet Fifth and Sixth
Rhodes Anthony, clerk, 402 Montgomery
Rhodes Anthony, waiter, dwl N s Oak nr Taylor
Rhodes Arthur, porter, St. Mary's Cathedral
Rhodes Charles, laborer, Sailors' Home, SW cor Battery and Vallejo
Rhodes Diggings Quartz M. Co. office 418 California
Rhodes Frank, machinist, Miners' Foundry, dwl 47 Clementina
Rhodes Frank W. machinist, dwl 39 Clementina
Rhodes Lucy (widow) dwl 810 Howard
Rhodes William, dwl 503 Jones
Rhodes William H. machinist, dwl 651 Mission
Ricard A. capitalist, off 640 Wash, dwl 1024 Stock
Ricard Peter, dwl 1510 Dupont
Ricaud *(J. Pierre)* & Raffour *(L.)* produce, 36 Metropolitan Market, dwl Bryant Place
RICCI PETER & CO. manufacturers punches, etc. and saloon, 635 Washington, dwl W s Montgomery bet Jackson and Pacific
Rice Adam, parasol maker, 1116 Dupont
Rice Barney, horse trainer, dwl Bay View
Rice Benjamin A. clock repairer, dwl W s Rassette Place No. 2
Rice C. B. cashier Naval Officer, Custom House, dwl 14 Quincy
Rice *(Charles R.)* & Somers *(Henry J.)* blacksmiths, 713 Mission, dwl 822 Post
Rice Daniel, carpenter, dwl S s Berry nr Mary Lane
Rice D. W. C. physician *(and Redington & Co.)* dwl 1122 Pine
RICE EDWARD, carpenter and treasure box maker, Leidesdorff nr California, dwl near cor McAllister and Buchanan
Rice Garrett, bar keeper with Thos. Quinn, dwl 251 Tehama
Rice George E. clerk with Macondray & Co. 206 Sansom, dwl 17 Third
Rice James, dwl 12 Kearny
Rice James, attorney at law, office 47 Montgomery Block, dwl 503 Dupont
Rice James, waiter, Miners' Restaurant, dwl W s Tyson Place
RICE *(James L.)* & CO. *(Holmes C. Patrick)* publishers and proprietors Weekly Record, office 538 Market, dwl 533 Howard
Rice James Mrs. (widow) dwl N s Welch bet Third and Fourth
Rice J. D. coach painter, dwl E s Park Avenue bet Bryant and Harrison
Rice Jerome, laborer with Dr. H. S. Gates, NE cor Sutter and Steiner
Rice John *(O'Brien & R.)* dwl 214 Fremont
Rice John D. painter, Knickerbocker Engine Co. No. 5
Rice John N. laborer, dwl 56 First
RICE JOHN R. M.D. surgeon and accoucheur, office and dwl 250 Fourth
Rice Joseph B. *(Piper & R.)* res California City
Rice L. engineer, Original House
Rice M. A. Mrs. millinery, 12 Kearny
Rice *(Michael)* & George *(Benoit)* butter, cheese, and eggs, 20 Metropolitan Market, dwl 25 Bush
Rice Michael, blacksmith, dwl 176 Clara, rear
Rice Michael, horse shoer with John Hart, dwl 321 Fifth
Rice Patrick, conductor, North Beach & M. R. R. Co. dwl 316 Fourth
Rice P. Henry *(O'Hara & Co.)* dwl cor Fourth and Louisa

Rice R. H. book keeper, Pacific Straw Works, dwl SE cor Dolores and Columbia
Rice Richard K. dwl SE cor Columbia and Dolores
Rice Susan Miss, domestic, 730 Post
Rice William P. clerk, 28 Montgomery
Rice W. R. clerk, dwl 13 Geary
Rice Zenas, locksmith and model maker, 114 Sansom, dwl S s Brannan bet Clinton and Geneva
Rich Abraham, laborer, dwl 14 Jane
Rich Abram, salesman, 514 Market, dwl 734 Howard
Rich Adolph, clerk, 524 Com, dwl 1 Hardie Place
Rich Albert, book keeper with S. Rich & Bro. dwl 214 Sansom
Rich Alexander *(S. Rich & Bro.)* res New York
Rich A. R. (widow) dwl 635 Market
Rich Charles, seaman, dwl 26 Sacramento
RICH D. W. jr. Club Rooms, 616 Sacramento
Rich Frederick, tailor, dwl 520 Vallejo
Rich George B. real estate agent, office 526 Montgomery, dwl cor Clay and Brenham Place
Rich Henry M. clerk with L. Keller, dwl 124 Austin
Rich Jacob, driver with George Ulshofer, dwl cor Douglas and Seventeenth
Rich Joseph, dwl 614 Bush
Rich Louis, merchant tailor, 1009 Stockton
RICH S. & BROTHER *(Alexander Rich)* hides and wool importers, office 220 California and Bay Warehouse, North Point, dwl 505 Bush
Rich Samuel, contractor, dwl 504 Howard
Richard Charles B. *(Joseph Boas & Co.)* res New York
Richard John, laborer, dwl W s Salmon bet Mason and Taylor
Richard Julius, dealer sacks, 112 Sacramento
Richard Margaret (widow) Oak Shade Nursery, W s Eleventh bet Harrison and Bryant
Richard Philippe, blacksmith, dwl 515 Green
RICHARDS & McCRAKEN *(John)* commission merchants and agents Oregon and California Packet Line, office 405 Front
Richards Alonzo, clerk, 213 Dupont, dwl 2 Martha Place
Richards Calvin *(Frost & R.)* dwl 307 Third
RICHARDS *(C. French)* & WHITFIELD *(William)* wholesale drugs and chemicals, etc. SW cor Sansom and Clay, dwl 732 Sutter
Richards Charles, actor, Maguire's Opera House, dwl 19 John
Richards Charles B. ornamental painter, dwl Chicago Hotel
Richards David M. collector with Barron & Co. dwl 507 Mason
Richards Ebenezer J. dwl N s Minna bet Second and Third
RICHARDS EZRA, proprietor Richards' Restaurant, 542–548 Clay, dwl 928 Clay
Richards Francis jr. with Kellogg, Hewston & Co. dwl 119 Natoma
Richards Isaac, bootblack with J. Lipman, dwl N s Pacific nr Powell
RICHARDS ISRAEL, contractor night work, 421 Kearny
Richards Jacob, merchant, bds 633 Broadway
Richards James E. clerk, 502 Sansom, dwl 17 Rincon Place
Richards James R. Mrs. (widow) dwl 1227 Wash
RICHARDS J. M. groceries and liquors, 213 Dupont, dwl 2 Martha Place
Richards John, astrologer, dwl 716 Broadway
Richards John, stone cutter, dwl 73 Natoma
Richards John E. bar keeper, dwl SW cor Kearny and Bay
Richards John H. carriage painter, bds 157 Minna
Richards Joseph, boatman, Fort Point, dwl N s Presidio Road nr Fillmore
Richards Margaret (widow) dwl with Hall Hanlon
Richards O. S. commission merchant, 223 Clay, bds American Exchange

Richards Robert R. longshoreman, dwl 116 Jackson
Richards Samuel, teacher, dwl 156 Minna
Richards Thomas G. real estate agent, office 517 Jackson, dwl 1020 Stockton
Richards Thomas P. baker, dwl 1112 Pacific
Richards William A. driver, Central R. R. Co. dwl 2 Martha Place
Richards William H. & Co. importers ale and porter, 708 Sansom, dwl 837 California
Richardson A. C. (widow) dwl 718 Stockton
Richardson Albert, cabinet maker, dwl 29 Minna
Richardson Albert, sash and blind maker with J. McGill & Co. dwl 663 Howard
Richardson Albert B. captain bark Almatia, dwl N s Sacramento bet Hyde and Leavenworth
Richardson Albert F. farmer, dwl S s Prospect Place nr Columbia
Richardson Edward A. clerk, office San Francisco City Directory, 612 Clay
Richardson George, dwl 18 First
Richardson H. F. Miss, assistant, Washington Grammar School, dwl 1108 Mason
Richardson J. hostler, Omnibus R. R. Co
Richardson *(Jacob M.)* & Daly *(John)* teamsters, Pier 3 Stewart, dwl SW cor Oak and Franklin
Richardson James, plumber and gas fitter, 616 Market, dwl 707 Howard nr Third
Richardson Jesse, wines and liquors, dwl cor Front and Vallejo
Richardson J. H. express wagon, cor Drumm and Clay
Richardson John, foreman Omnibus R. R. Co.'s Stable, dwl 245 Tehama
Richardson John C. driver, Eclipse Bakery, dwl 522 Union
Richardson John H. accountant with W. J. Stringer, dwl 109 Powell
Richardson Julia Miss, domestic with H. B. Congdon, N s Thirteenth nr Mission
Richardson Lewis C. drayman, 209 Front
Richardson Mary (widow) dwl 1119 Taylor
Richardson Mary E. Miss, dress maker, dwl 707 Howard
Richardson M. M. port warden, office 716 Front, bds Russ House
Richardson Prescott V. milkman, dwl NW cor Dolores and Nineteenth
Richardson Samuel W. milk ranch, NW cor Dolores and Nineteenth
Richardson Sarah (widow) dwl 707 Howard
Richardson Sarah J. Miss, dwl 247 Second, nr Folsom
Richardson S. O. miner, dwl 559 Market
Richardson S. S. *(Fuquay & R.)* 19 Geary
Richardson Warren, carpenter, dwl SW cor Folsom Avenue and Folsom
Richardson William, with Dickson, DeWolf & Co. dwl 829 Bush
Richardson William, book keeper with Austin & Co. NE cor Montgomery and Sutter
Richardson William, carpenter, dwl 155 Third
Richardson William J. teamster, 22 Stewart, dwl S s Ellis bet Webster and Fillmore
Richardson W. L. house mover, 613 Market, dwl 613 Mission
Richel Adolph, stock broker, dwl 808 Stockton
Richet Charles, jeweler, 1220 Dupont, dwl 633 Sac
Richet Jennie Madame, corset maker, 633 Sac
Richit Eugenie (widow) liquor saloon, E s Valencia bet Fifteenth and Sixteenth
Richland G. M. Co. office 529 Clay
Richmond Ellen (widow) dwl Mont nr Lombard
Richmond H. W. assistant assessor, U. S. Internal Revenue, NW cor Battery and Commercial, dwl Occidental Hotel
Ricbon Nicholas, money and exchange broker, 611 Commercial, dwl N s Eighteenth nr Guerrero
Richter August, basket maker, dwl N s Bryant bet Sixth and Garden

Richter Charles, printer, dwl SW cor Dupont and Broadway
Richter George, porter with R. Hall & Co. dwl W s Taylor nr Lombard
Richter Max, baker with Charles Frank
Richter William, barber, N s Bryant bet Sixth and Garden
Richter William H. drayman, 323 Battery, dwl E s Seventh bet Bryant and Brannan
Rick Harry, gas fitter with J. K. Prior, 730 Montgomery, dwl 609 Stockton bet Cal and Pine
Rick John G. boot maker, dwl 121 Pacific
Rick Seigmund, brewer, dwl S s Sixteenth bet Valencia and Mission
Rickard Michael, laborer, Excelsior Iron Works, dwl Harrison nr Main
Rickards Ellen Mrs. furnished rooms, Mead House 305 Montgomery
RICKARDS JAMES, Golden City House, Four Mile House, San Bruno Road
Ricketson John, merchant, dwl 811 Pacific
Rickett William, dwl 9 Geary
Ricketts A. Herbert, clerk with A. Roman & Co. dwl 41 Tehama
Rickey John, painter, dwl Bay State House
Ricklefson Gregory, dyer, 1408 Stockton
Rickmann John, porter, dwl N s Bush bet Stockton and Dupont
Riddell George H. dwl 20 Market
Riddell James (Crane & Brigham) dwl Government House room 39
Riddell Spear, paying teller with Parrott & Co. dwl NW cor Montgomery and Sacramento
Riddell Thomas C. carpenter, dwl 15 Langton
Riddle David M. (Starr & R.) dwl 358 Jessie
Riddle George, shoe maker, dwl 103 Stewart
Riddle James, California Engine Co. No. 4
RIDDLE JAMES L. & CO. (I. Ward Eaton) real estate, office 523 Mont, dwl Tehama House
Riddle Margaret H. (widow) domestic, 1024 Minna
Riddle Robert A. sash and blind maker with Geo. Robinson & Co. dwl 806 Clay
Rider Henry, shoe maker, dwl 32 Folsom
RIDER, (J. B.) SOMERS (H. C.) & CO. (Joshua Chadbourne) hay and grain, 22 and 24 Market and 15 and 17 Sac, dwl 215 Prospect Place
Rider L. A. (Stevens & R.) dwl 32 John
Rider W. M. assistant registry clerk, Post Office, dwl 215 Prospect Place
Rider, see Ryder
Ridgway William P. book keeper, Lick House
Ridley Albert E. stencil plate cutter with F. M. Truworthy 321 Front
Ridley Joseph, machinist, Union Works, dwl N s Mission bet Twelfth and Thirteenth
Ridley Kate Miss, domestic, NW cor Powell and Jackson
Ridley R. porter, steamer Senator
Ridley Robert (col'd) musician, dwl 7 Broadway
Rieck Henry, cooper, dwl 817 Battery
Riedel Frank, waiter, 230 Kearny
Riedel Gustave, dwl 1015 Mason
Rigelhaupt P. Mrs. fancy dry goods, 312 Third
Riegelbuth Conrade, cabinet maker with Goodwin & Co. dwl W s Julia bet Howard and Minna
Riegelhuth Jacob, basket maker, dwl 6 Virginia Place
Riehm Mathias, molder, dwl 71 Natoma
Riehn, (Charles F.) Hemme (August) & Co. assayers, 432 Montgomery, dwl 4 Martha Place
Rielly Patrick, cartman, dwl 119 Stevenson
Rielly Patrick, wines and liquors, dwl 428 Greenwich
Rielly Rose Miss, domestic, 806 Bush
Riemann Rudolph, salesman with M. Gray, 613 Clay, dwl S s Kearny bet Pine and Bush
Riemer Edward, laborer, dwl Slice Bar Exchange
Riepe John A. engraver with Lemme Bros. dwl 409 Dupont

Riepe Joseph H. jeweler with Lemme Brothers, dwl 409 Dupont
Ries Louis, sexton Jewish Cemetery, dwl 1510 Dupont
Riese Ernst, car builder, S. F. & San José R. R. Co. dwl S s Nineteenth bet Capp and Howard
Rieser Aaron, dwl S s Francisco bet Mason and Taylor
Riesner Antone, cabinet maker, dwl 1205 Dupont
Riesselmann Henry S. soap maker with J. P. Dyer, dwl 1413 Mason
Rietow Henry cabinet maker with J. B. Luchsinger, dwl 1339 Dupont
Rieux Louis A. clerk with J. D. Roberts, dwl 730 Union
Rigaud Francis, cooper with Henry Shuman, 121 Sacramento
Rigby Richard, laborer, dwl 56 Stevenson
Riggan Cornelius, ship carpenter, dwl SE cor Minna and Second
Rigney James, laborer, dwl N s Alta bet Sansom and Battery
Rihn Joseph, waiter, dwl 502 Kearny
Riker H. H. wines and liquors, 539 Washington, dwl 1 Chatham Place
Riker James, steward, steamer Orizaba
Rikert I. F. deck hand, steamer Josie McNear
Riley Ann Miss, domestic, 11 First Avenue
Riley Benjamin, shipping clerk, dwl 210 Jackson
Riley Bernard, blacksmith, S. F. & San José R. R. Co. dwl 129 Clara
Riley Bernard, laborer, dwl SE cor Sacramento and Drumm
Riley Bernard, plasterer, dwl 520 Mission
Riley Bernard, porter, 317 Sacramento
RILEY C. C. drugs and medicines, NW cor Second and Howard, dwl 236 Jessie
Riley Cornelius, wines and liquors and proprietor Yacht Saloon, 314 and 316 Clay
Riley Daniel, teamster, dwl United States Hotel, 706 Battery
Riley Edward, engineer, Pacific Mill, dwl W s Folsom Avenue, nr Folsom
Riley Frederick, workman, S. F. & P. Sugar Co. dwl Harrison nr Eighth
Riley George, bar keeper, dwl Manhattan Engine House
Riley George, foreman, Pacific Mail S. S. Co. dwl 203 Stewart
Riley Hazen K. conductor, Central R. R. Co. dwl 1004 Pine
Riley James, dwl W s Fifth nr Folsom
Riley James, dwl 1½ miles SW Lake Honda
Riley James, boot mkr with C. Joseph, 804 Kearny
Riley James, cattle dealer, dwl SW cor Natoma and Fifth, up stairs
Riley James, engineer, Pacific Flour Mills
Riley James, molder, Vulcan Iron Works, dwl 16 Jessie
Riley James, night inspector, Custom House, dwl 510 Sacramento
Riley James, stevedore, Monumental Engine Co. No. 6
Riley James, workman with John M. Mitchell
Riley James A. carpenter, Knickerbocker Engine Co. No. 5
Riley James F. porter, 211 Battery, dwl 252 Third
Riley James T. blacksmith, dwl 184 Stevenson
Riley James T. saloon keeper, Independence H. & L. Co. No. 3
Riley Jennie Miss, domestic, 927 Market
Riley J. H. superintendent Italian Fish Market, dwl 320 Kearny
Riley John, blacksmith, dwl 15 First
Riley John, blacksmith helper, S. F. & San José R. R. Co. dwl 16 Jessie
Riley John, boarding, 50 Beale
Riley John, clerk with Edwin Lewis, dwl 1004 Pine

Riley John, laborer, dwl 312 Ritch
Riley John, laborer, dwl 29 Jessie
Riley John, teamster, Monumental Engine Co. No. 6
Riley John G. boarding, 115 Jackson
Riley John G. waterman, Broadway nr Stockton
Riley John J. carpenter, dwl W s Dupont bet Washington and Jackson
Riley John W. blacksmith, dwl 184 Stevenson
Riley J. T. blacksmith, Independence H. & L. Co. No. 3
Riley Julia Miss, domestic, 26 O'Farrell
Riley Kate Miss, domestic, 22 John
Riley Kate Miss, domestic, 911 Sutter
Riley Kate Miss, domestic, 1805 Powell
Riley M. Mrs. (widow) dwl 135 Shipley
Riley Margaret, domestic, St. Mary's Hospital
Riley Margaret Miss, domestic with C. S. Lord, Grove Avenue nr Bryant
Riley Mary Miss, domestic, SW cor Pine and Mason
Riley Michael, dwl 416 Stevenson
Riley Michael, laborer, dwl S s Vallejo bet Montgomery and Sansom
Riley Michael, laborer, dwl 115 First
Riley Michael, molder, Union Foundry, dwl W s First bet Mission and Jessie
Riley Michael, porter, dwl 515 Sacramento
Riley Michael, vegetable pedler, dwl 717 Lombard
Riley Owen, milkman with Cornelius Conahan
RILEY P. & CO. (Edward Commins) importers and jobbers wines and liquors, 519 Front, dwl 428 Greenwich
Riley Patrick, blacksmith, dwl 184 Stevenson
Riley Patrick, blacksmith, dwl 266 Jessie
Riley Patrick, cartman, dwl 121 Stevenson
Riley Patrick, express wagon, cor Sansom and Commercial
Riley Patrick, gardener, dwl W s Guerrero nr Fifteenth
Riley Patrick, hostler, dwl 1614 Stockton
Riley Patrick, laborer, dwl 49 Jessie
Riley Patrick, laborer, dwl SW cor Clinton and Brannan
Riley Patrick, laborer, dwl E s Eighth bet Bryant and Brannan
Riley Patrick, laborer, dwl NW cor Twentieth and Florida
Riley Patrick, waiter, Russ House
Riley Patrick, waterman, 609 Market
Riley Peter, laborer, dwl Francisco bet Powell and Mason
Riley Philip, carpenter, dwl 310 Folsom
Riley Philip, waiter, dwl 551 Howard
Riley Richard, laborer, dwl W s Sansom bet Union and Filbert
Riley Richard, stone cutter, dwl 323 Dupont
Riley Susan Miss, domestic, 1112 Powell
Riley Terrence, gardener, dwl W s Guerrero nr Fifteenth
Riley Thomas, blacksmith with Kimball & Co. dwl Columbian Engine House
Riley Thomas, laborer, dwl Greenwich bet Montgomery and Sansom
Riley Thomas, machinist, Miners' Foundry, dwl 331 Bush
Riley Thomas, mason, dwl N s Willow Avenue bet Van Ness Avenue and Franklin
Riley (Thomas D.) & Vest (George) hay and grain, etc. 569 and 571 Market, dwl S s Howard bet First and Second
Riley William, laborer, dwl 19 St. Mark Place
Riley William, steward, Richard's Restaurant, dwl 213 Post
Riley, see O'Reily Reiley, Reilly, and Rieley,
Rimar Henry, with H. Ernst, dwl Butcher's Home, Potrero Avenue
Rimass Emanuel, boots and shoes, 932 Dupont
Rimers Jacob, steward, Zeile's Baths, 517 Pacific
Rimmington James W. with G. C. Eldridge, dwl 564 Mission

Rin Frank, butcher, dwl 115 First
Rinaldi C. R. upholsterer with W. M. Hixon
Rindge H. A. salesman with William E. Loomis, dwl 622 Greenwich
Rines James P. carpenter with O. Bergson, dwl 26 Battery
Rines Joshua R. fruits, 1237 Stockton
Ring Daniel, laborer with David B. Hughes, dwl S s Lombard bet Taylor and Jones
Ring David, milk ranch, N s Lombard nr Laguna
Ring F. David, diamond setter with F. R. Reichel, dwl SW cor Second and Stevenson
Ring George E. brick maker, cor Union and Polk
Ring Jeremiah W. stevedore, dwl E s Harrison Avenue nr Folsom
RING PETER, groceries and liquors, SW corner Lombard and Powell
Ring (R. G.) & Lunt (D. S.) butter, cheese, etc. 2 Wash Market, dwl 704 Howard nr Third
Ring Richard, groceries and liquors, 128 First
Ring William, miner, dwl 33 Turk
Ringel Celestin, with Kellogg, Hewston & Co. dwl 673 California
Ringley Frederick, steward, Brooklyn Hotel
Ringot Joseph, shipwright and calker, 109 Market, dwl 928 Bush
Rink Frederick, mariner, dwl 436 Fremont
Rinn Thomas, plasterer, dwl 256 Third
Rinsella John, boot maker, 252 Third, dwl 638 Mission
Rio Chico S. M. Co. office 30 Exchange Building
Riordan Daniel, boot maker, dwl W s Bryant Avenue nr Eighth
Riordan Edward, boot maker, dwl W s Bryant Avenue nr Eighth
Riordan Ellen (widow) dwl 14 Brooks, rear
Riordan Gerald S. clerk with Murphy, Grant & Co. dwl 219 Minna
Riordan James, salesman with Murphy, Grant & Co. dwl 1109 Powell
Riordan John, shoe maker with Abraham Keatz, dwl Freelon nr Fourth
Riordan John, shoe maker, dwl 323 Sutter
Riordan John M. bottler, dwl E s Powell nr Lombard
Riordan John P. with Fred. Collier, dwl 313 Mason
Riordan Mary Miss, domestic, 423 Post
Riordan Michael, laborer, dwl W s Jones bet Ellis and O'Farrell
Riordan Michael, marble polisher, dwl SW cor Jones and O'Farrell
Riordan Michael, wool washer, Mission Woolen Mills, dwl W s Shotwell bet Nineteenth and Twentieth
Riordan Owen, stone cutter, bds 707 Front
Riordan Richard, Dupont Street Wood and Coal Yard, 222 Dupont, dwl 616 Lombard
Riordan Samuel, salesman, 327 Sansom, dwl 1009 Powell
Rioton John, paper hanger, dwl 3 Thomson Av
Ripley (Edward L.) & Kimball (Charles H.) pianoforte and melodeon warerooms, 417 Montgomery, dwl NE cor Geary and Stockton
Ripley H. carpenter, dwl 116 Sansom
Ripley Lewis, mechanic, S. F. Gas Co
Rippe Hermann, bar keeper, Cliff House
Ris Gustave (Voizin, Ris & Co.) dwl Essex Place
Risdon John N. (Coffey & R. and Main Street Wharf Co.) dwl 213 Harrison
Risdon Orange jr. boiler maker with Coffey & Risdon, bds Bailey House
Rising Alfred, clerk with George F. & William H. Sharp, dwl 137 Townsend
Rising David B. broker, office 606 Merchant, dwl 137 Townsend
Rising Sarah A. Miss, dwl 137 Townsend
Risley Arthur A. tailor with R. T. Houston, dwl Selina Court nr California
Risley Hesidah, ship carpenter with John G. North

Rispaud Jean, liquor saloon, 634 Pacific
Rissel William F. carpenter, S. F. & San José R. R. Co. dwl cor Sixteenth and Folsom
Ritcher Adolph, cigar box maker, dwl Mary Lane bet Dupont and Kearny
Ritchie James, captain, office Pier 10 Stewart
Ritchie M. J. Miss, assistant, Fourth St. School, dwl 704 Howard
Ritson Edward J. painter with J. W. Denny
Ritt Harry, liquor saloon, 643 Pacific
Ritter Charles Aug. book keeper with F. R. Reichel
RITTER L. E. & CO. real estate agents, office 608 Sacramento, dwl 417 Dupont
Ritter William, clerk with H. M. Newhall & Co
Rivard Alphonse, waiter, 28 Mont, dwl 619 Market
Rivas Frances Miss, dwl S s Sixteenth bet Valencia and Guerrero
RIX ALFRED, attorney at law, office 11 Court Block 636 Clay, dwl 737 Pine
Rix Hale, attorney at law, office 230 Bush, dwl W s Potter nr Market
Rixon John, laborer, dwl W s Sansom bet Union and Filbert
Roach Dennis C. laborer, dwl 210 Stevenson
Roach Edward, liquor saloon, 421 Cal, dwl 320 Post
Roach James, laborer, dwl W s Montgomery bet Filbert and Union
Roach John, boot maker, dwl N s Greenwich nr Taylor
ROACH JOHN, optician and mathematical instrument maker, 413 Washington, dwl 820 Union
Roach John, teamster with Nelson & Stevens, dwl Potrero Avenue
Roach (John F.) & Co. (Martin Roach) cooperage, NW cor Commercial and Drumm
Roach Lawrence, job wagon, cor Mission and Second, dwl 848 Folsom, rear
Roach Lawrence, teamster, Mt. St. Joseph
Roach Martin (Roach & Co.) dwl 104 Sacramento
Roach Mary Miss, domestic, 30 Minna
Roach Mary Miss, domestic, 1063 Howard
Roach Mary E. Miss, dress maker, dwl 405 Bush
ROACH PHILIP A. wholesale wines and liquors, NW cor Jackson and Sansom, dwl 820 Union
Roach Thomas, express wagon, cor Sansom and Pac
Roach Tobias M. contractor and builder, 15 Leidesdorff, dwl 415 Post
Roach William, laborer, dwl 334 Third, rear
Roaches Henry, baker, dwl 717 Pacific
Roake James, groom, dwl 342 Brannan
Roake John, molder, dwl 519 Mission
Roalfe William (Anderson & R.) dwl 22 Clarence
Roan Bridget Miss, domestic, 706 Taylor
Roarke Bernard, boiler maker with Coffey & Risdon, dwl 10 Front
Robb James, core maker, Vulcan Iron Works, dwl Shipley nr Fifth
Robb J. C. salesman with Carle & Gorley, dwl W s Montgomery bet Pacific and Broadway
Robbin Benjamin, employé, Occidental Restaurant, dwl Muhr's Hotel
Robbins Alexander, blacksmith, dwl 12 Sutter
Robbins Charles F. book and job printing, and importer and dealer printers' material, 416 Battery, dwl 530 Pine
Robbins Charles F. engineer, 416 Mont, dwl 535 Cal
ROBBINS JAMES J. agent Nicolson Pavement, office 619 Montgomery, dwl Lick House
Robbins John, carpenter, Metropolitan Theater
Robbins John, wholesale and retail produce, 122 Clay, dwl NE cor Turk and Van Ness Avenue
Robbins Philip A. (Atchinson & Co.) Occidental Market, dwl 1 Winter Place
Robbins William J. drayman, cor Market and Stewart, dwl 611 Sutter
Robbins, see Robins
Roben Jean, dwl 721 Pacific
Robert Abraham, with James Laidley, Easton's Laundry

Robert Frank, gardener, dwl 716 Pacific
Robert J. D. shawl depôt, 119 and 121 Montgomery, dwl 825 Washington
Robert Joseph, gardener with Charles Duisenberg, S s Harrison bet Sixth and Seventh
Roberts Amos, with William Pixley, 216 Sutter
Roberts Charles G. foreman dyeing, Mission Woolen Mills, dwl W s Shotwell bet Nineteenth and Twentieth
Roberts Charles R. poll tax collector, City Hall
Roberts Charlotte Miss, waitress, SW cor Dupont and Broadway
Roberts (Clovis) & Co. (François Mercier) wheelwrights, 249 Fourth
Roberts David, rigger, dwl 316 Beale
Roberts D. S. stock broker, office 606 Merchant, dwl 139 Townsend
Roberts E. laborer, Pacific Foundry, dwl 28 Battery
Roberts Edward W. accountant, office 664 Mission, dwl 660 Howard
Roberts Eli, carpenter, dwl S s Minna nr Eighth
Roberts George W. clerk, Bank California, dwl 13 Stockton
Roberts H. laborer, dwl Original House
Roberts Henry, ship carpenter, bds Sacramento Hotel 407 Pacific
Roberts Hugh, painter, dwl 11 Verona Place
Roberts James, dwl 34 Eddy
Roberts James, fruits, 103 Kearny, dwl NE cor Polk and Eddy
Roberts James. superintendent Mission Woolen Mills, dwl N s Folsom nr Twelfth
ROBERTS (James B.) MORRISON (James W.) & CO. (Wickham C. McNish) importers boots and shoes and agents J. Miles & Son, Philadelphia, 216 and 218 California, dwl 230 Green
Roberts John, carpenter, dwl E s Dora nr Harrison
Roberts John, glazier with Wilson & Bro. dwl Meyers' Hotel
Roberts John, laborer, dwl 10 Hunt
Roberts John, metal roofer with H. G. & E. S. Fiske, dwl 407 Tehama
Roberts John, night inspector, Custom House, dwl NE cor Ellis and Gough
Roberts John E. harness maker with M. McColgan, dwl 15 Battery
Roberts John G. clerk with C. B. Grant, King near Third
Roberts Julius, carpenter, dwl 161 Beale
Roberts M. (col'd, widow) machine sewing, dwl 909 Washington
Roberts Mary Mrs. midwife, dwl 34 Eddy
Roberts M. R. dwl 1001 Washington
Roberts Napoleon, with Roberts & Co. 249 Fourth
Roberts Newton H. waterman, 709 Market
Roberts N. M. book keeper with Falkner, Bell & Co. dwl Union Club Rooms
Roberts Richards, baker, 1424 Stockton
Roberts R. T. cupeller, Assayers' Department U. S. Branch Mint, dwl SW cor Geary and Powell
Roberts S. A. shoe maker, dwl 6 First
Roberts Samuel S. clerk with Brooks & Whitney, 10–12 Exchange Building
Roberts Thomas, sail maker with John Harding, dwl 500 Howard
Roberts Thomas T. foreman Eureka Powder Works, dwl 12 Third
Roberts W. H. waterman, 609 Market
Roberts William, N. drayman with Webb & Holmes, dwl 500 Howard
Robertson Alexander, stone cutter, Fort Point
Robertson Anne M. groceries and liquors, San Bruno Road 3 miles from City Hall
Robertson C. O. proprietor Union House, 32 Stewart
Robertson E. R. clerk with H. M. Newhall & Co
Robertson Frederick, cabinet maker with John D. Bruns, 840 Mission
Robertson George, painter, dwl SW cor First and Market
Robertson H. miller, dwl 419 Vallejo

Robertson J. D. photographic gallery, 32 Kearny
Robertson John P. clerk with R. H. Bennett, dwl N s Harrison nr Sixth
Robertson J. R. dwl 639 Washington
Robertson Mary Mrs. dress maker, 210 Bush
Robertson Mary (widow) dwl 2 Chelsea Place
Robertson Robert, mariner, dwl 1046 Folsom
Robertson Stephen (col'd) domestic, Brevoort House
Robertson William, florist, W s Folsom bet Nineteenth and Twentieth
Robertson William R. mining superintendent, dwl E s Jones bet Jackson and Pacific
Robertson William R. pressman with Towne & Bacon, dwl 63 Clementina
Robinett (Frank) & Linn (Jacob) Verandah Saloon NE cor Wash and Kearny, dwl 28 Geary
Robinett John, plumber with John Kehoe, dwl E s Eleventh nr Mission
Robinett Roger, clerk, Chelsea Laundry, dwl 542 Brannan
Robinette Theodore J. with Frank Merrill, dwl 26 Scott
Robins Frank, liquor saloon, 726 Pacific
ROBINS GEORGE, justice of the peace Fourth Township, office 230 Bush, dwl SW corner Post and Jones
Robins John, painter, S. F. & San José R. R. Co. dwl S s Sixteenth bet Valencia and Mission
Robins Matthew, dwl W s Jones bet Post and Geary
Robins W. M. calker, dwl 14 Tehama Place
Robinson Aaron, wood turner, cor Mission and Fremont, dwl 765 Mission
Robinson Albert W. laborer, dwl San Bruno Road nr Santa Clara
Robinson Amelia J. (widow) dwl NE corner Sansom and Vallejo
Robinson Ann Miss, domestic with Thomas Reynolds, N s Fifteenth nr Mission
Robinson Annie J. Miss, dwl 143 Silver
Robinson Ansel, clerk, 217 Wash, dwl 43 Minna
Robinson August, book keeper with D. C. Mitchell & Co. dwl N s Vallejo nr Mason
Robinson C. B. dwl 112 Geary
Robinson Charles, clerk, dwl 129 Third
Robinson Charles K. dwl 129 Third
Robinson Charles L. railroad contractor, dwl 41 Minna
Robinson David N. dwl 43 Minna
Robinson E. A. Mrs. dwl 3 Dupont
Robinson Edward Mott, estate of, proprietor Robinson's California Line Clipper Ships, office 305 Front
Robinson Edwin, printer with Towne & Bacon, dwl 21 Howard Court
Robinson Edwin J. book keeper, dwl 561 Howard
Robinson Eli, carpenter, dwl S s Minna bet Seventh and Eighth
Robinson Elizabeth (widow) dwl 407 Filbert
Robinson F. H. bricklayer, dwl N s Presidio Road nr Laguna
Robinson Francis H. miner, dwl SE cor Hyde and Filbert
Robinson George & Co. (Howard Chapman) manufacturers sash, doors, blinds, moldings, etc. 30 and 32 California
Robinson George, drayman, 215 Sac, dwl 52 Clara
Robinson H. Loomis, mining, dwl 760 Harrison
Robinson Isaac S. bricklayer, dwl 714 Sansom
Robinson Jacob, carpenter, dwl 43 Jane
Robinson James, deck hand, steamer Sacramento
Robinson James, metal roofer with John Kehoe, 228 Bush
Robinson James, porter, 321 Sutter
Robinson James (col'd) whitewashing, dwl S side Broadway bet Kearny and Dupont
Robinson James F. boot fitter, dwl 315 Montgomery
Robinson James H. metal roofer with H. G. & E. S. Fiske
Robinson J. Calvin, laundryman, dwl 419 O'Farrell

Robinson J. L. C. builder, dwl 714 Sansom
Robinson John, miller, dwl 419 Vallejo
Robinson John, miner, dwl 843 Mission
Robinson John, plasterer, bds Cambridge House, 304 Pacific
Robinson John, produce, dwl N s Turk nr Van Ness Avenue
Robinson John, seaman, dwl 20 Commercial
Robinson John C. delivery clerk, Post Office, dwl 823 Jackson
Robinson John C. driver, Chelsea Laundry
Robinson John E. express wagon, NW cor Dupont and Pacific, dwl N s Post nr Laguna
Robinson John R. dwl 924 Mission
Robinson Jordan, waiter, dwl E s Varenne near Union
Robinson Joseph, box maker with Hobbs, Gilmore & Co. dwl 335 Ritch
ROBINSON JOSEPH, importer and jobber paints, oils, paper hangings, etc. 509 Sansom, dwl 713 Bush, rear
Robinson Joshua C. dwl 45 Everett
Robinson J. R. agent collection bounty claims, 626 Montgomery, dwl 924 Mission
Robinson Julius, clerk with Voizin, Ris & Co. dwl 219 Mason nr O'Farrell
Robinson Kate Mrs. dwl 1007 Powell
Robinson L. B. tailor, 610 Montgomery
Robinson L. L. trustee, Market St. R. R. Co. office SE cor Mont and Jackson, dwl 806 Stockton
Robinson Margaret Miss, dwl 334 Third, rear
Robinson Martin, laborer, dwl 140 Stewart
Robinson Mary C. Mrs. dwl 728 Bush
Robinson Matilda Mrs. dress and cloak maker, dwl NW cor Stockton and Green
Robinson (Michael) & Rosenthal (Joseph) stoves and tinware, 3 Commercial, dwl 1304 Stockton
Robinson Milo, proprietor Bay State House, NE cor Front and Sacramento
Robinson Peter, ship ballaster, dwl W s Battery bet Green and Union
Robinson R. A. dwl 619 Bush
Robinson Robert, carriage maker, dwl 541 Mission
Robinson Robert A. dwl 818 Post
Robinson Richard G. machinist, S. F. Iron Works, dwl 6 Auburn
Robinson Richard P. reporter, dwl 6 Auburn
Robinson Robert W. drayman, 215 Sacramento
Robinson Ruel (Veasey & R.) SE cor Taylor and Clay
Robinson Samuel, laborer, dwl S s Green bet Montgomery and Sansom
Robinson S. E. (widow) dwl 117 Taylor
Robinson Thomas A. professor mathematics City College, dwl 6 Martha Place
Robinson Thomas B. stevedore (and Tripp & R.) dwl 6 Qniney
Robinson Ward E. broker, dwl 112 Montgomery
Robinson William, dwl 608 Market
Robinson William, laborer, dwl W s Battery bet Filbert and Union
Robinson William, ship joiner, dwl S s Hayes nr Franklin, Hayes' Valley
Robinson William H. laborer, dwl S s Commercial bet Drumm and East
Robinson William H. tinsmith with D. S. Weaver, dwl 38 Battery
Robinson William J. X. painter with Sweett & Gadsby, dwl 311 Fremont
Robinson W. J. printer, Eureka Typographical Union, 625 Merchant
ROBINSON'S CALIFORNIA LINE CLIPPER SHIPS, Henry B. Williams agent, off 305 Front
Robison Charles F. salesman with I. S. Van Winkle & Co. dwl 27 Minna
Robitscheck Herman, with Pollack Bros. 421 Sacramento, dwl Steckler's Exchange
Robl John, butcher with L. Miller & Co. dwl W s August Alley bet Green and Union

Robly Thomas, ship carpenter, dwl 446 Brannan
Robson Henry, gas fitter, dwl N s Head nr Octavia
Robson James, boot maker, 412 Third
Rocchiccoli Raneri F. electrotyper, silver plater, engraver, and brass founder, 523 California
Roch Jane (widow) hat trimmer, dwl 611 Jackson
Rocha Jean B. with Peter Bonzi, 515 Merchant
Rocha Pablo, clerk, Mexican Loan Office, dwl 120 Fourth
Rocha William C. express wagon, cor Montgomery and Sutter
Rochbrane Alfred, molder, Pacific Foundry
Roche Antoine, waiter, 623 Commercial
Roche Charles, marble worker, 673 Market, dwl Pacific bet Dupont and Stockton
Roche James, steward Phil's Exchange, dwl with Herman Hedrick
Roche James M. porter, 411 Front
Roche James V. butcher, dwl 904 Stockton
Roche John, law student with Shafter, Goold & Dwinelle, dwl Virginia Place nr Jackson
ROCHE THOMAS, wholesale dealer wines and liquors, SW cor Pacific and Sansom, dwl 516 Pacific
Rochebrune Alfred, drayman, 323 Clay, dwl 632 Geary
Rochford Ann (widow) dwl 1232 Pacific
Rochford James H. special policeman, dwl 709 Lombard
Rochon Louis, waiter, steamer Yosemite
Rock Mary Miss, domestic, 926 Sacramento
Rock John, dwl 1522 Mason
Rockland Rose Miss, domestic, 410 Geary
ROCKWELL E. A. editorial department, Morning Call, dwl 641 Washington
ROCKWELL, (Walter M.) COYE (Hiram L.) & CO. importers and jobbers hardware, SW cor Pine and Battery, dwl 749 Howard
Rockwitz George W. bar keeper, Faust Cellar, SE cor Clay and Montgomery, dwl 20 Everett
Rodderman J. driver, Omnibus R. R. Co
Rode Christian, machinist, dwl 1109 Pacific
Rode Christian, seaman, bds 7 Washington
Rode Edward, cabinet maker with Joseph Mayer, dwl E s Garden bet Harrison and Bryant
Rode John, seaman, bds 7 Washington
Rodecker Elias (Gallagher & R.) dwl 31 Second
Rodemerk Albert D. workman, Pacific Glass Works, dwl S s Mariposa nr Mississippi
Roden A. G. (Wright & R.) dwl 31 Natoma
Rodenbeck Charles, porter steamer Yosemite, dwl 509 Vallejo
Roderer John, shoe maker with George Burkhardt, dwl 4 Milton Place
Roderigues Antonio, merchant, dwl 864 Mission
Rodey John, local policeman, dwl cor Fulton and Laguna
Rodgers A. mate, steamer Julia
Rodgers A. K. carpenter, Miners' Foundry, dwl Howard House
Rodgers Annie Miss, domestic, 504 Third
Rodgers Augustus F. assistant, U. S. Coast Survey, dwl 116 Eddy
Rodgers Charles L. waiter, dwl 116 Jackson
Rodgers E. laborer, dwl 140 Stewart
Rodgers Frank, confectioner, 131 Fourth
Rodgers Frank, milk ranch, San Miguel Ranch, Ocean House Road
Rodgers George, dwl 220 Third
Rodgers George, jeweler with Mathewson & Bucklin, dwl — Stockton
Rodgers James, painter, dwl S s Filbert bet Leavenworth and Hyde
Rodgers James D. carpenter, dwl 60 Beale
Rodgers J. Graham, with Rodgers, Meyer & Co. dwl NE cor Powell and Pine
Rodgers Nathaniel, ship master, dwl 238 Stewart
Rodgers P. A. (B. M. Atchinson & Co.) dwl Martha Place

Rodgers Patrick, laborer, dwl S s Folsom bet Main and Spear
RODGERS, (Robert) MEYER (William) & CO. commission merchants and agents West India & Pacific Steamship Co. and Mexican Dispatch Line Packets, office 314 Wash, res Liverpool
Rodgers Robert jr. with Rodgers, Meyer & Co. dwl NE cor Powell and Pine
Rodgers Thomas, lamplighter, S. F. Gas Co. dwl 432 Clementina
Rodgers T. R. blacksmith, dwl 741 Folsom
Rodgers Uriah, fruits, 932 Folsom
Rodgers Wm. B. express wagon, dwl S s Grove bet Laguna and Octavia
Rodgers ———, wagon maker, dwl 761 Mission
Rodick Elizabeth D. Mrs. dwl 358 Jessie
Rodman Daniel B. superintend't with Morris Greenberg
Rodola Frederick, carpenter, dwl 1012 Battery
Rodouan Alfred, clerk with C. François, 605 Sansom
Rodovich Theodore, express wagon, 420 Davis
Rodrigues A. dwl 918 Jackson
Rodrigues Catalina (widow) dwl E s Lagoon
Rodrigues Francisco, workman with Antonio Flores
Rodrigues Jacinto, lab, dwl NW cor Pac and Mason
Rodrigues John B. printer, dwl 627 Vallejo
Rodwell Vie Miss, dress maker, dwl N s Pine bet Powell and Stockton
Roe A. S. music teacher, dwl 740 Howard
Roe Charles, clerk, 10 First
Roe James, laborer, dwl 63 Minna
Roe M. J. Mrs. milliner and dress maker, 106 Second
Roe Patrick, hog ranch, NW cor Sixteenth and Nebraska
Roe W. S. amalgamator, 269 First
Roeben George, boarding, 37 Pacific and liquor saloon, 1029 Dupont, dwl 1405 Mason
Roeding Frederick (R. Feuerstein & Co.) office 212 Front
Roehrle Charles C. neatsfoot oil manufacturer, N s Sixteenth nr Rhode Island
Roemer Christian, tailor, dwl 1517 Dupont
Roemer Frederick, tailor, dwl 1 Vallejo Place
Roes Louis, clerk, NW cor Mason and Post
Roesch Cristoph F. baker, dwl 716 Pacific
Roesler Henry A. (Hotop, Garling & Co.) 116 Jackson
Roesmon Thomas J. blacksmith with J. Claffrich, dwl S s Minna nr Eighth
Roethel Edward, boot maker, 156 Third
Rof Peter, butcher with H. Watkins, 452 Third
Roffat Simon, watch maker, 1114 Dupont
Roge Louis, Union Restaurant, 339 Third cor Verona
Rogers A. Mme. dress maker, 1209 Dupont
Rogers Abram T. (col'd) tailor, 319 Bush
Rogers Anthony R. mate, steamer Julia, dwl S side Moulton Place nr Montgomery
Rogers Charles, scenic artist, Maguire's Opera House, dwl N s Vallejo bet Powell and Mason
Rogers Daniel, attorney at law, office 614 Merchant, dwl 355 Brannan
Rogers E. K. chief engineer. steamer Orizaba, dwl 1107 Mason
Rogers Evan T. shoe maker, 126 Bush
Rogers Ford H. book keeper with O. B. Fogle, dwl 714 Mission
Rogers Frank, dairyman, dwl San Miguel Ranch nr Ocean House Road
Rogers George E. clerk, 512 Cal, dwl 115 Dupont
Rogers George H. contractor, dwl N side Presidio Road cor Octavia
Rogers George P. clerk with R. B. Swain & Co. dwl 108 Prospect Place
Rogers Harriet L. (widow) dwl 714 Mission
Rogers Henry, merchant, office 240 Montgomery, dwl 548 Howard
Rogers Henry, sign and ornamental painter, 611 Market, dwl NE cor Sansom and Bush

Rogers Henry (col'd) shaving saloon, Francisco nr Powell, dwl Kearny nr Bush
Rogers Henry D. physician, office and dwl 719 Clay
Rogers H. P. (widow) dwl 108 Prospect Place
Rogers Isabella Miss, fancy goods, 846 Washington
Rogers James, clerk, Surveyor's Department Custom House, dwl 558 Howard
Rogers James, plasterer, dwl S side Broadway bet Kearny and Dupont
Rogers James A. mariner, dwl N s Presidio Road cor Octavia
Rogers James C. block maker, dwl N s Bernard bet Jones and Leavenworth
Rogers James H. butcher, dwl SE cor Dupont and Bay
Rogers James J. book keeper, Brooklyn Hotel
Rogers J. Henry, butcher with G. M. Garwood & Co
Rogers John, with James Cunningham, dwl cor Vallejo and Dupont
Rogers John, laborer, dwl E s Margaret Place
Rogers John H. seaman's boarding, Front nr Vallejo
ROGERS J. P. physician, office rooms 3 and 4 Mercantile Library Building
Rogers Levi, pork packer, 57 Metropolitan Market, dwl cor Clara Lane and Bush
Rogers Louisa (widow) dwl 421 East
Rogers M. (widow) dwl 13 Front
Rogers M. (widow) dwl 1214 Clay
Rogers M. A. B. (widow) furnished rooms, 1024 Stockton
Rogers Matilda, domestic with G. Treat, S s Twenty-Fourth bet Folsom and Howard
Rogers Michael, cook with Herman Buerfind
Rogers Michael H. laborer with David B. Hughes, dwl N s Filbert bet Montgomery and Kearny
Rogers Nathan, storage, 818 Battery, dwl Presidio Road nr Devisidero
Rogers Neil, laborer, Pacific Coal Yard, dwl SE cor Kearny and Lombard
Rogers O. F. dwl 209 Clara
Rogers Peter, ranchman, Lake Merced
Rogers Peter K. policeman, City Hall, dwl 417 Bush
Rogers Philip, shoe making, 502 Kearny, dwl Market nr Brady
Rogers P. T. proprietor Omnibus Railroad House, W s Dolores op Sixteenth, Mission Dolores
Rogers Ralph H. merchant, dwl 830 Mission
Rogers R. K. milkman, W s Noe bet Sixteenth and Seventeenth
ROGERS ROBERT C. court commissioner Twelfth Judicial District, office 614 Merchant, dwl 355 Brannan
Rogers Robert H. deputy collector and store keeper Custom House, dwl 613 Geary
Rogers Russell K. milkman, dwl W s First Avenue nr Sixteenth
Rogers S. M. Co. office 103 California
Rogers Thomas, ex-pilot, dwl 1112 Kearny
Rogers T. Scott, dwl 6 Martha Place
Rogers William, deck hand, steamer Cornelia
Rogers William H. carpenter, dwl 1618 Stockton
Rogers Zachariah, wharfinger, Lombard Dock, dwl Union bet Montgomery and Kearny
Rogers, see Rodgers
Rogison Thomas, waiter, Franklin House SW cor Broadway and Sansom
Rohde H. B. *(Muhlenbrink & R.)* dwl SE cor Sutter and Taylor
Robe John F. *(Classen & Co.)* dwl 1008 Market
Rohen Catherine Miss, dwl 606 Third
Rohl Julius, clerk, dwl 7 Anthony
Rohrer Fred, clerk, 541 Kearny
Rohrer John S. laborer with John Smith
Rohrs Deidrick, clerk, NE cor Mission and Beale
Rohte Emil *(Kruse & Euler)* dwl 1014 Stockton
Rohte Peter, boat maker, dwl 450 Kearny
Rojar Joseph, waiter, 526 Clay
Rokatalita Jean B. vegetable garden nr Hunter's Point

Rokobl D. *(Dyer, Badger & R.)* dwl Lick House
Roland Francis, dwl NW cor Dupont and Filbert
Roland James, laborer, dwl 10 Louisa
Rolen Henry *(Leedes & R.)* dwl 46 Stewart
Rolinat Jean, musician, dwl 1114 Stockton
Rolf Christian, laborer, Bay Sugar Refinery, dwl SW cor Battery and Broadway
Rolfe Asa T. merchant, dwl 28 Geary
Rolland Jules, manufacturer and dealer furniture, 837 Dupont
Rolland Louis, dyer, dwl 735 Clay
Roller T. R. carpenter, dwl 625 Third
Rollier Catharine (widow) dwl 421 Dupont
Rollins F. M. capt. brig Hugh Barclay, office Pier 10 Stewart, dwl Stevenson bet Fourth and Fifth
Rollins Francis, ship master, dwl 355 Jessie
Rollins George, with C. S. Navigation Co. Broadway Wharf
Rollins Lott M. salesman with Goodwin & Co. 636 Market, dwl 536 Washington
ROLLINS WILLIAM, real estate dealer, office 46 Exchange Building, dwl 27 Clementina
ROLLINSON'S LINE NEW YORK PACKETS, Henry B. Williams agent, 305 Front
Rolls Thomas (col'd) cook, dwl SW cor Stockton and Sacramento
Rolph James, book keeper with F. J. Thibault, dwl 719 California
ROMAN A. & CO. importers, publishers, and dealers books, 417 and 419 Mont, res New York
Roman Robert, seaman, bds N s Pacific bet Davis and East
Romano A. fish, 4 Washington Fish Market
Romano Mariano, laborer, dwl 1318 Kearny
Romer Frank, varnisher with Goodwin & Co. dwl 1014 Kearny
Romer John L. clerk, C. S. Navigation Co. dwl 959 Folsom
Romera Antonio, laborer with Edward J. Quirk
Romley Simon, porter, Cosmopolitan Hotel
Romoser Harry, seaman, dwl 20 Commercial
Ronan Bridget Miss, domestic, 722 Post
Ronan Catherine Miss, domestic, 505 Bush
Ronan James, laborer, S. F. & San José R. R. Co
Ronan James M. butcher, dwl NE cor Bryant and Eighth
Ronan Mary, domestic with H. Myers, 818 Kearny
Ronan Thomas, cooper, dwl 31 Ecker
Roncati F. merchant, dwl 703 Greenwich
Roncovieri Alfreda, chorister, dwl 33 Hinckley
Rondel Edward, lapidary, 622 Clay, dwl 1013 Sutter
Roney Elizabeth Miss, domestic, 110 Ellis
Ronge Harry, deck hand, steamer Julia
Ronband Hippolyte John, dwl 215 Fourth
Ronn Weiland, laborer, dwl 315 Bush
Ronon John, laborer, bds with Joseph Seale, N s Turk nr Fillmore
Rontet Mathias, groceries and liquors, SW cor Dupont and Green
Rood A. N. & Co. *(I. N. Hudson)* advertising agents, 626 Mont, dwl International Hotel
Rooin Richard, dwl 414 Market
Roome John D. drayman, dwl 111 Turk
Rooney Bernard P. carpenter, S s Perry bet Fourth and Fifth
Rooney Edward, laborer, dwl W s Hyde bet Union and Filbert
Rooney Elizabeth (widow) dwl 229 Sutter
Rooney Ellen H. assistant teacher, Grace Institute, dwl 710 Taylor
Rooney *(James J.)* & Reilly *(Hugh)* hog ranch, and dwl S s Sixteenth nr Rhode Island
Rooney John, waiter, Russ House
Rooney Mary M. Miss, dwl with William Magorty S s Shipley nr Harrison Avenue
Rooney Peter, drayman, Main St. Wharf, dwl Hayes' Valley
Rooney Thomas, wood turner, dwl 158 First

Rooney William, workman and dwl S. F. Cordage Factory

Roos Adolph *(Charles Dahlmann & Co.)* dwl 515 Sacramento

Roos Hyppolite, clerk, 520 Sac, dwl 515 Sac

ROOS JOSEPH, engravings and artists' materials, 219 Montgomery, dwl 612 Pine

Root Datus E. dwl 335 Sixth

Root E. M. *(P. J. White & Co.)* dwl NW cor Pacific and Stockton

Root Homer F. dwl 221 Seventh

Root Ira C. janitor, Masonic Temple, dwl W s Downey nr Bryant

Root John W. wagon maker with Benjamin A. Fisher, dwl Bailey House

Root Warren D. mining secretary, office 338 Montgomery, dwl 1001 Powell

Root William, carpenter, dwl 333 Fourth

Rooti Henry, seaman, dwl 20 Commercial

Roper Daniel, clothing, 405 Com, dwl 513 Hyde

Roper Edward, Cooper's Institute, 658 and 660 Mission

Roper Edward, painter with Snow & Co

Roper William (col'd) steward, dwl N s Card Place

Roper W. P. steward, steamer Cornelia

Roperson Johan, laborer with Louis Ancenhofer

Ropke Arand, clerk, NW cor Post and Kearny

Rorke F. M. produce commission, 130 and 132 Clay, dwl 1 Leroy Place

Rosa Adolph *(Carrau & R.)* 8 New Market

Rosa Antonio, cook, Atlantic House, 210 Pacific

Rosa Salvator, music and musical instruments, 615 Montgomery, dwl 1328 Stockton

Rosar Bartholomew, with Arguelas Bernal

Roschold Gustavus, steward, Cliff House

Rose Albert J. watch maker and jewelry, 3 Montgomery Masonic Temple

Rose Alex. compositor, Daily Examiner, dwl 73 Natoma

Rose Alexander, with Edward Uncelin, junction Market and Dolores

Rose August, liquor saloon, 919 Kearny

Rose Charles *(Miller & R.)* dwl 106 Stewart

Rose David, carpenter, dwl 677 Mission

Rose Frederick, clerk, Crescent Engine Co. No. 10

Rose George W. local policeman and deputy marshal U. S. dwl 113 Virginia

Rose Gold M. Co. (Mariposa Co.) office 338 Mont

Rose H. Hebrew school, 666½ Mission

Rose Henry, dwl 529 Greenwich

Rose Henry, book binder with Buswell & Co. dwl 815 Montgomery

Rose Henry, foreman India Rice Mill, dwl E s Howard bet Eighteenth and Nineteenth

Rose Henry, shoe maker, 647 Merch, dwl 423 Fourth

Rose Herman H. sash and blind maker with J. McGill & Co. dwl 536 Tehama

Rose John, laborer, Bay Sugar Refinery, dwl 813 Battery

Rose Linda, mining and manufacturing co. office 606 Montgomery

ROSE L. S. stock and money broker, 617 Montgomery, dwl 921 Stockton

Rose Lucy (widow) dwl 640 Howard

Rose Mary (widow) dwl 1425 Dupont

Roseback Henry, butcher, dwl 132 Minna

Rosehart Frank, painter, dwl 4 Central Place

Rosekamp Henry, clerk, NE cor Fourth and Jessie

ROSEKRANS H. & CO. *(Samuel Read)* importers, jobbers, and dealers hardware, 135 Montgomery, dwl 132 Turk

Rosekrans Henry M. painter, 626 Commercial, dwl 469 Minna

Roseman Richard B. laborer, dwl 11 St. Mary

ROSENBAUM A. S. & CO. *(Joseph Brandenstein and Moses Rosenbaum)* importers and jobbers cigars and tobacco, SE cor Battery and Clay, res New York

Rosenbaum Catharine Miss, domestic, 721 Lombard

Rosenbaum Frederick H. & Co. *(C. Nordon)* importers French plate glass, mirrors, etc. 421 and 423 Battery

Rosenbaum Isidor, dwl 404 Stockton

Rosenbaum John, agent, coffee and oyster saloon, 935 Kearny

Rosenbaum Joseph, salesman with Neustader Bros. dwl 427 Sacramento

Rosenbaum Leopold *(Martin L. Haas & Co.)* dwl 113 Taylor

Rosenbaum Meta Miss, domestic, 533 O'Farrell

Rosenbaum Moses *(A. S. Rosenbaum & Co.)* dwl 127 Eddy

Rosenbaum *(Sigmund D.)* & Friedmann *(Edward)* importers and jobbers fancy goods, embroideries, etc. 316 Sacramento, res New York

Rosenbaum Valentine, salesman, 316 Sacramento, dwl 39 Mason

Rosenberg Augustus A. professor music, dwl 321 Powell

Rosenberg G. & Co. *(H. Rosenberg)* importers hats and caps, 412 and 414 Sacramento, dwl SW cor Ellis and Hyde

Rosenberg H. *(G. Rosenberg & Co.)* res New York

Rosenberg *(Hermann)* & Hencken *(Claus)* Commerce Market, NW cor Vallejo and Powell, dwl 1605 Powell

Rosenberg Isaac, with Stahle Bros. dwl 323 Sutter

Rosenberg Louis, meat market, SW cor Taylor and Post, dwl 532 O'Farrell

Rosenberg M. & Co. butchers, 3 Occidental Market, dwl cor Clementina and Ecker

Rosenberg M. Mrs. ladies' nurse, dwl 332 Sutter, rear

Rosenberg Morris, dwl 332 Sutter, rear

Rosenberg Morris, physician, office and dwl 507 Pine

Rosenberg Nathan, cigar manufacturer, 408 Sacramento, dwl 261 Tehama

Rosenblatt Joseph B. salesman, 125 Montgomery, dwl 632 Market

Rosenblatt M. A. dwl Lick House

Rosenblatt S. Palace of Fashion, 125 Montgomery, dwl 131 Montgomery

Rosenblatt Simon, miller, dwl 515 Market

Rosenblum Joseph, boots and shoes, 623 Davis

Rosenblum Morris, crockery, 10 Fourth

Rosenbohm John H. liquor saloon, E s Potrero Av

Rosenbohm Max A. carpenter, dwl W s Fourth bet Howard and Everett

Rosendahl *(Charles)* & Anderson *(Andrew)* boarding, 1816 Powell

Rosendale P. dwl 236 Clara

Rosener Charles, dwl 812 Howard

Rosener Hermann, tailor, 414 Third

Rosener Levi, merchant, dwl 812 Howard

Rosener Simon, tailor, 817 Jackson, dwl 111 Prospect Place

Rosenfeld Anthony *(Borker & R.)* dwl 111 Natoma

Rosenfeld Emanuel, salesman, 318 Sansom, dwl 616 O'Farrell

Rosenfeld Henry, carpets, 14 Third

Rosenfeld John, dwl 307 Folsom

Rosenfeld John, coal yard, NE cor Folsom and Spear, dwl SW cor Fulton and McAllister

Rosenfeld Julius, dwl 317 Geary

Rosenfeld Lipman K. importer and jobber fancy dry goods, 318 Sansom, dwl 616 O'Farrell

Rosenfeld Susman W. clerk, 517 Sacramento, dwl 1014 Bush

Rosenfelder Ludwig, cabinet maker with John Wigmore, dwl 210 Sutter

Rosenfield Solomon *(Jacobs & R.)* res New York

Rosengarn John H. clerk, SW cor Mkt and Stewart

Rosenham Jacob, express wagon, 828 Union

Rosenheim Abraham, dwl 318 Davis

Rosenheim Jacob, fruit peddler, dwl 1326 Pacific

Rosenheim Joel, merchant, dwl 631 Post

Rosenkrang John, seaman, bds 7 Washington

Rosenmuller George, liquors, 8 Washington

Rosenshine Matthias *(Friedberg & R.)* dwl 214 Pac

Rosenstein Henry *(Kraft & R.)* dwl 1015 Kearny
Rosenstein Samuel, liquor dealer, dwl 323 Pine
ROSENSTOCK *(Samuel W.)* & PRICE *(Benja. min)* importers and jobbers boots and shoes, 210 and 212 Battery, res New York
Rosenthal Abraham *(M. Rosenthal & Co.)* dwl 259 Stevenson
Rosenthal Abraham, locksmith, dwl Rassette Pl No. 3
Rosenthal B. dwl 225 Post
Rosenthal Davis, dwl 243 Stevenson
Rosenthal Herman, tailor, 621 Mission
Rosenthal Isaac *(Ackerman & Co.)* dwl 769 Mission
Rosenthal Jacob, peddler, dwl 5 Berry
Rosenthal Jacob, tailor, dwl 1304 Stockton
Rosenthal Joseph *(Robinson & R.)* dwl 1304 Stockton
Rosenthal M. & Co. *(A. Rosenthal)* boots and shoes, 406 Com and 340 Kearny, dwl 259 Stevenson
Rosenthal *(Marcus)* & Simon *(J.)* shaving saloon, 709 Clay, dwl 1304 Stockton
Rosenthal Marcus, tailor, dwl 137 Third
Rosenthal Max, boys' clothing, 14 Second, dwl 275 Minna
Rosenthal P. express wagon, cor Market and Second, dwl cor Mission and Ninth
Rosenthal Samuel J. *(J. Vogelsdorff & Co.)* dwl 447 Bryant
Rosenzweig Philip, shoe dealer, dwl 246 Stevenson
Roskamp Frederick, groceries and liquors, NE cor Fourth and Jessie
Roskamp John, clerk, dwl NE cor Fourth and Jessie
Ross Adam, ship joiner, dwl 446 Brannan
Ross Alexander L. confectioner, 119 Third
Ross Anna Miss, dwl 523 Howard
Ross Charles L. dwl N s Pine bet Powell and Stockton
Ross Daniel, carpenter, dwl 424 O'Farrell
ROSS *(Daniel L.)* DEMPSTER *(C. J.)* & CO. importers and commission merchants, SW cor Battery and Pacific, (office 240 Broadway, N.Y.) res New York
Ross Daniel, carpenter, 14 Broadway, dwl 424 O'Farrell
Ross David G. engineer, dwl 728 Market
Ross D. C. dwl 10 Sutter
Ross Duncan, waiter, Pacific Temperance House, 109 Pacific
Ross Frank, house mover, dwl 265 Minna
Ross George, gymnast, Wilson's Circus
Ross H. F. bookbinder, dwl 14 John
Ross Hinrich, laborer, Bay Sugar Refinery, dwl Sansom bet Union and Filbert
Ross Horace D. blacksmith with Samuel F. Ross, dwl 9 Powell
Ross Isaac, carpenter, dwl 832 Harrison
Ross James, cabinet maker with J. Peirce, dwl 731 California
Ross James, steward, American Exchange, dwl 46 Ritch
Ross John, molder, dwl 547 Mission
Ross John, plasterer, dwl 229 Stevenson
Ross John, wood and coal, 315 First
Ross John E. drayman, with M. G. Searing, 401 Battery, dwl 510 Sacramento
Ross John W. printer, dwl 15 Second
Ross Joseph, plasterer, dwl 242 Jessie
Ross Leopold, dwl 750 Folsom
Ross Leopold Mrs. millinery, 641 Clay, dwl 750 Folsom
Ross Maggie Miss, milliner, 40 Fourth, dwl 71 Fourth
Ross Margaret Miss, domestic, 514 Dupont
Ross Nathan, book keeper, 314 California
Ross Peter, bds Mission Exchange
Ross Richard, shoe maker with I. M. Wentworth & Co. 210 Pine
Ross Samuel F. carriage making, 72 Powell, dwl 9 Powell
Ross Thomas, plumber and gas fitter, 319 Bush, dwl 71 Fourth

Ross William, longshoreman, dwl N s Filbert bet Montgomery and Sansom
Ross William, marble cutter, 67 Fourth, dwl 621 Geary
Ross William C. contractor, Howard Engine Co. No. 3
Ross William G. dwl NW cor McAllister and Devisidero
Ross William H. carriage painter with Samuel F. Ross, dwl 9 Powell
Ross William M. farmer, dwl Ocean House Flat, nr Ocean House
Ross William S. carpenter, dwl 621 Geary
Ross W. Q. machinist, Union Foundry, dwl St. Charles Hotel
Rossbach Herman, pork and preserved meats, 40 Occidental market, dwl 132 Minna
Rosseter George R. *(Rosseter & Co.)* dwl 716 Howard
ROSSETER *(John H.)* & CO. *(George R. Rosseter)* wines and liquors, SW cor Market and Third, dwl 716 Howard
Rossi Andres, fruits, SE cor Jackson and Dupont
Rossi Angelo, with Vincent Squarza, 120 Leidesdorff
Rossi C. dwl 1014 Washington
Rossi Charles, broker, dwl SW cor Dupont and Broadway
Rossi Nicolas, silver plater, 236 Kearny
Rossi Pietro, fruits, SE cor Kearny and Merchant
Rossignol Charles, dwl nr San Bruno Road 3¼ miles from City Hall
Rossiter James, window shade and awning manufacturer, N s Francisco nr Dupont
Rostron James, fireman, steamer Julia
Rotenberg Abraham, dry goods, 113 Fourth
Roth George, carrier, Evening Bulletin and Morning Call
Roth John, boots and shoes, dwl N s Pacific bet Sansom and Battery
Roth John, carrier, Bulletin, dwl 728 Market
Roth John, coffee saloon, 150 Stewart
Roth John A. butcher, Pacific Market, dwl SW cor Pacific and Powell
Roth Joseph, wines and liquors, 805 Montgomery, dwl 719 Green
Roth Renly F. book keeper, 515 Market, dwl 20 Rouse
ROTH SAMUEL, trader, dwl 16 St. Mary
Rothe William, dwl 319 Bush
Rother Robert, tailor, 17 Fourth
Rothermel Philip *(Nagel & R.)* dwl 626 Vallejo
Rothfeld Joseph, book keeper with B. Hamburger & Bro. 308 Sacramento
Rothganger Frederick, carriage maker, dwl 834 Harrison
Rothland Henry, cartman, dwl W s Beale bet Folsom and Howard
Rothman Herman J. express wagon, dwl W s Bower Place
Rothman Isaac, fruit peddler, dwl E s Sonoma Place nr Union
Rothold John, dwl 239 Sutter
Rothschild Baruch, actuary, Occidental Insurance Co. dwl 935 Folsom
Rothschild Henry, variety store, 112 Third, dwl 734 Folsom
Rothschild Jacob S. merchant, office 517 Sacramento, dwl 267 Tehama
Rothschild Moses, assistant book keeper with B. Hamburger & Bro. dwl 935 Folsom
Rothschild Samuel, dwl 417 Sutter
Rotrosky William, harness maker with William Trumbull, dwl N s Turk bet Buchanan and Webster
Rottanzi Antonio, physician, office and dwl SE cor Folsom and Third
Rottanzi G. dwl SE cor Folsom and Third
Rottanzi Leopold, manuf punches and liquor saloon, 635 Wash, dwl SE corner, Folsom and Third

Roturier Charles, chemist and apothecary, SW cor Dupont and Pacific, dwl 1029 Dupont

Rotusky Henry, express wagon, cor Clay and San Rouge Frank, butcher, dwl 1318 Stockton

Roughen Catherine, domestic, NE cor Fourth and Silver

Rougler William, fruit vender, bds Franklin Hotel SE cor Sansom and Pacific

Ronhaud Hippolyte, clerk, French Consulate, dwl 215 Fourth

Rouleau François A. *(Brooks & R.)* searcher records, dwl 729 Harrison

Roullier Henri, compositor, Courrier de San Francisco, 607 Sansom, dwl 27 Kearny

Roullier Jules, compositor, Courrier de San Francisco, 617 Sansom, dwl 27 Kearny

Roullier Victoire, dwl 27 Kearny

Roulstone A. J. shipping merchant and real estate agent, office 6 and 7 Armory Hall

Roulstone John W. with Edward S. Spear & Co. dwl 414 Pine

Roun John, laborer, dwl 315 Bush

Rounan Thomas R. cooper, dwl 31 Ecker

Rounds Samuel A. *(Corbett & R.)* dwl W s Sixth bet Brannan and Townsend

ROUNTREE *(Jas. O.)* & McMULLIN *(Geo. O.)* wholesale grocers, 323 Front, dwl 423 Second

Rountree Sarah S. (widow) boarding, 122 Fourth

Rourke Bernard, compositor, American Flag, dwl Eureka Lodging House

Rourke Bridget B. (widow) dwl 509 Pine

Rourke Charles, cabman, Plaza, dwl S s Jackson bet Leavenworth and Hyde

Rourke Hugh, clerk, NW cor Jessie and Fourth, dwl 273 Jessie

Rourke John, laborer, dwl 1626 Dupont

Rourke John, molder, dwl 547 Mission

Rourke John, tailor with J. L. Brooks, dwl 528 Bush

Rourke Mary Ann (widow) dwl 422 Powell

Rousch Agatha (widow) dwl 1124 Folsom

Rouse Charles F. show card painter, dwl 741 Mission

Rouse Henry M. dwl 18 Ellis

Roussel Isadore W. carpenter, dwl 1007 Market

Roussel O. L. carpenter, dwl 1007 Market

ROUSSET PAUL, commission merchant, 811 Mont

Roux *(A.)* & Silvestre *(John)* wines and liquors, 538 Broadway, dwl 615 Dupont

Roux Charles, laborer, dwl 632 Pacific

Roux Felix, perfumer, dwl NE cor Bdwy and Mason

Roux F. cabinet maker, SE cor Everett and Fourth

Roux Josephine Mme. domestic, 907 Clay

Roux Rosalie Mrs. millinery, SE cor Everett and Fourth

Rovegno Stephen, wood and coal, 1015 Washington, bds 27 Natoma

Rovere Edward *(Etienne & Co.)* dwl 825 Dupont

Roviere Frank, sausage maker, 1303½ Dupont

Rowan Belle (widow) furnished rooms, 842 Mission

Rowan Chas. waiter, Oriental Hotel, dwl 114 Bush

Rowan George P. with Charles C. McDonald, dwl S s Broadway bet. Montgomery and Kearny

Rowan Sarah J. Miss, dwl S s Townsend bet Third and Fourth

Rowan Winefred Miss, domestic with I. N. Thorne, W s Howard bet Sixteenth and Seventeenth

Rowane George P. *(McDonald & Co.)* dwl 523 Clay

Rowe A. A. Miss, special primary assistant, Mission Grammar School, dwl N s Fifteenth nr Dolores

Rowe Albert, ship carpenter with John G. North, dwl 118 Silver

Rowe Catharine Mrs. domestic, 1028 Clay

Rowe Charles L. shoe maker, 215 and 225 Sansom

Rowe Edward, butcher, dwl N s Fifteenth between Guerrero and Dolores

Rowe Edwin, bar keeper with George Sawyer, 327 Sansom, dwl 517 Pine

Rowe George (col'd) porter, dwl 13 Virginia Place

Rowe Harriet M. Mrs. teacher, Select School, 616 Post, dwl 220 Stockton

Rowe James, stevedore, dwl 35 Main

Rowe John, grocer, dwl 309 Eddy

Rowe Joseph A. agent Lee & Ryland, dwl N s Sixteenth nr Howard

Rowe Lewis, carpenter and builder, dwl E s Larkin bet Green and Union

Rowe Rufus, butcher, dwl N s Fifteenth nr Dolores

Rowe W. Maj. dwl 660 Howard

Rowe William, carpenter, dwl SW cor Hyde and O'Farrell

Rowe William B. *(Simmons, R. & Co.)* dwl 819 Filbert

Rowe William M. planer with James Brokaw, dwl N s Stevenson bet Sixth and Seventh

ROWELL CHARLES, physician, office 515 Kearny, dwl 522 Folsom

ROWELL ISAAC, president and professor chemistry, Medical Department University Pacific and physician and supervisor Third District, office and dwl 520 Kearny

Rowell John, gas fitter, dwl 1026 Montgomery

Rowell Joseph Rev. pastor Mariners' Church, Clarke nr East, dwl 1106 California

Rowell W. K. assistant, San Francisco Latin School, res Alameda Co

Rowen Sarah (widow) dwl 440 Jessie

Rowland Charles A. bricklayer, dwl 412 Bush

Rowland Henry, local policeman, dwl N s Barry Place nr Eighth

Rowland James, gardener, dwl 10 Louisa

Rowland Margaret T. Mrs. dress maker, dwl N s Barry Place nr Eighth

ROWLAND, *(Richard E.)* WALKER *(Andrew)* & CO. *(M. Klinkofstrom)* wholesale groceries and provisions, 505 Front and 647 Clay, dwl N s Lombard bet Mason and Taylor

Rowland R. W. harness making, 105 Sansom, dwl 133 Stevenson

Rowland William, contractor, dwl NE cor Valencia and Sixteenth

Rowlandson Thomas, mining and agricultural engineer, dwl W s Potrero Avenue nr Sixteenth

Rowley Charles M. *(Brunk & R.)* attorney at law, office 7 and 8 Armory Hall, dwl 537 Howard

Rowley R. G. law student with Tompkins & Crane, dwl 537 Howard

Rowley William H. book keeper with J. R. Stewart & Co. 417 Battery, dwl 2 Milton Place

ROXBURY HOUSE, James Curley proptr, 318 Pac

Roxbury G. & S. M. and Tunnell Co. office 308 Front

Roxbury Robert, marine surveyor, San Francisco Underwriters, office 308 Front, dwl 806 Bush

Roy David, carpenter, dwl 182 Jessie

Roy John, laborer, dwl Dolores Hall W s Valencia nr Sixteenth

Roy John A. *(N. H. Roy & Brother)* dwl San Bruno Road 3 miles from City Hall

ROY N. H. & BRO. *(John A. Roy)* milk ranch, San Bruno Road 3 miles from City Hall, depôt S s Mission nr Third

Roy Silvan, tailor, dwl 715 Vallejo

Roy W. F. dwl 314 Sutter

Royal Eagle Cliff G. & S. M. Co. office 423 Wash

ROYAL MAIL STEAM PACKET CO. via West Indies and Southampton, W. L. Booker agent, office 428 California

Royall J. P. book keeper with J. A. McClelland & Co. dwl NW cor First and Folsom

Royer A. C. physician, office and dwl 9 Geary

Royer B. F. engineer, dwl 1 Harlan Place

Royer Herman, machinist, Union Foundry, dwl 13 Dupont

Rraimers Margaret Mrs. domestic, NE cor Taylor and Greenwich

Ruaud A. physician, dwl 804 Jackson

RUBBER CLOTHING CO. (New York and Chicago) Joseph Fraser agent, manufacturers and wholesale dealers rubber clothing, druggists and stationery goods, 118 Montgomery

Rubin Mary Miss, domestic, SW cor Washington and Taylor

Ruby John, washing, N s Grove bet Laguna and Octavia

Ruby John H. actor, Maguire's Opera House, dwl 19 John

Ruckert Louis, with Gustave Leipnitz, dwl 107 Post

Ruckwardt Edward, cook, 424 Sacramento

Rudden John, tinsmith, bds 761 Mission

Ruddock Ellen Miss, domestic, 710 Folsom

Ruddock George, wood and coal, SW cor Sixth and Minna, dwl S s Minna bet Sixth and Seventh

Rudduck Catherine, domestic, 215 Sixth

Ruddy Fanny, laundress, Lick House

Ruddy Sarah, domestic, 1021 Battery

Rudel Charles, waiter, dwl SE corner Market and Stewart

Rudgens R. broker, dwl SW cor Dupont and Bdwy

Rudman Edwin, salesman, Pier 14 Stewart, dwl 521 Folsom

Rudman John *(Coffin & R.)* dwl 521 Folsom

Rudock John, miner, dwl Bartol nr Vallejo

Rudolf John, with Andrew Kohler, 424 Sansom, dwl NW cor Sacramento and Stockton

Rudolph Adam, cooper with Timothy Lynch, 219 Washington, dwl 222 Sutter

Rudolph Edward, jeweler with Lemme Brothers, dwl 216 Pacific

Rudolph Jacob, deputy superintendent streets, dwl W s Larkin bet Union and Filbert

Rudolph L. proprietor St. Lawrence House, 615 and 617 Market

Rudolph Lémuel, hackman, NW cor Washington and Mason

Rudolph William, gunsmith, dwl 216 Pacific

Rudolphi Herman, brewer, Philadelphia Brewery

Ruef Meyer, fancy goods, 1341 Dupont

Ruehl Charles, editor California Chronik, office NW cor Kearny and Sacramento, dwl 621 California

Ruen Richard, wool worker, Broadway Wool Depôt, dwl 414 Market

Ruep Simon, workman with J. H. C. Portmann

Ruet Frederick, machinist, Pacific Foundry, dwl Harlan Place

Ruez Adam, cabinet maker, dwl 33 Ritch

Rufener Susette, dress maker, 213 Fourth

Ruffier Henry, with J. W. Brittan & Co. dwl 621 Union

Ruffine François, W s Dolores bet Fifteenth and Sixteenth

Ruffley John, dwl 707 Mission

Ruffley Thomas E. hay dealer, 707 Mission

Ruffner James, plasterer, dwl S s Minna bet Second and Third

Rugen Henry, Golden Gate House, North Beach & Fort Point Road cor Fillmore

Ruggles Arvilla Miss, furnished rooms, 2 Hardie Pl

Ruggles David S. laborer, dwl 414 Folsom

Ruggles D. W. (col'd) stove dealer, 310 Jackson, dwl NE cor Mason and Broadway

Ruggles George, milkman with J. W. Cudworth

Ruh Anthony *(Christian, Wahl & Co.)* dwl 415 Bush

Ruiz Franquilino, dwl 1435 Taylor

Ruiz Macedonia, tailor, dwl S s Dupont Alley

Ruje Antonio, porter with B. Davidson & Berri

Rule John W. clerk, dwl 29 Minna

Rulo Louis L. driver with A. Lusk & Co. dwl 34 Silver

Rulofson William H. *(Bradley & R.)* dwl 1020 Washington

Rulofson William H. jr. clerk with Bradley & Rulofson, dwl 1020 Washington

Rume Joseph, blacksmith, S. F. & P. Sugar Co. dwl S s Boyd nr Chesley

Rumley Catherine, domestic, 727 O'Farrell

Rummelin George P. furrier with Adolph Muller, dwl E s Harrison Avenue nr Folsom

Rumsley William (col'd) laborer, dwl 1004 Jackson

Rumsplager Clemence, cook, bds Meyer's Hotel, 814 Montgomery

Rundell William M. *(Jones & Bendixen)* dwl 109 St. Mark Place

Rundle Richard T. *(Turner & R.)* dwl cor Salano and Kentucky

Runge Frederick, groceries and liquors, NW cor Kearny and Green

Runk Lewis W. drayman, 414 Front, dwl 1317 Jackson

Runkle Richard, groom, Wilson's Circus

Runnels H. (colored) chimney sweep, 364 Third

Runstedt Charles, cabinet maker, dwl 833 Pacific

Rupp Lizzie Miss, domestic, 716 Post

Ruppe Michael, cook, Phil's Exchange, dwl Grove bet Laguna and Octavia

Ruppel Charles, watch maker with Herman Wenzel, 303 Montgomery

Ruppelius William, watch maker with William Nolte, 103½ Montgomery, dwl 735 Pine

Ruppental J. C. cooperage, 508 Davis

Rusack William, picture frame maker, dwl 114 Kearny

Rusar Frederic, carpenter, dwl W s Folsom near Twenty-Third

Rusar John T. carpenter, dwl W s Folsom near Twenty-Third

Rusar Mary (widow) dwl W s Folsom nr Twenty-Third

Ruseck William, shoe maker, dwl Kearny bet Sutter and Post

Rush Edward H. driver, Omnibus R. R. Co. dwl 215 Tehama

Rush Hugh, compositor, American Flag, dwl 624 Commercial

Rush James, bar keeper, 226 Montgomery

Rush Michael, butcher, dwl N s Bernard bet Taylor and Jones

Rushmore Albert, contractor, office 316 Montgomery, dwl 312 Seventh

Ruskamp Henry, steward Independence Hook and Ladder Co. No. 3, dwl 28 Fourth

Russ Adolp G. dwl E s Columbia bet Harrison and Folsom

Russ Augustus P. dwl NW cor Sixth and Harrison

Russ Christiana (widow) dwl NW cor Sixth and Harrison

Russ George H. carpenter, dwl 762 Folsom

Russ Henry, real estate, dwl E s Columbia bet Folsom and Harrison

Russ Henry B. with C. F. Mebius, dwl 28 Belden Block

RUSS HOUSE, H. H. Pearson & Co. proprietors, W s Montgomery bet Pine and Bush

Russ J. A. *(Jackson & R.)* dwl 408 Beale

Russ Joseph, carpenter, dwl W s Kearny bet Bush and Sutter

Russ Joachim, dwl 219 Kearny

Ruseack William, shoe maker, dwl 116 Kearny

RUSSELL & ERWIN MANUFACTURING CO. (hardware) Joseph W. Stow agent, 106 and 108 Battery

Russell Adelia, chambermaid, Lick House

Russell Alfred, dwl 629 Clay

Russell Andrew, machinist, Union Foundry, dwl 17 Natoma

Russell Anna A. (widow) dwl 125 St. Mark Place

Russell Charles F. clerk, 305 California, dwl 545 Howard

Russell David, carrier, Daily Examiner, dwl 17 Natoma

Russell Edward, porter with Dodge & Phillips, dwl E s O'Farrell Alley

Russell Ellen Miss, dress maker, dwl 17 Natoma

Russell George, clerk, 616 Sacramento

Russell George, liquor saloon, SE cor Jackson and Battery, dwl 1027 Washington

Russell George H. deputy county recorder, office SE cor Wash and Kearny, dwl 1008 Powell

Russell George T. printer with Francis, Valentine & Co

Russell George W. butcher, dwl 921 Post

Russell Henry P. ranch, dwl NW cor Stockton and Pacific

Russell Horatio H. salesman with R. A. Swain & Co. dwl 1516 Mason

Russell Isidor W. carpenter, dwl S s Market bet Sixth and Seventh, rear

Russell James, stevedore, dwl 1332 Pacific

Russell J. F. painter, dwl 11 Stockton Place

RUSSELL *(J. M.)* & CO. *(C. T. Forrest)* proprietors United States Restaurant, 507 and 509 Clay, dwl 327 Minna

Russell John, laborer, dwl E s Bryant bet First and Fremont

Russell John, meat market, NE cor Vallejo and Montgomery, dwl 5 Oregon

Russell John A. stevedore, dwl 3 Telegraph Place

Russell John B. *(Bosworth & R.)* dwl 1018 Clay

Russell *(John B.)* & Bouton *(Francis G.)* fruits and poultry, 38 and 39 Occidental Market, dwl Sixth nr Folsom

Russell Joseph G. northern coast messenger Wells, Fargo & Co. dwl 629 Clay

Russell M. dwl SE cor Mission and First

Russell Mary (widow) dwl with J. P. Hawkins E s Mission bet Twenty-Fifth and Twenty-Sixth

Russell Mary B. superior St. Mary's Hospital

Russell Michael, seaman, dwl 29 Ecker

Russell Monson, foreman with James Brokaw, dwl 133 Tehama

Russell Norman, assistant with James Brokaw, dwl First St. House

Russell Onomas L. carpenter, dwl S s Market bet Sixth and Seventh, rear

Russell Thomas S. book keeper with R. A. Swain & Co. dwl 1516 Mason

Russell Thomas S. dealer hair oil, dwl Tremont H

Russell William W. dwl 416 Bryant

Russelman F. captain schooner Sneezer, dwl 140 Stewart

Russen John M. fruit, 123 Fourth

Russi Louis, milker, dwl 315 Bush

RUSSIAN AMERICAN COMMERCIAL CO. office SE cor Battery and Broadway

Russo Joseph, molder, Golden State Iron Works, dwl 160 Jessie

Rust Henry, driver, dwl 115 Jessie

Rutenberg John H. office 220 Battery, dwl 1313 Stockton

Rutger Joseph, cook, dwl 624 Commercial

Ruthardt Victor *(Schwergerle & Co.)* dwl 411 Post

Rutherford A. J. captain schooner Arizona, dwl 254 Fourth

Rutherford Andrew, boiler maker, Vulcan Iron Works, dwl 62 Shipley

Rutherford *(Andrew H.)* & Clifford *(Thomas C.)* teamsters, 430 Pine, dwl 712 O'Farrell

Rutherford David, car builder, S. F. & San José R. R. Co. dwl 16 Natoma

Rutherford *(Frank A.)* & Hathaway *(Abraham N.)* painters, N s Sixteenth bet Mission and Valencia, dwl W s Howard bet Eighteenth and Nineteenth

Rutherford Joseph W. packer, Golden Gate Mills, dwl 406 Post

Rutherford Thomas, City Market, 117 Fourth, dwl 302 O'Farrell

Rutherford Thomas, receiver, Spring Valley W. W. Co. dwl 514 Bush

Rutherford Thomas L. *(Grosh & R.)* dwl 810 Wash

Rutherford William, laborer, dwl 269 Stevenson

Ruthrauff Alonzo T. book keeper with William Shew, dwl E s Garden nr Bryant

Ruthrauff Lizzie M. Miss, dwl 6 Sansom

Rutledge Mary Mrs. lodgings, dwl 518 Pacific

Rutman John, tinsmith, dwl 425 Pine

Rutmann Isaac, market wagon, dwl 8 Sonoma Pl

Ruttenberg Hermann, dwl 1313 Stockton

Ruttle David, conductor, Central R. R. Co. dwl 160 Shipley

Ryan Agnes Miss, dress maker, dwl 71 Minna

Ryan Andrew F. bar keeper with Cahill & McElroy, cor Bush and Kearny

Ryan Anthony, plumber with Lane & Gordon, dwl 719 Howard

Ryan Bridget Miss, domestic, 12 Quincy

Ryan Catherine Miss, dress maker, SW cor Third and Stevenson

Ryan Charles, express wagon, cor Sac and Market, dwl N s Twelfth bet Howard and Folsom

Ryan Charles, lamplighter, S. F. Gas Co

Ryan Cornelius, laborer with Hey & Meyn, dwl E s Chesley nr Harrison

Ryan Daniel, porter, dwl 114 William

Ryan Daniel, wood chopper, dwl W s Castro near Fourteenth

Ryan Daniel L. shoe maker, 536 Commercial

Ryan Dennis *(Kene & R.)* dwl 123 Silver

Ryan Dennis, blacksmith with Belduke & Co. dwl 123 Silver

Ryan Dennis, currier with W. H. Warren, dwl Folsom bet Eighteenth and Nineteenth

Ryan Dennis, laborer, dwl 11 Bay State Row

Ryan Edward, laborer with Hey & Meyn

Ryan Edward, laborer with B. Bonnet & Co

Ryan Edward, teamster, dwl Dora bet Harrison and Folsom

Ryan Edward W. carpenter, dwl 11 Berry

Ryan George, boiler maker, Pacific Foundry, dwl S s Stevenson nr Fourth

Ryan Hannah Miss, domestic. 13 Post

Ryan Hannah Miss, furnished rooms, 1016 Stockton

Ryan James, dwl 16 Taylor

Ryan James, apprentice, Pacific Foundry

Ryan James, cartman, cor Market and Kearny

Ryan James, clerk, Washington Hose Co. No. 1

Ryan James, driver, bds Cambridge House 304 Pac

Ryan James, groceries and liquors, SW cor Hyde and Pacific

Ryan James, horseshoer with Patrick Brannan, dwl cor Stevenson and Ecker

Ryan James, laborer, Spring Valley W. W

Ryan James, laborer, dwl 12 Anthony

Ryan James, laborer, dwl W s First Av nr Fifteenth

Ryan James, spinner, S. F. P. Woolen Mills, dwl cor Francisco and Van Ness Avenue

Ryan James E. book keeper, 13 Washington Market, dwl 1217 Washington

Ryan James K. clerk with Ryan & Waterman, dwl 1226 Pacific

Ryan James M. miner, bds Franklin Hotel, SE cor Sansom and Pacific

Ryan James N. architect, dwl 1 White Place

Ryan J. D. dwl 71 Clementina

Ryan John *(Taaffe & Co.)* dwl Russ House

Ryan John, dwl 910 Pine

Ryan John, bricklayer, Volunteer Engine Co. No. 7

Ryan John, butcher with Mrs. M. O'Brian, dwl 1217 Washington

Ryan John, door keeper, Maguire's Opera House

Ryan John, hackman, dwl 1808 Powell

Ryan John, job wagon, dwl W s Jansen bet Greenwich and Lombard

Ryan John, laborer, dwl 33 Frederick

Ryan John, liquor saloon, 228 Commercial

Ryan John, stair builder with N. P. Langland, dwl NE cor Mission and Jane

Ryan John, tanner with Davis & Sedgley, dwl Mission Creek nr Sixteenth

Ryan John B. harness maker with Main & Winchester, dwl 417 Stockton

Ryan John P. dwl 24 Sansom

Ryan Kate Miss, dwl 74 Tehama

Ryan Katie Miss, domestic, 530 Vallejo

Ryan Lawrence, book keeper with Levi Keller, dwl 3 Calhoun

Ryan Lawrence M. book keeper with Conroy & O'Connor, dwl W s Leav bet Wash and Clay
Ryan Margaret Miss, domestic, 757 Howard
Ryan Margaret Miss, domestic with Joseph H. Atkinson
Ryan Margaret (widow) dwl 403 Geary
Ryan Martin, express wagon, dwl W s Jansen bet Greenwich and Lombard
Ryan Mary, chambermaid, Occidental Hotel
Ryan Mary Miss, domestic, 518 Third
Ryan Mary Miss, domestic, 727 Vallejo
Ryan Mary Miss, dress maker, 71 Minna
Ryan Mary Miss, seamstress, dwl 2 Green
Ryan Mary (widow) dwl Higgins Place
Ryan Mary (widow) dwl W s Jansen nr Greenwich
Ryan Mary Ann Miss, domestic, S s Pine bet Mason and Taylor
Ryan Michael, bar keeper, 530 Sac, dwl 1248 Sac
Ryan Michael, bill poster with Way & Keyt, dwl 412 Vallejo
Ryan Michael, cartman, W s Jansen nr Greenwich
Ryan Michael, conductor, Omnibus R. R. Co. dwl 719 Howard
Ryan Michael, door keeper, Maguire's Opera House
Ryan Michael, fireman, steamer Chrysopolis
Ryan Michael, fireman, steamer Contra Costa
Ryan Michael, hostler, 317 Pine
Ryan Michael, laborer, dwl 234 Fourth
Ryan Michael, laborer, dwl Atlantic House 210 Pac
Ryan Michael, laborer, dwl 412 Vallejo, rear
Ryan Michael, stone cutter, dwl 12 Sutter
Ryan Nora Miss, domestic, 1017 Bush
Ryan *(P.)* & Waterman *(Joseph)* produce commission, 111 Clay, dwl 1226 Pacific
Ryan Patrick, carpenter, dwl 840 Market
Ryan Patrick, carriage painter with Albert Folsom, dwl N s Vallejo bet Montgomery and Sansom
Ryan Patrick T. plasterer, dwl with Andrew Turner E s Eleventh nr Mission
Ryan Peter A. book keeper, dwl 313 Tehama
Ryan Peter N. books and stationery, 54 Fourth
RYAN R. F. attorney at law, office 34 and 35 Exchange Building
Ryan Rosa Miss, domestic, 1013 Pine
Ryan Thomas, boot maker, 505 Kearny
Ryan Thomas, groceries and liquors, 21 Hinckley
Ryan Thomas, hackman, Plaza, dwl 1016 Stockton
Ryan Thomas, laborer with William Buckley
Ryan Thomas, laborer, dwl NE cor Broadway and Van Ness Avenue
Ryan Thomas, laborer, Fort Point, dwl Pacific nr Devisidero
Ryan Thomas, proprietor Continental House, 519 Mission
Ryan Thomas, shoe maker, dwl 12 St. Mark Place
Ryan Timothy, clerk Adjutant General's Department, dwl 214 Prospect Place
Ryan Timothy, hackman, Plaza, dwl 30 Clara, rear
Ryan Timothy, waiter, stm Constitution, dwl NE cor Folsom and Fourth
Ryan Timothy, wool puller, dwl 23 Natoma
Ryan Ursula (widow) dwl cor Wash and Octavia
Ryan *(William)* & Purcell *(Michael)* liquor saloon, 714 Market, dwl 21 Ann
Ryan William, coal oil peddler, dwl 129 Clara, rear
Ryan William, fireman, dwl N s Oregon nr Front
Ryan William, laborer, Fort Point
Ryan William, laborer with Conroy & Tobin
Ryan William, laborer, dwl 21 Everett
Ryan William, miner, dwl 122 Minna
Ryan William J. boiler maker, dwl Manhattan Engine House
Ryan William P. *(Rankin & R.)* SE cor Tehama and Sixth
Ryberg Charles G. dwl International Hotel
RYCKMAN G. W. real estate, office 15 Montgomery Block, dwl 1913 Stockton
Ryckman William, dwl 1314 Powell

Ryder C. B. wines and liquors, 412 Jackson
Ryder Charles, clerk, dwl 226 Sansom
Ryder Charles C. cooper with Timothy Lynch, dwl 140 Minna
Ryder Charles H. laborer, C. H. dwl 226 Sansom
Ryder Daniel S. bookbinder with Buswell & Co. dwl 106 Sixth
Ryder George W. *(Brennan & R.)* dwl 10 John nr Powell
Ryder J. C. foreman Shoe Department Industrial School, Old Ocean House Road
Ryder Joseph N. Poydras Market, 709 Pacific, dwl 716 Pacific
Ryder Margaret, domestic, Franklin Hotel cor Sansom and Pacific
Ryder William G. treasurer Olympic, dwl John nr Powell
Ryer W. F. S. miner, dwl 632 Market
Ryland Richard, bricklayer, Volunteer Engine Co. No. 7
Rynn Daniel, driver with Louis Jaffe, 133 Sutter
Ryno Marcus L. with Healy, Carleton & Co. dwl 9 Sherwood Place

S

SAALBURG *(Siegfried)* & Brodek *(Samuel)* hairdressing saloon, 107 Kearny, dwl 608 Powell
Saalburg William, business agent Hebrew Observer, office 511 Sacramento, dwl 263 Stevenson
Saany Elizabeth (widow) dwl 260 Stevenson
Saba John, merchant tailor, dwl 323 Pine
Sabash Antoine, waiter, NW cor Stewart and Mission
SABATIE A. E. & CO. *(Philip G. Sabatie and Henry Maubec)* importers and jobbers groceries, provisions, and liquors, 617 and 619 Sansom, dwl N s Burritt bet Stockton and Powell
Sabatie Philip G. *(A. E. Sabatie & Co.)* dwl 716 O'Farrell
Sabine John, carpenter, dwl 430 Brannan
SABINS A. C. shipping and commission merchant, 209 Sacramento, dwl 516 Green
Sablich John, fruits, NE cor Stockton and Wash
Sabordie Jean B. carver, dwl 1432 Stockton, rear
Sachs John, dwl 541 California
SACHS L. & M. & CO. *(William Heller)* importers and jobbers dry goods, Yankee Notions, etc. 312 and 314 California, dwl 308 Stockton
Sachs Martin *(L. & M. Sachs & Co.)* dwl 306 Stockton
Sachs Rebecca Mrs. fruits, 541 California
Sachs Samuel, salesman, 516 Sac, dwl 508 Sutter
SACK JOHN C. optician and mathematical instrument maker, 203 Montgomery (Russ Block) dwl 507 Bush
Sackett C. C. Mrs. furnished rooms, NE cor Montgomery and Pacific
Sackett Frederick A. book keeper with Church & Clark, dwl 619 Bush
Sackmann Frederick, sheet iron worker, Union Foundry, dwl 1006 Folsom
Sacramento & Meredith M. Co. office 1 Court Block
Sacramento Hotel, M. Hoffman proprietor, 407 Pac
SACRAMENTO LINE PACKETS, Frederick P. Green agent, office NW cor Sac and Front
SACRAMENTO LINE PACKETS, Jonathan Williams agent, office 413 East
SACRAMENTO LINE STEAMERS, California Steam Navigation Co. Broadway Wharf, office NE cor Front and Jackson
SACRAMENTO VALLEY R. R. office 734 Mont
Saddlemire David J. house carpenter, dwl 1008 Jackson
Saddler Daniel, dwl SE cor Sacramento and Davis
Saenger Leopold, dress maker, 415 Bush
Saenger Louis, dress maker, 415 Bush
Saes Mary Mrs. furnished rooms, 716 Dupont
Safford Henry F. clerk, dwl 523 Bush, rear

Safford J. R. waterman, 609 Market
SAGE LEWIS P. proptr Cowell's Warehouse and Wharf, NE cor Battery and Union, dwl S side Presidio Road nr Presidio House
Sage Robert M. book keeper, Alta California, 536 Sacramento
Sagehorn Charles. butcher, dwl 323 Kearny
SAGEHORN HERMAN, groceries and liquors, 520 Union
Sagord James, seaman, dwl 44 Sacramento
Sahling Theodore, porter with R. H. McDonald & Co. dwl 1 Milton Place
Sahlmann Carsten, liquor saloon, 2208 Powell
SAHNKE (Hermann G.) & McCUNE (John B.) groceries and liquors, SW cor Howard and Sumner
SAILORS' HOME, SW cor Battery and Vallejo
Saint Cyr Victor, clerk, dwl 1204 Dupont
Saint Jean Baptiste Society (Canadian Institute) office 585 Market
Saint John, French laundry, dwl 1751 Powell
Saip Edward, meat market, Union Court nr Kearny
Sajous J. wholesale and retail wines and liquors, NW cor Post and Dupont
Sala August, with François Lermitte, 526 Clay
Sala Joseph, mathematical instrument maker with John Roach, dwl 9 Stockton
Salaman Aaron, watch maker, 15 Fourth
Salambo Copper M. Co. office 804 Montgomery
Salamin Lemuel, lab, dwl Spring Valley House, rear
Salander Frederick, fireman, dwl NE cor Sacramento and Davis
Salari Germimus, fruit dealer, dwl 1314 Dupont
Salas Librado, dwl 1009 Jackson
Salasar Domingo, porter, 612 Sacramento, dwl Pacific bet Dupont and Kearny
Salberg M. gents' furnishing goods, 530 Jackson, bds International Hotel
Salenger F. baker, Cosmopolitan Hotel
Salgado John. porter, Empire State Restaurant
Salinger William, salesman, 504 Commercial, dwl 426 Kearny
Salisbury Guy, compositor, Youth's Companion, dwl 116 Dupont
Salisbury Mary A. Miss, assistant, Post St. Primary School, dwl cor Minna and Second
Salisbury William, glass blower, Pacific Glass Works, dwl W s Tennessee nr Mariposa
Saulisbury, see Saulsburry
Sall Henry, butcher, dwl Pacific Exchange
Sallerreuw Julien, cook, St. Francis Restaurant, dwl SW cor Dupont and Vallejo
Salmon Adolph, foreman with G. Venard, 625 Front
Salmon Eleanora (widow) dwl 310 Stockton
SALMON J. & W. C. mining machinists and amalgamators, S. F. Iron Works, NE cor Mission and Fremont
Salmon James, engineer, dwl 259 Jessie
Salmon John C. porter with Goodwin & Co. dwl N s Lombard bet Larkin and Polk
Salmon John F. machinist, S. F. Iron Works, dwl 609 Pine
Salmon Nicholas, teamster, dwl 233 Beale
Salmon Peter (Chiousse & S.) dwl E side Lagoon
Salmon W. C. (J. & W. C. S.) dwl 609 Pine
Salna Edouard & Co. garden, Presidio Road corner Union
Salna Fidele, garden, cor Vallejo, Presidio Road
Salomon A. (widow) fortune teller, dwl 417 Kearny
Salomon George, boatman, dwl 510 Howard
Salomon J. groceries and liquors, SW cor Hyde and O'Farrell
Salomon (L. G.) & Co. (L. J. F. Moigneu and F. P. Masson) steam candy manufactory, 211 Sutter, dwl 17 Dupont
Salomon Reuben, salesman, 20 Montgomery
Salomon S. boots and shoes, 1412 Stockton
Salomon Sylvain, salesman with Lazard Freres, 115 Battery

Salomons F. P. (Heynemann & Co.) dwl 807 Pac
Salter Charles, cook with J. W. Cudworth
Salter J. W. foreman with Francis Cassin, dwl 24 Sansom
Saltsien Herman, engineer, S. F. P. Woolen Mills, dwl cor North Point and Van Ness Avenue
Salvatore Ghisla, tinsmith, dwl W s Pacific Alley
Sam Kee (Chinese) dealer teas, 723 Sacramento
Sam Lee (Chinese) washing, 144 Fourth
Sam Lee Yon (Chinese) garden, NW cor Brannan and Eighth
Sam Lung (Chinese) washing, 1406 Stockton
Sam Sing (Chinese) garden, S s Brannan bet Seventh and Eighth
Sam Sing (Chinese) garden, S s Sixteenth nr Rhode Island
Sam Sing (Chinese) washing, 122 Pacific
Sam Son (Chinese) washing, 617 California
Samblanet François, liquor saloon, 718 Stockton
Samengo (Orazio) & Mazzoni (Lewis) liquor saloon, E s Drumm bet Clay and Washington
Sammis Almena (widow) dwl NE cor Valencia and Sixteenth
Sammis Edson, upholsterer with John C. Bell, dwl 18 Dupont
Sammis Julia (widow) dwl with Levi Burr
Sample Samuel S. clerk, 718 Mont, dwl 10 Central Pl
Sampson Eliza A. Mrs. domestic, 1411 Stockton
Sampson Frederick W. book keeper with J. C. Merrill, dwl W s Guerrero bet Sixteenth and Seventeenth
Sampson Henry, stevedere, dwl 514 Green
Sampson Henry F. porter, U. S. Branch Mint, dwl NE cor Mason and John
Sampson James (col'd) laborer, dwl S s Bernard bet Taylor and Jones
Sampson John, blacksmith with Charles Steinweg, dwl Hubbard nr Howard
Sampson John (col'd) express wagon, cor Washington and Battery, dwl 24 John
Sampson John A. watchman, U. S. Quartermaster's Department, dwl SW cor Post and Taylor
Sampson Leon, driver, dwl 6 Jasper Place
Sampson Rosalia Miss, teacher German, City Female Seminary
Samson Antonio B. dwl 1126 Pine
Samuel Henry, physician, dwl 906 Stockton
Samuel Joseph, with Samuel Bros. dwl 1510 Powell
Samuel Joseph, dress and cloak maker, 623 Mission
Samuel Louis, hat and cap maker, 1104 Dupont
Samuel Morris, expressman, cor Clay and Sansom, dwl W s Bower Place
Samuel Moses, boots and shoes, 926 Dupont, dwl Hall Court
Samuels Adolph, compositor, Abend Post, dwl 225 Post
Samuels Brothers (David and Samuel) dry goods, 119 and 121 Montgomery
Samuels John L. mining secretary, dwl 1114 Stock
Samuels Joseph, crockery, 110 Geary
Samuels Julius (Samuels Bros.) dwl 1015 Powell
San Bruno Turnpike Co. office 626 Clay
San Carlos Exploring & M. Co. office 404 Mont
SAN DIEGO STEAMSHIP LINE, C. S. Navigation Co. office NE cor Front and Jackson
San Francisco Cotton Mills, G. Falkenstein proprietor, N s King bet Third and Fourth
SAN FRANCISCO & ALAMEDA RAILROAD CO. office SW cor Sansom and Jackson
SAN FRANCISCO & ATLANTIC RAILROAD CO. office 405 Front
San Francisco & Castle Dome M. Co. office 326 Clay
SAN FRANCISCO & OAKLAND RAILROAD CO. office 535 Clay
SAN FRANCISCO & PACIFIC LEAD PIPE AND SHOT WORKS, Thomas H. Selby & Co. proprietors, SE cor Howard and First
SAN FRANCISCO & PACIFIC SUGAR CO. works cor Harrison and Eighth, office 310 Com

San Francisco and Point Lobos Road Co. office 6 Government House 502 Washington
San Francisco & San José Baggage Express, M. G. Kennedy proprietor, office 679 Market
SAN FRANCISCO & SAN JOSE RAILROAD CO. office SE cor Sansom and Halleck, H. M. Newhall president, depôt N side Brannan bet Third and Fourth
SAN FRANCISCO BENEVOLENT ASSOCIATION, office 410 Pine
SAN FRANCISCO BULLETIN CO. (J. W. Simonton, George K. Fitch, estate of James Nisbet, and estate of F. Tuthill) editors and proprietors Evening Bulletin daily, weekly, and steamer office 620 Mont, editorial rooms 517 Clay
SAN FRANCISCO BUSINESS DIRECTORY AND COMMERCIAL GUIDE, Henry G. Langley proprietor, office 612 Clay
SAN FRANCISCO CHEMICAL WORKS CO. (Egbert Judson & J. L. N. Shepard) NW cor Valencia and Fifteenth, office 327 Commercial
SAN FRANCISCO CORDAGE CO. Potrero, two miles SE Brannan St. Bridge, Tubbs & Co. office 613 Front
San Francisco Dredging Co. B. M. Hartshorne agent, office NE cor Front and Jackson
SAN FRANCISCO DRY DOCK CO. foot Second, H. B. Tichenor & Co. proprietors
San Francisco Female Seminary, Miss M. Butler principal, NE cor Jackson and Mason
San Francisco G. & S. M. Co. office 611 Clay
SAN FRANCISCO GAS CO. works First and Beale, Howard and Natoma, office NE cor First and Natoma
San Francisco Homestead Association, office 5 Government House, 502 Washington
SAN FRANCISCO INSURANCE CO. George C. Boardman president, office Donohoe, Kelly & Co.'s Building, SE cor Montgomery and Sac
SAN FRANCISCO LADIES' PROTECTION & RELIEF SOCIETY, Franklin, Post, and Geary
San Francisco Letter Express Co. office 316 Mont
San Francisco Macadamizing Co. office Market St. Wharf
San Francisco Machine & Iron Works Co. Devoe, Dinsmore & Co. proprietors, NE cor Mission and Fremont
SAN FRANCISCO MARKET ST. RAILROAD, depôt W s Valencia bet Fifteenth and Sixteenth office SE cor Montgomery and Jackson
SAN FRANCISCO MEDICAL JOURNAL (monthly) Henry Gibbons M.D. editor, office SW cor Clay and Sansom
SAN FRANCISCO NEWS LETTER and California Advertiser, Frederick Marriott editor and proprietor, office 528 Clay
SAN FRANCISCO OLYMPIC CLUB, rooms 35 Sutter bet Montgomery and Sansom
San Francisco Petroleum Co. (Humboldt) office 605 Montgomery
SAN FRANCISCO PIONEER WOOLEN FACTORY, Black Point bet Polk and Van Ness Avenue, Heynemann & Co. agents, office 311 and 313 California
SAN FRANCISCO SAVINGS UNION, office 529 California
SAN FRANCISCO STOCK AND EXCHANGE BOARD, Exchange Building, NW cor Montgomery and Washington
San Francisco Verein Club, rooms 534 Kearny
San José & Alviso Line Steamers, Bdwy Wharf
San José G. & S. M. Co. office 6 Montgomery Blk
San Leandro Line Packets, Clay St. Wharf
San Lorenzo Paper Mills, office 421 Clay
San Luis Rey G. & S. M. Co. office 338 Mont
San Marcial Silver M. Co. office 8 Stevenson House
San Mateo Line Packets, Central Wharf, foot Com
San Miguel Homestead Association, office 1 Government House

San Pablo Line Packets, Clay St. Wharf
San Rafael Line Packets, Clay St. Wharf
San Rafael Steamer, Vallejo St. Wharf
Sanbelch Nicholas, waiter, NW cor Stewart and Mission
SANBORN (Joseph T.) & HARMON (James A.) produce commission, 404 and 406 Davis, dwl 408 Geary
Sanborn Nestor H. lumber surveyor, dwl 416 Bryant
Sanborn O. A. miner, dwl 829 Clay
SANBORN T. C. & CO. stock and exchange brokers, office 613 Mont, dwl 828 Sacramento
Sanches Angel, dwl W s Margaret Place
Sanchez Louisa (widow) dwl N s Sixteenth bet Guerrero and Dolores
Sanchez Pedro, dwl N s Sixteenth bet Guerrero and Dolores
Sanchez Randolph, carpenter, dwl 13 Ellis
Sanchez Theodora (widow) dwl N s Sixteenth bet Guerrero and Dolores
Sand Ferdinand (Sand Bros.) dwl 272 Jessie
Sand Brothers (Joseph and Ferdinand) baths and hairdressing saloon, 50 Fourth, dwl 268 Jessie
Sand Max, truss maker, dwl SW cor Green and Powell
Sandberg Axel, seaman, dwl 20 Commercial
Sandborn Frank, teamster with S. Higgins, dwl 1051 Howard
Sandelin Beda Miss, dwl with C. I. Janson, W s Mission bet Twentieth and Twenty-First
Sander Jacob, fruit, W s Sixth bet Folsom and Harrison
Sander Peter, fruit, 116 Fourth
Sander Robert, druggist, NW cor Mission and Third
Sanders (Amos A.) & Bushman (William) dancing academy, NE cor Fourth and Jessie
Sanders A. N. waterman, 609 Market
Sanders H. E. fruit, 31 Third
Sanders Henry S. drug clerk, 330 Montgomery, dwl 226 Stevenson
Sanders Honora J. J. lodgings, 577 Howard
Sanders John P. proprietor Sanders' Hotel, 26 Sac
Sanders P. express wagon, 116 Fourth
Sanders Stephen P. photographer, dwl E s First Avenue bet Fourteenth and Fifteenth
Sanderson A. Mrs. dwl 540 Bryant
Sanderson Annie, domestic, 841 Howard
Sanderson Edward H. dwl E s Howard bet Fifteenth and Sixteenth
Sanderson E. L. clerk with Hayward & Coleman, dwl 12 Ellis
Sanderson Frederick W. clerk, 43 Occidental Market, dwl 540 Bryant
Sanderson George F. wharfinger, East St. Wharf, dwl 19 Clementina
Sanderson George H. (Weaver, Wooster & Co.) dwl W s Fremont bet Folsom and Harrison
Sanderson Henry M. machinist with E. T. Steen, dwl 58 Minna
Sanderson J. B. principal Fifth St. Colored School, dwl NE cor Sacramento and Yerba Buena
Sanderson John, dwl 902 Clay
Sanderson John H. family groceries, 23 Third, dwl 517 Tehama
Sanderson L. A. book keeper with Dickinson & Gammans, dwl 1325 Powell
Sanderson Lizzie Miss, dwl 638 Howard
Sanderson Robert, dwl 1325 Powell
Sanderson Samuel A. (Callahan & S.) dwl 1911 Howard
Sanderson Thomas, night watchman, dwl 726 Howard
Sandford William F. cabinet maker, dwl 777 Market
Sandine William, seaman, dwl 26 Sacramento
Sandison John A. gold beater with John F. Furley, dwl 367 Howard
Sando Antonio, with Joseph Silva, dwl nr Laguna de la Merced

Sandoval Andres, bakery, 527 Broadway
Sands Anna M. teacher, Private School, 903 Post
Sands Antonio, rigger, dwl 225 Beale
Sands Samuel G. merchant, office 120 California, dwl 903 Post
Sands Thomas, dwl 223 Stevenson
Sandstrom John, blacksmith, Golden State Iron Works, dwl NE cor Minna and Second
Sandtmann Augusta Miss, domestic, 1213 Mason
Sane Nicholas, hostler, 16 Sutter, dwl 34 Webb
Sanford A. J. cooper, dwl 116 Sansom
Sanford Henry L. salesman, 223 Montgomery
Sanford J. L. commission merchant, office 310 Washington, dwl NW cor Mary and Natoma
Sanford J. S. watchman, Custom House
Sanford T. G. & Co. estate of, clothing, 223 Mont
Sanford William, plasterer, dwl 8 Virginia Place
SANGER CHARLES W. secretary Western Pacific Railroad Company, office 409 Cal, dwl 1002 Pine
Sanger Nelson, carriage painter with Thomas Stackpole, 113 Bush
Sanguenetti A. peddler, dwl Washington bet Powell and Mason
Sanguenetti Schumann, fisherman, dwl NE cor Clay and Drum
Sanguinetti Domingo, deck hand, stmr Josie McNear
Sangninetti Joseph, wood dealer, S s Brannan foot Eighth
Sanguinetti Simone, fisherman, 40 Italian Fish Mkt
Sanjurjo, (Francisco) Bolado (Joaquin) & Pujol (Domingo) commission merchants and importers cigars, 713 Sansom
Sankey Charles A. (Fraser & Co.) dwl 16 Sansom
Sankey James, painter, dwl 16 Sansom
Sansman A. R. clerk, Empire Lodgings, 636 Com
Sansom Thomas, clerk, Mount Hood House, 54 Sac
Sansot Francis, shoe maker, 549 Merchant, dwl Morey Alley
Sansuparie Antoine, sawyer, dwl Meeks Place
Santa Anna Petroleum Co. (Los Angeles) office 702 Washington
SANTA BARBARA, SAN PEDRO, AND SAN LUIS OBISPO LINE STEAMERS, California Steam Navigation Company, office NE cor Front and Jackson
Santa Clara G. & S. M. Co. office 338 Montgomery
Santa Cruz Line Packets, office NE cor Front and Washington
Santa Cruz Petroleum Oil Works Co. off 415 Mont
Santa Cruz S. M. Co. (Lower California) office 652 Washington
SANTA CRUZ TANNING COMPANY, A. D. Ing & Co. agents, 312 Commercial
Santa Rita G. & S. M. Co. office room 1 Government House 502 Washington
Santa Rosa G. & S. M. Co. office 1 Government House 502 Washington
Santiago M. Co. office 804 Montgomery
Santif Joseph (Santif & Brother) dwl SW cor Howard and Fifth
Santif (Nicholas) & Brother (Joseph Santif) groceries and liquors, SW cor Howard and Fifth
Santini Catharine (widow) dwl 826 Broadway
Santry Daniel, harness maker with John O'Kane, dwl Clementina nr Fifth
Santry Michael, laborer, dwl N s Stevenson bet Sixth and Seventh
Sauty Andrew, laborer, dwl 8 s Hayes nr Franklin
Sanvers Henry, stock broker, dwl 226 Stevenson
Sapelle L. clerk with P. Fridach, dwl 619 Davis
Sapin Charles G. clerk with Charles Roturier, dwl Gautier's House 516 Pacific
Saratoga Petroleum Co. (Colusa) office 302 Mont
Sargent August, laborer, dwl Hodges Place
Sargent Bailey, real estate, dwl 1019 Washington
Sargent Edward O. painter, dwl SW cor Clay and Dupont
SARGENT JOHN W. proprietor American Exchange Hotel, 323-327 Sansom cor Halleck

Sargent T. E. dwl What Cheer House
Sargent Timothy, dwl 1606 Taylor nr Broadway
Sarle Benonia, millwright, Miners' Foundry, dwl 128 Fourth
Sarles W. H. accountant with A. C. Dietz & Co. 519 Front
Sarowski Frederick, watchman, steamer Julia
Sarrail Bernard, farmer, Hunter's Point
Sarraut Emile, éook, dwl 825 Dupont
Sarrfeldt Charles, tanner with S. Bloom, S s Brannan nr Sixth
Sarsfield Cornelius, painter, dwl 345 Tehama
Sarsfield Michael, tailor, 816 Montgomery, dwl 5 Stockton Place
Sarthon Jean, works with Arguelas Bernal
Sassenberg Charles, fresco painter, dwl 263 Jessie
Sassman Isabella Mrs. dwl 53 Sacramento
Satchwell John, cooper with Lyon & Co. dwl 159 Jessie
SATHER (Peder) & CO. bankers, NE cor Montgomery and Commercial, dwl 346 Second
Satterlee Helen Miss, assistant, Montgomery Street School, dwl 714 Pine
SATTERLEE JOHN. attorney at law, office 45 Mont Block, dwl NW cor Howard and Twelfth
Satterlee William, cook, Market St. Restaurant, dwl 619 Market
Satterlee William, door keeper, U. S. Branch Mint, dwl 714 Pine
Satterlee William R. register clerk Twelfth District Court, dwl 714 Pine
Saucelito Water and Steam Tug Co. office 326 Clay
Saucelito Water Co. Charles Goodall agent, office SW cor Merchant and East
Saul Edmond (Black & S.) dwl 24 Geary
Saul James B. dwl N s Tehama nr Fifth
Sauley J. M. express wagon, cor Kearny and Vallejo
SAULMANN (August J.) & LAUENSTEIN (Frederick L.) coffee saloon, restaurant and confectionery, and agents Caviar and Westphalia hams, 506 Mont, dwl SE cor Post and Hyde
Saulnier John & Co. (Aristide Brand) importers French wines and liquors, 719 Sansom, res Bordeaux, France
Saulsbury Edmund J. local policeman, dwl 813 Washington
Saulsbury Mary A. Miss, teacher, dwl 220 Third
Saunders C. R. Mrs. actress, Maguire's Opera House
Saunders Cyrus G. dwl SE cor Sixteenth and Rhode Island
Saunders David, dwl 927 Bush
Saunders Duke, physician, off and dwl 1102 Dupont
Saunders Henry, third cook steamer Pacific
Saunders James D. dwl 927 Bush
SAUNDERS JOHN H. City and County Attorney, office 13 City Hall third floor, dwl 927 Bush
Saunders M. H. (widow) dwl 919 Jackson
Saunders Philip, miner, dwl 251 Clementina
Saunders William, compositor, Alta California, dwl 8 Virginia Place
Saunders William T. peddler, dwl 70 Jessie
Saunders, see Sanders
Sauvage Claude, employé, Metropolitan Restaurant, 715 Montgomery
Savage James, blacksmith with Nelson & Doble, dwl 110 Sutter, rear
Savage James D. upholsterer with Goodwin & Co. dwl NW cor Clay and Davis
Savage Robert W. blacksmith, dwl 1112 Kearny
SAVAGE S. M. CO. office 712 Montgomery
Save Placide, florist, 319 Bush
SAVINGS AND LOAN SOCIETY (bank) office 619 Clay, E. W. Burr president, C. W. Carmany secretary
Savio N., S.J. St. Ignatius College, S s Market bet Fourth and Fifth
Savory Benjamin L. produce, dwl Russ House
Sawin (George W.) & Bradley (Thomas W.) wood and coal, 608 Broadway, dwl 605 Bdwy

Sawtelle G. & S. M. Co. office 302 Montgomery
Sawtelle Henry A. Rev. pastor Second Baptist Church, dwl 463 Minna nr Fifth
SAWYER A. F. physician and surgeon, office and dwl 13 Post
Sawyer Charles, liquor saloon, dwl SW cor Dupont and Broadway
Sawyer Charles H. attorney at law with Haight & Pearson, dwl SW cor Stockton and Pacific ·
Sawyer Charlotte A. Mrs. teacher, Industrial School, Old Ocean House Road
Sawyer E. D. Judge Fourth District Court, room 14 City Hall third floor, chambers 16 third floor, dwl 819 Bush
Sawyer Ethan A. carpenter, dwl 510 Dupont
Sawyer George, billiards and liquors, American Exchange, 327 Sansom, dwl NW cor Dupont and Broadway
Sawyer Jesse L. painter, dwl 12 Louisa
Sawyer Leander, contractor, dwl 307 Minna
Sawyer Lewis F. ship carpenter, dwl 243 Fremont
Sawyer Lewis W. tinsmith with Locke & Montague, dwl 251 Clara
Sawyer M. G. registry clerk, Post Office, dwl SW cor Ritch and Clara
SAWYER OTIS V. notary public and commissioner deeds, SW cor Montgomery and Clay, dwl SW cor Sacramento and Hyde
Sawyer Philena Miss, assistant, Mission Grammar School, dwl 317 Minna
Sawyer Samuel, engineer, S. F. & San José R. R. Co. res San José
Sawyer Samuel T. lather, dwl 444 Minna
Sawyer Seward N. carpenter, dwl 111 Washington
Sawyer Simeon, pile driver, dwl E s Mission bet Nineteenth and Twentieth
Sawyer S. S. carpenter, dwl 111 Washington
Sawyer Thomas, dwl 935 Mission
Sawyer W. D. attorney at law, office 625 Merchant
Sawyer William M. salesman with John R. Crouse, dwl Central Place
Saxby I. T. dwl 712 Sutter
Saxon Allen, shoe maker, 8 Bay State Row
Saxton Thomas A. clerk with Voizin, Ris & Co. 219 Sansom, dwl N s Camp bet Second Avenue and Guerrero
Saxtorph Henry, janitor Scandinavian Society Rooms, 320 Sansom
Sayer Edward, seaman, dwl 255 Beale ·
Sayer George, waiter, Russ House, dwl 284 Minna
Sayer Reuben S. drayman with Charles Hare, dwl W s Nevada nr Folsom
Sayers Hugh, teamster, dwl S s Sacramento bet Powell and Mason
Sayers John, clerk, dwl S s Sacramento bet Powell and Mason
Sayre E. E. gas fitter, S. F. Gas Co
Sayre John H. secretary Baltimore American G. & S. M. Co. 33 Montgomery Block, dwl SW cor Market and Third
Sayres Agnes (col'd, widow) dwl 829 Vallejo
Sayres Benjamin S. painter, dwl S s Perry between Fourth and Fifth
Sayward John H. bar keeper, SW cor Mission and Sixteenth
Sayward W. T. shipping and real estate, dwl 1232 Stockton
Sazer Jonas L. clerk with Greenhood, Newbauer & Klein
Sbarboro Andrea (B. Sbarboro & Bro.) dwl 924 Stockton
SBARBORO B. & BROTHER (Andrea Sbarboro) wholesale dealers groceries, provisions, and liquors, 531 Washington
Sbarboro Jeremiah, salesman, 531 Washington, dwl 531 Washington
Sbarboro John, fruit peddler, dwl 1506 Dupont
SBARBORO JOHN B. groceries and liquors, SW cor Folsom and Fifth

Sbarboro Joseph, oysters, 610 Clay
Sbizza Giacomo & Co. fishermen, 34 and 35 Italian Fish Market
Scales Amanda M. (widow) dwl E s Larkin nr Mission
Scalmanini (Carlo) & Frapolli (Batista) importers groceries, liquors, etc. 424 Front, dwl S s Filbert bet Taylor and Jones
Scammon C. M. Capt. dwl 409 Folsom
Scammon Jefferson H. wheelwright, 715 Folsom, dwl 535 Tehama
SCANDINAVIAN SOCIETY, rooms 320 Sansom
Scanlan James O. D. salesman, 11 Montgomery, dwl cor Fifth and Jessie
Scanlan Morris, dwl 156 Jessie
Scanlan P. Rev. assistant, St. Patrick's Church
Scanlin Catharine (widow) vegetables, dwl NW cor Jackson and Battery
Scanlin Daniel, salesman with Helbing, Greenebaum & Co. dwl Brooklyn Hotel
SCANLIN (Francis) & BRUNS (Frederick) groceries and liquors, 2 Second
SCANLIN (Francis) & DOSCHER (Henry) groceries and liquors, NW cor Bush and Jones, dwl W s Jones bet Bush and Pine
Scanlin Hannah Mrs. dwl 43 Baldwin Court
Scanlin Michael, shoe maker, dwl 232 Sutter
Scanlin Patrick T. coachman, dwl 912 Bush
Scanlin Thomas, laborer, dwl 14 Bay State Row
Scanlon Kate C. Miss, domestic, 1109 Stockton
Scanlon Mary Miss, dress maker, dwl 146 Minna
Scanlon Mike, cook, What Cheer House Restaurant
SCANNELL DAVID, chief engineer S. F. Fire Department, office and dwl 3 City Hall third floor
Scannell Eugene, plasterer, dwl 269 Stevenson
Scannell John, shoe maker with Mary Louis, 536 Commercial, dwl 909 Post
Scannell Michael, shoe making, 317 Dupont, dwl 232 Sutter
Scellier Louis (Verdier, Kaindler, S. & Co.) dwl N s Francisco bet Stockton and Dupont
Scerena Fred, carpenter, dwl W s Nevada nr Folsom
Schaap Charles A. L. bookbinder with Edward Bosqui & Co. dwl NW cor Green and Taylor
Schaap Mary A. (widow) dwl NW cor Green and Taylor
Schaar A. upholsterer, dwl 207 Tehama
Schad William, dwl with H. Schwerin, Visitacion Valley
Schadde William, cooper, S. F. & P. Sugar Co. dwl 1025 Minna
Schade John, boots and shoes, 16 Sansom
Schadek M. Mrs. milliner, dwl 313 Pine
Schadt William, bar keeper, 219 California
Schaefer Bartolomy, maltster, Philadelphia Brewery
Schaefer Charles G. porter with J. Y. Hallock & Co. dwl 1812 Mason
Schaefer Charlotte, midwife, dwl 606 Broadway
Schaefer George, machinist, dwl 110 Jessie
Schaefer John, dwl 606 Broadway
Schaefer Mary (widow) dwl S s Filbert bet Mason and Taylor
Schaetzl Zaver, tailor with Colman Bros. dwl Trinity bet Montgomery and Kearny
Schafer Francis, laborer, dwl 120 Sutter, rear
Schafer George F. tailor, 409 Bush
Schafer George G. dwl 726 Howard
Schafer Henry, hog butcher, E s Ninth bet Bryant and Brannan, dwl 124 Dora
Schafer Henry F. B. carpenter, dwl 138 Fourth
Schafer H. H. (Schafer & Bro. and J. F. & H. H. Schafer and Davis & Schafer) dwl 720 Wash
Schafer John, carriage maker with H. Casebolt & Co. dwl 228 Sutter, rear
Schafer John, waiter, German Hospital, Brannan
Schafer (John F.) & Brother (H. Henry Schafer) importers and manufacturers clothing, 509 Sacramento, res New York

SCHAFER J. F. & H. H. manufacturers beds, bedding, and furniture and importers pulu, 504 and 506 Sansom, res New York
Schaffer Louis, butcher with M. Selig & Co. dwl S s El Dorado nr Potrero Avenue
Schaeffer, see Shafer
Schaffner Frederick, cook, Cosmopolitan Hotel, dwl N s Church Place
Schallich Lucas, cabinet maker, 523 Kearny
Scham Andrew, carpenter, dwl Rassette Place No. 2
Schambaen Louis, boatman, dwl 15 Stewart
Schammel Henry, vinegar factory, 1820 Powell
Schauder John F. pilot, Old Line, 5 Vallejo, res Oakland
Schauley Patrick, carpenter and dwl Cincinnati Brewery Valencia nr Sixteenth
Schapper Florence, tinsmith with Johnston & Reay, 319 California, dwl 777 Clay
Scharlach C. M. physician, office 521 Pacific
Scharmann George, boot maker, 1320 Powell, dwl 714 Broadway
Schburg William, liquor saloon, E s Valencia bet Fifteenth and Sixteenth
Schedel George, groceries and liquors, NE cor Jessie and Ecker
Scheeline Nathan, merchant, dwl 738 Green
Scheffer Carl, statuary, dwl 619 Pacific
Scheibeler William, laborer, Lone Mountain Cemetery
Scheider Jacob, jeweler, NW cor Kearny and Jackson
Scheider Peter, laborer, Bay Sugar Refinery, dwl S s Vallejo bet Dupont and Kearny
Scheidler Joseph, engineer, Bay Sugar Refinery, dwl 32 Rousch
Scheifer Batal, laborer, dwl 123 Tehama
Scheimall Rudolph, dwl 955 Howard
Scheinberger Frederick W. porter, dwl 423 East
Schell Theodore L. (Woodworth, Schell & Co.) dwl 506 Second
Schellentrager Frances, domestic, 544 Bryant
Schellhorn Jacob, dealer grain, dwl 315 Bush
Schemmel Edward, clerk, French Savings and Loan, 533 Commercial
Schenck Cornelius, clerk, office 523 Montgomery third floor, dwl 51 Stevenson House
Schenck D. W. inspector, Custom House
Schenck G. Everett, real estate, dwl Pioneer Bdg
Schenck John, tailor with George Brodwolf, 319 Bush
Schenk Charles, tailor, dwl Reed Place bet Montgomery and Kearny
Schenk Ernst, porter, dwl 633 Broadway
Schenk Hugo, dwl S s Hayes bet Gough and Octavia
Schenk John, teaser, Pacific Glass Works, dwl Potrero
Schenk Michael & Co. (William Herzberg) Eureka Malt House, 1610 Stockton
Schenkelberger Francis, shoe making, SW cor Bush and Taylor
SCHEPER CHRISTOPHER, groceries and liquors, NW cor Montgomery and Sutter
SCHEPER MARTIN, groceries and liquors, SW cor Pine and Sansom
Schera Pascal, clerk, 746 Washington
Scherb Annie Mrs. dress maker, dwl 673 Mission
Scherb Francis (Stein, Link & S.) dwl 673 Mission
Scherer John, machinist, dwl cor Bush and Trinity
SCHERR FERDINAND, importer and dealer in hops, corks, etc. 511 Sac. dwl 9 Stockton Place
Scherr Joseph, tailor, dwl N s Minna bet Eighth and Ninth
Scherrebeck Mary Mrs. dwl S s Mission bet Sixth and Seventh
Scherrer John, shoe making, 503 Bush
Schesler Ernest, hog ranch, dwl W s Nevada nr Folsom

Schetter (Hermann) & Pearse (Charles H.) produce commission, 123 Clay
Scheu Frederick, shoe maker, 421 O'Farrell
Scheuring George, tailor, dwl NW cor Kearny and Jackson
Schezer Joseph, machine sewing, dwl NE corner Union and Kearny
Schieffer Christian H. shoe maker with Jacob Nagel, 222 Kearny, dwl 132 Sutter
Schierhold John F. foreman with Lowis Bros. dwl E s August Alley nr Union
Schiesler Christian, hatter, dwl 1235 Dupont
Schiess Louis, butcher, bds Meyer's Hotel, 814 Montgomery
Schiff Carrie Mrs. saleswoman, 16 Second, dwl 124 Jessie
Schiffmann Siegfried, book keeper with J. Lowenhelm & Co. dwl 323 Sutter
Schilling Adam, machinist, dwl 315 Montgomery
Schilling Charles, Excelsior Laundry, E s Lagoon
Schilling Regina (widow) dwl with T. Hellenschmidt E s Hampshire nr Sixteenth
Schilperoort Leendert, lab with John Warburton
Schimp John W. ex-policeman, Monumental Engine Co. No. 6
Schinck John H. workman, Pacific GlassWorks, dwl cor Mariposa and Indiana
Schindler Casper, tailor, dwl 320 Broadway
Schindler W. F. R. regimental quartermaster and commissary Second Infantry C. V. Presidio
Schindler William, butcher, 14 Jane
Schinkel Peter, hog butcher, cor Tenth and Bryant, dwl W s Eleventh nr Folsom
Schintz J. H. cutter, dwl 525 Broadway
Schirott William, liquor saloon, 716 Pacific
Schisler Louis, butcher, dwl 1622 Stockton
Schissler John, drayman, dwl 111 Turk
Schitts William, bedstead maker, dwl Chicago Hotel
Schlage Frederick, cook, 416 Kearny
Schlam (James) & Dunn (Willet) tailor's trimmings, 818 Montgomery
Schlechtwey Charles, farmer, dwl 323 Pine
SCHLEICHER JACOB, proprietor New England House, 205 Sansom
Schleiden William, commission and agent Mexican Line Packets, 324 Wash, dwl 1210 Kearny
Schleif John, seaman, bds 7 Washington
Schleimann Fred. laborer, South Park Malt House, bet Fifth and Sixth
Schlesinger Louis, salesman, 212 Battery, dwl Stevenson House
Schlesinger Oscar (Joseph Isaac & Co.) dwl 1307 Stockton
Schlesselmann John H. clerk with Schroder & Hashagen
Schley Daniel (Martenet & S.) 633 Market, dwl 509 Dupont
Schlidder D. ship carpenter, bds Sacramento Hotel, 407 Pacific
Schlinghyde Bernard, salesman, 633 Clay, dwl 258 Jessie
Schlink Thomas, driver, American Bakery, 1027 Dupont, dwl 711 Pacific
Schliechens Henry A. porter with Wormser Bros. 201 California, dwl 17 Ritch
Schloss (Louis) & Michal (Michael) butchers, 364 Third
Schloss Louis, broker, dwl 45 Belden Block
Schlosser Jacob, dwl 132 Sutter
Schlotte Ernest, musician, Maguire's Opera House, dwl 608 Green
Schlotter Egetus, hog butcher, dwl cor Tenth and Bryant
Schlotterback Charles, gunsmith with A. J. Plate, 411 Sansom
Schlueter Charles, clerk, SE cor Third and Hunt
Schlueter (Edward) & Leege (William) groceries and liquors, SE cor Third and Hunt, dwl 139 Minna

Schlueter Edward, clerk, 14 Third, dwl 81 Everett
Schlussel Alexander, office 323 Cal, dwl 652 Market
Schluter John H. fruit dealer, 152 Second
Schmaus Franz, shoe maker, dwl 135 Post
Schmedes Catherine Miss, domestic, 174 Clara
Schmedes John J. groceries and liquors, 642 Jackson
Schmeelk William (Bardenhagen & Co.) NE cor
    Folsom and Sixth
SCHMID JACOB, proprietor Helvetia Hotel, 431
    and 433 Pine
Schmid Martin, confectioner, dwl 431 Pine
Schmid Nicolaus, confectioner, dwl 431 Pine
Schmidt Adam, carpenter, dwl 28 Natoma
Schmidt A. F. bar keeper, 521 Merchant
Schmidt Albert, jeweler with Lemme Bros. 534
    Commercial, dwl 336 Bush
Schmidt Ambrose, clerk, dwl 7 Monroe
Schmidt Carl, musician, dwl 827 Vallejo
Schmidt Casper, tailor, 758 Clay
Schmidt Christian & Henry, cigars and tobacco,
    NE cor Wash and Kearny, dwl 806 Kearny
Schmidt Christopher, hairdressing saloon, 3 Fourth,
    dwl 776 Folsom
Schmidt Christopher, laborer with M. C. Hillyear,
    SW cor Gough and Sutter
Schmidt Frank, seaman, dwl N s Sixteenth bet Va-
    lencia and Mission
Schmidt Frederick, butcher, dwl 1321 Stockton
Schmidt George, tailor, dwl 315 Bush
Schmidt Godfried, painter with F. Tillman, dwl 820
    Montgomery
Schmidt Gregory, laborer, dwl 5 Pennsylvania Av
Schmidt Henry (C. & H. Schmidt) dwl 806 Kearny
Schmidt Henry, clerk, NE cor Minna and Fourth
Schmidt Henry, clerk with Claus Hadler, NW cor
    Clay and Mason
Schmidt Henry, musician, dwl 1513 Mason
Schmidt Henry, seaman, bds 7 Washington
Schmidt Henry W. chemist and apothecary, 542
    Kearny, dwl 719 Broadway
Schmidt (Ignaz) & Fretz (F. H.) pickle manufac-
    turers, 104 Commercial, dwl S s Bush nr Taylor
Schmidt James, vinegar factory, dwl 409 Stockton
Schmidt John, bar keeper, SW cor Kearny and St.
    Mark Place, dwl 13 Geary
Schmidt John, carpenter, dwl 637 Broadway
Schmidt John C. major Second Infantry C. V. Pre-
    sidio
Schmidt John M. (Schneider & Co.) dwl 12 Sac
Schmid Joseph, bar keeper, dwl 431 Pine
Schmidt Louis, cook, dwl 619 Pacific
Schmidt Louis, professor music, dwl 119 O'Farrell
Schmidt Louis, upholsterer, bds Meyer's Hotel 814
    Montgomery
Schmidt Mary (widow) dwl 5 St. Mary
Schmidt Michael, brass finisher, dwl 406 Dupont
Schmidt Mme. fortune teller, 302 Jackson
Schmidt Mrs. midwife, dwl 5 Pennsylvania Avenue
Schmidt Peter, milkman with George W. Hatman
Schmidt P. R. (Hoffman & S.) dwl 1913 Stockton
Schmidt S. (widow) dwl 719 Broadway
Schmidt William, groceries and liquors, NW cor
    Harrison and Ritch
Schmidtt Christian, baker, dwl 16 Langton
SCHMIEDELL HENRY, stock broker, office 705
    Mont, dwl N s Bryant bet Sixth and Seventh
Schmierer, Gottlieb & Co. (J. F. Eugster) liquor
    saloon, 427 Kearny
Schmit John, broker, dwl 1112 Stockton
Schmit Joseph, with Jacob A. Maison
Schmith Barbara (widow) dwl Eighteenth nr York
Schmith Charles L. boot and shoe maker, S s Bush
    nr Octavia
Schmith Christian, wholesale butcher, Potrero Av,
    dwl N s Broadway bet Kearny and Dupont
Schmitt August, porter, 323 Sacramento, dwl NE cor
    Broadway and Kearny
Schmitt B. L. stock and exchange broker, 605
    Washington, dwl 1016 Powell

Schmitt Charles (Godchaux Bros. & Co.) dwl 1509
    Stockton
Schmitt Charles, carpenter, bds Sacramento Hotel
    407 Pacific
Schmitt Charles, cook, 205 Sansom
Schmitt Charles, printer, Abend Post, dwl E s Fif-
    teenth nr Howard
Schmitt Emile, clerk, 54 Second, dwl 5 Milton Place
Schmitt Fannie Mrs. dwl NE cor Kearny and Bdwy
Schmitt George, butcher, dwl 319 Brannan
Schmitt George, hairbraider, dwl 233 Sutter
Schmitt George, proprietor Newark Market, junction
    Market and Sacramento, dwl 12 Sacramento
Schmitt George F. beer saloon, NE cor California
    and Kearny, dwl Belden nr Pine
Schmitt Henry (Godchaux Bros. & Co.) res Paris
Schmitt Henry, groceries and liquors, SW cor Russ
    and Howard
Schmitt John, cabinet maker with W. G. Weir, dwl
    Golden Eagle Hotel
Schmitt Joseph F. beer saloon, SE cor Pine and
    Kearny
Schmitt Louisa Miss, domestic, 306 Stockton
Schmitt Nicholas, carpenter with John Center, dwl
    NW cor Sixteenth and Folsom
Schmitt Peter, cook, Golden Eagle Hotel, 219
    Kearny
Schmitt William, blacksmith, dwl 711 O'Farrell
Schmitz Christoph, musician, dwl 6 Monroe
Schmitz John B. express wagon, 709 Market
Schmitz John J. clerk, 719 Market
Schmitz John P. liquors and wines, 719 Market
Schmitz Joseph L. leader orchestra Maguire's Opera
    House, dwl 6 Monroe
Schmitz Otto (Kohler & Frohling) res Los Angeles
Schmolz Adolphus, assistant coiner, U. S. Branch
    Mint, dwl 515 Union
SCHMOLZ WILLIAM, coiner U. S. Branch Mint,
    office 608 Commercial, and mathematical instru-
    ment maker, 430 Montgomery, dwl 24 O'Farrell
Schnabel J. chorus singer, Academy Music
Schnaittacher Charles J. book keeper with Max
    Morgenthau, dwl St. Nicholas Hotel
Schnefelt C. dwl What Cheer House
Schneider Albert, shoe maker with M. Rosenthal &
    Co. 340 Kearny
Schneider Alois, gunsmith with John Bach, dwl 4
    Virginia
Schneider Benjamin, blacksmith with Kimball &
    Co. dwl 113 Bush
Schneider Edward W. book keeper with Boswell &
    Shattuck, dwl 815 Union
Schneider Frank, employé, Washington Baths, 624
    Washington
Schneider Francis J. dwl 137 Clara
Schneider George, cigar maker, dwl 1 Vallejo Place
Schneider Gustin, waiter, Clipper Restaurant
Schneider Jacob, baker, dwl 46 Ritch, rear
Schneider Jacob, employé, Washington Baths, 624
    Washington
Schneider John J. proprietor Washington Baths and
    hairdressing saloon, 624 Washington
Schneider Louis, dwl 815 Union
Schneider Louis, steward, 44 Clay, dwl 308 Minna
Schneider M. & Co. (John Schmidt) Star Restau-
    rant, 12 Sacramento, dwl 5 St. Mary
Schneider Martin, laborer, dwl 5 St. Mary
Schneider Nicholas, shoe maker with Michael Reu-
    bold, 135 Kearny
Schneider Philip, barber, dwl NE cor Broadway
    and Scott
Schneider Richard, dwl NE cor Bdwy and Scott
Schneiter Philip, coffee saloon, E s Fourth bet Stev-
    enson and Jessie
Schnelle Charles, bar keeper, dwl 731 Vallejo
Schnoering Julius, dwl 110 Sutter
Schnoor Christian, locksmith, 1306 Stockton, dwl
    1513 Stockton
Schnyder John, hackman, Plaza

Scho Teresa (widow) dwl 602 Third
Schober Frederick, blacksmith with August Pritzel, dwl 1 St. Mary
Schoder Joseph, salesman, 106 Battery
Schoemann Otto *(Gottig & S.)* res La Paz Lower California
Schoen J. J. agent Wash Brewery, dwl 135 Post
Schoen Louis L. hairdresser, 43 Jackson
Schoen Paul, hairdresser with Henderson & Brown, dwl 406 Dupont
Schoen Samuel, bar keeper, Continental Hotel
Schoenau Henry, dwl 141 Minna
Schoenfeld Louis, bar keeper, NE cor Bush and Kearny, dwl E s Dupont nr Pine
Schoenmachers Charles, builder and contractor, dwl S s Chestnut bet Stockton and Powell
Schoenner J. R. tailor, dwl 641 Pacific
Schofield Anson, machinist Fulton Foundry, dwl 152 Natoma
Schofield Richard (col'd) night watchman, dwl 16 Hawthorne
Scholl F. W. F. clerk with ,P. G. Bauch, dwl 900 Vallejo
Scholl *(Louis)* & Mall *(Adam)* butchers, 34 Occidental Market, dwl 873 Mission
Scholl Michael, carpenter, dwl 900 Vallejo
Schollars Andrew, box maker with Hobbs, Gilmore & Co. dwl St. Charles Hotel
Scholle Abraham *(Scholle & Bros.)* res New York
Scholle Anthony, waiter, Richards' Restaurant, dwl SE cor Union and Kearny
Scholle F. C. first officer steamer Sierra Nevada, office SW cor Front and Jackson
Scholle Isaac, clerk, dwl 642 Folsom
Scholle Jacob, *(Scholle & Bros.)* dwl 640 Folsom
SCHOLLE *(William)* & BROTHERS *(Jacob and Abraham)* importers and manufacturers clothing, dry goods, etc. 405–409 Sacramento, dwl 642 Folsom
Scholten Henry, baker, dwl 619 Pacific
Schomaker Christian, laborer, Bay Sugar Refinery, dwl 19 Hinckley
Schonberg Julius, cook, bds 7 Washington
Schönfeld *(Selig & Co.)* dwl 811 Mission
Schonfeld *(Jonas)* & Bremer *(Hermann)* cigars and tobacco, 413 Pine, dwl 262 Jessie
Schonwald Francis, barber, 346 Third
Schonwasser Samuel *(Manheim, S. & Co.)* dwl 405 O'Farrell
SCHORD LOUIS G. wines and liquors, 721 Davis, dwl 219 California
SCHORTEMEIR HERMANN H. groceries and liquors, NE corner California and Prospect Place
Schott J. inspector, Custom House, dwl 329 Fremont
Schott Peter, farmer, dwl S s Spring Valley Road, 3 miles from City Hall
Schottler Antone, clerk with H. C. Evers, dwl SE cor Vallejo and Montgomery
Schottler Henry, clerk with J. A. Zabowski, dwl W s Potrero Avenue nr Sixteenth
Schou Andrew H. carpenter, dwl W s Prospect Avenue nr Twenty-Ninth
Schrack John T. laborer, dwl 32 Stewart
Schrader Adolphus, milkman, dwl SW cor Geary and Octavia
Schrader August, cabinet maker with A. Conrad, dwl Capp nr Twenty-First
Schrader *(Charles)* & Gerken *(Claus)* groceries and liquors, SW cor Fifth and Stevenson
Schrader Emily (widow) dwl 1326 Dupont
Schrader Ferdinand, peddler, dwl 633 Broadway
Schrader Sophie (widow) dwl 630 Green, rear
Schramm Adolph, engineer, Jackson Foundry, dwl 1109 Pacific
Schramm H. *(H. Siegfried & Co.)* Odeum Garden and Hall, Mission Dolores
Schraubstadter William, musician, dwl 337 Bush
Schreiber C. *(J. & C. Schreiber)* dwl 406 Sansom

Schreiber Christian, confectioner with M. Bernheim, 408 Clay
Schreiber Frederick, carpenter, dwl 514 Hyde
Schreiber Herman, dwl W s Stewart nr Market
SCHREIBER J. & C. wholesale and retail furniture and bedding, 406 Sansom, dwl 411 Ellis
Schreiber John *(Goetz & S.)* dwl 333 Pine
Schreiber L. trimmings and lace, 202 Second
Schreiber Louis, dwl S s Card Place
Schreiber Philip jr. salesman with J. & C. Schreiber, dwl N s Shipley bet Seventh and Eighth
Schreiber Phillipe, tailor, dwl 2 Quincy Place
Schreiner Hubert, musician, dwl 18 Sansom
Schrekett Charles, dwl N s Bryant bet Fifth and Sixth
Schriefer Christien, clerk, SE cor Folsom and Ritch
Schriefer Diedrich H. *(Ogle & S.)* dwl 155 Natoma
Schrimm Frank, carpenter, dwl 14 Bay State Row
Schriver William, hats and straw goods, 141 Fourth
Schroder Adam, boiler maker with Coffey & Risdon
Schroder Adrien, clerk with H. Schroder & Co. res Oakland
Schroder August, cabinet maker with Conrad, Pine, dwl with I. F. Markt W s Capp bet Twenty-First and Twenty-Second
Schroder Bernard, shoe maker, dwl 514 Mission
Schroder Charles, bar tender, bds St. Louis Hotel 11 Pacific
Schroder F. A. proprietor Senator Saloon, NE cor Powell and Francisco
Schroder Frederick, groceries and liquors, SE cor Sacramento and Drumm, dwl 958 Mission
Schroder Henry & Co. *(Bernard Bert)* importers French wines and liquors and agents Bordeaux Board Underwriters. 811 Mont, res Oakland
Schroder Henry, groceries and liquors, NE corner Grove and Gough
Schroder Henry, clerk with Claus W. Brauer, dwl NE cor Sansom and Pacific ·
Schroder Hermann, groceries and liquors, 330 Vallejo
Schroder *(John)* & Hashagen *(John H.)* groceries and liquors, NW cor Stockton and Vallejo
Schroder John H. clerk, dwl 330 Vallejo
Schroeder *(A.)* & Lloyd *(John)* dealers brick, office Rincon Point Wharf, dwl 15 Stockton, rear
Schroeder J. Louis, proprietor Blue Anchor Boarding House, 7 and 9 Washington, dwl 11 Wash
Schroeder John, proprietor Telegraph House, SW cor Battery and Green
Schroeder Louis *(Heimbnrg & S.)* 11 and 13 Pac
SCHROTH CHARLES, German Bakery and Coffee Saloon, 230 Kearny, dwl 214 Stockton
Schubach Jacob, driver, Mason's Brewery, dwl 620 Lombard
Schubart Auguste, millwright, bds Meyers' Hotel, 814 Montgomery
Schubart Elias, salesman, 304 Battery ·
Schubert Charles, carrier, California Demokrat, dwl 209 Third
Schuch Adolph, meerschaum pipe maker with Louis Schuch, 12 Sansom
Schuch Louis, manufacturer meerschaum pipes and cigars and tobacco, 12 Sansom
Schuerg George, shoe maker, 134 First
Schuetz *(Charles)* & Wochatz *(Charles)* Musik Halle Saloon, 607 Jackson, dwl 713 Vallejo
Schuetze Edward, tailor, dwl 824 Pacific
Schuff Ferdinand, blacksmith, dwl 507 Pacific
Schufflin Bridget Miss, domestic, 1419 Taylor
Schuldt *(Herman)* & Knoche *(Henry)* groceries and liquors, 120 Second, dwl Hubbard bet Second and Third
Schulenburg A. clerk with Henschel & Maurice, dwl 809 Larkin cor Geary
Schuler George, carpenter, dwl 315 Bush
Schull Valentine, baker, dwl 18 Langton
Schuller Louis, butcher, dwl 741 Broadway ·
Schulte F. W. liquor saloon, NE cor Clay and Kearny, dwl 521 Green

Schulte J. Herman, bar keeper, SW cor East and Market

Schulte John, liquor saloon, 610 Jackson

Schulte John G. W. *(George Osmer & Co.)* dwl 318 Folsom

Schulte Theodore, laborer, dwl W s Valencia bet Fifteenth and Sixteenth

Schulteis Henry, groceries and liquors, SW cor First and Clementina

Schultheis William, shoe maker with George Burkhardt, dwl 228 Second

Schultheiss Peter, laborer, NW corner Kearny and Jackson

Schultz Adolph, marble polisher with John Daniel, dwl Philadelphia House

Schultz Charles, professor music, dwl 704 Dupont

Schultz Charles H. bar keeper, dwl 9 Washington

Schultz Frederick, clerk, SE cor Dupont and Geary

SCHULTZ *(George)* & VON BARGEN *(Henry)* wholesale wines and liquors, SE cor California and Front *(and Pacific Distillery Co.)* dwl 606 Geary nr Jones

Schultz Henry, tailor with J. L. Brooks, dwl S s Clay bet Powell and Mason

Schultz Herman, salesman, 300 Battery

Schultz John, shoe maker, dwl 633 Mission

Schultz Julius, baker with H. Hoesch, dwl 612 Clay

Schultz Lazar, dwl 1018 Stockton

Schultz Louis E. J. book keeper, Pacific Distillery

Schultz Minnie Miss, domestic, 719 Post

Schultz Molly (widow) dwl 840 Vallejo

Schultz Otto, confectioner, dwl 606 Jackson

Schultz Peter, seaman, dwl 20 Commercial

Schultz Philip, hairdresser with Proschold & Rauch, dwl 315 Bush

Schultz Richard *(Sparks & S.)* dwl SE cor Harrison and Spear

Schultz William, groceries and liquors, SE cor Dupont and Geary, dwl 25 Dupont

Schultz William, groceries and liquors, SW cor First and Bryant

Schultz William, shoe maker, 109 Leidesdorff

Schultz William, silversmith with F. R. Reichel, dwl 613 Mission

Schultz William, waiter, dwl 431 Pine

SCHULTZE FRANCIS, commission merchant and agent National Life and Travellers' Insurance Co. New York, office see Supplementary Names

Schultze *(Herman)* & Harms *(John)* groceries and liquors, SE cor Kearny and Union

Schultze Louis, clerk with Herman Schultze, dwl SE cor Union and Kearny

Schultze Louis, shoe maker, dwl 6 Berry

Schulz John, bar keeper, dwl 767 Clay

Schulz John, clerk with Lewis Adler, 714 Market

Schulze Fred, wholesale and retail cigars and tobacco, 540 Commercial

Schulze Louis, boots and shoes, 402 Bush

Schumacher Albert, driver with Marden & Folger, dwl Union bet Powell and Mason

SCHUMACHER ANTHONY, importer and jobber leather and shoe findings, 634 Clay and 639 Merchant, dwl 1103 Mason

Schumacher August, dwl 1103 Mason

Schumacher Diedrich, porter with John Van Bergen & Co. dwl 48 Ritch

Schumacher F. A. dwl 1103 Mason

SCHUMACHER FREDERICK, Two Brothers Saloon, 44 Stewart

Schumacher John, proptr Post St. House, 207 Post

Schumacher Lewis, importer and jobber guns, pistols, and notions, 19 Sansom, dwl NE cor Grove and Gough

Schumacher R. professor music, dwl 211 Post

Schuman Charles A. gardener with R. B. Woodward, NW cor Mission and Fourteenth

Schuman Frederick, Junction Restaurent, SE cor Market and Stewart

Schuman Henry, cooper, dwl N s Heron nr Eighth

Schuman Henry, hatter with Triest & Friedlander, dwl 727 Broadway

Schumann Charles, gardener with R. B. Woodward, dwl Cincinnati Brewery, Valencia

Schumann Frederick, butcher, dwl Empire House

Schumann Hermann, cigars and tobacco, SE corner Mont and Cal and SW cor Kearny and Cal

Schumann Louis, clerk, SW cor Stockton and Bush

Schumann Valentine, waiter, Empire State Restaurant, dwl 242 Sixth

Schumann William, groceries and liquors, NW cor Fourth and Minna

Schun Wo (Chinese) cigar maker, 705 Sacramento

Schunemann Edward, cabinet maker, 429 Kearny

Schunemann Frank, blacksmith and wagon maker, 1625 Powell

Schunhoff Bernhard, clerk with C. L. Wilhelm, NE cor Howard and Fourth

Schunhoff B. H. salesman with Max Morganthau, dwl 820 Pacific

Schuntenhaus Julius, waterman, 609 Market

Schuntenhaus R. waterman, 609 Market

Schupback Jacob, express wagon, Chestnut bet Powell and Mason

Schuppert Adam, California Brewery, NE corner Stockton and Jackson

Schurr George, hairdresser, Montgomery Baths, dwl Kearny above Union

Schusler Israel, Empire Market, 1235 Dupont

Schusler John, hatter, dwl 631 Broadway

Schussler H. draftsman, Spring Valley W. W

Schussler Israel, drayman, SE cor Sacramento and Sansom, dwl 108 Turk

SCHUSTER *(John)* & BROTHER *(Joseph S. Schuster)* stoves and tin ware, 102 Kearny, dwl 214 Fremont

Schuster Joseph S. *(Schuster & Brother)* dwl 214 Fremont

Schutt Henry, drayman with Tillman & Co. dwl 11 St. Mark Place

Schutt William, clerk, SE cor Sacramento and Davis

Schutte Henry, carpenter with J. Center, dwl W s Folsom bet Nineteenth and Twentieth

Schutte Henry, cook, dwl 728 Market

Schutz ——, silversmith, dwl 613 Mission

Schutz Charles, saloon, dwl 713 Vallejo

Schuyayert A. D. runner, dwl NW cor Kearny and Jackson

Schuyler Charles, driver with G. M. Garwood & Co

SCHUYLER, *(J. R.)* HARTLEY, *(M.)* GRAHAM *(M.)* & CO. William A. Whitehorne agent, importers and jobbers guns, pistols, jewelry, military goods, etc. 409 Battery, res New York

Schuyler Nicholas, clerk, dwl 114 Prospect Place

Schuyler Thomas J. box maker, dwl 51 Second

Schwab Frederick, butcher, 519 Geary

Schwamm Sebastian, bakery, 114 Third

Schwartz Abraham, peddler, dwl 517 Clay

Schwartz *(C.)* & Husing *(R.)* liquor saloon, SE cor Mission and Eighteenth

SCHWARTZ *(Charles)* & WINKLER *(William)* Harmony Hall Liquor and Billard Saloon, 601 Sacramento SW cor Mont, dwl 1512 Powell

Schwartz *(Claus)* & Husing *(Rogers)* saloon, SE cor Eighteenth and Mission

Schwartz D. groceries and liquors, NE corner St. Charles and Kearny, dwl 1020 Kearny

Schwartz F. W. carpenter, dwl NE cor Tehama and Fourth

Schwartz George, clerk, 607 Commercial, dwl 230 O'Farrell

Schwartz Henry, dwl 728 Folsom

Schwartz Henry, cigars and tobacco, 607 Commercial, dwl 230 O'Farrell

Schwartz Henry, laborer, San Francisco Chemical Works, dwl N s Fifteenth nr Guerrero

Schwartz John, porter, 404 Front, dwl St. Charles Place

Schwartz Joseph, jeweler with Braverman & Levy, dwl Bootz's Hotel

Schwartz *(Lazarus)* & Sinay *(Elie)* retail dry goods, NW cor Pacific and Stockton, dwl SW cor Vallejo and Powell

Schwartz Nicholas J. molder, dwl 551 Tehama, rear

Schwartz William F. druggist with J. N. Hume, dwl NE cor Fourth and Tehama

Schwarz Joseph A. driver, dwl 1100 Stockton

Schwarzbach Bruno B. dwl 403 California

SCHWARZE *(Hermann)* & CO. *(John H. Reiners)* groceries and liquors, NW cor Kearny and Geary

Schwarzschild Louis, salesman with Thurnauer & Zinn, dwl 621 California

Schwergerle *(John)* & Co. *(Victor Ruthardt)* wines and liquors, 636 Com, dwl 1507 Dupont

Schweinle Louis, tailoring, 31 Kearny

Schweiss Philip, laborer, dwl 9 Harlan Place, rear

Schweitzer, *(Bernard)* Stiefel *(Louis)* & Co. *(Samuel Schweitzer)* importers and jobbers fancy goods, 307 Sacramento, dwl 608 Leav

Schweitzer Gottleib, cook with Henry Hoesch, dwl 612 Clay

Schweitzer John, salesman, Philadelphia Brewery, dwl 228 Second

Schweitzer Samuel *(Schweitzer, Stiefel & Co.)* bds 424 Sacramento

Schweitzer Sebastian, carpenter, dwl 8 Hartmann nr Greenwich

Schwenke Charles, tobacco and cigars, dwl 16 Stewart

Schwerdt Conrad, carpenter, dwl Eagle Hotel SW cor Kearny and Bush

Schwerdt Jacob, cabinet maker with John Wigmore, dwl 708 Market

Schwerdt Philip, boots and shoes, 708 Market, dwl W s Sixth bet Harrison and Bryant, rear

Schweria August, Columbia Bakery, 1129 Dupont

Schwerin Edward, cigar manufactory, 419 Brannan

Schwerin Henry, milk ranch. Visitacion Valley

Schwert William, laborer, Pacific Distillery

Schwetze Charles, Musik Halle, NE cor Dupont and Wash, dwl S s Green bet Stock and Powell

Schwitzer Joseph, foreman Mason Brewery, N s Chestnut bet Mason and Powell

Schycoff Frank, porter, dwl Bootz's Hotel

Sciuttich P. P. clerk with N. Trobock, 416 Davis

Scmadec J. Henry, Bull's Head Market, NE cor Folsom and Twenty-Second

Scollay Jeremiah, stone cutter, dwl S s Filbert bet Montgomery and Sansom

SCOLLAY WILLIAM A. wines and liquors, 1522 Stockton

Scoofy Peter M. dwl 338 Seventh

Scotchler James, dwl 2107 Mason

Scotchler John J. book keeper with Shattuck & Hendley, dwl 211 Seventh between Howard and Folsom

SCOTCHLER JOSEPH B. book keeper, U. S. Branch Mint and secretary Merchants' Mutual Marine Insurance Co. office 206 Front, res Oakland

Scotchler S. M. Miss, assistant, Greenwich Street School, dwl 2107 Mason

Scotland Robert, ship carpenter, dwl 206 Harrison

Scotland Thomas. carpenter, dwl 336 Bush

SCOTT *(Abel F.)* & CO. *(Lewis C. Hunter and Jeremiah J. Hanifin)* ship brokers, S s Vallejo nr Front, dwl 73 Clementina

Scott Albert W. *(C. L. Place & Co.)* dwl 225 Harrison

Scott Charles, clerk with Haight & Pearson, dwl Occidental Hotel

Scott Chalmers. with Haight & Pearson, dwl Cosmopolitan Hotel

Scott Charles, laborer, Spring Valley W. W.

Scott Charles, workman with J. Treat, dwl nr cor Twenty-Fourth and Potrero Avenue

Scott Charles P. plasterer, dwl 651 Mission

Scott D. C. dentist, office and dwl 617 Clay

SCOTT EDMUND, real estate agent, office NW cor Mont and Commercial, dwl 1815 Stockton

Scott Edward J. carpenter, dwl 14 Everett

Scott Francis (col'd) chief cook steamer Sacramento, dwl 44 Jessie

Scott George, butcher, 154 First

Scott George, carpenter, dwl 517 Greenwich

Scott George, second engineer steamer Yosemite

Scott George A. brickmason, dwl 327 Fourth

Scott George R. compositor with T. G. Spear, dwl 517 Greenwich

Scott George R. plumber, dwl 14 Everett

Scott Gustavus A. music teacher, office 3 Montgomery, dwl 55 South Park

Scott Harshaw, publisher, dwl 8 Langton

Scott Herschel, collector, dwl 8 Langton

Scott Hiram H. salesman, 212 Cal, dwl 207 Powell

Scott Hugh, seaman, dwl 26 Sacramento

Scott I. M. *(H. J. Booth & Co.)* dwl 237 Seventh nr Folsom

Scott J. Mrs. furnished rooms, 616 Mission

Scott Jacob H. N. mariner, dwl 33 John

Scott James, mariner, dwl SW cor Dupont and Bdwy

Scott James, salesman with Kerby, Byrne & Co. dwl 471 Jessie

Scott *(James G.)* & Hall *(Samuel)* James Market, SE cor Fifth and Shipley

Scott Jane (col'd, widow) dwl 1606 Powell

Scott John, assayer, 424 Battery, dwl 919 Pacific

Scott John, steward, Franklin Hotel, SE cor Sansom and Pacific

Scott John B. (col'd) laborer, dwl 1214 Pacific

Scott John H. manufacturer and importer cutlery, 29 and 31 Battery, res New York

Scott John J. carpenter, dwl S s Sixteenth bet Valencia and Guerrero

SCOTT *(John S.)* & GLOVER *(George F. M.)* stock and exchange brokers, 304 Montgomery, dwl NE cor Shotwell and Sixteenth

Scott J. S. record clerk, office Custom House third floor, dwl 427 Third

Scott M. & Exploring Co. office 804 Montgomery

Scott Maggie Miss, domestic, 1018 Clay

Scott Maggie B. Miss, milliner with Mrs. G. M. Nichols, 661 Clay

Scott Moses, averager adjuster, dwl 11 Tehama

Scott Moses jr. accountant with T. N. Cazneau, 504 Battery

Scott Norbourn B. dwl 13 Powell

Scott R. F. clerk, office U. S. Surveyor General, dwl 503 Dupont

Scott Richard, carpenter and builder, dwl 725 Ellis

SCOTT R. N. lieutenant colonel U. S. A. assistant adjutant general D. P. office 418 California, dwl Occidental Hotel

SCOTT ROBERT C. wines and liquors, 323 Wash

Scott Robert P. book keeper with William A. Green, Greenwich Dock Warehouse, dwl S s Broadway bet Montgomery and Sansom

Scott Sophia M. Miss, milliner with Mrs. G. M. Nichols, 661 Clay

Scott Stephen H. chief engineer stm Moses Taylor, dwl 170 Clementina

Scott Thomas, laborer, Spring Valley W. W.

Scott Thomas, machinist, Union Foundry, dwl 558 Bryant

Scott Thomas A. dwl 24 Sansom

Scott Walter, clerk, S. F. & P Sugar Co. dwl W s Mission bet Twelfth and Thirteenth

Scott Warehouse, James C. King & Co. proprietors, cor Greenwich and Sansom

Scott William, attaché, Maguire's Opera House

Scott William, boiler maker, dwl Vale bet Guerrero and Dolores

Scott William, engineer, dwl Verona Place

Scott William, laborer, dwl N s Grove bet Gough and Octavia

Scott William, laborer, dwl 335 Broadway
Scott William, workman with D. Hudson, Bay View
Scott William A. exchange clerk, bank Wells, Fargo & Co. dwl Occidental Hotel
Scott William G. sash and blind maker with George Robinson & Co. dwl 512 Taylor
Scott W. R. photographer with Hamilton & Kellogg, dwl 335 Broadway
Scottish Chief G. & S. M. Co. office 625 Clay
Scouler James, cabinet maker, E s Wallace Place, dwl 830 Vallejo
SCOVERN JAMES G. livery and sale stable, 739 Market
Scoville George W. waterman, 609 Market, dwl King bet Third and Fourth
Scoville William H. machinist, dwl W s Shotwell bet Twenty-First and Twenty-Second
Scran Charles, workman with J. O. Taplin, San Bruno Road
Scranton Charles, dwl 408 Market
Scriber William E. clerk, dwl 932 Montgomery
Scrimgeour James, salesman with J. R. Mead & Co. dwl 22 John
Scrimgeour Joseph, dwl SW cor Bdwy and Mont
Scriven William, hostler, 679 Market, dwl Jessie bet Second and Third
Scroggs George A. actor, dwl Pacific bet Montgomery and Kearny
Scudder Francis V. book keeper with William H. Martin, dwl N s Vallejo bet Powell and Mason
Scudder George. merchant, dwl 655 Washington
Scudder Henry M. Rev. pastor Howard Presbyterian Church, dwl 1 Vernon Place
Scudders August, nurse, U. S. Marine Hospital
Sculler Daniel, painter, dwl 441 Clementina, rear
Sculley John, groom, dwl 59 Stevenson
Sculley Patrick, driver, Central R. R. Co. dwl SE cer Brannan and Seventh
Sculley Peter, drayman with Bryant & Morrison, dwl N s Green bet Leavenworth and Hyde
Sculling Henry F. machinist, Union Foundry, dwl Bay State House
Scully Elizabeth Miss, domestic with George J. Griffing
Scully J. E. driver, Central R. R. Co. dwl SE cor Brannan and Seventh
Scully Patrick, workman, S. F. Sugar Refinery, dwl W s Chesley nr Harrison
Scunderhaus Julius, tailor with Julius Tammeyer, dwl 127 Jackson
Seaborn (Thomas) & Frei (Andrew) wood and ivory turners, 409 Mission, dwl 112 Tehama
Seaders C. fruit peddler, dwl SW cor Dupont and Broadway
Seal Joel A. dwl 619 Pacific
Seale Joseph, contractor, dwl N s Turk nr Fillmore
Seale Thomas, miner, dwl N s Tehama nr Fourth
Sewley Charles, bricklayer, dwl 119 Minna
Seally Patrick, workman, S. F. & P. Sugar Co. dwl Mary nr Chesley
Seals Daniel (col'd) real estate, dwl 421 Green
Seaman B. Mrs. millinery, 20 Montgomery
Seaman Charles, salesman, 424 Sansom, dwl 20 Mont
Seaman David, express wagon, corner Dupont and Jackson
Seaman George M. chair maker, dwl Howard En-House No. 3
Seaman Henry, mariner, dwl W s Kimball nr Sac
Seaman Victor, wharfinger, Vallejo St. Wharf, dwl SE cor Powell and Lombard
Seamans Job M. jeweler, 604 Merch, dwl 112 Geary
Seang Kee (Chinese) butcher, 733 Sacramento
Searell Allen, miller, Golden Age Flour Mills, dwl Chicago Hotel
Searing Henry L. book keeper with T. Ellsworth, SE cor Market and East
Searing Matthew G. drayman, 401 Bat, dwl 39 Clara
Searle A. T. butcher with Bookstaver & Weller, dwl 548½ Tehama

Searle William, butcher, dwl 1119 Clay
Searles Samuel, butcher with Harrington Bros. dwl cor Brannan and Ninth
Searles William A. straw hat manufacturer, dwl 1123 Taylor
SEARLS ANSON, carriage factory, 417 and 419 Market, dwl Russ House
Searls Ella Miss, domestic, 805 Filbert
Searls John, butcher, dwl E s Eighth bet Howard and Folsom
Sears G. & S. M. Co. office 302 Montgomery
Sears George C. second lieut. Co. I, C. V. Fort P
Sears J. Frank, clerk, County Recorder's Office, dwl 527 Bush
Sears Thomas H. book keeper with Miller & Co. 123 Clay, dwl 924 Mission
Seary Anna Miss, domestic, 408 Eddy
Seary Bridget Miss, domestic, 819 Bush
Seaton Daniel M. W. law student, dwl N s Erie nr Howard
Seaton George W. attorney at law, dwl N s Erie nr Howard
Seaton Mining Co. office 712 Montgomery
Seaton William M. dwl E s Second bet Mission and Howard
Seaver Freeman, conductor, North Beach & M. R. R. Co. dwl 172 Minna
Seaver William H. plasterer, dwl 5 Perry
Seavey Charles, waiter, What Cheer House
Seavey James E. C. carpenter, dwl S s Brannan nr Seventh
Seavey Otis L. laundryman, dwl N side Sacramento bet Jones and Leavenworth
Seawell James M. attorney at law, office 11 Montgomery Block, dwl 1312 Pine
Seawell Thomas, gardener, dwl W side Taylor bet Green and Union
Seawell Washington, col. U. S. A. commissary musters, office 418 Washington, dwl SE cor Taylor and Eddy
Sebastian M. musician, dwl 1314 Dupont
Sebert Charles, laborer, dwl E s Beale bet Market and Mission
Sebreras Fidel, saddler, dwl 1535 Broadway
Secchi Gaspar, bakery, 1233 Stockton
SECURITY FIRE INSURANCE CO. (New York) Bigelow & Brother agents, 505 Montgomery
Sedgeley John R. teamster, SE cor California and Davis, dwl S s Twelfth bet Howard and Folsom
SEDGLEY ABNER, carpenter and builder, office 316 Pine, dwl 318 Sutter
SEDGLEY (Joseph) & DAVIS (Franklin A.) wool dealers, Mission Creek nr Mariposa, office 536 Kearny
Sedgley Joseph, stock dealer and wholesale butcher, office 536 Kearny, dwl 837 Mission
Seegelken (A. D.) & Winckelmann (Henry) groceries and liquors, NE cor Davis and Commercial
Seegelken Diedrich, farmer, Ocean House Flat near Ocean House
Seeger Frederica (widow) dwl corner Shasta and Michigan
Seekamp George, musician, Bella Union, dwl 711 Filbert
Seelig Simon (A. Hollub & Co.) dwl 616 O'Farrell
Seeligsohn Max, dry goods, 512 Sacramento, dwl 732 Howard
Seeligsohn Solomon, with Max Seeligsohn, dwl 732 Howard
Seely Charles, cooper, dwl What Cheer House
Sefton Stephen, longshoreman, dwl 112 Jackson
Segale Peter, dwl 1506 Dupont
Segbers Albert, dwl 1523 Mason
Segbers Bernard, foreman with McMillan & Kester, dwl 1523 Mason
Segbers Joseph H. teamster with Lyon & Co. dwl 247 Minna
Segelhorst Augustus, seaman, bds 7 Washington

Seger George, dwl SW cor Taylor and Vallejo
Segers John, cook, Bootz's Hotel
Segord James, seaman, dwl 26 Sacramento
Segui Baltasar, restaurant, 723 Davis
Seguine Boont, dwl cor Sixteenth and Rhode Island
Sehabiague L. night attendant, French Hospital
Scheuring George, tailor, dwl NW cor Jackson and Kearny
Seib Herman, clerk, dwl 205 Sansom
Seibel Frederick, butcher, 3 New Market, dwl 1708 Stockton
Seibel Philip, meat market, 35 Geary
Seiberlich A. & Sons *(F. Anthony and F. H. Seiberlich)* importers and manufacturers boots and shoes, 214 California, res New York
Seiberlich F. Anthony *(A. Seiberlich & Sons)* dwl 214 California
Seiberlich F. H. *(A. Seiberlich & Sons)* res Philadelphia
Seidel William, clerk, 232 Montgomery
Seidenberg Charles, tailor, 529 East
Seifert Adam, cabinet maker with Goodwin & Co
Seifert M. L. machinist, Union Foundry, dwl 546 Mission
Seifert Nicholas, waiter, New York Bakery, dwl 132 Sutter
Seiferth Morris, medal maker, dwl Chicago Hotel, 220 Pacific
Seigmund Edward, coppersmith with J. G. Ils, dwl Meyer's Hotel
Seigmund William, clerk, bds Meyer's Hotel, 814 Montgomery
Sein Cung (Chinese) washing, 707 Union
Seine Joseph, market wagon, Washington Market
Seipp Conrad, laborer, Pacific Flour Mills
Seitz Christian, dwl 209 Ellis
Seivers William, mariner, dwl 14 Stewart
Selby Prentiss, salesman with Thomas H. Selby & Co. dwl 618 Harrison
SELBY THOMAS H. & CO. *(Peter Naylor)* importers metals, 116 and 118 California, and proprietors S. F. Shot Tower and Lead Pipe Manufactory, dwl 618 Harrison
SELBY'S WAREHOUSE, SW cor Market and Main
Seldner Louis, book keeper, 414 Sacramento, dwl 112 Stevenson
Self Julia (widow) dwl 1311 Stockton
Selfridge Edward H. book keeper, North America Life Insurance Co. 240 Montgomery, dwl NE cor Second and Minna
Selig Brothers *(Abraham and Samuel)* groceries and liquors, SE cor Minna and Jane
Selig I. gents' furnishing goods, 214 Montgomery, dwl 315 Bush
Selig Jetty (widow) dwl SE cor Minna and Jane
Selig *(Moses)* & Co. *(Jacob Schonfeld)* wholesale butchers, Potrero Avenue, dwl 811 Mission
Selig Samuel *(Selig Bros.)* dwl SE cor Minna and Jane
Seligman Abraham *(J. Seligman & Co.)* dwl 1706 Stockton
Seligman Frank, furniture, 1226 Dupont
SELIGMAN J. & CO. *(Leopold and Abraham Seligman)* importers and jobbers clothing, 111 Battery, res New York
Seligman Leopold *(J. Seligman & Co.)* dwl 1710 Stockton
Seligsberg William, book keeper, 111 Battery, dwl SW cor Washington and Powell
Selk James, groom, dwl Ritch bet Bryant and Brannan
Selka Rosa Miss, domestic, 724 Post
Selkirk James, tanner with McKenna & Tunsted, W s Lagoon
Selleck J. W. conductor, North Beach & M. R. R. Co
Selleck Mathew, bricklayer, dwl 26 Geary
SELLECK SILAS, photographic art gallery, 415 Montgomery, dwl 30 Minna

Sellen Christoph, blacksmith, dwl 630 Broadway
Seller Hiram, hostler, White House, W s Mission bet Twenty-Third and Twenty-Fourth
Seller J. H. dwl 119 Powell
Seller Joseph *(Goldstein & S)* dwl 113 Powell
Seller Louisa (widow) dwl W s Mason bet Chestnut and Lombard
Sellers *(James C.)* & McPherson *(S. G.)* house painters, 405 Kearny, dwl SW cor Broadway and Leavenworth
Sellinger Lawrence, night inspector, Custom House, dwl 426 Green
Selna Ubaldo *(Bulletti & Co.)* dwl E s Dupont bet Lombard and Greenwich
Sels Henry R. merchant, dwl 507 Greenwich
Semler A. carpenter, dwl Trinity nr Sutter
Semler Frederick, shoe maker, dwl 135 Post
Semmes Joseph, laborer, Clipper Restaurant
Semple James, laborer, Custom House, dwl SE cor Kearny and Lombard
Senechal Paul, laborer, McMillan & Kester, dwl City Laundry South Park
Senram Frederick, shoe making, 28 Kearny, dwl 219 Kearny
Senstack Harm H. laborer, Bay Sugar Refinery, dwl 813 Battery
Senter Moses S. carrier, Evening Bulletin and Call, dwl 522 Howard
Sepetin Baptiste, workman with L. L. Lefebvre, dwl Florida nr Twentieth
Sepulveda John, dwl S s Francisco bet Dupont and Stockton
Seran Gustave *(Blanc & S.)* 109 Fourth
Seregni F. professor ornamental penmanship and teacher public schools, office and dwl 606 Montgomery
Serin Julia Josephine (widow) dwl 1106 Wash
Sesnon Robert P. drayman, 211 Cal, dwl 10 Clara
Seanor Catherine, ironer, Chelsea Laundry
Sesser Peter, teamster, 315 California, dwl cor Sixth and Market
Sessions Charles A. clerk with S. B. Whipple, dwl 10 Clarence Place
Sessions E. C. *(Osborn & S.)* res Oakland
Sessions Josiah, teamster, dwl 810 Powell
Sessions Milton P. teamster, NW cor Battery and California, dwl 12 Clarence Place
Sessions William W. job wagon, SE cor Battery and California, dwl 12 Clarence Place
Setchell Dan, manager Academy of Music
Seth William H. (col'd) porter with G. C. Shreve & Co. dwl 12 Auburn
Seully Firmin *(Mercado & S.)* dwl 424 Greenwich
Severance Charles C. P. laborer, National Mills, dwl 142 Shipley
Severance Charles W. book keeper, 613 Sacramento, dwl 142 Shipley
Severance William, carpenter, dwl W s Dolores bet Twenty-Second and Twenty-Third
Severance William, stone cutter, bds Brooklyn Hotel
Severene Robert, dwl 109 First
Severin Theodore, gunsmith and sporting materials, 524 Kearny
Severin Theodore jr. gunsmith with Theodore Severin, dwl Olney nr Townsend
Severing Otto, lab, dwl cor Green and August Alley
Seversen Christian, seaman, dwl 26 Sacramento
Sevey L. J. laborer, dwl 163 Tehama
Sevier Francis, liquor saloon, NW cor Sacramento and Drumm
Seward George, carpenter, dwl 10 O'Farrell
Sewell John, carpenter, dwl 26 Hunt
Sexton Anna Miss, domestic, 314 Stockton
Sexton John, laborer, 4 Jessie
Sexton John, waiter, dwl 147 Minna
Sexton Thomas, laborer, dwl 12 Sutter
Seybold William F. bar keeper, 324 Sansom, dwl 172 Minna

Seyden Henry, drayman, 312 Front, dwl 6 Telegraph Place
Seymore Samuel, pantryman, steamer Senator
Seymour *(Alfred)* & Shillaber *(Levi)* fruit, 266 First, dwl 310 Folsom, rear
Seymour Charlotte (col'd, widow) dwl 30 Stone
Seymour F. M. (widow) dwl 30 Stanly Place
Seymour House, John Doyle proprietor, 24 Sansom
Seymour Simon H. with H. H. Pearson & Co. Russ House
SHABER J. F. furniture and bedding, 21 Second
SHABER JOHN A. furniture and bedding, 622 Market *(and Field & S.)* dwl 623 Market
Shaber William R. *(Field & S.)* dwl 623 Market
Shackerley Ann M. (widow) dwl 1716 Dupont
Shackleton John, molder, Miners' Foundry, dwl cor Pine and Kearny
Shackleton William T. molder, Miners' Foundry, dwl 256 Clementina
Shaddock Thomas, picture frame maker, 650 Market, dwl 9 Morse
Shaefer C. clerk with Morris Speyer, dwl SE cor Broadway and Stockton
Shaefer Henry, butcher, dwl 130 Dora
Shaeffer John W. cigar inspector, U. S. Internal Revenue *(and J. Macdonough Foard & Co.)* dwl 1508 Leavenworth
Shaen Joseph, tailoring, 332 Bush, dwl 41 Jessie
Shafer Henry, bar keeper, corner California and Kearny, dwl 636 Commercial
Shafer Jacob, teamster, 717 Bat, dwl 134 Minna
Shafer John Henry, contractor, dwl 14 Mason
Shafer O. L. dwl 615 Market
Shafer W. L. compositor, American Flag, dwl 624 Commercial
Shaff S. W. cook, New Wisconsin Hotel, 411 Pacific
Shaffer John, helper, Pacific Foundry
Shaffer Peter, butcher, dwl Potrero Avenue
Shaffner Frederick, dwl 16 Third
Shaffner Marshall, clerk, 411 Sacramento, dwl with F. Shaffner
Shaffrey Julia, domestic, 434 Second
SHAFTER, *(James McM.)* GOOLD *(Edmond L.)* & DWINELLE *(John W.)* attorneys at law, office 11 Montgomery Block, dwl S s Chestnut bet Hyde and Larkin
Shafter Oscar L. attorney at law, office 11 Montgomery Block, res Oakland
Shairlock John, dwl 269 Stevenson
Shakespear Benjamin F. bricklayer, dwl 509 Dupont
Shalaboy Joseph, cigar maker, dwl 353 Jessie
Shalte George T. driver, Central R. R. Co. dwl E s Eighth bet Bryant and Brannan
Shanabrook Isaac L. carriage painter with Larkins & Co. dwl 669 Mission
Shanahann John, hackman, dwl 176 Clara, rear
Shandel John, cook, 107 Tehama
Shane Jane Miss, dress making, 330 Bush
Shang Hun & Ah Kee (Chinese) cigar makers, 745 Sac
Shankey William, boots and shoes, 704 Union, dwl 2012 Powell
Shankland James W. receiver U. S. Land Office, office 625 Merchant, dwl 1 Essex Place
Shankland Robert, dwl 43 Clara
Shanley Eliza (widow) dwl 227 Bush
Shanly James H. molder, Pacific Foundry, dwl 227 Bush
Shannahan Ellen (widow) dwl 119 Stevenson
Shannon August, shoe maker, dwl 1113 Kearny, rear
Shannon Dominick, hostler, 669 Market, dwl Stevenson bet First and Second
Shannon James, hostler, 669 Market, dwl Winthrop House
Shannon James, laborer, 546 Clay, dwl 35 Sac
Shannon Jerry, plasterer, dwl NW cor Jessie and Anna
Shannon John, hackman, Plaza
Shannon John, porter with Robert Sherwood, dwl 107 Tehama

Shannon Joseph, dwl 727 Vallejo
Shannon Kate Miss, domestic, Ladies' Protection and Relief Society
Shannon Michael, printer with Frank Eastman, dwl W s Eighth bet Howard and Folsom
Shannon Rosa (widow) dwl 14 Stockton Place
Shannon Robert, dwl Original House
Shannon Thomas, bricklayer, dwl Davis St. House
SHANNON THOMAS B., U. S. Surveyor port San Francisco, office second floor Custom House, dwl 533 Post
Shantery Jeremiah, laborer, dwl United States Hotel, 706 Battery
Shanty Mary Miss, domestic, 537 Pine
Shapeare Abraham, asst teacher, Hebrew School, dwl cor Montgomery and Pacific
Sharkey Adelia A. Miss, domestic with W. L. Perkins, E s Eleventh bet Market and Mission
Sharkey Anna Miss, domestic, 11 Hampton Place
Sharkey Bernard, hostler, bds with Isaac Stone Lone Mountain
Sharkey Daniel F. marble worker, 673 Market, dwl 243 Stevenson
Sharkey Edward *(Toland & S.)* dwl W s Fifth Avenue nr Harrison
Sharkey James, laborer, C. S. Nav. Co. dwl SW cor Green and Sansom
Sharkey James, liquor saloon and boarding, 132 Folsom
Sharkey J. F. marble works, 673 Market
Sharkey J. M. physician, office and dwl SE cor Dupont and Washington
Sharkey William, laborer, dwl S s Stevenson near Fifth
Sharlen Rose, domestic, 843 Howard
Sharp Ann (widow) dwl 414 Union
Sharp Frederick, dwl 46 Sutter
SHARP GEORGE F. & WILLIAM H. attorneys at law, office 529 Clay, dwl Lick House
Sharp James D. book binder with Edward Bosqui & Co. dwl 414 Union
Sharp Jesse, laborer, dwl Dolores Hall W s Valencia nr Sixteenth
Sharp John, machinist, dwl 820 Dupont
Sharp Lawrence, carpenter, bds Manhattan House, 705 Front
Sharp Morris, merchant, dwl 716 Leavenworth
Sharp R. J. machinist, Union Foundry, dwl 18 Natoma
SHARP *(Sol. A.)* & LLOYD *(R. H.)* attorneys at law, office 17–19 Court Block, 636 Clay, dwl Russ House
Sharp William, book binder with Hicks & Co. dwl 414 Union
Sharp William, molder, Union Foundry, dwl 28 Bat
Sharp William, watch and clock maker, 837 Clay
Sharp William H. *(George F. & William H. Sharp)* attorney at law, office 529 Clay, dwl 517 Sutter
Sharpe John A. carpenter, dwl 31 Tehama, rear
Sharpe William, book keeper with Phil. Caduc, dwl 717 Green
SHARPSTEIN *(John R.)* & SMYTH *(J. H.)* attorneys at law, 24 and 25 Exchange Building, dwl 304 Stockton
Shath John, shoe maker, 215 Dupont
Shattuck Anna B. (widow) dwl 122 Geary
Shattuck D. D. *(Boswell & S.)* dwl 18 Prospect Pl
Shattuck Gilbert, dwl N s Fulton nr Fillmore
Shattuck Jane B. (widow) dwl 1313 Powell
Shaughnessy Ann Miss, nurse, 822 Folsom
Shaughnessy John, coal passer, steamer Senator
Shaughnessy John, printer, dwl 728 Market
Shaughnessy Lawrence, deck hand, stm Washoe
Shaughnessy Michael, carpenter, dwl 546 Bryant
Shaw A. M. (widow) lodgings, 40 Natoma
Shaw Anna (widow) dwl 41 Tehama
Shaw B. F. salesman with George Hughes, dwl 16 Perry

Shaw Charles, conductor, Omnibus R. R. Co
Shaw Charles H. contractor and builder, dwl 619 Mission
Shaw E. A. Miss, assistant, Denman Grammar School, dwl 716 Stockton
Shaw E. B. (Northup & S.) dwl 200 Stockton
Shaw Edward, clerk, dwl 510 Sacramento
Shaw E. H. broker, dwl 16 Perry
Shaw Elizabeth (widow) dwl 1808 Taylor
Shaw E. M. Miss, assistant, Fourth St. School, dwl 4 Essex
Shaw Frederick, mate, Sierra Nevada, dwl 13 Tehama
Shaw George H. ship joiner with John G. North, Potrero, dwl 446 Brannan
Shaw George T. carpenter, 320 Jackson, dwl 133 Stevenson
Shaw Hannah Mrs. dwl NE cor Broadway and Kearny
Shaw John, commission merchant, 207 Clay, dwl 926 Sacramento
Shaw John, laborer, dwl 605 Third
Shaw John, printer, dwl Golden Gate Hotel
Shaw J. S. clerk with R. B. Swain & Co. dwl Mission nr Fourth
Shaw LeFevre A. sign painter with James Donovan, dwl 16 Perry
Shaw Louis, butcher, Occidental Market, dwl 873 Mission
Shaw Mathias, stone cutter, dwl cor First and Folsom
Shaw Mrs. (widow) dwl 518 Bryant
Shaw N. W. clerk, dwl 28 Hunt
Shaw Oliver B. carpenter, dwl 702 Jones
Shaw S. W. portrait painter, SE cor Montgomery and California
Shaw T. C. millwright, Miner's Foundry, dwl SW cor First and Stevenson
Shaw Theodore, molder, dwl 7 Stevenson
Shaw Thomas L. contractor, dwl 633 Market
Shaw Thomas O. dwl International Hotel
Shaw Tobias, dwl 1027 Dupont
Shaw Tobias, pawnbroker, 913 Dupont, dwl 530 Geary
Shaw William, compositor, dwl 1808 Taylor
Shaw William, shoe maker, 7 Trinity
SHAW WILLIAM J. attorney at law, dwl cor Folsom and Thirteenth
Shaw William M. with Charles M. Plum, 22 Mont
Shaw William P. carpenter, dwl 111 Sixth
SHAWL MORRIS, Pavilion Liquor and Billiard Saloon, SE cor Post and Stockton
Shay James, lab, dwl N s Tyler bet Hyde and Larkin
Shay Mary Miss, domestic, 716 O'Farrell
Shea Annie Miss, domestic, 820 Howard
Shea Cornelius, peddler, dwl 2 Lick Alley
Shea Dennis H. express wagon, dwl W s Fifth Avenue bet Bryant and Harrison
Shea Edward, shoe maker, dwl 514 Front
Shea Elihu, with E. G. Allen, 513 Bush, dwl 12 Harlan Place
Shea Elizabeth (widow) dwl E s Grove Avenue bet Bryant and Harrison
Shea Ellen Miss, domestic, 892 Sutter
Shea Ellen Miss, domestic, 832 California
Shea Henry, with Herman Buerlind
Shea James, porter with Sullivan & Cashman, dwl Taylor bet Hyde and Larkin
Shea James, proprietor Brooklyn Hotel Coaches, 120 Sansom
Shea John, junk dealer, dwl S s Chambers bet Battery and Front
Shea John, laborer, dwl 258 Clementina
Shea Julia, domestic, 341 Minna
Shea Julia, domestic, 59 Stevenson
Shea Julia Miss, domestic, 619 Geary
Shea Margaret Miss, domestic, 21 Post
Shea Michael, carpenter, dwl cor Greenwich and Polk

Shea Morris, laborer with B. Bonnet & Co
Shea M. S. dwl 66 First
Shea Patrick, porter, dwl 12 Sutter
Shea Robert, boarding, 618 Mission
Shea Robert, laborer, dwl NE cor First and Bryant
Shea Timothy, laborer, dwl 174 Stevenson
Sheahan Morris, tailor, dwl 329 Kearny
Shean David, laborer, dwl cor Third and Folsom
Shean James E. printer, dwl 511 Pine
Shean Jeremiah F. printer, dwl 511 Pine
Shean John, laborer, dwl 113 Dora, rear
Shean John, workman, S. F. & P. Sugar Co. dwl E s Sumner nr Howard
Sheun M. Miss, regalia maker, dwl 18 Minna
Shear A. M. dwl SW cor Mission and Sixteenth
SHEAR CHARLES H. Five Mile House, Old San José Road 5 miles from City Hall
SHEAR EDWIN E. agent Folsom's New England Sewing Machines, 8 Montgomery, dwl 6 Mont
Shear Mary Mrs. millinery, 106 Third
Shear William, Nightingale Hotel, SW cor Mission and Sixteenth
Shear William H. blacksmith, dwl SW cor Mission and Sixteenth
Shearer Alexander, drayman, Miners' Foundry
Shearer Lewis, attorney at law, office 29 Exchange Building, dwl Guy Place
Shearer Mary (widow) dwl S s Thirteenth nr Mission
Shearer Sextus jr. student with Lewis Shearer, dwl Guy Place
Shears John, wheelwright with Black & Saul, dwl 906 Post
Sheba G. & S. M. Co. office 712 Montgomery
Sheble G. carpenter and cabinet maker, 741 Pacific
Scheck William, bricklayer, dwl 109 Pine
SHED (Charles D.) & WRIGHT (Henry C.) ship chandler and ship stores, 54 and 56 Stewart, dwl 816 Sutter
Sheddy James E. stone cutter with John Daniel, 421 Pine
Shee Kee (Chinese) groceries, 810 Sacramento
Sheehan Daniel, drayman, office 405 Front, dwl 459 Minna
Sheehan Daniel, laborer, bds Roxbury House 318 Pacific
Sheehan Daniel, laborer, dwl N s Clara bet Fifth and Sixth
Sheehan Daniel, teamster, dwl 459 Minna
Sheehan Daniel, waiter, What Cheer House Restaurant
Sheehan David, laborer, dwl 713 Folsom
Sheehan John, steward, Brooklyn Hotel
Sheehan Lawrence, workman, S. F. & P. Sugar Co. dwl cor Beale and Mission
Sheehan Mary, domestic, 548 Folsom
Sheehan Mary Miss, domestic with P. L. Murphy, E s Howard bet Fifteenth and Sixteenth
Sheehan Morris, boot maker, 264 Third
Sheehan Morris, laborer, dwl cor Berry and Mary Lane
Sheehan Morris, shoe maker, cor Folsom and Third, dwl 30 Ritch, rear
Sheehan Patrick F. painter with James R. Kelly, dwl 455 Jessie
Sheehan Timothy, laborer, dwl Lincoln Avenue
Sheehey Patrick, miner (Boise River) dwl 254 Jessie
Sheely John, workman, S. F. & P. Sugar Co. dwl Sumner nr Howard
Sheeran Daniel, dwl 12 Sutter
Sheeran Nicholas, bricklayer, dwl 256 Third
Sheffield Charles, upholsterer. dwl 125 Fremont
Sheffield (Charles P.) & Patterson (James) importers and manufacturers saws and files, NE cor Jackson and Battery
Shehan Charles, night watchman, American Exch
Shehan John, driver, North Beach & M. R. R. Co
Shehan John, farmer, dwl 116 Jackson
Shehan John, seaman, dwl 123 Tehama
Shehan Kate Miss, chambermaid, Russ House

Sheideker John, carpenter, dwl 1619 Dupont, rear
Sheifer Frank, brewer, dwl Pioneer Malt House Stockton nr Francisco
Sheil Annie Miss, ironer, Davis Laundry, W s Harriet bet Howard and Folsom
Shein Kate, domestic, 47 Frederick
Sheiuhardt Henry, Metropolitan Bakery, 226 Pac
Sheiva John, brass finisher, dwl 507 Market
Shelby Jennings T. blacksmith, Mission Woolen Mills, dwl Carolina nr Mariposa
Sheldon Bishop *(David Hays & Co.)* dwl 52 Second
Sheldon Catherine (widow) dwl 36 Louisa
Sheldon D. L. carpenter, dwl W s Mission bet Twenty-Fourth and Twenty-Fifth
Sheldon H. B. carpenter, 571 Mission, dwl 567 Mission
Sheldon Hiram A. contractor, dwl W s Mission bet Twenty-Fourth and Twenty-Fifth
Sheldon John K. bricklayer, dwl 36 Louisa
Sheldon John P. *(Armstrong, Sheldon & Davis)* dwl N s Guy Place
Sheldon Joseph (col'd) dwl 1017 Clay
Sheldon R. O. metal roofer with H. G. & E. S. Fiske, dwl 407 Tehama
Sheldon Samuel, drayman, 414 Clay
Sheldon *(S. G.)* & Lloyd *(Wm. O.)* teachers dancing, SW cor Market and Second, dwl 745 Clay
Shellard Benjamin, organ builder, dwl E s Montgomery bet Green and Union
Shelley John, upholsterer, dwl 248 Clara
Shelley William N. pilot, 805 Front, dwl N s Chestnut bet Dupont and Stockton
Shelly John F. upholsterer with Goodwin & Co. dwl 249 Clara
Shelly Peter, drayman, cor Battery and Bush, dwl N s Austin bet Franklin and Van Ness Avenue
Shelly William, laborer with John Center, NW cor Sixteenth and Folsom
Shelton Charles *(James Anderson & Co.)* dwl SE cor Battery and Union
Shelton Henry A. dwl 752 Howard
Shelton Samuel (col'd) cartman, dwl 1618 Dupont, rear
Shepard A. M. with T. C. Hanson & Co. 832 Market, dwl 761 Mission
Shepard D. W. dwl 219 California
Shepard George, dwl SW cor Vallejo and Davis
Shepard James *(Shepard & Sons)* dwl W s Ninth bet Market and Mission
SHEPARD J. L. N. *(San Francisco Chemical Works Co.)* office 327 Commercial, res Oakland
Shepard John, carpenter, dwl 200 Dupont
Shepard Samuel, toll collector Washington St. Wharf, dwl 761 Mission
Shepard *(William)* & Sons *(William jr. and James)* gas fitters and plumbers, 631 Market, dwl W s Ninth bet Market and Mission
Shepard William, laborer, dwl W s Nevada bet Folsom and Harrison
Shepard William jr. *(Shepard & Sons)* dwl W s Ninth bet Market and Mission
Shepeard Albert, street contractor, dwl cor Clay and Brenham Place
Sheperd William, laborer with Hey & Meyn
Shephard Alfred, engineer, dwl 1904 Powell
Shephard Joseph, with Thomas & Twing, cor Market and East
Shephard Mary (widow) dwl 121 Dupont
Shepheard John J. 1st Lieutenant Co. A Second Infantry C. V. Presidio
SHEPHEARD PHILIP W. judge Police Court, room City Hall first floor, chambers 13 second floor, dwl 1018 Powell
Shepheard William, grader, dwl W s Nevada nr Folsom
Shepherd Ansel J. first engineer stm Chrysopolis, dwl SW cor Mason and Filbert
Shepherd James, cutter, dwl 525 Greenwich
Sheppard John, tailor, dwl I. Goulet, dwl 1026 Clay

Sheppard John, tailor, S. F. P. Woolen Mills, dwl Sheppard Place nr Mason
Sheppard John W. law student, bds American Exch
Sheppard Mary (widow) liquor saloon, 720 Pacific
Shepperd Emily Mrs. dwl 316 Beale
Shepperd John, miner, dwl 76 Natoma
Shepston Catherine (widow) dwl with John A. Shepston
Shepston John A. farmer, dwl Old San José Road 6 miles from City Hall
Shepston William, dwl with John A. Shepston
Sheran Barney, hostler, 126 Fourth, dwl S s Minna bet Third and Fourth
Sherer Louis, trimmer with Kimball & Co. dwl 219 Kearny
Sherer Thomas, mason, dwl W s Gilbert bet Brannan and Townsend
Sheridan Andrew, laborer, dwl 6 Freelon
Sheridan Edward, laborer, dwl 6 Ecker
Sheridan Eliza, domestic, 753 Howard
Sheridan James, deck hand, steamer Yosemite
Sheridan James, expressman, dwl E s Hampshire nr Sixteenth
Sheridan James, fireman, steamer Orizaba
Sheridan James, seaman, dwl 60 Clementina
Sheridan James C. laborer, dwl 132 Stevenson
Sheridan James F. dwl 8 O'Farrell
Sheridan John, cooper, 708 Front, bds 306 Broadway
Sheridan John, milk ranch, Serpentine Avenue nr San Bruno Road
Sheridan Margaret Miss, domestic, 702 Lombard
Sheridan Patrick J. with Jones, Wooll & Sutherland, dwl 249 Jessie
Sheridan Patrick T. laborer, dwl 304 Pine
Sheridan Peter, shoe maker with P. F. Dunne, dwl NE cor Dupont and Francisco
Sheridan Robert, carpenter, dwl Buckley's Ranch Lone Mountain
Sheridan Thomas, actor, Olympic, dwl 445 Bush
Sheridan Thomas, coachman with Henry P. Coon, dwl N s Bush bet Gough and Franklin
Sheridan Thomas, machinist, Vulcan Iron Works, dwl 219 Beale
Sheridan William T. expressman, dwl E s Hampshire nr Sixteenth
SHERIFF CITY AND COUNTY, office 8 City Hall third floor
Sherman Ann, dwl 229 Jessie
Sherman Benjamin F. mason and builder, dwl SW cor California and Polk
Sherman C. A. Miss, assistant, Denman Grammar School, dwl 13 Harlan Place
Sherman Charles H. dwl DeBoom nr Second
Sherman Christopher, with James Brokaw, dwl 257 Clementina
Sherman David B. drayman, 34 Market, dwl 237 Beale
Sherman David S. porter with Wightman & Hardie, dwl NE cor Clay and Montgomery
Sherman Francis, assayer with Kellogg, Hewston & Co. dwl 616 Taylor
Sherman Frank, captain schooner L. B. Hasting, dwl NW cor Brannan and Third
Sherman George, driver with N. H. Roy & Bro. San Bruno Road, 3 miles from City Hall
Sherman George, vegetable peddler, dwl N s Pacific bet Larkin and Polk
Sherman Harry, compositor, Alta California, dwl 913 Clay
Sherman Hiram, milkman with Benjamin P. Jenkins
Sherman I. V. watch maker with Alfred Barrett, dwl 321 Minna
Sherman Jacob, cabinet maker, 304 Dupont, dwl 13 Harlan Place
Sherman James, conductor, Central R. R. Co. dwl 427 Sixth
Sherman James E. seaman, dwl 26 Sacramento
Sherman John, carpenter, dwl 511 Dupont

Sherman John, laborer, dwl S s Harrison bet Main and Spear
Sherman Leander S. silversmith with Vanderslice & Co. dwl 13 Harlan Place
Sherman O. D. express wagon, dwl NE cor Montgomery and Clay
Sherman Otis M. carpenter, dwl W s First near Bryant
Sherman S. S. Miss, assistant, Union Grammar School, dwl 13 Harlan Place
Sherman Thomas B. book keeper with Marsh, Pilsbury & Co. dwl 1112 Kearny
Sherman Thompson, carpenter, dwl W s First near Bryant
Sherman *(Walter B.)* & Brown *(James W.)* furniture, 402 Folsom
SHERMAN WILLIAM & CO. manufacturers, importers, and retailers clothing, gents' furnishing goods, trunks, valises, etc. 412 and 414 Sansom
Sherman William E. book keeper with Wm. P. Harrison & Co. dwl W s Guerrero bet Sixteenth and Seventeenth
Sherrett Thomas, carpenter, dwl W s White Place nr Bryant
Sherry Bernard, packer, Eclipse Bakery, 1412 Dupont
Sherry Eugene, tailor with Peter Anderson, 541 Merchant
Sherry James, ship carpenter, dwl 56 Main
Sherry John, milk ranch, N s Precita Avenue near Mission
Sherwood B. F. merchant, 712 Mont, bds Lick House
Sherwood Edwin H. *(Sherwood, Bulkley & Co.)* dwl SW cor Third and Market
Sherwood Elisha J. foreman sewing room, S. F. P. Woolen Mills
Sherwood George E. dwl 1512 Powell
SHERWOOD ROBERT *(late Barrett & S.)* importer and retailer watches, diamonds, jewelry, chronometers, etc. 517 Mont, dwl 21 Stanly Pl
Sherwood, *(Samuel B.)* Bulkley *(Milton)* & Co. *(Edwin H. Sherwood)* shipping and commission merchants, office 326 Clay cor Bat, dwl 17 Perry
Sherwood W. E. dwl 414 Market
Sherwood William J. apprentice, dwl N s Pine bet Powell and Stockton
Shetts Sidney, workman with John Henry, dwl W s Valencia bet Fifteenth and Sixteenth
Sheunamann Frank, blacksmith, dwl 323 Tehama
SHEW JACOB *(C. A. Marston)* photographic gallery, 315 Montgomery, dwl 759 Market
Shew Laura F. Miss, adjuster, U. S. Branch Mint, bds with J. B. Harmstead E s Howard between Eighteenth and Nineteenth
Shew Leonard M. cooper, dwl 708 Front
Shew Myron, with William Shew, 421 Montgomery, dwl 759 Market
SHEW WILLIAM, photographic art gallery, materials, picture frames, etc. 421 and 423 Mont
Shewbridge Thomas, laborer with Conroy & Tobin
Sheyer Solomon *(Toklas, Wise & Co.)* res New York
Shick J. H. glass blower, Pacific Glass Works, dwl Potrero
Shiel Margaret, domestic, 829 Mission
Shiel William, real estate, office 319 Bush, dwl 530 O'Farrell
Shields Alice E. Mrs. cook, Industrial School, Old Ocean House Road
Shields Ann (widow) dwl 518 Bryant
Shields Anna E. (widow) dwl 29 Jessie
Shields B. Miss, dwl 109 Geary
Shields Bessie Mrs. domestic, 505 Bush
Shields Daniel J. blacksmith, Phœnix Iron Works, dwl 13 Clementina
Shields George, laborer with Louis Ancenhofer
Shields James Capt. dwl 58 Clementina
Shields James Gen. dwl E s Howard bet Twelfth and Thirteenth

Shields John W. policeman, City Hall, dwl 113 Natoma
Shields Matthew, driver with Charles H. Killey
Shields Robert, with Owen Keating
Shields Robert, molder, Union Foundry, dwl 41 Minna
Shields Thomas, lather, dwl Minna bet Second and Third
Shields Timothy, liqnor saloon, 229 Bush
Shiels' Block, 608 Market and 9 Post
Shiels W. D. comedian, Metropolitan Theater
Shiffell Henry, lab, What Cheer House Restaurant
Shiler Charles, hostler with William Black
Shillaber George, carpenter, dwl 7 Everett
Shillaber Levi *(Seymour & S.)* dwl 266 First
Shillaber Theodore, dwl N s Harlan Place
Shillcott Henry, book keeper, dwl 704 Folsom
Shilling Joseph, tailor, 207 Fourth
Shilling Levi, hides and wool, 103 California, dwl 111 O'Farrell
Shilling Louis, handcartman, dwl 39 Jessie
Shillinger Joseph D. bar keeper, White House, W s Mission bet Twenty-Third and Twenty-Fourth
Shindler Casper, carriage painter with Albert Folsom, dwl Meyers' Hotel
Shine Ellen, domestic, 620 Howard
Shine James G. butcher, 343 Fourth
Shine John P. porter with L. B. Benchley & Co. dwl 238 Sutter
Shine Michael, lather, dwl 25 Perry
Shipley A. J. & Co. *(J. W. Chinn)* stock brokers, 617 Montgomery, dwl 1433 Taylor
Shirek *(Adolph)* & Co. *(Samuel Shirek)* variety stores, 19 Third and 1125 Stock, dwl 1112 Stock
Shirek Louis, laborer, dwl 125 Kearny
Shirek Samuel *(Shirek & Co.)* dwl 19 Third
Shirley Benjamin F. boot fitter, dwl 929 Greenwich
Shirley Francis, fruits, 206½ Fourth
Shirley John, dwl 1112 Stockton
Shirley John, boot fitter, dwl 1408 Kearny
Shirley John, merchant, office 524 Sansom, dwl W s Jones bet Washington and Jackson
Shirlock James, lather, dwl Jessie bet Third and Fourth
Shirpser Isadore, furrier, 106 Mont, dwl 744 Folsom
Shissler Ernest, hog butcher with Peter Schinkel, dwl W s Nevada nr Folsom
Shiverick Nathaniel, stock broker, dwl 916 Bush
Shlaberg Charles, boiler maker, Vulcan Iron Works, dwl 3 Chatham Place
Shloss E. Madame, millinery, 138 Montgomery, dwl 757 Howard
Shloss Marx, dry goods, 138 Mont, dwl 757 Howard
Shmidt John, laborer with Augustus Lind
Shneiter Phillip, coffee saloon, 31 Fourth
Shocken Abraham L. cigars and tobacco, 510 Kearny, dwl 1 St. Mary
Shocken Samuel H. hats and caps, 17 Second
Shockley Flournoy, dwl 48 Tehama
Shoebridge Frederick, drayman, 5 Washington, dwl Larkin bet Pacific and Broadway
Shoemaker Charles, dwl 121 Sixth
Shoemaker Fred'k *(Welsh & S.)* dwl 1761½ Mission
SHOEMAKER JOHN W. wharfinger Pacific Wharf, dwl 834 Clay
Shoen James, express wagon, cor Stock and Dupont
Shoenberg Lewis, cigars and tobacco, 32 Clay and SW cor East and Jackson
Shong Chong & Co. (Chinese) market, 720 Jackson
Shorb J. Campbell, physician, office 210 Bush
Short Bridget A. Miss, millinery, 106 Third, dwl Geary above Powell
Short David M. clerk, dwl 87 Stevenson
Short Emily Mrs. matron, County Jail, Broadway nr Dupont
Short Henry C. japanner with J. G. Ills, dwl W s Thirteenth nr Mission
Short John, jail keeper Broadway, dwl N s Broadway bet Dupont and Stockton

Short John, laborer, Lone Mountain Cemetery
Short John jr. pound keeper, SE cor Union and Van Ness Avenue, dwl N s Pacific nr Leavenworth
Short Mary (widow) dwl 3 Pollard Place
Short Patrick, drayman, 121 Clay, dwl 320 Geary
Short Peter, tailor, dwl N s Austin bet Gough and Octavia
Shortell Mary Miss, domestic, 1006 Clay
SHORTT LAWRENCE H. civil engineer and sur. veyor, office 302 Montgomery, dwl 320 Brannan
Shoshone G. M. Co. office 529 Clay
Shotwell J. M. secretary Gould & Curry S. M. Co. office NE cor Mont and Jackson, dwl 710 Leav
Shoule William, waiter, Richards' Restaurant, dwl SE cor Union and Kearny
Shoulters Henry, engineer, office 326 Clay, dwl 325 Fifth
Shove Mortimer G. carpenter, dwl 209 Tehama
SHRADER ANDREW J. butcher, cor Brannan and Ninth and supervisor Ninth District, office Pacific Fruit Market, dwl 413 Brannan
SHREVE GEORGE C. & CO. (Lucius Thompson) watches, diamonds, jewelry, and silver ware, etc. 525 Montgomery, dwl 412 Second
Shreve George W. carpenter, Potrero Rope Walk, dwl nr cor Sierra and Indiana
Shrom Ellen (widow) dwl N s Harrison bet Seventh and Eighth
Shroup Elizabeth, dwl with Conrad Riegelhuth, W s Julia nr Minna
Shultis Edward, painter, dwl 517 Bush
Shults Christian, laborer with Hey & Meyn
Shults Frederick, gardener with T. J. A. Chambers
Shultz Henry, handcartman, cor Stewart and Mission
Shultz Jacob S. carpenter, 208 Commercial, dwl 510 Bush
Shultze Christian, laborer, dwl W s Rousch bet Howard and Folsom
Shultze Oscar, cabinet maker, dwl N s Fulton near Octavia
Shuman Henry, cooperage, 120 Sacramento, dwl Heron nr Eighth
Shumann Peter, tinsmith, dwl 1 Auburn
Shumann William, groceries and liquors, NW cor Mission and Fourth
Shussler J. drayman, cor Stockton and Jackson
Shusvitz Mathias, dwl NW cor Kearny and Jackson
Shute C. E. with F. Gracier, dwl SE cor Mission and First
Shute Daniel S. (Shute & Bro.) dwl 1004 Pine
Shute (Henry M.) & Brother (Daniel S.) carriage and spring making, 539 Market, dwl 312 Pine
Shuvan Cornelius, dwl 822 Pacific
Shwartz Joseph, driver, Broadway Brewery, dwl 631 Broadway
Shyne James, Trinity Market, SE cor Fourth and Louisa
Sibley A. dwl 606 Montgomery
Sibley Nicholas, restaurant and wines, NW corner Broadway and Davis
Sibley William, dwl Summer St. House
Sichel Gustav, pile medicine, 614 Sacramento, dwl 502 Union
Sichel Marx, dentist, office 650 Washington, dwl 1701 Dupont
Sickels Colorado Prospecting Co. office 338 Mont
SICKLER CALEB M. stoves and tinware, 422 Kearny, dwl 528 Pine
Sickler Charles H. tinsmith with Caleb M. Sickler, dwl 516 Bush
Sickler John L. compositor with Agnew & Deffebach, 511 Sansom
Sickles Solomon, shoe maker, dwl 511 Union
Sicot C. cook, French Hospital
Sicotte Rogers (Belduke & Co.) dwl SE cor Fourth and Clementina
Siddel Benjamin, cigar maker, dwl SW cor Dupont and Broadway
Siebach John, dwl 2 Vallejo Place

Siebe Frederick C. confectioner with Ehrenpfort & Co. 24 Stockton
Siebe (John) & Co. (Martin Burfeind) proprietors Railroad Exchange, SW cor Powell and Francisco and SE cor Powell and Union
SIEBE JOHN & CO. (John Wessel) groceries and liquors, SE cor Union and Powell
Siebe Richard, liquor saloon, SW cor Kentucky and Sixteenth
Siebeck John, ship carpenter, bds 7 Washington
Siebenhauer Levi, student, dwl 688 Geary
Sieberst Henry G. clerk with Spencer & Jarboe, dwl SW cor Grove and Franklin
Siebert Frederick, cigars and tobacco, 218 Kearny
Siebrecht Franz, waiter, 416 Kearny
Siedenburg Herman, groceries and liquors, 520 Vallejo
Siedentopf Charles, book keeper with George Howes & Co. dwl E s Howard nr Fourteenth
Siegber Benjamin, laborer with McMillan & Kester, dwl 1523 Mason
Siegel Louis, policeman, City Hall, dwl 6 Harlan Pl
SIEGFRIED H. A. & CO. (H. Schramm & T. Haltirn) proprietors Odeum Garden and Concert Hall, NW cor Dolores and Fifteenth
SIEGFRIED H. A. proprietor Lutgen's Hotel, 228 Montgomery
Siegly Gottlieb, blacksmith with Gebhard & Boynton, dwl 1123 Dupont
Siegmund William, clerk, Adj't General's office, dwl Montgomery Place
Siegmundt Charles H. groceries and liquors, 825 Kearny
Siegrist August, gymnast, Gilbert's Museum, dwl 563 Mission
Siegrist Mary Miss, domestic, dwl 824 Mission
Siel August, dwl 354 Brannan
Sielark John, vegetable garden, Bay View
Siemers Wigmann, waiter, 614 Clay, dwl 612 Clay
Siems John H. groceries and liquors, 409 Union
Sier Dominique, milkman, dwl 1231 Dupont
Sier Philip, carriage maker, dwl 1231 Dupont
Siere James, bakery, NW cor Union and Dupont
Sierens Charles, L'Esperance Restaurant, 647 Com
Siering Herman (Locan & Co.) res Berlin Prussia
Sierp Frederick W. hatter with R. J. Tiffany, dwl N s Dorland nr Church
Sierra Madre G. & S. M. Co. (San Bernardino) office 611 Clay
Sierra Nevada Hotel, Niggle & Laurberg proprietors, 528 Pacific
Sierra Nevada S. M. Co. office 40 Montgomery Block
Sierra S. M. Co. office 103 California
Sierra Valley G. & S. M. Co. office 607 Washington
Sies Philip, express wagon, cor Sansom and Sac
Sievers Francis, accountant with R. Feuerstein & Co. dwl SE cor Stockton and Jackson
Sievers John H. clerk, 504 Mont, dwl Lutgen's Hotel
Siff George, laborer, dwl S s St. Charles nr Kearny
Sigel John, cooper, Pacific Distillery
Sigerson James, laborer, dwl 146 Stewart
Sigmund Carl, seaman, dwl 20 Commercial
Sigmund Geo. bar keeper, dwl Manhattan Engine H
Silberkohl Dorotha Mrs. machine sewing, 106 Kearny
Silberkohl Henry, hair dresser, dwl 106 Kearny
Silberman Gottlieb, clerk with L. Strauss, dwl 714 Vallejo
Silicks John, butcher, San Rafael Market, 311 Bdwy
Silk James, stableman, dwl 212 Ritch
Silk Thomas, laborer, dwl 20 St. Charles nr Kearny
Sillem William (Godeffroy & S.) dwl 1411 Powell
Silsby Margaret A. (widow) dwl E s Leavenworth bet Pacific and Broadway
Silva Aaron, waiter, steamer Petaluma
Silva Antonio, porter, steamer Cornelia, dwl 2 Sonoma Place
Silva Antouio, workman with Peter Casson & Co. nr Bay View Park

Silva Antonio, works with Joseph Silva
Silva Emanuel, deck hand, steamer Petaluma
Silva Francis, deck hand, steamer Petaluma
Silva Frank, barber, 102 Pacific, dwl Commercial Hotel 125 Pacific
Silva Joseph, boatman, Fort Point
Silva Joseph, deck hand, steamer Oakland, res Brooklyn
Silva Joseph, farmer, Lake Merced nr Ocean House
Silva Joseph, seaman, dwl N s Oregon nr Front
Silva Joseph T. photographic gallery, 402 Kearny cor Pine, dwl N s Filbert bet Hyde and Leav
Silva Lenardri D. laborer, dwl S s Pacific bet Montgomery and Kearny
Silva Manuel, waiter, Manhattan House 705 Front
Silva Manuel J. hair dresser, dwl Pacific Temperance House
Silver Abraham, porter, steamer Julia
Silver Age G. & S. M. Co. office 606 Montgomery
Silver Age S. M. Co. (Reese River) office 3 Odd Fellows' Hall
Silver Circle M. Co. office 529 Clay
Silver Emanuel D. carpenter, dwl SE cor Taylor and Filbert
Silver Frank, deck hand, steamer Julia
Silver Morris, clerk with Tobias Shaw
Silver Queen M. Co. office 608 Merchant
Silver Wilhelm, seaman, dwl 26 Sacramento
Silver William J. printer with Towne & Bacon, dwl cor Washington and Sansom
Silverberg Simon (E. N. Fish & Co.) dwl 16 Mason
Silverman Solomon, job wagon, cor California and Kearny, dwl 145 Post
Silverstein Louis, shoe maker, dwl 720 Front
Silverstein Mark, butcher, 505 Broadway
Silverston Harris, boots and shoes, 1138 Dupont
Silverston Harris, furniture wagon, dwl S s Francisco bet Mason and Taylor
Silverstone Solomon, dwl 816 Vallejo
Silverthorn W. H. under-sheriff, City Hall, dwl NE cor Filbert and Hyde
SILVESTER GEORGE F. seeds and agricultural tools, 317 Washington, dwl 82 Natoma
Silvester Leander, clerk, 319 Washington, dwl 82 Natoma
Silvestre John (Roux & S.) 538 Broadway.
Silvey Adolphe, dwl 709 Commercial
Silvey Anthony, trader, dwl 8 s Townsend bet Third and Fourth
Silvey Raymond, watchman, S. F. Cotton Factory, dwl Broderick Engine Co. No. 1
Silvey Robert, marine reporter with T. E. Baugh, office Meiggs' Wharf, dwl S s Pfeiffer Place
Silvis William, dwl 403 Union
Simay Lucian, cook, 143 Montgomery
SIME JOHN & CO. (B. F. Hastings) bankers, NW cor Mont and Clay, dwl 813 Jackson
Simen John, cabinet maker, Bush bet Sansom and Battery, dwl 749 Mission
Simeon Peter (col'd) restaurant, 223 Kearny
Simi Pietro & Co. (Antonio Descalzo) New World Restaurant, 1013 Dupont
Simmen John, cabinet maker with J. B. Luchsinger, dwl 749 Mission
Simmons Alonzo R. (Simmons, Rowe & Co.) dwl Central Place nr Pine
Simmons Andrew, workman, S. F. Cordage Factory, dwl NW cor Kentucky and Humboldt
Simmons Annie Miss, domestic, 1010 Powell
Simmons C. F. operator, Fire Alarm and Police Telegraph, City Hall, dwl 964 Mission
Simmons Charles, night inspector, Custom House, dwl 2 White Place
Simmons Ferdinand, musician, dwl 720 Vallejo
Simmons George A. dwl 107 Leidesdorff
Simmons Henry, driver, North Beach & M. R. R. Co. dwl N s Bryant nr Fifth
Simmons J. printer, Eureka Topographical Union, 625 Merchant

Simmons James, waiter, 626 Kearny
Simmons John, dwl 107 Leidesdorff
Simmons John B. book keeper with Wilson & Son, SE cor First and Market
SIMMONS, (Joseph S.) ROWE (William B.) & CO. (Alonzo R. and Philip Simmons) importers and jobbers hardware, 204 and 206 Pine and 34 Clay, dwl 819 Filbert
Simmons Leeson G. shooting gallery, Ocean House
Simmons Philip (Simmons, Rowe & Co.) dwl 819 Filbert
Simmons Samuel D. local policeman, dwl 1709 Leav
Simmons T. C. blacksmith helper, Vulcan Iron Works. dwl E s Seventh nr Brannan
Simmons William, carriage painter with M. P. Holmes, dwl 519 Filbert
Simmons William, rigger, dwl NE cor Mission and Beale
Simms Charles, waiter, Brooklyn Hotel
Simms William, actor, Maguire's Opera House
Simon Anne Mrs. dwl 1157 Mission
Simon Benjamin (Meetz & Co.) dwl SE cor Post and Dupont
Simon G. A. distiller and manufacturer syrups, 540 Washington, dwl Harrison bet Third and Fourth
Simon Hermann L. (Stein, S. & Co.) dwl 1806 Stockton
Simon J. (Rosenthal & S.) dwl 709 Clay
Simon Jacob, bar keeper, New York Hotel
Simon (John) & Nagle (Jacob) Pacific Coffee Saloon, 631 Pacific
Simon Joseph, boot maker, 511 East
Simon Joseph, furniture, 1214 Dupont
Simon Levi, broker, dwl 928 Mission
Simon Louis, laborer with G. A. Simon, 540 Washington, dwl Harrison bet Third and Fourth
Simon Louis, tailor, 51 Third
Simon Marks, barber, dwl 526 Vallejo
Simon Moritz, hats, dwl Continental Hotel
Simon S. with Lazard Freres, 115 Battery
Simon Seraphine, dwl 1124 Folsom
Simon S. I. merchant, dwl 406 Post
Simon Simon, merchant, dwl 1526 Powell
Simon Thomas, carpenter and joiner with Stevens & Rider, 256 Clementina
SIMON, (Ulrich) DINKELSPIEL (Lazarus) & CO. (Jonas Adler) importers and jobbers dry goods, SW cor Cal and Battery, res New York
Simondi Victoria Miss, embroideress, 745 Clay
Simonds E. S. miner, dwl 728 Market
Simonds Hazen K. carpenter, dwl 116 Sansom
Simonds James M. peddler, dwl 209 Dupont
Simonds Nathan, milkman cor Bay View Park and Hunter's Point Road
Simonds O. C. (widow) dwl 619 Post
Simonds Schuyler P. workman with N. Simonds, cor Bay View Park and Hunter's Point Road
Simonds S. D. principal colored school, dwl NE cor Filbert and Mason
Simonin Henry, with Frank Cereni, dwl cor Pacific and Virginia
Simons Alfred, clerk, Assistant Adjutant General's Office P. D. dwl Angel Island
Simons E. S. carpenter, dwl 728 Market
Simons Eugene, porter, 410 Front, dwl 679 Harrison
Simons Hiram C. notice server with City and County Treasurer, dwl 510 Leavenworth
Simons James M. fruits and produce, 209 Dupont
Simons L. D. attorney at law, office 655 Washington, dwl 1117 Montgomery
Simons Lewis C. H. with Kellogg, Hewston & Co. dwl 908 Union
Simons Louisa (widow) dwl 802 Stockton
Simons (Samuel) & Callender (John) boarding, S s Clark, bet Front and Davis
Simons Walter, dwl N s Brannan bet Sixth and Seventh
Simonsen David, saddlery, etc. 143 Fourth, dwl 21 St. Mark Place

Simonton James W. *(S. F. Bulletin Co.)* Occidental Hotel

Simonton L. M. carpenter, dwl St. Mark Place

Simoud John *(Ralston & Co.)* dwl cor Sansom and California

Simpson Abraham, dwl 188 Jessie

Simpson Andrew C. hairdressing saloon, 520 Market, dwl 19 Dupont

Simpson C. S. captain brig Arago, office Pier 11, dwl 209 Harrison

Simpson Cyrus H. carpenter with George Robinson & Co. 31 California, dwl N s Shipley, nr Harrison Avenue

Simpson David, plumber, dwl 1026 Montgomery

Simpson Edward, laborer, dwl N s Twentieth bet Valencia and Guerrero

Simpson Edward, laborer, Market St. R. R. Co. dwl cor Napa and Guerrero

Simpson George, job wagon, cor Clay and Front, dwl 266 Minna

Simpson George, waiter, steamer Orizaba

Simpson Henry M. expressman, dwl W s Fillmore bet Turk and Eddy

Simpson J. carpenter dwl 17 Third

Simpson James, dwl 248 Fourth

Simpson James, dwl 329 Broadway

Simpson John, carpenter with James Brokaw

Simpson John, longshoreman, dwl 531 Vallejo

Simpson *(Josiah R.)* & Pratt *(Frederick H.)* repackers and stampers matches, 105 Commercial, dwl SE cor Eighth and Mission

Simpson Leon, express wagon, Kearny nr Bdwy

Simpson Lionel D. clerk, 310 Commercial

Simpson Maria Mrs. private school, 266 Minna

Simpson Mary A. Miss, domestic, 11 Harlan Place

Simpson Peter G. hatter with B. F. Mead & Co. dwl Mead House

Simpson Richard, gardener, San Francisco Ladies' Protection and Relief Society

Simpson Thomas, grainer with Hopps & Kanary, dwl S s Filbert bet Larkin and Polk

Simpson Thomas B. clerk with C. V. Gillespie, dwl 921 Powell nr Clay

Simpson William, blacksmith, Pacific Foundry, dwl 144 Natoma

Simpson William, boiler helper, Pacific Foundry, dwl 532 Folsom

Simpson William, druggist and apothecary, dwl 609 Davis

Simpson William, laborer, dwl 1618 Dupont, rear

Simpson William, plasterer, dwl N side Vallejo bet Montgomery and Sansom

Simpson William, workman with S. Crim, dwl E s Mission bet Twenty-First and Twenty-Second

Simpton Charles J. W. surveyor, California Engine Co. No. 4

Sims George H. (col'd) porter, dwl 9 Perry

Sims John, photographer, dwl 109 Pacific

SIMS JOHN R. manufacturer iron doors and shutters, S s Oregon bet Front and Davis, dwl 1010 Jackson

Sims John W. clerk with John R. Sims, dwl 1010 Jackson

SIMSON ROBERT, attorney at law, office 804 Montgomery

Sin Kee & Co. (Chinese) merchants, 709 Jackson

Sin Kim Yek (Chinese) washing, 412 Brannan

Sin On (Chinese) washing, W s Montgomery bet Green and Union

Sin Wng Hing (Chinese) washing, 713 Commercial

Sin Yung (Chinese) washing, 739 Folsom

Sinay Elie *(Schwartz & S.)* dwl E s Stockton nr Pacific

Sinclair Archy *(Mather & S.)* dwl 415 Pine

Sinclair Collin R. porter with Ross, Dempster & Co. dwl 824 Union

Sinclair Elizabeth D. (widow) dress maker, 60 Everett

Sinclair Harry, actor, Maguire's Opera House

Sinclair Henry, G. bar keeper, Occidental Hotel, dwl 812 Stockton

Sinclair James, bar keeper, dwl SW cor Dupont and Broadway

SINCLAIR *(John)* & MOODY *(Joseph L.)* agents Bellingham Bay Coal Co. office 212 Clay, dwl 113 Prospect Place

Sinclair John. carpenter with John Center, NW cor Sixteenth and Folsom

Sinclair John A. drayman, 119 Clay, dwl 363 Minna

SINCOCK *(Henry)* & TREMBATH *(John)* proprietors New Wisconsin Hotel, 411 Pacific

Sindel Jacob *(Kirsch & S.)* dwl E s Montgomery bet Broadway and Vallejo

Sing Hop (Chinese) washing, 214 Commercial

Sing Sang (Chinese) washing, 734 Broadway

Sing Wing Chong (Chinese) washing, 135 Third

Sing Yuen (Chinese) washing, 12 Washington

Singer Aaron, carpenter, dwl 325 Dupont

SINGER MANUFACTURING CO. importers and manufacturers Singer's Sewing Machines, office 139 Montgomery

Singleton Daniel, blacksmith with Casebolt & Co. dwl 532 Mission

Sinion Gustave A. distiller, 540 Washington, dwl 712 Harrison

Sinkwitz William, liquors, 814 Kearny

Sinn John G. watchman, Kellogg, Hewston & Co.'s Refinery

Sinnett John, laborer, dwl 811 Battery, rear

Sinon William, carpenter, dwl W s Hyde nr Union

Sinram Fritz, shoe maker, dwl 219 Kearny

Sinsheimer Simon, crockery and glass ware, 149 Second

Sinteri Andrea, fish, 6 Washington Fish Market

Sinton Richard H. *(Cobb & S.)* commissioner deeds for Nevada, office 406 Montgomery, dwl 1109 Stockton

Sinton William, dwl 633 Market

Sion Lee (Chinese) washing, 1007 Dupont

Siple Charles, butcher with Rosenberg & Hencken

Sipples Richard *(Higgins & S.)* Shakspeare Hotel, 219 Pacific

Sirey John S. conductor, Central R. R. Co. dwl E s Gilbert nr Brannan

Siri Bernar *(Siri Bros.)* dwl Bay View

Siri Brothers *(John and Bernar)* vegetable gardeners, Bay View Park

Skahen John, laborer. dwl 12 Ecker

Skanks Jacob (col'd) barber, dwl 339 Union

Skelding George, hairdresser with Stephen G. Brown, Brooklyn Hotel

Skelly Catherine (widow) dwl 207 Minna

Skelly Frank, clerk with Crane & Brigham, dwl 207 Minna

Skelly John, blacksmith, dwl E s Mason nr Green

Skelly John R. clerk with Crane & Brigham, dwl 207 Minna

Skelly Michael, superintendent North Beach & M. R. R. Co. office cor Folsom and Fourth *(and Fagin, Bliven & S.)* dwl 565 Howard

Skelly Patrick, workman, S. F. & P. Sugar Co. dwl Everett nr Third

Skelly P. F. clerk with Crane & Brigham, dwl 207 Minna

Skelly Timothy, sash maker with Smith, Ware & Co. 22 California, dwl 78 Natoma

Skerrett Nicholas, dry goods, 11 Montgomery Lick Block, dwl 608 Sacramento

Skerritt John, laborer, bds Golden Age Hotel, 127 Pacific

Skiffington Francis, peddler, dwl 53 Everett

Skillings H. C. sawyer with J. S. Gibbs, dwl 156 Tehama

Skillman Peter, architect, dwl 259 Tehama

Skinner Elisha C. dwl 101 Prospect Place

Skinner Frank W. clerk, steamer Cornelia

Skinner James A. Rev. pastor First Presbyterian Church, dwl 816 Powell

Skinner *(Robert)* & Duncan *(George)* patent mastic roofers, S s Sixteenth nr Guerrero
Skinner Robert, mason, dwl 176 Minna
Skinner W. R. pattern maker, Union Foundry
Skivington John F. pattern maker, Union Foundry, dwl 625½ Mission
Skupinsky Adelbert, tailor, dwl 1111 Sacramento
Slack Ellen Miss, domestic with Samuel C. Bigelow, NW cor Steiner and McAllister
Slason William M. driver, Wells, Fargo & Co. dwl 510 Sacramento
Slately Angenette Miss, dwl 728 Howard
Slater Patrick, plasterer, dwl W s Sixth nr Brannan
Slattery Ellen Miss, fancy dry goods, dwl 256 Third
Slattery John, clerk, 734 Market
Slattery Richard, laborer, bds Cambridge House, 304 Pacific
Slattery Mary Miss, domestic, 830 Mission
Slattery Mary Miss, domestic, 504 Dupont
Slattery Morris, student, Mission Dolores Church
Slattery William Reverend, pastor Mission Dolores Church
Slavan A. E. Miss, principal Eighth St. School, dwl 865 Mission
Slaven John, liquor saloon, NE. cor Hayes and Laguna
Slaven Patrick, teamster, dwl E s Mission bet Seventeenth and Eighteenth
Slaven Thomas, laborer, dwl 309 Tehama
Slayback A. D. carpenter, dwl Howard Engine House
Sleet Sarah Miss, domestic with H. P. Coon
Sleison Louisa Miss, domestic, 217 Sixth
Slevin Daniel, carpenter, dwl 1335 Dupont
Slevin Patrick, teamster, Pier 5 Stewart
Slevin Frank, baker with James Donnelly, 109 Sansom
Sley Daniel, bricklayer, dwl 509 Dupont
Slicer, Dorsey J. brick mason, dwl 310 Minna
Sliter Richard G. bar keeper, dwl Pennsylvania Engine Co. No. 12
SLOAN *(E. W. F.)* & PROVINES *(R. R.)* attorneys at law, office 38 and 39 Exchange Bdg
Sloan John, car builder, S. F. & S. José R. R. Co. dwl SW cor Bryant and Ritch
Sloan John S. miner, dwl SE cor Jones and Bdwy
Sloan John W. bricklayer, dwl 236½ Jessie
Sloan Mary (widow) dwl 231 Stevenson
Sloan William R. clerk with M. A. Braly, dwl SE cor Geary and Hyde
Sloanaker I. N. *(C. P. Rank & Co.)* dwl 1109 Howard
Slocomb Henry B. quartz worker, dwl N s Austin bet Franklin and Van Ness Avenue
Slocum Henry, carpenter, dwl 110 Virginia
Slopsky Louis, express wagon, dwl 165 Minna
SLOSS, LOUIS & CO. *(Lewis Gerstle and Simon Greenewald)* mining stocks, etc. office 3 Donohoe, Kelly & Co.'s Building SE cor Montgomery and Sacramento, dwl 427 Post
Slosson Edward, teamster, dwl 457 Bryant
Slosson *(James W.)* & Ladd *(Wilbur J.)* groceries and liquors, SW cor First and Folsom
Slosson R. D. driver, North Beach & M. R. R. Co
Slyter Charles F. steward, dwl 619 Pacific
Smadeke William, clerk, NE cor Fourth and Folsom
Small Agnes Miss, domestic, 1102 Pine
Small Arosco G. cabinet maker, dwl 220 Third
Small Dominick, carpenter, dwl N s Harrison nr Sixth
Small *(I. H.)* & Redmond *(J. H.)* machinists, SE cor Market and Beale, dwl Second nr Folsom
Small Mary Jane Miss, domestic, 313 Sutter
Small William P. ship carpenter with John G. North, Potrero, dwl SW cor Louisiana and Sierra
Smalley L. D. first officer steamer America
Smallwood Joseph (colored) hairdressing saloon, 640 Clay, dwl 555 Howard

Smart George C. workman with S. C. & L. H. Talcott
Smedley Emma Mrs. dwl W s Old San José Road nr Navy
Smidt Edward, painter, dwl 507 Broadway
Smiley Charles W. driver with John McDivit, dwl N s Broadway bet Stockton and Powell
SMILEY GEORGE W. agency sale petroleum lands, office 419 Montgomery, dwl Russ House
Smiley James, stock broker, office 607 Clay, dwl 634 Broadway
Smiley T. J. L. merchant, office 519 Montgomery, dwl 1707 Powell
Smiley William T. Mission Laundry, S s Sixteenth bet Valencia and Mission
Smilie Elton R. physician and dentist, office and dwl 640 Washington
Smith A. B. Rev. (colored) pastor Zion Wesley Church, dwl 1419 Mason
Smith Adam, bowling alley, 536 Market, dwl 515 Sacramento
Smith Adam, carpenter, dwl 28 Natoma
Smith Adam jr. (colored) porter, dwl 1419 Mason
Smith A. G. jr. waiter, Lick House
Smith Ahimaaz B. horse dealer, dwl 262 First
SMITH, *(Alexander)* WARE *(James)* & CO. *(Samuel Ransom)* manufacturers sash, doors, blinds, etc. 22 and 24 Cal, dwl 623 Howard
Smith Alexander, mariner, dwl 32 Stewart
Smith Alexander, mariner, dwl 221 Beale
Smith Alexander D. compositor, Alta California
Smith Alfred, dwl 226 Sansom
Smith Alfred, carpenter, dwl What Cheer House
Smith Alfred J. plumber, 33 and 35 Webb, dwl N s Fell bet Franklin and Van Ness Avenue
Smith Algernon Custom House broker, dwl 624 Sac
Smith Amanda (widow) dwl with Charles Courtenay
Smith Amelia (widow) seamstress, 223 Fourth
Smith Andrew, boiler maker, Pacific Foundry, dwl 166 Perry
Smith Andrew, captain schooner Maria Nelson, dwl W s Main bet Harrison and Bryant
Smith Andrew D. court room clerk Twelfth District Court, dwl NE cor Powell and Lombard
Smith Andrew V. restaurant, 519 East, dwl 630 O'Farrell
Smith Anna (widow) dress maker, 409 Sutter
Smith Asher, farmer, Bay View Turnpike nr Hunter's Point
Smith B. Miss, dress maker, dwl 74 Tehama
Smith Barlow J. hygienic physician and surgeon, office 13 Armory Hall
Smith Benjamin, capitalist, dwl Union Club Rooms
Smith Benjamin F. K. clerk, 704 Market, dwl 13 Ellis
Smith Benjamin R. teamster with Selig & Co. dwl El Dorado nr Potrero Avenue
Smith Bridget (widow) nurse with Mrs. Edward G. Beckwith, E s Mission bet Fourteenth and Fifteenth
Smith C. A. laborer, dwl 424 Beale
Smith Caroline (widow) fancy goods, N s Sixteenth nr Valencia
Smith Carrie L. Miss, assistant, Market St. School, dwl 528 Greenwich
Smith Catharine (widow) dwl 5 Milton Place
Smith Catherine Miss, domestic, 28 Ellis
Smith Charles, dwl 1509 Stockton
Smith Charles, builder, dwl 1027 Dupont
Smith Charles, carpenter, dwl 46 Sutter
Smith Charles (colored) caterer, 1410 Stockton
Smith Charles, confectioner with Canty & Wagner
Smith Charles, drayman with F. Putzmann, dwl Bitter's Hotel
Smith Charles, hairdresser with Aaron Creamer, dwl 112 Liedesdorff
Smith Charles, harness maker with J. C. Johnson & Co. dwl 814 Montgomery

Smith Charles, musician, dwl 827 Vallejo
Smith Charles, seaman, dwl 26 Sacramento
Smith Charles, stevedore, dwl S s Union bet Montgomery and Calhoun
Smith Charles, store keeper with Alsop & Co. dwl 62 Jessie
Smith Charles, workman with Smith & Brown, dwl New Potrero
Smith Charles E. machinist, dwl 28 Sansom
Smith Charles F. with Yates & Stevens, dwl S side Union bet Powell and Mason
Smith Charles F. silversmith with Vanderslice & Co. dwl 922 Washington
Smith Charles G. carpenter, dwl 447½ Tehama
Smith Charles H. clerk, Bank California, dwl 1015 Stockton
Smith Charles H. longshoreman, dwl N s Alta bet Montgomery and Sansom
Smith Charles H. varnisher, dwl Pacific Temperance House
Smith Charles J. clerk with H. M. Newhall & Co. dwl 568 Howard
Smith Charles K. dwl Union Club Rooms
Smith Charles N. carpenter and builder, dwl S side Mission bet Eighth and Ninth
Smith Charles N. Mrs. private school, S s Mission bet Eighth and Ninth
Smith Charles O. compositor, Golden Era, dwl NW cor Folsom and First
Smith Charles P. porter, dwl 62 Jessie
Smith Charles W. (Graves & S.) dwl N s Union bet Hyde and Larkin
Smith Charles W. shutter maker with J. R. Sims, dwl 109 Hyde
SMITH CHARLES W. wines, liquors, and cigars, 538 Merchant, dwl 427 Fourth
SMITH (Christian) & CO. (Joseph Genth) wholesale butchers and packers, W s Potrero Avenue, packing house 539 Broadway
Smith Christian, laborer with John A. Shepston
Smith Christian, seaman, dwl 44 Sacramento
Smith Christian W. clerk, 401 Bat, dwl 735 Market
Smith Christopher, baker with J. Chadbourne, dwl Mission nr Eighth
Smith Clara (widow) dwl 607 Post
Smith Cornelius R. boot maker, cor Jackson and Davis, dwl 317 Vallejo
Smith C. W. match factory, SW cor Howard and Beale
Smith C. W. M. patent agent, office 423 Washington room 9 (and Dewey & Co.) dwl 1108 Mason
Smith Cyrus B. boatman, U. S. Boarding Office, dwl 113 Post
Smith Daniel, dwl 5 Hardie Place
Smith David, dwl 6 Montgomery
Smith David, clerk with C. E. Hinckley & Co. dwl S s Greenwich nr Dupont
Smith David, gilder with William Shew, dwl Sherwood Place
Smith David, sash maker with Smith, Ware & Co. dwl 729 Mission
Smith David F. clerk, 49 Market
Smith David P. gilder, dwl 6 Dupont
Smith David W. inspector, Custom House, dwl 528 Green
Smith D. C. clerk with Taaffe & Co. bds Brooklyn Hotel
Smith Dedrick, laborer, dwl 228 First
Smith E. A. dwl What Cheer House
Smith Ebenezer J. dwl NW cor Utah and Sixteenth
Smith Edward W. cashier Pacific Bank, office NE cor Montgomery and California, dwl cor Dupont and St. Mark Place
Smith Edward, laborer, dwl S s Filbert bet Mason and Taylor
Smith Edward, steward American Exchange
Smith Edward D. physician, office 4 Fourth
Smith Edward L. furniture, SE cor Pine and Montgomery, dwl 115 Fourth

Smith Edwin L. stock broker, 528 Clay, dwl 114 Natoma
Smith E. L. & Co. (E. P. Bowers) furniture and bedding, 49 and 51 Third
Smith E. L. & Co. (J. H. Crockett) furniture and bedding, NE cor Mont and Pine, dwl 115 Fourth
Smith E. L. (Marchant & S.) 104 Dupont
Smith Eliza Miss, domestic, 809 Bush
Smith Eliza Miss, domestic, 698 Geary
Smith Eliza Miss, domestic, 1020 Stockton
Smith Eliza C. Miss, dwl NW corner Utah and Sixteenth
Smith Elizabeth (widow) dwl 1112 Powell
Smith Ella C. (widow) lodgings 783 Market
Smith Ellen, domestic, Rincon House
Smith Ellen Mrs. restaurant, W s Main bet Harrison and Bryant
Smith Ellen (widow) dwl Higgins Place
Smith Emilia (widow) lodgings, 63 Tehama
Smith Ephraim, drayman with Davis & Cowell, NE cor Front and Washington
Smith Eynaud, teamster with S. B. Hanson
Smith F. & Co. importers and jobbers wines and liquors, 210 Sacramento, dwl 328 Bryant
Smith F. ship carpenter, dwl SW cor California and Drumm
Smith F. fireman, steamboat Contra Costa
Smith Fannie Mrs. nurse, NW cor Guerrero and Seventeenth
Smith Francis, gilder, dwl SW corner Dupont and Broadway
Smith Francis, produce, 203 Wash, dwl 808 Union
Smith Francis L. dwl 808 Union
Smith François, watch case manufacturer, 619 Mont
Smith (Frank) & Co. publishers and proprietors California Youths' Companion, office 505 Clay, dwl 808 Howard
Smith Frank, boatman, dwl E s Davis bet Pacific and Jackson
Smith Frank, paver, North Beach & M. R. R. Co
Smith Frank, seaman, dwl W s First Avenue near Sixteenth, rear
Smith Frank, waiter, Lick House
Smith Frank H. driver, dwl E s Powell bet Chestnut and Francisco
Smith Frank W. confectioner with Charles Schroth, dwl 1904 Powell
Smith Fred, fireman, steamer Orizaba
Smith Frederick, confectionery and fruits, 1511 Stockton and 1330 Dupont
Smith Frederick A. laborer, dwl SW corner Sacramento and Larkin
Smith Frederick A. waterman, 609 Market, dwl NE cor Polk and Austin
Smith Frederick G. paying teller with John Sime & Co. dwl NE cor Howard and Third
Smith (Frederick S.) & Kittredge (John R.) ship chandlers, 26 Clay, dwl 721 California
Smith Freeman, captain schooner Storm Cloud, office Pier 11 Stewart
Smith Gardner H. clerk, 404 Davis, dwl 1031 Mont
Smith G. E. & Co. brass founders, 417 Mission, dwl 724 Harrison
Smith George, dwl 718 Stockton
Smith George, clerk, Mexican Loan Office, dwl 120 Fourth
Smith George (col'd) boarding, 28 Stone
Smith George, express wagon, 530 Broadway
Smith George, job cart, cor Market and Sacramento
Smith George, laborer, dwl 13 Washington
Smith George, machinist, Fulton Foundry, dwl 120 Fourth
Smith George, waiter, Occidental Hotel
Smith George B. machinist, S. F. & San José R. R. Co. dwl NE cor Sixteenth and Valencia
Smith George H. hackman, Lick House, dwl 117 O'Farrell
Smith George H. tailor, 548 Washington, dwl West End Hotel

Smith George J. painter with J. T. O'Neil, dwl 29 Natoma
Smith George M. cooper, S. F. & P. Sugar Co. dwl 32 Rousch
Smith George M. Mrs. (widow) dwl 545 Folsom
Smith George N. J. jeweler, dwl E s Harriet bet Fifteenth and Sixteenth
Smith George O. jr. cashier U. S. Internal Revenue Office, dwl SW cor Powell and Geary
Smith George S. cook with John A. Shepston
Smith George W. (Hostetter, Smith & Dean) res Pittsburgh, Pa
Smith George W. foreman with Wightman & Hardie, dwl 314 Broadway
Smith Georgie Miss, saloon, 302 Dupont
Smith G. Frank (Pixley & S.) attorney at law, res Oakland
Smith Gilbert S. S. carriage maker with Black & Saul, dwl 670 Mission
Smith Godfrey, musician, dwl 827 Vallejo
SMITH (Harmon) & WILKINS (Harry) wines and liquors, 709 Davis, dwl S s Broadway bet Montgomery and Sansom
Smith Harry, fruit dealer, 115 Third
Smith Henry, carpenter and builder, dwl 606 Howard
Smith Henry, laborer Bay Sugar Refinery, dwl NW cor Battery and Jackson
Smith Henry, laborer, dwl E s Tyson Place
Smith Henry, musician, dwl 827 Vallejo
Smith Henry, musician, dwl 1513 Mason
Smith Henry, pickled and dried fish, 320 Davis, dwl cor Filbert and Varenne
Smith Henry, salesman with N. Curry & Bro. dwl 108 Tehama
Smith Henry, seaman, dwl 207 Pacific
Smith Henry, steward stm America, dwl 731 Bdwy
Smith Henry C. (Funk & S.) dwl 104 Pacific
Smith Henry L. clerk with Ben Holladay, dwl SW cor Hyde and Sacramento
Smith Henry N. bar keeper, 332 Montgomery
Smith Henry S. foreman machine shop Palmer, Knox & Co. dwl 221 Seventh
Smith Henry W. clerk, dwl SE cor Stockton and Jackson
Smith Henry W. plumber with J. H. O'Brien & Co. 706 Mont, dwl N s Clementina nr Eighth
Smith Henry W. soap maker, dwl W s Polk near Bush
Smith Hiram G. drayman, 104 Clay, dwl 104 Market
Smith Holland, assistant postmaster San Francisco, dwl 1414 Taylor
Smith Horace F. carrier, Call and Examiner, dwl 108 Valparaiso
Smith H. R. hairdressing saloon, junction Market and Geary
Smith H. R. W. printer, dwl 417 Bush
Smith H. S. wines and liquors (Sacramento) dwl 536 Washington
Smith Hugh, iron molder, Vulcan Iron Works, dwl 365 Jessie
Smith Hugh, works with Hugh McGrea
Smith Hugh D. lumberman, bds Franklin Hotel SE cor Sansom and Pacific
Smith Isaac G. drayman, 123 Clay, dwl W s Larkin bet Green and Union
Smith J. A. truckman, 3 Clay
Smith Jacob A. oil dealer, dwl SE cor Union and Leavenworth
Smith Jacob J. poultry, 44 Occidental Market, dwl Sutter bet Kearny and Dupont
Smith Jacob M. calker, dwl 510 Sacramento
SMITH (James) & BROWN (Benjamin W.) hide dealers, New Potrero, dwl 437 Sixth
SMITH (James) & Wilson (Charles) butchers, 27 Metropolitan Market, dwl NW cor Guerrero and Twenty-Second
Smith James (Turnbull & S.) dwl 108 Prospect Pl
Smith James, office 308 Front
Smith James, book keeper, dwl 720 Market

Smith James, contractor, dwl E s Mason bet Clay and Washington
Smith James, cook, 612 Market
Smith James, deck hand, stm Yosemite, dwl S s Vallejo bet Front and Davis
Smith James, groceries and liquors, NW cor Dupont and Chestnut
Smith James, laborer, rancho Laguna de Puerca, Ocean House Road
Smith James, laborer, Vulcan Foundry, dwl O'Farrell bet Gough and Octavia
Smith James, laborer, dwl 7 St. Mary
Smith James, laborer, dwl 112 Sacramento
Smith James, liquor saloon, 706 Pacific
Smith James, longshoreman, dwl NE cor Battery and Commerce
Smith James, plasterer, dwl Niantic Hotel
Smith James, printer, dwl International Hotel
Smith James, sail maker, dwl 5 Trinity
Smith James, salesman with A. Roman & Co. bds Lick House
Smith James, seaman, steamer Orizaba
Smith James, teamster with McKenna Bros.' & Co. dwl Sacramento nr Drumm
Smith James, trunk maker, 107 Sansom, dwl 1 Telegraph Place
Smith James D. finisher, Pacific Foundry, dwl 117 Natoma
Smith James E. receiving clerk, California State Telegraph Co. 507 Mont, dwl 103 Dupont
Smith James F. butcher with H. C. Dean, dwl cor Bryant and Park Avenue
Smith James F. clerk, dwl E s Park Avenue bet Harrison and Bryant
Smith James O. laborer, steamer Princess
Smith James P. carpenter, dwl SW cor Valencia and Nineteenth
Smith James R. drayman, 218 Front, dwl W s Hyde bet Post and Sutter
Smith June (widow) dwl W s Battery bet Vallejo and Broadway
Smith Jane L. Mrs. lodgings, 226 Sansom
Smith Jasper F. auctioneer, dwl 600 Pine
Smith J. Buck, clerk, Pier 4 Stewart, dwl 49 Market
Smith J. Clark, wood yard, Mission St. Wharf, dwl 240 Fremont
Smith J. Duncan, blacksmith, Vulcan Iron Works, dwl 20 Tehama
Smith Jennie Miss, assistant, Stevenson St. School, dwl 427 Fourth
Smith Jennie Miss, domestic, 119 Powell
Smith Jeremiah, dwl 410 Union
Smith Jesse, confectionery, 1404 Stockton
Smith Jesse R. book keeper with Glidden, Colman & Co. dwl 515 Jones
Smith Jessie Miss, assistant, Mission Grammar School, dwl 427 Fourth
Smith J. G. drayman, 124 Clay
Smith J. Hammond, clerk with Bradshaw & Co. dwl 257 Stevenson
Smith J. Henry, wharfinger, Howard St. Wharf, dwl 427 Second
Smith John (George & S.) dwl 737 Green
Smith John, dwl What Cheer House
Smith John, blacksmith, dwl 228 First
Smith John, bricklayer, dwl 200 Stockton
Smith John, carpenter, dwl N s Lombard bet Mason and Taylor
Smith John, carpenter, dwl What Cheer House
Smith John, conductor, Omnibus R. R. Co
Smith John, cook, 335 East
Smith John, farmer, Ocean House Road nr Ocean House
Smith John, groceries, 16 Clay, dwl 405 O'Farrell
Smith John, laborer, San Francisco Iron Works, dwl S s Stevenson bet Second and Third
Smith John, laborer, Vulcan Iron Works
Smith John, laborer, dwl Zoe Place
Smith John, laborer, dwl 9 Sherwood Place

Smith John, laborer, dwl 756 Harrison
Smith John, machinist helper, Vulcan Iron Works
Smith John, miner (Mexico) dwl 321 Sixth
Smith John, mining stocks, dwl 721 California
Smith John, poultry, Occidental Market, dwl W s Rassette Place No. 1
Smith John, seaman, dwl 26 Sacramento
Smith John, shoe maker with I. M. Wentworth & Co. dwl Lick House
Smith John, smutter, Golden Gate Mills, 430 Pine
Smith John, stone cutter with Phil Caduc, dwl 1021 Battery
Smith John A. drayman, dwl 11 Park Avenue
Smith John B. dwl 211 Minna
Smith John B. carpenter, dwl 25 Market
Smith John D. blacksmith, dwl 220 First
Smith John F. butcher, dwl E s Park Avenue bet Harrison and Bryant
Smith John H. engineer, Pacific Salt Works, dwl Isthmus House
Smith John H. liquor saloon, junction Market and Eddy
Smith John H. tinsmith, dwl Chicago Hotel 220 Pacific
Smith John L. contractor, dwl 144 Shipley
Smith John W. drayman, 101 California, dwl 21 Dupont
Smith Joseph (Poultney & S.) dwl 342 Brannan
Smith Joseph, boiler maker, dwl 408 Market
Smith Joseph, liquor saloon, 206 Leidesdorff
Smith Joseph, machinist, dwl 408 Market
Smith Joseph, seaman, dwl 44 Sacramento
Smith Joseph A. Melter and Refiner's Department, U. S. Branch Mint, dwl 525 Geary
Smith Joshua, merchant, dwl 1 Telegraph Place
Smith Josiah F. (col'd) with J. W. Brittan & Co. dwl W s Jones bet Sacramento and California
Smith J. R. furnished rooms, Dolan's Building, NE cor Third and Hunt
Smith J. S. ship carpenter, dwl 670 Market
Smith J. T. miner, dwl 608 Market
Smith Julia Miss, domestic, 712 Bush
Smith Julia F. (widow) dwl cor Octavia and Greenwich
Smith L. A. Mrs. lodgings, 52 Second
Smith Lawrence, laborer, dwl N s Alta nr Mont
Smith Lewis, porter, dwl SW cor Dupont and Broadway
Smith M. (widow) dwl 917 Pacific
Smith Maggie Miss, domestic, 915 Clay
Smith Margaret (widow) dwl S s Perry bet Fourth and Fifth
Smith Margaret Mrs. (widow) dwl 365 Jessie
Smith Mark P., Kellogg, Hewston & Co.'s Refinery, dwl E s Mission bet Twenty-Third and Twenty-Fourth
Smith Martin, seaman, dwl 20 Commercial
Smith Mary, domestic, 714 Mission
Smith Mary Miss, domestic with J. J. Haley S side Sixteenth bet Folsom and Howard
Smith Mary Mrs. ladies' nurse, dwl NW cor Bush and Powell
Smith Mary (widow) dwl W s Buenaventura nr California
Smith Mary Ann Miss, domestic, 830 Union
Smith Mathew, trap tender, U. S. Branch Mint, dwl Minna
Smith Matthew F. clerk, 122 Clay, dwl W s Harriet nr Sixteenth
Smith M. F. Miss, assistant, Stevenson St. School, dwl 427 Fourth
Smith Michael, laborer, dwl 207 Pacific
Smith Michael, machinist, dwl 406 Dupont
Smith Michal, dwl What Cheer House
Smith Mighill, constable third township, office 526 Montgomery, dwl SW cor Hyde and Sacramento
Smith M. W. inspector, Custom House
Smith (Nathan) & Norton (George F.) (colored) bootblacking, 115 Kearny, dwl 1 Card Alley

Smith Nicholas, carpenter with John Center, NW cor Sixteenth and Folsom
Smith Nicholas, laborer, Vulcan Iron Works, dwl S s O'Farrell nr Gough
Smith Nicholas, plasterer, dwl N s Vallejo bet Van Ness Avenue and Franklin
Smith N. Proctor, conveyancer and commissioner deeds, office 526 Montgomery, dwl 1004 Sutter
Smith O. B. (McHenry & S.) 11 Washington
Smith Oliver, stevedore, dwl NW cor Union and Powell
Smith P. (Robert Murdoch) pawnbrokers, 647 Sac
Smith P. teamster with Rider, Somers & Co
Smith Pardou T. clerk, cor Mariposa and Indiana
Smith Patrick, gardener, dwl 472 Jessie
Smith Patrick, laborer with Conroy & Tobin
Smith Patrick, laborer with Hey & Meyn
Smith Patrick, laborer, dwl 108 St. Mark Place
Smith Patrick, retortman, S. F. Gas Co
Smith Patrick J. laborer, dwl W s Eighth bet Howard and Clementina
Smith Peter, boiler maker, Union Foundry, dwl 3 Minna
Smith Peter, carpenter, dwl 116 Sansom
Smith Peter, lab, Bay Sugar Refinery, dwl 813 Bat
Smith Peter, miner, dwl Presidio
Smith Peter A. (P. L. Smith & Son) dwl SW cor Valencia and Nineteenth
Smith Peter L. & Son (Peter A.) carpenters, dwl SW cor Valencia and Nineteenth
Smith Phillip, molder, Vulcan Iron Works, dwl 365 Jessie
Smith Philip R. bar keeper, dwl 4 Central Place
Smith P. P. dwl Cosmopolitan Hotel
Smith Reginald H. mining secretary, office 606 Montgomery, dwl Russ House
Smith Reuben H. gilder, Manhattan Engine Co. No. 2
Smith Richard, with Hopps & Kanary, dwl 422 Tehama
Smith Richard, nurse, City and County Hospital
Smith Richard H. dwl N s Grove nr Laguna
Smith R. L. Mrs. furnished rooms, 52 Second
Smith (Robert) & Adams (James) hay and grain, 325 Davis, dwl 23 John
Smith Robert, blacksmith, dwl NE cor Washington and Stockton
Smith Robert, blacksmith, dwl NE cor Tay and Sac
Smith Robert, carpenter, S. F. & San José R. R. Co. dwl Brannan nr Fourth
Smith Robert, helper, dwl S s Clay nr Powell
Smith Robert, laborer, Crescent Engine Co. No. 10
Smith Robert, wagon maker, dwl S s Perry bet Fourth and Fifth
Smith Robert P. searcher records, 604 Merchant
Smith Rosa Miss, domestic, 277 Minna
Smith Rosa Miss, domestic, Union Court nr Kearny
Smith Rufus N. shipmaster, dwl 238 Stewart
Smith Ruth (widow) dwl 266 Minna
Smith Samuel, clerk, Independence H. & L. Co. No. 3
Smith Samuel, mason and builder, dwl 330 Green
Smith Samuel, seaman, dwl 20 Commercial
Smith Samuel B. foreman, Fort Point, dwl cor Francisco and Fillmore
Smith Samuel E. (Renton, S. & Co.) dwl 44 Tehama
Smith Sarah (widow) dwl 103 Perry
Smith Selah, waterman, dwl 70 Minna
Smith Sidney M. book keeper with Cutting & Co. dwl 328 Bryant
SMITH SIDNEY V. attorney at law, office 630 Sacramento
Smith (Silas) & Williams (John) wood and coal, NE cor Folsom and Seventh
Smith Simeon F. roofer, dwl N s Fourteenth nr Guerrero
Smith S. J. clerk with William M. Higgins, 534 Sac
Smith S. L. ship carpenter with John G. North, Potrero

Smith Stephen, ship carpenter, dwl SW cor Louisiana and Sierra
SMITH STEPHEN wholesale grocer, NE cor Front and Clay, dwl 900 Powell
Smith Stephen H. salesman with Stephen Smith, dwl 900 Powell
Smith Stephen M. clerk with Murphy, Grant & Co. dwl SE cor Howard and Second
SMITH STEPHEN S. hard lumber, 111 Market, dwl 633 Sutter
Smith Stewart, real estate agent, office 606 Montgomery, dwl 655 Howard
Smith Susan Miss, dwl 607 Sutter
Smith Susan Mrs. dwl 655 Howard
Smith S. W. conductor, Omnibus R. R. Co. dwl 721 Howard
Smith S. Wilson T. broker, dwl 320 Davis
Smith T. harness maker, dwl 20 First
Smith T. G. carpenter, dwl 414 Market
Smith T. G. M. shoe maker with W. Wolf & Co. 115 California
Smith Theodore C. teacher, Industrial School, Old Ocean House Road
Smith Theodore E. salesman with Hobart, Dunbar & Co. dwl 545 Folsom
Smith Thomas, dwl 620 Howard
Smith Thomas, with John Hall & Son, dwl 327 Third
Smith Thomas, bricklayer, dwl 7 Tehama
Smith Thomas, cook, 335 East
Smith Thomas, fireman, steamer Sacramento, dwl 11 Louisa, rear
Smith Thomas, flour packer, dwl 28 Hunt
Smith Thomas, laborer, Rincon Point Warehouse
Smith Thomas, laborer, dwl 311 Bryant
Smith Thomas, machinist, Vulcan Iron Works, dwl 835 Clementina
Smith Thomas, seaman, dwl 54 Sacramento
Smith Thomas, tinner, dwl 17 Ritch
Smith Thomas, wharfinger, Howard St. Wharf, dwl Second bet Harrison and Bryant
Smith Thomas, workman, S. F. Cordage Factory
Smith Thomas, workman with S. Crim, dwl W s Howard bet Nineteenth and Twentieth
Smith Thomas C. longshoreman, dwl N W cor Green and Battery
Smith Thomas V. bricklayer, dwl 6 Eddy
Smith Walter O. T. porter with Wilson & Bro. dwl Howard Engine House
Smith W. C. R. salesman, 220 Davis, dwl 16 Drumm
Smith Willard M. produce, 33 Clay, dwl 13 Monroe
Smith William, blacksmith with Lawton & Co. dwl 711 O'Farrell
Smith William (col'd) bootblack, Dunbar Alley, dwl E s Varenne nr Union
Smith William, brewer, dwl 423 Fourth
Smith William, butcher, SE cor Sixth and Mission
Smith William, carpenter, dwl 156 Silver, rear
Smith William, compositor, Alta California, dwl 815 Montgomery
Smith William, gymnast, Wilson's Circus, bds Brooklyn Hotel
Smith William, hat presser, dwl 250 Jessie
Smith William, hostler, North Beach & M. R. R. Co. dwl S s Shipley nr Fifth
Smith William, lab, dwl SE cor Harrison and Main
Smith William, mariner, bds SW cor Sierra and Georgia
Smith William, plumber with P. McKewn & Son
Smith William, quartermaster Golden Age, dwl 817 Battery
Smith William, rigger, dwl W s Main bet Harrison and Bryant
Smith William, salesman, 320 Davis, dwl 318 Davis
Smith William, sash and door maker, dwl 325 Third
Smith William, seaman, dwl 62 Clay
Smith William, seaman, dwl 117 Sacramento
Smith William, seaman, dwl S s Sacramento bet Davis and Drumm

Smith William, stevedore, dwl NW cor Front and Broadway
Smith William, stone cutter, dwl 1021 Battery
Smith William, teamster, 100 Stewart, dwl E s Dupont bet Sutter and Post
Smith William, teamster with William Gavigan, dwl N s Turk bet Jones and Leavenworth
Smith William, waiter, steamer Moses Taylor, dwl 5 Natoma
Smith William, wholesale butcher, Potrero, dwl 26 Rousch
Smith William A. dwl 409 Mason
Smith William B. clerk with August King
Smith William C. cabinet maker, dwl 1063 Bdwy
SMITH W. H. & CO. (H. Drew) stair builders, 409 Mission, dwl 1207 Clay
Smith (William H.) & Irving (Robert) soap manufacturers, N s Sixteenth nr Rhode Island, dwl S s Bush nr Larkin
Smith William H. cook with John Center, NW cor Folsom and Sixteenth
Smith William H. fruits, 65 Fourth
Smith William H. laborer, dwl SE cor Third and Hunt
Smith William H. mining and petroleum, dwl American Exchange
Smith William H. printer, 533 Clay, dwl 636 Com
Smith William H. teamster, dwl N s Greenwich bet Montgomery and Sansom
Smith William J. (S. H. Tyler & Co.) bds Cosmopolitan Hotel
Smith William J. picture frame maker with Jones, Wooll & Sutherland, dwl 118 Fifth
Smith William J. plasterer, dwl 12 Noble Place
Smith William L. quartz miner, dwl 539 Howard
Smith William M. (col'd) barber, dwl 908 Pac, rear
Smith William N. special policeman, dwl 510 Sac
Smith William S. messenger San Francisco Savings Union, dwl N s Lombard bet Mason and Taylor
Smith William W. carpenter, dwl cor Columbia and Prospect Place
Smith William W. gardener with G. S. Hall, W s Old San José Road bet Twenty-Third and Twenty-Fourth
Smith Windsor Fay, drayman, dwl N s Perry bet Fourth and Fifth
Smith W. J. printer with Calhoun & Son, dwl 326 Mason
Smith W. P. waterman, 609 Market
Smith W. Wallace, wood carver, dwl 512 Jones
Smithson Berthulia (widow) dwl 52 Minna
Smitten Walter, minstrel, Olympic, dwl 1112 Kearny nr Broadway
Smoky Valley G. & S. M. Co. office 36 Exchange Building
Smyth Charles F. book keeper, Bank California, dwl 923 Howard
Smyth Dennis C. book keeper with Taaffe & Co. dwl cor Howard and Third
Smyth Edward T. clerk with Conroy & O'Connor, dwl 872 Mission
Smyth J. H. (Sharpstein & S.) attorney at law, dwl N s Bush bet Buchanan and Webster
Smyth John, blacksmith, dwl 704 Broadway
Smythe Thomas, first lieut. Co. D, C. V. Fort Point
Snabel Anice, musician, dwl 1513 Stockton, rear
Snapper S. & Co. (Thomas Cohen) cap makers, 427 Pine, dwl SE cor Stockton and Sacramento
Snapper Samuel, hairdresser, 636 Washington, dwl 619 Union
Sneads Giles (col'd) bootblack, 421 California
SNEATH R. G. importer and wholesale grocer, 408 Front, dwl 646 Folsom
Sneeda Jirus (col'd) bootblack, dwl W s August Alley bet Green and Union
Sneider Augustus, waiter, dwl 147 Minna
Sneider (John) & Horstmann (Henry) billiard and bowling alley, 647 Pacific and NE cor Dupont and Jackson, dwl 731 Vallejo

Snelgrove Artamar, carpenter, dwl 741 Market
Snell George W. clerk with Redington & Co. dwl 24 Hawthorne
Snibley John, dwl 6 Sansom
Snively David, carpenter, dwl 519 Minna
Snook Edward C. plumber with G. & W. Snook, dwl 210 Dupont
SNOOK G. & W. tin, copper, and sheet iron workers and plumbers, 806 Mont, dwl 1306 Kearny
Snook John A. (McDonald & Co.) dwl N s Thirteenth nr Mission
Snook Josephine (widow) dwl 427 Union
Snook Otto, cook, Blue Anchor, 7 Washington
Snook W. S. (G. & W. Snook) dwl 724 Filbert
Snow Augustine, local editor Evening Bulletin, dwl 109 Montgomery
Snow Chester J. carpenter, dwl 704 Bush
Snow Eliza T. Miss, teacher, dwl 3 Martha Place
SNOW (Frank C.) & CO. engravings, picture frames, etc. SE cor Wash and San, and house and sign painting, 414 Merchant, dwl 1018 Stock
SNOW JOHN F. coloring and cleansing gloves, silks, feathers, and agent patent medicines, 24 Post
Snow William, physician, office 10 Sutter
Snowball Robert Y. compositor, Morning Call, dwl 417 Montgomery
SNYDER ALBERT A. architect, carpenter, and builder, 62 Halleck
Snyder Andrew J. register U. S. Land Office (Marysville) dwl 1410 Larkin
Snyder Augustus W. salesman with A. R. Baldwin & Co. dwl 834 Clay
Snyder Christopher, cooper, dwl 639 Bdwy, rear
Snyder G. assistant machinist, Maguire's Opera H
Snyder George, laborer, dwl 637 Broadway
Snyder Jacob, engineer, Spring Valley W. W. Black Point, dwl N s Bay nr Hyde
Snyder Jacob B. butcher with Johnson & Co. dwl cor Brannan and Ninth
Snyder Joseph H. dwl 504 Dupont
Snyder Kate Miss, domestic, 115 Powell
Snyder Louis, with Cornelius Riley, 316 Clay
Snyder Lyman R. carpenter, 116 Kearny
Snyder Mary (widow) dwl 566 Howard
Snyder Mary A. (widow) nurse, dwl Montgomery Pl
Snyder Peter, waterman, dwl St. Lawrence House
Snyder Teresa (widow) dwl 921 Sacramento
Snyder, see Schneider
SOCIETE FRANCAISE DE BIENFAISANCE MUTUELLE, office 649 Sacramento
Sockum H. W. seaman, dwl W s Beale bet Howard and Folsom
Soggs Eugene, dwl International Hotel
Soggs Nelson, dwl International Hotel
Sober Louis, physician, dwl 20 Sansom
Sohn Edward, barber, dwl S s Pacific bet Powell and Mason
Solari August, job cart, 416 Front, dwl Clement Pl
Solbinger Joseph, laborer, What Cheer House Restaurant
Sole George E. saloon, dwl 1506 Mason
Solera Serafino, fancy goods and toys, 1140 Dupont
Soley William J. packer with Reid & Brooks, dwl NE cor Jackson and Virginia
Solg Joseph, laborer, dwl 333 Bush
Solius August, clerk, dwl 417 Sutter
Solomanson J. dry goods, 53 Second, dwl 126 Jessie
Solomon Abraham, professor German Academic Seminary, dwl 1503 Dupont
Solomon Albert, dwl St. Nicholas Hotel
SOLOMON B. L. & SONS (Solomon B. and Isaac S. Solomon) importers, manufacturers, and jobbers carpets, upholstery goods, etc. NW cor Pine and Battery, res New York
Solomon Eve Miss, assistant, Sutter St. Primary School, dwl 1805 Stockton
Solomon Hyman, liquor saloon, NW cor Geary and Dupont, dwl 106 Geary

Solomon Isaac S. (B. L. Solomon & Sons) res New York
Solomon Israel, groceries and liquors, NW corner Stockton and Ellis, dwl 1805 Stockton
Solomon Jacob, cigars and tobacco, SW corner East and Washington, dwl 230 Pacific
Solomon Jacob, clerk, 648 Market
Solomon Levi D. clerk, dwl 963 Howard
Solomon Louis, clothing, 48 Stewart
Solomon Otto F. with Hoelscher & Wieland, dwl 510 Howard
Solomon P. L. Mrs. (widow) dwl 963 Howard
Solomon Solomon B. (B. L. Solomon & Sons) dwl 1114 Stockton
Solomon Thomas, salesman, 109 Battery
Solomon S. D. conductor, Omnibus R. R. Co
Solomons Seixas, book keeper with Simon, Dinkelspiel & Co. dwl 718 Green
Solon A. drayman, 416 Front
Solon A. drayman, 416 Front
Soltsien Herman A. engineer, S. F. P. Woolen Factory
Somerindyke G. W. dwl 621 Union
Somers Austin P. (Clough & S.) dwl 422 Third
Somers D. C. (Loop & S.) dwl N s DeBoom bet First and Second
Somers Frank, cook, Railroad House
Somers H. C. (Rider, S. & Co.) dwl E side Third bet Market and Mission
Somers Henry, seaman, dwl 26 Sacramento
Somers Henry J. (Rice & S.) dwl 623 Market
Somers W. J. Melter and Refiner's Department U. S. Branch Mint, dwl 119 Ellis
Somerville Alexander, dwl 505 Jones
Somerville Annie Miss, domestic, 1201 Sacramento
Somerville Mary Miss, ladies' hair dresser, 530 Bush
Sommer Dora (widow) dwl 206 Sutter
Sonmerfield S. dry goods, 18 and 20 Second, dwl 269 Minna
Sommers Charles, groceries and liquors, SE corner Sixth and Natoma
Sommers, see Somers and Summers
Sommerville A. with S. S. Culverwell, 20 Fremont
Sommerville William, boarding, 116 Stewart
Sompa Peter, vegetable garden, Visitacion Valley
Son Adolph A. cigars and tobacco, 426 Montgomery, dwl N s Post bet Jones and Leavenworth
Son Albert A. clerk with Adolph A. Son, dwl NE cor Sacramento and Sansom
Sonary Joseph, cook, dwl 829 Washington
Song Lee (Chinese) groceries, NW cor Jackson and Dupont
Song Tie (Chinese) washing, 503 Clay
Sonnenberg Louis B. groceries, 16 Kearny
Sonnichsen James, dwl 7 Dupont
Sonntag Charles C. clerk, Assessor's Department U. S. Internal Revenue, dwl Folsom bet Thirteenth and Fourteenth
Sonntag Henry A. florist, NW corner Folsom and Fourteenth
Sonntag Henry B. salesman with Henry A. Sonntag, dwl NW cor Folsom and Fourteenth
Sonntag Julius, commission merchant, dwl 1523 Powell
SONNTAG JULIUS H. commission merchant, dwl 1523 Powell
Sonoma Ledge G. M. Co. office 529 Clay
Sononini Dominique, porter, 497 California
Soong Sing & Co. (Chinese) cigars, 808 Sacramento
SORBIER J. E. & CO. proprietors Occidental Restaurant, 536 Washington, dwl 752 Howard
Soren George S. salesman with T. H. Selby & Co. dwl 15 Powell
Soria Morland M. dwl 639 Clay
Sornin Alexander, watches and jewelry, 605 Washington, dwl W s Stockton nr Vallejo
Soscevelli Becenti, laborer, dwl W side Sanson bet Green and Vallejo
Souc Peter, butcher, 245 Fourth

Soucaze Gustave, painter, dwl 424 Powell
Soul Marcus, tailor with S. Reinstein, dwl NE cor Sacramento and Sansom
SOULE A. G. visiting physician, City and County Hospital, office and dwl 514 Kearny
Soule Elden A. dwl 277 Stevenson
SOULE FRANK, collector U. S. Internal Revenue, office NW cor Battery and Commercial, dwl S s Chestnut bet Leavenworth and Hyde
Soule Harrison G. boot fitter, dwl 40 More
Soule Horace, cabinet maker, 518 Front, dwl 215 San
Soule John A. coppersmith with Graves & Smith, dwl 113 Post
Soule Samuel, lumber, dwl 59 Tehama
Soule William, farmer, dwl E s Mission bet Twelfth and Thirteenth
Soulé William, janitor Hayes' Valley School
Sour John, sheet iron worker, S. F. & P. Sugar Co. dwl cor Folsom and Eighth
Sourian D. washman, French Hospital
Soussingeas Louis & Co. (*L. Racouillat*) wines and liquors, 430 and 432 Jackson, dwl 515 Filbert bet Dupont and Stockton
South Eclipse M. Co. office 1 Government House, 502 Washington
South Oakland Homestead Association, office 30 Exchange Building
SOUTH PARK MALT HOUSE, John Winter agent, office 208 California
South San Francisco Homestead and Railroad Association, office 528 Clay
Southard E. P. dwl 511 Mission
Souther A. F. captain sch Harriet Roe, 32 Stewart
Souther Horace, plasterer, dwl 253 Stevenson
Souther John S. ship carpenter, dwl 2106 Mason
SOUTHER JOSEPH N. receipt clerk, U. S. Branch Mint, dwl 24 Hawthorne
Souther (*Joseph W.*) & Northey (*Thomas F.*) draymen, 120 California, dwl 39 Louisa
Southerland Robert, boiler maker, Union Foundry, dwl S s Stevenson bet Sixth and Seventh
SOUTHERN DISPATCH LINE PACKETS, San Diego and intermediate ports, Capt. Nelson Pierce proprietor, office 321 Front
Southern Light G. & S. M. Co. office 228 Front
Southwell George, carpenter and joiner, 761 Clay, dwl 727 Broadway
Southwick John, dwl 216 Stockton
Southwick John, machinist, Union Foundry, dwl 187 Jessie
Southwick Willet, secretary North Beach & M. R. R. Co. dwl 1104 Howard
Southworth Alden L. dwl Brevoort House
Southworth George, blacksmith with William Kerr, dwl 903 Battery
Southworth John J. tailor, dwl 178 Minna
Sove William, musician, dwl 130 Minna
Sowle Nathaniel, mariner, dwl 1040 Folsom
Spalding C. L. A. folder, Easton's Laundry, W s Lagoon
Spanagle George, shoe maker, 506 Clay, dwl corner Washington and Dupont
Spangenberg E. M. (widow) dwl 128 Stevenson
Spanier Joseph, teamster with Israel Schussler, dwl West End Hotel
Spannhaake Henry (*F. Behre & Co.*) dwl 1414 Kearny
Spanutius John M. stock broker, dwl NW cor Powell and Filbert
Spark (*J. G.*) & Schultz (*R.*) Eureka Saloon, SE cor Harrison and Spear, dwl 308 Beale
Sparks Thomas, drayman, U. S. Appraiser's Store
Sparks William, captain schooner J. A. Haskins, office 413 East, dwl 132 Natoma
Sparks William, porter with Bryant & Beadle, dwl Sailors' Home, Davis nr Washington
Sparks Z. W. real estate, office 614 Merchant, dwl 11 O'Farrell
Sparrell James, fireman, steamer Petaluma

Sparrow Albert R. compositor, Alta California, dwl 835 Vallejo
Sparrow E. dwl 32 Natoma
Sparrow Joseph, laborer, dwl Ecker bet First and Second
Sparrow S. J. stock broker, 622 Montgomery, dwl 111 St. Mark Place
Sparrow Walter, stock broker, 622 Montgomery, dwl 111 St. Mark Place
Spat Frederick, butcher, dwl 665 Mission
SPAULDING C. A. attorney at law and collector, office 328 Mont, dwl NW cor Clay and Leav
Spaulding Celia (widow) boarding, 521 Pine
Spaulding George, compositor with Dewey & Co. dwl 24 Langton
Spaulding Henry, rigger, dwl 409 Pacific
Spaulding J. & Co. carpet beating machine, 113 Fremont, dwl S s Clay bet Polk and Van Ness Avenue
Spaulding Jerome, sawsmith with N. W. Spaulding, 113 Pine, dwl 115 Ellis
Spaulding John A. carrier, Evening Bulletin and Call, dwl S s Clay bet Polk and Van Ness Av
Spaulding Julia A. Miss, nurse, dwl N s Riley near Taylor
Spaulding Lydia (widow) dwl with N. W. Spaulding, W s First Av bet Fifteenth and Sixteenth
Spaulding M. mason, Spring Valley W. W
Spaulding Madison, sawsmith with N. W. Spaulding, 113 Pine, dwl 115 Ellis
SPAULDING NATHAN W. sawsmith and importer and dealer saws, 113 Pine, dwl First Avenue bet Fifteenth and Sixteenth
Spaulding Philip, carpenter, dwl 407 Hyde
Spear Dudley, laborer, dwl SE cor Bush and Stock
SPEAR EDWARD S. & CO. (*Joseph S. Spear*) auctioneers and commission merchants, 433 California, dwl 811 Bush
Spear Frederick A. dwl W s Sixth nr Brannan
Spear James, machinist, Miners' Foundry, dwl with William Thackeray, W s Folsom bet Sixteenth and Seventeenth
Spear John I. jr. (*Hickox & S.*) dwl 728 Sutter
Spear John W. clerk with Joseph R. Clayes
Spear Joseph S. (*Edward S. Spear & Co.*) dwl 811 Bush
Spear Joseph S. jr. clerk, 433 Cal, dwl 811 Bush
Spear Samuel, liquors, cor Kearny and Francisco
Spear T. Dudley, trimmer with Nathaniel Gray, dwl NE cor Bush and Stockton
Spear Thomas G. book and job printing, NE cor Clay and Montgomery, dwl Pioneer Building
Spear T. R. dentist, office and dwl 202 Bush
Spearman Stephen, machinist, Union Foundry, dwl 13 Ohio
Specht George, miner, dwl N s Oregon bet Front and Davis
Specht Jacob, waterman, 609 Market
Specht William, cabinet maker, dwl 319 Bush
Speck Joseph, carrier, Daily Examiner, dwl 5 Margaret Place
Specker Peter, express wagon, corner Kearny and Washington
Speckles William, student, Mission Dolores Church
Speckmann Frederick, clerk, SW cor Folsom and Fourth
Speckter Henry (*Henry Struss & Co.*) dwl 141 Second
Speed Walter R. drug clerk with H. Adolphus, dwl 423 Fourth
Speer Charles, cabinet maker with J. B. Luchsinger, dwl cor Battery and Green
Speier Bernhard (*I. Speire & Bro.*) dwl 110 Stevenson
Speier (*I.*) & Brother (*Bernhard Speier*) fancy goods, 100 Kearny, dwl Dresdener House
Spellecy Ellen Miss. domestic, 803 Bush
Spellman Joseph, tailor, 511 Commercial, dwl E s Ecker bet Market and Stevenson

Spellman Thomas, workman, S. F. & P. Sugar Co. dwl S s Mary nr Harrison
Spellmeyer Charles *(Hencken & S.)* 719 Pacific
Spelman Henry J. boatman, dwl W s Battery bet Green and Vallejo, rear
Spelty F. interpreter, dwl Trinity nr Bush
Spence John, molder with Cock & Flynn, dwl 511 Mission
Spence W. A. fish, 9 and 10 Washington Fish Market, dwl 345 Brannan
Spencer Aaron G. machinist, Miners' Foundry, dwl 28 Perry
SPENCER *(Charles)* & JARBOE *(John R.)* attorneys at law, office 24–26 Court Block 636 Clay, dwl 431 Minna
Spencer Charles, seaman, dwl 20 Commercial
Spencer Christopher, ship wright, dwl 238 Stewart
Spencer David, saloon, NW cor Folsom and Beale
Spencer David, second officer stm Moses Taylor
Spencer Eliza (widow) dwl 337 Union
Spencer Frank, harness maker, dwl St. Charles Hotel
Spencer George, bricklayer, dwl 116 Sansom
Spencer James, boatman, bds City Front House, 625 Davis
Spencer J. C. *(R. H. McDonald & Co.)* dwl 506 Third
Spencer John D. dwl 908 Powell
Spencer Lowell B. porter with George Howes & Co. dwl Essex Place
SPENCER MICHAEL M. physician and surgeon, office 800 Howard cor Fourth, dwl 743 Howard
Spencer William, foreman Rincon Hose Co. No. 6, NW cor Folsom and Beale
Spencer William H. porter with E. Ayers, dwl 415 Pine
Spencer William V. *(Cobleigh & S.)* dwl N s Clay bet Polk and Van Ness Avenue
Sperry W. L. dwl 538 Commercial
Speyer David E. book keeper, 304 California, dwl 327 O'Farrell
Speyer Ernestina Mrs. cook, New York Hotel
SPEYER MORRIS, importer fancy goods and agent Hamburg Fire Insurance Co. office 526 Washington, dwl 716 Post
Speyer Bernard, clerk with S. Kohlman, dwl 220 Stevenson
Spieckerman Henry, gardener with James Dyer
Spielan John, laborer, dwl 231 Pacific
Spielmann George, jeweler with Mathewson & Bucklin, dwl 625 Vallejo
Spienette Guiseppe, vegetable garden, nr Bay View Park
Spier Richard P. *(Allen & S.)* dwl 719 California
Spiers James, draftsman, Miners' Foundry
Spies F. painter and paper hanger, 330 Bush
Spiese Joseph, shoe maker with Jacob Hess, dwl Belden nr Pine
Spillane John, orderly with Gen. H. W. Halleck
Spillcock Henry, with Hucks & Lambert, dwl 704 Folsom
Spiller F. Frank, policeman, City Hall, dwl 151 Natoma
Spindler Jacob, hairdresser with E. Boisse, dwl St. Charles nr Kearny
Spiner Alexander, laborer with Lyon & Co. dwl 649 Mission
Spinnetta M. Mrs. dwl S s Francisco bet Mason and Taylor
Spinney George R. secretary Empire Mill and Mining Co. office 240 Mont, dwl 213 Powell
Spinney Waldron S. foreman San Francisco Cordage Factory, dwl cor Iowa and Humbolt
SPIRIT OF THE TIMES AND FIREMAN'S JOURNAL (weekly) office SW cor Sansom and Jackson, Chase & Boruck editors and proprietors
SPLIVALO AUG. D. attorney at law, office 430 Jackson

Spoerndli J. M. watch maker with Theodore Hartung, 216 Kearny
Spofford *(John L.)* & Spooner *(Alden)* ship joiners, office Main Street Wharf, dwl N s Grove bet Franklin and Gough
Spohn Joseph, butcher, 45 Jackson, dwl 35 Jackson
Spohr Andrew, musician, dwl 1511 Mason
Spolier Alphonse, laundry, 1425 Dupont
Spooner Alden *(Spofford & S.)* dwl 308 Beale
Spooner Benjamin F. watchman Maguire's Opera House, dwl 24 Stone
Spooner John, architect, dwl 308 Beale
Spooner John P. photographer with Bradley & Rulofson, dwl 308 Beale
Spori Louis, tailor, 737 Pacific
Spotorno *(Jean B.)* & Auradou *(Leon)* poultry, 507 Merchant
Spottiswood Catherine Miss, domestic, SW cor Sixteenth and Howard
Spottiswood Mary Miss, domestic, SW cor Howard and Fifteenth
Spottiswood Rebecca Miss, domestic, 1713 Powell
Sprague Adna *(Loring & S.)* dwl 8 Quincy
Sprague Alfred P. trunk maker with E. Galpen & Co. dwl St. Francis H. & L. Co
Sprague Charles J. Maj. paymaster U. S. A. office 742 Washington, dwl 76 Clementina
Sprague Elisha M. carpenter with E. Galpen & Co. dwl St. Francis H. & L. Co
Sprague John, carpenter, dwl NW cor Stevenson and Third
Sprague Joseph, carpenter, dwl 145 Perry
Sprague Samuel S. with Bradshaw & Co. dwl 37 Natoma
Sprague Samuel S. jr. clerk Evening Bulletin, 620 Montgomery
SPRECKELS *(Claus)* & CO. *(Peter Spreckels and Claus Mangels)* proprietors Albany Brewery, 71–75 Everett, dwl SE cor Howard and Sixteenth
Spreckels Henry, driver, Albany Brewery, dwl 75 Everett
Spreckels Peter *(Spreckels & Co.)* dwl 72 Everett
Spreen William *(Nolting & Spreen)* dwl 640 Market
SPREEN WILLIAM, groceries and liquors, NE cor Brannan and Ninth
Spriggs George, clerk, Custom House, dwl 1 Bagley Place
Spriggs Harry, minstrel, dwl 508 Broadway
Spring Francis S. office 705 Sansom, res Oakland
Spring John R. office 705 Sansom, dwl 613 Stockton
Spring M. L. Miss, teacher, City Female Seminary, dwl S s Sixteenth bet Valencia and Mission
SPRING VALLEY WATER WORKS CO. office SE cor Montgomery and Jackson
Springer A. engineer, dwl Oriental Hotel
Springman Edward, cabinetmaker with W. G. Weir, dwl 520 Green
Springmiller John, seaman, dwl 14 Lewis Place
SPROAT *(Gilbert M.)* & WELCH *(Andrew)* commission merchants and agents for Anderson, Thomson & Co. London, 525 Front cor Jackson, res London
Sproul Andrew *(Grant, Averell & Co.)* dwl Warm Spring Landing, Alameda Co
Sproul Bridget Miss, domestic, NE cor Pacific and Mason
Sproul J. physician, office and dwl 108 Dupont
Sproul James A. hackman, Crescent Engine Co. No. 10
Sproul J. R. dwl 113 Minna
Sprowl Frederick S. carpenter, rms 3 Milton Place
Sprowl John, policeman, dwl ½ mile SW Lake Honda
Spruance J. & J. groceries and provisions (Folsom City) office 415 Front *(and J. C. Horan & Co.)* dwl Russ House
Spruance John *(J. & J. Spruance)* res Folsom
SPRUEGEL CHRISTIAN, California Beer Saloon and furnished rooms, 621 California

Spruban Walter, tailor, dwl 533 Jackson
Sprung David, assistant engineer Market St. R. R. Co. dwl Valencia bet Sixteenth and Seventeenth
Sprung Fred. actor, Bella Union, dwl International Hotel
Sprung *(Hiram)* & McArron *(Charles)* carriage makers, 579 Market, dwl W s Valencia near Seventeenth
Squarza Petroleum Co. (Humboldt) office 528 Clay
SQUARZA VINCENT, wines and liquors and manufacturer Squarza's Punches, Cordials and Bitters, 118 and 120 Leidesdorff, dwl 402 Mont
Squire Henry C. insurance broker, office 238 Mont, dwl S s Fell bet Franklin and Van Ness Av
SQUIRE HORATIO N. deputy county assessor, 22 City Hall first floor, dwl 824 Bush
Squire O D. book keeper with Tallant & Co. dwl 1005 Clay
Squires George, cook, Tremont House
Squires Nathaniel, with Church & Clark, dwl Vallejo bet Powell and Mason
Squires Sarah (widow) dwl 812 Vallejo
Sroufe John *(Dodge Bros. & Co.)* bds Russ House
St. Clair Consolidated M. Co. office 540 Washington
St. Dennis Jules *(E. Dubourque & Co.)* dwl S s Jackson bet Kearny and Dupont
St. Francis Hotel, Alphonse Mathieu proprietor, SW cor Dupont and Clay
ST. IGNATIUS' COLLEGE, S s Market bet Fourth and Fifth
St. John Benj. G. real estate agent, dwl 467 Minna
St. John B. G. Mrs. private school, 467 Minna
St. John's House, 639 Clay
St. Lawrence Central Tunnel & M. Co. office 1 Government House, 502 Washington
St. Lawrence House, 615 and 617 Market
St. Louis Brewery, E s Valencia bet Sixteenth and Seventeenth
St. Louis G. & S. M. Co. office 40 Montgomery Blk
St. Louis Hotel, Heimburg & Schroeder proprietors, 11 and 13 Pacific
St. Louis M. Co. (Reese River) office 6 Mont Block
St. Mary Francis, billiard keeper, Occidental Hotel
ST. MARY'S COLLEGE, Old San José Road 4½ miles from City Hall, Rev. P. J., Grey president
ST. MARY'S HOSPITAL, NW cor First and Bryant
St. Mathew John H. correspondent, dwl W s Kentucky bet Sixteenth and Santa Clara
St. Nicholas S. & S. M. Co. office 1 Government House, 502 Washington
ST. NICHOLAS HOTEL, Levi Hess proprietor, SW cor Sansom and Commercial
St. Petersburg Petroleum Co. office NE cor Clay and Battery
Staacke George, accountant with Barron & Co. dwl 1231 Stockton
Staats John, teamster, dwl Post St. House
Stacey D. B. Cashier's Department Wells, Fargo & Co. dwl 915 Stockton
Stacey Isaac, waiter, steamer Orizaba
Stacey Martin V. B. dwl with Nahum Poland, W s Ninth bet Howard and Mission
Stack John, workman, Mission Woolen Mills, dwl Mission Creek nr Sixteenth
Stack Thomas, laborer, dwl San Bruno Road 3½ miles from City Hall
Stackhouse John L. scenic artist Olympic Melodeon, dwl 414 Green
Stackhouse Robert, machinist, Maguire's Opera H
Stackpole B. B. boiler maker, Vulcan Iron Works, dwl 99 Stevenson
Stackpole Charles E. salesman with Edward Hall & Co. dwl 506 Dupont
Stackpole Thomas, carriage painting, 113 Bush, dwl 204 Montgomery
Stadermann Charles, musician, dwl 621 California
Stadler Louis, laborer, dwl 42 Sacramento
Stadtfeld Christian, musician, dwl 606 Jackson

Stadtfeld Jacob, melter, U. S. Branch Mint, dwl 106 Turk
Stacber George, book keeper, Revere House, 323 Pine
Staehl Frederick, cook, dwl 205 Sansom
Staffelbach Albert, barber, stm America, dwl 108 Stewart
Staffelbach Edward, barber, dwl 108 Stewart
STAFFELBACH XAVIER, hairdressing saloon, 108 Stewart
Stafford Henry, ship carpenter, dwl 114 Freelon
Stafford John, carpenter, bds Franklin Hotel, SE cor Sansom and Pacific
Stagg Catherine (widow) dwl 151½ Silver
Stagg Cornelius, deputy collector, U. S. Internal Revenue, office NW cor Battery and Commercial, dwl 151½ Silver
Staglich Frank, landscape gardener, dwl 813 Stock
Stahl Christian G. hatter, dwl 9 Virginia
Stahl Frederick, cook, 324 Montgomery, dwl New England House
Stahl John, waiter, Government House Restaurant, dwl 720 Geary
Stahl Theodore A. tobacconist with R. G. Gelien, SE cor California and Front
STAHLE BROTHERS *(Henry W. and John)* hairdressing saloon, SE cor Montgomery and California, dwl 12 Virginia
Stahle Edward, hairdresser with Stahle Bros. dwl 7 Tay
Stahle Frederick H. hairdresser, Vigilant Engine Co. No. 9
Stahle John *(Stahle Bros.)* dwl 28 John
Stahler Barbara Mrs. dwl 420 Bush
Stahmann Albert, clerk, NW cor Green and Dupont
Staib Conrad, shoe maker, 335 Bush, dwl 115 Geary, rear
Stair Alexander, clerk, dwl What Cheer House
Stalder Joseph, clerk, 7 Occidental Market, dwl 221 Dupont
Stalk John, dyer, Mission Woolen Mills
Stallman James S. book keeper, 314 Sacramento, dwl 319 Kearny
STALLMANN CHRISTIAN, merchant tailor, 543 Sacramento, dwl 414 Dupont
Stamer Julius *(Klemeier & S.)* dwl NW cor Jackson and Battery
Stamm Ferdinand, ranch hand with Justus Bepler
Stamm Louis, shoe maker with Hinders & Kast, dwl 207 Post
Stamper Joseph, bar keeper, Revere H, 325 Pine
Stamper Joseph, laborer, 614 Clay
Stampfli Frank, foreman with Henry Manneck, dwl 205 Sansom
Stamplemann Henry, clerk, 623 Pacific
Stanage Lucinda Mrs. lodgings, 217 Third
Stanage Philip, piano forte maker, dwl 217 Third
Standard Soap Co. *(R. P. Thomas and J. P. Cogswell)* office 207 Commercial
Standerwick James S. painter with Snow & Co. dwl 29 Third
Standish Sarah Miss, millinery, 406 Kearny
Staner Mrs. (widow) dwl S s Sixteenth nr Guerrero
Stanford Ann Miss, domestic, 716 Pine
Stanford A. P. *(Stanford Bros.)* dwl 24 Ellis
STANFORD BROTHERS *(Charles, Josiah, and A. P.)* importers and jobbers oils, lamps, etc. 121 and 123 Cal, and Pac Oil and Camphene Works, NE cor Chestnut and Taylor, res New York
Stanford Charles P. clerk with H. H. Bancroft & Co. dwl N s Union nr Hyde
Stanford Elijah, mining superintendent. dwl N s Union nr Hyde
Stanford H. glass blower, Pacific Glass Works, dwl Potrero
Stanford Josiah *(Stanford Bros.)* dwl 607 Bush
Stanford W. T. clerk with M. L. McDonald, dwl 245 Stevenson
Stangenberger Augustus, piano maker, 755 Mission

Stangroom Mark L. assistant engineer, Western Pacific R. R. Co. office 409 Cal, dwl 1825 Stockton
Staniels John S. bar keeper, 539 Washington, dwl 610 Filbert
Staniels William H. *(Stanyan & Co.)* dwl 510 Taylor
Stanislaus Copper M. Co. office 620 Washington
Stanley Benjamin, laborer with Galloway & Boobar, dwl E s Crook, bet Brannan and Townsend
Stanley Charles, clerk, 653 Sacramento, dwl corner Stockton and Market
Stanley Charles, machinist, Market St. R. R. Co. dwl First Avenue bet Fourteenth and Fifteenth
Stanley Charles A. engineer, steamer Cornelia, dwl 422 Third
Stanley Frederick H. reporter, dwl 322 Ritch
Stanley James, hackman, Plaza, dwl 265 Jessie
Stanley James H. (col'd) waiter, stm Chrysopolis
Stanley Jerome M. fruits, 107 Geary, dwl 109 Geary
Stanley Jerome M. painter, dwl SE cor Kearny and Vallejo
Stanly Charles, dwl 116 Post
Stanovich M. fruits, dwl 532 Commercial
Stanovich Pietro, fisherman, 42 Italian Fish Market
Stans John H. (col'd) dwl 445 Clementina
Stansa Ellen Miss, domestic, 615 Taylor
Stansbury William C. painter, dwl 460 Jessie
Stansfield Joseph, bricklayer, dwl 1110 Pine
Stanson Thomas, mariner, bds Clinton Temperance Hotel 311 Pacific
Stanton Anne Miss, dwl with Mrs. J. Stanton, W s Mission nr Fifteenth
Stanton A. P. cutter, U. S. Branch Mint, dwl Greenwich bet Fillmore and Steiner
Stanton G. F. teamster, dwl West End Hotel
Stanton Henry L. clerk, dwl NW cor Stockton and Jackson
Stanton James, laborer, dwl 334 Third, rear
Stanton James, miner, dwl W s Mission nr Fifteenth
Stanton Patrick, carpenter, dwl 41 Minna
Stanton Silas S. Coiner's Department U. S. Branch Mint
Stanton William, laborer with William Kerr, dwl 903 Battery
Stanwick James S. painter, 29 Third
Stanyan Albert P. clerk with Stanyan & Co
Stanyan *(Charles H.)* & Co. *(William H. Staniels)* teamsters, 17 California and Pier 4 Stewart and supervisor Twelfth District dwl W s Polk bet Clay and Sacramento
Stanyenwall Jeffroy, steward, Tremont House
Staples Alpheus, mining, office 7 Stevenson House, res Oakland
Staples Charles, bargeman, C. H. dwl 529 Pine
Staples D. J. Port Warden, office 706 Front, dwl N s Geary bet Jones and Leavenworth
Staples Edwin H. watch maker with William Geist, dwl Sumner nr Howard
Staples Ellen (widow) dwl 712 Pine
Staples Joseph, porter, 117 Clay, dwl 14 Clay
Staples William B. blacksmith, dwl 636 Commercial
Stapleton Catharine Miss, domestic, 806 Green
Stapleton Catherine Miss, domestic, 609 Bush
STAPLETON JOHN, proprietor Grotto Liquor Saloon, 530 Sacramento, dwl W s Mary bet Howard and Bush
Stapleton Margaret Miss, domestic, 931 Market
Stapleton Margaret Miss, nurse, St. Mary's Hospital
Stapleton Richard, hostler, Half-Way House, Ocean House Road
Stapleton William, shipwright, dwl 56 Stewart
Stappenbeck William, tailor, dwl 1205 Dupont
Star Line Packets, J. N. McCune agent, office 117 Clay
Star Soap and Candle Works, Fielding & Osgood agents, 221 Sacramento
Starbuck George, toll collector, Mission St. Wharf, dwl 266 Minna

Stark Alexander, engineer, dwl N s Folsom bet Seventh and Eighth
Stark Hannah, domestic, 246 Jessie
Stark John W. stair builder with N. P. Langland, dwl 356 Brannan
Stark William R. cigar maker with E. Goslinsky, dwl 475 Jessie
Starkey Joseph N. butcher, dwl N s Brannan bet Eighth and Ninth
Starkey J. R. (col'd) barber, 102 Stewart, dwl 406 Green
Starkweather George R. with C. W. Thomas, 22 Cal
Starr E. S. *(Jones & S.)* dwl 30 Silver
Starr G. R. laborer, C. H. dwl 1022 Montgomery
Starr *(Mordecai)* & Riddle *(David M.)* wood, coal, hay, and grain, 16 Drumm, dwl 358 Jessie
Starr Thomas N. *(Deeth & S.)* dwl S s Sixteenth bet Folsom and Howard
Starrs William, dwl 19 Moss
STATE ALMANAC AND HAND BOOK OF STATISTICS, annually, Henry G. Langley proprietor, office 612 Clay
STATE AND PACIFIC COAST BUSINESS DIRECTORY, Henry G. Langley proprietor, office 612 Clay
State Gauger, office 321 Front
STATE GEOLOGICAL SURVEY, office 90 Montgomery Block
STATE HARBOR COMMISSIONERS, board of, office 302 Montgomery
STATE REGISTER, annually, Henry G. Langley proprietor, office 612 Clay
State Stamp Inspector, office 424 Battery
Statts Christina Mrs. dwl 1314 Dupont
Statzon George, blacksmith with Benjamin A. Fisher, dwl cor Sansom and Market
Staub Edward, physician, office 519 Pacific
Stauch George, tailor, dwl 1005 Kearny
Staud Francis, dwl 521 Bush
Stand J. N. wood and coal, 211 Dupont, dwl 212 Dupont
Stauffer Rudolf, market, NE cor Brannan and Ritch
Staugard Cicilie Miss, domestic, SW cor Vallejo and Powell
Staunton Bridget Miss, domestic, 919 Jackson
Staunton Mary Miss, milliner, dwl 1713 Mason
Stead George, merchant, dwl 702 Vallejo
Steadman James, waiter, Lick House
Stealey Thomas, builder, dwl SE cor Seventeenth and Guerrero
Stearns Charles A. telegraph operator, dwl 1015 Powell
Stearns Joseph H. *(Kellogg, Hewston & Co.)* dwl 416 Montgomery
Stearns Mason, miner, dwl 113 Tehama
Stearns Myron J. laborer, 626 Kearny
Stearns Robert E. C. secretary Board State Harbor Commissioners, off 302 Mont, dwl 515 Geary
Stearns William, milkman, dwl 514 O'Farrell
Stebbins Adelia Mrs. furnished rooms, 6 Mont
Stebbins Henry L. messenger with Truman & Co. res San José
Stebbins Horatio Rev. pastor First Unitarian Church, dwl 930 Clay
Stebbins James C. attorney at law, office 803 Montgomery room 1, dwl 814 Bush
Stebbins T. dwl What Cheer House
Stebbins William P. C. contractor and builder, dwl 607 Stockton
Stecher Charles, shoe maker with George Spanagle, dwl Bootz's Hotel
Stecher Philip, carpenter, dwl 429 Minna
Steck Anna (widow) nurse, dwl with James Christy, W s Mississippi nr Mariposa
Steckler Henry, butcher, 146 Second, dwl 571 Howard
Steckler Isaac E. Steckler's Exchange, SE cor California and Sansom

Stedman Charles, printer, dwl 100 Stockton
Stedman Charles, tinsmith, dwl S s Broadway bet Stockton and Powell
Stedman Jane Miss, adjuster, U. S. Branch Mint, dwl E s Howard nr Sixteenth
Steele Charles H. bar keeper, Pennsylvania Engine Co. No. 12
Steele Edward, clerk with C. Adolphe Low & Co. dwl 933 Sacramento
Steele Edwin R. bar keeper, SE cor Sixth and Folsom
Steele Henry, blacksmith, 107 Leidesdorff
Steele James, carpenter, dwl 28 Sansom
Steele James G. chemist with W. H. Keith & Co. dwl NE cor Washington and Dupont
Steele William, boiler maker helper, Vulcan Iron Works, dwl Davis St. House
Steele William, fireman, dwl Davis St. House
Steele William A. (Edward Galpen & Co.) dwl 319 Harrison
Steele William H. clerk Pennsylvania Engine Co. No. 12
Steen Edward T. Novelty Iron Works and Machine Shop, 39 and 41 Fremont and 42 and 44 Beale, dwl 202 Post
Steen J. F. watchman, U. S. Branch Mint, dwl E s Yerba Buena bet Clay and Sacramento
Steen Joseph, dwl 7 Garden
Steen Joseph, barber, dwl 532 Mission
Steere Thomas F. waterman, 609 Market
Steffani C. (Mariani & S.) dwl 1006 Dupont
Steffen Charles (Steffen & Bro.) dwl Post St. House
Steffen (Jacob) & Brother (Charles Steffen) hairdressing saloon, 722 Market, dwl Post St. House
Steffens Charles, broom maker with L. Van Laak, 14 Drumm
STEFFENS DEIDRICH (Mangels & S.) dwl SE cor Folsom and Main
Steffens Henry, clerk, dwl 570 Mission
Steffens Joseph, book keeper, 223 Front, dwl 664 Howard
Steffens Mary A. J. dwl NE cor Mission and Thirteenth
Stege Henry, restaurant, W s Sixth bet Harrison and Bryant
Stege John, clerk, 7 Washington Market, dwl Bootz's Hotel
Stegmann Ferdinand, musician, dwl 62 Clay
Steguer George, waiter, 546 Clay
Steiger Alexander, machinist, Vulcan Foundry, dwl 322 Beale
Steiger Charles R. (Vulcan Iron Works Co.) secretary, dwl 942 Mission
Steiger W. H. pattern maker, Vulcan Iron Works, dwl 32 Minna
Steil, (Henry) Wehn (Charles F.) & Co. merchant tailors, Occidental Hotel, dwl 214 Sansom
Steillen Henry, waiter, 28 Montgomery
Stein Charles, clerk, NW cor Fifth and Shipley
Stein, (Charles W.) Link (Valentine) & Scherb (Francis) Union Carriage Factory, 743 Market, dwl 252 Stevenson
Stein Elizabeth (widow) dwl S s Sixteenth bet Valencia and Mission
Stein Frank, watchman, U. S. Branch Mint
Stein George, shoe maker, 413 East, dwl 18 Ohio
Stein Henry, shoe maker, 413 East, dwl 18 Ohio
STEIN, (Henry W.) SIMON (Hermann L.) & CO. (Alex. Weill) importers and dealers cloths, cassimeres, tailors' goods, etc. 632 and 634 Sac and 631 and 633 Com, dwl 1321 Powell
Stein Jacob, butcher with W. F. Witzemann, 425 East
Stein Meyer, cigars and tobacco, dwl 103 Pacific
Stein Paulina (widow) fancy goods, 1339 Dupont
Stein Samuel, cigars, SW cor Davis and Pacific
Steinbach Emil, real estate, office 38 Government House, 502 Washington, dwl 809 Stockton

Steinbach Fred'k, hairdresser, Montgomery Baths, dwl E s Dupont nr Sacramento
Steinberg Adam, gas fitter, dwl N s St. Charles near Kearny
Steinberg Charles, tailor, dwl 316 Ritch
Steinbrink Bernard, news dealer, 35 Second
Steinbrink Samuel, meter inspector with M. Kenny, dwl 618 Post
Steinck Samuel, laborer, dwl 511 Davis
Steincke William, carver, dwl S side Stevenson bet Sixth and Seventh
Steindler Meyer, groceries and liquors, NW cor Shipley and Willow, dwl 462 Natoma
Steinegger Henry (Britton & Co.) dwl 2 Gustavus
Steiner Barbara (widow) midwife, dwl 221 Dupont
Steiner Samuel (Steiner & Koneman, Silver City) office 421 Sacramento, dwl 36 Turk
Steinert Edward, trimmer, dwl W s Seventh near Brannan
Steinert Felix, salesman with Pollack Bros. dwl Steckler's Exchange
Steinfeld J. cigars and tobacco, 223 Pacific
Steinfort Frederick, carpenter with J. Center, dwl W s Florida nr Twentieth
STEINHART BROTHERS (Frederick, Sigmund, and Ignace) importers and jobbers foreign and domestic dry goods, 300 and 302 California, res New York
Steinhart Ignace (Steinhart Bros.) dwl 1509 Stock
Steinhart Israel (W. & I. Steinhart) dwl 711 Leav
Steinhart Falk, salesman, 316 Sac. dwl 518 Stock
Steinhart Frederick, carriage painter, dwl 121 Shipley
Steinhart Sigmund (Steinhart Bros.) dwl 1509 Stockton
Steinhart W. & I. importers and jobbers clothing and gents' furnishing goods, 321 and 323 Sacramento, dwl 711 Leavenworth
Steinhofer Philip, laborer, dwl 212 First
Steinhoff (Herman) & Co. (H. H. W. Stroecker) groceries and liquors, SW cor Bush and Trinity
Steinle Emil, professor music, dwl 211 Post
Steinle Henry, barber, SE corner Valencia and Sixteenth
STEINMANN JOHN, proprietor Revere House, 323 and 325 Pine
Steinweg Charles, blacksmith and wheelwright, 109 Pine, dwl 571 Minna
Steitzer George, blacksmith, dwl 6 Sansom
Steler P. watch maker and jeweler, 804 Washington
Stellberger George A. gas fitter, dwl 424 Pacific
Stemler Jacob, mariner, 32 Stewart
Stemmler P. L. varnisher with W. G. Weir, dwl 212 Sutter
Stenbiht W. musical director and pianist, Bella Union
Stenger Emil, clerk, dwl 820 Clay
Stenson Jane Miss, domestic, 324 Fremont
Stenson Robert J. salesman, NW cor Pine and Battery, dwl 129 Shipley
Stepf Michael (Perey & S.) dwl 1220 Pacific
Stephan John G. butcher, 56 Washington Market, dwl 809 Harrison
Stephens Andrew, porter with Redington & Co. dwl 308 Tehama
Stephens Anna Miss, domestic, 625 Harrison
Stephens Charles, book keeper with J. Mora Moss, dwl 614 California
Stephens Frances E. Mrs. dwl NE cor Filbert and Montgomery
Stephens Horace H. dwl 914 Vallejo
Stephens John, cook, S s Folsom bet Fifth and Sixth
Stephens John C. painter, dwl 636 Commercial
Stephens Samuel, clerk with Jones & Bendixen, dwl 20 Oak
Stephens Samuel, ship carpenter, dwl 24 Frederick
Stephens William Z. machinist, dwl 117 William
Stephenson James W. attorney at law, 5 Court Block 636 Clay

Stepney Richard (col'd) bootblack, Russ House
Steppacher Meyer, sexton synagogue Emanu-El and Nove Sholem Cemetery, dwl 820 Broadway
STERETT BENJAMIN F. book and job printing, 533 Clay, dwl 518 Howard
Sterett M. pattern maker, Vulcan Iron Works, dwl 36 Battery
Sterett William I. with Benjamin F. Sterett, dwl 518 Howard
Sterling Geo. W. salesman, 206 Pine, dwl Central Pl
Sterling Hiram, at Bay City Laundry, 1142 Folsom
Sterling Peter, actor, Bella Union, dwl 259 Jessie
Sterling Philip, miner, dwl 84 Natoma
Sterling William, cigar maker, 419 Brannan, dwl 186 Jessie
Sterling, see Stirling
Stern Celia Miss, domestic, NW corner Powell and Ellis
Stern Charles, confectioner, dwl 630 Green, rear
Stern Daniel, painter, dwl 315 Bush
Stern David (Wangenheim, Sternheim & Co.) dwl S s Fulton bet Franklin and Gough
Stern David (Levi Strauss & Co.) dwl 317 Powell
Stern Jacob (Adler & S.) dwl 221 Third
Stern M. importer and jobber hats and caps, 226 Bat
Stern Martin, merchant (Gold Hill) dwl 845 Sutter
Stern Philip, furniture, 232 Third
Stern Simon H. merchant, dwl 115 Mason
Sternheim Samuel (Wangenheim, S. & Co.) dwl 222 Minna
Sternitzski Charles, carpenter, dwl 415 Bush
Sterrett H. dwl What Cheer House
Stetson Alva M. engineer, dwl 131 First
Stetson Francis H. teamster, dwl 206 Fifth
Stetson James B. (Osgood & S.) dwl 1045 Howard
Stetson Josiah, carpenter, dwl 10 Sutter
Stetson W. W. accountant, dwl 810 Washington
Stenart Thomas, waiter, Occidental Hotel
Stevenot Gabriel K. real estate, office 606 Montgomery, dwl 475 Jessie
Stevens A. waiter, steamer Senator
Stevens Alvin C. drayman, 312 Clay
Stevens Augustus K. book keeper, Railroad House
Stevens Calvin C. drayman, 309 Clay, dwl 679 Harrison
Stevens Charles, fruits, dwl 615 Pacific
Stevens Charles, insurance broker, Occidental Insurance Co. dwl NE cor Howard and Fourth
Stevens Charles, book keeper with M. C. Hillyer & Co. dwl 1009 Powell
Stevens Coleman, milkman, N s Brannan bet Fifth and Sixth
Stevens D. A. wharfinger, Mission St. Wharf
Stevens (Dudley O.) & Rider (L. A.) sash and blind makers, SW cor Market and Fifth, dwl 453 Jessie
Stevens Edwin A. printer, Christian Advocate, dwl 211 Minna
Stevens Elisha & Co. produce commission, 204 Clay, dwl 825 Bush
Stevens Ernest E. carpenter with J. Brokaw, dwl W s Fremont bet Harrison and Bryant
Stevens Francis H. conductor, North Beach & M. R. R. Co. dwl 264 Tebama
Stevens George, clerk, 1024 Battery, dwl 1021 Bat
Stevens George, tin roofer with H. G. & E. S. Fiske, dwl 1505 California
Stevens George F. store keeper, Occidental Hotel
Stevens George W. & Co. (David Gorman) book and job printing, 511 Sacramento, res Clinton, Alameda Co
Stevens Geo. W. (Wilson & S.) dwl 10 Hardie Pl
Stevens Horatio N. operator, California State Telegraph Co. dwl 507 Montgomery
Stevens J. driver, Omnibus R. R. Co
Stevens James, carpenter and joiner, dwl 938 Mission
Stevens James, wagon maker with Gallagher & Farren, 112 Bush
Stevens J. H. dwl Occidental Hotel

Stevens Joseph, fireman, steamer Yosemite
STEVENS, (Levi) BAKER (Colin C.) & CO. (Judah Baker jr.) shipping and commission merchants, office 215 Front, dwl 4 Essex
Stevens Louis, fisherman, dwl 29 Commercial
Stevens L. S. captain ship Christopher Mitchell, office Pier 1 Stewart
Stevens Mary Miss, domestic, 716 Stockton
Stevens Mary F. Miss, dress maker, 308 Third
Stevens Martin V. builder, dwl W s Eleventh bet Folsom and Harrison
Stevens N. L. carpenter, dwl 116 Sansom
Stevens R. H. secretary, dwl 1109 Stockton
Stevens Richard H. salesman with G. W. Conkling, 714 Montgomery, dwl 353 Jessie
Stevens Robert, engineer, dwl 34 Clementina
Stevens Samuel S. carpenter and builder, dwl N s Austin bet Gough and Octavia
Stevens (Thomson H.) & Oliver (Oliver B. Huff) coffee saloon and bakery, 28 Montgomery
Stevens W. D. dwl 2 Thomson Avenue
Stevens William, boots and shoes, 544 Third
Stevens William, captain schr Falmouth, dwl 153 Natoma
Stevens William, porter with Davis & Witham, dwl cor Leavenworth and Green
Stevens William, shoe maker, dwl 604 Third
Stevens William E. contractor, dwl 264 Tehama
Stevens William H. secretary Home Mutual Insurance Co. 630 Montgomery, dwl 1109 Stockton
Stevens, see Stephens
Stevenson A. J. proprietor Stevenson House, office and dwl SW cor Montgomery and California
Stevenson Andrew, contractor, dwl 1122 Howard
Stevenson David, cook, steamer Yosemite
Stevenson House, A. J. Stevenson proprietor, SW cor Montgomery and California
STEVENSON JONATHAN D. notary public, attorney at law, commissioner deeds, solicitor patents, etc. office 614 Merch, dwl 615 Stockton
STEVENSON SAMUEL C. Arbor Liquor Saloon, 313 Montgomery, dwl 537 Mission
Stevenson William, with Charles Harley & Co. dwl Stevenson bet Fourth and Fifth
Stevenson William, treasurer Maguire's Opera House, dwl 310 Union
Steventon Frederick, cooper, dwl Montgomery bet Lombard and Chestnut
Steward Archibald, stevedore, dwl 1907 Dupont
Steward David H. seaman, dwl E s Sonoma Place nr Green
Steward Edwin, carpenter, 196 Stevenson
Steward Elizabeth Miss, domestic, 512 Dupont
Steward James (col'd) dwl W s Sonoma Pl nr Union
Stewart A. H. with Hobbs, Gilmore & Co. dwl 51 Second
Stewart Alexander, carpenter, 14 Broadway, dwl 507 Jones
Stewart Catharine (widow) dwl 810 Greenwich
Stewart Charles, with Warren A. Stewart
Stewart Charles, butcher, dwl 1011 Jackson
Stewart Charles, carpenter, dwl 33 Geary
Stewart Charles A. with Thomas Adam, cor Montgomery and Market, dwl 12 U. S. Court Bdg
Stewart Daniel, butcher with W. Smith, dwl 26 Rousch
Stewart Daniel, drayman with Haynes & Lawton, dwl S s Union bet Jones and Leavenworth
Stewart Daniel, seaman, dwl 337 Fourth
Stewart David, dwl N s Bush nr Laguna
Stewart David, drayman, dwl N s Ellis bet Van Ness Avenue and Franklin
Stewart David, drayman with E. Jaudin & Co. dwl 261 Tehama
Stewart Edwin, carpenter, dwl 274 Minna
Stewart (Edwin F.) & Daley (John H.) wines and liquors, 808 Kearny, dwl West End Hotel
Stewart E. F. Mrs. actress, Maguire's Opera House, dwl West End Hotel

Stewart Ellen ♠. Mrs. furnished rooms, U. S. Court Building
Stewart *(Frederick)* & Collie *(William)* florists and gardeners, NE cor O'Farrell and Broderick
Stewart George, groceries and provisions, NW cor Stockton and Clay
Stewart George W. clerk, office A. A. Provost Marshal General, dwl SW cor Mission and Twelfth
Stewart George W. merchant, dwl Cosmopolitan H
Stewart Hamilton, carpenter, dwl S s Boyd nr Chesley
Stewart Henry *(Collie & S.)* dwl SE cor Geary and Broderick
Stewart Henry, dwl 17 Anthony
Stewart Henry, clerk, 75 Washington Market, dwl 704 Battery
Stewart Isaac H. gardener with C. J. Janson, W s Mission bet Twentieth and Twenty-First
Stewart James, with T. N. Cazneau, dwl 624 Cal
Stewart James, accountant, Contra Costa Laundry, dwl 626 California
Stewart James, boiler maker, Pacific Foundry, dwl 27 Ritch
Stewart James, seaman, dwl 54 Sacramento
Stewart James A. machinist, dwl 116 Sansom
Stewart James F. superintendent Sailor's Home, SW cor Battery and Vallejo
Stewart Jesse C. waiter, steamer Julia
Stewart John, calker, dwl 258 Folsom
Stewart John, laborer, dwl 32 Folsom
Stewart John, ship carpenter, dwl SE cor Folsom and Beale
Stewart John W. *(Moulton & S.)* dwl N s Nineteenth bet Guerrero and Dolores
Stewart Joseph, captain Co. H Third U. S. Artillery, Fort Point
Stewart Joseph jr. operator, Fire Alarm and Police Telegraph, City Hall, dwl City Hall
Stewart Joseph M. laborer, dwl 55 Beale
STEWART J. R. & CO. *(Elisha T'. Peck)* auction and commission merchants, 417 Battery, dwl W s Shotwell bet Howard and Folsom
Stewart L. machinist, Fulton Foundry, dwl 17 Minna
Stewart M. (widow) dwl E s Harrison Av nr Folsom
Stewart Paton jr. fencing academy, 530 Merchant, dwl 612 Powell
Stewart Percilla Mrs. (col'd) assistant teacher Broadway School, dwl 1110 Pacific
Stewart R. & Co. *(Seth Milligan)* butter, cheese, and eggs, 54 Metropolitan Market, dwl N s Bernard nr Jones
Stewart Theresa, cook, New England Laundry, N s Brannan, bet Fifth and Sixth
Stewart Thomas, fruits, 521 Merch, dwl 72 Tehama
Stewart Thomas, salesman with Kerby, Byrne & Co. dwl 210 Jones, rear
Stewart Thomas, stevedore, dwl S s Union bet Battery and Sansom
Stewart Wallace, dwl 1027 Bush
Stewart Warren A. Powell St. Meat Market, SE cor Powell and Washington, dwl 1312 Pac
Stewart William, clerk, NE cor Mission and Fourth
Stewart William, engineer, dwl 814 Montgomery
Stewart William, porter with E. Martin & Co. dwl S s Green bet Dupont and Kearny
Stewart William W. superintendent, dwl 44 Minna
Stewart see Stuart
Sthall Teresa B. Miss, dwl 503 Sutter
Stickle Elizabeth (widow) dwl 13 Hinckley
Stickle S. B. horseshoeing, 326 Bush, dwl 350 Jessie
Stickney A. A. *(Californian P. Co.)* dwl 439 Jackson
Stickney B. Miss, dress making and patterns, 112 Second
Stickney Charles T. clerk with Main & Winchester, dwl SE cor Mission and First
Stickney Eleanor (widow) dwl NW cor Union and Sansom

Stickney John B. carpenter, dwl 20 Sutter
Stickney Samuel C. clerk with Joseph Peirce, dwl S s Sacramento bet Larkin and Polk
Stiessberg Frank, engineer, Zeile's Vapor Baths, 517 Pacific
Stifler Jacob, dwl S s Folsom bet Sixth and Seventh
Stiefel Louis *(Schweitzer, S. & Co.)* res New York
Stile Antonio, gardener, with John Stile, Lagoon
Stile John, garden, Presidio Road nr Lagoon
Stiles Anson G. office with S. A. Wood, 212 California, dwl 4 Vernon Place
Stiles John C. painter dwl S s Pacific bet Stockton and Powell
Stiles John M. carpenter, dwl N s St. Mark nr Stockton
Stiles Richard D. painter, dwl W s Hyde bet Union and Filbert
Still James P. watchman, Industrial School, Old Ocean House Road
Still John, laborer, dwl NW cor Main and Harrison
Still John H. news agent, dwl W s Hyde bet Bush and Pine
Still Mary (widow) dwl 14 Noble Place
Still Volney W. paper carrier, dwl W s Capp bet Eighteenth and Nineteenth
Stilley Henry G. carpenter, dwl 13 Everett
Stilley L. C. printer with Towne & Bacon, dwl 13 Everett
STILLMAN J. D. B. physician, office 15 Post, dwl 17 Post
Stilwell *(B. F.)* & Co. *(J. H. Gilmore)* publishers and advertising agents, office 511 Sansom, dwl 1123 Howard nr Eighth
Stilwell George W. real estate, dwl NE cor Folsom and Eleventh
Stimpson Joseph E. *(Thorndike & S.)* dwl 51 Natoma
Stinlar Jacob, handcartman, 211 Clay
Stinson N. H. miner, dwl Oriental Hotel
Stinson Perry, carpenter with Wm. H. Eastman, dwl 1913 Stockton
Stinson William, laborer, dwl E s Mission bet Twenty-First and Twenty-Second
Stiorda B. G. peddler, dwl 1508 Dupont
Stippler Henry, merchant tailor, dwl 623 Geary
Stirling John F. book keeper with Cox & Arnold, 240 Montgomery, dwl 127 Perry
Stirling Mathew R. with G. W. Bell, 512 California, dwl E s Van Ness Avenue bet Clay and Sac
Stitt James, rigger, dwl SW cor Mission and Beale
Stitt Robert, wheelwright, Third bet Folsom and Harrison, dwl 40 Everett
Stivers Charles A. physician, office and dwl 514 Kearny
Stivers Daniel A. wharfinger, Mission Street Wharf, dwl SW cor Union and Polk
Stivers Henry F. lumber surveyor, office Mission St. Wharf dwl S s Filbert bet Hyde and Larkin
Stivers Lafayette, dwl NE cor Vallejo and White
Stjernefeldt Charles, clerk with C. J. Janson, 210 Pine
Stochen Louis, photographic artist, dwl 315 Bush
STOCK CIRCULAR (weekly) Titus F. Cronise proprietor, office 536 Clay
Stock Edward, clerk, dwl 57 Shipley
Stock Ernest C. clerk with J. Stock & Co. dwl 23 Government House
STOCK JOHN & CO. *(Louis Pouzadoux)* Clipper Restaurant, 508 Washington, 611 Sansom, and 411 Jackson, dwl 23 Government House
Stockey John, carpenter, dwl 23 Geary
Stockfleth Catherine (widow) dwl 5 St. Ann
Stocking William D. dwl 108 Virginia
Stockinger Philip, blacksmith with Kimball & Co. dwl Columbian Engine House
Stockman John M. cabinet maker, dwl 353 Jessie
Stockton Elizabeth (widow) dwl 1016 Pine
Stockton James, store keeper, U. S. Bonded Warehouse North Point Dock, dwl 217 Third

STOCKTON LINE STEAMERS, Broadway Wharf, California Steam Navigation Company, office NE cor Front and Jackson
Stoddard A. B. captain schooner Ella Florence, office Pier 11, dwl 610 Pine
Stoddard James, machinist, Union Foundry, dwl 49 Jessie
Stoddard John, machinist, Union Foundry, dwl 49 Jessie
Stoddard Nathaniel K. compositor, Alta California, dwl 503 Dupont
Stoddard Russell R. trader, dwl Bagley Place
Stoddard Samuel, machinist, Union Foundry, dwl 49 Jessie
Stoddard S. B. salesman with Ross, Dempster & Co. res Oakland
Stoddard William, machinist, dwl 50 Beale
STODDART DAVID, Stoddart's Iron Works, 114 Beale, dwl 220 Fremont
Stodole Emily (widow) proprietress New York Hotel, SW cor Battery and Commercial
Stoelzle Constant, cabinet maker, dwl 638 Vallejo
Stoerk Jacob, restaurant, 530 merchant
Stoffer Thomas, lighterman, Pier 15 Stewart
Stohlmann William, bakery, SE cor Dupont and St. Mark Place
Stohr Albert F. musician, dwl 323 Pine
Stohr Matilda, furnished rooms, 611 and 613 Mission
Stokes Debby Miss, domestic, 923 Jackson
Stokes Mary Miss, domestic, 526 Green
Stokes William, dwl 510 Stockton
Stoler Augustine, fruits, 802 Kearny, dwl W side Kearny bet Washington and Jackson
Stolz Aaron, dry goods, 540 Kearny, dwl 712 Folsom
Stolz Abraham (Stolz Bros.) dwl 279 Stevenson
Stolz Brothers (Tobias, Abraham, and Joseph Stolz) toys and fancy goods, 530 Kearny and 8 Second, dwl 540 Mission
Stolz Joseph, dry goods, 8 Second (and Stolz Bros.) dwl 279 Stevenson
Stolze Conrad, livery and sale stable, 211 and 213 Pine
Stombs Charles A. tinsmith with G. & W. Snook, dwl 209 Second
Stone Charles L. mining secretary, dwl SE corner Geary and Jones
Stone Edward, workman, S. F. Cordage Factory
STONE EDWARD F. (Morgan, S. & Co.) dwl Union Club Rooms
Stone Edwin, laborer, dwl 35 Freelon
Stone Elise Mrs. physician, dwl 757 Mission
Stone Frank H. paper hanger, 506 Front
Stone George (Laws & Co.) dwl 757 Mission
Stone George, seaman, dwl 132 Folsom
Stone G. W. machinist, Vulcan Iron Works, dwl 1011 Mason
Stone K. B. foreman wool sorting Mission Woolen Mills
Stone Henry, carpenter, dwl 247 Jessie
Stone Isaac, proptr Lone Mountain House, NW cor Geary and Cemetery Avenue
Stone Jacob L. principal Hebrew School, 10 Stock
Stone John H. dwl S s Sixteenth bet Valencia and Mission
Stone Joseph (Clark & S.) dwl 625 Market
Stone K. L. dry goods, 6 Virginia Block, dwl SE cor Pacific and Stockton
Stone Lucius D. salesman with Stone & Heyden, dwl 500 Sutter
Stone Morris, clothing, 411 Commercial
Stone Napoleon B. ass't assessor, U. S. Int. Rev. NW cor Battery and Com, dwl Lick House
Stone Nathan J. teacher, Industrial School, Old Ocean House Road
Stone Patrick, laborer, dwl W s Salmon bet Mason and Taylor
STONE (Rockwell) & HAYDEN (Peter) importers and jobbers saddlery, hardware and leather dealers, 418 Battery, dwl cor Powell and Sutter

Stone Sherold D. dwl W s Harriet bet Howard and Folsom
Stone Silas A. dwl 531 Tehama
Stone Walter W. carpenter, dwl 1011 Mason
Stone William I. ship carpenter, dwl nr cor Illinois and Shasta
Stoneaker Henry, with James Brokaw
Stoner Abram, book keeper, Tremont H, 418 Jackson
Stoobach Henry, printer, dwl 323 Pine
Stopp Max H. watch maker, 541 Sacramento
Stoppelkamp A. H. (widow) groceries and liquors, SE cor Stockton and Union
Stoppenback Ernest, clerk, NW cor Ritch and Clara, dwl 28 Ritch
Storck (Charles L.) & Hendy (John H.) Fourth St. Market, 202 Fourth
Storer August, with John Toner, S s Brannan bet Fifth and Sixth
Storer James B. carpenter, 31 Webb, dwl 718 Union
Storer John F. compositor, Alta California, dwl N s Ellis bet Larkin and Polk
Stores Hollister, waiter, What Cheer House
Storey Sarah Miss, domestic, 313 Sutter
Storey William B. clerk with Wells, Fargo & Co. dwl N s California bet Hyde and Larkin
Storm Charles, hairdressing saloon, 327 Bush
STORM CORNELIUS, coal, 115 Sacramento, dwl 945 Mission
Stormes N. J. with Thomas C. Williams, 534 Market, dwl 49 Clementina
Storms Henry E. salesman, 304 Sansom, dwl cor Perry and Third
Storms S. H. stevedore, dwl 56 Tehama
STORY CHARLES R. tax collector city and county, office 1 City Hall first floor, dwl 30 McAllister opposite Seventh
Story Stephen C. butcher, 98 Occidental Market, dwl SW cor Ellis and Van Ness Avenue
Stoesser Frederick, baker, SE cor Mission and Fourth
STOTT ALEXANDER, lamps and oils, 512 Sansom, dwl 921 Powell
STOTT CHARLES, petroleum oil works, NW cor Chestnut and Taylor
Stott John, porter with A. C. Dietz & Co. 519 Front
Stoudt Charles, dwl E s Alameda bet Nebraska and El Dorado
Stoughton Henry, asphaltum roofer, dwl N s Bernard bet Taylor and Jones
Stover W. R. painter, dwl 623 Howard
Stout Arthur B. physician, office and dwl 832 Wash
Stout C. H. Mrs. principal Market St. School, dwl 527 Bush
Stout John, varnisher, dwl 116 Virginia
Stout M. J. Mrs. adjuster, U. S. Branch Mint, dwl 220 Third
Stoutenborough Charles H. book keeper, 219 Front, dwl 923 Jackson
Stoutenborough John H. clerk with J. W. Brittan & Co. dwl 2109 Mason
Stover Charles B. carpenter and builder, dwl 563 Howard
Stover W. R. painter, dwl 623 Howard
Stow Henry M. real estate, dwl 816 Mission
STOW JOSEPH W. agent Russell & Erwin Manufacturing Co. 106 and 108 Battery, dwl 528 Harrison
Stow William W. (Patterson, Wallace & S.) attorney at law, office 513 Jackson, dwl 1013 Pine
Stowe C. M. Mrs. clairvoyant physician, office and dwl room 14 Mead House
Stowell Charles E. Sazarac Saloon, 765 Clay and mate steamer Chrysopolis
Stowell Fannie Miss, ass't, Hayes' Valley School, dwl 124 Geary
Stowell M. E. Miss, assistant, Rincon School, dwl 124 Geary
Stowell Perry, machinist, Union Foundry, dwl 243 Tehama
Stowell P. M. Miss, assistant, Tehama St. School, dwl 104 O'Farrell

STOWELL WILLIAM H. merchandise broker, office 206 Front, dwl 522 Sutter
Strachun James, boots and shoes, 1104 Stockton
Strade Thomas, clerk, dwl 1231 Dupont
Strahan Samuel, wood carver, dwl 811 Market
Strahan Simon *(Bryant & Co.)* dwl 811 Market
Strahle Jacob, billiard table manufacturer, 537 Sacramento, dwl 606 Howard
Strahle Jacob, fringe maker with Daniel Norcross, dwl 320 Dupont
Strahle Paul, upholsterer, dwl 315 Pine
Strain Robert R. architect, dwl 6 Martha Place
Strait S. Y. machinist, S. F. Iron Works, dwl 11 Front
Strannhan David, laborer, 836 Washington, dwl 1120 Kearny
STRASSBURGER LEWIS, importer watches, 623 Washington, res New York
Strassburger Sigmund, salesman, 516 Sacramento, dwl 308 Stockton
Strasser Abraham, groceries, 426 Green
Strasser Augustus, poultry, 503 Merchant, dwl 426 Green
Strasser George, pipe layer, Spring Valley W. W. Co. dwl N s Page bet Franklin and Gough
Strasser Leopold *(L. Strasser & Son)* dwl 3 Card Alley
Strasser L. & Son *(Leopold Strasser)* poultry, eggs, butter, etc. 6 and 8 Clay St. Market, dwl 722 Vallejo
Stratford Thomas, blacksmith, Union Foundry, dwl 566 Mission
Strathern James, lithographic printer with George H. Baker, 522 Montgomery, dwl St. Francis H. & L. House
Stratman Ann Mrs. dwl W s Stockton bet Sacramento and California
STRATMAN JOHN, news agent, periodicals, books, and stationery, cor Washington and Sansom, dwl 804 Broadway
STRATTON A. W. & BROTHERS *(John S. and Edwin Stratton)* contractors raising and moving buildings, office 724 Harrison, dwl 742 Harrison
Stratton Ebenezer N. clerk, 524 California, dwl S s Sixteenth nr Bryant
Stratton Edward, clerk with O. T. Ames, dwl 718 Green
Stratton Edwin *(Stratton Bros.)* dwl 742 Harrison
Stratton Frank J. book keeper, 106 Bat, res Oakland
Stratton James, principal Washington Grammar School, dwl 1108 Mason
Stratton J. Smith *(Stratton Bros.)* dwl NE corner Minna and Second
Stratton R. F. workman with Casebolt & Co
Stratton Richard S. cabinet maker, dwl 20 O'Farrell
Stratton William, salesman with Needham & Co. dwl 58 Third
Straub Michael, clerk, 238 Kearny
Straub ———, carpenter, dwl 205 Sansom
Straus B. job wagon, NW cor Sacramento and Battery, dwl W s Dupont bet Sutter and Post
Straus E. *(Helbing, Greenebaum & Co.)* dwl St. Nicholas Hotel
Straus Henry, manager Concordia Club Rooms, NE cor Bush and Kearny, dwl W side William bet Post and Geary
Straus Marx, clothing, 6 Third, dwl 320 Sutter
Straus Max *(Homburger, M. & Co.)* 30 Second, dwl 333 Minnie
Strauss Amelia Miss, domestic, 1510 Powell
Strauss B. Queen City Market, 37 Third
Strauss Frank, truckman, 409 Sacramento
Strauss Henrietta (widow) dwl 31 St. Mark Place
Strauss Jacob *(Kahn & S.)* res New York
Strauss Kaufman, drayman, 409 Sac, dwl 24 Turk
STRAUSS LEVI & CO. *(David Stern and Louis Strauss)* importers and jobbers clothing, dry goods, etc. 315 and 317 Sac, dwl 317 Powell

Strauss Louis *(Levi Strauss & Co.)* dwl 427 Sacromento
Strauss Louis, dry goods, 7 and 8 Virginia Block, dwl 714 Vallejo
Strauss Moses, boots and shoes, 18 Fourth, dwl 18 Fourth
Strauss Samuel, broker, dwl 522 O'Farrell
Strausher G. laborer, Spring Valley W. W
Straut William E. salesman with Meeker, James & Co. 14 Pine
Stray Frederick, clerk with H. Schroder & Co. dwl S s Green bet Powell and Mason
Streboat William *(Meyers & S.)* dwl 13 Third
Street E. A. varnisher, dwl 732 Green
Street Harriet (widow) dwl 1209 Bush
STREET JAMES, general agent U. S. Pacific Telegraph Co. office 2 Armory Hall, 502 Mont
Street Nathan J. contractor, dwl 1017 Powell
Street Peter, express wagon, Kearny nr Market
Street Thomas, machinist, Vulcan Iron Works, dwl Tiger Engine House
Streeter Robert M. dwl 216 Tehama
Strehl Charles, butcher, 35 Occidental Market, dwl 34 Sutter
Strehl Jacob, United States Market, SE cor Sixth and Mission
Strehl Philip, hairdresser with Louis Hemprich, 18 Kearny
Strei J. Herman, blind maker with S. S. Culverwell, 29 Fremont, dwl NE corner Folsom and Fourth
Strei William G. L. carpenter, dwl NE cor Folsom and Fourth
Streib Julius, hairdresser with Adam Grimm, dwl 337 Bush
Streib William, hair dresser with Adam Grimm, dwl 337 Bush
STRELITZ J. & CO. *(D. Morris)* Metropolitan Coffee and Spice Mills, 25 Second
Strelitz Jacob, clothing, 11 Stewart, dwl 25 Second
Streuly John J. agent Philadelphia Brewery, dwl 18 Stockton Place
Striby Catherine, dwl with Dr. M. Heiniman, S side Creek Lane nr Folsom
Striby William, music school, 870 Mission
Strickland George, drayman, cor Market and Second, dwl 160 Silver, rear
Strickland Otis, ditch owner, dwl 603 Bush
Striegel Conrad, bricklayer, dwl E s Gilbert nr Brannan
Striker F. dwl SE cor Mission and First
Stringer Robert J. butcher, 9 Clay St. Market, dwl NW cor Dolores and Twenty-Second
Stringer William, longshoreman, dwl St. Francis Engine House
Stringer William, lubricating oils, etc. 118 Jackson, dwl 1904 Mason
Stringer W. J. furniture and carpets, 520 Washington, dwl 1904 Mason
Strittenberger Christopher, milk ranch, SE cor Union and Fillmore
Strobel Henry, dwl 1107 Kearny
STROBEL, *(Jacob F.)* FLEIG *(Kasimer)* & CO. *(F. Cooper)* meat market and pork packers, 1129 Folsom
Strober Max O. dwl 756 Folsom
Strobridge Addison, salesman with J. R. Mead & Co. NE cor Mont and Bush, dwl SE cor Folsom and First
Stroch S. T. dwl SW cor Kearny and Pacific
Stroecker H. H. W. *(Steinhoff & Co.)* dwl SW cor Bush and Trinity
Strohsahl William, clerk, 225 Sutter
Strolin E. F. & Co. *(August Ackerman)* cigars, tobacco, etc. SW cor Kearny and Pacific
Strombeck John, laborer, dwl SW cor Louisiana and Sierra
Stromburg Nicholas Rev. pastor Evangelical Lutheran Church

Strommeier Joseph, shoe maker with Hinders & Kast, dwl 221 Dupont, rear
Strong Charles L. compositor, American Flag
Strong Charlotte (widow) dwl with Lewis V. H. Howell, E s Eleventh nr Market
Strong C. O. Miss, teacher, San Francisco Ladies' Protection and Relief Society
Strong Edward Y. compositor, Alta California, dwl 409 Tehama
Strong Harvey, drayman with Davis & Cowell, dwl 508 Front
Strong Joseph D. Rev. pastor Larkin St. Presbyterian Church, dwl N s Union bet Hyde and Larkin
Strong William, painter with E. H. Wilkey, cor Commercial and Davis
Stross Henry H. J. dwl 29 Third
Strother Fleet F. attorney at law, 47 Third
Strothoff Richard *(C. Duveneck & Co.)* Exchange Building, NW cor Montgomery and Wash
Strouble Mary Miss, domestic with James R. Bolton
Stroud John R. clerk with H. P. Wakelee, dwl 2 Hardie Place
Stroud William, dwl 115 Ellis
Strub Carl, tailor with M. Brandhofer, dwl SW cor Sacramento and Leavenworth
Struck Henry, bar keeper, dwl NW cor Second and Townsend
Struckmeyer Henry, captain schooner San Pablo, bds 7 Washington
Struths Catherine Miss, dwl 337 Minna
Struttbloff Christoph, piano maker, dwl 1426 Dupont
Struve Fritz, waiter, dwl 323 Pine
Struver Justus, book-keeper, City Hall, dwl City Hall
Struwe Henry, seaman, dwl 20 Commercial
Strybing C. H. importer and commission merchant, 212 Jackson, dwl 1212 Mason
Stuart Charles, bar keeper, 550 Clay, dwl 911 Vallejo
Stuart Charles V. real estate, W s Montgomery nr Wash, dwl SE cor Sixteenth and Capp
Stuart James, boot maker with James Noble
STUART JAMES F. & CO. real estate agents, office 621 Montgomery, dwl 1012 Montgomery
Stuart John, clerk, Pacific Mail S. S. Co. NW cor Sacramento and Liedesdorff
Stuart John A. bricklayer, Columbia Engine Co. No. 11
Stuart Mary (widow) dwl 5 Trinity
Stuart Thomas, laborer, dwl 7 Haywood
Stuart William A. book keeper with T. H. Hatch & Co. dwl 1012 Montgomery
Stuart, see Stewart
Stubbs Jesse, engineer steamer Washoe, dwl N s Grove nr Franklin
Stuber Morris, real estate broker, dwl 621 Pine
Studte Frederick, gunsmith, 648 Commercial
Studley George, clerk, Pacific Weekly, NE cor Clay and Front
Studley Smith S. with Thomas & Twing, cor Market and East, dwl 102 East
Studley Warren, carpenter with Pratt & Jacobs, bds 6 Front
Studzinsky Benjamin *(Benjamin & Brown),* dwl 305 Kearny
Stuli Jacom, vegetable garden, Bay View Park
Stuli John, vegetable garden, Bay View Park
Stulz *(Charles) & Co. (John Hasslinger and John Leritter)* hairdressing saloon, 937 Kearny, dwl 1321 Kearny
Stumcke Charles, clerk with L. J. Ewell, dwl S s Sheppard Place
Stumcke Charles F. carpenter, dwl 1320 Jackson
Stumer John, blacksmith, Union Foundry, dwl 57 Jessie
Stureken Edward H. sail maker, dwl 4 Central Pl
Sturdivant Robert O. broker, office 526 Montgomery, dwl 338 Seventh
Sturgeon Henry T. workman with S. Crim, dwl W s Howard, bet Nineteenth and Twentieth

Sturm Isaac, porter, 317 Sacramento
Sturms Julius, upholsterer with W. M. Hixon, dwl 1332 Dupont
Sturtevant George, salesman with James E. Damon, dwl 813 Vallejo
Sturtevant Irving, lamps and oils, NE cor Broadway and Dupont, dwl 1603 Mason
Sturtevant J. Lawrence, with Kellogg, Hewston & Co. dwl 416 Montgomery
Sturtevant N. Miss, assistant, Market St. School, dwl 751 Howard
Stuss Henry & Co. *(Henry Speckter)* groceries and liquors, 141 Second
Stuttmeister Rudolph, physician, office and dwl 1126 Dupont
Stuttmeister Victor, salesman, 1122 Dupont
Stutzbach Augusta F. midwife, dwl 679 Mission
Stutzbach Frank, physician, dwl 679 Mission
Styes Lewis, waiter, steamer Orizaba
Styles Henry, physician, dwl N W cor Taylor and Green
Su Lee (Chinese) washing, 1312 Dupont
Subetez August, dwl 425 Powell
Sublett William, speculator, dwl San Bruno Road nr Twentieth
Sublett William A. dentist, dwl San Bruno Road nr Twentieth
Subrieto Camilo, musician, dwl 8 Hinckley
Succor G. & S. M. Co. office 6 Montgomery Block
Such Augustus, vender, dwl 1024 Buttery
Suckert Leon, physician, office and dwl 402 Kearny cor Pine
Sudden Robert, capt stm Salinas, dwl SE cor Mission and Erie
Suden Thomas, carrier, Evening Bulletin
Sue Woo & Co. (Chinese) groceries, 941 Dupont
Suess Adolph, mathematical instrument maker with Wm. Schmolz, dwl Helvetia Hotel
Suffrian James, cook, dwl 30 Jessie
Suhling Henry, drayman, 709 Sac, dwl 338 Third
Suich Jerome, porter with Louis Lacour, dwl 21 Ritch
Suifer Nicholas, waiter, 626 Kearny
Suisun City Flouring Mills, J. P. Raymond & Co. agents, office 119 Clay
Suit Lemoine, clerk, dwl 119 Second
Sukoff William, tailor, dwl 407 Third
Sullivan Ann Miss, domestic, 1122 Pine
Sullivan Ann Miss, domestic, 1806 Stockton
Sullivan Ann Miss, domestic with Sam'l C. Bigelow, NW cor Steiner and McAllister
Sullivan Bridget Miss, domestic, 211 Post
Sullivan Bridget Miss, domestic, 517 Sutter
Sullivan Bryan, fruits, 545 Kearny
Sullivan Catharine, domestic with James McM. Shafter
Sullivan Catharine Miss, domestic, 1108 Sacramento
Sullivan Catharine Miss, domestic, 932 Clay
Sullivan Catharine (widow) dwl 830 Pacific
Sullivan Catherine Mrs. embroidery, 214 Kearny
Sullivan Catherine (widow) dwl 220 Ritch
Sullivan Catherine (widow) dwl 358½ Jessie
Sullivan Catherine (widow) dwl 120 Jessie
SULLIVAN *(C. D. O.)* & CASHMAN *(William F.) (and H. Dimond)* importers and jobbers wines and liquors, SW cor Front and Jackson, dwl 1023 Bush
Sullivan Cornelius, deck hand, stm Chrysopolis
Sullivan Cornelius, laborer, dwl 26 Fourth
Sullivan Cornelius, shoe maker, dwl 26 Fourth
Sullivan Cornelius P. fruits and vegetables, SW cor Taylor and Geary
Sullivan Daniel, architect, dwl 605 Sacramento
Sullivan Daniel, blacksmith with Kimball & Co. dwl 15 Moss
Sullivan Daniel, coppersmith, 506 Front, dwl S s Vallejo nr Kearny
Sullivan Daniel, gilder with Nile & Kollmyer, dwl 120 Jessie

Sullivan Daniel, job wagon, SW cor Third and Market, dwl S s Freelon bet Third and Fourth
Sullivan Daniel, laborer, dwl N s Brannan nr Sixth
Sullivan Daniel, porter, 410 Front, dwl Calhoun nr Green
Sullivan Daniel, seaman, dwl 20 Commercial
Sullivan Daniel J. with R. F. Rocchiccoli, dwl 723 Market
Sullivan Daniel T., U. S. Commissioner deputy clerk U. S. District Court, office 17 U. S. Court Block, dwl W s Eleventh bet Market and Mission
Sullivan David (P. F. Bayliss & Co.) dwl W s Kearny bet Sutter and Bush
Sullivan Dennis & Co. (Peter O'Neil) groceries and liquors, NE cor Fifth and Clara
Sullivan Dennis, apprentice, Pacific Foundry, dwl 47 Ritch
Sullivan Dennis, blacksmith, dwl Bryant Place
Sullivan Dennis, laborer, dwl E s Sansom bet Broadway and Pacific
Sullivan Dennis, ship carpenter, dwl 515 Tehama
Sullivan D. M. coppersmith, Crescent Engine Co. No. 10
Sullivan Donald, blacksmith, dwl 15 Moss
Sullivan Ellen, chambermaid, American Exchange
Sullivan Ellen Miss, domestic, 829 Bush
Sullivan Ellen Miss, domestic, 726 California
Sullivan Ellen (widow) dwl 84 Stevenson
Sullivan Eugene, laborer, Fort Point
Sullivan Eugene L. office 50 Exchange Building, dwl Ashland Place N s Mission bet Eleventh and Twelfth
Sullivan F. J. laborer, S. F. Gas Co
Sullivan Florence, fruits, 232 Fourth
Sullivan Florence, laborer, dwl 129 Pacific
Sullivan Honora Miss, dress maker, 843 Clay
Sullivan James, blacksmith, dwl 120 Jessie
Sullivan James, carpenter, dwl Sullivan Place bet Minna and Mission
Sullivan James, compositor, Hebrew, dwl 512 Post
Sullivan James, hostler, 431 Cal, dwl 268 Stevenson
Sullivan James, job wagon, dwl S s Austin bet Van Ness Avenue and Franklin
Sullivan James, laborer with David B. Hughes, dwl S s Lombard bet Taylor and Jones
Sullivan James, laborer, dwl 223 Sutter
Sullivan James, laborer, dwl S s Brannan bet Seventh and Eighth
Sullivan James, Montreal House, dwl 29 Pacific
Sullivan James, shoe maker, 218 Pine, dwl 269 Stevenson
Sullivan James, shoe maker, dwl Ecker nr Stevenson
Sullivan James, trunk maker with E. Galpen & Co. dwl 214 Kearny
Sullivan Jeremiah, dwl with Daniel T. Sullivan W s Eleventh bet Mission and Bryant
Sullivan Jeremiah, laborer, dwl 29 Geary
Sullivan Jeremiah, laborer, dwl S s Chambers bet Battery and Front
Sullivan Jeremiah D. clerk, 202 Kearny, dwl Welsh nr Fourth
Sullivan Jeremiah J. tailor with S. Reinstein, dwl 25 Hunt
Sullivan J. F. butcher with Owen Connolly, SE cor Laguna and Waller
Sullivan J. Jerome, assistant assessor U. S. Internal Revenue, NW cor Bat and Com, dwl 319 Kearny
Sullivan Johanna Miss, domestic, SW cor Jackson and Taylor
Sullivan Johanna Miss, with Adolph Muller, 107 Montgomery, dwl 9 Natoma
Sullivan John, with Charles Harley & Co. dwl cor Sacramento and Davis
Sullivan John, boiler maker, Union Foundry, dwl Thompson Avenue nr Brannan
Sullivan John, carpenter, dwl 206 Stewart
Sullivan John, coachman, 1050 Mission
Sullivan John, deck hand, steamer Relief
Sullivan John, hackman, dwl 1226 Stockton

Sullivan John, laborer, S. F. Gas Co. dwl NW cor Jessie and Anna
Sullivan John, laborer, dwl 12 Howard Court
Sullivan John, laborer, dwl 16 Natoma
Sullivan John, laborer, dwl 149 Beale
Sullivan John, laborer, dwl S s Chambers bet Battery and Front
Sullivan John, marble cutter, 67 Fourth, dwl 775 Market
Sullivan John, messenger, U. S. Commissary Department, dwl Beale nr Harrison
Sullivan John, policeman, dwl 303 Davis
Sullivan John, waiter, Lick House
Sullivan John D. merchant, dwl 358½ Jessie
Sullivan John F. blacksmith with Kimball & Co. dwl Sumner nr Eighth
Sullivan John F. laborer, dwl Boston Place
Sullivan John J. gas fitter with J. H. O'Brien & Co. 706 Mont, dwl N s Vallejo bet Mont and Kearny
Sullivan John J. laborer, dwl cor Mission and Beale
Sullivan John J. tailor, 232 Fourth
Sullivan John L. laborer, dwl 805 Howard
Sullivan John M. laborer, dwl 106 Beale
Sullivan John P. laborer, dwl E s White nr Green
Sullivan Joseph, carpenter, bds 89 Everett
Sullivan Josephine, domestic, 314 Green
Sullivan Julia Miss, domestic, 26 Fourth
Sullivan Julia (widow) domestic, 1007 Mason
SULLIVAN J. W. bookseller and news agent, 516 Washington, dwl 119 Sixth
Sullivan Kate Miss, principal, Post St. Primary School, dwl 739 Howard
Sullivan Louisa (col'd, widow) dwl 916 Pacific
Sullivan Margaret, cook, Western Hotel, 306 Bdwy
Sullivan Margaret Miss, domestic, 1018 Jackson
Sullivan Margaret Miss, domestic, SW cor Francisco and Dupont
Sullivan Mary Miss, domestic, 509 Bryant
Sullivan Mary Miss, domestic, 415 O'Farrell
Sullivan Mary Miss, domestic, 1020 Stockton
Sullivan Mary Miss, domestic, 1517 Stockton
Sullivan Mary Miss, domestic, 1108 Mason
Sullivan Mary Miss, domestic, 442 Greenwich
Sullivan Mary Miss, domestic, 1 Lick Alley
Sullivan Mary Miss, dress maker, dwl 16 Natoma
Sullivan Mary (widow) dwl N s Day bet Guerrero and Dolores
Sullivan Mary A. assistant teacher, Parochial School, Mission Dolores, dwl N s Day between Guerrero and Dolores
Sullivan Mary C. Miss, domestic, 1812 Stockton
Sullivan Mary E. Miss, domestic, 119 Mason
Sullivan Mathew, laborer, dwl N s Oregon nr Front
Sullivan Michael, bar keeper, dwl 116 Stewart
Sullivan Michael, butcher with B. E. Arnold, dwl cor Tenth and Bryant
Sullivan Michael, laborer, dwl 27 Natoma Place
Sullivan Michael, laborer, dwl 25 Everett
Sullivan Michael, laborer, dwl 231 Pacific
Sullivan Michael, laborer, dwl 256 Clementina
Sullivan Michael, laborer, dwl 429 Clementina
Sullivan Michael, laborer, dwl cor Larkin and Francisco
Sullivan Michael, laborer, dwl cor Bryant and Ritch
Sullivan Michael, laborer, dwl E s Valencia near Thirteenth
Sullivan Michael, miner, dwl cor Polk and Francisco
Sullivan Michael, pressman with George W. Stevens & Co. dwl Sherwood Place
Sullivan Morris, laborer, dwl N s Welch bet Third and Fourth
Sullivan Murty, laborer, dwl 25 Jane
Sullivan Murty, stone cutter, dwl Fourth St. House
Sullivan Owen, laborer, dwl 314 Vallejo, rear
Sullivan Patrick, blacksmith with Nelson & Doble
Sullivan Patrick, hackman, Plaza, dwl 915 Folsom
Sullivan Patrick, laborer, dwl 10 Sherwood Place
Sullivan Patrick, laborer, dwl 9 Natoma
Sullivan Patrick, laborer, dwl 124 Minna

Sullivan Patrick, laborer, dwl E s Sansom between Broadway and Pacific
Sullivan Patrick, lab, dwl SW cor Jessie and Annie
Sullivan Patrick, pressman with Francis, Valentine & Co. dwl Original House
Sullivan Patrick, upholsterer, 871 Folsom
Sullivan Patrick, waiter, dwl 31 St. Mark Place
Sullivan Peter, hairdresser with Adam Grimm, 17 Montgomery
Sullivan Peter, laborer, dwl 178 Stevenson
Sullivan Peter J. principal Parochial School, Mission Dolores, dwl N s Day bet Guerrero and Dolores
Sullivan Philip H. stone cutter, dwl 29 Geary
Sullivan Robert, carpenter, dwl 21 Langton, rear
Sullivan Samuel, captain schooner, dwl Meek Place
Sullivan Samuel, laundry, Spring Valley House, rear
Sullivan T. & Co. (Mrs. H. E. Booker) cloaks, 24 Montgomery, dwl 29 Minna
Sullivan Thomas, bottle dealer, dwl 512 Post
Sullivan Thomas, fireman, steamer Senator
Sullivan Thomas, form carrier with Francis, Valentine & Co
Sullivan Thomas, laborer, Market St. R. R. Co. dwl N s Fulton bet Gough and Octavia
Sullivan Thomas, laborer, dwl 9 St. Mary
Sullivan Thomas, laborer, dwl 52 Minna
Sullivan Thomas, pressman, 511½ Clay, dwl Original House
Sullivan Thomas, seaman, dwl 132 Folsom
Sullivan Thomas, ship calker, dwl W s Thirteenth nr Market
Sullivan Thomas, trackman, Market S. R. R. Co. dwl Fulton, Hayes' Valley
Sullivan Thomas A. hackman, dwl Montgomery Pl
Sullivan Thomas D. laborer, dwl 254 Jessie
Sullivan Thomas N. hostler, dwl SW cor Jackson and Leavenworth
Sullivan Timothy, dwl S s Liberty bet Townsend and Brannan
Sullivan Timothy, cartman, dwl 540 Howard
Sullivan Timothy, lab with William J. Kingsley
Sullivan Timothy, laborer, dwl 223 Sutter
Sullivan Timothy, laborer, dwl 446 Natoma
Sullivan Timothy, laborer, dwl S s Clara nr Fifth
Sullivan Timothy, packer with J. P. McKenna & Co. Garden bet Harrison and Bryant
Sullivan Timothy, with Henry Bocken, dwl 334 Third
Sullivan Timothy, workman, S. F. & P. Sugar Co. dwl Harrison nr Eighth
Sullivan Timothy J. couchman, dwl 8 William
Sullivan Timothy J. messenger, Custom House, dwl 67 Minna
Sullivan William (col'd) dwl 1428 Stockton, rear
Sullivan William, boot maker, dwl 1513 Leav
Sullivan William, cartman, dwl corner Fourth and Mission
Sullivan William J. brass founder, dwl 115 First
Sullivan W. L. dwl 303 Davis
Sully John, plumber with J. K. Prior, dwl 6 Winter Place
Sulsberg Charles, broom maker with L. Van Laak, dwl 22 Spear
Sum Yuen (Chinese) washing, 29 Commercial
Summerfield A. salesman with S. Summerfield, 20 Second
Summerfield S. dry goods, 20 Second, dwl 1113 Dupont
Summerville Alexander, apprentice, dwl 115 First
Sumner Charles R. conductor, Central R. R. Co. dwl W s Garden nr Bryant
Sumner G. & S. M. Co. (Cove Dist. Tulare Co.) office 7 Stevenson House
Sumner J. H. Mrs. assistant, Stevenson St. School, dwl 62 Natoma
Sumner John H. straw hat finisher, 603 Market, dwl 155 Perry
Sumner Joseph, tinsmith, dwl 14 Russ

Sumner William A. wool puller and dealer pelts, N s Townsend bet Third and Fourth, dwl 3 Liberty
Sumner William B. hides and leather, office 31 Battery, dwl 147 Perry
Sun Chong Hee & Co. (Chinese) merchants, 710 Sac
Sun John W. clerk, dwl 83 Everett
Sun Kee & Co. (Chinese) teas, 639 Jackson
Sun Waa (Chinese) washing, 33 Ritch
Sun Wo Yee & Co. (Chinese) grocers, 727 Sac
Sun Yout Sing (Chinese) washing, 522 Green
Sunberry Michael, dwl N s Mission bet Third and Fourth
Suncook Mill & M. Co. office 424 Battery
SUNDAY MERCURY (weekly) J. Macdonough Foard & Co. publishers and proprietors, office and editorial rooms, 420 Montgomery up stairs
Sandberg Antoine, seaman, dwl 20 Commercial
Sandell William, seaman, dwl 44 Sacramento
Sander George, book keeper with Thomas Taylor & Co. dwl 214 Tehama
Sandermeyer William, tanner with Jacob Beisel, dwl Mississippi nr Mariposa
Sandland Wilson, job wagon, cor Clay and Battery, dwl 137 Natoma
Sundquist Ernest, seaman, dwl 20 Commercial
Sunet Charles, dwl N s Cliff House Road 3 miles W from City Hall
Sung Lee (Chinese) washing, 1510 Stockton
SUPERINTENDENT INDIAN AFFAIRS, State of California, office 423 Washington
SUPERINTENDENT PUBLIC SCHOOLS, office 23 City Hall second floor
SUPERINTENDENT STATE IMMIGRATION, office NE cor Washington and Battery
SUPERINTENDENT STATE PUBLIC INSTRUCTION, office 734 Montgomery
SUPERINTENDENT STREETS AND HIGHWAYS, office 12 City Hall first floor
SUPERVISORS, BOARD OF, office 3 City Hall second floor
Supple David, seaman, dwl NW cor Green and Bat
Supple Edward, porter, 516 Sac, dwl 3 Hardie Pl
Supple Mary Miss, domestic, 24 Turk
SURVEYOR CITY AND COUNTY, office 11 City Hall third floor
SURVEYOR GENERAL (U. S.) office 808 Mont
SURVEYOR OF THE PORT (U. S.) office Custom House second floor
Susenbeth J. C. merchant, dwl Bee Hive Building
Suskind Nathan, express wagon, dwl 838 Vallejo
Susmon Thomson, cigar maker, 527 East
Sutcliffe Daniel, spinner, S. F. P. Woolen Factory
Sutcliffe Richard S. carpenter, What Cheer House
Sutherd E. P. mariner, dwl 511 Mission
Sutherland Edwin (Jones, Woell & S.) dwl 516 O'Farrell
Sutherland E. G. seaman, dwl Spear nr Folsom
Sutherland F. E. attorney at law, office 606 Montgomery, dwl SE cor Mason and Sacramento
Sutherland George, carpenter, Fort Point
Sutherland James G. clerk, tax collector, City Hall, dwl W s Polk bet Market and Page
Sutherland John, butcher with George J. Haxe, 4 Metropolitan Market, dwl Brooklyn Hotel
Sutherland Thomas L. boatman, dwl 719 Davis
Sutherland William, dwl 516 O'Farrell
Sutherland William S. (Grain & S.) Bank British North America, 411 California
Sutkamp Bernardina Miss, teacher, St. Boniface School, 122 Sutter, dwl 417 Post
Sutliff Thomas, cigars and tobacco, 819 Kearny
SUTRO CHARLES, gold dust and exchange dealer, 427 Montgomery, dwl 619 Montgomery
Sutro Hugo, jeweler with Mathewson & Bucklin, dwl 147 Silver
Sutter A. dwl Original House
Sutter Atham, baker, 1412 Dupont
Sutter Emile V. notary public, 626 Clay, dwl 329 Bush

Sutter Joseph M. boot maker, 529 Jackson, dwl W s Kearny bet Jackson and Washington

Sutter Samuel, machinist, dwl 9 Hartman nr Greenwich

Sutton Alice Miss, domestic, 694 Geary

Sutton Charles, mariner, dwl Verona Place

Sutton Charles jr. salesman with Davis & Schafer, dwl E s Dupont bet Lombard and Chestnut

Sutton David S. Capt. dwl 200 Stockton

Sutton Fowler, carpenter, dwl Post bet Jones and Taylor

Sutton Jesse, dwl 54 Belden Block

Sutton John, helper, dwl E s Mission bet First and Second

Sutton Joseph, 1st officer Pacific Mail S. S. Co. dwl 250 Beale

Sutton O. P. secretary Pacific Bank, office NE cor California and Montgomery, dwl 736 Howard

Sutton Robert, laborer, dwl Dolores Hall W s Valencia nr Sixteenth

Sutton William, book keeper, Pier 10 Stewart, dwl 449 Natoma

Suydam T. dwl What Cheer House

Swain Aaron, carpenter, Mission Woolen Mills, dwl with P. L. Murphy E s Howard bet Fifteenth and Sixteenth

SWAIN (A. E.) & BROWN (William H.) proprietors Brown's Bakery, 5 Kearny

Swain Charles,·cook, Sierra Nevada Hotel, 528 Pac

Swain Charles A. mariner, dwl 1410 Leavenworth

Swain Daniel W. deputy marshal U. S. dwl 525 Union

Swain D. L. (widow) dwl 576 Folsom

Swain Frederick, express wagon, 109 Mission

Swain Harry F. book keeper, 641 Sac, dwl 709 Union

Swain Henry, waiter, dwl 166 Tehama

Swain Isaac, broker, dwl 909 Clay

Swain James, mariner, dwl 126 St. Mark Place

SWAIN JAMES H. & CO. boot and shoe making, 204 Bus'h, dwl 513 Lombard

Swain Josiah H. Bay City Stable, 413 and 415 Market, dwl 325 Folsom

Swain Laban W. laborer, 636 Commercial

Swain L. S. Miss, assistant, Lincoln School, dwl 1305 Stockton

Swain Maggie Miss, dwl W s Dolores bet Sixteenth and Seventeenth

SWAIN R. A. & CO. (William J. Mack) importers and wholesale and retail crockery and glassware, NE cor Pine and San, dwl 934 Howard

SWAIN R. B. & CO. commission merchants and insurance agents, 206 Front, dwl 814 Powell

Swain Reuben M. clerk with William Meyer & Co. dwl 1410 Leavenworth

SWAIN RINALDO R. bakery, confectionery, and ice cream saloon, 140 Second cor Natoma and 913 Stockton, dwl 103 Natoma

SWAIN ROBERT B. superintendent U. S. Branch Mint, office 610 Commercial, dwl 814 Powell

Swain Sarah (widow) dwl 29 Hunt

Swain Sarah C. (widow) Eureka Institute, 1420 Powell, dwl W s Dolores bet Sixteenth and Seventeenth

Swain Stephen, blacksmith, dwl E s Cushman bet California and Sacramento

Swain William B. (Humphrey & Co.) dwl 730 Green

Swan Edward S. clerk, 73 Washington Market, dwl 108 Prospect Place

Swan George, longshoreman, dwl SW cor Davis and Pacific

Swan James S. molder, Pacific Foundry, dwl SW cor First and Stevenson

Swan John, liquor saloon, NW cor Third and King

Swan Orrin, second pilot steamer Chrysopolis

Swan Peter, blacksmith, Pacific Foundry, dwl N s Vallejo nr Stockton

Swan Samuel B. teamster, National Flour Mill, dwl 44 Clara

Swansea John, stevedore, dwl 14 Clay

Swansea M. Co. office 6 Montgomery Block

Swanton Thomas, molder, Union Foundry, dwl 38 Tehama

Swarbrick Robert (Haller & S.) dwl NE cor Folsom and Beale

Swarty Nicholas, molder, Fulton Foundry, dwl 441 Tehama

Swasey Benjamin, photographic gallery, 205 Third

SWASEY E. T. J. general engraver, 605 Sacramento, dwl 537 California

Swayne William Y. cabinet maker, dwl 404 Geary

Swearingen A. S. broker, dwl 20 Ellis

Sweeney Anne J. Miss, nurse with Mrs. J. Stanton, W s Mission nr Fifteenth

Sweeney Christopher, tinsmith with W. M. Walmsley, dwl NE cor Brannan and Sixth

Sweeney D. & Co. (H. C. Olsen) auctioneers and stock yard, NW cor Stockton and Post, dwl N s Webster

Sweeney D. drayman, dwl W s Sixth nr.Brannan

Sweeney Daniel, stock dealer, dwl bet Lake Honda and Central Gravel Road

Sweeney. Ellen, Cook, 26 Fourth

Sweeney James, plumber with McNally & Hawkins, dwl SW cor First and Clementina

Sweeney James, works with Cornelius Conahan

Sweeney Jane Miss, dwl 72 Natoma

Sweeney Jennie Miss, with S. Reinstein, dwl 23 Ritch

Sweeney (John) & Downey (John) marble workers, 816 Market, dwl 254 Jessie

Sweeney John, carpenter, dwl 11 Sherwood Place

Sweeney John, tailor, dwl 180 Stevenson

SWEENEY J. P. & CO. (James McCloskey) seed warehouse, 406 Cal, dwl 266 Tehama

Sweeney Lawrence, tinsmith with Felix Daly, dwl cor Ecker and Stevenson

Sweeney Lorenzo H. with Boswell & Shattuck, dwl 107 Powell

Sweeney M. contractor, San Miguel Station 7 miles from City Hall

Sweeney Margaret (widow) dwl 673 Harrison

Sweeney Mary Miss, domestic, 19 Rousch

Sweeney Michael, foreman, San Francisco Gas Co. dwl 110 William

Sweeney Michael, wagon maker with Nelson & Doble, dwl 42 Louisa

Sweeney M. M. tinsmith with Locke & Montague, dwl 116 Sansom

Sweeney Roger, laborer, dwl 1026 Market

Sweeney Thomas W. dwl N s Brannan nr Sixth

Sweeney William, laborer, dwl W s Seventh nr Brannan

Sweeney William, paver, dwl 1514 Leavenworth

Sweeny Ann (widow) dwl SE cor Stevenson and Ecker

Sweeny Catherine Miss, domestic, 808 Fourth

Sweeny Daniel, cattle dealer, dwl 445 Bryant

Sweeny Dennis, coachman with Louis McLane, dwl 32 Ritch

Sweeny Edward, laborer, San Francisco Gas Co

Sweeny Edward, laborer, dwl NE cor Howard and Twenty-First

Sweeny Edward, laborer, dwl 254 First

Sweeny George, brass finisher, dwl NE cor Stevenson & Ecker

Sweeny Jane (widow) dwl 72 Natoma

Sweeny John, laborer, Atlantic House, 210 Pacific

Sweeny John, coachman, dwl 572 Folsom

Sweeny Mary, dwl S s Chambers bet Bat and Front

Sweeny Michael, engineer, dwl 66 Minna

Sweeny Michael, wheelwright, dwl 42 Louisa

SWEENY MYLES D. & CO. (Upton M. Gordon) importers and jobbers wines and liquors, 709 Sansom, dwl 905 Broadway

SWEENY NICHOLAS, merchant tailor, 143 Second

Sweeny P. C. plumber, Spring Valley W. W. dwl N s Post bet Kearny and Dupont

Sweeny Peter, cooper with Handy & Neuman, dwl 535 Howard
Sweeny William, clerk, dwl 228 Battery
Sweet Henry, seaman, dwl 54 Sacramento
Sweet Israel, captain schr Florence, dwl 321 East
Sweet John D. *(H. C. Moors & Co.)* physician, dwl 761 Howard
Sweet Mowry P. carpenter, dwl 719 Clay
Sweet Rodman, clerk, dwl 230 Sixth
Sweet Samuel S. book keeper, 609 Market, dwl 609 Folsom above Second
Sweet Solomon, merchant, office 217 Front, dwl 732 Post
Sweet Vengeance G. & S. M. Co. office 705 Sansom
Sweetland James, paper hanger, dwl 111 Stevenson
Sweetser A. J. & Co. fish, 22 Occidental Market, dwl 20 Sutter
SWEETT *(George W.)* & GADSBY *(Elijah H.)* paints, oils, and paper haugings, 28 Third, dwl 5 Hampton Place
Swenson August, seaman, dwl 44 Sacramento
Swett A. M. Mrs. clairvoyant, dwl 820 Mission •
Swett Daniel, printer, dwl 820 Mission
Swett Dwight, printer, dwl 4 Natoma
Swett Ebon, butcher with Anderson & Kline
Swett Elizabeth Mrs. proprietress First St. House, NW cor First and Mission
Swett Frederick P. contractor, dwl 1212 Clay
SWETT JOHN, State Superintendent Public Instruction, office 734 Montgomery cor Jackson, dwl 41 Everett
Swett John C. clerk, 54 Washington Market, dwl NW cor Mission and First
Swett Lorenzo, carpenter, dwl 217 Brannan
Swett Orlo F. milkman, dwl Old San José Road cor Navy
Swezey Samuel I. C. attorney at law, office 734 Montgomery, and secretary Citizens' Gas Co. 702 Washington, dwl 708 Mission
Swift Francis, molder, Monumental Engine Co. No. 6
Swift Jacob, laborer, dwl 4 Virginia
Swift James, bung maker, Chace's Mill, dwl Hayes' Valley
Swift James F. *(Loomis & S.)* dwl 329 Bush
SWIFT JOHN F. register Land Office and pension agent U. S. office 625 Merchant
Swift John H. second lieut. Co. F Second Infantry C. V. Presidio
Swift Joseph, drayman, dwl Bryant nr Third
Swift L. E. Mrs. dress maker, dwl 753 Mission
Swift Patrick, teamster with Preston & Kimball, dwl N s Natoma bet Eighth and Ninth
Swift Thomas, driver, North Beach & M. R. R. Co
Swift William H. street contractor, dwl 753 Mission
Swigert Adam, stoves and tinware, 873 Folsom
Swigert Edward, tinsmith, N s Folsom nr Sixth
Swim Robert, dwl 286 Stevenson
Swinerton Henry M. dwl 5 Fourth
Swinlock James, molder, 24 Stevenson
Swinson Gustavus, mariner, dwl 533 Bryant
Switzer Samuel C. salesman, 300 Mont, dwl 21 Minna
Sword John B. dwl 8 s Jackson bet Taylor and Jones
Swordstream John E. groceries and liquors, SE cor Louisa and Fourth
Sydney M. carpenter, dwl 18 Noble Place
Sykes C. H. painter, dwl 103 Montgomery Block
Sykes Charles, driver, Omnibus R. R. Co. dwl 161 Minna
Sykes Mary C. (widow) dwl 474 Jessie
Sykes Rowland, wool grader, Mission Woolen Mills
Sylva Gherkin, shoe maker, 417 East
Sylvester Daniel *(Sylvester & Bro.)* dwl 9 St. Mark Place
Sylvester Harry, dwl 67 Minna
Sylvester Henry, butcher, 307 Sixth
Sylvester Hinchman, pile driver, dwl 16 Anthony
Sylvester *(John)* & Brother *(Daniel Sylvester)* Kearny St. Market, 9 Kearny, dwl 9 St. Mark Pl

Sylvester Leander, dwl 82 Natoma
Sylvester Leon, stoves and hardware, 921 Dupont, dwl 813 Pacific
Sylvester Louis *(Roux & S.)* dwl 538 Broadway
Sylvia John F. bargeman, Custom House, dwl SW cor Vallejo and Dupont
Sylvia Joseph, dwl 213 Broadway.
Symes Effa J. seamstress, dwl 664 Howard
Symes Josiah, waterman, dwl N s Mission nr Jane
Symonds George D. copyist, 8 Court Block
Syms Charles, driver with J. W. Cudworth
Synnott Thomas, carpenter, dwl 56 Shipley
Synon Augusta Mrs. & Sister *(Henrietta Bartol)* embroideries, 318½ Third
Synon Patrick Henry, carpenter, dwl 318½ Third

T

TAAFFE G. O'Hara, consul for Denmark and commission merchant, office 430 Cal, dwl 420 Mont
Taaffe Thomas D. salesman with Taaffe & Co. dwl N s Lombard bet Powell and Mason
Taaffe William, butcher with Joseph Lawler, dwl Potrero Avenue
TAAFFE *(William P.)* & CO, *(John Ryan and E. L. Goldstein)* importers and jobbers staple and fancy dry goods, 107 Battery, retail 9 Montgomery, dwl SW cor Jones and Chestnut
Taber Charles A. waterman, dwl 43 Everett
Taber Charles W. bar keeper, 650 Sacramento
Taber George, driver, North Beach & M. R. R. Co. dwl 21 Louisa
Taber Hannah Mrs. private school, 43 Everett
Taber Isaiah W. photographer with Bradley & Rulofson, dwl 716 Stockton
Taber Jacob S. salesman with Dodge & Phillips, dwl 10 Silver
Taber Joseph E. paper hanger, dwl W s Mason bet Vallejo and Green
Taber William H. carpenter, dwl 116 Silver
Table Frederick, drayman, dwl Mason bet Clay and Merchant
Table Mountain C. M. Co. office 436 Jackson
Tabor Isaac, broker, dwl 7 Perry
Tacey Arnaud, laundryman with Charles Schilling
Tack Mary, chambermaid, Lick House
Tadini J. Rev., S.J. professor moral philosophy St. Ignatius College, S s Mkt bet Fourth and Fifth
Taft Benjamin D. baker, 1412 Dupont, dwl 1217 Kearny
Taft Charles, carpenter, dwl 8 Moss
Taft Edson H. book keeper, 56 Clay
Taft Gilbert, cigar maker, 46 Fourth
Taggard Edwin W. book keeper, U. S. Assistant Treasurer, res Oakland
Taggard John L. broker, dwl 462 Natoma
Taggert Patrick, hog ranch, W s Florida nr Solano
Tairney Thomas, laborer, dwl E s Folsom Avenue bet Seventh and Eighth
Tait Augustus, farmer, Old San José Road nr St. Mary's College
Tait George, seaman, dwl 4 Lick Alley
Talbert A. D. with James Glasgow
Talbot Alexander, Mountain House, 269 Stevenson
Talbot Frederick, laborer, dwl 140 Stewart
Talbot Henry, express wagon, cor Cal and Mont
Talbot James, hostler, dwl 112 Shipley, rear
Talbot J. C. variety store, 103 Second, dwl Frank's Building
Talbot Robert C. shoe maker, 412 Folsom, dwl 238 Fremont
Talbot Samuel C. machinist, Vulcan Iron Works, dwl 509 Howard
Talbot Thomas G. clerk, Mariner's Home, 306 Clark
Talbot William, teamster, dwl 17 Scott
Talbot William, waiter, steamer Yosemite
Talbot William C. *(Pope & T.)* Pier 12 Stewart, dwl 610 Folsom

Talcott Jonathan, driver with S. C. & L. H. Talcott
Talcott Lewis H. *(S. C. & L. H. Talcott)* dwl nr Industrial School
Talcott S. C. & L. H. milk ranch, 5¼ miles from City Hall nr Industrial School
Tulford Frank, driver, Chelsea Laundry
TALLANT *(Drury J.)* & CO. *(John McKee)* bankers, 321 Battery, dwl 517 Dupont
Tallant Patrick, deck hand, steamer Washoe
Talliet Alexis, machinist, Pacific Foundry
Tallon Michael, mate, steamer Washoe
Tallulah G. & S. M. Co. office 622 Montgomery
Tully Mary (widow) dwl with James Shields, E s Howard bet Twelfth and Thirteenth
Talty William, cook, steamer Yosemite
Tamm Edward, waiter, dwl 116 Jackson
Tammeyer Julius, merchant tailor, 325 Bush, dwl 315 Bush
Tams Sampson *(Rodmond Gibbons & Co.)* dwl 1116 Stockton
Tanck Nicolaus, boatman, dwl 2013 Mason
Tandler *(Abram)* & Lang *(Jacob L.)* proprietors Continental Hotel, SE cor San and Commercial
Taner P. hostler, Omnibus R. R. Co
Taney James, foreman sash maker with S. S. Culverwell, 29 Fremont, dwl SE cor Mission and Jane
Taney Josiah D. sash maker with S. S. Culverwell, 29 Fremont, dwl 208 Second
Tangstrom Adolph, seaman, dwl 26 Sacramento
Tannan John, teamster with James McDevitt, dwl W s Sansom bet Broadway and Vallejo
Taniere August, employé, Metropolitan Restaurant, 715 Montgomery
Taniere Battiste, employé, Metropolitan Restaurant, 715 Montgomery
Tannebann Bernard, dwl S s Chestnut bet Mason and Taylor
Tanner John, job wagon, dwl 12 Stockton
Tannian *(John)* & Waterman *(John)* blacksmiths, 665 Howard, dwl 12 Valparaiso
Tannian Patrick J. job wagon, NE cor Bush and Montgomery, dwl 112 Post
Tannyan Annie Miss, domestic, 724 Filbert
Taplin John O. milk ranch, opposite second toll gate San Bruno Road
Tappeiner John, liquor saloon, 104 Sansom, dwl 906 Pacific
Tarbett Foster B. harbor policeman, dwl 106 Freelon
Tarbox Clara G. (widow) dress and cloak maker, 32 Second
Tardiff William, ship carpenter, dwl 312 Beale
Tarnay Patrick, laborer, dwl E s Sansom bet Broadway and Pacific
Tarpey Dominick, with Taaffe & Co. 9 Montgomery
Tarpey John, book keeper with M. Tarpey & Co. dwl Howard nr Sixth
Tarpey M. & Co. produce commission, 102 Clay, dwl 957 Howard
Tarpey Pat, laborer, S. F. & San José R. R. Co
Tarpley L. B. carrier, Daily Examiner, dwl cor Hayes and Franklin
Tarr Alvin B. carpenter with Joshua E. Johnson, dwl E s Folsom bet Twenty-First and Twenty-Second
Tasheira George S. book keeper, 413 Sansom, dwl 422 Second
Tasker Josiah, dish washer, City and County Hospital
Tasker T. Arthur, assistant lighthouse keeper, Farallone Island, dwl 777 Market
Tasney John, job wagon, SW cor Third and Folsom, dwl 16 Stanford
Tate Robert H. dwl E s Tyson Place nr Wash
Tate Stanger, deputy manager S. F. & P. Sugar Co. dwl NE cor Ninth and Folsom
Taubmann Conrad, butter, cheese, and eggs, 15 and 16 Metropolitan Market, dwl 228 Sutter
Tangstrom Frank, seaman, dwl 26 Sacramento

Tauner John, express wagon, cor Kearny and Sutter
Taureck Charles, laborer, dwl 150 Stewart
Taurus M. Co. office 405 Front
Taussig *(Ludwig)* & Lederer *(D. L.)* wholesale dealers wines and liquors, 723 Sansom
Tantphaus Jacob, bowling saloon, dwl 230 First
Tantphaus Peter, butcher, dwl 230 First
Tavalaro G. *(Ossalino & Co.)* dwl cor Sixth and Howard
Tavlin John, wool puller, dwl cor Ritch and Bryant
TAX COLLECTOR, office 1 City Hall first floor
Taxler Willim, carpenter, dwl 728 Market
TAY, *(George H.)* BROOKS *(Henry B.)* & BACKUS *(Oscar J.) (and Charles J. Fox)* importers and jobbers stoves, metals, etc. 8W cor Wash and Front, dwl W s Calhoun nr Green
Tayac Lucian, wines and liquors and saloon, 19 Kearny
Tayker John J. collector, Mercantile Library Association, 202 Montgomery
Taylor Allen, blacksmith, Union Foundry, bds Franklin Hotel SE cor Sansom and Pacific
Taylor Arthur C. deputy U. S. Marshal, dwl 66 Jessie
Taylor Augustus, physician, dwl 719 Bush
TAYLOR *(Augustus C.)* & IREDALE *(Alfred S.)* stoves and tin ware, 410 Market, dwl 1112 Clay
Taylor C. miner, bds United States Hotel
Taylor Calvin, brick mason, dwl 12 Everett
Taylor Charles, clerk, Alta California, dwl Alta California Building
Taylor Charles D. office 723 Mont, dwl 1108 Stock
TAYLOR C. L. & CO. *(Edward Babson jr.)* shipping and commission merchants, 33 Cal, and harbor commissioner, dwl 512 Dupont
Taylor C. Lassell, salesman, 22 Montgomery, dwl N s California bet Hyde and Larkin
Taylor Cyrus D. wood turner, dwl 38 Tehama
Taylor Daniel, ship carpenter with John G. North, dwl N s Crook bet Townsend and Brannan
Taylor David, rigger, dwl 26 Stewart
Taylor David W. warehouse entry clerk, Custom House, dwl 277 Jessie
Taylor Dorcas B. (widow) dwl 603 Pine
Taylor Edward, cashier, Pacific Mail S. S. Co. res San Mateo
Taylor Edward, porter, dwl 113 Minna
Taylor Edward P. clerk with H. H. Bancroft & Co. dwl N s California bet Hyde and Larkin
Taylor Edward T. porter with Weaver, Wooster & Co. 218 Front
TAYLOR *(Edward W.)* & HASTINGS *(Horace M.)* attorneys at law, office 621 Clay, dwl 751 Howard
Taylor Edwin, steward, dwl NW cor Stock and Pac
Taylor Edwin L. clerk with Hickox & Spear, dwl 630 Sutter
Taylor Edmund, bds Franklin Hotel, SE cor Sansom and Pacific
Taylor Eliza Miss, ladies' nurse, dwl with Mrs. S. M. Lumborm, E s First Avenue bet Fourteenth and Fifteenth
Taylor Eliza Miss, nurse, 124 Silver
Taylor Ellen Mrs. lodgings, NW cor Sacramento and Stockton
TAYLOR F. B. & CO., J. R. Whitney & Co. agents, office 405 Front, res New York
Taylor F. M. dwl 636 Commercial
Taylor Francis A. carpenter, dwl N s California bet Hyde and Larkin
Taylor Frederick, laborer, dwl 146 Stewart
Taylor Frederick A. book keeper with H. H. Bancroft & Co. dwl N s Cal bet Hyde and Larkin
Taylor George, coachman, dwl 807 Stockton
Taylor George (colored) seaman, dwl 27 John
Taylor Gilbert H. apprentice, dwl 1214 Clay
TAYLOR GUSTAVUS, physician, office 324 Bush, dwl 719 Bush

Taylor Harrison A. waiter, dwl 12 Stewart
Taylor Holmes, deputy U. S. Drayman, dwl 1234 Dupont
Taylor H. P. printer with Francis, Valentine & Co, dwl 938 Folsom
Taylor James, blacksmith with Belduke & Co. dwl 268 Stevenson
Taylor James, ship carpenter with John G. North, Potrero, dwl SW cor Georgia and Sierra
TAYLOR JAMES M. attorney at law, court commissioner Fourth District and commissioner Mass. and Nevada, office 32 Court Block 636 Clay, dwl SE cor Bush and Steiner
Taylor James S. clerk with Voizin, Ris & Co. dwl Bee Hive Building
Taylor James S. veterinary surgeon and livery stable, 257 Clementina, dwl cor Harrison and Twenty-Second
Taylor J. Mont. bricklayer, 687 Market
TAYLOR JOHN & CO. (J. H. Page) importers druggists' and chemical glassware and assayers' materials, 512 and 514 Wash, dwl 1520 Mason
Taylor John (colored) whitewasher, 204 Sutter
TAYLOR JOHN, liquor saloon, 52 Third, dwl 246 Jessie
Taylor John, waiter, 335 East
Taylor John B. draftsman with Kenitzer & Farquharson, dwl 2006 Powell
Taylor John B. foreman with Tay, Brooks & Backus, dwl 8 s Washington bet Stockton and Powell
Taylor John B. produce, 408 Davis, dwl N s California bet Hyde and Larkin
Taylor John E. minstrel, dwl International Hotel
Taylor (John F.) & Turley (John) blacksmiths, 26 Folsom, dwl W s Main bet Folsom and Harrison
Taylor John G. assistant entry clerk, Custom House, dwl 546 Howard
Taylor John McL. major and commissary subsistence U. S. A. Division of the Pacific, office 418 California, dwl Occidental Hotel
Taylor John Q. A. drayman, 421 Washington
Taylor Jonathan, agent Nicolson Pavement California and Oregon, dwl 602 Sutter
Taylor Joseph, auctioneer, dwl Clementina bet Second and Third
Taylor Joseph night inspector, C. H. dwl 711 Cal
Taylor Joseph S. clerk, dwl 809 Kearny
Taylor M. second steward, steamer Pacific
Taylor Margaret (widow) dwl 713 Filbert, rear
Taylor Maria Miss, dress maker, 320 Kearny
Taylor Maria (widow, colored) dwl 714 Stockton
Taylor Mateo, truckman, cor Oregon and Davis
Taylor Michael D. butcher with O. H. Willoughby
Taylor Oliver, broker, dwl 601 Greenwich
Taylor Oliver, carpenter, dwl W s Seventh near Howard
Taylor Peter, book keeper, 17 and 18 Stewart, dwl 810 Second
TAYLOR PHILIP W. collector, office 723 Mont
Taylor Richard, laborer, dwl Grove House, SW cor Steiner and Tyler
Taylor R. L. (John Bamber & Co.) dwl SW cor Montgomery and Broadway
Taylor Robert, with Helbing, Greenebaum & Co. dwl 412 Folsom
Taylor Sanford W. blacksmith, dwl W s Main bet Folsom and Harrison
Taylor Sarah Miss, dress maker, 320 Kearny
TAYLOR S. P. & CO. proprietors Pioneer Paper Mill, office 322 Clay and junk 111 and 113 Davis, dwl S s Green bet Mont and Sansom
Taylor Stewart, hostler, E s Morse bet Pine and Bush
Taylor Sumner J. wharfinger, Jackson St. Wharf, dwl N s Austin bet Franklin and Van Ness Av
TAYLOR, THOMAS & CO. importers and jobbers wines and liquors, 413 and 415 Clay, dwl 716 Union
Taylor Thomas, peddler, dwl 8 Jessie

Taylor Thomas (colored) porter, Q. M. Dep't, dwl 1224 Sacramento bet Taylor and Jones
Taylor Thomas A. carpenter, dwl SE cor Mission and First
Taylor (Truman) & Co. Horse Radish Depôt, 53 Occidental Market, dwl 1006 Stockton
Taylor W. cook, 506 Montgomery, dwl 433 Bryant
Taylor Washington, trunk maker with E. Galpen & Co. dwl 36 Battery
Taylor W. G. (widow) dwl 809 Kearny
Taylor William, cook, 506 Mont, dwl 976 Harrison
Taylor William, proprietor Cosmopolitan Hotel Coaches, dwl 55 Natoma
Taylor William, waiter, dwl 433 Bryant
Taylor William C. foreman Flint's Warehouse, dwl cor Battery and Greenwich
Taylor William H. produce, 408 Davis, dwl N s California bet Hyde and Larkin
Taylor William J. Cashier's Department Wells, Fargo & Co. dwl 828 Sacramento
Taylor William M. printer with Francis, Valentine & Co. dwl 938 Folsom
Taylor William P. salesman with J. Peirce, dwl 1821 Stockton
Taylor William W. machinist, Pacific Foundry, dwl 327 Bryant
Taylor W. M. contractor, office 402 Montgomery
Taylor Wyman, painter, dwl 155 Third
Tayson John J. laborer, Fort Point, dwl W s Hartman nr Lombard
Teackle Elisha W. broker, office 32 Montgomery Block, dwl 32 Natoma
Teague E. teamster with Blair & Co. 28 Wash
Teague Henry, with Yates & Stevens, dwl 30 Clay
Teal Henry J. dwl 537 Mission
Teal J. M. sash and blind maker with J. McGill & Co. dwl 325 Dupont
Tebbe Henry, laborer with Wm. J. Kingsley
Techattucup S. & G. M. Co. office 702 Washington
Tecoripa M. Co. office SW cor Front and Jackson
Tedford A. C. mechanic with James Brokaw, dwl 135 Tehama
Teed Albert, carpenter, dwl S s Clay bet Taylor and Jones
Teens Casper, works with John Herrmann
Tees William, laborer, Bay Sugar Refinery, dwl 813 Battery
TEESE LEWIS jr. wines and liquors, SE cor California and Kearny
TEHAMA HOUSE, George W. Frink proprietor, 410 California
Teimann Henry, cigar maker with E. Goslinsky, dwl What Cheer House
Teiney Patrick, waiter, dwl 269 Stevenson
Teisseire Armand, portrait painter, dwl 29 Ritch
Teitgen Richard, groceries and liquors, NE corner Pacific and Battery
Teitman A. C. (H. D. Ellerhorst & Co.) dwl 306 Tehama nr Fourth
Teitman Sophia (widow) dwl 1014 Kearny
Teitterle Chris. F. carriage maker, dwl cor Capp and Twenty-Third
Telegraph House, John Schroeder proprietor, SW cor Green and Battery
Telfer James, wood carver, dwl 12 Sutter
Tell Elizabeth (widow) domestic, SE cor Stockton and Union
Teller Antoine, bar keeper, 635 Washington, dwl W s Montgomery bet Jackson and Pacific
Teller John D. P. broker, office 327 Front, dwl 745 Howard
Tellurium G. & S. M. Co. office 529 Clay
Tellyr John, liquor saloon, W s Mission bet Twenty-Third and Twenty-Fourth
Tempany Maria T. preceptress select school, dwl N s Chestnut bet Dupont and Stockton
Temple Isaac J. butcher, dwl 715 Greenwich
Temple John, broker, office 19 Exchange Building, dwl 617 Bush

Temple Rufus, calker, dwl 570 Howard
Templeton C. L. Mrs. boarding, dwl 5 Dixon's Blk
Templeton Herman S. clerk, 10 Occidental Market, dwl 569 Mission
Templeton Kate, chambermaid, Railroad House
Tence Charles & Co. *(Eugene Huet)* importers and jobbers French millinery goods, 514 Sac
Tennent Richard, workman, S. F. & P. Sugar Co. dwl Harrison nr Eighth
Tennent Robert J. groceries and liquors, NE corner Ellis and Larkin
TENNENT THOMAS, nautical instrument maker, SE cor Battery and Oregon, dwl NE cor Jones and Pacific
Tenney John, groom, dwl 5 Minna
Tenney Richard P. book keeper with Wm. McColl, dwl 1717 Leavenworth
Tenthorey Peter *(Tschantz, T. & Co.)* dwl 558 Mission
Teny John, laborer, dwl 7 Minna
Tercini Peter, gardener, Bay View
Terlonge Louis, tailor, with Francis Killpatrick, dwl cor Clay and Waverly Place
Terme Marie Madame, theatrical costumer, 534 Jackson, dwl SW cor Pacific and Sansom
Terpsichore Hall, NW cor Pacific and Virginia
Terry Caleb C. carpenter with Stevens & Rider, dwl 271 Clara
Terry James A. laborer with Wm. J. Kingsley
Terry Joseph T. clerk with Henry B. Williams, 305 Front
Terry Lineas, tinsmith with Osgood & Stetson, 219 Commercial
Terry Orrin, stevedore, dwl N s Oregon bet Front and Davis
Terry Thomas, hose maker with Cook & Son, dwl E s Sansom bet Broadway and Vallejo
Terry William N. ship carpenter, dwl S s Greenwich bet Hyde and Leavenworth
Terwilliger E. P. sash and blind maker with J. McGill & Co. dwl SE cor Sixth and Howard
Terwilliger Napoleon B. dwl 143 Fourth
Teschemacher Henry F. real estate, office 523 Montgomery, dwl Union Club Rooms
TESMORE *(Solomon)* & MAYES *(George)* fish, 33 and 34 Washington Market, dwl 208 Dupont
Tesoro and James River Consolidated M. Co. office 619 Merchant
Testa Dominic, fisherman, dwl Merchant bet Drumm and East
Tetgen Henry, clerk with Charles Duveneck, NW cor Dolores and Seventeenth
TETLOW SAMUEL, proprietor Bella Union Melodeon and saloon, 706 and 708 Washington
Teubner *(Gustav)* & Hoffman *(William)* showcase manufacturers, 431 Kearny
Teutonia Mount Diablo Coal M. Co. office 652 Wash
Tevens Patrick, hostler, Willows, SW cor Mission and Eighteenth
Tevis Lloyd *(Haggin & T.)* attorney at law, office 1 and 2 Court Block, dwl 1316 Taylor
Tew Daniel R. jeweler with R. B. Gray & Co
Tew George, carpenter, dwl 116 Sansom
Tew George W. carpenter, dwl E s Valencia bet Sixteenth and Seventeenth
Tewksbury Marcus R. physician, office and dwl 635 Market
Tgel Ludwig, confectionery, 1319 Stockton
Thackery William, foreman spinning Mission Woolen Mills, dwl N s Folsom bet Sixteenth and Seventeenth
Than Benedict, musician, dwl 735 Pine
Thatch Rufus, painter with Sweett & Gadsby
Thatcher H. M. book keeper, California Foundry, dwl Oriental Hotel
Thatcher Horatio, flour packer, dwl S s Geary bet Kearny and Dupont
Thaule William, waiter, Richards' Restaurant, dwl E s Vincent nr Green

Thayer Amasa, hatter, dwl E s Dupont nr Francisco
Thayer Andrew E. attorney at law, office 537 Washington, dwl Greenwich bet Mont and Sansom
THAYER B. B. chemist and State Assayer, SE cor Montgomery and Bush and NW cor Howard and Third, dwl 534 Howard
Thayer E. N. actor, Maguire's Opera House
Thayer George, ship joiner with John G. North, Potrero
Thayer Henry N. blacksmith with Nelson & Doble, 321 Pine
Thayer Hiram, bar keeper, dwl 445 Bush
Thayer Ignatius E. measurer, Custom House, dwl 20 Taylor
Thayer John S. with L. P. Cooley, Old San José Road, nr junction San José R. R.
Thayer Pierpont, actor, Maguire's Opera House
Thayer Sarah (widow) dwl 415 Green
Thayer S. C. E. salesman, dwl 37 Belden Block
Thayer Wales, nurse, City and County Hospital
Thryer William, dwl 612 California
Theas Philippe, clerk with D. Ghirardelli & Co. 417 Jackson
Theblask Henry, maccaroni manufacturer, dwl 558 Mission
Theisen Adolphine Mrs. teacher music, 15 Stockton, rear
Theisen Joseph, dwl 15 Stockton, rear
Theiss J. H. baker with Charles Frank, dwl 115 St. Mark Place
Theller Arnold, mining stocks, 605 Montgomery, dwl 402 Montgomery
THELLER SAMUEL L. real estate agent, 702 Washington, dwl SW cor Taylor and Vallejo
Theobald John V. manufacturer hair dye and restorative, 808 Market
Theobalds *(William W.)* & Co. *(Adam Magee)* publishers California Leader, office 625 Merchant, dwl NE cor Montgomery and Broadway
Theodel Theodore, porter, 623 Commercial
Theodore John (col'd) dwl S s Dupont Alley
Theodore Jules, clerk with Joseph Isaac & Co. dwl 522 Union
Theodore Samuel, clerk with Joseph Isaacs & Co. dwl 522 Union
Therkelsen Lauritz, carpenter, dwl Sierra Nevada Hotel, 528 Pacific
Thearen David, machinist, dwl 115 First
THIBAULT FREDERICK J. notary public and commissioner deeds, office 605 Montgomery, dwl 921 Jackson
Thickbroom J. second-hand furniture, SE cor Third and Tehama
Thiel John P. clerk, dwl 205 Sutter
THIELE A. LOUIS, proprietor Faust Cellar, SE cor Clay and Montgomery, dwl 417 Mont
Thiele Julius, hats and caps, 625 Commercial
Thiele Robert, cabinet maker with Andrew Conrad, 414 Pine
THIELE THEODORE & CO. editors and proprietors Le National, office 533 Commercial
Thielpape August, cook, Bootz's Hotel, dwl 308 Mason
Thies Henry, drayman, 743 Sacramento, dwl 1707 Dupont
Thoburn Hannah T. (widow) furnished rooms, NE cor Montgomery and Sutter
Thode Henry, cooperage, S s Vallejo bet Battery and Front
Thode Julius, clerk, 641 Pacific
Thoder Hermann, laborer, Bay Sugar Refinery, dwl 813 Battery
Thom James, calker, dwl SE corner Sacramento and Davis
Thom Lucinda (widow) plain sewing, 16 Ritch
Thomann Frederick, wagon maker, 214 Sutter
Thomann Henry, bar keeper, SW cor Clay and East
Thomas A. B. entry clerk Naval Office, C. H. dwl cor Minna and Second

Thomas Alfred, mariner, dwl 1608 Powell
Thomas Andrew, importer and dealer leather and shoe findings, 738 Market
Thomas Casper, dwl W side Valencia bet Sixteenth and Seventeenth
Thomas Charles, carpenter, dwl 712 O'Farrell
Thomas Christian, laborer, Pacific Glass Works, dwl W s Carolina nr Mariposa
Thomas Curtis, foreman with Hey & Meyn, dwl S s Folsom nr Eleventh
THOMAS C. W. planing mill and bellows manufactory, 22 and 24 California, dwl 611 Pine
Thomas (David) & Conway (John) billiard and liquor saloon, Brooklyn Hotel, dwl 226 Jessie
Thomas Dawson, ship carpenter, dwl 102 Dupont
Thomas Edward, engineer, 511½ Clay, dwl E side Leavenworth bet Greenwich and Lombard
Thomas Edwin W. local policeman, dwl 1703 Dupont
Thomas Eleazer Rev. editor California Christian Advocate, dwl 1106 Mason
Thomas Elijah, workman with G. Treat, S s Twenty-Fourth bet Folsom and Howard
Thomas Elizabeth (col'd, widow) dwl 923 Greenwich
Thomas Evan, miner, dwl E side Ninth bet Bryant and Brannan
Thomas Evan, third officer steamer Orizaba, dwl E s Market bet Twelfth and Thirteenth
Thomas F. watchman, steamer Clinton
Thomas François, dyer, 734 Washington
Thomas (Frank E.) & Twing (Daniel H.) wood and coal, cor Market and East and 122 Sacramento, dwl 465 Jessie
Thomas F. W. laundry, 431 Sutter bet Stockton and Powell
Thomas George H. clerk with Samuel F. Butterworth, 205 Battery, dwl W s Ridley nr Mission
Thomas George W. clerk, 518 Kearny
Thomas Henrietta F. Mrs. dwl 300 Stockton
Thomas Henry, blacksmith with Kimball & Co. carriage makers, dwl 106 Eddy
Thomas Henry, car builder, S. F. & San José R. R. Co. dwl E s Mission bet Eighteenth and Nineteenth
Thomas Henry, cooper with J. P. Meyer, dwelling Wright's Hotel, 210 Broadway
Thomas J. drayman with H. W. Bragg & Co
Thomas James, dwl What Cheer House
Thomas James, calker, dwl SE cor Sac and Davis
Thomas James, waiter, Brevoort House
THOMAS J. B. importing, shipping, and commission merchant, 619 Front
Thomas J. Henry, glass blower, Pacific Glass Works, dwl W s Carolina nr Mariposa
Thomas John, employé, Manhattan House, 705 Front
Thomas John, laborer, dwl NW cor Buchanan and Page
Thomas John, painter, dwl 414 Market
Thomas John (col'd) solder maker, dwl E s Seventh bet Brannan and Townsend
Thomas Johnson J. painter, dwl 1014 Clay
Thomas J. P. (Standard Soap Co.) res Oakland
Thomas Mary E. (col'd, widow) dwl 823 Sac
Thomas Mme. (col'd, widow) dwl 632 Broadway
Thomas Patrick, laborer, S. F. & San José R. R. Co
Thomas Patrick, plasterer, dwl 12 William
Thomas P. J. compositor, Evening Bulletin, dwl S s Vallejo nr Hyde
Thomas Samuel, dwl What Cheer House
Thomas Shepherd A. with H. C. Hudson & Co. dwl 22 Minna
Thomas Victor, cook, Government House Restaurant, 504 Washington
Thomas Vipoint, seaman, dwl 54 Sacramento
THOMAS WILLIAM, groceries and liquors, SE cor Sixth and Clementina
Thomas William, stevedore, dwl 36 Battery

Thomas William, washer, Chelsea Laundry
Thomas William B. clerk with G. H. Hopper, dwl Vernon House, Jackson
Thomas William D. dwl E s First Av nr Fifteenth
Thomas William D. machinist, Pacific Foundry
Thomas W. R. butter, cheese, eggs, etc. 24 Occidental Market, dwl 417 Howard
Thomason John, carpenter, dwl with Philip Rodgers E s Market bet Twelfth and Thirteenth
Thomasson O. K. laborer, dwl W s Sansom bet Green and Vallejo
Thomen Henry, dwl 431 Pine
Thomet Narcissus, hatter with Adams & Brother
Thomford Chris, clerk, 815 Jackson
Thomford (Henry A.) & Klein (Ernst) groceries and liquors, NW cor Powell and Filbert
Thompson A. fireman, Occidental Hotel
Thompson A. J. seaman, dwl 27 Frederick
Thompson Alexander, driver, Central R. R. Co. dwl Park Avenue
Thompson Andrew, mason, dwl N s Fifteenth nr Dolores
Thompson Andrew J. poultry, fish, etc. 12 and 13 New Market, dwl 429 Sixth
Thompson Anna Miss, dwl 92 Stevenson House
Thompson Bridget Miss, domestic with O. J. Preston, S s Mission nr Eleventh
Thompson Charles, captain schr J. Mora Moss, Caduc's Line, foot Washington
Thompson Charles, laborer, dwl 140 Stewart
Thompson Charles, seaman, dwl 26 Sacramento
Thompson Charles A. teamster, Pier 1 Stewart, dwl 65 Jessie
Thompson David, porter, dwl E s Varenne nr Union
Thompson David (col'd) waiter, stm Chrysopolis
Thompson D. W. C. insurance broker, office 224 California, dwl 12 Hawthorne
Thompson Esther Miss, domestic, 725 California
Thompson Frederick, milker with Murray & Noble
Thompson George, cook, Marysville Hotel, 414 Pacific
Thompson George, machinist, Vulcan Iron Works, dwl 19 Park Avenue
Thompson George C. Union Mineral Water Works, 526 Union, dwl 527 Union
Thompson George H. deputy surveyor, U. S. dwl 509 Powell
Thompson George W. B. with James Bowman
Thompson Hannah (widow) dwl N s Pinkham Place nr Eighth
Thompson Harriet L. (widow) dwl N s Riley nr Taylor
Thompson H. C. foreman Spirit of Times, dwl 308 Union
Thompson Helen Miss, head assistant Rincon School, dwl 124 Geary
Thompson Henry, seaman, steamer Pacific
Thompson Henry D. comedian, Metropolitan Theater, dwl W s Wetmore Place
Thompson Henry W. (Pacific Straw Works) dwl 62 Natoma
Thompson Hettie (widow) dwl E s Mission nr Thirtieth
THOMPSON I. D. wines and liquors, 321 Montgomery. dwl 768 Harrison
Thompson Isabella Miss, domestic, 725 California
Thompson Jacob, seaman, dwl N s Oregon bet Davis and Drumm
Thompson Jacob (col'd) waiter, dwl 16 Scott
Thompson J. Alden, clerk with Parrott & Co. dwl 716 Stockton
Thompson James (col'd) cook, dwl 7 Broadway
Thompson James, fireman, dwl 150 Natoma
Thompson James, plasterer, dwl Golden Gate Hotel
Thompson James, retortman, S. F. Gas Co
Thompson James, upholsterer with John C. Bell, dwl 626 California
Thompson James G. joiner with Stevens & Rider, dwl 73 Natoma

Thompson James W. with George F. Parker, dwl SW cor Montgomery and California
Thompson *(John)* & Co. *(William M. Hinton and Frank Mahon)* book and job printers, 505 Clay, dwl 1908 Mason
Thompson John *(Forsyth, Morrison & Co.)* dwl N s Perry bet Second and Third
Thompson John, with Charles Harley & Co. dwl cor Sacramento and Drumm
Thompson John, carpenter, dwl NW cor Kearny and Broadway
Thompson John, clerk with H. P. Wakelee, dwl 632 Market
Thompson John, drayman, dwl W s Montgomery bet Greenwich and Filbert
Thompson John, drayman, cor Mission and Stewart
Thompson John, drayman, dwl 551 Market
Thompson John, express wagon, cor Cal and Mont
Thompson John, fireman, steamer Senator
Thompson John, laborer, dwl NW cor Sacramento and Drumm
Thompson John, longshoreman, dwl NW cor Commerce and Battery
Thompson John, longshoreman, dwl 120 Freelon
Thompson John, waiter, dwl 132 Sutter
Thompson John, waiter, dwl 44 Stevenson
Thompson John B. calker, dwl E s Tennessee nr Solano
Thompson John D. carpenter, dwl 6 Winter Place
Thompson John R. machinist, Vulcan Iron Works, dwl 19 Park Avenue
Thompson Joseph P. real estate, office 523 Montgomery, dwl Union Club Rooms
Thompson Lewis H. with I. D. Thompson, dwl 768 Harrison
Thompson Lucius *(Geo. C. Shreve & Co.)* dwl 412 Dupont nr Pine
Thompson M. (widow) dwl 822 Clay
Thompson M. Mrs. nurse, 102 Minna
Thompson M. A. (widow) dwl 309 Third
Thompson Madaline (widow) dwl 783 Market
Thompson Malcolm, wines and liquors, 21 Pacific
Thompson Marion (widow) dwl NE cor Pine and Hyde
Thompson Mary Miss, seamstress, dwl 73 Tehama
Thompson Mary (widow) dwl 626 Mission
Thompson Mary A. Miss, domestic, 616 Greenwich
Thompson Mary Ann Miss, domestic, 745 Howard
Thompson Matilda Miss, seamstress, dwl 73 Tehama
Thompson M. E. Miss, dwl 112 Sutter
Thompson Michael, laborer, dwl S s Eddy bet Larkin and Polk
Thompson Mira (widow) dwl 1005 Stockton
Thompson M. J. (widow) dwl 303 Third
Thompson M. T. (widow) dwl 716 Stockton
Thompson Nicholas, laborer with B. Bonnet & Co.
THOMPSON R. A. & CO. *(Bernard Peyton)* Central Coal Yard, 126 Sutter, dwl W s Eleventh nr Market
Thompson R. Aug. attorney at law, office 2 Federal Building, dwl W s Eleventh nr Market
Thompson Robert, baker, dwl 1138 Folsom
Thompson Robert. warehouse clerk with Wm. Alvord & Co. dwl 748 Harrison
Thompson Rufus W. clerk with Thomas H. Selby & Co. dwl 1225 Clay
Thompson Samuel, conductor, U. S. Branch Mint, res Oakland
Thompson Samuel, machinist, Pacific Foundry, dwl 421 Folsom
Thompson Samuel, painter, dwl 19 Park Avenue
Thompson Samuel P. miner, dwl 321 Minna
Thompson S. B. carpenter and builder and school director Ninth District, dwl 373 Brannan
Thompson S. M. (widow) homeopathic physician, dwl 640 Howard
Thompson Thomas, clerk, dwl SW cor Broadway and Montgomery
Thompson Thomas, drayman, 107 Clay

Thompson Thomas, molder, dwl 18 Oak
Thompson Thomas, newsman, dwl 21 Baldwin Court
Thompson Thomas, waiter, Miners' Restaurant
Thompson Thomas, waiter, Lick House
Thompson Thomas A. seaman, dwl 27 Frederick
Thompson Thomas H. waterman, dwl SW cor Jones and Greenwich
Thompson Thornton, machinist, Pacific Foundry, dwl 47 Clementina
Thompson Wildes T. pilot commissioner, dwl 411 Powell
Thompson William, dwl U. S. Court Building, SW cor Montgomery and Jackson
Thompson William, dwl 1027 Kearny
Thompson William, blacksmith, Union Foundry, dwl 21 Baldwin Court
Thompson William, boarding and liquors, 112 Pac
Thompson William, cooper with Handy & Neuman, dwl S s Linden bet Octavia and Laguna
Thompson William, deck hand, Sancelito Water Boat
Thompson William, laborer bds 8 Jackson
Thompson William, mason, dwl 414 Market
Thompson William, seaman, dwl 26 Sacramento
Thompson William, seaman, dwl W s Battery bet Green and Vallejo, rear
Thompson William, tanner, dwl 130 Perry
Thompson William, teamster with Tiernan & Kershaw, dwl E s First Avenue nr Fifteenth
Thompson William jr. mining, office 519 Jackson
Thompson William B. laborer, dwl 214 Commercial
Thompson William B. painter, dwl Ws Florence nr Vallejo
Thompson William D. dwl 527 Union
Thompson William G. laborer with C. O'Donnell, dwl 126 Perry
Thompson William H. cook, steamer Julia
Thompson William L. Medical Purveyor's Office, 805 Sansom
Thompson William O. ironer, Chelsea Laundry
Thompson William P. secretary Napoleon C. M. Co. office 19 Stevenson House, dwl 1028 Minna
Thompson William S. carriage smith, 749 Market, dwl Ss Turk bet Jones and Leavenworth
Thompson W. T. pilot examiner
Thoms C. cooper, with Cutting & Co. dwl SE cor Stockton and Bush
Thomsen William, express wagon, dwl NE cor Sacramento and Davis
Thomson James, dwl 205 Fourth
THOMSON JAMES S. secretary Industrial School Department, office 9 City Hall third floor, res Oakland
Thomson John, machinist with E. T. Steen, dwl 154 Tehama
Thomson John D. carpenter, dwl 207 Fourth
Thomson John G. with A. C. Dietz & Co. SW cor Clay and Kearny, dwl 12 Perry
Thomson M. A. Miss, saleswoman, 125 Montgomery, dwl 245 Second
Thomson Peter & Co. *(Samuel Dixon)* gents' furnishing goods, 607 Sacramento, res Oakland
Thomson Samuel S. book keeper, Pacific Insurance Co. 436 California, res Oakland
THOMSON THOMAS, artesian well borer, 28 Third, dwl 262 Clementina
Thomson Thomas B. salesman with G. W. Conkling, 714 Montgomery, dwl SW cor Montgomery and Broadway
Thomson William, laundryman, dwl 316 Ritch
Thomson William, liquor saloon, NE cor Davis and Sacramento
Thomson William A. dwl S s Sixteenth, Mission Creek
Thomson William M. plasterer, dwl National Hotel, Market
Thone Christopher, carpenter, dwl 634 Second
Thonges Philip, German Bakery, NW cor Hartman Place and Greenwich
Thorick Carsten, laborer, dwl 619 Pacific

Thorley Thomas W. conductor, North Beach & M. R. R. Co. dwl Shipley nr Harrison Avenue
THORN PHILIP, bakery, 22 Dupont
Thornagel George, laborer, dwl Meeks Place
Thorndike *(Charles N.)* & Stimpson *(Joseph E.)* plasterers and bricklayers, office 741 Market, dwl SW cor Howard and Hubbard
Thorndike E. P. Mrs. dwl 1711 Dupont
Thorne Alicia M. Mrs. actress, Maguire's Opera House
Thorne Ann (widow) dwl 219 Minna
Thorne Charles, captain steamer Senator, C. S. Navigation Co. office NE cor Front and Jackson
Thorne Charles R. jr. actor, Maguire's Opera House, dwl 112 Sutter
Thorne I. N. attorney at law, office 535 Clay, dwl NW cor Howard and Seventeenth
Thornhill Joseph, driver, dwl 810 Green
Thornquist Charles, boarding and lodging, 20 Com
THORNTON ABEL, proprietor Columbia Hotel, 741 Market
Thornton Henry, coachman, NW cor Franklin and Post
Thornton James D. *(Williams & T.)* attorney at law, dwl SE cor Stockton and Sutter
Thornton Lucy C. (widow) dwl 26 O'Farrell
Thornton Mary E. Miss, dwl 1020 Minna
Thorp P. carpenter, dwl Original House
Thorra Frederick, mate, dwl 26 Stewart
Thour Catharine, domestic with William Harper
Thrall H. H. surgeon dentist, office 715 Clay, dwl 1024 Clay
Thresher M. S. salesman with Jacob Underhill & Co. dwl N s Guy Place
Throckmorton Samuel R. real estate, dwl 716 Mission
Thum George, baker, dwl 717 Pacific
Thurbach Julius, porter, 310 Sacramento
Thurber Albert E. milk ranch, cor Larkin and Pine
Thurber James A. laborer, dwl 7 Monroe
Thurbus Edward, wagon maker, dwl Natoma bet Second and Third
Thurman J. W. *(J. A. McClelland & Co.)* dwl 730 Filbert
Thurn Cipriano, attorney at law, dwl 919 Powell
Thurnauer Joseph, book keeper with Thurnauer & Zinn, dwl St. Nicholas Hotel
THURNAUER *(William)* & ZINN *(Henry)* importers and dealers baskets, toys, and willow ware, 320 and 322 Battery, res Bavaria
Thurston C. F. coaches, American Exchange
Thurston Christian, lodgings, dwl 57 Jessie
Thurston Edwin R. clerk, 605 Mkt, dwl 32 Tehama
Thurston Martha N. physician, dwl nr SE cor Folsom and Twenty-Second
Thurston Nathaniel, vegetable garden, nr SE cor Folsom and Twenty-Second
Thurton S. E. Miss, assistant, Powell St. School, dwl 909 Clay
Thwaites Joseph, photographic printer, Selleck's Gallery, 415 Montgomery
Thyarks Henry *(Tillmann & Co.)* dwl SW cor Washington and Stockton
Thyes John B. with Mayrisch Bros. dwl 23 Rousch
Thyson Adam, laborer, Mason's Brewery
Ti Loe & Co. (Chinese) merchants, 634 Jackson
Ti Loe (Chinese) washing, 25 Pacific
TIATIEN *(John H.)* & BOLKE *(Wilhelm)* groceries and liquors, SW cor Brannan and Ritch
Tibbet Edward, clerk, dwl 615 Pacific
Tibbetts Charles M. dwl Russ House
Tibbetts S. M. physician, dwl SE cor Jackson and Stockton
Tibbetts Edward, runner, Sailor's Home, SW cor Battery and Vallejo
Tibbey Alexander, clerk, dwl 533 Green
Tibbey Edney S. note clerk, Bank California, dwl 923 Howard
Tibbey E. M. Miss, assistant, Union Grammar School, dwl 533 Green

Tibbey Henry S. student with Doyle & Barber, dwl 533 Green
Tibbey M. A. (widow) dwl 533 Green
Tibbits Jane (widow) dwl with Charles A. Lanpher NE cor Brannan and Ninth
Tibbits R. P. machinist, Union Foundry, dwl Original House
Tice Alanson, foreman brick maker with E. Morrell, dwl NE cor Twentieth and Florida
Tice Andrew Jackson, dwl 152 Third
Tice Annie C. Mrs. dry goods, 152 Third
Tice Elbridge J. brick molder with E. Morrell, dwl NE cor Twentieth and Florida
Tice Henry M. book keeper with Grant, Averell & Co. dwl Harrison near Sixteenth
Tichenor DeWitt C. bar keeper, SW cor First and Mission, dwl 143 Natoma
TICHENOR H. B. & CO. *(Robert G. Byxbee)* San Francisco Dry Dock, foot Second, lumber, Navarro, and Russian River Packets, 221 Stewart Pier 21, dwl S s DeBoom nr Second
Tichenor Stephen J. porter, 415 Front, dwl 341 Jessie
Ticbit Rosalie Miss, domestic, 512 Union
Tichner John, painter, dwl 316 Beale
Tichner Louis, broker, dwl 308 Sutter
Tichner Solomon, clerk, dwl 824 Jackson
Tidball Scott, artist, Bradley & Rulofson's Gallery, dwl 31 O'Farrell
Tidball T. carpenter, dwl 842 Clay
Tiddens Lucas, clerk with Kennedy & Bell, dwl 17 Third
Tie Sang Tong (Chinese) merchants, 929 Dupont
Tiedemann *(Henry H.)* & Menckhoff *(Gustave)* liquors, Lombard nr Sansom, dwl 323 Jessie
Tiedemann John H. dwl N s Folsom bet Tenth and Eleventh
Tiedemann Martin, with Erzgraber & Goetjen, 120 Davis
Tiedemann Peter, groceries and liquors, NW cor Folsom and Rousch
Tiegel F. W. machinist, Miners' Foundry, dwl 163 First
Tiemann Henry, cigar manufacturer, bds Sacramento Hotel 407 Pacific
Tienken Benjamin *(Louis Miller & Co.)* dwl 725 Jackson
Tiernan John, laborer, dwl 7 Minna
Tiernan John, ship carpenter, dwl S s Brannan nr Sixth
Tiernan Mary Miss, domestic, SW cor Jackson and Taylor
Tiernan Michael, cartman, cor Battery and Vallejo
Tiernan Patrick, boiler maker, dwl 24 Clara
Tiernan Patrick H. ship builder, cor Kentucky and Mariposa, dwl nr cor Iowa and Mariposa
Tiernan Richard *(Teirnan & Co.)* dwl W s First Avenue nr Fifteenth
Tiernan Richard & Co. *(Marsden & Kershaw)* hay and grain, Valencia nr Sixteenth, dwl W s First Avenue bet Fourteenth and Fifteenth
Tiernan William, ship carpenter, dwl cor Mariposa and Indiana
Tiernay Michael, laborer, dwl 41 Louisa
Tiernay Peter, hostler, dwl 13 Clara
Tiernay Thomas, laborer, dwl 319 Tehama, rear
Tierney E. P. clerk, Medical Purveyor's Office, dwl 951 Folsom
Tierney James, bar keeper, 211 Sansom
Tierney James, laborer, dwl N s Filbert near Montgomery
Tierney John, liquor saloon, 211 Sansom
Tierney Patrick, express wagon, cor Broadway and Davis
Tierney Patrick, lab, dwl Seventeenth nr Dolores
Tierney Thomas, workman, S. F. Gas Co. dwl E s Folsom Avenue nr Folsom
Tierney W. dwl 331 Bush
Tieroff Augustus, groceries, 1118 Kearny
Tietjen A. (widow) dwl 1625 Powell

Tietjen Diedrick, groceries and liquors, NE cor Tehama and Fourth
Tietjen Emma, laundress, dwl 321 Tehama
Tietjen Henry *(Bulke & T.)* dwl SW cor Brannan and Ritch
Tietjen Henry *(Peterson & T.)* dwl SW cor Leavenworth and Broadway
Tietjen *(Hermann)* & Co. *(John Von Staden)* groceries and liquors, NE cor Pine and St. Mary
Tietjen Henry, with Edward McDevitt, 216 Davis
Tietjen Henry T. *(Peter Madel & Co.)* dwl NE cor Mission and Stewart
Tietjen John, car builder, S. F. & San José R. R. Co. dwl cor Sixteenth and Mission
Tietjen William, job cart, 401 Front, dwl NW cor Bush and Powell
Tietz Henry F. clerk, 542 Kearny
Tietzer Henrich, laborer, Bay Sugar Refinery, dwl 813 Battery
Tievers T. H. clerk, dwl Lutgen's Hotel
Tiffany Henry, porter with Wells, Fargo & Co. dwl NW cor Montgomery and California
Tiffany Margaret Miss, domestic, Brevoort House
Tiffany Owen, waiter, Occidental Hotel, dwl S s Union bet Hyde and Larkin
TIFFANY ROBERT J. proprietor Eagle Hat Store, 627 Washington (old stand) dwl SW cor Stockton and Clay
Tift Morgan, commission agent, dwl 629 Market
Tifts Edward, clerk, 15 Montgomery
Tift E. W. carpenter, dwl 654 Mission
Tighe Catherine Miss, domestic, 314 Jessie
Tighe John, attorney at law, office 606 Merchant
Tighe John, fireman, steamer America, dwl W s Beale bet Howard and Folsom
Tighe Kate Miss, chambermaid, Russ House
Tighe Mary (widow) dwl 69 Stevenson
Tighe Owen, porter, Russ House
Tighe William J. & Co. *(John Davis)* butchers, cor Mason and O'Farrell, dwl 111 William
Tilden & Fowler Petroleum Co. office NE cor Clay and Battery
Tilden Charles L. carpenter, dwl 8 Quincy
Tilden H. N. merchant, office 221 Clay, dwl 639 Clay
TILDEN *(Joseph)* & BREED *(H. L.)* stock and money brokers (successors to John Perry jr.) 611 Mont cor Merchant, dwl 1014 Stockton
Tilden Samuel, printer with Charles F. Robbins, dwl 417 Filbert
TILESTON FRED. L. agent Wheeler & Wilson Sewing Machine Co. 439 Mont, dwl Russ House
Tilford James W. dwl 12 Sutter
Tilghman Thomas H. clerk, dwl W s Devisidero bet McAllister and Tyler
Tilgner Francis, Pioneer Malt House, Stockton nr Francisco, dwl N s Francisco nr Stockton
Tilley Charles B. clerk with R. G. Sneath, 408 Front, dwl 430 Post
Tilley William J. salesman with R. G. Sneath, 408 Front, dwl 430 Post
TILLINGHAST WILLIAM H. agent North British and Mercantile Insurance Co. office 404 California, and sub manager Bank British Columbia, dwl 1218 Folsom
Tilliston F. L. dwl Russ House
Tillman August, foreman with Hyde & McClennen, 210 Pine, dwl 729 Mission
Tillman Charles, miner, dwl 728 Market
Tillman Clemens, liquor saloon, 729 Mission
TILLMAN F. agent Tilton & McFarland's Fireproof Safes, 318 Battery, dwl 521 Green
Tillman George, Monitor Saloon, 1009 Kearny
Tillman John, painter, dwl 202 Stockton
Tillman Mathew, laborer, dwl Kearny nr Bdwy
Tillman Thomas, dwl W s Devisidero nr Tyler
Tillman William (colored) cook, Bailey House
Tillmann *(Frederick)* & Co. *(Henry Thyarks and Charles Neuhaus)* wholesale grocers, 407 and 409 Clay, dwl SE cor Gough and Fulton

Tillmann William J. saddlery, 703 Mission, dwl 729 Mission
Tillot R. Washington, waiter, 718 Market, dwl Golden Gate Hotel
Tillson Charles, painter, dwl 304 Minna
Tilson Joseph, butcher, dwl 34 St. Mark Place
Tilson Joseph, cook, 626 Kearny
Tilton A. M. blacksmith, Pacific Glass Works
Tilton Charles H. toll collector, Clay St. Wharf, dwl 625½ Mission
Tilton Charles S. assistant, City and County Surveyor, dwl with Stephen S. Tilton
TILTON STEPHEN S. harbor commissioner, office 302 Montgomery, dwl cor Scott and Presidio Road
Timlin James, laborer, dwl 326 Tehama, rear
Timmerman L. Mrs. dwl 917 Clay
Timmins Francis, plasterer, dwl 108 St. Mark Place
Timmins Mary Miss, domestic, NE cor Folsom and Eleventh
Timmons Bartlett, driver with G. M. Garwood & Co. dwl NE cor Broadway and Kearny
Timny James, with Church & Clark, dwl N s Stevenson bet Seventh and Eighth
Tin, Youk & Co. (Chinese) groceries, 740 Sac
Tingley G. B. (widow) dwl 27 Hawthorne
Tingley Mary Miss, assistant teacher, Charlemagne College, dwl 27 Hawthorne
Tinis John, dwl What Cheer House
Tinkbam Myron M. driver with Bowen Bros. dwl 117 Natoma
Tinnaut William, artesian well borer, dwl SW cor Post and Powell
Tinney James, second steward steamer Orizaba
Tinnihan Bridget, domestic with M. B. Callahan, 431 Sixth nr Bryant
Tinsou Margaret Miss, domestic, 1105 Folsom
Tipper William, machinist, 120 Fremont, dwl Original House
Tipple William, watchman, City and County Hospital
Tipson W. H. printer, Eureka Typographical Union, 625 Merchant
Tirnin Michael, teamster, dwl W s Battery bet Broadway and Pacific
Tirrell C. & P. H. importers boots and shoes, 419 Clay, res South Weymouth, Mass
Tirrell Prince H. *(C. & P. H. Tirrell)* dwl 618 Market
Tisdale T. Rolph, clerk, dwl 136 Minna
Tisdall E. W. book keeper with Peter Donahue, dwl 511 Sixth
Tishler George, clerk, dwl 39 Second
Tishler H. Mrs. furnishing goods, 39 Second
Tishler Solomon, tailor, 610 Montgomery
Tissot Paul, salesman, 123 Montgomery, dwl N s Sixteenth bet Guerrero and Dolores
Tissott Jerome, lithographer with Britton & Co. dwl 533 Commercial
TITCOMB A. H. produce commission and agent Button & Blake's Fire Engines and Meneely's Bells, and supervisor First District, office 121 Clay, dwl 107 O'Farrell nr Powell
Titcomb Henry, dwl 759 Market
TITCOMB JOHN H. clerk Police Court, office City Hall first floor, dwl 759 Market
Tittel August, bricklayer, dwl E s Mission bet Fourteenth and Fifteenth
Tittel Augusta (widow) dwl 401 Bush
Tittel Charles, bricklayer, dwl 415 Bush
Tittel Conrad, real estate, dwl 401 Bush
Tittel Ernest, paper hanger, dwl 425 Bush
Tittel Frederick G. E. real estate, dwl 227 Kearny
Titus John T. plumber with McNally & Hawkins, dwl West End Hotel
Tiven Owen, steward, American Exchange
Tobelmann Frederick, clerk, NW cor Kearny and Geary
Tobey John, carpenter, dwl 513 Howard

TOBEY WILLIAM H. & CO. *(D. S. Cutter)* petroleum and mining agents, room 28 Government House, 502 Washington, dwl W s Sixteenth bet Howard and Folsom

Tobias Albert I. broker, dwl 423 Montgomery

Tobias M. cutter with S. Reinstein, dwl 3 Garden

TOBIN BROTHERS *(Thomas)* & DAVISSON *(Robert G.)* importers and jobbers fancy and millinery goods, SW cor Sacramento and Battery, dwl Cosmopolitan Hotel

Tobin Edward J. salesman with Tobin Bros. & Davisson

Tobin Edwin, packer with J. Chadbourne, dwl NW cor Broadway and Kearny

Tobin James, merchant, dwl Brevoort House

To·in Johanna Miss, domestic, 632 Post

Tobin John, dyer, Mission Woolen Mills

Tobin John, lab, dwl NE cor Harrison and Main

Tobin John, laborer, dwl 65 Stevenson

Tobin John, laborer with Hey & Meyn

TOBIN JOHN H. merchant tailor, 616 Sacramento, dwl Cosmopolitan Hotel

Tobin John W. mariner, dwl 247 Clementina

Tobin Mark, wool dealer, dwl S. F. & San José R. R. nr Mariposa

Tobin Patrick, laborer, dwl S s Perry bet Fourth and Fifth

Tobin Patrick, retortman, San Francisco Gas Co

Tobin Richard *(Conroy & T.)* dwl Ocean House Valley

TOBIN RICHARD, attorney at law, office room 17 NE cor Montgomery and Jackson, dwl 7 O'Farrell

Tobin Richard, clerk with H. M. Newhall & Co. bds Brooklyn Hotel

Tobin Richard, laborer, dwl 753 Mission, rear

Tobin Richard C. salesman, 634 Market, dwl 222 Montgomery

TOBIN ROBERT J. justice of the peace First Township, office 536 Pacific, dwl 1425 Stockton

Tobin Thomas, dwl Russ House

Tobin Thomas, gardener with Louis McLane, dwl 161 Silver

Tobriner M. book keeper with L. & M. Sachs & Co. dwl 320 Sutter

Toby John, laborer, dwl cor Mariposa and Indiana

TOBY *(Martin)* & DECKER *(Martin)* Club House, SW cor Third and King

TODD A. H. & CO. *(A. W. Cook)* produce commission merchants, 45 Clay cor Drumm, dwl 635 Second

Todd Amelia J. (widow) dwl 79 Clementina

Todd Charles, waiter, 712 Kearny

Todd F. A. San José messenger Wells, Fargo & Co

Todd George W. machinist, Miners' Foundry, dwl Union Hotel

Todd John, boots and shoes, office with H. M. Newhall & Co. dwl E s Beale bet Harrison and Bryant

Todd John, laborer, dwl N s Brannan bet Eighth and Ninth

Todd John M. attorney at law, office 422 Montgomery, dwl 314 Broadway

Todd John Mrs. boarding, N s Brannan bet Eighth and Ninth

Todman Robert, seaman, steamer Pacific

Toelken Hermann, cigars and tobacco, 58 Second and 538 Market

Tober John, laborer, dwl 122 Folsom

Toinet Pierre, with F. L. A. Pioche, 806 Stockton

Toklas Jacob, salesman, 308 Cal, dwl 220 Stevenson

TOKLAS, *(M.)* WISE *(Morris)* & CO. *(Solomon Sheyer)* importers and jobbers clothing and furnishing goods, 308 Cal, dwl 20 Sansom

Tolabella J. S. J. professor ancient and modern languages, St. Ignatius' College, S s Market bet Fourth and Fifth

Toland Frank, hostler with Craig, Golden & Yung, dwl 238 Jessie

TOLAND H. H. physician and surgeon, office 27–29 Naglee's Building cor Montgomery and Merchant, dwl 810 Jackson

TOLAND MEDICAL COLLEGE, H. H. Toland president, E s Stock bet Chestnut and Francisco

Toland *(Michael)* & Sharkey *(Edward)* draymen, NW cor California and Davis

Tolbart Henry (col'd) job wagon, NE cor Clay and Mont, dwl S s Greenwich bet Jones and Taylor

Tolbert James, coachman with Richard T. Maxwell, dwl 110 Shipley

TOLER WILLIAM P. clerk, U. S. Clothing Depôt, 34 California, dwl 452 Natoma

Tolle Henry A. dwl 30 Eddy

Tolle Matilda (widow) embroidering, dwl 30 Eddy

Tolles Harriet M. (widow) dwl 611 Harrison

Tolles *(William R.)* & Howard *(George)* stoves and tin ware, 724 Market

Tolley William W. bricklayer, dwl 22 Clara

Tollner Albert *(Waldenberg & T.)* dwl SE corner Battery and Pine

Tom Benton G. & S. M. Co. office 404 Front

Tombs A. M. dwl 24 South Park

Tomkins William H. carrier, Mining and Scientific Press, dwl 44 Jessie

Tomkinson James, Pennsylvania Livery Stable, 60 and 62 Minna, dwl 64 Minna

Tomler Hermann, shoe maker, dwl 5 Market

Tomlinson Charles A. carpenter with A. A. Snyder, dwl 271 Stevenson

Tomlinson John S. fish, 1 Washington Fish Market, dwl SW cor Washington and Drumm

Tomlinson William, fisherman, dwl SW cor Washington and Drumm

Tomlinson William, sawsmith with N. W. Spaulding, 113 Pine

Tommazini Joseph, with Frank Cereni, dwl 1308 Montgomery

Tompkins A. L. collector, office 302 Montgomery rm 9, dwl 626 California

Tompkins Benjamin G. peddler, dwl N s Brannan bet Sixth and Seventh

TOMPKINS *(Edward and William C.)* & CRANE *(A. M.)* attorneys at law, office 620 Merchant, res Oakland

Tompkins James, waterman, dwl 60 Minna

Tompkins M. M. exchange clerk, Bank of California, dwl SE cor Jones and Sutter

Tompkins Thomas B. butcher with Smith & Co. dwl Central Place

Tompkins Walter H. attorney at law, office 23 Exchange Building, bds Russ House

Tompkins William C. *(Tompkins & Crane)* attorney at law, office 620 Merchant, res Oakland

Tomkinson Joseph, clerk with Haynes & Lawton, dwl 925 Post

Tompson Charles, boatman, dwl 636 Pacific

Tonawanda G. & S. M. Co. office 702 Washington

Toner Eliza, confectionery, E s Sixth nr Brannan

Toner Henry, laborer, steamer Orizaba

Toner John, soap maker, S s Brannan bet Fifth and Sixth

Toner Margaret Miss, domestic, 1803 Stockton

Toner Mary Miss, domestic, 1607 Powell

Tong Chang (Chinese) washing, 715 Green

Tong Gin (Chinese) washing, 571 Mission

Tong Soong & Co. (Chinese) merchants, 732 Sac

Tong Wo & Co. (Chinese) merchants, 722 Sac

Tong Wo (Chinese) washing, 827 Pacific

Tong Yoong & Co. (Chinese) merchants, 730 Sac

Tonick David, clerk, 312 Com, dwl 639 Mission

Tonjes John, fruits, 529 Broadway

Tonine Jhaudinae, dwl 1013 Dupont

Tonkin Samuel, machinist, dwl 72 Minna

Toohill P. E. conductor, North Beach & M. R. R. Co. dwl 127 Clara

Tool Daniel, waiter, What Cheer House, dwl 54 Stevenson

Toole Christopher, carpenter, dwl 820 Green

Toole George, painter, dwl 12 Sutter
Toole Patrick, bricklayer, dwl 12 Sutter
Toomey J. J. clerk with T. N. Cazneau, dwl 160 Minna
Toomey John, clerk, dwl 266 Stevenson
Toomey J. W. carpenter, dwl 160 Minna
Toomey Patrick, helper, Union Foundry, dwl 112 Tehama
Toomey Richard, laborer, dwl Dolores Hall, W s Valencia nr Sixteenth
Toomey William, laborer, dwl 7 Natoma
Toomy Dennis, glass blower, Pacific Glass Works, dwl S s Mariposa nr Mississippi
Toothaker (J. H.) & Myers (Benjamin) blacksmiths, 116 Washington, dwl N side Pacific bet Hyde and Leavenworth
Toplitz Fabian, importer hats and millinery goods, 512 Sac, dwl N s Turk bet Jones and Leav
Topmann Conrad, dwl 228 Sutter
Topping Ambrose, teller with Wells, Fargo & Co. dwl 14 Kearny
Torento Elizabeth, Mrs. room 42 Government House, 502 Washington
Tormey George, teacher, dwl S s Filbert bet Mason and Taylor
Tormey John, waiter, Russ House
Tormey William, laborer, dwl S s Filbert bet Mason and Taylor
Tornado G. & S. M. Co. office 338 Montgomery
TORNING A. & T. house, sign, and ornamental painters, 528 California, dwl 810 Pacific
Torning Thomas A. (A. & T. Torning) dwl 930 Montgomery
Torpey Margaret, dwl 13 Laurel Place
Torpey Michael, shoe maker, dwl 206 First
Torpey Thomas, finisher, Mission Woolen Mills, dwl W s Shotwell bet Nineteenth and Twentieth
Torr George W. watchman, U. S. Branch Mint, dwl Federal Building
Torras V. printer, Eureka Typographical Union, 625 Merchant
Torre Paul, dwl 502 Stockton
Torrence John, carpenter, dwl 12 Quincy
Torrence John S. actor, dwl 12 Quincy
Torrens George, contractor, dwl N s Clay bet Hyde and Larkin
Torres B. dwl 448 Jessie
Torres Frank, handcartman, cor Sac and Front
Torres N. compositor, 417 Clay
Torres Vincent, compositor, dwl 1809 Stockton
TORREY ERASTUS N. carpenter, 439 Jackson, commissioner widening Kearny Street and supervisor Sixth District, dwl 516 Dupont
Torrey Henry, wood and coal, 8 Ecker
Torrey James M. toll collector, Vallejo St. Wharf, dwl 516 Dupont
Torrus Francisco, laborer, dwl 11 Ohio
Tostmann Henry, tobacco and cigars, 118 Second
Tothill John (Bayly & T.) dwl NW cor Powell and Union
Touaillon Jules, teacher private school, 911 Pacific
Touchard Gustave, secretary California Lloyds Marine Insurance and Rhodes' Diggings Quartz Mining Co. office 418 Cal, dwl 702 Lombard
Toudy Julius C. jeweler with Tucker & Co. dwl 248 Clementina
Toukin Samuel, machinist, Golden State Iron Works, dwl 72 Minna
Tourbous François, works with Arguelas Bernal
Tourny Julius, clerk with Adelsdorfer Bros. dwl 661 Howard
Tourny Louisa Miss, music teacher, dwl 661 Howard
Tourtellott Cassius, teamster, dwl 329 Pine
Tourtelott Emma (widow) dwl 816 Green
Toussantfort Borrey F. dairyman, Visitacion Valley
Toussin Emile, professor music, dwl 2 St. Mary
Toutdin Felix, saddle and harness, 533 Broadway
Tower Peter, express wagon, Brannan bet Fifth and Sixth

Toohill David, stair builder with B. H. Freeman & Co. dwl 49 Everett
Toohill Maurice, stair builder with B. H. Freeman & Co. dwl O'Farrell bet Jones and Leavenworth
Towan Stephen, clerk, dwl NE cor Union and Mason
Towle Charles B. accountant, dwl E s Dupont bet Francisco and Chestnut
Towle Frank B. milkman with S. C. & L. H. Talcott
Towle William J. clerk, 627 Commercial
Towmey, Julia, domestic with John Wiseman, E s Twelfth nr Folsom
Town H. A. carpenter, dwl Philadelphia House
TOWNE (James W.) & BACON (Jacob) book and job printers, 536 Clay op Leidesdorff, dwl N s Thirteenth bet Howard and Mission
Towne N. W. machinist, Union Foundry, dwl 11 Hunt
Towne William H. photographer with A. Edouart, 634 Washington, dwl 964 Mission
Towner Frederick, carpenter, dwl S s Brannan bet Fifth and Sixth
Towns W. E. porter, steamer Princess
Townsend Benjamin, captain Lucy Ann, dwl 327 Beale
Townsend Catherine, domestic, 863 Mission
Townsend Edward, carpenter, dwl N s Bryant bet First and Fremont
Townsend Edward, laborer, N s Valparaiso bet Mason and Taylor
Townsend Emanuel, cooper, Mason's Brewery
Townsend Frederick, accountant, Bank British Columbia, dwl 335 Pine
Townsend George, drayman wtth W. B. Lazalier, 401 Front
TOWNSEND JAMES B. attorney at law, room 5 NW cor Montgomery and Jackson
Townsend James S. clerk, U. S. Subsistence Department 208 Sansom, dwl 51 Tehama
Townsend Joseph, bricklayer, dwl 109 Sansom
TOWNSEND LOUIS R. architect, office 420 California, dwl 807 Stockton
Townsend Martin P. sail maker with James A. Wright, dwl 715 Howard
Townsend Sarah Miss, nurse, 12 Ritch
Townsend William T. carpenter, dwl 73 Natoma
Toy Daniel, merchant, dwl 209 Powell
Toy Harriet (widow) dwl 210 O'Farrell
Toy Lung & Co. (Chinese) washing, SW cor Mason and Kent
Tozer Charles H. physician, office 904 Kearny
Traass William, upholsterer, dwl 18 Sansom
Tracksler Robert, carpenter, dwl 504 Howard
Tracy Archibald, painter, dwl 315 First
Tracy Asa C. drayman, Pier 10 Stewart, dwl 49 Everett
Tracy C. C. civil engineer, dwl Oriental Hotel
Tracy Cornelius, laborer with C. Bernard, dwl 5 Sherwood Place
Tracy Daniel J. grainer and sign painter, dwl 315 First
Tracy Edward, workman, S. F. & P. Sugar Co. dwl Bryant nr Eighth
Tracy Edward, lumber wagon, Pier 2 Stewart, dwl 407 Natoma
Tracy Frances (widow) dwl 322 Sutter
Tracy James, boot maker, dwl 108 Pacific
Tracy James, carpenter, dwl 12 Sutter
Tracy James L. stevedore, dwl 754 Mission
Tracy John, liquors, 322 Pacific
Tracy John, plasterer, dwl 47 Jane
Tracy John J. boot maker, 231 Fourth, dwl 322 Pacific
Tracy Mary Miss, domestic, 617 Green
Tracy Mary (widow) dwl 140 Minna
Tracy Patrick, stone cutter, dwl 24 Sansom
Tracy P. W. boot maker, dwl 920 Kearny
Tracy Thomas, First St. Exchange Saloon, 132 First

Tracy William, baker, dwl 315 First
Trade Peter, laborer, dwl N s Stevenson bet Sixth and Seventh
Trainor Isabella Miss, domestic, 711 Taylor
Trainor James J. foreman with George D. Nagle
Trainor John, hostler, 532 California, dwl 16 Sutter
Trainor John, saddle and harness maker, 622 Mission
Trainor Joseph, laborer, dwl Dolores Hall W s Valencia nr Sixteenth
Trainor J. W. carpenter, dwl 165 Tehama
Trainor M. F. steward, Brooklyn Hotel
Trainor Patrick, laborer, dwl E s Cemetery Avenue bet Sutter and Post
Trainor Thomas, coachman, dwl 349 Fremont
Trainor Thomas, laborer with William Buckley
Trainor Thomas, seaman, dwl 106½ Clay
Tranfield Mrs. dwl W s Buchanan bet Bush and Sutter
Trant Mary (widow) dwl 361 Minna
Traute Mary (widow) dwl 561 Bryant
Trapani Salt Works Co. office 421 Washington
Trapnick Frederick, watch maker, 622 Clay
Trapp John, wheelwright with Kimball & Co. dwl 12 Dupont
Trapper William, maltster, Philadelphia Brewery
Trashar E. carpenter, bds Meyer's Hotel, 814 Mont
Trask Edward, physician, office Michel's Building, cor Montgomery and Market, dwl 226 Second
Trask Freeman, captain ship Amethyst, 212 Clay, dwl 28 Rousch
Trask James L. bds 704 Howard
TRASK JOHN B. physician, office and dwl 206 Kearny
Trask Josiah C. carpenter, dwl W s Folsom bet Twenty-Second and Twenty-Third
Trask Samuel, laborer, dwl W s Stewart nr Market
Trask Seth R. machinist, Miners' Foundry, dwl Bailey House
Traube Hartwig, watch maker, 717 Clay, dwl 821 Jackson
Traube Henry, watch maker, 717 Clay, dwl 821 Jackson
Trauger Lewis T. teamster with C. Patton, dwl nr St. Mary's College
Traunge Lewis, receiving clerk with Philip Caduc, dwl 29 Perry
Trautman John, farmer, dwl 323 Pine
Trautman William, cook, Occidental Hotel, dwl 36 Battery
Trautner August, tailor, dwl 409 Bush
Trautner Charles, hair dresser, 624 Washington
Trautner Gustave, tailor with J. L. Brooks, 710 Montgomery
Trautvetter Andrew, boot maker, 231 Fourth
Trautvetter Otto, carpenter, dwl W s Treat Avenue nr Twenty-Second
TRAVELLER'S INSURANCE COMPANY, Hartford, R. H. Magill general agent, L. B. Dell local agent, office 603 Commercial cor Mont
Traver G. W. (M. E. Traver & Brother) dwl 81 Natoma
Traver M. E. & Brother, general agents Eureka Wringer, 81 Natoma
Traver Oscar, fruit and vegetables, dwl 81 Natoma
Travers George, waiter, Russ House
Travers James R. carriage maker, dwl 1415 Kearny
Travers James R. hackman, Plaza
Travers John, compositor, dwl Original House
Travers Lawrence, workman with John Henry, dwl Dolores Hall
Traverse George W. boatman, dwl N s Union bet Montgomery and Sansom
Traverse Michael, engineer, dwl S s Francisco bet Taylor and Jones
Traves C. (Traves Freres) res Bordeaux, France
Traves Freres (J. and C.) importers wines and liquors and marble, off 606 Front, dwl 931 Clay
Travis George W. stock raiser, dwl Stevenson House

Traylor William W. general merchandise, 720 Montgomery, dwl 924 Jackson
Treadwell J. J. book keeper, 626 Clay, dwl Enterprise House
Treadwell John B. broom maker with Thomas Ward, 27 Drumm
TREADWELL J. P. attorney at law, office and dwl 528 Clay
TREADWELL (Leonard L.) & CO. (George R. Carter) importers and jobbers hardware and agricultural implements, NE cor Battery and California, warehouse SW cor Market and Fremont, dwl 204 Battery
Treanor James, workman, S. F. Gas Co. dwl W s Ritter nr Harrison
Treanton Paul, boatman, dwl NE cor Clay and Drumm
TREASURER CITY AND COUNTY, office 3 City Hall, first floor
TREAT GEORGE, farmer, S s Twenty-Fourth bet Folsom and Howard
Treat H. H. Mrs. principal Fairmount School, dwl San Bruno Road nr San Bruno School
Treat James W. painter, bds Meyer's Hotel
Treat John, farmer, dwl cor Twenty-Fourth and Potrero Avenue
Trebe Bruno, cook, Potrero Hotel, cor Louisiana and Sierra
Treier Theodore, tailor, 136 First
Trembath John (Sincock & T.) New Wisconsin Hotel, 411 Pacific
TREMONT HOUSE, E. S. Woolley proprietor, 418 and 420 Jackson
Tremper Peter, ship carpenter, nr cor Shasta and Michigan
Trendle Mary J. Miss, dress maker, dwl 30 Stone
Trengore Thomas C. machinist, 25 Natoma
Trenkle Emil, physician and surgeon, office 611 Washington, dwl 612 Mission
Trennese John, dwl 7 Pollard Place
Trenor Eustace, physician, office and dwl 202 Bush
Trent Mary (widow) dwl 561 Bryant
Trestler Vincent, cook with T. Adam, dwl 6 Auburn
Triber F. locksmith, 635 Howard
Tribon H. N. teamster, dwl E s Grove Avenue nr Bryant
Trickle Ezekiel C. fish, 19 Metropolitan Market, dwl Leavenworth bet Bush and Sutter
Tricou Henry P. teller with Parrott & Co. dwl E s Taylor bet Ellis and Eddy
Triebe Bruno, cook, dwl SW cor Louisiana and Sierra
Trieber Conrad, hardware, 302 Jackson, dwl 210 Jackson
TRIEST (Bernhard) & FRIEDLANDER (Herman) importers hats, caps, etc. 218 Battery, dwl 728 Vallejo
Trigge J. periodicals, etc. 611 Davis, dwl NE cor Montgomery and Broadway
Trim William, longshoreman, dwl 57 Jessie
Trim William T. laborer, dwl 1028 Market
Trimble John, book keeper with A. Crawford & Co. 27 Market
Trinder John H. with Russell & Erwin Man. Co. dwl 615 Bush
Trinidad & San José S. M. Co. office 404 Mont
Tripp George S. cooper, dwl 12 Sutter
Tripp G. F. dwl What Cheer House
Tripp John, stone mason, dwl 10 Mason
Tripp Lorett M. (widow) dwl 411 Tehama
Tripp P. F. (Powell & T.) dwl NE cor Third and Hunt
TRIPP (Silas G.) & ROBINSON (Thomas B.) pyrotechnists, E s Polk bet Green and Vallejo, office S s Washington opposite Post Office, dwl NW cor Broadway and Kearny
Tristram Simon, weaver, dwl SW cor Pac and San
Triunfo G. & S. M. Co. office 24 Government House, 502 Washington

Trobock N. importer California wine and brandy, 416 Davis
Trocen Pauline Mrs. dwl 632 Broadway
Trofatter George L. clerk with I. Friedlander, dwl 8 s Bush nr Octavia
Troll John, driver, Bavaria Brewery
Troll Matthew, brewer, Bavaria Brewery, dwl 1406 Kearny
Trolliet Henry P. porter with Lazard Freres, 115 Battery
Troost Charles, cigars and tobacco, 1322 Dupont
Trotter Lucy (colored, widow) dwl 1408 Dupont
Trouette Hypolite, physician, office 528 Clay, dwl N s Chestnut bet Dupont and Stockton
Trouin Theodore L. machinist, Pacific Foundry, dwl 249 Third
Troulson John, miller, Pacific Flour Mills
Troutman Fritz, cook, Occidental Hotel
Troutt H. J. M. carpets and paper hangings, 618 Market, dwl cor Steiner and Tyler
Trovieu Teresa, dwl 916 Montgomery
Troy Maggie Miss, domestic with Henry L. Kohn (No. 2)
Troy Patrick, laborer, dwl Sac bet Larkin and Hyde
Troy William H. dwl S s Precita Avenue nr Mission
Trozet John, laborer, Spring Valley W. W
Trüb Henry, bar keeper, dwl Summer nr Mont
Trub Rudolph, engineer, Philadelphia Brewery dwl 141 Minna
Truebody John, real estate, dwl 1000 Washington
Truell W. F. workman with Casebolt & Co
Truent Theodore, machinist, dwl 255 Third
Truesdell Orrin P. printer with Towne & Bacon, dwl 759 Howard
Truett F. G. Kellogg, Hewston & Co.'s Refinery, dwl NE cor Howard and Sixth
Truffo Fr. S.J. St. Ignatius' College, S s Market bet Fourth and Fifth
TRUMAN & CO. *(J. D. Burdick and W. B. Gould)* S. F. & San José R. R. express, office SE cor Front and Washington
Truman Henry, dwl 448 Clementina
Trumbull R. J. photographic views, 302 Montgomery room 2 third floor
Trumbull William, saddlery, NW cor Davis and Commercial
Trump William, packer with J. Chadbourne, dwl N s Vallejo bet Dupont and Stockton
Trustey Joseph A. (colored) dwl E s Bower Place
TRUWORTHY FRANCIS M. stencil plate cutter, 321 Front
Truworthy Thomas E. Capt. dwl NW cor Washington and Leavenworth
Tryon Charles W. carpenter, dwl W s Washington bet Howard and Mission
Tschantz *(Jacob)* Tenthorey *(Peter)* & Co. *(Edward Marcuet and Francis Mermoud)* pioneer macaroni and vermicelli manuf, 558 Mission
Tscher John, dish washer, dwl 431 Pine
Tsoy On (Chinese) washing, 14 Sutter
Tsun Kee (Chinese) washing, 815 Sacramento
TUBBS *(A. L.)* & CO. *(Hiram Tubbs)* ship chandlers and proprietors S. F. Cordage Manufactory Potrero, office 611 and 613 Front, and 349 Fremont cor Harrison
Tubbs Hiram *(Tubbs & Co.)* res Brooklyn, Alameda County
Tubbs Michael, dwl 117 Second
Tucholsky Gustave, chemist with M. Greenberg & Co. dwl 30 Tehama
Tucholsky Julius, porter, 317 Sacramento
Tuck Aaron, stevedore, dwl 14 Clay
Tuck John, dwl San Bruno Road 3 miles from City Hall
Tucker Edward, driver with A. Lusk & Co. dwl 913 Washington
Tucker E. S. carpenter, dwl Original House
Tucker Eugene, machinist, Miners' Foundry, dwl 275 Minna

Tucker Henry Capt. dwl 4 Clarence Place
Tucker Isaac N. gas fitter, dwl 121 Natoma
Tucker James, laborer with David B. Hughes, dwl 8 s Lombard bet Taylor and Jones
Tucker J. N. salesman with Thomas Day, 732 Montgomery, dwl 121 Natoma
Tucker John, plasterer, dwl 275 Stevenson
Tucker John, proprietor New York House, 840 Market
TUCKER *(John W.)* & CO. *(John H. Baird and George O. Ecker)* importers and retailers watches, diamonds, jewelry, etc. 505 Montgomery, dwl NW cor Harrison and Beale
Tucker Mary E. Miss, assistant teacher, Third St. School, dwl SW cor Stockton and Jackson
Tucker N. R. mason, dwl 508 Mason
Tucker Sarah Mrs. dwl 275 Minna
Tucker William, carpenter and builder, 614 Green
Tucker William W. carriage maker with M. P. Holmes, dwl 687 Market
Tue Hing (Chinese) washing, 408 O'Farrell
Tue Lung (Chinese) washing, 333 Sutter
Tueatulus Carlos, fish, 16 Washington Fish Market
Tufts Albert, wool puller, dwl 446 Brannan
Tufts Harry, carpenter. dwl 18 First
Tuggey William, laundryman, U. S. Marine Hospital, dwl Mississippi nr Solano
TUHTE *(Rudolph)* & REINERS *(Charles)* proprietors Pacific Exchange Hotel, 26 Stewart
Tuite Bernard, steward, American Exchange
Tukey Frank jr. delivery clerk, P. O. dwl 822 Clay
Tulare M. Co. office 1 Government House 502 Wash
Tuli Angelo, vegetable garden, Bay View
Tully Bridget Miss, domestic with Thomas L. Bridges, W s Eleventh bet Market and Mission
Tully *(Coleman)* & Durkin *(Edward)* produce dealers, 215 Clay, dwl 45 Natoma
Tully Elizabeth Miss, domestic, 113 O'Farrell
Tully Hugh, lab, dwl NW cor Eddy and Devisidero
Tully James, ship joiner with John G. North, Potrero
Tully John, drayman, dwl W s Sansom bet Union and Filbert
Tully Lucas, machinist, S. F. Cordage Factory, dwl nr S. F. Cordage Factory
Tully Peter, steamboat solicitor, dwl Manhattan Engine House
Tully Peter J. L. painter, dwl SE cor Bush and Powell
Tum Suden J. H. *(Henry Decker & Co.)* dwl 409 Montgomery
Tumpka Philip, liquor saloon, dwl SW cor Dupont and Broadway
Tung Chong & Co. (Chinese) grocers, 743 Sac
Tung Foo (Chinese) butcher, 729 Sacramento
Tung Thai (Chinese) washing, 827 Clay
Tung Tie & Co. (Chinese) dealers teas, 822 Dupont
Tung Yu & Co. (Chinese) merchants, 739 Sac
Tunnock Andrew, tobacconist, dwl 639 Mission
Tunsted Thomas *(McKenna & T.)* dwl W s Lagoon
Tuolumne Mountain G. & S. M. Co. office 22 Court Block
Tuomy Mary Miss, domestic, 1107 Folsom
Tupman Theodore, harness maker with Hyde & McClennen, 227 Montgomery
Turel Jean, with Lemoine, Gambert & Co. dwl 433 Pacific
Turk H. baker, dwl 827 Vallejo
Turkington Richardson R. machinist, Miners' Foundry, dwl 1517 Howard
Turkington William, foreman with Nathaniel Gray, dwl 1517 Powell
Turlach Frederick, watch maker with C. F. Mohrig, dwl NW cor Kearny and Sutter
Turley John *(Taylor & T.)* dwl 222 Fremont
Turn Verein Hall, Charles A. Janke proprietor, N s Bush bet Stockton and Powell
Turnack Joseph, engineer with E. T. Steen, dwl 44 Beale

Turnbull Benjamin C. clerk with Bigelow & Brother, 505 Montgomery, dwl 520 Minna
Turnbull John, carpenter, dwl SE cor Minna and Third
Turnbull Thomas *(England & T.)* dwl 456 Clementina
Turnbull *(Walter)* & Smith *(James)* book and job printers, 612 Commercial, dwl 108 Prospect Pl
Turner Albion G. Letter Department, Wells, Fargo & Co. dwl 608 Pine
Turner Andrew, lab, dwl E s Eleventh nr Mission
Turner Andrew, painter with A. & T. Torning, dwl 926 Montgomery
Turner Andrew J. salesman with Meiggs & Gawley, Pier 1 Stewart, dwl 320 Beale
Turner Anna Key (widow) private boarding, 933 Sacramento
Turner August, workman, S. F. & P. Sugar Co. dwl Heron nr Eighth
Turner *(Cephas jr.)* & Co. *(John E. Fitzpatrick)* Pioneer Soda Works, 529 Jackson, dwl 832 Cal
TURNER *(Charles O.)* & MARSH *(E. B.)* importers and jobbers wines and liquors, 221 California, dwl 16 Guy Place
Turner Daniel, plasterer, dwl 313 Geary, rear
Turner Daniel, Sacramento messenger, Wells, Fargo & Co. dwl 933 Sacramento
Turner Emma J. Mrs. (col'd) dwl 508 Green
Turner Frederick, porter with Falkenstein & Co. dwl cor Howard and Eighth
Turner George, attorney at law, office 15 and 16 Wells' Building 605 Clay, dwl Occidental Hotel
Turner George, mattress maker with J. Peirce, dwl N s Washington nr Powell
TURNER *(George R.)* & WATSON *(W. S.)* civil and mining engineers, 505 Montgomery cor Sacramento, dwl 1313 Vallejo
Turner Harry, artist with Silas Selleck, dwl 127 Montgomery
TURNER *(Horatio N.)* & RUNDLE *(Richard T.)* lumber, coal, and produce, cor Sixteenth and S. F. & San José R. R. dwl W s Folsom bet Sixteenth and Seventeenth
Turner Jerome, machinist, Vulcan Iron Works, dwl 634 Sutter
Turner Job, carpenter, dwl E s Selina Place
Turner John, carpenter, dwl 728 Market
Turner John, job wagon, NW cor Sutter and Kearny, dwl 12 Stockton Place
Turner John, laborer, dwl 14 Hunt
Turner John, Melter and Refiner's Department U. S. Branch Mint, dwl 229 Stewart
Turner John, molder, dwl 25 Louisa
Turner John, workman with H. Schwerin, Visitacion Valley
TURNER *(Joseph)* & LEWIS *(Edwin)* proprietors Empire House, S s Vallejo bet Front and Battery
Turner Joseph, brass finisher, dwl W s Haven Pl
Turner Lucy D. Miss (col'd) dwl SE cor Pacific and Jones
Turner Matthew, gilder with Jones, Wooll & Sutherland, dwl S s Bush nr Sansom
Turner Peter, folder, Chelsea Laundry
Turner Robert, pressman with John A. T. Overend, dwl Original House
Turner Robert D. butcher with F. Siebel, dwl 145 Fourth
Turner Seth, watchman, 431 Cal, dwl 415 Pine
Turner T. L. salesman, 418 Montgomery, dwl 7 Bagley Place
Turner William, carpenter, dwl 1021 Battery
Turner William, watch maker with Joseph McGregor, dwl 20 Dupont
Turner William H. machinist, Pacific Foundry, dwl 509 Leavenworth
TURNER *(William J.)* & HARVEY *(Alfred A.)* wood, coal, and brick, Robison's Wharf, E side Drumm bet Jack and Pac, dwl Robison's Wharf

Turney Andrew, book keeper with McAran & Kelly, dwl 603 Pine
Turney B. hostler, Omnibus R. R. Co
Turney J. H. bricklayer, dwl St. Lawrence House
Turney John H. teller with Donohoe, Kelly & Co. dwl SW cor Clay and Stockton
Turney T. hostler, Omnibus R. R. Co
Turot Phillip, shoe maker, dwl W s Bower Place
Turrell L. laborer, Spring Valley W. W
Turrell O. B. printer with Francis, Valentine & Co. dwl 938 Folsom
Tusarrat Jean, boot maker, 714 Pacific
Tustin Fernando, blacksmith with H. Casebolt & Co
Tustmann Louis, waiter, 614 Clay, dwl 612 Clay
Tuthill F. Estate of *(S. F. Bulletin Co.)* 620 Mont
Tutman Theodore, saddler, dwl 51 Natoma
Tuttle J. B. carpenter, bds Franklin Hotel SE cor Sansom and Pacific
Tuttle W. S. mariner, dwl 249 Stevenson
TWELFTH DISTRICT COURT, City Hall
Twelker Charles, bar keeper with Hauck & Marquard, dwl 22 Wells' Building
Twbig Mary Ann Miss, domestic, 421 Stevenson
Twiggs Susan (widow) lodgings, 834 Clay
Twilhill John, hostler, dwl 177 Jessie
Twichell William L. physician, dwl S s Sixteenth bet Valencia and Mission
Twing Daniel H. *(Thomas & T.)* dwl 468 Jessie
Twing Nathaniel, carriage trimmer, 579 Market, dwl 606 Kearny
Twohig David, hostler, Bay View Park
Twohig Jeremiah, foreman, 655 Sacramento, dwl 11 O'Farrell Alley
Twombly Charles H. real estate, dwl 816 Clay
Tylarker William, hackman, Plaza
Tyler Asher, dwl N s Lombard bet Mason and Taylor
TYLER BROTHERS *(Charles W. and Edward S.)* books, stationery, etc. 632 Washington, dwl 1006 Clay
Tyler Charles, dwl 657 Howard
TYLER CHARLES M. & Co. *(Samuel Tyler)* lumber and produce, Dewey's Wharf foot Third and real estate, etc. 626 Clay, dwl 1021 Bush
Tyler Edward S. *(Tyler Brothers)* dwl 1006 Clay
Tyler *(George W.)* & Cobb *(M. G.)* attorneys at law, office 31 Court Block 636 Clay, dwl cor Vallejo and Lincoln
Tyler George W. *(Forsaith & T.)* dwl 222 Stock
Tyler John, cook, Magnolia Restaurant, dwl 159 Silver
Tyler Samuel *(Charles M. Tyler & Co.)* dwl 1021 Bush
TYLER S. H. & CO. *(William J. Smith)* Eagle Salt Mills 110 Fremont, office and depôt SE cor California and Front, dwl 910 Howard
Tyler William M. printer, dwl 938 Folsom
Tynan William D. tailor, 125 Bush
Tyrell *(Jacob)* & Merritt *(R. D.)* Oakland Express, Oakland Ferry, Davis nr Broadway
Tyrrall Joseph, laborer, dwl 1121 Folsom
Tyrrell Michael, deck hand, steamer Julia
Tyson Jacob, express wagon, cor Clay and Sansom, dwl 4 Scotland

U

UBRICH Charles H. drayman, 104 Commercial, dwl 60 Everett
Ueffenger George, cabinet maker, dwl 121 Prospect Place
Uhl Adolph, shoe maker with Philip Schwerdt, 708 Market
Uhl George, shoe maker with Philip Schwerdt, 708 Market
Uhl X. Frank, butcher, dwl W s Sixth bet Harrison and Bryant
Uhler C. with Pease & Grimm, dwl 652 Market
Uhler J. Clein, dwl 652 Market

Uhley Fred, mariner, dwl S s Pacific nr Leav
UHLFELDER *(Samuel)* & CAHN *(Leopold)*
(and A. Blockman and Israel Cahn) importers
and jobbers foreign and domestic dry goods, 309
and 311 Sacramento, res New York
Ubrig Christian A. storage. Lazard Freres' Ware-
house cor Battery and Filbert, dwl 930 Howard
UHRLANDT HERMAN E. post sutler, Fort Point
Ule Henry, seaman, dwl 20 Commercial
Uleau Henry, clerk, Assistant U. S. Quartermaster,
dwl 516 Third
Ulerich Diedrich, laborer, Bay Sugar Refinery, dwl
813 Battery
Ulhorn Jno. Frederick, clerk, Quartermaster's De-
partment U. S. A. dwl 115 Stockton
Ulhorn J. S. dwl 115 Stockton
Ullman Daniel, apprentice with Thomas O. Malley,
646 Market
Ullmann M. real estate, office 423 Washington
Ulm Adam, baker with Charles Frank
Ulmer Alexander, drayman, cor California and Bat
Ulmer Moses, cigars and tobacco, 605 Kearny, dwl
323 Pine
Ulrich Jacob, barber, dwl 507 Dupont
Ulrich Mary Ann (widow) dwl 130 St. Mark Place
Ulricht Charles, drayman, 228 Front
Ulshofer George, milk ranch, cor Douglas and
Seventeenth
Umbsen Henry, groceries and liquors, NE cor Fol-
som and Moss, dwl 41 Moss
Unal Pierre, gardener, Old San José Road nr In-
dustrial School
Uncelin Edward, L'Ermitage Saloon, junction Mar-
ket and Dolores
UNCLESS THOMAS T. proprietor Portsmouth
House, NW cor Clay and Brenhan Place
Unckless T. T. keeper Point Bonita Light House
UNCLE SAM S. M. CO. office 519 Jackson
Underbill G. E. furniture and bedding, 624 Market,
dwl 216 Stockton
UNDERHILL JACOB & CO. importers and
jobbers hardware, 118 and 120 Battery, dwl
Lick House
Underhill J. I. lamplighter, S. F. Gas Co. dwl S s
Fern Avenue nr Polk
Underwood Isaac, carpenter, dwl 1116 Pacific
Underwood Warner L. attorney at law, room 7
302 Mont, dwl NE cor Fillmore and McAllister
UNDERWRITERS—Bordeaux, Henry Schröder
& Co. 811 Montgomery; Boston, T. H. & J.
S. Bacon 308 Front; Bremen, C. F. Mebius 223
Sacramento; French, J. E. Réne 716 Montgom-
ery; Hamburg, Ziel, Bertheau & Co. 122 Cali-
fornia; London (Lloyds), Falkner, Bell & Co.
430 California; New York, A. T. Fletcher 308
Front; Marine Board 318 California
Ungemach John M. cabinet maker, 146 Third
Unger Adolph *(Unger & Bro.)* dwl 26 Rincon Pl
Unger *(Herman)* & Brother *(Adolph Unger)* im-
porters and jobbers hats and caps, 412 Sacra-
mento, res New York
Unger Herman, miller, dwl 939 Folsom
Unger Marcus, tailor, 748 Market
Union Brewery, A. Kosta & Bro. proprietors, Clem-
entina bet Fourth and Fifth
Union City Flour Mills, I. H. Ham agent, office 211
Clay
UNION CITY LINE PACKETS, H. D. Eller-
horst & Co. agents, office 64 Clay
UNION COLLEGE, Dr. R. Townsend Huddart
Principal, 501 Second cor Bryant
UNION FOUNDRY, H. J. Booth & Co. proprie-
tors, NE cor First and Mission
Union Homestead Association, office 302 Mont
UNION INSURANCE COMPANY, Caleb T. Fay
president, Charles D. Haven secretary, office
416 California
UNION MARITIME SOCIETY (France) O. Chau-
vin agent, office 730 Montgomery

Union Mattole Oil Co. (Humboldt Co.) office 517
Jackson
Union Packet Line to Petaluma, T. F. Bayliss &
Co. agents, office foot Commercial
Union Salt Works, A. B. Winegar proprietor, 22
and 24 California, office 210 Front
Union Soap Manufactory, Henry Heilmann pro-
prietor, S s Brannan bet Fifth and Sixth
UNION STATE CENTRAL COMMITTEE, Al-
fred Barstow secretary, office 24 Mont Block
UNION THEATER (Bert's New Idea) S s Com-
mercial bet Kearny and Dupont
Union Warehouse, NW cor Battery and Union,
Koopmanschap & Co. proprietors
UNITED ANAHEIM WINE GROWERS' AS-
SOCIATION, depôt 321 Montgomery
United Ledges G. & S. M. Co. office 606 Merchant
United Reese River S. M. Co. office 402 Front
UNITED STATES ARMY, headquarters Military
Division of the Pacific 418 California
UNITED STATES ARMY OFFICERS AND
HEADQUARTERS, Dept. California 742 Wash
UNITED STATES ARMY, Commissary of Sub-
sistence, office 418 California, depôt 208 Sansom
UNITED STATES ARMY, paymaster, office 742
Washington
UNITED STATES ARMY, Quartermaster's De-
partment, office 742 Washington
UNITED STATES ARMY, Subsistence Depart-
ment Division of the Pacific, office 418 Cal
UNITED STATES ASSESSOR (internal revenue)
office NW cor Commercial and Battery
UNITED STATES ASSISTANT TREASURER,
office United States Branch Mint, 608 Com
UNITED STATES BARGE (revenue service) office
SW cor Pacific and Davis
UNITED STATES BRANCH MINT (superin-
tendent) office 612 Commercial
UNITED STATES CIRCUIT COURT (clerk)
office 6 United States Court Building
UNITED STATES CLOTHING DEPOT, 34 Cal
UNITED STATES COAST SURVEY, office Cus-
tom House third floor
UNITED STATES COLLECTOR (internal rev-
enue) office NW cor Commercial and Battery
UNITED STATES COLLECTOR (port San Fran-
cisco) office Custom House
UNITED STATES COMMISSIONER, office SW
cor Montgomery and Jackson
UNITED STATES COURT BUILDING, SW cor
Montgomery and Jackson
UNITED STATES CUSTOM HOUSE, NW cor
Washington and Battery
UNITED STATES DISTRICT ATTORNEY,
office 3 and 4 SW cor Montgomery and Jackson
UNITED STATES DISTRICT COURT (clerk)
office 17 United States Court Building
UNITED STATES ENGINEER'S OFFICE, 37
Montgomery Block
United States G. & S. M. Co. (Reese River) office
302 Montgomery
United States Hotel, 304 Beale
United States Hotel, P. C. Curley proptr, 706 Bat
UNITED STATES INDIAN AGENCY (Califor-
nia District) office 423 Washington
UNITED STATES INSPECTOR BOILERS,
office Custom House third floor
UNITED STATES INSPECTOR HULLS, office
Custom House third floor
UNITED STATES INSPECTOR INTERNAL
REVENUE, Pacific Coast, office NW corner
Battery and Commercial
UNITED STATES INTERNAL REVENUE,
agent, office NW cor Battery and Commercial
UNITED STATES LAND OFFICE, 625 Merch
UNITED STATES LIGHT-HOUSE (Department
Pacific Coast) office Custom House third floor
UNITED STATES MAIL AGENT, office Post-
Office, basement

UNITED STATES MARINE CORPS, assistant quartermaster, office 516 Third
UNITED STATES MARINE HOSPITAL, Rincon Point nr Main
UNITED STATES MARSHAL, office SW cor Montgomery and Jackson
United States Mining Co. office 7 Government House
UNITED STATES NAVAL OFFICE, C. H
UNITED STATES NAVY AGENT, office 432 Cal
UNITED STATES PACIFIC TELEGRAPH CO. James Gamble general supt, off 2 Armory Hall
UNITED STATES PENSION AGENT (Army) office 625 Merchant
UNITED STATES POST-OFFICE, NW cor Washington and Battery
UNITED STATES RECEIVER PUBLIC MONEYS, office 625 Merchant
United States Restaurant, Russell & Co. proprietors, 507 and 509 Clay
UNITED STATES SANITARY COMMISSION (California Branch) off SE cor Mont and Pine
UNITED STATES SPECIAL AGENT, office Custom House third floor
UNITED STATES SUPERVISING AGENT STEAMBOATS, office C. H. third floor
UNITED STATES SURVEYOR-GENERAL, office 808 Montgomery
UNITED STATES SURVEYOR PORT, office Custom House second floor
UNIVERSAL LIFE INSURANCE CO. H. S. Homans agent, 609 Clay
Upp John, clerk, dwl 13 Second
Upper Lander G. & S. M. Co. office 36 Exchange Building
Uppington James T. carriage trimmer with Black & Saul, dwl W s Russ bet Howard and Folsom
UPSON LAUREN, U. S. Surveyor-General California, office 808 Montgomery, dwl 706 Cal
Upstone John *(Nutting & U.)* 123 Bush
Upton Eugene A. printer with Towne & Bacon, dwl S s Washington bet Taylor and Jones
Upton James, bar keeper with Joseph Goetz, dwl 631 Davis
Upton John P. printer, Alta Job Office, dwl S s Fella Place nr Powell
UPTON MATHEW G. Editorial Department Alta California, dwl S s Folsom bet Eleventh and Twelfth
Urbain Roy, workman with Peter Casson & Co. nr Bay View Park
Urbais John, carpenter, dwl San Bruno Road op Flume House
Urban Ferdinand, jeweler with Lemme Bros. dwl SW cor Bush and Kearny
Urban Joseph, manufacturer violins, guitars, etc. SW cor Kearny and Bush, dwl 401 Bush
Urband *(Richard)* & Co. *(Henry Jurgans)* groceries and liquors, NW cor Howard and Fifteenth, res Mexico
Uri Felix, butcher, 16 and 17 New Market, dwl 27 Turk
Urie James S. pilot, office 5 Vallejo, dwl W s Jones bet Lombard and Chestnut
Urmy John B. captain Co. C Second Infantry C. V. Presidio
Urquhart James, operator, California State Telegraph Co. dwl SW cor Montgomery and Pine
Urquhart S. F. lamps and oils, 512 Sansom, dwl 921 Powell
Urton William L. wharfinger, Fillmore St. Wharf, dwl Allen nr Hyde
Uszynski B. Mrs. hairbraiding, 21 Geary
Uszynski John, watch maker and jeweler, 406 Kearny, dwl 21 Geary
Utica Gold M. Co. (Angels Camp) office 3 Odd Fellows' Hall
Utt Henry, dwl What Cheer House
Uzavich John, restaurant and liquors, 621 Davis, dwl 621 Davis

Uzeta Conrado, compositor, La Voz DeMejico, dwl 522 Commercial
Uzeta Eugenio musician, dwl N s Sixteenth bet Guerrero and Dolores

V

VACHE P. seaman, Lafayette H. & L. Co. No. 2
Vacinty José, cook, dwl cor Ecker and Mission
Vagts George, porter, 123 California *(and Dixon & V.)* dwl 1428 Stockton
Vail Charles H. insurance agent, dwl 1133 Folsom
Vail James N. workman with E. E. Moore, dwl SW cor Twenty-First and Florida
Vaillant Charles, dwl 1112 Stocton
Vaillant Clark, dwl 19 Dupont
Vaillant Edmund, carpenter, dwl 6 Lafayette Place
Vaillant J. office 728 Montgomery
Valadie François, restaurant and liquors, 721 Pacific
Valulee Theresa (widow) dwl 736 Pacific, rear
Valdavice Ricardo, laborer, dwl NE cor Kearny and Broadway
Vale Charles, blacksmith with Kimball & Co. dwl 12 Turk
Vale Charles jr. oil and lamps, 802 Dupont, dwl 12 Turk
Vale William, mining secretary, office 36 Exchange Building, dwl 12 Turk
Valein Margaret (widow) dwl 227 Fourth
Valencia Candelario, dwl SW corner Guerrero and Sixteenth
Valencia José, farmer, dwl corner Sixteenth and Dolores
Valente Louis *(Pagannini & V.)* dwl 523 Bdwy
Valentine Andrew, vegetable garden nr Bay View Park
Valentine Andrew W. teamster with John Center, NW cor Sixteenth and Folsom
Valentine Anton, carpenter, N s Sutter nr Kearny
Valentine C. machinist, dwl 39 First
Valentine Charles, lodgings, 726 Pacific
Valentine Charles, shoe maker with H. M. Beers, 313 Pine
Valentine Charles E. batteryman, California State Telegraph Co. dwl 507 Montgomery
Valentine Emanuel, commission merchant, 112 and 114 California, dwl 30 South Park
Valentine Frederick *(Valentine & Bro.)* 7 First
Valentine *(John)* & Brother *(Frederick)* bottling establishment, 7 First
Valentine John, bds 336 Bush
Valentine John, dwl cor Twentieth and Harrison
Valentine John, produce, dwl 333 East
Valentine John Y. Alta Copper Mine, office 728 Montgomery, dwl 46 Sutter
Valentine Levina R. (widow) dwl N s Hayes near Octavia
Valentine Matthew, helper, Vulcan Iron Works, dwl St. Charles Hotel
Valentine S. D. *(Francis, V. & Co.)* dwl 809 Mission
Valentine T. B. office 517 Clay
Valentine William, machinist, dwl 569 Mission
Valentine William T. brass molder, dwl Howard Engine House
Valenzuela Isabella (widow) dwl 10 Auburn
Valette Emile, driver with Amadee Leroux, dwl 103 Dupont
Vallerga Bartholomew, laborer. dwl 427 Filbert
Vallely Edward, carpenter, dwl S s Montgomery Court nr Montgomery
Valley Forge G. & S. M. Co. office 36 Exchange Building
Valley Forge Tunnel Co. office 36 Exchange Bdg
VALLIANT ADAM C. dealer hay, S s Brannan nr Fourth
Valliant Joseph B. clerk, S s Brannan nr Fourth
Valory Louis *(Bellanger & V.)* dwl 530 Clay

Valverde S. M. Co. (Reese River) office 405 Front
VAN ALEN WILLIAM K. agent Mutual Life Insurance Co. office 6 Government House, 502 Washington, dwl 115 Dupont
Van Allen L. E. (widow) dwl 442 Greenwich
Van Antwerp Annie (widow) dwl 17 Howard Court
Van Antwerp Jacob F. carpenter, dwl 116 Sansom
Van Arman *(John)* & Newman *(B. B.)* attorneys at law, Old Hall Records cor Washington and Brenham Place, dwl Occidental Hotel
Van Bergen Augustus H. bar keeper, Old Corner, 516 Montgomery
VAN BERGEN JOHN & CO. *(Nicholas Van Bergen)* importers and jobbers wines and liquors, 524 Washington
Van Bergen Nicholas *(John Vanbergen & Co.)* 524 Washington, dwl 518 Third
Van Brock Frederick, wood turner, 520 Stockton
Van Brock Henry, cigar maker, dwl 520 Stockton
Van Brunt H. C. carpenter, 114 Dupont, dwl cor Valencia and Market
VAN BRUNT R. N. secretary Occidental Insurance Co. office SW cor Montgomery and California, dwl 1310 Pine
Van Buskirk Harriet (widow) dwl 264 Jessie
Van Buskirk Howard, dock builder, dwl Salmon Place nr Larkin
Van Court James E. book keeper with William Shew, dwl 216 Stevenson
Van Court John F. carriage trimming, 119 Pine, dwl 109 Pine
Van Court John W. shoe maker with Thomas Dolliver, dwl E s Laguna nr McAllister
Van Crombugghe Alfred, clerk, Market St. R. R. Co. dwl 27 Kearny
Van DeCasteele X. lithographer with Britton & Co
Van Denburgh Alison, dentist with D. Van Denburgh, dwl 200 Stockton
VAN DENBURGH D. dentist, office 134 Geary, dwl N s Folsom bet Eighth and Ninth
Van Derheyden Richard, longshoreman, dwl Sansom bet Vallejo and Green
Van Deursen Ann (widow) dwl with W. Drury, E s Valencia bet Sixteenth and Seventeenth
Van Deusen M. M. broker, office 320 Montgomery, dwl 729 California
Van Deventer Frank, merchant, dwl S side Seventeenth bet Guerrero and Dolores
Van Doren Jonathan E. teller with Banks & Co. 513 Montgomery, dwl American Exchange
VAN DOREN JOSEPH, groceries and meat market, NE cor Bush and Mason, dwl 627 Union
Van Doren Samuel M. clerk, 105 Battery, dwl 504 Second
Van Dorn A. civil engineer, dwl Oriental Hotel
Van Dorn Charles H. drayman, dwl 11½ Howard Court
Van Duerson John H. blacksmith with Casebolt & Co. dwl cor Hyde and Tyler
Van Dusen Edward, painter, dwl 439 Jackson
Van Dusen Hubert, milkman with Henry H. Edmunds
Van Dusen William, milkman with J. W. Cudworth
Van Duyn Edward C. dwl 231 Stevenson
Van Duyn Theodore D. clerk, dwl NE corner Bush and Mason
Van Dyke James, carpenter, dwl 132 Sutter
VAN DYKE WALTER, attorney at law, office 31 and 32 Court Block, 636 Clay, dwl 11 First Avenue nr Sixteenth
Van Dyke W. B. dwl Tehama House
Van Eps Frederick, musician, dwl SW cor Dupont and Broadway
Van Geistefield H. Louis, shaving saloon, 647 Pacific, dwl 533 Broadway
Van Gulpen Carlton, saloon, 606 Greenwich
Van Hagen I. P. dwl 964 Mission
Van Hagan James B. dwl 964 Mission

Van Hess Christopher, carpenter, dwl 34 Silver
Van Horn Jerome B. printer, dwl Bailey House
Van Housen William, Banner Meat Market, NE cor Eddy and Mason
Van Hovenburg George, watchman with Wilson & Stevens, dwl Potrero
Van Laak L. broom manufactory, 14 Drumm
Van Ness Cornelius, manufacturer blacksmiths' bellows, 30 California
Van Ness Henry, pilot, 895 Front, dwl 826 Pacific
Van Ness J. P. mason and contractor, dwl 747 Howard
Van Noorden William, with J. Steinmann, 325 Pine
Van Norden R. T. *(George L. Kenny & Co.)* 608 Montgomery
Van Nostrand Daniel C. clerk, Pacific Mail S. S. Co. dwl 15 Park Avenue
Van Orden David T. mason, dwl 1520 Stockton
Van Pelt B. D. Capt. dwl 428 Bush
Van Pelt Cornelius V. clerk, C. S. Navigation Co. Broadway Wharf, dwl 917 Clay
Van Pelt David Capt. superintendent C. S. Navigation Co.'s Repair Shop, dwl 1010 Washington
Van Pelt Mary A. (widow) boarding and lodging, 112 Mason
Van Pelt Peter, book keeper with H. M. Newhall & Co. dwl 909 Bush
Van Pelt William B. collector with W. H. Miller, dwl 1010 Washington
Van Pick J. Madame, milliner, 42 Geary
Van Prang Samuel, book keeper with Ciprico & Cook, Cosmopolitan Hotel
Van Read James H. real estate agent, 7 Montgomery Block, dwl 908 Howard
Van Riper James, carpenter and builder, dwl 906 Jackson
Van Schaack Chancy P. commission and auctioneer, 706 Kearny, dwl SW cor Mont and Broadway
Van Schaack William, carpenter, Market St. R. R. Co. dwl Ridley nr Brannan
Van Straaten Benjamin E. *(Bender & Co.)* dwl SE cor Hayes and Laguna
Van Straaten Jacob H. drugs and medicines, 309 Davis, dwl New York Hotel
Van Syckle Albert S. assistant impost book keeper, Custom House, dwl 247 Tehama
Van Syckle Renslaer W. messenger, Custom House, dwl 247 Tehama
Van Tanten Evariste, with Belloc Frères, dwl 535 Clay
Van Tassel Alexander, boiler helper, Pacific Foundry, dwl 60 Clementina
Van Tassell Philip, engineer, stm Moses Taylor, dwl 342 Third
Van Tassell Theodore, salesman with Young & Co. dwl 208 Stockton
Van Velsor Jessie H. with George Morrow, dwl N s Filbert bet Mason and Taylor
Van Vleck *(Durbin)* & Keith *(William)* wood engravers, 611 Clay, dwl NW corner Folsom and First
Van Vorhees William *(McKinstry & V.)* dwl 933 Sacramento
Van Voorhees George, special policeman, Bella Union, dwl 815 Kearny
Van Wie Arie, carpenter, dwl 31 Kearny
Van Winkle Edward, pattern maker, Union Foundry, dwl 141 Silver
VAN WINKLE I. S. & CO. importers iron, steel, and coal, NE corner Battery and Bush, dwl 29 Silver
Van Winkle Matthew, with G. B. & I. H. Knowles, 17 California
Van Wyck Peter S. book keeper with W. K. Van Alen, dwl 1009 Powell
Van Wyck Thomas W. bar keeper with W. K. Van Alen, dwl 1009 Powell
Van Zandt J. W. physician and druggist, 629 Front, dwl NE cor Geary and Larkin

Vance Isaac H. waterman, 609 Market
Vance Joseph, with Barton & Bro. 218 Sacramento
Vance Katy Miss, domestic with Alfred Clark, dwl 1028 Kearny
Vance William, conductor, North Beach & M. R. R. Co. dwl 1810 Taylor
Vanden Bergh John P. P. physician, office NW cor Leavenworth and Sutter
Vander William, cook, 546 Clay
Vandercook Frank A. merchant, dwl NW cor Steiner and Fulton
Vandercook Robert, carpenter, dwl NW cor Steiner and Fulton
Vanderhoof Hannah (widow) dwl with George L. Kenny
Vanderpool Jacob (col'd) porter, 122 Battery, dwl 910 Powell
Vanderslice James, silversmith with Vanderslice & Co. dwl 5 Auburn
Vanderslice W. K. & Co. manufacturers silverware, etc. 810 Montgomery, dwl NE cor Washington and Powell
Vandervoort James, engineer, dwl E s Jansen bet Greenwich and Lombard
Vandervoort *(James A.)* & Co. *(N. P. Copp)* fruits and groceries, 30 Third, dwl 30 Langton
Vandervoort J C. dwl 641 Folsom
Vandervoort John D. salesman, 216 Battery, dwl 345 Minna
VANDEWATER R. J. merchant, office 540 Clay, dwl SE cor Mason and Filbert
Vangon August, billiard saloon, 611 Pacific
Vanier Charles, agent with D. Ghirardelli & Co. dwl SW cor Kearny and Pine
Vaninhoff Madame, dwl 52 Government House 502 Washington
Vanna Mathalia, molder, dwl 849 Clay
Vanston Thomas, Vanston's Dining Rooms, 42 Mkt
VANTINE J. & CO. *(David Dick)* produce commission merchants, SE cor Clay and Davis, dwl 325 Dupont
Varat Maurice, cook, 647 Com, dwl Miles Court
Varenne Madame, dress maker, 828 Washington
Varian Catharine Miss, domestic, 812 Bush
Varicas Lionel, engineer, dwl 752 Harrison
VARIETIES (weekly) J. Walter Walsh proprietor, office 517 Clay
Varndell William P. restaurant and chop house, 2197 Powell
Varnet Julius, employé, Metropolitan Restaurant, 715 Mont, dwl Filbert bet Dupont and Kearny
Varney L. painter, dwl Hall Court
Varney Lebbeus H. house carpenter, dwl 611 Powell
Varney Robert, dwl E s First Avenue nr Sixteenth
Varney Thomas, real estate and mining machinery, office 127 First, dwl 1012 Clay
Varweack Charles, express wagon, cor Mason and Broadway
Vasa Giovanni, fisherman, 18 Italian Fish Market
Vasconcellos J. J. *(Howland & V.)* dwl Mission bet Third and Fourth
VASSAULT FERDINAND, real estate agent, office 604 Merchant
Vasselin Hypolité, toys and fancy goods. 22 Fourth
Vasselin Jules, cabinet maker, dwl N s Berry nr Clara
Vater J. cook, Original House Restaurant
Vaughan William, mariner, dwl 903 Sacramento
Vaughn Edward, carpenter, dwl 759 Mission
Vaughn George, carpenter, dwl 570 Howard
Vaughn J. H. with I. D. Thompson, dwl 22 Mont
Vaughn Michael, cook, Miners' Restaurant, dwl 310 Vallejo
Vaughn William, laborer, dwl 255 Beale
Veasey *(Perley)* & Robinson *(Ruel)* Taylor St. Mkt, SE cor Taylor and Clay, dwl 1123 Taylor
Veatch James J. Coiner's Department U. S. Branch Mint
Veatch S. M. Co. office 712 Montgomery

Veeder P. V. principal City College, SE cor Stockton and Geary
Vega Placidi Gen. dwl Brenham Place W s Plaza
Veiger Lizzie (widow) dwl with Charles Bibend S s Twelfth bet Howard and Folsom
Veiller August, dwl 735 Folsom
Veiller James & Louis, wines and liquors, 606 Front, dwl 735 Folsom
Veiller Louis *(J. & L. Veiller)* dwl 735 Folsom
Veirs Jesse, accountant, dwl N s Allen nr Hyde
Veitch Perry, boot maker, 264 Third
Velasco Florenzio, dwl W s Havens Place
Velbert Peter H. groceries and liquors, SW cor Howard and First
Vellimiro C. with Rudolph Hochkofler, 208 Front, dwl 1621 Powell
Vellinger George, saddler with Main & Winchester, dwl Commercial nr Davis
Velly Louis D. clerk with A. E. Sabatie & Co. 617 and 619 Sansom
Venard Auguste, mattress maker, 404 Third
VENARD P. G. Chartres coffee, spices, etc. 625 and 627 Front, dwl 512 Union
Venassier Emile, dwl 8 s Lombard bet Powell and Mason
Vencel Lewis, dwl SE cor Vallejo and Montgomery
Vencel R. C. Mrs. dwl SE cor Vallejo and Mont
Venerhorn Frederick, machinist, dwl 511 Mission
Venner Wolf, job wagon, dwl 79 Stevenson
Venney John, butcher, 546 Clay, dwl 7 Central Place
Vensano Alexander, accountant with F. Daneri & Co. dwl 1115 Montgomery
Veoels Henry, waiter, dwl 315 Bush
VerMehr. Alfred, clerk with W. B. Johnston, dwl 1213 Pine
Verburgh Hendrick, ship carpenter, dwl Old Sailor's Home 18 Davis
Verbowe Benoit, tailor, dwl 1104 Washington
Verdinal D. F. *(J. M. & D. F. V.)* attorney at law, office 22 Court Block 636 Clay, dwl 273 Minna
VERDINAL J. M. & D. F. attorneys at law, office 22 Court Block 636 Clay, dwl 1234 Dupont
VERDIER *(Emile)* KAINDLER *(Gustave)* SCELLIER *(Louis)* & CO. *(Adolphe E. Lelièvre)* importers and wholesale and retail dry goods and millinery goods, 633 and 635 Clay, res Paris
VERDIER ERNEST, mineral water, 311 Dupont, dwl 609 Sacramento
Verdier Joseph, laborer with G. Venard, 625 Front
Verdier Pauline Mme, French milliner, 609 Sac
Verdiguel Miguel, printer, La Voz de Mejico, dwl N s Berry nr Clara
Verdin Adolph, French boot maker, 803 Montgomery
Vermehren Theodore H. A. porter Society California Pioneers, dwl Pioneer Hall
Vermilya Armenia (widow) dwl 31 Natoma
Vernon Charles, collector, dwl 812 Stockton
Vernon Flouring Mills, J. P. Raymond & Co. agents, office 119 Clay
Vernon Joseph P. salesman with Geo. C. Johnson & Co. dwl 72 Natoma
Vernon Joseph W. painter, dwl 759 Folsom
Verriez Albert Starr *(V. J. Blanckeart & Co.)* dwl 911 Dupont
Vervliet Charles, laborer, 53 Third
Very James H. hackman, Plaza, dwl 544 Third
Verzi Alexander, fisherman, Wash Hose Co. No. 1
Vessing Henry F. *(Drodge & V.)* dwl NE cor Natoma and Jane
Vest George *(Riley & V.)* dwl 558 Howard
Vetter Alfred, sign and ornamental painter, 205 Kearny, dwl 211 Kearny
Veuilliod Julius, butcher with Gabriel Dastugue, dwl 4 Quincy
Veuve Hypolite, clerk, 431 Battery
Veyrat François *(François Betuel & Co.)* dwl SW cor Pine and Dupont

Veyrat Jean, attendant, French Hospital, Bryant nr Fifth
Veyrat Morris, cook, dwl W s Oneida Place
Viadero Damasco, salesman with A. S. Rosenbaum & Co. dwl N s McAllister bet Buchanan and Webster
Vially Antonette Miss, domestic, 613 Kearny
Viard Prudon. toys, 1105 Stockton
Vibe Claus, seaman, dwl 26 Sacramento
Vibert Maximillian, fruits, 412 Brannan
Vicardo Giuseppo, dwl Garibaldi House, NE cor Broadway and Sansom
VICE THOMAS, boat builder, North Point foot Montgomery, dwl 157 Minna
Vick R. S. carpenter, dwl 741 Market
Vickerman John, laborer, dwl Dolores Hall, W s Valencia nr Sixteenth
Vickers Jerome G. printer, dwl 17 Noble Place
Victor Gustave, trunk maker with E. Galpen & Co. dwl 36 Battery
Victor Montague, confectionery, dwl 1013 Dupont
Victor Naede, brick molder with William Buckley
VICTORIA & OREGON STEAMERS, California Steam Nav. Co. office NE corner Front and Jackson
VICTORIA & PUGET SOUND PACKETS, Pope & Talbot, Pier 12 Stewart, and Amos Phinney & Co. agents, Pier 9 Stewart
Victoria & Puget Sound Packets (Merchants' Line) R. F. Pickett agent, 214 Sacramento
Victoria Packets (Pioneer Line) office 311 East
Vidal I. store keeper with Henry Schroder & Co. dwl Stockton bet Sacramento and California
Vidal Stephen, clerk with Buessard Neulens
Vidala Mary (widow) dwl N s Oregon nr Front
Vie Henry, cook, dwl 821 Kearny
Viera Manuel, shoe making, 417 East
Viera Vicente, fisherman, 47 Italian Fish Market
Viers Albert, dwl Union bet Hyde and Larkin
Vietor F. (John A. Bauer) 644 Washington
Vigneaud Henry, washer, New England Laundry, Brannan nr Fifth
Vignier Ami, clerk, 431 Battery, dwl 214 Sansom
Vigoreux A. W. physician, office and dwl 109 Third
Vigoreux P. M. wharfinger, Pacific Mail S. S. Co. Folsom St. Wharf, dwl 17 Clementina
Villar Louis, wines and liquors, SW cor Dupont and Broadway
Villard C. packer with Mercado & Seully, dwl cor Broadway and Dupont
Villaverde Atanasio, cigars and tobacco, 535 Bdwy
Villavicencio Lazaro, restaurant, 1033 Kearny
Villegia Leopold, gunsmith, 730 Washington
Villeneuve Eugene, merchant, dwl SW cor Dupont and Broadway
Villeneuve J. M. French importer, 1119 and 1121 Dupont, dwl Pollard Place
VILLIGER B. Rev. S.J. president St. Ignatius' College, S s Market bet Fourth and Fifth
Villimet M. L. teacher French, California Collegiate Institute
Vinal John, flour packer, National Mills
Vincen Jean Baptiste, workman with L. Artigues, dwl NW cor Sixteenth and Rhode Island
Vincenot (Peter) & Gautier (Anatole) Union Restaurant, 523 Merchant, dwl 222 Stevenson
Vincent Albert, carpenter with S. S. Culverwell, 29 Fremont, dwl 537 Tehama
Vincent Arthur, dwl 612 Larkin
Vincent Daniel, carpenter, dwl 612 Larkin
Vincent D. B. physician, office and dwl 515 Kearny
Vincent George, saloon, stm Amelia, dwl Cal Hotel
Vincent George T. clerk, 520 Montgomery
Vincent Henry, carpenter and builder, dwl 616 Cal
Vincent John P. carpenter, dwl 612 Larkin
Vincent Lucea, liquor saloon, 1230 Dupont
Vincent Margaret (widow) dwl 3 Francisco
Vincent Sevin & Co. seeds, New Market, res San Antonio

VINCENT WILLIAM H. proprietor American Theater Saloon, 314 Sansom
Viner Henry, butcher, dwl 229 Third
Viner John H. peddler, dwl 13 Pinckney Place
Vines Daniel B. auctioneer, dwl 1013 Washington
Vineyard Homestead Association, office 528 Clay
Vinken Frederick (Cordes & V.) dwl cor King and Third
Vinsohaler Ellen (widow) dwl S s Sheppard Place
Vinterburg Adolph, tailor, dwl S s Sacramento bet Mason and Taylor
Vinzent Charles, stock broker, office 605 Montgomery, dwl 1155 Mission
VIRGINIA BLOCK, NW cor Stockton and Pac
Visard Samuel, watchman, bds 127 Pacific
Vischer Edward, agent and commission merchant, office SW cor Front and Jackson, dwl 602 Stock
Vissner James, clerk, 626 Kearny
Vivian Richard, with Hart & Goodman, dwl W s Sansom bet Filbert and Greenwich
Vivian Robert, rigger, dwl NW cor Main and Folsom
Vivier Charles, paper box maker, dwl W s Taylor bet California and Sacramento
Vizard Joseph, blacksmith, dwl NE cor Third and Mission
Vizina Charles, with Locke & Montague, dwl 624 Vallejo
Voege Peter, seaman, bds 7 Washington
Voerekel Hermann, baker, dwl Minerva House 123 Jackson
Vogel Jacob, tailor, 337 Kearny
Vogelsdorff Jacob, importer and manuf cigars and leaf tobacco, 421 and 423 Bat, dwl 28 Tehama
Vogely Charles C. clerk, 114 Third
Vogle Benjamin M. tailor, 761 Clay
Vogle J. Mrs. domestic, 521 Post
Voight Berthold, machinist, dwl New England House
Voigt Christian H. (Eggers & Co.) dwl 1016 Stock
Voigt Ernst (John Zimmermann & Co.) dwl Butcher's Home, E s Potrero Av nr El Dorado
Voigt Gosche, cellar master with Kobler & Frohling, dwl cor Washington and Brenham Place
Voigt John E. with Joseph Roos, dwl Helvetia Hotel
VOIZIN, (Theodore) RIS (Gustave) & CO. auctioneers and commission merchants, 219 and 221 Sansom, dwl 856 Mission
Vokitch John, fruits, dwl 715 Davis
Volberg Charles, upholsterer with Kennedy & Bell, dwl 430 Natoma
Volckers Joseph, cook, dwl 538 Market
Vold Peter, seaman, dwl 13 Commercial
Voll F. A. cook, Railroad House, 319 Clay
Voller Nicholas, laborer, Bay Sugar Refinery, dwl Broadway bet Dupont and Stockton
Vollers Henry, groceries and liquors, NW cor Market and Powell
Vollers Maggie Miss, domestic, 1012 Clay
Vollbardt Jacob, boot maker, 210 Third
Vollbardt Peter, boot maker with J. Vollbardt, dwl 210 Third
Vollmer H. (J. & H. Vollmer) dwl SE cor Sacramento and Davis
VOLLMER J. & H. groceries and liquors, SE cor Sacramento and Davis
Vollmer Mathew, butcher, 1235 Dupont
Vollmer Reinhart, laborer, dwl 411 Sutter
Volmer Christian, ship carpenter, dwl 238 Stewart
Volz John, drayman, SW corner Sacramento and Front, dwl 612 Post
Volz Peter, carriage maker with Samuel F. Ross, dwl Golden Gate Hotel
Von Ahn Adolp, painter, dwl 827 Vallejo, rear
Von Arx Joseph, miner, dwl 819 Vallejo, rear
Von Bargen Henry (Schultz & Von B. and Pacific Distillery Co.) dwl 29 Hawthorne
Von Borstel Theodore, carpenter, dwl 26 St. Mark Place

Von Carnap Robert, book keeper with J. J. Robbins, dwl Garden nr Bryant

Von Deilen John H. butcher, SE cor Harrison and Main

Von Der Meden Ferdinand E. agent, office 422 California, dwl 405 California

Von Der Meden Rudolph, book keeper with Godeffroy & Sillem, 535 Clay

Von Glahn F. clerk, SE cor Clementina and Ecker

Von Glahn John, groceries and liquors, 226 Minna and 225 Sutter, dwl S s Harlan Pl nr Dupont

Von Glahn ——, laborer, Bay Sugar Refinery, dwl S s Harlan Place nr Dupont

Von Hadeln John, groceries and liquors, NW cor Green and Powell

Von Olhafen Frederick, draftsman, dwl 46 Beale

Von Pfister Francis M. book keeper with Lyon & Co. dwl Cosmopolitan Hotel

Von Poser Henry, ornamental plasterer, 614 Market, dwl O'Farrell bet Dupont and Stockton

VON RHEIN O. F. & CO. *(Henry J. Hyland)* employment and real estate agency, 105 Montgomery, dwl 28 Silver

Von Richthofen B ron, dwl 913 Dupont

Von Ronn Frederick, laborer, dwl SW cor Chestnut and Mason

Von Ronn *(William)* & Co. *(A. Kissling)* restaurant and bakery, 905 Kearny, dwl SW corner Union and Montgomery

Von Schawrz Joseph, teacher German, Union College

Von Seggen Henry, tannery, Lagoon

Von Staden Henry, clerk, NE cor Pine and St. Mary

Von Staden John *(Tietjen & Von S.)* dwl NE cor Pine and St. Mary

Vonach Bernard, waiter, 826 Market, dwl cor Market and O'Farrell

Vonbroch F. ede ick, wood turner, dwl SW corner Stockton and Pine

Vonhatten Paul, potter with V. Wackenreuder, San Bruno Ro d

Voorman Henry *(Pacific Distillery Co.)* dwl 512 Third

Voos Quirin, waiter, dwl 1226 Dupont

Vorbe Ephraim, cashier with Hentsch & Berton, dwl 440 Greenwich

Vorbe Joseph F. grain and produce, 120 Clay, dwl 440 Greenwich

Vordal John, broker, dwl 1432 Stockton

Vornbrock Henry, cigar maker, 819 Kearny, dwl 619 Pacific

Vorrath Christian C. Philadelphia Bakery, NE cor Mission and Thirteenth

Vorrath *(Henry)* & Co. *(Henry Meierdierks)* groceries, SE cor O'Farrell and Taylor

Vorrath Marx D. painter, dwl 29 St. Mark Place

Vorrath T. painting and paper hanging, 437 Bush, dwl 29 St. Mark Place

Vorwerck Charles H. salesman with Charles Bernard, 707 Sansom

Vorwerck Mary Mrs. ladies' nurse, dwl NW corner Mason and Broadway

Vosburg Isaac N. salesman with Meeker, James & Co. dwl 27 Ritch

Vosburgh William, clerk with D. E. Appleton, dwl Brenham Pl ce nr Washington

Voss *(Charles)* & Harding *(George)* liquor saloon, 637 Pacific

Voughan William, janitor Rincon Grammar School

Vrangnizan Joseph *(Francisco Matthew & Co.)* dwl SE cor Pacific and Davis

Vreeland E. B. dwl Russ House

Vroom P. Q. *(Anderson & V.)* 13 Jackson

Vuiovich Elias, cook, NE cor Com and Leidesdorff

VULCAN IRON WORKS CO. *(N. D. Arnot president, Samuel Aitken vice-president, Charles R. Steiger secretary, Richard Ivers treasurer, Joseph Moore superintendent)* foundry and machine works, 137 and 139 First

Vulcan Mining Co. (Lander Co. Santa Fé) office 405 Front

Vulicevich Mark S. *(J. Ivancovich & Co.)* dwl 325 Union

Vulliod Julius, tailor, dwl 5 Quincy Place

W

Wa Kee (Chinese) washing, E s Pacific Alley

Wa Lee (Chinese) washing, 512 Front

Waas Henry, bung and facet maker, 409 Mission, dwl S s Oak nr Franklin

Wachtel Henry, piano maker with Jacob Zech, dwl E s Kearny bet Bush and Pine

Wachtel John V. clerk, dwl 563 Mission

Wachter Conrad, cabinet maker, 307 Market, dwl 11 Pacific

Wachter H. carpenter, bds St. Louis Hotel 11 Pac

Wackenreader Vitus, surveyor and manufacturer pottery, San Bruno Road 3 miles from City Hall

Waddell George, waiter, NE cor Folsom and Main

Waddell Margaret (widow) dwl 2 Clementina

Waddell Margaret (widow) dwl 12 Natoma

Waddell William, chief engineer, Pacific Mail S. S. Co. dwl 248 Third

Waddell W. W. lumber dealer, bds Brooklyn Hotel

Waddy Anthony (col'd) laborer, dwl 1328 Pacific

Wade Abby T. Miss, dwl cor Shasta and Michigan

Wade Abel, merchant, dwl 302 Jessie

Wade Albert, seaman, dwl 26 Sacramento

Wade Catherine (widow) boarding, cor Shasta and Michigan

Wade Charles H. trunk maker with E. Galpen & Co. dwl 36 Battery

Wade David P. tobacconist, dwl 318 Davis

Wade Elizabeth (widow) dwl 407 Stevenson

Wade Ephraim H. blacksmith, dwl cor Shasta and Michigan

Wade James, with Swain & Brown, dwl 639 Mission

WADE *(James W.)* & HOWARD *(James G.)* attorneys at law, office 606 Montgomery

Wade J. C. wharfinger, North Point Dock, dwl 522 O'Farrell

Wade John *(Buchan & W.)* attorney at law, 537 Washington, dwl S s Wash bet Leav and Hyde

Wade John H. dwl cor Shasta and Michigan

Wade Joseph L. with S. H. Wade, res Brooklyn, Alameda County

Wade Maggie Miss, assistant, Powell St. School, dwl Washington W Leavenworth

Wade Patrick, clerk, dwl NE cor Market and Ecker

Wade Phil William, painter, dwl W s Sixth bet Stevenson and Jessie

Wade S. H. book and job printing, NE cor Washington and Kearny, res Brooklyn, Alameda Co

WADE THOMAS, dentist, office 26 Montgomery, dwl 716 Mission

Wade William, painter with James R. Kelly, dwl W s Sixth bet Mission and Stevenson

Wade William N. livery stable, 710 Broadway

Wadhams Luman, drayman, dwl W s Leavenworth bet Union and Green

Wadleigh Andrew S. machinist, S. F. & San José R. R. Co. dwl cor Sixteenth and Valencia

Wadleigh J. W. mining, dwl 130 Turk

Wadleigh Maria (widow) boarding and lodging, 8 Ellis and 5 Stockton

Wadsworth Benjamin C. *(Wadsworth & Son)* res Arizona

Wadsworth Charles Rev. D.D. pastor Calvary Presbyterian Church, dwl 920 Pine

WADSWORTH WILLIAM R. & SON *(B. C. Wadsworth)* commercial brokers and commission merchants and secretary Chamber Commerce, office 402 Front, dwl 759 Market

Wael Julius H. teacher, dwl 634 Pacific

Waest Frederick, painter, dwl 14 Baldwin Court

WAGENER F. O. & CO. cigars and tobacco, 504 Montgomery, dwl E s Eighth bet Howard and Folsom
Wagener John, hog ranch, dwl E s Ninth bet Bryant and Brannan
Wager D. C. lieutenant-colonel U. S. A. assistant inspector general D. P. office 418 California, dwl Occidental Hotel
Wagner (Adam) & Burffend (Chris) milk ranch, nr SE cor Seventeenth and Castro
Wagner Adam J. hairdresser, 417 Pacific, bds New Wisconsin Hotel, 411 Pacific
Wagner Adolph, cabinet maker with J. Peirce, dwl 304 Pine
Wagner Calvin, porter with Davis & Cowell, bds Pacific Temperance House
Wagner Catherine Mrs. groceries, N s Twentieth bet Guerrero and Dolores
Wagner Christian, real estate, dwl NE cor Hyde and Lombard
Wagner Ernest, carpenter, dwl 282 Stevenson
Wagner Ferdinand, liquor saloon, 1232 Dupont
Wagner Frederick (Engelberg & W.) dwl 416 Kearny
Wagner Henry, Our Market, 1440 Stockton
Wagner Jacob, bricklayer, dwl 417 Sutter
Wagner Jacob, driver, North Beach & M. R. R. Co. dwl E s Russ bet Howard and Folsom
Wagner (John) & Co. (Michael Kelly) wood and coal, 8 Waverly Place, dwl N s Pacific bet Dupont and Stockton
Wagner John, dwl N s Seventeenth bet Dolores and Church
Wagner Joseph, painter, dwl 625 Pacific, rear
Wagner Joseph, wood and coal, 716 Pacific
Wagner Louis, beer saloon, 652 Sacramento, dwl 13 St. Mark Place
Wagner Margaret Mrs. confectionery, 362 Third
Wagner Samuel (Brown & W.) dwl 214 Sansom
Wagner William (Canty & W.) dwl 399 Jessie
Wagner William, clerk, 503 Sansom
Wagner William J. ship carpenter, dwl 508 Howard
Wagoner H. B. local policeman, dwl NE cor Bryant and Sixth
Wah Hang (Chinese) washing, NW cor Pratt Court and California
Wah Lee (Chinese) washing, 33 Jackson
Wah Loong (Chinese) washing, N s Chestnut bet Stockton and Powell
Wah Sing (Chinese) washing, 633 Post
Wahl, Christian & Co. (Anthony Ruh) beer saloon, SW cor Bush and Clara
Wahler Joseph, watch maker with John Revalk, 510 Montgomery
Wahlgren Victor, machinist, Union Foundry, dwl 243 Tehama
Wahmuth Henry, driver, Albany Brewery, dwl N s Grove bet Octavia and Laguna
Waign Huign (Chinese) washing, 17 Geary
Wainwright Edward, laborer with Hey & Meyn, dwl N s Folsom bet Tenth and Eleventh
Wainwright James, bar keeper, 323 Washington, dwl W s Mariposa nr Harrison
Wainwright John, machinist, dwl 341 Tehama
Wainwright Robert, machinist, dwl 341 Tehama
Wainwright William, oysters and liquors, 219 California, dwl 233 Third
Wait Jerome, dwl 1065 Howard
Waite Abraham, laborer, dwl E s Garden bet Harrison and Bryant
Waite William F. superintendent laborers, Western Pacific R. R. Co. dwl 11 Perry
Waitt A. C. book keeper with Weaver, Wooster & Co. dwl W s Yerba Buena nr Clay
Waize Rudolph, musician, Academy Music
Waizmann Max, paper box manufacturer, 414 Sacramento, dwl 258 Jessie
Wakefield Benjamin, assistant, Montgomery Baths, dwl 36 Battery

Wakelee Benton, salesman with Blake & Co. dwl 116 Dupont
Wakelee C. H. real estate broker, office and dwl 518 Pacific
WAKELEE H. P. druggist, SE cor Montgomery and Bush and NW cor Howard and Third, dwl 311 Harrison
Wakelee T. H. B. clerk with Blake & Co. dwl 116 Dupont
Wakeman Alonzo C. dwl 51 Tehama
Wakeman Edgar, captain steamship John L. Stephens, office SW cor Front and Jackson, resides Brooklyn, Alameda County
Wakeman F. O. claim agent and sec'y Point Arena Oil Co. 12 Phœnix Building, dwl 402 Fremont
Wakeman Mary E. Miss. domestic, 1051 Howard
Walbert Henry, butcher with C. Schmith, dwl Potrero Avenue
Walbridge S. D. miller, Golden Age Flour Mill, dwl 335 Broadway bet Montgomery and Kearny
Walby Charles, butcher with Baldwin & Moffat, dwl cor Ninth and Brannan
Walby Nathan, butcher with Baldwin & Moffat, dwl cor Ninth and Brannan
Walch William, barber, dwl 33 Jane
Walck Ellen Miss, domestic, 822 Pacific
Walcom George, upholster with W. M. Hixon, dwl N s Bush bet Fillmore and Steiner
Walcom (Jacob) & Gowan (Edward) carriage painters, 717 Market, dwl Bush bet Steiner and Fillmore
Walcott Asa A. musician, dwl S s Bush bet Leavenworth and Hyde
Walcott Edward, boiler maker, dwl Meeks Place
Walcott G. W. boiler maker with Coffey & Risdon
Waldeier Charles, furniture wagon, SW cor Montgomery and California, dwl 18 Mission
Walde Daniel, brewer, Philadelphia Brewery
Walden Kate Miss, domestic, 223 Jessie
WALDENBERG (Charles J.) & TOLLNER (Albert) Old Whitehall Exchange Liquor Saloon, 311 Battery, dwl 533 California
Waldenstein Betsie Miss, 316 Third
Waldenstein Louis, carrier, Abend Post, dwl 914 Washington
Waldren Benjamin, machinist, Union Foundry, dwl 81 Natoma
Waldron John, workman, S. F. & P. Sugar Co. dwl S s Minna bet Eighth and Ninth
Waldron Westbrook, baker with J. Chadbourne, dwl 346 Third
Waldstein A. & Co. (E. Ehlin) cigar box factory, 407 Mission, dwl 316 O'Farrell
Wale Daniel, with S. S. Culverwell, 29 Fremont
Waler Charles, bar keeper, dwl 514 Pine
Wales G. W. dwl 76 Stevenson House
Walfish Louis S. clerk, 16 Third, dwl 209 Mason
Walker Abner (George W. Gildersleeve & Co.) dwl 13 Ellis
Walker Albert R. box maker with Hobbs, Gilmore & Co. dwl 73 Fourth
Walker Alfred, liquors, 116 Pacific
Walker Andrew (Rowland W. & Co.) dwl 818 Powell
Walker August, gilder with Snow & Co. dwl cor Commercial and Leidesdorff
Walker Charles, steward, dwl 35 Essex
Walker Edward, weigher, dwl W s Jones bet Lombard and Chestnut
Walker E. E. ship carpenter, dwl St. Lawrence House
Walker Erasmus D. dwl with W. B. Parsons, W s Folsom bet Sixteenth and Seventeenth
Walker Frederick, tinsmith with Osgood & Stetson, dwl 222 Sutter
Walker George, shoe maker, 530 California, dwl 4 O'Farrell nr Jones
Walker George C. clerk with J. B. Dorr & Co. dwl Railroad House

Walker George R. molder, dwl SE cor Minna and Second
Walker George W. carpenter, dwl 432 Jessie
Walker George W. first lieutenant Co. I. 9th U. S. Infantry, Fort Point
Walker James, mastic roofer, dwl 2 Hardie Place
Walker James, workman with Stratton Bros. dwl 28 Ritch
WALKER JAMES D. manager Bank of British Columbia, office 412 California, dwl cor Seventh and Folsom
Walker James I. *(N. P. Perine & Co.)* dwl 2 Hardie Place
Walker June (widow) domestic, 1117 Stockton
Walker John, dwl W s Garden bet Harrison and Bryant
Walker John, boarding, 215 Broadway
Walker John, clerk, 647 Clay, dwelling 2 Chelsea Place
Walker John, wire rope maker with A. S. Hallidie & Co. dwl Sailors' Home
Walker J. W. dwl 228 Stevenson
Walker Martin, engineer, dwl SW cor King and Third
Walker R. laborer, Bay Sugar Refinery, dwl N s Greenwich bet Sansom and Montgomery
Walker Solomon (colored) laundry, N s Broadway bet Leavenworth and Hyde
Walker Thomas, news dealer, dwl 215 Sansom
Walker William with John Howes, 502 Sansom
Walker William, clerk with Robert T. Payne, dwl 1026 Montgomery
Walker William, laborer, dwl 128 St. Mark Place
Walker William, laborer, Vulcan Iron Works, dwl Filbert nr Union
Walker William C. Golden Gate Nursery, 825 Folsom
Walker William H. news collector with T. E. Baugh, dwl Meigg's Wharf
Walker William J. foreman with Wilson & Stevens, dwl W s Fell bet Octavia and Laguna
Walker W. J. revenue agent U. S. office NW cor Battery and Commercial, res Oakland
Walkheim Otmar, waiter, What Cheer House Restaurant
Walkington George F. tinsmith with J. G. Ils, dwl 141 Silver
Walkington J. F. tinsmith with J. G. Ils, dwl 141 Silver
Walkington Samuel B. machinist, dwl 141 Silver
Wall Ann Miss, 334 Third
Wall Bridget (widow) dwl 515 Taylor
Wall Ellen Miss, domestic, dwl 1063 Howard
Wall James H. boiler maker with Coffey & Risdon, dwl SW cor Shasta and Michigan
Wall Johanna (widow) domestic with C. Kerr, Mission Creek nr Brannan St. Bridge
Wall John, pilot, dwl 408 Vallejo
Wall John J. drayman, dwl 1314 Jackson
Wall Michael, liquor saloon, 8 First
Wall Peter, dwl 1021 Clay
Wall Thomas, laborer, bds Western Hotel
Wallace Andrew, ship carpenter, dwl E s Harwood Alley
Wallace Anna Miss, dress maker, dwl 109 Mont
Wallace Benjamin, plasterer, dwl 649 Mission
Wallace Catharine Miss, domestic, 411 Lombard
Wallace Charles, laborer, dwl SW cor Taylor and Greenwich
Wallace Elizabeth Miss, domestic, 208 Jones
Wallace George, secretary San Francisco & Atlantic Railroad Co. office 338 Montgomery room 7, dwl 109 Montgomery
Wallace Hiram, seaman, dwl 20 Commercial
Wallace James, dwl S s Columbia nr Valencia
Wallace James, clerk with Chas. Bernard, dwl E s Harwood Alley
Wallace James, driver, North Beach & M. R. R. Co
Wallace James, laborer with Edward J. Quirk

Wallace James, laborer, North Point Warehouse, dwl 9 Natoma
Wallace James, lamplighter, S. F. Gas Co
Wallace James H. book keeper with Irvine & Co. dwl 33 Louisa
Wallace John, laborer, dwl 9 Natoma
Wallace John, laborer, dwl 203 Broadway
Wallace John, porter, 22 Battery
Wallace Joseph, cook, Golden Gate Hotel
Wallace Joseph M. butcher with A. J. Shrader, dwl cor Ninth and Brannan
Wallace Kate Miss, seamstress, dwl 531 Mission
Wallace Kinsley, dwl E s Geneva bet Bryant and Brannan
Wallace L. dwl What Cheer House
Wallace Margaret (widow) dwl 9 Natoma
Wallace Mary (widow) dwl 529 Greenwich
Wallace Mary (widow) dwl 14 Ritch
Wallace Michael, dwl N s Valencia bet Market and Ridley
Wallace Patrick, machinist, Union Foundry, dwl Francisco bet Dupont and Kearny
Wallace Robert, salesman with Taaffe & Co
Wallace Robert W. porter, dwl 632 Second
WALLACE THOMAS, office 523 Montgomery Howard's Building, res Oakland
Wallace Thomas, machinist, Miners' Foundry, dwl 134 Dora
Wallace William, seaman, dwl 26 Sacramento
Wallace William, supt. and sexton Mount Calvary Cemetery
Wallace William H. boiler maker, dwl Beale bet Howard and Mission
Wallace William M. agent California Leader, dwl 820 Washington
Wallace William T. *(Patterson, W. & Stow)* dwl NW cor Post and Leavenworth
Wallach Philip, waiter, 205 Sansom
Wallack James, carver with Snow & Co. dwl 515 Pine
Waller Charles A. bar keeper, 538 Merchant, dwl 514 Pine
Waller George C. attorney at law, office 6 Montgomery Block, dwl E s Montgomery nr Green
Waller George C. clerk with George C. Waller
Waller John, laborer, dwl 622 Vallejo
Waller Joseph, gas fitter, dwl W s Prentice nr Courtlandt Avenue
Waller *(L. P.)* & Jacobi *(Leopold)* auction and commission mchts, 306 Kearny, dwl 228 Sixth
Waller Moses, clerk, 424 Mont, dwl 517 Folsom
Waller R. H. attorney at law, office 6 Montgomery Block, dwl E s Montgomery nr Green
Wallick Martin, bar keeper, Empire House, S s Vallejo bet Front and Battery
Wallingford Elbridge, clerk, 110 California, dwl 37 Ritch
Wallmann *(Christian)* & Brother *(Julius Wallmann)* watchmakers and jewelers, 212 Mont
Wallmann Julius *(Wallmann & Bro.)* dwl 212 Montgomery
Walls John, driver with Daniel McGlynn, dwl 721 Market
Walls John, laborer, dwl NW cor Jessie and Annie
Wallworth Geary, commission mcht, dwl 38 Natoma
WALMSLEY WM. WALLACE, stoves and tin ware, 112 Fourth
Walnut Creek Petroleum Co. office 111 Clay
Walquest Frederick, seaman, dwl 312 Union
Walrath Austin *(J. Martenstein & Co.)* dwl 740 Howard
Walsh Bartholomew, laborer, Market St. R. R. Co. dwl E s Kearny nr Sutter
Walsh Charles J. waiter, Lick House
Walsh Cornelius, plumber, dwl 709 Stockton
Walsh E. seaman, dwl 140 Stewart
Walsh Edward, carder, Mission Woolen Mills
Walsh Edward, drayman, dwl NE cor Lombard and Kearny

Walsh Edward, gas fitter with McNally & Hawkins, dwl 14 Sutter
Walsh Edward, laborer, dwl 530 Mission
Walsh Edward, laborer, dwl 529 Mission
Walsh James, blacksmith, 606 Mission
Walsh James, carpenter, dwl 832 Vallejo
Walsh James, laborer, dwl 53 Beale
Walsh James, laborer, Fort Alcatraz, dwl W s Jansen bet Greenwich and Lombard
Walsh James, orchardist, E s Folsom bet Thirteenth and Fourteenth
Walsh James M. blacksmith helper, Vulcan Iron Works, dwl St. Charles Hotel
Walsh Jane (widow) dwl 3 Stockton Place
Walsh Johanna Miss, chambermaid, Brooklyn Hotel
Walsh John, waiter, 626 Kearny
Walsh John A. gas fitter with J. K. Prior, dwl cor Mission and Beale
Walsh John F. driver, Central R. R. Co. dwl SW cor Fourth and Jessie
WALSH J. WALTER, publisher and proprietor Varieties, office 517 Clay, dwl 331 Broadway
Walsh Kitty Miss, domestic; 811 Hyde
Walsh Lawrence M. molder, Fulton Foundry, dwl Eureka Hotel
Walsh Lewis, milkman, dwl W s Fifth nr Minna
Walsh Margaret Mrs. dress maker, 1308 Dupont
Walsh Margaret Mrs. machine sewing, dwl 205 Jessie
Walsh Martin, lather, dwl 114 Bush
Walsh Martin, soda bottler, Empire Soda Works, dwl NE cor Harrison and Third
Walsh Mathias, calker, dwl cor Stockton and Greenwich
Walsh Maurice D. painter with Hopps & Kanary
Walsh Michael, bar keeper, 624 Merchant
Walsh Michael, boots and shoes, 211 Pacific
Walsh Michael, drayman, cor Front and Jackson, dwl 34 Rousch
Walsh Michael, shoe maker with P. F. Dunne, 316 Battery
Walsh Michael, shoe maker, 408 O'Farrell
Walsh Michael, steward, 624 Merchant, dwl 2 Natoma
Walsh Michael, workman, S. F. & P. Sugar Co. dwl 110 Dora
Walsh P. Rev. St. Mary's Cathedral, dwl 602 Dupont
Walsh Patrick, architect, office and dwl 104 Sutter
Walsh Patrick, carpenter, dwl N s Jessie bet Second and Third
Walsh Richard, tailor, Spring cor Summer, dwl 11 Noble Place
Walsh Richard F. salesman, Pier 14 Stewart
Walsh Robert, jeweler with Lemme Bros. 534 Com
Walsh Robert, porter with Geo. C. Johnson & Co
Walsh S. F. real estate agent, 619 Merchant, dwl 149 Silver
Walsh Timothy, laborer, S. F. Sugar Co. dwl W s Ritter nr Harrison
Walsh W. boiler maker apprentice, Vulcan Iron Works
Walsh Walter, accountant, with D. J. Oliver, dwl NW cor Jones and Chestnut
Walsh William, bar keeper, Eureka Hose Co. No. 4
Walsh William, carpenter, dwl 608 O'Farrell
Walsh William, carrier, Evening Bulletin, Sacramento steamers
Walter Alois, tailor, 427 Bush
Walter Augustus, apprentice, NE cor Powell and Broadway
WALTER D. N. & E. & CO. (Herman, Moritz, and I. Newton Walter) importers and dealers carpets, oil cloths, etc. 303 and 305 California, dwl 628 Sutter
Walter Emanuel (D. N. & E. Walter & Co.) res New York
Walter Edward, with D. R. Provost & Co. dwl NW cor Sacramento and Stockton
Walter Frank, proprietor West End House, Old San José Road 6 miles from City Hall

WALTER G. FORREST & CO. merchant tailors, 611 Sacramento, dwl 913 Market
Walter Herman (D. N. & E. Walter & Co.) res Portland, Oregon
Walter I. Newton (D. N. & E. Walter & Co.) res Portland, Oregon
Walter John H. seaman, dwl 26 Sacramento
Walter Julia (widow) dwl 804 Union
Walter M. dwl 214 Sansom
Walter Moritz (D. N. & E. Walter & Co.) dwl 628 Sutter
Walter Stanislaus T. tailor, 120 Dupont, dwl NW cor Bush and Dupont
Walter Thomas, dwl 824 Folsom
Walters John, plasterer, dwl 3 Jane
Walters Louis, tailor, dwl 32 Webb
Walther Frederick, butcher, dwl 12 Ritch
WALTHER FREDERICK G. job printer and proprietor Die Montags Zeitung, 621 Sansom, dwl 1021 Clay
Walton A. B. Mrs. dwl 740 Howard
Walton David H. steamship agent, dwl 1116 Leav
Walton (E. M. Mrs.) & Wills (M. A. Miss) female seminary, corner Mason and Jackson, dwl 1007 Powell
Walton Fannie A. dwl with Ossian C. Mitchell, W s Eleventh bet Market and Mission
Walton George W. dwl 740 Howard
Walton James, farmer, dwl with James H. Bullard
Walton Jesse, collector, Spring Valley W. W. Co. dwl NE cor Third and Hunt
Walton Julia Mrs. dwl 303 Sutter
WALTON N. C. rosin, pitch, etc. 29 Market, dwl 31 Minna
Walton N. C. jr. clerk, dwl 31 Minna
Walton Thomas, annealer U. S. Branch Mint, dwl W s Telegraph Place
Walton William J. lumber surveyor, dwl 32 Frederick
Walworth M. seaman, dwl 307 Beale
Walz G. druggist, dwl Lutgen's Hotel
Walz John, Mount Hope Market, 741 Broadway
Wamuth H. agent Albany Brewery, dwl N s Grove bet Laguna and Octavia
Wand David (Wand & Co.) dwl 75 Clementina
Wand (Samuel) & Co. (David Wand) dry goods, 22 Second, dwl 75 Clementina
Wand Thomas N. (Hunter, W. & Co.) dwl E side Sixth bet Bryant and Brannan
Wandell John, laborer, dwl NW corner First and Mission
Wandelt Gottlieb, butcher with O. H. Willoughby, dwl N s Sixteenth nr Nebraska
Wanderer Henry, boot maker, 523 Kearny
Wandesforde Juan B. portrait and landscape painter, 513 Montgomery, dwl N s DeBoom nr Second
Wands James, hair dresser, Montgomery Baths, dwl 91 Stevenson
WANGENHEIM, (A. L.) STERNHEIM (Samuel) & CO. (David Stern) importers and jobbers crockery and glassware, SE cor California and Sansom, res New York
Wangenheim Amiel, book keeper with Wangenheim, Sternheim & Co. dwl 632 Market
Wangenheim Solomon, merchant, office SE cor Sansom and California, dwl 211 Powell
Wapler C. Adolph, book keeper with B. Eugene Auger, 704 Sansom, dwl 1213 Mason
Warburton John, milk ranch, N s Presidio Road nr Half-Way House
Ward A. C. dwl Franklin House, SW cor Sansom and Broadway
Ward Albert, broom maker with T. Ward, 27 Drumm
Ward Alexander H. jr. book keeper with Geo. C. Johnson & Co. dwl 1121 Sacramento
Ward Andrew J. (col'd) hairdresser, 916 Kearny, dwl 19 Scott
Ward Burnett, laborer, dwl S s Union bet Sansom and Calhoun

Ward Catharine Mrs. dwl 72 Natoma
Ward Christopher, merchant tailor, 127 Bush, dwl 4 Stockton Place
Ward Daniel, clerk with James H. Widber, corner Kearny and Market
Ward Edward, tinner, dwl 319 Bush
Ward Francis J. laborer, What Cheer House Restaurant, dwl 619 Mission
Ward George B. broom maker with Thomas Ward, 27 Drumm
Ward Geo. James, with Provost & Co. dwl S s Fell nr Octavia
Ward George W. (S. W. H. Ward & Son) dwl 200 Post
Ward Henry, paper hanger, 132 Third
Ward Isaac M. policeman, City Hall, dwl 313 Ritch
Ward James (O'Brien & W.) dwl 64 Stevenson
Ward James, molder, Union Foundry, dwl 427 Union
Ward James D. conductor, North Beach & M. R. R. Co. dwl 317 Tehama
Ward James J. stone cutter, dwl S side Filbert bet Leavenworth and Hyde
Ward John, boot and shoe maker, dwl Moulton Pl
Ward John, laborer, dwl 29 Ecker
Ward John, painter, dwl Clementina bet Second and Third
Ward John, printer, dwl 24 Minna
Ward John, tinner with Cutting & Co. dwl 1415 Kearny
Ward John C. stevedore, dwl W s Sansom between Greenwich and Filbert
Ward John H. painter, bds SW corner Sierra and Georgia
Ward John Murray, oil dealer, dwl 249 Second
Ward Joseph, seaman, dwl 26 Sacramento
Ward L. laborer, American Exchange
Ward Mary Miss, milliner, dwl 18 Minna
Ward Mary Mrs. furnished rooms, 15 Sutter and 510 Market
Wark Michael, dwl cor Hyde and Ellis
Ward Nathaniel, wood carver, dwl NE corner Polk and Filbert
Ward O. F. employé with Chas. Mathias, 114 Wash
Ward Patrick, painter, dwl 29 Ritch
Ward Patrick F. clerk, 14 Metropolitan Market, dwl NE cor Eighth and Howard
Ward Peter, dwl 510 Market
Ward Peter, carpenter, dwl 116 Sansom
Ward Philip J. carpenter, dwl Telegraph Hill, Mont
Ward Phineas P. laborer, dwl S side Brannan near Seventh
Ward Robert, carriage painter with Patrick J. O'Brien, dwl S s Bryant between Seventh and Eighth
Ward Robert, lamplighter, S. F. Gas Co. dwl 41 Minna
WARD S. W. H. & SON (George W. Ward) gents' furnishing goods, 323 Montgomery, res New York
Ward Theresa Miss, milliner, 128 Third, dwl 33 Minna
Ward Thomas, broom manufacturer, 36 Beale
Ward Thomas, workman, S. F. & P. Sugar Co. dwl N s Natoma bet Seventh and Eighth
WARD T. M. D. Rev. pastor African M. E. Church, dwl 532 Bush
Ward (William) & Kenny (Thomas) Metropolitan Exchange Liquor Saloon, 522 Market, dwl 154 Natoma bet Second and Third
Ward William, hostler, Omnibus R. R. Co. dwl 440 Jessie
Ward William, plasterer, dwl S s Sutter nr Taylor
Wardell Abraham, house mover, dwl 8 Russ
Warden David, waterman, 609 Market, dwl 106 Mason
Warden Hugh, trunk maker, dwl S s Mission bet Third and Fourth
Warden John, bar keeper with John Walker, dwl 215 Broadway

Warden Oscar, waterman, dwl 106 Mason
Warden William H. waterman, 609 Market, dwl 106 Mason
Wardlaw William, with James Laidley, Easton's Laundry
WARDWELL CHARLES O. attorney at law, office 604 Merchant, dwl 931 Sacramento
Ware Charles, ironer, Chelsea Laundry
Ware George A. compositor, Evening Bulletin, dwl 34 Second
Ware George W. merchant, dwl 317 Lombard
Ware Henry L. book keeper with J. Ivancovich & Co. dwl 3 Quincy Place
Ware James (Smith, W. & Co.) dwl 724 Harrison
Ware John, porter, dwl 20 Silver
Ware Joseph, hostler, Bay View
Ware Thomas, pork packer, dwl N s Brannan bet Eighth and Ninth
Ware William, clerk, dwl 912 Washington
Ware William, steam engines and machinist, 517 Market (and Main St. Wharf Co.) dwl 800 Howard
Warfield James (col'd) bootblack, 630 Kearny, dwl 508 Kearny
Warfield John (Oliver & W.) dwl 508 Kearny
Warfield J. P. physician, office 402 Montgomery, res Alameda
Waring S. H. steerage steward steamer Pacific
Warmby Thomas, machinist, Miners' Foundry, dwl 532 Folsom
Warmouth (Nicholas) & Baker (Henry) stock commission agents, 423 Pacific
Warnake Anne, domestic, 6 Langton
Warneke Louis, farmer, bds 7 Washington
Warner A. B. miner, dwl 103 Dupont
Warner Abraham, Meiggs' Wharf Saloon, NW cor Francisco and Lumber
Warner Adolph, tinsmith, dwl 209 Minna
Warner Catharine Miss, dwl 419 Union
Warner Charles, distiller, Pacific Distillery
Warner Charles H. with Tay, Brooks & Backus, dwl 5 Central Place
Warner James, musician, dwl NW cor Francisco and Lumber
Warner Phillip, express wagon, cor Jackson and Kearny
Warner William, purser steamer Petaluma, dwl 845 Dupont
Warner Wilson, nurse, City and County Hospital
Warren Albert T. printer with Frank Eastman, dwl 255 Third
Warren Augustus, weigher with A. H. Todd & Co. 45 Clay, dwl 26 Rousch
Warren C. C. T. (widow) dress maker, 405 Bush
Warren Charles E. laborer, Custom House
Warren E. A. sawyer with S. S. Culverwell, 29 Fremont, dwl SE cor Sansom and Bush
Warren E. D. book keeper with Fargo & Co. 214 Front
Warren E. W. clerk, dwl 858 Mission
Warren Henry S. compositor, Morning Call, dwl 217 Post
Warren James H. Rev. agent American Home Missionary Society, office 402 Front, res San Mateo
Warren James L. (Pover & W.) dwl 104 Natoma
Warren James M. milkman, dwl SE cor Ellis and Fillmore
Warren J. E. dwl 413 Folsom
WARREN (J. L. L. F.) & CO. editors and proprietors California Farmer, office 320 Clay, dwl SE cor Mason and Pacific
Warren John, dwl 834 Clay
Warren John, seaman, dwl 54 Sacramento
Warren John E. clerk, dwl 404 Post
Warren John K. clerk with Cameron, Whittier & Co. dwl E s Dolores bet Sixteenth and Seventeenth
Warren Joseph, bricklayer, dwl 13 Front
WARREN O. P. physician, office and dwl 836 Mkt

Warren Russell, carpenter, dwl 963 Mission
Warren Russell A. compositor, Morning Call, dwl 963 Mission
Warren Samuel, dwl 215 Sansom
Warren Timothy, carrier, Morning Call, dwl 30 Clara
Warren William B. dwl SE cor Ellis and Fillmore
WARREN WILLIAM H. tanner, Folsom between Eighteenth and Nineteenth
Warren Wyman, dwl 28 Sansom
Warrin John W. broker, office 618 Merchant
Warrington S. R. contractor, dwl 273 Clara
Warschbauer Teresa A. Mrs. proprietress Irving House, 568 Mission cor Anthony
Warshawski Albin *(J. Warshawski & Bro.)* dwl 322 Jessie
Warshaweki J. & Brother *(Albin Warshawski)* & Co. *(Max Weiner)* gents' furnishing goods, 656 Washington, dwl 322 Jessie
Warshawski Jacob, clerk, 528 Sac, dwl 236 Minna
Warshawski M. dwl 322 Jessie
Warshawski Oscar, dwl 322 Jessie
Warszauer Herman *(Jakubowski & W.)* dwl 342 Kearny
Warszauer Manheim, salesman, 538 Clay
Warwick James H. actor, Metropolitan Theater, dwl 563 Mission
Warwick *(Thomas)* & Brown *(John)* hatters, 207 Third
Wash John M. compositor, California Leader, dwl 603 Post
Wash Mary A. (widow) dwl 18 Jessie
WASHBURN E. H. stock broker, 622 Montgomery, dwl 932 Pacific
Washburn Georgia Mrs. assistant, colored school, dwl 804 Pine
Washburn Henry, milkman, dwl 66 Everett
Washburn J. M. *(Miller & W.)* 131 Third corner Sherwood Place
Washburn Leonard *(Reynolds & Co.)* dwl 66 Everett
Washburn M. A. Mrs. music teacher, 624 Market
Washburn Reuben W. Exchange Departm't Wells, Fargo & Co. dwl Tehama House
Washburne William M. mason, dwl SW cor Garden and Harrison
WASHINGTON B. F. editor Daily Examiner, office 535 Washington, dwl U. S. Court Building
Washington Brewery, Mangels & Co. proprietors, SE cor Lombard and Taylor
WASHINGTON FIRE INSURANCE CO. (New York) Bigelow & Brother agents, 505 Montgomery
Washington Francis (col'd) drayman with H. M. Newhall & Co. dwl 626 Vallejo
Washington G. & S. M. Co. office 529 Clay
Washington John, machinist, Union Foundry
WASHINGTON MARKET, S s Washington bet Montgomery and Sansom
WASHINGTON MARINE INSURANCE CO. New York, C. J. Janson agent, office 210 Pine
Washington R. B. attorney at law, office 4 Armory Hall, dwl 723 Sutter
WASHINGTON SALT MILLS, S. Klein proprietor, 29 Fremont, office 225 Clay
Washington St. Wharf, office foot Washington
Washington William (col'd) dwl 423 Union
Washington William, cook, steamer Petaluma
Washoe G. & S. M. Co. office 338 Montgomery
Wason Archibald, house and sign painter, 613 Sansom, dwl SW cor Geary and Larkin
Wass A. H. mate, stm Oakland, res Brooklyn
Wass Ambrose C. carpenter with C. W. Thomas, dwl N s Washington bet Leav and Hyde
Wass Andrew D. captain bark Jane A. Falkenberg, dwl 218 Stockton
Wass George, hairdressing saloon, 744 Market
Wass Henry, hairdresser, 744 Market
Wasser Thomas, engineer, stm Paul Pry, dwl SE cor Montgomery and Filbert

WASSERMANN A. & CO. importers and commission merchants, dealers in hides, wool, and furs, 429 Sacramento, dwl 515 Post nr Mason
Wasserman Elkan, clerk, 429 Sacramento, dwl 307 Eddy
Watchlet J. V. clerk, dwl 663 Mission
Waterdol Peter, drayman, cor Kearny and Jackson, dwl N s Green bet Sansom and Battery
Waterford Joseph, sail maker, dwl 1134 Pacific
WATERHOUSE *(C.)* & LESTER *(J. W.)* importers and dealers carriage and wagon stock, 29 and 31 Battery, dwl 1413 Larkin bet Sacramento and California
Waterhouse Fred. A. book keeper, 29 Battery, dwl 1413 Larkin
Waterhouse George, employé with Bayley & Cramer, 618 and 620 Washington
Waterman Alexander, cap maker with Wolf Fleisher, dwl 505 Kearny
Waterman Daniel M. salesman, 105 Battery, dwl 109 Sansom
Waterman Edwin R. flour inspector, office SW cor Clay and Davis, dwl NE cor Leav and Green
Waterman F. H. attorney at law, office 9 Montgomery Block, dwl Cosmopolitan Hotel
Waterman James M. with G. B. & I. H. Knowles, 17 California
WATERMAN JOHN G. groceries and liquors, NW cor Folsom and Sixth
Waterman John, blacksmith, dwl 309 Tehama
Waterman Joseph *(Ryan & W.)* dwl 526 Post
WATERMAN M. produce commission, 111 Clay, dwl 526 Post
WATERMAN MOSES, dry goods, 119 Second, dwl 204 Ellis
Waterman Richard, foreman Empire Brewery, dwl W s Vallejo Place
Waterman Robert H. inspector hulls, office Custom House third floor
Waterman William, musician, dwl 522 Filbert
Waters Arthur, drayman, 409 Front, dwl 519 Pine
Waters Donald S. business agent, La Voz de Mejico, dwl 223 First
WATERS E. D. proprietor Mercantile Gazette and Shipping Register, office 536 Clay, res Oakland
Waters E. D. jun. *(Dewey, Waters & Co.)* dwl 19 Tehama
Waters Frank, clerk, dwl SE cor Fifth and Shipley
Waters Frederick C. printer with Towne & Bacon, dwl 19 Tehama
Waters George, draftsman, dwl 109 Minna
Waters George L. broker, dwl Cosmopolitan Hotel
Waters James, brick maker, dwl SE cor Hyde and Union
Waters John, street sprinkler, dwl Union Place nr Green
Waters Joseph N. H. express wagon, 414 Clay, dwl 429 Clementina
Waters Mary Miss, domestic, 1103 Powell
Waters Mary Miss, dress maker, dwl 110 Kearny
Waters N. Ellis, Howard Engine Co. No. 3
Waters Patrick, laborer with S. Bloom, dwl 442 Natoma
Waters R. dwl What Cheer House
Waters Roger, laborer, Spring Valley W. W. Co. dwl 508 Post
Waters Samuel J. waterman, dwl 723 Ellis
Waters William, with Thomas Drinkwater, 437 Bush, dwl 331 Bush
Waters William, machinist, Miners' Foundry
Waterson A. R. blind maker with J. Brokaw, dwl 633 Market
Watkin Henry, contractor, dwl 325 Lombard
Watkin William B. policeman, City Hall, dwl 325 Lombard
Watkins A. A. book keeper with Locke & Montague, 112 Battery
Watkins Carlton E. photographer, 425 Montgomery
Watkins Henry, butcher, 452 Third, dwl 450 Folsom

Watkins James T. captain Pacific Mail S. S. Colorado, dwl 58 South Park

Watkins *(John)* & Co. contractors raising and moving buildings, 403 Mason, dwl 630 Post

Watkins John, contractor, dwl 325 Lombard

Watkins Joseph, teamster with James Brokaw

Watkins Joseph E. calker, dwl 20 Clementina

Watkins William T. clerk, dwl 111 Washington

Watson Alexander R. workman with Lawrence & Houseworth, dwl E s Prospect Avenue nr California Avenue

Watson Charles, machinist, Vulcan Iron Works, dwl 6 Natoma

Watson Dudley L. carpenter, Mission Woolen Mills, dwl W s Folsom bet Sixteenth and Seventeenth

Watson F. laborer, Miners' Foundry

Watson Frank, merchant, dwl 19 Jessie

Watson Frederick, fireman, steamer Washoe

Watson George, dwl 78 Clementina

Watson George, drayman, 213 Clay, dwl 24 Scott

Watson Henry, collector, Spring Valley W. W. Co. dwl 1110 Mason

Watson Horace H. jr. Capt. office 305 Front, dwl 440 Second

Watson James, commission merchant and agent Coast Whaling Co.'s, office 8 Clay, dwl N s Mission nr Tenth

Watson James, engineer, stm Sacramento, dwl 213 Minna

Watson James M. Capt. U. S. N. inspector 12th L. H. District, office Custom House third floor, res Mare Island

Watson James T. gauger's clerk, Custom House, res Alameda

Watson J. D. stm Chrysopolis, dwl Lick House

Watson Joseph (col'd) barber, dwl 823 Pacific

Watson Mary B. (widow) dwl 911 Clay

Watson Nicholas E. broker, dwl 108 Stockton

Watson Richard, seaman, dwl 26 Sacramento

Watson S. T. *(Henry & W.)* bds 4 O'Farrell

Watson Thomas, baker, 546 Clay, dwl 1407 Stock

Watson Thomas, carpenter, dwl 552 Tehama

Watson Thomas, tinsmith with J. G. Ils, dwl N s Vallejo bet Powell and Mason

Watson Thomas K. stone mason, dwl 1513 Leav

WATSON W. C. real estate, office 50 Exchange Building, dwl Ashland Place N s Mission bet Eleventh and Twelfth

Watson William, engineer, Mission Woolen Mills, dwl W s Folsom bet Sixteenth and Seventeenth

Watson William, workman with F. McKenna, N s Precita Avenue nr San Bruno Road

Watson William E. *(Joseph R. Rollinson & Co.)* successor E. Mott Robinson, office 305 Front

Watson William H. clerk, 606 Clay, dwl 920 Stock

Watson William P. steamboatman, dwl 45 Louisa

Watson William S. *(Turner & W.)* 505 Montgomery, dwl Russ House

Watson W. M. painter, dwl 2 Chelsea Place

Watt George, helper, Vulcan Iron Works

Watt Robert, carpenter, bds 761 Mission

Watt Samuel F., Kellogg, Hewston & Co.'s Refinery, dwl NE cor Market and Kearny

Watterlot Louis *(Pecqueux & W.)* dwl 1111 Kearny

Watterson George T. dwl 1109 Howard

Watts A. D. captain bark Jane A. Falkinburg, office 405 Front

Watts B. dwl What Cheer House

Watts Charles, machinist, Union Foundry, dwl 211 Minna

Watts Evan, carpenter, dwl 275 Jessie

Watts George, drayman, 213 Clay, dwl 24 Scott

Watts Isaac B. carpenter, dwl W s Eighth between Mission and Howard

Watts John, machinist, dwl 331 Bush

Watts Life C. shipwright, dwl 235 Beale

Watts Oscar, porter, Railroad House, 319 Clay

Watts Samuel F. silver refiner, dwl 652 Market

Watts W. dwl What Cheer House

Wattson Samuel B. salesman with B. C. Horn & Co. dwl 1322 Jackson

Wau Hup (Chinese) washing, 535 Kearny

Wau Yune & Co. (Chinese) merchants, 739 Com

Wauer Adam, baker with Charles Schroth, 230 Kearny

Waugh Alexander, laborer, dwl 655 Mission

Waugh John, laborer, dwl NW cor Jessie and Annie

Waugh Michael, cook, Miners' Restaurant

Waugh William (col'd) cook, dwl 909 Pacific

Waw Sing (Chinese) washing, 323 Pacific

Way Charles A. map and chart mounter, Summer nr Montgomery, dwl 232 Stevenson

WAY *(Charles S.)* & KEYT *(Abner C.)* bill posters, office 535 Merchant, dwl 925 Wash

WAY DANIEL E. Japanese Bazaar, 206 Montgomery, dwl W s First bet Harrison and Folsom

Wead Edward N. teacher book keeping, 229 Bush

Weams James, clerk with L. J. Ewell, dwl 514 Filbert

Weatherup Samuel, shipsmith's helper, dwl 118 Shipley

Weaver C. Mrs. nurse, dwl 1511 Stockton, rear

Weaver Caroline (widow) dwl 935 Clay

Weaver Daniel, workman, Pacific Glass Works, dwl S s Mariposa nr Mississippi

WEAVER DWIGHT S. importer and retail stoves, tin ware, sheet iron, copper, etc. 505 Sansom, dwl SE cor Washington and Sansom

Weaver George D. ship carpenter, dwl 639 Mission

Weaver George H. book keeper with Castle Bros. dwl Second Avenue nr Sixteenth

Weaver Henry, harness making, 644 Market, dwl 650 Howard

Weaver H. L. Mrs. head assistant Washington Grammar School, dwl 22 John

WEAVER, *(P. L.)* WOOSTER *(J. B.)* & CO. *(George H. Sanderson)* (successors to Moses Ellis & Co.) importers and wholesale groceries, 218 Front, dwl cor Laurel Place and Essex

Weaver James, physician, office and dwl 6 Mont

Weaver John, porter with Tay, Brooks & Backus, dwl 5 Morse

Weaver Kate M. Miss, with Grover & Baker Sewing Machine Co. 329 Mont, dwl 522 Howard

Weaver Maggie Miss, seamstress, Davis' Laundry

Weaver N. stucco worker, 627½ Market, dwl 650 Howard

WEBB ANDREW C. hardware and crockery, 779 and 781 Market and salesman with J. Underhill & Co. dwl S s Ellis bet Hyde and Leav

Webb A. W. printer with Towne & Bacon, dwl 8 Virginia Place

Webb C. C. commissioner, widening Kearny Street, office 410 Kearny, dwl 826 Bush

Webb C. H. editor, dwl Occidental Hotel

WEBB DANIEL E. librarian Mercantile Library Association, dwl 822 Bush

Webb Elizabeth A. (widow) dwl SE cor Eddy and Mason

Webb Francis A. drayman, 120 Bat, dwl 521 Ellis

Webb George, carpenter, dwl 753 Mission

Webb George W. boatman, dwl 753 Mission

WEBB *(Henry)* & HOLMES *(Henry T.)* lime and cement, NW cor Davis and Sacramento, dwl 318 Fremont

Webb Henry, molder, Vulcan Iron Works, dwl 25 Natoma

Webb James, dwl 152 Stewart

Webb John, seaman, dwl 152 Stewart

Webb John M. book keeper, dwl S s Bryant bet Seventh and Eighth

Webb Joseph W. clerk with A. C. Webb, dwl 521 Ellis

Webb Margaret Mrs. dress maker, 753 Mission

Webb Peter L. *(Littlefield, W. & Co.)* dwl 408 Geary

Webber Calvin E. *(C. W. Ham & Co.)* dwl 17 John

Webber C. E. waterman, dwl Greenwich bet Dupont and Stockton
Webber C. H. box maker with Hobbs, Gilmore & Co. dwl 181 Jessie
Webber Ezra J. dwl SE cor Alta and Calhoun
Webber George E. quartz miner, dwl W s Jones bet Sutter and Post
Webber Miranda Mrs. domestic with Frank McDermott
Webber Thomas, seaman, dwl 54 Sacramento
Webe Augusta (widow) dwl 145 Post
Webe William, hairdresser, dwl 145 Post
Weber Adolph C. civil engineer, 505 Montgomery, dwl 840 Folsom
Weber Albin, dwl 16 Geary
Weber Charles, dwl 240 Stevenson
Weber F. Mrs. midwife, dwl 1428 Dupont
Weber Frederick, shoe maker, 311 Davis, dwl 217 Commercial
Weber Frederick, steward, Zeile's Vapor Baths, 517 Pacific
Weber Gabriel & Co. *(William Branschied)* boots and shoes, 638 Commercial
Weber George, longshoreman, dwl 210 Commercial
Weber George, musician, dwl 631 Broadway
Weber John, butcher with John Mengel
Weber Louis, bar keeper, SW cor East and Market, dwl 318 Folsom
Weber Tanias H. groceries and liquors, SE corner Broadway and Mason
Weber Wilhelmina Mrs. millinery, 16 Geary
Webster A. B. salt mill and water works, 521 Market, res Brooklyn, Alameda County
Webster Catherine (widow) dress maker, dwl 7 Baldwin Court
Webster Charles F. real estate, dwl SE cor Fifth and Harrison
Webster F. E. New York Department Wells, Fargo & Co. dwl 28 Stanly Place
Webster Horace, merchant, office 410 Front, dwl 526 Howard
Webster James K. sail maker, dwl 8 Clay
Webster John N. internal revenue stamps, 608 Montgomery, res Alameda
Webster N. B. pantryman, Original H Restaurant
Webster P. clerk and student with C. A. Johnson
Webster Samuel, printer, Eureka Typographical Union, 625 Merchant
Webster William A. millwright, dwl 305 First
Webster William T. blacksmith with N. W. Spaulding, dwl 340 Fremont
Weby John T. butcher with Crummie & O'Neill, dwl cor Brannan and Ninth
WECK L. E. & CO. *(Bernard Getleson)* importers and jobbers leather and shoe findings, 415 Clay, dwl 609 Pine
Wedde Henry, musician, dwl E s Vallejo Place
Wedderspoon John *(Cross & Co.)* 625 Sansom, res Oakland, Alameda County
Wedekind George, turner with Mathias Gray, dwl NE cor Bush and Larkin
Wedemeir Claus, workman, Albany Brewery
Wedemeyer Henry, brewer, Union Brewery
Wedgwood William O. carpenter, dwl N s Bush bet Polk and Van Ness Avenue
Wedtel John, handcartman, cor Davis and Pacific, dwl 207 Pacific
Weed Alexander, contractor, dwl American Exchange Hotel
Weed George, laborer, dwl N s Sixteenth near Nebraska
Weed Joseph, store keeper, Griffing's Bonded Warehouse, dwl 1401 Powell
Weed Joseph H. *(Gallagher, W. & White)* dwl W s Leavenworth bet Clay and Sacramento
Weed W. W. operator, California State Telegraph Co. 507 Montgomery, dwl 842 Clay
Weeden Ellen H. Miss, associate teacher, private school, W s First Avenue, dwl 22 First Avenue

Weedmar Rudolph, dwl 17 Everett
WEEKS E. JOHN, steamboat agent, office 405 Front, dwl 1325 Powell
Weeks F. F. physician, office and dwl 47 Second
Weeks Frank S. compositor with Dewey, Waters & Co. res Oakland
Weeks George P. bag maker, dwl N s Vallejo bet Larkin and Polk
Weeks Martin B. engineer, S. F. Cordage Factory, dwl 5 Dixon's Block
Weeks Thomas D. gilder with Jones, Wooll & Sutherland, dwl 249 Jessie
Weerbrouk Frederick, porter, 410 Pine
Wegener Albert, cook, Union Brewery
Wegener Frederick O. real estate agent, office 415 Montgomery, dwl 174 Clara
Wegener Leonora Mrs. dwl S s Eddy bet Jones and Leavenworth
WEGENER RICHARD accountant and mining secretary, office 415 Montgomery, dwl 274 Clara
Webmoller William, cooper, S. F. & P. Sugar Co. dwl Russ bet Folsom and Harrison
Wehn Charles F. *(Steil, Wehn & Co.)* dwl 908 Post
Wehr Fred. carpenter, bds St. Louis Hotel 11 Pac
Wehr Henry, carpenter, bds St. Louis Hotel 11 Pac
Weichbart John, safe and tool maker, 17 Fremont
Weid Ivar A. clerk with Miller & Cutter, dwl S s California nr Kearny
Weideman John, laborer, Miners' Foundry
Weidemuller Frederick *(Bresrasher & Co.)* dwl 1012 Dupont
Weidenrich *(Solomon)* Lehman *(Lipman)* & Co. clothing etc. 414 Commercial, dwl 814 Vallejo
Weiderhold Eunice (widow) dwl 652 Mission
Weidler George W. purser, dwl Occidental Hotel
Weidman John, cooper, 141 Third
Weigel Henry, superintendent Hayes' Park Pavilion
Weighland H. cook, International Hotel
Weigold John, waiter, Bootz's Hotel
Weihe August *(Hobe & W.)* res Stockton San Joaquin Co
Weihe Otto, cartman, cor Washington and Mont
Weil Abraham *(Godchaux, Weil & Co.)* dwl 1522 Powell
Weil David *(Elfelt, Weil & Co.)* dwl 1016 Stockton
Weil Henry L. book keeper, 312 Sac, dwl 339 Minna
Weil Hermann, bakery, 114 Third
Weil J. cigars and tobacco, 1016 Stockton
WEIL *(L.)* & CO. *(Julius Beer and Joseph Aron)* imptrs and jobbers cigars and tobacco, 226 Front
Weil *(Meyer)* & Levy *(Solomon A.)* importers and jobbers stationery and fancy goods, NW cor Battery and Sacramento, dwl 625 O'Farrell
Weil Theodore, dwl 214 Sansom
Weil Theodore, clerk, 400 Sac. dwl 616 Bush
Weiland C. musician, dwl cor Market and Kearny
Weiler Isaac S. salesman, 125 Mont, dwl 1008 Bush
Weill Alexander *(Stein, Simon & Co. and Lazard Freres)* dwl 1018 Bush
Weill E. & Son *(Maurice Weill)* importers cloths, cassimeres, tailors' trimmings, etc. 630 Sacramento, res Paris
Weill Emile, interpreter, City and County Hospital
Weill Henry, salesman, 609 Sacramento
Weill Maurice *(E. Weill & Son)* dwl 1321 Powell
Weill Raphael *(J. W. Davidson & Co.)* dwl 1509 Stockton
Weill Sylvain, salesman with Stein, Simon & Co. 632 Sacramento
Weimeyer Lizzie (widow) domestic, 845 Sutter
Weiner Aaron, fancy goods, 824 Market
Weiner F. deck hand, steamer Petaluma
Weiner Isaac, clothing, dwl 236 Minna
Weiner John, porter with Hecht Bros
Weiner Max *(J. Warshawski Bro. & Co.)* 656 Wash
Weiners Bernard, workman, S. F. & P. Sugar Co. dwl Rousch nr Folsom
Weinmann *(John)* & Bruder *(William)* liquor saloon, 612 Pacific

Weinschenk A. merchant, dwl 405 Taylor
Weintraub Samuel, clerk, 314 Davis
Weintraub W. dwl 211 Clay
Weintraut Charles H. harness maker, 429 Pacific, dwl N s Greenwich bet Stockton and Powell
Weir James, with Redington & Co. dwl What Cheer House
Weir James, blacksmith, Vulcan Iron Works, dwl 6 Natoma
Weir James, carpenter, dwl 840 Mission
Weir John, baker, dwl S s Bush bet Van Ness Avenue and Franklin
Weir John, porter with Conroy & O'Connor, dwl 20 Silver
Weir Thomas, butcher with Wilson & Stevens, dwl Brannan St. Bridge
WEIR WILLIAM G. furniture manufacturer, 638 Market, dwl E s Second Avenue nr Sixteenth
Weise J. captain schooner Flora, office 413 East
Weisenborn Frederick, Presidio H, Presidio Road
Weisler Alexander, Rev'd, pastor Congregation Emanu-El, dwl 1818 Powell
Weismann Henry, cabinet maker, 719 Mission, dwl Meyer's Hotel
Weiss Bernard, dwl 13 Dupont
Weiss George, brewer, dwl 1100 Stockton
Weiss (H. William) & Zwiesdele (George) Plaza Restaurant, 712 Kearny, dwl Lincoln Place
WEISS JACOB, Philadelphia Coffee Saloon, 308 Montgomery, dwl 314 Sixth
Weiss John, waiter, 143 Mont, dwl 40 St. Mark Pl
Weiss John P. carpenter, dwl 505 Union
Weiss M. toys and fancy goods, 324 Kearny, dwl 13 Dupont
Weisse Henry, gardener, Lafayette H. & L. Co. No.2
Weissenberg Joseph, miner, dwl 323 Pine
Weissich W. O. job wagon, SW cor Washington and Bat, dwl S s Post bet Gough and Octavia
Weithermei Bertha Miss, domestic, 961 Howard
Weitner Charles A. fruits, 740 Market
Weitzel Henry, shoe maker, dwl N s Francisco bet Powell and Mason
Welbern Henry, laborer, S. F. & San José R. R. Co
Welbrock Henry, clerk with Scanlin & Bruns, dwl 2 Second
Welch Andrew (Sproat & W.) dwl Occidental Hotel
Welch Andrew, iron founder, dwl NW cor Front and Broadway
Welch Charles, workman with N. Simonds, cor Bay View Park and Hunter's Point Roads
Welch Charles W. carrier, Call and Bulletin, dwl 817 Post
Welch David, musician, dwl S s Chambers bet Battery and Front
Welch Edward, plumber, dwl 14 Sutter
Welch Edward, laborer, Mission Woolen Mills, dwl N s Fifteenth nr Howard
Welch H. H. book keeper, 540 Clay, dwl 608 Pine
Welch James, cartman, cor Jones and Greenwich
Welch James, laborer, Lone Mountain Cemetery
Welch James, laborer, dwl 2 Stockton Place
Welch James, laborer, dwl 1224 Kearny
Welch James, laborer, dwl N s Vallejo bet Leavenworth and Hyde
Welch James, milkman with Charles H. Killey
Welch James, operator with Thomas J. Higgins, dwl S s Jessie nr Sixth
Welch James H. dwl SE cor Valencia and Sixteenth
Welch James H. carrier, Alta California, dwl 428 Fremont
Welch James M. captain of police, City Hall, dwl 721 Bush
Welch James M. jr. porter with J. W. Brittan & Co. dwl 351 Minna
Welch Jane Miss, domestic, 821 Post
Welch Jerome, shoe maker with David Hauser, dwl 412 Post, rear

Welch John, calker, dwl 222 Ritch
Welch John, laborer, Pioneer Woolen Mills, dwl SE cor Jones and Francisco
Welch John, shoe maker, dwl S s Berry nr Mary Lane
Welch Julia Miss, domestic, 688 Geary
Welch Lawrence, hackman, Plaza, dwl 425 Clementina
Welch Lewis, carpenter, dwl 1330 Washington
Welch Margaret Miss, domestic, 1012 Bush
Welch Margaret (widow) dwl nr cor Folsom and Kosciusko
Welch Mary Miss, domestic, 818 Kearny
Welch Mary Miss, domestic, 810 Jackson
Welch Mary A. Miss, domestic, 728 Howard
Welch Michael, blacksmith, Omnibus R. R. Co
Welch Michael, laborer, dwl N s Hayes nr Polk, rear
Welch Michael, tailor with Heuston, Hastings & Co. dwl 85 Stevenson
Welch Michael. wool sorter, S. F. P. Woolen Mills, dwl SW cor Francisco and Jones
Welch Patrick, express wagon, Stevenson nr Second
Welch Peter, helper, Pacific Foundry, dwl E s Beale nr Howard
Welch Richard, dwl What Cheer House
Welch Richard, laborer, dwl 13 Ohio
Welch Samuel G. with D. Greninger, 116 Third, res San José
Welch Stephen, express wagon, cor Broadway and Davis, dwl 325 Broadway
Welch Thomas, laborer, dwl 761½ Mission
Welch Thomas, laborer, dwl 1330 Washington
Welch Thomas, laborer, dwl 127 Shipley
Welch Thomas, milkman with Charles H. Killey
Welch William, laborer, S. F. P. Woolen Mills, dwl North Point bet Polk and Van Ness Avenue
Welch William, blacksmith, dwl E s Park Avenue bet Bryant and Harrison
Welch William, laundryman, dwl SE cor Lombard and Jones
Welch, see Walsh and Welsh
Weldon Christopher, clerk, dwl 304 Fremont
Welker William, sauerkraut manuf, 753 Mission
Wellenkamp Ernest H. clerk, dwl 719 Pacific
Weller Charles L. attorney at law, dwl 302 Stock
Weller Gottfried, butcher, bds 7 Washington
Weller Herman, dwl 821 Bush
Weller John B. dwl Cosmopolitan Hotel
Weller Peter H. (Bookstaver & W.) dwl 709 Howard
Wellhoff Brothers (Isaac and Meyer) dry goods, 328 Kearny, dwl Belden nr Pine
Wellhoff Meyer (Wellhoff Bros.) dwl Belden nr Pine
Welling C. G. proprietor Hayes' Park Pavilion, Hayes' Valley
Wellington E. L. clerk, dwl Original House
Wellington John, oysterman with Adam Smith, 536 Market, dwl 115 Dupont
WELLMAN, (B.) PECK (John M.) & CO. importers and wholesale grocers, 404 Front, dwl NW cor First and Laurel Place
Wells Asa R. (Brown & W.) dwl SW cor Market and Third
Wells Benjamin H. maltster with Thomas Lea, 430 Pine
WELLS' BUILDING, SW cor Mont and Clay
Wells Charles, blacksmith, dwl 511 Market
Wells Chester W. drayman, 216 Jackson, dwl W s Leavenworth bet Union and Green
WELLS, FARGO & CO. Express and Banking Co. office NW cor Montgomery and California, Louis McLane general agent, Samuel Knight superintendent
Wells Francis H. attorney at law, office 402 Mont
Wells George G. captain bark Emily Banning, office 305 Front

Wells George R. clerk with D. S. & S. M. Wilson, dwl 764 Mission
Wells G. F. A. laborer with Hobbs, Gilmore & Co. dwl 515 Market
WELLS HENRY H. (col'd) liquor saloon, 917 Washington
Wells Henry J. justice of the peace Second Township, office 623 Merchant, dwl 908 Jackson
Wells Henry R. clerk with Alfred S. Lowndes, 311½ Battery
Wells Isadore, with Jacob A. Maison
Wells James, bar keeper, Eureka Theater, dwl Summer St. House
Wells Joseph, dwl 29 Third
Wells Joseph W. with C. W. Thomas, 22 California
Wells Levi, horse shoeing, 19 Sutter, dwl 920 Clay
Wells M. A. Miss (Walton & W.) cor Jackson and Mason
Wells Mortimer, carriage painter with Samuel F. Ross, dwl Montgomery House
Wells Revello, book keeper with S. S. Culverwell, dwl 47 Second
Wells Samuel P. Port Warden's office, 716 Front, dwl 202 Bush
Wells T. C. milkman with Murray & Noble
Wells T. M. actor, Bella Union
Wells Walter, longshoreman, dwl 77 Jessie
Wells William F. (Freeman & Co.) dwl with F. A. Hanson
Wells William P. dwl N s Francisco bet Stockton and Powell
Wellsford Charles H. dwl 651 Howard
Wellvor G. & S. M. Co. office 338 Montgomery
Welsh Andrew, laborer, Miners' Foundry, dwl 149 Beale
Welsh Charles Capt. dwl S s Chestnut bet Leavenworth and Jones
Welsh Charles H. Knickerbocker Engine Co. No. 5
Welsh Daniel, helper, Miners' Foundry, dwl Beale nr Folsom
Welsh Daniel, milkman, dwl N s Turk bet Fillmore and Steiner
Welsh Frank, boiler maker helper, Vulcan Iron Works, dwl 543 Mission
Welsh James, fireman, steamer Orizaba
Welsh James, laborer, dwl N s Sutter bet Laguna and Buchanan
Welsh James, laborer, dwl 39 First
Welsh James H. dwl cor Valencia and Sixteenth
Welsh John C. laborer, dwl 23 Minna Place
Welsh John L. calker, dwl NW cor First and Frederick
Welsh J. P. painter, dwl 64 Tehama
Welsh Kate (widow) dwl 144 Natoma
Welsh Mary Miss, laundress, dwl 133 Stevenson
Welsh Michael, boarding, 49 Stevenson
Welsh Michael, boot maker, dwl 132 First
Welsh Michael, laborer, dwl S s Market bet Sixth and Seventh
Welsh Michael, shipsmith with W. S. Phelps & Co. dwl 49 Stevenson
Welsh Michael, tailor, dwl 91 Stevenson
Welsh Patrick, laborer with Edwd. J. Quirk
Welsh Patrick, waiter, dwl 156 Natoma
Welsh Peter, laborer, dwl 209 Beale
Welsh Richard, laborer, dwl 17 Main
Welsh Robert, porter, dwl 120 Geary
WELSH (Thomas) & SHOEMAKER (Frederick) stoves, tin ware, etc. 29 Market, dwl 761½ Mission
Welsh Thomas, waiter, dwl 6 Boston Place
Welsh Thomas, workman, S. F. & P. Sugar Co. dwl 37 Everett
Welsh Timothy, workman S. F. & P. Sugar Co. dwl Dora nr Seventh
Welsh Walter, carriage painting, 115 Bush and 119 Pine, dwl W s Leav bet Geary and O'Farrell
Welsh, see Walsh and Welch
Welton Amy Miss, dwl SW cor Larkin and Sutter

Welton Bartholomew, blacksmith helper, S s Grove nr Polk
Welton Garrett, contractor, dwl 752 Howard
Welton Lamson S. (M. Welton & Son) dwl cor Larkin and Sutter
Welton Merritt & Son (L. S. Welton) real estate agents, office 420 Montgomery, dwl SW corner Larkin and Sutter
Wemble T. driver Omnibus R. R. Co
Wempke Henry, tinsmith with E. Ayers, dwl 247 Clara
Wempke Henry jr. tinsmith with Cutting & Co. 247 Clara
Wenck Charles, porter, 624 Sacramento
Wendel David, laborer, dwl 137 Clara
Wendel John, cook, 826 Market, dwl 753 Mission
Wendell William G. salesman, 106 Battery, dwl 1219 Clay
Wendling George, clerk, 531 Kearny
Wendt Herman, groceries and liquors, NE corner Third and Folsom
Wendt John, carpenter, Brown Alley nr Pine
Wendt William, clerk, cor Third and Folsom
Wenger Joseph, boot maker, 1103 Stockton
Wenig Charles, drayman, Front nr Washington
Wenner Wolf, butcher, 77 Stevenson
Wennerhold Christian, with Kellogg, Hewston & Co. dwl 834 Folsom
Wensinger F. S. office 511 Front, dwl S s Sutter bet Jones and Leavenworth
Wentworth Daniel B. lamplighter, S. F. Gas Co. dwl 310 Mason
WENTWORTH I. M. & CO. manufacturers and jobbers boots and shoes, 210 Pine, dwl 5 Stockton nr Market
Wentworth Jackson J. engineer, Golden Gate Flour Mills, dwl N s Vallejo bet Mont and Kearny
Wentworth J. P. H. real estate, dwl Second Avenue Mission Dolores
Wentworth Nathan, dwl 231 Seventh
Wenz John D. butcher, SW cor Folsom and Ritch
Wenzel Edw. (Procureur & W.) dwl 431 Natoma
Wenzel George L. cooper, dwl 82 Jessie
Wenzel Herman, watch maker and jeweler, 303 Montgomery, dwl SW cor Seventh and Folsom
Wenzel Lizzie Miss, domestic, 31 Turk
Wenzner Peter, restaurant, dwl 222 Stevenson
Wepfler Joseph, hog ranch, dwl E s Ninth bet Bryant and Brannan
Werber Frederic, compositor, Courrier de San Francisco, 617 Sansom
Werber Frederick, shoe maker, 311 Davis, dwl 219 Commercial
Werber Mme. French dress maker, 616 Bdwy, rear
Werch William, blacksmith with Black & Saul, dwl 186 Jessie
Werli S. mechanic, dwl 431 Pine
Werlin J. G. boots and shoes, 532 Commercial, dwl 258 Stevenson
Werner Charles, dwl E s Rassette Place No. 1
Werner C. H. baker, dwl 140 Second
Werner Christian H. barber, 113 Third
Werner Hermann, watchmaker with Joseph McGregor, dwl NW cor First and Howard
Werner Jacob, shoe maker, dwl 113 Commercial
Werner William, barber with C. Schmidt, dwl 38 Clara
Wernham F. Miss, teacher pianoforte, dwl 1809 Powell
Wernicki J. A. visiting physician French Hospital, office and dwl 42 Geary
Wernstrom E. G. seaman, dwl 20 Commercial
Wertheimber Philip, merchant, dwl 721 Lombard
Wertheimer E. (L. & E. Wertheimer) dwl St. Nicholas Hotel
Wertheimer John F. assistant weigber and measurer, Custom House, dwl 105 Prospect Place
Wertheimer L. & E. importers and jobbers cigars and tobacco, NW cor Front and Sacramento

Wertheimer Louis *(Erlanger & W., Washoe City)* office NW cor Front and Sacramento, dwl St. Nicholas Hotel

Wertheimer Louis, merchant, dwl S s Howard near Sixth

Wertheimer Louis, distiller, 721 Lombard

Wertheimer Michael, butcher, dwl 1006 Market

Wertheman Arthur, civil engineer, dwl 417 Dupont

Wertheman Edmond, professor chemistry, dwl 417 Dupont

Wertheman Rudolph, real estate, office 28 Exchange Building, dwl 417 Dupont

Wesby John R. *(Hicks & Co.)* dwl 1417 Kearny

Wescott Elliot, shoe maker, 313 Pine

Wescuss Mary Cecelia (widow) dwl N s Sixteenth bet Guerrero and Dolores

Wesenberg Peter, with John H. Cook, dwl S s Vallejo nr Mason

Wesh Michael, laborer, dwl 16 Jessie

Wesley Hurley E. horse shoer with Levi Wells, dwl 12 Sutter

Wesley Willis C. at Newhall & Brooks, dwl 353 Jessie

Wessel Frank, express wagon, SW cor Montgomery and Cal, dwl cor Geary and Leavenworth

Wessel John *(J. Siebe & Co.)* dwl SE cor Union and Powell

Wessel William, hatter, dwl N s Pacific bet Stockton and Powell

Wessels Herman, carpenter, dwl 114 Dupont

Wessenberg Peter F. clerk, 48 Washington Market, dwl S s Filbert bet Taylor and Mason

Wessling William, groceries and liquors, SE corner Folsom and Fourth

Wesson *(Joseph W.)* & Magilton *(Thomas)* lumber dealers, Hathaway's Wharf NE cor Bryant and Main, dwl NW cor Polk and Green

West Benjamin, engineer, dwl 141 Fourth

West C. B. dwl Niantic Hotel

West Charles, laborer, dwl 308 Folsom

West Charles, longshoreman, SW cor Montgomery and Greenwich

West Charles, mariner, dwl N s Grove bet Gough and Octavia

West Charles H. stock broker, office 606 Merchant, dwl 214 Ellis

West Edwin O. carpenter and builder, dwl S s Sixteenth bet Mission and Valencia

West Edwin W. clerk, dwl S s Sixteenth bet Mission and Valencia

West Ellen H. Mrs. dress maker, 141 Fourth

WEST END HOTEL, J. H. Daley proprietor, Brenham Place W s Plaza

West Frank, furniture wagon, SW cor Montgomery and Cal, dwl S s Geary nr Franklin and Gough

West Frederick, captain, schr Three Brothers, dwl 9 Park Avenue

West George (col'd) porter, 409 California

West Henry, laborer, dwl 424 Geary

WEST INDIA AND PACIFIC STEAMSHIP COMPANY, Rodgers, Meyer & Co. agents, office 314 Washington

West James E. sail maker, dwl W s Thirteenth nr Valencia

West James E. sash and blind maker, dwl SE cor Ritch and Bryant

WEST LOUIS, groceries and liquors, NW cor Fifth and Shipley

West Mary W (widow) dwl 721 Howard

West Samuel, carpenter, dwl 1209 Bush

West T. J. clerk, dwl Niantic Hotel

West William, hair dresser with C. Diehl, dwl S s Clay bet Stockton and Waverly Place

WEST W. W. secretary Pacific Ore Company, office 240 Montgomery, res San Mateo

Westall Edward *(Hicks & Co.)* dwl 1417 Kearny

Westcott Elmer, purser steamer Del Norte, dwl Russ House

Weste Amanda C. dwl NW cor Eddy and Buchanan

Westedd William, liquors, dwl 820 Battery

Westerfeld Henry, dwl 114 Eddy

Westerfeld Joseph, cigar maker with John Claussen, 121 Kearny

Westerfeld Louis, with Charles Schroth, 230 Kearny, dwl 512 Bush

Westerheid Charles, porter, 210 California, dwl Lutgen's Hotel

Westerholdt Charles, shoe maker, dwl 5 Brooklyn Place

Westerling John, seaman, dwl 26 Sacramento

Westerman J. tailor, 804 Clay

WESTERN HOTEL, John Higgins proprietor, 306 Broadway

WESTERN PACIFIC RAILROAD COMPANY, president Charles N. Fox, secretary Charles W. Sanger, office 409 California

Westevelt Ellsworth, clerk with C. Adolphe Low & Co. dwl Brevoort House

Westfall Albert H. drayman with Peter Sesser, dwl cor Sixth and Market

Westfall John C. carpenter, dwl 1014 Larkin

Westfall Julius, drayman with Peter Sesser, dwl cor Sixth and Market

Westheimer John F. clerk, dwl 105 Prospect Place

Westheimer John F. weigher, dwl 105 Prospect Pl

Westhouse Ferdinand, tailor, dwl 327 Minna

Weston Aaron, teacher music, dwl N s Geary nr Leavenworth

WESTON C. W. & CO. *(O. P. Goodhue)* wholesale commission fruits, Pacific Fruit Market, dwl 1922 Taylor

WESTON JOHN, wholesale and retail wines and liquors, 536 Jackson, bds Russ House

Weston Nathaniel, photographic artist, 14 Second, dwl First Avenue bet Fourteenth and Fifteenth

Weston Ryland K. assistant cashier, Custom House, office second floor, dwl 577 Howard

Westover S. H. assayer, dwl Howard Engine House No. 3

WETHERBEE *(Colvin H.)* & COOK *(Isaac)* foreign and domestic lumber, Pier 2½ Stewart and 21 and 23 California, dwl S s Eddy bet Taylor and Jones

Wetherbee Charles E. merchant, dwl 725 O'Farrell

Wetherbee Henry *(Macpherson & W.)* dwl Occidental Hotel

Wetherbee Seth H. commissioner immigration, office NE cor Battery and Washington *(and Blyth & W.)* dwl 343 Beale

Wetherell John H. salesman with J. R. Hughes, dwl Delavan House

Wetherill Samuel E. treasurer Maguire's Opera House, dwl S s Wash bet Dupont and Stockton

Wetmore W. M. foreman with James Brokaw, dwl 44 Second

Wetmore W. N. Mrs. ladies' and children's furnishing goods, 44 Second

Wetteg Minna (widow) dwl 202 Dupont, rear

Wetterman August, musician, dwl 114 Post

Wettstein William, paper hanger and painter, 819 Jackson

Wetzel Theodore, mining secretary, office 611 Clay, dwl 717 Howard

WETZLAR GUSTAVUS, real estate and money broker, office 420 Mont room 3, dwl 109 Silver

Wexel A. S. glazier with Wilson & Bro. dwl N s Minna bet Third and Fourth

Wey John W. handcartman, corner Jackson and Drumm

Weydemann Henry, furniture, 238 Fourth

Weygant F. E. jr. dwl International Hotel

WEYGANT FRANK E. proprietor International Hotel, 530–534 Jackson

Weyl Abram, dwl 24 Everett

Weyl Cerf, book keeper, 307 Sac, dwl 24 Everett

Weyl Henry J. cooper with C. Bingenheimer, dwl 3 Lafayette Place

Weyl Jerome, clerk, 307 Sacramento, dwl 24 Everett

Weyl Junius, apprentice, dwl 24 Everett
Weyle James, steward, dwl 731 Broadway
Weymouth Orrin, teamster, Pier 17 and 18 Stewart
Whalan Larry, cook, Railroad House, 319 Clay
Whalen Charles, steward, Clipper Restaurant
Whalen Hannah Miss, domestic, 816 Powell
Whalen James, cooper, dwl Manhattan House
Whalen Jerry, clerk, Board Port Wardens, office 716 Front, dwl NE cor Jackson and Kearny
Whalen John, cooper with Timothy Lynch, 219 Washington
Whalen John, salesman, 1 Montgomery, dwl 28 Post
Whalen Thomas, coupé, dwl 321 Jessie
Whaley Andrew, laborer, dwl 540 Mission
Whaley Thomas (DeBloin & Co.) dwl 651 Folsom
Whalon Alice (widow) dwl NE cor Tehama and Fourth
Whalon Charles, waiter, dwl 122 Jessie
Whalon James, laborer with Alexander Lemore
Whaland Andy, laborer, dwl 553 Mission
Whannell Peter B. expressman, S. F. & P. Sugar Co. dwl cor Eighth and Market
Wharton John H. book keeper with John C. Bell
WHAT CHEER HOUSE, R. B. Woodward proprietor, 525–529 Sacramento
WHAT CHEER LAUNDRY, Miller & Cutter proprietors, What Cheer House
Whearty James, miner, dwl S s Perry bet Fourth and Fifth
Whearty Martin, express wagon, cor Pacific and Davis, dwl SW cor Green and Sansom
Whearty Michael, miner, dwl N s Perry bet Fourth and Fifth
WHEATLEIGH CHARLES, lessee Metropolitan Theater, W s Montgomery bet Washington and Jackson, dwl 504 Dupont
Wheaton Benjamin F. stair builder, 315 Mission, dwl 628 Geary
Wheaton Horace E. book keeper with Wilson & Stevens, dwl Hardie Place
Wheaton William H. porter with Tay, Brooks & Backus, dwl 5 Morse
WHEATON WM. R. city and county assessor, office 22 City Hall first floor, dwl 920 Jackson
Wheatty C. H. merchant, dwl 518 Pacific
Wheelan Margaret Miss, domestic, 504 Third
WHEELAN (Peter) & CO. Alta Flour Mills, N s Stevenson nr First
Wheelan Rosa Miss, domestic, 202 Ellis
Wheelan Thomas, calker, dwl SW cor California and Drumm
Wheeland James, bar keeper with Hoadley & Co. dwl Vernon House 210 Jackson
Wheeland Samuel, molder, Vulcan Iron Works, dwl 43 Clementina
Wheelen Charles. jobber, dwl 1921 Mason
WHEELER & WILSON SEWING MACHINE CO. F. L. Tileston agent, 435 Montgomery cor Sacramento
Wheeler Alfred, attorney at law, office 34 Montgomery Block, dwl 403 Bryant
Wheeler D. drayman, Clay bet Front and Davis
WHEELER E. D. attorney at law, office 402 Montgomery; res Alameda
Wheeler Edward A. salesman with William Alvord & Co. dwl 211 Prospect Place
Wheeler Francis B. Rev. pastor First Congregational Church, dwl 33 South Park
Wheeler Frank, dwl 32 Second
Wheeler Frank, tinsmith with G. & W. Snook, dwl N s Union bet Jones and Leavenworth
Wheeler Frederick A. hairdresser, dwl 934 Kearny
Wheeler Harry, salesman with Jacob Underhill & Co. dwl 521 Ellis
Wheeler Henry, groceries and liquors, SW cor Howard and Langton
Wheeler Hiram S. carpenter, dwl 649 Mission
Wheeler H. T. assistant entry clerk, Custom House, dwl 915 Market

Wheeler H. Z. assistant U. S. Appraiser, office Custom House, dwl 915 Market
Wheeler John, builder, dwl 423 Sutter
Wheeler (M. A.) & Gallagher (S. C.) stock and money brokers. office 302 Montgomery
Wheeler Martha Mrs. lodgings, dwl 934 Kearny
Wheeler Osgood C. secretary California Branch U. S. Sanitary Commission. office SE cor Montgomery and Pine, dwl Russ House
Wheeler Preston, hat presser, dwl 567 Mission
Wheeler R. F. Mrs. milliner, 32 Second
Wheeler R. H. carpenter and builder, 439 Jackson, dwl S s Columbia bet Guerrero and Dolores
Wheeler T. Wright, carrier, Alta California, dwl King bet Third and Fourth
Wheeler Willard S. carpenter, dwl Berry nr Dupont
Wheeler William P. Pioneer Liquor Saloon, NE cor Sixteenth and Dolores
Wheelock Anna (widow) dwl NE cor Dupont and Jackson
Wheelock D. laborer, Custom House
Wheelock Harrison, collector, dwl 3 Milton Place
Wheelock Jay (Munson & W.) dwl 3 Milton Pl
Wheelock Joanna (widow) dwl 916 Stockton
Wheelock Joseph, with Samuel Johnson, 33 Geary
Wheelock Samuel D. carpenter, dwl 3 Milton Place
Whelan Catherine, dwl with William Green, S s Mission bet Eleventh and Twelfth
Whelan Dennis, boot maker, 17 Fourth
Whelan Dennis, drayman, 210 Clay, dwl 1220 Stock
Whelan Frank, ship joiner, dwl 446 Brannan
Whelan Honora Miss, domestic, 2002 Powell
Whelan Jeremiah, laborer, S. F. & San José R. R. Co
Whelan Johanna Mrs. dress making, 1203 Bush
Whelan John, laborer, dwl 1203 Bush
Whelan John, laborer, W s Leavenworth between Vallejo and Broadway
Whelan John A. ship joiner, dwl 446 Brannan
Whelan John R. (McLennan, W. & Grisar) Broadway Wool Depôt, bds Franklin House
Whelan Kate (widow) dwl E s Sumner nr Howard
Whelan Malachi, workman, Mission Woolen Mills, dwl with P. Whelan W s Shotwell between Nineteenth and Twentieth
Whelan Margaret Mrs. dress maker, dwelling 1220 Stockton
Whelan Patrick, sexton St. Joseph's Church, dwl W s Tenth bet Folsom and Howard
Whelan Patrick, workman, Mission Woolen Mills, dwl with P. Whelan, W s Shotwell bet Nineteenth and Twentieth
Whelan Thomas, coupé, Plaza
Whelden Isaac, dwl 38 Silver
Whelpley James, dwl 1323 Stockton
Whicher Harvey F. printer with Calhoun & Son, 320 Clay
WHIPPLE ALBERT, private club rooms, 630 Com
Whipple Edwin E. dwl 630 Commercial
Whipple Hugh L. cashier with Charles W. Brooks & Co. dwl 441 Minna
Whipple Ithemar C. assistant store keeper, Custom House, dwl 1807 Powell
Whipple Louis, box maker with Hobbs, Gilmore & Co. dwl 124 Fourth
Whipple Samuel W. salesman with G. W. Conkling, 714 Montgomery, dwl 18 Stockton
WHIPPLE S. B. agent Union Coal Co. (Mount Diablo) depôt Mission bet Fremont and Beale, offices 203 Sansom and cor Mission and Fremont, res San Mateo
Whipple Stephen B. carpenter, dwl W s Eleventh bet Market and Mission
Whipple Willard, contractor, dwl 321 Clementina
Whitaker J. K. office 405 Front
Whitaker John C. real estate, dwl 1010 Bush
Whitaker John W. painter, 637 California, dwl 4 Virginia Place
Whitaker Margaret L. Miss, dwl 1010 Bush
Whitaker, see Whittaker

WHITCOMB A. C. attorney at law and president Citizen's Gas Co. office NW cor Washington and Kearny. dwl 605 Clay room 23·

Whitcomb Baker, real estate agent, 472 Montgomery, dwl 286 Stevenson

Whitcomb Charles G. with Reynolds, Howell & Ford, dwl 624 Commercial

Whitcomb George, seaman, dwl 26 Sacramento

Whitcomb Henry H. jeweler, dwl NE cor Seventeenth and Church

Whitcomb J. B. broker, dwl 200 Stockton

Whitcomb *(Nathan T.)* & Dyer *(James J.)* dentists, office 205 Third

White and Murphy G. & S. M. Co. office 620 Wash

White Adonijah A. salesman with Jones, Dixon & Co. dwl 1209 Taylor

White Albert E. engineer, dwl 687 Market

White Anthony C. carpenter, dwl 21 John

White Benjamin, livery stable, dwl 626 California

White Charles, mariner, dwl 29 Pacific

White Charles, seaman, dwl 111 Washington

White Charles, waiter, 623 Commercial

White Charles W. variety store, 40 Clay, dwl 810 Green

White Charles W. jr. Vigilant Engine Co. No. 9

White Charlotte Miss, dress maker, dwl 18 Minna

White David, engineer, dwl 128 Perry

White David, laborer, dwl 472 Jessie, rear

White Dennis, laborer, dwl E s Geneva nr Brannan

White D. W. porter, Falkner, Bell & Co. dwl 449 Bryant

White E. & Co. *(S. Gumbinner)* hot pies, 114 Dupont

White Eben D. stone cutter, dwl 219 Minna

White Ebenezer D. porter, 206 California, dwl Mission bet First and Second

White Edward, deck hand, steamer Chrysopolis

White Edward P. proprietor Davis' Laundry, W s Harriet bet Howard and Folsom

White Elijah, physician, office and dwl 639 Market

White Eliza (widow) dwl S s Filbert bet Mason and Taylor

White Ellen (widow) liquor saloon, 609 California

White Emma Miss, dwl with George R. Turner

White Emma A. (widow) dwl 137 Fourth

White E. N. Miss, assistant, Second St. School, dwl 21 Minna

White F. B. actor, Gilbert's Melodeon, dwl NE cor Kearny and Clay

White Frederick, clerk, dwl 517 Pine

White F. T. mechanic with James Brokaw, dwl NW cor First and Mission

White George, bricklayer, dwl Chestnut bet Van Ness Avenue and Franklin

White George, engineer, dwl W s Mont nr Vallejo

White George, mining stocks, dwl 626 California

White George, tinsmith, dwl Chicago Hotel, 220 Pacific

White George C. master bark Fremont, dwl 238 Stewart

White George D. salesman with Stanford Bros. dwl 923 Bush

White George H. clerk, dwl 842 Mission

White George R. photographic operator with Addis & Koch, dwl 5 Hardie Place

White Harvey G. ship joiner, dwl 256 Stevenson

White Henry, cook, 117 Sacramento

White Henry, salesman with LeGay & Co. dwl 3 Adona Place

White Henry L. dwl 926 Market

White I. K. manufacturer cigars and dealer furs, 221 Sacramento

White J. dwl 1000 Market

White Jacob W. collar maker with Calvin Ewing, 324 Davis

White James, dwl What Cheer House

White James, carpenter, dwl 430 Geary

White James, machinist, dwl E s Beale bet Market and Mission

White James, proprietor Museum, Meiggs' Wharf, dwl 618 Lombard

White James, seaman, dwl Clay bet Drumm and East

White James F. foreman with Louis & Neville, dwl cor Pacific and Leavenworth

White James H. mineralogist, dwl 1615 Dupont

White James M. painter, dwl 1233 Pacific

White James T. salesman with H. H. Bancroft & Co. dwl 516 Greenwich

White James W. ironer, Davis' Laundry, W s Harriet bet Howard and Dolsom

White J. C. lumber, dwl 47 Minna

White Jeremiah, with Goodwin & Co. dwl W side Beale bet Mission and Howard

White John, advertising clerk, Evening Bulletin, 620 Montgomery, dwl 1807 Stockton

White John, editor, dwl Occidental Hotel

White John, laborer, North Beach & M. R. R. Co

White John, watchman, New Wisconsin Hotel, 411 Pacific

White John C. dwl 424 Bryant

White John D. carpenter, dwl SE cor Vallejo and Kearny

White Joseph, with Rodgers, Meyer & Co. dwl 723 Sutter

White Joseph, stair builder, dwl SE cor Twenty-Third and Valencia

White Joseph K. house and sign painter, 644 Market, dwl 315 First

White Josiah H. conductor, dwl American Exchange

White Lina Miss, domestic, 912 Jackson

White Louisa R. Mrs. machine sewing, 926 Market

White Lovell *(J. S. Day & Co.)* dwl 5 Stockton

White Margaret Miss, domestic, 107 Fourth

White Margaret (widow) dwl 1807 Stockton

White Martin, attorney at law, dwl 33 Government House 502 Washington

White Mary (widow) dwl 150 Clara

White Mary S. Mrs. dwl 279 Minna

White Matthew, boots and shoes, 530 Commercial, dwl 336 Union

White M. C. physician and druggist, NE cor Jackson and Kearny, bds International Hotel

White Michael, laborer, dwl 721 Market

White Michael P. *(Morrison & W.)* dwl E s Thirteenth bet Howard and Folsom

White M. W. door keeper, U. S. Marine Hospital

White Nicholas, dwl W s Florida nr Twentieth

White Nellie Miss, domestic, 1319 Powell

White Patrick, laborer, dwl 25 Natoma Place

White Peter, wheelwright with Kimball & Co. dwl 777 Market

White Philo, jeweler, dwl 114 Geary

WHITE P. J. & CO. *(E. M. Root)* wholesale grocers, 412 Front, bds Brooklyn Hotel

WHITE *(Robert)* & BAUER *(Emile)* news agents, 413 Washington, dwl 1807 Stockton

White Robert, carpenter, dwl N s Welch bet Third and Fourth

White Robert N. clerk, U. S. Clothing Depôt, 34 Cal

White Rover G. & S. M. Co. office 6 Mont Block

White Samuel *(Gallagher, Weed & W.)* dwl 547 Market

White Samuel, office with George W. Chapin, 338 Montgomery

White Samuel, laborer, Lone Mountain Cemetery

White Samuel A. with S. B. Whipple, coal, 203 Sansom, dwl 850 Howard

White Samuel S. farmer, Old San José Road near county line

White S. J. Miss, assistant, Washington Grammar School, dwl 850 Howard

White Sarah J. Miss, with California Straw Works, dwl 358 Jessie

White Stephen, stevedore, dwl 29 Main

White Thomas, boot maker, dwl 23 Pacific

White Thomas, carpenter with S. S. Culverwell, dwl 108 Sutter

White Thomas, brick mason, dwl 45 Minna
White Thomas, driver, Central R. R. Co. dwl SE cor Brannan and Seventh
White Thomas, engineer, Market St. R. R. Co. dwl W s Polk bet Hayes and Fell
White Thomas, hostler with Central R. R. Co. dwl W s Gilbert bet Seventh and Eighth
White Thomas, spar maker. dwl 308 Beale
White Thomas A. dwl 126 Silver
White Thomas H. clerk with Weaver, Wooster & Co. dwl American Exchange
White Thomas N. carpenter with S. S. Culverwell, 29 Fremont, dwl cor Mission and Annie
White Thomas W. molder, dwl 102 Fourth
White Timothy, boiler maker with Coffey & Risdon, dwl 61 Natoma
White William, with Lewis & Neville, dwl cor Pacific and Leavenworth
White William, laborer, dwl 140 Stewart
White William A. clerk with H. M. Newhall & Co. dwl 325 Fremont
White William C. tinsmith with E. Ayers, dwl 320 Ritch
White William H. cashier with Dibblee & Hyde, dwl 613 Pine
White William H. driver, Swain's Bakery, dwl 557 Howard.
White William H. second engineer Chelsea Laundry
WHITE WILLIAM M. livery and sale stable, 431 California
White, see Wight
Whitehead John, with C. F. Powell, 610 Clay, dwl 524 Union
Whitehead Samuel, cabinet maker, dwl 1116 Pac
Whitehead Samuel B. driver with David Dolben, dwl 14 Stockton Place
Whitehill John, straw hat presser, dwl 605 Market
Whitehill Morris, straw hat presser, dwl 605 Market
WHITEHORNE WILLIAM A. importer, agent Schuyler, Hartley, Graham &. Co. New York, office 409 Battery, dwl 225 Second
Whitehouse Moses C. painter, 241 Sutter, dwl 8 s Post bet Polk and Van Ness Avenue
Whitehurst Henry, cook, Market St. Restaurant, dwl 136 Stevenson
Whiteley William H. liquidating clerk Naval Office Custom House, dwl 335 Jessie
Whiteman Joseph R. millwright, dwl 845 Market
Whitesides Charles, printer, dwl 7 Stevenson
Whitesides Charles H. carriage trimmer, dwl 408 Market
Whitesides James H. printer with Edward Bosqui & Co. dwl 420 Montgomery
Whitett James, tinsmith, dwl Pacific bet Larkin and Hyde
Whitey James, waiter, steamer Orizaba
Whitfield Robert A. blacksmith, dwl 56 Clementina
Whitfield William (Richards & W.) dwl 732 Sutter
Whiting Augustus H. clerk with George F. Hooper, 308 Front, dwl SE cor Stockton and Pacific
Whiting B. G. (widow) dwl 410 Stockton
Whiting B. G. (widow) dwl 612 Bush
Whiting Emma (widow) dwl E s Russ bet Howard and Folsom
Whiting James W. drayman, 325 Front, dwl 24 O'Farrell
Whiting M. S. merchant, office 535 Clay, dwl 1213 Taylor
Whiting Thomas, mastic roofing, 320 Clementina
Whiting W. J. dwl NW cor Pacific and Powell
Whiting W. P. C. (Crockett, W. & Wiggins) attorney at law, office 3 Exchange Building, dwl W s Howard bet Eighth and Ninth
Whitland (William) & Karsten (Henry) butter, cheese, etc. 45 and 46 Washington Market, dw N s Jackson nr Leavenworth
Whitlatch G. & S. M. Co. office 402 Front
Whitlatch Yankee Blade G. & S. M. Co. office 402 Front

Whitley Mary Mrs. domestic, W s Jones bet Filbert and Greenwich
Whitman Charles, brewer with Mangels & Co
Whitman C. Sidney, professor natural sciences, Union College
Whitman G. & S. M. Co. office 505 Montgomery
Whitman Henry (Nauland & W.) dwl NW cor Union and Powell
Whitman Mercy G. (widow) dwl 1122 Sacramento
WHITMAN S. P. property, general agency, and business house, 313 Mont bet Cal and Pine
Whitman Wm. W. clerk with Miller & Co. 123 Clay
Whitmarsh Edward G. salesman, 727 and 729 Market, dwl NW cor Jessie and Annie
Whitmars John, clerk, dwl NW cor Jessie and Annie
Whitmore Horace M. real estate, office 540 Clay, dwl 618 California
Whitmore Sylvester S. dwl 5 Calhoun
WHITNEY (A. D.) & CO. (A. C. Gordon and A. M. Ellsworth) forwarding merchants, 405 Front, res Sacramento
Whitney Ann Miss, domestic, 609 Sutter
Whitney A. W. (Noyes & W.) bds Cosmopolitan Hotel
Whitney Charles, salesman, 219 Front, dwl 505 Jackson
Whitney Charles B. gardener with J. W. Cox, N s Thirteenth nr Howard
Whitney C. S. (widow) dwl 345 Fremont
Whitney Edgar B. salesman with S. W. H. Ward & Son, dwl 648 Howard
Whitney Frank E. R. deputy sheriff, City Hall, dwl 252 Fourth
Whitney George, stevedore, dwl NW cor Grove and Van Ness Avenue
Whitney George E. (Brooks & W.) attorney at law, office 10 Exchange Building, dwl 20 Ellis
Whitney George O. mining, office 2 Odd Fellows' Hall, dwl 1015 Clay
Whitney G. H. laborer, dwl cor Hayes and Franklin
Whitney Henry M. dwl 317 Sixth
WHITNEY JAMES jr. president C. S. Navigation Co. office NE cor Front and Jackson, dwl 628 Harrison
WHITNEY JAMES D. physician, office and dwl 4 Brenham Place
Whitney James O. clerk with James Wilson, dwl 605 Clay, room 16
WHITNEY JAMES P. physician, 4 Brenham Pl, dwl 304 Stockton
WHITNEY J. D. State Geologist, office 90 Montgomery Block
Whitney John N. mariner, dwl 43 Natoma
Whitney Joseph, clerk, dwl 670 Mission
WHITNEY J. R. & CO. (T. Ellard Beans) commission merchants, office 405 Front, dwl 311 Clementina
Whitney Mary A. (widow) liquor saloon, NE cor Powell and Chestnut
Whitney Nathaniel P. dwl N s Greenwich bet Montgomery and Sansom
Whitney N. J. tinsmith, dwl 6 Central Place
Whitney Pliny, dwl 509 Bush
WHITNEY SUMNER, dealer law books, office with H. H. Bancroft and Co. dwl 98 Mont Blk
Whitney W. B. (widow) dwl 648 Howard
Whitney, William K. dwl 304 Stockton
Whittaker R. F. farmer, Old Ocean House Road
Whittaker J. F. carpenter. dwl 107 Leidesdorff
Whittaker J. K. book keeper, dwl 417 Dupont
Whittaker John G. local policeman, dwl SE cor William and Geary
Whittaker Kate (widow) dwl 1804 Stockton
Whittam Matthew, carpenter, dwl W s Montgomery bet Vallejo and Green
Whitted James, tinner, dwl 120 Stewart
Whittell George, clerk with Murphy, Grant & Co. bds Occidental Hotel

Whittemore Daniel H. deputy superintendent streets, dwl 810 Second

Whittemore James B. compositor, Alta California, dwl 419 Folsom

Whittey Henry, cook, dwl 621 Pacific

Whittier Charles A. brevet brigadier general U. S. Vols. office 418 California, dwl Occidental Hotel

Whittier Richard, carpenter, 208 Washington, dwl W s Leidesdorff bet California and Sacramento

Whittier Simon P. clerk with Cameron, Whittier & Co. 425 Front

Whittier Thomas J. molder, Golden State Iron Works, dwl 30 Clementina

Whittier W. Frank *(Cameron, W. & Co.)* 425 Front

Whittle Deering, porter with William Alvord & Co. dwl 919 Howard

Whittle Joseph. grainer, office 507 Kearny, dwl nr Lake Honda

Whittle Thomas, dwl with Joseph Whittle, ¼ mile SW from Lake Honda

Whitton Abel, printer with Towne & Bacon, dwl Pacific bet Taylor and Jones

Wholer Nicholas, cook, St. Nicholas Hotel

Whooller Daniel, mariner, dwl SW cor Dupont and Broadway

Whoriskey Richard, stone cutter, dwl Central House 814 Sansom

Whyland David H. dwl 216 Tehama

Whyte John P. carpenter, 21 Sutter, dwl S s Fell nr Franklin

Wiance Newell, clerk, dwl 63 Natoma

Wibler Henry, carpenter, dwl Sierra Nevada Hotel 528 Pacific

Wichelhausen H. & Co. merchants (Ukiah) office SE cor Battery and Clay, dwl 112 Taylor

Wichelhausen R. clerk with Brooks & Rouleau

Wicht Louis, clerk, NW cor Folsom and Twenty-Second

Wickan Carsten *(Lohaus & W.)* dwl 42 Stewart

Wickenhauser Frederick, carpenter, dwl 415 Bush

Wickersham J. M. machinist, Union Foundry, dwl 619 Mission

Wickes A. M. clerk, 612 Washington

Wickes Augustus L. painter, dwl Philadelphia H

Wickes Luther C. salesman with R. H. McDonald & Co. dwl 1 Clarence Place nr Townsend

Wickman Andrew, seaman, dwl 423 East

Wickman William *(Edgerly & W.)* dwl 21 Essex

Widber Jacob, carpenter, Board Education, dwl 740 Mission

WIDBER JAMES H. druggist, NE cor Market and Kearny, dwl 740 Mission

Wide West G. & S. M. Co. (Silver Mountain, Cal.) office 410 Montgomery

Wide West Mining Co. office 103 California

Widman Adolph, refiner. Kellogg, Hewston & Co.'s Refinery, dwl cor Santa Clara and San Bruno Road

Widman Frederick W. carpenter, dwl 420 Union

Widmann Herman G. butcher with Barney Horn, dwl SW cor Santa Clara and Potrero Avenue

Widmann John, dwl SW cor Santa Clara and San Bruno Road

Widmann Rudolph, machinist, Miners' Foundry, dwl SW cor Santa Clara and San Bruno Road

WIDOWS' AND ORPHANS' BENEFIT LIFE INSURANCE CO. H. S. Homans agent, office 607 Clay

Wieals W. dwl 323 Pine

Wiebar Nicholas, groceries and liquors, NW cor Third and Everett, dwl NW cor Second and Natoma

Wiebcke Henry, boot maker, dwl NE cor Montgomery and Broadway

Wiebe William, hairdresser with Louis Hemprich, dwl SE cor Post and Dupont

Wiechern Herman. waiter, 506 Montgomery, dwl Montgomery Block

Wiechert Charles, shoe maker with A. F. W. Melchert, dwl Golden Eagle Hotel

Wiedach P. restaurant and liquors, dwl 621 Davis

Wiederhold Charles, salesman with A. Kohler, 622 Washington, dwl 712 Harrison

WIEDERO OTTO & CO. *(Pierre Frontier and Eugene Deviercy)* watches, jewelry, diamonds, etc. 433 Montgomery, dwl 614 Taylor

Wiegand Jacob, musician. dwl 722 Broadway

Wiegels William, boot maker, dwl 847 Clay

Wiegmann Martin, tinsmith, dwl S s Hayes bet Octava and Laguna

Wiehe Caroline E. Mrs dwl 726 Folsom

Wieland Catharine (widow) saloon, SW cor California and Kearny

Wieland Conrad & Co. *(Nicholas Daleth)* beer saloon, NE cor Kearny and Mkt, dwl 742 Mkt

Wieland F. & Co. *(John H. Ahlers)* groceries and liquors, SW cor Vallejo and Powell

Wieland Jacob, salesman, Philadelphia Brewery, dwl 228 Second

Wieland John *(Hoelscher & W.)* dwl 228 Second

Wiemeyer K. F. compositor, Abend Post, dwelling Mead House

Wiener Aaron, carrier, Hebrew Observer

Wiener Aaron, cigars and tobacco, 303 Kearny

Wiener Aaron, clerk, 505 Commercial, dwl Sutter nr Montgomery

Wiener Adolph, salesman, 416 Sacramento, dwl 1022 Stockton

Wiener Isaac, clerk, dwl 155 Minna

Wiener Isaac, salesman, SE cor Commercial and Leidesdorff, dwl N s Sutter, nr Montgomery

Wiener Jacob, clerk, 420 Sansom, dwl 515 Sac

Wiener Jacob, salesman with I. & A. Froomberg, dwl 424 Sacramento

Wiener Jacob A. pawnbroker, 1134 Dupont

Wiener Mina (widow) dwl 813 Harrison

Wieners John H. clerk, dwl 234 Ritch

Wiese Peter, upholsterer, dwl 232 Minna

Wiess Henry, carpenter, dwl 26 Jessie

Wiggin Charles L. secretary, Mayor City and County, office 2 City Hall, dwl 9 Minna

Wiggin Thomas, plasterer, dwl 3 Delaware Court

Wiggin W. B. machinist, Fulton Foundry, dwl 566 Mission

Wiggin William K. house and sign painter, dwl 1623 Powell

Wiggins D. S. clerk, U. S. Clothing Depôt, dwl 422 Bush

Wiggins William H. fireman, dwl 337 Union

Wiggins W. W. *(Crockett, Whiting & W.)* attorney at law, office 3 Exchange Building, dwl 46 South Park

Wight George J. attorney at law, office City Hall, rear, dwl 38 Moss Place

Wight Jason, farmer, dwl Old San José Road 6 miles from City Hall

Wightman G. F. miner, dwl W s Garden bet Harrison and Bryant

Wightman James, book keeper with Winant & Co. dwl 548 Mission

WIGHTMAN *(John)* & HARDIE *(Dietrich)* importers and jobbers foreign and domestic dry goods, carpets, oil cloths, etc. 414 and 416 Clay, dwl 983 Harrison nr Sixth

Wightman John, clerk with James H. Cutter, 511 Front, dwl 548 Mission

Wigmore Alfred, cabinet maker with John Wigmore, dwl California bet Hyde and Larkin

Wigmore Arthur, cabinet maker, dwl S s California bet Hyde and Larkin

Wigmore James E. local policeman, dwl 9 Front

WIGMORE JOHN, cabinet maker and furniture dealer, 423 California, manufactory NE corner Leidesdorff and Halleck, dwl S s California bet Hyde and Larkin

Wilbar Charles, agent Contra Costa Laundry, 744 Washington, dwl 279 Jessie

Wilbar Marshall, contractor and builder, 509 Bush, dwl 179 Jessie

Wilber Albert, book keeper, dwl 652 Market

Wilber George, box maker, dwl 177 Jessie

Wilber *(George B.)* & Engleman *(E. R.)* carriage painters, 535 and 537 Market, dwl 315 Sixth

Wilber H. C. newspaper carrier, Tiger Engine Co. No. 14

Wilber J. C. butcher, dwl 179 Jessie

Wigram George, seaman, dwl 26 Sacramento

Wilbert Jacob, varnisher with Goodwin & Co. dwl SE cor Pacific and Dupont

Wilbur George B. teamster with Stanyan & Co. 17 California

Wilbur Rozel M. book keeper with William Alvord, 652 Market

Wilcocks Benjamin, collector and insurance agent, office 410 Montgomery, dwl 295 Clementina

Wilcott James, ship carpenter, dwl 417 Folsom

Wilcox Charles S. clerk, County Recorder's office, dwl 408 Market

Wilcox James H. mining, dwl 408 Market

Wilcox Samuel, seaman, dwl 44 Sacramento

Wilcox Silas, surveyor, dwl W s Fillmore bet Hayes and Grove

Wilcox William, carpenter, dwl 633 Market

Wilde Charles W. book keeper with Charles W. Hathaway, dwl 1521 Leavenworth

Wilde Daniel, asphaltum worker, 216 Sansom, dwl 413 Mason

Wilde George, asphaltum worker, dwl 226 Sutter

Wilde John, seaman, bds 7 Washington

Wilde Otis, laborer, dwl 26 McAllister

Wilde Thomas, baker with Swain & Brown, 5 Kearny

Wilder Charles, painter, dwl Sailors' Home SW cor Battery and Vallejo

Wilder David, dwl What Cheer House

WILDER DAVID, secretary Front St., Mission & Ocean R. R. Co. office and dwl 529 Clay

Wilder Frederick A. surveyor, Pacific Railroad, dwl 333 Fourth

Wilder H. milk ranch, Old San José Road 5 miles from City Hall

Wilder Henry, dwl What Cheer House

Wilder N. Cornelius, harness maker, NE cor Front and Market, dwl 73 Natoma

Wilder William A. book keeper with Thomas O'Malley, 646 Market

Wildermuth Julius, waiter, dwl Dresdener House

Wildes J. H. principal draftsman U. S. Surveyor General's office. dwl 339 Bryant nr Stanly Pl

Wildt Valentine, brass finisher, dwl 315 Bush

Wiley Addison, seaman, dwl 54 Sacramento

Wiley Austin *(J. J. Ayers & Co.)* dwl SW cor Turk and Fillmore

Wiley Charles, laundryman, dwl N side Perry bet Fourth and Fifth

Wiley Elizabeth J. (widow) dwl 74 Minna

Wiley Isaac, captain bark Legal Tender, office Pier I Stewart, dwl SW cor Hubbard and Howard

Wiley James, dwl W s Mason bet Filbert and Greenwich

Wiley James Capt. assistant quartermaster U. S. Marine Corps, office 516 Third, dwl W s Second Avenue bet Sixteenth and Seventeenth

Wiley John, laborer, dwl 607 Market

Wiley Joseph, workman, St. Mary's College

Wiley Nathan, laborer, dwl W s Gaven nr Filbert

Wiley W. A. house mover, dwl 5 Thomson Avenue

Wilhelm August, physician, office and dwl 6 Brenham Place

WILHELM CARL L. druggist, NE cor Howard and Fourth

Wilhelm John, cooper with Henry Shuman, dwl 33 Ritch

Wilke Frederick, painter, dwl SW cor Stevenson and Second

Wilke Louis *(Nolting & W.)* dwl Stockton Place

Wilkerson J. F. carpenter, dwl W s Battery near Green

Wilkey John, ship joiner, dwl SW cor Louisiana and Sierra

Wilkey E. H. sign painter, SE cor Commercial and Davis, dwl SE cor Turk and Polk

Wilkie Frederick, broker, office 423 Washington

Wilkie Thomas, cabinet maker, dwl SW cor Sutter and Kearny

Wilkie Thomas, cabinet maker with J. & J. Easton

Wilkie William, carpenter, dwl 525 East

Wilkin Charles, laborer, dwl Pacific Exchange

Wilkin D. G. Mrs. dwl 1031 Pacific

Wilkins B. P. gents' furnishing goods, 654 Market

Wilkins F. A. groom, dwl 417 Folsom

Wilkins Harry *(Smith & W.)* dwl S s Broadway bet Montgomery and Sansom

WILKINS HENRY, attorney at law, office 803 Montgomery room 1, dwl NW cor Seventeenth and Second Avenue

Wilkins James M. & Co. groceries, NE cor Second and Natoma, dwl 643 Folsom

Wilkins John (col'd) bootblack, 653 Merchant, dwl NE cor Pacific and Stockton

Wilkins Milton V. (widow) dwl 1114 Pacific

Wilkinson Charles, waiter, International Hotel

Wilkinson Elizabeth (widow) dwl 23 Ritch

Wilkinson Isaac, tailor with George B. Davis, 522 Montgomery

Wilkinson James M. (col'd) porter, dwl 728 Mont

Wilkinson James W. cooper, S. F. & P. Sugar Refinery, dwl 31 Moss

Wilkinson John J. cooper, S. F. & P. Sugar Co. dwl 6 Eddy

Wilkinson Joseph, engineer, dwl 328 Bryant

Wilkinson Mary Miss, dwl 23 Ritch

Wilkinson Philetus C. policeman, City Hall, dwl 557 Howard

Wilkinson Sarah Miss, upholsteress with W. M. Hixon, dwl 23 Ritch

Wilkinson William, laborer, dwl W s Gough near Grove

WILL *(Frederick A.)* & FINCK *(Julius)* surgical instrument makers, locksmiths, and bell hangers, 613 Jackson, dwl 504 Vallejo

Will John D. bar keeper, 316 Pine

Willard E. dwl International Hotel

Willard H. Augusta Miss. assistant, Denman Grammar School, dwl 713 Bush

Willard Harriet Mrs. matron Protestant Orphan Asylum

Willard William P. mining secretary, office 522 Montgomery, dwl 933 Sacramento

Willcox Joseph, dwl Oriental Hotel

WILLCUTT JOSEPH L. secretary San Francisco and San José Railroad, office SE cor Sansom and Halleck, dwl 1302 Pine

Willett A. P. shoe maker, dwl 6 First

Willett Edward W. miscellaneous bond clerk, Custom House, dwl 521 Folsom

Willett Ellen (widow) dwl 1405 Kearny

Willey John M. physician, dwl 113 Dora

Willey Charles J. *(J. T. Jones & Co.)* dwl 108 Prospect Place

Willey Gustavus B. shoe maker, 538 Market, dwl S s Natoma bet First and Second

WILLEY O. F. & CO. importers and jobbers carriages, harness, etc. 316 Cal, dwl 522 Third

Willey W. H. H. clerk, 73 Washington Market

Willey William, office 94 Montgomery Block, dwl 308 Minna

Willey William, teamster, dwl 109 Sansom

WILLIAM TELL HOUSE, Martin Fenstermacher proprietor, 315 and 317 Bush

Williams A. dwl 331 Bush

Williams Abraham, dwl 408 Lombard

Williams A. L. molder, Pacific Foundry, dwl 117 Natoma

Williams Albert Rev. dwl 706 California

WILLIAMS ANDREW, attorney at law and commissioner of deeds, office 535 Clay, dwl 18 South Park
Williams A. S. (widow) dwl 143 Jessie
Williams Benjamin F. ship joiner, dwl cor Michigan and Shasta
Williams B. B. ship broker, office S s Oregon near Battery, dwl 604 Filbert nr Stockton
Williams Brothers *(Thomas and Henry)* stock brokers, 79 Montgomery Block
Williams Catharine C. Miss, domestic, NE cor Page and Laguna
Williams Charles, cook, dwl 636 Commercial
Williams Charles, draftsman, Miners' Foundry
Williams Charles, quartermaster Revenue Cutter Joe Lane, dwl N s Francisco nr Stockton
Williams Charles, teamster with Stanyan & Co. 17 California, dwl N s Sacramento bet Franklin and Van Ness Avenue
Williams Charles A. stevedore, dwl 218 Mission
Williams Charles H. *(H. C. Hudson & Co.)* dwl 826 Folsom
Williams Charles H. foundryman, dwl 506 Brannan
Williams Charles S. captain schooner Isabella, dwl 1920 Mason
Williams Charles W. first lieutenant Co. B. Second Infantry, C. V. Presidio
Williams *(Chauncey B.)* & Law *(William)* hay and grain, NW cor Front and Broadway, dwl cor Church and Dorland, Mission Dolores
Williams C. L. druggist, SE cor Folsom and Third
Williams Clarence A. dwl 604 Filbert
Williams C. M. porter, 424 California, dwl 424 Cal
Williams Cyril, cashier with Falkner, Bell & Co. dwl 430 California
Williams Daniel D. with Hosmer, Goewey & Co. dwl 517 Howard
WILLIAMS *(Edward)* & GUTHRIE *(Jonathan)* proprietors Golden City Billiard Saloon, 429 Montgomery cor Sacramento, dwl 1113 Stock
Williams Edward, porter, Brooklyn Hotel
Williams Edward B. with H. C. Hudson & Co. dwl 32 Frederick nr First
Williams Edward W. employé with Tay, Brooks & Backus, dwl with G. H. Tay, W s Calhoun nr Green
Williams Edwin A. clerk, dwl 231 Stevenson
Williams Elizabeth (widow) dwl S side Geary bet Franklin and Gough
Williams Ellen M. Miss, teacher private school, dwl 1017 Mason
Williams Evan, druggist, dwl 515 Kearny
Williams F. O. A. compositor, Evening Bulletin, dwl 1623 Powell nr Union
Williams Francis, stone yard, junction Market and Pine, dwl 27 Eddy
Williams Frank, with Andrew J. Thompson, dwl 429 Sixth
Williams Frank, laborer with Edward J. Quirk
Williams Frank, second officer, Pacific Mail S. S. Co
Williams Franklin (col'd) bootblacking, 231 Bush, dwl Dupont nr Broadway
Williams G. & S. M. Co. office 404 Front
Williams George, book keeper, 711 Montgomery, dwl 22 Dupont
Williams George, broker, dwl 12 Rousch
Williams George, clerk with Michael Jarpa.
Williams George, drayman with Taaffe & Co. 107 Battery
Williams George, porter, dwl 535 Folsom
Williams George, saloon keeper, dwl 206 Kearny
Williams George A. with Thomas H. Selby & Co. 116 California
Williams George F. boot maker, N s Market opposite Stewart, dwl East bet Clay and Wash
Williams *(George M.)* & Kempf *(George W.)* furniture, 117 Third, dwl Rousch nr Folsom
Williams Harriet (col'd, widow) dwl E s Taylor nr Clay

Williams Henry *(Williams Bros.)* 79 Montgomery Block, dwl 451 Bryant
Williams Henry, musician, dwl 110 Virginia
Williams Henry, porter, Bank of British Columbia, dwl W s Dupont bet Lombard and Chestnut
Williams Henry, waiter, steamer Senator
Williams Henry, waterman, 609 Market
Williams Henry B. carpenter, dwl 21 Rousch
WILLIAMS HENRY B. shipping and commission merchant and agent Rollinson's California Line Clipper Ships, office 305 Front, dwl 705 Stock
WILLIAMS HENRY F. real estate, office 626 Clay, dwl 1022 Pine
Williams Henry P. teamster with John R. Sedgley, dwl S s Twelfth bet Howard and Folsom
Williams Isaac J. carpenter, dwl 21 Rousch
Williams Jacob S. compositor with M. D. Carr & Co. 410 Clay, dwl 515 Sacramento
Williams James *(Bloomer & Co.)* dwl 322 Sutter bet Dupont and Stockton
Williams James (col'd) whitewasher, dwl 825 Pac
Williams J. E. second officer, Pacific Mail S. S. Co
Williams J. M. shipwright, dwl 12 Tehama
Williams J. O. (widow) water colorer, 25 Third, dwl Brogan's Building 313 Fifth
Williams John *(Smith & W.)* dwl Geneva near Brannan
Williams John, dwl What Cheer House
Williams John, clerk, Adjutant General's Office, dwl S s Montgomery Court nr Montgomery
Williams John, deck hand, steamer Clinton
Williams John, driver with C. B. Folsom
Williams John, jeweler with R. B. Gray & Co. dwl 32 John
Williams John, laborer, dwl 255 Beale
Williams John, laborer, dwl S s Filbert nr Sansom
Williams John, stone cutter with Francis Williams, dwl 454 Jessie
Williams John, watchman, steamer Pacific, dwl 515 Greenwich
Williams John B. attorney at law, dwl 1010 Stock
Williams John C. artist, dwl SW corner Broadway and Dupont
Williams John H. accountant, dwl 1016 Stockton
Williams *(John J.)* & Thornton *(James D.)* attorneys at law, office 8 and 9 Exchange Building, dwl 1112 Bush
Williams John L. collector, dwl Federal Building
Williams John L. poll tax collector, City Hall, dwl N s Vallejo bet Montgomery and Kearny
Williams John V. driver with John Agnew, 26 Kearny
Williams Jonathan, shipping and commission, agent Sacramento Line Packets, 413 East
Williams Joseph, broker, dwl 911 Sacramento
Williams Joseph, captain bark Samuel Merritt, office 405 Front, dwl 1 Auburn
Williams Joseph, carpenter, Miners' Foundry, dwl 506 Brannan
Williams Joseph, clerk with Joseph Maciel, dwl 200 Front
Williams Joseph, cook, NW cor Stockton and Pac
Williams Joseph, fruits, 215 Pacific
Williams Joseph, ship carpenter, dwl 12 Tehama Pl
Williams Joseph, stone cutter, dwl 27 Eddy
Williams Joseph, tinner, dwl 802 Sansom
Williams M. Mrs. dwl N s Sutter bet Polk and Van Ness Avenue
Williams Margaret (widow) dwl 434 Bush
Williams Martin, helper, Union Foundry, dwl 10 Brannan
Williams Mary Miss, domestic, 776 Folsom
Williams Mary Miss, assistant, Denman Grammar School, dwl 21 Rousch nr Folsom
Williams Mary Mrs. saloon, 8 Dupont
Williams Mary Jane (widow) dwl 36 Valparaiso
Williams Mary J. (widow) dwl 130 Third
Williams Michael, cabinet maker, 518 Front, dwl 1063 Broadway

Williams, Morris, drayman, corner Sacramento and Sansom, dwl 47 Jessie
Williams Nathaniel T. (col'd) dairdresser, dwl 21 Dupont, rear
Williams Oscar, coachman with Robert J. Polk
Williams Oscar, driver with F. R. Amos & Co. dwl 505 O'Farrell
Williams Penny (widow) fruits, 106 Dupont
Williams Peter, laborer, dwl 29 Jessie
WILLIAMS RICHARD, proprietor Mechanics' Hotel, 8W cor Kearny and Pacific
Williams Ross, dwl 624 Commercial
Williams Samuel (J. McGill & Co.) dwl 128 Eighth
Williams Samuel, pattern maker, Pacific Foundry, dwl 117 Natoma
Williams S. E. seaman, dwl 26 Sacramento
Williams Stephen G. groceries and liquors, SW cor Jessie and Fourth, dwl 364 Jessie
WILLIAMS STEPHEN H. architect, office 505 Montgomery, dwl SW cor Wash and Larkin
Williams Sylvester M. photographic printer with Bradley & Rulofson
Williams T. G. attorney at law, office 23 Court Blk 636 Clay, dwl 132½ Pacific
Williams T. H. sexton Trinity Church, dwl 831 Clay
Williams Thomas, commission merchant, dwl 627 Folsom
Williams Thomas, cook, steamer Senator
Williams Thomas, liquor saloon and coffee stand, NW cor East and Merchant
Williams Thomas, seaman, steamer Orizaba
Williams Thomas, seaman, dwl 32 Stewart
Williams Thomas C. oyster saloon, 534 Market, dwl 439 Clementina
Williams Virgil M. artist, room 15 Mercantile Library Building, bds 218 Bush
Williams W. dwl 10 Sutter
Williams Warren H. architect with S. H. Williams, dwl SW cor Washington and Larkin
Williams William (Eddy & W.) dwl N side Union bet Dupont and Stockton
Williams William, dwl 1016 Stockton
Williams William (col'd) dwl 109 Pine
Williams William, boatman, dwl 525 Filbert
Williams William, stone cutter, dwl 27 Eddy
Williams William B. foreman Eureka Match Factory, dwl SE cor Folsom and Twelfth
Williams William C. painter with James Donovan, dwl Howard bet Fourth and Fifth
Williams William H. carpenter, dwl 21 Rousch
Williams William M. weaver, S. F. P. Woolen Mills, dwl N s Bay bet Leav and Hyde
Williams William O. Rev. dwl SW cor Kearny and Pacific
Williams William P. with L. F. Baker, SE corner Davis and Washington
Williams William W. sutler's clerk, Fort Point
WILLIAMS W. J. G. principal Williams' Academy, 871 Mission
Williams ——, physician, office 18 Belden Block
Williamson (Andrew) & McMillan (Daniel) wholesale and retail salt, 217 Davis, dwl SW cor Seventh and Harrison
Williamson Charles, seaman, dwl 48 Beale
Williamson Duncan, dwl 656 Second
Williamson Edmund, compositor, dwl 815 Mont
Williamson John, laborer, dwl 8W cor Louisiana and Sierra
Williamson Martin, laborer, dwl 8 s Brannan near Sixth
Williamson Mary (widow) dwl N side Oregon bet Davis and Drumm
Williamson M. N. dwl 627 California
Williamson Peter S. Rev. pastor Reformed Dutch Church, 629 California
Williamson R. J. maj. U. S. A. quartermaster, office 742 Washington
Williamson Robert S. maj. U. S. A. Engineers, Dep. Cal. office 728 Montgomery, dwl 319 Kearny

Williamson Thomas, dwl Bay State House
Williamson William, carpenter, dwl 207 Ritch
WILLIAMSON WILLIAM F. proprietor Bay View Trotting Park, E side San Bruno Road 3 miles from City Hall
Williamson William P. carpenter, dwl SE cor Garden and Harrison
Willing Mining and Exploring Expedition, office 6 Armory Hall
Willis Charles, hairdresser, dwl 535 California
Willie G. W. dwl What Cheer House
Willie H. G. driver, dwl 72 Howard
Willis James B. laborer, Broadway Wool Depôt, bds Franklin House 8W cor Bdwy and Sansom
Willis John, lamplighter, S. F. Gas Co. dwl 11 William
Willis John F. book keeper, Chelsea Laundry, dwl 805 Mission
Willis Milton E. book keeper, Mission Woolen Mills, dwl 8 Virginia Place
Willis Robert, lamplighter, S. F. Gas Co. dwl 11 William
Willis Thomas, laborer, dwl 612 Clay
Willis William, jobber, dwl 204 Sutter
Willis William, mining secretary, office 712 Montgomery, dwl 762 Howard
Willis William H. porter, dwl 510 Sacramento
Willis William M. local policeman, dwl 13 Stewart
Willis W. W. musician, office 138 Montgomery, dwl NE cor Clementina and Third
Williston Cory, shipping and forwarding merchant, office 424 Battery, dwl 40 Minna
Willoughby Charles, captain bark Narremisic, office Pier 10 Stewart
Willoughby Elizabeth (widow) lodgings, 82 Natoma
Willoughby James R. butcher, dwl 653 Howard
Willoughby J. B. seaman, dwl 54 Sacramento
Willoughby Louis D. dwl with O. H. Willoughby N s Sixteenth nr Hampshire
WILLOUGHBY OTIS H. beef and pork packer, 151 Third, dwl N s Sixteenth nr Hampshire
Willow Cosolidation G. & S. M. Co. office 1 Government House, 502 Washington
Willows Brewery, 8W cor Mission and Nineteenth, Kleinclaus & Fauss proprietors
Willows, Frank Kelly proprietor, 8W cor Mission and Eighteenth
Wills James jr. ship joiner with John G. North, Potrero
Wills John, ship joiner, 8 Drumm, dwl 420 Filbert
Wills Mary A. Miss, dwl 1007 Powell
Willson G. carpenter and joiner, dwl Oriental Hotel
Willson J. F. livery and sale stables, 807 and 809 Montgomery, bds International Hotel
Willson Robert, farmer, dwl N s Boyd nr Chesley
Willstatter Bernard, book keeper with Heynemann & Co. dwl 307 Seventh
Wilmos Louis, waiter, dwl SW cor Dupont and Broadway
Wilmerding J. C. (Fargo & Co.) dwl 127 Mont
Wilmot W. F. & Co. (John M. Burrell) saddlery and harness, 315 Battery, dwl 225 Second
Wilmot William, clerk, dwl 227 Beale
Wilson A. D. box maker, dwl 181 Jessie
Wilson Adair, reporter, American Flag, dwl 402 Fremont
Wilson Adelbert, drayman with Boswell & Shattuck, dwl 309 Sutter
Wilson A. L. miner, dwl Railroad House
Wilson Albert, harness maker with John S. Wilson, 310 Davis
Wilson Albion D. box maker, dwl 181 Jessie
Wilson Alexander, molder, Pacific Foundry, dwl SE cor Hyde and O'Farrell
Wilson Alfred, clerk, 13 Stewart Pier 1
Wilson A. M. Mrs. dwl 36 Stevenson House
Wilson Andrew, livery stable, 739 Folsom
Wilson Andrew, watchman, steamer Oakland, res Brooklyn

WILSON BENJAMIN D. & SON *(John B. Wilson and Adolph Everhart)* California Native Wines and Brandies, depôt SE cor First and Market, res Los Angeles

Wilson C. seaman, dwl 54 Sacramento

Wilson Charles *(Smith & W.)* res Virginia City

Wilson Charles, captain bark Sireta, dwl 605 Taylor

WILSON CHARLES, Lick House Liquor Saloon, dwl 329 Broadway

Wilson Charles, porter, dwl NW cor Kearny and Broadway

Wilson Charles, seaman, dwl 26 Sacramento

Wilson Charles stock broker, dwl 308 Green

Wilson Charles C. salesman with J. Vantine & Co. dwl 312 Jessie bet Fourth and Fifth

Wilson Charles M. with Yates & Stevens, dwl 925 Washington

Wilson Charles T. foreman California Farmer, 320 Clay

Wilson Charles W. apothecary, 632 Mission, dwl 757 Mission

Wilson Copper M. Co. office 611 Clay

Wilson C. Wheeler, salesman with Wilson & Stevens, dwl 6 Martha Place

Wilson Cyrus *(Wilson & Co.)* dwl 343 Bryant

Wilson Daniel, mariner, dwl 32 Stewart

Wilson David S. *(S. M. & D. S. W.)* attorney at law, office 2 and 3 Mont Block, dwl 220 Third

Wilson Dayton J. with Wey & Keyt, dwl 527 O'Farrell

Wilson Edmund, policeman, City Hall, dwl 309 Sutter

Wilson Edward A. harness maker with John S. Wilson, dwl 805 Union

Wilson E. H. secretary Eel Run Oil Co. office 436 Jackson, dwl 632 Market

WILSON *(Ezekiel)* & BAKER *(Henry)* liquor saloon, 550 Clay, dwl Point Lobos Road 3 miles from Plaza

Wilson F. J. clerk, California Lloyds, 418 Cal

Wilson Francis, helper, Vulcan Iron Works, dwl Sailors' Home

Wilson George, dwl SW cor Kearny and Pacific

Wilson George, cook, 28 Montgomery, dwl NW cor Greenwich and Mason

Wilson George, soap maker with J. P. Dyer, dwl 1413 Mason

Wilson George, tinsmith with Taylor & Iredale

Wilson George H. *(Bruns & Co.)* dwl 201 Com

Wilson *(George O.)* & Brother *(N. Irving Wilson)* manufacturers and dealers doors, windows, and blinds, NE cor Cal and Drumm, dwl 328 Fremont

Wilson H. actor, Maguire's Opera House

Wilson H. B. carpenter, dwl 431 Pine

Wilson Henry, cook, dwl 12 Stewart

Wilson Henry, salesman with Taaffe & Co. dwl 825 Bush

Wilson Henry C. farmer, dwl S s Cliff House Road, 3 miles W from City Hall

WILSON *(H. H.)* & EVANS *(John R.)* gunsmiths and sporting materials, 513 Clay, dwl SW cor Jones and Broadway

WILSON ISAAC, milk depôt, 637 Kearny

Wilson Israel (col'd) bootblack, 624 Washington, dwl S s Broadway bet Stockton and Powell

Wilson James, office 14 Wells' Building, 605 Clay

Wilson James, boiler maker, dwl 606 Third

Wilson James (col'd) bootblack with Lee & Keating, dwl 30 John

Wilson James, carpenter, dwl 1426 Pacific

Wilson James, gas fitter with McNally & Hawkins, dwl 188 Jessie

Wilson James, molder, Miners' Foundry, dwl SW cor Mission and Fifth

Wilson James Mrs. dwl 742 Pine

Wilson James Mrs. dwl 18 Ellis

Wilson James, seaman, dwl 20 Commercial

Wilson James H. with W. T. Coleman & Co. dwl 605 Clay

Wilson James Hepburn, grocer, dwl 113 Ellis

Wilson J. Burrough, carpenter, dwl 124 Ellis

Wilson J. D. dwl First St. House

Wilson Jed. professor music, office 430 Montgomery, dwl Brooklyn Hotel

Wilson J. N. painter, 928 Washington

Wilson John, attorney at law, office 620 Washington room 16, dwl 402 Fremont

Wilson John, blacksmith, dwl 44 Jessie

Wilson John, boatman, dwl SE cor Sac and Davis

Wilson John, bricklayer, dwl 419 Sutter

Wilson John (col'd) carpenter, dwl 431 Filbert

Wilson John, employé, Occidental Hotel

Wilson John, hair dresser, Original House, dwl 405 Geary

Wilson John, harness maker with John S. Wilson, 310 Davis

Wilson John, machinist, Union Foundry, dwelling Wright's Hotel 210 Broadway

Wilson John, mariner, dwl 206 Stewart

Wilson John, miner, dwl E s Wetmore Place

Wilson John, seaman, dwl 26 Sacramento

Wilson John, seaman, dwl E s Main bet Market and Mission

Wilson John, proprietor Wilson's Circus, dwl 67 Natoma

Wilson John, seaman, dwl 44 Sacramento

Wilson John, washer, Chelsea Laundry

Wilson John B. *(B. D. Wilson & Son)* dwl SE cor First and Market

Wilson John D. St. Francis H. & L. Co. No. 1

Wilson John Downes, mining stocks, dwl E s Mission bet Fourteenth and Fifteenth

Wilson John E. porter with Weaver, Wooster & Co. 218 Front, dwl 21 Silver

Wilson John G. harness maker, dwl Bush nr San

Wilson John H. B. boot maker, 1228 Dupont

Wilson John L. blacksmith with Devoe, Dinsmore & Co. dwl 44 Jessie

Wilson *(John N.)* & Moulton *(Josiah)* painters, paints and oils, 516 Davis, dwl 251 Minna

Wilson John R. book keeper with A. Massey, dwl 109 Montgomery

Wilson John Robert, clerk with H. & C. McAllister

WILSON JOHN S. *(Wilson & Son)* dwl 210 Bush

WILSON *(John Y.)* & STEVENS *(George W.)* pork packers, Lobos Square, office 506 Market and 7 Sutter, dwl 612 California

Wilson J. T. attorney at law, dwl W s Buenaventura nr California

Wilson Joseph, clerk, dwl 911 Bush

Wilson Joseph, machinist, Union Foundry, dwl 4 Beale Place

Wilson Joseph, molder, dwl 47 Clementina

Wilson Joseph L. Melter and Refiner's Department U. S. B. Branch Mint, dwl cor Van Ness Avenue and Union

Wilson Isaiah S. (col'd) steward, dwl NE cor Montgomery and Market

Wilson Julius, laborer, dwl 29 Natoma Place

Wilson Letitia, dress maker, dwl 625½ Mission

Wilson Marion A. porter, 223 Front, dwl 526 Pine

Wilson Mary Ann Mrs. liquors, 308 Pacific

Wilson Mary Ann (widow) lodgings, 606 Third

Wilson N. Irving *(Wilson & Brother)* dwl 347 Fremont

Wilson O. moving and raising buildings, dwl E side Willow bet Folsom and Shipley

Wilson Pehr A. billiards and liquors, NW corner Davis and Jackson

Wilson Peter, pile driver, 56 Stewart

Wilson Peter, seaman, dwl 26 Sacramento

Wilson Peter L. painter, S. F. & San José R. R. Co. dwl cor Sixteenth and Folsom

Wilson R. A. painter, dwl SE cor Mission and First

Wilson Richard, seaman, dwl 26 Sacramento

Wilson Robert, laborer, dwl Minna Place nr Beale

Wilson Robert, seaman, dwl 117 Sacramento

Wilson Robert, student, dwl 402 Fremont

Wilson Robert G. ship builder, dwl N s Thirteenth nr Mission
WILSON SAMUEL M. & DAVID S. attorneys at law, office 1–3 Montgomery Block, dwl 764 Mission
Wilson Sarah Mrs. dwl 51 Natoma
Wilson Sarah C. Miss, private school, N s Thirteenth nr Mission
Wilson S. D. & Co. *(David F. Dodge)* yankee notions, 541 Kearny, res New York
Wilson Stephen, bar tender, 717 Davis, dwl SW cor Davis and Pacific
Wilson Thomas, seaman, dwl 26 Sacramento
Wilson V. V. book keeper, 647 Clay, dwl 818 Powell
Wilson Wallace, pharmaceutist, office and dwl 632 Mission
Wilson William, dwl N s Court Building SW cor Montgomery and Jackson
Wilson William, baker with Deeth & Starr, dwl 32 Valparaiso nr Taylor
Wilson William (col'd) barber, dwl 15 Virginia Pl
Wilson William, bricklayer, dwl 306 Dupont
Wilson William, carpenter, dwl 6 Front
Wilson William, carpet weaver, dwl 214 Commercial
Wilson William, clerk, dwl 752 Washington
Wilson William, laborer, dwl N s Filbert bet Stockton and Powell
Wilson William, marble worker, dwl 126 Post
Wilson William, painter, cor Leidesdorff and California, dwl 636 Commercial
Wilson William, porter with D. C. Mitchell & Co. dwl S s Filbert bet Stockton and Powell
Wilson William, seaman, dwl 524 Broadway
Wilson William, teacher dancing, 220 Mont, dwl 18 Sansom
Wilson William B. marble worker, dwl 128 Post
Wilson William F. gas fitter with J. H. O'Brien & Co. 706 Montgomery, dwl 630 Post
Wilson William H. carpenter with Pratt & Jacobs, dwl 6 Front
Wilson *(William O.)* & Co. *(Cyrus Wilson)* produce dealers, 219 Clay, dwl 717 Broadway
Wilson William P. blacksmith with Pollard & Carvill, dwl 7 Central Place
Wilson William L. lather, dwl 445 Minna
Wilson, see Willson
Wiltse William, 2d lieut. Co. K, C. V. Fort Point
Wilzinski Max, with Stahl Brothers, dwl 41 Jackson
Wilzinski T. tailor, dwl 41 Jackson
Wimble Thomas, driver, Omnibus R. R. Co. dwl 79 Clementina
Wimmer Andrew, hairdresser, 636 Washington, dwl cor Mission and Jane
WINALL *(Stuart A.)* & CLAPP *(Jason)* wagon makers and blacksmiths, 505 Market, dwl 311 Fremont
Winans J. C. broker, office 521 Clay, dwl 573 Harrison
WINANS *(Joseph W.)* & BELKNAP *(David P.)* attorneys at law, office 604 Merchant, and president Board Education, dwl 1319 Powell
Winant J. J. *(Winant & Co.)* dwl 35 Clara
Winant Mark, oysters, 75 Washington Market and 24 Metropolitan Market, dwl 736 Harrison
WINANT *(S.)* & CO. *(J. J. Winant and H. P. Dissosway)* wholesale oysters, 24 Metropolitan Market, dwl 756 Harrison
Winant William, oysterman, dwl 730 Harrison
Winants Newell, warehouse entry and liquidating clerk, Custom H, dwl S s Harrison nr Fifteenth
Winberg Julia Mrs. fancy goods, 5 Virginia Block
Winbigler David N. carpenter, dwl NW cor Sixth and Bryant
Winchester Ezra H. *(Main & W.)* 216 Battery
Winchester John P. clerk, 216 Battery, dwl Tehama House
Winchester Jonas, dwl 1421 Taylor
Winchester S. F. agent life insurance, dwl 19 Stanly Place

Winckelmann Henry *(Seegelken & W.)* dwl NE cor Davis and Commercial
Winckler William, butcher, Vigilant Engine Co. No. 9
Wind M. L. R. bedstead manuf'r, dwl 510 Dupont
Winder William A. capt. Co. D 3d U. S. Artillery, dwl Black Point
Windle William, groom, dwl 16 Clementina
Windlir Charles H. butcher, dwl Brannan St. Bridge
Windsor Norman E. clerk, Phœnix Insurance Co. 603 Commercial, dwl 6 Russ nr Howard
Windsor Phineas, mariner, dwl 6 Russ
Windsor Walter, mariner, dwl 275 Jessie
Windsor William, laborer, Assayer's Department U. S. Branch Mint, dwl 743 Mission
Winegar A. B. proprietor Union Salt Works and dealer salt, 308 and 310 Front, dwl 438 Natoma
Winegar Charles E. clerk, 310 Front, dwl 927 Howard
Winegar Henry S. with J. B. Winegar, dwl 118 Jessie
Winegar Jesse P. southern coast messenger, Wells, Fargo & Co. dwl SE cor Montgomery and Cal
Winehill Sophia J. (widow) dwl 1217 Powell
Wing Chong Lung (Chinese) merchant, 706 Dupont
Wing Fung & Co. (Chinese) merchants, 745 Sac
Wing Hi (Chinese) washing, 14 Fourth
Wing Hing (Chinese) washing, 248 Stevenson
Wing Jeremiah C. workman S. F. & P. Sugar Co. dwl 16 Rousch
Wing Kee (Chinese) washing, 814 Stockton
Wing Lee (Chinese) washing 271 First
Wing Lee (Chinese) washing, 118 Fourth
Wing Sing (Chinese) washing, 211 Dupont
Wing Sing (Chinese) washing, 9 Second
Wing Soong & Co. (Chinese) merchants, 714 Sac
Wing Wo Sang & Co. (Chinese) merchants, 720 Sac
Wing Yune & Co. (Chinese) merchants, 818 Dupont
Wingard Adam, boat builder, dwl 536 Second
Wingard James, ship joiner, dwl Second nr Brannan
Wingard Thomas B. clerk with Adam Wingard, W s Second rear South Park
Wingerter C. J. dwl 224 Stockton
Wingot Philip, barber, dwl 315 Kearny
Winkle Adam, baker with Henry Winkle, dwl SE cor Vallejo and Battery
Winkle Henry, master teazer, Pacific Glass Works, dwl cor Mariposa and Indiana
WINKLE HENRY, proprietor Winkle's Bakery, SE cor Battery and Vallejo
Winkle Herman, baker, Winkle's Bakery, dwl SE cor Battery and Vallejo
Winkle William, shooting gallery, NW cor Kearny and Jackson
Winkleman Bernard, laborer, dwl 560 Mission
Winkleman *(Thomas)* & Carroll *(Patrick)* wood yard, 560 Mission
Winkler Charles, musician, dwl 709 Filbert
Winkler William *(Schwartz & W.)* dwl 709 Filbert
Winkler William, butcher with G. M. Garwood & Co
Winks James, machinist, dwl 606 Third
Winlock James, molder, Pacific Foundry, dwl 24 Stevenson
WINN A. M. Gen. real estate dealer, office 622 Clay room 11, dwl 704 Powell
Winn C. S. with F. Gilbert, dwl 619 Market
Winn Daniel, dwl with James Faulkner, 332 Green
Winn Marshal, Siegel Coffee Saloon, 603 Market
Winn Marshall, mining agent, dwl 136 Sutter
Winn Mary, domestic, N s Alta bet San and Battery
Winn S. A. waiter, dwl SE cor Mission and First
Winn, see Wynne
Winnea John L. builder, dwl Summer St. House, Summer nr Montgomery
Winning Louisa D. Mrs. dwl 641 Broadway
Winrow Christopher, butcher, dwl E s Mission bet Twenty-Eighth and Twenty-Ninth

Winrow Joseph, dwl E s Mission bet Twenty-Eighth and Twenty-Ninth
Winrow Richard, butcher, dwl E s Mission bet Twenty-Eighth and Twenty-Ninth
Winship Edward, teacher, dwl 810 Washington
Winship Thomas, chief engineer Shubrick, dwl E s Dupont bet Francisco and Bay
Winslow Edward, ship carpenter, dwl 410 Beale
Winslow Julius C. adjutant Second Infantry California Volunteers, Presidio
Winslow Michael, boiler maker, dwl 56 Main
Winslow Terry, dwl Zoe Place
Winson Thomas, dwl 845 Dupont
Winter Casimer, with John Winter, 208 California, dwl SW cor Pine and Dupont
Winter Charles, real estate, dwl 715 Bush, rear
Winter C. book keeper, 517 Jackson, dwl 708 Green
Winter Daniel *(Currier & W.)* dwl 620 Market
Winter Emma Miss, dwl 920 Sutter
Winter Frederick, dwl 425 Green
Winter George, painter, dwl 620 Market
Winter George, sign painter, dwl 5 Winter Place
WINTER JOHN, importer and jobber hops, corks, brewers' materials, etc. and agent South Park Malt House, office 208 California
Winter John, hostler, Fort Point
Winter John, laborer, Bay Sugar Refinery, dwl SW cor Union and Sansom
Winter John F. clerk with Geo. W. Menomy & Co. dwl SE cor Lombard and Jansen
WINTER J. W. dentist, 649 Clay, dwl 1030 Bush
Winter Michael, tobacconist, dwl 514 Post
Winter Paul, tailor, 409 Bush
Winter Robert, artist, studio 605 Sacramento, dwl 715 Bush, rear
Winter William, sign and ornamental painter, 805 Washington, dwl 5 Winter Place
Winter William C. cook with W. Hall, Old San José Road, county line
Winterburn Francis, printer, dwl What Cheer H
Winterburn Joseph, printer with William P. Harrison, dwl 765 Howard
Winters Christopher, tinsmith, dwl 21 Valparaiso
Winters James, driver, Central R. R. Co. dwl N s Brannan bet Sixth and Seventh
Winters Peter, hostler with Central R. R. Co. dwl Gilbert nr Brannan
Winters Silas, laborer, Main St. Wharf, dwl 26 Stewart
Winterson Ann (widow) dwl 36 Tehama
Winterson Kate Miss, domestic, 320 Mason
Winterson Michael, pressman with Towne & Bacon, dwl N s Hayes bet Franklin and Gough
Winterton Frank, with William Meyer & Co. dwl 614 Powell
Winterton John D. salesman, 309 Sacramento, dwl 614 Powell
Winterton John R. job wagon, 423 California, dwl 614 Powell
Wintjens Francis, shutter maker, dwl 4 Margaret Pl
Wintringer Leander, assistant superintendent Central R. R. Co. office 116 Taylor, dwl 427 Sixth
Wintrobe Samuel, clerk, dwl 531 Mission
Wire John, laborer, dwl 333 Bush
Wirt Adam, driver, Omnibus R. R. Co
Wischbusen Diedrich, liquor saloon, Potrero Av
Wisconsin Tunnel Co. office 36 Exchange Building
Wise Charles H. tinsmith with Tolles & Howard, dwl 1014 Clay
Wise George, brass finisher, dwl 2 Auburn
Wise George, laborer, dwl S s Folsom bet Main and Spear
Wise James, photographic art gallery, 417 Montgomery, dwl 467 Clementina
Wise John, steward, dwl 40 Jessie
Wise John H. *(Christy & W.)* dwl S s Sheppard Pl
Wise Morris *(Toklas, Wise & Co.)* dwl 510 Sutter
Wise Tully R. attorney at law, office 637 Washington, dwl S s Sheppard Place nr Mason

Wisely John, carpenter, dwl 728 Market
Wiseman John J. foreman with Hey & Meyn, dwl N s Twelfth bet Folsom and Harrison
Wiseman Julia Miss, dwl Mead House
Wiseman Robert (col'd) porter, dwl 927 Broadway
Wishaw James, carpenter with John Center, dwl NW cor Sixteenth and Folsom
Wissel Albert, book keeper, 210 Cal, dwl 139 Silver
Wissel Charles, blacksmith with Kimball & Co. dwl 217 Broadway
Wissil Julius, trimmer with Kimball & Co. dwl 11 Perry
Wissing Jacob, Wissing's Market NW cor Clementina and First
Wissing William, Seventh Ward Market, 232 First
Wissinger Henry L. dwl 554 Tehama
Wissinger John W. carpenter and builder, 408 Jackson, dwl 1116 Kearny
Wiswell Sarah P. (widow) dwl 109 Stevenson
Witbeck Howard T. deputy collector U. S. Internal Revenue, office NW cor Battery and Commercial, dwl N s Jackson bet Hyde and Leav
Witbeck Peter, Melter and Refiner's Department U. S. Branch Mint, dwl 815 Mission
Witchert Harvey, printer, dwl 515 Sacramento
Witfeld Gustavus, clerk, 429 California
Witgen Diedrick, groceries and liquors, NW corner Dupont and Broadway
Witgen Peter, laborer, dwl 39 Clay
Witham George, teamster, dwl 530 Market
Witham William L. *(Davis & W.)* dwl cor White Place and Jones
Withen Frank, cook, dwl 115 First
Wither Nathaniel, watchman, Dow's Distillery, dwl 752 Harrison
Witherbee C. E. with George Hughes, East St. Wharf, dwl S s O'Farrell bet Hyde and Larkin
Witherby Daniel S. book keeper, dwl 512 Geary
Witherby L. B. clerk with A. Kohler, dwl 622 Wash
Witherby Mary (widow) lodgings, SW cor First and Folsom
Witkowski *(Adolph)* & Wurkheim *(Max)* fancy goods and shoes, 725 Montgomery, dwl W side Montgomery bet Jackson and Pacific
Witkowski Elias, auctioneer, dwl 815 Montgomery
Witkowski Isidor, book keeper, 512 Sacramento
Witkowski Sarah (widow) dwl 35 Hinckley
Witkowsky Elias, clerk, dwl 658 Mission
Witkowsky Elias, dry goods, dwl 844 Folsom
Witkowsky I. *(N. Witkowsky & Bro.)* dwl corner Dupont and St. Mark Place
Witkowsky N. & Brother *(I. Witkowsky)* hairdressing saloon, Oriental Hotel, dwl cor Dupont and St. Mark Place
Witt Julius, drayman, 220 California, dwl 271 Minna
Witte C. E. clerk with T. Lemmen Meyer
WITTE CHARLES, groceries and liquors, corner Shasta and Michigan
Witte Diedrich, dwl N s Folsom bet Tenth and Eleventh
Witte Henry, seaman, bds 7 Washington
Witte Herman, hairdresser with Proschold & Rauch, dwl Clara nr Bush
Witte William, clerk, 126 Minna
Wittenburg Adolph, porter with Redington & Co. dwl Fourth nr Everett
Witter William, gymnast, Wilson's Circus
Wittman George, with J. Sorbier & Co. dwl 809 Washington
Wittmeier George, beer saloon, 614 Jackson
Wittmeier Sevrin, bar keeper, dwl 614 Jackson
WITTRAM CHARLES, attorney at law, office 39 Montgomery Block, bds Lick House
WITTRAM FREDERICK, attorney at law, office 39 Montgomery Block, bds Lick House
Witta William, plasterer, dwl 617 Post
Witzemann W. F. meat market, 425 East
Wilzinski Marks, tailor with S. Reinstein, dwl Stockton nr Broadway

Wlecke John F. clerk with August F. Wolbern
Wo Hing Lung & Co. (Chinese) merchants, 729 Com
Wo Hop (Chinese) washing, 506 Kearny
Wo Kee & Co. (Chinese) teas, 939 Dupont
Wo Sang (Chinese) washing, SE cor Eddy and Mason
Wo Shong (Chinese) washing, 111 Davis
Wo-Tsun Yeun (Chinese) physician, 741 Clay
Wochatz Charles *(Schuetz & W.)* dwl 607 Jackson
Wochatz Charles, confectioner, dwl 5 Trinity
Woeldecke Fred'k, cigars and tobacco, 504 Kearny
Wohler Herman, real estate, office 415 Montgomery
WOHLERS HENRY, Precito Valley House, SW cor Mission and Thirtieth
Wohlfeld Glucksman, cigars and tobacco, dwl 13 Everett
Wohltmann Hinrich, waterman, dwl 613 Battery
Wohn Wendall C. carpenter, dwl 17 John
Wohrden Theodore Thom. clerk, SE cor Mission and Fifth
Wolbern August F. groceries and liquors, 8 Clay and SE cor Broadway and Powell
Wolbern Jacob D. groceries and liquors, SE cor Dupont and Greenwich
Wolcott Charles P. assistant assessor, U. S. Internal Revenue, NW cor Battery and Commmercial, dwl 295 Clementina
Wolcott James L. dwl S s Washington bet Leavenworth and Hyde
Wold Iver, boot maker, 510 Jackson, dwl SW cor Broadway and Dupont
Wold Peter, boot maker, dwl SE cor Broadway and Dupont
Woldeier Theodore, boot crimper, 200 Sutter
Wolf Aaron, clothes renovator, 109 Leidesdorff
Wolf Aaron, salesman, 619 Sacramento
Wolf August, boot maker, 627 Broadway
WOLF BROTHERS *(Abraham and Philip)* coal yard, and agents Manhattan Coal Company (Mount Diablo) 19 and 21 Bat, dwl 620 Green
Wolf Caspar, dwl 8 Harlan Place
Wolf Charles, wood turner with Cameron & Kuenzi, dwl 325 Pine
Wolf D. & Co. *(C. A. Fletcher)* merchants, (Virginia City) office NE cor Battery and Pine, dwl 13 Stockton
Wolf David, superintendent Clay St. Market, dwl 13 Stockton
Wolf Desire, painter, 1432 Stockton
Wolf Edward, tailoring, 35 Geary
Wolf Frederick, broker, dwl 920 Market
Wolf Frederick, watch maker, 622 Clay
Wolf Frederick, wood turner, dwl 323 Pine
Wolf George, tailor, dwl 425 Bush
Wolf Henry, handcartman, NW cor Sac and Battery, dwl N s Natoma bet Second and Third
Wolf Henry, watch maker, bds Meyer's Hotel, 814 Montgomery
Wolf Herman, salesman, 308 Cal, dwl 35 O'Farrell
Wolf Jacob, glazier, dwl 419 Union
Wolf John, salesman with Daniel Norcross, dwl 273 Minna
Wolf John, hairdressing saloon, 404 Market, dwl Trinity nr Sutter
Wolf John G. cook, dwl 111 Washington
Wolf Julius S. salesman, 10 Mont, dwl 920 Market
Wolf J. W. *(Almy & W.)* res Oakland
Wolf Louis, compositor, California Demokrat, dwl 435 Minna
Wolf M. dwl 21 Dupont
Wolf Michael, millwright, City Flour Mills, dwl 32 Third
Wolf Morris, express wagon, cor Clay and Dupont
Wolf Morris, tailor, dwl N s Pacific bet Montgomery and Sansom
Wolf Philip *(Wolf Brothers)* dwl 1321 Powell
WOLF SEBASTIAN Rev. pastor St. Boniface Church, N s Sutter bet Montgomery and Kearny, dwl 122 Sutter

Wolf Simon, dwl 819 Vallejo
Wolf Simon, clerk, 10 Clay
Wolf W. & Co. *(Samuel Bloom)* boot and shoe manufacturers, 115 California, dwl 619 Sac
Wolf William, cloaks and mantillas, 619 Sacramento
Wolfarth John M. boot maker, dwl 1213 Pacific
Wolfe George H. driver with Swain & Brown, dwl 525 Geary
Wolfe Henry, dwl 1804 Stockton
Wolfe James E. architect, office 402 Montgomery, dwl 525 Geary
Wolfe James E. jr. *(Beardsley & W.)* dwl 525 Geary
Wolfe John H. dwl 525 Geary
Wolfe Meyer, tailor, 539 Kearny
Wolfe Samuel A. photographer with J. M. Ryan, dwl 611 Clay
Wolff August, clerk with W. A. Spence, dwl 929 Greenwich
Wolff Bernard, fruit dealer, Washington Hose Co. No. 1
Wolff Bernhard, hair dresser with C. Diehl
Wolff Harris, collector, dwl S s Olive Avenue bet Polk and Van Ness Avenue
Wolff M. dwl 119 Kearny
Wolff Marcus, tinner with Adam Swiegert, dwl NE cor Polk and Ellis
Wolff Max, fancy goods, 116 Kearny
Wolff Michael, drayman, 311 Sac, dwl 705 Hyde
Wolff Morris, dwl N s Ellis nr Van Ness Avenue
Wolff Peter, cabinet maker, dwl 2 Trinity
Wolfinger Charles, waiter, Clipper Restaurant
Wolford Lans H. engineer with Wilson & Stevens, dwl Potrero
Wolfson Joseph, salesman, 523 Sac, dwl 417 Mont
Wollard ——, fruits. Italian Fish Market
Wollatz Frederick, baker with Charles Schroth, 230 Kearny
Wolleb Edward, assayer with G. W. Bell, 512 California, dwl 35 McLaren Lane
Wollitz Fred, baker with Charles Schroth, 230 Kearny
Wollitz Theodore, San Francisco Bakery, 1321 Dupont and 16 Fourth
Wollstein Theodore, book keeper with A. Kunast, dwl 214 Sansom
Wolmsley Ellen (widow) dwl 7 Hinckley
Wolrad Wilhelmina, cook, 619 Kearny
Wolters John J. groceries and liquors, SE cor Folsom and Ritch
Wolzen Henry, clerk with Dahnken & Bose
Won Lee (Chinese) washing, 10½ Broadway
Wong Chong (Chinese) washing, 106 Sansom
Wong Kee (Chinese) employment office, 834 Dupont
Woo Lee (Chinese) washing, 320 Dupont
Woo Yek (Chinese) washing, E s Sixth nr Tehama
Woo Yek (Chinese) washing, N s Pacific bet Jones and Leavenworth
Wood A. G. adjuster accounts, office 338 Montgomery, dwl 1012 Taylor
Wood Alfred, salesman with D. E. Appleton & Co
Wood Andrew B. clerk, 760 Clay, dwl NE cor Sacramento and Taylor
Wood Anne, domestic, dwl 1024 Kearny
Wood Benjamin, clerk, 507 Com, dwl 348 Third
Wood Charles, carpenter, dwl 17 Stockton Place
Wood Charles, carpenter, dwl 1005 Clay
Wood Charles, laborer, dwl 214 Commercial
Wood Charles, law student, dwl 765 Mission
Wood Charles, millwright, U. S. Branch Mint, dwl Clay above Powell
Wood Charles, planer with Hobbs, Gilmore & Co. dwl 61 Tehama
Wood Charles H. (col'd) porter, dwl 1004 Wash
Wood Charles S. book keeper with John G. Hodge & Co. dwl 300 Stockton
Wood Courtland, dwl 652 Market
Wood D. H. artist, 659 Clay, dwl 1133 Clay
Wood Ezra R. stevedore, dwl 1504 Leavenworth

Wood Frank, merchant, dwl 215 Geary
Wood Frank G. clerk with A. G. Wood, dwl 1012 Taylor
Wood Fred. B. clerk with Charles Geddes, dwl 1012 Taylor
Wood George (col'd) hair dresser stm Chrysopolis, dwl 309 Eddy
Wood George A. captain brig Glencoe, office 36 Stewart
Wood George B. bar keeper, 711 Montgomery, dwl 815 Montgomery
Wood George H. plumber with Thomas Day, 732 Montgomery
Wood George M. engraver and stencil plate cutter, 508 Montgomery, dwl 725 Bush
Wood Harris, drayman, NW cor Sacramento and Battery, dwl 16 Louisa
Wood Harrison, compositor with Dewey, Waters & Co. dwl 728 Folsom
Wood Henry, drayman, 310 Sansom, dwl 16 Louisa
Wood Henry, tailor, dwl 11 Baldwin Court
Wood Henry C. nurse, U. S. Marine Hospital
Wood Henry F. book keeper, 224 Battery, dwl 310 Stockton
Wood Henry H. carpenter and builder, 936 Market
WOOD HORACE V. Hyde St. Market, SW cor Hyde and Geary
Wood Hugh, cabinet maker with W. G. Weir, dwl 541 Mission
Wood Israel, mattress maker, dwl 707 Mission
Wood James P. *(William Wood & Son)* dwl 521 Mission
Wood J. Henry, proprietor Napa Soda Springs, office 232 Bush, res Napa Springs
Wood John, shoe maker, 9 Stewart
Wood John F. machinist, dwl W s Leavenworth bet California and Pine
Wood John H. night inspector, Custom House, dwl 280 Minna
Wood John K. clerk, Pacific Mail S. S. Co. dwl N s Turk bet Van Ness Avenue and Franklin
Wood Jonas, mariner, dwl 809 Vallejo
WOOD JOSEPH, deputy sheriff, City Hall, dwl SW cor Sacramento and Gustavus
Wood Joseph M. farmer, cor Steiner and Vallejo
Wood J. T. machinist, Golden State Iron Works, dwl 1011 Leavenworth
Wood L. H. miner, dwl 280 Minna
Wood Miles L. clerk, 6 Kearny, dwl 1011 Leav
Wood P. A. clerk with Crane & Brigham, dwl NW cor Turk and Eddy
Wood Robert, pile driver, dwl 113 Minna
Wood S. mining, dwl American Exchange
Wood S. Austin, stone cutter with Francis Williams, dwl 27 Geary
WOOD SAMUEL A. importer boots and shoes, etc. 212 California, dwl Cosmopolitan Hotel
Wood Samuel P. tin roofer with John Kehoe, dwl 9 Ritch
Wood Sarah Miss, dwl 809 Vallejo
Wood *(Thomas)* & Leszinsky *(Henry)* brick yard, cor Fillmore and Presidio Road
Wood Thomas, conductor, Central R. R. Co. dwl SE cor Harrison and Sixth
Wood William & Son *(James P. Wood)* poultry and game, 37 Occidental Mkt, dwl 521 Mission
Wood William, butcher, 17 and 18 Washington Market, dwl 1320 Kearny
Wood William, stevedore, Volunteer Engine Co. No. 7
Wood William C. sail maker, dwl W s Stanford bet Townsend and Brannan
Wood William E. *(J. G. Jackson & Co.)* dwl 911 Sutter
Wood William G. attorney at law, office 625 Merch
Wood William H. drugs and medicines, 111 Second, dwl 177 Minna
Wood Zephaniah, architect, office 410 Montgomery, dwl NE cor Sacramento and Taylor

Woodaff William, dwl N s Chestnut bet Stockton and Powell
Woodard John, manager Olympic, dwl 116 Natoma
Woodbridge E. A. with John S. Lohse, 318 Cal
Woodbridge S. apothecary, U. S. Marine Hospital
Woodbridge William H. fruit peddler, dwl 318 Davis
Woodbury Calvin E. pilot, 805 Front, dwl NW cor Washington and Polk
Woodbury Enos A. with Church & Clark, dwl Everett bet Third and Fourth
Woodbury John, machinist, dwl 419 Fremont
Woodbury Thomas Y. bag maker, dwl 551 Howard
Wooden William H. bricklayer, dwl 226 Stevenson
Woodhams Oscar, book keeper, New Orleans Warehouse, dwl 719 California
Woodhead George, musician, Olympic, dwl 215 Stevenson
Woodhull Fred, actor, Maguire's Opera House
Woodis John E. (col'd) calker, dwl S s California bet Jones and Leavenworth
Woodleaf Henry *(H. Cohn & Co.)* dwl 424 Post
Woodley William, engineer, dwl 33 Jackson
Woodman George E. express wagon, 125 Wash
Woodruff Elihu, merchant, office 206 Front, bds 618 California
Woodruff Michael H. janitor Union School, dwl SW cor Filbert and Montgomery
Woods Amos, pattern maker, dwl 70 Tehama
Woods C. D. dwl 154 Tehama
Woods Charles B. clerk, Dann & Landesman
Woods D. C. first officer steamer John L. Stephens, office SW cor Front and Jackson
Wood Edward P. seaman, dwl 45 Sacramento
WOODS *(Francis H.)* & CHEESMAN *(Morton)* stock, note, and loan brokers, office SW cor Montgomery and Clay, dwl S s Pine bet Mason and Taylor
Woods Frederick, drayman, 101 Cal, dwl 605 Stock
Woods James H. carder, S. F. P. Woolen Mills, dwl North Point bet Polk and Van Ness Avenue
Woods John C. brick molder, dwl 130 Second
Woods Mary A. Miss, dress maker, dwl 629 Clay
Woods Samuel, major U. S. A. paymaster, office 742 Washington, res Oakland
Woods Samuel D. teacher English, City College, dwl 765 Mission
Woods William H. machinist, S. F. & San José R. R. Co. dwl E s Carolina nr Mariposa
Woodside Elbridge, carriage maker, dwl 516 Bush
WOODSON JOSEPH A. attorney at law, office 604 Merchant, dwl Verona Place
Woodthorpe John, book keeper, dwl E s Columbia nr Sixteenth
Woodward A. B. dwl What Cheer House
Woodward Charles J. clerk, What Cheer House Restaurant, dwl 404 Post
Woodward Charles W. traveling agent, dwl 151 Silver
Woodward G. dwl Cosmopolitan Hotel
WOODWARD GEORGE F. surgeon U. S. Pension Bureau, and physician, office and dwl 112 Sutter
Woodward Henry T. carpenter, dwl E s Eighth bet Folsom and Howard
Woodward Jessie, dwl 273 Clara
WOODWARD ROBERT B. proprietor What Cheer House 525–529 Sac, res Napa Co
Woodward Warren, ship carpenter, dwl N s Drury Lane nr Seventh
WOODWARD WILLIAM A. *(Frederick Mac-Crellish & Co.)* dwl SW cor Pine and Mason
Woodward James Rev. city missionary, dwl 411 Tehama
WOODWORTH, SCHELL *(Theodore L.)* & CO. importers and manufacturers piano fortes, organs, etc. 12 Post, Masonic Temple
Woodworth James D. dwl S s Sixteenth, bet Folsom and Howard
Woodworth John, wines and liquors, 509 Jackson

Woodworth Joseph, mining stocks, dwl 636 Folsom
Woodworth Selim E., U. S. N. dwl 611 Folsom
Woodworth Willard F. driver, North Beach & M.
    R. R. Co. dwl San Bruno Road 3¼ miles from
    City Hall
Woolf Elias, dwl 1217 Powell
Woolf Hermann, ship carpenter, dwl 1816 Powell
Woolf John, laborer, dwl 273 Minna
Woolfe Bernard, fruits, NW cor Stockton and Green,
    dwl 1511 Stockton, rear
Wooll John *(Jones, W. & Sutherland)* dwl 1300
    California
WOOLLEY E. S. proprietor Tremont House, 418
    ana 420 Jackson
Woolley John C. blacksmith, Spring Valley W. W.
    dwl 26 Clementina
Woolley John, engraver, dwl 912 Powell
Woolley Lell. H. groceries, 8W cor Taylor and Clay,
    dwl 1211 Taylor
Woolser A. H. dwl 138 Fourth
Woolsey John L. laborer, dwl N s Welch bet Third
    and Fourth
WOOSTER DAVID, physician and surgeon, office
    314 Kearny, dwl NE cor Sutter and Jones
Wooster Dexter, clerk, NE cor Sutter and Sansom,
    dwl 6 Sutter
Wooster Henry E. planer with James Brokaw,
    dwl Geary bet Broderick and Devisidero
Wooster J. B. *(Weaver, W. & Co.)* dwl S s Mis-
    sion bet Eleventh and Twelfth
Wooster Lathrop, carpenter, dwl 528 Pine
Wooster Thomas, teamster with James Brokaw
Worden Stephen J. carpenter, dwl 202 Fourth
Wording Dean W. night inspector, Custom House,
    dwl 1513 Stockton, rear
Worell Charles H. Pennsylvania Engine Co. No. 12
Worford William, liquors, 106 Pacific, dwl 462 Pac
Work John W. merchant, dwl NW cor Bush and
    Leavenworth
WORLD'S CRISIS (semi-monthly) office NE cor
    Clay and Montgomery
Worms Charles, steward, dwl 15 Spofford
WORMSER BROTHERS *(Isaac and Simon A.)*
    importers and jobbers liquors, and consul for
    Wurtemburg, SW cor California and Front, dwl
    121 Powell cor O'Farrell
Wormser Isidor *(William Meyer & Co.)* dwl 524
    Sutter
Wormser Louis *(William Meyer & Co.)* dwl 736
    Vallejo
Wormser Simon *(William Meyer & Co.)* dwl 524
    Sutter
Wormser Simon A. *(Wormser Bros.)* SW cor Cali-
    fornia and Front
WORN GEORGE A. real estate agent, office 519
    Montgomery, dwl 210 Powell
Worn James W. salesman with Robert Sherwood,
    517 Montgomery, dwl 210 Powell
Worn Thomas (col'd) porter, dwl Broadway bet
    Kearny and Dupont
Worrell William, theatrical manager, dwl 39 Minna
Worres Jacob, hats and caps, 609 Washington, dwl
    611 Washington
Wort Henry, carpenter, C. S. Navigation Co. 14
    Broadway, dwl 1415 Taylor
Worth Charles, dwl E s Selina Place
Worth Charles A. drayman with Badger & Linden-
    berger, dwl 528 O'Farrell
Worth Edwin, book keeper with Davis & Schafer,
    dwl 1118 Sacramento
Worth Francis, leather and shoe findings, 338 Bush,
    dwl 6 Berry nr Dupont
Worth Francis M. waterman, dwl E s Selina Place
Worth George F. chief deputy and book keeper, U.
    S. Marshal's office, dwl 708 Lombard
Worth Obed, carpenter, dwl E s Selina Place
Worth R. painter, dwl 1610 Stockton
Worth Reuben G. drayman, SW cor Dupont and
    Jackson, dwl N s Sac bet Jones and Leav

Worth W. E. *(Cameron & W.)* dwl 770 Howard
Worth William H. machinist, Fulton Foundry, dwl
    641 Mission
Worthington William, paints, oils, etc. 735 Market,
    dwl 919 Market
Worthley Lewis, with J. O. Taplin, San Bruno Road
WORTHLEY T. R. & CO. grain and produce, 10
    Washington, dwl 9 Sutter
Wray Edward Mrs. dwl 5 Stevenson
Wray Jacob, butcher, 11 Washington Market, dwl
    N s Turk W Jones
Wrede Claus *(Pfirter & W.)* dwl E s Larkin bet
    Geary and Post
WREDE DEIDRICH, groceries and liquors, NW
    cor Sansom and Sutter, dwl 453 Jessie
WREDE GEORGE, liquor saloon, NW cor Stew-
    art and Mission, dwl 417 Fremont
Wrede William, cigars and tobacco, 705 Clay
Wren Batholomew, laborer, dwl cor Greenwich and
    Webster
Wren John, blacksmith helper with Coffey & Ris-
    don, dwl 1152 Folsom
Wren Mary Mrs. dress maker, dwl 1152 Folsom
Wright Andrew, painter, dwl S side O'Farrell bet
    Webster and Fillmore
Wright Anna Miss, dwl 934 Kearny
Wright Anna (widow) dwl NE cor Leavenworth
    and Francisco
Wright Anson, laborer, Fulton Foundry, dwl 24
    Clementina
Wright B. C. local editor Evening Bulletin, dwl
    910 Vallejo
Wright Charles, baker with J. Chadbourne, dwl St.
    Charles Place
Wright Charles, laborer, dwl W s Battery bet Fil-
    bert and Union
Wright Charles J. P. dwl N side Filbert bet Taylor
    and Jones
Wright Daniel F. photographic operator with James
    Wise, dwl 909 Clay
Wright Elisha, ship carpenter, dwl 13 Front
Wright Frances Mrs. teacher private school, dwl N s
    Filbert bet Taylor and Jones
Wright Frank S. clerk, 646 Clay
Wright Frederick F. clerk with C. H. Bradford, dwl
    566 Howard
Wright George, liquor commission merchant, dwl
    735 Market
Wright *(George H.)* & Roden *(A. G.)* livery and
    sale stable, 405 Kearny, dwl 3 Central Place
Wright George H. trunk maker with James Long-
    shore, 208 Bush
Wright George W. carrier, Sunday Mercury, dwl
    732 Green
Wright Harriet (widow) dwl Malvina Pl nr Mason
Wright Henry C. *(Shed & W.)* dwl 620 Pine
Wright Isaac N. mining stocks, dwl S s Filbert bet
    Hyde and Larkin
Wright James, cartman, cor Pacific and Larkin
Wright James, driver, Omnibus R. R. Co
Wright James, wood polisher, dwl 238 Jessie
Wright James A. Mrs. (widow) dwl 15 Clementina
Wright J. B. & Co. *(Eliphalet Grover)* carpenters
    and builders, SE corner Powell and Union, dwl
    732 Green
Wright J. D. ship carpenter, dwl 925 Broadway
Wright John, carpenter, dwl 613 Mission
Wright John, laborer, dwl 41 Louisa, rear
Wright John, pick manufacturer, 511 Market, dwl
    N s Camp bet Second Avenue and Guerrero
Wright Joseph G. supt. Guiboth Olam (Jewish)
    Cemetery, dwl 1112 Stockton
Wright Joseph W. book keeper, Seymour House,
    24 Sansom
Wright Maria (widow) dwl 12 Harlan Place
WRIGHT MARY Mrs. Wright's Hotel, 210 Bdwy
Wright Mary Mrs. dwl 1719 Powell
Wright Mary (widow) dwl N s Washington bet Ma-
    son and Taylor

Wright Mary (widow) stewardess steamship Sacramento, dwl S s Bernard bet Jones and Leav

Wright Owen, retortman, S. F. Gas Co. dwl W s Clinton bet Brannan and Bryant

Wright S. A. first officer Pacific M. S. S. Sacramento

Wright Selden S. attorney at law, office 625 Merchant, dwl S s Lombard bet Taylor and Jones

Wright William, carpenter with Stevens & Rider

Wright William, lather, dwl W s Larkin bet Green and Union

Wright William, stevedore, dwl Montgomery bet Chestnut and Lombard

Wright W. H. steerage steward, steamer Senator

Wright William J. book keeper with Badger & Lindenberger, dwl SW cor Third and Market

Wright William W. porter, steamer Chrysopolis

Wrigley Elizabeth Mrs. Yacht Saloon, E s Mission bet Nineteenth and Twentieth

Wrigley Joseph, foreman Boiler Shop Pacific Foundry, dwl cor Mission and Thirteenth

Wrin Michael J. *(Freeman & W.)* dwl 314 Rich

Wubrmann Henry *(H. Droger & Co.)* dwl SE cor Sixth and Harrison

Wulburn Claus *(J. Wulburn & Bro.)* dwl 734 Broadway

Wulburn J. & Brother *(Claus Wulburn)* groceries and liquors, 734 Broadway

Wulferdingen Charles, pile driver, Tiger Engine Co. No. 14

Wulzen Albert H. with Martin & Folger, dwl 138 Fourth

Wulzen Frederick, dwl 24 Park Avenue

Wulzen John, clerk, dwl 342 Third

Wunch Henry, waiter with H. Stege, W side Sixth bet Harrison and Bryant

Wunderlich Julius, clerk with Maurice Bernheim, dwl 314 Sixth

Wunderlich Reinhold, druggist, German Benevolent Association Hospital

Wunderlich Reynolds, sign painter, dwl 845 Dupont

WUNNENBERG *(N. H.)* & CO. *(Charles Hafner)* proprietors New York Brewery, SE cor Powell and Francisco, res Alameda

Wurkheim Max *(Witkowski & W.)* dwl W side Montgomery bet Jackson and Pacific

WURKHEIM MORRIS, cloaks and trimmings, 613 Sacramento

Wustfeld Frederick, fruit dealer, SE cor Market and Second

Wuth G. F. G. *(Folmer & Co.)* SW cor Louisiana and Sierra

Wuth Louis B. steward, dwl 324 Fremont

Wuthe William, beer saloon, NW cor California and Kearny

Wuthrich John *(Michel & Co.)* dwl 329 Geary

Wyatt Christopher B. Rev. pastor Trinity Church, dwl 812 Bush

Wyatt John, leader orchestra, Bella Union

Wyatt William J. agent Golden Era, office 543 Clay, dwl 522 California

Wyckoff ———, 679 Market

Wyer Elizabeth Mrs. memorandum clerk, U. S. Branch Mint, dwl 100 O'Farrell

Wyman B. H. dwl 18 South Park

Wyman Freeman C. painter, dwl 29 Third

Wyman George D. sign and ornamental painter, 320 California

Wyman John, cabinet maker, dwl 512 Kearny

Wyman John A. cabinet maker with Goodwin & Co. dwl 512 Vallejo

Wyman Matthew F. carpenter, dwl cor Potrero and Napa

Wyman Oliver, carpenter and builder, 106 Davis, dwl 331 Fremont

Wyman Philip, laborer, dwl West End House Old San José Road

Wymer Sarah (widow) dwl 109 Third

Wyndham J. C. printer, Eureka Typographical Union, 625 Merchant

Wyneken Ernest, draftsman with L. R. Townsend, dwl 7 Prospect Place

Wynn Ann Miss, domestic, 1013 Clay

Wynn Bridget Miss, boarding, 1105 Powell

Wynn Jane M. Miss, domestic, 1024 Bush

Wynn J. B. cashier Commercial Bank of India, dwl 503 Powell

Wynn Williams, machinist with E. T. Steen, dwl 115 Bush

Wynne Nicholas, clerk, 306 Kearny, dwl 316 Fourth

Wynne Nicholas, waiter, Lick House, dwl 611 Post

Wynne Patrick, carpenter, dwl N s Ellis bet Jones and Leavenworth

Wynne William, groceries and liquors, NW cor Fourth and Louisa

Wynjents F. iron door and shutter maker with J. R. Sims, dwl S s Broadway bet Leav and Hyde

Wyre Charles, captain schooner Alpha, office 8 Clay

Wysham Frances Mrs. (col'd) dwl 536 Green

Wythe J. H. Rev. pastor Powell St. M. E. Church, dwl 1008 Washington

Y

YABLONSKY John, gas fitter, S. F. Gas Co

Yager Henry, baker, Miners' Restaurant, dwl 320 Dupont

Yale Abraham, butcher, dwl 649 Broadway

YALE *(Gregory)* & McCONNELL *(J. R.)* attorneys at law, office 520 Mont, dwl 35 South Park

Yale Jeremiah S. dwl 1129 Folsom

Yale Lawrence B. butcher, dwl 1129 Folsom

Yan On Chong & Co. (Chinese) merchants, 734 Sac

Yankee Blade Tunnel Co. office 305 Montgomery

Yaukee Thomas, driver with Barry & Patten, 413 Montgomery

Yarans George, barber, dwl 6 Broadway

Yarbrough S. M. Co. office 302 Montgomery

Yard Charles D. upholsterer with Wightman & Hardie, dwl 19 John

Yarrington Halsey J. veterinary surgeon, dwl 810 Union

Yarrington Jacob T. book keeper, Bank Wells, Fargo & Co. dwl N s Mission nr Twelfth

Yarskio Mendel, tailor, 110 Geary

Yarver George, cook, dwl Oriental Hotel

Yates Alexander O. butcher, 41 Occidental Market, dwl 809 Mission

Yates Charles M. clerk with M. Miner & Co. NW cor Front and Washington, dwl 663 Mission

Yates Elizabeth Miss, domestic with Isaac Lankershim

Yates G. Clement, salesman, 224 Battery, dwl Brevoort House

Yates Jacob (col'd) seaman, dwl 407 Union

Yates John, dwl 113 Stockton

Yates John, dwl SE cor Hayes and Pierce

Yates Joseph, express wagon, corner Howard and Hubbard

Yates M. H. Mrs. proprietress Brevoort House, NW cor Mission and Fourth

Yates R. P. steward, steamer Princess

YATES W. H. & CO. produce commission merchants, 208 Clay, dwl 911 Bush

Yates William, fireman, dwl N s Vallejo bet Montgomery and Sansom

Yates William H. (col'd) steward, steamer Chrysopolis, dwl 1421 Pacific

Ye Wah (Chinese) washing, 666 Howard

Yeager Joseph, clerk, dwl E s Washington Avenue nr Howard

Yeager Thomas T. fruit dealer, 43 Third

Yeamans Annie Mrs. actress, Metropolitan Theater

Yearson Ernst, boatman, dwl 1027 Dupont

Yeary A. G. dwl What Cheer House

Yeates John L. clerk, dwl 820 Dupont

Yeaton Oliver T. North Point Meat Market, SE cor Battery and Filbert

Yeazel A. H. salesman, 15 Third, dwl 609½ Howard
Yee Chy Tong (Chinese) druggist, 810 Dupont
Ye Lay (Chinese) washing, 708 Broadway
Ye Wo & Co. (Chinese) merchants, 805 Dupont
Yehagan Richard, laborer, dwl 4 Lick Alley
Yehl Abraham, butcher with Felix Uri, dwl SE cor Broadway and Stockton
Yek Wan (Chinese) washing, 349 Third
Yellott George, clerk dwl NW cor Sansom and Pine
Yellow Monster G. & S. M. Co. office room 1 Government House, 502 Washington
Yeo Wm. H. boot maker, 737 Market, dwl 177 Minna
Yerkes Isaac, salesman, 206 Mont, dwl 626 Cal
Yerkes Joseph, dwl 626 California
Yerman John, wheelwright and blacksmith, 1116 Howard
Yerworth William, compositor with B. F. Sterett, 533 Clay
Yet Kie (Chinese) washing, 642 Commercial
Yetes Joseph, junk and bottles, dwl SE cor Howard and Hubbard
Yik Yune & Co. (Chinese) merchants, 823 Dupont
Yontz William R. chief operator California State Telegraph Co. 507 Montgomery, dwl 713 Bush
Yop Shin (Chinese) washing, 751 Mission
Yore J. P. boot maker, dwl 322 Pacific
Yore Mary (widow) dwl W s Sansom nr Union
York Charles, stevedore. dwl 224 Mission
York John, cooper with H. Thode, dwl 454 Jessie
York William, stevedore, dwl 26 Stewart
York William R. painter, dwl 120 Ellis
Yost Daniel Z. clerk, Gould & Curry M. Co. dwl 632 Market
Yost Henry D. engineer, dwl 27 Ritch
Yost William, carpenter, dwl 41 Clara
Young Abell W. ship joiner, dwl 73 Natoma
Young A. J. carpenter, dwl S s Columbia bet Guerrero and Dolores
Young Alexander, workman with Cutting & Co. dwl S s Harrison bet Seventh and Eighth
Young Andrew, Metropolitan Restaurant, 154 and 156 Second
Young Andrew S. pilot, office 5 Vallejo
Young Charles B. engraver with Lemme Bros. dwl 135 Tehama nr Second
Young Christopher C. with Herman W. Massey, 1014 Market
Young Conrad, laborer, dwl 8 Virginia Place
Young Crist T. blacksmith, dwl 608 Powell
Young George, dwl E s Dupont nr Francisco
Young George, carpenter, dwl SW cor Laguna and Oak
Young George, teamster, dwl 62 Clay
Young George A. collector, S. F. Gas Co. dwl 728 Bush
Young George W. janitor Mission School, dwl with Ambrose P. Hodgdon
Young Henry, pile driver, dwl NW cor Townsend and Third
Young Henry, porter, 208 California
Young Henry C. teamster, dwl N s Francisco bet Stockton and Powell
Young Henry D. with Wm. Faulkner & Son, dwl 1414 Stockton
Young Henry J. clerk, S. F. & San José R. R. Co. cor Sansom and Halleck, dwl 704 Howard
Young James, driver, Omnibus R. R. Co
Young J. J. broker, dwl 815 Post
Young John, with Charles Schroth, dwl 815 Mont
Young John, bar keeper, dwl 619 Pacific
Young John, contractor, office 405 Front
YOUNG *(Mansfield)* & CO. hats, 336 Montgomery, dwl 1018 Clay
Young Mary (widow) dwl 761 Mission
Young Maxima (widow) dwl 711 Pine
Young McP. engineer, S. F. Gas Co
Young Men's Benevolent Society, hall 9 Scott
YOUNG MEN'S CHRISTIAN ASSOCIATION, rooms 526 California, John Dunn librarian

Young Men's Homestead Union, office 305 Mont
Young Michael, dwl 577 Howard
Young Nahum E. cooper with Handy & Neuman, dwl E s Eighth bet Mission and Minna
Young Nelson, carpenter, dwl W s Larkin between Union and Filbert
Young Nicholas, foundryman, dwl 1203 Sacramento
Young Richard, blacksmith, Phœnix Iron Works, dwl 9 Bagley Place
Young Richard, groceries and liquors, NE cor Larkin and Clay
Young Robert, boiler maker, Pacific Foundry, dwl 314 Beale
Young Samuel, cabinet maker, 625 Market, dwl 405 Union
Young Samuel, captain schooner, dwl 30 Frederick
Young Sarah Miss, domestic, SW cor Dupont and Broadway
Young S. T. boiler maker, dwl 314 Beale
YOUNG THOMAS, city and county recorder, office SE cor Kearny and Washington, dwl NE cor Sutter and Van Ness Avenue
Young Thomas, stair builder with B. H. Freeman & Co. dwl 525 Bush
Young Thomas, stevedore, dwl E s Harrison Avenue nr Folsom
Young Thomas D. machinist, Vulcan Iron Works, dwl 303 Bryant
Young Walter, teller, Bank of British Columbia, dwl 335 Pine
Young Willet C. drug clerk, dwl 1020 Minna
Young William, clerk, dwl 1906 Powell
Young William, laborer, dwl 29 Baldwin Court
Young William E. carpenter, dwl SE cor Guerrero and Thirteenth
Young William E. cigars and tobacco, 902 Kearny
Young Wo Tong & Co. (Chinese) merchants, 733 Commercial
Younger Alexander J. student with Dr. W. J. Younger, dwl 316 Green
Younger Alexander T. dwl with Dr. W. J. Younger, 316 Green
Younger Annie E. Miss, assistant, Union St. Primary School, dwl NE cor Green and Vincent
Younger William J. physician and dentist, office 315 Montgomery, dwl 316 Green
Youst Richard, carpenter, 16 Freelon
Yslas Florence, pressman with Towne & Bacon, dwl 1311 Stockton
Yu Yuen, Ching Kee & Co. (Chinese) merchants, 734 Sacramento
Yuba G. & S. M. Co. office 210 Pine
Yue Yee & Co. (Chinese) merchants, 728 Sac
Yuisitra Rafael S. tailor, dwl 631 Green, rear
Yung Michael, with G. Groezinger, NW cor Pine and Battery
Yung Nicholas, Railroad Iron Works, 28 Fremont *(and Craig, Golden & Y.)* dwl 1203 Sac
Yung Son (Chinese) washing, 216 Sansom
Yunker A. R. musician, dwl 1511 Mason
Yunker Frederick, cutter with J. H. Tobin, dwl 818 Pacific
Yust John, seaman, dwl 524 Vallejo

Z

ZABORWSKI JOHN A. cigar maker, W s Potrero Avenue nr Sixteenth
Zabriskie James C. attorney at law, office 528 Clay, dwl 1109 Stockton
ZABRISKIE WILLIAM M. attorney at law, office rear City Hall
Zabriski Z. peddler, dwl cor Powell and Filbert
Zacharias Henry, watch maker and jeweler, 538 Kearny, dwl 110 Stevenson
Zadig Hermann, salesman, 513 Sac, dwl 610 Pine
Zadig Phillip, city agent Bigelow & Brother, 505 Montgomery, dwl Sophie Terrace

Zaepffel William, confectionery, 1208 Dupont
Zahn Adam. hairdresser with Ciprico & Cook
Zahn Charles, workman, Potrero Rope Walk, dwl cor Shasta and Michigan
Zahn Ernest, clerk with Alfred Borel, dwl 809 Pac
ZAHN HENRY, groceries and liquors, 823 Vallejo
Zamut Frank, with B. Miller, dwl Merchant bet Montgomery and Sansom
Zander Jacob *(Hayden & Z.)* dwl 542 Wash
Zander L. T. Cashier's Department Wells, Fargo & Co. dwl 409 Bryant
Zane John P. dwl 320 Kearny
Zaninovich Marino, broom maker with Palmer, Gillespie & Co. 205 Davis
Zawskey Thomas, upholsterer with Goodwin & Co. dwl 229 Jessie
Zebf Henry, hose and belt maker, Sixth St. Tannery, dwl 132 Townsend
Zech Frederick, pianoforte manufacturer, 212 Post
ZECH JACOB, pianoforte manufactory, 416 Market
Zeglio *(David)* & Moore *(Thomas)* marble works, 24 Fourth, dwl SW cor Fifth and Stevenson
Zeh Bros. *(Louis and Theodore)* Eclipse Market, SE cor Union and Dupont, dwl 417 Union
Zeh Gottlieb, butcher, 433 Union
Zeh John *(Girzikowsky & Z.)* dwl 20 Hinckley
Zeh Theodore *(Zeh Bros.)* dwl 417 Union
Zebfuss William, cabinet maker, dwl 5 Trinity
Zeigler Frank E. clerk, 532 Sac, dwl 24 Dupont
Zeile Charles D, druggist and apothecary, 517 Pac
Zeile Frederick, physician, office 517 Pacific
ZEILE JOHN, proprietor Pacific Flour Mills, 508 Pacific, dwl W s Mont bet Vallejo and Green
Zeile Robert, agent Pacific Flour Mills, 508 Pacific
Zeis John, shoe making, 5 Dupont
Zeiseniss Christian, cabinet mkr, dwl 19 Dupont, rear
Zeitfuchs Edward, engraver with Lemme Bros. dwl SW cor Mary and Minna
Zeitler Edmund, laborer with William Fruhling
Zeitska Henry, merchant tailor, 415 Montgomery, dwl 419 Bryant
Zella Henry, clerk, NW cor Tehama and Second
Zephyr Louis, master schooner Union, office 413 East, dwl N s Townsend bet Second and Third
Zerga Stephen, with Vincent Squarza, dwl 1508 Dupont
Zermendez Eloy, waiter, Miners' Restaurant, dwl 810 Stockton
Ziegelmeyer Anton, groceries and liquors, 629 Mission cor Jane
Ziegenfuss Thomas H. sawsmith with N. W. Spaulding, dwl Thirteenth nr Valencia
Ziegenbirt Brothers *(Henry and Louis Ziegenbirt)* ladies' dress trimmings, 639 Sac, dwl 214 Tehama
Ziegenbirt Louis *(Ziegenbirt Brothers)* dwl 744 Howard
Ziegenisz C. with Henry Bocken
Zieglmayr Ferdinand, dwl 219 Pacific

Ziegler Anthony S. hairdresser with C. Diehl, dwl 24 Dupont
Ziegler J. Louis *(Dodge & Z.)* dwl 517 Minna
Ziegler Joseph, boot maker, NE cor Clay and Powell
ZIÉL, *(Gustavus)* BERTHEAU *(Cesar)* & CO. *(C. A. Balzer)* importers merchandise, 122 Cal, consulate Hamburg and Hessia and agents Hamburg Underwriters, dwl 354 Brannan
Ziess Friedrick, waiter, Union Club Rooms
Ziff John, laborer, Bay Sugar Refinery, dwl S s St. Charles bet Broadway and Pacific
Zihn Andrus, dwl 156 Silver
Zimlin J. harness maker, Omnibus R. R. Co
Zimmer Charles K. hairdresser with Aaron Creamer, dwl 6 Milton Place
Zimmer Jacob, tailor, dwl 425 Green
Zimmer L. blacksmith, NE cor Powell and Bdwy
Zimmerman Henry, wholesale butcher, Potrero Av, dwl SW cor Santa Clara and San Bruno Road
ZIMMERMAN JOHN & CO. *(Ernst Voigt)* wholesale butchers, Brannan St. Bridge, dwl N s Sixteenth nr Rhode Island
Zimmerman Leonard, musician, dwl 1117 Kearny
Zimmerman Mathew, fruit, 136 Second
Zimmerman Simon, beer saloon, SE cor Pine and Kearny
Zimmett Joseph, cook, Excelsior Restaurant, 25 Third
Zinn Henry *(Thurnauer & Z.)* dwl 20 Mont
Zinnamon Abraham, tailor, 362 Third, dwl 362 Third
Zinns Christian, cutter with J. L. Brooks, dwl SE cor Post and Jones
Zinton James, dwl 331 Bush
Zmitt Antonio, poultry dealer, dwl E s Beale bet Market and Mission
Zmitt Joseph, cook, dwl N s Mission nr Beale
Zoller John A. Pacific Market, SW cor Pacific and Powell
Zollner W. R. shoe maker, dwl 707 Broadway
Zott Nickolas, boot maker, dwl S s Dupont Alley
Zowaski Thomas, upholsterer, dwl 229 Jessie
Zschiesche Christian, boot maker, 1329 Dupont
Zuckerman Jacob, dwl 1818 Stockton
Zurmblen Augustus, stone mason, dwl 120 Sutter, rear
Zurmuhlen Henry, dwl E s Hyde bet Filbert and Greenwich
Zwahlen Julius, furnished rooms, 1414 Stockton
Zweig Louis, handcartman, SW cor Sansom and California, dwl 605 Broadway
Zweybrück Christian F. cigars, dwl 357 Jessie
ZWICK *(Charles)* & LOEVEN *(Emil)* manufacturers extract of coffee and French and German mustard, 725 Vallejo
Zwieg Herman, proprietor South Park Malt House, N s Brannan bet Fifth and Sixth
Zwiesle George *(Weiss & S.)* dwl Whitehall Exchange

PUBLIC STREETS, AVENUES, SQUARES, ALLEYS, ETC.*

[COMPILED FROM OFFICIAL AND AUTHENTIC SOURCES.]

THE principal streets south-east of Market, and running parallel to Fifth, have been, by an Ordinance of the city, changed, and they are to be designated hereafter numerically, as follows: Simmons to be Sixth, Harris as Seventh, Price as Eighth, Johnston as Ninth, and so on, as far as such parallel streets continue. †

ADA, opens S s Lombard bet Stockton and Dupont
Ada Court, N s O'Farrell bet Leavenworth and Hyde
Adelaide Place, W s Taylor bet Post and Geary
Adele Place, N s Jackson bet Stockton and Powell
Adelphi Place, E s Jones bet Post and Geary
Adler, E s Dupont bet Broadway and Pacific
Adona Place, N s Washington bet Mason and Taylor
Agnes Lane, N s Vallejo bet Dupont and Stockton
Alabama, Potrero Nuevo
Alameda, W from the bay to Channel
Alamo Square, bet Hayes, Steiner, Fulton, and Scott
Alcatraces Square, bet Jefferson, Franklin, North Point, and Gough
Allen, W s Hyde bet Union and Filbert
Almera, N s Clay bet Leavenworth and Hyde
Alta (now Twenty-First) W s Folsom bet Twentieth and Twenty-Second, to Castro
Alta Place, E s Montgomery bet Union and Filbert
Alta Plaza, bet Clay, Steiner, Jackson, and Scott
Andrew, S s Mission bet Fifth and Sixth
Ankeny Place, E s Powell bet Bush and Sutter
Ann, N s Folsom bet Fourth and Fifth
Anna, N s Eddy bet Powell and Mason
Annie, S s Market bet Second and Third
Anthony, N s Mission bet First and Second
Antonio, W s Jones bet O'Farrell and Ellis
Arkansas, Potrero Nuevo
Army, W s Valencia nr Duncan
Ashburton Place (or Lincoln Avenue) E s Dupont bet Sutter and Post
Ashland Place, N s Mission bet Potter and Eleventh
Auburn, N s Jackson bet Taylor and Mason
August Alley, N s Green bet Powell and Mason
Austin, W s Larkin bet Bush and Pine

BAGLEY PLACE, N s O'Farrell bet Dupont and Stockton
Bailey Alley, S s Bush bet Montgomery and Kearny
Baker, W of Devisidero from Market N to the bay
Balance, N s Jackson bet Montgomery and Sansom
Baldwin Court, N s Folsom bet First and Fremont
Bannam Place, N s Green bet Dupont and Stockton
Baright Place, op 27 O'Farrell
Barret Alley, S s Bush bet Stockton and Dupont
Barry Place, W s Eighth bet Howard and Clementina

Bartlett Alley, N s Jackson bet Kearny and Dupont
Bartol, N s Broadway bet Montgomery and Sansom
Battery, N s Market nr First, N to Lombard
Bay, W s Kearny (North Point) W to Devisidero
Bay Avenue, S s Bryant bet First and Second
Bay View Place, N s Union bet Leavenworth and Jones
Beach, W s Powell bet North Point and Jefferson, W to Devisidero
Beale, S s Market (junction Pine and Davis) to Brannan
Beale Place, E s Beale bet Folsom and Harrison
Bedford Place, N s Jackson bet Powell and Stockton
Belden, S s Pine bet Kearny and Montgomery
Bellair Place, N s Chestnut bet Dupont and Stockton
Benton or Devisidero, junction Ridley and Castro, N to the bay
Benzi, S s Howard bet Eighth and Ninth
Bernard, W s Taylor bet Broadway and Pacific
Berry, E s Dupont bet Bush and Sutter
Berry, W s Second bet Channel and King, SW to Seventh
Bertha, W s Beale bet Mission and Howard
Bestole, N s Vallejo bet Montgomery and Sansom
Beverly Place, N s O'Farrell bet Dupont and Stock
Billings Place, N s Vallejo bet Dupont and Stockton
Birch, W s Larkin bet Grove and Fulton
Bluxome, E s Sixth bet Brannan and Townsend
Bluxome East, W s First bet Brannan and Townsend
Bone Alley, N s Green bet Montgomery and Kearny
Boston Place, E s First bet Folsom and Harrison
Bower Place, S s Green bet Dupont and Stockton
Boyd, N s Seventh bet Harrison and Bryant
Brady, S s Market bet Herman and Potter SE to Mission
Brady Place, E s Larkin bet Union and Green
Brandon Alley, S s Washington bet Powell and Stockton
Brannan, W s Beale bet Bryant and Townsend, SW to Channel
Brenham Place, N s Clay bet Kearny and Dupont
Broadway, W s Davis bet Pacific and Vallejo, W to Devisidero
Broderick, from Market W of Baker, N to the bay
Broderick Avenue, S s Market bet Eleventh and Potter
Brooklyn Place, S s Sac bet Stockton and Dupont

---

* Reference is frequently made in the Register of Names to the following, and which are located as follows, viz.: Hoadley's Addition, situated west of Grant or Pierce between Geary and Washington: Horner's Addition, south and near the Mission Dolores; Western Addition, west of Larkin: San Miguel Ranch, south-west and near the Mission Dolores: and Bernal Heights, near the San Bruno Road and south of the Potrero Nuevo. See, also, Prominent Places, page 476.

† The names of the principal streets west of Larkin have been changed upon an unofficial map of this city recently published, viz.: Gough to Lafayette Avenue, Octavia to Jefferson Avenue, Laguna to Clinton Avenue, Buchanan to Monroe Avenue, Webster to Webster Avenue, Fillmore to Fillmore Avenue, Steiner to Madison Avenue, Pierce to Hamilton Avenue, Scott to Scott Avenue, and Devisidero to Devisidero Avenue. As these alterations have not yet been sanctioned by the Board of Supervisors, the original names have been retained in the canvass for the work.—[COMPILER.

BIGELOW & BROTHER, Agents Fire, Life, Marine, and Accidental Insurance.

Brooks, N s Market bet Dupont and Kearny
Brown (now Twelfth) S s Mission bet Eleventh and Thirteenth
Brown Alley, S s Pine bet Kearny and Dupont
Bryan Place, N s Bush bet Sansom and Montgomery
Bryant, W s Spear bet Harrison and Brannan, SW to Channel
Bryant Avenue, N s Bryant bet Eighth and Ninth
Buchanan (now Lincoln) junction Market and Ridley N to Lewis
Buenaventura, N s Cal bet Kearny and Dupont
Buena Vista, N s Cal bet Stockton and Powell
Burgoyne Place, S s Pacific bet Hyde and Leavenworth
Burritt, S s Bush bet Powell and Stockton
Bush, junction Battery and Market W to Devisidero
Butte, W from the bay to Channel

CADELL ALLEY, N s Union bet Stockton and Dupont
Calhoun, N s Green bet Sansom and Montgomery
California, junction Drumm and Market W to Devisidero
Camille Place, N s Washington bet Jones and Taylor
Camp, E s Guerrero bet Sixteenth and Seventeenth
Campbell, E s Dolores bet Sixteenth and Seventeent
Capp, S s Fourteenth bet Howard and Mission
Card Alley, W s Stockton bet Vallejo and Green
Carlos Place, S s O'Farrell bet Mason and Powell
Carolina, Potrero Nuevo
Caroline, N s Lombard bet Jones and Leavenworth
Caroline, S s Folsom bet Sixth and Seventh
Caroline Place, E s Powell bet Jackson and Pacific
Carr Place, S s Chestnut bet Taylor and Mason
Castle Avenue (or Pennsylvania Avenue) W s Kearny bet Pacific and Broadway
Castro, S s Ridley W of Noe
Catarro Place, W s Taylor bet Post and Geary
Catharine, E s Sixth bet Harrison and Bryant
Cazneau, N s Thirteenth nr Howard
Cedar, N s Clay bet Davis and Washington
Cedar Avenue, W s Larkin bet Post and Geary
Cemetery Alley, W side Dolores bet Sixteenth and Seventeenth
Cemetery Avenue, W Lyon, Hoadley's Extension
Center (now Sixteenth) from the bay W to Market bet Fifteenth and Seventeenth
Center, S s Bryant SE to South Park
Central Place, S s Pine bet Dupont and Kearny
Chambers, W s Front bet Pacific and Broadway
Channel, W s Third bet Berry and Hooper SW to Seventh, thence W to Eleventh, thence S to Twenty-Second
Charles, N s Taylor bet Leavenworth and Hyde
Charles, N s Harrison bet First and Second
Chatham Place, N s Bush bet Dupont and Stockton
Chattanooga, S side Twenty-First bet Dolores and Church
Chelsea Place, S s Bush bet Stockton and Powell
Chesley, S s Harrison bet Seventh and Eighth W to Devisidero
Church, S s Ridley bet Dolores and Sanchez
Church Place, W s Dupont bet Lombard and Greenwich
Clara, W s Fifth bet Folsom and Harrison
Clara Lane, N s Sutter bet Kearny and Dupont
Clarence, N s Townsend bet Second and Third
Clarice Place, N s Townsend bet Second and Third
Clarissa Place, N s Tyler bet Leav and Hyde
Clark, E s Front bet Jackson and Pacific
Clary, E s Fourth bet Folsom and Harrison
Clay, W s East bet Washington and Commercial W to Devisidero
Clay Avenue, N s Clay bet Stockton and Powell
Cleaveland, W s Columbia Square bet Folsom and Harrison
Clement Place, N s Green bet Stockton and Dupont

Clement Place, N s Tyler bet Leav and Hyde
Clementina, W s First bet Folsom and Tehama
Clementina Place, W s Fourth bet Folsom and Harrison
Clinton, S s Brannan bet Sixth and Seventh
Codman Place, N s Clay bet Powell and Mason
Cohen Place, S s Ellis bet Leavenworth and Hyde
Cohn Place, S s Jackson bet Leav and Hyde
Columbia, E s Dolores bet Eighteenth and Nineteenth
Columbia, Potrero Nuevo
Columbia, S s Folsom bet Sixth and Seventh
Columbia Square, bet Folsom, Sixth, Harrison, and Seventh
Commerce, E s Battery bet Union and Green
Commercial, W s East bet Clay and Sacramento W to Dupont
Connecticut, Potrero Nuevo
Cooper Alley, S s Jackson bet Kearny and Dupont
Corbett (now Seventeenth) E s Market bet Sixteenth and Eighteenth E to Mission Creek
Cormick, S s Pacific bet Hyde and Larkin
Cottage, S s Pacific bet Mason and Taylor
Courtlandt Avenue, Potrero
Creek Lane, W s Folsom bet Thirteenth and Fourteenth
Crook, N s Townsend bet Third and Fourth
Cushman, S s Sacramento bet Mason and Taylor
Custom House Place, N s Washington bet Sansom and Battery

DALE, S s Tyler bet Leavenworth and Hyde
Dall, S s Ellis bet Leavenworth and Hyde
Davis, N s Market bet Drumm and Front N to Vallejo
Day, E s Dolores nr Mission Church
DeBoom, E s Second bet Bryant and Brannan
Decatur, S s Bryant bet Seventh and Eighth
Delaware, Potrero Nuevo
Delaware Court, N s Sutter bet Mason and Powell
Delgardo, E s Hyde bet Green and Union
Dent Place, N s Jackson bet Stockton and Powell
Dexter, S s Howard bet Main and Spear
Devisidero, junction Ridley and Castro N to Lewis
Dikeman Place, W s Mason bet O'Farrell and Ellis
Dock, W s Front bet Filbert and Union
Dodge, S s Turk bet Hyde and Larkin
Dolores, S s Market bet Church and Guerrero
Domett Alley, S s Bush bet Stockton and Dupont
Dora, S s Folsom bet Seventh and Eighth
Dorland Lane (now Day) W s Dolores nr Mission Church
Douglas Place, E s Beale bet Folsom and Harrison
Dow Place, W s Second bet Folsom and Harrison
Downey, S s Bryant nr Seventh
Drumm, N s Market bet Davis and East N to Pacific
Duane, W s Jones bet Chestnut and Lombard
Dunbar Alley, rear City Hall
Duncan, W s Valencia nr Army
Duncan Court, W s Broadway bet Dupont and Stock
Dunn Alley, E s Kearny bet Broadway and Vallejo
Dupont, junction of Market and O'Farrell N to the bay
Dupont Alley, W s Dupont bet Jackson and Pacific
Dupont Place, E s Dupont bet Post and Sutter

EAGLE (now Nineteenth) W s Folsom bet Eighteenth and Twentieth W to Castro
East, from Folsom N to Pacific fronting the bay
East, Little, S s Sacramento bet Drumm and East
Ecker (now Jones) S s Market bet First and Second and N s Folsom bet First and Second
Eddy, junction Powell and Market W to Devisidero
Eddy Place, S s Eddy bet Powell and Mason
Edward, N s Bush bet Larkin and Hyde
Eighteenth (late Falcon) W s Folsom bet Seventeenth and Nineteenth W to Castro
Eighth (late Price) S s Market bet Seventh and Ninth, SE to Channel

El Dorado, W from the bay to Channel
Eleventh (late Wood) S side Market bet Tenth and Twelfth, SE to Mission Creek
Eliza, N s Union bet Taylor and Jones
Eliza Place, N s Washington bet Taylor and Jones
Elizabeth, S s Harrison bet Third and Fourth
Ellen (now Thirteenth) S s Mission bet Twelfth and Fourteenth SE to Harrison
Ellen, S s Folsom bet Seventh and Eighth
Ellick Alley, N s Pacific bet Dupont and Stockton
Ellick Lane, N s California bet Stockton and Powell
Ellis, junction Market and Stockton W to Devisidero
Elm Avenue, W s Larkin bet Turk and Tyler
Emma, E s Stockton bet Pine and Bush
Emma Place, S s Chestnut bet Stockton and Powell
Emmet Place, W s Stockton bet California and Sacramento
Erie, W s Howard bet Thirteenth and Fourteenth
Essex, S s Folsom bet First and Second
Essex Place, W s Essex bet Folsom and Harrison
Everett, W s Third bet Mission and Howard
Ewer Place, W s Mason bet Sacramento and Clay

Fair Oaks, S side Twenty-First bet Guerrero and Dolores
Falcon (now Eighteenth) W s Folsom bet Seventeenth and Nineteenth W to Castro
Falcon Place, E s Taylor bet Broadway and Vallejo
Fay, S s Sacramento bet Powell and Mason
Fell, junction Market and Polk W to Devisidero
Fella Place, E s Powell bet Bush and Pine
Fern Avenue, W s Larkin bet Bush and Sutter
Fifteenth (late Sparks) N s Folsom bet Fourteenth and Sixteenth W to Castro
Fifth, S side Market bet Fourth and Sixth, SE to Hooper
Fifth Avenue, bet Fifth, Sixth, Folsom, and Harrison
Figg (now Twenty-Seventh) W s Valencia bet Duncan and Army
Filbert, W side Front bet Greenwich and Union to Devisidero
Filbert Place, N s Union bet Kearny and Dupont
Fillmore, N s Ridley bet Webster and Steiner N to Lewis
First, S s Market bet Fremont and Second
First Avenue, N s Sixteenth bet Mission and Valencia
Flint Alley, W s Battery bet Broadway and Vallejo
Florence, N s Broadway bet Taylor and Jones
Florida, Potrero Nuevo
Folsom, W s East bet Howard and Harrison SW to Fourteenth, thence S to Twenty-Second
Folsom Avenue, S s Folsom bet Eighth and Ninth
Folsom Avenue, S s Folsom bet Seventh and Eighth
Forsyth, W s Leavenworth bet O'Farrell and Ellis
Fort Place, S s Pacific bet Hyde and Larkin
Fourteenth (late Tracy) W s Folsom bet Thirteenth and Fifteenth W to Market
Fourth, junction Market and Ellis SE to Channel
Francisco, W s Montgomery W to Devisidero
Frank Place, W s Mason bet California and Pine
Franklin, junction Market and Page N to Lewis
Frederick, W s First bet Brannan and Bryant
Freelon, W s Zoe bet Brannan and Welsh
Fremont, S side Market bet First and Beale SE to Brannan
Fremont Court or Clay St eet Avenue, S s Clay bet Stockton and Powell r
Front, junction Fremont and Mkt N to Greenwich
Fuller Alley, E s Kearny to Webb bet California and Pine
Fulton, W s Larkin bet McAllister and Grove W to Devisidero

Gaines, N s Green bet Sansom and Battery
Galinto, N s Sixteenth bet Guerrero and Dolores
Garden, S s Harrison bet Sixth and Seventh
Gardner, N s Post bet Dupont and Kearny

Gaven, S s Greenwich bet Powell and Mason
Gay, S s Bush bet Larkin and Hyde
Geary, junction Market and Kearny W to Devisidero
Geneva, S s Bryant bet Sixth and Seventh ·
George, block Irwin, Hubbell, Fifth and Sixth
Gerard Avenue, block Howard, Mission, Ninth, and Tent
Gerke Alley, E s Dupont bet Greenwich and Filbert
Gibb, W s Maiden Lane bet Jackson and Wash
Gibson. E s Larkin bet Union and Green
Gilbert, S s Bryant bet Sixth and Seventh
Glenwood Place, S s Howard bet Twelfth and Thirteenth
Gold, E s Montgomery bet Jackson and Pacific
Good Children, S s Lombard bet Dupont and Kearny
Gordon, N s Harrison nr Ninth
Gough, junction Market and Haight N to Lewis
Grady, N s Mission nr Twelfth
Graham Place, N s Union bet Stockton and Dupont
Grand Avenue, S s Mission bet Ninth and Tenth
Grand Place, N s Filbert bet Dupont and Kearny
Grant (late Pierce) N s Waller bet Scott and Steiner N to Lewis
Green, W s Front bet Vallejo and Union W to Devisidero
Greenwich, W s Front bet Filbert and Lombard W to Devisidero
Grove, W s Larkin bet Fulton and Hayes W to Devisidero
Grove Avenue, S s Harrison bet Fifth and Sixth
Guerrero, S s Market bet Valencia and Dolores
Gustavus, N s California bet Powell and Mason
Guy Place, W s First bet Folsom and Harrison

Haight, junction Market and Gough W to Devisidero
Hall Alley, S s Vallejo bet Montgomery and Sansom
Hall Court, opens at 923 Dupont
Halleck, W s Battery bet Sacramento and California W to Leidesdorff
Hamlin, N s Green bet Leavenworth and Hyde
Hamlin Place, E s Larkin bet Vallejo and Broadway
Hamilton Square, bet O'Farrell, Steiner, Post, and Scott
Hamlin, N s Green bet Leavenworth and Hyde
Hamlin Place, W s Larkin bet Bdwy and Vallejo
Hammond, S s Townsend bet Second and Third
Hampshire, Potrero Nuevo
Hampton Place, N s Harrison bet Second and Third
Hancock, W s Dolores bet Falcon and Eagle
Hardie Place, E s Kearny bet Bush and Sutter
Harlan Place, W s Dupont bet Bush and Sutter
Harrick, N s Folsom bet Sixth and Seventh
Harriet, S s Howard bet Sixth and Seventh
Harriet, N s Sixteenth bet Valencia and Guerrero
Harris (now Seventh) S s Market bet Sixth and Eighth SE to the bay
Harrison, W s Stewart bet Folsom and Bryant SW to Fourteenth
Harrison Avenue, S s Folsom bet Seventh and Eighth
Harrison Place, Harrison bet Seventh and Eighth
Hartman, S s Lombard bet Mason and Taylor
Harwood Alley, S s Filbert bet Dupont and Kearny
Havens, W s Leavenworth bet Filbert and Union
Hawes, S s Folsom bet Tenth and Eleventh
Hawthorne, S s Folsom bet Second and Third
Hayes, W s Larkin bet Grove and Fell W to Devisidero
Hayes, W s Leavenworth bet Pacific and Broadway
Haywood, N s Harrison bet Third and Fourth
Haywood Alley, opens at 431 Filbert
Helen, S s California bet Leavenworth and Hyde
Henry, N s Lombard bet Hyde and Larkin
Hermann, S s Market bet Brady and Ridley E to Mission
Hermann Place, N s Sutter bet Montgomery and Sansom

Heron, E s Eighth bet Folsom and Harrison
Heyn Place, S s Clay bet Hyde and Leavenworth
Hickory, Potrero
Hickory, W s Market bet Oak and Fell
Higgins Place, N s Pacific bet Mason and Powell
Hinckley, W s Kearny bet Broadway and Vallejo
Hodges Court, W s Spear bet Market and Mission
Hodges Place, N s Vallejo bet Mont and Sansom
Hoff Avenue, S s Sixteenth bet Mission and Valencia
Hooper, W s Fifth bet Channel and Irwin SW to
  Seventh
Houston, W s Taylor bet Chestnut and Francisco
Howard, W s East SW to Twelfth, thence S to
  Twenty-Second
Howard Court, N s Howard bet Fourth and Fifth
Hubbard, S s Howard bet Second and Third
Hubbell, W s Fifth bet Irwin and South SW to
  Seventh
Hunt, E s Third bet Howard and Sherwood Place
Hyde, N s McAllister bet Larkin and Leavenworth
  N to the bay

INDIANA, Potrero Nuevo
Iowa, Potrero Nuevo
Irwin, E s Fifth bet Hooper and Hubbell SW to
  Seventh
Isdel Place, S s Bush bet Montgomery and Kearny

JACKSON, W s East bet Washington and Pacific W
  to Devisidero
Jackson Place, E s Montgomery bet Vallejo and
  Green
Jacobi, N s California bet Leavenworth and Hyde
Jane, S s Jessie bet Second and Third
Jane Place, N s Pine bet Mason and Taylor
Jansen, N s Greenwich bet Mason and Taylor
Jasper Place, N s Union bet Dupont and Stockton
Jefferson, W s Powell N of Beach to Devisidero
Jefferson Square, bet Tyler, Gough, Eddy, and La-
  guna
Jersey, Potrero Nuevo
Jessie, W s First bet Market and Mission
Jewett, W s Fourth bet Townsend and King
John, W s Powell bet Pacific and Jackson
John (now Twenty-Second) W s Folsom S of Twen-
  ty-First W to Castro
Johnson, S s Harrison bet Main and Spear
Johnston (now Ninth) junction of Market and Lar-
  kin SE to Mission Creek
Joice, N s Pine bet Stockton and Powell
Jones, junction of Market and McAllister to the bay
Jones, S s Bryant bet First and Second
Jones Alley, N s Washington bet Sansom and Mont-
  gomery
Jones Place, N s Pine bet Mason and Taylor
Joyful Alley, E s Jones bet Post and Geary
Julia, S s Bryant bet First and Second
Julia, S s Minna bet Seventh and Eighth
Julia Court, N s O'Farrell bet Dupont and Stockton
Julius, N s Lombard bet Kearny and Dupont
Juniper, S s Folsom bet Tenth and Eleventh

KANSAS, Potrero Nuevo
Kate, S s Bryant bet Seventh and Eighth
Kate, junction Laguna and Market W to Devisidero
Kearny, junction Geary and Market N to North
  Point
Kensington Place, W s Howard bet Nineteenth and
  Twentieth
Kent, W s Mason bet Filbert and Union
Kentucky, Potrero Nuevo
Keyes Alley, N s Pacific bet Mason and Powell
Kimball, N s Sacramento bet Leav and Hyde
King, S s Second bet Townsend and Berry SW to
  Seventh
Kisling Place, S s Folsom op Thirteenth
Kosciusko, Potrero Nuevo
Kramer Place, S s Greenwich bet Dupont and
  Stockton

LAFAYETTE AVENUE, S s Mission bet Eleventh and
  Twelfth
Lafayette Place, N s Green bet Kearny and Dupont
Lafayette Square, bet Sacramento, Gough, Wash-
  ington, and Laguna
Laguna, junction Market and Kate N to Lewis
Langton, N s Folsom bet Seventh and Eighth
Larkin, junction Market and Hayes N to the bay
Laskie, N s Mission bet Eighth and Ninth
Latham Place, W s Mason bet O'Farrell and Ellis
Laura, N s Ellis bet Jones and Taylor
Laura Place, S s Pine bet Montgomery and Sansom
Laurel Avenue, W s Larkin bet Turk and Eddy
Laurel Place, W s First bet Folsom and Harrison
Leavenworth, N s McAllister bet Jones and Hyde
  N to the bay
Leidesdorff, S s Clay bet Montgomery and Sansom
Leroy Place, S s Sacramento bet Jones and Leaven-
  worth
Lestrade Place, N s Pacific nr Kearny
Lewis, W s Polk N of Tonquin
Lewis Place. W s Taylor bet Sutter and Post
Liberty, N s Townsend bet Ritch and Crook
Lick, W s First bet Mission and Jessie
Lick Place, N s Post bet Montgomery and Kearny
Lima, N s Filbert bet Leavenworth and Hyde
Lincoln (late Buchanan) junction Market and Ridley
  N to Lewis
Lincoln, W s Taylor bet Union and Green
Lincoln Avenue, opens at 210 Dupont
Lincoln Place. E s Fremont nr Folsom
Linden, N s Market bet Hayes and Fell
Lobos Square, bet Laguna, Bay, Webster, and
  Chestnut
Lombard, W s Battery bet Chestnut and Greenwich
  W to Devisidero
Lombard Place, S s Lombard bet Stockton and
  Powell
Lone Mountain Avenue, from Hayes' Pavilion NW
  to Lone Mountain Cemetery
Louisa, E s Fourth bet Folsom and Harrison
Luconia, W s Third bet Harrison and Bryant
Lumber, N s Francisco nr Mason
Luning Alley, N s Vallejo nr Stockton
Lynch, W s Leavenworth bet Pacific and Broadway
Lyon, S s Bush to Geary, Hoadley's Extension

M, W s Valencia bet Twenty-Second and Horner
Mahon Place, N s Geary bet Hyde and Larkin
Maiden Lane, S s Jackson bet Mont and Kearny
Maiden Lane, N s Vallejo bet Powell and Stockton
Main, S s Market bet Spear and Beale SE to Bryant
Malvina Place, W s Mason bet Clay and Sacramento
Margaret, N s Mission bet Eighth and Ninth
Margaret Place, N s Vallejo bet Dupont and Kearny
Margaret Place, N s Turk bet Mason and Taylor
Maria, N s Howard bet Seventh and Eighth
Mariposa, W from the bay to Channel
Mariposa Terrace, N s Harrison bet Seventh and
  Eighth
Market, junction Sacramento and East SW to Mis-
  sion Dolores
Martha Place, S s Geary bet Mason and Taylor
Martin Alley, block Stockton, Dupont, Geary, and
  O'Farrell
Mary, S s Mission bet Fifth and Sixth
Mary, S s Chesley bet Bryant and Harrison
Mary Lane, N s Sutter bet Kearny and Dupont
Mason, junction Turk and Market N to the bay
Massett, W s Seventh bet Mission and Howard
Mathew or June, N s Howard bet Second and Third
Mathew Lane or West Mathew, N s Post between
  Kearny and Dupont
Mathews Place, W s Mason bet Clay and Wash
McAllister, junction Market and Jones W to Devis-
  idero
McCormick, S s Pacific bet Hyde and Larkin
McLaren Lane, W s Folsom bet Thirteenth and
  Fourteenth

Mecham Place, S s Post bet Hyde and Larkin
Meeks Place, W s Main bet Market and Mission
Mellus, W s Fremont bet Mission and Howard
Merchant, E s Kearny bet Clay and Washington E to Front and from E s Drumm to the bay
Middle, E s Sixth bet Irwin and Hubbell
Midway, N s Francisco bet Dupont and Stockton
Midway East, N s Francisco bet Kearny and Dupont
Midway West, N s Francisco bet Stock and Powell
Miles Court, N s California bet Stockton and Powell
Miles Place, N s Sacramento bet Stock and Powell
Miller, W s Powell bet Pacific and Broadway
Mills Place, W s Dupont bet Post and Sutter
Mills Place, S s Lombard bet Stockton and Dupont
Mills Place. S s Sutter bet Dupont and Stockton
Milton Place, N s Bush bet Kearny and Dupont
Minna, W s First bet Mission and Natoma
Minna Place, W s Beale bet Mission and Howard
Minnesota, Potrero Nuevo
Mission, W s East bet Market and Howard SW to Potter, thence S to Twenty-Second
Mission Plaza, bet Mission, Potter, Ridley, and Mkt
Mississippi, Potrero Nuevo
Missouri, Potrero Nuevo
Monroe, N s Bush bet Stockton and Powell
Montgomery, junction Market and Post N to the bay
Montgomery Court, W. s Montgomery bet Pacific and Broadway
Montgomery Place, W s Montgomery bet Union and Filbert
Mooney Place, W s Harrison Avenue bet Folsom and Harrison
Moore, N s Union bet Hyde and Larkin
Moore Place, N s Clay bet Hyde and Larkin
Moore Place, S s Broadway bet Leav and Hyde
Morel Place, N s Pacific bet Larkin and Hyde
Morey Alley, N s Broadway bet Stock and Powell
Morse, S s Pine bet Kearny and Dupont
Morse Place, S s Broadway bet Hyde and Leav
Moss, S s Howard bet Sixth and Seventh
Moss Place, N s Folsom bet Sixth and Seventh
Moulton Place, W s Montgomery bet Union and Green
Myrtle, W s Leavenworth bet O'Farrell and Geary

NAPA (now Twentieth) W s Folsom bet Nineteenth and Twenty-First W to Castro
Nassau Place, S s Harrison bet Second and Third
Natoma, W s First bet Howard and Mission
Natoma East, E s First bet Howard and Mission
Natoma West, W s Fifth bet Mission and Howard
Nebraska, Potrero Nuevo
Necropolis Avenue, W s Dolores bet Sixteenth and Seventeenth
Nevada, S s Folsom bet Eleventh and Twelfth
New Anthony, N s Mission bet First and Second
Newell, N s Lombard bet Mason and Taylor
Newell, W s Mason bet Chestnut and Lombard
Newell, W s Stockton bet Chestnut and Lombard
New Orleans Avenue, N s Green bet Hyde and Leavenworth
Nineteenth (late Eagle) W s Folsom bet Eighteenth and Twentieth W to Castro
Ninth (late Johnston) junction Market and Larkin E to Mission Creek
Noble Alley, S s Green bet Montgomery and Kearny
Noe, S s Ridley bet Castro and Sanchez
North Avenue, Potrero
North Point, W s Kearny bet Beach and Bay W to Devisidero

OAK, junction Van Ness Avenue and Market W to Devisidero
Oak, W s Mason bet Geary and Post
Oak Park, S s Harrison bet Fifth and Sixth
Octavia, junction Waller and Market N to Lewis
O'Farrell, junction Market and Dupont W to Devisidero
O'Farrell Alley, N s O'Farrell bet Powell and Mason

O'Heron, W s Eighth bet Folsom and Harrison
Ohio, N s Pacific bet Montgomery and Sansom
Olive Avenue, W s Larkin bet Ellis and O'Farrell
Olney Place, N s King bet Second and Third
Oneida Place, S s Sacramento bet Stockton and Dupont
Oregon, E s Battery bet Washington and Jackson and E s Front bet Washington and Jackson
Orleans Avenue, N s Green nr Leavenworth

PACIFIC, W s East bet Jackson and Broadway W to Devisidero
Pacific Alley, W s Pacific bet Dupont and Stockton
Page, junction Franklin and Market W to Devisidero
Palmer Alley, W s Kearny bet Jackson and Washington
Panmure Court, E s Fremont bet Market and Mission
Park Avenue, N s Bryant bet Fifth and Sixth
Park Avenue, S s Harrison bet Fifth and Sixth
Park Place, E s Second bet Folsom and Harrison
Pauls Court, W s Dupont bet Jackson and Washington, rear
Pennsylvania, Potrero Nuevo
Pennsylvania Avenue, W s Kearny bet Pacific and Broadway
Perley Place, E s First bet Folsom and Harrison
Perry, E s Third bet Harrison and Bryant
Pfeiffer, W s Dupont bet Francisco and Chestnut
Phelan Place, E s Hyde bet Pacific and Jackson
Pierce (now Grant) N s Waller bet Scott and Steiner N to Lewis
Pierce Row, S s Union bet Stockton and Dupont
Pike or Waverly Place, S s Washington bet Dupont and Stockton
Pinkham Place, W s Eighth bet Howard and Folsom
Pinckney Place, N s Broadway bet Kearny and Dupont
Pine, junction Market and Davis W to Devisidero
Polk, junction Market and Fell N to Lewis
Polk Lane, E s Stockton bet Broadway and Pacific
Pollard Place, N s Vallejo bet Kearny and Dupont
Pomona Place, W s Dupont bet Jackson and Washington
Porter, N s O'Farrell bet Powell and Stockton
Portsmouth Square, bet Washington, Kearny, Clay, and Brenham Place
Post, junction Montgomery and Market W to Devisidero
Post Office Place, N s Washington bet Sansom and Battery
Potrero, Potrero Nuevo
Potter, S s Market bet Eleventh and Twelfth
Powell, junction Market and Eddy N to the bay
Pratt Court, N s California bet Stockton and Powell
Precita Avenue, San Bruno Road
Price (now Eighth) S s Market bet Seventh and Ninth SE to Channel
Priest, N s Clay bet Jones and Leavenworth
Prospect, E s Ninth bet Bryant and Brannan
Prospect Place, S s Clay bet Stockton and Powell

QUINCY, N s Pine bet Kearny and Dupont

RAILROAD AVENUE, E s Dolores bet Sixteenth and Seventeenth
Randall Place, N s Greenwich bet Hyde and Leavenworth
Rassette Place, Nos. 1, 2, and 3 S s Sutter bet Kearny and Dupont
Reed, N s Clay bet Jones and Leavenworth
Reed Place, S s Green bet Kearny and Montgomery
Rhode Island, Potrero Nuevo
Richard, S s Sutter nr Jones
Richmond, W s Front bet Sacramento and California
Ridley, W s Mission bet Hermann and Fourteenth W to Devisidero
Riley, W s Taylor bet Sacramento and Clay ... N
Rincon Court, W s Main bet Folsom and Harrison

Rincon Place, S s Harrison bet First and Second
Ritch, S s Folsom bet Third and Fourth
Ritter, S s Harrison bet Seventh and Eighth
Roach, W s Zoe bet Bryant and Harrison
Roach Alley, N s Filbert bet Taylor and Jones
Robbins Place, N s Union bet Kearny and Dupont
Rose Alley, Jane to Annie bet Mission and Jessie
Ross (Stout Alley) N s Washington bet Stockton and Dupont
Rousch, N s Folsom bet Seventh and Eighth
Russ, S s Howard bet Sixth and Seventh
Russ Alley, N s Sutter bet Montgomery and Kearny

SACRAMENTO, junction Market and East W to Devisidero
Salmon, N s Pacific bet Mason and Taylor
Salmon Place, E s Larkin bet Broadway and Vallejo
Salmon Place, N s Gleen bet Mason and Taylor
Sanchez, S s Ridley bet Church and Noe
Sand, N s Sacramento bet Powell and Mason
San Luis Alley, S s Jackson bet Dupont and Stockton
Sansom, junction Market and Sutter N to Chestnut
Santa Clara, W from the bay to Channel
School Alley, E s Montgomery bet Union and Filbert
Scotland, N s Filbert bet Powell and Mason
Scott, N s Ridley bet Pierce and Devisidero N to Lewis
Scott Place, N s Pacific bet Powell and Mason
Second, junction Market and Montgomery SE to Berry
Selina Place, N s California bet Dupont and Stockton
Serpentine Avenue, E s San Bruno Rroad 3½ miles from City Hall
Seventeenth (late Corbett) E s Market bet Sixteenth and Eighteenth E to Mission Creek
Seventh (late Harris) S s Market bet Sixth and Eighth SE to the bay
Sharp Place, N s Green bet Leavenworth and Hyde
Sheppard Place, E s Mason bet Clay and Washington
Sherman, W s Columbia Square, bet Sixth and Seventh
Sherwood Place, E s Third bet Howard and Minna
Shotwell, S s Sixteenth bet Howard and Folsom
Shipley, E s Sixth bet Folsom and Harrison
Silver, W s Second bet Harrison and Bryant
Simmons (now Sixth) junction Market and Tyler SE to the bay
Sixteenth (late Center) from the bay op South W to Market bet Fifteenth and Sixteenth
Sixth (late Simmons) junction Market and Tyler SE to the bay
Solano, W from the bay to Channel
Sonoma or Sonora Place, N s Green bet Kearny and Dupont and S s Green bet Kearny and Dupont
Sophie Terrace, N s Pine bet Dupont and Stockton
South Park, W s Second bet Bryant and Brannan
Sparks (now Fifteenth) W s Folsom bet Fourteenth and Sixteenth W to Castro
Spear, S s Market bet Stewart and Main, SE to Bryant
Spofford, N s Clay bet Waverly Place and Stockton
Spring, S s California bet Kearny and Montgomery
St. Ann, N s Eddy bet Powell and Mason
St. Charles, E s Kearny bet Pacific and Broadway
St. Charles Place, W s Montgomery bet Pacific and Broadway
St. Charles Place, W s Kearny bet Vallejo and Green
St. Louis Alley, S s Jackson bet Dupont and Kearny
St. Mark Place, W s Kearny bet Post and Geary
St. Mary Place, N s Post bet Stockton and Powell
St. Mary Place, N s Pine bet Dupont and Kearny
St. Vincent, N s Green bet Montgomery and Kearny
Stanford, N s Townsend bet Second and Third
Stanly Place, S s Harrison bet First and Second
Steiner, junction Ridley and Sanchez N to Lewis
Steveloe E s Jones bet O'Farrell and Ellis
Stevenson, W s First bet Market and Mission and W s Third bet Market and Mission

Stewart, S s Market bet East and Spear SE to Rincon Point
Stockton, junction Market and Ellis N to Bay
Stockton Alley, E s Stockton bet Sutter and Post
Stockton Place, E s Stockton bet Union and Filbert
Stone, N s Washington bet Stockton and Powell
Stout Alley (now Ross) N s Washington bet Dupont and Stockton
Strawberry Alley, N s Pacific between Dupont and Stockton
Sullivan Alley, N s Jackson bet Dupont and Stockton
Sullivan Alley, S s Mission bet First and Second
Summer, W s Montgomery bet California and Pine
Sumner, E s Howard bet Seventh and Eighth
Susan, S s Harrison bet Sixth and Seventh
Sutter, junction Market and Sansom W to Devisidero
Sweet, N s Broadway bet Taylor and Jones

TAY, N s Sacramento bet Powell and Mason
Taylor, junction Market and Tyler N to the bay
Tehama, W s First bet Clementina and Howard
Tehama Place, E s First bet Folsom and Howard
Telegraph Place, N s Greenwich bet Dupont and Kearny
Tennessee, Potrero Nuevo
Tenth (late Thorne) S s Market between Ninth and Eleventh
Texas, Potrero Nuevo
Third, junction Market and Kearny SE to Channel
Thirteenth (late Ellen) S s Mission bet Twelfth and Fourteenth
Thirteenth East, S s Folsom bet Twelfth and Thirteenth
Thompson Avenue, S s Brannan bet Second and Third
Thompson Place, S s Washington bet Stockton and Powell
Thorne (now Tenth) S s Market bet Ninth and Eleventh SE to Channel
Tilford, W s Fifth bet Bryant and Brannan
Tonquin, from Larkin bet Lewis and Jefferson W to Devisidero
Touchard Alley, S s Pine bet Jones and Leavenworth
Townsend, W s First bet Brannan and King W to Channel
Tracy (late Fourteenth) W s Folsom bet Thirteenth and Fifteenth W to Devisidero
Treat Avenue, Twenty-Fifth bet Folsom and Channel
Trinity, N s Sutter bet Montgomery and Kearny
Trinity Court, W s Trinity bet Bush and Sutter
Truett, W s Mason bet Washington and Clay
Turk, junction Market and Mason W to Devisidero
Twelfth (late Brown) S s Mission bet Eleventh and Thirteenth SE to Harrison
Twentieth (late Napa) W s Folsom bet Nineteenth and Twenty-First W to Castro
Twenty-First (late Alta) W s Folsom bet Twentieth and Twenty-Second W to Castro
Twenty-Second (late John) W s Folsom S of Twenty-First W to Castro
Tyler, junction Market and Taylor W to Devisidero
Tyson Place, S s Washington bet Stockton and Powell

UNION, W s Front bet Filbert and Greenwich W to Devisidero
Union Alley, from Union Place
Union Court, E s Kearny bet Sutter and Post
Union Place, N s Green bet Dupont and Stockton
Union Square, bet Stockton, Powell, Geary, and Post
Utah, Potrero Nuevo

VALENCIA, S s Market bet Mission and Guerrero
Vallejo, W s Davis bet Green and Broadway W to Devisidero
Vallejo Place, N s Vallejo bet Stockton and Powell
Valparaiso, W s Mason bet Filbert and Greenwich
Vandewater, W s Powell bet Francisco and Bay

Van Ness Avenue, junction Oak and Market N to Lewis
Varenne, N s Green bet Kearny and Dupont
Vassar Place, S s Harrison bet Second and Third
Ver Mehr, E s Kearny bet Post and Sutter
Vermont, Potrero Nuevo
Vernon Place, W s Second bet Folsom and Harrison
Vernon Place, E s Hyde bet Union and Green
Vernon Place, S s Jackson bet Mason and Taylor
Verona Place, S s Folsom bet Second and Third
Vincent or St. Vincent, N s Green bet Montgomery and Kearny
Virginia, N s Washington bet Stockton and Powell
Virginia Alley, W s Dupont bet Pine and California
Virginia Place, N s Pacific bet Stockton and Powell
Vischer Place, E s Beale bet Market and Mission

WALL PLACE, N s Jackson bet Leav and Hyde
Wallace Place, N s California nr Kearny
Waller, junction Market and Octavia W to Devisidero
Washington, W s East bet Jackson and Clay W to Devisidero
Washington Alley, N s Washington bet Dupont and Kearny
Washington Avenue, S s Mission bet Ninth and Tenth
Washington Square, bet Stockton, Filbert, Powell, and Union
Washoe Place, N s Vallejo bet Powell and Mason
Water, W s Mason bet Francisco and Chestnut
Waverly Court, S s Washington bet Dupont and Stockton, rear

Waverly Place, N s Sacramento bet Dupont and Stockton
Webb, S s Sacramento bet Montgomery and Kearny
Webb Place, W s Mason bet Union and Filbert
Webster, N s Lombard bet Kearny and Montgomery
Webster, N s Ridley bet Fillmore and Buchanan N to Lewis
Wells Court, S s Lombard bet Dupont and Stockton
Welsh, W s Zoe bet Bryant and Brannan
Wetmore Place, N s Clay bet Powell and Mason
White, N s Vallejo bet Hyde and Larkin
White Place, E s Jones bet Bush and Sutter
White Place, S s Bryant bet Seventh and Eighth
Whitney, N s Sixteenth bet Howard and Mission
William, N s O'Farrell bet Jones and Taylor
William Place, W s Davis bet California and Sacramento
William South, E s Fourth bet Harrison and Bryant
Williams Place, N s California bet Stockton and Dupont
Willow, S s Folsom bet Fifth and Sixth
Willow Avenue, W s Larkin bet Ellis and Eddy
Winter Place, N s O'Farrell bet Powell and Mason
Winters Alley, E s Mason bet Union and Green
Wisconsin, Potrero Nuevo
Wood (now Eleventh) S s Market bet Tenth and Twelfth SE to Mission Creek

YERBA BUENA, N s Sac bet Mason and Taylor
York, Potrero Nuevo

ZOE, N s Bryant bet Third and Fourth
Zoe Place, S s Folsom bet Fremont and Beale

BUILDINGS, BLOCKS, ROWS, WHARFS, ETC.

PUBLIC BUILDINGS.

CITY HALL, Kearny from Washington to Merchant
County Hospital, cor Stockton and Francisco
County Jail, N s Broadway bet Kearny and Dupont
Custom House, NW cor Washington and Battery
Hall of Records, SW cor Kearny and Washington
Industrial School, six miles S City Hall
Post Office, NW cor Washington and Battery
United States Appraiser's Store, SE cor Battery and Jackson
United States Branch Mint, N s Commercial nr Mont
United States Marine Hospital, Harrison bet Main and Spear

BUILDINGS.

ALSOP's BUILDING, 411 and 413 California
Alta California Building, 536 and 538 Sacramento
Apel's Building, 410 Kearny bet California and Pine
Armory Hall Building, NE cor Mont and Sac
Athenæum Building, SE cor California and Mont
Bee Hive Building, NE cor Washington and Dupont
Bella Union, Washington op Portsmouth Square
Bernis' Building, 626 California
Bofer's Building, SW cor California and Kearny
Bolton & Barron's Building, NW cor Montgomery and Merchant
Brogan's Building, cor Third and Hunt.
California Exchange Building, NE corner Clay and Kearny
Callaghan's Building, W s Dupont bet Clay and Wash
Citizens' Gas Co.'s Building, cor Second and King
Cogswell's Building, 610 Front cor Chambers
Cross' Iron Buildings, Battery bet Pac and Jackson
Cunningham's Building, cor Market and Third
Czapkay's Building, 651 Washington
Davidson's Building, NW cor Mont and Commercial

Donohoe, Kelly & Co.'s Building, SE cor Montgomery and Sacramento
Exchange Building, NW cor Mont and Washington
Express Building, NE cor California and Mont
Federal Building (late Merchant's Exchange) Battery op Post Office
Franks' Building, W s Brenham Place op Plaza
Government House, NW cor Wash and Sansom
Grissim's Building, S s Bush bet Mont and Sansom
Grogan & Lent's Building, NW cor Sansom and Jackson
Helvetic Bazaar, NE cor Market and Sansom
Hentsch's Building, NW cor Jackson and Mont
Horber's Building, SW cor Mont and Summer
Howard's Building, 521 and 523 Montgomery
Hyatt's Building, SW cor Market and Third
Lecount's Building, 417 and 419 Montgomery
Lucas, Turner & Co.'s Building, NE cor Montgomery and Jackson
Lyceum or Metropolitan Building, NW cor Montgomery and Wash (now Exchange Building)
Maguire's Building, 618 and 620 Washington
Masonic Building (Reese's) 722 Washington
Masonic Hall Building, 420 Montgomery
Maynard's Building, NW cor California and Bat
McCreery's Buildings, cor Montgomery and Pine
Mead's Building, NW cor Montgomery and Pine
Mechanics' Institute Building, S side California bet Montgomery and Kearny
Mercantile Library Building, NE cor Montgomery and Bush
Metropolitan (now Exchange Building) or Lyceum Building, NW cor Montgomery and Wash
Michel's Building, NE cor Montgomery and Market
Naglee's Building, SW cor Mont and Merchant
Newhall's Buildings, cor Sansom and Halleck
Parrott's Building, NW Sac and Montgomery
Parsons' Building, N s Clay bet Mont and Sansom

Patterson, Wallace & Stow's Building, 513 Jackson
Phœnix Building, SW cor Sansom and Jackson
Pioche & Bayerque's Building, SE cor Montgomery and Jackson
Pioneer Building, E s Mont bet Jackson and Pacific
Popper's Building, SE cor Mission and Third
Rabe's Building, 609–613 Clay
Reese's Building, 716–722 Washington
Riddle's Building, 511–521 Clay
San Francisco Gas Co.'s Building, First, Howard, and Natoma
Sargent's Building, 129 Montgomery
Sherman's Building, 606 and 608 Montgomery
Specht's Building, 635 and 637 Broadway
Stevenson's Building, SW cor Montgomery and California
Sullivan's Building, SW cor Dupont and Pacific
Thayer's Building, SW cor Mont and Sacramento
Tittel's Building, SW cor Bush and Kearny
Truett's Building, E s Front bet California and Sacramento
Ullmann's Building, SE cor Washington and Sansom
Union Building, NE cor Market and Kearny
United States Court Building (now Federal Building) Battery cor Washington and Oregon
United States Court Building (new) SW cor Montgomery and Jackson
Verandah Building, NE cor Washington and Kearny
Wells' Building, SW cor Montgomery and Clay
Whiting's Building, SE cor Sansom and Pine
Wright's Building (see Hentsch's Building)

HALLS.

Apollo Hall, N s Pacific nr Stockton
Assembly Hall, NW cor Kearny and Post
Barra's Hall, NW cor First and Minna
Blumenthal Hall, S s Pine bet Mont and Sansom
Bachelors' Hall, 131 Mont bet Sutter and Bush
City Hall, Kearny op Portsmouth Square
Dashaway Temperance Hall, S s Sutter bet Kearny and Dupont
Hall of Records, SE cor Washington and Kearny
James' Hall, SE cor Fifth and Shipley
Masonic Hall, cor Stockton and Polk Lane
Masonic Temple, junction Montgomery, Market, and Post
Mechanics' Hall, SW cor First and Stevenson
Merriman's Hall, Mission bet Second and Third
Minerva Hall, SW cor California and Kearny
New Music Hall (Platt's) Montgomery nr Bush
Odd Fellows' Hall, 323–327 Montgomery
Philharmonic Hall, NE cor Stockton and Jackson
Riggers' & Stevedores' Hall, S s Pacific nr Mont
Terpsichorean Hall, N s Pacific nr Stockton
Teschemacher's Hall, N s Commercial bet Sansom and Battery
Turn Verein Hall, N s Bush bet Stockton and Powell
Union Hall, S s Howard bet Third and Fourth

BLOCKS.

Belden's Block, SW cor Bush and Montgomery
Broadway Block, NW cor Broadway and Kearny
Brokers' Block, NW cor Mont and Washington
California Block, SE cor California and Battery
Court Block, 634–638 Clay
Custom House Block, SE cor Sansom and Sac
Dixon's Block, SW cor Natoma and Jane
Empire Block, California bet Sansom and Battery
Front Street Block, E s Front from Clay to Washington
Howard's Block, Sansom, Commercial, and Clay
Howard's Block, 627 Third
Hungarian Block, 655 Washington
Lick House Block, W s Mont from Post to Sutter

Metropolitan Block, NW cor Wash and Mont
Montgomery Block, E s Montgomery from Merchant to Washington
Moore & Folger's Block, Davis bet Cal and Pine
O'Donnell's Block, NE cor Vallejo and Dupont
Park's Block, N s Pacific bet Front and Jackson
Russ House Block, W s Mont from Bush to Pine
Shiels' Block, cor Montgomery and Post
Union Block, NE cor Market and Kearny
Virginia Block, NW cor Stockton and Pacific

ROWS.

Bay State Row, Sansom bet Bush and Pine
Commercial Row, Clay Street Wharf cor Drumm
Howard's Row, NW cor Mission and Third
Maynard's Row, SE cor Pine and Battery
Orleans Row, NW cor California and Davis
South Park Row, Third bet Bryant and Brannan
Trainer's Row, SE cor Kearny and Sutter

WHARFS.

Abernethy, Clark & Co.'s Wharf, Stewart bet Market and Mission
Batchelder's Wharf, Stewart bet Market and Mission
Brannan's Wharf, Stewart bet Mission and Howard
Broadway Wharf, foot of Broadway
Burnham's Wharf, Pier 2 Stewart
California Street Wharf, see Market Street Wharf
Central Wharf, foot of Commercial
Clay Street Wharf, foot of Clay
Cowell's Wharf, extends from Battery bet Union and Filbert
Cunningham's Wharf, continuation of Front Street cor Green
Dewey's Wharf, foot of Third
East Street Wharf, bet Clay and Washington
Fillmore Street Wharf, foot of Fillmore
Folsom Street Wharf (Pacific M. S. S. Co.'s) foot of Folsom
Greenwich Dock, continuation of Battery Street
Griffing's Wharf, continuation of Battery bet Filbert and Greenwich
Ham & Hathaway's Wharf, Spear cor Harrison and Rincon Point
Howard Street Wharf, extends from Howard cor Stewart
India Dock, foot of Battery
Jackson Street Wharf, foot of Jackson
Lombard Dock, continuation of Lombard Street from Sansom to Battery
Market and California Street Wharf, foot of Market
Mastick's Wharf, Stewart bet Mission and Howard
Meiggs' Wharf, from Francisco bet Powell and Mason, North Beach
Mission Street Wharf, extends from Mission cor Stewart
Nelson's Wharf, East between Market and Central wharfs
North Point Dock, continuation of Sansom from Lombard to Chestnut
Pacific M. S. S. Co.'s Wharf, foot of Folsom
Pacific Wharf, foot of Pacific
Pennell & Brown's Wharf, Stewart nr Howard
Pope's Wharf, Stewart nr Howard
Rand's Wharf, East bet Clay and Central wharfs
Rincon Dock, foot of Stewart
Rincon Point Dock, opposite Rincon Point
Robison's Wharf, extends from Clark bet Jackson and Pacific
Roussett's Wharf, Stewart nr Howard
Shaw's Wharf, see Cowell's Wharf
Smith's Wharf, Stewart cor Howard
Vallejo Street Wharf, foot of Vallejo
Washington Street Wharf, foot of Washington

A. ROMAN & CO., 417 and 419 Montgomery Street, Photograph Albums, Gift Books, Etc.

PLACES OF AMUSEMENT.

ACADEMY OF MUSIC, N s Pine bet Mont and Sansom
American Theater, E s Sansom bet California and Sacramento
Bella Union Melodeon, N s Washington nr Kearny
Chinese theaters, E s Dupont bet Clay and Wash and N s Jackson bet Dupont and Stockton
Eureka theater, E s Mont bet California and Pine
Gilbert's Museum, N s Market bet Mont and Sansom
Hayes' Park Pavilion, cor Laguna and Hayes
Maguire's Opera House, N s Washington nr Montgomery
Metropolitan Theater, W s Montgomery bet Washington and Jackson
Odeum Garden, NW cor Dolores and Fifteenth
Olympic Melodon, NE cor Clay and Kearny
Pacific Museum of Anatomy, 320 Montgomery
Union Theater, S s Com bet Kearny and Dupont
Willows, Valencia nr Mission Dolores

PROMINENT PLACES.

BAY VIEW PARK, Race Course, nr Hunter's Point
Black Point, W Leavenworth and N Francisco
Clark's Point, foot of Broadway
Cliff House, 7 miles W Plaza
Fort Point, 2 miles W Presidio
Hayes' Valley, NW Mission and W Larkin
Hunter's Point, 2¼ miles S Mission Dolores
Kensington, Howard bet Twenty-First and Twenty-Fifth
Lagoon, bet Lombard and Francisco W Larkin
Lone Mountain, head Bush 3 miles from Plaza
Mission Bay Bridge, foot Third
Mission Creek, from Mission Dolores SE to San Francisco Bay
Mission Dolores, 2¼ miles SW City Hall
North Beach, foot Powell N to Black Point
North Point, foot Francisco
Ocean House, Ocean Road 6 miles from Plaza
Point Lobos, 6 miles W Plaza
Potrero Nuevo, 2 miles S Plaza
Presidio, 3 miles W Plaza
Race Course Ocean, 6½ miles SW City Hall
Race Course Pioneer, SE and nr Mission Dolores
Race Course Willows, SE and nr Mission Dolores
Rincon Point, foot Harrison
Russian Hill, head Vallejo bet Taylor and Jones
San José Point, W Lagoon
San Quentin Point, SW Mission Bay
South Park, bet Second, Third, Bryant, and Brannan
Spring Valley, nr and S Lagoon
St. Ann's Valley, NW Market bet Stockton, Mason, and O'Farrell
Steamboat Point, foot of Second
Telegraph Hill, Montgomery from Broadway N to the Bay
Visitacion Valley, nr the Bay and San Mateo County Line
Willows, ¼ mile E Mission Dolores
Yerba Buena Park, Market, McAllister, and Larkin

KEY TO PUBLIC OFFICES.

FEDERAL.

AGENT, SPECIAL, United States Custom House
Agent U. S. Internal Revenue, office NW corner Battery and Commercial
Army U. S. Clothing Department, 34 California
Army U. S. Commandant Department of California, 742 Washington
Army U. S. Commandant Division of the Pacific, 418 California
Army U. S. Deputy Quartermaster General, office 742 Washington
Army U. S. Engineers, Harbor Fortifications, office 37 Montgomery Block
Army U. S. Engineers, Department of California, 728 Montgomery
Army U. S. Medical Director, 742 Washington
Army U. S. Medical Purveyor, 805 Sansom
Army U. S. Paymaster's Department, 742 Wash
Army U. S. Quartermaster's Department, 742 Wash
Army U. S. Subsistence Department, 418 California
Assessor Internal Revenue, office NW cor Battery and Commercial
Barge Office, SW cor Pacific and Davis
Clerk Circuit Court, 15 U. S. Court Building
Clerk District Court, 17 U. S. Court Building
Coast Survey, Custom House Building third floor
Collector Internal Revenue, NW cor Bat and Com
Collector Port, Custom House Building third floor
Commissioner U. S. 15 and 17 U. S. Court Building
Courts District and Circuit, U. S. Court Building
District Attorney, 3–5 U. S. Court Building
Indian Agency, U. S. California, 423 Wash cor San
Inspector Boilers, Custom House third floor
Inspector Drugs, SW cor Jackson and Battery
Inspector Hulls, Custom House third floor
Inspector U. S. Internal Revenue, Pacific Coast, NW cor Battery and Commercial
Land Office, 625 Merchant
Light-House Department Pacific Coast, Custom House Building third floor
Mail Agent Special, Post Office basement
Marine Corps U. S. Ass't. Q. M. Dep't, 576 Third
Marine Hospital, Rincon Point nr Main
Marshal U. S. 13–14 U. S. Court Building
Mint Branch U. S. Superintendent, 610 Commercial
Naval Officer, Custom House second floor
Naval Store Keeper, office Mare Island
Navy Agent, 432 California
Pension Agent U. S. A. 625 Merchant
Post Office, NW cor Battery and Washington
Purser U. S. N. 432 California
Purveyor U. S. 742 Washington
Receiver Public Moneys, 625 Merchant
Supervising Ins'r Steamboats U. S. C. House 3d floor
Surveyor-General U. S. for California, 810 Mont
Surveyor of the Port, Custom House second floor
Treasurer Assistant U. S., U. S. Branch Mint, 608 Commercial nr Montgomery

STATE.

ASSAYER STATE, SE cor Montgomery and Bush
Commissioner in Equity, 614 Merchant
Gauger of Liquors, 405 Front
Harbor Commissioners, 302 Montgomery
Immigration Superintendent, 504 Battery
Inspector Gas Meters, 612 Commercial
Inspector Stamps, SE cor Washington and Battery
Land Locating Agent, 328 Montgomery
Pilot Examiners, 521 Clay
Pilots, office cor Vallejo and Davis, and 805 Front
Port Wardens, 716 Front
Sealer Weights and Measures, 321 Front
Superintendent Public Instruction State, SE corner Montgomery and Jackson

COUNTY AND CITY.

Assessor County, City Hall 22 first floor
Attorney and Counselor, City Hall 13 second floor
Attorney District, City Hall 20 second floor
Attorney Police, City Hall second floor
Auditor County, City Hall 6 first floor
Board Commissioners widening Kearny Street, 410 Kearny
Board Equalization, City Hall 2 second floor
Board Supervisors President of, and Mayor City and County, City Hall 2 first floor
Board Supervisors Clerk of, City Hall 4 second floor
Clerk County, City Hall 18 first floor
Coroner County, 636 Clay
Education Board, City Hall cor Merchant
Funded Debt Commissioners 1851, NW cor Montgomery and Sacramento
Fire Alarm and Police Telegraph, City Hall 11 third floor
Fire Department Board Delegates, City Hall 1 third floor
Fire Department Engineer, City Hall 3 first floor
Fire Department Secretary Board Delegates, City Hall 2 third floor
Fire Marshal, City Hull 7 third floor
Fire Wardens, City Hall 2 third floor
Grand Jury Rooms, City Hall 20 third floor

Harbor Master, SW cor East and Merchant
Harbor Police, cor Pacific and Davis
Health Officer, 121 Montgomery.
Industrial School Secretary, City Hall 8 third floor
Judge County. City Hall 8 second floor
Judge Fifteenth District Court, City Hall 16 second floor
Judge Fourth District Court, City Hall 10 second floor
Judge Probate Court, City Hall 18 second floor
Judge Twelfth District Court, City Hall 1 second floor
Physician City and County, office County Hospital
Police Chief, City Hall 9 first floor
Police Commissioners, City Hall first floor
Police Judge, City Hall 13 first floor
Pound Keeper, NW cor Filbert and Larkin
Public Administrator, 35 Montgomery Block
Recorder County, SE cor Washington and Kearny
Sheriff County, City Hall 8 first floor
Streets and Highways Sup't, City Hall 12 first floor
Station House, City Hall basement
Superintendent Public Schools, City Hall cor Merchant 23 second floor
Surveyor County, City Hall 11 third floor
Tax Collector, City Hall cor Merchant 1 first floor
Treasurer County, City Hall 3 first floor
Weigher of Coal (vacant)

NUMERICAL DIRECTORY OF THE PRINCIPAL STREETS,

IN ACCORDANCE WITH THE NEW NUMBERS.

[COMPILED EXPRESSLY FOR THIS WORK.]

☞ *For Alphabetical List of Streets, Avenues, etc. see page 468.*

NEW NUMBERS.—The Ordinance for renumbering the buildings of this city p o   es that—"Market Street shall be the starting point for the numbers on all buildings fronting on the streets running therefrom in a northerly direction, and also for those running therefrom in a southwesterly direction. The streets laid down in the official map of the city as forming the water front thereof, shall be the starting point for numbers on all streets running westerly and south-westerly therefrom, except upon such streets running westerly commencing from Market Street, and upon all such streets Market Street shall be the starting point for numbers. On all streets the numbers on the northerly or north-easterly sides thereof shall be even numbers, and on the southerly or south-westerly sides thereof shall be odd numbers. One hundred numbers, or as many thereof as may be necessary, shall be allotted to each block bounded by principal streets; numbers 100, 200, and 300 being respectively the numbers for commencing the blocks distant one, two, and three streets from the starting point on the side designated for even numbers, and numbers 101, 201, and 301 in similar manner for the opposite side of the street, throughout its extent; so that the initial figure of the number placed on a building at any street-crossing shall indicate the number of main streets, such street-crossing is from the starting point. Not less than twenty feet in frontage of all vacant lots of ground shall be allowed for each number. On all cross or intermediate streets the numbering shall commence where said streets begin, and shall conform to the plan specified in this order."*

By this new decimal system of numbering buildings, the exact location of any number is readily ascertained : for instance, if you want to find 624 Montgomery, it is on the east side of the block extending from Clay to Washington, which is the seventh from Market—Commercial and Merchant being private streets. Again : 825 Clay is above the eighth block from the water front, which is the one extending from Dupont to Stockton. It must be borne in mind that 100 numbers are allowed on each block between principal streets.

(a) End of street. (b) Not opened. (c) Fractional Blocks, one hundred numbers allowed for first two blocks. (d) Fronting the bay.

BATTERY.

Commences at Market and runs North to Lombard.

East.	Street.	West side.
2	Market and Bush	1
100	Pine	101
200	California	201
300	Sacramento	301
314	Commercial	315
400	Clay	401
416	Merchant	417
500	Washington	501
600	Jackson	601
700	Pacific	701
800	Broadway	801
900	Vallejo	901
1000	Green	1001
1100	Union	1101
1200	Filbert	1201
1300	Greenwich	1301
1400	Lombard	1401

BAY.

Runs West from Kearny.

North.	Street.	South side.
2	Kearny	1
100	Dupont	101

200	Stockton	201
300	Powell	301
400	Mason	401
500	Taylor	501
600	Jones	601
700	Leavenworth	701
800	Hyde	801
900	Larkin	901

BEACH.

Runs West from Dupont.

North.	Street.	South side.
2	Powell	1
100	Mason	101
200	Taylor	201
300	Jones	301
400	Leavenworth	401
500	Hyde	501
600	Larkin	601

BEALE.

Runs South-East from Market.

South-West.	Street.	North-East.
2	Market	1
100	Mission	101
200	Howard	201
300	Folsom	301

400	Harrison	401
500	Bryant	501
600	Brannan	601

BERRY.

Runs South-West from Second.

North-West.	Street.	South-East.
2	Second	1
100	Third	101
200	Fourth	201
300	Fifth	301
400	Sixth	401
500	Seventh	501

BRANNAN.

Runs South-West from Beale.

North-West.	Street.	South-East.
2	Beale	1
100	Fremont	101
200	First	201
300	Second	301
400	Third	401
500	Fourth	501
600	Fifth	601
700	Sixth	701
800	Seventh	801
900	Eighth	901

* The streets running East and West, North of Market, are numbered to Larkin, and those running South-West, South of Market, are numbered to Tenth.

| 1000 | Ninth | 1001 |
| 1100 | Tenth | 1101 |

BROADWAY.
Runs West from Davis.

North.	Street.	South side.
2	Davis	1
100	Front	101
200	Battery	201
300	Sansom	301
400	Montgomery	401
500	Kearny	501
600	Dupont	601
700	Stockton	701
800	Powell	801
900	Mason	901
1000	Taylor	1001
1100	Jones	1101
1200	Leavenworth	1201
1300	Hyde	1301
1400	Larkin	1401

BRYANT.
Runs South-West from Spear.

North-West.	Street.	South-East.
2	Spear	1
100	Main	101
200	Beale	201
300	Fremont	301
400	First	401
500	Second	501
600	Third	601
700	Fourth	701
800	Fifth	801
900	Sixth	901
1000	Seventh	1001
1100	Eighth	1101
1200	Ninth	1201
1300	Tenth	1301

BUSH.
Runs West from junction Market and Battery.

North.	Street.	South side.
2	Market	1
100	Battery	101
200	Sansom	201
300	Montgomery	301
400	Kearny	401
500	Dupont	501
600	Stockton	601
700	Powell	701
800	Mason	801
900	Taylor	901
1000	Jones	1001
1100	Leavenworth	1101
1200	Hyde	1201
1300	Larkin	1301

CALIFORNIA.
Runs West from junction Drumm and Market.

North.	Street.	South side.
2	Drumm	1
100	Davis	101
200	Front	201
300	Battery	301
400	Sansom	401
424	Leidesdorff	421
500	Montgomery	501
600	Kearny	601
700	Dupont	701
800	Stockton	801
900	Powell	901
1000	Mason	1001
1100	Taylor	1101

1200	Jones	1201
1300	Leavenworth	1301
1400	Hyde	1401
1500	Larkin	1501

CHESTNUT.
Runs West from Sansom.

North.	Street.	South side.
2	Sansom	1
(c)	Montgomery	(c)
100	Kearny	101
200	Dupont	201
300	Stockton	301
400	Powell	401
500	Mason	501
600	Taylor	601
700	Jones	701
800	Leavenworth	801
900	Hyde	901
1000	Larkin	1001

CLAY.
Runs West from East.

North.	Street.	South side.
2	East	1
100	Drumm	101
200	Davis	201
300	Front	301
400	Battery	401
500	Sansom	501
(a)	Leidesdorff	527
600	Montgomery	601
700	Kearny	701
800	Dupont	801
900	Stockton	901
1000	Powell	1001
1100	Mason	1101
1200	Taylor	1201
1300	Jones	1301
1400	Leavenworth	1401
1500	Hyde	1501
1600	Larkin	1601

CLEMENTINA.
Runs South-West from First.

North-West.	Street.	South-East.
2	First	1
100	Secon	101
200	Thirdd	201
300	Fourth	301
400	Fifth	401
500	Sixth	501
600	Seventh	601
700	Eighth	701
800	Ninth	801
900	Tenth	901

COMMERCIAL.
Runs West from East.

North.	Street.	South side.
2	East	1
100	Drumm	101
200	Davis	201
300	Front	301
400	Battery	401
500	Sansom	501
524	Leidesdorff	525
600	Montgomery	601
700	Kearny	701

DAVIS.
Runs North from Market.

East.	Street.	West side.
2	Pine	1
100	California	101

200	Sacramento	201
214	Commercial	215
300	Clay	301
(b)	Merchant	(b)
400	Washington	401
500	Jackson	501
600	Pacific	601
700	Broadway	701
(d)	Vallejo	801

DRUMM.
Runs North from Market.

East.	Street.	West side.
2	California	1
100	Sacramento	101
116	Commercial	115
200	Clay	201
214	Merchant	(b)
300	Washington	301
400	Jackson	401
500	Pacific	501

DUPONT.
Runs North from Market.

East.	Street.	West side
2	Mkt and O'Farrell	1
100	Geary	101
200	Post	201
300	Sutter	301
400	Bush	401
500	Pine	501
600	California	601
700	Sacramento	701
714	Commercial	(b)
800	Clay	801
900	Washington	901
1000	Jackson	1001
1100	Pacific	1101
1200	Broadway	1201
1300	Vallejo	1301
1400	Green	1401
1500	Union	1501
1600	Filbert	1601
1700	Greenwich	1701
1800	Lombard	1801
1900	Chestnut	1901
2000	Francisco	2001
2100	Bay	2101
2200	North Point	2201
2300	Beach	2301

EAST.
Runs North from Folsom.

East.	Street.	West side.
(d)	Folsom	1
(d)	Howard	101
(d)	Mission	201
(d)	Market	301
(d)	Clay	401
(d)	Washington	501
(d)	Jackson	601
(d)	Pacific	701

EDDY.
Runs West from junction Market and Powell.

North.	Street.	South side.
2	Mkt and Powell	1
100	Mason	101
200	Taylor	201
300	Jones	301
400	Leavenworth	401
500	Hyde	501
600	Larkin	601

EIGHTH.
Runs South-East from Market.

South-West.	Street.	North-East.
2	Market	1
100	Mission	101
200	Howard	201
300	Folsom	301
400	Harrison	401
500	Bryant	501
600	Brannan	601
700	Townsend	70J

ELLIS.
Runs West from junction Market and Stockton.

North.	Street.	South Side.
2	Mkt and Stockton	1
100	Powell	101
200	Mason	201
300	Taylor	301
400	Jones	401
500	Leavenworth	501
600	Hyde	601
700	Larkin	70l

FIFTH.
Runs South-East from Market.

South-West.	Street.	North-East.
2	Market	1
100	Mission	101
200	Howard	201
300	Folsom	301
400	Harrison	401
500	Bryant	501
600	Brannan	601
700	Townsend	701

FILBERT.
Runs West from Front.

North.	Street.	South side.
2	Front	1
100	Battery	101
200	Sansom	201
300	Montgomery	301
400	Kearny	401
500	Dupont	501
600	Stockton	601
700	Powell	701
800	Mason	80l
900	Taylor	901
1000	Jones	1001
1100	Leavenworth	1101
1200	Hyde	1201
1300	Larkin	1301

FIRST.
Runs South-East from Market.

South-West.	Street.	North-East.
2	Market	1
100	Mission	101
200	Howard	201
300	Folsom	301
400	Harrison	401
500	Bryant	501
600	Brannan	601
700	Townsend	701

FOLSOM.
Runs South-West from East.

North-West.	Street.	South-East.
2	Stewart	1
100	Spear	101
200	Main	201
300	Beale	301
400	Fremont	401
500	First	501
600	Second	601
700	Third	701
800	Fourth	801
900	Fifth	901
1000	Sixth	1001
1100	Seventh	1101
1200	Eighth	1201
1300	Ninth	1301
1400	Tenth	1401

FOURTH.
Runs South-East from Market.

South-West.	Street.	North-East.
2	Market	1
100	Mission	101
200	Howard	201
300	Folsom	301
400	Harrison	401
500	Bryant	501
600	Brannan	601
700	Townsend	701

FRANCISCO.
Runs West from Montgomery.

North.	Street.	South side.
2	Montgomery	1
(c)	Kearny	(c)
100	Dupont	101
200	Stockton	201
300	Powell	301
400	Mason	401
500	Taylor	501
600	Jones	601
700	Leavenworth	701
800	Hyde	801
900	Larkin	901

FREMONT.
Runs South-East from Market.

South-West.	Street.	North-East.
2	Market	1
100	Mission	101
200	Howard	201
300	Folsom	301
400	Harrison	401
500	Bryant	501
600	Brannan	601

FRONT.
Runs North from Market.

East.	Street.	West side.
2	Bush	1
100	Pine	101
200	California	201
300	Sacramento	301
318	Commercial	317
400	Clay	401
416	Merchant	(c)
500	Washington	501
600	Jackson	601
700	Pacific	701
800	Broadway	801
900	Vallejo	901
1000	Green	1001
1100	Union	1101
1200	Filbert	1201
(d)	Greenwich	1301

GEARY.
Runs West from junction Market and Kearny.

North.	Street.	South side.
2	Market and Kearny	1
100	Dupont	101

GREEN.
Runs West from Front.

North.	Street.	South side.
2	Front	1
100	Battery	101
200	Sansom	201
300	Montgomery	301
400	Kearny	401
500	Dupont	501
600	Stockton	601
700	Powell	701
800	Mason	801
900	Taylor	901
1000	Jones	1001
1100	Leavenworth	1101
1200	Hyde	1201
1300	Larkin	1301

GREENWICH.
Runs West from Front.

North.	Street.	South side.
2	Front	1
(c)	Battery	(c)
100	Sansom	101
200	Montgomery	201
300	Kearny	301
400	Dupont	401
500	Stockton	501
600	Powell	601
700	Mason	701
800	Taylor	801
900	Jones	901
1000	Leavenworth	1001
1100	Hyde	1101
1200	Larkin	1201

HARRISON.
Runs South-West from Stewart.

North-West.	Street.	South-East.
2	Stewart	1
100	Spear	101
200	Main	201
300	Beale	301
400	Fremont	401
500	First	501
600	Second	601
700	Third	701
800	Fourth	801
900	Fifth	90l
1000	Sixth	1001
1100	Seventh	1101
1200	Eighth	1201
1300	Ninth	1301
1400	Tenth	1401

HOWARD.
Runs South-West from East.

North-West.	Street.	South-East.
2	East	1
(c)	Stewart	(c)
100	Spear	101
200	Main	201
300	Beale	301
400	Fremont	401
500	First	501
600	Second	601
700	Third	701

800	Fourth	801
900	Fifth	901
1000	Sixth	1001
1100	Seventh	1101
1200	Eighth	1201
1300	Ninth	1301
1400	Tenth	1401

HYDE.
Runs North from McAllister.

East.	Street.	West side.
2	McAllister	1
100	Turk	101
200	Tyler	201
300	Eddy	301
400	Ellis	401
500	O'Farrell	501
600	Geary	601
700	Post	701
800	Sutter	801
900	Bush	901
1000	Pine	1001
1100	California	1101
1200	Sacramento	1201
1300	Clay	1301
1400	Washington	1401
1500	Jackson	1501
1600	Pacific	1601
1700	Broadway	1701
1800	Vallejo	1801
1900	Green	1901
2000	Union	2001
2100	Filbert	2101
2200	Greenwich	2201
2300	Lombard	2301
2400	Chestnut	2401
2500	Francisco	2501
2600	Bay	2601
2700	North Point	2701
2800	Beach	2801
2900	Jefferson	2901

JACKSON.
Runs West from East.

North.	Street.	South side.
2	East	1
(c)	Drumm	(c)
100	Davis	101
200	Front	201
300	Battery	301
400	Sansom	401
500	Montgomery	501
600	Kearny	601
700	Dupont	701
800	Stockton	801
900	Powell	901
1000	Mason	1001
1100	Taylor	1101
1200	Jones	1201
1300	Leavenworth	1301
1400	Hyde	1401
1500	Larkin	1501

JEFFERSON.
Runs West from Powell.

North.	Street.	South side.
(d)	Powell	1
(d)	Mason	101
(d)	Taylor	201
(d)	Jones	301
(d)	Leavenworth	401
(d)	Hyde	501
(d)	Larkin	601

JESSIE.
Runs South-West from First.

North-West.	Street.	South-East.
2	First	1
100	Second	101
200	Third	201
300	Fourth	301
400	Fifth	401
500	Sixth	501
600	Seventh	601
700	Eighth	701
800	Ninth	801
900	Tenth	901

JONES.
Runs North from junction Market and McAllister.

East.	Street.	West side.
2	McAllister	1
100	Tyler	101
200	Turk	201
300	Eddy	301
400	Ellis	401
500	O'Farrell	501
600	Geary	601
700	Post	701
800	Sutter	801
900	Bush	901
1000	Pine	1001
1100	California	1101
1200	Sacramento	1201
1300	Clay	1301
1400	Washington	1401
1500	Jackson	1501
1600	Pacific	1601
1700	Broadway	1701
1800	Vallejo	1801
1900	Green	1901
2000	Union	2001
2100	Filbert	2101
2200	Greenwich	2201
2300	Lombard	2301
2400	Chestnut	2401
2500	Francisco	2501
2600	Bay	2601
2700	North Point	2701
2800	Beach	2801
2900	Jefferson	2901

KEARNY.
Runs North from Market.

East.	Street.	West side.
2	Geary	1
100	Post	101
200	Sutter	201
300	Bush	301
400	Pine	401
500	California	501
600	Sacramento	601
632	Commercial	627
700	Clay	701
720	Merchant	(a)
800	Washington	801
900	Jackson	901
1000	Pacific	1001
1100	Broadway	1101
1200	Vallejo	1201
1300	Green	1301
1400	Union	1401
1500	Filbert	1501
1600	Greenwich	1601
1700	Lombard	1701
1800	Chestnut	1801
1900	Francisco	1901
2000	Bay	2001
2100	North Point	2101

LARKIN.
Runs North from Market.

East.	Street.	West side.
2	Market	1
(c)	Hayes	(c)
100	Grove	101
200	Fulton	201
300	McAllister	301
400	Tyler	401
500	Turk	501
600	Eddy	601
700	Ellis	701
800	O'Farrell	801
900	Geary	901
1000	Post	1001
1100	Sutter	1101
1200	Bush	1201
1300	Pine	1301
1400	California	1401
1500	Sacramento	1501
1600	Clay	1601
1700	Washington	1701
1800	Jackson	1801
1900	Pacific	1901
2000	Broadway	2001
2100	Vallejo	2101
2200	Green	2201
2300	Union	2301
2400	Filbert	2401
2500	Greenwich	2501
2600	Lombard	2601
2700	Chestnut	2701
2800	Francisco	2801
2900	Bay	2901
3000	North Point	3001
3100	Beach	3101
3200	Jefferson	3201

LEAVENWOTRH.
Runs North from McAllister.

East.	Street.	West side.
2	McAllister	1
100	Tyler	101
200	Turk	201
300	Eddy	301
400	Ellis	401
500	O'Farrell	501
600	Geary	601
700	Post	701
800	Sutter	801
900	Bush	901
1000	Pine	1001
1100	California	1101
1200	Sacramento	1201
1300	Clay	1301
1400	Washington	1401
1500	Jackson	1501
1600	Pacific	1601
1700	Broadway	1701
1800	Vallejo	1801
1900	Green	1901
2000	Union	2001
2100	Filbert	2101
2200	Greenwich	2201
2300	Lombard	2301
2400	Chestnut	2401
2500	Francisco	2501
2600	Bay	2601
2700	North Point	2701
2800	Beach	2801
2900	Jefferson	2901

LEIDESDORFF.
Runs North from Pine.

East.	Street.	West side.
2	Pine	1

100	California	101
200	Sacramento	201
300	Commercial	301
400	Clay	401

LOMBARD.
Runs West from Battery.

North.	Street.	South Side.
2	Battery	1
(c)	Sansom	(c)
100	Montgomery	101
200	Kearny	201
300	Dupont	301
400	Stockton	401
500	Powell	501
600	Mason	601
700	Taylor	701
800	Jones	801
900	Leavenworth	901
1000	Hyde	1001
1100	Larkin	1101

MAIN.
Runs South-East from Market.

South-West.	Street.	North-East.
2	Market	1
100	Mission	101
200	Howard	201
300	Folsom	301
400	Harrison	401

*MARKET.
Runs South-West from East.

N. W.	Street.	S. E.	Street.
2	East	1	East
(c)	Stewart	(c)	Stewart
100	Drumm	101	Spear
200	Davis	201	Main
300	Front	301	Beale
400	Battery	401	Fremont
500	Sansom	501	First
600	Montgomery	601	Second
700	Kearny	701	Third
800	Dupont	801	Fourth
900	Stockton	901	Fifth
1000	Powell	1001	Sixth
1100	Mason	1101	Seventh
1200	Taylor	1201	Eighth
1300	Jones	1301	Ninth
1400	Leav'w'rth	1401	Tenth
1500	Hyde	1501	Eleventh
1600	Larkin	1601	Twelfth

MASON.
Runs North from Market.

East.	Street.	West side.
2	Turk and Market	1
100	Eddy	101
200	Ellis	201
300	O'Farrell	301
400	Geary	401
500	Post	501
600	Sutter	601
700	Bush	701
800	Pine	801
900	California	901
1000	Sacramento	1001
1100	Clay	1101
1200	Washington	1201
1300	Jackson	1301
1400	Pacific	1401
1500	Broadway	1501

*The want of uniformity in the numbers of Market Street is occasioned by the difference in the frontage of the blocks on each side of the street.

1600	Vallejo	1601
1700	Green	1701
1800	Union	1801
1900	Filbert	1901
2000	Greenwich	2001
2100	Lombard	2101
2200	Chestnut	2201
2300	Francisco	2301
2400	Bay	2401
2500	North Point	2501
2600	Beach	2601
2700	Jefferson	2701

McALLISTER.
Runs West from Market.

North.	Street.	South side.
2	Market and Jones	1
100	Leavenworth	101
200	Hyde	201
300	Larkin	301

MERCHANT.
Runs West from East.

North.	Street.	South side.
2	East	1
(b)	Drumm	(b)
(b)	Davis	(b)
300	Front	301
400	Battery	401
500	Sansom	501
600	Montgomery	601
700	Kearny	701

MINNA.
Runs South-West from First.

North-West.	Street.	South-East.
2	First	1
100	Second	101
200	Third	201
300	Fourth	301
400	Fifth	401
500	Sixth	501
600	Seventh	601
700	Eighth	701
800	Ninth	801
900	Tenth	901

MISSION.
Runs South-West from East.

North-West.	Street.	South-East.
2	East	1
(c)	Stewart	(c)
100	Spear	101
200	Main	201
300	Beale	301
400	Fremont	401
500	First	501
600	Second	601
700	Third	701
800	Fourth	801
900	Fifth	901
1000	Sixth	1001
1100	Seventh	1101
1200	Eighth	1201
1300	Ninth	1301
1400	Tenth	1401

MONTGOMERY.
Runs North from Market.

East.	Street.	West side.
2	Post	1
100	Sutter	101
200	Bush	201
300	Pine	301
400	California	401

500	Sacramento	501
518	Commercial	513
600	Clay	601
622	Merchant	613
700	Washington	701
800	Jackson	801
900	Pacific	901
1000	Broadway	1001
1100	Vallejo	1101
1200	Green	1201
1300	Union	1301
1400	Filbert	1401
1500	Greenwich	1501
1600	Lombard	1601
1700	Chestnut	1701
1800	Francisco	1801

NATOMA.
Runs South-West from First.

North-West.	Street.	South-East.
2	First	1
100	Second	101
200	Third	201
300	Fourth	301
400	Fifth	401
500	Sixth	501
600	Seventh	601
700	Eighth	701
800	Ninth	801
900	Tenth	901

NINTH.
Runs South-East from Market.

South-West.	Street.	North East.
2	Market	1
100	Mission	101
200	Howard	201
300	Folsom	301
400	Harrison	401
500	Bryant	501
600	Brannan	601
700	Townsend	701

NORTH POINT.
Runs West from Kearny.

North.	Street.	South side.
2	Kearny	1
(c)	Dupont	(c)
100	Stockton	101
200	Powell	201
300	Mason	301
400	Taylor	401
500	Jones	501
600	Leavenworth	601
700	Hyde	701
800	Larkin	801

O'FARRELL.
Runs West from Market.

North.	Street.	South side.
2	Dupont	1
100	Stockton	101
200	Powell	201
300	Mason	301
400	Taylor	401
500	Jones	501
600	Leavenworth	601
700	Hyde	701
800	Larkin	801

PACIFIC.
Runs West from East.

North.	Street.	South side.
2	East	1
(c)	Drumm	(c)

100	Davis	101
200	Front	201
300	Battery	301
400	Sansom	401
500	Montgomery	501
600	Kearny	601
700	Dupout	701
800	Stockton	801
900	Powell	901
1000	Mason	1001
1100	Taylor	1101
1200	Jones	1201
1300	Leavenworth	1301
1400	Hyde	1401
1500	Larkin	1501

PINE.
Runs West from Market.

North.	Street.	South side.
2	Davis	1
100	Front	101
200	Battery	201
300	Sansom	301
318	Leidesdorff	(b)
400	Montgomery	401
500	Kearny	501
600	Dupont	601
700	Stockton	701
800	Powell	801
900	Mason	901
1000	Taylor	1001
1100	Jones	1101
1200	Leavenworth	1201
1300	Hyde	1301
1400	Larkin	1401

POST.
Runs West from Market.

North.	Street.	South side.
2	Market and Mont	1
100	Kearny	101
200	Dupont	201
300	Stockton	301
400	Powell	401
500	Mason	501
600	Taylor	601
700	Jones	701
800	Leavenworth	801
900	Hyde	901
1000	Larkin	1001

POWELL.
Runs North from Market.

East.	Street.	West side.
2	Eddy and Market	1
100	Ellis	101
200	O'Farrell	201
300	Geary	301
400	Post	401
500	Sutter	501
600	Bush	601
700	Pine	701
800	California	801
900	Sacramento	901
1000	Clay	1001
1100	Washington	1101
1200	Jackson	1201
1300	Pacific	1301
1400	Broadway	1401
1500	Vallejo	1501
1600	Green	1601
1700	Union	1701
1800	Filbert	1801
1900	Greenwich	1901
2000	Lombard	2001
2100	Chestnut	2101
2200	Francisco	2201
2300	Bay	2301

2400	North Point	2401
2500	Beach	2501
2600	Jefferson	2601

SACRAMENTO.
Runs West from East.

North.	Street.	South side.
2	East	1
100	Drumm	101
200	Davis	201
300	Front	301
400	Battery	401
500	Sansom	501
522	Leidesdorff	525
600	Montgomery	601
700	Kearny	701
800	Dupont	801
900	Stockton	901
1000	Powell	1001
1100	Mason	1101
1200	Taylor	1201
1300	Jones	1301
1400	Leavenworth	1401
1500	Hyde	1501
1600	Larkin	1601

SANSOM.
Runs North from Market.

East.	Street.	West side.
2	Sutter	1
100	Bush	101
200	Pine	201
300	California	301
400	Sacramento	401
416	Commercial	417
500	Clay	501
514	Merchant	515
600	Washington	601
700	Jackson	701
800	Pacific	801
900	Broadway	901
1000	Vallejo	1001
1100	Green	1101
1200	Union	1201
1300	Filbert	1301
1400	Greenwich	1401
1500	Lombard	1501

SECOND.
Runs South-East from Market.

South-West.	Street.	North-East.
2	Market	1
100	Mission	101
200	Howard	201
300	Folsom	301
400	Harrison	401
500	Bryant	501
600	Brannan	601
700	Townsend	701

SEVENTH.
Runs South-East from Market.

South-West.	Street.	North-East.
2	Market	1
100	Mission	101
200	Howard	201
300	Folsom	301
400	Harrison	401
500	Bryant	501
600	Brannan	601
700	Townsend	701

SPEAR.
Runs South-East from Market.

North-West.	Street.	South-East.
2	Market	1

100	Mission	101
200	Howard	201
300	Folsom	301
400	Harrison	401
500	Bryant	501

SIXTH.
Runs South-East from Market.

South-West.	Street.	North-East.
2	Market	1
100	Mission	101
200	Howard	201
300	Folsom	301
400	Harrison	401
500	Bryant	501
600	Brannan	601
700	Townsend	701

STEVENSON.
Runs South-West from First.

North-West.	Street.	South-East.
2	First	1
100	Second	101
200	Third	201
300	Fourth	301
400	Fifth	401
500	Sixth	501
600	Seventh	601
700	Eighth	701
800	Ninth	801
900	Tenth	901

STEWART.
Runs South-East from Market.

South-West.	Street.	North-East.
2	Market	1
100	Mission	101
200	Howard	201
300	Folsom	301
400	Harrison	401

STOCKTON.
Runs North from Market.

East.	Street.	West side.
2	Ellis and Market	1
100	O'Farrell	101
200	Geary	201
300	Post	301
400	Sutter	401
500	Bush	501
600	Pine	601
700	California	701
800	Sacramento	801
900	Clay	901
1000	Washington	1001
1100	Jackson	1101
1200	Pacific	1201
1300	Broadway	1301
1400	Vallejo	1401
1500	Green	1501
1600	Union	1601
1700	Filbert	1701
1800	Greenwich	1801
1900	Lombard	1901
2000	Chestnut	2001
2100	Francisco	2101
2200	Bay	2201
2300	North Point	2301
2400	Beach	2401

SUTTER.
Runs West from Market.

North.	Street.	South side.
2	Sansom and Market	1

100	Montgomery	101
200	Kearny	201
300	Dupont	301
400	Stockton	401
500	Powell	501
600	Mason	601
700	Taylor	701
800	Jones	801
900	Leavenworth	901
1000	Hyde	1001
1100	Larkin	1101

TAYLOR.
Runs North from Market.

East.	Street.	West side.
2	Taylor and Market	1
100	Turk	101
200	Eddy	201
300	Ellis	301
400	O'Farrell	401
500	Geary	501
600	Post	601
700	Sutter	701
800	Bush	801
900	Pine	901
1000	California	1001
1100	Sacramento	1101
1200	Clay	1201
1300	Washington	1301
1400	Jackson	1401
1500	Pacific	1501
1600	Broadway	1601
1700	Vallejo	1701
1800	Green	1801
1900	Union	1901
2000	Filbert	2001
2100	Greenwich	2101
2200	Lombard	2201
2300	Chestnut	2301
2400	Francisco	2401
2500	Bay	2501
2600	North Point	2601
2700	Beach	2701
2800	Jefferson	2801

TEHAMA.
Runs South-West from First.

North-West.	Street.	South-East.
2	First	1
100	Second	101
200	Third	201
300	Fourth	301
400	Fifth	401

500	Sixth	501
600	Seventh	601
700	Eighth	701
800	Ninth	801
900	Tenth	901

THIRD.
Runs South-East from Market.

South-West.	Street.	North-East.
2	Market	1
100	Mission	101
200	Howard	201
300	Folsom	301
400	Harrison	401
500	Bryant	501
600	Brannan	601
700	Townsend	701

TOWNSEND.
Runs South-West from First.

North-West.	Street.	South-East.
2	First	1
100	Second	101
200	Third	201
300	Fourth	301
400	Fifth	401
500	Sixth	501
600	Seventh	601

TURK.
Runs West from Market.

North.	Street.	South side.
2	Mason and Market	1
100	Taylor	101
200	Jones	201
300	Leavenworth	301
400	Hyde	401
500	Larkin	501

TYLER.
Runs West from Market.

North.	Street.	South side.
2	Taylor and Market	1
100	Jones	101
200	Leavenworth	201
300	Hyde	301
400	Larkin	401

UNION.
Runs West from Front.

North.	Street.	South side.
2	Front	1

100	Battery	101
200	Sansom	201
300	Montgomery	301
400	Kearny	401
500	Dupont	501
600	Stockton	601
700	Powell	701
800	Mason	801
900	Taylor	901
1000	Jones	1001
1100	Leavenworth	1101
1200	Hyde	1201
1300	Larkin	1301

VALLEJO.
Runs West from Davis.

North.	Street.	South side.
2	Davis	1
(c)	Front	(c)
100	Battery	101
200	Sansom	201
300	Montgomery	301
400	Kearny	401
500	Dupont	501
600	Stockton	601
700	Powell	701
800	Mason	801
900	Taylor	901
1000	Jones	1001
1100	Leavenworth	1101
1200	Hyde	1201
1300	Larkin	1301

WASHINGTON.
Runs West from East.

North.	Street.	South side.
1	East	1
101	Drumm	101
201	Davis	201
301	Front	301
401	Battery	401
501	Sansom	501
601	Montgomery	601
701	Kearny	701
801	Dupont	801
901	Stockton	901
1001	Powell	1001
1101	Mason	1101
1201	Taylor	1201
1301	Jones	1301
1401	Leavenworth	1401
1501	Hyde	1501
1601	Larkin	1601

A BUSINESS DIRECTORY

OF THE

CITY OF SAN FRANCISCO:

In which the different Trades and Professions are Classified and Arranged.

[COMPILED EXPRESSLY FOR THIS WORK.]

Accountants.
Ashton Charles, 405 Pine
Beck A. G. 116 Stevenson
Blake H. C. 436 Jackson
Cadiz J. G. 536 Washington
Culverwell W. 619 Merchant
Doolittle W. G. 328 Montgomery
Evans G. 406 California
Ingols N. L. 32 Montgomery Block
Wegener R. 415 Montgomery
Wood A. G. 338 Montgomery

Adjusters Marine Losses.
CAZNEAU T. N. 504 Battery (see adv. p. xlviii)
Evans G. 406 California
JOHNSTON W. B. 412 Montgomery
Moore E. J. 425 Washington

Acids. *Manufacturers.*
S. F. Chemical Works Co. office SE cor Battery and Commercial
[See Chemists.]

Advertising Agents.
BOYCE THOMAS, NE cor Mont and Washington (see adv. p. 648)
Fisher L. P. 629 Washington
Knowlton J. J. & Co. 402 Montgomery
Lake W. B. 502 Washington
McBoden A. 315 Montgomery
Rood A. N. & Co. 626 Montgomery
Stilwell & Co. 511 Sansom
Tobey W. H. 28 Government House

Agricultural Stores.
AMES PLOW CO. over Quincy Market, Boston (see adv. p. cvi)
Arnold N. S. & Co. 306 Battery
Arthur J. D. & Son, SW cor California and Davis
BENCHLEY L. B. & CO. 206 Battery
François C. 605 Sansom
Hawley & Co. SE cor Battery and Cal
Kellogg C. L. (seeds) 427 Sansom
Moore E. E. (seeds) 425 Washington
Moore S. W. (seeds) 414 California
Perkins D. E. (seeds) 216 Washington
Silvester G. F. (seeds) 317 Washington
Sweeney John P. & Co. (seeds) 406 Cal
Treadwell & Co. NE cor Bat and Cal
Vincent S. & Co. New Market
[See Hardware.]

Ale and Porter.
Richards W. H. & Co. 708 Sansom
[See Liquors, Wines, Etc.]

Amalgamating Machines.
SALMON J. & W. C. cor Mission and Fremont (see adv. p. lxi)
Varney T. 127 First

Anchors, Chains, Etc.
Richard N. 209 Stewart
Hare Charles, 11 Stewart
[See Junk Dealers.]

Apothecaries.
Adams Samuel, SE corner Bush and Powell
Adolphus H. 511 Jackson
Barbat J. 910 Pacific
Bauer J. A. 644 Washington
Bayley & Tothill, 512 Kearny
Bennett H. W. 21 Third
Bruns C. 429 California
Bryan W. J. cor Mission and Second
Bummer J. cor Mason and Post
Burnett G. G. 330 Montgomery
Chevalier V. (French) 739 Clay
Clapp G. H. cor Howard and Sixth
Cunningworth J. B. 228 Pacific
Curtis J. S. 42 Second
Dickey G. S. cor Third and Folsom
Dwyer J. 2 Sacramento
Eaton E. B. cor Folsom and Caroline
Emery R. 760 Clay
Flinn R. P. 5 Stewart
Gomer N. B. corner Valencia and Sixteenth
Griswold George, 106 First
Gros A. 720 Washington
Gros E. cor Green and Stockton
Guirado R. C. 210 Bush
Higgins W. M. 534 Sacramento
Hinckley C. E. & Co. SE cor Clay and Kearny
Jungcart T. 1317 Dupont
Keith W. H. & Co. 521 Montgomery
Kote W. 605 Merchant
Krug A. 1125 Dupont
Lefevre & Co. (French) SE cor Washington and Dupont
Leipnitz G. 312 Kearny
Mayhew W. E. cor Howard and Fourth
Miller W. C. cor Pacific and Stockton
Parker R. 164 First
Pfeiffer E. cor Post and Dupont
Pickering W. cor Stockton and Bdwy
Polastri V. 619 Vallejo
Reilly P. J. 535 Commercial
Richards & Whitfield, cor Clay and San
Riley C. C. 156 Second
Rottanzi A. cor Third and Folsom
Roturier C. 1031 Dupont
Sander R. NW cor Third and Mission
Schmidt H. W. 542 Kearny
Simpson W. 609 Davis
Van Straaten J. H. 309 Davis
Van Zandt J. W. 629 Front
Wakelee H. P. SE cor Mont and Bush and cor Third and Howard
White M. C. cor Jackson and Kearny
Widber J. H. Kearny cor Market
Wilhelm Carl, cor Howard and Fourth
Williams C. L. cor Folsom and Third
Wilson C. W. 632 Mission
Wood Wm. H. 111 Second
Zeile C. D. 517 Pacific
[See Drugs.]

Architects.
Bayless Jos. 20 Montgomery
Bayless W. H. 20 Montgomery
Boardman J. Naglee's Building
Bordwell George, 214 Montgomery
Bugbee S. C. 74 Montgomery Block

Butler M. F. 73 Montgomery Block
Cleaveland H. W. 505 Montgomery
CRAINE WM. 632 Washington (see advertisement, p. lxi)
Cummings G. P. 131 Montgomery
Eisen A. F. SE cor Mont and Cal
England & Turnbull, 528 Clay
Gaynor J. P. 402 Montgomery
Geddes C. 315 Montgomery
Gosling J. 204 Montgomery
Grob T. cor Dupont and Harlan Place
Hoagland & Newsom, 328 Montgomery
Hoffman & Schmidt, 240 Montgomery
Huerne & Harant, cor Mont and Sac
Hyatt C. 5 Post
Johnston T. J. Shiel's Block
JORDAN A. H. 410 Kearny (see adv. p. lxi)
Kenitzer & Farquharson, 428 Cal
Kutzbock A. 204 Montgomery
Levy T. S. 325 Montgomery
Macy H. C. 315 Montgomery
McDougal & Marquis, 328 Mont
Miller W. P. 204 Montgomery
Mooser W. 28 Exchange Building
O'Connor P. J. 571 Howard
Olney J. N. jr. 630 Sacramento
Patton W. 620 Washington
Petit A. P. Haves' Park
Portois P. 620 Merchant
Reynolds L. E. 328 Montgomery
Snyder A. A. 62 Halleck
Stevens S. S. cor Wash and Polk
Townsend L. R. NE cor Cal and Leid
Walsh P. 104 Sutter
Williams S. H. NW cor Mont and Sac
Wolfe J. E. 402 Montgomery
Wood Z. 410 Montgomery

Aquarians.
Jacobs A. 217 Washington

Artesian Well Borers.
Cowing T. 323 First
THOMSON T. 28 Third (see advertisement, p 653)

Artists.
[See Painters, Teachers, etc.]

Artists' Materials.
Bradley W. H. 620 Clay
COOKE WM. B. & CO. 624 Montgomery (see adv. front cover)
GENSOUL ADRIEN, 511 Montgomery (see adv. p. xxix)
HITCHCOCK G. B. cor Sansom and Commercial (see adv. p. cxii)
JONES, WOOLL & SUTHERLAND, 312 Mont (see adv. p. xxxvi)
Roos Joseph, 219 Montgomery
Shew W. 423 Montgomery

Asphaltum Workers.
Bonnet B. & Co. corner Third and Stevenson
Easton O. W. 316 Montgomery
FITZGIBBON M. E. 204 Bush (see advertisement, p. lix)

Perine N. P. & Co. 135 Montgomery
Wilde D. 216 Sansom
Wilde G. W. 318 Bush

Assayers.

BELL G. W. 512 California (see advertisement, p. xlix)
California Copper (Smelting) 540 Clay
Dexter A. G. 108 Kearny
Goldsmith Bros. 472 Montgomery
Hanks H. G. 622 Clay
HENTSCH & BERTON, cor Clay and Leidesdorff (see adv. p. xxviii)
KELLOGG, HEWSTON & CO. 416 Montgomery (see adv. p. l)
MOLITOR A. P. 611 Commercial (see adv. p. xliii)
Riehn, Hemme & Co. 432 Montgomery
Scott John, 424 Battery
Thayer B. B. (State) SE corner Montgomery and Bush

Astrologers.

Cohen S. 520 California
DeBerrio W. 816 Stockton
DeCassins Mme. 723 Broadway
Richards John, 718 Broadway
Salomon A. Mrs. 417 Kearny
Schmidt Madame, 302 Jackson
Schworer M. Mrs. 403 Bush

Attorneys at Law.

Allen W. H. 6 Armory Hall
Applegate J. H. 702 Washington
Bachelder J. W. 625 Merchant
Bachelder T. F. 625 Merchant
Baldwin Lloyd, 10 Montgomery Block
Barber W. Wells' Building
Barde D. NW cor Mont and Merchant
Barnes W. H. L. 436 California
Barstow A. 24 Montgomery Block
Barstow D. P. 24 Montgomery Block
Barstow George, 432 Montgomery
Bartlett C. 325 Montgomery
Bartlett Earl. 34 Montgomery Block
Bartlett W. 325 Montgomery
Batchelor E. P. 9 Montgomery Block
Bates A. 636 Clay
Belknap D. P. NW cor Montgomery and Merchant
Bell O. 5 Montgomery Block
Bennett N. 31 Exchange Building
Benzen G. A. 22 Exchange Building
Bergin M. 40 Exchange Building
Bergin T. I. 23 Exchange Building
Billings Frederick, 42 Mont Block
Biter J. cor Wash and Brenham Place
Blake M. C. City Hall
Blanding Lewis, cor Mont and Cal
Blanding William, 604 Montgomery
Blatchley J. S. 40 Montgomery Block
Blood J. H. 7 Montgomery Block
Booraem H. Toler, 519 Montgomery
Botts C. T. 19 Montgomery Block
Bowman James F. 417 Clay
Boyd James T. 8 Wells' Building
Brackett C. H. 432 Montgomery
Brandon J. R. 522 Montgomery
Brewer J. H. 40 Montgomery Block
Bristol J. D. 970 Harrison
Broderick J. C. 614 Merchant
Brodie S. H. 614 Merchant
Brooks B. S. NW cor Mont and Wash
Brooks E. L. B. 629 Washington
Brown H. S. cor Battery and Com
Brumagim John W. 35 Mont Block
Brunk D. D. 7 Amory Hall
Bryan H. 611 Clay
Buchan P. G. 537 Washington
Budd J. H. 625 Merchant
Bugbee J. S. cor Mont and Clay
Bullock W. H. 502 Montgomery
Burbank C. 6 Wells' Building
Burnett W. C. 20 and 22 Court Block
Burnett P. H. 404 Montgomery
Byrne H. H. 30 Court Block
Campbell Alex. 710 Montgomery
Campbell Alex. 540 Clay
Campbell R. C. 710 Montgomery
Campbell T. 35 Montgomery Block
Capp C. S. 543 Clay
Carpentier E. R. 606 Washington
Carpentier H. W. 507 Montgomery
Cary J. C. 604 Merchant
Casserly E. 436 California
Chadbourne J. 502 Montgomery
Chipman E. S. 17 Exchange Building
Chipman J. S. 110 Kearny
Chipman W. W. 17 Exchange Bdg
Chittenden N. W. 804 Montgomery
Clark L. S. 636 Clay

Clark W. H. 72 Exchange Building
Clarke D. 31 Exchange Building
Clarke H. K. W. 606 Washington
Clarke J. 11 Court Block
Clarke S. J. Jr. 604 Merchant
Clement J. 710 Washington
Clement R. P. 58 Exchange Building
Cobb M. G. 636 Clay
Cohen A. A. cor Sansom and Jackson
Collins A. L. 58 Exchange Building
Colton D. D. 402 Montgomery
Coombs J. cor Mont and Jackson
Cook E. 33 Exchange Building
Cope W. 5 U. S. Court Building
Cornwell W. A. 48 Exchange Building
Cowles S. 8 City Hall
Crane A. M. 620 Merchant
Crane W. W. 605 Clay
Creigh J. D. 604 Merchant
Crockett J. B. 2 Exchange Building
Crosby D. A. 619 Bush
Culver W. H. 722 Washington
Currey John, 535 Clay
Cutter S. L. Jr. 34 Exchange Building
Daingerfield W. P. cor Montgomery and Jackson
Dame T. 409 California
Dameron J. P. 35 Exchange Building
Dann F. P. 604 Merchant
Delany Chas. McC. 519 Montgomery
Dempsey P. 604 Merchant
Doyle J. T. 11 Wells' Building
Drake E. B. 420 Montgomery
Drum T. J. 606 Washington
Drummond W. W. 620 Washington
Dupré E. 606 Merchant
Dwinelle J. W. 10 Montgomery Block
Dwinelle S. H. 17 City Hall
Drummond W. W. 620 Washington
Ely Alex. 16 Wells' Building
Emmet C. T. NW cor Mont and Com
Fabens F. A. 46 Montgomery Block
Felton J. B. 25 Court Block
Field S. J. 2 U. S. Court Building
Finkler C. C. 639 Washington
Finn J. T. 36 Montgomery Block
Fitch W. S. Ocean House
Fletcher J. A. 502 Montgomery
Freelon T. G. 28 Court Block
Galan C. F. 9 Montgomery Block
Gardner C. 604 Merchant
George Julius, NW cor Mont and Sac
Gillespie G. V. 655 Washington
Gitchell J. M. Custom House
Gluyas G. C. 625 Merchant
Goold E. L. 11 Montgomery Block
Gray G. H. 621 Clay
Greeley A. D. SE cor Mont and Sac
Grey C. V. 523 Montgomery
Grimwood A. D. 16 City Hall
Gunnison A. J. NW cor Merchant and Montgomery
Hager J. S. Occidental Hotel
Haggin J. B. 2 Court Block
Haight H. H. 510 Jackson
Hale W. 52 Metropolitan Block
Halleck H. W. 42 and 43 Mont Block
Halsey Charles, NW cor Washington and Montgomery
Hambleton J. D. 6 U. S. Court Block
Hambly T. C. NE cor Mont and Sac
Harmon J. B. cor Mont and Cal
Harrison E. 402 Montgomery
Hart J. B. 21 Exchange Building
Hastings B. M. 621 Clay
Hastings S. C. 3 Court Block
HASTINGS W. 436 Jackson (see advertisement, p. xliii)
Hawes Horace, cor Folsom and Ninth
Haycock J. 622 Clay
Hayes Wm. NW cor Clay and Mont
Head E. F. 46 Montgomery Block
Henry S. H. 606 Montgomery
Hent R. W. 22 Exchange Building
Heslep A. M. cor Mont and Sacramento
Heydenfeldt S. 712 Montgomery
Highton H. E. 540 Clay
Hinchman A. F. 19 Exchange Building
Hittell T. H. 636 Clay
Hoffman O., U. S. Court Building
Hoge George, 625 Merchant
Hoge Joseph P. 5 Montgomery Block
Holladay S. W. 614 Pine
Holland N. Wells' Building
Howard J. E. 606 Montgomery
Howe D. J. 606 Montgomery
Hoyt James T. 34 California
Hubbard J. F. 7 Hampton Place
Hubert N. 51 Montgomery Block
Hyde G. 721 Geary
Inge S. W. 408 Stockton
Irving H. P. 604 Merchant

James G. F. 624 Merchant
James H. B. 622 Clay
Jarboe J. R. 636 Clay
Johnson C. A. cor Mont and Sac
Johnson E. 204 Stockton
Johnson S. L. 523 Montgomery
Johnson O. Pen. U. S. Court Building
Johnston W. B. 412 Montgomery
Joice E. V. NE cor Battery and Wash
Jones E. 829 Howard
Jones W. C. 20 Exchange Building
Judah C. D. 657 Howard
Lake D. 3 U. S. Court Building
Landesman J. 604 Merchant
Lane O. L. 502 Montgomery
Lawrence E. A. 620 Washington
Larkin F. R. 622 Clay
Latham M. S. 412 Montgomery
Lawton W. W. NE cor Mont and Cal
Lies E. 18 Exchange Building
Lloyd R. H. 636 Clay
Louderback D. City Hall
Loewy W. City Hall
Loughborough A. H. NW cor Montgomery and Sacramento
Love H. S. 540 Clay
Love J. L. 540 Clay
Luli L. R. 424 Battery
Lupton S. L. 604 Clay
Mackinley E. 502 Montgomery
Manchester J. B. cor Mont and Mont
Mastick E. B. NE cor Mont and Com
Maxson W. B. NW cor Montgomery and Merchant
McAllister C. 540 Clay
McAllister H. 540 Clay
McAllister M. H. 423 First
McCabe James, 625 Merchant
McCeney J. Tehama House
McConnell J. R. 520 Montgomery
McDougall J. A. 636 Clay
McGrew W. K. Valencia nr Sixteenth
McHenry J. 212 Broadway
McKinstry E. W. 434 Jackson
McLellan R. G. 305 Montgomery
Mee James, 625 Merchant
Meeks W. 523 Montgomery
Merrill A. 58 Exchange Building
Merrill G. B. 529 Montgomery
Miller C. W. 622 Clay
Mills J. J. 509 Bush
Moffatt W. P. rear City Hall
Moon J. W. 668 Harrison
Moore B. F. 522 Montgomery
Moore E. J. 77 Montgomery Block
Moore H. K. 630 Sacramento
Moore Joseph H. 77 Mont Block
Morrison R. F. 4 Court Building
Mott G. N. 911 Jackson
Muller H. G. 228 Montgomery
Mulville M. B. 604 Merchant
Murphy B. D. 636 Clay
Murphy Daniel J. 10 Court Block
Neumann P. 803 Montgomery
Newhall H. C. 636 Clay
Newman B. B. 629 Washington
Newmark M. J. 529 Clay
Nichols J. 614 Merchant
Northrop D. B. 43 Montgomery Block
Norton E. 502 Montgomery
O'Connor H. T. 45 Montgomery Block
Papy J. J. NW cor Mont and Merch
Parburt G. R. 41 Exchange Building
Parker C. H. 8 Montgomery Block
Parker S. H. 238 Montgomery
Parsons L. 702 Washington
Patterson D. W. 26 Exchange Building
Patterson W. H. 513 Jackson
Payne R. T. 522 Montgomery
Peachy A. C. 44 Montgomery Block
Perkins R. F. cor Wash and Battery
Peyton B. jr. 618 Sutter
Phelps A. 537 Washington
Pierson W. M. 510 Jackson
Pixley F. M. 52 Exchange Building
Platt S. 626 Merchant
Plunkett W. A. 636 Clay
Porter Nathan, 620 Washington
Pout F. 21 Montgomery Block
Pratt James, NW cor Mont and Wash
Pratt O. C. City Hall
Pringle E. J. 23 Court Block
Provines R. R. 38 Metropolitan Block
Ransom L. 302 Montgomery
Ransom A. 436 California
Raphall J. M. 614 Merchant
Redman R. A. 402 Montgomery
Reichert J. A. 636 Clay
Reynolds J. NW cor Mont and Wash
Reynolds S. F. NW cor Mont and Wash
Rice J. 57 Montgomery Block
Rix A. 19 Court Block

Rix H. 230 Bush
Rogers Daniel, 814 Merchant
Rogers R. C. 614 Merchant
Rowley C. M. 502 Montgomery
Ryan R. F. 35 Exchange Building
Satteriee J. 45 Montgomery Block
Saunders J. H. 13 City Hall
Sawyer C. H. 622 Clay
Sawyer E. D. City Hall
Sawyer W. D. 625 Merchant
Seaton G. W. Erie nr Howard
Scawell J. M. 10 Montgomery Block
Shafter J. McM. 11 Montgomery Block
Shafter O. L. 11 Montgomery Block
Sharp G. F. 529 Clay
Sharp Sol. A. 636 Clay
Sharp W. H. 529 Clay
Sharpstein J. R. 24 Exchange Building
Shaw W. J. Thirteenth nr Mission
Shearer L. NW cor Mont and Wash
Shearer S. NW cor Mont and Wash
Shepheard P. W. City Hall
Shields James, Howard nr Twelfth
Simons L. D. 655 Washington
Simson R. 804 Montgomery
Sloan E. W. F. NW cor Montgomery
  and Washington
Smith G. F. 52 Exchange Building
Smith S. V. 630 Sacramento
Smyth J. H. 24 Exchange Building ·
Spaulding C. A. 328 Montgomery
Spencer Charles, 636 Clay
Spilvalo A. D. 430 Jackson
Stebbins J. C. 803 Montgomery
Stephenson J. W. 5 Court Block
Stevenson J. D. 604 Merchant
Stow W. W. 513 Jackson
Strother F. F. 29 Third
Sullivan D. T. 3 U. S. Court Building
Sutherland F. E. 606 Montgomery
Swezey S. I. C. 734 Montgomery
Swift J. F. 625 Merchant
Taylor E. W. 621 Clay
Taylor J. M. 636 Clay
Tevis L. 3 Court Block
Thayer A. E. 537 Washington
Thompson R. A. 2 Federal Building
Thorne I. N. 535 Clay
Thornton J. D. NW cor Montgomery
  and Washington
Thurn C. 919 Powell
Tighe J. 604 Merchant
Tobin R. cor Mont and Jackson
Tompkins E. NW cor Montgomery and
  Merchant
Tompkins W. C. 620 Merchant
Tompkins H. J. 23 Exchange Building
Todd J. M. 422 Montgomery
Townsend J. B. NW cor Montgomery
  and Jackson
Treadwell J. P. 528 Clay
Turner G. 605 Clay
Tyler G. W. 536 Clay
Underwood W. L. 302 Montgomery
Van Arman J. cor Washington and
  Brenham Place
Van Dyke W. 636 Clay
Verdenal D. F. 22 Court Block
Verdenal J. M. 22 Court Block
Voorhees J. H. 639 Market
Wade J. W. 606 Merchant
Wade John, 537 Washington
Wallace W. T. 513 Jackson
Waller G. C. 6 Montgomery Block
Waller R. H. 6 Montgomery Block
Wardwell C. O. NW cor Montgomery
  and Merchant
Washington B. F. 535 Washington
Washington R. S. 502 Montgomery
Waterman F. H. 9 Montgomery Block
Weller C. L. 302 Stockton
Wells F. H. NE cor Mont and Cal
Wells H. J. 623 Merchant
Wheaton W. R. City Hall
Wheeler A. 34 Montgomery Block
Wheeler E. D. 10 Express Building
Whitcomb A. C. cor Wash and Kearny
White M. 502 Washington
Whiting W. P. C. 3 Exchange Building
Whitney G. E. 11 Exchange Building
Wiggins W. W. 3 Exchange Building
Wight G. J. rear City Hall
Wilkins Henry, cor Mont and Jackson
Williams A. 535 Clay
Williams J. B. 1010 Stockton
Williams J. J. NW cor Montgomery
  and Washington
Williams T. G. 636 Clay
Wilson D. M. 2 Montgomery Block
Wilson James, 14 Wells' Building
Wilson John, 620 Washington
Wilson J. T. Buenaventura nr Cal ·

Wilson S. M. 2 Montgomery Block
Winans J. W. 604 Merchant
Wise T. R. 637 Washington
Wittram C. 39 Montgomery Block
Wittram F. 39 Montgomery Block
Wood W. G. 625 Merchant
Woodson J. A. 604 Merchant
Wright S. S. 625 Merchant
Yale G. 520 Montgomery
Zabriskie J. C. 528 Clay
Zabriskie W. M. City Hall, rear

Auctioneers.
*Real Estate.

Baker H. E. 413 Kearny
Butterfield & Bro. 408 Pine
Carle & Gorley, 724 Montgomery
*Cobb & Sinton, 408 Montgomery
Conkling G. W. & Co. 714 Montgomery
Davega Joseph & Labatt, 318 Pine
*Dore Maurice & Co.*327 Montgomery
Dyer, Rokohl & Butler, 300 Mont
Edwards, Olney & Co. 626 Montgomery
Froomberg Bros. 813 Kearny
Geib & Ludorff, 15 Third
Goldsmith & Davis, 6 Fourth
Jones & Bendixen, 207 California
Keller Levi, 537 California
Lasky & Lamson, 524 California
Levy N. 823 Kearny
Marks & Bro. 521 California
MERRILL J. C. & Co. 204 California
*Middleton John & Son, 404 Mont
Myers, Goldstone & Co. 36 Third
Newhall H. M. & Co. cor Sansom and
  Halleck
Newhall & Brooks, 722 Montgomery
Spear E. S. & Co. 433 California
Stewart J. R. & Co. 417 Battery
Sweeney D. & Co. (live stock) cor
  Stockton and Post
Van Schaack C. P. 706 Kearny
Voizin, Ris & Co. 219 Sansom
Witkowski & Co. 19 Third
Waller & Jacobi, 306 Kearny

Axle Grease, Patent.

HUCKS & LAMBERT, 320 Jackson
  (see advertisement, p. 652)

Bag Makers.

Bardwell & Co. 105 Clay
Dakin E. 33 Clay
Doherty & Co. 215 Davis
Elias R. 116 Clay
Johnson E. C. cor Jackson and Battery
Lavielle D. 318 Davis
Lewis & Neville, 113 Clay
Meyer & Co. 314 Davis
  [See Machine Sewing.]

Bakers and Bakeries.

Adler A. 316 Third
Albrecht Richard, 1006 Folsom
Backer W. Sandy Hill, cor Clay and
  Mason
Barnett J. cor Fourth and Jessie
Bateman M. C. 45 Stevenson
Bereaud Bros. cor Third and Stevenson
Blebrach F. 819 Sansom
Bordenave J. 433 Pacific
Boudin & Gleizes, 434 Green
Bresrasher & Co. 1012 Dupont
Brower D. R. cor Vallejo and Stockton
Brown D. T. 1223 Stockton
Burkhardt C. 1516 Stockton
Cameron James, 509 Third
Caraffa D. & Co. 1309 Dupont
Carroll J. C. Eureka, 5 Jessie
Chadbourne J. (steam cracker) 433 Jack
Chadbourne & Co. Eclipse, 1418 Du-
  pont
D'Arcy John, cor Third and Perry
Deeth & Starr, 205 Sacramento
Dellwig & Bro. cor Fourth and Mission
Dempsey P. 127 Fourth
Deuwel & Co. 627 Broadway
Donnelly J. 108 Sansom
Doud P. Franklin, 256 First
Druffel F. H. Empire, cor Bush and
  Mason
Eades William, 1434 Stockton
Engelberg & Wagner, German, 416
  Kearny
Feldbush J. D. cor Dupont and Berry
Francis J. 1412 Dupont
Frank Charles, Belden nr Pine
Guerim F. 1510 Dupont
Hall, Hunt & Malone, New York, 628
  Kearny

Hefter C. B. 776 Folsom
Hessler W. 715 Pacific
Horr William, 719 Battery
Jallee F. 613 California
Kapp J. 1314 Dupont
Larimer A. (widow) 913 Stockton
Love W. 120 Third
Malatesta L. 427 Pacific
McDevitt James, 108 First
Miller S. W. cor Third and Clementina
Milliman D. P. cor Bdwy and Scott
Mysell & Kobicke, Sixteenth nr Guer-
  rero
Nichols & Co. 819 Sansom
O'Regan P. D. cor Fourth and Jessie
Ott John & Co. 1017 Pacific
Patek & Co. 836 Mission
Poehlman W. 104 Second
Sandoval A. 527 Broadway
Schroth Charles, 230 Kearny
Schwamm S. 114 Third
Schwerin A. 1129 Dupont
Secchi G. 1223 Stockton
Sheinhardt H. 226 Pacific
Stohlmann W. cor Dupont and St.
  Mark Place
Sutter A. 1412 Dupont
Swain & Brown, 5 Kearny
Swain R. 140 Second and 913 Stockton
Thonges P. corner Hartman Place and
  Greenwich
Thorn Phil, 22 Dupont
Von Ronn & Co. 905 Kearny ·
Vorrath C. cor Mission and Thirteenth
Weil H. 141 Third
White E. & Co. 114 Dupont
Winkle H. cor Battery and Vallejo
Wollitz T. 1321 Dupont
  [See Restaurants.]

Ball Courts and Alleys.

Cullen T. 543 Market

Bankers.

Alsop & Co. 411 and 413 California
Banks & Co. SW cor Mont and Com
Belloc Fréres, 515 Clay
Borel A. cor Montgomery and Jackson
BOURS & CO. Stockton, Cal (see ad-
  vertisement, p. cii)
Davidson B. & Berri, NW cor Mont-
  gomery and Commercial
Donohoe, Kelly & Co. cor Montgom-
  ery and Sacramento
Grain & Sutherland, agents Bank
  British North America, 413 Cal
Guy Abel, 411 Washington
HENTSCH & GERION, cor Clay and
  Leidesdorff (see adv. p. xxviii)
Luning & Co. 428 California
Newby R. agent Commercial Bank of
  India, 408 California
Parrott & Co. NW cor Montgomery
  and Sacramento
PIOCHE & BAYERQUE, SE corner
  Jackson and Montgomery
Ritter L. E. & Co. 608 Sacramento
Sather & Co. cor Mont and Com
Sime John & Co. NW cor Montgomery
  and Clay
Tallant & Co. 321 Battery
WALKER JAMES D. Bank of British
  Columbia, 412 Cal (see adv. p. xxv)
WELLS, FARGO & CO. cor Mont and
  California (see adv. p. viii)

Banks

BANK OF BRITISH COLUMBIA, 412
  California (see adv. p. xxv)
Bank of British North America, 411
  and 413 California
BANK OF CALIFORNIA, cor Bat
  and Washington (see adv. p. ll)
British and Californian (Limited) 424
  California
Commercial Bank, Corporation of In-
  dia and the East, 408 Cal
Pacific Bank, 400 Montgomery
LONDON & SAN FRANCISCO, Lim-
  ited, 412 Mont (see adv. p. 16)

Banks—Savings and Loan.

French Savings & Loan Mutual, 533
  Commercial
HIBERNIA SAVINGS AND LOAN,
  506 Jackson (see adv. p. lii)
SAN FRANCISCO SAVINGS UNION,
  513 California (see adv. p. xxxvii)
SAVINGS AND LOAN SOCIETY, 619
  Clay (see adv. p. xxxix)

Barbers.
[See Hairdressers.]

Baths.

Andrews H. S. Mrs. 10 Post
Anthes & Diehl, 533 Sacramento
Bagley J. B. 611 Howard
Bonneau T. C. Railroad House
Bourne G. M. Water Cure, 10 Post
Chapman G. W. Apollo, 687 Market
Ciprico & Cook, Cosmopolitan Hotel
Corraud E. New York, 738 Pacific
Diehl Chr. 533 Sacramento
Drucker A. Eureka, 328 Pacific
Ewald Edward, Montgomery, 621 Mont
Greif John, San Francisco, 636 Wash
Henderson & Brown, Cochituate, 217 Sansom
Houck J. M. South Beach
Johnson J. E. cor Larkin and Beach
King M. Mrs. (vapor) 174 Minna
Lipman & Korn, 406 Pine
Sand Bros. 50 Fourth
Schneider J. J. Washington, 624 Wash
Swimming Bath Co. cor Powell and Filbert
Zelle F. Russian, 517 Pacific

Bedding. *Manufacturers.*

Banks William (comforter) 400 Sac

Beds and Bedding.
* Importers.

Clark H. 625 Market
Fuhr C. A. 626 Market
Goodwin & Co. 528 Washington and 636 Market
Lloyd R. R. & Co. 727 Market
PEIRCE J. 417 Cal (see adv. p. iii)
Raddy F. 735 Washington
SCHAFER J. F. & H. H. (manufacturers) 504 and 506 Sansom (see advertisement, p. 654)
*SCHREIBER J. & C. 406 Sansom (see advertisement, p. lxx)
Shaber J. A. 622 Market
Shaber J. F. 31 Second
Smith E. L. & Co. 49 Third
Underhill G. E. 624 Market
[See Furniture; Mattress Makers.]

Bedsteads. *Manufactures.*

Emanuel L. 11 Beale
Field & Shaber, 407 Mission
Miller John, 307 Market
[See Cabinet Makers; Furniture, Etc.]

Bell Hangers.

Browning & McNamara, 806 Wash
Crowe T. 659 Mission
Mark & Fleishel, 18 Post
Marwedel & Otto, 329 Bush
Will & Finck, 613 Jackson
[See Brass Founders; Locksmiths.]

Bellows. *Manufacturers.*

Mandeville E. 218 Mission
Thomas C. W. 22 California
Van Ness C. 30 California
[See Machinists, Etc.]

Billiard Balls and Cues.

Doerger C. & Co. 539 Sacramento
Hughes M. E. 730 Montgomery
Meyer J. G. H. 228 Montgomery
PARKER GEORGE F. SE cor Wash ington and Montgomery
Strahle J. & Co. 537 Sacramento

Billiard Saloons.

Brown A. B. 328 Montgomery
Croyade A. 713 Pacific
Fitch & Merritt, Eureka, 314 Mont
Harter & Fitch, 219 Bush
Lynch John, Cosmopolitan Hotel
Martin L. cor Stockton and Jackson
PARKER G. F. Bank Exchange, cor Montgomery and Washington
Pearson & Armstrong, Russ House
Williams & Guthrie, 429 Montgomery
[See Liquors.]

Billiard Table Manufacturers.

Clees P. 515 Jackson
Echart H. 821 Montgomery
HUGHES M. E. 730 Montgomery (see advertisement, p. 653)

LIESENFELD PETER, 612 Battery (see advertisement, p. liv)
Strahle Jacob, 539 Sacramento

Bill Posters.

Way & Keyt, 537 Merchant

Bitters.

Hostetter, Smith & Dean, 401 Battery
Jacobs N. B. & Co. 423 Front
Keller M. 609 Front
McMillan & Kester, 718 Front
[See Wines, Etc.]

Blacksmiths.

Andresen Bros. 119 Sansom
McGlauflin & Moholy, Brannan near Seventh
Barber William, 118 Bush
Brannan P. cor Spring and Summer
Burns P. 12 Geary
Campbell T. cor Bush and Market
Cunningham Z. H. & Co. 581 Market
Donlan Thos. 3 Powell
Doran & Ford, 121 Bush
Ducommon & Lowney, 535 Market
Dunn & McDonald, Oregon nr Front
Dunnigan & Flynn, 575 Market
Dupuy & Co. 528 Broadway
English and Lothrop, 203 Sansom
Fisher B. A. 115 Bush
Fleury P. 713 Dupont
Flintoff & O'Neill, cor Halleck and Leidesdorff
Fogarty D. 671 Mission
Foster Dan. 164 Stewart
Gallagher & Rodecker, 115 Pine
Glinden James. 38 Webb
Godkin Thos. 715 Folsom
Hahn & Vizina, 516 Front
Hart John, 419 Pine
Hayes & Grimes, 17 Battery
Herold F. H. 967 Folsom
Hicks W. B. 118 Bush
Holmes M. P. 417 Pine
Horgan & Kenny, 665 Howard
Juillion J. B. 421 Kearny
Keller J. 210 Sutter
Kenny J. cor Third and Howard
King J. M. Mission nr Sixteenth
Kittlewell J. R. 269 First
Klapperich J. S. Wash Av nr Howard
Knight G. W. & Co. Potrero Avenue
Maugeot C. cor Howard and Ninth
McAntee O. 322 Third
McCarthy J. 815 Market
McGlauflin & Moholy, Brannan near Seventh
McLaughlin & Feisel, 121 Bush
McTernan T. & H. cor Drumm and Commercial
Misgill & Cooper, 815 Market
Muller F. 212 Sutter
Nelson & Doble, 321 Pine
Nicholas J. & Co. 19 Fremont
Nutting & Upstone, 123 Bush
Rice & Somers, 713 Mission
Rosendahl & Anderson, 1816 Powell
Schuemann F. 1625 Powell
Steele H. 107 Leidesdorff
Steinweg C. 109 Pine
Stickney S. B. 326 Bush
Toothaker & Meyers, 116 Washington
Tanian & Waterman, 665 Howard
Taylor & Turley, 26 Folsom
Thickbroom J. cor Third and Tehama
Thompson W. S. 749 Market
Wells Levi, 19 Sutter
Winall & Clapp, 505 Market
Yerman J. 1116 Howard
Zimmer L. cor Powell and Broadway
[See Foundries; Machinists, etc.]

Blank Books. *Manufacturers.*
[See Bookbinders.]

Blinds.
[See Doors, Etc.]

Block and Pump Makers.

Currier C. H. 29 Market
Hanson J. C. 6 California
Mitchell T. F. 22 Drumm
[See Pumps.]

Block Letter Makers.

Wyman G. D. 320 California

Boarding Houses.

Alexander Mathew, 504 Howard

Alton J. A. (widow) 904 Jackson
Anderson J. P. Drumm nr Clark
Angelis Edward, 18 Sansom
Baker C. F. (widow) 800 Howard
Bannett Harris. 532 Commercial
Barber Wm. 215 Broadway
Baumeister J. & Co. 425 Pine
Bell S. J. Mrs. 742 Howard
Bishop L. Valencia nr Sixteenth
Blackmore T. 321 Beale
Bowley S. (widow) 54 Third
Branger J. 821 Kearny
Brown M. A. Mrs. 321 Minna
Brown W. 152 Stewart
Brunn D. (widow) 1022 Stockton
Calender J. T. (colored) 907 Pacific
Cameron E. Mrs. 312 Beale
Carson John, 10 Anthony
Chamberlain L. 115 Dupont
Chapman S. Bay nr Kearny
Clark Wm. 71 Tehama
Cox A. M. Mrs. 138 Fourth
Davis Anna P. 746 Howard
Delahanty M. 127 St. Mark Place
Dennison M. J. (widow) 704 Howard
Doyle E. G. 308 Beale
Dubbs A. J. (widow) cor Jackson and Stockton
Falkenberg H. cor Jessie and Anna
Fernandez B. Senora, 7 O'Farrell
Fisher P. 777 Market
Glynn M. (widow) 79 Jessie
Graves M. A. (widow) Brannan near Eighth
Griffin M. Miss, Virginia Block
Hagan M. E. (widow) 1009 Powell
Hannah Harriet, 734 Mission
Hayes E. C. Mrs. 14 Sansom
Holbrook L. E. (widow) 1123 Stockton
Holden T. Mrs. 749 Market
Hollahen E. Mrs. 16 Third
Hopkinson M. (widow) 29 Minna
Hughes J. Miss. 15 Ecker
Hurley D. J. 704 Front
Hutchison W. 110 Prospect Place
Jensen C. H. 32 Rousch
Jessel S. (widow) 286 Stevenson
Johnson A. 117 Sacramento
Johnson C. E. cor Third and Market
Johnson J. E. cor Larkin and Beach
Johnson John, cor Sierra and Georgia
Jones M. (widow) 120 Fourth
Ozedeavliar & Alves, 114 Jackson
Kane E. (widow) 530 Bush
Kelly M. 112 Jessie
Kilday Wm. 23 Hunt
Lathrop Lydia A. 719 Market
Lehrke H. cor Mariposa and Indiana
Leland S. A. (widow) 618 California
Lelevier T. 725 Pacific
Lovely G. S. 607 Pine
Lyons J. (widow) 17 Fourth
Maguire C. (widow) 613 Pine
Mahoney D. cor Sixth and Bryant
Mahoney T. Union Court nr Kearny
Mall Adam, 13 Geary
Mann C. N. Mrs. 218 Bush
Mast H. Potrero Avenue
Matzenback W. B. 18 First
McArdie M. 57 Stevenson
McCaffrey M. (widow) 14 Sutter
McCann J. Washington nr Davis
McCarthy O. Union Court nr Kearny
McEleny A. Mise. 277 Minna
Mitrovich P. & Co. 715 Davis
Moneypenny C. 138 Natoma
Murdock G. L. 24 Battery
O'Brien C. Mrs. 64 First
O'Connor Dan, 26 Fourth
Ochs S. (widow) 427 Sacramento
Olmstead S. (widow) 759 Market
Patten A. (widow) 174 Jessie
Peck & Cox (col'd) 5 Broadway
Platt E. (widow) 248 Fourth
Poly S. 424 Sacramento
Price J. C. Battery nr Vallejo
Quinn J. B. 206 Pacific
Rassette E. (widow) 630 Market
Reardon M. Mrs. 97 Stevenson
Riley J. 50 Beale
Riley J. G. 115 Jackson
Roeben G. 37 Pacific
Rogers J. H. Front nr Vallejo
Rogers P. T. Dolores nr Sixteenth
Rountree S. S. (widow) 122 Fourth
Sharkey J. 133 Folsom
Shea R. 648 Mission
Simons & Callender, Clark nr Davis
Smith G. (col'd) 28 Stone
Somerville W. 116 Stewart
Spaulding C. (widow) 521 Pine
Talbot A. 269 Stevenson

Templeton C. L. Mrs. 5 Dixon Block
Thompson W. 112 Pacific
Thornquist C. 20 Commercial
Todd J. Mrs. Brannan nr Eighth
Turner A. K. (widow) 933 Sacramento
Van Pelt M. A. (widow) 112 Mason
Wade C. (widow) corner Shasta and
  Michigan
Wadleigh M. (widow) 5 Stockton
Walker J. 215 Broadway
Welsh M. 49 Stevenson
Wynn B. Miss, 1105 Powell
[See Hotels; Lodgings; Restaurants,
  etc.]

Boat Builders.

Duerden J. R. cor Spear and Mission
Gilman J. 20 Commercial
Griffin & Cooper, Clark nr Davis
Vice Thomas. foot Montgomery
[See Shipwrights; Ship Builders.]

Boiler Makers.

Coffey & Risdon, cor Market and Bush
BOOTH H. J. & CO. Union Foundry,
  cor First and Mission (see adver-
  tisement, p. lviii)
GODDARD & CO. Pacific Foundry,
  127 First (see adv. p. x)
HINCKLEY & CO. Fulton, 47 First,
  (see advertisement, p. 640)
HOWLAND, ANGELL & KING, Min-
  ers', 247 First (see advertisement,
  pp. 642 and 643)
MOYNIHAN & AITKEN, Portland,
  311 Mission (see adv. p. 641)
PALMER, KNOX & CO. Golden State,
  19-25 First (see adv. p. 639)
Steen E. T. Novelty Works, 39 Fremont
VULCAN IRON WORKS CO. corner
  First and Natoma (see adv. p. 638)

Bone Factories.

Ohlandt & Co. New Potrero

Bonnet Bleachers.

Burton J. 1317 Stockton
California Straw Works, 45 Third
Pacific Straw Works Co. 603 Market

Bonnets and Straw Goods.

[See Millinery, etc.]

Bookbinders.

Ball D. H. 408 Clay
Bartling & Kimball, 505 Clay
Bateman H. C. 202 Kearny
BOSQUI E. & CO. 517 Clay (see ad-
  vertisement, p. xciii)
BUSWELL ALEX. & CO. 509 Clay and
  508 Commercial (see adv. p. 680)
Cortis A. J. 522 Montgomery
Hicks & Co. 543 Clay
Laurent A. 522 Clay

Booksellers.

* Importers.

*Allen & Spier, 542 Clay
Appleton D. E. cor Clay and Kearny,
  California and Kearny, Sacramen-
  to and Leidesdorff, and 508 Mont
Arnold E. F. 538 Market
Aubrey C. F. 310 Third
Bailey & Hillis, 767 Market
*Bancroft H. H. & Co. 609 Montgomery
Barkhaus F. W. & D. 321 Kearny
Beach C. 34 Montgomery
*BELL G. H. SW corner Merchant and
  Montgomery (see adv. p. lxix)
*Betge R. J. 217 Montgomery
Blake & Myers, 702 Montgomery
Bowen & Hart, 620 Market
Boyd T. C. 300 Montgomery
Brooks W. H. 51 Third
Carrie Jos. A. & Co. 404 Battery
Choynski J. N. cor Market and Second
*COOKE W. B. & CO. 624 Montgom-
  ery (see advertisement, cover)
Dewing & Co. (agents) 511 Sacramento
Fella P. 224 Kearny
Flood M. (Catholic) 428 Kearny
Freund & Co. 511 Clay
*GENSOUL A. (Foreign) 511 Mont-
  gomery (see adv. p. xxix)
Hass M. L. & Co. cor Front and Sac
Hardy J. 138 Montgomery
Herrera F. 126 Second
*Hodge John G. & Co. 418 and 420 Clay
*Kenny George L. & Co. 608 Mont

Larrabee & Braser (stand) SE. corner
  Commercial and Montgomery
Laws, Brewer & Co. 409 Jackson
Martenet & Schley, 633 Market
Mathor & Sinclair (stand) Metropolitan
  Market
*Mendheim H. 631 Clay
Mosse & Son, 639 Kearny and 618 Wash
Nicol W. (stand) cor Mont and Sac,
  Clay and Mont, and Clay and East
Obergh J. A. 158 Third
Payot Henry (Foreign) 640 Wash
Pike Thomas (stand) SE cor Commer-
  cial and Leidesdorff
Pitts H. A. 408 Third
Pries R. F. 760 Washington
*ROMAN A. & CO. 419 Montgomery
  (see advertisement, pp. 56 to 531)
Stratman John, cor Wash and Sansom
Sullivan J. W. 516 Washington
Triggs J. (stand) 611 Davis
Tyler Bros. 632 Washington
Whitney S. 609 Montgomery

Boots and Shoes. *Importers and Wholesale.*

Benkert George F. 210 Pine
Claflin A. & Co. 406 Front
Deering J. H. 419 Clay
Einstein Bros. 207 and 209 Battery
Hecht Brothers, 417 Sacramento
Hobart, Dunbar & Co. 223 California
Hudson N. 217 Front
ROBERTS, MORRISON & CO. 216 Cal-
  ifornia (see adv. p. xviii)
Seiberlich A. & Sons, 214 California
Tirrill C. & P. H. 419 Clay
Wood S. A. 212 California

Boots and Shoes. *Importers and Jobbers.*

Benkert George F. (agent) 210 Pine
Claflin A. & Co. 406 Front
Einstein Bros. 207 and 209 Battery
Hecht Bros. 417 Sacramento
Rosenstock & Price, 210 and 212 Bat
Todd John, cor Sansom and Halleck

Boots and Shoes. *Makers and Repairers.*

Ackley Lawrence, 114 Kearny
Alexander Isidor, 306 Sansom
Augerer Charles, 126 Post
Arriveto John, 631 Pacific
Auerbach L. cor Bdwy and Kearny
Axt Louis, 640 Broadway
Barrett A. 528 Pacific
Barry M. Cemetery Avenue nr Post
Bateman & Phillips, 219 Davis
Beck Henry, 320 Dupont
Beers H. M. 313 Pine
Bender F. 29 Ritch
Bloch William, 1022 Dupont
Blucher S. C. 1504 Stockton
Bostrom John, 305 Davis
Bosworth C. W. 153 Third
Brack O. 606 Post
Bray M. 341 Third
Broderick D. 252 Stewart
Buckingham T. H. 416 Battery
Buhler J. F. 529 Jackson
Burkhardt G. 323 Bush
Cahalan J. 831 Washington
Campbell A. D. 319 Kearny
Cardiff M. 513 Bryant
Carroll M. 646 Commercial
Cazaux B. 710 Pacific
Chaplin H. 1150 Folsom
Cohn Jacob, 37 Pacific
Coleman J. 1020 Market
Cornor C. W. 304 Pine
Coyle H. 356½ Third
Curtis J. 264 Third
Dempsey J. Brannan nr Sixth
Dennehy D. 7 Sansom
Deucher A. 704 Pacific
Doerfler J. cor Howard and Eighth
Dolliver T. (ladies') 108 Sutter
Donohoe O. 629 Merchant
Dorn Peter, 34 Geary
Dreg J. 1124 Dupont
Dugan M. M. 102 Second
Dugan P. S. 110 Leidesdorff
DUNNE P. F. 316 Battery (see adver-
  tisement, p. 657)
Eberts M. 648 Washington
Ehret J. M. 230 Sutter
Ehrhardt C. 1332 Dupont
Fellheimer B. 215 Fourth
Fengeler H. 527 East

Fennell H. 511 Mason
Fernbach J. 420 Market
Finan B. 777 Folsom
Fish Charles, 555 Market
Fisher M. 802 Dupont
Flynn James, 47 Second
Fogler G. P. 4 Sutter
Forsyth & Son, 803 Market
Francis J. Market nr East
Frankenbury J. 20 Post
Freeman E. 646 Commercial
Freidel F. 104 Stewart
Frisholz M. 546 Washington
Frixen A. 426 Dupont
Gaetz Daniel, 103 Stewart
Gerber J. B. 507 Jackson
Gerlach C. 335½ Kearny
Goldschmidt I. 807 Clay
Grady M. 204 Davis
Gutberlet J. 648 Washington
Hagerty J. 515 Kearny
Haney J. Jackson nr Sansom
Healy Thomas, 105 Kearny
Hempel F. 409 Bush
Hobson A. 543 Kearny
Hoffman F. 737 Mission
Holes John, 915 Pacific
Huth Charles, 504 Green
Irwin John, 12 Clay
Jeannin A. 229 Bush
Johnson E. 50 Sacramento
Johnson J. 23 Fourth
Johnson John, 40 Sutter
Johnston W. H. 306 Third
Jones J. J. cor Pacific and Sansom
Katz A. 100 Dupont
Kaufman A. 216 Pacific
Keenan P. 105 First
Kelly H. P. 112 Sansom
Kelly John, 23 Fourth
Kelly P. 729 Clay
Kennedy T. 204 Second
Kenny M. 110 Leidesdorff.
Kline B. 812 Montgomery
Komer E. 611 Mission
Kramer F. 157 Second
Kramer F. 217 Davis
Kramer R. 232 Commercial
Laib J. cor Stockton and Jackson
Lando & Marks, 327 Sacramento
Larson H. Belden nr Pine
Lavergne A. cor Sac and Kearny
Leberski A. 425 California
Lehman A. 1111 Dupont
Leugenfelzer J. 418 Brannan
Leuzen J. J. 200 Sutter
Leonhardt C. 125 Bush
Lester G. 18 Stewart
Louis M. 536 Commercial
Lowback W. 6 First
Lucke H. 648 Washington
Lyng James, 238 Third
Maguire E. cor Mission and Main
Mandron J. 729 Pacific
Marshall A. 218 First
Mason John, 7 Second
May John, 507 Jackson
Maynard E. 18 Stewart
McAntee O. 682 Market
McArthur T. 510 Jackson
McCardle P. 618 Pacific
McCarthy P. 227 Jackson
McElroy W. R. 339 Bush
McGinnis P. 723 Mission
McGravy J. 317 Battery
Meagher W. F. 313 Pine
Meiness R. 406 Market
Melchert A. F. W. 429 Bush
Meshaw J. P. (colored) 539 California
Metzger G. 39 Jackson
Meyer C. 1111 Dupont
Miller W. H. 413 East
Monahan P. 620 Mission
Morrison A. cor Brannan and Ninth
Motta C. 815 Washington
Munnin Bros. 820 Kearny
Murphy Dennis, 158 First
Neary N. 7 Sutter
Nelson N. P. 640 Pacific
Nicolay L. 112 Dupont
Noble J. City Hall, rear
Nolan P. 205 Stevenson
O'Brien J. 317 Battery
O'Conner W. 152 First
O'Toole J. Davis nr Broadway
Ohm Fred. 103 Sansom
Oppenheimer W. 647 Merchant
Pahl R. 77 Fourth
Palmtag A. 18 Stewart
Paul R. 77 Fourth
Perry & Damon, 604 Mission
Peterl J. 8 Summer

Plouf F. 1205 Dupont
Prince J. 224 Sansom
Quinn R. 244 Sixth
Raw F. 174 Dupont
Renhold M. 135 Kearny
Rinsela J. 252 Third
Robson James, 412 Third
Roethel E. 156 Third
Rogers E. T. 126 Bush
Rogers F. 502 Kearny
Rose H. 647 Merchant
Rowe C. L. 215 Sansom
Ryan D. L. 538 Commercial
Ryan T. 505 Kearny
Sensot F. 549 Merchant
Saxon A. 110 Sansom
Scannell M. 517 Dupont
Scharmann G. 1326 Powell
Schenkeberger F. cor Bush and Taylor
Scherrer J. 503 Bush
Scheu F. 421 O'Farrell
Schnerg G. 134 First
Schultz W. 109 Leidesdorff
Senram F. 28 Kearny
Shath J. 115 Dupont
Shaw W. 7 Trinity
Sheehan M. 264 Third
Simon J. 511 East
Smith C. R. cor Jackson and Davis
Spanagle G. 505 Clay
Stalb C. 335 Bush
Stein G. 413 East
Stein H. 413 East
Sullivan J. 218 Pine
Snitzer J. M. 529 Jackson
Swain J. R. & Co 204 Bush
Sylva G. 417 East
Talbot E. C. 412 Folsom
Tracy J. 231 Fourth
Trautvetter A. 231 Fourth
Tusarrat J. 714 Pacific
Veltch P. 264 Third
Verdin A. 300 Montgomery
Viera M. 417 East
Vallhardt J. 210 Third
Walker G. 530 California
Walsh M. 408 O'Farrell
Wanderer H. 523 Kearny
Weber F. 311 Davis
Wenger J. 1103 Stockton
Wentworth H. M. & Co. 210 Pine
Werber F. 311 Davis
Wescott E. 313 Pine
Wheelan D. 17 Fourth
Willey G. B. 538 Market
Williams G. F. Market or East
Wilson J. H. B. 1228 Dupont
Woid I. 510 Jackson
Woldeier T. 200 Sutter
Wolf A. 627 Broadway
Wolf W. & Co. 115 California
Wood J. 8 Stewart
Yeo W. H. 737 Market
Zschiesche C. 1329 Dupont
Zeigler J. cor Clay and Powell

Boots and Shoes. *Retail.*

Alvarus & Levy, 325 East
Adler & Stern, 221 Third
Allen John, 733 Pacific
Barrett A. 528 Pacific
Broderick T. J. 225 Montgomery
Burke W. F. cor Mont and Pine
Caxanx B. 710 Pacific
Dunne F. F. 316 Battery
Dupont J. H. 822 Washington
Ehlhart & Hemmer, 542 California
Fridolin M. 546 Washington
Frohmann S. 196 Third
Gerhaud A. 1310 Dupont
Goldmann & Adler, 330 Kearny
Guerin M. cor Commercial and Battery
Harkins M. 151 Fourth
Hauser D. 504 Commercial and corner Bush and Kearny
Becker H. 328 Commercial
Hess J. 746 Market
Hinders & Kast, 332 Kearny
Hirsch & Marks, 50 Second
Holcombe Bros. cor Wash and Kearny
Hortkorn C. 528 Kearny
Hughes James, 47 Second
Hughes J. R. cor Mont and Sutter
Joseph C. 504 Kearny
Kehoe F. 238 Third
Koenig Bros. 817 Washington
Kohler H. 514 Commercial
L'Hote E. 902 Dupont
Lardner W. 211 Pacific
Leddy John, 119 Fourth
Levy A. 19 Second
Levi U. 414 Commercial

Linehan C. 27 Ecker
Litman J. 103 Second
Lowenstein Isaac, 1208 Stockton
Maas H. F. 1411 Powell
Magnes A. 6 and 115 Second
Martin J. 419 East
Meyer S. 926 Dupont
Meyers & Strebost, 13 Third
Mitzner M. 322 Kearny
Munnin Bros. 820 Kearny
Nagel J. 272 Kearny
Newdorfer H. 524 Commercial
Newkom S. 42 Fourth
Phillips S. 15 Pacific
Prescott & Israel, 460 Kearny
Repenn F. 630 Commercial
Reiter G. S. 215 Second
Rimasa E. 932 Dupont
Rosenblum J. 623 Davis
Rosenthal M. & Co. 406 Commercial and 340 Kearny
Roth J. Pacific nr Sansom
Salomon S. 1412 Stockton
Samuel M. 926 Dupont
Schade J. 16 Sansom
Schulze L. 402 Bush
Schwerdt P. 703 Market
Shankey W. 704 Union
Silverston H. 1138 Dupont
Stevens W. 544 Third
Strachan J. 1104 Stockton
Strauss M. 18 Fourth
Walsh M. 231 Pacific
Weber G. & Co. 638 Commercial
Werlin J. G. 632 Commercial
White M. 530 Commercial
Witkowski & Wurkheim, 725 Mont

Botanists.

Schulte J. G. W. cor Market and East
[See Aquarians.]

Bottle Dealers.

Cereol F. 207 Davis
Contie M. A. Jasper nr Filbert
Kane J. Commercial or Drumm
Miller & Bro. 655 Mission
Reardon J. M. 2008 Powell
Yetes J. cor Howard and Hubbard
[See Junk Dealers.]

Bowling Alleys.

Bilay A. F. Valencia nr Sixteenth
Goetz & Schreiber, 335 Pine
Hoehler N. 827 Pacific
Lozier Peter, 201 Bush
Palm Edw. 403 Pine
Smith A. 336 Market
Snelder & Horstman, 647 Pacific

Box Makers. *Cigars.*

Korbel F. 33 Fremont
Waldstein A & C. 407 Mission

Box Makers. *Jewelry.*

Breidenstein L. 650 Washington

Box Makers, *Packing.*

Gibbs John S. 309 Market
HOBBS, GILMORE & CO. 217 Market
(see adv. p. liv)
Racouillet L. cor Market and Beale

Box Makers. *Paper.*

Entoine E. cor California and Kearny
Levy & Mochet, 408 Sacramento
Manneck H. & Co. cor San and Pine
Walzman M. 414 Sacramento

Box Makers. *Specie.*

Hennesay Peter, 816 Front
RICE E. Leidesdorff nr California

Box Makers. *Tin.*

Osgood & Stetson, 219 Commercial
Weaver D. S. 805 Sansom
[See Stoves and Tinware.]

Box Makers, *Treasure.*

Rice Edw. Leidesdorff nr California
(see advertisement, p. 662)

Brand Manufacturers.

Hall J. F. cor Front and Commercial
Trueworthy F. M. 324 Front
[See Stencil Cutters.]

Brass Founders. *Finishers.*

BOOTH H. J. & CO. Union cor First and Mission
GALLAGHER & WEED, 125 First (see advertisement, p. 644)
Garratt W. T. 507 Market
Greenberg M. 120 Bush
Smith G. E. & Co. 417 Mission
[See Coppersmiths.]

Bread Manufacturers.

[See Bakers.]

Brewers.

Albrecht & Co. Broadway, 627 Bdwy
Armstrong C. M. & Co. Mission Street, cor Mission and Second
Durkin & Co. Mission Street, 698 Mission
FORTMANN F. Pacific, 271 Tehama (see advertisement, p. 568)
Gluck & Hansen, National, cor O'Farrell and William
Green Thomas, Jackson, 23 First
Gundlach J. Bavaria, 630 Vallejo
Hock H. Mission Railroad, Valencia nr Sixteenth
HOELSCHER & WIELAND, Philadelphia, 230 Second (see adv. p. 646)
Huant F. & Co. Lafayette, 735 Green
Jullitz Herman, 511 Green
Kleinelaus & Fauss, Willows, cor Mission and Nineteenth
Koris H. & Co. St. Louis, 147 Third
Koster L. & Bro. Union, Clementina nr Fourth
Lyon & Co. Empire, 139 Jessie
Mangels & Co. Washington, cor Lombard and Taylor
Mason J. Mason's, Chestnut nr Powell
Metzler C. Golden Gate, 713 Greenwich
Meyer A. Cincinnati, Valencia nr Sixteenth
Schuppert A. California, 1100 Stockton
SPRECKELS BROTHERS, Albany, 71 Everett (see advertisement, p. 647)
WUENENBERG & CO. New York, cor Powell and Francisco (see advertisement, p. 847)

Brick Yards.

Bonnet B. & Co. Larkin nr Vallejo
Buckley James, office 528 Mont
California Patent Brick Making Co. 28 Government House
Colby & Barker, Howard nr Eighteenth and foot Third
Lemere A. cor Polk and Union
Morrell E. Sixteenth nr Dolores
NAGLE GEORGE D. office 302 Montgomery, see advertisement, p. xlvi)
Piper & Rice, Spear nr Harrison
Schroder & Lloyd, Rincon Wharf
Wood & Leszinsky, cor Fillmore and Presidio Road

Brokers. *Bullion.*

Hickox & Spear, NE cor Montgomery and Sacramento
Richon N. 511 Commercial
Sutro C. 427 Montgomery

Brokers. *General.*

Bluxom I. (coal and iron) 208 Front
Bonney George, cor Clay and Mont
Bowden Charles S. 213 Clay
Broughton N. L. 605 Montgomery
Burling W. cor Mont and Wash
Buzzolini D. 415 Jackson
Cantin & Everett, 614 Montgomery
Dow J. G. cor Front and Clay
Fortune H. W. 605 Montgomery
Gladwin Bros. 604 Montgomery
Gould J. 526 Montgomery
Gwin J. R. 607 Washington
Heatley E. D. 412 Battery
Holl Z. 618 Merchant
Howell M. D. cor Front and Clay
Jaszynsky L. 612 Merchant
Johnson John, 438 Jackson
Jones T. J. 728 Montgomery
Marina E. J. de Sta. 697 Clay
Moore J. M. 77 Montgomery Block
Reeve C. B. & Co. 33 Montgomery Blk
Sturdivant R. O. 528 Montgomery
Wilson E. H. 438 Jackson
Winans J. C. 321 Clay

Brokers. *House.*

Adams & Root, 410 Montgomery
Bryan W. J. 420 Montgomery
Carter R. W. 713 Montgomery
Daly & Hawkins, 220 Montgomery
Dam G. W. 422 Montgomery
Hoogs & Madison, 316 Montgomery
Kimball C. P. 629 Market

Brokers. *Insurance.*

Garvey W. V. 519 Montgomery
Knapp J. G. 609 Clay
Odell J. cor Front and California
Squire H. C. 238 Montgomery
Thompson D. W. C. 224 California

Brokers. *Merchandise.*

Byrne Thomas, 306 Front
Cohn M. 218 Battery
Farish & Co. 221 Davis
Gilmor J. W. A. 206 Front
Hochkofler R. 203 Front
Jones C. C. 323 Front
Ottenheimer W. 322 Commercial
Pavillier A. (liquors) 610 Front
Peat S. F. 327 Commercial
Stowell W. H. 206 Front
Trayler W. W. 720 Montgomery
Wadsworth W. R. & Son, 402 Front
Whitman S. P. 313 Montgomery

Brokers. *Mining Stocks and Money.*

Abbot C. E. 302 Montgomery
Abbott O. 613 Merchant
Adsit L. B. 604 Montgomery
Ames O. T. 618 Montgomery
Anderson John, 622 Clay
Argyras B. 423 Front
Arlington N. O. 626 Montgomery
Badlam E. B. 504 Montgomery
Barkeloo J. 705 Montgomery
Bates J. & Co. 524 Montgomery
Beard J. R. 707 Montgomery
Benjamin F. A. 605 Montgomery
Boilleau F. cor Mont and Jackson
Bonney G. SW cor Mont and Clay
Borker & Rosenfeld, 602 Montgomery
Bosworth & Russell, cor Montgomery and Merchant
Bowley S. C. & H. L. 621 Montgomery
Bradford C. H. 609 Clay
Brown L. A. 706 Montgomery
Budd C. P. 707 Montgomery
Budd W. C. & Co. 707 Montgomery
Cantin & Everett, 614 Montgomery
Cavallier J. B. E. 619 Washington
Chapelie A. M. 619 Merchant
Chapin G. W. 338 Montgomery
Chapman W. S. 76 Montgomery Block
Child E. F. 606 Montgomery
Clark J. E. 46 Exchange Building
Clark J. P. 46 Exchange Building
Clements L. G. 48 Exchange Building
Cobb & Sinton, 406 Montgomery
Cook & Peckham, cor Montgomery and Clay
Corcoran F. E. 605 Montgomery
CORNWALL P. B. 608 Merchant (see advertisement, p. 664)
Critcher H. 606 Merchant
Crosby L. 36 Exchange Building
Cumming John, 622 Montgomery
Darnell Henry Y. 6 Montgomery Blk
Davies J. S. 723 Montgomery
DePass J. M. 55 Exchange Building
Downer A. J. Government House
Duncan W. L. & Co. 605 Montgomery
Ehrlich M. 20 Montgomery Block
Ferris D. C. 6 Maguire's Building
Gallagher W. R. 728 Montgomery
Galland A. 411 Montgomery
Gildemeester A. H. 605 Washington
Gladwin Bros. 604 Montgomery
Greene A. P. 605 Montgomery
Grimes N. E. 502 Washington
Haley C. M. & Co. 604 Montgomery
Haley J. J. 604 Montgomery
HENRIQUES D. 612 Merchant (see advertisement, p. lxviii)
Hill Thomas, 622 Montgomery
Hillyer M. C. & Co. 706 Montgomery
Hinchman & Co. 723 Montgomery
Holt & Bowley, 605 Montgomery
Hugg H. 108 California
Hutchins U. P. 712 Montgomery
Hyman P. C. 712 Montgomery
Jamynsky L. 612 Merchant
Jenkins I. S. 723 Montgomery
Johnson J. 436 Jackson

Jones T. J. 728 Montgomery
Koenig A. cor Mont and Jackson
Kunast A. 540 Washington
Logan H. C. 706 Montgomery
Loveland L. F. 707 Montgomery
Lubeck S. 529 Clay
Lawton F. Exchange Building
Lissak A. H. jr. 613 Montgomery
Livingston F. 32 Montgomery Block
Livingston M. 32 Montgomery Block
Marina E. J. D. S. 607 Clay
Marina J. G. D. S. 607 Clay
Mathews & Fall, 723 Montgomery
Mayer S. 623 Montgomery
McDonald M. L. 621 Montgomery
McElwain J. 626 Montgomery
McKenty A. J. 605 Washington
Miller J. H. 404 Montgomery
Minturn J. 528 Montgomery
Moore J. M. 77 Montgomery Block
Murdock A. H. 623 Montgomery
Newell L. W. & Co. 626 Montgomery
Noyes & Whitney, 608 Montgomery
Otis Stephen & Co. 509 Clay
PACIFIC BOARD, 606 Washington
PEASE & GRIMM, 709 Montgomery (see advertisement, p. lvi)
Pierce H. & W. 728 Montgomery
Pool C. W. 606 Sacramento
Reeve G. B. & Co. 33 Montgomery Blk
Richards T. G. 517 Jackson
Rising D. B. 606 Merchant
Robbins James J. 619 Montgomery
Roberts D. S. 606 Merchant
Rose L. S. 617 Montgomery
S. F. STOCK & EXCHANGE BOARD, NW cor Montgomery and Wash
Sanborn T. C. & Co. 613 Montgomery
Schmiedell H. 705 Montgomery
Schmitt B. L. 607 Washington
Scott & Glover, 304 Montgomery
Shipley A. J. & Co. 611 Montgomery
Sloss Louis & Co. cor Mont and Sac
Smiley G. W. 419 Montgomery
Smiley James, 607 Clay
Smith E. L. 528 Clay
Sparrow S. J. 622 Montgomery
Sparrow W. 622 Montgomery
Sturdivant R. O. 526 Montgomery
Swain Isaac, 606 Merchant
Tabor I. 502 Montgomery
Taggard J. L. 612 Montgomery
Teackle E. W. 32 Montgomery Block
Teller I. D. P. 327 Front
Temple John, 19 Exchange Building
Theller A. 605 Montgomery
Tilden & Breed, 611 Montgomery
Van Deusen M. M. 320 Montgomery
Vinzent Charles, 605 Montgomery
Warmonth & Baker, 423 Pacific
Warrin J. W. & Co. 618 Merchant
Washburn E. H. 622 Montgomery
West C. H. 606 Merchant
Wheeler & Gallagher, 302 Montgomery
Wilkie F. 423 Washington
Woods & Cheesman, cor Mont and Clay

Brokers. *Produce.*

[See Flour; Merchants—Produce Commission.]

Brokers. *Real Estate.*

* Stocks and Money.

Abbot C. E. 302 Montgomery
Abrams & Greenberg, 321 Montgomery
Adams & Root, 410 Montgomery
Anderson F. C. & Co. 537 Washington
Atkinson N. 2 Mead House
Barkeloo J. 705 Montgomery
Barnard I. D. 410 Montgomery
Barrett James, 420 Montgomery
Bigelow & Bowman, 202 Montgomery
Boyd & Davis, 321 Front
Brewer F. A. 40 Montgomery Block
Brocklebank & Co. 302 Montgomery
Brown E. O. cor Battery and Com
Brown H. S. 18 Naglee's Building
Bryan W. J. 420 Montgomery
*Carter C. D. 610 Merchant
Carter R. W. 713 Montgomery
*Cavallier J. B. E. 619 Washington
Chapelie A. M. 619 Merchant
CHAPIN GEO. W. & CO. 338 Montgomery
*Charles T. C. 605 Merchant
Child E. F. 602 Washington
Clark R. 338 Montgomery
*Cobb & Sinton, 406 Montgomery
Coombs W. jr. 626 Clay
Courtis Thomas, 515 Bush
Daly & Hawkins, 220 Montgomery

Dam G. W. 422 Montgomery
DePass J. M. 55 Exchange Building
Dewey S. P. & Sons, 410 Montgomery
Dorr R. S. 605 Montgomery
*DRESCHFELD H. SE cor Montgomery and Merchant
Duncan W. L. 605 Montgomery
Dupre E. 606 Merchant
Eaton C. S. 708 Kearny
Elveena C. 610 Clay
Flanagan E. 606 Montgomery
Gately M. 19 Geary
Gauley J. A. 625 Merchant
Gunn W. J. 502 Washington
Hancock S. & Co. 203 Montgomery
Hassey F. A. 524 Montgomery
HENRIQUES D. 612 Merchant
Higgins J. B. 624 Merchant
*Higgins W. L. 723 Montgomery
*Himmelman A. 637 Washington
Holmes A. 304 Montgomery
Hoogs & Madison, 316 Montgomery
Hurlbut I. 420 Montgomery
Hutchinson J. C. & Co. 626 Mont
Kimball C. P. 629 Market
Kower E. 605 Montgomery
Lafargue J. B. 306 Davis
Leffingwell H. 25 Montgomery Block
*Leffingwell W. 619 Montgomery
Leonard W. 402 Front
Lindsey W. 536 Washington
Loveland L. F. 605 Washington
Manrow J. P. 606 Merchant
Martel James L. 8 Court Block
Mason F. 33 Montgomery Block
Masten N. K. 619 Montgomery
Mathewson T. D. 606 Montgomery
McDougall J. 604 Merchant
Meeks W. N. 804 Montgomery
Moon G. C. cor Merchant and Mont
Morison S. A. 302 Montgomery
*Moulton & Stewart, 522 Clay
Olbrecht A. 338 Montgomery
Osborn & Sessions, 619 Merchant
*Otis S. & Co. 509 Clay
Parker W. C. 517 Jackson
Partridge P. G. cor Mont and Jackson
Paterson J. 602 Montgomery
Pearkes G. Selina Place
Pearson C. T. 423 Washington
PEASE & GRIMM, 709 Montgomery
Pforr J. 328 Montgomery
Pickett J. 619 Merchant
Pierce H. & W. 728 Montgomery
Piper A. D. 52 First
Piper J. Q. 606 Montgomery
Piper W. A. 606 Montgomery
Polack J. S. 420 Montgomery
Price & Page, 626 Clay
*Randall A. 536 Washington
Rawson J. A. 338 Montgomery
Reed J. L. 526 Montgomery
Reynolds C. H. & Co. 334 Montgomery
Richards T. G. 517 Jackson
Riddle J. L. & Co. 523 Montgomery
Ritter L. E. & Co. 608 Sacramento
Rollins W. 46 Metropolitan Block
Roulstone A. J. 502 Montgomery
Ryckman G. W. 15 Montgomery Block
Schmiedell Henry, 708 Montgomery
Scott E. NW cor Com and Mont
Shiel William, 319 Bush
*Smith C. K. 401 Montgomery
Smith*Stewart, Naglee's Building, 606 Montgomery
Smith W. Melvin, 79 Mont Block
Sparks Z. W. 624 Merchant
Steinbach E. 502 Montgomery
Stuart C. V. NE cor Mont and Merch
Stuart J. F. & Co. 621 Montgomery
Sullivan E. L. NW cor Mont and Wash
Teller S. L. 702 Washington
Thompson J. P. 523 Montgomery
Van Read J. H. 7 Montgomery Block
*Vassault F. 604 Merchant
Von Rhein O. F. & Co. 105 Mont
Wakelee C. H. 518 Pacific
Walsh S. F. 619 Merchant
Walton W. F. 518 Merchant
Warrin John W. & Co. 618 Merchant
Wegener F. O. 415 Montgomery
Welton M. & Son, 546 Merchant
Wertheman R. 28 Exchange Building
Wetzel T. 611 Clay
Wetzlar G. 420 Montgomery
Whitcomb B. 472 Montgomery
Whitman S. P. 313 Montgomery
Williams Bros. 79 Montgomery Block
Winn A. M. 622 Clay
Wohler H. 415 Montgomery
Worn George A. 519 Montgomery
[See Real Estate Dealers.]

Brokers. *Ship.*

Baker J. G. & Co. Front nr Vallejo
Grimes G. T. 708 Montgomery
Scott & Co. Vallejo nr Front
Williams B. B. Oregon nr Battery
[See Shipping Offices.]

Brokers. *Ship and Custom House.*

Bauch P. G. 506 Battery
Baum Charles, SE cor Oregon and Bat
Bunker H. S. & Co. cor Bat and Wash
DeFremery H. S. 413 Washington
Doyle W. H. 502 Washington
Hassbach O. 502 Battery
Henschel & Maurice, 506 Battery
Hughes & Hunter, Federal Building, 504 Battery
MacCann W. & Co. 610 Front
Nicholson J. Y. Davis nr Pacific
Schleiden W. 224 Washington
Wadsworth W. R. & Son, 402 Front
Williams B. B. 2 Oregon nr Battery

Brokers. *Stock and Money.*

Boileau F. cor Mont and Jackson
Glidemeester A. H. 605 Montgomery
Hickox & Spear, NE cor Mont and Sac
Holt Z. 618 Merchant
Noyes & Whitney, 608 Montgomery
PEASE & GRIMM, 709 Montgomery (see advertisement, p. lvi)
Peckham E. P. 8W cor Mont and Clay
Ritter L. E. 608 Sacramento
Sloss L. & Co. cor Mont and Sac
Sutro C. 427 Montgomery
Vassault F. 604 Merchant
West C. H. 606 Merchant
Wetzlar G. 420 Montgomery
Woods & Cheesman, SW cor Clay and Montgomery

Broom Makers.

* *Importers.*

*ARMES & DALLAM, 215 Sacramento (see advertisement, p. 644)
*Elam & Howes, 310 Clay
Gracier F. J. (handles) 309 Market
Hotop, Garling & Co. 116 Jackson
Palmer, Gillespie & Co. Eureka, 205 Davis
Van Laak L. 14 Drumm
Ward T. 36 Beale

Brush Manufacturers.

Newman Brothers, 406 Battery

.. Bung Makers.

Gracier F. J. 309 Market
Waas H. cor Mission and Fremont

Butchers.

Adler D. 3 Stockton
Adler M. 302 Beale
Alexander Eli, 241 Sutter
Ambrose S. NE cor Pine and Dupont
Anderson & Kline, cor Stock and Wash
Andre P. 19 Metropolitan Market
Andrews E. O. cor Fremont and Folsom
Arms M. C. cor Sac and Waverly Pl
Arnitz X. cor Dupont and Green
Artigues L. 17 New Market
Baker & Randahl, cor Folsom and Nevada
Baraty F. 7 Clay St. Market
Barrie H. D. 904 Stockton
Bazille A. Sixteenth nr Rhode Island
Bazille John, 30 Washington Market
Bellocy A. 1224 Dupont
Bender & Co. cor Hayes and Laguna
Berghofer & Dodge, 203 Stewart
Bernede J. 5 Clay St. Market
Boland J. 39 Metropolitan Market
Bookstaver & Weller, 82 Washington Market
Brackett & Keyes, 50 Stewart
Brady D. cor Jessie and Fifth
Breiling Bros. 335 Bush
Brown & Brown, 406 Folsom
Burdick & Dooley, Brannan St. Bridge
Camerden M. 36 Occidental Market
Carrau & Rosa, 8 New Market
Clough & Somers, corner Bryant and Ritch
Conniff W. cor Howard and Sumner
Creighton P. 240 Fourth
Cronan M. cor Folsom and Folsom Av
Crowley J. J. Sixteenth nr Valencia

Cutter R. S. & Co. corner Second and Howard
Danos J. B. cor Laguna and Waller
Dastugue G. 4 New Market
Dean H. C. 1 Occidental Market
Dereins H. 3 Clay St Market
Desmn J. 1202 Dupont
Dinger & Berthold, 703 Battery
Dodge E. A. cor Sixteenth and Mission
Dolet A. 18 New Market
Douillard F. 1224 Dupont
Duck W. B. & Co. corner Second and Tehama
Duffy W. Ninth nr Brannan
Dullon P. & L. 705 Pacific
Duran J. 14 New Market
Dutertre B. 2 O'Farrell
Dwyer P. J. & E. 56 First
Earle E. Sixth nr Bryant
Eckhardt H. cor Jackson and Leav
Elias A. 100 Occidental Market
Elston S. cor Bryant and Rincon Place
Engleskind L. cor Beale and Mission
Fallon D. G. cor Jones and O'Farrell
Faubel F. 307 Sixth
Fields T. cor Stockton and Greenwich
Finck H. 117 Jackson
Flack J. 721 Greenwich
Fleishmann L. 48 Metropolitan Market
Flynn M. W. cor Sixth and Brannan
Fogarty J. 55 Metropolitan Market
Frechette J. 735 Pacific
Freeborn W. cor Jessie and Ecker
Freeborn W. H cor Kearny and Union
Fuller E. J. cor Taylor and Geary
Fulton J. M. 451 East
Fulton W. 80 Washington Market
Garwood G. M. & Co. 84 Washington Market
Geantit A. 621 Pacific
Geggus C. cor Third and Everett
Gerhardy P. 323 Kearny
Gibbons J. cor Taylor and Greenwich
Glaser A. 244 Third
Goldman J. 1202 Stockton
Goodwin C. 6 Occidental Market
Gottgetren H. cor Hyde and Union
Grattan W. 203 Stewart
Gray W. 29 Metropolitan Market
Guikenheimer M. 4 Clay St. Market
Hahn William, 1000 Pacific
Hall & Aitken, 6 Washington
Harris Dan, 3 Clay St. Market
Hartmeyer L. cor Post and Dupont
Haxe G. J. 4 Metropolitan Market
Heister W. 513 Pacific
Henderson W. P. 1 Metropolitan Mkt
Henings M. A. cor Mason and Bdwy
Hertz H. cor Stevenson and Ecker
Hickson H. 104 First
Hill H. O. 1113 Clay
Hirleman P. cor Mission and Stewart
Holst J. H. 45 Jackson
Hook C. cor Mason and Union
Hooper A. J. cor Mission and Twenty-Fourth
Hurley J. 4 Occidental Market
Iffert L. cor Dolores and Sixteenth
James W. T. 317 Fifth
Josse E. 1318 Stockton
Kaeb J. A. cor Mont and Union
Katz F. 617 Jackson
Kearns P. & Co. 36 Fourth
Keates George, 811 Fifth
Keller Fred. 513 Pacific
Kelly & Hanlon, 903 Howard
Kerrigan & Cardiff, cor Minna and Jane
Kerrigan J. 1098 Market
Knowles James, 154 First
Lafferty O. 546 Third
Lamaison M. 523 Pine
Laroche F. 1524 Stockton
Lauterwasser F. P. cor Clark and Davis
Lawlor G. W. 432 Third
Lemaitre F. 1402 Stockton
Lewis A. J. 240 Sixth
Lewis & Kearns, 36 Fourth
Litchfield W. D. 53 Washington Mkt
Loeb H. cor Stockton and Broadway
Maradins R. 645 Pacific
Marron J. cor Second and Tehama
McGlynn E. corner Harrison and Fifth Avenue
McInerney T. 311 Broadway
McMenomy J. W. 343 Fourth
Mengel J. cor Stockton and Sutter
Menges & Frankenheimer, 30 Metropolitan Market
Merchant T. S. 822 Jackson
Merkelbach W. 51 Everett
Merron J. cor Second and Tehama
Meyer A. 55 Sacramento

Meyer J. C. Gilbert nr Brannan
Meyer L. Larkin nr Pine
Meyer W. 258 Third
Meyerholz W. & Co. 702 Bush
Michel & Co. 329 Geary
MILLER L. & CO. 12 and 60 Washington Market (see adv. p. 656)
Miller W. X. cor Mason and Bdwy
Mocker W. cor O'Farrell and Mason
Mogan J. 47 Metropolitan Market
Molt J: P. 432 Third
Monbrone B. 310 Fifth
Moritz J. C. & Co. cor Powell and Filbert
Murr C. H. 215 Kearny
Nagel & Rothermel, cor Dupont and Green
Nauland & Whitman, cor Union and Powell
Neustadt L. 505 Broadway
Newman A. 2 Metropolitan Market
Nobmaun F. & Co. cor Sac and Leav
O'Brian M. (widow) 14 Wash Market
O'Brien M. cor Mission and Ninth
O'Neill R. 16 Washington Market
O'Rourke P. cor Minna and Jane
Ochs S. 10 Dupont
Oswald W. 1005 Pacific
Pensam J. J. Eighth nr Howard
Peterson S. B. & Co. cor Market and Stewart
Popp A. 1703 Stockton
Powers & Co. cor Folsom and Fremont
Raabe G. A. cor Ritch and Folsom :
Rosenberg & Hencken, cor Vallejo and Powell
Rosenberg L. cor Taylor and Post
Rosenberg M. & Co. 3 Occidental Mkt
Russell J. cor Montgomery and Vallejo
Rutherford Thos. 117 Fourth
Ryan M. J. 33 Everett
Ryder J. N. 709 Pacific
Saip E. Union Court nr Kearny
Schloss & Michal, 364 Third
Schmitt G. cor Sac and Market
Scholl & Mall, 34 Occidental Market
Schussler I. 1235 Dupont
Schwab F. 519 Geary
Smadec J. H. cor Folsom and Twenty-Second
Scott & Hall, cor Fifth and Shipley
Seibel E. 3 New Market
Seibel F. 33 Geary
Shine J. G. 343 Fourth
Shyne J. cor Fourth and Louisa
Silverstein M. 505 Broadway
Smith & Wilson, 27 Metropolitan Mkt
Smith W. cor Sixth and Mission
Souc Peter, 245 Fourth
Spohn J. 45 Jackson :
Stauffer R. cor Brannan and Ritch
Steckler H. 146 Second
Stephan J. G. 56 Washington Market
Stewart W. A. cor Wash and Powell
Storck & Hendy, 202 Fourth
Story S. C. 98 Occidental Market
Strauss B. 37 Third
Strehl C. 35 Occidental Market
Strehl J. cor Sixth and Mission
Stringer K. J. 9 Clay St. Market
Strobel & Fleig, 1129 Folsom
Sylvester H. 307 Sixth
Sylvester & Bro. 9 Kearny
Tighe W. J. & Co. corner Mason and O'Farrell
Uri F. 16 New Market
Van Doren J. cor Bush and Mason
Van Housen W. cor Mason and Eddy
Veasey & Robinson, corner Clay and Taylor
Wagner H. 1440 Stockton
Walz J. 741 Broadway
Watkins H. 452 Third
Wenner W. 77 Stevenson
Wenz J. D. cor Folsom and Ritch
Willoughby O. H. 151 Third
Willson & Stevens, 506 Market
Wissing J. cor First and Clementina
Wissing W. 232 First
Witzemann W. F. 425 East
Wood H. V. cor Hyde and Geary
Wood W. 18 Washington Market
Wray J. 11 Washington Market
Yates A. O. 41 Occidental Market
Yeaton O. T. cor Battery and Filbert
Zeh Bros. cor Union and Dupont

Butchers—Cattle. *Wholesale.*

Baldwin & Moffat, Ninth nr Brannan
Bazille J. Sixteenth nr Rhode Island
Burdick & Dooley, Brannan St. Bridge
Cabanness & Co. Brannan St. Bridge

Connolly N. Potrero Avenue
Conway John, Potrero
Crummie & O'Neill, Potrero
Hebert Z. Santa Clara nr Jersey
Horn Barney, cor Mariposa and Florida
Johnson & McCann, Brannan nr Ninth
Kerr Charles, Potrero
Lumes X. Sixteenth nr Rhode Island
Miller & Lux, 536 Kearny
Metzger & Co. Potrero
O'Brien W. Ninth nr Brannan
Peres L. & Co. Potrero Avenue
Selig M. & Co. Potrero
Shrader A. J. 534 Clay
Smith & Co. Potrero
Zimmerman H. Potrero
Zimmerman J. & Co. Potrero

Butchers—Hog. *Wholesale.*

Andrews Oliver, Ninth nr Brannan
Arnold Benjamin E. 536 Kearny
Arnold F. D. cor Bryant and Tenth
Kelly Peter, El Dorado nr Potrero Av
Schafer H. Ninth nr Brannan
Schinkel Peter, cor Tenth and Bryant
Willoughby J. R. Potrero

Butchers—Sheep. *Wholesale.*

Baca & Co. 402 Montgomery
Dulhorn & Barker, Potrero
Harrington Bros. cor Alameda and Potrero
Larroche Vincent, cor Fifteenth and Potrero
Lawler Joseph, Brannan St. Bridge
Mahoney Dennis, Pacific nr Larkin
O'Donnell William, Potrero
Penguillam Eugene & Bro. Sixteenth nr Potrero Avenue
Regan Bros. cor Tenth and Bryant
Reiner A. Potrero Avenue
Schmith C. Potrero Avenue
Sedgley Joseph, 536 Kearny
Smith Wm. Potrero

Butter. *Importers.*

Cutter J. H. 511 Front
Dodge Bros. & Co. 406 Front
Newton J. B. & Co. 108 California
Patrick J. & Co. 617 Battery
Smith Stephen, 400 Front
Strybing C. H. 212 Jackson
[See Commission Merchants; Groceries; Produce.]

Cabinet Makers.

Aubrey F. O. 302 Third
Boisnce A. 3 Stockton
Bryant & Co. 313 Market
Buckley J. cor Vallejo and Polk
Buckner C. 719 Mission
Cohen N. Clara nr Bush
Collins D. J. 613 Mission
Conrad A. 414 Pine
Davies Shadrach, 904 Clay
Easton & Bro. 725 Market
Erkins W. 611 Jackson
Foster J. & Co. 314 Pine
Hanson J. P. 1502 Stockton
Haussler & Fonemann, 231 Jackson
Heinzenberger J. A. cor August Alley and Union
Hometz J. 757 Mission
Johnson C. 213 Kearny
Keller L. 305 Pine
Kerner P. 132 Sutter
Kind R. C. T. 612 Battery
Luchsinger J. B. 116 Bush
Ludwig J. A. 757 Mission
Miller J. M. 329½ Kearny
Moore B. P. 314 Pine
PEIRCE J. 415 California
Provines W. 303 Third
Rolland J. 837 Dupont
Roux F. cor Fourth and Everett
Schallich L. 523 Kearny
Schuemann E. 429 Kearny
Scouler J. Wallace Place
Sheble G. 741 Pacific
Sherman J. 304 Dupont
Simen J. Bush nr Sansom
Soule H. 518 Front
Ungemach J. M. 146 Third
Wachter C. 307 Market
Weismann H. 719 Mission
Wigmore John, 423 California
Williams M. 518 Front
Wyman O. 106 Davis
Young S. 625 Market
Zeis John, 5 Dupont

Calkers.
[See Shipwrights.]

Camphene Distillers.

DAY THOMAS (importer) 732 Mont
Dietz & Co. (oil) 519 Front and 56 Second
HARRISON C. H. 517 Front
Hollub & Co. cor Front and Wash
McMahon F. P. & Co. 404 Front
Stanford Brothers, Pacific, 125 Cal
Stott C. cor Chestnut and Taylor

Candle Manufacturers.
[See Soap.]

Cap Manufacturers.

Alexander S. 1110 Dupont
Fleisher W. 405 California
Kalisher S. & Co. 414 Sacramento
Lang C. Mrs. 728 Washington
Lust S. 408 Sacramento
MEUSSDORFFER K. 635 Commercial
Rosenberg G. (army and navy) 410 Sac
[See Hats and Caps.]

Car Manufacturers.

Casebolt H. & Co. cor Market and Fifth
Kimball G. P. & Co. Market nr Fourth
STEPHENSON JOHN, 27 East Twenty-Seventh Street, New York (see advertisement, p. cviii)
[See Carriage and Wagon Manufacturers.]

Cards—Machine.

EARLE T. K. & CO. Worcester, Mass. (see advertisement, p. cli)

Carpenters and Builders.

Alexander D. G. 227 Bush
Allen J. D. 196 Stevenson
Ashmead G. S. 318 Dupont
Ballentine J. cor Sansom and Halleck
Bergson Ole, 111 Leidesdorff
Bovyer W. L. 417 Pine
Brooks E. L. 763 Mission
Brown & Hussey, Summer nr Mont
Brown J. 208 Washington
Buckley F. Fifth nr Howard
Burrows J. 763 Mission
Caldwell C. M. 607 Market
Clapp M. W s Leidesdorff bet Pine and California
Clark J. cor Third and Harrison
Collins B. 627 California
Comins P. B. 1067 Broadway
Connell J. D. 1026 Pacific
Conrad A. 414 Pine
Consolez D. 949 Howard
Corcoran William, 325 Pine
Cottle F. D. 42 Fremont
Curry E. L. 809 Jackson
Curtis J. P. 320 Jackson
Cutter A. J. 806 Clay
Danner F. A. 757 Mission
Downey J. H. cor Third and Harrison
Doyle J. J. 812 Pacific
Duncan J. W. 1216 Taylor
Eastman W. H. 637 California
Eckert & Carruthers, Summer nr Mont
Edgerly C. L. 319 Bush
Ford Elisha, Seal Rock House
Gale John, 17 Fourth
George L. F. 905 Stockton
Giles F. M. 435 Jackson
Grant John, 623 Dupont
Gunner C. 421 Sansom
Hargitt G. 17 Geary
Harlow J. 109 O'Farrell
Harvey C. L. 114 Dupont
Hutchinson C. & W. 304 Pine
Hynes W. H. 71 Fourth
Ivory J. T. 571 Mission
Jorres W. 525 California
Josclyn J. B. 152 Tehama
Keith J. W. 730 Harrison
Kells W. F. 408 Jackson
Keyes J. A. cor Mason and Jackson
Lacey C. 714 Sansom
Lowry J. & McLagan, 129 Second
Meyers A. 729 Pacific
Miller A. Leavenworth nr California
Muhs D. 501 Broadway
Murray R. J. 670 Market
Nunan Edward, 321 Pine
Packard C. 320 Jackson

Pinkham F. W. 818 Clay
Pratt & Jacobs, 118 Washington
Quackenbush T. M. 534 Jackson
Quinn & McConnell, 450 Natoma
Reese E. A. 194 Geary
Renault J. P. 610 Vallejo
RICE EDWARD, Leidesdorff nr California (see advertisement, p. 662)
Roach T. M. 15 Leidesdorff
Sedgly A. 316 Pine
Shaw G. T. 320 Jackson
Sheldon H. B. 571 Mission
Smith P. L. & Son, cor Valencia and Nineteenth
Snyder A. A. 62 Halleck
Southwell G. 761 Clay
Storer J. B. 31 Webb
Torrey E. N. 439 Jackson
Tucker W. 614 Green
Valentine A. Sutter nr Kearny
Van Brunt H. C. 114 Dupont
Wheeler R. H. 439 Jackson
Whittier R. 208 Washington
Whyte J. P. 21 Sutter
Widber J. 740 Mission
Wissinger J. W. 408 Jackson
Wood H. H. 936 Market
Wright J. B. & Co. cor Powell and Union

Carpets.
* Importers.

*BELL JOHN C. SW cor California and Sansom (see adv. p. xlv)
*EDWARDS F. G. 646 Clay (see adv. front cover)
Fuhr C. A. 626 Market
*Gullixon & Nelson, 336 Kearny
*Hixon William M. 606 Clay
*KENNEDY & BELL, SW cor Mont and Cal (see adv. front cover)
Lenhardt A. 1232 Stockton
*LOUGHRAN P. F. & Co. 403 Sansom (see advertisement, p. xxx)
McElwee & Ackerman, 235 Mont
Morgan W. 1224 Stockton
Plum C. M. 22 Montgomery
Rosenfeld H. 14 Third
Solomon B. L. & Sons, cor Pine and Battery
Stringer W. J. 520 Washington
Troutt H. J. M. 618 Market
*WALTER D. N. & E. & CO. 303 and 305 California (see adv. p. cxli)
*WIGHTMAN & HARDIE, 416 Clay (see advertisement, p. xlix)

Carriage and Wagon Depots.

Casebolt H. & Co. corner Market and Fifth
Eells R. S. & Co. cor Front and Pine
Hill & Eastman, 618 Battery
Kimball & Co. Market nr Fourth
MEEKER JAMES & CO. 12 Pine (see advertisement, p. xl)
Waterhouse & Lester, 29 Battery
Willey O. F. & Co. 316 California

Carriage and Wagon Manufacturers.
* Importers.

Andreasen Bros. 119 Sansom
Andrews C. N. cor Main and Howard
Bath & Morrison, 118 Bush
Belduke & Co. 820 Folsom
Black & Miller, 717 Market
Brown W. R. Grand Av nr Mission
Burnham A. W. 321 Pine
*Casebolt H. & Co. corner Market and Fifth
Dacoumon & Lowney, 535 Market
*Eells R. S. & Co. cor Front and Pine
Folsom & Hiller, 531 California
Gallagher & Farren, 112 Bush
Gallagher & Rodecker, 115 Pine
Gebbard & Boynton, 113 Bush
Holmes M. P. 417 Pine
*Kimball G. P. & Co. Market nr Fourth
Larkins & Co. cor Summer and Spring
Lawton & Co. 932 Market
Matthai J. C. H. 607 Battery
McGivern P. 29 Webb
McLaughlin & Feisel, 121 Bush
*MEEKER JAMES & CO. 12 Pine (see advertisement, p. xl)
Pollard & Carvill, 37 Webb
Ross S. F. 72 Powell
*Rudman & Co. cor Pine and Front
Searls A. & Co. 417 Market
Shute & Bro. (springs) 539 Market

Sicotte & Roberts, 249 Fourth
Sprung & McArron, 579 Market
Stein, Link & Scherb, 743 Market
Vosburgh & Hicks, Folsom nr Fourth
*Willey O. F. & Co. 316 California
Winall & Clapp, 505 Market

Carriage and Wagon Smiths.
[See Blacksmiths.]

Carriage and Wagon Stock.
Casebolt G. T. & Co. 214 Pine
Eells R. S. & Co. cor Front and Pine
Hill & Eastman, 618 Battery
Kimball P. & Co. Market nr Fourth
Mann G. S. 207 Market
MEEKER JAMES & CO. 12 Pine
Searls A. & Co. 417 Market
WATERHOUSE & LESTER, 29 Battery (see adv. p. xlv)

Carvers and Gilders.
Bryant & Co. (ornamental) 313 Beale
Gereau W. B. (ship) Drumm nr Pac
Hofer H. G. 838 Clay
JONES, WOOLL & SUTHERLAND, 312 Montgomery (see adv. p. xxxvi)
Moise H. (restorer old paintings) 181 Jessie
NILE & KOLLMYER, 312 Bush (see advertisement, p. xlvii)
Parkinson & Mahony, 415 Kearny
Power & Warren, 27 Fremont
ROOS JOSEPH, 219 Montgomery
Shaddock W. 650 Market
SNOW & CO. corner Washington and Sansom (see adv. p. lxviii)

Cask Manufacturers.
[See Coopers.]

Caviar Manufacturers.
Saulmann & Lauenstein, 506 Mont

Cement.
Adams S. cor Market and Main
Davis & Cowell, cor Front and Wash
Walton N. C. 29 Market
Webb & Holmes, cor Davis and Sac
[See Lime and Cement.]

Cemetery Fences.
[See Carpenters.]

Cement Pipe.
BROWELL J. 530 Clay (see advertisement, p. xlviii)

Charcoal.
[See Wood and Coal.]

Chemical Works.
San Francisco Chemical Works Co. office SE cor Battery and Com

Chemists.
Dickey G. S. (pharmaceutical) corner Howard and Third
Hanks H. G. 622 Clay
Hewston J. jr. (analytical) 416 Mont
Hucks J. J. Francisco nr Mason
Keith W. H. & Co. 521 Montgomery
KELLOGG, HEWSTON & CO. (analytical) 416 Montgomery
Steele J. G. (manufacturing) 521 Mont
Thayer B. B. cor Mont and Bush
Wilson W. 632 Mission

Chinese Goods.
[See Chinese Merchants.]

Chiropodists.
Kennedy B. C. 12 Montgomery
Rosenberg M. 507 Kearny

Chocolate.
[See Coffee; Spices, Etc.]

Chronometers.
BARRETT & SHERWOOD, 517 Montgomery (see adv. inside cover)
McGREGOR J. 409 Sansom (see advertisement, p. lxx)
Pace C. 613 Battery

Rack J. C. 203 Montgomery
SCHMOLZ WM. 430 Montgomery (see advertisement, p. 669)
SHERWOOD R. 517 Montgomery (see advertisement, p. 11)
SHREVE G. C. & CO. 525 Montgomery (see advertisement, p. xliv)
Tennent Thos. cor Battery and Oregon
[See Watches.]

Cider Dealers.
Cutting & Co. 202 Front
Erzgraber & Goetjen, 120 Davis
McNamee M. & Co. 129 Pacific
Myers B. K. cor Santa Clara and Connecticut
Oakley & Jackson, 320 Front
Provost D. R. & Co. 413 Front
[See Vinegar, Etc.]

Cigars.   Importers and Jobbers.
Cassou P. 713 Sansom
Crozat P. 613 Sansom
Drinkhouse J. A. & Co. 228 Front
EMERY C. G. 518 Battery (see advertisement, p. 652)
Fahlsten C. J. E. 434 Jackson
Hirstel E. cor Montgomery and Clay
Horn B. C. & Co. SW cor Front and Clay
Mayblum M. cor Sac and Front
Morgenthau M. 418 Sacramento
Oppenheimer & Bro. 311 Clay
Patrick & Co. 617 Battery
ROSENBAUM A. S. & CO. SE corner Battery and Clay (see adv. p. lxviii)
Sanjurjo, Bolado & Pujol, 713 Sansom
Weil & Co. 226 Front
Wertheimer L. & E. cor Front and Sac

Cigars.   Makers.
Boyle F. R. 705 Davis
Brand H. 408 Clay
Caspar I. & Co. 526 Merchant
Cohen King, 942 Kearny
Crown H. 414 Sacramento
Eisenberg E. 723 Sansom
EMERY C. G. 518 Battery
Engelbrecht & Mayrisch Brothers, 314 Front
Esberg M. & Co. cor Sac and Front
Friedberg & Rosenshine, 214 Pacific
Gensler L. & Co. 309 East
Goslinsky E. 316 Front
Graff S. & Co. 1102 Dupont
Harris J. 419 Brannan
Inslee & Joseph, 326 Montgomery
Kalmuk M. 414 Sacramento
Kuhlmeyer H. 228 Third
Lewis Bros. 421 Clay
Lichtenstein M. 19 Pacific
Mann A. 232 Montgomery
Michaelsen & Elfers, 300 Jackson
Modry M. cor Bush and Devisidero
Moran P. & T. 710 Battery
Morris J. 744 Commercial
Rosenberg N. 408 Sacramento
Schonfeld & Bremer, 311 Pine
Schwerin E. 419 Brannan
Troost C. 1322 Dupont
Vogelsdorff J. 421 Battery
White I. K. 221 Sacramento
Zaborwski J. A. Potrero Avenue near Sixteenth

Cigars.   Retail.
Arnheim S. S. 322 Montgomery
Auerbach L. What Cheer House
Baker F. W. 705 Davis
Bearwald T. 714 Kearny
Becker Bros. 714 Washington and cor Montgomery and Clay
Benrimo J. Occidental Hotel
Berroa A. 613 Pacific
Bingham Edw. cor Sutter and Sansom
Brand E. Cosmopolitan Hotel
Breslauer B. 314 Sansom
Charpentier A. 710 Market
Chenot E. cor Fourth and Folsom
Claussen J. 121 Kearny
Cohn E. 627 Clay
Cohn J. 228 Battery
Cox J. 210 Montgomery
Crown H. 414 Sacramento
Davidson & Poppe, cor Com and Bat
Davis Daniel, 612 Washington
Diller G. W. 621 Montgomery
Eckstein A. 15 Montgomery
Eliasar A. 929 Kearny
Emery S. S. 614 Montgomery

Falconer H. cor Third and Market
Frey Sam, 46 Fourth
Freidberg M. 56 Third
Friedlander P. cor Market and Fourth
Glick K. 254 Third
Goldstein S. 336 Sansom
Graaff S. & Co. 539 Clay and 1102 Dupont
Gruaz M. 1438 Stockton
Gumpertz G. 650 Sacramento
Hansen·F. 525 East
Heiman L. American Exchange
HEUCK H. H. 233 Kearny (see advertisement, page 660)
Hirstel E. cor Montgomery and Clay
Hirstel N. A. Russ House
Hobe & Weihe, cor Wash and Dupont
Hoffman S. 338 Third
Holst J. C. 321 Montgomery
Howell M. C. 616 Montgomery
Imhaus L. cor Sansom and Com
Inslee & Joseph, 326 Montgomery
Irvine G. 704 Market
Jacoby G. cor Front and Sacramento
Jurgens A. 10 First
Koehler Bros. 804 Market
Kosminsky Bros. 322 Sansom
Krohn F. 317 Pacific
Kuetner L. cor Jackson and Kearny
Laporte J. B. 706 Market
Latz J. 413 Montgomery
Leavy & Bro. 526 Montgomery
Levy J. 262 Jessie
Lipman L. cor Clay and Kearny
Magauran P. H. 252 Fourth
Mann A. 232 Montgomery
Mattat M. 916 Dupont
McFarland A. 635 Pacific
Medau J. & P. cor Dupont and Pacific
Medau J. J. cor Davis and Broadway
Meyer A. 629 Kearny
Meyer & Brother, 335 Pine
Mitchell J. E. 4 Second
Morelos A. 646 Pacific
Morton S. P. 226 Montgomery
Moss E. W. Bank Exchange
Nicol W. 532 Sacramento
Oehlert H. 7 Stewart
Ohrt C. 521 Clay
Pargo A. 717 Montgomery
Pilitzer M. 209 Fourth
Plagemann, Kanzee & Co. 4 Kearny
Pratt N. 112 Sansom
Prinz John, 49 Second
Raphael I. & Co. 430 Kearny
Schmidt C. & H. cor Wash and Kearny
Schonfeld & Bremer, 311 Pine
Schuch L. 12 Sansom
Schulze F. 540 Commercial
Schumann H. corner Montgomery and California and Kearny and Cal
Schwartz H. 607 Commercial
Shocken A. L. 510 Kearny
Shoenberg L. 22 Clay
Siebert F. 218 Kearny
Smith C. W. 538 Merchant
Solomon J. cor East and Washington
Son A. A. 426 Montgomery
Stein S. cor Davis and Pacific
Steinfeld J. 223 Pacific
Strolin E. F. & Co. cor Kearny and Pac
Sutliff Thos. 832 Kearny
Toelken H. 58 Second
Tostmann H. 118 Second
Troost C. 1322 Dupont
Ulmer M. 605 Kearny
Villaverde A. 535 Broadway
Wagener F. O. & Co. 504 Montgomery
Weil J. 1016 Stockton
Wiener A. 308 Kearny
Woeldecke F. 504 Kearny
Wrede W. 705 Clay
Young W. E. 902 Kearny

Claim Agents.
Fogle O. B. 617 Montgomery
RANSOM L. 625 Merchant (see advertisement, p. lxix)
Robinson J. R. 626 Montgomery
Stevenson J. D. 604 Merchant
Wakeman F. O. Phœnix Building

Clergymen.
Aerden James H. Rev. pastor Saint Bridget's Church, Van Ness Av nr Broadway
Afferbach C. H. pastor German M. E. Church
Alemany Joseph S. Most Rev. (R. C.) Archbishop S. F., St. Mary's Cathedral, dwl 602 Dupont

Andolshek Andrew Rev. ass't pastor St. Boniface's Church, Sutter nr Montgomery
Bartlett W. C. Rev. 536 Clay
Beckwith E. G. Rev. Third Congregational Church, dwl Mission bet Fourteenth and Fifteenth
Benton J. A. Rev. Second Congregational Church, dwl 1032 Pine
Bertolio J. M. St. Ignatius' Church
Bissell E. C. Rev. pastor Fourth Congregational Church, dwl cor Dupont and Lombard
Blain J. D. Rev. dwl 451 Natoma
Brennan R. P. Rev. vice president St. Mary's College
Brotherton T. W. Rev. St. John's Church, Mission Dolores, dwl Ashland Place
Brueck H. Rev. pastor German M. E. Church, dwl Folsom nr Fourth
Buchard J. M. Rev. St. Ignatius' College
Buehler J. M. Rev. First German Evangelical Lutheran Church, dwl 29 O'Farrell
Buel F. Rev. 757 Market
Burrowes George Rev. D.D. SE cor Geary and Stockton
Caldwell E. J. Rev. ass't pastor St. Bridget's Church, cor Broadway and Van Ness Avenue
Cheney D. B. Rev. D.D. pastor First Baptist Church, dwl Taylor nr Pac
Cian A. Rev. St. Ignatius' College
Clark O. Rev. D.D. dwl NE cor Washington and Jones
Clarke Chas. Russell Rev. cor Mason and O'Farrell
Cohn E. Rev. Emanu-El, 235 Post
Conglato N. Rev. St. Ignatius' College
Cotter J. Rev. St. Francis' Church, dwl 519 Green
Croke James Very Rev. V.G. rector St. Mary's Cathedral
Deininger C. F. Rev. 635 Mission
Derham H. Rev. O.S.D. St. Francis' Ch
Dierking C. Rev. German M. E. dwl 858 Folsom
Duggan M. R. O.S.D. ass't pastor St. Bridget's Church
Durham H. Rev. ass't pastor St. Francis' Church, dwl 519 Green
Easton G. A. Rev. ass't pastor Grace Cathedral, dwl 1006 Pine
Fackler J. G. Rev. pastor Central Presbyterian Church, dwl 37 Fifth
Fitzgerald O. P. Rev. pastor Minna St. M. E. Church, dwl Francisco nr Dupont
Gallagher H. P. Rev. St. Joseph's Church, dwl Tenth nr Folsom
Gallagher J. A. Rev. pastor St. Joseph's Church, dwl Tenth nr Folsom
Gibney Thomas Rev. ass't St. Patrick's Church
Goodwin H. Rev. ass't Grace Cathedral, dwl 828 California
Grey P. J. Rev. St. Mary's College
Harker G. M. Rev. pastor Wesleyan Church, dwl corner Hickory and North Avenue
Harrington J. Rev. St. Mary's Cathedral
Henry H. A. Rev. Sherith Israel, dwl 736 Green
Hill J. B. Rev. pastor Central M. E. Church, dwl 524 Tehama
Hodges J. R. Rev. ass't St. Francis' Church, dwl 519 Green
Howell Thomas Rev. (colored) pastor Third Baptist Church, dwl Oak bet Taylor and Mason
Loomis A. W. Rev. Chinese Missionary, dwl NE cor Stockton and Sac
Ludlow J. P. Rev. pastor Post St. Baptist Church, dwl Hyde nr Bush
Maraschi A. Rev. S.J. St. Ignatius, dwl S s Market bet Fourth and Fifth
McAllister F. Marion Rev. Church of the Advent, dwl 421 First
McMonagle J. H. Rev. Army Chaplain, dwl 109 Powell
Molinier J. Rev. Notre Dame des Victoires, dwl Bush nr Stockton
Moore J. J. Rev. (colored) M. E. Zion, dwl 331 Union
Mooshake F. Rev. German Lutheran, dwl 245 Stevenson
Neri J. Rev. St. Ignatius' College
O'Ferrall M. E. Rev. St. Ignatius' College

O'Neill Thos. Rev. pastor St. Bridget's Church, cor Broadway and Van Ness Avenue
Peck J. T. Rev. D.D. pastor Howard St. M. E. Church, dwl Hubbard nr Howard
Prendergast John Rev. St. Francis' Church, Mission Dolores
Rowell Joseph Rev. Mariners' Church, dwl 1106 California
Sawtelle H. A. Rev. pastor Second Baptist Church, dwl 463 Minna
Scudder H. M. Rev. pastor Howard Presbyterian Church, dwl 1 Vernon Place
Skinner J. A. Rev. pastor First Presbyterian Church, dwl 816 Powell
Slattery W. Rev. pastor Mission Dolores' Church
Smith A. B. Rev. (col'd) pastor Zion Church, dwl 1419 Mason
Stebbins Horatio, Rev. pastor (Unitarian) Geary nr Stock, dwl 930 Clay
Stromburg N. Rev. German Lutheran, dwl 709 Stockton
Strong J. D. Rev. Larkin Street Presbyterian, dwl Union nr Hyde
Thomas E. Rev. dwl 1106 Mason
Wadsworth Charles Rev. D.D. pastor Calvary Presbyterian Church, dwl 920 Pine
Ward Thomas M. D. Rev. (col'd) M. E. dwl 532 Bush
Warren J. H. Rev. 402 Front
Weisler A. Rev. pastor Congregation Emanu-El, dwl 1818 Powell
Wheeler F. B. Rev. pastor First Congregational Church, dwl 33 South Park
Williams Albert Rev. dwl 706 Cal
Williamson P. S. Rev. pastor Dutch Reformed Church, dwl 629 Cal
Wolf S. Rev. St. Boniface (R. C. German) 122 Sutter
Wyatt C. B. Rev. Trinity Church, dwl 812 Bush
Wyatt C. B. Rev. St. M. E. Church, dwl 1008 Wash

Cloaks and Mantillas.

Berkowitz M. 626 Sacramento
Ehrhard A. 648 Sacramento
Eisen & Co. 104 Montgomery
Goldsmith H. 625 Sacramento
Leszynski L. 638 Sacramento
Meyer & Jonasson, 10 Montgomery
Morgenstern M. 410 Kearny
Ney J. L. 14 Montgomery
Sullivan Thomas & Co. 24 Montgomery
Wolf W. 619 Sacramento
Wurkheim M. 615 Sacramento
[See Millinery Goods.]

Clocks. *Importers.*

Haynes & Lawton, NE cor Sansom and Merchant
Lehmann Geo. 525 Sacramento
Parker G. H. 303 Montgomery
Swain S. & Co. cor Sansom and Pine
[See Watches; Jewelry, Etc.]

Clothing. *Wholesale Jobbers.*

*Importers.
Alexander J. & Co. 312 Sansom
*BADGER & LINDENBERGER, 415 Battery (see adv. p. xliii)
Baum J. 407 and 409 Commercial
*Cohn Henry & Co. 413 and 415 Sac
*Fechheimer, Goodkind & Co. 521 Sac
Haas S. & Co. 322 Commercial
*Heuston, Hastings & Co. cor Battery and Pine
*Jennings & Brewster, 222 and 224 Bat
*King L. & Bro. 213 and 215 Battery
*Kohn M. & Co. cor Battery and Sac
*Mayer S. & Bro. 307 California
*MEAD J. R. & CO. NW cor Sansom and Washington, and 200 Montgomery (see advertisement cover)
*Meyer Wm. & Co. cor Sac and San
*Rubber Clothing Company (rubber) 118 Montgomery
*Schafer & Bro. 509 Sacramento
*Scholle Bros. 405 and 407 Sacramento
*Seligman S. & Co. 121 Battery
*Steinhart W. & I. 321 Sacramento
*Strauss L. & Co. 315 Sacramento
Toklas, Wise & Co. 308 California
Weidenrich & Lehmann, 414 Com

Clothing. *Boys or Children.*

Clements M. Miss, 152 Third
Cohen H. Mrs. 240 Third
Dannenberg A. Mrs. (Infants') 618 Sac
Durning T. Miss, 10 Second
Fletcher C. A, 1 Montgomery
Lion J, Miss (Infants') 857 Clay
LOCKWOOD H. M. & Co. 624 Clay
Rosenthal & Co. 14 Second

Clothing. *Retail.*

* Importers.
Abrahams L. 10 Clay
Alexander S. O. SE cor Jackson and Dupont
Arnheim S. 315 Pacific
Asher S. 14 Stewart
Badt M. 505 and 527 Commercial
Baum J. 407 Commercial
Baum J. & Bro. 424 Mont
Benjamin & Brown, 305 Kearny
Blum I. 411 Montgomery
Brodek Bros. 339 Kearny
Caro S. 54 Third
Citron M. L. 181 Pacific
Clayburgh A. & Co. 418 Montgomery
Cline S. 409 East
Cohen M. 516 Commercial
Cohn L. 417 Commercial
Cohn L. B. 921 Kearny
Cohn M. 413 Commercial
Cohn M. B. 181 Jackson
Cohn S. 509 and 525 Commercial
Coleman M. 110 Third
*Colman Bros. cor Mont and Wash
Cowen H. & B. 327 East
Dahlmann C. & Co. 526 Sacramento
Dake E. C. 541 Washington
Davis & Schafer, Quincy Hall 545 Wash
Davis Max, 607 Pacific
Eaton J. 822 Kearny
Estrem J. 506 Washington
Farrell P. 222 Pacific
Feder Louis, 254 Stewart
Fisher S. 527 Jackson
Fletcher C. A, 1 Montgomery
Foulk Levi, 261 Third
Frank E. 213 Pacific
Franklin D. 511 Davis
*Fraser J. (agent Rubber) 118 Mont
Froomberg Bros. 419 Commercial
Gilbert M. & Co. 58 Third
Gilbert Michael, 22 Third
Goldberg P. 421 East
Goodman & Linder, 235 Kearny
Green H. 105 Pacific
Haas S. & Co. 428 Montgomery
Harris Isaac, 613 Davis
Harris S. 212 Stewart
*Heuston Hastings & Co. cor Montgomery and Sutter
Hintze Isaac, 20 Sutter
Hudson G. B. & Co. 327 Sansom
Hyams G. J. S. 431 Montgomery
Ichon E. F. 325 Sansom
Isaaca A. 903 Kearny
Isaacs M. 1032 Dupont
Jacobs A. 227 Pacific
Jakubowski & Warszaur, 538 Clay and 342 Kearny
Joseph I. & Co. cor Mont and Pine
Karn F. Mrs. cor Mont and Pacific
Kirsky & Bro. 617 Pacific
Kohlman & Galinger, 637 Market
Kohn E. S. 651 Washington
Kopp F. 723 Clay
Levi A. 403 Commercial
Levy H. 110 Third
Levy M. 11 Jackson
Levy M. B. & Bro. 333 East
Lindenberg I. 52 Stewart
LOCKWOOD H. M. & Co. 624 Clay (see adv. p. xliv)
Loebenstein J. 220 Kearny
Lohmann & Moesta, 644 Clay
*Loveland I. & Co. 211 Montgomery
Lovich C. 40 First
Marks H. 24 Stewart
Martin J. M. 528 Sacramento
MEAD J. R. & CO. cor Mont and Bush and Washington and Sansom (see advertisement, back cover)
Meyer J. C. 915 Kearny
Meyerstein H. 313 Kearny
Meyerstein & Lowenberg, 301 Kearny
Michael S. 129 Pacific
Morganstern S. cor Pacific and Front
Nathan S. 112 Stewart
Pelser I. & N. 201 Montgomery
Peyser H. 405 Pacific
Plato D. 307 East

Plåtshek & Co. 537 Commercial
Roper D. 405 Commercial
Sanford T. G. 223 Montgomery
SHERMAN WM. & CO. 414 Sansom
(see advertisement, p. xxxviii)
Solomon L. 48 Stewart
Stone M. 411 Commercial
Straus M. 6 Third
Strelitz J. 11 Stewart
Warshawski J. & Bro. 656 Washington
Weidenrich, Lehman & Co. 414 Com

Clothing.   Oil.

Appel S. & Co. 322 Commercial

Cloths and Woolen Goods.

*Importers.

Goldsmith L. 612 Sacramento
*LANZENBERG & CO. 628 Clay (see advertisement, p. xlv)
Levy M. 608 Sacramento
*STEIN, SIMON & CO. 632 Sacramento and 631 Com (see adv. p. xxx)
*Well E. & Son, 630 Sacramento
[See Dry Goods.]

Coal Oil.   Lamps, Etc.

*Importers.

*Dietz A. C. & Co. 519 Front, cor Clay and Kearny and 56 Second
Hemenway & Merrill, 215 Sacramento
*Hollub A. & Co. 501 Front
Levitzsky D. & Co. 54 Second
Owens J. B. 10 Third
*Stanford Bros 125 California
*Swain R. A. & CO. cor Pine and San
Urquhart S. F. 512 Sansom
Vagts G. 1428 Stockton

Coal Yards.

Anderson Thomas, 737 Jackson
Doyle J. R. 413 Pacific
Dwyer & Co. 539 California
Ebbets A. M. 115 Sacramento
Glas F. 25 Washington
GREENHOOD, NEWBAUER & KLEIN, cor Market and Main and 209 Sansom (see adv. p. 662)
Haste & Kirk, 515 Cal and 35 Beale
Henderson J. 836 Washington
Jaffe L. 133 Sutter
Johnson J. M. 215 Jackson
Ramsdell B. H. 110 Jackson
Rosenfeld John (scales and storage) cor Folsom and Spear
Sinclair & Moody, 212 Clay
Storm C. 115 Sacramento
Thompson R. A. & Co. 126 Sutter
Van Winkle I. S. & Co. cor Battery and Bush
Whipple S. B. Mission nr Beale
Wolf Brothers, 19 Battery
[See Wood and Coal.]

Coffee Factories.

BERNARD C. 707 Sansom (see advertisement, p. xl)
Gates H. Eagle, 110 Fremont
Ghirardelli D. & Co. 415 Jackson
Marden & Folger, 220 Front
Strelitz J. & Co. 25 Second
Tyler S. H. 110 Fremont
VENARD P. G. 627 Front (see advertisement, p. 665)
Zwick & Loeven (extract) 725 Vallejo

Coffee Houses.

Antonuvich F. cor Clay and East
Besson F. & G. 520 Merchant
Boghischich & Metrovich, 715 Davis
Brown C. P. 517 East
Carubino & Louis, 939 Kearny
Clark F. 12 Stewart
Costudia G. cor Com and Leidesdorff
Ellich J. cor Commercial and East
Johnson & Peterson, 531 East
Jury John & Bro. 524 Merchant
Lastreto L. 513 Commercial
Lelong J. 413 Davis
Luxich & Drobaz, 503 East
Matich N. cor Market and East
Mauletti & Co. cor San and Merchant
Moron & Ratto, 10 Stewart
Peterson L. 628 Broadway
Radovich A. cor Stewart and Mission
Roth John, 150 Stewart
Shneder P. 31 Fourth
Simon & Nagle, 631 Pacific
Williams T. cor Merchant and East
[See Restaurants.]

Coffin Warehouses.

GRAY N. 641 Sacramento (see advertisement, p. 658)
MASSEY A. 651 Sacramento (see advertisement, p. 657)

Colleges.

California Collegiate Institute, Miss M. Lammond, 64 Silver
Charlemagne (private) Broadway nr Stockton
City, Rev. Dr. Burrowes, cor Geary and Stockton
Pacific Business, M. K. Laudenslager, 747 Market
SANTA CLARA, Santa Clara County (see advertisement, p. xvii)
ST. IGNATIUS', Market near Fourth (see advertisement, p. xvi)
ST. MARY'S, Old San José Road (see advertisement, p. lxii)
Toland Medical, Stockton nr Chestnut
UNION, Dr. R. T. Huddart, 501 Second (see advertisement, p. xviii)
[See Teachers; Schools.]

Collectors.

Arnold O. B. 626 Clay
Ashton Charles, 415 Pine
Bibbins & Garland, 540 Clay
Blake P. H. 613 Market
Buffandeau E. B. 528 Clay
Childs C. W. 528 Montgomery
Dessaa J. 617 Clay
Drew H. P. 604 Merchant
Fogle O. B. 617 Montgomery
Fraser & Co. cor Clay and Battery
Gardner C. A. 604 Merchant
Gay Charles, 415 Pine
Gushee F. A. 528 Montgomery
Hoffman J. A. & Co. 604 Merchant
Hoogs & Madison, 424 Montgomery
Kaiser M. 604 Merchant
LeMare J. J. 626 Clay
Linn H. T. F. 35 Exchange Building
McLaughlin M. P. 604 Merchant
Miller J. H. 404 Montgomery
Miller W. H. 538 Clay
PULVERMAN B. 526 Montgomery (see advertisement, p. 651)
Spaulding C. A. 328 Montgomery
Taylor F. W. 723 Montgomery
Tompkins A. L. 402 Montgomery
Wilcocks B. 410 Montgomery

Commercial Agencies.

[See Mercantile Agencies.]

Commission Merchants.

[See Merchants.]

Commissioners Deeds.

Andrews W. O. 630 Montgomery
Barstow A. 24 Montgomery Block
Blood J. H. 7 Montgomery Block
Brenham C. J. 205 Halleck
Congdon E. B. 620 Washington
CORNWALL P. B. 608 Merchant (see advertisement, p. 664)
Garniss J. R. 526 Washington
Gould A. S. 528 Clay
Knox G. T. 613 Montgomery
Quarles W. A. 327 Montgomery
Sawyer O. V. cor Clay and Mont
Sinton B. H. 406 Montgomery
Smith N. P. 526 Montgomery
Stevenson J. D. 604 Merchant
Taylor J. M. 636 Clay
Thibault P. J. 605 Montgomery
Williams A. 535 Clay
[See Notaries Public.]

Confectioners.

Albrecht R. 1006 Folsom
Baker & Co. 1125 Dupont
Baker J. Dupont nr Broadway
Behre H. C. 210 Stockton
Bernheim M. (manufac'r) 408 Clay
Booth N. B. & Co. 20 Kearny
Brack G. A. 1228 Stockton
Canty & Wagner (manuf) 113 Mont
Close H. A. Mrs. 828 Market
Coley & Dearborn, 121 Fourth
Ehrenpfort & Co. 22 Stockton
Garland M. H. 765 Market
Gerhard S. 12 Dupont
Gjel L. 200 Third
Good C. & Co. 738 Washington
Hanson A. G. 826 Washington

Lelong J. 413 Davis
McGann T. 442 Brannan
Mercer C. H. 127 Second and 518 Kearny
Poehlman W. 102 Second
Rathbun & Co. 430 Sansom
Ross A. L. 119 Third
Salomon & Co. 211 Sutter
Smith F. 1426 Stockton and 1330 Dupon
Smith Jane Mrs. 1404 Stockton
Swain R. R. 146 Second and 913 Stock
Tgel L. 1319 Stockton
Toner E. Sixth nr Brannan
Wagner M. Mrs. 362 Third
Zaepffel W. 1208 Dupont

Consuls.

Austria, R. Hochkofler, 203 Front
Bavaria, C. F. Mebius, 223 Sacramento
Belgium, E. Berri, NW cor Montgomery and Commercial
Bremen, C. A. C. Duisenberg, 205 Cal
Chili, C. B. Polhemus, SE cor Sansom and Halleck
Costa Rica, S. H. Greene, 609 Front
Denmark, G. O'Hara Taaffe, 430 Cal
Ecuador, Daniel Woolf (absent)
France, C. F. DeCazotte, 434 Jackson
Guatemala, S. H. Greene, 609 Front
Great Britain, W. L. Booker, 428 Cal
Hamburg, G. Ziel, 122 California
Hanover, C. F. Mebius (acting) 223 Sac
Hawaiian Islands, C. E. Hitchcock, 405 Battery
Hessia, G. Ziel, 122 California
Hesse Cassel, C. F. Mebius, 223 Sac
Honduras, William V. Wells (absent)
Italy, E. Perri (acting) cor Montgomery and Commercial
Japan, C. W. Brooks, SW cor Battery and Pine
Lubeck, C. F. Mebius, 223 Sacramento
Mecklenburg Schwerin, J. DeFremery, 407 Merchant
Mexico (Republic) J. A. Godoy, 517 Bush
Mexico (Empire) M. Guillien, 502 Wash
Nassau, C. C. Finkler, 637 Wash
Netherlands, J. DeFremery, 407 Merch
New Granada, A. H. Gildemeester, 605 Washington
Norway, George C. Johnson, 33 Bat
Oldenburg, H. Hanssmann, 220 Front
Peru, B. Barrolihet, 535 Clay
Portugal, H. N. Byfield, 607 Dupont
Prussia, H. Hanssmann, 220 Front
Russia, M. Klinkofstrom, 505 Front
San Salvador, R. W. Heath, 609 Front
Sardinia, B. Davidson, cor Montgomery and Commercial
Saxony, H. Michels, cor Montgomery and Market
Saxony Anhalt, H. Behr, 639 Wash
Spain, C. Martin, 412 Montgomery
Sweden, George C. Johnson, 33 Bat
Switzerland, H. Hentsch, cor Clay and Leidesdorff
United States of Colombia, F. Herrera, 126 Second
Wurtemburg, I. Wormser, cor California and Front

Contractors.

Bateman M. C. City Hospital
Battles W. W. 652 Market
Berger, G. 212 Post
Blasdell G. W. 650 Howard
Blattner J. J. 425 Third
Bones J. W. 40 Minna
Bowman W. O. corner Townsend and Crook
Brennan M. T. 11 Ritch
BRIDGE M. 319 Bush (see adv. p. 653)
Brooks & Hughes, 804 Bush
BROWELL J. 530 Clay (see advertisement, p. xlviii)
Brown J. (night work) 115 Kearny
Brown W. H. (night work) Rassette Place No. 3
Buckley James, 528 Montgomery
Cochrane J. 223 Fourth
Corcoran William, 325 Pine
Cox & Arnold (Western Pacific R. R.) 240 Montgomery
Dore Benjamin, 728 Montgomery
Elveene C. 610 Clay
Evans W. 306 Clay
Feaster & Co. (night work) 213 Pine
Fowler A. G. 413 Sansom
Galloway & Boobar, dock builders, cor Stewart and Howard
Hendrick C. S. Chestnut nr Kearny
Henry J. cor Valencia and Sixteenth

Hewes D. (steam paddy) cor Third and Market
Hey & Meyn, cor Folsom and Twelfth
Houston A. H. 302 Montgomery
Howe William, 730 Bush
HYDE & CHESTER, 619 Mission (see advertisement, p. 655)
Johnson Sam (night work) 33 Geary
Jordan Dan, cor Kearny and Geary
Kimball Bros. 122 Natoma
Kyson E. F. 604 Merchant
Lathrop & Whipple, 402 Montgomery
Lind J. O. cor Mason and Geary
Lufkin J. Merchant nr East
McGlynn D. C. 246 Third
McLaughlin C. 40s California
Mitchell W. (night work) 140 Sutter
Moors H. C. & Co. 423 Washington
NAGLE G. D. 302 Montgomery (see advertisement, p. xlvi)
Nutting J. E. 714 Sansom
Patridge H. C. 604 Merchant
Patton J. H. cor Folsom and Sixteenth
Perry H. E. 619 Market
Platt H. B. 302 Montgomery
Prindle D. S. 109 Kearny
Richards I. (night work) 421 Kearny
Richardson W. L. 613 Market
Rushmore A. 316 Montgomery
Stratton A. W. & Bros. 724 Harrison
Sweeney M. San Miguel Station
Taylor W. M. 402 Montgomery
Watkins & Co. 403 Mason
Wilbar M. 506 Bush
Wilson O. Willow nr Folsom
Young J. 405 Front

Conveyancers.

Bell J. P. 23 Exchange Building
Bryant A. H. 528 Montgomery
Cook & Peckham, cor Mont and Clay
Laurie B. 55 Exchange Building
Roberts S. S. 11 Exchange Building
Smith N. P. 526 Montgomery
[See Records.]

Cooking Ranges.

LOCKE & MONTAGUE, 112 Battery (see advertisement, p. xlvii)
[See Stoves; Metals, Etc.]

Coopers.

Arnold F. W. 708 Front
Bingenheimer C. 106 Davis
California Wine Cooperage Co. corner Sacramento and Drumm
Eck Florent, 1235 Stockton
Fulda M. cor Sacramento and Drumm
Gunn William, 508 Battery
Handy & Cathcart, 41 Commercial
Handy & Neuman, 216 Commercial
Jensen C. 154 Second
Kramer B. H. 206 Davis
Landry T. 110 Davis
Lynch T. 219 Washington
McIntyre M. 508 Front
Meyer J. P. cor Battery and Bdwy
Murdock A. Oregon nr Davis
Neagle T. F. & Co. 221 Washington
Palecki J. Washington nr Front
Powers J. 117 Pine
Regan J. R. 215 Washington
Roach & Co. cor Com and Drumm
Ruppental J. C. 508 Davis
Sheridan J. 708 Front
Sherman H. 120 Sacramento
Thode H. Vallejo nr Front
Weidman J. 141 Third

Coppersmiths.

Bepler F. G. 421 Mission
Graves & Smith, 520 Davis
Macken James, 226 Fremont
Nell W. 35 Sacramento
Perey & Stepf, 114 Bush
Reynolds Thomas, 506 Front
SNOOK G. & W. 806 Montgomery
Sullivan D. 506 Front
[See Machinists; Gas Fitters; Plumbers.]

Copyists.

Symonds G. D. 636 Clay
[See Teachers—Penmanship.]

Cordage.

SAN FRANCISCO CORDAGE MANUFACTORY, Potrero, Tubbs & Co. office 613 Front (see adv. p. xii)
[See Ship Chandlers.]

Corks.

Scherr F. 511 Sacramento
WINTER JOHN, 208 California (see advertisement, p. xlvii)
[See Drugs.]

Corsets.

Besson & Pons M'mes, 629 Sac
Protols F. M'me, 755 Clay
Richet J. Miss. 633 Sacramento
[See Millinery and Dress Makers.]

Costumers.

Campioni E. 712 Washington
Fell C. (widow) 710 Washington
Terme M. Madame, 534 Jackson

Crockery and Glassware.

*Importers.
Austin John, 212 First
Bailey J. H. 1513 Stockton
Baker Joseph, cor Dupont and Sutter
Berman E. 127 Third
Bernard Isaac, 426 Third
*Bisagno Bros. 420 Battery
Blanchard J. 26 Third
Bouchard H. 1330 Dupont
*Brignardello & Bro. 622 Pacific
Brown William, 508 Market
*Callahan & Sanderson, 310 Battery
Dixon & Vagts, 144 Fourth
Greenberg & Mandel, 524 Sacramento
Harris B. 253 Third
*Haynes & Lawton, cor Sansom and Merchant
*HELBING, GREENEBAUM & CO. cor Battery and Pine (see advertisement, p. xxiv)
*Heynemann M. D. 409 California
Hughes R. 213 Third
Jacobs M. 208 First
Johnson F. 231 Kearny and 109 Second
Kalthoff A. 352 Third
Lavington A. 8 Kearny
Levitzky D. & Co. 54 Second
Mariani & Steffani, 1006 Dupont
*NATHAN B. 616 Kearny (see advertisement, p. xxvi)
Newman C. L. 111 Third
Oppenheim B. 1111 Dupont
Page J. M. 42 Clay
*Reid & Brooks, 524 Sansom
Rosenblum M. 10 Fourth
Sinsheimer S. 149 Second
*Swain R. A. & Co. cor San and Pine
TAYLOR JOHN (druggists' glassware) 514 Washington (see adv. p. lvi)
*Wangenheim, Sternheim & Co. cor California and Sansom
Webb A. C. 781 Market

Curriers.

[See Tanneries.]

Cutlers.

Kesmodel F. 817 Kearny
Ortet J. 223 Leidesdorff
Price M. 110 Montgomery
Will & Finck, 605 Jackson

Cutlery.

Adelsdorfer Bros. cor Sac and San
Appleton D. E. & Co. 508 Montgomery
Arnold N. S. 306 Battery
Bisagno Bros. 420 Battery
Clatworthy F. (agent) 29 Battery
COOKE W. B. & CO. 624 Montgomery
DAY THOS. 732 Montgomery (see advertisement, front cover)
GENNOUL A. 511 Montgomery (see advertisement, p. xxix)
Haynes & Lawton, cor San and Merch
HICKMAN L. M. (Stockton, California, see adv. p. cl)
HITCHCOCK G. B. & CO. cor Sansom and Commercial (see adv. p. cxli)
LAWRENCE & HOUSEWORTH, 317 Montgomery (see adv. cover)
LECOUNT J. P. & CO. cor Montgomery and Sacramento
Nathan B. 616 Kearny
Ortet J. 223 Leidesdorff
Oxenham A. H. 19 Sansom
Scott J. H. 29 Battery
SPEYER M. 526 Washington
Swain R. A. & Co. cor Pine and San

Daguerreian, Ambrotype, and Photographic Materials.

Bradley H. W. 620 Clay
Shew W. 421 Montgomery

Daguerreians.

[See Photographic Galleries.]

Dental Goods.

BIDDLE JOHN, 207 Centre St. New York (see advertisement, p. cx)
FOLKERS J. H. A. 218 Montgomery (see adv. p. xxxix)
McDONADD R. H. & Co. cor Pine and Sansom (see adv. inside back cover)
WHITE S. S. Philadelphia, Pa. (see adv. pp. civ and cv)

Dentists.

Austin Henry, 634 Washington
Beers J. B. & Son, 127 Montgomery
Belle Edward, 408 Pine
Bennett George, 653 Clay
Birge J. J. Mead House
Blake C. E. cor Clay and Kearny
Bouquin Charles, 426 Kearny
Boyle G. S. 625 Clay
Boyle W. A. 625 Clay
Brown C. F. cor Third and Hunt
Brown G. H. 137 Third
Bunnell E. F. 611 Clay
Burbank D. 505 Montgomery
Burdell G. 625 Clay
Bush & McAllister, 606 Kearny
Calvert W. 19 Post
Chesley C. P. 12 Montgomery
Cogswell J. L. 117 Second
Cole R. E. 715 Clay
Crawford & Dutch, 415 Montgomery
Davis C. E. cor Third and Hunt
Dennis B. W. 652 Market
Esterle B. M. Belden Block
Fox H. B. 515 East
Gunn J. 502 Montgomery
Hayden G. G. 727 Clay
HEALD J. 12 Stevenson House (see advertisement, p. 661)
Howenstein W. M. cor Third and Hunt
Hutchinson D. S. 107 Natoma
Kellum W. C. 649 Clay
Knowles & Clarke, 121 Montgomery
Knox H. E. 715 Clay
Lancaster C. E. 912 Dupont
LIBBEY M. L. 109 Montgomery (see advertisement, p. 637)
Lundborg J. A. W. 131 Montgomery
Lyon I. W. 663 Howard
Lysnar F. R. 634 Washington
Paine & Adams, 522 California
Parker A. H. 3 Brenham Place
PARKER T. H. 3 Brenham Place (see advertisement, p. 661)
Scott D. C. 617 Clay
Sichel M. 650 Washington
Spear T. R. 202 Bush
Thrall H. H. 715 Clay
Van Denburgh D. 134 Geary
Wade Thomas, 26 Montgomery
Whitcomb & Dyer, 205 Third
Winter J. W. 649 Clay
Younger W. J. 315 Montgomery

Dermatologists.

Kennedy B. C. 12 Montgomery

Diamonds.

BARRETT & SHERWOOD, 517 Mont
Bruhl M. 563 Clay
Crosby F. W. & Co. 638 Clay
Joseph Brothers, 607 Montgomery
Josephi I. S. & Co. 641 Washington
Levison Brothers, 629 Washington
Lipman J. 203 Montgomery
SHERWOOD R. 517 Montgomery
SHREVE G. C. & CO. 525 Mont
Tucker & Co. 505 Montgomery
WIEDERO OTTO & CO. 433 Mont

Diamond Setters.

Malmgren & Nordgren, 608 Sacramento
[See Jewelers, Etc.]

Die Sinkers.

KUNER A. 521 Wash (see adv. p. 663)
[See Engravers.]

Distillers.

Bepler J. San José Road 7 m. fr'm Plaza
DOWS JAMES & Co. Mission Creek, office 205 Sac (see adv. p. 681)
Henry G. B. 42 Commercial
Pacific Distillery Co. Presidio Road
Simon G. A. Harrison nr Third
Wertheimer L. Lombard nr Taylor
[See Brewers; Camphene; Liquors.]

Dock Builders.

Galloway & Boobar, cor Stewart and Howard

Docks.

San Francisco Dry Dock, H. B. Tichenor & Co. foot Second

Doors, Sashes, and Blinds.
*Manufacturers.

*Brokaw James, corner Mission and Fremont
*CULVERWELL S. S. 20 and 29 Fremont (see advertisement, p. xlvi)
Doe B. & J. S. (importers) junction California and Market
Hall John & Son (importers) 11 Cal
Hopkins S. J. 112 Washington
*McGILL & CO. cor Market and Beale (see advertisement, p. 665)
*Robinson George & Co. 30 California
Rossiter J. (Venetian blinds) cor Dupont and Francisco
*Smith & Ransom, 22 California
Stevens & Rider, cor Market and Fifth
*Ware & Co. 26 California
*Wilson & Bro. cor Cal and Drumm

Doors and Shutters. Iron.

KITTREDGE JONATHAN, 6 and 8 Battery
KITTREDGE & LEAVITT, 588 Jackson and 603 Bat (see adv. p. cxi)
Nutting & Upstone, 123 Bush
Fritzel A. 416 Market
Shute H. M. (shutters and springs) 312 Pine
Sims J. R. Oregon nr Front
[See Foundries; Machinists.]

Draymen.

Beach J. D. C. 401 Front
Chadbourne C. F. 216 California
Davis & Clifford, 430 Pine
Farnsworth & Glynn, 210 California
Garrison L. B. 215 Front
Graham R. J. (U.S.) Custom House
Hays D. & Co. cor Front and Sac
Lazalier W. B. 401 Front
Morrison & White, 217 Market
Morton R. & J. 205 Battery
Nibbe & Gibson, cor Front and Cal
Reynolds & Co. cor Bat and Bdwy
Richardson & Daly, Pier 3 Stewart
Sessions M. F. 205 Battery
Souther & Northey, 120 California
Stanyan & Co. 17 California, 49 Stewart, and Pier 4 Stewart
Toland & Sharkey, cor Cal and Davis

Dress Makers.

Aldrich L. A. Miss, Stevenson House
Altamirem S. Mrs. 206 Dupont
Augier C. Madame, 620 Sacramento
Barter A. B. (widow) 517 Howard
Bascombe A. Miss, 912 Market
Belden M. S. Mrs. 32 Second
Billett M. (widow) 419 Stockton
Bodkin E. Miss, 246 Sixth
Boisse H. Madame, 625 Sacramento
Bourdais Miss, 15 Second
Brown E. J. Mrs. 528 California
Bruns H. Mrs. 713 Folsom
Buchanan M. Miss, 243 Stevenson
Burns E. Miss, 31 Everett
Butler M. Mrs. 503 Sutter
Carey M. A. Miss, 127 Montgomery
Carity M. Mrs. 212 Third
CHAPMAN C. M. Mss. 218 Third (see advertisement, p. 667)
Chase E. (widow) 127 Fourth
Chevalier Madame, 213 Dupont
Clark R. R. & S. Misses, 962 Howard
Clark S. E. (widow) 715 Howard
Clement C. Mrs. 415 Powell
Clinton M. Miss, 15 Ritch
Close H. A. (widow) 828 Market
Clough F. Miss, 21 Langton

Coleman M. M. Mrs. 400 Kearny
Collins P. (widow) 627 Sacramento
Colvin L. Mrs. 644 Mission
Curtis M. Mrs. 27 Stockton
Daly A. Miss, 422 Third
Dense J. A. (widow) 619 Mission
Desneufbour Madame, 843 Clay
Dillon M. A. Miss, 406 Third
Doran J. Mrs. 242 Sixth
Draheim M. Miss, 8 Clara
Dyson M. Mrs. 112 Dupont
Edstrom A. Mrs. 113 Dupont
Favre C. Miss, 435 Bush
Flood A. B. Mrs. 302 Dupont
Foerster E. (widow) 124 Post
Fuller M. Mrs. 615 Mission
Gage H. E. Miss, 12 Montgomery
Gallagher E. Miss, 753 Mission
Gendar A. M. Mrs. 810 Market
Glaze A. C. 116 Dupont
Green E. Miss, 8 Turk
Gregory E. Mrs. 211 Tehama
Groom L. Mrs. 835 Clay
Guiraud Madame, 626 California
Hansch G. 733 Clay
Hargrave E. A. Miss, Union Court
Haskell S. L. (widow) 356 Third
Hayes M. (widow) 433 Bush
Henderson M. Mrs. 430 Geary
Herting E. Miss, 416 Stevenson
Hervey C. B. Mrs. 10 Stockton
Hezlep M. A. Mrs. 410 Third
Hifti R. Mrs. 717 Clay
Hill O. W. Mrs. 79 Clara
Hodnett M. Miss, 15 Ritch
Kennedy S. Miss, cor Mission and Fifth
Kornfeld C. 733 Clay
Lake F. Miss, 732 Folsom
Lamarche A. Madame, 113 Post
Lamarche E. Madame, 22 Mont
Lavrock G. Mrs. 106 Third
Leavitt H. N. (widow) 43 Second
Lebars J. Madame, 8 Sansom
Lee Ellen Miss, 713 Folsom
Leggett M. (widow) 31 Everett
Lenfest E. Mrs. 52 Tehama
Madden Kate Miss, 27 Stevenson
Mathews M. Mrs. 25 Geary
McFarland O. Mrs. 1119 Folsom
Molloy H. Mrs. 248 Minna
Morris L. A. 1110 Pacific
Morrison M. Miss, 687 Market
Norwald P. Miss, 13 St. Mark Place
O'Brien C. L. Miss, 112 Post
O'Neil M. Miss, 46 Beale
Ozanne M. (widow) 713 Dupont
PIPER E. Mns. 624 Market (see adv. p. 659)
Priebatch A. Miss, 46 Everett
Protois F. Madame, 749 Clay
Quimby M. Miss, 608 Market
Quinn A. (widow) 20 Montgomery
Rabeux L. Mrs. 723 Broadway
Reynolds J. Miss, 141 Third
Robertson M. Mrs. 230 Bush
Rogers A. Madame, 1209 Dupont
Ryan C. Miss, cor Third and Stevenson
Ryan M. Miss, 71 Minna
Saenger L. 415 Bush
Samuel J. 623 Mission
Shane J. Miss, 330 Bush
Sinclair E. D. (widow) 60 Everett
Smith A. (widow) 409 Sutter
Stevens M. F. Miss, 308 Third
Stickney B. Miss, 112 Second
Sullivan H. Miss, 843 Clay
Tarbox C. G. (widow) 32 Second
Taylor M. Miss, 320 Kearny
Taylor S. Miss, 320 Kearny
Varenne Madame, 828 Washington
Walsh M. Miss, 1306 Dupont
Warren C. C. T. (widow) 405 Bush
Webb M. Mrs. 753 Mission
Werber Madame, 616 Broadway
West E. H. Mrs. 141 Fourth
Whelan J. Mrs. 1203 Bush

Dress Trimmings.
*Importers.

Berkowitz M. 626 Sacramento
Bernstein S. 1012 Stockton
Bolling G. K. Mrs. 1009 Folsom
*Dexter, Lambert & Co. 105 Battery
*Hornberger M. cor Bush and Kearny
Kerlin R. Mrs. 114 Second
Krone L. 1018 Stockton
Norcross D. Mrs. 5 Montgomery, Masonic Temple
Schreiber L. 202 Second
Wheeler A. Mrs. 32 Second
Zeigenbirt Bros. 637 Sacramento
[See Cloaks; Millinery, Etc.]

Drugs and Medicines.

Bauer J. A. 644 Washington
CRANE & BRIGHAM, SE cor Front and Clay (see adv. p. lxiii)
Hall Edward & Co. 309 Front
Hall R. & Co. cor Sansom and Com
Hostetter, Smith & Dean, 401 Battery
Langley, Crowell & Co. cor Clay and Battery
McDONALD R. & CO. cor Pine and San (see adv. inside back cover)
Pugh E. 210 Bush
Redington & Co. 416 and 418 Front
Reilly P. J. 535 Commercial
Richards & Whitfield, cor Clay and Sansom
Rubber Clothing Co. 118 Montgomery
Wakelee H. P. cor Mont and Bush
[See Apothecaries.]

Dry Docks.

Tichenor H. B. & Co. foot Second
[See Ship Builders.]

Dry Goods. *Importers and Jobbers.*
*Retail.

AUSTIN & CO. SE cor Montgomery and Sutter (see adv. p. xxvi)
Bachman Brothers, 304 California
Breslauer H. 310 California
Flood B. S. & Co. 308 California
Funkenstein J. 308 California
Glass & Levy, 305 Battery
Glaser C. & Co. 207 Battery
Godchaux Brothers, 109 Battery
*Godchaux, Verdier & Co. 61 Second
Goodman Simon, 517 Sacramento
Hamburger B. 306 Sacramento
Heller M. & Bros. 425 Sacramento
Herrmann S. & Co. 310 Sacramento
HEYNEMANN & Co. 311 and 313 Cal
Hoffman & Co. 312 Sacramento
HUGHES HENRY, 220 Battery
*Kerby, Byrne & Co. 7 Montgomery
LAZARD FRERES, 115 Battery
Meagher, Taaffe & Co. 107 Battery
Milburn J. & Co. 313 Sacramento
MURPHY, GRANT & CO. NW cor Sansom and Sac (see adv. p. xxx)
Pollack Brothers. 421 Sacramento
Rank C. P. & Co. 314 Sacramento
*Rosenthal S. & Co. 618 Kearny
Sachs L. & M. & Co. 312 California
Scholle Bros. 407 and 409 Sacramento
Seeligsohn M. 512 Sacramento
Seligman & Co. 111 Battery
Simon, Dinkelspiel & Co. 301 Cal
Steinhart Brothers, NW cor California and Battery
Strauss L. & Co. 315 and 317 Sac
Uhlfelder & Cahn, 309 and 311 Sac
*VERDIER, KAINDLER, SCELLIER & CO. 633 Clay (see adv. p. xxxi)
WIGHTMAN & HARDIE, 414 Clay (see advertisement, p. xlix)
Ziel, Bertheau & Co. 122 California
[See Fancy Goods; Furnishing Goods.]

Dry Goods. Retail.
*Importers.

Abrahams E. 23 Second
Ackerman Brothers, 19 Montgomery
*AUSTIN & CO. SE cor Montgomery and Sutter (see adv. p. xxvi)
Bergstein L. 303 Sixth
Blaisdell E. F. Mrs. 329 Dupont
Blass M. 58 Second
Bloch J. 3 Virginia Block
Bonnard Thomas, 425 Fourth
Bornstine H. 731 Montgomery
Brennan & Co. 16 Third
Breslauer B. & Co. 50 Third
Cahn J. 326 Third
CANNAVAN M. 902 Dupont and 805 Kearny (see adv. front cover)
Castle S. W. 619 Montgomery
Charles I. & H. 153 Fourth
Clements M. Miss, 152 Third
Coblentz & Brother, 1023 Dupont
Conkling G. W. 714 Montgomery
*Curtin C. 48 Second
*Davidson J. W. & Co. 609 Sacramento
Doyer J. 104 Third
Edelkamp B. Mrs. 424 Third
Elias & Kutner, 136 Kearny
Friedlander Brothers, 628 Sacramento
Friedlander M. 2 Montgomery
Galland B. 60 Third
Glaser C. & Co. 207 Battery

*Godchaux, Well & Co. 61 Second
Goldman I. A. 634 Market
Goldsmidt N. 651 Clay
Goldsmith G. 318 Kearny
Goldsmith L. 612 Sacramento
Goldsmith S. & Co. 630 Sacramento
Gorfinkel S. Mrs. 1136 Dupont
Henderson S. 105 Fourth
Hicks R. M. 110 Second
Hirsch L. 1122 Dupont
Homberger M. & Co. 30 Second
Irvine W. & Co. 34 Second
Jacobs P. Mrs. 203 Kearny
Jeremias G. & Co. 207 Battery
Joseph & Co. 643 Clay
Kennedy & Driscoll, 108 Third
*Kerby, Byrne & Co. 7 Montgomery
Kline L. 1004 Stockton
Knibbe H. W. 266 Kearny
Kohlman C. 915 Dupont
Kohlman & Galinger, 637 Market
Kohn & Co. 8 Fourth
Kohn H. L. (No. 2) 628 Market
Kuttner N. 350 Third
Landers D. 4 Third
Landsberger J. 606 Mission
Langstadter S. 211 Fourth
Lazarus S. & H. cor Third and Minna
Leahy M. Mrs. 154 Third
Lezinsky A. 21 Kearny
Levy G. 307 Battery
Levy L. & Co. 618 Kearny
Levy J. & Brother, 1106 Stockton
Levy L. 12 Second
Levy M. & Bro. 4 Montgomery
Levy M. B. & Bro. 333 East
Levy & Cohn, 45 Second
*Meagher, Taaffe & Co. 9 Montgomery
Metzger C. 134 Second
Mosgrove and Blakely, 222 Third
Myers N. 646 Sacramento
Popper L. Mrs. 101 Third
Quinton & Lane, 217 Fourth
Regan A. 52 Fourth
*Rosenblatt S. 127 Montgomery
Rotenberg A. 113 Fourth
Schwartz & Sinay, cor Stock and Pac
Shioss M. 138 Montgomery
Skerritt N. 11 Montgomery
Samuels Bros. 630 Market
Solomanson J. 53 Second
Stolz A. 540 Kearny
Stolz J. 8 Second
Stone K. L. 6 Virginia Block
Strauss L. 8 Virginia Block
Summerfield S. 20 Second
Tke A. C. Mrs. 52 Third
*VERDIER, KAINDLER, SCELLIER & CO. 633 Clay (see adv. p. xxx)
Wand & Co. 22 Second
Waterman M. 109 Second
Wellhoff Brothers, 328 Kearny

Dyers.

Barton P. (widow) 213 Kearny
Christian R. R. 808 Market
Goux J. B. 212 Third
Rauck F. W. 148 Third
Ricklefson G. 1408 Stockton
Snow J. F. (gloves and feathers) 24 Post
Thomas F. 734 Washington

Dye Stuffs, Chemicals, Etc.

[See Apothecaries; Chemists, Etc.]

Egg Dealers.

[See Produce.]

Electrotypers.

Clark W. H. T. 228 Kearny
Kellogg A. 517 Jackson
Rocchiccoli R. F. 523 Clay
[See Silver Platers and Stereotypers.]

Embroideries.

* Importers.

*Anderson & Prosergue, 111 Mont
Bigot Madame, 828 Washington
Bolander Mrs. 60 Second
Buffum R. V. E. 422 Third
Dannenberg A. Mrs. 618 Sacramento
Duden Freres, 629 Clay
*Heller M. & Bros. 425 Sacramento
Hendricks E. Mrs. 627½ Mission
*HUGHES HENRY, 218 Battery
*Jones, Dixon & Co. NE cor Sacramento and Sansom
Lion Julia Miss, 657 Clay
Marchal L. 729 Clay

Merzbach J. 412 Kearny
Mortensen E. Mrs. 212 Fourth
*Rosenbaum & Friedman, 316 Sac
*Sachs L. and M. & Co. 312 California
Sullivan C. Mrs. 214 Kearny
Synon A. Mrs. & Sister, 318½ Third
Tobin Bros. & Davisson, SW cor Sacramento and Battery
Tolle M. Mrs. 30 Eddy
*Uhlfelder & Cahn, 309 Sacramento

Engine Builders.

Devoe, Dinsmore & Co. cor Mission and Fremont
BOOTH H. J. & CO. Union Foundry, NE cor Front and Mission
GODDARD & CO. Pacific Foundry, 127 First
HINCKLEY & CO. Fulton Foundry, 47 First
HOWLAND, ANGELL & KING, Miners' Foundry, First nr Folsom
Lochhead J. 111 Beale
STEEN E. T. Novelty Works, 39 Fremont
VULCAN IRON WORKS CO. First nr Natoma
Ware William, 517 Market

Engineers. Civil.

Bielawski C. 728 Montgomery
Black G. 528 Clay
Boynton C. W. 240 Montgomery
Brady J. B. 423 Washington
Bridgens R. P. 528 Clay
Brooks Thad R. City Hall
Clayton H. 543 Clay
Ellis C. B. 49 Montgomery Block
Gardiner J. J. City Hall
Gaynor J. P. 402 Montgomery
Gird R. 302 Montgomery
Goodyear & Blake, 127 Montgomery
Harris R. L. 72 Montgomery Block
Hoffman C. F. 90 Montgomery Block
Hoffman J. D. 728 Montgomery
Humphreys W. P. 50 Mont Block
Keith S. D. (mechanical) Sixteenth nr Folsom
Lacy T. J. P. City Hall
Parkinson T. D. City Hall
Poett A. 728 Montgomery
Shortt L. H. 302 Montgomery
Shoulters H. 326 Clay
Steen Edward T. (mechanical) 35 Fremont
Turner & Watson, 505 Montgomery
Von Schmidt A. W. SE cor Montgomery and Jackson
Wackenreuder V. San Bruno Road nr Flume
Weber A. C. 505 Montgomery

Engineers. Mechanical.

Brodie & Radcliff, 402 Montgomery

Engineers. Mining.

Day S. 57 Montgomery Block
Goodyear & Blake, 127 Montgomery
Janin H. cor Montgomery and Jackson

Engravers.

Baker G. H. 522 Montgomery
Beekman H. 325 Pine
Boyd T. C. 300 Montgomery
Carson B. 539 Sacramento
Deaves E. (wood) 214 Fourth
Eastman H. (wood) SE cor Montgomery and California
Fenn F. C. 58 (card, etc.) 637 Howard
Genot S. (seal) 622 Clay
Gihon T. 522 Montgomery
Goldsmith W. E. 505 Montgomery
Joiner J. J. 648 Sacramento
Klumpp W. (metal) 637 Washington
KUNER A. (seal) 621 Washington (see advertisement, p. 663)
Loomis & Swift, (wood) 617 Clay
Pages J. F. (jewelry) 622 Clay
Procureur & Wenzel (watch case, etc.) 622 Clay
Rocchiccoli R. F. 523 California
Steinbrink B. 33½ Second
Swasey E. T. J. 605 Sacramento
Van Vieck & Keith, 611 Clay
Wood G. M. 508 Montgomery

Engravings.

Franco-American Commercial Co. 215 Bush

GENSOUL ADRIEN, 511 Montgomery
Hausmann D. & Co. 535 Clay
LAWRENCE & HOUSEWORTH, (photographic) 319 Montgomery
Roos J. 219 Montgomery
SNOW & CO. cor Washington and Sansom (see adv. p. lxviii)

Exchange. By Telegraph.

Bank of California, cor Bat and Wash
COLEMAN WM. T. & CO. 417 Battery
Donohoe, Kelly & Co. cor Montgomery and Sacramento
LONDON & S. F. LIMITED, 412 Mont
Sather & Co. cor Mont and Com
[See Bankers.]

Expresses.

Baker I. F. (Potrero) cor Mont and Cal
Bamber & Co. (Contra Costa) 719 Davis
California Letter (city) 424 Mont
City Letter, 423 Washington
Couch J. (Mission) 716 Kearny
Dorland Brothers (Mission Dolores) cor Merchant and Kearny
Half-Moon Bay and Pescadero, 679 Market
Kennedy M. G., S. F. & San José, 679 Market
San Francisco & San José, Troman & Chapman, cor Front and Wash
San Francisco & San José, M. G. Kennedy, 679 Market
Tyrrell & Merritt (Oakland) Davis nr Broadway
WELLS, FARGO & CO. (California, New York, and European) NW cor Mont and Cal (see adv. p. viii)

Fancy Goods. Importers and Jobbers:

Adelsdorfer Bros. cor San and Sac
Bachman Bros. 304 California
Berliner H. 414 Sacramento
Boas J. & Co. 513 Sacramento
Brigham S. O. (Paris fashions) 111 Montgomery
Brown A. F. 308 Battery
Falkenau Bros. 629 Washington
Franco-American Commercial Co. 215 Bush
Glaser C. & Co. 207 Battery
Glass & Levy, 305 Battery
Godchaux Bros. 109 Battery
Hamberger B. 306 Sacramento
Heller M. & Bros. 425 Sacramento
Herrmann H. 205 Battery
Herzberg M. 314 Sacramento
Hoffman & Co. 312 Sacramento
HUGHES HENRY, 220 Battery
Jones, Dixon & Co. NE cor Sacramento and Sansom
Kohler A. 424 Sansom
Krause W. E. F. (toilet, etc.) cor Front and Jackson
LAZARD FRERES, 115 Battery
Manheim, Schonwasser & Co. 113 Bat
Meagher, Taaffe & Co. 107 Battery
Michels A. W. & Bro. 304 Battery
Moss R. & Co. 207 Battery
Neustadter Bros. NE cor Bat and Sac
Oxenham A. H. & Co. 19 Sansom
Pecqueux & Watterlot, 511 Sac
Pevser S. A. & Co. 424 Sacramento
Pollack Bros. 421 Sacramento
Rank C. P. & Co. 314 Sacramento
Rosenbaum & Friedman, 316 Sac
Rosenfeld L. K. 318 Sansom
Sachs L. and M. & Co. 312 California
Schweitzer, Stiefel & Co. 307 Sac
SPEYER M. 526 Washington
SWAIN R. A. & CO. cor Sansom and Pine
Steinhart Bros. NE cor Cal and Bat
TOBIN BROTHERS & DAVISSON, SW cor Battery and Sacramento (see adv. p. xxxv)
Uhlfelder & Cahn, 309 and 311 Sac
Wasserman A. 429 Sacramento
Well & Levy, cor Battery and Sac
Whitehorne W. A. (agent) 409 Battery
[See Dry Goods; Millinery, Etc.]

Fancy Goods. Retail.

* Importers.

Alexander L. 16 Second
Aubrey F. 310 Third
Blaisdell E. F. Mrs. cor Dupont and Bush

Blockman E. Fourth nr Jessie
Bolander H. N. Mrs. 60 Second
Bolling G. K. Mrs. 1009 Folsom
*Breslauer H. 310 California
Brown W. & Co. 108 Third
Buyer & Reich, cor Stock and Jackson
Cannavan M. cor Dupont and Wash
Connor H. cor Harrison and Chesley
Dannenbaum & Katzenstein, 20 Mont
Delande S. 60 Clay
*Dexter, Lambert & Co. 105 Battery
Dietch L. Mrs. 212 Third
Durning A. Mrs. 10 Second
Ehrlich L. 126 Third
Eisman A. 646 Market
Elgutter B. Mrs. 18 Second
*Feldbush & Co. 207 Mont and 307 Cal
Frey W. A. 404 Kearny
Friedlander & Basthelm, 8 Mont
*Gensoul A. 511 Montgomery
Glave & Co. 11 Second
Goldsmith S. & Co. 19 Montgomery
Harris M. 153 Second
Hodea A. 321 East
Jacoby S. 1108 Stockton
Landsberger J. 606 Mission
Leon S. 214 Second
Levy A. N. 26 Fourth
*LOCAN & CO. 623 Clay (see adv. p. xxxi)
Lowe & Mansbach, 116 Second
Mansbach & Bine, 56 Second
Marks A. 1018 Dupont
Martin J. 1106 Dupont
*Mayers R. 242 Montgomery
Merzbach J. 412 Kearny
Michael I. 200 Fourth
Newhall & Brooks, 722 Montgomery
Nolan M. Mrs. 256 Third
Norcross D. Mrs. 5 Montgomery
Pasquale B. 550 Washington
Reuben G. 511 Sacramento
Roe M. J. Mrs. 108 Second
Riegelhaupt P. Mrs. 312 Third
Rogers J. Miss, 846 Washington
*Rosenblatt S. 125 Montgomery
Rothschild H. 112 Third
Ruef M. 1341 Dupont
Shirek & Co. 16 Third and 1125 Stock
Slattery E. 256 Third
Soleroz S. cor Dupont and Broadway
Spier & Bro. 100 Kearny
Stein P. (widow) 1339 Dupont
Stolz Bros. 530 Kearny and 8 Second
Talbot J. C. 103 Second
Weiner A. 824 Market
Weiss M. 324 Kearny
White C. W. 40 Clay
Winberg J. Mrs. 5 Virginia Block
Witkowski & Wurkhelm, 725 Mont
Wolff M. 116 Kearny

Faucet Makers.

GRACIER F. J. Chace's Mills
Waas H. 409 Mission
·[See Turners—Wood, Etc.]

Feather Dealers.

Pecqueux & Watterlot, 511 Sac
[See Fancy Goods.]

Feed Stores.

Barraclough J. & Co. 39 Clay
Driscoll T. cor Sixteenth and Mission
Dulip & Waddington, 534 Broadway
Dutton Henry & Son, 109 Stewart
Eudes & Co. 53 Third
Garret, Averell & Co. 41 Sacramento
Holmes J. B. & Co. 108 Market
Lea T. 430 Pine
Leperca H. Pacific nr Taylor
Mathison A. C. cor Leav and Bdwy
McKenna Bro. & Co. cor Clay and Drumm
Melbourn J. & Co. 1219 Powell
Miner T. E. Commercial Street Wharf
Morrow Geo. 21 Clay
Paine J. A. Fourth nr Mission
Place C. L. Folsom Street Wharf
Reilly & Clancy, 751 Mission
Rider & Somers, 24 Market
Ruffley T. 707 Mission
Tiernan & Turk, First Avenue nr Fifteenth
[See Hay and Grain.]

Ferries.

Alameda, cor Davis and Broadway
Contra Costa, foot Broadway
San Quentin, cor Davis and Broadway

File Makers.

Hall E. C. Pacific, 19 Fremont
Sheffield & Patterson, cor Jackson and Battery
[See Saw Makers.]

Fire Bricks. *Makers.*

[See Brick Yards.

Fire Works.

CHURCH & CLARK, 407 Front (see adv. p. xli)
Tripp & Robinson, 409 Washington
[See Pyrotechnists.]

Firemen's Caps.

[See Cap Makers.]

Fishing Tackle.

Curry N. & Bro. 317 Battery
Hall R. & Co. cor Sansom and Com
KLEPZIG I. C. E. 733 Washington
Liddle R. & Co. 538 Washington
Plate A. J. 411 Sansom
[See Cutlers and Gunsmiths.]

Fishmongers.

Aime G. 33 Italian Fish Market
Alsma F. & Co. 29 Italian Fish Market
Barbetto F. 38 Italian Fish Market
Bardellini A. & Co. 50 Italian Fish Mkt
Barretto P. 37 Italian Fish Market
Bennett F. B. 2 Washington Market
Berce & Wolf, 31 Washington Market
Brascocci M. 10 Italian Fish Market
Camiano A. 15 Italian Fish Market
Camiano B. 20 Italian Fish Market
Camiano G. 1 Italian Fish Market
Capatorno G. 2 Washington Market
Cardillo G. 7 Washington Market
Cardinet E. H. 25 and 26 Wash Market
Carlton & Co. 34 Metropolitan Market
Cbesi P. 5 Washington Market
Cieffo M. 12 Washington Fish Market
Cignione P. 17 Italian Fish Market
Cleopatra Co. 30 Italian Fish Market
Coscibicci A. 3 Italian Fish Market
Conte V. 11 Italian Fish Market
D'Lucca F. 46 Italian Fish Market
Deletti V. 3 Italian Fish Market
Edwards M. 4 Italian Fish Market
Fabriani G. 15 Washington Fish Mkt
Francesca F. 16 Italian Fish Market
Frau T. 11 Washington Fish Market
Glavigni L. 41 Italian Fish Market
Griffin L. (salt) 321 Davis
Harry B. & Co. 24 Washington Market
Harvey J. 19 Occidental Market
Hogan M. 45 Metropolitan Market
Kasson Joe, 43 Italian Fish Market
Kessing J. H. 7 Clay Street Market
Larco A. 44 Italian Fish Market
Luigetto J. R. 7 Italian Fish Market
Macchiavello A. 14 Italian Fish Mkt
Maggio P. 12 Italian Fish Market
Malta A. 36 Italian Fish Market
Mavagliano L. 6 Italian Fish Market
May P. 23 Italian Fish Market
Mela G. 8 Washington Fish Market
Mibelli L. 46 Italian Fish Market
Moreeno F. 5 Italian Fish Market
Napolitana G. A. 14 Italian Fish Mkt
Palmieri A. 2 Italian Fish Market
Pancho O. 13 Washington Fish Mkt
Paoletti G. 45 Italian Fish Market
Pardini N. 32 Italian Fish Market
Parmasano L. 8 Italian Fish Market
Pascalaqua B. 13 Italian Fish Market
Patata Co. 22 Italian Fish Market
Prucitano L. 39 Italian Fish Market
Romano A. 4 Washington Fish Market
Sanguinetti S. 4 Italian Fish Market
Sbizza G. & Co. 34 Italian Fish Mkt
Sintera A. 6 Washington Fish Market
Smith H. (dried) 320 Davis
Spence W. A. 10 Washington Fish Mkt
Stanovich P. 42 Italian Fish Market
Sweeiser A. J. & Co. 22 Occidental Market
Tesmore & Mayes, 34 Washington Mkt
Thompson A. J. 12 New Market
Tomlinson J. S. 1 Wash Fish Mkt
Trickle E. C. 19 Metropolitan Market
Tucatulus C. 16 Washington Fish Mkt
Vasa G. 18 Italian Fish Market
Viera V. 47 Italian Fish Market

Florists.

Chiousse & Salmon, 716 Washington
Coillic & Stewart, 27 Geary
Culver W. Sans Souci Valley
Hourcade A. 1337 Dupont
Lauzezeur & Habert, cor Market and Powell
O'Hare J. cor Folsom and Fifteenth
Reimer E. L. Folsom nr Fifteenth
Robertson W. Folsom nr Twentieth
Save P. 319 Bush
Sonntag H. A. cor Folsom and Fourteenth
Staeglich Frank & Co. 414 California
[See Nurseries.]

Force Pumps.

HARRISON C. H. 517 Front (see advertisement, p. 851)
Underhill J. & Co. 118 Battery

Flour Dealers.

Bassett J. (agent Clinton Mills) 213 Clay
Bray Brothers (agents Alviso & Granite Mills) NE cor Front and Clay
Brennan & Co. (agents Santa Cruz Mills) 106 Clay
Clayton C. & Co. (agents Santa Clara Mills) 223 Clay
Conro F. D. & Co. Golden Age Mills, 717 Battery
Davis H. & Co. Golden Gate Mills, 430 Pine
Davis & Witham, 406 Davis
DeForest J. 222 Clay
Delabigne J. B. 323 Clay
Eisen Bros. Pioneer Mills, 515 Market
Everding J. & Co. 64 Clay
Freidlander I. 114 California
GROSH & RUTHERFORD, Commercial Mills, NE cor First and Natoms (see adv. p. 660)
Ham I. M. 211 Clay
Hunt C. A. & Co. 222 Clay
Kennedy & Hopkins, Genessee Mills, Gold nr Sansom
Lewis Edwin, 124 Clay
Lick J. 422 Clay
Martenstein J. & Co. National Mills, 561 Market
Raymond J. P. & Co. 7 Clay
Ryan & Co. 210 Clay
Waterman M. (agent Orange and San José City) 210 Clay
Wheelan & Co. Alta Mills, 12 Stevenson
Zeile J. Pacific Mills, Pacific nr San
[See Commission Merchants; Produce; Mills—Flour, Etc.

Foundries.

Brodie Wm. & Co. Cal. 16 Fremont
BOOTH H. J. & CO. Union, cor First and Mission (see adv. p. lviii)
CHASE, SHARPE & THOMSON, 209 North Second St. Philadelphia (see advertisement, p. cvii)
Dunn, McHaffie & Co. Atlas, 26 Fremont
GALLAGHER & WEED (brass) 125 First (see adv. p. 644)
Garratt W. T. (brass) 507 Market
GODDARD & CO. Pacific, 127 and 131 First (see advertisement, p. x)
HICKOK W. O. Eagle, Harrisburg, Penn. (see adv. p. cxiii)
HINCKLEY & CO. Fulton, 47 and 49 First (see advertisement, p. 640)
HOWLAND, ANGELL & KING, Miners', First nr Folsom (see advertisement, p. 643)
Ils J. G. Jackson, 628 Washington
Kittredge J. Phœnix, 708 Battery
KITTREDGE & LEAVITT, Pioneer, 389 Jackson (see adv. p. cxi)
McKibbin Wm. Eureka, 41 First
PALMER, KNOX & CO. Golden State, 19 First (see advertisement, p. 639)
Steen E. T. Novelty Iron Works, 39 Fremont
VULCAN IRON WORKS CO corner First and Natoma (see adv. p. 638)
Yung N., R. R. Iron Works, 28 Fremont
[See Brass Founders; Machinists, Etc.]

Frame Makers. *Looking Glass and Picture.*

[See Carvers and Picture Framers.]

Fruits.

*Importers.

Ahrens J. SW cor Battery and Cal
Aillon F. & Co. NE cor Second and Folsom
Bacigalupi D. 910 Dupont
Baily William, 403 Davis
Baldwin O. D. 418 Third
Barnstein G. 235 Third
Barto C. 1220 Powell
Battista J. 235 Jackson
Bell George, 257 Third
Bello Vincent, 1328 Stockton
Borchers & Poska, 423 Davis
Bornheimer F. 226 Third
Boyer D. cor Commercial and East
Boylen C. 1436 Stockton
Bricket J. B. 940 Market
Brown C. 624 Jackson
Brown C. F. 1218 Stockton
Brown & Avery, 42 Washington Mkt
Bryant M. 203 Third
Bulletti & Co. Pacific Fruit Market
Bunner A. (widow) 727 Mission
Cadesi John, 204 Second
Carnell R. 129 Kearny
Caswell A. M. 267 Third
Catanich P. & Co. 525 Davis
Catlin P. H. 13 Fourth
Chapman R. 147 Second
Cheyne R. 140 First
*CHURCH & CLARK, 407 Front (see adv. p. xli)
Claffey J. cor Fourth and Tehama
Clayton W. cor Sansom and Bush
Colby Z. E. Meiggs' Wharf
Coley & Dearborn, 121 Fourth
*Conrad J. & D. 419 Washington
Cosgrove P. 356 Third
Cousens G. W. 817 Clay
Criggins T. 125 Third
Croce & Glamboni, cor Stock and Clay
Crou & Co. 18 Occidental Market
Dabovich E. 1122 Stockton
Dabovich N. 420 Davis
Daley A. 546 Mission
Davis J. S. Sixth nr Tehama
Dejen L. 439 Kearny
Dejort A. 1620 Stockton
Denegri A. 329 Kearny
Denis Z. 1307 Dupont
Denning H. (widow) 938 Market
Devoto A. 802 Kearny
Dolan M. & Co. 538 Wash
Dolan T. cor Davis and Pacific
Dominique & Gonella, 1112 Dupont
Donnelly M. Mrs. cor Fourth and Silver
Doolittle F. 668 Howard
Dornay P. cor Bush and Kearny
Drake & Emerson, 312 Washington
Drouet V. 1622 Stockton
Ducatel A. Mrs. 10 Washington Mkt
Elwood F. H. 262 Third
Englander W. 105 Fourth
Evans P. J. 513 Broadway
Ewell L. J. cor Wash and Sansom
Feig Alex. 49 Third
Fitzpatrick J. Mrs. 106 Sixth
Fox M. Union nr Stockton
Freeman & Co. 2 Occidental Market
French E. cor Fifth and Stevenson
Freud M. 124 Second
Funk & Smith, 104 Pacific
Fusari & Gregovich, cor California and Kearny
Gill Robt. 326 Sansom
Gillespie M. (widow) 241 Sutter
Goetslhe J. cor Davis and Pacific
Goldsmith M. 826 Market
Hall & Brigham, 74 Washington Mkt
Ham C. W. & Co. 7 Washington Mkt
Hassel & Huber, 47 Washington
Henry & Kaskell, 614 Washington
Hickey J. 805 Market
Hodge Alex. 304 Third
Hohenschild G. 22 Washington Mkt
Holland S. cor Mont and Jackson
*Hughes Geo. cor Sansom and Clay
Isimini H. 445 Bush
*Ivancovich J. & Co. 405 Davis
Jacobs A. 217 Washington
Jarpa M. cor Powell and Vallejo
Jefts J. M. 419 Washington
Johnson J. Fifth nr Folsom
Johnson J. cor Washington and Bat
Jones I. W. 205 Fourth
Kennedy & Hayden, 146 Fourth
LaSever S. 720 Dupont
Label H. cor Dupont and Bush
Laporte J. B. 706 Market
Lavenburg S. 134 Third

Lincoln B. B. 712 Washington
Lusk A. & Co. Pacific Fruit Market
Martin A. & Co. Pacific Fruit Market
Martini R. 104 Stewart
Mattovich M. 746 Washington
Mattovich S. 624 Kearny
McCabe P. 34 Fourth
McCarthy J. 539 Sacramento
McDade G. 335 Fourth
McDonogh J. Pacific Fruit Market
McGuire E. Mrs. 812 Market
McPherson W. Davis nr Pacific
Meyer L. 61 Washington Market
Moore Z. W. & Co. 9 Washington Mkt
Morgan A. 512 Montgomery
Morgan & Co. cor Third and Bryant
Mudrogna A. 28½ First
Nicholas J. D. 26 Sansom
Nicholas N. G. cor Jackson and Bat
Nichols J. 1438 Pacific
Norman M. (widow) Sixteenth nr Mission
O'Brien J. cor Pacific and Larkin
O'Dowd M. 924 Market
Page F. H. 605 Market
Perich J. cor Clay and Dupont
Pisani R. 230 Montgomery
Podd J. 601 Post
Precht & Eggers, Pacific Fruit Market
Pudd J. 739 Broadway
Rehm P. N. 27 Fourth
Rines J. R. 1237 Stockton
Roberts J. 103 Kearny
Rogers U. 932 Folsom
Rossi A. cor Dupont and Jackson
Rossi P. cor Kearny and Merchant
Russell & Bouton, 38 Occidental Mkt
Russen J. M. 123 Fourth
Sablich J. cor Wash and Stockton
Sand J. Sixth nr Folsom
Sander P. 116 Fourth
Sanders H. E. 31 Third
Schuller J. H. 152 Second
Seymour & Shillaber, 266 First
Sherman & Brown, 402 Folsom
Shirley F. 206½ Fourth
Simon J. 1214 Dupont
Smith E. L. & Co. cor Pine and Mont
Smith F. 1511 Dupont
Smith H. 115 Third
Smith W. 65 Fourth
Stanley J. M. 107 Geary
Stewart T. 521 Merchant
Stoler A. 802 Kearny
Sullivan B. 545 Kearny
Sullivan C. P. cor Taylor and Geary
Sullivan F. 232 Fourth
Tonjes J. 529 Broadway
Vandevoort & Co. 30 Third
Vibert M. 412 Brannan
Weitzner C. A. 740 Market
Weston C. W. & Co. Pacific Fruit Mkt
Williams J. 215 Pacific
Williams P. (widow) 8 Dupont
Woolfe B. cor Stockton and Green
Wustfield F. cor Market and Second
Yeager T. T. 43 Third
Zimmerman M. 136 Second

Fur Dealers.

Liebes H. & Co. 105 and 413 Mont
Mayer I. C. & Sons, 129 Montgomery
MULLER A. 107 Montgomery (see advertisement, back cover)
Shirpser I. 106 Montgomery
Wasserman A. & Co. 429 Sacramento
White I. K. 221 Sacramento

Furnaces and Ranges.

Brittan J. M. 114 Front
De la Montanya James, 216 Jackson
Johnston & Reay, 111 Battery
LOCKE & MONTAGUE, 112 Battery
Tay, Brooks & Backus, SW cor Front and Washington
Weaver D. S. 505 Sansom
[See Stoves.]

Furnished Rooms.

[See Lodgings; Boarding, Etc.]

Furnishing Goods. Gents'.

*Importers.

Ash & Hurley, 602 Kearny
*Atkinson L. & Co. 509 Sacramento
Block A. B. 1107 Dupont
Block John, 532 Kearny
Blum H. 304 Montgomery
Blum I. 411 Montgomery

CANNAVAN M. corner Dupont and Washington (see adv. front cover)
Godfrey W. A. H. 105 Second
*Goldstone, Barnett & Co. 814 Cal
Harris M. 802 Kearny
*Heuston, Hastings & Co. cor Montgomery and Sutter
*Hughes Henry, 220 Battery
Ichon E. F. 321 Sansom
Kuhn S. 200 Kearny
Lohmann & Moesta, 644 Clay
Loveland I. & Co. 211 Montgomery
*MEAD J. R. & CO. 200 Montgomery and cor Sansom and Washington (see advertisement, back cover)
*Meagher, Taaffe & Co. 107 Battery
*Menderson W. & Co. 304 Battery
Meyers I. 36 Third
*Morgenthau M. 418 Sacramento
*MORISON, HARRIS & CO. 329 San
Myers, Goldstone & Co. 36 Third
*Neustadter Bros. 300 Battery
Orr & Atkins, 415 Montgomery
Salbery M. 530 Jackson
Selig I. 214 Montgomery
SHERMAN WM. & CO. cor Sansom and Com (see adv. p. xxxviii)
*Steinhart W. & I. 321 Sacramento
Thomson P. 607 Sacramento
*Toklas, Wise & Co. 308 California
*WARD S. W. H. & SON, 323 Mont (see advertisement, back cover)
Warshawski & Bro. 656 Washington
Wilkins B. P. 654 Market
[See Clothing.]

Furnishing Goods. Ladies'.

Edwardes E. Mrs. 559 Mission
Hoffman M. Mrs. 22½ Montgomery
Lion J. Mrs. (infants') 657 Clay
Meagher M. Mrs. 1320 Stockton
Simmons L. Mrs. 1108 Dupont
Tishler H. Mrs. 39 Second
Wetmore W. N. Mrs. 44 Second
[See Dress Makers; Millinery, Etc.]

Furniture.

*Importers.

Ackley & Bergstrom, 417 Mission
Baum G. 919 Dupont
Bennett Sam, 1019 Dupont
Bernard B. 1120 Stockton
Bernstein M. C. 841 Pacific
Beuchamp J. 215 Second
Bird Adam, 243 Third
Borren K. 246 Third
Bowers E. P. 31 Third
Burnstine J. 838 Market
Bush N. 708 Pacific
Castel F. C. 811 Clay
Clark H. 695 Market
*Cole N. P. & Co. 518 Front
Cook A. 226 Sutter
Cornish H. C. (col'd) 622 Battery
Courcelle A. 320 Washington.
Cullens J. W. 30 First
Davis M. 1316 Dupont
Doud A. 113 Sansom
Eichel C. 106 Fourth
*Foster J. & C. (manuf) 314 Pine
Frank H. 217 Commercial
Fuhr C. A. 626 Market
*Goodwin & Co. 528 Washington and 636 Market
Hall E. 106 Jackson
Harris B. 253 Third
Henry S. 707 Pacific
Hinckley W. H. 823 Clay
Holt W. (school) Mead House
Horstmann H. & Co. 740 Washington
Hyman M. 606 Broadway
Kempney C. P. 1311 Dupont
Levy A. N. 33 Market
Levy D. 607 Mission
Levy S. 26 Geary
Levy S. 37 Second
Lewis M. 1302 Dupont
Lloyd R. R. & Co. 727 Market
Luchsinger J. B. (manuf) 116 Bush
Lynch F. 522 Broadway
Lynch J. T. 814 Pacific
Marchebout C. Madame, 1115 Dupont
McCarty D. 223 Sutter
Mogan & Co. 900 Market
Murphy D. J. 732 Market
O'Brien & Rice, 107 Second
*PEIRCE J. 417 California (see advertisement, p. iii)
Ralle M. Folsom nr Stewart
Regan J. 29 Second

Shaber J. F. 21 Second
Shaber John A. 672 Market
SCHAFER J. F. & H. H. 504 Sansom (see advertisement, p. 854)
*SCHREIBER J. & C. 406 Sansom (see advertisement, p. lvi)
Seligman F. 1226 Dupont
Stern P. 232 Third
Stringer W. J. 520 Washington
Underhill G. E. 624 Market
Weir W. G. (manufacturer) 638 Market
Weydemann H. 238 Fourth
Wigmore J. (manuf) 423 California
Williams & Kempf, 117 Third

Furriers.

[See Fur Dealers.]

Galvanic or Electrical Machines.

[See Opticians.]

Game.

[See Produce—Game.]

Gardens—Public.

Hayes' Park, junction Market St. and Hayes Valley R. R.
Odeum, H. Siegfried & Co. cor Dolores and Fifteenth
Willows, F. Kelly, Mission bet Eighteenth and Nineteenth, Mission Dolores

Gas Fitters.

* Importers.

Collins E. S. 825 Montgomery
*DAY THOMAS, 732 Montgomery (see advertisement, cover)
Eccles J. 667 Mission
Kane J. 641 Market
Lane & Gordon, 11 Post
McKewen & Son, 618 Clay
McNALLY & HAWKINS, 104 Mont and 83 Sutter (see adv. p. 650)
McNiel & Burton, 817 Kearny
Moore H. J. 406 Montgomery
O'Brien J. H. & Co. 706 Montgomery
O'Brien P. R. 641 Market
O'Malley Thomas, 646 Market
*PRIOR J. K. 730 Montgomery (see advertisement, p. lx)
Richardson J. 616 Market
Ross Thos. 319 Bush
Shepard & Sons, 631 Market
Smith A. J. 35 Webb
SNOOK G. & W. 806 Montgomery (see advertisement, p. 663)

Gas Meter Manufacturers.

Dobrzensky M. 417 Mission

Gas Works.

Citizens' Gas Co. office 702 Wash
San Francisco Gas Co. office NE cor First and Howard

Geyser Water.

Wood J. H. 232 Bush

[See Soda.]

Gilders.

[See Carvers and Gilders.]

Glass. Plate.

Cameron, Whittier & Co. 425 Front
Rosenbaum F. H. & Co. 423 Battery

Glass Cutters.

Mallon John & Co. 14 Beale
McDermott, Graham & McCarty, 120 Fremont

Glass Stainers. Ornamental.

Bowen James B. 12 Fourth

Glassware.

Langley, Crowell & Co. (chemical) cor Clay and Battery
TAYLOR J. (chemical) 514 Washington
[See Crockery and Glassware.]

Glass Works.

Newman & Brannan, S. F. Flint, Crook nr Brannan

PACIFIC GLASS WORKS, Potrero, office 621 Clay, H. Hanssmann, agent (see adv. p. xxxii)

Gloves.

Hughes Henry, 220 Battery

Glue Manufacturers.

BAEDER & ADAMSON, Philadelphia, (see advertisement, p. cii)
DANA G. S. Pacific, cor Gough and Lombard (see adv. p. xxxvii)
[See Soap Manufacturers.]

Gold Beaters.

Furley J. F. 641 Commercial
Riley Thomas, 641 California

Gold Dust Dealers.

Richon N. 611 Commercial
Sutro C. 427 Montgomery
[See Assayers; Bankers; Brokers.]

Gold Pen Manufacturers.

Haight A. J. 434 California
Kenney W. B. J. 502 Montgomery
Pearce H. D. 606 Montgomery

Granite Yards.

Cadue P. foot Sansom
Grant C. B. cor Third and King
HEVERIN M. 783 Market (see advertisement, p. 659)
[See Stone Yards.]

Grocers. Wholesale and Jobbers.

Athearn & Morrison, 8 Clay
Bowen & Bro. 421 Battery
Bradshaw & Co. NE cor Cal and San
Brady Benjamin, 120 California
Breed & Chase, NE cor Clay and Bat
Burnap J. 425 Davis
Cahn A. & Co. 205 California
Callaghan J. 121 Front
Castle Bros. 213 and 215 Front
Coghill J. H. & Co. SW cor Front and Commercial
Crouse J. R. cor Clay and Sansom
Cutter J. H. 511 Front
Day J. S. & Co. 306 Clay
Dellapaine & Co. 426 Battery
Dickinson & Gammans, NW cor Front and Clay
Dodge Bros. & Co. 408 Front
Dodge & Phillips, 325 Front
Eggers & Co. 210 California
Fordham & Jennings, 600 Front
Goldstein & Seller, 217 Front
Hemmenway & Merrill, 215 Sac
Hendley A. C. & Co. 204 Front
Herrmann S. & Co. 310 Sacramento
Hodges W. 223 Sacramento
Irvine & Co. 224 Front
Jennings T. 402 Sansom
Jennings & Austin, 223 Sacramento
Jones & Co. 205 Front
Kruse & Euler, 209 and 211 Front
Larco N. 432 Jackson
Levi H. & Co. 222 California
Lewis H. L. 208 Sacramento
Marks E. & Co. 311 Commercial
McKay D. 427 Davis
Rountree & McMullin, 323 Front
Rowland, Walker & Co. 505 Front
Sahatie A. E. & Co. 617 and 619 San
Sbarboro Bros. 531 Washington
Scalmanini & Frapolli, 424 Front
Smith S. 400 Front
SNEATH R. G. 408 Front (see advertisement, p. lv)
Strybing C. H. 212 Jackson
Tillman & Co. 407 Clay
Weaver, Wooster & Co. 218 Front
Wellman, Peck & Co. 404 Front
White P. J. & Co. 412 Front

Grocers. Retail.

Albers A. 825 Stevenson
Albers & Foege, 641 Pacific
Alcayga J. NE corner Vallejo and Dupont
Allsgood & Miller, corner Jackson and Drumm
Arimond J. cor Fillmore and Presidio Road
Arps John, cor Geary and Hyde
Asher E. cor Bush and Battery
Athearn & Morrison, 8 Clay

Atkins H. B. cor O'Farrell and Jones
Badenhop H. Mission nr Twelfth
Bañeos John, cor Dupont and Union
Bahrs A. cor Jackson and Davis
Balke & Tietjen, cor Ritch and Brannan
Bardenhagan & Co. cor Folsom and Sixth
Beck Peter, cor Mission and Beale
Becker Wm. cor Mont and Green
Behrens Jos. cor Brannan and Sixth
Benard A. cor Fourth and Howard
Benker F. cor Third and Folsom
Berbe Louis, Potrero Avenue
Berge O. E. Green nr Montgomery
Bermingham Thos. corner Taylor and Turk
Berry F. G. cor Jackson and Stockton
Berthon E. 523 Union
Betuel F. & Co. cor Pine and Dupont
Beverson C. 570 Mission
Bigley C. 134 Clay
Blohm P. 42 Webb
Bockman R. H. cor Folsom and Eighth
Bockman & Mangels, cor Freelon and Fourth
Bogel C. H. cor Wash and Waverly Pl
Bohanan P. cor Natoma and Mary
Bohlken & Bremer, cor Third and Harrison
Bolan James, 328 Third
Bollo Thos. cor Stockton and Vallejo
Borella A. cor Seventh and Cleveland
Boschen N. & Co. cor Fifth and Minna
Bowen Bros. 340 Montgomery
Bradshaw & Co. 300 Sansom
Braghi R. cor Brannan and Seventh
Brander J. S. cor Mission and Fourth
Brandt O. 1040 Market
Brauer C. W. cor Pacific and Sansom
Brickwedel A. D. cor First and Market
Brickwedel J. cor Clay and Waverly Pl
Briordy John, 60 First
Brommer & Bro. cor Sixth and Bryant
Bronstrup W. cor Folsom and Dora
Brown W. P. cor Clay and Dupont
Brunings H. & Co. cor Third and Mission
Brunjes D. 425 Bush
Brunjes H. cor Fourth and Harrison
Bruns & Bro. cor Folsom and Spear
Bruns & Co. 201 Commercial
Bruns H. cor San José Road and Thirtieth
Bruns N. Guerrero nr Sixteenth
Buhsen B. 727 Davis
Burmeister A. cor Cal and Leav
Burmeister C. H. cor Beale and Mission
Burmeister Chr. 31 Main
Burnap J. 425 Davis
Bush S. cor Pacific and Kearny
Buttenop H. 625 Pacific
Butler R. cor Harrison and Eighth
Butt & Kuchmeister, cor Pacific and Kearny
Byrne & Castree, corner Howard and Twelfth
Campe H. cor Second and Tehama
Campe J. & Magnus, cor First and Folsom
Carroll & Bro. cor Third and Minna
Carroll R. cor Harrison and Garden
Carson J. opposite Presidio House
Carsten F. cor Bush and Dupont
Carsten C. cor Dupont and O'Farrell
Castagnet D. 708 Broadway
Clayes J. R. 913 Washington
Cline H. 5 Mission
Connell M. cor Moss and Folsom
Cook E. G. & Co. cor Second and Minna
Cooney J. Union nr Montgomery
Corbett D. E. cor Mason and O'Farrell
Corby J. cor Sixth and Stevenson
Cordes A. J. F. cor Pacific and Powell and Broadway and Octavia
Cordes & Vinken, cor King and Third
Cordes W. 128 Stewart, Main nr Harrison, and cor Bush and Pierce
Cornahrens H. cor Howard and Sixth
Cox W. B. cor Third and Bryant
Croskey & Howard, cor Hayes and Franklin
Crouse J. B. cor Clay and Sansom
Crus Henry, 56 Clay
Curry Luke, 734 Market
Dacey J. 1426 Stockton
Dahlen Francis, cor Dupont and Sutter and Ritch and Clara
Dahmke F. cor Wash and Drumm
Daley M. cor Sansom and Greenwich
DeCosta J. N. Green nr Larkin
Dellapaine & Co. cor Wash and Bat

Delventhal W. cor Jackson and Davis
Denmark & Horning, cor Pacific and Taylor
Detels M. cor Harrison and Main
Dettmer & Luhrsen, cor Montgomery and Filbert
Dicaud J. H. cor Dupont and Vallejo
Dietrich J. cor Vallejo and Mason
Dimmer N. 815 Pacific
Donzelmann J. F. 409 Pine
Doscher & Co. 138 Second
Doscher H. H. cor Braunan and Seventh
Doscher J. D. cor Bush and Sansom
Downs J. cor Fourth and Stevenson
Doyle M. cor Hayes and Van Ness Av
Dreyer & Ebbighausen, cor Gilmore and Kentucky
Droge & Vessing, cor Natoma and Jane
Droge G. F. C cor Natoma and Jane
Droge H. cor Pacific and Front
Droger H. & Co. cor Pine and Battery
Drollet J. A. 1396 Dupont
Drucker A. 624 Mission
Druckert E. cor Clay and Stockton
Druhe J. H. cor Market and Stewart
Dulip & Waddington, cor Dupont and Broadway
Dunn W. cor Pacific and Leavenworth
Dunning Thomas, 253 Clara
Ebbinghausen H. corner Folsom and Fourth
Efford N. C. 309 East
Eggers F. cor Dupont and Vallejo
Ehlers W. 49 Hinckley
Evers H. C. cor Mont and Vallejo
Expert A. cor Pacific and Leavenworth
Fahrenkrug W. cor Tehama and Third
Feehan & Byrnes, corner Fourth and Jessie
Feehan J. cor First and Natoma
Fehnemann B. cor Larkin and Green
Feidbush J. H. 108 Sutter
Fichen J. cor Dupont and Pacific
Fielitz W. cor Fourth and Folsom
Fink H. & Co. cor Powell and Union
Fishback & Brother, 1501 Mason
Fisk & Barber, Howard Court nr Howard
Fitschen J. H. cor Fourth and Stevenson
Flynn E. cor Fourth and Bryant
Flynn J. cor Hyde and Ellis
Flynn P. T. cor Howard and Eighth
Foley M. cor Stevenson and Ecker
Fonda A. cor Third and Howard
Fredericks W. cor Battery and Bdwy
Freie H. cor Dupont and Sacramento
Friedrich J. G. corner Sixteenth and Second Avenue
Friesenhausen J. 220 Sutter
Frisch J. W. cor Fifth and Mission
Fromhelm W. cor Third and Townsend
Fusilier J. cor Jones and Geary
Gallagher J. A. cor Sixth and Shipley
Garronne & Hutaf, cor Dupont and Cal
Gassert W. cor Mission and Ninth
Gately J. cor Mason and Geary
Gehreis W. A. cor Sixth and Mission
Geils H. W. cor Kearny and Sutter
Geraghty B. cor Mason and Turk
Gerdes A. cor Third and Stevenson
Gerhow F. cor Mission and East
Gerken F. cor Mission and Main
Girzikowsky & Zeh, 20 Hinckley
Gleason & Hurley, corner Dupont and O'Farrell
Gobener G. H. cor Third and Brannan
Gordeau A. 1220 Dupont
Godfrey J. Mrs. 614 Broadway
Gordon J. H. 243 Minna
Gotze & Borchers, cor Cal and Kearny
Gould & Co. cor Third and Silver
Greenberg C. 12½ Fourth
Gremke H. cor Clark and Davis
Grimm F. W. cor Fourth and Clementina
Grosbauer & Fitschen, cor Folsom and Haywood
Grote F. cor Geary and Broderick
Grotheer H. cor Fourth and Brannan
Gudehaus F. & C. cor Clara and Berry
Gunther J. 1421 Dupont
Haake J. C. 100 Stewart
Haase F. cor Folsom and Beale
Hacke C. W. cor Sac and Waverly Pl
Hadler C. cor Clay and Mason
Hahn W. B. 1016 Clay
Hamman J. H. 828 Clay
Hanavan P. cor Sixth and Tehama
Hans J. cor Stockton and Greenwich
Hardigan P. 162 First

Harjes F. cor Greenwich and Jones
Harms H. corner Folsom and Twenty-Second
Hartman C. cor Dupont and St. Mark Place
Hartmann & Hillebrandt, corner Third and Brannan
Hashagen J. cor Stockton and Bdwy
Haskell G. S. & Co. 514 Market and 15 Sutter
Hasshagen J. & Co. 322 Jackson
Hawley C. J. & Co. 42 Second
Hayburn J. C. cor Fifth and Shipley
Hayes, B. D. cor Eighth and Clementina
Healy M. cor Leavenworth and Mason
Heeseman G. F. corner Second and Brannan
Heidhoff A. H. cor Stockton and Sac
Heins & Eden, cor Battery and Bdwy
Helms C. cor Folsom and Sixteenth
Helms E. A. cor O'Farrell and Hyde
Hencke & Co. cor Wash and Dupont
Hencke & Spellmeyer, 719 Pacific
Hencken & Muller, corner Powell and Vallejo
Hencken W. H. 417 Third
Hermann Isaac, 619 Post
Heuer P. cor Lombard and Jansen
Hey & Meyn cor Folsom and Twelfth
Heye & Luttig, corner Lombard and Mason
Heyer A. cor Third and Bryant
Hildebrandt & Knop, cor Montgomery and Broadway
Hildebrandt H. cor Kearny and Sutter
Hillebrandt C. cor Brannan and Gilbert
Hobe A A. cor Eighth and Minna
Hoelscher & Rau, cor Eddy and Mason
Hoger E. 525 Washington
Holm T. cor Stockton and Sutter
Holtmler H. cor Filbert and Taylor
Holtz W. & Co. cor Mont and Pacific
Hoppe W. 814 Jackson
Horstmann J. cor Bush and Powell
Hosling A. cor Fifth and Mission
Humphrey J. cor Geary and William
Iburg W. cor Pine and Kearny
Inderstruth J. cor Bryant and Rincon Place
Jacobs C. cor Stockton and Green
Jacobs E. cor Dupont and Harlan Pl
Jacobson T. 2013 Mason
Jenkins Isaac, cor Polk and Austin
Jensen & Harnkin, cor Francisco and Midway
Johnson & Brandon, cor Jones and Pac
Jones W. cor Fourth and Silver
Joost Bros. cor Eleventh and Mission
Kahman J. G. cor Kearny and Post
Kappke H. F. cor Union and Mason
Keely J. cor Pacific and Leavenworth
Kennedy B. cor Ellis and Larkin
Kennedy & Bro. cor Taylor and O'Farrell
Kenny J. cor Sixth and Minna
Keulen H. cor Union and Mason
Kiszler H. 619 Broadway
Klein Bros. cor Kearny and Bdwy
Kleine H. 5 Mission
Klemeier & Stamer, cor Jack and Bat
Koen C. 926 Folsom
Kohlmoos C. cor Mission and First
Kohlmoos H. cor Fourth and Tehama
Kohn H. & Co. 408 Folsom
Koller J. 816 Washington
Koopman H. cor Franklin and Austin
Korff M. (widow) cor Mission and Thirteenth
Korten B. cor Mason and Greenwich
Koster & Co. cor Jones and O'Farrell
Koster H. cor Third and Howard
Koster H. cor Townsend and Crook
Kramer J. cor Dupont and Greenwich
Kriete H. cor Pine and Larkin
Kroning W. cor Sac and Kearny
Kruger & Hollings, corner Mason and Geary
Kuechler A. cor Jessie and Annie
Lammers & Lilienthal, cor Hyde and Bush
Lange F. W. & Co. cor Stockton and Bush
Lankenau F. cor Powell and Ellis
Lebatard & Brother, 513 Washington
Lehinkuhl H. cor Fourth and Minna
Lehrke H. cor Mariposa and Indiana
Lemkau A. cor First and Minna
Levin S. 220 First
Levingston L. J. cor Dupont and Geary
Levy H. 523 Pacific
Lewellyn R. 1008 Pacific

Liebenberg C. cor Pacific and Battery
Lindsey J. H. Sansom nr Greenwich
Lohaus & Wickan, 42 Stewart
Longlitz J. 906 Pacific
Loop & Somers, cor Second and Bryant
Ludorff J. & Co. cor Mont and Jack
Luhmensen W. cor Sixth and Harrison
Madel P. & Co. cor Mission and Stewart
Magner T. cor Broadway and Scott
Mallon J. cor Pacific and Scott
Mangels & Claussen, 313 Dupont
Mangels & Co. cor Howard and Fourth
Mangels & Steffens, corner Folsom and Main
Marks J. J. & Co. 6 Clay
Marks S. 658 Mission
Marlow Owen, cor Third and Mission
Martens D. & Bro. cor Sac and Stock
Martin M. cor Hyde and Pacific
Martin W. cor Second and Howard
Marx A. cor Green and Stockton
Matthias L. cor Dupont and Union
Maume J. (widow) 150 First
McCabe B. cor Jessie and Anthony
McComb J. cor Sixth and Jessie
McConnell M. (widow) 81 Stevenson
McCraith D. cor Front and Pacific
McGee P. 1014 Jackson
Medel P. cor Mission and Stewart
Meetz & Co. cor Post and Dupont
Mehrtens A. cor Mason and Filbert
Mehrtens H. cor Front and Oregon
Meier & Knippenberg, cor Stevenson and Ecker
Meier H. cor Stockton and Francisco
Meierderks A. Co. cor Post and Powell
Menke H. cor Battery and Commerce
Mentel W. cor Broadway and Stock
Merz & Greiner, cor Sutter and Powell
Meyer Bros. cor Folsom and Fremont
Meyer & Molk, cor Dupont and Green
Meyer H. cor Dupont and Filbert
Meyer H. W. 210 Stewart
Meyer J. H. cor Wash and Powell
Meyer W. F. cor Mission and Beale
Michaelis F. 238 Kearny
Michelson F. cor Davis and Jackson
Miller & Brunning, corner Jessie and Annie
Miller & Washburn, 131 Third
Miller L. & Co. 725 Jackson
Miller J. J. cor Sutter and Leav
Milliman D. F. cor Bdwy and Scott
Mindermann H. 520 Broadway
Mitchell J. 174 Stevenson
Mitchell J. F. cor Post and Hyde
Mohrmann F. cor Kearny and Bdwy
Monje A. G. 13 Stewart
Morrisey P. H. cor Fifth and Tehama
Muhlenbrink & Rohde, cor Sutter and Taylor and Post and Taylor
Murken M. cor Ecker and Clementina
Murphy J. cor Folsom and Baldwin Court
Murphy M. C. cor Sixteenth and First Avenue
Nelson I. M. Twentieth nr Guerrero
Neumann L. cor Stock and O'Farrell
Neunebar & Co. cor Folsom and Beale
Neuval F. 83 Union
Nobmann C. cor Bush and Mason, and Sacramento and Leavenworth
Nobman J. Francisco nr Powell
Nolan M. 87 Stevenson
Noite C. R. cor Mission and Twenty-Fourth
Noltmeyer F. cor Harrison and Chesley
Norman & Co. cor Valencia and Sixteenth
Nunan M. cor Bryant and Ritch
O'Brien Bros. cor Stock and Vallejo
O'Keefe D. cor Harrison and Dora
O'Reilly & Brady, cor Mission and Sixth
Offerman & Co. cor Dupont and Pac
Offerman J. H. cor Fourth and Mission
Ogle & Schriefer, 155 Natoma
Ohlandt H. & N. cor Powell and Pac
Onfray Madam, 1204 Dupont
Orr W. H. cor Harrison and Fifth Av
Ortmann J. F. 815 Jackson
Pastene A. 20 Lewis Place
Pestner E. cor Fourth and Clementina
Peterson C. A. cor Mont and Union
Peterson & Tietjen, cor Leav and Bdwy
Peterson P. cor Washington and East
Petterman H. 533 California
Piper J. cor Second and Howard
Plath H. 431 Union
Plege & Hoffman, cor Post and Taylor
Pope & Bruns, cor Fillmore and Steiner
Postel P. J. cor Fourth and Everett

Powers J. cor Union and Hyde
Princivalle G. Sixteenth nr Dolores
Puckhaber J. cor Post and Mason
Puvogel J. cor Mason and Filbert
Raffetto L. 623 Broadway
Ranken & Ryan, cor Sixth and Tehama
Reardon D. cor Washington and Leav
Reed R. 455 Jessie
Reese H. cor Powell and Greenwich
Reilly B. cor Sixth and Clara
Reimers C. cor Mason and O'Farrell
Richards J. M. 213 Dupont
Ring P. cor Lombard and Powell
Ring R. 128 First
Robertson A. M. San Bruno Road three miles from Plaza
Rontet M. cor Dupont and Green
Roskamp F. cor Fourth and Jessie
Runge F. cor Kearny and Green
Ryan J. cor Pacific and Hyde
Ryan T. 21 Hinckley
Sagehorn H. 520 Union
Sahnke & McCune, cor Howard and Sumner
Salomon J. cor O'Farrell and Hyde
Sanderson J. H. 23 Third
Santif & Bro. cor Howard and Fifth
Sbarboro & Brother, 531 Washington
Sbarboro J. B. cor Folsom and Sixth
Scanlin & Bruno, 2 Second
Scanlin & Doscher, cor Bush and Jones
Schedel G. cor Jessie and Ecker
Scheper C. cor Mont and Sutter
Scheper M. cor Pine and Sansom
Schlueter & Leege cor Third and Hunt
Schmedes J. J. 542 Jackson
Schmidt W. cor Harrison and Ritch
Schmitt H. cor Howard and Russ
Schortemeier H. H. cor California and Prospect Place
Schrader & Gerken, cor Fifth and Stevenson
Schroder F. cor Sac and Drumm
Schroder H. cor Grove and Gough
Schroder R. 330 Vallejo
Schroder & Hashagen, cor Stockton and Vallejo
Schuldt & Knoche, 120 Second
Schulteis H. cor First and Clementina
Schultz W. cor Dupont and Geary
Schultze & Harms, cor Kearny and Union
Schumann W. cor Fourth and Minna
Schwartz D. corner Kearny and St. Charles
Schwarze & Co. cor Kearny and Geary
Seegelken & Winckelmann cor Davis and Commercial
Selig Bros. cor Minna and Jane
Shumann W. cor Fourth and Mission
Siebe J. & Co. cor Union and Powell
Siedenberg H. 520 Vallejo
Siegmundt C. H. 825 Kearny
Siems J. H. 409 Union
Slosson & Ladd, cor First and Folsom
Smith J. cor Dupont and Chestnut
Smith John, 16 Clay
Solomon I. cor Stockton and Ellis
Sommers C. cor Sixth and Natoma
Sonnenberg L. B. 16 Kearny
Spreen W. cor Brannan and Ninth
Steindler M. cor Shipley and Willow
Steinhoff & Co. cor Bush and Trinity
Stewart G. cor Stockton and Clay
Stoppelkamp A. H. cor Stockton and Union
Strasser A. 426 Green
Stuss H. & Co. 141 Second !
Sullivan D. & Co. cor Fifth and Clara
Swordstream J. E. cor Fourth and Louisa
Teltgen R. cor Pacific and Battery
Tennent R. J. cor Ellis and Larkin
Thomas W. cor Sixth and Clementina
Thomford & Klein, cor Powell and Filbert
Tiatien & Bolke, cor Brannan and Ritch
Tiedemann P. cor Folsom and Rousch
Tieroff A. 1118 Kearny
Tietjen D. cor Fourth and Tehama
Tietjen & Co. cor Pine and St. Mary
Uhrlandt H. E. Fort Point
Umbsen H. cor Folsom and Moss
Urband & Co. cor Howard and Fifteenth
Van Doren J. cor Bush and Mason
Vandevoort & Co. 30 Third
Velbert P. H. cor First and Howard
Voliers H. cor Powell and Market
Vollmer J. & H. cor Sac and Davis
Von Glahn J. 226 Minna and 225 Sutter

Von Hadeln J. cor Powell and Green
Vorrath & Co. cor Taylor and O'Farrell
Wagner C. Mrs. Dolores nr Twentieth
Waterman J. G. cor Folsom and Sixth
Weber T. H. cor Broadway and Mason
Wendt H. cor Third and Folsom
Weasling W. cor Fourth and Folsom
West Louis cor Fifth and Shipley
Wheeler H. cor Howard and Langton
Wiebar N. cor Third and Everett
Wieland F. & Co. cor Powell and Vallejo
Wilkins J. M. & Co. cor Second and Natoma
Williams S. G. cor Fourth and Jessie
Witgen D. cor Dupont and Broadway
Witte C. cor Shasta and Michigan
Wolbern A. F. 8 Clay
Wolbern J. D. cor Dupont and Greenwich
Wolters J. J. cor Folsom and Ritch
Woolley L. H. cor Clay and Taylor
Wrede D. cor Sansom and Sutter
Wulburn J. & Bro. 734 Broadway
Wynne W. cor Fourth and Louisa
Young R. cor Clay and Larkin
Zahn H. 823 Vallejo
Ziegelmeyer A. 629 Mission

Gunny Bags.
[See Bag Makers; Sacks.]

Gunpowder.
California Powder Works, office 320 California
California Powder Co. office 728 Mont
Eureka Blasting, 227 Commercial
Gibbons Rodmond & Co. (Dupont) 214 California
Parker E. H. (Hazard) 224 California

Gunsmiths.
Bach John, 408 Commercial
Blewitt & Johnson, 507 Commercial
Curry N. & Bro. 317 Battery
Harris W. & Co. 208 Leidesdorff
Herget J. 114 Pacific
KLEPZIG I. C. E. 733 Washington (see advertisement, p. 649)
Lagoarde B. 730 Washington
Liddle R. & Co. 538 Washington
Meyer C. H. J. 604 Pacific
Newhoff F. 208 Leidesdorff
Plate A. J. 411 Sansom
PROVIDENCE TOOL CO. Providence, R. I (see adv. p. c)
Rudolph W. 216 Pacific
Severin T. 524 Kearny
Studte F. 648 Commercial
Wilson & Evans, 513 Clay

Guns and Sporting Materials.
Bach John, 408 Commercial
Blewitt & Johnson, 507 Commercial
Curry N. & Bro. 317 Battery
Hall R. & Co. (importers) cor Sansom and Commercial
HICKMAN L. M. Stockton, Cal. (see advertisement, p. cl)
Klepzig I. C. E. 733 Washington
Liddle R. & Co. 538 Washington
Oxenham A. H. 19 Sansom
Plate A. J. 411 Sansom
PROVIDENCE TOOL CO. Providence, R. I. (see adv. p. c)
Schuyler, Hartley & Graham, 409 Bat
Severin T. 524 Kearny
Wilson & Evans, 513 Clay

Gymnasium.
Olympic Club, Sutter bet Montgomery and Sansom

Gymnasium. Ladies.
Aldrich J. Miss, 115 Stevenson
Wheeler F. cor Second and Market

Hair Dressers.
Allen Asa, 136 Fourth
Alves A. J. 833 Pacific
Barbara R. 538 Commercial
Baskerville R. D. 305 Davis
Bass C. (col'd) 925 Kearny
Belliere E. 756 Clay
Bergst L. E. 944 Market
Beyer L. 805 Battery
Blak & Denison, 615 Merchant
Blodes T. 602 Market
Boisse E. 526 Commercial

Bonneau T. C. Railroad House
Brennan A. Mrs. (ladies') 705 Howard
Brooks R. F. 302 Kearny
Brown S. G. Brooklyn Hotel
Campbell J. 426 Folsom
Cary I. G. 640 Clay
Castera C. 1026 Dupont
Ciprico & Cook, Cosmopolitan Hotel
Clark S. P. (col'd) 159 Second
Cordan A. C. 129 Third
Costa F. 703 Front
Cox C. Madame (ladies) 441 Bush
Creamer A. American Exchange
Davis & Koffel, 44 Sutter
Deitz Adam, 416 Folsom
Diehl C. 533 Sacramento
Dobelman & Elsen, 9 Second
Elwell C. 530 California
Ewald E. 621 Montgomery
Fischer & Koch, 408 Kearny
Francis R. (col'd) 234 Bush
Froell C. cor Clay and Dupont
Fugaze J. F. 509 Kearny
Garissere F. 532 Jackson
Gies Adam, 315 Kearny
Gies K. 822 Montgomery
Godfrey N. A. (col'd) Occidental Hotel
Gorfinkel W. 105 Jackson
Grandi G. 506
Greif John, 536 Washington
Gressler C. A. 307 Pine
Grimm Adam, Lick House
Grote F. 906 Kearny
Gutzeit H. 631 Kearny
Guyod V. 712 Pacific
Hammerschmidt & Huck, 129 Third
Hayden & Zander, 550 Washington
Held G. & Brother, 331 Pine
Hemprich L. 18 Kearny
Henderson & Brown, 215 Sansom
Henderson W. International Hotel
Hertel G. 20 Clay
Hirschfeld & Maleton, 303 Mont
Hirschfeld & Moritz, 32 Montgomery
Hock T. 532 Jackson
Hubert C. 603 Montgomery
Jackson H. 23 Sansom
Jensen C. 683 Pacific
Jung W. 43 Second
King B. 235 Pacific
King H. 3 Stewart
Kock M. 417 Kearny
Koelzer A. 136 Fourth
Laville E. 13 Washington
Lawton S. W. Miss (ladies') 319 Powell
Lebert & Brougham, 918 Dupont
Lemke C. H. 1430 Stockton
Lipman J. What Cheer House
Lipman & Korn, 406 Pine
Messerle C. 1212 Stockton
Monie G. 307 Montgomery
Morton H. R. 109 Pacific
Murphy C. J. 214 Fourth
Obenauer G. 43 Second
Oppenheimer E. cor Union and Powell
Patrick G. (col'd) Folsom nr Sixth
Patrick W. C. 1503 Stockton
Pfister C. Russ House
Pilling J. 105 Jackson
Pimentel J. 105 Jackson
Pimentel J. 218 Pacific
Proschold & Rausch, 310 Bush
Puyvou P. 610 Kearny
Rogers H. (col'd) Francisco nr Powell
Rosenthal & Simon, 709 Clay
Saalburg & Brodek, 107 Kearny
Sand Brothers, 50 Fourth
Schmidt Chris. 3 Fourth
Schneider J. J. 624 Washington
Silva F. 102 Pacific
Simpson A. C. 520 Market
Smallwood J. (col'd) 640 Clay
Smith H. R. cor Market and Geary
Somerville M. Miss (ladies') 530 Bush
Staffelbach X. 108 Stewart
Stahle Brothers, cor Mont and Clay
Starkey J. E. (col'd) 102 Stewart
Steffen & Bro. 722 Market
Steinle H. cor Valencia and Sixteenth
Storm C. 321 Bush
Stulz & Co. 937 Kearny
Van Geistenfeld H. L. 647 Pacific
Ward A. J. (col'd) 916 Kearny
Wass G. 744 Market
Witkowski N. & Bro. Oriental Hotel
Wolf J. 404 Market

Hair Restorative.
CHAPMAN S. M. Mrs. 218 Third (see advertisement, p. 667)
Ciprico George (Ciprico's) Cosmopolitan Hotel

Howard M. (col'd) 315 Montgomery
Theobald J. 808 Market

Hair Workers.

Bolander A. M. Mrs. 60 Second
Cook C. Mrs. 645 Clay
Dagger C. 521 Market
Mohrhardt F. F. 251 Third
Usynski R. Mrs. 21 Geary

Hardware.
* Importers.

*Alvord William & Co. 122 Battery
AMES PLOW CO. over Quincy Market, Boston (see adv. p. cvi)
*Arnold N. S. 306 Battery
*BENCHLEY L. B. & CO. 206 and 208 Battery (see adv. p. lxv)
*Bisagno Bros. 420 Battery
Blanchard J. 26 Third
*Bofer William & Co. 610 Sacramento
Brignardello Bros. 623 Pacific
*Butcher G. H. 421 Battery
*Caire Bros. 530 Washington and 1028 Dupont
Clark J. H. 117 Sansom
Clark P. B. 412 Merchant
*CONROY & O'CONNOR, 107 Front and 208 Pine (see adv. p. xi)
COX & NICHOLS (tanners) 422 Battery (see advertisement, p. lxv)
Dillon T. 38 Kearny
*Doty W. R. (agent) 113 Pine
Glein C. F. & Co. 317 Kearny
Guion G. W. 7 Post and 606 Market
*Hawley & Co. SE cor Cal and Bat
*Helmken J. T. 816 Kearny
HICKMAN L. M. (Stockton, California, see adv. p. ci)
*Hooker & Co. 117 California
*Johnson George C. & Co. 35 Battery
*Kennedy L. W. (agent) 210 Bush
*LOCKE & MONTAGUE, 112 and 114 Battery (see adv. p. xlvii)
Long C. 604 Washington
Mariani & Steffani, 1006 Dupont
*MARSH, PILSBURY & CO. cor Front and Pine (see adv. p. xcv)
Marwedel & Otto. 329 Bush
Merrill R. A. 14 First
Miller T. S. 729 Davis
Newman C. L. 111 Third
Osborn R. F. & Co. 751 Market
Page J. M. 42 Clay
Patrick J. C. 122 Battery
*Rockwell, Coye & Co. cor Battery and Pine
Rosekrans H. & Co. 135 Montgomery
*RUSSELL & ERWIN MANUFACTURING CO. 106 Battery (see advertisement, p. lxvi)
*SELBY T. H. & CO, 118 California (see adv. p. xii)
*Simmons, Rowe & Co. 204 Pine and 34 Clay
*SPEYER M. 826 Washington
*Tay, Brooks & Backus, SW cor Washington and Front
*Treadwell & Co. NE cor Cal and Bat
Trieber C. 302 Jackson
*Underhill J. 118 and 120 Battery
*Van Winkle I. S. & Co. cor Bush and Battery
Webb A. C. 781 Market

Harness and Saddlery.
* Importers.

Carlos T. 525 Pacific
Carmelich G. 230 Sansom
Castany A. 563 Market
*Clark J. H. 107 Sansom
Conway M. G. 721 Market
Cram W. R. 557 Market
Cronin P. J. 719 Davis
Dornett J. W. 20 First
Fennell D. 520 Battery
Frankenberg J. 1110 Dupont
Hamilton J. 243 Third
Hanson L. 901 Sansom
Helke C. 139 Third
Hurlbutt J. M. & Co. 407 Battery
Hyde & McClennen, 227 Montgomery
*JOHNSON J. C. & Co. 520 and 522 Sansom (see adv. p. lxxviii)
Jones C. 741 Folsom
Jones H. 437 Kearny
Juguet & Perrin, 208 Kearny
Kreits & Cosbie (collars) 36 Battery
Lawless M. 506 Sansom

*MAIN & WINCHESTER, 214 and 216 Battery (see adv. p. xxxviii)
McColgan M. 225 Washington
*Mead C. H. SE cor Jackson and Front
Mead & Son. 224 Sansom
O'Kane J. 526 Kearny and 14 Sutter
*Peet Francis & Son, 508 Battery
Phillips & Co. 407 Battery
Rowland R. W. 105 Sansom
Simonsen D. 143 Fourth
*Stone & Hayden, 418 Battery
Tillman W. J. 703 Mission
Toutdin F. 533 Broadway
Trainor J. 622 Mission
Trumbull W. cor Davis and Com
Weaver M. 644 Market
Weintraut C. H. 429 Pacific
Wilder N. C. cor Front and Market
*Willey O. F. & Co. 316 California
Wilmot W. F. 315 Battery

Hat and Cap Manufacturers.

Adams & Brother, 647 Washington
Blake & Co. 524 Montgomery
Booth William & Co. 314 Sacramento
Cranert F. 510 Bush
Gaidon M. 239 Sutter
Harris I. 716 Market
Kallisher & Diamant, 414 Sacramento
Lang C. Mrs. 728 Washington
Laurent A. 1222 Stockton
LeGay & Co. 614 Commercial
Lipson J. 619 Sacramento
Lust S. 408 Sacramento
Snapper S. & Co. 427 Pine
Tiffany R. J. 627 Washington
[See Caps.]

Hat Block Makers.

Grush & Co. 29 Fremont
Johnson J. B. cor Fremont and Mission

Hats. *Straw.*

Hats and Caps. *Importers.*

Berwin P. & Bros. 319 Sacramento
Booth William & Co. 314 Sacramento
Badger & Lindenberger, 415 Battery
Cohn H. & Co. 413 Sacramento
Jacobs A. & Co. 325 Sacramento
Kline & Co. 420 Sacramento
Lanzenberg M. & Co. 626 Clay
LeGay & Co. 614 Commercial
Meussdorffer J. C. 628 Commercial
Rosenberg G. & Co. 410 Sacramento
Stern M. 226 Battery
Toplitz F. 512 Sacramento
Triest & Friedlander, 218 Battery
Unger & Bro. 412 Sacramento
Young & Co. 336 Montgomery
Pacific Straw Works Co. 603 Market

Hatters.

Adams & Brother, 647 Washington
Arnold Caspar, 14 Geary
Blake & Co. 524 Montgomery
Boysen Charles, 314 Pine
Boysen Julius, 314 Pine
Contet & Plege, 721 Clay
Coupland W. F. 514 California
Danglada A. 641 Commercial
Desmond C. Cosmopolitan Hotel
Glass J. 1018 Dupont
Kaskal M. 617 Commercial
LeGay & Co. 614 and 616 Commercial
Mangeot G. 423 Kearny
McGann P. & Co. 654 Washington
Mead B. F. 309 Montgomery
MEUSSDORFFER K. 635 and 637 Commercial (see adv. p. 654)
Nickerson C. 209 Montgomery
Rebard Bros. 630 Washington
Samuels L. 1104 Dupont
Schriver W. 141 Fourth
Shocken s. H. 17 Second
Thiele J. 625 Commercial
Tiffany R. J. Eagle, 627 Washington
Warwick & Brown, 207 Third
Worres J. 609 Washington
Young & Co. 336 Montgomery

Hatters' Stock.

LANZENBERG M. & Co. 626 Clay
Meussdorffer J. C. 628 Commercial
STEIN, SIMON & CO. 632 Sacramento

Hay Presses.
[See Machinists.]

Hay and Grain.

Barraclough J. & Co. 39 Clay
Blair & Co. 28 Washington
Boquilion A. A. 53 Third
Brown M. 204 Washington
Dutton Henry & Son, Pier 7 Stewart
Grant, Averell & Co. 41 Sacramento
Holmes J. B. & Co. 108 Market
Leperco H. Pacific nr Taylor
Maver R. 120 Fourth
McKenna Bro. & Co. corner Clay and Drumm
Meng T. Brannan nr Ninth
Miller & Hall, 418 Market
Miner T. E. cor Commercial and East
Morrow George, 21 Clay
Place C. L. & Co. Folsom Street Wharf
Rider & Somers, 24 Market
Riley & Vest, 569 Market
Smith & Adams, cor Wash and Davis
Starr & Riddle, 16 Drumm
Tiernan R. & Co. Valencia nr Sixteenth
Vaillant A. C. Brannan nr Fourth
Williams & Law, cor Front and Bdwy

Hides and Wool.

Burke F. G. 220 Front
COX & NOCHOLS, 422 Battery
Ernst H. 15 Davis
Farish A. T. & Co. 221 Davis
Feuerstein R. & Co. 212 Front
McLennan, Whelan & Grisar, Rincon Dock
Mitchell T. S. 38 California
Moore & Co. Davis nr California
Mulholland J. & Co. 11 Davis
Read M. G. 11 Davis
Rich S. & Bro. 220 California
Ross, Dempster & Co. 427 Battery
Shilling L. 103 California
Smith & Brown, Potrero
Sumner W. B. 31 Battery
Taylor C. L. & Co. 38 California
Wassermann A. & Co. 429 Sacramento

Hoop Skirts.

Alexander L. (manuf) 16 and 20 Second
Jacobs & Rosenfield, 24 Second
[See Dry Goods; Fancy Goods.]

Hops.

Scherr F. 511 Sacramento
WINTER J. 208 Cal (see adv. p. xlvii)

Hose and Belting. *Manufacturers.*

Cook & Son. cor Battery and Bdwy
COX & NICHOLS, 422 Battery (see adv. p. lxv)
Free W. 17 First
Howard S. (colored) 326 Davis
[See Leather; Tanners.]

Hosiery and Gloves.

Austin & Co. cor Mont and Sutter
Hughes Henry, 220 Battery
Meagher, Taafe & Co. 9 Montgomery
TOBIN BROS. & DAVISSON, 219 Battery (see adv. p. xxxv)
[See Dry Goods; Furnishing Goods.]

Hospitals.
[See Appendix.]

Hotels, Etc.

Abbey Hotel, Old San José Road 7 miles from Plaza
Abbey Hotel, McLaren Lane near Folsom
Albion House, 559 Market
Albion House, A. Furlong, 208 Stewart
American Exchange, J. W. Sargent, 323 and 325 Sansom
Atlantic House, John McManus, 210 Pacific
Baily House, A. H. Baily, 116 Sansom
Bay State House, M. Robinson, corner Front and Sacramento
Beatty's, nr Pioneer Race Course
Belle Vue House, T. L. Planel, 1018 Stockton
Benton House, F. J. Hanlon, cor First and Mission
Bitter's Hotel, W. Bitter, cor Kearny and Jackson
Blue Anchor, J. L. Schroeder, 7 Wash
Bootz's Hotel, J. Baumeister & Co. 435 Pine

Brevoort House, Mrs. M. H. Yates, cor Fourth and Mission
Brown's Hotel, J. F. Brown, cor Stockton and Filbert
Brooklyn Hotel, J. Kelly Jr. cor Sansom and Pine
Brooklyn House, J. Gately, 217 Bdwy
Brunswick House, 761 Market
Brunswick House, J. F. Johnson, 761 Mission
Burnet House, T. Buckley, 34 Webb
Bush St. House, J. McNamara, 333 Bush
California Hotel, Gaillard Bros. corner Commercial and Dupont
Cambridge House, L. McKeone, 304 Pacific
Carroll & Resing, Old San José Road
Central House, J. Cornynn, 814 San
Central House, M. Cornynn, 115 First
Chicago Hotel, E. W. Helmburg & Co. 720 Pacific
City Front House, H. Bernhammer, 625 Davis
Cliff House, J. G. Foster, Point Lobos
Clinton Temperance House, M. Hartsel, 311 Pacific
Commercial Hotel, W. H. Norton, 125 Pacific
Columbia House, Leedes & Rolen, 46 Stewart
Columbia House, Bdwy nr Davis
Columbia House, Clark nr Front
Columbia Hotel, A. Thornton, 741 Market
Continental Hotel, Tandler & Lang, cor Commercial and Sansom
Continental House, T. Ryan, 519 Mission
Cosmopolitan Hotel, Adelphi Hotel Co. cor Bush and Sansom
Coso House, L. J. Ewell, 627 Com
Dresdener House, T. Brown, 337 Bush
Dublin House, P. Melehan, 228 First
Eagle Hotel, Beale nr Folsom
Empire House, corner Jackson and Drumm
Empire House, Turner & Lewis, Vallejo nr Front
Eureka Hotel, J. Levy, 20 Sansom
First St. House, Mrs. E. Swett, corner First and Mission
Five Mile House, C. A. Bohner, San Bruno Road
Five Mile House, C. H. Shear, Old San José Road
Flume House, J. E. Biggs, San Bruno Road
Franklin Hotel, H. Curran, cor Sansom and Pacific
Franklin House, C. Maloney, cor Sansom and Broadway
Gamba House, Mrs. F. Gamba, 518 Sac
Garibaldi House, B. Daneri, cor Broadway and Sansom
Georgia Hotel, 919 Kearny
German Hall, E. Angelis, 16 and 18 Sansom
Golden Age Hotel, T. Gibbons, 127 Pac
Golden City Four Mile House, J. Rickards, San Bruno Road
Golden Eagle Hotel, C. Dittmer, 219 Kearny
Golden Gate Hotel, H. H. Meyer, 728 Market
Golden Gate House, Mrs. E. Graham, 510 Davis
Golden State House, J. W. McCormick, 135 Jackson
Government House, J. C. Collins, cor Washington and Sansom
Grass Valley House, T. Madden, Sixth nr Market
Great Eastern, 9 Broadway
Great Western, cor Wash and Drumm
Green's House, W. Green, 1027 Dupont
Half-Way House, S. Costello, Ocean House Road
Harbor View House, F. Hermann, Fort Point Road
Helvetia Hotel, J. Schmid, 431 Pine
Hibernia House, 518 Pacific
Howard St. House, 504 Howard
International Hotel, F. E. Weygant, 532 Jackson
Irving House, Mrs. T. A. Warschauer, 508 Mission
Isthmus House, W. J. Bally, 54 First
Keystone House, E. Hostkamper, 127 Jackson
Lick House, Alstrom & Johnson, Montgomery bet Sutter and Post

Londonderry House, G. McLaughlin, 12 Broadway
Lutgen's Hotel, H. A. Siegfried, 228 Montgomery
Manhattan House, D. McCarthy, 705 Front
Mansion House, P. Backus, Dolores op Sixteenth
Mariners' Home, H. Brown, 306 Clark
Marysville Hotel, E. McNabb, 414 Pac
Mechanics' Hotel, 539 Market
Mechanics' Hotel, R. Williams, 605 Pac
Meyers' Hotel, N. Gartner, 814 Mont
Miners' Hotel, 516 Pacific
Mission House, Miss A. Harrington, 520 Mission
Mission St. House, 511 Mission
Minerva House, F. W. Pauplitz, 123 Jackson
Montgomery House, W. Perkins, 623 Market
Montreal House, 622 Pacific
Morning Light House, P. J. Cody, cor Mission and Twenty-Ninth
Mount Hood House, A. Jackson, 54 Sacramento
Muh's Hotel, N. Muh, 716 Pacific
National House, Dunning & Herbert, 414 Market
New Atlantic Hotel, Bucholtz & Kock, 619 Pacific
New England House, J. Schleicher, 205 Sansom
New Branch Hotel, M. O'Neil, 12 Sutter
New Orleans House, J. Hopkins, 222 Commercial
New Wisconsin Hotel, Sinock & Trembath, 411 Pacific
New York & Baltimore House, Mrs. J. Jillard, 29 Jackson
New York Hotel, Mrs. E. Stodole, cor Commercial and Battery
New York House, J. Tucker, 840 Market
Niantic Hotel, Miss B. Mooney, corner Clay and Sansom
Nightingale Hotel, W. Shear, cor Mission and Sixteenth
Occidental Hotel, Lewis Leland & Co. cor Montgomery and Bush
Ocean House, J. R. Dickey, 3 miles S W City Hall
Olive Branch House, cor Sacramento and Drumm
Oregon House, Mrs. B. Cunningham, 38 Stewart
Oriental Hotel, Bailey & Hyatt, corner Battery and Bush
Original House, E. & L. Lazar, 531 Sac
Pacific Exchange, Tuhte & Reiners, 26 Stewart
Pacific House, Pinner & Laflin, 35 Pac
Pacific Railroad House, Brannan near Fourth
Pacific Temperance House, Wm. Jackson, 109 Pacific
Palm's House, Kroger & Muloch, 633 Broadway
Philadelphia House, J. Knack, 336 Bush
Phoenix House, F. Harrington, 721 San
Point San Quentin House, R. A. Follmer, cor Louisiana and Sierra
Portsmouth House, T. T. Uncless, NW cor Clay and Brenham Place
Post St. House, J. Schumacher, 207 Post
Potomac House, W. Denny, Folsom nr Spear
Precita Valley House, H. Mohlers, cor Mission and Thirtieth
Queen City Hotel, W. Cummings, 627 Davis
Railroad House, C. B. Green, 318 and 320 Commercial
Revere House, J. Steinmann, 323 and 325 Pine
Rincon House, J. B. Price, cor First and Folsom
Roxbury House, J. Curley, 318 Pacific
Russ House, H. H. Pearson & Co. Montgomery bet Pine and Bush
Sacramento Hotel, M. Hoffman, 409 Pacific
Sailors' Home, cor Bat and Vallejo
Sanders' Temperance House, J. P. Sanders, 24 Sacramento
Scandinavian House, J. Johnson, 41 Jackson
Seymour House, J. Doyle, 24 Sansom
Shakespeare Hotel, Higgins & Sipples, 219 Pacific

Sierra Nevada Hotel, Niggle & Laurberg, 528 Pacific
Spring Valley House, J. Evans, cor Union and Presidio Road
St. Charles Hotel, D. C. Plimpton, 29 First
St. Francis Hotel, A. Mathieu, cor Clay and Dupont
St. John's House, Mrs. W. F. Lapidge, 639 Clay
St. Lawrence House, L. Rudolph, 615 Market
St. Louis Hotel, Helmberg & Schroder, 11 Pacific
St. Nicholas Hotel, L. Hess, cor Sansom and Commercial
Steckler's Exchange, J. E. Steckler, cor Sansom and California
Tehama House, G. W. Frink, 410 Cal
Telegraph House, J. S. Schroder, cor Green and Battery
Tremont House, E. S. Woolley, 420 Jackson
Tri-Mountain House, M. O'Connell, 545 Market
Union House, R. B. Butler, 511 Mission
Union House, C. O. Roberts, 32 Stewart
United States Hotel, P. C. Curley, 706 Battery
United States Hotel, M. Gregg, 304 Beale
Victoria Hotel, 409 Pacific
Washington House, J. Donnelly, 412 Davis
West End Hotel, J. H. Daley, Plaza
Western Hotel, J. Higgins, 306 Broadway
Western House, H. Fortmann, 140 Stewart
What Cheer House, R. B. Woodward. 529 Sacramento
White House, R. Beatty, cor Mission and Twenty-Third
Whitehall Exchange, L. Maurer, cor Spring and Market
William Tell House, M. Fenstermacher, 317 Bush
Winchester House, 409 Pacific
Winthrop House, P. Denehy, 524 Mission
Wright's Hotel, Mrs. M. Wright, 210 Broadway
[See Boarding Houses.]

House Brokers.

[See Brokers — House; Real Estate, Etc.]

House Raisers.

Dodge & Ziegler, 668 Mission
HYDE & CHESTER, 619 Mission (see advertisement, p. 655)
Merriman R. 639 Mission
Richardson W. L. 613 Market
Stratton A. W. & Bros. 724 Harrison bet Third and Fourth
Watkins J. & Co. 403 Mason
[See Contractors.]

Ice.

American Russian Commercial Company, 718 Battery

India Rubber Goods.

BADGER & LINDENBERGER, SW cor Battery and Merchant
Rubber Clothing Co. 118 Montgomery
Scholle Bros. 405 and 409 Sacramento
[See Clothing.]

Ink Manufacturers.

DONALD W. G. & CO. 9 Spring Lane, Boston (see adv. p. cvi)
MAYNARD & NOYES, Boston, Mass. (see advertisement, p. cix)
[See Stationers.]

Inspectors. *Provisions.*

Anthony E. T. & Co. cor Sacramento and Battery
Coffin A. State, junction Pine and Mkt
Deeth J. (State stamp) 424 Battery
Gallagher & Co. 17 Beale
Lull L. R. (State stamp) 424 Battery
Waterman E. R. (flour) 406 Davis
[See Packers of Goods.]

Instrument Depots.

Kesmodel F. (surgical) 817 Kearny

Koehler A. 750 Washington
LAWRENCE & HOUSEWORTH, 317 Montgomery
Roach J. 413 Washington
Sack J. C. 203 Montgomery
SCHMOLZ WM. 430 Montgomery (see advertisement, p. 669)
Tennent Thos. cor Battery and Oregon
[See Cutlers; Opticians.]

Insurance Adjusters. *Marine.*

CAZNEAU T. N. 436 California (see advertisement, p. xlviii)
Moore E. J. 425 Washington

Insurance. *Agents Underwriters.*

Bacon T. H. & J. S. Boston, 216 Front
FALKNER, BELL & CO. Lloyds, 430 California
Fletcher A. T. New York, 216 Front
Mebius C. F. Bremen, 223 Sacramento
Rene J. E. French, 716 Montgomery

Insurance Companies.
Foreign.

ACCIDENTAL N. Y., Bigelow & Bro. agents, 505 Mont (see adv. p. xcvii)
ÆTNA, E. H. Parker agent, 224 California (see adv. p. lxxvi)
ARCTIC FIRE, N. Y., Bigelow & Bro. agents, 505 Montgomery
BRITISH & FOREIGN MARINE, Liverpool, Falkner, Bell & Co. agents, 430 Cal. (see adv. p. 637)
CHARTER OAK LIFE, H. P. Coon, agent, 2 City Hall (see adv. p. xcv)
COLUMBIA FIRE, N. Y., R. B. Swain & Co. agents, 206 Front (see advertisement, p. 637)
CONNECTICUT MUTUAL LIFE, Hartford, Bigelow & Bro. agents, 505 Montgomery
CONTINENTAL, N. Y., C. A. Low & Co. agents, 426 California (see advertisement, p. 634)
EQUITABLE LIFE. N. Y., Bigelow & Bro. agents, 505 Montgomery
German Mutual Fire, 58 Mont Block
GERMANIA LIFE, B. Gattel agent, 519 Montgomery (see adv. p. lxxi)
GUARDIAN LIFE, J. R. Garniss agent, 526 Washington (see adv. p. lxxix)
HAMBURG & BREMEN FIRE, M. Speyer agent, 526 Washington (see advertisement, p. xxiii)
HARTFORD FIRE, Bigelow & Bro. agents, 505 Montgomery
HOME, N. Y., Bigelow & Bro. agents, 505 Montgomery
IMPERIAL FIRE & LIFE, London, Falkner, Bell & Co. agents, 430 California (see adv. p. xxxvi)
LIVERPOOL & LONDON & GLOBE, W. B. Johnston agent, 414 Montgomery (see adv. p. 633)
LONDON & LANCASHIRE FIRE ASSOCIA'N, H. Dreschfeld agent, 623 Mont (see adv. p. xiii)
MANHATTAN FIRE, N. Y., R. B. Swain & Co. agents, 206 Front (see advertisement, p. 637)
MANHATTAN LIFE, N. Y., J. Landers, agent, SW cor Montgomery and Clay (see adv. p. 635)
MUTUAL LIFE, H. S. Homans, agent, 609 Clay (see adv. p. 635)
NATIONAL LIFE & TRAVELERS'. F. Schultze agent, 623 Montgomery (see adv. p. xcvi)
NEW YORK LIFE, R. N. Van Brunt agent, SW cor Mont and Cal (see advertisement, p. lxxviii)
NIAGARA FIRE, N. Y., J. Landers agent, SW cor Montgomery and Clay (see adv. p. 636)
NORTH AMERICA LIFE, J. A. Eaton & Co. agents, 240 Montgomery, (see advertisement, back cover)
NORTH AMERICAN FIRE. N. Y., C. A. Low & Co. agents, 426 California (see adv. p. 634)
NORTH BRITISH & MERCANTILE, W. H. Tillinghast agent, 414 California (see advertisement, p. xxiii)
NORTH CHINA MARINE, Koopmanschap & Co. agents, 1101 Battery (see advertisement, p. 636)
NORTHERN ASSURANCE FIRE & LIFE, London, W. L. Booker agent, 428 Cal (see advertisement, p. 634)

PACIFIC MUTUAL, C. A. Low & Co. agents, 426 Cal (see adv. p. 634)
PHENIX FIRE, N. Y., Bigelow & Bro. agents, 505 Montgomery
PHŒNIX, Hartford, R. H. Magill agent, 603 Commercial (see advertisement, pp. 467 and 484)
SECURITY FIRE, N. Y., Bigelow & Brother agents, 505 Montgomery
TRAVELLERS, Hartford, R. H. Magill agent, 603 Commercial (see advertisement, p. xxxiii)
UNIVERSAL LIFE, H. S. Homans agent, 609 Clay (see adv. p. 635)
WASHINGTON FIRE, N. Y. Bigelow & Bro. agents, 505 Montgomery
Washington Marine N. Y., C. J. Janson agent, 210 Pine
WIDOWS' & ORPHANS' BENEFIT LIFE, H. S. Homans agent, 609 Clay (see advertisement, p. 635)

Insurance Companies. *Foreign—Agents.*

BIGELOW & BROTHER, NW corner Mont and Sac (see adv. pp. 9 to 631)
BOOKER W. L. 428 California (see adv. pp. xxiv and 634)
COON H. P. Charter Oak, 2 City Hall (see advertisement, p. xcv)
DELL L. B. Phœnix, etc. cor Mont and Com (see adv. pp. 467 and 484)
DRESCHFELD H. London and Lancashire, 623 Mont (see adv. p. xiii)
EATON J. A. & CO. North America Life, 240 Mont (see adv. back cover)
FALKNER, BELL & CO. Imperial Fire and Life, 430 California (see adv. pp. xxxvi and 637)
GARNISS J. R. Guardian Life, 526 Washington (see adv. p. lxxix)
GATTEL B. Germania Life, 519 Montgomery (see adv. p. lxxi)
HOMANS H. S. Mutual Life, etc. 609 Clay, (see adv. p. 635)
JOHNSTON W. B. Liverpool, London, and Globe (see adv. p. 633)
KOOPMANSCHAP & CO. North China, 1101 Battery (see adv. p. 636)
LANDERS JOHN, Manhattan Life, 527 Montgomery (see advertisement, p. 636)
LOW C. A. & CO. Fire and Marine, 426 Cal (see adv. p. 634)
MAGILL R. H. Phœnix, SW cor Mont and Com (see adv. pp. 467 and 484)
PARKER E. H. Ætna, 226 California (see advertisement, p. lxxvi)
SCHULTZE F. National, Life, and Travelers', 623 Montgomery (see advertisement, p. xcvi)
SPEYER M. Hamburg-Bremen, 526 Washington, (see adv. p. xxiii)
SWAIN R. B. & CO. 206 Front (see advertisement, p. 637.)
TILLINGHAST W. H. North British. 414 California (see adv. p. xxiii)
Van Alen W. K. Life, 502 Washington
VAN BRUNT R. N., Y. Life, SW cor Mont and Cal (see adv. p. lxxviii)

Insurance Companies. *Home.*

CALIFORNIA HOME, 224 California (see advertisement, p. xx)
CALIFORNIA LLOYDS MARINE, 416 Cal (see adv. p. lxxxvii)
FIREMAN'S FUND, 238 Montgomery (see advertisement, p. ii)
German Mutual Fire, 58 Mont Block
HOME MUTUAL 630 Montgomery (see advertisement, p. 477)
MERCHANTS' MUTUAL MARINE, 206 Front (see adv. p. xx)
OCCIDENTAL, SW cor Montgomery and California (see adv. p. iii)
PACIFIC, 406 Cal (see adv. p. xxi)
SAN FRANCISCO, SE cor Montgomery and Sac (see adv. p. xcviii)
UNION, 416 Cal (see adv. p. lxxvii)

Intelligence Offices.

Brady Thomas, 623 Kearny
Curran Thomas, 138 Sutter
Eaton C. S. 708 Kearny
Fish F. & Co. 522 Montgomery
Hills Henry & Co. 5 Second
O'Brien E. M. Mrs. 108 Montgomery
O'Brien & Ward, cor Mont and Clay
Von Rhein O. F. & Co. 105 Mont
WHITMAN S. P. 313 Montgomery

Interpreters of Languages.

Carvalho C. (Chinese) Police Court
DeClairmont B. 855 Washington
Hartog E. City Hall, rear
Lussey John (French and Spanish) Police Court
Splivalo A. D. 430 Jackson
[See Translators; Teachers.]

Iron and Steel.

CONROY & O'CONNOR, 107 Front and 208 Pine (see adv. p. xi)
Gabeldu & Meyer, 25 Fremont
Johnson George C. & Co. 33 and 35 Bat
SELBY T. H. & CO. 116 and 118 California (see adv. p. xii)
Van Winkle I. S. & Co. cor Battery and Bush
[See Hardware and Stoves.]

Iron Railings, Fences, Etc.

McKibben W. (Eureka) 41 First
Sims J. R. Oregon nr Davis
[See Machinists, Etc.]

Japanese Goods.

Way D. E. 206 Montgomery

Jewelers. *Importers.*

BARRETT & SHERWOOD, 517 Mont (see adv. front cover)
BRAVERMAN & LEVY, 621 Washington (see adv. front cover)
Crosby F. W. & Co. 636 Clay
Dinkelspiel S. B. 607 Washington
Falkenau Bros. (chains and bracelets) 629 Washington
Gray R. B. & CO. 616 Merchant
Heringhi B. 635 Kearny
Jordan M. 625 Montgomery
Joseph Bros. 607 Montgomery
Josephi I. S. 641 Washington
Kahn & Strauss, 619 Washington
Levison Brothers, 629 Washington
Lippman J. 203 Montgomery
Mathewson & Bucklin, 519 Mont
SHERWOOD R. 517 Montgomery (see advertisement, p. ii and cover)
SHREVE GEO. C. & CO. 525 Montgomery (see adv. p. xliv)
Tucker & Co. 505 Montgomery
WIEDERO OTTO & CO. 433 Montgomery (see advertisement, p. lii)

Jewelers.
Importers.

Ahrens C. 836 Dupont
Anderson David, 58 Clay
Baldwin M. M. 311 Montgomery
*BARRETT & SHERWOOD, 517 Mont (see adv. inside front cover)
Barrett A. 33 Second
*BRAVERMAN & LEVY, 621 Washington (see adv. front cover)
Burkhardt G. 209 Pacific
Campbell J. 335 Kearny
Carmaix A. 707 Clay
Collins C. E. 602 Montgomery
*Crosby F. W. & Co. 638 Clay
Drapnick F. 622 Clay
Eckart C. 620 Merchant
Finberg A. 911 Kearny
Friedlander W. 41 Third
Geist W. 205 Montgomery
Green W. 538 Kearny
Hain C. H. & Co. 321 Montgomery
Hammond W. A. 57 Second
Hartung T. 216 Kearny
Heinz F. 504 Market
Heinz F. 848 Washington
Helzman A. 406 Commercial
Helzman L. 521 Kearny
Heringhi B. 635 Kearny
Isson S. 639 Pacific
*Joseph Bros. 607 Montgomery
Kling G. W. 227 Jackson
Knowlton W. H. 648 Sacramento
Lang E. 102 Pacific
Lehmann G. What Cheer House
Lewis H. M. & M. 655 Clay
Magnus F. A. cor Sac and Davis
Marks F. 1024 Dupont
Mathewson & Bucklin, 519 Mont
Mathieu G. 724 Washington
McGREGOR J. 409 Sansom (see advertisement, p. lxx)
Miller L. H. 216 Clay
Milisner L. 707 Clay
Mohrig C. F. 613 Washington

Mund William, 750 Market
Newman H. 13 Second
Nolte W. 1034 Montgomery
O'Connell D. A. 155 Third
Ohm E. F. 615 Montgomery
Pace C. 613 Battery
Peckford J. 309 Sixth
Rahwyler A. 927 Kearny
Revalk J. 510 Montgomery
Richet C. 1220 Dupont
Roffat S. 1114 Dupont
Rose A. J. 3 Montgomery
Scheider J. cor Kearny and Jackson
Sharp W. 837 Clay
*SHERWOOD ROBERT. 517 Montgomery (see adv. cover and p. li)
*SHREVE G. C. & CO. 525 Montgomery (see advertisement, p. xliv)
Sornin A. 605 Washington
Steler P. 804 Washington
Stopp M. H. 541 Sacramento
Trappnick F. 622 Clay
Traube H. 717 Clay
*Tucker & Co. 505 Montmery
Usynski J. 406 Kearny
Wallmann & Bro. 212 Montgomery
Wenzel H. 303 Montgomery
WIEDERO OTTO & CO. 433 Montgomery (see advertisement lii)
Wolf F. 622 Clay
Zacharias H. 538 Kearny
[See Watchmakers.]

Jewelers. *Manufacturing.*

BARRETT & SHERWOOD, 517 Mont
Bohm William, 614 Merchant
BRAVERMAN & LEVY, 621 Wash
Eckart C. 620 Merchant
Frontier & Deviercy, 740 Commercial
Gray R. B. & Co. 616 Merchant
Hubash J. 409 Sansom
Joseph Brothers, 607 Montgomery
Kling O. W. 227 Jackson
Laird D. W. 620 Merchant
Lemme Bros. 534 Commercial
Letellier A. 620 Merchant
Mathewson & Bucklin, 519 Mont
Miller L. 614 Sacramento
MORRIS B. & CO. 643 Sacramento (see advertisement, p. 649)
Perrochon E. 622 Clay
Pohlmann & Co. 516 Clay
Reichel F. R. 620 Merchant
Rondel E. 622 Clay
Seamans J. M. *04 Merchant
SHERWOOD ROBERT, 517 Montgomery (see adv. p. li and cover)
SHREVE G. C. & CO. 525 Montgomery (see advertisement, p. xliv)
Tucker & Co. 505 Montgomery
Vanderslice & Co. 810 Montgomery
WIEDERO OTTO & CO. 433 Montgomery (see adv. p. lii)

Joiners.

[See Carpenters; Shipwrights.]

Junk Dealers.

Barnstead T. S. 113 Commercial
Bichard N. 209 Stewart
Dettelbrach M. 417 Brannan
Hallel C. 111 Washington
Hare Charles, 34 Stewart
Harley Charles & Co. 116 Davis
Hashagen M. 102 Sacramento
Klaus, Bowman & Co. 728 Mission
Ludeman W. 567 Market
Madden C. cor Mission and Annie
Taylor S. P. & Co. 113 Davis
Yetes J. cor Howard and Hubbard
[See Bottles and Sacks.]

Kerosene.

[See Oil; Lamps; Coal Oil.]

Laces.

* *Importers.*

*Anderson & Pronsergue, 105 Mont
Bigot Madame, 828 Washington
*Duden Freres, 629 Clay
Elgutter M. 18 Second
Merzbach J. 412 Kearny
[See Dry Goods; Fancy Goods; Millinery.]

Lamp Dealers.

* *Importers.*

*Dell, Cranna & Co. 513 Front

---

*Dietz A. C. & Co. 519 Front and cor Clay and Kearny
Dixon & Vagts, 144 Fourth
Dow M. & Co. 62 Second
*Hayward & Coleman. 414 Front
*Hollub A. & Co. 501 Front
Levitzsky D. & Co. 54 Second
McCarty A. 850 Washington
Owens J. B. 10 Third
*Stanford Brothers, 121 California
*Swain R. A. & Co. cor Pine and San
*Taylor F. B. & Co. 511 Front
Urquhart S. F. 512 Sansom
Vale C. Jr. 802 Dupont
[See Crockery and Glassware.]

Land Agents. *Bounty.*

RANSOM L. 625 Merchant (see advertisement, p. lxix)
Robinson J. R. 626 Montgomery
Stevenson J. D. 604 Merchant
[See Attorneys; Notaries, etc.]

Lapidaries.

Cartier & Co. 532 Broadway
GRAY R. B. & CO. 616 Merchant
Rondel E. 622 Clay
SHERWOOD R. 517 Montgomery
[See Jewelers.]

Lash and Whip Makers.

MAIN & WINCHESTER, 214 Battery
Murphy J. 12 First
[See Harness, etc.]

Last Makers.

Hetkes John, cor Bdwy and Kearny

Laundries.

Auger M. A. (widow) 777 Clay
Aureau F. Miss, 26 Post
Barbier Andrew, 841 Clay
Battles S. Pacific bet Mont and San
Berard Brothers, 638 Broadway
Berson A. Mrs. 828 Washington
Boudan A. 2111 Mason
Boutard C. 178 Jessie
Bovee, Hallett & Bartlett (Contra Costa) 113 Broadway
Bowret J. Sixth nr Brannan
Bufford S. F. (Bay City) Sixth near Brannan
Burscough H. 505 Third
Chelsea, James Laidley, Lagoon
Cole William, 106 Dupont
Collibeaux P. Madame, 335 Bush
Couch A. A. 1140 Folsom
Contra Costa, 13 Broadway
Covet F. Bush nr Brannan
Croze Aug. 231 Ritch
Darriman L. Fern Avenue nr Polk
Duff T. 705 Commercial
Dumas L. 416 Dupont
Dunand A. cor Stockton and Jackson
Eude M. Madame, 1320 Stockton
Fleury A. 503 Powell
Gassman J. B. 406 Union
Gray E. C. 624 Commercial
Grethen P. Madame, 409 Bush
Haercade J. Bush nr Polk
Hay Aug. 1419 Dupont
Jantzen E. (widow) 615 California
Jardon M. (widow) 922 Stockton
Jusset C. 11 Virginia
Kehoe T. Brannan nr Sixth
Kene & Ryan, 123 Silver
Laidley J. (Easton's and Chelsea) office 321 Sansom
Larue A. Quincy Place nr California
Lemaitre A. E s Lagoon
Lemaitre P., E s Lagoon
Lowenstein J. H. 906 Powell
May S. (Bay City) 1140 Folsom
Miller & Cutter (What Cheer) 125 Leidesdorff
Minor L. 1130 Folsom
Pacaud M. 178 Jessie
Pinckney W. J. 36 Clay
Portal J. B. cor California and Kearny
Pougel J. (widow) 604 Broadway
Reynolds J. M. Jones nr Pacific
Schilling C. E s Lagoon
Smiley W. T. Valencia cor Sixteenth
Spoiler A. 1425 Dupont
Thomas F. W. 431 Sutter
Tolford & Cole (Star) 115 Sansom
White E. P. Harriet nr Howard
Wiley C. Perry nr Fourth

Leather Collar Manufacturers.

Cook & Son, cor Broadway and Bat.,
Ewing C. 794 Davis
Kreitz & Cosbie, 26 Battery
[See Harness and Saddlery.]

Leather Dealers.

* *Importers.*

Bender C. 114 Sutter
COX & NICHOLS, 422 Battery (see advertisement, p. lxv)
Delabigne J. B. 323 Clay
*DUDLEY & GERHARDY, 422 Battery (see adv. p. lv)
*HEIN JOHN G. 416 Battery (see advertisement, p. xxxv)
ING A. D. & CO. 312 Commercial (see advertisement, p. xxxv)
Lumsden W. 643 Merchant
*Schumacher A. 634 Clay
Stone & Hayden. 418 Battery
Thomas A. 738 Market
*Weck L. E. & Co. 415 Clay
Worth F. 338 Bush
[See Boots; Shoes; Tanners.]

Leg. *Artificial.*

Jewett Jarvis (Palmer's) 629 Wash

Libraries. *Circulating.*

Bowen & Hart, 620 Market
Boyd T. C. 300 Montgomery
Mather & Sinclair, Metropolitan Mkt
Payot H. 640 Washington
[See Literary Institutions—Appendix.]

Lime and Cement.

Adams Samuel, cor Market and Main
Benicia Cement Company, 629 Clay
Davis & Cowell, cor Front and Wash
Hanna John jr. 215 Clay
Webb & Holmes, cor Sac and Davis

Liquors. *Importers and Wholesale.*

* *Ale and Porter.*

Altschul L. & Co. 723 Sansom
Baldwin A. R. & Co. 219 Front
Barra & Galvin, 118 First
*Barry & Patten, 413 Montgomery
Behrens James, 429 Battery
Beiden F. C. 612 Sacramento
Bradshaw & Co. NE cor Cal and San
Brickwedel Henry & Co. 208 Front
Bryant & Morrison, 614 Front
Cahn A. & Co. 205 California
Carroll John, 305 and 307 Front
Cassin F. 520 Front
Castera J. E. & Co. 540 Washington
Chauche & Martin, 608 Front
*Commeseel H. L. 307 California
Cutter W. T (agent) 111 California
Dames & Lohse, 608 Sansom
Daneri F. & Co. 615 Front
Deney A. & Co. 623 Sansom
DeRutte E. (estate of) 431 Battery
DICKSON, DeWOLF & CO. 410 Bat
Dolheguy B. 507 Front
DOWS JAMES & CO. 205 Sacramento (see advertisement, p. 678)
Enqvist A. A. cor Davis and Clark
Fahlsten C. J. Edwards, 434 Jackson
Fargo & Co. 214 and 216 Front
Favre & Mendesolle, 605 Front
Fenkhausen A. 309 Montgomery
Field & Co. 422 California
Finley T. E. 113 Leidesdorff
Flanagan J. & Co. 421 Front
Fox & Porter, 531 Clay
Funkenstein J. & Co. 323 California
Gale A. B. 404 Front
Groezinger Geo. cor Battery and Pine
Horan J. C. & Co. 415 Front
Hosmer, Goewey & Co. 411 Front
Hotaling A. P. & Co. NE cor Sansom and Jackson
Hunter, Wand & Co. 612 Front
Irwin J. 30 Montgomery
Jacobs N. B. & Co. 423 Front
Jaudin E. & Co. 522 Front
Kelly & Egan, 604 Battery
Lacour L. & Co. 206 Jackson
Larco M. 432 Jackson
LeRoy T. 540 Washington
Livingston & Hickey, 221 California
Loewe Bros. 309 California
*Lumley D. 1024 Battery

Lyons E. G. & Co. 510 Jackson
MARTIN E. & CO. 606 Front (see advertisement, p. xxxvii)
Maury P. jr. 710 Sansom
May P. 725 Clay
McAran & Kelly, 618 Front
Meinecke C. 213 Front
Melville John, 613 Commercial
Menu J. H. 728 Montgomery
MERCADO & SEULLY, 506 Jackson
NUDD, LORD & CO. 419 Front (see advertisement, p. lxiii)
O'Connor J. & Bro. 512 Battery
O'Connor M. 605 Front
O'Neil M. J. 312 Jackson
PARKER GEORGE F. cor Washington and Mont (see adv. p. 668)
Pascal, Dubedat & Co. 426 Jackson
Patrick James & Co. 617 Battery
Phelan J. 616 Front
Poursillie A. 605 Sansom
Putzmann F. (distiller) 213 Jackson
*Richards & Co. 708 Sansom
Riley P. & Co. 519 Front
Roach P. A. NW cor San and Jackson
Roche T. cor Sansom and Pacific
Roth J. 805 Montgomery
Sabatie A. E. & Co. 617 Sansom
Saulnier & Co. 719 Sansom
Sbarboro Bros. 531 Washington
Scalminini & Frapoli, 424 Front
Schroder & Co. 811 Montgomery
Schultz & Von Bargen, cor California and Front
Schwergerie & Co. 636 Commercial
Smith F. & Co. 210 Sacramento
Soussingeas L. & Co. 430 Jackson
SPEYER MORRIS, 926 Washington (see advertisement, p. xii)
Strybing C. H. 212 Jackson
Sullivan & Cashman, SW cor Front and Jackson
Sweeny M. D. 709 Sansom
Taussig L. 723 Sansom
Taylor Thos. & Co. 415 Clay
Traves Freres, 606 Front
Trobock N. 416 Davis
Turner & Marsh, 221 California
Van Bergen J. & Co. 524 Washington
Weston J. 536 Jackson
Wormser Bros. SW cor Cal and Front
[See Wines : Syrups, Etc.]

Liquors. *Retail.*

Adam Thomas, 516 Montgomery and cor Montgomery and Market
Adler L. 714 Market
Albers A. 825 Stevenson
Albers & Foege, 641 Pacific
Albert C. 931 Kearny
Allen A. C. 702 Pacific
Allen E. W. 724 Pacific
Alsgood & Miller, cor Jack and Drumm
Aitschul Louis, 723 Sansom
Anderson John, 8 Jackson
Anderson John, Front nr Vallejo
Andrezjowski J. W. cor Bush and Mont
Anthes John & Anthea, cor Sacramento and Kearny
Antonio J. Mission nr Twenty-First
Appel S. cor Stockton and O'Farrell
Arimond J. cor Fillmore and Presidio Road
Arnold A. (widow) 1211 Dupont
Asps John, corner Geary and Hyde
Asher E. cor Bush and Battery
Atkins H. B. cor O'Farrell and Jones
Atkinson James, 538 Market
Aureau L. cor Com and Kearny
Badenhop H. Mission nr Twelfth
Bañeos John, cor Dupont and Union
Bagnall Bridget, B's Pacific nr Mont
Bahrs A. cor Jackson and Davis
Bailey & Co. 320 Montgomery
Bailey Frank, 109 Washington
Balke & Tietjen, cor Ritch and Brannan
Ballinger P. 545 California
Bardenhagen & Co. corner Folsom and Sixth
Barra & Galvin, 118 First
Barry & Patten, 413 Montgomery
Batteaux D. cor Kearny and St. Mark Place
Bauer John, 47 Third
Baumount J. 310 Pacific
Beard George, 52 First
Becherer E. Mrs. Mountain Lake
Beck Peter, cor Mission and Beale
Becke William, cor Mont and Green
Beer & Co. 547 California
Behrens Jos. cor Brannan and Sixth
Bell Thomas, 218 Clay

Bellanger & Valory, 530 Clay
Renard A. cor Fourth and Howard
Bening G. F. cor Wash and East
Benker F. cor Third and Folsom
Berbe Louis, Potrero Avenue
Berge O. E. Green nr Montgomery
Bermingham Thomas, cor Taylor and Turk
Berry F. G. cor Jackson and Stockton
Berthon E. 523 Union
Betuel F. & Co. cor Pine and Dupont
Beverson Charles, 570 Mission
Bird Thomas, 160 First
Bizard E. 712 Market
Blake J. (colored) 734 Pacific
Blanc & Seran, 109 Fourth
Blanckeart V. J. & Co. 911 Dupont
Blohm P. 42 Webb
Bloomer & Co. Oriental Hotel
Bock Charles, 769 Clay
Bockman R. H. cor Folsom and Eighth
Bockman & Mangels, cor Freelon and Fourth
Bogel C. H. cor Washington and Waverly Place
Bohanan P. cor Natoma and Mary
Bohlken & Bremer, corner Third and Harrison
Bolan James, 328 Third
Bolger M. cor Davis and Sacramento
Bollo T. cor Stockton and Vallejo
Boite H. cor Dupont and Broadway
Boosma A. 923 Kearny
Borbeck J. 404 Market
Borella A. cor Third and Tehama
Boschen N. & Co. cor Fifth and Minna
Bose & Dahnken, cor Clay and Davis
Bottcher R. 641 Pacific
Bourgade C. 247 Third
Boyne Thomas, 521 East
Braddock A. Mrs. cor Jackson and Davis
Brader H. 611 Battery
Braghi R. cor Brannan and Seventh
Brander J. S. cor Mission and Fourth
Brandt O. 1040 Market
Brauer C. W. cor Pacific and Sansom
Bredhoff & Cordes, cor Pac and Drumm
Bredhoff & Co. 423 East ;
Brennan & Rider, cor Clay and Kearny
Brewer C. cor Front and Chambers
Brickwedel A. D. cor First and Market
Brickwedel C. H. & Co. 253 Stewart
Brickwedel J. cor Clay and Waverly Place
Briordy John, 60 First
Brommer & Bro. cor Sixth and Bryant
Bronstrup W. cor Folsom and Dora
Brower A. J. 532 Green
Brown A. Mrs. 912 Kearny
Brown A. B. 328 Montgomery
Brown J. D. 112 First
Brown Louis, 204 Stewart
Brown W. P. cor Clay and Dupont
Brunings H. & Co. cor Third and Mission
Brunjes D. 425 Bush
Brunjes H. cor Fourth and Harrison
Brunner L. cor Mont and Summer
Bruns & Bro. cor Folsom and Spear
Bruns H. Old San José Road nr Thirtieth
Bruns & Co. 201 Commercial
Bruns N. Guerrero nr Sixteenth
Brunsen M. 612 Montgomery
Bryan Bros. 322 Sansom
Bryan J. M. 704 Howard
Buchanan H. 324 Commercial
Buhsen D. 727 Davis
Buis & Giubetich, 605 Davis
Burckhardt & Klebs, 634 Commercial
Burkhardt & Faas, 1214 Stockton
Burmeister A. cor California and Leav
Burmeister O. H. cor Beale and Mission
Burmeister Chr. 31 Main
Burr Levi, Bay nr Dupont
Bush N. cor Pacific and Kearny
Butenop H. 625 Pacific
Butler R. cor Harrison and Eighth
Butler E. B. 511 Mission
Butt & Kuchmeister, cor Pacific and Kearny
Byrne & Castree, cor Howard and Twelfth
Byrne M. J. (widow) Sac nr Davis
Caffrey D. 210 First
Cahill & McElroy, cor Bush and Kearny
Cahill J. cor Brannan and Fourth
Cahill J. C. cor Dupont and St. Mark Place
Callaghan J. 130 Pacific

Callahan J. cor Jones and Francisco
Calnon P. cor First and Mission
Campe H. cor Second and Tehama
Campe J. & Magnus, cor . First and Folsom
Carolin & McArdle, 215 Tehama
Carristy R. Sixteenth nr Dolores
Carroll & Bro. cor Third and Minna
Carroll R. cor Harrison and Garden
Carson J. cor Presidio House
Carsten F. cor Bush and Dupont
Carter J. cor Dupont and O'Farrell
Carteron C. 605 Sansom
Casey P. C. 930 Market
Castagnet D. 709 Broadway
Castagnetto F. 609 Pacific
Cavaletti C. 537 Broadway
Cella L. cor Dupont and Vallejo
Chamberlin J. P. 318 Bush
Chapelle P. 936 Kearny
Chenot E. cor Fourth and Folsom
Chielovich A. cor Cal and Drumm
Chincovich P. cor Drumm and Pacific
Chopart J. 4 Market
Christian L. 1420 Stockton
Claresy V. Madame, 607 Jackson
Cline H. 8 Mission
Cline Henry, Mission St. Wharf
Coleman & Burditt, 650 Sacramento
Coleman J. P. 1005 Kearny
Combes J. C. 526 Montgomery
Coneo & Pizello, 1313 Dupont
Conley L. cor Geneva and Brannan
Connell M. cor Moss and Folsom
Connolly John, cor Dupont and Mkt
Cook E. G. & Co. corner Second and Minna
Corney & Beirne, 417 Powell
Corbett D. E. cor Mason and O'Farrell
Corbett James, 10 Sutter
Corbett John, 865 Market
Corby J. cor Sixth and Stevenson
Cordes A. J. F. cor Pacific and Powell and Broadway and Octavia
Cordes C. H. 17 Fremont
Cordes C. H. 1007 Battery
Cordes John, cor Powell and Pacific
Cordes & Yinken, cor King and Third
Cordes Wm. Main cor Harrison and cor Bush and Pierce
Cordouan R. 643 Broadway
Core Thomas, Folsom nr Beale
Cornahrens H. cor Howard and Sixth
Costa G. 314 Pacific
Cowen W. J. 500 Battery
Cox W. B. cor Third and Bryant
Craig William, 805 Dupont
Cronan J. 719 Battery
Cronan T. 119 Kearny
Cronin J. Miss, 249 Third
Croskey & Howard, cor Hayes and Franklin
Cullen T. 543 Market
Cunningham A. cor Sutter and Sansom
Curry Luke, 734 Market
Dahlen F. cor Dupont and Sutter and Ritch and Clara
Dahmke F. cor Wash and Drumm
Daley M. cor Sansom and Greenwich
Dalrymple & Irvin, 32 Stewart
Daney M. 616 Washington
Daryes Richard, 21 First
Decker H. & Co. cor Bush and Sansom
Decker J. cor Bush and Cemetery Av
Delafont L. cor Pine and Kearny
Delventhal W. cor Jackson and Davis
Denham W. cor Kearny and Pacific
Denmark & Horning, cor Pacific and Taylor
Dennis J. 616 Pacific
Desprez C. 520 Clay
Detels M. cor Harrison and Main
Detjens H. 704 Davis
Dettner & Luhrsen, cor Montgomery and Filbert
Deuher A. 819 Kearny
Dicaud J. H. cor Dupont and Vallejo
Diederichsen C. 540 Jackson
Diehl & Hause, 1126 Dupont
Dietrich J. cor Vallejo and Mason
Dillmann G. F. 825 Kearny
Dillon & Chandler, 212 Bush
Dillon J. 671 Market
Dimmer N. 815 Pacific
Dixon C. Summer nr Montgomery
Donahue Phil. 417 Front
Donaldson J. cor Market and Ecker
Donohoe J. 88 Stevenson
Donohue & Phelan, 31 Second
Donzelmann J. 349 Pine
Dorgeloh & Meyer, 775 Clay

Dorsey E. Mrs. 133 Folsom
Dorsey George, 7 Broadway
Doscher H. F. cor Brannan and Ninth
Doscher & Co. 138 Second
Doscher H. H. corner Brannan and Seventh
Doscher J. D. cor Bush and Sansom
Dow & Desebrock, corner Fourth and Brannan
Downs J. cor Fourth and Stevenson
Doyle M. cor Hayes and Van Ness Av
Doyle T. 535 Sacramento
Dreyer & Ebbighausen, cor Gilmore and Kentucky
Dreyer J. cor Clay and East
Driscoll & Jellings, 426 Montgomery
Driscoll J. (widow) 512 Mission
Droge & Vessing, cor Natoma and Jane
Droge G. F. A. cor Natoma and Jane
Droge H. cor Pacific and Front
Droger D. North Point
Droger H. & Co. cor Pine and Battery
Drollet J. A. 1336 Dupont
Drucker A. 624 Mission
Druckert E. cor Clay and Stockton
Druhe J. G. cor Mission and Eighteenth
Druhe J. H. cor Market and Stewart
Dulip & Waddington, cor Dupont and Broadway
Dundas Thomas, 328 Pine
Dunham W. 934 Kearny
Dunn W. cor Pacific and Leavenworth
Dunning Thomas, 253 Clara
Duveneck C. & Co. cor Mont and Wash
Earle J. H. cor Clay and Drumm
Ebbinghausen H. corner Folsom and Fourth
Eddy & Williams, cor Mont and Pac
Edgerly H. 6 Merchant
Efford N. C. 309 East
Eggers F. cor Dupont and Vallejo
Ehlers W. 19 Hinckley
Ehmann H. 525 Kearny
Ehricks D. cor Battery and Vallejo
Emerson & Bailey, 531 Sacramento
Ernst V. Mrs. Mission nr Precita Av
Evans J. R. 621 Pacific
Everard W. 214 Stewart
Evers H. C. cor Mont and Vallejo
Expert A. cor Pacific and Leav
Fagan M. (widow) 585 Market
Fahrenkrug W. cor Tehama and Third
Farley B. Sixth nr Brannan
Farr A. cor Third and King
Farrell P. E. cor Valencia and Sixteenth
Feehan & Byrnes, cor Fourth and Jessie
Feehan J. cor First and Natoma
Fehnemann B. cor Larkin and Green
Feldbush J. H. 108 Sutter
Fernier M. (widow) Powell nr Chestnut
Ferriere A. Mme, 620 Jackson
Ficheu J. cor Dupont and Pacific
Fielitz W. cor Fourth and Folsom
Fink H. & Co. cor Powell and Union
Fischback & Bro. 1501 Mason
Finley T. E. 113 Leidesdorff
Fisk & Barber, Howard Court nr Howard
Fitschen J. H. cor Fourth and Stevenson
Fitter E. H. cor Clay and Davis
Fitch & Merritt 314 Montgomery
Flinn P. T. cor Howard and Eighth
Flood & O'Brien, 509 Washington
Floyd W. 511 Pacific
Flynn E. cor Bryant and Fourth
Flynn J. cor Hyde and Ellis
Flynn P. T. cor Howard and Eighth
Foley D. cor Octavia and Presidio Road
Foley M. cor Stevenson and Ecker
Fonda A. cor Third and Howard
Forthman J. A. 160 Stewart
Fox & Porter, 531 Clay
Foye F. Battery nr Green
Franc Alex. 1021 Dupont
Francisco M. & Co. cor Pacific and Davis
Frederick & Lorber, corner Pine and Kearny
Frederick W. cor Battery and Broadway
Freie H. cor Dupont and Sacramento
Friedrich J. G. cor Sixteenth and Second Avenue
Friesenhausen J. 220 Sutter
Frisch J. W. cor Fifth and Mission
Fromheim W. cor Third and Townsend
Fruchtnicht J. 266 Stewart
Fuselier J. cor Jones and Geary
Gallagher J. A. cor Sixth and Shipley
Garcia F. 718 Montgomery
Gardner & Co. 707 Davis

Gardner Sam. 765 Clay
Garronne & Hutaf, cor Dupont and Cal
Gasley M. (widow) 418 Brannan
Gately J. cor Mason and Geary
Gaussall B. 630 Pacific
Gautier L. M. 516 Pacific
Gehrels W. A. cor Mission and Sixth
Geils H. H. cor Kearny and Sutter
George P. nr St. Mary's College
Geraghty B. cor Mason and Turk
Gerdes A. cor Third and Stevenson
Gerhow F. cor Mission and East
Gerken P. cor Mission and Main
Ghilardi L. & Co. 534 Commercial
Ghio A. & Co. 927 Washington
Glandoni J. 1402 Dupont
Gibb James, 617 Merchant
Giblen T. cor Folsom and Beale
Gill Owen, cor Folsom and Stewart
Girzikowsky & Zeh, 20 Hinckley
Gleason & Hurley, corner Dupont and O'Farrell
Gleason P. H. Francisco nr Powell
Gnlaio M. L. 3 Broadway
Gobener G. H. cor Third and Brannan
Goetz & Schreiber. 335 Pine
Goodman & Duffy, 857 Washington
Gore Charles, 129 Third
Gotze & Borchers, cor Cal and Kearny
Gould & Co. cor Third and Silver
Gould & Capprise, 18 Clay
Graefner M. King nr Third
Green G. W. 616 Montgomery
Grenoke H. cor Clark and Davis
Grimler M. Mrs. 331 Kearny
Grimm C. 1421 Pacific
Grimm F. W. cor Fourth and Clementina
Grooez G. 538 Broadway
Grosbauer & Fitschen, cor Folsom and Haywood
Gross J. F. cor Front and Broadway
Grote F. cor Geary and Broderick
Grotheer H. cor Fourth and Brannan
Gudehaus F. & Co. cor Clara and Berry
Guillennin J. N. 207 Kearny
Gschwind R. Valencia nr Sixteenth
Gunther J. 1421 Dupont
Haake J. C. 100 Stewart
Haase F. cor Folsom and Beale
Hacke C. W. corner Sacramento and Waverly Place
Hadler C. cor Clay and Mason
Hagemann & Detels, Niantic Hotel
Hahn W. B. 1016 Clay
Hamman J. H. 828 Clay
Hampshaw W. H. 220 Washington
Hanavan P. cor Sixth and Tehama
Haney W. W. (Gem) cor Front and Sac
Hans J. cor Stockton and Greenwich
Hardigan P. 162 First
Harjes F. cor Greenwich and Jones
Harms H. corner Folsom and Twenty-Second
Harms H. 2 California
Harris J. N. 432 California
Harrison J. cor Wash and Dupont
Harter & Fitch, 319 Bush
Hartman C. cor Dupont and St. Mark Place
Hartmann & Hillebrandt, cor Third and Brannan
Hashagen J. cor Stockton and Bdwy
Hashagen J. & Co. 322 Jackson
Hauck & Marquard, 541 Clay
Hawley C. J. & Co. 42 Second
Hay & Coates, 37 Sutter
Hayden J. G. cor Mont and Wash
Hayes B. H. cor Fifth and Clementina
Hayburn J. C. cor Fifth and Shipley
Healey M. cor Jackson and Leav
Heck John, 619 Jackson
Heesman G. F. cor Second and Brannan
Heidhoff A. H. cor Stockton and Sac
Heimburg E. W. & Co. Grove near Laguna
Helns & Eden, cor Battery and Bdwy
Heinsohn & Hammann, cor Washington and Davis
Heinz Jacob, 636 Pacific
Heinz C. cor Folsom and Sixteenth
Helms E. A. cor O'Farrell and Hyde
Hencken & Co. cor Wash and Dupont
Hencken & Spellmeyer, 719 Pacific
Hencken & Muller, corner Powell and Vallejo
Hencken W. H. 417 Third
Henderson T. 2206 Powell
Hermann Isaac, 619 Post
Hermann R. Harbor View House

Herteman E. 822 Pacific
Hess G. B. cor Clay and Brenham Pl
Heuer & Koop, corner Howard and Stewart
Heuer P. cor Lombard and Jansen
Hey & Meyn, cor Folsom and Twelfth
Heye & Luttig, cor Lombard and Mason
Heyer A. cor Third and Bryant
Higgins & Ladd, 711 Montgomery
Hildebrand J. H. 505 Pacific
Hildebrandt & Knop, cor Montgomery and Broadway
Hildebrandt H. cor Kearny and Sutter
Hillebrandt C. cor Brannan and Gilbert
Hoadley & Co. 617 Montgomery
Hobe A. A. cor Eighth and Minna
Hobi K. (widow) Mission nr Twenty-First
Hochgurtel N. 1624 Powell
Hodgkins W. cor Third and Howard
Hoehler N. 627 Pacific
Hoelscher & Rau, cor Eddy and Mason
Hoffman C. W. 525 Pacific
Hohendorff H. cor Pine and Mont
Hoin P. P. 418 Jackson
Holchler I. C. 142 Stewart
Holje H. & Co. cor Jackson and East
Holland H. 541 Broadway
Holland J. G. 621 Merchant
Holm T. cor Stockton and Sutter
Holmes T. Lone Mountain
Holtmier H. cor Filbert and Taylor
Holtz W. & Co. cor Mont and Pacific
Hons Fred. 206 Stewart
Hooper J. F. 2 Jackson
Hopkins D. Mrs. 35 Jackson
Hoppe W. 814 Jackson
Hopper G. H. cor Pacific and Davis
Horstmann J. cor Bush and Powell
Hosting A. cor Fifth and Mission
Houck J. M. 126 California
Howard G. Broadway nr Montgomery
Huber & Anthes, 603 Kearny
Hughes James, 14 Clay
Hughes W. A. 515 Clay
Humphrey J. cor Geary and William
Hunter & Myers, 332 Montgomery
Hutaf H. 230 Commercial
Iburg W. cor Pine and Kearny
Inderrroth J. cor Bryant and Rincon Place
Irwin James, 30 Montgomery
Isaacs K. S. (widow) cor Sac and Bat
Israel I. G. jr. Cosmopolitan Hotel
Jack & Bushnell. 300 Dupont
Jackson A. M. 214 Commercial
Jacobs C. cor Stockton and Green
Jacobs E. cor Dupont and Harlan Pl
Jacobson P. 2019 Mason
Janus W. Sixteenth nr Dolores
Jennings Isaac, cor Polk and Austin
Jensen & Harnkin, cor Francisco and Midway
Johnson & Peterson, 531 East
Johnson & Brandon, cor Jones and Pac
Johnson & Holje, 28 Clay
Johnson R. M. 614 Montgomery
Jones J. T. & Co. cor Mont and Cal
Jones W. cor Fourth and Silver
Joost Bros. cor Eleventh and Mission
Joyce M. Mrs. Folsom nr Main
Kahman J. G. cor Kearny and Post
Kamps W. cor California and Davis
Kane M. 125 Fremont
Kappke H. F. cor Union and Mason
Keating M. J. 624 Merchant
Keating P. 71 Stevenson
Keely J. cor Pacific and Leavenworth
Kelbing C. cor Sutter and Kearny
Kelly E. 533 Kearny
Kelly Frank, Willows
Kelly T. cor Fourth and Market
Kennedy B. cor Ellis and Larkin
Kenney M. near City Hall
Kenney P. 112 Leidesdorff
Kenney, Maroney & Co. 623 Front
Kenny J. 923 Kearny
Kenny J. cor Sixth and Minna
Kerr J. W. cor Jackson and Kearny
Keulen H. V. cor Union and Mason
Keyes R. Mrs. 930 Kearny
Kibbe M. cor Montgomery and Commercial and Mont and Market
Kihlmeyer L. cor Kearny and Jackson
Kinsle M. J. cor First and Tehama
Kiszler H. 619 Broadway
Klein Bros. cor Kearny and Bdwy
Klein J. 634 Pacific
Kleine H. 5 Mission
Kleinschroth & Mohr, 650 Commercial
Klemeier & Stamer, cor Jack and Bat
Knell J. cor California and Kearny

Knop C. F. cor Montgomery and Wash
Knop & Co. cor Market and Beale
Koen C. 926 Folsom
Koeppel W. Sixteenth nr Dolores
Kohler G. F. 826 Montgomery
Kohlmoos C. cor Mission and First
Kohlmoos H. cor Fourth and Tehama
Kohlwin B. 440 Bush
Kohn H. & Co. 408 Folsom
Koller J. H. 916 Washington
Koopman H. cor Franklin and Austin
Korber H. 722 Pacific
Korten B. cor Mason and Greenwich
Koster & Co. cor Jones and O'Farrell
Koster H. cor Third and Howard
Koster H. cor Townsend and Crook
Kraft & Rosenstein, cor Mont and Sac
Kramer J. cor Dupont and Greenwich
Kraus F. cor Mont and Market
Kriete H. cor Pine and Larkin
Kruger C. 648 Pacific
Kruger & Hollings, corner Mason and Geary
Kuechler A. cor Jessie and Annie
L'Ecuyer M. 732 Market
Labinski W. 322 Montgomery
Lange F. W. & Co. cor Stock and Bush
Lankenau F. cor Ellis and Powell
Lannigan P. Folsom nr Main
Lapouble F. 1304 Dupont
Lauricella J. 16 Washington
Lazarque F. cor Pacific and Mont
LeRay Joseph, 11 Sutter
Leddy John, foot Powell
Lee N. A. cor Clay and Waverly Pl
Lehmkuhl H. cor Fourth and Minna
Lehrke H. cor Mariposa and Indiana
Lemkau A. cor First and Minna
Leroux C. 1008 Dupont
Levi S. 220 First
Levingston L. J. cor Dupont and Geary
Levin L. 29 Fourth
Levy H. 523 Pacific
Levy N. cor Montgomery and Cal
Lewellyn R. 1008 Pacific
Lewis C. 32 Sacramento
Lewis L. 29 Fourth
Liebenberg C. cor Pacific and Battery
Liebling & Brandt, cor Pac and Kearny
Liekefeld A. 404 Montgomery
Lindsey J. H. Sansom nr Greenwich
Lohaus & Wickan, 42 Stewart
Longlitz J. 906 Pacific
Loring & Sprague, 534 Merchant
Lottritz J. Sixteenth nr Mission
Lozier Peter, 221 Bush
Ludorff J. & Co. cor Mont and Jackson
Luesmann E. 326 Dupont
Luhmensen W. cor Sixth and Harrison
Lumley G. 1024 Battery
Lund H. N. cor Stock and Geary
Luttringer J. 810 Clay
Lynch M. cor Broadway and Davis
Mackie D. & 400 Third
Madden M. (widow) 30 Stewart
Madel P. & Co. corner Mission and Stewart
Magner T. cor Broadway and Scott
Mallon J. cor Pacific and Scott
Maloney T. 309 Third
Manchester & O'Neil, 627 Pacific
Manslet J. P. 448 Brannan
Mangels & Claussen, 313 Dupont
Mangels & Cuttrell, corner Clay and Davis
Mangels & Co. cor Howard and Fourth
Mangels & Steffens, corner Folsom and Main
Manning J. M. cor Market and Powell
Marcel A. 132 Fourth
Marion A. 107 Jackson
Marion & Henderson, 321 East
Marks S. 658 Mission
Marlow Owen, cor Third and Mission
Marony J. Brannan nr Sixth
Marshall & Johnson, 614 Montgomery
Marshall R. 733 Howard
Martens D. & Bro. cor Sac and Stock
Martens M. 18 Sutter
Martin & Horton, 545 Clay and 534 Mont
Martin Lewis, cor Stock and Jackson
Martin M. cor Hyde and Pacific
Martin Phil. 510 Kearny
Martin W. cor Second and Howard
Marx A. cor Green and Stockton
Matich M. foot Jackson
Matthias L. cor Dupont and Union
Maume J. (widow) 150 First
May J. H. 615 Washington
Mavrisch E. 619 Kearny
McCabe B. cor Jessie and Anthony
McCarthy J. D. 1009 Dupont

McCarthy T. 612 Washington
McCarty E. D. 608 Howard
McCauley C. 425 Pacific
McComb J. cor Sixth and Jessie
McConnell M. (widow) 81 Stevenson
McCormick & Luhrs, 521 Merchant
McCraith D. cor Front and Pacific
McCrum Hugh, 611 Kearny
McCully J. cor Second and Minna
McGee P. 1014 Jackson
McGinnis R. cor Howard and Beale
McGovern P. cor Market and Geary
McGuirk & Farry, 518 Market
McKenzie & Fairman, 716 Kearny
McLane A. foot Fillmore
McLane C. Mrs. Presidio Road
McLaughlin M. Presidio Road corner Fillmore
McLea Donald, 534 California
McMahon P. J. Russ House
McManna T. 5 Broadway
McParland M. 225 Kearny
McPyke H. W. 631 Merchant
McQuade M. N. cor Fourth and Minna
McQuinn M. 234 First
Medel P. cor Mission and Stewart
Meehan W. cor Kearny and Com
Meetz & Co. cor Post and Dupont
Mehrtens A. cor Filbert and Mason
Mehrtens H. cor Front and Oregon
Meier H. cor Stockton and Francisco
Meier & Knippenberg, cor Stevenson and Ecker
Meierdierks & Co. cor Post and Powell
Meloney W. B. jr. corner Sixth and Brannan
Menant L. cor Clay and Kearny
Mendes D. 319 Commercial
Menke H. cor Battery and Commerce
Mentel W. cor Stock and Broadway
Merill F. cor Pacific and Stockton
Merz & Greiner, cor Sutter and Powell
Mewes C. 611 Pacific
Meyer Bros. cor Folsom and Fremont
Meyer & Molk, cor Dupont and Green
Meyer H. cor Filbert and Dupont
Meyer H. W. 310 Stewart
Meyer J. H. cor Wash and Powell
Meyer W. F. cor Mission and Beale
Michaelis F. 238 Kearny
Michelsen F. cor Davis and Jackson
Middlehoff G. cor Grove and Laguna
Miller A. Mrs. 603 Kearny
Miller & Rose, 106 Stewart
Miller G. cor Mission and Fremont
Miller & Washburn, 131 Third
Miller J. J. cor Sutter and Leav
Miller & Brunning, corner Jessie and Annie
Miller L. & Co. 725 Jackson
Milliman D. P. cor Bdwy and Scott
Mills L. R. 16 Sutter
Mindermann M. 520 Broadway
Mish Wolff, 420 Commercial
Mitchell James, 609 Battery
Mitchell John, 174 Stevenson
Mitchell John F. cor Post and Hyde
Mitchell W. H. cor Bush and Sansom
Mohrmann F. cor Kearny and Bdwy
Monje A. G. 13 Stewart
Mooney Con. cor Com and Kearny
Moore G. cor Sacramento and Market
Moore W. 40 Jackson
Morales E. 728 Pacific
Morken H. F. 316 Pine
Morrisey P. H. cor Fifth and Tehama
Moser & Smith, Valencia nr Sixteenth
Moutry James, 313 East
Mueckenhoff A. 516 Pacific
Muhlenbrink & Rohde, cor Sutter and Taylor and Post and Taylor
Muller H. 917 Kearny
Mulloy J. cor Broadway and Davis
Murken M. cor Ecker and Clementina
Murphy A. 36 First
Murphy J. cor Folsom and Baldwin Court
Murphy M. C. cor Sixteenth and First Avenue
Murray M. 216 Washington
Myer Fred. 611 Jackson
Myers John, 226 Montgomery
Nelson I. M. corner Twentieth and Guerrero
Neulens B. 811 Dupont
Neuman L. cor Stockton and O'Farrell
Neunaber & Co. cor Folsom and Beale
Neuval F. 518 Union
Nichols W. M. foot Powell
Nobmann C. cor Bush and Mason and Sacramento and Leavenworth
Nobmann J. Francisco nr Powell

Nolan M. 87 Stevenson
Nolte C. R. cor Mission and Twenty-fourth
Noltmeyer F. cor Harrison and Chesley
Nolting J. C. A. cor Wash and Kearny
Nolting & Wilke, cor Bush and Kearny
Norland P. 32 Sacramento
Norman & Co. cor Valencia and Sixteenth
Nunan M. cor Bryant and Ritch
O'Brien Bros. cor Stock and Vallejo
O'Brien J. cor First and Stevenson
O'Brien J. E. Brannan St. Bridge
O'Brien M. cor Vallejo and Davis
O'Brien P. cor Folsom and Stewart
O'Donnell James, 6 Drumm
O'Keefe D. cor Harrison and Dora
O'Neil J. cor Kearny and Pacific
O'Reilly & Brady, corner Mission and Sixth
Offerman & Co. cor Dupont and Pacific
Offerman J. H. cor Fourth and Mission
Ogle & Schriefer, 155 Natoma
Ohlandt H. & N. cor Powell and Pac
Oipherts & Bergin, cor Kearny and Jackson
Olsen J. E. 107 Washington
Orr W. H. cor Harrison and Fifth Av
Ortmann J. F. 815 Jackson
Osmer G. & Co. 1 Market and cor Folsom and Stewart
Pagannini & Valente, cor Montgomery and Pacific
Palm E. 403 Pine
PARKER G. F. cor Mont and Wash
Parker J. C. cor Sacramento and East
Pascal & Co. 1127 Dupont
Pastor S E. 518 Battery
Patterson G. 2195 Powell
Pedichio D. Vallejo nr Davis
Perrier H. 205 Third
Pestner E. cor Fourth and Clementina
Petersen C. A. cor Mont and Union
Peterson A. G. 504 Davis
Peterson C. 10 Sacramento
Peterson F. cor Washington and East
Petterman H. 533 California
Phair E. Mrs. Bay Shore Road
Piper J. cor Second and Howard
Plath H. 421 Union
Plege & Hoffman, cor Post and Taylor
Pless & Lindner, 425 Sansom
Pope & Bruns, cor Filbert and Steiner
Postel P. J. cor Fourth and Everett
Porter A. A. 520 California
Porter Horace, 605-Commercial
Powell C. F. 610 Clay
Powers J. cor Union and Hyde
Preda G. 727 Montgomery
Princivalle G. Sixteenth nr Dolores
Prinz John, 49 Second
Puckhaber J. cor Post and Mason
Puvogel J. cor Mason and Filbert
Purcell T. 210 Commercial
Quinn J. cor Sutter and Market
Ranken & Ryan, cor Sixth and Tehama
Ratliff H. cor Pacific and Davis
Rattol C. F. 10 Stewart
Raymond C. 51 Sacramento
Reardon D. cor Washington and Leav
Reese H. cor Powell and Greenwich
Reilly B. cor Sixth and Clara
Reilly E. cor Fourth and Freelon
Reilly J. L. cor Market and Fourth
Reimers C. cor Mason and O'Farrell
Reynolds J. H. cor Third and Jessie
Ricci & Co. 635 Washington
Richards J. M. 213 Dupont
Richit E. (widow) Valencia near Sixteenth
Richardson J. cor Front and Vallejo
Riker H. H. 539 Washington
Riley C. 316 Clay
Ring P. cor Powell and Lombard
Ring Richard, 128 First
Rispaud J. 834 Pacific
Ritt H. 842 Pacific
Roach E. 421 California
Robertson & Linn, cor Washington and Kearny
Robins F. 726 Pacific
Roeben G. 1029 Dupont
Ronit M. cor Dupont and Green
Rose A. 919 Kearny
Rosenbohm J. H. Potrero
Rosenmuller G. 8 Washington
Roskamp F. cor Fourth and Jessie
Rosseter & Co. cor Market and Third
Rottanzl L. 635 Washington
Roux & Silvestre, 536 Broadway
Rugen H. foot Fillmore
Runge F. cor Kearny and Green

Russell G. cor Jackson and Battery
Ryan & Purcell, 714 Market
Ryan J. cor Hyde and Pacific
Ryan J. 228 Commercial
Ryan T. 21 Hinckley
Ryder C. B. 412 Jackson
Sagehorn H. 520 Union
Sahlmann C. 2208 Powell
Sahnke & McCune, cor Howard and Sumner
Sajous J. cor Post and Dupont
Salomon J. cor O'Farrell and Hyde
Samblanet F. 718 Stockton
Samengo & Mazzoni, Drumm nr Clay
Santif & Bro. cor Howard and Fifth
Sawyer G. 327 Sansom
Sharboro J. B. cor Folsom and Sixth
Scanlin & Bruns, 2 Second
Scanlin & Doscher, cor Bush and Jones
Schbarg W. Valencia nr Sixteenth
Schedel G. cor Jessie and Ecker
Scheper C. cor Mont and Sutter
Scheper M. cor Pine and Sansom
Schirott W. 716 Pacific
Schueter & Leega, cor Third and Hunt
Schmedes J. J, 642 Jackson
Schmidt W. cor Harrison and Ritch
Schmierer O. & Co. 427 Kearny
Schmitt G. F. cor Cal and Kearny
Schmitt H. cor Howard and Russ
Schmitt J. P. cor Pine and Kearny
Schmitz J. P. 719 Market
Schord L. G. 721 Davis
Schortemeier H. H. cor California and Prospect Place
Schrader & Gerken, cor Fifth and Stevenson
Schroder F. A. cor Powell and Francisco
Schroder Fred, cor Sac and Drumm
Schroder H. cor Grove and Gough
Schroder H. 330 Vallejo
Schroder & Hashagen, cor Stockton and Vallejo
Schuetz & Wochatz, 607 Jackson
Schuldt & Knoche, 120 Second
Schulte F. W. cor Clay and Kearny
Schulte J. 610 Jackson
Schulteis H. cor First and Clementina
Schultz W. cor Dupont and Geary
Schultz W. cor First and Bryant
Schultze & Harms, cor Kearny and Union
Schumacher F. 44 Stewart
Schumann W. cor Fourth and Minna
Schwartz & Husing, cor Mission and Eighteenth
Schwartz & Winkler, cor Mont and Sac
Schwartz D. cor Kearny and St.Charles
Schwarze & Co. cor Kearny and Geary
Schwergerle & Co. 636 Commercial
Schwetze C. cor Dupont and Wash
Scollav W. A. 1522 Stockton
Scott Robert C. 323 Washington
Seegelken & Winckelmann, cor Davis and Commercial
Selig Bros. cor Minna and Jane
Sevier F. cor Sacramento and Drumm
Sharkey J. 132 Folsom
Shawl M. cor Post and Stockton
Sheppard M. (widow) 720 Pacific
Shields T. 229 Bush
Shumann W. cor Fourth and Mission
Sibley N. cor Broadway and Davis
Siebe & Co. cor Powell and Francisco
Siebe J. & Co. cor Union and Powell
Siebe R. cor Sixteenth and Kentucky
Siedenburg H. 520 Vallejo
Siegfried H. A. cor Dolores and Fifteenth
Siems J. H. 409 Union
Sinkwitz W. 814 Kearny
Slaven J. cor Hayes and Laguna
Slosson & Ladd, cor First and Folsom
Smith C. W. 538 Merchant
Smith G. Miss, 302 Dupont
Smith & Wilkins, 709 Davis
Smith J. cor Dupont and Chestnut
Smith J. 706 Pacific
Smith H. cor Market and Eddy
Smith Joseph, 206 Leidesdorff
Sneider & Horstmann, 647 Pacific
Solomon H. cor Geary and Dupont
Solomon I. cor Stockton and Ellis
Sommers C. cor Sixth and Natoma
Spark & Schultz, corner Harrison and Spear
Spreen W. cor Brannan and Ninth
Spruegel C. 621 California
SQUARZA N. 120 Leidesdorff
Stapleton J. 530 Sacramento
Steindler M. cor Shipley and Willow

Steinhoff & Co. cor Bush and Trinity
Stevenson S. C. 313 Montgomery
Stewart J. Daley, 808 Kearny
Stone I. Geary Lone Mountain
Stoppelkamp A. H. cor Stockton and Union
Stowell C. E. 765 Clay
Stuss H. & Co. 141 Second
Sullivan D. & Co. cor Fifth and Clara
Swan J. cor Third and King
Swordstream J. E. corner Fourth and Louisa
Tappeiner J. 104 Sansom
Tayac L. 19 Kearny
Taylor John, 52 Third
Teese L. jr. cor California and Kearny
Teitgen R. cor Pacific and Battery
Tellyr J. Mission nr Twenty-Fourth
Tennent R. J. cor Ellis and Larkin
Tetlow S. 708 Washington
Thiele A. L. cor Clay and Mont
Thomas & Conway, Brooklyn Hotel
Thomas W. cor Sixth and Clementina
Thomford & Klein, corner Powell and Filbert
Thompson I. D. 321 Montgomery
Thompson M. 21 Pacific
Thompson W. 112 Pacific
Thomson W. cor Davis and Sac
Tiatien & Bolke, corner Brannan and Ritch
Tiedemann P. cor Folsom and Rousch
Tierney John, 211 Sansom
Tietjen D. cor Fourth and Tehama
Tietjen & Co. cor Pine and St. Mary
Tillman C. 729 Mission
Tillman G. 1009 Kearny
Toby & Decker, cor Third and King
Tracy J. 222 Pacific
Tracy T. 132 First
Uhrlandt H. E. Fort Point
Umbsen H. cor Folsom and Moss
Uncelin E. cor Market and Dolores
Urband & Co. corner Howard and Fifteenth
Uzavich J. 621 Davis
Valadie F. 721 Pacific
Valentine & Bro. 7 First
Van Doren J. cor Bush and Mason
Van Gulpen C. 606 Greenwich
Yangon A. 611 Pacific
Veiller J. & L. 606 Front
Velbert P. H. cor First and Howard
Villar L. cor Dupont and Broadway
Vincent L. 1230 Dupont
Vincent W. H. 314 Sansom
Vollers H. cor Powell and Market
Vollmer J. & H. cor Sac and Davis
Von Glahn J. 226 Minna and 225 Sutter
Von Hadeln J. cor Powell and Green
Vorrath & Co. cor Taylor and O'Farrell
Voss & Harding, 631 Pacific
Wagner P. 1232 Dupont
Wagner L. 652 Sacramento
Wahl C. & Co. cor Bush and Clara
Wainwright W. 219 California
Waldenberg & Tollner, 311 Battery
Walker A. 116 Pacific
Wall M. 8 First
Ward & Kenny, 522 Market
Warner A. North Beach
Weber T. H. cor Broadway and Mason
Weinmann & Bruder, 612 Pacific
Weisenborn F. Presidio House
Welling C. G. Hayes' Park
Wells H. (colored) 917 Washington
Wendt H. cor Third and Folsom
Wessling W. cor Fourth and Folsom
West Louis, cor Fifth and Shipley
Westedd W. 820 Battery
Weston J. 536 Jackson
Wheeler H. cor Howard and Langton
Wheeler W. P. cor Dolores and Sixteenth
White E. (widow) 609 California
Whitney M. J. (widow) corner Powell and Chestnut
Wiebar N. cor Third and Everett
Wiedach P. 621 Davis
Wieland C. (widow) cor California and Kearny
Wieland C. & Co. corner Kearny and Market
Wieland F. & Co. corner Powell and Vallejo
Williams & Guthrie, 429 Montgomery
Williams M. Mrs. 8 Dupont
Williams S. G. cor Fourth and Jessie
Williams T. cor East and Merchant
Wilson Charles, Lick House
Wilson & Baker, 550 Clay
Wilson P, A. cor Jackson and Davis

Wischhusen D. Potrero Avenue
Witgen D. cor Dupont and Broadway
Wittmeier G. 614 Jackson
Wolbern A. F. 8 Clay
Wolbern J. D. cor Dupont and Greenwich
Wolters J. J. cor Folsom and Ritch
Woodworth J. 509 Jackson
Worford W. 106 Pacific
Wrede D. cor Sansom and Sutter
Wrede G. cor Stewart and Mission
Wrigley E. Mrs. Mission nr Nineteenth
Wulburn J. & Bro. 734 Broadway
Wuthe W. cor California and Kearny
Wynne W. cor Fourth and Louisa
Young R. cor Clay and Larkin
Zahn H. 823 Vallejo
Ziegelmeyer A. 629 Mission
Zimmerman S. cor Pine and Kearny
[See Hotels, Etc.]

Lithographers.

Baker G. H. 522 Montgomery
Britton & Co. 533 Commercial
Brown G. T. 543 Clay
Butler B. F. 338 Montgomery
DeMontpreville C. 803 Montgomery
Fletcher Edward, 308 Front
Harnett E. 543 Clay
Jump E. 116 Montgomery Block
Moody E. King nr Third
Nagel L. King nr Third
Nahl Brothers, 121 Montgomery

Lock Dealers.

Doty W. R. 118 Pine
[See Hardware.]

Locksmiths.

Bien J. 322 Commercial
Browning & McNamara, 806 Wash
Crowe T. 659 Mission
Dexter A. G. 108 Kearny
Duncan H. 114 Dupont
Fogel F. 605 Jackson
GALLAGHER WEED & WHITE, 125 First (see advertisement, p. 644)
Grussell F. 70 Jessie
Harris W. (colored) 208 Leidesdorff
Herget J. 114 Pacific
KLEPZIG I. C. E. 733 Washington
Markt & Fleishel, 18 Post
Marwedel & Otto, 329 Bush
Nauman E. 218 Commercial
Pfeiffer J. W. 759 Clay
Rice Z. 114 Sansom
Schnoor C. 1306 Stockton
Weichart J. 22 Fremont
Will & Finck, 613 Jackson
[See Bell Hangers; Safes.]

Lodgings.

Allen E. (widow) 829 Sacramento
Andrews John, 13½ Second
Babcock A. B. 624 Commercial
Babcock A. Mrs. corner Dupont and Washington
Baldwin M. (widow) 812 Sacramento
Ballard C. cor Com and Leidesdorff
Baron V. Madame, corner Dupont and Jackson
Barrett M. Miss, 1206 Stockton
Barry H. Mrs. 200 Stockton
Bartet W. cor Kearny and Bdwy
Begin Mary, 613 Kearny
Bellenger G. Madame, 736 Pacific
Benoit A. Mrs. cor Mont and Jackson
Beston E. (widow) 106½ Clay
Bird I. Mrs. 820 Washington
Black A. F. (widow) 445 Bush
Blair L. Mrs. 737 Market
Bolander C. (widow) 736 Market
Boyd A. Miss, 11 Stockton
Boyd C. (widow) 325 Dupont
Bradley E. Mrs. 1014 Stockton
Brewster J. Summer nr Montgomery
Brown M. Mrs. cor Mission and Second
Buckler M. C. (widow) 32 Natoma
Budd J. H. Mrs. 652 Howard
Burdick F. 732 Pacific
Buster M. Mrs. 131 Montgomery
Butler S. S. 528 Com and 511 Wash
Campbell S. T. Mrs. 642 Sacramento
Carlton H. C. (widow) 327 Bush
Cassidy C. (widow) 110 Kearny
Caznolt E. 303 Sutter
Champlin J. A. 524 Howard
Chapman G. W. cor Third and Tehama
Charplot M. Mrs. 938 Dupont
Chauvin E. Mrs. 403 California

Chittenden H. W. Mrs. 406 Market
Church W. A. 636 and 640 Commercial
Clahan M. (widow) 24 Minna
Clark E. (widow) 815 Dupont
Clark E. (widow) 67 Clementina
Cook J. (widow) 6 Sansom
Cooke M. M. (widow) 32 Second
Crawford A. Mrs. cor Second and Stevenson
Cummings A. M. (widow) 17 Third
Curtis C. (widow) 118 Post
Dangler J. (widow) 413 Kearny
Davis N. P. Mrs. 629 Clay
Dubois J. A. (widow) cor Montgomery and Jackson
Duffy John, 10 Sutter
Dunn E. (widow) 421 Dupont
Dutertre L. cor Dupont and Broadway
Dutton J. Miss, 62 Clay
Fisher A. (widow) 812 Clay
Fitzgerald G. 815 Kearny
Flager J. 551 Market
Fleishman J. cor Mont and Market
Fleury D. Madame, 921 Stockton
Foley M. Miss, 36 Natoma
Forbes Jennie, 614 Mission
Fore E. E. (widow) 73 Natoma
Gautier L. M. 516 Pacific
Gillis A. 44 Minna
Gillony D. A. (widow) 803 Howard
Girod J. 809 Clay
Gleeson M. E. (widow) 22 Montgomery
Gonzales J. Miss, 1211 Powell
Gordon E. Mrs. (col'd) cor Second and Mission
Grattan M. (widow) 18 Minna
Griffin M. Miss, Virginia Block
Hager G. D. 559 Market
Hammersmith J. Mrs. Belden Block and Stevenson House
Hancock S. A. (col'd, widow) 102 Dupont
Harrington M. C. 29 Second
Harrison H. E. cor Kearny and Bdwy
Hazilquist L. 812 Jackson
Heren J. (widow) 154 First
Higgins E. J. (widow) 506 Market
Holmes S. D. Miss, 522 California
Hoyd S. E. (widow) 202 Second
Hunt M. J. (widow) 522 Dupont
Inches Robert, 10 Jane
Irwin M. Miss, 173 Minna
Jacquenot V. (widow) 745 Clay
James S. 538 Commercial
Jillard M. (widow) 111 Wash
Johnson C. E. cor Third and Market
Jones K. A. (widow) 53 Clementina
Journet A. Madame, 120 Post
Kieffer S. (widow) 607 Jackson
Kennedy E. (widow) 1006 Clay
Kenney A. (widow) 526 Pine
Kinchela J. cor Mission and Second
Koster J. cor Kearny and Broadway
Lapidge W. F. Mrs. 639 Clay
Lauman L. (widow) 8 and 14 Kearny
Lee M. A. Mrs. 828 Montgomery
Leek M. Mrs. cor Sac and Davis
Levy F. Mrs. 335 Pine
Levy R. Mrs. 214 Sansom
Lockwood C. (widow) 284 Minna
Lykins J. E. (widow) 109 Montgomery
Lynch E. (widow) Mercantile Library Building
Mackle C. (widow) 177 Minna
Maher M. (widow) 3 Hardie Place
Maitre T. Mrs. 626 California
Mathison F. Madame, 615 Dupont
Mauge A. Mrs. cor Kearny and Jackson
McConnell E. Mrs. 820 Dupont
McDonald Eva A. Mrs. 652 Market
McGuire M. Mrs. 521 Union
McMurtry E. (widow) 609½ Howard
Meegan A. (widow) 417 Stockton
Melick C. 300 Fourth
Merrill Parker, 27 Minna
Mocker W. cor Kearny and St. Mark Pl
Morris R. S. (widow) 720 Market
Mowry N. B. Mrs. 28 Sansom
Mullen B. Miss, 633 California
Murdock G. L. 24 Battery
Murray F. (widow) 116 Post
Nichols M. (widow) 29 Post
Noonan W. 114 Bush
O'Brien M. 47 Jackson
O'Connor M. Mrs. 188 Stevenson
Olmste d L. cor Third and Hunt
Parkell H. H. Mrs. 318 Pine
Parker R. J. (widow) 216 Stockton
Pate Ellen, 670 Mission
Pinkham C. L. B. 23 Kearny
Potter E. A. (widow) 6 Sutter
Potter J. (widow) 22 Kearny

Poulet P. 540 Washington
Powell C. F. Mrs. 819 Montgomery
Rainey B. (widow) 303 Davis
Rassette E. (widow) 639 Market
Rickards E. Mrs. Mead House
Robinson M. cor Front and Sacramento
Rogers M. A. B. (widow) 1024 Stockton
Rowane B. (widow) 842 Mission
Ruggles A. Miss, 2 Hardie Place
Rutledge M. Mrs. 818 Pacific
Ryan H. Miss, 1016 Stockton
Sackett C. C. Mrs. cor Mont and Pac
Sacs M. Mrs. 716 Dupont
Sanders H. J. J. 577 Howard
Scott J. Mrs. 616 Mission
Shaw A. M. (widow) 40 Natoma
Smith E. C. (widow) 783 Market
Smith E. (widow) 63 Tehama
Smith J. L. Mrs. 226 Sansom
Smith L. A. Mrs. 52 Second
Stanage L. Mrs. 217 Third
Stebbins A. Mrs. 6 Montgomery
Stewart E. A. Mrs. cor Montgomery and Jackson
Stohr M. Mrs. 611 Mission
Taylor E. Mrs. cor Sac and Stockton
Thoburn H. T. (widow) cor Montgomery and Sutter
Thornquist C. 20 Commercial
Thurston C. 57 Jessie
Twiggs S. (widow) 834 Clay
Valentine C. 726 Pacific
Van Pelt M. A. (widow) 113 Mason
Wadleigh M. (widow) 5 Stockton
Ward M. Mrs. 510 Market
Wheeler M. Mrs. 934 Kearny
Willoughby E. (widow) 82 Natoma
Wilson M. A. Mrs. 308 Pacific
Witherby M. (widow) corner First and Folsom
Zwahlen J. 1414 Stockton
[See Boarding; Hotels, Etc.]

Looking Glasses, Mirrors, etc.

Hausmann D. & Co. 537 Clay
JONES, WOOLL & SUTHERLAND, 312 Mont (see adv. . xxxvi)
NILE & KOLLMYER, 312 Bush (see advertisement, p. xlvii)
ROSENBAUM F. H. 423 Battery (see advertisement, p. lxxiv)
Swain R. A. & CO. cor San and Pine
[See Picture Frames, Etc.]

Lumber.

Ackerson & Russ. Hathaway's Wharf
Adams, Blinn & Co. Pier 17 Stewart
Amos, Phinney & Co. Pier 9 Stewart
ARMSTRONG, SHELDON & DAVIS, cor Cal and Davis (see adv. p. 662)
Badger T. W. 424 Battery
Blyth & Wetherbee, 101 Market
Burnham G. M. 509 Clay
Coffin & Rudman, Pier 14 Stewart
Crooks & Magilton, corner Folsom and Main
Dolbeer & Carson, 36 Stewart
Ellsworth T. cor East and Market
Glidden, Colman & Co. Pier 22 Stewart
Godeffroy & Sillem, 535 Clay
Halsted & Frav, 26 Market
Hanson C. 54 Stewart
Heywood & Harmon, Pier 4 Stewart
Hooper C. A. & Co. Townsend bet Third and Fourth
Hooper F. J. & A. J. 49 Market
Hopkins S. J. 112 Washington
Jackson J. G. Pier 2 Stewart
Johnston J. & Co. 39 Market
Kentfield J. Pier 10 Stewart
KNOWLES G. B. & I. H. 17 California and Piers 13 and 19 Stewart (see advertisement, p. xlvi)
Macpherson & Wetherbee, Pier 20 Stewart
Mann G. S. 205 Market
Mastick S. L. & Co. Pier 10 Stewart
Meigs & Gawley, Pier 119 Stewart
Patridge R. K. foot Powell
Pennell J. T. Pier 11 Stewart
Pennell Robert & Co. 32 Market
Perkins S. Pier 11 Stewart
Pope & Talbot, Pier 12 Stewart
Preston & McKinnon, Pier 8 Stewart
Renton, Smith & Co. Pier 3 Stewart
Simpson A. M. Pier 11 Stewart
Smith S. S. 111 Market op California
Tichenor & Co. Pier 21 Stewart
Turner & Rundie, San José Road cor Sixteenth
Tyler C. M. & Co. foot Third

WATERHOUSE & LESTER, 29 Battery (see adv. p. xlv)
Wesson & Magilton, cor Bryant and Main
Wetherbee & Cook, 21 and 23 California and Pier 2½ Stewart
[See Mills.]

Maccaroni and Vermicelli.

Brignardello, Macchiavello & Co. 706 Sansom
Tschantz, Tenthorey & Co. 558 Mission

Machine Sewing.

[See Bag Makers; Sewing Machines; Dress Makers.]

Machinists.

AMES' PLOW CO. over Quincy Market, Boston (see adv. p. cvi)
Bacon F. N. 113 Pine
BOOTH H. J. & CO. cor First and Mission (see adv. p. lviii)
Breen Thomas, 120 Fremont
Brodie William & Co. California, 16 Fremont
Cameron & Worth, Neptune, 46 Fremont
CHASE, SHARPE & THOMSON, 209 North Second St. Philadelphia, (see advertisement p. cvi)
Cock & Flynn, Empire, 221 Mission
COFFEY & RISDON, cor Market and Bush (see adv. p. 664)
Devoe, Dinsmore & Co. cor Mission and Fremont
Disney M. 28 Fremont
Doane M. Shotwell nr Twenty-First
DUDGEON E. cor Eighth and Minna (see advertisement, p. 645)
Dunn, McHaffie & Co. Atlas, 26 Fremont
Free W. 17 First
Gallagher & Kenny, 712 Sansom
Garcin L. P. 32 Sutter
GODDARD & CO. Pacific Foundry, 127 First (see adv. p. x)
Hall D. C. Idaho, 9 First
HICKOK W. O. Eagle, Harrisburg, Penn. (see adv. p. ciii)
Hicks J. L. (sewing machines) 55 Second
HINCKLEY & CO. 47 First (see advertisement, p. 640)
HOWLAND, ANGELL & KING, Miners' Foundry, First nr Folsom (see advertisement, pp. 642 and 643)
Jolnet V. 620 Clay
KITTREDGE J. 6 and 8 Battery (see advertisement, p. 655)
KITTREDGE & LEAVITT, 308 Jackson and 603 Battery (see adv. p. cxi)
Kleinclaus & Clerc, 632 Vallejo
Lockhead J. 111 Beale
Marwedel & Otto (steam gauges) 329 Bush
McKIBBIN W. 41 First
Mooney J. H. 111 Montgomery, rear
MONYIHAN & AITKEN, 311 Mission (see advertisement, p. 641)
Nutting & Upstone, 123 Bush
PALMER, KNOX & CO. 19 First (see advertisement, p. 639)
PRACY G. T. 109 Fremont (see advertisement, p. 644)
Pretzel A. 416 Market
Quick J. W. (quartz screens) 137 First
SALMON J. & W. C. cor Mission and Fremont (see adv. p. lxi)
Sims J. R. Oregon nr Front
Small & Redmond, cor Market and Beale
Steele B. 107 Leidesdorff
Steen E. T. 35 Fremont
Stoddart D. 114 Beale
Talbot S. C. 313 Market
VULCAN IRON WORKS, 137 First (see advertisement, p. 638)
Ware W. 517 Market
Yung N. Railroad, 28 Fremont
[See Blacksmiths.]

Map Mounter.

Way C. A. Summer nr Montgomery

Malt Manufacturers.

Andrews T. J. Brannan nr Fourth
Bush P. Brannan nr Eighth
Lea Thomas, 430 Pine, rear
Schenk M. & Co. 1610 Stockton

Tilgner F. & Co. Stock nr Francisco
WINTER J. (agent) 208 California
Zwieg H. Brannan nr Fifth
  [See Brewers.]

Manufacturers, Eastern. *Agts.*

Clntworthy F. 29 Battery
Doty W. K. 113 Pine
MARSH, PILSBURY & CO. cor Front
and Pine (see adv. p. xcv)
  [See Hardward, Etc.]

Mantel Grates. *Manufacturers of.*

PALMER, KNOX & CO. Golden State
Iron Works, 19 First (see adv. p. 639)
[See Marble; Machinists, Etc.]

Maps, Etc.

Bancroft H. H. & Co. 609 Mont
GENSOUL A. Pacific Map Depôt, 511
  Montgomery (see adv. p. xxix)
Holt W. 2 Mead House

Marble Yards.

Daniel John, 421 Pine
Grant C. B. King nr Third
Grant John, Lone Mountain
Hayes & Pritchard, 536 California
Hennessey A. 507 O'Farrell
HEVERIN M. 783 Market (see advertisement, p. 659)
Kell F. 67 Fourth
Kelly & Sweeney, 816 Market
Murphy P. 722 Market
Myers Leon R. & Co. 747 Market
PALTENGHI & LARSENEUR, 422
  Jackson (see adv. p. 660)
Sharkey J. F. 673 Market
Sweeney & Downey, 816 Market
Zeglio & Moore, Fourth nr Market

Market Men.

[See appropriate heads.]

Markets.

Adler M. Rincon Point, 302 Beale
Ambroise S. Lafayette, cor Pine and
  Dupont
Anderson & Kline, Fulton, cor Stockton and Washington
Andrews E. O. Tremont, cor Howard
 . and Fremont
Arms M. C., Waverly, cor Sacramento
  and Waverly Place
Arnitz X., Essex, cor Dup and Green
Barris H. D., Philadelphia, 904 Stock
Berghofer & Dodge, Crescent, 203
  Stewart
Brackett & Keyes, Stewart Street, 50
  Stewart
Brelling Bros., Franklin, 335 Bush
Brown & Brown, Brown's, 406 Folsom
M. Cronan, Clay Street, 524 Clay
Cutter R. S. & Co., Howard, cor Second and Howard
Desmu J., Prospect, 1202 Dupont
Dinger & Berthold, Fell's Point, 703
  Battery
Dodge E. A., Excelsior, cor Sixteenth
  and Mission
Douillard F., Orient, 1224 Dupont
Duck W. B. & Co., Tehama, cor Second and Tehama
Duljon F. & L., New Orleans, 705 Pac
Dwyer P. J. & E., Faneuil Hall, 56 First
Fallon D. G., Center, cor Jones and
  O'Farrell
Fields T., Emmet, cor Stockton and
  Greenwich
Folsom Street, cor Folsom and Fol Av
Freeborn W. H., Star, cor Kearny and
  Union
Fulton J. M., Oriental, 451 East
Geantit A., Lyon, 521 Pacific
Gerhardy P. San Francisco, 323 Kearny
Hahn W., Harbor View, 1000 Pacific
Hartmeyer L., Monroe, cor Post. and
  Dupont
Heister W., Keller's, 513 Pacific
Henings M. A., Russian Hill, corner
  Mason and Broadway
Hickson, First Street, 104 First
Hill H. O., Alta, 1113 Clay
Hirleman P., New York, cor Mission
  and Stewart
Hook C. Gen. Taylor, cor Union and
  Mason
Italian Fish, cor Clay and Leidesdorff

Katz T., Jackson, 617 Jackson
Kearns P. & Co. New York, 36 Fourth
Kelly & Hanlon, Liberty, 903 Howard
Kerrigan J., St. Ann's, 1038 Market
Laroche F., Quincy, 1524 Stockton
Lauterwasser F. P. Golden Gate, cor
  Clark and Davis
Loeb H., Jefferson, cor Stock and Bdy
McInerney T. San Rafael, 311 Bdwy
Mengel J., St. Louis, cor Stockton and
  Sutter
Merchant T. S., Virginia, 822 Jackson
Metropolitan, N s Market bet Montgomery and Sansom
Meyerholz W. & Co. King Philip, 702
  Bush
Michel & Co. Eighth Ward, 329 Geary
Molt J. P. South Park, 432 Third
Moritz J. C. & Co. Camanche, corner
  Powell and Filbert
Murr C. H. Sand Hill, 215 Kearny
Nagel & Rothermel, El Dorado, corner
  Dupont and Green
Nauland & Whitman, Buffalo, corner
  Powell and Union
Neustadt L. Telegraph, 505 Broadway
New Market, 518 Clay
Occidental, Market to Sutter between
  Montgomery and Sansom
Oswald W. Harbor View, 1005 Pacific
Pacific Fruit Market, 532 Clay
Peterson S. B. & Co. Golden State, cor
  Market and Stewart
Popp A. Alcatraz, 1703 Stockton
Powers & Co. Fremont, corner Folsom
  and Fremont
Rosenberg & Hencken, Commerce,
  Vallejo nr Powell
Rutherford T. City, 117 Fourth
Ryder J. N. Poydras, 709 Pacific
Schmitt G. Newark, cor Sac and Mkt
Scmadec J. H. Bull's Head, cor Folsom and Twenty-Second
Scott & Hall, James', corner Fifth and
  Shipley
Strauss B. Queen City, 37 Third
Strehl J., U. S., cor Sixth and Mission
Van Housen W. Banner, corner Mason
  and Eddy
Walz A'. Mount Hope, 741 Broadway
WASHINGTON, cor Washington and
  Sansom (see adv. p. 677)
Wood H. V. Hyde Street, corner Geary
  and Hyde
Zeh Bros. Eclipse, corner Union and
  Dupont
Zoller J. A. Pacific, cor Pac and Powell
  [See Butchers.]

Masonic Goods.

JOHNSON T. RODGERS, 325 Mont
  (see adv. inside back cover)
NORCROSS D. Masonic Temple (see
  advertisement, p. lxxix)

Match Manufacturers.

Allen J. F. 201 Beale
JESSUP WM. & CO. corner Harrison
  and Nevada (see adv. p. 648)
Morres & Cohen, Minna nr Fifth
Smith C. W. cor Howard and Beale

**Mathematical, Nautical, and
Philosophical Instrument
Makers.**

LAWRENCE & HOUSEWORTH, 319
  Montgomery (see adv. back cover)
Roach John, 413 Washington
Sack J. C. 203 Montgomery
SCHMOLZ W. 430 Montgomery (see
  advertisement, p. 669)
Tennent Thomas, cor Bat and Oregon
  [See Instruments; Opticians, Etc.]

Mattress Makers.

Marchant & Smith, 104 Dupont
SCHAEFER J. F. & BRO. 504 Sansom
SCHREIBER J. & C. 406 Sansom
Venard A. 404 Third
  [See Beds and Bedding.]

Medicines. *Patent.*

Brandreth W. F. 118 Montgomery
CRANE & BRIGHAM, cor Front and
  Clay (see adv. p. lxiii)
Hall Edward & Co. 309 Front
Hostetter, Smith & Dean, 401 Battery
Redington & Co. 416 Front
Richards & Whitfield, cor Clay and San
  [See Apothecaries; Drugs, etc.]

Mercantile Agencies.

Bradstreet J. M. & Son, cor Montgomery and Sacramento
Fraser & Co. 205 Battery

Merchants.

Adams L. S. 405 Front
Adler H. 207 Battery
Allen & Lewis. NW cor Front and Cal
Andrade G. 403 Jackson
Arnold John & Co. 405 Front
Barker T. L. cor Front and Clay
Batties W. W. 652 Market
Berggren Aug. 415 Montgomery
Bernheim R. 304 California
Bettman M. 305 California
Blanchard H. P. 214 California
Block A. & Co. (San Juan) 300 Battery
Bohm S. H. 117 Battery
Booker W. L. 428 California
Booth Newton, 405 Front
Borel A. cor Montgomery and Jackson
Bowman C. C. 728 Montgomery
Brady Benjamin, 120 California
Broderson J. B. 611 Clay
Burnham G. M. 509 Clay
Burr E. W. 619 Clay
Burton C. H. 405 Front
Byrne J. M. 426 Jackson
Cahn A. & Co. 409 California
Callaghan J. 421 Front
Cerf J. 517 Sacramento
Chambariere L. 426 Jackson
Clark P. B. 520 Montgomery
Clifford G. 290 Front
Cobliner A. 422 California
Coghill A. J. & Co. 313 Front
Cohn Louis, 207 Battery
Cook A. 207 Battery
Cramer V. & Co. 310 Sacramento
Crane A. E. 8 Government House
Cronise W. H. V. 536 Clay
Dart P. C. 419 Front
Davidson M. 314 California
Dean J. T. 314 Merchant
Deering C. J. 419 Clay
Derby E. M. cor Front and Clay
Dole J. S. 115 Prospect Place
Elfelt & Well, 308 Front
Ellis Moses, 218 Front
Elwell D. A. & Co. 405 Front
Fassett N. C. 402 Front
Fleishaker A. cor Mont and Sac
Frank Joseph, 315 Clay
Frankenau S. A. 217 Front
Franki L. 321 Washington
Freeborn J. cor Mont and Market
French J. M. 419 Front
Giffin O. F. & Bro. 240 Montgomery
Gilman A. M. 409 Front
Glazier I. & Brother, 311 Clay
Gottig & Schoemann, 226 Front
Griffith W. T. cor O'Farrell and Market
Hahn S. 302 California
Hanna J. jr. 215 Clay
Haseltine Wm. 524 California
Hensley S. J. 205 Battery
Hollenbeck J. C. 523 Front
Hull E. 405 Front
Ide J. A. Stevenson House
Janson C. J. 210 Pine
Kedon M. 319 Davis
Kenyon W. P. 14 First
Klopenstine A. J. 405 Front
Kohn I. 308 Front
Kraner E. H. 401 Front
Ladd J. W. 419 Front
Langermann W. 519 Montgomery
Lankershim I. 407 Sacramento
Lengfeld L. 302 California
Lichte L. 109 Battery
Levy S. W. 302 California
Lewis P. 207 Battery
Lord & Co. 405 Battery
Lynch F. E. 430 Jackson
Maynard A. S. 206 Front
McRuer D. C. 204 California
Meininger L. 420 Sacramento
Merritt S. 240 Montgomery
Meyer Daniel, 207 Battery
Michelssen E. 327 Front
Milliken J. M. 405 Front
Mitchell R. 405 Front
Morris A. 310 California
Peirce O. 417 California
Perkins O. M. 308 Battery
Perry R. 102 California
Peters W. B. 308 Battery
Polhemus C. B. cor San and Halleck

Pratt W. P. 218 California
Reinhart B. 218 Battery
Rogers H. 240 Montgomery
Rothschild J. S. 517 Sacramento
Sands S. G. 129 California
Sherwood B. F. 308 Montgomery
Shirley J. 324 Sansom
Sloss Louis & Co. cor Mont and Sac
Smiley T. J. L. 519 Montgomery
Spruance J. & J. 415 Front
Steiner S. 421 Sacramento
Stiles A. G. 212 California
Sweet S. 217 Front
Taylor F. B. & Co. 405 Front
Traylor W. W. 720 Montgomery
Vandewater R. J. 540 Clay
Von Der Meden F. E. 422 California
Wangenheim S. cor Cal and Sansom
Webster H. 410 Front
Wensinger F. S. 511 Front
Wertheimer L. cor Front and Sac
Whitaker J. K. 405 Front
Whiting M. S. 535 Clay
Wichelhausen H. & Co. cor Clay and
    Battery
Woodhuff E. 206 Front
[See Dry Goods; Fancy Goods; Gro-
    ceries, Etc.]

Merchants. Commission.
* Importers.

Abbott Oscar, 723 Montgomery
*Agard, Foulkes & Co. 412 Front
*Allen & Lewis, 807 Sansom
*ALSOP & CO. 411 and 413 California
*Auger B. E. 704 Sansom
*Bacon T. M. & J. S. 216 Front
*BADGER & LINDENBERGER, cor
    Battery and Merchant
Ballard & Hall, 224 Clay
*Bandmann, Nielsen & Co. 210 Front
*Barron & Co. NE cor Jackson and
    Montgomery
*Behrens James, 429 Battery
*Belloc Fréres, 535 Clay
Blake G. O. 609 Front
Blood L. L. 225 Clay
*Borel A. cor Jackson and Mont
Bowne W. F. 311 East
Brady B. 120 California
*Bragg G. F. & Co. 111 California
Bray & Bro. NE cor Front and Clay
*BROOKS C. W. & Co. 511 Sansom
    (see advertisement, p. vii)
Bull Alpheus, NW cor Clay and Front
Bunker, Greaves & Co. 424 Battery
Burnap J. 425 Davis
Butterfield & Bro. 408 Pine
Buzzolini D. 417 Jackson
Byrne J. M. 426 Jackson
Carle & Gorley, 724 Montgomery
Cazalis E. 308 Commercial
*Chauvin O. 730 Montgomery
Christy & Wise (wool) 610 Front
Clark & Perkins (wool) 402 Front
Clark P. B. 520 Montgomery
Clifford G. 200 Front
*COLEMAN W. T. & CO. 417 Battery
    (see advertisement, p. xi)
Commeseel H. L. 307 California
*Connell D. 547 Sacramento
COX & NICHOLS, 422 Battery (see
    advertisement, p. lxv)
*Cramer V. & Co. 310 Sacramento
Crane E. J. 308 Commercial
Crane I. 308 Commercial
*Cross & Co. cor Sansom and Jackson
*Cummings W. B. 124 California
*Dana Bros. & Co. NE cor Clay and
    Battery
Dart P. C. 419 Front
Davega, Joseph & Labatt, 318 Pine
Davidson & Co. SE cor Mont and Cal
*DeFremery J. 409 Merchant
Delabigne J. B. 323 Clay
Derby E. M. NE cor Front and Clay
Dewar John, 311 East
*DeWitt, Kittle & Co. cor California
    and Front
*Dibblee & Hyde, 108 Front
*Dickson, DeWolf & Co. 410 Battery
Dorn R. & Co. cor Pine and Battery
*Doty W. R. 113 Pine
Doyle W. H. 502 Washington
*Duisenberg Charles & Co. 205 Cal
DYER, ROKOHL & BUTLER, 300
    Montgomery (see adv. p. lxxii)
Edwards, Olney & Co. 626 Mont
*FALKNER, BELL & CO. 430 Cal
Farish A. T. & Co. 221 Davis
Felton H. F. & Co. 225 Clay
*Feuerstein R. & Co. 212 Front

Feusier & Son, 221 Clay
Fielding & Osgood, 221 Sacramento
Fisk R. cor Front and Clay
*FLINT, PEABODY & CO. 716 Front
    (see advertisement, p. xi)
*Forbes, Bros. & Co. Front nr Vallejo
Friedlander I. 114 California
*Frisius F. A. 524 Washington
Geib & Ludorff, 15 Third
Gibbs C. E. 404 Front
Gildemeister W. 840 Washington
Goldschmidt J. 318 Sacramento
Griffith & Ellis, 225 Washington
*Grimes G. T. 708 Montgomery
*Grogan A. B. NW cor Jackson and
    Sansom
Groezinger G. cor Pine and Battery
*Guy Abel, Washington op Post Office
Haas S. 322 Commercial
*Hanssmann H. 220 Front
Harker J. W. 402 Front
HARRISON S. L. 23 Sansom (see ad-
    vertisement, p. lxxii)
Harrold J. 619 Front
*Haynes T. J. 404 Front
*Heath & Langhorne, 609 Front
*Hellman Bros. & Co. cor Front and
    Jackson
Holderness S. & S. M. NW cor Front
    and Clay
Hooper G. F. cor Front and Com
*Howes George & Co. 309 Clay
*Iken F. 525 Front
Jacobs J. cor Front and Washington
Jaudin E. & Co. 523 Front
Jee A. W. 523 Front
Jones J. H. 708 Montgomery
Jones & Bendixen, 207 California
Keller L. 535 California
King J. C. & Co. cor Bat and Filbert
Kohn H. 419 Sacramento
*KOOPMANSCHAP & CO. 1101 Bat
Koshland S. 308 Sacramento
Lasky & Lamson, 524 California
Lawrence C. B. 304 Montgomery
*Lent W. M. 712 Montgomery
Levy M. 414 Sacramento
Linforth James, 206 Battery
*LOW C. ADOLPHE & CO. 426 Cal
*LOWENHELM J. 220 Front (see ad-
    vertisement, p. cx)
McCann & Co. 402 Front
*MACONDRAY & CO. 204 and 206 San-
    som (see advertisement, p. ix)
Marks & Bro. 521 California
Martinon A. 811 Montgomery
*Maury P. jr. 710 Sansom
McCarty L. P. 528 Montgomery
*MEADER, LOLOR & CO. 405 Front
    (see advertisement, p. ix)
*Mebius C. F. 223 Sacramento
Mecartney A. 220 Davis
*Meinecke C. 215 Front
*Mel John, cor Front and Jackson
*Mendheim M. 631 Clay
MERRILL J. C. & CO. 206 California
    (see advertisement, p. lxxi)
Messer W. D. 206 Front
*Meyer T. L. 815 and 817 Sansom
*Milburn F. & Co. 313 Sacramento
Moore & Co. 17 Davis
*Morgan, Stone & Co. 108 Front
Moritz M. 209 Sansom
Moss J. Mora, 418 California
Muecke G. cor Front and Jackson
Newhall H. M. & Co. cor Sansom and
    Halleck
Newhall & Brooks, 722 Montgomery
*Newman J. P. 401 Sacramento
*Newton J. B. & Co. 108 California
O'Callaghan D. J. 106 Clay
Olcovich Bros. 403 California
Osgood & Co. 214 California
Paige Calvin, NW cor Cal and Battery
PALMER W. A. & CO. 19 First
*PARKER E. H. 224 California
*Patrick James & Co. 617 and 619 Bat
Perkins W. L. 404 Front
Pierce H. & W. 728 Montgomery
Pierce Nelson, 321 Front
*PIOCHE & BAYERQUE, SE corner
    Montgomery and Jackson
*Price S. & Co. 436 Jackson
Price T. 406 California
Pugh E. 210 Bush
Raimond R. E. 515 Front
Redmond J. R. 413 Washington
Reed H. R. 321 Washington
*Réne J. E. 716 Montgomery
*Rich S. & Bro. 220 California
Richards & McCraken, 405 Front
Richards O. S. 223 Clay

*Ritter L. E. & Co. 608 Sacramento
*ROBERTS, MORRISON & CO. 216
    California
*Rodgers, Meyer & Co. 314 Wash
*Ross, Dempster & Co. 425 and 427 Bat
Rousset P. 811 Montgomery
Sabins A. C. 209 Sacramento
Sanjurjo, Bolado & Pujol, 713 Sansom
Schleiden W. 324 Washington
SCHULTZE F. 623 Montgomery
Shaw John, 207 Clay
Sherwood, Bulkley & Co. 326 Clay
Spear E. S. & Co. 433 California
Sproat & Welch, 525 Front
Stanford Brothers, 121 California
*Stevens, Baker & Co. 215 Front
Stewart J. R. & Co. 411 Battery
Strybing C. H. 212 Jackson
*SWAIN R. B. & CO. 206 Front
Taaffe G. O'H. 430 California
Taylor C. L. & Co. 38 California
*Thomas J. B. 619 Front
*Union Maritime Society, 730 Mont
Valentine E. 114 California
Van Schaack P. 706 Kearny
Vischer E. cor Front and Jackson
Voizin, Ris & Co. 219 and 221 Sansom
Wadsworth W. R. & Son, 402 Front
*Walton W. F. 618 Merchant
*Wassermann A. 429 Sacramento
Watson J. 8 Clay
Weston C. W. & Co. Pacific Fruit Mkt
Whitney & Co. 405 Front
Whitney J. R. & Co. 405 Front
WILLIAMS H. B. 305 Front (see ad-
    vertisement, p. x)
Williams J. 413 East
Willistun C. 424 Battery
WINTER JOHN, 208 California
Yates W. H. & Co. 202 Clay
*Ziel, Bertheau & Co. 122 California

Merchants. Commission Produce.

Amos F. R. & Co. cor Com and Front
Bailey W. 407 Davis
Baker L. F. cor Wash and Davis
Bassett J. 213 Clay
Bennett R. H. 3 Clay
Blood L. L. & Co. 225 Clay
Booth & Co. 36 Clay
Boswell & Shattuck, cor Front and
    Commercial
Bray & Bro. NE cor Front and Clay
Brennan & Co. 206 Clay
Brocas & Perkins, 52 Clay
Bryant & Beadle, 316 Davis
Burke M. & Bro. 010 Clay
Campbell J. W. H. foot Commerce
Campbell & Fairbanks, cor Front and
    Washington
Chamberlin & Balch, 210 Clay
Clark & Co. 62 Clay
Clayton & Co. 223 Clay
Cohn I. H. & Son, 607 Sansom
Conger & Gray, 212 Washington
Crosby G. O. 104 Clay
Cummings H. K. 415 Davis
Cunningham J. 204 Clay
Curtis & Allen, 313 Davis
Davis & Witham, 406 Davis
DeBlois & Co. 421 Davis
DeForest J. 221 Clay
Delabigne J. 323 Clay
Dorman & Wolf, 101 Clay
Drake & Emerson, 312 Washington
Dutard B. 217 Clay
Ellerhorst & Co. 64 Clay
Everding J. & Co. 56 Clay
Ewell L. J. cor Washington and San
Forsaith & Tyler, 309 Commercial
Gale J. W. & Co. 409 Davis
Giorgiani A. 421 Washington
Graves & Williams, 534 Clay and 529
    Merchant
Green A. 107 Clay
Gutridge & Curtin, 128 Clay
Hall & Brigham, 73 and 74 Wash Mkt
Ham I. H. 211 Clay
Harlow & Parker, cor Wash and Davis
Harms & Joost, 410 Clay
Hatch T. H. & Co. 319 Washington
Hathaway & Co. 7 Clay
Howes John, 502 Sansom
Hughes George, NW cor Clay and San
Humphrey & Co. 104 Clay
Hunt C. A. & Co. 222 Clay
Jones H. F. 107 Clay
Kessing J. F. 56 Clay
Keyes G. 112 Clay
Kirk W. H. 46 Clay
Knapp & Grant, 310 Washington
Lane & Kelly, 124 Clay

Leonard J. B. 5 Washington
Lewis E. 124 Clay
Lewis H. L. 209 Sacramento
Linsley E. W. & Co. 225 Clay
Littlefield, Webb & Co. 202 Wash
Loucks O. & Co. 108 Clay
Lowry W. J. cor Wash and Davis
Lusk A. & Co. Pacific Fruit Market
Mahan Henry & Co. 219 Washington
Markley Levi, 107 Clay
Matthews E. G. & Co. corner Clay and Drumm
McClelland J. A. & Co. 123 Clay
McColl Wm. 62 Clay
McCune J. N. 117 Clay
McHenry & Smith, 11 Washington
McKee John, 48 Clay
McNear & Bro. 39 Clay
Miller & Co. 124 Clay
Molloy & O'Connor, 64 Clay
Moran & Co. 114 Clay
Moulton Brothers, 5 Washington
O'Callaghan D. J. 112 Clay
Olmstead & Knowles, 405 Front
Peake W. B. & Co. 101 Clay
Pearse C. H. 46 Clay
Ralston & Co. 507 Sansom
Raymond J. P. & Co. 119 Clay nr East
Reynolds & Murray, 202 Clay
Reynolds, Howell & Ford, 313 Davis
Robbins J. 122 Clay
Robison D. N. cor Davis and Wash
Rorke F. M. 130 Clay
Ryan & Waterman, 111 Clay
Sanborn & Harmon, 406 Davis
Sanford J. L. 310 Washington
Schetter & Pearse, 123 Clay
Smith W. M. 33 Clay Street Wharf
Stevens E. & Co. 204 Clay
Tarpey M. & Co. 102 Clay
Taylor W. H. 408 Davis
Titcomb A. H. 121 Clay
Todd A. H. & Co. 45 Clay
Tully & Durkin, 215 Clay
Tyler C. M. & Co. foot Third
Vantine J. & Co. SE corner Clay and Davis
Vorbe J. F. 120 Clay
Warmouth & Baker, 423 Pacific
Waterman E. R. 406 Davis
Waterman M. 210 Clay
Williamson & McMillan, 217 Davis
Wilson & Co. 219 Clay
Worthley T. R. & Co. 10 Washington
Yates W. H. 208 Clay
[See Fruit; Provisions; Vegetables.]

Merchants. *Shipping and For-warding.*
[See Shipping and Forwarding.]

Merchants. *Chinese.*

Chang Ning Tuck Kee, 704 Dupont
Chue Yuen & Co. 832 Dupont
Chung Hay, 632 Jackson
Chung Lung & Co. 709 Sacramento
Chung Sing & Co. 723 Sacramento
Chung Shung & Co. 806 Sacramento
Chung Wo Tong (druggist) 933 Dupont
Chy Lung & Co. (crape and shawls) 642 Sacramento
Foo Kee, 834 Dupont
Fook On, 731 Commercial
Hip Wo & Co. 707 Dupont
Hong Yuen & Co. 708 Sacramento
Hop Kee & Co. 705 Dupont
Hop Wo Co. 726 Commercial
Hop Wo, 744 Sacramento
Hop Yik & Co. 705 Sacramento
Kee Song Tong, 742 Sacramento
Kong Yuen & Co. 724 Commercial
Kwong Ye & Co. 734 Sacramento
Lun Sing & Co. 706 Sacramento
Lung Wo & Co. 716 Sacramento
Quong Lung & Co. 719 Sacramento
Quong Le Toong & Co. 631 Jackson
Quong Shay Lung & Co. 812 Dupont
Quong Sung, 711 Commercial
Quong Tong Yon, 703 Dupont
Quong Yee & Co. 734 Sacramento
Quong Ying Kee & Co. 718 Com
Sam Kee, 723 Sacramento
Seong Kee & Co. 710 Sacramento
Sin Kee & Co. 708 Jackson
Sing Kee & Co. 727 Sacramento
Song Lee, 943 Dupont
Soong Sing, 808 Sacramento
Sue Woo & Co. 942 Dupont
Sun Chung Kee Co. 711 Sacramento
Sun Kee & Co. 639 Jackson
Sun Wo Yee & Co. 727 Sacramento
Ti Loe, 634 Jackson

Tie Sang Tong, 929 Dupont
Tin Yonk & Co. 740 Sacramento
Tong Soong & Co. 731 Sacramento
Tong Wo & Co. 722 Sacramento
Tong Yung & Co. 728 Sacramento
Tung Chong & Co. 743 Sacramento
Tung Tie & Co. 822 Dupont
Tung Yu & Co. 739 Sacramento
Wau Tuen, 733 Commercial
Wing Chong Lung, 708 Dupont
Wing Fung & Co. 745 Sacramento
Wing Lung, 1208 Stockton
Wing Soong & Co. 714 Sacramento
Wing Wo Lang & Co. 720 Sacramento
Wing Yune & Co. 818 Dupont
Wo Hing Lung & Co. 729 Commercial
Wo Kee & Co. 939 Dupont
Yan On Chong & Co. 734 Sacramento
Ye Wo & Co. 806 Dupont
Yik Yune & Co. 823 Dupont
Young Wo Tong & Co. 733 Commercial
Yu Yuen Ching Kee & Co. 734 Sac
Yue Yee & Co. 728 Sacramento

Metal Dealers.
[See Iron and Steel; Hardware.]

Metallurgical Works.

Electro Metallurgical Co. 616 Merch
KELLOGG, HEWSTON & CO. Seventh nr Brannan, office 416 Montgomery (see adv. p. 1)
Kimball & Co. 539 Bryant
Pacific Metallurgical Works, J. Mosheimer, 238 Montgomery
Pacific Mineral Co. office 325 Mont
[See Assayers.]

Midwives.

Bothe S. Mrs. 437 Pine
Chateau M. Madame, 26 Geary
Collin S. L. Mrs. Pacific nr Hyde
Delbanco F. Madame, 232 Kearny
Giraux A. Mrs. 730 Vallejo
Hartung W. Mrs. 207 Dupont
Hund C. (widow) 337 Fourth
Kiel D. Mrs. 34 Third
Korb L. Mrs. 28 Natoma
Labohm H. G. Mrs. 433 Sutter
Ledwith F. A. Mrs. 502 Bush
McKenley R. A. Mrs. 172 Minna
Plum M. Mrs. 635 Howard
Roberts M. Mrs. 34 Eddy
Schmitt G. Mrs. 5 Pennsylvania Av
Smith M. Mrs. 165 Tehama
Steiner A. Mrs. 221 Dupont
Stone E. Mrs. 157 Mission
Stutzback A. F. Mrs. 879 Mission
Thompson M. D. Mrs. 122 Fourth
Thurston M. N. Mrs. cor Folsom and Twenty-second
Weber F. Mrs. 1428 Dupont
[See Nurses.]

Military and Regalia Goods.

JOHNSON T. RODGERS, 325 Montgomery (see adv. inside back cover)
NORCROSS D. Masonic Temple (see advertisement, p. lxxix)
Schuyler, Hartley & Graham, 409 Bat

Milk Dealers.

Adam J. 735 Pacific
Bateman W. A. 329½ Kearny
Brommer & Bro. cor Sixth and Bryant
Bruhns W. 1209 Dupont
Cobleigh & Spencer, Clay nr Polk
Conahan C. Lake Merced
Cosgrove P. Folsom nr Precita Av
Cook M. M. cor Bush and Pierce
Cudworth J. W. cor Laguna and Presidio Road
Doran J. cor Felsom and Kosciusko
Edmunds H. H. nr Presidio House
Fellows G. W. Fourth nr Brannan
Frank R. nr Bay View Park
Green A. F. & Brother, 116 Fourth
Hatman G. W. nr Lagoon
Heath P. cor Courtland and North Av
Hendricks S. cor Larkin and Pine
Hutchinson Bros. Fourth nr Brannan
Jackson J. Lombard nr Fillmore
Jenkins B. F. Presidio Road nr Scott
Johnson E. Pres'o Road nr Devisdero
Jones & Starr, 429 Third
Jury L. & Co. near Protestant Orphan Asylum
Kelly P. University Mound
Killey C. H. Presidio Road nr Webster
Knight E. H. cor Filbert and Fillmore

Leonard T. San José Road nr St. Mary's College
Llepsic & Loudon, San Miguel Ranch
Lustenberger H. nr Mission Church
Mills & Evans, 6 Jane
Murray & Noble, cor Thirteenth and San José Road
Owen A. W. nr Presidio House
Richardson S. W. cor Dolores and Sixteenth
Ring D. Lombard nr Laguna
Rodgers F. San Miguel Ranch, San Bruno Road
Rogers R. K. Noe nr Sixteenth
Roy H. N. & Bro. Mission nr Third
Schwerin H. Visitacion Valley
Sheridan J. Serpentine Avenue
Sherry J. Precita Avenue nr Mission
Simonds N. Bay View Park
Stevens C. Brannan nr Fifth
Strittenberger C. cor Union and Fillmore
Talcott S. C. & L. H. nr Industrial School
Taplin J. O. San Bruno Road
Thurber A. E. cor Pine and Larkin
Ulshofer G. cor Douglass and Seventeenth
Wagner & Burfiend, cor Castro and Seventeenth
Warburton J. Presidio Road
Wilder H. Old San José Road, 5 miles
Wilson Isaac, 637 Kearny
[See Produce; Butter, Eggs, Etc.]

Milliners.

Altenberg R. Mrs. 302 Kearny
Altenburg P. Mrs. 828 Washington
Altshuler H. Mrs. 1105 Dupont
Appel S. Mrs. 204 Kearny
Barde C. Mme. 928 Dupont
Baumann S. A. Miss, 40 Fourth
Bert A. Miss, 44 Fourth
Butler M. A. Mrs. 136 Montgomery
Constant Mme. 634 Vallejo
Desmond J. Miss, 167 Third
Diamond Mrs. and Miss, 404 Kearny
Dixon & Putnam, 615 Clay
Dundas L. Miss, 40 Fourth
Forbes J. A. Mrs. 410 Third
Foutz M. Mrs. 1018 Stockton
Galavotti E. Mme. 725 Market
Hinchman H. E. Miss, 637 Sacramento
Hubbard & Freeman, 23½ Second
Jordan Mme. 1318 Dupont
Laurent Mme. & Co. 828 Washington
Laurent C. Mme. 407 Bush
Maurer Mme. 634 Vallejo
O'Donnell A. Miss, 1434 Stockton
Picot J. H. Mme. 22 Montgomery
Racouillat H. Mrs. 626 Vallejo
Reed M. & A. Misses, 231 Third
Roe M. J. Mrs. 106 Second
Ross M. Miss, 40 Fourth
Verdier P. Madame, 609 Sacramento
Ward T. Miss, 128 Third
Wheeler R. F. Mrs. 32 Second
[See Dress Makers.]

Millinery Goods. *Importers.*

Dexter, Lambert & Co. 105 Battery
Hamburger B. & Bro. 306 Sacramento
Held Bros. 416 Sacramento
Heller M. & Bro. 425 Sacramento
Hoffman W. & Co. 427 Sacramento
HUGHES HENRY, 218 Battery
Jones, Dixon & Co. NE cor Sacramento and Sansom
LAZARD FRERES, 115 Battery
Manheim, Schonwasser & Co. 113 Bat
Moss R. & Co. 207 Battery
Pecqueux & Watterlot, 511 Sac
Peyser S. A. & Co. 424 Sacramento
Rosenbaum & Friedman, 216 Sac
Sachs L. and M. & Co. 1312 California
Tence Charles & Co. 514 Sacramento
TOBIN BROTHERS & DAVISSON, SW cor Sacramento and Battery (see advertisement, p. xxxv)
Toplitz F. 512 Sacramento
Uhlfelder & Cahn, 309 Sacramento
VERDIER, KAINDLER, SCELLIER & CO. 633 Clay (see advertisement, p. xxxi)
[See Fancy Goods.]

Millinery Goods. *Retail.*

Altenberg R. Mrs. 308 Kearny
Appel S. Mrs. 204 Kearny
Barde C. Mme. 928 Dupont
Blockman E. 40 Fourth

Blood M. Mrs. 8 Montgomery
Butler M. A. Mrs. 136 Montgomery
Campbell E. T. Mrs. 128 Third
Carroll A. G. Miss, 24 Kearny
CHAPMAN C. M. Mrs. 218 Third (see advertisement, p. 667)
Chewning E. Miss, 44 Fourth
Cohen H. Mrs. 240 Third
Cohen M. Mrs. 1009 Stockton
Collins C. E. Mrs. 755 Clay
Diamond Mrs. and Miss. 404 Kearny
Dixon & Putnam, 615 Clay
Egan J. Mrs. 32 Third
Ferrenbach L. H. Mrs. 804 Washington
Flynn M. Miss, 940 Dupont
Forbes J. A. Mrs. 410 Third
Foute M. Mrs. 1018 Stockton
Goldberg C. Mrs. 124 Kearny
Gorman E. J. & K. Misses, 1221 Stock
Herrick E. J. Mrs. 106 Kearny
Holahan & Holahan, 424 Kearny
Jansou M. Mrs. 240 Third
Jenkins A. Mme. 1130 Dupont
Jordan A. 1016 Stockton
Kennedy & Conning, 62 Third
Landesman M. Mrs. 141 Montgomery
Lane E. (widow) 749 Clay
Marks S. Mrs. 617 Sacramento
McCrum E. Mrs. 604 Kearny
Michaelis B. (widow) 46 Second
Mish S. Mrs. 6 Kearny
Mitchell Mrs. 59 Second
Nally E. T. 1221 Stockton
Neumann M. Mrs. 612 Kearny
Newby J. H. & S. H. Misses, 1006 Stockton
Nichols G. M. 661 Clay
Norcross D. Mrs. 8 Montgomery
Plunkett L. Mrs. 122 Third
Rebstock J. Mrs. cor Bush and Dupont
Regan E. Mrs. 129 Second
Rice M. A. Mrs. 12 Kearny
Ross U. Mrs. 641 Clay
Roux R. Mrs. cor Fourth and Everett
Seaman R. Mrs. 20 Montgomery
Shear M. Mrs. 106 Third
Shloss E. Mrs. 138 Montgomery
Short B. A. Miss 106 Third
Standish S. Miss, 406 Kearny
Van Pick J. Madame, 42 Geary
Verdier F. Mrs. 609 Sacramento
Weber W. Mrs. 16 Geary

Mills. *Cotton.*
Greenburg M. & Co. 120 Bush

Mills. *Flour.*
Alta, Wheelan & Co. 12 Stevenson
CAPITOL, Mallory & Leihy, 115 Commercial (see adv. p. lxxii)
COMMERCIAL, Grosh & Rutherford, NE cor First and Natoma (see advertisement, p. 660)
Genessee, Kennedy & Hopkins, Gold nr Sansom
Golden Age, F. D. Conro & Co. 717 Battery, office 127 Clay
Golden Gate, H. Davis & Co. 430 Pine
National, J. Martenstein & Co. 561 Mkt
Pacific, J. Zeile, 508 Pacific
Pioneer, Elsen Bros. 515 Market
[See Flour; Groceries, Etc.]

Mills. *Paper.*
Harrison W. P. agent San Lorenzo, 421 Clay
TAYLOR S. P. Pioneer, 322 Clay (see advertisement, p. xlix)

Mills. *Quartz and Crushing.*
Howland S. W. 22 California
Woodward & Wilson, 537 Market

Mills. *Rice.*
Greenwood W. M. India, 39 Beale
FLINT, PEABODY & CO. W s Sansom nr Greenwich

Mills. *Salt.*
Barton B. F. & Co. Pioneer, 213 Sac
Barton John, Pacific, 218 Sacramento
Klein S. Washington, 29 Fremont
Tyler S. H. & Co. Eagle, 110 Fremont
Webster A. B. 321 Market
Winegar A. B. Union, 319 Front
[See Salt Stores.]

Mills. *Saw.*
Brokaw Jas. cor Mission and Fremont

CHACE'S, Macdonald Bros. cor Market and Beale (see adv. p. 666)
CULVERWELL S. S. 29 Fremont
HOBBS, GILMORE & CO. Market nr Beale (see adv. p. liv)
Macdonald Bros. 311 Market
Metcalf S. A. cor Mission and Fremont
Smith & Ransom, 24 California
Thomas C. W. 22 California
Ware & Mosher, 26 California

Mills. *Woolen.*
MISSION, cor Folsom and Sixteenth, Lazard & McLennan proprietors. office 217 Battery (see advertisement, p. ix)
S. F. PIONEER, Black Point, Heynemann & Co. agents, office 311 California (see advertisement, p. xl)
WADDING MANUFACTORY, J. H. Bacon proprietor, office 1 Union St. Boston (see advertisement, p. xcix)

Mining Agencies.
[See Brokers.]

Mining Companies.
[See Register Names.]

Mining Stocks.
[See Brokers.]

Mirrors.
Hausmann D. & Co. 535 Clay
Hirschfelder A. & Co. 427 Montgomery
JONES, WOOL & SUTHERLAND, 312 Montgomery (see adv. p. xxxvi)
ROSENBAUM F. H. 423 Battery (see advertisement, p. lxxiv)
Swnin R. A. & CO. cor San and Pine

Model Makers.
Grush & Co. 24 Fremont
Kallenberg T. 416 Market
Lewis & Culver, 509 Market
Meyer G. 531 Market
[See Carvers and Sculptors.]

Music Dealers.
Bowers J. T. 138 Montgomery
Feldbush & Co. 307 California
FREY W. A. 404 Kearny (see advertisement, p. 650)
Frisbee W. B. & Co. 3 Montgomery
GRAY M. 613 Clay (see advertisement, p. xiii)
Kohler A. 630 Wash and 424 Sansom
Rosa S. 615 Montgomery
WOODWORTH, SCHELL & CO. Masonic Temple, Post (see adv. p. cx)

Museums.
Gilbert's, Market bet Mont and Sansom
Pacific, L. J. Jordan, 318 Montgomery

Musical Instruments. *Importers.*
Bowers J. T. 131 Montgomery
FREY WILLIAM A. 404 Kearny (see advertisement, p. 650)
Frisbee W. B. & Co. 3 Montgomery
GRAY M. 613 Clay (see adv. p. xiii)
Kohler A. 630 Washington and 424 San
Pierce W. S. & Co. 26 Montgomery
WOODWORTH, SCHELL & CO. Masonic Temple (see adv. p. cx)

Musical Instruments. *Makers.*
Keene C. C. (accordeons and flutes) 103 Montgomery
Lang J. F. 1306 Stockton
MAYER J. (organs) Page nr Octavia (see advertisement, p. 664)
Mojica D. 1026 Kearny
Pfaff G. (flutes) 614 Sacramento
Ripley & Kimball, 417 Montgomery
Urban J. cor Kearny and Bush
WOODWORTH, SCHELL & CO. (organs and piano fortes) Masonic Temple (see advertisement, p. cx)

Mustard Mills.
Hudson H. C. & Co. corner Pine and Front
Marden & Folger, 220 Front
Zwick & Loeven, 725 Vallejo
[See Coffee; Spices, Etc.]

Native Wines.
Anaheim, B. Dreyfus agent, 321 Mont
Burkhardt & Klebs, 634 Commercial
FINLEY THOMAS E. (agent) 113 Leidesdorff (see adv. p. x)
Groezinger s. cor Battery and Pine
Harazsthy & Giovanari (Sonoma) Thos. E. Finley agent, 113 Liedesdorff
HOADLEY & CO. 617 Montgomery (see advertisement, p. 658)
Jacobs N. B. & Co. 423 Front
Jaudin E. & Co. 523 Front
Keller M. 609 Front
KOHLER & FROHLING, 626 Montgomery (see adv. front cover)
Loane J. M. cor First and Market
LOWNDES A. S. 311½ Battery (see advertisement, p. lvi)
MERCADO & SEULLY, 506 Jackson (see advertisement, p. xxxii)
McMillan & Kester, 714 Front
Schwergerie & Co. 636 Commercial
Wilson B. D. & Son, cor First and Mkt

Newspapers and Periodicals.
Abend Post, Leo Eloesser & Co. 517 Clay
Alta California, Fred MacCrellish & Co. 536 Sacramento
American Flag, D. O. McCarthy, 528 Montgomery
California Christian Advocate, 711 Mission
California Chronik, Charles Ruehl, N W cor Sacramento and Kearny
California Demokrat, Fredk. Hess & Co. N W cor Sac and Kearny
California Farmer, Warren and Co. 320 Clay
California Leader, Theobalds & Co. 625 Merchant
California Police Gazette, F. S. Harlow & Bro. 424 Battery
California Rural Home Journal, T. Hart Hyatt & Co. 3-6 Sansom
California Teacher, 536 Clay
California Youths' Companion, Smith & Co. 505 Clay
Californian, 532 Merchant
Christian Spectator, Rev. O. P. Fitzgerald, Francisco nr Stockton
Courrier de San Francisco, 617 San
Die Montags Zeitung, F. G. Walther, 621 Sansom
Dramatic Chronicle, G. & C. de Young, 417 Clay
El Correo de San Francisco, 619 San
EL NUEVO MUNDO, F. P. Ramirez, 603 Front (see adv. p. 684)
Elevator, cor Sansom and Jackson
Evangel, Stephen Hilton, 523 Clay
Evening Bulletin, 620 Montgomery
Examiner, Wm S. Moss, 535 Wash Clay
Golden Era, Brooks & Lawrence, 543 Clay
Guide, J. B. Faitoute & Co. 411 Clay
Hebrew, Philo Jacoby, 509 Clay
Hebrew Observer, Rev. Julius Eckmann, 511 Sacramento
Irish News, Jeffrey Nunan, 510 Clay
Irish People, 502 Washington
L'Independent, Neuval & Chamon, 617 Commercial
La Voz de Mejico, A. Mancillas, NW cor Montgomery and Jackson
Le National, Theodore Thiele & Co. 533 Commercial
Mercantile Gazette and Shipping Register, E. D. Waters, 536 Clay
Mining and Scientific Press, Dewey & Co. 505 Clay
Monitor, Thomas A. Brady, 622 Clay
Morning Call, J. J. Ayers & Co. 612 Commercial
New Age, John F. Pynch & Co. 235 Merchant
Our Mazeppa, T. de M. Hylton, 423 Washington
Pacific, NE cor Clay and Front
Pacific Medical and Surgical Journal, 505 Clay
Puck, Loomis & Swift, 617 Clay
Record, Rice & Co. 538 Market
San Francisco News Letter and California Advertiser, Fred'k Marriott, 528 Clay
Spirit of the Times and Fireman's Journal, Chase & Boruck, cor Sansom and Jackson
Stock Circular, T. F. Cronise, 536 Clay
Sunday Mercury, J. MacDonough Foard & Co. 420 Montgomery

Varieties, J. Walter Walsh, 517 Clay
World's Crisis, John L. Hopkins, NE cor Clay and Montgomery
[See Appendix.]

Newspaper and News Agents.

Anthony G. W. Occidental Hotel
Arnold E. F. 538 Market
Bamber & Co. 716 Davis
Bell G. H. 611 Montgomery
Betge R. J. 217 Montgomery
BOYCE T. NE cor Washington and Montgomery (see adv. p. 649)
Brooks W. H. 51 Third
Fisher L. P. 629 Washington
Knowlton J. J. & Co. 402 Montgomery
Lake W. B. 502 Washington
Loomis W. E. cor Wash and Sansom
Marks L. cor Kearny and Pine
Mosse & Son, 639 Kearny and 618 Wash
Newburgh O. cor Market and Second
Payot H. 640 Washington
Steinbrink B. 33½ Second
STRATMAN J. cor Washington and San (see advertisement, p. lxxiii)
Sullivan J. W. 516 Washington
Tyler Brothers, 632 Washington
White & Bauer, 413 Washington

Notaries Public.

Andrews W. O. 630 Montgomery
Blood J. H. 7 Montgomery Block
DREschFELD H. 623 Montgomery
Gorman John, 619 Merchant
Gould A. S. 528 Clay
Haight Henry, 607 Clay
Hassey F. A. 524 Montgomery
HOMANS H. S. 609 Clay
Huefner William, 619 Merchant
Joice E. V. NE cor Battery and Wash
Knox G. T. NW cor Mont and Merch
Lawton W. W. 404 Montgomery
McKenzie J. W. 406 Montgomery
Milliken I. F. 608 Merchant
Murphy S. S. 520 Montgomery
Parker W. C. 517 Jackson
Peckham E. P. cor Clay and Mont
Sawyer O. V. cor Clay and Mont
Sutter E. V. 626 Clay
Thibault F. J. 605 Montgomery
Waller G. C. 6 Montgomery Block

Nurseries.

Chiousse & Salmon, 716 Washington
Collie & Stewart, 27 Geary
Culver William, Sans Souci Valley
McElroy W. C. Presidio Road
Meheren Thos. agent, cor Battery and Oregon
Meyer W. F. Post nr Lone Mountain
O'Hare J. cor Harrison and Tenth
Patterson W. San Brano Road, 3 miles from City Hall
Reimer E. L. NW cor Folsom and Fifteenth
Sonntag H. A. NE cor Sixteenth and First Avenue
Walker W. C. cor Folsom and Fourth
Walsh J. Folsom nr Thirteenth

Nurses.

Blake M. L. Mrs. LeRoy Place nr Sac
Connell H. Miss, cor Stockton and Pac
DeRoos F. Mrs. 309 Dupont
Deutler A. (widow) 1308 Kearny
Eustis H. (widow) 228 Minna
Ferry E. 318 Jessie
Flynn D. T. (widow) 15 Monroe
Hayes E. (widow) 210 Third
Heise M. (widow) 319 Bush
Higgins J. (widow) Lincoln Avenue
Howes E. Mrs. Leavenworth nr Sac
Johnson A. Mrs. Natoma nr Seventh
Kerby E. Mrs. 32 Geary
Ladd C. (widow) 516 Bush
May M. Mrs. cor Dupont and Bdwy
McCarty S. Miss, 869 Mission
Miller C. Mrs. 816 Filbert
Nixon M. (widow) 228 Minna
Otto P. Mrs. 55 Fifth
Reynolds A. Miss, Taylor nr Pacific
Rosenberg M. Mrs. 332 Sutter
Smith M. Mrs. cor Bush and Powell
Spaulding J. A. Miss, Riley nr Taylor
Taylor E. Mrs. 124 Silver
[See Midwives.]

Oakum. Manufacturers.

TUBBS & CO. 611 Front (see advertisement, p. xli)

Observatories.
McGREGOR J. Telegraph Hill

Oculists and Aurists.
DeCastro F. 620 Market
Dunning O. 515 Sacramento
Pardee E. H. 767 Clay
[See Physicians.]

Oil Clothing.
Appel S. & Co. 322 Commercial
Rubber Clothing Co. 118 Montgomery
[See Clothing.]

Oil Cloths.
* Importers.

*BELL JOHN C. cor California and Sansom (see advertisement, p. xiv)
*EDWARDS F. G. 646 Clay (see advertisement, front cover)
Gullixson & Nelson, 336 Kearny
Hixon W. M. 606 Clay
*KENNEDY & BELL, cor Montgomery and Cal (see adv. front cover)
*LOUGHRAN P. F. & CO. 403 Sansom (see advertisement, p. xxx)
*WALTER D. N. and E. & Co. 305 California (see advertisement, p. cxli)
*WIGHTMAN & HARDIE, 416 Clay (See advertisement, p. xlix)

Oil Dealers. Lamps.
* Importers.

*Cameron, Whittier & Co. 425 Front
Deane J. R. 318 Clay
*Dell, Cranna & Co. 513 Front
*Dietz A. C. & Co. 521 Front
Dixon & Vagts, 144 Fourth
Dow M. & Co. 62 Second
*Fuller & Heather, 223 Front
*Gibb G. & W. 527 Kearny
HARRISON C. H. Phoenix, 517 Front
*Hayward & Coleman, 414 Front
*Hollub A. & Co. 501 Front
Kelly J. R. 38 California
McCarty A. J. 850 Washington
*McMahon F. P. & Co. 404 Front
Oliver D. J. 318 Washington
Owens J. B. 10 Third
*Redington & Co. 418 Front
Robinson Joseph, 509 Sansom
Roehrle C. C. (manufacturer neat's-foot) Potrero
*Stanford Bros. 121 California
Stringer W. 118 Jackson
Sturtevant I. cor Bdwy and Dupont
SWEETT & GADSBY, 28 Third
Urquhart S. F. 512 Sansom
Vale C. jr. 802 Dupont
[See Coal Oil; Lamps and Oils.]

Opticians.
Kahn & Strauss, 619 Washington
LAWRENCE & HOUSEWORTH, 317 Montgomery (see adv. back cover)
Muller C. 3 Montgomery
Roach John, 413 Washington
Sack J. C. 203 Montgomery
[See Mathematical Instrument Makers.]

Ores and Metals.
California Copper Smelting, Contra Costa County, 540 Clay
California Mining and Metallurgical Company, 509 Clay
Davidson Donald & Co. 338 Mont
Martin & Co. cor Mont and California
Pacific Mineral Co. W. F. Bryant, 325 Montgomery
Penrose W. 228 Montgomery
[See Assayers.]

Organ Builders.
MAYER J. Page nr Octavia (see advertisement, p. 664)
Pierce W. S. & Co. (importers) 26 Mont
Shellard B. Montgomery nr Union
WOODWORTH, SCHELL & CO. Post, Masonic Temple

Oysters. Dealers in.
Anderson & Roalfe, 32 Wash Market
Guesti J. 26 Metropolitan Market
Ladium A. 624 Howard
Ladium J. C. 624 Howard

McDonald C. C. & Co. cor Clay and Leidesdorff
Morgan & Co. 31 Wash Market
Nolting & Spreen, 640 Market
Winant M. 75 Washington Market
Winant & Co. 24 Metropoliton Market

Oyster Saloons.
Conrades & Co. 612 Market
Egan W. cor Third and Howard
Haney J. 612 Washington
Harkness J. J. cor Second and Tehama
Howard H. S. 324 Sansom
Johnson G. O. North Beach
Kutter H. 221 Bush
Lahusen Henry, 324 Montgomery
Lee N. A. cor Clay and Waverly Place
McCormack John, cor Mont and Wash
McDonald & Co. cor Clay and Leidesdorff
Nolting & Spreen, 640 Market
Quinn Samuel (stand) corner Clay and Kearny
Sbarboro J. (stand) 610 Clay
Stormes N. J. 25 Third
Walnwright W. 219 California
Williams T. C. Occidental Market
Winant W. W. (stand) 24 Metropolitan Market

Packets.
Albion & Noyo, Pier 20 Stewart
Alviso and San José (West's) Central Wharf
Alviso and San José (Union) Central Wharf
Amos, Phinney & Co. 123 Stewart
Australian and Melbourne, Battery nr Washington
Benicia and Martinez, Clay St. Wharf
Boas J. & Co. (Hamburg) 513 Sac
Bodega Line, Washington St. Wharf
Bolinas, Jackson Street Wharf
BOOKER W. LANE (Royal Mail Steam) 428 Cal (see adv. p. xxiv)
Bordeaux, 431 Battery
BOSTON, 405 and 716 Front
Caduc's Line, foot Washington
California and Victoria, 123 and 129 Stewart
California, Oregon & Mexican (steamship) cor Front and Jackson
COLEMAN'S CALIFORNIA & NEW YORK, 417 Battery (see adv. p. xi)
Colorado River, 308 Front
Coose Bay, Pier 11 Stewart
Eden Landing, Clay Street Wharf
Freeport, Washington Street Wharf
Glidden & Williams' California Line, Flint, Peabody & Co. agents, 716 Front
Guaymas, 314 Washington
Guaymas (steam) SW cor Front and Jackson
Hamburg Line, 513 Sacramento
HAWAIIAN LINE TO HONOLULU, C. W. Brooks & Co. 511 Sansom (see adv. p. vii)
Hongkong, cor Battery and Union and 204 Sansom
HONOLULU REGULAR DISPATCH LINE, J. C. Merrill & Co. 204 California and 511 Sansom
Humboldt and Puget Sound, Pier 10 Stewart
Liverpool, Australia, etc. Dickson, De-Wolf & Co. agents, 414 Battery
Mazatlan, N. Larco, 432 Jackson
McCune J. N. (Star Line) 817 Clay
MEADER, LOLOR & CO. 405 Front (see advertisement, p. ix)
Mendocino, J. T. Fennell, Pier 11 Stewart
Merchants' Transportation, cor Battery and Clay
Merchants' Express Line, DeWitt, Kittle & Co. cor Cal and Front
Merchants' Line for Victoria and Portland, R. F. Pickett, 214 Sac
Mexican and South American, 324 Washington
Mexican Dispatch, 314 Washington and 424 Battery
Napa City, foot Commercial
New York and Marsh Landing, Mission Street Wharf
NEW YORK LINE, 427 Battery, 106 and 200 Cal, 305 Front and 309 Clay
Noyo and Albion River, A. W. Macpherson, pier 20 Stewart
Oregon Line, pier 3 Stewart

Oregon and California, Richards & Mc-
 Craken, 405 Front
Pacheco Line, 11 Clay
Petaluma, 48 Clay ·
Pioneer Line, Victoria, 311 East
Puget Sound, pier 17 Stewart
Port Orford, Navarro, and Russian
 River, pier 21 Stewart
Portland, 214 Sac and 405 Front
Puget Sound, piers 17 and 1 Stewart
Robinson's Line, H. B. Williams, 305
 Front
ROYAL MAIL STEAM PACKET CO.
 428 California (see adv. p. xxiv)
Salt Point, Stewart Street piers
Sacramento, Broadway Wharf
Sacramento Dispatch Line, 413 East
Sacramento (Green's) cor Front and
 Sacramento
San José and Alviso (steamers) Broad-
 way Wharf
San Leandro, Clay Street Wharf
San Mateo, Central Wharf
San Pablo, Clay Street Wharf
San Rafael, Clay Street Wharf
Santa Cruz, cor Front and Wash
Southern Dispatch Line, N. Pierce,
 cor Market and East
Southern Dispatch Line, N. Pierce
Star Line, J. N. McCune, 117 Clay
Stockton Line, Clay Street Wharf
Suisun Line, Clay Street Wharf
Union City, Clay Street Wharf
Union Line, foot Commercial
Union Maritime, 730 Montgomery
Victoria and Port Townsend, 615 Bat
Victoria and Puget Sound, piers 9, 12,
 and 17 Stewart, 214 Sacramento,
 and 311 East
Victoria, Pioneer Line, 311 East
West India and Pacific Steamship Co.
 Rodgers, Meyer & Co. 314 Wash
 [See Shipping, Etc.]

Pail and Tub Manufacturers.

ARMES, DALLAM & CO. 22 California (see adv. p. 644)

Painters. *Coach.*

Begeman & Bonn, cor· Mission and
 Ninth
Kimball G. P. & Co. Market nr Fourth
O'Brien P. J. cor Pine and Morse
Stackpole T. 113 Bush
Weber M. 626 Sansom
Welsh W. 115 Bush
Wilber & Engleman, 535 Market

Painters. *House, Sign, and Ornamental.*

Addison & Macomber, 311 Bush
Armor J. G. 427 California
Armstrong & Kelly, 611 Market
Arons M. 3 Summer
Barker Y. W. 212 Fourth
Barron C. 644 Market
Barry & Kennedy, 4 Summer
Bartlett J. D. Dolores op Sixteenth
Beatty J. J. 132 Third
Beguhl A. 222 Fourth
Belinder C. 725 Market
Bernard C. A. 617 Clay
Bernard W. R. 511 Commercial
Bose R. 235 Sutter
Boyd, McAuliffe & Co. 412 Pine
Brandt B. L. 322 Commercial
Brewster & Son, 237 Bush
Cathcart T. 670 Howard
Cherry J. W. 626 Commercial
CHURCH W. S. 823 Montgomery (see
 advertisement, p. lxx)
Clough & Ellis, 85 Everett
Coleman J. E. W. 412 Tehama
Cooney J. jr. 830 Market
Corliss W. P. 156 Perry
Courtenay Charles, 10 Sutter
Currier & Winter, 620 Market
Cutting E. 759 Mission
Davis R. E. 731 Mission
Delauney H. 632 Pacific
Denike W. J. 805 Washington
Denny J. W. 617 Montgomery
Donovan J. 312 Davis
Doyle J. 507 Broadway
Dubourque E. & Co. 703 Sacramento
Duff John, 642 Clay
Fisher J. Brannan nr First
Frank A. W. 507 Kearny
Fredoya H. 571 Mission

Frost & Richards, 13 Post
Fulton W. G. 13 Post
Fuquay & Richardson, 19 Geary
Giles & Dunbar, 403 Bush
Hammerschmidt H. A. 230 Sutter
Hastings E. S. 203 Commercial
Henry & Watson, 535 Market
Holm H. 305 Pine
Hopps & Kanary, 216 Sansom
Hopps & Downing, 110 Sutter
Hopps & Chapman, 628 Commercial
Ickelheimer H. 15 Dupont
Jones T. L. 604 Jackson
Jump E. 116 Montgomery Block
Lancy T. C. 822 Montgomery
Lang C. E. 216 Washington
Longley A. C. & Son, 922 Howard
Lougee J. W. 516 Davis
Luhr E. 238 Ritch
Mansell Fred. 420 California
McAlpin T. 3 Broadway
McCorkell A. 347 Third
McCoy & Mason, 611 Market
McFarland B. L. 624 Front
Melendy H. B. 341 Bush
Morsch Fred. 527 Kearny
Noble & Gallagher, 437 Jackson
Nutz Fred. 525 California
O'Neil J. T. 10 Sutter
Rogers H. 611 Market
Rosekrans H. M. 626 Commercial
Rouse C. F. 741 Mission
Rutherford & Hathaway, Sixteenth nr
 Mission
Sellers & McPherson, 405 Kearny
Snow & Co. 414 Merchant
Spies F. 330 Bush
SWEETT J. S. 29 Third
SWEETT & GADSBY, 28 Third (see
 advertisement, p. xxxiv)
TORNING A. & T. 528 California (see
 advertisement, p. 656)
Vetter A. 205 Kearny
Vorrath T. 437 Bush
Walcolm & Gowan, 717 Market
Wason A. 613 Sansom
Wettstein W. 819 Jackson ·
Whitaker J. W. 637 California
White J. K. 644 Market
Whitehouse M. C. 241 Sutter
Wilkey E. H. cor Com and Davis
Wilson J. N. 928 Washington
Wilson & Moulton, 516 Davis
Wilson W. cor Cal and Leidesdorff
Winter W. 805 Washington
Wunderlich R. 845 Dupont
Wyman G. D. 920 California

Painters. *Portraits, Etc.*

Arriola F. 338 Montgomery
Brooks S. M. 611 Clay
Burgess Geo. H. 423 Montgomery·
Butman F. A. (landscape) 240 Mont
Chittenden A. Union College
Claveau A. & F. (scenic) 912 Market
Claveau M. Hayes' Park
Denny G. J. 338 Montgomery
Eastman H. 338 Montgomery
Frey Henry J. 649 Clay
Hill Thomas jr. 202 Montgomery
Jewett W. S. 612 Clay
Johnson N. T. 429 Montgomery
Kaltschmidt O. 410 Kearny
Kipps A. K. 618 Washington
McClellan C. B. 240 Montgomery
Nahl Bros. 121 Montgomery
Perry E. W. jr. 202 Montgomery
Shaw S. W. cor Montgomery and Cal
Wandesforde J. B. 315 Montgomery
Williams W. 202 Montgomery
Winter Robert, 605 Sacramento

Paints, Oils, and Glass.
 * Importers.

*Cameron, Whittier & Co. 425 Front
Deane J. R. 318 Clay
*Fuller & Heather, 223 Front and 305
 Sacramento
*Gibb J. W. 521 Kearny
*Hallock J. Y. & Co. 525 Front
Kelly James R. 38 California
Lebouc F. 1181 Dupont
McDonald John, 103 Stevenson
*Oliver D. J. 318 Washington
*Redington & Co. 418 Front
*Robinson Joseph, 509 Sansom
*ROSENBAUM F. H. 423 Battery
SWEETT & GADSBY, 28 Third
Wilson & Moulton, 516 Davis
Worthington W. 735 Market

Paper Boxes.
 [See Boxes.]

Paper Hangings.
 *Importers.

*BELL JOHN C. SW cor California
 and Sansom (see adv. p. xiv)
*Clark G. W. NE cor Clay and San
Day E. & Co. 823 Montgomery
Duff John. 642 Clay
EDWARDS FRANK G. 646 Clay (see
 advertisement, front cover)
Fricke Louis, 423 Bush
*Gullixson & Nelson, 336 Kearny
*Hixon W. M. 606 Clay
*KENNEDY & BELL, SW cor Mont-
 gomery and California
*McElwee & Ackerman, 236 Mont
*Plum C. M. 22 Montgomery
*Robinson J. 509 Sansom
SOLOMON B. L. & SONS, NW cor
 Pat and Pine (see adv. p. lxvi)
SWEETT & GADSBY, 28 Third
Troutt H. J. M. 618 Market
*WALTER D. N. & E. & CO. 303 Cali-
 fornia (see adv. p. cxli)
*WIGHTMAN & HARDIE, 416 Clay
 (see advertisement, p. xlix)
 [See Carpets; Upholsterers.]

Paper Warehouses. *Printing.*

Blake & Moffitt, 533 Washington
Harrison W. P. 421 Clay
ISAAC JOS. & CO. 513 Sansom (see
 advertisement, p. xlviii)
Manneck H. 210 Pine
TAYLOR S. P. (manufacturer) Pioneer
 Mills 322 Clay (see adv. p. xlix)
*TOWNE & BACON, 536 Clay (see
 advertisement, p. 8)
 [See Stationers.]

Patent Agency. ·

Dewey & Co. 505 Clay
Smith C. W. M. 423 Washington
Stevenson J. D. 604 Merchant

Pattern Makers.

Culver J. H. 509 Market
Grush & Co. 24 Fremont
Lewis O. 509 Market
 [See Carvers; Cabinet Makers.]

Pawnbrokers.

Coney A. 813 Dupont
Craner A. P. & Co. 110 Kearny
Franklin A. 809 Kearny
Funkenstein J. 843 Dupont
Heyman W. 25 Kearny
Hyman H. 741 Washington
Jacobs C. 708 Dupont
Jacoby J. 615 Kearny
Jaffe S. & Co. 341 Kearny
Kamsler J. 729 Washington
Lewis S. 15 Kearny
Lichtenstein M. B. 629 Commercial
Michael A. 835 Dupont
Milsner L. & Co. 752 Washington
Murdock R. 647 Sacramento
Myers H. 632 Com and 818 Kearny
Myers J. 827 Dupont
Shaw T. 911 Dupont
Smith F. 647 Sacramento
Wiener J. A. 1134 Dupont

Perfumery.

Fayard J. B. 711 Clay
Hinckley C. E. & Co. cor Clay and
 Kearny
Krause W. E. F. (agent Rowland &
 Sons) cor Front and Jackson
Oppenheim M. Chestnut nr Powell

Perfumery. *Manufacturers.*

Oppenheim M. Chestnut nr Powell
 [See Apothecaries; Fancy Goods, Etc.]

Petroleum Refineries.

Pacific, Stanford Bros. cor Chestnut
 and Taylor
Stott Charles, cor Chstnut and Taylor

Photographic Galleries.

Addis & Koch, 425 Montgomery
Bayley & Cramer, 618 Washington
Bayley M. F. cor Kearny and Com

BRADLEY & RULOFSON, 429 Montgomery (see adv. p, 659)
Bryan J. M. 611 Clay
Bush H. 9 Post
DYER & LUDERS, 612 Clay
Edouart Alex. 634 Washington
Hamilton & Kellogg, 513 Montgomery
Higgins T. J. 659 Clay
Hord J. R. 143 Fourth
Howland & Vasoncelles, 25 Third
Johnson A. P. 649 Clay
McGinn A Miss, 2 O'Farrell
Olsen H. 650 Washington
Perkins & Foss, 606 Kearny
Pilliner W. H. 14 Second
Robertson J. D. 119 Third
Selleck Silas, 415 Montgomery
Shew Jacob, 315 Montgomery
Shew William, 421 and 423 Mont
Silva J. T. 402 Kearny
Swasey Benj. 205 Third
Watkins C. E. 425 Mont
Weston N. 14 Second
Wise J. 417 Montgomery

Physicians.

Adolphus H. 511 Jackson
Alers A. 521 Pacific
Aronstein Adolphe, 810 Washington
Avery A. L. Mrs. 158 Second
Ayer Washington, 605 Sacramento
Ayres W. O. 613 Howard
Badarous Camillo, 732 Washington
Baldwin A. S. cor Clay and Kearny
Baldwin H. S. 612 Clay
Ball Albert, Government House
Barbat J. 910 Pacific
Beck F. E. S. 706 Montgomery
Beckford D. R. 731 Clay
Behr H. 639 Washington
Behrens H. C. F. 754 Washington
Bennett Thomas, cor Sutter and Mont
Benton H. A. 109 Montgomery
Berg C. NE cor Kearny and Jackson
Berthier A. 814 Washington
Bertody Charles, 807 Washington
Blake James, 206 Bush
Borchers J. C. 343 Kearny
Bowie A. J. 672 Clay
Brown J. N. 46 Sutter
Bruner W. H. cor Mont and Market
Bryant E. G. 415 Montgomery
BRUNS C. 434 Cal (see adv. p. 661)
Buffum A. C. 652 Market
Burke M. J. 930 Clay
Burrill C. Geary nr Stockton
Bush J. P. 605 Sacramento
Cachot M. St. Mary's Hospital
Calef J. S. 726 Washington
Caman A. 106 Fourth
Carman William, 616 Howard
Cashnel M. St. Mary's Hospital
Celle E. 829 Washington
Chapin S. F. 338 Montgomery
Chase R. P. 436 Bush
Clapp G. H. cor Howard and Sixth
Cleburne J. cor Stockton and Bdwy
Cohn D. 642 Washington
Coit Benjamin B. cor Mont and Mkt
Cole R. Beverly, cor Stock and Bdwy
Conroy B. 505 Pacific
Coon Henry P. cor Geary and Hyde
D'Assonville D. 934 Dupont
Damour F. 402 Kearny
Davis N. R. 131 Montgomery
DeCourcillon E. 737 Clay
Dean B. D. SW cor Bush and Mont
Deane C. T. 414 Bush
Demarest J. D. cor Jack and Kearny
Desch C. 814 Washington
Dietrich H. B. Bush nr Kearny
D'Oliveira E. 812 Washington
Doherty W. E. 515 Sacramento
Douglass W. A. Mission nr Fourth
Dunlevy J. cor Dupont and Kearny
Dunning O. 636 Sacramento
Eaton E. B. cor Folsom and Caroline
Eckel J. N. (homeopathic) 228 Post
Eidenmiller G. SW cor Washington and Brenham Place
Elliot S. F. 636 Clay
Elliott T. W. 574 Mission
Fantini J. 1020 Dupont
Farrar E. 4 Brenham Place
Favor K. 131 Third
Finigan H. 608 Jackson
Flinn R. P. 5 Stewart
Floto J. H. 400 Kearny
Fourgeaud V. J. 325 Bush
Fox J. V. W. (homeopathic) 643 Com
Garwood W. T. City and County Hospital

Gates H. S. 526 Merchant
Gautier L. P. 402 Montgomery
Geary J. F. (homeopathic) 632 Howard
Gerry S. R. 817 Washington
Gibbon J. F. 619 Kearny
Gibbons H. 6 Montgomery
Gibbons H. jr. 6 Montgomery
Gilbert J. 503 Davis
Green Thomas, 738 Mission
Grover W. A. 27 Post
Hahn F. 122 Post
Haine J. 132 Geary
Hale W. F. 520 Kearny
Hall S. H. 402 Montgomery
Hamelin L. 224 Stevenson
Hammond W. 202 Bush
Hardy B. F. 762 Mission
Harris S. R. 12 Court Block
Harville J. W. Sixteenth nr Valencia
Hastings John, U. S. Marine Hospital
Hathaway B. W. 82 Montgomery Blk
Hathaway E. V. 38 South Park
Hayne A. P. 748 Washington
Heiniman M. 804 Montgomery
Henkenius H. 639 Washington
Henry L. J. 745 Clay
Hewston G. 652 Folsom
Hinckley G. E. cor Second and Stevenson
Hitchcock C. M. 214 Bush
Holman F. A. cor Mont and Sutter
Holmes S. 646 Washington
Horner J. C. 644 Pacific
Howard P. 648 Washington
Huard A. cor Dupont and Wash
Hume J. N. cor Fourth and Mission
Hunt H. 12 Montgomery
Hyams L. 659 Clay
Hyde J. T. cor Sansom and Jackson
Hylton T. 423 Washington
Jordan L. J. 211 Geary
Josselyn B. F. 540 Washington
Josselyn J. H. (electropathic) 645 Washington
Journe J. cor Sixth and Stevenson
Kafka J. 343 Kearny
Keeney C. C. 562 Folsom
Kellogg A. 511 Bush
Kiser D. 1714 Dupont
Kisfy Z. S. 809 Kearny
Lane L. C. 664 Mission
Levison L. 398 Greenwich
Lind J. Y. 759 Market
Lindop W. cor Front and Jackson
Loehr F. cor California and Quincy
Low L. I. 528 Folsom
Mackintosh R. 128 Second
Malech G. 105 Post
Maxwell R. T. 124 Sutter
May W. B. 1114 Clay
Mayerhofer F. V. cor Stevenson and Third
McCormick C. 410 Kearny
McDonald A. R. 518 Green
McMillan R. 722 Washington
McNulty J. M. 414 Bush
Merritt S. 240 Montgomery
Meyers J. S. cor Mont and Pine
Miller L. 619 Market
Moore C. W. 643 Commercial
Moreno A. M. 305 Montgomery
Morison J. 219 First
Morse J. F. 10 Brenham Place
Mouser S. M. 324 Bush
Murphy James, 859 Clay
Murray R. 805 Sansom
Newell W. A. 632 Mission
Neuberger S. cor Kearny and Jackson
O'Donnell C. 537 California
O'Neill O. H. 652 Market
Ober Benjamin, 109 St. Mark Place
Otto G. 5 St. Mark Place
Pardee E. 767 Clay
Parker W. 548 Folsom
Paugh W. J. O'Farrell nr Jones
Pawlecki L. 617 Commercial
Perrault J. 502 Montgomery
Perrin B. 109 Montgomery
Peyraud P. 904 Kearny
Pigne J. B. 1007 Stockton
Pissis J. E. 316 Sutter
Polastri V. 619 Vallejo
Pond M. B. City Hospital
Quinlin A. G. 610 Front
Randle P. W. 737 Harrison
Regensburger J. 652 Washington
Reilly P. J. 535 Commercial
Repiton R. A. J. 816 Montgomery
Reynolds W. cor Mont and Sutter
Rice D. W. C. 1122 Pine
Rice J. W. 250 Fourth

Ringgold F. M. 12 Hawthorne
Rogers H. D. 719 Clay
Rogers J. P. 294 Montgomery
Rosenberg M. 507 Pine
Rottanzi A. cor Folsom and Third
Rowell C. 515 Kearny
Rowell I. 520 Kearny
Royer A. C. 9 Geary
Ruaud A. 804 Jackson
Samuel H. 906 Stockton
Sanders D. 1102 Dupont
Sawyer A. F. 13 Post
Schariach C. M. 521 Pacific
Sharkey J. M. cor Dupont and Wash
Shorb J. C. 210 Bush
Smilie E. R. 640 Washington
Smith B. J. 502 Montgomery
Smith E. D. 4 Fourth
Snow William, 10 Sutter
Soltmann F. 542 California
Soule A. G. 514 Kearny
Sproul J. 108 Dupont
Staub E. 519 Pacific
Stillman J. D. B. 15 Post
Stivers C. A. 514 Kearny
Stout A. B. 832 Washington
Stuttmeister R. 1128 Dupont
Stutzbach F. 679 Mission
Suckert J. 402 Kearny
Styles H. C. cor Taylor and Green
Sweet J. D. 761 Howard
Taylor G. 324 Bush
Tewksbury M. R. (eclectic) 637 Market
Tibbitts S. M. cor Stock and Jackson
Toland H. H. Merchant cor Mont
Tozer C. H. 904 Kearny
Trask E. cor Montgomery and Market
Trask J. B. 206 Kearny
Trenkle E. 611 Washington
Trenor E. 202 Bush
Trouette H. 528 Clay
Twitchell W. S. Sixteenth nr Mission
Van Zandt J. W. 629 Front
Vandenberg J. P. P. cor Leavenworth and Sutter
Vigoreaux A. W. 109 Third
Vincent D. B. 515 Kearny
Warfeld J. P. 402 Montgomery
Warren O. F. 336 Market
Weaver J. 6 Montgomery
Weeks F. F. 47 Second
Wernicki J. A. 42 Geary
White E. 639 Market
White H. C. cor Jackson and Kearny
Whitney J. D. 4 Brenham Place
Whitney J. P. 4 Brenham Place
Wilhelm A. 6 Brenham Place
Willey J. M. 113 Dora
Williams W. cor Mont and Bush
Woodward G. F. 112 Sutter
Wooster D. 314 Kearny
Younger W. J. 315 Montgomery
Zeile F. 517 Pacific

Physicians. *Botanic.*

Vincent D. B. 515 Kearny

Physicians. *Electro-Magnetic.*

Benton H. A. 109 Montgomery
Josselyn J. H. 645 Washington

Physicians. *Female.*

Avery A. L. Mrs. (homeopathic) 158 Second
Beman M. E. (clairvoyant) Washington nr Taylor
Button S. Miss (clairvoyant) 3 St. Mark Place
Giraud A. Madame, 732 Vallejo
Hayden L. M. (widow) 87 Jessie
Howard R. A. Mrs. 220 Stockton
Stone E. Mrs. 757 Mission
Stowe C. M. Mrs. Mead House
Swett A. M. Mrs. 820 Mission
Thompson S. M. (widow, homeopathic) 648 Howard
Thurston Martha N. Mrs. cor Folsom and Twenty-Second
Warren L. W. Mrs. cor Mason and Pac

Physicians. *Water Cure.*

Bourne G. M. 10 Post
Smith B. J. 502 Montgomery

Piano Fortes.

BADGER & LINDENBERGER, 415 Battery (see advertisement, p. xliii)

Bowers J. T. 131 Montgomery
GRAY MATTHIAS, 613 Clay (see advertisement, p. xlii)
Maury P. jr. 710 Sansom
Kohler A. 424 Sansom
Pierce W. S. & Co. 26 Montgomery
Ripley & Kimball, 417 Montgomery
Rosa S. 615 Montgomery
WOODWORTH, SCHELL & CO. Post, Masonic Temple (see adv. p. cx)
[See Musical Instruments.]

Piano Forte Makers.

Curtaz Benjamin, 123 Kearny
WOODWORTH, SCHELL & CO. Masonic Temple
Stangenberger A. 755 Mission
Zech F. 212 Post
ZECH JACOB, 416 Market (see advertisement, p. 649)

Pickles.

Cutting & Co. 202 Front
Erzgraber & Goetjen, 120 Davis
Mitchell C. 114 Sacramento
Oakley & Jackson, 320 Front
Provost D. R. & Co. 413 Front
Schmidt & Fretz (manuf) 104 Com
[See Groceries; Vinegar, Etc.]

Pick Makers.

Wright John, 511 Market
[See Blacksmiths, Etc.]

Picture Frames.

Currier & Winter, 620 Market
Hausmann D. & Co. 535 Clay
Hirschfelder A. & Co. 427 Montgomery
JONES, WOOLL & SUTHERLAND, 312 Mont (see adv. p. xxxvi)
McQUILLAN B. 211 Leidesdorff (see advertisement, p. 652)
NILE & KOLLMYER, 312 Bush (see advertisement, p xlvii)
Roos Joseph, 219 Montgomery
Shaddock Thomas, 650 Market
SNOW & CO. cor Mont and Sansom (see advertisement, p. lxviii)
Swain R. A. & Co. cor Sansom and Pine
[See Carvers and Gilders.]

Pile Drivers.

Galloway & Boobar, cor Howard and Stewart
Hildebrandt F. 2 California

Pilots.

[See Appendix, p. 592.]

Pistol Galleries.

[See Gunsmiths.]

Plaster Cast Figures and Plaster Paris Workers.

Basham F. & Son, 28 Geary
Kellett S. 761 Market
Kellett W. F. 627½ Market
Lucchesi G. & Co Summer nr Mont
Mancarini D. 421 Pine
Mancarini D. & Co. 743 Clay
Paterson John, 316 Dupont

Plasterers.

Davis James, 338 Montgomery
Fisher H. E. 338 Montgomery
Henderson A. W. 861 Mission
Irwin S. M. & Co. 792 Market
Kellett S. 761 Market
Kellett W. F. 627½ Market
Mulrein D. 406 Montgomery
Poser H. Von, 614 Market

Plumbers.

Clark T. 641 Market
Collins E. S. 825 Montgomery
DAY T. 732 Montgomery (see advertisement, front cover)
Ecclas J. 667 Mission
Graves & Smith, 520 Davis
Johnston & Reay, 319 California
Jorgensen J. E. 28 Third
Lane & Gordon, 11 Post
McKewen P. & Son, 618 Clay
McNALLY & HAWKINS, 104 Montgomery and 38 Sutter (see advertisement, p. 650)
McNeil & Burton, 617 Kearny

Moore H. J. 406 Montgomery
O'Brien John H. & Co. 706 Mont
O'Brien P. K. 641 Market
O'Malley T. 646 Market
PRIOR J. K. 730 Montgomery (see advertisement, p. lx)
Reynolds T. 506 Front
Richardson J. 616 Market
Shepard & Sons, 631 Market
Smith A. J. 33 Webb
SNOOK G. & W. 806 Montgomery (see advertisement, p. 663)
[See Gas Fitters.]

Potteries.

Chabot J. (cement pipe) Francisco nr Taylor
Barman J. San Bruno Road 4 miles from City Hall
Herzer H. (crucibles) 9 St. Mark Place
Wackenreuder V. San Bruno Road 3½ miles from Plaza

Powder Agency.

GIBBONS, RODMOND & CO. 214 California
Eureka Blasting Powder Co. 327 Com
Lohse, J. F. California Powder Works, 318 California
[See Gunpowder.]

Preserved Meats.

Andereau J. 9 Metropolitan Market
Aurado & Bunker, 507 Merchant
Bailly F. 40 Washington Market
Bazille J. & Co. (tripe) 4 Clay Street Market
Bunker & Auradon, 9 Clay St. Market
Camerden M. 39 Occidental Market
Charrau M. Mrs. 6 New Market
Cholet J. 69 Washington Market
Cutting & Co. 202 Front
Dick William, 65 Washington Market
Dietrich W. M. 54 Washington Market
Estabrook John, 145 Second
Hartley William, 2 Merchant
Harvey & Co. 234 Third
McGARVEY & CO. 433 Stevenson (see advertisement, p. 650)
McKenna J. P. & Co. Garden nr Harrison
Provost D. R. & Co. 413 Front
Reinle F. 32 Metropolitan Market
Rogers L. 57 Metropolitan Market
Rossbach H. 40 Occidental Market
Secchi A. 9 New Market
Slocomb R. W. & Co. 151 Third
Smith & Co. 539 Broadway
Strobel & Fleig, 1129 Folsom
Willoughby O. H. 151 Third
Wilson & Stevens, 506 Market

Presses. Hydraulic.

DUDGEON E. cor Minna and Eighth (see advertisement, p. 645)

Printers. Book and Job.

Agnew & Deffebach, 511 Sansom
Albin L. 533 Commercial
BOSQUI EDW. & CO. 517 Clay (see advertisement, p. xciii)
Bruce D. 534 Commercial
Calhoun C. A. & Son, 320 and 322 Clay
Carr M. D. & Co. 410 Clay
Clark F. 520 Merchant
Dewey, Waters & Co. 505 Clay
Dunn & Campbell, 538 Market
Eastman Frank, Franklin, 415 Wash
Eluesser L. 517 Clay and 514 Com
Francis, Valentine & Co. 517 Clay and 514 Commercial
Jacoby P. 509 Clay
Lafontaine A. J. 627 Merchant
Moore R. C. Alta California Office
Painter & Co. 510 Clay
Robbins C. F. 416 Battery
Spear T. G. NE cor Clay and Mont
Stevens G. W. & Co. 511 Sacramento
Thompson & Co. SW cor Clay and San
TOWNE & BACON, Excelsior, 536 Clay (see advertisement, p. 8)
Turnbull & Smith, 612 Commercial
Wade S. H. cor Wash and Kearny
Walther F. G. 621 Sansom

Printers. Power Press.

Eastman Frank, 415 Washington
Francis, Valentine & Co. 514 Com

Overend J. A. T. 511½ Clay
Painter & Co. 510 Clay
TOWNE & BACON, 536 Clay

Printers' Materials.

Faulkner William & Son, 411 Clay
Harrison W. P. & Co. 421 Clay
Painter & Co. 510 Clay
Robbins C. F. 416 Battery

Printers' Rollers.

Newell William W. 530 Merchant

Produce. Butter, Cheese, Eggs, Etc.

Amos F. R. & C. cor Com and Front
Atchinson B. M. & Co. 7 Occidental Market
Beardsley & Wolfe. 29 Occidental Mkt
Boswell & Shattuck, 319 Front
Browning & Kohlmoos, 505 Wash
Cocks W. H. 104 Mission
Cohn I. H. & Son, 607 Sansom
Connolly T. 4 New Market
Deloche & Corthay, 9 New Market
Donnelly J. 119 Occidental Market
Donnelly & Bro. 20 Occidental Market
Field & Cummings, 16 Occidental Mkt
Forsaith & Tyler, 30 Commercial
French & Hall, 8 Washington Market
Gaughran P. 44 Washington Market
Gough J. T. 20 Washington Market
Hanley M. F. 64 Washington Market
Hanson T. C. & Co. 832 Market
Hatch T. H. & Co. 319 Washington
Harms & Joost, 410 Clay
Hart & Goodman, 66 Washington Mkt
Kane C. H. 8 Occidental Market
Kelly R. G. 24 Occidental Market
Kingon R. 123 Occidental Market
Leahy D. 17 Metropolitan Market
Lemoine, Gambert & Co. 2 New Mkt
Lewis M. A. 30 Occidental Market
Martens & Bredhoff, 58 Wash Market
McIlwain J. & Co. 21 Metropolitan Mkt
Menomy G. W. & Co. 3 Wash Market
Mitchell & Plege, 50 Washington Mkt
Morlock F. 23 Metropolitan Market
Nauman A. Mrs. 507 Sansom
Nichols & Horton, 142 Fourth
Northup & Shaw, 76 Washington Mkt
Rice & George, 20 Metropolitan Market
Ring & Lunt, 2 Washington Market
Spotorno & Aurado, 507 Merchant
Stewart R. & Co. 54 Metropolitan Mkt
Strasser A. 503 Merchant
Strasser L. & Son, 6 Clay St. Market
Taubmann C. 16 Metropolitan Market
Thomas W. R. 24 Occidental Market
Whitland & Karstens, 46 Wash Market
[See Merchants. Commission Produce.]

Produce. Game.

Arnold & Heywood, 11 Metropolitan Market
Card R. & Co. 62 Washington Market
Connolly T. 4 New Market
Cook J. H. 48 Washington Market
Cunningham J. 14 Metropolitan Mkt
Hart & Goodman, 66 Wash Market
Louderback A. 5 Washington Market
Miller R. 7 Metropolitan Market
Russell & Bouton, 38 Occidental Mkt
Schmitt J. J. 44 Occidental Market
Spotorno & Aurado, 507 Merchant
Strasser A. 503 Merchant
Strasser L. & Son, 8 Clay St. Market
Thompson A. 12 New Market
Wood J. P. 37 Occidental Market

Produce. Vegetables.

Baker L. F. cor Wash and Davis
Behre & Co. 515 Merchant
Bennett R. H. 3 Clay
Bergerot J. A. & Co. 10 Clay St. Mkt
Booth & Co. 38 Clay
Brown & Avery, 42 Washington Mkt
Campbell & Fairbanks cor Front and Washington
Carroll M. 203 Washington
Chamberlin & Baich, 210 Clay
Conger & Gray, 212 Washington
Donner P. 1306 Dupont
Dorman & Wolf, 101 Clay
Ducatel A. Mrs. 10 Washington Mkt
Dutard B. 217 Clay
Ewell L. J. cor Washington and San
Freem J. 2 Occidental Market
Gallagher & Gaven, 26 Occidental Mkt

Griffith & Ellis, 225 Washington
Hall & Brigham, 74 Washington Mkt
Ham C. W. & Co. 1 Washington Mkt
Harris & Bernhard, 25 Metropolitan Market
Hassell & Huber, 47 Washington Mkt
Hohenschild G. 22 Washington Mkt
Howes John, 502 Sansom
Laws & Co. 8 Metropolitan Market
Litchfield B. Harrison nr Fifth
Littlefield, Webb & Co. 202 Wash
Lysett & Co. 27 Metropolitan Market
Maginnis E. & Co. 503 Sansom
Messinger S. 34 Metropolitan Market
Meyer L. 61 Washington Market
Moore Z. W. & Co. 9 Washington Mkt
Morris E. (widow) 10 Metropolitan Mkt
Morris M. P. 10 Occidental Market
Mortimer and Maginnis, 503 Sansom
Nauman A. Mrs. 507 Sansom
Nichols & Co. 31 Metropolitan Mkt
Nolan T. cor Anna and Ellis
Podd J. 601 Post
Rattie G. cor Sansom and Merchant
Reillay P. 775 Folsom
Ricaud & Raflour, 38 Metropolitan Mkt
Simonds J. M. 299 Dupont
Smith F. 203 Washington
Taylor J. B. 408 Davis
Taylor & Co. (horse radish) 53 Occidental Market
[See Merchants — Commission; Produce.]

Provisions.

Athearn & Morrison, 8 Clay
Boswell & Shattuck, 319 Front
Bowen Bros. 427 Battery
Bradshaw & Co. 300 Sansom
Breed & Chase, cor Clay and Battery
Castle Brothers, 215 Front
Coghill J. H. & Co. cor Front and Com
Dickinson & Gammans, cor Front and Clay
Dodge Bros. & Co. 408 Front
Dodge & Phillips, 325 Front
Dolbeguy B. 507 Front
Eggers & Co. 210 California
Goldstein & Seller, 217 Front
Hendley A. C. & Co. 204 Front
Jones & Co. 205 Front
Kruse & Euler, 211 Front
Larco N. 432 Jackson
Levi B. & Co. 222 California
Sabatie A. E. & Co. 617 and 619 Sansom
Sbarboro B. & Bro. 531 Washington
SNEATH R. G. 408 Front (see advertisement, p. iv)
Wellmann, Peck & Co. 404 Front
Wensinger F. S. 511 Front
White F. J. & Co. 412 Front
Wilson & Stevens, 506 Market
[See Flour; Groceries, Etc.]

Provisions. Repackers.

Dick W. & Co. 65 Washington Market
Dietrich W. K. 54 Washington Market
Gallagher E. A. T. 17 Beale
Harvey & Co. (pork) 236 Third
McGARVEY W. & CO. Stevenson nr Fifth (see advertisement, p. 650)
McKenna & Co. 505 Mission
Nichols & Alden, 142 Fourth
Simpson & Pratt (matches) 105 Com
Wilson & Stevens (pork) 506 Market
[See Packers; Inspectors.]

Publishers.

Appleton D. E. 508 Montgomery
Bancroft H. H. & Co. 609 Montgomery
COOKE W. B. & CO. (law blanks) 624 Mont (see adv. front cover)
GENSOUL A. 511 Montgomery (see advertisement, p. xxix)
Kenny G. L. & Co. 608 Montgomery
LANGLEY HENRY G. State Register, City Directory, State Almanac, etc. 612 Clay
Payot H. 640 Washington
ROMAN A. & CO. 419 Montgomery (see advertisement, pp. 55–632)
Stilwell & Co. 511 Sansom
[See Booksellers.]

Pulu.

SCHAEFER J. F. & H. H. 506 Sansom
SCHRIEBER J. & C. 406 Sansom
[See Beds; Furniture; Mattresses, Etc.]

Pumps. Force.

HARRISON C. H. 517 Front (see advertisement, p. 651)
Hunt E. O. 28 Second

Pumps. Manufacturers.

Currier C. H. 29 Market
Hanson J. C. 6 California
HARRISON C. H. 517 Front (see advertisement, p. 651)
Mitchell T. F. 22 Drumm
[See Blockmakers, Etc.]

Pyrotechnists.

CHURCH & CLARK, 407 Front (see advertisement, p. xli)
TRIPP & ROBINSON, Howard near Twenty-Fourth (see adv. p. lix)

Quartz Amalgamators.

GODDARD & CO. Pacific Foundry, 127 First (see adv. p. x)
HOWLAND, ANGELL & KING, Miners', 241 First (see adv. p. 642)
PALMER, KNOX & CO. Golden State, 19 First, (see adv. p. 639)
SALMON J. & W. C. cor Mission and Frement (see adv. p. lxi)
Varney Thomas, 127 First
[See Foundries.]

Quartz Screens.

Quick J. W. 137 First

Quicksilver. Agents.

Butterworth S. F. (New Almaden) 205 Battery

Race Courses.

BAY VIEW PARK, W. F. Williamson, Hunter's Point, 5½ miles from City Hall. San Bruno Road
Ocean, J. M. Daniels, 6½ miles SW City Hall

Railroad Companies.

Central R. R. Co. office 116 Taylor nr Turk
City R. R. Co. office 326 Clay
Front Street, Mission & Ocean R. R. Co. 523 Clay
Market St. & Mission R. R. Co. office 734 Montgomery
North Beach & Mission, cor Fourth and Louisa
Omnibus R. R. Co., 8 s Howard bet Third and Fourth
Sacramento Valley R. R. 734 Mont
S. F. & Alameda, cor Jackson and San
S. F. & Atlantic R. R. Co. office 405 Front
S. F. & Oakland, office 535 Clay
S. F. & San José R. R. Co. office cor Sansom and Halleck
S. F. Market, Valencia nr Sixteenth
Western Pacific R. R. Co. office 409 Cal

Razor Strop Makers.

Hillman & Severence, 151 Shipley

Real Estate.

Ashbury M. 202 Montgomery
Atkinson J. H. 621 Clay
Babcock W. F. 412 Montgomery
Barkeloo John, 705 Montgomery
Belden Josiah, 202 Montgomery
Bergin Thomas, cor Powell and Green
Billings F. 43 Montgomery Block
Blumenberg J. H. 315 Pine
Bolton James R. 618 Merchant
Boyd & Davis, 321 Front
Braly M. A. 405 Front
Brannan S. 420 Montgomery
Brown H. S. cor Bat and Commercial
Bull A. 405 Front
Center John, cor Sixteenth and Folsom
Cheesman M. 402 Montgomery
Cogswell H. D. 610 Front
Cunningham F. 673 Market
Cunningham T. B. 55 Mont Block
Dana Bros. & Co. 326 Clay
Davis Erwin, 44 Montgomery Block
Dewey S. P. & Sons, 410 Montgomery
Dumartheray F. 34 Mont Block
Elliott F. A. 522 Clay
Emeric Joseph, 606 Montgomery

Fish J. H. 606 Montgomery
Franklin E. 7 Montgomery Block
Fry J. D. 803 Washington
Gates H. S. 526 Merchant
Gaven D. 520 Montgomery
Green W. A. 918 Market
Greene William, Mission nr Twelfth
Grissim W. T. 219 Bush
Grogan A. B. cor San and Jackson
Haggin J. B. 536 Clay
Halleck, Peachy & Billings, 43 Montgomery Block
Hastings S. C. 536 Clay
Hawes Horace, cor Folsom and Ninth
Hayes Thomas & Michael, Hayes' Park
Head A. E. 32 Montgomery Block
Hearst G. 712 Montgomery
Highton E. R. 540 Clay
Hinckley Barney, 205 Battery
Horber J. 315 Montgomery
Howard G. H. 523 Montgomery
Jobson D. 1010 Montgomery
Johnson J. 625 Clay
Keesing B. 1012 Bush
Klumpke J. G. 522 Clay
Lander P. C. 17 Exchange Building
Le Roy Theodore, 716 Montgomery
Lent William M. 712 Montgomery
Leonard E. 505 Montgomery
Leonard W. 402 Front
Lincoln Jerome, 205 Battery
Mahoney D. cor Pacific and Larkin
Manrow J. P. 606 Merchant
Manson John S. 206 Front
Mathews H. 338 Montgomery
Maynard Lafayette, 205 Battery
Mayne Charles, 535 Clay
McCarthy D. C. 610 Merchant
McCreery Andrew B, 602 Commercial
McKee W. R. cor Mont and Clay
Meeks W. N. 804 Montgomery
Merritt Samuel, 405 Front
Morison S. A. 302 Montgomery
Morrow R. F. 32 Montgomery Block
Moss J. Mora, 418 California
Murphy D. 338 Montgomery
Naglee Henry M. 605 Merchant
Nichols Asa C. 422 Battery
O'Donnell H. cor Vallejo and Dupont
Page N. 206 Front
Paige C. 205 Battery
Partridge P. G. 801 Montgomery
Payne W. R. 618 Merchant
Pearsons H. 23 Montgomery Block
Phelan James, 616 Front
Randolph B. 315 Montgomery
Ray J. H. 15 Montgomery Block
Reese Michael, 410 Montgomery
Sargent Bailey, American Exchange
Shiel William, 319 Bush
Stevenot G. K. 606 Montgomery
Stevenson A. J. cor Mont and Cal
Sullivan Eugene L. 52 Exchange Bdg
Teschemacher H. F. 523 Montgomery
Tevis Lloyd, 636 Clay
Thompson Joseph P. 523 Montgomery
Throckmorton S. R. 716 Mission
Watson W. C. cor Mont and Jackson
Williams H. F. 626 Clay
Whipple S. B. 630 Commercial
Whitmore H. M. 540 Clay
Wohler H. 415 Montgomery
[See Brokers; Merchants — Commission.]

Records. Searchers of.

Adams H. Q. 420 Montgomery
Beatty S. G. 604 Merchant
Brooks & Rouleau, 620 Washington
Clement E. B. 710 Washington
Clement J. 710 Washington
Garvey J. P. 618 Merchant
GILLESPIE|C. V. 655 Washington (see advertisement, p. 664)
Hart C. B. 21 Exchange Building
Smith R. P. 604 Merchant
[See Notaries; Attorneys, Etc.]

Regalia.

JOHNSON T. RODGERS, 323 Montgomery (see advertisement, inside back cover)
NORCROSS D. 5 Montgomery (see advertisement, p. lxxix)
[See Military Goods.]

Repackers. Merchandise.

Anthony E. T. & Co. cor Sacramento and Battery
[See Provisions—Repackers.]

Reporters—Phonographic.

Marsh A. J. City Hall
O'Doherty G. City Hall
[See Accountants; Copyists, Etc.]

Restaurants.

Alphonsa G. 532 Pacific
Anderson & Husban, cor Jackson and Drumm
Benkelmann A. Brannan St. Bridge
Bertucci L. & Co. 512 Clay
Bocken C. 643 Washington
Bonzi P. 515 Merchant
Boyd O. D. 428 Sansom
Boyle M. cor Sansom and Merchant
Brady J. 625½ Mission
Branch & Colver, 923 Kearny
Branger J. 821 Kearny
Brickwedel C. H. & Co. 253 Stewart
Brown John, 638 Pacific
Buia & Gliubetich, 605 Davis
Cabannes E. cor San and Merchant
Carson W. S. 116 Jackson
Chardine A. cor Clay and Dupont
Chielovich A. cor Cal and Drumm
Collier G. W. 923 Kearny
Deschaseaux F. 507 Washington
Dingeon L. (Barnum's) 621 Com
Donahue Phil, 417 Front
Dryer C. (Fashion) 820 Clay
Engelberg & Wagner, 416 Kearny
Enright & Dwyer, 706 Market
Etienne & Co. 825 Dupont
Etienne T. 715 Montgomery
Field H. E. 619 Market
Finance Alexander & Co. 825 Dupont
Fogarty & O'Rourke, 204 Fourth
Forret & Mortier, 620 Pacific
Fowler T. S. cor Third and King
Franklin A. 514 Washington
Gatinelle L. 1222 Stockton
Goetz Joseph, 631 Davis
Good C. & Co. 738 Washington
Hall, Hunt & Malone (New York) 628 Kearny
Harris S. M. 30 Clay
Hirth J. & Co. 531 Commercial
Hoesch Henry, 614 Clay
Hohenschild & Melstedt, 720 Market
Job Peter, cor Montgomery and Bush
Jury J. & Bro. 524 Merchant
Keenan J. Oriental Hotel
Lake H. 813 Montgomery
Lastreto L. 513 Commercial
Lermitte F. 526 Clay
Mandege P. cor Mission and Stewart
Marchand & Laurent, 607 Kearny
Marion S. 335 East
Marshall J. 304 Front
Messersmith G. 826 Market
Mandolet & Etienne, 837 Dupont
Morgan B. cor Fourth and Clementina
Namur P. cor Dupont and Commercial
Nelson A. N. & Co. 1025 Dupont
Ossalino & Co. 528 Market
Pickett E. H. 619 Market
Pipes J. G. 603 Market
Poets J. C. 407 California
Porter Horace (Clayton's) 605 Com
Powell & Tripp, 143 Third
Quinn A. Dolores nr Sixteenth
Radovich A. cor Mission and Stewart
Rety F. 907 Dupont
Richards Ezra, 548 Clay
Roge Louis, 339 Third
Russell & Co. 507 Clay
Saulmann & Lauenstein, 506 Mont
Schneider M. & Co. 12 Sacramento
Schroth Charles, 230 Kearny
Schuman F. Market nr Stewart
Seguy B. 723 Davis
Sierens C. 647 Commercial
Simeon P. (colored) 223 Kearny
Smith A. V. 519 East
Smith E. Mrs. Main nr Harrison
Sorbier J. E. & Co. 536 Washington
Stege H. Sixth nr Harrison
Stevens & Oliver, 28 Montgomery
Stock J. & Co. 508 Washington
Stoerk J. 530 Merchant
Uzavich J. 621 Davis
Valadie F. 721 Pacific
Vanston T. 42 Market
Varndell W. P. 2197 Powell
Villavicencio L. 1033 Kearny
Vincenot & Gautier, 523 Merchant
Von Ronn & Co. 905 Kearny
Weiss & Zwiesdele, 712 Kearny
Weiss Jacob, 308 Montgomery
Wiedach P. 621 Davis
Winn M. 603 Market

YOUNG A. 612 Montgomery (see advertisement, p. lxxiv)
[See Boarding.]

Rice Dealers.

FLINT, PEABODY & CO. 716 Front
Greenwood W. M. India Mill, 35 Beale
MACONDRAY & CO. 204 Sansom
[See Groceries; Provisions.]

Riding Academies.

Herman & Lohse, Ellis nr Stockton
Poultney & Smith, 346 Brannan
[See Stables.]

Riggers and Stevedores.

Hazeltine Chas. E. & Co. 36 Stewart
Morton E. H. 621 Front
[See Contractors.]

Roofing.

Fiske H. G. & E. S. (metal) 820 Kearny
FITZ-GIBBON M. E. (asphaltum) 204 Bush (see adv. p. lix)
Kehoe John (metal) 228 Bush
Kone D. C. 126 Sutter
Myers John & Co. (New England) cor Montgomery and Jackson
Perine N. P. & Co. (Boston) 135 Mont
Skinner & Duncan, Sixteenth nr Guerrero
Smith S. F. (asphaltum) 500 Market

Rope Manufacturers.

TUBBS & CO. 613 Front (see advertisement, p. xii)

Sack Dealers.

Doherty A. & H. 215 Davis
Duchange M. cor Com and Drumm
Guyamard G. L. 112 Sacramento
Kane J. Commercial nr Drumm
McDevitt Edw. 216 Davis
Miller & Bro. 655 Mission
Richard J. 112 Sacramento
[See Junk.]

Safes. Iron.

RUSSELL & ERWIN MANUFACTURING CO, 106 Battery (see advertisement, p. lxvi)
TILLMAN F. 318 Battery (see advertisement, p. 672)
Weichart J. 17 Fremont
[See Hardware.]

Sail Makers.

Beckman, Aiken & Co. 516 Davis
Blakiston J. S. cor Clay and East
Brandt G. B. 27 Sacramento
Branson & Bell, Broadway nr Front
Byrne Chas. & Co. 7 Clay
CRAWFORD A. & CO. 27 Market (see adv. p. 655)
Fisher M. East nr Jackson
Funk C. C. East nr Jackson
Harding John, 215 Front
Morgan J. A. 221 Davis

Salt Stores.

Barton B. F. & Co. Pioneer, 213 Sac
Barton & Bro. Pacific, 218 Sacramento
Blumberg J. F. Washington, 308 Com
Oakley & Jackson, 320 Front
Tyler S. H. (manufac'r) 110 Fremont
Williamson & McMillan, 217 Davis
Winegar A. B. 310 Front

Sash Makers.

[See Doors.]

Sawing and Planing.

Brokaw James, cor Mission and Fremont
CULVERWELL S. S. 20 and 29 Fremont (see adv. p. xlvi)
MACDONALD BROS. Chace's, cor Market and Beale (see adv. p. 666)
Metcalf S. A. cor Mission and Fremont

Saw Manufacturers.

Berney W. 318 Jackson
Gabbs W. H. 116 Kearny
Hendy J. (agent) 402 Montgomery
Linforth A. 318 Jackson
Munson & Wheelock, 28 Kearny

Roberts A. 116 Kearny
Rollins J. B. 834 Kearny
Sheffield & Patterson, cor Jackson and Battery
SPAULDING N. W. 113 Pine (see advertisement, p. cxi)

Scavengers.

Brown J. 115 Kearny
Brown W. H. Rassette Place nr Sutter
Feaster & Co. 213 Pine
Johnson S. 33 Geary
Mitchell W. 140 Sutter
Richards I. 421 Kearny
[See Contractors.]

Scales.

Fairbanks & Hutchinson, 334 Mont
[See Hardware.]

School Furniture.

Derby J. L. Mission nr Third
Easton & Bro. 725 Market
Holt W. 305 Montgomery
[See Furniture; Cabinet Makers.]

Schools.

BATES G. University, Post bet Stockton and Powell (see adv. p. xiv)
Beverly J. Miss, Hayes' Valley
Blanchard S. J. Miss, 928 Bush
Bouton W. Miss, cor Green and Dupont
Brier C. Institute cor Geary and Mason
Bryant A. M. Miss, 272 Clementina
Buttner F. 918 Pacific
Clarke C. R. Rev. Female Seminary, cor Mason and O'Farrell
Cleveland E. A. Miss, First Avenue nr Sixteenth
Cohn E. Rev. Academic Seminary, 135 Post
Eaton S. T. Miss, Folsom nr Sixth
Fisher B. V. Q. 135 Post
Foster M. Miss, 124 Perry
Gilmore J. B. Mrs. 336 Fifth
Glasby J. K. Mrs. 355 Third
Goodwin H. Rev. Grace Female Institute, cor Stockton and California
Harris M. R. Miss, 410 Stockton
Herrera M. Mrs. 438 Second
Higgins M. Miss, 8 Anthony
Hildebrand G. W. 753 Mission
Hogan E. A. (widow) 219 Sixth
Hooper A. J. 3 Monroe
Kennedy J. Miss, 563 Bryant
Lammond M. Miss, Collegiate Institute, 64 Silver
Miel Charles, 54 South Park
Moore N. W. 725 Bush
Nichols B. C. Miss, cor Powell and Washington
Rose H. 666½ Mission
Rowe H. M. Mrs. 616 Post
S. F. Seminary, Miss M. Butler, cor Jackson and Mason
Sands A. M. 903 Post
Simpson M. Mrs. 266 Minna
Smith C. M. Mrs. Mission nr Eighth
St. John B. G. Mrs. 467 Minna
State Normal, Post nr Dupont
Swain S. C. (widow) Eureka Institute, Dolores nr Sixteenth
Taber H. Mrs. 43 Everett
Touaillon J. 911 Pacific
Walton & Wills, cor Jackson and Mason
Williams W. J. G. 871 Mission
Wilson S. C. Miss, Thirteenth nr Mission
[See Colleges; Teachers.]

Sculptors.

Bacon L. S. SW cor Pine and Morse
Basham F. & Son, 28 Geary
Mezzara P. (cameo) 436 Jackson
PALTENGHI & LARSENEUR, 422 Jackson (see advertisement, p. 660)
Paterson John, 316 Dupont
[See Marble; Plaster, Etc.]

Sewing Machines.

Florence, S. Hill agent, 111 Mont
Folsom, E. E. Shear agent, 8 Mont
Grover & Baker, J. W. J. Pierson agent, 329 Montgomery
Hicks J. L. 47 Second
Howe's, Deming & Co. agents, 3 Mont
Ladd, Webster & Co. J. L. Willcutt agent, 32 Montgomery

New England, P. C. Craig & Co. 305 Third
Singer's, Wm. Broderick agent, 139 Montgomery
Wheeler & Wilson, F. L. Tileston agent, cor Montgomery and Sac
Williams & Orvis', J. Greenwood ag't, cor Jackson and Battery

Shells, Etc.

Cohn M. A. 822 Market
[See Fancy Goods; Toys.]

Shingle Machines.

HOWLAND, ANGELL & KING, Miners' Foundry
· [See Machinists.]

Ship Bread.

[See Bakers.]

Ship Builders.

Cousins J. C. North Point Dock
Farnham J. N. Mission nr Stewart
Gilman J. (boats) Mission nr Spear
Glidden A. M. cor Mission and Main
Griffin & Cooper, (boats) Clark nr Davis
Goodsell D. C. M. corner Mission and Main
Herrick W. A. (boats) N s Clark near Davis
Hillert F. W. 131 Townsend
Irelan Wm. 164 Stewart
Murphy A. Drumm nr Pacific
North J. G. Potrero
Owen H. cor Michigan and Shasta
Parker S. (boats) Merchant nr East
Vice Thos. (boats) cor Chestnut and Montgomery
Watts L. C. 235 Beale
[See Boat Builders and Shipwrights.]

Ship Chandlers.

Bichard N. Pier 15 Stewart
Cathcart & Coffin, 415 East
CRAWFORD A. & CO. 29 Market (see advertisement, p. 655)
Edgerly & Wickman, 407 East
Efford N. C. 309 East
Farwell J. D. & Co. 307 Clay
Hare C. 34 Stewart
Haseltine H. & Co. 710 Front
Hubert C. & Co. 517 Davis
Josselyn Jas. M. 36 Market
Marks J. J. & Co. 6 Clay
Mitchell D. C. & Co. Bdwy nr Battery
Shed & Wright, 54 Stewart
Smith & Kittredge, 26 Clay
TUBBS & CO. 611 and 613 Front
[See Grocers.]

Ship Joiners.

Bigley Thos. 31 Market
Duncan J. Drumm nr Jackson
Galloway J. D. 10 Broadway
Parent C. L. 232 Fremont
Robinson W. Commercial nr East
Spofford & Spooner, Main St. Wharf
Wills J. 8 Drumm

Shipping and Forwarding Merchants.

Allen & Lewis, NW cor Front and Cal
Allen W. R. (Stockton) 517 Davis
Anderson J. & Co. cor Pac and Davis
Ballard & Hall, 224 Clay
Bichard N. 209 Stewart
Boas J. (Hamburg) S. S. Co.) 513 Sac
Bourn W. B. 222 Sacramento
Bowne W. F. 311 East
Brennan & Co. (Santa Cruz) 206 Clay
BROOKS C. W. & CO. (Honolulu) 511 Sansom (see adv. p. vii)
Bunker H. S. & Co. (Mexican) 424 Bat
Caduc P. Washington St. Wharf
CALIFORNIA STEAM NAVIGA- TION CO. NE cor Jackson and Front (see adv. pp. v and vi)
Card S. (Merchants' Transportation Co.) 326 Clay
COLEMAN W. T. & CO. (New York) 417 Battery (see adv. p. xi)
DeWar John (Victoria) 311 East
DeWitt, Kittle & Co. (New York) cor California and Front
Dibblee & Hyde, 106 Front
Dickson, DeWolf & Co. (Liverpool, Australia, etc.) 410 Battery

Emory F. A. (N. Y. & Phil. S. S. Line) 302 Montgomery
ELDRIDGE OLIVER (P. M. S. S. CO.) NW cor Sacramento and Leidesdorff (see adv. p. iv)
FLINT, PEABODY & CO. (Boston) 716 Front (see adv. p. xi)
Forbes Bros. & Co. Front nr Vallejo
Gibbs C. E. 404 Front
Goodrum George. 424 Battery
Greaves B. H. 424 Battery
Green F. P. (Sacramento) SE cor Front and Sacramento
HOLLADAY BEN. (Oregon S. S. Line) NW cor Front and Jackson (see advertisement, p. lxlV)
Hooper, G. F. 308 Front
Howes George & Co. 309 Clay
Hughes & Hunter (Australia) 504 Bat
Joice E. V. (Suisun Steamers) NE cor Battery and Washington
Kentfield J. 129 Stewart
King James C. & Co. cor Battery and Filbert
KOOPMANSCHAP & CO.(Hongkong) 1101 Battery (see adv. p. 636)
LOW C. ADOLPHE & CO. 426 Cali- fornia (see adv. p. 634)
Larco M. 430 Jackson
MacCann W. & Co. 402 Front
Macpherson & Wetherbee, (Noyo Riv- er) Pier 20 Stewart
MACONDRAY & CO. 204 Sansom (see advertisement, p. ix)
Mastick S. L. & Co. (Humboldt Bay) 10 Stewart
MEADER, LOLOR & CO. (Boston) 405 Front (see adv. p. ix)
Meigs & Gawley (Puget Sound) 1 Stew- art
MERRILL J. C. & CO. 206 California (see advertisement, p. lxxi)
Minturn Charles (Contra Costa and Petaluma Steamers) 9 Vallejo
Moore & Co. 17 Davis
Newton J. B. & Co. 108 and 110 Cal
Pennell J. T. (Mendocino) Pier 11 Stewart
Perkins W. L. 404 Front
Pickett & Co. (Victoria, etc.) 214 Sac
Pierce N. Capt. (Southern Line) 321 Front
Pope & Talbot, Pier 12 Stewart
Raimond R. E. 515 Front
Ramsdell & Peck, 110 Jackson
RAYMOND L W. (Central American Transit Co.) cor Battery and Pine
Reed H. B. 221 Washington
Richards & McCraken, 405 Front
Rodgers, Meyer & Co. 314 Washington
Rollinson J. R. & Co. 305 Front
Ross, Dempster & Co. 425 and 427 Bat
Roulstone A. J. 502 Montgomery
ROYAL MAIL STEAM PACKET CO. 428 California (see advertisement, p. xxiv)
Schleiden W. 324 Washington
Sherwood, Bulkley & Co. 326 Clay
Simpson A. M. (Coose Bay) 11 Stewart
Stevens, Baker & Co. 215 Front
Swain R. B. & Co. 206 Front
Taylor C. L. & Co. 38 California
Thomas J. B. 619 Front
Tichenor & Co. foot of Second
Weeks E. J. 405 Front.
West India and Pacific Steamship Co. office 314 Washington
Whitney & Co. 405 Front
Whitney J. R. & Co. 405 Front
Williams H. B. (agent) 305 Front
Williams Jonathan, 413 East
Willistun C. 424 Battery

Shipping Offices.

Allen W. R. 617 Davis
Anderson James & Co. cor Pacific and Davis
Baker James G. Vallejo nr Front
Nicholson J. S. Davis nr Vallejo
Nickels W. 23 Market
Willistun C. 305 Sacramento
[See Shipping and Forwarding.]

Shipsmiths.

Burns I. Market nr Stewart
Coleman D. R. 706 Front
Grant & Coon, 136 Stewart
Hendry W. M. foot Second
McTernan T. & H. corner Commercial and Drumm
Muir A. 1015 Battery

Phelps W. S. & Co. 34 Drumm
Taylor & Laughlin, Folsom nr Spear

Shipwrights.

Allen L. S. Folsom nr Stewart
Foster D. cor Howard and Stewart
Houseman J. S. Vallejo nr Front
MacPhun W. 40 Clay
Ringot J. S s Market nr Main
Watts L. C. & Co. 212 Beale
[See Ship Builders.]

Shirts and Collars.

Atkinson L. & Co. 509 Sacramento
Menderson W. & Co. 308 California
Morgenthau M. 418 Sacramento
Morison, Harris & CO. 329 Sansom
Noustadter Bros. NE cor Battery and Sacramento
Orr & Atkins, 415 Montgomery
PIPER E. Mrs. (manuf) 624 Market (see advertisement, p. 659)
Thomson P. 607 Sacramento
WARD S. W. H. & SON, 323 Mont- gomery (see adv. back cover)
[See Clothing; Furnishing Goods, Etc.]

Shoe Blacking.

COX & NICHOLS, 422 Battery (see advertisement, p. lxv)

Shoe Findings.

* Importers.

Bender C. 114 Sutter
COX & NICHOLS, 422 Battery (see advertisement, p. lxxv)*
*DUDLEY & GERHARDY, 422 Bat- tery (see adv. p. lv)
*HEIN J. G. NE cor Battery and Wash- ington (see adv. p. xxxv)
ING A. D. & CO. 312 Commercial (see advertisement, p. xxxv)
Lumsden W. 643 Merchant
*Schumacher A. 634 Clay
Thomas A. 738 Market
*Weck L. E. & Co. 415 Clay
Wood S. A. 212 California
Worth F. 338 Bush
[See Boots; Leather; Tanners.]

Shooting Galleries.

Frickens H. North Beach
Heintz Aug. Willows
Schmidt F. 643 Jackson
Winkle W. cor Jackson and Kearny

Shot Towers.

S. F. & PACIFIC, T. H. Selby & Co. 118 California

Show Cases. *Manufacturers.*

Miller J. M. Fell near Laguna, Hayes' Park
Teubner & Hoffman, 431 Kearny
[See Cabinet Makers.]

Silk Goods.

[See Dry and Fancy Goods.]

Silver Platers.

Bofinger J. 433 Kearny
Browning & McNamara, 806 Wash
Clark, W. H, T. 228 Kearny
Ekelund A. 733 Washington
Fenn F. C. M. 637 Howard
Lawler W. 530 Merchant
MARTELL JOHN, 619 Kearny (see ad- vertisement, p. 645)
Oakley O. B. 106 Leidesdorff
Reynaud F. 131 Kearny
Rocchiccoli R. F. 523 California
Rossi N. 236 Kearny

Silversmiths.

Reichel F. R. 622 Merchant
Vanderslice & Co. 810 Montgomery
[See Jewelers.]

Silver Ware.

BARRETT & SHERWOOD, 517 Mont
BRAVERMAN & LEVY, 621 Wash
Crosby F. W. & Co. 638 Clay
Falkenau Bros. 629 Washington
Gray R. B. & Co. 616 Merchant
Joseph Bros. 607 Montgomery
Mathewson & Bucklin, 519 Mont

SHERWOOD ROBERT, 517 Mont
SHREVE G. C. & CO. 525 Mont
Tucker & Co. 505 Montgomery
Vanderslice W. K. & Co. 810 Mont
WIEDERO OTTO & CO. 433 Mont
[See Jewelers; Watchmakers, Etc.]

Skirt Supporters.

Read M. S. (widow) 109 Montgomery

Snuff Makers.

[See Tobacconists, Etc.]

Soap Manufacturers.

Bergin J. J. cor Green and Powell
Brown & Cook, Eureka, 207 Sac
Burdick E. B. & Co. Potrero
Cogswell & Thomas, Standard, 207
  Commercial
DANA G. S. (Pacific Glue Manufactory) Lagoon
Dyer J. P. corner Nebraska and Sixteenth
Fay John, Chestnut nr Mason
Hellmann H. Brannan nr Sixth
Leiphart F. cor Third and Ritch
Lucy & Hymes, 181 Beale
PORTMANN J. H. C. Potrero (see adv. p. 656)
Rohrie C. C. Potrero
Smith & Irving, Potrero
Standard Soap Co. Com nr Front
Star Soap & Candle Works, Austin nr
  Larkin
Toner J. Brannan nr Fifth

Soap Stone.

Dougherty J. (mills) 311 Market
Patterson J. (worker) 420 Market

Soda Manufacturers.

Brader Henry, Excelsior, 738 Bdwy
Classen & Co. 115 Jessie
Fagan, Bliven & Skelly, Empire, cor
  Third and Harrison
McEwen J. California, 190 Stevenson
Thompson W. D. (mineral) 526 Union
Turner & Co. 529 Jackson
Verdier E. 311 Dupont
Wood J. H. (natural) 232 Bush

Spectacles.

Kahn & Strauss, 619 Washington
Lawrence & Houseworth, 317 Mont
Muller C. 3 Montgomery

Spice Manufacturers.

BERNARD C. 707 Sansom (see advertisement, p. xi)
Hudson H. C. & Co. corner Pine and
  Front
Marden & Folger, 220 Front
Tyler S. H. Eagle Mills, 110 Fremont
VENARD P. G. 627 Front (see advertisement, p. 665)
[See Coffee; Mustard, Etc.]

Stables. *Livery.*

Agnew John, Dashaway, 26 Kearny
Allen J. M. Market Street, 669 Market
Banks G. S. & Co. 577 Market
Barker & Bro. 739 Folsom
Berry Thomas, 16 Clementina
Blair & Scovern, 739 Market
Bridge Wm. E. Black Hawk, 317 Pine
Brown James (col'd) 318 Broadway
Carroll W. cor Washington and Mason
Coburn L. 1016 Stockton
Code J. 818 Mission
Collier F. 655 Sacramento
Crittenden C. S. Mission nr Fourth
Domett C. H. Union, 13 Stevenson
Dorr J. B. & Co. 408 Bush
Eggleton G. 121 Jackson
Herman & Garness, Ellis nr Stockton
Hopkins N. 679 Market
Kemp & Owen, 126 Fourth
Kenny John, Union, 726 Union
Killip & O'Connor, 704 Commercial
Kruse F. 628 Pacific
Lemon F. H. & Co. 115 Kearny
Leonard & Brophy, 527 Pacific
Lusk C. D. 535 Jackson
May & Byington, 328 Bush
McDevitt J. 712 Broadway
Moffat O. 325 Mission
Morshead, 233 Bush
O'Donnell B. 1808 Powell

O'Nell M. 12 Sutter
Parker & Jones, 532 California
Porter & Covey, 16 Sutter
Poultney & Smith. 344 Brannan
Scovern J. G. 739 Market
Stolze C. 211 Pine
Swain J. H. 413 Market
Taylor J. S. 257 Clementina
Tompkinson J. Pennsylvania, 60 Minna
Wade W. N. 710 Broadway
White W. M. 431 California
Willson J. F. 807 Montgomery
Wilson A. 739 Folsom
Wright & Roden, 405 Kearny

Stair Builders.

BROWN & WELLS, 535 Market (see
  advertisement, p. 654)
Dillon & Hanlon, cor Fifth and Natoma
FREEMAN B. H. & CO. cor Market
  and Beale (see adv. p. 666)
Frick A. cor Hyde and Green
LANGLAND N. P. 49 Beale (see advertisement, p. 665)
Payson C. N. 1216 Taylor
Plumer W. P. Vallejo nr Leavenworth
Smith & Co. 407 Mission
Wheaton B. F. 315 Mission

Stamps. *Hand.*

[See Stencil Cutters.]

Starch Dealers.

Hallock J. Y. & Co. corner Front and
  Jackson

Starch Manufacturers.

Everding J. & Co. Pioneer, 56 Clay

Stationers. *Wholesale.*

Bancroft H. H. & Co. 609 Montgomery
Carrie J. A. & Co. 404 Battery
COOKE WM. B. & CO. 624 Mont
Frank & Co. 404 Sacramento
Haas M. L. cor Front and Sacramento
Hodge J. G. & Co. 418 and 420 Clay
ISAAC J. 529 Sansom (see advertisement, p. xlviii)
Kenny George L. & Co. 608 Mont
Lecount J. P. corner Sacramento and
  Montgomery
Rubber Clothing Co. 118 Montgomery
Weil & Levy, cor Sac and Battery

Stationers. *Retail.*
* Importers.
*Allen & Spier, 542 Clay
Appleton D. E. 508 Montgomery
Arnold E. F. 538 Market
Aubrey C. F. 310 Third
Bailey & Hillis, 767 Market
*Bancroft H. H. & Co. 609 Mont
Barkhaus F. W. & D. 321 Kearny
Beach C. 24 Montgomery
BELL G. H. SW corner Merchant and
  Montgomery (see adv. p. lxix)
Betge R. J. 217 Montgomery
Blake & Myers, 702 Montgomery
Bowen & Hart, 620 Market
Boyd T. C. 300 Montgomery
Brooks W. H. 51 Third
*Carrie J. A. & Co. 404 Battery
Carter J. W. 215 California
Clark C. 149 Fourth
Carter J. W. 215 California
Coleman E. (manufacturer envelopes)
  775 Market
*COOKE W. B. & CO. (law blanks) 624
  Montgomery, Montgomery Block
  (see advertisement, front cover)
Damon J. E. & Co. 421 Sansom
*Faulkner Wm. & Son, 411 Clay
Fella P. 224 Kearny
Flood M. 428 Kearny
Freund & Co 511 Clay
Friedman S. 1108 Stockton
*GENSOUL A. 511 Montgomery (see
  advertisement, p. xxix)
*Haas M. L. SW cor Front and Sac
Hardy J. 138 Montgomery
Herrera F. 126 Second
*HITCHCOCK G. B. 413 Sansom (see
  advertisement, p. cxii)
*Hodge John G. & CO. 418 and 420 Clay
Hoin & Brother, cor Mont and Jackson
Holz L. 311 Battery
Hutchinson E. I. cor Geary and Kearny
*ISAAC JOS. & CO. 513 Sansom (see
  advertisement, p. xlviii)

*Kenny George L. & Co. 608 Mont
Lecount J. P. & Co. cor Mont and Sac
Loomis W. E. cor Sansom and Wash
Macatee A. M. Mrs. 352 Third
Magauran P. H. 252 Fourth
Martenet & Schley, 633 Market
Mendheim H. & Co. 631 Clay
Mitchell B. J. 414 Sacramento
Mosse & Son, 639 Kearny and 618 Wash
Obergh J. A. 158 Third
Payot H. 640 Washington
Pitts H. A. 408 Third
Ryan P. N. 54 Fourth
STRATMAN JOHN, cor Washington
  and Sansom
Tyler Brothers, 632 Washington
  [See Booksellers.]

Steam Gauges.

Marwedel & Otto, 329 Bush

**Steamship and Steamboat
Lines.**

Alameda Rail Road Line, A. A. Cohen
  superintendent, cor Jackson and
  Sansom
CALIFORNIA, OREGON & MEXICAN, Ben Holladay, cor Front and
  Jackson (see adv. p. lxiv)
CALIFORNIA STEAM NAVIGATION CO. Portland, O., and Victoria, cor Front and Jackson (see
  advertisement, p. vi)
CALIFORNIA STEAM NAVIGATION CO. Sacramento, Marysville,
  Stockton, etc. cor Front and Jackson (see adv. p. v)
CENTRAL AMERICAN TRANSIT
  CO. New York via Nicaragua, I. W.
  Raymond agent, cor Battery and
  Pine
CRESCENT CITY, EUREKA, AND
  TRINIDAD, Ben Holladay, corner
  Front and Jackson (see adv. p. lxiv)
Liverpool, New York and Philadelphia, F. A. Emory agent, 302 Mont
MEXICAN COAST, Cape St. Lucas,
  Mazatlan, Guaymas, and La Paz,
  Ben Holladay, cor Front and Jackson (see adv. p. lxiv)
Napa City, L. J. Weeks agent, 405
  Front
Oakland and San Antonio, A. A. Cohen
  superintendent, cor Sansom and
  Jackson
PACIFIC MAIL STEAMSHIP CO.
  New York via Panama, Oliver Eldridge agent, cor Sacramento and
  Leidesdorff (see adv. p. iv)
Petaluma, McNear & Bro. agents, 37
  Clay
SAN FRANCISCO AND CHINA, Pacific Mail S. S. Co. O. Eldridge
  agent, cor Sac and Leidesdorff
San Pablo and San Quentin, C. Minturn agent, Vallejo St. Wharf
SANTA BARBARA, SAN DIEGO,
  AND SAN LUIS OBISPO, California Steam Navigation Co. cor
  Front and Jackson (see adv. p. vi)
West India and Pacific, Rodgers, Meyer
  & Co. agents, 314 Washington

Stencil Cutters.

Argenti T. 402 Third
Burns H. J. What Cheer House
Castle D. H. 260 First
Hall John F. cor Front and Com
Hoffman G. 327 Commercial
Kellogg A. cor Mont and Jackson
Truworthy F. M. 321 Front
Wood G. M. 508 Montgomery
  [See Engravers, Etc.]

Stereoscopic Goods.

LAWRENCE & HOUSEWORTH, 317
  Mont (see adv. back cover)

Stereotypers.

Kellogg A. cor Mont and Jackson
  [See Electrotypers; Silver Platers.]

Stone Yards.

Brady M. 213 Mission
Caduc P. foot Sansom
Grant C. B. King nr Third
Grant John, Lone Mountain
Williams F. junction Pine and Market
  [See Granite; Marble.]

A. ROMAN & CO., 417 and 419 Montgomery Street, School, Law, and Medical Works.

Storage Warehouses.

Alsop & Co. Pine nr Sansom
Bay Warehouse, Sansom nr Lombard
Bonded Warehouse, cor Filbert and
    Battery
Bonded Warehouse, New Orleans, cor
    California and Davis
Bonded Warehouse, 22 Battery, C. E.
    Peters & Co. proprietors
Bonded Warehouse, corner Front and
    Vallejo, A. K. Durbrow
California Steam Nav. Co.'s Ware-
    house, Front nr Broadway
Carlton's Warehouse, Beale nr Mar-
    ket, Carlton & Harris
Central, 210 and 212 Sacramento, Dana
    & Dick
City Warehouse, Lombard Dock, How-
    ard & Pool
Clark's Point Warehouse, cor Broad-
    way and Battery, W. S. Clark
Cowell's Warehouse, cor Battery and
    Union, L. P. Sage
Dibblee A. Commerce nr Front
Cunningham's Warehouse, bet Front,
    Battery, Green, and Commerce, F.
    Read
Eagle Warehouse, Davis nr Pine, N.
    R. Lowell
Empire Warehouse, Beale cor Market
Falkner, Bell & Co. corner Union and
    Battery
Flint, Peabody & Co.'s Warehouse,
    Battery nr Filbert, T. B. Ludlum
Forbes' Warehouse, Front nr Vallejo
Gibbs' Warehouse, corner Front and
    Vallejo
Granite Warehouse, 35 Sacramento, T.
    H. Selby & Co
Greenwich Dock Warehouse, NW cor
    Bat and Greenwich, W. A. Green
Guy Abel, warehouse, 916 Battery
Howard's U. S. Bonded, cor Front and
    Broadway, Howard & Pool
Howes & Co.'s Warehouse, 1013 Bat
Lazard's Warehouse, cor Filbert and
    Battery
Lombard Warehouse, corner Lombard
    and Sansom
Loning & Feuerstein, Union nr Front
New Orleans Warehouse, California nr
    Davis, T. B. Ludlum
New York Warehouse, cor California
    and Davis
North Point Dock Warehouse, corner
    Sansom and Lombard, C. R. Pe-
    ters & Co
Pacific Warehouse, cor Battery and
    Broadway
Rincon Point Warehouse, Rincon Pt.
    D. & G. W. Hardy
Resenfeld J. (coal) corner Folsom and
    Spear
Rogers N. 818 Battery
Scott's Warehouse, cor Greenwich and
    Sansom, J. C. King & Co
Union Warehouse, NW cor Union and
    Battery, Koopmanschap & Co
Vallejo St. Bonded Warehouse, corner
    Front and Vallejo

Stoves and Tinware.
Importers.

Abrahamson P. 439 Bush
Alvey C. W. 907 Kearny
Armstrong & Bertram, Fort Point
Atherton W. F. 15 Second
*Austin B. C. 324 Clay
*Ayers E. 417 Washington
Bohn John, 1218 Dupont
*Brittan J. W. & Co. 118 and 120 Front
Brown Archibald, 214 Third
Brown Charles, 34 Kearny
Brydges M. C. Sacramento nr East
Bucknam E. T. 22 Stewart
Bullard &Battles (petroleum) 316 Mont
CHASE, SHARPE & THOMSON, 209
    North Second St. Philadelphia (see
    advertisement p. cvii)
Colson A. 530 Dupont
Corey T. 204 Pacific
Daly D. J. 814 Market
David A. 1204 Stockton
*De la Montanya J. 216 Jackson
Engela H. A. 602 Mission
Fiske H. G. & E. S. 807 Market
Freeman & Wrin, 342 Third
Friel & Mann, 69 Fourth
Gebler T. 825 Clay
Giffin J. 1413 Stockton
Goldstein A. S. 214 Fourth

Greninger D. 116 Third
Groffman C. P. 48 Jackson
Haythrop E. 510 Sansom
HICKMAN L. M. Stockton Cal. (see
    advertisement p. cl)
Howell T. 290 Third
Hoy A. 730 Jackson
Hughes R. 213 Third
*Ils J. G. 628 Washington
Johnston & Reay, 319 California
*Kohler Jacob, foot Battery
Kone D. C. 126 Sutter
Little & Lawson, 214 Jackson
*LOCKE & MONTAGUE. 112 Battery
    (see advertisement. p. xlvii)
Mayer J. 155 Second
McCormack W. 820 Market
Moenning G. 140 Fourth
Murtha W. O. cor Market and Powell
O'Shea James, 1322 Stockton
Pape A. 1204 Dupont
Prag M. 125 Clay
Robinson & Rosenthal, 3 Commercial
Ruggles D. M. (col'd) 310 Jackson
Schuster & Bro. 102 Kearny
Sickler C. M. 422 Kearny
Swigert A. 873 Folsom
Sylvester L. 921 Dupont
*TAY, BROOKS & BACKUS, corner
    Front and Washington
Taylor & Iredale, 410 Market
Tolles & Howard, 724 Market
WALMSLEY W. W. 112 Fourth (see
    advertisement, p. cxl)
Weaver D. S. 505 Sansom
Welsh & Shoemaker, 29 Market

Straw Goods.

California Straw Works, 45 Third
Hoffman, W. & Co. 427 Sacramento
Jones, Dixon & Co. cor Sacramento
    and Sansom
Pacific Straw Works, 603 Market
Peyser S. A. 424 Sacramento
Schriver W. 141 Fourth
    [See Millinery; Hats, Etc.]

Stucco Workers.
[See Plasterers; Cement, Etc.]

Sugar Refineries.

BAY SUGAR REFINERY, cor Bat-
    tery and Union (see adv. p. 645)
S. F. & PACIFIC SUGAR CO. cor
    Eighth and Harrison (see advertise-
    ment, p. lvii)

Surgical Instrument Makers.

FOLKERS J. H. A. 218 Montgomery
    (see advertisement, p. xxxix)
Kesmodel F. 817 Kearny
Price M. 110 Montgomery
WHITE S. S. 528 Arch St. Philadelphia
    (see advertisement, pp. civ and cv)
Will & Finck, 613 Jackson
    [See Cutlers.]

Surveyors.

Brown Harry S. (marine) 504 Battery
Humphreys W. P. 49 Mont Block
Noyes Amos (marine) cor Washington
    and Battery
Potter G. C. (City and County) City
    Hall
Roxby Robert (marine) 306 Front
Stivers H. F. (lumber) Mission Street
    Wharf
Shortt L. H. 302 Montgomery
Wackenreuder V. San Bruno Road
    [See Engineers—Civil.]

Suspension Bridge Builders.

HALLIDIE A. S. & CO. 412 Clay (see
    advertisement, p. 671)
    [See Wire Rope, Etc.]

Syrups and Wines.

Cassin F. 520 Front
Crevolin & Co. 510 Jackson
Ghio A. & Co. 527 Washington
Lyons E. G. & Co. 510 Jackson
McMillan & Kester, 714 Front
Nichols A. R. 225 Clay
Ricci & Co. 635 Washington
Rottanzi L. 635 Washington
Simon G. A. Harrison nr Third
Squarza V. 118 Leidesdorff
    [See Liquors; Native Wines.]

Tailors.

Abraham G. 35 Second
Adler B. 27 Pacific
Albrecht John, 339 Bush
Alexander S. 144 Stewart
Anderfuren J. 24 Dupont
Assion & Bro. 205 Montgomery
Bargon M. 409 Bush
Barry E. M. Trinity nr Sutter
Bazin V. 445 Bush
Benas B. 13 Kearny
Berg J. A. 50 Sacramento
Bergholte & Baloun, 819 Clay
Berwin Isaac, 115 Leidesdorff
Bird William, 126 Bush
Blum Isaac, 104 Bush
Bolian M. 108 Sansom
Borkheim H. (regt.) 236 Sutter
Bornheim G. 102 Sansom
Boucher E. 537 Sacramento
Boyes C. (merchant) 42 Sutter
Boyle W. 308 Sansom
Brandhofer M. 628 Merchant
Brennan J. E. 223 Montgomery
Brenner Bros. 401 Bush
Brodwolf G. (merchant) 319 Bush
Brooks J. L. (merchant) 710 Mont
Canty T. 548 Washington
Chisholm D. 414 Pine
Cohen Louis, 70 First
Cohen S. 110 Leidesdorff
Cohn Louis, 312 Pacific
Cohn N. 672 Mission
Cohn S. 312 Pacific
Collins B. 416 Folsom
Corcoran D. P. 104 Bush
Cordiner C. L. (merchant) 208 Bush
Cordiviola S. 1106 Dupont
Coulon E. 1213 Dupont
Crosby J. 610 Montgomery
Curran B. 206 Bush
Dannheimer L. (merchant) 310 Mont
Davis I. (merchant) 635 Market
Dejonghe P. 104 Sutter
Dettmer H. 104 Sutter
Dietch S. 212 Third
Dixey F. (merchant) 825 Washington
Drought R. 304 Pine
Duparque L. Powell nr Chestnut
Eisenberg I. (merchant) 206 Bush
Elwell F. (merchant) 316 Bush
Erb M. 1416 Stockton
Erenberg L. 202 Bush
Feig Louis, 10 Sansom
Fitzgerald A. 619 Sacramento
Freeman Louis, 34 Sutter
Fuhrmann H. 26 Dupont
Futter J. 1210 Sacramento
Gallagher P. 229 Bush
Geimann W. (military) 633 Wash
Generlich J. 409 Bush
Giesemann H. 204 Dupont
Goldstein M. 625 Commercial
Goodman L. 922 Kearny
Goulet Isidore (merchant) 1103 Mont
Gray Simon, 112 Kearny
Gruenwald A. 654 Pacific
Guillot J. 606 Vallejo
Hager J. 318 Third
Harris A. 504 Mission
Harris M. 646½ Pacific
Harshall G. 219 Third
Harshall Gus, 144 Third
Heffernan M. cor Spring and Summer
Henry H. cor Spring and Summer
Houston R. T. 645 Merchant
Hubbard H. W. 333 East
Hughes J. 1220 Stockton
Hunter G. 619 Sacramento
Hussey J. cor Spring and Summer
Imbrie A. C. 215 California
Isaac M. 233 Third
Isaacs M. 7 Summer
Isaacs S. 16 First
Jacob A. 504 Pine
Jacobs D. 315 East
Jacoby J. 714 Commercial
Jennings W. 404 Folsom
Jonas B. 337 Kearny
Kalisky S. 333 Kearny
Kaliner S. 468 Pine
Kaul S. 324 Commercial
Keagel F. 136 First
Kelly R. 549 Merchant
Kesper M. 611 Mission
Keyser M. 321 Bush
Killpatrick F. (merchant) 25 Sansom
Kirby John, 109 Jessie
Knoll C. F. 420 Market
Kramer A. 526 Merchant
Kratz H. 409 Bush
Kron & Co. 763 Clay

Kruger C. 704 Pacific
Langdon R. 651 Merchant
Levin L. 733 Mission
Levy B. 613 Pacific
Levy B. W. 619 Pacific
Levy M. 91 Stevenson
Levy S. 235 Jackson
Lobree E. 530 Commercial
Mann David, 108 Market
Marcuse H. L. 1314 Stockton
Marks H. 504 Market
Marks J. 809 Washington
Matavron J. C. 614 Sacramento
Mayer J. 226 First
McArthur A. 431 Bush
McCarty M. 713 Folsom
McDermott M. 73 Stevenson
McGeary H. 126 Bush
Mendelson M. 6 Sutter
Mengelkamp B. cor Pine and Battery
Menne C. 533 Jackson
Meyer J. 311 Davis
Meyer L. 347 Third
Meyers C. 602 Broadway
Meyers M. J. 805 Clay
Michael H. 739 Pacific
Michael L. 607 Davis
Michaelis B. 1432 Stockton
Michel A. 221 Pacific
Miller A. 200 Sutter
Miller & Meister, 426 Third
Moroni E. 1231 Dupont
Morris H. 125 Fourth
Motzenbecker P. 22 Sansom
Moy E. 1163 Dupont
Munter A. 214 First
Neeb H. 629 Merchant
O'Neil C. 210 Leidesdorff
Outman T. 731 Pacific
Pauba A. 409 Bush
Peiser J. 241 Third
Peyser M. cor Pine and Dupont
Phillips J. 305 Pine
Pincus M. 302 Pacific
Planz H. 319 Commercial
Raclet W. 1206 Dupont
Raphael A. 129 Fourth
Regelhaupt P. 504 Market
Reinstein S. 312 Sansom
Repensky P. 909 Kearny
Reynolds G. L. 518 California
Rich L. 1009 Stockton
Rogers A. T. (colored) 319 Bush
Rosener H. 414 Third
Rosener S. 817 Jackson
Rosenthal H. 621 Mission
Rother R. 17 Fourth
Sarsfield M. 816 Montgomery
Schafer G. F. 409 Bush
Schmidt C. 758 Clay
Seidenberg C. 529 East
Shaen J. 332 Bush
Shilling J. 207 Fourth
Simon L. 51 Third
Smith G. H. 548 Washington
Spellman J. 511 Commercial
Spori L. 737 Pacific
Stallmann C. (merchant) 543 Sac
Steil, Wehn & Co. (merchant) Occidental Hotel
Sullivan J. J. 232 Fourth
Sweeney N. (merchant) 143 Second
Tammeyer J. (merchant) 325 Bush
Tobin J. H. (merchant) 616 Sacramento
Treier T. 136 First
Tynan W. D. 125 Bush
Unger M. 748 Market
Vogle B. M. 761 Clay
Walter A. 427 Bush
Walter G. F. & Co. (merchant) 611 Sac
Walter S. T. 120 Dupont
Ward C. 127 Bush
Westerman J. 804 Clay
Wolf A. 109 Leidesdorff
Wolf E. 35 Geary
Wolfe M. 539 Kearny
Yarskio M. 110 Geary
Zeitska H. (merchant) 415 Mont
Zinnamon A. 362 Third
[See Clothing, Etc.]

Tailors' Trimmings.

Hammond W. 321 Bush
LANZENBERG M. & CO. 628 Clay
Schiam & Dunn, 818 Montgomery
STEIN, SIMON & CO. 634 Sacramento
Weill E. & Son, 630 Sacramento

Tallow.

Burdick E. B. Potrero
COX & NICHOLS, 422 Battery

Dyer J. P. cor Nebraska and Sixteenth
Ernst Herman, 15 Davis
[See Hides and Wool; Soap.]

Tanners and Tanneries.

Bissell J. Potrero
Bloom S. Brannan nr Sixth
Cook & Co. Greenwich nr Octavia
COX & NICHOLS (agents) 422 Battery (see advertisement, p. lxv)
Degen P. Old San José Road nr Industrial School
Duncan J. Brannan nr Eighth
Grady J. J. cor Eighteenth and Folsom
ING A. J. D. & CO. (agents) 312 Commercial (see adv. p. xxxv)
King J. F. cor Santa Clara and Connecticut
Lein H. cor Folsom and Eighteenth
McKenna & Tunsted, W s Lagoon
Muir & McLean, Ninth nr Brannan
Von Seggen H. w s Lagoon
Warren W. H. Folsom nr Eighteenth
[See Leather, Etc.]

Tanners' Tools.

COX & NICHOLS, 422 Battery (see advertisement, p. lxv)

Taxidermists.

Lorquin E. F. 522 Pine

Teachers. *Book Keeping.*

Beck A. G. 116 Stevenson
DeSequeira A. L. 204 Montgomery
Heald E. P. 202 Montgomery
Luty J. S. 305 Montgomery
Wead E. N. 229 Bush

Teachers. *Dancing.*

Cogill Mr., Mrs. & Sons, 320 Bush
Fitzgibbon D. Assembly Hall, corner Kearny and Post
Fuller & McCarty, 727 Market
Galavotti T. 725 Market
Sanders & Fuller, corner Fourth and Jessie
Sheldon & Lloyd, corner Market and Second
Wilson W. 222 Montgomery

Teachers. *Drawing.*

Coulon A. 410 Kearny
Grob T. 306 Dupont

Teachers. *Fencing.*

Monastery T. 534 Kearny
Stewart P. jr. 530 Merchant

Teachers. *Fine Arts.*

[See Painters; Portraits.]

Teachers. *Languages.*

DeClairmont R. 1518 Stockton
Hasback & Bro. 719 Vallejo
Hungerford E. Mrs. 626 California
JOSSET J. 634 Vallejo
Keeler B. 124 Silver
Lannay V. (widow) 444 Third
Willey M. B. Mrs. 113 Dora
[See Colleges; Schools, Etc.]

Teachers. *Music.*

Anderson M. A. 812 Stockton
Andres C. 320 Kearny
Barrette M. E. (widow) 12 Stockton
Beutler J. B. 613 Mission
Bianchi E. 714 Vallejo
Carnaud J. 1013 Mission
Chandler C. (widow) 638 Howard
Chapman S. Mrs. 574 Mission
Coad S. 561 Mission
Cohen W. Madame, 1505 Stockton
Damon F. Mrs. 828 Folsom
DeHaga J. 714 Vallejo
Dimpfel J. Miss, 1221 Clay
Dohrmann J. H. 706 Bush
Doison A. E. Miss, Laskie nr Eighth
Dresser T. E. 507 Bush
Elliott W. 158 Second
Evans George T. cor Mason and O'Farrell
Ferrer M. Y. 1710 Mason
Fleury J. 607 Dupont
Frederick L. Madame, 712 Wash
Gabbs P. Miss, 209 Fourth
Goodrich J. A. 1024 Stockton

Goodrich J. B. 1024 Stockton
Griswold J. A. 1129 Folsom
Grob H. G. 106 Geary
Hahn A. 153 Third
Hammerschmidt A. J. 626 California
Hartmann E. 522 Dupont
Hauser H. Union nr Hyde
Hekmgu L. 1624 Dupont
Henn J. Mrs. 423 Stevenson
Herold Rudolph, 211 Post
Holzhauer H. 69 Everett
Hooper L. M. Mrs. 3 Monroe
Ken E. Mrs. 155 Third
Klingeman C. 1607 Powell
Koppitz G. 32 Everett
Kuhne A. 613 Clay
Lapfgeer A. W. 659 Howard
Leach S. W. 607 Folsom
Liebert B. 265 Minna
Loomis A. Miss, 317 Minna
Lyle E. A. C. Miss, cor Howard and Washington Avenue
Lynch Kate Miss, corner Montgomery and Broadway
MacDougall W. J. cor Mont and Pac
Martini J. 917 Sacramento
Miller E. L. 708 Sutter
Minot J. Polk Alley
Mitchell F. K. 131 Montgomery
Mueller C. 828 Vallejo
Neidinger W. A. 617 Union
Norcross W. F. Mrs. 11 Ellis
Patrick J. D. 326 Mason
Pettinos G. F. 426 Second
Pindell A. Miss, cor Kearny and Bdwy
Pique E. 1484 Dupont
Quevedo V. 519 Vallejo
Rosenberg A. A. 321 Powell
Schmidt Louis, 119 O'Farrell
Schultz Charles, 704 Dupont
Schumacher R. 211 Post
Scott G. A. 3 Montgomery
Steinle E. 211 Post
Striby W. 870 Mission
Theisen A. Mrs. 18 Stockton
Tourny L. Miss, 661 Howard
Touissin E. 2 St. Mary
Washburn M. A. Mrs. 624 Market
Wernham F. Miss, 1809 Powell
Weston A. Geary nr Leavenworth
Willey M. B. Mrs. 113 Dora
Wilson Jed, 430 Montgomery

Teachers. *Penmanship.*

Beck A. G. 116 Stevenson
Burgess H. Public Schools
Doolittle W. G. 328 Montgomery
DeSequeira A. L. 204 Montgomery
Josset J. 634 Vallejo
Seregni F. 606 Montgomery

Teachers. *Private Schools.*

[See Colleges and Schools.]

Tea Stores.

Belden F. C. 612 Sacramento
Bradshaw & Co. cor Sansom and Cal
Haskell George S. & Co. 514 Market
Haynes J. W. (jobber) 404 Front
Kell E. & Co. 631 Washington
[See Groceries; Provisions.]

Telegraph Offices.

California State Telegraph Co. 507 Montgomery
Fire and Police, City Hall
U. S. and Pacific, 502 Montgomery

Tin Plate, Sheet Iron, and Tin Importers.

Brittan J. W. & Co. 118 Front
Kohler Jacob, foot Battery
LOCKE & MONTAGUE, 112 Battery (see advertisement, p. xlvii)
MARSH, PILSBURY & CO. cor Front and Pine (see adv. p. xcv)
SELBY T. H. & CO. 118 California (see advertisement, p. xii)
Van Winkle I. S. & Co. cor Battery and Bush
[See Hardware; Stoves, Etc.]

Tin and Sheet Iron Workers.

[See Stoves and Tinware.]

Tobacco Dealers. *Wholesale.*

Drinkhouse J. A. & Co. 228 Front
EMERY C. G. 518 Battery (see advertisement, p. 652)

Engelbrecht & Mayrisch Brothers, 314 Front
Falkenstein & Co. 315 Clay
GELIEN R. G. cor California and Front (see advertisement, p. 663)
Heath & Langhorne, 609 Front
Horn B. C. & Co cor Front and Clay
Maybium M. 230 Front
Oppenheimer & Bro. 311 Clay
Rhine C. 407 Merchant
ROSENBAUM A. S. & CO. cor Clay and Battery (see adv. p. lxviii)
WEIL & CO. 226 Front (see advertisement, p. xli)
Wertheimer L. & E. cor Front and Sac [See Cigars.]

Tobacconists.

EMERY C. G. 518 Battery (see advertisement, p. 652)
Engelbrecht & Mayrisch Brothers, 314 Front
Freidberg M. 56 Third
GELEIN R. G. cor Front and California (see advertisement, p. 663)
Hamma J. B (snuff) 604 Battery
Heerdink & Baumgartner, 33 Fremont
Moran Brothers, 708 Battery
ROSENBAUM A. S. & CO. cor Clay and Battery (see adv. p. lxviii)
[See Cigars.]

Toilet Articles.

Krause W. E. F. cor Front and Jackson [See Apothecaries; Fancy Goods.]

Tool Manufacturers.

PROVIDENCE TOOL CO. (Providence, R. I., see adv. p. c)

Toys.

*Importers.

Allen John, 733 Pacific
Argenti E. Mrs. 402 Third
Brown & Wagner 134 Kearny
Delande S. 60 Clay
Dodge D. F. 229 Kearny
Dunagnou L. 1105 Stockton
*Feldbush & Co. 207 Montgomery and 307 California
Friedman S. 1108 Stockton
Gaubert J. 1312 Stockton
*Gensoul A. 511 Montgomery
Gingras M. Mrs. 1303 Stockton
Harris J. F. 265 Third
Heilbron M. & Bro. 27 Third
*Kohler A. 630 Washington
Pasquale B. 650 Washington
Solera S. 1140 Dupont
Stolz Bros. 530 Kearny and 8 Second
*THURNAUER & ZINN, 320 Battery (see advertisement, p. 644)
Vasselin H. 22 Fourth
Viard P. 1105 Stockton
Weiss M. 324 Kearny
Wilson S. D. & Co. 541 Kearny [See Fancy Goods.]

Translators.

[See Interpreters.]

Trunk Makers.

Aubry J. 713 Clay
Galpen E. & Co. 222 Sansom
HARRIS J. 513 Kearny (see advertisement, p. 659)
LONGSHORE JAMES, 208 Bush (see advertisement, p. 657)
Smith James, 107 Sansom

Truss Manufacturers.

FOLKERS J. H. A. (agent) 218 Montgomery (see adv. p. xxxix)
KOEHLER A. 718 Washington (see advertisement, p. 666)

Turners. *Ivory and Wood.*

Cameron & Kuenzi, 309 Market
Coppi V. 309 Pine
Davis & Seaborn, 409 Mission
Doerger Charles & Co. 539 Sacramento
FREEMAN B. H. & CO. SW cor Market and Beale
Haller & Swarbrick, 31 Fremont
JELLINEK A. 14 California (see advertisement, p. 660)
LANGLAND N. P. 227 Market

Pearce C. G. 837 Washington
Robinson A. 37 Fremont
Seaborn & Frei, 409 Mission
Thomas C. W. 22 California
Van Brock F. 920 Stockton

Turpentine, Pitch, Etc.

Walton N. C. 29 Market

Type. *Agents.*

[See Printers' Materials.]

Type Founders.

Kellogg A. 517 Jackson

Umbrella Makers.

Alsop J. 334 Bush
Barr J. D. 625 Mission
Costello T. 116 Minna
Rice A. 1116 Dupont

Undertakers.

Craig, Golden & Yung, 705 Market
Crowe & Farrell, 709 Market
GRAY N. 641 Sacramento (see advertisement, p. 658)
MASSEY A. 651 Sacramento (see advertisement, p. 657)
McGinn & Mullins, 733 Market

Underwriters. *Agents of.*

Bacon T. H. & J. S. (Boston) 216 Front
FALKNER, BELL & CO. (London Lloyds) 430 California
Fire Board, office 414 California
Fletcher A. T. (New York) 216 Front
Marine Board 318 California
Mebius C. F. (Bremen) 223 Sacramento
Rène J. E. (French) 706 Montgomery
Schroeder H. & Co. (Bordeaux) 811 Montgomery
Ziel, Bertheau & Co. (Hamburg) 122 California
[See Insurance.]

Upholsterers and Paper Hangings.

*Importers.

Aldrich G. C. 618 Mission
Beal S. 527 California
*BELL JOHN C. SW cor California and Sansom (see adv. p. xiv)
Burbank E. A. 727 Market
Burnham W. F. 101 Second
*Clark C. W. NE cor Clay and Sansom
Duff John, 642 Clay
*EDWARDS F. G. 646 Clay (see advertisement, front cover)
Fuhr Charles A. 636 Market
*Gullixson & Nelson, 334 Kearny
*Hixon W. M. 606 Clay
*KENNEDY & BELL, cor Montgomery and Cal (see adv. front cover)
Lenhardt A. 1292 Stockton
*LOUGHRAN P. F. & CO. 403 Sansom (see advertisement, p. xxx)
*McElwee & Ackerman, 236 Mont
*Plum C. M. 22 Montgomery
*Robinson Joseph, 509 Sansom
SOLOMON B. & SONS, cor Battery and Pine (see adv. p. lxvi)
Troutt H. J. M. 618 Market
*WIGHTMAN & HARDIE, 416 Clay

Upholstery Goods.

BELL JOHN C. cor Sansom and Cal
SOLOMON B. L. & SONS, cor Pine and Battery (see adv. p. lxvi)
WALTER D. N. and E. & CO. 203 California (see advertisement, p. cxli)
WIGHTMAN & HARDIE, 416 Clay
[See Carpets; Dry Goods.]

Varnishers and Polishers.

[See Painters.]

Varnishes.

Walton N. C. (petroleum) 29 Market
[See Paints.]

Veterinary Surgeons.

Bonis P. 214 Stevenson
Claussen H.H. 211 Pine
Cooper A. F. 815 Market
Delaney M. 733 Market

DeTavel A. 427 Pine
Maquart F. Mission Dolores
Taylor J. S. 257 Clementina
Yarrington H J. 810 Union

Vinegar Manufacturers.

Cutting & Co. 202 Front
Erzgraber & Goetjen, 120 Davis
Mitchell & Co. 114 Sacramento
Oakley & Jackson, 320 Front
Pholey J. Brannan nr Eighth
Provost D. R. & Co. (importers) 413 Front
Schammel H. 1320 Powell
[See Pickles.]

Wagon Grease. *Manufacturers.*

HUCKS & LAMBERT, 146 Natoma (see advertisement, p. 652)

Warehouses.

[See Storage.]

Washing Machines.

Arnold N. & Co. (agents) 306 Battery
Traver M. E. & Bro. (patent wringer) 81 Natoma
[See Machinists; Hardware, Etc.]

Watches. *Importers of.*

* Retail.

*BARRETT & SHERWOOD, 517 Mont
*BRAVERMAN & LEVY, 621 Wash
*Collins C. E. 602 Montgomery
Crosby F. W. & Co. 638 Clay
Dinkelspiel S. B. 607 Washington
Dirking A. 621 Washington
Falkenau Bros. 629 Washington
Gerard V. agent, 629 Clay
Huguenin V. J. 619 Montgomery
*Jordan M. 625 Montgomery
*Joseph Brothers, 607 Montgomery
Josephi I. S. 641 Washington
Kahn & Strauss, 619 Washington
Levison Bros. 629 Washington
*Lippman J. 203 Montgomery
*Revalk J. 510 Montgomery
*SHERWOOD R. 517 Montgomery
*SHREVE G. C. & CO. 525 Mont
Strassburger L. 623 Washington
*Tucker & Co. 505 Montgomery
*WIEDERO, OTTO & CO. 433 Mont

Watch Makers.

Ahrens C. 836 Dupont
Anderson David, 58 Clay
Baldwin M. M. 311 Montgomery
Barrett A. 33 Second
BARRETT & SHERWOOD, 517 Montgomery (see advertisement, p. li)
BRAVERMAN & LEVY, 621 Washington (see adv. front cover)
Burkhardt G. 209 Pacific
Campbell J. 335 Kearny
Carmatz A. 707 Clay
Clark W. H. T. 228 Kearny
Collins C. E. 602 Montgomery
Crowley J. 422 Folsom
Drapnick F. 622 Clay
Finberg A. 911 Kearny
Friedlander W. 41 Third
Geist W. 205 Montgomery
Golly A. 717 Clay
Green William, 538 Kearny
Hain C. H. & Co. 321 Montgomery
Hammond W. A. 57 Second
Hartung T. 216 Kearny
Hauser F. 504 Market
Heinz F. 848 Washington
Heizman L. 521 Kearny
Heizman J. 408 Commercial
Heringhi B. 635 Kearny
Hudson J. 15 Fourth
Isson S. 639 Pacific
Kling O. W. 227 Jackson
Knowlton W. H. 648 Sacramento
Lamaure T. 526 Commercial
Lang E. 102 Pacific
Lehmann G. What Cheer House
Lewis H. M. & M. M. 655 Clay
Magnus F. A. cor Sac and Davis
Marks F. 1024 Dupont
Mathieu G. 724 Washington
Mayer L. 1020 Dupont
McGREGOR J. 409 Sansom (see advertisement, p. lxx)
Miller L. H. 210 Clay
Milsner L. 707 Clay
Mohrig C. F. 613 Washington

Mund William, 750 Market
Newman H. 13 Second
Nolte W. 103½ Montgomery
O'Connell D. A. 155 Third
Ohm E. F. 615 Montgomery
Pace C. 613 Battery
Pecktord J. 308 Sixth
Rahwyler A. 927 Kearny
Revalk J. 510 Montgomery
Richet C. 1220 Dupont
Roflat S. 1114 Dupont
Rose A. J. 3 Montgomery
Salaman A. 15 Fourth
Scheider J. cor Kearny and Jackson
Sharp W. 837 Clay
SHERWOOD ROBERT, 517 Montgomery (see advertisement, p. li)
SHREVE G. C. & CO. 525 Montgomery (see advertisement, p. xliv)
Sornin A. 605 Washington
Steler P. 804 Washington
Stopp M. H. 841 Sacramento
Trapnick F. 622 Clay
Traube H. 717 Clay
Tucker & Co. 505 Montgomery
Usynski J. 406 Kearny
Wallmann & Bro. 212 Montgomery
Wenzel H. 303 Montgomery
WIEDERO, OTTO & CO. 433 Montgomery (see advertisement, p. lii)
Winkleman & Carroll, 560 Mission
Wolf F. 622 Clay
Zacharias H. 538 Kearny
[See Jewelers.]

Watchmakers' Materials.

Dirking A. 621 Washington
Josephi I. S. 641 Washington
Levison Brothers, 629 Washington

Watch Case Makers.

Giannini P. A. 622 Clay
Falco A. 622 Clay
Smith F. 619 Montgomery

Water Works.

Fountain Head, 537 Market
Hunt E. O. 108 Jessie
Keating G. 609 Market
Saucelito Co. cor Merchant and East
SPRING VALLEY W. W. CO office SE cor Montgomery and Jackson (see advertisement, p. liii)
Webster A. B. 521 Market

Well Borers.

THOMSON T. 28 Third (see advertisement, p. 653)

Wheelwrights.

Gallagher & Rodecker, 115 Pine
James E. 415 Third
Kimball G. P. & Co. Market nr Fourth
King J. M. Mission nr Sixteenth
Knight G. W. & Co. Potrero Avenue
Larkins & Co. cor Spring and Summer
Roberts & Co. 249 Fourth
Scammon J. H. 715 Folsom
Shute H. M. 539 Market
Sier P. 528 Broadway
Steinweg C. 109 Pine
Stitt R. Third nr Folsom
Thornan F. 214 Sutter
Yerman J. 1116 Howard
[See Blacksmiths; Carriage Makers.]

Whip Makers.

MAIN & WINCHESTER, 214 Battery
Murphy James, 12 First

Wig and Toupee Makers.

Hubert C. 603 Montgomery
Monie G. 307 Montgomery
Pfister C. 221 Montgomery
Puyoou P. 610 Kearny
[See Hair Dressers.]

Willow Workers and Wares.

ARMES & DALLAM, 215 Sacramento (see advertisement, p. 644)
Elam & Howes (importers) 310 and 312 Clay
Heilborn Brothers, 27 Third
Navelet V. 221 Leidesdorff
THURNAUER & ZINN (importers) 320 and 322 Battery (see advertisement, p. 644)

Wind Mills.

Atwood & Bodwell, 222 Mission
Hunt E. O. 28 Second
Johnson J. B. corner Fremont and Mission

Window Glass.

[See Paints; Oils; Glass.]

Window Shades.

Edwards F. G. 646 Clay
Rossiter J. Francisco nr Dupont
TORNING A. & T. 528 California (see advertisement, p. 656)
[See Paper Hangings.]

Wines and Brandies.

Meinecke C. 215 Front
[See Liquors.]

Wines and Brandies. *Native.*

[See Native Wines.]

Wire Rope Manufacturers.

HALLIDIE A. S. & CO. 412 Clay (see advertisement, p. 671)

Wire Goods and Workers.

GRAVES H. T. 412 Clay (see advertisement, p. 670)
HALLIDIE A. S. & CO. 412 Clay
MARSH, PILSBURY & CO. corner Front and Pine (see adv, p. xcv)

Wood and Coal.

Allen E. G. 513 Bush
Anderson Thomas, 737 Jackson
Audiffred & Male, Market St. Wharf
Browning & Klein, 629 Broadway
Caffrata & Larebarde, 1823 Powell
Cahill M. Waverly Place nr Clay
Callan Thomas, Fifth nr Howard
Corbett & Rounds, 735 Brannan
Cruze & Co. 531 Pine
Delano Thomas, 233 Fourth
Delano W. H. 326 Geary
Doyle J. R. 413 Pacific
Driscoll T. cor Mission and Sixteenth
Dunn Edward, 502½ Third
Dwyer & Co. 539 California
Edelkamp B. cor Stewart and Folsom
Fales Edward, 419 Post
Forsyth, Morrison & Co. Howard St. Wharf
Fuegelsberger A. cor Kearny and Bdwy
Garibaldi J. 8 Pollard Place
Gatt & Gionazzo, 510 Green
Gavigan W. Commercial St. Wharf
George & Smith, 430 Pine
Giavonini & Brother, 816 Pacific
Gildersleeve & Co. 607 Market
GREENHOOD, NEWBAUER & KLEIN, 207 Sansom (see advertisement, p. 662)
Hamilton S. 414 Brannan
Hartnet M. 30 Fourth
Haste & Kirk, 515 California
Healey, Carlton & Co. 429 Pine
Henderson J. 836 Washington
Henry & Dunn, 1626 Powell
Heyfron M. 716 Folsom
Horabin T. Washington nr Stockton
Hurles D. D. cor Mission and Seventeenth
Jaffe L. 133 Sutter
Johnson J. M. 215 Jackson
Kentzel W. H. Broadway nr Mont
Kershaw M. Valencia nr Sixteenth
Klaber G. 866 Howard
Lauterwasser & Peters, Sixth nr Tehama
Maguire & Co. cor Hayes and Van Ness Avenue
Maisch J. 38 Geary
Mallett & Edwards, 803 Stockton
Massey H. W. 1014 Market
Mathias C. 114 Washington
McCaull M. 631 Green
McErlain P. 159 Shipley
McKew J. 431 Union
McMullen D. cor Third and Silver
Melbourn J. & Co. 1219 Powell
Mervey J. 1417 Stockton
Moore A. 1012 Powell
Moore John, 662 Mission
Morrison C. foot Howard
Munroe George, 16 Stockton
Neulens J. B. Sansom nr Pacific

O'Connell J. foot Mission
O'Grady & Flynn, 831 Howard
O'Hara & Co. 133 Post
Peck G. 11. cor Broadway and Sansom
Penniman J. 645 Mission
Pezzoni & Coppi, Taylor nr Lombard
Pixley W. 216 Sutter
Prior C. 911 Folsom
Quinn J. C. 325 O'Farrell
Raubinger B. 130 Geary
Ramsdell B. H. 110 Jackson
Reilly J. S. 751 Mission
Renault J. 713 Pacific
Riordan R. 222 Dupont
Ross John, 315 First
Rovegno S. 1015 Washington
Ruddock G. cor Sixth and Minna
Sanguinetti J. foot Eighth
Sawin & Bradley, 608 Broadway
Smith J. C foot Mission
Smith & Williams, corner Folsom and Seventh
Starr & Riddle, 16 Drumm
Staud J. N. 211 Dupont
Storm C. 115 Sacramento
Thomas & Twing, cor Market and East
Thompson R. A. & Co. 126 Sutter
Torrey H. 8 Ecker
Turner & Harvey, Drumm nr Jackson
Turner & Rundle, San José Road cor Sixteenth
Van Winkle I. S. & Co. cor Battery and Bush
Wagner & Co. 8 Waverly Place
Wagner J. 716 Pacific
Whipple S. B. 203 Sansom and corner Mission and Fremont
Wolf Brothers, 19 Battery
[See Coal and Coal Yards,]

Wood and Willow Ware.

ARMES & DALLAM, 215 Sacramento (see adv. p. 644)
Elam & Howes, 310 Clay
Feldman L. & Co. 211 California
Navelet V. 221 Leidesdorff
Newman Bros. 406 Battery
THURNAUER & ZINN, 320 Battery (see adv. p. 644)
[See Willow Ware.]

Wool Dealers.

Burke F. G. 220 Front
California Wool Growers' Association, 402 Front
Christy & Wise, 610 Front
Clark & Perkins, NE corner Front and Clay
Ernst H. 15 Davis
Farish A. T. & Co. 221 Davis
HEYNEMANN & CO. 311 California (see adv. p. xl)
LAZARD & McLENNAN, 217 Battery (see advertisement, p. ix)
McLennan, Whelan & Grisar, cor Sansom and Broadway
Sedgley & Davis, 536 Kearny
[See Hides and Wool.]

Woolen Goods.

LOCAN & CO. 623 Clay (see advertisement, p. xxxi)
MISSION WOOLEN MILLS, Lazard & McLennan, 217 Battery (see advertisement, p. ix)
S. F. PIONEER MILLS, Heynemann & Co. 311 California (see advertisement, p. xl)
STEIN, SIMON & CO. 532 Sacramento and 531 Commercial (see advertisement, p. xxx)
[See Clothes and Woolen Goods.]

Woolen Manufacturers.

MISSION WOOLEN MILLS, Lazard & McLennan, office 217 Battery (see adv. p. ix)
S. F. PIONEER MILLS, Heynemann & Co. office 311 California (see advertisement, p. xl)

Worsted Goods.

LOCAN & CO. 623 Clay (see advertisement, p. xxxi)
Meagher, Taaffe & Co. 107 Battery
[See Fancy Goods, Etc.]

Yeast Powder Manufacturers.

Callaghan D. (Donnolly's) 121 Front

WM. BARTLING.   HENRY KIMBALL.

BARTLING & KIMBALL,

BOOKBINDERS,

PAPER RULERS,

AND

BLANK BOOK MANUFACTURERS,

505 Clay Street, South-West cor. Sansom,

SAN FRANCISCO.

Every variety of Bookbinding done at as low rates, and in a better manner than any other establishment on this coast.

TO BE PUBLISHED JULY 1st, 1866.

THE

Pacific Coast Business Directory,

CONTAINING THE

NAMES, BUSINESS, AND ADDRESS

OF ALL

MERCHANTS, MANUFACTURERS, AND PROFESSIONAL MEN

IN THE STATES OF

CALIFORNIA, OREGON, AND NEVADA,

AND THE TERRITORIES OF

WASHINGTON, MONTANA, AND IDAHO.

ALSO, LISTS OF

Mining, Manufacturing, Petroleum, Banking, and Insurance Companies, Institutions of Learning, etc. with such other items of information as will render the work a

VALUABLE AND RELIABLE MEDIUM OF REFERENCE.

ONE VOLUME, 8 VO.

Henry G. Langley,

PUBLISHER,

612 Clay Street, San Francisco.

APPENDIX.

The Consolidation Act, with the Amendments now in Force.

AN ACT

TO REPEAL THE SEVERAL CHARTERS OF THE CITY OF SAN FRANCISCO, TO ESTAB-
LISH THE BOUNDARIES OF THE CITY AND COUNTY OF SAN FRANCISCO, AND
TO CONSOLIDATE THE GOVERNMENT THEREOF.

The People of the State of California,
Represented in Senate and Assembly, do enact as follows:

ARTICLE I.

SECTION 1. The corporation, or body politic and corporate, now existing and known as the City of San Francisco, shall remain and continue to be a body politic and corporate, in name and in fact, by the name of the City and County of San Francisco, and by that name shall have perpetual succession, may sue and defend in all courts and places, and in all matters and proceedings whatever, and may have and may use a common seal, and the same may alter at pleasure, and may purchase, receive, hold, and enjoy real and personal property, and sell, convey, mortgage, and dispose of the same for the common benefit. The boundaries of the City and County of San Francisco shall be as follows : Beginning in the Pacific Ocean, three miles from shore, and on the line (extended) of the United States survey, separating townships two and three south (Mount Diablo meridian), and thence running northerly and parallel with the shore so as to be three miles therefrom opposite Seal Rock; thence in the same general direction to a point three miles from shore, and on the northerly side of the entrance to the Bay of San Francisco ; thence to low water mark on the northerly side of the said entrance, at a point opposite Fort Point ; thence following said low water mark to a point due north-west of Golden Rock ; thence due south-east to a point within three miles of the natural high water mark on the eastern shore of the Bay of San Francisco ; thence in a southerly direction to a point three miles from said eastern shore, and on the line first named (considered as extending across said bay) ; and thence along said first-named line to the place of beginning.* The islands in said bay, known as the Alcatraces and Yerba Buena, and the islands in said ocean known as the Farallones, shall be attached to and form a part of said city and county ; *provided*, however, that all rights and liabilities of the corporation heretofore and now known as the City of San Francisco, shall survive to, and continue against, the corporations continued by this act. The district or districts of said city and county, bordering upon the southern line thereof, as heretofore established, shall be extended to the southern line of said city and county, as established in this act.—[Amendment, April 18, 1857.

SEC. 2. The public buildings, lands, and property, all rights of property and rights of action, and all moneys, revenues, and income, belonging or appertaining either to the corporation of the City of San Francisco, or to the County of San Francisco, are hereby declared to be vested in, and to appertain to, the said City and County of San Francisco ; and the moneys in the treasury of said City, and in the treasury of said County of San Francisco, and all the revenues and income from whatsoever source arising, including delinquent taxes upon persons and property appertaining to the said city or to the said county, shall be handed over, paid, and received into the treasury of the City and County of San Francisco as a part of the General Fund ; or where the said moneys, revenues, and income, or any part thereof, have been heretofore and still remain set apart and dedicated by lawful authority to the use of a Special Fund, the necessity and objects of which still continue, the same shall continue to be received, held, and disbursed for the same use, unless it is otherwise provided in this or some other act.

---

* By the Act of the Legislature, April 25, 1860, the boundaries of Marin County have been extended so as to include the islands of Los Angeles, Dos Hermanos, and Marin.—COMPILER.

SEC. 3. The records, books, and papers in the custody of the said City Treasurer, shall be handed over to and received into the custody of the Treasurer of the said city and county, and all other books, records, and papers of the said corporation, shall be delivered and received into the custody of the Clerk of the Board of Supervisors of said city and county, and shall not be withheld under any claim of a lien thereon for arrears of salary, fees, services, or advances, nor under any other pretense whatsoever. Suits and actions may be brought and maintained in the name of the City and County of San Francisco, for the recovery of any property, money, or thing belonging thereto, or the enforcement of any rights of, or contracts with, said city and county. And from any judgment rendered against the said city and county in any Court, an appeal may be taken by the said city and county, where such appeal is allowed by law, without the giving of any appeal bond or undertaking, on complying with the other requisites prescribed by law.

SEC. 4. All the existing provisions of law, defining the powers and duties of county officers, excepting those relating to Supervisors and Boards of Supervisors, so far as the same are not repealed or altered by the provisions of this act, shall be considered as applicable to officers of the said City and County of San Francisco, acting or elected under this act. Provision shall be made from the revenues of the said city and county for the payment of the legal indebtedness of the former city corporation and of the County of San Francisco. The taxes which may be levied and collected under the provisions of this act, shall be uniform throughout the said City and County of San Francisco; but in case it should hereafter be found necessary, for the purpose of providing for the said city indebtedness, to increase taxation beyond the rate of the county tax levied upon property in said County of San Francisco, during the year one thousand eight hundred and fifty-five, such increased taxation, over and above the rate aforesaid, shall be levied and assessed exclusively upon the real and personal property situated within the limits defined in the second section of the act entitled "An Act to Reincorporate the City of San Francisco," passed May fifth, one thousand eight hundred and fifty-five, and not upon such property situated without those limits.

SEC. 5. ˙ Immediately after the passage of this act, the present City Attorney, Surveyor-General, and C. K. Garrison, shall proceed to lay off the said city and county into twelve convenient districts, equal in population as near as conveniently may be, giving a distinct name to each district, the boundaries of which they shall accurately define by reference to public streets, roads, or other permanent monuments, and shall cause a map to be made representing the said districts, with their names and boundaries so fixed. The act of said officers establishing said districts, signed by them or a majority of them, shall be recorded in the office of the County Recorder of said city and county, and the original deposited in the office of the County Clerk, and the map shall be deposited with the said County Surveyor. Each of said districts shall constitute an election precinct.

SEC. 6. [Amended April 18 and 29, 1857, April 22 and May 3, 1861, and May 2, 1862 :] There shall be elected, hereafter, for the City and County of San Francisco, by the qualified electors thereof at the time thereinafter mentioned, and in the manner prescribed by law for the election of State and county officers, one Mayor, who shall be *ex officio* President of the Board of Supervisors; a County Judge, County Clerk, Police Judge, Chief of Police, Sheriff, Coroner, Recorder, Treasurer, Auditor, Tax Collector, Assessor, Public Administrator, Surveyor, Superintendent of Common Schools, Superintendent of Public Streets and Highways, District Attorney, and Harbor Master, who shall continue in office for two years next after their election and qualification, unless otherwise provided for in this act. There shall be elected in each of the twelve election districts of said city and county, by the qualified electors thereof, one Supervisor and one School Director ; and in each of the six townships of said city and county, one Justice of the Peace and one Constable, who shall continue in office for two years ;* and in each of the twelve districts, one Inspector and two Judges of Elections, who shall continue in office for one year, and until their successors are elected and qualified.—[Act April 22, 1861, Sec. 1.] And all vacancies in the office of Supervisor or School Director, where the term of the office will not expire at the next ensuing general election, shall be then filled by an election, in the proper district, for the unexpired term ; and for the interval between the happening of any such vacancy and the general election next ensuing, any vacancy in the office of Supervisor shall be filled by appointment by the President of the Board of Supervisors, by and with the advice and consent of a majority of the Supervisors then in office ; and any vacancy in the office of School Director shall be filled by appointment by the Superintendent of Common Schools, by and with the advice and consent of a majority of the School Directors then in office ; and such appointees shall hold office respectively until the general election next ensuing,

* Justices of the Peace shall be elected by the electors of their respective townships or cities, at the special elections to be held for the election of Justices of the Supreme Court, and shall hold their offices for two years from the first day of January next following their election. All vacancies to be filled by appointment of the Board of Supervisors of the County.—*Act April 20, 1863.*

and the election and qualification of their successors in office. But no such appointment shall be valid unless the appointee be, at the time of his appointment, an elector of the district wherein the vacancy occurred.—[Act April 29, 1857.] All elections for city and county officers, under this act. shall be held in said city and county on the third Tuesday of May in each year ; the first of which elections shall be held on the third Tuesday of May, eighteen hundred and sixty-one, at which time, and every two years thereafter,* there shall be elected a Mayor, who shall be *ex officio* President of the Board of Supervisors; County Clerk, Sheriff, Coroner, District Attorney, Recorder, Treasurer, Assessor, Surveyor, Superintendent of Common Schools, and Harbor Master ; also, in the second, fourth, sixth, eighth, tenth, and twelfth districts, by the qualified electors thereof, one Supervisor and one School Director. There shall also be elected, at the first election under this act, and every year thereafter, in each of the twelve districts,† one Inspector and two Judges of Elections, who shall be elected in the manner prescribed in section two of " An Act amendatory of and supplementary to an Act to repeal the several Charters of the City of San Francisco, to establish the Boundaries of the City and County of San Francisco, and to consolidate the Government thereof," approved April eighteenth, eighteen hundred and fifty-seven.—[Act April 22, 1861, Sec. 2.] In all elections for Inspectors and Judges of Elections, each qualified voter shall vote for one Inspector and one Judge of Election only, and the person having the highest number of votes for Inspector shall be declared 'elected Inspector, and the two having the highest number of votes for Judges shall be the Judges of Elections for the respective districts. There shall also be elected, at the general election‡ next preceding the expiration of the terms of the present Justices for the said city and county, six Justices of the Peace and six Constables. For that purpose, the Board of Supervisors shall lay off the city and county into six townships, in such manner as not to divide any district in the formation of such township, in each of which townships there shall be elected, by the qualified electors thereof, one Justice of the Peace and one Constable, to continue in office two years, and until their successors are elected and qualified. The Justices of the Peace so elected shall have jurisdiction coextensive with the city and county, but shall hold their Courts within the townships for which they were chosen respectively.—[Act April 18, 1857.] At the second election held under this act, on the third Tuesday of May, eighteen hundred and sixty-two, and every two years thereafter, there shall be elected a Police Judge, Chief of Police, Auditor, Tax Collector, Public Administrator, and Superintendent of Public Streets and Highways; and in each of the six townships, one Justice of the Peace and one Constable; and in the first, third, fifth, seventh, ninth, and eleventh districts, one Supervisor and one School Director ; and at the election next preceding the expiration of the term of office of the present incumbent, a County Judge, who shall continue in office for four years, and until his successor is elected and qualified.—[Amended, Act May 3, 1861.] The Police Judge, Chief of Police, Auditor, Tax Collector, Public Administrator, Superintendent of Public Streets and Highways, Justices of the Peace,§ Constables, Supervisors, and School Directors, who shall be elected for the City and County of San Francisco at the election to be held on the third Tuesday of May, in the year eighteen hundred and sixty-two, shall hold their office from the time of the expiration of the terms of office of their immediate predecessors, and until the first of July in the year eighteen hundred and sixty-four, or until their successors are elected and qualified.—[Act May 2, 1862.] The official terms of all officers elected under this act are hereby declared to commence on the first day of July next succeeding their election, excepting, however, that of the Assessor, whose official term shall commence on the first day of September ; and any and all of the present city and county officers, whose official terms shall not have expired previous to the first two elections provided for in this act, shall continue in office during the entire term for which they were elected ; *provided*, that their successors shall not continue in office after the first day of July, eighteen hundred and sixty-three, or until their successors are elected and qualified ; and no officer elected or appointed to fill a vacancy which may, in any manner, occur, shall serve only except during the balance of. the unexpired term of his predecessor.—[Act April 22, 1861, Sec 4.] It is hereby made the duty of the Mayor, to issue his proclamation, by publication in not less than three daily newspapers published in said city and county, at least ten days previous to the third Tuesday of May, in each year, calling upon the qualified voters of said city and county to meet in their respective districts for the purpose of electing such officers as are provided for in this act, reciting in such proclamation, the different officers to be elected at such election.—[Act April 22, 1861, Sec. 5.]

SEC. 7. By the term "qualification of officers," as used in this act, is to be understood their having taken the oath of office, given the official bond, where it is required by law, and complied with all the requisites prescribed by the statutes of this State, to entitle and qualify them to exercise the functions of their offices.

* A State Harbor Commissioner, who shall hold his office for two years, shall be elected at the election for municipal officers in May, 1863. The term of his successor shall be four years.—*Act April 24, 1863.*
† The Act of April 4, 1864, authorizes the Board of Supervisors to divide the Twelfth Election District into two voting precincts.   ‡ Amended. See Note, page 532.   § Amended. See Note, page 532.

SEC. 8. The Sheriff, County Clerk,* County Recorder, Treasurer, District Attorney, Auditor, Tax Collector, Superintendent of Public Streets and Highways, Surveyor, Harbor Master, and Clerk of the Board of Supervisors of said city and county, shall keep public offices, which shall be kept open for the transaction of business every day in the year except Sundays, Christmas, New Year's, Fourth of July, Thanksgiving, the twenty-second of February, and on any days during which a general election shall be held, between the hours of nine o'clock, A.M. and four o'clock, P.M.—[Amendment May 14, 1861.]

SEC. 9. Whenever vacancies occur in any elective office of the said city and county, and provision is not otherwise made in this or some other act for filling the same until the next election, the Board of Supervisors shall appoint a person to discharge the duties of such office until the next election, when the vacancy shall be filled by election for the term. All persons so appointed shall, before entering upon their duties, take the oath of office and give bond as required by law. But in an action or proceeding where the Sheriff of said city and county is a party, or is interested, or otherwise incapacitated to execute the orders or process therein, the same shall be executed by a suitable person, residing in said city and county, to be appointed by the Court, and denominated an "Elisor," who shall give such security as the Court in its discretion may require, and shall execute the process and orders in the same manner as the Sheriff is required to execute similar process and orders in other cases.†

SECS. 10 and 11.—[Amended April 18, 1857 and May 17, 1861] : Salaries shall be allowed and paid to the following officers of the City and County of San Francisco, as in this act provided, and not otherwise, and shall be in full compensation for all official services required of them by law :

To the County Judge, five thousand dollars per annum.

To Associate Justices of the Court of Sessions, five dollars per day for each day's actual attendance, not to exceed six hundred dollars per annum each.

SUPPLEMENTAL I.—*An Act providing for an Attorney and Counselor in and for the City and County of San Francisco.*—Approved March 25, 1862.

SECTION 1. There shall be elected, hereafter, for the City and County of San Francisco, by the qualified electors thereof, on the third Tuesday of May, eighteen hundred and sixty-two, and every two years thereafter, one Attorney and Counselor, learned in the law, who shall hold his office for two years, and until his successor shall have been duly elected and qualified, and shall be paid by said city and county, a salary of five thousand dollars per annum, to be audited and paid monthly, in the same manner as the salary of the County Judge is by law audited and paid. Said Attorney and Counselor shall perform such duties as Attorney and Counselor in and for the said city and county as the Board of Supervisors of said city and county shall from time to time prescribe.—[Amendment, Act April 27, 1863.]

To the District Attorney, five thousand dollars per annum.—[Amendment April 4, 1863.]

To the Clerk of the District Attorney, one hundred and twenty-five dollars per month.—[Amendment April 4, 1863.]

To the Police Judge, four thousand dollars per annum.

To the Clerk of the Police Court, two hundred dollars per month.

To the Prosecuting Attorney for the Police Court, two hundred and fifty dollars per month.

To three [Act April 4, 1864] Interpreters and Translators of foreign languages, to be appointed by the County Judge, Police Judge, and President of the Board of Supervisors, if they deem them necessary, one hundred and twenty-five dollars each per month, subject, however, to be reduced by an order of the Board of Supervisors, if in their opinion such reduction is proper.

To the City and County Attorney, five thousand dollars per annum.

To the Clerk of the City and County Attorney, one hundred and twenty-five dollars per month.—[Amendment April 4, 1863.]

To the County Clerk, four thousand dollars per annum.

To the Deputy County Clerks ‡ for the Twelfth District Court, as follows :

To one Register Clerk, one hundred and seventy-five dollars per month.

To one Court Room Clerk, one hundred and seventy-five dollars per month.

To one Copying Clerk, one hundred and fifty dollars per month.

To the Deputy County Clerks for the Fourth District Court, as follows :

To one Court Room Clerk, one hundred and seventy-five dollars per month.

To one Register Clerk, one hundred and seventy-five dollars per month.

To one Copying Clerk, one hundred and fifty dollars per month.

---

* The Act of March 16, 1863, fix the hours of the County Clerk and County Recorder, from nine o'clock, A.M. to five o'clock, P.M.—COMPILER.
† By the act of the Legislature, Feb. 19, 1859, the Coroner is authorized to act as an "Elisor."
‡ The Deputy Clerks for the Fifteenth District Court are provided for by resolution of the Board of Supervisors.

·To the Deputy County Clerks for the County Court, Court of Sessions, and Probate Court, as follows:

The County Clerk may appoint two Deputies for the County Court, one of whom shall receive a salary of one hundred and seventy-five dollars per month, and the other a salary of one hundred and fifty dollars per month. The said County Clerk may also appoint two Deputies for the Probate Court, one of whom shall receive a salary of one hundred and seventy-five dollars per month, and the other a salary of one hundred and fifty dollars per month. [Amendment March 2, 1864.]

[SUPPLEMENTAL II.—*An Act concerning the Office of County Clerk of the City and County of San Francisco.*—Approved May 15, 1862.

SECTION 1. The County Clerk of the City and County of San Francisco is hereby authorized to employ, from time to time, as many copyists as he, the said County Clerk, may deem necessary to perform promptly the duties of his office, who shall be paid at a rate not exceeding six cents per folio of one hundred words, for each and every folio of all matter either recorded or copied by him ; *provided*, that the amount so expended in any one month shall not exceed the sum of one hundred and fifty dollars.

SEC. 2. The said County Clerk shall certify, monthly, under oath, the number of folios copied by each one of said copyists, and such certificate of said Clerk shall be conclusive and sufficient evidence to authorize and require the Auditor of said city and county to audit severally the accounts of said copyists, monthly, and the payments of said demands by the County Treasurer out of the Special Fee Fund, as is provided for the payment of other officers of said city and county.]

To the Sheriff, eight thousand dollars per annum.

To one Under Sheriff, two hundred dollars per month.

To six Deputy Sheriffs, each one hundred and fifty dollars per month.—[Amendment April 4, 1864.]

To four Deputies, acting as Jail-Keepers, each one hundred and twenty-five dollars per month.

To one Book-Keeper for the Sheriff's office, one hundred and fifty dollars per month.

The Sheriff may appoint, if deemed necessary by the Board of Supervisors, a Matron and Assistant Matron for the female department of the County Jail, at a salary not exceeding one hundred dollars per month.—[Act April 4, 1864.]

To the Coroner,* four thousand dollars per annum ; he shall also be allowed and paid, as fees, fifty dollars per month, for chemical analyses, and ten dollars for each interment made by him—[Act of April 8, 1862] ; and he shall likewise receive for the interment of deceased persons payment at the same rate, each, as is allowed for the interment of deceased hospital patients in said city and county, not to exceed ten dollars for each interment made by him. The compensation allowed by this act shall be paid out of the General Fund, and shall be audited and paid in the same manner as the salaries of officers for the said city and county ; *provided*, that the said Coroner shall make oath that he has received no compensation for any of the items charged in his demand ; and that the interments charged in his demand, if any have been made by him, and that the bodies interred were proper subjects for burial by the Coroner.—[Act Feb. 19, 1859.]

To the Mayor, three thousand dollars per annum.

To the Clerk of the Mayor, one hundred and fifty dollars per month.—[Amendment, April 4, 1864.]

To the City and County Surveyor, five hundred dollars per annum, which shall be in lieu of all fees or other charges for official services, which would otherwise be a city and county charge, and he shall charge and collect, for services rendered individuals, such fees as may be prescribed and allowed by the Board of Supervisors.

The Assessor shall receive, for all services required of him by law, a salary at the rate of four thousand dollars per annum, which salary shall be in full for all services required of him, and for all contingent expenses of his office, except necessary books ; and he shall devote his whole time, during office hours, to the business of his office, and shall keep his office open to the public during the same hours provided by law for the City and County Auditor. To assist him in making his assessments, he shall be allowed, from the first of February in each year until the first of May, seven Deputies, and from the first of May until the assessment roll is finally completed and handed over to the Auditor, he shall be allowed but three Deputies, after which time, during the balance of the year, he shall be allowed one Deputy only, except as hereinafter provided. The said Deputies shall be paid at the rate of one hundred and fifty dollars per month each.†

In addition to the number now provided by law, the Assessor shall be allowed, at such times as he

---

* The salary of the Coroner, after the expiration of the present term, is fixed at two thousand dollars per annum, and a sum not exceeding fifty dollars per month for chemical analyses. He shall likewise receive, for the interment of deceased persons, the same rate each as is allowed for hospital patients, not exceeding ten dollars each.—*Act March 13, 1864.*

† The Act of April 4, 1864, allows a salary of two hundred dollars per month to be paid to the Chief Clerk or Deputy Assessor.

may require, between the first day of February and the first day of July in each year, five Deputies; the term for which such additional Deputies shall be paid shall not exceed an average of three months each, at a salary not exceeding one hundred and fifty dollars per month each.—[Act February 6, 1864.] The Assessor shall also be allowed such Deputies as he may require to collect poll taxes, who shall be allowed for their services only such fees and per centages as may be allowed by law for the collection of poll taxes.

To the Clerk of the Board of Supervisors, two hundred dollars per month.—[Amendment April 4, 1863.]

To three Porters,* not to exceed seventy-five dollars each per month.—[Act April 4, 1864.]

To the Auditor, four thousand dollars per annum.

To one Clerk of Auditor, one hundred and twenty-five dollars per month.

To the Tax Collector, four thousand dollars per annum.† During the entire year the Tax Collector shall be allowed two Deputies—one at two hundred dollars per month, and one at one hundred and seventy-five dollars per month; during six months he shall be allowed two Clerks, in addition to said Deputies, and during five months he shall be allowed three additional Clerks. Said clerks shall be paid at the rate of one hundred and fifty dollars per month, each. He shall also be allowed one Auctioneer, to conduct tax sales, whose compensation for sales of real estate delinquent for taxes, in any one year, shall not exceed the sum of two hundred dollars. All fees, commissions, per centages, and other compensation, of whatever nature or kind, heretofore allowed by law, or which may hereafter be allowed by law, as the compensation of the Tax Collector of said city and county, for the collection of State and County taxes, shall be paid into the Special Fee Fund.—[Amendment April 10, 1862.]

To the Treasurer, four thousand dollars per annum.

To one Deputy Treasurer, one hundred and seventy-five dollars per month; and to one additional Deputy, one hundred and twenty-five dollars per month.—[Amendment April 4, 1863.]

To the County Recorder, four thousand dollars per annum.

To one Chief Deputy Recorder, one hundred and seventy-five dollars per month.—[Act of April 26, 1862.] For an additional Deputy, one hundred and fifty dollars per month.—[Amendment April 4, 1863.] The Recorder may also employ as many Deputy Clerks as he may deem necessary to duly perform the duties of his office, and they shall be paid at the rate of twelve cents per folio of one hundred words for all matters either registered or copied by them respectively. The Recorder or his Chief Deputy, when any papers are presented for registration, or to be copied, shall write on the margin of each paper so presented the number of folios paid for; and shall, in his monthly return to the Treasurer, certify under oath the number of folios copied or registered by each one of said Deputy Clerks; and such certificate of the Recorder or his Chief Deputy shall be conclusive evidence to authorize the Auditor to audit such certified accounts of such Deputy Clerks, monthly.

To one Porter, or Watchman, for the Recorder's Office, not to exceed seventy-five dollars per month.

To the Harbor Master, three thousand dollars per annum.

To the Superintendent of Common Schools, four thousand dollars per annum.

To the Clerk of the Superintendent of Common Schools, who shall also act as Secretary of the Board of Education, one hundred and twenty-five dollars per month, payable from the School Fund, as now provided for by law.

To the Superintendent of Public Streets and Highways, four thousand dollars per annum.

To the Deputies of the Superintendent of Streets and Highways,‡ one hundred and fifty dollars per month, each.

FIRE DEPARTMENT.

To the Chief Engineer, four thousand dollars per annum.

To the First, Second, and Third Assistant engineers, each fifty dollars per month.

To the Secretary of the Board of Delegates, as such, and also as Clerk of the Chief Engineer, one hundred and fifty dollars per month.

POLICE DEPARTMENT.

To Chief of Police, four thousand dollars per annum.

To four Captains of Police one hundred and fifty dollars per month, each.

To Policemen, not exceeding one hundred, the number to be determined from time to time by order of the Board of Supervisors, one hundred and twenty-five dollars per month, each.—[Act April 4, 1864]; provided, that one of the same, detailed for Clerk in the office of the Chief of Police, to be appointed by him, shall receive one hundred and fifty dollars per month.

* To the principal Porter, ninety dollars per month.—Act April 4, 1864.
† And fees on delinquent taxes, poll taxes, and levies on delinquent personal property.—COMPILER.
‡ The act of April 28, 1862, allows the Superintendent of Streets and Highways, at the discretion of the Board of Supervisors, not less than three nor more than five Deputies, to be by him appointed from time to time.

To the Resident Physician of the City and County Hospital, two hundred dollars per month, in full compensation for all duties as such, and also for his attendance on the Small-Pox Hospital, County Jail, and City Prison.—[Act May 17, 1861, Sec. 1.]

To the Visiting Physician and Surgeon of the County Hospital, one hundred dollars per month, each.—[Act April 27, 1860.]

The several officers named in this act, who are entitled to charge and collect, or receive any fees, commissions, per centages, or other compensation, of whatever nature or kind, allowed by law for services rendered by them or their Deputies, in their several official capacities, or for the performance of duties appertaining to said offices, shall collect and safely keep the same, and on each Monday they shall pay the total amount by them received to the Treasurer of said city and county, who shall set apart the same as a Special Fee Fund, for the payment of the respective salaries of the several officers entitled to charge and collect fees, commmissions, or other compensation. And the salaries of all other officers shall be paid out of the General Fund ; *provided*, that the Assessor, so far as relates to the collection of poll tax, and the City and County Surveyor, shall be exempt from the provisions of this section. It shall be, and is hereby made, the duty of all such officers who are entitled to charge and collect or receive fees, commissions, or other compensation for their official services, to keep a book or books, in which shall be entered by items the amount received for all official services performed by them or their Deputies, showing the date and nature of such services, and the amount received therefor, which book or books shall, at all office hours, be open to the inspection of the Board of Supervisors or any citizen ; and each of said officers shall, at the expiration of each month, make out and verify by oath, and file with the Auditor, a full and accurate transcript, from his said book or books, of the entries for the preceding month.—[Act May 17, 1861, Sec. 2.] It shall be the duty of the Treasurer of said city and county to receive, receipt for, and safely keep all moneys paid over to him under the provisions of this act, and to make up, on the first day of October, eighteen hundred and sixty-one, and quarterly thereafter, an accurate statement of said Special Fee Fund, showing the actual condition of the same up to such time, when, if any balance remain in said fund, after satisfying all demands payable out of the same, the Treasurer shall transfer such balance to the General Fund ; but should such Special Fee Fund be insufficient to satisfy all of the demands payable therefrom, then the Treasurer shall, at the request of the holder, register such unpaid demands against, and pay the same in their order of registration out of the General Fund, as in other cases.—[Act May 17, 1861, Sec. 3.] All demands upon the treasury, allowed by this Act, shall, before they are authorized to be paid, be duly audited, as in other cases of demands lawfully payable out of the treasury. The several salaries named shall be payable monthly by the Treasurer upon the audit of the County Auditor, who is hereby directed to audit the salaries herein provided for.—[Act May 17, 1861, Sec. 4.] The Board of Supervisors may, from time to time, authorize the appointment of such additional Deputies, for any of the various city and county offices, and for such period of time as in their judgment may be necessary for the proper and faithful discharge of the duties of such office. Deputies appointed under the provisions of this section, shall receive not to exceed one hundred and fifty dollars per month, each ; but in no case shall the aggregate pay of such Deputies exceed three thousand dollars per annum.—[Act May 17, 1861, Sec. 5.] The fees receivable by the several officers named in this act, shall be payable in advance.—[Act May 17, 1861, Sec. 6.] It shall be the duty of the Sheriff to bestow the advertising of his office on either of the three daily papers having the largest circulation in the county, who will do the same at the lowest rates. He shall, every six months, publish three successive times in one or more daily papers published in the County of San Francisco, for such bids, and the daily paper offering to do the work at the lowest price shall be awarded the contract for such advertising ; *provided*, it be one of the three papers having the largest circulation, and the proprietors or Chief Clerk of said papers are hereby required to verify, under oath, the amount of their circulation ; and, *provided*, also, that no bids so made shall exceed seventy-five cents for one square of three hundred ems for the first insertion, and fifteen cents for each subsequent insertion. Should the proprietors of the aforesaid papers decline to do said advertising at the prices as aforesaid, then the Sheriff shall advertise and give the same to the daily papers published in the English language offering the most favorable terms for doing such advertising.—[Amendment March 1, 1864.] For a willful neglect, or refusal to comply with any of the provisions of this act, by any officer or officers herein named, he or they shall be deemed guilty of felony, and, on conviction thereof, in the Court of Sessions, be subject to a fine not to exceed five thousand dollars, and a forfeiture of office, or to imprisonment in the State Prison not less than one nor more than three years, or to both such fine and imprisonment; *provided*, that nothing herein shall be held to release such officer from the obligation to give the official bond required by law, or from any civil responsibility arising from his official duties.—[Act May 17, 1861, Sec. 8.] All requisitions for books, blanks, and stationery, for any of the offices named in this act, shall be made by such officers respectively, upon the Board of Supervisors, stating the amount and description thereof, and that the same are essential and necessary for the use of such office, which statement shall be verified by the oath of such officer, and, upon their approval thereof, the said Board shall order the cost of the same paid out of the Special Fee Fund.—[Act May 17, 1861, Sec. 9.] The Inspectors, Judges, and Clerks of Elections, shall be paid out of the General Fund, such reasonable compensation for their services as such, as may be fixed and allowed by the Board of Supervisors, not exceeding twenty-five dollars each for all services at any one election.—[Act May 17, 1861, Sec. 10.]

SEC. 12. Neither the Board of Supervisors, the Board of Education, or any officer of the said city and county, or of any district, shall have any power to contract any debt or liability, in any form whatsoever, against the said city and county; nor shall the people or tax-payers, or any property therein, ever be liable to be assessed for, or on account of, any debt or liability hereafter contracted, or supposed or attempted to be contracted, in contravention of this section.

SEC. 13. Balie Peyton, E. J. Moore, J. B. Crockett, Louis McLane, Jr., and E. R. Carpentier, shall appoint, in each of the districts to be erected in said city and county, as aforesaid, one Inspector and two Judges of Election, by whom the first election under this act shall be held. The term of office of all officers elected under this act, shall commence on Monday following the day of election, unless otherwise already provided by law. [Amended, see Sec. 6.]

SEC. 14. All officers of the said city and county must, before they can enter upon their official duties, give bond as required by law. The bonds and sureties of such officers must be approved by the County Judge, Auditor, and President of the Board of Supervisors. Where the amount of such official bond is not fixed by law, it shall be fixed by the Board of Supervisors. No banker residing or doing business in said city and county, nor any such banker's partner, clerk, employé, agent, attorney, father, son, or brother, shall be received as surety for the Treasurer, President of the Board of Supervisors, Sheriff, Auditor, nor any officer having the collection, custody, or disbursement of money. No person can be admitted as surety on any such bond, unless he be worth, in fixed property, including mortgages, situated in said city and county, the amount of his undertaking, over and above all sums for which he is already liable, or in any manner bound, whether as principal, indorser, or security, and whether such prior obligation or liability be conditional or absolute, liquidated or unliquidated, certain or contingent, due or to become due. All persons offered as sureties on official bonds may be examined on oath touching their qualifications. The official bond of the Auditor shall be filed and kept in the office of the Clerk of said city and county. All other official bonds shall be filed and kept in the office of the Auditor. All officers continued in office under this act shall be required to execute new bonds, conformable to laws heretofore existing, and in case of default on the part of any officer of doing so within two days after the first meeting of the Board of Supervisors, the said Board shall declare his office vacant.—[Amendment March 28, 1859.]

ARTICLE II.
PUBLIC ORDER AND POLICE.

SEC. 15. The Department of Police of said city and county shall be under the direction of the Chief of Police, in subjection to the laws of this State, and the rules and regulations, not in conflict therewith, which may be established by competent authority, under the powers granted in this act. In the suppression of any riot, public tumult, disturbance of the public peace, or organized resistance against the laws, or public authorities in the lawful exercise of their functions, he shall have all the powers that now are, or may hereafter be conferred upon Sheriffs by the laws of this State, and his lawful orders shall be promptly executed by all Police officers, Watchmen, and Constables, in the said city and county; and every citizen shall also lend him aid, when required, for the arrest of offenders and maintenance of public order.

SEC. 16. The Chief of Police shall keep a public office, which shall be open, and at which he, or in case of his necessary absence, a Captain of Police, or Police Officer, by him designated for that purpose, shall be in attendance at all hours, day and night. In case of his necessary absence from his office, it shall be made known to the Police Officer in attendance where he can be found, if needed, and he shall not absent himself from the city and county without urgent necessity, and leave obtained in writing from the President of the Board of Supervisors, Police Judge, and County Judge, or two of them, who shall, at the time of granting the same, appoint a person to act during his absence, with all his powers, duties, and obligations. If such absence from the city or county be on any other than business immediately connected with his office, he shall lose his salary for the time of such absence, of which account shall be taken by the Police Judge.

SEC. 17. The Chief of Police shall designate one or more out of the number of Police Officers to attend constantly upon the Police Judge's Court, to execute the orders and process of the said Court; he may order to be arrested and to be taken before the Police Judge, any person guilty of a breach of the peace or a violation of the general regulations established by the Board of Supervisors under the authority granted in this act; he shall supervise and direct the Police force of said city and county, and shall observe and cause to be observed the provisions of this act and the regulations established by the Board of Supervisors in relation thereto ; he shall see that the lawful orders and process issued by the Police Judge's Court are promptly executed ; and shall exercise such other powers connected with his office as head of Police, as may be prescribed in the general regulations adopted by the Board of Supervisors.

SEC. 18. The Chief of Police shall acquaint himself with all the statutes and laws in force in this State defining public offenses and nuisances and regulating criminal proceedings, and shall procure and keep in his office the statutes of this State and of the United States, and all necessary elementary works on that subject ; he shall give information and advice touching said laws, gratuitously, to all Police officers and Magistrates asking it.

SEC. 19. Repealed by the following :

SUPPLEMENTAL III.—*An Act to prescribe the Jurisdiction of the Police Judge's Court of the City and County of San Francisco.*—Approved January 27, 1864.

The Police Judge's Court of the City and County of San Francisco shall have jurisdiction :
First. Of an action or proceeding for the violation of any ordinance of the City and County of San Francisco.
Second. Of proceedings respecting vagrants and disorderly persons.

The said Court shall have jurisdiction of the following public offenses when committed in the said city and county :
First. Petit larceny, receiving stolen property, when the amount involved does not exceed fifty dollars
Second. Assault and battery, not charged to have been committed upon a public officer in the discharge of his duties, or with intent to kill.
Third. Breaches of the peace, riots, affrays, committing willful injury to property, and all misdemeanors punishable by fine not exceeding five hundred dollars, or imprisonment not exceeding six months, or by both such fine and imprisonment.

The Justices of the Peace within the limits of the City and County of San Francisco shall not have power to try and decide any cases of the classes mentioned in this section.

The Judge of said Court shall also have power to hear cases for examination, and may commit and hold the offender to bail for trial in the proper Court, and may try, condemn, or acquit, and carry his judgment into execution, as the case may require according to law, and shall have power to issue warrants of arrests, subpenas, and all other process necessary to the full and proper exercise of his power and jurisdiction. All fines imposed by the Police Judge not exceeding twenty dollars, exclusive of costs, shall be final and without appeal.   *   *
His Court shall be a Court of Record ;* a Clerk shall be appointed therefor by the Board of Supervisors, with a salary of two hundred dollars per month, who shall give bond as required by law, and hold his office during the pleasure of said Board.—[Amendments, April 18, 1857, and March 25, 1862.]

SEC. 20. Proceedings in the Police Judge's Court shall be conducted in conformity with the laws regulating proceedings in the Recorder's Court. The said Court shall be open daily, Sundays excepted, and may be held by any Justice of the Peace of the city and county, in case of the temporary absence of the Police Judge or his temporary inability to act from any cause. In case of a vacancy in the office of Police Judge, the Board of Supervisors shall have power to appoint any Justice of the Peace of said city and county to fill the vacancy until the next election, when the office shall be filled by election for a full term.

SEC. 21. The Clerk of the Police Judge's Court shall keep a record of its proceedings, issue all process ordered by said Court, receive and pay weekly into the treasury of the city and county all fines imposed by said Court, and render to the County Auditor, monthly, and before any amount can be paid him on account of salary, an exact and detailed account, upon oath, accompanied with an exhibition of said record, of all fines imposed and moneys collected since his last account rendered. He shall prepare bonds, justify and accept bail, when the amount has been fixed by the Police Judge, in cases not exceeding one thousand dollars, and he shall fix, justify, and accept bail, after arrest, in the absence of the Police Judge, in all cases not amounting to felony, in the same manner and to the same effect as though the same had been fixed by the Police Judge. The said Clerk shall remain at the court-room of said Court, in the City Hall, during the hours named in section eight of the act of which this is amendatory, and during such reasonable hours thereafter as may be necessary for the purpose of discharging his said duties.—[Amendment May 18, 1861, Sec. 1.]

SEC. 22. All fines imposed by the Police Judge's Court, Court of Sessions of said city and county, or any Justice's Court, shall be paid into the treasury thereof, as part of the Police Fund ; in cases where, for any offense, the said Courts are authorized to impose a fine or imprisonment in the county jail, or both, they may, instead thereof, sentence the offender to be

---

* Declared not to be a Court of Record.—*Act April 27, 1863.*

employed in labor upon the public works of said city and county, for a period of time equal to the term of imprisonment which might be legally imposed, and may, in case of imposing a fine, embrace as a part of the sentence, that in default of payment of such fine, the offender shall be employed to labor on said public works at one dollar a day till the fine imposed is satisfied. By the "public works," as used in this act, is understood the construction, or repair, or cleaning, of any street, road, dock, wharf, public square, park, building, or other works whatsoever, which is authorized to be done by and for the use of the said city and county, and the expense of which is not to be borne exclusively by the individuals or property particularly benefited thereby.

Sec. 23. The Chief of Police, in conjunction with the President of the Board of Supervisors and the Police Judge, the concurrence of two of them being necessary to a choice, shall appoint four Captains of Police, each from a different district, and as many Police Officers, not exceeding one hundred, [Amendment April 4, 1864] as the Board of Supervisors shall determine to be necessary.* Thereof an equal number in proportion to population, as near as may be, shall be selected from each district that shall be situated, wholly or partly, within the limits specified in section second of the act now repealed, entitled "An Act to Re-Incorporate the City of San Francisco," passed May sixth, one thousand eight hundred and fifty-five.

Sec. 24. No person can be appointed Captain of Police or Police Officer, unless he be a citizen of the United States and of this State, and a resident and a qualified voter of the city and county; and, in case of each Police Officer, a resident of the district from which he is chosen, and also before his appointment, shall produce to the said President of the Board of Supervisors, Chief of Police, and Police Judge, a certificate signed by at least twelve freeholders and qualified voters of the said city and county, who, in case of application for appointment of a Police Officer, must also be residents of the district from which he is to be appointed, stating that they have been personally and well acquainted with the applicant for one year or more, next preceding the application, and that he is of good repute for honesty and sobriety, and they believe him to be, in all respects, competent and fit for the office. All the certificates so produced, shall be carefully preserved in the office of Chief of Police.

Sec. 25. Police Captains and Officers may be suspended from office by the Chief of Police, and, with the concurrence of the President of the Board of Supervisors and Police Judge, removed from office for official negligence, inefficiency, or misconduct, under such general rules and regulations, not contrary to law, as may have been established by the Board of Supervisors; they shall receive from the treasury of said city and county, payable out of the Police Fund, such compensation as may be fixed by the Board of Supervisors, not exceeding one thousand eight hundred dollars a year, each, for Captains, and one thousand two hundred dollars a year, each, for Police Officers.†

Sec. 26. Neither the Chief of Police, Captains, or any officer of Police, shall follow any other profession or calling, become bail for any person charged with any offense whatever, receive any present or reward for official services rendered, or to be rendered, unless with the knowledge and approbation of a majority of the Police Commissioners, to wit: the Police Judge, President of the Board of Supervisors, and Chief of Police of the City and County of San Francisco—such approbation to be given in writing; nor be allowed pay for any period during which they shall absent themselves from public duty, unless such absence necessarily result from indisposition or disability occasioned by injuries suffered while in the discharge of official duty. Police Officers in subjection to the orders of the respective Captains, and all under the general direction of the Chief of Police, shall be prompt and vigilant in the detection of crime, the arrest of public offenders, the suppression of all riots, frays, duels, and disturbances of the public peace, the execution of process from the Police Judge's Court, in causing the abatement of public nuisances, the removal of unlawful obstructions from the public streets, and the enforcement of the laws and regulations of Police—[Amendment March 24, 1859.]

Sec. 27. In case of great public emergency or danger, the Chief of Police may appoint an additional number of Policemen, of approved character for honesty and sobriety, who shall have the same powers as other Police Officers for twenty-four hours only, but without pay. The Chief of Police, Captains, and every officer of the permanent force, shall provide themselves with a uniform and badge of office, to be prescribed by regulations of the Board of Supervisors, which shall be worn by them upon all occasions, with such exceptions as may be permitted by the Chief of Police in the performance of detective duty.

Sec. 28. Charges of oppression or official misconduct, when presented by any citizen of the said city and county, against any Police Captain or officer, and verified on oath, setting forth the specific acts complained of, shall be received and attentively considered and determined by the Police Judge, President of the Board of Supervisors, and Chief of Police, giving to the accused due notice, and an impartial hearing in defense. The Chief of Police, Police Judge, and

---

* The Police Commissioners may be empowered by the Board of Supervisors to appoint and regulate local Policemen whenever necessary, provided that no money shall be paid out of the city and county treasury for their services.—[Act April 4, 1864.
† Salary of officers increased to $1,500 per annum.—Act April 4, 1863.

all other officers now acting or hereafter to be elected or appointed under the provisions of this act, may be accused, tried, and removed from office in the mode prescribed by the laws of this State for the removal of civil officers otherwise than by impeachment.

SEC. 29. The Board of Supervisors shall, from time to time, establish a convenient number of Police Stations; determine within what districts the Police Officers and Captains shall usually be distributed and employed; designate the prisons to be used for the reception of all persons arrested or convicted and sentenced for public offenses, in cases not provided for by law; [and] appoint, during the pleasure of the Board, the keeper of such prisons.

SUPPLEMENTAL IV.—*An Act to provide for a Police Contingent Fund.*—Approved February 28, 1859.

SECTION 1. The Board of Supervisors of the City and County of San Francisco, shall annually set apart from the General Fund, in the treasury of said city and county, the sum of three thousand six hundred dollars, to constitute a special fund, to be called the Police Contingent Fund.

SEC. 2. The Police Commissioners of the City and County of San Francisco, or a majority of them, are hereby authorized to allow, out of the Police Contingent Fund of said city and county, any and all orders signed by the Chief of Police of said city and county; *provided,* that the aggregate of said orders shall not exceed the sum of three thousand six hundred dollars per annum.

SEC. 3. The Auditor of said city and county is hereby authorized to audit, and the Treasurer of said city and county to pay, out of the Police Contingent Fund, any and all orders so allowed by the Police Commissioners, not exceeding, in the aggregate, the sum of three thousand six hundred dollars per annum.

SEC. 4. At the end of each fiscal year, any sum remaining in the Police Contingent Fund, upon which no order shall [have] been allowed, shall be returned to the credit of the General Fund.

SUPPLEMENTAL V.—*An Act to establish Police Regulations for the Harbor of the City and County of San Francisco, etc.*—Approved April 4, 1864.

SECTION 1. No person shall board or attempt to board any vessel arriving in the harbor of the City and County of San Francisco before said vessel has been made fast to the wharf, without obtaining leave from the Master or person having charge of said vessel, or permission, in writing, from the owner or owners, or the Agent thereof, or having boarded such vessel, shall refuse or neglect to leave the same upon request of the Master or other person in charge thereof, under the penalty prescribed in the next succeeding section of this act.

SEC. 2. Any person violating section one of this act shall be deemed guilty of a misdemeanor, and upon conviction thereof before the Police Judge's Court of said city and county, shall be punished for each offense by a fine not exceeding one hundred dollars, or imprisonment in the County Jail of the City and County of San Francisco for a term not exceeding fifty days, or both, in the discretion of the Judge of the said Police Judge's Court, which Court shall have jurisdiction in such cases.

SEC. 3. The provisions of the last two foregoing sections shall not apply to any Pilot or public officer visiting a vessel in discharge of his duty.

SEC. 4. No person shall entice or persuade nor attempt to entice or persuade any member of the crew of any vessel arriving in said harbor, or of any vessel in said harbor, to leave or desert said vessel before the expiration of his term of service in such vessel. Any person guilty of so doing shall be deemed guilty of a misdemeanor, and upon conviction thereof shall be subject to the penalty prescribed in section two of this act.

SEC. 5. No person shall knowingly and willfully persuade or aid any person who shipped on any vessel for a voyage from said port, and receive any advance wages there desert or willfully neglect to proceed on such voyage. Any person guilty of so doing shall b deemed guilty of a misdemeanor, and upon conviction thereof before the Police Judge's Cour of said city and county, shall be punished for each offense by a fine not exceeding one hundrec dollars, or imprisonment in the County Jail of the City and County of San Francisco for a term not exceeding fifty days, or both, in the discretion of the Judge of said Police Judge's Court which Court shall have jurisdiction in such cases.

SEC. 6. Any person offending against any provision of this act may be arrested, with o without warrant, as provided in other cases of misdemeanor, by any officer qualified to serv criminal process in the said City and County of San Francisco; *provided,* the person so arreste shall be forthwith brought before said Police Judge's Court or admitted to bail, as in othe cases of misdemeanor committed in said City and County of San Francisco.

SEC. 7. The word "Harbor," as used in this act, shall be held to mean and include all th waters of the Bay of San Francisco within the limits of the said City and County of San Fran cisco; and the word "Vessel," as used in this act, shall be held to mean and include all vessel propelled by steam or sails, plying or bound on a voyage between the said port of San Francisco and any other port in this State, or in any other State of the United States, or in any foreign country.

SEC. 8. The Board of Supervisors of said City and County of San Francisco shall cause this act to be printed in cheap pamphlet form, and it shall be the duty of each and every Branch Pilot of the port of San Francisco to obtain from the Clerk of the Board of Supervisors of said city and county a reasonable supply of said pamphlets, and to deliver one copy of the same to the Master or person in charge of each and every vessel boarded by him as a Pilot, whether the said Pilot is employed to bring such vessel into said port or not.

SEC. 9. Any Branch Pilot refusing or neglecting to perform the requirements set forth in the last preceding section shall be deemed guilty of a misdemeanor, and shall upon conviction thereof before the Police Judge's Court of said city and county be fined in the sum of ten dollars, or be imprisoned in the County Jail for the term of twenty-five days, or both, in the discretion of the Judge of said Police Judge's Court, which said Court is hereby given jurisdiction in such cases.

ARTICE .III.

PUBLIC INSTRUCTION.

[Sections 30 to 35 are repealed by the following act, approved April 27, 1863.]

An Act to establish and define the powers and duties of the Board of Education of the City and County of San Francisco, and to repeal former Acts regulating the same, and to confer further Powers upon the Auditor and Treasurer of said City and County.

SECTION 1. The Board of Education of the City and County of San Francisco, shall consist of the School Directors elected for the several election districts of said city and county. The said Board shall organize annually, on the first Tuesday in July, by electing a President from among its members, and shall hold meetings monthly thereafter, and at such other times as the Board may determine. A majority of all the members elect shall constitute a quorum to transact business, but a smaller number may adjourn from time to time. The Board may determine the rules of its proceedings. Its sessions shall be public, and its records shall be open to public inspection.

SEC. 2. The Board of Education shall have sole power :

First. To establish and maintain Public Schools, and to establish School Districts, and to fix and alter the boundaries thereof.

Second. To establish Experimental and Normal Schools, either separately or in connection with the State Normal School.

Third. To employ and dismiss Teachers, Janitors, and School Census Marshals, and to fix, alter, allow, and order paid, their salaries or compensations ; and to employ and pay such mechanics and laborers as may be necessary to carry into effect the powers and duties of the Board ; and to withhold, for good and sufficient cause, the whole or any part of the salary or wages of any person or persons employed as aforesaid.

Fourth. To make, establish, and enforce all necessary and proper rules and regulations, not contrary to law, for the government and progress of Public Schools within the said city and county, the pupils therein, and the Teachers thereof, and for carrying into effect the laws relating to education ; also to establish and regulate the grade of schools, and determine what text-books, course of study, and mode of instruction shall be used in said schools.

Fifth. To provide for the School Department of said city and county, fuel, lights, water, blanks, blank books, printing, stationery, and such other articles, materials, or supplies as may be necessary and appropriate for use in the schools or in the office of the Superintendent, and to incur incidental expenses not exceeding twenty-five hundred dollars per annum.

Sixth. To build, alter, repair, rent, and provide school-houses, and furnish them with proper school furniture, apparatus, and school appliances, and to insure any and all school property.

Seventh. To lease for a term not exceeding ten years, any unoccupied property of the School Department not required for school purposes.

Eighth. To receive, purchase, lease, and hold in fee, in trust for the City and County of San Francisco, any and all real estate, and to hold in trust any personal property that may have been acquired, or may hereafter be acquired, for the use and benefit of the public schools of said city and county ; *provided,* the lots to be purchased under the provisions of this section do not exceed ten in number ; and all conveyances heretofore made to the said Board of Education are hereby legalized and declared valid, and the property therein conveyed vested in said Board in trust as aforesaid.

Ninth. To sell or exchange the following lots of land, or any part thereof, situate in the City and County of San Francisco, to wit : Fifty-vara lot number four hundred and sixty-two, on the corner of Filbert and Kearny streets ; fifty-vara lot number seven hundred and thirty-two, on the corner of Harrison and Fremont streets ; one-half of one hundred-vara lot number one hundred and twenty-eight, corner of Market and Fifth streets ; one hundred-vara lot number one hundred and seventy-four, corner of Harrison and Fourth streets ; fifty-vara lot number six hundred and sixty-three, corner of Taylor and Vallejo streets ; and the lots, or any portion thereof, which were set aside for School purposes by the Commissioners appointed by the Van Ness Ordinance, ratified and confirmed by the Legislature by an act entitled "An Act concerning the City of San Francisco, and to ratify and confirm certain Ordinances of the Common Council of said City," approved March eleventh, eighteen hundred and fifty-eight, and good and valid deeds therefor to make and execute; *provided*, that no real estate shall be sold or exchanged without the consent of seven members of the Board of Education, and seven members of the Board of Supervisors, of said city and county ; and, *provided*, further, that the proceeds of such sales shall be applied exclusively to the purchase of other lots or the erection of school-houses.

Tenth. To grade, fence, and improve school lots, and in front thereof to grade, sewer, plank, or pave, and repair streets, and to construct and repair sidewalks.

Eleventh. To sue for any and all lots, lands, and property belonging to or claimed by the said School Department, and to prosecute and defend all actions, at law or in equity, necessary to recover and maintain the full enjoyment and possession of said lots, lands, and property, and to employ and pay counsel in such cases; *provided*, the amount of fees paid to such counsel shall not exceed one thousand dollars in any one year ; and further, to do any and all lawful acts necessary thereto.

Twelfth. To determine, annually, the amount of taxation, not exceeding thirty-five cents on each one hundred dollars valuation upon the assessment roll, to be raised by tax upon the real and personal property within the said city and county, not exempt from taxation, for the establishment and support of Free Public Schools therein, and for carrying into effect all the provisions of law regarding Public Schools ; and the amount so determined by the said Board of Education shall be reported in writing to the Board of Supervisors of said city and county on or before the third Monday of April of each year ; and the said Board of Supervisors are hereby authorized and required to levy and cause to be collected, at the time and in the manner of levying State and other city and county taxes, the amount of taxation so determined and reported to them by the said Board of Education, as a school tax upon all taxable property of said city and county ; and said tax shall be in addition to all other amounts levied for State, and city, and county purposes.

Thirteenth. To establish regulations for the just and equal disbursement of all moneys belonging to the Public School Fund.

Fourteenth. To examine and allow, in whole or in part, every demand payable out of the School Fund, or to reject any such demand for good cause, of which the Board shall be sole judge.

Fifteenth. To discharge all legal incumbrances now existing upon any school property.

Sixteenth. To order paid from the School Fund of the said city and county, a sum not exceeding one hundred dollars per month, until the first day of July, eighteen hundred and sixty-four, and no longer, for rent of an office and rooms for the Superintendent and said Board, and a further sum, not exceeding five hundred dollars, to fit up such office and rooms.

Seventeenth. To prohibit any child under six years of age from attending the Public Schools.

Eighteenth. And, generally, to do and perform such other acts as may be necessary and proper to carry into force and effect the powers conferred on said Board.

SEC. 3. The President of the Board of Education shall have power to administer oaths and affirmations concerning any demand upon the treasury payable out of the School Fund, or other matters relating to his official duties.

SEC. 4. At the last regular session of the Board, in September, December, March, and June, of each year, before proceeding to other business, each Director shall be called on to report the condition of the school or schools in his district, and the circumstances and wants of the inhabitants thereof, in respect to education, and to suggest any defect he may have noted and improvement he would recommend in the school regulations. The reports to be made in December and June, shall be in writing.

SEC. 5. Before giving out any contract or incurring any liability to mechanics or laborers, or for expenditures authorized by section two, subdivisions three, five, and six, respectively, to any amount exceeding two hundred dollars, the Board of Education shall cause notice to be published for five days, inviting sealed proposals for the object contemplated. All proposals offered shall be delivered to the Superintendent of Public Schools, and said Board shall, in open session, open, examine, and publicly declare the same, and award the contract to the lowest responsible bidder ; *provided*, said Board may reject any and all bids, should they deem it for the public good, and also, the bid of any party who may have proved delinquent or unfaithful in any former contract with said city and county or said Board, and cause a republication of the notice for proposals as above specified.—[Amendment March 12, 1864.]

SEC. 6. No School Director or Superintendent shall be interested in any contract pertaining in any manner to the School Department of said city and county. All contracts in violation of this section are declared void, and any Director or Superintendent violating or aiding in the violation of the provisions of this section shall be deemed guilty of a misdemeanor.

SEC. 7. No teacher shall be employed in any of the Public Schools without having a certificate issued under the provisions of this act. For the purpose of granting the certificates required, the Board of Education, either as a body, or by committee, or by the Superintendent, shall hold examinations of teachers. No certificate shall be issued except to a person who shall have passed a satisfactory examination in such branches as the Board may require, and shall have given evidence of good moral character, ability, and fitness to teach. The said certificate shall be in force for two years; *provided*, that the person to whom it is granted is continuously employed in the schools in teaching.

SEC. 8. The Board may, in its discretion, renew, without reëxamination, the certificate of any person so employed. It shall have power to revoke the certificate of any teacher upon evidence of immoral or unprofessional conduct; and any School Director, with the consent and advice of the Superintendent, may, for good and sufficient cause, provisionally withdraw the certificate of any teacher employed in the schools of his district until the next regular meeting of the Board.

SEC. 9. The Superintendent of Public Schools of the City and County of San Francisco is hereby declared and constituted *ex officio* a member of the Board of Education, without the right to vote.

SEC. 10. The said Superintendent is hereby authorized to appoint a Clerk, subject to the approval of the Board of Education, who shall act as Secretary of the Board, and who shall be paid a salary, to be fixed by the said Board, not to exceed the sum of one hundred and fifty dollars per month. The said Clerk shall be subject to removal at the pleasure of the Superintendent, and shall perform such duties as may be required of him by the Board or the Superintendent.

SEC. 11. The Superintendent shall report to the Board of Education, annually, on or before the twentieth day of June, and at such other times as they may require, all matters pertaining to the expenditures, income, and condition and progress of the Public Schools of said city and county, during the preceding year, with such recommendations as he may deem proper.

SEC. 12. It shall be the duty of the Superintendent to visit and examine each school at least once in three months; to observe and cause to be observed such general rules for the regulation, government, and instruction of the schools, not inconsistent with the laws of the State, as may be established by the Board of Education; to attend the session of the Board, and inform them at each session of the condition of the Public Schools, School-Houses, School Funds, and other matters connected therewith, and to recommend such measures as he may deem necessary for the advancement of education in the city and county. He shall acquaint himself with all the laws, rules, and regulations governing the Public Schools in said city and county, and the judicial decisions thereon, and give advice on subjects connected with the Public Schools gratuitously, to officers, teachers, pupils, and their parents and guardians.

SEC. 13. Any vacancy in the office of School Director shall be filled by appointment by the Superintendent, by and with the consent of a majority of the School Directors then in office; and such appointees shall hold office, respectively, until the municipal election next ensuing, and the election and qualification of their successors in office. But no such appointment shall be valid, unless the appointee be at the time of his appointment an elector in the district wherein the vacancy occurred.

SEC. 14. In case of a vacancy in the office of Superintendent, the Board of Education may appoint a person to fill the vacancy until the regular election then next following, when the office shall be filled by election of the people.

SEC. 15. The School Fund* of the City and County of San Francisco shall consist of all moneys received from the State School Fund; of all moneys arising from taxes which shall be levied annually by the Board of Supervisors of said city and county for school purposes; of all moneys arising from the sale, rent, or exchange of any school property; and of such other moneys as may, from any source whatever, be paid into said School Fund; which fund shall be kept separate and distinct from all other moneys, and shall only be used for school purposes under the provisions of this act, and for the payment of the interest and redemption of the principal of the school bonds, according to law. No fees or commissions shall be allowed or paid for assessing, collecting, keeping, or disbursing any school moneys; and if, at the end of any fiscal year, any surplus remains in the School Fund, such surplus money shall be carried forward to the School Fund of the next fiscal year, and shall not be, for any purpose whatever, diverted or withdrawn from said fund, except under the provisions of this act.

* The Act of March 5, 1864, authorizes the transfer of $60,000 from the General to the School Fund for the purchase of lots and the erection of school-houses, at such points as may be selected by the Board of Education; and the Act of April 4th, 1864, empowers the transfer of the City and County Hospital Building to the Board of Education whenever the same shall not be required for a hospital.

Sec. 16. The said School Fund shall be used and applied by said Board of Education for the following purposes, to wit:

First. For the payment of the salaries or wages of teachers, janitors, school census marshals, and other persons who may be employed by the said Board.

Second. For the erection, alteration, repair, rent, and furnishing of school houses.

Third. For the expenses of Model and Normal schools.

Fourth. For the purchase money or rent of any real or personal property purchased or leased by said Board.

Fifth. For the insurance of all school property.

Sixth. For the payment of interest due on school bonds, and for the redemption of the same.

Seventh. For the discharge of all legal incumbrances now existing on any school property.

Eighth. For lighting school rooms and the office and rooms of the Superintendent and the Board of Education.

Ninth. For supplying the schools with fuel, water, apparatus, blanks, blank-books, and necessary school appliances, together with books for indigent children.

Tenth. For supplying books, printing, and stationery for the use of the Superintendent and Board of Education, and for the incidental expenses of the Board and Department.

Eleventh. For the payment of the salary of the Secretary of the Board of Education.

Twelfth. For grading, fencing, and improving school lots, and for grading, sewering, planking, or paving, and repairing streets, and constructing and repairing sidewalks in front thereof.

Sec. 17. All claims payable out of the School Fund, excepting the coupons for interest and the School Bonds, shall be filed with the Secretary of the Board, and after they shall have been approved by a majority of all the members elect of the Board, upon a call of yeas and nays, which shall be recorded, they shall be signed by the President of the Board and the Superintendent of Public Schools, and be sent to the City and County Auditor. Every demand shall have indorsed upon it a certificate of its approval by the Board, showing the date thereof and the law authorizing the same, by title, date, and section. All demands for teachers' salaries shall be payable monthly.

Sec. 18. Demands on the School Fund may be audited and approved in the usual manner, although there shall not at the time be money in the treasury for the payment of the same; *provided,* that no demand on said fund shall be paid out of or become a charge against the School Fund of any subsequent fiscal year; and, further, *provided,* that the entire expenditures of the said School Department for all purposes shall not in any fiscal year exceed the revenues thereof for the same year.

Sec. 19. The City and County Auditor shall state, by indorsement upon every claim or demand audited on the School Fund, the particular money or fund out of which the same is payable, and that it is payable from no other source.

Sec. 20. Audited bills for the current fiscal year for wages or salaries of the teachers in the Public Schools, shall be receivable for school taxes due upon real estate.

Sec. 21. All demands authorized by this act shall be audited and approved in the usual manner ; and the Auditor and Treasurer of said city and county are respectively authorized and required to audit and pay the same when so ordered paid and approved by the said Board ; *provided,* that the said Board shall not have power to contract any debt or liability in any form whatsoever against the said city and county, in contravention of this act.

Sec. 22. The teachers in the Industrial School in said city and county shall be exempt from the provisions of this act.

Sec. 23. This act shall take effect and be in force from and after its passage, and all laws and parts of laws, so far as they are consistent with or a repetition of the provisions of this act, are hereby repealed.

ARTICLE IV.

PUBLIC STREETS AND HIGHWAYS.

[Sections 36 to 64, inclusive, of the original act are repealed by the following which is substituted therefor.]

SUPPLEMENTAL VI.—*An Act amendatory of Article Fourth of an Act entitled An Act to repeal the several Charters of the City of San Francisco, to establish the Boundaries of the City and County of San Francisco, and to consolidate the Government thereof, approved the nineteenth day of April, eighteen hundred and fifty-six, repealing sections thirty-six to sixty-four, inclusive, and Acts and parts of Acts amendatory and supplementary thereof, and substituting this Act for said Article Four.*—Approved April 25, 1862.

SECTION 1. All the original streets, as laid down upon the map now in the office of the City and County Surveyor of the City and County of San Francisco, signed by C. H. Gough, Michael Hayes, and Horace Hawes, Commissioners, and by John J. Hoff, Surveyor, and generally known as the " Van Ness Map," and all other streets, lanes, alleys, places, or courts, now dedicated to public use, or which shall be hereafter dedicated to public use, lying between the

Bay of San Francisco and Johnston and Larkin streets, including the two last-named streets, are hereby declared to be open public streets, lanes, alleys, places, or courts, for the purposes of this law ; and the Board of Supervisors of said city and county are hereby authorized to employ the City and County Surveyor to ascertain and establish the lines and width of all or any of said streets, lanes, and alleys, and the sizes of said places, or courts, when they shall deem it necessary so to do.

Sec. 2. The Board of Supervisors shall have power to lay out and open new streets, within the corporate limits of the City and County of San Francisco, and west of Larkin and southwest of Johnston streets, in accordance with the conditions of the ordinance of the Common Council of said city, approved June twentieth, eighteen hundred and fifty-five, entitled An Ordinance for the Settlement and Quieting of Land Titles, but shall have no power to subject the city and county to any expense therefor, exceeding the sum of one thousand dollars, and, when so laid out and opened, the provisions of this act shall be applicable thereto.

Sec. 3. The Board of Supervisors are hereby authorized and empowered to order the whole, or any portion of the said streets, lanes, alleys, places, or courts, graded, or regraded, to the official grade, planked, or replanked, paved, or repaved, or macadamized, piled, or repiled, capped, or recapped, and to order sidewalks, sewers, cesspools, manholes, culverts, curbing, and crosswalks, to be constructed therein, and to order any other work to be done which shall be necessary to make and complete the whole, or any portion of said streets, lanes, alleys, places, or courts, and they may order any of the said work to be improved. The work provided for in this act shall not be deemed to be " specific improvement," within the meaning of section sixty-eight, Article V, of Chapter One Hundred and Twenty-Five, of the act entitled " An Act to repeal the several Charters of the City of San Francisco, to establish the Boundaries of the City and County of San Francisco, and to consolidate the Government thereof," approved April nineteenth, eighteen hundred and fifty-six. Nor shall the ordinances or resolutions passed by the said Board of Supervisors, under the provisions of this act, be deemed to be such ordinances or resolutions as are mentioned in said section of sixty-eight.

Sec. 4. The Board of Supervisors may order any work authorized by section three of this act to be done, after notice of their intention so to do, in the form of a resolution, describing the work, and signed by the Clerk of said Board, has been published for the period of ten days ; and it shall not be lawful for any property owner to become exempt from assessment by the performance after the first publication of the said notice of intention of any work included in such notice. At the expiration of any notice of intention, as herein before provided, the Board of Supervisors shall be deemed to have acquired jurisdiction to order any of the work to be done, or to be afterwards improved, which is authorized by section three of this act ; and all owners of lands, or lots, or portions of lots, who may feel aggrieved, or who may have objections to any of the subsequent proceedings of the said Board in relation to the work mentioned in such notices of intentions, shall file with the said Clerk a petition or remonstrance, wherein they shall state in what respect they feel aggrieved, or the proceedings to which they object. Said petition or remonstrance shall be passed upon by the said Board of Supervisors, and their decisions thereon shall be final and conclusive. The owners of more than one-half in frontage of the lots and lands fronting on the work proposed to be done and designated in said resolutions, may make written objections to grading, and to piling, capping, and planking, within ten days after the first publication of said resolution of intention ; said objections shall be delivered to the Clerk of the said Board of Supervisors, who shall indorse thereon the date of the reception by him, and such objections, so indorsed, shall be a bar to any further proceedings in relation to said grading for a period of six months, unless the owners aforesaid shall sooner petition for said grading to be done ; provided, that when one-half or more of the grading of any street lying between two main street crossings has been already performed, the Board of Supervisors may order the remainder of such grading to be done, notwithstanding the objections of any property owners. Before passing any order for the construction of sewers, plans, and specifications, careful estimates shall be furnished to the said Board of Supervisors by the Superintendent of the Public Streets and Highways of the City and County of San Francisco, if required by them.—[Amendment April 25, 1863.]

Sec. 5. The owners of more than one-half in frontage of lots and lands fronting on any street, lane, alley, place, or court, mentioned in sections one and two of this act, or their duly authorized agents, may petition the said Board of Supervisors to order any of the work mentioned in section three of this act, to be done, and the Board of Supervisors may order the work mentioned in said petition to be done, after notice of their intention so to do has been published, as provided in section four of this act. No order or permission shall be given to grade or pile and cap any street, lane, alley, place, or court, in the first instance, or any portion thereof, without extending and completing the same throughout the whole width of such street, lane, alley, place, or court ; when any such work has heretofore been done, or when any such work shall hereafter be done, in violation of this section, neither the lots or portions of lots, in front of which such work has been or may be done hereafter, nor the owners thereof shall be exempt from assessments made for the payment of the work afterwards done to complete said street, lane, alley, place, or court, to its full width, as provided in section eight of this act.

SEC. 6. Before giving out any contracts by the Board of Supervisors, for doing any work authorized by section three of this act, the Board of Supervisors shall cause notice to be conspicuously posted in the office of the Superintendent of Public Streets and Highways, and also published for five days, inviting sealed proposal for the work contemplated. All proposals offered shall be delivered to the Clerk of the Board of Supervisors, and said Board shall, in open session, open, examine, and publicly declare the same, and award said work to the lowest responsible bidder ; *provided*, said Board may reject any and all bids, should they deem it for the public good, and also the bid of any party who may have proved delinquent or unfaithful in any former contract with said city and county. All proposals shall be accompanied with a bond in the sum of two hundred dollars, signed by the bidder and two sureties, who shall justify in the manner hereinafter provided, conditioned to pay to the Street Department Fund the full sum of two hundred dollars as liquidated damages, if the bidder to whom the contract is awarded shall fail or neglect to enter into a contract, as hereinafter provided. It shall be the duty of said City and County Attorney to sue on said bonds, in the name of said city and county, and to pay the amount recovered over to said fund. The Board of Supervisors shall have power to relieve the contractor from the performance of the conditions of said bond, when good cause is shown therefor. All persons (owners included) who shall fail to enter into contracts, as herein provided, are hereby prohibited from bidding a second time for the same work. Notice of such awards shall be published for five days. The owners of the major part of the frontage of lots and lands liable to be assessed for said work, shall not be required to present sealed proposals, but may, within said five days after the first publication of notice of such award, elect to take said work, and enter into a written contract to do the whole work at the price at which the same may have been awarded. Should said owners fail to commence the work within ten days after the first publication of the notice of said award, and prosecute the same with due diligence, to completion, it shall be the duty of the Superintendent of Public Streets and Highways to enter into a contract with the original bidder to whom the contract was awarded, and at the price the same may have been awarded him ; but if said bidder neglect, for fifteen days after the first publication of the notice of said award, to enter into the contract, then the Board of Supervisors shall again publish for said five days, and pursue the steps required by this section, the same as in the first instance. If the owners who may have taken said contract, do not complete the same within the time limited in the contract, or within such further time as the Board of Supervisors may give them, said Superintendent shall report such delinquency to the Board of Supervisors, who may relet the unfinished portion of said work, after having pursued the formalities of this section as stated aforesaid. All such contractors shall, at the time of the execution of the contract, also execute a bond to the satisfaction of said Superintendent, with two or more sureties, payable to the City and County of San Francisco, in such sums as the said Superintendent shall deem adequate, conditioned for the faithful performance of the contract, and the sureties shall justify, before any officer competent to administer an oath, in double the amount mentioned in said bond, over and above all statutory exemptions. Any person suffering damages, by reason of the breach of said contract, may sue on such bond in his own name. It shall be the duty of the Superintendent to collect from the contractors, before the contract is signed by him, the cost of publication of the notices required under the proceedings prescribed in this act.

SEC. 7. The Superintendent of Public Streets and Highways is hereby authorized, in his official capacity to enter into all written contracts, and to receipt all bonds authorized by this act, and to do any other acts, either expressed or implied, that pertain to the Street Department under this act ; and said Superintendent shall fix the time for the commencement and completion of the work under all contracts entered into by him, and may extend the time so fixed from time to time under the direction of the Board of Supervisors. And in all cases where the Superintendent, under the direction of said Board, has extended the time for the performance of contracts, the same shalll be held to have been legally extended. And whenever, in any contract heretofore made, the said Superintendent has fixed the time for doing the work, or has extended the same, such acts shall be deemed and held to have been legally done, and it shall be so held in all the Courts of this State ; but this provision shall not apply to any contracts the work under which has not been commenced. The work provided for in section three of this act must, in all cases, be done under the direction and to the satisfaction of the Superintendent, and the materials used shall be such as are required by the said Superintendent ; and all contracts made therefor must contain this condition, and also express notice that in no case (except where it is otherwise provided in this act) will the city and county be liable for any portion of the expense, nor for any delinquency of persons or property assessed. The assessment and apportionment of the expenses of all such work, in the mode herein provided, shall be made by the said Superintendent of Public Streets and Highways.—[Amendment April 25, 1863.]

Sec. 8. *One.* The expense incurred for any work authorized by section three of this act, shall be assessed upon the lots and lands fronting thereon, except as hereinafter specially provided, each lot or portion of lot being separately assessed, in proportion to its frontage, at a rate per front foot sufficient to cover the total expense of the work.

Two. The expense. of all improvements (except such as done by contractors under the provisions of section fourteen of this act) until the streets, street crossings, lanes, alleys, places, or courts, are finally accepted, as provided in section twenty-one of this act, shall be assessed upon the lots and lands as provided in this section, according to the nature and character of the work, and after such acceptance, the expense of all work thereafter done thereon shall be paid by said city and county out of the Street Department Fund ; and if said Fund shall not be sufficient to defray such expenses, the Board of Supervisors may transfer from the General Fund to the Street Department Fund sufficient money to meet any deficiency.

Three. The expense of work done on main street crossings, excepting such as are provided for in subdivision eight of this section, shall be assessed upon the four quarter blocks adjoining and cornering on the crossing ; and each lot, or part of a lot, in such quarter blocks, fronting on such main streets, shall be separately assessed, according to its proportion of frontage on the said main streets.

Four. Where a main street terminates at right angles in another main street, the expense of the work done on one-half the width of the street opposite the termination shall be assessed upon the lots in each of the two quarter blocks adjoining and cornering on the same, according to the frontage of such lots on said main streets, and the expense of the other half of the width of said street upon the lots fronting on the latter half of the street opposite such termination.

Five. Where any small or subdivision street crosses a main street, the expense of all work done on said crossing shall be assessed on all the lots or portions of lots half way on said small streets to the next crossing, or intersection, or to the end of said small or subdivision street, if it does not meet another.

Six. The expense of work done on the small or subdivision street crossings, shall be assessed upon the lots fronting upon such small streets on each side thereof, in all directions, half way to the next street, place, or court, on either side, respectively, or to the end of such street, if it does not meet another.

Seven. Where a small street, lane, alley, place, or court terminates in another street, lane, alley, place, or court, the expense of the work done on one-half the width of the street, lane, alley, place, or court, opposite the termination, shall be assessed upon the lot fronting on such small street, lane, alley, place, or court, so terminating, according to its frontage thereon, half-way on each side, respectively, to the next street, lane, alley, place, or court, or to the end of such street, lane, alley, place, or court, if it does not meet another, and the other one-half of the width upon the lots fronting such termination.

Eight. The map now in the office of the said Superintendent of Public Streets and Highways, showing the street crossings, or spaces formed or made by the junction or intersection of other streets with Market Street, also showing other street crossings adjoining fractional or irregular blocks (all which said crossings or spaces are colored on said map, and numbered from one to seventy, inclusive) and heretofore certified by said Superintendent, and adopted by a resolution of the Board of Supervisors, Number Fifteen Hundred and Seventy-Eight, approved on the sixteenth day of December, eighteen hundred and sixty-one, which resolution is copied on the face of said map, shall be deemed and held to be an official map for the purposes of this act, and the same is hereby approved ; and the expenses incurred for work done on the said crossings of spaces formed by the junction and intersection of East Street with Market Street, and of other streets with Market Street, on the northerly side of the same, and not squarely in front of and not properly assessable to lots fronting on such streets, and for work done on said other street crossings and spaces, all of which are colored on said map, shall be assessed on the contiguous, adjacent, and neighboring irregular or quarter blocks or lots of land which are of the same color as the crossings or spaces, and which have a number thereon corresponding with the number of the crossing or space on which the work has been done.

Nine. In all the streets constituting the water front of the City and County of San Francisco, or bounded on one side by the property of said city and county, or crossings cornering thereon, or on the water front, the expense of work done on that portion of said streets, from the center line thereof to the said water front, or to such property of the city and county bounded thereon, and of one-fourth of their crossings, shall be provided for by the said city and county ; but no contract for any such work shall be given out except to the lowest responsible bidder, after an observance of all the formalities required by this act.

Ten. Where any work mentioned in section three of this act (sewers, manholes, cesspools, culverts, crosswalks, crossings, curbings, grading, piling, and capping excepted) is done on one side of the center line of said streets, lanes, alleys, places, or courts, the lots or portions of lots fronting on that side only in front of which said work is done shall be assessed to cover the expenses of said work according to the provisions of this section.

Eleven. The assessment made to cover the expenses of the grading mentioned in the proviso in section four of this act, shall be assessed upon all the lands, lots, and portions of lots, fronting on either side of said street, lying and being between the said main street crossings, in the manner provided in subdivision one of this section. Before any work is done under a contract to complete the grading of a partially graded street, lane, alley, place, or court, under the provisions of section four of this act, the City and County Surveyor shall ascertain, as near as possible, the number of cubic yards of grading done previous to the letting of the contract in front of each lot or parcel of land fronting upon the work under contract, and also ascertain the number of cubic yards of grading necessary to complete the work included in the contract, and certify such estimates to the Superintendent of Public Streets and Highways before the completion of the work included in said contract. And when any owner of a lot or lots fronting on said partially graded street, lane, alley, place, or court, has graded a part of the same, and such grading in cubic yards or measurement equals the proportional amount of grading which such owner would be obliged to do if no grading had been done on such street, lane, alley, place, or court, then such owner and his lot or lots shall be exempted from assessment for the remaining work. And if the grading done by such owner is less than his proportional share, then the work required to be done in front of his lot or lots, according to the original profile of the land previous to any grading thereon, shall be included in the assessment, and the work he shall be determined to have done at his own expense shall be credited to him at the contract rate; *provided*, that in making the assessment to cover the expense of any work mentioned in this section, the said Superintendent may deviate from its provisions, and assess such lots and lands fronting on any street, lane, alley, place, or court, as he may decide liable to assessment for said work, which decision may be appealed from as hereinafter provided.

Twelve. Section one of an Act entitled "An Act amendatory of and supplementary to an Act to provide Revenue for the support of the Government of this State," approved April twenty-ninth, eighteen hundred fifty-seven, approved April nineteenth, eighteen hundred and fifty-nine, shall not be applicable to the provisions of this section, but the property therein mentioned shall be subject to the provisions of this act, and to be assessed for work done under the provisions of this section.—[Amendment April 25, 1863.]

SEC. 9. After the contractor of any street work has fulfilled his contract to the satisfaction of the Superintendent or Board of Supervisors, on appeal, the Superintendent shall make an assessment to cover the sum due for the work performed and specified in such contracts (including incidental expenses, if any), in conformity with the provisions of the preceding section, according to the character of the work done, or, if any directions and decision shall be given by said Board on appeal, then in conformity with such direction and decision; which assessment shall briefly refer to the contract, the work contracted for and performed, and shall show the amount to be paid therefor, together with the incidental expenses, if any; the rate per front foot assessed; the amount of each assessment; the name of the owner of each lot, or portion of a lot (if known to the Superintendent); if unknown, the word "unknown" shall be written opposite the number of the lot, and the amount assessed thereon; the number of each lot, or portion of a lot, assessed; and shall have attached thereto a diagram, exhibiting each street, or street crossing, lane, alley, place, or court, on which any work has been done, and showing the relative location of each distinct lot, or portion of a lot, to the work done, numbered to correspond with the numbers in the assessments, and showing the number of feet fronting assessed for said work contracted for and performed.

SEC. 10. To said assessment shall be attached a warrant, which shall be signed by the Superintendent, and countersigned by the Auditor of said city and county, who, before countersigning it, shall examine the contract, the steps taken previous thereto, and the record of assessments, and must be satisfied that the proceedings have been legal and fair. The said warrants shall be substantially in the following form:

FORM OF THE WARRANT.

"By virtue hereof, I [name of Superintendent], Superintendent of Public Streets and Highways of the City and County of San Francisco, and State of California, by virtue of the authority vested in me as said Superintendent, do authorize and empower [name of contractor] [his or their] agents or assigns, to demand and receive the several assessments upon the assessment and diagram hereto attached, and this shall be [his or their] warrant for the same. San Francisco, [date], 186—. [Name of Superintendent], Superintendent of Public Streets and Highways. Countersigned by [name of Auditor] Auditor."

Said warrant, assessment, and diagram shall be recorded. When so recorded, the several amounts assessed shall be a lien upon the lands, lots, or portions of lots, assessed respectively, for the period of two years from the date of said recording, unless sooner discharged; and from and after the date of said recording of any warrant, assessments, and diagrams, all persons mentioned in section twelve of this act shall be deemed to have notice of the contents of the record thereof. After said warrant, assessment, and diagram are recorded, the same shall be delivered to the contractor, or his agent or assigns, on demand, but not until after the payment to the said Superintendent of the incidental expenses not previously paid by the contractor, or his assigns. And by virtue of said warrants, said contractor, or his agents or assigns, shall be authorized to demand and receive the amount of the several assessments made to cover the sum due for the work specified in such contracts and assessment.

SEC. 11. The contractor, or his agent or assigns, shall call upon the persons so assessed, or their agents, if they can conveniently be found, and demand payment of the amount assessed to each. If any payment be made, the contractor or his agent shall receipt the same upon the assessment, in presence of the person making such payment, and shall also give a separate receipt, if demanded. Whenever the persons so assessed, or their agents, cannot conveniently be found, or whenever the name of the owner of the lot is stated as "unknown," on the assessment, then the said contractor, or his agent or assigns, shall publicly demand payment on the premises assessed; the warrant shall be returned to the Superintendent within ten days after its date, with a return indorsed thereon, signed by the contractor, or his agent or assigns, verified upon oath, stating the nature and character of the demand, and whether any of the assessments remain unpaid, in whole or in part, and the amount thereof; thereupon the Superintendent shall record the return so made, in the margin of the record of the warrant and assessment, and also the original contract referred to therein, if it has not already been recorded at full length in a book to be kept for that purpose in his office, and shall sign the record. All warrants, assessment lists, and diagrams heretofore issued or delivered by said Superintendent to any person or persons, shall be returned to said Superintendent within sixty days from and after the approval of this act, and in all cases where warrants shall not be returned within the sixty days limited as aforesaid, any liens created thereby shall be and are hereby released and discharged, as if the same had been paid; *provided*, however, that in case any warrant is lost, upon proof of such loss a duplicate can be issued, upon which a return may be made. The Superintendent is authorized at any time to receive the amounts due upon any assessment list and warrant issued by him, and give a good and sufficient discharge therefor; and he may release any assessment upon the books of his office on the production to him of the receipt of the party, or his assigns, to whom the assessment and warrant was issued; and if any contractor shall fail to return his warrant within the time and in the form provided in this section, he shall thenceforth have no lien upon the property assessed.—[Amendment April 25, 1863.]

SEC. 12. The owner, contractor, or his assigns, and all persons, whether named in the assessment or not, and all persons directly interested in any work provided for in this act, or in the said assessment, feeling aggrieved by any of the acts or determinations aforesaid of the said Superintendent in relation thereto, or having or making any objection to the correctness or legality of the assessment, shall, within fifteen days after the date of the warrant, appeal to the Board of Supervisors, as provided in this section, by briefly stating their objections in writing, and filing the same with the Clerk of said Board. Notice of the time and place of the hearing, briefly referring to the work contracted to be done, or other subject of appeal, and to the acts or determinations objected to or complained of, shall be published for five days. The said Board may correct, alter, or modify said assessment in such manner as to them shall seem just, and may instruct and direct the Superintendent to correct said warrant, assessment, or diagram, in any particular, and to make and issue a new warrant, assessment, and diagram, to conform to the decisions of said Board in relation thereto, at their option. All the decisions and determinations of said Board upon notice and hearing as aforesaid, shall be final and conclusive upon all persons entitled to an appeal under the provisions of this section as to all errors and irregularities which said Board could have remedied and avoided. The said warrant, assessment, and diagram shall be held *prima facie* evidence of the regularity and correctness of the assessment, and of the prior proceedings and acts of the said Superintendent, and of the regularity of all the acts and proceedings of the Board of Supervisors upon which said warrant, assessment, and diagram are based.—[Amendment April 25, 1863.]

SEC. 13. At any time after the period of fifteen days from the day of the date of the warrant as hereinbefore provided, or if an appeal is taken to the Board of Supervisors, as is provided in section twelve of this act, any time after five days from the decision of said Board, or after the return of the warrant or assessment, after the same may have been corrected, altered, or modified, as provided in section twelve of this act (but not less than fifteen days from the date of the warrant), the contractor or his assignee may sue, in his own name, the owner of the lands, lots, or portions of lots assessed, on the day of the date of the recording of the warrant, assessment, and diagram, or on any day thereafter during the continuance of the lien of said assessment, and recover the amount of any assessment remaining due and unpaid. Suit may be brought in any Court in said city and county having jurisdiction of the amount to recover which suit is brought; said Courts are hereby clothed with jurisdiction to hear and determine such actions. The said warrant, assessment, and diagram, with the affidavit of demand and non-payment, shall be *prima facie* evidence of such indebtedness, and of the right of the plaintiff to recover in the action. The Court in which suit shall be commenced shall have power to adjudge and decree a lien against the premises assessed, and to order such premises to be sold on execution, as in other cases of sale of real estate by the process of said Courts; and on appeal, the Appellate Courts shall be vested with the same power to adjudge and decree a lien, and to order to be sold such premises on execution or decree, as is conferred on the Court from which an appeal is taken. Such premises, if sold, may be redeemed as in other cases. In all suits now pending, or hereafter to be brought, to recover street assessments, the proceedings therein shall be governed and regulated by the provisions of this act, and also, when not in conflict herewith, by the Civil Practice Act of this State. This act shall be liberally construed to effect the ends of justice.—[Amendment April 25, 1863.]

SEC. 14. The Superintendent of Public Streets and Highways may require at his option, by notice in writing, to be delivered to them personally, or left on the premises, the owners, tenants or occupants, of lots, or portions of lots, liable to be assessed for work done under the provisions of this act, to improve forthwith any of the work mentioned in section three of this act, in front of the property of which he is the owner, tenant, or occupant, to the center of the street, or otherwise, as the case may require, specifying in said notice what improvement is required. After the expiration of three days, the said Superintendent shall be deemed to have acquired jurisdiction to contract for the doing of the work or improvements required by said notice. If such improvement be not commenced within three days after notice given as aforesaid, and diligently and without interruption prosecuted to completion, the said Superintendent may enter into a contract with any suitable person applying to make said improvements, at the expense of the owner, tenant, or occupant, at a reasonable price, to be determined by said Superintendent; and such owner, tenant, or occupant shall be liable to pay the same. After the certificate referred to in section fifteen shall have been recorded, the sum contracted to be paid shall be a lien, the same as provided in section ten of this act; and may be enforced in the same manner.

SEC. 15. If the expenses of the work and material for such improvements, after the completion thereof, be not paid to the contractor so employed, or his agent, or assignee, on demand, the said contractor or his assigns, shall have the right to sue the owner, tenant, or occupant, under the provisions of this act, for the amount contracted to be paid, and the certificate of the Superintendent that the work has been properly done, and that the charges for the same are reasonable and just, shall be *prima facie* evidence of the amount claimed for said work and materials, and of the right of the contractor to recover for the same in such action.

SEC. 16. In addition, and as cumulative to the remedies above given, the Board of Supervisors shall have power, by resolution or ordinance, to prescribe the penalties that shall be incurred by any owner or person liable, or neglecting, or refusing to make improvements when required, as provided in section fourteen of this act, which fines and penalties shall be recovered for the use of the city and county, by prosecution in the name of the People of the State of California, as in other cases provided for in subdivision eleven of section fifteen, Chapter Four Hundred and Ninety-Three, on page five hundred and forty-four of the Statutes of said State, approved May eighteenth, eighteen hundred and sixty-one, and may be applied, if deemed expedient by the said Board, in payment of the expenses of any such improvements, when not otherwise provided for.

SEC. 17. The person owning the fee, or the person in possession, of lands, lots, or portions of lots, or buildings under claim, or exercising acts of ownership over the same, shall be regarded, treated, and deemed to be the " owner " (for the purposes of this law), according to the intent and meaning of that word as used in this act; and in case of property leased, the possession of the tenant or lessee, holding and occupying under such person, shall be deemed to be the possession of such owner, and the person so defined to be such owner shall be personally liable for the payment of any charge or assessment lawfully made or assessed upon said lands, lots, or portions of lots, by said Superintendent, or contracted to be paid to the contractor for improvements to cover the expenses of any work done under and authorized by the provisions of this act.

SEC. 18. Any tenant or lessee of the lands or lots liable, may pay the amount assessed against the property of which he is the tenant or lessee, under the provisions of this act, or he may pay the price agreed to be paid, under the provisions of section fourteen of this act, either before or after suit brought, together with costs to the contractor, or his agent, or assigns; or he may redeem the property, if sold on execution or decree, for the benefit of the owner, within the time prescribed by law, and deduct the amounts so paid from the rents due, and to become due, from him; and for any sum so paid beyond the rents due from him, he shall have a lien upon, and may retain possession of the said lands and lots, until the amount so paid and advanced be satisfied, with legal interest, from accruing rents or by payment by the owner.

SEC. 19. The records, kept by the Superintendent of Public Streets and Highways, in conformity with the provisions of this act, and signed by him, shall have the same force and effect as other public records, and copies therefrom, duly certified, may be used in evidence, with the same effect as the originals. The said records shall, during all office hours, be open to the inspection of any citizen wishing to examine them, free of charge.

Sec. 20. Notices in writing which are required to be given by the Superintendent, under the provisions of this act, may be served by any Police officer, with the permission of the Chief of Police, and the fact of such service shall be verified by the oath of the person making it, taken before the Superintendent (who is hereby authorized to administer oaths), Police Judge, or any Judge, or Justice of the Peace; or such notices, whether verbal or written, may be delivered by the Superintendent himself. The Superintendent shall keep a record of the fact of giving such notices, when delivered by himself, personally, and also of the notices and proof of services, when delivered by any other person.

Sec. 21. When any street or portion of a street has been or shall hereinafter be constructed to the satisfaction of the Committee on Streets, Wharfs, and Public Buildings, of the Board of Supervisors, and the Superintendent of Public Streets and Highways, under such regulations as said Board shall adopt, the same shall be accepted by the Board of Supervisors and thereafter shall be kept open and improved by the said city and county, the expenses thereof to be paid out of the Street Department Fund; *provided,* that the Board of Supervisors shall not accept of any portion of the street less than the entire width of the roadway (including the curbing, and one block in length, or one entire crossing). The Superintendent of Public Streets and Highways shall keep in his office a register of all accepted streets, the same to be indexed so that reference may be easily had thereto.—[Amendment April 25, 1863.]

Sec. 22. The said Superintendent shall keep a public office in some convenient place, to be designated by the Board of Supervisors, and his office shall be kept open as in this act required. He shall not, during his continuance in office, follow any other profession or calling, but shall be required to devote himself exclusively to the duties of his office. He shall be allowed, at the discretion of the Board of Supervisors, not less than three nor more than six Deputies, to be by him appointed from time to time; three of said Deputies shall receive a salary not exceeding one hundred and fifty dollars each and three a salary not exceeding one hundred and twenty-five dollars per month. It shall be lawful for the said Deputies to perform all or any of the duties conferred by this act upon the Superintendent of the Public Streets and Highways, under the direction of the said Superintendent, except the acceptance or approval of work done. The Superintendent of Public Streets and Highways, or his Deputies, shall superintend and direct the clearing of all sewers in the public streets, and the expenses of the same shall be paid out of the Street Department Fund in the same manner as provided for the improvements of streets that have been finally accepted as in this act provided.—[Amendment April 25, 1863.]

Sec. 23. It shall be the duty of the said Superintendent to see that the laws, orders, and regulations relating to the public streets and highways, are carried into execution, and that the penalties therefor are rigidly enforced. It is required that he shall keep himself informed of the condition of all public streets and highways, and also of all public buildings, parks, lots, and grounds, of the said city and county, as may be prescribed by the Board of Supervisors. He shall, before entering upon the duties of his office, give bonds to the city and county, in such sum as may be fixed by the Board of Supervisors, conditioned for the faithful discharge of the duties of his office; and should said Superintendent fail to see that the laws, orders, and regulations, relating to the public streets and highways, are carried into execution, after notice from any citizen of a violation thereof, the said Superintendent and his sureties shall be liable upon his official bond, to any person injured in his person or property in consequence of said official neglect.

Sec. 24. No recourse shall be had against said city and county for damages to person or property suffered or sustained by or by reason of the defective condition of any street or public highway of said city and county, whether originally existing, or occasioned by construction, excavation, embankment, or want of repair of such street or public highway, and whether such damage be occasioned by accident on said street or public highway, or by falling from or upon the same. But if any person, while carefully using any street or public highway of said city and county graded, or in course of being graded, or carefully using any other street or public highway leading into or crossing the same, be injured, killed, lost, or destroyed, or any horses, animals, or other property, be lost, injured, or destroyed, through any defect in said street or public highway, graded, or in course of being graded as aforesaid, or by reason of any excavation or embankment in or of the same, or by falling from or upon such embankment or excavation, then the person or persons upon whom the law may impose the duty either to repair such defect or to guard the public from the excavation, embankment, or grading aforesaid, and also the officer or officers through whose official neglect such defect remained unimpaired, or said excavation or embankment remained ungraded, as aforesaid, shall be jointly and severally liable to the person or persons injured for the damage sustained.—[Amendment April 25, 1863.]

SEC. 25. *First.* The City Surveyor shall be the proper officer to do the surveying and other work which may be necessary to be done under sections one and two of this act, and to survey, measure, and estimate the work done under contracts for grading streets, and every certificate of work done by him, signed in his official character, shall be *prima facie* evidence, in all the Court, in this State, of the truth of its contents. He shall also keep a record of all surveys made under the provisions of section one of this act, as in other cases. The Superintendent shall measure and determine any other work which may be done under the provisions of this act.

Second. The words "improve," "improved," and "improvement," as used in this act, shall include all necessary repairs of all work mentioned in section three of this act, and also the reconstruction of all, or any portion, of said work.

Third. The term "main street," as used in this act, means such street or streets as bound a block. The term "street," shall include crossings. ·.

Fourth.· The word·"block" shall mean the blocks which are known and designated as such on the map and books of the Assessor of said city and county.

Fifth. The term "incidental expenses" shall mean the expense for work done by the City Surveyor, under the provisions of this act; also, the expense of printing, advertising, and measuring, the work done under contracts for grading, and the expense of superintendence of sewers, and of piling and capping.

Sixth. The publication of notices, required by the provisions of this act, shall be published daily, (Sunday excepted) in the newspaper doing the printing by contract for said city and county,

SEC. 26. *First.* All assessments hereafter to be made, to cover the expense of work provided for by contracts awarded prior to the first day of June, eighteen hundred and sixty-one, and after George T. Bohen became the acting Superintendent, shall be assessed as provided by the law in relation thereto, and in force at the time said work was awarded; and all assessments heretofore made by George T. Bohen, as Superintendent, under said laws, to cover the expense of such work, shall be deemed and held to have been assessed under the proper law. ·. · ·ı ·

Second. All assessments hereafter to be made to cover the expense of work provided for by contracts awarded on and after the first of June, eighteen hundred and sixty-one, shall be assessed according to the provisions of this act.

The Board of Supervisors, upon receiving a petition for that purpose from the owners of a majority of the property on any one or more blocks, estimating the property by the front foot, in that portion of the City and County of San Francisco lying west of Larkin Street and south-west of Ninth Street, may order the grading or other improvement of such street or streets in accordance with the prayer of the petitioners, and without reference to the official width or grade of such street or streets, and in the same manner as other street improvements provided for in this act; *provided,* that no street shall be raised above or cut below the official grade.—[Amendment April 25, 1863, Sec. 10.] · · · · i

SEC. 27. The Superintendent shall appoint a person or persons, suitable to take charge of and superintend the construction and improvement of each and every sewer, and of piling and capping, whose duty it shall be to see that the contract made for doing said work is strictly fulfilled in every respect, and in case of any departure therefrom, to report the same to said Superintendent. He shall be allowed, for his time actually employed in the discharge of his duties, such compensation as shall be just, but not to exceed five dollars per day. The sum to which the party so employed shall be entitled, shall be deemed to be "incidental expenses," within the meaning of those words, as defined in this act; *provided,* that the owners of more than one-half in frontage of the lots and lands fronting on the work proposed to be done under this section, may, within forty-eight hours after the work has been commenced, appoint their own Superintendent of the work, and provide for his compensation by private agreement.

SEC. 28. All notices, orders, resolutions, advertisements, or other matters required or authorized by any law of this State to be published, the publication of which was by order of any Court of this State, or by contract with the said city and county, commenced in either the Daily or Weekly Mirror, or Weekly San Francisco Herald, newspapers published in the said city and county, and subsequently continued and ended in the Daily or Weekly Herald and Mirror, also published in said city and county; as the case may be, shall be taken, deemed, and held, by all the Courts in the State, to have been legally published, the same as if the publication had been completed in the paper in which it was originally commenced; and when any such publication shall hereafter be completed and ended in said Daily or Weekly Herald and Mirror, the same shall be taken, deemed, and held by said Courts to have been legally published, as aforesaid, and all notices, orders, resolutions, advertisements, or other matters, required or authorized by any law of this State to be published, and which H. Wheelock, the proprietor of the Daily and Weekly Mirror (a newspaper lately published in the City and County of San Francisco), agreed to publish, by virtue of a contract made with said city and county, may be published in the Daily and Weekly Herald and Mirror, as the case may require, a newspaper now published in said city and county, during the existence of said contract; and all such notices, orders, resolutions, or other matters which have been heretofore published, or which are now being published, or which shall hereafter be published, in said Herald and Mirror, during the existence of said contract, shall be taken, deemed, and held, to be legal and valid in all the Courts of this State, to all intents and purposes, the same as if they had been published in the Daily or Weekly Mirror, and the said Daily Mirror and the San Francisco Herald had not been consolidated, under the name of Herald and Mirror.

SEC. 29. Article four, embracing sections from thirty-six to sixty-four, inclusive, of an act entitled An Act to repeal the several Charters of the City of San Francisco, to establish the Boundaries of the City and County of San Francisco, and to consolidate the Government thereof, approved April nineteenth, eighteen hundred and fifty-six, and sections three, four, five, six, seven, eight, nine, ten, eleven, twelve, thirteen, and fourteen of an act entitled An Act amendatory to an Act entitled An Act to repeal the several Charters of the City of San Francisco, to establish the Boundaries of the City and County of San Francisco, and to consolidate the Government thereof, approved April nineteenth, A.D. eighteen hundred and fifty-six, approved March twenty-eighth, eighteen hundred and fifty-nine, and sections two, three, four, five, six, seven, eight, nine, ten, eleven, twelve, thirteen, sixteen, and seventeen of an act entitled An Act amendatory of an Act entitled An Act to repeal the several Charters of the City of San Francisco, to establish the Boundaries of the City and County of San Francisco, and to consolidate the Government thereof, approved the nineteenth day of April, eighteen hundred and fifty-six, and of an act amendatory and supplementary thereof, approved the eighteenth day of April, eighteen hundred and fifty-seven, and of an act amendatory thereof, approved the twenty-eighth day of March, eighteen hundred and fifty-nine, and supplementary to said acts, approved May eighteenth, eighteen hundred and sixty-one—all and singular, and all acts, or parts of acts, in conflict with this act, are hereby repealed ; and this act shall be deemed to be substituted in place of the sections under the head of said Article IV, and as amendatory of this act first above recited in this section, and held as part thereof, and shall be taken and deemed a public act, to take effect from and after its passage. All proceedings which may have been taken under the law for which this law is a substitute, and which are pending at the time this law shall take effect, may be continued and completed under this law ; and all advertisements being published at the date of the passage of this act, shall be published for the respective periods provided by the law in force at the time the publication may have been commenced.

ARTICLE V.

SUPERVISORS.

SEC. 65. The Supervisors, in their respective districts, shall vigilantly observe the conduct of all public officers, and take notice of the fidelity and exactitude, or the want thereof, with which they execute their duties and obligations, especially in the collection, custody, administration, and disbursement of public funds and property ; for which purpose the books, records, and official papers of all officers and magistrates of such districts, shall at all convenient times be open to their inspection. They shall take care that the books and records of all officers in their districts are kept in legal and proper form. They shall have power, and it shall be their duty, every month, to examine the accounts of any officer of their respective districts, having the collection and custody of the public funds, to examine and count over the moneys remaining in the hands of such officers, and shall note any discrepancy or defalcation that may be discovered, or reasonably suspected, and report the same forthwith, together with any willful official negligence or misconduct on the part of any such officer, to the President of the Board of Supervisors.

SEC. 66. At every regular session of the Board of Supervisors, before proceeding to other business, each member shall be called upon to report, orally, upon the matters specified in the preceding section ; to give information of the condition of his district, in regard to public schools, streets, roads, and highways, health, police, industry, and population ; and to suggest any defects he may have noticed in the laws and regulations, or the administration thereof, and the means of remedying them.

SEC. 67. The Supervisors shall meet within five days after each annual election, and also on the first Monday of January, April, July, and October, of each year, and at such other times as specially required by law ; or they may, for urgent reasons, be specially convoked by the President of the Board of Supervisors. A majority of all the Supervisors to be elected in the several districts shall constitute a quorum to do business ; and no regulation, resolution, ordinance, or order of the Board can pass without the concurrence of a majority of all the members elected ; but a smaller number may adjourn from day to day. All the sessions, acts, and resolutions of the Board shall be public. The President of the Board of Supervisors, elected by the city and county at large, shall preside at all the sessions of the Board, without the right to vote. In his absence, during any session, the Board shall appoint a President *pro tempore*, who shall, however, have the same vote as other members. The Board of Supervisors shall be the judge of election returns, and qualifications of its own members, and shall order and provide for holding elections in the proper districts, to fill vacancies which may happen or exist more than six months previous to the next general election ; at which general election such office shall be filled by election for the full term of two years. The Board of Supervisors shall determine the rules of its proceedings, keep a record of its acts and resolutions, and allow the same to be published ; and the yeas and nays on any question shall, at the request of any member, be entered on its journals. The Board of Supervisors shall appoint a Clerk with a salary of twenty-one hundred dollars a year, [Amendment Act April 26, 1862] to hold office during the pleasure of the Board, who shall be *ex officio* Clerk of the Board of Equalization, without any additional salary as such, except as provided in section eleven, and shall be required to take the constitutional oath of office, and give bond for the faithful discharge of the duties of his office.* He shall have power to administer such oaths and affirmations as may be required by law or the regulations, or the orders of the Board, relating to any demands upon the treasury or other business connected with the government of the city and county ; and shall also have power to certify and authenticate copies of all records, papers, and documents in his official custody. The powers of the Board of Supervisors are those granted in this act ; and they are prohibited to exercise any others.—[Amendment April 18, 1857.]

SEC. 68. It shall be the duty of the President of the Board of Supervisors, vigilantly to observe the official conduct of each Supervisor in his district, and of all public officers of the city and county, and take note of the fidelity and exactitude, or the want thereof, with which they execute their duties and obligations, especially in the collection, custody, administration, and disbursement of the public funds and property ; for which purpose the books, records, and official papers of all officers and magistrates of said city and county, shall at all convenient times be open to his inspection. He shall take especial care to see that the books and records of all such officers are kept in legal and proper form ; and any official defalcation, or willful neglect of duty, or official misconduct, which he may have discovered, or which shall have been reported to him by any Supervisor, shall, at the earliest opportunity, be laid before the Grand Jury, in order that the officer in default may be proceeded against according to law. Every ordinance or resolution of the Board of Supervisors, providing for any specific improvement, the granting of any privilege, or involving the lease, or other appropriation of public property, or the expenditure of public moneys, (except for sums less than five hundred dollars) or laying tax or assessment, and every ordinance or resolution imposing a new duty or penalty shall, after its introduction in the Board, be published, with the ayes and nays, in some city daily newspaper, at least five successive days before final action of the Board upon the same ; and every such ordinance, after the same shall pass the Board, shall, before it takes effect, be presented to the President of the Board for his approval. If he approves, he shall sign it ; if not, he shall return it within ten days, to the Board, with his objections in writing. The Board shall then enter the objections on the journals, and publish them in some city newspaper. If at any stated meeting thereafter, two-thirds of all the members elected to the Board, vote for such ordinance or resolution, it shall then, despite the objections of the President, become valid. Should any such ordinance or resolution not be returned by the President, within ten days after he receives it, it shall become valid the same as if it had received his signature.

SEC. 69. All contracts for building† and printing to be done for the said city and county, and ordinary supplies for subsistence of prisoners, must be given by the Board of Supervisors to the lowest bidder offering adequate security, after due public notice for not less than five days, in at least two newspapers in said city and county. All contracts for subsistence of prisoners must be given out annually, at a fixed price per day, not exceeding twenty-five cents *per diem*, for each person connected with the prison ; [Amendment Act April 26, 1862] and the advertisement for proposals to be published as aforesaid by the Board of Supervisors, shall specify each article that will be required, the quantity thereof, the quantity for each person, and the existing and probable number of prisoners to be supplied. All articles of food supplied for prisoners must be of a sound and wholesome quality, and subject to the inspection and approval of the keeper of the prison, and also the President of the Board of Supervisors and Police Judge of said city and county, all of which must be expressed in the contract therefor to be entered into.

SEC. 70. The Board of Supervisors shall have power to hear and determine appeals from the executive officers of said city and county, in the cases provided in this act ; and in all cases of an appeal taken to the Board of Supervisors, or Board of Education, from the order or decision made by any other officer or officers, such officer or officers shall furnish the Board with a statement of his or their reasons for the orders or decisions so appealed from, and the party appealing

---

* The Act of April 23, 1858, authorizes the Clerk to appoint an assistant, who shall be paid by him. The Clerk of the Board is also Clerk of the Finance Committee.—*Act Legislature, April 10*, 1857.
† Inapplicable to the Board of Education and the property of the School Department.—*Act Legislature, April 26*, 1858. —[COMPILER.

shall be heard briefly, but without the observance of any technical or other formalities, not necessary in the discretion of the Board, to a just decision; which shall, after ascertaining the true state of the case, be given without delay.

SEC. 71. On or before the first Monday of May, annually, the Board of Supervisors of said city and county shall levy the amount of taxes for State, city, and county purposes, required by law to be levied upon all property in said city and county, not exempt from taxation, such amount as they may deem sufficient to provide for the payment of all demands upon the treasury thereof, authorized by law to be paid out of the same; *provided*, that such taxation, exclusive of the State tax and any special tax shall not, in the aggregate, for all the purposes of said city and county tax, exceed the rate of two dollars and thirty-five cents upon each one hundred dollars' valuation; *provided*, further, that the Board of Supervisors shall, in making the levy of said taxes, apportion and divide the taxes so levied, collected, and applied, to specific purposes, as hereinafter provided :

First. For the Corporation Debt Fund, not to exceed one dollar twelve and one-half cents upon each one hundred dollars' valuation, as aforesaid, which shall be applied to the payment of demands authorized under the fourth, fifth, sixth, seventh, eighth, and tenth, subdivisions of section ninety-five of the act as amended April eighteenth, eighteen hundred and fifty-seven, and of section seven of an act entitled " An Act for the funding and payment of the Outstanding Unfunded Claims against the City of San Francisco and against the County of San Francisco, as they existed prior to the first day of July, A.D. eighteen hundred and fifty-six, approved April twentieth, A.D. eighteen hundred and fifty-eight."

Second. For the School Fund not to exceed thirty-five cents upon each one hundred dollars' valuation aforesaid, which shall be applied to the payment of demands authorized under the second and ninth subdivisions of section ninety-five of the act as amended April eighteenth, eighteen hundred and fifty-seven.

Third. For the General Fund, not to exceed seventy cents upon each one hundred dollars' valuation, as aforesaid, which shall be applied, first, to the payments of demands authorized under the first, third, eleventh, twelfth, thirteenth, and fourteenth subdivisions, of section ninety-five of the act as amended April eighteenth, A.D. eighteen hundred and fifty-seven, and for the payment of any sum authorized by any special act; and for the payment of any demands, not exceeding eight thousand dollars* in any fiscal year, for the purchase and erection of hydrants, under the first section of an act entitled An Act to provide for the purchase and erection of Hydrants in the City and County of San Francisco, approved March seventh, eighteen hundred and fifty-nine ; and after all the foregoing demands are provided for and satisfied, for the payment of demands authorized under the fifteenth subdivision of section ninety-five of the act as amended April eighteenth, eighteen hundred and fifty-seven ; *provided*, that all repairs for hydrants shall be paid out of the eighteen thousand dollars as aforesaid.

Fourth. For the Street Light Fund, not to exceed seven and one-half cents upon each one hundred dollars, which shall be paid for lighting the streets of said city with gas, and for the repair of lamps and posts, in pursuance of the provisions of the present contract of said city and county with the San Francisco Gas Company, upon demands to be audited and allowed.

Fifth. For the Street Department Fund, not to exceed ten cents upon each one hundred dollars, which shall be paid for repairing and cleaning the streets and sewers which may have been accepted by the Board of Supervisors, for constructing street crossings, the salary of the Assistant Superintendent of Public Streets and Highways, and for such other objects relating to streets as shall be directed by law to be paid therefrom. All moneys received from licenses on wheeled vehicles, from the income on street railroads, and all fines received from the violation of any law or laws, of any city and county ordinances regulating the public streets, shall be paid into said Street Department Fund; and no money shall be transferred from either of the said funds to another, nor used in paying any demands upon such other fund, until all the indebtedness arising in any fiscal year and payable out of said funds, so raised for said fiscal year, shall have been payed and discharged.—[Act May 18, 1861, Sec. 14.]

SEC. 72. The said Board of Supervisors shall also constitute a Board of Equalization for said city and county, and as such shall have the powers conferred by the general laws regulating the assessment and collection of taxes, when not inconsistent with the provisions of this act.† Appointments of officers or public agents required by existing statutes, not repealed by this act, to be made on the nomination of the Mayor, and confirmation by the Common Council of the City of San Francisco, shall, after this act takes effect, be made in like manner on the nomination of the President of the Board of Supervisors and a confirmation by said Board.

SEC. 73. It shall be the duty of the Auditor, the Superintendent of Common Schools, the

---

* Amount increased to ten thousand dollars. See Act April 4, 1863, page 509.
† The assessment and taxation of property in the City and County of San Francisco are altogether regulated by special amendments to the General Public Revenue Act, approved May 17, 1861. See Statutes, 1859, Chap. CCCXV, pages 343-351.

Superintendent of Public Streets and Highways, Chief of Police and Chief Engineer of the Fire Department of said city and county, to report to the Board of Supervisors on the first Monday in February of each year, the condition of their respective departments, embracing all their operations and expenditures during the preceding year, and recommending such improvements in them as they may deem necessary. The Auditor shall also present to the Board of Supervisors at each quarterly session, and must also publish the same, a statement of the exact condition of the finances of said city and county, which must show the receipts into, and disbursements made from the treasury during the preceding quarter, the amount of money on hand, and the amount of audited demands outstanding. Immediately after the first Monday in February, the Board of Supervisors shall make up and publish an abstract from these several reports and other sources of the operations, expenditures, and conditions of all departments of governments of the said city and county.

SEC. 74. The Board of Supervisors of the City and County of San Francisco shall have power, by regulation or order [Amendment April 25, 1863] :

First. To regulate the police and police force of said city and county, and to prescribe their powers and duties.—[Amendment April 25, 1863.]

Second. To provide for the security, custody, and administration of all property of said city and county, without any power to sell or encumber the same, or lease any part thereof for more than three years, except, however, that such personal property belonging to the fire, street, or other departments, as they deem unsuited to the uses and purposes for which the same was designed, or so much worn and dilapidated as not to be worth repairing, may be sold, or exchanged, by order or resolution.

Third. To authorize and direct the summary abatement of nuisances ; to make all regulations which may be necessary or expedient for the preservation of the public health and the prevention of contagious diseases ; to provide, by regulation, for the prevention and summary removal of all nuisances and obstructions in the streets, alleys, highways, and public grounds of said city and county ; and to prevent or regulate the running at large of dogs, and to authorize the destruction of the same when at large contrary to ordinance.—[Amendment April 25, 1863.]

Fourth. To provide for cases omitted in this act, and in conformity with the principles adopted in it for opening, altering, extending, constructing, repairing, or otherwise improving, of public streets and highways, at the expense of the property benefited thereby, without any recourse, in any event, upon the city and county, or the public treasury for any portion of the expense of such works, or any delinquency of the property-holders, or owners.

Fifth. Providing for lighting the streets.—[Amendment Act April 26, 1862.]

Sixth. To regulate market-houses and market-places.

Seventh. To provide for the erection, repair, and regulation of wharfs and docks, and fixing the rates of wharfage thereat.

Eighth. To provide for inclosing, improving, and regulating all public grounds of the city and county, at an expense not to exceed two thousand dollars per annum.

Ninth. To prohibit the erection of wooden buildings, or structures, within any fixed limits where the streets have been established and graded, or ordered to be graded ; to regulate the sale, storage, and use of gunpowder, or other explosive, or combustible materials and substances, and make all needful regulations for protection against fire.

Tenth. To make such regulations concerning the erection and use of buildings as may be necessary for the safety of the inhabitants.

Eleventh. To determine the fines, forfeitures, and penalties that shall be incurred for the breach of regulations established by the said Board of Supervisors, and also for a violation of the provisions of this act, where no penalty is affixed thereto, or provided by law, but no penalty to be imposed shall exceed the amount of one thousand dollars, or six months' imprisonment, or both ; and every violation of any lawful order, or regulations, or ordinance, of the Board of Supervisors of the City and County of San Francisco, is hereby declared a misdemeanor, or public offense, and all prosecutions for the same shall be in the name of the people of the State of California.

Twelfth. To regulate and provide for the employment of prisoners sentenced to labor on the public works of said city and county.

Thirteenth. To license and regulate hackney-coaches, carriages, and other public vehicles, and to fix the rates to be charged for the transportation of persons, baggage, and property, therein ; and also to license and regulate porters employed in conveying baggage for persons arriving in and departing from said city and county, and to prohibit the exercise of those employments without such licenses.

Fourteenth. To license and regulate all such callings, trades, and employments, as the public good may require to be licensed and regulated, and are not prohibited by law.—[Amended, see Act April 27, 1863, Sec. 1, Sub. 1.]

Fifteenth. To prohibit and suppress, or exclude from certain limits, all houses of ill-fame, prostitution, and gaming ; to prohibit and suppress, or exclude from certain limits, or to regulate, all occupations, houses, places, pastimes, amusements, exhibitions, and practices, which are against good morals, contrary to public order and decency, or dangerous to the public safety.—[Amendment April 25, 1863.]

Sixteenth. To provide for the erection of a work-house, house of refuge, or house of correction, and for the regulation and government of the same.

Seventeenth. To direct and control the fire department of said city and county in conformity with the laws.

Eighteenth. To fix the fees and charges to be collected by the Surveyor of said city and county for certificates of surveys for buildings, or other purposes, and by the Superintendent of Streets and Highways, and any and all other municipal officers, where their fees are not otherwise fixed by law.

Nineteenth. To provide, by regulation, where it may be necessary, for carrying the provisions of this act into effect.

Twentieth. To provide for the care and maintenance of the indigent sick of said city and county.

Twenty-First. To provide for the construction and repair of hydrants, fire-plugs, cisterns, and pumps in the streets, for public security and convenience.

Twenty-Second. [Repealed, Act of April 26, 1862.]

Twenty-Third. To provide ways and means for the prosecution of the claims, in the name of the City of San Francisco, to the public lands, now pending for the same.

Twenty-Fourth. To permit the laying down of railroad tracks, and the running of cars thereon, along any street, or portion of street, for the sole purpose of excavating and filling in a street or portion of a street, or adjoining lots, and for such limited time as may be necessary for the purposes aforesaid, and no longer.—[Act May 18, 1861, Sec. 15.]

The term "construction of a street," as used in this act, shall include any, or all, of the following, viz. : Grading, sewering, paving, piling, and capping, planking, excavating, filling in, and other incidental matters, necessary to make a street, or part of a street, in perfect condition in the first instance, including sidewalks, crosswalks, street-crossings, or intersections of streets. The term " repairs of streets," as used in this act, includes all manner of necessary improvements of any street, or part of a street, including sidewalks and crossings, or intersections of streets, and, also, keeping the same in order, after the same has been accepted as in this act provided. The term " main streets," as used in this act, mean such streets as bound a block. The word " block ", shall mean the blocks which are known and designated as such on the map and books of the Assessor of said city and county.—[Act May 18, 1861, Sec. 16.]

The publication of all notices required by the provisions of this act, shall be made in the newspaper doing the printing for said city and county.—[Act May 18, 1861, Sec. 17.]

The following additional powers have been granted by the Legislature of the State, viz. :

To allow and order paid out of the General Fund, not exceeding the sum of six thousand dollars, in any one fiscal year, for the maintenance of an almshouse.—[Act May 17, 1861.]

To fix limits in said City and County of San Francisco, within which the burning of bricks shall be prohibited, and to make such rules and regulations in relation to the burning of bricks in any part of said city and county as they may deem advisable.—[Act April 15, 1861, Sec. 1.]

To allow and order paid out of the General Fund, a sum not to exceed fifty thousand dollars, for the purchase of a lot and building adjoining the City Hall in said city and county, and for repairs thereon.—[Act April 4, 1863, Sec. 1, Sub. 23.]

The said Board of Supervisors are authorized and empowered, in their discretion, to allow to the Clerk of said Board an increase of salary,* to the amount of twenty-five dollars per month, to be paid out of the General Fund, and to allow said Clerk to appoint an assistant, who shall be paid by said Clerk for all services said assistant may render him.—[Act April 23, 1858, Sec. 1, Sub. 24.]

To allow and order paid out of the General Fund, not exceeding the sum of five thousand dollars, for any one fiscal year, for the employment of special counsel.—[Act May 17, 1861, Sec. 5.]

To allow and order paid out of the General Fund, a sum not exceeding ten thousand dollars, in addition to the amount now allowed by law, for straightening, widening, and otherwise improving, that portion of the county road south of the Pioneer Race Course, and north of the county line of San Mateo County.—[Act April 26, 1862, Sec. 1, Sub. 18.]

To allow and order paid out of the General Fund, a sum not to exceed one hundred and fifty dollars per month, to be expended at the instance of the President of the Board of Supervisors, for contingent expenses other than those heretofore provided for, and of which he shall make a quarterly report to the Board.—[Act May 17, 1861, Sec. 1, Sub. 1.]

* Increased to two hundred dollars per month; also, Clerk of Finance Committee.

To appropriate the sum of five thousand dollars, in payment of so much money agreed to be paid by said city and county to John W. Dwinelle and Delos Lake, pursuant to the terms of a contract in that behalf, bearing date on November tenth, in the year eighteen hundred and sixty-two, for conducting certain special litigation in behalf of said city and county ; which said contract is hereby confirmed, and the said Board of Supervisors is hereby authorized to appropriate and allow the Auditor of said city and county to audit, and the Treasurer of said city and county to pay, the sums of money so appropriated and allowed by said Board in discharge of such contract, as fast as they become due, out of the General Fund of said city and county.—[Act April 4, 1863, Sec. 1, Sub. 11.]

To have power to appoint an Assistant Prosecuting District Attorney, who shall hold said office during the pleasure of said Board. The said Assistant shall also be the Prosecuting Attorney for the Police Court of said city and county, and shall receive a salary as such Assistant and Prosecuting Police Attorney of twenty-four hundred dollars per annum,* payable monthly out of the General Fund, which shall be in full for all services rendered for said city and county, or for either of them.—[Act April 23, 1858, Sec. 1, Sub. 22.]

To allow and order paid out of the General Fund, for the election expenses of said city and county, not to exceed seventy-five dollars for each Election District for each election in said city and county.—[Act April 4, 1863, Sec. 1, Sub. 5.]

To divide the Twelfth Election District into two voting precincts ; to designate two places for holding election polls in said district ; to appoint two additional Judges and one additional Inspector of Election for said district ; and to appropriate and order paid from the General Fund the necessary expenses of such additional polling place and of the elections held thereat, whenever they may deem the same necessary ; provided, that if said district is divided as aforesaid, provision shall be made for the election of Judges and Inspectors to preside at subsequent elections, as in other districts in said city and county.—[Act April 4, 1864, Sec. 1, Sub. 27.]

To allow and order paid out of the General Fund, not to exceed four thousand dollars per month, for the entire expenses of the Fire Department for said city and county.—[Act April 4, 1863, Sec. 1, Sub. 9.]

The Board of Supervisors of the City and County of San Francisco are hereby authorized and empowered to purchase and erect such hydrants, with the connecting pipes and appendages, as they may deem necessary and expedient. And the Auditor of said city and county is hereby authorized to audit, and the Treasurer to pay, the demands so authorized.—[Act March 7, 1859, Sec. 1.]

To allow and order paid out of the General Fund, a sum not to exceed twenty thousand dollars for the current year, and ten thousand annually thereafter, for the erection and construction of hydrants and cisterns in said city and county.—[Act April 4, 1863, Sec. 1, Sub. 7.]

The expense of the purchase and erection of said hydrants shall be paid out of the General Fund, over and beyond the amount already allowed for the maintenance of the Fire Department.—[Act March 7, 1859, Sec. 1.]

To allow and order paid to the San Francisco City Water Works Company, a sum not to exceed fourteen hundred dollars, out of the General Fund, for furnishing and setting hydrants in said city and county, in the years eighteen hundred and sixty-one and eighteen hundred and sixty-two, if, upon due investigation by them, each claim shall be found to be equitable and just.—[Act April 4, 1864, Sec. 1, Sub. 22.]

To allow and order paid out of the General Fund, not to exceed six thousand dollars annually, for rent of buildings for hose and engine companies in said city and county.—[Act April 4, 1863, Sec. 1, Sub. 8.]

To allow and order paid out of the General Fund, the sum of one thousand dollars, for the purpose of compromising conflicting titles to engine house lots, if the legal advisers of the said city and county shall deem such compromise expedient ; this sum to be in addition to the amount now allowed by law.—[Act April 4, 1864, Sec. 1, Sub. 3.]

To compromise upon such terms as to the said Board may seem proper, pending action, or actions, or claims, for the possession of the lot upon which the engine house of Broderick Engine Company, Number One, is now erected, in said City and County of San Francisco ; and for that purpose to appropriate, allow, and order paid, out of the General Fund, a sum not to exceed one thousand dollars.—[Act April 4, 1864, Sec. 1, Sub. 20.]

To purchase lots and erect engine houses for such fire company or companies as said Board may deem proper and advisable, to remove from their present location to other parts of the city and county, and for such purpose to allow and order paid out of the General Fund such sum or sums of money as may be required ; provided, that all sums expended under this provision shall not exceed twenty-five thousand dollars in addition to such sums as may be received for engine houses and lots sold as in this act provided ; and, provided, further, that no fire company shall

* Increased to two hundred and fifty dollars per month.—Act April 16, 1862.

be required to remove from their present location until a suitable and proper building shall be provided for such company.—[Act April 4, 1863, Sec. 1, Sub. 28.]

To allow and order paid out of the General Fund for the removal and building of engine houses in said city and county, a sum not to exceed twenty thousand dollars in addition to the amount now allowed by law.—[Act April 4, 1864, Sec. 1, Sub. 4.]

To establish and construct a complete system of fire alarm telegraph in the City and County of San Francisco, and to purchase and obtain materials and suitable apparatus therefor ; to connect the same to as many heavy bells as may be deemed expedient by them ; and to combine with said fire alarm telegraph a complete system of police telegraph, and for that purpose to allow and order paid out of the General Fund a sum not to exceed fifteen thousand dollars in addition to the amount now allowed by law for that purpose.* And said Board of Supervisors are hereby allowed, if in their judgment deemed necessary, to withdraw by order from the treasury of said city and county the sum of twenty-five thousand dollars, or so much thereof as may be necessary, to be paid and appropriated for the purposes hereinbefore mentioned, and for purchasing in the Atlantic States, for cash, suitable apparatus and materials for erecting and completing said fire alarm and police telegraph ; *provided,* that said sum of twenty-five thousand dollars, or so much thereof as may be withdrawn as aforesaid from the treasury as aforesaid, be deposited with some banking-house in said City and County of San Francisco, to be designated by said Board of Supervisors, subject to the drafts from time to time, as may be necessary for the purposes herein set forth, of the person or persons contracting with said city and county for the erection and completion of said fire alarm and police telegraph ; and, *provided,* further, that said person or persons so contracting as aforesaid, execute to the City and County of San Francisco, and deliver to the Treasurer of said city and county, a good and sufficient bond, with at least two good and sufficient sureties, (the bond and sureties to be approved by the Mayor and Treasurer of said city and county) in double the amount so deposited, conditioned for the just and faithful and proper use of said sum of twenty-five thousand dollars, or so much thereof as may be necessary for the erection, completion, and furnishing with apparatus and suitable materials, said fire alarm and police telegraphs.—[Act April 4, 1864, Sec. 1, Sub. 18.]

To appoint, when deemed necessary by said Board during the erection or upon the completion of said system of fire alarm and police telegraphs, one Superintendent for said telegraphs, and three Assistants therefor, in lieu of the Bell Ringers now employed for the watch tower of the City Hall of said city and county ; and to allow and order paid out of the General Fund, when by said Board deemed necessary, one hundred and fifty dollars per month as a salary to said Superintendent, and to allow and order paid in the same manner and out of the same fund as now provided for by law for payment of the aforesaid Bell Ringers, a sum not to exceed one hundred dollars per month, each, to said Assistants as salary.—[Act April 4, 1864, Sec. 1, Sub. 19.]

To allow and order paid out of the General Fund, a sum not to exceed three thousand dollars in any year, for the celebration in said city and county of the anniversary of our National Independence.—[Act April 4, 1863, Sec. 1, Sub. 4.]

To allow and order paid out of the General Fund, to the Secretary of the Board of Funded Commissioners, one hundred and twenty-five dollars per month, for clerk hire and office expenses, in addition to the amount now allowed by law.—[Act April 4, 1864, Sec. 1, Sub. 1.]

To order paid out of the General Fund, any deficiency that may occur in the Street Light Fund, for lighting the public streets.—[Act April 26, 1852, Sec. 1, Sub. 7.]

To audit, allow, and pay, the bills of the San Francisco Gas Company, rendered after the passage of this act, at the end of each calendar month, in pursuance of the original contract made with James Donahue & Co., by the City of San Francisco.—[Act March 6, 1858, Sec. 2.]

In case the Board of Supervisors of the City and County of San Francisco shall order any gas for the City Hall, engine houses, or any other public buildings, they are hereby authorized to audit and pay for the same out of the General Fund of the City and County of San Francisco as herein provided.—[Act March 6, 1858, Sec. 3.]

The payments authorized to be made by this act, when ordered by the Board of Supervisors, shall be made out of the General Fund, and in addition to the payments specified in section eleven of an act entitled " An Act amendatory of and supplementary to Section Ninety-Five of an Act to repeal the several charters of the City of San Francisco, to establish the Boundaries of the City and County of San Francisco, and to consolidate the government thereof," approved April nineteenth, one thousand eight hundred and fifty-six, said act approved April eighteenth, one thousand eight hundred and fifty-seven, and said section eleven being an amendment of section ninety-five or the said original act, approved April nineteenth, one thousand eight hundred and fifty-six.—[Act March 6, 1858, Sec. 4.]

---

* The Act of April 4, 1863, appropriates ten thousand dollars to erect a bell tower or to establish a system of Fire Telegraph.—[COMPILER.

The amounts authorized to be paid by the Act of April 4, 1864, shall be the only amounts to be paid for the respective purposes for which they are authorized to be paid under the provisions thereof, except when otherwise expressly provided therein, and excepting an allowance of two thousand dollars per annum, heretofore provided by law, for inclosing, improving, and regulating all public grounds in said city and county; and said Board of Supervisors are hereby authorized and empowered to direct and have executed the work, building, services, and improvements thereinbefore mentioned and provided to be paid for.—[Act April 4, 1861, Sec. 3.]

To allow and order paid out of the General Fund, not to exceed the sum of five thousand dollars per month, for the support of the indigent sick, and the contingent expenses of the City and County Hospital of said city and county; and out of the same fund, not to exceed the sum of six thousand dollars for any one year, for the support of the Small Pox Hospital of said city and county.—[Act April 4, 1863, Sec. 1, Sub. 13.]

To allow and order paid out of the General Fund, not to exceed six thousand dollars, for repairs to the City and County Hospital; and also, out of said fund, not to exceed the sum of twelve thousand dollars, to furnish said hospital.—[Act April 4, 1863, Sec. 1, Sub. 19.]

Also to allow and order paid out of the General Fund, such sums as are now due, or may become due, to the physicians of the City and County Hospital.—[Act April 27, 1860, Sec. 1, Sub. 17.]

To improve and enlarge the present City and County Hospital buildings and property, in said city and county, and if by them deemed expedient, to that end to purchase and receive additional land in said city and county, and to allow and order paid out of the General Fund, and for the purposes mentioned in this section, such sums of money as in the aggregate shall not exceed the sum of twenty-five thousand dollars.—[Act April 4, 1863, Sec. 1, Sub. 18.]

SUPPLEMENTAL VI.—*An Act to give further Powers to the Board of Supervisors of the City and County of San Francisco.*—Approved April 17, 1862.

SECTION 1. The Board of Supervisors of the City and County of San Francisco are hereby authorized and empowered, with the assent of the respective creditors of said city and county, hereinafter mentioned and referred to, and in the manner hereinafter provided, to settle, compound, and compromise, and adjust, certain indebtedness of said city and county, existing by certain final judgments against the City of San Francisco, or against said city and county, in favor of the purchasers, or assignees of purchasers, of certain property known as the "City Slip Property;" and also, any final judgment that may hereafter be rendered in favor of any other of such purchasers or assignees; and also, the claim in suit in Fourth District Court, in the name of Felix Argenti, against the said city; and also, the judgment in the Twelfth District Court in the name of Lucas, Turner & Co., against said city; and also, the judgment of H. W. Seale, against the said city in said Twelfth District Court; and also, a certain judgment in favor of Nathaniel Holland, against the City of San Francisco, rendered in the Twelfth Judicial District Court, in and for the City and County of San Francisco, on the seventh day of January, eighteen hundred and fifty-six, for four thousand eight hundred and sixty-eight dollars, and costs, with interest thereon, the same as if said judgment remained in full force and effect, and unreversed; and to close, adjust, and settle, all controversies respecting the title to said property, known as the "City Slip Property," upon such terms as the said Board may deem just and equitable; and the said Board is further hereby authorized and empowered to sell, on such terms and conditions as it may deem proper, the said property called the "City Slip Property," and, if deemed by it expedient, to apply the proceeds thereof to the payment of said judgments and indebtedness, or either or any of them, or any part thereof, in such sums and proportions as said Board shall deem best, and to issue, or cause to be issued, in such manner and form, and with such terms and conditions, redeemable in twenty years, as may be approved by said Board, bonds of said city and county, in payment of said indebtedness and judgments, or any or either of them, or of so much thereof as shall remain unpaid after the application and payment, as aforesaid, of said proceeds of sale, if said Board shall conclude to sell said city slip property, and appropriate the proceeds as aforesaid; and said bonds so issued shall be good and valid securities against said city and county, for the amounts for which the same shall be issued in pursuance of this act; *provided*, the interest on said bonds shall not, in any instance, exceed the sum of seven per cent. per annum; and the said Board are further authorized and empowered to levy and collect, from time to time, and in any settlement, as aforesaid, as herein provided, to provide for the future levy and collection of such tax, not to exceed one-half of one per cent. per annum, upon the taxable property in said city and county, as may be deemed necessary to pay the interest, and, eventually, the principal of said bonds, when said interest and principal shall respectively, become due; which tax shall be levied and collected in the same manner, and with like remedies, as other taxes are levied and collected in said city and county; *provided*, that in all cases where the purchase money has been paid for any of said lots, and the purchasers may elect to receive deeds for the same, in lieu of any judgment recovered, or claim for a return of the purchase money, the Mayor of said City and County of San Francisco is hereby authorized to make and execute deeds to such purchasers, or their assigns, without any additional consideration, which deeds shall convey all the title in said lots which the city and county has therein ; *provided*, further, that the Mayor of said city and county is also authorized to make and execute deeds for certain slip lots, to such purchasers or their grantees, as paid in full, and receive deeds from the Treasurer of said city and county, under, and by virtue of An Act to authorize the Treasurer of the City and County of San Francisco to execute certain Deeds and cancel Claims, approved April twenty-sixth, eighteen hundred and fifty-eight, and an act amendatory of said act, approved April sixth, eighteen hundred and sixty, without additional compensation, which deeds shall convey all the title in said lots, which the city and county has therein.

SEC. 2. *Be it further enacted*, That in the settlement and adjustment of such indebtedness the said Board shall have full power to require and take such assurances, indemnities, and satisfactions as the said Board may deem necessary for the protection of the interests of said city and county.

SEC. 3. *Be it further enacted*, That this act shall not be construed to divert, diminish, or impair, any power heretofore possessed by said Board of Supervisors.

To allow and order paid out of the General Fund, not exceeding the sum of ten thousand dollars in any one fiscal year, for the redemption of such property belonging to the City and County of San Francisco as may have been or may hereafter be sold for taxes or judgments.— [Act May 17, 1861, Sec. 1, Sub. 1.]

To prescribe by order the time and place of sale, and to cause to be sold at public auction, after advertisement [for] twenty days, in two or more daily papers printed in said city and county, the lot and building on the corner of Brenham Place and Washington Street, in said city and county, known as the "Hall of Records ;" also, such engine houses and lots in said city and county, not exceeding six in number, as said Board may deem it expedient to sell ; and upon such sale or sales, the Mayor of said city and county is hereby empowered to sign, seal, execute, and deliver to the purchaser or purchasers thereof such deed or deeds as may be necessary to perfect such sale or sales ; and the money received for such sale or sales as may be made by virtue hereof, shall be paid to the Treasurer of said city and county, and by him placed in the General Fund of said city and county.—[Act April 4, 1863, Sec. 1, Sub. 26.]

To appropriate all sums of money received from the sale of the Hall of Records, as authorized by subdivision twenty-six of an act to confer, etc., approved April fourth, eighteen hundred and sixty-three, for the repairs of a building to be used as the Hall of Records, in addition to the amount now authorized by law.—[Act April 4, 1864, Sec. 1, Sub. 23.]

To allow and order paid out of the General Fund, not to exceed twenty-five hundred dollars, for repairs to the Hall of Records of said city and county.—[Act April 4, 1863, Sec. 1, Sub. 3.]

To allow and order paid out of the General Fund, a sum not to exceed fifty thousand dollars, for the purchase of a lot and building for a Hall of Records, and for repairs thereon, or for the purchase of a lot and erection of a building for that purpose.—[Act April 4, 1863, Sec. 1, Sub. 27.]

SUPPLEMENTAL VII.—*An Act to empower the Board of Supervisors of the City and County of San Francisco to appropriate certain Moneys for the Purchase of a Lot and Building adjoining the City Hall, in said City and County, and for alterations and repairs thereof.*—Approved January 30, 1864.

SECTION 1. The Board of Supervisors of the City and County of San Francisco are hereby authorized and empowered : To appropriate, allow, and order paid. out of the General Fund, in addition to the sum of fifty thousand dollars provided by Article Twenty-Third of Section One of an Act to confer additional powers upon the Board of Supervisors of the City and County of San Francisco, and upon the Auditor and Treasurer thereof, and to authorize the appropriations of money by said Board, approved April fourth, eighteen hundred and sixty-three, the further sum of thirty thousand dollars for the purchase of a lot and building adjoining the City Hall in said city and county, and for alterations and repairs thereof, for the accommodation of the public offices of the city and county.

SEC. 2. All sums lawfully appropriated and expended under the provisions of the preceding section, shall be paid out of the General Fund, on demands duly audited in the mode prescribed by law for auditing other demands on the treasury.

SEC. 3. From and after the first day of June, eighteen hundred and sixty-four, and after the purchase aforesaid, it shall not be lawful to pay out of the treasury of the City and County of San Francisco, or out of any public funds thereof, any money for rent of rooms or offices for Judges' Chambers, the City and County Attorney, the Board of Education, the Board of Delegates of the Fire Department, or for any other officer or officers of the said city and county ; *provided*, that this section shall not impair any contract now existing.

To allow and order paid to the President and Treasurer of the Home for the Care of the Inebriate, for the support of said institution, out of the Police Fund of said city and county, the sum of two hundred and fifty dollars per month.—[Act April 25, 1863.]

To allow and order paid out of the General Fund, such sums as are now due, or may become due, for burying the indigent dead.—[Act April 27, 1860, Sec. 1, Sub. 6.]

To improve and enlarge the present City and County Hospital buildings and property in said city and county, and if by them deemed expedient to that end, to purchase and receive additional land in said city and county, and to erect new buildings for the City and County Hospital in said city and county, and to allow and order paid out of the General Fund, and for the purposes mentioned in this section, such sums of money as in the aggregate shall not exceed the sum of one hundred and twenty-five thousand dollars in addition to the amount now allowed by law.—[Act April 4, 1864, Sec. 1, Sub. 9.]

To transfer to the Board of Education of said City and County, for Public School purposes, the building now occupied as a County Hospital, whenever the same shall not be required for a Hospital.—[Act April 4, 1864, Sec. 1, Sub. 4.]

To allow and order paid out of the General Fund a sum not to exceed three hundred dollars per annum for medical attendance upon the inmates of the Industrial School in said city and county.—[Act April 4, 1864, Sec. 1, Sub. 26.]

To allow and order paid out of the General Fund, such sums as are now due, or may become due, for expenses of conveying insane persons to the State Hospital, at Stockton.—[Act April 27, 1860, Sec. 1, Sub. 6.]

To improve, alter, and enlarge the present jail building and property of said city and county, and if by them deemed expedient, for that purpose to purchase and receive additional land in said city and county, and to allow and order paid out of the General Fund, sums not to exceed the aggregate sum of twenty thousand dollars, for the purposes mentioned in this section.—[Act April 4, 1863, Sec. 1, Sub. 20.]

SUPPLEMENTAL VIII.—*An Act to confer further Powers upon the Board of Supervisors of the City and County of San Francisco.*—Approved April 27, 1863.

SECTION 1. The Board of Supervisors of the City and County of San Francisco shall have power, by regulation or order :

First. To license and regulate all such callings, trades, and employments, as the public good may require to be licensed and regulated, and as are not prohibited by law. And all licenses granted in pursuance of the provisions of this act, or the powers therein delegated, shall be signed by the Auditor of said city and county.

Second. To authorize the Auditor of said city and county to deliver, from time to time, to either the Treasurer or to the License Collector, as many of such licenses as may be required, and to sign the same, and charge them to the officer receiving them, specifying in the charge the business and amounts named in the licenses and class of licenses.

Third. To regulate and compel the payment to the County Treasurer, of all moneys received by any License Collector or Deputy License Collector ; and to fix the amount of the bonds to be required from such License Collector or Deputy.

Fourth. To appoint, instead of the present License Collectors, one person as Collector of Licenses, whose salary shall not exceed one hundred and seventy-five dollars per month, and two persons as Deputy Collectors of Licenses, whose salaries shall not exceed one hundred and twenty-five dollars per month each, the amount of each such salary to be fixed by the said Board of Supervisors ; which said Collector of Licenses and Deputy Collectors of Licenses shall have and exercise the same powers as Police Officers in serving process or summons and in making arrests ; also, shall have and exercise the power to administer such oaths and affirmations as shall be necessary in the discharge and execution of their official duties. The said Board of Supervisors shall have power to make all needful rules and by-laws regulating the official conduct or duty of said persons who shall be appointed Collector of Licenses and Deputy Collectors of Licenses, and alter or amend the same from time to time, in such manner as they may deem proper.—[Act April 27, 1863.]

To license and regulate hackney coaches, and other public passenger vehicles, and to fix the rates to be charged for the transportation of persons, baggage, and property, or either, therein ; and to license and regulate all vehicles used for the conveyance of merchandise, earth, and ballast, or either ; and also, to license and regulate persons and parties employed in conveying baggage, property, and merchandise, or either, to or from any of the wharfs, slips, bulkheads, or railroad stations within the limits of the City and County of San Francisco ; to appoint and license one Collector, in addition to the two now authorized by law, [amended, see preceding section] at a salary not to exceed one hundred and twenty-five dollars per month, which License Collector, and also those now authorized by law to be appointed, shall each have and exercise the same powers as Police Officers in serving process of summons and making arrest ; to fix and establish the amount of every license paid into the City and County Treasury for city and county purposes, at such rate as said Board shall determine, not exceeding the amount fixed by law ; and, *provided*, said Board shall have no power to entirely abolish any license fixed by law, or to reduce the proportions of each license collected, which by law is paid into the City and County Treasury for State purposes.—[Act April 25, 1863, Sec. 1, Sub. 4.]

SUPPLEMENTAL IX.—*An Act to authorize the Board of Supervisors of the City and County of San Francisco to regulate and license Intelligence Offices in said City and County.*—Approved May 17, 1861.

SECTION 1. The Board of Supervisors of the City and County of San Francisco are hereby authorized to direct the Auditor of said city and county to issue licenses to so many and to such persons as they shall deem properly qualified to keep intelligence offices in said city and county.

SEC. 2. Each license shall designate the house in which the person or persons licensed shall keep his or their office, and said license shall be paid for quarterly, in advance, and shall continue and be in force during the current quarter and no longer, unless revoked by order of the Board of Supervisors.

SEC. 3. Every person so licensed, under and by virtue of the provisions of this act, shall pay to the Treasurer of said city and county the sum of fifty dollars per quarter, one-half for the use of said city and county and the other half for State purposes.

SEC. 4. Each and every keeper of an intelligence office, licensed under the provisions of this act, shall keep his books in the English language, and, on the receipt of any money from any person applying for a situation, or other intelligence, for which fees are demanded, shall furnish to the said applicant a statement in writing of the amount received, on what account received, and what the intelligence office keeper agrees to do for and on account of said payment, with the date thereof, and to be signed by the said intelligence office keeper with his signature.

SEC. 5. Any person violating the provisions of this act, or keeping an intelligence office within the limits of said city and county, without being duly licensed, or after the same shall have been revoked by order of the Board of Supervisors of said city and county, or at any other house or place than is designated in such license, shall be deemed guilty of a misdemeanor, and, on conviction thereof, shall be fined not less than fifty dollars nor more than five hundred dollars, or imprisonment in the County Jail for not less than twenty days nor more than three months.

SEC. 6. Any person who shall obtain information or employment from an intelligence office keeper, and who shall communicate the same to another person, or send another person in his or her stead, with intent fraudulently to obtain the return of the money paid for such information, shall be deemed guilty of a misdemeanor, and, on conviction thereof, shall be punished by fine not exceeding one hundred dollars.

To allow and order paid out of the General Fund, for the fiscal year of eighteen hundred and sixty and eighteen hundred and sixty-one, not exceeding the sum of ten hundred dollars, for compiling and publishing the laws and ordinances relating to the City and County of San Francisco ; and for any fiscal year thereafter a further sum, not exceeding three hundred dollars, for the same purpose.—[Act May 17, 1861, Sec. 3.]

To designate one of their number, who shall, in the absence of the Mayor, or during his inability from any cause, perform the duties required by law of the Mayor of said city and county.—[Act April 25, 1863, Sec. 1, Sub. 7.]

The said Board of Supervisors may make all needful rules and police regulations for the safety and well ordering of all omnibus lines in the City and County of San Francisco.—[Act April 23, 1858, Sec. 1, Sub. 23.]

To regulate the Police and Police force of said city and county, and to prescribe their powers and duties.—[Act April 25, 1863, Sec. 1, Sub. 1.]

To increase the salary of each member of the Police force of said city and county twenty-five dollars per month, and to diminish the same again at pleasure to the present salary of said Police force ; which said increase of salary, if made, shall be paid as the salaries of the Police force are now paid, and out of the same fund.—[Act April 4, 1863, Sec. 1, Sub. 16.]

To increase the Police force of said city and county, as from time to time may be deemed necessary by the said Board of Supervisors, to not exceeding one hundred members, including the number now allowed by law, a portion of which increase may constitute a Harbor Police in and for the said city and county, and to allow and order paid out of the General Fund the salaries of said additional Police force, not to exceed the sum of one hundred and twenty-five dollars per month, or any less sum which they may deem proper for each member of said additional Police force.—[Act April 4, 1864, Sec. 1, Sub. 11.]

To authorize and empower the Police Commissioners of said city and county to appoint and to regulate local Policemen, whenever in their judgment the necessities of said city and county require it; *provided*, that no money shall be paid out of the treasury of the said city and county to said local Policemen.—[Act April 4, 1864, Sec. 1, Sub. 12.]

To purchase boats, tackle, and apparatus for the use of the Harbor Police, and to allow and order paid out of the General Fund, for that purpose, a sum or sums not in the aggregate to exceed one thousand dollars.—[Act April 4, 1864, Sec. 1. Sub. 16.]

To order constructed a common pound for estrays, and to provide for the taking up and impounding of all animals running at large within the streets of said city and county, north of Johnston Street and east of Larkin Street; [jurisdiction extended over the entire limits of the City and County of San Francisco.—Act May 14, 1861] *provided*, the cost of the construction of said pound shall not exceed five hundred dollars, which sum, or so much thereof as may be necessary, may be paid out of the General Fund by order of said Board of Supervisors. The said Board shall have power to make all needful rules and regulations necessary for the proper management and control of said pound, and may appoint one or more Pound Keepers, who shall be paid out of the fines imposed and collected of the owners of any animals impounded, and from no other source.—[Act April 23, 1858, Sec. 1, Sub. 14.]

To allow and order paid to Interpreter of the German language for the Police and County Courts, to be appointed by the County Judge, Police Judge, and President of the Board of Supervisors, one hundred and twenty-five dollars per month, to be paid from the General Fund. —[Act April 4, 1864, Sec. 1, Sub. 28.]

To allow and pay, out of the General Fund, a sum not to exceed five hundred dollars per annum, for deficiency in the salary of the Pound Keeper in said city and county.—[Act April 4, 1864, Sec. 1, Sub. 5.]

To provide for the safe keeping and disposition of all lost, stolen, or unclaimed property of every kind which may be in the possession or under the control of the Chief of Police of said city and county, or which may hereafter come into the possession of the Police of said city and county.—[Act April 25, 1863, Sec. 1, Sub. 10.]

To allow and order paid, out of the General Fund, not to exceed the sum of six thousand dollars, in addition to the amount now allowed by law, for repairing and improving roads south of Navy Street, in said city and county.—[Act April 4, 1864, Sec. 1, Sub. 10.]

To compromise and settle all claims upon the part of the Western Pacific Railroad and the Central Pacific Railroad, for cash or other security, in place of bonds claimed by said companies of said city and county, under an Act to authorize the Board of Supervisors of the City and County of San Francisco to take and subscribe one million dollars to the capital stock of the Western Pacific Railroad Company and the Central Pacific Railroad Company of California, and to provide for the payment of the same, and other matters relating thereto, approved April twenty-second, eighteen hundred and sixty-three; *provided*, that the power to make such compromise shall rest in said Board of Supervisors only after and in case said Board of Supervisors shall be compelled by final judgment of the Supreme Court to execute and deliver the bonds specified in said act.—[Act April 4, 1864, Sec. 1, Sub. 5.]

To allow and order paid, out of the General Fund, for the repairs to the outer half of streets constituting the water front of said city and county, as provided in section thirty-eight of " An Act to repeal the several Charters of the City of San Francisco, to establish the Boundaries of the City and County of San Francisco, and to consolidate the Government thereof," approved April nineteenth, one thousand eight hundred and fifty-six; the Auditor to audit, and the Treasurer to pay, sums not exceeding in the aggregate, three thousand dollars [increased to six thousand dollars.—Act April 27, 1860] during any one fiscal year.—[Act April 18, 1858, Sec. 1.]

To allow and order paid out of the General Fund, not exceeding the sum of twelve thousand dollars, in any one fiscal year, for repairs to, and improvements upon, streets and sewers in front of property belonging to the city, other than those mentioned in the previous subdivision of this section.—[Act April 27, 1860, Sec. 1, Sub. 2.]

To require, by ordinance, all contractors for street work, or other persons lawfully undertaking to improve, grade, or alter streets or public highways in the City and County of San Francisco, to erect fences or other suitable barriers, to protect the public from damage, loss, or accident, by reason of such grading, alteration, or improvement, and to determine and prescribe the fines and penalties that shall be incurred for breach of such regulations and ordinances as may be passed by virtue hereof.—[Act April 25, 1863, Sec. 1, Sub. 6.]

SUPPLEMENTAL X.—*An Act to confer further Powers upon the Board of Supervisors of the City and County of San Francisco.*—Approved April 25, 1863.

SECTION 1. That the Board of Supervisors of the City and County of San Francisco, shall have full power and authority to provide, by order, for laying out, opening, extending, widening, straightening, or closing up, in whole or in part, any street, square, lane, or alley, within the bounds of said city, which, in their opinion, the public welfare or convenience may require; to provide for ascertaining whether any, and what amount in value of damage will be caused thereby, and what amount of benefit will thereby accrue to the owner or possessor of any ground or improvements within said city and county, for which such owner or possessor ought to be compensated, or ought to pay a compensation, and to provide for assessing and levying either generally on the whole assessable property within said city, or specially on the property of persons benefited, the whole, or any part of the damages and expenses which they shall ascertain will be incurred in locating, opening, extending, widening, straightening, or closing up the whole or any part of any street, square, lane, or alley, in said city and county; to provide for granting appeals to the County Court of the City and County of San Francisco, from the decisions of any Commissioners, or other persons, appointed in virtue of any ordinance, to ascertain the damage which will be caused, or the benefit which will accrue to the owners or possessors of grounds or improvements, by locating, opening, extending, widening, straightening, or closing up, in whole or in part, any street, square, lane, or alley, within said city and county, and for securing to every such owner and possessor, the right, on application, within a reasonable time, to have decided, by a jury trial, whether any damage has been caused, or any benefit has accrued to them, and to what amount; to provide for collecting and paying over the amount of compensation adjudged to each person entitled, and to enact and pass all orders, from time to time, which shall be deemed necessary and proper to exercise the powers and effect the objects above specified; *provided*, nevertheless, that before the Board of Supervisors of the City and County of San Francisco proceed to execute any of the powers vested in them by this act, at least thirty days' notice shall be given of any application which may be made for the passage of any order, by advertisement in at least two of the daily newspapers of the City and County of San Francisco having the largest circulation; *provided*, further, that whenever any street or part of any street in the said city and county, occupied or used by the track of any railroad company, shall require to be altered or widened for the convenience of public travel, and proceedings for the altering or widening the same shall have been taken under the provisions of this act, it shall be lawful for the Commissioners appointed as in this act provided, and whose duty it may be, to make a just and equitable assessment of the whole amount of costs, damages, and expenses of such altering or widening, among the owners of all the lands and real estate intended to be benefited thereby, to assess such portion of said costs, damages, and expenses, upon the corporation or company owning or using said railroad track, as shall to them seem equitable and just, and such assessment shall be a lien upon any property of said corporation or company in the said city and county, and may also be enforced in the same manner as the assessment upon such owners of lands and real estate intended to be benefited thereby.

SEC. 2. That before any Commissioners, appointed by any order to be passed in virtue of this act, shall proceed to the performance of their duty, they shall give notice in at least two of the daily newspapers, published in the City of San Francisco, having the largest circulation, of the object of the order under which they propose to act, at least ten days before the time of their first meeting to execute the same.

SEC. 3. That upon the return of any assessment to be made under any ordinance to be passed in virtue of this act, the Clerk of the Board of Supervisors of the City and County of San Francisco shall cause a copy of said assessment to be published for ten days, in at least two daily newspapers of said city and county having the largest circulation.

SEC. 4. That the time within which any appeal is to be made from any assessment, shall be computed from and after the expiration of the ten days mentioned in the preceding section.

SEC. 5. All the expenses resulting from locating, opening, widening, straightening, or closing up, in whole or in part, any street, square, lane, or alley, within said City and County of San Francisco, shall be paid out of the moneys derived from the assessments upon the property benefited by such locating, opening, extending, widening, straightening, or closing up, in whole or in part, any street, square, lane, or alley, within said city and county; and the City and County of San Francisco shall not be liable for any expense caused by the same.

SEC. 6. This act shall take effect and be in force from and after its passage.

SUPPLEMENTAL XI.—*An Act to declare and regulate the power of the Board of Supervisors of the City and County of San Francisco to take Private Lands for certain Public Improvements, and to prescribe the manner of its Execution.*—Approved April 4, 1864.

SECTION 1. The Board of Supervisors of the City and County of San Francisco shall have power to determine, by order, to lay out, open, extend, widen, or straighten, any street, alley, square, park, road, or highway, in said city and county, and that it will be necessary to take private lands for that purpose, and for that purpose they shall enter in their minutes a resolution or ordinance declaring such determination, containing a description of the lands so deemed necessary, and also of that part or portion of said city and county, and those railroad companies and corporations, if any which they adjudge will be benefited by said improvement, and which ought to bear the expense thereof; such descriptions to be made with like certainty as is required by law in complaints in actions of ejectment, to refer to all such lands by the adjoining streets, and the numbers of the lots of which they are composed or form a part, as the same are or shall be laid down upon the official map of said city and county, if the same are so laid down on said map, or if not so laid down, to refer to the sections, half sections, quarter sections, or fractional sections, of which the same are composed or form a part, as the same are laid down on the official map of the United States. The said Board of Supervisors shall thereupon make an order directing some officer or officers of said city and county, to be designated in said order, to ascertain and report to them an estimate of the whole expense of the said improvements. Upon such report being made, the said Board of Supervisors shall pass an order requiring all persons interested in the subject matter of the said improvement to attend the said Board of Supervisors at a time fixed by the said Board of Supervisors, and to be specified in said order for that purpose. The said Board of Supervisors shall cause all such orders, resolutions, ordinances, and reports, to be published together daily, for one week, in two daily newspapers, published in the said City and County of San Francisco. After the completion of such publication, and upon proof thereof, and at the time appointed therefor as aforesaid, the said Board of Supervisors shall proceed to hear the allegations of the owners and occupants of the houses, lots, and lands, situated within the portion or part of the said city and county so described as aforesaid, and after hearing the same, shall make such further order in respect to such improvement as they shall deem proper.

SEC. 2. If the said Board of Supervisors shall determine to proceed with such contemplated improvement, they shall thereupon pass and enter in their minutes a final ordinance or resolution, declaring such determination, containing a description of the land deemed necessary to to be taken therefor, and also of that portion of the said city and county and those railroad corporations and companies, if any, which will be benefited by said improvement, and upon which the expense thereof is to be assessed, which description shall contain the certainty and particularity required in that behalf in the next preceding section of this act.

SEC. 3. The said Board of Supervisors may purchase the whole or any part of the land so finally declared to be necessary for such public improvement, of the owner or owners, and make such compensation therefor as the said Board may deem reasonable, and shall thereupon receive from such owner or owners a conveyance of said land to said city and county. In case all the land so declared necessary for such public improvement shall be so purchased and conveyed to said city and county, and the expense of such improvement shall have been declared in manner aforesaid to be a benefit to and the expense thereof to be assessed upon the whole of said city and county, the said Board of Supervisors shall cause the expenses of the said contemplated public improvement to be assessed upon the whole of the taxable property of said city and county, and to be included in and form a part of the next general assessment roll of said city and county, being stated in a separate column thereof, and with the like effect in all respects as if the same formed a part of the State and county taxes; and when the same shall have been collected the said Board of Supervisors shall cause the said contemplated public improvement to be forthwith made and completed.

SEC. 4. The said Board of Supervisors shall cause a map of said contemplated public improvement to be made, designating on such map the lots, tracts, and parcels of land which shall have been declared necessary to be taken for the same as aforesaid, and showing the commencement, boundaries, and determination of such contemplated improvement, and also the part and portion of said city and county, the corporations and companies as aforesaid, declared to be benefited by the same, and to be assessed therefor, with the like certainty as required by the first section of this act, which map shall be filed in the office of the Clerk of said Board of Supervisors.

SEC. 5. In case a part or portion of said city and county, and not the whole of said city and county, shall [have] been declared to be benefited by such contemplated improvement, and to be assessed for the expense thereof, as hereinbefore provided, the said Board of Supervisors shall cause to be published daily for one week, in the official newspaper of said Board in said city and county, a notice specifying and describing the land so declared necessary for such public improvement, and the portion of the said city and county, corporations and companies, so declare to be benefited by the making thereof, and to be assessed for the expenses thereof, and that the damages and recompense to which the owner or owners of such land may be entitled for the same, will be inquired into and determined, and that such damages and recompense, together with the costs and charges of the proceedings for the purpose of acquiring title to such lands and making appointment [apportionment] thereof, will be apportioned and assessed upon the owners and occupants of houses, lots, and other real estate, corporations, and companies, to be benefited thereby, by Commissioners to be appointed by the County Court of the County of San Francisco in the exercise of its civil jurisdiction, at a day in some term thereof to be specified in such notice, not more than ten nor less than three weeks from the first publication thereof. The Said Board of Supervisors shall cause a copy of such notice to be served upon each of the aforesaid corporations and companies, and each of the owners of the respective parcels of land to be taken for such improvement, and of the lands and tenements within the territory declared to be benefited by such improvement, who are residents of said city, so far as the same can be ascertained, and upon each of the occupants of each of said parcels, if such there be, and upon the usual Agents and Attorneys who shall theretofore have had charge of such lands of such owners as may be nonresidents of the said city and county, if such Agents or Attorneys may be found in said city and county; and in case any of such parcels of land are vacant, then by affixing a copy of such notice in some conspicuous place thereon, at least ten days previous to the day specified in said notice for the appointment of such Commissioners by the said County Court. The service and posting of such notices may be proved by the affidavit of any male citizen of this State, of full age, and disinterested in the proceedings, taken and certified by any officer authorized to administer affidavits to be read in Courts of Justice in this State, or by the certificate of the Sheriff of said city and county, as in proceedings in civil cases, and such affidavit and certificate in the respective case shall be received as evidence of the circumstances required by this section to be shown in regard to such service as alternative with personal service or as a substitute therefor.

SEC. 6. Upon the filing in the said County Court a copy of all the proceedings had by the said Board of Supervisors, as hereinbefore provided, certified by the Clerk of said Board, under the corporate seal of said city and county, and also, of all original affidavits showing publications of notices, and of all original affidavits and certificates showing service and posting of notices, and the original map, made as hereinbefore provided, in the said County Court, the said Court shall thereupon have and take jurisdiction of said proceeding as a special proceeding, and shall act therein and continue and determine the same after the manner of cases of equitable cognizance. At the day in such notice specified, or on any other day to which the same may be adjourned by the said Court, the said Court, after ascertaining to its own satisfaction that said notices have been duly served and published, or that sufficient reason for nonservice thereof, personally, has been shown by affidavit or Sheriff's certificate, as hereinbefore provided, and upon hearing the Attorney and Counsel for the said city and county, and any parties interested who may appear for that purpose, shall appoint three discreet freeholders of said city and county, not interested in any of the lands and tenements described in the said notice, nor of kin to any owner or occupant thereof, Commissioners of Appraisal and Assessment. The said Court may at any time remove any or all of said Commissioners for cause, upon reasonable notice and hearing, and may fill any vacancies occurring among them for any causes.

SEC. 7. The said Commissioners shall be sworn faithfully to discharge their duties according to the provisions of this act without favor or partiality; they shall proceed to view the lands and tenements mentioned and described in the notice, ordinances, resolutions, and map aforesaid, and may examine witnesses on oath, to be administered by any one of them, and shall keep minutes of the testimony so taken by them. In case of any controversy or doubt respecting any legal principle involved in their proceedings, or in any determination to be made by them, they shall apply to the said County Court for instructions, and shall enter upon their minutes the substance of any charge or instruction given them by the Court. They shall appraise the damages which the owner or owners, and if there be any occupants who are not owners, which such occupants of the lands and tenements to be taken for such public improvement will severally sustain by being deprived thereof, and shall apportion and assess the whole amount of such damages, together with the costs and charges of the Board of Supervisors in the proceedings to be taxed and allowed by the said Court, upon all the owners and occupants of lands and houses within the territory deemed by the resolution of the Board of Supervisors to be benefited by such improvement, as near as may be in proportion to the benefit which each shall be deemed to acquire by the making thereof; *provided*, that no damage shall be allowed for the injury, removal, or demolition of any building erected on any of said lands after the filing of said map; and, *provided*, further, that when any street, or part of any street in the said city and county occupied or used by the track of any railroad company shall require to be altered or widened for the convenience of public travel, and proceedings for the altering or widening the same shall have been taken under the provisions of this act, it shall be lawful for the Commissioners appointed as in this act provided, and whose duty it may be to make a just and equitable assessment of the whole amount of costs, damages, and expenses of such altering or widening among the owners of all the lands and real estate intended to be benefited thereby, to assess such portions of such costs, damages, and expenses upon the corporation or company owning or using said railroad track, as shall to them seem equitable and just, and such assessment shall be a lien upon any property of said corporation or company in the said city and county, and may also be enforced in the same manner as the assessment upon such owners of lands and real estate intended to be benefited thereby.

SEC. 8. The said Commissioners shall make a report thereof under their hands, or the hands of a majority of them, to the said County Court, in which report they shall describe, with all practicable certainty, the several pieces and parcels of land taken for such improvement, and the names and residences of the owner or owners thereof, respectively, and the rights of such owners, so far as they can be ascertained, designating unknown owners, if any such there be, and the sum of money which should be paid to each of the owners and occupants of the said several parcels of land, or his or their recompense for being deprived thereof, or of his or their estate and interest therein, including any and all lands purchased by, and conveyed to said city and county, for the purposes of said improvement, as hereinbefore provided, and the cost and expense thereof. They shall also in such report specify, in the form prescribed by law for assessment rolls in said City and County of San Francisco, the sums of money which each and every owner or occupant of houses and lands, corporation or company, deemed to be benefited by such improvement, whether known or unknown, as aforesaid, should pay towards the expense of making the same, and the lands in respect to which he shall be deemed by them to be so benefited; and in case the land in respect to which any person shall be deemed benefited, shall be the same of which any portion held by him under the same title shall be taken for such improvement, that fact shall be stated in their report; they shall also file a duplicate of such report in the office of the Clerk of said city and county.

SEC. 9. Upon the filing of such report, the said Court shall assign a day for hearing objections to the confirmation thereof; and on the day assigned, or on such other day or days to which the same shall be adjourned by said Court, shall hear the allegations of all persons interested, and may take proof in relation thereto, from time to time, and shall confirm the said report; or may set the same aside and refer the matter to the same or to new Commissioners, who shall thereupon proceed as hereinbefore provided.

SEC. 10. Upon the confirmation of the report of Commissioners of Appraisal and Assessments, the said County Court shall enter an order that the City and County of San Francisco shall be entitled to take the lands and tenements specified in the report of such Commissioners as necessary for the making of such public improvement, on paying the amount of damages assessed to the owners and occupants thereof, in such report; and where any damages shall be awarded, and any assessments for benefits of the improvements in respect to which such damages are awarded, shall be made upon the same person or persons, or in respect to the ownership of any entire parcel of land, a part of which shall be taken for such improvements, in that case the said City and County of San Francisco shall become vested with the title of such lands, (free from all incumbrances) upon paying or depositing, according to the law, the amount of the difference between the sums of money so awarded and assessed.

SEC. 11. The said Commissioners shall be entitled to compensation for their services, under this act, to be certified by the said County Court, and taxed by said Court as a part of the expenses of the proceedings.

SEC. 12. Any person conceiving himself aggrieved by any part of such report that shall have been confirmed by said County Court, may, within one month after such confirmation, give notice to the said Board of Supervisors and to the Clerk of said County Court, of his intention to appeal to the Supreme Court, to review the said report, or the proceedings of the said Commissioners, or of the said County Court, or of any or of all of them, upon matters of law, and to correct the said report. Said notice shall specify the grounds of such appeal with sufficient certainty, and shall be accompanied by the undertaking or deposit provided for in section three hundred and forty-eight of the act to regulate proceedings in Courts of Justice in this State, commonly known as the Civil Practice Act. When the party appealing shall desire a statement to be annexed to the record, the same shall be prepared as in other appeals in civil cases, with the like effect, and any portion of the testimony taken by the Commissioners or Judge, or of the minutes of the Commissioners pertinent to the appeal, may be inserted in such statement.

SEC. 13. The giving of such notice and filing of such undertaking, or making such deposit, shall suspend all further proceedings of the Board of Supervisors in relation to the taking of the lands and tenements which shall be the subject of such notice, until a decision thereon, as hereinafter provided. The Supreme Court shall proceed to hear such appeal, giving the same such procedure as may be consistent with the dispatch of public business in the said Court, and may confirm, correct, modify, or set aside such report, in whole or in part; may direct the Commissioners to proceed and revise the same upon principles declared by the said Supreme Court; and in case a new report is made by the Commissioners under such direction, the same shall be subject to the same confirmation by the County Court, and to the like appeal, with the like effect, respectively, as hereinbefore provided.

SEC. 14. In case the said report so made and confirmed as aforesaid in the said County Court shall be confirmed in the Supreme Court, the obligors in the undertaking given to the said city and county as before provided, shall be liable to pay all the taxable costs necessarily incurred on said appeal; and in case the said report shall be corrected or modified, the Supreme Court shall determine under the circumstances of the case whether the appellant shall be entitled to his costs and expenses; and if the same be awarded to such appellant they shall be paid on taxation by the Board of Supervisors of said city as part of the contingent expenses of the proceeding.

SEC. 15. Whenever the amount of damages for taking any lands as aforesaid and assessment thereof shall be finally ascertained and fixed, either by confirmation of the County Court as aforesaid, and no notice and undertaking being given as hereinbefore prescribed, or by the confirmation, correction, or modification of the report of the Commissioners by the Supreme Court, the Mayor of the said city shall cause a transcript to be made, and in the form used for assessment rolls in said city, except that in such assessment roll to be made from such report as confirmed shall be set down in separate columns :

First. The names of all persons, corporations, and companies assessed, when known, and if not known, then that fact to be stated.

Second. The description of the land in respect to which they are assessed.

Third. The amount to which such persons shall respectively be assessed.

Fourth. The amount of damages, if any, to which such persons are respectively entitled by the award of the Commissioners.

Fifth. The amount of the excess, if any, to be collected ; to which said transcript, when so made, the Mayor shall annex his warrant, and the same shall be thereupon collected in the manner then prescribed by law for the collection of general taxes in said city and county, and shall in like manner be a lien upon the respective tracts and parcels of land, corporations, and companies, as aforesaid.

SEC. 16. The expenses of any public improvement herein authorized shall be defrayed by assessment on the owners and occupants of houses and lands, corporations and companies, that may be benefited thereby.

SEC. 17. Whenever the amount of any damages for taking any lands as aforesaid shall be finally ascertained and fixed, either by confirmation of the County Court as aforesaid, and no notice and undertaking being given within the time above prescribed, or by the confirmation thereof by the Supreme Court, it shall be the duty of the said Board of Supervisors to cause the said damages and the other expenses of said improvement to be collected upon the said assessment roll as aforesaid, and when so collected they shall forthwith pay the amount of such damages to the owners and occupants of lands and tenements, or to persons having any liens thereon to whom the same shall have been allowed ; and in case such owners be unknown non-residents of the said city, married women, infants, idiots, or lunatics, or the rights and interests of persons claiming the same shall, in the opinion of the Board of Supervisors, be doubtful, it shall be lawful for the said Board of Supervisors in any such case to pay the amount of such damages into the office of the Clerk of the said County Court, accompanied by a statement of the facts and circumstances under which said payment is made, and describing the lands and tenements taken by the said City and County of San Francisco for which such damages have been awarded ; but the City and County of San Francisco shall not be liable for any expense of such public improvement beyond the moneys actually collected for the same, except as hereinbefore provided.

SEC. 18. Until such damages shall be paid as aforesaid, it shall not be lawful for the said Board of Supervisors or any of their officers or Agents to take or enter upon any lands or tenements for the taking of which any such damages shall have been allowed.

SEC. 19. Upon any such damages being paid into the said County Court, the said Court shall take order for the investment thereof and of the interest arising thereupon after the manner of Courts of Equity in regard to trust funds deposited therein, and shall cause the securities taken on such investments to be transferred, and the money on hand to be paid over to the persons entitled to such damages, their guardians, or legal representatives, in the manner prescribed by law respecting moneys belonging to doubtful or unknown owners, and deposited in District Courts, and the same proceedings in all respects shall be had to ascertain the rights and interests of such persons.

SEC. 20. If any title attempted to be acquired by virtue of this act shall be found to be defective from any cause, the said Board of Supervisors may again institute proceedings to acquire the same, as in this act provided, or if proceedings have been had in the said County Court in regard to such public improvements as herein provided, may summon the owner, occupant, or claimant of such lands to appear, in the first instance in such County Court and show cause why Commissioners should not be appointed and proceedings thereafter had from that point in and by said Court in relation to said lands as herein provided. Upon the return of such new proceedings so had by the Board of Supervisors as hereinbefore provided, or upon the return of a summons duly served in the respective case, the said County Court shall have and take jurisdiction of the proceedings, and such proceedings shall be thereafter had in the same by said Court from that point as hereinbefore provided, and with the like effect. At any stage of such new proceedings, or of any proceedings under this act, the said County Court, or the Judge thereof at Chambers, may, by an order made in that behalf, authorize the said city and county, if already in possession of any of such lands, to continue in such possession and the use thereof for the purposes of such improvements ; *provided,* said city and county shall pay a sufficient sum into Court, or give security, to be approved by said County Court or Judge, to pay the compensation in that behalf when ascertained.

. SEC. 21. This act shall not be construed to repeal An Act to confer further Powers upon the Board of Supervisors of the City and County of San Francisco, passed April twenty-fifth, eighteen hundred and sixty-three, but the provisions of that act shall be held not to apply to the proceedings provided for in this act. This act shall be deemed a public act, and shall be liberally construed, and the said Board of Supervisors and the said County Court shall have all powers necessary to carry the same into execution. All presumptions attaching to the proceedings of Courts of general jurisdiction shall apply to the proceedings had in the said County Court under the provisions of this act; *provided*, it shall appear that its jurisdiction originally attached in the same, and such jurisdiction shall be deemed to attach upon the filing in the said County Court of the proceedings, map, affidavits, and certificates mentioned in the sixth section of this act, notwithstanding any defect of form or of substance not appearing on the face of the proceeding or papers. This act shall take effect immediately.

To order paid out of the General Fund, not to exceed seven thousand five hundred dollars, for cleaning sewers, cesspools, and street crossings, in any one fiscal year.—[Act April 26, 1862, Sec. 1, Sub. 9.]

To allow and order paid out of the General Fund, not to exceed eight thousand dollars per annum, in addition to the sum now allowed by law, for cleaning the streets, sewers, crosswalks, and highways of said city and county.—[Act April 4, 1863, Sec. 1, Sub. 6.]

To allow and order paid out of the General Fund a sum not to exceed three thousand dollars, for grading and improving Columbia Square, in said city and county.—[Act April 4, 1864, Sec. 1, Sub. 2.]

To appropriate, allow, and order paid out of the General Fund, a sum not to exceed ten thousand dollars, for grading and fencing Hamilton Square, in said city and county.—[Act April 4, 1864, Sec. 1, Sub. 24.]

To allow and order paid out of the General Fund, a sum not to exceed five thousand dollars, for improving Washington, Union, and Portsmouth squares, in said city and county.—[Act April 4, 1864, Sub. 3.]

To settle claims for the refunding of taxes collected under the levy decided to be illegal by the Supreme Court in the case of Crosby et al. vs. Patch; *provided*, the aggregate amount of claims so settled shall not exceed the portion of such taxes levied for city and county purposes.—[Act April 4, 1864, Sec. 1, Sub. 25.]

SUPPLEMENTAL XII.—*Act to Establish the Lines and Grades of Streets in the City and County of San Francisco.*—Approved April 4, 1864.

SECTION 1. The City and County of San Francisco is authorized, as in this act provided, to establish the lines and grades of the streets in said city and county lying within the corporate limits of the City of San Francisco as defined in an act entitled An Act to Incorporate the City of San Francisco, passed April fifteenth, eighteen hundred and fifty-one, and for that purpose a Board of Civil Engineers is hereby constituted, composed of the City and County Surveyor, and Thaddeus R. Brooks, who shall be known as the " Board of City Engineers," who shall proceed, as soon as practicable, to survey and to complete surveys already commenced of all the streets and fix the lines thereof within the limits above mentioned, and to make a map or maps thereof, showing thereon the width of every street, to fix monuments for the preservation of the street lines so established, and to prepare and file in the office of the City and County Surveyor a complete record of the monument so fixed; and the lines so established by said Board shall conform as far as possible with the original base lines of the city survey.

SEC. 2. Said Board shall, after making a careful survey thereof, make profiles of all the streets within said limits west and south of Larkin and Johnson or Ninth streets, and legibly designate on said profiles such lines of elevation or grade as they shall deem suitable to establish a permanent grade for said streets.

SEC. 3. The Board having completed their survey, maps, and profiles, or either, shall deliver the same with a written report to the Board of Supervisors of said city and county, who shall thereupon publish a notice for three weeks, stating that such report has been made, and that the same, with the maps or profiles, are open for public inspection in the office of the Clerk of the Board of Supervisors, where the same shall be kept during the publication of said notice. Any property owner dissatisfied with such maps or profile may at any time within three weeks after the first publication of said notice, file with the Clerk of the Board of Supervisors objections thereto in writing, stating specifically the grounds and reasons of such objections, and the Clerk shall indorse thereon the date of such filing. After the expiration of said notice, in case such objections are so filed, the Clerk shall cause said maps or profiles, together with the written objections thereto, to be returned to said Board of City Engineers, who may, after duly considering such objections, modify their report, maps, and profiles, if they deem proper. In case no written objections are so filed or being filed, and the same being thus considered by the Board of City Engineers, the said maps or profiles, or both, shall be finally submitted to the

Board of Supervisors, who shall approve or reject the same; and if the same shall be finally approved and adopted by an order of the said Board of Supervisors, then such maps and profiles shall stand as the legal and valid official plan of said city, to determine the lines of the streets and the grades thereof.

SEC. 4. In making the survey of that part of the city to the west and south of Larkin and Johnson or Ninth streets, said Board shall make the same conform, as far as possible, to the official plan or map of the Western Addition, made by the Commissioners appointed by Ordinance Number Eight Hundred and Forty-Five, of the City of San Francisco, conforming also to the lines and grades, as far as practicable, of the streets to the east and north-east of the streets last named, observing the original base lines of the city survey, so far as they can be ascertained.

SEC. 5. The maps and profiles, when approved by the Board of Supervisors, shall also be certified by said Board of City Engineers, by their certificate indorsed thereon, and by them subscribed. All their surveys, field notes, and records, and the map or maps designating the lines of the streets, and the width of the same, and the size of each block, on the completion of their duties, as herein prescribed, shall be deposited with and kept by the City and County Surveyor, as a part of the records of his office, and shall be and remain the property of the City and County of San Francisco.

SEC. 6. The Board of Supervisors shall determine the amount of compensation to be paid to said Board of Engineers, and shall also allow them the necessary assistants, and provide suitable rooms for their use while engaged in the work authorized by this act, and furnish the necessary instruments, books, stationery, and office furniture, and also furnish suitable monuments, of iron, stone, or wood, for the purposes mentioned in section one of this act; all of which shall be obtained by said Board of Engineers, by their requisition upon the Board of Supervisors, in the mode prescribed in section nine of the act entitled "An Act to fix and regulate the Salaries of Officers in the City and County of San Francisco," approved May seventeenth, eighteen hundred and sixty-one ; *provided*, that no payments shall be made by said Engineers on account of their compensation until after the completion of their duties as herein provided ; and, *provided*, further, that no compensation shall be allowed or paid to said Engineers for any services performed after the first day of August, A.D. one thousand eight hundred and sixty-four. Every item of expense authorized by this act, before it becomes a claim or debt against said city and county, shall first be allowed and ordered paid by the Board of Supervisors, and audited by the Auditor, when the same shall be paid by the Treasurer, out of the General Fund of the City and County of San Francisco ; *provided*, further, that the amount of money expended under the provisions of this act, including salaries of Engineers, shall not exceed eight thousand dollars.

SEC. 7. In case of vacancy in said Board of City Engineers, the Mayor shall fill such vacancy by the appointment of some competent Civil engineer, which appointment shall be subject to the approval of the Board of Supervisors.

SEC. 8. All acts and parts of acts in conflict with this act are hereby repealed.

SEC. 9. This act shall take effect and be in force from and after the date of its passage.

To ordain, procure, and use, a common seal, to be used at pleasure, as the official seal of the said City and County of San Francisco, the cost of which seal shall not exceed fifty dollars, to be paid out of the General Fund, by order of said Board of Supervisors.—[Act April 23, 1858, Sec. 1, Sub. 20.]

To expend and order paid out of the General Fund, not to exceed two thousand dollars per month, for objects of urgent necessity.—[Act April 26, 1862, Sec. 1, Sub. 10.]

To provide for the summary removal and disposition of any or all vehicles found during certain hours of the day and night, to be designated by said Board, in the streets, highways, and public squares of said city and county, or such of them as said Board may designate ; and, in addition to all other remedies, to provide, by regulation, for the sale or other disposition of said vehicles so found in said streets, highways, or public squares, as aforesaid.—[Act April 25, 1863, Sec. 1, Sub. 5.]

Also, to remove the remains of the dead from the Yerba Buena Cemetery to some other burial ground, and to dedicate the land now known as the Yerba Buena Cemetery for such purpose of a public nature as they may deem proper, and to allow and order paid out of the General Fund, a sum not to exceed ten thousand dollars.—[Act April 27, 1860, Sec. 1, Sub. 14.]

To allow and order paid out of the General Fund, for grading, improving, and erecting a monument in Yerba Buena Park, a sum not to exceed ten thousand dollars, in addition to the amount now allowed by law for that purpose.—[Act April 4, 1864, Sub. 1.]

To allow and order paid out of the General Fund, to the Clerk of the Mayor of said city and county, the sum of one hundred and fifty dollars per month in lieu of the present salary allowed by law to said Clerk.—[Amendment April 4, 1864, Sec. 1, Sub. 8.]

To allow and order paid out of the General Fund, to the Porter of the City Hall of said city and county, a sum not to exceed ninety dollars per month in lieu of the salary now allowed to him by law.—[Amendment April 4, 1864, Sec. 1, Sub. 14.]

To appoint an additional Assistant Porter for the City Hall of said city and county, after the same shall be enlarged, and to allow and order paid out of the General Fund a salary to him not exceeding the sum of seventy-five dollars per month.—[Amendment April 4, 1864, Sec. 1, Sub. 13.]

To allow and order paid out of the General Fund, in lieu of their present salary, the sum of one hundred and fifty dollars per month to three Deputies of the Sheriff of said city and county, which Deputies now receive one hundred and twenty-five dollars per month.—[Amendment April 4, 1864, Sec. 1, Sub. 15.]

SUPPLEMENTAL XIII.—*An Act to define the Powers and Duties of the Board of Supervisors, etc.*— Approved April 10, 1857.

SECTION 1. The Board of Supervisors of the City and County of San Francisco shall have power to appoint a committee, consisting of three members of said Board, to be denominated the " Finance Committee," and to fill all vacancies which may happen in said committee by new appointments, from time to time. Said committee, in addition to the ordinary duties of the Finance Committee of said Board, shall have the power as hereinafter specified.

SEC. 2. The Clerk of the Board of Supervisors shall be Clerk of the Finance Committee, after the expiration of six months from the passage of this act, and during said intermediate period of six months, the said committee shall have power to appoint a Clerk, who, during the time that he shall be actually employed, shall receive a salary of two hundred dollars a month, which amount shall be understood to cover all expenses for books, stationery, lights, fuel, and contingencies, which may be necessary for the use of said committee, and shall be paid out of the General Fund, upon demand, of the treasury of said City and County of San Francisco, after being first approved by the committee, and allowed and registered by the Auditor, like other similar demands.

SEC. 3. The Clerk of said committee shall keep a record of its proceedings, with the names of witnesses examined, and a substantial account of the evidence taken. It shall be the duty of the Sheriff, or any Constable, or Policeman, of said city and county, to execute the lawful process and orders of the said committee. The said committee may visit any of the public offices when, and as often, as they think proper, and make their examinations and investigations therein, without hindrance. In the exercise of its functions, the concurrence of two members of the committee shall be deemed sufficient.

SEC. 4. It shall be the duty of the committee to proceed forthwith to examine and settle all the accounts and transactions of the Treasurer of said city and county, and to make out and state two distinct accounts, the one embracing his transactions from the first Monday in October, 1855, to the first day of July, 1856, and the other embracing those of the period from the said first day of July to the time of said settlement; and the said committee shall ascertain, determine, and state the true balance of said accounts.

SEC. 5. After the settlement of the accounts and transactions of the present Treasurer of said city and county, the said committee shall proceed in like manner to investigate and settle the transactions and accounts of the Treasurers, Auditors, Controllers, and Tax Collectors of the City and of the County of San Francisco, who were in office during the two terms next preceding those of the present incumbent; and also of the present Auditor and President of the Board of Supervisors.

SEC. 6. The said committee shall hereafter, as often as may be required, by order of the Board of Supervisors, investigate the transactions and accounts of all officers having the collection, custody, or disbursement of public money, or having the power to approve, allow, or audit demands on the treasury, and report thereon to the Board of Supervisors, and for the purpose, shall continue to have and exercise all the powers granted in this act. But nothing in this act contained shall be construed to relieve the Auditor, President of the Board of Supervisors, or other officers, from any of the duties and obligations now imposed on them by law.

SEC. 7. The said committee and the Clerk, shall have free access to any records, books, and papers in all public offices. And said committee shall have the same power as courts of record, to administer oaths and affirmation, to examine witnesses, and compel their attendance before them, by subpena, and attachment for contempt, in case of their refusal to appear or to testify when lawfully required, and shall have the like power to punish as for contempt, any officer, ex-officer, or other person, who shall refuse or neglect, when required in writing, by said committee, to exhibit any official records, books, or papers in his custody, or to explain the same, or any official transaction of his own, or of any other officer so far as he may be able.

SEC. 8. If, from the examination made by the Finance Committee, in pursuance of the powers granted by this act, it shall appear that a misdemeanor in office, or a defalcation has been committed by any officer of said city and county, whose accounts and transactions they are authorized to examine as aforesaid, said committee shall immediately report the same to the President of the Board of Supervisors, who shall immediately cause said report to be published, in at least two daily newspapers, published in the City of San Francisco, for the period of three days.

SUPPLEMENTAL XIV.—*An Act to create certain Road Districts in the City and County of San Francisco, and to provide for the repair and improvment of Roads therein.*—Approved May 20, 1861.

SECTION 1. It shall be the duty of the Board of Supervisors of the City and County of San Francisco, within sixty days from and after the passage of this act, to divide that portion of the eleventh and twelfth districts in said city and county, being southerly and westerly of the line formed by Center, Dolores, Market, and Larkin streets, into two road districts; they shall cause each district to be numbered, and the boundaries of the same to be accurately defined by reference to public streets or highways, or other permanent monuments, and shall cause such description of boundaries, with their numbers, to be entered on their minutes.

SEC. 2. The said Board of Supervisors shall, as soon as they have established the road districts before named, appoint some qualified person, a resident and legal voter in each road district, Roadmaster, and whenever thereafter a vacancy in said office may occur; each Roadmaster shall hold his office for the term of one year from and after the date of his appointment, and until his successor is appointed and qualified.

SEC. 3. Said Roadmasters shall each take and subscribe the proper oath of office and give bond conditioned on the faithful discharge of the duties of his office, in such sum, not exceeding fifteen hundred dollars, and with such sureties as the Board of Supervisors may direct.

SEC. 4. It shall be the duty of each Roadmaster to carefully examine all the public roads in his district and report the condition of the same from time to time, to the Board of Supervisors; *provided,* that from the month of November to May, inclusive, of each year such report shall be made on the first Monday of each month; said report shall specify the kind of repairs and the portion or portions of the district in which they are required, together with an estimate of the cost thereof.

SEC. 5. Upon presentation to the Board of Supervisors of the estimate of the Roadmaster of any district, as herein provided, the said Board of Supervisors shall appropriate a sum of money not exceeding the amount of said estimate; *provided,* that the amount of all appropriations authorized by this act shall not exceed four thousand dollars for any one fiscal year. All sums so appropriated shall be faithfully applied for the purposes specified in such appropriation; and upon the presentation of the sworn certificate of the Roadmaster of any district, any sum or sums, not exceeding such appropriation, shall be allowed and ordered paid out of the General Fund, in like manner as other demands are allowed and ordered paid.

SEC. 6. For the purposes of this act, public roads and highways shall include all roads that have been open to the public and used as public highways long enough to evince their utility and necessity, but shall not include any street established by any authorized survey of the city, or City and County of San Francisco, or any part thereof, unless such street shall have been or may hereafter be established across or along such public road or highway, or some part thereof.

SEC. 7. Each Roadmaster is hereby authorized to purchase all necessary timber, planks, or other material for the construction or repair of bridges or culverts, and to hire, at just and reasonable rates, all necessary labor, tools, or implements, for widening, straightening, grading, or otherwise improving such roads and highways. Each Roadmaster shall receive a reasonable compensation, to be paid out of the General Fund, not to exceed five dollars per day for each day's service rendered in the discharge of the duties of his office; *provided,* that no Roadmaster shall be entitled to receive more than three hundred dollars for all services he may render as such officer, in any one fiscal year.

SUPPLEMENTAL XV.—*Act Concerning Roads, Etc.*—Approved April 16, 1859.

SECTION 1. The provisions of an act entitled "An Act concerning Roads and Highways," approved April twenty-eighth, one thousand eight hundred and fifty-five, and the provisions of an act entitled "An Act to amend An Act entitled An Act concerning Roads and Highways," passed April twenty-eighth, one thousand eight hundred and fifty-five, approved April nineteenth, one thousand eight hundred and fifty-six, are hereby declared to be applicable to the City and County of San Francisco, and all roads and highways in that portion of said city and county that was not included in the City of San Francisco as the boundaries of the same, established by an act entitled "An Act to Reincorporate the City of San Francisco," passed April fifteenth, one thousand eight hundred and fifty-one, shall be laid out, opened, constructed, and repaired, as aforesaid in the said acts; *provided,* that all streets within the said former City of San Francisco, as the boundaries thereof, were established by an act entitled "An Act to Reincorporate the City of San Francisco," passed April fifteenth, one thousand eight hundred and fifty-one, shall be, and they are hereby, excepted from the operations of this act.

SUPPLEMENTAL XVI.—*An Act in relation to the Exempt Fire Company of the City and County of San Francisco.*—Approved March 26, 1863.

SECTION 1. The Board of Supervisors of the City and County of San Francisco are hereby authorized and empowered, in their discretion, to designate and set apart for the use of the Exempt Fire Company in said city and county, the building now occupied by the Manhattan Engine Company, Number Two, situated on Jackson Street, near Montgomery, in said city and county; *provided*, a suitable building be first procured for the use of said Manhattan Engine Company, Number Two, now occupying the building to be so set apart or designated for the use of the said Exempt Fire Company.

SEC. 2. Said Board of Supervisors are also authorized and empowered, in their discretion, to allow and order paid out of the General Fund in the Treasury of the City and County of San Francisco, a sum not to exceed eight thousand dollars, for repairs to such building, and for the purchase of apparatus for the Exempt Fire Company; and the Auditor is hereby directed to audit, and the Treasurer to pay, such sums as are authorized to be paid by this section.

ARTICLE VI.

FINANCE AND REVENUE.*

SEC. 75. All fines, penalties, and forfeitures, imposed for offenses committed within the said city and county, shall be received by the Clerk or Magistrate of the respective court and paid into the treasury thereof, as a part of the Police Fund; forty per cent. of all poll taxes collected in said city and county, or any other proportion of such poll taxes which may be hereafter assigned to said city and county, by law, shall also be paid and received into the treasury thereof, as a part of the Police Fund. All demands payable out of said fund, may, in case there be not sufficient money in the treasury arising from the sources specified in this section, be paid out of the General Fund of said city and county.

SEC. 76. The School Fund of said city and county, shall consist of all moneys received from the State School Fund; all moneys arising from taxes upon property which shall be levied each year for that use, by the Board of Supervisors, and which shall in no case exceed the rate of thirty-five cents on each hundred dollars' valuation of all property, real and personal, liable to be assessed. The General Fund consists of all moneys in the treasury not designated and set apart by law to a specified use, and of the overplus of any Special Fund remaining after the satisfaction of all demands upon it. The Surplus Fund consists of any moneys belonging to the General Fund remaining in the treasury after the satisfaction of all demands due and payable, which are specified in the first fourteen subdivisions in section ninety-five. The fiscal year shall be the same as that of the State.

SEC. 77. All taxes assessed upon real and personal property in said city and county, shall be payable and be paid directly to the Treasurer thereof; and in default of such payment before the time when the Tax Collector may be authorized by law to seize and sell the property therefor, the said Tax Collector shall proceed to collect such taxes, together with his legal fees, by seizure and sale of the property liable in the mode prescribed by law for the collection of such State and county taxes. The taxes due, however, may be paid to the said Treasurer at any time before the property is sold, and on production to the Tax Collector of the proper receipt, and payment of his legal fees for services rendered up to that time, such property shall be discharged.

SEC. 78. The Tax Collector, upon the final settlement to be made by him as such Tax Collector, according to the requirements of the law, shall be charged with, and shall pay into the hands of the Treasurer, the full amount of all taxes by him collected and not previously paid over, without any deduction of commissions, fees, or otherwise; he shall also be charged with and be deemed debtor to the treasury for the full amount of all taxes due upon the delinquent list delivered to him for collection, unless it be made to appear that it was out of his power to collect the same by levy and sale of any property liable to be seized and sold therefor; if the impossibility to collect any portion of such delinquent taxes have resulted from an irregularity or defect in the assessment, then the Assessor, whose duty it was to make the assessment, shall be liable and be deemed debtor to the treasury for the amount remaining uncollected for that cause.

SEC. 79. The Treasurer of said city and county shall receive and safely keep in a secure fireproof vault, to be prepared for the purpose, all moneys belonging to, or which shall be paid into the treasury, and shall not loan, use, or deposit the same, or any part thereof, with any banker or other person, nor pay out any part of said moneys, except upon demands authorized by this act, and after they have been duly audited; he shall keep the key of said vault and not suffer the same to be opened except in his presence. At the closing up of the same, each day, he shall take

---

* The Public Revenue Act, with its various amendments relative to San Francisco, should also be referred to.

an account and enter in the proper book, the exact amount of money on hand, and at the end of every month shall make and publish a statement of all receipts into, and payments from, the treasury, and on what account. If he violate any of the provisions of this section, he shall be considered a defaulter, and shall be deemed guilty of a misdemeanor in office, and be liable to removal, and shall be proceeded against accordingly; if he loan or deposit said moneys, or any part thereof, contrary to the provisions of this section, or apply the same to his own use or to the use of any other person, in any manner whatsoever, or suffer the same to go out of his personal custody, except in payment of audited demands upon the treasury, he shall be deemed guilty of felony, and on conviction thereof, shall suffer imprisonment in the State Prison for a period not less than three or more than ten years.

SEC. 80. The Treasurer shall keep the moneys belonging to each fund separate and distinct, and shall, in no case, pay demands chargeable against one fund out of the moneys belonging to another, except as otherwise provided in this act, without an express order of the Board of Supervisors, which can only be made at or after the third regular session, held during the fiscal year, by a vote of two-thirds. The said Treasurer shall give his personal attendance at his public office during the office hours fixed in this act; and if he absent himself therefrom, except on account of sickness or urgent necessity, during such office hours, he shall lose his salary for the entire day on which he was absent.

SEC. 81. Repealed. [See Act of the Legislature, March 28, 1859.]

SEC. 82. No payment can be made from the treasury or out of the public funds of said city and county, unless the same be specifically authorized by this act, nor unless the demand which is paid, be duly audited, as in this act provided, and that must appear upon the face of it. No demand upon the treasury shall be allowed by the Auditor in favor of any person or officer in any manner indebted thereto, without first deducting the amount of such indebtedness, nor to any person or officer having the collection, custody, or disbursement of public funds, unless his account has been duly presented, passed, approved, and allowed, as required in this act; nor in favor of any officer who shall have neglected to make his official returns or his reports, in writing, in the manner and at the time required by law, or by the regulations established by the Board of Supervisors; nor to any officer who shall have neglected or refused to comply with any of the provisions of this or any other act of the Legislature, regulating the duties of such officer, on being required in writing, to comply therewith, by the President of the Board of Supervisors, or the Supervisor of the respective district; nor in favor of any officer for the time he shall have absented himself without lawful cause, from the duties of his office during the office hours prescribed in this act; and the auditor may examine any officer, receiving a salary from the treasury, on oath, touching such absence.

SEC. 83. The term "audited," as used in this act with reference to demands upon the treasury, is to be understood their having been presented to, and passed upon, by every officer and Board of officers, and finally allowed as required by law; and this must appear upon the face of the paper representing the demand, or else it is not audited. The term "law or laws," as used in this act, is never to be understood as applicable to any regulation of the Board of Education, or of the Board of Supervisors, or Board of Delegates of the Fire Department, but only applicable to the constitution and the laws made or adopted by the Legislature in pursuance thereof.

SEC. 84. Every demand upon the treasury, except the salary of the Auditor, and including the salary of the Treasurer, must, before it can be paid, be presented to the Auditor of the city and county to be allowed, who shall satisfy himself whether the money is legally due and remains unpaid, and whether the payment thereof from the treasury in the city and county is authorized by law, and out of what fund. If he allow it he shall indorse upon it the word "allowed," with the name of the fund out of which it is payable, with the date of such allowance, and sign his name thereto; but the allowance or approval of the Auditor, or of the Board of Supervisors, or any other Board, or officer, of any demand, which upon the face of it appears not to have been expressly made by law payable out of the treasury or fund to be charged therewith, shall afford no warrant to the Treasurer or other disbursing officer for paying the same. No demand can be approved, allowed, audited, or paid, unless it specify each several item, date, and value composing it, and refer to the law by title, date, and section authorizing the same.

SEC. 85. The demand of the Auditor for his monthly salary shall be audited and allowed by the President of the Board of Supervisors. All other monthly demands on account of salaries fixed by law, and made payable out of the treasury of said city and county, may be allowed by the Auditor without any previous approval. All demands payable out of the School Fund must, before they can be allowed by the Auditor, or paid, be previously approved by the Board of Education, or by the President thereof, and Superintendent of Common Schools, acting under the express authorization of said Board. Demands for teachers' wages or other expenses appertaining to any school, cannot be approved, allowed, or audited, to an amount exceeding the share of school money which such school will be entitled to have apportioned to it during the current fiscal year. Demands for monthly pay of Police Captains and Officers must, before they can be allowed by the Auditor or paid, first be approved by the Police Judge and Chief of Police, or if they refuse or cannot agree, then by the Board of Supervisors. All other lawful demands payable out of the treasury, or any public funds of said city and county, and not hereinbefore in this section specified, must, before they can be allowed by the Auditor, or in any manner be recognized or paid, be first approved by the Board of Supervisors ; or, if the demand be under two hundred dollars, by the President and two members thereof, appointed by the Board for that purpose, with power to act under and subject to its instruction and regulations during recess of the said Board. The Auditor must number and keep a record of all demands on the treasury allowed by him, showing the number, date, amount, and name of the original and present holder ; on what account allowed, out of what fund payable, and, if previously approved, by what officer, officers, or Board it has been so approved ; and it shall be deemed a misdemeanor in office for the Auditor to deliver any demand with his allowance thereon, until this requisite shall have been complied with.—[Amendment April 18, 1857.]

Sec. 86. The President of the Board of Supervisors, Auditor, Chief of Police, President of the Board of Education, and each Supervisor, shall have power to administer oaths and affirmations concerning any demand on the treasury, or otherwise relating to their official duties. Every officer who shall approve, allow, or pay any demand on the treasury not authorized by this act, shall be liable to the city and county, individually, and on his official bond, for the amount of the demand so illegally approved, allowed, or paid. Every citizen shall have the right to inspect the books of the Auditor, Treasurer, and Clerk of the Board of Supervisors, at any time during business hours. Copies, or extracts from said books, duly certified, shall be given by the officer having the same in his custody, to any citizen demanding the same, and paying or tendering sixteen cents per folio of one hundred words for such copies or extracts.—[Amendment April 18, 1857.]

Sec. 87. The Auditor is the head of the Finance Department of the city and county, and as such is required to be constantly acquainted with the exact condition of the treasury, and every lawful demand upon it. He shall keep a public office, and give his personal attendance there daily, during the office hours fixed in this act, and shall not be permitted to follow or engage in any other occupation, office, or calling, while he holds said office ; if he absents himself from his office during such office hours, except on indispensable official business, or urgent necessity, he shall lose his salary for the day, and it shall be a part of his official duty to keep account of the times and occasions when he shall be so absent from duty.

Sec. 88. Every lawful demand upon the treasury, duly audited, as in this act required, shall in all cases be paid on presentation and canceled, and the proper entry thereof be made, if there be sufficient money in the treasury belonging to the fund out of which it is payable ; but if there be not sufficient money belonging to said fund to pay such demand, then it shall be registered in a book to be kept by the Treasurer for that purpose, showing its number, when presented, date, amount, name of the original holder, and on what account allowed, and out of what fund payable ; and being so registered, shall be returned to the party presenting it with an indorsement of the word " registered," dated and signed by the Treasurer.

Sec. 89. Whenever any audited demand has been presented to the Treasurer and not paid, and it be made known to the President of the Board of Supervisors, he shall proceed immediately to investigate the cause of such non-payment ; and if it be ascertained that the demand has been illegally and fraudulently approved or allowed, he shall cause the officer guilty of such illegal and fraudulent approval or allowance, to be proceeded against for misconduct in office. If he ascertain that the demand has been duly audited, and that the Treasurer has funds applicable to the payment thereof, which, without reasonable grounds for doubt as to the legality of such payment, he refuses to apply thereto, he shall proceed against him as a defaulter ; if it be ascertained that the demand was not paid for want of funds, then he shall cause the Sheriff or Tax Collector, or other officer or person or persons, who ought to have collected or to have paid the money into the treasury, if they have been grossly negligent therein, to be proceeded against according to law, and without any delay.

Sec. 90. The salaries, fees, and compensations of all officers, including policemen and employés of all classes, and all teachers in common schools, or others, employed at fixed wages, shall be payable monthly ; and any demand whatsoever upon the treasury hereafter accruing, shall not be paid, but shall be forever barred by limitation of time, unless the same be presented for payment, properly audited, within one month after such demand became due and payable ; or if it be a demand which has to be passed and approved by the Board of Supervisors, or Board of Education, then, within one month after the regular session of the proper Board, held next after the demand accrued, or unless the Board of Supervisors shall, within six months after the demand accrued as aforesaid, on a careful investigation of the facts, certify that the same is in all respects just and legal, and that the presentation of it as above required was not in the power either of the original party interested, or his agent, or the present holder, in which case it shall be barred in the same manner, unless presented for payment within twenty days thereafter.

Sec. 91. The Treasurer, for money received into the treasury, and all other officers of said city and county receiving money from the Treasurer for disbursement, shall give receipt for all moneys by them received, which receipt shall be presented to, and countersigned by the Auditor. The Auditor, before countersigning any such receipt, shall number it, and make an entry in a book of record, to be kept in his office for that purpose, of the number, date, and amount, by whom, and in whose favor given, and on what account. No such receipt shall be valid as evidence in favor of the person or officer receiving it, till presented to the Auditor and countersigned as aforesaid; and any person or officer using, or offering to use, such receipt as evidence, in favor of such person or officer, of the payment specified in it, without being first countersigned as above required, shall forfeit to the said city and county double the amount of money specified in such receipt.

Sec. 92. If any person feel aggrieved by the decision of the Auditor, or other proper officer or officers of said city and county, except the Board of Education, in the rejection of, or refusal to approve or allow, any demand upon the treasury, presented by such person, he may appeal, and have the same passed upon by the Board of Supervisors, whose decision thereon shall be final; and if the said Board shall approve and allow the demand, it shall afterwards be presented to the Auditor, and entered in the proper book in like manner as other demands allowed by him and an indorsement must be made of its having been so entered before it can be paid; *provided*, that from the decision of the President of the Board of Education and Superintendent of Common Schools refusing or not agreeing to allow any demand, payable out of the School Fund, the appeal shall be taken to the Board of Education, whose decision thereon shall be final.

Sec. 93. In all cases of such appeals to the Board of Supervisors, or the Board of Education, the opinion of the District Attorney thereon, shall be required in writing, read and filed; and upon such appeal, and in all other cases upon the approval or allowance of any demand upon the treasury, or School Fund, the vote shall be taken by yeas and nays, and entered upon the records.

Sec. 94. The President of the Board of Supervisors, in conjunction with the County Judge and Auditor of said city and county, shall, every month, examine the books of the Treasurer, and other officers of said city and county, having the collection and custody of public funds, and shall be permitted, and it shall be their duty to see and count over all the moneys remaining in the hands of such Treasurer, or other officer. If they ascertain *clearly* that such Treasurer or other officer, is a defaulter, they shall forthwith take possession of all funds, books, and papers, belonging to such officer, and appoint a person to fill the same, until the said defaulting officer can be proceeded against according to law, which shall be done without delay. The person so appointed shall give bond and take the oath of office, in the same manner as was required of the officer whose place he is appointed to fill. If the Treasurer, or other officer so charged as a defaulter, be acquitted thereof, he shall resume his duties.

Sec. 95. Payments of demands on the treasury of said city and county may be made for the following objects, and none others:

First. Out of the Police Fund, the fixed salaries of Police Captains and Officers, Chief of Police, Police Judge, and Clerk of Police Court.

Second. Out of the School Fund, the salaries or wages of teachers in the common schools, rents, repairs, building, and furnishing of school-houses, as provided by law.

Third. Out of the General Fund, the fixed salaries or compensation of the Assessor and his deputies, the salaries fixed by law, and other officers of said city and county, and of officers of the Fire Department, and the legal fees of jurors and witnesses in criminal cases, when the same by law are payable out of the County Treasury.

Fourth. Out of the General Fund, coupons for interest due upon the "San Francisco City Stock," duly issued in pursuance of the act entitled "An Act to authorize the Funding of the Floating Debt of the City of San Francisco, and to provide for the Payment of the same," passed May first, eighteen hundred and fifty-one.

Fifth. Out of the General Fund, coupons for interest due on the bonds duly issued by the Board of Fund Commissioners, in pursuance of the provisions of the act entitled "An Act to provide for the Funding of the Legal and Equitable Debt of the City of San Francisco, and for final redemption of the same," passed May seventh, eighteen hundred and fifty-five.

Sixth. Out of the General Fund, coupons for interest due on bonds duly issued by the Commissioners for Funding the Floating Debt of the County of San Francisco in pursuance of an act entitled "An Act to fund the Floating Debt of the County of San Francisco," passed May fourth, eighteen hundred and fifty-two.

Seventh. Out of the General Fund, coupons for interest due upon the bonds known as the "Fire Bonds," issued to the amount of "two hundred thousand dollars," by the corporate authorities of the City of San Francisco, and bearing date December first, eighteen hundred and fifty-four.

Eighth. Out of the General Fund, the certificates of stock and bonds, after maturity, which have been duly issued, referred to in the four next preceding subdivisions of this section.

Ninth. Out of the School Fund, coupons for interest due on the bonds known as the "School Bonds," dated May fourth, eighteen hundred and fifty-four, and amounting in the aggregate to the sum of sixty thousand dollars, issued by the corporate authority of the City of San Francisco, together with the sum of five thousand dollars, annually, as a Sinking Fund, for the redemption of said bonds, and the sum or sums due on each and every of the said bonds at maturity, and also the amount necessary to discharge legal incumbrances now existing on school-houses and school-house lots.

Tenth. Out of the General Fund the sum of fifty thousand dollars, annually, for the redemption of the certificates of stock, mentioned in the fourth subdivision of this section, when the same shall be offered for redemption at the treasury, and after first applying to that use the money now belonging to said "Sinking Fund," remaining in the hands of the Fund Commissioners. Also, the sum of sixteen thousand six hundred and sixty-seven dollars, annually, for the redemption of said "Fire Bonds," mentioned in the seventh subdivision of this section, when the same shall be offered at the City and County Treasury for redemption, and after first applying to that use the money now belonging to this "Sinking Fund."

Eleventh. Out of the Police Fund, bills for the subsisting of prisoners previously authorized by the Board of Supervisors, as in this act provided, and duly audited, which bills must minutely specify each several item composing the demand.

Twelfth. Out of the General Fund, the amount due upon the mortgage upon the City Hall shall be paid off immediately, and in preference to any other demand whatsoever, not previously registered by the Treasurer, under this act.

Thirteenth. Out of the General Fund, bills duly audited for expenditures in the care and maintenance of the indigent sick of the city and county, previously authorized by the Board of Supervisors, and not exceeding the amount in this act, limited for that purpose.

Fourteenth. [Amended, see Powers of the Board of Supervisors; sec. 74, page 557.]

Fifteenth. Out of the Surplus Fund, expenditures previously authorized by the Board of Supervisors, in the lawful exercise of their powers, for objects other than those specified in the preceding fourteen subdivisions of this section, may be paid out of the Surplus Fund, as specified in sections ninety-seven and ninety-eight, but not otherwise. At the end of each fiscal year, and after every lawful demand on the treasury then due and payable, or to accrue for that year, shall have been actually paid, taken up and 'canceled, and record thereof made in the proper books, or cash in the treasury shall have been set apart and reserved, equal to the amount of said demands that may then be outstanding, or to accrue for that year, and a surplus of money shall still remain in the treasury, then, and in such case, but not otherwise, the Board of Supervisors may, out of such Surplus Fund, and from no other source whatever, make appropriations for the various objects embraced within their lawful powers, other than those specified in the first fourteen subdivisions of this section, and may, in case the revenue of the year then next ensuing, will, in their opinion, be amply sufficient to satisfy all demands upon the General Fund and Police Fund, set apart and reserve the moneys so appropriated, to be expended from time to time, during such succeeding year, subject, however, to the provisions of section ninety-six. Every contract whereby any money is to be paid out of the treasury for other objects than those specified in the first fourteen subdivisions of this section, shall be null and void as against the city and county, if made before such Surplus Fund exists in the treasury, and unless it be in writing, with a printed copy of sections ninety-five, ninety-six, ninety-seven, and ninety-eight of this act attached to it, and in such case, the officer or officers executing the same, in behalf of the city and county, in contravention of this provision, shall alone be liable in his or their individual capacity, to the other contracting party, for the fulfillment of such contract.—[Amendment April 18, 1857.]

SEC. 96. The demands specified in the first fourteen subdivisions of section ninety-five, shall be paid out of any moneys in the treasury, in preference to any and all other demands whatsoever; and in case of any deficiency of funds for the payment of any of the said demands, when presented, then all such demands, being presented and registered by the Treasurer, as in this act required, shall be paid out of any moneys afterward coming into the said treasury, applicable thereto, in the order in which the same are registered.

SEC. 97. The Board of Supervisors, Board of Education, and each and every officer of the said city and county, being absolutely prohibited to contract any debt or liability, in any form, against the said city and county hereafter, the powers of the Board of Supervisors, enumerated in this act, so far as the exercise thereof may involve the expenditure of money otherwise than for the objects and demands referred to in the preceding section, shall be deemed to extend only to authorizing the appropriation and application of any surplus moneys remaining in the treasury, during any one fiscal year, to the objects specified in such numeration of powers, after the demands mentioned in the first fourteen subdivisions of section ninety-five, due and payable during such fiscal year, shall have been paid, and the several Sinking Funds shall have been provided and reserved for the redemption of said bonds and certificates of stock, to the amount hereinbefore specified.

SEC. 98. If any expenditures not authorized by this act, be incurred, they can never be paid out of the treasury, nor shall they be deemed to constitute, or lay the foundation of any claim, demand, or liability, legal, equitable, or otherwise, against the said city and county. If expenditures be incurred, which are authorized by this act to be paid out of the surplus funds in the treasury, but not for the preferred objects specified in section ninety-six, such expenditures can only be paid out of such surplus funds and revenues strictly appertaining to the fiscal year in which such expenditures have been ordered, or the contracts therefor entered into, and cannot be carried forward and paid out of any revenues accruing and receivable into the treasury for any subsequent year; nor shall any demand for, or arising out of, any such expenditure, contract, or consideration, be deemed to be a legal nor equitable claim or liability against the said city and county, or the treasury thereof, or the taxable property or tax payers, otherwise than as in this section provided; and no demand preferred against the said city and county, or the treasury thereof, which is not legally obligatory under the provisions of this act, can be recognized, assumed, or legalized, so as to give it any validity, or authorize the payment thereof.

SEC. 99. [Repeals former acts, and provides that all laws and parts of laws defining the powers and duties of Supervisors or Boards of Supervisors, are declared inapplicable to the said City and County of San Francisco, except such as are expressly referred to in, and made applicable thereto by the provisions of this act; also, all laws and parts of laws, as far as they conflict with the provisions of this act. The schedule to the act provides for the organization of San Mateo County, and is therefore omitted.]

SUPPLEMENTAL XVII.—*An Act to provide for the Collection of the Taxes on Personal Property in the City and County of San Francisco.*—Approved May 9, 1862.

SECTION 1. On or before the first Monday in June, in each year, the Assessor of the City and County of San Francisco shall deliver to the Clerk of the Board of Supervisors of said city and county, a list containing the names of all persons, firms, corporations, and associations, who have given in a sworn statement, or whose personal property has been finally assessed, as provided for in section three of An Act to provide Revenue for the Support of the Government of this State, approved April twenty-ninth, eighteen hundred and fifty-seven, and the acts amendatory thereof and supplementary thereto, and the amount of the tax on personal property assessed to each of said persons, firms, corporations, and associations. Said list shall be certified by the Assessor ; *provided*, however, that the Assessor may, at any time prior to the last Saturday in October, in each year, specially assess any property which shall not be on the regular list, as provided in section eleven of said act, approved April twenty ninth, eighteen hundred and fifty-seven. As soon as the Clerk of the Board of Supervisors shall receive said list, he shall give notice of the fact, specifying therein the time of the meeting of the Board of Equalization, for the correction of errors in the assessment of personal property, as provided in section two of this act, by publication in one or more daily newspapers published in said city, and he shall keep said list open in his office, for public inspection.

SEC. 2. The Board of Equalization of said city and county, as constituted by section eight of An Act to provide Revenue for the support of the Government of this State, approved April twenty-ninth, eighteen hundred and fifty-seven, shall meet on the first Monday in June, in each year, for the correction of errors in the assessment of personal property, and shall continue in session, from time to time, until such errors brought to their notice shall be corrected ; *provided*, however, that they shall not sit after the third Monday in June. Said Board shall have power to determine such complaints only as shall be made to them upon sworn statements in writing in regard to the assessed value of any property, and may change and correct any such valuation, either by adding thereto, or deducting therefrom, if the sum fixed in the assessment roll is proven to be too small or too great. During the session of the Board, the Assessor may be present, and shall have liberty to make any statement touching questions before the Board. During the session, or as soon as possible after the adjournment of the Board, the Clerk shall enter upon said assessment roll all the changes and corrections made by the Board, and thereupon deliver the assessment roll, so corrected, to the Auditor of said city and county, whose duty it shall be to add up the columns of valuation, and on or before the first Monday in July he shall deliver to the Tax Collector a true copy of the corrected roll, to be styled a " Duplicate Assessment List of Personal Property," with the total of taxes to each person, firm, corporation, and association, carried out in separate money columns, which said duplicate assessment list shall be duly certified by said Auditor.—[Amendment February 27, 1864.]

SEC. 3. The personal property assessment list referred to in section one of this act, and the copy thereof named in section two of this act, shall be made in the form and bound in the manner now provided by law.

SEC. 4. Upon receiving the tax list of personal property from the Auditor, the Tax Collector shall immediately give notice, by publication in three daily newspapers published in the county, that the taxes on personal property are due and payable, and such notice shall be continued until the first Monday of August next succeeding; he shall also cause a notice to the like effect to be addressed to each person, firm, corporation, or association, named in said list, and shall deposit the same in the post-office in said city, for delivery, the names of the persons, firms, corporations, or associations, alone to be considered a full address for the purposes of this act.

SEC. 5. All taxes on personal property remaining due and unpaid on the first Monday of August in each year shall then become delinquent, and the Tax Collector shall, at the close of his official business for that day, enter upon the personal property tax list a statement that he has made a levy upon all the property assessed in said list upon which the taxes have not been paid, and thereafter he shall charge two and one-half per cent. on the amount of such delinquent taxes, and on the first Monday in September then next following he shall charge two and one-half per cent. additional on all such delinquent taxes on personal property then remaining, due and unpaid. The taxes on special assessments of personal property, provided for in section one of this act, shall become delinquent, and be subject to the additional charges above named, and the property assessed to be levied upon in the form and manner hereinbefore described at the expiration of thirty days after notice to the persons, firms, corporations, or associations assessed, that such tax is due and payable. The additional charges on delinquent taxes provided for in this section shall be paid into the County Treasury, for the use of the city and county; *provided*, that the delinquent taxes on personal property shall not be chargeable in addition to the per centage above imposed, with the five per cent. now imposed by law in section thirteen of said Act of April twenty-ninth, eighteen hundred and fifty-seven.

SEC. 6. At any time after the first Monday in August of each year, the Tax Collector is authorized and required, in person or by deputy, to seize and take possession of any personal property on which the assessed taxes have not been paid, or any personal property belonging to any person, firm, corporation, or association, delinquent for taxes on personal property, and to sell, at public auction, sufficient thereof to satisfy the taxes due, and the costs of seizure and sale, upon giving notice of the time and place of sale, by publication once in any newspaper published in the county; said time and place of sale shall be such as the Tax Collector may select, and shall be authorized to employ an Auctioneer to conduct said sales, all expenses being chargeable to the party or parties delinquent.

SEC. 7. In seizing and selling property in accordance with section six of this act, the Tax Collector shall be governed by his judgment as to the quantity necessary to satisfy the taxes due, and costs; and should the quantity taken by him prove more than necessary for the purpose named, the portion remaining unsold may be left at the place of sale, at the risk of and subject to the order of the person or persons delinquent, and all proceeds of sales, over and above the amount due for taxes and costs, shall be returned by the Tax Collector to the person or persons on whose account the sale was made; and in case said person or persons cannot be found, or shall decline to receive said balance, then the Tax Collector shall deposit the amount with the County Treasurer, subject to the order of said person or persons; and if the same be not demanded within six months from the date of deposit, then the Treasurer shall pay the same into the County Treasury. And when no sufficient visible property can be found to pay said taxes or costs, or when the Tax Collector is in doubt whether said visible property is owned by the party taxed, or whether he has a legal right to seize the same, or when the property of an incorporated company shall be assessed, and the owner or owners of such personal property, seizable under section six of said Act of May ninth, eighteen hundred and sixty-two, or such incorporated companies do not pay said taxes on or before the first Monday in August of each year, it shall be the duty of the Tax Collector to commence an action against the owner or owners of such personal property, or against the person or persons taxed, or such incorporated company or companies, in the name of the People of the State of California, in any Court in said city and county of competent jurisdiction, for the amount of taxes against said personal property, or said persons, or said companies. And it is hereby made the duty of the District Attorney of said city and county to prosecute said action whenever required by the Tax Collector aforesaid; and if judgment shall be obtained against the defendants in said action, ten per cent. over and above the amount due shall be taxed and added to the costs against the defendants, for Attorney's fees, and all other costs of prosecution; said ten per cent. to be paid into the Urgent Necessity Fund of said city and county.—[Amendment April 4, 1864.]

SEC. 8. For seizing or selling personal property, as provided in this act, the Tax Collector shall be entitled to charge and retain in each case, the sum of three dollars, and the same mileage that a Sheriff would be entitled to receive for traveling to the place to make a levy, the same to be added to the costs, and to be recovered from the delinquent party.

SEC. 9. The bill of sale of the Tax Collector shall vest full title to the property sold in the purchaser.

· Sec. 10. Sections six, seven, eight, and nine, of this act, shall apply and take effect in relation to the collection of all taxes on personal property due to said city and county, and unpaid at the time of the passage of this act.

Sec. 11. So much of sections three, seven, nine, twelve, thirteen, and forty-four, of the Act to provide Revenue for the Support of the Government of this State, approved April twenty-ninth, eighteen hundred and fifty-seven, and so much of sections two, five, and nine, of the act amendatory thereof and supplementary thereto, approved April nineteenth, eighteen hundred and fifty-nine, and also so much of section one of an act entitled "An Act to amend An Act for the Support of the Government of this State," approved April twenty-ninth, eighteen hundred and fifty-seven, and of an act amendatory of and supplementary to said act, approved April nineteenth, eighteen hundred and fifty-nine, approved March eighteenth, eighteen hundred and sixty-two, as conflict with the provisions of this act, are declared to be inoperative so far as they apply to the City and County of San Francisco, and in so much are hereby appealed.

SUPPLEMENTAL XVIII.—*Act to provide for the prevention of Conflagrations and the protection of Property saved from Fire in the City and County of San Francisco.*—Approved April 1, 1864.

SECTION 1. It shall be lawful for the Board of Fire Underwriters in the City and County of San Francisco to nominate, and, with the approval of the Board of Police Commissioners, to appoint an officer, to be known as the Fire Marshal, who shall serve for one year, unless sooner removed, as provided in this act. He shall execute a bond to the State of California, in the sum of five thousand dollars, conditioned for the faithful discharge of his duties, with two sureties, to be approved by the County Judge, and his salary shall be fixed from time to time and paid by said Board of Underwriters. Any person aggrieved by any misconduct of said officer, may bring an action in his own name on such official bond, to recover any damages sustained by him.

SEC. 2. It shall be the duty of said officer to attend at all fires that may occur in said city and county, with a badge of office conspicuously displayed, upon which his official title shall be legibly printed, and he shall take possession of all property saved from fire for which no owner can be found ; shall, as far as practicable, prevent property from being injured at fires, and regulate and direct, when necessary, the removal of goods, merchandise, and other property, to a place of safety. He shall also exercise the functions of a Peace Officer of said city and county. Any person who willfully hinders or obstructs said officer in the performance of any of the duties of his office shall be deemed guilty of a misdemeanor, and shall, on conviction, be punished by imprisonment in the County Jail, for not more than three months, or by fine not exceeding five hundred dollars.

SEC. 3. It shall be the duty of the Fire Marshal to institute investigations into the cause of such fires as occur in said city and county, and, for this purpose, he shall have power to issue subpenas and administer oaths, and compel the attendance of witnesses before him by attachment and otherwise. All subpenas issued by him shall be in such form as he may prescribe, and shall be directed to and served by any Police Officer, or by any Peace Officer of said city and county. Any witness who refuses to attend, or testify, in obedience to such subpena, shall be deemed guilty of contempt, and be punishable by him as in cases of contempt in Justices' Courts in civil cases: *provided*, that said officer shall not have jurisdiction to try any person charged with commission of a crime for the purpose of inflicting punishment therefor, but shall make a written report of the testimony to the District Attorney or Assistant District Attorney, and institute criminal prosecutions in all cases in which there appears to be a reasonable and probable cause for believing that a fire has been caused by design.

SEC. 4. It shall be the duty of the Fire Marshal to aid in the enforcement of the fire ordinances of said city and county, and, for this purpose, to examine all buildings in process of erection, and institute prosecutions for all violations of the ordinances of the city and county which relate to the erection, alteration, and repairs of buildings, and the prevention of fires. He shall exercise such additional powers as may be conferred by the ordinances of said city and county.

SEC. 5. Any person who saves from fire, or from a building endangered by fire, any article of personal property, who willfully neglects, for two days, to give notice to the Fire Marshal, or to the owner, of his possession thereof, shall be deemed guilty of grand or petit larceny, as the case may be ; and any person who shall be guilty of false swearing in an investigation referred to in section second, shall be deemed guilty of perjury, and liable to punishment as in other cases.

SEC. 6. No person shall be entitled to any property in the hands of the Fire Marshal, saved from fire, until the actual expenses paid by said officer for saving and keeping the same shall be paid to him, such expenses to be determined, in case of dispute, by the Police Judge of said city and county.

SEC. 7. It shall be lawful for said Board of Underwriters, at any time, to remove said Fire Marshal, and to fill any vacancy in said office caused by such removal, or by resignation, death, or absence from the city, in the same manner as provided in section first of this act.

THE MUNICIPAL GOVERNMENT

CITY AND COUNTY OF SAN FRANCISCO.

STATE ELECTION,*

FIRST WEDNESDAY

OF

SEPTEMBER,

MUNICIPAL ELECTION,

THIRD TUESDAY

OF

MAY.

MAYOR OF THE CITY AND COUNTY—HENRY P. COON, *ex officio* President of the Board of Supervisors. Term expires July 1st, 1867. Salary, $3,000 per annum.
CLERK—CHARLES L. WIGGIN, appointed by the Mayor. Salary, $1,800 per annum.

BOARD OF SUPERVISORS—1865-66.

Term of office two years—one-half elected annually. Term expires first Monday of July. Weekly meetings every Monday evening. Quarterly meetings first Monday in January, April, July, and October. Special meetings at the discretion of the President.
President—HENRY P. COON (Term expires July 1st, 1867). Salary, $3,000 per annum.
Clerk—JAMES W. BINGHAM, appointed by the Board. Salary, $2,400 per annum.
Sergeant-at-Arms—B. S. Blitz. Salary, $600 per annum.

MEMBERS.

First District	A. H. TITCOMB,		Seventh District	CHAS. CLAYTON,
Second "	R. P. CLEMENT,		Eighth "	G. W. BELL,
Third "	ISAAC ROWELL,		Ninth "	A. J. SHRADER,
Fourth "	WM. S. PHELPS,		Tenth "	J. H. REYNOLDS,
Fifth "	MONROE ASHBURY,		Eleventh "	FRANK McCOPPIN,
Sixth "	E. N. TORREY,		Twelfth "	CHAS. H. STANYAN.

STANDING COMMITTEES.—*Judiciary*, McCoppin, Clement, Bell. *Finance and Auditing*, Bell, Clayton, McCoppin. *Fire and Water*, Titcomb, Shrader, Phelps. *Streets, Wharfs, Grades, and Public Squares*, Ashbury, McCoppin, Stanyan. *Public Buildings*, Phelps, Torrey, Stanyan. *Health and Police*, Clayton, Rowell, Clement. *Licenses and Orders*, Clement, Shrader, Reynolds. *Hospital*, Rowell, Clayton, Ashbury. *Printing and Salaries*, Shrader, Torrey, Titcomb. *Special Auditing*, Reynolds, Phelps, Rowell. *Industrial School*, Stanyan, Ashbury, Reynolds. *Fire Alarm and Police Telegraph*, Torrey, Titcomb, Bell.

CITY AND COUNTY OFFICERS—1865-66.

County Judge—HON. SAMUEL COWLES; term expires January, 1866; salary, $5,000 per annum.

District Attorney—NATHAN PORTER; term expires July, 1867; salary, $5,000 per annum. *Clerk*—H. B. Congdon; salary, $1,500 per annum.

Probate Judge—MAURICE C. BLAKE; term expires January, 1868; salary, $5,000 per annum.

* The State Election takes place biennially, on the first Wednesday of September, except the year of the Presidential Election, when it takes place on the same day. A special election for Justices of the Supreme Court, District Judges, County Judges, and all other judicial officers, required by law, and a State Superintendent of Public Instruction, takes place on the third Wednesday in October, 1867, and every two years thereafter.

City and County Attorney and Counselor—JOHN H. SAUNDERS; term expires July, 1866; salary, $5,000 per annum. *Clerk*—H. C. Hyde; salary, $1,500 per annum.

County Clerk—WILLIAM LOEWY; term expires July, 1867; Salary, $4,000 per annum. *Deputies*— Fourth District Court: James E. Ashcom, Register Clerk, salary, $175 per month; L. J. Lee, Assistant Register Clerk, $150 per month; John F. Boden, Court Room Clerk, $175 per month. Twelfth District Court: William R. Satterlee, Register Clerk, salary, $175 per month; Giles C. Letcher, Assistant Register Clerk, $150 per month; Andrew D. Smith, Court Room Clerk, $175 per month. Fifteenth District Court: A. D. Grimwood, Court Room Clerk, $175 per month. County Court: Joseph Naphtaly, Court Room Clerk, $175 per month; William Harney, Register Clerk, $150 per month. Probate Court: A. J. Jeghers, Court Room Clerk, $175 per month; Levi P. Peck, Office Clerk, $150 per month; Copyists, Bertrand McNulty and William Ledlie, paid at the rate of six cents per folio.

Sheriff—HENRY L. DAVIS; term expires July, 1867; salary, $8,000 per annum. William H. Silverthorn, Under Sheriff, $200 per month; Justus Struver, Book-Keeper, $150 per month. *Deputies*— Henry D. Lammot and George Childs, each $150 per month; S. C. Ellis, Fourth District Court, Joseph Wood, Twelfth District Court, $150 per month, each; F. E. R. Whitney, County and Probate Courts, $150 per month; A. V. Lammot, District Attorney and Grand Jury, $150 per month. *Jail Keepers*—H. P. Grinnell, James H. Demerest, H. Fitzgerald, and John Short, $125 per month, each. *Matron County Jail*—Mrs. John Short, salary, $900 per annum.

Recorder—THOMAS YOUNG; term expires July, 1867; salary, $4,000 per annum. *Deputies*—Geo. H. Russell, $2,100 per annum, and R. D. Blauvelt, jr., $1,800 per annum. *Deputy Clerks*—E. Bonnell, P. O. Barry, W. P. Merriam, T. Penniman, jr., John F. Sears, Gideon M. Berry, W. L. Cazneau, T. M. Young, Charles S. Wilcox, John McQuade, T. H. Henderson, J. C. Edwards, and Henry Casey; paid twelve cents per folio of one hundred words. *Porter and Watchman*—A. F. Norring, salary, $900 per annum.

Treasurer—JOSEPH S. PAXSON; term expires July, 1867; salary, $4,000 per annum. *Deputy*— Avery T. Harris, $2,100 per annum. *Assistant Deputy*—Charles H. Paxson, $1,500 per annum. *Notice Servers*—Charles Neff and Hiram C. Simons; salary, $900 per annum, each. All fees and commissions received by the officers of the county are paid into the "Special Fee Fund" weekly.*

Assessor—WILLIAM R. WHEATON; term expires September, 1867; salary, $4,000. *Deputy*— Horatio N. Squire, $1,800 per annum. Special Deputies, $1,800 per annum, each.

Auditor—HENRY M. HALE; term expires July, 1866; salary, $4,000 per annum. *Clerk*—John Pettee; salary, $1,500 per annum.

Tax Collector—CHARLES R. STORY; term expires July, 1866; salary, $4,000 per annum. *Deputies*—John Hanna, $200 per month; George B. Bayley, $175 per month. *Clerks*—William Stanwood, J. W. Collins, A. S. Eldredge, James N. Hume, and E. L. Hall, $150, each, per month.

Surveyor—GEORGE C. POTTER; term expires July, 1867; salary, $500 per annum and fees. *Deputies*—James J. Gardiner, and Thomas J. P. Lacy. *Assistants*—S. M. Farran and J. S. Fake. *Draftsman*—Malcom G. King.

Board of State Harbor Commissioners—C. L. TAYLOR, term expires November, 1867; S. S. TILTON, term expires November, 1868, and JAMES LAIDLEY, term expires November, 1869. Salary, $2,400 per annum, each. *Secretary*—R. E. C. Stearns, salary, $2,400 per annum.

Coroner—STEPHEN R. HARRIS; term expires July, 1867. Salary, $2,000 per annum and fees.

Public Administrator—JOHN W. BRUMAGIM; term expires July, 1866. Salary, fees.

Superintendent Public Streets and Highways—GEORGE COFRAN; term expires July, 1866; salary, $4,000 per annum. *Deputies*—D. McLaren, D. H. Whittemore, and D. S. Dikeman, each $1,800 per annum; Jacob Rudolph, James N. Burson, and H. L. King, jr., $1,500 per annum, each.

Weigher of Coal—(Vacant).

Superintendent of Common Schools—JOHN C. PELTON; term expires July, 1867. Salary, $4,000 per annum.

Secretary Board of Education—DANIEL LUNT. Salary, $1,800 per annum.

Police Judge—PHILIP W. SHEPHEARD; term expires July, 1867. Salary, $4,000 per annum.

Chief of Police—MARTIN J. BURKE; term expires July, 1866. Salary, $4,000 per annum.

Board of Commissioners for the Widening of Kearny and Third Streets—E. N. Torrey, C. C. Webb, and A. B. Forbes. *Secretary*—R. P. Lewis. Salaries to be fixed by the County Court.

Fire Alarm and Police Telegraph—MONROE GREENWOOD, Superintendent; term regulated by the Board of Supervisors; salary, $1,800 per annum. *Operators*—Charles F. Simmons, Joseph Stewart, jr., and Stephen D. Field; salary, $1,200 per annum, each. *Line Repairer*—John Bigley; salary, $1,200 per annum.

---

* The County Surveyor receives fees for surveying private property, and the Tax Collector, for collections on delinquent and poll taxes.—[COMPILER.

Clerk Police Court—JOHN H. TITCOMB; term regulated by the Board of Supervisors. Salary, $2,400 per annum.

Assistant District Attorney—DAVIS LOUDERBACK, JR.; term regulated by the Board of Supervisors. Salary, $3,000 per annum.

Court Commissioners—Fourth District, JAMES M. TAYLOR; Twelfth District, ROBT. C. ROGERS; Fifteenth District, HARLOW S. LOVE. Salary, fees.

District Court Reporters—GEO. O'DOHERTY, Reporter Fourth and Twelfth Districts; A. J. MARSH, Reporter Fifteenth District. Salary, fees.

Interpreters Police Court—CHARLES CARVALHO, Chinese Interpreter; JOHN LUSSEY, French Interpreter: (vacant) German Interpreter. Salary, $1,500 per annum, each.

Harbor Master—MARCUS HARLOE; term expires July, 1867. Salary, $3,000 per annum.

License Collector—EDWARD P. BUCKLEY; term regulated by the Board of Supervisors; salary, $2,100 per annum. *Deputies*—Cornelius Hoyer and T. A. Mudge; $1,500 per annum.

Pound Keeper—JOHN SHORT, JR. Salary, $900 per annum and fees.

Roadmasters—First District, P. J. CODY; Second District, HUGH McSHERRY. Salary, not to exceed $300 per annum.

Porters City Hall—FREDERICK KILIAN; salary, $1,080; A. H. HENDERSON and EDWARD DEVITT; salary, $900, each, per annum.

Industrial School Superintendent—GEORGE L. LYNDE, acting Superintendent; salary, $1,500 per annum. *Secretary*—James S. Thomson, $1,500 per annum.

Health Officer—J. M. McNULTY; term regulated by the Board of Supervisors. Salary [not yet fixed].

Hospital Resident Physician—WILLIAM T. GARWOOD; term regulated by the Board of Supervisors. Salary, $2,400 per annum.

Hospital Visiting Surgeon—F. A. HOLMAN. Salary, $1,200 per annum.

Hospital Visiting Physician—A. G. SOULE. Salary, $1,200 per annum.

DISTRICT OFFICERS—1865-66.

TERMS OF OFFICE—*School Directors*, two years; one-half elected annually. *Justices of the Peace* and *Constables*, two years. *Inspectors* and *Judges of Elections*, each, one year.

Districts.	School Directors.	Justices Peace.*	Constables.	Inspectors Election.†	Judges of Election.
1st	Levi B. Mastick..			C. Hanson...........	H. Gill............
2d	H. T. Graves......	R. J. Tobin	Patrick Crowley.	Wm. Snook..........	B. Shellard .... H. Lawrence........
3d	Washington Ayer			E. E. Norris	M. C. Conroy...... Wm. P. Dewey......
4th	Jos. W. Winans..	Alfred Barstow..	Sam'l C. Harding	Geo. F. Bragg	H. G. Laugley..... R. G. Brown........
5th	W. A. Grover....			Jacob Underhill.....	J M. Johnson..... E. V. Suttor........
6th	A. C. Nichols....	J. C. Pennie	Mighill Smith....	W. G. Wendell	A J. Moon......... J. C. Harvey.......
7th	W. G. Badger....			C. S. Hobbs........	H. R. Johnson...... B. C. Howard.......
8th	George C. Hickox	E. B. Drake......	Joshua Hilton....	J. W. Crosby........	C. A. Hawley...... C. Stetman........
9th	S. B. Thompson..			James Dows.........	Jacob Lynn........ N. K. Masten......
10th	S. B. Bugbee.....	J. P. Van Hagen.	John Groesbeck..	G. W. Snell..........	E W. Roberts...... D. P. Belknap .....
11th	M. Lynch........			O. H. Willoughby ..	John E. Rose...... H. N. Turner.......
12th	C. M. Plum......	W. H. Bell.......	Martin Fennell ..	J. B. Marston, 1st prec	W. O. Andrews... Wm F. Canham...
				C. P. Kimball, 2d "	Thos. Bolster ...... E. Heath .... W. Culver.........

* The city and county is now divided into six Judicial Townships, each composed of two Wards, to each of which is attached a Constable: term of office, two years from January 1st, 1866; salary, fees.

† The Act of April 4th, 1864, authorizes the Board of Supervisors to divide the Twelfth District into two election precincts.

A. ROMAN & CO., 417 and 419 Montgomery St., Booksellers, Importers, and Publishers.
38

STATE CONGRESSIONAL DISTRICTS:

First District—The Counties of San Diego, Los Angeles, San Bernardino, Santa Barbara, San Luis Obispo, Tulare, Monterey, Fresno, Merced, Mariposa, Stanislaus, Santa Clara, Santa Cruz, San Mateo, and San Francisco.

Second District—The Counties of Contra Costa, Alameda, San Joaquin, Tuolumne, Mono, Calaveras, Amador, El Dorado, Sacramento, Placer, Nevada, and Alpine.

Third District—The Counties of Marin, Sonoma, Napa, Lake, Solano, Yolo, Sutter, Yuba, Sierra, Butte, Plumas, Tehama, Colusa, Mendocino, Humboldt, Trinity, Shasta, Siskiyou, Klamath, and Del Norte.

At the election for Presidential Electors, in the year 1864, and every two years thereafter, there shall be elected from each district one Representative to the Congress of the United States.

ELECTION DISTRICTS—as established by Act of the Legislature, March 21st, 1864:

First District—Shall be bounded by Washington Street on the South, Kearny Street on the east, and the Bay of San Francisco on the north and east.

Second District—Shall be bounded by Kearny Street on the east, Vallejo Street on the south, Larkin Street on the west, and the Bay of San Francisco on the north.

Third District—Shall be bounded by Washington Street on the North, Kearny Street on the west, California Street on the south, and Market Street and the Bay of San Francisco on the east.

Fourth District—Shall be bounded by Vallejo Street on the north, Kearny Street on the east, Washington Street on the south, and Larkin Street on the west.

Fifth District—Shall be bounded by California Street on the north, Kearny Street on the west, and Market Street on the south and east.

Sixth District—Shall be bounded by Kearny Street on the east, Pine Street on the south, Larkin Street on the west, and Washington Street on the north.

Seventh District—Shall be bounded by Harrison Street on the south, Second Street on the west, Market Street on the north, and the Bay of San Francisco on the east.

Eighth District—Shall be bounded by Kearny Street on the east, Market Street on the south, Larkin Street on the west, and Pine Street on the north.

Ninth District—Shall be bounded by Harrison Street on the North, Seventh Street on the west, and the Bay of San Francisco on the south and east.

Tenth District—Shall be bounded by Market Street on the north, Seventh Street on the west, Harrison Street on the south, and Second Street on the east.

Eleventh District—Shall be bounded by Seventh Street on the east, by Market Street and Ridley Street, in a direct line to the Pacific Ocean, on the north, by the Pacific Ocean on the west, and by the line of San Mateo County and the Bay of San Francisco to the line of Seventh Street, on the south and east.

Twelfth District—Shall be bounded by Larkin Street on the east, by Market Street and Ridley Street, in a direct line to the Pacific Ocean, on the south, and by the Pacific Ocean and the Bay of San Francisco on the west and north.

All the islands in the Bay of San Francisco or in the Pacific Ocean, within the limits of said city and county, shall, for all election purposes, be included in the First District.

Police Department, Nov. 1st, 1865.*

Chief of Police—MARTIN J. BURKE.

Commissioners—Mayor—*Ex officio* President Board of Supervisors, Police Judge, and Chief of Police.

Captains of Police—Isaiah W. Lees, James M. Welch, William Y. Douglass, and Stephen N. Baker.

Regular Policemen—J. M. Ball, A. P. Barker, Edward Barnard, Thomas D. Barnstead, B. S. Blitz, J. F. Billings, B. F. Bohen, G. G. Bradt, W. P. Brant, A. D. Brown, D. B. Brown, G. F. Brown, William L. Carpenter, J. G. Chappell, Alfred Clarke, John Colter, John Coffey, J. H. Conway, J. R. Conway, Charles Cook, George W. Curtis, Martin Van Buren Dana, George W. Duffield, H. H. Ellis, L. Englander, John Evatt, James Evrard, Henry P. Fogarty, J. B. Forner, F. O. Fuller, Henry Gardenier, F. W. Gibbons, Andrew Glover, Sheldon S. Gordon, John Greer, P. R. Hunna, James H. Hesse, Mortimer Hopkins, A. J. Hoyt, Richard Ingham, N. L. Jebu, James Kavanagh, D. Keefe, Thomas King, J. Knower, Edw. J. Levy, M. Lindheimer, A. Marsh, W. Martin, Cornelius Martin, Patrick McCormick, John McCraith, C. McMillan, William McWilliams, J. Meagher, W. F. Miles, F. J. Mineon, R. B. Monks, James Moore, J. A. Moore, Thomas Nolan, C. Perry, E. W. Pike, Spencer Poole, F. L. Post (property clerk) Benjamin Pratt, S. O. Richardson, P. K. Rogers, J. W. Shields, L. Siegel, F. Spiller, John Sproul, Appleton W. Stone, F. B. Tarbett, Reuben Tucker, Isaac M. Ward, James D. Ward, W. B. Watkins, Philetus C. Wilkinson, and Edmund Wilson.

Special or Local Policemen—Thomas Ansbro, A. Barbier, David F. Bachelder, N. Bachelder, C. F. Becherer, George W. Birdsall, Joseph H. Bogle, W. H. Buckingham, Christian F. Callundan, P. Carty, William Close, Thomas Cody, W. A. Cook, Emanuel de Levere, C. W. Denny, W. Devine, George A. Dunham, J. H. Earl, W. J. Evatt, Edward Flaherty, S. C. Fleming, W. Fredericks, C. M. Gaskin, George Harman, H. W. Hendrickson, J. B. Hodgdon, T. B. Hotchkiss, Jeremiah Keefe, D. Lawlor, Henry E. Lewis, H. J. Lewis, William Little, H. Lorentzen. John E. Magary, Michael McLaughlin, Henry J. Mellus, John C. Morgan, Thomas O'Brien, W. H. J. Piper, D. H. Rand, James Rocheford, John Rodey, George W. Rose, Henry Rowland, E. J. Saulsbury, J. W. Schimp, S. D. Simmons, W. N. Smith, E. W. Thomas, H. B. Wagoner, John G. Whittaker, James Wigmore, and W. M. Willis.

Fire Alarm and Police Telegraph.†

Superintendent—Monroe Greenwood.
Operators—Charles F. Simmons, Joseph Stewart, and Stephen D. Field.

SIGNAL-BOX STATIONS.

1. Corner Stockton and Francisco streets.
2.   "   Mason and Lombard streets.
3.   "   Stockton and Greenwich streets.
4.   "   Sansom and Greenwich streets.
5.   "   Kearny and Union streets.
6.   "   Jones and Filbert streets.

* Number of Captains provided by law, four; salary, $1,800 per annum, each: number of policemen limited by law to one hundred; salary, $1,500 per annum, each. Salary of Chief's Clerk, $1,800 per annum. In addition to the regular force of the department, there are a number of local officers deputized, for duty in particular sections of the city, who are paid by the owners of property on their respective beats.

† Established April 24th, 1865. Cost of Telegraph and Machinery, $20,000; two extra Bells, and three Bell Towers. $4,300. Total expense of construction, $24,300.

7. West End Engine House, Union Street, bet Hyde and Larkin streets.

8. Corner Powell and Union streets.

9. Hose Company No. 1, Dupont Street, bet Union and Green streets.

12. Corner Montgomery and Green streets.

13. " Front Street and Broadway.

14. " Stockton Street and Broadway.

15. " Leavenworth and Pacific streets.

16. " Mason and Pacific streets.

17. " Kearny and Pacific streets.

18. " Sansom and Jackson streets.

19. " Davis and Washington streets.

21. City Hall.

23. Corner Taylor and Clay streets.

24. " Powell and Clay streets.

25. " Dupont and Clay streets.

26. " Battery and Clay streets.

27. " Montgomery and Commercial streets.

28. " Leavenworth and Sacramento streets.

29. " Stockton and California streets.

31. Engine No. 3, California Street.

32. Corner Drumm and California streets.

34. " Mason and Pine streets.

35. " Hyde and Bush streets.

36. Engine House No. 11, Bush Street, between Dupont and Kearny streets.

37. Engine House No. 4, Market Street, between Sansom and Battery streets.

38. Corner Montgomery and Sutter streets.

39. " Stockton and Sutter streets.

41. Engine House, Sutter Street, near Jones Street.

42. Hose Co. No. 4, Geary Street, near Mason Street.

43. Engine House No. 2, O'Farrell Street, near Dupont Street.

45. Corner Hyde and O'Farrell streets.

46. " Jones and Turk streets.

47. " Market and Powell streets.

48. " Gough and Grove streets (Hayes' Park).

49. " Mission and Stewart streets.

51. " Folsom and Spear streets.

52. " Mission and Fremont streets.

53. " Folsom and First streets.

54. Engine House No. 14, Second Street nr Howard.

56. Corner Harrison and Second streets.

57. " Brannan and Second streets.

58. " Townsend and Third streets.

59. Engine House, No. 12, Bryant St., near Third St.

61. Corner Howard and Third streets.

62. Hose Co. No. 2, Fourth St. nr Everett St.

63. Corner Harrison and Fourth streets.

64. " Howard and Fifth Streets.

65. " Mission and Sixth streets.

67. Engine House, Sixth Street, near Folsom Street.

68. Corner Harrison and Seventh streets.

69. " Howard and Eighth streets.

71. " Mission and Eleventh streets.

72. " Mission and Thirteenth streets.

73. " Folsom and Sixteenth streets.

74. Engine House No. 13, Sixteenth Street.

Directions for Key-Holders.—Upon the discovery of a fire near your signal box, turn the crank slowly and steadily about twenty-five or thirty times; then wait a few moments, and if you hear no ticking in the box, or alarm on the large bells, turn as before. If you still hear no alarm, go to the next box, and give the alarm from that. Never open the box, or touch the crank, except in case of fire. Never signal for a fire seen at a distance. Be sure your box is locked before leaving it.

Keys of the signal boxes are deposited in the vicinity of each box, at such places as are indicated upon cards placed thereon.

The telegraphic apparatus consists of thirty-seven miles of wire, divided into ten circuits, of which five are signal circuits, or circuits running to the signal boxes; twenty alarm gongs, located in the different engine, book and ladder, and hose houses, each connected with the central office by the five alarm circuits, and three alarm bells for striking the number of the alarm box, located as follows: one on the City Hall, one on Pennsylvania Engine House, on Sixth Street, and one on Washington Hose House, on Dupont Street. The bells and gongs are each struck at the same time by electrical machinery. The

police apparatus consists of nine stations, each communicating with the central office in the City Hall, where a constant watchfulness is exercised by the attending operator.

Public Schools.*

Superintendent of Public Schools—JOHN C. PELTON.

Board of Education.

President—Joseph W. Winans.

Secretary—Daniel Lunt.

School Directors—1st District, L. B. Mastick; 2d District, H. T. Graves; 3d District, Washington Ayer; 4th District, Joseph W. Winans; 5th District, W. A. Grover; Sixth District, A. C. Nichols; 7th District, W. G. Badger; 8th District, George C. Hickox; 9th District, S. B. Thompson; 10th District, S. B. Bugbee; 11th District, M. Lynch; 12th District, C. M. Plum.

Fire Department.

The Fire Department of the City and County of San Francisco is composed of fourteen Engine, three Hook & Ladder, and three Hose Companies, numbering 826 members.† There are in service in addition to the hand apparatus, four steam engines. Number of feet of hose, 10,000—of which 4,000 feet is of an ordinary quality. Number of hydrants—409. Expenditures of the Department, per annum, including the salaries of the officers and of the Department, repairs, etc., $48,000.

Chief Engineer—David Scannell.‡

First Assistant Engineer—Charles D. Connell.

Second Assistant Engineer—Cornelius Mooney.

Third Assistant Engineer—Thomas Finerty.

BOARD OF DELEGATES.—President, A. J. Houghtaling; Secretary, Michael Lynch; Treasurer, John Stratman.

Members—Broderick 1, John Stratman, James G. Carson; Manhattan 2, Edward Giles, James Price; Howard 3, James L. Fink, Edward Daltou; California 4, John J. Conlin, B. J. Cosgrove; Knickerbocker 5, Stephen Bunner, T. McCarthy; Monumental 6, Wm. G. Olwell, J. J. Creery; Volunteer 7, Thomas J. Shields, John Ryan; Pacific 8, Frank McGlynn, R. W. Brannan; Vigilant 9, John Brougham, Eugene Casanova; Crescent 10, Samuel Rainey, Jr., James E. Connolly; Columbian 11, Robert Cushing, William E. Duffy; Pennsylvania 12, John H. Gardiner, D. S. Garwood; Young America 13, Edward Ewald, P. McAtee; Tiger 14, A. J. Houghtaling, George B. Hudson; St. Francis H. & L. 1. George H. Baker, Henry A. Chase; Lafayette H. & L. 2, Dr. Joseph Haine, Paulin Huaut; Independence H. & L. 3, Warren R. Payne, Fred. Roskamp; Washington Hose 1, Richard Chute; Liberty Hose 2, Thomas Sawyer; Eureka Hose 4, Daniel Bigley.

Trustees Fire Department Charitable Fund—William McKibbin, Louis Cohn, M. G. Searing, Edw. S. Spear, and Jas. H. Cutter; Treasurer, Jas.

*For the progress and present condition of the Public Schools of San Francisco, see GENERAL REVIEW at the commencement of the work.

†In addition to the regular force of the Department, there are four independent companies, viz.: West End Engine, and Rincon, Hayes' Valley, and Central Hose companies.

‡The salary of the Chief Engineer is $4,000 per annum; Assistant Engineers, $600 per annum, each. Secretary of the Board of Delegates, $1,800 per annum. The amount provided by the Consolidation Act for the maintenance of the Department is $48,000 per annum.—[COMPILER.

H. Cutter. Amount of fund November 2d, 1865, $91,630.87. Amount paid for relief from November 8th, 1864, to November 2d, 1865, $6,414.77.

Board of Physicians and Surgeons — (Whose services are given gratuitously)— ———, President; Dr. A. B. Stout, Secretary; Dr. F. A. Holman, Dr. H. H. Toland, Dr. A. J. Bowie, Dr. A. F. Sawyer, Dr. Charles Bertody, Dr. John Hastings, Dr. C. M. Hitchcock, Dr. William Hammond, Dr. Isaac Rowell, Dr. S. R. Harris, Dr. Jos. Haine, Dr. J. R. Boyce, Dr. James Murphy, Dr. Wm. H. Bruner, Dr. G. F. Woodward, and Dr. L. J. Henry.

Board of Fire Wardens — The Chief Engineer and Assistants, Secretary of the Board of Delegates, and Fire Marshal.

Board of Foremen—President: Wm. B. Fairman, of Knickerbocker No. 5: Secretary : M. Lynch, of Young America No. 13; Treasurer: Mark Harris, of St. Francis H. & L. No. 1.

Location, Capacity, and Condition of Public Cisterns—Taylor, cor Clay, brick, †45,000 gallons; Powell, cor Filbert, brick, †20,000; Powell, corner Green, brick, 30,000; Powell, cor Broadway, brick, 30,000; Powell, cor Pacific, brick, 30,000; Powell, cor Jackson, brick, 30,000; Powell, cor Washington, brick, 30,000; Powell, cor Bush, brick, †30,000 (in bad order); Powell, cor Ellis, brick, †25,000; Stockton, cor Union, brick, †30,000; Stockton, cor Green, cement, †21,000; Stockton, corner Vallejo, brick, †20,000; Stockton, cor Broadway, brick, †20,000; Stockton, cor Pacific, brick, †35,000; Stockton, cor Washington, cement, †20,000; Stockton, cor Clay, cement, †20,000; Dupont, cor Union, brick, 20,000; Dupont, cor Green, brick, 32,000; Dupont, cor Vallejo, brick, 30,000; Dupont, cor Broadway, brick, 35,000; Dupont, cor Pacific, brick, †31,000; Dupont, cor Jackson, wood, †25,000; Dupont, cor Washington, cement, †25,000; Dupont, corner Clay, cement, †25,000; Dupont, cor California, brick, 30,000; Dupont, cor Bush, brick, 29,000; Kearny, cor Pacific, brick,†30,000 (in bad order); Kearny, cor Merchant, brick, †30,000; Kearny, corner Sacramento, brick, 30,000; Kearny, corner California, brick, †30,000; Kearny, cor Bush, brick, †27,000; Kearny, cor Post, brick, †30,000 (in bad order); Montgomery, cor Pacific, brick, 30,000; Montgomery, cor Commercial, brick, †32,000; Montgomery, cor Washington, brick, †25,000; Montgomery, cor California, brick, 33,000; Montgomery, cor Bush, brick, †22,000; Sansom, cor Pacific, wood, 25,000 (in bad order); Sansom, corner Bush, brick, †30,000; Battery, corner Bush, brick, 26,000; First, cor Jessie, wood, 25,000; First, cor Folsom, brick, †29,000; Mission, cor Third, brick, †30,000 (in bad order); Ecker, cor Stevenson, brick, †29,000; Broadway, cor Ohio, brick, †40,000; Sixteenth, cor Mission, brick, †29,000; Dolores, cor Sixteenth, brick, †42,000; Donahue's, First bet Mission and Market, wood, 20,000; junction Market and First, wood, 18,000; Folsom, corner Second, brick, 51,000. Total number cisterns, 48. Total number gallons, 1,470.000.

No. 1, Broderick Engine Company.—House situated on the north side of Bryant Street west of Third. Company organized April 14th, 1850; admitted into the Department June 4th, 1850. The building occupied by the company is a new two story frame building recently erected at the expense of the city. This company has two engines, one a new second class, built by James Smith of New York, size of cylinders, eight and one-half inches; stroke, nine inches; purchased by the company at an expense of $2,500. The other engine is of the Worth style and cost the city $5,000. The company has thirty-five active members on the roll. Stated meetings, first Friday in each month. The first foreman of No. 1 was David C. Broderick, who was succeeded by John A. McGlynn, Geo. W. Green, David Scannell, John Martin, Edward B. Cotter, and M. McLaughlin.

Officers—Foreman, Robert Howard; Assistant, Thos. Mitchell; Secretary, James G. Carson; Financial Secretary, W. G. Hambly; Treasurer, John O'Kane.

No. 2, Manhattan Engine Company.—House situated on the north side of Geary Street near Market. Company organized January 31st, 1854; admitted into the Department February 4th, 1854. The house now occupied by the company is situated on the north side of O'Farrell Street, between Dupont and Stockton. It is of the Italian style of architecture, twenty-two and a half feet wide by sixty-three feet deep, three stories in hight, exclusive of the basement; built of brown stone and pressed brick; cost, including the price paid for the lot, $12,000—the entire amount paid by the city. The company have now in service a new second class engine built by Cowing & Co., Seneca Falls, N. Y. Size of cylinders, eight and a half inches; stroke, seven and a half inches. Cost $2,000; is the property of the city. Stated meetings, first Monday of each month. The company has forty-six active members on the roll. The first foreman was David L. Beck, succeeded by Mathew McIntire, as acting foreman, and Ira Cole, D. L. Beck, Thomas J. Smith, John D. Swift, L. Stivers, Cornelius Mooney, and the present foreman.

Officers—Foreman, A. C. Imbrie; First Assistant, C. Gunnond; Second Assistant, J. Lynch; Secretary, J. E. Kirby; Treasurer, Samuel Apple.

No. 3, Howard Engine Company.—House situated on the south side of California Street, near Sansom. Company organized June 15th, 1850; founded by Samuel Brannan, W. D. M. Howard, and J. L. Folsom, and admitted into the Department June 16th, 1850. The house now occupied by the company is a commodious three-story building recently erected at a cost of, including the furniture, $14,400; of which the city paid $8,500. Size of building, twenty-three feet front by sixty feet deep. Cost of lot $7,000, purchased by the city. Hunneman style of engine, cost $3,000, and is the property of the city. Size of cylinders, six inches; capacity, 409·91 cubic inches. No. 3 has fifty-seven active members on the roll. Stated meetings, first Wednesday in each month. The first foreman was J. S. Eagan, who was succeeded respectively by F. E. R. Whitney, George Mellus, F. E. R. Whitney, (second term) Jacob Wells, Caleb Clapp, W. H. Patten, F. E. R. Whitney (third term), W. T. Chase, D. W. Crane, Frederick L. Tyler, H. W. Burckes, and F. E. R. Whitney (fourth term), who was succeeded by the present foreman.

Officers—Foreman, H. W. Burckes; First Assistant, Joseph Austin; Second Assistant, E. Cain; Secretary, B. Ordenstein; Financial Secretary, W. H. Friend; Treasurer, Edward Babson.

No. 4, California Engine Company.—House situated on the north side of Market Street near Battery. Company organized September 7th, 1850; admitted into the Department Sept. 9th, 1850. The house is two stories in hight, built of brick, cemented; the lot is sixty-two feet six inches in depth by twenty-seven feet in width; purchased by the city, and cost $5,000. The house was built by the city at a cost of $7,200, of which amount the company paid $700. This company have received and have now in use a Button & Blake's third class steam engine. Size of cylinder, nine inches; stroke, nine inches; weight, 3,546 pounds; cost, $3,760. The company have also a Hunneman engine. Size of cylinders, six and a quarter inches; capacity, 411 cubic inches; cost, $4,200, and is the property of the company. Stated meetings held last Monday of each month. No. 4 has fifty active members on the roll. The first foreman was George M. Garwood, who was succeeded by George N. Shaw, Herman R. Haste, Charles R. Bond, Charles S. Simpson, Augustus J. Ellis, Isaiah W. Lees, W. S. O'Brien, John W. Farran, P. A. O'Brien, and C. H. Ackerson, respectively.

Officers—President, William Osborn; Foreman, J. K. Coady; First Assistant, H. D. Claffey; Second Assistant, C. J. Gilbert; Secretary, A. Hertz Treasurer, Charles H. Williams; Engineer, P. H. Fleming.

No. 5, Knickerbocker Engine Company.—House situated on the north side of Sacramento Street near Sansom. Company organized October 17th, 1850; admitted into the Department October 19th, 1850. The new building recently completed by the company is of the modern style of architecture, three stories in hight, exclusive of the basement, and is most admirably adapted to the purposes of the company. The interior arrangements provide every convenience for the members, and its general appearance is not only an ornament to the Department, but to the city whose interests the company is organized to protect; entire cost of building $11,000, of which the city paid $9,500. The lot is sixteen and two-thirds feet by fifty-nine feet two inches, and was purchased by the city at an expense of $5,000. The engine used by this company is one of Jeffers' second class recently received from the East. Stated meetings held first Monday of each month. Number of active members, fifty-seven. The first foreman of the company was James H. Cutter, who was succeeded by Charles E. Buckingham. The third foreman was James E. Nuttman, who was followed by Edward S. Spear, who was succeeded by E. B. Vreeland, James E. Nuttman (second term), William B. Fairman, Lafayette Stivers, E. Jacob Chase, and William N. Smith.

Officers—Foreman, William B. Fairman; First Assistant, Edward Flaherty; Second Assistant, John E. Ross; Secretary, E. D. Norris; Treasurer, Henry R. Reed.

No. 6, Monumental Engine Campany.—House situated on Brenham Place, between Washington and Clay streets. Company organized September -10th, 1850; admitted into the department September 12th, 1850. The house is two stories in hight, the first of granite, the second of free-stone, and is of the Corinthian style of architecture. The lot is twenty-five by sixty-five feet, purchased by the city for $16,000; the house, which contains a fine library of over one thousand volumes, was built by the city and cost $10,500, of which amount the company expended $4,000. This company has a steam engine, built by Lee & Larned, Novelty Works, New York city, annular boiler, rotary pumps; weight, 6,300 pounds. Cost $5,500. This is the pioneer steam-engine of the State, it having been received by way of Panama, per "John L. Stevens," Sept. 2d, 1860, and placed in active service February 2d, 1861. The company has forty-three active members on the roll.' Stated meetings first Tuesday of each month. The first foreman of No. 6 was George H. Hossefross, who was succeeded by W. H. Silverthorn, John L. Durkee, and Walter J. Bohen.

Officers—Foreman (vacant); First assistant, W. D. L. Hall; Second Assistant, Wm. F. Findley; Recording Sec'y, D. D. McClennan; Financial Sec'y, J. J. Creery; Treasurer, A. P. Hotaling.

No. 7, Volunteer Engine Company.—House situated on the south side of Sutter, between Jones and Leavenworth streets. Company organized June 17th, 1854; admitted into the department June 20th, 1854. The house is a two-story frame, twenty-five and a half feet front by sixty-five feet deep, recently erected at the expense of the city. The engine in use by the company is a new second class Hun-

neman. Size of cylinders, six and a half inches; stroke sixteen inches. Cost, $1,653, paid by the city. The company has thirty-three active members on their roll. Stated meetings first Monday of each month. The first foreman of No. 7 was Caleb Clapp, who was succeeded by John M. Haskell, in whose place J. C. Lane was elected, who was succeeded by W. O. Farnsworth, John J. Fenton, M. G. Searing, G. W. Knowlton, Richard Ryland, Peter McCormick, and the present foreman.

Officers—President, John S. Wilson; Foreman, Dennis Manning; First Assistant, Edward Butler; Second Assistant, Peter Dunnigan; Secretary, R. L. Massey; Treasurer, Charles Field.

No. 8, Pacific Engine Company.—House situated on the north side of Jackson, between Davis and Front streets. Company organized August 2d, 1853; admitted into the department, September 19th, 1853. The lot is twenty-two feet six inches by eighty feet, and was purchased by the city for $6,000. The house is two stories in hight; built of brick, cemented, and is in the Corinthian order of architecture; it was built by the city at a cost of $7,600, of which amount the company expended $1,100. Style of engine Jeffers' side stroke, nine-inch cylinder and nine-inch stroke. Cost $3,000, and is the property of the city. Stated meetings first Tuesday of each month. The company has thirty-nine active members on the roll. The first foreman of No. 8 was Brierly Oakley, who was succeeded by Cornelius Walsh, M. S. Neefus, J. H. Gilchrist, P. H. Daly, Andreas Bahrs, and the present foreman.

Officers—President, A. Bahrs; Foreman, P. H. Daly; First Assistant, George White; Second Assistant, G. Black; Secretary, Charles Black; Treasurer, J. Dreyer.

No. 9, Vigilant Engine Company.—House situated on westerly side of Stockton, between Broadway and Pacific streets. Company organized February 22d, 1852; admitted into the department April 8th, 1852. The house is two stories high, built of brick, front cemented; Gothic style of architecture. The lot is twenty-two feet six inches front by eighty feet deep; bought by the city for $6,000. The house was also built by the city at a cost of $7,300, of which amount the company expended eight hundred dollars. The Jeffers' engine formerly used by this company, having been sold, a new second-class apparatus, by the same maker, has been purchased, and placed in service. Stated meetings first Monday of each month. The company has forty members. Martin R Roberts was the first foreman of the company, and was succeeded by Wm. H. Bovee, John Short, J. E. Fitzpatrick, John Short (second term), Peter Brader, H. D. Hudson, J. C. Cotter, and the present foreman.

Officers—President, John Short, Sr.; Foreman, Daniel T. Brown, Jr.; First Assistant, B. H. Schunhoff; Second Assistant, Frank Schneider; Recording Secretary, William J. Jenkins; Financial Secretary, L. G. Kohler; Treasurer, Nicholas Brignardello.

No. 10, Crescent Engine Company.—House situated on east side Stockton between Greenwich and Lombard streets. Company organized October 25th, 1852; admitted into the department November 4th, 1852. The house is two stories in hight; built of brick, and was erected during the present year at the expense of the city. The company have in service a new second-class engine, made by Cowing & Co., Seneca Falls, N. Y., purchased at an expense of $2,300, of which the city paid $1,500. Size of cylinders, 8¼; stroke, 7¼ inches, the property of the city. The company has fifty-two active members on the roll. Stated meetings first Tuesday of each month. The first foreman was James Herbert, succeeded by Jas. P. Casey, in whose place Jas. Herbert was elected, who was succeeded by J. C. Curry, Wm. Free, F. Evans, and the present Foreman.

Officers—Foreman, Charles McCann; First Assistant, Samuel Newman; Second Assistant, Michael Fitzgerald; Secretary, L. Morse; Treasurer, Henry Rick.

No. 11, *Columbian Engine Company.*—House situated north side Bush between Kearny and Dupont streets. Company organized October 12th, 1852; admitted into the Department, November 3d, 1852. The lot is twenty-four by sixty feet, owned by the city, costing $4,000. The house is two stories in hight, the first of freestone, the second of pressed brick; the amount expended in its construction was $7,100, of which amount the company appropriated $600; the building belongs to the city; New York style of engine, piano deck, cost $3,200, and is owned by the city; size of cylinder, scant 8-inch; capacity, 412.73 cubic inches. The company has forty-six active members on the roll. Stated meetings first Wednesday of each month. The first foreman was John D. Brower, who was succeeded respectively by Daniel N. Tucker, J. D. Brower (second term), A. Devoe, C. Gray, Wm. Brannan, Robert Cushing, Alex. Devoe, John Pennycock, Robert Cushing, B. C. Donnellan, Peter O'Riley, and the present foreman.

Officers—President, Robert Cushing; Foreman, Henry J. Hussey; First Assistant, William H. Driscoll; Second Assistant, John A. Stout; Secretary, William J. Hogan; Financial Secretary, John P. Shine; Treasurer, A. A. Louderbach.

No. 12, *Pennsylvania Engine Company.*—House situated on east side Sixth near Folsom. Company organized September 14th, 1852; admitted into the Department November 4th, 1852. The house is a new two story frame, twenty-three feet front by seventy deep, erected at the expense of the city. The company are the owners of a powerful steam apparatus built by Neafie & Levy, Philadelphia, which is drawn by horse power. This steamer was received by the company on the 17th day of January, 1861, under contract authorized by a resolution passed March 7th, 1860. Cylinder eight-inch bore, twelve-inch stroke; pump four and a half-inch bore, twelve-inch stroke.

Also a hose carriage capable of carrying 1,000 feet of hose. Cost of engine, $4,339.25; carriage, $761.30; of which amount the company contributed the sum of $2,800, the balance having been subscribed by the citizens of the city. Stated meetings first Wednesday of each month. Number of active members, fifty-three. The first foreman of the company was H. S. Brown, the second Robert B. Quayle, who was succeeded by Edward T. Battars, John Hanna, Robert Pollock, Frank G. Edwards, John Hanna (second term), and the present incumbent.

Officers—President, Franklin L. Jones; Foreman, John Robbins; First Assistant, E. A. Stevens; Secretary, I. D. Barnard; Treasurer, John H. Gardiner.

No. 13, *Young America Engine Company.*—House situated on Sixteenth between Guerrero and Valencia streets, Mission Dolores. Company organized February 7th, 1854; admitted into the Department April 12th, 1854. The house and inclosure were built by the city at a cost of $8,300, of which amount the company appropriated $500. It is two stories in hight, built of granite, in the Elizabethian style of architecture. The lot, twenty-two by eighty-five feet, cost $600, bought by the city. Style of engine, New York, constructed by Cowing & Co., cost $2,625, purchased by the company; size of cylinders, eight-inch, with eight-inch stroke. The company has sixty-four active members on the roll. Stated meetings first Friday of each month. The first foreman was James G. Denniston, who was suc-

ceeded by S. Courtier, in whose place M. Hayes was elected, who was succeeded by Arthur Quinn.

Officers—Foreman, Isaac V. Denniston; First Assistant, Patrick McAtee; Second Assistant, Edward Daly; Secretary, M. F. Smith; Treasurer, Edward Ewald.

No. 14, *Tiger Engine Company.*—House situated on westerly side Second between Howard and Natoma streets. Company organized February 22d, 1855; admitted into the Department December 17th, 1855. The house is a brick building, and cost, to complete, $7,500. Size of lot, twenty-five feet wide by eighty feet in depth. This company own a powerful Hunneman engine, purchased at an expense of $3,500; size of cylinders, six and five-sevenths inches. This company have recently received and have now in service one of Button & Blake's third-class steam engines. Size of cylinder, nine inches; stroke, nine inches; weight 3,720 pounds; cost, $4,143. Number of members on the roll, thirty-nine. Stated meetings first Monday of each month. The first foreman of the company was Caleb Clapp, who was succeeded by P. C. Wilkinson, John Carroll, A. J. Houghtaling, John Carroll (second term), and the present foreman.

Officers—Foreman, M. G. Searing; First Assistant, John Barr; Second Assistant, T. J. Muldoon; Recording Secretary, Geo. Pierce; Financial Secretary, J. B. Taylor, Jr.; Treasurer, C. M. Plum.

No. 1, *St. Francis Hook & Ladder Company.*—House situated on Dupont, westerly side, between Clay and Sacramento streets. Company organized June 15th, 1850; admitted into the Department June 17th, 1850. The house is two stories in hight, built of brick, cemented. Style of architecture, a combination of Ionic and Corinthian. Cost of building, $7,000, of which amount the company appropriated five hundred dollars; it is owned by the city. The lot is twenty-three by sixty feet, purchased by the city for $5,000. Truck constructed in San Francisco, cost $4,500, paid for by the city. The company has thirty-seven active members on the roll. Stated meetings first Wednesday of each month. The first foreman was Joseph C. Palmer, who was succeeded respectively by J. P. Buckley, G. W. Gibbs, L. H. Robie, George A. Worn, Jacob Ezekiel, C. Schultz, C. A. Crane, and the present foreman.

Officers—President, George H. Baker; Foreman, Mark Harris; First Assistant J. H. Baker; Second Assistant, Henry Wood; Recording Secretary, Henry A. Chase; Financial Secretary, Mark Ettling, Treasurer, Irving H. Knowles.

No. 2, *Lafayette Hook & Ladder Company.*—House situated on the southerly side of Broadway, between Stockton and Dupont streets. Company organized June 1st, 1853; admitted into the Department September 19th, 1853. The house is two stories in hight, built of brick, cemented. Italian style of architecture; cost $7,100, of which amount the company appropriated six hundred dollars; owned by the city. Lot twenty-two feet five inches by one hundred and thirty feet; bought by the city for $4,000. The truck was constructed in San Francisco; cost $4,500, paid for by the city. The company has forty-three active members on the roll. Stated meetings held first Tuesday of each month. The first foreman was H. A. Cobb, who was succeeded by T. A. Mitchell, D. Bovrat, L. Prudon, and the present foreman.

Officers—President, Chas. DeCazotte; Foreman, Paulin Huant; First Assistant, Alexander Bourgeois; Second Assistant, Pierre Perrin; Secretary, Joseph Begue; Treasurer, P. Bidau.

No. 3, *Independence Hook & Ladder Company.*—

House situated west side Fourth between Market and Jessie. Organized as an independent company April 1st, 1863; admitted into the Department July 18th, 1864. Number of members thirty-five. Stated meetings first Sunday of each month.

Officers—President, W. R. Payne; Foreman, F. Roskamp; Assistant Foreman, N. B. Adams; Secretary, D. J. Lucy; Treasurer, William Stewart.

No. 1, Washington Hose Company.—Organized Aug. 10th, 1860; admitted into the Department June 17th, 1862. The building occupied by the company is situated on the west side of Dupont between Green and Union. It is twenty feet wide by fifty feet deep, and was erected during the year 1864 at an expense of $8,000. The carriage used by the company is one of Button & Blake's, and was recently purchased by the company for $1,486. Number of members, twenty-one. Stated meetings, first Wednesday of each month.

Officers—Foreman, James S. Allen; First Assistant, Jeremiah Driscoll; Secretary, John F. Lyons; Treasurer, Frank Ansalda.

No. 2, Liberty Hose Company.—Organized February 2d, 1861; admitted June 17th, 1862. The company own their own house, lot, and apparatus; entire cost, $4,000. House situated 147 Fourth. Number of active members twenty. Stated meetings of the company first Thursday of each month. The first foreman was Thomas Sawyer, who was succeeded by John D. Rice, W. C. Fox, Thomas Sawyer (second term), Thomas H. Fox, and the present foreman (second term).

Officers—President, I. J. Casebolt; Foreman, John W. Holmes; Assistant Foreman, John Cain; Secretary, R. H. Bockman; Treasurer, A. Benard.

No. 4, Eureka Hose Company.—House situated on the easterly side of Mason, between Sutter and Post. Company organized 1863; admitted into the Department October 19, 1863. Number of members, twenty-one. Stated meetings first Thursday of each month.

Officers—President, Daniel Bigley; Foreman, (vacant); Assistant Foreman, M. J. Dolans; Secretary, H. A. Irving; Treasurer, A. P. Raye.

Exempt Fire Company.—Organized in accordance with Section 15 of an Act of the Legislature "To regulate the Fire Department of the City of San Francisco," approved March 25th, 1857, which reads as follows: "Exempt members of the Department may organize themselves to be known and designated as the *Exempt Fire Company, etc.* and shall be entitled to equal relief from the Fire Department Charitable Fund; but they shall have *no vote,* or other representation in the Department." The Legislature of the State, March 16, 1863, passed an act appropriating $8,000 to be expended in repairing the building now occupied by Manhattan Engine Company No. 2, which is set apart for the use of the company, and for the purpose of a suitable apparatus.

Officers—President, Wm. McKibbin; Vice President, M. E. Fitz Gibbon; Treasurer, James H. Cutter; Secretary, William Martin. Annual election of officers, third Monday in October. Stated meetings, third Monday in every month. Admission fee, five dollars; quarterly dues, one dollar. Number of members, two hundred and eighty.

In addition to the regularly constituted force of the Department, there are several independent organizations located in sections of the city remote from the protection of other companies, viz.:

West End Engine Company.—House situated on south side Union between Hyde and Larkin. Com-

pany organized August, 1863. Number of members, forty-five. Stated meetings the first Tuesday of each month.

Officers—Foreman, John Mulholland; First Assistant, C. Lane; Second Assistant, J. W. Kenzel; Secretary, Maurice Tobin; Treasurer, Martin Daney.

No. 3, Hayes' Valley Hose Company.—House situated on the corner of Larkin and Grove. Company organized July 6th, 1864. Number of members, thirty. Stated meetings, first Saturday of each month.

Officers—Foreman, Henry Schroeder; Secretary, James Hughes; Treasurer, Thomas Gilmore.

No. 6, Rincon Hose Company.—House erected on south side Folsom near Beale. Company organized April, 1864. The house occupied by the company is a new and convenient structure, erected at an expense of $1,500, which was defrayed by private subscription. The hose carriage used by the company is one of the best in the State, and was formerly owned by Confidence, No. 1, of Sacramento. Number of members, thirty. Stated meetings held second Tuesday in each month.

Officers—President, Robert Cleary; Foreman, William H. Spencer; Assistant, S. W. Taylor; Secretary, F. K. Krauth; Treasurer, C. Dunker.

FEDERAL AND STATE OFFICERS.

Federal Officers.

Agent, Special, of the United States.—J. M. Gitchell; office, Custom House.

Army U. S. Division of the Pacific.—Maj. Gen. H. W. HALLECK, Commanding. Lieut. Col. R. N. Scott, Assist. Adj't.-Gen.; Lieut. Col. D. C. Wager, Asst. Inspector Gen.; Maj. John McL. Taylor, Chief Commissary; 1st Lieut. H. A. Huntington, 4th Arty., A. D. C.; head quarters, 418 California.

Army, U. S., Commandant Department California.—Major-General Irvin McDowell, U.S.A.; office 742 Washington.

Army U. S., Subsistence Department.—Major J. McL. Taylor, Commissary of Subsistence; office 418 California; depot, 208 Sansom.

Army U. S., Adjutant-General.—Colonel Richard C. Drum, Assistant Adjutant-General U. S. A., Chief of Staff; office 742 Washington.

Army U. S.—Col. Washington Seawell, U. S. A., Commissary of Musters; office 418 Washington.

Army, U. S., Medical Director.—Surgeon Charles McCormick; office 408 Market.

Army, U. S., Paymaster.—Lieut.-Colonel Hiram Leonard, Deputy Paymaster-General U. S. A., office 742 Washington.

Army, U. S.—Provost Marshal, Major Alfred Morton; head office 416 Washington.

Army, U. S., Purveyor Medical Department, Robert Murray, Surgeon U. S. A.; William N. Thompson, clerk; Robert Dwinelle, laborer; office 805 Sansom.

Army, U. S.—U. S. Engineers Harbor Fortifications; office 37 Montgomery Block. Brevet Brig.-Gen. E. DeRussy, Fort Point; Lieut. G. H. Elliot, Alcatraz. R. S. Williamson, Light-House Department Pacific Coast, office 728 Montgomery.

Army, U. S., Quartermaster's Department.—Colonel E. B. Babbitt, U. S. A., Deputy Quartermaster-General; Major R. W. Kirkham, U. S. A.; office 742 Washington.

Court, Circuit.—Hon. Stephen J. Field, Judge: George C. Gorham, clerk; C. W. Rand, U. S. Marshal; Court Room, U. S. Court Building.

Court, District.—Hon. Ogden Hoffman, Judge; George C. Gorham, Clerk; C. W. Rand, U. S. Marshal; Court Room, U. S. Court Building.

Coast Survey, Western Coast Division.—Officers of the different departments: W. E. Greenwell, Assistant Primary and Secondary Triangulation; Julius Kincheloe, Sub-Assistant Primary and Secondary Triangulation; James L. Lawson, Sub-Assistant Secondary Triangulation and Topography; Augustus F. Rodgers, Asst. in charge of Topography; Alexander Chase, Aid in Topographical Party; Edward Cordell, Assistant in charge of Hydrography; Lieut. G. H. Elliot, U. S. Engineer, in charge of the Tidal Observations; G. Farquhar, Draftsman; office Custom House, third floor.

Internal Revenue.—Office north-west corner Battery and Commercial. Assessor's Department: Lewis C. Gunn, Assessor; Gordon Backus, B. L. Bartlett, Wm. H. Baxter, O. F. Briggs, George W. Bryant, John B. F. Davis, Charles L. Farrington, William S. Hughson, William C. Johnson, Fred. Lux, Lewis E. Morgan, Andrew J. Morrison, Edwin S. Perkins, John F. Perry, H. W. Richmond, Napoleon B. Stone, J. Jerome Sullivan, and Chas. P. Wolcott, Assistant Assessors; Henry Baker and John W. Shaeffer, Cigar Inspectors; Henry C. Mallory, Chief Clerk; Charles C. Sonntag, Clerk Assessor's Department; John Costigan, Messenger. Collector's Department: Frank Soulé, Collector; Cornelius Stagg and Howard T. Witbeck, Deputies; George O. Smith, Jr., Cashier; A. Noel Blakeman and Milo Calkin, Clerks; Samuel C. Beaver, Stamp Clerk; James S. Kennedy, Inspector; John Costigan, Messenger. P. W. Randle, Inspector Pacific Coast, office NW corner Battery and Commercial. W. J. Walker, U. S. Revenue Agent, office NW corner Battery and Commercial.

Collector of the Port.—J. F. Miller; office Custom House.

Commissioner, U. S.—Geo. C. Gorham; office 10 U. S. Court Building.

District Attorney.—Delos Lake; office 4 U. S. Court Building.

Indian Agent.—Charles Maltby, Superintendent; office SE corner Washington and Sansom.

Inspector of Boilers.—C. C. Bemis; office Custom House, third floor.

Inspector of Hulls.—R. H. Waterman; office Custom House, third floor.

Land Office.—John F. Swift, Register; J. W. Shanklin, Receiver, 625 Merchant.

Light-House Department, Pacific Coast.—Twelfth L. H. District: Capt. Jas. M. Watson, U. S. N., Inspector of the District; Maj. R. S. Williamson, U. S. Eng., Engineer; H. R. Crosby, Clerk; office Custom House, third floor. J. F. Miller, ex officio Superintendent of Lights. Hartford Joy, Keeper Alcatraz Island; T. T. Uneckless, Keeper Point Bonita; T. Blanchard, Keeper Fort Point; A. Blanchard, Assistant Keeper; Thomas Tasker, Keeper Farallone Islands.

Mail Agent.—R. C. Gaskill; office Custom House, basement.

Marine Corps, U. S.—Captain James Wiley, Asst. Q. M.; office 516 Third.

Marine Hospital, U. S.—J. Hastings, M.D., Surgeon and Physician.

Marshal U. S.—C. W. Rand. Deputies: George

F. Worth (chief and book-keeper), D. W. Swain, A. C. Taylor, and John Drum; office 13 and 14 U. S. Court Building.

Mint, Superintendent of Branch.—Robt. B Swain; office 610 Commercial near Montgomery.

Navy Agent.—E. C. Doran, Acting: office 434 Cal.

Pension Agent, U. S. A.—J. W. Shanklin; office 625 Merchant.

Post Office.—R. F. Perkins, Postmaster; Holland Smith, Assistant Postmaster; office Post Office.

Purser, U. S. N.—E. C. Doran, Acting; office 434 California.

Receiver U. S. Public Moneys.—J. W. Shanklin; office 625 Merchant.

Supervising Agent Steamboats.—William Burnett; office Custom House, third floor.

Surveyor-General for California.—L. Upson; Edward Conway, Chief Clerk; office SW corner Washington and Battery.

Treasurer, U. S. Assistant.—D. W. Cheesman; office U. S. Branch Mint.

State Officers.

Assayer, State.—B. B. Thayer, SE cor Montgomery and Bush.

Commissioner in Equity.—C. McC. Delany, 519 Montgomery.

Funded Commissioners 1851.—Office NW corner Montgomery and Sacramento, W. M. Lent, Wm. Hooper, Samuel Knight, and C. M. Hitchcock.

Gauger of Liquors.—G. H. Cushing, 321 Front.

Inspector of Gas Meters.—M. Kenney, 612 Com.

Inspectors of Stamps.—Louis R. Lull and Jacob Deeth; office SW corner Battery and Wash.

Land Locating Agent.—Leander Ransom; office 625 Merchant.

Notaries Public.—Andrews W. O. 630 Montgomery.
Barstow A. 24 Montgomery Block.
Cook C. W. 607 Clay.
Dreschfeld Henry, 623 Montgomery.
Gorman John, 619 Merchant.
Gould A. S. 528 Clay.
Haight Henry, 607 Clay.
Homans H. S. 607 Clay.
Huefner William, 619 Merchant.
Joice E. V. NE cor Battery and Washington.
Knox George T. NW cor Mont and Merchant.
Lawton W. W. 404 Montgomery.
McKenzie J. W. 406 Montgomery.
Milliken I. T. 608 Merchant.
Murfey S. S. 520 Montgomery.
Parker William C. 517 Jackson.
Peckham E. P. 607 Clay.
Sawyer O. V. SW cor Montgomery and Clay.
Sutter Emile V. 626 Clay.
Thibault F. J. 605 Montgomery.

Pilots, Board of Examiners.—Office Merchants' Exchange; N. Pierce, H. S. Brown, and W. T. Thompson, Examiners; W. N. Shelly, A. A. Buckingham, W. E. Domett, Chas. Mayo, John Mahan, J. F. Schander, John May, W. H. Jolliffe, F. Murphy, Thos. J. Reddish, Andrew S. Young, S. C. Nathan, H. Van Ness, John Delavan, and O. S. Calott, Pilots; Charles W. Kellogg, Secretary.

Pilots, Benicia and Mare Island.—C. H. Harrison, (resident) 517 Front.

Pilots, Old Line.—Office 5 Vallejo (up stairs). Charles Mayo, S. C. Nathan, John Mahan, J. F. Chander, T. J. Reddish, W. H. Jolliffe, and F. Murphy, Pilots; Boat: J. C. Cousins.

Pilots, Opposition Line.—Office 895 Front (up stairs). Wm. N. Shelley, W. E. Domett, A. A. Buckingham, Henry Van Ness, John Delavan, A. S. Young, O. S. Calott, and J. A. May, Pilots; Boats: Caleb Curtis and Fanny.

Port Wardens.—Office 716 Front; Geo. S. Porter, S. P. Wells, M. M. Richardson, and D. J. Staples; Jerry Whalen, Secretary.
Superintendent of Immigration.—Seth H. Wetherbee; office NE cor Battery and Washington.
Superintendent of Public Instruction. — John Swett; office SE cor Montgomery and Jackson.

Custom House.

North-West cor Washington and Battery : open daily from 9 o'clock, A.M. to 4, P.M. (Sundays excepted).
J. F. MILLER, Collector.
J. Frank Miller, Deputy Collector and Auditor.
L. M. Kellogg and E. Burke, Deputy Collectors.

COLLECTOR'S OFFICE.

Benj. E. Babcock, Cashier; R. K. Weston, Assistant Cashier; F. G. Bornemann, Cashier to Assistant Treasurer; E. W. Taggard, Book Keeper; J. W. Foard, Entry Clerk; J. J. Martin, Assistant Auditor; J. M. Good, Liquidating Entry Clerk; J. S. Church, Impost Book Keeper; A. A. Vansyckle, Assistant Import Book Keeper; J. A. Perkins, Statistical Clerk; B. Hall, Assistant Statistical Clerk; R. S. Miller, Recording Clerk; T. J. Blakeney, Miscellaneous Bond Clerk; H. T. Wheeler, W. J. Pixley, and John G. Taylor, Assistant Entry Clerks; W. Pearson, Register Clerk; F. McCarthy, Entrance and Clearance Clerk; W. W. Morrow, Debenture and Abstract Clerk; J. Mathis, Assistant Liquidating Clerk; F. W. Redding, Invoice Clerk; W. Lattimore, Weigher's Clerk; E. Collins, Assistant Weigher's Clerk; J. T. Watson, Gauger's Clerk; R. W. Van Sickle, T. J. Sullivan, and E. A. Colson, Messengers; M. Hall, J. S. Sanford, and J. Lynn, Watchmen.

APPRAISER'S STORE.

S. J. Bridge and H. M. Miller, Appraisers; Henry Marshall and H. Z. Wheeler, Assistant Appraisers; C. A. McNulty, Examiner; C. Burrill, Special Examiner of Drugs; T. O. Lewis, Abstract Clerk; Isaiah Eakins, Messenger; D. J. Hogan, J. Feeny, J. Semple, and N. B. Hoyt, Laborers.

NAVAL OFFICE.

NOAH BROOKS, Naval Officer.
Edward Hunt, First Entry Clerk and Acting Deputy; Charles B. Rice, Cashier; W. H. Whitely, Liquidating Clerk; Arthur B. Thomas, Entry Clerk; W. E. McArthur, Assistant Entry Clerk; Thomas Reynolds, Bond Clerk; J. M. Ainsa, Warehouse Clerk; P. G. Clark, Clerk; Cheney Moulton, Messenger.

SURVEYOR'S OFFICE.

THOMAS B. SHANNON, Surveyor.
J. Burke Phillips and A. W. Genung, Deputy Surveyors; I. E. Thayer, Measurer of Vessels; Thomas Finegan, Messenger.

WEIGHERS AND MEASURERS.

DANIEL CONY, Weigher; Zenas Coffin, J. F. Westheimer, and P. McIntire, Assistants; C. E. Warren, J. Kinnear, James Cunningham, and W. Dargan, Laborers.

WAREHOUSE DEPARTMENT.

ROBERT H. ROGERS, Deputy Collector and Storekeeper.
W. A. Darling, Bond Clerk; R. Frank Clark, Warehouse Book Keeper; D. W. Taylor, Warehouse Entry Clerk; H. B. Chambers, Abstract Clerk; N. Winants, Warehouse Entry Liquidating Clerk; G. McDonald, Assistant Warehouse Entry Liquidating Clerk; N. S. Pettit, Assistant Storekeeper Appraiser's Store; L. M. Manzer, Delivery Clerk; C.

C. Redington, Receiving Clerk; Joseph Weed, J. Stockton, J. W. Mason, M. Flynn, P. H. Patton, D. K. Meacham, and R. K. Piotrowski, Assistant Storekeepers; DeWitt C. Dolson, and I. H. Perry, Messengers, D. Gallagher and E. Holbrook, Watchmen; D. Barclay, T. Callaghan, L. H. Daily, J. F. Hack, D. McIntosh, C. H. Ryder, T. R. Starr, and D. Wheelock, Laborers.

GAUGER.

J. W. PROBASCO, Gauger.
Henry Lion and M. A. Cornwall, Laborers.

INSPECTORS.

R. D. Arms, John Banning, P. E. Bowman, O. T. Baldwin, W. O. Bradley, T. C. Nye, E. H. Coe, W. Fenn, C. M. Hall, W. Horton, T. W. Lawrence, G. Laws, J. C. Low, Anna McGlauthlen, J. McNeil, J. Humphreys, C. W. Phelps, T. P. Vallean, S. B. Reed, G. E. Schenck, J. Schott, D. W. Smith, and M. W. Smith, Revenue Boat; C. Hansen, Boarding Officer; J. S. Bates, Assistant Boarding officer; C. Staples, H. F. Davoue, C. F. Holland, C. Johnson, J. Hall, C. B. Smith, J. T. Sylvia, and C. O'Neil, Bargemen.

NIGHT INSPECTORS.

C. D. Connell, T. H. Fox, T. Finnerty, J. W. Greenlow, C. W. Reed, C. Simmons, L. Sellinger, J. Taylor, D. W. Wording, J. A. Hill, L. Morse, and J. Roberts.

MARINE HOSPITAL.

J. HASTINGS, Surgeon and Physician.
S. Woodbridge, Apothecary; T. G. W. Luyster, Steward; W. Christmas, Cook.

United States Treasury,

North Side of Commercial, near Montgomery.

Office hours from 9, A.M. to 2, P.M.

D. W. CHEESMAN, Assistant Treasurer.
F. G. Bornemann, Cashier; Edwin W. Taggard, Book keeper; T. H. Bornemann, Ass't Book keeper; O. Macy, Messenger.

U. S. Branch Mint,

North Side of Commercial, near Montgomery.

The law for the establishment and regulation of the United States Mint, and the branches thereof, provides that any person may deposit with the officers in charge of the same, gold and silver in bullion, grain, or lumps, which, if requested, shall be refined, assayed, and cast into bars or coined, as speedily as possible after the receipt thereof, the bars to be stamped in said mint or branches, in such manner as shall indicate the weight, fineness, and value of the same; the expense incurred to be retained from each deposit so made, at such rates and charges, and under such regulations, as may from time to time be established. The said charges not to exceed the actual cost of refining, casting, and forming said bars, including labor, wastage, use of machinery, material, etc., or ¼ per cent. for coinage, to be received by the Treasurer of the Mint at which the deposit was made, and by him accounted for to the Treasurer of the United States.
Office hours from 9 o'clock, A.M. to 2, P.M. Gold Bullion received daily from 9 o'clock, A.M. to 12, M.; Silver Bullion from 12, M. to 1, P.M. Visitors admitted daily from 9 o'clock, A.M. to 12, M.
ROBERT B. SWAIN, Superintendent.

TREASURER'S DEPARTMENT.

D. W. CHEESMAN, Treasurer.
William Macy, Cashier; J. B. Scotchler, Book Keeper; John H. Beardsley, Abstract Clerk; Jos. P. Cochran, Weigh Clerk; J. N. Souther, Receipt Clerk; William M. Noyes, Superintendent's Clerk; Robert T. Polk, Internal Revenue Clerk; James H. Cills, Computing Clerk; Mrs. Elizabeth Wyer, Memorandum Clerk; George W. Torr, Watchman.

GENERAL DEPARTMENT.

FRANK BRET HARTE, Secretary.
Oliver P. Allen, General Clerk; M. Gallagher, Warehouseman; Charles Wood, Millwright; Samuel Thompson, Conductor; William Satterlee and Andrew Kurtz, Door-keepers; S. D. Cunningham, N. Haskell, E. H. Morton, Jacob Odell, and Cornelius Schenck, Watchmen; Henry F. Sampson, Janitor.

ASSAYER'S DEPARTMENT.

B. T. MARTIN, Assayer.
H. H. LAWRENCE, Deputy Assayer.
George Parry, Treasurer's Clerk; William H. Martin, Registrar; John Evans, Sampler; T. R. Butler, George H. Fillmore, Wirt Hopkins, Alexander H. Martin, and William T. Riley, Beammen; W. P. Prescott, Foreman Laboratory; Oliver Hawes and R. T. Roberts, Cupellers; Frank Kennedy and James Ogelsby, Boilers; Patrick Durkin, Helper; William Windsor, Laborer.

MELTER AND REFINER'S DEPARTMENT.

JOHN M. ECKFELDT, Melter and Refiner.
CHARLES S. COUSINS, Assistant Melter and Refiner.
W. K. Benjamin, Treasurer's Clerk; Timothy H. Rearden and A. B. Falkenburgh, Clerks; John Feix, Samson Liou, Jacob Stadtfeld, and J. M. Gardner, Melters; Frederick M. Benner, C. W. Cornor, Geo. Curtis, Charles Gibbs, Wm. Edmonds, John Turner, and Joseph Wilson, Helpers; Archibald Cooper, Foreman Refinery; James S. Blaikie, Henry Cromer, W. S. Eaton, E. E. Elliott, R. P. Franklin, J. S. Ottignon, Joseph A. Smith, W. J. Somers, James S. Handlin, and Peter Witbeck, Refiners.

COINER'S DEPARTMENT.

WILLIAM SCHMOLZ, Coiner.
ADOLPHUS SCHMOLZ, Assistant Coiner.
John A. Collison, Chief Adjuster; Granville Hosmer, Assistant Adjuster; Mrs. A. W. Bunnell, Mrs. Mary Comstock, Miss M. M. Eschenburg, Miss Maria Fernald, Miss C. L. Frost, Mrs. Anna Heydenfeldt, Miss H. S. Lovekin, Mrs. Abby L. Marble, Miss J. A. McLean, Miss Charlotte Pilkington, Mrs. E. B. Rankin, Miss Laura F. Shew, Miss Jane Steadman, Mrs. M. J. Stout, and Miss Isabella Gallagher, Adjusters; Warren C. Butler, Foreman Cutting Room; B. H. Campbell, A. P. Stanton, and James J. Veatch, Cutters; E. C. Bowen, Foreman Coining Room; W. M. Boyd, Assistant Foreman; D. W. Davies, James C. Harvey, and S. B. Mowry, Rollers; Thomas Higgins, C. W. Kittredge, and Thomas Walton, Annealers; Mathew Smith, Trap-tender; J. B. Harmstead, Machinist; Lewis Henry, Chief Engineer; Peter Mott, Assistant Engineer; Silas S. Burt, Foreman.

U. S. Surveyor-General.

LAUREN UPSON, Surveyor-General.
Office 810 Montgomery Street. Office hours from 10 o'clock, A.M. to 4 o'clock, P.M.
Edward Conway, Chief Clerk; R. C. Hopkins, Keeper of Archives; J. H. Wildes, Principal Draftsman; C. Bielawski and R. Gibbons, Draftsmen; John Clar and R. F. Scott, Clerks.

Post Office.

North-west cor Washington and Battery. Office hours from 8 o'clock, A.M. to 4, P.M., and 7 to 8½, P.M.
RICHARD F. PERKINS, Postmaster.
HOLLAND SMITH, Assistant Postmaster.
W. C. Dougherty, Secretary; Edward C. Palmer, Mail Clerk; Frank E. Dyer, Overland Mail Clerk; William W. Bryant, John A. Clapp, and Daniel O'Connor, Assistant Mailing Clerks; M. G. Sawyer, Registry Clerk; John Crowley, Assistant Registry Clerk; Jas. Murphy, Stamp Clerk; Warren P. Adams, Box Clerk; F. B. Cassas, John E. Gorham, E. B. Jerome, Samuel H. Jones, James F. Madden, John C. Robinson, and Frank Tukey, Jr., Delivery Clerks; James F. Breed, M. C. Conroy, F. N. Gutierrez, Charles Lembcke, and William M. Rider, Night Clerks; Henry W. Butler, Newspaper Clerk; Charles M. Prodger, Assistant Newspaper Clerk; Daniel McSwiggin, Messenger; William H. Kirby, Janitor.

Great Overland Mail from San Francisco to St. Joseph, Mo., via Salt Lake, leaves daily (except Sundays) at 4 o'clock, P.M. Mail closes at 3½, P.M.
English Closed Mail closes Wednesdays and Saturdays at 3 o'clock, P.M.
Mails for Sacramento and the Northern Mines close daily at 3:45, P.M.; for Benicia, Vallejo, etc., at the same hour.
Mails for Stockton and the Southern Mines close daily at 3:45, P.M.
Mails for San José, etc., close daily at 7:30, A.M. and, 4 P.M.
Mails for Petaluma leave daily at 1½ o'clock, P.M.
Mails for Eureka, via Petaluma, leave Mondays and Thursdays at 1:40 o'clock, P.M.
Mails for Santa Barbara, Los Angeles, and San Diego, are dispatched at 7½, A.M. Monday, Wednesday, and Friday.
Mails for Acapulco, Panama, and South America, are forwarded on the 10th, 20th, and 30th of each month, and close at 9 o'clock on the morning of the sailing of the steamer.
Mails for China, the Sandwich Islands, and Australia, are forwarded from the Post Office by every suitable opportunity, containing all letters and papers, the inland postage of which is prepaid to San Francisco, leaving the sea postage to be collected in the ports where the mails are delivered.
Letters should be fully prepaid by stamps. Drop Letters must be prepaid by postage stamps. Letters will not be sent with stamps cut from stamped envelopes.
All printed matter is now forwarded to the East by steamer, on 10th, 20th, and 30th of each month.
The Post Office opens at 8 o'clock, A.M. and closes at 4 o'clock, P.M. every day, except Sundays.
Open Sundays from 9 to 10 o'clock, A.M.
The General Delivery will be open from 7 to 8½ o'clock every evening, except Sundays.
One window will be kept open ALL NIGHT every night, except Sundays.
Boxes for the reception of mail matter, secured by U. S. mail locks, are placed at the following points in charge of a competent person, who will take therefrom all letters, etc. at the hours named, and deposit the same to be dispatched by the four o'clock, P.M. mails:

NE corner of Broadway and Dupont	1.00 P.M.
SE corner of Pacific and Stockton	1.03 "
SE corner of Powell and Union	1.08 "
NE corner of Pacific and Larkin	1.30 "
NW corner of Bush and Jones	1.35 "
SW corner of Geary and Taylor	1.40 "
NE corner of Mission and Sixth	1.43 "
SW corner of Sixteenth and Valencia	1.55 "
SW corner of Twelfth and Howard	2.00 "
SW corner of Sixth and Folsom	2.15 "
San José Railroad Depot, Brannan	2.25 "
SE corner of Third and Howard	2.33 "
SE corner of Fourth and Market	2.38 "

Junction of Geary and Market...........2.41 P.M.
Metropolitan Market, Market. A..........3.33 "
Book store adjoining the Museum, Market.3.33 "
SE corner of California and Montgomery..3.30 "
Oriental Hotel, cor of Bush and Battery..3.35 "
SW corner of Howard and First...........2.50 "
SE corner of Mission and Stewart.........2 55 "
Junction of California and Market........3 00 "
SW corner of California and Front........3.40 "
SE corner of Clay and Davis..............3.43 "

COURTS.

United States District Court—Northern District.
—Regular terms held in San Francisco first Monday
of April, second Monday of August, and first Monday of December. Special terms at the discretion
of the Court. Hon. Ogden Hoffman, Judge; Delos
Lake, Attorney; C. W. Rand, Marshal; Geo. F.
Worth, D. W. Swain, John Drum, and A. C. Taylor, Deputies.

*United States Circuit Court—District of Cali-
fornia.*—Regular terms held in San Francisco first
Monday of February, second Monday of June and
first Monday of October. Special terms at the dis-
cretion of the Court. Hon. Stephen J. Field,
Judge; Hon. Ogden Hoffman, Associate; Delos
Lake, Attorney; George C. Gorham, Clerk; C. W.
Rand, Marshal; Deputies (as above).

Supreme Court of California.—Regular terms
held at Sacramento first Monday in January, April,
July, and October. John Curry, Chief Justice; Lo-
renzo Sawyer, A. L. Rhodes, O. L. Shafter, and S.
W. Sanderson, Judges; J. G. McCullough, Attorney
General; W. D. Harriman, Clerk; A. Tuttle, Rep'r.

District Court—Fourth District.—Regular terms
first Monday of February, May, August, and November. Hon. E. D. Sawyer, Judge; William
Loewy, Clerk. Deputies: James E. Ashcom, Register Clerk; L. J. Lee, Assistant Clerk, and John F.
Boden, Court Room Clerk; H. L. Davis, Sheriff;
Samuel C. Ellis, Bailiff; Geo. D'Doherty, Reporter.

District Court—Twelfth District.—Regular terms
first Monday of January, April, July, and October.
Hon. O. C. Pratt, Judge; William Loewy, Clerk.
Deputies: William R. Satterlee, Register Clerk; G.
C. Letcher, Assistant Clerk, and Andrew D. Smith,
Court Room Clerk; Joseph Wood, Bailiff; George
O'Doherty, Reporter.

District Court — Fifteenth District. — Regular
terms first Monday of March, June, September, and
December. Hon. S. H. Dwinelle, Judge; William
Loewy, Clerk; A. D. Grimwood, Court Room
Clerk; John Hill, Bailiff; A. J. Marsh, Reporter.

County Court.—Regular terms first Monday of
January, and of each alternate month thereafter.
Hon. Samuel Cowles, Judge; William Loewy,
Clerk; William Hurney, Deputy; H. L. Davis,
Sheriff; H. D. Lamott, Bailiff.

Probate Court.—Regular terms first Monday of
each month. Hon. M. C. Blake, Judge; William
Loewy, Clerk; A. J. Jeghers, Deputy; Joseph
Wood, Bailiff.

Police Court.—Sessions held daily. P. W. Shepheard, Judge; D. Louderback, Jr., Prosecuting, Attorney; John H. Titcomb, Clerk; J. Lussey and C.
Carvalho, Interpreters; Capt. James M. Welch,
Bailiff.

JUSTICES' COURTS.*

(SESSIONS DAILY.)

First Township—First and Second Wards.—
R. J. Tobin, Justice; P. Crowley, Constable; office
536 Pacific near Kearny.

Second Township—Third and Fourth Districts.
—Henry J. Wells, Justice; Samuel C. Harding,
Constable; office 623 Merchant.

Third Township—Fifth and Sixth Districts.—
C. Cornell, Justice; Migbill Smith, Constable; office
528 Montgomery.

*Fourth Township—Seventh and Eighth Dis-
tricts.*—George Robins, Justice; Joshua Hilton, Constable; office 230 Bush near Montgomery.

Fifth Township—Ninth and Tenth Districts.—
J. A. Coolidge, Justice; John Groesbeck, Constable; office 613 Market near Second.

*Sixth Township—Eleventh and Twelfth Dis-
tricts.*—Martin W. Lamb, Justice; Martin Fennell,
Constable; office Valencia nr Sixteenth.

CHURCHES.

BAPTIST.

First Baptist Church.

Rev. D. B. CHENEY, D.D., pastor; location, north
side Washington near Stockton. Pastor's residence
and study, 1417 Taylor Street, near Jackson.

This church was organized in June, 1849, under
the labors of its first pastor, Rev. O. C. Wheeler.
The church lot was purchased in the spring of the
year for the sum of $10,000. The first house of
worship was dedicated in August, 1849, and was the
first Protestant house of worship erected in California. Mr. Wheeler's pastorate ended in November,
1851, who was succeeded by Rev. B. Brierly in
May, 1852. In the summer and fall of 1853, the
wooden building was removed, and the basement of
the present edifice was erected at a cost of $13,000.
In this, the church worshiped until September,
1857, when it dedicated its newly-finished building
which it had completed, for the sum of $16,000, in-
cluding upholstery. During the administration of
the present pastor, who commenced his labors in
July, 1859, large accessions, both to the church and
congregation, have been made, and its heavy debt
has been paid.

Number of communicants, three hundred and
twenty-three. The Sunday School has an average
attendance of about three hundred and fifty. Number of enrolled about five hundred. The library
contains over three thousand volumes.

Sabbath services morning and evening; Sabbath
School at 1, P.M. Prayer meeting every Wednesday
evening; Young People's Meeting held on three
Friday evenings of each month, conducted by the

*At the election held October 18th, 1865, the following
named were elected Justices of the Peace for the term commencing January 1st, 1866: R. J. Tobin, First Township;
Alfred Barstow, Second Township; J. C. Penny, Third
Township; E. B. Drake, Fourth Township; I. P. Van
Hagan, Fifth Township, and William H. Bell, Sixth Township.

Pastor; Church Covenant Meeting the Friday evening preceding the First Sabbath in each month.

This church, in connection with the Second Baptist Church in this city, has recently established a Mission interest on Post Street, near Larkin. A chapel has been built at a cost of about $4,000. A Sunday School has been organized with about one hundred members, and preaching is maintained by Rev. James P. Ludlow.

Officers—John F. Pope, D. N. Breed, Abraham Hobson, and Isaac Lankershim, Deacons; A. B. Forbes, P. Sather, John F. Pope, and Isaac Lankershim, Trustees; Edmond Worth, Clerk; D. C. Breed, Treasurer; B. T. Martin, Superintendent of Sunday School; A. B. Forbes, Assistant Superintendent; Cassius M. Conro, Secretary and Treasurer; R. W. Thompson, Librarian.

Second Baptist Church.

The house of worship is located on the corner of Fifth and Jessie streets. Rev. Henry A. Sawtelle, Pastor. Residence 463 Minna, bet Fifth and Sixth.

This church was organized December 22d, 1862. At the present time (October, 1865) it has a membership of one hundred and twenty-four. During the past year it has received, by baptism and otherwise, thirty-eight new members, and has dismissed twenty-three.

Officers—S. A. Bemis, L. L. Alexander, and John Reynolds, Deacons; Thomas Day, S. Benson, J. S. King, John Reynolds, and H. B. Angell, Trustees; J. W. Olmstead, Treasurer; John Daniel, Clerk.

Services are held each Sabbath at 11, A.M., and at 7½, P.M. Prayer meetings on Wednesday evening, and also on Sunday a half hour before evening preaching. A Sunday School, with an average attendance of two hundred and twenty-five, and with a library of eight hundred volumes, is connected with the church. L. L. Alexander, Superintendent; J. Daniel, Secretary and Treasurer; A. E. Knowles, Librarian. The school meets Sunday, P.M., at a quarter before 1 o'clock.

Third Baptist Church (Colored).

Rev. THOMAS HOWELL, Pastor: location, east side of Dupont Street, between Filbert and Greenwich; residence of the Pastor, north side of Oak Street, near Taylor. Services at 11, A.M. and 3 and 7½ o'clock, P.M.

This church was organized in 1854. It owns its church property free of debt. The present pastor, who was ordained in 1861, began to supply the church some five years ago. Under his ministry the church has been much prospered and increased in numbers and efficiency. It has about eighty members. Church Clerk, vacant.

Sabbath School—eight teachers, forty-four scholars.

Post St. Baptist Mission Chapel.

Location, near NW corner Post and Larkin streets. Rev. James P. Ludlow, Missionary officiating; residence, west side Hyde between Bush and Sutter. Hours of service, 11, A.M. and 7½, P.M. every Sunday, with a weekly prayer meeting on Tuesday evening. Sunday School meets at 9½, A.M.

This house of worship was consecrated August 20th, 1865, the Missionary preaching the sermon, and the Rev. Messrs. O. C. Wheeler, O. M. Briggs, H. Richardson, and Stephen Hilton participating in the exercises. The mission was projected about a year ago by the First and Second Baptist Churches of this city. The chapel is of wood, forty-four by sixty feet, and presents a neat and tasty appearance. It will seat about four hundred, and cost, with lot, about seven thousand dollars. A Sunday School with about eighty scholars was organized on the Sunday following the dedication, and the following officers elected:

Officers—J. A. Eaton, Superintendent; E. Worth, Secretary and Treasurer; Harvey Mount, Librarian.

Central Baptist Mission Chapel.

Commenced holding worship in Congress Hall, Bush St. near Montgomery on Sunday, November 5th, 1865, with the Rev. O. W. Briggs, present officiating for this nucleus of the new Baptist Church.

CONGREGATIONAL.

First Congregational Church.

Location, south-west corner of California and Dupont. Pastor (vacant).

Preaching every Sabbath at 11 o'clock, A.M. and 7½, P.M.; Lecture every Wednesday evening at 7½ o'clock; Sabbath School immediately after morning service.

Officers of Church—L. B. Benchley, W. O. Ayers, M.D., Lyman Dickerman, J. W. Clark, M.D., and J. T. Boyd, Deacons; A. C. Nichols, Henry Dutton, and A. G. Stiles, Standing Committee.

Officers of the Society—Ira P. Rankin. Moderator; A. G. Stiles Clerk; A. C. Nichols, Treasurer; H. L. Dodge, William A. Dana, A. C. Nichols, Ira P. Rankin, A. G. Stiles, and W. N. Hawley, Trustees.

This church, or congregation, was organized July 29th, 1849, when Thomas Douglas and Frederick S. Hawley were chosen Deacons, and inducted into office on the following Sunday by Rev. T. D. Hunt, assisted by Rev. A. Williams. The society met in the school-house, on the Plaza, until it was required for other purposes, when the members were deprived of a regular place of meeting for several months. As early as practicable, however, efforts were made for the erection of a suitable house of worship, which resulted in the building of a commodious frame structure, twenty-five by fifty feet, on the corner of Jackson and Virginia streets, which was dedicated to the worship of God, February 10th, 1850. Rev. T. D. Hunt was chosen Pastor, and installed June 26th, 1850, who, in this connection, it is proper to state, was the first Protestant clergyman, located as such, in the State, having arrived at San Francisco as early as October 29th, 1848, and was immediately invited by the citizens, in a meeting called for the purpose, to act as their chaplain for one year, commencing November 1st, 1848, in which capacity he was laboring at the time of the organization of this church. The congregation increased so greatly as to require a larger house; accordingly measures were adopted, in the summer of 1852, for the erection of the present substantial brick edifice, which was dedicated on the tenth of July, 1853. Rev. E. S. Lacy was installed as Pastor July 6th, 1856.

The whole number of members admitted to the church since its organization is five hundred and twenty-four. The present membership is over four hundred. The cost of the present church property, including lot, building, and repairs, has been about $70,000.

Sunday School—L. B. Benchley, Sup't; Charles S. Eaton, Assistant. Number at present connected with the Sabbath School, scholars and teachers, is about five hundred and ninety; average attendance, three hundred and eighty. A valuable and instructive library of over 1,000 volumes is attached to the Sabbath School.

Second Congregational Church.

Rev. J. A. BENTON, Pastor; residence 1032 Pine Street. Services held every Sabbath at 11 o'clock A.M. and 7½ o'clock, P.M. The Sabbath School and Bible Classes meet immediately after the morning service. Lecture room prayer meeting in the church every Sunday evening at 6½ o'clock. Weekly prayer meeting and lecture every Wednesday evening; teachers' meeting every Friday evening.

The neat and commodious church edifice, recently erected and now occupied by this society, is on Taylor Street, south of Geary. It presents a fine appearance and is very accessible, the Central Railroad passing in front of it.

Officers—S. S. Smith, L. C. Gunn, and J. M. Craig, Deacons.

Third Congregational Church.

Rev. E. G. BECKWITH, Pastor. Location, Fifteenth Street, just above Mission. Services at 11, A.M. and 5, P.M. Sabbath School immediately after morning service. Weekly prayer meeting, Wednesday evening.

Green Street Congregational Church.

Location, south side Green, between Stockton and Powell. Rev. E. C. BISSELL, Pastor; residence, north-east corner Lombard and Dupont streets.

This church was organized February, 1863, with a membership of twenty-six persons. The Rev. J. M. Caldwell was first connected with this enterprise, and was succeeded by the Rev. Wm. C. Bartlett and the Rev. E. C. Bissell, the present incumbent of the Pastorate. The building occupied by this society is of wood, and is neatly finished and tastefully furnished. It was designed by S. C. Bugbee & Son. The cost was about $5,000, exclusive of the amount, $5,000, paid for the lot. The hours of Sabbath service are 11, A.M. and 7¼, P.M. The weekly prayer meeting is held on Wednesday, at 7¼, P.M. The Sabbath School meets immediately after the morning service. The school numbers four hundred members.

The Trustees are H. H. Lawrence, C. P. Stanford, James L. Cogswell, Timothy Sargent, and Jno. Archbald.

EPISCOPAL.

Grace Cathedral.

Officiating Clergy—The Right Rev. Bishop KIP, D.D., Rev. H. GOODWIN, Rev. G. A. EASTON, and O. CLARK, D.D. Location, corner California and Stockton streets.

Public services every Sunday at 11, A.M. and 7¼, P.M.; Sunday School at half-past nine in the morning. The congregation was organized in 1849, the statistics of which may be summed up as follows: Communicants, three hundred; the Sunday School numbers about two hundred scholars, and has a library of over one thousand volumes. The first Rector of the church was Dr. J. L. Ver Mehr, who preached his first sermon in California at the house of Mr. Merrill, in this city, September 10th, 1849. A chapel was next built toward the close of 1849, at the corner of John and Powell streets, which was first opened for divine services December 30th, 1849. This was the first Grace Church. It was sixty feet long by twenty wide, and cost eight thousand dollars. On the twenty-eighth of April, 1850, Grace Church was formally organized. E. Bryant and D. S. Turner were elected Wardens, and Dr. Ver Mehr chosen Rector. The first vestry meeting was held on May 20th, 1850. In February, 1851, the contract was made to build the former Grace Church on Powell Street, which was finished that summer. Dr. Ver Mehr preached the first sermon in this edifice. Bishop Kip arrived in San Francisco January 29th 1854, and on the twenty-fifth of February following, assumed the Rectorship, at which time Dr.

Ver Mehr resigned. The Bishop continued to officiate until Palm Sunday, April 5th, 1857, when F. C. Ewer was ordained, and on the next Sunday he preached his first sermon. On the fourteenth of April Mr. Ewer was elected to be Assistant Minister, and on the twentieth of the same month he took charge of the parish, the Bishop having departed for the Atlantic States. The Bishop having returned and resigned the Rectorship, Mr. Ewer was elected Rector of the Church, December 15th, 1857, and retained that position until April, 1861, when he resigned. At the earnest solicitation of the Vestry, Bishop Kip again became Rector, and served as such until October, 1864, since which date the clergyman at present officiating have had pastoral charge.

The corner-stone of Grace Cathedral was laid by Bishop Kip in May, 1860. The building is one hundred and thirty-five feet deep and sixty-two feet wide. Hight, from floor to apex of roof, sixty-six feet. The edifice was first opened for public worship September 28th, 1862. Its cost, when completed, will be about $90,000.

Officers—Wm. Blanding, Senior Warden; Geo. W. Gibbs, Junior Warden; Edward Pringle, Stephen Smith, Alex. Ely, H. F. Williams, H. C. Parker, Joseph S. Winans, Nathaniel Holland, R. J. Van Dewater, H. B. Williams, and W. M. Rockwell, vestryman.

Trinity Church.

The Rev. CHRISTOPHER B. WYATT, Rector. Pastor's residence, No. 812 Bush Street. Church located north side of Pine between Montgomery and Kearny. Organized, 1849.

Public worship every Sunday at 11, A.M. and 7½, P.M.; Wednesday at 11, A.M., and Friday at 4, P.M.; Sunday School at 9, A.M.

Officers—J. D. Hawks, Senior Warden; B. H. Randolph, Junior Warden; W. F. Babcock, James Bell, Jacob Underhill, J. T. Dean, H. S. Dexter, and L. H. Allen, Vestrymen.

St. John's Church, Mission Dolores.

Rev. T. W. BROTHERTON, Rector.

This church was established in November, 1857—the Rev. John Chittenden, President of the San Francisco College, then a lay reader, licensed by the Bishop of the Diocese, officiating as its Minister. The parish, of which this is the church, was instituted in February, 1858. The inhabitants are indebted mainly to the liberality of a few individuals and to the Rev. John Chittenden for the first introduction of this church service into the neighborhood. The Rev. J. Cameron, ordained in April, 1840, officiated as Curate—the Rev. J. Chittenden being his Rector. By the energy of the Curate, assisted by his brother clergymen, he has established the Episcopal Church permanently in this vicinity. Services are held at 11, A.M. and 7½, P.M. Sundays. It is worthy of being noted that the ministers, organist, choir, and other assistants, give their services gratuitously. The present Rector took charge on the first of August, 1861. The first of August, 1862, a church edifice was commenced, on a lot presented by the ladies of the congregation to the Vestry, which was finished in November of the same year. The new church is built in the early English First pointed style, at a cost of $8,500, with furniture, etc., and is capable of accommodating two hundred and fifty persons. The Sunday School numbers about one hundred and twenty scholars and fifteen teachers. Number of volumes in the library, 800.

Officers—W, O. Andrews, Senior Warden; Wm, Greene, Junior Warden; Charles E. Gibbs, Treasurer; J. W. Haynes, Secretary; Theodore E. Smith, J. B. Williams, C. Christiansen, L. V. H. Howell, J. Martenett, J. R. Jarboe, and R. A. Thompson, Vestrymen.

Church of the Advent.

Rev. F. MARION McALLISTER, Rector.

The parish was established, with its first and present Rector, June, 1858.

This church is located on Howard Street between Second and Third. It was completed and consecrated February 24th, 1861.

Services every Sunday at 11, A.M. and 7½, P.M.; Sunday School at 9, A.M.

Officers—C. Langley and Cutler McAllister, Jr.; Wardens; L. A. Garnett, C. A. Eastman, E. B. Benjamin, John Kiloh, T. R. Johnson, Hall McAllister, and James Palache, Vestrymen.

The new church, with its lofty steeple, forms a conspicuous object in the southern part of the city. The architecture is nearly pure Gothic. Some modifications in the Romanesque style have been introduced, adding materially to the light and graceful effect. The exterior is of a rich dark brown, and, with its lofty lantern, reminds one of "St. Dunstan's in the East," London, built by Sir Christopher Wren, and copied by him from the fine old church of St. Nicholas, New Castle, England.

The interior is plain and elegant, and offering an auditorium in the clear of fifty feet by eighty, or one hundred and twenty feet in depth with the chancel. The walls are painted in imitation of stone; the ceiling, which is divided with delicate tracery, springs gradually to the apex of the roof, and is painted light blue. The chancel is a model of neat, unpretending architecture, and with the pulpit, which is very high, is much in the old English style. A very attractive feature is the Ten Commandments, which fill up the niches at the rear of the chancel. The windows are lofty and divided into diamond-shaped sections by a lattice work of wood on the inside.

The lot, with the edifice and furniture, cost the society $27,000.

METHODIST EPISCOPAL.

Powell Street Church.

Rev. J. ASBURY BRUNER, Pastor.

Residence, 1008 Washington Street.

Location, west side of Powell Street between Washington and Jackson.

Services Sunday morning at 11 o'clock, and in the evening at 7¼. Sunday School at 2¼, P.M.

This is the oldest M. E. church in the city, having been organised in 1849 by Rev. Wm. Taylor. Some of the members of this church have witnessed the spread of their denomination in California, from its feeble beginning among them, until it now numbers over 4,000 communicants and about 40,000 hearers.

The present officers of the church are as follows: Revs. E. Thomas, D.D., S. D. Simonds, Charles D. Cushman, H. B. Sheldon, Rob. Beeching, and G. W. B. McDonald, Resident Ministers; John Truebody, Annis Merrill, John Sims, A. A. White, A. Walker, R. P. Spier, J. M. Brown, R. C. Harrison, J. T. McLean, J. M. Johnson, and J. W. Cherry, Stewards and Trustees; Dr. J. T. McLean, Superintendent of Sunday School.

The opening of the conference year (Oct. 1865) has shown a decided improvement in church attendance and the spiritual status of the society.*

* Methodist Episcopal Church statistics of the City of San Francisco, prepared by Rev. J. Asbury Bruner:

Number of churches	7
Number of members and probationers	844
Value of church property	$110,850
Number of Sunday Schools	8
Number of officers and teachers	200
Number of volumes in the libraries	5,000
Number of Sunday School Advocates	1,445
Expenses of schools	$2,113

Number of Ministers in California Conference of M. E. Church, 91; No. of Stations and Circuits, 94.

Howard Street Methodist Episcopal Church.

Rev. JESSE T. PECK, Pastor; residence, Hubbard Street, in rear of church. Location Howard Street, between Second and Third. Sunday morning and evening service at the usual hours. Sunday School at 2, P.M. Prayer meeting, etc., on Wednesday evening.

The society, organized in 1852, under the superintendence of Rev. Isaac Owen, erected and dedicated December 5th, 1853, a plain, but substantial, neatly furnished house of worship. The building is gothic of the fourteenth century, ninety-six feet long by fifty-eight feet wide. It will seat 1,000 persons. Value, including lot, and parsonage, $64,000. After setting off the Central and Mission Street Churches, there are now more than three hundred communicants, and two Sunday Schools, numbering seventy-nine officers and teachers, eight hundred and thirty scholars, with an average attendance of five hundred and seventy-eight, and a library of 1,653 vols.

Officers—Charles Goodall, Wm. H. Gawley, W. H. Coddington, Robert McElroy, James Harlow, J. W. Whiting, S. H. Hancock, Robert G. Byxbee, and W. H. Howland, Trustees. Charles Goodall, President Board Trustees and Superintendent Sabbath School.

Bethel Methodist Episcopal Church.

Rev. R. W. WILLIAMSON, Pastor; residence, 520 Howard Street. Location, Mission, between First and Second streets.

This church was organized early in 1851, under the pastoral charge of Rev. W. Taylor. Service was then held in the ship Panama, on Davis Street. Subsequently, the ship was moved to the foot of Mission Street, and a church built on deck. Early in 1857, the church was taken down and rebuilt in its present eligible situation.

During the past year this church has enjoyed a constant prosperity. Its membership is over one hundred.

Services at the usual hours on Sabbath morning and evening. Sabbath School at 9½, A.M. Number of volumes in library, four hundred and fifty; officers and teachers, sixteen; scholars, one hundred. Prayer meeting, every Wednesday and Saturday evening; class meeting, every Sabbath morning at 12½ o'clock, and every Tuesday, Thursday, and Friday evening.

Officers—Israel Richards, Joseph B. Firth, Henry Mahan, James G. Fulmer, James Woods, Peter Miller, Peter Johnson, and John A. Bergner, Trustees; Joseph Ware and P. Johnson, Officers.

Central Methodist Episcopal Church.

Rev. JOHN B. HILL, Pastor; residence, 524 Tehama Street. Location, corner Sixth and Minna streets. Services on Sabbath at 11, A.M., and 7¼, P.M. Sabbath School meets at 9, A.M.

The building occupied by this congregation is a neat and commodious structure, forty by sixty, and will accommodate about four hundred persons. It was erected by the Trustees of the Howard Street Methodist Church, in connection with their Pastor, the Rev. J. D. Blain, and dedicated September 18th, 1864. During the past year the building was removed to its present location, the lot having been purchased within that time at an expense of $10,250.

The society now numbers, in full connection, sixty-five; probationers, twelve; total, seventy-seven. The Sabbath School numbers, including teachers, about three hundred.

Officers—W. B. Holcomb, W. H. Gawley, Edward Farnam, J. M. Buffington, J. Harlow, E. Burke, and N. Poland, Trustees; W. B. Holcomb, H. H. Morgan, L. McLaughlin, N. Poland, W. H. Porter, W. O. Grey, J. W. Nye, J. F. Smith, and J. R. Culin, Stewards.

Mission Street Methodist Episcopal Church.

Rev. C. H. LAWTON, Pastor. Location, Mission Street, opposite the Willows.

Services on Sabbath at 11, A.M.; and 7½, P.M. Sabbath School meets at 2½, P.M. Prayer meetings on Thursday evenings, at 7½ o'clock.

The building occupied by this church is a neat and substantial frame structure, with a lecture room fifty by fifty-two feet, and so constructed that it can be extended whenever the wants of the society demand it.

Minna Street M. E. Church, South.

Rev. O. P. FITZGERALD, Pastor; residence, northeast corner Stockton and Lombard streets. Location, south side Minna, between Fourth and Fifth streets.

This church was organized in October, 1858, by the present Pastor, the Rev. O. P. Fitzgerald. Revs. W. R. Gober, Morris Evans, and Samuel Brown, have severally had pastoral charge of the congregation. The present house of worship was dedicated August 7th, 1864. The building is in the Gothic style of architecture, fifty-five by seventy-five feet.

Regular service on Sabbath at 11 o'clock, A.M. and at 7, P.M. Sabbath School at close of morning service. Class meeting at 9½, A.M. Prayer meeting on Wednesday evenings.

Officers—C. L. Newman, Class Leader; Charles Spencer, P. W. Taylor, Rufus K. Cain, J. A. McClelland, Richard Lariemore, C. A. Klose, and John C. Ayres, Trustees.

German Methodist Episcopal Church.

Rev. C. H. AFFLERBACH, Pastor; residence in rear of church. Organized February 29th, 1859. Location, north side Broadway, between Stockton and Powell. Services every Sunday at 10½, A.M., and 7½, P.M. Sunday School at 9, A.M. Services also every Wednesday evening at 7½ o'clock.

German Methodist Episcopal Church.

Rev. HERMAN BRUCK, Pastor; residence in rear of church. Organized April 4th, 1858. Location, Folsom Street, between Fourth and Fifth. Services every Sunday at 10½, A.M., and 7½, P.M., in the German language. Services also every Thursday evening at 7½ o'clock. Sunday School at 9, A.M.

African Methodist Episcopal Church.

Rev. T. M. D. WARD, Pastor; residence, 532 Bush. Location, west side Powell, between Jackson and Pacific. Services each Sabbath at 11, A.M., 2½, P.M. and 7½, P.M.

The society worshiping here was organized in 1850, and is the same that formerly occupied the St. Cyprian Church. Under the pastorship of Rev. T. M. D. Ward they reorganized in 1856, and purchased the Scott Street Church property, where they continued to worship until March, 1862, when they purchased the property which up to that time had been known as Grace Church, for $5,500. Having paid the debt in March, 1864, on the first of January, 1865, the society made extensive necessary repairs, requiring the sum of $6,500; $3,200 of that has been paid, leaving a balance on the main debt of $3,300, and a floating debt amounting to $550—total, $3,850. Rev. J. B. Sanderson was Pastor from May, 1857, to June, 1859, since which time the society has been under the care of the present Pastor. During the year three deacons were ordained by Right Rev. Jabez P. Campbell, Bishop of California.

Officers—Barney Fletcher, John Sampson, J. Pierson, J. Warfield, J. B. Sanderson, Edward Quinn, A. Gross, J. H. Scott, C. D. Armstead, Trustees.

Zion Wesleyan Methodist Church (Colored).

Rev. JOHN J. MOORE, Pastor; residence, 331 Union, between Taylor and Jones. Location, west side Stockton near Sacramento.

The congregation was organized by Rev. John J. Moore, August 1st, 1852. In April, 1863, they purchased the Unitarian Church on Stockton Street, for $15,500, on which there is a debt of $5,500; attached, there is a Sabbath School of six teachers and forty scholars, and a library of three hundred volumes; R. T. Houston, Superintendent. Services every Sabbath at 11, A.M. and 3 and 7½, P.M. Sabbath School at 1, P.M.

PRESBYTERIAN.

First Presbyterian Church.

Rev. W. C. ANDERSON, D.D., late Pastor. Location, Stockton Street nr Clay. Services on Sabbath at 11, A.M. and 7½, P.M. Sabbath School and Bible Class at 1, P.M. Lecture on Wednesday evening at 7½ o'clock.

This church was organized May 20th, 1849, under the direction of Rev. Albert Williams, and was the first Protestant Church organized in San Francisco. W. W. Caldwell, Frederick Billings, Dr. George F. Turner, Mrs. Sarah B. Gillespie, Mrs. Ann Hodgson, and Mrs. Margaret A. Geary, were the original members: Capt. B. Simmons, E. Woodruff, and H. Grimes, were the first Trustees.

During the summer of 1849, the congregation worshiped in a tent on Dupont Street, afterward in a store-room of the Custom House, and in the Superior Court Room, City Hall, until January 19th, 1851, when a neat Gothic edifice, capable of holding seven hundred persons, was dedicated. This house was destroyed by the great fire of June 22d, 1851. A plain building was immediately erected, in which the congregation worshiped until August, 1857; and from that time until May, 1858, their meetings were held in the Chinese Mission Chapel. Their present fine house of worship was built in the summer and autumn of 1857, at a cost of about $50,000, including the lot, furniture, and fixtures. It is in the Gothic style of architecture throughout. The main building is one hundred and seventeen feet long, or to the outside of the tower, one hundred and twenty-three feet, and is sixty-one feet wide. Rooms for the Pastor's study and social meetings are on the same floor with the audience room, which last is eighty-one by fifty-eight feet, with a ceiling thirty-nine feet high. A Sabbath School room, fifty-seven by thirty-six, is over the front apartments; on the north-east corner of the house is a brick tower, ninety-six feet in hight. There is an organ gallery that will seat a choir of forty persons. In all its arrangements the edifice is admirably adapted to its purpose, and at the same time is in accordance with true architectural taste.

In 1863, a valuable organ was added to the church, at an expense of $5,000, and the Church debt of over $13,000 had been canceled, leaving the congregation entirely free from any liability.

Officers—Rev. W. C. Anderson, D.D., late Pastor; R. H. Waller, N. Gray, S. Hopkins, John D. Arthur, and J. K. S. Latham, Elders. Trustees: James Bowman, President; W. H. Miller, Secretary; G. E. Rogers, Treasurer; S. B. Stoddard, D. Van Pelt, J. B. Painter, Ira Warden, W. H. Knight, and Gerritt W. Bell.

The church is in a very prosperous condition. Present number of communicants, two hundred and fifty. S. B. Stoddard Superintendent Sabbath School. Number of scholars, four hundred; number of teachers, forty-two; average attendance, three hundred and fifty. A fine library of over 2,000 volumes is attached to the school.

Calvary Presbyterian Church.

Rev. CHARLES WADSWORTH, D.D., Pastor; residence 920 Pine Street between Mason and Taylor. Location north side of Bush Street between Montgomery and Sansom. Services every Sabbath at 11, A.M. and 7, P.M. in winter months, and at 7½, P.M. in summer. Public Lecture Wednesday evening; Prayer Meeting Sabbath evening, one hour before the evening service. Young Men's Prayer Meeting on Friday evening. Sabbath School every Sabbath at 9½, A.M., James B. Roberts, Superintendent.

Officers—R. McKee, Henry P. Coon, James B. Roberts, Elders; Edward Hagthrop, Deacon; F. Henderson, Alexander Campbell, James B. Roberts, H. H. Haight, Thomas H. Selby, C. Wittram, H. H. Bigelow, C. Clayton, and H. M. Newhall, Trustees.

The church was erected in the fall of 1854, at a cost, including the lot, of about $70,000. On its completion the property was largely in debt, but the debt was gradually reduced, and finally wholly extinguished. The whole property is now entirely free from debt; and the income of the church, now some $13,000, from pew rents and Sabbath collections, is ample to meet all its current expenses. The church has a splendid organ, built by Henry Erben, of New York, which cost over $8,000. This is, in all respects, the largest and most costly organ on the Pacific coast, and it has few superiors even in the Atlantic States. It has forty-six stops and over 2,000 pipes. The greatest variety of combinations can be made by the use of the various stops and couplings; and for excellence of workmanship and sweetness of tone it has been pronounced by judges to be unsurpassed. The choir is under the efficient management of Mr. Washington Elliot, Mr. Gustave A. Scott being the organist.

The church building will seat comfortably 1,000 persons. The number of communicants is now about four hundred and seventy-five. The number of scholars and teachers in the Sabbath School is about three hundred; number of volumes in the library, 1,000, which were selected with great care, and form a very complete library. Connected with the church is a depository of the books of the Presbyterian Board of Publication, in which there is kept a variety of the standard books and tracts published by that Board.

Howard Presbyterian Church, (N. S.)

Pastor, Rev. HENRY M. SCUDDER, M.D., D.D.; residence, No. 1, Vernon Place. Location, corner of Natoma and June streets. Services every Sabbath at 11, A.M. and 7½, P.M. in summer months, and at 7½, P.M. in winter. Prayer meeting and lecture Wednesday evening. Prayer meeting Sabbath evening, one hour before the evening service. Sabbath School every Sabbath at 1 P.M.; Wales L. Palmer, Superintendent. Teachers' meeting every Friday evening. Number of teachers and scholars, about 450. Volumes in library, about 1,500.

The church was organized September, 1850, to supply a portion of the city then destitute of religious privileges, under the auspices of the Rev. S. H. Willey, who continued in the pastorate for twelve years. The building at present occupied by the congregation was dedicated June 17th, 1851, and was enlarged and thoroughly repaired in 1864. In the early part of 1864, the church building was found inadequate to the wants of the increasing congregation, then under the pastoral care of the Rev. A. E. Kittredge, and the Sabbath services were held in Platt's Hall, Montgomery Street, for several months, until about the end of July, when the pastor's health requiring a journey to the Atlantic States, the old location was reoccupied.

The present pastor, who was for many years a missionary in India, was installed by the Presbytery of San Francisco July 23d, 1865, and has commenced his work with every prospect of great success. The church edifice is crowded, and measures have been taken to speedily erect a large and convenient building for the use of the congregation on Howard Street, near the present site. It is hoped that the new church will be ready for use during the coming year.

Officers—W. A. Palmer, E. Bigelow, Geo. W. Armes, Samuel I. C. Swezey, Elders; Cyrus Palmer, I. E. Davis, C. W. Armes, Charles Geddes, S. C. Bugbee, Samuel I. C. Swezey, Trustees.

Larkin Street Presbyterian Church, (O. S.)

Location, corner of Larkin and Pacific streets. Rev. J. D. STRONG, Pastor.

Officers—H. P. Coon, H. H. Haight, G. L. Kenny, S. H. Williams, E. R. Waterman, F. Leppien, and Robert Irwin, Trustees.

This enterprise was commenced by its present pastor, in the Spring Valley School House, in April, 1862. A Union Sabbath School, under the superintendence of E. R. Waterman, had previously existed in the neighborhood for more than two years, but was not formally connected with the church movement till near the close of that year, when an effort was made to erect a house of worship, but failed for want of the requisite funds. During the following summer the effort was revived, and in September, 1863, a Board of Trustees was incorporated, a lot purchased at an expense of $1,000, plans and specifications prepared by S. H. Williams, and the contract for building the church edifice let to J. W. Duncan. On the 4th September, 1864, the building was completed and dedicated. It is of wood, seventy-two feet long by forty-two wide, and has seats for about four hundred persons. Its architecture is plain and unpretending, but neat and tasteful, and it is one of the most substantial and thoroughly constructed wooden churches in the State. Its whole cost was a little over $10,000.

Central Presbyterian Church, (O. S.)

Rev. JOHN G. FACHLER, Pastor. Location, Mission Street, between Fifth and Sixth. Pastor's residence, 37, Fifth street. Sabbath services are held at 11 o'clock, A.M.; evening services at 7 o'clock in winter, and 7½ o'clock in summer. Prayer meeting every Thursday at 7½ o'clock, P.M. Sabbath school at 9½ o'clock, A.M.

The church organization was effected May 14th, 1865, with sixty-one members. Its total membership October 1st, 1865, was seventy-two. The house of worship is a handsome frame of two stories. In the first story there are four rooms to be used for lectures and weekly services, library, Sabbath school, and pastor's study. The main audience room is forty by eighty feet, with a handsomely arched ceiling of nearly thirty feet pitch. It will seat about five hundred persons. The whole cost of the building, including gas fixtures, upholstering, carpeting, etc., exclusive of the ground, will be something more than $9,000, the payment for nearly all of which has been provided for, leaving the congregation with a merely nominal debt.

Officers—Stephen Franklin, Esq. and James D. Thornton, Esq. Elders; James D. Thornton, John W. Thurman, A. T. Furrish, Charles H. Reynolds, R. R. Provines, William Glaskin, Henry Steele, George K. Gluyas, and A. Hemme, Trustees.

ROMAN CATHOLIC.

St. Mary's Cathedral.

Most Rev. JOSEPH S. ALEMANY, Archbishop; Very Rev. James Croke, V.G. Rector; Revs. John

F. Harrington and O. Reilly, D.D., Assistants; Rev. W. Bowman, Secretary; Rev. P. Walsh; Archi-episcopal and pastoral residence, Dupont Street, adjoining the Cathedral. Location, NE corner California and Dupont streets. Masses, Sundays at 6½, 8, 9, and 11 o'clock, A.M.; week days, 6, 6½, 7, and 7½ o'clock, A.M.; Vespers, at 7 o'clock Sunday evenings, in Winter, and 7½ in Summer.

The erection of this noble structure was commenced on the seventeenth of July, 1853, during which year the basement portion was built, and the work was resumed the July following. Dedicated December 25th, 1854. The church is seventy-five feet wide, fronting on California Street, by one hundred and thirty-one feet on Dupont Street, being the largest church in the State. Service was begun at midnight on December 24th, 1854. The basement portion, is lighted from both sides and well ventilated. The present expenditure on the building is $175,000. The church portion is forty-five feet high in the clear, and contains spacious galleries and an organ loft. The ceilings are vaulted with a series of groined arches which are decorated, and every means has been resorted to for accommodation, light, and ventilation. The church can seat twelve hundred persons. The tower is at present one hundred and thirty-five feet high, and when completed, with the spire, will be two hundred feet high. The edifice is of Gothic architecture, which has been carried out in every detail through the building. In all the arrangements for the erection of the church, the greatest attention has been paid to the selection of the best materials, and to the combination of strength and durability, which are admirably effected in its construction. William Craine, architect.

The present dimensions of the Cathedral not being sufficiently large for the vast congregation that attends it, it is intended to add about thirty feet more to its length. An Archi-episcopal and pastoral residence on California Street, as also a beautiful and spacious Baptistery, are now in course of erection, and will be completed during this fall.

Attached to the Cathedral is a large day school for boys, conducted by the Brothers of St. Francis, Rev. John McMahon, Principal; average attendance, four hundred and fifty.

St. Francis.

Rev. JAMES H. AKRDEN, O.P., Pastor; Rev. Hyacinth Derham, O.P., Assistant Pastor. Pastoral residence south side Green near Dupont. Location north side Vallejo bet Dupont and Stockton. Services, Sunday at 6½, 8½, and 11, A.M.; Sunday School at 2 o'clock, P.M.; and evening devotions at 7 o'clock, P.M.; at 8½ o'clock, A.M. the sermon is in Spanish.

This church was organized by Very Rev. Anthony Langlois, in the spring of 1849, through whose efforts a commodious frame building was erected in the month of December, 1849, and was the first Roman Catholic Church organized in San Francisco. Its ground base was forty by one hundred feet, one story in hight. During the years 1859–60, a large and commodious church was erected, which was dedicated on the seventeenth March, 1860. Its design is of the Gothic order, prevalent in the fourteenth century, presenting an illustration of the Christian architecture of that period. The principal features of this imposing structure are the towers, which project beyond the body of the church, and present in their elevation four divisions, rising to a hight of ninety feet from the ground. The entrance porch, or vestibule, has two side aisles, a semi-octagonal sanctuary, and two sacristies, and is approached by a flight of ten steps, ascending to the vestibule, from which, at each side, are entrances to the galleries and baptistery, and in front are the pointed arched doorways which lead to the nave and aisles. In the central space, between the towers, are the three doorways communicating with the vestibule, and thence with the interior. Over the central door there is a large and elegant three-compartment window, and in the gable a highly decorated rose window. Over each side door there is a lofty and spacious niche, which rises from richly molded brick corbels; there are also three marble panels, with appropriate inscriptions, recessed in the brick work immediately over the doorway and gable; the work is finished with a massive and richly decorated cross.

The east and west sides of the structure are divided by buttresses into eight spaces, in each instance; seven of which contain the large, pointed, arched windows, which light the church. Beneath the floor of the church there is a large, well-lighted basement, which is used as a school room, and also as a place of meeting for the parishioners. The extreme length of the building is sixty-six by one hundred and thirty-seven and one-half feet; from the floor to the foot of the rafters is thirty-five feet. The cost, when completed, will be nearly $100,000.

St. Patrick's Church.

Rev. PETER J. GREY, Pastor; Revs. Thomas Gibney and P. Scanlan, Assistants. Location, south side Market Street, between Second and Third Streets; pastoral residence, Market Street, adjacent to the church. Masses: Sundays, at 6, 8, 9, and 11, A.M.; during the week, daily, at 6½ and 7½, A.M.; evening service at 7½ o'clock. A boys' school is kept in the basement, at which there is an average attendance of nearly four hundred pupils.

St. Boniface Church (German).

Rev. SEBASTIAN WOLF, Pastor; Rev. Andrew Andolshek, Assistant Pastor; residence, Sutter, near Montgomery Street. Location, north side Sutter, between Montgomery and Kearny streets. Dedicated April 5th, 1860. Services—Mass: Sundays, at 8 and 10½ o'clock, A.M., and Vespers 7 o'clock, P.M.; week days, 7 o'clock, A.M.

St. Ignatius' Church.

Served by the Fathers of the Society of Jesus connected with St. Ignatius' College. Location, north side Market Street between Fourth and Fifth streets. Masses: Sundays, at 5, 5¾, 6½, 7¼, 8, 8¾, 9½, and 11 o'clock, A.M.; Vespers at 7 o'clock, P.M. in winter, and 7½, P.M. in summer; week days, 5, 5¾, 6½, 7¼, and 8 o'clock, A.M. The old building dedicated July 15th, 1855, being found too small for the rapidly-increasing congregation, the new Hall of the College is at present used as a Church, and accommodates about 2,000 persons. The church will afterwards be built on the site of the old one. The present portion of the institution, recently erected, cost about $120,000.

Notre Dame des Victoires.

Rev. FATHER MOLINIER, Pastor. Location, north side Bush between Dupont and Stockton streets. Services at 7½, A.M. every day. Sundays at 7 and 11, A.M.; also, Vespers at 3½, P.M. The congregation was organized May, 1856, and its splendid edifice dedicated on the fourth of the same month. The building was constructed by a society of Baptists, and at the date above given was disposed of to the present owners. It has a ground base of fifty by one hundred feet, is a very beautiful and massive brick structure, and with its basement, which is intended for school rooms connected with the church, has a capacity of comfortably seating seven hundred persons.

Mission Dolores.

Rev. JOHN J. PRENDERGAST, Pastor; Rev. Thos. Cushing, Assistant. Services at 8 and 11 o'clock, A.M., on Sundays and Festivals. This adobe church is located on the south-west corner of Sixteenth and Dolores streets; was dedicated on the ninth of October, 1776, although projected in 1769, by Father Junipero Serra, the Father of the California Missions. The first Friar who had charge was Francisco Palou, who was assisted in his labors by Benito Cambon. At the organization of this Mission, and for its protection, there were fifteen soldiers located at the Presidio, under the command of S. Flores. A cemetery is attached to the church, in which the first interment was made in September, 1776. The first Indian convert was baptized on the twenty-seventh December, in the same year. In the introductory portion of the San Francisco Directory for 1862, page, 5, will be found further details connected with the history of this Mission. Attached to this church is the Seminary of St. Thomas and a large day school.

St. Joseph's Church.

Rev. H. P. GALLAGHER, Pastor; residence, next door to the church. Location, Tenth Street between Folsom and Howard. Services on Sundays and Festival days. Mass at 8 o'clock, A.M.; High Mass at 11 o'clock, A.M.; Catechism at 3, and Vespers at 7 o'clock, P.M.; Mass, week days, at 7 o'clock, A.M. St. Joseph's Church was opened for divine service on the eighth day of December, 1861. The building is a neat and substantial one story frame, sixty feet long by thirty-seven feet wide, and stands on the one hundred-vara lot donated by Horace Hawes, Esq., for the future Cathedral of the Arch Diocese. The forementioned building, removed back for a school, has been replaced by a new edifice, over thrice the size of the above. It is cruciform gothic, and elegantly finished. The new building is designed to be, as nearly as possible, earthquake and panic proof, the ceiling being done in finely finished wood, and the large entrance door to slide on rollers.

St. Rose's Church.

Pastor—(Vacant). Attended from the Cathedral. Location, Bryant Street. Mass: Sundays, at 8 o'clock, A.M. St. Rose's Church was dedicated on the Festival of Pentecost, June 8th, 1862. There is a vacancy in the Pastorship, which will be in a short time filled. There is connected with the church a ol for girls, in charge of the Sisters of St. Dominic, which contained, within one month after its establishment, one hundred and fifty-six pupils. There are now more than three hundred girls in regular attendance.

St. Bridget's Church.

Rev. THOMAS O'NEILL, O.P., Pastor; Rev. Mannes Duggan, O.P., Assistant; residence, rear of church. Location, SW corner Van Ness Avenue and Broadway. The building occupied by this church was completed in February, 1864. It is a one-story wooden structure, forty by seventy-six feet, erected upon a valuable lot purchased by Archbishop Alemany, at a cost of $5,000. Services, Sundays, 8 and 11, A.M., and 7½, P.M.; week days, 7, A.M. The services for the burial of the dead at Calvary Cemetery, is attended by the clergymen of St. Bridget's Church, from 3 to 5, P.M., from March to October, and from 2½ to 4, P.M., from November to April. St. Bridget's Church is the first established in the Western Addition. Services first held in February, 1864.

SWEDENBORGIAN.

Church of the New Jerusalem.

Public service held every Sabbath morning at 11 o'clock, A.M., in the room of the Twelfth District Court, City Hall. Administration of the Sacrament of the Lord's Supper, at the residence of Thomas

S. Miller, 823 Bush Street, on the first Sundays of January, April, July, and October, at 2½ o'clock, P.M.

This society purchased, two years ago, an eligible and beautiful lot on O'Farrell between Mason and Taylor, measuring fifty-feet front by one hundred and thirty-seven and a half feet in depth, at a cost of four thousand one hundred dollars. In May last they commenced to erect thereon a neat Gothic church, which is now nearly completed, capable of seating three hundred persons. It is one of the neatest little churches in the city. Designed and superintended by S. C. Bugbee, architect, and will cost when finished about six thousand dollars. It has a Chancel, in the rear of which is a Tabernacle, as a Depository of the Holy Word, and on each side of this are two Tablets, on which will be inscribed the Law of the Ten Commandments, the Lord's Prayer, and the Ten Blessings. On one side of the church is the Pastor's study, and on the other side is a room for the organ and choir.

Officers—Thomas S. Miller (President) Benjamin Hobart, James Kellogg, C. C. Webb, Charles Pace, Oliver Eldridge, and J. H. Purkitt, Trustees; J. H. Purkitt, Reader; Dr. A. Kellogg, Librarian; Jas. Kellogg, Treasurer; John Pettee, Secretary; Benj. Shellard, Chorister; J. H. Purkitt (Chairman) Thos. S. Miller, L. L. Blood, Benj. Shellard, and Jas. Kellogg, Church Committee.

A library, containing all the Scientific and Theological works of Swedenborg, recently greatly enlarged by a valuable donation of all Swedenborg's Works in Latin and English, together with a large collection of the collateral works of the New Church, both English and American, is kept constantly on hand.

The church was organized in 1851.

UNITARIAN.

First Unitarian Church.

Rev. HORATIO STEBBINS, Pastor. Location, south side Geary below Stockton. Services Sunday at 11, A.M., and 7½, P.M. Sabbath School, Sunday at 1, P.M.

This society was organized September 1st, 1850. The first edifice owed by the society was erected in 1852, on Stockton Street between Clay and Sacramento. The first regular pastor, the Rev. Joseph Harrington, arrived August 27th, 1852, and died November 2d of same year, of Panama fever. The second regular pastor, Rev. F. T. Gray, arrived June, 1853, and left in June, 1854, and died in Boston in February, 1855. The third regular pastor, the Rev. R. P. Cutler, arrived August 31st, 1854, and continued his ministrations without intermission until June 1st, 1859, at which time he resigned his charge and left for New York. The Rev. John A. Buckingham then officiated as temporary pastor until April 5th, 1860. The late pastor, Rev. Thomas Starr King, arrived here with his family, April 28th, 1860, and commenced his ministrations the following day (Sunday) before one of the largest congregations ever assembled in this city.

During the period of Mr. King's ministry, the society extinguished a long standing debt of twenty thousand dollars, and erected a new church on Geary Street near Stockton, at a cost of one hundred and fifteen thousand dollars, all of which has been paid. It is one of the most beautiful structures our city contains, and is remarkable for the purity of its architectural design and its interior beauty.

Upon the death of Thomas Starr King, on the fourth of March, 1864, Rev. Dr. Henry W. Bellows, of All Saints Church, New York, President of the Sanitary Commission, and one of the most distinguished and influential ministers of the denomination, responded to an earnest call from the society, and left New York within a few weeks to fill the pulpit thus vacant, for a period of six months.

The Rev. Horatio Stebbins of Porland, Maine, who had received a unanimous call from the society, became the permanent pastor the following September. Since then the society has enjoyed its accustomed prosperity. At the annual renting of pews in January every seat was taken, and, a premium secured above the regular assessments of ten thousand dollars, thus assuring an income for the year of nearly twenty-seven thousand dollars.

The pews of the Church are not owned by individuals, but belong to the society, whose organic law requires that they shall be rented annually at auction to the highest bidder. A clause in the new Constitution of the society provides that the property shall never be pledged, mortgaged, or incumbered for any purpose whatever.

Officers—R. B. Swain, Moderator; Charles Wolcott Brooks, Treasurer; George C. Hickox, Secretary; Charles L. Low, J. A. Coolidge, Nathaniel Page, Samuel C. Bigelow, Henry Kimball, and Levi Stevens, Trustees.

MISCELLANEOUS.

Chinese Mission House.

Rev. A. W. Loomis, Pastor; residence, north-east corner Stockton and Sacramento; location north east corner Stockton and Sacramento streets.

Religious services in the Chinese language on each Sabbath afternoon and evening, and also on Thursday evening. A day and evening school is kept throughout the week, also a Sabbath School. The house is brick, and was built by the liberality of the citizens of San Francisco, and by funds from a Board of Missions in New York, by which the Mission to the Chinese in California is supported. The house contains school-rooms in the basement; on the first floor a chapel which will seat two hundred persons, and on the second, apartments for the accommodation of the Missionary family.

The Mariners' Church.

Rev. J. Rowell, Pastor; residence, 1106 California Street; location, Clark Street, near Pacific Wharf.

This church was organized with six members, in December, 1858, and now numbers eighty-three. Public worship every Sabbath at 3 o'clock, P.M. There is connected with the church a Sabbath School and Bible Class, numbering more than ninety teachers and scholars. The house of worship is a commodious wooden building, on Clark Street, near Drumm. It was erected some years since by contributions from merchants and other citizens of San Francisco.

Officers—Rev. J. Rowell, Pastor and Chaplain of the American Seaman's Friend Society, who has labored here since August, 1858; James F. Stewart, Henry Chester, and John B. Tulloch, Deacons.

This church finds a wide field for usefulness, in the usual church services, a large Bible Class for seamen and strangers, a Sabbath religious reading room, weekly prayer meetings in several sailors' boarding houses, preaching on the Sabbath and personal labor during the week at the U. S. Marine Hospital; distribution of bibles and tracts on ship board, boarding houses, and elsewhere, and missionary labors about the streets, wharfs, and shipping, and on board several men-of-war, and other sea-going vessels. It is an undenominational missionary church.

During the year 1860 a society was formed among the business men of San Francisco, having for its object the moral improvement of seamen, called the San Francisco Port Society. It seeks to attain its object by sustaining the preaching of the Gospel, and other missionary labors, in connection with the Mariners' Church.

The officers of the society for the present year, are: Ira P. Rankin, President; R. B. Swain, Vice President; J. Rowell, Secretary; A. C. Nichols, Treasurer; Dr. H. P. Coon, Dr. J. T. McLean, A. C. Nichols, Nathaniel Gray, J. F. Pope, Cyrus Palmer, Louis McLane, J. Rowell, and James F. Stewart, Trustees.

Church of Christ.

The Church of Christ (Disciples) meet every Lord's day morning, at 11 o'clock, in the University School Hall, Post Street, between Stockton and Powell. Sunday School from 10 to 11, A.M.

German Evangelical Lutheran Church.

Rev. F. Mooshake, Pastor; residence, 245 Stevenson, near Third. Location, Sutter Street, between Stockton and Dupont. Services every Sabbath at 11 o'clock, A.M. Sunday School at 10 o'clock, A.M. There is, during the week, a day school for girls and boys, under the charge of Mr. Zahn.

German Evangelical Lutheran St. Mark's Church.

J. M. Buehler, Pastor; residence 29 O'Farrell Street, between Market and Stockton. Location, south side of Geary Street, between Stockton and Powell. Public worship every Sunday at 10½, A.M. and 7¼, P.M., also on Wednesday evenings at 7¼.

This church was organized in the fall of 1860. Divine services were first held in the northern part of the city, when the growing wants of the congregation made the selection of a more conveniently located place of worship necessary. The society therefore purchased its present lot on Geary Street, fronting on Union Square, and measuring fifty-five feet front by one hundred and thirty-seven feet and a half feet in depth. A large and commodious basement building, which, after the completion of the entire edifice, will be devoted to school purposes alone, has already been erected, and is now used for public worship. The corner stone of the church proper was laid October 31st, 1863, with appropriate services, and the entire building will soon be finished, A German and English day school, superintended by a School Board, with Mr. G. H. Labohm as principal teacher, is connected with this congregation.

Officers—F. Rutenberg, President; H. Hanssmann, Vice President; H. Buttner, Secretary; Ch's Meinecke, Treasurer; W. Reinhardt, M. Mangels, and H. Putzmann, Trustees.

First German Evangelical Lutheran Church.

F.'Hansen, Pastor; location, north side Greenwich, between Dupont and Stockton. Services in the German language, each Sabbath, at 10½ o'clock, and Sunday School at 9½ o'clock, A.M.

Officers—F. Maass, President; L. Schneider, Vice President; H. Buttner, Secretary; M. Lammers, Treasurer; F. Kramer, A. Marks, and W. Reinhardt, Trustees.

Swedish Evangelical Lutheran Church.

N. Stromberg, Pastor. Services every Sunday at 11, A.M., in the Mariners' Church on Clark Street.

Friends of Progress.

Meet at the hall corner of Fourth and Jessie streets. Conference meetings at 11, A.M. every Sunday morning. Children's Progressive Lyceum at 2, P.M. Lecture at 8, P.M.

Church of Christ.

The reorganized Church of Jesus Christ of Latter-Day Saints hold public worship at Mechanics' Hall, Bush Street, next door to the Occidental Hotel, every Sunday, at 11, A.M. and 7½, P.M.

Disciples of Christ.

Congregation of Disciples of Christ (Christian Church) meets every Lord's Day morning at 11 o'clock, in the University School Hall, Post Street, opposite Union Square. Sunday School from 10 to 11, A.M.

HEBREW.

The Congregational Sherith Israel.

Rev. Dr. H. A. HENRY, Minister and Rabbi Preacher; residence 736 Green. Location of Synagogue, East side Stockton, between Broadway and Vallejo. L. Ries, Sexton.

Officers—Israel Solomon, President; C. Meyer, Vice President; L. King, Treasurer; F. Pulvermacher, P. Funkenstein, P. Berwin, J. M. Martin, A. Reinstein, Trustees; Isaiah Cohen, Secretary.

Congregation Emanu El.*

ELKAN COHN, Minister; residence, 117 Taylor, between Turk and Eddy. Location, north side Broadway, between Powell and Mason streets. Organized April, 1851. The present building was erected in 1854, at a cost of $35,000; it is a noble edifice, and will seat about 800 persons. The school for the religious education of youth is now conducted in the school building of the pastor, north side Post Street, between Dupont and Stockton.

Officers—L. Sachs, President; M. Heller, Vice President; Jacob Greenebaum, Treasurer; B. Hagan, Secretary; M. Steppacher, Sexton and Collector; L. Cohn, I. T. Bloch, M. Mayblum, Ab. Seligman, B. Price, A. Hirschfelder, and L. Dinkelspiel, Trustees.

Congregation Ohabai Shalome.*

Rev. ————— —————, Minister; residence,————— —————. Location of synagogue, east side Mason, between Post and Geary. Charles Greenberg, Sexton.

Officers—B. Hamburger, President; S. Wand, Vice President; H. Greenberg, Treasurer: M. Waterman, Secretary; S. Wangenheim, S. Hahn, J. Baum, S. Wolf, and L. Kullman, Trustees.

SOCIETIES.

Religious.

CALIFORNIA BIBLE SOCIETY.—Organized October 30th, 1849, with John M. Finley as President; and the Revs. J. L. Ver Mehr, Albert Williams, and W. Taylor, Vice Presidents; and T. D. Hunt as Secretary. Depository, 757 Market Street. Meetings of the Board of Trustees are held by appointment on the Tuesday after the first Sunday of each month. The first building of the soci-

ety, on Stockton Street, was destroyed by fire April 26th, 1853, when a new one was erected on the same site at an expense of $7,000. The corner stone of the new building of the Society, 757, 759, and 761 Market Street, was laid with appropriate ceremonies on the second day of May, 1862. The edifice is an ornament to the city, a marked feature of the enterprise and foresight of the Board of Trustees; having disposed of the property owned by the Society on Montgomery Street, they selected this location on a growing thoroughfare, in hopes that the future income of the property will enable the respected agent, Rev. F. Buel, to more fully extend the circulation of the Holy Scriptures in this State, and the Pacific Coast. The building is fifty feet by seventy-five, three stories high, with stores on the ground floor. One of them is now occupied as the depository of the society. The name of the society was changed by Act of the Legislature, 1859, from the San Francisco Bible Society to its present title. New constitution adopted November, 1860.

Officers—Rev. J. T. Peck, D.D., President; Reverends A. Williams, D. B. Cheney, D.D., S. D. Simonds, F. M. McAllister, J. Rowell, J. A. Benton, John D. Blain, all of San Francisco, Rev. S. H. Willey, Rev. Lucius Hamilton of Oakland, Rev. M. C. Briggs, Rev. W. C. Pond of Downieville, Rev. W. H. Hill of Sacramento, Rev. C. C. Pierce of Placerville, Rev. J. W. Ross of Yreka, Rev. George Moore of Oakland, Hon. H. P. Coon of San Francisco, Rev. John Braley of Santa Clara, Rev. Isaac Owen of Sacramento, and Rev. Peter Veeder of Napa, Vice Presidents; C. Wittram, Treasurer; William R. Wadsworth, Secretary; the President, Treasurer, Secretary, Agent, Annis Merrill, Elijah Bigelow, John Reynolds, E. P. Flint, and Nathaniel Gray, Trustees.

INDEPENDENT ORDER OF GOOD TEMPLARS.—Grand Lodge organized May 29th, 1860. Jurisdiction embraces the States of California, Oregon, and Nevada, and Territories of Utah, Idaho, New Mexico, and Washington. Annual sessions held at Sacramento City, fourth Tuesday in September. Number of working Lodges, one hundred and forty-one. Total membership, about 6,000. Office of Grand Worthy Secretary, rooms 5 and 6 Garwood's Building, J Street, between Fifth and Sixth, Sacramento.

Officers—Fiscal year ending September, 1866. Hon. C. S. Haswell, Nicolaus, G.W.C.T.; Mrs. E. R. Anderson, Santa Rosa, G.W.V.T.; F. A. Hornblower, Placerville, G.W.C.; William H. Mills, Sacramento, G.W.S.; Mrs. M. C. Heald, Napa City, G. W.A.S.; Mrs. E. W. Frasier, Sacramento, G.W.T.; P. Y. Baker, San Francisco, G.W.M.; Miss Ada M. Hazen, Martinez, G.W.D.M.; J. L. Cook, Souoma, G. W.Mess.; J. McIlmoil, Yuba City, G.W.I.G.; G. M. Stratton, Chico, G.W.O.G.; Rev. A. F. White, Carson City, G.W.Chap.; Hon. J. L. Downing, Santa Rosa, P.G.W.C.T.; A. C. McDougall, W. V. Frasier, R. E. Comins, P. Conway, W. K. Forsyth, B. S. McLafferty, W. J. Johnson, T. W. Smith, Wm. H. Payne, and H. W. Briggs, Grand Lecturers and Organizing Officers.

CALIFORNIA LODGE, No. 7.—Hall, Merriman's Building, Mission Street, between Second and Third. Meet every Friday evening.

Officers—James Pennycook, W.C.T.; Miss Carrie A. George, W.V.T.; Charles H. Warner, W.S.; Richard Merriman, W.F.S.; Mary A. Casebolt, W.T.; Geo. W. Mower, W.M.; Henry Hess, W.I.G.; J. R. Ripes, W.O.G.; Geo. W. Gildersleeve, D.D.G.W.C.T.

EVENING STAR LODGE, No. 114.—Meets every Wednesday evening at Merriman's Hall.

Officers—James Thomson, W.C.T.; Jane Parker, W.V.T; D. C. Porter, W.S.; T. G. McCammant,

---

* During the present year the congregations of the Emanu El and Ohabai Shalome have each erected commodious and elegant houses of worship, which are fully described in our introductory article, "Progress of the City," at the commencement of the work.

W.F.S.; E. Green, W.T.; Ann Black, W.M.; F. Gill, W.I.G.; G. W. Rolph, W.O.G.; George Beanston, W.C.; Lewis Green, P.W.C.T.; Peter Beanston, D.D.G.W.C.T.

STAR SPANGLED BANNER LODGE, No. 123.—Meets every Tuesday evening at the Presidio.
Officers—A. P. Kelly, W.C.T.; S. Brown, W.V. T.; E. Lehe, W.S.; C. Lange, W.T.; D. S. Collins, W.F.S.; A. Taylor, W.M.; P. Farrell, W.D.M.; D. Brown, W.A.S.; T. P. Hastie, W.Chap.; C. Miltenberger, W.I.G.; Jas. Dickey, W.O.G.; M. Lewis, W.R.H.S.; Kate Kernahan, W.L.H.S.; W. N. Glenn, P.W.C.T.

ORIENTAL LODGE, No. 150.—Meets every Tuesday evening at Merriman's Hall, Mission Street, between Second and Third.
Officers—T. H. Lufkin, W.C.T.; Miss A. S. Farnham, W.V.T.; Miss Mary Miller, Sec'y; C. Leonard, Financial Sec'y; W. C. Forsyth, Treasurer; Ira Cook, Marshal; Miss Sarah Forsyth, Inside Guard; —— Fripp, Outside Guard; C. Leonard, Deputy.

HOME FOR THE CARE OF THE INEBRIATE.—Organized May 24th, 1859. The society has recently purchased the property known as Pfeiffer's Building, north-east corner Stockton and Chestnut, at an expense of $7,500.
The Legislature of the State, session of 1863, authorized the Board of Supervisors to appropriate $250 per month for the support of this institution.
Officers—Rev. Horatio Stebbins, President; R. A. Redman, Secretary; Alexander Stott, Treasurer; Rev. J. D. Blain, William A. Kollmyer, J. B. Badger, Frank G. Edwards, Royal Fish, and Jacob Deeth, Trustees; John Armitage, Superintendent; Mrs. John Armitage, Matron.

PARENT DASHAWAY ASSOCIATION.—Organized January 2d, 1859. Number of members who have joined the association since that time, 6,200. The society occupy their new and commodious building on Post Street, near Dupont, built by the association at a cost, including lot, of $22,000, nearly two-thirds of which debt has been liquidated up to the present time. Public meetings are held on Sunday and Thursday evenings. Business meeting, Tuesday evening.
Officers—E. T. Batturs, President; Jos. B. Badger, First Vice President; C. E. B. Howe, Second Vice President; J. Madison Platt, Secretary; S. A. Thomas, Treasurer; David Hunter and J. H. Lawton, Trustees.

SABBATH SCHOOL UNION. — Reorganized May, 1857. The union meets quarterly, alternately at the different churches whose schools are represented in the union, when reports from the different schools, showing the average attendance of scholars and teachers for the previous month are presented. [See General Review.]
Officers—J. W. Stow of Calvary Church, President; B. T. Martin of First Baptist Church, L. B. Benchley of First Congregational Church, Captain Charles Goodall of Howard Methodist Episcopal Church, Wales L. Palmer of Howard Presbyterian Church, Hon. E. D. Sawyer of Second Congregational Church, and Dr. J. C. Spencer of Second Baptist Church, Vice Presidents; Samuel Pillsbury of First Congregational Church, Secretary and Treasurer.

SAN FRANCISCO PORT SOCIETY.—Organized March, 1860.
The object of the society is the moral improvement of seamen, and others connected with the sea, in this port, by aiding the American Seamen's Friend Society of New York in sustaining the Mariners'

Church of San Francisco, and in such enterprises connected therewith as the society may approve. This society is organized and sustained on the principle that it belongs properly to the people of San Francisco to provide religious privileges and instruction for the sailors belonging to and visiting this port. Any person may become a member by paying five dollars a year, or a life member by the payment at one time of fifty dollars.
Officers—Ira P. Rankin, President; R. B. Swain, Vice President; J. Rowell, Secretary; A. C. Nichols, Treasurer: A. C. Nichols, Henry P. Coon, Louis McLane, J. B. Thomas, Nathaniel Gray, Cyrus Palmer, J. Rowell, J. F. Pope, and James F. Stewart, Trustees.

SAN FRANCISCO TRACT SOCIETY.—Auxiliary to the American Tract Society; Depository at C. Beach's Book Store, 34 Montgomery Street, near Sutter. Organized August 16th, 1852.
Officers—Samuel I. C. Swezey, President; Rev. Jos. Rowell, Dr. H. M. Scudder, and Dr. J. H. Wyathe, Vice Presidents; Thomas B. Ludlum, Secretary; J. K. S. Latham, Treasurer; and a Board of Directors composed of one delegate from each Evangelical Church in the city.

SODALITY OF THE B. V. M.—Organized in December, 1861. Meetings held every Sunday morning at 9½ o'clock, at the hall, on Market Street, between Fourth and Fifth, belonging to St. Ignatius' College. Organizations of the above order have existed for the past two hundred years. This society was founded in this city by the Rev. J. M. Buchard, S.J., having for its object the moral and intellectual improvement of its members. It is governed by a Prefect and two assistants, together with a Secretary, Treasurer, and twelve Consultors; there is also a Chaplain attached to the society. It has a library of about one thousand volumes, which is being increased as the funds of the society will permit. Number of members, from three to four hundred.
Officers—James R. Kelly, Prefect; —— McKenny, 1st Assistant Prefect; John B. Oliver, 2d Assistant Prefect; Prof. —— McCurry, Secretary; Francis A. Durning, Treasurer; James J. O'Malley and Henry Bowie, A.B., Marshals; Rev. J. M. Buchard, S.J., Chaplain.

SONS OF TEMPERANCE.—Office of the Grand Scribe, No. 302 Montgomery Street, room No. 1. Annual Session Grand Division held at Santa Cruz, fourth Tuesday in October, 1866.
Officers of the Grand Division—H. A. Scofield, G.W.P.; Jesse Hobson, G.W.A.; Wm. Hollis, G.S.; J. J. Hucks, G.T.; Rev. Thomas Welsh, G.Chap.; B. F. Tucker, G.C.; D. R. Jayne, G.S.; H. H. Rhees, P.G.W.P.
EXCELSIOR DIVISION, No. 6.—Meets at Merriman's Hall, Mission Street, between Second and Third, every Monday evening.
Officers—F. Shoemaker, W.P.; B. F. Kennedy, R.S.; G. W. Gildersleeve, D.G.W.P.
GOLDEN GATE, No. 12.—Meets 302 Montgomery Street, every Thursday evening.
Officers—William Sutton, W.P.; A. C. Flemming, R.S.; J. J. Hucks, D.G.W.P.
OCCIDENTAL DIVISION, No. 3.—Meets corner Sixteenth and Valencia, every Friday evening.
Officers—T. H. Lufkin, W.P.; A. B. Perry, R.S.
PHŒNIX DIVISION, No. 100.—Meets every Tuesday evening at Merriman's Hall, Mission Street.
Officers—John Gorman, W.P.; J. A. Woodson, R.S. and D.G.W.P.
RISING SUN DIVISION, No. 1.—Meets every Tuesday evening at 203 Montgomery Street.
Officers—John F. Coffey, W.P.; P. Beanston, R.S.

UNIVERSAL ISRAELITISH UNION.—Pacific Branch. Office 522 Montgomery Street. The objects of the union are, to promote everywhere the emancipation and moral progress of the Israelite; to render aid to those who suffer persecution as Israelites, and to encourage every publication tending to assist the union in its efforts.

Officers—Rev. Elkan Cohn, President.

YOUNG MEN'S CHRISTIAN ASSOCIATION. —Established in 1853, having for its object the moral, social, and intellectual improvement of young men of all denominations, by means of a Reading Room, supplied with all the leading religious and secular papers, magazines, and periodicals, domestic and foreign, together with a well selected Library of more than two thousand volumes. [See Historical and General Review.]

The third Monday evening of each month is devoted to literary exercises and debates, open to all. A Prayer Meeting, to which all of every denomination are welcome, is held at the rooms every Saturday evening from 8 to 9 o'clock.

The rooms of the Association are at 526 California Street, which are open the year round from 8, A.M. to 10, P.M. The Library is open every day (Sundays excepted) from 3 to 10, P.M.

Officers—Ralph C. Harrison, President; H. L. Chamberlain, Samuel Irving, John Daniel, J. Watkins Jones, and F. S. Page, Vice Presidents: Charles J. King, Recording Secretary; R. J. Trumbull, Corresponding Secretary; R. G. Davisson, Treasurer; John Dunn, Librarian; Chas. S. Eaton, C. W. Moulthrop, Chas. G. Roberts, Philo Mills, James Kirkpatrick, J. H. Applegate, jr., John Lowry, E. A. Upton, E. R. Hawley, E. R. Watermann, Irvine Blakely, H. H. Morgan, Chas. Spencer, Wm. Krug, G. L. Plympton, John Reynolds, Edward Barry, George H. Bell, and James F. Stewart, Board of Managers.

Benevolent.

ASSOCIATION OF THE DAUGHTERS OF ISRAEL.—This society was organized April, 1864, for benevolent purposes, and meets monthly at the residence of some member of the society. Number of members, twenty-five.

Officers—Mrs. G. Scholle, 640 Folsom Street, President; Mrs. Hagan, Post Street near Eleventh, Secretary; Mrs. Loewy, Hayes' Valley, Treasurer.

A. J. O. K. S. B.—HAR HARMORIAH LODGE, No. 3.—Meets every Sunday evening. Hall, 726 Montgomery Street.

Officers—Ch. Baund, W.A.; W. Mayer, N.; P. Levy, Arch.

MOUNT HOREB LODGE, No. 7.—Meets every Wednesday evening. Hall, 726 Montgomery Street.

Officers—L. Strasser, W.A.; B. E. Van Straaten, N.; M. Davis, Arch.; J. Lipson, Al.; F. Phillips, Sf.; A. Cohen, Ass't. Sf.; J. Levy, Sh.; B. M. Blum, Sh.H.; Charles Brown, G.b.

REHOBOTH LODGE, No. 6.—Meets every Tuesday evening. Hall, 726 Montgomery Street.

Officers—Meyer Mish, W.A.; A. Franklin, N.

ZION LODGE, No. 4.—Meets every Thursday evening. Hall, 726 Montgomery Street.

Officers—M. Schloss, W.A.; S. May, N.

B'NAI B'RITH—DISTRICT GRAND LODGE, No. 4.—Meetings held quarterly, at Covenant Hall, Sacramento Street, between Montgomery and Leidesdorff.

Officers—William Steinhart, M.W.Gr.N.A.; B. Kozminsky, W.Gr.Y.; Louis Kaplan, W.Gr.S.;

Elias Newburger, W.Gr.B.H.; S. Rosener, W.Gr. S.H.; B. Rothschild, Past Gr.N.A.; J. Greenebaum, Past Gr.N.A.

OPHIR LODGE, No. 21.—Meets every Wednesday evening, at Covenant Hall, Sacramento Street, between Montgomery and Leidesdorff.

Officers—Simon Wolf, President; William Saalburg, Vice President; Louis Sherk, Secretary; Joseph Stolz, Financial Secretary; Wolf Caro, Treasurer; L. Seldner, Monitor; Levi Kaplan, Assistant Monitor; F. Triber, Guardian.

MODIN LODGE, No. 42.—Meets every Tuesday evening, at Covenant Hall, Sacramento Street, between Montgomery and Leidesdorff.

Officers—Emanuel Levy, President; L. Godchaux, Vice President; M. Waterman, Secretary; Samuel Haas, Treasurer: L. Tichner, Monitor; M. Sichel, Warden; M. Zeller, Guardian.

PACIFIC LODGE, No. 48.—Meets every Thursday evening, at Covenant Hall, Sacramento Street, between Montgomery and Leidesdorff.

Officers—M. Badt, President; G. Goldsmith, Vice President; Alexander L. Badt, Secretary; S. S. Arnheim, Financial Secretary; Louis Kaplan, Treasurer; Henry Abpel, Warden; J. Warshawsky, Monitor; Julius Solomon, Assistant Monitor; M. Isaacs, Guardian.

MONTEFIORE LODGE, No. 51.—Meets every Sunday evening, at Covenant Hall, Sacramento Street, between Montgomery and Leidesdorff.

Officers—Julius Platchek, President; J. Wolfsohn, Vice President; N. Levy, Secretary; J. H. Shocken, Financial Secretary; G. Rosenburg, Treasurer; J. Mathias, Monitor; M. Isaacs, Guardian.

BRITISH BENEVOLENT ASSOCIATION.— This society was established in July, 1865, with the object of assisting British born subjects in distress or sickness. Meetings are held on the second Tuesday of every month, temporarily at the St. Andrew's Society Rooms, No. 522 Market Street. Number of members, three hundred and thirty.

Officers—W. Lane Booker, H. B. M. Consul, President; A. Forbes, First Vice President; J. B. Wynn, Second Vice President; John Archbald, Treasurer; Thos. Hulbert, Secretary; Edward Briant, Assistant Secretary; Chas. F. H. Gillingham, M.D., Physician; James Bell, H. A. Fox, Robert Roxby, John Wedderspoon, John Mason, Gomer Evans, John Landale, and Thos. B. Simpson, Board of Trustees: T. P. Bevans, R. Mayers, C. Ashton, and H. E. Highton, Board of Relief.

CALIFORNIA CONTRABAND RELIEF ASSOCIATION (colored).—Organized February, 1863. Meetings held in Scott's Hall, first Wednesday evening of each month. Number of members, thirty.

The object of this Association is to relieve the freedmen who are made so by the recent war.

Officers—Rev. T. M. D. Ward, President; Barney Fletcher, Vice President; J. B. Sanderson, Recording Secretary; Rev. John J. Moore, Corresponding Secretary; A. B. Smith, Treasurer.

CHEBRA ACHIM RACHMONIM ASSOCIATION.—Organized October 26th, 1862. Meetings held in Platt's Hall the third Sunday of each month. Number of members, sixty. Their object is to relieve and care for the sick, infirm, and disabled members of the society, etc. The funds and property of the society are to constitute a Charity Fund, in which no member will have an individual interest.

Officers—M. Meyer, President; L. Licht, Vice President; H. Peiser, Recording Secretary; L. Ehrlich, Financial Secretary; G. Rosenbaum, Treasurer; L. Levy, Messenger.

CHEBRA BIKUR CHOLIM UKÈDISHA SOCIETY.—Organized February, 1857, to assist needy and sick brethren with medicine, attendance, and all necessaries required in case of disease. Meetings held every second Sunday in the month, at Platt's Hall.

Officers—Fitel Phillips, President; P. Abrahamson, Vice President; Wm. Meyer, Recording Secretary; Isaiah Cohn, Permanent Secretary; M. Blass, Treasurer; J. Meyer, D. Plato, Wm. Geist, A. S. Goldstein, and I. Charles, Trustees; Th. Born, Messenger.

CHEBRA B'NAI LESSLA.—Organized June 19th, 1864, at San Francisco. Meetings held every third Sunday in the month. Object of the society, to aid and assist all members or natives of Lessla, Prussia, and to aid the sick, etc.

Officers—S. Morgenstern, President; Jacob Cohen, Vice President; W. Wilson, Secretary; M. Dobrzynsky, Treasurer; T. Wilzinski, H. Asher, and M. Harris, Trustees.

CHEBRA B'RITH SHALOME.—Meet corner of Bush and Kearny, first Sunday of each month. Number of members, one hundred and twenty-five.

Officers—S. Brodek, President; P. S. Meyer, Vice President; B. Pulverman, Recording Secretary; J. Jacobson, Financial Secretary; Charles Morganstern, Treasurer; M. J. Harris, F. Seligman, H. Salomon, and J. Linderbaun, Trustees; S. Samuels, Messenger.

CHINESE BENEVOLENT ASSOCIATION.—Established 1862. Sustained by the Hop Wo Company, 736 Commercial Street. Shung Gee, Agent. The object of this association is to assist Chinese coming to this State; to assist them when desiring to return to China; to minister to the sick, bury the dead, and return their corpses to their native land.

CONGREGATION AND BENEVOLENT SOCIETY, BETH YISRAEL.—Organized September, 1861. Meetings held the last Sunday of every month, and religious services held daily, at 108 Dupont Street.

Officers—Adolph Samuels, President; J. Caspar, Vice President; S. Snalburg, Secretary; S. Tichner, Treasurer; S. Goldman, J. Friedman, J. Salomonson, M. Louis, and M. Wolff, Trustees; H. Wolff, Messenger.

EUREKA BENEVOLENT SOCIETY.—Established October, 1850, to assist poor and needy Hebrews, in want or in sickness. Number of members, three hundred, who pay one dollar each per month, besides a small additional sum to accumulate as a sinking fund for the support of widows and orphans. The society has a capital of $25,000, partly invested in real estate and partly on interest.

Officers—W. Steinhart, President; M. Heller, Vice President; J. Greenebaum, Secretary; M. Mayblum, Treasurer; J. Cerf, E. Newburger, J. Adler, H. Woodleaf, S. W. Levy, and Nathan Bachman, Trustees.

FENIAN BROTHERHOOD.*—State Officers—Elected October 17th, 1865: John Hammill, State Center; Timothy McCarthy, State Secretary; Myles D. Sweeny, Treasurer; J. Cerf, E. Hughes, all of San Francisco, J. McGuire of Sacramento, F. S. McGuire of San José, and M. Colbert of Allison Ranch, State Central Council.

EMMETT CIRCLE, No. 1.—Organized September, 1859. Number of members, two hundred and fifty.

* Large additions are daily being made to this association.

Meet every Tuesday evening, corner California and Kearny streets.

Officers—Thomas Hare, Center; Timothy McCarthy, Secretary; Timothy Nunan, Treasurer.

SARSFIELD CIRCLE, No. -.—Organized April, 1864. Number of members, seventy-five. Meet every Monday evening, at room 18 Platt's Hall.

Officers—Philip Markey, Center; John Mullen, Secretary; John Wightman, Treasurer.

O'MAHONY CIRCLE, No. -.—Organized August, 1865. Number of members, sixty. Meet first and third Monday in each month, at Barra's Hall, corner First and Minna streets.

Officers—M. C. Smith, Center; P. J. Casey, Secretary; J. D. Brown, Treasurer.

FIRST HEBREW BENEVOLENT SOCIETY.—Established in 1849, to assist needy Hebrews in sickness and in want. Reorganized, 1853; incorporated, 1862. Number of members, three hundred and five.

Officers—Charles Meyer, President; J. Baum, Vice President; B. Isaacs, Secretary; J. Funkenstein, Treasurer; J. P. Newmark, Saul Marks, F. Pulvermacher, M. Brown, and John Alexander, Trustees.

FRENCH BENEVOLENT SOCIETY, (Société Française de Bienfaisance Mutuelle).—Established December 28th, 1851. This is a Mutual Relief Society, established for the purpose of affording assistance to its members in case of sickness. The office of the society is located at 649 Sacramento Street. A new and commodious hospital has been recently erected on Bryant Street between Fifth and Sixth, which forms a very important addition to the charitable institutions of the city. Office of the Secretary, 533 Commercial Street.

Officers—E. Lazard, President; A. Cavayé and E. Kohn, Vice Presidents; L. G. Martin and A. Simon, Secretaries; E. Pascal, Treasurer; N. Guillemin, R. Bayerque, J. Traves, H. Dereins, E. Jaudin, B. Maitre, J. B. Lemoine, F. Lebouc, and A. Coulon, Trustees.

FRENCH RELIEF SOCIETY.—Organized August 7th, 1859. Office, 252 Jessie Street.

Officers—Hon. Charles F. de Cazotte, French Consul, President; Gustave Touchard and Theo. LeRoy, Vice Presidents; Alexander Weill, Secretary; Gustave Dussol, Treasurer; A. Caselli, Louis Scellier, John Hahn, and J. Caire, Directors; Henri J. Hellmann, Agent.

GERMAN CLERK'S RELIEF SOCIETY.—Organized 1864. Meets 410 Kearny.

Officers—J. Gutte, President; W. Weill, Treasurer; A. Cohen, Secretary.

GERMAN GENERAL BENEVOLENT SOCIETY OF SAN FRANCISCO (styled in German, Die Allgemeine Deutsche Unterstuetzungs Gesellschaft), is one of the largest and most efficient charitable associations in the State. It was organized on the seventh of January, 1854, with one hundred and five members, and has rapidly increased until now it numbers thirteen hundred and forty-two city members, and four hundred and eighty in the interior. Only Germans and persons speaking German are admitted to membership. The chief purpose of the association is mutual assistance in case of sickness, and when sick every member has a right to demand support and medical attendance from the society. The society has a second purpose of doing charity to Germans not members of the association, but especially to German immigrants newly arrived. The society has a hospital situated on Brannan Street near Third, built of brick, two stories high, with a basement, one hundred and twelve and one-half feet front, fifty feet deep, with a wing in the rear of twenty-three feet front, one hundred and twenty-two feet deep, furnished with steam, sulphur, hot, and cold water and shower baths, and other conveniences for the treatment of the sick. The wards are smaller than in any other hospital in the city, so that not many patients are put together in a room. The lot upon which the hospital is built is one hundred and thirty-seven feet six inches wide by two hundred and seventy-five feet long, the whole surrounded by a high fence and cultivated in a fine garden, a part planted with ornamental flowers and shrubs and a part with kitchen vegetables. The property of the society, including the lot and hospital buildings, is worth about $40,000. The revenue of the society amounted in 1864 to $23,560.65, derived chiefly from a monthly assessment of one dollar levied on each member. The expenses of the hospital in the year 1864 amounted to $22,631.32. The society has as paid servants in the hospital, a superintendent, an apothecary, a gardener, a cook, and five waiters.

Officers—C. F. Mebius, President; Jacob Gundlach and Herman Pflueger, Vice Presidents; A. Wapler, Recording Secretary; Theodore Helmken, Financial Secretary; H. Nielsen, Treasurer; A. Küner, Wm. Kroning, A. Mayrisch, A. Müller, J. Everding, Christian Seitz, I. H. Rutenberg, Directors; Drs. Loehr, Regensberger, and Scharlach, Physicians.

The office of the society is at 625 Merchant Street, between Montgomery and Kearny streets, where the principal agent, Julius Barckhausen, can be found from 8, A.M. to 5, P.M., on week days. All applications for admission into the society, or for charitable relief, and to furnish employment, or servants to applicants, should be addressed to the agent. No charge for applications.

HEBREW SELF-PROTECTING ASSOCIATION.—Organized July, 1863. This is a charitable and benevolent society, organized under the laws of the State concerning corporations. The objects and purposes of the association are to support the afflicted, to relieve the distressed, to attend to the dying, and to bury the dead of the members of the society. The funds and property are to constitute a charity fund, in which no member is to have an individual interest, and shall be disbursed in carrying out the objects and purposes of the society. The time of the existence of the society shall be fifty years.

Officers—Joseph Wolfson, S. Goldberg, S. H. Shocken, W. H. Krause, Isadore Charles, S. Liebreich, M. Fuchs, J. Goslinsky, and R. Prag, Trustees.

HIBERNIAN SOCIETY.—This society is composed of citizens of Irish birth, and numbers fifty members. Organized February 3d, 1852. The object of the organization is to perpetuate generosity by extending relief to Irish immigrants.

Officers— ———— ————, President; M. Guerin, Treasurer; Thomas O'Hare, Secretary.

INDUSTRIAL SCHOOL.—Organized by Act of the Legislature, 1858. Located on the Ocean House Road. Office City Hall, No. 9 third floor.

Officers—William G. Badger, President; Jacob Deeth, Vice President; John Archbald, Treasurer; James S. Thomson, Secretary; George L. Lynde, Superintendent; Theodore C. Smith, Nathan J. Stone, Mrs. Charlotte A. Sawyer, Teachers; Mrs. John Fountain, Matron; John Fountain, Janitor; John Abeel, Farmer; J. P. Still, Watchman; J. C. Ryder, Foreman of Shoe Shop; Benj. D. Dean, Physician.

Number of inmates June 6th, 1865, 153.

IRISH AMERICAN BENEVOLENT SOCI-ETY.—Organized May, 1860. Meet first and third Mondays of each month. Hall SW cor California and Kearny.

Officers—John M. Ahern, President: Charles O'Neil, Vice President; James G. Hayden, Treasurer; John M. Farrell, Recording Secretary; Peter McCrink, Corresponding Secretary; Hugh Gallagher, Martin White, John Sheridan, Michael Farrell, Miles Bulger, and Charles O'Neil, Trustees.

ITALIAN BENEVOLENT SOCIETY.—(Societa Italiana di Mutua Benificenza.)—Organized October 17th, 1858. This is a mutual relief society, established for the purpose of affording assistance to indigent sick Italians. The sick are cured at the expense of the society in St. Mary's Hospital, where ample accommodation is provided. Dr. E. D'Oliveira, Physician. Office NW cor Montgomery and Jackson.

Officers—G. B. Cerruti, President; N. Larco and F. Daneri, Vice Presidents; A. Sbarboro, Secretary; G. Brignardello, Treasurer.

LABORERS' UNION BENEVOLENT AND PROTECTIVE ASSOCIATION.—Meetings held every Monday evening at the hall on Battery Street, between Broadway and Vallejo. Number of members, one hundred and fifty.

Officers—Bernard Monaghan, President; Patrick Carroll, Vice President; John Cogan, Recording Secretary; Dennis F. Driscoll, Financial Secretary; James Callaghan, Treasurer; D. F. Driscoll, John Clark, and Morty Clark, Trustees.

LADIES' PROTECTION AND RELIEF SOCIETY.—Established August 4th, 1853. Incorporated August 9th, 1854. The society has under its supervision a Home where friendless or destitute girls under the age of fourteen and over three years of age, and boys under ten and over three years old, abandoned by their parents, may be received and provided for until permanent homes in christian families can be secured. The adults are embraced in two classes: first, those able to labor, who are received temporarily until employment can be obtained; second, those who by reason of age or infirmity are incapacitated for labor, without means or friends to care for them.

The building is situated on Franklin Street between Post and Geary. It is two stories high, with full basement and French roof (equal to four stories). The walls are of the best hard-burned brick. It was commenced October 1st, 1863, and completed April 20th, 1864. It is forty-eight by eighty-one feet, contains forty-seven rooms with all the modern improvements, gas, water, etc. The cost of the edifice, including grading, fencing, etc., was $23,000. S. C. Bugbee & Sons, architects, designed and superintended the building, and with the contractor, Garrett Welton, rendered most efficient service. It is an ornament to the city and cannot be surpassed for convenience, cheapness, or substantial work.

Application for admission should be made to the President. Letters and communications should be addressed to the Secretary, Mrs. E. Thomas. Donations of money, etc., should be sent to the Treasurer, Mrs. J. H. Flint, 1312 Powell Street, between Broadway and Pacific.

Officers—Mrs. A. G. Stiles, President; Mrs. J. H. Applegate, Vice President; Mrs. E. Thomas, Secretary; Mrs. Jane H. Flint, Treasurer; Mrs. J. Archbald, Mrs. E. B. Babbitt, Mrs. T. P. Bevans, Mrs. S. C. Bugbee, Mrs. D. Cony, Mrs. J. W. Cox, Mrs. A. Dam, Mrs. J. Deeth, Mrs. N. Gray, Mrs. J. Hooper, Mrs. J. King, Mrs. Dr. Mouser, Mrs. Dr. Ober, Mrs. M. Parker, Mrs. N. P. Perine, Mrs. J. Reynolds, Mrs. W. Stringer, Mrs. John Taylor, Mrs. A. G. Turner, Mrs. H. Wattson, Managers; J. W. Stow, President, R. B. Swain Secretary, J. B.

Roberts, S. C. Bugbee, G. W. Dam, Nathaniel Gray, John Archbald, Trustees; Miss C. A. Harmon, Matron.

LADIES' SEAMEN'S FRIEND SOCIETY.— Organized March 26th, 1856. This society is the offspring of the great philanthropic movement on behalf of seamen which has peculiarly distinguished the last half century. The "men of the sea," an invaluable class to all mercantile countries, are subjected, by the nature of their avocations, to hardship and deprivation, moral, social, and intellectual. To ameliorate their condition by supplying them with a *Home*, when on shore, surrounded by remedial influences, and affording them protection from imposition is the object of the society. [See Historical Review for a statement of the operations of this society.]

Their present "Sailor's Home" is situated at the corner of Vallejo and Battery streets. Capt. James F. Stewart, Sup't; Albert Worth, Chaplain.

Officers—Mrs. C. D. Knight, First Directress; Mrs. R. H. Lambert, Second Directress; Mrs. E. T. Schenck, Corresponding Secretary; Miss L. A. Smith, Recording Secretary; Mrs. C. E. Cogswell, Treasurer.

LADIES' SOCIETY OF ISRAELITES (Der Israelitisher Frauen Verein).—For the purpose of assisting Hebrew women under all circumstances of want. Established August 12th, 1855.

Officers—Mrs. B. Regensburger, President; Caroline Newburger, Vice President; L. Seligman, Secretary; Caroline Wolf, Treasurer; Jeannette Steppacher, Mrs. S. Haas, Mrs. S. Epstein, Mrs. M. Mayblum, Mrs. M. Morganthau, Trustees; J. Regensburger, L. Tichner, and L. Sachs, Counselors.

LADIES' UNION BENEFICIAL SOCIETY (Colored).—Incorporated April 8th, 1861. The objects of the society are to aid its members when sick and to bury them when dead.

Officers—Mrs. Cornelia Depee, President; Mrs. Jane A. Jackson, Vice President; Barney Fletcher, Secretary; Mrs. Martha L. Jones, Treasurer; Mrs. H. Harron, Chaplain; Mrs. Jane Jackson (President), Mrs. L. George, Mrs. Elizabeth Scott, Mrs. Susan Westermore, Mrs. Ellen Bell, Mrs. Elizabeth Fletcher, Mrs. Hager Harron, Mrs. Charlotte C. Davis, Board of Managers.

LADIES'· UNITED HEBREW BENEVO-LENT SOCIETY.—Established 1855. Meets first Wednesday of every month, at 3, P.M. The objects of the society are to support the afflicted, to relieve the distressed, to attend the dying, and to bury the dead females of the Israelitish faith. The affairs of the society are managed by a Board of officers and an adjuncta of three Councilmen.

Officers—Mrs. Fanny Tandler, President; Mrs. Caroline Rosenberg, Vice President; Mrs. Hannah Seligsohn, Treasurer; Mad. Sophie Waldow Cohen, Secretary; Leopold King, M. Seligsohn, and S. R. Cohen, Councilmen; Mr. Kafka, Collector.

MAGDALEN ASYLUM.—Under the charge of the Sisters of Mercy. Location, San Bruno Road. During the past year a large and commodious building, three stories in hight, has been erected for the accommodation of the inmates of the asylum. Since the foundation of this institution nearly one hundred females have been received, most of whom have been reformed by the influence and attention of those in charge. At the present time there are sixty penitents, attended by seven Sisters of Mercy. Officiating clergyman, Rev. H. P. Gallagher, assisted by T. Cushing.

MANCHESTER UNITY—Union Lodge, No.

4,694, I.'O. F. M. U.—San Francisco District, California, Jeremiah Browell, Pro.G.M., office 530 Clay Street.

ORPHAN ASYLUM (CATHOLIC).—Market near Kearny Street. Organized March 23d, 1851, and placed under the care of the Sisters of Charity. A frame building for this purpose was commenced in July, and completed in September, 1851. It was occupied in part for a school, and a portion was temporarily used as a church, under the pastoral charge of Rev. John Maginnis. The present capacious brick building was completed in November, 1854, at a cost of $45,000. It is a source of gratification to behold the consoling appearance presented by the three hundred and twenty little ones now provided for in the institution, which speaks audibly of the benign influence of their guardian sisters, and of the true liberality of our community in their noble efforts to lend a helping hand to the fatherless. Another spacious brick building, of the same dimensions as that erected in 1854, was completed in January, 1859, for a school, in which five hundred and fifty children, day scholars, receive a useful education. The asylum is conducted under the sole management of Archbishop Alemany, and the Sisters of Charity. The dilapidated condition of the frame building erected in 1851, and since used for kitchen refectories and clothes rooms, etc., has of late become unsafe for the use of the children, therefore a large and commodious brick building has been commenced, fronting on Market Street, measuring sixty-eight by seventy-three feet, and an addition is in course of erection in the rear of the asylum.

A farm of fifty-three acres has been purchased at Hunter's Point, where a branch Orphan Asylum has been established for very young children. A large and commodious brick edifice will soon be erected thereon.

ORPHAN ASYLUM SOCIETY (PROTES-TANT).—Organized January 31st, 1851, and incorporated February 10th, 1851.

Original Officers—Mrs. Albert Williams, President; Mrs. S. H. Willey, Vice President; Mrs. E. A. Warren, Secretary; Mrs. Boring, Treasurer; Mrs. R. H. Waller, Mrs. C. V. Gillespie, Mrs. Taylor, Mrs. Joice, Mrs. A. Dubbs, and Mrs. O. C. Wheeler, Managers; Charles Gilmore, D. L. Ross and S. Franklin, Trustees.

It originally occupied the building on the corner of Second and Folsom streets, owned by Gen. H. W. Halleck, whence they removed the children in March, 1854, to the present building, just then completed at a cost of $30,000. This house, built of stone and brick, expressly for the purpose, is highly creditable to the institution, and one of the noblest monuments of San Francisco benevolence. During the year 1862-'63, a large and convenient addition was made to the present building, at an expense of $30,000, which, together with the main building, will accommodate two hundred and fifty children. As a compliment to the Sansom Hook & Ladder Co., who, upon disbanding, donated to the asylum the building and lot owned by them, the new addition is called the "Sansom Wing." The number of children under the care of the asylum is one hundred and sixty-four, of which eighty-nine are boys and seventy-five girls.

Officers—Mrs. Ira P. Rankin, President; Mrs. R. J. Vandewater, Vice President; Mrs. S. R. Throckmorton, Treasurer; Mrs. F. MacCrellish, Secretary; Mrs. J. C. Davis, Mrs. A. J. Downer, Mrs. C. O. Gerberding, Mrs. C. V. Gillespie, Mrs. Henry Haight, Mrs. Annis Merrill, Mrs. John Middleton, Mrs. Isaac Swain, Mrs. J. B. Thomas, Mrs. R. H. Waller, Mrs. A. C. Wakeman, and Mrs. Dr. Keeney, Managers; S. R. Throckmorton, Frederick Billings, R. J. Vandewater, J. B. Thomas, and James Otis, Trustees;

Mrs. Willard, Matron; Miss Adams, Assistant Matron; Miss E. Adams, Teacher; Benjamin D. Dean, M.D., Physician.

RUSSIAN SCLAVONIC BENEVOLENT SOCIETY.—Organized April 6th, 1864. Meets 512 Battery, for the purpose of erecting church, hospital, and school; meetings subject to call of the President.

Officers—M. Klinkofstrom, President and Treasurer *pro tem.*; Charles Baum, Secretary; Andrew Chalovich, Peter Rudovitch, and Geo. Lazarovitch, Trustees.

SAN FRANCISCO BENEVOLENT ASSOCIATION.—Organized 1865. Office of the association, 410 Pine Street. The design of the association is to improve the condition of the indigent, and so far as is compatible, the relief of their necessities. [For a statement of the operations of this benevolent and praiseworthy organization, see Historical Review, at the commencement of the work.]

Officers—Robert B. Swain, President; J. W. Stow, Treasurer; Dr. L. C. Gunn, Corresponding Secretary; I. S. Allen, General Agent and Secretary; R. G. Sneath, J. W. Stow, R. B. Swain, and L. Sachs, Advisory Committee; R. B. Swain, R. G. Sneath, Louis Sachs, Capt. Levi Stevens, Moses Ellis, W. C. Ralston, J. W. Stow, Eli Lazard, D. W. C. Rice, M.D., Wm. Norris, and Louis McLane, Trustees.

SAN FRANCISCO MUSICAL FUND SOCIETY.—Organized November 1st, 1863. Incorporated January 20th, 1864. Meets at Platt's Upper Hall. Number of members, eighty-five.

The object of this society is to assist sick and disabled members and their families.

Officers—F. A. Stoehr, President; Ferdinand Eggers, C. Schwartz, Vice Presidents; Jacob Zeck, Treasurer; William Crocker, Secretary; H. A. Siegfried, John Wyatt, and —— Woodhead, Trustees; J. E. Metz, Registrar; J. Wiegand, Librarian; —— Hammerschmidt, —— Seecamp, F. Kaufmann, G. Kunemann, W. Waterman, E. Schmidt, and H. Wedde, Committee of Relief.

Has no library, as yet, except music.

SCANDINAVIAN BENEVOLENT SOCIETY.—Organized February 28th, 1859. The object of this society is to support their sick countrymen, and to have a private hall and adjoining rooms for monthly meeting and library.

Officers—B. A. Hendrikson, President; C. J. Edwards Fahlsten, Vice President; W. Lubeck and W. Lundberg, Secretaries; H. Saxtorph, Librarian; J. Jorgensen, Treasurer.

SLAVONIH ELLIRIH MUTUAL BENEVOLENT SOCIETY.—Organized November 17th, 1857. Number of members, one hundred and forty. Meets first Tuesday of every month, corner of Front and Jackson streets.

Officers—Samuel Marion, President; John Sabliza, Vice President; M. Somascievich, Secretary; M. Gnalo, Collector; Peter Mitrovich, Luca Zenovisch, and A. Mudrayna, Trustees; B. W. Boghiscich, Treasurer.

SONS OF THE EMERALD ISLE.—Organized March 17th, 1852; reorganized April 6th, 1856. Hall 239 Bush.

Officers—Jos. Kelly, President; Daniel Kearny, Vice President; James O'Connell, Treasurer; John D. Farrell, Recording Secretary; James M. Roche, Corresponding Secretary; T. Wm. McDonald, Michael Doyle, John Collins, Thomas Flaherty, Daniel Desmond, Edward Matthews, Dennis O'Day, Jas. Burke, and Felix O'Hanlon, Trustees.

ST. ANDREW'S SOCIETY (Scottish Benevolent Society).—Organized September 21st, 1863, for the purpose of affording temporary relief to destitute Scotchmen or their families. The society at present consists of three hundred and thirty members, and meets every Monday evening, at 8 o'clock, at its rooms, 522 Market Street.

Officers—Thomas Anderson, President; John Craik and Thomas Ross, Vice Presidents; Robert Gowenlock, Treasurer; Alexander Stott, Financial Secretary; George Davidson, Recording Secretary; John McCombe, Assistant Secretary; Hugh Davidson, Librarian; Robert Mackintosh, Physician; Rev. F. M. McAllister, Chaplain; David Hunter, John Bain, and John McHaffie, Trustees; John Kiloh, A. C. Simpson, Hugh Cowan, James Pollock, and Andrew Torning, Board of Relief.

ST. JEAN BAPTISTE MUTUAL BENEVOLENT SOCIETY.—Organized July 4th, 1865. Place of meeting, 585 Market Street. Open every evening.

The object of this society is to assist poor and needy Canadians and members of the society, and to obtain for them employment. Connected with the ball is an institute where papers from all parts of Canada can be seen.

Officers—P. Larseneur, President; Dr. J. Perrault, Vice President; Joseph Couture, Secretary and Treasurer; F. A. Gravel, Commissary; J. B. LeBlanc, S. Gadouas, F. Plouf, Ed. Parberon, and J. Prould, Directors.

ST. JOSEPH'S BENEVOLENT SOCIETY (R. C.)—Established 1860. The objects of this society are to extend assistance to each other in the time of sickness, by corporeal aid and spiritual consolation; for providing their deceased brethren with a decent and christian interment in accordance with their Holy Faith; for the relief of the families they may leave after them; as also for stimulating each other to a more constant observance of the duties of religion and the general promotion of moral and intellectual improvement.

Officers—Thomas Golden, President; Hugh Duffy, Vice President; J. R. Kelly, Secretary; Rev. J. Cotter, Chaplain; M. Guerin, Treasurer. Meetings held third Sunday of each month in the basement of St. Mary's Cathedral. Number of members, two hundred.

ST. MARY'S LADIES' SOCIETY.—Adjoining St. Mary's Hospital in St. Mary's Hall, a wooden building sixty by thirty feet, erected by the St. Mary's Ladies' Society for their meetings. St. Mary's Society, which was founded by the Sisters of Mercy, 1859, for the purpose of promoting piety among the Catholic females, has recently been converted into a Mutual Benevolent Society. It numbers between eight and nine hundred members. The officers of the society are selected from the Sisters of Mercy. Rev. M. O'Reilly, Chaplain.

STATE DEAF, DUMB, AND BLIND ASSOCIATION.—Located corner of Mission and Fifteenth streets. Organized 1860. Number of pupils, fifty-three, of which nineteen are blind. The total appropriations by the State of California to the first of January, 1863, toward the building of the institution, amount to $20,000. The appropriation by the City of San Francisco toward the purchase and improvement of the lots upon which the buildings are erected amounts to $7,000. About $2,000 derived from private charity have been expended upon furniture and necessary fixtures. The present value of the buildings and grounds is estimated at $42,000. It is a State institution, under the charge and control of a Board of Trustees and Lady Managers, who are ready to receive all children of this unfortunate class. Among all the charitable institutions so liberally sustained by the wealthy and benevolent, none is more worthy of support than this. The school will be free to all; yet it is expected of parents and guardians of children, who have the ability, to pay $250 per annum, which includes everything except clothing; an allowance of $250 for each pupil is provided for by Legislative enactment.

The Managers propose to receive all of suitable age to commence their education, and it is considered better to send the deaf mutes young, say five years old, as it is essential they should learn the Sign language correctly at the commencement.

The Legislature of the State, at the session of 1863, passed an Act submitting to the people of the State, an act authorizing the issue of State bonds to the amount of $75,000 for the completion and furnishing of this institution. The operation of this act was, by the Legislature of 1864, we are sorry to say, suspended until further action.

Officers—Mrs. P. B. Clark, President; Mrs. J. P. Whitney, Vice President; Mrs. B. H. Randolph, Treasurer; Mrs. O. C. Pratt, Secretary; Dr. J. P. Whitney, B. H. Randolph, Ira P. Rankin, Rev. J. A. Benton, and George Tait, Trustees.

STEAMSHIP FIREMEN'S BENEVOLENT SOCIETY.—Organized, 1864. Meets at Mechanics' Hall, 239 Bush Street. Number of members, one hundred.

Officers—Thomas Mulcahy, President; James G. Hayden, Vice President; John Eagan, Treasurer; James Pratt, Recording Secretary; J. F. Meagh, Corresponding Secretary; Miles Bulger, Richard Redy, and John Stapleton, Trustees.

SWISS BENEVOLENT SOCIETY.—Organized 1849. The object of this society is to support their sick countrymen, and to procure employment for those who are in want of it.

Officers—Alfred Borel, President; E. Fehlman, Vice President pro tem.; Ant. Borel, Treasurer; A. Vignier, French Secretary; A. Konig, German Secretary; A. Rottanzi and E. Staub, Physicians; E. Bourquin, Collector.

THE YOUNG MEN'S UNION BENEFICIAL SOCIETY (Col'd).—Organized, 1861; incorporated, 1864. Objects of the society, to render aid and protection to its sick members and bury their dead.

Officers—Barney Fletcher, President; James Carter, Vice President; A. F. Phillips, Secretary; R. T. Houston, Treasurer; Samuel Davis, Marshal; James Ross, Messenger.

UNITED ANCIENT ORDER OF DRUIDS.— Grand Grove of the State of California—

Officers — Fred Sieg, N.G.A.; Jacob Weiss, D.G.A.; H. Louis Van Geistefield, W.G., Secretary; Joseph Lingenfelzer, G.T.; Fred Eiser, G.M.; Theodore Eisfeld, G.W.; Wm. Krahner, G.H.

SAN FRANCISCO GROVE, No. 3.—Organized March 27th, 1864. Meets every Monday evening corner of Bush and Kearny streets.

Officers—Edward Schuetze, N.A.; John Freie, V.A.; Christ. Roemer, Secretary; C. W. Lomier, Financial Secretary; Charles Schwenke, Treasurer.

EUREKA GROVE, No. 4.—Organized June 25th, 1865. Meets every Friday evening, 333 Pine.

Officers—A. Winterberg, N.A.; F. C. Schmidt, V.A.; William Hesse, Secretary; C. A. Landenberger, Financial Secretary; Theodore Hartung, Treasurer.

U. O. R. M. UNABHAENGIGER ORDEN DER ROTH-MAENNER (exclusive German Order).—The Gross-Stamm of the State of California, meets every last Sunday of the month at 2, P.M., at the Red Men's Hall, in Pine Street, opposite the Academy of Music.

Officers—Sam. Polack, Grand O. Ch.; Sam. Brodeck, Grand U. Ch.; D. Gendes, Grand B. Ch.; T. B. Reinhardt, Grand P.; Charles Metzler, Grand Treasurer; Wm. Saalburg, Grand Secretary.

PACIFIC STAMM. No. 66 meets every Monday evening at Red Men's Hall, Pine Street, opposite the Academy of Music.

CALIFORNIA STAMM No. 70 meets every Friday evening in Covenant Hall, No. 537 Sacramento Street.

GOLDEN GATE STAMM No. 74 meets every Wednesday evening at Red Men's Hall, Pine Street, opposite Academy of Music.

SAN JOSE STAMM No. 77 meets every Thursday evening at Odd Fellows' Hall, in San José.

JOHANNIS STAMM No. 78 meets every Tuesday evening at Red Men's Hall, Pine Street, opposite Academy of Music.

SAN FRANCISCO STAMM No. 83 meets every Thursday evening at Red Men's Hall, Pine Street, opposite the Academy of Music.

The summer time of meeting is at 8, P.M., and in winter 7½, P.M.

U. S. SANITARY COMMISSION.—California Branch. Office south-east corner Montgomery and Pine.

Officers—His Excellency F. F. Low, President; R. G. Sneath, Treasurer; D. C. McRuer, Chairman Executive Committee; O. C. Wheeler, Secretary. [See General Review for a history of this truly benevolent organization.]

WAITERS', UNION BENEVOLENT SOCIETY.—Organized July 2d, 1863. Meetings held at Metropolitan Hall the first Monday evening of each month. Number of members, three hundred. The object of this union is the maintenance of a fair rate of wages, the encouragement of good workmen, the prompt payment of their earnings, and to prevent all persons in their line of business from working for less than the established rates of wages; a charitable regard for the sick and disabled, and the burial of the dead.

Officers—James McKew, President; Bernard Tuite, Vice President; Edward Phelan, Treasurer; Cornelius McAleer, Secretary.

Masonic.

THE GRAND LODGE OF FREE AND ACCEPTED MASONS OF THE STATE OF CALIFORNIA.—Assembles annually at the City of San Francisco, on the second Tuesday in October. Its officers from October, 1865, to October, 1866, are—

M.·.W.·. Gilbert B. Claiborne, Grand Master, Stockton;

R.·.W.·. William A. Davies, Deputy Grand Master, Columbia;

" " Isaac S. Titus, Senior Grand Warden, Placerville;

" " Henry H. Hartley, Junior Grand Warden, Sacramento;

V.·.W.·. James Laidley, G.T., San Francisco:

" " Alexander G. Abell, G.S., San Francisco,

V.·. Rev. William H. Hill, G.C., Sacramento;

W.·. Leonidas E. Pratt, G.O., Downieville;

" Lawrence C. Owen, A.G.S., San Francisco;

" Henry M. Beach, G.M., San Francisco;

" William D. Newton, G.S.B., Jamestown;

" Edgar Mason, G.S.B., Crescent City;

" Thomas Beck, S.G.D., Watsonville;

W∴ Francis F. Ensign, J.G.D., Yreka;
" William K. Creque, ⎰ Grand ⎰ Pilot Hill;
" Thomas Johnson, ⎱ Stewards ⎱ Cloverdale;
" William Horton, G.O., San Francisco;
" Daniel J. Edgar, G.P., Chinese Camp;
" James Oglesby, G.T., San Francisco.
There are now in existence under the jurisdiction of this body one hundred and forty-three subordinate Lodges, with a membership of 6,000, of which thirteen are in the City of San Francisco, as follows:

CALIFORNIA LODGE, NO. 1.—Meets every Thursday evening, in King Solomon's Hall.
Officers—George T. Grimes, Master; James Scrimgeour, Senior Warden; John McComb, Junior Warden; Edward Taylor, Treasurer; Elisha W. Bourne, Secretary; Charles D. Haven, Senior Deacon; George L. Waters, Junior Deacon; Henry H. Thrall, Marshal; William Craig and William J. Stringer, Stewards; William Horton, Organist; Lewis Peck, Tyler. Two hundred and seventy-five members.

LOGE LA PARFAITE UNION, NO. 17.—Meets every Friday evening in St. John's Hall.
Les Officiers—Hippolite Rauhaud, Maître; Michel Lebatard, 1er Surveillant; Emile Kohn, 2de Surveillant; Henri Lucké, Tresorier; Bernard Levy, Secretaire; Edouard R. Dubourque, Orateur; E. N. Deney, 1er Diacre; Andre Secchi, 2de Diacre; Joseph Alexandre, Maréchal; Christian Gutt, Charlemagne Leroux, Maîtres des Cerémonies; Joel Noah (de la Loge Occidental, No. 22) Couvreur. Sixty-three members.

OCCIDENTAL LODGE, NO. 22.—Meets every Monday evening in King Solomon's Hall.
Officers—Alexander D. McDonald; Master; Harrison Jones, Senior Warden; Wilfred W. Montague, Junior Warden; Thomas L. Rutherford, Treasurer; Robert Irwin, Secretary; Rev. Joseph H. Wythe, Chaplain; Jabez B. Knapp, Senior Deacon; Frederick N. Giles, Junior Deacon; Joseph Winterburn, Marshal; Chas. Lyman and Edward Bannon Stewards; Joel Noah, Tyler. Two hundred members.

GOLDEN GATE LODGE, NO. 30.—Meets every Tuesday evening in King Solomon's Hall.
Officers—Thomas Bigley, Master; Edward M. Cottrell, Senior Warden; James Patterson, Junior Warden; Calvin H. Wetherbee, Treasurer; Adolphus A. Hobe, Secretary; James B. Dobbie, Senior Deacon; Joseph Knowland, Junior Deacon; Edward X. Field, Marshal; Henry Brickwedel and Henry Blyth, Stewards; Charles O. Robertson, Tyler. One hundred and twenty-one members.

MOUNT MORIAH LODGE, NO. 44.—Meets every Wednesday evening in King Solomon's Hall.
Officers—Edwin S. Perkins, Master; John W. Shaeffer, Senior Warden; Davis Louderback, Junior Warden; Wm. Melvin Smith, Treasurer; Charles L. Wiggin, Secretary; Rev. Eleasor Thomas; Chaplain; Charles H. Packman, Senior Deacon; Donald Bendle, Junior Deacon; Albert Solomon Marshal; Lell H. Woolley and D. N. Lunt, Stewards; Ira C. Root, Tyler. One hundred and eighty-four members.

FIDELITY LODGE, NO. 120.—Meets every Thursday evening in St. John's Hall.
Officers—Mendel Esberg, Master; Julius Platshek, Senior Warden; Moses Heller; Junior Warden; Elias Newburger, Treasurer; Seixas Solomons, Secretary; Charles Glass, Senior Deacon; Adolph Koenigsberger, Junior Deacon; Saul Marks, Marshal, Seigmund Bettmann and Max Wurkheim, Stewards; Joel Noah, Tyler. One hundred and twenty-five members.

PROGRESS LODGE, NO. 125.—Meets every Monday evening in St. John's Hall.
Officers—Bennett Pulverman, Master; I. N. Choynski, Senior Warden; William Geist, Junior Warden; Moritz Kalmuk, Treasurer; Louis Kaplan, Secretary; Alexander L. Badt, Senior Deacon; Herman Stern, Junior Deacon; Frederick Cohen, Marshal; B. N. Boghiscich and Louis Abrams, Stewards; Louis Sherek, Tyler. Eighty-nine members.

HERMANN LODGE, NO. 127.—Meets every Thursday evening in the Upper Hall.
Officers—John G. Andresen, Meister; Christian H. Voight, Erster Autsehr; Charles E. Hansen, Zweiter Aufsher; H. C. Bebre, Shatmeister; O. L. Becker, Secretair, Martin Henken, Erster Schaffner; Christian H. Lange, Zweiter Schaffner; Henning Koester, Marschall; Nicholas Lohse and Herman Wendt, Stewards; Christian G. Stahl, Waechter. Sixty-seven members.

PACIFIC LODGE, NO. 136.—Meets every Friday evening in King Solomon's Hall.
Officers—Thomas Anderson, Master; John H. Stoutenborough, Senior Warden; Henry B. Forester, Junior Warden; James Ballentine, Treasurer; Edward C. Lovell, Secretary; L. Kullman, Senior Deacon; Frederick W. Kamps, Junior Deacon; Joseph Frazier, Marshal; Henry Hickie and W. Fischel, Stewards; William Canham, Tyler. One hundred and thirty-four members.

CROCKETT LODGE, NO. 139.—Meets every Wednesday night in the Upper Hall.
Officers—Henry M. Beach, Master; Andrew J. Bryant, Senior Warden; Samuel McCullough, Junior Warden; Peter Johnson, Treasurer; Wm. H. Richards, Secretary; Charles D. Hayes, Senior Deacon; Wm. F. Bamber, Junior Deacon; Charles P. Chesley, Marshal; Emile V. Sutter and William Carham, Stewards; Joel Noah, Tyler. Seventy-seven members.

ORIENTAL LODGE, NO. 144.—Meets every Tuesday evening in St. John's Hall.
Officers—James R. Richards, Master; Alfred C. Waitt, Senior Warden; John Bell, Junior Warden; Dustin D. Shattuck, Treasurer; Henry E. Matthews, Secretary; Edward F. Bent, Senior Deacon; John W. Carter, Junior Deacon; Thomas Young, Marshal; Edward Barry and George H. Russell, Stewards; Ira C. Root, Tyler. One hundred and thirteen members.

EXCELSIOR LODGE, NO. 166.—Meets every Wednesday evening in St. John's Hall.
Officers—Thomas Kyle, Master; Theodore E. Smith, Senior Warden; Seymour B. Clark, Junior Warden; William H. Davis, Treasurer; Thomas Y. McNally, Secretary; Horatio H. Russell, Senior Deacon; James A. Brown, Junior Deacon; Stewart Menzies, Marshal; John G. Gay and James Davis, Stewards; James Ogelsby, Tyler. One hundred members.

MISSION LODGE, NO. 169.—Meets ——
Officers—Edson Sammis, Master; Nathan W. Spaulding, Senior Warden; Frank A Rutherford, Junior Warden; James H. Welch, Treasurer; Irvin S. Lamb, Secretary; Alexander Eaton, Senior Deacon; Madison Spaulding, Junior Deacon; Benj. F. Ogden, Marshal; Wm. L. Twichell and Thomas Livesay, Stewards; Joseph McQuoid, Tyler. Thirty members.

THE GRAND CHAPTER OF ROYAL ARCH MASONS OF THE STATE OF CALIFORNIA.

—Assembles annually at the City of San Francisco, on the Monday next succeeding the second Tuesday in October. Its officers from October, 1865, to October, 1866, are:

M∴E∴ John Kirkpatrick, G.H.P., Downieville;
R∴E∴ Charles Marsh, D.G.H.P., Nevada;
" William A. Davies, G.K., Columbia;
" Isaac S. Titus, G.S., Placerville;
" P. W. Shepheard, G.T., San Francisco;
" Lawrence C. Owen, G.S., San Francisco;
Rev. Arthur E. Hill, G.C., Sonora;
E∴ John W. Harville, G.C. of the Host, Todd's Valley;
E∴ George T. Grimes, G.R.A.C., San Francisco;
Comp. Lewis Peck, G.G, San Francisco.

There are now in existence under the jurisdiction of this body thirty-four subordinate Chapters with a membership of twelve hundred and fifty, of which the two following named are in the City of San Francisco:

SAN FRANCISCO CHAPTER, NO. 1.—Meets every Monday evening in the Chapter Hall, Masonic Temple.

Officers—Theodore E. Smith, High Priest; John R. Jarboe, King; Joseph Clement, Scribe; William H. Davis, Captain of the Host; Thomas Kyle, Principal Sojourner; Henry J. Burns, Royal Arch Captain; David Furquharson, Master of Third Vail; Louis Wormser, Master of Second Vail; John H. Stoutenborough, Master of First Vail; Thomas Anderson, Treasurer; Thomas Y. McNally, Secretary; Lewis Peck, Guard. One hundred and sixteen members.

CALIFORNIA CHAPTER, NO. 5.—Meets every Tuesday evening in the Chapter Hall, Masonic Temple.

Officers—Charles L. Wiggin, High Priest; George T. Grimes, King; William T. Reynolds, Scribe; William E. Moody, Captain of the Host; James Scrimgeour, Principal Sojourner; Charles Wilson, Royal Arch Captain; Henry H. Thrall, Master of Third Vail; William H. Harvey, Master of Second Vail; William W. Stetson, Master of First Vail; Ebenezer E. Morse, Treasurer; Elisha W. Bourne, Secretary; William Horton, Organist; Lewis Peck, Guard. One hundred and fifty members.

THE GRAND COUNCIL OF ROYAL AND SELECT MASTERS OF THE STATE OF CALIFORNIA.—Assembles annually at the City of San Francisco, on the second Wednesday after the second Tuesday in October.

Officers (October, 1865, to Obtober, 1866)—M.P. Anderson Seavy of Marysville, Grand Master; R. P. Louis Cohn of San Francisco, Deputy Grand Master; R.P. William A. January of Placerville, Grand Illustrious Master; R.P. Alvin B. Preston of Jamestown, Grand Principal Conductor of the Works; R.P. James Laidley of San Francisco, Grand Treasurer; R.P. Lawrence C. Owen of San Francisco, Grand Recorder; Rev. Arthur E. Hill of Sonora, Grand Chaplain; Comp. Daniel P. Bystle of Shasta, Grand Captain of the Guards; Comp. George T. Grimes of San Francisco, Grand Steward; Comp. Lewis Peck of San Francisco, Grand Sentinel.

There are seven chartered Councils under the jurisdiction of the Grand Council, their membership being five hundred. There are seven subordinate Councils now under its jurisdiction, one of which is in San Francisco.

CALIFORNIA COUNCIL, NO. 2.—Meets first Saturday in each month in Chapter Hall, Masonic Temple.

Officers—Lawrence C. Owen, Thrice Illustrious Master; Samuel S. Arnheim, Deputy Illustrious Master; Seymour B. Clark, Principal Conductor of the Works; William H. Lyon, Treasurer; Elisha W. Bourne, Recorder; Thomas Kyle, Captain of the Guards; James Laidley, Conductor; George T. Grimes, Marshal; Geo. W. Paget, Steward; Lewis Peck, Sentinel. One hundred and forty-two members.

THE GRAND COMMANDERY OF KNIGHTS TEMPLAR OF THE STATE OF CALIFORNIA.—Assembles annually on the second Thursday after the second Tuesday in October.

Officers (from October, 1865, to October, 1866)—R. E. Sir Henry Holcombe Rhees of Marysville, Grand Commander; V.E. Sir William M. Rundell of San Francisco, Deputy Grand Commander; E. Sir Theodore F. Tracy of Placerville, Grand Generalissimo; E. Sir William W. Traylor of Columbia, Grand Captain-General; E. Sir Charles Caleb Peirce of Placerville, Grand Prelate; E. Sir Frederick F. Barss of Placerville, Grand Senior Warden; E. Sir Andrew J. Kellogg of San Francisco, Grand Junior Warden; E. Sir Elisha W. Bourne of San Francisco, Grand Treasurer; E. Sir Lawrence C. Owen of San Francisco, Grand Recorder; E. Sir Anderson Seavy of Marysville, Grand Standard-Bearer; E. Sir William F. Knox of Sacramento, Grand Sword-Bearer; E. Sir John Kirkpatrick of Nevada, Grand Warder; Sir James Oglesby of San Francisco, Grand Captain of the Guards.

There are seven subordinate Commanderies in the State, of which the following named are in San Francisco:

CALIFORNIA COMMANDERY, NO. 1.—Meets every Friday evening in Masonic Temple.

Officers—Sir William Norris, Commander; Sir William M. Rundell, Generalissimo; Sir Andrew J. Kellogg, Captain-General; Sir Charles L. Wiggin, Prelate; Sir George Tempest Knox, Senior Warden; Sir Lawrence C. Owen, Junior Warden; Sir William H. Lyon, Treasurer; Sir Elisha W. Bourne, Recorder; Sir Ebenezer E. Morse, Standard-Bearer; Sir Frank Eastman, Sword-Bearer; Sir Eugene E. Dewey, Warder; Sir James Oglesby, Sentinel. One hundred and eleven members.

There are also in this city three colored Lodges, viz.:

HANNIBAL LODGE, NO. 1.—Organized, 1852. Meets Wednesday evenings of each week. Hall, north-east corner Mason and Broadway.

Officers—Bros. George A. Duval, W.M; Ezekiel Cooper, S.W.; Anthony Osborne, J.W.; A. B. Smith, Treasurer; Sam'l A. Smith, S.D.; James R. Starkey, J.D.; J. B. Scott, Tyler; Barney Fletcher, Secretary; Rev. T. M. D. Ward, Chaplain; Henry C. Cornish and James Wilkinson, Stewards; J. Madison Bell, Marshal.

VICTORIA LODGE, NO. 3.—Organized, 1853. Meets every Monday evening, north-east corner Mason and Broadway.

Officers—Bros. D. W. Ruggles, W.M.; E. P. Hilton, S.W.; L. H. Brooks, J.W.; James Johnson, Treasurer; S. P. Clark, S.D.; James Wilkinson, J.D.; J. B. Scott, Tyler; S. Howard, Secretary; Rev. A. B. Smith, Chaplain; George Roe and Geo. Toogood, Stewards; J. Madison Bell, Marshal.

OLIVE BRANCH LODGE, NO. 5.—Meets Tuesday evenings of each week. Hall, Stockton Street, between Pacific and Broadway.

Officers—Nelson Cook, W.M.; Ed. Quinn, S.W.; Alexander Cochrane, J.W.; R. M. Cleary, Secretary; H. Tolbert, Treasurer; J. H. Bell, Tyler.

Under the charter of the United Grand Lodge of New York, March 3d, 1855. Organized April 5th, 1855. Number of members, ninety.

MASONIC CEMETERY ASSOCIATION—Organized January 26th, 1864. Office, Masonic Temple. *Officers*—W. R. Wheaton, President; Thomas Young, Vice President; George J. Hobe, Secretary; Thomas Anderson, Treasurer; D. B. Arrowsmith, Joseph Clement, Peter Craig, Thomas Young, B. H. Freeman, Wm. R. Wheaton, Thomas Anderson, E. L. Smith, and James Laidley, Trustees.

MASONIC HALL ASSOCIATION.—Incorporated 1859. Office Masonic Temple, north-west corner of Montgomery and Post streets. *Officers*—Alexander G. Abell, President; Adolphus Hollub, Vice President; Louis Cohn, Isaac E. Davis, James Laidley, William Norris, James R. Richards, Dustin D. Shattuck, and William Melvin Smith, Trustees; Henry M. Newhall, Treasurer; Lawrence C. Owen, Secretary.

MASONIC LIBRARY ASSOCIATION.—Organized 1864. Rooms, Masonic Temple, corner Montgomery and Post streets. *Officers*—Thomas Anderson, President; I. N. Choynski, Secretary.

I. O. O. F.

GRAND OFFICERS OF THE R.W. GRAND LODGE OF THE STATE OF CALIFORNIA, FOR THE TERM COMMENCING MAY 7TH, 1865.—C. O. Burton, M.W. Grand Master, Stockton; I. N. Randolph, R.W. Deputy Grand Master, Jackson, Amador County; Chas. N. Fox, R.W. Grand Warden, San Francisco: T. Rodgers Johnson, R.W. Grand Secretary, San Francisco; M. Heller, R.W. Grand Treasurer, San Francisco; Nathan Porter, R.W. Grand Representative, elect, San Francisco; Charles Marsh, R.W. Grand Representative, elect, Nevada; Rev. Wm. H. Hill, Worthy Grand Chaplain, Sacramento; Prescott Robinson, Worthy Grand Marshal, Sacramento; C. S. Haswell, Worthy Grand Conductor, Nicolaus; C. F. Pousland, Worthy Grand Guardian, Benicia; Isaac Frank, Worthy Grand Herald, San Francisco.

Past Grand Masters.—S. H. Parker, San Francisco; John F. Morse, San Francisco; H. M. Heuston, San Francisco; W. H. Watson, Gold Hill, Nev.; J. Van Bokkelen, Virginia, Nev.; J. A. McClelland, San Francisco; L. L. Alexander, San Francisco; W. M. Allen, San Francisco; T. R. Kibbe, Grass Valley; J. A. J. Bohen, San Francisco; D. Kendall, Sacramento.

District Deputy Grand Patriarchs.

District No. 1, Davis Louderback, P.C.P., San Francisco, comprising Encampments Nos. 1 and 23
District No. 2, Samuel Cross, P.C.P., Sacramento City, comprising Encampments Nos. 2 and 24.
District No. 3, R. E. Wilhoit, P.C.P., Stockton, comprising Encampment No. 3.
District No. 4, Jas. Letford, P.C.P., Sonora, comprising Encampment No. 4.
District No. 5, C. C. Pierce, P.C.P., Placerville, comprising Encampment No. 5.
District No. 6, M. W. Shuster, P.C.P., Marysville, comprising Encampment No. 6.
District No. 7, N. Heitman, P.C.P., San Francisco, comprising Encampment No. 7.
District No. 8, Z. W. Keyes, P.C.P., Downieville, comprising Encampment No. 8.
District No. 9, W. G. Long, P.C.P., St. Louis, comprising Encampment No. 9.
District No. 10. H. J. Tilden, P.C.P., Mokelumne Hill, comprising Encampments Nos. 10 and 18.
District No. 12, F. A. Young, P.C.P., Weaverville, comprising Encampment No. 12.

District No. 14, Samuel Isaacks, P.C.P., Shasta, comprising Encampment No. 14.
District No. 15, C. E. Burrows, P.C.P., Yreka, comprising Encampment No. 15.
District No. 16, J. B. Russell, P.C.P., Forest Hill, comprising Encampment No. 16.
District No. 17, I. N. Randolph, P.C.P., Jackson, comprising Encampments Nos. 17 and 19.
District No. 18, Philip R. Pearson, P.C.P., Oroville, comprising Encampment No. 22.
District No. 19, Ellis Reiser, P.C.P., Red Bluff, comprising Encampment No. 21.
District No. 20, Thos. B. Harper, P.C.P., Lincoln, comprising Encampment No. 20.
District No. 21, Ezra St. John, P·C.P., Portland, comprising Encampments Nos. 1 and 2, Oregon.
District No. 22, Isaac Pforzheime, P.C.P., Virginia City, Nev., comprising Encampment, No. 1, Nevada.

District Deputy Grand Masters.

District No. 1, A. D. Meacham, San Francisco, comprising Lodges Nos. 1, 3, 15, 17, 29, 71, 112.
District No. 2, Christopher Diehl, San Francisco, comprising Lodges Nos. 13, 116.
District No. 3, Wm. H. Hill, Sacramento, comprising Lodges Nos. 2, 4, 8, 62, 87, 111.
District No. 4, S. B. Wyman, Lincoln, comprising Lodges Nos. 7, 107.
District No. 5. L. T. Crane, Marysville, comprising Lodges Nos. 5, 45.
District No. 7, L. E. Yates, Stockton, comprising Lodges Nos. 6, 11, 98, 102.
District No. 8, W. L. Sears, Sonora, comprising Lodges Nos. 10, 21, 58, 82, 97.
District No. 9, T. R. Kibbe, Grass Valley, comprising Lodges 12, 16, 67.
District No. 11, O. A. Pearce, Moore's Flat, comprising Lodge No. 48.
District No. 12, A. Siesbuttel, Diamond Springs, comprising Lodges Nos. 9, 20, 27, 37, 56, 63, 72, 89.
District No. 13, John B. Russell, Todd's Valley, comprising Lodges Nos. 14, 38, 40, 55, 73, 108, 120.
District No. 14, Henry Coster, Napa, comprising Lodges Nos. 18, 28.
District No. 15, Richardson Long, Vacaville, comprising Lodges Nos. 78, 83.
District No. 16, Lewis Burnham, Cherokee Flat, comprising Lodges Nos. 47, 59, 92, 113.
District No. 17, W. G. Long, St. Louis, comprising Lodges Nos. 49, 80, 91.
District No. 18, C. J. Lee, Forest City, comprising Lodges Nos. 24, 32, 54.
District No. 19, Isaac Tripp, Jackson, comprising Lodges Nos. 25, 31, 36, 51, 79, 95.
District No. 20, C. N. Fox, San Francisco, comprising Lodges Nos. 37, 52, 109.
District No. 21, J. O. Lovejoy, Mariposa, comprising Lodges Nos. 39, 99, 104, 110.
District No. 22, Samuel Isaacs, Shasta, comprising Lodges Nos. 57, 75.
District No. 23, T. C. Harvey, Angels Camp, comprising Lodges, Nos. 33, 68, 86, 106.
District No. 24, George Buck, La Grange, comprising Lodge No. 65.
District No. 25, G. Warner, Petaluma, comprising Lodges Nos. 30, 53, 64.
District No. 26, D. Lawton, Yreka, comprising Lodges Nos. 19, 70, 115.
District No. 27, H. Orman, Jr., Crescent City, comprising Lodge No. 41.
District No. 28, Ellis Reiser, Red Bluff, comprising Lodge No. 76.
District No. 29, J. A. Whaley, Arcata, comprising Lodges Nos. 77, 85.
District No. 30, John Turner, Los Angeles, comprising Lodge No. 35.
District No. 31, Detlef Hanson, Weaverville, comprising Lodges Nos. 61, 84.

District No. 32, T. Eisfeldt, Jr., Placerville, comprising Lodge No. 74.

District No. 33, B. F. Wilcoxen, Watsonville, comprising Lodges Nos. 90, 96.

District No. 34, W. C. Jains, Campo Seco, comprising Lodges Nos. 44, 50, 66.

District No. 36, T. O. Hopkins, Alvarado, comprising Lodges Nos. 93, 114.

District No. 38, Geo. W. Bigelow, Sawyer's Bar, comprising Lodge No. 101.

District No. 39, Wm. Wright, Red•Dog, comprising Lodges Nos. 46, 81.

District No. 40, C. W. Wilcox, Nicolaus, comprising Lodge No. 100.

District No. 41, Frank Denver, Virginia City, Nevada, comprising Lodges Nos. 1, 3, 7, 10.

District No. 42, Chas. Schwartz, Sacramento, comprising Lodge No. 105.

District No. 43, E. B. Rail, Carson City, Nevada, comprising Lodges Nos. 4, 8.

District No. 44, J. G. Canfield, Aurora, comprising Lodge No. 6.

District No. 45, E. X. Willard, Austin, comprising Lodge No. 9.

District No. 46, J. S. Drummond, Victoria, V. I., comprising Lodge No. 1.

District No. 47, W. C. Park, Hawaiian Islands, comprising Lodge No. 1.

District No. 48, Henry Morris, Markleeville, comprising Lodge No. 119.

District No. 49, Wm. Haydon, Dayton, Nevada, comprising Lodges Nos. 2, 5.

District No. 50, C. F. Pousland, Benicia, comprising Lodges Nos. 22, 43, 117.

Regular Committees.

Credentials.—Geo. M. Garwood, of No. 17, D. Louderback, of No. 15, E. W. Bradford, of No. 73.

Finance.—H. B. Brooks, of No. 3, Wm. T. Gibbs, of No. 37, C. T. Pidwell, of No. 17, C. Langley, of No. 15, W. L. Sears, of No. 10.

Correspondence.—T. Rodgers Johnson, of No. 3, J. H. Gregory, of No. 34, Robert Porter, of No. 77.

Appeals.—A. A. Sargent, of No. 16, G. R. Moore, of No. 4, J. L. Browne, of No. 7, W. W. Broughton, of No. 96, D. McLaren, of No. 2.

Laws of Subordinates.—J. F. Miller, of No. 17, John Phillips, of No. 112, H. F. Swain, of No. 3, T. C. Harvey, of No. 33, A. B. Armstrong, of No. 8.

Petitions.—B. W. Barns, of No. 80, Samuel Miller, of No. 110, G. P. Loucks, of No. 117, D. B. Woolf, of No. 7, Nevada, H. Bentley, of No. 98.

State of the Order.—L. L. Alexander, of No. 15, C. W. Dannals, of No. 67, C. V. D. Hubbard, of No. 5, Wm. Haydon, of No. 5, Nevada, E. E. Hathaway, of No. 78.

Legislative.—J. H. McKune, of No. 8, M. M. Estee, of No. 87, T. R. Kibbe, of No. 12, M. W. Shuster, of No. 45, A. D. Meacham, of No. 1.

All Subordinate Lodges I. O. O. F. of the City of San Francisco meet at the Hall, 325 Montgomery Street, on the following evenings, viz:

CALIFORNIA LODGE, No. 1.—Meet Monday evenings. W. C. Mead, N.G.; H. W. Byington, V. G.; M. P. Holmes, Recording Secretary; G. E. Underbill, Treasurer; James Davis, Permanent Secretary.

SAN FRANCISCO LODGE, No. 3.—Meet Friday evenings. William Bartling, N.G.; A. S. Baldwin, M.D., V.G.; George H. Lovegrove, Recording Secretary; H. I. Hellman, Treasurer; P. G. Ularchand, Permanent Secretary.

HARMONY LODGE, No. 13.—Meet Tuesday evenings. Theodore Van Borstel, N.G.; Joseph Meyer, V.G.; Charles Quast, Recording Secretary; F. Fortman, Treasurer; F. V. Meyerhofer, Permanent Secretary.

YERBA BUENA LODGE, NO. 15.—Meet Thursday evenings. John M. Hepworth, N.G.; E. C. Gray, V.G.; W. P. Adams, Recording Secretary; Henry C. Squire, Treasurer; P.G. Franklin Williams, Permanent Secretary.

TEMPLAR LODGE, NO. 17.—Meet Wednesday evenings. J. D. B. Stillman, N.G.; James B. Johnson, V.G.; Fred. Leippien, Recording Secretary; Robert Cairns, Treasurer; P.G. C. T. Pidwill, Permanent Secretary.

MAGNOLIA LODGE, NO. 29.—Meet Tuesday evenings. Alex. Hoy, N.G.; Thos. Sterns, V.G.; Joseph Luffkin, Recording Secretary; E. Suskind, Treasurer; A. Morganstern, Permanent Secretary.

BAY CITY LODGE, NO. 71.—Meet Monday evenings. H. Robitcheck, N.G.; B. Hagen, V.G.; Wm. Fisbel, Recording Secretary; J. L. Lang, Treasurer; Julius Adler, Permanent Secretary.

ABON BEN ADHEM LODGE, NO. 112.—Meet Thursday evenings. A. W. Genung, N.G.; Orrin Pulsipher, V.G.; Jos. P. Cochrane, Recording Secretary; John Phillips, Treasurer; A. G. Moore, Permanent Secretary.

GERMANIA LODGE, NO. 116.—Meet Wednesday evenings. A. Fenkhausen, N.G.; Ernest Lomler, V.G.; Andrew Bahrs, Recording Secretary; Charles Metzler, Treasurer; Charles W. Lomler, Permanent Secretary.

Address of Grand Officers.

M.W. Grand Patriarch, Lewis Sober, San Francisco; M.E. Grand High Priest, A. B. Asher, Downieville; R.W. Grand Sen. Warden, W. A. Gilman, Freeport; R.W. Grand Scribe, T. Rodgers Johnson, San Francisco; R.W. Grand Treasurer, Philo White, San Francisco; R.W. Grand Jun. Warden, B. W. Barns, La Porte; R.W. Grand Rep. Elect, D. Norcross, San Fran'co; W.G. Sentinel, D. Louderback, San Francisco; W.D.G. Sentinel, Thos. Jamison, Auburn.

Past Grand Patriarchs—S. H. Parker, San Francisco; Prescott Robinson, Sacramento; David Kendall, Sacramento; A. S. Iredale, San Francisco; M. K. Shearer, Placerville; J. A. McClelland, San Francisco; A. J. Lucas, Marysville; W. N. Hall, Gold Hill, Nev.; D. McLaren, San Francisco; J.A. J. Bohen, San Francisco; C. L. Thomas, Marysville.

ODD FELLOWS' CEMETERY ASSOCIATION.—Incorporated September 26th, 1865. Office 325 Montgomery.

Officers—Charles Langley, President; William Hayes, Vice President; Henry C. Squire, Secretary; David Hunter, Treasurer; George T. Bohen, Henry B. Brooks, James Adams, George Fritsch, Royal Fisk, Benjamin Price, Alex. Hoy, and J. G. Mysell, Trustees.

ODD FELLOWS' HALL ASSOCIATION.—Organized 1858. Capital stock $50,000, increased in 1863 to $150,000. This association own that fine building corner of Montgomery and Summer streets, known as "Odd Fellows' Hall," where they now meet.

Officers—J. A. J. Bohen, President; Henry B. Brooks, Vice President; T. Rodgers Johnson, Secretary; A. Himmelmann, Treasurer; Thomas Sleaty, George T. Bohen, J. S. Reed, S. H. Parker, W. A. Woodward, A. D. Meacham. M. Heller, A. Block, P. Sander, H. Kimball, A. A. Waters, J. G. Mysell, W. K. Benjamin, Samuel G. Beatty, Jr., I. Frank, W. Saalburg, and H. C. Squire, Directors.

ODD FELLOWS' LIBRARY ASSOCIATION. —Organized, 1855. Rooms, Odd Fellows' Hall, 327 Montgomery Street.
Officers—S. H. Parker, President; J. D. B. Stillman and H. B. Brooks, Vice Presidents; H. C. Squire, Secretary; A. Himmelmann, Treasurer; John Phillips, Librarian; J. Q. Piper, Henry Kimball, Chas. Quast, J. A. J. Bowen, W. R. Satterlee, Alex. Hov, J. Vogelsdorff, W. K. Benjamin, E. Lomler, Philo White, Henry Briel, and W. J. Gunn, Directors.
This library now contains over 14,000 volumes in the various departments of literature, including one of the most extensive collections of works in the early history of the Pacific coast. It also contains what is believed to be the most complete and valuable cabinet of minerals, etc., in the State.

ODD FELLOWS' SAVINGS AND HOMESTEAD ASSOCIATION.—Incorporated September 1st, 1862. Number of shares, seventy-seven. Capital stock, $120,000. To continue in existence five years from date of organization. This association own two valuable lots situated on Van Ness Avenue.
Officers—Henry B. Brooks, President; Henri J. Hellmann, Secretary; Henry Michaels, Treasurer; Samuel H. Parker, A. D. Meacham, David Hunter, Henry C. Squire, Columbus Bartlett, and Joseph Winterburn, Directors.

Protective.

ANTI-COOLIE ASSOCIATION.— Organized 1859. Meet at the call of the President.
Officers—Samuel H. Henry, President; J. W. Wilkinson, Vice President; A. Buetelle, Secretary; John Schuster, Treasurer; J. B. Quinn, Sergeant-at-Arms.

BARBERS' AND HAIRDRESSERS' PROTECTIVE ASSOCIATION.—Organized June 21st, 1864. Meetings held in basement old Odd Fellows' Hall, corner Bush and Kearny, on the first Monday in each month. Number of members, fifty.
Officers—Charles Proschold, President; Herman Kirchner, Vice President; Isaac Adams, Recording Secretary; Chris Heider, Financial Secretary; Geo. Obenauer, Treasurer; S. W. Lipman, Wm. Henderson, Jacob Ulrich, Samuel Schnapper, and H. Gutzeit, Trustees.

BAY VIEW PARK STOCK ASSOCIATION.— Organized July 1st, 1865. Rooms, 219 Bush Street. Regular meetings held on the first Saturday of each month, at 7 o'clock, P.M. Special meetings may be called by the President, or at the request of ten members, by giving one week's notice through the Secretary. The objects of this society are the improvement of our breed of horses and the encouragement of those friendly contentions and rivalries which characterize field sports. Number of members, one hundred and three.
Officers—Alexander Gamble, President; E. M. Skaggs, E. T. Pease, G. B. Gammans, R. F. Morrow, and F. Collier, Vice Presidents; Charles M. Chase, Secretary; Alex. Gamble, Charles Hosmer, W. T. Grissim, H. R. Covey, and Wm. Hendrickson, Executive Committee.

BOILER MAKERS' ASSOCIATION.—Organized November 22d, 1863. Meetings second and fourth Wednesdays of each month at Barra's Hall, corner First and Minna streets.
Officers—J. Cully, President; John Bush, Vice President; James Allison, Recording Secretary; William W. Canty, Financial Secretary; Joseph Plunkett, Treasurer; William Brady, Wm. Thompsom, and James Hannon, Trustees.

BREWERS' ASSOCIATION.— Organized in 1860.
Officers— Claus Spreckles, President; Charles Armstrong, Secretary.

BRICKLAYERS' PROTECTIVE ASSOCIATION.— Organized September, 1863. Meets first Thursday in each month at Minerva Hall, corner California and Kearny streets. Number of members two hundred.
Officers— D. T. Van Orden, President; B. F. Sherman, Vice President; John D. Cavanagh, Secretary; Joseph Jones, Treasurer; Abram T. Enos, James A. Hale, and Cornelius Martin, Trustees.

BUILDERS' ASSOCIATION.—Organized October 1st, 1865. Meetings held every Monday evening at Mechanics' Institute (upper hall).
Officers—J. B. Morton, President; G. Welton, Vice President; F. X. Murray, Secretary; C. W. Davis, Treasurer.

CALIFORNIA BUILDING AND LOAN SOCIETY.—Organized in 1861. Office 406 Montgomery Street.
The objects of this society are to assist industrious persons in procuring homesteads, and improving the same by the erection of dwellings, etc., and receive payments from borrowers in monthly installments, extending over a period of years, as may be agreed on—thus converting rent into capital. This society has now a capital of $300,000—over four hundred partners.
Officers — Thomas Mooney, President; L. R. Townsend, Secretary.

CARTMAN'S PROTECTIVE AND RELIEF SOCIETY.—Organized March 8th, 1862. Meetings held first Monday in each month at Barra's Hall, corner First and Minna. Number of members sixty-five.
Officers — William Green, President; Michael McDevitt, Treasurer; Thomas Egan, Secretary.

CENTRAL PARK HOMESTEAD ASSOCIATION.—Organized June 7th, 1864. Capital, $72,000. Location, north beach of Hunter's Point. office, 302 Montgomery.
Officers — William Hollis, President; Edward Barry, Secretary and Treasurer; A. Crawford, William H. Martin, Jno. F. Coffey, and R. S. Eells, Directors.

CENTRAL POLISH SOCIETY OF THE PACIFIC COAST.—Organized May 1st, 1863. Meetings held monthly in the Russ House. Number of members, seventy-five.
Officers—C. Bielawski, President; R. C. Piotrowski, Vice President; C. Meyer, Political Agent; Martin Prag, Treasurer; J. W. Andrzejowski, Secretary; F. Woyeiscihowski, Dr. Pawlicki, and M. Schloss, Trustees.

CHAMBER OF COMMERCE.—Rooms at Merchants' Exchange, 521 Clay Street. Organized April, 1850. Regular meetings second Tuesday of each month, except when the same falls on steamer day, then the day previous. Annual meeting for the election of officers in May.

Officers—Joseph A. Donohoe, of Donohoe, Kelly & Co., President; William Meyer, of Rodgers, Meyer & Co., 1st Vice President; Charles Wolcott Brooks, of C. Wolcott Brooks & Co., 2d Vice President; W. R. Wadsworth, of William R. Wadsworth & Son, Secretary, Treasurer, and Librarian; R. G. Sneath, L. B. Benchley, of L. B. Benchley & Co., and Albert Miller, Executive Committee; President or one of the Vice Presidents ex officio Chairman, George H. Kellogg, Adam Grant, C. J. Dempster, Charles B. Polhemus, and E. Lazard, Committee of Appeals. W. Frank Ladd, Chairman to May, 1866; members retiring August, 1865. Abraham Seligman, E. H. Jones, Cornelius Koopmanschap, Nicolas Reynolds, Committee of Arbitration.

COLLEGE HOMESTEAD ASSOCIATION.— Organized August 25th, 1864. Office south-west corner Front and Jackson. Capital stock, $62,500.
Officers— William Sherman, President; W. C. Ralston, Treasurer; T. B. Bigelow, Secretary; John W. Dwinelle, William Sherman, L. B., Benchley, Rev. E. B. Walsworth, William Alvord, Ira P. Rankin, and T. B. Bigelow, Trustees.

COTTAGE SAVINGS AND HOMESTEAD ASSOCIATION. — Incorporated December 5th, 1861. Capital, $40,250.
Officers—A. B. Stout, M.D., President; H. A. Cobb, D. P. Belknap, Thomas H. Agnew, James Scrimgeour, John J. Hucks, and D. Murphy, Trustees; A. B. Stout, Secretary and Treasurer.

EUREKA HOMESTEAD ASSOCIATION.— Organized August 29th, 1862. Meetings of shareholders first Monday in January, and meeting of Directors last Monday in each month.
Officers—D. P. Belknap, President; C. C. Webb, Vice President; H. B. Congdon, Secretary; James S. Hutchinson, Treasurer. Office 620 Washington.

EUREKA TYPOGRAPHICAL UNION, NO. 21.—Reorganized September 4th, 1859. Hall, No. 625 Merchant Street, room 4. Regular monthly meeting held on the last Saturday of each month.
Officers—Fred. K. Krauth, President; George T. Russell, 1st Vice President; A. C. Hiester, 2d Vice President; F. O. A. Williams, Recording Secretary; John F. Brown, Financial Secretary; Daniel Damrell, Treasurer; I. W. Carpenter, Sergeant-at-Arms. John J. Kelly, Job Court, J. M. McCreary, R. Y. Snowball, M. Shannon, J. T. Barry, and E. P. Hill Directors; William Harper, G. K. Hilton, and William Murray, Trustees.

FISHERMEN'S ASSOCIATION. — Organized October 18th, 1864. Number of members, 305.
Officers—Aug. D. Splivalo, President; A. Bardellini and D. Fio, Vice Presidents; P. Berretta, Secretary; L. Mibelli, Treasurer.

FRENCH SAVINGS AND LOAN SOCIETY.— Organized 1860. Office 533 Commercial Street.
Officers—G. Drouaillet, President; A. R. Favre, Vice President; Camilo Martin, Treasurer; G. Mabé, Director.

GAS FITTERS' PROTECTIVE UNION.—Organized March, 1864. Meets corner California and Webb streets, every first Monday in each month.
Officers—John Rhawl, President; Geo. W. McDonald, Treasurer; Edward Groves, Secretary.

GERMAN MUTUAL FIRE INSURANCE COMPANY.—Organized July 12th, 1858. Office 58 Montgomery Block. Office hours 2 to 3 o'clock, P.M. Number of members, 200.
Officers—H. Geils, President; J. Dreyer, Vice President; T. Meetz, Secretary; P. Meyer,

Treasurer; H. H. Geils, C. Brauer, G. Waterman, Wm. Mentel, H. Holje, J. Dreyer, and Charles Reimers, Directors.

GERMANIA HOMESTEAD ASSOCIATION. —Meetings first Tuesday of each month, at the hall south-west corner Kearny and Bush.
Officers—John Pforr, President; Fred. G. E. Tittel, Vice President; J. C. Lutz, Treasurer; Geo. Strasser, Financial and Cor. Secretary; G. Moenning, Philip Siebel, Frederick Gebhard, Charles Alpers, William Schulz, and Jacob Zech, Directors.

GERMANIA SOCIETY.—Is composed of musicians, principally, from the Philharmonic Society, for the purpose of giving concerts on Sunday evenings. It has no regular organization and liable to be disbanded at any moment.
Joseph L. Schmitz, Leader; Chris Andres, Agent.

GOLDEN CITY HOMESTEAD ASSOCIATION.—Incorporated January 2d, 1864. Capital, $100,000, in five hundred shares. Office 734 Mont.
Officers—Earl Bartlett, President; William H. Moor, Vice President; Isaac T. Milliken, Treasurer; Samuel I. C. Swezey, Secretary; Earl Bartlett, Charles Elliot, John Stock, William Blackwood, T. R. Brooks, E. M. Casey, L. Brunner, F. Dumartheray, and Samuel I. C. Swezey, Directors.

HAT FINISHERS' ASSOCIATION.—Organized February 8th, 1853. Meetings held quarterly.
Officers—Horatio J. Lothrop, President; R. G. Simpson, Vice President; Samuel McAlester, Secretary; G. W. Miller, Treasurer; A. Jackson and G. Hawkins, Trustees.

HIBERNIA SAVINGS AND LOAN SOCIETY. —Office 506 Jackson Street. The object for which this association is formed, are, that by its operations the members thereof may be enabled to find a secure and profitable investment for small savings, and may have an opportunity of obtaining from it the use of a moderate capital, on giving good and sufficient security for the payment of the same
Officers—M. D. Sweeny, President; C. D. O'Sullivan, Vice President; Edward Martin, Treasurer; Richard Tobin, Attorney.

HOUSE AND SIGN PAINTERS' PROTECTIVE UNION.—Organized 1864. Meets in Lower Dashaway Hall every Wednesday evening.
Officers—W. R. Storer, President; John Dugan, Vice President; E. D. Norris, Secretary; W. J. Hughes, Financial Sec.; A. M. Gray, Treasurer.

IRON MOLDERS' PROTECTIVE UNION.— Organized June, 1863. Number of members, 145. Meets at Barra's Hall every second and fourth Thursday of each month.
Officers—Henry Morgan, President; Wm. Fields, Vice President; Harvey Kellum, Financial Sec.; ——, Recording Sec.; Jacob Hartman, Treasurer.

LABORERS' PROTECTIVE AND BENEVOLENT ASSOCIATION.—Meets at the hall 222 Montgomery Street, on the third of each month.
Officers—James Cahill, President; John McGowan, Vice President; P. T. Sheridan, Recording Secretary; M. Kairns, Secretary; M. Donavin, Treasurer.

LUMBER DEALERS' ASSOCIATION.—Incorporated December 22d, 1862. Meetings held at their rooms, Pier 3, Stewart Street Wharf. Number of members, 28, embracing all the lumber dealers of San Francisco.
The objects of the association are for mutual information, protection, and benefit in business; to

keep a record of all events and statistics of interest to the trade; to keep an account of all imports and exports of lumber, state of the market, etc.

Officers—Wm. H. Gawley, President; J. E. de la Montagnie, Sec'y; J. J. McKinnon, Treasurer.

MERCHANTS' ASSOCIATION.— Office 623 Montgomery.

METROPOLITAN HOMESTEAD ASSOCIATION.—Organized April 20th, 1864. Capital, $7,200. Office 302 Montgomery.

Officers—Wm. Irvine, President; Edward Barry, Secretary and Treasurer.

NEWSPAPER CARRIERS' ASSOCIATION.—Organized in 1858. Number of members, 60. Hall of association, 528 Clay Street.

Officers—Wm. Fletcher, President; Henry Meyer, Vice President; Walter J. Johnson, Secretary; Henry Meyer, Treasurer; H. B. Meyers, Auditor.

NORTH OAKLAND HOMESTEAD ASSOCIATION.—Organized August 5th, 1864. Capital stock, $20,000. Office SW cor Front and Jackson.

Officers—W. W. Crane, Jr., President; T. B. Bigelow, Secretary; W. W. Crane, Jr., Thomas Basse, John G. Dawes, J. S. Emery, D. N. Hawley, E. Bigelow, and T. B. Bigelow, Trustees.

NORTH SAN FRANCISCO HOMESTEAD AND RAILROAD ASSOCIATION.—Incorporated 1864. Office 24 Montgomery Block.

Officers—Caleb T. Fay, President; J. T. Boyd, Vice President; Alfred Barstow, Secretary; N. Luning, Treasurer; Caleb T. Fay, J. W. Stewart, N. Luning, B. F. Moulton, and J. T. Boyd, Trustees.

OPERATIVE BOOT MAKERS.—Organized 1864. Stated meetings, second Tuesday of each month. Hall south-west corner Kearny and California. Number of members, fifty-five.

Officers—John Welch, President; Michael Radford, Treasurer; Edward Barrett, Secretary.

PACIFIC ACCUMULATION LOAN COMPANY.—Incorporated February 4th, 1863. Capital, $5,000,000. No. shares, 50,000. Office 400 Mont.

Officers—Peter H. Burnett, President; George F. Bragg, Vice President; Edward W. Smith, Cashier; Samuel Brannan, Treasurer; O. P. Sutton, Secretary; Joseph W. Winans, Attorney; Sam'l Brannan, Peter H. Burnett, John W. Brumagim, R. B. Woodward, Sam. J. Hensley, Christian Reis, Joseph W. Winans, J. M. McDonald, and George F. Bragg, Directors.

PACIFIC GLASS WORKS CO.—Organized September 29th, 1862. Present capital, $125,000.

Officers—Giles H. Gray, President; H. Hanssmann, Secretary; Giles H. Gray, Albert Miller, John Archbald, M. B. Callahan, and S. D. Gilmore, Trustees; Giles H. Gray, Manager and Financial Agent, office 621 Clay Street.

Articles of manufacture are confined to hollow ware, and green or black glass.

PACIFIC MACHINISTS' UNION.—Organized in 1864. Meets at Barra's Hall.

Officers—R. A. Marden, President; Henry Sanderson, Vice President; Jos. McElroy, Recording Sec.; F. B. Tarbett, Corresponding Sec.; B. B. McAllister, Treasurer; M. Kelly, Sergeant-at-Arms.

PLASTERERS' PROTECTIVE UNION.—Organized 1862. Meets monthly at Mechanics' Hall, 239 Bush Street, near Occidental Hotel.

Officers—Wm. Simpson, President; David Hunter, Treasurer; Thomas Bodkin, Secretary.

PLEASANT VALLEY HOMESTEAD ASSOCIATION.—Organized January 19th, 1865. Capital, $8,000, divided into eighty shares. Office 528 Clay Street.

Officers—James Laidley, President; E. D. Waters, Vice President; A. S. Gould, Secretary; S. H. Wetherbee, Treasurer; James Laidley, E. D. Waters, Henry Baker, S. H. Wetherbee, and R. P. Franklin, Directors.

PLUMBERS' PROTECTIVE UNION.—Organized 1864. Meets in Mechanics' Hall, Bush Street, near Occidental Hotel, every first Tuesday in each month.

Officers—George E. Reid, President; R. J. Carduff, Secretary.; Wm. Enwright, Treasurer.

RAILROAD HOMESTEAD ASSOCIATION.—Incorporated Nov. 1st, 1864. Capital, $60,000. Office 543 Clay Street.

Officers—James L. Blaikie, President; John R. Mead, Vice President; Charles S. Capp, Secretary; William R. McKee, Treasurer; William W. Morgan, James Heron, John R. Mead, William H. Silverthorne, Charles S. Capp, John Landers, N. W. Spaulding, John H. O'Brien, Edward Galpen, William R. McKee, and James L. Blaikie, Trustees.

RIGGERS' AND STEVEDORES' UNION ASSOCIATION OF SAN FRANCISCO.—Rooms 431 Pacific. Organized July 25th, 1853; for the regulation of wages and protection of each other; number of members, one hundred and fifty-five. Meets every Monday evening.

Officers—Wm. C. Cummings, President; Wm. A. Adams, Vice President; Francis Durham, Financial Secretary; George Monroe, Recording Secretary; John P. Byers, Treasurer; John Hublow, Warden; Abram Hugbes, Tyler; John Phillips, James Orr, and John A. Russell, Trustees.

SADDLE, HARNESS, AND COLLAR MAKERS' PROTECTIVE ASSOCIATION.—Organized September 3d, 1865. Meets at Barra's Hall, north-west cor First and Minna streets, the first Tuesday night in each month. Number of members, forty-eight.

Officers—C. Jones, President; J. Miller, Vice President; M. McColgan, Treasurer; Charles J. Jones, Secretary; J. Roberts, Corresponding Secretary.

SAN FRANCISCO ARCHITECTURAL SOCIETY.— Organized 1861. Office Metropolitan Block. The object of the society is to promote and preserve the artistic, scientific, and practical knowledge of its members; to facilitate their intercourse and good fellowship; to elevate the standing and sustain the dignity of the sublime profession, and to unite the efforts of those engaged in the practice of architecture, for the general advancement of the truthful art.

Officers—Wm. Craine, President; Henry Kenitzer, Vice President; P. J. O'Connor, Recording Secretary; P. Huerne, Treasurer.

SAN FRANCISCO BAY DISTRICT AGRICULTURAL SOCIETY.—Organized in 1860. The annual meeting for 1865 will take place in San José during the month of November.

SAN FRANCISCO HOMESTEAD ASSOCIATION.—Incorporated April 7th, 1864. Term of duration, three years.

This association purposes to purchase lots within the City of San Francisco, and divide the same among the members.

Officers—N. P. Perine, President; William J. Gunn, Secretary; A. Himmelman, Treasurer; N.

P. Perine, William J. Gunn, John Pforr, Davis Louderback, W. M. Pierson, Samuel Irving, and Wm. Bitter, Directors.

SAN FRANCISCO INDEPENDENT MUSICAL CLUB.—Organized 1865. Musical Headquarters, Pioneer Hall, corner Bush and Montgomery streets.
Officers—Jacob Wiegand, President; Peter Johannsen, Secratary; George Kineman, Treasurer; John Wyatt, Conductor.

SAN FRANCISCO SAVINGS UNION.—Incorporated June 18th, 1862.
This association offers to the public a secure depository for small savings, and facilities for obtaining loans on real estate, on terms very advantageous to those wishing to procure homesteads of moderate value. Security is insured to its depositors by a cash capital, paid in by its stockholders, which, under the statute, can in no case be withdrawn until all its liabilities are discharged, even though this should exhaust every dollar both of the Capital and of the Reserved Fund. The statute also positively prohibits any purchase or investment which would bring the corporation into debt. Office 529 California Street, Mechanics' Institute Building.
Officers—James DeFremery, President; Albert Miller, Vice President; Washington Bartlett, Thos. P. Bevans, George C. Potter, C. Adolphe Low, Robert B. Swain, Edward P. Flint, and Charles Pace, Directors; John Archbald, Cashier and Secretary.

SAN MIGUEL HOMESTEAD ASSOCIATION.—Incorporated September 1st, 1865. Capital Stock, $26,000, in 200 shares of $130 each. Office 1 Government House.
Officers—Louis H. Bonestel, President; James E. Damon, Vice President; William J. Gunn, Secretary; L. H. Bonestel, J. E. Damon, W. Hamill, G. W. McNear, D. J. O'Callaghan, W. Gunn, Daniel C. Breed, S. S. Piper, and J. Ivancovich, Directors.

SAVINGS AND LOAN SOCIETY.—Incorporated July 23d, 1857.
The object for which this society is formed is that by means of it the members may be enabled to find a secure and profitable investment for small savings. Deposits received from two and a half dollars up to any amount. Deposits are invested in mortgages of real estate. Amount of capital paid in, nearly $1,500,000, invested exclusively on first bond and mortgage. The society have recently erected, for the accommodation of their increasing business, a fine three-story brick building, 619 Clay Street.
Officers—E. W. Burr, President; Benjamin D. Dean, Vice President; James O. Dean, Auditor; Cyrus W. Carmany, Secretary; Giles H. Gray, Attorney.

SHIP AND STEAMBOAT JOINERS' ASSOCIATION.—Organized March 21st, 1857. Reorganized April 25th, 1864. Meetings at Barra's Hall, corner First and Minna streets, second Fridays of each month.
Officers—Robert Bragg, President; Henry A. Foster, Vice President; George M. Thayer, Treasurer; D. S. Lindley, Financial and Recording Secretary; Henry S. Loane, John Dougherty, and Henry Guion, Trustees; A. A. Pike, Sergeant-at-Arms.

SHIP CALKERS' ASSOCIATION.—Organized 1861; reorganized March 21st, 1864. Meets second Tuesday of each month at Barra's Hall, north-west corner Minna and First.
Officers—H. D. Hudson, President; W. H. Car-

dinell, Vice President; J. L. Cornynn, Treasurer; J. Veeder, Secretary; J. N. Smith, Sergeant-at-Arms.

SHIPWRIGHTS' JOURNEYMEN ASSOCIATION.—Organized April 26th, 1857. Number of members, three hundred and fifteen. Meets at Barra's Hall, north-west corner Minna and First, on the first and Third Thursdays of each month.
The object of this association is to procure a fair and uniform rate of wages for the trade.
Officers—P. R. Marine, President; R. R. Bartlett and W. D. Delany, Vice Presidents; A. Stewart, Treasurer; J. F. Banfield, Sergeant-at-Arms.

SOUTH SAN FRANCISCO HOMESTEAD AND RAILROAD ASSOCIATION.—Incorporated November 15th, 1861. Capital, $150,000. Number of shares, five hundred. Office 528 Clay. This association are the owners of a valuable parcel of land, situated at Hunter's Point.
Officers—Henry F. Williams, President; Alex. G. Abell, Vice President; A. S. Gould, Secretary; J. B. Knapp, Joseph DeForest, H. B. Brooks, H. N. Tilden, Henry Webb, Joseph L. Bardwell, Thos. Anderson, Wm. W. Neal, and Joseph Frazier, Directors.

STONE CUTTERS' (JOURNEYMEN) ASSOCIATION.—Organized May 30th, 1863. Meetings first Wednesday in each month, at Barra's Hall, corner First and Minna.
Officers—William Johnson, President; Robert Giles, Vice President; Richard Bishop, Treasurer; Philip H. Sullivan, Secretary.

TRADERS' ASSOCIATION.—Organized May 13th, 1862. Meets quarterly.
Officers—A. J. Bryant, President; H. Bockman, 1st Vice President; John Myers, 2d Vice President; A. A. Hobe, Recording Secretary; H. Schwartz, Corresponding Secretary; A. Kloppenburg, Treasurer; A. Meyers, Sergeant-at-Arms.

TRADES' UNION OF SAN FRANCISCO.—Organized October, 1863. Meets at Old Odd Fellows' Hall, corner Bush and Kearny.
Officers—A. M. Kenaday, Typographical Union, President; George E. Reid, Plumbers' Union, Vice President; John A. Russell, Riggers' and Stevedores' Association, Recording and Corresponding Secretary; Thomas Anderson, Riggers' and Stevedores' Association, Treasurer; P. Ryan, Plasterers' Protective Union, Sergeant at Arms; J. F. Gormley, James Johnston, and H. W. Smith, Trustees.

VINEYARD HOMESTEAD ASSOCIATION.—Organized July 25th, 1865. Capital stock, $24,000. Number shares, one hundred. Office, 528 Clay.
Officers—Thomas Anderson, President; Samuel Tyler, Vice President; Henry F. Williams, Treasurer; A. S. Gould, Secretary; Edwin L. Smith, Chas. W. Neuman, Henry F. Williams, Thos. Anderson, J. J. Birge, James E. Damon, William W. Neale, Samuel Tyler, and Henry O. Howard, Directors.

YOUNG MEN'S HOMESTEAD ASSOCIATION.—Office 305 Montgomery Street. John S. Luty, Secretary.

Literary, Historical, Etc.

ACADEMY OF NATURAL SCIENCES.—Rooms 622 Clay. Organized April 22d, 1853.
Officers—Leander Ransom, President; J. N. Eckel, M.D., and J. B. Trask, M.D., Vice Presidents; W. O. Ayres, M.D., Corresponding Secre-

tary ; T. H. Bloomer, Recording Secretary; Prof. J. D. Whitney, Librarian ; Samuel Hubbard, Treasurer ; Curators ; Henry G. Hanks, of Mineralogy; W. M. Gabb, of Palæontology ; H. N. Bolander, of Botany; E. F. Lorquin, of Zoölogy ; R. E. C. Stearns, of Conchology ; H. Behr, M.D., of Entomology. Col. Leander Ransom, Dr. J. N. Eckel, and Dr. J. B. Trask, Trustees.

ADDISONIAN LITERARY SOCIETY. — Organized December, 1864. Meets every Friday evening in basement of the Howard Street M. E. Church, room No. 1.
Officers—Edwin Goodall, President; J. W. Bluett, Vice President; George M. Ciprico, Secretary ; H. H. Noble, Treasurer.

CALIFORNIA ART UNION. — Incorporated January 12th, 1865. Hall, 312 Montgomery Street. Annual meeting to be at such time and place as may be appointed by the Executive Committee. Objects of the association, to promote the cultivation and taste of the fine arts. Number of subscribers, five hundred and twenty-two.
Officers—Hon. F. F. Low, President; W. C. Ralston, Treasurer; L. F. Ireland, Secretary ; George H. Howard, Robert C. Rogers, M. Cheesman, Maj. R. W. Kirkham, U. S. A., William Norris, C. Wolcott Brooks, D. P. Belknap, R. B. Woodward, C. T. Meader, N. A. H. Ball, R. J. Vandewater, Dr. V. J. Fourgeaud, and A. H. Houston, Trustees; Rob't C. Rogers, George H. Howard, R. J. Vandewater, William Norris, and C. Walter Brooks, Executive Committee : Dr. V. J. Fourgeaud, M. Cheesman, William Hooper, S. W. Shaw, and Virgil Williams, Examining Committee; J. Oliver, Custodian.

CALIFORNIA PIONEERS' SOCIETY.—Organized in August, 1850. Rooms north-east corner of Montgomery and Gold streets, near Jackson. The President, Secretary, and Treasurer are *ex officio* members of the Board of Directors and Trustees of the society. The expressed objects of the society are to collect and preserve information connected with the early settlement and subsequent conquest of the country, and to perpetuate the memory of those whose sagacity, energy, and enterprise induced them to settle in the wilderness and become the founders of a new State. All who were in California *prior* to the first day of January, 1850, are eligible to membership. Any who have rendered distinguished or important services to the society, the State, or the United States, may be admitted as honorary members. The roll of the society embraces the names of nearly eight hundred members. Regular meetings of the society take place on the first Monday of each month. Annual election of officers on the seventh day of July, the anniversary of the Conquest of California, and of the raising of the American Flag on its soil. Annual celebration on the ninth of September, the anniversary of the Admission of California into the Union. The society is possessed of an excellent library, many curious and interesting relics of the "Early Times," trophies from Vicksburg, Port Hudson, and Gettysburg, and a cabinet of minerals.
Officers—P. B. Cornwall, President; Wm. H. Clark and E. L. Sullivan of San Francisco, James Lick, of Santa Clara, Andrew Goodyear of Solano, and J. C. Birdseye of Nevada, Vice Presidents ; Louis R. Lull, Secretary ; John H. Turney, Treasurer; R. J. Tiffany, O. P. Sutton, B. O. Devoe, J. H. Gardiner, R. C. Moore, Wm. L. Duncan, and Jacob Shew, Directors ; A. G. Randall, Marshal.

GERMAN SOCIETY OF NATURAL SCIENCES.—Organized in 1861. Meetings held every Wednesday evening, at their rooms, 517 Clay Street. Fifty members.

Officers—Dr. J. N. Eckel, President; Dr. J. Regensburger, Vice President; E. Kruse, Treasurer; J. A. Bauer, Corresponding Secretary ; A. E. Koels, Recording Secretary ; Julius George, Librarian; Curators : Zoölogy, F. Gruber; Assistants : Entomology, J. Behrens; Conchology, J. A. Bauer and N. Bolander; Ornithology, F. Gruber; Botany, J. Bauer; Mineralogy, Charles F. Riehn; Assistant, A. C. Weber.

MECHANICS' INSTITUTE.—Organized March 29th, 1855. Rooms 529 California Street, between Montgomery and Kearny. This association has recently purchased a commodious and desirable building on California Street, and have dedicated it to the purposes of the organization. The objects of the Institute, are the establishment of a library, reading-room, collection of a cabinet, scientific apparatus, works of art, and other literary and scientific purposes. The society has a reading-room well supplied with the leading scientific and literary periodicals of the day, and a valuable library, containing over seven thousand volumes. During the years 1858, 1860, 1864, and 1865 this Institute presented to the attention of the people of California their second, third, fourth, and fifth annual exhibitions, each of which was attended with the most complete success.
Officers—Charles M. Plum, President; Josiah Moulton, Vice President ; P. B. Dexter, Recording Secretary ; C. S. Higgins, Corresponding Secretary ; Edward Nunan, Treasurer ; A. A. Snyder, H. K. Cummings, W. W. Hanscom, James R. Deane, David Dwyer, D. A. MacDonald, and J. W. Reay, Directors.

MERCANTILE LIBRARY ASSOCIATION.—Mercantile Library Building, north-east corner of Montgomery and Bush streets. Organized January 24th, 1853. The rooms of the association are commodious and well arranged. The library contains about 20,000 volumes, and the reading-rooms are amply supplied with papers and magazines from the Eastern States and Europe. The terms of membership are two dollars initiation fee and one dollar per month—dues payable quarterly in advance.
Officers—G. W. Bell, President; C. W. Brooks, Vice President; David Wilder, Recording Secretary ; Henry S. Homans, Corresponding Secretary : J. G. Clark, Treasurer ; J. H. Wildes, James W. Cox, Adam T. Green, George Hewston, Frederick L. Castle, Arthur M. Ebbets, F. D. Kellogg, Charles R. Bond, and Daniel Rogers, Trustees; Daniel E. Webb, Librarian; John A. Haugh, Janitor; J. J. Tayker, Collector.
[See General Review for a notice of this useful and deservedly popular institution.]

MERCHANTS' EXCHANGE.—Theodore E. Baugh, proprietor, 521 Clay Street, south side, between Sansom and Montgomery. The Merchants' Exchange was opened by Messrs. Sweeny & Baugh in March, 1852, on Sacramento Street, one square south of its present location, and in September, 1853, they completed a line of Telegraph to Point Lobos, (south head), enabling them to report as soon as they could be signalized at sea, the names of inward-bound vessels. The Telegraph Line is the pioneer on the Pacific coast. In July, 1855, the Exchange was located in its present rooms, where can be found files of the leading newspapers, foreign and domestic.

NATIONAL DEMOCRATIC ASSOCIATION READING ROOMS.—622 Clay Street. Organized July 24th, 1865.
Officers—W. D. Sawyer, President; Henry H. Parkell, First Vice President ; W. L. Bromley, Second Vice President ; Frank V. Scudder, Recording Secretary ; W. A. Henry, Corresponding Secre-

tary;·Marcus A.·Braly, Treasurer; W. P. Kirkland, Janitor; Geo. W. Degear, Sergeant-at-Arms.

SOCIAL LITERARY SOCIETY, Y. M. C. A.—Organized November 3d, 1862. Meets every Tuesday evening in the rooms of the Young Men's Christian Association, for the purpose of debate, literary exercise, and improvement in elocution.
Officers—Donald Bruce, President; F. S. Page, Vice President; H. D. Gates, Secretary; E. A. Carrique, Editor; A. J. Hindes, Associate Editor; C. F. Whitton and Geo. A. Hubbard, Executive Committee.

Social.

AVONITES.—Organized 1865. Meetings held every Wednesday evening, at Room 15, Mead House. This is an Amateur Dramatic Society, organized in 1855.
Officers—Harry Gordon, President; J. E. Carton, Secretary; Leon Amy, Treasurer; Frank Wilton, Stage Manager.

CONCORDIA SOCIETY.—Organized November, 1864. Meets at old Odd Fellows' Hall, corner of Bush and Kearny. Number of members, one hundred. The object of this society is to promote sociability and literature.
Officers—M. Essberg, President; S. Solomon, Vice President; J. Naphtaly, Recording Secretary; M. Hyman, Corresponding Secretary; A. Block, Treasurer; M. Taklas, Sig. Greenbaum, M. Tobriner, M. Haas, L. Hildburghamer, J. Goldsmith, and A. S. Ulsell, Directors.

EAGLE BASE BALL CLUB.—Organized 1860.
Officers—John L. Durkee, President; John Calvert, Vice President; John M. Fisher, Treasurer; C. S. Ashton, Secretary; Robt. Grigleitti, Robert Gunn, Thomas Peel, Ed. Kerrigan, and C. S. Ashton, Directors.

EUREKA TURN VEREIN.—Organized October 26th, 1863. Number of members, 44. Pupils, 45. Regular meetings, first Monday of each month. The object of this association is to encourage morality and improve health. Hall, 541 Broadway.
Officers—Felix Marcuse, President; Ed. Ehrenfort, Secretary; F. G. Hartman, Treasurer; Wm. Koch, 1st Turnwart; P. Landgraf, 2d Turnwart; Hans Wedel, Zungwart.

GARIBALDI HARMONIE SOCIETY.—Meet Monday and Thursday of each week. Hall, 619 Broadway.

GERMAN CLUB.—Organized December, 1850. Number of members, thirty-five. Rooms north-west corner Kearny and Sacramento.
Officers—Geo. L. J. Bendixen, President; Ernest Zahn, Treasurer; Charles Mayne, Secretary; V. Cramer, Augustus Ahlers, M.D., and C. Scharlach, M.D., Directors.

HARMONIE, THE.—The object of this association is for the cultivation and improvement of music. Number of members, eighty; fifty active singers. Meetings held every Monday evening at the corner of California and Kearny streets.
Officers—H. Brand, President; C. Schaefer, Vice President; A. Braun, Secretary; L. Breidenstein, Treasurer; C. Fluhr, Librarian; Rudolph Herold, Director.

ITALIAN PHILHARMONIC SOCIETY.—Organized June 2d, 1864. Meets 619 Broadway, on the last Thursday of each month. Object, musical instruction. Number of members, eighty.
Officers—Nicola Brignardello, President; Guiseppe Sala and L. Costa, Vice Presidents; Giovanni Sbarboro, Treasurer; Andrea Sbarboro, Secretary.

PACIFIC CLUB.—Rooms, 633 Commercial, containing library and reading rooms, supplied with all the domestic and foreign newspapers and periodicals. Number of members, one hundred.
Officers—Ogden Hoffman, President; D. J. Tallant, Treasurer; George B. Gammans, Secretary.

PACIFIC SAENGERBUND.—This is the name of an organization of all the Singing Clubs of California, except the San Francisco Harmonie, and has for its object the cultivation of singing in general, to facilitate as much as possible the establishment of new singing clubs, and furnishing to them music at a cheap rate, by publishing in print, the best known songs, and giving them any information touching the objects of their organization. Furthermore, to accomplish any kind of commission in this line without charge, when it is within reach of the Board.
The association is represented by a board of five Boardmen, of whom one is President, one Secretary, and one Cashier.
Officers—E. Schnabel, President; E. J. Pfeiffer, Secretary; J. C. Sack, Cashier; J. Heismann and X. Huber, Boardmen.
The following societies compose the Saengerbund: Maennerchor, San Francisco; Turn Verein, Stockton; Liederkranz, Marysville: Maennerchor, San José; Quartette, Oroville; Liedertaefel, Yreka; Gesangverein, Vallecito; Orpheus, Weaverville; Teutonia, Los Angeles; Liederkrans, Anaheim; Eintracht, Stockton; Germania, Victoria, V. I.; and Germania, Virginia City.

PACIFIC TURNER BUND.—Organized 1859. Rooms, Turn Verein Hall, Bush Street, between Stockton and Powell streets. Meetings at the call of the President.
This is an organization of the different Turn Vereins on the Pacific coast, and has for its object the cultivation of gymnastic exercises in general, to facilitate as much as possible the establishment of new Turn Vereins, and to impart information on the subject of their organization to the different associations constituting the Pacific Turner Bund.
The following societies constitute the Pacific Turner Bund: Socialer Turn Verein, San Francisco; Sacramento Turn Verein, Sacramento; Marysville Turn Verein, Marysville; Stockton Turn Verein, Stockton; Gold Hill Turn Verein, Gold Hill.
The association is represented by a board of the following five officers: Aug. Anferman, President; Fr. Marks, Vice President; H. Hinrichs, Recording Secretary; A. F. Marquardt, Corresponding Secretary; Emil Steinle, Treasurer.

PIONEER CRICKET CLUB. — Organized March 23d, 1857. Number of members, thirty.
Officers—Charles Boyes, President; Henry Havelock, Vice President; Henry Fox, Treasurer; Edward Pugh, Secretary.

SAN FRANCISCO AMATEURS.—Organized February, 1861. Regular meetings held first and third Tuesdays in each month. Place of meeting, Turn Verein Hall. Number of regular members, fourteen. The object of this association is the study of the drama and mutual improvement.
Officers—H. P. Taylor, President; Robert Fulford, Stage Manager; Edwin R. Bow, Business Manager; Samuel A. Wolfe, Secretary; Robert Fulford, Treasurer.

SAN FRANCISCO CRICKET CLUB.—Organized July 28th, 1864. Number of members, seventeen.
Officers—D. W. Davis, President; John W. Harrison, Vice President; J. M. Fisher, Treasurer; R. B. Bulmore, Secretary.

SAN FRANCISCO GERMAN RIFLE CLUB.—Organized November 7th, 1860. Meetings held monthly, at the NW corner of Bush and Kearny streets. Number of members, twenty.
Officers—George Schmitt, 1st Shooting Master; Wm. Ehrenpfort, 2d Shooting Master; John Bach, Treasurer; Adolph Hertz, Secretary; Theodore Severin, Assistant Secretary.

SAN FRANCISCO MAENNERCHOR.—Organized 1865. Meets every Monday evening at Philharmonic Hall, NE corner Stockton and Jackson streets. Monthly contribution, one dollar. Number of members, forty. The object of this association is the cultivation of music.
Officers—John C. Sack, President; Henry Newman, Vice President; Herman Royer, Secretary; H. Helguth, Treasurer; P. Theas, Librarian; M. Schumacher, Leader.

SAN FRANCISCO OLYMPIC CLUB.—Organized in 1860. Rooms 35 Sutter near Montgomery. Number of members, five hundred.
Officers—R. H. Lloyd, President; Arthur K. Hawkins, Vice President; W. H. Eldridge, Treasurer; D. Wilder, Secretary; H. W. A. Nahl, Leader; S. W. Holladay, G. S. Haskell, E. M. Furbush, and J. W. Coleman, Directors.
The Olympic Club is at present in a very flourishing condition, having regularly organized classes in gymnastics, boxing, and fencing, the two former being taught by J. S. Winrow, and the latter by Col. Monstery. The new rooms of the association are most admirably adapted to the purposes of the organization. The apparatus is extensive and complete, and the accommodations are on a scale commensurate with its increasing importance.

SAN FRANCISCO PHILHARMONIC SOCIETY.—Organized January 16th, 1865. Meetings held quarterly. Rehearsals every Tuesday. Number of members, twenty-five. Object, to promote the cultivation and taste of music.
Officers—Joseph L. Schmitz, President; James Kendall, Vice President; Alexander Hildebrand, Secretary; George Koppitz, Treasurer; Charles Schultz, A. Wiese, und A. Mueller, Trustees; F. Boehme, Librarian.

SAN FRANCISCO TURN VEREIN.—Organized 1852. Rooms, Turn-Verein Hall, Bush Street, near Powell. The object of this society is the cultivation of gymnastic exercises in general, to encourage morality, to improve health, to cultivate music, and to entertain and cultivate free religious and political sentiments. Stated meetings first and third Wednesday evenings of each month. Number of members, seventy-five, of which about thirty are attached to the vocal department. Besides this, there exists, in connection with the association a school for boys from seven to eighteen years, which numbers seventy pupils. Exercises for the pupils every Monday and Thursday evenings, from 7 to 8½ o'clock, and for members every Tuesday and Friday evenings, from 8 to 10 o'clock.
Officers—Jacob Weiss, President; Emil Steinle, Vice President; A. F. Marquardt, First Leader; H. Hinrichs, Second Leader; G. H. Behrens, Recording Secretary; C. Hubert, Corresponding Secretary; H. Gotte, Financial Sec'y; H. Plagemann, Treasurer; W. Koch, Propertywart; H. Planz, Singwart; Emil Steinle, Musical Director; Aug. Aufermann, Jacob Weiss, and H. Plagemann, Trustees.

SAN FRANCISCO VEREIN.—Organized October 2d, 1853. Rooms SE corner Kearny and Sacramento streets. Library numbers 3,000 volumes. Reading room is supplied with thirty different newspapers, and all the current magazines and periodicals. Number of members, ninety.
Officers—Dr. J. Regensburger, President; R. Vonder Meden, Secretary; J. G. Ils, Treasurer; C. Bürkner, Librarian.

SWISS RIFLE CLUB.—Organized September 1st, 1861. Meetings held monthly at Helvetia Hotel. Number of members, thirty-five.
Officers—Ernest Zahn, President; M. Stuber, Vice President; P. A. Gianinni, Shooting Master; Antoine Borel and E. DeRutte, Secretaries.

Military.

MILITARY DIVISION OF THE PACIFIC.—Including the Department of California and the Department of the Columbia.
Major-General H. W. HALLECK, U. S. A. Commanding;
Major Robert N. Scott, Assistant Adjutant General;
Major D. C. Wager, Acting Assistant Inspector General;
Major John McL. Taylor, Chief Commissary;
Brevet Capt. H. A. Huntington, Aide-de-Camp.
Headquarters, 418 California Street.

DEPARTMENT OF CALIFORNIA.—Major-General IRVIN McDOWELL, U. S. A., Commanding.
Staff—Col. Richard C. Drum, Assistant Adjutant General and Chief of Staff; Col. E. B. Babbitt, Deputy Quartermaster-General; Lieut.-Col. Hiram Leonard, Deputy Paymaster General; Col. Washington Seawell, Commissary of Musters; Major C. J. Sprague, Paymaster U. S. A.; Surgeon Charles McCormick, Medical Director; Lieut.-Col. Charles C. Keeney, Medical Inspector; Lieut.-Col. R. E. DeRussy, Engineer Corps; Major R. W. Kirkham, U. S. A., Quartermaster and Chief Commissary of Subsistence; Lieut.-Col. E. W. Hillyer, Judge Advocate; Surgeon Robert Murray, Medical Purveyor; Major Alfred Morton, Provost Marshal. Headquarters, 742 Washington Street.

Commissary Musters, U. S. A.—Col. Washington Seawell. Office, 418 Washington Street.

Medical Department U. S. A.—Surgeon Charles McCormick, Medical Director; office 410 Kearny Street. Lieut.-Col. Charles C. Keeney, Medical Inspector; office 742 Washington Street. Surgeon Robert Murray, Medical Purveyor; William N. Thompson, Clerk; office and depôt, 805 Sansom Street.

Paymaster's Department U. S. A.—Lieut.-Col. Hiram Leonard, Deputy Paymaster General; Majors Samuel Woods, Charles J. Sprague, Cary H. Fry, Hiram C. Bull, and E. C. Kemble. Paymaster's office, 742 Washington Street.

Provost Marshal U. S. A.—Major Alfred Morton, Provost Marshal, office 416 Washington.

Quartermaster's Department U. S. A.—Col. E. B. Babbitt, Deputy Quartermaster General, office 742 Washington; Captain James T. Hoyt, Assistant Quartermaster, office and depôt 34 California; William P. Toler, Clerk; John M. Hoyt, Store Keeper.

Subsistence Department U. S. A.—Major J. McL. Taylor, Commissary of Subsistence U. S. A., Chief Commissary Military Division of the Pacific, office

418 California Street; Richard C. Alden, Chief Clerk; Frank Bryan, Clerk; Captain S. A. Ballou, Commissary of Subsistence U. S. V. Depôt Commissary and Chief Commissary Department of California, office 208 Sansom Street; James S. Townsend, Clerk; M. I. Morgan, Store Keeper. Warehouses, 210 and 212 Sansom Street.

CALIFORNIA MILITIA.* — Commander-in-Chief, Governor F. F. Low.
Staff—Gen. George S. Evans, Adjutant General; Col. Solon, S. Pattee, Paymaster; Col. W. H. L. Barnes, Judge Advocate; Lieut.-Col. Wm. Harney, Chief Aid-de-Camp; John T. Mosely, Aid.
Major-General Lucius H. Allen, Commanding. Headquarters San Francisco.
Staff—Lieut.-Col. S. Cladius Ellis, Assistant Adjutant-General; Lieut.-Col. S. O. Houghton, Inspector; Lieut.-Col. A. W. Von Schmidt, Engineer; Lieut.-Colonel Robert Simson, Ordnance Officer; Lieut.-Col. J. H. Stearns, Quartermaster; Lieut.-Col. A. H. Houston, Commissary; Lieut.-Col. Daniel Norcross, Paymaster; Lieut.-Col. J. W. Brumagim, Judge Advocate; Lieut.-Col. George M. Hewston, Surgeon; Major S. P. Middleton and Major T. A. Mudge, Aids.

Second Brigade (comprising the counties of Santa Cruz, Santa Clara, San Mateo, San Francisco, Alameda, Contra Costa, Marin, Sonoma, Solano, Napa, and Lake)—Brig.-Gen. John Hewston, Jr., Commanding. Headquarters 416 Montgomery Street.
Staff—John Hewston, Jr., Brigadier-General; Major George W. Smiley, Ass't Adjutant-General and Chief of Staff; Major C. L. Wiggin, Quartermaster; Major Charles E. Hinckley, Commissary; Major Thomas J. P. Lacy, Engineer; Major W. Frank Ladd, Ordnance Officer; Major M. M. Richardson, Paymaster; Major Adolphus D. Grimwood, Judge Advocate and Act'g Ass't Adjutant-General; Major Samuel R. Gerry, Surgeon, and Capt. Octavius Bell, Aid-de-Camp.

FIRST REGIMENT INFANTRY.—Joseph Wood, Colonel; T. B. Ludlum, Lieutenant-Colonel; Edwin Lewis, Major; Lieut. Stephen Smith, Adjutant; Edwin Harris, Quartermaster; Capt. Isaac Rowell, Surgeon; Lieut. Joseph Haine, Ass't Surgeon; Lieut. Andrew B. Wood, Paymaster; George Childs, Sergeant-Major; John Markell, Q. M. Sergeant; R. C. Hanson, Principal Musician—
Composed of the following companies, viz.: A, State Guard; B, City Guard; C, National Guard; D, San Francisco Guard; E, Sherman Guard; F, Light Guard; I, Sumner Guard; K, Ellsworth Rifles.

SECOND REGIMENT INFANTRY.—M. C. Smith, Colonel; James T. Hyde, Lieut.-Colonel; R. F. Ryan, Major; Lieut. Thomas Callan, Adjutant; Capt. James M. Sharkey, Surgeon; William Barton, Sergeant-Major; Thomas Kelly, Quartermaster-Sergeant. Regimental Armory, 577 Market.
Composed of the following companies, viz.: A, Montgomery Guard; B, McMahon Grenadier Guard; C, Shields Guard; D, Wolfe Tone Guard; E, Meagher Guard; F. Emmett Rifles (Petaluma); G, Sarsfield Guard (Benicia); H, Emmett Life Guard; K, O'Neil Guard; L, Seaward Guard.

SIXTH GERMAN REGIMENT.—F. G. E. Tittel, Colonel; Henry Hasbach, Lieutenant-Colonel; Peter Sesser, Major; Lieut. Henry Schmidt, Adjutant; Lieut. A. G. Russ, Quartermaster; Lieut. Gustave Malech, Surgeon; Henry Lion, Sergeant-Major; A. Hemmelman, Quartermaster-Sergeant—

*The Act of the Legislature, April 25th, 1863, organizes the militia of the State into six brigades.—[COMPILER.

Composed of the following companies, viz.: A, California Fusileers; B, Sigel Rifles; C, Ellis Guard; D, California Grenadiers; E, Steuben Guard, F, San Francisco Tiralleurs; G, Germania Guard; H, California Musketeers; I, Tittel Zouaves; K, San Francisco Jagers.

The following infantry companies are unattached, viz.: Mission Guard; Sherman Guard, Ellsworth Zouave Cadets, Federal Guard, Governor's Guard, and Hibernia Greens.

SECOND INFANTRY BATTALION.—Major R. P. Lewis, Commanding—Composed of the following companies, viz.: A, Lincoln Guard; B, Grant Guard; C, Sheridan Guard; D, California Tigers.

FIRST REGIMENT HEAVY ARTILLERY.—Head Quarters, 406 Montgomery Street. John W. McKenzie, Colonel; James Brown, Lieut. Colonel; John Stratman, Major; (vacant) Junior Major, Lieut. H. H. Thrall, Adjutant; Capt. Jas. Murphy, Surgeon; Lieut. E. Irving Smith, Quartermaster; (vacant) Sergeant Major; Albert Haulon, Quartermaster Sergeant—
Composed of the following companies, viz.: A, Union Guard; B, Ellsworth Guard Zouaves; C, Oakland Guard; D, Washington Guard; E, Franklin Guard; F, Liberty Guard; G, Excelsior Guard; H, Mechanic Guard; I, Eureka Guard; K, San Francisco Cadets. Regimental Armory, 416 Commercial.

FIRST REGIMENT CAVALRY.—Charles L. Taylor, Colonel; Alfred McCall, Lieut. Colonel; John H. Marston, Major; H. M. Leonard, Junior Major; Lieut. S. B. Pike, Adjutant; Lieut. John Crowley, Quartermaster; Capt. H. S. Baldwin, Surgeon; F. Steinhart, Sergeant Major; John Carroll, Quartermaster Sergeant—Composed of the following companies, viz.: A, First Light Dragoons (San Francisco); B, San Francisco Hussars (San Francisco); C, Jackson Dragoons (San Francisco); D, Suisun Cavalry (Suisun City); E, Redwood Cavalry (Santa Clara); F, Santa Cruz Cavalry (Santa Cruz); G, Contra Costa Guard (San Pablo); H, Jefferson Cavalry (Redwood City); I, Burnett Light Horse Guard (San José); K, New Almaden Cavalry (New Almaden); L, Napa Rangers (Napa City); M, Lincoln Cavalry (Tomales). Regimental Armory, 722 Montgomery.

CALIFORNIA FUSILEERS.—Organized September 9th, 1856. Number of members, 65. Armory, corner Sacramento and Kearny streets.
Officers—John Obenauer, Captain; Jacob Zech, 2d Lieutenant; Abraham Mayer, Brevet 2d Lieutenant; J. Bohn, Orderly; J. Ackerman, Treasurer; John Berghofer, Secretary.

CALIFORNIA GRENADIERS—Company D.—Organized March 3d, 1864. Number of members, 70. Armory, corner Bush and Montgomery.
Officers—S. Lion, Captain; J. W. Andrzejowski, 1st Lieutenant; Francis Worth, 2d Lieutenant; Bruno Triebe, 3d Lieutenant.

CALIFORNIA MUSKETEERS—Company H.—Organized April 25th, 1864. Number of members, 46. Armory, 525 Kearny.
Officers—R. Meiners, Captain; C. H. W. Hewelke, 1st Lieutenant; Joseph Behrens, 2d Lieutenant; M. Langensee, 3d Lieutenant.

CALIFORNIA TIGERS.—Organized 1865. Number of members, 48.
Officers—E. McDevitt, Captain; Charles Broad, 1st Lieutenant; Joseph Dougherty, Senior 2d Lieutenant; D. M. Coleman, Junior 2d Lieutenant.

CITY GUARD—Company B, 1st Regiment C. M.—Organized 1852; reorganized as Independent City Guard, 1856; reorganized as City Guard, March 11th, 1859. Number of members, 60. Armory, north-west cor Montgomery and California streets.
Officers—W. C. Little, Captain; Wm. M. Noyes, 1st Lieutenant; Geo. W. Grannis, 2d Lieutenant; Theodore Van Tassell, Junior 2d Lieutenant; Thos. Penniman, Jr. Secretary; John Bray, Treasurer.

ELLIS GUARD.—Organized June 23d, 1863. Armory, Turn Verein Hall, N s Bush nr Stockton.
Officers—F. Michaelis, Captain; J. Thierbach, 1st Lieutenant; J. Lenhart, 2d Lieutenant; C. Waldenberger, Junior 2d Lieutenant; F. Carstens, Orderly Sergeant; J. Lenhart, Secretary.

ELLSWORTH GUARD ZOUAVES—Organized June 23d, 1861. Number of members, 48. Armory, rear Metropolitan Theater.
Officers—Charles McMillan, Captain; John Middleton, Jr. 1st Lieutenant; R. G. Robinson, 2d Lieutenant; Gilbert Clayton, Brevet 2d Lieutenant; John P. Jourden, Orderly; T. H. Bloomer, Secretary; J. P. Jourden, Treasurer.

ELLSWORTH RIFLES.—Organized October 22d, 1861. Number of members, 51. Armory, 729 Market Street.
Officers—Edward C. Newhoff, Captain; James G. Carson, 1st Lieutenant; John Sampson, 2d Lieutenant; E. C Fogarty, Brevet 2d Lieutenant; J. C. Mayerhofer, Secretary; J. G. Carson, Treasurer.

ELLSWORTH ZOUAVE CADETS.—Organized 1865. Number of members, 51. Armory, 751 Market.
Officers—George Birdsall, Jr. Captain; Lawrence Dunn, 1st Lieutenant; John A. Ledden, Senior 2d Lieut.; James W. Hentsel, Junior 2d Lieut.

EMMETT LIFE GUARDS.—Organized November 18th, 1862. Number of members, 65. Armory, south-west corner Front and Jackson.
Officers—Thomas O'Neil, Captain; Robert Cleary, 1st Lieutenant; James Leonard, 2d Lieutenant; Thomas Kenny, 3d Lieutenant; James Quinn, Orderly; J. Flanagan, Secretary; Thomas O'Neil, Treasurer.

EUREKA GUARD.—Organized 1865. Number of members, 60.
Officers—Robert G. Gilmore, Captain; Wallace T. James, 1st Lieutenant; Henry Moffat, Senior 2d Lieutenant; John C. Heenan, Junior 2d Lieutenant.

EXCELSIOR GUARD.—Organized January 1st, 1863. Number of members, 65. Armory, east side of Fifth, near Harrison.
Officers—Jas. W. Wilkinson, Captain; Roger Robinett, 1st Lieutenant; Thomas Sawyer, 2d Lieutenant; I. W. Russell, Junior 2d Lieutenant; Roger Robinett, Secretary; (vacant) Treasurer.

FEDERAL GUARD.—Organized 1865. Number of members, 47.
Officers—Joseph Steward, Captain; William J. Dutton, Jr. 1st Lieutenant; George A. Brush, Senior 2d Lieutenant; (vacant) Junior 2d Lieutenant.

FIRST LIGHT DRAGOONS.—Organized June 24th, 1862. Number of members, 70. Armory, 722 Montgomery Street.
Officers—David Moore, Captain; Jacob Browning, 1st Lieutenant; Francis Blake, 2d Lieutenant; M. H. Carter, 3d Lieut.; Francis Blake, Treasurer.

FIRST CALIFORNIA GUARD (LIGHT BATTERY).—Organized July 27th, 1849. Number of members, 138. Armory, south side of Pine, between Montgomery and Sansom streets.
Officers—W. C. Burnett, Captain; R. G. Brush, 1st Lieutenant; Geo. W. Blasdell, Senior 2d Lieutenant; Marcus Harloe, Junior 2d Lieutenant; D. H. Haskell, Q. M.; (vacant) Surgeon; D. H. Haskell, 1st Sergeant and Sec'y; C. Storm, Treasurer.

FRANKLIN GUARD — Company E.—Organized June 3d, 1861. Number of members, 72. Armory, 727 Market Street.
Officers—John McComb, Captain; Louis Cohn, 1st Lieutenant; James Ware, 2d Lieutenant; James McDonnell, Jr. Brevet 2d Lieutenant; B. K. Michaels, Secretary; John McComb, Treasurer.

GERMANIA GUARD—Company G.—Organized March 25th, 1864. Number of members, 50. Armory, Market near Third.
Officers—H. Mund, Captain; L. Herzer, 1st Lieutenant; Wm. Miller, 2d Lieutenant; Wm. Huntemann, 3d Lieutenant.

GOVENOR'S GUARD.—Organized 1865. Armory, north side Commercial, between Sansom and Battery streets. Number of members, 50.
Officers—J. S. Henshaw, Captain; J. E. Purdy, 1st Lieutenant; James M. Hoyt, Senior 2d Lieutenant; C. H. Eldredge, Junior 2d Lieutenant.

GRANT GUARD. — Organized 1865. Number of members, 65.
Officers—Hugh A. Gorley, Captain; John McH. Hay, 1st Lieutenant; John H. Dougherty, Senior 2d Lieut, (vacant) Junior 2d Lieut.

HIBERNIA GREENS — Organized 1865. Armory, 567 Market Street. Number of members, 46.
Officers— P. R. Hannah, Captain; James McQuirk, 1st Lieutenant; R. B. Butler, Senior 2d Lieutenant; Lawrence Kelly, Junior 2d Lieutenant.

JACKSON DRAGOONS. — Organized March 16th, 1863. Armory, 722 Montgomery Street. Number of members, 60.
Officers—Patrick R. O'Brien, Captain; Michael Miles, 1st Lieutenant; John Doyle, 2d Lieutenant; Michael Nunan, Junior 2d Lieutenant; F. McCarthy, 1st Sergeant; James McGinn, Secretary; Arthur Quinn, Treasurer.

LIBERTY GUARD.—Organized 1865. Number of members, 52. Armory, 416 Commercial.
Officers — Thomas J. Dixon, Captain; John D. Rice, 1st Lieutenant; Patrick Flynn, Senior 2d Lieutenant; Thomas Brown, Junior 2d Lieutenant.

LIGHT GUARD. — Organized October, 1858. Number of members, 59. Armory, 636 Market.
Officers — C. H. Simpson, Captain; Daniel T. Phelps, 1st Lieutenant; M. G. Shove, 2d Lieutenant; W. L. Caznean, Brevet 2d Lieutenant; Ira Cook, Orderly; C. A. Lampe, Secretary; W. W. McDevitt, Treasurer.

LINCOLN GUARD.—Organized December 3d, 1864. Number of members, 53.
Officers—Charles H. Weintraut, Captain; S. P. Rines, 1st Lieutenant; M. S. de Larue, Senior 2d Lieutenant; T. F. Dailey, Junior 2d Lieutenant.

McMAHON GRENADIER GUARDS.—Organized December, 1859. Number of members, 60. Armory, 567 Market Street.
Officers — Thomas N. Cazneau, Captain; John Cahill, 1st Lieutenant; Patrick O'Brien, 2d Lieutenant; Wm. Love, Brevet 2d Lieutenant; J. H. Dillon, Orderly Sergeant; John Cahill, Treasurer; William Burns, Secretary.

MILITARY. 625

MEAGHER GUARD. — Organized May 17th, 1862; reorganized, 1863. Armory, 567 Market Street. Number of members, 53.
Officers — John W. Winters, Captain; Timothy Collins, 1st Lieutenant; M. C. Bateman, 2d Lieutenant; Henry C. Bateman, Brevet 2d Lieutenant; J. A. Kelly, Orderly; H. C. Bateman, Secretary; J. W. Winters, Treasurer.

MECHANIC GUARD.—Organized 1865. Number of members, 52.
Officers—Stillman H. Davenport, Captain; Francis B. Harrington, 1st Lieutenant; Charles E. Dusenberg, Senior 2d Lieutenant; Eugene J. Mullen, Junior 2d Lieutenant.

MISSION GUARD.—Organized 1865. Armory, 567 Market Street. Number of members, 51.
Officers—Peter E. Farrell, Captain; John P. Griffith, 1st Lieutenant; Patrick Gray, Senior 2d Lieutenant; Thomas J. Dargin, Junior 2d Lieutenant.

MONTGOMERY GUARDS. — Organized December 23d, 1859. Number of members, 63. Armory, 567 Market Street.
Officers—C. Quinn, Captain; William Lee, 1st Lieutenant; James Mathews, 2d Lieutenant; J. F. Cahill, Brevet 2d Lieutenant; P. H. Lawlor, Orderly; John Casey, Secretary; William Lee, Treasurer.

NATIONAL GUARD.—Organized, 1855; reorganized January 3d, 1859. Number of members, 95. Armory, Post Street, opposite Union Square.
Officers—Benjamin Pratt, Captain; George Humphrey, 1st Lieutenant; Frederick A. Will, 2d Lieutenant; A. D. Moulton, Junior 2d Lieutenant; J. H. Baker, Secretary; Edward Babson, Treasurer.

O'NEIL GUARD.—Organized May 6th, 1863. Number of members, 44. Armory, 567 Market.
Officers—M. W. Higgins, Captain; N. Sweeney, 1st Lieutenant; E. A. Williams, 2d Lieutenant; Thomas Flemming, 3d Lieutenant; Michael Kerns, Orderly; Nicholas Sweeney, Treasurer; J. McMahon, Secretary.

PACIFIC GUARD.—Organized February, 1864. Armory, Pioneer Hall. Number of members, 30.
Officers—Joseph Stewart, Captain; W. J. Dutton, 1st Lieutenant; George Brush, Orderly Sergeant.

POLICE MILITARY ORGANIZATION (Independent).— Organized April 15, 1863. Number of members, 77. Armory, basement City Hall.
Officers—Martin J. Burke, Captain; William Y. Douglas, 1st Lieutenant; S. N. Baker, Senior 2d Lieutenant; G. G. Bradt, 1st Sergeant; Benjamin Pratt, 2d Sergeant; P. McCormick, 3d Sergeant.

SAN FRANCISCO CADETS.—Organized August, 1863. Armory, 326 Bush.
Officers—C. E. S. McDonald, Captain; G. Bigley, 1st Lieutenant; W. Pickett, Senior 2d Lieutenant; Thomas Carew, Junior 2d Lieutenant.

SAN FRANCISCO GUARD.—Organized June, 1863. Armory, south-west corner California and Kearny. Number of members, 69.
Officers—J. V. McElwee, Captain; Henry Cooper, 1st Lieutenant; David Thomas, Senior 2d Lieutenant; John R. Regan, Junior 2d Lieutenant.

SAN FRANCISCO GUARD (Independent.)— Organized 1862. Number of members, 86. Armory, 416 Commercial.
Officers—Robert Simpson, Captain; W. McDonald, 1st Lieutenant; H. J. Burns, Senior 2d Lieutenant; Jabish Clement, Junior 2d Lieutenant; A.

P. Flint, 1st Sergeant; E. W. Smith, Secretary and Treasurer.

SAN FRANCISCO HUSSARS.—Organized 1857. Number of members, 68. Armory, 722 Montgomery.
Officers—G. G. Bradt, Captain; Jacob Strahle, 1st Lieutenant; William Moker, 2d Lieutenant; Jas. Irwin, 3d Lieutenant; Jno. Schreiber, Orderly Sergeant and Treasurer; Wm. Dick, Secretary.

SAN FRANCISCO TIROLLEURS, COMPANY F.—Organized March 10th, 1864. Number of members, 63. Armory, 525 Kearny Street.
Officers—R. Van Senden, Captain; Charles Segehorn, 1st Lieutenant; William Bohme, 2d Lieutenant.

SAN FRANCISCO YAGERS, COMPANY K.—Organized September 14th, 1864. Number of members, 46. Armory, Bush, near Powell.
Officers—Louis Hartmayer, Captain; August Melchers, 1st Lieutenant; Jonas Brandt, 2d Lieutenant.

SEWARD GUARD.—Organized, 1865. Number of members, 45.
Officers — Patrick Creighton, Captain; John J. Hayden, 1st Lieutenant; John Conroy, Senior 2d Lieutenant; John Gilmore, Junior 2d Lieutenant.

SHERIDAN GUARD.—Organized, 1865. Number of members, 64.
Officers—Gerard Brigaerts, Captain; I. D. Lawton, 1st Lieutenant; ———, Senior 2d Lieutenant; F. X. Murray, Junior 2d Lieutenant.

SHERMAN GUARD. — Organized 1865. Number of members, 51. Armory, N side Post opposite Union Square.
Officers — Stephen Barker, Captain; Samuel A. Rounds, 1st Lieutenant; John D. Bartlett, Senior 2d Lieutenant; Frank B. Kennedy, Junior 2d Lieutenant.

SHIELDS' GUARDS. — Organized December 21st, 1861. Number of members, 64. Armory, 567 Market Street.
Officers — George T. Knox, Captain; Jeremiah Baldwin, 1st Lieutenant; W. Barry, 2d Lieutenant; Wm. Barry, Brevet 2d Lieutenant; P. Ryan, Orderly; Geo. T. Knox, Treasurer; P. Boyle, Secretary.

SIGEL RIFLES.—Organized September 25th, 1861. Number of members, 59. Armory, south-west corner California and Kearny.
Officers—Anton Ewald, Captain; Charles Goger, 1st Lieutenant; Charles Belender, 2d Lieutenant; N. Dimmer, Brevet 2d Lieutenant; C. Manderscheid, Orderly; Jacob Knell, Treasurer; C. W. Lomler, Secretary.

STATE GUARD.—Organized November 24th, 1863. Armory 729 Market. Regular drill night, Wednesday evening. Number of members, 80.
Officers—John G. Dawes, Captain; John H. Carmany, 1st Lieutenant; Samuel L. Cutter, Jr., Senior 2d Lieutenant; Fred. C. Gummer, Junior 2d Lieutenant; Josiah Hand, 1st Sergeant; George T. Vincent, Secretary; John H. Carmany, Treasurer.

STATE GUARD CADETS.—Organized July 4th, 1864. Armory 729 Market. Regular drill night, Saturday evening. Number of members, 30.
Officers—Charles H. Thomas, Captain; George W. Studley, 1st Lieutenant; A. F. Cornell, 1st Sergeant.

STEUBEN GUARD, COMPANY E.—Organized March 4th, 1864. Number of members, 50. Armory, Platt's Music Hall.

Officers—Charles Wochatz, Captain; E. Hartman, 1st Lieutenant; F. Wuckenhauser, 2d Lieutenant; John Shisler, 3d Lieutenant.

SUMNER LIGHT GUARD.—Organized October 14th, 1861. Number of active members, 76. Armory, Turn-Verein Hall, north side Bush between Stockton and Powell.

Officers—Abram Moger, Captain; Rufus W. Thompson, 1st Lieutenant; Charles H. Daly, 2d Lieutenant; J. F. Steen, Brevet 2d Lieutenant; Frs. A. Taylor, 1st Sergeant; W. A. Plunkett, Recording Secretary; David H. Penne, Financial Secretary; Cyrus W. Carmany, Treasurer.

A class for military instruction, known as the Sumner Guard Cadets, is connected with the above company. All boys from fourteen to eighteen years of age, five feet four inches high, and well recommended, are eligible. The Cadets are under the management of a Board of Trustees, composed of the commissioned officers and 1st Sergeant of the Sumner Light Guard. The rules and regulations governing the Cadets were adopted April 4th, 1864.

TITTEL ZOUAVES, COMPANY I.—Organized July 22d, 1864. Number of members, 46. Armory, Bush Street near Powell.

Officers—John Schneider, Captain; August Janke, 1st Lieutenant; George Dockendorff, 2d Lieutenant; John Plath, 3d Lieutenant.

UNION GUARDS.—Company A, 1st Regiment C. M.—Organized April, 1861. Number of members, 60. Armory, 722 Montgomery Street.

Officers—S. D. Simmons, Captain; P. B. Quinlan, 1st Lieutenant; Daniel Gorham, 2d Lieutenant; John Mason, Brevet 2d Lieutenant; E. Casey, Orderly; (vacancy) Secretary; H. R. Reed, Treasurer.

WOLF TONE GUARD.—Organized April 12th, 1862. Number of members, 69. Armory, 567 Market Street.

Officers—Archibald Wason, Captain; (vacant) 1st Lieutenant; T. Noonan, 2d Lieutenant; D. Callaghan, Brevet 2d Lieutenant; William Simpson, Orderly; Richard McCabe, Secretary; T. Noonan, Treasurer.

WASHINGTON GUARD.—Organized December 15th, 1855. Number of members, 62. Armory, 326 Bush Street.

Officers—James B. Storer, Captain; J. M. Hurlbutt, 1st Lieutenant; Joseph Cloyes, Senier 2d Lieutenant; P. W. Barton, Junior 2d Lieutenant; H. O. Souther, Orderly Sergeant; P. W. Barton, Treasurer; C. H. Engles, Secretary.

Newspapers.

ABEND POST—German; Daily; Leo Eloesser & Co.; office 517 Clay.

ALTA CALIFORNIA—Independent; daily, weekly, and steamer; Fred'k MacCrellish & Co., 536 Sacramento.

AMERICAN FLAG—Republican; daily and weekly; D. O. McCarthy, 528 Montgomery.

CALIFORNIA CHRISTIAN ADVOCATE—Religious; weekly; M. E. Church, 711 Mission.

CALIFORNIA CHRONIK—German; weekly; Chas. Ruebl, cor Sacramento and Kearny.

CALIFORNIA DEMOKRAT—German; daily; F. Hess & Co., corner Sacramento and Kearny.

CALIFORNIA FARMER—Agricultural; weekly; Warren & Co., 320 Clay.

CALIFORNIA LEADER—Weekly; Theobalds & Co., 625 Merchant.

CALIFORNIA POLICE GAZETTE—Criminal; weekly; F. S. Harlow & Bro., 424 Battery.

CALIFORNIA RURAL HOME JOURNAL—Monthly; T. Hart Hyatt & Co., 306 Sansom.

CALIFORNIAN—Literary; weekly; Californian Publishing Co., 532 Merchant.

CALIFORNIA YOUTHS' COMPANION—Weekly; Smith & Co., 505 Clay.

CHRISTIAN SPECTATOR—Religious; weekly; Rev. O. P. Fitzgerald, Francisco near Stockton.

COURRIER DE SAN FRANCISCO—French; daily, weekly, and steamer; 617 Sansom.

DIE MONTAGS ZEITUNG—German; weekly; F. G. Walther, 621 Sansom.

DRAMATIC CHRONICLE—Daily; G. & C. DeYoung, 417 Clay.

ELEVATOR—Weekly; P. A. Bell, corner Sansom and Jackson.

EVANGEL—Religious; semi-monthly; Rev. Stephen Hilton, 528 Clay.

EVENING BULLETIN—Independent; daily, weekly, and steamer; S. F. Bulletin Co., 620 Mont.

EXAMINER—Political; daily; W. S. Moss, 535 Washington.

GOLDEN ERA—Literary; weekly; Brooks & Lawrence, 543 Clay.

GUIDE—Weekly; J. B. Faitoute & Co., 411 Clay.

HEBREW—Weekly; P. Jacoby, 505 Clay.

HEBREW OBSERVER—Religious; weekly; Rev. J. Eckman, 511 Sacramento.

IRISH NEWS—Political; weekly; J. Nunan, 510 Clay.

IRISH PEOPLE—Political; weekly; 502 Wash.

L'INDEPENDENT—French; Nueval & Chamon, 617 Commercial.

LA PAROLA—Italian; weekly; A. D. Splivalo & Co., 430 Jackson.

LA VOZ DE MEJICO—Mexican; tri-weekly; A. Mancillas, cor Montgomery and Jackson.

LE NATIONAL—French; weekly; Theo. Thiele & Co., 533 Commercial.

MERCANTILE GAZETTE AND SHIPPING REGISTER—Commercial; tri-monthly; E. D. Waters, 536 Clay.

MINING AND SCIENTIFIC PRESS—Mining; weekly; Dewey & Co., 505 Clay.

MONITOR—Catholic; weekly; Thos. A. Brady, 622 Clay.

MORNING CALL—Independent; daily; J. J. Ayers & Co., 612 Commercial.

NEW AGE—Temperance; weekly; John F. Pynch & Co., 532 Merchant.

NUEVO MUNDO—Spanish; tri-weekly; F. P. Ramirez, 603 Front.

OUR MAZEPPA—Weekly; T. de M. Hylton, 423 Washington.

PACIFIC—Religious; weekly; NE cor Front and Clay.

PACIFIC APPEAL—Political; weekly; P. Anderson, publisher, 541 Merchant.

PUCK--Literary; monthly; Loomis & Swift, 617 Clay.

RECORD—Weekly; Rice & Co., 538 Market.

SAN FRANCISCO NEWS LETTER AND CALIFORNIA ADVERTISER — Weekly; F. Marriott, 528 Clay.

SPIRIT OF THE TIMES AND FIREMAN'S JOURNAL—Independent; weekly; Chase & Boruck, SW corner Sansom and Jackson.

STOCK CIRCULAR—Brokers'; weekly; T. F. Cronise, 536 Clay.

SUNDAY MERCURY—Literary; weekly; J. Macdonough Foard & Co., 420 Montgomery.

VARIETIES—Weekly; J. Walter Walsh, 517 Clay.

WORLD'S CRISIS—Spiritual; semi-monthly; John L. Hopkins, NE cor Clay and Montgomery.

Periodicals, Etc.

CALIFORNIA TEACHER — Educational; Monthly; office, 734 Montgomery.

PACIFIC COAST BUSINESS DIRECTORY—Annually; Henry G. Langley, 612 Clay.

PACIFIC MEDICAL AND SURGICAL JOURNAL—J. Thompson & Co., Publishers: office, south-west corner Clay and Sansom.

SAN FRANCISCO DIRECTORY AND BUSINESS GUIDE — Annually; Henry G. Langley, Publisher and Proprietor; office, 612 Clay.

STATE ALMANAC AND HAND-BOOK OF STATISTICS—Annually; Henry G. Langley, Editor and Publisher; office, 612 Clay.

STATE REGISTER AND YEAR-BOOK OF FACTS—Annually; Statistical; Henry G. Langley, Editor and Publisher; office, 612 Clay.

Insurance Companies.

ACCIDENTAL INSURANCE COMPANY—New York; Capital, $250,000; Bigelow & Brother, Agents, 505 Montgomery.

ÆTNA INSURANCE COMPANY—Hartford; Capital and Assets, $4,000,000; Edward H. Parker, Agent, 224 California.

ARCTIC FIRE INSURANCE COMPANY—New York; Capital, $600,000; Bigelow & Bro., Agents, 505 Montgomery.

BRITISH AND FOREIGN MARINE INSURANCE COMPANY—Liverpool and London; Capital, $5,000,000; Falkner, Bell & Co., Agents, 430 California.

CALIFORNIA HOME INSURANCE COMPANY — Capital, $300,000; Benjamin F. Lowe, President; John G. Parker, Jr., Secretary; office, 224 California.

CALIFORNIA INSURANCE COMPANY — Capital, $200,000; Albert Miller, President; C. T. Hopkins, Secretary; office, 318 California.

CALIFORNIA LLOYDS—Office, 418 California.

COLUMBIA FIRE INSURANCE COMPANY—New York; Capital and Surplus, $600,000; R. B. Swain & Co., Agents, 206 Front.

CONNECTICUT MUTUAL LIFE INSURANCE COMPANY—Hartford; Accumulated Capital, $9,000,000; Bigelow & Bro., Agents, NW cor Montgomery and Sacramento.

CONTINENTAL INSURANCE COMPANY—New York; Capital, $1,600,000; C. Adolphe Low & Co., Agents, 426 California.

EQUITABLE LIFE ASSURANCE COMPANY—New York; Assets, $500,000; Bigelow & Bro., Agents, NW corner Mont and Sacramento.

FIREMAN'S FUND INSURANCE COMPANY—San Francisco; Capital, $500,000; S. H. Parker, President; C. R. Bond, Sec.; office, 238 Mont.

GERMANIA LIFE INSURANCE COMPANY—B. Gattel, Agent, 519 Montgomery.

GERMAN MUTUAL FIRE INSURANCE COMPANY—San Francisco; office, 58 Montgomery Block; office hours, 2 to 3 o'clock, P.M.

GUARDIAN LIFE INSURANCE COMPANY—New York; Capital, $250,000; James R. Garniss, Agent, 526 Washington.

HAMBURGH AND BREMEN FIRE INSURANCE COMPANY — Capital, $1,000,000; Morris Speyer, Agent, 526 Washington.

HARTFORD FIRE INSURANCE COMPANY—Hartford; Assets, $1,500,000; Bigelow & Bro. Agents, NW cor Montgomery and Sacramento.

HOME INSURANCE COMPANY—New York; Capital, $3,500,000; Bigelow & Bro., Agents, NW cor Montgomery and Sacramento. .

HOME MUTUAL FIRE, LIFE, AND MARINE INSURANCE COMPANY -- San Francisco; Capital, $1,000,000; Geo. S. Mann, President; Wm. H. Stevens, Secretary; office, 630 Mont.

IMPERIAL FIRE AND LIFE INSURANCE COMPANY — London; Capital, $8,000,000; Falkner, Bell & Co., Agents, 430 California.

LIVERPOOL AND LONDON AND GLOBE FIRE AND LIFE INSURANCE COMPANY—

Capital, $15,000,000; invested in the United States, $1,500,000; W. B. Johnston, Agent, 414 Mont'ry.

LONDON AND LANCASHIRE FIRE IN-SURANCE COMPANY—Capital, $5,000,000; H. Dreschfeld, Agent, 623 Montgomery.

MANHATTAN FIRE INSURANCE COMPANY—New York; Capital and Assets, $826,000; R. B. Swain & Co., Agents, 206 Front.

MANHATTAN LIFE INSURANCE COMPANY—New York; Capital, $2,000,000; John Landers, Agent, SW cor Montgomery and Clay.

MERCHANTS' MUTUAL MARINE INSURANCE CO.—San Francisco; Capital, $500,000; J. P. Flint, President; J. B. Scotchler, Secretary; office, corner California and Front.

MUTUAL LIFE INSURANCE COMPANY—New York; Capital and Assets, $13,500,000; H. S. Homans, General Agent, 609 Clay.

MUTUAL LIFE INSURANCE COMPANY—New York; Capital and Assets, $13,500,000; W. K. Van Alen, Agent, corner Washington and Sansom.

NEW YORK LIFE INSURANCE COMPANY—New York; Accumulated Capital, $4,250,000; R. N. Van Brunt, Agent, corner Mont and California.

NIAGARA FIRE INSURANCE COMPANY—New York; Capital, $1,000,000; John Landers, Agent, south-west corner Montgomery and Clay.

NORTH AMERICA LIFE INSURANCE CO.—New York; J. A. Eaton & Co., General Agents; Samuel Pillsbury, Agent, 240 Montgomery.

NORTH AMERICAN FIRE INSURANCE COMPANY—New York; Capital, $700,000; C. Adolphe Low & Co. Agents, 426 California.

NORTH BRITISH AND MERCANTILE INSURANCE COMPANY—Capital, $10,000,000; W. H. Tillinghast, Agent, 414 California.

NORTHERN ASSURANCE COMPANY—London and Aberdeen; Capital, $10,000,000; W. L. Booker, Agent, 428 California.

OCCIDENTAL INSURANCE COMPANY—San Francisco; Capital, $300,000; Henry B. Platt, President; R. N. Van Brunt, Secretary; office, south-west corner Montgomery and California.

PACIFIC INSURANCE COMPANY — San Francisco; Capital, $750,000; J. Hunt, President; A. J. Ralston, Secretary; office, 436 California.

PHENIX FIRE INSURANCE COMPANY—New York; Capital, $1,000,000; Bigelow & Bro. Agents; north-west corner Mont and Sacramento.

PHŒNIX INSURANCE COMPANY—Hartford; Capital and Assets, over $1,000,000; R. H. Magill, General Agent; L. B. Dell, Agent; office, south-west corner Montgomery and Commercial.

ROYAL FIRE AND LIFE INSURANCE COMPANY — Liverpool and London; Capital, $10,000,000; Alsop & Co. Agents, 411 California.

SAN FRANCISCO INSURANCE COMPANY—Capital, $250,000; office, 432 Montgomery; G. C. Boardman, President; P. McShane, Secretary.

SECURITY FIRE INSURANCE COMPANY

—New York; Assets, $2,000,000; Bigelow & Bro. Agents, north-west corner Montgomery and Sacramento.

TRAVELERS' INSURANCE COMPANY—Hartford; (Insurance against Accidents); Capital, $500,000; R. H. Magill, General Agent; L. B. Dell, Agent; office, south-west cor Mont and Commercial.

TRAVELERS' INSURANCE CO.—New York; Capital, $500,000; Francis Schultze, General Agent, 623 Montgomery.

UNION INSURANCE COMPANY—Capital, $750,000; Caleb T. Fay, President; Charles D. Haven, Secretary; office, 416 California.

UNIVERSAL LIFE INSURANCE COMPANY—New York; Capital, $2,000,000; H. S. Homans, General Agent, 609 Clay Street.

WASHINGTON FIRE INSURANCE COMPANY—New York; Capital, $600,000; Bigelow & Bro. Agents, north-west corner Mont and Sac.

WASHINGTON MARINE INSURANCE CO.—New York; Capital, $500,000; C. J. Janson, Agent, 210 Pine.

WIDOWS AND ORPHANS BENEFIT LIFE INSURANCE COMPANY—New York; Capital, $200,000; H. S. Homans, General Agent, 609 Clay.

Telegraph Lines.

CALIFORNIA STATE TELEGRAPH COMPANY—Capital Stock, $2,500,000; office, 507 Montgomery Street; office hours from 8, A.M. to 10, P.M. Sundays 1, P.M. to 4, P.M.

Officers—H. W. Carpentier, President; J. Mora Moss, Vice President; Frederick MacCrellish, Lloyd Tevis, J. Mora Moss, H. W. Carpentier, H. H. Haight, W. C. Ralston, and J. M. McDonald, Board of Directors; R. E. Brewster, Treasurer; Geo. S. Ladd, Secretary; Geo. S. Ladd, General Superintendent; R. R. Haines and W. R. Yontz, Assistant Superintendents. This line extends to the following places, and connects at Salt Lake with the lines for the Atlantic States:

California—Auburn, Benicia, Bowers, Coloma, Camptonville, Columbia, Chico, Calistoga Springs, Callahan's, Copperopolis, Centreville, Colfax, Downieville, Donner Lake, Drytown, Dutch Flat, El Dorado, Folsom, Forest City, Fort Tejon, Forest Hill, Fort Jones, Friday's, Georgetown, Grass Valley, Gilroy, Healdsburg, Ione City, Iowa Hill, Jackson, Kingston, Los Angeles, Lincoln, Latrobe, Marysville, Martinez, Mokelumne H., Markleeville, Murphy's, Monterey, Monitor, Napa, Nevada, Oakland, Oroville, Petaluma, Placerville, Redwood, Rough and Ready, Red Bluff, Siskiyou, Sugar Loaf, San Francisco, San José, San Juan, N., San Juan, S., San Andreas, San Leandro, San Mateo, Santa Rosa, Santa Cruz, Santa Clara, Sacramento, Stockton, Sonora, Smartsville, Suisun, Shasta, Strawberry, Shingle Spring, Silver City, Sonoma, San Rafael, Sportsman's H., Sutter Creek, Silver Mountain, Todd's Valley, Trinity Centre, Timbuctoo, Tehama, Volcano, Visalia, Vallejo, Watsonville, Washoe, Weaverville, Warm Springs, Yank's Station, Yreka, and Yankee Jim's.

Oregon—Albany, Corvallis, Canyonville, Eugene City, Grave Creek, Jacksonville, Mountain House, Oakland, Oregon City, Portland, Roseburg, and Salem.

Nevada—Austin, Aurora, Carson, Dayton, Egan

Cañon, Fort Churchill, Genoa, Ophir, Ruby Valley, Star City, Unionville, Virginia City, West Gate, Wellington, and Williamsburg.

Washington Territory — Drew's, Monticello, Martin's Bluffs, Olympia, Point Elliott, San Juan Island, Seattle, Steilacoom, Suniahmoo, Swinomish, Tulalip, and Vancouver.

Utah Territory—Deep Creek, Ft. Crittenden, Fish Springs, and Salt Lake City.

British Columbia — N. Westminster, Victoria, and Vancouver's Island.

UNITED STATES PACIFIC TELEGRAPH COMPANY—(In the course of construction) James Gamble, General Superintendent; James Street, General Agent; office, 2 Armory Hall.

Railroads.*

CENTRAL RAILROAD CO.—Office east side Taylor, bet Turk and Eddy.

CITY RAILROAD CO.—Office 326 Clay.

FRONT STREET, MISSION, AND OCEAN RAILROAD.—Office 529 Clay.

MARKET STREET AND MISSION DOLORES.—Office corner Montgomery and Jackson.

NORTH BEACH AND MISSION RAILROAD CO.—Office corner Fourth and Louisa.

OMNIBUS RAILROAD. — Office south side Howard between Third and Fourth.

SACRAMENTO VALLEY RAILROAD CO.— Office 734 Montgomery.

SAN FRANCISCO AND ALAMEDA RAILROAD.—Office SW corner Sansom and Jackson.

SAN FRANCISCO AND ATLANTIC RAILROAD CO.—Office 405 Front.

SAN FRANCISCO AND OAKLAND RAILROAD.—Office 535 Clay.

SAN FRANCISCO AND SAN JOSE RAILROAD.—Office corner Sansom and Halleck.

WESTERN PACIFIC RAILROAD.—Office 409 California.

Ocean Steamers.

CHINA, JAPAN, AND THE SANDWICH ISLANDS.—Pacific Mail Steamship Co. Monthly. Oliver Eldridge, Agent. Office NW corner Sacramento and Leidesdorff.

LIVERPOOL, NEW YORK, AND PHILADELPHIA.—F. A. Emory, Agent. Office 302 Montgomery.

MEXICAN COAST.—Mexican Steamship Line. For Cape St. Lucas, Mazatlan, Guaymas, and La Paz, monthly. Steamer John L. Stephens. Ben Holladay, proprietor. Office SW corner Front and Jackson.

NEW YORK *via* PANAMA.—Pacific Mail

Steamship. Co.; tenth, twentieth, and thirtieth of each month. When either of these dates falls on a Sunday, the departure takes place on the following day. Steamers Constitution, Golden Age, Golden City, Colorado, and Sacramento. Oliver Eldridge, Agent. Office NW corner Sac and Leidesdorff.

NEW YORK.—People's Opposition *via* Nicaragua. Central American Transit Co. Steamers Moses Taylor and America. I. W. Raymond, Agent, NW corner Battery and Pine.

NORTHERN COAST.—California and Oregon Steamship Co. For Eureka (Humboldt Bay), Trinidad and Crescent City. Semi-monthly. Steamers Del Norte and Panama. Ben. Holladay, proprietor. Office SW corner Front and Jackson.

NORTHERN COAST.—California and Oregon Steamship Line. For Portland, Oregon, and Victoria, V. I. Steamers Oriflamme, Sierra Nevada, and Oregon. Ben. Holladay, proprietor, SW corner Front and Jackson.

NORTHERN COAST.—California Steam Navigation Co.'s Steamship Line. For Portland, Oregon, and Victoria, V. I. Steamers Pacific and Orizaba. California Steam Navigation Company, proprietors. Office NE corner Front and Jackson.

ROYAL MAIL STEAM PACKET CO.—W. L. Booker, Agent. Office 428 California.

SOUTHERN COAST.—California Steam Navigation Co.'s Steamship Line. For San Luis Obispo, Santa Barbara, San Pedro, and San Diego. Steamer Senator. California Steam Navigation Company, proprietors. Office NE corner Front and Jackson.

WEST INDIA AND PACIFIC STEAMSHIP CO.—Rodgers, Meyers & Co., Agents, 314 Wash.

Steamboats, Etc.

ALAMEDA FERRY. — Leaves Pacific Street Wharf, daily, at stated hours. Alfred A. Cohen, Superintendent. Office SW corner Jackson and Sansom.

ALCATRAZ FERRY.—Hourly; foot Meiggs' Wharf.

NAPA, MARE ISLAND, AND VALLEJO.— Leaves Broadway Wharf every Tuesday, Thursday, and Saturday, at 11, A.M. E. J. Weeks, Agent, 405 Front.

OAKLAND FERRY.—Leaves the corner of Pacific and Davis streets, daily, at stated hours. George Goss, Superintendent.

PETALUMA, BODEGA, SANTA ROSA, BIG RIVER, UKIAH, ETC.—Steamer Josie McNear. Leaves East near Wash, Tuesdays, Thursdays, and Saturdays. McNear & Brother, Agents, 37. Clay.

PETALUMA.—Steamer Relief. Leaves Commercial Street Wharf, Tuesdays, Thursdays, and Saturdays. T. F. Bayliss & Co. Agents, Petaluma.

SACRAMENTO, MARYSVILLE, AND THE NORTHERN MINES.—California Steam Navigation Co.'s steamers, leave Broadway Wharf, daily, at 4, P.M. Office NE corner Front and Jackson.

SAN PABLO AND SAN QUENTIN FERRY. —Steamer leaves corner of Broadway and Davis

---

* See General Review for a description of the various roads now in course of construction.

streets, daily, at 8, A.M. and 2, P.M.   C. Minturn, Agent, Vallejo Street Wharf.

SANTA CRUZ AND SALINAS.—Office 204 Clay.

SONOMA *via* LAKEVILLE AND PETALUMA.—Steamer leaves Vallejo Street Wharf, daily. C. Minturn, Agent, Vallejo Street Wharf.

STOCKTON AND SOUTHERN MINES.—California Steam Navigation Co.'s steamers leave Broadway Wharf, daily, at 4, P.M. Office NE corner Front and Jackson.

SUISUN AND BENICIA. — Steamer leaves Broadway Wharf every Tuesday, Thursday, and Saturday, at 10, A.M.

Incorporated Companies.*

AMERICAN RUSSIAN COMMERCIAL COMPANY.—Office, 718 Battery.

BAY SUGAR COMPANY.—Capital $250,000. Office, south-west corner Battery and Union. H. Meese, Manager.

CALIFORNIA BUILDING, LOAN AND SAVINGS SOCIETY.—Thomas Mooney, President ; L. R. Townsend, Secretary ; Samuel Crim, A. Rosenfield, C. A. Janke, L. R. Townsend, J. G. Wier, John W. McCormick, Robert Lewellyn, Thomas Mooney, and John Dunn, Directors. Office, 406 Montgomery.

CALIFORNIA COAL MINING COMPANY.— Capital, $5,000,000.
Officers—F. L. A. Pioche, President ; J. H. Applegate, Secretary. Office, south-east corner Montgomery and Jackson.

CALIFORNIA MINING BUREAU ASSOCIATION.—Incorporated October 19th, 1865. Office, south-east corner Montgomery and Pine.
Officers—A. J. Snyder, President ; J. B. Whitcomb, Recording Secretary ; J. F. Lintbicum, Corresponding Secretary.

CALIFORNIA STATE TELEGRAPH COMPANY.—Capital Stock, $2,500,000 ; office, 507 Montgomery ; office hours from 8, A.M. to 10, P.M. ; Sundays, 1, P.M. to 4, P.M.

CALIFORNIA STEAM NAVIGATION CO.— Organized March 1st, 1854. Capital, $2,500,000.
Officers—James Whitney, Jr., President ; B. M. Hartshorne, Vice President ; S. O. Putnam, Secretary ; Samuel J. Hensley, James Whitney, Jr., Alfred Redington, Wm. Norris, W. H. Moor, B. M. Hartshorne, John Bensley, N. C. Paddock, and C. L. Low, Trustees; Alfred Redington and Wm. H. Taylor, Sacramento, G. P. Jessup, Marysville, J. B. Andrus, Red Bluff, and Arthur Cornwall, Stockton, Agents. Office, 602 Front.

CENTRAL AMERICAN TRANSIT CO.—I. W. Raymond, Agent, north-west corner Battery and Pine.

CENTRAL RAILROAD.—Incorporated 1861. Capital, $500,000 ; office, Taylor between Turk and Eddy.
Officers—R. J. Vandewater, President ; S. C.

* For Mining Companies see Register of Names ; for other Incorporated Companies see appropriate heads.

Bigelow, Vice President ; John T. Hoyt, Secretary ; A. J. Gunnison, Treasurer ; John A. McGlynn, Superintendent ; J. Whitney, jr., B. M. Hartshorne, George H. Davis, Charles Main, E. H. Winchester, A. J. Gunnison, and John A. McGlynn, Directors.

CITIZENS' GAS COMPANY. — Incorporated December, 1862. Capital, $2,000,000. Office, 702 Washington.
Officers—A. C. Whitcomb, President ; Samuel I. C. Swezey, Secretary ; Calvin Paige, John Benson, R. M. Jessup, John Bensley, and A. C. Whitcomb, Trustees.

CITY RAILROAD COMPANY.—Incorporated May 20th, 1863. Capital, $1,000,000. Office, 326 Clay.
Officers—Isaac Rowell, President ; J. P. Whitney, Vice President ; E. W. Casey, Secretary ; O. F. Willey, Treasurer ; Isaac Rowell, J. P. Whitney, Michael Fennell, H. Kimball, George Barstow, A. J. Gladding, and Crayton Winton, Directors.

FRANCO AMERICAN COMMERCIAL COMPANY.—Office, 215 Bush. J. A. Getze, F. C. Hagedorn, John Bioren, W. H. Clay, and F. A. Gentze, Trustees.

FRONT STREET, MISSION, AND OCEAN RAILROAD COMPANY.—Incorporated May 23d, 1863. Capital Stock, $1,000,000. Office, 529 Clay.
Officers—H. H. Haight, President ; H. P. Coon, Vice President ; John Barton, Treasurer ; David Wilder, Secretary ; H. H. Haight, H. P. Coon, John Barton, G. W. Dam, J. T. Godfrey, H. P. Herrick, and S. S. Tilton, Directors.

HIBERNIA SAVINGS AND LOAN SOCIETY. —Incorporated April 12th, 1859. Office, 506 Jackson, near Montgomery.
Officers—M. D. Sweeny, President ; C. D. O. Sullivan, Vice President ; Edward Martin, Treasurer ; Richard Tobin, Attorney.

NORTH BEACH AND MISSION RAILROAD COMPANY.—Incorporated August 23d, 1862. Capital, $1,000,000. Office, west side Fourth corner Louisa.
Officers—Dr. A. J. Bowie, President ; James T. Boyd, Vice President ; Willet Sonthwick, Secretary ; Michael Reese, Treasurer ; M. Skelly, Superintendent ; Dr. A. J. Bowie, Michael Reese, James T. Boyd, Michael Skelly, Andrew L. Morrison, Henry A. Lyons, John S. Hager, and Alpheus Bull, Directors.

OMNIBUS RAILROAD COMPANY.—Incorporated, 1861. Capital, $1,000,000. Office, south side Howard between Third and Fourth.
Officers—Peter Donahue, President ; E. Casserly, Vice President ; W. H. Lyons, Treasurer ; James O'Neil, Secretary ; John Gardner, Superintendent ; Peter Donahue, Eugene Casserly, H. M. Newhall, Wm. H. Lyon, Wm. Thompson, Jr., J. O. Eldridge, and John Gardner, Directors.

PACIFIC ACCUMULATION LOAN COMPANY.—Capital, $5,000,000. Office, 400 Montgomery Street.

PACIFIC GLASS WORKS COMPANY.—Potrero, two miles from Brannan Street Bridge. Office, 621 Clay. Giles H. Gray, Agent.

PACIFIC MAIL STEAMSHIP COMPANY.— Office, north-west cor Sacramento and Leidesdorff.

QUICKSILVER MINING COMPANY.—Office, 205 Battery.

SAN BRUNO TURNPIKE COMPANY.—Office, 626 Clay.

SAN FRANCISCO AND ALAMEDA RAILROAD COMPANY.—Office, south-west corner Sansom and Jackson.
Officers—F. D. Atherton, President; A. A. Cohen, Superintendent and Secretary.

SAN FRANCISCO AND ATLANTIC RAILROAD COMPANY.—Capital, $20,000,000. Office, 405 Front.

SAN FRANCISCO AND OAKLAND RAILWAY.—Incorporated 1862. Capital, $500,000; office 535 Clay.

SAN FRANCISCO AND PACIFIC SUGAR COMPANY.—Capital, $800,000. Office, Eighth between Folsom and Harrison.
Officers—George Gordon, President; N. Luning, W. C. Ralston, Charles DeRo, and R. Feuerstein, Trustees; George Gordon, Manager; R. Feuerstein, Commercial Agent, 310 Commercial.

SAN FRANCISCO AND SAN JOSE RAILROAD.—Incorporated July 21st, 1860. Capital, $2,000,000. Office, south-east corner Sansom and Halleck.
Officers—H. M. Newhall, President; John T. Doyle, Vice President; D. O. Mills, Treasurer; Joseph L. Willcutt, Secretary; Charles B. Polhemus, General Superintendent; H. M. Newhall, John T. Doyle, D. O. Mills, C. B. Polhemus, F. D. Atherton, Peter Donahue, and S. J. Hensley, Directors.

SAN FRANCISCO GAS COMPANY.—Organized August, 1852. Capital, $2,000,000.
Original Officers—Beverly C. Sanders, President; John Crane, Secretary.
Present Officers—Peter Donahue, President; Joseph A. Donohoe, Vice President; Joseph G. Eastland, Secretary; Peter Donahue, Joseph A. Donohoe, Joseph G. Eastland, Louis McLane, and James Bell, Trustees; Tyler Sabbatton, Engineer and Superintendent; William G. Barrett, Cashier; Norton Bush and Arthur K. Hawkins, Clerks; George A. Young, John B. Gallagher, George H. Lovegrove, James Brereton, Thomas O'Brien, James Fitzpatrick, and J. W. O'Kane Collectors.

SAN FRANCISCO MARKET STREET RAILROAD.—Incorporated 1857. Office, south-east cor Montgomery and Jackson.
Officers—A. Caselli, President; Frank McCoppin, Levi Parsons, R. Bayerque, and Henry Pichoir, Directors. Superintendent's office, west side Valencia near Sixteenth.

SAN FRANCISCO SAVINGS UNION.—Office, 529 California.

SAVINGS AND LOAN SOCIETY.—Incorporated July 23d, 1857. Office, 619 Clay.

SPRING VALLEY WATER WORKS COMPANY.—Capital, $3,000,000.
Officers—William F. Babcock, President; Wm. T, Coleman, Vice President; Henry Wattson, Secretary; Calvin Brown, Treasurer; William F. Babcock, Lloyd Tevis, S. C. Bigelow, Nicholas Luning, Charles Mayne, H. S. Dexter, and John Parrott, Trustees. Office, south-east corner Montgomery and Jackson.

THE BANK OF CALIFORNIA.—South-west corner Battery and Washington streets. Capital stock, $2,000,000, with the privilege of increasing to $5,000,000. D. O. Mills, Pres't; W. C. Ralston, Cash.

VULCAN IRON WORKS COMPANY.—Nos. 137 and 139 First. Capital, $250,000.
Officers—N. D. Arnott, President; Sam'l Aitken, Vice President; Richard Ivers, Treasurer; Charles R. Steiger, Sec'y; Joseph Moore, Superintendent.

WELLS, FARGO & CO.—This is a joint stock company, with a capital of $2,000,000. Principal office in New York, 84 Broadway. Principal office in California, in Parrott's Building, corner Montgomery and California streets. This company has branch express offices in all the principal cities and towns in California, Oregon, Nevada, Idaho, and Washington Territories, and banking offices at Sacramento and Stockton, California; Portland, Oregon; Victoria, V. I.; Virginia and Carson, Nevada; connecting in their express business with all the principal express companies in the Atlantic States and Europe. Established branch in California, July 13th, 1852.
Officers—D. N. Barney, President; C. F. Latham, Treasurer; Louis McLane, General Agent; Samuel Knight, Superintendent Express and Banking Departments.

WESTERN PACIFIC RAILROAD.—Incorporated December 11th, 1862. Capital, $5,400,000. Office, 409 California.
Officers—Charles N. Fox, President; Erastus S. Holden, Vice President; Charles W. Sanger, Secretary; B. F. Mann, Treasurer; M. L. Strangroom, Chief Engineer; Charles McLaughlin, Contractor; Charles N. Fox, B. F. Mann, John Center, E. T. Pease, Charles W. Sanger, S. O. Houghton, and E. S. Holden, Directors.

Consuls.

[See Business Directory, p. 496.]

Boards of Brokers.

SAN FRANCISCO STOCK AND EXCHANGE BOARD—Organized Sept. 11th, 1863. Number of members, 76. Rooms, north-west corner Montgomery and Washington.
Officers—J. B. E. Cavallier, President; Franklin Lawton, Secretary; Henry Schmiedell, Treasurer.

AUTHORIZED SCALE OF COMMISSION.
[Adopted January 7th, 1864.]

MISCELLANEOUS.

Funded Debt, on par	⅛ per cent.
Insurance Stocks, on par	½ "
Gas Stocks, on par	½ "
Railroad Stocks, on par	½ "
Steamboat Stocks, on par	½ "
Telegraph Co. Stocks, on par	½ "
Water Co. Stocks, on par	½ "
Legal Tender Notes and Bonds, on par	⅛ "
Bills of Exchange, on net amount	⅛ "
Mint Certificate, on net amount	⅛ "
Specie, on net amount	⅛ "

COMMISSION ON MINING SHARES.

Sale at 1 dollar up to 10 dollars	$0 25 per foot.
Sale at 10 dollars up to 25 dollars	50 "
Sale at 25 dollars up to 50 dollars	1 00 "
Sale at 50 dollars up to 100 dollars	1 50 "
Sale at 100 dollars up to 200 dollars	2 50 "
Sale at 200 dollars up to 400 dollars	5 00 "
Sale at 400 dollars up to 600 dollars	6 00 "
Sale at 600 dollars up to 800 dollars	7 50 "

From $800 to $3,000 per foot, one per cent. on the amount of purchase or sale.
Anything above $3,000 per foot, three-quarters of one per cent. on the amount of purchase or sale.

PACIFIC BOARD OF BROKERS—Organized July, 1863. No. members, 40. Rooms, 606 Wash.
Officers—Minor S. Martin, President; James H. Gager, Secretary; E. L. Smith, Treasurer.

Stages.

HALFMOON BAY.—Tuesday, Thursday, and Saturday, at 9 o'clock, A.M. Office SE corner Washington and Kearny.

NEW ALMADEN, ETC.—Via San José R. R. connect at San José daily—summer at 8, A.M., and winter at 9, A.M. for Gilroy, San Juan, Watsonville, Guadalupe Mines, New Almaden Mines, and Warm Springs.

PESCADERO, ETC.—Via San José R. R. connect at San Mateo, daily at 8, A.M., summer, and 9, A.M., winter, for Crystal Springs, Spanish Town, Halfmoon Bay, and Pescadero.

PLACERVILLE (CALIFORNIA), AND ST. JOSEPH (MO.)—Great Overland Mail, via Salt Lake City, daily, at 4 o'clock, P.M. Office NW corner Montgomery and California.

PRESIDIO AND FORT POINT. — Hourly, daily. Office Kearny Street opposite Plaza.

SEAL ROCK, POINT LOBOS, ETC.—Hourly, connecting with the Central Railroad cars at Lone Mountain.

VISALIA, ETC.—Via San José R. R. Stage connects at San José Mondays, Wednesdays, and Fridays, with the trains which leave at 8, A.M., summer, and 9, A.M., winter, for Monterey, Natividad, Hot Springs, San Luis Obispo, Santa Barbara, Los Angeles and Visalia.

Expresses.

CITY LETTER EXPRESS.—Office SE corner Washington and Sansom.

CONTRA COSTA EXPRESS.—Bamber & Co. Office 719 Davis between Broadway and Vallejo

MISSION DOLORES EXPRESS.—J. & H. Dorland and John Couch. Leaves Stage Office, corner Kearny and Merchant, at 2, P.M. and 5, P.M., daily.

SAN FRANCISCO AND SAN JOSE EXPRESS.—Truman & Co. Office SE corner Washington and Front.

SAN FRANCISCO AND SAN JOSE EXPRESS (BAGGAGE).—M. G. Kennedy. Office 679 Market.

WELLS, FARGO & CO.'S EXPRESS.—Daily, to all parts of California, Nevada, and Eastern States, per Overland Mail (for letters only). Weekly, to Crescent City, Oregon, Washington Territory, Vancouver's Island, and the Southern Coast, and tri-monthly to the Atlantic States and Europe. Office, north-west corner California and Montgomery streets.

Hospitals.

COUNTY HOSPITAL.—South-west corner Francisco and Stockton. W. T. Garwood, M.D., Resident Physician; F. A. Holman, M.D., Visiting Surgeon; A. G. Soule, M.D., Visiting Physician; M.

B. Pond, Apothecary. Average number of patients, three hundred and seventy; daily admission, four. Deaths about ten per cent. per annum.

BRITISH HOSPITAL.—Sustained by the British Benevolent Society. [See Benevolent Associations.]

FRENCH HOSPITAL.—Sustained by the French Benevolent Society; Brannan between Fifth and Sixth. [See Benevolent Associations.]

GERMAN HOSPITAL.—Sustained by the German Benevolent Society; Brannan and Third. [See Benevolent Associations.]

HOSPITAL OF THE SISTERS OF MERCY. —Corner Bryant and First. Conducted by the Sisters of Mercy. Sister Mary B. Russell, Superior; Drs. H. H. Toland and J. P. Whitney, Visiting Physicians; Dr. J. Lee, Resident Physician.

ITALIAN HOSPITAL.—Sustained by the Italian Mutual Benevolent Society. [See Benevolent Associations.]

UNITED STATES MARINE HOSPITAL.— Rincon Point, between Main and Spear. Organized March 16th, 1852.
Officers—John Hastings, Surgeon and Resident Physician. Daily admittance, three; deaths per month, two, average number of patients, one hundred and five.

Cemeteries.*

CEMETERY, HEBREW.—"Hills of Eternity" (Gibboth Olom) Dolores, Nineteenth, Twentieth, and Church, Mission Dolores. Jacob Rich, Secretary, 638 Sacramento.

CEMETERY, HEBREW.—"Home of Peace," (Nevai Shalome) Dolores, Eighteenth, Nineteenth, and Church, Mission Dolores. David Stern, Secretary, south-east corner California and Sansom.

CEMETERY, HEBREW.—North-side Broadway, between Franklin and Gough, Presidio.

CEMETERY, LONE MOUNTAIN.—Two and a half miles west from Montgomery, and opposite California. Nathaniel Gray, Jos. H. Atkinson, and Charles C. Butler, Proprietors; W. K. Van Alen, Treasurer; Frederick Mowe, Superintendent. Office No. 6 Government House.

CEMETERY, MASONIC.—Near Lone Mountain. George J. Hobe, Secretary; office, Masonic Temple.

CEMETERY, ODD FELLOWS.—Near Lone Mountain. H. C. Squire, Secretary; office, 325 Montgomery.

CEMETERY, ROMAN CATHOLIC.—Mission Dolores, Burial Ground adjoining the Church, Mission Dolores.

CEMETERY, ROMAN CATHOLIC.—Mount Calvary, adjoining Lone Mountain Cemetery. The burial services are attended to by the clergymen of St. Bridget's Church, from 3 to 5, P.M., from March to October, and from 2½ to 4, P.M., from November to April.

* See General Review, for a detailed description of the different Cemeteries.

MARINE INSURANCE.

THE BRITISH AND FOREIGN

MARINE INSURANCE CO.,

OF LIVERPOOL AND LONDON.

CAPITAL, $5,000,000.

The Undersigned having been appointed Agents at this Port for the Company above named, are now prepared to effect

INSURANCE ON MERCHANDISE, SPECIE, AND FREIGHT,

To and from all parts of the world.

LOSSES PAID IN GOLD COIN.

FALKNER, BELL & CO.,

No. 430 California Street.

FIRE INSURANCE.

MANHATTAN

FIRE INSURANCE COMPANY,

OF NEW YORK,
INCORPORATED, 1821.

Cash Capital, ... $500,000
Surplus, over 250,000
    Total Assets, over $750,000

COLUMBIA

FIRE INSURANCE COMPANY,

OF NEW YORK.
INCORPORATED, 1858.

Cash Capital, ... $500,000
Surplus, over 70,000
    Total Assets, ... $570,000

The above named responsible and well known Companies have complied with the law of the State of California, and have each deposited **$75,000** as additional security for policy holders.
  Buildings, Merchandise, Furniture, and other property, Insured against loss or damage by Fire, on the most favorable terms. Losses promptly adjusted, and paid in UNITED STATES GOLD COIN.

R. B. SWAIN & CO.,
206 FRONT STREET,   General Agents, San Francisco.

PALMER, KNOX & CO.

GOLDEN STATE

IRON WORKS,

Nos. 19, 21, 23, and 25 First Street,

SAN FRANCISCO.

Manufacture all kinds of

MACHINERY,

Steam Engines and Quartz Mills;

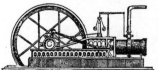

DUNBAR'S IMPROVED
SELF ADJUSTING PISTON PACKING,

Requires no springs or screws; is always steam-tight; without excessive friction, and never gets slack or leaky.

Wheeler & Randall's

NEW GRINDER AND AMALGAMATOR;

HEPBURN & PETERSON'S AMALGAMATOR AND SEPARATOR;

Tyler's Improved Water Wheel,

Giving the greatest power, at lower cost, than any Wheel in use. There are over 1,500 running, giving universal satisfaction.

KNOX'S AMALGAMATORS,

WITH PALMER'S PATENT STEAM CHEST,

Superior for working either Gold or Silver Ores.

GENUINE WHITE IRON STAMP SHOES AND DIES.

Having been engaged for the past eight years in quartz mining, and being conversant with all the improvements, either in Mining or Milling, we are prepared to furnish, at the shortest notice, the most perfect machinery for reducing ores, or saving either Gold or Silver.

Interior View of one of our Quartz Mills for Silver.   Miners' Foundry and Machine Works, First Street, San Francisco.

VAN VLECK

PHILADELPHIA

BREWERY

Corner of Second and Folsom Streets,

SAN FRANCISCO.

WE TAKE THE PRESENT OPPORTUNITY OF THANKING OUR
Friends and Customers for the liberal support heretofore extended to the

PHILADELPHIA BREWERY,

And notify them that we have added to our Establishment

NEW AND EXTENSIVE BUILDINGS,

By which we hope, through the greatly increased facilities, now possessed by us,
to furnish, as usual,

A SUPERIOR ARTICLE OF BEER,

That shall not only equal that previously furnished by us, but convince them
that we are determined to merit their continued patronage and support.

.A½.

HOELSCHER & WIELAND.

C. H. HARRISON,

PHŒNIX OIL WORKS

[ESTABLISHED 1850,]

517 FRONT STREET, BETWEEN WASHINGTON AND JACKSON,

Manufacturer, Importer of, and Dealer in

SPERM, LARD, POLAR, KEROSENE, AND OTHER OILS.

Also, Office of Benicia and Mare Island Pilot.

HARRISON'S ECCENTRIC PUMP.

This Pump is designed for throwing large quantities of water, either as a wrecking pump, a mining pump, or for irrigation. Its principal advantages are that it is light and compact, very durable, and not at all liable to choke or get out of order. It has no valves and no packing. It is a suction and force pump, and has sucked the water up over 27½ feet.

It can be run fast or slow, and according to its speed is the quantity of water discharged.

All sizes, capable of throwing from 100 to 5,000 gallons per minute, for sale by

C. H. HARRISON,
Phœnix Oil Works, 517 Front Street, S. F.

B. PULVERMAN,

COLLECTOR OF BILLS, NOTES, RENTS, ETC.,

No. 526 Montgomery Street, San Francisco,

Near Clay, over the Blue Wing.

SUITS INSTITUTED AND ATTENDED FOR CLAIMANTS.

Office Hours—From 1 to 3 o'clock, P. M.

BY PERMISSION REFERS TO

Hon. ALEX. CAMPBELL, late Judge Twelfth District Court. | W. H. RICHARDS & CO., Sansom St.
Hon. P. W. SHEPHEARD, Police Judge. | LEO ELOESSER, Esq.; Editor Abend Post.

DR. LIBBEY,

SURGICAL AND MECHANICAL DENTIST,

109 Montgomery Street, Between Bush and Sutter,

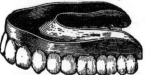

OPERATES IN EVERY DEPARTMENT OF DENTISTRY,

As low and as well as any good Dentist in the State.

☞ *All operations guaranteed to give satisfaction.*

109 MONTGOMERY STREET,

SAN FRANCISCO.

EMPORIUM OF FASHION.

New and Elegant Millinery & Dress-Making Establishment

MRS. C. M. CHAPMAN

Takes this method of announcing to the Ladies that she has established a

FIRST-CLASS MILLINERY AND DRESS-MAKING HOUSE

AT No. 218 THIRD STREET, IN COLTON BUILDING.

Mrs. Belden and *Mrs. Akin* have charge of the MILLINERY DEPARTMENT, and will be pleased to see their friends at all times.

Miss Gage, from MME. DEMOREST'S great Emporium of Fashion, in New York, has charge of the DRESS-MAKING DEPARTMENT.

☞ MISS GAGE is the only authorized Agent of Mme. Demorest's Emporium of Fashion on this coast, and guarantees to give perfect satisfaction, as heretofore, to all who may favor her with their work.

C. M. CHAPMAN'S

Celebrated Hair-Dyeing and Hair-Restoring Establishment

No. 218 THIRD STREET, SAN FRANCISCO.

Ladies can have their Hair beautifully *Dyed and Colored,* a perfect BLACK OR BROWN, or any desired shade, without coloring the skin, the operation being completed within an hour. Guaranteed to defy detection. The process and Coloring Material are entirely new and being of a vegetable nature, does not injure the Hair, but makes it

SMOOTH, YOUTHFUL AND LIVELY.

Persons having thin Hair, or bald, can have a thick coat of Hair in a very short time. Also,

SECRETS OF LADIES' TOILETS; OR, HOW TO BEAUTIFY THE SKIN!

It removes all blotches from the face and skin, leaving the skin perfectly SMOOTH, SOFT, CLEAR AND WHITE. I guarantee to remove all Freckles and Pimples from the skin and leave it Smooth and Clear. Also,

Shampooing, Hair Dressing and Cleaning neatly done. Call and Examine for Yourselves.

Also, constantly on hand, a full supply of VEGETABLE HAIR WASH. Hair Dressing done by Ladies from Boston, either at the Store or their Residences.

F. GRACIER,

MANUFACTURER OF

SCROLL SAWING, BUNGS, DECK PLUGS,

Broom Handles, Rosewood Faucets, Pick Handles, Etc.

81 FREMONT STREET,

Between Market and Mission.

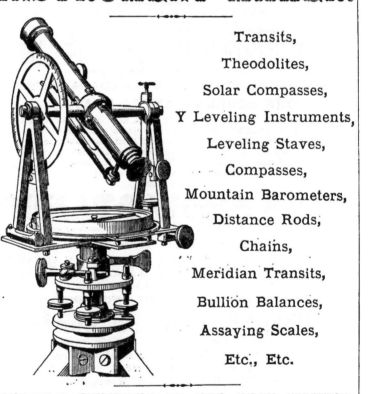

PACIFIC MUSEUM
—OF—
ANATOMY AND SCIENCE
EUREKA THEATER, 320 MONTGOMERY ST.

THE WONDERS OF THE WORLD, AND BEAUTIES OF NATURE,
HITHERTO HIDDEN, NOW REVEALED,
Showing that the handicraft of Man follows the heels of Nature.

Wonders of the Brain and Pons Varolii, where the seat of Mind or Soul is supposed to be; Wonders of the Five Senses, Seeing, Hearing, Smelling, Taste and Touch; Extraordinary Freaks of Nature, together with wonders from Paris, Florence, Munich and England; THE WONDERFUL CYCLOPS CHILD, the most remarkable lusus naturæ of the present century; Wonders of Life, actually showing *Hidden Life within Life*; Wonders of Accouchment; Wonders in Hermaphrodites; Wonderful Child, with one head united to two bodies; Wonders in Obstetrics; Wonders of Osteology; Wonders of Embryology, displaying from the earliest to the full period of gestation; Wonders of Comparative Anatomy; Wonders of the Digestive Organ; Wonders of Incubation, showing the Chicken from the second hour of incubation to the full time or twenty-second day; Wonders of the Human Frame, displaying at one glance innumerable portions of the body; WONDERFULLY BEAUTIFUL FLORENTINE VENUS, the acme of Anatomical Skill and Science, pronounced by competent authorities the finest specimen of indefatigable talent in the world; The MONSTER CHILD, unparalleled wonders, phenomena and striking unheard-of sights, never before seen by the public, spirit-inspiring and almost fabulous in the annals of the world.

It is the Most Wonderful, Scientific and Beautiful Institution in the World.

The Medical and General Press are unanimous in their approval of this truly valuable Scientific Collection. More may be learned by one visit than weeks of reading would impart.

Lectures every evening, at 8 o'clock, on important subjects connected with our Health.

Open Daily, for Gentlemen only, from 9 o'clock A.M. till 10 P.M.

ADMISSION, - - - ONE DOLLAR.

WASHINGTON MARKET.

THIS, the most extensive **MARKET**, and one of the features of our commercial metropolis, is located in the immediate vicinity of the great thoroughfare, MONTGOMERY STREET. It can be approached from Washington, Sansom and Merchant Streets, upon which it has a frontage of 95, 80 and 177½ feet respectively, with a depth of 120 feet. Few enterprises in San Francisco have been conducted with a greater success than this Market, and its popularity must continue to increase so long as its management is intrusted to the same energetic and enterprising gentlemen who have so ably conducted it from its first opening to the present time.

E. JACOB CHASE,
Superintendent.

HENRY F. WILLIAMS & CO.
Proprietors.

DIRECTORY.

Butchers. STALL.
Bookstaver & Weller.......82
Deitrich, W. K......53 and 54
Fulton, W.................80
Garwood, G. M. & Co.......84
Litchfield, W. D...........53
Miller & Co......12, 59 and 60
O'Brian, Michael Mrs.13 and 14
O'Niell, Richard...15 and 16
Wood, William.....17 and 18
Wray, Jacob & Co..........11

Oysters.
Anderson & Roalfe.........82
Morgan & Co...............31
Winant, M.................70

Game.
Card, R. & Co.......62 and 63
Cook, John H.......48 and 49

STALL.
Hart & Goodman...........66
Louderback, A. A......5 and 6

Fish.
Baltimore Harry & Co.23 and 24
Cardinet, E...........25 to 28
Fishermen's Association.1 to 16
Spence, W. A........9 and 10
Tesmore & Mayes....33 and 34
Wolff, A....................4

Hams, Sausages, Etc.
Bazille, J. (tripe).....29 and 30
Cholet, J. & Co...........69
Dick, William.............65

Butter, Cheese, Eggs, Etc.
French & Hall.........7 and 8
Gaughran, Peter...........44

STALL.
Gough, J. T...............20
Hadley, M. F..............71
Howard & Kneller.........68
Martens & Bredhoff..57 and 58
Menomv, G. W. & Co........3
Mitchell & Plege.....50 and 51
Ring & Lunt................2
Whitland, William.........45

Fruits and Vegetables.
Brown & Avery......41 and 42
Ducatel, A. Mrs...........10
Hall & Brigham.....73 and 74
Ham, C. W. & Co...........1
Hassel & Huber............47
Hohenschild, Henry..21 and 22
Meyer, L. Mrs.............61
Moore, Z. W. & Co.........9
Northup & Shaw...........76

DOWS' DISTILLERY,

MISSION CREEK,

SAN FRANCISCO.

THE PROPRIETORS OF THE ABOVE ESTABLISHMENT ARE NOW MANUFACTURING about THREE THOUSAND gallons of WHISKY daily, and are prepared to furnish the trade with ALCOHOL, PURE SPIRITS and HIGH WINES, of a quality equal, if not superior, to any imported, as Wheat alone is used for their manufacture. Purchasers can be supplied with lots to suit, at the depot, **No. 208 SACRAMENTO STREET.**

DOWS' DISTILLERY,

J. DOWS & CO., Proprietors,

Office, No. 208 Sacramento Street.